P9-DEH-559

DICTIONARY OF
THE HISTORY OF IDEAS

DICTIONARY
OF THE HISTORY
OF IDEAS

Studies of Selected Pivotal Ideas

PHILIP P. WIENER
EDITOR IN CHIEF

Index

CHARLES SCRIBNER'S SONS · NEW YORK

1 3 5 7 9 11 13 15 17 19 M|P 20 18 16 14 12 10 8 6 4 2

PRINTED IN THE UNITED STATES OF AMERICA

Library of Congress Catalog Card Number 72-7943

SBN 684-16422-1 (pbk.)   Volume I
SBN 684-16423-X (pbk.)   Volume II
SBN 684-16424-8 (pbk.)   Volume III
SBN 684-16425-6 (pbk.)   Volume IV
SBN 684-16426-4 (pbk.)   Index
SBN 684-16418-3 (pbk.)   Set

Index

All references include volume numbers shown in bold-face Roman numerals, page numbers shown in Arabic numerals, and left or right columns shown by the letters "a" and "b" respectively. Birth and death dates are given for major historical figures when they appear as main entries.

A

Aarne, Antti, folklore, III 238b, 239a
Aaron (Bible)
  music, III 265a
  mythology, III 277a, 277b, 282b
Aaron ben Elijah of Nicodemia (1300–1369), atomism, I 496a
Abarbanel, Jehudah
  aesthetics, IV 354b
  Platonism, III 509a, 510b, 512a–512b, 514a
Abbasid period, II 640b, 641a
Abbot, Francis Ellingwood (1836–1903)
  Orientalism, III 429a, 434b
  pragmatism, III 556b, 558a
  transcendentalism, III 429a, 434b
Abbt, Th.
  aesthetics, IV 356a
  taste, IV 356a
Abdiashirta, freedom of speech, II 254a
Abel (Bible)
  mythology, III 279a, 281b
  Saint Augustine and, IV 63a
Abélard, Peter (1079–1142)
  abstraction, I 3a, 3b
  aesthetics, II 217b
  analogy, I 65b–66a
  Chain of Being, I 326a
  dignity, IV 139b, 140a
  God, I 326a; II 343a
  heresy, II 418a
  love, III 98a, 98b, 103a, 107b
  methodology, III 382a
  Middle Ages, I 65b–66a
  rationalism, III 382a
Aberration of light, IV 77b
Abinavagupta, I 464a
Abiogenesis, IV 307a, 308b, 312a
Abraham (Bible)
  loyalty, III 108b
  mythology, III 275b, 277a, 280a, 280b, 281a, 283a, 284a
  prophecy, III 659a, 666b
  religion, IV 119a
  social contract, IV 252a
Abraham, Pol, Gothic, II 373a
Abrams, M. H.
  art, II 310b
  organicism, III 426b
  romanticism, IV 196a
Absolute
  infinity, II 606a, 611b

irrationalism, II 637a
  metaphor, III 199b
  necessity, III 357a
  pragmatism, III 556b
Absolute location, relativity, IV 76a
Absolute materialism, communism, II 561a–561b
Absolute rest, relativity, IV 76a, 78a, 80a, 95b
Absolute space
  Clark, IV 302b
  Leibniz, IV 302b
  measurement, IV 403b
  Newton, III 183b; IV 302b
Absolute time, IV 403b
Absolute velocity, relativity, IV 75b, 76a, 78a, 79a
Absolution, heresy, II 420a
Absolutism
  Austria, I 593a
  Bodin, III 19b
  common law, II 695b
  Denmark, I 593b
  despotism, I 1a, 8a
  education, II 82b–83b
  fascism, III 332a
  France, I 593b
  general will, II 276b
  Germany, I 593b
  Hegel, II 414a; III 556b
  Hobbes, IV 256b, 257a
  law, II 686a
  Louis XIV, II 8a
  loyalty, III 113a, 115a
  Machiavellism, III 117a 119b, 120a, 120b, 122b
  Milan, I 593a
  nationalism, III 322b, 325a, 329b, 332a
  natural law, III 19b, 21b
  revolution, IV 157b, 160a
  romanticism, IV 207b
  Rousseau, III 21b
  Russia, I 593b
  Schlegel, IV 207b
  social contract, IV 256b, 257a
  socialism, IV 291b
  totalitarianism, IV 406b, 407a, 408a, 408b
Abstentionism, revisionism, IV 272b, 273a, 273b
Abstraction
  Alexander of Aphrodisias, I 3a
  Al-Ghazali, I 4a–4b
  Aquinas, I 5a–6a, 6b
  Aristotle, I 1a–2b, 3a, 3b, 5a, 6b; III 190a
  art, II 528a–529b
  Atomists, I 1a
  Averroës, I 4b

Avicenna, I 3b–4a, 4b
Bergson, II 636b
Berkeley, I 4a, 7a–9a
Boethius, I 1a, 1b, 3a, 3b
Cantor, I 8b
concept formation, I 1a–9b
Democritus, I 1a
Descartes, I 6b–7a
determinism, II 18b–19a
Duns Scotus, I 4a, 5b–6a
Epicureanism, I 1a, 2b
Epicurus, I 2b
Franciscans, I 4b–5a
Frege, I 8a–9a
Galileo, IV 361a
Grosseteste, I 4b
historiography, II 18b–19a
Hobbes, I 4a
Hume, I 6b, 7a–9a
Husserl, I 8a
iconography, II 525b, 534a, 539a
idea, II 542a–542b, 546b, 599b–600b, 601b
ideal, II 551a, 551b
idealism, I 8a
impressionism, II 580b–581a
individualism, II 599b–600b, 601b
infinity, II 609a
introduction of the term, I 1a
John of Saint Thomas, I 6b
John of Salisbury, I 3a–3b
Kant, II 551b
language, II 665a
Locke, I 7a
Maimonides, I 4b
mathematics, III 184b
matter, III 187a, 190a
Matthew of Aquasparta, I 4b–5a
Mill, I 8a
mountains in literature, III 253b
mythology, III 272a, 273a, 293a
natural law, III 20a, 22a
naturalism in art, III 344a
necessity, III 360a
Newton, III 398a
nominalism, I 4a, 4b
numbers, III 403b, 406a, 406b
optics, III 398a
painting, IV 470a, 474a
perennial philosophy, III 462b
philosophy, II 551a, 551b
Plato, I 1a–1b, 3a, 3b; III 273a
Plotinus, I 3b

poetry, II 580b–581a; IV 470a, 474a
Pope, III 398a
Proclus, I 3b
Russell, I 8b–9a
Santayana, I 8a
Suarez, I 6b
symbolism, IV 344a, 345a
technology, IV 361a
verbal terms, I 2a
Whitehead, I 8a
William of Ockham, I 6a–6b
Abu Bišr, poetics, III 528a–528b
Abu Mansur Muwaffak, alchemy, I 30a
Abu Ma'shar (805–886), astrology, I 120b, 122b, 124a, 124b
Abu'l-Barakāt, mechanics, II 201b, 202a
Abu'l Kalam Azad, nationalism, III 338a
Academic freedom, I 9b–17a
  Africa, I 10a
  American Association of University Professors, I 13b–15b, 16a–16b
  anti-intellectualism, I 16a
  Australia, I 14a
  beginning of, I 9b–10a
  Brennan, I 12a
  Canada, I 14a
  Cold War, I 16a
  commerce, I 10a
  communism, I 10a, 16a
  Declaration of Principles, I 11b
  defined, I 9b
  described, I 10b
  dictatorship, I 10a, 15a
  Far East, I 10a
  France, I 16b
  Frankfurter, I 12a
  Germany, I 10b
  Great Britain, I 10a, 14a
  institution, I 10a
  Jackson, I 13a–13b
  Japan, I 16b
  Joint Statement on Rights and Freedoms of Students, I 11a
  Lovejoy, I 11b
  Mexico, I 16b
  Middle East, I 10a
  as a modern phenomenon, I 9b
  Newman, I 11a–11b
  political activity, I 15b
  Portugal, I 10a
  racial prejudice, I 16a–16b
  salaries, I 14a–15b
  Scandinavia, I 14a
  Spain, I 10a

State, I 10a
Statement on Government of College and Universities, I 14b–15b
Statement of Principles, I 12b–13a
students, I 10b–11a, 16b
teaching, I 10a–16b
tenure, I 12b–14a
two uses of the term, I 10a
U.S., I 10a–16b
United States Supreme Court, I 11b–13b
Warren, I 11b–12a
See also Education
Acceleration
Einstein, IV 86a–86b, 89a, 89b
relativity, IV 75b–76a, 76b, 77a, 82b, 86a–86b, 89a, 89b
Accidentalism, ambiguity, I 54b–56a
See also Chance Images
Accursius, Francesco, law, II 685b
Accusatorial proceedings, III 7b
Achaemenids, freedom of speech, II 254b
Achan (Bible), IV 226b
Achilles (myth), III 308a
death, I 634b
historiography, II 504b
human nature, III 571b, 572a
infinity, II 608b
law, II 675b, 676b, 677b
metaphor, III 203b
neo-classicism in art, III 368a
religion, III 203b
tragic sense, IV 412b
Achilles Tatius, primitivism, III 579b
Acmeists
classicism, I 455b
symbolism, IV 343a
Acontius, Jacobus (1492?–?1565), religion, IV 119a
Acoustics
art, I 459a
Galileo, III 263a
mathematics, III 387b
music, III 260b, 263a, 264a
psychology, IV 12a
Pythagoras, III 260b–261a
Acquired characteristics, II 617a–622a, 623b, 624a
adaptation, II 618a, 618b
agriculture, II 618a, 620a, 621a–621b
animals, II 617b
Aristotle, II 617b–618a

atomism, II 618b
Bagehot, II 620a
Bertalanffy, II 619a
Brumbaugh, II 617b
Bukharin, II 620b
Cannon, II 619a
class, II 620b, 622a
Comte, II 620a
Correns, II 619a
cytology, II 618b, 619a
Darlington, II 617b
Darwin, II 618a–618b, 620a
Darwinism, II 620b
De Vries, II 619a
Diderot, II 618a
Dobzhansky, II 622a
Engels, II 620a, 620b
environment, II 618a–618b, 619b
Epicurus, II 617b
eugenics, II 620b
evolution, II 617b–618b, 619a, 620a
genetics, II 617b–619b, 620b, 621a, 621b
Germany, II 620b
Great Britain, II 617b
ideology, II 620b
individualism, II 622a
Kautsky, II 620a, 620b
Kidd, II 620a
Lamarckism, II 617a–622b
Lenin, II 620b, 621b
Lysenko, II 619a–621b
Mackintosh, II 620a
Marxism, II 619b–621b
materialism, II 620a
medicine, II 620b
Mendel, II 617b–621a
Michurin, II 621a
modes of acquisition, II 623b
natural selection, II 618b, 620a
Nazism, II 620b
Neo-Darwinism, II 619a
Neo-Lamarckism, II 619a
pangenesis, II 623b
peasantry, II 617b, 620b, 621b
pessimism, II 620b
philosophy, II 617a, 617b, 620b
phylogenesis, II 618a
Plekhanov, II 620b
proletariat, II 620b
psychology, II 620b
Pythagoreans, II 617b
race, II 618a, 620b, 622a
revolution, II 619b–620a, 621b
Saint Thomas Aquinas, II 617b

Shakespeare, II 617a–617b
sin, II 617b
society, II 619b–620a, 621b–622a
sociology, II 620a, 621a, 622a
Spencer, II 620a
Stalin, II 620b, 621b
teleology, II 618a, 618b, 619b, 620a
Timiriazev, II 620b
Tschermak, II 619a
U.S.S.R., II 617b, 619a–621b
variation, II 617b–619a
vitalism, II 619a
Waddington, II 619a
Weismann, II 618b–619a
Zirkle, II 617b
Acteon (myth), III 297a
Acting, as an art, I 458a
Activism
determinism, IV 271b–273b
expressionism, II 206b
nationalism, III 331b
revisionism, IV 271b–273b
Thoreau, III 431a
totalitarianism, IV 408a
U.S., III 430a, 431a
Acton, Lord (1834–1902)
Christianity, I 408b, 409a
cycles, I 626a
ethnic groups, III 328b
historiography, II 496b
individualism, II 599a
liberty, III 328b
modernism, I 419b
nationalism, III 328b, 329b
politics, III 328b
power, I 626a
progress, III 636a
race, III 328b
Saint Thomas Aquinas and, I 382a
Adages, common law, II 692b
Adalbert, Saint, iconography, II 527b
Adam (Bible)
children, III 595b
Christianity, III 590b
Clement of Alexandria, III 582b
dignity, IV 145b
envy, III 583a
evil, III 582b, 583a
Gnosticism, II 327b
good, III 582a, 583a
Gregory of Nyssa, III 583a
idea, II 546b
language, II 669a
linguistics, III 65a–65b
longevity, III 90a
microcosm, III 131a
mountains in literature, III

254b–255a, 257b
mythology, III 277a–277b, 278b–279b
Nature, III 350a
primitivism, III 581b, 582a, 583a, 583b, 584a, 589b, 590b, 593a, 595b, 596b
psychology, IV 16b, 17a
reformation, IV 63a
religion, IV 119a
Saint Ambrose, III 583b
Saint Augustine, III 584a–584b
Saint Basil, III 583a–583b
sin, IV 227a, 230a
social contract, IV 257b
Stoics, III 583a
temptation, III 583a
tragic sense, IV 415b, 416a
witchcraft, IV 521b
women, III 596b
work, IV 531a
Adam, Robert (1728–1792)
art, II 308a
genius, II 308a
mimesis, III 229b
neo-classicism in art, III 364a, 365a, 365b, 366b, 369a
Adam of Bremen, primitivism, III 592b
Adamites, primitivism, III 593b
Adams, Brooks (1848–1927), conservatism, I 484a
Adams, Henry (1838–1918)
Buddhism, III 437a
conservatism, I 484a
crisis in history, I 591a
determinism, II 23b, 24a–24b
entropy, II 116a
evolution, II 24a
history, II 23b, 24a–24b
mythology, III 276b
Orientalism, III 437a
Adams, John (1735–1826)
authority, I 660a
constitutionalism, I 488b
democracy, I 659b, 660a
Jefferson and, IV 21b
psychology, IV 21b, 22a
State, I 660a
Adams, John Couch (1819–1892), cosmology, I 552b
Adams, John Quincy (1767–1848), social contract, IV 262b–263a
Adams, Samuel (1722–1803), social contract, IV 260b
Adanson, Michel, primitivism, III 603b
Adaptation
acquired characteristics, II 618a, 618b

Darwin, II 180a, 180b, 181a
evolutionism, II 180a, 180b,
181a, 185a
Lamarck, II 618a
Mendel, II 618b
pragmatism, III 552a
Addams, Jane (1860-1935),
sociology, IV 27a
Addison, Joseph (1672–
1719)
art, II 306b, 307b
attitude toward antiquity, I
80a, 83a–83b, 85a
beauty, I 202a–202b
Burnet and, III 259a
Chain of Being, II 446b
cosmic voyages, I 529b
creativity in art, I 587b,
588a
deism, I 651a
Enlightenment, II 89b, 91b
genius, II 294b–295a,
306b, 307b
hierarchy, II 446b, 447b
Milton and, III 300a
mountains in literature, III
259a
mythology, III 300a–300b
Newton and, III 392a, 396b,
397b–398a, 398b
optics, III 392a, 396b,
397b–398a, 398b
sublime in external nature,
IV 334a–335a, 335b, 336b
taste, IV 355b
ut pictura poesis, IV 471a,
471b
virtuoso, IV 488a, 489a–
489b
Adelard of Bath, II 646b
Adler, Alfred (1870–1937),
classification of the
sciences, I 465b
psychology, IV 14a
Adler, M. J., education, II 83a
Adler, Max (1873–1937),
Marxism, III 164b
Admetus (myth), love, III 96a
Adonis (myth), II 335a–335b,
341a; III 281a, 284a, 296b,
297a
religion, IV 96a, 104b
salvation, IV 228b
Adorno, T., historicism, II 463b
Adrasteia (myth), II 229a
Adrian Leverkühn (fiction),
Faust (legend), III 252a
Adriani, Giovanni Battista
(1513–1579), genius, II
293b
Adultery
primitivism, III 580b
prophecy, III 661a
Rome (ancient), II 688b

Advaita Vedānta, salvation, IV
232a
Adventists, eschatology, II
157a
Adversary proceedings, III 7b,
10a
Aegisthus (myth), law, II 683a
Aegyptus, King (myth), historiography, II 499b
Aelian (3rd century A.D.), theriophily, IV 384b, 388b
Aelius Theon, ut pictura poesis,
IV 468b
Aelred of Rielvaux (1109?–
1166), analogy, I 65b
Aeneas (myth), III 287a
Aenesidemus of Crete, skepticism, IV 234a, 235a,
236b–237a, 238b, 240a,
241a
Aeschines (389–314 B.C.)
freedom of speech, II 258a
law, II 684b
temperance, IV 368a, 370b
Aeschylus (525–465 B.C.)
ambiguity, I 50a–50b
anarchy, IV 366b
anthropology, III 625a,
625b
art, III 625b, 626a
biology, I 231b
catharsis, I 267a
comedy, I 468b
culture, I 608b; III 625b,
626a
democracy, IV 366b
disease, II 399a
divination, III 625a, 625b
evolution, III 625a
evolution of literature, II
171b
freedom, IV 366b
freedom of speech, II 259a–
259b
God, III 574b
health, II 399a
heroes, IV 366b
history, III 625a
human nature, III 571b,
573a, 574b
hybris, IV 366b
idea, II 545a
imagination, III 208b
justice, I 653a; IV 366b
law, II 681a–683a, 684a;
III 625b
masculinity, IV 366b
mathematics, III 180a
metaphysics, III 208b
motif, III 240b
mythology, III 272b
philanthropy, III 487a
piety, IV 366b
progress, III 625a–626a

reason, III 625b
science, III 625a, 625b
society, III 625b
space, IV 296a
symbolism, III 626a
symmetry, IV 348a
temperance, IV 366b–367a,
368b
thought, III 625a
tragedy, I 267a; IV 366b
tragic sense, IV 413b
tyranny, IV 366b
virtue, IV 366b–367a, 368b
wisdom of the fool, IV 517a
Aesculapius (myth), III 274a,
287a
Aesop (620–560 B.C.)
analogy, I 68b
eighteenth century view of,
I 81a, 82a
mythology, III 275a, 275b
theriophily, IV 384b
Aesthetics
Abbt, IV 356a
Abélard, II 217b
Addison, IV 355b
Alain de Lille, II 217b
Albert the Great, II 222b
Alberti, L.B., II 218a–218b
Alembort, IV 355a
anarchy, IV 223b
architecture, II 216a, 216b,
217a, 218b, 221b, 224a
Ariosto, IV 354b
Aristotelianism, II 220a–
220b, 222b
Aristotle, I 463a; II 216b,
217a, 222a, 222b
arrangement, II 216a,
216b–219b
art, II 216a–225b, 575b,
576a, 583a, 583b; IV 353b,
355b, 356a
art versus non-art, III 88b
Aschenbrenner, II 219a
Augustinianism, II 222b
Austria, II 223b
Baldinucci, II 222b
Balguy, III 233a
Balzac, IV 354b
Batteux, II 550a; IV 355a
Baumgarten, IV 356a
beauty, I 208b; II 216b–
219a, 221a, 222b–223b; IV
353b–356b
behavior, IV 354b
Bell, Clive, II 221a
Bembo, II 218b
Bernard of Clairvaux, II
218a
Blondel, II 218b
Bodmer, IV 356a
Bosse, II 218b
Bouhours, IV 355a

Burke, Edmund, IV 355b
Burnet, I 512a–512b; III
258a
Carbano, II 218b
Cassirer, II 222a
Castelvetro, II 220a
catharsis, I 268b
cathedrals, II 546a
causation, II 223a
Caxton, IV 355b
Cellini, IV 354b
Cicero, II 217a, 219b–220a
Clarembaldus of Arras, II
217b
classicism, IV 353b, 355b
classification of sciences, I
463a
color, II 221b, 222a, 224a;
III 396b
common sense, IV 355b,
356a
communication, II 219b
conceptual essence, II
216b, 222a–223a
Congreve, IV 355b
context, II 216a, 220b, 221a
convention, II 224a
Cosmic Fall, I 512a
cosmic images, I 513b,
514a
Crates, II 220a
creativity in art, I 587a, 588a
Crousaz, IV 355a
Crusius, IV 356a
Dacier, IV 355a
Dante, II 222b
de Quincy, II 218b
deism, I 651a
Demetrius, II 219b, 220a
Deonna, II 223b
Dewey, III 568b, 569b
Diderot, II 549b–550a; III
217a; IV 355a
disposition, II 216a, 216b–
219b
Dolce, IV 354b
Donne, I 512a
drawing, II 221b–222a,
222b
Du Fresnoy, II 218b
dualism, II 218a, 220b,
221a
Dubos, Abbé, IV 355a, 355b
Duff, I 588a
Duns Scotus, II 217b–218a
Ebreo, IV 354b
education, IV 354a, 355a
Einstein, Albert, IV 88b
Eliot, I 602a; IV 195a
empathy, II 85b–86a
enlightenment, II 97b–98a
entelechy, II 216b, 223a
Ettorri, IV 354b
evil, II 166b

3

evolution of literature, II 171b, 173b

expressionism, II 206a, 206b

Faust, (legend), III 249a

feeling, IV 353b, 354a, 354b, 355a, 356b

Feijóo, IV 354b

Félibien, II 218b

Ferber, II 551a

Ficino, II 218a

Fidler, II 223b

Filarete, IV 354a

Focillon, II 221a

forms, II 216a–225b

Fracastoro, II 220a

France, II 216a, 218b, 221a, 221b–222a, 224a; IV 354b–355b

France, Anatole, II 575b

Franciscans, II 222b

gardening, II 224a

genius, II 223b, 315b, 316a, 316b, 318b, 322b–323a, 323b, 325b; IV 356b

Gerard, IV 355b–356a

Germany, II 216a; IV 356a–356b

Ghyka, II 219a

Goethe, IV 124b

good, IV 182b, 184a, 354a, 355a, 356a, 356b

Goodman, I 512a

Gothic, II 367a–374a

Gottsched, IV 356a

Gracián, IV 354b

Graziani, IV 354b

Great Britain, II 219a, 221a; IV 355a, 355b–356a

Greece (ancient), II 216b, 217a–217b, 218a, 219a, 220a, 222a, 222b–223a

Greville, I 512a

Grosseteste, II 218a, 224b

Hakewill, I 512a

Hamann, IV 356b

happiness, II 374b, 380b, 386a

harmony, II 216b, 217a, 217b, 219a, 222a

Hartley, III 234b; IV 356a

Heracleodor, II 220a

Herbart, II 218b, 223b

Herder, IV 356b

Hildebrand, II 223b

Hume, III 232a, 232b–233a; IV 355b, 356a

Hutcheson, I 588a; III 230b–231a; IV 355b

idea, II 223a, 546a, 548b

ideal, II 549a–550a, 551a–551b

impressionism, II 219b,

575b, 576a, 583a, 583b

irrationalism, IV 355a, 355b, 356b

Isidore of Seville, II 217b

Italy, II 216a, 218a–218b, 221b, 224a

Johnson, Samuel, IV 356a

judgment, IV 354a, 354b, 355a, 355b, 356a, 356b

Jung, III 597a

Kames, II 221a; III 234b

Kandinsky, II 221a

Kant, I 588a; II 216b, 218b, 221a, 223a–223b, 551a, 551b; IV 356a, 356b

knowledge, II 223a, 223b; IV 354a, 355a

König, IV 356a

La Bruyère, IV 355b

La Fontaine, IV 354a

La Rochefoucauld, IV 354b

Lalande, II 221a

Le Corbusier, II 219a, 221a

Lebrun, II 221b

Leibniz, IV 356a

Lessing, IV 124b; 356a

light, II 218a

literary criticism, I 596a, 597b–598a, 602a, 602b–603a, 603b, 606a, 606b

literature, II 216a, 219b–220b, 224a; III 82b, 85a, 85b, 86a, 87b, 88a–88b; IV 330b, 331b, 332b

Lovejoy, III 552b

luster, II 222b

Malebranche, IV 355a

Malevitch, II 221a

Mandeville, IV 356a

Marburg School, II 223a

Mathieu of Vendôme, II 220a

matter, II 216a, 216b, 221b–222a, 222b

meaning, IV 353b

Meier, IV 356a

Mendelssohn, IV 356a

Mengs, IV 356a

Méré, IV 354b

metaphor, III 196b–197a, 198b, 199a

metaphysical imagination, III 218b

Mexico, III 544b

Michelangelo, IV 354b

Middle Ages, II 217b–218a, 220a, 222a–222b, 223a, 224a

Milton, IV 355b

mimesis, III 228a, 229b

mind, II 216b, 223a–223b, 224b; IV 354a, 355b

Mingard, IV 355a

Molière, IV 354b

Mondrian, II 221a, 222b

Monet, II 220b

Monod-Herzen, II 219a

Montesquieu, IV 355a

moral sense, III 230b, 232a, 232b–233a, 234b–235a

morality, IV 354b, 355b, 356a, 356b

motif, III 237a, 238a

mountains in literature, III 256b, 258a

Muratori, IV 354b

music, II 216a, 216b, 219b, 220b, 224a, 315b, 316a, 316b, 318b, 322b–323a, 323b, 325b; III 267b, 271b

mythology, III 289b, 292a, 305a

nationalism, III 336b

naturalism in art, III 343a, 343b

Nature, III 347a, 350a, 350b; IV 355b

neo-classicism, IV 354a

neo-plasticism, II 221a

Netherlands, II 221a

Newton, III 396b

Nicholas of Cusa, II 223a

Nicholson, Ben, II 222b

Norris, IV 355b

optics, III 396b

oratory, II 220a

order of parts, II 216a, 216b–219b

organicism, III 421a–422b, 425a–426b

painting, II 217a, 219b, 220b, 221b, 224a, 575b, 576a, 583a, 583b; IV 465b, 466b, 467a, 469a, 471b, 472a, 473b, 474a

paleography, II 219b

Palladio, II 218b

Pater, II 576a

Peirce, III 568b, 569b

perfectibility, III 463b, 467b; IV 356a, 356b

philanthropy, III 491b, 492a

Philodemus, II 219b

philosophy, II 549a–550a, 551a–551b; III 196b–197a, 198b, 199a; IV 356a, 356b

Pico della Mirandola, II 218a

Piles, II 222b

Pino, II 221b

Plato, II 217a, 221a, 223a; III 502a

Platonism, II 218a; III 496a, 502a, 514b, 516b, 518b, 523b, 524a, 524b

pleasure, II 374b, 380b, 386a; IV 354a, 354b

Plotinus, II 217a–217b, 218a

poetics, III 525b, 527b, 531a

poetry, II 216a, 219b–220a, 224a; IV 465b, 466b, 467a, 469a, 471b, 472a, 473b, 474a

Poland, II 216a, 219a, 221a, 222a

Pope, I 588a

Porrée, II 217b, 224a–224b

Posidonius, II 219b

positivism, III 538a

Poussin, II 218b

pragmatism, III 552b, 568b, 569b

Price, III 233a

Priestley, IV 356a

primitivism, III 596b–597a

proportion, II 217b, 218a, 222b

Pseudo-Dionysius, II 218a, 222b

psychology, IV 24a, 27b

purism, II 221a

Pythagoreans, I 514a; II 217a, 219a

Quintilian, II 219b

Racine, II 550a

Rapin, IV 355a

rationalism, IV 355b, 356a

realism in literature, IV 51b, 55b

reason, III 232a; IV 353b, 354a, 354b, 355a, 355b, 356a, 356b

relativism, IV 356a

relativity, IV 75a, 80a, 88b, 89a

religion, IV 106b, 108b

Renaissance, II 218a–218b, 220a, 221b, 222a, 223a; IV 124b, 128a, 354a–354b, 439b–440a, 442b

Richelet, II 222b

Riedel, IV 356b

Riehl, II 223b

right, IV 182b, 184a

Rinuccini, IV 354b

Robert, II 221b

Robortello, II 220a

Rollin, IV 355a

romanticism, II 224a; IV 188b, 191b, 193b, 195b, 202a, 205a, 210a

Rome (ancient), II 216a, 219b–220a

Rubenists, II 222a

Russia, II 216a, 221a

Saint Augustine, II 217b, 218a, 219a

Saint Bonaventura, II 219b, 222b, 224b

Saint-Evremond, IV 354b–355a

Saint Thomas Aquinas, II 218a

Schiller, Friedrich, III 569b

Schlosser, II 223b

scholasticism, II 217b, 219a, 220a, 222b

Schramm, IV 356a

science, IV 354a, 356a

sculpture, II 216b, 217a, 220b, 221b, 224a, 224b

senses, II 216a–216b, 219b–221b; IV 355a, 355b

Shaftesbury, I 588a; IV 355b, 356a

space, II 223a

Spain, II 216a; IV 354b

Stoicism, II 217a

structure, II 219a

Strzemiński, II 222a

style, IV 330b, 331b, 332b

subjectivism, IV 355b, 356b

sublime in external nature, IV 334a, 335a, 336b, 356a

Sulzer, II 551a; IV 356b

symbolism, IV 338a, 338b, 339b, 340a, 341b, 343b, 345a

symmetry, II 217b; IV 347b, 348b, 351b

temperance, IV 368a, 369a, 369b, 370a

Testelin, II 218b, 221b–222a

theodicy, IV 381a

Thomasius, IV 356a

tradition, II 224a

tragedy, II 224a

transcendentalism, IV 24a

truth, IV 354a, 355a, 356a

Ulrich of Strassburg, II 222b

unism, II 221a

U.S., II 219a

universal man, IV 439b–440a, 442b

universality, IV 354a–356b

utility, IV 355a, 355b, 356a

value, IV 354a

Varchi, IV 354b

Vasari, II 221b

Vauvenargues, IV 355a

Vilate, IV 355a

virtue, IV 355b, 356b

vision, II 223b

Vitruvius, II 217a

Voltaire, IV 355a

Webb, IV 355b

William of Ockham, II 218a

Winckelmann, II 218b, 550a; IV 124b

Witkiewicz, II 219a

Wolf, IV 124b

Wölfflin, II 223b

work, IV 533b

Worringer, II 223b

Zimmermann, II 217a, 218b

Zuccaro, II 221b, 222b

Zuccolo, IV 354b

Aether drag, IV 78b, 79a, 83b

Einstein, IV 80b, 81a–81b, 89b

Maxwell, IV 80b

measurement, IV 405a

Poincaré, IV 80a, 80b

relativity, IV 78a–81b, 83a, 89b

time, IV 405a

Afanasyev, A. N., folklore, III 239a

Affligemensis, Johannes, musical genius, II 314a

Afghanistan (ancient), Buddhism, I 247b, 248a

Africa

academic freedom, I 10a

art, III 597a

crisis in history, I 593a–593b

fetishism, III 301a, 303b

missionaries, I 376a

mythology, III 301a, 303b, 313b, 314a

nationalism, III 335a–338b

numbers, III 399b

primitivism, III 596b, 597a, 598b, 599a, 603b, 604a, 604b

Protestantism, III 490b

religion, IV 94a

technology, IV 361a

witchcraft, IV 521a, 523a

Africanus, Julius (3rd century A.D.), historiography, II 471a

Agamemnon (myth)

human nature, III 571b, 573a

law, II 675a, 676b

sin, IV 228a

tragic sense, IV 413a

Agapē, II 209b, 210a

love, III 97b, 103b, 106a–106b, 107a

Neo-Platonism, III 377a

pragmatism, III 560b

progress, III 635b

Agatharchides (2nd century B.C.)

historiography, II 509b

progress, III 630a

Agatharchos, creativity in art, I 582a

Agathocles the Sicilian, *virtù*, IV 480a, 482b

Agave (myth), III 496b

Agbar of Edessa, King, historiography, II 478b

Age of Heroes (myth), primitivism, III 578a, 578b, 579a, 580a

Agesilaus, King, historiography, II 503a

Aggression

morality, II 383b

right, IV 174a

war, IV 507a, 507b, 508a

Agni (myth), II 343b

Agnosticism, I 17a–27a

atheism, I 19a, 22a, 24a

Christianity, I 17a–27a

Clifford, I 19a

Darwin, IV 107b

defined, I 17a

Dewey, I 18a

empiricism, I 19a, 19b, 23a, 23b, 24a–24b

Flint, I 17a

free will, II 246b

gnosticism, I 19a

Hägerström, I 26a

Hamilton, I 17b, 18a

Hick, I 24a

humanism, II 520a

Hume, I 19a, 20a, 23b

Huxley, T. H., I 17a–19a, 20a, 20b–21a, 22b–23a

idealism, I 22b–23a

James, William, I 17a–17b; III 563a

Judaism, I 17a–27a

Kant, I 18a, 19a, 23b; II 246b

knowledge, I 17a–27a

Mansel, I 19b

materialism, I 22b–23a

monism, I 23b–24a

Neo-Platonism, III 373a, 373b

Newman, I 19b

Orientalism, III 438b

Plantinga, I 23b–24a

Popper, I 23a

pragmatism, III 561b, 563a

Price, I 24a, 24b–25a

religion, IV 106b, 107b, 120b

Russell, Bertrand, I 22b

science, I 17a–27a

Smart, I 22b, 23a–23b

Spencer, I 25b; III 438b

Stebbing, I 24b

Stephen, I 17b, 18b–21a, 22b–23a

theistic, I 17b

Ward, I 17a, 22b–23a

Wright, III 561b

Agricola, George (1494–1555), I 176a

Agricola, Rudolph (1444–1485)

geology, III 255b, 256a

humanism, II 519a

Ramus and, IV 43a

Agriculture

acquired characteristics, II 618a, 620a, 621a–621b

anarchy, III 674a

Aristotle, I 654a

art, I 458a; II 313b

Bible, III 279a, 279b, 281a, 282a

China, I 366b, 367b, 372b

classification of sciences, I 464b

conservation, I 472a, 475a

cosmology, I 535b, 537a

culture, I 609b, 611a–611b

democracy, I 654a

economic history, II 47b, 57a

Enlightenment, II 90b, 93b, 98b

Germany, III 651b

Great Britain, III 600a

Lucretius, III 587b

Marxism, III 152b, 155a, 166a, 166b

as mechanical art, II 313b

monopoly, II 57a

mythology, III 279a, 279b, 281a, 282a, 312a

nationalism, III 334b

natural liberty, II 62b, 69a

peace, III 442b, 446b, 447a

peasantry, III 595a

Poland, III 166b

primitivism, III 579a, 580a, 580b, 583a, 584b, 587b, 595a, 600a, 600b

private property, III 650b, 651a, 651b, 652b, 653a, 653b, 654a, 655a, 656a

progress, III 625a, 631b, 635a

protest movements, III 672b, 674a

religion, IV 96a, 104b

revolution, IV 161a, 162b

Rome (ancient), III 651b, 652a

Saint Augustine, III 635a

Stalin, II 621b

syndicalism, III 674b

time, IV 402a

U.S.S.R., II 620a, 621a–621b; III 653b

U.S., I 367b, 371b; II 69a

utility, IV 453a

Utopia, IV 462b

war, IV 500b, 501b

welfare state, IV 511a

Yugoslavia, III 166a

Agrippa, Cornelius (Agrippa

von Nettesheim) (1486?–1535),
Bacon and, I 174a, 174b
Counter-Enlightenment, II 101a
demonology, I 669b–670a
Faust (legend), III 246a
harmony, II 389b, 393b, 394a
hierarchy, II 435b
linguistics, III 74b
literary paradox, III 79a
mythology, III 290b
primitivism, III 591a, 595a
skepticism, IV 234a, 238a, 242a, 243a
wisdom of the fool, IV 519b
Ahab (Bible), prophecy, III 660b, 661a
Aharonov, Y., indeterminacy, II 591a
Ahriman, II 339a–340a
  dualism, II 39a–40a
  evil, II 162b, 165a
  sin, IV 231a–231b
Ahura Mazdà, II 339a–340a
  dualism, II 39a–40a, 162b
  kings, II 254a–254b
  sin, IV 231a–231b
Ainalov, D. V., iconography, II 535b
Ajax (myth)
  cynicism, I 628a
  law, II 681b
  Sophocles, IV 367a
  temperance, IV 367a
Akedah (Bible), loyalty, III 108b
Akenside, Mark (1721–1770)
  Newton, III 395a, 396b, 398a
  sublime in external nature, IV 335a, 335b–336a, 336b, 337a
Akhmatova, Anna, symbolism, IV 343a
Akhnaton, King, city, I 428a
Akiba, Rabbi, equity, II 151b–152a
Akkad
  freedom of speech, II 253a
  impiety, II 564a
Akkadian language, III 278a
Alain of Lille (1114?–?1203)
  aesthetics, II 217b
  analogy, I 65b
  Antisthenes and, III 590b
  Bible, III 590b
  Christianity, III 590b
  cynicism, III 590b
  dignity, IV 140a
  iconography, II 526a–526b
  mimesis, III 227b

Nature, III 590b
primitivism, III 590b
Pythagorean cosmos, IV 41a
Seneca and, III 590b
skepticism, IV 250a
Al-'Āmiri, II 645a
Alan the Englishman, nationalism, III 320b
Alaric the Goth, II 341a
Al-Ashari (873–?935), causation, I 273b–274a, 286b
Albalat, Antoine, IV 332b
Albani, Cardinal, neo-classicism in art, III 366b
Albania
  communism, III 334a
  Marxism, III 169a
  nationalism, III 334a
  U.S.S.R., III 334a
Al-Bāqillānī, Abū Bakr, II 642a
Albee, Edward (1928–   ), tragic sense, IV 414a
Albert the Great, *see* Albertus Magnus, Saint
Albert of Saxony
  humanism, IV 134a
  matter, III 192a
  medieval science, II 201b, 202a–202b, 203b
Alberti, Leone Battista (1404–1472)
  aesthetics, II 218a–218b
  art, II 301a, 308a, 309b; III 228a
  chance images, I 345a–346a, 346b, 347a, 351a
  city, I 430a–430b
  deism, I 650b–651a
  fortune, II 235a; IV 478a
  genius, II 293b, 301a, 308a, 309b, 317b
  Gothic, II 367b
  happiness, IV 478a
  harmony, II 390b; IV 41b
  hermeticism, II 433b
  humanism, II 522a; IV 437b–438a, 439a–442b
  iconography, II 528a, 528b
  mimesis, III 227b, 228a
  music, II 317b, 390b
  temperance, IV 377b
  universal man, IV 437b–438a, 439a–442b
  ut pictura poesis, **IV 467b, 468a, 469a, 469b**
  virtue, II 234b–235a; IV 478a
  wisdom of the fool, IV 519b
  work, IV 532a
Alberti, Rafael, symbolism, IV 342a
Albertus Magnus, Saint (1193? or 1206? –1280)

alchemy, I 30b
Chain of Being, I 326b
astrology, II 232a, 233a
beauty, I 585b; II 22b
causation, II 232a, 232b
chance images, I 343a
creativity in art, I 585b
determinism, II 232a
environment, II 129a
forms in aesthetics, II 222b
fortune, fate, and chance, II 232a, 232b, 233a
medieval science, II 197a
mind, II 232a
natural law, III 18b
Nature, II 197a
providence, II 232a
Albigensian crusade, II 423a; III 670b
  Cathars, II 423a
  heresy, II 423a
  love, III 102b
  Middle Ages, II 423a
  perfectibility, III 468a
  protest movements, III 670b
Al-Birūnī (973-1050?), I 546b; II 647a
Albumazar (805–885), double truth, II 35b–36a
Alcestis (myth), love, III 96a
Alchemy, I 27a–34a
  Abu Mansur Muwaffak, I 30a
  Aquinas, I 30b
  Arabia, III 91a
  Arabic texts on, I 29b–30a
  Aristotle, I 28a, 29b, 30a, 30b
  Babylonia, I 27b–28a
  Bacon, Francis, I 174a–174b
  Bacon, Roger, I 31a, 32b
  Boyle, I 28b, 31a, 33a; III 190b
  China, I 27a, 29a, 33a; III 91a
  cosmic images, I 516a
  Creation, I 28a–28b, 31b–32b
  early Western, I 30a–31b
  Egypt (ancient), I 28b–29a, 29b, 33a
  Fallopius, I 31a
  Far East, I 27a–29a
  Faust (legend), III 245a, 246a
  Fludd, I 32b, 33b
  French, John, I 32b
  Galen, I 29b
  Gassendi, I 32b
  Gesner, I 31b
  Glauber, I 33a
  Greece (ancient), I 28a–29a, 29b

harmony, II 392b
Helmont, I 32b, 33a
Henry IV, I 31a
Hermes Trismegistus, I 28b, 29b
Holmyard, I 29b
humanism, II 521a
India, I 27a, 29a
Islam, I 29a–30a, 33a; II 641a, 646a, 646b
Jabir ibn Hayyan (Geber), I 29b, 30b; III 91a
John of Rupescissa, I 31a–31b
John XXII (Pope), I 31a
Kepler, I 32b
Khalid ibn Yazid, I 29b, 30a
Ko Hung, I 29a
Leiden papyri, I 28a
Libavius, I 32b
longevity, III 91a–91b
macrocosm and microcosm, I 27b, 28a
Manget, I 31b
Maria the Jewess, I 28b
matter, III 190b–191a, 192a
medicine, I 27b, 32a–32b, 33a
Mersenne, I 32b
Middle Ages, II 197b; III 190b–191a, 192a
Nature, I 27b, 28a
Near East, I 27a–29a
Neo-Platonism, I 28a; III 91a
Newton, I 33a; III 190b
Paracelsus, I 28b, 31b–32a, 33b; III 91b
Petrus Bonus of Ferrara, I 30b
Plato, I 28a
Pliny the Elder, I 29a
Ptolemy, I 29b
Renaissance, I 28b, 31b–32b
Robert of Chester, I 30a–30b
Rome (ancient), III 91b
Ruska, I 29b
Savonarola, I 31a
science, II 641a, 646a, 646b
Sennert, I 32b
skepticism, IV 242a
Stockholm papyri, I 28a
Stoics, I 28a
Sylvius, I 33a
Taoism, III 91a
technology, IV 358a, 360a
Webster, John, I 32b
Western civilization, III 91a
Zetzner, I 31b
Zosimos, I 28b, 29b
Alcherus of Clairvaux, dignity, IV 140a

Alciati, Andrea
  iconography, II 530b
  mythology, III 290a, 296a
Alcibiades (450?–404 B.C.),
  law, II 683b
  literary paradox, III 78b
Alcinous (myth), law, II 684b
Alcmaeon (6th century B.C.),
  analogy, I 62b
  biology, I 230b
  dualisms, IV 346b
  health, II 397b; III 574a
  human nature, III 574a
  Man-Machine, III 132a
  psychology, IV 2a
  Pythagoreans, IV 34a
  symmetry, IV 346b
Alcoholism
  law, III 34b
  Victorianism, IV 219a–219b
Alcott, Bronson (1799–1888),
  psychology, IV 24a
  transcendentalism, IV 24a
Alcuin (735–804), temper-
  ance, IV 371a
  vox populi, IV 498a–498b
  work, IV 531b
Al-Din Shīrāzī, Sadr, II 651b
Aldrovandi, Ulise (1522–
  1605), chance images, I
  343b
Alembert, Jean Le Rond d'
  (1717?–1783)
  aesthetics, IV 355a
  anticlericalism, III 536a,
  538a, 544a
  astronomy, III 535b
  axiomatization, I 166a
  Bacon, Francis, I 177b
  Bible, II 353a
  classification of the
  sciences, I 464b
  Comte and, III 532b, 533a
  Counter-Enlightenment, II
  101b
  despotism, II 10b
  Enlightenment, II 89b–90a,
  91b, 93a, 96a–96b, 99b,
  100a
  genius, II 294b
  mathematics, III 179b
  methodology, III 378b
  music, III 263b
  Newton and, III 378b
  positivism, III 532b, 533a
  probability, III 606b
  reason, II 96a–96b
  revolution, IV 154b
  rhetoric, IV 172a
  society, II 99b
  space, IV 302b
  taste, IV 355a
  universal man, IV 443a
  Utopia, IV 462a

Alexander, Franz, psychology,
  IV 29a
Alexander, Samuel (1859–
  1938)
  beauty, I 209b
  Creation, I 576a
  evolutionism, II 183b–184a,
  186a
  God, I 576a
  romanticism, IV 210b
  Schelling and, IV 210b
  time, IV 396b
Alexander of Aphrodisias (fl.
  about 200 A.D.)
  abstraction, I 3a
  Aristotle and, I 639b; II
  203b; III 380b–381a
  atomism, I 130b
  axiomatization, I 164a
  creativity in art, I 580b
  double truth, II 34b, 36b
  ethics, IV 322a
  geometry, III 380b–381a
  Islam, II 644a
  mathematics, I 580b
  soul, I 36b
  Stoicism, IV 322a
Alexander of Villedieu, linguistics, III 63a
Alexander the Great (356–323
  B.C.), II 234b, 254a
  analogy, I 68b
  art, II 299b
  Buddhism, I 254b
  classicism, I 451b
  cosmic voyages, I 527a
  Cynicism, I 628a–628b,
  631b, 632a, 633b
  despotism, II 3a
  Diogenes of Sinope and, I
  633b
  Epicureanism, IV 7a
  ethics, IV 320a–320b
  Faust (legend), III 247a
  freedom of speech, II 257b
  historiography, II 469a,
  504a, 504b–505b, 508b
  law, II 574a
  longevity, III 90a–90b
  loyalty, III 111a
  periodization in literary history, III 481b
  philanthropy, III 487a
  primitivism, III 592a, 592b
  psychology, IV 7a
  Stoicism, IV 320a–320b
  Stoics, IV 7a
  war, IV 502b
Alexander I, Tsar (1777–
  1825)
  conservatism, I 482b
  international peace, III 453a
Alexander IV, Pope (d. 1261),
  witchcraft, IV 522a

Alexander VII, Pope (1599–
  1667), China, I 357b
Alfanus, dignity, IV 137b
Al-Fārābī (870?–950 A.D.),
  causation, I 273b, 287a,
  288a
  classification of the
  sciences, I 463b
  Islam, II 643a, 644a–644b,
  645a, 649a, 649b
Alfieri, Cesare (1796–1869),
  classicism, I 452a
  nationalism, III 336b
  neo-classicism in art, III
  370b
Algarotti, Francesco (1712–
  1764)
  iconography, II 533a
  periodization in literary history, III 482a
  ut pictura poesis, IV 472b
  virtuoso, IV 489a
Algebra
  Condillac, IV 435b
  empiricism, III 549a
  Leibniz, IV 435b
  mathematics, III 173a, 174a,
  175a, 175b, 178a, 178b,
  179a, 183b, 184a
  methodology, III 379b,
  380b
  necessity, III 355b
  Newton, III 379b, 380b
  numbers, III 403a, 404b,
  405a, 406a
  probability, III 609a, 614a
  Ramism, IV 42b
  Renaissance, III 178a
  Sumer-Babylonia, III 171a
  unity of science, IV 435b,
  436a
Algeria, nationalism, III 338a
Al-Ghazālī (1058–1111)
  abstraction, I 4a–4b
  atomism, I 496a
  Avicenna and, I 288b–289a
  causation, I 274a, 277a,
  286b–287a, 288a–289a
  discontinuity, I 496a
  God, I 288b, 289a
  Hume and, I 274a
  Islam, II 642b, 648a, 648b,
  649b, 650b
  Malebranche and, I 274a
  skepticism, IV 241b
Al-Hallaj of Bagdad, love, III
  99b
Alhazen (965?–?1039), II
  198b
  optics, III 409a–409b, 410a
Al ibn abi al-Rijāl, I 124b
Alien and Sedition Laws, III
  114a

Alienation
  Albigensians, I 35b
  Bauer, I 37b, 38a
  bureaucracy, III 168b
  capitalism, III 168b
  Christianity, I 34a–37a
  determinism, II 25a
  existentialism, III 158b–
  159b
  Feuerbach, I 37b–38a, 38b
  Gnosticism, I 35b–36a
  Hegel, I 37a–41a
  Hess, I 38a
  historiography, II 25a
  ideology, II 557b
  Judaism, I 34a–34b
  labor, I 38b–40b
  Lukács, III 168b
  Luther, I 36b
  Manicheism, I 35a, 35b
  Marx, I 37a–41a, 620b;
  II 25a; III 158b–159b,
  168b
  Mill, I 38b, 40a, 40b
  Neo-Platonism, I 34b
  romanticism, I 36b, 620b
  Saint Paul, I 35a–35b, 36a
  scholasticism, I 36a–36b
  socialism, III 168b
  theology, I 34a–37a
  Utopia, IV 463b
  Wordsworth, I 36b
Alison, Archibald (1757–
  1839), beauty, I 202b–203a
Al-Juwaynī, II 642b
Al-Kindī (fl. 9th century A.D.)
  causation, I 273b
  experimental science, II
  197b
  Islam, II 643a–643b, 644a
  macrocosm and microcosm,
  III 129a
  Neo-Platonism, III 377b
  optics, III 409a
Al-Kūdat Hamadānī, Ain
  Islam, II 650b
Allāf, Islam, II 641b
Allah (myth), II 344b–345a;
  III 282b
Allat (myth), III 282b
Allegory, I 41a–48b
  Aristophanes, I 42a
  art, II 525b, 526a, 527a,
  530b, 531a–531b, 532a,
  532b–533b, 534a
  Bible, III 282b
  Cabbala, II 42b
  Chapman, III 294b
  cosmos, I 46a–47a
  Dante, I 41b, 42b, 46b
  decorum, I 47b–48a
  Demetrius, I 41b
  Enlightenment, I 47b
  Euhemerus, I 47b

Euripides, I 42a
expressionism, II 208b
Greece (ancient), III 526b
Christianity, I 43a–48a,
51b–53a
Clement of Alexandria, I
44a, 45a, 46b
Gregory of Nazianzus, I 44a
Heraclitus, I 42b, 44b, 61a–
61b
Herder, III 305a
Homer, I 42b, 43a, 44b, 46a
Horace, I 41b–42a
humanism, II 520a
iconography, II 525b, 526a,
527b, 530b–534a
irony, II 628b, 630b, 634a
Isidore of Seville, I 41a–
41b
jealousy, I 42b
Jesuits, III 293a–293b
Joachim of Floris, I 47a
Judaism, I 43a–44a, 46a,
47a–48a
Kafka, I 47b–48a
language, I 41a
Leibniz, I 47b
macrocosm and microcosm,
III 130a
as a means of structuring
language, I 41a
metaphor, I 42a; III 203b–
204b, 205b–206b
millenarianism, III 224b
mimesis, III 228b
mountains in literature, III
253b
music, III 266a, 270a, 271a
Origen, I 44a, 46b
origin of the term, I 41b
Philo Judaeus, I 42a, 45a–
45b, 46a
Plato, I 42a, 42b–43b, 46b
Platonism, III 505a, 513b,
514b, 522b
Plotinus, I 43b, 46b
Plutarch, I 42a
poetry, III 526b, 528b,
529b
progress, III 626b
prophecy, I 45a–45b; III
657b, 666b
Prudentius, I 47a
Ptolemy, I 47b
Pythagoras, I 42b
Quintilian, I 41b
Ramism, IV 44a
religion, III 203b, 204a,
204b, 205b, 206a, 206b;
IV 94a
Renaissance, I 46b, 47a–
47b
rhetoric, IV 170b

Saint Augustine, I 42a, 44a,
46b
Shelley, I 47a
Spenser, I 41b
symbolism, I 41a, 42a; IV
338a, 339a, 341b, 342a,
342b, 344a, 345a
syncretism, I 43b–46a
synonyms for, I 42a
temperance, IV 377b
theology, I 41b
time, I 47a–47b
ut pictura poesis, IV 469a,
470a, 471a, 473b
William of Ockham, I 46b
Wulf, I 46b
Xenophon, I 42a
See also mythology
Allegorical portraiture, II 532a
Allen, C. K., legal precedent,
III 31a
Alliances
international peace, III
448b, 452a
Machiavellism, III 122b
All-India National Congress,
III 338a
Allport, G. W.
happiness, II 385a
psychology, IV 15a
Al-Majriti, II 646b
Al-Ma'mūn, II 641b
Almeida-Garrett, João Bap-
tista da Silva Leitão (1799–
1854), romanticism, IV
191a
Almohads, Islam, II 648b
Al-Nazzām (d. ca. 848), divine
justice, I 287a–287b
Alonso, Dámaso
baroque in literature, I 192a
symbolism, IV 342b
Alpatov, M., iconography, II
535b
Alphabet
language, II 661a, 666a
mathematics, III 180b
numbers, III 401b, 402a
writing, III 180b
Alphonsus of Liguori, Saint
(1696–1787)
casuistry, I 263a–263b,
264b
the Wesleys, I 263a–263b
Al-Qasrānī, astrology, I 124b
Al-Rāzī, Fakhr al-Dīn, II 642b,
643a, 647a, 648a–648b
Al-Rāzī, Muhammad ibn Zaka-
rīyā', II 646b–647a
Al-Rijāl, 'Alī ibn abī, astrology,
I 124b
Al-Sādiq, Imam Ja-far, II 641a
Al-Saymarī, astrology, I 124b
Al-Shīrāzī, Qutb al-Dīn, II 651b

Al-Sijistānī, II 644b
Alsted, John Henry, perennial
philosophy, III 460a
Alt, Rudolph von, naturalism in
art, III 341a
Al-Tabari, historiography, II
474b
Altdorfer, Albrecht (1480?–
1538), iconography, II 531b
Altenstein, Karl von (1770–
1840), Hegel and, II 411b
Althusius, Johannes (1557–
1638), social contract, IV
254b
Althusser, Louis, structuralism,
IV 329a–329b
Altizer, T. J., God, II 363b–
364a
Altruism, III 644a, 647a, 648b–
649a
Al-Tūsī, Khwājah Nasīr al-Dīn,
II 651a–651b
Alving, Oswald (fiction), tragic
sense, IV 416b–417a
Ambiguity, I 48b–58b
accidentalism, I 54b–56a
Aeschylus, I 50a–50b
Aristophanes, I 50b
Bach, I 57a
Bacon, Francis, I 55a
Butterfield, I 54a–54b
Camoës, I 58b
Christianity, I 52a–54b
Cosmic Fall, I 505a
Dante, I 53b–54a
Darwin, I 58b
Descartes, I 58b
drama, I 50a–51a, 54b–56a
Euripides, I 50b
Greece (ancient), I 48b–
52a
Hamlet, I 54b–56a
Haydn, I 57a–58a
Homer, I 49b
Isaiah (Bible), I 51b
Jesus Christ, I 51b
Joseph (Bible), I 52a
Judaism, I 51a–52a
Leeuwenhoek, I 57a
Leonardo da Vinci, I 56a–
56b
Montaigne, I 54a
Moses (Bible), I 51b
music, I 57a–58a
Newton, I 58b
oracular utterances, I 49a
painting, I 56a–57a
Panofsky, I 52a–52b
Philo Judaeus, I 51a, 52a,
54a
Pindar, I 49a–50a
poetry, I 49a–50a, 54b–
56a, 58a–58b
Polanyi, I 59b

Rabelais, I 54a
Renaissance, I 54b–56a,
58a–58b
riddles, I 49a
Rome (ancient), I 50b–51a,
51b
science, I 54a–54b, 58a
Scientific Revolution, I 54a–
54b, 58a
Sewell, I 59b
Shakespeare, I 54b–56a
Solomon, I 52a
Sophists, I 50b
typology, I 51a–51b
Vergil, I 50b–51a, 53b–54a
Virgin Mary (Bible), I 52b–
53a
Zola, I 55a
Ambition
freedom, II 242a
human nature, III 576a
progress, III 631a, 639b
Ambrose, Saint (340?–397),
Adam (Bible), III 583b
Christianity, I 378b; III
589a–589b
dignity, IV 138a, 139a, 140a
Eve (Bible), III 583b
God, III 589b
knowledge, III 589b
mythology, III 288a
natural law, III 17b
Nature, III 589b
perfectibility, III 467a
philanthropy, III 489a
predestination, II 26b
primitivism, III 583b, 584a,
589a–589b
Saint Augustine and, III
589b
socialism, IV 286a
temperance, IV 370b, 372b
vice, III 589b
American Association for the
Advancement of Science, I
475b
American Association for
Higher Education, I 13b
American Association of University Professors, academic
freedom, I 11a–16b
American Civil Liberties Union,
I 13b
American Civil War, III 225b,
450a
American Council on Education, I 14b–15b
American Missionary Association, I 436b
American Oriental Society, III
434b
American Peace Society, III
448b, 453a

American Revolution
  crisis in history, I 590a, 593a
  democracy, I 656a, 658b–660b
  economic history, II 45a
  equality, II 143a, 145a
  Great Britain, I 658b–660b
  international peace, III 453a
  law, III 7b
  perfectibility, III 472a
  private property, III 654b
  revolution, IV 155b–156a, 156b, 160b
  social contract, IV 252a, 260b
  war, III 453a
American Society of International Law, III 451a
American Society for Judicial Settlement of International Disputes, III 451a
American Society for the Prevention of Cruelty to Animals (A.S.P.C.A.), IV 388a
Ames, E. S., God, II 359a
Ames, Van Meter, Buddhism, I 256b
Ames, William, casuistry, I 263a
Amici, Giovan Battista (1786?–1863), microscope, III 415b
Amino acid sequences, I 239a, 239b–241b, 245b–246a
Amitābha Buddha, I 248b
Am-mut (myth), IV 225b
Amos (Bible)
  metaphor, III 202a
  philanthropy, III 487b
  prophecy, III 661b, 663a
Ampère, A. M. (1775–1836), classification of the sciences, I 465a, 465b
Ampère, J. J. (1800–1864), literature, III 84a
  romanticism, IV 201a
Amphinomus (legend), law, II 676a
Amphion (myth), music, III 266a
Amulets, mythology, III 287b
Anabaptists
  Bible, I 390b
  Christianity, III 670b
  class, I 442b
  city-state, I 395a
  communism, IV 287a
  equality, II 142a, 142b
  eschatology, II 156b–157a
  heresy, II 425b, 426a, 427b
  love, III 107b
  millenarianism, III 225a
  polygamy, IV 287a

progress, III 635b
protest movements, III 670b
Reformation, IV 67b
socialism, IV 287a
Anabiosis, prolongevity, III 92a
Anacharsis (fl. 600 B.C.), Nature, III 348b
  primitivism, III 591b, 592a
Anacreon (572?–?488 B.C.), law, II 681a
Anacreontea, *ut pictura poesis*, IV 471a
Analogy
  Abélard, I 65b–66a
  Aesop, I 68b
  Alcmaeon, I 62b
  Alexander the Great, I 68b
  Aristophanes, I 68a
  Aristotle, I 61b, 62a, 62b, 63b, 66a, 68a; III 189b–190a
  Bacon, Francis, I 76b, 77b
  biology, I 241b–242a
  body politic, I 67a–69b
  Boethius, I 65a, 67a
  Calvin, I 70a
  Carlyle, I 70a
  Christianity, I 64a–67a, 68b–69b, 70a
  Cicero, I 68b
  Clement of Alexandria, I 64a
  cosmos, I 60b–63a, 65h
  Dante, I 64a, 65b
  Demosthenes, I 68b
  Denis, I 64b, 65b
  Duns Scotus, I 67a
  Eckhart, I 67a
  Empedocles, I 60b–61a, 62a
  Erigena, I 65b
  Eudoxus of Cnidos, I 63a
  Fortescue, I 69a
  free will, II 246b–247a
  Greece (ancient), I 60a–63b, 68a–68b
  harmony, II 389a
  Heraclitus, I 61a–61b
  Hippocrates, I 61b–62a
  Hugh of St. Victor, I 65b
  hylozoism, I 61b, 68a, 70a
  iconoclasts, I 65a–65b
  India, I 68a
  John of Salisbury, I 69a
  language, II 664b, 665a, 671b
  law, III 29b
  Livy, I 69b
  logic, I 63a–63b
  Macrobius, I 65b
  macrocosm and microcosm, I 27b, 28a, 29a
  matter, III 189b
  metaphor, III 198b, 205b, 206a, 207a
  metaphysical imagination,

III 209a, 216b
  methodology, III 379b
  Middle Ages, I 65b–67a, 69a
  Milton, I 69b
  music, II 389a
  mythology, III 273a, 273b, 274a
  necessity, III 361a, 361b
  Newton, III 379b
  Nicholas of Cusa, I 67a
  Origen, I 64a
  Parmenides, I 60b
  patristic period, I 64a–65b, 68b–69a
  Philip II, I 68b
  Philo Judaeus, I 64a, 68b
  philosophy, III 198b
  Plato, I 61a, 62a–63b, 68a; III 273b
  Plotinus, I 64b
  Plutarch, I 69b
  political images, I 60a–61b
  predication, I 66b
  Proclus, I 64b
  rationalism, IV 46b
  Saint Augustine, I 64b–65a, 68b–69a
  Saint Bonaventure, I 66a–66b
  Saint John Damascene, I 65a
  Saint Paul, I 68b, 69a
  Saint Thomas Aquinas, I 66a, 66b–67a, 69a; III 206a
  Seneca, I 68b
  Shakespeare, I 69b
  social images, I 60a–61b
  Socrates, I 68b
  Spengler, III 361a
  State, I 67b–70b
  technological images, I 60b, 62a
  vitalism, I 60b, 61b–62a
  Xenophon, I 68b
Ananke (myth), III 272b
Ananus, I 413b
Anarcho-communism, I 71b–72a
Anarchy, I 70a–76b
  Aeschylus, IV 366b
  agriculture, III 674a
  American Declaration of Independence, I 74a
  American Indians, I 71a
  artists, I 71b
  Bakunin, I 71b, 74a–74b, 75a
  Bentham, I 437b
  bureaucracy, III 673b
  collectivism, I 71b
  Christianity, I 72a
  civil disobedience, I 435a, 436b

democracy, I 656b, 664b
Diderot, I 71a
dualism, II 40a
economic history, II 59a, 59b
education, I 71b
Engels, I 72b
equality, II 145b, 147b
ethics, III 445a, 446a
evolution, IV 180b
federalism, I 72b
Fourier, I 73a
freedom, III 470a
freedom of speech, II 256b
Gandhi, I 72a
general will, II 280b
Godwin, I 72b–73a
good, III 470a; IV 180b
Hegel, I 74a
Henry, Emil, I 72a
Hobbes, I 656b
Humboldt, I 71a
Hume, I 437b
ideology, III 674a
individualism, I 71b; II 594b, 595a, 597b
industry, III 673b
Kropotkin, I 71b–72a, 74b–75a, 75b
Lahontan, I 71a
law, II 688a; III 20a
liberalism, I 71a. III 51b, 56b, 58a, 58b
Lorenz, Konrad, I 74b
loyalty, III 112a
Malatesta, I 74b–75a
Marx, I 72b, 74b, 409a; IV 162a
Marxism, III 160b
morality, III 470a
Mumford, I 75b
Mussolini, III 597a
Nature, III 348b
New Left, I 160a–161a
Nietzsche, IV 485a
organization, III 673b
Owen, I 73a
peace, III 445a, 446a
perfectibility, III 470a–471a
Plato, I 71a
primitivism, III 597a, 597b
progress, III 638a, 641a
Proudhon, I 73a–73b, 74a; II 280b
revisionism, IV 271a
revolution, IV 152b, 157b, 158b, 162a, 165a, 166b
right, IV 180b
romanticism, IV 202b
Rome (ancient), II 688a
Russian Revolution (October 1917), I 75a
Shelley, I 73a

Social Darwinism, I 70a–70b

socialism, I 72a–72b; IV 290a

society, III 470a, 470b–471a, 673b

Spain, III 674a, 676b

Spanish Civil War, I 75a–75b

Spencer, I 70a–70b

Stalin, I 75a

State, III 470a–470b, 673b

Stirner, I 73b

temperance, IV 366b

theorists. I 72a–75b

Thompson, William, I 73a

Thoreau, I 72a, 436b

Tolstoy, I 72a

trends, I 71b–72a

Tucker, I 73b–74a

U.S., I 74a

Vaillant, Auguste, I 72a

Victorianism, IV 223b

violence, I 72a; III 673b

virtù, IV 485a–485b

Warren, Josiah, I 74a

Zeno of Citium, I 71a

Anatolia (ancient), God, II 333b

Anatomy
evolutionism, II 177a, 179b
linguistics, II 427b
macrocosm and microcosm, III 126a, 128b
Man-Machine, III 132b, 135a–135b
medicine, II 400b, 401a–401b, 404a
naturalism in art, III 340a–340b
phrenology, IV 23b
rationalism, IV 48a
recapitulation, IV 56b–57a
Renaissance, IV 440a
revolution, IV 155b
uniformitarianism, IV 427b
universal man, IV 440a

Anaxagoras (500?–428 B.C.),
analogy, I 60b, 63b
atomism, I 126b–127a, 128b
biology, I 231b, 233b, 234a
causation, I 271a
conservation, I 472a
cosmos, I 539a; III 573b; IV 3a, 50a
culture, I 609a, 610b
cynicism, I 631a
Democritus and, IV 3a
design argument, I 671a, 671b
dualism, II 40b; IV 346b
Empedocles and, IV 3a
freedom of speech, II 258b

human nature, III 573b, 574b, 575a, 575b

impiety, II 565b

intelligence, III 626b

matter, III 187a

metaphor, III 203a, 203b

mind, IV 50a

natural law, III 15a

nous, IV 3a

pangenesis, II 622b

Plato and, IV 34a

progress, III 626b, 627a

psychology, IV 3a

Pythagoreans, IV 34a

rationalism, IV 48b, 50a

realism, IV 3a

religion, III 203a, 203b; IV 93a

skepticism, IV 234b

Socrates and, I 671a

space, IV 297a

symmetry, IV 346b

theriophily, IV 385b

time, IV 390a

Anaxarchos (fl. about 350 B.C.)
Buddhism, I 254b
skepticism, IV 234a, 234b

Anaximander (611–547 B.C.),
analogy, I 60b–61a, 63a
apeiron, IV 298a
Aristotle and, I 671a
causation, I 271a, 290b
conservation, I 472a
continuity, I 502b
cosmos, III 573b
design argument, I 670b–671a
dualism, IV 346b
harmony, IV 38b
historiography, I 502b; II 499a
human nature, III 573b
infinity, II 604b, 605a, 608b, 609a
justice, I 290b; II 653a
law, II 677a
mythology, III 273a
perfectibility, III 464a
Pythagoreans, IV 38b
rationalism, IV 46b
space, IV 297a, 298a
spontaneous generation, IV 307b
symmetry, IV 346b, 348a
theodicy, IV 380a
time, IV 390a
universe, IV 38b

Anaximenes (6th century B.C.),
analogy, I 61b, 62a
causation, I 271a
continuity, I 502b
cynicism, I 628a–628b
design argument, I 671b
evolutionism, II 175a

historiography, I 502b

human nature, III 574a

matter, III 186b

mythology, III 273a

psychology, IV 2a

rationalism, IV 46b, 47a

spontaneous generation, IV 307b

Ancestor worship
China, I 360b, 362a
China (ancient), II 344b
Leibniz, I 360b
mythology, III 309a
Orientalism, III 434a
religion, IV 93a

Anchorites, I 377b–378a

Ancients and moderns, I 76b–87b
Bacon, Francis, and Descartes, I 76b–77b
eighteenth century, I 76b–87b
Encyclopédie, I 77b
Paine, Tom, I 77b
Renaissance, I 77b

Andocides (b. 440 B.C.), law, II 680b

André, Père (1675–1764)
beauty, I 198a, 198b
Diderot and, I 199b
genius, II 294a
Newton and, I 198a

Andreae, Johann
Campanella and, IV 461b–462a
Utopia, IV 461b–462a

Andreas of Isernin (d. 1316), heresy, II 425a

Andreski, S., war, IV 507a

Androcentrism, women, IV 524a, 524b, 525b, 527a

Andromache (myth)
neo-classicism in art, III 368a, 368b
temperance, IV 365b

Angell, James R. (1869–1949), I 116b; IV 27b

Angell, Norman, war, IV 507a–507b

Angelo of Clareno, III 668b, 669a

Angels
children, III 595b
demonology, I 667b, 669a, 669b
dignity, IV 138b, 140b, 141a, 146a
fortune, fate and chance, II 232b–233a
Gnosticism, II 329a, 330b
harmony, II 393b, 394a, 394b; IV 40b–41a
hierarchy, II 435b, 439b, 441b

humanism, IV 132a

love, III 101b

millenarianism, III 223b

music, II 393b, 394a, 394b; III 265a, 265b, 266a, 269a, 269b, 270a, 270b; IV 40b–41a

mythology, III 277b, 280a, 282b

Nature, III 346b, 347b

Platonism, III 510b, 512a

Pomponazzi, II 36b, 37a

primitivism, III 582b, 595b

prophecy, III 657b, 658a, 666b, 668b

Pseudo-Dionysius, I 668a–668b

psychology, IV 16a

Pythagoreans, IV 40b–41a

Renaissance, IV 132a, 138b, 140b, 141a, 146a

Saint Augustine, IV 138b

Saint Thomas Aquinas, I 669b; IV 140b

sin, I 669b

universe, IV 40b–41a

witchcraft, IV 521b, 523a

work, IV 533b

Angelus Silesius (1624–1677)
baroque in literature, I 193a
eschatology, II 158a
Islam, II 651a

Anglicanism
Berkeley, IV 20a
Calvinism, IV 20a
Church, I 418a
idealism, IV 20a
Johnson, IV 19b–20a
psychology, IV 16b, 19b–20a
Puritanism, IV 19b

Anglicus, Bartholomaeus, music, II 388a

Animals
acquired characteristics, II 617b
art, III 596a
behaviorism, I 220b–221b; II 584b–585a, 585b, 586a
biology, III 596a
Cartesianism, III 596a
catastrophism, IV 418b, 419b, 420a, 421b
children, III 596a
conservation, I 472b–473a, 474a, 475b, 476a
culture, III 596a
cynicism, III 585b
Diogenes of Sinope, III 596a
ethics, IV 319b
evolution, III 596a
game theory, II 262a–273b

Germany, III 651b
human nature, III 573b, 574b
Humane Societies, IV 388a
intelligence, III 596a
law, II 677a, 682a, 682b; III 33a
linguistics, IV 425b, 427b
Machiavelli, IV 480b, 481b–482a
macrocosm and microcosm, III 126a, 127a, 128b
metaphor, III 198b
Middle Ages, III 596a
Montaigne, III 594b
music, III 265a, 266b, 268a–268b
Mussolini, III 597a
mythology, III 273b, 275a, 279b, 280a, 296a, 303b, 308a–309a, 309b, 310a, 310b, 315a, 317b
natural law, III 14b, 18b, 19b
Nature, III 347b, 348b, 349a, 596a
Nazis, III 597a
philanthropy, III 491a
philosophy, III 198b
Platonism, III 510a
poetry, II 87b
primitivism, III 578a, 580b, 581b, 583b, 585b, 594b, 596a, 597a, 597b, 599b, 604a, 605a
private property, III 650b, 651a, 651b, 655a
progress, III 627a, 627b
prophecy, III 665a
psychology, IV 5a, 6b, 10a, 11a, 14b–15a, 17a, 17b, 20a, 25a, 25b, 28a
Pythagoreans, IV 31a, 31b, 33a
recapitulation, IV 56b–57a, 59a
religion, IV 95a–95b, 96a, 100a, 107b
Renaissance, III 596a
rights, III 596a
Rousseau, III 599b
sex, III 596a
soul, II 390b, 391a; III 596a
Stoicism, IV 319b
suffering, IV 415b
symbolism, IV 338b
temperance, IV 370a, 371b, 373a, 377a–377b
territorial imperative, III 597b
theriophily, IV 384a–389a
uniformitarianism, IV 418b,
419b, 420a, 421b, 425b, 427b
U.S.S.R., III 655a
virtù, IV 480b, 481b–482a
war, III 596a
See also Theriophily
Animism
anthropomorphism, I 87b–91a
dualism, II 38b
empathy, II 87b
metaphor, III 198b
mythology, III 308a–310b, 315a, 317b
Platonism, III 510a
poetry, II 87b
religion, IV 95a–95b, 96a
Annals
Assyria (ancient), II 465b–466a
China (ancient), II 480a
Egypt (ancient), II 465a
historiography, II 465b–466a, 468b, 469a, 469b, 474a, 474b, 475a, 476a, 476b, 480a, 481b, 482a, 484a, 496b
Hittites, II 465b
Rome (ancient), II 468b
Anne, Queen (1665–1714), periodization in literary history, III 483a
Annensky, Innokenty, symbolism, IV 343b
Annius of Viterbo, historiography, II 485b
Anomalism, language, II 664b, 671b
Anomie, II 565a
Anouilh, Jean (1910–   ), comedy, I 469b
Anquetil-Duperron, Abraham-Hyacinthe (1731–1805), despotism, II 13a–13b, 17a
Montesquieu and, II 13a
Oriental thought, III 428a, 429a
Anselm, Saint (1033–1109), appearance and reality, I 95a
causation, I 273b
chance images, I 342b
Creation, I 573a
design argument, I 672b
God, I 573a, 672b; II 343a
ontological argument, II 546b
primitivism, III 591a
Anselmi, Giorgio, Pythagorean cosmos, IV 41a
Anstruther-Thompson, C., empathy, II 86b
Anthony, Saint (c. 250–350), as an anchorite, I 378a

freedom of speech, II 262a
Anthony, Susan B. (1820–1906), women, IV 526b
Anthropocentrism, I 88a–88b
Aristotle, I 88a, 88b
Boyle, I 88a
Bruno, III 510a
Ficino, III 510a
mythology, III 274a
Anthropology
Aeschylus, III 625a, 625b
Aristotle, III 354a
beauty, I 213b–214a
Boas, Franz, III 153b
Counter-Enlightenment, II 103a
dignity, IV 138b, 139b, 145a, 145b
dualism, II 38a
Engels, III 153b
Enlightenment, II 90a, 97a–97b, 100a
ethics, III 443a; IV 70b, 71a
evolutionism, II 186b, 187a
Greece (ancient), IV 96b
individualism, II 603b
Islam, II 651a
law, III 28b
Lévi-Strauss, IV 324a–327b
Locke, III 598b
Marx, II 450a–450b, 451a, 454a
Marxism, III 153b, 168a
materialism, II 450a–450b, 451a, 454a
metaphysical imagination, III 210a
Morgan, Lewis, III 153b
motif, III 238a, 238b, 240a–240b
mythology, III 279a, 308a, 309a, 310b, 311a, 312b, 316a, 316b–317b
necessity, III 352b, 354a, 357a, 362a
Oriental scholarship, III 435a
peace, III 443a
Posidonius, III 630b
primitivism, III 598b
progress, III 625a, 625b, 626b, 627a–627b, 629a, 629b, 630b
psychology, IV 14a, 15b, 29a; II 384a
Ramism, IV 45b
recapitulation, IV 58a
relativism, IV 70b, 71a
religion, IV 95a, 95b, 96a, 96b, 97a, 107b
Renaissance, IV 138b, 139b, 145a, 145b
romanticism, IV 201b, 202b

satire, IV 212a
Saussure, IV 324a
structuralism, III 316b–317b; IV 323a–327a, 329b
symbolism, IV 341a
Volksgeist, IV 496a
war, IV 508a
witchcraft, IV 522b
women, IV 523b, 525b
Anthropomorphism, I 87b–91a
animism, I 87b
Bacon, Francis, I 88b
characteristics of, I 87b–88a
defined, I 87a
Einstein, I 90a
Faraday, I 90a
Galileo, I 89b
Gassendi, I 85b
Gilbert, William, I 89a
Greece (ancient), II 652b
Helmholtz, I 89b
justice, II 652b
metaphor, III 202b, 206a
mythology, III 273a, 278a
Newton, I 89a–89b
parochialism, I 88b, 90a
perfectibility, III 464a
picture theory of language, I 90a
psychology, IV 14b
religion, III 202b, 206a; IV 92b
Stoics, I 89a
symbolism, IV 338b
Tyndall, I 89b
Wittgenstein, I 90a
Antichrist
Franciscans, II 421b
heresy, II 418a, 419a, 421b
millenarianism, III 224a, 224b, 225a
mythology, III 276b
papacy, I 390a; III 225a
prophecy, III 664b–666a, 667a–669b
socialism, IV 286b
Anticlericalism, IV 120b
France, III 538a
intolerance, IV 120b
Mexico, III 544a
protest movements, III 670b
Antigone (myth)
law, II 683a
loyalty, III 110b
Sophocles, IV 367a
tragic sense, IV 412b
Anti-industrialism
Christianity, III 676a
class, III 676a
liberalism, III 676a
Luddism, III 676a
Nazism, III 676a
Nietzsche, III 676a

protest movements, III 676a
romanticism, III 676a
socialism, III 676a
student unrest, III 676a
violence, III 676a
Anti-intellectualism
academic freedom, I 16a
Christianity, III 590b–591a
Freud, III 597a
Middle Ages, III 590b–591a, 595a
Montaigne, III 595a
primitivism, III 582b, 587a, 590b, 595a, 597a, 599b, 604a
Rousseau, III 595b, 599b
Saint Bernard, III 591a
Antilochus (myth), law, II 676b
Antimatter
space, IV 297a
symmetry, IV 351a
Antiochus of Ascalon (1st century B.C.)
Neo-Platonism, III 372a
skepticism, IV 234a
Antiochus Epiphanes (d. 163 B.C.), I 52a
Antiochus VI (d. 142 B.C.), impiety, II 566a
Antipater
skepticism, IV 239b
temperance, IV 369b
Antiphon (fl. 5th century B.C.),
Counter-Enlightenment, II 101a
cynicism, I 629a, 629b, 631a
human nature, III 575a, 575b–576a
justice, III 575b–576a
morality, I 629b
rationalism, IV 48b
work, IV 530b
Antiprimitivism
biology, III 604a
Blacks, III 604a
Bosman, III 604a
climate, III 604a
Cook, III 604a
Falconer, III 604a
Goldsmith, III 604a
Hottentots, III 604b, 605a
Ignoble (Ugly) Savage, III 604a–605a
Johnson, III 604b
Lessing, III 604b
literature, III 604a
Ovington, III 604b
Petty, III 604b
Polyphemus (myth), III 604a
Shakespeare, III 604a
slavery, III 604a

Thicknesse, III 604a
Voltaire, III 604b–605a
Anti-Semitism
communism, III 157b
conservatism, I 483a
intolerance, IV 114a
Judaism, IV 114a
millenarianism, III 225a
protest movements, III 672a, 674a
religion, IV 114a
See also Nazism
Antisthenes (444?–after 371 B.C.)
Alain of Lille and, III 590b
cynicism, I 627b–631a, 632a–633b; III 585a, 590b
morality, I 629b
mythology, III 273b
pacifism, I 630b–631a
pain, I 632a–632b
Plato and, I 630a; III 518a
pleasure, II 375b
primitivism, III 585a, 590b
temperance, IV 367a
Antonelli, G., utility, IV 456b, 457a
Antoninus, Saint (1389–1459)
art, II 305a
casuistry, I 261b–262a
Anu (myth), II 335b
Anubis (myth)
religion, IV 104b
judgment, IV 225b
Anxiety
Fromm, II 384a
mental health, II 384a
Niebuhr, Reinhold, III 467a
perfectibility, III 465a, 467a
pleasure, II 383b, 384a
progress, III 630a
Anytus, cycles, I 623a–623b
Apeiron
Anaximander, IV 298a
Aristotle, IV 298a
Greece (ancient), II 604b, 605a, 607a–607b
infinity, II 604b, 605a, 607a–607b, 608b, 609b; IV 298a
matter, IV 298a
Apelles (4th century B.C.),
chance images, I 341a
creativity in art, I 582a
genius, II 299a, 299b
neo-classicism in art, III 365b
Aphrodite (myth), II 333b; III 272b, 496b
cynicism, III 585b
human nature, III 571b, 572b
law, II 681a

love, III 94b, 95a
macrocosm and microcosm, III 126b
primitivism, III 585b
religion, IV 93a
Aphtonius, rhetoric, IV 468b
Apianus, Petrus (1501?–1552), cosmology, I 545a, 549a; II 436b, 437a
Apocalypse
Christianity, III 223b–224a
eschatology, II 154b–155a
Ezra, III 224a
Germany, I 391a
heresy, II 420b, 421b
Judaism, III 223b–224a
literature, III 202b
millenarianism, III 223b–224a, 224b
mythology, III 277a, 283b, 304a
prophecy, III 664a–669b
reformation, IV 61a, 65a, 66a
socialism, IV 286a, 288a, 293b
Apollinaire, Guillaume (1880–1918), ut pictura poesis, IV 471a
Apollo (myth), III 272b, 274a, 282b, 289a, 292a, 294a, 296b, 305b, 500b
disease, II 397b
hubris, IV 366a
law, II 675b, 682b
metaphor, III 203b
morality, IV 365b–366a
music, III 268b
poetics, III 530a
Pythagoras, IV 31a, 35a
religion, III 203b
temperance, IV 365b, 366a, 367a
tragic sense, IV 415a
Apollodorus (fl. 5th century B.C.)
creativity in art, I 582a
mythology, III 289b
Apollonius, (1st century B.C.),
infinity, II 611a
mathematics, III 178b, 182b, 183a
space, IV 295a
Spengler, III 251a
Apollonius Dyscolus (fl. c. 180 A.D.), language, II 664b, 665a, 665b
Apollonius of Perga (3rd century B.C.)
cosmology, I 541a
Halley and, III 380b
mathematics, III 380a
methodology, III 380a
science, II 203a

Apollonius of Tyana (1st century A.D.)
alchemy, I 29b
Buddhism, I 254b
Apologism
aging, III 89b
Aristotle, III 90a
Avicenna, III 90a
Bible, III 90a
Buddhism, III 90a
death, III 89b
disease, III 90a
Epicureanism, III 89b
Frazer, III 89b
Galen, III 90a
gerontology, III 89b–90a
Gilgamesh (myth), III 89b
Hesiod, III 89b
Hinduism, III 90a
Huxley, III 89b
Juvenal, III 89b
longevity, III 89a, 89b–90a, 92b
Lucretius, III 89b
Marcus Aurelius, III 89b
meliorism, III 89a
mythology, III 89b
Pandora (myth), III 89b
prolongevity, III 89b
Prometheus (myth), III 89b
religion, III 90a
Stoicism, III 89b
Swift, III 89b
Tennyson, III 89b
Tithonus (myth), III 89b
Vedanta, III 90a
Wilde, III 89b
Yoga, III 90a
Apophis (myth), II 38b, 335a, 335b
Apostasy
Calvin, IV 67b
God, II 337a
prophecy, III 661a, 662a, 662b
Reformation, IV 67b
Apostles
Christianity, III 591b
Nature, III 347a
primitivism, III 591b, 595a
Saint Bernard, III 591a
Apotelestic art, I 458a
Appearance and reality, I 94a–99b
atomism, I 94a
Beckett, I 98b–99a
Berkeley, I 97a–97b
Blake, I 97a
Bradley, F. H., I 94b
Broad, I 98a
Coleridge, I 97b
Deism, I 96a–97a, 98a
Democritus, III 187b–188b
Descartes, I 95a–95b

existentialism, I 98b
Hegel, I 94b, 98a–98b
human nature, III 575b
Husserl, I 98b
James, I 98a
Kant, I 97b–98a
Leibniz, I 95b
Locke, I 95b, 97b
Lucretius, I 94a
matter, III 187b, 188a, 188b, 190b, 192b
Moore, G. E., I 98a
Parmenides, I 94a, 94b, 95a, 95b, 96a, 99a
Plato, I 94a–95a, 97a–97b; III 188b
Plotinus, I 95a
Price, H. H., I 98a
Russell, Bertrand, I 98a
Saint Anselm, I 95a
Sartre, I 98b
Schiller, Friedrich, I 97b
skepticism, IV 236a–236b, 238b–239a, 246a
Socrates, I 94b
Spinoza, I 94a–98a
time, IV 394a, 394b
Wordsworth, I 96b–97a, 98a, 98b
Zeno of Citium, I 94a, 94b
Approval
  justice, III 232a, 232b
  moral sense, III 230a–234b
Apsu (myth), III 278a
Apuleius (2nd century A.D.),
  art, II 310a
  cynicism, I 630b
  dignity, IV 139a
  ekphrasis, IV 469a
  fate, II 228a, 232a
  humanism, III 292b
  mythology, III 291a, 296a
  religion, IV 93b
Aquhat (myth), III 281b
Aquila, Serafino dall', II 320a
Aquinas, Saint Thomas
  (1225?–1274)
  abstraction, I 5a–6a, 6b
  acquired characteristics, II 617b
  Acton and, I 382a
  aesthetics, II 218a
  alchemy, I 30b
  alienation, I 36a
  analogy, I 66a, 66b–67a, 69a; III 206a
  angels, I 669b; IV 140b
  Aristotelianism, II 210b–211a, 211b
  Aristotle and, I 259b–260a, 274b, 384b, 644a, 672b–673a; II 343a; III 19a; IV 432a, 434b, 435a, 525a–525b

art, III 227b
art and play, I 103a
atomism, I 496a
authority, I 148a
Bacon and, I 173b
beauty, I 197b–198a, 585b
Being, IV 432a
casuistry, I 259b–260a
causation, I 274b–275a, 292a; II 232a–233a
Chain of Being, I 326b
chance, I 336b, 338b; II 232a–233a
charity, II 210b–212a, 213a
choice, II 237b, 238a
Christianity, IV 114a
Church, I 417b
class, I 445b, 446a; III 11a
classification of the arts, I 458a
common nature, I 4a
constitutionalism, I 487b
Creation, I 574a–574b; IV 392a
creativity in art, I 585b; II 320a
cycles, IV 392a
death, I 644a–644b
demonology, I 669b
design argument, I 672b–673b, 674b
determinism, II 238a
dignity of man, IV 140b
discontinuity, I 496a
dualism, I 673a
education, II 74b, 81a
environment, II 120b, 127b, 129a, 129b
equality, III 11a; IV 525a
ethics, III 441a, 441b; IV 392a
evil, I 164b
evolution, III 19a
faith, II 210b–212a, 213a; IV 134b, 392a
Fall, III 466b
fate, II 232a–233a
Faust (legend), III 246b
fortune, II 232a–233a
free will, II 238a, 245a, 245b; IV 392a
friendship, II 210b–211a
genius, II 320a
God, I 260a, 274b–275a, 384b, 574a–574b, 585b, 669b, 673a–673b; II 201b, 211a, 232a–233a, 238a, 320a, 343a; III 466b–467a; IV 140b, 392a, 525a–525b
good, II 212a; IV 176b
grace, III 466b
Grotius and, III 20a
happiness, II 212a, 238a
heresy, II 425a

hierarchy, II 440b
hope, II 210b–212a, 213a
humanism, II 515a; IV 129b, 134a
iconography, II 536b
imagination, III 210a
immortality, I 644a–644b
imprinting, II 584a
individualism, II 598a
infinity, II 605b, 614b
Islam, II 644a, 645a, 645b, 649b, 651b
justice, II 655a, 656b–657a
knowledge, IV 432a
law, I 292a; III 11a, 19a
learning, II 584a
liberalism, III 37a
longevity, III 90a
loyalty, III 112b
Man-Machine, III 136a
matter, III 191b
metaphor, III 200a
metaphysics, III 210a; IV 432a
Middle Ages, I 66a, 66b–67a, 69a
mimesis, III 227b
mind, II 120b
morality, III 466b
Moses (Bible) and, III 466b–467a
mythology, III 288a
nationalism, III 323a
natural law, I 487b; III 19a, 20a, 23a
Nature, I 673a; III 19a, 227b
necessity, II 238a
occasionalism, I 496a
optics, III 408b, 410a
paganism, IV 114a
peace, III 441a, 441b
perfectibility, III 466b–467a, 467b
philosophy, III 200a
Plato and, I 259b, 673a
Platonism, II 210b
predestination, IV 392a
private property, III 654a
providence, II 232a, 232b
Pseudo-Dionysius and, III 467b
psychology, IV 16b, 17b, 18a
Puritanism, IV 16b, 18a
reason, III 19a; IV 134b
religion, IV 114a, 116a
resurrection, I 644a–644b
right, IV 176b
Roman Catholic Church, III 654a, 654b; IV 525a
Saint Augustine and, III 466b

Saint Paul and, III 466b–467a; IV 525b
scholasticism, I 383a, 384b, 406a
science, II 197a
sensation, II 120b
sin, I 669b; III 466b
slavery, II 213a
social contract, IV 253a
society, III 11a, 19a
soul, I 644a–644b; II 36b, 211a; III 191b
species, I 574a
spontaneous generation, IV 308b
stars, III 288a
supernaturalism, I 669b
temperance, IV 372b
theodicy, IV 380b, 381a, 382a
theriophily, IV 386b
time, IV 392a, 393b
unity of science, IV 432a, 434b, 435a, 436a
universal man, IV 441a
universality, IV 432a
universe, III 19a
value, IV 452a
virtue, I 259b; II 211a, 211b–212a; III 466b
women, IV 525a–525b
Arabia
  alchemy, III 91a
  Christianity, I 374b
  freedom of speech, II 254a
  health and disease, II 398b
  infinity, II 609b
  love, III 99b, 100b
  mathematics, III 181a, 184b–185a
Arator (fl. 6th century A.D.),
  poetics, III 528b
Aratus (c. 315–c. 245 B.C.),
  primitivism, III 579a, 579b, 580a, 585b
  progress, III 630a
Arbitration, international
  peace, III 449b–450b, 451b, 452b, 453b, 454a
Arbrissel, Robert d', love, III 98a, 99a, 99b, 100a
Arbuthnot, John (1667–1735)
  chance, I 337b–338a
  environment, II 129b
Arcesilaus (316–241 B.C.),
  Platonism, III 504a, 504b
  Pythagoreans, IV 37b
  skepticism, IV 234a–235b, 238b–241a
Archashir I (c. 226–241 A.D.), I 122b
Archebiosis, spontaneous generation, IV 311a, 311b

Archelaus (fl. 5th century B.C.),
  culture, I 609a
  human nature, III 575a
  natural law, III 16a
  progress, III 626b
Archeology
  art, II 535a
  Asia Minor, III 363a
  Castel de Guido, III 364a
  Gabii, III 364a
  God, II 331b–333a, 343b
  Greece, III 363a
  Hadrian's Villa, III 364a
  Hamilton, III 364a
  Herculaneum, III 363b,
  367b
  holy, II 513b
  humanism, II 516a
  iconography, II 535a
  linguistics, III 69a, 69b; IV
  430a
  mathematics, III 181a
  mimesis, III 229b
  Monte Cagnolo, III 364a
  mythology, III 274a, 274b,
  289b, 291b
  neo-classicism in art, III
  363a–364b, 367a, 368b
  Oriental scholarship, III
  435a
  Ostia, III 364a
  Paestum, III 365a, 365b,
  370b
  Pompeii, III 364a
  progress, III 648a
  religion, IV 97a, 98a–98b
  Schliemann, III 363a
  Tor Colombaro, III 364a
  uniformitarianism, IV 430a
Archilochus (7th century B.C.),
  law, II 674b, 679a
  satire, IV 212a
  skepticism, IV 234b
Archimedes (287?–212 B.C.),
  axiomatization, I 163b, 164b
  continuity, I 499b
  equilibrium, III 134a
  geometry, III 134a
  humanism, IV 133a
  infinity, II 609a–611a
  Islam, II 640b
  Man-Machine, III 134a–
  134b
  mathematics, III 178b,
  182b–184b
  matter, III 193b
  mechanics, II 197b, 203a,
  204b, 205a
  physics, III 134a
  pragmatism, III 555b
  progress, III 630a–630b,
  633a
  space, IV 295a, 295b

Architecture
  aesthetics, II 216a, 216b,
  217a, 218b, 221b, 224a
  art, I 456b, 457b–461b
  Austria, I 398b
  baroque, I 398b
  Boullée, III 366a
  censorship, III 499a
  China, I 355a, 363b
  Christianity, I 417b
  city, I 427a–434b
  creativity in art, I 581a
  culture, I 610b
  Doric order, III 365a, 366b,
  368b, 370b
  Egypt (ancient), III 365a
  ethics, II 372a–372b
  Germany, I 398b
  Goethe, II 371b
  Gothic, II 367a–374a
  Greece (ancient), I 428a;
  III 350b
  happiness, II 374b
  harmony, IV 41a–41b
  hierarchy, II 440b–441a,
  441b
  humanism, II 521b; IV
  133a
  impressionism, II 578a
  infinity, II 612b
  Italy, I 398b
  law, II 687a
  Ledoux, III 366a
  macrocosm and microcosm,
  III 130a
  mimesis, III 226a
  motif, III 237a, 238a
  music, III 265a, 266b, 270a
  mythology, III 283b, 288b,
  296b, 297a, 314a
  Nature, III 350b
  neo-classicism in art, III
  362b, 363a, 363b, 365a,
  365b, 366b, 367b, 368b,
  369b, 370a, 370b
  Palladio, II 218b
  Plato, I 457b, 581a; III
  497b, 498b, 499a; IV 41b
  Platonism, III 497b, 498b,
  499a
  Poland, I 398b
  Portugal, I 398b
  primitivism, III 588b
  progress, III 632b
  Pythagoreans, IV 41b
  rationalism, IV 46a
  Renaissance, IV 122b,
  123a, 124a, 127a, 133a,
  439b, 440a
  revolution, IV 165a, 165b
  Roman Catholic Church, I
  398b
  romanticism, IV 201a
  Seneca, III 588b

  Soane, III 366a
  space, IV 298b
  Spain, I 398b
  Spengler, IV 298b
  sublime in external nature,
  IV 334b
  temperance, IV 373a, 377a
  universal man, IV 439b,
  440a
  Vasari, II 367b–368a
  Vitruvius, II 217a
Archives, historiography, II
  475a, 476b, 479b–480a,
  486b, 493a–493b, 494b,
  496a, 496b
Archytas of Tarentum (fl. 400–
  365 B.C.)
  classification of the
  sciences, I 462b
  Great Year (myth), IV 400b
  harmony, IV 38a
  measurement, IV 400b
  Plato and, III 516a; IV 32b–
  33a
  Pythagoreans, IV 32b–33a,
  37a–37b, 38a
  time, IV 390b, 400b
Ardens, Radulphus, classification of the arts, I 459a
Arendt, Hannah, totalitarianism, IV 409b
Arendt, Karl, China, I 367b
Areopagus, the (myth), law,
  II 681a, 681b, 684b
Ares (myth), macrocosm and
  microcosm, III 126b
Aretaeus (fl. 1st to 2nd century A.D.), disease, II 398b
Aretino, Pietro (1492–1556),
  art, II 304b–305a, 308b
  genius, II 304b–305a, 308b,
  317b, 320a
  music, II 317b, 320a
  poetry, III 530b
Argand, J. R. (1768–1822),
  numbers, III 405b
Argentina
  nationalism, III 335b
  positivism, III 543b–544a
Argonauts, the (myth), III
  275b
  culture, I 608b
Argumentation
  common law, III 31a
  Greece (ancient), III 7a
  law, III 7a, 25a, 28a, 31a
  Ramism, IV 43a–43b
  Renaissance, IV 129a
  rhetoric, IV 167b–170b,
  172b
  skepticism, IV 235a–237a,
  239b, 245a
  Sophists, IV 49a
Ariadne (myth), III 272b, 291a

Arianism, I 377b, 379a
  heresy, II 417a
Ariosto, Lodovico (1474–
  1533)
  aesthetics, IV 354b
  baroque in literature, I 189a,
  190a
  Gothic, II 368b
  iconography, II 531a
  mythology, III 298a
  Platonism, III 514b
  poetics, III 531a
  romanticism, IV 187a,
  187b, 188a, 190b, 192a,
  193b
  taste, IV 354b
  ut pictura poesis, IV 468b,
  469a
  wisdom of the fool, IV 519b
Aristaeus the Elder, mathematics, III 380a
Aristarchus (fl. c. 100 B.C.),
  cosmology, I 543b, 544a
  language, II 664b
  literary criticism, I 596b
Aristides Quintilianus (4th
  century B.C.?)
  musical genius, II 313a
  Pythagorean cosmos, IV
  39a–40b
Aristippus (435?–356 B.C.),
  love, III 95b
  Plato and, III 516a, 518a
  pleasure, II 375b, 378a
Aristocles, skepticism, IV 238a
Aristocracy
  Aristotle, II 259a
  art, II 570a, 578b, 581b
  Cicero, I 655a, 655b
  Counter-Enlightenment, II
  107a
  de Staël, II 14a–14b
  deism, I 647b, 649a
  democracy, I 654a, 655a,
  656b, 657a, 659b
  despotism, II 1a, 6a, 8a–
  8b, 11a–11b, 14a–14b
  elective, II 11a–11b
  Enlightenment, II 91a, 94a,
  97b
  equality, II 143b, 146b
  Fénelon, II 8b
  freedom of speech, II 253b,
  254a, 259a, 259b, 260b–
  261a
  general will, II 276a
  genius, II 320b
  good, IV 175a, 180b
  Gothic, II 369b
  Greece (ancient), II 675a
  hereditary, II 11a–11b
  historiography, II 468b,
  469b, 470a
  Hobbes, I 656b; II 6a

humanism, II 519b
impressionism, II 570a, 578b, 581b
law, II 675a, 687b, 690a; III 28b–29a
mercantile, II 254a
Mill, J. S. I 154a
music, II 320b
natural, II 11a
painting, II 570a, 578b, 581b
Plato, IV 175a
Platonism, III 505b, 520b
Polybius, I 625b, 626a
pragmatism, III 553b–554a
Renaissance, IV 441b
revolution, IV 152b, 154b, 161a
right, IV 175a, 180b
romanticism, IV 207a
Rome (ancient), II 260b–261a, 468b, 687b, 690a; IV 154b
Rousseau, II 11a–11b; III 276a
Saint-Pierre, II 11a
Santayana, III 553b–554a
universal man, IV 441b
Victorianism, IV 218a, 218b, 220a–220b
Voltaire, II 11a
war, IV 501b, 504b
work, IV 530b
Aristodemus, theriophily, IV 385b
Ariston of Chios, temperance, IV 369b
Aristophanes (448–?380 B.C.), allegory, I 42a
ambiguity, I 50b
analogy, I 68a
comedy, I 468b, 469a
education, II 80a, 80b
freedom of speech, II 259b, 260a
historiography, II 506a
human nature, III 574a, 575b, 576a
irony, II 630b
law, II 681a, 682b, 684b; III 576a
love, III 95a
mythology, III 275b
peace, III 440a
periodization in literary history, III 481b
Platonism, III 496a, 497b, 512a, 524a
rationalism, IV 48b
religion, IV 100a
satire, IV 212b, 214a, 214b, 215b
Socrates and, IV 48b
theriophily, IV 385b

Utopia, IV 464a
Aristophanes of Byzantium (257?–?180 B.C.), linguistics, III 62b
Aristotelianism
aesthetics, II 220a–220b, 222b
Augustinianism, IV 109a
Bruno, III 194a
catharsis, III 500b
cosmic images, I 515a
Cynicism, III 585b
dignity, IV 139b, 140b, 141b, 146a
double truth, II 32a, 34b, 36a, 36b, 37b
empiricism, III 20a
Enlightenment, II 90a, 94a
equality, II 138b
ethics, IV 320b, 322a
faith, hope, and charity, II 210b–211b
fortune, fate, and chance, II 229b–231b, 232b, 233a, 234a
free will, II 245a
friendship, II 210b–211a
Gnosticism, II 329b
God, II 347a–347b, 363a
good, II 231b; IV 176b
harmony, II 389b
Hegel, II 454a
heresy, II 418a, 427a
historiography, II 468a, 471b, 488a, 509a
humanism, II 520a, 521a, 521b; IV 130a, 131b, 132a, 133a, 134a, 134b, 135a
iconography, II 526b, 532b
idea, II 545a, 547a
imitation, II 306a
Islam, II 641a, 642b, 643b, 646a, 646b, 647b, 650a
language, II 666b
law, III 1b
literary criticism, I 597b, 604a
literature, IV 330b
Man-Machine, III 133b, 135a, 137a
materialism, II 454a
mathematics, III 174a
matter, III 190b, 191b, 192a, 192b, 194a, 194b, 196a
mechanics, II 199a, 199b, 201b, 205a
metaphor, III 198b
metaphysical imagination, III 211b, 215a
Middle Ages, II 666b
mimesis, III 227b–228a, 229a, 229b
modernism, I 422b

music, II 389b
natural law, III 14a, 19b, 20a, 23a
natural rights, III 17a
necessity, III 354b, 355a, 355b
Newton, III 194b
numbers, III 406a
organicism, III 422a, 422b, 424b, 425a, 426b
perennial philosophy, III 458b, 459b
periodization in history, III 480b
Platonism, III 500b, 510a, 513a, 514a, 520a
Plotinus, III 423b
poetics, III 529a–529b, 531a
pragmatism, III 554b, 567a
primitivism, III 585a, 585b
progress, III 633a
psychology, IV 6b, 16b
Puritanism, IV 16b
Ramus, IV 42b, 43a, 44b
rationalism, IV 51a
religion, IV 109a
Renaissance, IV 130a, 131b, 132a, 133a, 134a, 134b, 135a, 139b, 140b, 141b, 146a
right, IV 176b
Saint Thomas Aquinas, II 210b–211a, 211b
science, II 196a, 203b
self-sufficiency, III 585a
skepticism, IV 243b, 244a, 244b
space, IV 304b
Stoicism, IV 320b, 322a
Strato, IV 6b–7a
style, IV 330b
temperance, IV 369a
time, IV 392a, 392b
women, IV 525a, 525b
Aristotle (384–322 B.C.)
abstraction, I 1a–2b, 3a, 3b, 5a, 6b; III 190a
acquired characteristics, II 617b–618a, 623a, 623b
aesthetics, I 463a; II 216b, 217a, 222a, 222b
alchemy, I 28a, 29b, 30a, 30b
Alexander of Aphrodisias and, III 380b–381a
analogy, I 61b, 62a, 62b, 63b, 66a, 68a; III 189b–190a
Anaximander and, I 671a
anthropocentrism, I 88a, 88b
anthropology, III 354a
apeiron, IV 298a

apologism, III 90a
Archytas and, IV 33a
aristocracy, II 259a
art, II 299b, 309a, 309b; III 189a, 226b, 227a, 365b–366a; IV 50b
art and play, I 100b, 101a–102b
artists, I 578a
atomism, I 127a–131a, 132b, 133a, 134b, 136a, 495a–495b; IV 390b
authority, I 148a
Avicenna and, I 4a
axiomatization, I 163a, 164a, 164b
Bacon and, I 173b; III 355b; IV 432a
beauty, I 196b, 200b, 578b, 580b, 583b, 584b; II 217a; III 226b
behaviorism, I 214a–216a, 228a; IV 5a, 49b
Being, III 189b; IV 431b, 432a
biology, I 230a, 231a, 231b–236a; II 623a; III 354a; IV 4b
body, IV 4b, 5b, 6b
Burke and, III 229b
Campanella and, IV 461b
casuistry, III 15b
catastrophes, III 628b
catharsis, I 102a, 264b–270a; IV 411b, 412a
causation, I 271b, 272a–272b, 273b, 274a, 274b, 275a, 286b, 287a, 288a, 288b, 289a, 290b, 300b, 301a, 302a–302b, 303b; II 230b, 233a, 282a; III 195a; IV 307b
Chain of Being, I 326a
chance, I 336a, 339b; II 226a, 227a, 227b–228a, 228b, 229b, 231b, 233a
chance images, I 341b
change, III 189b, 190a; IV 390b
chaos, III 15b
choice, II 237a
chora, IV 299b, 301b
Cicero and, IV 169a
city, I 428a
city-state, III 629b
class, I 443a, 443b, 444a, 449a
classicism, I 453a
classification, I 233a–233b, 456b–458a, 463a, 465b
climate, II 3a
cognition, I 1b–2b
comedy, I 467b, 468a; II 169b, 506a; III 528a

commodities, **IV** 451b–452a

common sense, **IV** 6a

communism, **IV** 285b

constitutionalism, **I** 487a, 488b

contemplation, **III** 465a

continuity, **I** 492b–493a, 495a–495b, 498a, 499a, 501a, 501b, 502b–503b

conventionalism, **III** 75b

Cosmic Fall, **I** 505b

cosmic images, **I** 515b, 516a–516b

cosmology, **I** 540a–541a, 543a, 544a, 545a, 546b, 622b; **III** 90a; **IV** 400b

cosmos, **II** 163a; **IV** 50b

Counter-Enlightenment, **II** 101a, 102b

craftsmanship, **III** 15b; **IV** 50b

Creation, **I** 585a

creativity in art, **I** 578a, 578b, 580a–580b, 583b, 584b–585b

culture, **I** 355a, 610b–611a, 611b, 612b; **III** 629b

custom, **III** 629b

cycles, **I** 621b, 622b, 623b, 625a–625b; **IV** 391a, 400b

Darwin and, **I** 676b

decision, **IV** 175b

deduction, **III** 380a

deism, **I** 647b

Demiurge, **I** 672b

democracy, **I** 625b, 653a–654b, 655a, 655b, 657a, 657b, 658a, 667a; **II** 249b; **III** 554a; **IV** 175b, 497a

Democritus and, **I** 495a, 495b; **II** 226a; **III** 189a

demonology, **I** 668a, 669b

Descartes and, **IV** 435b

design argument, **I** 671a, 672a–673a, 676b

desire, **IV** 5a, 5b

despotism, **II** 1b, 2a–3a, 4a, 4b, 5a, 6a, 7b, 16a

determinism, **II** 19b, 135a, 236b–237a; **III** 189b

Dewey and, **III** 554b

dignity, **IV** 140b, 141b, 143b

Dionysius Thrax and, **II** 665a

discontinuity, **I** 495b

double truth, **II** 31b, 32a, 33a–35a, 36b–37b

dualism, **I** 673a; **II** 41a; **IV** 34a

education, **II** 77b, 78a, 81a–81b, 83a, 84a; **IV** 123b

eighteenth century view of, **I** 76b–77a, 78b, 83a, 83b

emotion, **IV** 5a

empathy, **II** 87b

empiricism, **II** 623a; **III** 189b

Enlightenment, **II** 96b

environment, **II** 120b

epics, **III** 527a

Epicureanism, **II** 135a, 135b, 137a; **IV** 7a

epigenesis, **II** 623a

epistemology, **IV** 4b

equality, **I** 449a; **II** 138b; **III** 11a, 15b; **IV** 285b

equity, **II** 149b–150b, 153b

essence, **I** 2a–2b

ethics, **I** 463a, **II** 149b–150b, 236b–237a; **III** 354a, 440a, 554b; **IV** 4b, 6b, 49b, 175b, 320a, 321a, 451b, 452a

etymology, **II** 663a

Euclid and, **III** 461a

Eurytos and, **I** 580a–580b

evil, **II** 163a, 167b; **IV** 36a, 411b, 412a

evolution, **II** 505b–507a; **III** 19a

evolutionism, **II** 175b–176a

excess, **IV** 369a

experience, **III** 554b

faith, hope, and charity, **II** 210b

fate, **II** 226a, 227a, 227b–228a, 228b, 229b, 231b, 233a; **IV** 412a

fear, **IV** 412a

First Teacher, **II** 644a

Flood, **I** 625b

Forms, **I** 639a, 672a–672b; **II** 163a, 175b; **III** 189a, 423b, 424a, 465a, 629a, 629b; **IV** 4b, 5a

fortune, **II** 226a, 227a, 227b–228a, 228b, 229b, 231b, 233a

four elements, **I** 230b–231a

free will, **II** 135a, 135b, 137a; **II** 236b–237a, 243a–243b

freedom, **I** 578b, 585a; **II** 249b

freedom of speech, **II** 254a, 258a, 259a, 260a, 260b

friendship, **III** 110b–111a, 112a

Galen, **III** 90a

genetic continuity, **II** 281b–282a

genetics, **I** 231b–232a

genius, **I** 584b, 585b; **II** 293b, 299b, 309a, 309b, 320b

geometry, **III** 380a

goals, **IV** 175a–175b

God, **I** 272a, 572a, 672b; **II** 32a, 163a, 339a, 339b, 341a, 377b; **III** 273b, 465a; **IV** 6b, 50b, 530b

good, **II** 227b–228a, 377a–377b; **III** 354a, 465a; **IV** 5a, 5b, 36a, 49b, 175a–175b, 176b, 180a, 436a, 451b

grammar, **II** 663a–663b

Great Year (myth), **III** 628b; **IV** 400b

Grosseteste and, **II** 196a–196b

hallucinations, **IV** 5b

handicrafts, **III** 15b

happiness, **II** 227a, 228a, 375a, 377a–378a, 379a, 380b, 387a; **III** 465a; **IV** 175b, 176b, 530b

harmony, **I** 580b; **II** 389b, 390a, 392b; **III** 15b, 92a; **IV** 38a, 40a

heaven, **III** 273b

Hegel and, **II** 407b, 408a, 409b

hierarchy, **II** 438a–438b, 443a–443b, 448a

Hippodamus of Miletus and, **I** 428a

historiography, **I** 502b–503a, 503b; **II** 19b, 468a, 474b, 486a, 505b–508b

history, **I** 400a; **II** 19b, 507a; **III** 354b

Hobbes and, **III** 20b, 75b

hubris, **IV** 413a

human nature, **II** 377a; **III** 554b, 574b; **IV** 285b

hylomorphism, **III** 187a–187b, 189a, 194a

immortality, **I** 639a–639b, 644a, 645b; **IV** 34a

impiety, **II** 565b

indeterminacy, **II** 228b, 587a

individualism, **II** 299b, 309a, 309b; **III** 37a, 598a; **IV** 49b, 175a–175b

induction, **III** 380a

inequality, **II** 140a; **III** 11a; **IV** 318a

infinity, **II** 604b–605b, 607b–609a, 610a, 611a–612b, 614a–615a

Islam, **I** 3b; **II** 639b, 640b, 643a, 644a–645b, 647a, 649a–650b; **IV** 6a, 34b, 285b

irony, **II** 627b, 628a, 628b

irrationalism, **II** 635a, 635b

judgment, **II** 243a; **IV** 238a

justice, **II** 150a, 653a–657a, 658b; **III** 1b, 15a–15b, 16b, 27b; **IV** 285b, 313a

knowledge, **I** 128a, 456b, 625b; **II** 196b; **III** 190a, 380a; **IV** 6b, 49b, 175b, 431b, 436a, 530a

language, **II** 661b, 663a–663b, 664a, 665a, 667b, 672b, 673a

law, **I** 290b, 487a; **II** 2a–2b, 149b–150a, 249b, 679b, 680b, 684b, 688a; **III** 11a, 15a–15b, 16b, 27b; **IV** 175b, 313a

learning, **IV** 530b

Leibniz and, **IV** 435a–435b

leisure, **I** 102a; **IV** 497b

Leucippus and, **I** 495a

liberalism, **III** 36b–37b, 46a, 47a

linguistics, **III** 62a, 75a, 75b

literary criticism, **I** 596a, 596b, 602a, 604a

literature, **IV** 330b, 331a

logic, **I** 316a, 382b, 463a; **II** 663a, 663b, 666b; **III** 162b–173a, 176b, 380b, 381b–382a, 554a, 554b; **IV** 135a

longevity, **III** 89b–90a

love, **II** 210b; **III** 95a, 95b, 110b–111a

loyalty, **III** 110b–112a

macrocosm and microcosm, **III** 126b, 127a, 127b

mathematics, **I** 1b–2b, 463a, 580a–580b; **III** 172a, 172b–173a, 173b, 180a, 184a, 380a, 380b, 554b; **IV** 38a, 400b

matter, **II** 41a, 163a; **II** 175b, 389b, 392b, 407b; **III** 187a–187b, 189a–190a, 190b, 191a, 192b, 195a; **IV** 4b, 5a

Mead and, **III** 554b

Mean, **IV** 369a

measurement, **IV** 400a–400b, 451b–452a

mechanics, **II** 196a, 197a, 197b, 199a, 200a, 201b, 202a, 204a, 204b

melancholy, **II** 309a, 320b

metaphor, **I** 585a–585b; **III** 200a, 205a, 206a, 207a

metaphysics, **II** 377a; **III** 354a, 355a; **IV** 4b, 6b

methodology, **III** 380a–381a, 382a, 387b, 554b; **IV** 434b

Middle Ages, **IV** 369a

mimesis, **II** 507a, 507b; **III** 226a–227a, 227b, 228a, 228b, 229b; **IV** 411b

mimetic art, **I** 578b, 585a

mind, II 120b, 226a; III 189b; IV 5a, 5b, 6a, 6b
moderation, IV 369a
monarchy, I 625b
money, I 396a–396b; IV 451b
morality, III 365b–366a; IV 49b, 175a, 175b
motion, I 463a, 498a; II 46a, 200a, 202a, 387a; III 273b; IV 34a, 50b, 76b, 390b, 391a
music, I 264b–265a, 266b, 578b, 587b; II 389b, 390a, 392b; III 226b, 260b, 261b, 263a
mythology, III 273b
nationalism, III 324b
natural law, I 487a; III 15a–15b, 16b, 17a, 19a, 20b, 23a; IV 175b
natural science, I 382b–383a
Nature, I 128b, 234a–234b, 382b, 672b, 673a; II 167b, 175b, 202a, 226a, 377a, 438b; III 15b, 189b, 222b, 273a, 350b, 355a, 380a, 429a, 629a, 629b; IV 4b, 50b, 175a, 436a
necessity, III 189b, 351b, 353a–354b, 355a, 355b; IV 50b, 411b–412a
neo-classicism in art, III 365b
Neo-Platonism, III 372a, 374a, 377a
Newton and, III 380a, 381a, 392a, 387b
numbers, IV 33a, 34a, 36a, 36b
oligarchy, I 625b, 654b; IV 175b
oratory, III 554b
order, II 438a–438b, 443a–443b, 448a; III 1b, 16b
organicism, III 421b–424b
painting, IV 467b, 468a, 469b, 473a
pangenesis, II 623a–623b
Parmenides and, IV 3a
peace, III 440a
Peirce and, III 555a, 567a
perception, I 1b–2a; IV 5a, 5b–6a
perennial philosophy, III 459a, 459b, 460b, 461a, 462a, 462b
perfectibility, III 464a, 465a, 473b
Petrarch and, IV 141b
phenomena, III 354a
philosophy, I 463a; II 408a, 661b, 666b; III 189b–190a,

200a; III 273b, 380a, 628b, 629b; IV 4b, 436a
physics, I 463a; II 666b; III 354b, 355b
physiology, IV 5b
pity, IV 411b, 412a
planets, I 540a–541a, 557a
Plato and, II 390a, 663a, 663b; III 189a, 459b, 461a, 500b, 503a, 509a, 509b, 510b, 512a, 514b, 516b, 554a; IV 4b, 5a, 6b, 33a, 33b, 34a–34b, 49b, 50b, 175b, 369a, 400b
Platonism, III 500b, 503a, 504a, 505a, 509a, 509b, 510b, 512a, 513b, 514a, 514b, 516b, 519a, 519b, 530b–531a
pleasure, I 585a; II 375a, 377a–378a, 379a, 380b, 387a; IV 5a, 369a, 412a
Plotinus and, III 372a, 374a
pluralism, III 190a, 190b, 554b
pneuma concept, I 231a, 232a
poetics, III 526a–528a, 529a–529b, 531a
poetry, I 265a, 457a; II 299b, 507a; III 226b, 354b, 526a–528a, 529a–529b; IV 467b, 468a, 469b, 473a
politics, I 463a; II 377b, 379b; III 354a, 554b; IV 175b, 313a, 314b
Porphyry and, III 377a
positivism, III 538b
potentiality, II 544a; IV 6a
Poussin and, III 365b
power, III 15b; IV 175b, 313a
pragmatism, III 554a, 554b, 555a, 555b
primitivism, III 586a
private property, IV 285b
probability, III 500b, 614b
progress, III 627a–630a
psychology, I 499a; II 135b, 236b–237a, 377a; IV 2a, 2b, 4b–6b, 7a, 8a, 9a, 9b, 10b, 16b, 17b
punishment, II 135a
Puritanism, IV 16b
purpose, III 354a, 355a
Pythagoras and, IV 31a
Pythagoreans, I 578b, 580a–580b; IV 31a, 31b, 33a–36a, 37a, 38a, 40a, 41a, 400b
Ramism, IV 43b
rationalism, IV 48a, 49a, 49b, 50b, 51a, 122a, 175b
realism, III 19a

reality, III 226b
reason, II 196b; III 1b, 380a, 381b, 440a, 586a; IV 49b, 175b
recapitulation, IV 56b
relativity, IV 74b, 76b
religion, III 205b, 206a, 207a
Renaissance, IV 369a
responsibility, II 236b–237a
revolution, IV 152b
rhetoric, III 500b; IV 168a–171b, 369a
right, III 15a–15b; IV 175a–175b, 176b, 180a
ritual, III 226b
Rome (ancient), IV 369a
rules, IV 175b
Saint Augustine and, IV 9a
Saint Thomas Aquinas and, I 259b–260a, 274b, 384b, 643a, 672b–673a; II 343a; III 19a; IV 432a, 434b, 436a, 525a–525b
Santayana and, III 554a
satire, IV 211a, 216a
science, I 463a; II 196a–197b, 199a, 200a, 201b, 202a, 203a–204b; III 189b–190a, 503a, 629b; IV 4b, 6b, 175b
sculpture, III 226b
senses, I 1a–1b; III 189b, 190a; IV 5a, 5b–6a, 34b, 530b
Shaftesbury and, III 365b
skepticism, III 503a; IV 234b, 238a, 239b, 244b
skill, III 628b, 629b
slavery, I 443a; II 2a, 2b–3a, 5a, 5b, 259a; III 440a; IV 530b
social contract, IV 252b
socialism, IV 285b, 292b
society, III 20b, 629b
Socrates and, III 226a–226b; IV 49a
soul, I 2a, 2b, 61b, 215b, 231b, 234b, 639a–639b; II 36b, 41a, 243a, 377a, 392b; IV 4b–5b, 6b, 33a, 34a, 36b, 49b, 56b, 301a
sound, II 389b
space, III 189a–189b; IV 295a, 296b–301b, 305b
species, I 232b–233a, 463a; IV 175a
speech, II 663a
Speusippus and, IV 35a–35b, 36a, 36b
spontaneous generation, II 281b–282a; IV 307b
stars, I 668a
State, I 625b, 653a–655b,

657a, 657b, 658a, 667a; IV 313a, 313b, 314b, 318a, 497a–497b
Stoicism, IV 320a, 321a
style, IV 330b, 331a
suffering, IV 412a
syllogistic logic, III 127a
symbolism, II 663a; III 273b
symmetry, IV 346b, 347a, 349a
sympathy, IV 412a
teleology, I 234a–236b, 272a, 300b, 301a, 302a–302b, 303b; II 623a; III 90a, 354a, 354b; IV 51a, 175a, 175b
temperance, IV 369a–369b, 375a, 377a
terror, IV 411b, 412a
theater, III 226b
theodicy, IV 380a
theology, IV 176b
Theophrastus and, IV 6b
theriophily, IV 384a, 384b, 385b, 388b
thermodynamics, I 495a
thought, IV 6a, 6b, 49b, 530b
time, I 492b–493a; II 170a, 664a; III 189a–189b; IV 301a, 349a, 390b–391a, 391b, 393a, 393b, 400a–400b
to pan, IV 300a
topos, IV 299b, 301b
totalitarianism, IV 406b
tragedy, I 265b–270a, 578b, 584b, 585a–585b, 611a; II 169b–170a, 506a, 507a, 544a–544b; III 423a, 527a, 527b, 629a; IV 411b–412a, 413a
transcendentalism, I 584b
truth, II 663a, 663b; IV 431b–432a
tyranny, I 625b; II 1b, 2a–2b, 4b
ugliness, I 585a, 586a, 586b
unity, I 501a; II 623a; III 423a, 527a, 527b, 531a
unity of science, IV 431a–432b, 433b, 434b–436a
universal man, IV 439a
universality, IV 49b, 175b, 431b
universe, II 175b, 438b; III 354a; IV 38a, 40a
urbanization, I 654b
utilitarianism, IV 444a
utility, IV 451b, 453b, 455b
Utopia, IV 459b, 460a, 461b
vacuum, I 495a
value, IV 450b, 451b–452a, 452b, 453a, 453b, 455b

verbal terms, I 2a
verse, III 531a
vice, II 237a
virtue, II 237a, 377a, 377b;
IV 49b, 175b, 369a, 375a,
477a, 530b
visible numbers, I 580b
voluntariness, II 236b–237a
vox populi, IV 497a–497b
war, IV 501b
wealth, I 624b, 653a
Wilkins and, I 310a
William of Ockham and, III
19a
Winckelmann and, III 365b,
366a
wisdom, IV 49b, 175b
work, IV 530b
writing, II 663a
Xenocrates and, IV 35a,
36b, 37a
Xenophanes and, III 464a
Zeno of Citum and, IV 301a,
320b
Aristoxenus (4th century B.C.),
music, II 313a; III 261b,
262a, 262b
Arithmetic
art, I 459a
genius, II 313b
harmony, II 390a; IV 38a,
39a, 40b, 42a
language, II 660a
Leibniz, IV 435b
mathematics, III 171b,
173a, 173b, 178a, 178b
mechanics, II 197b, 200a
methodology, III 379b,
389b
music, II 313b, 390a; III
260b, 270b
Newton, III 379b, 389b
Plato, I 462b–463a; IV 39a
pragmatism, III 560a
probability, III 606a, 617a
progress, III 625a
Pythagoreans, IV 31a, 32a,
33a, 38a, 40a, 41a
Ramism, IV 42b
Renaissance, III 178a; IV
438b
rules, II 660a
unity of science, IV 431b,
435b
universal man, IV 438b
universe, IV 38a, 39a, 40b,
42a
Arius (d. 336 A.D.), God, I
377a–377b
Arkwright, Richard (1732–
1792), technology, IV
362b–363a
Armageddon
millenarianism, III 223b

mythology, III 276b, 282a
Armenian language, III 62a
Armenini, G. B.
individualism in art, II 303a
mythology, III 293a, 295b,
299a
Arminianism
Calvinism, I 399a
predestination, I 397b
psychology, IV 19b, 20a
Arminius, Jacob (1560–1609)
free will, II 245b
predestination, II 28b
Armstrong, W. E., social welfare, IV 280b
Arnauld, Antoine (1612–
1694)
casuistry, I 262a–262b
China, I 360a
Descartes and, I 7a
language, II 667b
Man-Machine, II 137a
methodology, III 384b
Port-Royal Logic, I 7a
probability, III 606b
skepticism, IV 245a
Arndt, Ernst Moritz (1769–
(1860), romanticism, IV
207a
Arnim, Achim von, romanticism, IV 189a, 190a, 196b
Arnobius (fl. 300 A.D.)
dignity, IV 138a, 140a
reformation, IV 62b
Arnold, Armin, expressionism,
II 208b
Arnold, Edwin (1832–1904),
Buddhism, I 256b; III 437a
Arnold, Gottfried
heresy, II 430a
Pietism, III 494a–494b
Arnold, Matthew (1822–
1888)
antiquity, I 81a
classicism, I 450a
comparative literature, III
83a
culture, I 617b
literary criticism, I 599b–
600a
literature, III 83a
modernism, I 422b
Platonism, III 507b
Victorian age, IV 222b
welfare state, IV 510a
Arnold, Thurman, private property, III 654b
Arnold of Brescia (1100?–
1155), heresy, II 418b,
419a
Arnold of Villanova (1235?–
?1312)
alchemy, I 31a
mechanics, II 197b

Arnulph of Orleans, mytho-
logy, III 288a
Aron, Pietro (fl. 1545)
music, II 314a, 317a
Aron, Raymond, war, IV 508a
Arp, Hans (1887–1966),
chance images, I 352b
Arrhenius, Svante (1859–
1927), cosmic images, I
518b, 522a, 523a–523b
Arrow, K. J., social welfare,
IV 282b–283a, 283b–284a
Art
Abrams, II 310b
abstract, I 352a
abstraction, II 525b, 534a
academicians, II 303b–
304a, 306b
Adam, II 308a
Addison, II 306b, 307b
Aeschylus, III 625b, 626a
aesthetics, II 216a–225b,
575b, 576a, 583a, 583b;
IV 353b, 355b, 356a
Africa, III 597a
Alberti, II 301a, 308a, 309b;
III 228a
Alexander the Great, II 299b
allegory, II 525b, 526a,
527b, 530b–534a
animals, III 596a
Apelles, II 299a, 299b
apotelestic, I 458a
appearance, I 460b–461a
Apuleius, II 310a
archaeology, II 535a
architecture, II 298a, 299a,
300a, 300b, 308a
Aretino, II 304b–305a,
308b
Ariosto, II 308b
aristocracy, II 570a, 578b,
581b
Aristotle, II 299b, 309a,
309b; III 189b, 226b, 227a,
365b–366a; IV 50b
Armenini, II 303a
artisans, II 300a
artists, II 297a, 299a–304b
Balzac, II 308b
Baudelaire, II 310b
beauty, I 461b
Bell, II 298b
Bernini, II 303a–303b,
309a
Blake, II 304a, 306b, 307a,
308a
Boccaccio, II 301a, 310a
Bohemians, II 303b–304a
Boileau, II 310a
Boucher, II 310b
bourgeois, II 570a, 580a
Bourget, II 310b
Brunelleschi, II 298a, 300b

Bruno, II 306a
Burckhardt, II 300a–300b
Castiglione, II 305a
Catullus, II 310a
Cennini, II 298a, 300b
censorship, III 497b–498a
Cézanne, II 614a
Chagall, II 304b
chance, II 230a
chance images, I 340b–
353b
Chardin, II 306a
Christianity, III 591a
Cicero, II 305a, 309b
city planning, I 461b
city-state, II 300b–302b
civilization, I 616a, 621a
class, II 576b, 581b, 583a
classicism, III 363b
classification, I 457a, 458a,
459a, 460a–461a, 461b
climate, IV 150a
Clovio, II 301b
Colbert, II 303b
Coleridge, II 307b
Colman, II 307a–307b
Colonna, II 303a
color, II 567b, 570a, 570b,
571a, 572a–572b, 574a,
574b, 577a, 577b, 578b,
579a, 579b, 580a, 580b,
582b, 583a
Comanini, III 228a
commemorative, I 460a
common sense, II 309b
competition, II 300b
composition, II 570a, 571a,
581b, 582b
conservatism, II 571a
Cosimo, II 302b
Counter-Enlightenment, II
101b–102a, 104a, 105b,
107a, 108b–109a, 109b
Courbet, II 298b
craftsmanship, I 456b,
457a, 458b, 459a, 459b,
460a, 461b; III 300a
creativity, II 297a, 297b,
307a–307b, 309a
criticism, II 572b, 573a,
573b, 574b, 575b–576a,
577a, 581a
Cubism, II 534a
culture, I 612a, 616a, 621a;
II 297a, 298b, 311a, 567b,
577a, 580b, 581b, 582b,
583a; IV 165b
cynicism, III 585b
decadence, II 575b, 582a
Delacroix, II 305a
democracy, II 583a
Democritus, III 226a
demonology, I 668b
Dewey, III 569b

dichotomy, II 309b–311a
Diderot, II 310a–310b
dignity, IV 136b, 141a
divisionism, II 570b
drawing, II 305b, 580b
Dryden, II 307a, 308b
Du Bos, II 309b
dualism, II 581b
Dürer, II 309a
education, II 299a–299b, 300a, 307b–308a, 583a; III 501a
Egypt (ancient), II 298b, 582b
elegant, I 460b
emotion, II 297b, 575a, 575b, 576b, 581a; III 501b
empathy, II 85b, 86a, 86b, 88a–88b, 297b
empiricism, II 576b, 580b, 581b, 582a, 583a
encyclic, I 457b, 458b
enigma, II 533a
Enlightenment, II 90a, 91a, 96b, 100a
enterprise, II 300b
environment, II 583a
Epicureanism, II 576a, 581a, 581b, 582a
Erasmus, II 302a
ethics, II 576a
evil, II 166b
evolution, II 297a, 581b, 583a
evolution of literature, II 170a–170b, 173b
experiments, II 567b; III 569b
expressionism, II 206a–208b
fate, II 230a, 232a, 234a, 235a
Faust (legend), III 249a
feeling, II 575b, 576b
Ficino, II 309a; III 229a
figurative, I 460a, 461a
Filarete, II 298a
fine, I 587a
Fiorentino, II 302b
Flaubert, II 310b
folklore, II 581a, 582b
fortune, II 230a, 232a, 234a, 235a
France, II 297b, 298b, 300b, 305a, 614a; III 366a
Franciabigio, II 302a
free, I 461a
freedom, II 297b, 298a, 300b, 304a–304b
freedom of speech, II 253a, 254b
Freising, II 300a
French Revolution, IV 165a

Freud, III 312b; IV 96b
Friedrich, II 309a
game theory, II 274b
genius, II 293a–295b, 297a–299a, 299b, 304b–311a, 313a–313b, 314a–316b, 318b, 325a, 326a
geometry, II 614a
Germany, II 305b, 306b, 307a
Ghiberti, II 298a, 301a
Giotto, II 298b
God, I 597b; II 297b, 300a, 308a–308b, 340 b, 574b, 582b; III 574b; IV 123a
Goethe, II 310b
Gothic, II 297b, 298a, 367a–374a, 527a
Goya, II 302a
grace, II 305a
grammar, I 456b, 459a
graphic, II 528a
Great Britain, II 297b, 298b, 300b, 303b, 305a, 305b, 306a, 308a, 310a
Greece (ancient), II 297b, 299a, 299b, 459a; III 363a, 365a–365b
Guarini, III 228a
guilds, II 300a–300b
Hadrian, II 299b
happiness, II 368a
harmony, II 388b, 390a
hedonism, II 575b
Hegel, II 408a
Herder, II 306b
heresy, II 427a
hermeticism, II 431a–431b, 433a
hierarchy, II 436a, 436b
hieroglyphic signs, II 529b, 530a, 530b, 531a
historians, II 297b
historicism, II 459a
historiography, II 577b; IV 148b, 149b, 150a
history, II 528a–529b, 576a–580b
Hogarth, II 300b, 306a
Hollanda, II 303a, 305a, 308b
Hugo, II 310b
human nature, III 574b
humanism, II 516a, 517a, 517b, 519b, 521b, 523a; IV 130b, 131a, 133a, 134b
hunting, II 313b
iconography, II 525b, 526a, 527a–528a, 530a–534a, 536a, 537b, 539b–540b
idea, II 544a, 544b, 547a–547b
ideal, II 549a–551b

ideology, II 555b, 582a, 583a
imagery, II 526a, 526b, 527a, 530a, 530b
imagination, II 304b, 307a–307b; III 217a, 219b, 221b, 222a, 222b; IV 334b
imitation, II 298a, 306a–306b, 582b; III 497b–498a
immutability, II 582b
impressionism, II 534a
individualism, II 297a–299a, 299b, 304b–311a, 567b, 570b, 572a, 574b, 577a, 577b, 581b, 582b
industry, II 580a
infinity, II 612b, 614a
ingenious, I 459b
Ingres, II 614a
innovation, II 577a, 579b
insanity, II 575b
inspiration, II 307a–307b
invention, II 304b, 307a–307b
irony, II 630b
irrationalism, II 305a, 636a
Islam, II 640a
Italy, II 297b, 298b, 299a, 300b–303b, 308b
judgment, II 297b
Kant, I 598; II 307a
Keble, II 310b
Klee, II 304b; III 597a
knowledge, I 456b
landscapes, II 567b, 571b, 572a, 573a, 574a, 577b–579a, 580a
Lebrun, II 303a
Leonardo da Vinci, II 298a, 298b, 301b, 302a, 304a, 308a, 529a
liberal, I 457b, 458b, 459a, 460a; II 313b
liberty, II 300b
light, II 567b, 570a–570b, 572a, 574a–574b, 578b, 579a, 580a–580b, 581b
line, II 570a, 581b
literary criticism, I 599a, 605a, 606b; II 297a, 306a, 318b
literature, II 298a, 299a, 301a–301b, 306a–307b, 528a–529a, 530a, 531a
Lomazzo, II 303a, 305a, 308a
Lombroso, II 308b
Longinus, II 304b
love, III 97b, 103b, 106a–106b, 107a
Lowell, II 305b
Lucian, II 299b
Lucretius, III 587b
Machiavellism, III 117b

madness, II 308b–309b
Mans, III 228a
Maoris, III 597a
Marcus Aurelius, II 299b
Marxism, III 148a, 152b, 153b
Masaccio, II 301b
mass, II 570a
mathematics, II 614a
matter, II 298b; III 189b
mechanical, I 459a, 459b, 460b, 461b; II 313b
mechanics, II 203b, 205b
Medici family, III 506a
medicine, II 313b
melancholy, II 308b–309b, 581a
Mendelssohn, Moses, II 550b
Mengs, A. R., II 306a
metaphor, I 460a; III 198b
metaphysics, III 217a, 219b, 221b, 222a, 222b
Michelangelo, II 298b, 302a–302b, 303a, 304a, 305a, 308b, 309a; IV 443a
Middle Ages, II 297b, 298a, 298b, 300a, 303b, 527a, 527b–528a; III 82b; IV 123b, 133a
military, I 458a
mimesis, III 225b–230a, 497b
mind, II 298b
Miró, III 597a
Moebius, II 308b
motif, III 235a, 236b, 241b
motion pictures, II 572a, 572b
music, II 313a–316b, 318b, 325a, 326a, 388b, 390a; III 269a–272a
mutability, II 581a–581b
mysticism, II 575b, 581b, 582a
Naples, II 297b
nationalism, II 579b; III 326a
natural science, II 576b
naturalism, II 571a, 573a, 575b, 576a, 576b, 578a, 578b, 579b, 580b, 581b, 582a, 582b, 583a; III 339a, 339b, 340b, 343a, 345a
necessity, III 360a, 362a
neo-classicism in art, III 363a, 363b, 364b, 365b, 366a, 367a, 368a, 369a, 369b, 370b, 371a
Neo-Platonism, II 308b, 576b
Netherlands, II 532a–532b
neuroses, II 575b
Nietzsche, II 307b

noble, I 460a
non finito, II 297b, 298b–299a
Northcote, II 303b, 309b
novelty in, II 315b
nude, II 531a
optics, III 408b–409a
order, II 436a, 436b
organic, I 458a
organicism, III 421a, 422b–425b, 426b, 427a
Orientalism, III 428a, 428b
originality, II 306a–306b
Ovid, II 310a
Pamphilos, II 299a–299b
Panofsky, II 308a
Parrhasios, II 299b
patrons, II 573a, 577a, 580a; IV 437b
Pausanias, II 299b
peasantry, III 595a
Peirce, III 569b
periodization in history, III 477b, 479b
periodization in literary history, III 482b, 483b, 484a–485b
perspective, II 570a, 577a, 612b, 614a; IV 302a
perversion, II 575b
Petrarch, II 302a
philosophy, II 549a, 549b, 550a–551b; III 198b
Philostratus, II 299b
photography, II 571a–572b
physics, II 580a–580b
Picasso, II 304b; III 230a, 597a
Piero di Cosimo, II 302b
Pini, II 309b
Pinkerton, II 306b
Piranesi, II 308a
Pisano, IV 123a
plastic, I 459b
Plato, II 299b, 308a, 309a, 309b, 582b; III 226b, 227a, 497a–502a
Platonism, II 298b, 308b, 310a, 310b; III 497a–502a, 506a, 510a, 511b, 512b, 513a, 524a
pleasure, II 386a, 582b
Pliny, II 299a–299b, 305a, 310a
Plutarch, II 299b
poetry, I 456b, 457a, 458a–461a; III 525b, 527a, 527b; IV 465b, 466a, 467a, 467b, 469a, 470a, 470b, 471b, 472a, 473b, 475a, 475b
poietic, I 458a, 458b
pointillism, II 567b
Pollock, II 304b
polyphonic, II 314b

Pontormo, II 301b, 302b
Pope, II 305a, 306a–306b
portraiture, II 532a
Portugal, II 303a
positivism, III 538a
power, II 576a–576b, 577a
practical, I 458a
pragmatism, III 555a, 568b, 569b
prestige, II 572b, 573a
primitive, III 597a
primitivism, III 577b, 578a, 580b, 582b, 585b, 587b, 588a, 588b, 591a, 593b, 595a, 596a, 596b, 597a, 597b, 599b
progress, III 625b, 626a, 628a, 630b, 631b, 632b, 635a, 637b, 638b, 639a, 642a, 642b, 644a, 644b
prophecy, III 658a
proto-Bohemians, II 304a
Pseudo-Dionysius, III 227a
psychology, II 297a, 304a–304b, 309b, 310b–311a, 575a, 580b, 583a
Quintilian, II 305a, 309b
Rainaldus, II 300a
Ramism, IV 44a, 45a, 45b
Raphael, II 298a, 302b–303a, 309a, 309b
rationalism, IV 46a, 46b, 49a, 50b
realism, II 532a–532b, 570a, 571a, 576b, 578b, 579a, 580a, 581b, 582b
realism in literature, IV 52a, 53b, 55b, 56a
reason, I 458b
relativity, IV 75a, 83b–84a, 92a
religion, II 575b, 576a, 576b, 581b, 582b; IV 96b
Rembrandt, II 309a
reproductive, I 461a
revolt, II 567b–570b, 577a, 581b
revolution, II 577a, 581b; IV 155b, 165a, 165b
Reynolds, II 300b, 303a–303b, 306a, 306b, 307b–308a, 309b
rhetoric, I 458a, 458b, 459a; IV 168a, 168b, 171b, 172a
Riedel, II 550b–551a
Riegl, II 297b
Rimbaud, II 308b
Robbia, II 301b
Rodin, II 299a
romanticism, II 298b, 304a–304b, 533b–534a, 575b, 578a, 578b, 579a, 580a, 581a, 581b; IV 196b, 199b,

200a, 201b, 202a, 202b, 208a, 209a
Rome (ancient), II 299b; III 365a–365b
Rousseau, III 599b
Rubens, II 303a, 309a
Ruskin, II 297b, 307a; IV 125b
Rustici, II 302a
Sacchetti, II 301a
Saint Antonio, II 305a
Saint Augustine, III 227a, 227b, 635a
Saint Bernard, III 591a
salvation, IV 233a
sanity, II 309b
Sarto, II 302b
Scaliger, II 308a; III 228a
Schiller, II 307b
Schlegel, IV 208a
Schopenhauer, II 308b
science, I 456b–458a, 459a, 461b; II 203b, 205b, 575b, 580a–580b, 581b, 582b, 583a; III 262b; IV 83b–84a
sculpture, II 299a, 299b, 300b–302a, 313b, 534a
Seneca, II 308b; III 588a
senses, II 574b, 575b, 576b, 580b, 582a, 583a–583b
Shaftesbury, II 308b
Shakespeare, II 306a–306b, 307a
Sharpe, II 307a
Sidney, II 306a
sin, IV 233a
skepticism, II 575b; IV 236a–236b
sociology, II 297a
Socrates, III 226a
space, IV 298b, 302a
spatial, I 461a
Spengler, IV 298b
spontaneity, II 307a–307b
Stahl, II 309b
Stalin, III 152b
State, II 570a, 576a, 582b
Stoicism, II 299b
structuralism, IV 327b, 328b
structure, II 219b
style, II 297b–298b, 567b, 570a–570b, 572a, 572b, 574a, 574b, 576a, 576b–577b, 580a, 580b, 581b, 583a
sublime in external nature, IV 334b, 336a, 336b
sunlight, II 567b, 570a–570b, 571b, 579a, 581a
supernatural, II 575b, 576b, 580b
symmetry, IV 348a

as a system, I 456b, 458b–459a
Taine, II 308b
taste, II 572b, 573a; IV 353b, 355b, 356a
technique, II 567b, 570a–570b, 574a, 580a, 581b, 583a
technology, IV 358b, 359b
temperance, IV 366a, 371a–378a
Temple, II 305b, 307b
temporal, I 461a
Theodorus of Samos, II 299a
theoretical, I 458a
theriophily, IV 385a, 385b
theory, III 343a
Tintoretto, II 302a
tomb decorations, II 525b, 531b
Torri, II 301b
trade, II 580a
tradition, II 577a–577b, 579b, 581b
Trilling, II 308b–309a
truth, I 460b–461a; II 571a, 575b, 576a–576b, 582b
Uccello, II 301b
ugliness, II 571a
unity, II 576a
unity of science, IV 431b
universal man, IV 437a, 437b, 438a, 439b, 440a, 441b, 442a, 443a
Utopia, IV 462b
value, II 576b, 577b
vanishing point, II 612b, 614a
Varchi, III 228a
Vasari, II 298a, 301b–303b, 305a–305b, 309b; IV 123a, 124a, 150a
Velázquez, II 309b
Venice, II 297b
vibrism, II 570b
Victorianism, IV 219b, 221a, 221b, 223a, 223b
Vida, II 306a
virtue, II 550b; IV 371a–378a
vision, II 223b
Voltaire, IV 124a
vox populi, IV 499a, 499b
vulgar, I 457b, 459a
wall-paintings, II 529b
Walpole, II 306a
Walzel, II 308b
war, II 577a, 580a; IV 504b
wealth, II 299b, 570a, 577a, 580a
Wellek, II 304b, 307a
Wieland, II 551b
Winckelmann, II 297b
wisdom of the fool, IV 519b

witchcraft, **IV** 522b
Wölfflin, **II** 297b
women, **III** 596b
Young, **II** 306b, 307a, 307b
Zeitgeist, **IV** 536b
Zeuxis, **II** 299b
See also Mythology, Nature, Painting, Renaissance, Symbolism
Art for art's sake, **I** 108a–111a
Bell, **I** 110b
Bradley, A. C., **I** 110b
Coleridge, **I** 109a
Constant, **I** 109b
Flaubert, **I** 109a
Fry, **I** 110b
Gautier, **I** 109b, 110a
Goethe, **I** 109a
Hanslick, **I** 110b
Hegel, **I** 108b
Herder, **I** 109a
Hugo, **I** 109b
Hume, **I** 108b
idealism, **I** 108b
Kant, **I** 108b, 109b
Mallarmé, **I** 109b
Pater, **I** 109b, 110a
Schelling, **I** 108b, 109b
Schiller, Friedrich, **I** 108b
Schlegel brothers, **I** 109a
Whistler, **I** 110a
Wilde, **I** 109b
Wordsworth, **I** 109a
Art Nouveau
naturalism in art, **III** 341a
painting, **III** 341b
Art and play, **I** 99b–107b
Freud, **I** 107a
Groos, **I** 106a–106b
Plato, **I** 100a–101b, 107a
pleasure, **I** 374b
Rousseau, **I** 105a
Schiller, **I** 103b, 105a–106a, 107b, 203b–204a
Spencer, **I** 106a, 106b
Vico, **I** 103b
Artaud, Antoine, irrationalism, **II** 638a
Artemis (myth), **III** 272b
Arthur, King (legend)
historiography, **II** 483b
millenarianism, **III** 224b
motif, **III** 240b
mythology, **III** 240b, 308a
Arthurs, E., indeterminacy, **II** 592a
Artificial language, linguistics, **III** 75a
Artists
anarchy, **I** 71b
Aristotle, **I** 578a
attributing works of, **II** 297b

autobiographies by, **II** 298a, 301a
Croce, **I** 588b
doodles, **II** 304b
evolution of literature, **II** 174a
experiments, **III** 569b
fame, **II** 300a
freedom, **I** 585a, 586b; **II** 300b, 304a–304b; **III** 569b
genius, **II** 297a, 299a–304b
gentlemen, **II** 302b–303b
God, **I** 577b–578a, 578b–579a, 585b, 586a–587b; **II** 551b
Greece (ancient), **III** 527a
guilds, **II** 300a–300b
hermeticism, **II** 432a
ideal, **II** 550b, 551a, 551b
imagination, **III** 209a, 221b
imitation, **II** 298a
individualism, **II** 297a, 299a–304b
influences on, **II** 579b
literary criticism, **I** 598a
literature, **II** 298a, 299a, 301a
Renaissance, **IV** 123a, 437b, 439b
revolt, **II** 567b, 577a
revolution, **IV** 165a
romanticism, **II** 298b; **IV** 199b, 200a, 201b, 208b, 210b
soul, **II** 551b
status, **II** 299a–300a, 303a–303b
style, **II** 297b
talent, **II** 304b–306a
technology, **IV** 359b
tragic sense, **IV** 412b
universal man, **IV** 437b, 439b
Utopia, **IV** 461a
virtue, **IV** 477b
Artusi, Giovanni Maria
music, **III** 262b
Zarlino and, **III** 262b
Arundel, Countess of, mythology, **III** 297a, 298a
Arundel, Earl of, Gothic, **II** 369a
Aryabhata (b. 476 A.D.), cosmology, **I** 543b
Asanga (c. 310–390 A.D.), **I** 248a
Asceticism
casuistry, **I** 260a–261b
Christianity, **IV** 371a
Cynicism, **I** 631b–633b
dignity, **IV** 141a
Diogenes of Sinope, **I** 631b–632a
disease, **II** 399a

ethics, **IV** 320b
evil, **II** 164a–164b, 166b
Gandhi, **III** 446a
Gnosticism, **II** 328a–328b
Greece (ancient), **I** 631b–632a
heresy, **II** 418b, 423b
humanism, **IV** 133b
India (ancient), **I** 631b–632a
love, **III** 96b, 99b
morality, **I** 260
Neo-Platonism, **III** 373a, 373b, 511a
Oriental thought, **III** 431a
perfectibility, **III** 467b
Platonism, **III** 509a, 511a
Pythagoras, **I** 632a
Pythagoreans, **IV** 31b
reformation, **IV** 63b
Renaissance, **IV** 133a, 141a
salvation, **II** 212b
socialism, **IV** 286b
Socrates, **I** 632a
Stoicism, **IV** 320b
Strabo, **I** 631b–632a
temperance, **IV** 371a
Thoreau, **III** 431a
Victorianism, **IV** 218b
work, **IV** 531b
Ascham, Roger (1515–1568), deism, **I** 648b
Gothic, **II** 368a
Platonism, **III** 507b
poetics, **III** 529b
Aschenbrenner, Karl, aesthetics, **II** 219a
Asclepiades (fl. 100 B.C.), disease, **II** 398b
Asclepian therapy, catharsis, **I** 264b, 269a
Asclepius (cult), creativity in art, **I** 578b
Ascoli, Grazindio I (1829–1907), linguistics, **III** 70a–70b
Asebeia, **II** 565b–566b, 567a
Ash'arism
causation, **I** 277a, 286b, 287a–289a
Islam, **II** 641b, 642b, 643a, 647b, 648b
Asherah (myth), **III** 282b
Ashley, William (1860–1927)
economic history, **II** 60b
historiography, **II** 495a
Ashmole, Elias (1617–1692), **I** 31b
Asia
Counter-Enlightenment, **II** 101b, 105b
equality, **II** 141a, 143b
religion, **IV** 93b, 94a
technology, **IV** 361a

Asia Minor, neo-classicism in art, **III** 363a
Aśoka (d. 232 B.C.)
Buddhism, **I** 247a, 247b, 252a, 252b, 253a
cycles, **I** 622a
philanthropy, **III** 487a
Aspasia (470?–410 B.C.), impiety, **II** 565b
Asquith, H., welfare state, **IV** 510b
Assassination, protest movements, **III** 673b
Assemblies
Aristotle, **II** 258a
Athens (ancient), **II** 256b–257a
Babylonia, **II** 253a
Crete (ancient), **II** 258a
Egypt (ancient), **II** 256a
freedom of speech, **II** 252b–255b, 256a, 256b–261b
Greece (ancient), **II** 256b–260b, 675b, 680a
Hittite Kingdom, **II** 252b
law, **II** 675b, 680a
Palestine (ancient), **II** 253b–256a
Rome (ancient), **II** 261a–261b
Association of ideas, **I** 111a–118a
genius, **II** 295a
Godwin, **I** 114a–114b
Hartley, **I** 111b, 113a–114a, 114b, 116a, 116b
Hobbes, **I** 111b
Hume, **I** 113b, 116a
Locke, **I** 111b–113b, 114b, 116a
Pavlov, **I** 116a
Watson, **I** 116b–117a
Wundt, **I** 116b
Associationism
behaviorism, **I** 222a–222b, 227b
empathy, **II** 88a
Mill, J. S., **I** 220a
Watson, **I** 214b–215a
Assonance, **III** 269a, 271a
Assumption, Virgin Mary (Bible), **III** 107a
Assur (myth), **II** 335b–336a
Assurbanipal (669–626 B.C.), freedom of speech, **II** 253a
Assyria
annals, **II** 465b–466a
astrology, **I** 538b
cosmology, **I** 538b
despotism, **II** 252b
freedom of speech, **II** 252b, 253a
God, **II** 335b–336a

historiography, II 465b–466a, 475a, 475b
impiety, II 564a
music, III 264b
mythology, III 279a, 280a, 281b
naturalism in art, III 340a, 340b
prophecy, I 538b
Ast, Friedrich (1778–1841), romanticism, IV 189a
Astarte (myth), II 333b; III 282b
Astraea (myth), III 291b
Astral mythology, III 310a–310b
Astrology, I 118a–126b
  catarchic, I 118b, 123b–124b
  Causation, III 287b–288a
  celestial omens, I 118b–119b
  Chaldaeans, I 125a
  chance, II 232a–233b, 234b, 235a
  Christianity, I 123a, 123b
  cosmology, I 538b–539a
  Critodemus, I 121a
  Dante, II 233b
  defined, I 118a
  determinism, II 36a, 232b
  divination, I 118b–119b, 124b
  Dorotheus of Sidon, I 120a–122b, 124a, 124b
  double truth, II 35b–36a
  Egypt (ancient), I 119a, 119b–120a
  fate, II 232a–233b, 234b, 235a
  Faust (legend), III 247a
  four categories of, I 118a–118b
  freedom of speech, II 261b
  general, I 118a–118b, 123a–123b
  genethlialogy, I 118a, 119b–123a
  Gnosticism, I 125a–125b
  Greece (ancient), I 119a–122b, 123a, 124b, 125a, 125b
  harmony, II 392b; IV 40b
  Hermes, I 122b
  Hermeticism, I 125a
  historiography, II 479b–480a
  humanism, II 517b, 520a, 521a
  India (ancient), I 119a–119b, 121b–122a, 123a, 124a, 124b, 125b
  interrogatory, I 118b, 124b–125a

Islam, I 122b–125b; II 644a, 646b
  Judaism, I 119a
  logos, III 74b
  macrocosm and microcosm, I 119b–120a; III 128a–128b, 130b, 131a
  measurement, IV 399a, 402b
  medicine, I 118b
  Mesopotamia, I 118b–120a, 122a–122b, 125a, 125b
  Middle Ages, IV 153a
  military, I 118b
  Mithraists, I 125a
  music, II 392b; III 260b
  mythology, III 287b–288a, 288b, 290a–290b, 291a
  Nature, III 347b, 350b
  necessity, III 354a
  Neo-Platonism, I 119b, 123a, 125a
  Persia (ancient), I 122a–122b, 125b
  Plato, I 462b–463a
  Platonism, III 506a, 507b
  Porphyrius, I 121a, 125a
  primitivism, III 579b
  progress, III 628b, 631b
  Ptolemy, I 119a, 121a
  Pythagoras, I 120a
  Pythagoreans, IV 40b
  rationalism, IV 46a
  reformation, IV 65a
  religion, I 125a–126a
  revolution, IV 155b
  Rome (ancient), I 121b, 123a
  Saint Albertus Magnus, II 232a, 233a
  science, II 644a, 646b
  scientific classification, I 462b–463a
  skepticism, IV 242a
  sphujidhvaja, I 121b, 124a
  Stoics, I 119b
  technology, IV 360a
  Theophilus of Edessa, I 124a
  Tiberius, I 121a
  time, IV 399a, 402b
  universe, IV 40b
  Utopia, IV 461b
  World Spirit, II 392b
  Zoroastrianism, I 122a–122b, 123a
Astronomy
  alchemy, II 521a
  art, I 457b, 458a, 459a
  Bode, IV 42a
  China, I 355a
  Comte, III 535b, 642a
  Copernican paradox, III 77a
  Copernicus, IV 153a
  Cosmic Fall, I 511b

cosmology, I 554a
  culture, I 608b
  cycles, I 621b
  defined, I 213a
  evolutionism, II 187b
  Faust (legend), III 246b, 247a
  free will, II 245b
  Galileo, III 356a
  game theory, II 264a
  genius, II 313b
  geology, III 255b
  harmony, II 389a–390a; IV 40b
  hierarchy, II 443a, 448a
  humanism, II 521a
  imagination, I 513a–523b
  Islam, II 639a, 640b, 647a, 651b
  Judaism, I 536b
  love, III 106b
  mathematics, III 180a, 182b
  matter, III 192a, 194b
  measurement, IV 399a, 399b, 401a, 402a, 403a, 405b
  mountains in literature, III 255b, 256a, 257a
  music, II 313b, 389a–390a; III 260b, 270b
  mythology, III 287b, 310b
  Nature, III 348b
  necessity, III 353b, 356a
  Newton, III 194b
  numbers, III 403a
  order, II 443a, 448a
  Plato, I 462b–463a, 539b
  Pons, I 76b
  primitivism, III 579b
  probability, III 611b, 613b, 619a
  progress, III 625a, 628a, 630b, 632b, 642a
  psychology, IV 12a
  Ptolemy, I 515b; III 77a
  Pythagoreans, IV 32b, 40b
  relativity, IV 74a, 77b–78a
  Renaissance, IV 438b, 440a, 441a
  revolution, IV 153a
  scientific classification, I 462b–463a, 463b, 464a, 465a, 465b
  space, IV 295b, 299b, 303a, 305b, 306a
  sublime in external nature, IV 336b
  symmetry, IV 348b
  time, IV 399a, 399b, 401a, 402b, 403a, 405b
  unity of science, IV 431b, 433b
  universal man, IV 438b, 440a, 441a

Victorian sensibility, IV 221b
  virtuoso, IV 489a, 489b
Astruc, Jean (1684–1766), deism, I 651b
  historiography, II 490b
Astruc, Zacharie, impressionism, II 573a
Asura, II 39a
Asymmetry
  body, IV 348b
  evolution, IV 349a
  psyche, IV 349a
  reason, IV 349a
  symmetry, IV 347b, 349a, 350b, 351a, 351b
  time, IV 349a, 349b
Atatürk, Kamal (1880–1938), nationalism, III 337a
Athanasius, Saint (293?–373), freedom of speech, II 262a
Atharva-Veda, disease, II 395b
Atheism, II 344b, 355b, 360b, 363b
  agnosticism, I 19a, 22a, 24a
  atomism, I 134b, 136b–137a, 495b, 496b
  Bayle, IV 120a
  Blake, II 412b
  Buddhism, II 344a
  China, I 360a
  deism, I 646b, 648a–648b, 650a
  discontinuity, I 495b, 496b
  eighteenth century, I 402a
  Epicureanism, II 137b
  evil, II 162a, 168a–168b
  evolutionism, II 180b
  existentialism, II 192b
  faith, hope, and charity, II 213a, 213b
  Faust (legend), III 246b
  Feuerbach, I 74a
  free will, II 137b, 246b–247a
  Garaudy, II 213b
  Greece (ancient), II 565b
  Hegel, IV 291a
  hierarchy, II 444b, 445a
  Hobbes, I 136b
  humanism, II 520a; IV 128a
  impiety, II 565b
  intolerance, IV 120a
  irrationalism, II 637a
  Kant, IV 209a
  Kierkegaard, II 192b
  liberalism, III 42b
  Locke, IV 120a
  Machiavelli, III 119b
  Man-Machine, III 141a, 141b, 142a
  Marx, IV 291a

Marxism, **II** 213b
More, **I** 137a
music, **III** 267a
positivism, **III** 540b
progress, **III** 625a
religion, **IV** 116b, 120a
Renaissance, **IV** 128a
romanticism, **IV** 208b, 209a
Sartre, **II** 192b, 637a
skepticism, **IV** 244a
social contract, **IV** 255b
socialism, **IV** 291a
spontaneous generation, **IV** 310b
symbolism, **IV** 345a
theodicy, **IV** 380b, 381b
unity of science, **IV** 432b
Victorian sensibility, **IV** 221a
Athena (myth), **III** 272b
Athenaeus (2nd–3rd century A.D.), wisdom of the fool, **IV** 516b
Athens (ancient)
 abstraction, **I** 9b
 assemblies, **II** 256b–257a
 democracy, **II** 259a, 683a, 686a
 freedom of speech, **II** 256b–257a, 258a–260a, 261b, 262a
 impiety, **II** 565b, 566b
 law, **II** 565b, 674a, 679b, 680a, 680b, 681b–685a; **III** 7a
 Machiavellism, **III** 116a
Atomism, **I** 61a, 126a–141a; **II** 137b
Aaron ben Elijah of Nicodemia, **I** 496a
abstraction, **I** 1a
acquired characteristics, **II** 618b
al-Ghazali, **I** 496a
anti-hypothetical view, **I** 139a–140b
appearance and reality, **I** 94a
Aristotle, **I** 127a–129a, 130a, 130b, 131a, 132b, 133a, 134b, 495a–495b; **IV** 390b
atheism, **I** 134b, 136b–137a, 496b
Averroës, **I** 130b, 131a, 496a
biology, **I** 233b–234a, 235a
Boyle, **I** 135a, 137a, 138a, 138b–139a, 140a, 310b; **III** 194b
Bradwardine, **II** 200a
Bruno, **I** 133a, 133b, 494b–495a

causation, **I** 272a, 303b; **II** 18b
chance, **II** 226a
change, **III** 187b
Cicero, **I** 497a; **II** 137a
continuity, **I** 494a–497b
creativity in art, **I** 583b
culture, **I** 610b
Cynicism, **I** 631a
death, **I** 635a, 640a
defined, **I** 126b
Democritus, **I** 126b, 127b–131a, 132b, 134a, 134b, 494b–497a; **II** 547b, 582a–582b; **III** 187b; **IV** 3a, 51a
Descartes, **I** 134b, 135b–136b, 137b–138b; **III** 193b
determinism, **II** 18b, 237b
discontinuity, **I** 495b–497b
disease, **II** 398b
emotion, **III** 187b
Engels, **I** 497a–497b
Epicureanism, **I** 272a; **IV** 7a, 7b, 175b
Epicurus, **I** 130b, 132b, 135b–136a, 137a, 496a–497a; **II** 136a–137a, 237b, 244a, 582a–582b, 586b–587a; **IV** 51a
ethics, **IV** 319a
evolution of literature, **II** 173b
evolutionism, **II** 181b–182a
free will, **II** 237b, 244a, 245b
Galileo, **I** 133a, 134a–134b
Gassendi, **I** 134b, 135b–138b, 306b, 310b
good, **IV** 175b
Greece (ancient), **I** 126a–131a, 494b–497a
Hariot, **I** 133a, 133b–134a, 134b
Hegel, **II** 414b
Heraclitus, **I** 127a, 127b–128a
Hero of Alexandria, **I** 134a, 134b
Herodotus, **I** 132b
Hobbes, **I** 134b, 135b, 136a–136b, 137b, 138a
Hooke, **I** 135a, 140a
humanism, **III** 187b
Huygens, **I** 138a
impressionism, **II** 547b, 582a–582b
indeterminacy, **II** 586b–587a
India (ancient), **I** 496b
individualism, **II** 603b
Islam, **I** 495b–497b; **II** 641b, 642a, 642b, 643a
Leibniz, **III** 193b
Lenin, **I** 497a–497b

Leonardo da Vinci, **I** 133a
Leucippus, **I** 126b, 132b, 494b, 495a; **III** 187b; **IV** 51a
Lucretius, **I** 130b, 132b–133a, 136b, 137a, 497a; **II** 137b, 237b; **IV** 51a
Maimonides, **I** 495b, 496a
Man-Machine, **III** 132a, 132b, 133a, 134b, 139a
Marxism, **I** 497a–497b
materialism, **II** 245b
matter, **III** 185a, 187a–190b, 191b, 192b, 193a, 193b, 194b, 195a
Mersenne, **I** 135b, 137b–138a
metaphor, **III** 203b
metaphysical imagination, **III** 213b
Middle Ages, **I** 127a, 129b, 132b
motion, **IV** 51a
Nature, **I** 543b
necessity, **III** 353a
Newton, **I** 137a, 138a, 139b, 140a–140b, 518a; **II** 137b; **III** 194b, 195a
Nifo, **I** 130b, 131a
Non-Being, **IV** 299a
organicism, **III** 425a
pain, **III** 187b
pangenesis, **II** 622b, 623a
Parker, **I** 138b
Parmenides, **I** 127a–128a
Patrick, **I** 132a–132b
Pell, **I** 135b
Petty, **I** 135b, 136b
Plato, **I** 127b–128a, 539b; **II** 586b; **III** 188b; **IV** 34a
Plutarch, **I** 497a
psychology, **IV** 3a, 7a–7b, 8a, 22b, 27b, 28a, 28b
Pythagoreans, **IV** 32a, 34a
Pythocles, **I** 132b
rationalism, **IV** 51a
reform, **I** 138a–139a
religion, **III** 187b–188a, 203b
Renaissance, **I** 132b–138a
right, **IV** 175b
Roberval, **I** 135b
Russell, **IV** 394b
Saint Thomas Aquinas, **I** 496a
Scaliger, **I** 131a
Sennert, **I** 131a–131b
sensations, **II** 547b
skepticism, **IV** 234b
soul, **I** 231a
space, **IV** 299a
Stoicism, **IV** 319a
structuralism, **IV** 324b
teleology, **I** 303b

time, **IV** 389b–390b, 394b
universe, **III** 187b
void, **III** 187b
Wren, **I** 138a, 139a–139b
Atonement
 dignity, **IV** 138a, 138b, 140a
 mythology, **III** 277a, 279a, 281b
 Renaissance, **IV** 138a, 138b, 140a
 Saint Augustine, **IV** 138b
Atterbury, Francis (1662–1732), periodization in literary history, **III** 483a
Atticus, Titus Pomponius (109–32 B.C.)
 Neo-Platonism, **III** 372a, 372b
 skepticism, **IV** 238b
Attis (myth), **II** 335a–335b, 341a; **III** 281a, 288a
 agriculture, **IV** 104b
 religion, **IV** 96a
 salvation, **IV** 228b
Atum (myth), **II** 334a, 334b; **III** 278a
Aubignac, Abbé d' (1604–1676), drama, **III** 529b
Aubigné, Théodore Agrippa d' (1552–1630), baroque in literature, **I** 193b
Audubon, John James (1785–1851), conservation, **I** 474a
Auenbrugger von Auenbrugg, Leopold (1722–1809), medicine, **II** 401b
Auerbach, Erich, literary criticism, **I** 606a; **IV** 54b, 55a
Auerbach, Felix, entropy, **II** 117b–118a
Auger, Louis S., romanticism, **IV** 191a
Augsburg Confession, eschatology, **II** 157a
Augustine, Saint (354–430),
 abstraction, **I** 4b
 aesthetics, **II** 217b, 218a, 219a
 agriculture, **III** 635a
 alienation, **I** 35b–36b
 allegory, **I** 41b, 42a, 44a, 46b
 analogy, **I** 68b–69a
 angels, **IV** 138b
 Aristotle and, **IV** 9a
 art, **III** 227a, 635a
 art and play, **I** 102b
 atomism, **III** 191b
 atonement, **IV** 138b
 authority, **I** 147a–147b
 Bayle and, **IV** 119b
 beauty, **I** 197a–197b, 198a,

23

impiety, II 566b
law, II 689b; III 29a
periodization in literary history, III 481b, 483a, 483b, 484b
temperance, IV 370b
Aulard, François V. A. (1849–1928), historiography, II 496b
Aulen, G., II 360a–360b
Aurispa, Giovanni (1369?–1459), humanism, II 516b
Aurora (myth), III 297b
Aury, Madame Dominique, baroque in literature, I 192b
Austen, Jane (1775–1817), IV 475a
Austin, John L. (1911–1960), obligation, IV 184b
utilitarianism, IV 448b
Austin, John (1790–1859), common law, III 31a
Hart and, III 2b
justice, III 1b
law, III 1b–2a, 2b, 31a
natural law, III 1b
positivism, III 1b
Australia
academic freedom, I 14a
common law, II 696a
mythology, III 309a
positivism, III 550a
religion, IV 97a, 100a
social welfare, IV 282a
time, IV 399a
Volksgeist, IV 495a
welfare state, IV 510b
Austria
absolutism, I 593b
aesthetics, II 223b
architecture, I 398b
balance of power, I 181a, 181b, 186a, 186b
baroque in literature, I 191a
conservatism, I 484b
Counter-Enlightenment, II 106a
crisis in history, I 593b
economic history, II 61a
equality, II 144a
international peace, III 449a, 453b
Marxism, III 164b
nationalism, III 329b, 332a, 333a, 338b
naturalism in art, III 341a
peasantry, II 144a
phrenology, IV 23a
private property, III 655b
protest movements, III 67aa, 674a
psychology, IV 23a
Reformation, I 390a, 394b
revisionism, IV 274a

romanticism, IV 207a, 207b
social welfare, IV 277b, 283a
war, IV 500b
Austria-Hungary, nationalism, III 328b
Austrian Civil Code, II 656a
Authority, I 141a–162a
Adams, John, I 660a
Argentina, III 544a
Boniface VIII (Pope), II 689b
Brown, Norman O., I 161b
Bruno, III 513b
Burke, Edmund, I 152b, 154b
Calvin, I 150a
charity, II 212a
Cicero, I 142b–144b
common law, II 692a, 692b, 693a; III 31a, 31b
Comte, I 152b, 155b–156a
Conciliarists, I 149a, 149b
democracy, I 655a, 657a, 660a, 660b, 666b
dictatorship, I 158b–160a
evolution, III 646b–647a
faith, I 148a, 148b; II 212a
family, II 678b
fascism, I 159a–159b, 161a; III 674a
Filmer, I 152b
freedom, II 249a–250a
God, I 146b, 147a, 147b, 148b, 150a; II 356a, 358b
Godwin, I 160b
Greece (ancient), II 678b, 680a, 681a, 681b, 682b
Hegel, I 152b, 154b–155b
Henry VIII, II 690a
hierarchical, I 146a
Hitler, I 159b–160a
Hobbes, I 151b–152a, 657a; III 20b
holy, II 512a, 513b
Holy Spirit, I 148b, 150a
hope, II 212a
impressionism, II 581b
incremental, I 142b, 144a
individualism, I 161a–162a; II 599b
James, III 565b
Justinian, III 29b
Kant, I 153a
Kropotkin, I 160b
law, I 141b–146b; II 249a, 249b–250a, 678b, 680a, 681a, 681b, 682b, 686a, 689b–690a; III 4b, 5b, 11a, 29a–29b, 31a, 31b, 32a, 33b, 34a
Lenin, I 158b
liberalism, I 154a–154b, 158a; III 39b, 673a

literary criticism, I 597
Locke, I 152b–153a, 657a
Luther, I 149b–150a
Machiavelli, I 151a–151b; IV 315a
Marx, I 152b, 153b, 155a, 158b; IV 534b
Marxism, III 152b
Mexico, III 544a
Middle Ages, I 141b, 146b–148b, 150a; III 528b
mythology, III 288a, 293b, 301a
nationalism, III 331b
natural law, III 23b, 24b
natural rights, III 25b
Oriental thought, III 436b
papacy, I 149a–150a; II 689b
Pascal, IV 118b
Peirce, C. S., III 555a
perennial philosophy, III 459a
personal, I 142b–143a, 144a, 146a
Platonism, III 513b
positivism, I 155b–156a, 156b; III 544a
pragmatism, III 552a, 553a, 555a, 565b, 568a
progress, III 646b–647a
prophecy, III 660b, 661a, 668a
protest movements, III 673a, 674a, 674b–675a
psychology, I 161a–162a; IV 18a–18b
Pufendorf, I 152a
Puritanism, IV 18a–18b
religion, IV 118a, 118b
Renaissance, III 11a
Robespierre, I 153b
Roman Catholic Church, I 146b–150b; II 212a, 689b
Rome (ancient), I 141b–146b; II 686a, 689b–690a
Rousseau, I 152b, 153a–153b
sacramental, I 149a
sacred, II 512a, 512b
satire, IV 212a
Stalin, I 158b; III 152b
State, III 37b–38a; IV 313a, 314a, 314b, 315a, 316a, 316b, 318a
totalitarianism, I 158b–160a, 161a; IV 407b
welfare state, IV 509a, 510a
wisdom of the fool, IV 516b
work, IV 534b
Zeitgeist, IV 536a
Autolycus (fl. c. 310 B.C.), primitivism, III 581b

Automatism
Descartes, III 135b, 136b, 138b
psychology, IV 11a
See also Man-Machine
Automorphism, IV 351a–351b, 352a, 352b
Autonomy
idea, II 598a–598b, 602b, 603a
India, III 337a
individualism, II 498a–598b, 602b, 603a
nationalism, III 329a, 337a, 338b
naturalism in art, III 343a
Plato, II 629a
progress, III 629a
Switzerland, III 329a
Autrecourt, Nicolas of (d. 1350), causation, I 289a
Avalokitesvara (myth), II 344b
Avarice, millenarianism, III 225a
Avaux, Jean-François Félibien des (1658–1733), Gothic, II 372b–373a
Avenarius, Richard (1843–1896), positivism, III 545b, 547b
Averroës (1126–1198)
abstraction, I 4b
atomism, I 130b, 131a, 496a
causation, I 274a, 289a
cosmology, II 199a
discontinuity, I 496a
double truth, II 31b, 32a–32b, 33a, 34b, 35a, 37a
God, II 32a
heresy, II 426b
hierarchy, II 441a
immortality, I 639b, 645b
Islam, II 642b, 644b, 645b, 646a, 648a, 649a–650a
mimesis, III 227b
Neo-Platonism, III 377b
occasionalism, I 496a
poetics, III 528a, 528b
pragmatism, III 555b
science, II 203a, 204a
soul, II 32b
unity, II 34b
Avicebron (1021?–?1058), causation, I 274a–274b
hierarchy, II 441a
Islam, II 648b
Avicenna, (Ibn Sina, 980–1037)
abstraction, I 3b–4a, 4b
alchemy, I 30a
Al-Ghazali and, I 288b–289a
Aristotle and, I 4a

biology, I 231b
causation, I 273b, 274a, 287a, 288a–289a
classification of the sciences, I 463b
common nature, I 4a, 5b
doctrine of distinctions, I 3b–4a
God, I 288a–288b
hierarchy, II 441a
humanism, II 521b
Islam, II 644b, 645a–645b, 646a, 647a, 648a, 649a, 650a, 651a–651b
longevity, III 89b–90a, 91b
mechanics, II 201b
psychology, I 3b, 4b
scholasticism, I 3b
soul, I 3b
Avienus, Rufus Festus (fl. 4th century A.D.), *auctores*, III 528b
Avignon papacy (1309–1377), IV 64a, 65a
despotism, II 3a
Axiomatization, I 162b–172b
Cartesianism, I 166a
categorical deduction, I 166b
defined, I 163a
Descartes, I 164b, 165a, 165b
Duhem, I 166b
Euclid, I 163b–164a, 165a, 167b; III 172b, 175b
formalization, I 169b–170a, 172a
Fourier, I 166b
Frege, I 168b, 169b
Galen, I 164b
Galileo, I 165b
Gassendi, I 165b
Gergonne, I 167b, 168a
Gödel, I 170a–170b
Hilbert, I 168a, 170a, 170b
Hippocrates, I 164a
hypothetical deduction, I 166b
Kelvin, I 171b
Lagrange, I 166b
law, I 165a–165b
Leibniz, I 163a, 165a, 165b, 169b
Lévi-Strauss, I 171b
Lukasiewicz, I 168b–169a
mathematics, III 172b, 174a, 174b, 175a, 176a, 176b, 177a, 180a
Maxwell, I 166b
Megaric-Stoic logic, I 164a–164b
meta-mathematics, I 170a–170b
Mersenne, I 165b

Newton, I 164b–165a, 166a, 166b
Osiander, I 166b
Pascal, I 165b–166a
Pasch, I 167a–167b, 168a
Peano, I 168a, 169b
Pieri, I 167a
Poincaré, I 166b
Poncelet, I 168a
Post, I 169a
Ptolemy, I 166a
Pufendorf, I 165a–165b
pure hypothetical deduction, I 166b
Riemann, I 167a
Roberval, I 165b
Russell, I 168b, 169b
Saccheri, I 164b
Spinoza, I 165a
symbolization, I 169b
Tarski, I 170b
Whitehead, I 168b
Wittgenstein, I 169a
Wolff, C. F., I 165b
Ayer, A. J. (1910–   )
agnosticism, I 24a–24b
behaviorism, I 219b
good, IV 184a
matter, III 195b
moral sense, III 234b–235a
perennial philosophy, III 462b
pragmatism, III 568a
Ayres, Clarence E., economic history, II 60b
Ayscough, Florence (1878–1942), China, I 369b
Azazel (Bible), III 284a
Azorín (1874–1967), symbolism, IV 342a

B

Baader, Franz von (1765–1841)
economics, IV 207b
Marx and, IV 207b
romanticism, IV 207b, 209b
Baal (myth), III 281b, 282b, 283b
religion, IV 104b
Baalat (myth), III 282b
Babbage, Charles (1792–1871), methodology, III 559b
Babbitt, Irving (1865–1933),
Buddhism, I 256a
China, I 369b
classicism, I 455a
conservatism, I 484a
irony, II 633b

literary criticism, I 603a
romanticism, IV 195a, 196b
ut pictura poesis, IV 474b
Babeuf, François-Noël Emile (1760–1797)
class, I 443b
communism, III 520b
equality, II 145b, 147a
Platonism, III 520b
socialism, IV 288b
Utopia, IV 463a
Babrius (1st century A.D.), theriophily, IV 384b
Babylon, I 427b–428a
Marduk (myth), IV 104a
Mesopotamia, IV 104a
New Year Festival, IV 104a
religion, IV 104a
Babylonia
alchemy, I 27b–28a
assemblies, II 253a
Code of King Hammurabi, III 6b
cosmic voyages, I 527a
cosmology, I 536b–539a
cycles, I 621b
death, I 634b, 644b
despotism, II 252b
dualism, II 39a
evil, II 163b
first interpretation of history, II 465a
freedom of speech, II 252b, 253a
geometry, III 171a–172b
God, II 335b–336a
hermeticism, II 431b
historiography, II 465a, 469a, 472a, 474a, 476b
Islam, II 639a
law, II 686b; III 6b
mathematics, III 171a, 171b, 173a, 180b, 182b
matter, III 186a
mythology, II 39a; III 275b, 279a, 280a–281b, 289a, 310a–310b, 311b
music, III 260b, 264b
nomos, II 683b
progress, III 628b
prostitution, II 683b
Pythagorean cosmos, IV 38b
reincarnation, I 644b
religion, IV 104a
writing, III 180b
Babylonian Captivity, Judaism, II 656a
Bacchius Senex (4th century A.D.?), music, II 313a
Bacchus (myth), III 291a, 297a

neo-classicism in art, III 365a
religion, IV 94a
Bach, Johann Sebastian (1685–1750)
baroque, II 321a–324a; III 267a–267b, 271a–271b
Christianity, I 404b
genius, II 321a, 324a
God, III 267a–267b
imagination, III 208a
romanticism, IV 209b
Bachelard, Gaston
cosmic images, I 513b, 522b
irrationalism, II 636b, 638b
metaphysics, III 209b, 210a, 212b
motif, III 242b
Bachofen, J. J.
matriarchy, III 313b
mythology, III 313a–313b
symbolism, III 313b
Bacon, Francis (1561–1626), I 80a, 81a, 83b, 172b–179b
Agrippa and, I 174a, 174b
Alembert and, I 177b
analogy, I 65b, 77b
alchemy, I 31a, 32b, 174a, 174b
ambiguity, I 55a
anthropomorphism, I 88b
antimetaphysics, III 213b
Aristotle and, I 173b; III 355b; IV 432a
atomism, I 135a–135b, 138a–139a
balance of power, I 182a, 183a
behaviorism, I 219a
Blake and, II 412b; III 398b
Boyle and, I 172b, 176b, 177a
Cardan and, I 173b, 174a, 174b
causation, I 276a, 290a, 292a, 294b–295a, 296a, 301a, 301b
certainty, I 304b, 306a, 311b
Cicero and, I 173b
classification of the sciences, I 464b
Comte and, I 172b, 178a
Copernicus and, I 176a, 178a; III 356a
cosmic fall, I 509b–510a
cosmic voyages, I 532a
Dalgarno and, I 176b
Deleyre and, I 177b
Della Porta and, I 174b
Descartes and, I 177a, 177b; III 215a–215b

Dewey and, I 172b, 174a, 178a
Diderot and, I 172b, 177b
Duns Scotus and, I 173b
emotion, IV 466b
empiricism, I 175a–175b; III 215a
Enlightenment, I 173b; II 90a, 96b, 100a; III 215b
Epicureanism, II 137b
equity, II 152b, 153b
eschatology, II 160a
evolution, III 559a
experiments, III 383b, 384b, 386b, 387a
Fontenelle and, I 176a
forms, I 294b; III 356a
as a founder of modern thought, I 173a
freedom of inquiry, I 10a
Galen and, I 173b
Galileo and, I 176a, 177a, 177b, 178b; III 356a
Gassendi and, I 176b, 177a
genius, II 295a
Giambattista and, I 176b
God, I 294b, 301b; II 349b, 355a; IV 434a
Hakewill and, I 510a
happiness, II 379b
harmony, II 393a
Hegel and, I 175b; II 412b
Heidegger and, I 179a
heresy, II 428a
historians, III 356a
historiography, I 503a; IV 148b, 151a
history, IV 434a, 467b
Hobbes and, I 216b
Husserl and, I 178b
idea, II 547a
ideology, II 553a
idola, II 553a–553b; III 212b–213a, 215a, 218a
induction, I 221b, 503a; III 384a
influences on, I 172b–173a
invention, IV 128a
Kant and, I 178a; III 218a
knowledge, I 173a; III 559a; IV 361b, 434a, 462a
language, II 667b; III 62b–63a, 73a–74b
law, I 290b, 292a; II 688b
learning, I 173a; IV 434a, 486b
Leibniz and, I 172b, 177a
Liebig, J. von, I 178a
literature, III 85a–85b
logic, III 355b; IV 434a
longevity, III 92a
Machiavelli and, I 173a
Machiavellism, III 121a–121b

magic, I 174a–174b
Maistre and, I 178a
Man-Machine, III 135b
Marx and, I 179a
materialism, IV 432a
mathematics, III 356a
matter, III 187a; IV 434a
memory, IV 434a
Mersenne and, I 176b
metaphysics, I 294b; III 211b, 212b–214a, 215a–215b, 216a, 217a, 218a, 218b, 219a, 221b, 222a; IV 434a
method, III 383b–384b, 385b, 386a–387b; IV 462a
Mill and, I 178a
mind, III 212b–213a, 215a
morality, IV 433b–434a
motion, I 294b–295a
music, III 393a; IV 466b
mythology, III 299a, 299b–300a
natural history, I 173b, 176a–176b
Nature, I 173a, 175b–176a, 219a; III 383b; IV 361b, 432a, 434a
necessity, III 355b–356a, 358a
Newton and, I 172b, 177a; III 383b–384b, 385b, 386b, 387a, 387b, 397a, 398b
optics, III 397a, 398b
painting, IV 466b
Paracelsus and, I 173b, 174b
Pascal and, I 176b
Peirce and, I 176b; III 558b–559a
perennial philosophy, III 459b, 460a, 461a
perfectibility, III 471b
phenomena, III 355b–356a
philosophy, IV 432a–432b, 433b–434a, 462a
physics, III 356a; IV 434a
Plato and, I 173b
Platonism, III 510b
Plutarch and, I 173b
poetry, IV 434a
politics, IV 361b, 433b–434a
positivism, I 173b; III 534a
pragmatism, III 355b, 356a, 558b–559a
progress, IV 433b
psychology, IV 19b, 23a
Ramus and, I 173b, 175b, 176a
reason, IV 434a
rhetoric, III 383b; IV 172a
Rousseau and, I 179a

Saint Thomas Aquinas and, I 173b
science, I 173b, 174a–174b; IV 462a
scientific method, II 553a
search for a method, I 173b, 175b–176a
Seneca and, I 173b
senses, IV 466b
skepticism, I 311b; IV 244b
socialism, IV 287b–288a
society, IV 361b, 462a
speculative thought, III 213a–213b
spontaneous generation, IV 308b
technology, I 173b, 174b–175b; IV 361a–363a, 364a, 364b, 462a
teleology, I 301a, 301b
Telesio and, I 173b, 545a
tradition, I 173b–174a
unity of science, IV 431a, 432a, 433b–434a
universal man, IV 443a
universality, IV 432a
utopianism, II 379b; IV 462a
Vico and, I 172b
view of antiquity, I 176a
virtuoso, IV 486b
Voltaire and, I 177b
Wallis and, I 177a
wealth, IV 361b
Whewell and, I 178a
Wilkins and, I 176b
work, IV 533b, 534a
Bacon, Roger (1214?–1294), I 77b
  Adamic language, III 74a
  alchemy, I 31a
  classification of the sciences, I 464b
  double truth, II 31b
  empiricism, III 73a–74b
  Enlightenment, II 90a
  grammar, III 62b
  Islam, II 645b, 650b
  language, III 62b–63a, 73a–74b
  linguistics, III 62b–63a, 73a–74a
  longevity, III 90a
  meliorism, III 91b
  method, II 197a; IV 434b
  pragmatism, III 555b
  scientific reform, III 73a–74a
  unity of science, IV 434b
  universal man, IV 441a
  Webster, John, III 74b
Baconianism, I 172b–179b
  See also Bacon, Francis
Bādarāyana, astrology, I 124b

Baer, Karl Ernst von (1792–1876)
  Darwin and, IV 57a
  evolutionism, II 179b
  recapitulation, IV 57a, 58a
  species, II 179b
Bagehot, Walter (1826–1877)
  acquired characteristics, II 620a
  association of ideas, I 115b
  progress, III 623b, 624a, 643a
  romanticism, IV 193a
Bahm, Archie, Buddhism, I 256b
Bahnsen, Julius, evil, II 166a, 167a
Bahr, Hermann (1863–1934), expressionism, II 206b–207a
Baif, Jean-Antoine de (1532–1589), Gothic, II 368a
Baillie, John, progress, III 636b
Bain, Alexander (1818–1903), association of ideas, I 116a
  behaviorism, I 219a
  evolutionism, II 184b
  Man-Machine, III 143a
  Peirce and, III 558a
  pragmatism, III 558a, 566a
Baird, James (1802–1876), symbolism, IV 341b
Baju, Anatole, symbolism, IV 340a
Bakunin, Michael (1814–1876)
  anarchism, I 71b, 74a–74b, 75a
  authority, I 160b
  communism, I 74a–74b
  Marx and, IV 166b
  Marxism, III 152a
  perfectibility, III 471a
  revolution, IV 166b
  socialism, IV 293a
  society, III 471a
Balance of payments, natural liberty, II 67a–68a, 70b
Balance of power, I 179b–188a
  antiquity, I 179b–180b, 184a
  Concert of Europe, I 186b
  Congress of Vienna (1815), I 186a, 187a
  defined, I 179b
  eighteenth century, I 184a–186b
  Fénelon, I 183b–184a
  Fox, I 187a
  France, I 181a–181b, 182b–184a, 186a–187b

Francis I, I 182a
Frederick the Great, I 186a
French Revolution, I 187a
Gentz, I 186a
Germany, I 181b, 186a, 186b, 187b
Gibbon, I 186a
Great Britain, I 181a, 181b, 183a, 184a, 186a–187a
Great Northern War, I 186a
Greece (ancient), I 180a
Grotius, I 182a, 184a, 184b
Guicciardini, I 181a, 181b, 182a, 183a
Habsburg dynasty, I 181b, 182b, 183a, 186a
Henry VIII, I 182a
Huguenots, I 182b
Hume, I 180a–180b
international peace, III 452a, 456a, 456b
Italy, I 180b–181b, 187a
liberty, I 185a–185b
Louis XIV, I 183a–184a
Louis XV, I 186a
Machiavelli, I 180a–182b
Mazarin, I 182b–183a
Medicis, I 180b
Metternich, I 187a
Napoleon I, I 186a, 186b
Netherlands, I 181b, 183a, 187a
nuclear weapons, I 187b
Ottoman Empire, I 186b
Renaissance, I 180b–181b
Richelieu, I 182b, 185a
Roman Catholic Church, I 182b
Rome (ancient), I 180a
Russia, I 186a, 186b, 187a–187b
Seven Years' War, I 186a
since 1815, I 186b–188b
Spain, I 181a, 181b, 182b, 183a
Talleyrand, I 186a
Third World, I 187b
Thucydides, I 180a
Treaty of Utrecht, I 183a, 184a
Treaty of Westphalia, I 184a
universal dominion, I 183a–183b, 184b–185a
Venice, I 180b, 181b, 182b
war, I 185a–185b; III 452a
War of the Spanish Succession, I 183a, 185b–186a
Wilson, Woodrow, I 187a
World War I, I 186b–187a, 187b; III 332a
World War II, I 187a
Balázs, N. L., entropy, II 116b
Balbiani, E. G. (1825–1899), genetic continuity, II 286b,

287a
Baldensperger, Fernand, baroque in literature, I 192a–192b
Baldinucci, Filippo (1624–1696)
  aesthetics, II 222b
  mimesis, III 229a
Baldur (myth), III 282b
Balguy, John (1686–1748)
  ethics, IV 72a
  Hutcheson and, III 233a
  moral sense, III 233a
  Shaftesbury and, III 233a
Balkans
  nationalism, III 329b, 330a, 336a
  protest movements, III 672a
Ball, John (d. 1381)
  socialism, IV 287a
  vox populi, IV 498a
Ballads
  historiography, II 464b
  vox populi, IV 498b–499a
Ballet
  Faust (legend), III 252a
  mythology, III 291a–291b
Baltrusaitis, Jurgis, chance images, I 343b
Balzac, Guez de (1597?–1654)
  genius, II 294a
  taste, IV 354b
Balzac, Honoré de (1799–1850)
  genius, II 308b
  literary criticism, I 601a
  literature, III 86a, 87b
  motif, III 237b, 239b, 242b
  realism in literature, IV 52a, 52b, 53b, 55a
  romanticism, IV 201b
  ut pictura poesis, IV 467a, 469a, 474b
Bancroft, George (1800–1891)
  historiography, II 493a
  psychology, IV 24a
  transcendentalism, IV 24a
  Volksgeist, IV 495b
Bandinelli, Baccio (1493–1560), mythology, III 291b
Banier, A.
  mythology, III 301b, 303a
  rationalism, III 301b, 303a
Banks, Joseph (1743–1820), primitivism, III 602a, 602b
Banks, Thomas (1735–1805), neo-classicism in art, III 370b
Baptism, I 413b; IV 102b
  mythology, III 282a, 283a, 284a, 291b

reformation, IV 61a, 61b, 62a
religion, IV 102b–103a, 113b, 114a–114b
Saint Paul, I 416a
Saint Peter, I 414a
salvation, IV 230a
Saxons, IV 113b
Barante, Baron de (1782–1866), romanticism, IV 203b
Barbarism
  Counter-Enlightenment, II 103a, 105b
  crisis in history, I 591a–591b
  culture, I 620a
  cynicism, I 629a, 632a
  despotism, II 1a–4a, 16b, 17a
  evolutionism, II 176a
  war, IV 501b, 502a
Barberini Panels, Master of, chance images, I 347a, 347b
Barberino, Francesco da (1597–1679), *virtù*, IV 477b
Barbeyrac, Jean
  despotism, II 4b
  natural law, II 20b
Barckley, Richard
  Chain of Being, I 511b
  cosmic fall, I 511b
  genius, II 294a
  hierarchy, II 435b
Bardesanes (154–223?), astrology, I 125a
  Buddhism, I 255a
Bardi, Giovanni de' (1534?–1612), cosmic harmony, IV 41a
Bardo Tödol, I 644b
Baretti, Giuseppe (1719–1789), literature, III 81b
Bar-Hillel, Y., pragmatism, III 553a, 557a
Barlaam (monk), humanism, II 516b
Barlach, Ernst (1870–1938), expressionism, II 206b
Barlow, Joel (1754–1812), psychology, IV 21a
Baroja, Pío (1872–1957), symbolism, IV 342a
Barolo, Conte Falleti di, romanticism, IV 190b
Baron, Hans, periodization in history, III 480a
Baronius, Cesare (1538–1607), historiography, II 484a, 485b
Baroque
  architecture, I 398b

disease, II 403b
expressionism, II 207b–208a
genius, II 321a–323a
Germany, III 483b, 484a
Gothic, II 368b, 373a
Gurlitt, I 189a
impressionism, II 582b
music, II 321a–323a; III 271a–271b
mythology, III 293b
naturalism in art, III 340b, 341a, 342a
neo-classicism in art, III 363a, 365b, 366b, 368a, 369a, 370b
periodization in history, III 479a
periodization in literary history, III 483b, 484a
sculpture, III 342a
temperance, IV 377b
Baroque in literature, I 188b–195b; IV 331b
Ariosto, I 189a, 190a
Aury, Mme, I 192b
Austria, I 191a
Baldensperger, F., I 192a–192b
Brie, I 191a
Browne, I 191a, 193b, 195a
Bunyan, I 193a
Burckhardt, I 188b, 189a
Calderón, I 190a, 195a
Camões, I 191a
Černý, I 192b–193a
Cervantes, I 190a–190b, 195a
Collins, I 193a, 195a
conceptism, I 190a
Corneille, I 192a
Crashaw, I 191b, 193a, 195a
Croce, I 191b–192a, 194b
D'Annunzio, I 189b, 194b
Donne, I 191b, 193a, 193b, 194b, 195a
d'Ors, Eugenio, I 194b–195a
Dryden, I 191a, 193b, 194b
Eliot, T. S., I 193a
Euripides, I 195a
expressionism, I 190a
Fletcher, I 192a, 193a, 193b
Ford, I 191a
France, I 189b, 190b–191a, 192a–192b, 193b, 194a, 195a
Friederich, I 191a
Garth, I 191a
Germany, I 189a–192a, 194a, 194b, 195a
Góngora, I 190a, 192a, 195a

28

Gongorism, I 190a, 195a
Gracián, I 189b, 190a
Great Britain, I 189b, 191a, 191b, 193a–195a
Guevara, I 190a, 195a
Gundulić, I 193a
Haerten, I 191b
Hatzfeld, I 190a–191a, 194a
Hungary, I 191a, 193a
Italy, I 189a–189b, 191a, 191b–192a, 194a, 195a
Jonson, Ben, I 191a
La Fontaine, 190b
Lebègue, I 192a–192b
Linné, I 195a
Lope de Vega, I 190b
Lyly, I 195a
Marino, I 190a, 194b, 195a
Menéndez y Pelayo, I 188b–189a
Michelangelo, I 189a
Milton, I 191a, 192a, 193a, 193b, 194b, 195a
Molière, I 190b
Montaigne, I 188b
Moret, I 192a
Netherlands, I 191b
Nietzsche, I 189a
Ortega y Gasset, I 192a
Peyre, I 192a–192b
Pfandl, I 190b
Pindar, I 192a
Poland, I 189a, 191a, 192b
Pope, I 191a
Praz, I 191b, 193a, 193b
Quevedo, I 190a, 192a, 195a
Rabelais, I 190b, 195a
Racine, I 190b, 192b, 193b, 195a
Rembrandt, I 191b
Reynold, Gonzage de, I 192a
Rimbaud, I 195a
Ronsard, I 192b, 195a
Rousseau, I 188b
Rousset, I 192b
Ruskin, I 194a–194b
Shakespeare, I 189b, 190a, 191a
Spain, I 188b–191a, 192a, 193b, 194a, 195a
Spitzer, Leo, I 190b
Spoerri, I 190a, 191b
Sponde, I 192b
Strich, I 189b, 192a
Sypher, I 193b
Tasso, I 189a, 190a, 192a, 195a
Taylor, Edward, I 194a
Thomson, I 191a, 193a
Tillyard, I 193a
Tirso de Molina, I 192a

U.S., I 193a, 193b–194a, 194b
Venturi, I 191b
Vives, I 188b
Wagner, Richard, I 189a
Walzel, I 189b, 194b
Wilamowitz-Moellendorff, I 189a
Wölfflin, I 189a–190a, 191a, 191b, 192b, 193b
Wordsworth, I 191a
Yugoslavia, I 191a, 193a
Zeigler, I 189b
Barraclough, G., periodization in history, III 479a
Barre, André, symbolism, IV 340a
Barreda, Gabino, positivism, III 544a
Barrès, Maurice (1862–1923), conservatism, I 483a
Barros, João de (1496–1570), China, I 354b
Barrow, Isaac (1630–1677), I 308b
atomism, I 139a, 139b–140a
causation, I 276a–276b
Gassendi and, IV 393a
mathematics, III 178b–179a, 388a–388b
measurement, IV 403a–403b, 405a
method, III 380b, 387a–388b
Newton and, III 380b, 387a–388b
time, IV 393a, 403a–403b, 405a
Barrows, John Henry, Oriental thought, III 435b
Barry, James (1741–1806), neo-classicism in art, III 364a
Bartas, Seigneur du (1544–1590)
baroque in literature, I 193a, 195a
music, II 391a, 391b, 392b
Barth, Karl (1886–1968), I 24a, 408a
Bible, II 359a
determinism, II 30b
eschatology, II 160b–161a
evil, II 168a
existentialism, II 192a
faith, II 213a, 359b
God, II 29a, 359b, 360a–360b, 363b; III 467a
grace, III 467a
holy, II 513b, 514a
Jesus Christ, II 29a
Lutheranism, I 408a
original sin, II 29a

perfectibility, III 467a
predestination, II 29a
sin, II 29a; III 467a
theodicy, IV 381b
time, II 160b–161a
women, IV 528a
Barthes, Roland
literary criticism, I 605a–605b
structuralism, IV 327b–328a, 328b
symbolism, IV 344b
Bartholdt, Richard, international peace, III 453b
Bartholomew, Saint, Machiavellism, III 117b
Bartlett, Phyllis, mythology, III 295a
Bartoli, Cosimo (fl. 1567), music, II 316b
Bartoli, Pietro Santi (c. 1635–1700), neo-classicism in art, III 363b
Bartolus of Sassoferrata, nationalism, III 321b
social contract, IV 253a
Barton, Bruce, mythology, III 276b
Bartram, William (1739–1823), conservation, I 474a
Basch, Victor, empathy, II 88a–88b
Bascom, John, psychology, IV 24b
Basedow, Johann Bernhard (1724?–1790), Pietism, III 495a
Basil the Great, Saint (330?–?379), I 44a, 68b, 378b
Adam (Bible), III 583a–583b
Christianity, III 589b–590b
community ideal of, I 378a
culture, II 127b
cynicism, III 590a–590b
dignity, IV 137a, 137b
environment, II 127b
Faust (legend), III 246b
health, III 590b
Hercules (myth), III 590b
Hesiod and, III 590a
humanism, II 520b
Nature, III 590b
Neo-Platonism, III 373b
pleasure, III 590b
primitivism, III 583a–583b, 589b, 590a–590b
Basile, Giambattista, baroque in literature, I 191b–192a, 195a
Basilides (d. about 140 B.C.), Buddhism, I 255a
ethics, II 329a–329b

Gnosticism, II 329a–329b, 330b
Basque language, III 63a
Basson, Sébastien, teleology, I 303b
Bastian, H. C. (1837–1915)
Jung and, III 312b
mythology, III 312b
spontaneous generation, IV 311a
Bastiat, Claude Frédéric (1801–1850), natural liberty, II 69a
Bateson, F. W.
baroque in literature, I 193a
evolution of literature, II 173a
Bateson, William (1861–1926), progress, III 646b
Bathsheba (Bible), prophecy, III 661a
Batista y Zaldívar, Fulgencio, positivism, III 545a
Batman, Stephen, music, II 388a
Batoni, Pompeo Girolamo (1708–1787), neo-classicism in art, III 369a
Bataille, Georges, irrationalism, II 638a, 638b
Batteux, Charles (1713–1780)
aesthetics, II 550a; IV 355a
classification of the arts, I 460a–460b
Counter-Enlightenment, II 109a
genius, II 294a, 295a, 324a
ideal, II 550a
mimesis, III 229a–229b
music, II 324a
taste, IV 355a
ut pictura poesis, IV 468a, 471b, 472b
Battifol, Pierre
modernism, I 421a
natural law, III 23a
Battle of the Books, poetics, III 531b
See also Ancients and Moderns
Baucis (myth), III 283a
Baudelaire, Charles Pierre (1821–1867), I 109b
art, II 310b
China, I 369a
ekphrasis, IV 469a
existentialism, II 194a
genius, II 310b
impressionism, II 571b, 573a, 574b, 578a, 581a
irony, II 633b

literary criticism, I 601a–601b, 605a
love, III 104a–104b
metaphysical imagination, III 212a, 212b
modernity, I 58b–59a
naturalism, IV 53b
photography, II 571b
realism in literature, IV 53b
romanticism, IV 196b, 209b
senses, II 574b
structuralism, IV 327b
symbolism, IV 338b, 339b, 340b, 342b, 344a, 344b, 345a
synaesthesia, IV 473a
Weltschmerz, IV 209b
Bauer, Bruno (1809–1882)
 alienation, I 37b, 38a
 Hegel and, IV 291a
 Marx and, IV 291a
 socialism, IV 291a
 work, IV 534b
Bauer, H., iconography, II 538b
Bauer, Walter, heresy, II 430a
Baugh, Albert C., baroque in literature, I 193b
Bauhaus, poetry, IV 475a
Baumgarten, Alexander Gottlieb (1714–1762)
 aesthetics, IV 356a, 471b
 beauty, I 202a
 genius, II 295a
 taste, IV 356a
Baur, F. C. (1792–1860), Strauss and, II 412b
Bavaria
 balance of power, I 181a
 Reformation, I 390a, 395a
Bavaria, Duke of, Counter-Reformation, I 395a
Baxter, Richard (1615–1691), demonology, I 670a
Bayer, G. S., China, I 367a
Bayes, Thomas (1706–1761),
 chance, I 338b–339a
 Laplace and, III 612b
 probability, III 608b, 609b–611b, 612b, 613a, 615a
Bayesian probabilities, game theory, II 265b
Bayeux Tapestry, iconography, II 528a
Bayle, Pierre (1647–1706), I 79b, 91a
 atheism, IV 120a
 Bible, II 353a
 China, I 360a
 conscience, III 42b
 Cosmic Fall, I 510b–511a
 deism, I 648a, 649a
 despotism, II 18a, 13b
 dualism, II 38a

Edict of Nantes, IV 119b
Enlightenment, II 89a, 91b, 94a
God, II 355b; IV 119b, 120a
heresy, IV 120a
Huguenots, IV 119b
ideal, II 549b
individualism, IV 119b
intolerance, IV 119b–120a
liberalism, III 42b, 43a
liberty of conscience, III 42b
literature, IV 124a
mythology, III 301b
Nature, II 94a
perennial philosophy, III 461b
periodization in history, III 479a
persecution, IV 119b
rationalism, III 301b
religion, IV 119b–120b
rhetoric, IV 172b
Roman Catholic Church, IV 120a
Saint Augustine and, IV 119b
skepticism, IV 241a, 245b–248a, 250b
Bayne, S. F., education, II 74b
Bazard, Saint-Amand (1791–1832)
 progress, III 641a–641b
 socialism, IV 290a
Bazarov, I. P., entropy, II 114b
Bazin, René (1853–1932), China, I 369a
Beachcroft, T. O., baroque in literature, I 193a
Beale, John, Bacon and, I 177a
Beard, Charles (1874–1948),
 historicism, II 462a
 Marxism, III 149b
 pragmatism, III 553b, 569a–569b
Beard, George (1839–1883), psychology, IV 28b
Beast-machine, III 135b–138a, 139b, 144a
Beatniks, progress, III 628b
Beattie, James (1735–1803),
 certainty, I 317a–317b
 classification of the arts, I 460b
 nature, I 317a
 truth, I 317a, 317b
Beaufort, Louis de, historiography, II 487a
Beaumanoir, Philippe de (1250–1296)
 common law, II 692b
 law, III 28a

nationalism, III 321a, 322b
Beaumont, Léonce Élie,
 baroque in literature, I 192a
 catastrophism, IV 418a
Beauty, I 195b–214a
 Addison, I 202a–202b
 adumbration, III 292a
 aesthetics, I 208b; II 216b–219a, 221a, 222b–223b; IV 353b–356b
 Albert the Great, II 222b
 Alberti, II 218b
 Alexander, Samuel, I 209b
 Alison, I 202b–203a
 anthropology, I 213b–214a
 Aristotle, I 196b, 200b, 578b, 580b, 583b, 584b; II 217a; III 226b
 art, I 461b
 art and play, I 203b–204a
 attributive view of, I 209b–210a
 Balguy, III 233a
 Baumgarten, I 202a
 Bell, Clive, I 207b
 Bellori, II 549b
 Bembo, II 218b
 benevolence, III 232b
 Bosanquet, I 207a, 207b
 Bruno, II 443a; III 513b
 Burke, I 202b, 211b
 Cardano, II 218b
 characteristic, II 551b
 Chernyshevsky, I 211a
 Child, I 213b–214a
 Cicero, II 217a
 clarity in, I 197b–198a
 classicism, I 200a–200b
 Coleman, I 209b
 color, IV 337a
 consonance in, I 197b–198a
 Copernicus, IV 75a
 cosmic images, I 519b, 521a
 Counter-Enlightenment, II 103a
 Cousin, I 198a
 as a creative force in man, I 205b
 creativity in art, I 578b, 579a, 580a–581b, 583a–584b, 585b, 586a
 Croce, I 207b
 Darwin, I 204a
 defined, I 195a–196b
 Definist view of, I 210a
 definiteness in, I 196b
 dependent, I 203b
 Desoir, I 212b
 Diderot, I 199b–200a
 dignity, IV 136a, 139a
 divine, II 550b
 Du Bos, I 202b

Ducasse, I 209b
Edwards, IV 110a
emotion, I 201a–201b
Empathy Theory, I 213a
Enlightenment, II 90a
evil, III 500b
expressionism, II 207b, 208a
Eysenck, I 213a
Fechner, I 212b
Fénelon, I 201b
Ficino, II 218a; III 511a
Flaubert, I 208a
Formalism, I 210b
fortune, II 228a
free, I 203a–203b
Fry, I 207b
genius, II 293a, 294a
Gilson, I 197b, 210a
God, I 197a–197b, 585b; III 368b
Goethe, I 203b
Gothic, II 370a
Grosseteste, II 218a
Guyau, I 213a
Hagedorn, II 550b
harmony in, I 197a, 199a, 205b–206a
Harvey, I 195a
health, II 399a
Hegel, I 204a–205a
Heidegger, I 212a
Hemsterhuis, II 550a
Herder, II 551a
Herskovits, I 213b
Hesiod, I 196b
hierarchy, II 443a, 446a, 447b
Hofstadter, I 212a, 212b
Hogarth, I 202b, 210b
Hölderlin, III 524a
Homer, I 196a
Horace, I 200b, 201b
humanism, IV 129b
Hume, I 201b, 202b; III 232b
Hutcheson, I 198b–199b; III 231a, 231b
idea, II 545b
ideal, II 218b, 549a–551b
idealism, I 203b, 207a
immediate perception, I 206a
impressionism, II 580b, 581a, 583a
integrity, I 197b–198a
Kames, II 221a
Kant, I 203a–203b; II 85b, 221a, 223a–223b
Keats, III 524a
Kepler, IV 75a
Klopstock, II 550b
knowledge, I 203a, 206a–206b

Koffka, I 213a
Lavater, II 551b
Leibniz, II 446a, 447b
Lenz, II 551b
Lipps, I 213a
literary criticism, I 597b
literature, IV 330b–332a
Locke, I 198b
Lomazzo, II 550a
love, I 205a–205b; III 231a
Maritain, I 210a
Marshall, I 209a
measure in, I 197a
Mendelssohn, Moses, II 550b
Mengs, II 550b
metaphysical foundation, I 205a–206a
Michelangelo, III 229a
Middle Ages, I 197b; II 217b–218a; IV 123b
mimesis, III 226b–229a
mind, I 201b
Mondrian, II 222b
monism, I 208b
Moore, G. E., I 209b–210b
moral sense, III 230b–233a
morality, III 512a
Müller-Freienfels, I 212b
music, III 269a–269b
mythology, III 274b, 291b, 292a
natural, II 550b, 551b
Nature, I 200a–200b; II 549b; III 347a, 350b
neo-classicism in art, III 367b, 368a, 368b
Newton, III 393a–394b, 398b
Nietzsche, I 200b
Nondefinist view of, I 210a–210b
objective conception of, I 200a–201a
objective existence of, I 196a–200a
objectivism, I 210b, 211a–211b
Ogden, I 208a, 209a
optics, III 393a–394b, 398b
order, I 196b, 197a, 198a, 199a; II 443a, 446a, 447b
organicism, III 422a, 423a, 425b, 426a
Palladio, II 218b
Pepper, I 208b, 209a
perfectibility, II 549b; III 465a
phenomenology, I 212a–212b
philosophy, I 212a; II 549a–551b
Plotinus, I 197a, 586a; II 217a–217b; III 423b; IV

347a
pluralism, I 208b
poetics, III 525b
poetry, III 394b, 526a
Polykleitos, I 196b
positivism, I 196a
pre-Socratics, I 196b
Price, III 233a
proportion, I 196a, 197a, 198a
Pseudo-Dionysius, II 218a, 222b; III 227a
psychology, I 212a, 212b–213a
Pyrrhonism, I 198a, 198b
Pythagoreans, I 196b; II 217a
relativity, IV 75a, 86a, 88b, 91a
religion, IV 110a
Renaissance, I 197b, 198a, 200b; II 218a–218b; III 508b, 510a, 511a, 511b, 512a, 513a, 513b, 514a; IV 122b, 126b, 129b, 136a, 139a, 440b
repudiation of, I 207a–208b
Reynolds, II 550a
Richards, I. A., I 208a, 209a
romanticism, I 203b, 207b
Ruskin, I 209a; IV 339a
Saint Albertus Magnus, I 585b
Saint Augustine, I 197a–197b, 198a; II 217b; III 227a; IV 139a
Saint Bonaventura, II 222b
Saint Thomas Aquinas, I 585b, 586b; II 218a
Santayana, I 209a; II 88b
Schelling, I 203b, 204b
Schiller, I 203b–204a
scholasticism, II 217b
Schueller, I 211a
Shaftesbury, I 201a, 205b
Shelley, III 524a
Sibley, I 207a–207b
Siroto, I 214a
smell, I 209b
sociology, I 212a, 213a–213b
Spencer, I 204a
Stace, I 211a
Stevenson, I 208a
Stoicism, II 217a
subjective approach to, I 201a–205a
sublime in external nature, IV 333b–337a
symbolism, IV 338a, 338b, 339a
symmetry, I 196a, 196b, 198a, 199a; IV 347a
taste, I 202a; IV 353b–356b

theater, I 208a
Tolstoy, I 209a
touch, I 209b
transcendentalism, I 207b
truth, I 212a–212b
Ulrich of Strassburg, II 222b
unity, I 198a, 199a
universal, II 550a–550b
universal man, IV 440b
usefulness, I 201a
utilitarianism, IV 446b, 447a, 448b
Valentine, I 212b
van Gogh, I 212a–212b
virtue, I 198b; III 231a, 233a
Vitruvius, II 217a
Wieland, II 550b
Winckelmann, I 200b; II 550a, 550b
Xenophon, I 196b, 201a
Zola, I 208a
See also Plato, Platonism
Beauvoir, Simone de
existentialism, II 191a
women, IV 523b, 529a
Beazley, J. D., mythology, III 286b
Bebel, August (1840–1913), revisionism, IV 264b, 265a
Beccaria, Cesare (1738–1794)
Enlightenment, II 89b
utilitarianism, II 380b
Bechterev, W. (1857–1927), psychology, IV 14a, 28a
Becker, Carl (1873–1945)
historicism, II 462a
pragmatism, III 553b
Becket, Thomas à (1118?–1170)
historiography, II 484a
nationalism, III 319b
tragic sense, IV 417a
Beckett, Samuel (1900–
)
appearance and reality, I 98b–99a
comedy, I 470a
death, I 637b
irony, II 633b
literature, III 88b
tragic sense, IV 414b
Beckner, Morton
nature of universals, I 237b
positivism, III 550b
Becoming
Chain of Being, I 332a–334a
evil, IV 414b
time, IV 390a, 390b, 391a–391b, 396b
tragic sense, IV 414b, 415a
work, IV 534a

Becquerel, Henri (1852–1908), cosmology, I 553a
Bede, Saint (673–735), I 380b
dignity, IV 139b
disease, II 399a
Gothic, II 367a
hierarchy, II 438a
historiography, II 473a, 478b
numbers, III 399b
work, IV 531b
Beecher, Henry Ward (1813–1887), psychology, IV 23b, 25b
Beeckman, Isaac (1588–1637)
atomism, I 133a–133b, 134b
music, III 262b
Beers, Henry A. (1847–1926), romanticism, IV 193b
Beethoven, Ludwig van (1770–1827), genius, II 325a, 325b
Beger, Lorenzo, neo-classicism in art, III 363b
Béguin, Albert, romanticism, IV 196b
Béguines
Augustinianism, IV 109a
heresy, II 423a
Behaviorism, I 214a–229b
animals, I 220b–221b; II 584b–585a, 585b, 586a
Aristotle, I 214a, 214b, 215a–216a, 228a; IV 5a, 49b
associationism, I 222a–222b, 227b
Bekhterev, I 218b, 222a
Berkeley, I 221b
Bernard, Claude, I 218a
Boerhave, I 220a
Bridgman, I 219b
Cabanis, I 220a
Condillac, I 220a
Darwin, I 214b, 220a
Descartes, I 217a–217b, 218b, 223a
Dewey, I 214b
Diderot, I 220a
empiricism, I 218b–220b
environment, II 123a–124a
Epicureanism, IV 8a
Fabre, I 221a
Fechner, I 219b
Galileo, I 224b
Greece (ancient), II 677b–678b, 682b
Guthrie, I 225b–226a, 227b
Hall, I 218a
Hartley, I 220a
Harvey, I 217b
Hobbes, I 214a, 214b,

216a–217a, 219b, 220a, 224b
Holmes, Justice, III 567a
Hull, I 214b, 217a, 223b, 227b–225b, 227a
Hume, I 219a–220a, 221b
imprinting, II 584a–586a
inductivism, I 221b–222a
James, I 214b, 222a–222b; III 562b–563a
Kant, I 219b
Keynes, I 219b
La Mettrie, I 214a, 218b, 220a
Lashley, I 223a–223b
law, II 677b–678b, 682b
learning, II 584a–586a
Lewin, I 224b
Locke, I 219a, 220a, 221b
Loeb, I 221a
McDougall, I 220b, 221a, 224a; II 382b
Magendie, I 218a
Man-Machine, III 134a, 139b, 140a, 143b, 144a, 144b, 145a
materialism, I 222b–223b
Mill, James, I 219a
Mill, John Stuart, I 219b, 220a
molar theory, I 217a, 223b, 224b–225a
Moore, G. E., I 219b
Morgan, Lloyd, I 221a
Pavlov, I 218a–218b, 222a, 224b
Peirce, C. S., I 214b
Piaget, I 229a
Pillsbury, I 220b, 221a
pleasure, II 382b
positivism, III 549a–549b
pragmatism, I 226b; III 552a, 557a, 562b–563a
Pratt, I 219b
rationalism, I 218b
reflexology, I 217b–218b
Romanes, I 221a
Russell, Bertrand, I 219b
Skinner, I 219b, 226a–228a
Spencer, I 218a
Stoicism, IV 8a
Taine, I 220a
Thorndike, I 218b, 221a, 224b, 225a, 226b, 227a
Titchener, I 221b
Tolman, I 217a, 223b–224b, 225a, 226a
Utopia, IV 464a
Watson, I 214a–215a, 216a, 217b, 218b, 220b–223b, 225a, 227a; II 382b
Weber, I 219b
Weiss, I 222b–223a, 223b
Wundt, I 221b; II 382b

Behn, Aphra (1640–1689)
cosmic voyages, I 528a
primitivism, III 601b, 603a
virtuosa, IV 488b
Being
Aristotle, III 189b; IV 431b, 432a
cosmic images, I 514b
dualism, II 40b
Edwards, IV 110b
existentialism, II 192b, 193b, 195a
Faust (legend), III 249b
God, II 361b, 363a, 363b, 364b, 365b
Heidegger, II 193b, 195a, 637b
Heraclitus, III 187a
hierarchy, II 445a, 446a
infinity, II 614a, 615a
irrationalism, II 637a, 637b
Kierkegaard, II 192b, 193a
Leibniz, IV 434b
macrocosm and microcosm, III 129a
matter, III 185b, 187a, 188a, 188b, 189b
necessity, III 359a
Neo-Platonism, III 375a, 376a–377b
Non-Being, IV 299a
Parmenides, I 493b, 495a; III 187a
perfectibility, III 464a–464b, 467b
Plato, II 40b; III 188a, 188b; IV 431b
Platonism, III 509a
pragmatism, III 555a
Pythagoreans, I 580a–580b
religion, IV 109a, 109b, 110b
romanticism, IV 204a
Saint Thomas Aquinas, IV 432a
Santayana, III 555a
Sartre, II 637a
science, I 465b
space, IV 299a, 305a
Spinoza, IV 434b
time, IV 389b, 390a, 391b, 393b, 395b, 398a
unity of science, IV 431b, 432a–432b, 434b
work, IV 535a
Zeitgeist, IV 536b
See also Chain of Being
Bekhterev, Vladimir (1857–1927), behaviorism, I 218b, 222a
Bekker, Balthasar (1634–1698), witchcraft, IV 522b
Bel (myth), III 281a
Belgium

balance of power, I 187a
capitalism, I 396a
conservatism, I 484b
impressionism, II 578a
language, II 660b
mythology, III 289a, 289b
nationalism, III 330b, 338b
protest movements, III 673a
revisionism, IV 274a
revolt against Joseph II, I 404a
war, IV 505a
Belief
emotion, III 562b
historiography, IV 147b
human nature, III 572a, 575b
liberalism, III 45a
Lovejoy, III 552b
metaphor, III 203a
Peirce, III 558a
Plato, IV 33b, 35b
pleasure, II 387a
pragmatism, III 552b, 558a, 562b
progress, III 625a, 632a, 635a, 636a, 636b, 637b, 641a, 641b, 642b
Pythagoreans, IV 33b, 35b
religion, III 203a; IV 105a
Renaissance, IV 147b
Speusippus, IV 35b
tragic sense, IV 412b, 414a
truth, III 562b
Waldensians, II 420a
Belinsky, Vissarion (1811–1848)
literary criticism, I 606b
naturalism, IV 53b
realism in literature, IV 53a, 53b
Belknap, Jeremy (1744–1798), democracy, I 660a
Bell, Charles (1774–1842), I 116a
behaviorism, I 218a
Man-Machine, III 142b
psychology, IV 24b
Bell, Clive (1881–1964), aesthetics, II 219a, 221a
art, II 298b
art for art's sake, I 110b
beauty, I 207b
individualism, II 298b
Bell, Daniel, ideology, II 556a–556b
Bellamy, Edward (1850–1898), Utopia, IV 463b
Bellamy, Joseph (1719–1790)
Edwards and, IV 110b
religion, IV 110b
Bellarmine, Cardinal Roberto (1542–1621)

Galileo, III 356a
necessity, III 356a
Platonism, III 513b–514a
skepticism, IV 242b
war, III 441b
Bellay, Joachim du (1522–1560)
literature, III 82b
Platonism, III 507b, 514a
Belleau, Rémy (1528–1577), literary paradox, III 77b
Bellerophon (myth)
law, II 681a
temperance, IV 366a
Bellers, Fulk, hierarchy, II 436b
Bellers, John, medicine, II 402a
Belles lettres
literary paradox, III 76a, 76b
literature, III 81b, 83a, 85a, 85b
primitivism, III 593b, 599b
Rousseau, III 599b
Bellini, Giovanni (1431–1516)
impressionism, II 577b
mythology, III 291b, 292b
Bellori, Giovanni Pietro (1636?–1700)
beauty, II 549b
iconography, II 528b, 534b
ideal, II 549b, 550a
naturalism in art, III 339a–339b
ut pictura poesis, IV 466a–466b, 469a
Bembo, Cardinal (1470–1547)
aesthetics, II 218b
love, III 512b
mimesis, III 229a
Petrarch and, III 512b
Platonism, III 510a, 511a, 512a, 512b, 514a
poetics, III 531b
Ben Azariah, Rabbi Elizer, equity, II 151b
Benda, Julien (1867–1956), classicism, I 455a
Benedetti, G. B. (1530–1590)
mechanics, II 205a
music, III 262a–262b
Benedict of Aniane, reformation, IV 63b–64a
Benedict of Nursia (480?–?543), I 378a
prophecy, III 667a
reformation, IV 63b, 64a, 64b
work, IV 531b
Benedict XV, Pope (1854–1922)
modernism, I 423b

Roman Catholic Church, IV 526b–527a
women, IV 526b
Benedictines, I 399a
historiography, II 473b
reformation, IV 63b–64a
Benevolence
Egypt (ancient), III 487a
good, IV 178a
happiness, II 380a
Hume, III 232a, 232b
Hutcheson, III 231a, 231b, 232a
millenarianism, III 223b
moral sense, III 231a–232b
religion, IV 111a, 111b
right, IV 178a
Victorian sensibility, IV 218b, 219b
utilitarianism, IV 444b, 447a, 447b
Bengel, Johann Albrecht (1687–1752)
Counter-Enlightenment, II 105a
eschatology, II 157a–157b
Benivieni, Girolamo (1453–1542), Platonism, III 511a, 511b–512a
Benlowes, Edward, music, II 394a–394b
Benn, Gottfried, expressionism, II 206a, 209a
Bentham, Jeremy (1748–1832)
anarchy, I 73a, 437b
antipathy, IV 178b
association of ideas, I 114a
causation, I 291a
certainty, I 317a, 317b–318a
civil disobedience, I 437b–438a
classification of the sciences, I 465b
common law, III 31a
common sense, III 234a
democracy, I 657b, 662a–663a
economics, IV 277b
Enlightenment, II 89b, 90b, 93a, 97b, 98b
equality, II 145a
evil, II 167b; III 470a
goals, IV 178b
good, IV 177b, 178b, 179a, 181b–182a, 185a
happiness, II 380b, 381a–381b; IV 454a
hedonism, II 167b, 381a; IV 277b, 454b
Hume and, I 317a, 317b–318a; III 234a
Hutcheson and, III 234a

individualism, II 596b, 597b, 602a
justice, IV 279a
Kant and, III 444b
knowledge, I 662b
language, I 317b–318a
law, I 291a; III 31a, 470a
liberalism, III 45a–45b, 46b
Marx and, II 381b
measurement, IV 181b–182a, 454a
Mill and, I 318a–318b; III 470a; IV 278b, 279a
moral sense, III 233b, 234a
natural law, III 22a, 234a
pain, II 167b, 381a–381b; III 470a; IV 178b, 277b, 451a, 451b
peace, III 444a–444b, 452b
Peirce and, III 558a
perfectibility, III 470a, 471b
pleasure, II 167b, 380b, 381a–381b; IV 178b, 181b, 277b, 431a, 451b, 454a
politics, II 98b
pragmatism, III 558a
prejudice, III 233b
private property, II 381a
psychology, IV 23a
rationalism, III 233b, 234a
right, IV 177b, 178b, 179a, 181b–182a, 185a
rights, I 437b–438a
romanticism, IV 277b
social welfare, IV 277a–277b, 278b–279a, 280a, 280b, 283a
State, I 657b, 662a–663a
sympathy, IV 178b
war, III 444b
wealth, II 381a; IV 277b
Weber and, I 260b
See also Utilitarianism
Bentley, Richard (1662–1742)
attitude toward antiquity, I 81a
Bruno and, IV 298a
mountains in literature, III 258b–259a
Newton and, I 311a
poetry, III 531b
space, IV 298a
Bentley, Robert, infinity, II 608a
Benz, Ernst, Buddhism, I 255a
Benz, Richard, romanticism, IV 197a
Berak (Bible), prophecy, III 660b
Berchet, Giovanni (1783–1851), romanticism, IV 190b
Berdyaev, Nicholai A. (1874–

1948)
love, III 98b
theodicy, IV 383a
Bergaigne, Abel, mythology, III 308a
Berger, Gaston, psychology, IV 15a
Bergh, Henry, theriophily, IV 388a
Bergman, Gustav
determinism, II 18b
positivism, III 545b, 549a
Bergson, Abram, social welfare, IV 279b, 280a, 283a, 283b
Bergson, Henri (1859–1941),
abstraction, II 636b
chain of Being, I 334a
consciousness, III 565a
Creation, I 576a
death, I 641b
emotion, III 565a
empathy, II 88b
Enlightenment, II 104b, 108b
entropy, II 118b
evolution, III 474a, 563a, 565a
evolution of literature, II 172b
evolutionism, II 182b, 183a–183b, 186a
existentialism, III 565a
experience, III 552b, 565a
God, I 576a; II 359a
imagination, II 209a, 212b, 221a–221b, 222a
immortality, I 641b
intuition, III 565a, 565b
irrationalism, II 636b
James and, III 565a, 565b; IV 396a, 396b
literary criticism, I 604b
Lovejoy and, III 552b
metaphor, III 207a
modernism, I 420a
motif, III 241a–241b
mythology, III 309b
perfectibility, III 474a
Platonism, III 523a
positivism, III 545a
pragmatism, III 552b, 563a, 564b, 565a, 565b
psychology, III 565a; IV 12b
realism in literature, IV 55a
religion, III 207a, 565b; IV 119b
romanticism, IV 210b
Schelling and, IV 210b
science, II 636b
space, IV 301a
spiritualism, III 563a, 565a, 565b

symbolism, IV 344a
symmetry, IV 349b
theodicy, IV 383a
theriophily, IV 388b
time, II 183a; IV 349b, 391b, 394b, 396a, 396b, 397a
universe, III 474a
violence, III 564b
vitalism, II 636b; III 565b
Bergstraesser, Arnold, Pietism, III 494b
Beria, Lavrenti, Marxism, III 157a
Berkeley, George (1685–1753)
abstraction, I 4a, 7a–9a
Anglicanism, IV 20a
appearance and reality, I 97a–97b
behaviorism, I 221b
causation, I 276b
certainty, I 312b, 317a, 317b
change, IV 395a
creation, I 572b
deism, I 651b
dualism, II 246a
environment, II 120b
free will, II 246a
God, I 276b, 572b; II 246a, 352a–352b
Hume and, I 312b
idea, II 547b
idealism, I 276b; III 561b
infinity, II 606a
knowledge, IV 246a
language, II 352b
mathematics, III 173a
matter, I 317a; II 120b; III 185b
Maxwell and, IV 80b
morality, II 352b
motion, IV 85b
Nature, II 352b
necessity, III 357b
Newton and, III 395b, 396a; IV 75b
optics, III 395b, 396a
perennial philosophy, III 457a
periodization in literary history, III 482a
Platonism, III 506b, 523b
pragmatism, III 561b
psychology, IV 19b, 20a
relativity, IV 75b, 80b, 85b–86a, 89b
rotation, IV 86a
sensation, II 120b
skepticism, IV 245b, 246a, 248b
space, IV 85b, 301b

sublime in external nature, IV 334b

time, IV 394b, 395a

utilitarianism, IV 448a, 449a, 449b

vision, IV 334b

Berkenhout, John, literature, III 82a

Berlin, Isaiah
    causation, I 286a
    individualism, II 599a

Berliner, R., iconography, II 538b, 540b

Berlioz, Hector (1803–1869), motif, III 236a
    romanticism, IV 208b
    ut pictura poesis, IV 473a

Bernard, Charles de (1804–1850)
    literary criticism, I 601a
    realism in literature, IV 52a

Bernard, Claude (1813–1878)
    behaviorism, I 218a
    cybernetic theory, II 126a
    disease, II 404a, 404b, 405a
    environment, II 125a–125b, 126a
    longevity, III 93a
    Man-Machine, III 142
    milieu intérieur, II 126a

Bernard, L. L., war, IV 507b

Bernard of Arezzo, I 275b

Bernard of Chartres (12th century), poetics, III 528b

Bernard of Clairvaux, Saint (1091–1153), I 46b, 53a
    aesthetics, II 218a
    anti-intellectualism, III 591a
    dignity, IV 140a
    God, III 591a
    heresy, II 417b
    knowledge, III 591a
    love, III 98b, 107b
    primitivism, III 591a
    reformation, IV 64b

Bernardin de Saint Pierre, Jacques Henri (1737–1814), environment, II 127b

Bernardino of Siena, Saint (1380–1444), chance, I 337a

Bernays, Jakob (1824–1881), catharsis, I 267a, 268a, 269b
    language, III 547b
    positivism, III 547b

Bernhardi, Friedrich von (1848–1930), war, IV 505a

Berni, Francesco (1497–1536), Platonism, III 513a

Bernini, Domenico, genius, II 303a

Bernini, Giovanni Lorenzo (1598–1680), I 398b
    genius, II 303a–303b, 309a
    iconography, II 530a, 538a
    ideal, II 549b
    mimesis, III 228b
    neo-classicism in art, III 369b

Bernoulli, Daniel (1700–1782)
    game theory, II 265b
    social welfare, IV 277a, 278a, 282a
    utility, IV 454a, 454b, 457a

Bernoulli, James (Jakob or Jacques; 1654–1705), chance, I 337b
    de Moivre and, III 609a
    De Witt and, III 607a
    direct problem, III 608b
    game theory, II 264b
    Huygens and, III 607a
    inverse problem, III 608b
    Laplace and, III 612a, 612b
    Law of Large Numbers, III 607a–609a
    Leibniz and, III 607a, 608b
    mathematics, III 179b
    probability, III 607a–609a, 610a, 612a, 614a

Bernoulli, Nicholas (1687-1759), game theory, II 264b

Bernoulli Theorem, III 608a, 609a, 611a, 612b, 614a, 618a–618b, 619a

Bernoulli trial, III 607b, 619a–619b

Bernoulli-de Moivre-Laplace theorem, III 611b

Bernoulli-Poisson theorem, III 614a, 615b

Bernstein, Eduard (1850–1932)
    capitalism, III 161b 162a, 162b, 163a, 164a
    class, III 162a, 162b
    cooperatives, III 163b
    democracy, I 664a, 664b
    economics, III 149a, 162a–162b, 163b
    empiricism, III 162b, 163a
    ethics, III 162b–163a, 164b
    evolution, III 161b, 162b, 163a
    Kant and, III 163a
    Kautsky and, III 164a
    Luxemburg and, III 162b
    Marxism, III 148a, 149a, 152b, 161a–164b, 165a, 165b, 166a, 167b, 168b, 169a, 169b; IV 266b–267b, 270a
    morality, III 163a
    revisionism, IV 266b–273a, 275a
    revolution, III 161b, 162b, 163a, 163b
    skepticism, III 163a
    socialism, I 663b; III 162b–164b
    surplus value, III 162b
    unions, III 163b
    value, III 162b
    Webb and, III 163b

Bertalanffy, L. acquired characteristics, II 619a

Berthelot, Marcelin (1827–1907), classification of the sciences, I 466a

Berthold of Regensburg, music, III 266a

Bertoni, Giulio, baroque in literature, I 191b

Bertrand, Louis Marie Émile (1866–1941), classicism, I 450b

Berzelius, Jöns Jakob (1779–1848), fermentation, II 283a, 283b

Bessarion, Johannes (15th century)
    dignity, IV 144b
    humanism, II 516b

Best, George, historiography, IV 149a

Bethmann-Hollweg, Moritz August von (1795–1877), war, IV 505a

Bettini, Mario, cosmology, IV 41b

Beudant, François Sulpice (1787–1852), natural law, III 22b

Bevan, Aneurin, welfare state, IV 513b, 514a

Beveridge, William, welfare state, IV 513a

Bevilaqua, Clóvis, positivism, III 541b

Beza, Theodore (1519–1605), heresy, II 424b, 425a
    Reformation, IV 67b

Bhagavad-Gita, theodicy, IV 379b

Bhairava (myth), II 344a

Bible
    agriculture, III 279a, 279b, 281a, 282a
    Alain of Lille, III 590b
    Alembert, II 353a
    alienation, I 34a–34b
    allegory, III 282b, 666b
    Anabaptists, I 390a
    authority, I 147a, 150a
    Buddhism, I 255a
    Calvin, I 392a; III 255a; IV 67a–67b
    Calvinism, I 395b–396a

catastrophism, IV 418a, 418b, 419b, 420a
catharsis, I 264b
causation, I 290a
chaos, IV 297a–297b
charity, II 209b, 210a
children, III 595b
Christianity, III 588b, 589a, 589b, 590b, 591a; IV 102b, 103a, 371a
city, I 427b, 429a
civilization, III 276b, 279a–279b
class, I 442a–442b
communism, I 396a; IV 286a
community, III 276b
continuism, I 503b
continuity, I 492b, 493a, 502b, 503b
Cosmic Fall, I 505a–505b, 506a
cosmic harmony, IV 38b, 40b
cosmic voyages, I 524a
cosmology, I 21a, 536b, 538b, 543a, 543b, 544a, 545b; III 281b
Counter-Enlightenment, II 103b, 104b, 105b
Creation, I 571a–571b
cults, III 276b, 277a, 282a, 284a
culture, II 127b, 128b
cycles, I 623b
death, I 639b, 640b, 644a; III 278b, 279a, 281a, 282b, 284a
deism, I 647b, 649a, 650b
demonology, I 668a, 668b, 669b
design argument, I 672b, 673a
determinism, II 26b
dignity, IV 136b–137a, 138a, 139b, 144a, 145b
disease, II 396b, 399a, 403a; III 279a
double truth, II 31b, 35b
dualism, II 39a, 42a–42b
economic history, II 47b, 58b
Eden-motif, I 607b
education, II 74b
Egypt (ancient), I 359a–359b
environment, II 127b, 128b
equality, II 140a–140b, 142a, 142b
equity, II 151a–152a
eschatology, II 154a–156b, 157b, 160a–161a
evil, II 163b–164a

evolutionism, II 176a, 176b, 180a
existentialism, II 192a
faith, II 209b, 210a
Faust (legend), III 246a
free will, II 244b
freedom, II 249b, 250a
freedom of speech, II 252a, 254b–256a, 262a
genetic continuity, II 281b
Geneva, III 255a
genius, II 316a
geology, III 255b
Gnosticism, II 327b, 328a, 328b–329a, 329b–330a
God, I 571a–571b; II 336a–337b, 341b, 342b, 349b, 353a, 358a, 359b, 360b, 361a, 363a, 365b, 366a
Gospel-books, IV 371b
Gothic, II 379a
happiness, II 375b, 378b
health, II 396b, 399a, 403a
Hegel, II 411a, 412a
heresy, II 416b, 417b, 418a, 419a, 419b, 420a, 421b, 422a, 425a, 426b, 427a, 428b
heroes, III 276b, 279b, 280b–282b
hierarchy, II 435b, 440a
history, I 359a–359b, 376b; II 156b–157b; III 275b–284b, 666a–666b
holy, II 512a–512b, 513b
humanism, II 517b, 520b; IV 135a
Huxley, I 18a–18b, 21a
iconography, II 527b, 528a, 539a
immortality, I 639b, 640b, 644a, 644b
impiety, II 564a, 565a
individualism, II 597a
infinity, II 604b
Israel (ancient), IV 226b–227b
Judaism, IV 103b, 104a
kingship, III 277a, 281a
language, II 669a
law, I 290a; II 249b, 250a; III 6b, 7a, 35b
liberalism, III 40b, 42a
linguistics, IV 423b–424a, 426a, 427a, 427b
literary criticism, I 596b
Locke, IV 258a
longevity, III 90a
love, III 96a–96b, 97a, 98a, 100a, 101a
loyalty, III 108b–109a, 112a, 115a
Luther, I 390a–390b, 392a, 394a

macrocosm and microcosm, III 127b, 129a, 130a
makom, IV 296a–296b
mathematics, III 180b
matter, III 186a–186b, 190b
metaphor, III 201b–202b, 204a–206b, 207b
migration, III 275b, 279a, 280b–281a
millenarianism, III 223b, 225a
misogyny, IV 524a
modernism, I 419a, 420b–421a, 422a
motif, III 237a, 240b, 242b
mountains in literature, III 253a–255b, 257b
music, II 316a, 394a; III 265a, 265b, 266a, 267a, 269b, 270a
mythology, III 275a–286a, 286b, 288a, 291a, 301a, 301b, 302b, 304a, 304b, 305b, 310b, 311b
nationalism, III 325a
natural law, III 17b, 18b
Nature, III 349a
necessity, III 354b, 355b
neo-classicism in art, III 370b
pain, III 278b, 284a
peace, III 440b, 441a, 445b
perfectibility, III 465b, 466a, 466b, 468b, 472a
periodization in history, III 476b, 477a
Persia (ancient), I 359a–359b
philanthropy, III 487b–489a
phrenology, IV 23b
Pietism, III 493b
Plato, IV 369a
Platonism, III 505a, 512a, 519a
pleasure, II 375b, 378b; III 278b
poetics, III 528b
primitivism, III 582b, 583a, 583b, 588b, 589a, 589b, 590b, 591a, 593a, 595a, 595b, 600a
progress, III 634b, 635a, 636a
prophecy, III 657a–664a, 664b, 666a–668a, 669b
protest movements, III 670b, 674b
Protestantism, I 395b–396a
psychology, IV 9a, 10a, 17b, 18b, 19a, 23b
punishment, III 283a
Pythagoreans, IV 38b, 40b
Ramism, IV 45a

realism in literature, IV 55a
reformation, IV 61a, 61b–62b, 63a, 64b
Reformation, IV 67a–67b, 68a
reincarnation, I 644a
Renaissance, IV 121b, 124a, 135a, 136b–137a, 138a, 139b, 144a, 145b
ritual, III 275b, 276b, 277a, 278a, 279b, 281a, 281b–282a, 282b, 284a, 284b
Roman Catholic Church, I 394a
romanticism, IV 198b, 200b
sacrifice, III 279a, 279b, 280a, 281b
Saint Augustine, IV 9a
salvation, IV 226b–227b, 229a–229b, 230a–230b
Septuagint, I 412b, 417a, 667a
sin, IV 226b–227b, 229a–229b, 230a–230b
skepticism, IV 242b, 246b–247a
social contract, IV 252a–252b, 258a
socialism, IV 286a, 287a, 291a
space, IV 296a–296b, 297a
spontaneous generation, IV 308b
State, IV 315b
Strauss, II 412b–413a
symmetry, IV 348a
temperance, IV 369a, 371a, 371b, 375a, 375b
theodicy, II 163b–164a
theriophily, IV 384a, 384b, 386a, 388a
time, IV 402a
tragic sense, IV 415b, 416a
translation into vernacular, I 387a, 390b
uniformitarianism, IV 418a, 418b, 419b, 420a, 423b–424a, 426a, 427a, 427b
universal man, IV 442b
Utopia, IV 460a–460b
virtues, IV 371b
Vivian, IV 371b
vox populi, IV 498b
wisdom of the fool, IV 517a–517b, 518a, 519a
witchcraft, IV 521a, 521b, 522a, 522b
women, IV 523b, 524a, 524b, 525b, 526b
work, IV 531a–531b
Wycliffe, I 387a
Zwingli, I 390b
See also Historiography, Religion

Bichat, Marie François Xavier (1771–1802)
  class, I 448b
  Comte and, III 534a
  disease, II 404a
  equality, I 448b
  positivism, III 534a
Biel, Gabriel, dignity, IV 141a
Big bang hypothesis, I 566b–567b, 569a
Bigelow, Sturgis, Buddhism, III 437a
Bilbao, Francisco, positivism, III 543b
Binary expansion, probability, III 619b
Binary stars, I 550b
Binet, Alfred (1857–1911), psychology, IV 13a
Biogenesis, spontaneous generation, IV 311a, 312a
Biogenetic Law, IV 56a, 57b–58a
Biogeography, culture and environment, II 131b
Biography
  humanism, II 518b
  literature, IV 333a
  poetry, IV 471a
  Rome (ancient), II 468a
Biological immortality, I 645b–646a
Biology, I 229b–246b, 465b
  acquired characteristics, II 618a–621a, 622a
  Alcmaeon, I 230b
  amino acid sequences, I 239b–241b, 245b–246a
  analogy, I 241b–242a
  anatomism, I 231a, 232a
  Anaxagoras, I 231b, 233b, 234a
  antiquity, I 229b–236a
  Aristotle, I 230a, 231a, 231b–236a; II 623a; III 354a; IV 4b
  atomism, I 233b–234a, 235a
  Avicenna, I 231b
  Bolton, I 240b–241a
  Britten, I 240b–241a, 241b
  classification, I 233a–233b
  Comte, III 535b
  conservation, I 473a
  continuity, I 492b, 498b–500b
  cosmology, I 232a
  culture, I 609a
  Darwin, I 236b, 237a
  De Beer, I 236b, 237a, 237b, 239b
  Descartes, I 242b–243a, 245b

determinism, I 245b–246b;
II 24a

Diderot, II 177a, 177b–
178a; III 217a

Diodorus Siculus, I 232a

Diogenes of Sinope, I 233b

disease, II 398a, 400a,
403b, 405b

DNA, I 238a, 239b–241b,
245b

Empedocles, I 233b

Epicureanism, I 235a, 236a

ethics, III 646b

evolution, I 236b–239a; III
646a, 646b

evolutionism, II 176b–180a,
181a, 182b, 183b, 184a,
184b, 186b

Faust (legend), III 248b

Fitch, I 241a, 241b

four elements, I 230a–231a

Galen, I 231a, 231b, 232a,
235a–235b

game theory, II 273a–273b

Gegenbaur, I 239b

genetics, I 231b–232a

Geoffrey St. Hilaire, I 236b–
237a

God, II 359a

Greece, I 229b–236a

happiness, II 375a, 382a–
384b

Hippocrates, I 230a

historiography, II 24a

history, I 236b–239a; II 24a

homologies, I 236b–242a

humanism, II 521b

hylozoism, I 229b, 234b

idealism, I 237a, 237b

inheritance, II 618a–621a,
622a, 623a, 623b, 624b–
625a, 626a, 626b

international peace, III 448b

La Mettrie, I 242b

language, II 669b

Lankester, I 237a–237b

Laplace, I 242b–243a

linguistic paleontology, IV
425a–425b

linguistics, IV 424a, 424b,
425b–427b, 428a, 429a

logical empiricism, III 548b,
549a, 550b

Lucretius, I 234a

Man-Machine, III 131b,
134b, 136a, 136b, 139a–
142a, 143a, 144a, 144b,
145a, 146a

Margoliash, I 241a, 241b

Marxism, II 620a, 621a

matter, III 192a, 194a

Maupertuis, II 177a–177b

models, I 242b–246b

nationalism, III 330a, 330b

necessity, III 354a, 355a,
360a, 360b

Neo-Platonism, I 235b

organicism, III 427a

organismic view of, II 121a

Owen, I 237a, 237b

pangenesis, I 231b; II 623a,
623b, 624b–625a, 626a,
626b

Pasteur, I 232a

perfectibility, III 471a, 475a

periodization in literary history, III 485b

Persia, I 231b

Picasso, I 239a

Plato, I 232a, 233a–235a;
III 354a

Platonism, I 237a, 237b

pleasure, II 375a, 382a–
384b

pneuma concept, I 231a,
232a

positivism, III 534a, 535b,
548b, 549a, 550b

pragmatism, III 552a, 553a

preformationism, I 231b

primitivism, III 596a

probability, III 612a, 613b,
615b, 618a

progress, III 629a, 646a,
646b

psychology, IV 4b, 7a, 11a,
12a, 12b, 16a, 26a, 29a

Pythagoreans, IV 35b

recapitulation, I 239b; IV
56a, 56b–57a, 58a, 59a

romanticism, II 178b–179a;
IV 196a, 201b

Saint Hilaire, I 236b–237a

scientific classification, I
465a, 466a

Simpson, I 236b–238a

Social Darwinism, III 646a,
646b

society, II 619b

species, I 232a–233a

spontaneous generation, IV
310a–310b, 312a

Stoicism, I 235a–235b

structuralism, IV 322b

teleology, I 233b–236a

Theophrastus, I 233a

uniformitarianism, I 492b,
499b–500b; IV 424a–
428a, 429a

utilitarianism, IV 445b

war, III 448b

Wilson, I 239b, 241a

women, IV 523b, 525b

Biomedicine, longevity, III
89a, 91a, 92b, 93a

Bion the Borysthenite (fl. 3rd
century B.C.), Cynicism, I
628b, 629a, 631b

Birbaum, O. J., China, I 369b

Birkhoff, George David (1884–
1944), game theory, II 266b

Bishop, C. W., China, I 369a

Bismarck, Otto Eduard Leopold von (1815–1898),
balance of power, I 186b

conservatism, I 480b

cycles, IV 157b

historiography, II 493b–
494a

Machiavellism, III 124a

modernism, I 424b

revolution, IV 157b, 160b

war, IV 505a

welfare state, IV 510a, 510b

Bisterfeld, John, perennial
philosophy, III 460a

Bisticci, Vespasiano da,
balance of power, I 180b

Bitnar, V., baroque in literature,
I 193a

Blache, Paul Vidal de la,
cultural geography, II 131a

Black, Duncan, social welfare,
IV 282b–283a, 283b

Black, Hugo (1886–   ),
due process, III 9b

Black, John, romanticism, IV
192a

Black, Joseph (1728–1799),
geology, IV 419a

technology, IV 362b

Black Death, I 635a

Black theater, repudiation of
beauty, I 207b–208a

Black-body radiation, II 590a

Blackmore, Richard (1650?–
1729), I 77a

attitude toward antiquity, I
81b–82a

mountains in literature, III
259b

Newton and, III 392a

optics, III 392a

Blackmur, Richard P.

literary criticism, I 603b

literature, III 88b

Brazil, III 540a, 541b, 542b

class, I 442a, 449a

equality, II 145a

Jefferson, IV 21b

loyalty, III 113b

migrations, I 594a

nationalism, III 328b–329a

positivism, III 540a, 541b,
542b

primitivism, III 600b, 603b,
604a

progress, III 639b

psychology, IV 20b, 21b,
27a

racial discrimination, I 439a,
440a–440b; III 12a, 13a

revolution, IV 166b

sculpture, II 577b

slavery, III 280b

spirituals, I 407a

U.S., I 442a, 449a, 594a;
III 12b, 13a, 113b, 328b–
329a

Volksgeist, IV 491b

vox populi, IV 497a

witchcraft, IV 523a

women, IV 529a

Blackstone, William (1723–
1780), I 488a

common law, II 695b, 696a

democracy, I 657b, 659a,
660a, 662a

loyalty, III 113b, 114a

sovereignty, I 659a

State, I 657b, 659a, 660a,
662a

Blackwell, Thomas

mythology, III 302a, 304a

poetics, III 530a

Bladud (legend), cosmic voyages, I 524a, 527a, 529a

Blair, Hugh (1718–1800),
catharsis, I 265b

literature, III 83a

pity, I 265b

Blake, William (1757–1827),
appearance and reality, I
97a

art, II 304a, 306b, 307a,
308a

atheism, II 412b

Bacon and, II 412b; III
398b

Counter-Enlightenment, II
107a, 108a

creativity in art, I 579b,
587b

Descartes and, III 398b

genius, II 304a, 306b, 307a,
308a

God, II 412b, 433b

Hegel and, II 412b

Hermeticism, II 432b, 433a,
433b

iconography, II 533b

individualism, II 304a, 306b,
307a, 308a

inspiration, II 307a

irrationalism, II 638a, 638b

Jesus Christ, II 412b

Locke and, II 412b; III 398b

metaphysical imagination,
III 208a, 209a, 211a

mythology, III 278b, 306b

neo-classicism in art, III
370b, 371a

Newton and, II 412b; III
398b; IV 199b, 201a

organicism, III 425b

philanthropy, III 490b

Platonism, III 523b, 524b
Pythagoras and, I 579b
recapitulation, IV 56b
romanticism, II 304a; IV
199b, 200b, 201a, 202a
spontaneity, II 307a
ut pictura poesis, IV 470b
Blanc, Louis (1811–1882),
individualism, II 595a
protest movements, III 672b
revolution, IV 160a
socialism, IV 289b–290a
Blancanus, Joseph
Descartes and, III 257a
mountains in literature, III
256b, 257a
Blanche of Castille (1187?–
1252), women, IV 525b
Blanche of Navarre (1331–
1398), women, IV 525b
Blanchot, Maurice
baroque in literature, I 192b
literature, III 88b
Blanot, Jean de, law, II 690a
Blanqui, Louis Auguste
(1805–1881)
class, I 443b
communism, II 559b
democracy, I 664b
ideology, II 559b
individualism, II 595a
Marxism, III 152a
protest movements, III 671b
revolution, IV 160a
socialism, IV 293a
Blanshard, Brand, God, II
358a
Blasius of Parma (d. 1416),
double truth, II 35a–36a,
37a
faith, II 35b
knowledge, II 35b
soul, II 35a, 35b
Bleibtreu, Karl (1859–1928),
Buddhism, I 256b
Bloch, Ernst
eschatology, II 159b
faith, II 213b, 214a
historicism, II 462b, 463a
Bloch, Ivan S., war, IV 504a,
504b, 507a, 508a
Block-universe, IV 395b–
396a
Blok, Alexander (1880–1921),
irony, II 632b
literary criticism, I 606b
revolution, IV 165b
symbolism, IV 343a, 344b
Blondel, François (1617–
1686)
aesthetics, II 218b
classification of the arts, I
460a
Blondel, Maurice (1861–

1949)
Bible, I 422a
Jesus Christ, I 421b, 422b
modernism, I 419a, 420a,
421b–422b, 423b, 425a,
426a
Bloom, Harold, romanticism,
IV 196a
Bloomfield, Leonard (1887–
1949)
language, II 672a, 672b
linguistics, III 71b
Blount, Charles (1654–1693),
deism, I 650a
mythology, III 301a
rationalism, III 301a
Blunt, A., iconography, II 538a
Bluntschli, J. C., international
peace, III 451a
Blyden, Edward (1832–1912),
nationalism, III 337b
Boas, Franz (1858–1942),
linguistics, III 71a–71b
Marxism, III 153b
mythology, III 316a
Boas, George
literary criticism, I 604a
progress, III 624a, 637a
socialism, IV 285a–285b
time, IV 395b
Boase, Alan, baroque in literature, I 192b
Bober, H., iconography, II
538b
Boccaccio, Giovanni (1313–
1375)
art, II 301a, 310a
Dante and, IV 122a
fame, II 234a
fortune, II 233b–234a
genius, II 293b, 301a, 310a,
317a
Giotto and, IV 122a
God, II 233b–234a
good, II 234a
handwriting, II 518a
humanism, II 518a
individualism, II 301a, 310a
literature, IV 188b
love, II 234a
motif, III 241a
mythology, III 288b, 289b,
290a, 292b, 299a
Platonism, III 512b
pleasure, II 234a
poetics, III 529b, 531b
romanticism, IV 188b
space, III 301a
virtue, IV 477a
Boccalini, Traiano (1556–
1613), Machiavellism, III
122b–123a
Bode, J. E. (1747–1826),
planets' distances, IV 42a

Bodin, Jean (1530–159),
absolutism, III 19b
authority, I 151b
climate, IV 150a
common law, II 19b
Counter-Enlightenment, II
101b
deism, I 648b
despotism, II 1a, 1b, 4a–4b,
5a, 5b, 6a, 7a, 7b, 10a
Enlightenment, II 90a
environment, II 129a–129b
God, II 355a
harmony, II 390–390b
historiography, II 486a; IV
149b–150a
individualism, III 19b
literary paradox, III 78a
monarchy, II 4a–4b
natural law, III 19b
Plato and, II 390a–390b
skepticism, IV 242a, 246b
sovereignty, IV 315b, 316a
State, III 19b; IV 315b,
316a
Ulpian and, III 19b
war, II 6a; IV 502a–502b,
507b
witchcraft, IV 522a
Bodkin, Maud
Faust (legend), III 251b
motif, III 242a
Bodmer, Johann Jakob
(1698–1783)
aesthetics, IV 356a
genius, II 295a
Body
Aristotle, IV 4b, 5a, 5b, 6b
asymmetry, IV 348b
Democritus, IV 3a
Epicureanism, IV 7a
imagination, III 212a, 214b
Man-Machine, III 132a–
133b, 135b, 139b–140a,
143b, 144b, 145a
numbers, III 404a
Plato, IV 3b, 4a, 4b
Plotinus, IV 8b, 9a
psychology, IV 1a–5b, 6b,
7a, 7b, 8b, 9a, 9b, 10b, 16b,
17a, 17b, 19b, 24a–24b,
25a
Pythagoras, IV 34a
Pythagoreans, IV 31b, 34a
religion, IV 95a
Renaissance, IV 439a
Saint Augustine, IV 9a
Seneca, III 128a
Socrates, IV 3b
Strato, IV 7a
symmetry, IV 348a–348b
tragic sense, IV 414b, 415a,
415b
unity of science, IV 432b,

434b
universal man, IV 439a
See also Health and Disease
Body politic, *see* State
Boeckh, August, Platonism,
III 519b, 520a, 521a
Boerhaave, Hermann (1668–
1738)
behaviorism, I 220a
Man-Machine, III 139b
Boethius, Anicius Manlius
Severinus (480?–?524),
abstraction, I 1a, 1b, 3a, 3b
analogy, I 65a, 67a
axiomatization, I 164a
cognition, I 3a
design argument, I 672b
dignity, IV 139a
fortune, fate, and, chance, II
231a–232a, 234b
genius, II 313a, 313b, 314a,
317a, 324b
good, II 231b–232a
harmony, IV 40b, 41a
idea, II 546a
logic, I 381a
mechanics, II 200a
Middle Ages, I 65a, 67a
music, II 313a, 313b, 314a,
317a, 324b; III 261a, 261b,
270b
Nature, II 231a
Neo-Platonism, III 377b,
378a
Pythagoreans, IV 40b, 41a
Ramism, IV 43b
soul, I 3a
work, IV 531b
Boethius of Dacia (13th century), double truth, II 31b,
33b–34a, 36b, 37b
Bogomils
dualism, II 43a
Gnosticism, II 327a
heresy, II 423a–423b
Boguet, Henri (fl. 1590),
witchcraft, IV 522a
Bohemia
heresy, I 387a
Magyars, I 381a
nationalism, III 328b
Reformation, I 395a
romanticism, IV 191a
Bohm, D., indeterminacy, II
591a
Böhm-Bawerk, Eugen (1851–
1914)
Marxism, III 164b
social welfare, IV 283a
Böhme, Jacob (1575–1624),
Bradley and, II 415a
eschatology, II 157a, 158a
Hermeticism, II 433a, 433b
imagination, III 212a

Islam, II 651b
linguistics, III 74b
Bohr, Niels (1885–1962),
ambiguity, I 59a
Einstein and, II 590a–591a
Fifth Solvay Congress, II
590a
game theory, II 273b
Heisenberg and, II 588b,
589a, 590a
indeterminacy, II 588b,
589a, 590a–591a
relativity, IV 91b
Schrödinger and, II 588b
Sixth Solvay Congress, II
590b
uncertainty principle, II
589a
Bohtlingk, O. (1815–1904),
linguistics, III 70b
Boiardo, Matteo Maria (1434–
1494), poetics, III 531a
Boileau-Despréaux, Nicolas
(1636–1711), I 77a
art, II 294a, 310a
attitude toward antiquity, I
79b
baroque in literature, I 190b,
191a
classicism, I 453a
Counter-Enlightenment, II
109a
Dryden and, I 453a
genius, II 294a
individualism, II 310a
irony, II 629a
organicism, III 424b
poetics, III 529b
Pope and, I 453a
style, IV 330b, 331b
sublime in external nature,
IV 333b
Boisrobert, François Le Métel
de (1592–1662), I 78a
Bolingbroke, Henry St. John
(1678–1751)
constitutionalism, I 486b
deism, I 650b–651a
Machiavellism, III 120a
theodicy, IV 382b
Bolívar, Simón (1783–1830),
nationalism, III 335a, 335b
revolution, IV 160b
Bolland, John (1596–1665),
historiography, II 486b
Bolshevik Party
Marxism, III 152b
U.S.S.R., II 559b–560a,
561a
Bolshevik-Leninism, Marxism,
III 148a, 150b, 152a–157b,
159b
Bolshevism, revolution, IV
163b, 164a, 164b, 165b,

166a
Boltwood, B. B. (1870–1927),
IV 426b
Boltzmann, Ludwig (1844–
1906)
entropy, II 114b–118b
indeterminacy, II 587b–
588a
positivism, III 545b
probability, III 620a
universe, II 117b
Boltzmann problem, II 118a–
118b
Bolyai, W. (1775–1856)
axiomatization, I 167a
cosmology, I 555a
relativity, IV 87a–87b
space, IV 302b, 304a
Bolzano, Bernhard (1781–
1848), infinity, II 606b
Bonald, L. G. A. de (1754–
1840)
Comte and, III 533b, 534a–
534b
conservatism, I 482a
Counter-Enlightenment, II
110a, 111b
counter-revolution concept,
III 534a
French Restoration, III 534a
individualism, II 600b; III
534a
law, III 22a
Maistre and, III 534a–534b
natural law, III 22a
positivism, III 533b, 534a–
534b
romanticism, IV 205b
sociology, III 534a
Bonaventura, Saint (1221–
1274)
aesthetics, II 219b, 222b,
224b
analogy, I 66a–66b
ambiguity, I 53a
happiness, II 379a
iconography, II 526b
matter, III 191b
Middle Ages, I 66a–66b
mimesis, III 227b
optics, III 410a
prophecy, III 668a
Bondi, Hermann
cosmology, I 567b–568a
space, IV 303b, 304a
Bonet, Pierre, psychology, IV
13b
Bonhoeffer, Dietrich
Christianity, II 213b
existentialism, II 192a
women, IV 528a
Boniface VIII, Pope (1235?–
1303)
authority, II 689b

challenge to monarchs, I
385a
heresy, II 421b
law, II 689b
nationalism, III 320b, 321a
prophecy, III 668b
reformation, IV 64a
State, IV 314a
Bonnet, Charles (1720–1793),
Chain of Being, I 333b
evolutionism, II 178a
genetic continuity, II 284a–
284b, 285a, 288b
spontaneous generation, IV
310b
Bonnet, Nicolas, time, IV 392a,
392b
Bonpland, Aimé Jacques
Alexandre (1773–1858),
environment, II 130a
Bonsignori, Giovanni di, mythology, III 289b
Bontekoe, William, China, I
356b
Boole, George (1815–1864),
pragmatism, III 555a
probability, III 610b
Booth, Charles (1840–1916),
welfare state, IV 510b, 511a
Booth, Wayne
irony, II 633a
rhetoric, IV 172b
Boothby, Penelope, neo-
classicism in art, III 370b
Bopp, Franz (1791–1867),
language, II 671a; III 67b–
68a
linguistics, III 67b–68a; IV
427b
mythology, III 306a
uniformitarianism, IV 427b
Borah, William E. (1865–
1940), law, III 9a
Borda, Jean-Charles de
(1733–1799), social wel-
fare, IV 281a–282b
Borel, Félix Édouard Émile
(1871–1956)
game theory, II 265a, 269b
probability, III 608b–609a,
619b
Borelli, Giovanni Alfonso
(1608–1679), cosmology, I
546b–547a, 548a, 549a
Borgia, Cesare (1476–1507),
Machiavellism, III 125a
power, IV 316b
universal man, IV 442a
virtue, IV 125a, 478a
Borinski, Karl, baroque in
literature, I 189b
Born, Max (1882–1970)
Einstein and, II 592b
entropy, II 114b

indeterminacy, II 592a–
592b
infinity, II 606b
Newton and, IV 302b
Borromeo, Federico, iconography, II 531a
Borromeo, Saint Carlo (1538–
1584), icononography, II
531a
Borromini, Francesco (1599–
1667)
baroque in literature, I 188b
Gothic, II 368b
Bosanquet, Bernard (1848–
1923)
beauty, I 207a, 207b
general will, II 280a–280b
God, II 358a
Hegel and, II 414b–415a,
415b
Mill and, II 414b
organicism, III 526a
Platonism, III 522a
State, II 280a–280b
Bosch, Hieronymus (1450?–
1516)
heresy, II 427a
music, III 266a–266b
ut pictura poesis, IV 467a
wisdom of the fool, IV 519b
Böschenstein, B., symbolism,
IV 342b
Boscovich, Ruggiero Giuseppe
(1711–1787)
cosmic images, I 518b
matter, III 185b
Bosman, William
antiprimitivism, III 604a
mythology, III 301a
Bosse, Abraham (1602–
1676), aesthetics, II 218b
Bossier de Sauvages (1706–
1767), disease, II 400a
Bossuet, Edmund, historiography, II 488b
Bossuet, Jacques Bénigne
(1627–1704)
axiomatization, I 163a
causation, I 279b–280a
China, I 365a
despotism, II 5a, 8b
Gallicanism, I 399b
God, I 279b
heresy, II 428b
literature, III 86a
modernism, I 419b
periodization in history, III
477b
progress, III 638b
religion, IV 109b, 112b
slavery, II 5a
Boswell, James (1740–1795),
literature, III 81b
primitivism, III 604b

Botany
  cosmology, I 230a
  mythology, III 287b
  realism in literature, IV 53b
Botero, Giovanni (1540–1617), Machiavellism, III 122b
Botticelli, Sandro (1444?–1510)
  chance images, I 346b, 349a, 350b
  iconography, II 529b
  mythology, III 291b–292a
  Neo-Platonism, III 511b
  temperance, IV 373b
Bottrigari, Ercole, music, III 262a
Boucher, François (1703–1770)
  China, I 363b–364a
  impressionism, II 572b
  individualism, II 310b
  neo-classicism in art, III 369a
Boucher de Crèvecour de Perthes, Jacques (1788–1868), chance images, I 351a
Bougainville, Louis Antoine de (1729–1811)
  Diderot and, III 603a
  primitivism, III 602a, 602b, 603a
Bouguereau, William Adolphe (1825–1905)
  as academic painter, II 570a
  impressionism, II 580a
Bouhours, Father
  aesthetics, IV 355a
  genius, II 294a
  literary criticism, I 597a
Bouillier, F., progress, III 643a, 644a
Boulainvilliers, Henri de (1658–1722), despotism, II 8b
Boulanger, Nicolas-Antoine, despotism, II 4a, 10a, 12a
  mythology, III 303a
Boulding, Kenneth E.
  natural liberty, II 65a
  war, IV 504b, 508a
Boullée, Étienne-Louis
  architecture, III 366a
  neo-classicism in art, III 366a, 369b
Bourdin, Pierre, skepticism, IV 245a
Bourgeois, Léon (1851–1925), social contract, IV 263a
Bourgeoisie

art, II 570a, 580a
Calvinism, IV 44b
Engels, IV 316b
Enlightenment, II 91a, 94a
equality, II 143a, 145a, 146a
good, IV 177a, 181a
historiography, IV 147b
humanism, II 521b–522a; IV 129b, 132b–133a
impressionism, II 570a, 580a
love, III 103b, 104a–104b, 105b, 106a
Marx, II 25a, 451b, 452a, 452b, 453a; IV 161b, 163a, 292a, 293a, 316b
Marxism, III 156a, 161b, 164a, 165b, 166a, 168a, 169a; IV 181a
materialism, II 451b, 452a, 452b, 453a
positivism, III 537a
pragmatism, III 565b
Ramism, IV 44b, 45a
Renaissance, IV 125a, 131a, 147b
revisionism, IV 264b, 266b, 270b, 272a, 274b
revolution, IV 161a, 161b, 162a, 163a, 163b, 164b
right, IV 177a, 181a
socialism, IV 291b, 292a, 293a
State, IV 316b
universal man, IV 441b, 442b
Volksgeist, IV 494b
vox populi, IV 499a, 500a
Bourget, Paul (1852–1935), genius, II 310b
  modernism, I 420a–420b
Bourne, Randolph (1886–1918), irony, II 633a
Bouterwek, Friedrich (1766?–1828)
  romanticism, IV 188a, 189a, 189b, 191b
  Schlegel and, IV 189b
Boutroux, Étienne Émile (1845–1921)
  indeterminacy, II 587a–587b
  modernism, I 420a
  time, IV 395b, 396a, 398a
Bouvet, Father Joachim
  Figurism, I 359b–360a
  perennial philosophy, III 461b
Bovin, Jean, attitude toward antiquity, I 83a
Bowen, Francis (1811–1890), psychology, IV 22b, 23a
Bowen, Howard, social wel-

fare, IV 283a
Bowlby, John, war, IV 507b
Bowne, Borden Parker (1847–1910), God, II 358a
Bowntree, Seebohm, welfare state, IV 510b, 511a
Boxer Rebellion, I 369a
Boyle, Charles (1676–1731), attitude toward antiquity, I 81a
Boyle, Robert (1627–1691), alchemy, I 28b, 31a, 33a; III 190b
  anthropocentrism, I 88a
  association of ideas, I 112a
  atomism, I 135a, 137a, 138a, 138b–139a, 140a, 310b; III 194b
  Bacon and, I 172b, 176b, 177a
  causation, I 294a, 294b, 296a–296b, 300b, 303b, 304a
  certainty, I 304b, 306b, 308a, 310a–311a
  cosmic voyages, I 532a
  cosmology, I 548b; IV 402b
  design argument, I 674a
  disease, II 400b
  Epicureanism, II 137b
  God, I 311a; II 352a, 355a
  matter, III 190b, 194a, 194b
  method, III 386b, 387a
  Newton and, III 386b, 387a
  perennial philosophy, III 461a
  psychology, IV 16b
  skepticism, I 304b, 306b, 308a, 310a–311a
  technology, IV 361b
  teleology, I 303b, 304a
  virtuoso, IV 487a, 487b, 488b
Boym, Father Michel, China, I 356a
Bracton, Henry de (d. 1268), common law, II 694a, 695a; III 30b–31a
  constitutionalism, I 488a
  law, II 690a
  nationalism, III 319b, 321a, 322a
Bradford, William (1590–1657)
  human nature, IV 17b, 18a
  Puritanism, IV 17b–18a
Bradley, Andrew Cecil (1851–1935)
  art for art's sake, I 110b
  organicism, III 422b
Bradley, F. H. (1846–1924), behaviorism, I 219a
  Böhme and, II 415a
  faith, II 415a

free will, II 240b–241a, 241b
  God, II 358a, 415b
  good, IV 181a
  happiness, II 381b
  Hegel and, II 414b–415a
  indeterminacy, II 587b
  individualism, II 600b
  Mill and, II 414b
  Platonism, III 506b, 522a
  pleasure, II 381b
  right, IV 181a
  State, II 415a
  time, IV 393b, 394a
  Trendelenburg and, II 415a
Bradley, James (1693–1762)
  aberration of light, IV 77b
  relativity, IV 77b
Bradley, Joseph P. (1813–1892), law, III 9a
Bradwardine, Thomas (1290?–1349)
  atomism, II 200a
  Islam, II 649a
  mechanics, II 197b, 199b–200a, 202a, 202b, 204a
Brahe, Tycho (1546–1601), cosmology, I 545a–545b, 548a
  hierarchy, II 442b
  mythology, III 299b
  skepticism, IV 242a
  symmetry, IV 348b
Brahmā (myth), II 344a
Brahmagupta (588–?660), cosmology, I 543b
Brāhmana
  dualism, II 39a
  evil, II 162a
  God, II 344a
  India (ancient), IV 104a
  love, III 100a
  reincarnation, I 644b
  religion, IV 104a
Brahmendra, Buddhism, I 254b
Brahmins, primitivism, III 592a–592b
Brameld, Theodore, education, II 83a
Brandão Júnior, F.A.
  Pereira Barreto, III 541b
  positivism, III 541b
Brandeis, Louis (1856–1941), law, III 9a–9b, 12b
Brandes, E., conservatism, I 481b
Brandes, Georg (1842–1927), periodization in literary history, III 485a
Brandis, Christian August (1790–1867), Platonism, III 521b
Brandl, Alois (1855–1940),

romanticism, **IV** 193b
Brandolini, Aurelio, dignity, **IV** 144a
Brandt, Sebastian, wisdom of the fool, **IV** 518a
Brans, C., cosmology, **I** 568b
Braque, Georges (1882–1963)
chance images, **I** 352a, 352b
impressionism, **II** 577b
metaphysical imagination, **III** 208a
Brattle, William, psychology, **IV** 18b
Braudel, Fernand
historicism, **II** 462b, 463a
periodization in history, **III** 480b
Braun, J., iconography, **II** 535b
Bray, J. S., economic history, **II** 60a
Bray, René, beauty, **I** 200b
Brazil
blacks, **III** 540a, 541b, 542b
Latin America, **III** 335b–336a
Marxism, **III** 540b
positivism, **III** 537a, 539b–543b, 544a, 545a
primitivism, **III** 599a, 599b
religion, **III** 541b, 543a, 543b, 545a
republicanism, **III** 539b, 541b, 542a, 542b, 543a, 543b, 545a
Roman Catholic Church, **III** 540b, 541b, 542b
slavery, **III** 541b, 542a, 543a
U.S., **III** 542b
Brecht, A., justice, **II** 658b
Brecht, Bertolt (1898–1956), culture, **IV** 165b
drama, **II** 87b
empathy, **II** 87b
expressionism, **II** 209a
revolution, **IV** 165b
satire, **IV** 214b, 215a
Bréhier, L. (1868–1951), iconography, **II** 535a
Breme, Lodovico di, romanticism, **IV** 190b
Brennan, William Joseph, Jr. (1906–   )
academic freedom, **I** 12a
justice, **II** 657b
Brentano, Clemens (1778–1842), romanticism, **IV** 189a, 190a, 196b, 197a
Brentano, Franz (1838–1917), psychology, **IV** 13b
Brethren of the Free Spirit,

IV 109a
Breton, André (1896–1966)
irrationalism, **II** 638a
metaphysical imagination, **III** 209a
Breton language, **III** 63a
Breuer, Josef (1842–1925), catharsis, **I** 268a
Brezhnev, Leonid (1906–   ), Marxism, **III** 167a
Bridges, Robert (1844–1930), beauty, **I** 207b
Bridgman, Elijah C., China, **I** 367a–367b
Bridgman, Percy Williams (1882–1961)
behaviorism, **I** 219b
knowledge, **III** 561b
methodology, **III** 559b
positivism, **III** 550b
pragmatism, **III** 551b, 553b, 557b, 559b, 561b
space, **IV** 304b
Bridgman, Raymond, international peace, **III** 453b
Brie, Friedrich
baroque in literature, **I** 191a
periodization in literary history, **III** 484a
Briggs, Charles (1841–1913), heresy, **II** 430b
Briggs, Henry (1556?–1631), mathematics, **III** 178b
Brightman, E.S.
Creation, **I** 576b
God, **I** 576b; **II** 359a
theodicy, **IV** 383a–384a
Brill, A. A. (1874–1948), psychology, **IV** 28b
Brillouin, Leon
entropy, **II** 116b
indeterminacy, **II** 592a
Brinkmann, Richard, realism in literature, **IV** 55a
Brissot de Warville, Jean-Pierre (1754–1793), socialism, **IV** 289b
British and Foreign Bible Society, **III** 63b
British Peace Society, **III** 448b
Britten, John, biology, **I** 240b–241a, 241b
Britton, John, Gothic, **II** 372a
Broad, C. D. (1887–   ), appearance and reality, **I** 98a
organicism, **III** 426a
time, **IV** 396b
Brochard, Victor, skepticism, **IV** 234b
Brodzinski, Casimir (1791–1835), romanticism, **IV** 191b

Brongniart, Alexandre (1770–1847), geology, **IV** 419b
Brooke, Henry (1703?–1783), hierarchy, **II** 446b
Newton and, **III** 395a
Brooke, Tucker, baroque in literature, **I** 193b
Brooks, Cleanth
irony, **II** 633a, 634a
linguistics, **IV** 425b
literary criticism, **I** 603b
organicism, **III** 426b
Brosses, Charles de (1709–1777)
myth, **III** 302a, 302b, 303a, 303b
religion, **IV** 94a
Brougham, Henry (1778–1868), balance of power, **I** 184a
Broussais, F. J. V. (1772–1838)
Comte and, **III** 534a
disease, **II** 404a
positivism, **III** 534a
Brouwer, L. E. J., mathematics, **III** 170b, 176b
Browder, Earl, Marxism, **III** 156b
Brown, Charles Brockden (1771–1810), psychology, **IV** 21a
Brown, John (1715–1766), evolution of literature, **II** 170a
Thoreau and, **III** 431a
utilitarianism, **IV** 444b, 445b
Brown, John (1735–1788), disease and health, **II** 402b, 404a
Brown, Norman
authority, **I** 161b
Buddhism, **I** 256b
irony, **II** 634a
perfectibility, **III** 475a
Brown, Robert (1773–1858), cells, **II** 285b
Brown, Robert McAfee, Reformation, **IV** 69a
Brown v. Board of Education, **I** 440a
Browne, Alexander, mythology, **III** 297b–298a
Browne, Moses, Newton and, **III** 395a
Browne, Thomas (1605–1682)
baroque in literature, **I** 191a, 193b, 195a
Cosmic Fall, **I** 510a
harmony, **II** 388a
hierarchy, **II** 436a
literary paradox, **III** 80a
music, **II** 388a

Brownian motion, **III** 620a
indeterminacy, **II** 588a
Browning, Elizabeth Barrett (1806–1861), classicism, **I** 450a
Browning, Robert (1812–1889),
romanticism, **IV** 193a
ut pictura poesis, **IV** 469a, 471a
Brown-Séquard, Charles (1817?–1894), longevity, **III** 93a
Brücke, Ernst Wilhelm von (1819–1892), physiology, **II** 404b
Brucker, Johann Jakob (1696–1770)
perennial philosophy, **III** 460a
Platonism, **III** 517a–518a
Brueghel, Pieter (the Elder) (1520?–1569)
iconography, **II** 529b, 531b, 538a
impressionism, **II** 578a
naturalism in art, **III** 346a
ut pictura poesis, **IV** 467a, 469b
Brueghel, Pieter (the Younger) (1564?–1638), *ut pictura poesis,* **IV** 467a
Brügmann, Karl (1849–1919), individualism, **II** 595b
language, **II** 671b
linguistics, **III** 71b; **IV** 425a
Brunelleschi, Filippo (1377?–1446), **II** 298a
individualism, **II** 300b
Bruner, Jerome, behaviorism, **I** 229a
Brunet, Jacques Charles (1780–1867), classification of the sciences, **I** 465b
Brunetière, Vincent de Paul Marie Ferdinand (1849–1906)
classicism, **I** 450a–450b
evolution of literature, **II** 171b, 172a, 172b
individualism, **II** 595a
literary criticism, **I** 600b–601a, 601b
naturalism, **IV** 54a
realism in literature, **IV** 54a
romanticism, **IV** 196b
style, **IV** 332b
Brunhes, Jean (1869–1930), environment, **II** 131a
Bruni, Leonardo (1369–1444)
as chancellor, **IV** 122b
city, **I** 429b–430a
despotism, **II** 4a

education, IV 124b
historiography, II 482a
humanism, II 517b, 518a, 519b, 522b, 522b, 523a; IV 129b, 132b–133a
Platonism, III 509b
Brunner, Emil, God, II 360a–360b
Brunner, O.
natural law, III 23a
periodization in history, III 478b
Bruno, Giordano (1548?–1600)
allegory, I 44a, 47b
anthropocentrism, III 510a
Aristotelianism, III 194a
atomism, I 133a, 133b, 494b–495a
authority, III 513b
beauty, II 443a; III 513b
Bentley and, IV 298a
Chain of Being, I 327a, 327b, 328b
change, IV 393a
continuity, I 494b–495a
Copernicus and, III 193b, 194a
cosmic images, I 515a, 516b, 517b–519b
cosmology, I 545a, 548a, 549b; III 193b; IV 298a–298b
Creation, II 433b
death, I 637b
demonology, I 669b–670a
dualism, IV 393b
Epicureanism, II 137b
ethics, II 347b, 348b
Euclid and, IV 298a
execution of, III 513b
Faust (legend), III 246a, 247a, 247b
genius, II 293b, 306a, 317a–317b
God, I 327b; II 347b–348b, 350b, 443a; III 194a, 510b
good, III 513b
heresy, III 193b, 194a, 513b
Hermeticism, II 433a, 433b
hierarchy, II 442a, 442b–443a, 445b
historiography, II 488a
hylomorphism, III 194a
immortality, I 645a, 645b
infinity, II 442b–443a, 605a, 607a, 608a; IV 298a, 298b
Inquisition, III 194a
Kant and, IV 298a
Kepler and, II 443a
knowledge, II 348a; III 212a
Leibniz and, II 445b
literary paradox, III 79a

love, III 513b
Lucretius and, III 193b, 194a
matter, III 193b–194a
mechanics, II 203b
metaphysical imagination, III 211b, 212a, 212b, 222a
Milne and, IV 298b
monads, II 445b
More and, IV 298a
motion, III 510b
music, II 317a–317b
Nature, I 517a; II 443a, 443b; III 194a, 351a
Neo-Platonism, III 212a
Nicolas of Cusa and, III 193b, 510b
pantheism, II 443a; III 194a
perennial philosophy, III 460b
philosophy, IV 298a
Platonism, III 510a, 510b, 513b
Plotinus and, III 193b
pluralism, II 443a; III 510b
poetics, III 530b
pre-Socratics, III 513b
psychology, IV 10b
Ramism, IV 44b
reality, IV 393b
reincarnation, I 645a, 645b
romanticism, IV 210b
Schelling and, IV 210b
space, IV 298a, 298b, 303b, 305a
Spinoza and, II 350b, 445b; III 194a
theory of mnemonics, III 212a
time, IV 392a–394a
as an undisciplined thinker, II 442b
universe, II 442b–443a; III 194a, 510b
virtuoso, IV 489a
work, IV 532a
Bruno of Cologne, Saint (1030?–1101), reformation, IV 64b
Brunschwig, Hieronymus, I 31b
Brunt, Samuel, cosmic voyages, I 528b–529a
Bryan, William Jennings (1860–1925), international peace, III 450b
Bryant, Jacob (1715–1804), mythology, III 306b
Bryant, William Cullen (1794–1878), Nature, III 349b
Bryce, Lord James (1838–1922)
constitutionalism, I 485b
individualism, II 596b

Brydges, Edgerton, romanticism, IV 192a
Bryusov, Valery, symbolism, IV 343a
Brzezinski, Z. K., totalitarianism, IV 409b
Buber, Martin (1878–1965), Tillich, III 158a
Buch, Leopold von (1774–1852), catastrophism, IV 418a, 421a–421b
Buchan, A., war, IV 507a
Buchanan, Joseph, psychology, IV, 21a
Buchdahl, H. A., entropy, II 114b
Bücher, Karl (1847–1930), economic history, II 60b
Buchez, Philippe, socialism, IV 290a
Büchner, Georg (1813–1837), Counter-Enlightenment, II 110a
irony, II 633b
Büchner, Ludwig (1824–1899)
matter, III 185a
psychology, IV 12a
spontaneous generation, IV 311a
Buck, C. D. (1866–1955), linguistics, II 72b
Buck, Pearl, China, I 372a
Buckland, Rev. William, catastrophism, IV 420a
Buckle, Henry Thomas (1821–1862)
causation, I 282a, 282b, 283b
Comte and, I 282a
culture, I 619a–619b; II 130a, 131b
determinism, II 22a
environment, II 130a, 131b
historicism, II 462a–462b
historiography, II 22a, 495b
history, I 282a, 282b, 283b; II 22a
Mill and, I 282a
necessity, III 360a
progress, III 640b, 644b
Buckley, Edmund, Oriental thought, III 435b
Buddha (563?–?483 B.C.), Buddhism, I 251a
Buddhism, I 247a–257b, 355a, 355b, 357a, 376a, 369b, 370b
Adams, Henry, III 437a
Afghanistan (ancient), I 247b, 248a
Alexander the Great, I 254b
Anaxarchos, I 254b
Apollonius of Tyana, I 254b

apologism, III 90a
Arnold, Edwin, I 256b
Aśoka, I 247a, 247b, 252a, 252b, 253a
atheism, II 344a
attitudes toward non-Buddhists, I 254a–254b
Bible, I 255a
bodhisattvas, IV 233a
Brahmendra, I 254b
Buddha, I 251a
Buddhist Society, I 256b
Burma, I 247b, 248b, 251b, 252b
Cambodia, I 248b, 251b, 252b
Canada, I 256b
capital punishment, I 253a
Carus, I 256b
causation, IV 232b
celibacy, I 251a–251b
Ceylon, I 247a, 247b, 248b, 249a, 252b
China, I 248b, 249a, 250b–251a, 252a–254a, 257a
China (ancient), I 247a, 248a–248b, 253b; II 481b; IV 476a
China (Communist), I 248b, 252a, 252b, 253a
Christianity, I 252a, 253b, 254b, 255b, 256a
Clement of Alexandria, I 255a
commerce, I 253b–254a
communism, I 249a, 252a, 252b, 253a
Confucianism, I 255b
cosmology, I 544b
Creation, II 344a
current, I 248b–249a
death, I 644b; IV 232b
democracy, I 253a
Deussen, I 255b–256a
diligence, I 253b–254a
discrimination, I 252b
Egypt (ancient), I 247b, 255a
Eightfold Path, IV 232b
Emerson, I 256a
Essenes, I 255a
ethics, I 252a–252b, 253b–254a; III 446a
evil, II 162a
evolutionism, II 174b
faith, I 249b
Fao-lin, I 247a
Fenollosa, III 437a
First Zen Institute of America, I 256b
Five Aggregates or Constituents, I 250a
founder of, I 247a–247b

four kinds of followers, I 251a
France, I 256a
fundamental attitude, I 249b–250a
Gandhi, III 446a
Garbe, I 255a
Gautama Siddhārtha, I 247a–247b
Germany, I 256b
Gjellerup, I 256b
Gnosticism, I 255a
God, I 251a, 256b; II 344a–344b
Great Britain, I 255a, 256b
Greece (ancient), I 254b
health, II 397a
Hearn, I 256b; III 437a–438b, 439a
Hesse, I 256b
Hinayāna, I 247b–248a
Hinduism, I 248a, 249a, 254a, 254b; IV 232b
Hiriyana, I 254b
historical development, I 247b–248b
historiography, II 481b
hospitals, III 487a
Huxley, Aldous, I 256b
ignorance, I 250a, 250b
immortality, I 644b
incarnation, IV 232b
India, I 247b–248a, 248b, 249a, 252b, 254a, 254b
India (ancient), I 247a–247b, 248a–248b, 250b, 253a, 253b, 254b, 255a
individualism, I 251b–252a
influence on the West, I 254b–257a
institution of, I 251a–252a
Iran, I 255a–255b
Isherwood, I 256a
Japan, I 248b, 249a, 250b–254b, 256b
Japan (ancient), I 247a, 248a–248b, 253b
karma, I 250b; IV 232b, 233a
Korea, I 248a, 248b, 249a, 251a–251b, 253a, 254a
Lamaism, I 248a, 249a, 253a
Laos, I 248b, 251b, 252b
liberation, IV 233a
longevity, III 90a
love, III 100a
Lowell, III 437a
Macedonia, I 247b
Mādhyamika school, I 248a
Mahāsanghika, I 253b
main teachings, I 250a–250b
Manicheism, I 255a; II 42b

Masson-Oursel, I 256a
Megasthenes, I 255a
metaphysics, IV 232b
mission of, I 252a
missionaries, I 248a, 252a, 257a
Mongolia, I 248b, 253a
monks, I 251a–251b, 253a, 253b
mythology, III 306a
Nāgārjuna, I 248a
nationalism, III 324b
Nature, IV 232b
Neo-Platonism, I 255a
Nepal, I 248b, 249a, 251a, 253b
Nirvāna, I 250a, 250b; II 344a; IV 232b–233a
non-ego teaching, I 250a
Northern (Mahāyāna), I 247a, 248b–249a, 249b, 250b, 251b, 253a, 253b, 255a
Origen, I 255a
Otto, I 256a
pacifism, I 253a–253b, 257a
Pāli Text Society, I 255b
Pantaenus, I 255a
peace, III 446a
perfectibility, III 464b, 465b, 466a
Persia (ancient), I 248a
philanthropy, III 487a
Philostratus, I 255a
Plotinus, I 255a
Plutarch, I 254b
Portugal, I 256b
Pyrrho of Elis, I 254b
racial prejudice, I 252b
reason, I 249b
reincarnation, I 644b
Renaissance, I 255b
Riepe, I 256b
Ripley, III 437a
Roman Catholic Church, I 255b
Rome (ancient), I 247b, 255a
salvation, IV 232b–233a
samsāra, IV 232b
Sanghabhadra, I 247a
Sarvāstivādin school, I 247b
Sasaki, I 256b
Schopenhauer, I 255b
Schweitzer, I 256a
scriptures, I 249a–249b
Senzaki, I 256b
Shōtoku, I 252b
Sikkim, I 248b, 249a
Slater, I 257a
soul, IV 232b, 233a
Southern (Theravāda), I 247a, 247b, 248b–249b,

252a, 253a, 253b, 255b
State, I 252b–253b
suffering, I 250a
Suzuki, I 256b
Sweden, I 255a
Thailand, I 248b, 251b, 252b
Thoreau, I 256a
Tibet, I 248b, 249a, 251a, 252a, 252b, 253a–254b
Tibet (ancient), I 248a
Tillich, I 257a
tolerance, I 254a
totalitarianism, I 253a
transcendentalism, IV 233a
transmigration, I 250b, 255a
Turkestan, I 255a–255b
U Thant, I 253b, 257a
U.S.S.R., I 253a
U.S., I 256a, 256b–257a; III 429a, 430b, 431a, 432b, 434b, 436a–439a
universal laws, I 249b–250a
universality, III 437a
universe, I 250b–251a; II 344a
Upanishadic period, IV 232b
Vajrayāna, I 248a, 249a
Vietnam, I 248b, 249a
Yogāoāra school, I 248a
Zen, I 248a–248b, 249a, 249b, 250b–251a, 253a, 253b, 256a, 256b–257a
Budé, Guillaume (1468–1540), historiography, II 486a
Buffon, Georges (1707–1788), I 85b
  Burnet and, III 259a
  Chain of Being, I 331b, 333b, 334b
  classification, I 331b
  conservation, I 473a, 473b
  cosmic images, I 520b
  Diderot, III 217a
  Enlightenment, II 91b, 92b–93a
  environment, II 128b, 132b
  evolution of literature, II 170a
  evclutionism, II 176b, 177a, 177b, 178b
  Faust (legend), III 248b
  geology, II 176b, 177a
  Man-Machine, III 141b, 142a
  mountains in literature, III 259a
  Nature, II 132b, 177a
  pangenesis, II 623b
  psychology, IV 21b
  reason, I 334b

species, II 177a
  spontaneous generation, IV 310b
  style, IV 330b, 331b, 332a
Buffum, Imbrie, baroque in literature, I 193b
Bühler, Karl
  empiricism, III 547a
  psychology, IV 13a
Bukharin, Nikolai I. (1888–1938)
  acquired characteristics, II 620b
  communism, II 560a
  ideology, II 560a
  Marxism, III 165b, 166a
Bulganin, Nikolai A. (1895–), Marxism, III 157a
Bulgaria
  Eastern Orthodox Church, I 409b
  Marxism, III 157b
Bulnes, Francisco, positivism, III 544a, 544b
Bultmann, Rudolf (1884–), I 408a
  eschatology, II 161a
  existentialism, II 192a
  faith, II 213a
  God, II 360–360b, 361a, 365b
  metaphor, III 207a
  mythology, III 307a
Bulwer-Lytton, Edward (1803–1873), romanticism, IV 193a
Bunge, Carlos Octavio, positivism, III 543b
Bunge, Mario, empirical sciences, III 550a
Bunyan, John (1628–1688), I 396b
  baroque in literature, I 193a
  tragic sense, IV 415a
Bunyan, Paul, mountains in literature, III 253b
Buonaiuti, Ernesto, modernism, I 424a
Buonamici, Francesco, Galileo, II 205a
Buonarroti, Filippo Michele (1761–1837), protest movements, III 671b
Buondelmonti, Cristoforo de', mythology, III 289b
Burckhardt, Jacob (1818–1897)
  art, II 300a–300b
  baroque in literature, I 188b, 189a
  China, I 370a
  civilization, IV 159a
  conservatism, I 483a

crisis in history, I 591a–592b, 595b
culture, I 591a–591b
eschatology, II 160a
Ferguson and, IV 126a, 126b
Franco-Prussian War, IV 159a
French Revolution, IV 159a
Goethe and, IV 126a
historicism, II 460b
historiography, II 495a
individualism, II 300a–300b, 595b–596a, 596b, 597b; IV 485a
Jung and, III 312b
Kugler and, IV 125b, 126a
mathematics, III 178a
mythology, III 312b
Nietzsche and, IV 485a
periodization in history, III 479a, 480a
Renaissance, III 479b; IV 124b, 125b–127a, 127b–128a, 437a–439b, 440a, 441a, 485a
revolution, I 591b–592a; IV 159a
universal man, IV 437a–439b, 440a, 441a
war, I 591b
Bureaucracy
alienation, III 168b
anarchy, III 673b
freedom of speech, II 256a
Marxism, III 168b, 169b
progress, III 630a
protest movements, III 673b, 675b
reformation, IV 64b
revisionism, IV 268a
revolution, IV 158a
socialism, IV 293b
syndicalism, III 673b
technology, IV 357b, 358a
totalitarianism, IV 410b
U.S.S.R., IV 158a
virtù, IV 483b
Bürger, Gottfried August (1747–1794), romanticism, IV 190b, 191b
Bürger, Jost, mathematics, III 178b
Burgundio of Pisa, dignity, IV 137b
Buridan, Jean (d. after 1358), causation, I 275b
double truth, II 34a–34b, 36b, 37b
humanism, IV 134a
matter, III 192a
mechanics, II 202a
Burke, Edmund (1729–1797), I 77b, 103b, 405a

aesthetics, IV 355b
Aristotle and, III 229b
authority, I 152b, 154b
balance of power, I 186a, 187a
beauty, I 202b, 211b
catharsis, I 265b
civilization, I 619b
Coleridge and, IV 203a
conservatism, I 477b, 480a, 481a–481b, 484a; IV 203a
Counter-Enlightenment, II 104b, 106b–107a
deism, I 651b
democracy, I 661a–661b
Enlightenment, IV 203a
equality, II 143b
French Revolution, IV 157b
historicism, II 458b
historiography, II 492a
history, IV 203a, 204a
individualism, IV 594a, 599a
justice, II 654a–654b
liberalism, III 44b, 45b
mimesis, III 229b
Montesquieu and, IV 203a
Nature, IV 203a, 204a
necessity, III 358b
pity, I 265b
power, I 154b
revolution, I 481a–481b; IV 157b, 158b, 203a
rhetoric, IV 172a
romanticism, IV 194a, 203a, 203b, 204a, 205b
Rousseau and, I 481b; IV 203a
Scott and, IV 203a
social contract, IV 262a–262b
State, I 661a–661b; IV 205b
sublime in external nature, IV 335a, 336b–337a
synaesthesia, IV 471b, 472a
taste, IV 355b
ut pictura poesis, IV 471b, 472a
Volksgeist, IV 491a
Burke, Kenneth
history, II 634b
irony, II 633a, 633b, 634b
literary criticism, I 603b
literature, III 88b
tragic sense, IV 412b
Burkert, W., Pythagoreans, IV 32b
Burley, Walter, motion, II 197a
Burma
Buddhism, I 247b, 248b, 251b, 252b
Burma Socialist Program Party, III 338a
nationalism III 337a, 338a

socialism, III 338a
Burnet, Gilbert (1643–1715), historiography, II 487b
Burnet, John (1863–1928), time, IV 390a
Burnet, Thomas (1635?–1715), I 80b
Addison and, III 259a
aesthetics, I 512a–512b
Buffon and, III 259a
catastrophism, IV 418b
Coleridge and, III 259a
Cosmic Fall, I 505a, 509b, 510b, 511a, 512a–512b
cosmic images, I 522b–523a
Diderot and, III 259a
Leibniz and, III 259a
mountains, III 257a–258b, 259a
primitivism, III 593a
Steele and, III 259a
sublime in external nature, IV 333b
Voltaire and, I 511a; III 259a
Wordsworth and, III 259a
Burnett, James, language, II 669a
Burnouf, Eugène, mythology, III 306a
Burns, Robert (1759–1796), primitivism, III 600b
romanticism, IV 195a
witchcraft, IV 522b
Burra, Peter, baroque in literature, I 193a
Burritt, Elihu, international peace, III 453a
Burton, Asa
psychology, IV 22b
religion, IV 112a
Burton, Robert (1577–1640), Cosmic Fall, I 508b
death, I 626a
deism, I 648b
demonology, I 668b
disease, II 399a
epistemology, III 81a
imagination, III 211b
literary paradox, III 80b
macrocosm and microcosm, I 508b
melancholia, III 80b
mountains in literature, III 255b–256a
mythology, III 295b–296a
style, IV 331b
Utopia, IV 462a
virtuoso, IV 486b
Burtt, Edwin A.
Buddhism, I 256b
Newton on, III 397b, 398a
Bury, John Bagnell (1861–

1927)
causation in history, I 283b
progress, III 634b, 636a–637a, 640a, 641b, 649a
Busenbaum, Hermann (1600–1668), casuistry, I 262b, 263b
Bush, Douglas
baroque in literature, I 193b
Chapman on, III 294b
mythology, III 294b, 295b, 299b, 300a
Bushnell, Horace (1802–1876)
heresy, II 429b
reformation, IV 69b
Butler, Bishop Joseph (1692–1752)
deism, I 651b
good, IV 178a
Hutcheson and, III 231a
individualism, IV 178a
moral sense, III 230b, 231a
perfectibility, III 469a
utilitarianism, IV 444a, 444b, 447b
Butler, Charles, music, II 392a, 394a
Butler, Philip, baroque in literature, I 192b
Butler, Samuel (1612–1680), cosmic voyages, I 528a
Butler, Samuel (1835–1902), chromosomes, II 288a
Darwin and, II 185b
evolutionism, II 181b, 185b
happiness, II 380a
Utopia, IV 464a
Bütschli, Otto (1848–1920), cell division, II 287a
Butterfield, Herbert
ambiguity, I 54a–54b
matter, III 194b
Butterfield, William (1814–1900), Gothic, II 372b
Byrd, William (1540?–1623), music, II 390a
Byres, James, neo-classicism in art, III 364a
Byron, George Gordon, Lord (1788–1824)
cosmic images, I 520a
Counter-Enlightenment, II 109a, 110a
evil, II 165a–165b
Faust (legend), III 250b
Goethe and, IV 192b
individualism, II 598a
irony, II 633b
love, III 507a
Macaulay and, IV 194b
melancholy, IV 204a
Musset and, IV 204a

Nature, III 350b
Newton and, IV 201a
periodization in literary history, III 485b
Platonism, III 507a
poetry, IV 192b
Pope and, IV 192b
romanticism, IV 192b, 193a, 194b, 195a, 196a, 201a, 204a, 205a, 208a, 209b
satire, IV 212b, 214a–214b, 215b
Schlegel and, IV 192b
Staël and, IV 192b
Weltschmerz, IV 204a, 209b
Byzantine Empire
Church Councils, II 526a
civilization, III 181a, 181b
crisis in history, I 591a
hierarchy, II 440b–441a
historiography, II 473a, 473b, 474b, 491a
iconography, II 526a, 535b, 539b
Islam, II 639b
mathematics, III 181a, 181b
Neo-Platonism, III 377b
periodization in history, III 480a
poetics, III 527b
prophecy, III 669a

C

Cabanel, Alexandre (1823–1889), impressionism, II 580a
Cabanis, Pierre J. G. (1757–1808)
behaviorism, I 220a
class, I 448b
death, I 641a
equality, I 448b
ideology, II 553a, 553b, 554a
immortality, I 641a
Jefferson and, IV 21a
Man-Machine, III 141b
metaphysics, III 216a
positivism, III 533a
psychology, IV 21a
skepticism, IV 242a, 243a
Cabbalism
hierarchy, II 441a
Platonism, III 507b
reincarnation, I 645a
Cabet, Étienne (1788–1856),
economic history, II 60a
individualism, II 595a
socialism, IV 289b, 290a
Cabral, Domingos Guedes,

positivism, III 541b
Cabrol, F., iconography, II 535b
Caelius Aurelianus (5th century A.D.), temperature, IV 370b
Caesaropapism, I 379b
Charlemagne, I 380b
determinism, II 30a
papacy, I 380b
Cage, John (1912–   ), I 58a
Cagniard de la Tour, Charles (1777–1859) fermentation, II 283a–283b
Cahier, C., iconography, II 535b
Cain (Bible)
motif, III 237a
mountains in literature, III 254b, 255a
mythology, III 278b, 279a, 279b, 281b
necessity, III 355b
reformation, IV 63a
Saint Augustine and, IV 63a
vox populi, IV 498a
Caird, Edward (1835–1908),
Hegel and, II 414a, 414b
Caird, John (1820–1898)
Hegel and, II 415a
modernism, I 420a
Cajetan, Saint (1480–1547), I 6b
Calculatores, II 201a, 201b, 204b
Calculus
Huygens, III 606b–607a
Leibniz, II 668b
linguistics, IV 430a
mathematics, II 610b; III 173a–173b, 174a, 177b, 178b, 182b
necessity, III 361b
numbers, III 406a, 406b
optics, III 420a
perfectibility, III 471b
pragmatism, III 561a
probability, III 606a, 606b–607a, 607b, 608a, 609b, 612a, 612b, 621a, 623a
science, III 178b
uniformitarianism, IV 430a
See also Axiomatization, Newton
Calder, Alexander (1898–   ), *ut pictura poesis*, IV 475b
Calderón de la Barca, Pedro (1600–1681)
baroque in literature, I 190a, 195a
Faust (legend), III 246b
motif, III 240b

periodization in literary history, III 482a
romanticism, IV 188a, 188b, 189a
Calderoni, Mario, pragmatism, III 551b, 564a
Calendar
cosmology, I 536a, 537a–537b
historiography, II 468b, 472b
lunar, I 537a–537b
time, IV 399b
Calhoun, John (1782–1850),
conservatism, I 484a
psychology, IV 22a
Callimachus (5th century B.C.),
linguistics, III 62a
poetics, III 527b
Callisthenes (360?–328 B.C.),
historiography, II 504b–505a
Callisto (myth), III 296a
Callistratus (3rd or 4th century A.D.)
mimesis, III 227a
ekphrasis, IV 468b, 469a
poetics, III 527a
Calmet, Dom, mythology, III 301b
Calvin, John (1509–1563), I 389b, 391a–392b
analogy, I 70a
apostasy, IV 67b
authority, I 150a
Bible, I 392a; III 255a; IV 67a–67b
casuistry, I 262a
city-state, I 395a
Cosmic Fall, I 506a
determinism, II 27b, 28a, 28b, 29a, 39b
equality, II 142a–142b
ethics, III 441b
faith, II 349a
free will, II 245a–245b
freedom, I 392b
God, I 262a, 392a; II 142b, 349a; III 271a; IV 67a, 533a
good, IV 67a
humanism, II 520b
individualism, II 597a, 598b, 602b, 603a
Jesus Christ, IV 67b
Luther and, II 142b; III 255a; IV 67b
mountains, III 255a
music, III 271a
Nature, III 255a
Olivetan and, IV 67a
peace, III 441b
perfectibility, III 467a, 468b–469a

philanthropy, III 489b
predestination, II 27b, 28a, 28b, 29a, 30b, 142b, 245b; IV 67a, 533a
pride, III 468b–469a
private property, II 142a
Reformation, IV 67a–67b
religion, IV 115a
revolution, I 392b
sacraments, I 392a
Saint Augustine and, II 27b; III 255a; IV 115a
salvation, II 245a; IV 67b
sin, I 506a; III 467a
skepticism, II 349a; IV 242a–242b
stabilizing effect of, I 391b
theodicy, IV 381b
Tories, I 392b
virtue, III 467a
war, II 441b
Whigs, I 392b
work, IV 533a
Calvinism, I 392a–392b
Anglicanism, IV 20a
Arminianism, I 399a
Bible, I 395b–396a
bourgeoisie, IV 44b
capitalism, I 396b
casuistry, I 262a, 262b–263a
causation, I 302b, 303b
certainty, I 305a
Creation, I 572b
deism, I 648a–648b, 649b
determinism, II 28b–29a, 30a–30b
Edwards, Jonathan, IV 110b
evil, II 164b
Five Points of, II 28b
God, I 572b; III 654a
good, IV 177a
heresy, II 424b, 425a, 425b, 427b, 428a
liberalism, III 40b, 42a–42b
liberty, I 392b
Lutheranism, III 654a
morality, I 262a; III 654a
Oriental thought, III 429a
phrenology, IV 23b
poetics, III 530a
poverty, III 654a
predestination, I 397b; II 28b–29a, 30a–30b
private property, III 654a
progress, III 643a
psychology, IV 16b, 19a, 19b, 20a, 22a, 23b
Puritanism, IV 16b
Ramism, IV 44b
religion, IV 109b, 110b
right, IV 177a
Saint Augustine, I 262a
salvation, IV 177a

skepticism, **IV** 242b, 244a
State, **I** 395a, 397b
Synod of Dordrecht, **I** 397b
Trinity, **I** 436b
TULIP formula, **II** 28b
U.S., **III** 429a
wealth, **III** 654a
Will, **III** 654a
witchcraft, **IV** 522b
Calypso (myth), **III** 273b
Camaldulians, reformation, **IV** 64b
Camargo, Joracy, positivism, **III** 542a
Cambodia
  Buddhism, **I** 248b, 251b, 252b
  nationalism, **III** 333a
Cambridge, R. O., irony, **II** 629a, 629b
Camden, William (1551–1623)
  historiography, **II** 483b
  mythology, **III** 296a
Camerini (legend)
  Christianity, **III** 592a
  primitivism, **III** 592a
Camillo, Giulio, hierarchy, **II** 436b
Camillus, Marcus Furius (d. about 365 B.C.), temperature, **IV** 377a
Camoës, Luiz Vaz de (1524–1580)
  ambiguity, **I** 58b
  baroque in literature, **I** 191a
Campana, Dino, symbolism, **IV** 342a
Campanella, Tommaso (1568–1639)
  Andreae and, **IV** 461b–462a
  Aristotle and, **IV** 461b
  Christianity, **IV** 461b
  city, **I** 431a–431b, 432b
  class, **I** 448a
  deism, **I** 649a
  Galileo and, **IV** 461b
  illuminists, **IV** 109a
  inequality, **I** 448a
  More and, **IV** 461b
  Platonism, **III** 510a–510b
  progress, **IV** 461b
  religion, **IV** 109a
  socialism, **IV** 287b–288a
  Utopia, **IV** 461b, 462a
  welfare, **IV** 461b
  work, **IV** 532a, 532b
Campbell, C. A., determinism, **II** 241a–241b
Campbell, George (1719–1796)
  catharsis, **I** 265b

pity, **I** 265b
Campbell, Joseph (1879–1944)
  motif, **III** 240a
  mythology, **III** 240a, 313a–313b
Campbell, R. J. (1867–1956), religion, **IV** 108a
Campbell, Thomas (1777–1844)
  romanticism, **IV** 192a
  Schlegel and, **IV** 192a
Campistron, Jean Gilberte de (1656–1723), literary criticism, **I** 601a
Camus, Albert (1913–1960), allegory, **I** 48a
  Christianity, **II** 213b, 215a
  death, **I** 637b
  existentialism, **II** 189b–190a
  God, **II** 364a
  irony, **II** 633a
  tragic sense, **IV** 414b
Canaan (Bible)
  God, **II** 336b, 337b
  mythology, **III** 280a, 280b, 281a–281b, 282b
Canada
  academic freedom, **I** 14a
  Buddhism, **I** 256b
  common law, **III** 31b
  constitutionalism, **I** 491a
  equality, **III** 13b
  freedom, **III** 13b
  law, **III** 13b, 31b
  nationalism, **III** 334b, 338b
  Roman Catholic Church, **III** 334b
  Volksgeist, **IV** 495a
Canisius, Saint Peter (1521–1597)
  catechism, **I** 394b
  Counter-Reformation, **I** 394b
Cannibalism
  cynicism, **III** 586a
  Montaigne, **III** 594a, 594b
  mythology, **III** 309a, 312a
  primitivism, **III** 586a, 588a, 594a, 594b, 599b
  progress, **III** 626b
  Swift, **III** 599b
  theriophily, **IV** 385a
Canning, George (1770–1827), balance of power, **I** 187a
Cannon, H. G., acquired characteristics, **II** 619a
Cannon, Walter Bradford (1871–1945)
  cybernetic theory, **II** 126a
  environment, **II** 125b, 126a
  homeostasia, **II** 404b

pragmatism, **III** 562b
Canon law, **II** 694a–694b, 695a
Canon of proportions, **I** 580a, 581b, 582a
Canova, Antonio (1757–1822)
  classicism, **I** 454b
  mimesis, **III** 229b
  neo-classicism in art, **III** 369a, 370a, 370b, 371a
Cantillon, Richard (1680?–1734), supply and demand, **IV** 452b
Cantor, Georg (1845–1918), abstraction, **I** 8b
  continuity, **I** 498b, 499b
  infinity, **II** 606b, 609b, 610a, 611a, 611b–612b
  mathematics, **III** 175b
  numbers, **III** 405b, 406a
  Peirce and, **III** 558a
  pragmatism, **III** 557b, 558a
  space, **IV** 301a, 304b
Cantor, Peter
  Christianity, **III** 590b
  primitivism, **III** 590b
Capital, **II** 47b, 49a
  Marx, **I** 39a–40b
Capitalism
  alienation, **III** 168b
  Belgium, **I** 396a
  Bernstein, **III** 161b, 162a, 162b, 163a, 164a
  Calvinism, **I** 396b
  China, **I** 368a
  Christianity, **I** 396a–397a
  class, **III** 148b
  communism, **II** 559a–559b
  community, **III** 148b
  Counter-Reformation, **III** 480b
  crises, **III** 161a–161b, 162a, 164a
  crisis in history, **I** 590b–591a; **III** 164a
  democracy, **I** 666a; **III** 148b
  economic history, **II** 59b
  economics, **III** 148a, 148b, 151b–152a
  employment, **III** 148a
  equality, **II** 146a
  ethics, **IV** 70a
  evolutionism, **II** 180b
  existentialism, **III** 158a, 158b–159a, 160a
  exploitation, **III** 162b
  fascism, **III** 331b, 674a
  freedom, **III** 646a
  Fromm, **III** 158a
  Germany, **I** 396a
  Great Britain, **I** 396a
  historiography, **IV** 147b, 151b

individualism, **II** 595b, 596a, 596b–597a
industry, **III** 148b
Lenin, **III** 156b
love, **III** 104a, 107b
Luther, **I** 396a
Marx, **I** 590b–591b; **II** 146a, 452b, 453a; **III** 149a, 154a, 158b–159a, 160a, 161b, 167b, 168b; **IV** 161b, 292a, 292b, 293a
Marxism-Leninism, **III** 478b, 479a
materialism, **II** 452b, 453a
Middle Ages, **III** 479a
nationalism, **III** 331b, 336b
natural liberty, **II** 69b, 70a, 70b
Netherlands, **I** 396a, 396b
periodization in history, **III** 478b, 479a, 480b
pessimism, **III** 645b
poverty, **III** 151b
power, **III** 160a
pragmatism, **III** 564b, 565b
private property, **III** 148b, 653a, 654b
production, **III** 148a, 148b
profit, **III** 148a
progress, **III** 643a, 645b, 646a
prosperity, **III** 151b
protest movements, **III** 674a
Protestantism, **I** 396a–397a
psychology, **IV** 28a
Puritanism, **I** 396a–397b, 656a
Reformation, **I** 396a–397a
religion, **IV** 115a
Renaissance, **IV** 147b, 151b, 442a
responsibility, **III** 646a
revisionism, **IV** 264b, 265a, 266b, 267a, 271b
revolution, **IV** 161a–163a, 164a, 166a
Russia, **III** 164b
Russian Revolution (October 1917), **IV** 164a, 164b
socialism, **I** 666a; **III** 148b; **IV** 292a, 292b, 293a
society, **III** 148a
Sorel, **III** 564b
Spain, **I** 396a
Stalin, **III** 156b–157a
surplus value, **III** 148a
Switzerland, **I** 396b
totalitarianism, **IV** 406b, 407b
unemployment, **III** 151b
U.S.S.R., **III** 151a, 155a; **IV** 166a
universal man, **IV** 442a
value, **III** 148a

45

Volksgeist, IV 494a
wages, III 151b
Weber, I 368a, 396a
welfare state, IV 510a, 512a
work, IV 533a
See also Marxism
Cappadocians, temperance, IV
370b
Capriano, G. P.
classification of the arts, I
460a
mimesis, III 229a
Capuana, Luigi (1839–1915),
realism in literature, IV 53a
Capuchins, I 394b
Caracalla, Emperor (188–217
A.D.), neo-classicism in art,
III 366a
Carathéodory, Constantin
(1873–1950), entropy, II
114b
Caravaggio, Michelangelo da
(c. 1565–1609), ideal, II
549b
Cardano, Girolamo (Cardan,
Jerome) (1501–1576)
aesthetics, II 218b
Bacon and, I 173b, 174a,
174b
chance, I 337a
gambling, III 605b
game theory, II 264a
genius, II 293b
historiography, IV 149a
Islam, II 644a
mathematics, II 205a
probability, III 605b
spontaneous generation, IV
308b
Cardinal numbers, I 8b–9a
Cardozo, Benjamin N. (1870–
1938)
justice, II 657b
legal precedent, III 32a
Carducci, Giosuè (1835–
1907), baroque in literature,
I 188b
Carducho, Vicente (c. 1578–
1638), Gothic, II 369b
Carey, Mathew (1760–1839),
nationalism, III 330a
Carion, John (1499–1537),
historiography, II 484b
Carlile, Richard (1790–1843),
deism, I 652a
Carlyle, Thomas (1795–1881),
analogy, I 70a
classicism, I 449b
Counter-Enlightenment, II
108b
democracy, I 663a
Diderot, IV 199a
economic history, II 58b
Enlightenment, IV 199a,

200b
French Revolution, IV 160a
heroes, IV 204a
history, I 283a
infinite, IV 200b
literary criticism, I 599a
Marxism, III 158b
religion, IV 200b
revolution, IV 160a
romanticism, IV 192b,
194a–194b, 199a, 200b,
201a, 204a, 210b
Schelling and, IV 210b
supernatural, IV 201a
symbolism, IV 339a, 344b
Carnap, Rudolf (1891–1970)
certainty, I 321b
metaphysics, III 220a–
220b, 221a
positivism, III 545b, 546a,
547b–550a
pragmatism, III 557a, 568a
probability, III 618b
unity of science, III 548a,
548b, 549b
Carneades (214?–129 B.C.),
causation, I 273a
Platonism, III 504b
skepticism, IV 234a, 235a,
235b–236a, 237a, 238b–
239a, 239b, 241a
Carnegie, Andrew (1835–
1919)
individualism, II 596b
international peace, III 453a,
453b
philanthropy, III 491b–492a
Carnot, Nicolas Léonard Sadi
(1769–1832)
entropy, II 113a
technology, IV 363b–364a
Carnot's Theorem, II 113a,
113b
Caroline minuscule
handwriting, II 518a
humanism, II 518a
Carolingian Renaissance, IV
127b
Carpenter, Joseph Estin
(1844–1927), Buddhism, I
255b
Carpenter, William Benjamin
(1813–1885)
association of ideas, I 116a
Man-Machine, III 143a
Carpocratians, primitivism, III
589a
Carr, E. H.
causation, I 285b–286a
progress, III 637b–638a
Carrel, Armand (1800–1836),
romanticism, IV 199a
Carriere, Moriz (1817–1895),
literature, III 84a

Carritt, E. F., moral sense, III
234b
Carroll, Lewis (1832–1898),
literary paradox, III 77b; IV
470b
Cartari, Vincenzo
Hermeticism, II 432b
iconography, II 530b
mythology, III 292b–293a,
298a, 299a
Carter, Elizabeth (1717–
1806), virtuosa, IV 489a
Carter, John, Gothic, II 372a
Cartesianism
animals, III 596a
axiomatization, I 166a
causation, I 302a–302b
Comte, III 535a
cosmic images, I 518a
Counter-Enlightenment, II
102a
deism, I 649a
determinism, II 19b
dualism, II 38a, 41b, 443b,
444a, 445b
Engels, I 453b
God, III 461a
hierarchy, II 444a, 444b,
445b
ideology, II 553a
impressionism, II 582a
irrationalism, II 635a, 638a
Man-Machine, III 135a,
136a–138b, 139b, 141b
Marx, II 450a–450b
materialism, II 450a, 450b,
453b
metaphor, III 198b
metaphysics, II 450a; III
217a
method, III 385a
motion, III 461a
mountains, III 257a
music, III 263a
mythology, III 302a–302b
necessity, III 356b, 357a,
359a
Newton, III 385a, 397a,
397b
optics, III 397a, 397b
perennial philosophy, III
461a
physics, II 450b
pleasure, II 387a
poetics, III 530a
positivism, III 535a
pragmatism, III 558a
primitivism, III 596a
progress, III 640a
psychology, IV 11a, 12b,
18b
Puritanism, IV 18b
Ramism, IV 42b
relativity, IV 87b, 88a

space, IV 304a
Spinoza, II 444b, 445b
structuralism, IV 328b, 329a
Vico, II 102a; III 357a
Carthage (ancient)
Aristotle, II 254a
constitution, II 254a
freedom of speech, II 254a
Carthusians, reformation, IV
64b
Carus, Paul (1852–1919),
Buddhism, I 256b
materialism, II 454b
Oriental thought, III 435b–
437a, 438a, 439a
Casaubon, Isaac (1559–
1614), satire, IV 213a
Case, John, music, II 390b,
391a
Caserio, Santo, I 72a
Casey, John, literary criticism,
I 602b
Caso, Antonio, positivism, III
544b
Cassian, John
literature, III 81b
temperance, IV 371a
Cassini, G. D. (1625–1712),
cosmic voyages, I 533b
Cassiodorus, Flavius Magnus
Aurelius (c. 540 A.D.),
Gothic, III 367a
literature, III 82b
Pythagoreanism, IV 41a
work, IV 532a
Cassirer, Ernst (1874–1945),
aesthetics, II 222a
genius, II 308b
iconography, II 536a
imagination, III 210a
indeterminacy, II 590a
infinity, II 611b
Islam, II 647b
linguistics, IV 428b
metaphysics, III 209b,
222a–222b
method, III 382b
mythology, III 315a
Newton, III 382b
romanticism, IV 209b
uniformitarianism, IV 428b
universal man, IV 440a,
441a, 443a
Castagnary, Jules Antoine,
impressionism, II 573b–
574a, 581a
naturalism in art, III 339b
Castanheda, Fernão Lopes de
(d. 1559), China, I 354b
Caste
class, I 442a
defined, I 442a
Egypt (ancient), III 10b
India, I 442a

progress, III 647a
U.S., I 442a
Castel, Père Louis Bertrand, III 396a
ocular clavecin, IV 473a
Castellion, Sebastian (1515–1563)
heresy, II 426a, 430b
liberalism, III 42a–42b
religion, IV 118b
Castelvetro, Lodovico (1505–1571)
aesthetics, II 220a
classification of the arts, I 460a
poetics, III 529a–531a; IV 467b
tragic sense, IV 412b
Castiglione, Baldassare (1478–1529)
art, II 305a
Cicero and, III 512b
genius, II 293b, 295a, 305a, 317a
literary paradox, III 80b
love, III 512b
music, II 317a
Platonism, III 507b, 512b
universal man, IV 439a, 442b
Castilhos, Júlio de, positivism, III 542a
Castra stativa, I 428b
Castres, L'Abbé Sabatier de, literature, III 82a
Castro, Américo, baroque in literature, I 192a
Castro, Eugenio de, symbolism, IV 341a
Castro, Fidel
positivism, III 544b
revolution, IV 165a
Casuistry, I 257b–264a
Ames, I 263a
Aristotle, III 15b
Arnauld, I 262a–262b
Ascetics, I 260a–261b
Busenbaum, I 262b, 263b
Calvinism, I 262a–263a
Christianity, I 258b–264a
Clavasio, I 262a
common law, III 31a
Cyprian, I 258b
d'Asti, I 259a
defined, I 257b
Enlightenment, I 263b
Escobar y Mendoza, I 262b
Frederick William II, I 263a
Greece (ancient), I 258a
Hessen, I 262b
historical appearance of, I 257b
Italy, I 260b
Jansenism, I 262a–263a

Jesuits, I 262a, 262b
Joseph II, I 263b
Judaism, I 258a
Kant, I 263a
König, I 262b
Koran, I 258a
law, III 30b, 31a
Luther, I 262a, 262b
Machiavellism, I 260b
Middle Ages, I 259b–260a
Mohammedanism, I 258a
natural law, III 15b, 17a, 23a
Olearius, I 262b
Pascal, I 262b
Pennaforte, I 259a
Peraldus, I 259a
perennial philosophy, III 459a
Perkins, I 262b–263a
philanthropy, III 489a
pragmatism, III 55a
Prierias, I 259a
punishment, I 258b
Protestantism, I 262a–263b
Reformation, I 262a
religion, IV 113a
Roman Catholic Church, I 258b–264a
Rome (ancient), I 258b
Thaumaturgus, I 258b
Cataclysms, time, IV 391a
Catastrophism, IV 417b–423b
animals, IV 418b, 419b, 420a, 421b
Aristotle, III 628b
basalt, IV 420a–420b
Bible, IV 418a, 418b, 419b, 420a
Bourbon restoration, IV 420a
Buch, IV 418a, 421a–421b
Buckland, IV 420a
Burnet, IV 418b
Canary Islands, IV 418a, 421a
Christianity, IV 419b
continuity, I 500a, 500b
Conybeare, IV 420a, 421b
Creation, IV 419b
Cuvier, IV 419b, 420a
Darwin, IV 422b–423a
defined, IV 417b
dignity, IV 142b
discontinuity, I 500a, 500b
earth, IV 417b–419b, 420b, 421b, 422a, 423a
electricity, IV 419a
elements, IV 423a
Enlightenment, IV 419b
evolution, IV 423a
Flood, IV 419b
fossils, IV 418b, 419b, 420a, 421a, 421b, 422a

France, IV 420a, 421a, 421b, 422a
French Revolution, IV 419b
Geikie, IV 423a
geography, IV 422a
geology, IV 417b, 418a, 418b, 419b, 420a, 420b, 422a, 422b, 423a
Germany, IV 418a
Great Britain, IV 418a, 418b, 419b–422a
heat, IV 419a, 423a
history, IV 417b, 418a, 420b, 421b, 423a
Hume, IV 419b
Hutton, IV 419a, 419b, 420a, 420b
Ireland, IV 420b
Isle of Wight, IV 420b
Italy, IV 418b, 420b, 421b, 422a
Kelvin, IV 423a
latent heat, IV 419a
liberalism, IV 419b
light, IV 419a
linguistics, IV 423b, 425a
Lyell, IV 421b–423a
Madeira, IV 421a
Mantell, IV 420a, 421b
matter, IV 419a
mineralogy, IV 418b
Moses (Bible), IV 419b
mountains, IV 417b–421a
Murchison, IV 422a
natural selection, IV 422b, 423a
Nature, IV 418a, 419b, 422b
Norway, IV 421a
origin of species, IV 422b–423a
paleontology, IV 420a, 421b
physics, IV 419a, 423a
plants, IV 421b
Plato, III 628b, 630b
Polybius, III 630b
progress, III 628a, 628b, 630b
radioactivity, IV 423a
rationalism, IV 419b
Ray, IV 418b
reactionism, IV 419b
religion, IV 419b, 420a
Renaissance, IV 142b
rocks, IV 418b, 419a, 420b, 421b, 423a
Rutherford, IV 423a
Saussure, IV 418b
science, IV 417b, 419b, 420a, 422a, 423a
scientists, IV 417b, 418b
Scotland, IV 419a, 419b, 420a, 421b
Sicily, IV 421a, 421b, 422a

space, IV 417b
specific heat, IV 419a
sum, IV 419a
Switzerland, IV 421b
time, IV 417b, 422b
uniformitarianism, I 500a; IV 423b, 425a
volcanoes, IV 417b–423a
Werner, IV 418b, 419b, 420a, 420b
Whewell, IV 418a, 420b
Categories
Hegel, III 358b–359a
Kant, III 357b
metaphor, III 198a–200a
necessity, III 357b, 358b–359a
philosophy, III 198a, 198b–200a
Cathars
Albigensian crusade, II 423a
death, I 645a
doctrine of, II 423a–423b
dualism, II 43a
Gnosticism, II 327a
heresy, II 417b, 423a–424a, 426b
immortality, I 645a
origin of, II 423a
Provence, II 423a
reincarnation, I 645a
Roman Catholic Church, II 423a–423b
socialism, IV 286b
Waldensians, II 423b
Catharsis, I 102a, 264a–270b
Aeschylus, I 267a
aesthetic, I 268b
Aristotelianism, III 500b
Aristotle, I 264b–270a; IV 411b, 412a
Asclepian therapy, I 264b, 269a
Bible, I 264b
Christianity, I 264b, 265b–266a, 269a
comedy, I 468a
Corneille, I 268a
dance, I 269a
Delphi, mystery cult of, I 264b
Democritus, I 269a
Dionysiac ritual, I 269a
Dodds, I 268b–269a
Dubos, I 268a
Eleusis, mystery cult of, I 264b
Else, I 266a, 266b, 268b, 269a
ethics, I 267b–268a
fear, I 264b–267b, 268b
Euripides, I 266b
Freud, I 268a

Greece (ancient), I 264a–270a
happiness, II 378b
Hesiod, I 264b
Hippocrates, I 264b, 267a, 269a
Homer, I 264b, 266b
Hume, I 266a, 268a, 268b
hysteria, I 269a
Iamblichus, I 269a, 270a
Kames, I 265b
Lessing, I 268a
love, III 98a, 98b, 99b, 100a, 107a
medical, I 264b, 266b, 267a, 268b–269a, 269b
melancholy, I 267a
Milton, I 267a
Minturno, I 267a
Molière, I 269b
music, I 264b–265a, 266b, 269a
Nicomachus, I 269a
Nietzsche, I 268a
origin of the term, I 264a–264b
Petrusevski, I 269b–270a
pity, I 102a, 264b–267b, 268b
Plato, I 264b, 266a, 268a, 268b–269a; III 501a
Platonism, III 500b
pleasure, II 378b
poetry, I 265a, 269a
Proclus, I 269a, 270a
psychology, I 268a, 269a
purgation, I 264b
Pythagoreans, I 269a
Racine, I 268a
reason, I 267b–268a
Renaissance, I 269a–269b
Saint Augustine, I 265b
Saint-Évremond, I 266b
Schopenhauer, I 268a
sin, I 264b
Smith, I 265b
Sophocles, I 264b, 269a
Theophrastus, I 269a
tragedy, I 264b–270a
tragic sense, IV 411b, 412a
Wilamowitz-Moellendorff, I 269a
wisdom, I 267b–268a
Cathedrals, I 417b
aesthetics, II 546a
Christianity, I 382b, 417b
Middle Ages, II 527a
music, III 265a, 266b, 270a
mythology, III 283b, 288b
Roman Catholic, I 382b
Catherine of Siena, Saint, (1347–1380)
prophecy, III 669b
women, IV 525b

Catherine II (Catherine the Great) (1729–1796)
Enlightenment, II 90b
free-thinkers, I 411a
Jesuits, I 403b
language, II 669b; III 64a
linguistics, III 64a
perfectibility, III 470a
periodization in literary history, III 483a
Catholic Reformation, see Counter-Reformation
Catlin, George (1796–1872), conservation, I 474a, 474b, 476a
Cato, Marcus Porcius (234–149 B.C.)
conservation, I 472a
historiography, II 469a, 469b
nationalism, III 323a
poetry, III 528b
Stoicism, IV 321b
temperance, IV 370a
Catt, Carrie Chapman (1859–1947), women, IV 526b
Cattaneo, Carlo (1801–1869), nationalism, III 329b
Cattaneo, Simonetta, Platonism, III 511b
Cattell, James McKeen (1860–1944), psychology, IV 12b, 25a–25b
Catullus, Gaius (c. 200 B.C.), art, II 310a
genius, II 310a
love, III 104a
mountains in literature, III 253b
mythology, III 298a
Cauchy, Augustin Louis (1789–1857)
continuity, I 494a, 498b
infinity, II 606b, 609b
mathematics, III 174a, 174b
Cauchy integrals, III 620b
Caumont, Arcisse de (1802–1873), Gothic, II 373a
Causation, I 270b–304a
accidental causes, II 230b, 233a, 235a
aesthetics, II 223a
Al-Ashari, I 273b–274a, 286b
Al-Farabi, I 273b, 287a, 288a
Al-Ghazali, I 274a, 277a, 286b–287a, 288a–289a
Al-Kindi, I 273b
Al-Nazzām, I 287a–287b
analytical approaches, I 284a–286a
Anaxagoras, I 271a
Anaximander, I 271a, 290b

Anaximenes, I 271a
Anselm, I 273b
antinomian view, I 282b–284a
Aristotle, I 271b, 272a–272b, 273b, 274a, 274b, 275a, 286b, 287a, 288a, 288b, 289a, 290b, 300b, 301a, 302a–302b, 303b; II 230b, 233a, 282a; III 195a; IV 307b
Ash'arites, I 277a, 286b, 287a–289a
astrology, III 287b–288a
atomism, I 272a, 287a, 289a, 303b; II 18b
Autrecourt, I 289a
Averroës, I 274a, 289a
Avicebron, I 274a–274b
Avicenna, I 273b, 274a, 287a, 288a–289a
Bacon, I 276a, 290b, 292a, 294b–295a, 296a, 301a, 301b
Barrow, I 276a–276b
Bentham, I 291a
Berkeley, I 276b
Bible, I 290a
Boethius, II 231a–231b
Bossuet, I 279b–280a
Boyle, I 294a, 294b, 296a–296b, 300b, 300b, 303b, 304a
Buckle, I 282a, 282b, 283b
Buddhism, IV 232b
Buridan, I 275b
Bury, I 283b
Calvinism, I 302b, 303b
Carneades, I 273a
Carr, I 285b–286a
Cartesians, I 302a–302b
causal laws, I 281a–282b
Chalcidius, II 230a
chance, II 226a–233b, 234b, 235a, 236a
Christianity, I 279b, 290b
Collingwood, I 284b, 285a, 285b
Comte, I 281a, 291a
conception of inertia, I 276a
contingent causes, II 232b
continuity, II 231a
Cordemoy, I 298b
Cournot, I 283b–284a
Crusius, I 301a
culture, I 611b
d'Ailly, I 275b
Dante, II 233a, 233b
Democritus, I 272a; II 135b, 136a–136b
Descartes, I 290b, 294a, 296b–299a, 302a, 302b, 303b
determinism, I 285b–286a; II 18a–19b, 21b–22a, 238a,

238b, 240a, 240b–241a
Dilthey, I 284a–284b, 285a
Diogenes Laërtius, I 273a
Duns Scotus, I 275a
Egypt (ancient), I 270b
Einstein, Albert, II 590a
Empedocles, I 271a
empiricism, I 291a; III 546b
Engels, I 282b; II 452b; III 643a
Epicureanism, I 272b–273a, 275b; II 135b, 136a–137a
Epicurus, I 271b, 273a; II 136a–136b, 587a
ethics, IV 320a
evolution of literature, II 172a, 174a
fate, II 226a–233b, 234b, 235a, 236a
final causes, I 300b–304a; II 587a
free will, II 135b–137a, 238a, 238b, 240a–241a, 245a–246a, 247b, 248a
freedom, I 285b–286a
Galileo, I 276a, 281a, 301b
Gassendi, I 301a, 303b
general will, II 275b
genetic continuity, II 282a
geometry, III 382a
good, IV 177a
Greece (ancient), I 271a–273a, 275b, 290b, 291b, 293b; II 18b
Grosseteste, I 274b
happiness, II 378a
Hegel, I 277b, 280a–281a
Heisenberg, I 278a; II 589b, 590a
Helmont, I 301a
Hempel, I 284b–285a
Heraclitus, I 271a
hierarchy, II 446b
Hippocrates, I 271b
historiography, II 18a–19b, 21b–22a, 480b, 489a, 501b–502a, 509b
history, I 279a–286b; II 18a–19b, 21b–22a
Hobbes, I 276a, 290b, 294b, 295a–296a, 301b, 303a; IV 177a, 434a
Holbach, I 281a
Honoré, I 293a
Ibn-Tofail, I 273b
idea, II 544a–544b, 548a–548b
imagination, III 213b
indeterminacy, II 586b, 587a, 587b, 588b, 589b, 590a
individualism, II 598b
inertia, I 276a
Islam, I 273a–274a, 277a,

286b–289b, 495b; II 642b, 643a
James, William, III 562a
Judaism, I 273a, 274a–274b, 290a
Kant, I 277b, 280a, 280b, 291a, 675a; II 240a; IV 433b
Kepler, I 281a
law, I 289b–294a; III 34a, 34b
Leibniz, I 276b–277a, 290b, 294b, 299a–300a, 300b, 302b, 303b–304a; II 446b; III 193a
Lenin, I 283b
Leucippus, I 272a; II 587a
liberalism, III 37b–41b
Locke, I 276b, 290b, 296a
logic, III 546b
loyalty, III 115a
Lucretius, I 273a, 301a–301b
macrocosm and microcosm, III 126a
Maimonides, I 289a
Maine de Biran, I 278a
Malebranche, I 274a, 276a, 296b, 297b–298b, 302b–303a; III 193a
Man-Machine, III 137a, 139b, 143b
Marx, I 282a–282b; II 452b
materialism, II 452b
matter, III 192b, 193a
medicine, I 271b
Melissus of Samos, I 271b
Mesopotamia (ancient), I 270b
metaphor, III 199a
metaphysics, I 279b–281a; III 213b
methodology, III 382a, 382b, 387a
Middle Ages, II 18a
Mill, J. S., I 272b, 291a, 295a, 295b
Molière, III 195a
moral sense, III 232b
Mu'ammar, I 287b
Mu'tazilites, I 287a–288a
mythology, III 287b–288a, 302a, 302b
mythopoeic, I 270b
Napoleon I, I 283b
natural causes, II 230b
natural law, III 16a
necessity, II 232b; III 352b, 357b, 360b
Neo-Platonism, I 273a–273b, 275b, 287a, 288a, 303b
Newton, I 281a, 294b, 299a–299b; III 193a, 382a,

382b, 387a
Nicholas of Autrecourt, I 275b, 277a
Nifo, III 382b
notion of cause, I 284a–285b
Occasionalism, I 274a, 276a, 277a, 286b, 289a, 296b, 302b
Parmenides, I 271a
Peirce, II 587b
perennial philosophy, III 459b
Petrarch, II 234b
philosophy, I 290a–291a; III 199a
physics, III 382a
Plato, I 271b–272a, 273b, 303b
pleasure, II 378a
Plekhanov, I 283a
pluralism, I 282b–284a
Plutarch, I 272b
Pollock, I 293a
Popper, I 281b
positivism, III 546b
power, II 231a
pragmatism, III 553a, 562a, 567a
pre-Newtonian philosophers, I 294b–296b
Pre-Socratics, I 290b
progress, III 624a, 638b, 643a
protest movements, III 674b
Protestantism, I 302b
Pythagoreans, IV 34a
Raei, I 302a–302b
rationalism, III 302a, 302b; IV 48a–48b, 50a, 50b
recapitulation, IV 57b
Regius, I 302b
Renaissance, I 275b–276a
right, IV 177a
Rome (ancient), I 290b, 291a, 291b, 293a
Saint Albertus Magnus, II 232a, 232b
Saint Augustine, I 273b, 279b; II 230a–231a, 232a–233a; IV 381a
Saint Thomas Aquinas, I 274b–275a, 292a
Saint-Simon, I 281a
salvation, IV 232b
Schlick, II 589b
scholasticism, I 300b–301a, 303b
science, II 199b, 201b
sin, IV 232b
skepticism, I 273a, 277b; IV 237a, 247b
socio-morphic, I 270b
Sophists, I 271b

Spencer, I 291a
Spinoza, I 276b, 290b, 296b, 298b–299a, 301a, 301b, 303a–303b; II 238b; III 193a; IV 434b
spontaneous generation, IV 307b
Stillingfleet, I 276b
Stoicism, I 272b–273a, 275b, 290b; IV 320a
substantive theories, I 279a–284a
teleology, I 300b–301a
Telesio, I 301a
theodicy, IV 381a
theology, I 279b–281a
time, IV 395b, 396a, 397a
Toynbee, I 283a
unity of science, IV 433b, 434a, 434b
Vico, I 280a–280b
Volksgeist, IV 496a
Whitehead, I 278a
William of Ockham, I 275a–275b
witchcraft, IV 521a
Zabarella, III 382b
See also Aristotle, God, Hume
Cave art, chance images, I 351a
Cavendish, Charles (1836–1882), I 135b, 136b
Cavendish, Henry (1731–1810)
cosmic voyages, I 532a
mathematics, III 179a
Cavendish, Margaret (1624?–1674)
cosmic voyages, I 528b
virtuosa, IV 488a–488b
Cavendish, William (1592–1676), I 135b
Caxton, William (1422?–1491), aesthetics, IV 355b
Caylus, Count de (1692–1765)
iconography, II 533a, 534b
mythology, III 302b
ut pictura poesis, IV 467a
Cazamian, Louis (1877–1965), classicism, I 450a
Celaya, Juan de (1490?–1558), logic, II 204a–204b
Celestine V, Pope (1215–1296), prophecy, III 668b
Cell division
Balbiani, II 286b
Bütschli, II 287a
genetic continuity, II 285b–287b
Hertwig, II 287a
Hofmeister, II 286a

Kölliker, II 286a
Nägeli, II 286a
Remak, II 286a–286b, 287a
Schleiden, II 285b, 286a
Schneider, Anton, II 287a
Virchow, II 286a
Wolff, C. F., II 285b
Cellarius, Christophus
periodization in history, III 477a, 478a, 480a, 481b
Reformation, IV 67a
Cellini, Benvenuto (1500–1571), taste, IV 354b
Celsus, Aulus Cornelius (1st century A.D.)
classification of the sciences, I 463b
disease, II 397b
Gnosticism, II 330a
heresy, II 426a
humanism, IV 133a
natural law, III 16b, 17b
paganism, I 647b
Celtes, Conradus (1459–1508), mythology, III 292b
Celtic language, III 66b
Celts
law, III 7a
longevity, III 90a
mythology, III 293a
Cennini, Cennino (c. 1370–c. 1440), genius, II 298a, 300b–301a
Censorship
architecture, III 499a
art, III 497b–498a
drama, III 497b–498a
Holmes, Justice, III 567b
law, III 567b
literature, III 497a–498a
love, III 106a
loyalty, III 113a
Mill, J. S., III 567b
music, III 499a
painting, III 499a
Plato, III 497a–498a, 499a, 501b, 554b
Platonism, III 497a–498a, 499a, 501b
poetry, III 499a, 501b
pragmatism, III 554b, 567b
protest movements, III 672a
satire, IV 214b
theater, III 497b–498a
U.S.S.R., III 153a
Victorian sensibility, IV 219b
Center of mass, IV 76a
Centlivre, Mrs. Susannah (1667?–1723), virtuosa, IV 490a–490b
Central American Court of International Justice, III 451a

49

Central Limit Theorem, **III** 609a–609b, 619a

Central Organization for a Durable Peace, **III** 454a

Cerberus (myth), historiography, **II** 499b

Cercidas of Megalopolis, cynicism, **I** 627b–628a

Ceremonies, game theory, **II** 264a

Ceres (myth), **III** 274a, 287a, 290a, 297a
  neo-classicism in art, **III** 365a

Cerinthus (1st century A.D.), millenarianism, **III** 224a

Černý, Václav, baroque in literature, **I** 192b–193a

Certainty, **I** 304a–325a
  absolutely infallible, **I** 307b–308a, 309a
  artists, **I** 322a
  Bacon, Francis, **I** 304b, 306a, 311b
  Beattie, **I** 317a–318b
  Bentham, **I** 317a–318a
  Berkeley, **I** 312b, 317a, 317b
  Boyle, **I** 304b, 306b, 308a, 310a–311a
  Calvinism, **I** 305a
  Carnap, **I** 321b
  Charron, **I** 304b, 305a
  Chillingworth, **I** 304b, 306a, 307a–309a, 310a–311b
  Comte, **I** 318a
  Condillac, **I** 318a
  conditionally infallible, **I** 307b, 309a
  Condorcet, **I** 318a
  Descartes, **I** 304b, 305a–306a, 307a, 308b, 311a, 311b, 314a
  Dewey, **I** 323b–324b
  d'Holbach, **I** 318a
  French Encyclopedists, **I** 318a
  Gassendi, **I** 304b, 306a, 306b–307a, 310a, 310b, 311b
  Glanvill, **I** 304b, 308a, 310a
  Goethe, **I** 322a
  Greece (ancient), **I** 304a
  Hegel, **I** 319a–319b
  Hobbes, **I** 306a
  Hooke, **I** 308a
  Hume, **I** 304b, 312a–318a, 319b, 320a, 321b, 323b
  Husserl, **I** 322a
  Huxley, T. H., **I** 318b
  indubitable, **I** 309a
  Kant, **I** 314a–316b, 317b, 319a, 319b, 321b, 324b
  knowledge, **I** 312a–325a

La Mothe Le Vayer, **I** 304b
Leibniz, **I** 312b, 314a, 315b
Locke, **I** 304b, 306a, 308a, 311b, 317b
  mathematics, **I** 309a, 312a–312b, 314b
Mersenne, **I** 304b, 305a, 306a–306b, 310a, 310b, 311b
Mill, J. S., **I** 318b
Montaigne, **I** 304a–305a
Moore, G. E., **I** 319b
  moral, **I** 307b–309b, 317b
  natural sciences, **I** 318a
Newton, **I** 304b, 310b–311b
Plato, **I** 316b
Popkin, **I** 305b
Popper, **I** 323a–323b
  positivism, **I** 318b, 321b–322a
  pragmatism, **III** 553a
  probability, **III** 608a–608b
  Protestantism, **I** 304a, 305a, 307a–308a
Reid, **I** 317a
  Roman Catholic Church, **I** 304a, 307a–308a
  Rule of Faith controversy, **I** 307a–308a
  Russell, Bertrand, I 319b–321b, 323b
  science, **I** 312a–325a
  Sextus Empiricus, **I** 304a
  skepticism, **I** 304a–311b
  Spencer, **I** 319a
  Tillotson, **I** 308a
  Veron, **I** 304b, 305a
  Wallis, **I** 308a
  Whewell, **I** 318b
  Wilkins, **I** 304b, 308a–310a, 311a
  Wittgenstein, **I** 320a, 321b–322a
Cervantes, Miguel de (1547–1616)
  baroque in literature, **I** 190a–190b, 195a
  comedy, **I** 470a
  Gothic, **II** 370a
  irony, **II** 629a, 629b, 630b, 632b
  motif, **III** 240b
  romanticism, **IV** 188a, 188b
  wisdom of the fool, **IV** 519b, 520a
Cesalpino, A. (1519–1603), spontaneous generation, **IV** 308b
Cessolis, Jacobus de, game theory, **II** 264b
Ceylon
  Buddhism, **I** 247a, 247b, 248b, 249a, 252b

common law, **III** 31b
discrimination, **III** 337a
Hindu-Tamil minority, **III** 337a
nationalism, **III** 337a, 338a
numbers, **III** 400b
racial prejudice, **III** 337a
Singhalese-Buddhist majority, **III** 337a
Cézanne, Paul (1839–1906), art, **II** 614a
  cubism, **II** 207a
  expressionism, **II** 207a
  iconography, **II** 538b
  impressionism, **II** 567b, 573a
  infinity, **II** 614a
  motif, **III** 241b
  perspective, **IV** 302a
  space, **IV** 302a
  ut pictura poesis, **IV** 467b, 475b
Chadwick, Edwin (1800–1890), disease, **II** 403a
Chadwick, John
  Oriental thought, **III** 429a
  transcendentalism, **III** 429a
Chaeremon, progress, **III** 626b
Chagall, Marc (1887–   ), genius, **II** 304b
  mythology, **III** 280a
Chain of Being, **I** 325a–335b
  Addison, **II** 446b
  Albert the Great, **I** 326b
  Aristotle, **I** 326a
  becoming, **I** 332a–334a
  Bergson, **I** 334a
  Bonnet, **I** 333b
  Bruno, **I** 327a, 327b, 328b
  Buffon, **I** 331b, 333b, 334b
  Christianity, **I** 326a–326b, 329b–330a
  continuity principle, **I** 333a–334a
  Cosmic Fall, **I** 511b–512a
  Darwin, **I** 335a
  Descartes, **I** 327b
  Diderot, **I** 333b
  dignity, **IV** 139b
  Erigena, **I** 326b
  ethics, **I** 328b–329a
  evil, **I** 512a
  evolutionism, **I** 334a–335a; **II** 178a, 184a
  Fichte, **I** 334b
  Fontenelle, **I** 327b, 332a
  Forms, **I** 325b–326a
  Franklin, B., **IV** 22a
  God, **I** 326b, 512a
  Goodman, **I** 511b, 512b
  Hakewill, **I** 512a
  harmony, **II** 389a
  heresy, **II** 427a
  hierarchy, **II** 440b, 446b–

448a
  Huxley, Julian, **I** 334b
  idealism, **I** 334b
  Johnson, Samuel, **I** 329b, 330a
  499a; **II** 447a–447b
  Kant, **I** 330a–331b, 332b, 334a
  La Mettrie, **I** 333b, 334b
  Lamarck, **I** 335a
  Leibniz, **I** 326a, 327b–329a, 330a, 331b, 332a, 333a, 499a–499b
  Linnaeus, **I** 332a
  Locke, **II** 446b
  Lovejoy, **I** 325b, 326a, 327b, 329a, 330a, 333a
  Lully, **I** 327a
  Macrobius, **II** 440b
  matter, **III** 193b
  Maupertuis, **I** 332b–333a
  music, **II** 389a
  mythology, **III** 277a
  Nature, **I** 326a–327b, 332a–334a
  Needham, J. T., **I** 333b
  Neo-Platonism, **I** 326a
  Newton, **I** 330a
  ontological basis, **I** 325a–325b
  papacy, **I** 329b
  Parkinson, **I** 334b–335a
  Plato, **I** 325a–325b, 326b, 330a, 333a
  Plotinus, **I** 325b
  pluralism, **I** 327b
  Pope, **I** 329a; **II** 447a
  Pseudo-Dionysius, **I** 326a
  psychology, **IV** 22a
  Pyrrhonism, **I** 331b
  Réaumur, **I** 332a
  Renaissance, **I** 326b–327a, 327b; **IV** 139b
  Robinet, **I** 331b–332a, 332b, 333b, 334a
  Saint Augustine, **I** 326a
  Saint Thomas Aquinas, **I** 326b
  Schelling, **I** 334b
  Schiller, Friedrich, **I** 334b
  science, **I** 326b–327b
  species, **I** 330b–333b
  Spinoza, **I** 326a, 329a
  Sprat, **I** 327a
  State, **I** 328b–329a
  theology, **I** 326a–326b
  Thomson, **II** 446b
  Tree of Life, **I** 334a–335a
  Trembley, **I** 331b
  two basic principles of, **I** 333a
  Vallisnieri, **I** 332a
  vitalism, **I** 334a

Voltaire, I 329a, 329b–330a; II 447a–447b
Wesley, II 446b
William of Conches, I 326b
Young, II 446b–447a
Zeno of Citium, I 329b
See also Continuity, Hierarchy, Plenitude
Chain of History, mythology, III 276b–284b
Chaitin, G. J., probability, III 623a
Chalcidius (fl. 335 A.D.)
Being, II 229a
causation, II 230a
chance, II 229a–230a, 233a
dignity, IV 139a
free will, II 229a, 229b–230a
God, III 381b
methodology, III 381b
Platonism, III 509b
Pythagorean cosmos, IV 39b
Chaldea
astrology, I 125a
hermeticism, II 431b
Islam, II 639a
mythology, III 272a
Pythagoreans, IV 38b
Chamberlain, Houston Stuart (1855–1927), China, I 370b
Chamberlin, Edward H., economic history, II 51b
Chambers, Robert (1802–1871)
deism, II 179a
evolutionism, II 179a, 182b
literature, III 82b
religion, IV 106a
romanticism, IV 195a
Schopenhauer and, II 182b
Chambers, William (1726–1796), nature, I 364a
Champfleury, J. H. (1821–1889)
mimesis, III 229b
realism in literature, IV 52a
Champier, Symphorien (c. 1472–1539)
humanism, III 514a
Platonism, III 507b, 514a
Chance, I 335b–340a; II 225b–236a
Adrasteia, II 229a
Alberti, II 235a
angels, II 232b–233a
Apuleius, II 228a, 232a
Arbuthnot, I 337b–338a
Aristotelianism, II 229b, 230a, 230b, 231a–231b, 232b, 233a, 234a
Aristotle, I 336a, 339b; II 226a, 227a, 227b–228a,

228b, 229b, 231b, 233a
art, II 230a, 232a, 234a, 235a
astrology, II 232a, 232b, 233a, 233b, 234b, 235a
atomism, II 226a
Augustinianism, II 230b
Bayes, I 338b–339a
beauty, II 228a
Bernoulli, I 337b
birth, II 226b, 228a, 228b, 232a, 233b
Boccaccio, II 233b–234a
Boethius, II 231a–232a, 234b
Bracciolini, II 235a
Bradley, II 587b
Cardano, I 337a
causation, II 226a–233b, 234b, 235a, 236a
celestial spheres, II 228b–229b, 232a–233b
Chalcidius, II 229a–230a, 233a
Christianity, I 336b–337a, 338b; II 229a–236a
Claudius, I 336a
cosmology, II 226a
courage, II 234a
Cournot, I 339b
Creation, II 226a, 226b, 231a
cycles, II 228a, 229b
Dante, II 233a–233b, 234b
death, II 226b
deism, II 227a
Democritus, II 226a–226b
destiny, II 225b, 228a, 233b
determinism, II 229b, 230a, 230b, 232a, 233b, 234b, 240a
dice-playing, I 336a–337a
dignity, II 231b
Dirac, I 339b
diviners, I 336a, 336b
Egypt (ancient), I 335b–336a
Einstein, I 336b
Epicureanism, II 231a
Epicurus, I 336a
ethics, II 226b–227b, 233a
evil, II 234a
fame, II 234a
fate, fortune, and, II 225b–236b
Fates, II 229a
fear, II 234b
Fermat, I 337b
Finetti, I 338b
Firmicius Maternus, II 232a
free will, II 226b–231b, 234a, 236a, 240a
freedom, II 227a, 229b

friendship, II 228a
Galileo, I 337a
gambling, I 336a–337a
game theory, II 264a–264b, 265a, 266a, 268b, 269b
glory, II 231b
God, I 336a, 336b; II 226b, 227b–231a, 232a–235a, 236a
good, II 227b–229a, 231b–235b
grace, II 233b
Greece (ancient), I 335b–336a; II 225b–228b
happiness, II 227a, 228a, 235a
harmony, II 229b
haruspication, I 336a
Heimarmene, II 229a
Hera, II 229a
heredity, II 228a
Hermes Trismegistus, II 232a
humanism, II 225b, 235a, 236a
Hume, I 339a
Huygens, I 337b
impulse, II 227b, 232b–233b, 234a, 234b, 235a
indeterminacy, II 225b–226b, 228b, 230b, 587b
instinct, II 227b
Islam, I 336b
James, William, IV 395b
Judaism, I 336a
justice, II 233b
Kant, II 240a
knowledge, II 226a–226b, 229b, 232b
Laplace, I 337b, 339a; III 612a–612b
law, II 226a, 226b, 227a, 228a, 229a, 229b, 231b, 235b
Lévy, Paul, I 336b
logic, II 230a, 230b, 231a
love, II 234a
luck, II 225b, 227a–227b, 234a–234b
Machiavelli, II 235b–236a
Martianus Capella, II 229a
mathematics, I 337a–337b
matter, III 187b
Middle Ages, II 227b, 232a
mind, II 226a, 227a, 229a, 232a, 233b, 233a
moon, II 233b
morality, II 229b, 231b–232a, 234a, 234b–235a
motion, II 229b, 231b
music, III 263b
mythology, II 226b, 228a, 229a
Nature, I 336a, 336b; II

225b, 226b, 227a, 227b, 228b, 229a, 229b, 231a, 233a, 233b; III 263b
necessity, II 225b, 226b, 228a, 229b, 230a, 230b, 232a, 234a
Neo-Platonism, II 229a
Nonsufficient Reason, I 339a
observation, II 226a
Orphism, II 226b
Pascal, I 337b
passions, II 233b
Peirce, II 587b; III 560b
perfectibility, III 470a
Petrarch, II 234a–235a
philosophy, III 612a
Plato, II 226b, 231b–232a; III 629a–629b
playing cards, I 337a
pleasure, II 234a
Pontano, II 235a
power, II 228a, 228b, 229a–229b, 230a, 231a, 231b, 233b, 235a, 235b, 236a
pragmatism, III 560b
predestination, II 225b
Principle of Indifference, I 339a
probability, I 337b–340a; II 226a; III 605b–607a, 612a–612b, 614b, 615b, 616a
Proclus, II 228b
progress, III 629a–629b
prudence, II 235a
psychology, II 227b
punishment, II 229b
Quételet, I 338a
radioactivity, I 339b
reason, II 225b–226a, 226b, 227b, 233a, 234a
reincarnation, II 226b, 227a
religion, II 227a
Renaissance, II 232a
reputation, II 228b
reward, II 229b
Roman Catholic Church, I 336b–337a
Rome (ancient), I 335b–336a; II 226a
Saint Albertus Magnus, II 232a, 232b
Saint Augustine, I 336b; II 230a–231a, 231b, 232a
Saint Bernardino of Siena, I 337a
Saint Cyprian of Carthage, I 336b–337a
Saint Thomas Aquinas, I 336b, 338b; II 232a–233a
Salutati, II 234b
Savage, I 338b
scholasticism, II 227b, 230a

science, II 225b
Seneca, II 228a
Simplicius, II 228a, 228b, 233a
soul, II 226b–230a, 233a–233b, 235b
space, II 231b
Spinoza, I 336b
stars, II 227a, 229b, 235a
statistics, I 338a
Stoicism, II 228a, 230a, 232a, 234a, 234b
success, II 228b, 233a
superstition, II 226a, 234b
Süssmilch, I 338a
Sybilline books, I 336a
Tacitus, I 336a
teleology, II 231a
time, II 231b, 232b, 233a; IV 395b, 398a
tragedy, II 228a
Venn, I 338b
virtue, II 225b, 227b, 231b, 233b, 234a, 234b, 235a
virtù, II 235b–236a
wealth, II 228a, 228b, 231b
Zeus (myth), II 229a
Chance images, I 340b–353b
Alberti, I 345a–346a, 346b, 347a, 351a
Albertus Magnus, I 343a
Aldrovandi, I 343b
Anselm of Canterbury, I 342b
Apelles, I 341a
Aristotle, I 341b
Arp, I 352b
Baltrusaitis, I 343b
Botticelli, I 346b, 349a, 350b
Braque, I 352a, 352b
cave art, I 351a
China, I 352b–353b
Christianity, I 342b–344b
Chrysostom, I 341a
Cicero, I 341a
Constable, I 350b
Correggio, I 347a, 348a
Cosimo, I 348a–348b, 349b
Cozens, I 349a–353b
Cubism, I 352
Dadaism, I 352b
Delacroix, I 350b
Duchamp, I 352b
Dürer, I 344b–345a, 345b
El Greco, I 347a, 348b
foliage masks, I 341b, 342a
fortune, I 340b, 341a, 341b
Freud, I 352b
Fuseli, I 350b
God, I 342a
Gothic, I 343a–345a
Grandville, I 350a
Greece (ancient), I 340b–

342b, 347a
Hugo, I 350b
ink blots, I 340b, 349b–351a, 353a
Japan, I 353a
Kerner, I 350b–351a, 351b
Kircher, I 343b
Ladendorf, I 341b, 343b, 345a
Leonardo da Vinci, I 346b, 347b–349a, 349b–350b
Lucretius, I 341b, 343a
Mantegna, I 345b, 346b–347a, 347b
Marbod of Rennes, I 343b
Master of Barberini Panels, I 347a, 347b
Middle Ages, I 342b–345a
Milanese Master (Bernardo Zenale?), I 347b–348a, 348b
Montaigne, I 349a
Nature, I 340b, 341a, 341b, 343a
Nealces, I 341a
Old Stone Age, I 340b, 351a
Ore, I 337a
painting, I 341a–353b
Perthes, I 351a
Philostratus, I 342a–342b
Picasso, I 352a–352b
Pliny, I 340b–341b, 342b, 345b
Protogenes, I 341a, 349a, 350b, 352b
Psellus, I 342b–343a
Pyrrhus, I 340b–341a, 341b, 345a, 346a, 349a
Raphael, I 347a
Renaissance, I 342b, 345a–349a
Retza, I 343a
Rome (ancient), I 341a, 341b, 347a
Rorschach, I 350b, 351a
Saint Médard, I 343b
sculpture, I 340b–341b, 345a–346a, 351a–353b
Turner, I 350b
Vasari, I 348a–348b
Wang Mo, I 352b–353a
Whistler, I 351a–352a
Chandler, A. R., beauty, I 212b
Chandrasekhar, S., entropy, II 114b
Channing, Edward Tyrrel, Orientalism, III 429a
Channing, William Ellery (1780–1842), Pietism, IV 111a
Channing, William Henry (1810–1884)
Orientalism, III 429a, 434b

transcendentalism, III 429a, 434b
Chantavoine, Henri (1850–1918), irony, II 633a
Chanteloup, Comte de, Enlightenment, II 98b
Chants, III 265b, 266a, 269b, 270a
Chaos
Aristotle, III 15b
Bible, IV 297a–297b
Comte, III 641a
Creation, III 281b
dignity, IV 138a, 141b, 142a
etymology, IV 296b
Greece (ancient), IV 296b, 297b
hermeticism, II 431a, 431b, 432a, 432b, 433a, 434a
Hesiod, IV 297a
hierarchy, II 444b
impressionism, II 582a
justice, III 15b
language, II 664b
Milton, III 393b
music, III 265b, 267a
mythology, III 281b, 284a–284b, 315a; IV 296b
natural law, III 14b, 15b
order, II 444b
Ovid, IV 297a
Plato, IV 296b–297a
pragmatism, III 560b
progress, III 641a
Renaissance, IV 138a, 141b, 142a
Saint-Simon, III 741a
socialism, IV 285a
space, IV 296b–297b
time, IV 390a
Chapelain, Jean (1595–1674)
literary criticism, I 597a
literature, III 81b
Chapin, Charles V., environment, II 124b
Chapman, George (1559?–1634)
allegory, III 294b
baroque in literature, I 194b
Bush and, III 294b
culture, III 294b
Donne and, III 294b
Drayton and, III 295b
ethics, III 294b
Greville and, III 294b
harmony, II 394b
humanism, III 294b
idealism, III 295a
individualism, III 294b, 295a
Jonson and, III 294b
Marlowe and, III 294b
morality, III 294b

music, II 394b
mythology, III 294b–295a, 295b, 297a, 299a
painting, III 294b
Platonism, III 295a
poetry, III 294b–295a
Roydon and, III 294b
Spenser and, III 294b
Chaptal, Jean Antoine (1756–1832), Enlightenment, II 98b
Character
genius, II 293a–293b, 295b
Man-Machine, III 133a–133b
motif, III 239b
psychology, IV 15a, 15b, 16a
Chardin, Jean Baptiste Siméon (1699–1779)
art, II 306a
impressionism, II 572b, 578b
individualism, II 306a
Charity, II 209b–216a
agapē, II 209b, 210a
Aristotelianism, II 210b–211a, 211b
Aristotle, II 210b
asceticism, II 212b
atheism, II 213a, 213b
Augustinianism, II 210b
authority, II 212a
Bible, II 209b, 210a
Bloch, II 213b, 214a
Bonaventure, II 210b
Bonhoeffer, II 213b
Camus, II 213b, 215a
Christianity, II 209b–215b
Cox, II 214b
deterioration of the meaning of, II 212b–213a
Dewart, II 214b
egocentric aspect of, II 209b
Erigena, II 210b
eros, II 209b, 210a, 210b
ethics, II 212b, 215a
faith, II 209b–216a
Feuerbach, II 213b
Freud, II 213b
friendship, II 210b–211a
Garaudy, II 213b, 214a
gnosis, II 210a
Gnosticism, II 210a
God, II 209b–214b
good, II 209b, 212a
grace, II 211a
Great Britain, III 489b
Greece (ancient), II 209b
Hobbes, II 212b
hope, II 209b–216a
humanism, II 214a, 215a
individualism, II 212b

Jesus Christ, II 211b, 214b
Judaism, III 487b, 488a
knowledge, II 210a, 211b
law, II 687a
love, II 209b, 210a, 210b, 212a, 215a
Luther, II 212a–212b
Lutheranism, II 212b, 213a
Marxism, II 213b–214a
Middle Ages, II 210a–212b
monasticism, II 212b
morality, II 212b, 213a
Nietzsche, II 213a
Pannenberg, II 214b
Pietism, III 493b
Plato, II 209b
Platonism, II 210b
private property, III 654a
Protestantism, II 212a–213a, 215b
Pseudo-Dionysius, II 210b
Reformation, II 212a–213a, 215b
Roman Catholic Church, II 210a–211b, 212b, 213a, 215a–215b; III 654a
Rome (ancient), II 687a
Saint Augustine, II 210a–210b, 213a
Saint John, II 210a
Saint Paul, II 210a, 211b
Saint Thomas Aquinas, II 210b–212a, 213a
salvation, II 210a, 212b
Sartre, II 213b
slavery, II 213a
society, II 212b, 213a
soul, II 211a
temperance, IV 372b, 374a, 375b
Tillich, II 211a
transubstantiation, II 212b
Victorian sensibility, IV 219b
virtue, II 211a–212b; IV 372b, 373a, 374a, 375b
Weber, II 211b, 212b
welfare state, IV 509b
See also Philanthropy
Charlemagne (742–814),
common law, II 691b
crowned by Leo III, I 418a
historiography, II 473a
humanism, II 515a
intolerance, IV 113b
Middle Ages, III 477a
periodization in history, III 477a, 477b, 480a
religion, IV 113b
Saxons, IV 113b
vox populi, IV 498a–498b
Charles I, King (1600–1649),
equality, II 142b
law, III 8a

Machiavellism, III 119b
mythology, III 297a, 297b
periodization in literary history, III 482b
revolution, IV 153b
social contract, IV 255a
virtuoso, IV 487b
Charles II, King (1630–1685),
I 649a
revolution, IV 153b
tolerance, I 401b
Charles V, Emperor (1500–1558)
balance of power, I 182a
Counter-Reformation, I 393b–394a
Faust (legend), III 247a
heresy, II 425b
historiography, II 484a
Lutheranism, I 390a
mythology, III 291a
Charles V, King (1337–1380),
despotism, II 3a
Charles IX, King (1550–1574),
mythology, III 290a
Charles X, King (1757–1836),
Cousin and, III 533b
Charleton, Walter (1620–1707),
atomism, I 137a, 138a
Charlier, C. V. I. (1862–1934),
space, IV 303b
Charlton, Joshua, virtuoso, IV 489b
Charpentier, François (1734–1817), attitude toward antiquity, I 78a–78b
Charron, Pierre (1541–1603),
causation, I 301b
certainty, I 304b, 305a
Counter-Enlightenment, II 101b
God, I 301b; II 349b
historiography, IV 150b
Mersenne and, I 301b
perfectibility, III 468b
skepticism, II 349b
teleology, I 301b
theriophily, IV 387b
Chartier, Émile Auguste (1868–1951), dualism, II 41b
Chartism
class, I 443b
deism, I 652a
equality, II 143a
Chasles, Philarète (1798–1873), literature, III 82b, 84a
Chastel, André, iconography, II 538a
Chastity
Christianity, IV 370b, 371a
heresy, II 418b, 421a
perfectibility, III 467a

temperance, IV 367b, 370a–371b, 372b, 373a, 377a
Victorian sensibility, IV 219a
virtue, IV 371a–371b, 372b, 377a
Chateaubriand, Francois René de (1768–1848)
classicism, I 452a
conservatism, I 477b
Counter-Enlightenment, II 110a
God, IV 201a
iconography, II 535a
literary criticism, I 599b
literature, IV 189b, 195b, 332b
Nature, IV 201a
primitivism, III 598b, 601b, 603b
religion, IV 201a
Roman Catholic Church, IV 200b
romanticism, I 404b–405a; IV 189b, 195b, 198a, 200b, 205a, 208b
Rousseau and, III 603b; IV 201a
style, IV 332b
Chatterton, Thomas (1752–1770), romanticism, IV 194b, 195a
Chaucer, Geoffrey (1340?–1400)
beauty, II 199b
comedy, I 469b
continuity, I 493a–493b
cosmic voyages, I 527a
periodization in literary history, III 485b
Platonism, III 507b
romanticism, IV 194b
symbolism, IV 341b
ut pictura poesis, IV 469a
Chebychev, P. L. (1821–1894), probability, III 620a
Chekhov, Anton (1860–1904), comedy, I 470a
Chemistry
Comte, III 535b
disease, II 400b, 401a
linguistics, IV 424b
Man-Machine, III 131b
mathematics, III 177a, 178a
positivism, III 535b, 548b
technology, IV 360a, 364a
uniformitarianism, IV 424b
Chénier, André (1762–1794),
classicism, I 454b
Chernyshevsky, Nikolai (1828?–1889), beauty, I 211a
Cherubim (myth), III 282b, 283b, 284a

Chéseaux, Phillipe Loys de, space, IV 303a
Chess, game theory, II 264b, 265a, 266a
Chesterton, G. K. (1874–1936), literary paradox, III 77b
Chevalier, H., irony, II 633a
Chevalier, Michel, individualism, II 596a
Chevreul, Michel-Eugène (1786–1889), impressionism, II 580a, 580b
Chigi, Agostino (1465?–1520), mythology, III 290a
Child, Irvin L., beauty, I 213b–214a
Child, Lydia Maria (1802–1880)
Orientalism, III 429a
transcendentalism, III 429a
Child, T., symbolism, IV 341a
Child labor, reformation, IV 68b
Childe, V. Gordon
creativity in art, I 582a
evolutionism, II 187a
Children
Adam (Bible), III 595b
Andersen, III 596a
angels, III 595b
animals, III 596a
Bible, III 595b
Christianity, III 595b
Cicero, III 595b
comedy, III 501a
degeneration, III 595b–596a
Earl, III 595b
educators, III 596a
Jesus Christ, III 595b
Jung, III 597a
Key, III 596a
law, II 686b, 688a
Locke, III 469b
Montaigne, III 595b
morality, III 596a
Nature, III 347a
pedagogy, III 595b
perfectibility, III 469b–470a, 471a
philanthropy, III 491a
Plato, III 471a, 501a
primitivism, III 595b–596a, 597a, 597b
recapitulation, IV 58b, 59a
rights, III 596a
Rome (ancient), II 686b, 688a
Rousseau, III 469b, 595b
suffering, IV 415b
Victorian sensibility, IV 219a, 221a
welfare state, IV 510b, 511a

wisdom of the fool, IV 516a
Wordsworth, III 596a
Chile, positivism, III 544a
Chiliasm, *see* Millenarianism
Chillingworth, William (1602–1644)
certainty, I 304b, 306a, 307a–308a, 308b, 309a, 310a, 311a, 311b
deism, I 649b
Rule of Faith controversy, I 307a–308a
skepticism, I 306a, 307a–308a, 308b, 309a, 310a, 311a, 311b; IV 245b
Chilon, temperance, IV 366a
China, I 353b–373a
agriculture, I 366b, 367b, 372b
alchemy, I 27a, 29a, 33a; III 91a
Alexander VII (Pope), I 357b
ancestor worship, I 360b, 362a; II 341b
architecture, I 355a, 363b
Arendt, I 367b
Arnauld, I 360a
astronomy, I 355a
atheism, I 360a
Ayscough, I 369b
Babbitt, I 369b
Barros, I 354b
Baudelaire, I 369a
Bayer, I 367a
Bayle, I 360a
Bazin, I 369a
Bible, I 358b–359b
Bierbaum, O. J., I 369b
Bishop, C. W., I 369a
Bontekoe, I 356b
Bossuet, I 365a
Boucher, I 363b–364a
Boxer Rebellion, I 369a
Boym, I 356a
Bridgman, E. C., I 367a–367b
Buck, I 372a
Buddhism, I 248b, 249a, 250b–251a, 252a–254a, 257a, 355a, 355b, 357a, 368a, 369b, 370b; II 481b; IV 476a
Burckhardt, I 370a
capitalism, I 368a
Castanheda, I 354b
Chamberlain, I 370b
chance images, I 352b–353b
Ch'ing dynasty, I 356b
Christianity, I 353b, 354a, 354b, 355a–361b
civil service, I 367b
classification of the scien-

ces, I 464a
Clemenceau, I 369a
Clement IV (Pope), I 357b
Commelin, I 356b
communications, I 354a
Confucianism, I 355a–358a, 360a, 361a, 362a, 368b, 372b
Costa, I 356a
Coulanges, I 371a
Couplet, I 358b, 359a, 456b
Creel, I 369b
crisis in history, I 594a
Cruz, I 354b
Culbertson, M. S., I 367b
culture, I 353b–355a, 355b
Dapper, I 356b–357a
De Tournon, I 357b
determinism, II 22b
Dewey, John, I 371a
d'Hervey Saint-Denys, I 367b
dictionaries, I 464a
Dominicans, I 354b, 357a–357b
drama, I 367a, 372a
dualism, II 41b–42a
Du Halde, I 360b, 361b, 365b
economics, III 154a
education, I 355a, 355b, 356b; II 75a–75b
Engels, I 366b, 369b
Enlightenment, I 353b–354a, 365a
Ernst, Paul, I 371a
Ferrari, Joseph, I 371a
figure poetry, IV 476a
Figurism, I 359b–360b
Flaubert, I 369a
Fourmont, I 367a
Franciscans, I 357a
games, II 264b
gardening, I 364a
Gautier, Judith, I 369a
Gautier, Théophile, I 369a
geography, I 355a
Giles, I 367a
Gobineau, I 370b
God, I 357a, 360a, 360b; II 344b
Goethe, I 365a, 368b
Goncourt, Edmond, I 369a
Goncourt, Jules, I 369a
Great Britain, I 367b
Gregory XIII (Pope), I 354b
Grimm, F. M., I 365a
Grousset, I 368a
Guimet, I 369a
Hagdorn, I 364a
health, II 369b, 397a; III 90b
Hegel, I 366a–366b, 370a
Heine, I 368b

Herbert of Cherbury, I 360a
Herder, I 365b
historiography, II 22b, 467b, 479b–482a, 488b
history, I 358b–359b, 367a–368b, 372a; II 22b
Hobart, I 372a
holy, II 513a
Horn, I 359a
Hugo, Victor, I 369a
influence on Western literature, I 364a–364b
influence on Western painting, I 363b–364a
Innocent X (Pope), I 357b
Intorcetta, I 356a–356b
Islam, I 354a; II 640b
Jansenism, I 357b
Japan, I 369a, 372a
Jesuits, I 353b, 354b, 355b–361b, 363b, 364b, 365a, 365b, 367a
Jews, I 360b
Johnson, Samuel, I 365a
Judaism, I 360b
Justi, I 362b
Kircher, I 358a
Klaproth, I 367a
La Mothe le Vayer, I 360a
lacquer ware, I 363a
language, I 354a–355b, 358a–358b, 362a, 366b–367a, 369b, 372a; II 661a, 661b, 668a, 669b
Lavisse, I 370a
law, III 7a, 28b
Le Comte, I 357b
Legge, I 367b, 370a
Leibniz, I 358b, 359b–360b, 361a, 362b
Lenin, I 372a, 372b
linguistics, II 661a, 661b
literature, I 364a–364b, 366b, 367a–367b, 368b–369b, 372a; IV 476a
Longobardi, I 357a
Loti, I 369a
Lowell, Amy, I 369b
McNeill, William, I 372a
Maffei, I 354b
Maigrot, I 357b
Mailla, I 361a
Malebranche, I 360a
Malthus, I 365b–366a
Marco Polo, I 354a, 365b
Martini, I 356a, 358b–359a
Marx, I 366b, 369b, 372a
Marxism, III 154a
mathematics, I 355a; III 180b; IV 399a, 401a, 402a
Meadows, I 367b, 371a
Mendoza, I 354b, 355a, 355b
Mill, J. S., I 369b

Ming policy of isolation, I 354b
missionaries, I 353b, 354a, 354b, 355a–361b, 383b
Montanus, I 356b–357a
Montesquieu, I 361b–362a, 365a
morality, I 355a, 356b, 357b, 361a–363a, 366a
Morrison, I 367a
Morse, H. B., I 367b
Müller, Max, I 368a
music, III 268b
mythology, III 302b
nationalism, III 332b, 333a, 334a
natural resources, I 370a
Navarrete, I 357b
Neo-Confucianism, I 356b
Nestorian monument, I 356a, 358a
Netherlands, I 356b–357a
Nicholas II, I 370b
Nieuhof, I 356b
Noël, I 356b
numbers, III 402b
Odoric of Pordenone, I 354a
opened to the West, I 369b
Orientalism, III 428a, 428b, 430a–431a, 433a–434b, 436a
painting, I 353b–354a, 363b–364a, 369a; IV 470b, 473a, 475b–476a
Pascal, I 360a
Pauthier, I 369a
Pearson, C. H., I 370b
peasants, I 371a, 372a–372b
Pelliot, I 368a
philanthropy, III 486b
Philippines, I 355a
Physiocrats, I 362b–363a
Pillement, I 364a
poetry, I 354a, 367a, 368b–369b; IV 470b, 473a, 475b
Polo, I 354a, 365b
population, I 365b–366a
porcelain, I 363a
Portugal, I 354a–354b
Pound, Ezra, I 369b
private property, III 651a
pragmatism, III 569a
progress, III 638b, 639b, 648a
Protestantism, I 360a, 360b, 366a, 367a, 368a, 369b–370a
Quesnay, I 362b–363a
Ranke, I 370a
religion, I 354a, 354b, 355a, 368a; IV 104a, 105a, 379b
Rémusat, I 367a

revisionism, IV 275a
Ricci, I 355b–356a, 357a
Richthofen, I 370a, 371a
Roman Catholic Church, I 353b, 354b, 355a–361b
Rome (ancient), I 354a
Rousseau, I 365a
Rückert, I 368b
Russell, Bertrand, I 371a–371b
Russia, I 371a
sacred, II 513a
science, I 355a
sculpture, I 369a
sea passage opened to, I 354a
Semedo, I 356a
Silhouette, I 358a
Simon, Eugène, I 371a
slavery, I 354b, 363a
Smith, Adam, I 365a–365b
social organization, I 355a, 361a, 370a
socialism, III 154a
Spengler, I 371b
Spinoza, I 360a
Staunton, George, I 365b
State, I 361a–363a, 365b, 370b
superstition, I 362a
Taiping rebellion, I 366b
Taoism, I 249a, 254a, 355a, 355b, 357a, 367a, 367b, 368a, 368b, 371a; IV 476a
Tawney, I 371b
technology, I 353b, 594a; IV 358b, 359b
Temple, William, I 364b
Tennyson, I 369a
textiles, I 363a
Thomasius, I 360a
Thoms, I 368b
time, IV 399a, 401a, 402a
Tolstoy, I 371a
Toynbee, I 371b–372a
trade, I 354a, 354b, 356b; III 428b
transcendentalism, I 368b
Treaty of Nerchinsk, I 360b
Trigault, I 355b
Trotsky, I 372a–372b
U.S., I 367b, 370b, 371b; III 428a, 428b, 430a–430b, 431a, 433a–434b, 436a
Unzer, I 368b
utilitarianism, III 433b
Utopia, IV 359a
Valignano, I 354b, 355b
Voltaire, I 361b, 362a, 365a; II 10b
Vosius, I 358b–359a
Wallace, H. A., I 371b
Weber, I 368a–368b, 372b

Wells, H. G., I 371b
Wilhelm, Richard, I 369b
William II, I 370b
Williams, S. Wells, I 367b
Wittfogel, I 372b
Wolff, Christian, I 361a–361b
writing, III 180b–181a
yin and yang doctrine, II 122b
China (Communist)
Buddhism, I 248b
communism, III 334a–334b
Constitution, I 486a
constitutionalism, I 486a
culture, I 372b; III 334a, 334b; IV 166a
democracy, III 334a
despotism, III 147b
freedom, I 486a
imperialism, III 161b, 167a, 334a
international peace, III 455b, 456a
Marxism, III 147b, 150b, 154b, 157a–157b, 161b, 166b, 167a, 157b, 169a
Marxism-Leninism, II 453b; III 334a, 334b
materialism, III 334a, 453b
morality, III 334a
nationalism, III 334a–334b
natural liberty, II 70a
peasantry, III 154b
pragmatism, III 565b
proletariat, III 154b
revolution, IV 166a, 166b
Stalin, I 372b
totalitarianism, IV 409b
tradition, III 334a
U.S.S.R., IV 166a–166b
war, IV 507a
Westernization, III 334b
Chinard, Gilbert, primitivism, III 593b–594a
Chinaware, neo-classicism in art, III 366b
Ch'ing dynasty, I 356b
Chirico, Giorgio de (1888–   ), creativity in art, I 583a
Chiron (myth), III 273b
Chivalry.
love, III 97a–100a, 101b, 102b
Middle Ages, II 530a
romanticism, IV 187b, 206b
Shaftesbury, III 598b
Choderlos de Laclos, Machiavellism, III 119a
Cholmondeley, Thomas, Orientalism, III 431a
Chompre, Pierre, mythology, III 303a

Chomsky, Noam
grammar, II 672b–673a
literature, III 88a
structuralism, IV 324b–325a, 326b
Chopin, Frédéric (1810–1849)
disease, II 403b
romanticism, IV 208b
Chora, IV 299b–301b
Chou dynasty, II 480a
historiography, II 480a
Chrétien de Troyes (12th century), love, III 102a
Christian Brotherhoods, Augustinianism, IV 109a
Christianity, I 373b–412b
Acton, I 408b, 409a
Age of Reason, I 400b–402a
agnosticism, I 17a–27a
Agrippa, III 591a
alienation, I 34a–37a
allegory, I 43a–48a, 51b–53a
ambiguity, I 52a–54b
analogy, I 64a–67a, 68b–69b, 70a
anarchy, I 72a
anti-industrialism, III 676a
anti-intellectualism, III 590b–591a
Arabia, I 378b, 380a
Arabs, I 401a
architecture, I 417b
Arianism, I 377b, 379a
art, III 591a
art and play, I 102b, 103a
asceticism, IV 371a .
astrology, I 123a, 123b
atomism, I 129b–130a, 136a–137a
authority, I 146b–150a
Bach, I 504b
Bible, III 588b, 589a, 589b, 590b, 591a; IV 102b, 103a, 371a
Bonhoeffer, II 213b
Brahmins, III 592a–592b
brotherhood, III 488b, 489b
Buddhism, I 252a, 253b, 254b, 255b, 256a
caesaropapism, I 379b, 380b
Camerini (legend), III 592a
Campanella, IV 461b
Camus, II 213b
capitalism, I 396a–397a
Carolingian Renaissance, I 380b
casuistry, I 258b–264a
catastrophism, IV 419b
catharsis, I 264b, 265b–266a, 269a

cathedrals, I 382b, 417b
causation, I 279b, 290b
Chain of Being, I 326a–326b, 329b–330a
chance, I 336b–337a, 338b; II 229a–236a
chance images, I 342b–344b
charity, II 209b–215b; III 488b, 489b
chastity, IV 370b, 371a
children, III 595b
China, I 353b, 354a, 354b, 355a–361b
Church, I 412b–426b
city, I 427b, 428b–429b
class, I 442a–443a, 443b, 446a, 449a; III 670b
common law, II 691a, 692a, 694a–694b
communism, I 379b, 407b; III 590b, 674b
consciousness, I 215a
conservatism, I 477b, 482a, 482b, 483a
continuism, I 503b
continuity, I 492b, 493a, 502b, 503b
corporations, III 589a
Cosmic Fall, I 504b–512b
cosmic voyages, I 524a, 625a, 532a
cosmology, I 542b–544a, 545b, 546b, 622b
cosmopolitanism, III 586b
Council of Constance, I 399b
Council of Constantinople, I 377b
Council of Trent, I 393b, 394a
Counter-Enlightenment, II 101b, 102a, 102b, 103b, 105b, 110a–112a
Counter-Reformation, I 392b–395a
Creation, I 543b, 571a–572b
creativity in art, I 585b, 586a
Crusades, I 383a, 418a
culture, I 375a; II 132a–132b
cycles, I 622b, 623a, 623b–624b
cynicism, I 631a; III 588b–591a
Darwin, I 405b
death, I 636a, 639b, 640b, 643b–645a; IV 229b, 230a
defined, I 373b
deism, I 402a, 403a, 646b, 647b–652a
democracy, I 653a, 661b

demonology, I 667b–670a
design argument, I 671a, 672b–673b
despotism, II 1b, 3a–4a, 8a, 10a, 10b, 14a–14b
determinism, II 19b, 20a, 22a, 26a–31a, 237b–238a
Diet of Worms, I 390b
dignity, IV 136a–146a
ditheism, II 342b
Donatist schism, I 377a
double truth, II 31a–37b
dualism, II 38b, 39a, 41a, 42a–43b; III 281b
Eastern Orthodox Church, I 409a–411b
ecclesiastical property, I 386b
economic history, II 45a, 46a–47a, 47b, 58b
education, I 379b, 388a; II 746, 806; III 591a
Egyptian anchorites, I 377b–378a
eighteenth century, I 402a–403a
emphasis on spiritual life, II 470b
Enlightenment, II 91a
environment, II 132a–132b
Epicureanism, II 137b
Epicurus, III 590a
equality, II 138a, 138b, 140b–143a; III 670b
eschatology, II 154b, 155b–157b, 158b, 159a, 160a, 160b–161a; IV 229a, 230a
ethics, III 440a, 441a, 441b, 445b, 446a; IV 176a–176b, 177a, 322a
evangelicalism, I 403a, 406b
evil, II 164a–165a, 167a, 168b; IV 229b
evolution, I 405b
evolutionism, II 176a, 177a
existentialism, II 189b, 190a, 190b, 191b, 192a–192b
faith, II 209b–215b
fate, II 229a–236a
Faust (legend), III 246a, 247a, 249b, 250b
Feuerbach, II 213b
fortune, II 229a–236a
free will, I 394b; II 137b, 237b–238a, 244a–245b
freedom, II 250a, 251a–251b
freedom of speech, II 262a
French Revolution, I 404a–404b, 408b–409a
Freud, II 213b
Gandhi, III 446a

Giotto, I 383a
Gnosticism, I 35a, 35b; II 42a–42b, 155b, 326b–331a; IV 229b
God, I 571a–571b, 572b; II 338a, 339b, 341b–343a, 345a, 349b, 354b–366b, 567a, 582b; III 588b, 589a, 590a, 590b, 592a
Golden Age (myth), III 590a
good, IV 174a–174b, 176a–177a
Gothic, II 371a, 371b–372a
grace, IV 370b
Greece (ancient), I 375a; IV 228a
Gregory I (the Great) (Pope), I 379b, 381b
Gregory VII (Pope), I 381b, 382a–382b
Gregory XI (Pope), I 385a
Guibertus the Venerable, III 591a
Guigo the Carthusian, III 590b
happiness, II 378b–379a
harmony, II 389a, 389b, 390b, 392b
health, II 399a, 406a
heaven, IV 230a
Hegel, II 408b, 410a–411b, 414a
Helinandus, III 591a
hell, IV 230a, 230b
Hellenization, I 374a–374b, 375a
Hercules (myth), III 590b
heresy, I 378b, 383a–383b, 386b–387a; II 42a–42b, 43a, 416b–430b, 566b, 567a; III 589a, 670b
hermeticism, II 431a, 432a, 433a; IV 229b
Hesiod, III 590a
hierarchy, II 438a, 439a–439b, 440b, 441a
Hildebert, III 591a
historicism, II 457a, 461a
historiography, I 503b; II 19b, 20a, 22a, 470b–472a, 473a, 474b, 477a, 478a, 483b, 488a, 491a
history, II 19b, 20a, 22a; III 626a; IV 60b, 61a
holy, II 511b–514b
Holy Roman Empire, I 375a–378b
Holy Trinity, I 376a
homoousion theory, I 377b
hope, II 209b–215b
hostels, III 488b
hostility to poetry, III 526b, 528b, 530a
Hugh of Saint Victor, III

592a
Huguenots, IV 113b, 117a
humanism, II 520a–520b; IV 129b, 130b, 131a, 132b, 134b, 135a
Iceland, III 592b
iconography, II 525b–526a, 533b
idealism, I 402b
idolatry, II 567a
immortality, I 639b, 640b, 643b–645a; IV 230b
impiety, II 564a, 564b, 565a, 566b, 567a
impressionism, II 582b
Incarnation, I 376a–376b, 377a; III 477a
individualism, I 400b; II 596b, 597a
indulgences, I 386b, 388b, 389b
industry, I 405b
infinity, II 615a
Innocent III, III 591a
institutionalized, II 215a
international peace, III 448a
intolerance, IV 113b, 114a
irony, II 630a, 632a
Islam, I 378b, 379a, 380b, 381a, 418a; II 639a–640b, 641b, 646a, 650a, 651a; IV 230b
Japan, I 357a
John (King), I 383a
John XIII (Pope), III 590b
Judaism, I 373b–375a; III 488a–488b, 591b; IV 114a
justice, II 656b, 657a; III 671a
language, II 666a, 667a, 669a
law, I 290b; II 250a, 251a–251b, 686b, 688a, 689a
Leibniz, II 471b–472a
liberalism, III 36a, 36b, 37a, 40b, 41b, 42a
literary paradox, III 80a
longevity, III 90a, 91b, 92b
love, III 96a–103b, 107a–107b
loyalty, III 109a, 115a
macrocosm and microcosm, III 129b
magic, III 246a
Manicheism, I 35a, 35b; II 42b–43a
Man-Machine, III 133a, 135a
Marcionites, III 589a
Martyr, III 589b
Marxism, II 213b–214a; III 146b, 160b
Mass, IV 103a
mathematics, III 182a

matter, III 190b
measurement, IV 402a
mechanics and science, II 197a, 199b, 201b–202a
metaphor, III 205a, 205b, 206a, 207a
metaphysical imagination, III 211b
Middle Ages, I 378b–387b, 401a; III 584b–585a, 670b; IV 153a, 153b, 230a, 371a
millenarianism, III 223a–225b, 477a, 488b
missionaries, I 255b, 353b, 354a, 354b, 355a–361b, 375a–376b, 383b
monasteries, I 377b–378a, 380b, 383b, 388a, 392b–393a; III 590a, 590b; IV 371a
monogamy, II 251a–251b
monotheism, II 342b
Montanism, I 375a–375b
morality, III 588b
More, IV 461a
Moses (Bible), III 590a
mountain-origin, III 254b–255a
mountains in literature, III 254a, 254b, 255a
music, I 404b, 407a; II 389a, 389b, 390b, 392b; III 265a–266b, 269a, 269b–271a
mythology, III 276a–277b, 281a–282b, 284a, 286a–294a, 295a, 301a–303b, 304b, 305a–308a, 314a
nationalism, I 385a, 386b, 395a–397a, 399b–400a; III 319b, 320b, 321a, 332b
natural law, III 17b–18b, 19a
natural liberty, II 62a, 64a–64b
natural science, I 405b
naturalism in art, III 342b
Nature, I 129b–130a; III 347a, 347b, 351a, 589a, 590b
Nazism, I 407b
necessity, III 354b–355b, 360b
needy, III 488b
Neo-Platonism, III 371b, 372b, 373a, 373b, 375b–378a; IV 371a
Nero, I 416a
Newman, I 406b
Nietzsche, II 213a
Nikon, Patriarch of Moscow, I 411a
nineteenth century, I 404b–407b

Noble Savage, III 591b–592b
Novalis, IV 207a
orators, III 590b
Orientalism, III 428b, 429a, 432a–434a, 436a, 436b
paganism; I 376a–376b, 377a–377b, 378b, 379a, 380a, 388b; II 341a; III 286b, 588b, 589a, 589b, 590a, 590b, 591b
Paul III (Pope), I 393a
peace, III 440b, 441a, 441b, 445b, 446a; IV 502a
peasantry, III 670b
perennial philosophy, III 457b, 458a, 459a, 459b, 461a
perfectibility, III 464a, 464b, 465b–469b, 471b–472a, 474b
periodization in history, III 476b, 477a, 477b, 478a, 478b
persecutions, I 377a
Persia, I 376a
philanthropy, III 487b, 488a–489a, 490a, 490b, 492a
Philip II, I 397b, 398a
Philip II (Augustus), I 383a
Philo Judaeus, III 590a
philosophers, III 590b
philosophy, III 588b, 591a
Pius VII (Pope), I 404b
Photius, I 409b
Platonism, I 375a; III 505a–506b, 509a–514b, 516a, 517a, 519a, 532a, 589a; IV 371a
pleasure, II 378b–379a
Plotinus, III 505a–505b
poetics, III 526b, 528b, 530a, 530b, 531a
Pole, Cardinal, I 393a, 393b
populism, III 505b
positivism, III 534b, 538b, 543b
poverty, III 590a
predestination, I 394a; II 26a–31a
pre-Reformation, I 388a–389a
primitivism, III 577b, 578a, 581b–585b, 586b, 587a, 588b–591a, 592a, 593a, 593b, 595b, 598b, 603a
private property, III 589a–589b, 654a
progress, III 626a, 634b–635b, 638b, 641a
prophecy, III 663b, 664a–669b
protest movements, III

670a–671a, 672a, 674a, 674b, 675a, 675b, 676a
Protestantism, III 670b, 671a; IV 230a–230b
Pseudo-Callisthenes, III 592a
psychology, IV 8b, 9a, 10b, 16b, 18b, 19b, 20b, 24a
punishment, I 258b
Puritanism, IV 16b
purity, IV 370b
Pythagoreans, IV 40b–41a
Ramism, IV 42b, 44b, 45a
rationalism, III 301a–303b
reformation, IV 60a–60b
Reformation, I 382a, 389a–397a; III 670b
reincarnation, I 645a
religion, III 205a, 205b, 206a, 207a; IV 93b, 94a, 96a, 98a, 102a–103a, 105a, 106a, 106b, 107b, 108a–108b, 110b, 113b, 114a, 114b, 115a, 115b, 117a, 118b, 119a
Renaisance, III 509a–514b; IV 121b, 122a, 123a, 125b, 126b, 128a, 129b, 130b, 131a, 132b, 134b, 135a, 136a–146a
resurrection, I 21b–22b; IV 102b, 230b
revelation, I 419b
revolution, IV 153a, 153b
right, IV 174a–174b, 176a–177a
ritual, IV 229b, 230a
Roman Catholic Church, IV 230a–230b
Roman Empire, I 375a–378b
romanticism, IV 188b, 192a, 195a, 201a, 206a, 207a, 207b
sacraments, I 390a, 391b–392a
Saint Ambrose, I 378b; III 589a–589b
Saint Anselm, III 591a
Saint Augustine, III 355a; IV 9a
Saint Basil, III 589b, 590a–590b
Saint Bernard, III 591a
Saint Jerome, III 590a, 591b
Saint John, III 592a
Saint Justin, III 589b
Saint Paul, I 414a–415b; III 589a, 589b, 590a; IV 102b, 103a
Saint Peter, III 590a, 590b
Saint Thomas Aquinas, IV 114a

Saint Vincent de Paul, I 399a
saints, III 589b, 590a
salvation, IV 224a, 226a, 228a, 229a–230b, 231b
Salvianus, III 592a
Savonarola, I 388a
Schlegel, IV 207
Schleiermacher, IV 201a
scholasticism, I 36a–36b, 382b–383a, 383b, 384b
science, I 401b, 402a; III 591a
Scythia, III 592a
Second Coming, III 488b
self-denial, IV 370b
self-sufficiency, III 590b
Seneca, III 590a, 590b
sin, III 591a; IV 102b, 224a, 226a, 228a, 229a–230b, 231b
skepticism, I 401b; IV 241b, 242a–244b, 245b, 246b–247a, 250b
slavery, II 250a
sobriety, IV 370b
social contract, IV 252b
socialism, III 670b, 674b; IV 285a, 286a–287b, 290a–290b, 291a
society, III 670b, 671a
soteriology, II 343a; IV 229a, 230a
soul, IV 230a
Spain, III 674b
spontaneous generation, IV 308a–308b
State, I 403a–404b, 405a–405b; III 671a; IV 314a, 317a
Stoicism, III 590a; IV 322a, 370b
Stoics, IV 8b
Strauss, II 412b–413a
suicide, III 80a
as a supra-national religious society, I 384a
symbolism, IV 341b
technology, IV 358b, 359b
temperance, IV 370b
Tertullian, III 589a, 590b
theodicy, II 164a–165a; IV 379b, 380b–381b
theology, I 17a–27a, 34a–37a, 52a–53a, 326a–326b; II 26a–31a; III 476b
theriophily, IV 384b, 386a
time, II 155b–156b; IV 391b–392a, 402a
tolerance, I 400b–401a
Toynbee, II 213a
tragic sense, IV 411b, 413a, 415a, 415b–417a

transcendentalism, IV 24a
transubstantiation, I 394b
Trinity, I 376a
truth, II 582b
twentieth century, I 407b–409a
uniformitarianism, IV 419b
U.S., III 428b, 429a, 432a–434a, 436a, 436b
universities, development of, I 382b
Urban VIII (Pope), I 398b
urbanization, I 376a, 405b
utility, IV 452a
Utopia, IV 460b, 461a, 461b, 462a, 462b
utopianism, III 670b
value, IV 452a
Vergil, III 589b
violence, III 670b, 671a
virtue, IV 370b–371a
vox populi, IV 498a–498b
war, III 448a; IV 502a, 505b
wealth, III 488b, 589b, 670b
wisdom of the fool, IV 516b, 517a–517b, 518a, 518b
witchcraft, IV 521a–523a
women, IV 524a, 524b, 525a, 526b
work, IV 531a–531b, 532b–533b
world periods, III 476b–477a
World War I, I 407b
World War II, I 407b
Wycliffe, I 386b–387a
Zoroastrianism, IV 231b
See also Eastern Orthodox Church; names of denominations; Protestantism; Roman Catholic Church
Christine de Pisan (1363?–1431), women, IV 526a
Christmas, mythology, III 282b
Christy, Arthur
  Buddhism, I 255a
  Oriental thought, III 431a
Chromosomes
  Balbiani, II 287a
  Butler, II 287a
  Bütschli, II 287a
  Darwin, II 286b, 287b, 288a–288b
  De Vries, II 289a–289b
  DNA, II 289a
  evolution, II 286b, 287b, 288a
  Flemming, II 286b, 287a–287b
  Fol, II 287a
  genetic continuity, II 286b–289b, 291b
  germplasm, II 288b, 289a
  Haeckel, II 288a

57

heredity, II 286b, 288a–288b
Hering, II 288a
Hertwig, II 287a, 289a
Heuser, II 287b
idioplasm, II 288a, 288b
Mendel, II 286b, 288a, 289b
Nägeli, II 287b–289a
Orr, II 288a
RNA, II 289a
Roux, II 287b
Schleicher, II 287b
Schneider, Anton, II 287a
Semon, II 288a
Spencer, II 288b
Strasburger, II 286b, 287b, 289a
Tschistiakoff, II 287a
van Beneden, II 287a, 287b
Weismann, II 288b–289a
Wilson, E. B., II 286b–287a
Chronicle
  historiography, II 465a, 472b, 473b, 475b, 478b, 479a, 481b, 482a, 484a, 484b
  mythology, III 287b
  periodization in history, III 477b
Chronology
  measurement, IV 400a
  periodization in history, III 476b
Chronometry, IV 403a, 404b
Chrysippus (c. 280–206 B.C.)
  matter, III 190a
  mythology, III 274a
  natural law, III 16a
  Platonism, III 504a
  primitivism, III 587b
  Stoicism, III 587b; IV 321b, 322a
  temperance, IV 369b
  theodicy, IV 380b
  theriophily, IV 384b
  time, IV 391b
  Zeno of Citium and, IV 321b
Chrysoloras, Manuel (1355?–1415), humanism, II 516b
Chrysostom, Saint John (345?–407)
  art and play, I 103a
  class, I 443a
  humanism, II 520b
Chu Hsi (1130–1200), I 356b, 361a
Chuang-Tzú (fl. 4th century B.C.)
  longevity, III 90b
  philanthropy, III 486b
Chubb, Thomas (1679–1746), deism, I 650b–651a

Church
  Anglicans, I 418a
  bishops, I 416a–416b, 417b
  Christianity, I 412b–426b
  conservatism, I 478b
  Constantine, I 416b, 417b
  Council of Chalcedon, I 416b
  Council of Nicaea, I 416b
  Dante, I 418a
  deacons, I 416a
  as divinely commissioned, I 416b–417a
  ecumenicalism, I 418b
  excommunication, I 416b
  Expectant, I 418a
  Germany, I 412b
  Greece (ancient), I 412b, 416b
  as an institution, I 412b–418b
  Israel (ancient), I 412b–416a, 417a
  Jerusalem, I 413a, 413b, 415a
  Jesus Christ, I 413a–416a, 416b, 417a, 418a
  Josephus, I 415b
  Judaic Christianity, I 412b–416a, 416b
  Judaism, I 412b, 413a, 413b, 417a
  Last Judgment, I 418a
  Lutheranism, I 418a
  Middle Ages, I 417b–418a
  Militant, I 418a
  missionaries, I 413b
  modernism, I 419b, 420b, 422b, 423b, 425a, 425b
  nationalism, I 412b
  origin of the term, I 412b
  paganism, I 417a
  papacy, I 417b, 418a
  Plato, I 417a
  Presbyterians, I 418a
  priesthood, I 416a
  Protestantism, I 418a
  Reformation, I 418a
  reunion of, I 418a–418b
  Rome (ancient), I 417b
  sacramental system, I 416a–416b
  Saint Augustine, I 417a, 418a
  Saint James, I 413b, 415b
  Saint John, I 412b
  Saint Mark, I 416a, 416b
  Saint Matthew, I 413a, 414a
  Saint Paul, I 413b, 414b–417b
  Saint Peter, I 413b, 414a
  Saint Thomas Aquinas, I 417b

  Socrates, I 417a
  teaching role of, I 416b
  Triumphant, I 418a
  Vincent of Lérins, I 416b
Church of England, I 406b
  conservatism, I 479b–480a
  deism, I 649b, 650a
  God, II 361b
  harmony, II 388b
  history, I 401a
  modernism, I 419a, 424b
  music, II 388b
  reformation, IV 68b
  salvation, IV 224a
  sin, IV 224a
  State, I 405a
  Victorian sentiment, IV 217b, 218a
Church Peace Union, III 449a
Churchill, Winston (1874–1965), welfare state, IV 510b, 511b
Cicero, Marcus Tullius (106–43 B.C.), I 41b, 64b, 79a; II 658b
  aesthetics, II 217a, 219b–220a
  analogy, I 68b
  aristocracy, I 655a, 655b
  Aristotle and, IV 169a
  art, II 305a, 309b
  art and play, I 102b
  atomism, I 497a; II 137a
  authority, I 142b–144b
  axiomatization, I 164b
  Bacon and, I 173b
  beauty, II 217a
  Castiglione and, III 512b
  chance images, I 341a
  children, III 595b
  classification of the arts, I 456b, 458a, 458b, 459b
  conservatism, I 479b
  constitutionalism, I 487a, 488b
  cosmic voyages, I 524a
  cosmology, I 622b–623a
  culture, I 613b; II 127b
  cycles, I 622b–623a
  death, I 644b
  deism, I 647b–648a
  democracy, I 655a
  desire, IV 50a
  dignity, IV 136a–136b, 138a, 139a, 141b, 142b, 143b
  education, II 81a–81b; IV 123b
  eighteenth-century view of, 83b
  environment, II 127b
  Epicureanism, II 137a, 137b
  equity, II 150b–151a
  ethics, III 16b; IV 319b,

321b, 322a
  evolution of literature, II 170a
  evolutionism, II 176a
  free will, II 137a, 137b
  freedom, II 249b–250a; IV 50a
  freedom of speech, II 261b
  friendship, III 112a
  genius, II 305a, 309b, 314b
  God, II 340b, 438b–439a
  good, IV 50a
  gratitude, III 16b
  happiness, IV 50a
  harmony, II 389b; IV 40a
  health, II 397b
  hierarchy and order, II 438b–439a
  historiography, II 469b, 470a
  humanism, II 515a, 515b, 516a; IV 129b
  immortality, I 644b
  impiety, II 566a
  indeterminacy, II 587a
  irony, II 627b, 628a, 628b; III 77a
  law, I 487b; II 150b–151a, 249b–250a; III 16b, 587b
  letter-writing, II 515b, 516a
  literary paradox, III 77a
  literature, III 81b, 82b, 86a; IV 330a, 330b, 331a
  longevity, III 91b
  loyalty, III 112a
  Machiavellism, III 116a
  mimesis, III 227a, 229a
  mind, IV 50a, 136a–136b
  monarchy, I 655a, 655b
  morality, III 116a; IV 50a
  music, II 314b, 389b
  mythology, III 274a, 274b, 287a, 289a
  nationalism, III 323a
  natural law, I 487b; III 16b
  natural rights, III 16b
  Nature, III 349a, 587b
  Neo-Platonism, III 372a
  oratory, II 170a; IV 169a–169b
  organicism, III 423b
  painting, IV 468a, 468b
  piety, III 16b
  Plato and, III 509b; IV 40a
  Platonism, III 509b, 512b
  pleasure, IV 136b
  poetics, III 526a, 527a, 528b, 529a
  pragmatism, III 554a
  prejudice, III 587b
  primitivism, III 579b, 587b, 589b, 591b, 595b, 599a
  progress, III 629b, 631b, 632a

psychology, IV 7b, 8a
Pythagoreans, IV 40a
Ramism, IV 43a, 44a, 44b
rationalism, IV 50a, 50b
reason, III 16b
reformation, IV 61b
reincarnation, I 644b
religion, III 16b
respect, III 16b
revolution, IV 152b
rhetoric, IV 169a–172a
skepticism, IV 234a, 234b,
235b, 236a, 236b, 238b,
239a, 239b, 241a, 243a
socialism, IV 286a
space, IV 301a
State, I 655a; IV 313b
Stoicism, II 340b; IV 50a,
319b, 321b, 322a
style, IV 330a, 330b, 331a
temperance, IV 365b, 370a–
370b, 371a, 375a
truth, III 16b, 227a, 587b
universal man, IV 439a,
440b
universe, IV 40a
Utopia, IV 460b
vengeance, III 16b
vice, IV 50a
virtù, IV 375a, 477b, 478a–
478b
vox populi, IV 497b, 498a
welfare, III 116a
Cieszkowski, August von,
Hegel and, II 414a–414b
Hess and, II 413b
Michelet and, II 413b
Cincinnatus, Lucius (b. about
519 B.C.), temperance, IV
377a
Cinema, see Motion pictures
Cinthio, Giraldi (1504–1573),
poetry, III 529a, 531a
Cinyras, King, religion, IV 93a
Circe (myth), III 273b, 291b,
296a
temperance, IV 365b
Circular universe, II 536b–
438b, 442b
Circularity, symmetry, IV
348b–350b
Circulatory system, Man-
Machine, III 135b
Circumcision
mythology, III 283a, 284a
Saint Paul, I 414a, 415a
Ciriaco of Ancona
humanism, II 516b
mythology, III 289b
Cistercians, reformation, IV
64b
Citizenship
democracy, I 652b, 653a,
654b, 655b, 658a, 660b–

661a
education, II 77a–77b, 99b
feudalism, I 655b
Rousseau, I 658a
City, I 427a–434b
Aigues-Mortes, I 429a
Alberti, I 430a–430b
ancient, I 427a–428b
architecture, I 427a–434b
Aristotle, I 428a
Babylon, I 427b–428a
Babylonia, I 427a–427b
Bethlehem, I 429b
Bible, I 427b, 429a
Bruni, I 429b–430a
Campanella, I 431a–431b,
432b
castra stativa, I 428b
Christianity, I 427b, 428b–
429b
culture and civilization, I
612b, 616b, 617a, 617b
Edward I, I 429a
Egypt (ancient), I 428a
Enlightenment, I 432a
Fichte, I 432a
Filarete, I 430b, 431a
France, I 429a, 432a–432b,
433a–434a
Garnier, I 433a
Germany, I 432a
Giorgio, I 431a
God, I 427b, 428b–429a,
430b
Great Britain, I 429a, 432a,
432b
Greece (ancient), I 427b,
428a–428b, 432a, 653b–
654b, 655b
gridiron scheme, I 428a,
428b
Hippodamic system, I 428a–
428b
Hölderlin, I 432a
Hyginus Gromaticus, I 428b
iconography, I 429b
India (ancient), I 427b,
428a
Italy, I 429b–430a, 430b
Jerusalem, I 427b, 428a,
428b–429a, 429b
Jesus Christ, I 429a
Judaism, I 427b
law, II 687a
Le Corbusier, I 432b, 433a–
434a
Ledoux, I 432a–432b
Leonardo da Vinci, I 430b–
431a
Macrobius, I 428a
Mecca, I 428a
Mesopotamia, I 428a
Middle Ages, I 428b–429b
modern, I 431b–434a

Mohenjo-Daro, I 428a
Montpazier, I 429a
Near East, I 427b–428a,
429a
Nicholas V, I 430b
organic growth of, I 429a
Pius II (Pope), I 430b
Plato, I 427b
Platonism, I 427b
Pliny, I 428b
Polybius, I 428b
Quattrocento, I 431a
Renaissance, I 429b–431b
Rome, I 430b
Rome (ancient), I 428a,
428b–429a; II 687a
Saint Augustine, I 428b–
429a
Saint Louis, I 429a
Sant'Elia, I 433a
Schiller, I 432a
Smith, Adam, I 432a
symbolism, I 427a–428a,
429a, 429b–431b
U.S., I 432b
utopianism, I 430a, 431a–
431b, 432b
Varro, I 428a
Venice, I 429b, 430a–430b
Voltaire, I 432a
Wright, F. L., I 433b
See also Urbanization
City planning
ancient, I 428a–428b
art, I 461b
classification of the arts, I
461b
happiness, II 374b
Middle Ages, I 429a, 429b
modern, I 431b–434a
Renaissance, I 429b–431b
urbanization, I 431b–434a
City-state
Aristotle, III 629b
art, II 300b–302b
ethics, IV 320a
freedom of speech, II 252b,
253b–254a, 256b–258a
genius, II 300b–302b
Greece (ancient), II 46b,
256b–258a, 674a, 679b,
681b, 682b; III 37b, 449b;
IV 228a, 313a–313b, 366b
historiography, II 482a,
482b, 483a
humanism, II 518b
individualism, II 300b–302b
Italy, IV 438a, 477a
law, II 674a, 679b, 681b,
682b
liberalism, III 37b
loyalty, III 110a, 111a,
111b, 112a
Middle Ages, IV 253a, 314a

nationalism, III 321a, 321b,
323b, 325a
Platonism, III 503b
progress, III 629b, 630a
Reformation, I 391a–392b
religion, IV 99a
Renaissance, III 321a, 321b,
323b; IV 122b, 123a–123b,
438a, 441b
Rome (ancient), III 37b; IV
313b–314a
sin and salvation, IV 228a
social contract, IV 253a
Stoicism, IV 320a
temperance, IV 365b, 366b,
368b, 373b
universal man, IV 438a,
441b
Utopia, IV 459b, 461a
war, IV 501a, 502a
Civil disobedience, I 434b–
441a
abolitionism, I 435a, 436a
anarchy, I 435a, 436b
Bentham, I 437b–438a
Christianity, I 436a–437a,
438a–439a
concept of, I 434b–435a
Curtis, I 436a
Denmark, I 438a
drama, I 434b
Emerson, I 436a
Fortas, I 439b–440b
Gandhi, I 435a, 438a, 438b,
439a
Garrison, W. L., I 436b
Germany, I 435a, 438a
God, I 435b–437a
Great Britain, I 435a
Greece (ancient), I 434b
Higher Law doctrine, I
435b–437a
Hobbes, I 437b
Hume, I 437b
India, I 435a
Jesus Christ, I 434b–435a
Judaism, I 434b
King, Martin Luther, I 438a,
438b–439a
law, I 435a–435b
Mahan, I 436a
Milton, I 435a
natural rights, I 435b, 437a–
438a
Nazis, I 435a, 438a
nonviolence, I 435a, 438a–
441a
Norway, I 438a
Oberlinites, I 436b–437a,
438b
Parker, Theodore, I 436a
Pius VI, I 404b
Protestantism, I 436a–437a
rights, I 435b, 437a–438a

South Africa, I 435a
Steinbeck, I 438a
Thoreau, I 434b, 435a, 436a–436b, 437a, 437b, 438b; III 431a
Tolstoy, I 435a, 438a–438b, 439a
transcendentalism, I 436a
Trinity, I 436a–436b
U.S., I 435a, 436a–439a, 439b–441a
Vietnam War, I 435a, 440b
violence, I 435b, 438a, 439a, 439b
World War II, I 435a
Civil law, II 691a, 692a, 692b, 693a, 693b, 694a, 695a, 696a; III 17, 18a–18b, 19b, 21a, 33b
perennial philosophy, III 460b
proximate cause, III 567a
Civil Rights Act of 1964, I 440a; IV 528b, 529a, 529b
Civil service
China, I 367b
Great Britain, I 367b
Hegel, II 409a
Renaissance, IV 123b
Civil war, III 450a
Great Britain, III 450a
international peace, III 450a
psychology, IV 23a, 24b
U.S., III 225b, 450a
Civilization, I 613b–621b
anthropology, I 618b, 619a
Arnold, Matthew, I 617b
art, I 616a, 621a
artifacts, I 618b
barbarism, I 620a
Bible, III 276b, 279a–279b
birth, I 614a
Buckle, I 620a–620b
burial, I 614a
Burckhardt, IV 159a
Burke, Edmund, I 619b
Byzantine Empire, III 181a, 181b
Cicero, I 613b
city, I 616b, 617a, 617b
climate, I 616a
Coleridge, I 617b
Collingwood, I 616a
common-origin theory, I 614a–616b
Comte, I 620a; II 23b–24a
Condorcet, I 619b–620a
continuity, I 619a
Crusades, III 181a
cyclical development theory, I 618a
cynicism, III 585b, 586b
determinism, II 21a–23b
Diderot, I 616b; III 603a

dignity, IV 142a
dissolution of, III 181a–182b
economy, I 618b
Eliot, I 619a
Engels, I 620b
Enlightenment, I 616a–616b, 617a
ethics, III 443b, 444a
evolution, III 646a
Fichte, I 619a
freedom, I 615b; III 183a
Freud, III 597a
Germany, I 613b–614a
Hegel, I 615b–616a, 619a, 619b
Hegelianism, III 473b
Herder, I 613b–614a, 615b, 616b, 617a, 618a–621a; III 326a
historiography, II 21a–21b, 22b–23b; IV 150a
history, II 21a–23b
humanism, IV 130a
ideology, II 557a
industry, III 182b
Islam, II 650a; III 181a
Jefferson, I 619b
Kant, I 614a, 616a, 617b, 619b; III 443b
knowledge, I 220a
language, I 615b
law, II 677a, 685b, 690b
love, III 100a–100b, 101b, 104a
loyalty, III 108b
Lucretius, III 587b
marriage, I 614a
Marx, I 619b, 620a–620b
Marxism, I 618b
mathematics, III 177b, 180a, 181a–182b
measurement, IV 399a
Mill, J. S., I 619a
Montaigne, III 594a
Montesquieu, I 616a, 616b
multiple-independent-origin theory, I 614a–616b, 618a
mythology, I 618b–619a, 619b, 620a; III 272a, 276b, 279a–279b, 287a, 291a, 301a, 302a, 302b, 303a, 306a, 308a, 312a
nationalism, III 326a, 327b, 330a, 332a, 332b, 335b, 336b, 337a, 338b
natural law, I 617a, 620b
Nature, III 347b, 348b
Nazis, III 597b
necessity, III 360b, 361a, 361b
numbers, III 399a, 406b
origin of, I 614a–615b

origin of the term, I 613b
Paine, I 619b
peace, III 443b, 444a
periodization in history, III 476b, 478b, 480a, 480b
philanthropy, III 486b, 488a, 491b
philosophy, I 615b, 617a, 619b, 620a
Plato, III 629a
poetics, III 526b
pragmatism, III 554a, 560b, 569b
primary, II 22b
primitivism, III 583a, 585b, 586b, 587b, 594a, 597a, 597b, 598a, 603a, 603b
private property, I 617a; III 650b, 651a
progress, III 626b, 628b, 629a, 630b, 631a, 631b, 636b, 638a, 638b, 644b, 646a, 647b
proletariat, III 183a
psychology, IV 18b, 24a, 26a
religion, I 614a, 618b, 619b, 620a; IV 94a, 115a
Renaissance, IV 130a, 142a, 150a
revolution, IV 158b, 165b, 166b
romanticism, IV 204a, 206b, 207b, 208a
Rome (ancient), I 613b; III 181a, 181b, 182b
Rousseau, I 616b–617a, 617b; III 598a
Schlegel, I 619a
science, I 620a, 621a
secondary, II 22b
Seneca, III 588b
skepticism, I 617b, 620a
slave labor, III 182b
Snow, C. P., I 617b
Social Darwinism, III 646a
society, I 615b–616a, 616b, 620a, 620b
sociology, I 619a
space, IV 298b, 301a
Spengler, I 616b, 617a–617b, 619a; III 251a
Stoicism, III 588a
technology, I 620a; IV 357b, 358a, 360b
teleology, I 619a
tertiary, II 22b
time, I 619a–619b; IV 399a
Toynbee, I 616a, 617b, 619a; II 21a–21b, 22b–23b; III 361a–361b
tradition, I 621a
transcendentalism, IV 24a
Tylor, E. B., I 617b–618a

urbanization, I 616b, 617a, 617b
Utopia, IV 459a
versus culture, I 616b–618a
Vico, I 614a–615b, 616b, 617a, 618a, 619b, 620a
Voltaire, I 616a–616b, 618a, 619b
war, IV 501b, 502a, 508a
Claims, II 676a–677a, 678b, 679a
Clairaut, A. C. (1713–1765), mathematics, III 179b
Clairvoyance, prophecy, III 658a
Claparède, Édouard, psychology, IV 13a, 27a
Clarembaldus of Arras, aesthetics, II 217b
Clarity, naturalism in art, III 345a
Clark, Grenville, international peace, III 451b
Clark, H. H., organicism, III 426b
Clark, John Bates (1847–1938), economic history, II 50b, 53b–54b
Clarke, James Freeman (1810–1888)
Johnson and, III 433a, 433b, 434a
Orientalism, III 429a, 431b–435b, 439a
slavery, III 432a
temperance, III 432a
transcendentalism, III 429a, 431b–433a, 433b, 434a, 435a–435b, 439a
women's suffrage, III 432a
Clarke, Samuel (1675–1729), deism, I 651a
God, II 352a
Leibniz and, I 327b–328a
moral sense, III 230b
Shaftesbury and, III 230b
space, IV 295b, 302b
theodicy, IV 382b
time, IV 394b
See also Newton
Clarkson, Laurence, mountains in literature, III 253a
Class, I 441b–449b
acquired characteristics, II 620b, 622a
Anabaptists, I 442b
anti-industrialism, III 676a
Aristotle, I 443a, 443b, 444a, 449a
Babeuf, I 443b
Bernstein, III 162a, 162b
Bible, I 442a–442b
Bichat, I 448b

Blacks, I 442a, 449a
Blanqui, I 443b
Cabanis, I 448b
Campanella, I 448a
capitalism, III 148b
caste, I 442a
Chartism, I 443b
Christianity, I 442a–443a,
443b, 446a, 449a; III 670b
Chrysostom, I 443a
common law, II 693a
communism, III 673b
Condillac, I 448a
culture, III 150b
cynicism, I 629a
Dahrendorf, I 446a
determinism, II 25a
dichotomous conceptuali-
zations, I 442a–443b
Diderot, I 448a
differentiation on basis of
social function, I 445b–
446b
Djilas, III 154b
Dreiser, I 445b
economics, III 151b
Engels, II 146a, 452a,
454b, 554b; III 22a, 156a
English Revolution, I 442a–
442b
Enlightenment, II 91a, 92a
equality, II 139b, 145a,
146a
equality of opportunity, I
448b–449a
eschatology, II 159a
evil, II 169a
evolution, III 646a, 646b
existentialism, III 160a
Fitzgerald, Scott, I 445b
Fourier, I 446a
France, I 441b, 443b; IV
500a
Galton, I 448a
general will, II 279a, 279b
Germany, I 441b; IV 500a
God, I 446a
good, IV 174b, 177a
gradations in, I 444a–445b
Great Britain, I 441b, 449a;
III 674b; IV 500a
Greece (ancient), I 443a
Hamilton, I 444a
Helvétius, I 448a
Hemingway, I 445b
historiography, II 25a
history, II 25a
humanism, II 521b
Ibn Khaldun, I 442b
ideology, II 555b
impressionism, II 576b,
581b, 583a
income, III 151a
Industrial Revolution, I 441b

inequality, I 448a–448b
IQ, II 620b
Islam, I 442a
James, Henry, I 445b
Jefferson, IV 21b
John of Salisbury, I 445b
Judaism, I 442a
Koran, I 442a
Lassalle, I 443b
law, III 11a, 11b, 12b
Lenin, II 561b–562a; III
156a–156b; IV 163b
Levellers, I 442b
liberalism, III 672b
Lipset, I 449a
literature, I 445b
Locke, I 448a, 448b
Luther, I 446a; III 11a
Lutheranism, I 446a
Malthus, I 441b
Marxism-Leninism, III
154a–154b
materialism, II 451b, 452a,
454b
measurement, IV 402a
Mexico, III 544a
Michels, III 151a
Middle Ages, I 442b, 445b–
446a, 447a
millenarianism, III 224a
multiple divisions, I 444a–
445b
nationalism, III 150b–151a,
673a
natural law, III 22a
necessity, III 359a
painting, II 576b, 581b,
583a
Pareto, I 448a; III 151a
philanthropy, III 489b, 490a,
491a
phrenology, IV 23a, 23b
Plato, I 443a; III 508b; IV
3b
positivism, III 544a
primitivism, III 595b
private property, I 448b;
III 651a, 651b, 652a, 652b,
653b
production, III 148a
progress, III 645b, 646a,
646b, 648a
protest movements, III 670a,
670b, 671a, 672a, 672b,
673a, 673b, 674b, 675b,
676a, 676b
psychology, IV 3b, 16a, 18a,
21b, 22a, 26b, 27a
Puritanism, IV 18a
radicalism, III 672b, 673a
religion, I 442a; IV 112b,
114b
Renaissance, IV 438a, 441b
revisionism, IV 264a, 264b,

265a, 266b, 270b, 271b,
272a
revolution, IV 158a, 159b,
160a, 160b, 161a, 162a,
163b, 165a, 166a
Ricardo, I 441b
right, IV 174b, 177a
romanticism, IV 199b, 207a
Rome (ancient), III 652a
Rousseau, I 448a–448b
Saint Augustine, I 442a; IV
286b
Saint Paul, I 446a
Saint Thomas Aquinas, I
445b, 446a; III 11a
Saint-Simon, I 443b, 448b,
449a
Shelley, I 442b–443a
Silone, I 442b
slavery, I 443a
Smith, Adam, I 444a, 446b,
447a–447b
social contract, IV 251b,
253b, 256a
Social Darwinism, III 646a
socialism, III 673b; IV 285a,
286a, 286b, 288a, 288b,
291a, 292a, 292b, 293b
society, III 150b
Stalin, III 154b
State, III 148b, 151b, 155a;
IV 314b, 316b, 318a
Stein, I 448b
temperance, IV 368b
time, IV 402a
totalitarianism, IV 407a,
407b, 408a, 408b, 410a,
410b
tripartite divisions, I 443b–
444a
Troeltsch, I 446a
U.S.S.R., III 154b, 155a; IV
158a
U.S., I 442a, 444a, 444b,
448b–449b; IV 499b–500a
universal man, IV 438a,
441b
Utopia, IV 459a, 459b,
461a, 462b
Victorian sensibility, IV
217a, 217b, 218a, 219a,
220a, 220b, 222b
virtuoso, IV 486a
Voltaire, IV 288a
vox populi, IV 497a–497b,
498b, 499b–500a
war, IV 502b, 503b, 504b,
505a, 506a
Weber, Max, I 444b–445a
welfare state, IV 509a, 513a,
514b
Winstanley, I 442a–442b
work, IV 534a, 534b
Young, I 449b

Yugoslavia, III 154b
See also Marx, Marxism
Classicism
Acmeists, I 455b
aesthetics, IV 353b, 355b
Alexander the Great, I 451b
Aristotle, I 453a
Arnold, I 450a
art, III 363b
Augustus, I 451b
Aulus Gellius, I 451a
Babbitt, I 455a
beauty, I 200a–200b
Benda, I 455a
Bertrand, I 450b
Boileau, I 453a
Brunetière, I 450a–450b
Canova, I 454b
Carlyle, I 449b
Cazamian, I 450a
Chateaubriand, I 452a
Chénier, I 454b
Corneille, I 451b, 452a
cycles, I 627a
Dante, I 451b, 452a, 452b
De Quincey, I 452b
Deschanel, I 450a
D'Olivet, I 451b
Dryden, I 450a, 452b, 453a,
454a
Eckermann, I 453b
Eliot, I 450b, 452a, 453a,
455a–455b
Enlightenment, I 454b
Faust (legend), III 249b
France, I 449b, 450a–450b,
451a, 451b, 452a–452b,
453a, 453b, 454a, 454b–
455b; III 366a, 483a, 483b
French Revolution, I 452a,
453b
Germany, I 450b–451a,
451b, 453a–454b, 455b; III
483b
Gervinus, I 454a
Gide, I 455a; IV 196b
Goethe, I 451a, 453a, 453b–
454b, 455a, 455b; IV 197a
Great Britain, I 450a, 450b,
451a–451b, 452a, 452b–
453a, 454a, 454b; III 483b
Greece (ancient), I 451a,
453a
Harnack, I 450b–451a
Heine, I 450a
Homer, I 452b
Hulme, I 450b, 452a,
455a–455b
iconography, II 539b
Italy, I 450a, 451b, 452a,
453a, 454a
jewelry, III 363b
Jonson, I 453a
Klopstock, I 453a

La Fontaine, I 452a
Lanson, I 450b
Lasserre, I 450b, 455a
Leo X (Pope), I 451b
Lessing, I 453a
literature, I 449b–456a; III 363b
Littré, I 450a
Macaulay, I 452b
Maritain, I 455a
Maurras, I 450b, 454b–455a
Middle Ages, I 451a; III 528a, 528b
Mill, J. S., I 449b
Milton, I 452b
Molière, I 452a, 453a
More, P. E., I 455a
Napoleon I, I 454b
nationalism, III 325a, 332b
naturalism in art, III 341a, 342a, 345a
necessity, III 355b
Necker de Saussure, I 451b
neo-classicism in art, III 363b, 364a, 364b, 366a, 366b, 368b, 369a, 369b, 370a, 371a
Netherlands, I 453a
Nisard, I 452a
organicism, III 421b
Pascal, I 452a
Pater, I 450a
periodization in literary history, III 483a, 483b
Phidias, I 455b
poetry, III 528a, 528b, 529a–531b
Ponsard, I 452a, 452b
Pope, I 450a, 451b, 452b, 453a, 454a, 454b, 455a
Racine, I 452a, 455a
Raphael, I 455b
realism, I 454b
realism in literature, IV 56a
relief, III 363b
Renaissance, I 451a, 452a; III 355b
rococo, I 454b
romanticism, I 449b, 451a, 453b–454a, 455a; IV 187b–192a, 193a, 193b, 195b–197a, 202b, 205a, 209a, 209b
Rome (ancient), I 451a
Ruskin, I 450a
Russia, I 454b, 455b
Sainte-Beuve, I 450a, 452b
Scaliger, I 453a
Schiller, I 449b, 451a, 453a, 453b–454b; IV 197a
Schlegel, August Wilhelm von, I 451b, 453b, 454a
Schlegel, Friedrich, I 450b,

451b, 453b, 454a, 454b
sculpture, III 363b
Shakespeare, I 451b, 452b, 454a
Sorel, I 455a
Spain, I 451b
Staël, I 451b
Stendhal, I 450a
Swift, I 453a
Taine, I 450a
taste, IV 353b, 355b
Titian, I 455b
U.S., I 450a, 453a, 455a
Valéry, I 455a; IV 196b
Vergil, I 455b
Vilmar, I 454a
Voltaire, I 451b
Vossius, I 453a
Wieland, I 453a–453b
Wölfflin, I 451a
Classification
antiquity, I 233a–233b
Aristotle, I 233a–233b
Buffon, I 331b
knowledge, I 462a–462b, 466a
law, III 1b–13b
mechanics and science, II 197a
mind, I 513b–514a
motif, III 237b
natural law, III 18a
Plato, I 233a–233b
Robinet, I 331b–332a
State, III 11a–12b
value, I 462a–462b
William of Ockham, I 330b
Classification of the arts, I 456a–462a
acoustics, I 459a
acting, I 458a
agriculture, I 458a
anti-novel, I 461b
antiquity, I 456a–458b, 459a–459b, 461a
architecture, I 456b–461b
Ardens, I 459a
Aristotle, I 456b, 457a, 457b, 458a, 458b
arithmetic, I 459a
astronomy, I 457b, 458a, 459a
athletics, I 458a
Batteux, I 460a–460b
Beattie, I 460b
Blondel, I 460a
Cicero, I 456b, 458a, 458b, 459b
cinema, I 461b
city planning, I 461b
dance, I 458a, 458b, 460a, 461a
Dionysius Thrax, I 458a
drawing, I 459b

Duns Scotus, I 458b
eloquence, I 458a
entertainment, I 459a
Ficino, I 459b–460a
Francesco de Hollanda, I 460a
Galen, I 456b, 457b, 458a, 459a
geometry, I 456b, 457b, 458a, 459a
Goclenius, I 459a
Goethe, I 460b
grammar, I 456b, 459a
Greece (ancient), I 456b–458b
handicrafts, I 456b, 457a, 458b–460a, 461b
Hegel, I 461a
Hugh of Saint Victor, I 458b–459a
Hume, I 460b
Hutcheson, I 460b
Kant, I 460b–461a
logic, I 459a
Lucius Tarrhaeus, I 458a
mathematics, I 456b, 457b, 459a
medicine, I 458a
Mendelssohn, Moses, I 460b
metaphor, I 460a
Middle Ages, I 457a, 458b–459a, 459b, 461a–461b
military, I 458a
modern, I 460b–461b
music, I 457a, 458a, 458b, 459a, 459b–460a, 460b, 461a, 461b
oratory, I 460b
painting, I 456b, 457b, 458a–461b
perfectibility, I 457a
photography, I 461b
Plato, I 456b–458b, 459b, 460b, 583a
pleasure, I 457a, 458b, 459a, 459b
Plotinus, I 458a–458b
Plutarch, I 457a–457b
poetry, I 456b, 457a, 458a–461a
Poliziano, I 459b
Pythagoreans, I 457a
Quintilian, I 456b, 457b–459a
Ramus, I 459a
Renaissance, I 457a, 459a–460b, 461b
rhetoric, I 458a, 458b, 459a
Saint Thomas Aquinas, I 458a
scholasticism, I 459a
science, I 456b, 457a, 457b, 458a, 459a, 461b

sculpture, I 456b, 458a, 459a–461b
Seneca, I 457b, 459a–459b
Sophists, I 457a–457b, 458a, 458b, 459a
Stoics, I 456b
Tesauro, I 460a
utility, I 457a, 458b, 459a, 459b
Varchi, I 459a
Vasari, I 459b
Vico, I 460b
Classification of the sciences, I 462a–467a
Abinavagupta, I 464a
aesthetics, I 463a
agriculture, I 464b
Al-Farabi, I 463b
Ampère, I 465a, 465b
Arabs, I 463b
Archytas of Tarentum, I 462b
Aristotle, I 463a, 465b
arithmetic, I 462b–463a, 464a
astrology, I 462b–463a
astronomy, I 462b–463a, 463b, 464a, 465a, 465b
Avicenna, I 463b
Bacon, Francis, I 464b
Bacon, Roger, I 464b
Bentham, I 465b
Berthelot, I 466a
biology, I 465a, 466a
chemistry, I 465a, 465b, 466a
China, I 464a
China (ancient), I 464a
Comte, I 465a, 466a
Cournot, I 465a–465b
d'Alembert, I 464b
Demetrius of Phalerum, I 463a–463b
Dilthey, I 465b
Djahiz, I 463b
drama, I 464b
ethics, I 463a, 464b, 465a
geometry, I 462b–463a, 464a
Gesner, I 465b
grammar, I 464b, 466b
Greece (ancient), I 462b–463b
Grosseteste, I 464b
Hegel, I 465b
Helmholtz, I 465b
history, I 465a
Hugh of Saint-Victor, I 464b
hunting, I 464b
Iamblichus, I 462b
Ibn Qutaibah, I 463b
idioscopy, I 466a
India, I 464a

62

India (ancient), I 464a
Islam, I 463b
language, I 465a, 466b
Leibniz, I 465a
Liu Hsi, I 464a
Locke, I 465a
logic, I 463a, 464b–466b
mathematics, I 463a, 463b, 464b, 465a, 466a
mechanics, I 465b
medicine, I 463b, 464b
Mei Ying-tsu, I 464a
metaphysics, I 464b, 466a
Middle Ages, I 464a–464b
Mill, J. S., I 465b
Moors, I 463b
Münsterberg, I 465b
music, I 464a
navigation, I 464b
nomology, I 466a
optics, I 465b
oratory, I 463b
Ostwald, I 465b
Pearson, I 465b
Peirce, I 465b
phenomenology, I 466a
philosophy, I 463a, 464b, 466a
physics, I 463a, 464b, 465a, 465b, 466a
Piaget, I 466a–466b
Plato, I 462b–463a
Pliny the Elder, I 463b
poetry, I 463b, 464b
Porphyry, I 462a
Proclus, I 462b
psychical science, I 466a
psychology, I 465b, 466a
Pythagoras, I 462b
Renaissance, I 464b
rhetoric, I 464b
Rome (ancient), I 463b
Schopenhauer, I 465b
sociology, I 465a, 466a
Somadeva, I 464a
Spain, I 463b
technology, I 465b
theology, I 464b
veterinary art, I 464a
Whittaker, I 465a
Wundt, I 465b
Clauberg, Johann (1622–1655), causation, I 302b
Claudel, Paul (1868–1955), symbolism, IV 340a, 340b, 344a
Claudian (c. 395 A.D.), evolution of literature, II 172a
Clausewitz, Carl von (1780–1831), war, IV 500b, 501a, 502a, 502b, 503a, 504a, 505b, 506b
Clausius, Rudolf Julius Emmanuel (1822–1888),

entropy, II 113a–114a
probability, III 619b–620a
State, II 113b–114a
technology, IV 363b
Claustrophobia
color, IV 335b, 336b, 337a
cosmic voyages, IV 335b, 336a–336b
sublime in external nature, IV 335a
Clavasio, Angelus de, casuistry, I 262a
Clayton, John (1685?–1773), cosmic voyages, I 532a
Cleanthes (3rd century B.C.),
creativity in art, I 580b
cycles, I 623a
determinism, II 237b
ethics, IV 321b
free will, II 237b
mythology, III 274a
primitivism, III 587b, 588a
providence, II 237b
Stoicism, III 587b, 588a; IV 321b
Cleisthenes (6th–5th century B.C.)
freedom of speech, II 258b, 259b
law, II 682a
Clemenceau, Georges (1841–1929), China, I 369a
Clement of Alexandria (150?–?220)
Adam (Bible), III 582b
analogy, I 64a
allegory, I 44a, 45a, 46b
Buddhism, I 255a
Christianity, III 592a
dignity, IV 137a
eschatology, II 157b
ethics, III 441a; IV 322a
faith, II 210a
Faust (legend), III 246a
metaphor, III 205b
music, III 266a
mythology, III 276b
patristic period, I 64a
peace, II 441a
perfectibility, III 466a
Philo Judaeus and, III 466a
primitivism, III 582b, 592a
Pythagoreans, IV 40b
religion, II 205b
Stoicism, IV 322a
temperance, IV 370b
Clement V, Pope (1264–1314), Great Schism, I 385a
Clement VIII, Pope (1536–1605), Platonism, II 513b
Clement XI, Pope (1649–1721), China, I 357b
Clement XIV, Pope (1705–1774), I 403b

Clements, Frederick (1874–1945), conservation, I 475b
Clements, R. S., iconography, II 537b
Cleon (5th century B.C.),
democracy, I 653b; II 260a
freedom of speech, II 260a
historiography, II 502b
imperialism, II 260a
Cleonides, music, III 261b
Clergy
Christianity, III 671a
equality, II 138b, 141a–141b, 142b
Edwards, Jonathan, IV 109b
impressionism, II 570a
language, II 666a, 667a
protest movements, III 671a
Cleveland, Grover (1837–1908), women, IV 526b
Clews, Henry (1834–1923), individualism, II 596b
Cliffe-Leslie, T. E., economic history, II 60b
Clifford, W. K. (1845–1879),
agnosticism, I 19a
cosmology, I 555a–555b
pragmatism, III 560a, 562b
relativity, IV 88a
space, IV 304a
Climate
antiprimitivism, III 604a
Aristotle, II 3a
art, IV 150a
Bodin, IV 150a
culture, I 616a
despotism, II 3a
Herder, IV 492a
historiography, IV 148a, 150a
linguistics, III 62a
Montesquieu, III 640a; IV 491a, 491b
mythology, III 304a
Orientalism, III 433b
primitivism, III 604a
probability, III 608b
progress, III 640a
rationalism, IV 48a
Renaissance, IV 148a, 150a
Toynbee, II 369b
Vasari, IV 150a
Volksgeist, IV 491a, 491b, 492a
Clitomachus of Carthage (2nd century B.C.), Skepticism, IV 234a
Clocks
atomic, IV 404a
measurement, IV 399a, 401a–401b, 402b, 403a, 404a
mechanical, IV 399a, 401a,

401b, 402b, 403a
shadow, I 536a
star, I 536a
water, IV 401a–401b, 403a
weight-driven, IV 359a–359b, 360b
Clothing, Pythagoreans, IV 31b
Clotho (myth), III 272b
Clotilde, Queen (475?–?545), women, IV 525b
Clovio, Giulio (1498–1578),
art, II 301b
genius, II 301b
Clytemnestra (myth), law, II 683b
Cobbett, William (1763–1835), Counter-Enlightenment, II 109b–110a
Cochlaeus, Johannes (1479–1552)
heresy, II 428a
Luther and, II 428a
Coclico, Adrian Petit, music, II 316b, 319a
Code of Gortyn, II 680a, 680b
Code of Hammurabi
justice, II 655b
Mesopotamia (ancient), IV 226b
salvation, IV 226b
Code of Justinian, heresy, II 425a
Code Napoléon, III 30b, 32b
justice, II 656a
Codex, II 685b
Coenogenetic embryos, IV 57b, 58a
Coercion
law, III 2b, 3a, 5a
society, III 3a
Cognition
Aristotle, I 1b–2b
Boethius, I 3a
Kant, I 103b–104a; III 218b
mathematics, III 183b, 184a, 184b
metaphor, III 197b, 198b, 199a, 199b, 200a–201a
metaphysical imagination, III 211a, 212a, 214b, 217b, 218b, 219a, 221b, 222b
philosophy, III 197b, 198b, 199a, 199b, 200a–201a
Plato, I 1a
sense objects compared to, I 1a
Cohen, Hermann (1842–1918)
Marxism, III 163a
Platonism, III 522b
Cohen, I. Bernard, optics, III 392a

Cohen, Leon, indeterminacy, II 592a
Cohen, Morris Raphael (1880–1947)
  continuity, I 502a–502b
  God, II 360a
Cohn, Ferdinand Julius (1828–1898)
  genetic continuity, II 284a
  spontaneous generation, II 284a
Cohnheim, Julius (1839–1884), disease, II 405b
Coing, Helmut, natural law, III 23a
Coke, Edward (1552–1634)
  common law, II 695b
  constitutionalism, I 487b, 488a–488b
  equity, II 153a
  freedom, II 250b–251a
  James I and, II 250b–251a
  law, II 250b–251a, III 7b
Colbert, Jean Baptiste (1619–1683)
  art, II 303b
  conservation, I 473a
  despotism, II 8b
  individualism, II 303b
  literature, III 83a
Cold War
  academic freedom, I 16a
  totalitarianism, IV 406b, 408b, 410b
Colds, disease, II 404b
Cole, George Douglas Howard (1889–1959)
  economic history, II 60a
  socialism, IV 289a
Colebrooke, H. T. (1765–1837), mythology, III 306b
Coleman, Francis J., beauty, I 209b
Coleridge, Samuel Taylor (1772–1834)
  appearance and reality, I 97b
  art, II 307b
  art and play, I 101b
  art for art's sake, I 109a
  association of ideas, I 117a
  Burke and, IV 203a
  Burnet and, III 259a
  Cosmic Fall, I 509b
  Counter-Enlightenment, II 108b, 109b–110a
  creativity in art, I 587b
  culture, I 617b
  democracy, I 663b
  genius, II 307b
  hierarchy, II 441a
  ideas, I 117a
  Kant and, I 617b; IV 199a, 200a, 202a

literary criticism, I 598a, 598b
literature, IV 191b, 192b, 193a, 195a, 196b
metaphysical imagination, III 222a
Mill and, IV 199a
motif, III 235b
mountains in literature, III 259a
neo-classicism, III 425b
Neo-Platonism, III 507b
organicism, III 421b, 422b, 425b, 526b, 427a
periodization in literary history, III 488b
Pietism, IV 111b
Platonism, III 507b, 523b–524a
Plotinus and, III 425b
religion, IV 111b
romanticism, IV 191b, 192b, 193a, 195a, 196b, 198a, 199a, 200a, 201a, 202a, 202b, 203a
Schelling and, IV 201a, 201b
Schlegel and, IV 191b
social contract, IV 263a
symbolism, IV 338b–339a, 344b, 345a
ut pictura poesis, IV 471a
Colet, John (c. 1466–1519), Platonism, III 507b, 514a–514b
Collectivism
  anarchy, I 71b
  communism, II 559b
  economics, III 151b–152a
  evolution, III 646b
  Marx, II 451a
  Marxism, III 151a, 151b–152a, 152b, 166a, 167a, 654a
  materialism, II 451a
  private property, III 654a
  progress, III 646b
  revisionism, IV 264a
  structuralism, III 326b
  U.S.S.R., III 151a, 152b
  U.S., III 151a
  welfare state, IV 510a, 510b, 511b, 512b
Colleoni, Bartolommeo (1400–1475), Ramism, IV 44a
Collier, Arthur (1680–1732), I 93a
Collingwood, R. G. (1889–1943)
  causation, I 284b, 285a, 285b
  civilization, I 616a
  creativity in art, I 582a, 588b

determinism, II 23b
historicism, II 461b–462a
historiography, II 23b
history, I 284b, 285a, 285b; II 23b
metaphysics, III 208b
necessity, III 354b, 360b
Zeitgeist, IV 536b–537a
Collins, Anthony (1676–1729), deism, I 650b
Collins, John Churton (1848–1908)
  baroque in literature, I 193a, 195a
  primitivism, III 601a
  romanticism, IV 195a
Colman, George (1732–1794)
  art, II 307a–307b
  individualism, II 307a–307b
  literature, III 82a
Colombe, Michel (1430?–1512), temperance, IV 375a
Colonialism
  despotism, II 1b, 16b–17a
  Greece (ancient), III 61b
  Great Britain, III 537a
  Hegel, II 16b
  Marx, II 16b–17a
  mythology, III 302a
  nationalism, III 329a, 673a
  periodization in literary history, III 483b
  philanthropy, III 490b
  positivism, III 537a
  Protestantism, III 490b
  religion, IV 94a, 95a, 113b
  revolution, IV 166a
  Roman Catholic Church, III 490b
  Rome (ancient), IV 113b
  U.S., III 7b–8a, 329a, 483b
Colonna, Francesco, iconography, II 529b
Colonna, Vittoria (1492?–1547)
  art, II 303a
  individualism, II 303a
Color
  aesthetics, II 221b, 222a, 224a; III 396b
  beauty, IV 337a
  Castel, III 396a
  colorimetry, III 418a
  Descartes, III 418a, 418b
  Grimaldi, III 418a, 418b, 419a
  harmony, III 395b
  Huygens, III 418a
  impressionism, II 567b, 570a, 570b, 571a, 572a–

572b, 574a, 574b, 577a, 577b, 578b, 579a, 579b, 580a, 580b, 582b, 583a
  mathematics, III 395b–396a
  methodology, III 386a–386b, 387a, 389a, 389b, 390a–390b
  motion, III 419b
  naturalism in art, III 346a
  Newton, I 140a; III 386a–386b, 387a, 389a, 389b, 390a–390b, 392a–398b, 418a, 418b, 419a
  optics, III 392a–398b, 407b, 410b, 416a, 417b, 418a–418b, 419a, 420b
  painting, II 567b, 570a, 570b, 571a, 572a–572b, 574a, 574b, 577a, 577b, 578b, 579a, 579b, 580a, 580b, 582b, 583a; III 350a; IV 473a
  photography, II 572a–572b
  photometry, III 418a
  physics, II 580a–580b
  Platonism, III 511b, 519a
  poetry, III 392a–398b; IV 473a
  precious stones, III 394a
  relativism, IV 71b
Colorimetry, III 418a
Columbus, Christopher (1451–1506)
  disease, II 399b
  humanism, IV 131a
  linguistics, IV 427b
  primitivism, III 592b, 593b, 601a
  skepticism, IV 241b
  uniformitarianism, IV 427b
Columella, Lucius Junius Moderatus (1st century A.D.), conservation, I 472a, 472b
Combe, George (1788–1858), phrenology, IV 23b
Combination tones, III 263b
Comedy, I 467a–470b
  Aeschylus, I 468b
  Anouilh, I 469b
  Aristophanes, I 468b, 469a
  Aristotle, I 467b, 468a; II 169b, 506a; III 528a
  Beckett, I 470a
  catharsis, I 468a
  Cervantes, I 470a
  Chaucer, I 469b
  Chekhov, I 470a
  children, III 501a
  Commedia dell'arte, III 238a
  content of, I 468b–470b
  Dante, I 470a

defined, I 467a, 467b
Dostoevski, I 469b
drama, III 238a, 527a, 528a, 531a
English Restoration, I 469b
ethics, III 440a
Euripides, I 468b
Fielding, I 469a
form of, I 467b–468b
freedom of speech, II 258b
Goethe, I 470a
Greece (ancient), I 467b, 468b, 469a–469b; III 61b
Homer, I 468b
human nature, III 574a
Huxley, Aldous, I 469b
Iamblicus, I 467b
irony, II 627a, 628b, 630a, 631a–632b, 633b, 634a, 634b
Jonson, I 469b
logic, I 467b
Menander, III 238a
Meredith, I 468a
Molière, I 468b–469a; III 238a
motif, III 238a
mythology, III 311a
painting, IV 468b
peace, III 440a
Plato, I 467b; III 498a, 501a
Platonism, III 498a, 501a
pleasure, I 467b, 468a
poetics, III 527a, 528a, 531a
poetry, III 527a, 528a, 531a; IV 468b
primitivism, III 579b
Proclus, I 467b
progress, III 628a
Rabelais, I 469b
rationalism, IV 48b
Rome (ancient), III 61b
Rouault, I 470a
satire, IV 211a, 212b, 215b, 216a
Shakespeare, I 468b, 469a, 470a
Socrates, I 467b, 468b, 469a–469b
Swift, I 469b
temperance, IV 370a
tragedy, I 467b–468a, 469b–470a
virtuoso, IV 488b
Wycherly, I 469b
Comenius, Amos (1592–1670)
   perennial philosophy, III 460a
   Pietism, III 493b, 495a
Comes, Natalis, mythology, III 295a, 299a, 299b

Comestor, Petrus, mythology, III 286b
Comets
   cosmology, I 545a–545b, 549a–549b
   determinism, II 18b–19a
   Newton, I 674a
Commedia dell'arte, comedy, III 238a
Commelin, Isaac, China, I 356b
Commemorative arts, I 460a
Commerce
   academic freedom, I 10a
   Buddhism, I 253b–254a
   ethics, I 253b–254a; III 443b
   international peace, III 451a
   mathematics, III 178b
   More, Thomas, IV 287b
   numbers, III 399b, 400a
   peace, III 443b
   periodization in history, III 480a
   primitivism, III 599a
   socialism, IV 286b, 287b, 290a
   virtuoso, IV 486a
Commission for Conventional Armaments, III 455b
Committee on the Cause and Cure of War, III 449b
Commodianus (3rd century A.D.), millenarianism, III 224a
Common law, II 691a–696b
   absolutism, II 695b
   adages, II 692b
   argumentation, III 31a
   Austin, III 31a
   Australia, II 696a
   authority, II 692a, 692b, 693a; III 31a, 31b
   Bartolus, II 692a
   Beaumanoir, II 692b
   Bentham, III 31a
   Blackstone, II 695b
   Bodin, III 19b
   Bracton, II 694a, 695a; III 30b–31a
   Canada, II 696a; III 31b
   Cardozo, III 32a
   casuistry, III 31a
   Ceylon, III 31b
   Charlemagne, II 691b
   Christianity, II 691a, 692a, 694a–694b
   class, II 693a
   Coke, II 695b
   common sense, II 691a
   communis opinio doctorum, II 692a
   constitutions, III 32a
   contracts, II 693a

Corpus Iuris Civilis, II 685b–690b, 691b, 692a
   courts, II 692a, 693a–694b, 696a; III 31a, 32a
   culture, II 692a
   custom, II 691a, 691b, 692b, 693a, 694a–696a; III 30b
   defined, II 691a
   economics, II 693a, 694b; III 32a
   education, II 691b, 692b, 693a, 694b–695a; III 32a
   equity, II 695a, 695b
   evidence, II 693b
   Fortescue, II 695a
   France, II 691b, 692b, 693a, 693b, 694a
   Frank, III 31b
   fraud, II 695a
   French Revolution, II 693b
   Gaius, II 691a
   Germany, II 691a–691b, 692b–693a, 693b
   Glanvil, II 694a, 694b
   Glossators, II 691b, 692b, 694a
   God, II 691b, 695b
   Great Britain, II 686a, 691a, 692a, 693b–695b, 696a; III 6b, 7b, 30b–31b, 32a, 32b
   Great Gloss of Accursius, II 691b–692b
   Henry II, II 693b
   heresy, II 691a
   hierarchy, III 31a, 31b
   Holy Roman Empire, II 691b–692a
   inequality, III 31b
   Innocent III (Pope), II 694b
   Inns of Court, II 694b–695a
   Italy, II 691b, 692a, 692b, 693a
   judges, II 692a–694b, 695b; III 31a, 31b, 32a
   judgment, III 31a
   jurors, II 692a, 693a, 695a; III 31a
   justice, II 693b, 695a
   Justinian, II 691a, 691b
   kingship, II 693b–696a
   language, II 691b, 692a
   lawyers, II 691a, 692a, 692b, 695a, 695b; III 30b–31a, 32a
   literature, II 694a
   Machiavellism, III 116b
   Maitland, II 694b, 695a
   maxims, II 692b
   merchants, II 694b
   national codes, II 693b
   national deviations, II 693a–693b

national origin, II 691b
   nationalism, II 695a
   New Zealand, II 696a
   ordeal, II 693b
   personal principle, II 691b
   philosophy, III 32a
   Pollock, II 694b, 696a
   positivism, II 693b
   professors, II 692b
   reason, II 691a, 692a, 693a, 695b
   Reception, II 692a, 692b
   as a relative motion, II 691a
   romanticism, II 693b
   Rome (ancient), II 685b–690b, 691a–691b
   rules, II 691a, 692b, 693a, 694a, 695a, 696a; III 31b
   St. Germain, II 695a–695b
   Scandinavia, II 692a
   science, II 695a
   Scotland, II 693a; III 31b
   society, II 692b, 693a, 696a; III 32a
   State, II 693a, 695b
   statutes, II 692a, 692b, 694b, 695b
   territorial principle, II 691a, 691b
   trade, II 694b
   U.S., II 696a; III 31b–32a
   unity, II 692b
   unwritten, II 694b, 695b
   William I, II 693b
   wills, II 691a
   writ, II 693b, 694a
   Year Books, II 694b, 695b
Common nature
   Avicenna, I 4a, 5b
   Duns Scotus, I 4a
   Richard of Campsall, I 4a
   Saint Thomas Aquinas, I 4a
   scholasticism, I 4a
   William of Ockham, I 4a, 6a–6b
Common sense
   aesthetics, IV 355b, 356a
   Aristotle, IV 6a
   art, II 309b
   Bentham, III 234a
   common law, II 691a
   education, II 77a
   genius, II 294a, 294b, 309b
   good, IV 183a, 183b
   Moore, G. E., I 319b
   moral sense, III 233b–234a
   morality, III 645a
   mythology, III 300b
   Orientalism, III 430a
   perennial philosophy, III 459b
   Platonism, III 516a
   progress, III 645a
   psychology, IV 6a

Ramism, IV 43a
Reid, Thomas, III 233b–234a
right, IV 183a, 183b
Russell, Bertrand, I 319b–320b
taste, IV 355b, 356a
technology, IV 361a
truth, I 319b
Victorian sensibility, IV 218a
virtù, IV 479a
Volksgeist, IV 491a
witchcraft, IV 522b
Commons, John R. (1862–1945), economic history, II 60b
Communication
aesthetics, II 219b
Counter-Enlightenment, II 103b
culture, I 608b
economic history, II 44a–44b, 50a
empathy, II 87a
empiricism, III 547a
Enlightenment, II 90b, 91a–91b, 93a
freedom, II 44a–44b
God, III 657a–661a
international peace, III 451a, 453a, 456b
language, II 660b, 661a, 661b, 668a, 668b; IV 325b–326a
Lévi-Strauss, IV 325b–326a
linguistics, IV 426a
logic, III 547a
love, III 507a
nationalism, III 325a, 328a, 332b
numbers, III 400a
philanthropy, III 490b
Platonism, III 507a
positivism, III 547a
progress, III 635a
prophecy, III 657a–664a
Saint Augustine, III 635a
structuralism, IV 325b–326a
totalitarianism, IV 406b, 407b, 409a, 410b
tragic sense, IV 411b, 414a, 414b
uniformitarianism, IV 426a
Communis opinio doctorum, II 692a
Communism
absolute materialism, II 561a–561b
academic freedom, I 10a, 16a
Albania, III 334a
Anabaptists, IV 287a

anarcho-, I 71b–72a
anti-Semitism, III 157b
Aristotle, IV 285b
Babeuf, III 520b
Bakunin, I 74a–74b
Bible, I 396a; IV 286a
Blanqui, II 559b
Buddhism, I 249a, 252a, 252b, 253a
Bukharin, II 560a
capitalism, II 559a–559b
China (Communist), III 334a–334b
Christianity, I 379b, 407b; III 590b, 674b
class, III 673b
collectivism, II 559b
Communist International (Comintern), II 562b, 563a
compromises, III 673b
crisis in history, I 592a
culture, IV 165b
Dewey, John, III 569a
economic history, II 59b
economics, III 673b
Eighth Congress of the Party, II 560a
eschatology, II 158b, 159b
ethics, IV 70a, 291b
existentialism, III 157b, ·158b
France, III 334a
French Workers Party, II 559a
German Social Democratic Party, II 559a
Germany, IV 268b, 273b
goals, II 561b
good, IV 181a
Hegel, II 413b
history, II 559b–563b
Hungary, III 334a
ideology, II 559a–563b
individualism, II 596a, 598a, 599b
Latin America, III 335b
Lenin, II 560a–560b
liberalism, III 59a, 59b
literary criticism, I 606b–607a
longevity, III 93a
loyalty, III 113a, 114b
Marx, II 450a, 450b, 451a; III 359b, 473b, 673b; IV 161b, 292a–292b
Marxism, II 559a; III 147b, 148a, 151a, 152a–157b, 645b–646a; IV 181a
materialism, II 450a, 450b, 451a
methods compared to Christianity, I 379b .
morality, III 22b
Moravia, I 391a

More, Thomas, IV 287b
Münzer, II 158b
mythology, II 562a, 563a–563b
nationalism, III 333a–334b, 335b, 336b, 338a, 338b
natural law, III 22b
natural liberty, II 69b
necessity, III 359b, 645b–646a
organization, III 673b
perfectibility, III 473b
Plato, III 520b; IV 285b
Platonism, III 520b
Plekhanov, II 559a
Poland, III 334a
polycentrism, III 157a–157b
power, III 646a
pragmatism, III 564b, 565b–566a, 569a
primitivism, III 589b, 590b
principles of, II 559b
private property, III 653a
progress, III 629a, 645b–646a, 647b–648a
proletariat, II 559a–559b; III 673b
protest movements, III 673a, 673b, 674b, 675a, 675b
rationalism, III 645b
realism in literature, IV 55b
rebellion, III 673b
reform, III 673b
relativism, IV 70a
religion, III 22b, 675a; IV 111a, 115b
responsibility, III 646a
revisionism, IV 268b, 273b, 274a–275a
revolution, III 673b; IV 157b, 161b, 164b, 165a, 165, 166a
right, IV 181a
Roman Catholic Church, I 379b; III 334b
Rumania, III 334a
Russia, II 559a
Russian Revolution (October 1917), IV 164b
Second Congress of Russian Social Democratic Workers Party, II 559a–559b
social revolution, II 559b, 561a
socialism, II 559a; III 673b; IV 285b–287b, 288b, 289a, 291b–292b
society, III 646a
Socrates, IV 285b
Spanish Civil War, I 75a–75b
State, III 646a
totalitarianism, IV 406b–409b, 410b

Toynbee, III 647b–648a
truth, III 22b
U.S.S.R., III 148a, 150b, 152a–157b, 333a–334a
U.S., III 151a
Utopia, IV 459b, 460b, 461b, 462b
Volksgeist, IV 494b
war, IV 506a
Yugoslavia, III 154b, 334a
Communist Party (Bulgaria), III 157b; (France), III 156b; (Germany), III 164a; (Italy), III 157b; (Poland), III 166b; (U.S.S.R.), I 665b; III 153b, 154b, 156a, 157a–157b; (U.S.), III 156b; (Yugoslavia), III 166a, 167a
Communitarianism, psychology, IV 21a
Community
Bible, III 276b
capitalism, III 148b
good, IV 175a, 176a, 178b, 179b
Greece (ancient), II 675a, 677a, 677b, 678b, 679b, 681a, 681b, 683a–683b, 685a
happiness, II 374b, 380b; IV 178b
holy, II 512b
humanism, IV 132b
Kant, IV 179b
language, II 660b
law, II 675a, 677a, 677b, 678b, 679b, 681a, 681b, 683a–683b, 685a, 687a, 690a; III 3b, 5a
Locke, III 21a
Machiavellism, III 116b
Marxism, III 148b, 154b
monasticism, I 378a
mythology, III 276b, 312a
natural law, III 19a, 21a
progress, III 625a, 627a
prophecy, III 659a, 662a, 663b
Protagoras, III 627a
reformation, IV 60a, 64b, 69a–69b
Renaissance, IV 132b
right, IV 175a, 176a, 178b, 179b
Rome (ancient), II 687a, 690a
satire, IV 211b
socialism, IV 285a, 287a, 289b, 294a
State, IV 313b, 314a, 314b
Stoicism, IV 176a
technology, IV 357b
value, IV 452b, 454a–454b

welfare state, **IV** 511a, 511b

Commynes, Philippe de (1447?–?1511), balance of power, **I** 181a–181b

Comparative Method, linguistics, **IV** 426b, 427a, 428a, 430a

Comparison,
linguistics, **III** 64a, 65b, 66a–66b, 67b–68a, 70b, 71a, 71b, 72b, 75a
naturalism in art, **III** 339b–340a

Compass, **IV** 360b

Compassion, genius, **II** 295b

Competition
art, **II** 300b
evolution, **III** 646b
individualism, **II** 300b, 384b, 596b
Machiavellism, **III** 122b
natural liberty, **II** 64a, 66b
progress, **III** 646b
religion, **II** 64a
Smith, Adam, **III** 11b
Social Darwinism, **III** 646b
technology, **IV** 358b

Completeness, infinity, **II** 614a–615b
See also Logic

Composers, **III** 261b, 262a, 262b, 263b, 271b
genius, **II** 313a, 314a–323a, 325b
impressionism, **II** 574b, 581a
music, **II** 313a, 388b
romanticism, **IV** 208b

Composition
Hals, **III** 344b
harmony, **II** 388b
impressionism, **II** 570a, 571a, 581b, 582b
Leibl, **III** 344b
music, **II** 388b; **III** 261a, 262b, 263b–264a, 270b, 271a
naturalism, **III** 340b, 341a, 341b, 344b, 346a

Compositional method, methodology, **III** 379a
Newton, **III** 379a

Compton effect, **II** 589a
indeterminacy, **II** 589a

Computers
feedback, **II** 660a
indeterminacy, **II** 592a
language, **II** 660a, 673a
law, **III** 32b
literature, **IV** 333a
Man-Machine, **III** 145b–146a
music, **III** 264a

mythology, **III** 316b
numbers, **III** 400a, 406b
psychology, **IV** 29a
Ramism, **IV** 44b
rules, **II** 660a
style, **IV** 333a
symmetry, **IV** 350b
Wiener, N. **III** 32b

Comte, Auguste (1798–1857)
acquired characteristics, **II** 620a
altruism, **III** 644a, 648b
astronomy, **III** 535b, 642a
authority, **I** 152b, 155b
biology, **III** 535b
Bichat and, **III** 534a
Bonald and, **III** 533b, 534a
Broussais and, **III** 534a
Buckle and, **I** 282a
Cartesianism, **III** 535a
causation, **I** 281a, 291a
certainty, **I** 318a
chaos, **III** 641a
chemistry, **III** 535b
Christianity, **III** 634b
civilization, **I** 620a; **II** 23b–24a
classification of the sciences, **I** 465a, 466a; **III** 533a, 534b, 535b
Condorcet and, **III** 532b, 533a, 640b
counter-revolution concept, **III** 534a
Cousin and, **III** 533b–534a, 534b
crisis in history, **I** 590a
d'Alembert and, **III** 532b, 533a
death of, **III** 536b, 540a
Descartes and, **III** 532b
determinism, **II** 23b–25b
Diderot and, **III** 533a
disciples of, **III** 536b–539a, 541b
Durkheim and, **III** 538b
eclecticism, **III** 534a
economics, **III** 644b
Eliot, George, **III** 539a
emotion, **III** 648b–649a
engineering, **III** 533b
Enlightenment, **II** 93b, 95a; **III** 532b, 533b
entropy, **II** 116a
Epicureanism, **II** 582a
ethics, **III** 644a
evolution, **II** 454b, 620a; **III** 641b
evolution of literature, **II** 171b
Floresta and, **III** 539b–540a

Fontenelle and, **III** 536b
French Revolution, **III** 533b, 534a, 534b
Gall and, **III** 534a, 537a
geometry, **III** 642a
God, **II** 356a, 415b; **III** 642a
happiness, **III** 637a, 644a
harmony, **III** 637a
Hegel and, **III** 533b
historical development, **III** 478a
historiography, **II** 23b–24a, 14b, 25b, 495b
history, **I** 281a; **II** 23b–25a, 451b; **III** 640a
Hobhouse and, **III** 538b
human nature, **III** 534b, 644a
idea, **II** 547b; **III** 535a, 535b
ideology, **III** 533b
impressionism, **II** 582a, 583a
individualism, **II** 600b, 601a; **III** 534a
industry, **III** 642a–642b
influence of, **III** 537b, 538a, 538b
instinct, **III** 644a, 648b–649a
knowledge, **II** 25b
laissez-faire, **III** 540a
Lamarck and, **II** 620a
law, **I** 291a; **III** 22a, 360a, 640a, 640b–642b
Law of the Three Stages, **III** 533a, 534b, 535b
legacy, **III** 538a
liberty, **II** 95a
Littré and, **III** 536b, 537b, 642b
logic, **III** 535a
longevity, **III** 93b
Loyola and, **III** 536b
Maistre and, **III** 533b–534b
Man-Machine, **III** 142b
Marx and, **II** 451b, 452a
materialism, **II** 451b, 452a, 454b
mathematics, **III** 535a, 535b
medicine, **III** 537a
messianic concept, **III** 534b, 535a, 536a
metaphysics, **III** 534b, 535b, 536b, 641b, 642a
Mill and, **I** 318b; **III** 536b, 537b, 641b, 642b
monotheism, **III** 641b–642a
Montesquieu and, **III** 533a, 640a
morality, **III** 533b, 534a
mythology, **III** 303b
Napoleon I and, **III** 540a
natural law, **III** 22a

natural science, **III** 534a–534b, 535b
naturalism, **II** 582a
Nature, **III** 642a
necessity, **III** 359b–360a, 643a
order, **III** 642a
passions, **III** 641b, 644a
peace, **III** 642a–642b
Peirce and, **III** 558a
Pereira Barreto and, **III** 540b
perennial philosophy, **III** 462b
periodization in history, **III** 478a
phenomena, **III** 360a
philosophy, **III** 534b, 535b, 536b
physics, **II** 451b; **III** 360a, 535b
positivism, **I** 318b; **II** 415b, 452a; **III** 359b–360a, 478a, 532b–542b, 544a–545b
pragmatism, **III** 556b, 558a, 566b
proletariat, **III** 537a
psychology, **III** 142b, 534a, 537a; **IV** 12a
rationalism, **III** 303b
realism in literature, **IV** 55a
reason, **III** 649a
religion, **III** 534a, 534b, 535a, 536a, 538b, 540a; **IV** 106b
Religion of Humanity, **III** 536a, 536b
Saint-Simon and, **III** 533b, 534b–535a, 535b
scholasticism, **III** 535a
science, **III** 641b–642a, 644b
Segond and, **III** 540a
Silva Gomes and, **III** 539b
society, **II** 22a, 640a, 641b, 642a, 642b, 643a, 644a, 644b
sociology, **III** 534a, 534b, 535a, 535b, 536a, 538a
space, **IV** 302b
species, **III** 640b
Spencer and, **III** 642a, 642b
State, **III** 642a
teachings of, **III** 535a–536b
theocracy, **III** 534b
theology, **III** 641b
thought, **III** 641b
Turgot and, **III** 533a
unity, **III** 641b–642a
Vaux and, **III** 536a, 536b, 537b
war, **III** 642a–642b
women, **IV** 526b
work, **IV** 534b

67

Concept formation
  abstraction, I 1a–9b
  Epicureanism, I 2b
  Kant, I 7a–8b
  Stoics, I 2b
Conception
  Greece (ancient), II 607b
  infinity, II 607b
  naturalism in art, III 343b
  necessity, III 352a, 352b, 353a, 357b, 358a, 361b
  Peirce, III 558a, 559b
  pragmatism, III 558a, 559b
Conceptual environment, II 123b–127a
Concert of Europe, III 453a
  balance of power, I 186b
Conciliar Movement
  Eastern Orthodox Church, I 410b
  Febronianism, I 403b
  Jansenism, I 404a
Conciliation
  international peace, III 450b
  mythology, III 291a
Condillac, Étienne Bonnot de (1715–1780)
  algebra, IV 435b
  association of ideas, I 113b
  behaviorism, I 220a
  certainty, I 318a
  class, I 448a
  Counter-Enlightenment, II 103a, 107b
  Descartes and, II 450a
  Enlightenment, II 96a
  equality, II 143b
  genius, II 294a
  happiness, II 381a
  human nature, III 643b
  idea, I 113b; II 547b
  ideology, II 553a–553b
  inequality, I 448a
  knowledge, I 318a
  language, II 669a; IV 435b–436a
  Man-Machine, III 141b
  materialism, II 450a
  metaphysical imagination, III 215b, 216a, 216b, 516a
  methodology, III 378b, IV 435b–436a
  Newton and, III 378b
  pain, II 381a
  Platonism, III 516a
  positivism, III 533a, 534a
  progress, III 643b, IV 435b
  psychology, IV 11a, 13a, 28a
  reason, II 96a
  romanticism, IV 202a
  signs, IV 435b
  social welfare, IV 277a

society, II 669a
theriophily, IV 388b
unity of science, IV 435b–436a
utility and value, IV 451a
Conditioning
  imprinting, II 585b
  learning, II 585b
  See also Behaviorism
Condorcet, M. J. de (1743–1794)
  attitude toward antiquity, I 79b–80a, 84b
  certainty, I 318a
  civilization, I 619b–620a
  Comte and, III 532b, 533a, 640b
  conservation, I 473b
  Counter-Enlightenment, II 101b, 106a
  cycles, I 625a
  economics, III 644a
  educational reform, III 533a
  Enlightenment, III 533a
  equality, II 144b–145a, 145b, 147a; III 644a, 648b
  eschatology, II 158b
  freedom, III 644a
  French Revolution, III 533a; IV 156a, 156b, 157a–157b
  game theory, II 272b
  historiography, II 488b
  human nature, III 644a
  idea, I 114a, 114b
  immortality, I 646b
  knowledge, II 472a, 644a
  Lagrange and, III 533a
  language, IV 436a
  longevity, III 92a, 92b
  mathematics, III 533a
  methodology, IV 436a
  morality, III 533a, 644a
  mythology, III 303b
  natural science, III 533a
  Nature, III 644a
  perfectibility, III 471b, 472a, 643b–644a
  positivism, III 532b, 533a
  probability, I 318a; III 609b, 614a
  progress, III 640b–641a, 643b–644a, 644b, 648b
  reason, III 614a
  revolution, IV 156a, 156b, 157a–157b
  Saint-Simon and, III 640b
  science, III 644a
  social welfare, IV 281a–282b, 283b, 284a
  socialism, IV 288b
  Utopia, IV 462b–463a
  women, IV 526a
Conductus, II 314b
Confession

heresy, II 420a, 425b, 428a, 430b
  soul, I 261a
Conformity
  intolerance, IV 114a
  Judaism, IV 114a
  loyalty, III 108a
  Nietzsche, I 468a
  religion, IV 114a
  State, IV 313a
  Victorian sensibility, IV 219a, 220a, 223b
Confucianism
  Buddhism, I 255b
  China, I 355a–358a, 360a, 361a, 362a, 368b, 372b
  God, I 356a, 357a, 360a, 360b
  historiography, II 480b
  Longobardi, I 357a
  pantheism, I 360a
  Ricci, I 355b–356a, 357a
  Roman Catholic Church, I 355b–356a, 357a–358a
Confucius (c. 551–479 B.C.), I 360a, 361a
  economics, I 371b
  Emerson and, I 369a
  evolutionism, II 174b
  Hegel and, I 366a
  historiography, II 480a–480b
  Legge and, I 369b–370a
  Orientalism, III 429a, 430a, 430b, 431a, 433b
  philanthropy, III 486b
  religion, IV 105a
  Ricci and, I 355b
  transcendentalism, III 430a, 430b, 431a
Congress of Vienna, III 453a
  balance of power, I 186a, 187a
Congreve, Richard (1818–1899)
  positivism, III 537a
  taste, IV 355b
Congreve, William (1670–1729), cosmic voyages, I 528a
Conjugality, love, III 100b
Conrad II, Emperor (990?–1039), law, III 7a
Conrad of Hirzau, temperance, IV 372b
Conscience
  Bayle, III 42b
  Egypt (ancient), IV 225a, 226a
  ethics, IV 70a, 71a
  genius, II 295b
  intolerance, IV 118a
  law, III 1a
  liberalism, III 37b, 40a, 42b,

43a
  Locke, III 42b, 43a
  moral sense, III 230b, 233b
  religion, IV 106b, 117b, 118a, 119a, 120a
  right and good, IV 178a
  sin, IV 225a, 226a
  Smith, III 233b
  Spinoza, III 42b
  Victorian sensibility, IV 218b
Consciousness
  Bergson, III 565a
  Christianity, I 215a
  Descartes, I 215b, 218b
  Empedocles, IV 3a
  Epicureanism, I 215a
  good, IV 173a, 178b, 179b–181b
  happiness, II 382b–383a
  history, IV 179b–181b
  human nature, III 574a
  individualism, I 215a–215b
  James, III 562a, 562b, 563a, 565a
  Kant, III 555b
  Man-Machine, III 140b, 143b
  metaphor, III 207a
  metaphysical imagination, III 208b, 209b, 210a
  perfectibility, IV 112a
  pleasure, II 382b–383a
  Plotinus, IV 9a
  pragmatism, III 553a, 553b, 555b, 562a, 562b, 563a, 565a
  psychology, IV 3a, 7a, 9a, 27b, 28a, 28b
  religion, III 207a; IV 96b, 97a, 97b, 98a
  right, IV 173a, 178b, 179b–181b
  romanticism, IV 202a, 208a, 208b
  Saint Augustine, I 215a–215b
  Santayana, III 553b
  Sartre, III 209b
  space, IV 301a
  Stoicism, I 215a
  Strato, IV 7a
  time, IV 389a, 391b, 394a, 396a
  Tolman, I 223b
Conservation, I 470b–477a
  agriculture, I 472a, 475a
  animals, I 472b–473a, 474a, 475b, 476a
  Audubon, I 474a
  Bartram, I 474a
  biology, I 473a
  Buffon, I 473a, 473b
  Catlin, I 474a, 474b, 476a

Cato, I 472a
Clements, I 475b
Colbert, I 473a
Columella, I 472a, 472b
Condorcet, I 473b
dams, I 476a
Darwin, I 473a
Dasmann, I 472a, 476b
defined, I 471a
ecology, I 475b
Egypt (ancient), I 472a
Elton, I 472a, 475b, 476a
Emerson, I 474a–474b
Empedocles, I 472a
Eskimos, I 471b
Evelyn, I 473a
Fairfield, I 471a
forest, I 473a, 474a, 475b–476a
France, I 473a
Glacken, I 471b, 472a, 472b
Godwin, I 473b
Goethe, I 473a
Graham, I 471b, 472b, 474a
Grant, I 475a
Great Britain, I 472b, 473a–473b
Greece (ancient), I 471b–472a, 472b
Harrison, I 475b
Hayes, I 475b
Humboldt, I 473a–473b
hunting, I 474a
Indians (American), I 471b, 474a
Lebanon, I 472b
Leopold, I 472b, 476a
Linnaeus, I 473a
Louis XIV, I 473a
Malthus, I 473b
Marsh, I 474b, 475b
Mather, I 475a
Muir, I 475a, 475b, 476a
Mumford, I 472b
natural history, I 473a
origin of the word, I 470b
Osborn, I 476a
Penn, I 474a
Phoenicians, I 472b
Pinchot, I 471a, 475b–476a
Plato, I 471b–472a
Pliny, I 472a, 472b
population explosion, I 471a, 473b, 475b, 476b
Powell, I 475a–475b, 476a
preservationist school, I 475a
Rome (ancient), I 471b, 472a–472b
Roosevelt, I 471a, 475b, 476a
Sennacherib, I 472b
Tacitus, I 472a–472b

Thoreau, I 474a–474b, 475a, 476a
Udall, I 471b, 475a, 476b
U.N., I 471a
U.S., I 471a–476b
wildlife, I 472b–473a, 474a, 475b, 476a
Conservatism, I 477a–485a
Adams, Brooks, I 484a
Adams, Henry, I 484a
Alexander I, I 482c
Anglo-Saxon, I 481a–481b
antirevolutionary, I 480a–481a
anti-Semitism, I 483a
art, II 571a
Augustus, I 477b
Austria, I 484b
authority, I 154a–154b, 480a–481a
Babbitt, I 484a
Barrès, I 483a
Belgium, I 484b
Bismarck, I 480b
Bonald, I 482a
Brandes, I 481b
Burke, I 477b, 480a, 481a–481b, 484a; IV 203a
Burkhardt, I 483a
Calhoun, I 484a
Chateaubriand, I 477b
Christianity, I 477b, 482a, 482b, 483a
Church, I 478b
Church of England, I 479b–480a
Cicero, I 479b
contemporary usage, I 477a–477b
cycles, I 627a
Disraeli, I 480b
Dostoevski, I 483a
economy, I 478b–479a
Enlightenment, I 479b, 480a
etymological summary, I 477b–478a
fascism, I 483b
France, I 477b, 480a, 480b, 481a, 482a, 483a, 484b
French Revolution, I 480a, 481a
Friedrich Wilhelm IV, I 482b
Gentz, I 477b, 481b
German Peasant War, I 479b
Germany, I 479b, 480b, 481a, 481b, 482b, 483a–483b, 484b
Glorious Revolution, I 479b
God, I 482a
Great Britain, I 477a, 477b–478a, 479a–480a, 481b

Greece (ancient), I 477b, 479b
Haller, I 482a–482b
Hamilton, I 484a
Holy Alliance, I 482b
Hoover, I 484a
ideology, I 480a
Italy, I 484b
Jacobinism, I 480a
Jefferson, I 483b–484a
Joseph II, I 480b
leadership, I 479a
liberalism, I 480a, 481a, 482b, 483b
Locke, I 483b, 484a
Luther, I 479b
Madison, I 484a
Maistre, I 480a, 482a
Maurras, I 483a
Metternich, I 480
Möser, I 481b
Napoleon I, I 477b
nationalism, I 482b–483a; III 328a
neo-, I 483a–483b
Netherlands, I 484b
Nietzsche, I 483a
nonideological, I 478a–479a
philanthropy, III 490a, 492a
Plato, I 582a
positivism, III 537a
prerevolutionary, I 479a–480a
Protestantism, I 408b
Prussia, I 482b
radicalism, I 479b–480a
Ranke, I 479b
Rehberg, I 481b
religion, IV 106a, 106b–107a, 115b, 117a
Renan, I 483a
restorationist, I 481b–482b
revolution, I 480a–482b; IV 157b, 158b, 160a
Rienzo, I 479b
Roman Catholic Church, I 482a, 483a, 484a, 484b
romanticism, I 482b–483a; IV 196b, 198a, 199b, 200a, 202b, 203a, 207b
Rome (ancient), I 477b, 479b
Russia, I 482b–483a
Scandinavia, I 477a, 484b
Schelling, I 482b
social contract, IV 256b, 257b, 262b
socialism, I 483b
Sophists, I 479b
Sorel, I 483a
Staël, I 477b
Stahl, I 481a
Stankević, I 482b–483a

Taine, I 483a
temperance, IV 367b
Tiberius Gracchus, I 479b
Tocqueville, I 481a
U.S., I 481b, 483b–484b
war, IV 502b, 504b–507a
Wellington, I 477b
women, IV 528a, 529b
Wycliffe, I 479b
Consonance, III 260b–263a, 269a
Descartes, III 262b
Galileo, III 263a
numbers, III 269a
Pythagoras, III 261a, 261b
Constable, John (1776–1837)
chance images, I 350b
impressionism, II 578a, 579a–579b; III 342a
naturalism in art, III 342a
romanticism, IV 201a
Schelling and, IV 201a
ut pictura poesis, IV 467a, 473b
Constant, Baron d'Estournelles de (1852–1924), international peace, III 453b
Constant, Benjamin (1845–1902)
art for art's sake, I 109b
despotism, II 2a, 4b, 13b, 14b–15a, 17a
Enlightenment, II 95a
freedom, II 15a
general will, II 279a–279b
individualism, II 599a
law, II 279b
liberalism, III 45b, 46a, 58a
liberty, II 95a
positivism, III 543a
romanticism, IV 190a
Rousseau and, II 279a–279b
usurpation, II 14b–15a
Constantine, J. R., antiprimitivism, III 604a
Constantine the African (c. 1020–c. 1087), methodology, III 381a
Constantine I, Emperor (280?–337)
Christianity, III 589b
conversion of, I 52a
Council at Nicaea, I 377a
God, I 376b
grants freedom to Roman Catholic Church, I 376b
holy, II 512b
historiography, II 471b
humanism, IV 130b
philanthropy, III 488b
primitivism, III 581b, 589b

Constitutionalism, I 485a–492a
Act of Settlement, I 488a, 490b
Act of Union, I 490b
Adams, I 488b
Aristotle, I 487a, 488b
Bill of Rights (Great Britain), I 490b
Bill of Rights (U.S.), I 490a
Bolingbroke, I 486b
Bracton, I 488a
Bryce, I 485b
Canada, I 491a
central element of, I 485b
China (Communist), I 486a
Cicero, I 487a, 488b
Coke, I 487b, 488a–488b
constitutions, I 485b–492a
Cromwell, I 491a
Davis, I 489b–490a
economics, I 490b
France, 404a–404b; III 7b
freedom, I 486a
Gladstone, I 491a
Graham, I 485b
Great Britain, I 487b–488b, 490b–491a, 491b
Greece (ancient), I 486b–487b, 488b
Grotius, I 488b
Harrington, I 488b
Henry III, I 488a
Heraclitus, I 486b
Hughes, I 490a
Israel, I 491a, 491b
Jackson, I 490a
James I, I 488a–488b
John of Salisbury, I 487b
Judicature Act, I 490b
law, I 485b–492a
Livy, I 488b
Local Government Act, I 490b
Locke, I 488b
McIlwain, I 485b, 486b, 488b
Magna Carta, I 487b–488a, 488b, 490b
Marshall, Justice, I 489a–489b
Middle Ages, I 487b–488a
nationalism, III 332a
natural law, I 487a–487b
Paine, I 486b
Parliament Act, I 490b
Plato, I 487a, 488b
principle of parliamentary supremacy, I 491a–491b
Pufendorf, I 488b
Representation of the People Act, I 490b
Rome (ancient), I 487b, 488b

Saint Thomas Aquinas, I 487b
Stalin, I 486a
State, I 485b–486b
Sutherland, Arthur, I 487b–488a
Sydney, Philip, I 488b
U.S.S.R., I 486a
U.S., I 488b–490b, 491a
U.S. Supreme Court, I 489a–490a
West Germany, I 491a
Constitutions
Bolingbroke, I 486b
Carthage (ancient), II 254a
China (Communist), I 486a
common law, III 32a
constitutionalism, I 485b–492a
Crete (ancient), II 254a
despotism, II 2b
France, I 491a–491b, 661b–662a; III 7b, 25b
Great Britain, I 487b–488b, 490b–491b, 657b–659b; II 410a
Greece (ancient), II 675a, 675b, 677b
Hegel, II 410a
Holmes, Justice, III 567b
India, I 491b; III 13b
law, I 486a–492a; II 675a, 675b, 677b, 686a; III 2a, 2b, 3a, 7b–10a, 11b, 12a, 32a
Machiavellism, III 123b–124a
Mexico, I 491b
natural law, III 21b
Nature, III 350a
Paine, I 486b; IV 261a
pragmatism, III 567b
Sparta (ancient), II 254a
U.S.S.R., I 468a; II 563a; III 334a
United States, see United States Constitution
Volksgeist, IV 492a, 492b, 493a
welfare state, IV 509a
West Germany, I 491a
Contarini, Cardinal (1483–1542), I 393a, 393b
Content
formalism, II 221a
naturalism in art, III 346a
organicism, III 423b, 424a, 426b
style in literature, IV 330b, 332a, 332b
ut pictura poesis, IV 466b, 470b, 471a
Context, aesthetics, II 216a,

220a, 220b, 221a
Conti, Natale, mythology, III 292b–293a
Continuism, I 503a–504a
Aristotle, I 503b
Bible, I 503b
Christianity, I 503b
continuity, I 503a–504a
Diogenes Laërtius, I 503b
Duhem, I 503b
Herodotus, I 503b
Judaism, I 503b
Newton, I 503b
Shakespeare, I 503b
Spengler, I 503b
Toynbee, I 503b, 504a
Continuity, I 492a–504b
Archimedes, I 499b
Aristotle, I 492b–493a, 495a–495b, 498a, 499a, 501a, 501b, 502b–503b
atomism, I 494a–497b
Bacon, Francis, I 503a
Bible, I 492b, 493a, 502b, 503b
biology, I 492b, 498b–500b
Bruno, I 494b–495a
Cantor, I 498b, 499b
catastrophism, I 500a, 500b
Cauchy, I 494a, 498b
causation, II 231a
Chain of Being, I 498a
Chaucer, I 493a–493b
Christianity, I 492b, 493a, 502b, 503b
civilization, I 619a
Cohen, M. R., I 502a–502b
continuism, I 503a–504a
Cosmic Fall, I 505a, 505b–509a
culture, I 619a
Darwin, I 499b
de Broglie, I 494b, 495a
Dedekind, I 499b
Democritus, I 494b, 495a, 502b, 503a
Descartes, I 498a
Diogenes Laërtius, I 503b
Dirichlet, I 498b
Du Bois Reymond, I 498b
duality, I 494b
Duhem, I 503b
Egypt (ancient), I 503b–504a
Einstein, II 590a
Euclid, I 498a
Eudoxus, I 499b
evolution, I 499b, 500b
evolutionism, II 185a, 187b
Fechner, I 501b–502a
Fresnel, I 494a
Gauss, I 494a
Gaussian law, I 494a

geology, I 492b, 498b–500b
Greece (ancient), I 492b–493b, 494b–495a, 497b–498a, 500b, 501a, 502b–503a
Green, G., I 494a
Hankel, I 498b
Hegel, I 502a
Helmholtz, I 494a–494b
Herbart, I 501a–501b
Herodotus, I 503b
Hertz, I 494a
historiography, I 493b, 502b–504a
history, I 492b
Homer, I 493a
humanism, IV 134b
Hutton, James, I 499b
indeterminacy, II 590a
inductivism, I 503a
infinity, II 605b
Johnson, Samuel, I 499a
Judaism, I 492b, 493a, 502b, 503b
Kant, I 501a, 502a
Kelvin, I 494a
Kirchhoff, I 494a
Lagrange, I 498b
Lamarck, I 499b
Laplace, I 498b
Leibniz, I 493b, 498a–499b, 501a–502b
Leucippus, I 494b, 495a, 503a
Lyell, I 499b, 500a–500b
mathematics, I 492b, 493b, 494a, 497b–498b, 500b–501a, 502b
Maxwell, I 494a
Melissus, I 503a
Mesopotamia (ancient), I 504a
Middle Ages, I 500b
monads, I 493b
music, III 269b
mythology, III 291b
Nature, I 500b–501a
Newton, I 492b, 493a, 503b
origin of the word, I 493a
Parmenides, I 493b, 503a
Peirce, I 501b, 502a–502b; III 560b
philosophy, I 493b, 494b, 500b–502b
physics, I 493b, 494a
Plato, I 500b
Poisson, I 494a
pragmatism, III 560b
probability, I 494a; III 620a
prophecy, III 667b
psychology, I 498b–499a
Pythagoreans, I 493b, 498b
Renaissance, IV 134b

Richard Rolle of Hampole, I 493a–493b

Riemann, I 498b

Russell, I 502b

Saint Augustine, I 500b

science, I 492b, 493b, 494a–495b

Shakespeare, I 503b

Spengler, I 498a, 503b

synechology, I 501b–502b

Thales, I 502b

theology, I 492b

Thucydides, I 502b

time, IV 390a

Toynbee, I 503b, 504a

transformism, I 499b, 500b

uniformitarianism, I 492b, 499b–500b

Valerio, I 498a

Whitehead, I 502b

Young, I 494a

Zeno of Elea, I 498b, 499a

Contracts
common law, II 693a
law, II 686b; III 2a
natural law, III 17a, 22b
Rome (ancient), II 686b
See also Social Contract

Convention
aesthetics, II 224a
general will, II 277b
law, III 1a
naturalism in art, III 341b
necessity, III 353b
See also Nature

Conway, Moncure (1832–1907)
Orientalism, III 429a, 431b, 434a–434b
transcendentalism, III 429a, 431b, 434a–434b

Conybeare, William Daniel (1787–1857), catastrophism, IV 420a, 421b

Cook, Captain (1728–1779), primitivism, III 598b, 602a, 602b, 603b, 604a

Cooley, Charles Horton
individualism, II 601a
psychology, IV 26b

Cooper, Anthony Ashley, *see* Shaftesbury, Third Earl of

Cooper, James Fenimore (1789–1851)
conservation, I 474a
primitivism, III 603b
transcendentalism, IV 24a

Cooper, Thomas (1805–1892), Jefferson and, IV 21a

Cooperatives
Bernstein, III 163b
Marxism, III 148b, 163b
See also Collectivism

Copernicus, Nicolaus (1473–1543)
astronomy, IV 153a
axiomatization, I 166b
Bacon, Francis, I 176a, 178a; III 356a
beauty, IV 75a
Bruno and, III 193b, 194a
cosmic images, I 515b–516a, 519a
cosmic voyages, I 527b
cosmology, I 543b–544b, 545b–546a, 546b, 548a, 550b; II 521a
cosmos, II 442b
design argument, I 673b
economic history, II 45a
Faust (legend), III 246b
game theory, II 272a
God, II 347b
gravity, III 194a
harmony, III 389b
heresy, II 428a
hierarchy, II 436b, 437b, 442a, 442b, 443b
historiography, IV 148b
Hobbes and, I 216b
humanism, II 521a; IV 134a
infinity, II 605a, 608a
Islam, II 646a, 651b
Kepler and, I 545b–546a
mathematics, II 442b, 443b, III 178a, 182b
matter, III 192b, 193b, 194a
mechanics, II 203b
metaphysical imagination, III 215a
music, II 389b
mythology, III 299b
necessity, III 356a
relativity, IV 74b, 75a, 76b
revolution, IV 153a, 162b
skepticism, IV 242a
socialism, IV 293b
space, IV 295b, 300b
symmetry, IV 348b
universe, II 442b

Copernicus paradox, literary paradox, III 77a

Copyists, humanism, II 516a, 516b

Copyrights, economic history, II 57a

Cordemoy, Géraud de
causation, I 298b
idea, II 548a
occasionalism, I 276a

Cordier, Henri (1849–1925), China, I 368a

Coriolanus, Gaius (5th century B.C.), law, II 690a–690b

Corman, Louis, psychology, IV 15a

Cornaro, Luigi (1467?–1566),

longevity, III 91b
catharsis, I 268a

Corneille, Pierre (1606–1684),
baroque in literature, I 192a
classicism, I 451b, 452a
evolution of literature, II 171b, 172a
genius, II 294b
neo-classicism in art, III 366a
poetics, III 529b, 530a

Cornell, Ezra (1807–1874), philanthropy, III 491b

Cornford, Francis MacDonald (1874–1943)
comedy, I 468a
mythology, III 307a, 311a
Pythagoreans, IV 32a
rationalism, IV 48a
tragedy, I 468a

Cornutus, Lucius Annaeus (1st century A.D.), mythology, III 274a

Coronations, humanism, II 517a

Corot, Jean Baptiste Camille (1796–1895)
impressionism, II 572b, 578a, 578b; III 342a
naturalism in art, III 342a

Corporations
Christianity, III 589a
law, II 686b–687a; III 11b, 13a
Middle Ages, III 320a–320b
nationalism, III 320a–320b
pragmatism, III 566a
private property, III 653a, 654b, 655a, 655b, 656a
romanticism, IV 206b
Rome (ancient), II 686b–687a
U.S.S.R., III 655a

Corpus Iuris Civilis, II 685b–690b, 691b, 692a

Correa, T., mimesis, III 228b

Correggio, Antonio (1494–1534)
chance images, I 347a, 348a
iconography, II 529a, 538a
mythology, III 290b

Correns, Karl Erich (1864–1933), acquired characteristics, II 619a

Cortés, Hernando (1485–1547), mythology, III 308b

Cortona, Pietro da (1596–1669), I 398b

Corvisart des Marets, Jean (1755–1821), disease, II 401b

Coryate, Thomas (1577?–

1617), mountains in literature, III 253b–254a, 258b

Cosmic Fall, I 504b–513a
aesthetics, I 512a
ambiguity, I 505a
Aristotle, I 505b
astronomy, I 511b
Bacon, I 509b–510a
Barckley, I 511b
Bayle, I 510b–511a
Bible, I 505a–505b, 506a
Browne, Thomas, I 510a
Burnet, I 505a, 509b, 510b, 511a, 512a–512b
Burton, Robert, I 508b
Calvin, I 506a
Chain of Being, I 511b–512a
Christianity, I 504b–512b
Coleridge, I 509b
continuity, I 505a, 505b–509a
Creation, I 505b, 516b
Donne, I 506a–506b, 507a, 512a
Drummond of Hawthornden, I 508b–509a
evil, I 512a
Flood, I 505a, 506a, 507a, 508b, 509a, 509b, 511a
Galen, I 508b
Galileo, I 511b
Glanvill, I 510b
God, I 505a–505b, 506a, 507a–508a, 509a, 510b, 511a, 512a, 512b
Goodman, G., I 505b, 506b–508b, 510a, 511b, 512a
Greece (ancient), I 505b, 512a
Greville, I 505b, 506b, 512a
Hakewill, I 506b, 507b–508b, 510a, 512a
Hardy, I 511b
Herbert, George, I 509a
human nature, I 504b, 507b
Hume, I 511b
Huxley, I 511b
Judaism, I 505a–505b
Keil, I 510b
Leopardi, I 511b
Lucretius, I 505b
Luther, I 505b–506a
macrocosm and microcosm, I 508b, 511a
Marvell, I 509b
Mill, J. S., I 511b
Milton, I 509a–509b
More, Henry, I 510a, 510b
Nature, I 504b–513a
Newton, I 511b
Plato, I 505b, 512a
power, I 510b
Purchas, I 506b

Raleigh, I 506b
Ray, John, I 510b
Saint Paul, I 505a
Senault, I 509a
sin, I 505a, 506a, 506b, 507a, 507b, 508b
Spencer, I 510b
Spenser, I 506a
Stubbes, I 505b
Swan, I 509a
teleology, I 511b
Trethowan, I 512b
Vaughan, I 509a
Voltaire, I 511a
Webb, C. C. J., I 512b
Wilkins, I 510a
Williams, I 512b
Young, I 509b
Cosmic Images, I 513a–523b
  aesthetics, I 513b, 514a
  alchemy, I 516a
  Aristotle, I 515b, 516a–516b
  Arrhenius, I 523a–523b
  astrophysics, I 513a
  Bachelard, I 513b, 522b
  beauty, I 519b, 521a
  Being, I 514b
  Boscovich, I 518b
  Bruno, I 515a, 516b, 517a, 518a
  Buffon, I 520b
  Burnet, I 522b–523a
  Byron, I 520a
  Copernicus, I 515b–516a, 519a
  Creation, I 514b
  Croll, James, I 523a
  death, I 522a–523b
  de Maillet, I 518a
  de Sales, I 519b, 523a
  Descartes, I 515a, 517a–517b, 518a, 519a, 520a
  discontinuity, I 514a
  d'Olivet, I 519b
  Donne, I 517a
  d'Ors, I 513b, 515a
  Einstein, I 515b
  Euler, I 519b
  Faye, I 521b, 522b, 523a
  Flammarion, I 516b, 518b, 520a, 522a, 522b, 523a
  France, I 517a–517b, 522a, 523a
  French Revolution, I 522a
  Galileo, I 513a, 515a, 516a–516b, 517a, 522b
  God, I 513a, 514b, 516a, 517a, 518a, 519a
  Great Britain, I 516b, 517b–519b, 522b–523a
  Greece (ancient), I 514b, 515b, 516a–516b
  Halley's comet, I 523a
  Heraclides of Pontus, I 515b
  Heraclitus, I 513b, 514a–514b, 515a, 516b–517a, 519b, 521a
  Herschel, I 519b, 521b
  hierarchy, I 514a
  Humboldt, I 520a
  Jeans, I 521b, 522a
  Kant, I 513b, 519a, 519b, 521a–521b, 522a
  Kepler, I 515a, 515b, 516a, 516b, 517a
  Koestler, I 513b, 514a, 515b–516a
  Laforgue, I 522a
  Lambert, I 519a
  Lamennais, I 521b
  Laplace, I 519b–520a, 521a, 521b
  Leibniz, I 515a
  Leopardi, I 520a
  Lovejoy, I 513b
  macrocosm and microcosm, I 513a
  Maeterlinck, I 523b
  Metzger, I 518b
  Milton, I 518b
  Mirandola, I 516a
  More, I 518a
  Moreux, I 523b
  Neo-Platonism, I 515a, 516a
  Newton, I 515a, 517a, 517b–519b, 520b
  Nichol, I 523a
  Nicolson, M. H., I 513b, 515b
  Parmenides, I 513b–516a, 517a, 519b, 520b, 521a, 522b
  Plato, I 514b
  Poe, I 519b, 523a
  Poincaré, I 523b
  psychology, I 515b, 522b
  Ptolemy, I 515b, 516a
  Pythagoreans, I 514a, 515b, 517a
  Ray, I 523a
  Renaissance, I 515a
  Restif de la Bretonne, I 519b, 522b–523a
  Reynaud, I 520a
  romanticism, I 520a
  Rousset, I 513b
  Saint-Simon, I 520a
  scholasticism, I 515a
  Schopenhauer, I 520b
  socialism, I 520a
  Svante, I 518b, 522a
  Swedenborg, I 520b
  telescopes, I 521b
  Tressan, I 518a
  Vico, I 519b
  Whitehead, I 513b
Wölfflin, I 513b
Wright, I 519a
Young, I 518b
Cosmic Voyages, I 524a–535b
  Addison, I 529b
  Alexander the Great, I 527a
  Babylonia, I 527a
  Bacon, Francis, I 532a
  Behn, I 528a
  Bible, I 524a
  Boyle, I 532a
  Brunt, I 528b–529a
  Cassini, I 533b
  Cavendish, Henry, I 532a
  Cavendish, Margaret, I 528b
  Chaucer, I 527a
  China (ancient), I 524a, 532b
  Christianity, I 524a, 526a, 532a
  Cicero, I 524a
  Clayton, I 532a
  Congreve, William, I 528a
  Copernicus, I 527b
  Cyrano de Bergerac, I 528a, 530a–531b
  Daedalus, I 524a, 529a, 529b
  Dante, I 524a, 527a
  Danti, I 529a–529b
  Defoe, I 528a, 528b, 532b–533a
  Denmark, I 534b
  D'Urfey, I 528a
  Fontenelle, I 525a, 528a
  France, I 527a, 530a–531b
  Galileo, I 524b–527a
  Gassendi, I 530a
  Gilbert, I 533b
  Glanvill, I 529b
  God, I 526b, 532a
  Godwin, I 527a–528a, 530b, 531b, 532b
  Great Britain, I 524a–525a, 527a–530a, 532a–534b
  Greece (ancient), I 524a–525a, 527a
  Guericke, I 532a
  Gusmão, I 532b
  Harding, I 529b–530a
  Hermes, I 524a
  Hodgson, I 532a
  Holberg, I 534b
  Hooke, I 529b
  Icarus, I 524a, 529a
  Israel (ancient), I 524a
  Italy, I 525a, 531b–532b
  Jesus Christ, I 524a
  Jonson, I 528b
  Judaism, I 524a
  Kepler, I 525a, 525b–526a, 527a, 527b–528a, 529a, 530b, 531b, 533a, 546a
  Kindermann, I 532b
  Kircher, I 526a
  Lana, I 531b–532b
  Leonardo da Vinci, I 524a
  Lucian, I 524a–524b, 530b
  Marco Polo, I 527a
  Martello, I 532b
  Mendoza, I 532a
  Milton, I 526a–526b, 531b
  Montgolfier brothers, I 532a
  Netherlands, I 525a
  Newton, I 528b, 529a, 533b
  Persia (ancient), I 527a
  Plato, I 524a
  Plutarch, I 524a–525a
  Poe, I 527a, 528a, 534b
  Portugal, I 532b
  Ptolemy, I 524b
  Rabelais, I 530b
  Renaissance, I 524a, 527a
  Robault, I 530a
  Roman Catholic Church, I 526a, 532a
  Rome (ancient), I 524b
  Satan, I 526b
  Schott, I 532a
  Settle, I 528a
  Sheba, Queen of, I 524a
  Shun, I 524a
  Spain, I 525a
  Steele, I 529b
  Swift, I 528a, 528b, 532b, 533a–534a
  U.S., I 534b
  Verne, I 526a, 527a, 528a, 534b
  Voltaire, I 526a, 534a–534b
  Welles, I 534b
  Wells, I 526a, 534b
  Wesley, I 528a
  Wilkins, I 525a, 528a–530a, 531b, 532b
  Wood, I 527a
  Wren, I 529b
  Zamagna, I 532b
  Zoroaster, I 526a
Cosmogony
  evolutionism, II 176a–176b, 185a
  Faust (legend), III 246b
  Hesiod, II 432a
  human nature, III 574a
  language, II 661b
  progress, III 627a
  psychology, IV 2a
  religion, IV 93b
  space, IV 299b
  spontaneous generation, IV 307b
  symmetry, IV 350b
  time, IV 399b, 400a
Cosmology, I 535b–570b; II 38a

Adams, John C., I 552b
agriculture, I 535b, 537a
al-Biruni, I 546b
Alfvén, I 570a
Alpher, I 566b
al-Shatir, I 544a
Anaxagoras, I 539a
Apian, I 545a, 549a
Apollonius of Perga, I 541a
Arabs, I 542b, 544a
Aristarchus, I 543b, 544a
Aristotle, I 540a–541a,
543a, 544a, 545a, 546b,
622b; III 90a; IV 400b
Aryabhata, I 543b
Assyria, I 538b
asteroids, I 552a
astrology, I 538b–539a
astronomy, I 554a
asymmetry, IV 349a
atomic energy, I 553a–
553b
atomism, I 539b–540a,
543b
Babylonia, I 536b–539a
Becquerel, I 553a
Bible, I 21a, 536b, 538b,
543a, 543b, 544a, 545b;
III 281b
biology, I 232a
Bolyai, I 555a
Bondi, I 567b–568a
Borelli, I 546b–547a, 548a,
549a
botany, I 230a
Boyle, I 548b
Brahe, I 545a–545b, 548a
Brahmagupta, I 543b
Bruno, I 545a, 548a, 549b;
III 193b; IV 298a–298b
Buddhism, I 544b
calendar, I 536a, 537a–
537b
Christianity, I 542b, 543a–
543b, 544a, 545b, 546b,
622b
Cicero, I 622b–623a
Clifford, I 555a–555b
comets, I 545a–545b,
549a–549b
constellations, I 538b, 541b
Copernicus, I 543b–546b,
548a, 550b; II 521a
Creation, I 536b, 539b,
543b
culture, I 609a
cycles, I 621b–624a
de Sitter, I 561b–562b
death, I 644b–645a
Democritus, I 540a, 549b
Descartes, I 546b; II 182a–
187b
Dicke, I 567a, 568b
Digges, I 544b–545a, 548a

dignity, IV 139b, 145b
Dirac, I 568b
Doppler, effect, I 553a,
562, 567a
earth, I 539a–540a, 542a,
543a–546b, 547b, 549b,
550b
Ecphantus, I 539b
Eddington, I 562b, 565b–
566a, 568a
Egypt (ancient), I 536a–
536b, 537a
Einstein, I 553b, 555a,
556a–562b, 564a–564b,
565b, 566a–566b, 567b,
568a, 570a; IV 306a
electromagnetism, I 554b
entropy, II 117b
environment, II 123a
Euclidean geometries, I
555b, 557b, 558b, 559a,
559b, 563a
Eudoxus, I 540a
Euler, I 554b
evolution, I 549b–550a,
553b
evolutionism, II 176a, 182a,
186b, 187a
Fabricius, I 550b
Faraday, I 554b
Ficino, III 510b–511a
fishing, I 535b
Fraunhofer, I 552b–553a
Friedmann, I 562b, 563a,
564a, 565a, 565b, 566b
Galileo, I 546b, 548a, 550b,
558a
Galle, I 552b
Gamow, I 565b, 566b–567a
Gauss, I 554b, 555a
Geminus, I 544b
God, I 543b, 549b; II
348a, 356a, 357a, 359a;
IV 306a
Gold, I 567b–568a
gravity, I 547a, 547b–548b,
549b–550b, 554a–554b,
555a, 556a, 557b–559b,
560b, 561a, 564b, 570a
Greece (ancient), I 538b,
539a–541a, 543a, 544b; II
117b, 674a
Grosseteste, III 191a
Halley, I 549a–549b
Hamilton, I 554b
harmony, IV 38b, 39a–39b,
41b
Hermes Trismegistus, IV
306a
hermeticism, II 431b
Herschel, William, I 550a–
552a
Hevelius, I 549a
Hinduism, I 539a, 543b

Hipparchus, I 541a
Hooke, I 547a–547b, 548a
Hoyle, I 567b, 568a
Hubble law, I 562a, 564a,
564b, 565a, 568a, 568b
humanism, II 520a, 521a;
IV 134a, 134b
Humason, I 565a, 567b
hunting, I 535b
Huygens, I 547b–548a,
550a
immortality, I 644b–645a
India (ancient), I 539a
inertia, I 547a, 548a, 558b
infinity, II 605a, 608a
Islam, I 542b, 544a; II
640a, 644b, 646a, 646b,
648b, 651a
Jeans, I 569b
John Philoponus, I 543b
Jordan, I 568b
Judaism, I 536b–537a,
538b, 539a, 543a, 543b,
622b
justice, IV 382b
Kant, I 549b–550a; II 182a,
187b; IV 382b, 383b
Kepler, I 545b–546a, 547a,
548a, 549a, 550b; IV 306a
Kirchhoff, I 553a
Koran, I 542b
Kuiper, I 570a
Lagrange, I 554b
Laplace, I 550a, 554b; II
182a, 187b
law, II 674a
Lemaître, I 562b, 565b,
567a
Leverrier, I 552b
light, I 553b, 554b, 555a,
557a
linear zigzag function, I
537b, 538a
Lobachevsky, I 555a
longevity, III 90a
lunar months, I 537a
matter, I 559b–560b, 561a,
562b; III 186b, 190a, 191a,
193b, 195b
Maxwell, I 554b, 555a
mechanics, II 199a
Mesopotamia (ancient), I
536b–539a
Metrodorus, I 540a
Michelson, I 555a, 557a
Milky Way, The, I 549b,
551a–551b
millenarianism, III 223b
Milne, I 568b; IV 306a
moon, I 535b, 536b–537a,
537b–538a, 539a, 539b,
540a, 542a, 546a, 546b,
549b
Morley, I 555a, 557a

motion, I 535b, 536a,
537b–538a, 539b, 542a,
543a–544a, 545a–546b,
548a–550a, 551a, 556b,
557a, 557b, 558b, 559a,
560b
music, III 260b, 268a, 268b,
269a, 270b, 271a, 271b
mythology, III 273a, 281b,
294a, 309a, 311a, 314b
Nature, I 542b, 543b, 556b,
558b; III 347b, 351a
Neo-Platonism, I 543a
Neumann, I 556a
Newton, I 548a–549a,
549b–550a, 550b, 553b,
554b–558b, 560b
Nicholas of Cusa, I 545a;
IV 306a
non-Euclidean geometries,
I 55a–55b, 559a–559b,
563a
numbers, I 537b–538a
numerical tables, I 537b–
538a
Olbers, I 552a, 555b–556a
Olbers paradox, I 555b–
556a
optics, I 554b, 556b, 557a,
557b
Oresme, I 544a
Parmenides, III 179b
Patrizzi, I 545a
Peebles, I 567a
Peirce, I 552b; III 558b,
559b, 561a, 562a
Penzias, I 567a
perfect cosmological principle, I 567b–568a
perfectibility, III 464a
perennial philosophy, III
459b
periodization in history, III
476b
Persia (ancient), I 536b
Philolaus, I 539b
photography, I 552b
physics, I 554a–554b,
555a, 556a–561b
Pico della Mirandola, IV
145b
planets, I 538a–552b
Plato, I 539b, 543a, 552b,
578b–579a, 624b; III 512a;
IV 39a–39b, 41b, 368b
Platonism, III 510b–511a,
512a
Pliny the Elder, I 541a
pragmatism, III 558b, 559b,
561a, 562a
prophecy, I 538a
psychology, IV 2a
pulsars, I 570a

Ptolemy, I 541a–542b, 543a, 544a–544b, 546a
Pythagoreans, I 539b; IV 38b, 39a–39b, 41b
quantum theory, I 555a, 568a
quasars, I 568a
radiation, I 550b, 553a–553b, 555a, 556a, 567a, 567b, 568a, 569b
radio sources, I 568a
rainfall, I 536b
rationalism, IV 46a
reformation, IV 60b, 61a
reincarnation, I 644b–645a
relativity, I 555a, 556a–559b; IV 89b
Renaissance, IV 134a, 134b, 139b, 145b, 440b, 442b
Riemann, I 555a
Robertson, I 562b, 563a, 565b
Roberval, I 546a, 548a
Roemer, I 551b
Roll, I 567a
Rome (ancient), I 544b
Sandage, I 565a, 567b
seasons, I 535b–536a, 540a, 544a
Seeliger, I 556a
Seneca, I 545a
Shapley, I 562a
Slipher, I 562a
solar years, I 547a
spectroscopy, I 553a
stars, I 535b, 536a, 537a–537b, 541a–541b, 542b, 543a, 544b–545a, 546b, 549a–549b, 550a–552a, 553b, 555b–556a, 566b, 569b–570a
Stoics, I 622b–623a
sun, I 535b, 536a, 543b, 545b, 546a, 547a, 551a, 552a
symmetry, IV 349a, 349b, 350b, 352b
technology, IV 364a
telescopes, I 546b
Telesio, I 545a
Teller, I 568b
temperance, IV 368b
theodicy, IV 380a, 382b, 383a
Tolman, I 565b
Tombaugh, I 552b
universal man, IV 440b, 442b
universe, I 536b, 541b, 542b, 544b, 545b, 554b–556a, 559b–562b, 568b, 569a; IV 38b–39b, 41b
urbanization, I 537a

Urey, I 570a
Venus, I 538a, 539a, 540a, 540b–541a, 542a, 542b, 544b, 546b
Xenophanes, I 539a–539b
zoology, I 230a
See also Cosmos, names of planets, Space, Time
Cosmopolitanism
Christianity, III 586b
Counter-enlightenment, II 106a
Herder, III 326a
nationalism, III 325a, 325b, 326b, 329b, 331a
primitivism, III 586b
Rousseau, II 276a
Stoicism, III 586b
Cosmos
allegory, I 46a
analogy, I 60b–63a, 65b
Anaxagoras, III 573b; IV 3a, 50a
Anaximander, III 573b
Aristotle, II 163a; IV 50b
Christianity, II 338a, 341b–343a, 345a, 349b
Copernicus, II 442b
Crooke, II 439b
cycles, I 621b–624b
Democritus, IV 3a
Digges, II 442b
dignity, IV 136b, 139a, 139b, 143a
equality, II 138b, 140a
eschatology, II 160a
evil, II 162b–163b; IV 413b, 414a
evolution, I 549b–550a; II 447b
evolutionism, II 174b, 178b, 179a, 181b, 182b, 184a, 184b, 185a, 188a
as finite, I 541a–543a, 544b, 545a
fortune, fate, and chance, II 226a
free will, II 243b, 244a
Gnosticism, II 329b
God, II 334a–336a, 338b, 340a–341a
good, IV 176a, 181a
Greece (ancient), III 94b
harmony, II 388a, 389a, 389b; III 270b; IV 38a–42a
Hegel, II 583a
Heraclitus, III 573b; IV 297b
hermeticism, II 432a, 433a
hierarchy, II 436a, 436b, 439a, 439b, 442b, 443b, 445a, 445b, 446b, 447b

Homer, IV 297b
human nature, III 573b
humanism, IV 131a
impressionism, II 583a
indeterminacy, II 586b
India (ancient), IV 104a
infinity, I 543b, 544b, 545a; II 604b, 606b, 608a
Kant, II 447b
Kepler, II 443b
Locke, II 446b
love, III 94a, 94b, 106b
macrocosm and microcosm, III 126a–129b
metaphor, III 198b, 199a, 199b
Middle Ages, IV 153a
mind, IV 50a
motif, III 239a
motion, IV 50b
music, II 388a, 389a, 389b; III 265a, 268b, 269a, 270b
mythology, III 273a, 287a, 287b, 290b, 315a
natural law, III 14b, 15a
naturalism in art, III 342b
numbers, III 269a
philosophy, III 198b, 199a, 199b
Plato, I 586b; II 162b–163a; IV 34a, 35b, 37b, 39a, 39b, 50a–50b
Platonism, III 510a
Plotinus, II 163a–163b
Plutarch, IV 38b
Porphyry, III 129a
primitivism, III 587b
prophecy, III 664b, 665a–665b, 668a, 668b
psychology, IV 2a, 2b, 3a
Pythagoras, I 579b; IV 39a, 47a, 50a
Pythagoreans, IV 34a, 35a–42a
rationalism, IV 46a, 47a, 50a–51a
reformation, IV 60b
regeneration, IV 60b
religion, IV 104a
Renaissance, IV 132b, 136b, 139a, 139b, 143a
revolution, IV 153a
right, IV 176a, 181a
romanticism, IV 201b
sin and salvation, IV 224b
socialism, IV 286b
space, IV 297b–298a
Spinoza, II 445a, 445b
spontaneous generation, IV 310a
Stoicism, I 62a–62b; II

340b; III 588a; IV 50a, 50b, 176a
tragic sense, IV 413b, 414a, 414b, 416b
See also Cosmology
Cossa, Francesco (1438?–1480), iconography, II 535b–536a
Costa, Ignatius da, China, I 356a
Cotes, Roger (1682–1716), Newton and, III 378b
Cotta, Bernhard (1808–1879), Hegel and, II 411b
Cotton, Charles (1630–1687), mountains in literature, III 254a
Cotton, John (1584–1652), Puritanism, IV 18a
Coulomb, C. A. (1736–1806), mathematics, III 179a
Council of Basel, I 386b
Council of Chalcedon, I 416b
Council of Constance, I 386a–386b, 399b
Council of Constantinople, I 377b
Council of Europe, III 113a
Council of Ferrara, I 386b
Council of Nicaea, I 416b
Council of Pisa, I 386b
Council of Trent, I 393b, 394a; IV 116b, 117a, 119a
Faust (legend), III 246b
heresy, II 425a, 427b–428a
iconography, II 531a
Counter-Enlightenment, II 100b–112b
Agrippa, II 101a
anthropology, II 103a
Antiphon, II 101a
aristocracy, II 107a
Aristotle, II 101a, 102b
art, II 101b–102a, 104a, 105b, 107a, 108b–109a, 109b
Asia, II 101b, 105b
Austria, II 106a
barbarism, II 103a, 105b
Batteux, II 109a
beauty, II 103a
Bengel, II 105a
Bergson, II 104b, 108b
Bible, II 103b, 104b, 105b
Blake, II 107a, 108a
Bodin, II 101b
Boileau, II 109a
Bonald, II 110a, 111b

Büchner, II 110a
Burke, II 104b, 106b–107a
Byron, II 109a, 110a
Carlyle, II 108b
Cartesianism, II 102a
Charron, II 101b
Chateaubriand, II 110a
Christianity, II 101b, 102a, 102b, 103b, 105b, 110a–112a
Cobbett, II 109b–110a
Coleridge, II 108b, 109b–110a
communication, II 103b
Condillac, II 103a, 107b
Condorcet, II 101b, 106a
cosmopolitanism, II 106a
creativity in art, II 108b–109a
Critias, II 101a
culture, II 102a, 102b–103a, 103b, 105b–106a, 109a
d'Alembert, II 101b
Descartes, II 101b, 109b
Diderot, II 106a
drama, II 107a, 108a
Elizabethan Age, II 101b
ethics, II 101a
existentialism, II 109b
faith, II 101b, 104a, 108b
family, II 110b
Fichte, II 108b
France, II 101a, 103b, 104b–107a, 108a, 109a–112a
Francke, II 105a
Frederick the Great, II 103b, 104b, 106b
free will, II 107b–108a
freedom, II 102a, 106b, 108a
French Revolution, II 109b–110a, 112a
Galileo, II 109b
genius, II 109a
Germany, II 103b, 104b, 106a–106b, 107a, 108a–109b
Gerstenberg, II 107a
God, II 102a, 102b, 103b, 104a, 108b, 111b
Goethe, II 104a, 107a, 108b
Great Britain, II 105a, 105b, 107a
Greece (ancient), II 101a, 102b, 103a, 111a
Hamann, II 103b–105a, 108b, 109b
happiness, II 101a, 102a, 108a
Hegel, II 108b
Heinse, II 107a–107b
Helvétius, II 106a, 107b,

110a
Herder, II 107a
history, II 102b–103a, 104b, 109a, 110a–110b, 111b
Holbach, II 106a, 107a, 110a
Homer, II 103a
Hugo, II 109a
human nature, II 101a, 108a, 111a
Hume, II 101b, 103b–104a, 109b, 110a
Hungary, II 106a
India, II 105b
individualism, II 111b
Italy, II 107a
Jacobean Age, II 101b
Jacobi, II 104b, 108b
Jansenism, II 101b
Judaism, II 102b
Kant, II 103b, 104a, 107b–108a, 109b
Kierkegaard, II 109b
Klinger, II 107a
knowledge, II 100b, 101b, 103b–104a, 104b, 108a
language, II 105a
Lavater, II 104a, 107a
law, II 102a, 102b, 106b, 108a
Leibniz, II 103a
Leisewitz, II 107a
Lenz, II 107a
literature, II 101b, 107a–107b
Locke, II 108a
logic, II 101b
Louis XIV, II 106b, 111b
Louis XVI, II 110b, 111b
Lutheranism, II 103b, 105b
Mably, II 102a
Maistre, II 110a–111b
mathematics, II 101b, 103a
Michelet, II 103a
Montaigne, II 101b
Montesquieu, II 101b, 103a, 109b
morality, II 101a, 105b, 107b, 108a, 110
Möser, II 104b, 106b, 107a
Müller, II 109b–110a
mythology, II 102b
nationalism, II 105b–106a, 109a
natural law, II 101a, 102a, 102b, 105a, 107b–108a
natural sciences, II 101b, 103a, 105a, 110a
Nature, II 101a, 102a–102b, 105a, 108b, 110a–110b
Newton, II 101a, 108a
Nietzsche, II 109b

Novalis, II 109b
Palestine, II 106b
Peter I (the Great), II 110b
philosophy, II 103a, 111a
Pietism, II 103b, 105a
Plato, II 103a, 108b
pluralism, II 103a, 106a
poetry, II 102b, 103a, 104b
politics, II 101a, 107a, 111b
positivism, II 107b
Protagoras, II 101a
Protestantism, II 101b, 102a, 103b
Prussia, II 103b, 104b
reason, II 100b, 104b, 106b, 107b, 110b
religion, II 100b, 101b, 102a, 102b, 105b, 106b–107a
Reynolds, II 108b–109a
Robespierre, II 111a–111b
Roman Catholic Church, II 101b, 102a, 110a–112a
romanticism, II 108b–110a
Rome (ancient), II 101b, 102b, 105b, 111a
Rousseau, II 102a, 104b–105a, 107b, 109b, 110a, 111a
Russell, II 103a
Russia, II 106a
Sade, II 107b
Sand, II 110a
Schelling, II 104b, 108b
Schiller, II 107a, 108a–108b
Schlegel, II 109b–110a
Schopenhauer, II 108b, 109b
Schubart, II 107a
science, II 101a, 101b–102a, 104a, 104b, 106b
Shaftesbury, II 104b
Shakespeare, II 104b
Shelley, II 110a
sin, II 110a
skepticism, II 101a–101b
society, II 101b, 102a, 102b–103a, 105a, 110a, 111a–112a
sociology, II 106b
Sophists, II 101a, 110b
Spinoza, II 108b
soul, II 103b
State, II 101a, 106b, 107a, 110b
Stirner, II 109b
Tieck, II 109b
travel, II 101b
truth, II 101a, 102a, 102b, 103a, 104b–105a
Turkey, II 106a
tyranny, II 106b

U.S., II 101b
universe, II 103a, 103b, 108b, 109b
utilitarianism, II 102b
Vico, II 102a–103b, 105b
virtue, II 101a, 102a, 106b, 108a
Voltaire, II 101b, 104b, 106a, 106b
wisdom, II 101a, 108a
Wordsworth, II 108b
Young, II 104b
zoology, II 110a
Counterpoint, II 314b, 316b, 319a, 321a–321b, 322b
Counter-Reformation, I 392b–395a
Canisius, I 394b
capitalism, III 480b
determinism, II 30b
Duke of Bavaria, I 395a
eschatology, II 157a
Faust (legend), III 246a
Habsburgs, I 394b
heresy, II 427a
iconography, II 526b, 532b, 538b
Jesuits, I 393a, 393b, 394b
Lutheranism, I 393a–393b, 394a, 395a
mythology, III 293a
papacy, I 394b–395a
perennial philosophy, III 457b
periodization in history, III 480b
poetry, III 529b, 530b
Reformation, IV 66a
religion, IV 116b
Renaissance, IV 126a; IV 130a, 135a
Spain, I 392b–395a
universal man, IV 442a, 442b
Wittelsbachs, I 394b
Counting, III 400b–401a, 402a, 403b, 405b
Couplet, Philippe, China, I 356b, 358b, 359a
Courage
ethics, IV 320b
fortune, fate and chance, II 234a
good, IV 174b
human nature, III 572a
loyalty, III 110a, 110b
Plato, III 110a
right, IV 174b
Stoicism, IV 320b
temperance, IV 366b, 368b, 369b, 370a
virtue, IV 366b, 368b, 371b
virtù, IV 477a, 477b, 478b, 484b

Courbet, Gustave (1819–1877)
concrete art, III 343a
Degas and, II 571a, 571b
impressionism, II 571a, 571b, 573a, 575b, 578a, 581b, 583a
individualism, II 298b
mimesis, III 229b
naturalism, II 583a; III 229b, 343a
painting, III 343a
politics, II 583a
realism in literature, IV 52a

Cournot, Antoine Augustin (1801–1877)
causation, I 283b–284a
chance, I 339b
classification of the sciences, I 465a–465b
economic history, II 57a
history, I 283b–284a
indeterminacy, II 587a
periodization in literary history, III 485b
probability, III 614b, 615a, 615b
progress, III 643a
utility, IV 452b

Courtenay, J. Baudoin de (1845–1929), linguistics, III 71a

Courtesy, love, III 102b

Courtly love, III 97b–100a, 101b, 102a, 102b, 103a, 104a, 107b

Courts, II 676b, 679b, 686a, 686b, 687b, 688b–689a; III 2a, 7a
common law, II 692a, 693a, 693b, 694a, 694b, 696a; III 31a, 32a
Greece (ancient), II 676b, 679b
law, III 15a, 27b–28a, 30a, 30b, 31a, 32a, 32b, 33b
pragmatism, III 566a, 567b
Rome (ancient), II 686a, 686b, 687b, 688b–689a

Courtship
love, III 95b, 99a, 100a
Platonism, III 95b

Cousin, Victor (1792–1867)
beauty, I 198a
Charles X and, III 533b
Comte and, III 533b–534a, 534b
eclecticism, III 533b
French Restoration, III 533b
Hegel and, II 411b
intellectualism, III 533b
liberalism, III 533b
morality, III 533b

natural science, III 534a
philosophy, III 533b
Platonism, III 521b, 522a
politics, III 533b
positivism, III 533b–534a, 534b, 538a, 538b
psychology, III 533b; IV 11b
spiritualism, III 534a

Couture, Thomas (1815–1879), as academic painter, II 570a

Covenant
Judaism, I 396a; II 656a, 656b, 657a
justice, II 656a, 656b, 657a
Middle Ages, III 112a
Puritanism, I 396a
social contract, I 396a; IV 251b, 252a, 252b, 254b

Covenanters, Augustinianism, IV 109a

Cowley, Abraham (1618–1667), harmony, II 390a, 391b

Cowper, Lord (1834–1905)
equity, II 153b
romanticism, IV 194b, 195a

Cox, George William (1827–1902), mythology, III 308a

Cox, Harvey, faith, hope, and charity, II 214b

Coxe, John, historiography, II 492a

Cozens, Alexander (d. 1786), chance images, I 349a–351b, 352b, 353a, 353b

Crackanthorpe, M. H., war, IV 504b

Craen, Nicolaus, music, II 316a, 319a

Craftsmanship
Aristotle, III 15b; IV 50b
art, I 456b, 457a, 458b, 459a, 459b, 460a, 461b
communism, III 653a
economic history, II 54b
genius, II 300a, 319b, 321b–322a, 323b
humanism, IV 133a, 134b
individualism, II 300a
Man-Machine, III 134b
matter, III 187a
mimesis, III 226a
music, II 319b, 321b–322a, 323b
optics, III 411a–411b, 420a
private property, III 652a
protest movements, III 672b, 674b
Ramism, IV 45a, 45b
rationalism, IV 46b, 49a, 50b
Renaissance, IV 133a,

134b, 437b, 441b
U.S.S.R., III 653b, 655a
universal man, IV 437b, 441b

Cramér, H. (1704–1752), probability, III 618b

Crane, H. R. (1907–   ), DNA, II 291a

Crane, Hart (1899–1932), symbolism, IV 341a, 344b

Crane, R. S.
irony, II 634a
literary criticism, I 604a
romanticism, IV 195b

Crashaw, Richard (1613?–1649)
baroque in literature, I 191b, 193a, 193b, 195a
harmony, II 391b

Crates (5th century B.C.), aesthetics, II 220a
literary criticism, I 596b
pacifism, I 630b–631a
Platonism, III 504a

Crates of Thebes (4th century B.C.), cynicism, I 628b, 630b–631a, 631b

Cratinus (520?–?423 B.C.), progress, III 627b

Cratippus (4th century B.C.), historiography, II 509a

Creation, I 571a–577a
alchemy, I 28a–28b, 31b–32b
Alexander, I 576a
annihilation, I 571b
Anselm, I 573a
Aristotle, I 572a, 585a
Bergson, I 576a
Berkeley, I 572b
Bible, I 571a–571b
Brightman, I 576b
Bruno, II 433b
Buddhism, II 344a
Buridan, II 34b
Calvinism, I 572b
catastrophism, IV 419b
chaos, III 281b
Christianity, I 543b, 571a–571b, 572b; III 476b, 477a
Cosmic Fall, I 505b, 506b
cosmic images, I 514b
cosmology, I 536b, 539b, 543b
creationism, I 573a–577a
Darwinism, IV 180a
Descartes, I 575a
dignity, IV 137a, 137b, 138a–139a, 140b, 142a, 144a, 145b
dualism, II 38b, 42a–42b
Egypt (ancient), I 536b
emanationism, I 572a
environment, II 127b

Erigena, I 573b–574a
evil, IV 415b
evolutionism, II 174b, 176a, 176b, 178a, 180a
ex nihilo, I 571a–573a, 575b–577a
fortune, fate, and chance, II 226a, 226b, 231a
freedom, I 571b, 575b, 576b
genetic continuity, II 281b
genius, II 293b
Gilson, I 574b
God, I 573a–577a; II 336a, 336b, 338b, 339a, 340a, 343b, 344a, 345a, 357a
good, IV 176b
Greece (ancient), I 571a, 571b–572a
harmony, IV 38b, 39a
Hartshorne, I 576a
hermeticism, II 431b–432a, 432b, 433a, 433b
hierarchy, II 438a, 439b, 445a, 447b
historiography, II 471a–471b
immortality, I 571b
India (ancient), I 571a
infinity, II 605b
Islam, I 571a, 571b; II 345a
Judaism, I 536b, 571a–571b
Kant, II 447b
Leibniz, I 572b; II 166a
linguistics, IV 423b, 424a, 426a
love, III 94a, 94b, 106b
Lucretius, I 573a
MacQuarrie, I 575b–576a
matter, II 186b, 190b, 193a
mechanics and science, II 196b
Mesopotamia (ancient), I 536b
millenarianism, III 224a, 224b, 225a
monism, I 571a, 572a, 572b
motif, II 239a
mountains in literature, III 254a–254b, 256a
music, III 265a, 268b, 271a
mythology, III 276a, 277a, 278a, 278b, 281b, 284a, 284b
Nature, I 572b, 574a, 574b–575a
pantheism, I 571a
perennial philosophy, III 459b, 460b

periodization in history, III 476b, 477a
Philo Judaeus, I 571b
Pico della Mirandola, IV 145b
Plato, I 539b, 571b–572a, 622b; IV 39a
Platonism, III 512a
Plotinus, I 572a
primitivism, III 593a
Protestantism, I 572b
Pythagoreans, IV 38b, 39a
rationalism, IV 46b
religion, IV 93b, 104b
Renaissance, IV 137a–140b, 142a, 144a, 145b
right, IV 176b
Saint Augustine, I 571b, 573a–573b, 575a; IV 138a–139a, 381a, 392a
Saint Thomas Aquinas, I 574a–574b; IV 392a
Schelling, IV 202a
socialism, IV 287b
soul, I 571b
Spinoza, I 572a; II 445a
spontaneous generation, IV 308b, 310a
symmetry, IV 349a, 350b
temporalistic personalists, I 576a 577a
Tennant, I 574b–575b, 576a
theism, I 571a–576a
theodicy, IV 381a, 381b
Thomism, I 572b, 574b–575b
Tillich, I 575b
time, IV 392a, 393a, 394b
tragic sense, IV 415b
uniformitarianism, IV 419b, 423b, 424a, 426a
U.S. Declaration of Independence, I 571a
universe, IV 38b, 39a
Ussher, II 176b
Ward, I 573b
Whitehead, I 576a
Creativity in art, I 577b–589b
Addison, I 587b, 588a
aesthetics, I 587a, 588a
Agatharchos, I 582a
Albertus Magnus, I 585b
Alexander of Aphrodisias, I 580b
Apelles, I 582a
Apollodorus, I 582a
architecture, I 581a
Aristotle, I 578a, 578b, 580a–580b, 583b, 584b–585b
Asclepius (cult), I 578b
atomism, I 583b

beauty, I 578b, 579a, 580a, 580b, 581a, 581b, 583a–584b, 585b, 586a
Blake, I 579b, 587b
Boutades, I 580b, 581a
canon of proportions, I 580a, 581b, 582a
chiaroscuro, I 582a
Childe, I 582a
Christianity, I 585b, 586b
Cleanthes, I 580b
Coleridge, I 587b
Collingwood, I 582a, 588b
Counter-Enlightenment, II 108b–109a
criticism, I 586b–588a, 588b
Croce, I 588a–588b
de Chirico, I 583a
Duff, I 588a
Dürer, I 580a
Egypt (ancient), I 580a, 580b, 581a
Empedocles, I 578b, 579a
Euphranor, I 582a
Euripides, I 585a–585b
Eurytos, I 580a–580b, 581a
Expressionism, I 588b
freedom, I 577b–578a, 578b, 582b, 583a, 584a, 585a, 586b, 588a
genius, I 577b, 578a, 584b, 585b, 586b–588b
God, I 577b–579a, 580a, 585b, 586a–587b
Grant, I 585a
Greece (ancient), I 578a–585b, 586a
harmony, I 579a–579b, 580b
Hauser, I 582a
Heraclitus, I 578b, 582a–582b
Hindemith, I 579b
Holst, I 579b
Hume, I 588a
Hutcheson, I 588a
imagination, I 586a, 586b, 588a
immortality, I 584a
inspiration, I 583b–584a
Judaism, I 585b, 586b
Kames, I 587b–588a
Kant, I 588a, 588b
Kepler, I 579b
Le Corbusier, I 580a
Leonardo da Vinci, I 580a, 585b
Leucippus, I 583b
Longinus, I 586a
Lucretius, I 584b
Lysippus, I 582a
macrocosm and microcosm, I 586b

Maritain, I 585b
mathematics, I 580a–581a, 583b, 584a, 584b
mimetic art, I 581a–581b, 582b–583a, 584a, 585a, 586a
music, I 578b, 579a, 581a, 584b
Nietzsche, I 588b
painting, I 580b–582a
perspective, I 580a, 582a, 582b
Phidias, I 581b, 582a, 586a
Philo Judaeus, I 578a, 586b
Philokles, I 580b
Philolaus, I 580a
Philostratus, I 578a, 586a
Plato, I 578a–584b, 585a, 586a, 586b, 587b, 588a
pleasure, I 585a
Pliny, I 580b
Plotinus, I 586a, 586b
Polycleitean Canon, I 580a, 581a
Polycleitus, I 581b
Pope, I 588a
Praxiteles, I 586a
Puttenham, I 587a–587b
Pythagoras, I 578b, 579a–581a
Renaissance, I 585b
Saint Augustine, I 578a, 579b, 586b–587a
Saint Thomas Aquinas, I 585b
Schiller, I 578a
sculpture, I 580b, 581a–582a
Shaftesbury, I 588a
Shorey, I 586b
Socrates, I 578b, 581b–582a, 583b
Sophists, I 578b, 582a–582b
soul, I 586a
Spingarn, I 588b
Swindler, I 582a
technique, I 577b, 578a–578b, 583b, 584a, 585a, 585b, 586a, 588b
Theophrastus, I 584b
tragedy, I 578b, 584b, 585a–585b
transcendentalism, I 578b, 583b, 584a–584b
ugliness, I 585a, 586a–586b
universe, I 580a
Webb, I 588a
Xenophon, I 581b
Yeats, I 579b
Young, I 587b
Creel, H. G., China, I 369a

Cremer, William Randal (1838–1908), international peace, III 448b
Creon (myth)
law, II 682b
tragic sense, IV 412b
Crescas, Hasdai, infinity, II 605a
Crete (ancient)
assemblies, II 258a
constitutions, II 254a
freedom of speech, II 254a
God, II 333a, 333b
mythology, III 272a, 272b, 275b
temperance, IV 366a
Creuzer, F. (1771–1858),
iconography, II 535a
mythology, III 305a, 306a, 306b
Platonism, III 521b
Crick, F. H. C. (1906–   ),
DNA, II 289b–291a, 291b
Crime
disease and health, II 400b
economic history, II 51b
Egypt (ancient), IV 225b
Enlightenment, II 89b
ethics, IV 70a
Great Britain, I 71b
Netherlands, I 71b
phrenology, IV 23b
psychology, IV 23b
recapitulation, IV 58a
relativism, IV 70a
sin, IV 225b
totalitarianism, IV 410b
U.S., I 71b
Utopia, IV 463b
witchcraft, IV 521a, 522a, 522b
Crisis in history, I 589b–596a
capitalism, I 590b–591a; III 164a
China, I 594a
communism, I 592a
culture, I 591a–591b, 592b, 594a–595a
economy, I 590a–591a, 593a
English Revolution, I 593a
eschatology, I 591a
fascism, I 592a
French Revolution, I 590a, 591b, 593a
genius, I 595b
genuine, I 591b, 592b
Germany, I 591a, 591b, 592b, 593b, 595a
Great Britain, I 592b, 593a
Industrial Revolution, I 590a
invasions, I 591a, 591b

Luther, I 592b
Malthus, I 590a
Marx, I 590b–591a, 593b–594a
meaning of the term, I 589b–590a
medicine, I 589b–590a, 594a
Metternich, I 591a
Middle Ages, I 592b
migrations, I 591a, 594a
Nazism, I 593b
Nietzsche, I 591a
Ottoman Turks, I 591a
Paine, Tom, I 590a
Reformation, I 591b, 592b
Renaissance, I 592b–593a, 594b
Renan, I 592a
revolution, I 590a, 591b–592a, 593a–593b
romanticism, I 594b–595a
Rome (ancient), I 591a, 591b, 592a
Russian Revolution (October 1917), I 593a, 593b
Saint-Simon, I 590a
Say, I 590a
Schumpeter, I 590b
as a sign of vitality, I 592a
Sismondi, I 590a
Spain, I 593b, 595a
Spengler, I 595a
surface, I 591b
technology, I 594a
test of, I 592a
Tocqueville, I 591a
U.S., I 590a, 593a, 593b, 594a
urbanization, I 594a
war, I 591b, 593b–594a, 594b
World War I, I 594b, 595b
World War II, I 595a
Critias (5th century B.C.),
Counter-Enlightenment, II 101a
deism, I 647b
God, III 575a
law, III 575a
progress, III 626b
Criticism
conventionalism, III 353b
creativity in art, I 586b–588a, 588b
Croce, I 588b
ethics, IV 321b
evolution of literature, II 172b–173a, 173b
Faust (legend), III 250b, 252b
France, II 575b–576a

genius, II 316a–316b, 318a, 325a
Goethe, III 237a
historiography, II 476a–479b, 480b, 481b, 484b–486a, 487b, 490a–492a, 499a, 500a
humanism, II 516a, 518b
iconography, II 534a–540b
impressionism, II 572b, 573a, 573b, 574b, 575b–576a, 577a, 581a
irony, II 629a, 632b–634b
law, II 676b
linguistics, III 73a–75a
literary paradox, III 77b
literature, III 82b, 83a, 84b, 86a; IV 332a, 333a
Marxism, III 146b, 147b, 168b, 169b
mathematics, III 179b
metaphor, III 205b, 206b, 207a
metaphysical imagination, III 210a, 216a, 219b, 220a, 221b
motif, III 237a, 238a, 241b, 242b
music, II 316a–316b, 318a, 325a
mythology, III 273a, 274a, 274b
naturalism in art, III 339b, 343b, 346a
New Critics, III 77b
Nietzsche, I 588b
Pater, II 575b, 576a
Plato, III 499a, 507a
Platonism, III 496a, 499a, 507a, 521b, 523a
poetry, III 527b, 529a, 530b, 531a, 531b
Porphyry, III 376b
positivism, III 550b
religion, III 205b, 206b, 207a; IV 107a, 107b, 11b
romanticism, IV 208a
Schlegel, IV 208a
social contract, IV 254a–254b, 261b
Stoicism, IV 321b
style, III 297b
totalitarianism, IV 406b, 408b, 409a
utilitarianism, IV 446b, 447a, 448b, 449b
Utopia, IV 462b
See also Literary Criticism
Crito (fl. 5th century B.C.),
death, I 638b, 642a
immortality, I 638b

Critodemus (1st century A.D.),
astrology, I 121a
Croce, Benedetto (1866–1952)
art and play, I 103b
baroque in literature, I 191b–192a, 194b
beauty, I 207b
creativity in art, I 588a
criticism, I 588b
empathy, II 87a
evolution of literature, II 172b
genius, I 588b; II 293b
historicism, II 457b, 461b, 462a
iconography, II 540a
language, I 588a–588b
literary criticism, I 605b–606a
literature, III 88a
Marxism, III 165a
motif, III 238b, 241b
organicism, III 425b, 426a
perennial philosophy, III 462a, 462b
pragmatism, III 564a
progress, III 638a
realism in literature, IV 55a
time, IV 394a
ut pictura poesis, IV 471a
Vico and, III 638a
Croesus, King (d. 576 B.C.),
historiography, II 500b
Croll, James (1821–1890),
cosmic images, I 523a
Croll, Morris W., baroque in literature, I 193b
Crollius, Oswald (1560–1609), hierarchy, II 435b
Crombie, A. C.
methodology, III 381b, 382a
science and mechanics, II 197a
Crombie, I. M., Platonism, III 523a
Crome, John (Old) (1768–1821), impressionism, II 579a
Cromwell, Oliver (1599–1658)
constitutionalism, I 491a
equality, II 142b
heresy, II 428a
Machiavellism, III 120a
revolution, IV 153b
social contract, IV 255a
Cronus (myth), III 274a, 308a, 309a
culture, I 608a, 609a

historiography, II 506b
law, II 674b, 675b, 677b
primitivism, III 578a, 578b–579a, 579b, 580a, 581a
progress, III 624b, 627b
religion, IV 93a
wisdom, I 612a
Crooke, Helkiah
cosmos, II 439b
hierarchy, II 436a–436b
Crosnier, A., iconography, II 535a
Cross, R.
common law, III 31b
Middle Ages, II 527a
Crucé, Émeric, international peace, III 452b
Crucifixion
history, III 276a
Jesus Christ, II 470b, 477b; III 276a, 281b, 282a, 283a; IV 402a
mythology, III 276a, 277a, 281b, 282a, 283a
Cruciger, Kaspar (1507–1548), language, II 671a
Cruelty
ethics, IV 72a
Machiavelli, IV 480a
Montaigne, III 594b
motif, III 239b
primitivism, III 594b
relativism, IV 72a
theater, I 208a
virtù, IV 480a
Crusades, I 418a
Albigensian, II 423a
beginning of, II 473a
Christianity, I 383a
First, I 382b, 410a
Fourth, I 410a
Innocent III (Pope), I 383a
international peace, III 452b
intolerance, IV 113b
Islam, II 651a
love, III 99b
Middle Ages, II 423a, 473a; III 452b
prophecy, III 666a
religion, IV 113b
Roman Catholic Church, I 383a
romanticism, IV 203b
war, III 452b
Crusius, Christian August (1758–1831), I 93a
aesthetics, IV 356a
causation, I 301a
taste, IV 356a
teleology, I 301a
Crusoe economy, II 52a, 52b, 53a–53b, 54b

Cruz, Gaspar da, China, I 354b

Cruz Costa, João, nationalism, III 335b

Cryptography
mythology, III 289b–290a
Renaissance, IV 441b
universal man, IV 441b

Ctesias (5th century B.C.), progress, III 628a

Ctesibios (2nd century B.C.), Man-Machine, III 134a

Cuba, III 544b
positivism, III 544b
primitivism, III 593b
revolution, IV 165a
U.S., III 565b
war, III 544b

Cubism, II 534a
Cézanne, II 207a
chance images, I 352a
expressionism, II 206b, 207a, 208b
iconography, II 534a
perspective, IV 302a
space, IV 302a
symbolism, IV 345b
ut pictura poesis, IV 470b, 475b

Cudworth, Ralph (1617–1688)
atomism, I 137a
design argument, I 674a
ethics, III 441a–441b
hierarchy, II 444a
Nature, II 444a
Neo-Platonism, III 506a
peace, III 441a–441b
Platonism, III 506b, 517a

Cujas, Jacques, law, III 3b

Culbertson, M. S., China, I 367b

Cullen, William (1710–1790), disease, II 400a

Cullmann, Oscar, eschatology, II 157b
God, II 363a

Cults
Bible, III 276b, 277a, 282a, 284a
holy, II 512b
human nature, III 573a
mimesis, III 226a
mythology, III 272b, 276b, 277a, 282a, 284a, 287b, 309a, 311b, 313b–314b
perfectibility, III 464b
phrenology, IV 23b
Platonism, III 505a
psychology, IV 23b
Pythagoreans, III 505a
Virgin Mary (Bible), III 107a

Cultural evolutionism, II 175a–175b, 178b, 181a, 184a, 184b, 187a

Culture, III 177b–185a
Aeschylus, I 608b; III 625b, 626a
agriculture, I 609b, 611a–611b
Albertus Magnus, II 129a
Anaxagoras, I 609a, 610b
animals, III 596a
anthropology, I 618b, 619a
antiquity, I 607b–613b
Arbuthnot, II 129b
Archelaus, I 609a
architecture, I 610b
Argentina, III 543b
Argonauts, I 608b
Aristotle, I 355a, 610b–611a, 611b, 612b; III 629b
Arnold, I 617b
art, I 612a, 616a, 621a; II 297b, 298b, 311a, 567b, 577a, 580b, 581b, 582b, 583a; IV 165b
artifacts, I 618b
astronomy, I 608b
atomism, I 610b
Augustus, I 612b
barbarism, I 620a
Basil the Great, II 127b
Bible, II 127b, 128b
biogeography, II 131b
biology, I 609a
birth, I 614a
Bodin, II 129a–129b
Bolshevism, IV 165b
Brazil, III 542b
Brecht, IV 165b
Brunhes, II 131a
Buckle, I 620a–620b; II 130a, 131b
Buffon, II 129b, 132b
Burckhardt, I 591a–591b
burial, I 614a
Burke, I 619b
causation, I 611b
Chapman, III 294b
China, I 354b–355a, 355b
China (Communist), I 372b; III 334a, 334b; IV 166a
Christianity, II 132a–132b
Cicero, I 613b; II 127b
city, I 612b, 616b–617b
class, III 150b
climate, I 616a
Coleridge, I 617b
Collingwood, I 616a
common law, II 692a
common-origin theory, I 614a–616b
communication, I 608b
communism, IV 165b
Comte, I 620a
Condorcet, I 619b–620a
content of, I 616b–619a
continuity, I 619a
cosmology, I 609a
Counter-Enlightenment, II 102a–103b, 105b–106a, 109a
Creation, II 127b
crisis in history, I 591a–591b, 592b, 594a–595a
Cronus, I 608a, 609a
cyclical development theory, I 618a
Daedalus, I 608b
Darwin, II 130b, 133a
Darwinism, II 130b
Demeter, I 608b
Democritus, I 610b, 611a, 611b, 612b–613a
Derham, II 132a
determinism, I 609b, 611b; II 22a–22b
development of, I 619a–621a
Dewey, III 555b, 556b
Dicaearchus, I 611a–611b
Dickens, II 133b
Diderot, I 616b
dignity, IV 141a, 141b, 142a, 143b
Diodorus Siculus, I 610b
disease, II 129a
ecology, II 128b, 131b, 133b
economic history, II 44b, 45b
economics, I 609b, 617b; IV 165b
Eden-motif, I 607b–608a, 612a
education, IV 165b–166a
Egypt (ancient), II 129a
Eliade, II 132a
Eliot, I 619a
Engels, I 620b
Enlightenment, I 616a–616b, 617a; II 90b, 91a, 92a, 95a, 130a
environment, II 123b–124a, 127a–134b
Epicureanism, I 610b, 611b
equality, II 141b
eschatology, II 128a
ethics, III 442b, 443b, 444a, 447a; IV 70a, 71a, 71b, 73a, 73b, 320a–320b
Euripides, I 611b; IV 367a
evolution, I 612b; II 127b, 128a, 128b, 130b, 581b; III 566b
Faust (legend), III 249a
Febvre, II 131a, 131b
Fichte, I 619a
free will, II 247a
freedom, I 615b
genius, II 297b, 298b, 311a
geography, II 129a–132a
Germany, I 613b–614a; III 250b, 252a; IV 165a, 165b
God, II 127b, 128a, 128b, 129a, 132b, 356a, 358a, 359b, 364a, 364b, 365b–366b
good, IV 173a, 174a, 174b, 180a, 180b
Gothic, II 367b–374a
Greece (ancient), I 607b–613a; II 127b, 129a; IV 367a
Gropius, IV 165a–165b
happiness, II 384a
harmony, II 128a, 128b
Hegel, I 615b–616a, 619a, 619b; III 555b, 556b, IV 180a
Herder, I 613b–614a, 615b, 616b, 617a, 618a–621a; II 105b–106a, 128a–128b; IV 203a
hermeticism, II 431b
Herodotus, II 129a
Hesiod, I 607b–608b
Hinduism, IV 231b
Hippocrates, II 129a
Hippodamus of Miletus, I 612b
historiography, II 22a–22b
history, II 22a–22b
holy, II 513b, 514a–514b
Homer, I 607b, 608a
human nature, III 574b–575a
humanism, II 515b, 520a; IV 129b, 130a, 130b
Humboldt, II 128b, 130a
Hume, II 128b, 129b
Huntington, II 131b
ideology, II 555b, 557a, 557b, 558a–558b
impiety, I 564b
impressionism, II 567b, 577a, 580b, 581b, 582b, 583a
incest, IV 327a
as an integral whole, I 616b, 618a–619a
international peace, III 451b, 456b
inventions, I 608b, 609b
Japan, III 438a
Jefferson, I 619b
Judaism, II 127b, 132a–132b
Jung, III 313a

79

Kant, I 614a, 616a, 617b, 619b; II 128b
knowledge, I 620a
language, I 610a, 611b, 615b; II 659b, 660a, 661a, 664b
Latin America, III 539b
law, II 677b; III 6a–6b, 12b, 35a
Le Roy, II 133a
Leibniz, II 128a, 130a
leisure as the basis of, I 102a
Lenin, IV 165b
love, III 94a, 100b, 104a, 104b, 106b
loyalty, III 108b, 113a–113b
Lucretius, I 610b, 611b
Lyell, II 133a
Malthus, II 128a, 130b
marriage, I 614a
Marsh, G. P., II 128a, 132b–133b
Marx, I 619b, 620a–620b; II 451a, 583a
Marxism, I 618b; III 146b, 148a, 149a, 150a, 150b; IV 165a, 165b
materialism, II 451a
mathematics, III 171a, 171b, 173a, 177a, 185a
medicine, I 608b
metaphor, III 198b, 203a, 207a
metaphysical imagination, III 210a, 212a, 222a, 222b
Mexico, III 544b
Middle Ages, I 609b; II 129a–129b, 132b
migrations, II 130b
Mill, J. S., I 619a
mind, II 129a
modern, I 613b, 621b
monasticism, I 380b
Montesquieu, I 616a, 616b; II 129b, 131b
morality, III 575a
Morris, William, II 133b
multiple-independent-origin theory, I 614a–616b, 618a
Nash, II 133b
nationalism, II 106a; III 324a, 324b, 325a, 327a, 328a, 330a, 330b, 333a, 334a, 334b, 336b, 337a
natural law, I 617a, 620b
naturalism, I 609b–610a
Nature, II 127b–128b, 130a, 132a, 132b, 133b
necessity, III 354b, 360b–361a
numbers, III 399a, 404a,

406a, 406b
order, II 128a
Orientalism, III 427b–439a
origin of, I 614a–615b
origin of the term, I 613b
painting, II 567b, 577a, 580b, 581b, 582b, 583a; IV 474a
Paley, II 127b
peace, III 442b, 443b, 444a, 447a
Peirce, III 555b
Pericles, I 612b
philanthropy, III 487a, 492b
Philip of Opus, I 611a, 611b
philosophy and, I 608b, 612a, 612b, 613a, 615b, 617a, 619b, 620a; II 127b; III 198b
Picasso, IV 165b
Plato, I 608b–609a, 611a, 611b–612b; II 127b, 129b
Platonism, I 610b; II 127b
pleasure, II 384a
pluralism, III 113a–113b
poetry, III 526a, 526b, 528a, 531b; IV 474a
politics, I 609b, 612b, 613a, 618b, 619b, 620a; III 575a; IV 165a
Polybius, I 610b; II 129a
Portugal, III 539b
Posidonius, I 611a; III 630b
positivism, III 533b, 539b, 542b, 543b, 544b
pragmatism, III 552a, 552b, 556b, 566b
Pre-Socratics, I 609a, 610b
primitivism, III 596a, 602b
private property, I 617a; III 656b
Prodicus, I 609b
progress, III 624b, 625a, 625b, 626a, 629b, 630a, 630b, 633a, 636b, 649a
Prometheus, I 608b
Protagoras, I 608b–609a, 609b
protest movements, III 671a
psychology, IV 14a, 15b, 24a, 28a, 29b
rationalism, IV 48a–48b
Ratzel, II 128a, 130b–131a, 131b
Ray, II 127b, 128a, 130a
realism, IV 165b
reformation, IV 60b–61a
Reformation, IV 68a
relativism, IV 70a, 71a, 71b, 73a, 73b
revisionism, IV 269b
revolution, IV 165a–166a
right, IV 173a, 174a, 174b,

180a, 180b
Ritter, II 128a, 130a
ritual, III 311a
romanticism, IV 198b, 201b, 203a, 205b, 208a, 208b, 209a, 210a
Rome (ancient), I 609a, 612b, 613a, 613b
Rousseau, I 616b–617a, 617b
Ruskin, II 127b, 133b
sacred, II 513b, 514a–514b
Saint Augustine, II 127b
Saint Thomas Aquinas, II 127b, 129a, 129b
Saint-Pierre, II 127b
salvation, IV 231b, 232b, 233a
Schelling, III 555b
Schlegel, I 619a
Schopenhauer, III 555b
science, I 608b, 620a, 621a; II 127b, 128a, 130a
skepticism, I 617b, 620a; IV 243a–243b, 250a
Snow, I 617b
social contract, IV 259a
Social Darwinism, II 130b
society, I 609b–610b, 612a, 612b, 615b–616a, 616b, 620a, 620b; IV 165a, 165b
sociology, I 619a
Sophism, I 608b, 609b
Sophocles, I 613a
Spain, III 539b, 544b
Spencer, IV 180b
Spengler, I 616b, 617a–617b, 619a; II 22a–22b, 131b; III 251a, 360b–361a
Spinoza, II 128b
as a state of transformation, I 607b
Stoicism, I 611a; II 127b; IV 320a–320b
Strabo, II 129a
structuralism, IV 322b, 326b, 327a–327b, 328a
technology, I 608b, 609a–609b, 611a, 611b–612b, 620a; IV 358b
Teilhard de Chardin, II 133a
teleology, I 609b, 611a–613a, 619a; II 128b, 129a
temperance, IV 367a
theodicy, IV 379b
Theophrastus, I 611b
Thucydides, I 609b
time, I 619a–619b; IV 399a
totalitarianism, IV 407a
Toynbee, I 616a, 617b, 619a; II 131b
tradition, I 621a

transcendentalism, IV 24a
Trotsky, IV 165b
Tylor, I 617b–618a
U.S.S.R., III 333b; IV 165a, 165b, 166a
U.S., III 328b, 427b–439a, 491b
unity, II 128a, 128b
unity of science, IV 431a
urbanization, I 612b, 616b, 617a, 617b
Utopia, IV 459a
Vernadsky, II 133a
versus civilization, I 616b–618a
Vico, I 614a–615b, 616b, 617a, 618a, 619b, 620a; II 102b–103a
Victorian sensibility, IV 217b, 219a, 222b
Vitruvius, I 610b
Volksgeist, IV 491b, 492b, 495a, 496a
Voltaire, I 616a–616b, 618a, 619b; II 129b
war, III 447a; IV 506a
web of life concept, II 128b, 133a
women, IV 523a, 523b, 524a
Xenophanes, I 608b; III 625a
Xenophon, I 611b
Zeus, I 608a
See also Mythology, Religion, Universal Man
Cumberland, Richard (1631–1718)
   happiness, II 380b
   natural law, III 20b
   utilitarianism, II 380b; IV 444a
Cummings, E. E. (1894–1962), *ut pictura poesis*, IV 470b
Cumont, Franz (1868–1947), iconography, II 540a
   mythology, III 292a
Cunha, Euclides da (1866–1909), nationalism, III 335b
Cupid (myth), III 290b, 297a
   neo-classicism in art, III 370b
Currier, Nathaniel (1813–1888), impressionism, II 579b
Curtis, George William (1824–1892)
   civil disobedience, I 436a
   transcendentalism, I 436a
Curtius, Ernst Robert (1886–1956)
   literary criticism, I 606a
   periodization in literary

history, **III** 484a
Cush (Bible), mythology, **III** 277b
Custom
Aristotle, **III** 629b
common law, **II** 691a, 691b, 692b, 693a, 694a–696a; **III** 30b
Democritus, **III** 575b
freedom of speech, **II** 261a
general will, **II** 277b
Germany, **II** 692b, 693a
Greece (ancient), **III** 347b
Hecataeus, **III** 575a
Herodotus, **III** 575a
human nature, **III** 574b, 575a, 575b
language, **II** 662b, 664b
law, **II** 681b–685a, 686a, 686b, 687b, 688a; **III** 3b, 6a–6b, 12a, 27b, 29b, 30b
Locke, **III** 598b
mythology, **III** 304a
natural rights, **III** 14b, 15a, 16a, 18a, 18b, 22a
Nature, **III** 346b, 347b
Orientalism, **III** 428b
Parmenides, **III** 575b
Plato, **II** 662b; **III** 15a
primitivism, **III** 598b, 599a, 603a
progress, **III** 624a 629b, 639a
rationalism, **IV** 48b
reformation, **IV** 66a
Rome (ancient), **II** 686a, 686b, 687b, 688a
Savigny, **III** 22a
skepticism, **IV** 238b, 243b, 247b, 248a
Volksgeist, **IV** 491a, 491b, 493a, 496a
Cuvier, Georges (1769–1832)
catastrophism, **IV** 419b, 420a
evolutionism, **II** 179b
linguistics, **III** 65b; **IV** 427b
literature, **III** 83a
realism in literature, **IV** 53b
uniformitarianism, **IV** 419b, 420a, 427b
Cuyp, Jacob (1594–?1651), impressionism, **II** 578a
Cybele (myth), **II** 333b; **III** 274b, 288a
Cybernetic theory
Bernard, **II** 126a
Cannon, **II** 126a
environment, **II** 126a–126b
Man-Machine, **III** 145b
Wiener, N., **II** 126a
Cycles, **I** 621b–627b

Acton, **I** 626a
Anytus, **I** 623a–623b
Aristotle, **I** 621b, 622b, 623b, 625a–625b; **IV** 391a, 400b
Asoka, **I** 622a
astronomy, **I** 621b
authoritarianism, **I** 627a
Babylonia, **I** 621b
Bible, **I** 623b
Bismarck, **IV** 157b
Christianity, **I** 622b, 623a, 623b–624b
Cicero, **I** 622b–623a
Cleanthes, **I** 623a
classicism, **I** 627a
Condorcet, **I** 625a
conservatism, **I** 627a
cosmology, **I** 621b–624b
cosmos, **I** 621b–624b
dignity, **IV** 138a
Diogenes Laërtius, **I** 623a
Egypt (ancient), **I** 625a
Empedocles, **I** 622a
Eudemus, **I** 623b
Flood, **I** 625a, 625b
fortune, fate, and chance, **II** 228a, 229b
free will, **I** 623b
French Revolution, **IV** 156a
God, **I** 623b, 624b
Great Year (myth), **IV** 401a
Greece (Ancient), **I** 621b, 622a–623b, 624b–626a
Guicciardini, **I** 626b; **IV** 150b
Hegel, **I** 627a
Heraclitus, **I** 622b
Hinduism, **IV** 232a
historiography, **IV** 148a, 150a–150b, 151b
history, **I** 52a; **II** 22a–23b, 154b,518b; **III** 624b, 627b, 628a, 630b, 633a, 640b; **IV** 148a, 150a–150b, 151b, 156a
human nature, **III** 572a
India (ancient), **I** 621b, 622a
Jesus Christ, **I** 624a
Judaism, **I** 622b, 623a, 624b
Machiavelli, **I** 626b; **IV** 150a
measurement, **IV** 399b, 400b, 401a, 402a, 403a
Meletus, **I** 623a–623b
Metternich, **IV** 157b
Middle Ages, **I** 626a
Montesquieu, **III** 640b
Moore, George, **I** 623b
music, **III** 262b
mythology, **I** 622a, 622b, 624b; **III** 290a, 291a

natural law, **III** 14b
Nietzsche, **I** 622a, 624a–624b, 626b
Origen, **I** 623b
Ovid, **I** 625a
Panaetius, **I** 623a
philosophy, **I** 622a–622b
Plato, **I** 621b, 622b, 623b, 624a, 624b–625a
Pliny, **I** 623a
Plutarch, **I** 623a
Polybius, **I** 625b–626b
progress, **III** 624b, 627b, 628a, 630b, 633a, 634a, 634b, 638a, 640b
Pythagoras, **I** 623b
Pythagoreans, **I** 621b, 623b; **IV** 31b
radicalism, **I** 627a
reformation, **IV** 60b, 61a
Renaissance, **I** 626a–626b; **IV** 138a, 148a, 150a–150b, 151b
revolution, **IV** 152b, 153b, 154a, 154b, 155a, 156a, 157b, 158a
romanticism, **I** 627a
Rome (ancient), **I** 622a–623b, 626a
Saint Augustine, **I** 624a
Saint Thomas Aquinas, **IV** 392a
salvation, **IV** 232a
Seneca, **I** 623a
Shelley, **I** 623b
skepticism, **I** 627a
Socrates, **I** 623b
Spengler, **I** 626b–627a
Stoicism, **I** 621b, 622b–624a
Tatian, **I** 623a–623b
time, **IV** 390a, 391a, 392a, 399b, 400b, 401a, 402a, 403a
Toynbee, **I** 626b–627a
Vasari, **IV** 150a
Vergil, **I** 623b
Villani, **I** 626a–626b
Volksgeist, **IV** 493a
Zeno of Citium, **I** 623a–623b
Cyclopes (myth), law, **II** 674b, 678b, 683a
Cynicism, **I** 627b–634a
Agrippa, **III** 591a
Ajax, **I** 628a
Alain of Lille, **III** 590b
Alexander the Great, **I** 628a–628b, 631b, 632a, 633b
Anaxagoras, **I** 631a
Anaximenes of Lampsacus, **I** 628a–628b
animals, **III** 585b

Antiphon, **I** 629a, 629b, 631a
Antisthenes, **I** 627b–631a, 632a–633b; **III** 585a, 590b
Aphrodite (myth), **III** 585b
Apuleius, **I** 630b
Aristotelianism, **III** 585b
art, **III** 585b
asceticism, **I** 631b–633b
atomism, **I** 631a
barbarians, **I** 629a, 632a
Bion the Borysthenite, **I** 628b, 629a, 631b
cannibalism, **III** 586a
Cercidas of Megalopolis, **I** 628b–629a
Christianity, **I** 631a; **III** 586b, 588b–591a
civilization, **III** 585b, 586b
class, **I** 629a
concord, **I** 629b
Crates of Thebes, **I** 628b, 630b–631a, 631b
Cynics, **III** 585b, 586a, 586b, 590a
Cynosarges, **I** 628a
Cyrus, **I** 632a, 633a, 633b
Dio Chrysostomus, **I** 633a–633b; **III** 586a
Diogenes of Apollonia, **I** 631a
Diogenes Laërtius, **I** 628a, 628b, 629b, 630a
Diogenes of Sinope, **I** 627b–629a, 630a–633b; **III** 585a–586b, 589b, 592b
drama, **I** 632a
Dümmler, **I** 627b
economics, **III** 586a
education, **I** 628a, 629a, 630a–631a, 632b–633a; **III** 585b
ethics, **I** 627b, 628a, 629b–630a, 633a, 633b; **IV** 320b
Eubulus, **I** 630a–630b
Euripides, **I** 630b, 632a
freedom, **I** 633a
God, **III** 585b
Golden Age (myth), **III** 586a–586b
Gorgias, **I** 628a, 629a
Greece (ancient), **I** 627b–633b; **III** 476b
happiness, **II** 375b
harmony, **I** 629b, 630a
hedonism, **I** 631b, 632a
Hercules (myth), **I** 628a, 630a, 630b, 632a–632b, 633a; **III** 590a
Herodorus of Heraclea, **I** 633a
ideology, **I** 632a–633b
incest, **III** 586a

James, William, III 563a
knowledge, I 629b
law, I 629a, 629b
Lucian, I 630b, 631b; III 586a
luxury, III 586a
morality, I 633a, 633b; III 585b
mythology, I 628a, 630a, 630b, 632a–632b
Nature, I 629a, 629b, 630a; III 347b, 585a, 586a
Odysseus, I 628a, 633a, 633b
origin of, I 627b–628a
pacifism, I 630b–631a
pain, I 632a–632b
Pericles, I 629a
periodization in history, III 476b
philosophy, III 586b
Plato, I 627b, 629b, 630a, 631b
Platonism, III 585b
pleasure, II 375b
polytheism, I 629b
pragmatism, III 563a
Protagoras, I 629a
reason, III 585b
religion, I 629a
rhetoric, I 632b
Saint Basil, III 590a–590b
science, I 631a–631b; III 585b
Seneca, III 588b, 590b
slavery, I 630a–630b, 633b
society, III 585b
Socrates, I 627b, 629a, 632a, 633b; III 585a, 586a
sophism, I 628a, 629a, 630a, 631a, 632a–633b
Stoicism, I 627b; III 585b, 587b–588a; IV 320b
tragedy, I 631a
truth, I 629a
U.S., III 347b–348a
virtue, I 629b–630a, 632b, 633a
See also Primitivism
Cynosarges, cynicism, I 628a
Cyprian, Saint (3rd century A.D.)
casuistry, I 258a
gambling, I 336b–337a
reformation, IV 62b
religion, IV 115b
Roman Catholic Church, IV 115b
socialism, IV 286a
Cyprus
Diaspora, I 414a
God, II 333b
international peace, III 454b

Cyrano de Bergerac, Savinien de (1619–1655)
cosmic voyages, I 528a, 530b–531b
deism, I 648b
Utopia, IV 462b
Cyrene, Diaspora of, I 414a
Cyril, Saint (827–869), I 409b
Cyrus (600?–529 B.C.), cynicism, I 632a, 633a, 633b
Cysarz, Herbert, baroque in literature, I 190a
Cytology, acquired characteristics, II 618b, 619a
Czechoslovakia
evolution of literature, II 173b–174a
Marxism, III 167a–167b, 168b, 169a, 169b
nationalism, III 328b
Peyre, I 192a–192b
prophecy, III 669b
revisionism, IV 274b
revolt in 1419, I 387a
romanticism, IV 191a–191b
socialism, IV 287a
symbolism, IV 343b

D

Da Barga, Antonia, dignity, IV 143a, 143b
Da Costa, Uriel (1590?–1647), skepticism, IV 246b
Dacie, Augustin de, I 47a
Dacier, Madame (1654–1720)
aesthetics, IV 355a
attitude toward antiquity, I 78b–79a, 82a
genius, II 294a
Dadaism
chance images, I 352b
expressionism, II 206b
repudiation of beauty, I 207b–208a
truth, I 322a
Daedalus (myth), III 272b
cosmic voyages, I 524a, 529a, 529b
culture, I 608b
Daguerre, Louis Jacques Mandé (1789–1851), impressionism, II 572a
Daguesseau, H. F. (1668–1751), Enlightenment, II 95b
Dahl, Robert, democracy, I 666a
Dahlke, Paul, Buddhism, I

256b
Dahlmann, Friedrich Christoph (1785–1860), French Revolution, IV 159b
Dahrendorf, Ralf, class, I 446a
Daiches, David, baroque in literature, I 193a
D'Ailly, Cardinal Pierre (1350–1420), causation, I 275b
Dale, Rev. Thomas, literature, III 84b
D'Alençon, Duc (1554–1584), Machiavellism, III 117b
Dalgarno, George (1626?–1687)
Bacon and, I 176b
linguistics, III 75a
Dalla, D. M., romanticism, IV 190b
Damascius (b. about 780 A.D.), irrationalism, II 635b
Damian, Peter (1007?–1072), heresy, II 418b, 419a
Damnation
Enlightenment, III 248a
Faust (legend), III 246b, 247a, 247b, 248a
God, II 345a, 359b, 361a
good, IV 174b, 176b
happiness, II 374b, 379a
Dams, conservation, I 476a
Danaos (myth), historiography, II 499b
Dance
art, I 458a, 458b, 460a, 461a
catharsis, I 269a
death, III 265b
demonology, III 264b, 265b, 266a
God, II 333a
Greece (ancient), IV 96b
mimesis, III 226a, 226b
music, III 264b, 265b, 266a, 266b–270a
mythology, III 291a–291b
Plato, III 226b, 500b
religion, IV 96b, 100a
Renaissance, IV 439a
ut pictura poesis, IV 467b, 470a, 475a
Dandyism, IV 223a
Daniel (Bible)
metaphor, III 202b
millenarianism, III 223b, 225a
mythology, III 283a, 283b
prophecy, III 657b, 664b, 666b
reformation, IV 61a
religion, III 202b
socialism, IV 287a

Daniel, Samuel (1562–1619), mythology, III 298a
Daniello, L.
painting, IV 467b, 468a
poetry, III 529a, 531a; IV 467b, 468a
Daniells, Roy
baroque in literature, I 193b
periodization in literary history, III 484a
Danilewski, Nikolai, crisis in history, I 595a
D'Annunzio, Gabriele (1863–1938)
baroque in literature, I 189b, 194b
symbolism, IV 341a, 343a
Dante Alighieri (1265–1321)
allegory, I 41b, 42b, 46b
ambiguity, I 53b–54a
analogy, I 64a, 65a
astrology, II 233b
Boccaccio and, IV 122a
causation, II 233a, 233b
Church, I 418a
classicism, I 451b, 452a, 452b
comedy, I 470a
cosmic voyages, I 524a, 527a
crisis in history, I 592a
Diaspora, III 63a
Ficino and, III 511a
fortune, fate, and chance, II 233a–233b, 234a
God, II 233a; III 511a
good, II 233a–233b; IV 176b–177a
grace, II 233b
grammar, III 63a
happiness, II 379a
harmony, IV 41a
heaven, IV 176b–177a
heresy, II 419a
hierarchy, II 440b; III 509b, 511a
historiography, II 482a
history, I 383a
humanism, II 517b; IV 132a
Intelligence, II 233a, 233b
irony, II 627a
knowledge, III 511a
language, II 667a; III 62b–63a, 63b
literature, III 86a; IV 331a
love, III 102b, 105b, 511a; IV 177a
metaphysical imagination, III 211b
Middle Ages, I 65b
mountains in literature, III 253b
music, III 265a, 270a, 270b

mythology, III 283b, 287b–288a
nationalism, III 320b
Nature, II 233a, 233b
neo-classicism in art, III 370a, 371a
Neo-Platonism, III 509b, 511a
organicism, III 424a
periodization in literary history, III 485b
Platonism, III 507a, 507b, 509b, 511a, 512a, 512b, 513a
poetry, III 529a, 529b, 530a, 530b, 531a, 531b
power, II 233b
providence, II 233a, 233b
Pythagoreans, IV 41a
realism in literature, IV 55a
reason, II 233a
right, IV 176b–177a
romanticism, IV 187b, 188b, 189b
senses, III 511a
sin, IV 176b–177a
soul, II 233a–233b; III 511a; IV 176b–177a
space, IV 301a
style, IV 331a
symbolism, III 511a; IV 341b
theology, III 511a
tragic sense, IV 415b
universal man, IV 442b
universe, II 233b; IV 41a
Utopia, IV 461a
vernacular, III 63a
virtù, IV 477a, 479b
virtue, II 233b; IV 176b–177a
Danti, Giovanni Battista, cosmic voyages, I 529a–529b
Danti, Vincenzo (1530–1576), aesthetics, II 222b
classification of the arts, I 459b
mimesis, III 228b
Danto, A. C.
determinism, II 19b
historiography, II 19b
Daphne (myth), III 290b, 296b
Dapper, Olfert, China, I 356b–357a
D'Argenson, Marquis, individualism, II 602a
Darío, Rubén (1867–1916), symbolism, IV 342a, 344b
Darius (558?–?486 B.C.)
freedom of speech, II 254b
law, II 683a
Dark Ages

law, II 685b
periodization in history, III 478b, 480a
science, II 196a
Darlington, C. D., acquired characteristics, II 617b
Darwin, Charles (1809–1882), I 80a, 405b
acquired characteristics, II 618a–618b, 620a
adaptation, II 180a, 180b, 181a
agnosticism, IV 107b
ambiguity, I 58b
Aristotle and, I 676b
Baer and, IV 57a
beauty, I 204a
behaviorism, I 214b, 220a
biology, I 236b, 237a
Butler and, II 185b
catastrophism, IV 422b–423a
Chain of Being, I 335a
Christianity, I 405b
chromosomes, II 286b, 287b, 288a–288b
conservation, I 473a
continuity, I 499b
culture, II 130b, 133a
design argument, I 676b–677a
determinism, II 24a, 24b
education, III 646a
environment, II 125a, 126a, 130b, 133a
eschatology, II 159b–160a
evolution, II 126a, 624a, 626a; III 360a, 360b, 473b, 646a
evolution of literature, II 171a
evolutionism, II 176a, 177b, 179a, 179b–181b, 182a, 183b, 184a, 185b, 186b, 187a
fitness, II 121b–122a
genetic continuity, II 285a, 286b, 287b, 288a–288b
God, II 356a
Haeckel and, IV 57b
heredity, II 285a
hierarchy, II 448a
Hippocrates and, II 624a
historiography, II 24a, 24b, 492b, 499b, 505b
Huxley and, I 318b
idea, I 115b, 116a
imprinting, II 584b
Lamarck and, II 618a–618b
language, II 669b, 670b; III 68b–69a
learning, II 584b
linguistics, III 68b–69a; IV

424a, 424b, 425a, 428b–429a, 429b
longevity, III 92b
Lyell and, II 176b, 180a; IV 422b–423a, 424a
Malthus and, I 89a; II 180a
Marx and, II 620a, 626a–626b; III 146b
modernism, I 419b
morality, III 646a
nationalism, III 330a
natural selection, II 180a, 180b, 181a, 182a, 184a, 185b, 186b, 448a, 618b; III 473b, 561a, 646a; IV 107b, 422b, 423a
necessity, III 360a, 360b
Nietzsche and, II 185b
order, II 448a
origin of species, IV 422b, 323a
pangenesis, II 624a–624b, 626a–626b
panmixis, II 624b
Peirce and, III 558a
perfectibility, III 473b, 474a
position effects, II 624b
pragmatism, III 556b, 558a, 561a–561b
progress, III 646a
psychology, IV 11b–12a, 13b, 25a, 25b, 26b
Ratzel and, II 130b
recapitulation, IV 56a, 56b, 57a–57b, 58a
religion, IV 107a–107b
romanticism, IV 204b
sacred, II 513b
Schleicher and, IV 428a
Shaw and, II 185b
species, II 180a
Spencer and, III 194a; IV 107b
theodicy, IV 383b
time, II 588a; IV 395b
tradition, II 646a
transformism, I 499b
Tree of Life, I 335a
uniformitarianism, IV 422b–423a, 424a, 424b, 425a, 428b–429a, 429b
variation, II 618b, 624a
Victorian sensibility, IV 221a, 221b, 222a
web of life concept, II 128b, 133a
Wright and, III 561a–561b
Darwin, Charles Galton (1887–1962)
free will, II 588a
law, II 588a; III 11b
Darwin, Erasmus (1731–1802)

association of ideas, I 114b, 115a, 116a
deism, II 179a
evolutionism, II 179a, 185b
idea, I 114b, 115a, 116a
poetry, IV 473a
romanticism, IV 201b
species, II 179a
spontaneous generation, IV 311a–311b
Darwinism
acquired characteristics, II 620b
Creation, II 180a
entropy, II 115b
environment, II 130b
evolution of literature, II 171a, 172a
evolutionism, II 171a, 179b–182a, 182b, 183a, 184a, 184b, 185a, 185b–186a, 186b
Haeckel, II 181b–182a
heresy, II 429a
Hitler, III 125a
Huxley, I 17b; IV 107a
Latin America, III 542b
linguistics, IV 428a
longevity, III 92b
Lysenko, II 620b
Machiavellism, III 125a
Man-Machine, III 143b
materialism, IV 107b
motif, III 243a
Mussolini, III 125a
Peirce, III 558a, 560b
positivism, III 542b
pragmatism, III 558a, 560b
religion, IV 107a
revolutionary impact of, II 180a
Social Darwinism, III 646a–646b
socialism, IV 293b
spontaneous generation, IV 311b, 312a
uniformitarianism, IV 428a
war, IV 501a, 503b, 505a, 505b
Wilberforce, IV 107a
D'Ascoli, Grazadei, time, IV 392b
Dasmann, Raymond, conservation, I 472a, 476b
D'Asti, Astexanus, casuistry, I 259a
Daubenton, Louis Jean Marie (1716–?1800), evolutionism, II 178b
Daubeny, Charles (1795–1867), catastrophism, IV 421b
Daubigny, Charles François

83

(1817–1878), impressionism, II 577b, 578a

Däubler, Theodor (1876–1934), expressionism, II 206b–207a, 207b

Daudet, Alphonse (1840–1897), naturalism, IV 54a

Daumier, Honoré (1808–1879), satire, IV 215b

Dauthendey, Max (1867–1918), symbolism, IV 342b

David (Bible)
freedom of speech, II 255a
God, II 336b
loyalty, III 108b
music, III 265a, 267a, 270b
mythology, III 275b, 277a, 277b, 281a, 282b, 283a, 284b
prophecy, III 658a, 659a, 661a
social contract, IV 252a–252b
temperance, IV 371b

David, Jacques Louis (1748–1825)
classicism, I 454b; III 341a
Géricault and, III 341a
iconography, II 533b
impressionism, II 572b, 577a, 577b
Ingres and, III 341a
naturalism in art, III 341a, 345a
neo-classicism in art, III 366a, 367a, 370b, 371a
synthesis of detail, III 341a

Davids, Caroline Augusta Foley (d. 1942), Buddhism, I 255b

Davids, Thomas William Rhys (1843–1922)
Buddhism, I 255b
Orientalism, III 434b

Davies, Edward
historiography, IV 151a
mythology, III 306b

Davies, John (1569–1626), common law, II 695b

Davis, David (1815–1886), constitutionalism, I 479b–490a

Davis, Hayne, international peace, III 453b

Davis, K., class, I 446a

Dawson, Christopher, periodization in history, III 480a

Dawson, J. P., law, III 28a, 29b–30a

Day, Thomas (1748–1789), primitivism, IV 600b

DDT, disease, II 406a

De Beer, G. R., biology, I 236b, 237a, 237b, 239b

De Broglie waves
space, IV 302a
symmetry, IV 349a, 350b–351a

De Broglie-Einstein equations, II 589a–589b

De Gaulle, Charles, nationalism, III 337a, 338b

De Jonge v. Oregon, I 490a

De Méré, Chevalier (1607–1684), probability, III 606a, 622a

De Moivre, Abraham (1667–1754)
Bernoulli and, III 609a
Laplace and, III 609a–609b, 612b
Montmort and, III 609a
perfectibility, III 471b
probability, III 609a–609b

De Morgan, Augustus (1806–1871), pragmatism, III 555a

De Mott, Benjamin
irony, II 633b
satire, IV 212a

De Quincey, Thomas (1785–1859)
classicism, I 452b
literature, III 83a; IV 332b
romanticism, IV 192a, 195a

De Quincy, Quatremère
aesthetics, II 218b
painting, IV 475a

De Sanctis, Francesco (1818–1883)
literary criticism, I 600a
literature, III 84a
organicism, III 426a
realism in literature, IV 52b

De Stilj, painting, IV 475a

De Vries, David Pietersen (1592?–1655), evolution of literature, II 172b

De Vries, Hugo (1848–1935), acquired characteristics, II 619a
genetic continuity, II 289a–289b

De Waldegrave, James, game theory, II 264b

De Witt, John (1625–1672), probability, III 607a

Dead, motif, III 238a

Dead Sea Scrolls, I 413b, 415b
mythology, III 279b

Dear, G. F., indeterminacy, II 592a

Death, I 634a–646b
apologism, III 89b
Aristotle, I 639a–639b, 644a, 645b

atomism, I 640a, 644a

Averroës, I 639b, 645b

Bardo Tödol, I 644b

Bergson, I 641b

Bible, I 639b, 640b, 644a; III 278b, 279a, 281a, 282b, 284a

Buddhism, I 644b; IV 232b

Burton, I 626a

cabbalism, I 645a

Camus, I 637b

Cathars, I 645a

Christianity, I 636a, 639b, 640b, 643b, 644a–644b, 645a; IV 229b, 230a

cosmic images, I 522a–523b

Crito, I 638b

dance, III 265b

deism, I 646b

determinism, II 27a

disease, II 396a, 397a, 401a, 401b, 402a, 404a

drama, I 635b

dualism, II 38b

economic history, II 56b

Egypt (ancient), I 644b; IV 224b–226a

Epicurus, I 635a–635b, 636b; III 274a

eschatology, II 156a

ethics, IV 70b, 71b

Eve (Bible), III 582a

evil, II 167a

existentialism, I 637b; II 193b

fortune, fate, and chance, II 226b

freedom, I 636b

Freud, I 634b, 636b

genius, II 320b, 323a, 324b

Gilgamesh Epic, I 634b

God, I 635b, 640b, 644a; II 333a, 335a–335b, 336a, 337b, 338b, 340b, 341a, 343b, 353b

Goethe, I 642a, 642b, 646a

Gnosticism, I 645a

Greece (ancient), I 634b–639b, 642a, 643b–645b; II 674a, 676a, 678a; IV 228a

happiness, II 378a, 383b, 384b

Hartmann, I 637b

hell, I 635a, 643b

Hemingway, I 637b

hermeticism, II 432b

Hinduism, I 644b, 645a

human nature, III 571b, 572a

immortality, I 635a, 635b, 636b–637a, 638a–643b

India (ancient), I 644b

law, II 674b, 676a, 678a

longevity, III 89b

love, III 96a, 98b, 104b

Man-Machine, III 132b, 133a

Mesopotamia (ancient), IV 226a

metaphysical imagination, III 209a

metempsychosis, I 644b

millenarianism, III 224a, 224b

music, II 320b, 323a, 324b; III 265a, 265b, 268b–269a, 271b

mythology, I 634b; III 273b, 274a, 278b, 279a, 281a, 282b, 284a, 286b, 310a, 315a

natural law, III 20b

Neo-Platonism, I 645a

Nietzsche, I 637b

Omar Khayyam, I 642b

Orphism, I 644b; II 226a

pain, I 635a, 638a

palingenesis, I 644b

Paul VI (Pope), I 643b

pessimism, I 635b

Pherecydes of Syros, I 644b

philosophy, I 637a–637b

Plato, I 635b, 636b, 637a–637b, 638b–639b, 643b, 644a, 645a; III 273b

pleasure, II 378a, 383b, 384b

Plotinus, I 645a

poetry, I 635b, 636a

Pomponazzi, I 640b

predestination, II 27a

primitive man, I 634a–634b

primitivism, III 582a, 583a

prophecy, III 661a, 662a, 663a, 663b, 664a

psychical research, I 642b–643b

psychology, I 634b, 637b–638a

Pythagoreans, I 645a

rebirth, I 644b

reformation, IV 60b

reincarnation, I 644b–646a

relativism, IV 70b, 71b

religion, I 637a; IV 94a, 98a, 98b, 100b, 101b, 102b, 104b, 113b

Renaissance, I 636a, 645a; IV 439b

resurrection, I 643b–644b

Roman Catholic Church, I 643b

romanticism, I 645b; IV 192a

Rome (ancient), I 635a, 646a

Saint Augustine, **IV** 381a
Saint Paul, **I** 644b–644a
Saint Thomas Aquinas, **I** 644a–644b
salvation, **IV** 224b–226a, 227b, 228a, 228b, 229b, 230a, 231a, 231b, 232b
Santayana, **I** 646a
Satan, **III** 265b
Saxons, **IV** 113b
Schopenhauer, **I** 634b, 637a, 637b
science, **I** 637b
Seneca, **I** 635b
Siger of Brabant, **I** 639b, 640b
sin, **IV** 224b–226a, 227b, 228a, 228b, 229b, 230a, 231a, 231b, 232b
skepticism, **I** 644a, 645a
sleep, **I** 636b
Socrates, **I** 636b, 638b, 642a; **IV** 415a
soul, **I** 634b, 635a, 637a–637b, 638b–644b
Spinoza, **I** 636a–636b, 637b, 645b
spiritualism, **I** 642b–643b
Stoicism, **I** 635b, 636a, 637b
theodicy, **IV** 381a
theology, **II** 27a
Tolstoy, **II** 193b
tragic sense, **IV** 414b, 415a
transmigration, **I** 644b, 645a
universal man, **IV** 439b
Utopia, **IV** 463b
Voltaire, **I** 634a
welfare state, **IV** 509b
witchcraft, **IV** 521a, 522a, 522b
Zoroastrianism, **IV** 231a, 231b
Deborah (Bible), prophecy, **III** 660b
Debordes-Valmore, Madame, literary criticism, **I** 601a
Debray, Regis, revolution, **IV** 166a
Debts, Greece (ancient), **II** 679a, 684b
Debussy, Claude (1862–1918), impressionism, **II** 575a, 580b
Decadence
  art, **II** 575b, 582a
  impressionism, **II** 575b, 582a
Decembrio, Pier Candido (1399–1477), humanism, **II** 522b
Decembrists, nationalism, **III** 328a
Deception
  genius, **II** 313b

music, **II** 313b
virtù, **IV** 477b
Decimal system
  mathematics, **III** 171a, 173a
  numbers, **III** 402b, 404a
Decision
  Aristotle, **IV** 175b
  game theory, **II** 263a–263b, 272a
  law, **III** 4a–5a, 6a
  right, **IV** 175b
Declaration of the Rights of Man and the Citizen, **I** 660b–661a; **II** 144b, 157b; **III** 7b, 11b, 12a, 21b, 23a, 25b
Decorum
  allegory, **I** 47b–48a
  neo-classicism in art, **III** 368b, 371a
Decreasing return, economic history, **II** 51a
Dedekind, Julius (1831–1916)
  continuity, **I** 499b
  mathematics, **III** 175b
  Peirce and, **III** 558a
  pragmatism, **III** 557b, 558a
  space, **IV** 301a
Deduction
  Aristotle, **III** 380a
  axiomatization, **I** 162a–172b
  Descartes, **III** 356a
  idea, **II** 543a
  methodology, **III** 386a, 388a, 390b
  necessity, **III** 356a, 356b
  Newton, **III** 386a, 388a, 390b, 392a
  optics, **III** 392a
Deerfield Massacre, primitivism, **III** 594b
Deffand, Madame du (1697–1780), love, **III** 103a
Defoe, Daniel (1659?–1731), cosmic voyages, **I** 528a, 528b, 532b–533a
  irony, **II** 629a
  Noble Savage, **III** 601b–602a
Degas, Edgar (1834–1917), Courbet and, **II** 571a, 571b
  impressionism, **II** 567b, 570b–571a, 571b, 572a, 573b, 574b, 580a
  naturalism in art, **III** 341b
  photography, **II** 571b, 572a
  Rodin and, **II** 574b
Degeneration
  children, **III** 595b–596a
  disease, **II** 404a
  evolution, **III** 646b
  historiography, **IV** 148a,

150a, 150b–151a
  Plato, **III** 629b
  primitivism, **III** 595b–596a
  Renaissance, **IV** 148a, 150a, 150b–151a
  See also Progress
Degérando, J. M., literature, **III** 83b
Dehio, Georg, **I** 189a
Dehumanization, Man-Machine, **III** 146a
Deianeira (myth), temperance, **IV** 367a
Deinhard, Ludwig, Buddhism, **I** 256b
Deioces, King, historiography, **II** 501a
Deism, **I** 646b–652b
  Chambers, **II** 179a
  chance, **II** 227a
  Chartism, **I** 652a
  Christianity, **I** 402a, 403a, 646b–652a
  Darwin, **II** 179a
  defined, **I** 646b
  Enlightenment, **I** 647b; **II** 91a
  Epicureanism, **I** 647b, 648a
  equality, **I** 651a
  Etherege, **I** 650a
  ethics, **I** 651a
  evolutionism, **II** 179a
  faith, **I** 648a
  fate, **II** 227a
  fideism, **I** 646b, 647a, 648b, 652a
  Fontenelle, **I** 651a
  fortune, **II** 227a
  France, **I** 648b, 649a, 651a, 651b
  freedom, **I** 647b
  Germany, **I** 649b, 651a
  Great Britain, **I** 648b, 649a–652a
  Greece (ancient), **I** 647b
  Herbert of Cherbury, **I** 360a, 648b, 649a, 649b, 650a
  Islam, **I** 648a, 650b
  Israel (ancient), **IV** 226b
  Italy, **I** 648a, 649a
  More, **I** 648b
  Mossner, **I** 652a
  mythology, **III** 301a–303a, 304b
  Napoleon I, **I** 651b
  natural law, **I** 646b, 648a, 648b, 651a
  naturalism, **I** 648a
  Nature, **I** 648a
  Neo-Platonism, **II** 244b
  Netherlands, **I** 649a
  optimism, **I** 647a–647b, 651a
  Pluche, **I** 651b; **III** 302a

pluralism, **I** 651b
  politics, **I** 649b, 651b; **III** 301b–302a
  primitivism, **III** 598a
  progress, **III** 641a
  propositions of, **I** 646b
  Protestantism, **I** 648a, 648b, 649b
  psychology, **IV** 20a, 22b
  Puritanism, **I** 649b, 650a
  Quakers, **I** 649b
  radicalism, **I** 651b
  rationalism, **III** 301a–303a
  reason, **I** 646b, 647a, 647b, 648a, 648b, 649a, 649b, 650b, 651a, 651b
  Reimarus, **I** 651a
  religion, **IV** 92b, 93a, 94b, 96a, 96b, 98b, 119a
  Renaissance, **I** 648a, 649a
  republicanism, **I** 647b, 649b
  Restoration, **I** 650a
  Robespierre, **I** 651b
  Roman Catholic Church, **I** 648b, 649a, 649b
  romanticism, **IV** 208b
  Rome (ancient), **I** 647b
  Rousseau, **I** 651b
  Saint Paul, **I** 647b
  St. Pierre, **I** 651a
  Saint-Évremond, **I** 649a
  Saint-Simon, **III** 641a
  salvation, **IV** 224a, 226b
  science, **I** 648a, 648b, 649a, 650a, 651b
  sin, **IV** 224a, 226b
  skepticism, **I** 647a, 648b
  Socinians, **I** 648a
  theodicy, **IV** 380b
  theology, **I** 647a, 647b, 648b, 649b
  Utopia, **IV** 462b
  utopianism, **I** 649a
  ut pictura poesis, **IV** 471b, 472a
  Viret, **I** 648a–648b
  vitalism, **I** 651b
  Voltaire, **I** 651a; **III** 302b, 303a
Dekker, Thomas (1572?–?1632), wisdom of the fool, **IV** 520a
Del Bene, G., mimesis, **III** 228b
Del Rio, Martin, witchcraft, **IV** 522a
Delacroix, Ferdinand Victor Eugène (1798–1863)
  art, **II** 305b
  chance images, **I** 350b
  Duff and, **II** 306b, 307a, 307b
  French Revolution (1789), **IV** 156b

genius, II 305b
iconography, II 538b
impressionism, II 572b,
578b, 579b, 580a
mythology, III 306b
revolution, IV 156b
romanticism, IV 204a, 208b
Weltschmerz, IV 204a
Delaunay, Robert
expressionism, II 207b
Gothic, II 372b
Delbos, Victor (1862–1916),
modernism, I 420a
Delbrück, B. (1842–1922),
language, II 672b
linguistics, III 71b
Deleyre, Alexandre, Bacon
and, I 177b
Delft, Dirk van, game theory,
II 264b
Deliberative rhetoric, IV 168b
Delilah (Bible), mythology, III
282a, 282b
Delille, Jacques (1738–1813),
primitivism, III 602b
Delolme, Jean-Louis (1740–
1806)
Enlightenment, II 94b, 98a
liberty, II 94b
Delphi
catharsis, I 264b
law, II 681b
temperance, IV 356b–366a
Delvaille, J., progress, III
634b–635a
Demand
economic history, II 48b,
51b, 54a, 57b
natural liberty, II 63a
supply, IV 452b
value, IV 452b, 453b
Demaratus, King (fl. 500 B.C.),
historiography, II 501a
Demeter (myth), III 272b
culture, I 608b
cynicism, III 585b
Greece (ancient), IV 102a
law, II 681b
metaphor, III 203b
primitivism, III 585b
religion, III 203b; IV 102a
salvation, IV 228b
Demetrius (1st century A.D.),
aesthetics, II 219b, 220a
allegory, I 41b
rhetoric, IV 169b, 170a,
171a
style, IV 330b, 331a
Demetrius Phalereus (345?–
283 B.C.), classification of
the sciences, I 463a–463b
Demetz, Peter, realism in
literature, IV 55b
Demiurge

Aristotle, I 672b
Gnosticism, II 327a
harmony, II 390b; IV 39a–
39b
indeterminacy, II 586b
Kant, I 676a
macrocosm and microcosm,
III 127a
Plato, I 325b, 333a, 571b–
572a, 579a, 672a, 673b; II
40b, 390b, 586b; III 127a,
505a; IV 39a–39b, 50a,
415a
Platonism, III 506a, 510b
Pythagoreans, IV 39a–39b
rationalism, IV 50a
romanticism, IV 205b
tragic sense, IV 415a
universe, IV 39a–39b
Democracy, I 652b–667b
Adams, John, I 659b,
660a
Aeschylus, IV 366b
agriculture, I 654a
American Revolution, I
656a, 658b–660b
anarchy, I 656b, 664b
aristocracy, I 654a, 655a,
656b, 657a, 659b
Aristotle, I 625b, 653a,
653b–654b, 655a, 655b,
657a–658a, 667a; II 249b;
III 554a; IV 175b, 497a
authority, I 655a, 657a,
660a, 660b, 666b
Bentham, I 657b, 662a–
663a
Buddhism, I 253a
Burke, I 661a–661b
capitalism, I 666a; III 148b
Carlyle, I 666a
China (Communist), III
334a
Christianity, I 653a, 661b
Cicero, I 655a
citizenship, I 652b, 653a,
654b, 655b, 658a, 660b–
661a
Cleon, I 653b; II 260a
Coleridge, I 663a
defined, I 652b
despotism, I 663b; II 6a,
14a, 17a–17b
Dewey, John, III 554a,
569b
Digges, I 656b
Durand, IV 65b
economic history, II 44a,
46b, 47a, 59a, 59b
economics, I 667a
education, II 83a
English Civil War, I 656a,
656b–657a, 658b
Enlightenment, I 657b–

658a; II 91a
Epictetus, I 655b
equality, II 140a, 142b,
143a–143b, 145a–145b,
146b, 147a, 260a
Fabianism, I 664b
fascism, I 665b
France, I 656a, 657b, 658b,
660b–662a
Franklin, I 660b
freedom, II 249b, 259a
freedom of speech, II 252b,
253a, 257a, 259a, 259b–
260a, 260b
French Revolution, I 656a,
658b, 660b–662a; IV 156b
Germany, I 661a, 665b; IV
264b, 265b, 266b, 267a,
268b, 272b, 274a
Girondins, I 661b
good, IV 175b, 175b
Great Britain, I 656a, 656b–
657b, 658b–660b, 661a,
661b, 662a–663a
Greece (ancient), I 652b–
655a, 655b, 657a, 657b,
658a, 658b, 667a; II 257a,
259a, 682a, 685a; III 11a
Harrington, I 657a
Helvétius, I 661a
Herodotus, I 653a–653b,
667a
Hobbes, I 656a–656b,
657a–657b; II 6a
impressionism, II 583a
individualism, I 664a; II
595a, 599a, 602a
international peace, III 449a,
451a
Italy, I 665b; III 674b
Jacobins, I 661a, 661b–
662a
James, III 554a, 563a
Jefferson, I 660a, 660b
law, II 249b, 682a, 685a,
686a; III 2a, 11a
League of Nations, I 665a
Lecky, I 655b–656a
Lenin, I 665a–665b; II 653a
Levellers, I 656b
liberalism, I 663a, 664a;
III 39b–40a, 44b–45a, 45b,
46a, 52b, 55a, 59a, 59b,
60a, 60b
liberty, I 655b; II 260a
Lilburne, I 656b
Locke, I 656a, 657a–657b,
659a
loyalty, III 113a
Machiavelli, I 652b, 656a
Madison, I 660b, 656a,
656b, 666a
majorities, I 666a
Marx, I 664a

Marxism, I 664a–664b; III
147b, 148b, 152a, 153a,
155b, 156a, 156b
Michels, I 664b, 665a
Middle Ages, I 655b, 656a
military, II 253a
Mill, James, I 662a, 662b
Mill, John Stuart, I 154a,
663a, 664a
Milton, I 657a
modernism, I 423b
monarchy, I 653a, 655a,
656b, 657b, 659b
Montesquieu, I 656a, 657b,
659a, 660a
Mosca, I 664b, 665a
nationalism, III 325b, 326b,
328a, 329a, 329b, 330a,
331b, 333a, 334a, 335a,
335b
natural liberty, II 67a, 70a
Nazism, I 665b
Newman, I 663a
oligarchy, I 653a, 654a,
654b, 656b, 657b, 664b,
665a
Paine, I 659a–659b, 661b
painting, II 583a
Pareto, I 664b, 665a
Pericles, I 653b, 654a, 658b
periodization in history, III
479a
philanthropy, III 487a, 490b
Plato, I 653a, 653b–654a,
655a, 658a; II 22a; III
554a, 629a; IV 175a, 497a
politics, I 652b, 655b,
657a–657b, 658b–660b,
666a–666b; III 148b
polyarchy, I 666a
Polybius, I 626a, 655a,
655b, 657b
Popular Sovereignty, I
437a–437b
pragmatism, III 554a, 563a,
565b, 569b
Price, Richard, I 661b
private property, I 656b
progress, III 629a, 636b,
647b
protest movements, III 673a,
674b
Proudhon, I 664b
psychology, IV 18a, 19b,
24a, 26b, 29a
Puritanism, I 656a, 656b–
657a
quietism, I 655b
radicalism, III 673a
rationalism, I 656a
realism in literature, IV 55a
religion, IV 114b
republicanism, I 657a
revisionism, IV 264b, 265b,

266b, 267a, 268b, 272b, 274a
revolution, IV 152b, 154b, 156b, 162a, 164a
right, IV 175a, 175b
Robespierre, I 661b–662a
Roman Catholic Church, I 661b
Rome (ancient), I 652b, 653a, 655a–655b, 657a, 658a; II 686a; IV 154b
Rousseau, I 656a, 657b–658a, 661a, 661b; II 323b
Rush, I 660a
Russia, I 665a–665b
Russian Revolution (October 1917), I 665b
Santayana, III 554a
Schumpeter, I 665b–666a
self-determination, III 147b
Sidney, I 657a
Sieyès, I 661a
slavery, I 652b
social contract, IV 251b, 253b, 255a, 256a, 257a, 257b, 263b
socialism, I 664b, 666a; III 155b; IV 285b, 291b, 293b, 294a
Socrates, IV 285b
Sorel, I 664b
sovereignty, I 656b, 657a, 659a–661a
Stalin, I 665b
State, IV 316b–317a
Stoicism, I 655a, 655b
suffrage, I 660a, 662a, 664b, 665a, 666a; II 70a
Switzerland, I 661a
syndicalists, I 664b
Taylor, John, I 660a–660b
temperance, IV 366b, 368a
Thucydides, I 653b, 655a, 656a
Tocqueville, I 663a–664a; II 17a–17b; IV 503a–503b
totalitarianism, III 147b; IV 407a, 408b, 409a, 409b, 410b
transcendentalism, IV 24a
tyranny, I 644a, 656b, 663b, 664a
U.S.S.R., I 665b
U.S., I 652b, 656a, 656b, 657b, 658a, 658b–660a, 663a–664a, 665a, 666a–667a
urbanization, I 654b
utility, I 653a
Utopia, IV 458b
virtue, I 652b, 653a, 655b
Voltaire, I 657b
vox populi, IV 497a, 500a
war, I 655b–656a, 665a; IV

501a, 501b, 503a, 503b, 505a, 505b, 506a, 506b, 507a
welfare state, IV 510b
Wilson, Woodrow, I 665a
Wollstonecraft, I 661b
World War I, I 665a
Democritus (5th and 4th century B.C.)
abstraction, I 1a
Anaxagoras and, IV 3a
appearance and reality, III 187b, 188b
Aristotle and, I 495a, 495b; II 226a; III 189a
art, III 226a
atomism, I 126b, 127b, 128a, 128b, 129a, 130a–130b, 131a, 132b, 134a, 134b, 494b, 495a, 495b, 496a–497a; II 199b, 547b, 582a–582b; III 187b; IV 3a, 51a
catharsis, I 269a
causation, I 272a; II 135b, 136a–136b
chance, II 226a–226b
continuity, I 494b, 495a, 502b, 503a
cosmology, I 540a, 549b
cosmos, IV 3a
creativity in art, I 583b
culture, I 610b, 611a, 611b, 612b–613a
custom, III 575b
death, I 635a
desire, III 576b
determinism, II 135b, 586b
discontinuity, I 494b, 495a, 495b, 496a–497a
dualism, IV 346b
education, I 613a; III 627a
eighteenth-century view of, I 85a
Enlightenment, II 96b
Epicureanism, II 135b, 136a–136b; IV 7a
ethics, IV 319a
evolutionism, II 175a–175b
fate, II 226a–226b
four elements, I 230a–230b
free will, II 135b, 136a–136b
freedom of speech, II 259b
good, III 576b
happiness, II 378a; III 576b, 577a
hedonism, III 576b
Heraclitus and, III 187b
historiography, I 502b, 503a; II 501b, 502a, 510b
human nature, III 571a, 573b, 575b, 576b–577a

idea, II 547b
impressionism, II 582a–582b
indeterminacy, II 586b
justice, III 576b
law, II 681b, 683b
love, III 106b
Man-Machine, III 132a
materialism, III 577a
matter, III 185b, 187a–187b, 188a, 188b, 189a, 192b, 195a, 196a
metaphor, III 199b, 203b
metaphysical imagination, III 213b
mimesis, III 226a, 226b, 227a, 230a
mind, III 576b–577a
morality, III 577a
motion, IV 51a, 389b–390a
Nature, I 613a; III 226a
necessity, III 353a
Non-Being, IV 299a, 299b
Parmenides and, III 187b
passions, III 576b
philosophy, III 199b
Plato and, III 188a, 188b
pleasure, II 378a; III 576b
poetics, III 526a
progress, II 626b, 627a, 627b, 631a, 631b
psychology, IV 3a, 7a, 9b, 28a
Pythagoreans, IV 34a
rationalism, IV 51a
religion, III 203b
senses, III 188b
skepticism, IV 234b, 235a, 239b
Socrates and, III 576b–577a
soul, I 215b; II 135b; III 576a–577a
space, III 188a, 189a; IV 299a, 299b
Stoicism, IV 319a
symmetry, IV 346b, 348a
temperance, III 576b
theriophily, IV 385b
time, IV 389b–390a
universe, II 135b
wisdom, III 576b
Demography, linguistics, III 70a
Demonax (2nd century A.D.), freedom of speech, II 260b
Demonology, I 667b–670a
Agrippa, I 669b–670a
angels, I 667b, 669a, 669b
Aristotle, I 668a, 669b
art, I 668b
Baxter, I 670a
Bible, I 668a, 668b, 669b

Bruno, I 669b–670a
Burton, I 557b
Christianity, I 667b, 668a, 668b, 669a–670a
dance, III 264b, 265b, 266a
defined, I 667b
Descartes, I 670a
disease, II 396a–396b, 397a
dualism, II 38b–39a, 39b
eschatology, II 156a
evil, I 668b; II 165a
exorcism, III 264b, 267a
Ficino, I 669b–670a; II 393b–394a
Glanvill, I 670a
Gnosticism, III 327a, 328a
God, I 667b, 668a, 669a, 669b–670a; II 336a, 337a, 342a
Greece (ancient), I 667b–669a
Gregory I (the Great), Pope, I 669b
harmony, II 390b, 392b, 393b–394a
heroes, I 669a
Hesiod, I 667b
Homer, I 667b
Judaism, I 667b, 668a–668b, 669a, 669b, 670a
Justin Martyr, I 668b
Luther, III 267a
Maxwell, I 670a
Middle Ages, I 668b, 669b
music, II 390b, 392b, 393b–394a; III 264a–267b, 268a
mythology, III 282b, 287b, 288a, 290a–291b
Neo-Platonism, I 667b, 668a, 669a, 669b, 670a
Otto, IV 97b
Philo Judaeus, I 668b
planets, I 669b
Plato, I 668a, 668b, 669a
Plotinus, I 669a
Plutarch, I 668b
Pomponazzi, II 36b, 37a
Proclus, I 669a
Pseudo-Dionysius, I 669a–669b
Pseudo-Platonism, I 668a
Pythagoreans, I 668a, 670a
religion, IV 97b
Renaissance, I 668b, 669b, 670a
Saint Augustine, I 668b
Saint Gregory, I 669b
Saint John Damascene, I 669b
Saint Paul, II 342a
Saint Thomas Aquinas, I 669b
Satan, I 668a, 668b, 670a
stars, I 669a, 669b

witchcraft, **IV** 521a, 521b, 522a, 522b
World Spirit, **II** 393b–394a
Xenocrates, **I** 668a, 669a
Demosthenes (385?–322 B.C.), **I** 79a
  analogy, **I** 68b
  evolution of literature, **II** 170a
  freedom of speech, **II** 260a
  irony, **II** 627b
  law, **II** 684b; **III** 7a
  oratory, **II** 170a
  philanthropy, **III** 487a
  rhetoric, **IV** 171b
Denham, John (1615–1669), romanticism, **IV** 194a
Denifle, Heinrich (1844–1905)
  heresy, **II** 428a, 430b
  Luther, **II** 428a
Denina, Carlo (1731–1813), literature, **III** 82b
Denis (3rd century A.D.), analogy, **I** 64b–65b
  patristic period, **I** 64b, 65b
Denmark
  absolutism, **I** 593b
  balance of power, **I** 182b–183a
  baroque in literature, **I** 189b
  civil disobedience, **I** 438a
  cosmic voyages, **I** 534b
  crisis in history, **I** 593b
  existentialism, **II** 190b, 191b
  language, **II** 671b, 672a, 672b
  naturalism in art, **III** 341a
Denning, W. E., probability, **III** 609b
Dennis, John (1657–1734), Don Juan (legend), **III** 350b
  Gothic, **II** 368a
  mountains in literature, **III** 259a
  Nature, **III** 350b
  sublime in external nature, **IV** 333b–334a, 335b
Denon, Baron Dominique (1747–1825), neo-classicism in art, **III** 364b
Density
  matter, **III** 192a
  probability, **III** 621a
Dentice, Luigi
  genius, **II** 316a–316b
  music, **II** 316a–316b
Deonna, W., aesthetics, **II** 223b
Deontic logic, **I** 172a; **IV** 183b
Deontology, **IV** 184b

Deprès, Josquin (1450?–1521), genius, **II** 319a, 320a–320b, 325b
  music, **II** 319a, 320a–320b, 325b
Depression of the 1930's, *see* Great Depression of the 1930's
Derathé, M., despotism, **II** 5a
Derham, William (1657–1735)
  culture, **II** 132a
  Newton and, **III** 393a
  Paley and, **II** 352a
Derrida, Jacques, structuralism, **IV** 329a
Desaguliers, J. T. (1683–1744), Newton and, **III** 393a
Desargues, Gérard (1593–1662), space, **IV** 302b
Descartes, René (1596–1650), **I** 76b, 77b, 85b
  abstraction, **I** 6b–7a
  ambiguity, **I** 58b
  appearance and reality, **I** 95a–95b
  Aristotle and, **IV** 435b
  Arnauld and, **I** 7a
  atomism, **I** 134b, 135b, 136a–136b, 137b–138a, 138b; **III** 193b
  automaticity, **III** 135b, 136b, 138b
  axiomatization, **I** 164b, 165a, 165b
  Bacon and, **I** 177a, 177b; **III** 215a–215b
  behaviorism, **I** 217a–217b, 218b, 223a
  bête machine doctrine, **III** 135b–136a, 136b, 137b
  biology, **I** 242b–243a, 245b
  Blake and, **III** 398b
  Blancanus and, **III** 257a
  causation, **I** 290b, 294a, 296b–299a, 302a, 302b, 303b
  certainty, **I** 304b, 305a–306a, 307a, 308b, 311a, 311b, 314a
  Chain of Being, **I** 327b
  change, **IV** 394b
  color, **III** 418a, 418b
  Comte and, **III** 532b
  Condillac and, **II** 450a
  consciousness, **I** 215b, 218b
  consonance, **III** 262b
  continuity, **I** 498a
  cosmic images, **I** 515a, 517a–517b, 518a, 519a, 520a
  cosmology, **I** 546b; **II** 182a,

187b
  Counter-Enlightenment, **II** 101b, 109b
  Creation, **I** 575a
  death, **I** 637b, 639b–641a
  deduction, **III** 356a
  deism, **I** 648b
  demonology, **I** 670a
  determinism, **II** 18b, 19b; **II** 239b
  dualism, **I** 217a–217b; **II** 41a, 381a, 443b, 445a; **III** 214a; **IV** 201a
  earth, **III** 257a
  economic history, **II** 45a
  Enlightenment, **II** 90a, 96a; **III** 248a
  evolutionism, **II** 176a, 182a, 187b
  experience, **IV** 432b
  extensio, **IV** 301b
  as a founder of modern thought, **I** 173a
  free will, **II** 239b, 245b, 246a
  Gassendi and, **II** 450a; **IV** 393a
  genius, **II** 294a
  geology, **III** 257a
  geometry, **IV** 304a, 435b
  God, **I** 276a, 296b, 297b, **302a**, 304b, 305a–306a, **575a, 639b**; **II** 349a–350a, **350b, 351a**, 355a, 444a; **III** 193a, 193b, 257a, 356a; **IV** 244b
  happiness, **II** 380b, 381a
  Harvey and, **I** 640a
  health, **II** 400b
  Hegel and, **III** 356b
  Helvétius and, **II** 450a
  heresy, **III** 136b
  hierarchy, **II** 443b, 444a, 444b
  historians, **III** 356b
  historiography, **II** 24a, 24b, 487b
  history, **II** 19b
  Hobbes and, **II** 450a
  humanism, **II** 523a
  Hume and, **III** 357b
  idea, **I** 111b–112a; **III** 561b
  imagination, **III** 213b–214b, 215a, 216b
  imprinting, **II** 584b
  inertia, **III** 193a
  infinity, **II** 605b, 606a, 608a
  irrationalism, **II** 635b, 638a
  James and, **III** 561b
  judgment, **IV** 244b
  knowledge, **I** 640a; **IV** 244b, 435b
  language, **II** 667b, 669a
  law, **I** 290b

  learning, **II** 584a
  Leibniz and, **III** 384b
  light, **III** 384a, 418a, 418b; **IV** 77b
  Locke and, **II** 450a
  logic, **III** 356a, 384b; **IV** 435b
  longevity, **III** 91b–92a
  Machiavelli and, **III** 356b
  Man-Machine, **III** 135b, 136a, 136b, 137a, 137b, 138a
  Marx and, **III** 356b
  materialism, **III** 193a
  mathematics, **III** 178b, 183a, 183b, 214b, 357a; **IV** 435b
  matter, **I** 517b; **II** 41a; **III** 185b, 192b–195b
  measurement, **IV** 402b
  mechanics, **II** 199a, 202b
  mechanism, **III** 357a
  meliorism, **III** 91b
  metaphor, **III** 199b
  metaphysics, **II** 450a; **III** 136a, 213b–214b, 215a, 216b; **IV** 432b
  methodology, **III** 384a–384b, 385b, 387b, 388a; **IV** 435b
  mind, **II** 41a; **III** 418a
  mind-body distinction, **I** 4a
  mind-matter dualism, **III** 199b
  morality, **IV** 432b
  More, H., and, **I** 297a–297b
  motion, **I** 297b; **III** 418a
  mountains in literature, **III** 257a, 259a
  music, **III** 262b, 263a
  mythology, **III** 300a
  natural sciences, **III** 357a
  naturalism in art, **III** 339a
  Nature, **II** 350b, 381a; **III** 348a
  necessity, **III** 355b, 356a–357a, 357b, 362b
  Newton and, **I** 518a; **III** 384a–384b, 385b, 387b, 388a, 395b, 398b
  numbers, **III** 403a, 404b, 405b
  occasionalism, **I** 276a, 296b
  optics, **III** 395b, 398b, 418a
  order, **II** 443b, 444a, 444b; **III** 561b; **IV** 435b
  organic machine, **III** 136a, 138a
  pain, **II** 381a
  passions, **II** 381a
  perennial philosophy, **III** 460b, 461a
  perfectibility, **III** 471b

philosophy, III 199b; IV 432b
physics, III 388a; IV 432b
planets, III 257a
Platonism, III 193a
pleasure, II 380b, 381a
pluralism, I 517b; IV 435b
Polybius and, III 356b
positivism, III 532b
pragmatism, III 557a, 561b
probability, I 305a
psychology, IV 9b, 11a, 16b, 17a
psychophysiology, III 137a
Ramism, IV 43b
rationalism, I 296b
reason, II 96a; III 384a–384b; IV 435b
refraction, III 384a, 418a
relativity, IV 75a, 77b
religion, IV 118a
rhetoric, IV 172b
robot, III 136b
romanticism, IV 201a
rules, III 384b
science, II 199a, 202b
senses, IV 244b
skepticism, I 304b, 305a–306a, 308b, 311b; IV 241a, 244b–245a, 245b, 247a, 248b, 249b
soul, I 638b–640a; II 381a; III 137b, 138a
space, IV 295b, 301b, 304a
Spinoza and, II 349b, 350a
structuralism, IV 328b
syllogism, III 356b
teleology, I 302a, 302b, 303b; II 381a
theory, III 356b
theriophily, IV 388a
time, IV 393a, 394b, 395a, 402b
truth, IV 244b, 432b
unity of science, IV 432b, 433a, 435b
universal man, IV 443a
universality, IV 435b
universe, IV 443b
vibration, III 262b
vision, III 418a
Volksgeist, IV 492a
Will, II 381a
world-scheme, III 257a
Deschanel, Émile (1819–1904), classicism, I 450a
Design argument, I 670b–677b
Aristotle, I 671a, 672a–673a, 676b
Bible; I 672b, 673a
Boethius, I 672b
Christianity, I 671a, 672b–673b

Copernicus, I 673b
Cudworth, I 674a
defined, I 670b
Diogenes of Apollonia, I 671b
evolution, I 676b–677a
Galen, I 672b
God, I 672b, 673a–676a
Greece (ancient), I 670b–673b
Heraclitus, I 671a, 671b
Hooke, I 674a
Hume, I 674b, 675a–676b
justice, I 671a
Kepler, I 673b–674a
logos, I 671a, 671b
Middle Ages, I 672b–673b
mind, I 671a
modern developments, I 673b–676a
natural science, I 673b–675a
Nature, I 672b, 673a
Neo-Platonism, I 674a
Newton, I 674a–674b, 675a, 676b
origins of, I 670b–672b
Paley, I 674b–675a, 676b
Plato, I 671a–673b, 674a, 674b, 676b
Platonism, I 674a
pre-Socratics, I 670b–671b
Saint Anselm, I 672b
Saint Thomas Aquinas, I 672b–673b, 674b
Socrates, I 671a, 671b
Spinoza, I 675b
Stoicism, I 671a
teleology, I 671b, 673a, 676b
universe, I 671b–672a, 672b
Whitehead, I 677a
Desire
Aristotle, IV 5a, 5b
choice, II 237a
Cicero, IV 50a
Democritus, III 576b
determinism, II 237a, 240a, 240b, 241b
Epicureanism, IV 8a
ethics, IV 72a
free will, II 237a, 240a, 240b, 241b, 244a
good, IV 173a, 173b, 177a–177b, 178a, 178b, 179a, 181a, 182b, 186b
happiness, II 375a, 380a, 380b
Hermeticism, II 432a
Hobbes, IV 177a–177b
human nature, III 576b
idea, II 548b
Kant, II 240a, 240b

law, III 1a
Mill, J. S., IV 179a
perfectibility, III 466b, 472a
Plato, III 498a, 499b
Platonism, III 498a, 499b, 512a
Plotinus, IV 9a
prophecy, III 664b
psychology, IV 3b, 4a, 5a, 5b, 8a, 9a
rationalism, IV 50a
relativism, IV 72a
religion, IV 99b
Saint Augustine, II 378b
Stoicism, IV 50a
utilitarianism, IV 446a
utility, IV 453a
Desmarest, N. (1725–1815), catastrophism, IV 420a
Desmarets de Saint-Sorlin, Jean (1596–1676), I 78a
Desnoyers, Fernand, impressionism, II 573a
Despotism, II 1a–18a
aristocracy, II 1a, 6a, 8a–8b, 11a–11b, 14a–14b
Aristotle, II 1b–5a, 6a, 7b, 16a
Assyria, II 252b
autocracy, II 1a
Avignon papacy, II 3a
Babylonia, II 252b
barbarism, II 1a–4a, 16b, 17a
Bayle, II 18a, 13b
Bodin, II 1a, 1b, 4a–4b, 5a, 5b, 6a, 7a, 7b, 10a
Bossuet, II 5a, 8b
China (Communist), III 147b
Christianity, II 1b, 3a–4a, 8a, 10a, 10b, 14a–14b
climate, II 3a
Colbert, II 8b
colonialism, II 1b, 16b–17a
concept of, II 1a
Constant, II 2a, 4b, 13b, 14b–15a, 17a
constitutions, II 2b
Declaration of Independence, II 1a
democracy, I 663b; II 6a, 14a, 17a–17b
dictatorship, II 1a
Diderot, II 10b, 12b
economics, II 9b, 12a
Edict of Nantes, II 7b–8a, 14b
education, II 9b
Egypt (ancient), II 15b, 252b
Engels, II 13a, 17a
Enlightenment, II 12a, 12b–13b

fear, II 6a, 6b, 9b, 12b, 13b–14a
Fénelon, II 8a, 8b
Ferguson, II 12b–13a
Filmer, II 4a, 5a, 5b, 6b, 7a, 7b
France, II 1a–1b, 2a, 3a–4a, 7b–15a
freedom, II 1a–17b
freedom of speech, II 252b, 259a
French Revolution, II 1a, 13b–14b; IV 156b
general will, II 278a
Germany, II 1a
Great Britain, II 5b–8a
Greece (ancient), II 1b, 2a–3a, 4a, 4b, 5a, 6a, 7b, 9a, 11b, 13a, 13b, 15b, 16a, 17a
Grotius, II 1a, 4a, 4b–5b, 6a, 7a, 11a
Hegel, II 2a, 4b, 13a, 15a–16b, 17a
Herodotus, II 2a
Hobbes, II 1a, 4a, 4b, 5a, 5b–7a, 9b, 11a
Holbach, II 10b, 12a, 12b
Holy Roman Empire, II 3a
Huguenots, II 7b–8a
humanism, II 4a
imperialism, II 1b
India (ancient), II 13a–13b
industry, II 12a
Jacobinism, II 15a
Jesus Christ, II 3b
Judaism, II 5a
kingship, II 1b, 2a, 3a, 3b, 4b, 5a, 8a, 8b, 13h–14a
La Bruyère, II 8a
law, II 1a, 2a–2b, 3b, 4a, 5a, 12a, 12b
Locke, II 4a–7b
Louis XIV, II 8a, 8b, 14a–14b
Mably, II 12a, 15a
Machiavellism, III 116a–125a
Marat, II 13b, 14a
Marsilius of Padua, II 3a; 3b–4a
Marx, II 2a, 4b, 13a, 16b–17a
Marxism, III 147b
Middle Ages, II 1b, 3a–4a
Monarchomachs, II 4b
monarchy, II 4a–4b, 6a, 8a, 9a, 10b–11a, 11b, 12a, 14a, 16a
Montesquieu, II 1a, 1b, 2a, 4b, 6a, 8a–12b, 13a, 13b, 16a
Napoleon I, II 13b–14b, 15a

Netherlands, II 7b–8a
Nimrod (Bible), II 4b
Oresme, II 4a, 7b
Orientalism, II 1a–3a, 4b–6a, 7b–8b, 11a, 12a, 13a–13b, 14b, 15a–17a
origin of the term, II 2a
Ottoman Empire, II 7b–8a
papacy, II 3a–4a
Persia, II 2a, 13a, 13b, 15b, 252b, 259a
Physiocrats, II 11a, 12a–12b
Plato, II 2a
power, II 1a–17b
primitivism, III 588a–588b
private property, II 12a, 13a–13b, 17a
Protestantism, II 14a–14b
psychology, II 9b
Pufendorf, II 1a, 4a, 4b–5b, 6a, 7a, 11a
Renaissance, II 4a
revolution, IV 156b, 157b, 160a, 160b
Robespierre, II 2a, 8b, 13b–14a
Roman Catholic Church, II 8a, 10b
Rome (ancient), II 4b, 10a, 11b, 13b
Rousseau, II 4a, 4b–5a, 8b, 10a, 11a–12b, 15a
Saint Just, II 2a, 8b, 13b, 14a
Saint-Pierre, II 8b, 11a, 12b
Saint-Simon, II 8b
Seneca, III 588a–588b
Sidney, II 1b, 7b
slavery, II 1b, 2a, 2b–3a, 4b, 5a–5b, 6b–7b, 9a, 9b–10b, 11a, 11b, 13b, 15b, 16a
socialism, II 17a
sovereignty, II 1a–17b
Staël, II 2a, 13b, 14a–14b
Tocqueville, II 1a, 2a, 17a–17b
totalitarianism, II 1a; IV 406b
Turgot, II 12a
Turkey, II 4b, 13a
tyranny, II 1a, 2a–2b, 8a, 10b, 11b–12a, 14a, 14b, 17a–17b
U.S.S.R., III 147b, 475a
U.S., II 1a, 7a–7b, 10a
usurpation, II 14b–15a
utopianism, II 12b
Voltaire, II 8a, 10a, 10b–11a, 13a, 13b
war, II 2a, 6a, 10a, 14a, 16a; IV 503a
wealth, II 12a

William of Moerbeke, II 3a, 4a
William of Ockham, II 3a–3b
Xenophon, II 2a
Zoroaster, II 13a
Dessoir, Max
beauty, I 212b
classification of the arts, I 461a
Destiny
chance, II 225b, 228a, 233b
ethics, III 442a; IV 319a
fortune, II 225b, 228a, 233b
God, II 336a
Hinduism, IV 231b
irrationalism, II 635a
necessity, III 360b
peace, III 442a
Rousseau, III 326a
Spengler, III 360b–361a
Stoicism, IV 319a
tragic sense, IV 414a
Zoroastrianism, IV 231a
Destutt de Tracy, Antoine Louis Claude (1754–1836), ideology, II 553a, 553b, 554a
Jefferson and, IV 21a
metaphysical imagination, III 216a
positivism, III 533a
psychology, IV 21a
Determinism, II 18a–31a
absolute idealism, II 20a–20b
abstraction, II 18b–19a
activism, IV 271b–273b
Adams, Henry, II 24a–24b
alienation, II 25a
Aristotle, II 19b, 135a, 236b–237a; III 189b
Arminius, II 28b
astrology, II 36a, 232b
atomism, II 18b, 237b
attitude, II 237a–237b
Augustinianism, II 27b
Barth, II 29a, 30b
Bible, II 26b
biology, I 245b–246b; II 24a
Boltzmann, II 587b–588a
Boutroux, II 587a–587b
Bradley, II 240b–241a, 241b
Buckle, II 22a
caesaropapism, II 30a
Calvin, II 27b, 28a, 28b, 29a, 30b
Calvinism, II 28b–29a, 30a–30b
Campbell, II 241a–241b
Cartesianism, II 19b

causation, I 285b–286a; II 18a–19b, 21b–22a, 238a, 238b, 240a, 240b–241a
China, II 22b
choice, II 237a, 238a–238b, 239a, 241a, 241b
Christianity, II 19b, 20a, 22a, 26a–31a, 237b–238a
civilization, II 21a–21b, 22b–23b
class, II 25a
Cleanthes, II 237b
Collingwood, II 23b
comets, II 18b–19a
compulsion, II 237a, 238a, 239a, 240a, 241a
Comte, II 23b–24a, 24b, 25b
Counter-Reformation, II 30b
culture, I 609b, 611b; II 22a–22b
Darwin, II 24a, 24b
death, II 27a
defined, II 18a
Democritus, II 135b, 586b
Descartes, II 18b, 19b, 239b
desire, II 237a, 240a, 240b, 241b
dignity, IV 144b–145a
duty, II 241b
Eastern Orthodox Church, II 30a
economics, III 569a
Einstein, II 590a
emotion, II 237b, 238b–239a
Engel-Janosi, II 20b
Engels, II 24b, 25a, 25b, 454b
Enlightenment, II 23b–24a
environment, II 22a, 23a
Epicureanism, II 135a–137a
Epicurus, II 135b–137a; II 237b
ethics, II 236b–237a
evil, II 26b, 27a, 236b–237b, 238a
evolution, II 24a
fatalism, II 29b, 30a
Fichte, IV 394a
Ficino, IV 144b–145a
foreknowledge, II 238a
fortune, fate, and chance, II 229b, 230a, 230b, 232a, 232b, 234b
France, II 30b
free will, II 26b, 27a, 29b, 30a, 135a–137a, 236b–242a, 247b–248a
freedom, I 93a; II 25b–26a, 135a
friendship, II 238b
Galileo, II 18b

Germany, II 20a–20b, 25a, 30b
Geyl, II 19a, 19b, 21b
Gibbs, phase rule, II 24b
God, II 19b, 20a, 20b, 21a, 21b, 24b, 25b–31a, 237b–238a, 240a
Gomarus, II 28a
good, II 237a, 237b, 238a–238b; IV 177b
Gottschalk of Orbias, II 27b
grace, II 27a, 238a
Great Britain, II 22a, 30b
Greece (ancient), II 18b, 19b, 22a, 22b, 24b
happiness, II 238a, 378a
hate, II 238b
Haydn, II 20b
Hegel, II 20a–20b, 21a, 25a
Hegelianism, II 24b
historicism, II 20a, 20b–21a
historiography, II 18a–25b
history, I 285b–286a; II 18a–25b
Huguenots, II 30b
Hume, II 238a, 239a, 239b–240a; III 357b
Huxley, T. H., II 24a
idealism, II 20a–20b
ignorance, II 236b, 237a, 238b
immorality, II 240b, 241b
impulse, II 237a
inclination, II 240a, 240b
indeterminacy, II 586b, 587a–588a, 589b, 590a
inevitability, II 20b–21a
intellect, II 238b, 239a
intention, II 237b
involuntarianism, II 236b
Islam, II 29b, 30b
Italy, II 22a, 23a, 23b
James, III 562a, 569a; IV 395b–396a
Jansenism, II 30b
Jesuits, II 30b
Jesus Christ, II 26b, 27a, 28b, 29a
Judaism, II 22a, 29b–30a
judgment, II 237b, 238a, 239a, 240a–240b
Julius Caesar, II 23b
justice, II 236b
Kant, II 240a–240b, 241a, 241b, 242a
Kautsky, II 25a
Kepler, II 23b
kismet, II 30b
knowledge, II 236b, 238b, 239a, 239b, 241a, 241b
Koran, II 29b

Lamarck, II 24a
Laplace, II 18b, 19a, 587a
law, II 237a, 240a, 240b, 241a
Leibniz, II 239a
Leverrier, II 23b
libertarianism, II 240b–241b, 242a, 248a
liberty, II 239b–240a, 241a
linguistics, IV 429a
Locke, II 239a–239b
logic, II 19b, 20a, 238b
love, II 237b, 238a, 238b
Lucretius, II 237b
Luther, II 27b
Man-Machine, III 139a, 144b
Marxism, II 24b–25a; III 149a, 149b, 150a, 152b, 162b, 163b, 168a–168b, 569b
materialism, II 237a, 454b
matter, III 189b
Melanchthon, II 28a
metaphysics, II 24a
Middle Ages, II 18a, 22b, 28a
Mill, J. S., II 241a
mind, II 238b, 239a
morality, II 237a–237b, 238a, 240b, 241a–241b
Muhammad, II 29b
music, III 262b
natural law, II 240a–240b
natural science, II 18b
Nature, II 18b, 20a, 237a, 237b, 238b
necessity, II 237b, 238a, 239a, 240b; III 361a
Netherlands, II 28a–28b, 30b
Newton, II 18b
Niebuhr, R., II 29a, 30b
Nowell-Smith, II 241b
origin of the term, II 18a
passions, II 236b
Peirce, II 587b
Pelagius, II 26b–27a
Petrarch, II 234b
philosophy, II 20a–20b, 23a–23b, 24a
physics, II 18b
planets, II 18b–19a
Plato, II 22a, 135a, 236b, 237a
Popper, Karl, II 20b–21a
positivism, II 241a
power, II 239a, 239b, 240a, 241b
pragmatism, III 553a, 562a, 569a
predestination, II 19b–20a, 21a
probability, III 620a

progress, III 630a, 643a
Protestantism, II 20a, 27b–29a, 30a–30b
providence, II 237a–237b
psychology, II 236b–237a, 238b, 239a, 239b, 240a; IV 12a
punishment, II 241a
Puritanism, II 30b
racism, II 22a
Ranke, II 20b
reason, II 26b, 236b, 237b, 238a, 238b, 239a, 240b
reformation, IV 60b, 61a
Reformation, II 28a, 30b
relativism, II 20b
religion, IV 107b
Renaissance, IV 144b–145a
responsibility, II 236b–238a, 240a, 241a
revisionism, IV 270a, 271b–273b
revolution, II 23b
rewards, II 241a
Roman Catholic Church, II 30a, 30b
Rome (ancient), II 22a, 22b
Saint Albertus Magnus, II 232a
Saint Ambrose, II 26b
Saint Augustine, II 19b, 26a–27b, 28a, 29a, 237b–238a
Saint John Chrysostom, II 26b
Saint Thomas Aquinas, II 238a
Salutati, II 234b
Schlick, II 239a, 241a
science, II 21b–22a, 24a–24b, 29a
sin, original, II 26a, 26b–27b, 29a, 236b
skepticism, II 25b
social contract, IV 263a
socialism, II 30b
society, II 22b–23b, 25a, 30a–31a
solar system, II 18b–19a
soul, II 26a, 26b, 236b
Spain, II 22a
Spencer, II 24a
Spengler, II 22a–22b, 23a, 23b
Spinoza, I 329a; II 237b, 238b–239a; IV 310a
spontaneous generation, IV 310a
State, II 20a, 22a
Stoicism, II 137a, 237a, 237b, 238b
synergism, II 28a
teleology, II 24a
theology, II 21a, 24a, 25b–

31a
Thirty Years' War, II 30b
time, II 240b; IV 393b, 394a, 395b–396a, 396b, 398a
Toynbee, II 21a–21b, 22a, 22b–23b
uniformitarianism, IV 429a
universality, II 18a–19b, 587b
universe, II 18a–19b
Veblen, III 150a
vice, II 237a, 237b
Vico, II 22a, 23a, 23b
virtue, II 237a, 237b
vitalism, II 238b
voluntariness, II 236b–237a, 239a
Zwingli, II 30b
Detzel, H., iconography, II 535b
Deucalion (myth), primitivism, III 579b
Deussen, Paul (1845–1919), Buddhism, I 255b–256a
Orientalism, III 434b
Deutero-Isaiah (Bible), metaphor, III 202b
Deutschbein, Max, romanticism, IV 197a
Deva, II 39a
Devlin, Lord, legal freedom, II 251a–251b
Dewart, Leslie
charity, faith, and hope, II 214b
God, II 365b
Dewey, John (1859–1952),
aesthetics, III 568b, 569b
agnosticism, I 18a
Aristotle and, III 554b
art, III 569b
association of ideas, I 116b
Bacon and, I 172b, 174a, 178a
behaviorism, I 214b; III 568b
certainty, I 323b–324b
China, I 371a
communism, III 569a
creativity, III 569b
culture, III 555b, 556b
democracy, III 554a, 569b
education, II 72b, 75a–75b, 81a, 82a, 82b, 83a, 83b; III 569a
emotion, III 568b
ethics, III 446b, 447a; IV 186a
evolutionism, II 184b–185a
experience, III 556b, 569a
fascism, III 565b, 569a
God, II 360a
good, IV 185b, 186a–186b

happiness, II 381b, 382b
Hegel and, III 556a–556b
history, III 556b
human nature, III 554b, 556b, 569b
idea, I 116b; III 568b
ignorance, III 569a
injustice, III 569a
instrumentalism, III 552b, 566a, 569a; IV 185b
James and, III 569a
judgment, III 556a, 568b–569a, 569b
justice, III 569b
Kant and, I 324b; III 555b
knowledge, I 323b–324b; III 561b, 568a, 568b
language, II 381b
literary criticism, III 569b
literature, III 88a
logic, I 184b
Lovejoy and, III 552b
Marxism, III 153b, 565b
metaphor, III 198a, 207a
methodological-monism, I 23a
mind, III 561b
morality, III 555b; IV 186a
natural law, I 324b
naturalism, III 554a
organicism, III 421a
pain, II 382b
peace, III 446b, 447a, 569a
perennial philosophy, III 462a
philosophy, III 198a
Platonism, III 554a
poverty, III 569a
pragmatism, I 323b–324b; II 184b–185a; III 551b, 552b, 553a, 553b, 554a, 555b, 556a–556b, 564a, 565b, 566a, 568a–569b
psychology, IV 27a–28a
religion, III 207a
revolution, III 569a
right, IV 185b, 186a–186b
romanticism, IV 210b
Russell and, III 446b
Santayana and, III 553b, 554a
Schelling and, IV 210b
society, III 556b, 564a
thought, III 568b
time, IV 396b
unity, III 556b
utilitarianism, II 382b; III 552b
value, III 556a, 568a, 568b–569a, 569b
Volksgeist, IV 494b
war, III 447a–447b, 569b

Di Casali, Giovanni, and Oresme, II 202b

Diacetto, Francesco da
harmony, II 394a
Platonism, III 512b–513a

Diachrony, IV 323b

Diagnosis, disease, II 396a

Diagoras (fl. 5th century B.C.), freedom of speech, II 258b

Dialect, II 660a, 660b, 671b, 691b; III 62b
history, II 660b
linguistics, III 62b, 63b, 67a, 70a, 70b, 73b
literature, III 62b

Dialectics
evolution of literature, II 170b
genius, II 313b
Hegel, III 199b, 358b
humanism, II 520b, 521b
idea, II 543a–543b
literary paradox, III 76a, 76b, 77a, 78a, 79b
music, II 313b
necessity, III 355b, 356b, 358b, 359a, 360b
periodization in history, III 478a
Renaissance, IV 438b, 441a

Diana (myth), III 290b, 291b, 297a
love, III 95a
witchcraft, IV 521a, 521b

Diaz, Porfirio (1830–1915), positivism, III 544a, 544b

Dicaerchus (4th century B.C.), culture, I 611a–611b
historiography, II 506b–507a, 508b, 510b
impiety, II 566a
progress, III 629b–630a

Dice-playing, I 336a–336b

Dicey, Edward (1832–1911), individualism, II 596b, 602a

Dicke, R. H., cosmology, I 567a, 568b

Dickens, Charles (1812–1870)
environment, II 133b
motif, III 237b, 239b, 242b
Nature, III 350a
realism in literature, IV 52b
Victorian sensibility, IV 221a, 221b, 222a
vox populi, IV 499b

Dictatorship
academic freedom, I 10a, 15a
authority, I 158b–160a
Brazil, III 542a, 543a, 545a
despotism, II 1a
Engels, III 155b
existentialism, III 158a

Latin America, III 540a
law, III 5a
Lenin, II 562b; III 146a
Machiavellism, III 125a
Marxism, III 147b, 155b–156a, 158a, 166b
Marxism-Leninism, III 155b–156a
Mexico, III 544a, 544b
nationalism, III 325a
natural law, III 5a
positivism, III 540a, 542a, 543a, 544a, 545a
progress, III 647b
proletariat, III 155b–156a, 166b
revolution, IV 157b
totalitarianism, IV 406a–410b
U.S.S.R., II 560b; III 647b
war, IV 505a

Dictionaries
China, I 464a
Gothic, II 369a
linguistics, III 63a, 67a
mythology, III 293a, 299a

Diderot, Denis (1713–1784), acquired characteristics, II 618a
aesthetics, II 549b–550a; III 217a; IV 355a
anarchy, I 71a
André and, I 199b
antimathematicism, III 142a
Aphra Ben and, III 603a
art, III 310a–310b
attitude toward antiquity, I 81a–81b, 83b–84a
Bacon and, I 172b, 177b
beauty, I 199b–200a
behaviorism, I 220a
biology, II 177a, 177b–178a; III 217a
Bougainville and, III 603a
Burnet and, III 259a
Carlyle and, IV 199a
Chain of Being, I 333b
Christianity, III 603a
civilization, I 616b; III 603a
class, I 448a
Comte and, III 533a
Counter-Enlightenment, II 106a
deism, I 651a, 651b
despotism, II 10b, 12b
Enlightenment, II 89b, 91b, 95a, 96b, 97b
Epicureanism, II 582a
evil, III 603a
evolutionism, II 177a, 177b–178a, 182b
Franklin and, III 603b
general will, II 276a
genius, II 294a–294b,

310a–310b
God, II 353a–353b
Hawkesworth and, III 603a
humanism, III 141a
Hutcheson and, I 199b
ideal, II 549b–550a
impressionism, II 582a, 582b
individualism, II 310a–310b, 600a–600b, 601a, 601b; III 644b
inequality, I 448a
justice, II 276a
Kant and, III 218b
knowledge, I 96b
liberty, II 95a
literary paradox, III 77b
Machiavellism, III 116a–125a
Man-Machine, III 140b, 141a, 141b, 142a
materialism, III 140b
mechanism, III 140b–141a
metaphysical imagination, III 215b–217b, 218b
morality, III 603a, 644b
mountains in literature, III 259a
naturalism, II 582a
Nature, I 333b; III 603a
neo-classicism in art, III 366a, 368b
optics, III 420b
philoprogenitiveness, III 603b
philosophy, II 549b–550a; Platonism, III 518a
positivism, III 533a
power, III 644b
primitivism, III 602a–603b
private property, III 603a
progress, III 644b
reason, II 96b; III 644b
revolution, IV 154b–155a
rhetoric, IV 172a
romanticism, IV 199a, 199b
Rousseau and, III 603a
Saint Paul and, III 603a
science, III 216b
sex, III 603a, 603b
Shaftesbury and, III 603a
society, III 644b
space, IV 302b
species, II 177b–178a, 618a
spiritualism, III 603a
spontaneous generation, IV 310b
structuralism, IV 328a
superstition, III 644b
Tahiti, III 603a–603b
taste, IV 355a
universal man, IV 443a
universe, II 177b
ut pictura poesis, IV 469a,

470a, 472b, 473a
utilitarianism, II 97b
Utopia, IV 462a, 462b
vice, III 603a
virtù, IV 484a–484b
women, IV 526a

Didron, A. N. (1806–1867), iconography, II 535a

Diego, Gerardo, symbolism, IV 342b

Diet
Empedocles, IV 32a
Pythagoreans, IV 31b, 32a

Diet of Augsburg (1548), IV 66b–67a

Diet of Worms, I 390b

Dietary laws, III 277a, 279b, 283a

Dietl, Josef, disease, II 404a

Dietrich, Paul Henri, Utopia, IV 462b

Dietrich of Niem (1340?–1418), reformation, IV 65b

Difference tone, III 263b

Diffraction
Grimaldi, III 418b, 419a
Newton, III 389b, 390a
optics, III 418b, 419a

Diffusionism, mythology, III 310b

Digby, Kenelm (1603–1665)
atomism, I 135b, 136a
inheritance, II 623b
metaphysical imagination, III 212a
pangenesis, II 623b

Digges, Thomas (d. 1595), cosmology, I 544b–545a, 548a; II 442b
hierarchy, II 436b, 437b, 442b

Dignity, IV 136a–147a
angels, IV 138b
anthropology, IV 138b, 139b, 145a, 145b
art, IV 136b, 141a
asceticism, IV 141a
atonement, IV 138a, 138b, 140a
beauty, IV 136a, 139a
Bible, IV 136b–137a, 138a, 139b, 144a, 145b
catastrophism, IV 142b
Chain of Being, IV 139b
chaos, IV 138a, 141b, 142a
chaos, IV 138a, 141b, 142a
Christianity, IV 136a–146a
Cicero, IV 136a–136b, 138a, 139a, 141b, 142b, 143b
Clement of Alexandria, IV 137a

cosmos, IV 136b, 139a, 139b, 143a

Creation, IV 137a, 137b, 138a–139a, 140a, 140b, 142a, 144b, 145b

culture, IV 141a, 141b, 142a, 143b

cycles, IV 138a

determinism, IV 144b–145a

divination, IV 144b, 145a, 145b

dualism, IV 138b

economics, IV 141a

Egypt (ancient), IV 139a

emotion, IV 142b

Epicureanism, IV 142b, 143a

epistemology, IV 139b

Erigena, IV 137b, 139b, 140a

eschatology, IV 137b, 138a

evil, IV 138b

existentialism, IV 142a

faith, IV 142a, 142b, 143a

Fall, IV 137a, 138a, 138b, 140a, 143a

fate, II 231b; IV 143a, 145a

Ficino, IV 139a, 144a–145b

fortune, II 231b; IV 142a, 143a

free will, IV 142b, 143a

freedom, IV 141a, 142a, 145a, 145b, 146a

Gnosticism, IV 138b

God, IV 136b–137b, 138a–139a, 140b, 142a, 142b–143a, 144a, 145a, 145b, 146a

good, II 231b; IV 138b, 143a

grace, IV 138a, 138b, 139a, 142a, 142b

Greece (ancient), IV 136a–136b, 137a–138a, 139a, 144a

Greek language, IV 143b

Gregory of Nyssa, IV 137a–137b, 139b

happiness, IV 143a

harmony, IV 142b

heaven, IV 142b, 143a

Hebrew language, IV 143b

heroes, IV 136b

hierarchy, IV 139b, 145a, 145b, 146a

history, IV 138a, 141a, 141b, 142a, 144a, 145b

Horace, IV 141b

human nature, III 572a; IV 142b–143a

humanism, IV 136b, 137b, 141a–146a

imagery, IV 138a–138b,

140b, 142b, 143a, 144a

imagination, IV 145a

immortality, IV 137a, 137b, 144b, 145a

Incarnation, IV 137a, 138a, 140a, 142a, 146a

Italy, IV 136a–146a

Jesus Christ, IV 137a, 140a, 142b, 146a

Judaism, IV 136b–137a, 139a, 143b, 145b

justice, IV 138a

knowledge, IV 139b

Lactantius, IV 138a, 139a, 140a

language, IV 143b

Latin language, IV 143b

literature, IV 141a, 142a, 146a

love, IV 138b, 142b–143a

magic, IV 145a, 145b

Marxism, III 148b

materialism, IV 141b, 142a

matter, IV 138b

memory, IV 138b

metaphysics, IV 140b

microcosm, IV 137b, 140a

Middle Ages, IV 139a–141a, 142a

Middle Platonism, IV 136b, 144a

mimesis, IV 137a

mind, IV 136a–138b

moral sense, III 231b

morality, IV 136a, 141a, 141b, 142a

mortality, IV 137a, 137b

mysticism, IV 137a, 138a, 138b

mythology, III 291b; IV 137a, 139a

Nature, IV 140b

Neo-Platonism, IV 137a, 139a, 139b, 140a, 140b, 144a, 144b, 145b

origin of the term, IV 136a

passions, IV 138b, 142b

Pelagianism, IV 138b

perfectibility, IV 144a

Peripateticism, IV 137a, 137b

Petrarch, IV 136b, 141b–142a, 142b, 143b

philosophy, IV 138a, 140b, 141a, 141b, 142a, 143b, 144a–144b, 145a, 146a

Pico della Mirandola, IV 139a, 145b

piety, IV 144b, 145b

Platonism, IV 137a, 137b, 138a, 139a, 139b–140a, 142a, 143b, 144a–145b, 146a

pleasure, IV 136b, 142b,

143a

poetry, IV 141a, 141b

poverty, IV 141a, 141b

power, IV 137b, 138b, 139a, 140b, 143a

progress, IV 144a

Protestantism, IV 146a

race, IV 136a–136b

rationalism, IV 136b, 142b

reason, IV 144b–145a

Reformation, IV 146a

religion, IV 136a–146a

Renaissance, IV 136a–147a, 439a, 441b

responsibility, IV 142a

rhetoric, IV 136a, 138a, 138b, 139a, 141a, 141b, 142a, 142b, 144a

Rome (ancient), IV 136b, 139a, 141b, 144a

Saint Augustine, IV 138a–139a, 139b, 140b, 141b–142a, 142b, 144a, 144b

salvation, IV 142a, 142b

sanctification, IV 140a

scholasticism, IV 140a–140b, 141b

science, IV 140b, 146a

secularism, IV 141a, 142a, 145b

Seneca, IV 141b, 142b

senses, IV 136b, 145a

skepticism, IV 140b–141a

society, IV 136a, 141a, 142a

Sophocles, IV 137b

soul, IV 137a, 138b, 140a, 140b, 143a

spiritualism, IV 142a

status, IV 141a

Stoicism, IV 136b, 137a, 137b, 138a, 139a, 142b, 143a, 144a, 146a

supernatural, IV 142b, 145a

syncretism, IV 144a

theology, IV 137b, 138a, 138b, 139b, 140b–141a, 141b, 142a, 142b, 143b, 144a, 144b, 145a

tradition, IV 144a, 145b

tragic sense, IV 413a, 414a, 417a

trinity, IV 138b, 140b, 141a

universal man, IV 439a, 441b

universality, IV 145a, 145b

universe, IV 136b, 137a, 138a, 138b, 139a, 140b, 142a, 145a, 146a

utilitarianism, IV 143a

vanity, IV 141b

Vergil, IV 141b

virtue, IV 136a, 137a, 138b, 141a, 143a

Will, IV 138b, 142b

wisdom of the fool, IV 519b

work, IV 136b, 531a, 532a, 533b, 534b

Dike, justice (Greek), II 674a–679b, 680a, 681b, 682a, 683a

Dilthey, Wilhelm (1833–1911)

causation, I 284a–284b, 285a

classification of the sciences, I 465b

empathy, II 85b, 86b–87a

evolution of literature, II 171a

historiography, II 496a

history, I 284a–284b, 285a

irrationalism, II 636b

literary criticism, I 600a

metaphysical imagination, III 208b, 209a, 219b, 220b, 222a

motif, III 237a–237b

necessity, III 354b, 360a, 360b, 361a

perennial philosophy, III 462a, 462b

psychology, IV 13b–14a

reformation, IV 69b

Dingler, Hugo, empiricism, III 546a

Dio Cassius (155?–after 230 A.D.), freedom of speech, II 261b

Dio Chrysostomus (40?–115 A.D.)

cynicism, I 632b–633b; III 586a

freedom of speech, II 261b

ideology, I 631b–632b

mimesis, III 227a

mythology, III 274a

primitivism, III 586a

progress, III 631b

Diodati, Giovanni (1576–1649), deism, I 647b

Diodorus Curtius, Enlightenment, II 95b

Diodorus Siculus (1st century B.C.)

biology, I 232a

culture, I 610b

human nature, III 573b, 574b

mythology, III 299b

progress, III 627a–627b, 631b

Diodotus

democracy, II 260a

freedom of speech, II 260a

Diogenes of Apollonia (5th century B.C.)

analogy, I 60b
cynicism, I 630a
design argument, I 670b
freedom of speech, II 258b
human nature, III 574a
metaphor, III 203b
religion, III 203b
Diogenes Laërtius (3rd century A.D.)
atomism, I 132b, 496b
causation, I 273a
continuity, I 503b
cycles, I 623a
cynicism, I 628a, 628b, 629b, 630a
Epicureanism, II 137b
free will, II 137b, 243b
historiography, I 503b
humanism, II 520a
infinity, II 604b
music, IV 38a
Platonism, III 516b
progress, III 630a
psychology, IV 7b
Pythagoreans, IV 35a, 36a, 38a
skepticism, IV 234b, 237b, 238a, 243a
Diogenes of Oenoanda, skepticism, IV 234b
Diogenes of Sinope (412?–323 B.C.)
Alexander the Great and, I 633b
animals, III 596a
asceticism, I 631b–632a
biology, I 233b
Christianity, III 589b, 590a
cynicism, I 627b–629a, 630a–632a, 632b, 633a, 633b; III 585a–585b, 586a, 586b, 589b, 592b
Cynics, III 503b
education, I 630a, 631a
ethics, IV 320b
freedom of speech, II 260b
ideology, I 632b, 633a
law, I 632a
mythology, III 273b–274a
Nature, I 632a; III 347b, 348a, 348b
Platonism, III 503b
primitivism, III 585a–585b, 586a, 586b, 589b, 590a, 592b, 596a
social contract, IV 252b
State, I 631b
Stoicism, IV 320b
temperance, IV 369b
theriophily, IV 384b–385a, 385b
tragedy, I 631a
Zeno of Citium and, IV 320b

Diomedes (4th century A.D.), poetics, III 526a
Dion, Léon, ideology, II 558a
Dionysian ritual, catharsis, I 269a
Dionysian tragic sense, IV 413a–414b
Dionysians, mimesis, III 226a
Dionysius the Areopagite (1st century A.D.)
Chain of Being, I 326a
demonology, I 667b, 669a–669b
harmony, IV 41a
Neo-Platonism, III 377b–378a
Pythagoreans, IV 41a
salvation, IV 228b
Dionysius Exiguus (6th century A.D.)
dignity, IV 137b
mathematics, III 182a
measurement, IV 402a
time, IV 402a
Dionysius of Fourna, iconography, II 526a
Dionysius of Halicarnassus (d. about 7 B.C.)
evolution of literature, II 170a
linguistics, III 62a
literature, IV 330b, 331a
oratory, II 170a
poetics, III 526a
rhetoric, IV 169b
style, IV 330b, 331a
Dionysius Thrax (fl. 100 B.C.), Aristotle and, II 665a
classification of the arts, I 458a
language, II 664b–665a
linguistics, III 62a
Dionysus (myth), III 272b, 282b, 305b, 496b, 500b; IV 96b
human nature, III 572b
metaphor, III 203b
motif, III 240b
music, III 268b
mythology, III 240b
perfectibility, III 464b
Pythagoreans, IV 31a
religion, III 203b; IV 96b
Dionysus-Zagreus (myth), II 341a
Diophantus (3rd century A.D.), mathematics, II 203a
Diopithes (5th century B.C.)
decrees, II 258b
impiety, II 565b, 566a, 566b
Dioscorides, Pedanius (1st century A.D.), I 29a
Diplomacy
game theory, II 264a

international peace, III 443b, 452a–452b, 454b, 456b
Kant, III 443b
U.N., III 454b
Dirac, Paul Adrien Maurice
chance, I 339b
cosmology, I 568b
entropy, II 118a
relativity, IV 91a
Dirac-Jordan transformation theory, II 588b
Dirichlet, Peter (1805–1859), continuity, I 498b
Disarmament, international peace, III 444b, 449b, 454a, 455a, 455b, 456a, 456b
Discipline
education, II 385b
happiness, II 385b
holy, II 512a
Machiavelli, IV 316a
reformation, IV 64a
socialism, IV 286b
State, IV 316a
temperance, IV 367b
work, IV 531b, 532a
Discontinuity, I 495b–497b
Aaron ben Elijah of Nicodemia, I 496a
al-Ghazali, I 496a
Aristotle, I 495b
atheism, I 495b, 496b
atomism, I 495b–497b
Averroës, I 496a
catastrophism, I 500a, 500b
Cicero, I 497a
cosmic images, I 514a
Democritus, I 494b–497a
Engels, I 497a–497b
Epicurus, I 496a–497a
Greece (ancient), I 495b–497a
humanism, IV 134b
Islam, I 495b–496b
Lenin, I 497a–497b
Lucretius, I 497a
Maimonides, I 495b, 496a
Marxism, I 497a–497b
occasionalism, I 496a
Plutarch, I 497a
probability, III 620a
prophecy, III 667b
Renaissance, IV 134b
Saint Thomas Aquinas, I 496a
theology, I 495b–497b
transformism, I 499b, 500b
uniformitarianism, I 492b, 499b–500b
Disease, II 395b–407b
Aeschylus, II 399a
air pollution, II 397b

Alcmaeon of Croton, II 397b
alcoholism, II 402b
anatomy, II 400b, 401a–401b, 404a
antibiotics, II 406a
anti-ontology, II 405a
Apollo (myth), II 397b
apologism, III 90a
apothecary, II 401a
Arabia (ancient), II 398b
Aretaeus, II 398b
Aristotelianism, II 398a, 399a, 400b
art, II 396a, 399a
asceticism, II 399a
Asclepiades, II 398b
Atharva-Veda, II 395b
atomism, II 398b
Auenbrugger, II 401b
bacillus (tubercle), II 405a
bacteriology, II 405a, 405b
baroque, II 403b
Bayle, II 403b
beauty, II 399a
Bede, II 399a
Bellers, II 402a
Bernard, Claude, II 404a–405a
Bible, II 396b, 399a, 403a; III 279a
Bichat, II 404a
biochemistry, II 404b
biology, II 398a, 400b, 403b, 405b
biophysics, II 404b
Bismarck, II 406a
body, II 397a–406b
Buddhism, II 397a
chemistry, II 400b, 401a
China (ancient), II 396b, 397a
cholera (Asiatic), II 403a
Chopin, II 403b
Christianity, II 399a, 406a
Cicero, II 397b
colds, II 404b
Columbus, II 399b
consumption, II 398b, 403b, 405a
contagious, II 399b, 400a
crime, II 400b
DDT, II 406a
De Haen, II 402b
death, II 396a, 397a, 401a, 401b, 402a, 404a
defined, II 395b, 396a–396b, 397a, 405a
degeneration, II 404a
demonology, II 396a–396b, 397a
Descartes, II 400b
Dewey, John, III 569a
diagnosis, II 396a

diphtheria, II 401b, 405a
dropsy, II 398b
Du Bois-Reymond, II 404b
Dürer, Albrecht, II 399a
Egypt (ancient), II 395b–396b
elements, II 398a
Elisha (Bible), II 396b
emotion, II 395b
empiricism, II 398b
endocrine glands, II 405a
Enlightenment, II 402b, 403a
environment, II 122b, 124a–125a, 125b, 126a, 129a
epidemics, II 397b, 399b, 400a, 402a, 403a–403b, 405a
epilepsy, II 398b
ethics, IV 321a, 321b
evil, II 395b, 396b
examinations, II 396a
faith, II 399a
fatigue, II 404b
four temperaments, II 398b, 399a
Fracastoro, II 399b
French disease, II 399b
Galen, II 398a–398b, 400b, 402a; III 381b
gastric ulcers, II 401b
Gehazi (Bible), II 396b
Germ Theory, II 284a, 405a
God, II 343b, 395b, 396a, 396b, 397a, 397b, 399a, 403a, 403b
Goethe, II 403b
good, II 397a, 398a, 403a, 406a
gout, II 403b
Graunt, II 402a
Greece (ancient), II 397a–399a
happiness, II 399a, 406b
harmony, II 397b
Harvey, II 400a, 400b, 401a
Helmholtz, II 404b
Helmont, II 400a, 400b–401a
hepatitis, II 398b
heresy, II 400b
Hesiod, II 395b
Hippocrates, II 396a, 397b, 398a–398b, 400a, 400b
homeostasis, II 404b
Homer, II 397b
hospital, II 401b–402a, 406a
human nature, III 574a
humours, II 398a–398b, 400a, 400b
hunger, II 404b
hygiene, II 397a–397b
immortality, II 397a, 402b

immunology, II 405a, 406a
India (ancient), II 395b–397a
indolence, II 397b
Industrial Revolution, II 403a, 403b, 405b–406a
infection, II 399b, 405a, 405b, 406a
inheritance, II 620b
injury, II 396a
insurance, II 406a
irritation, II 404a
Israel (ancient), II 396b
Jenner, II 403a
Jesus Christ, II 399a
joy, II 397a
Judea (ancient), II 398b
Justinian, II 399b
Keats, II 403b
kidneys, II 398b
knowledge, II 396a
Koch, II 405a, 405b
laboratory, II 402a–402b, 405a, 406a
Laennec, II 401b, 403b
League of Nations, II 406a
leprosy, II 396b, 399a, 399b
Linné, II 400a
liver, II 398a, 398b
logic, II 396b
longevity, III 90a
luxury, II 397b
macrocosm and microcosm, II 397a
Magendie, II 404a
magic, II 396b, 397b
Mann, II 406b; III 252a
Mark (Bible), II 399a
masturbation, II 403a
Mather, II 403a
Matthew (Bible), II 399a
Medicaid, II 406a
melancholia, II 399a, 403b
mental illness, II 395b, 397b, 400b, 403b, 404b
Mesopotamia (ancient), II 396a–396b
methodology, III 381b
microbes, II 405a, 406a
Middle Ages, II 399b
mind, II 397a, 399a, 402b, 406b
Miriam (Bible), II 396b
morality, II 396b
Morgagni, II 401a–401b, 404a
multiple sclerosis, II 401b
mythology, II 395b, 397b; III 279a
Nature, II 397b, 398a, 400a, 400b, 402a, 402b, 403a, 403b, 404b, 406b
Newton, III 396a

Nirvana, II 397a
nominalism, II 406b
nosology, II 400a, 401a, 404b
Novalis, II 403b
Oedipus (myth), II 397b
omens, II 396a
onanism, II 403a
ontology, II 399b–400a, 404a, 404b
Origen, II 399a
pain, II 396a, 398a
Paracelsus, II 400a, 400b, 401a
passions, II 397a, 398a
Pasteur, II 405a, 405b
pathology, II 400b, 405b
Persia (ancient), II 398b
philanthropy, II 406a
philosophy, II 395b, 396b, 397a, 397b, 398b, 399a
physicians, II 395b, 396a, 397a, 397b, 398a, 398b, 400a, 400b, 401a, 401b, 402a, 402b, 404a, 405b
physics, II 400b
physiology, II 404a–404b, 406b
Pinel, II 400a
plague, II 399b
Plato, II 399a, 399b–400a
Platonism, II 398a
pleurisy, II 398b
pneumonia, II 398b, 401b
Poe, II 403b
poetry, II 399a
Polybius, III 574a
power, III 574a
pragmatism, III 569a
primitivism, III 583a
prognosis, II 396a
progress, III 649a
prophecy, III 659a, 660b
Pseudo-Aristotelianism, II 399a
psychology, II 397a, 398a
punishment, II 396b
rationalism, II 395b, 396b; IV 48a
realism, II 406b
reductionism, II 404b
religion, II 396b, 397a, 406a
remedies, II 397a
Renaissance, II 399b, 403b
romanticism, II 403b
Rousseau, II 402b, 403b
Rufus of Ephesus, II 398b
salvation, II 397a, 399a, 406b
sin, II 395b, 396b, 399a, 400b, 403a
smallpox, II 403a
society, II 396a, 403a, 403b, 406b

somatic, II 397b
Sophocles, II 397b
sorcery, II 396b
soul, II 397b, 398a, 400b, 401a
stars, II 399b
stethoscopes, II 401b
Stoicism, II 397b, 398a, 399a; IV 321a, 321b
sulfonamides, II 406a
sun, II 397b
superstition, II 396b
surgeons, II 401a, 401b
surgery, II 406a
Sutrasthana, II 397a
Sydenham, II 400a
symmetry, II 399a
symptoms, II 396a–396b, 398b, 400a
syphilis, II 399b, 403a, 403b
Syria (ancient), II 398b
Taoism, II 397a
teleology, II 398a
temperance, II 398b–399a
Thebes, II 397b
Theognis, II 397a
thermometers, II 402a, 402b
thirst, II 404b
time, II 398b
truth, II 397a
tuberculosis, II 403b, 405a
typhoid fever, II 401b
universe, II 396b
Utopia, IV 463b
vaccination, II 403a
value, II 397b
variolation, II 403a
venereal, II 402b
Vesalius, II 400b, 401a, 402a
vice, II 402b
Virchow, II 403a, 404a, 404b, 405b
virtue, II 397a, 397b, 399a
wealth, II 397a
Will, II 400b
wisdom, II 399a
witchcraft, IV 523a
Wordsworth, II 403b
work, II 395b, 403a
World Health Organization (U.N.), II 406a
yin and yang, II 397a
See also Medicine
Dispersion
  Newton, III 418b–419a
  optics, III 418b–419a, 420b
Disraeli, Benjamin (1804–1881), conservatism, I 480b
Distribution
  economic history, II 46a–46b, 49b, 54a

good, **IV** 179a
justice, **IV** 179a
Mill, **IV** 179a
probability, **III** 610b, 612b–613a, 616b, 619a, 620a
Smith, Adam, **II** 49b
Victorian sensibility, **IV** 217b, 218a, 218b, 220b, 222a
Ditheism, Christianity, **II** 342b
Divination
Aeschylus, **III** 625a, 625b
astrology, **I** 118b–119b, 124b
dignity, **IV** 144a, 145a, 145b
Egypt (ancient), **III** 11a
ethics, **IV** 320a
Faust (legend), **III** 250a
Ficino, **IV** 144b, 145a
fortune, **II** 226a, 227a, 230b, 231a, 232a, 236a
good, **IV** 179b, 180a
Greece (ancient), **II** 675a–675b, 676a, 679b, 680a, 680b, 682b
impiety, **II** 564b
infinity, **II** 605a
law, **II** 675a–675b, 676a, 679b, 680a, 680b, 682b; **III** 11a
light, **III** 410a
Machiavellism, **III** 116b, 119a
matter, **III** 186a
music, **III** 264b, 267b–272a
mythology, **III** 286b
natural law, **III** 15a, 18a, 19a
Pico della Mirandola, **IV** 145b
progress, **III** 625b, 625b, 626a
prophecy, **III** 657b, 658a, 663a
Pythagoreans, **IV** 31a, 32a
Renaissance, **IV** 144b, 145a, 145b
skepticism, **IV** 235b–236a
Stoicism, **IV** 320a
tragic sense, **IV** 413a
witchcraft, **IV** 521a
Divini, Eustachio (1620–1695), optics, **III** 420a
Dixmerie, Nicolas Bricaire de La, Rousseau and, **III** 602b
Djahiz ('Amr Ibn Bahr Jahiz) (773?–869), classification of the sciences, **I** 463b
Djilas, Milovan
class, **III** 154b
Khrushchev and, **III** 166a
Marxism, **III** 154b
DNA, **I** 239a, 239b–241b,

245b
chromosomes, **II** 289a
Crane, **II** 291a
Crick, **II** 289b–291a, 291b
Doty, **II** 291a
genetic continuity, **II** 286b, 289a, 289b–292b
heredity, **II** 289b–292b
Kornberg, **II** 291a
La Mettrie, **II** 292a
Levinthal, **II** 291a
Marmur, **II** 291a
Meselson, **II** 291a–291b
Stahl, **II** 291a–291b
Taylor, **II** 291b
Watson, **II** 289b–291a, 291b
Dobrzeniecki, T., iconography, **II** 538b
Dobzhansky, Theodosius
acquired characteristics, **II** 622a
inheritance, **II** 622a
Dodds, E. R.
catharsis, **I** 268b–269a
Neo-Platonism, **III** 373a
Pythagoreans, **IV** 31a
rationalism, **IV** 46a
Dodgson, C. L., social welfare, **IV** 282b
Dodsworth, Roger, Gothic, **II** 369a
Dogma
heresy, **II** 424b, 425b, 426a, 426b, 427b, 429a, 429b, 430b
idea, **II** 546a–546b
necessity, **III** 354b, 357a, 359b
Neo-Platonism, **III** 372a, 373a
religion, **IV** 107a, 107b–108a, 116a, 117a, 118b, 119a, 120b
skepticism, **IV** 235a–236a, 237a, 238b, 239b, 240a, 244a, 245a
Voltaire, **IV** 118b
Dolce, B.
aesthetics, **IV** 354b
mimesis, **III** 229a
ut pictura poesis, **IV** 467b
Dolce, Lodovico (1508–1568)
art, **II** 305a
genius, **II** 305a
D'Olivet, Fabre, cosmic images, **I** 519b
D'Olivet, Pierre-Joseph Thoulier, classicism, **I** 451b
Dollard, John
behaviorism, **I** 223a
war, **IV** 507b
Döllinger, Johann (1799–

1890)
excommunication of, **I** 424a
modernism, **I** 419b
Dollond, John (1706–1761), optics, **III** 420a
Dominic, Saint (1170–1221), **I** 383b
heresy, **II** 419b
humanism, **IV** 132b
Dominicans
China, **I** 354b, 357a–357b
grace, **I** 394a–394b
scholasticism, **I** 383b
Domitian (51–96 A.D.), freedom of speech, **II** 261b
Don Juan (legend)
love, **III** 103a
motif, **III** 241a
mythology, **III** 241a
Nature, **III** 350b
Don Quixote (fiction), organicism, **III** 422a
Donation of Constantine
heresy, **II** 419a, 420b
historiography, **II** 485a
Middle Ages, **II** 419a, 420b
Roman Catholic Church, **II** 419b, 420b, 520b
Donatists
heresy, **II** 417a, 418b
reformation, **IV** 62b–63a
schism, **I** 377a
Donatus, Aelius (4th century A.D.)
language, **II** 665a, 666b, 667a
poetry, **III** 528b
Dondi, Giovanni di (fl. 1400), clocks, **IV** 402b
Doni, Antonfrancesco (1513?–1574), on artistic personality, **II** 321a
Doni, Giovanni Battista (1594–1647), on counterpoint, **II** 321a–321b
Donne, John (1573–1631), aesthetics, **I** 512a
baroque in literature, **I** 191b, 193a, 193b, 194b, 195a
Chapman and, **III** 294b
Cosmic Fall, **I** 506a–506b, 507a, 512a
cosmic images, **I** 517a
harmony, **II** 394b
hierarchy, **II** 434b, 443b
literary paradox, **III** 77b, 78b, 80a, 80b
mountains in literature, **III** 254b, 256a
music, **II** 394b
mythology, **III** 294b
periodization in literary history, **III** 485b
Saint Paul and, **III** 80a

suicide, **III** 80a
universe, **II** 443b
Doppler, Christian (1803–1853), cosmology, **I** 553a
Doppler effect
cosmology, **I** 553a, 562a, 567a
space, **IV** 305b
Doresse, J., Gnosticism, **II** 327b
Dörffel, Georg Samuel, cosmology, **I** 549a
Dorfles, Gillo, mythology, **III** 315b
Doric order, architecture, **III** 365a, 366b, 368b, 370b
Dorn, Gerhard, **I** 28b
Dorotheus of Sidon (6th century A.D.), astrology, **I** 120a–121b, 122a, 122b, 124a, 124b
D'Ors, Eugenio
baroque in literature, **I** 194b–195a
cosmic images, **I** 513b, 515a
Dort, synod of, **II** 28b
Dositheus, **I** 411a
Dosso Dossi (1479?–1542), iconography, **II** 529b
Dostoevski, Fëdor (1821–1881)
comedy, **I** 469b
conservatism, **I** 483a
literature, **III** 86a
motif, **III** 241b
realism in literature, **IV** 53a
tragic sense, **IV** 416b
wisdom of the fool, **IV** 520a
Doty, Paul, DNA, **II** 291a
Double truth, **II** 31a–37b
Albumazar, **II** 35b–36a
Alexander of Aphrodisias, **II** 36b
Arabic doctrines, **II** 31b, 32a, 32b
Aristotelianism, **II** 32a, 34b, 36a, 36b, 37b
Aristotle, **II** 31b, 32a, 33a, 34b, 35a, 36b, 37a, 37b
astrology, **II** 35b–36a
Augustinianism, **II** 32a
Averroës, **II** 31b, 32a–32b, 33a, 34b, 35a, 37a
Bacon, Roger, **II** 31b
Bible, **II** 31b, 35b
Blasius of Parma, **II** 35a–36a, 37a
Boethius of Dacia, **II** 31b, 33b–34a, 36b, 37b
Buridan, **II** 34a–34b, 36b, 37b
Christianity, **II** 31a–37b
Duns Scotus, **II** 36b

excommunication, II 31b
faith, II 33a. 33b, 34a, 34b, 35b
Gerson, II 34a
God, II 32a–37a
Greece (ancient), II 31b, 32a, 32b, 33a
Gregory IX (Pope), II 31b
heresy, II 31b
Islam, II 35a
John of Jandun, II 32b 34b–35a, 35b, 37a, 37b
Judaism, II 35b
Middle Ages, II 31b–37b
Nature, II 33a, 34b
Neo-Platonism, II 32a
paganism, II 31b, 32a, 33a, 34a
philosophy, II 31a–37b
Pomponazzi, II 36b–37a
probability, II 33b, 34a–34b
psychology, II 32a–32b
reason, II 33a, 33b, 34a, 34b, 36b
revelation, II 34a, 34b
Roman Catholic Church, II 31a–31b, 36a–36b, 37a
Saint Augustine, II 31b
Saracens, II 35b
Siger of Brabant, II 31b, 32b–34a, 34b, 36a, 36b, 37b
soul, II 32b, 34a, 34b, 35a, 35b
Tempier, II 31a–31b
theology, II 31a–37b
universe, II 32a
See also Truth
Douglas, Stephen (1813–1861), popular sovereignty, I 437a–437b
Douglas, William O. (1898–), law, III 9a, 9b
Dowries, law, II 686b
Draco (c. 600 B.C.), law, II 674a, 679a, 680b, 681a, 681b
Drake, Nathan (1766–1836), romanticism, IV 192a
Schlegel and, IV 192a
Drama
ambiguity, I 50a–51a, 54b–56a
art and play, I 101b–102a, 102b–103a
Brecht, II 87b
censorship, III 497b–498a
China, I 367a, 372a
civil disobedience, I 434b
comedy, III 238a, 527a, 528a, 531a
counter-Enlightenment, II 107a, 108a

cynicism, I 632a
death, I 635b
empathy, II 87a–87b
ethics, III 440a
evolution of literature, II 171a–171b, 172b
expressionism, II 206b, 208a–208b, 209a
Faust (legend), III 247b, 248a–250a
France, II 529b, 531a
genius, II 323b
Germany, II 206b, 208a–208b, 209a
God, II 340b
Great Britain, II 208b; III 482b, 483b, 530a, 531a
Greece (ancient), III 112a, 527a, 527b
Hamlet problem, I 54b–56a
humanism, II 517b
irony, II 627a, 629b, 631a, 631b, 633b–634a
Italy, III 531a
loyalty, III 112a
Machiavellism, III 118a–119a, 121b
Marlowe, III 247b–248a
Middle Ages, III 528b
Mill, J. S., IV 199a
motif, III 238a
music, II 323b
mythology, III 277a, 281b, 307a
pastoral, III 531a
peace, III 440a
periodization in literary history, III 482b, 483a
Plato, III 497b–498a, 500a
Platonism, III 497b–498a, 500a
poetry, III 527a, 527b, 528b, 529b, 530a, 531a
primitivism, III 601b, 602a, 602b
realism in literature, IV 54b
religion, IV 100a
romanticism, IV 189a, 189b, 190a, 199a
satire, III 527a
Spain, III 531a, 601b
symbolism, IV 340b, 344b
tragedy, III 527a, 527b, 531a
tragicomedy, III 531a
U.S., II 208b
unity, III 527a, 527b, 531a
ut pictura poesis, IV 467a–468a, 472b, 475a
Draper, John W. (1811–1882)
recapitulation, IV 58b

religion, IV 107a
Drawing
aesthetics, II 221b–222a, 222b
art, I 495b; II 305b, 580a
genius, II 305b
impressionism, II 580a
mythology, III 291b, 296b, 298b
naturalism in art, III 342a, 346a
Dray, W. H., causation, I 285a
Drayton, Michael (1563–1631)
Chapman and, III 295b
hermeticism, II 432a
mythology, III 295a, 295b, 296b–297a
Dreams
mythology, III 312b–313a, 315a
prophecy, III 657b, 659b, 664b
romanticism, IV 196b, 201b, 202a
Dreiser, Theodore (1871–1945), class, I 445b
Dreyfus, Alfred (1859–1935), romanticism, IV 196b
Droysen, Johann Gustav (1808–1884)
historicism, II 461a
historiography, II 494a–494b
symmetry, IV 347a–347b
Drugs
happiness, III 475a
law, III 34b
perfectibility, III 475a
virtue, IV 476b
Drummond, Henry (1851–1897)
eschatology, II 160a
evolution, III 474b
God, III 474b
perfectibility, III 474b
Drummond of Hawthornden (1585–1649)
Cosmic Fall, I 508b–509a
hierarchy, II 436a
Drury, John, reunion of Protestants and Catholics, I 398b
Dryden, John (1631–1700)
art, II 307a, 308b
art and play, I 103b
attitude toward antiquity, I 78a, 80a
baroque in literature, I 191a, 193b, 194b
Boileau and, I 453a
classicism, I 450a, 452b, 453a, 454a

death, I 635b, 636b
deism, I 650a
Eliot and, I 453a
genius, II 307a, 308b
Gothic, II 368a
literary criticism, I 596a
mythology, III 298b, 300a
neo-classicism in art, III 362a, 369b
periodization in literary history, III 481b, 482a
primitivism, III 601a
Puritanism, I 650a
romanticism, IV 193a, 194a, 195a
satire, IV 214a, 214b
Du Bois-Reymond, Emil (1818–1896)
disease, II 404b
empiricism, III 546a
linguistics, IV 428b
positivism, III 546a
uniformitarianism, IV 428b
Du Bois-Reymond, Paul (1831–1889), continuity, I 498b
Du Fresnoy, Charles Alphonse (1611–1688)
aesthetics, II 218b
Gothic, II 368a
ideal, II 549b
mythology, III 298b–299a
neo-classicism in art, III 369b
Du Halde, J. B., China, I 360b, 361b, 365b
Du Perron, Cardinal, skepticism, IV 242a
Du Pont de Nemours, Pierre Samuel (1739–1817), Enlightenment, II 98b
Dualism, II 38a–44a
aesthetics, II 218a, 220b, 221a
Alain, II 41b
Alcmaeon of Croton, IV 346b
anarchy, II 40a
Anaxagoras, II 40b; IV 346b
Anaximander, IV 346b
animism, II 38b
anthropology, II 38a
Aristotle, I 673a; II 41a; IV 34a
art, II 581b
Avesta, II 38a, 39b
Bayle, II 38a
Berkeley, II 246a
Bible, II 39a, 42a–42b
Bogomils, II 43a
Brâhmana, II 39a
Bruno, IV 393b

Cartesianism, II 38a, 41b, 443b, 444a, 445b
Cathari, II 43a
China (ancient), II 41b–42a
Christianity, II 38b, 39a, 41a, 42a–43b; III 281b
continuity, I 494b
cosmology, II 38a
Creation, II 38b, 42a–42b
de Broglie, I 495a
death, II 38b
Democritus, IV 346b
demonology, II 38b–39a, 39b
Descartes, I 217a–217b; II 41a, 381a, 443b, 445a; III 214a; IV 201a
dignity, IV 138b
Egypt (ancient), II 38b–39a
Empedocles, II 40b; IV 346b
empiricism, III 549b
Epicureanism, II 41a
equity, II 148a–148b
error, II 38a
eschatology, II 40a, 154b, 155a
evil, II 38a, 38b, 39a–40a, 40b–41a, 43a, 162b, 164a, 164b, 165a
existentialism, III 159a, 159b
falsity, II 39a
Faust (legend), III 246a
Fichte, II 41b
free will, II 246a
Galileo, IV 393b
geometry, IV 304a
Germany, II 39a
Gnosticism, II 38b, 42a–43a
God, II 38a, 38b–39a, 40b, 41a, 42a–42b, 43a, 335b, 337a, 338b, 339b, 344b
good, II 38a, 38b, 39a–40a, 43a; IV 180a
Greece (ancient), II 39a, 40a–41a, 42a, 42b, 164a, 164b
happiness, II 381a, 382b, 387a
Hegel, II 41b; III 159b; IV 180a, 291a
Heraclitus, II 40b; IV 346b
Herder, I 618b
heresy, II 42a–42b, 43a
hierarchy, II 443b, 444a, 445b
Hyde, II 38a
Iamblichus, IV 346b–347a
impressionism, II 581b

India (ancient), II 39a, 41b
Indians (American), II 38b
Iran, II 155a
Iran (ancient), II 39a–40a, 42a
Islam, II 42b
Jansenism, II 43b
Judaism, II 39a, 42a–42b; III 281b
justice, II 657b–658a
Kant, II 41a–41b; III 436b
kinds of, II 38a
knowledge, II 38a
legends, II 38b–40a, 43a
Leibniz, II 38a, 41a
Lovejoy, II 41b
Luther, II 43b
Manicheism, II 38b, 42b–43a
Man-Machine, III 138a, 138b, 143a, 145a, 145b
Marxism, III 159a, 159b
matter, II 38a, 38b, 41a, 43a
metaphysical imagination, III 220b
Middle Ages, II 43a, 218a
mind, II 38a, 41a
monism, II 40a, 41a, 41b
monotheism, II 42a
morality, II 40a, 41b
mountains in literature, III 253a, 255a
music, III 264b–265a, 270b
mythology, II 38b–40a, 43a; III 281b, 283a, 306a
naturalism, II 581b; III 342a
Nature, II 38b, 43b; III 350b–351a
neo-classicism in art, III 371a
Neo-Platonism, III 373a, 375a
Orientalism, III 436b
origin of the term, II 38a
Pahlavi, II 38a, 40a
Parmenides, II 40b; IV 346b
Parsees, II 40a
Paulicians, II 43a
perennial philosophy, III 458b, 460b
Persia (ancient), II 38a, 42b–43a
Philo Judaeus, II 42a
philosophy, II 38a–38b, 40a–42a
Plato, II 40a–41a; III 507a, 508b; IV 3b, 4a, 4b, 34b
Platonism, II 41b, 42a, 42b; III 504a, 505a, 507a, 508a, 508b, 509a
pleasure, II 381a, 382b,

387a
Plotinus, IV 8b
pre-Gnostic, II 42a
probability, III 614a, 621b
prophecy, III 665b, 667a–667b
psychology, IV 3b, 4a, 4b, 8b, 11a, 16b, 21a, 25a, 27b
Puritanism, IV 16b
Pythagoreans, IV 34a–34b, 346b
Pythagoras, II 40a–40b
religion, II 38a–40a, 42a–43b
Renaissance, II 41a, 218a; IV 138b
right, IV 180a
Roman Catholic Church, II 42b
romanticism, IV 201a, 204a, 207a
Saint Augustine, II 43a–43b
Saint John, II 43a
Saint Paul, II 43a
Saint Thomas Aquinas, I 673a
salvation, IV 229a, 231a
Satan, II 38a
Schlegel, III 306a
Set (myth), II 39a
Shelley, III 508a
socialism, IV 291a
Socrates, II 40b
Sophists, IV 346b
soul, II 38a, 40b–41a
space, IV 295b, 296a, 299a, 304a
Spinoza, II 41a, 445b; IV 393b
spiritualism, II 38b
Stoicism, II 41a
symmetry, IV 346a–347a, 350b–351a
systematic, II 39a–39b
theodicy, IV 379a, 379b, 380a, 380b
time, IV 391b, 393b
totalitarianism, IV 409a, 410a
tragic sense, IV 414b, 415a
truth, II 39a
two principal meanings, II 38a
Veda, II 39a, 39b, 41b
Volksgeist, IV 495a
witchcraft, IV 521b, 522a, 522b, 523a
Wolff, II 38a
work, IV 530b, 532a
yin and yang, II 41b–42a
Zeus, II 39a
Zoroaster, II 39b, 40a

Zoroastrianism, II 38a–43a; IV 231a
Zurvân, II 40a
Dubcek, Alexander
  Marxism, III 169b
  revisionism, IV 274b
Dubislav, Walter, empiricism, III 546a
Dubois, Pierre (1852?–1925), international peace, III 452b
Dubos, Jean Baptiste (1670–1742)
  aesthetics, IV 355a, 355b
  art, II 309b
  attitude toward antiquity, I 82b–83a, 83b, 85a, 86a
  beauty, I 202b
  genius, II 294a, 309b
  mimesis, III 228a
  painting, IV 471b
  poetics, III 530b
  poetry, III 228a, 530b; IV 471b
Dubos, René (1901–   ), catharsis, I 268a
Ducasse, C. J.
  beauty, I 209b
  immortality, I 644a
  reincarnation, I 644a
Ducasse, Pierre (1813–1893), positivism, III 532b
Duchamp, Marcel (1887–1968)
  chance images, I 352b
  ut pictura poesis, IV 475b
Duchesne, Louis (1843–1922), modernism, I 420b
Duck, Stephen, primitivism, III 600b
Duclos, Jacques, Marxism, III 156b
Due process, III 6a–10b
  justice, II 654b–655a
Duff, William (1732–1815)
  art, II 306b, 307a, 307b
  creativity in art, I 588a
  genius, II 295a, 306b, 307a, 307b
Dugas, Charles, mythology, III 286a–286b
Dugdale, Richard (1841–1883), psychology, IV 26b
Dugdale, William (1605–1686), Gothic, II 369a
Duhem, Pierre (1861–1916), axiomatization, I 166b
  continuity, I 503b
  entropy, II 114b, 118b
  historiography, I 503b
  humanism, IV 130a
  infinity, II 609b
  matter, III 192a
  pragmatism, III 553b, 555a, 564b

science, II 201b; III 555a
Dühring, Karl Eugen (1833–1921)
historicism, II 457a
perfectibility, III 474a
Dullaert, John, science, II 204a
Dumas, Alexandre (1824–1895), realism in literature, IV 52a
Duméry, Henry, theodicy, IV 383a
Dumézil, Georges
mythology, III 313b, 315a
religion, IV 94b–95a
Dümmler, Ferdinand, cynicism, I 627b
Dumortier, B. C., genetic continuity, II 285b
Dumuzi (myth), II 335b
Dunbar, William (1460?–?1520), death, I 637a
Dundes, Alan, mythology, III 316a, 316b
Duns Scotus, John (1265?–?1308)
abstraction, I 4a, 5b–6a
aesthetics, II 217b–218a
analogy, I 67a
authority, I 148b
Bacon and, I 173b
causation, I 275a
classification of the arts, I 458b
common nature, I 4a, 5b–6a, 6b
double truth, II 36b
God, I 275a
heresy, II 426a
Middle Ages, I 67a
Peirce and, III 555a
soul, II 36b
space, IV 301b
time, IV 392a
value, IV 452b, 453b
Dunton, John (1659–1733), virtuoso, IV 489a
Duplessis-Mornay, Philippe de (1549–1623), social contract, IV 254a
Dupuis, Charles François (1742–1809)
mythology, III 302a, 303b, 306b
rationalism, III 301a, 302a, 309b
religion, IV 94a
Dupuit, Jules, economic history, II 50b
value, IV 454a
Durand, Gilbert, mythology, III 315b
Durand, William (d. 1330), reformation, IV 65a

Durandus, Gulielmus (William) (1237?–1296), I 52b
iconography, II 527a
Durandus of Huesca, heresy, II 419b
Durante, Francesco (1684–1755)
genius, II 323a
music, II 323a
Duranty, Edmond
impressionism, II 573b
realism in literature, IV 52a
Durbin, E. F. M., war, IV 507b
Dürer, Albrecht (1471–1528), art, II 309a
canon of proportions, I 580a
chance images, I 344b–345a, 345b
creativity in art, I 580a
disease, II 399a
genius, II 309a
iconography, II 529b, 530b
Leibl and, III 345a
mimesis, III 228a, 228b
mythology, III 290b, 292b
naturalism in art, III 345a
D'Urfey, Thomas (1653–1723), cosmic voyages, I 528a
Duris of Samos (7th century B.C.)
art, II 299b
historiography, II 507a–507b
individualism, II 299b
Durkheim, Émile (1858–1917)
authority, I 156b–157a
Comte and, III 538b
historiography, II 497a
individualism, II 601a, 603b
love, III 97b
mythology, III 307a, 309b–310a, 311a–311b, 315a
positivism, III 538b
religion, IV 96b
ritual, III 311b
sacred, II 513b
structuralism, IV 325b
Dusch, T. von
genetic continuity, II 283b
spontaneous generation, II 283b
Dutch Guiana, primitivism, III 601b
Dutch language, III 63a
Dutens, Louis (1730–1812), attitude toward antiquity, I 85a–85b
Duty
Balguy, III 233a
determinism, II 241b

existentialism, III 160a
free will, II 241b
freedom, II 249a
Hart, III 2b–3a
Hegel, III 160a
Hume, III 232b
Judaism, III 487b
Kames, III 234b
Kant, III 472b; IV 179b
law, II 249a; III 1b, 2b–3a, 5a, 27b
Marxism, III 160a
moral sense, III 232b, 233a, 233b, 234a, 234b
morality, III 644b
natural law, III 22b
perfectibility, III 472b
philanthropy, III 487b
Price, Richard, III 233a
progress, III 630b, 644b, 649a
rationalism, IV 50a
Reid, III 234a
relativism, IV 71a
right, IV 173b, 176a, 179b, 180a, 182a, 183b, 186a
Smith, Adam, III 233a
Stoicism, IV 50a, 176a
sympathy, III 232b
Victorian sensibility, IV 217b, 218a, 218b, 220b, 222a
Volksgeist, IV 495b
welfare state, IV 511b
Duwe, Willi, symbolism, IV 342b
Dvořák, Max
naturalism in art, III 339a
periodization in literary history, III 484a
Dyad
Plato, IV 34a, 34b
Pythagoreans, IV 34a–35b
Speusippus, IV 35b
Dyer, John (1700?–1758), primitivism, III 600a
Dynamics, II 201b–204a
Dynamism
romanticism, IV 196a, 197a
totalitarianism, IV 408b
Dynasties
mythology, III 287a
nationalism, III 332a
World War I, III 332a

E

Ea (Enki), II 335b
Earle, John (1824–1903), primitivism, III 595b
Earth

acceleration, IV 76b
age of, II 176b
catastrophism, IV 417b, 418a, 418b, 419a, 419b, 420b, 421b, 422a, 423a
Descartes, III 257a
determinism, II 19a
distance from the moon, I 540a
Empedocles, IV 2b
evolutionism, II 174b, 176b
geology, III 254b, 255a, 255b, 256b
harmony, II 389b–390a
hermeticism, II 432b–433a
historiography, II 19a
linguistics, IV 424a, 424b, 426b
macrocosm and microcosm, III 128a, 129b
motion, I 544a, 545a, 545b, 546b, 550b; IV 74a, 74b, 76a–76b, 78a–78b
mountains in literature, III 254b, 255a, 255b, 256b, 257a, 257b, 259a, 259b
music, II 389b–390a
orbits, I 544a, 544b, 545b, 550b; IV 74b, 79a
psychology, IV 2b, 7b
relativity, IV 74a, 74b, 75a, 75b, 76a–76b, 78a–78b, 79a, 90a–90b
Seneca, III 128a
shape of, I 539a–539b, 543a, 547b
size of, I 543b
Stoics, IV 7a
time, IV 404a, 405a, 405b
uniformitarianism, IV 417b, 418a, 418b, 419a, 419b, 420b, 421b, 422a, 423a, 424a, 424b, 426b
velocity, IV 76b, 79a
See also Cosmology
Eastern Orthodox Church,
Bulgaria, I 409b
Conciliar Movement, I 410b
determinism, II 30a
economic history, II 46b
education, I 409b
Egypt, I 411a
filioque clause, I 410a
Greece, I 409b, 410a, 410b, 411a
humanism, II 515a, 516b
Lebanon, I 411a
Mass, IV 103a
missionaries, I 409b
mysticism, I 409b, 410b
mythology, III 276b
nationalism, I 411a–411b; III 324b
Patriarchate of Constanti-

nople, I 409a–409b, 410b, 411a–411b, 417b
Peter the Great, I 411a
Phanariots, I 411a
philanthropy, III 488b
Platonism, III 510a
Poland, I 411a
predestination, II 30a
religion, IV 103a
Roman Catholic Church, I 409a–411b
Russia, I 417b
Syria, I 411a
theology, II 30a
Turkey, I 409a–411b
Eastlake, Lady (1809–1893), romanticism, IV 193b
Eastman, George (1854–1932), philanthropy, III 491b
Ebbinghaus, Hermann (1850–1909)
association of ideas, I 116b
psychology, IV 13a
Ebeling, Gerhard, God, II 365b
Eberhard, Johann August (1739–1809)
genius, II 295b
romanticism, IV 191b
Ebionites, millenarianism, III 224a
Eble of Ventadour and Marcabru, Viscount, love, III 99b
Ebreo, Leone, see Abarbanel, Jehudah
Echtermeyer, T. (1805–1844), Hegel and, II 413a–413b
Eckermann, Johann Peter (1792–1854)
classicism, I 453b
Goethe and, IV 188a
motif, III 237a
Eckersberg, Wilhelm (1783–1853), naturalism in art, III 341a
Eckhart, Johannes (1260?–1327)
analogy, I 67a
Free Spirit, foundation of, II 422b
Hegel and, II 412b
heresy, II 417b, 418a, 422b, 426b
Islam, II 651a
Middle Ages, I 67a
mysticism, II 417b
perfectibility, III 467b
Eclecticism
Comte, III 534a
Cousin, III 533b
Orientalism, III 429b, 431a
perennial philosophy, III 458b–461b, 462b
Platonism, III 516b–517b,

521b, 522a
revisionism, IV 269b, 270b
Stanley, III 516b–517a
transcendentalism, III 429b
Eclipses, I 537b–538a, 539a, 539b, 540a
Ecology
conservation, I 475b
culture, II 128b, 131b, 133b
environment, II 122a, 128b, 131b, 133b
natural liberty, II 64b
technology, II 122a
Economic history, II 44a–61b
Age of Reason, II 45a
agriculture, II 47b, 57a
American Revolution, II 45a
anarchism, II 59a, 59b
Ashley, II 60b
assets, II 56a
Austria, II 61a
Ayres, II 60b
balance of trade, II 45b
Bible, II 47b, 58b
booms, II 58a–58b
Bray, II 60a
Bücher, II 60b
business cycle, II 57a–58b
Cabet, II 60a
capital, II 47b, 49a, 49b, 50a, 53a, 54a, 54b–57a
capitalism, II 59b
Carlyle, II 58b
Chamberlin, II 51b
Christianity, II 45a, 46b–47a, 47b, 58b
Clark, J. B., II 50b, 53b–54b
Cliffe-Leslie, II 60b
Cole, G. D. H., II 60a
Commons, J. R., II 60b
communication, II 44a–44b, 50a
communism, II 59b
consumption, II 52b, 53a
Copernicus, II 45a
copyrights, II 57a
cost, II 48b, 51a, 52a
Cournot, II 57a
craftsmanship, II 54b
crime, II 51b
Crusoe economy, II 52a, 52b, 53a–53b, 54b
culture, II 44b, 45b
death, II 56b
decreasing return, II 51a
demand, II 48b, 51b, 54a, 57b
democracy, II 44a, 46b, 47a, 59a, 59b
Descartes, II 45a
distribution, II 46a–46b, 49b, 54a
divisions of economic science, II 52a–53a

Dupuit, II 50b
Eastern Orthodox Church, II 46b
economic system concept, II 51b–52a
economics as a science, II 50a–51a
economizing, II 50a
education, II 47b
Edward VII, II 60a
Enlightenment, II 45a, 45b, 47a
enterprise-economy, II 54b–55b
entrepreneur, II 49b, 54b, 55a, 55b
error, II 51b
evolution of economic thought, II 46b–47b
fallacy of political economists, II 47b–50a
fallacy of three productive factors, II 51a–51b
family, II 54b
feedback principle, II 55a, 57b
feudalism, II 46b–47a, 54b
Fisher, Irving, II 48b, 57a
Fourier, II 60a
Foxwell, II 60b
France, II 45a, 47a, 49b, 57b
free social-economic order, II 53b–54b
freedom, II 44a–44b, 45b, 46a, 47a, 47b, 50a, 53a, 55a, 59a
French Revolution, II 45a, 57b
Galileo, II 45a
Garnier, II 50b
Germany, II 45a, 60b, 61a
Gibbon, II 46b
Gilbert, William, II 45a
gold, II 57b
goods, II 49a, 50b, 51a, 51b, 52a, 52b, 53a
Gossen, II 50b
Gray, John, II 60a
Great Britain, II 44b, 45a, 45b, 46a, 47a, 60a, 60b
Great Depression of the 1930's, II 58a, 58b
Greece (ancient), II 44b, 45a, 45b, 46b
handicrafts, II 54b
Hegel, II 61a
Hildebrand, II 60b
historicism, II 60b
Hume, II 45a–45b, 57b
idea of economics, II 45a–45b
idealism, II 46b
income, II 46b, 49a–49b,

52b–53b, 55a
increasing returns, II 51a
individualism, II 45b, 46b, 47a, 59a
industry, II 49a
inflation, II 57b
institutions, II 60b
interest, II 45b, 49b, 53b, 54a, 54b–58b
international trade, II 45b, 57a
investment, II 51a, 51b, 53a–53b, 54, 56a–56b
Islam, II 46b
Jefferson, II 44b, 46a
Jevons, II 47a, 50b, 52b
Keynes, II 58b
Knies, II 60b
labor, II 47b, 48a–48b, 49a, 49b, 50a, 51a, 52b, 54a, 57a, 59b–60a
laissez-faire, II 47a, 55b, 58b–59a
land, II 48a–48b, 49a, 49b, 50a, 51a, 52b, 54a
Landauer, II 60a
land rent, II 46b
law, II 51a, 59a
Leonardo da Vinci, II 45a
liberalism, II 47a–47b
Lincoln, II 44b
Lloyd, W. F., II 50b
loans, II 55a, 56a, 58a
Locke, II 45b, 57b
Longfield, II 50b
Luther, II 45a
Maine, II 61a
Malthus, II 49a, 49b
manufacturing, II 49a
marginalism, II 50b
market economic order, II 54b–57a
Marshall, II 48b, 50b, 53b–54b, 55a, 55b, 56b, 57a
Marx, II 49b, 59b, 60a
Marxism, II 49b, 55a, 59b
materialism, II 46b
materials, II 52b
meaning of the topic, II 44a–45a
mechanism, II 50a
Menger, II 47a, 50b, 52b, 60a, 61a
mercantilism, II 47b
Middle Ages, II 45a, 45b, 46b
Mill, J. S., II 48b, 49b–50a, 54a, 55a, 57a, 57b, 60a
Mitchell, W. C., II 60b
mobility, II 51a
modern cultural revolution, II 45b–46b
Molière, II 46a
money, II 45a–45b, 47b,

49a, 52b, 54b, 57a–58b
money-lending, II 55a, 56a, 58a
monopoly, II 48b, 51b, 57a
Montesquieu, II 60b
morality, II 51a
movements opposed to analytical economics, II 58b–61a
nationalism, II 47a
natural resources, II 51b
Newton, II 45a
North, Dudley, II 45b
oligopoly, II 51b
Owenism, II 59b, 60a
patents, II 57a
Petty, William, II 45b
Physiocrats, II 49b
population theory, II 49a
prices, II 46a–46b, 48a, 48b, 49a, 51b, 57b–58a
private property, II 47b, 49b
production, II 48b, 49a, 50b–51b, 52a, 52b, 53a, 54b, 58a
products, II 55a
profit, II 46b, 48b–49a, 49b, 50a, 54b–57a, 58a, 60a, 63b
Protestantism, II 46b–47a
Proudhon, II 49b
qualifications of economic analysis, II 57a
Reformation, II 46b–47a
Renaissance, II 45a, 45b, 46b
rent, II 48b, 49a, 49b, 51b, 54a, 54b–57a, 57b
resources, II 51b
Ricardo, II 48a, 48b, 49b, 50a, 54a, 57a, 59a
risk, II 55b–56a
Roman Catholic Church, II 45a, 46b–47a
Rome (ancient), II 44b, 45b, 46b
Roscher, II 60b
Rousseau, II 44b
Savigny, II 60b
savings, II 49a, 53a
Schmoller, II 60b, 61a
Senior, N. W., II 48b, 50b, 69a
services, II 53a, 55a
silver, II 57b
Sismondi, II 58b–59a
slavery, II 53a
Smith, Adam, II 45b–50a, 53a, 55a, 57a, 57b, 58b, 59a
socialism, II 59b–60b
society, II 44a–44b, 53a, 53b–54b
Spann, II 60b

State, II 47a
Steuart, II 46a
stock, II 48a, 49a
supply, II 48b, 51a, 51b, 54a, 57b
Tawney, II 60b
taxes, II 45b
technology, II 46a, 49a, 51a, 51b, 52b, 54a, 56b
Thompson, II 60a
Thünen, II 50b
trade, II 45b, 57a
unemployment, II 58a, 58b
U.S.S.R., II 59b
U.S., II 44b, 45a, 46a, 47a, 58b, 60b
utility, II 48a, 51b, 52b, 59a
utopianism, II 59b–60a
value, II 48a–48b
Veblen, II 60b
Vesalius, II 45a
wages, II 45b, 46b, 48b–49a, 49b, 50a, 54a, 54b–57a
Walras, II 47a, 50b, 52a, 52b
wealth, II 45a–45b, 49b, 53a, 56b, 58b, 60b
Webb, Beatrice, II 60a
Webb, Sidney, II 60a
Weber, Max, II 46b
Wickstead, II 50b
Wycliffe, II 45a
Xenophon, II 45a
Economic theory of natural liberty, II 61b–71b
advertising, II 67a
agriculture, II 62b, 69a
balance of payments, II 67a–68a, 70b
banking, II 64b, 68a, 70b
Bastiat, II 69a
Boulding, II 65a
capitalism, II 69b, 70a, 70b
China (Communist), II 70a
Christianity, II 62a, 64a–64b
communism, II 69b
competition, II 64a, 66b
degrading aspect of trade, II 69a–69b
democracy, II 67a, 70a
demand, II 63a
Depression of the 1930's, II 70a–70b
ecology, II 64b
education, II 63b–64a, 64b, 71a
feedback principle, II 63b
Ford, Henry, II 66b
France, II 62a, 69a
free trade, II 67a–68a
Friedman, Milton, II 68a

Galbraith, II 66b–67a, 70a
Galton, II 65b
Germany, II 69a
Germany (Nazi), II 70a, 70b
God, II 62a, 63a
gold standard, II 68b–69a
government, II 67a, 68b–69a, 71a
Great Britain, II 63b, 69a
Greece (ancient), II 61b
Gross National Product, II 70b
Haiti, II 70a
Hitler, II 70b
Hobbes, II 61b, 62a
Hume, II 64a
income, II 62a, 63b, 65a–65b, 66b, 69b, 71a
international trade, II 67a–68a
judiciary, II 63b
Keynes, II 70b
Keynesian concept, II 62a, 70a, 70b–71a
labor, II 65b, 69a–69b
laissez-faire, II 61b, 69a
Liberman, II 70a
licensing, II 67a
List, II 68b
Locke, II 62a
Lutheran Church, II 64a–64b
manufacturing, II 62b
Mao Tse-tung, II 70a
Marx, II 69b
Marxism, II 69a–69b
Middle Ages, II 62a, 69b
Mill, James, II 69a
monarchy, II 62b
money, II 67b, 69b
natural law, II 62a, 63a
Newton, II 62a
Physiocrats, II 62a–62b
Plato, II 61b
pollution, II 64b
power, II 65a–65b, 66b–67a
prices, II 62b–63b, 68b, 69a, 69b, 70a
private property, II 62a, 65b, 69b
production, II 62b–63a, 64b, 65b, 67a, 69a–69b
profit, II 63b
public works, II 65a, 71a
Quesnay, II 62a
quotas, II 67a
religion, II 63b, 64a–64b
revised sequence, II 66b–67a, 70a
Ricardo, II 67b, 68a–68b, 69a
Rousseau, II 62a
savings, II 65b

Scandinavia, II 64a–64b
Senior, N. W., II 69a
slavery, II 65b
Smith, Adam, II 61b–66a, 67a, 67b, 68a, 69a
socialism, II 69a–69b, 70a
society, II 61b–71a
Stalin, II 70a
State, II 62a, 64a
suffrage, II 70a
tariffs, II 67a, 68a, 69a
technology, II 63b
Turgot, II 62b
tyranny, II 70a
unemployment, II 70a–70b, 71a
U.S.S.R., II 70a
U.S., II 63b–64a, 66b, 67a, 69a, 70a–70b
Vietnam War, II 67a
wealth, II 65a–65b, 66b
World War II, II 70b
Yugoslavia, II 70a
See also Economic History

Economics
Baader, IV 207b
Bentham, IV 277b
Bernstein, III 149a, 162a–162b
capitalism, III 148a, 148b, 151b–152a
China, III 154a
civilization, I 618b
class, III 151b
collectivism, III 151b–152a
common law, II 693a, 694b; III 32a
communism, III 673b
Comte, III 644b
Condorcet, III 644a
Confucius, I 371b
conservatism, I 478b–479a
constitutionalism, I 490b
crisis in history, I 590a–591a, 593a
culture, I 609b, 618b; IV 165b
cynicism, III 586a
democracy, I 667a
despotism, II 9b, 12a
determinism, III 569a
dignity, IV 141a
education, II 72a
Engels, II 452a, 452b; III 22a, 156a
Enlightenment, II 90b
equality, II 145a
equity, II 148a
ethics, III 442a, 444a, 445b, 446b
evil, II 169a
evolutionism, II 180b–181a
existentialism, III 157b, 158b–159a, 160b

fascism, III 674a

freedom, II 250a

game theory, II 266a, 266b, 270b, 271a, 272a

good, IV 177a, 179a, 180b–181a, 181b–182a, 182b

happiness, II 374b, 379b, 381b, 384b–385a

Hegel, II 408b, 409a, 415b

hierarchy, II 442a

historiography, II 494b–495a, 495b, 497a; IV 147b, 148a, 151b

human nature, III 576a, 644a

humanism, IV 129b

ideology, II 554a–554b

individualism, II 602a–602b

international peace, III 448b, 454a, 454b

intolerance, IV 120a–120b

law, II 250a; III 6b, 9a–9b, 10b, 11b, 13b, 28a, 30b, 32a

Lenin, II 562a; III 153b–154a

liberalism, III 672b

Locke, IV 259a

love, III 104a, 104b

Luxemburg, III 162b

Machiavellism, III 117b, 123a, 124b

Marx, II 451b, 452b, 453a, 453b; III 22a, 149a, 156a, 359b; IV 161b, 163a, 290a–290b, 292a, 534a

Marxism, III 146b–170a, 646a; IV 180b–181a

materialism, II 451b, 452a, 452b, 453a, 453b

mathematics, III 178a, 178b

millenarianism, III 225a

Montesquieu, II 9b

morality, III 644b, 645a

nationalism, III 324a, 330a, 330b, 333a, 334b, 335a, 336a, 336b, 337a

natural law, III 22a

necessity, III 359b

order, II 442a

Orientalism, III 428a, 428b, 434a

peace, III 442a, 444a, 445b, 446b

perfectibility, III 472a, 473b, 644a

periodization in history, III 478a, 478b, 479a

philanthropy, III 489b, 490a

pleasure, II 374b, 379b, 381b, 384b–385a

politics, III 154a

positivism, III 542b

power, III 151b

pragmatism, III 569a, 569b

primitivism, III 578b, 586a, 596b, 599b

private property, III 650b, 651a–653b, 654b, 655a, 655b, 656a, 656b, 657a

progress, III 624a, 625b, 629a, 630a, 638b, 639a, 644a, 644b, 645a, 646a, 647b

protest movements, III 672b, 673b, 674a, 674b, 676b

psychology, IV 16a, 16b, 17b, 23a

reformation, IV 63b, 65b

religion, IV 96a, 100a, 115a, 115b, 120a–120b

Renaissance, IV 122b, 129b, 141a, 147b, 148a, 151b, 440a, 441a, 442a–442b

revisionism, IV 264a, 266a, 266b, 269a, 269b, 270a, 271b–272a

revolution, IV 160a, 161a, 161b, 162b, 163a, 165a, 165b, 166a, 166b

Ricardo, II 453a

right, IV 177a, 179a, 180b–181a, 181b–182a, 182b

romanticism, IV 206a, 206b, 207b

Russia, III 154a

Schulze-Gävernitz, III 162a

science, II 50a–51a

skepticism, IV 250a

Smith, Adam, II 453a; III 11b

social contract, IV 259a, 263a

social welfare, IV 276a, 276b, 277b, 279a, 279b, 281a, 283a

socialism, III 673b; IV 286b–290b, 292a, 292b

State, III 151b–152a

technology, IV 358a, 359b, 364a

time, IV 402a

Tolstoy, II 169a

totalitarianism, IV 407a, 407b, 409b

Trotsky, III 153b–154a

U.S.S.R., III 150b, 151a, 153b, 154b–155b, 655a

U.S., I 490b; III 9a–9b, 151a, 428a, 428b, 434a

universal man, IV 438a, 439b, 442a

utilitarianism, IV 447a

utility, IV 450a–458b

Utopia, IV 459a, 461a, 461b, 462b, 463b

value, IV 450a–458b

Victorian sentiment, IV 218a–218b, 221a, 222a, 222b

virtù, IV 477a

Volksgeist, IV 494a–494b

vox populi, IV 499b–500a

war, III 157b, 448b; IV 504a, 504b, 506a

welfare state, IV 509a, 509b, 510a, 510b, 511a, 511b–512b, 514a, 514b, 515a

Wolf, Julius, III 162a

women, III 596b; IV 523a, 523b, 524a

work, IV 531a, 534a

Zeitgeist, IV 536a

Ecphantus, cosmology, I 539b

Ecstasy, prophecy, III 658b

Ectropy, entropy, II 117b–118a

Ecumenical Movement, Church, I 418b; IV 68b

modernism, I 425a, 426a

Eddington, Arthur (1882–1944)

cosmology, I 562b, 565b–566a, 568a

metaphor, III 198b

Pythagorean cosmos, IV 42a

space, IV 297a, 305b

time, IV 397a

Eddy, Mary Baker (1821–1910), millenarianism, III 225b

Edelstein, Ludwig, progress, III 623b, 628a, 629a, 630b, 631a, 631b, 632b, 634b

Eden, Frederick Morton, Enlightenment, II 98b

Eden, Richard, historiography, IV 149a

Eden, Robert, philanthropy, III 490a

Eden-motif
culture, I 607b–608a, 612a
Zeus, I 608a

Edgerton, Franklin, Buddhism, I 255b

Edgeworth, F. Y. (1845–1926)
social welfare, IV 279a, 283a
utility, IV 451b, 454b, 455b–456a, 457b

Edict of Nantes, IV 113a, 116a, 116b, 117b, 119a, 119b

despotism, II 7b–8a, 14b

heresy, II 424b, 428a

Huguenots, II 428a

Renaissance, II 424b, 428a

revoked, I 401a

Edman, Irwin (1896–1954), pragmatism, III 553b

Edschmid, Kasimir, expressionism, II 207a, 208b, 209a

Education, II 71b–85a
absolutism, II 82b–83b
Adler, M. J., II 83a
anarchy, I 71b
Argentina, III 543b
Aristophanes, II 80a, 80b
Aristotle, II 77b, 78a, 81a–81b, 83a, 84a; IV 123b
Bayne, II 74b
Bible, II 74b
Brameld, II 83a
Brazil, III 540a, 541a, 541b, 542b, 543b
Brougham, II 99b
Bruni, IV 124b
as a business, II 72a
China, II 75a–75b
China (ancient), I 464a
Christianity, I 379b, 388a; II 74b, 80b; III 591a
Cicero, II 81a–81b; IV 123b
citizenship, II 77a–77b, 99b
common sense, II 77a
common law, II 691b, 692b, 693b, 694b–695a; III 32a
concept of, II 72a–73b, 74b–75a, 75b
Condorcet, III 533a
culture, IV 165b–166a
curriculum, II 83b, 84a–84b
cynicism, I 628a, 629a, 630a–631a, 632b–633a; III 585b
Darwin, Charles, III 646a
democracy, II 83a
Democritus, I 613a; III 627a
despotism, II 9b
Dewey, John, II 72b, 75a–75b, 81a–83b; III 569a
Diogenes Laërtius, I 630a
Diogenes of Sinope, I 630a–631a
discipline, II 385b
Eastern Orthodox Church, I 409b
economic history, II 47b
economics, II 72a
Eliot, T. S., II 72b, 75a–77b, 78b, 81a, 82b, 84a
emotion, III 500b
empiricism, III 550b
Enlightenment, II 90b, 91a, 98a, 99b–100a
equality, II 138b, 143b, 144b, 146b, 147a
Erasmus, IV 124b, 526a
ethics, II 77a–77b, 78b; III 440a

evil, II 168b
evolution, II 75b; III 474a, 646a
faith, II 79b–80a
Fellenberg, II 99b
Feltre, II 519a–519b
free, II 74a
freedom, II 249b
Froebel, II 99b
Garfield, Pres., II 72b, 75a
general will, II 276b, 277a, 278a, 278b, 279a
genius, II 294b–295a, 299a–299b, 300a, 307b–308a
Germany, I 388a; II 99b
God, II 74b, 79a
Godwin, III 643b
Great Britain, IV 510b, 511a
Greece (ancient), I 258a; II 74b, 75a–76a, 76b–77a, 77b, 78a, 79b–82a, 83a, 84a, 84b, 339b; IV 367a
Guarino of Verona, II 519a–519b
guilds, II 300a
Hadas, II 71b
happiness, II 374b, 380a, 382a, 385a, 385b
Helvétius, III 470a
hermeticism, II 432a
history, II 79a–85a
Homer, II 80a; III 496a, 497a
Hopkins, Mark, II 72b
human nature, III 643b
humanism, II 515a–515b, 516a, 519a–519b, 522a, 523a; III 129b, 130b; IV 438b–440a, 440b, 441a
Hutchins, R. M., II 73b, 83a
Huxley, T. H., III 474a
idea, II 72a–73a, 75a–75b, 79b
importance of, II 72a
imprinting, II 584a, 584b–585a, 585b, 586a
indoctrination, II 74a, 77a–77b
international, II 72a
international peace, III 448b, 449a
Isocrates, II 81a–81b
Jefferson, IV 21b
Jesuits, III 293a–293b
Kant, II 72a, 75a–75b, 80b, 82b, 83a, 83b, 84a
kinds of, II 75b
knowledge II 73b, 78b, 81b
Latin America, III 541a
law, II 249b, 687a, 690a; III 3b, 4b, 5a, 12b, 13b, 32a

learning, II 584a, 584b–585a, 585b, 586a
Leonardo da Vinci, IV 440b
liberalism, II 147a
Locke, III 469b
logic, III 550b
love, III 106a
Lucian, I 630b
Lucretius, III 587b
Marrou, II 82b, 83a
Mead, G. H., III 569a
Melanchthon, IV 123b
Merton, Thomas, II 79a
Mexico, III 544a
Middle Ages, IV 123b
Mill, James, III 470a
Mill, John Stuart, II 76b, 82b
Montaigne, III 595a
Montesquieu, II 9b
morality, II 73b, 74a, 75a, 75b, 76b–77a, 77b, 84a
music, II 76b–77a, 77b
mythology, III 288a, 293a–293b
nationalism, III 324b, 325a, 326b, 328a, 333a, 334b
natural law, III 15a
natural liberty, II 63b–64a, 64b, 71a
Nature, III 348b, 350a
Netherlands, I 388a
Newman, Cardinal, II 79a
pain, II 385b
painting, II 583a
peace, III 440a; IV 500b
Pereira Barreto, III 541a
perfectibility, III 465a, 466b, 469a–470a, 470b, 472a, 474a, 474b
periodization in history, III 480b
periodization in literary history, III 485a–485b
Pestalozzi, II 99b
Petrarch, IV 124b
Phenix, II 83a
philanthropy, III 488b, 490a, 491a, 491b, 492a, 492b
philosophy, II 71b, 74b, 76a, 76b, 78a, 78b, 81a–81b, 82b, 83a
physical, II 75b
Pietism, III 493b, 494a, 495a
Pindar, II 75b
Plato, II 74b, 75a–76a, 77b, 79b, 80b–81b, 83a, 99b; III 465a, 466b, 469a–469b, 497a, 498b, 500b, 501a, 502a; IV 49b, 368b
pleasure, II 374b, 380a, 382a, 385a, 385b
poetry, III 496a, 497a, 525b,

526a, 527b, 528b
positivism, III 533a, 538a, 540a, 541a, 541b, 542b, 543a, 543b, 544a, 550b
pragmatism, III 569a, 569b
Priestley, III 472a
primitivism, III 585b, 587b, 591a, 595a, 595b, 597b, 598a, 600a
progress, III 627a, 630a, 636b, 639a, 643b, 646a
Protagoras, II 80b, 81a–81b
protest movements, III 670b, 672a, 675b, 676a
psychology, II 71b, 83a; IV 18b–19b, 20b, 21a, 21b, 22b, 23a, 24a, 25a, 27b
public, II 75b
Puritanism, IV 18b–19b
Quintilian, II 81a–81b
Rabelais, I 54a
Ramism, IV 42b, 43b, 44a, 44b, 45a, 45b
Ramus, IV 42b, 43a
rationalism, IV 48b, 49b
relativism, II 82b–83b, 84a
religion, II 74b, 78b–79a, 80b
Renaissance, IV 121b, 122a, 123b, 124b, 127a, 127b, 128a, 129b, 130b, 437a, 437b, 438b–440a, 440b, 441a, 441b
revolution, IV 165b–166a
rhetoric, IV 168b, 169a, 170a, 172a–172b
Roman Catholic Church, I 379b, 388a
Rome (ancient), II 84b, 687a, 690a
Rousseau, II 73a, 74a–74b, 75a, 80b, 83a, 99b, 276b, 277a, 278a, 278b, 279a; III 469b, 595b, 600a
Saint Thomas Aquinas, II 74b, 81a
Schiller, Friedrich, III 569b
self-, II 72a, 72b
Shaftesbury, III 598a
Smith, Adam, II 63b–64b
Snow, C. P., II 81b
society, II 82a, 83a
Socrates, II 75b, 79b, 80a–80b, 81a–81b; III 496a
Sophists, I 629a; II 75b, 81a–81b; IV 48b
Spencer, Herbert, II 81b
Spinoza, IV 434b
State, III 469b–470a
taste, IV 354a, 355a
teaching, II 72b, 73b, 75b, 80a–80b, 81a–81b
technology, IV 358a, 360a

temperance, IV 368b
theology, II 79a
theory of, II 76a–79a
tradition, II 77a
transcendentalism, IV 24a
Trilling, II 81a
truth, II 81b
U.S., I 15b–16a, 440a, 440b; II 63b–64a, 83a, 147a; III 4b, 9b, 12b, 491b, 495a
unity of science, IV 431a, 434b
universal man, IV 437a, 437b, 438b–440a, 440b, 441a, 441b
Utopia, IV 463a
virtue, II 80a–80b, 249b
virtuoso, IV 490a, 490b
vocational, II 75b, 77b
Volksgeist, IV 494b
Vox populi, IV 499b
war, IV 500b, 505a, 508a
welfare state, IV 510b, 511a, 512a, 513b, 515a
wisdom of the fool, IV 517a
women, IV 490a, 490b, 523b, 524b, 525a, 526a, 527a, 528a
Woodward, W. H., II 83a
work, IV 531b, 532b
Zeno of Citium, III 630a
See also Academic freedom
Edward I, King (1239–1307)
city, I 429a
nationalism, III 321a
Edward III, King (1312–1377)
law, III 7b
nationalism, III 323b
Edward VII, King (1841–1910), economic history, II 60a
Edwards, Jonathan (1703–1758)
beauty, IV 110a
Being, IV 110b
Bellamy and, IV 110b
Calvinism, IV 110b
Christianity, IV 110b
clergy, IV 109b
emotion, IV 110a
Enlightenment, IV 109a–111b
followers of, IV 110b–112a
God, IV 109b, 110a
good, IV 109b
grace, IV 110a, 111a
Great Awakening, IV 110a
harmony, IV 110a
history, I 402b
Holy Spirit, IV 110a
illuminists, IV 109a, 109b–110a, 110b
James and, IV 112a
light, IV 110a

literature, **IV** 109b, 110b
Locke and, **IV** 109b
love, **IV** 109b, 110a, 111a
millenarianism, **III** 225b
morality, **IV** 110a
philosophy, **IV** 110a
Pietism, **IV** 110b
psychology, **IV** 16b, 19a–19b, 22b, 24b, 110b, 112a
Puritanism, **IV** 16b, 19a–19b, 109b
religion, **IV** 109a, 109b–110b, 111a, 111b
sin, **IV** 110b
soul, **IV** 109b
utopianism, **III** 225b
virtue, **IV** 109b, 110a, 111a
Will, **IV** 109b, 110a
Eggli, M. Edmond, romanticism, **IV** 190a
Egidio da Viterbo
dignity, **IV** 145b–146a
mythology, **III** 291b
Egoism
Buddha, **II** 162a
evil, **II** 162a
Fichte, **IV** 209b
good, **IV** 178a, 185a
happiness, **II** 383a, 383b
nationalism, **III** 329b
pleasure, **II** 383a, 383b
right, **IV** 178a, 185a
romanticism, **IV** 209b
time, **IV** 395a
tragic sense, **IV** 415b
utilitarianism, **IV** 445b
Victorian sentiment, **IV** 218a
Volksgeist, **IV** 494a
Egypt
Eastern Orthodox Church, **I** 411a
nationalism, **III** 332b, 337b, 338a
Neo-Platonism, **III** 373b, 377a
numbers, **III** 401a
Egypt (ancient)
alchemy, **I** 28b–29a, 29b, 33a
Anchorites, **I** 377b–378a
annals, **II** 465a
architecture, **III** 365a
assemblies, **II** 256a
astrology, **I** 119a, 119b–120a
art, **II** 298b, 582a
Atum-Rē (myth), **IV** 100b
benevolence, **III** 487a
Bible, **I** 359a–359b
Book of the Dead, **IV** 101a
Buddhism, **I** 247b, 255a
canon of proportions, **I** 580a, 581b

caste, **III** 10b
causation, **I** 270b
chance, **I** 335b–336a
city, **I** 428a
conscience, **IV** 225a, 226a
conservation, **I** 472a
continuity, **I** 503b–504a
cosmology, **I** 536a–536b, 537a
Creation, **I** 536b
creativity in art, **I** 580a, 580b, 581a
crime, **IV** 225b
cycles, **I** 625a
death, **I** 644b; **IV** 224b–226a
despotism, **II** 15b, 252b
dignity, **IV** 139a
disease, **II** 395b–396b
divination, **III** 11a
dualism, **II** 38b–39a
eloquence, **II** 256a
environment, **II** 124a, 129a
freedom, **II** 249b
freedom of speech, **II** 252a, 252b, 253a, 254a, 256a–256b
furniture, **III** 364b–365a
Gnosticism, **II** 327a, 328b, 329a
God, **II** 331b, 333b–335b, 336b, 340a, 341b, 345a, 564b; **III** 11a; **IV** 225b
Greece (ancient), **IV** 228b
harmony, **II** 389a, 393b
hedonism, **II** 256a
heredity, **III** 10b
hermeticism, **II** 431a, 431b
historiography, **II** 465a–467b, 469a, 475a, 476b
iconography, **II** 530a
immortality, **I** 644b
impiety, **II** 564a–564b, 566a
Isis (myth), **IV** 100b
Judaism, **II** 656a
justice, **IV** 224b, 225b
language, **II** 669b
law, **II** 249b, 686b; **III** 6b–7a, 10b, 11a, 249b; **IV** 226a
Leyden papyrus, **II** 256a
literary criticism, **I** 596b
mathematics, **III** 180a, 180b, 182b
Mesopotamia (ancient), **IV** 226a
millenarianism, **III** 224a
morality, **IV** 224b
mortuary ritual, **IV** 101a, 101b, 102a, 102b
music, **II** 389a, 393b; **III** 260b, 268a
mythology, **II** 38b–39a; **III** 272a, 275a, 275b, 278a,

281a, 281b, 282b, 292b, 303b, 305b, 310b, 311b; **IV** 224b–225a, 225b
naturalism in art, **III** 340a, 340b
neo-classicism in art, **III** 363a, 364b, 365a, 368b
Nephthys (myth), **IV** 100b
non finito, **II** 298b
Osiris (myth), **IV** 100b–101a, 101b, 102a, 102b
peasantry, **II** 256a
perennial philosophy, **III** 459a
pharaohs, **III** 487a
philanthropy, **III** 487a
polytheism, **II** 333b
private property, **II** 686b
progress, **III** 648a
prophecy, **III** 660a
Pyramid Texts, **IV** 100b–101a
pyramids, **III** 364b
reincarnation, **I** 644b
religion, **II** 582b; **IV** 93a, 93b, 94b, 98a, 100b–101b, 102a, 102b, 104b, 105a
Renaissance, **IV** 139a
revival, **III** 364b–365a
ritual, **IV** 225a–225b, 226a
salvation, **IV** 224b–226a, 228b
sculpture, **I** 580a, 581a
Set (myth), **IV** 100b
slavery, **II** 466a
sphinx, **III** 364b
suicide, **II** 256a–256b
symbolism, **IV** 338b
technology, **IV** 358a–358b
time, **IV** 401a
transcendentalism, **IV** 224b
witchcraft, **IV** 521a
writing, **III** 180a–180b
Egyptian-Pharaonic nationalism, **III** 337b
Ehrenberg, C. G. (1795–1876)
cell division, **II** 285b
genetic continuity, **II** 285b
Ehrenfest, Tatiana, entropy, **II** 117a
Ehrenreich, P., mythology, **III** 310a
Ehrenstrahl, David Klöcker, iconography, **II** 533a
Ehrlich, Eugen, law, **III** 3b–4a
Eichendorff, Josef von (1788–1857), romanticism, **IV** 205b, 207b
Eichhorn, J. G. (1752–1827), literature, **III** 84b; **IV** 187b
Eichrodt, L. (1827–1892), periodization in literary history, **III** 483b

Eiffel, Gustave (1832–1923), Gothic, **II** 373a
Einem, H. von, iconography, **II** 538a
Einstein, Albert (1879–1955),
absolute rest, **IV** 80a
acceleration, **IV** 86a–86b, 89a, 89b
aesthetics, **IV** 88b
aether, **IV** 80b, 81a–81b, 89b
ambiguity, **I** 59a
anthropomorphism, **I** 90a
Bohr and, **II** 590a–591a
Born and, **II** 592b
causation, **II** 590a
chance, **I** 336b
continuity, **II** 590a
cosmic images, **I** 515b
cosmology, **I** 553b, 555a, 556a–562b, 564a–564b, 565b, 566a–566b, 567b, 568a, 570a; **IV** 306a
de Sitter and, **I** 561b–562b
determinism, **II** 590a
electromagnetic radiation, **IV** 84a
empiricism, **III** 545b, 546b, 549a
energy, **IV** 84a, 86b
energy-time uncertainty relation, **II** 590b, 591a
ethics, **III** 445b, 446b–447a
extensio, **IV** 301b
Fifth Solvay Congress, **II** 590a
Freud and, **III** 446b
general theory of relativity, **IV** 85b–87a, 88a–88b, 89b–90a, 91a, 91b, 92a
gravity, **I** 557b–559b, 560b, 561a; **IV** 83b, 86a, 86b–87a, 88a, 89a, 89b, 91b
harmony, **II** 448b
hierarchy, **II** 448b
indeterminacy, **II** 590a–591a, 592b
inertia, **IV** 84a, 86a, 86b, 89a, 89b
light, **IV** 81a, 81b, 83b
Lorentz and, **IV** 80a
Mach and, **IV** 86a
mass, **IV** 84a, 86a, 86b
mathematics, **IV** 83a, 84a
matter, **I** 559b–560b, 561a, 562b
measurement, **II** 590a, 590b; **IV** 404b–405a
motion, **I** 556b, 557a, 558b, 559a, 560b; **IV** 80a, 81a–81b, 91b
Nature, **I** 556b, 558b

Newton and, I 557a
nuclear power, III 446b
pacifism, III 447a
peace, III 445b, 446b–447a
photon-box thought-experiment, II 590b
Poincaré and, IV 79b–81a
principle of equivalence, I 558a–558b; IV 86b, 89a, 90a
principle of general covariance, IV 88b, 89b
probability, III 620a
relativity, I 555a, 556a–559b; IV 74a, 74b, 79b–84a, 85b–87a, 88a–90a, 90b–92a
Russell and, III 446b
simultaneity, IV 81b, 82a–82b
Sixth Solvay Congress, II 590a–590b
society, III 446b
space, I 556b, 557a–557b, 558b, 559a, 559b, 560b, 561b; II 590a, 590b; IV 80b, 88b–89a, 89b, 90a, 90b, 92a, 297b, 301b, 306a
special theory of relativity, IV 87a, 88a, 88b, 89b–90a, 91a
time, I 556b, 557a–557b, 558b, 559a, 559b, 561b; II 590a, 590b–591a; IV 81b, 85b, 88b–89a, 89b, 90a, 90b, 92a, 397a, 404b–405a
uncertainty principle, II 590a–591a
universe, I 559b–562b, 565b, 566a–566b
war, III 446b–447a
Whittaker and, IV 79b–80a
See also Relativity
Einthoven, W. (1860–1927), indeterminacy, II 588a
Eisenmann, K., indeterminacy, II 589a
Ekphrasis, IV 466a, 467a, 468b, 469a, 469b
El (myth), II 336b; III 281b
El Greco (1548?–1614), chance images, I 347a, 348b
impressionism, II 577b
El-Amarna letters, freedom of speech, II 253b–254a
Elbern, V., iconography, II 538b
Eldon, Lord (1751–1838), equity, II 153b
Eleanor of Aquitaine (1122?–1204)
love, III 102a
women, IV 525b
Eleatics

literary paradox, III 76b
mathematics, III 171b
matter, III 187a
Pythagoreans, III 171b
rationalism, IV 47b
skepticism, IV 234b
time, IV 389b, 390a, 390b, 391b, 393b, 394a
Eleazar ben Arach, Rabbi, impiety, II 565a
Electra (myth)
Sophocles, IV 367a
temperance, IV 367a
Electricity
catastrophism, IV 419a
mathematics, III 179a
matter, III 195a
Newton, III 195a
Electrodynamic field theory, empiricism, III 549a
Electromagnetic radiation, Einstein, IV 84a
Electromagnetic waves, optics, III 419b, 420a
Electromagnetics
cosmology, I 554b
empiricism III 548b, 549a
optics, III 419b
relativity, IV 74b, 78b, 79a, 79b, 80a–80b, 84a, 91a
space, IV 302a
symmetry, IV 349a
technology, IV 364a
time, IV 405a, 405b
Electronic music, III 264a
Electronics, Man-Machine, III 145b
Electrons
acausal behavior, II 588a
free will, II 588a
indeterminacy, II 588a, 589a, 591b
measurement, II 589a
symmetry, IV 351a, 353a
unpredictable behavior, II 588a
Eleusis, mystery cult of, catharsis, I 264b
Elgar, Edward (1847–1934), ambiguity, I 57a
Elgin Marbles, neo-classicism in art, III 363a–363b
Eliade, Mircea
culture, II 132a
motif, III 242b
mythology, III 314b–315a
Eligius, S. (d. 658), art, II 300a
Elijah (Bible)
mythology, III 275b, 277b, 281b, 283b, 284a, 284b
prophecy, III 658b, 660b, 661a
Eliot, Charles W. (1834–1926), psychology, IV 26b

Eliot, George (1819–1880),
association of ideas, I 115a, 117a
Comte and, III 539a
irony, II 633b
motif, III 240a
mythology, III 240a
naturalism, IV 54a
Nature, III 349a
positivism, III 539a
realism in literature, IV 54a
Victorian sensibility, IV 219b
Eliot, John (1604–1690)
psychology, IV 18a
Puritanism, IV 18a
Ramism, IV 44b
Eliot, T. S. (1888–1965),
aestheticism, IV 195a
antiromanticism, IV 195a
baroque in literature, I 193a
classicism, I 450b, 452a, 453a, 455a–455b
culture, I 619a
Dryden and, I 453a
education, II 72b, 75a, 75b, 76a, 77a, 77b, 78b, 81a, 82b, 84a
evolution of literature, II 172b–173a
historiography, IV 147a
literary criticism, I 602a, 602b, 603a, 604b
literature, IV 147a
Maurras and, I 455a
motif, III 236b
Shelley and, IV 195a–195b
symbolism, IV 341a, 344b
tragic sense, IV 417a
Wagner and, III 236a
Elisha (Bible)
disease, II 396b
music, II 394a
mythology, III 283b
prophecy, II 394a; III 658a–658b, 660b, 661a
Elisha ben Abujah, impiety, II 565a
Elite
good, IV 175a
Machiavellism, III 125a
Marxism, III 154b
perfectibility, III 465a
Plato, III 465a; IV 175a
Renaissance, IV 123b
right, IV 175a
State, IV 318a–318b
Elizabeth I, Queen (1533–1603)
periodization in literary history, III 482a–483a
historiography, II 484a

Ellesmere, Lord, equity, II 153b
Ellinwood, Frank Field, Orientalism, III 435b
Ellipses, symmetry, IV 348b–349a
Ellis, Edwin, symbolism, IV 340b
Ellis, R. L., probability, III 615a, 615b, 616a, 616b
Elmes, James, motif, III 236b
Elohim (myth), Gnosticism, II 329a
Eloquence
art, I 458a
Egypt (ancient), II 256a
freedom of speech, II 256a, 262a
genius, II 317b
humanism, II 519a; IV 129b
language, IV 168a
music, II 317b
Renaissance, IV 129b, 438b–439a
rhetoric, IV 168a, 169b, 171b–172a
Rome (ancient), II 262a
universal man, IV 438b–439a
Elpenor (myth), III 296a
Else, Gerald F., catharsis, I 266a, 266b, 268b, 269a
Elton, Charles, conservation, I 472a, 475b, 476a
Ely, Richard T. (1854–1943), welfare state, IV 512a
Elyot, Thomas (1490?–1546)
Erasmus and, IV 526a
hierarchy, II 434b
women, IV 526a
Emanationism
Creation, I 572a
Epicureanism, III 505b
Emancipation
nationalism, III 326a
peace, III 444b
primitivism, III 596b
women, III 596b; IV 526a, 526b, 527a
Emblems, mythology, III 289b, 290a, 290b, 293b, 295b–296b
Embryology
evolutionism, II 177a, 178a, 179b, 182a
primitivism, III 597b
recapitulation, IV 56a–56b, 57a, 58a, 59a
Emergent evolutionism, II 183b–184a
Emergentism, empiricism, III 548b–549a
Emerson, Mary Moody, transcendentalism, III 429b

Emerson, Ralph Waldo (1803–1882)
  Buddhism, I 256a
  civil disobedience, I 436a
  environment, II 122b–123a
  ethics, III 430a, 430b
  freedom, III 430b
  heresy, II 429b
  individualism, I 596a
  literary criticism, I 599a
  literature, III 86a
  Marxism, III 158b
  materialism, III 430a
  morality, III 430b
  mysticism, III 430a, 430b
  Nature, I 464a–474b; III 349b
  Neo-Platonism, III 430a
  organicism, III 426b
  Orientalism, III 429a, 429b–430b, 431b–433b, 439a
  phrenology, IV 23b
  Plato and, III 430a, 502b
  Platonism, III 502b, 522a–522b
  pragmatism, III 553b
  psychology, IV 23b, 24a
  romanticism, IV 210b
  Schelling and, IV 210b
  self-reliance, II 596a
  symbolism, IV 339a, 341b, 344b
  Thoreau and, I 474a–474b; III 430b–431a
  transcendentalism, I 436a; III 429a, 429b–430b, 431b, 432a–433b, 439a; IV 24a
  Upaniṣads and, I 256a
Emilio, Paolo (d. 1529), historiography, II 508a
Eminent domain, private property, III 656a
Emmons, Nathanael, religion, IV 111a, 112a
Emotion
  Aristotle, IV 6a
  art, II 297b, 575a, 575b, 576b, 581a; III 501b
  atomism, III 187b
  Bacon, Francis, IV 466b
  beauty, I 201a–201b
  belief, III 562b
  Bergson, III 565a
  Comte, III 648b–649a
  determinism, II 237b, 238b–239a
  Dewey, John, III 568b
  dignity, IV 142b
  disease, II 395b
  education, III 500b
  Edwards, IV 110a
  empathy, II 85b, 88a
  free will, II 237b, 238b–239a, 244a

genius, II 294b, 295b, 297b, 313b, 316a, 316b, 318b, 319a–319b, 323a, 323b, 324a
good, IV 176a, 177b, 184a
historiography, IV 147b
holy, II 513a
human nature, III 572a, 575b
impressionism, II 575a, 575b, 576b, 581a
individualism, II 297b, 603a
James, III 562b–563a, 565a
Jung, IV 97a
Kant, II 324a
Lange, III 562b
Leibniz, II 239a
Lewis, C. I., III 568b
love, III 94a
Lovejoy, III 552b
matter, III 187b
music, II 313b, 316a, 316b, 318b, 319a–319b, 323a, 323b, 324a, 393a; III 271b
mythology, III 272a, 302a, 317a
painting, II 575a, 575b, 576b, 581a; IV 466a, 466b, 472a, 472b, 474b
Plato, III 496b, 497b, 498a, 499a, 500a, 500b, 501b; IV 4b
pleasure, II 382b
poetry, II 575b; III 501b, 572b; IV 466a, 466b, 472a, 472b, 474b
positivism, III 537a, 550a
pragmatism, III 552b, 562b–563a, 565a, 568a, 568b
progress, III 648b–649a
psychology, IV 1a, 1b, 2b, 3a, 4b, 5a, 7a, 8a, 22b, 23a, 23b, 27a, 27b
rationalism, IV 50a
realism in literature, IV 53b
religion, IV 97a, 98b, 99b, 105a, 110a, 112a
Renaissance, IV 142b, 147b, 438a
rhetoric, IV 168a, 169b
right, IV 176a, 177b, 184a
romanticism, IV 208a
Saint Augustine, III 584a
Spinoza, II 238b–239a; IV 177b, 381b, 434b
State, IV 315a, 316b, 318b
Stoicism, IV 50a, 176a
Stoics, IV 8a
Strato, IV 7a
theodicy, IV 381b
truth, III 562b
unity of science, IV 434b
universal man, IV 437b
Victorian sensibility, IV

217a, 217b, 219b, 221b, 222a
vox populi, IV 499a, 500a
Empathy, II 85a–89a
  aesthetics, II 85b–86a
  animism, II 87b
  Anstruther-Thompson, II 86b
  Aristotle, II 87b
  art, II 85b, 86a, 86b, 88a–88b, 297b
  associationism, II 88a
  Basch, II 88a–88b
  beauty, I 213a
  Bergson, II 88b
  Brecht, II 87b
  communication, II 87a
  Croce, II 87b
  defined, II 85a–85b, 88a
  Dilthey, II 85b, 86b–87a
  drama, II 87a–87b
  emotion, II 85b, 88a
  Endell, II 88b
  ethics, II 85b
  experience, II 86a–86b, 88a
  France, II 88a–88b
  freedom, II 86b
  genius, II 323a, 323b
  Germany, II 85b–87a, 88a, 88b
  Great Britain, II 86b, 88a
  Greece (ancient), II 87b
  Groos, II 88a
  Hegelianism, II 85b
  Herbartians, II 85b
  Homer, II 87b
  Hume, II 88a
  as an intuited fact, II 86a
  Kames, II 87b
  Kant, II 85b–86a
  Langfield, II 88b
  Lipps, II 86a, 86b, 87a, 88a, 88b
  music, II 323a, 323b
  Nature, II 86a
  necessity, III 351a, 359b–360b
  Nietzsche, II 88b
  origin of the term, II 85b
  Paget (Vernon Lee), II 86b
  philosophy, II 85b–86a
  Plato, II 87b
  pleasure, II 86b
  poetry, II 87b
  popular idea of, II 87a, 87b
  psychology, II 87b, 88b
  Ruskin, II 88a
  Santayana, II 88b
  Schiller, Friedrich, II 85b
  social sciences, II 85b, 88b
  style, II 297b
  sympathy, II 87b
  three levels of, II 86b
  Titchener, II 85b

U.S., II 88b
Vico, II 87a
Vischer, Friedrich, II 86a
Vischer, Robert, II 85b, 86a
Volkelt, II 88a
Weber, Max, II 85b, 86b–87a
Empedocles (5th century B.C.),
  analogy, I 60b–61a, 62a, 63a
  Anaxagoras and, IV 3a
  atomism, I 126b, 128a
  biology, I 233b
  causation, I 271a
  consciousness, IV 3a
  conservation, I 472a
  creativity in art, I 578b, 579a
  cycles, I 622a
  diet, IV 32a
  dualism, II 40b; IV 346b
  elements, IV 2b
  evolutionism, II 175a
  harmony, II 390a
  hate, III 187a
  historiography, I 503a
  human nature, III 573a, 574a–574b, 575b
  law, II 683b
  light, III 407a
  love, II 94b, 95a, 187a; IV 2b
  macrocosm and microcosm, III 126b
  Man-Machine, III 132a, 133a
  matter, III 187a, 188b
  music, II 390a
  mysticism, IV 2b
  mythology, III 273a
  Nature, III 347a
  optics, III 407a
  Orpheus (myth), IV 2b
  Parmenides and, IV 3a
  perfectibility, III 464b
  physicalism, IV 2b
  Plato and, III 188b
  poetry, IV 2b
  primitivism, III 579a, 579b, 581a
  progress, III 627b
  psyche, IV 2b
  psychology, IV 2b–3a
  Pythagoras, IV 2b, 31b–32a
  Pythagoreans, IV 31b–32a, 37a
  science, IV 2b
  skepticism, IV 234b
  soul, I 215a, 622a; III 573a; IV 2b, 31b–32a
  spontaneous generation, IV 307b
  strife, IV 2b

symmetry, **IV** 346b, 348a
time, **IV** 390a
Empiricism
acquired characteristics, **II** 621b
agnosticism, **I** 19a, 19b, 23a, 23b, 24a–24b
algebra, **III** 549a
Aristotelianism, **III** 20a
Aristotle, **II** 623a; 189b
atomic theory, **III** 548b
Australia, **III** 550a
authority, **I** 152b–153a, 157b
Avenarius, **III** 545b, 547b
Bacon, **I** 175a–175b; **III** 215a
beauty, **I** 196a, 202b, 206a; **II** 580b
behaviorism, **I** 218b–220b; **III** 549a–549b
Bentham, **III** 233b
Berlin Society of Scientific Empiricists, **III** 545b, 546a–550b
Bernays, **III** 547b
Bernstein, Eduard, **III** 162b, 163a
biology, **III** 548b, 549a, 550b
Boltzmann, **III** 545b
Bridgman, **III** 550b
Bühler, **III** 547a
Carnap, **III** 545b, 546a, 547b–548a, 548b, 549a, 549b
causation, **I** 291a; **III** 546b
chemistry, **III** 548b
communication, **III** 547a
criticism, **III** 550b
disease, **II** 398b
Du Bois-Reymond, **III** 546a
dualism, **III** 549b
education, **III** 550b
Einstein, **III** 545b, 546b, 549a
electrodynamic field theory, **III** 549a
electromagnetics, **III** 548b, 549a
emergentism, **III** 548b–549a
emotion, **III** 550a
epistemology, **III** 547b, 548a
ethics, **III** 443b
Feigl, **III** 546a, 550a, 550b
Feyerabend, **III** 550b
Frank, **III** 546a, 548a
Frege, **III** 545b, 547b, 548a, 550a
geometry, **III** 547a
God, **II** 351b–353a, 355b
Gödel, **III** 545b
good, **IV** 178b, 179b, 184a

Great Britain, **II** 351b–353a; **III** 550b; **IV** 199b
Grelling, **III** 546a
Hahn, **III** 545b, 548a, 548b
Hegel, **II** 407b, 414b
Hegelianism, **III** 546a
Helmholtz, **III** 545b
Hempel, **III** 546a, 550a
Hertz, **III** 545b
Hilbert, **III** 545b, 547b
historicism, **II** 456b, 457a
Hull, **III** 549a
human nature, **III** 643b
humanism, **II** 521a; **IV** 134a, 135a
Hume, **I** 291a, 296b, 319b; **II** 582a; **III** 231b, 233a, 545b, 546b, 547a, 550b
Husserl, **III** 550a
Hutcheson, **III** 231b
idea, **II** 547a–547b
ideal, **II** 549a, 549b, 551a, 551b
indeterminacy, **II** 587b, 591b
individualism, **II** 603b
induction, **III** 550a
intuition, **III** 547b
James, **III** 546b, 552b, 559a, 561b, 562a
Kames, **III** 234b
Kant, **II** 407b, 551b; **III** 233b, 358a, 547a, 547b, 556b, 562a; **IV** 248b–249a, 382b, 433b
knowledge, **I** 218b–219a; **III** 547b, 548a, 549b
Köhler, **III** 549a
language, **II** 667b, 669b, 672b; **III** 546a, 546b, 547a, 547b, 548a, 549b, 550b
Lavoisier, **III** 546b
law, **I** 291a; **III** 2a, 3a, 4a
Leibniz, **III** 195b
Leonardo da Vinci, **IV** 440b–441a
linguistics, **III** 73a–74a
Locke, **III** 195b, 546b; **IV** 199a
logic, **I** 24a–24b, 219b
Lorentz, **III** 546b
Mach, **III** 545b, 546a, 547b, 550b
Man-Machine, **III** 132a, 138b, 139a, 146a
Marxism, **III** 147a, 160b, 162a, 162b, 163a
materialism, **II** 455a
mathematics, **III** 547b, 548a
matter, **III** 188a, 189b, 190b, 195b, 546b
Meehl, **III** 550b

Menger, **III** 545b
metaphor, **III** 201a
metaphysical imagination, **III** 211b, 212b, 215a, 216b, 218a–219b, 221a, 547a, 551a
methodological-monism, **I** 23b
Mill, J. S., **III** 545b
Mises, Richard von, **III** 546a
molecular biology, **III** 549a
monism, **III** 549b, 550a
moral sense, **III** 230b, 231b, 233a, 233b, 234b, 235a
Morris, **III** 547a
music, **III** 262a
mythology, **III** 302b
Nagel, Ernest, **III** 550a
natural law, **III** 15a, 20a
natural science, **III** 549b, 550a
Nature, **III** 547a, 548b, 549a
necessity, **III** 351b, 356b, 357b–358a, 359b, 360a
Neurath, **III** 545b, 548b
neurophysiology, **III** 549b, 550a
Newton, **III** 546b, 549a
operationalism, **III** 550b
optics, **III** 548b
organicism, **III** 422a, 425a
Orientalism, **III** 436b
painting, **II** 576b, 580b, 581b, 582a, 583a
pangenesis, **II** 623a
peace, **III** 443b
Peirce, **III** 546b, 559a, 559b
perennial philosophy, **III** 457a, 460a, 462b
perfectibility, **III** 471a–471b, 643b
phenomenalism, **III** 548a, 548b, 549b, 550b
philosophers, **III** 545b, 546a, 550b
philosophy, **II** 549a, 549b, 551a, 551b; **III** 201a, 546a, 547b, 548b, 549b, 550a, 550b, 551a
physicalism, **III** 549a
physics, **III** 547b, 548b, 549a, 549b, 550a
Plato, **III** 15a, 497a, 500b, 546b
Popper, **III** 545b, 550b
positivism, **III** 545b–551a
Pratt, **III** 550b
probability, **III** 550a, 606b, 612a, 613a, 614a, 615a, 615b
progress, **III** 631a, 643b
psychology, **III** 548a, 548b,

549a, 549b, 550b; **IV** 2b, 3b, 11a, 11b, 13a, 24b
quantum mechanics, **III** 548b, 549a, 550b
Quine, **III** 547a, 550b
Ramism, **IV** 45a
rationalism, **III** 302b
realism, **III** 548a–548b, 550b
reason, **I** 91b; **III** 547a–547b
reductionism, **III** 547b–550a
Reichenbach, **III** 546a, 547b, 548a, 550a, 550b
Reid, Thomas, **III** 233b
Reidemeister, **III** 545b
religion, **IV** 106a
Renaissance, **IV** 134a, 135a
revisionism, **IV** 269b, 270b
Riemann, **III** 545b
right, **IV** 178b, 179b, 184a
romanticism, **IV** 199a, 199b, 203b, 209a
Royce, **III** 561a
Russell, **I** 319b; **III** 545b, 547b, 548a, 549a
Ryle, **III** 549a, 549b
Schlick, **III** 545b, 548a
science, **III** 546b, 547b, 548a, 548b, 549a, 549b, 550a, 550b, 551a
skepticism, **IV** 234a, 236b, 240a, 244a, 247b, 248b–249a, 249b–250a
Skinner, **III** 549a–549b
Smith, Adam, **III** 233a, 233b
social science, **III** 548b, 549a
space, **III** 546b, 550a
spontaneous generation, **IV** 309a–309b, 310a
technology, **IV** 361b, 363a, 364b
theodicy, **IV** 382b
thermodynamics, **III** 548b
Thomism, **III** 20a
thought, **III** 550a
time, **III** 546b, 550a; **IV** 395a–395b
unity, **III** 548a, 548b, 549a, 549b
unity of science, **IV** 433a, 433b, 434b
value, **III** 567b–568a
Vienna Circle of Logical Positivists, **III** 545b, 546a–550b
virtue, **IV** 178b
vitalism, **III** 548b–549a
Volksgeist, **IV** 496a
Voltaire, **I** 220a
Waismann, **III** 545b
Watson, J. B., **III** 549a

Watson, W. H., **III** 550b
welfare state, **IV** 512b
Wertheimer, **III** 549a
Whitehead, **III** 545b, 547b, 548a
wisdom of the fool, **IV** 515b
Wittgenstein, **III** 545b, 546a, 546b, 548a, 549b, 550b
Wright, **III** 558a, 561a, 562a
Zilsel, **III** 545b
See also Pragmatism
Employment
capitalism, **III** 148a
equality, **II** 144b
happiness, **II** 385a
Marxism, **III** 148a
welfare state, **IV** 509b, 512a, 513a
Empson, William, irony, **II** 633a, 634a
Encapsulation theory, evolutionism, **II** 178a
Endell, August, empathy, **II** 88b
Endocrine glands, disease, **II** 405a
Endocrinology
longevity, **III** 93a
Man-Machine, **III** 144b
Energy
conservation of, **II** 612b
Einstein, **IV** 84a, 86b
entropy, **II** 112b–120a
hermeticism, **II** 431a, 431b, 432a, 432b
matter, **III** 185b
mythology, **III** 305a
relativity, **IV** 82b, 84a, 85b, 86b, 91a, 91b
space, **IV** 296b, 297a, 302a, 303a, 303b
symmetry, **IV** 349a, 352b
time, **IV** 395b
Energy-time uncertainty relation, **II** 589a, 590b, 591a
Einstein, **II** 590b, 591a
Heisenberg, **II** 589a, 590b, 591a
Enfantin, Barthélemy-Prosper (1796–1864), socialism, **IV** 290a
Engelbert of Volkersdorf (1250–1311), social contract, **IV** 253b
Engel-Janosi, F.
determinism, **II** 20b
historiography, **II** 20b
Engelmann, Woldemar, justice, **III** 28b
Engels, Friedrich (1820–1895)
acquired characteristics, **II** 620a, 620b
anarchism, **I** 72b

anthropology, **III** 153b
atomism, **I** 497a–497b
authority, **I** 153a
bourgeois, **IV** 316b
Cartesianism, **II** 453b
causation, **I** 282b; **II** 452b; **III** 643a
China, **I** 366b, 369b
class, **II** 146a, 452a, 454b, 554a; **III** 22a, 156a
culture, **I** 620b
despotism, **II** 13a, 17a
determinism, **II** 24b, 25a, 25b, 154b
dictatorship, **III** 155b
discontinuity, **I** 497a–497b
economics, **II** 452a, 452b; **III** 22a, 156a
equality, **II** 146a
Erfurt Program, **III** 148b
ethics, **III** 159b
evolution, **II** 454b, 620a; **III** 153b; **III** 473b
existentialism, **II** 191b
false consciousness, **II** 554b
Hegel and, **II** 413b, 453b, 454a, 454b, 455a
Hess and, **II** 413b
history, **I** 282b; **II** 24b, 25a, 25b, 450a, 452a, 454a–454b; **III** 643a
Hobbes and, **II** 453b
ideology, **II** 554a–554b, 559b, 560b
individualism, **III** 643a
industry, **III** 153b
law, **III** 22a
Lenin and, **II** 454b–455a
logic, **II** 454b, 455a
love, **III** 104b
Lysenko and, **II** 620b
Marx and, **III** 359a; **IV** 292a, 293a
materialism, **II** 450a, 452a, 452b–453a, 453b–455a; **III** 153a
matter, **II** 455a
metaphysics, **II** 455a
monism, **II** 455a
motion, **II** 454b
natural law, **III** 22a
natural science, **II** 455a
Nature, **II** 450a, 454a–454b
necessity, **III** 149a, 359a
ontology, **II** 450a, 454b, 455a
perfectibility, **III** 473b
periodization in history, **III** 478b
philosophy, **II** 452b, 453b
Plekhanov and, **II** 455a
positivism, **II** 454b
private property, **IV** 316b
production, **II** 25b, 452a

progress, **III** 629a, 643a
proletariat, **II** 559b; **III** 155b
realism in literature, **IV** 53a
revisionism, **IV** 265a, 265b, 266a, 266b, 267b, 268a–268b, 269a, 269b, 270a
revolution, **II** 452b; **IV** 163b, 293a
Ruge and, **II** 413b
science, **II** 455a
socialism, **II** 452a, 454b; **III** 154a, 155b; **IV** 292a, 293a
society, **II** 452a, 452b, 454b
State, **IV** 316b
structuralism, **IV** 326a
theology, **III** 473b
truth, **III** 22a
universe, **II** 455a
war, **IV** 506a
women, **IV** 529b
See also Marxism
English Civil War
democracy, **I** 656a, 656b–657a, 658b
social contract, **IV** 254b–255a
English Revolution
class, **I** 442a–442b
crisis in history, **I** 593a
equality, **II** 138b, 143a
French Revolution, **IV** 159b
English language, **II** 661a, 670b; **IV** 466b
Engnell, Ivan, mythology, **III** 311b
Enki (myth), **II** 335b
Enlightenment, **II** 89a–100b
Addison, **II** 89b, 91b
aesthetics, **II** 97b–98a
Age of Reason, **III** 479b
agriculture, **II** 90b, 93b, 98b
Alembert, **II** 89b–90a, 91b, 93b, 96a–96b, 99b, 100a
allegory, **I** 47b
anthropology, **II** 90a, 97a–97b, 100a
aristocracy, **II** 91a, 94a, 97b
Aristotelianism, **II** 90a, 94a
Aristotle, **II** 96b
art, **II** 90a, 91a, 96b, 100a
Bacon, Francis, **I** 173b; **II** 90a, 96b, 100a; **III** 215b
Bacon, Roger, **II** 90a
Bayle, **II** 89a, 91b, 94a
beauty, **II** 90a
Beccaria, **II** 89b
Bentham, **II** 89b, 90b, 93b, 97b, 98b
Bodin, **II** 90a
bourgeois, **II** 91a, 94a
Buffon, **II** 91b, 92b–93a
Burke, **IV** 203a

Carlyle, **IV** 199a, 200b
casuistry, **I** 263b
catastrophism, **IV** 419b
Catherine the Great, **II** 90b
central dogma of, **II** 102a
Chanteloup, **II** 98b
Chaptal, **II** 98b
China, **I** 353b–354a
Christianity, **II** 91a; **III** 671a
city, **I** 432a
class, **II** 91a, 92a
classicism, **I** 454b
climax of, **II** 89b
communications, **II** 90b, 91a–91b, 93a
Comte, **II** 93b, ´95a; **III** 532b, 533b, 534a
Condillac, **II** 96a
Condorcet, **III** 533a
conservatism, **I** 479b, 480a
Constant, **II** 95a
Counter-, **II** 100b–112b
culture, **I** 616a–616b, 617a; **II** 90b, 91a, 92a, 95a, 130a
Daguesseau, **II** 95b
damnation, **III** 248a
deism, **I** 647b; **II** 91a
Delolme, **II** 94b, 98a
democracy, **I** 657b–658a; **II** 91a
Democritus, **II** 96b
Descartes, **II** 90a, 96a; **III** 248a
despotism, **II** 12a, 12b–13b
determinism, **II** 23b–24a
Diderot, **II** 89b, 91b, 95a, 96b, 97b
disease, **II** 402b, 403a
Diodorus Curtius, **II** 95b
Du Pont de Nemours, **II** 98b
economic history, **II** 45a, 45b, 47a
economics, **II** 90b
Eden, **II** 98b
education, **II** 90b, 91a, 98a, 99b–100a
electricity, **III** 179a
environment, **II** 130a
Epicureanism, **II** 90a
Epicurus, **II** 90a
equality, **II** 138a, 143a–144a, 145a
eschatology, **II** 158b–159a, 159b, 160a
ethics, **II** 90a, 96b
evil, **III** 248a
evolution, **II** 93a–94a
Faust (legend), **III** 248a, 248b, 249a
Fellenberg, **II** 99b
Ferguson, **II** 89b, 92b, 93a, 93b, 94b, 99b
Filmer, **II** 95a

France, **II** 89a, 89b, 91a, 91b, 94b, 98b
Franklin, **IV** 22a, 22b
Frederick the Great, **II** 90b
free will, **II** 92a
French Revolution, **II** 89a, 91a, 94b
Froebel, **II** 99b
George II, **II** 89b
Germany, **II** 89a, 89b, 91b, 99b
Gibbons, **II** 89b, 90a, 90b, 92a, 93a, 94b
God, **II** 353a–354a, 355b–359a, 364a
Godwin, **II** 98b, 99b
Goethe, **III** 343a
Goguet, **II** 93a
Gothic, **II** 371a
Gottsched, **II** 89b
Great Britain, **II** 89a, 89b, 90b, 91a, 91b, 94b, 95a, 98b
Greece (ancient), **II** 90a
Grotius, **II** 90a
happiness, **II** 96b–98a, 99a
Hegel, **II** 93b, 95a
Helvétius, **II** 94b
Herder, **II** 89b
heresy, **II** 427a, 428b, 429a
historicism, **II** 457a, 458b, 459a
historiography, **II** 23b–24a, 491a, 492a
history, **II** 23b–24a
Hobbes, **II** 90a, 94a, 98a
holy, **II** 512b
human nature, **II** 91b–92b, 93a, 96b–98a, 98b, 100a
humanism, **II** 90a
Hume, **II** 89b, 91a, 92a, 92b, 93a, 93b, 94a, 95a, 96a, 97a, 98a, 99a, 100a
Hutcheson, **II** 89b, 97b–98a, 100a
iconography, **II** 533a, 533b
idealism, **II** 96a
ideology, **II** 554a
individualism, **II** 89a, 90a, 594a, 595a, 595b, 598b, 600b
industry, **II** 90b
infinity, **II** 611a
influence of, **I** 403b
international peace, **III** 452b
irrationalism, **II** 635b
Italy, **II** 89b, 91b, 98b
Jefferson, **IV** 22b
Jesuits, **II** 91a
Joseph II, **II** 90b
justice, **II** 94a
Kafka, **II** 99a
Kant, **II** 89b, 93a, 98b; **III** 326b, 343a, 479b; **IV** 209a

Kierkegaard, **II** 99a
knowledge, **II** 90a, 96b
La Mettrie, **II** 96a
labor, **II** 90b, 99a
Lamarck, **II** 91b
language, **II** 667a–669b
law, **II** 90b, 91b–92b, 93a; **III** 11a–11b
Leibniz, **II** 89b, 90a; **III** 248a
Leopold II, **II** 90b
Lessing, **II** 89b; **III** 248a, 343a
liberty, **II** 90a, 91a, 92a, 94a, 94b–95b
Linguet, **II** 99b
linguistics, **IV** 428b
literature, **II** 91a–91b, 96b, 98b–99a, 100a
Locke, **II** 89a, 89b, 90a, 95a, 95b–96a, 96b; **IV** 120a
longevity, **III** 91b, 92a
love, **III** 107b
Mably, **II** 99b
Macaulay, **II** 95b
Mandeville, **II** 94b
Man-Machine, **III** 135b, 138b–141b, 142a
manufacturing, **II** 90b, 93b
Marivaux, **II** 96b
Marx, **II** 99a
materialism, **II** 450a, 450b
mathematics, **III** 179a–179b
matter, **III** 193b, 194a–195a
mechanics, **III** 179b
Mendelssohn, **II** 89b
Meslier, **II** 99b
metaphysical imagination, **III** 215b, 216a
Methodism, **II** 91a
Middle Ages, **II** 93b
Mill, **IV** 199a, 200a
Millar, **II** 93a, 93b, 94b, 98a, 99b
modernism, **I** 423a–423b, 425b–426a
monarchy, **II** 91a
Montesquieu, **II** 89b, 93a, 93b, 95a, 98a, 100a
Morelly, **II** 99b
Moreri, **II** 91b
Möser, **II** 89b
music, **III** 263b, 271b
nationalism, **III** 324b, 326b, 327b, 329a, 331b, 332a
naturalism in art, **III** 343a, 343b
Nature, **II** 90a, 92a, 94a–94b
Neo-Platonism, **II** 97b
Newton, **II** 90a, 96b, 100a
Niebuhr, **II** 93b
Nietzsche, **II** 99a

optics, **III** 179a
Paine, **II** 99b
papacy, **II** 91a
passions, **III** 248a
peace, **III** 446a
perennial philosophy, **III** 459b–461b
perfectibility, **II** 92b–93a; **III** 469a–469b, 471b–472a, 473a–473b, 474b
periodization in history, **III** 477b, 478a, 478b, 479b
Pestalozzi, **II** 99b
philosophy, **II** 89b, 90a, 91a, 93a, 97a–97b
physics, **III** 179b
Pietism, **II** 91a, 97b; **III** 494a, 495a
Plato, **II** 90a, 99b
Platonism, **III** 516a
Plutarch, **II** 90a, 95b
politics, **II** 90a, 90b, 96b, 98a–99a
Popper, **II** 94a
positivism, **III** 532b, 533a, 533b, 534a, 536a, 538a, 545b
pragmatism, **III** 553a, 554a
Prevost, **II** 96b
Priestley, **II** 93a
production, **II** 90b
progress, **II** 92b–93a; **III** 634a, 643a
protest movements, **III** 671a, 672b, 675b
Protestantism, **II** 429a
psychology, **IV** 20b, 21b, 22a, 22b, 23b
Puritanism, **II** 94a; **IV** 20b
Quakers, **IV** 20b
rationalism, **III** 494a
reason, **II** 94a, 95b–96b
reform, **II** 89b, 90a–91a, 98b
reformation, **IV** 68b
Reformation, **II** 89a, 90a; **IV** 68a
religion, **II** 90a, 91a, 100a; **IV** 120a
Renaissance, **II** 89a, 90a; **IV** 124a
revolution, **IV** 154b, 155b
Robertson, **II** 89b, 93b, 94b
Rollin, **II** 95b
Roman Catholic Church, **II** 91a
romanticism, **III** 479b; **IV** 198b, 199a, 200a, 200b, 201a, 201b, 202b, 203a, 203b, 204a, 206a, 206b, 207b, 208a, 208b, 209a
Rome (ancient), **II** 90a
Rousseau, **II** 89b, 91a, 91b, 93a, 93b, 94b, 98a, 99b

Russell, **III** 446a
Sade, **II** 94b
St. Pierre, **II** 90b
Schiller, Friedrich, **II** 94b; **III** 343a
Scotland, **II** 89b, 91b, 94a, 100a
Seneca, **II** 90a
sensationalism, **II** 96a
Shaftesbury, **II** 89b, 96b, 97b
Sismondi, **II** 95a, 98b–99a
skepticism, **II** 96a
slavery, **II** 95a
Smith, Adam, **II** 89b, 91b, 92b, 93a–93b, 94b, 95a, 97a, 98a, 99a–99b
social welfare, **IV** 277a
socialism, **IV** 285a, 288a–288b, 290b
society, **II** 90a–90b, 91a, 92a, 93b, 99a–100a
sociology, **II** 98b
spontaneous generation, **IV** 308a, 310a, 310b
Staël, **II** 100a
Steele, **II** 89b, 91b
Stewart, **II** 99b, 100a
Stoicism, **II** 90a, 99a
Switzerland, **III** 329a
technology, **II** 90b, 91a
theodicy, **IV** 382a–383b
Thucydides, **II** 95a
trade, **II** 90b, 93b
travel, **II** 90b
truth, **III** 248a
Turgot, **II** 90b, 93a, 93b, 98b
uniformitarianism, **IV** 419b, 426a
utilitarianism, **II** 94a, 96b–98a; **IV** 450b–451a, 452a
Utopia, **IV** 462b
Vergil, **II** 90a
Verri, Alessandro, **II** 89b, 91a
Verri, Pietro, **II** 89b
Vico, **II** 102a–103b
virtù, **IV** 484b
Voltaire, **II** 90a, 91a, 91b, 94b, 95a–95b, 97a–97b, 98a; **IV** 155b
wealth, **II** 91a, 99b
Whitney, **II** 99a
Winckelmann, **II** 89b; **III** 343a
work, **IV** 534a
Wundt, **II** 93b
Xenophon, **II** 95a
Young, **II** 98b
Zeno of Citium, **II** 90a
Enlil (myth), **II** 335b
Ennemoser, Joseph, witchcraft, **IV** 522b

Enoch (Bible)
  Islam, II 640a
  mythology, III 277b, 279b, 283b, 284a
Ense, Varnhagen von, Hegel and, II 412a
Entelechy, aesthetics, II 216b, 223a
Entomology, theriophily, IV 388b
Entrepreneur, the, economic history, II 49b, 54b, 55a, 55b
Entropy, II 112b–120a
  Adams, Henry, II 116a
  Bergson, II 118b
  Boltzmann, II 114b–115b, 116a, 117a–117b, 118a–118b
  Boltzmann problem, II 118a–118b
  Born, II 114b
  Broglie, II 118b
  Carathéodory, II 114b
  Carnot's Theorem, II 113a, 113b
  Clausius Theorem, II 114a
  Comte, II 116a
  cosmology, II 117b
  Darwinism, II 115b
  Dirac, II 118a
  Duhem, II 114b, 118b
  ectrophy, II 117b–118a
  Ehrenfest, Paul, II 117a
  Ehrenfest, Tatiana, II 117a
  energy, II 112b–120a
  eschatology, II 160a
  extrascientific applications, II 118b
  Gibbs, II 113a–113b, 114b, 116a
  Gibbs thermodynamic potential, II 114b
  Greece (ancient), II 117b
  heat death theory, II 115b
  Heisenberg, II 116b
  Helmholtz, II 113a, 114b, 115b, 116a, 117b
  immediate consequences of, II 115b–116a
  Joule, II 113a
  Kelvin, II 113a, 113b, 115b, 116a, 116b, 117a
  Lagrange, II 117a
  Laplace, II 117a
  limits of the conception, II 117b–118a
  Lorentz, II 114b
  Maxwell, II 114b, 115a, 116a–117a
  Mayer, II 113a
  music, III 263b
  Nernst, II 114b
  Newton, II 117a

Nietzsche, II 117b
Pauli, II 118a
Planck, II 113a, 113b
Plato, II 117b
Poincaré cycle, II 117b
Poisson, II 117a
probability, III 620a
Pythagoreans, II 117b
Renaissance, II 116a
restrictions of the conception, II 116a–117b
reversibility objection, II 117a
sorting demon, II 116a–117a, 117b
state function, II 113b–114a
statistical definition of, II 115a–115b
Stoicism, II 117b
symmetry, IV 349b, 350a
Szilard, II 116b
Tait, II 116a
thermal death theory, II 115b
thermodynamic definition, II 112b–114b
thermodynamics, II 112b–120a
Tyndall, II 116a
universe, II 115b, 117b
Wells, H. G., II 116a
Zermelo, II 117a–117b, 118b
Environment, II 120b–127a
  acquired, II 122a, 124a
  acquired characteristics, II 618a–618b, 619b
  Albertus Magnus, II 129a
  Aristotle, II 120b
  art, II 583a
  Athena (goddess), II 122b
  behaviorism, II 123a–124a
  Berkeley, II 120b
  Bernard, Claude, II 125a–126a
  Bible, II 127b, 128b
  biogeography, II 131b
  Bodin, II 129a–129b
  Buckle, II 130a, 131b
  Buffon, II 128b, 132b
  Cannon, W. B., II 125b, 126a
  China (ancient), II 122a–122b
  Christianity, II 132a–132b
  Cicero, II 127b
  conceptual, II 123b–127a
  cosmology, II 123a
  Creation, II 127b
  culture, II 123b–124a, 127a–134b
  cybernetic theory, II 126a–126b

Darwin, II 125a, 126a, 130b, 133a
Darwinism, II 130b
Derham, II 132a
determinism, II 22a, 23a
Dickens, II 133b
disease, II 122b, 124a–125a, 125b, 126a, 129a
ecology, II 122a, 128b, 131b, 133b
Egypt (ancient), II 124a, 129a
Emerson, II 122b–123a
Enlightenment, II 130a
environmentalism, II 131a–131b
environmentalists, II 122b–123a
eschatology, II 128a
evolution, II 125a, 126a–127a, 127b, 128a, 128b, 130b; III 646b
existentialism, II 194b
external, II 124a–125b
extrasensory perception, II 123b
geography, II 129a–132a
Germany, II 124b
God, II 122b, 127b, 128a, 128b, 129a, 132b
Great Britain, II 124a, 124b
Greece (ancient), II 120b, 122b, 127b, 129a
harmony, II 128a, 128b
Henderson, II 121b–122a, 125b
Herder, II 128a, 129b–130a; III 639a
Herodotus, II 129a
Hippocrates, II 122b, 124a–124b, 125a, 125b, 129a
historiography, II 22a, 23a
homeokinesis, II 125b–127a
homeostasis, II 125b–127a
human nature, III 643b
Hume, II 120b, 128b, 129b
Huntington, II 131b
Hygeia (myth), II 122b
Indians (American), II 122b
individualism, II 125b–127a
Industrial Revolution, II 124b
internal, II 124a–125b
James, William, II 125b
Jefferson, IV 21b
Judaism, II 127b, 132a–132b
Kant, II 120b, 128b
Lamarck, II 618a, 623b–624a
language, II 660a, 665a
Leibniz, II 128a, 130a
Locke, II 120b

loyalty, III 110b
Lyell, II 133a
Malthus, II 128a, 130b
Marsh, II 128a, 132b–133b
Marx, II 451a
materialism, II 451a
matter, III 191b
Mendel, II 126a
Middle Ages, II 129a–129b, 132b
migrations, II 130b
milieu intérieur concept, II 125a–125b
mind, II 120b–121a, 122a, 123b, 129a
Montesquieu, II 129b, 131b
natural law, II 122b; III 14a
natural selection, II 125a
Nature, II 127b–128b, 130a, 132a, 132b, 133b
Neo-Darwinism, II 126a
Netherlands, II 124a
order, II 128a
organicism, II 120b–123a
Owen, IV 289b
painting, II 583a
Paley, II 127b
pangenesis, II 623b–624a, 625b
perception, II 123a–123b
perfectibility, III 471a–471b, 643b
Philo the Jew, II 132a
philosophy, II 127b
physiochemical, II 122a, 123a–123b
Plato, II 127b, 129b
Platonism, II 127b
pollution, II 122a
Polybius, II 129a
pragmatism, III 558a, 562a
progress, III 637a, 639a, 640a, 643b, 646b
psychology, IV 21b, 23b, 24b, 25a, 26a, 26b, 27a, 27b, 28b
rationalism, IV 48a
Ratzel, II 128a, 130b–131a, 131b
Ray, II 127b, 128a, 130a
religion, II 127b, 128b; IV 107b
Renaissance, II 129a–129b
Ruskin, II 127b, 133b
Saint Augustine, II 127b
Saint Thomas Aquinas, II 120b, 127b, 129a, 129b
Saint-Pierre, II 127b
Sartre, II 194b
science, II 127b, 128a, 130a
Semple, II 131a
Social Darwinism, II 130b
socialism, IV 289b

Spengler, II 131b
Spinoza, II 128b
spiritualism, II 123b
Stoicism, II 127b
Strabo, II 129a
superego, II 123b–124a
Taine, II 583a
technology, IV 364b
Teilhard de Chardin, II 133a
teleology, II 128b, 129a
total, II 123a–124a
Toynbee, II 23a, 131b
U.S., II 124b
unity, II 128a, 128b
urbanization, II 124a
Victorians, IV 217a, 218b–219a, 222a, 223a
Voltaire, II 129b
web of life concept, II 128b, 133a
Wiener, Norbert, II 126a
yin and yang, II 122b
Environmentalism
culture, II 131a–131b
equality, II 143b
Environmentalists, II 122b–123a
Epaminondas (418?–362 B.C.), historiography, II 504b
Ephialtes (d. 469 B.C.), temperance, IV 366b
Ephorus of Cumae (4th century B.C.)
historiography, II 503b–504a, 507a–508a
progress, III 628a
Ephraem Syrus (died 373 A.D.), music, III 266a
Epics
Aristotle, III 527a
freedom of speech, II 253a
Greece (ancient), II 466b
historiography, II 464b–465a, 465b, 466b, 472b, 476b, 491b, 504b, 507a
humanism, II 517b
literature, III 87b, 241b; IV 331b
mimesis, III 226b
mythology, III 272b, 273a, 279a, 279b–280a, 304a, 304b, 307a, 308a, 309a, 315a
organicism, III 424a
painting, IV 465b, 469b, 473b
Plato, III 226b, 497b, 501a
Platonism, III 496a, 497b, 501a, 513b
poetry, III 527a, 527b, 530b, 531a; IV 465b, 469b, 473b
progress, III 624b
romanticism, IV 188b–189a
satire, IV 211a, 214b

temperance, IV 365b
Epictetus (c. 50–c. 138 A.D.)
Christianity, III 590a
death, I 635b
democracy, I 655b
ethics, IV 319a, 321b, 322a
freedom of speech, II 261b
humanism, II 520a
loyalty, III 111a, 111b
primitivism, III 590a
State, I 655b
Stoicism, III 590a; IV 319a, 321b, 322a
Epicureanism, II 134b–138a
abstraction, I 1a, 2b
Alexander the Great, IV 7a
anti-intellectualism, III 587a
apologism, III 89b
Aristotle, II 135a, 135b, 137a; IV 7a
art, II 576a, 581a–582a
atheism, III 137b
atomism, I 272a; II 135b, 136a–137a, 137b; IV 7a, 7b, 175b
Bacon, Francis, II 137b
behaviorism, IV 8a
biology, I 235a, 236a
body, IV 7a
Boyle, II 137b
Bruno, II 137b
causation, I 272b–273a, 275b; II 135b, 136a–137a
chance, II 231a
Christianity, II 137b; IV 8b
Cicero, II 137a, 137b
Comte, II 582a
concept formation, I 2b
consciousness, I 215a
culture, I 610b, 611b
Cynics, III 587a
deism, I 647b, 648a
Democritus, II 135b, 136a–136b; IV 7a
desire, IV 8a
determinism, II 135a–137a
Diderot, II 582a
dignity, IV 142b, 143a
Diogenes Laërtius, II 137b
dualism, II 41a
Enlightenment, II 94a
Epicurus, II 134b–137b; III 587a, 587b, 590a; IV 7a
ethics, IV 8a, 319a
evil, II 163a, 167a
fate, II 231a
Faust (legend), III 247a
fortune, II 231a
free will, II 244a
freedom of speech, II 260b
Gassendi, I 306b
good, II 378a; III 587b; IV 175b–176a
Greece (ancient), II 135a;

IV 7a
happiness, II 378a
hedonism, II 137b; III 587a
Hobbes, II 137b
humanism, II 520a
idea, IV 7b
indeterminism, II 136a–137a
joy, IV 175b
justice, II 656b
knowledge, IV 7b, 8a
literary paradox, III 79b
longevity, III 89b
Lucretius, II 134b–135a, 136a, 136b, 137b; III 587a–587b
Man-Machine, III 132a, 132b, 133a, 134a, 138a, 139a
Marxism, I 497a
materialism, IV 7a, 8a, 175b
matter, III 187b, 190a
Mill, J. S., II 137b
mind, IV 7b, 8a
monism, II 41a
morality, IV 7a
More, Thomas, III 79b
mortality, IV 176a
motivation, IV 8a
mysticism, II 581b
mythology, III 292a–292b
natural law, III 16a–16b
naturalism, II 581b
Neo-Platonism, III 373a
optics, III 408a, 408b
pain, II 137b, 378a; IV 8a, 175b
painting, II 576a, 581a, 581b, 582a
Pater, II 137b, 576a
peace, IV 175b
philosophy, IV 7a, 53b
Plato, II 135a, 135b; III 504a; IV 7a
Platonism, III 504a, 524a
pleasure, II 137b, 378a; III 587a; IV 8a, 175b
poetry, III 526a, 526b
pragmatism, III 555b
pre-Socratics, IV 7b
primitivism, III 585a, 586a, 586b–587b
progress, III 630a, 630b, 633a
psychology, IV 7a–8b
psychosomatics, IV 8a
punishment, II 135a; IV 176a
realism in literature, IV 53b
reason, I 91b; III 586a
Renaissance, II 137b; IV 142b, 143a
right, IV 175b–176a
Rome (ancient), II 134b–

137b
Saint Augustine, II 137a
Saint-Évremond, II 137b
self-sufficiency, III 585a, 587a
sensation, IV 7b
skepticism, IV 236a, 239b–240a, 241a
soul, IV 7a
spontaneous generation, IV 308a
Stoicism, II 137a; IV 319a
supernatural, III 587b
superstition, IV 176a
swerve theory, II 136a–137a
teleology, IV 175b
temperance, IV 369b, 375b
theodicy, IV 380b
thought, IV 7b
Valla, II 137b; IV 142b, 143a
Voltaire, II 137b
Epicurus (342?–270 B.C.),
abstraction, I 2b
acquired characteristics, II 617b
atomism, I 130b, 132b, 135b–136a, 137a, 496a–497a; II 136a–137a, 237a, 244a, 582a 582b, 586b–587a; IV 51a
causation, I 271b, 273a; II 136a–136b, 587a
chance, I 336a
choice, II 244a
Christianity, III 590a
Cicero and, II 137a
death, I 635a–635b, 636b; III 274a
Democritus and, II 135b, 136a–136b
determinism, II 135b–137a, 237b
discontinuity, I 496a–497a
Enlightenment, II 90a
Epicureanism, II 134b–137b; III 587a, 587b, 590a; IV 7a
ethics, IV 321b
free will, II 134b–137b, 237b, 243b–244a, 245b
freedom of speech, II 260b
God, III 274a
happiness, II 378a; III 465a
humanism, II 520a; IV 133b
impressionism, II 582a–582b
indeterminacy, II 586b–587a, 590a
individualism, II 594b
Islam, II 642b
justice, II 654b, 656b
love, III 95b
Man-Machine, III 132a

Marxism, I 497a
matter, II 244a; III 187b
motion, IV 51a
mythology, III 274a
Nature, II 136a, 137a
pain, II 137b, 378a, 465a
perception, I 2b
perfectibility, III 465a–465b, 468b
Plato and, III 274a
pleasure, II 137b, 378a
primitivism, III 587a, 587b, 590a
progress, III 630a, 631a, 631b
psychology, IV 7a, 10b
punishment, II 135a
rationalism, IV 51a
reason, II 244a
religion, IV 93a
Saint Augustine and, II 137a
science, III 630a
skepticism, IV 234a, 234b, 236a, 240a
social contract, IV 252b
society, III 468b
Stoicism, IV 321b
soul, I 231a; II 244a; III 274a
swerve theory, II 136a–137a
temperance, IV 375b
theodicy, IV 380a–380b
time, IV 389b
wisdom of the fool, IV 518b
Epicycles, IV 74b
planets, I 541a, 541b, 542a, 544a
Epideictic rhetoric, IV 168a, 168b, 171b
Epidemics, II 397b, 399b, 400a, 402a, 403a–403b, 405a
Epigenesis
Aristotle, II 623a
evolutionism, II 178a
pangenesis, II 623a, 623b
Epigrams
humanism, II 516a, 517b
literary paradox, III 79b
Epimenides the Cretan (6th century B.C.), literary paradox, III 76b
Epiphanes, Gnosticism, II 328a
Epiphany, mythology, III 280b, 281b, 314a
Epiphenomenalism, happiness, II 382b
See also Mind
Epistemology
Aristotle, IV 4b

Burton, III 81a
dignity, IV 139b
empiricism, III 547b, 548a
France, II 515b
Hegel, II 414b
human nature, III 572a, 575b
humanism, II 515a, 515b
idea, II 603b
ideology, II 553a–554a, 554b, 555a
indeterminacy, II 589b, 590a
individualism, II 603b
Kant, III 218a, 218b, 219b, 233b
language, II 661a, 661b
linguistics, III 75a
literary paradox, III 77b, 81a
Man-Machine, III 138b, 140a, 145a
metaphor, III 206a
moral sense, III 230b, 233b, 234b
naturalism in art, III 339b
necessity, III 351b, 356a–357a
Platonism, III 505b
Plotinus, III 505b
pragmatism, III 565a, 565b
primitivism, III 589a, 595a, 596a
psychology, IV 4b, 11b, 24b
Reid, Thomas, III 233b
religion, III 206a
Renaissance, IV 139b
skepticism, IV 236b, 237a, 240a, 243b, 246a
social welfare, IV 277a, 278a
structuralism, IV 326b
time, IV 390b, 395a
work, IV 533b
Epithalamium, love, III 98a
Equal protection in law, III 10b–13b
Equality, II 138a–148a
aliens, II 140a
American Revolution, II 143a, 145a
Anabaptists, II 142a, 142b
anarchism, II 145b, 147b
aristocracy, II 143b, 146b
Aristotelianism, II 138b
Aristotle, I 449a; II 139a, 139b, 140a; III 11a, 15b; IV 285b
Asia, II 141a, 143b
Austria, II 144a
Babeuf, II 145b, 147a
Bentham, II 145a
Bible, II 140a–140b, 142a,

142b
Bichat, I 448b
Blacks, II 145a
bourgeois, II 143a, 145a, 146a
Burke, Edmund, II 143b
Cabanis, I 448b
Calvin, II 142a–142b
Canada, III 13b
capitalism, II 146a
Charles, I, II 142b
Chartists, II 143a
Christianity, II 138a, 138b, 140b–143a; III 670b
class, II 139b, 145a, 146a
clergy, II 138b, 141a–141b, 142b
competition, III 11b
Condillac, II 143b
Condorcet, II 144b–145a, 145b, 147a; III 644a, 648b
cosmos, II 138b, 140a
Cromwell, II 142b
culture, II 141b
deism, I 651a
democracy, II 140a, 142b, 143a–143b, 145a–145b, 146b, 147a, 260a
Diggers, II 143a
economics, II 145a; III 10b, 11b
education, II 138b, 143b, 144b, 146b, 147a
employment, II 144b
Engels, II 146a
English Revolution, II 138b, 143a
Enlightenment, II 138a, 143a–144a, 145a
environmentalism, II 143b
ethics, II 142a
Euclid, II 138b
Euripides, II 140a
family, II 145a
feudalism, II 141a, 143b, 144b
force, II 138b
France, II 138a, 139b, 141b, 143a, 143b–145b; III 11b
Franklin, IV 22a
freedom, II 146b
freedom of speech, II 260a
French Revolution, II 138a, 139b, 141b, 143a, 144b–145b, 146a
Galileo, II 138b
general will, II 277a, 277b, 278b, 279b
Germany, II 141a, 142a; III 11a–11b
God, II 138a–138b, 140a–141a, 142a, 142b, 143b
Great Britain, II 138b, 142a, 142b–143a, 144a, 145a; III

11a
Greece (ancient), II 138a, 138b, 140a, 140b, 144b; III 11a
Helvétius, II 143b
Herodotus, II 144b
history, II 146b
Hobbes, II 144a
human nature, III 644a
humanitarianism, II 143b, 144a
Hutterites, II 142a
income, II 146a
income taxes, II 145b
India, II 141a; III 12a, 13b
Indians (American), II 143b, 145a
instinct, III 644a
Ireland, II 145a
Jacobins, II 143a
Jefferson, III 317b
Jesus Christ, II 140b, 142a
Judaism, II 138a–138b, 140a–140b
justice, II 141a, 147a–147b; III 15b, 27b, 28a
Kant, II 279b
kingship, II 138b
Kosciuszko, II 144b
labor, II 145b, 146a
law, II 140a, 140b, 142b, 144a, 145a, 145b, 687b, 688b; III 10b–13b, 15b, 27b, 28a
Levellers, II 142b, 143a, 144a
liberalism, II 146a–147a; III 55b–60b
liberty, II 140a, 146a, 147b
Lilburne, II 142b
Locke, I 448b; II 143a, 143b; III 11a, 21a
Luther, II 141b–142a, 142b
majorities, II 139a
Marx, II 145b–146a
Marxism, II 142a; III 148b
mathematics, II 138b, 140b
matter, II 138b
Mennonites, II 142a
Middle Ages, II 141a–141b; III 11a
Mill, J. S., II 146b
millenarianism, III 225a
monotheism, II 140b
Montesquieu, II 143b
morality, II 144a
Moravians, II 142a
motion, II 138b
Münzer, II 142a
nationalism, III 326b, 327a, 328b, 329a, 329b, 331b, 332a
natural law, II 140a, 142b; III 15b, 21a, 21b, 25b

Nature, II 144a
Netherlands, II 142a
nobility, II 138b, 144a
opportunity, I 448b–449b
Paine, II 140a
papacy, II 141a, 141b
Peace of Westphalia, II 138b
Peasant Rebellion, II 142a
Philippines, III 13b
philosophy, II 139b, 143b–144a
Plato, I 449a; II 140a
Poland, II 139a, 144a, 144b
politics, II 138b, 143a, 145a–145b; III 11a–11b, 15b
poverty, II 145a
power, II 141b, 142a
predestination, II 140b–141a, 142b
primitivism, III 589a
private property, II 142a, 144a, 145a; III 650b, 653b, 654a, 657a
progress, III 637b, 644a, 648b
proletariat, II 146a
protest movements, III 670b
Protestantism, II 138a, 138b, 141b–143a
Prussia, II 144a
psychology, IV 22a
Ptolemy, II 138b
Puritanism, II 142b–143a
race, II 139a–139b, 144b
Rainborough, II 142b, 143a, 144a
Reformation, II 138a
Renaissance, IV 438a
Restoration, II 143a
Rhodesia, III 13a
Robespierre, II 144b, 145a
Roman Catholic Church, II 138b, 141a–141b, 142a
romanticism, IV 205a, 206a
Rome (ancient), II 140a, 140b, 687b, 688b; III 11a
Rousseau, I 448b, 658a; II 143b–144a, 277a, 277b, 278b; III 21b
Saint Augustine, II 140b
Saint Paul, II 140b, 144b
Saint Thomas Aquinas, III 11a; IV 525a
Saint-Simon, I 448b, 449a
science, II 140b; III 11b
Seneca, II 140a
sex, II 139a, 140a, 144b
skepticism, II 140b
slavery, II 140a, 140b, 141a, 144b
Smith, Adam, III 11b
social contract, IV 251b, 255b

social welfare, IV 279a
socialism, II 143a, 145b–146a, 147a; IV 285a, 285b, 288a, 288b, 293b, 294a
society, II 138b, 141a–141b, 145a, 146a–146b
Socrates, IV 285b
soul, II 141a
State, II 143a, 145b; IV 313b–314a, 316b–317a, 317b, 318a
Stoicism, II 140a, 140b; IV 285b
suffrage, II 138b–139a, 145a, 145b
Switzerland, III 329a
Tawney, II 147a
taxation, II 144a, 144b, 145b; III 11b
third estate, II 138b
Tocqueville, II 139b, 146a–146b
totalitarianism, IV 407b
tyranny, II 146b
U.S.S.R., II 147a
unions, II 145b
U.N., II 138b, 140a, 147b; III 12a
U.S., II 138b, 139a–139b, 142a, 143b, 145a, 146b, 147a; III 11b, 12a–13a, 329a
universal man, IV 438a
universe, II 138b
utilitarianism, IV 447a, 449b
Utopia, IV 462b
Voltaire, II 143b; IV 288a
wages, II 146a
war, IV 503b
wealth, II 139a, 143a, 144a, 145a
welfare state, IV 510b, 511a
Winstanley, II 143a
wisdom, II 139a
Wolff, III 11b
women, IV 524b, 525b, 526b, 527a, 527b, 528a, 528b, 529a
work, IV 532b
Young, II 146b–147a
See also Equity
Equicola
mythology, III 291a
Platonism, III 514a
Equity
Akiba, II 151b–152a
Aristotle, II 149b–150b, 153b
Bacon, Francis, II 152b, 153b
ben Azariah, II 151b
Bible, II 151a–152a
Cicero, II 150b–151a

Coke, II 153a
common law, II 695a, 695b
Cowper, II 153b
defined, II 148a
dualism, II 148a–148b
economics, II 148a
ethics, II 148a–154a
God, II 151a
Great Britain, II 148a, 152a–154a
Greece (ancient), II 148a–150b, 151a, 153b
Hadrian, II 151a
Israel, II 152a
James I, II 152b, 153a
Judaism, II 151a–152a, 153a
judges, II 149a–149b, 153b
justice, II 150a, 150b, 151b, 656a, 656b
kingship, II 152a–153a
law, II 148a–154a
Lehmann, II 153b
Maimonides, II 151b
Maine, II 151a
morality, II 151a
More, Thomas, II 153b
Nature, II 150b
Nottingham, II 152b, 153a–153b
oratory, II 150a–150b
philosophy, II 151a
Plato, II 148a–149b, 150a, 150b
Puritanism, II 152b–153a
Quintilian, II 151a
reason, II 150b
Roman Catholic Church, II 152a
Rome (ancient), II 150b–151a, 152a
society, II 149a
Stoicism, II 150b, 151a
U.S., II 148a, 152a, 153a
women, IV 522a–530a
yosher, II 151a–152a
Equivalence principle, IV 397b
Er (myth)
harmony, II 389b; IV 38b, 39b, 41a
music, II 389b
Pythagorean cosmos, IV 38b, 39b, 41a
Erasistratus (3rd century B.C.), rationalism, IV 48a
Erasmus, Desiderius (1466?–1536)
education, IV 124b, 526a
Elyot and, IV 526a
eschatology, II 158b
genius, II 293b, 302a, 315b
God, II 348b
heresy, II 426a, 427a, 429a
history, I 393a, 397b

humanism, II 520a, 520b; III 514b; IV 135a
iconography, II 530a
individualism, II 302a, 599a
intolerance, IV 118b
irony, II 629a
liberalism, III 42a
literary criticism, I 596b
literary paradox, III 78a, 78b
literature, IV 124a
Luther and, II 348b–349a
mimesis, III 229a
More and, IV 526a
music, II 315b
periodization in literary history, III 482a
persecution, IV 118b
Platonism, III 514b
primitivism, III 595a
reformation, IV 63a
religion, IV 118b
satire, IV 213b
science, II 203a
skepticism, IV 242b, 247b, 248b–249a, 250b
war, IV 118b
wisdom of the fool, IV 518a–519b
women, IV 526a
Erastianism
faith, IV 119a
Hobbes, IV 119a
mysticism, IV 119a
religion, IV 117b–118a, 119a
Spinoza, IV 119a
Eratosthenes (3rd century B.C.), technology, IV 358a
Ercole of Ferrara, genius in music, II 320a
Erdmann, J. E. (1805–1892), Platonism, III 522a
Erffa, H. M. von, iconography, II 538a
Erfurt program, revisionism, IV 265a–265b
Erigena, John Scotus (9th century)
analogy, I 65b
Chain of Being, I 326a
death, I 640b
dignity, IV 137b, 139b, 140a
faith, hope, and charity, II 210b
God, I 573b–574a; II 210b
hierarchy, II 441a
iconography, II 526a
logos, I 574a
love, II 210b
methodology, III 381b
Nature, I 574a; III 351a
Pythagoreans, IV 41a

wisdom of the fool, **IV** 517b

Erikson, Erik, psychology, **IV** 29a

Ernst, Paul (1866–1933), China, **I** 371a
classicism, **I** 455b
genius, **II** 295b

Eros (love), **III** 94b, 95a, 274b, 498a, 499a
faith, hope, and charity, **II** 209b, 210a, 210b
Neo-Platonism, **III** 377a
Plato, **III** 95a

Eroticism
Diderot, **III** 603a
love, **III** 94a, 96b, 104a, 106a, 107a, 107b
motif, **III** 241a
mythology, **III** 291a
neo-classicism in art, **III** 365b
primitivism, **III** 603a

Error
deism, **I** 647a
dualism, **II** 38a
economic history, **II** 51b
evil, **II** 162b
indeterminacy, **II** 587b, 592b
measurement, **II** 587b; **III** 613a
perennial philosophy, **III** 458b, 459a
Platonism, **III** 506a
probability, **III** 613a–613b, 619a, 619b
progress, **III** 635b, 636b
prophecy, **III** 658b
rationalism, **IV** 48a, 51a
utilitarianism, **IV** 447a

Esau (Bible), mythology, **III** 279a, 280b

Eschatology, **II** 154b–161b
abandonment of, **II** 160a–160b
Adventists, **II** 157a
Anabaptists, **II** 156b–157a
Angelus Silesius, **II** 158a
apocalypse, **II** 154b–155a
Augsburg Confession, **II** 157a
Bacon, **II** 160a
Barth, **II** 160b–161a
Bible, **II** 154b–155a, 155b, 156a, 156b, 157b, 160a, 160b–161a; **IV** 229a, 230a
Böhme, **II** 157a, 158a
Bultmann, **II** 161a
Burckhardt, **II** 160a
Christianity, **II** 154b, 155b–157b, 158b, 159a, 160a, 160b–161a; **IV** 229a, 230a
class, **II** 159a

Clement, **II** 157b
communism, **II** 158b, 159b
concept of, **II** 154b
Condorcet, **II** 158b
cosmos, **II** 160a
Counter-Reformation, **II** 157a
crisis in history, **I** 591a
culture, **II** 128a
Darwin, **II** 159b–160a
death, **II** 156a
demonology, **II** 156a
dignity, **IV** 137b, 138a
dualism, **II** 40a, 154b, 155a
Enlightenment, **II** 158b–159a, 159b, 160a
entropy, **II** 160a
environment, **II** 128a
Erasmus, **II** 158b
ethics, **II** 159a
evil, **II** 154b, 155a
evolution, **II** 159b–160a
existentialism, **II** 161a
faith, **II** 156a, 158b, 160b
Fichte, **II** 158a
Gnosticism, **II** 155a–155b, 157b
God, **II** 154b–156a, 157a–161a, 337a–337b, 339a, 365b, 366a
good, **II** 154b, 155a–155b
Greece (ancient), **II** 155a–155b, 160a
Hegel, **II** 158a–158b, 159a
Heidegger, **II** 161a
history, **II** 154b–161b
Hobbes, **II** 160a
hope, **II** 214b
humanism, **II** 158b, 159b
Hume, **II** 160a
idealism, **II** 157b–158b, 159b
Iran, **II** 154b, 155a
Islam, **II** 154b
Israel, **II** 155a
Jehovah's Witnesses, **II** 157a
Jesus Christ, **II** 155b, 156a, 156b, 157a, 157b, 159a, 160b, 161a
Joachim of Floris, **II** 156b
Judaism, **II** 29b, 154b–155a
Kant, **II** 159a
Kierkegaard, **II** 160b, 161a
Kingsley, **II** 159a
knowledge, **II** 158a–158b
Lessing, **II** 158b–159a
Locke, **II** 160a
Löwith, **II** 157b
Luther, **II** 156b, 157a, 160b, 161a; **III** 270b–271a
McCosh, **II** 160a
Marx, **II** 159a–159b

Marxism, **II** 160a
millenarianism, **II** 158b, 159a; **III** 225a
Montanism, **II** 156b
Münzer, **II** 157a, 158b
music, **III** 270b–271a, 271b
mythology, **II** 154b; **III** 276b, 277b
Neo-Platonism, **II** 155b
Nicholas of Lyra, **II** 156b
Nietzsche, **II** 159a, 160a, 160b
nihilism, **II** 160b
nuclear power, **II** 160a
Origen, **II** 157b, 158a
pacifism, **II** 158b
papacy, **II** 156b
perennial philosophy, **III** 458b, 459b, 461a
periodization in history, **III** 477b
philosophy, **II** 155b, 158b, 159b, 160a
Pietism, **II** 157a
Platonism, **II** 157b
positivism, **II** 158b
progress, **III** 634b–635a
prophecy, **III** 663b, 664a, 666a
Protestantism, **II** 156b, 160b; **III** 270b–271a, 271b
purgatory, **II** 156a
reason, **II** 158a, 158b
Reformation, **II** 156b, 157a
relativism, **II** 160a–160b
Renaissance, **IV** 137b, 138a
Roman Catholic Church, **II** 156a–157b, 160b
Russell, **II** 157a
Saint Augustine, **II** 156b, 160b
Saint John, **II** 156a, 156b
Saint Luke, **II** 157b
Saint Mark, **I** 416a
Saint Paul, **II** 156a
salvation, **IV** 226a, 229a, 230a, 231b
Satan, **II** 155a, 155b
Schelling, **II** 159b
Schleiermacher, **II** 158b
Schweitzer, **II** 160b–161a
secularization, **II** 158b–159b, 160a
socialism, **II** 159b
soul, **II** 156a, 157b
Spener, **II** 157a
technology, **II** 159b
Teilhard de Chardin, **II** 160a
teleology, **II** 156a
theodicy, **IV** 380b
Thirty Years' War, **II** 157a
Ticonius, **II** 156b
time, **II** 155b–156a, 160b–161a

Turgot, **II** 158b
Zoroastrianism, **II** 339a; **IV** 231b
Zwingli, **II** 156b

Escobar y Mendoza, Antonio (1589–1669), casuistry, **I** 262b

Eskimos
conservation, **I** 471b
primitivism, **III** 596b

Esotericism
hermeticism, **II** 431a, 431b, 434a
Islam, **II** 648b, 650b, 651a

Esperanto language, **II** 669a

Espinas, Alfred, individualism, **II** 601a

Espionage Act, **III** 114a

Essence
Aristotle, **I** 2a–2b
naturalism in art, **III** 342b
symbolism, **IV** 338b

Essenes
Buddhism, **I** 255a
Christianity, **III** 590a
primitivism, **III** 590a

Essex, Countess of, mythology, **III** 294b

Eternal Return (myth)
irrationalism, **II** 635a, 638a
progress, **III** 624b, 628b
time, **IV** 392a, 395b

Eternity
infinity, **II** 604b
macrocosm and microcosm, **III** 128a
Middle Ages, **III** 477a
periodization in history, **III** 477a
romanticism, **IV** 196a, 202a
sublime in external nature, **IV** 336b
time, **IV** 392a, 393b, 400a
utilitarianism, **IV** 444b

Etherege, George (1635?–?1691)
deism, **I** 650a
Puritanism, **I** 650a

Ethics, **III** 440a–457a; **IV** 70a–74a
abortion, **IV** 70a
aggression, **III** 446b, 447a
agriculture, **III** 442b
Alexander the Great, **IV** 320a–320b
altruism, **III** 644a
anarchy, **III** 445a, 446a
animals, **IV** 319b
anthropology, **III** 443a; **IV** 70b, 71a
architecture, **II** 372a–372b
Aristophanes, **III** 440a
Aristotelianism, **IV** 320b, 322a

Aristotle, I 463a; II 149b–150b, 236b–237a; III 354a, 440a, 554b; IV 4b, 6b, 49b, 175b, 320a, 321a, 451b, 452a
asceticism, IV 320b
atomism, IV 319a
Basilides of Alexandria, II 329a–329b
behaviorism, IV 72b, 73a
Bellarmine, III 441b
Bentham, III 444a–444b
Bernstein, Eduard, III 162b–163a, 164b
Bible, III 440b, 441a, 445b
biology, III 646b
birth, IV 322a
Bruno, II 347b, 348b
Buddhism, I 252a–252b, 253b–254a; III 446a
Burnet, III 258a
Calvin, III 441b
capitalism, IV 70a
catharsis, I 267b–268a
Cato, IV 321b
causation, IV 320a
Chain of Being, I 328b–329a
chance, II 226b, 227a, 227b, 233a
Chapman, III 294b
charity, II 212b, 215a
China, III 430a, 430b
Christianity, I 407b; III 440b, 441a, 441b, 445b, 446a; IV 176a–176b, 177a, 322a
Chrysippus, IV 321b, 322a
Cicero, III 16b; IV 319b, 321b, 322a
city-state, IV 320a
classification of the sciences, I 463a, 464b, 465a
Cleanthes, IV 321b
Clement of Alexandria, III 441a; IV 322a
color, IV 71b
comedy, III 440a
commerce, I 253b–254a; III 443b
communism, IV 70a, 291b
Comte, III 644a
conscience, IV 70a, 71a
Counter-Enlightenment, II 101a
courage, IV 320b
crime, IV 70a
criticism, IV 321b
cruelty, IV 72a
Cudworth, III 441a–441b
culture, III 442b, 443b, 444a, 447a; IV 70a, 71a, 71b, 73a, 73b, 320a–320b

cynicism, I 627b, 629a, 629b–630a, 633a, 633b; IV 320b
death, IV 70b, 71b
deism, I 651a
Democritus, IV 319a
desire, IV 72a
destiny, III 442a; IV 319a
Dewey, III 446b, 447a; IV 186a
Diogenes of Sinope, IV 320b
diplomacy, III 443b
disarmament, III 444b
divination, IV 320a
Doukhobors, III 441a
drama, III 440a
dueling, IV 70a
duty, IV 71a
economics, III 442a, 444a, 445b, 446b
education, II 77a–77b, 78b; III 440a
egoistic interpretation of, III 231a, 231b, 233a
Einstein, III 445b, 446b–447a
emancipation, III 444b
Emerson, III 430a, 430b
emotion, IV 72a
emotive theory, III 234b–235a
empathy, II 85b
empiricism, III 443b
Engels, III 159b
Enlightenment, II 90a, 96b; III 446a
Epictetus, IV 319a, 321b, 322a
Epicureanism, IV 8a, 319a
Epicurus, IV 321b
equality, II 142a
equity, II 148a–154a
eschatology, II 159a
Euripides, III 440a
evil, II 162b, 163a, 163b, 165a, 167a–167b; IV 70b, 71a, 72b, 319a, 320a, 321a
evolution, III 646b, 647a; IV 71a, 180a, 181a
evolutionism, II 181a
existentialism, II 192a; III 158a, 158b, 159b, 160a
faith, II 212b, 215a
fascism, III 674a
fate, II 226b, 227a, 227b, 233a
Faust (legend), III 251a
fear, IV 71b
Ficino, III 506a
Fichte, IV 209a
fortune, II 226b, 227a, 227b, 233a
Fox, III 441a

France, III 444b
free will, II 236b–237a; IV 320b
freedom of speech, II 259a
Freud, III 445b, 446b, 447a; IV 96b
Galen, IV 321b
game theory, II 273a
Gandhi, III 441b–442a; IV 73a
Genghis Khan, IV 73a
Gnosticism, II 328a–328b, 331a
God, II 334b, 347b, 348b; III 440b; 441a, 441b, 445b; IV 70b, 72a, 319a–320b
good, IV 70b, 71b, 72b, 173b–186a, 319b, 320a, 320b, 321a, 321b
Gothic, II 372a–372b
Great Britain, III 538a
Greece (ancient), III 353a, 440a, 440b, 585a; IV 319a, 320a–320b
Grotius, III 441b–442a
happiness, II 374b–375a, 375b, 378a, 379a, 379b, 380a, 380b, 381b, 383a; IV 70b, 319a, 320a, 321a, 321b
harmony, II 390b
health, IV 321a, 321b
Hector (myth), III 440a
Hegel, II 408b; III 445a; IV 180a, 290b
Heraclitus, IV 320b
hierarchy, II 444a
Hillel, III 440b
history, III 440a, 440b, 443b, 444a, 445a; IV 320a–320b
Hitler, IV 73a
Hobbes, III 441b, 442b, 443a, 443b, 445b, 446a; IV 72a, 72b, 177a–177b
Hobhouse, IV 71b
holy, II 512a, 513a, 513b
Homer, III 440b
homosexuality, IV 70a, 70b
hope, II 212b, 215a
human nature, III 442b, 443b, 446a, 577a, 644a; IV 72a, 72b
human sacrifice, IV 71a
humanism, III 446a; IV 129b
humanitarianism, III 441a
Hume, III 231b, 232a, 233a, 233b, 235a, 444a; IV 70a–70b, 71b, 72a, 72b
Hutcheson, III 231a–232a; IV 70b, 71b–72b
idea, II 544b, 548b, 603a–603b

ideal, II 549a, 550b, 551a
idealism, III 443a, 443b, 444a, 445b
ideology, II 554a
imperialism, III 445a
impressionism, II 576a
India, III 446a
individualism, II 603a–603b; IV 49b
industry, III 445a, 445b, 446a
infanticide, IV 70a
injury, IV 71a
internationalism, III 442a, 444b, 446a
intolerance, III 446b
Jainism, III 446a
James, William, III 447a
joy, IV 321b
Judaism, III 440b, 487b, 488a; IV 176a
judgment, IV 71b, 72a, 73a; IV 321a
justice, III 443a, 444b; IV 320b
Kames, III 234b
Kant, II 551a; III 233b, 442a–442b, 443a–444a, 444b, 445a, 445b, 555b–556a, 639b; IV 179a–179b, 181a, 322a
kindness, IV 72a
knowledge, IV 71b, 321a
Kropotkin, III 445a
language, IV 72b, 319b, 321b
law, III 1a, 2a, 6a, 440b, 441b, 442a, 443a–444b, 445b, 447a; IV 72b
Lecky, IV 70b, 71b
Leibniz, III 442a, 443b
Leonardo da Vinci, IV 442a–442b
Lévy-Bruhl, IV 70b–71a
Lieber, III 444a
Lincoln, III 444a
logic, III 568b; IV 319a, 319b–320a, 320b, 322a
logos, III 440b; IV 319a, 320a, 320b, 321b
love, III 440b, 441a, 445b, 447a
Lovejoy, III 552b
Luther, III 441b
lying, IV 71a, 72b
Machiavelli, III 116a–125a, 441b
Mandeville, III 231a
Marcus Aurelius, III 440b; IV 321b, 322a
Maritain, III 441a, 445b
Marxism, III 148a, 151b, 158a, 158b, 159b, 160a,

162b–163a, 163b, 164b,
167b, 168a–168b; IV 180b
materialism, II 450b, 452a
matter, IV 319a
metaphysics, III 440b, 444a
Middle Ages, III 116b
military, III 440a, 441a,
443b, 444a, 445b, 446b,
447a
Molière, II 153b
moral sense, III 230b–235a
motif, III 235b, 237a
murder, IV 71a
music, II 390b
mythology, III 282a, 283a,
288b, 294b, 309a, 312a
nationalism, III 445a, 446b
nation-state, III 441b–445b
natural law, III 16a, 16b,
22b, 23a
Nature, III 348a, 348b,
349b, 350b, 440b, 442a,
444a, 446b; IV 72b, 319a,
319b, 320a, 320b, 321a
navigation, III 442b
necessity, III 353a, 354a
nuclear power, III 446b
Orientalism, III 430a–430b,
436b
Origen, III 441a
over-population, III 446b,
447b
pacifism, III 441a, 441b,
445a, 445b, 447a
pain, IV 320a, 321a
painting, II 576a; IV 473b
Panaetius, IV 321b
Pater, II 576a
patriotism, III 445a, 445b
Pax Romana, III 440b, 441b
peace, III 440a–447a
Peirce, III 556a, 568b
perennial philosophy, III
460a
perfectibility, III 644a
philanthropy, III 486b,
487b, 488a, 489a
philosophy, II 549a, 550b,
551a; III 442a, 443a, 443b,
444a; IV 70a, 71b, 319a
physics, IV 319a–319b,
320a, 320b, 322a
Pietism, III 493b, 495a
Plato, II 148a–149b, 375b;
III 440a; IV 33b, 49a–
49b, 175a, 320a, 320b,
321a
Platonism, III 441a, 503b,
504a, 505b, 506a, 507b,
523a; IV 319b, 320b
pleasure, II 374b–375a,
375b, 378a, 379a, 379b,
380a, 380b, 381b, 383a;
IV 320a, 321a

Plotinus, IV 322a
Plutarch, IV 321b
pneuma, IV 319a, 320a
poetry, III 527b, 531a; IV
473b
politics, III 116a–125a,
441a, 443a, 444a, 445a,
446a, 446b; IV 320a, 320b,
321b
pollution, III 447b
Pope, III 397a
Posidonius, IV 321b
positivism, III 538a, 540b;
IV 183b–184a
poverty, III 447b; IV 70a,
70b, 321a
power, III 445a, 446a
pragmatism, III 552b, 554b,
555b–556a, 558a, 564b,
567a, 568a, 568b
primitivism, III 585a, 586a,
597a
prisoners of war, III 441b
progress, III 636a, 639b,
644a, 645a, 646b, 647a,
648a–648b
protest movements, III 672a,
674a
Protestantism, III 441b; IV
177a
providence, IV 319a
psychology, III 447a; IV
1a, 1b, 4b, 6b, 8a, 23a,
23b, 27b
Pythagoras, IV 37a
Pythagoreans, IV 32a, 33b,
37a
Quakers, III 441a
race, IV 70b
rationalism, III 233a; IV
49a–50a, 319a, 320a, 320b,
321a
reason, III 442a–443b,
444b, 446a, 586a; IV 319a–
321b
Reid, III 233b, 234a
relativism, IV 70a–74a
religion, III 444a, 445b,
446b; IV 70b, 71a, 96b,
111b, 117a, 118b, 119a
Renaissance, IV 129b,
440b–441a, 442b, 443a
republicanism, III 443a–
443b
revisionism, IV 269b, 273a
rhetoric, IV 168a–168b,
169a, 170a
right, IV 70b, 71a, 72a,
73a, 73b, 173b–186b
romanticism, IV 195b, 209b
Rome (ancient), III 440b,
441b, 585a; IV 71b, 321b–
322a
Rousseau, III 442a, 445b

Russell, III 445b, 446a–
446b; IV 70a
Saint Augustine, III 441b;
IV 176a–176b
Saint Francis of Assisi, IV
73a
Saint Justin, III 441a, 441b,
443a, 446b
Saint Paul, III 440b
Saint Thomas Aquinas, III
441a, 441b; IV 392a
Saint-Pierre, III 442a
satire, IV 214b
science, III 442b, 443b,
444a, 446b, 447b; IV 70b
scientific classification, I
463a, 464b, 465a
Scipio Africanus, IV 321b–
322a
security, III 445a
self-control, IV 320b
self-realizationist, II 381b
Semitism, IV 320b
senses, IV 72a
Sermon on the Mount, III
441a, 441b, 445b, 446a
sex, IV 71a
Sextus Empiricus, IV 320a
skepticism, IV 236a, 237a,
241a
Simon Magus (Bible), II
328a
sin, IV 70a, 225a, 225b,
227a
slavery, III 441a
Smith, III 233a, 233b, 444a
Social Darwinism, III 646b
socialism, III 445a; IV 287a,
287b, 290b, 291b
society, III 440a, 440b,
442a–443b, 445b, 446b,
447a; IV 70b, 71a, 72a,
72b, 320a, 320b, 322a
sociology, III 445a, 445b,
446a, 447a, 447b; IV 72a
Socrates, III 577a; IV 49a–
49b, 320b
sophism, I 629a
Sorel, III 564b
soul, III 441a
Spencer, II 383a; III 445a;
IV 180b
Spinoza, II 273a; IV 177b
State, III 441a, 441b, 443a,
446b
Stoicism, III 440b–441b;
IV 8a, 176a, 319a–322b
suicide, IV 70a
superstition, IV 71a
taxation, III 441a
technology, III 445a, 445b,
446b
temperance, IV 369b, 378a
theft, IV 71a

theodicy, IV 379a, 380b
theriophily, IV 385a
Thirty Years War, III 441b
Thoreau, III 446a
time, IV 392a, 395b
Tolstoy, III 441a, 445b–
446a
tragedy, III 440a
tragic sense, IV 413a, 415b,
416a
transcendentalism, III 444a
treaties, III 444b
tribes, IV 71a, 72b
Trojan War, III 440a
truth, IV 72b
U.S., III 430a–430b, 436b,
444a, 444b, 446b, 447a
unity, III 441b, 648a–648b
universal man, IV 440a,
441a, 442a–442b
utilitarianism, III 441a
utility, IV 451b, 452a
value, III 568a, 568b; IV
320b–321b, 451b, 452a
Vattel, III 442a
vice, IV 321a
Victorians, IV 218a, 218b
violence, IV 71a
virtue, I 629b–630a; IV
320b–322a, 478b, 483b
war, IV 70a, 506a
wealth, IV 321a, 321b
Weber, I 260b
welfare state, IV 512a
Westermarck, IV 71a
wife-lending, IV 70a
wisdom, IV 320b
work, IV 533b, 534b
wrong, IV 71a, 72a–73b
Zeno of Citium, III 440b;
IV 319a, 320a, 320b, 321b,
322a
See also Evil, Good, Happiness, Morality
Ethiopia
Greece (ancient), III 591a
international peace, III 454a
primitivism, III 590a
Ethnic nationalism, III 328a–
329b, 336b, 337a
Ethnology
psychology, IV 22b
religion, IV 95a, 96b–97a
structuralism, IV 325a,
326b, 327b, 329a
Ethology
imprinting, II 584a, 585a–
585b
psychology, IV 15a
Etiology, longevity, III 91b
Etruscan language, III 61b
Ettori, C., aesthetics, IV 354b
Etymology
Aristotle, II 663a

chaos, **IV** 296b
Greece (ancient), **II** 675a, 676a, 679b–681a, 682a
language, **II** 662a–663a, 664b, 666a, 671b
law, **II** 675a, 676a, 679b–680a, 680b–681a, 682a
linguistics, **III** 61b, 66a, 67a, 68a, 75a
mimesis, **III** 226a
mythology, **III** 274a, 301a, 306b, 308a, 316b
ouranos, **IV** 300b
Plato, **II** 662a–662b
space, **IV** 296b, 300b
structuralism, **IV** 323b
wisdom of the fool, **IV** 515b–516a

Eucken, Rudolf (1846–1926), modernism, **I** 420a

Euclid (fl. about 300 B.C.), Aristotle and, **III** 461a
axiomatization, **I** 163b–164a, 165a, 167b; **III** 172b, 175b
Bruno and, **IV** 298a
continuity, **I** 498a
despotism, **II** 12a
equality, **II** 138b
geometry, **III** 380b; **IV** 304a
humanism, **IV** 135a–135b
Islam, **II** 640b, 647b
mathematics, **III** 172b, 174a, 174b, 178b, 179a, 179b, 180a, 182b, 184b, 380a
medieval sciences, **II** 198b, 200a, 203a
methodology, **III** 380a, 380b
music, **III** 261b
Newton and, **III** 380b; **IV** 302b
optics, **III** 408a, 410a, 415b
perennial philosophy, **III** 461a
postulate, **III** 172b
pragmatism, **III** 557b, 559b
probability, **III** 605b
Proclus and, **I** 163b
Pythagorean cosmos, **IV** 39b
rationalism, **IV** 47b
relativity, **IV** 87a
space, **IV** 295a, 298a, 299b–300a, 302a–304a
symmetry, **IV** 346b
technology, **IV** 359b

Euclidean geometry
cosmology, **I** 555b, 557b, 558b, 559a, 559b, 563a
mathematics, **III** 174a, 175b

Euclideanism
metaphysical imagination, **III** 214b
necessity, **III** 356a

Eudemus of Rhodes (4th century B.C.)
axiomatization, **I** 163b
cycles, **I** 623b
God, **II** 339a
time, **IV** 390b

Eudoxus of Cnidos (408–355 B.C.)
analogy, **I** 63a
axiomatization, **I** 163b, 164a
continuity, **I** 499b
cosmology, **I** 540a
infinity, **II** 604b
mathematics, **III** 172b, 173b, 175a, 380a
methodology, **III** 380a
symmetry, **IV** 349a

Eugene III, Pope (d. 1153), reformation, **IV** 64b

Eugenics
acquired characteristics, **II** 620b
health, **II** 620b
Marxism, **II** 620b
psychology, **IV** 26b
U.S.S.R., **II** 620b

Euhemerism, **III** 286b, 287a, 294a, 301b, 302b, 303a, 306b

Euhemerus (late 4th century B.C.)
allegory, **I** 47b
religion, **IV** 93a
Utopia, **IV** 460a

Euler, Leonhard (1707–1783), cosmic images, **I** 519b
cosmology, **I** 554b
infinity, **II** 611a
mathematics, **III** 179b
music, **III** 263b
probability, **III** 609b

Eumelus (myth), law, **II** 676b

Euphorion (fiction), Faust (legend), **III** 249a, 250a

Euphranor (4th century B.C.), creativity in art, **I** 582a

Euripides (5th century B.C.), allegory, **I** 42a
ambiguity, **I** 50b
baroque in literature, **I** 195a
catharsis, **I** 266a
comedy, **I** 468b
creativity in art, **I** 585a–585b
culture, **I** 611b; **IV** 367a
cynicism, **I** 630b, 632a
equality, **II** 140a
ethics, **III** 440a
evolution of literature, **II** 171b
freedom of speech, **II** 259a, 259b, 260a
heroes, **IV** 367a
historiography, **II** 506a

human nature, **III** 571a, 573a
idea, **II** 545a
justice, **III** 573a
law, **II** 681a–684b
love, **III** 94b, 96a
Machiavellism, **III** 116a
mythology, **III** 272b
passions, **III** 573a
peace, **III** 440a
periodization in literary history, **III** 481b
Plato and, **III** 500a
politics, **III** 116a
pre-Socratics, **IV** 367b
progress, **III** 626a
rationalism, **IV** 49a; **IV** 367a
satire, **IV** 212b
self-restraint, **IV** 367b
skepticism, **IV** 234b
Sophists, **IV** 367b
soul, **III** 573a
temperance, **IV** 367a–367b
Thucydides and, **IV** 367b
tragedy, **I** 266b; **IV** 367a–367b
tragic sense, **IV** 413b
virtue, **IV** 367a–367b

Europa (myth), **III** 289b, 290b

Eurydice (myth), **III** 96a

Eurystheus, King (myth), historiography, **II** 499b

Eurytos, creativity in art, **I** 580a–580b, 581a

Eusebius (260?–?340)
historiography, **II** 471b, 472a, 473a, 474b, 478a–478b, 488b
history, **I** 378a
religion, **IV** 93b
skepticism, **IV** 234b

Evagrius Ponticus (536?–600), temperance, **IV** 371a

Evangelicalism
conservative, **I** 21a–21b
history, **I** 403a, 406b
individualism, **II** 596a
love, **III** 96b
philanthropy, **I** 403a
Pietism, **III** 493b, 494b
reformation, **IV** 68b, 69a
religion, **IV** 109a, 111a
U.S., **II** 596a
utilitarianism, **IV** 218b–219a
Victorian sentiment, **IV** 217b–220a, 221a, 222b

Evans, Joseph, beauty, **I** 210a

Eve (Bible)
Christianity, **III** 591a
death, **III** 582a
evil, **III** 582a
mountains in literature, **III**

254b, 255a, 257b
mythology, **III** 278a, 278b, 279a, 294a
primitivism, **III** 581b, 582a, 583b, 584b, 591a, 596b
prophecy, **III** 582a
psychology, **IV** 17a
Saint Ambrose, **III** 583b
Saint Bernard, **III** 591a
salvation, **IV** 227a
sin, **IV** 227a
tragic sense, **IV** 416a
war, **III** 582a
women, **III** 596b; **IV** 524a, 524b

Evelyn, John (1620–1706), conservation, **I** 473a
genius, **II** 294b
mountains in literature, **III** 254a, 258b
virtuoso, **IV** 486a, 486b–487a

Everard, J., hermeticism, **II** 431b

Everett, Alexander Hill (1790–1847), Orientalism, **III** 429a

Everett, Charles Carroll (1829–1900), Orientalism, **III** 435b

Everett, Edward (1794–1865), Orientalism, **III** 429a

Evidence
common law, **II** 693b
pragmatism, **III** 562b

Evil, **II** 161b–169b
Adam (Bible), **III** 582a, 583a
aesthetics, **II** 166b
Ahriman, **II** 162b, 165a
aristocracy, **II** 162b
Aristotle, **II** 163a, 167b; **IV** 36a, 411b, 412a
art, **II** 166b
asceticism, **II** 164a–164b, 166b
atheism, **II** 162a, 168a–168b
atomism, **II** 163a
Babylonia, **II** 163b
Barth, **II** 168a
beauty, **III** 500b
becoming, **IV** 414b
Bentham, **II** 167b; **III** 470a
Bible, **II** 163b–164a
Brahmanism, **II** 162a
Buddha, **II** 162a, 165a
Byron, **II** 165a–165b
Calvin, **IV** 381b
Calvinism, **II** 164b
Chain of Being, **I** 512a
chance, **II** 234a
Christianity, **II** 164a–165a, 167a, 168b; **IV** 229b
class, **II** 169a
Cosmic Fall, **I** 512a

cosmos, II 162b–163b; IV 413b, 414b
Creation, IV 415b
death, II 167a
demonology, I 668b; II 165a
determinism, II 26b, 27a, 236b–237b, 238a
Diderot, III 603a
dignity, IV 138b
disease, II 395b, 396b
dualism, II 38a, 38b, 39a–40a, 40b–41a, 43a, 162b, 164a, 164b, 165a
economics, II 169a
education, II 168b
egoism, II 162a
Enlightenment, III 248a
Epicureanism, II 163a, 167a
error, II 162b
eschatology, II 154b, 155a
ethics, II 162b, 163a, 163b, 165a, 167a–167b; IV 319a, 320a, 321a
Eve (Bible), III 582a
existentialism, II 168a–168b
fate, II 234a; IV 413b, 416a
fortune, II 234a
free will, II 236b–237b, 238a
Gnosticism, II 327a, 328b, 329a
Goethe, II 165b
good, II 161b–169b; IV 174b, 177a, 180b
Greece (ancient), II 162b–163b, 167b, 674b, 677a
hagiography, II 165a
happiness, II 167a–167b, 374b, 375b, 376b, 379a
harmony, II 388a
hedonism, II 167a–167b
Hegel, II 167a, 167b, 408a, 408b
Herder, III 639a
heresy, II 164b
hermeticism, II 431b, 432a, 432b, 433b
Hobbes, III 20b
human nature, II 162b; III 571b, 572a, 575a, 577a, 643b
humanism, IV 133b
Hume, IV 382b
immortality, II 167a
India (ancient), II 162a
individualism, II 595a–595b
irony, IV 411b
irrationalism, II 167b
Jefferson, IV 21b
Jerusalem, II 163b
Jesus Christ, II 164a, 165a
Judaism, II 30a, 163b–

164a, 165a
justice, II 163b, 166b
Justinian, III 17b
Kant, III 472b; IV 382b
Kierkegaard, II 168a
knowledge, II 162b, 167a, 168b, 169a
law, II 674b, 677a
Leibniz, I 329a; II 166a–166b; IV 378b, 381b–382a
Leopardi, II 166a
literature, II 162a, 169a
Locke, III 469b
love, III 104b
Luther, IV 381b
Machiavelli, III 116a–125a; IV 482a, 483a
Manichaeism, II 164b
Marxism, III 147a
matter, II 43a, 163a, 163b, 164a, 164b
Mesopotamia (ancient), IV 226a
metaphysics, II 162b, 166b–167a; IV 382a
Middle Ages, II 165a
millenarianism, III 223b, 224a
Milton, II 165a–165b
mind, II 38a
monotheism, II 163b–165a
Montaigne, II 167b–168a
morality, II 165b, 166b, 168a; IV 382a
music, II 388a; III 264b, 265a, 265b
mythology, II 165a; III 278b, 315b; IV 412b–417a
nationalism, II 169a
natural, IV 382a, 383b
natural law, III 17b, 20b
naturalism, II 161b, 162b
Nature, I 575a; II 161b–163b, 164b, 166b, 167a, 167b; IV 383b
necessity, IV 381a
Neo-Platonism, II 163a–163b; III 373a
Nietzsche, IV 180b
nuclear power, II 169a
pain, II 163a, 167a–167b
pantheism, II 162a
Pascal, II 168a; IV 381b
passions, II 163a
peasantry, III 595b
Pelagianism, II 164b
Pelagius, II 26b
perennial philosophy, III 458b, 459a
perfectibility, III 469b, 470a, 470b, 472b, 474a, 475a, 643b
Persia (ancient), II 162b
pessimism, II 163b, 166b–

167b, 169a
philosophy, II 162a, 163a, 165b, 169a
Pietism, II 165a
Plato, II 40b–41a, 162b–163a, 236b, 376b; III 496b–497a, 498a, 500b, 501b; IV 380b
Platonism, II 162b; III 496b–497a, 498a, 500b, 501b, 513a
pleasure, II 163a, 167a–167b, 374b, 375b, 376b, 379a
Plotinus, II 163a–163b; IV 380a
Plutarch, IV 380b
poetry, II 165a–166a
Pope, II 165b
population explosion, II 169a
predestination, II 26b, 27a
primitivism, III 582a–584a, 588a, 588b, 595b, 596b, 599b, 603a
private property, III 653b
progress, III 626a, 632a, 635b, 636a, 639a, 642b, 643b, 648a, 648b
prophecy, III 664b, 665b
Protestantism, II 164b
psychology, IV 17b, 19a, 20a, 21b
Pythagoreans, IV 36a
racial prejudice, II 169a
rationalism, II 162b, 163a, 166b, 167a, 168a
reason, II 162b, 163a, 163b, 164a, 164b, 168a
reformation, IV 65b
reincarnation, II 162a
religion, II 161b–162a, 162b, 163a, 165a, 168b, 169a–169b; IV 112b
Renaissance, IV 133b, 138b
Renouvier, II 162a
revolution, IV 159b, 166b
right, IV 174b, 177a, 180b
romanticism, iV 209b, 210b
Rome (ancient), II 163a
Rousseau, II 168b; III 599b
Saint Augustine, II 164b–165a, 169b, 238a; III 584b; IV 138b, 379b, 380b–381a, 381b
Saint Paul, II 164a
Saint Thomas Aquinas, II 164b
Sartre, II 168a–168b
Satan, II 163b, 165a–165b
satire, IV 211b, 214a
science, III 642b, 648a
Seneca, III 588b
Shaftesbury, II 166a

167b, 169a
sin, II 164a–166a; IV 224a, 226a, 228b, 229b, 231a, 231b, 233a
skepticism, II 164a, 167b–168a; IV 235b
society, III 147a
Socrates, II 162b, 167b; III 496b–497a, 577a; IV 174b
soul, II 162a, 163b, 164a; IV 414b
Spencer, III 474a
Speusippus, IV 36a
Spinoza, IV 381b
Stoicism, II 163a; III 588a; IV 319a, 320a, 321a
superstition, II 165a, 168b
symmetry, IV 348a
technology, II 168b; III 648a
temperance, IV 371a
theodicy, II 162b–165a, 166a; IV 378b–383b
theology, II 26b, 27a
theriophily, IV 386a–386b
Thomson, II 167b
Tolstoy, II 168b–169a
tragic sense, IV 411a–417a
truth, II 161b–162a, 162b
universe, II 162a
utilitarianism, IV 447b, 448a, 448b, 449a
Utopia, IV 463b
vanity, II 164a, 164b
virtù, IV 482a, 483a
Voltaire, II 166b
vox populi, IV 498a
war, IV 502a, 506a, 507a, 508a
Weltschmerz, IV 209b
wisdom, IV 412b
witchcraft, IV 521a, 521b, 522b, 523a
women, III 596b
work, IV 534b
Zeus (myth), III 571b
Zoroaster, II 162b
Zoroastrianism, II 162b, 164b, 165a; IV 231a, 231b
See also God, Morality, Sin
Evolution
acquired characteristics, II 617b–618b, 620a
Adams, Henry, II 24a
Aeschylus, III 625a
anarchy, IV 180b
animals, III 596a
Aristotle, II 505b–507a; III 19a
art, II 297a, 581b, 583a
asymmetry, IV 349a
authoritarianism, III 646b–647a
behavior, IV 180a

Bergson, III 474a, 563a, 565a

Bernstein, Eduard, III 161b, 162b, 163a

biology, I 236b–239a; III 646a, 646b

catastrophism, IV 423a

Christianity, I 405b

chromosomes, II 286b, 287b, 288a

class, III 646a, 646b

collectivism, III 646b

competition, III 646b

Comte, II 454b, 620a; III 641b

continuity, I 499b, 500b

cosmology, I 549b–550a, 553b; II 447b

culture, I 612b; II 127b, 128a, 128b, 130b, 581b; III 566b

Darwin, II 126a, 624a, 626a; III 360a, 360b, 473b, 646a

degeneration, III 646b

design argument, I 676b–677a

determinism, II 24a

Diderot, III 140b

Drummond, III 474b

earth, I 549b

education, II 75b, 583a; III 474a, 646a

Engels, II 454b, 620a; III 153b, 473b

Enlightenment, II 93a–94a

environment, II 125a, 126a–128b, 130b; III 646b

eschatology, II 159b–160a

ethics, III 646b, 647a; IV 180a, 181a

freedom, IV 181a

genetic continuity, II 281b, 286b, 287b, 288a, 292a, 292b

genius, II 297a

goals, IV 180a, 181a

God, I 352a

good, IV 179b–181b, 183a, 185b, 186b

happiness, II 383a

hedonism, IV 180a–180b

Hegel, II 583a

heresy, II 429a, 430b

hierarchy, II 447b, 448a

historiography, II 24a, 505b–507a

history, II 24a

holy, I 513b

human nature, III 575b

humanism, II 518b

Huxley, Julian, III 474a

Huxley, T. H., III 474a, 647a

indeterminacy, II 587b

individualism, II 126b–127a, 297a; III 646b

inequality, III 646b

instinct, IV 180a

international peace, III 448b

Joachim of Floris, IV 286b

Kant, I 521a

Kautsky, II 454b

Lamarck, II 620a, 623b, 624a

language, II 669b, 670b; III 68b; IV 323a–323b

law, III 24b–25a, 26a, 35a, 566b; IV 180a

liberalism, III 672b

linguistics, III 68b; IV 424a, 424b, 429a

Lyell, IV 424b

Man-Machine, III 140b, 143b

Marx, II 454a, 583a

Marxism, III 149a, 149b, 153b, 161b, 162b, 163a, 163b, 167b, 169b; IV 180b–181a

materialism, II 177b, 180b, 188a, 454a, 454b; III 140b, 433b; IV 180b

Mendel, II 126a, 618b

moon, I 549b

morality, III 646a, 647a

mutation, II 125a

mythology, III 274b

natural law, III 19a, 24b–25a, 26a, 646a

natural selection, II 24a, 125a; III 646a, 646b

naturalism, IV 181a, 182a

necessity, III 360a, 360b

Neo-Darwinism, II 126a

Nietzsche, III 474a

order, II 447b, 448a

Orientalism, III 433b, 434a, 435a, 438a–438b, 439a

painting, II 581b, 583a

pangenesis, II 623b, 624a, 626a

Pearson, III 646a

Peirce, III 562a

perfectibility, III 473b–474b

periodization in history, III 476b, 478a, 479a, 480b

periodization in literary history, III 482b, 484b

pleasure, II 383a; IV 180a–180b

politics, III 646b

primitivism, III 596a, 596b

progress, II 178a–179b, 182a, 182b; III 625a, 629a, 634a, 637a, 641b, 643a, 646a–647a

protest movements, III 672b, 673b

psychology, IV 12a, 13b, 25a, 25b, 26a, 27a

race, III 646a

rationalism, III 646b

recapitulation, IV 56a–56b, 57a–57b, 58a

religion, III 435a; IV 95a, 95b, 96a, 106a, 107b, 108a

revisionism, IV 266b, 269b, 270b

revolution, IV 160a

right, IV 179b–181b, 183a, 185b, 186b

Rodin, II 574b

Saint Thomas Aquinas, III 19a

science, II 196a

Social Darwinism, III 646a–646b

socialism, III 646b, 673b; IV 286b, 293b, 294a

society, II 454a; III 153b, 566b, 646b–647a; IV 180b–181a

space, IV 297a

Spencer, II 620a, 363a, 454b; III 473b–474a, 637a, 643; IV 180b, 395a, 395b

spontaneous generation, IV 310b, 311b, 312a

stars, I 553b; II 187b

structuralism, IV 323a–323b

superman, III 474a

symmetry, IV 349a, 349b, 353a

synthetic theory of, II 186b–187a

Teilhard de Chardin, III 474b

teleology, II 170a; III 149b; IV 180a

theodicy, IV 383b

time, IV 395a–395b

totalitarianism, III 646b–647a

tradition, III 646a, 646b

tragic sense, IV 413a

transcendentalism, III 433b, 434a

uniformitarianism, IV 423a, 424b, 429a

U.S., III 433b, 434a, 435a, 438a–438b, 439a

utilitarianism, IV 180a–180b

Wallace, William, III 473b

war, III 448b

Wright, Chauncey, III 561a–561b

Evolution of literature, II 169b–174a

Aeschylus, II 171b

aesthetics, II 171b

Aristotle, II 169–170a

art, II 170a–170b, 173b

artists, II 174a

atomism, II 173b

Bergson, II 172b

Brunetière, II 171b–172b

Buffon, II 170a

causation, II 172a, 174a

Cicero, II 170a

Claudian, II 172a

Comte, II 171b

Corneille, II 171b, 172a

criticism, II 172b–173b

Croce, II 172b

Czechoslovakia, II 173b–174a

Darwinism, II 171a, 172a

De Vries, II 172b

Demosthenes, II 170a

dialectics, II 170b

Dilthey, II 171a

Dionysius of Halicarnassus, II 170a

drama, II 171a–171b, 172b

Eliot, T. S., II 172b–173a

Euripides, II 171b

Formalism, II 173b

France, II 171b–172b

Futurism, II 173b

genius, II 171a, 172a

Germany, II 170b, 171a

Great Britain, II 171a–171b, 173a

Greece (ancient), II 169b–170a, 171b

Grimm, Jacob, II 170b

Grimm, Wilhelm, II 170b

Hegel, II 170b–171a, 171b, 172a, 173b

Herder, II 170b

historiography, II 173a

history, II 171a–174a

Homer, II 172b

Hugo, II 172a, 172b

Italy, II 171b

Leibniz, II 170b

Lucretius, II 171b

Marxism, II 173b

Mérimée, II 172b

Middle Ages, II 172b

novel, II 172b

oratory, II 170a, 172a

painting, II 171b

philosophy, II 172b

poetry, II 170a–172a, 173a

Quintilian, II 170a

Racine, II 172a

Renaissance, II 170a, 172a

Rome (ancient), II 170a, 171b–172a

Rousseau, II 170a

Russia, II 173a–173b
Sainte-Beuve, II 170a
Scherer, II 171a
Schlegel, August Wilhelm von, II 171a
Schlegel, Friedrich, II 170b, 171a
society, II 171b
Spencer, II 171a, 171b, 172b
Symonds, II 171a–171b
time, II 174a
tragedy, II 169b–172a
U.S., II 171b, 173a
Vico, II 170a
Vigny, II 172b
Voltaire, II 171b, 172a
Wellek, II 173b–174a
Winckelmann, II 170a
Evolutionism, II 174a–189a
adaptation, II 180a, 180b, 181a, 185a
Agassiz, II 179b
Alexander, S., II 183b–184a, 186a
anatomical studies, II 177a, 179b
Anaximander, II 175a
Anaximenes, II 175a
anthropology, II 186b, 187a
anti-, II 175b–176a
Aristotle, II 175b–176a
astronomy, II 187b
atheism, II 180b
atomism, II 181b–182a
Baer, II 179b
Bain, II 184b
barbarism, II 176a
Bergson, II 182b, 183a–183b, 186a
Bible, II 176a, 176b, 180a
biochemistry, II 186b
biology, II 176b–180a, 181a, 182b, 183b, 184a, 184b, 186b
Bonnet, II 178a
Buddhism, II 174b
Buffon, II 176b, 177a, 177b, 178b
Butler, Samuel, II 181b, 185b
capitalism, II 180b
Chain of Being, I 334a–335a; II 178a, 184a
Chambers, II 179a, 182b
chemical, II 187a
Childe, II 187a
China (ancient), II 174b
Christianity, II 176a, 177a
Cicero, II 176a
Confucius, II 174b
continuity, II 185a, 187b
cosmogony, II 176a–176b, 185a

cosmology, II 176a, 182a, 186b, 187a
cosmos, II 174b, 178b, 179a, 181b, 182b, 184a, 184b, 185a, 188a
Creation, II 174b, 176a, 176b, 178a, 180a
cultural, II 175a–175b, 178b, 181a, 184a, 184b, 187a
Cuvier, II 179b
Darwin, Charles, II 176a, 177b, 179a, 179b–181b, 182a, 183b, 184a, 185b, 186b, 187a
Darwin, Erasmus, II 179a, 185b
Darwinism, II 171a, 179b–186b
Daubenton, II 178b
defined, II 174a–174b
deism, II 179a
Democritus, II 175a–175b
Descartes, II 176a, 182a, 187b
Dewey, II 184b–185a
Diderot, II 177a, 177b–178a, 182b
earth, II 174b, 176b
economics, II 180b–181a
eighteenth century, II 176b–178a
embryology, II 177a, 178a, 179b, 182a
emergent, II 183b–184a
Empedocles, II 175a
encapsulation theory, II 178a
environment, II 179a, 184b, 185b
epigenesists, II 178a
ethics, II 181a
Fisher, R. A., II 186b
Flood, II 176b, 180a
fossils, II 176b, 180b
free will, II 247a
French Revolution, II 180b
genetics, II 177a, 186b
geology, II 176b, 180a, 182b
Germany, II 181b
Gide, II 183a
God, II 176a, 178b, 179a, 180a, 183b, 184a, 185a, 186a, 359a
Gray, Asa, II 180b
Great Britain, II 180b–181b
Greece (ancient), II 175a–176a
Haeckel, II 181b–182a, 182b
Haldane, J. B. S., II 186b, 187a
Hegel, II 184b

Herder, II 178b
heredity, II 177a, 177b–178a, 186b
homologies, I 237b–239a
Horace, II 176a
Huxley, T. H., II 180a–180b, 183b, 186b, 187a, 187b, 188a
India (ancient), II 174b
James, II 183a, 184b, 186a
Kant, II 176a, 178a, 182a, 187b
Kropotkin, II 181a
laissez-faire, II 180b
Lamarck, II 178a, 179a, 179b, 182a, 185b
language, II 175b
Laplace, II 176a, 182a, 187b
Leibniz, II 176b, 177a, 178a
Life Force, II 186a
Linnaeus, II 177a
Lovejoy, II 177a, 177b, 178a, 182b–183a
Lucretius, II 176a
Lyell, II 176b, 180a, 180b
Maine, II 187a
Malthus, II 180a, 180b
Mansel, II 182a
Marx, II 180b
materialism, II 177b, 180b, 188a
mathematics, II 187b
matter, II 175b, 177b, 182b, 183a, 184a
Maupertius, II 177a–178a
Mead, G. H., II 184b
mechanistic, II 181b–182b
Mendel, II 186b
metaphysics, II 178b, 181b–185a, 187b
modernism, I 420a
Monboddo, II 178a–178b
morality, II 184a
Morgan, Conway Lloyd, II 183b
Morgan, Lewis Henry, II 187a
motion, II 181b
mutations, II 177b
mythology, II 174b
natural sciences, II 176a
natural selection, II 177b, 180a–182a, 184a, 185a, 185b, 186b, 187b
Nature, II 174b–177a, 178b, 179a, 181a, 182b–185a
Neo-Platonism, II 178a, 178b
Newton, II 176a–176b
Nietzsche, II 185b–186a
nominalism, II 176b–177a
Oken, II 178b

ontogeny, II 178a
Oparin, II 187a
organicism, II 174b, 175a, 177a–177b, 178a, 179a–179b, 180a, 181a, 182b, 183a, 184a, 187a–188a
paleontology, II 176b, 179b
Paley, II 180a, 180b
Peirce, II 181a, 184b, 185a
philosophy, II 176b–177a, 179a, 181a, 181b, 182b, 184a–185a, 186b, 187b
Plato, II 175b
Platonism, II 175b, 177a, 178a, 181a
population explosion, II 180b
pragmatism, II 184a–185a
preformationism, II 178a
pre-Socratics, II 175a
progressionism, II 178a–179b, 182a, 182b
proto-, II 174b–175b
Proust, II 183a
rebirth of, II 176a–176b
Robinet, II 178b, 183a
Roman Catholic Church, II 177a, 180b
Romanes, II 180b
romanticism, II 178b–179a, 182b, 183b
Rousseau, II 178a–178b
Schelling, II 178b, 185a
Schopenhauer, II 182b–183a, 183b
scientific method, II 184a–184b
Shaw, II 181b, 183a, 185b–186a
Simpson, G. G., II 188a
social, II 175a–175b, 178b, 181a
Social Darwinism, II 181a
socialism, II 181a
solar system, II 174b, 176a, 182a
soul, II 174b
Spallanzani, II 178a
species, II 174b, 175b, 177a–180a, 182a
Spencer, I 319a; II 177b, 181a, 182a–182b
spontaneous generation, II 178a
State, II 180b
Sumner, W. G., II 181a
survival of the fittest, II 182a, 187a
Taine, II 183a
Taoism, II 174b
taxonomy, II 175b
Teilhard de Chardin, II 188a
teleology, II 178b, 182b, 183a

Tennyson, II 181b
theology, II 186a
time, II 183a
transformism, II 177b, 178a, 178b, 179a
transmutation, II 183b
Tylor, E. B., II 187a
Tyndall, II 187a
uniformitarianism, II 176b
U.S., II 181a
universe, II 174a–174b, 175b, 176a–176b, 177b, 181b, 183b, 184b, 188a
Ussher, II 176b
vitalism, II 182b–183b, 185b–186a
Voltaire, II 176b
Wallace, William, II 180b
wealth, II 180b
Whitehead, II 186a
Will, II 182b
Wright, Chauncey, II 184b
zoology, II 179b
Excommunication, II 420a, 420b
Church, I 416b
double truth, II 31b
heresy, I 416b; II 420a, 420b, 425b
intolerance, IV 117b
modernism, I 423b
religion, IV 117b
Waldensians, II 420b
Eximeno, Antonio, music, III 263b
Existentialism, II 189a–195b
alienation, III 158b–159b
appeal of, II 190b–191a
appearance and reality, I 98b
atheism, II 192b
Barth, II 191a
Baudelaire, II 194a
Beauvoir, II 191a
Being, II 192b, 193b, 195a
Bergson, III 565a
Bible, II 192a
Bonhoeffer, II 192a
Bultmann, II 192a
Camus, II 189b–190a
capitalism, III 158a, 158b–159a, 160a
Christianity, II 189b, 190a, 190b, 191b, 192a–192b
class, III 160a
commodities, III 158b–159a
communism, III 157b, 158b
Counter-Enlightenment, II 109b
death, I 637b; II 193b
Denmark, II 190b, 191b
dictatorship, III 158a
dignity, IV 142a
dualism, III 159a, 159b

duty, III 160a
economics, III 157b, 158b–159a, 160b
Engels, II 191b
environment, II 194b
eschatology, II 161a
ethics, II 192a; III 158a, 158b, 159b, 160a
evil, II 168a–168b
expressionism, 206b
faith, II 192a, 192b, 194a, 194b
Faust (legend), III 252a–252b
France, II 190b, 191a, 194b
free will, II 246b
freedom, II 193b, 194a, 194b; III 157b, 158a, 160a
Genet, II 194a
God, II 189b, 192a, 192b, 193b, 359a, 360a, 362b
Hegel, II 191b
Heidegger, II 189a, 190a, 192b–195a
Hinduism, IV 232a
history, III 159a, 159b–160a
human nature, III 159b
humanism, III 158a, 160a
Husserl, II 192b, 193b, 194a
idealism, III 158a
individualism, II 189b, 191a, 603a
industry, III 158b, 160b
irrationalism, II 635b
Islam, II 651b, 652a
Jesus Christ, II 190b, 192a
judgment, III 160a
Kierkegaard, II 189a–190b, 191b–192b, 193b
knowledge, II 189b, 192a
law, II 191b–192a
Lenin, III 158a
literary criticism, I 606a
love, III 160a
Marcel, II 189b, 191b
Marx, II 191b; III 157b–160a, 160b
Marxism, II 191a, 194a, 194b, 195a; III 147a, 148a, 157b–161a, 164b, 168a
materialism, III 158a, 159a
Merleau-Ponty, II 189b; III 158a
metaphor, III 207a
morality, II 190b, 193a, 194a, 195a; III 160a
Nature, III 159a–159b
Nietzsche, II 192b
norms, III 160a
Pascal, II 189b
perennial philosophy, III 462b
phenomenology, II 192b,

193b
philosophy, II 651b, 652a; III 157b, 158b–159a, 159b
positivism, III 546a
power, III 160a
pragmatism, III 565a
private property, III 158b, 159b
production, III 158a–160a
psychoanalysis, II 194a
psychology, III 158b, 159a, 159b; IV 14a
realism in literature, IV 54b, 55a, 56a
religion, III 159a, 207a
Renaissance, IV 142a
revolution, III 160b
romanticism, IV 210b
Saint Augustine, II 189b
Sartre, II 189a–191a, 192b, 193a–195a; III 158a, 160b, 161a
Schelling, II 191b; IV 210b
science, III 159a, 160b
sin, IV 232a
skepticism, IV 250a
socialism, III 158a–160a
society, III 157b, 158b, 159b, 160b
sociology, III 158a, 158b, 160b
Stalin, III 158a
structuralism, IV 327b, 329b
teleology, II 192a
Tillich, II 192a
time, II 189b, 193a
Tolstoy, II 193b
truth, III 160b
utopianism, III 160a
value, III 159a
virtue, II 192a
voluntarism, III 158a
Exner, Franz, statistical concept of laws, II 588a
Exodus, mythology, III 276b, 277a, 280b
Exogamy
Freud, IV 96a
religion, IV 96b
Exorcism
demonology, III 264b, 267a
music, III 264b, 267a
Experience
Aristotle, III 554b
Bergson, III 552b, 565a
Descartes, IV 432b
Dewey, III 556b, 569a
empathy, II 86a–86b, 88a
game theory, II 267a
good, IV 177a, 177b
Hegel, III 556a, 556b
Herder, IV 492a
Hobbes, IV 177a, 177b
humanism, IV 134a

idea, II 547a–547b, 548a
Kant, III 555b, 556a; IV 248b–249a, 382b–383a, 433b
knowledge, III 565a
Leonardo da Vinci, IV 134a, 440a, 440b
Lovejoy, III 552b
Mead, III 569a
metaphysical imagination, III 209a
Papini, III 563b
Peirce, III 556b, 559a
progress, III 626b
psychology, IV 27b
relativity, IV 75b
religion, IV 97b, 98a
Renaissance, IV 134a, 440a, 440b, 441a, 443a
right, IV 177a, 177b
Saint Augustine, IV 381a
Santayana, III 554a; IV 250a–250b
senses, IV 435a
skepticism, IV 242b, 247b, 248b–249a, 250b
technology, IV 361a
theodicy, IV 381a, 382b–383a
time, IV 396a
unity of science, IV 432b, 433b, 435a
universal man, IV 440a, 440b, 441a, 443a
Volksgeist, IV 492a, 496a
wisdom of the fool, IV 519a
work, IV 533b
Zeitgeist, IV 536b
See also Empiricism, Pragmatism
Experiments
art, II 567b; III 569b
artists, III 569b
Bacon, III 383b, 384b, 386b, 387a
Dewey, III 556b, 569b
Galileo, III 382b–383b, 385b; IV 361a, 533a
Hegel, III 556b
Hooke, III 387a
impressionism, II 567b
indeterminacy, II 587b
James, III 561b, 562a
music, III 262b
Nature, III 349b
Newton, II 389b
optics, III 410b, 411a–415a, 416a–416b, 417a
Peirce, III 554a, 555a, 558a, 559a, 559b, 560b, 561a
Power, III 386b
pragmatism, III 553a, 553b, 554a, 555a, 555b, 556b, 557a, 557b, 558a, 559a,

559b, 560b, 561a, 561b, 562a, 564b, 569b
Ramism, IV 45a
rationalism, IV 48a
recapitulation, IV 58a, 59a
relativity, IV 75b, 78a–81a, 86a, 88a
skepticism, IV 247b
spontaneous generation, IV 309a–309b, 310b, 311a
technology, IV 361a
time, IV 395a
Exploration
genius, II 293a
religion, IV 93b, 94a, 95a
Expressionism
activism, II 206b
aesthetics, II 206a, 206b
allegory, II 208b
Arnold, II 208b
art, II 206a, 206b–207b, 208a, 208b
baroque, II 207b–208a
baroque in literature, I 190a
beauty, II 207b, 208a
Brecht, II 209a
Cézanne, II 207a
creativity in art, I 588b
cubism, II 206b, 207a, 208b
dadaism, II 206b
existentialism, II 206b
France, II 207a, 208b
futurism, II 206b, 207a, 208b
Galsworthy, II 207b
Germany, II 206a–207a, 208b–209a; III 483b
Great Britain, II 208b
history, II 206a, 206b–207a
Hulme, II 208b
impressionism, II 206a–207a
Kandinsky, II 208a
literature, II 206a–209b
Lovejoy, II 206a
Marc, II 207b
Middle Ages, II 207b
naturalism, II 206a, 207a
O'Neill, II 208b
painting, II 206a, 207a, 207b, 208a, 208b
periodization in literary history, III 483b
philosophy, II 206a
Platonism, II 207a
poetry, II 206b, 208a, 208b, 209a
positivism, II 206b–207a
Pound, II 208b
realism, II 207a
reason, II 208a
Rilke, II 206b, 208a
romanticism, II 206a, 207b–

208a
surrealism, II 206a, 206b
symbolism, IV 345a
ugliness, II 208a
U.S., II 208b
van Gogh, Theo, II 207a
van Gogh, Vincent, II 207a
Wellek, II 206a
Worringer, II 207b, 208a, 208b
Extension, IV 301a–302a
Extrachromosomal inheritance, II 619a
Extrasensory perception, environment and, II 123b
Extremism
fascism, III 332a
nationalism, III 331a, 332a
Extroversion, psychology, IV 23a
Eye, See Optics
Eysenck, H. J., beauty, I 213a
Ezekiel (Bible)
law, III 35b
metaphor, III 202b
music, III 269b
mythology, III 277a, 281a, 283b, 284b
Ezra (Bible)
apocalypse, III 224a
freedom of speech, II 255a
loyalty, III 108b

F

Fabians, II 454a
democracy, I 664b
perfectibility, III 470a
revisionism, IV 269b, 272a
socialism, I 664b
Fabini, Mario, literary criticism, I 606a
Fabius Maximus (d. about 290 B.C.), virtù, IV 481a, 482a
Fables
mythology, III 286b, 288a, 290a, 291a, 293a, 293b, 299b, 307a, 307b, 315a, 316a
ut pictura poesis, IV 468b, 469b
Fabre, Jèan Henri (1823–1915)
behaviorism, I 221a
theriophily, IV 388b
Fabricius, David (1564–1617), cosmology, I 550b
Facio, Bartolomeo, dignity, IV 143a–143b
Fairchild, James H. (1817–

1902), civil disobedience, I 436b
Fairholt, F. W. (1814–1866), motif, III 236b
Fairweather, Eugene, God, II 361b
Fairy tales
music, III 266a, 267a, 270a
mythology, III 275b, 315a, 315b, 316b
Faith, II 209b–216a
agapē, II 209b, 210a
Aristotelianism, II 210b–211a, 211b
Aristotle, II 210b
asceticism, II 212b
atheism, II 213a, 213b
Augustinianism, II 210b
authority, I 148a, 148b; II 212a
Barth, II 213a, 359b
Bible, II 209b, 210a
Blasius of Parma, II 35b
Bonaventure, II 210b
Buddhism, I 249b
Bultmann, II 213a
Buridan, II 34b
Calvin, II 349a
Camus, II 213b, 215a
charity, II 209b–216a
Christianity, II 209b–215b
Clement of Alexandria, II 210a
Counter-Enlightenment, II 101b, 104a, 108b
Cox, II 214b
deism, I 648a
dignity, IV 142a, 142b, 142b, 143a
double truth, II 33a, 33b, 34a, 34b, 35b
education, II 79b–80a
egocentric aspect of, II 209b
Erastianism, IV 119a
Erigena, II 210b
eros, II 209b, 210a, 210b
eschatology, II 156a, 158b, 160b
ethics, II 212b, 215a
existentialism, II 192a, 192b, 194a, 194b
Feuerbach, II 213b
fortune, II 232a
Freud, II 213b
friendship, II 210b–211a
Gnosticism, II 210a
good, II 209b, 212a
grace, II 211a
Greece (ancient), II 209b
Hamann, II 104a
happiness, II 378b
health, II 399a

Hegel, II 411a, 412a; IV 290b
heresy, II 416b, 424a, 426a
historiography, IV 147b
Hobbes, II 212b
holy, II 513b
hope, II 209b–216a
humanism, II 214a, 215a; IV 134b, 135a
individualism, II 212b
James, William, III 563b
Jaspers, II 213a
Jesus Christ, II 211b, 214b
John of Jandun, II 34b
Kant, I 316a; IV 383a
Kierkegaard, II 192a, 192b
knowledge, II 210a, 211b
law, II 689a; III 10b
liberalism, III 41a, 42b
love, II 209b, 210a, 210b, 212a, 215a
Luther, I 390a, 394a; II 160b, 212a–212b; IV 66b, 381b
Lutheranism, II 212b, 213a
Marxism, II 213b–214a
Middle Ages, II 210a–212b
modernism, I 421b–423a
monasticism, II 212b
morality, II 212b, 213a
mythology, III 303a, 314b
Nietzsche, II 213a
paganism, II 34a
Pascal, IV 381b
perennial philosophy, III 458b, 459a, 461b
perfectibility, III 465b–466a
Petrarch, IV 142a
Philo Judaeus, III 465b–466a
Pietism, III 493b
Plato, II 209b
Platonism, II 210b
pleasure, II 378b
politics, II 212b, 213a, 214b, 215a
pragmatism, III 563b
progress, III 632a, 633a, 634a, 636a
prophecy, III 665a
Protestantism, II 212a–213a, 215b
Pseudo-Dionysius, II 210b
reason, I 384b–385a; III 458b
reformation, IV 61b, 62a, 62b, 66b, 68a, 68b, 69b
Reformation, II 212a–213a, 215b
religion, IV 103a, 106b, 113b, 114b, 116b, 119a
Renaissance, IV 134b, 135a, 142a, 142b, 143a, 147b

Roman Catholic Church, II 210a–211b, 212b, 213a, 215a–215b
romanticism, IV 200b, 206a
Saint Augustine, II 210a–210b, 213a; IV 286b
Saint John, II 210a
Saint Paul, II 210a, 211b
Saint Thomas Aquinas, II 210b–212a, 213a; IV 134b, 392a
salvation, II 210a, 212b
Sartre, II 194a, 194b, 213b
Schleiermacher, II 358b
Siger of Brabant, I 639b; II 33a, 33b
skepticism, IV 243a, 243b, 244a, 248a, 250a–251a
socialism, IV 286b, 290b
society, II 212b, 213a
soul, II 211a
Teilhard de Chardin, II 214a
temperance, IV 372b, 375b
theodicy, IV 379b, 380b, 381b, 383a
theriophily, IV 386b
Tillich, II 211a
time, IV 392a
tragic sense, IV 412b, 415b, 416a–416b
transubstantiation, II 212b
truth, III 563b
universal acceptance of, I 382b
Victorian, IV 217b, 218b
virtue, II 211a–212b; IV 372b, 375b
Weber, II 211b, 212b
work, IV 531a
See also God
Falconer, William (1732–1769), primitivism, III 604a
Falconet, Étienne-Maurice (1716–1791), neo-classicism in art, III 369a
Fall
Calvin, IV 381b
dignity, IV 137a, 138a, 138b, 140a, 143a
Luther, IV 381b
mythology, III 277a–279a, 284b, 288a, 315b
Nature, III 347b
perennial philosophy, III 459b
perfectibility, III 466a–466b
primitivism, III 578a, 581b, 595b, 596a
progress, III 634b
Renaissance, IV 137a, 138a, 138b, 140a, 143a
Saint Augustine, III 466a–466b; IV 138b, 381a
Saint Thomas Aquinas, III

466b
theodicy, IV 381a, 381b
tragic sense, IV 415b, 416a
women, IV 524a
See also Cosmic Fall
Fallopius, Gabriel (1523–1562), alchemy, I 31a
Falstaff (fiction), literary paradox, III 78b
Fame
Boccaccio, II 234a
chance, II 234a
Family
authority, I 157b, 158b; II 678b
Counter-Enlightenment, II 110b
economic history, II 54b
equality, II 145a
Greece (ancient), II 674b, 677b, 678a, 678b
Hegel, II 408b–409a
law, II 674b, 677b, 678a, 678b, 686b
love, III 100b
Victorian sentiment, IV 217b–222a
Fanshawe, Richard (1608–1666), mythology, III 295b
Fantasy
metaphor, III 197b, 198b
metaphysics, III 220b, 221b
mythology, III 312b–313a, 315a, 315b, 317b
naturalism in art, III 342b, 344a
philosophy, III 197b, 198b
surrealism, III 342b
Fao-lin (572–640), Buddhism, I 247a
Faraday, Michael (1791–1867)
anthropomorphism, I 90a
cosmology, I 554b
Maxwell and, I 89b
relativity, IV 78b
religion, IV 108a
Tyndall and, I 89b
Farel, Guillaume (1489–1565), heresy, II 427b
Farmasb, astrology, I 122b
Farrer, Austin, God, II 361b
Fascism
absolutism, III 332a
authority, I 159a–159b, 161a; III 674a
capitalism, III 331b, 674a
conservatism, I 483b
crisis in history, I 592a
defeat of, III 675b
democracy, I 665b
economics, III 674a
efficiency, III 331b

ethics, III 674a
extremism, III 332a
Germany, III 331b–332a
ideology, III 674a
labor, III 674a
League of Nations, III 332a
liberalism, III 331b
loyalty, III 112a
Machiavellism, III 125a
Marxism, III 147a, 166a
morality, III 331b
Mussolini, III 597a
nationalism, III 674a
Nazis, III 674a
New Left, I 160a
organization, III 674a
Platonism, III 520b
plutocracy, III 331b
positivism, III 542a
power, III 674a
pragmatism, III 564b–565a, 565b, 569a
primitivism, III 597a
protest movements, III 673a, 673b, 674a, 675b
racism, III 674a
revolution, IV 164a, 164b, 165a
romanticism, IV 203a
society, III 674a
Sorel, III 565b
totalitarianism, IV 406a–408b, 409b, 410b
violence, III 674a
war, IV 505a, 505b
Fatalism
determinism, II 29b, 30a
Islam, II 29b
mythology, III 288a, 306a
Stoicism, II 137a
Fate, II 225b–236a
Adrasteia, II 229a
Alberti, II 235a
angels, II 232b–233a
Apuleius, II 228a, 232a
Aristotelianism, II 229b–231b, 232b, 233a, 234a
Aristotle, II 226a, 227a–228b, 229b, 231b, 233a; IV 412a
art, II 230a, 232a, 234a, 235a
astrology, II 232a–233a, 234b, 235a
atomism, II 226a
Augustinianism, II 230b
beauty, II 228a
birth, II 226b, 228a, 228b, 232a, 233b
Boccaccio, II 233b–234a
Boethius, II 231a–232a, 234b
Bracciolini, II 235a
causation, II 226a–233b,

234b, 235a, 236a
celestial spheres, II 228b, 229a, 229b, 232a, 232b–233a, 233b
Chalcidius, II 229a–230a, 233a
chance images, I 340b
Christianity, II 229a–236a
cosmology, II 226a
courage, II 234a
Creation, II 226a, 226b, 231a
cycles, II 228a, 229b
Dante, II 233a–233b, 234b
death, II 226b
deism, II 227a
Democritus, II 226a–226b
destiny, II 225b, 228a, 233b
determinism, II 229b, 230a, 230b, 232a, 232b, 234b
dignity, II 231b; IV 143a, 145a
Epicureanism, II 231a
ethics, II 226b, 227a, 227b, 233a
evil, II 234a; 413b, 416a
fame, II 234a
Fates, II 229a
Faust (legend), III 251b
fear, II 234b
Ficino, IV 145a
Firmicius Maternus, II 232a
free will, II 226b–231b, 234a, 236a, 243b, 245b
freedom, II 227a, 229b
friendship, II 228a
game theory, II 271b
glory, II 231b
God, II 226b, 227b–235a, 236a; III 571b
good, II 227b–229a, 231b–234a, 235a, 235b
grace, II 233b
Greece (ancient), II 225b–228b
happiness, II 227a, 228a, 235a
harmony, II 229b
heredity, II 228a
Hermes Trismegistus, II 232a
human nature, III 571b, 573a
humanism, II 225b, 235a, 236a
impulse, II 227b, 232b–233b, 234a, 234b, 235a
indeterminacy, II 225b, 226a–226b, 228b, 230b
instinct, II 227b
irony, II 627a, 632a
justice, II 233b

knowledge, II 226a–226b, 229b, 232b

law, II 226a, 226b, 227a, 228a, 229a, 229b, 231b, 235b

logic, II 230a, 230b, 231a

love, II 234a

luck, II 225b, 227a–227b, 234a–234b

Machiavelli, II 235b–236a

Martianus Capella, II 229a

Middle Ages, II 227b, 232a

mind, II 226a, 227a, 229a, 232a, 232b, 233a

moon, II 233b

morality, II 229b, 231b–232a, 234a, 234b–235a

motion, II 229b, 231b

mythology, II 226b, 228a, 229a

nature, II 225b–227b, 228b–230a, 231a, 233a, 233b

necessity, II 225b, 226b, 228a, 229b, 230a, 230b, 232a, 234a

Nemesis, II 229a

Neo-Platonism, II 229a

observation, II 226a

Orphism, II 226b

passions, II 233b

Petrarch, II 234a–235a

Plato, II 226b, 231b–232a; IV 415a

pleasure, II 234a

Pontano, II 235a

power, II 228a–230a, 231b, 233b, 235a–236a; IV 413a

predestination, II 225b

probability, II 226a

Proclus, II 228b

prudence, II 235a

psychology, II 227b

punishment, II 229b

Pythagoras, IV 31a

reason, II 225b–226a, 226b, 227b, 233a, 234a

reincarnation, II 226b, 227a

religion, II 227a

Renaissance, II 232a; IV 143a, 145a

reputation, II 228b

reward, II 229b

Rome (ancient), II 226a

Saint Albertus Magnus, II 232a, 232b, 233a

Saint Augustine, II 230a–231a, 231b, 232a

Saint Thomas Aquinas, II 232a–233a

Salutati, II 234b

scholasticism, II 227b, 230a

science, II 225b

Seneca, II 228a

Simplicio, II 228a, 228b, 233a

skepticism, IV 236a

soul, II 226b–230a, 233a–233b, 235b

space, II 231b

stars, II 227a, 229b, 235a

Stoicism, II 228a, 230a, 232a, 234a, 234b

success, II 228b, 233a

superstition, II 226a, 234b

teleology, II 231a

theodicy, IV 379a

time, II 231b, 232b, 233a

tragedy, II 228a

tragic sense, IV 412a–415a, 416a, 416b

virtue, II 225b, 227b, 231b, 233b–236a

wealth, II 228a, 228b, 231b

Zeus (myth), II 229a

See also Providence, Universe

Fates (myth), III 274a

chance, II 229a

fortune, II 229a

Fatigue, disease, II 404b

Faulkner, William (1897–1962)

death, I 637b

mythology, III 277a

realism in literature, IV 55a

symbolism, IV 341a, 343a, 344b

Faust, Johann, III 245a

Faust (legend), III 244b–252b

Absolute, III 250b

Adrian Leverkühn (fiction), III 252a

aestheticism, III 249a

Agrippa, III 246a

alchemy, III 245a, 246a

Alexander the Great, III 247a

ambivalence, III 250b–252b

amoralism, III 252a

archetypes, III 251a, 251b, 252a

Aristotle, III 245a

art, III 249a

aspiration, III 252b

astrology, III 247a

astronomy, III 246b, 247a

atheism, III 246b

ballet, III 252a

Basil of Caesarea, III 246b

Being, III 249b

Bible, III 246a

biology, III 248b

Bruno, III 246a, 247a, 247b

Buffon, III 248b

Byron, III 250b

Calderón de la Barca, III 246b

Charles V, III 247a

Christianity, III 246a, 247a, 249b, 250b

classicism, III 249b

Clement of Alexandria, III 246a

Copernicus, III 246b

cosmogony, III 246b

Council of Trent, III 246b

Counter-Reformation, III 246a

criticism, III 250b, 252b

culture, III 249a

damnation, III 246b, 247a, 247b, 248a

discontent, III 250a

divination, III 250a

Doctor Faustus (fiction), III 245a

drama, III 247b, 248a–250a

dualism, III 246a

Enlightenment, III 248a–248b, 249b

Epicureanism, III 247a

ethics, III 251a

Euphorion (fiction), III 249a, 250a

existentialism, III 252a–252b

fate, III 251b

Faustianism, III 244b, 251a, 252a

folklore, III 245b, 248b

frailty, III 250b

France, III 250b

Frankenstein legend, III 245b

free will, III 246b

freedom, III 249b

Freud, III 251b

Fust, III 247a

Germany, III 245a, 247a, 248a, 250b, 251a, 251b, 252a

Gnosticism, III 246a

God, III 246a, 247a, 248a, 248b, 251b

Goethe, III 248a–252b

good, III 248b

Gutenberg, III 247a

Heine, III 252a

Helen of Troy (myth), III 246a, 247a–249a

hell, III 247a, 247b, 248b

heresy, III 245b, 246b

Hertz, III 251a

Hesse, III 251a

historical figure, III 244b–245a

history, III 249a, 251a, 252a

Hitler, III 251b

Homunculus (fiction), III 249a, 250a

humanism, III 246b

idealism, III 249b

ideology, III 252a

Jesus Christ, III 245a, 247b

Jung, III 251a

Kierkegaard, III 250b

Lamarck, III 248b

Lessing, III 248a

liberalism, III 250b

libertinism, III 246b

literature, III 244b–253a

Luther, III 245a, 246b, 247a, 248a

magic, III 246a, 247a, 247b, 248b, 249b, 251a

magus, III 245b, 246b, 251a

Manichaeism, III 246a, 246b

Mann, III 251a, 252a

Margarete (fiction), III 248b, 249a, 249b, 250a, 251b

Marlowe, III 247b–248a

Marxism, III 252a

medicine, III 247a

Melanchthon, III 245a

Menelaus (myth), III 249a

metamorphosis, III 248b

meteorology, III 247a

Middle Ages, III 246b

morality, III 247b–248a

motif, III 240b–241a

Mudt, III 245a

Müller (Friedrich), III 250a

music, III 250b, 252a

mythology, III 240b–241a, 244b, 249a, 250b, 251a, 252a, 305a

nationalism, III 251b, 252a

natural science, III 246a

Nature, III 248b, 347a

Nazism, III 251b, 252a

necromancy, III 247b

Neo-Platonism, III 246b

Nietzsche, III 251a

nihilism, III 251b, 252a

novel, III 250a

optimism, III 249b

paganism, III 246b

Pansophism, III 246b

paradox, III 252b

Peter (Bible), III 246a

philosophy, III 246b, 249a, 250a, 252a

Plato, III 245a

poetry, III 248b, 250a

politics, III 252a

pre-Goethean, III 252a

printing, III 247a

Prometheus (myth), III 251a

Protestantism, III 246b–247a

psychology, III 252a
Pushkin, III 250a
Reformation, III 245a, 246a, 246b
religion, III 249b, 250b
Renaissance, III 245b, 247b
Roman Catholic Church, III 246a, 249a
romanticism, III 249b, 250a, 250b
Saint Thomas Aquinas, III 246b
salvation, III 250a
Santayana, III 250b
Satan, III 245a, 247a, 247b, 248b, 249a, 249b, 250a, 251b, 252a
Schelling, III 250a
science, III 249a, 250b, 251a, 252a
self-regeneration, III 250a, 251b
Shakespeare, III 248a, 251b
Shelley, III 250b
Simon Magus (Bible), III 246a
soul, III 250b, 252a
Spengler, III 251a
spiritualism, III 247a, 250b
Staël, III 250b
Steiner, III 251a
Superman, III 250b
supernatural, III 245a, 245b, 247b, 249b
Sylvester II (Pope), III 245b
symbolism, III 248a, 249a, 251a, 252b
technology, III 250b, 251a
theology, III 247a, 251a, 252a
Theophilus of Cilicia, III 246b
tragedy, III 249b–250a, 251b, 252b
tragic sense, IV 416a–416b
Trinity, III 246b
Unitarianism, III 246b
Urfaust, III 248b, 250a
Valéry, III 251b–252a
Virgin Mary (Bible), III 246b, 249b
Walpurgisnight, III 249a
Will, III 250a
witchcraft, III 245b, 246b
World War II, III 252a
Zeitgeist, IV 536a–536b
Zoroaster, III 251a
Faust-books, III 245b, 247b, 252a
motif, III 241a
Favorinus of Arles (2nd century A.D.), skepticism, IV 240a

Fawkes, Alfred, modernism, I 424b
Faye, Hervé (1814–1902), cosmic images, I 521b, 522b, 523a
Fear
Aristotle, IV 412a
atomism, III 187b
catharsis, I 264b–267b, 268b
death, I 635b–637a, 638a, 641a
despotism, II 6a, 6b, 9b, 12b, 13b–14a
ethics, IV 71b
general will, II 278a
God, III 575a
good, IV 174a, 181a
happiness, II 378a, 384b
hell, II 62a
Hobbes, II 9b; III 20b
human nature, III 575a, 576a, 576b
Machiavelli, IV 481a, 481b
matter, III 187b
Montesquieu, II 9b, 13b
mythology, III 290b, 302a 302b, 304b
natural law, III 20b
perfectibility, III 465a
Plato, IV 3b
pleasure, II 378a, 384b
psychology, IV 3b
relativism, IV 71b
religion, IV 93b
revolution, IV 157a, 157b, 159b, 162a
right, IV 174a, 181a
Robespierre, II 13b–14a
romanticism, IV 206a
sublime in external nature, IV 333b
technology, IV 358a
tragic sense, IV 412a, 413a, 415a
Victorian sensibility, IV 220a, 222a, 222b
virtù, IV 481a, 481b
welfare state, IV 513a
Febronianism, I 403b
Conciliar Movement, I 403b
Gallican Movement, I 403b
Febvre, Lucien (1878–1956)
environment, II 131a, 131b
historicism, II 462b, 463a
Fechner, Gustav Theodor (1801–1887)
beauty, I 212b
behaviorism, I 219b
continuity, I 501b–502a
irrationalism, II 636b
linguistics, IV 429b
probability, III 616b

psychology, IV 12b, 13a, 24b
psychophysics, II 636b
uniformitarianism, IV 429b
utility, IV 454b
Feder, J. G., ideal, II 551a
Federalism
anarchism, I 72b
Augustinianism, IV 109a
nationalism, III 329b
religion, IV 109a
Federigo, Duke of Urbino, dignity, IV 137b
Feedback, computers, II 660a
Feedback principle
economic history, II 55a, 57b
natural liberty, II 63b
Feeling
aesthetics, IV 353b, 354a, 354b, 355a, 356b
Balguy, III 233a
good, IV 174a
happiness, II 382b, 383a, 386b
Hartley, III 234b
historiography, IV 147b
holy, II 513a, 514a
human nature, III 643b
Hume, III 230a–230b, 232a, 232b–233a
Hutcheson, III 230a–230b, 231a, 231b, 232b
ideal, II 550a
impressionism, II 575b, 576b
Kames, III 234b
Kant, III 234b
literary criticism, I 597a, 598a
Man-Machine, III 137b
metaphysical imagination, III 208b
moral sense, III 230a–234b
music, III 267b
perfectibility, III 643b
Pietism, IV 68b
Plato, III 498a
Platonism, III 498a
pleasure, II 382b, 383a, 386b
progress, III 638a, 642b, 643b, 648b
reformation, IV 68b
Renaissance, IV 147b
right, IV 174a
Victorian sensibility, IV 217a, 217b, 218a, 221a, 221b
Fehr, Bernhard, baroque in literature, I 191a
Feigl, H., empiricism, III 546a,

550a, 550b
Feijóo, Benito (1676–1764), aesthetics, IV 354b
attitude toward antiquity, I 85a
Feininger, Lyonel (1871–1956), Gothic, II 372b
Feldmann, Wilhelm, symbolism, IV 343b
Félibien, André (1619–1695), aesthetics, II 218b
iconography, II 534b
ideal, II 549b
mythology, III 299a
neo-classicism in art, III 368a
ut pictura poesis, IV 470a
Fellenberg, Philipp Emanuel von (1771–1844)
education, II 99b
Enlightenment, II 99b
Fellowship of Reconciliation, III 449b
Femininity
love, III 107a
women, IV 523b, 524b, 526a, 526b, 528a, 529a, 529b
Fénelon, François de Salignac de La Mothe (1651–1715)
aristocracy, II 8b
attitude toward antiquity, I 82a, 83a
balance of power, I 183b–184a
baroque in literature, I 195a
beauty, I 201b
despotism, II 8a, 8b
illuminists, IV 109a
irrationalism, II 638a
periodization in literary history, III 483a
religion, IV 109a, 109b
Fenigstein, Berthold, baroque in literature, I 91b
Fenollosa, Ernest (1853–1908)
Buddhism, III 437a
Orientalism, III 428b, 437a
Ferber, J. C. C., aesthetics, II 551a
Ferdinand II, King (1578–1637)
Counter-Reformation, I 392b–395a
Machiavelli and, IV 502a
Ferguson, Adam (1723–1816)
art, II 307b
despotism, II 12b–13a
Enlightenment, II 89b, 92b, 93a, 93b, 94b, 99b

genius, II 307b
literature, III 82a
society, II 99b
Ferguson, James (1710–1776), Newton and, III 393a
Ferguson, Wallace K.
Burckhardt and, IV 126a, 126b
periodization in history, III 479b
Fergusson, Francis, tragic sense, IV 412b
Fermat, Pierre de (1601–1665)
chance, I 337b
frequency, III 606a
Pascal and, III 606a–606b
probability, III 606a–607b
Fernandez, Ramon, literary criticism, I 604b
Ferrari, Joseph (1812–1876), China, I 371a
Ferrier, David (1843–1928), association of ideas, I 116a
Fertility
love, III 100b
religion, IV 98b, 100a, 104b
Festivals
mythology, III 281a, 281b, 311a, 311b, 312a–312b
Plato, III 500b
socialism, IV 286a
Festus Avienus, primitivism, III 579b
Fet, Afanasi A. (1820?–1892), symbolism, IV 343a
Fête de Fous, IV 516b, 519b
Fetishism
Africa, III 301a, 303b
Brosses, III 303b
mythology, III 301a, 303b, 309b
progress, III 641a
religion, IV 94a
Saint-Simon, III 641a
Feudalism
citizenship, I 655b
economic history, II 46b–47a, 54b
equality, II 141a, 143b, 144b
feudal contract, III 112a, 112b
freedom, II 250a–250b
land, II 692a
law, II 250a–250b, 692a
loyalty, III 112a
Marx, IV 161b
Marxism-Leninism, III 478b
Middle Ages, III 112a, 112b, 319a–319b, 321b, 322a, 322b; IV 253b

millenarianism, III 225a
nationalism, III 319a–319b, 321b, 322a, 322b, 333a
papacy, III 225a
periodization in history, III 478b
philanthropy, III 488b, 489b
pragmatism, III 566b
private property, III 650b, 652a
progress, III 641a
revolution, IV 161b, 163a
romanticism, IV 206b, 207a
social contract, IV 253b
war, IV 501a, 503b
women, IV 525b
Feuerbach, Anselm (1829–1880), naturalism in art, III 341b
Feuerbach, Ludwig Andreas (1804–1872)
alienation, I 37b–38a, 38b
atheism, I 74a
Christianity, II 213b
death, I 637b
faith, hope, and charity, II 213b
God, II 356a
Hegel and, I 38a; II 414a
historicism, II 456b
immortality, I 646a
Marx and, I 38a; II 450b, 451b
materialism, II 450b, 451b
revisionism, IV 270a
socialism, IV 291a
Stirling and, II 414b
work, IV 534b
Feydeau, Ernest (1821–1873), realism in literature, IV 52a
Feyerabend, Paul K., empiricism, III 550b
Feyerabend; Sigmund, hierarchy, II 435b
Fichte, Johann Gottlieb (1762–1814)
antinomy, I 93a
Chain of Being, I 334b
city, I 432a
Counter-Enlightenment, II 108b
culture, I 619a
determinism, IV 394a
dualism, II 41b
egoism, IV 209b
eschatology, II 158a
ethics, IV 209b
free will, II 246b
freedom, II 407b; III 473a; IV 209b
general will, II 279a
Hegel and, II 279a, 407a
historicism, II 457a

idea, II 548a, 548b
idealism, II 158a, 158b, 407b
individualism, IV 209b
irony, II 630a
literary criticism, I 598a
love, III 473a
modernism, I 420a
natural law, III 22a
necessity, III 358b
perfectibility, III 473a, 475a
psychology, IV 11b
romanticism, IV 202b, 205b, 208a, 210a
Rousseau and, II 279a
Schelling and, IV 210a
Schlegel and, IV 208a
Schleiermacher and, IV 202a
skepticism, IV 249a, 249b
social contract, IV 261a
society, III 473a
sociology, IV 209b
sovereignty, II 279a
Strauss and, II 413a
theodicy, II 383a
time, IV 393a–394a, 394b
unity, III 473a
war, IV 502a
work, IV 534a
Zeitgeist, IV 536a
Ficino, Marsilio (1433–1499),
aesthetics, II 218a
alchemy, I 31b
anthropocentrism, III 510a
art, II 309a, 310a; III 229a
atomism, I 132b
beauty, II 218a; III 511a
classification of the arts, I 459b–460a
cosmology, III 510b–511a
Dante and, III 511a
demonology, I 669b–670a; II 393b–394a
determinism, IV 144b–145a
dignity, IV 139a, 144a–145b
divination, IV 144b, 145a
ethics, III 506a
fate, IV 145a
free will, IV 131b, 132a
friendship, III 511a
genius, II 309a, 310a, 320b
God, II 347a, 442a; III 511a; IV 145a
harmony, II 389a, 389b, 393a, 393b, 394a; IV 39b, 41a
hierarchy, II 442a, 442b; III 511a
humanism, II 520a, 521b; IV 131b–132a, 144a–145b
idea, II 547a
imagination, IV 145a

immortality, IV 144b, 145a
individualism, II 597b
knowledge, III 511a, 513a
love, II 442a; III 510b, 511a, 511b, 512b
magic, IV 145a
matter, III 192b
medieval science, II 203a
Michelangelo and, III 513a
mimesis, III 229a
morality, III 511a
music, II 320b, 389a, 389b, 393a, 393b, 394a, 521b
mythology, III 290b, 295a
Nature, III 229a
Neo-Platonism, III 510b, 511a, 511b, 516a; IV 144b, 145b
Nicholas of Cusa and, III 510b
painting, IV 470b
perennial philosophy, III 459b
periodization in literary history, III 482a
piety, IV 144b, 145b
Platonism, III 506a, 506b, 507b, 509b, 510a, 510b–511b, 512a, 512b, 513a, 514a–516a; IV 131b–132a, 144a–145b
Plotinus and, III 510b, 511a
poetry, III 529b, 530a; IV 475b
pragmatism, III 555a
Pythagoreans, IV 39b, 41a
reason, IV 144b–145a
senses, III 511a
skepticism, IV 242a
soul, II 442a, 442b; III 511a
space, IV 301b–302a
supernatural, IV 145a
syncretism, IV 126b
tone, II 389b
universality, IV 145b
universe, II 442a, 442b; IV 39b, 41a
work, IV 532a, 532b
Fiction
irrationalism, II 636a
mimesis, III 228b
mythology, III 275b, 307a, 307b, 308b
Nature, III 348a
poetry, III 525b, 531a
prose, III 82b
romanticism, IV 187b, 188b, 191b, 208b
U.S., III 348a
Fideism
deism, I 646b, 647a, 648b, 652a
God, II 355b, 356a
Jacobi, II 412a

Luther, IV 381b
Montaigne, IV 243b
perennial philosophy, III 459a
pragmatism, III 563b
skepticism, IV 243b, 244a, 246b, 248a, 249a, 250b
theodicy, IV 381b, 383b
Fiedelson, Charles, symbolism, IV 341b
Fiedler, Konrad
aesthetics, II 223b
naturalism in art, III 343b
Field, David Dudley (1781–1867)
equity, II 153a
international peace, III 451a
Fielding, Henry (1707–1754),
comedy, I 469a
irony, II 629a
Machiavellism, III 119a
satire, IV 215a
Figgis, J. N., State, IV 314a
Figurative arts, I 460a, 461a
Figurative mythology, III 286a–286b, 296b
Figurism
Bouvet, I 359b–360a
China, I 359b–360b
God, I 359b, 360a, 360b
Leibniz, I 359b–360b
Ramsay, I 359b, 360a, 360b
Zoroaster, I 359b
Filarete, Antonio di Pietro Averlino (1400?–1470),
aesthetics, IV 354a
art, II 298a
city, I 430b, 431a
genius, II 298a
Gothic, II 367b
virtù, IV 477b
Filelfo, Francesco (1398–1481), humanism, II 516b, 519b
Filiozat, Jean, Buddhism, I 256b
Filla, Emil, iconography, II 534a
Filmer, Robert (d. 1653),
authority, I 152b
despotism, II 4a, 5a, 5b, 6b, 7a, 7b
Enlightenment, II 95a
liberty, II 95a
Locke and, IV 258a
patriarchalism, I 479b
social contract, IV 257b, 258a
Finck, F. N. (1867–1910), linguistics, III 71a
Finck, Hermann (1527–1558)
genius, II 318a–318b
music, II 318a–318b

Findlay, J. N., time, IV 394a
Finetti, Bruno de, chance, I 338b
Finger numbers, III 399b, 400a, 403b, 404a, 406b
Finland
folklore, III 238b, 239a
language, II 660b
nationalism, III 328b
Finlay, Carlos (1833–1915), Pereira Barreto and, III 541a
positivism, III 541a
Finley, M. I., Jr., temperance, IV 365b
Finney, Charles (1792–1875),
civil disobedience, I 436b
Pietism, IV 111b
psychology, IV 24a
reformation, IV 68b
religion, IV 111b
transcendentalism, IV 24a
Finno-Ugric language, III 64b, 71a
Fiorentino, Graffione
art, II 302b
individualism, II 302b
Fioretti, Benedetto, literary criticism, I 597a
Firmicus Maternus (4th century A.D.)
astrology, I 121a, 124a, 124b
fate and fortune, II 232a
Firth, Raymond
beauty, I 213b
relativism, IV 71a
Fischer, E., periodization in history, III 479b
Fisher, Irving (1867–1947),
economic history, II 48b, 57a
social welfare, IV 277b
utility value, IV 456a
Fisher, R. A.
evolutionism, II 186b
genetics, II 186b
probability, III 610b, 618b
Fishing, cosmology, I 535b
Fiske, John (1842–1901),
pragmatism, III 558a, 566b
psychology, IV 26a
reformation, IV 69a
Volksgeist, IV 495b
Fitch, J. E. Crawford, baroque in literature, I 193a
Fitzgerald, F. Scott, class, I 445b
Fitzneale, Richard (d. 1198), nationalism, III 319b
Five Power Treaty, III 455b
Flacius Illyricus, Matthias (1520–1575)
historiography, II 484a

reformation, IV 67a
Flake, Otto, expressionism, II 206a–206b, 208b–209a
Flammarion, Camille (1842–1925), cosmic images, I 516b, 518b, 520a, 522b, 523a
Flaubert, Gustave (1821–1880)
art, II 310b
art for art's sake, I 109a
beauty, I 208a
China, I 369a
genius, II 310b
irony, II 633b
literature, IV 332b
naturalism, IV 54a
realism in literature, IV 52a, 52b, 54a, 55a
style, IV 332b
Flavio Biondo (1388–1463),
historiography, II 484b–485a, 485b
Flaxman, John (1755–1826),
mimesis, III 229b
neo-classicism in art, III 369a, 370a, 370b, 371a
Fleming, J. M., social welfare, IV 280a, 280b
Flemming, W. (1843–1906)
cell division, II 286b
chromosomes, II 286b, 287a–287b
genetic continuity, II 286b, 287a–287b
Fletcher, Angus, symbolism, IV 342a
Fletcher, Giles (the elder) (1548?–1611)
baroque in literature, I 193a, 193b
mythology, III 295a–295b
Fletcher, Giles (the younger) (1588?–1623), mythology, III 295a
Fletcher, John (1579–1625), baroque in literature, I 192a
Fletcher, Joseph, equity, II 153b
Fletcher, Phineas (1582–1650)
baroque in literature, I 191a
mythology, III 295a
Flint, Robert (1838–1910),
agnosticism, I 17a
progress, III 634b
Flood
Aristotle, I 625b
Blasius of Parma, II 35b
catastrophism, IV 419b
Cosmic Fall, I 505a, 506a, 507a, 508b, 509a, 509b, 511a
cycles, I 625a, 625b

evolutionism, II 176b, 180a
historiography, II 472b, 487b
linguistics, IV 423b, 424a, 426a
mountains in literature, III 255a, 255b, 256b, 257b
mythology, III 276a, 278b, 279a–280b
Plato, I 625a
spontaneous generation, IV 308a
sublime in external nature, IV 333b
uniformitarianism, IV 419b, 423b, 424a, 426a
Florence, I 429b–430b
art, II 300a–302b, 303b
balance of power, I 180b–181b
casuistry, I 260b
genius, II 300b–302b, 303b
idealism, I 593a
Platonism, III 506a, 506b–507a, 507b, 510a, 511a–511b, 512b, 515a–515b
Renaissance, IV 122a–124a
Floresta, Nísia
Comte and, III 539b–540a
humanitarianism, III 540a
Napoleon I and, III 540a
Oliveira Lima, III 539b
positivism, III 539b–540a
religion, III 540a
Vaux and, III 540a
Flourens, Pierre (1794–1867), Man-Machine, III 142b
Flournoy, Théodore (1854–1920), psychology, IV 12b–13a
Fludd, Robert (1574–1637),
alchemy, I 32b, 33b
harmony, II 390a; IV 41b
hierarchy, II 437a
Islam, II 646b
linguistics, III 74b
metaphysical imagination, III 212a
music, II 390a; III 271a
Foch, General Ferdinand (1851–1929), war, IV 504a
Focillon, H., aesthetics, II 221a
Fock, V. A., indeterminacy, II 591a
Fodor, J. (1752–1828)
language, II 668b
Foerster, Norman
literary criticism, I 603a
realism in literature, IV 54a
Foggazzaro, Antonio (1842–1911)
modernism, I 424a
mysticism, I 424a

Fogle, R. H., organicism, III 426b

Fogliano, Lodovico, music, III 261b

Foigny, Gabriel de, Utopia, IV 462b

Fol, Hermann (1845–1892)
cell division, II 287a
genetic continuity, II 287a

Folengo, Teofilo (1496?–1544), wisdom of the fool, IV 519b

Foliage masks, I 341b, 342a

Foliot, Gilbert, nationalism, III 319b

Folk songs, II 317b, 323b

Folklore, Aarne, III 238b, 239a
Afanasyev, III 239a
Faust (legend), III 245b, 248b
Finland, III 238b, 239a
Frazer, James, III 238b
Germany, III 265a
Grimm, Jacob Ludwig Karl, III 236b, 239a, 239b
Grimm, Wilhelm Karl, III 236b, 239a
Herder, IV 209a
impressionism, II 581a, 582b
millenarianism, III 224b
morphology, III 240a
motif, III 235a–235b, 238a–240a, 240b, 241b
music, III 265a
mythology, III 275a–275b, 279a, 304a, 306a, 307a, 307b, 314b, 315a, 315b, 316a–316b
nationalism, III 337b
Propp, III 239a
reformation, IV 60b
romanticism, IV 207a, 208b, 209a
taxonomy, III 240a
theriophily, IV 384b
Thompson, Stith, III 238b, 239a–239b, 241b
Tomashevsky, III 239a
U.S.S.R., III 239a, 333b
Volksgeist, IV 491a, 492a, 494a, 495a
witchcraft, IV 521a, 521b, 522b

Fonseca, Marshal Diodoro de (1827–1892), positivism, III 543a

Fontaine, Pierre-François (1762–1853), neo-classicism in art, III 365b

Fontana, Francesco (1580–1626), optics, III 420a

Fonte, Bartolomeo della, poetics, III 529a

Fontego, Sylvestro Ganassi del, genius, II 320a

Fontenelle, Bernard Le Bovier de (1657–1757), I 77b, 79a–79b, 80b, 85a
Bacon and, I 176b
Chain of Being, I 327b, 332a
Comte and, III 536b
cosmic voyages, I 525a, 528a
deism, I 651a
Epicureanism, II 137b
genius, II 324a–324b
morality, III 644a–644b
mountains in literature, III 582b
music, II 324a–324b
mythology, III 301a, 301b, 302a, 302b
Nature, I 332a
passions, III 644b
poetics, III 530a
positivism, III 536b
progress, III 644a–644b
rationalism, III 301a, 301b, 302a, 302b
skepticism, I 401b
virtuoso, IV 488b, 489a

Fool, see Wisdom of the fool

Force
equality, II 138b
Hobbes, IV 484a
human nature, III 573b
law, III 2b
Lenin, III 156a
Machiavelli, III 116b, 122a; IV 315a
Marxism, III 155b, 156a, 169b
matter, III 192a, 194b, 195a, 196a
Newton, III 194b, 195a
progress, III 641b, 642b
relativity, IV 82b, 90a
State, IV 313a, 313b, 315a, 315b, 316b, 317a, 318a, 318b
virtù, IV 479a, 484a, 485a

Ford, Henry (1863–1947), natural liberty, II 66b

Ford, John (1586?– after 1638), baroque in literature, I 191a

Foreign policy, Machiavelli, III 117a, 122a–123a; IV 484a

Forensic rhetoric, IV 168b

Forest conservation, I 473a, 474a, 475b–476a

Forgeries, historiography, II 481b, 485a, 485b

Formalism
aesthetics, II 219b, 220a, 221a

beauty, I 210b
content, II 221a
evolution of literature, II 173b
forms, II 219b, 220a, 221a
indeterminacy, II 588b, 590b–491a, 592a
Kant, I 104b
Le Corbusier, II 221a
mathematics, II 588b
matter, III 187a
mythology, III 316a–316b
naturalism in art, III 341a, 341b
organicism, III 424a
Orientalism, III 430b
Platonism, III 518b
symbolism, IV 343a, 343b

Forms
mathematics, III 176b
metaphor, III 200a
Neo-Platonism, III 372b, 374a, 375a, 375b
organicism, III 421a, 421b, 424a, 424b, 425b, 426b
Plato, I 271b, 505b, 571b–572a, 639a, 672a–672b; III 188a–188b, 211a, 353b, 354a, 464b–465a, 498b–499a, 499b, 500b, 501a, 502a, 504b, 507a, 508a, 577a, 628b–629a; IV 3b, 4a, 6a, 47a–47b, 49b, 369a, 431b
Platonism, III 498b–499a, 499b, 500b, 501a, 502a, 503b, 504a, 504b, 507a, 508b, 513b
plentitude of, I 325b–326a
Plotinus, III 423b; IV 8b
Socrates, III 499a; IV 436a
Stoicism, III 504a; IV 319b

Forms in aesthetics, II 216a–225b
Abélard, II 217b
abstraction, II 223b
Alain of Lille, II 217b
Albert the Great, II 222b
Alberti, II 218a–218b
ambiguity, II 216a
architecture, II 216a, 216b, 217a, 218b, 221b, 224a
Aristotelianism, II 220a–220b, 222b
Aristotle, II 216b, 217a, 222a, 222b
arrangement, II 216a, 216b–219b
art, II 216a–225b
Aschenbrenner, II 219a
Augustinianism, II 222b
Austria, II 223b
Baldinucci, II 222b

Bell, II 219a, 221a
Bembo, II 218b
Bernard of Clairvaux, II 218a
Blondel, II 218b
Bosse, II 218b
Cardano, II 218b
Cassirer, II 222a
Castelvetro, II 220a
causation, II 223a
Cicero, II 217a, 219b–220a
Clarembaldus of Arras, II 217b
classicism, II 223b
color, II 221b, 222a, 224a
commonly accepted, II 224a
communications, II 219b
conceptual essence, II 216b, 222a–223a
context, II 216a, 220a, 220b, 221a
convention, II 224a
Crates, II 220a
crystalline, II 223b
Danti, II 222b
De Quincy, II 218b
Demetrius, II 219b, 220a
Deonna, II 223b
disposition, II 216a, 216b–219b
drawing, II 221b–222b
Du Fresnoy, II 218b
dualism, II 218a, 220b, 221a
Duns Scotus, II 217b–218a
empathy, II 223b
entelechy, II 216b, 223a
evil, II 163a
evolutionism, II 175b
Félibien, II 218b
Ficino, II 218a
Fiedler, II 223b
Focillon, II 221a
Formalism, II 219b, 220a, 221a
formism, II 221a
Fracastoro, II 220a
France, II 216a, 218b, 221a, 221b–222a, 224a
Franciscans, II 222b
gardening, II 224a
genius, II 223b
Germany, II 216a
Ghyka, II 219a
Great Britain, II 219a, 221a
Greece (ancient), II 216b, 217a–217b, 218a, 219a, 220a, 222a, 222b–223a
Grosseteste, II 218a, 224b
haptic, II 223b
harmony, II 216b, 217a, 217b, 219a, 222a
Heracleodor, II 220a

Herbart, II 218b, 223b
Hildebrand, II 223b
idea, II 223a, 544a–544b, 545a, 545b
impressionism, II 219b
Isidore of Seville, II 217b
Italy, II 216a, 218a–218b, 221b, 224a
Kames, II 221a
Kandinsky, II 221a
Kant, II 216b, 218b, 221a, 223a–223b
kinesthetic, II 223b
knowledge, II 223a, 223b
Lalande, II 221b
Le Corbusier, II 219a, 221a
Lebrun, II 221b
light, II 218a
literature, II 216a, 219b–220b, 224a
luster, II 222b
Malevitch, II 221a
Marburg School, II 223a
Mathieu of Vendôme, II 220a
matter, II 216a, 216b, 221b–222a, 222b
meanings of the term, II 216a
Middle Ages, II 217b–218a, 220a, 222a–222b, 223a, 224a
mind, II 216b, 223a–223b, 224b
Mondrian, II 221a, 222b
Monet, II 220b
Monod-Herzen, II 219a
music, II 216a, 216b, 219b, 220b, 224a
Neo-Platonism, II 221a
Netherlands, II 221a
Nicholas of Cusa, II 223a
Nicholson, II 222b
optical, II 223b
oratory, II 220a
order of parts, II 216a, 216b–219b
organicism, II 223b
painting, II 217a, 219b, 220b, 221b, 224a
paleography, II 219b
Palladio, II 218b
perennial philosophy, III 458b
Philodemus, II 219b
Pico della Mirandola, II 218a
Piles, II 222a
Pino, II 221b
Plato, II 217a, 221a, 223a
Platonism, II 218a
Plotinus, II 217a–217b, 218a
pluralism, II 223b

poetry, II 216a, 291b–220a, 224a
Poland, II 216a, 219a, 221a, 222a
porcelain, II 224a
Porrée, II 217b, 224a–224b
Posidonius, II 219b
pottery, II 224a
Poussin, II 218b
primitive, II 223b
printing, II 224a
proportion, II 217b, 218a, 222b
Pseudo-Dionysius, II 218a, 222b
purism, II 221a
Pythagoreans, II 217a, 219a
Quintilian, II 219b
Renaissance, II 218a–218b, 220a, 221b, 222a, 223a
Richelet, II 222b
Riehl, II 223b
Robert, II 221b
Robortello, II 220a
romanticism, II 224a
Rome (ancient), II 216a, 219b–220a
Rubenists, II 222a
Russia, II 216a, 221a
Saint Augustine, II 217b, 218a, 219a
Saint Bonaventura, II 219b, 222b, 224b
Saint Thomas Aquinas, II 218a
scholasticism, II 217b, 219a, 220a, 222b
Schlosser, II 223b
sculpture, II 216b, 217a, 220b, 221b, 224a, 224b
senses, II 216a–216b, 219b–221b
sophism, II 219b
space, II 223a; IV 296a
Spain, II 216a
Stoicism, II 217a
structure, II 219a
Strzemiński, II 222a
substance, II 223a
suprematism, II 221a
symmetry, II 217b
tactile, II 223b
Testelin, II 218b, 221b–222a
time, II 223a, 223b
tinctorial, II 224a
tools, II 223b–224a
tradition, II 224a
tragedy, II 224a
Ulrich of Strassburg, II 222b
unism, II 221a
U.S., II 219a
Vasari, II 221b

vision, II 223b
Vitruvius, II 217a
William of Ockham, II 218a
Winckelmann, II 218b
Witkiewicz, II 219a
Wölfflin, II 223b
Worringer, II 223b
Zimmermann, II 217a, 218b
Zuccaro, II 221b, 222b
Formschneider, Hieronymus, genius, II 318a
music, II 318a
Forssman, E., iconography, II 539b
Forster, E. M., Utopia, IV 464a
Forster, Georg (1754–1794), revolution, IV 158b
Fortas, Abe
civil disobedience, I 439b–440b
King and, I 440a
Fortescue, John (1394?–?1476)
analogy, I 69a
common law, II 695a
Fortitude, temperance, IV 366b, 368b, 369b, 370a–375b, 377a, 377b
Fortoul, Hippolyte, realism in literature, IV 52a
Fortunate Islands (myth), III 591a
Fortune, II 225b–236a
as the absence of intentionality, II 232b
Adrasteia, II 229a
Alberti, II 235a; IV 478a
angels, II 232b–233a
Apuleius, II 228a, 232a
Aristotle, II 226a, 227a–228b, 229b, 231b, 233a
art, II 230a, 232a, 234a, 235a
astrology, II 232a, 232b, 233a, 233b, 234b, 235a
atomism, II 226a
Augustinianism, II 230b
beauty, II 232a
birth, II 226b, 228a, 228b, 232a, 233b
Boccaccio, II 233b–234a
Boethius, II 231a–232a, 234b
Bracciolini, II 235a
causation, II 226a, 226b, 227a–233b, 234b–236a
celestial spheres, II 228b, 229a, 229b, 232a, 233b
Chalcidius, II 229a–230a, 233a
chance images, I 340b, 341a, 341b
Christianity, II 229a–236a
cosmology, II 226a

courage, II 234a
Creation, II 226a, 226b, 231a
cycles, II 228a, 229b
Dante, II 233a–233b, 234b
death, II 226b
Democritus, II 226a–226b
destiny, II 225b, 228a, 233b
determinism, II 229b, 230a, 230b, 232a, 233b, 234b
dignity, II 231b; IV 142a, 143a
divination, II 226a, 227a, 230b, 231a, 232a, 236a
Epicureanism, II 231a
ethics, II 226b, 227a, 227b, 233a
evil, II 234a
faith, II 232a
fame, II 234a
Fates, II 229a
fear, II 234b
Firmicius Maternus, II 232a
free will, II 226b–231b, 234a, 236a
freedom, II 227a, 229b
friendship, II 228a
glory, II 231b
God, II 226b–231a, 232a–235a, 236a
good, II 227b–229a, 231b–235b
grace, II 233b
Greece (ancient), II 225b–228b
happiness, II 227a, 228a, 235a
harmony, II 229b
Heimarmene, II 229a
Hera, II 229a
heredity, II 228a
Hermes Trismegistus, II 232a
historiography, II 470b
human nature, III 572a
humanism, II 225b, 235a, 236a, 519b
impulse, II 227b, 232b–233b, 234a, 234b, 235a
indeterminacy, II 225b, 226a–226b, 228b, 230b
instinct, II 227b
irrationality, II 227b
justice, II 233b
knowledge, II 226a–226b, 229b, 232b
law, II 226a, 226b, 227a, 228a, 229a, 229b, 231b, 235b
logic, II 230a, 230b, 231a
love, II 234a
luck, II 225b, 227a–227b, 234a–234b
Machiavelli, II 235b–236a;

129

IV 479b, 480b–481b, 482a, 482b

Martianus Capella, II 229a

Middle Ages, II 227b, 232a

mind, II 226a, 227a, 229a, 232a, 232b, 233a

moon, II 233b

morality, II 229b, 231b–232a, 234a, 234b–235a

motif, III 239b

motion, II 229b, 231b

mythology, II 226b, 228a, 229a

Nature, II 225b, 226a–227b, 228b–230a, 231a, 233a, 233b

necessity, II 225b, 226b, 228a, 229b, 230a, 230b, 232a, 234a; IV 481b

Nemesis, II 229a

Neo-Platonism, II 229a

observation, II 226a

Orphism, II 226b

passions, II 233b

Petrarch, II 234a–235a; IV 478a

Plato, II 226b, 231b–232a

pleasure, II 234a

politics, II 235b–236a

Pontano, II 235a

power, II 226a, 228a–230a, 231a, 231b, 233b, 235a–236a; IV 480b

predestination, II 225b

probability, II 226a

Proclus, II 228h

providence, II 225b–236a

prudence, II 235a

psychology, II 227b

punishment, II 229b

reason, II 225b–226a, 226b, 227b, 233a, 234a

reincarnation, II 226b, 227a

religion, II 227a

Renaissance, II 232a; IV 142a, 143a

reputation, II 228b

rewards, II 229b

Rome (ancient), II 226a

Saint Albertus Magnus, II 232a, 232b, 233a

Saint Augustine, II 230a–231a, 231b, 232a

Saint Thomas Aquinas, II 232a–233a

Salutati, II 234b

scholasticism, II 227b, 230a

science, II 225b

Seneca, II 228a; IV 478a

Simplicius, II 228a, 228b, 233a

space, II 231b

stars, II 227a, 229b, 235a

Stoicism, II 228a, 230a,

232a, 234a, 234b

success, II 228b, 233a

superstition, II 226a, 234b

teleology, II 231a

time, II 231b, 232b, 233a

tragedy, II 228a

tragic sense, IV 413a, 416b

universe, II 225b–236a

wealth, II 228a, 228b, 231b

Zeus (myth), II 229a

See also Virtù

Fosdick, Harry Emerson, heresy, II 430b

Fossils

catastrophism, IV 418b, 419b, 420a, 421a, 421b, 422a

evolutionism, II 176b, 180b

geology, III 255b

language, II 660b

linguistic paleontology, IV 425a

linguistics, IV 425a, 425b

mountains in literature, III 255b

species, II 618a, 660b

uniformitarianism, IV 418b, 419b, 420a, 421a, 421b, 422a, 425a, 425b

Foster, John (1770–1843), romanticism, IV 191b

Foster, W. Z. (1881–1961), Marxism, III 156b

Foucault, Jean Bernard Léon (1819–1868), relativity, IV 80b

Foucault, Michel

irrationalism, II 637b

structuralism, IV 323a, 328b–329a, 329b

Foucher, Simon (1644–1696)

philosophy, III 458a, 461a

skepticism, IV 245a–246a

Foulcher of Chartres, historiography, II 473b

Foundations, philanthropy, III 489b, 492a–492b

Fourier, Francois Marie Charles (1772–1837)

anarchy, I 73a; III 22a

axiomatization, I 166b

class, I 446a

economic history, II 60a

happiness, II 380a

individualism, II 595a

law, III 22a

liberalism, III 58a

love, III 104a

natural rights, III 22a

perfectibility, III 470b

progress, III 640b–641a

romanticism, IV 203b

socialism, IV 289b, 290a,

293a, 293b

society, III 22a

Utopia, III 22a; IV 463a

utopianism, I 433b; II 380a

Fourier, Joseph (1768–1830)

mathematics, III 174b, 175b

Fourier transformation, II 588b

Fourmont, Étienne (1683–1745)

China, I 367a

mythology, III 302b

Fourth dimension, IV 84b, 85b, 88b, 91a

Fowler, H. W. (1858–1933), irony, II 632b

Fowler, O. S., phrenology, IV 23b

Fox, Charles James (1749–1806)

balance of power, I 187a

French Revolution, IV 156a–156b

Fox, George (1624–1691), peace, III 441a

Foxe, John (1516–1587), historiography, II 484a; IV 149a–149b

Foxwell, H. S., economic history, II 60a

Fra Angelico (1387–1455), neo-classicists' attitude to, III 370a

Fracastoro, Girolamo (1483–1553)

aesthetics, II 220a

disease, II 399b

genius, II 293b

mimesis, III 227b, 228b

mountains in literature, III 255b

ut pictura poesis, IV 467b

France

absolutism, I 593b

academic freedom, I 16b

aesthetics, II 216a, 218b, 221a, 221b–222a, 224a; IV 354b–355b

anticlericalism, III 538a

architecture, I 398b

art, II 297b, 298b, 300b, 305a, 614a; III 366a

balance of power, I 181a–181b, 182b–184a, 186a–187b

baroque in literature, I 189b, 190b–191a, 192a–192b, 193b, 194a, 195a

Buddhism, I 256a

Capuchins, I 394b

catastrophism, IV 420a, 421a, 421b, 422a

cave art, I 351a

city, I 429a, 432a–434a

class, I 441b, 443b; IV

500a

classicism, I 449b–455b; III 366a, 483a, 483b

Code Napoléon, II 656a; III 30b, 32b

common law, II 691b, 692b, 693a, 693b, 694a

communism, III 334a

conservation, I 473a, 477b, 480a, 480b, 481a, 482a, 483a, 484b

Conspiracy of Equals, II 145b

Constitution, I 491a–491b, 661b–662a; III 7b, 25b

constitutionalism, I 404a–404b; III 7b

cosmic images, I 517a–517b, 522a, 523a

cosmic voyages, I 527a, 530a–531b

Counter-Enlightenment, II 101a, 103b, 104b, 105a, 106a, 106b, 107a, 108a, 109a–112a

crisis in history, I 590a, 591b, 593a, 593b, 595a

Declaration of the Rights of Man and the Citizen, I 660b–661a; II 144b, 157b; III 7b, 11b, 12a, 21b, 23a, 25b

deism, I 648b, 649a, 651a, 651b

democracy, I 656a, 657b, 658b, 660b–662a

despotism, II 1a–1b, 2a, 3a–4a, 7b–15a

determinism, II 30b

drama, III 529b, 531a

economic history, II 45a, 47a, 49b, 57b

empathy, II 88a–88b

encyclopedias, I 464b

Enlightenment, II 89a, 89b, 91a, 91b, 94b, 98b

epistemology, II 515b

epistolography, II 515b

equality, II 138a, 139b, 141b, 143a, 143b–145b

ethics, III 444b

evolution of literature, II 171b–172b

existentialism, II 190b, 191a, 194b

expressionism, II 207a, 208b

Faust (legend), III 250b

February revolution (1848), IV 158a, 158b

freedom, II 250b, 251a

Freud, IV 96b–97a

Fifth Republic, III 534b

Gallicanism, I 399b–400a

genius, II 294a–294b, 297b, 298b, 300b, 305a, 315b, 317b, 322b–323a
geology, III 256a–256b
Great Britain, III 537a; IV 106b
guilds, II 300b
harmony, II 388b
historiography, II 485a–485b, 486a, 494b
history, III 366a
Huguenots, IV 113a, 119a
humanism, II 515a, 521b, 522b; IV 131a
ideal, II 549a, 549b–550a
impressionism, II 567b–583b
international peace, III 449a, 453b, 455b, 456a
intolerance, IV 113a, 119a
Jansenism, I 400a
Jesuits expelled, I 403b
July revolution (1830), IV 158a, 158b
justice, II 657b
language, II 670a, 671b
Latin America, III 539b
law, II 250b, 251a, 673b, 687b, 690a; III 3b, 5b, 7b, 11b, 12a, 28a, 30a–30b, 32b
leadership, III 337a
League of Peace, III 449a
liberalism, III 45b, 52b
literary criticism, I 596b–601a, 604b–605b, 606b
literature, IV 331a–332b
love, III 97b–100a, 102a, 103a
Machiavellism, III 117a–119b, 120b, 123a–123b
Man-Machine, III 139a–139b
Marxism, I 664a–664b; III 150b–151a, 156b, 158b, 165a, 167a, 167b
materialism, II 450a, 450b, 451a–451b; IV 106b
mathematics, III 178b
medieval science, II 196a, 197b, 201b–202b, 203b, 204a–204b
methodology, III 382a
mimesis, III 227b, 228a, 228b
modernism, I 419b, 420a, 420b, 421b–422b, 423b, 424a. 426a
mountains in literature, III 256a–256b
music, II 315b, 317b, 322b–323a, 388b; III 267a, 271b
mythology, III 289a, 289b, 290a, 291a–291b, 292b,

295a, 298b–299a, 304a, 305b, 306b, 315b
nationalism, II 690a; III 319a–322b, 326b, 327a, 328a, 330b, 333b, 334a–338b; IV 125a, 493b
natural law, III 21a–22a
natural liberty, II 62a, 69a
naturalism, IV 53b, 54a
naturalism in art, III 339a, 341a
Neapolitan revolution (1820), IV 158a
neo-classicism in art, III 366a, 368b
novel, II 172b
numbers, III 404a
oratory, II 172a
organicism, III 424b
Orientalism, III 429a, 432a
Pact of Paris, III 452a
painting, III 366a; IV 467a, 468b, 471b, 473b, 475a
Pan-Latinism, III 338b
peace, III 444b
peasantry, IV 500a
periodization in history, III 478a, 479b
periodization in literary history, III 481b, 482a, 483a, 483b, 485b
philanthropy, III 489b
philosophy, III 366a; IV 106b
Platonism, III 506a, 507a–507b, 514a, 520b, 521b
poetry, III 529b, 530a, 531a; IV 467a, 468b, 471b, 473b, 475a
politics, III 21b, 366a, 676b
positivism, III 532b, 537a, 538a, 539b, 542b, 543b; IV 532b, 533b, 534b, 537a, 538a, 539b, 542b, 543b
pragmatism, III 557a, 557b, 560a, 564a–566a
predestination, II 30b
primitivism, III 593a, 597a, 601b, 602a, 602b
private property, III 654b, 655b, 656a
probability, III 620a
progress, III 538a, 634a, 639b, 642b, 643a, 643b, 644b
proletariat, III 537a
prophecy, III 667a, 668a
protest movements, III 671b–672b, 673a, 676b
psychology, IV 11a, 12a, 12b, 13a, 21b, 22b
psychopathology, III 537a
Quietism, I 595a

radicalism, III 52b, 673a
Ramism, IV 44b, 45a
realism in literature, III 483b; IV 51b–52b, 53b, 54a
Reformation, I 394b, 395b; IV 68a
religion, I 397b–398a; III 543b; IV 100a, 106b, 107b, 109a, 113a, 116b, 119a
Renaissance, II 294a–294b; III 479b, 483b; IV 121b, 124a, 124b–125b, 131a
revisionism, IV 272a, 273b, 274a
revolution, IV 155a, 156a, 156b, 158a, 159b, 160a, 164a
rhetoric, IV 171b–172a, 172b
romanticism, III 304a, 305b, 306b, 483b, 485b; IV 187a, 187b, 189b, 190a, 191a, 192a, 193a, 193b, 194a, 196a, 196b, 198a, 198b, 199a, 199b, 200a, 203a, 203b, 204a, 205a, 206b, 207a
sacred, II 512a
satire, IV 214b
science, IV 106b
scientific method, IV 106b
skepticism, IV 242b–245b, 248a
slavery, II 144b
social contract, IV 253b, 254a, 261a, 263a
social welfare, IV 277b
socialism, III 165a; IV 272a, 273b, 274a, 285a, 288a–289a, 291b, 292a, 293b
space, IV 300b–301a, 302a
State, I 397b–398a, 398b–400a, 656a, 657b, 658b, 660b–662a; IV 315a, 316a
structuralism, IV 323a, 324b, 327b–329b
style, IV 331a, 331b, 332b
sublime in external nature, IV 333a–333b, 334b
suffrage, I 662a
symbolism, III 483b; IV 339a–344a, 345a
syndicalism, III 676b
taste, IV 354b–355b
technology, IV 362a, 363a, 363b
temperance, IV 371b, 372b, 373a, 374b, 375a, 378a
theology, II 30b
Third Republic, III 537a
time, IV 401b
toleration, I 401b; IV 112b–

121a
tragedy, II 171b–172a
truth, IV 106b
Tunisia, III 537a
Ultramontanism, I 405a
uniformitarianism, IV 420a, 421a, 421b, 422a
utilitarianism, IV 444a
utility, IV 453a
Utopia, IV 462a, 463b
virtuoso, IV 486a, 488b
Volksgeist, IV 493b, 494a, 495b
vox populi, IV 499a, 500a
war, IV 500b, 501a, 502b, 503a, 504a, 504b, 505b, 506a
welfare state, IV 510b, 514a
Weltschmerz, IV 204a
witchcraft, IV 522b
women, IV 526a, 528a
France, Anatole (1844–1924),
    aesthetics, II 575b
    criticism, II 575b–576a
    equality, III 11b
    impressionism, II 575b–576a
    irony, II 632b, 633a
    justice, II 655b
    law, III 11b
    literary criticism, I 597b, 600b, 605a
    Schlegel and, IV 190a, 192a
Francesco di Giorgio (1439–1502)
    city, I 431a
    Pythagorean cosmos, IV 41b
Francesco de Hollanda, classification of the arts, I 460a
Franciabigio, Francesco (1482?–1525)
    art, II 302a
    genius, II 302a
Francis of Assisi, Saint (1182–1226)
    ethics, IV 73a
    heresy, II 418a, 419b, 420a, 420b, 421a, 421b
    history, I 383b
    humanism, IV 132b
    humility, IV 64b
    love, III 98b; IV 65a
    Nature, IV 127b
    philanthropy, III 489a
    poverty, III 668a, 668b; IV 64b
    prophecy, III 668a, 668b
    reformation, IV 64b–65a
    wisdom of the fool, IV 517b
Francis I, King (1494–1547),
    balance of power, I 182a
    hierarchy, II 436b

131

Platonism, III 507a–507b
Franciscans
abstraction, I 4b–5a
aesthetics, II 222b
antichrist, II 421b
China, I 357a
Community (Conventuals),
II 420b–421b
Fraticelli, II 421b
heresy, II 417b, 418b, 419a,
419b, 420b–421b, 422a
history, I 383b
holy, II 513a
love, III 98b
Observantine section of, I
394b
poverty, II 420b–421b
prophecy, III 667a, 667b,
668a–669b
reformation, IV 65a, 65b
Roman Catholic Church, II
421a–421b
socialism, IV 286b, 287a
Spirituals, II 420b–421b
Franciscus de Marchia, mechanical science, II 201b–
202a
Francke, August Hermann
(1663–1727)
Counter-Enlightenment, II
105a
Pietism, III 493b–495a
Franco, Francisco (1892–
), totalitarianism, IV
409b
Franco of Cologne (fl. 1260),
music, II 314b
François I, King (1494–
1547)
iconography, II 529b, 538a
wisdom of the fool, IV 516b
Franco-Prussian War (1870),
Burckhardt, IV 159a
revolution, IV 159a
Francus (myth), III 287a
Frank, E., Pythagoreans, IV
36a
Frank, Jerome (1889–1957),
common law, III 31b
equity, II 153b
law, II 153b; III 4b
pragmatism, III 553b
Frank, Johann Peter (1745–
1821), disease, II 403a
Frank, Philipp
positivism, III 546a, 548a
relativity, IV 79b
Frankenstein legend, III 245b
Frankfort, H., mythology, III
311b
Frankfurter, Felix (1882–
1965)
academic freedom, I 12a
law, III 12a

Frankl, Paul (1878–1962),
Gothic, II 369a, 372b, 373b
Franklin, Benjamin (1706–
1790)
Chain of Being, IV 22a
deism, I 651b
democracy, I 660b
Diderot and, III 603b
Enlightenment, IV 22a, 22b
equality, IV 22a
human nature, IV 22a
Jefferson and, IV 22a–22b
longevity, III 92a
morality, IV 22b
nationalism, III 325b
philanthropy, III 490b–
491a
philoprogenitiveness, III
603b
pragmatism, III 553b; IV
22a
primitivism, III 598b, 600b,
603b
psychology, IV 20a, 22a–
22b
religion, III 603b
sin, IV 22a
work, IV 534b
Fraud
common law, II 695a
Hobbes, IV 484a
law, II 688b
Rome (ancient), II 688b
virtù, IV 477b, 484a
Fraunhofer, Joseph von
(1787–1826)
cosmology, I 552b–553a
mathematics, III 179a
Fraunhofer lines, cosmology, I
552b–553a
Frazer, James George (1854–
1941)
Eden myth, III 89b
folklore, III 238b
longevity, III 89b
motif, III 238b, 240a
mythology, III 240a, 277a,
278b, 279a, 279b, 280b,
281a, 282b
religion, IV 95b–96a
Fréart, Roland, mythology, III
298a, 298b, 299a
Fréart de Chambray, ideal, II
549b
Frederick I, Emperor (1123?–
1190)
historiography, II 474a
law, II 689b
as legend, III 224b, 225a
millenarianism, III 224b,
225a
nationalism, III 320b
Frederick II, Emperor (1194–
1250)

heresy, II 425b
humanism, II 515a
law, II 689b
Machiavellism, III 121b–
122a
mythology, III 287b–288a
prophecy, III 668b, 669a
socialism, IV 286b
witchcraft, IV 522a
Frederick III, Emperor (1463–
1525)
heresy, II 421b
prophecy, III 668b, 669a
reformation, IV 66a
Frederick the Great (1712–
1786)
balance of power, I 186a
Counter-Enlightenment, II
103b, 104b, 106b
Enlightenment, II 90b
historiography, II 493b–
494a, 495a, 496b
Jesuits, I 403b
Machiavelli and, IV 484a
Machiavellism, III 120a,
121b–122a
perfectibility, III 470a
periodization in literary
history, III 482a, 483a
probability, III 609b
virtù, IV 484a
war, IV 501a, 502b, 504a,
505a
Frederick William I, King
(1688–1740), Pietism, I
361b
Frederick William II, King
(1744–1797), casuistry, I
263a
Frederick William IV, King
(1795–1861), conserva-
tism, I 482b
Free Religious Association, III
434a–434b, 436a
Free Spirit
heresy, II 422a–423a
Meister Eckhart, II 422b
millenarianism, III 225a
papacy, II 422b–423a
socialism, IV 286b
Free will, II 134b–138a, 236b–
248b
agnosticism, II 246b
analogy, II 248b
Aristotelianism, II 245a
Aristotle, II 135a, 135b,
137a, 236b–237a, 243a–
243b
Arminius, II 245b
astronomy, II 245b
atheism, II 137b, 246b–
247a
atomism, II 135b–137b,
237b, 244a, 245b

attitude, II 237a–237b
Augustinianism, II 246b
Berkeley, II 246a
Bible, II 244b
Boethius, II 231a, 231b
Bradley, II 240b–241b
Calvin, II 245a–245b
Campbell, II 241a–241b
causation, II 135b–137a,
238a, 238b, 240a–241a,
245a–246a, 247b, 248a
Chalcidius, II 229a, 229b–
230a
chance, II 226b, 227a,
228a–231b, 234a, 236a,
240a
choice, II 237a, 238a–238b,
239a, 241a, 241b, 243a,
244a, 244b, 248a–248b
Christianity, I 394b; II 137b,
237b–238a, 244a–245b
Cicero, II 137a, 137b
Cleanthes, II 237b
compulsion, II 237a, 238a,
239a, 240a, 241a
constraint, II 242b
cosmos, II 243b, 244a
Counter-Enlightenment, II
107b–108a
culture, II 247a
cycles, I 623b
Darwin, II 588a
defined, II 242a
Democritus, II 135b, 136a–
136b
Descartes, II 239b, 245b,
246a
desire, II 237a, 240a, 240b,
241b, 244a
determinism, II 26b, 27a,
29b, 30a, 135a–137a,
236b–242a, 247b–248a
dignity, IV 142b, 143a
Diogenes Laërtius, II 137b,
243b
dualism, II 246a
duty, II 241b
electrons, II 588a
emotion, II 237b, 238b–
239a, 244a
Enlightenment, II 92a
Epicureanism, II 244a
Epicurus, II 134b–137b,
237b, 243b–244a, 245b
ethics, II 236b–237a; IV
319b
evil, II 236b–237b, 238a
evolutionism, II 247a
existentialism, II 246b
fate, II 226b–231b, 234a,
236a, 243b–245b
Faust (legend), III 256b
Fichte, II 246b
Ficino, IV 131b

foreknowledge, II 238a
fortune, II 226b–231b, 234a, 236a
Freud, II 246b
friendship, II 238b
Gnosticism, II 244a
God, I 586b; II 237b, 238a, 240b, 243b–248b, 343a, 345a
good, II 237a–238b, 243a, 243b, 244b, 245a; IV 176b
grace, II 238a, 244b, 245a, 245b
Greece (ancient), II 135a, 245b
happiness, II 238a
harmony, II 236b
hate, II 238b
hedonism, II 137b
Hegel, II 246b, 408b, 409a, 414a
heresy, II 417a
Hinduism, IV 232b
Hobbes, II 246a
humanism, II 245b; IV 131a–131b, 132a
Hume, II 238a, 239a, 239b–240a, 246a
ignorance, II 236b, 237a, 238b
immorality, II 240b, 241b
impulse, II 237a
inclination, II 240a, 240b
indeterminacy, II 587a, 588a, 589b
intention, II 237b
international peace, III 452b
Islam, II 29b, 245a, 345a, 641b; IV 230b
James, III 562a, 563a, 563b
judgment, II 237b, 238a, 239a, 240a–240b, 243a
Julian, II 244b
Jung, II 246b
justice, II 236b, 653a, 656a, 656b
Kant, II 240a–242a, 246a–247a; III 555b, 562a, 640b
Kierkegaard, II 246b
kingship, II 242b
knowledge, II 236b, 238b, 239a, 239b, 241a, 241b, 246b, 247b
law, II 237a, 240a, 240b, 241a, 242b, 247a
Leibniz, II 239a
libertarianism, II 240b–241b, 242a, 248a
liberty, II 239b–240a, 241a, 248a
linguistics, II 247a–248b
Locke, II 239a–239b
logic, II 238b

love, II 237b, 238a, 238b, 244a
Lucretius, II 134b–135a, 136a, 136b, 137b, 237b
Luther, II 245a–245b
Machiavelli, II 236a
Manetti, IV 131a–131b
Manichaeism, II 244a
Man-Machine, III 135a, 139a, 140b–141a
Marcus Aurelius, II 243b
Marx, II 246b
Marxism, II 246b
materialism, II 237a
mathematics, II 245b, 246b
Melden, II 241b–242
Mill, II 241a
mind, II 238b, 239a, 245a, 246a
Mohammed, II 245a
morality, II 237a–238a, 240a–241b, 242b, 247a
mythology, III 287b, 288a
natural law, II 240a–240b; III 14b, 15a
Nature, II 237a, 237b, 238b, 245b, 246a, 246b
necessity, II 237b, 238a, 239a, 240b, 243a, 243b
Neo-Aristotelianism, II 245a
Neo-Platonism, II 244a, 244b, 245a
Newton, II 246a
Nicholas V (Pope), II 137b
Nowell-Smith, II 241b
pain, II 137b
Papini, III 563b
passions, II 236b, 242b
Pelagianism, II 245a
Pelagius, II 244b; III 469a
perfectibility, III 467a, 469a
Philo Judaeus, I 586b
physicalism, II 245b–246b
Pico della Mirandola, IV 131b
Plato, I 586b; II 135a, 135b, 236b, 237a, 242b–243b
pleasure, II 137b, 238b
positivism, II 241a
power, II 239a, 239b, 240a, 241b, 244a, 246a, 247a
pragmatism, III 555b, 562a, 563a, 563b
predestination, II 26b, 27a, 29b, 30a, 245a, 245b
progress, III 628b, 637b, 640b, 649a
Protestantism, II 245a–245b
Proudhon, III 637b
providence, II 237a–237b, 243b
psychology, II 236b–237a,

238b–240a, 243a, 244a, 246a, 246b
punishment, II 135a, 241a
reason, II 236b, 237b, 238a, 238b, 239a, 240b, 242b, 243a, 243b, 244a
reconciliationism, II 238a, 239a, 240a, 241a, 241b, 242a
Reformation, II 245a–245b
Renaissance, II 137b; IV 131a–131b, 132a, 142b, 143a
responsibility, II 236b–238a, 240a, 241a, 244b, 245a
rewards, II 241a
right, IV 176b
Roman Catholic Church, I 394b; II 245a, 245b
romanticism, II 247a
Rome (ancient), II 134b–137b
Saint Augustine, I 573; II 27a, 137a, 230a–230b, 231a, 237b–238a, 244a–145a; III 584a
Saint Paul, II 245a
Saint Thomas Aquinas, II 238a, 245a, 245b; IV 392a
salvation, II 244b–245b; IV 230b, 231a, 232b
Sartre, II 246b–247a
Schelling, II 246b
Schlick, II 239a, 241a
scholasticism, II 245a
Schopenhauer, II 246b
science, II 245b–246b
sin, II 236b, 243b; IV 230b, 231a, 232b
social contract, IV 255b
social science, II 246b
society, II 242b
Socrates, II 242b
Sophists, II 242b
soul, II 236b, 243a, 243b, 244b
sovereignty, II 242b–243a, 244b, 245a, 248b
Spinoza, II 237b, 238b–239a, 246a
stars, II 245b
State, II 243a
Stoicism, II 137a, 237a, 237b, 238b, 243b, 244a, 246b; IV 320b
swerve theory, II 136a–137a
theism, II 244b
theodicy, IV 379b
theology, II 26b, 27a, 29b, 30a, 242a–248b
time, II 240b; IV 392a
tragic sense, IV 411b–412a

universe, II 243b
vice, II 237a, 237b
virtue, II 237a, 237b
vitalism, II 238b
Voltaire, II 137b
voluntariness, II 236b–237a, 239a, 242b, 247b, 248a
work, IV 532a, 532b, 533b, 534a
Wright, Chauncey, III 562a
Zoroastrianism, IV 231a
Freedom, II 248b–263a
action, II 44a
Aeschylus, IV 366b
ambition, II 242b
anarchy, III 470a
Aristotle, I 578b, 585a; II 249b
art, II 297b, 298a, 300b, 304a–304b
artists, I 586b; II 300b, 304a–304b; III 569b
authority, II 249a, 249b–250a
Bible, II 249b, 250a
Calvin, I 392b
Canada, III 13b
capitalism, III 646a
causation, I 285b–286a
chance, II 227a, 229b
China (Communist), I 486a
Christianity, II 250a, 251a–251b
Cicero, II 249b–250a; IV 50a
civilization, I 615b; III 183a
Coke, II 250b–251a
communication, II 44a–44b
Condorcet, III 644a
conduct, II 44a
Constant, II 15a
constitutionalism, I 486a
Counter-Enlightenment, II 102a, 106b, 108a
Creation, I 571b, 575b, 576b
creativity in art, I 577b–578a, 578b, 582b, 583a, 584a, 585a, 586b, 588a
Cuba, III 544b
cynicism, I 633a
de Staël, II 14b
death, I 636b
deism, I 464b
democracy, II 249b, 259a
despotism, II 1a–17b
determinism, I 93a; II 25b–26a, 26b, 135a
Devlin, II 251a–251b
dignity, IV 141a, 142a, 145a, 145b, 146a
duty, II 249a
economic history, II 44a–

133

44b, 45b, 46a, 47a, 47b, 50a, 53a, 55a, 59a
economics, II 250a
education, II 249b
Egypt (ancient), II 249b
Emerson, III 430b
empathy, II 86b
equality, II 146b
evolution, IV 181a
existentialism, II 193b, 194a, 194b; III 157b, 158a, 160a
expression, II 44a
fate, II 227a, 229b
Faust (legend), III 249b
Fichte, II 407b; III 473a; IV 209b
fortune, II 227a, 229b
France, II 250b, 251a
freemen, II 249a
French Revolution, II 250b, 409a–409b; IV 157a, 220a
general will, II 276b, 277a, 278b, 279a, 279b
genius, II 295a, 296a, 297b, 298a, 300b, 304a–304b, 313b, 316a, 316b, 320b
Gnosticism, II 328b
God, I 571b, 575b, 576b, 577b, 586b; II 249b, 250a, 251a, 360b, 361b, 364a
good, IV 177b, 179b, 180a, 181a
Great Britain, II 44b, 250b–251a
Greece (ancient), II 44b, 249b, 684b
Grotius, II 250b
happiness, II 379b
Hegel, I 37b; II 16a, 407b–410b, 413b–415b; IV 180a
Heidegger, II 193b
Herder, I 615b
historiography, IV 147b, 152a
history, I 285b–286a
Hobbes, II 250a; IV 256b
human nature, III 644a
humanism, IV 130a, 131a–131b, 135b
Hume, II 240a
idea, II 548a
immunities, II 249a, 250b
individualism, II 297b, 298a, 300b, 304a–304b, 596a–596b, 598a, 598b
international law, II 250b
Jefferson, II 44b
Judaism, II 249b
justice, II 249a
Kant, I 104a, 588a, 641a; II 240a–240b, 242a, 279b, 407b, 548a; III 21b–22a, 47b–48a, 637a, 639b; IV

179b
law, II 248b–251b, 684b, 686a, 687b; III 1a, 12a, 13b, 35b
Leibniz, II 239a; IV 382a
liberalism, III 36a–60b
liberty, II 248b–249a, 249b, 250b
Lincoln, II 44b
Locke, II 239a; III 21a
Luther, I 389b–390a
Machiavelli, II 250a; III 117a, 123b
Machiavellism, III 117a, 120b–121a, 123b
Marat, II 14a
Marx, II 159a; III 473b; IV 291a, 292a
Marxism, III 147a, 148b–149a, 152a, 155b, 156a, 157b, 158a, 160a, 167b, 168a–168b, 645b–646a; IV 181a
metaphor, III 199a
metaphysical imagination, III 210b, 217b, 219a
Michelet, II 414b
Middle Ages, IV 254a
Mill, J. S., II 251a
Montesquieu, II 9a–9b, 251a; III 21a
morality, II 249a, 251a–251b; III 645a
mythology, III 305a, 315b
natural law, II 249a, 250a; III 17a, 21a–22a, 23a, 25b
Nature, II 250a
necessity, II 237b; III 305a
as a negative idea, II 46a
Orientalism, III 430b
perennial philosophy, III 459b
perfectibility, III 470a, 472b, 473a, 473b, 475a, 644a
philosophy, III 199a
Plato, I 578b, 583a, 584a; II 243a, 249b
pleasure, II 379b
popular concept of, II 248b
positivism, III 544b
power, I 577b; II 249a, 250a, 250b, 251a
pragmatism, III 553a, 567b, 569b
predestination, II 25b–26a, 26b
of press, III 45a–47a
private property, III 653b, 654b, 656b
progress, III 635b, 637a, 637b, 639b, 644a, 645a, 645b–646a, 647b, 649a
protest movements, III 672a

Protestantism, II 409b; III 23a
rationalism, IV 50a
reason, II 250a
reformation, IV 60b, 61a
Reformation, I 648b
religion, II 44b, 64a; III 40a–40b; IV 113a, 119a
Renaissance, IV 130a, 131a–131b, 135b, 141a, 142a, 145a, 145b, 146a, 147b, 152a, 438a
research, I 10b
revolution, IV 157b, 158a
right, IV 177b, 179b, 180a, 181a
Roman Catholic Church, II 250a
romanticism, IV 203a, 205a, 209a, 209b, 210a, 210b
Rome (ancient), II 44b, 249b–250a, 686a, 687b
Rousseau, II 44b, 250b, 276b, 277a, 278b, 279a; III 21b, 156a; IV 260a
sacraments, I 390a
Saint Augustine, I 573a; II 250a; IV 381a
Saint Paul, II 250a
Sartre, II 193b, 194a, 194b; III 210a
Saul (Bible), II 249b
Schiller, I 578a
Schlegel, IV 209a
Schleiermacher, IV 210a
science, I 10a
self-discipline, II 251b
sin, II 250a
slavery, II 242b, 249a–250b
Smith, II 58b–59a
social contract, IV 254a, 255b, 256b, 257b, 260b
socialism, IV 289a, 290b, 291a, 292a
society, II 249a, 249b; III 475a
Solon, II 249b, 259a
Sophists, I 582b, 583a
sovereignty, II 250a–250b
speech in antiquity, II 252a–263a
Spinoza, II 238b–239a; IV 177b
State, IV 317b
Stoicism, IV 50a
syncretism, I 45b
temperance, IV 366b
theodicy, IV 380b–383b
theology, II 25b–26a, 26b
theriophily, IV 385a
Thirty Years War, II 250b
thought, II 44a

three major forms of, II 44a
time, IV 392a
totalitarianism, IV 407a, 410b
tragic sense, IV 414a, 417a
tyranny, II 250a, 250b
U.S.S.R., I 486a; III 155a, 155b
U.N., III 12a
U.S., II 251a
universal man, IV 438a
Utopia, IV 459b, 460, 463b, 464b
Volksgeist, IV 495b
Voltaire, II 11a
wisdom of the fool, IV 516a, 516b
work, IV 531b, 532a
Zeitgeist, IV 536b
See also Academic freedom
Freedom of speech in antiquity, II 249a, 252a–263a
Abdiashirta, II 254a
abuse of, II 252a
Achaemenids, II 254b
administrative processes, II 253a
Aeschines, II 258a
Aeschylus, II 259a–259b
Agga, II 252b
Ahura Mazdā, II 254a–254b
Akkad, II 253a
Alexander the Great, II 257b
Amenemope, II 256b
anarchism, II 256b
Anaxagoras, II 258a
Ani, II 256b
Arabia, II 254a
aristocracy, II 253b, 254a, 259a, 259b, 260b–261a
Aristophanes, II 259b, 260a
Aristotle, II 254a, 258a, 259a, 260a, 260b
art, II 253a
Artemisia, II 254b
assemblies, II 252b–255b, 256a, 256b–261b
Assurbanipal, II 253a
Assyria, II 252b, 253a
Assyriologists, II 253a
astrology, II 261b
Athanasius, II 262a
Athens (ancient), II 256b–257a, 258a–258b, 259a, 259b, 260a, 261b, 262a
Augustus, II 261a, 261b
Babylonia, II 252b, 253a
Bible, II 252a, 254b–256a, 262a
blasphemy, II 252a
bureaucracy, II 256a
Carthage (ancient), II 254a
Christianity, II 262a
Cicero, II 261b

city-state, II 252b, 253b–254a, 256b–258a
Cleisthenes, II 258b, 259b
Cleon, II 260a
comedy, II 258b
correspondence, II 252a
councils, II 253a–255b, 258b
Crete (ancient), II 254a
custom, II 261a
Darius, II 254b
David (Bible), II 255a
democracy, II 252b, 253a, 257a, 259a, 259b, 260a, 260b
Democritus, II 259b
Demonax, II 260b
Demosthenes, II 260a
despotism, II 252b, 259a
Diagoras, II 258b
Dio Cassius, II 261b
Dio Chrysostom, II 261b
Diodotus, II 260a
Diogenes of Apollonia, II 258b
Diogenes of Sinope, II 260b
Diopeithes, II 258b
Domitian, II 261b
Egypt (ancient), II 252a, 252b, 253a, 254a, 256a–256b
El-Amarna letters, II 253b–254a
eloquence, II 256a, 262a
epics, II 253a
Epictetus, II 261b
Epicureanism, II 260b
Epicurus, II 260b
equality, II 260a
ethics, II 259a
Euripides, II 259a, 260a
Ezra (Bible), II 255a
foreigners, II 260a, 261a
Gilgamesh, II 252b
God, II 253a, 254b, 255a–255b, 256a, 258b, 262a
Greece (ancient), II 252a, 252b, 254b, 256b–260b, 261b
Hattushilish I, II 253a–253b
hedonism, II 256b
heresy, II 252b, 256a
Herodotus, II 254b, 259a, 259b
Hesiod, II 259a
Hezekiah (Bible), II 255a
Hittites, II 252a, 252b, 253a–253b
Holmes, Justice, III 567b
Homer, II 257a–257b, 259a
Horace, II 260b
imperialism, II 260a
impiety, II 252b
Ipu-wer, II 256a

Isagoras, II 259b
Isaiah (Bible), II 255b–256a
Isocrates, II 260a, 262a
Israel (ancient), II 253b–254a, 254b–256a
Jephthah (Bible), II 254b
Jeremiah (Bible), II 255b–256a
Jeroboam (Bible), II 255a
Jesus Christ, II 262a
Jezebel (Bible), II 255b
Joash (Bible), II 255a
Josephus, II 262a
Joshua (Bible), II 255a
journalism, II 252a
Judah (Bible), II 254b, 255a
Judaism, II 254b–256a, 256b, 262a
Judea (ancient), II 252a
justice, II 252b, 253b, 255a
Juvenal, II 261b
Kantuzilish, II 253b
kingship, II 252b–259a
Labaja, II 254a
law, II 252b, 253a, 255a, 256a, 258b, 259a, 261a
Leontius, II 257b
libel, II 252a
liberty, II 258b–259a, 260a, 262a
Lycurgus, II 257b
Macedonia, II 257b, 260a
Marcus Aurelius, II 260b
Mardonius, II 254b
Marduk, II 253a
Medes, II 254b
Menander, II 260a
Mesopotamia (ancient), II 252a, 252b–253a
Middle Ages, II 262a
military, II 253a, 253b, 257b, 261a
modern, II 252a
Moses (Bible), II 255a
Naboth (Bible), II 255b
Naevius, II 261a
Near East, II 252a, 252b, 253a, 254a, 255a
obscenity, II 252a
oligarchy, II 260b
Palestine (ancient), II 253b–254a, 254b–256a
Pericles, II 259a, 260a, 261b
Persia (ancient), II 252a, 252b, 254a–254b, 259a, 259b
petition, II 252a
Phaedrus, II 261b
Philip II, II 257b
Philip V, II 257b
Philo Judaeus, II 260b,

261b, 262a
Philodemus, II 260b
philosophy, II 260b
Phoenicia (ancient), II 252a, 254a, 257a
Pindar, II 259b
Pisistratus, II 260a
Plato, II 258b, 260a
pleasure, II 256b
Plutarch, II 257b, 258a, 260b, 261b
poetry, II 252b, 259a
Polybius, II 257b, 260b
power, II 252b
pragmatism, III 566b
Prah-hotep, II 256a
prayer, II 253a
Prometheus, II 259a
propaganda, II 254a
prophecy, II 255a–256a
Protagoras, II 258b
Pseudo-Xenophon, II 259b
public meetings, II 252a
publishing, II 252a
Quintilian, II 261b
rabbi, II 256a
reason, II 260a
rebellion, II 254b
Rehoboam (Bible), II 255b
religion, II 252a, 252b, 253b, 254b, 256b, 262a
reticence, II 259a
Rome (ancient), II 252a, 252b, 260b–262a
Saint Anthony, II 262a
Saint John Chrysostom, II 262a
Saint Paul, II 262a
Samuel (Bible), II 254b, 255a
sedition, II 252a
Shuppiluliumash I, II 253b
Sicily (ancient), II 254a
silence, II 256b, 259a
skepticism, II 256b
slander, II 252a, 258b, 259b, 261a
slavery, II 256a, 259a, 260a
sneering, II 258b
society, II 252a, 252b, 253a, 253b, 261a
Socrates, II 258b
Solon, II 258a, 259a
Sophocles, II 259b
Sparta (ancient), II 254a, 256b, 257a, 257b
State, II 252a, 252b
suffrage, II 261a
Sulla, II 261a
Sundwall, II 260a
Syracuse, II 258a
Syria (ancient), II 253b–254a, 254b
Tacitus, II 260b, 261b–

262a
teaching, II 252a–252b, 258b
Telepinush, II 253a–253b
theater, II 258b, 259b, 261a
Theognis, II 259a
Thersites (myth), II 259a
Thucydides, II 258a, 259a, 259b–260a
Tiberius, II 261b
tradition, II 260a
truth, II 254b
Tutankhamen, II 253b
tyranny, II 259a
Tyrtaeus, II 258a
Vespasian, II 261b
virtue, II 256b, 259a, 260a
war, II 259a
wealth, II 260a, 261a
Wen-Amon, II 254a
Wilson, J. A., II 254a
wisdom, II 256b
women, II 255a, 256a
worship, II 252a
Xenophon, II 258a
Xerxes, II 254b
Zeno of Citium, II 260b
Freeling, Nicholas, literary paradox, III 77b
Freeman, Edward Augustus (1823–1892), Gothic, II 369b
Frege, Gottlob (1848–1925)
    abstraction, I 8a–9a
    axiomatization, I 168b, 169b
    empiricism, III 545b, 547b, 548a, 550a
    infinity, II 611b
    mathematics, III 175b, 176a
    pragmatism, III 557b
Freiberg, Dietrich von mechanical science, II 198a, 198b–199a
Freige, Johann Thomas, Ramism, IV 44a
Freising, Bishop Otto von
    art, II 300a
    genius, II 300a
French, John, alchemy, I 32b
French Civil Code, II 693b
French Linguistic Atlas, III 70a
French Revolution (1789)
    art, IV 165a
    balance of power, I 187a
    Burckhardt, IV 159a
    Burke, IV 157b
    Carlyle, IV 160a
    catastrophism, IV 419b
    Christianity, I 404a–404b, 408b–409a
    classicism, I 452a, 453b
    common law, II 693b
    Comte, III 533b, 534a, 534b

Condorcet, III 533a; IV 156a, 156b, 157a–157b
conservatism, I 480a, 481a
cosmic images, I 522a
Counter-Enlightenment, II 109b–110a, 112a
crisis in history, I 590a, 591b, 593a
cycles, IV 156a
Delacroix, IV 156b
democracy, I 656a, 658b, 660b–662a; IV 156b
despotism, II 1a, 13b–14b; IV 156b
economic history, II 45a, 57b
English Revolution, IV 159b
Enlightenment, II 89a, 91a, 94b
equality, II 138a, 139b, 141b, 143a, 144b–146a
evolutionism, II 180b
fall of the Bastille, IV 156a–156b
Fox, C. J., IV 156a–156b
freedom, II 250b, 409a–409b; IV 157a
general will, II 278b–279a, 280b–281a
Gentz, IV 158b
Guizot, IV 159b
Hegel, II 409a–409b, 410a; IV 156b
history, III 671b
ideology, III 671b
impressionism, II 577a, 581b
Jansenism, I 400a
Lamartine, III 671b
law, II 250b
liberty, II 94b
linguistics, III 64b
literature, III 671b
Locke, IV 156b
Machiavellism, III 123a–123b
Marx, IV 162a
Marxism, IV 499a
Mazzini, I 408b–409a
Michelet, IV 159b
Mignet, IV 159b
nationalism, III 323b, 325a, 325b, 326a, 326b, 327a, 331a
neo-classicism in art, III 366a
papacy, I 404a–404b
periodization in history, III 478a, 479a, 480a
periodization in literary history, III 483a, 485b
philanthropy, III 490a
Platonism, III 520b

positivism, III 533a–534b, 537a, 538a, 538b
power, IV 157a
prelude to, I 404a
Price, IV 156b
progress, III 634a, 639b, 642b; IV 156b
protest movements, III 671b, 672a
reason, II 409a–409b
Renaissance, IV 124b
republicanism, IV 156b
revolution, IV 152a, 156a–158a, 159b, 160a, 160b, 162a, 164b, 165a
Robespierre, IV 157a, 157b
Roman Catholic Church, I 404a–404b
romanticism, I 450b; IV 195a, 196b, 199b, 203a, 204a, 205a, 206b
Rousseau, II 326a
Saint-Simon, III 534b
Schiller, IV 156b–157a
Scott, II 512a
social contract, IV 255a, 260a, 261a, 262a, 262b
socialism, III 671b; IV 288a, 288b, 293b
society, IV 156a
State, IV 156a, 157a
Stendhal, IV 157b
terror, IV 157a–157b
Thermidor, IV 157b
Thiers, III 671b
Tocqueville, IV 158b–159a
totalitarianism, IV 408a
tribunals, IV 157a
tyranny, II 409a–409b
uniformitarianism, IV 419b
U.S., IV 156a, 160b
Utopia, IV 463a
violence, IV 156b, 157a, 157b
vox populi, IV 499a
war, IV 500b, 501a, 502b
Weltschmerz, IV 204a
French Revolution (1830), protest movements, III 671b, 672a
French Revolution (1848), protest movements, III 671b, 672a
Freneau, Philip (1752–1832), psychology, IV 21a
Frequency
Fermat, III 606a
Pascal, III 606a
probability, III 606a, 606b, 607b, 611a, 614a–618b, 621a, 622a, 623a
Fréret, Nicolas (1688–1749), mythology, III 302b, 303a, 304a

Frescoes
music, III 270a
mythology, III 276b, 289a, 291a
neo-classicism, III 364b
Fresnel, Augustin (1788–1827)
continuity, I 494a
mathematics, III 179a
optics, III 419a–419b
relativity, IV 78a–78b, 79a, 80a, 83b
Freud, Nicholas, literary paradox, III 77b
Freud, Sigmund (1856–1939)
aggression, II 383b
anti-intellectualism, III 597a
anxiety, II 383b
art, III 312b; IV 96b
art and play, I 107a
authority, I 161b
catharsis, I 268a
chance images, I 352b
Christianity, II 213b
civilization, III 597a
death, I 634b, 636b; II 383b
death instincts (Thanatos), II 557a
ego, II 383b
Einstein and, III 446b
ethics, III 445b, 446b, 447a; IV 96b
exogamy, IV 96b
faith, hope and charity, II 213b
Faust (legend), III 251b
free will, II 246b
guilt, II 383b; IV 96b
Hall and, III 562b
happiness, II 383a–384a
hedonism, II 383b
holy, II 513b
id, II 383b
idea, I 116b; II 544b, 548b
ideology, II 555b. 556b–557b
imprinting, II 584b, 585b
incest, IV 96b
individualism, II 601b
instinct, II 383b
irony, II 634a
irrationalism, II 636a, 637a
James and, III 562b, 563a
Jung and, III 312b–313a; IV 97a
learning, II 584b, 585b
life instincts (Eros), II 557a
longevity, III 92b
love, III 104b–105b, 106a
masochism, II 383b
metaphysics, II 383b; III

216a, 221a
morality, II 383b; III 312b
motif, III 240b, 242a
mythology, III 281a, 307a, 309b, 312a–312b
neurosis, IV 96b
Oedipus complex, III 312b; IV 96b
pain, II 383b
peace, III 445b, 446b, 447a
Plato and, II 383b
pleasure, II 383a–384a
pragmatism, III 562b, 563b
primitivism, III 597a; IV 96b
psychoanalysis, IV 96b
psychology, IV 13b, 14a, 28b, 96b
reality principle, II 383b
religion, II 556b–557b; III 216a, 312a–312b; IV 96b–97a
repression, II 383b
revolution, IV 163a
romanticism, IV 204b
Russell and, III 446b
sadism, II 383b
satire, IV 214a
Schiller and, I 105a
sex, IV 97a
skepticism, IV 250a
society, II 383b; III 312a–312b; IV 96b
structuralism, IV 328b
superego, II 383b
Surrealism, I 352b
taboos, IV 96b
totemism, IV 96b
value, IV 250a
war, III 447a; IV 507b
women, IV 528a
Freudianism
good, IV 185a
irrationalism, II 637a–637b
literature, III 242a
love, III 105b
Man-Machine, III 144b
psychology, IV 14a, 28b–29a
right, IV 185a
wisdom of the fool, IV 516a
Frey, Dagobert
Gothic, III 373b
symmetry, IV 348a
Freytag, Gustav (1816–1895), motif, III 235b
Fried, Alfred H. (1864–1921), international peace, III 449a
Friedan, Betty, women, IV 529a
Friederich, Werner P., baroque in literature, I 191a
Friedländer, P., indeterminacy, II 586b

Friedländer, W., iconography, II 538a

Friedman, Milton
individualism, II 597a
natural liberty, II 68a

Friedrich, Carl Joachim,
periodization in history, III 479b
totalitarianism, IV 409b

Friedrich, Caspar David (1774–1840)
art, II 309a
melancholy, II 309a
naturalism in art, III 341a
romanticism, IV 206a
Schelling and, IV 201a

Friends of God, Augustinianism, IV 109a

Friendship
Aristotelianism, II 210b–211a
Aristotle, III 110b–111a, 112a
Cicero, III 112a
determinism, II 238b
faith, hope, and charity, II 210b–211a
Ficino, III 511a
fortune, fate, and chance, II 228a
Greece (ancient), III 112a
happiness, III 377b, 378a
free will, II 238b
love, III 94a, 94b
loyalty, III 110b, 111a, 112b
Plato, III 112a, 554a; IV 285b
Platonism, III 507a, 511a
pleasure, II 377b, 378a
Saint Thomas Aquinas, II 210b–211a
socialism, IV 285b
Socrates, III 554a
Spinoza, II 238b
utilitarianism, IV 445a

Frobenius, Leo (1873–1938), mythology, III 307a, 313a–313b, 314a, 317b

Froebel, Friedrich Wilhelm, (1782–1852)
education, II 99b
Enlightenment, II 99b

Fromm, Erich (1900–   ),
anxiety, II 384a
authority, I 158a, 161a
capitalism, III 158a
happiness, II 384a
Marxism, III 158a
perfectibility, III 475a
pleasure, II 384a
psychology, IV 14a, 29a
socialism, III 158a

Frommichen, K. H., ideal, II 551a

Frothingham, Octavius Brooks
Orientalism, III 429a, 434b
transcendentalism, III 429a, 434b

Froude, James (1818–1894), reformation, IV 60a

Froumenteau, Nicolas, Machiavellism, III 117a

Fry, Roger (1866–1934)
art for art's sake, I 110b
beauty, I 207b

Frye, Northrop
irony, II 634b
literary criticism, I 604a–504b
motif, III 242a
symbolism, IV 337b, 341b

Fu Hsi (fl. c. 2800 B.C.),
Figurism, I 359b, 360a

Fuchs, Klaus, God, II 365b

Fugue, the, II 322b

Fulgentius, mythology, III 288a, 296a, 299b

Fuller, Lon
law, III 5b
natural law, III 26a
pragmatism, III 566a

Fuller, Margaret (1810–1850)
literary criticism, I 599a
transcendentalism, IV 24a

Fuller, Thomas (1608–1661), philanthropy, III 489b

Fun, happiness, II 385b

Functionalism, mythology, III 276b
Newton, III 184a
psychology, IV 27a, 27b, 28a, 28b
structuralism, IV 325b

Fundamentalism
conservative, I 21a–21b
heresy, II 429b, 430a
Marxism, III 169a
metaphor, III 206b–207a
millenarianism, III 225a
modernism, I 419a
mountains in literature, III 255b
religion, III 206b–207a
U.S., II 429b, 430a

Furies (myth), temperance, IV 367a

Furniture
Egypt (ancient), III 364b–365a
neo-classicism in art, III 364b–365a, 368b

Fuseli, Henry (1741–1825)
chance images, I 350b
neo-classicism in art, III 371a

Fust, Johann (1400?–?1466),

Faust (legend), III 247a

Fustel de Coulanges, Numa Denis (1830–1889), China, I 371a

Futurism
evolution of literature, II 173b
expressionism, II 206b, 207a, 208b
revolution, IV 165a
symbolism, IV 343b, 345a

Fux, Johann Joseph (1660–1741), painting, III 350a

Fyodorov, Nicholas F. (1828–1903), longevity, III 92b

G

Gad (prophet), III 659a

Gaelic language, II 660b

Gaetano da Thiene, Saint (1480–1547), medieval sciences, II 204a

Gafori, Franchino (1451–1522), also Gaffurio
music, III 261a, 261b
Pythagoreans, IV 41a

Gaia (myth), III 273b

Gainsborough, Thomas (1727–1788), landscapes, III 349b

Gaius (2nd century A.D.)
common law, II 691a
law, III 17a
natural law, III 17a, 19b

Galaxies
space, IV 303b, 305b
time measurement, IV 405b

Galbraith, J. K.
natural liberty, II 66b–67a, 70a
power, II 66b

Galen (fl. 2nd century A.D.),
alchemy, I 29b
animal spirits, III 133b
apologism, III 90a
Aristotle, III 90a
axiomatization, I 164b
Bacon and, I 173b
biology, I 231a, 231b, 232a, 235a–235b
classification of the arts, I 456b, 457b, 458a, 459a
Cosmic Fall, I 508b
design argument, I 672b
dignity, IV 137b
ethics, IV 321b
four temperaments, III 133b
Galileo and, III 382b
health, II 398a–398b, 400b,

402a; III 381b
humanism, II 521b; IV 133a
literary criticism, I 596b
logic, III 381a
longevity, III 89b–90a, 91b
Man-Machine, III 133b, 134a, 134b
medicine, III 133b, 381a–381b, 382a
methodology, III 381a–382a
Newton and, III 381a–382a
observation, III 381a
perennial philosophy, III 461a
progress, III 632b
psychology, IV 8b
Ramism, IV 43b
skepticism, IV 236a, 237a, 239a, 240a
Stoicism, IV 321b
teleology, I 235a–235b
virtù, IV 480b

Galiani, Abbot Ferdinando (1728–1787)
social welfare, IV 277a
utility, IV 450a, 452a–453b

Galilean transformation, IV 79b, 84b

Galilei, Vincenzo, music, III 261a, 261b, 262a, 262b

Galileo (Galileo Galilei) (1564–1642)
abstraction, IV 361a
acoustics, III 263a
anthropomorphism, I 89b
astronomy, III 356a
atomism, I 133a, 134a–134b
axiomatization, I 165b
Bacon and, I 176a, 177a, 177b, 178b; III 356a
behaviorism, I 224b
Bellarmine and, III 356a
Campanella and, IV 461b
causation, I 276a, 281a, 301b
chance, I 337a
conception of inertia, I 276a
consonance, III 263a
cosmic images, I 513a, 515a, 516a–516b, 517a, 522b
Cosmic Fall, I 511b
cosmic voyages, I 524b–527a, 530a
cosmology, I 546b, 548a, 550b, 558a
Counter-Enlightenment, II 109b
determinism, II 18b
economic history, II 45a
equality, II 138b

137

experiments, III 382b–383b, 385b; IV 361a, 533b
as a founder of modern thought, I 173a
as the founder of modern science, III 415b
Galen and, III 382b
gambling, III 605b
game theory, II 264a
genius, II 293b
God, I 301b; II 346b–347a, 352a; IV 393b
heresy, II 428a
heterodoxy, III 356a
hierarchy, II 436b, 443b
historiography, II 18b
humanism, II 521a, 523a; IV 130a, 133a, 134a, 134b, 135b
hypotheses, III 356a
indeterminacy, II 587a
Inquisition, I 546b; III 356a
intuition, IV 361a
Islam, II 649a
Kepler and, III 414a–415a
kinematics, III 383a
language, II 667b
light, II 587a; IV 77b
mathematics, III 193a, 356a, 383a, 385b; IV 134a, 361a
matter, III 193a, 194a
mechanical experiments, II 196b, 197b, 198a, 202a, 202b, 203b–205a
metaphysical imagination, III 218a
methodology, III 382b–383b, 385b, 386a–388a
motion, II 46a, 205a, 587a; III 383a
mountains in literature, III 256a, 256b
music, III 261a, 262b–263a
mythology, III 299b
Nature, I 281a; III 349b; IV 361a
necessity, III 353b, 354a, 355b, 356a, 357a–358a
Newton and, III 382b–383b, 385b–388a
numbers, III 405b, 406a
observation, III 382b, 385b
optics, III 411b, 414a–415b, 420a
philosophy, III 382b, 388a
physics, II 521a
Plato and, III 353b
Platonism, II 521a; III 356a, 510b; IV 361a
pragmatism, III 555a, 557b
probability, III 383b, 605b, 606a, 606b
psychology, IV 11a
ratio, III 263a

relativity, IV 74a, 75a, 76b–77a, 77b, 86a
revolution, IV 162b
space, IV 302a
speed, II 587a
technology, IV 361a–361b, 362a, 363b
teleology, I 301a
telescope, III 414a–415b, 420a
time, IV 393b, 402b–403b
universe, III 193a
Utopia, IV 461b
vibration, III 263a
virtuoso, IV 489a
work, IV 533b
Gall, Franz Joseph (1758–1828)
Comte, III 534a, 537a
Man-Machine, III 142b
phrenology, IV 23a
positivism, III 534a, 537a
Galle, Johann Gottfried (1812–1910), cosmology, I 552b
Gallicanism, I 399b–400a
Bossuet, I 399b
Febronianism, I 403b
heresy, II 428b
Jansenism, I 404a
Louis XIV, I 399b
Napoleon I, I 404b
Galsworthy, John (1867–1933), expressionism, II 207b
Galton, Francis (1822–1911), class, I 448a
inequality, I 448a
natural liberty, II 65b
perfectibility, III 471a
psychology, IV 13b, 25a, 26b
Galuppi, Baldassare (1706–1785), musical genius, II 324a
Gama, Vasco da (1469?–1524), I 58b
Gambling and probability
Bernoulli, IV 454a, 457a
Cardano, III 605b
chance, I 336a–337a
De Méré, III 606a
Fermat, III 606a–606b
Galileo, III 605b
Pascal, III 606a–606b
utility, IV 454a, 457a
Game theory, II 263a–275b
animals, II 263b
applications, II 272a–273b
art, II 274b
astronomy, II 264a
basic concepts, II 268b–272a
Bayesian probabilities, II

265b
Bernoulli, Daniel, II 265b
Bernoulli, James, II 264b
Bernoulli, Nicholas, II 264b
biology, II 273a–273b
Birkhoff, II 266b
Bohr, II 273b
Borel, II 265a, 269b
business, II 263b, 268a
Cardano, II 264a
ceremonies, II 264a
Cessolis, II 264b
chance, II 264a–264b, 265a, 266a, 268b, 269b
chess, II 264b, 265a, 266a
China (ancient), II 264b
Condorcet, II 272b
Copernicus, II 272a
de Waldegrave, II 264b
decisions, II 263a–263b, 272a
Delft, II 264b
descriptive theory of, II 268a–268b
diplomatic customs, II 264a
economics, II 266a, 266b, 270b, 271a, 272a
ethics, II 273a
experience, II 267a
fate, II 271b
future, II 263b
Galileo, II 264a
Gauss, II 264b
geometry, II 266b
God, II 263b
Gödel, II 263b
Great Britain, II 264a
Heisenberg, II 273b
history, II 263b–265a
human action, II 266a–267a
Hurwicz, II 272a
Huygens, II 264a
imputation, II 270a–271a
Japan (ancient), II 264b
Laplace, II 264a, 272a
law, II 263b, 267a
Leibniz, II 264a–264b, 265a, 274b
Leonardo da Vinci, II 274b
liturgies, II 264a
logic, II 263b, 266b
Lucas, II 271a
mathematics, II 263b–265b, 266b, 271a, 273a, 274a
Michelangelo, II 274b
military, II 263b, 266a, 272b
minimax strategy concept, II 264b, 265a, 269b
money, II 264b, 265a–265b
morality, II 265b
Morgenstern, II 265a, 265b, 267a, 269a, 271a, 272b

normative theory, II 268a–268b
organicism, II 263b–264a
origin of games, II 263b
Pareto, II 271a
Pascal, II 264a
philosophy, II 264a, 265a, 265b, 266a, 267a, 273b–274b
physics, II 264a, 271b, 273a
poker, II 266a
politics, II 264b, 265b, 266a, 268a, 270b, 272b
present, II 263a–263b
probability theory, II 264a, 265b, 269b–270a
programming theory, II 273a
Ptolemy, II 272a
Ramsey, II 265b
reason, II 267a–268a, 273b–274a
Reiss, II 264b–265a
Remond, II 264b
Rome (ancient), II 264a
rules, II 268b–269a
saddle points, II 269a
Savage, II 272a
science, II 263b, 264a, 266a–266b, 267a, 268a
social equilibrium, II 270a
society, II 264a, 266b, 267a, 268a–272a, 274a, 274b
sociology, II 272b
Spinoza, II 273a
statistics, II 272a
stock market, II 264b
strategy, II 264b, 265a, 266a, 266b, 268a, 268b, 269a–269b, 272b
subjective probability, II 265b
utilitarianism, II 265a–266a
variables, II 267b
Ville, J., II 265a
von Neumann, II 265a, 265b, 266b, 269a–269b, 272b
Wald, A., II 265a, 272a
war, II 264a
Zermelo, II 265a
Games, III 605a–607a, 608b, 609a, 610a, 612a, 615b, 617a
social welfare, IV 278b, 283a
Gamliel II, Rabbi, impiety, II 565a
Gamma-ray microscopic experiment, II 588b–589a, 591b
Gamow, George (1904–

1968), cosmology, I 565b, 566b–567a

Gandhi, Mahatma (1869–1948)
anarchism, I 72a
asceticism, III 446a
Buddhism, III 446a
Christianity, III 446a
civil disobedience, I 435a, 438a, 438b, 439a
ethics, III 445b, 446a; IV 73a
humanism, III 446a
industry, III 446a
Jainism, III 446a
King and, I 439a
morality, III 446a
peace, III 445b, 446a
power, III 446a
relativism, IV 73a
Sermon on the Mount, III 446a
Thoreau and, III 446a
Tolstoy and, III 446a
violence, III 446a
war, III 446a

Gans, Eduard (1798–1839), Hegel and, II 411b, 412a

Gansfort, Wessel (c. 1420–1489), Luther and, IV 65b

Garasse, François, skepticism, IV 244a–244b

Garaudy, Roger, atheism, II 213b

Garbe, Richard von (1857–1927)
Buddhism, I 255a
Orientalism, III 436a

García Lorca, Federico (1899–1936), symbolism, IV 342a

Garcilaso de la Vega (1503–1536), periodization in literary history, III 482a

Gardening
aesthetics, II 224a
China, I 364a
Gothic, II 368b, 370a, 370b
sublime in external nature, IV 334b

Gardiner, Samuel Rawson (1829–1902), nationalism, III 331a

Gardner, Helen, literary criticism, I 602b

Garfield, James Abrams (1831–1881), education, II 72b, 75a–75b

Garibaldi, Giuseppe (1807–1882), revolution, IV 160b

Garin, Eugenio
universal man, IV 440a
Utopia, IV 461a

Garland, Hamlin (1860–1940), impressionism, II 574a

Garland, John, style, IV 331a

Garnett, Richard (1835–1906), realism in literature, IV 54a

Garnier, Clement Joseph (1813–1882), economic history, II 50b

Garnier, Tony, city, I 433a

Garrigou-Lagrange, R., God, II 361b

Garrison, William Lloyd (1805–1879)
civil disobedience, I 436b
slavery, I 436b

Garth, Samuel (1661–1719), baroque in literature, I 191a

Gärtner, Eduard, naturalism in art, III 341a

Garzoni, Benedetto, dignity, IV 143b–144a

Gaskell, Elizabeth Cleghorn (1810–1865), *vox populi*, IV 497b, 499a, 499b

Gassendi, Pierre (1592–1655)
alchemy, I 32b
anthropomorphism, I 85b
association of ideas, I 112a
atomism, I 134b, 135b–138b, 306b, 310b; II 137b
axiomatization, I 165b
Bacon and, I 177a
Barrow and, IV 393a
causation, I 301a, 303b
certainty, I 304b, 306a, 306b–307a, 310a, 310b, 311b
Descartes and, II 450a; IV 393a
Epicureanism, I 306b
God, I 303b
hedonism, II 137b
heresy, II 428a
imprinting, II 584a
learning, II 584a
Man-Machine, III 139a
materialism, II 450a
methodology, III 387b
Newton and, III 387b; IV 393a
skepticism, I 306a, 306b–307a; IV 244a, 244b, 245a, 250b
teleology, I 301a, 303b
time, IV 394b

Gaster, Theodor H., mythology, III 307a, 312a

Gāthās, II 39b, 40a

Gathy, August, genius, II 324b, 325a

Gaudi, Antonio (1852–1926), Gothic, II 372b

Gaulli, Giovanni Battista (1639–1709), temperance, IV 377b

Gauss, Christian (1878–1951)
symbolism, IV 341b
Wilson and, IV 341b

Gauss, Karl Friedrich (1777–1855)
continuity, I 494a
cosmology, I 554b, 555a
game theory, II 264b
infinity, II 611a, 613a–613b
Laplace and, III 613b
mathematics, III 179a
numbers, III 405b
probability, III 613b, 619a, 619b
relativity, IV 87a–87b, 88a, 88b

Gauss integral, III 612b

Gaussian distribution, II 588b

Gaussian law, III 613b
continuity, I 494a

Gautama Siddhārtha (436–383 B.C.)
Buddhism, I 247a–247b
Jesus Christ and, I 255a
philanthropy, III 487a

Gautier, Judith (1850–1917), China, I 369a

Gautier, Théophile (1811–1872)
art for art's sake, I 109b, 110a
China, I 369a
naturalism in art, III 343b

Gay, John (1685–1732)
approval, III 233a
happiness, II 380b
Hartley and, III 234a
honor, III 233b
Hutcheson and, III 233a
idea, I 112a, 112b, 113a
moral sense, III 233a–233b
pleasure, II 380b; III 233a–233b
satire, IV 215a
utilitarianism, II 380b

Gay, Peter, God, II 355b

Geertz, Clifford, ideology, II 558a

Gegenbaur, Karl (1826–1903), biology, I 239b

Gehazi (Bible), disease, II 396b

Geikie, Archibald (1835–1924), uniformitarianism, IV 423a

Geiringer, H., probability, III 622a, 622b

Gelasius I, Pope (492–496), authority, I 148b, 149a

Gellert, Christian Fürchtegott (1715–1769), genius, II 295a

Gelli, Giovanni Battista (1498–1563), theriophily, IV 386b–387a

Gellius, Aulus (2nd century A.D.)
classicism, I 451a
humanism, IV 129b

Genealogy
language, III 63a, 65b
linguistics, III 65b, 66b, 68b, 71b

General Theory of Relativity, *See* Einstein, Albert

General will, II 275b–281b
absolutism, II 276b
anarchism, II 280b
aristocracy, II 276a
Bosanquet, II 280a–280b
causation, II 276b
class, II 279a, 279b
Constant, II 279a–279b
conventions, II 277b
craftsmanship, II 300a
custom, II 277b
despotism, II 278a
Diderot, II 276a
education, II 276b, 277a, 278a, 278b, 279a
equality, II 277a, 277b, 278b, 279b
fear, II 278a
Fichte, II 279a
freedom, II 276b, 277a, 278b, 279a, 279b
French Revolution, II 278b–279a, 280b–281a
God, II 275b
good, II 277a, 280a
grace, II 275b
Gravina, II 275b
Great Britain, II 275b
Greece (ancient), II 276a
Green, T. H., II 280a
happiness, II 277a
Hegel, II 279a, 280a, 280b
Hobbes, II 276a–276b
individualism, II 275b–280b
inequality, II 277a, 277b, 278a, 278b
instinct, II 277a
justice, II 276a, 278a, 279b, 280b
Kant, II 279b–280a
law, II 275b, 276a, 277a, 277b, 278a, 278b, 279b
liberalism, II 278b, 280b
liberty, II 276a, 277a, 279b
Locke, II 277a
Lycurgus, II 277a
majorities, II 278b, 280b
Malebranche, II 275b

military, II 278b
mind, II 276b
minorities, II 278b
Montesquieu, II 275b, 276a
morality, II 276b, 278a, 279b
mores, II 278a
Nature, II 276b
necessity, II 277a
passions, II 276b
patriotism, II 278a
politics, II 275b, 278a–279b, 280b–281a
poverty, II 276b, 277a, 277b, 279a
power, II 276b, 278a
Proudhon, II 280b
prudence, II 278a
psychology, II 276b, 277a, 279b
public opinion, II 278a, 280a
Pufendorf, II 276a–276b
reason, II 280a
revolution, II 278b–279a
Rome (ancient), II 275b
Rousseau, II 275b–280b
Saint-Lambert, II 276a
Sieyès, II 279a
socialism, II 278b, 280b
society, II 276a–281a
sovereignty, II 276b, 278a, 279a
Sparta (ancient), II 276a, 279a
State, II 276a–276b, 277b, 278a, 279a, 279b, 280a–280b
stupidity, II 277b
suffrage, II 277b, 279b
talent, II 276b
tyranny, II 276a
vanity, II 278a
voluntarism, II 280b
wealth, II 276b, 277a, 277b, 278a, 279a
Genes
acquired characteristics, II 620b
genetic continuity, II 289a, 289b
perfectibility, III 471a
recapitulation, IV 58a
Genet, Jean (1910–   ),
existentialism, II 194a
literary criticism, I 605a
Genetic continuity, II 281b–293a
Aristotle, II 281b–282a
Balbiani, II 286b, 287a
Berzelius, II 283a, 283b
Bible, II 281b
Bonnet, II 284a–284b, 285a, 288b

Brown, Robert, II 285b
Butler, II 288a
Bütschli, II 287a
Cagniard de la Tour, II 283a–283b
causation, II 282a
cell division, II 285b–287b
Cell Theory, II 285a, 285b, 286b
cells, II 285b–292b
chromosomes, II 286b–289b, 291b
Cohn, Ferdinand, II 284a
Crane, H. R., II 291a
Creation, II 281b
Crick, II 289b–291a, 291b
Darwin, II 285a, 286b, 287b, 288a–288b
De Vries, II 289a–289b
DNA, II 286b, 289a, 289b–292b
Doty, II 291a
Dumortier, II 285b
Dusch, II 283b
Ehrenberg, C. G., II 285b
evolution, II 281b, 286b, 287b, 288a, 292a, 292b
fermentation, II 283a–283b
final cause, II 282a
Flemming, II 286b, 287a–287b
Fol, II 287a
formal cause, II 282a
genes, II 289a, 289b
genetic code, II 286b
Germ Theory of Disease, II 284a
germplasm, II 288b, 289a
Greece (ancient), II 281b–282a
Haeckel, II 288a
heredity, II 281b–293a
Hering, II 288a
Hertwig, II 287a, 289a
Heuser, II 287b
Hofmeister, II 286a
hybridization, II 285a
idioplasm, II 288a, 288b
interbreeding, II 285a
Joblot, II 282b–283a
Kölliker, II 286a
Kornberg, II 291a
La Mettrie, II 292a
Lavoisier, II 283a
Law of Biogenesis, II 281b
Leeuwenhoek, II 282b
Levinthal, II 291a
Liebig, II 283a, 283b
logos, II 282a
Malpighi, II 282b
Marmur, II 291a
material cause, II 282a
Maupertuis, II 284b–285a, 288a

meaning of, II 281b
Mendel, II 286b, 288a, 289b
Meselson, II 291a–291b
Meyen, II 285b
Mohl, II 285b
motive cause, II 282a
Nägeli, II 286a, 287b–288a, 288b, 289a
Orr, II 288a
Pasteur, II 282a, 283b
Pouchet, II 283b
preformation, II 284a
Redi, II 282a, 282b
Remak, II 286a–286b, 287a
RNA, II 289a
Roux, II 287b
Samson (Bible), II 281b
Schleicher, II 287b
Schleiden, II 285b, 286a
Schneider, II 287a
Schröder, II 283b
Schulze, II 283b
Schwann, II 283a–283b, 285b, 286a
Semon, II 288a
Spallanzani, II 283a
species, II 281b, 282a, 285b
Spencer, II 288b
spontaneous generation, II 281b–285b
Sprengel, II 285b
Stahl, II 291a–291b
sterilization, II 283b–284a, 289a
Strasburger, II 286b, 287a, 287b, 289a
Swammerdam, II 282a–282b
Taylor, II 291b
technology, II 292a
Trembley, II 284a–284b
Tschistiakoff, II 287a
Turberville, II 283a
Turpin, II 285b
Tyndall, II 283b–284a
Unger, II 286a
Vallisneri, II 282b
van Beneden, II 287a, 287b
Virchow, II 286a
viruses, II 285a–285b
Watson, J. D., II 289b–291b
Weismann, A., II 288b–289a
Wilson, E. B., II 286b–287a
Wöhler, II 283b
Wolff, Friedrich, II 285b
Genetic homology, I 239b
Genetics
acquired characteristics, II 617b–619b, 620b–621b
antiquity, I 231b–232a
Aristotle, I 231b–232a
evolutionism, II 177a, 186b

Fisher, R. A., II 186b
Haldane, II 186b
humanism, II 518b
morality, III 645a
pangenesis, II 624b, 625b, 626a
perfectibility, III 471a, 474b
probability, III 616a, 616b, 617b, 620a
progress, III 645a, 646b
recapitulation, IV 56a–56b, 58a
society, II 619b–620a
spontaneous generation, IV 307a
U.S.S.R., II 619b–620a, 620b, 621a, 621b
Volksgeist, IV 491a, 496a
Genghis Khan (1162–1227), ethics, IV 73a
Genius, II 293a–326b
Abrams, II 310b
academicians, II 303b–304a, 306b
Adam, II 308a
Addison, II 294b–295a, 306b, 307b
Adriani, II 293b
aesthetics, II 223b, 315b, 316a, 316b, 318b, 322b–323a, 323b, 325b; IV 356b
Affligemensis, II 314a
Alberti, II 293b, 301a, 308a, 309b, 317b
Alembert, II 294b
Alexander the Great, II 299b
André, II 294a
Apelles, II 299a, 299b
Aquila, II 320a
architecture, II 298a, 299a, 300a, 300b, 308a
Aretino, II 304b–305a, 308b, 317b, 320a
Aribo Scholasticus, II 314a, 317b
Ariosto, II 308b
Aristides Quintilianus, II 313a
aristocracy, II 320b
Aristotle, I 584b, 585b; II 293b, 299b, 309a, 309b, 320b
Aristoxenus, II 313a
arithmetic, II 313b
Aron, II 314a, 317a
art, II 293a–295b, 297a–299b, 304b–311a, 313a–318b, 325a, 326a
association of ideas, II 295a
astrology, II 293b
astronomy, II 313b
Bacchius Senex, II 313a
Bach, II 321a, 324a
Bacon, Francis, II 295b

Baeumler, II 295a
Balzac, II 294a, 308b
baroque, II 321a–323a
Baudelaire, II 310b
Baumgarten, II 295a
beauty, II 293b, 294a
Beethoven, II 325a, 325b
Bell, Clive, II 298b
Bernini, II 303a–303b, 309a
Bertram, II 295a
Bible, II 316a
Blake, II 304a, 306b, 307a, 308a
Boccaccio, II 293b, 301a, 310a, 317a
Bodmer, II 295a
Boethius, II 313a, 313b, 314a, 317a, 324b
Bohemians, II 303b–304a
Boileau, II 294a, 310a
Boucher, II 310b
Brunelleschi, II 298a, 300b
Bruno, II 293b, 306a, 317a–317b
Burckhardt, II 300a–300b
Cardano, II 293b
Carvallo, II 293b
Cassirer, II 308b
Castiglione, II 293b, 295a, 305a, 317a
Catullus, II 310a
Cennini, II 298a, 300b–301a
Chagall, II 304b
character, II 293a–293b, 295b
Chardin, II 306a
Cicero, II 305a, 309b, 314b
city-state, II 300b–302b
Coclico, II 316b, 319a
Colbert, II 303b
Coleridge, II 307b
Colonna, II 303a
common sense, II 294a, 294b, 309b
compassion, II 295b
competition, II 300b
composers, II 313a, 314a–325b
Condillac, II 294a
Condivi, II 293b
conscience, II 295b
Corneille, II 294b
Cosimo, II 302b
Counter-Enlightenment, II 109a
Courbet, II 298b
Craen, II 316a, 319a
craftsmanship, II 300a
Creation, II 293b
creativity, II 295a, 296a, 297a, 297b, 307a–307b, 309a, 319b–320a, 321a–321b, 326a

creativity in art, I 577b, 578a, 584b, 585b, 586b, 587a, 587b, 588a, 588b
crisis in history, I 595b
criticism, II 316a–316b, 318a, 325a
Croce, I 588b; II 293b
culture, II 297b, 298b, 311a
death, II 320b, 323a, 324b
deception, II 313b
defined, II 297a
Delacroix, II 305b
Deprès, II 319a, 320a–320b, 325b
Descartes, II 294a
dialectics, II 313b
dichotomy, II 309b–311a
Diderot, II 294a–294b, 310a–310b
diligence, II 293b, 296a
discoveries, II 293a, 295a
as divine, II 293b, 294b, 295a, 295b
Dolce, II 305a
Doni, Antonfrancesco, II 321a
Doni, Giovanni Battista, II 321a–321b
drama, II 323b
drawing, II 305b
Dryden, II 307a, 308b
Dubos, II 294a, 309b
Dürer, II 309a
Duris of Samos, II 299b
education, II 294b–295a, 299a–299b, 300a, 307b–308a, 313b, 314a, 317a, 323b
Egypt (ancient), II 298b
eloquence, II 317b
emotion, II 294b, 295b, 297b, 313b, 316a, 316b, 318b, 319a–319b, 323a, 323b, 324a
empathy, II 323a, 323b
enterprise, II 300b
enthusiasm, II 293b, 294a, 294b, 295a, 295b, 318a–318b
Erasmus, II 293b, 302a, 315b
Ercole of Ferrara, II 320a
Evelyn, II 294b
evolution, II 297a
evolution of literature, II 171a, 172a
exploration, II 293a
fancy, II 307a–307b
Ficino, II 309a, 310a, 320b
Filarete, II 298a
Fiorentino, II 302b
Flaubert, II 310b
Fontenelle, II 324a–324b
Formschneider, II 318a

Fracastoro, II 293b
France, II 294a–294b, 297b, 298b, 300b, 305a, 315b, 317b, 322b–323a
Franciabigio, II 302a
Franco of Cologne, II 314b
freedom, II 295a, 296a, 297b, 298a, 300b, 304a–304b, 313b, 316a, 316b, 320b
fundamental trait of, II 293a
Galileo, II 293b
geometry, II 313b
Gerard, II 295a, 306b, 307a
Germany, II 295a, 295b–296a, 305b, 306b, 307a, 315b, 317b, 323a
Gesualdo, II 320b–321b
Ghiberti, II 298a
Giotto, II 298b
Giovio, II 293b
Glareanus, II 315b, 316a, 317b–318a, 319b, 320a, 325b
Gluck, II 324a
God, II 293b, 297b, 300a, 308a–308b, 313a, 319b–320a
Goethe, II 296a, 301b
Gothic art, II 297b, 298a
Goya, II 307a
grace, II 305a
Gracián, II 293b–294a
grammar, II 313b
Grappin, II 294a, 295a, 295b, 296a
Great Britain, II 294b–295a, 297b, 298b, 300b, 303b, 305a, 305b, 306a, 308a, 310a, 315b, 322a
Greece (ancient), II 297b, 299a, 299b, 312b–313a, 315b, 317b–318a, 318b
Guido of Arezzo, II 313b, 314a
guilds, II 300a–300b
Guillaume de Machaut, II 315a
Hadrian, II 299b
Hamann, II 295b
harmony, II 313b, 314a, 315a, 315b, 322b, 323a, 324a
Helvétius, II 294b
Herder, II 295b, 306b, 324a–324b
Herrera, II 293b
Heyden, II 315b
history, II 297a–297b
Hoffman, II 324b
Hogarth, II 300b, 306a
Hollanda, II 293b, 303a, 305a, 308b
Homer, II 294b, 317a, 318a

Huarte, II 293b
Hugo, I 599b; II 310b
Huygens, II 294b
ideal, II 551a
idiosyncracies, II 297b, 301b–303a
imagination, II 294a, 294b, 295a, 304b, 307a–307b, 322a–323a, 323b
imitation, II 294a, 294b, 298a, 306a–306b, 317a, 323b, 324a
inclination, II 318a–318b
independency, II 295b
as an innate capability, II 293a, 293b
innovation, II 315b
inspiration, II 293b, 294a, 294b, 295a, 295b, 307a–307b, 316b, 318b, 323b–324a
instinct, II 294a, 295a, 295b, 314a, 317a, 325a
intuition, II 295b
invention, II 293a–295a, 304b, 307a–307b, 314b, 317b–318b, 319b
irrationalism, II 293a–293b, 294b, 295a, 295b, 305a, 318b
Italy, II 293b, 297b, 298b, 299a, 300b–303b, 308b, 315b, 323a–323b
James II, II 322a
Johnson, Samuel, II 307b
judgment, II 294a, 294b, 295a, 296a, 297b, 313a, 314a, 317a, 318a, 318b, 322b, 323a
Kant, I 588a; II 223b, 295b–296a, 317b, 323b–324a
Keble, II 310b
Klee, II 304b
Klopstock, II 295b
knowledge, II 294b, 295b, 313a
Lamb, II 309b
language, II 313b
Lasso, II 319a, 320a
Leo, II 323a
Leonardo da Vinci, II 298a, 298b, 301b, 302a, 304a, 308a, 317b
Lessing, II 295b
liberty, II 300b
Lipenius, II 293b, 295a
literary criticism, I 599b, 600a; II 297a, 306a, 318b
literature, II 298a, 299a, 301a–301b, 306a–307b
Locke, II 294b
Lomazzo, II 303a, 305a, 308a

Lombroso, II 308b
Longinus, II 304b
Lowell, J. R., II 305b
Lucian, II 299b
Luscinius, II 315b–316a, 317b, 319a
macrocosm and microcosm, II 313b
madness, II 294a, 308b–309b
magic, II 313a
Marcus Aurellus, II 299b
Masaccio, II 301b
matter, II 298b
mechanical aspect, II 294b
melancholy, II 308b–309b, 320a–321b
memory, II 293b, 294b
Mendelssohn, Moses, II 295b
Michelangelo, II 293b, 298b, 302a–302b, 303a, 304a, 305a, 308b, 309a, 320a
Middle Ages, II 297b, 298a, 298b, 300a, 303b, 313a–314b, 315a, 316b, 317b, 320a, 325b
Milton, II 295a
mind, II 293b, 298b, 324a
Moebius, II 308b
Monteverdi, II 321b
morality, II 295b, 314b
Mozart, II 324a, 325a
music, II 312b–326b
Naples, II 297b
nationalism, II 295b; IV 125a
natural laws, II 294a
Nature, II 294a, 294b, 295a, 295b, 307a, 318b, 321a, 324a
Neo-Platonism, II 308b
Nero, II 299b
Netherlands, II 295a–295b
Nietzsche, II 307b, 318b, 325a–325b
non finito, II 297b, 298b–299a
North, R., II 318b, 322a
Northcote, II 303b, 309b
Odo of Cluny, II 314b
Ogilvie, II 295a
organicism, III 422b
originality, II 295b, 306a–306b, 317b, 318a, 320b, 321a, 323b, 324a
Orpheus (myth), II 313a, 316a
Ovid, II 310a
painting, II 298a–298b, 299b, 300b, 301a, 301b, 304a, 305a–305b, 306a, 307b–308a, 317b–318a,

321a
Palestrina, II 321b
Pamphilos, II 299a–299b
Panofsky, II 308a
Parrhasios, II 299b
passions, II 294a
patrons, II 320b
Pausanias, II 299b
Pellegrini, II 293b
Pepys, II 322a
performances, II 293a
performers, II 313a, 313b, 314a, 316a
Perrault, II 294a
Petrarch, II 293b, 302a, 317a
philosophy, II 294b, 313a, 313b, 551a
Philostratus, II 299b
Picasso, II 304b
Piccolomini, II 293b
Pico, II 293b
Piero di Cosimo, II 302b
Plato, I 578a; II 293b, 295a, 299b, 308a, 309a, 309b, 317b–318a, 318b, 320b
Platonism, II 293a–293b, 298b, 308b, 310a, 310b
Pliny, II 299a–299b, 305a, 310a
Plutarch, II 299b
poetic license, II 319a
poetics, II 293a–293b, 304b
poetry, II 294a, 294b, 295a, 295b, 299b, 302a–302b, 304b, 310b, 312b–313a, 314a, 316a, 317b–318a, 318b, 319a, 320a, 321a, 323b
Poliziano, II 293b
Pope, II 305a, 306a–306b
Portugal, II 293b, 303a
power, II 294a, 294b, 295a, 295b
proto-Bohemians, II 304a
Pseudo-Aristotle, II 320b
psychology, II 294a, 295a, 297a, 304a–304b, 309b, 310b–311a, 320a, 320b–321a
Quintilian, II 305a, 309b
Racine, II 294b
Rameau, II 322b–323a, 323b
Raphael, II 298a, 203b–303a, 309a, 309b
Rapin, II 294a
rationality, II 318b
reason, II 294a, 294b, 295a, 295b, 296a, 307b
reincarnation, I 645b
Rembrandt, II 309a
Renaissance, II 293a, 293b,

294a–294b, 297b, 298a, 298b, 300a–302b, 303b–304a, 304b, 305a, 306a, 307b, 308a, 308b, 309a, 310a, 314a, 315a–321a, 325b; IV 125a, 128a
Reynolds, II 301b, 303a–303b, 306a, 306b, 307b–308a, 309b
rhetoric, II 313b
Rimbaud, II 308b
Robbia, II 301b
Rodin, II 299a
romanticism, II 298b, 304a–304b, 322a, 323a–326a; IV 201b, 202a, 202b, 205b
Rome (ancient), II 299b
Rousseau, II 322a, 322b, 323a–323b, 324a–324b
Rubens, II 303a, 309a
rules, II 294a, 294b, 295a, 295b, 317a, 319a, 319b, 323b, 325b
Ruskin, II 297b, 307a
Saint Augustine, II 320a
Saint Thomas Aquinas, II 320a
Saint-Evremond, II 294a
sanity, II 309b
Sarto, II 302a
Scaliger, II 308a, 320a
Schiller, II 307b
Schlegel, J. A., II 295a
Schopenhauer, II 308b
Schubart, II 324a
science, II 293b, 294a, 294b, 295a, 295b, 313a, 313b, 314a
sculpture, II 299a, 299b, 300b, 301a, 301b–302a, 317b–318a, 321a
Seneca, II 308b
senses, II 294a, 313b
Shaftesbury, II 294b, 308b, 320a
Shakespeare, II 294b, 306a–306b, 307a
Sidney, II 306a
singers, II 313b, 314a, 314b, 315a, 316a, 316b, 317b
skill, II 295b
sociology, II 297a
Socrates, II 293b, 317b–318a
Spain, II 293b–294a
Spataro, II 316b, 318a
spontaneity, II 293a, 294a, 295a, 307a–307b, 320b
Stahl, II 309b
Stoicism, II 299b
style, II 316a, 321a, 321b
Sulzer, II 295a–295b
as supernatural power, II

293b
Taine, II 308b
talent, II 293a, 293b, 294a, 295b, 304b–306a, 314a, 316b, 318a–318b, 319b, 320b, 323b–324a, 325a
taste, II 294a, 294b, 295a, 296a, 323b; IV 356b
Temple, II 294b, 305b, 307b
Theodorus of Samos, II 299a
Thüme, II 293b, 294a, 294b, 295a
Timotheus, II 313a, 316b
Tinctoris, II 315a, 315b, 316a, 316b
Tintoretto, II 302a
Tonelli, II 294b, 295a, 296a
Torricelli, II 293b
Trilling, II 308b–309a
truth, II 313b
Uccello, II 301b
uncertainty, II 313b
union in, II 209b–311a
Vasari, II 293b, 298a, 301b–303b, 305a–305b, 309b
Vauvenargues, II 294a
Velázquez, II 309b
Venice, II 297b
Vergil, II 295a
Vico, II 293b
Vida, II 306a
Volksgeist, IV 491a, 491b, 493a, 493b
Voltaire, II 294b
Vossius, II 295a
Wagner, Richard, II 325a
Walpole, II 306a
war, II 293a
wealth, II 299b
Wellek, II 304b, 307a
Wieland, II 295a
Wilhelm V, II 320b
Winckelmann, II 297b
Wolff, Christian, II 295a
Wölfflin, II 297b
Young, II 295a, 295b, 306b, 307a, 307b
Zarlino, II 319a, 319b
Zeitgeist, IV 535b, 536a
Zeuxis, II 299b
Zilsel, II 293b, 294a, 295a, 317b

Genossenschaft, III 651b
  See Property
Genotype, acquired characteristics, II 618a, 619a, 622a
Gentile, Giovanni (1875–1944)
  authority, I 159a–159b
  Platonism, III 510a
  totalitarianism, IV 408b
Gentili, Alberico (1552–

1608), Machiavellism, **III** 121a

Gentillet, Innocent, Machi-avellism, **III** 117b

Gentleman, virtuoso, **IV** 486a, 486b

Gentz, Friedrich von (1764–1832)
  balance of power, **I** 186a
  conservatism, **I** 477b, 481b
  French Revolution, **IV** 158b
  romanticism, **IV** 207a

Geocosm, harmony, **II** 389a

Geodesic line, **IV** 90a, 91b

Geoffroy, Julien-Louis (1743–1814), literary criticism, **I** 599a

Geoffrey of Monmouth (1100?–1154), historiog-raphy, **II** 483b

Geoffroy St. Hilaire, Étienne (1772–1844), evolution-ism, **I** 236b–237a

Geoffroy de Vinsauf (c. 1210),
  poetry, **III** 528b
  style, **IV** 331a

Geography,
  Bonpland, **II** 130a
  Brunhes, **II** 131a
  China, **I** 355a
  environment, **II** 129a–132a
  Febvre, Lucien, **II** 131a
  Herder, **II** 129b–130a
  humanism, **II** 521b
  Humboldt, Alexander von, **II** 130a
  Newbigin, **II** 130b
  progress, **III** 632b
  Renaissance, **IV** 440a
  Ritter, **II** 130a
  universal man, **IV** 440a

Geological Society of London, **IV** 419b

Geological Survey, U.S., **I** 475b

Geology
  Agricola, **III** 255b, 256a
  astronomy, **III** 255b
  Bible, **III** 255b
  Buffon, **II** 176b, 177a
  catastrophism, **IV** 417b, 418a, 418b, 419b, 420a, 420b, 422a, 422b, 423a
  continuity, **I** 492b, 498b–500b
  Descartes, **III** 257a
  earth, **III** 254b, 255a, 255b, 256b
  evolutionism, **II** 176b, 180a, 182b
  fossils, **III** 255b
  France, **III** 256a–256b
  God, **II** 359a
  Great Britain, **III** 256a–

256b
  Islam, **II** 645b
  linguistic paleontology, **IV** 425a–425b
  linguistics, **IV** 423b–424b, 425a–427b, 429a
  Lyell, **II** 180a; **IV** 424b
  Maillet, **II** 176b
  mathematics, **III** 178a
  mountains in literature, **III** 255b–257a, 259b
  religion, **IV** 106a
  science, **II** 645b
  Steno, **III** 255b, 256a
  symmetry, **IV** 352b–353a
  uniformitarianism, **I** 492b, 499b–500b; **IV** 417b, 418a, 418b, 419b, 420a, 420b, 422a, 422b, 423a, 423b–424b, 425a–427b, 429a
  Varenius, **III** 256b
  Victorians, **IV** 221b

Geometrical universe, **II** 443a–443b

Geometry
  Alexander of Aphrodisias, **III** 380b–381a
  Archimedes, **III** 134a
  Aristotle, **III** 380a
  art, **I** 456b, 457b, 458a, 459a; **II** 614a
  Babylonia, **III** 171a–172b
  Bolyai-Lobachevsky non-Euclidean, **IV** 304a
  causation, **III** 382a
  Comte, **III** 642a
  Descartes, **IV** 304a, 435b
  dualism, **IV** 304a
  empiricism, **III** 547a
  Euclid, **III** 380b; **IV** 304a
  game theory, **II** 266b
  genius, **II** 313b
  harmony, **II** 390a; **IV** 38a, 39a, 40a, 41b
  La Grange, **IV** 304a
  mathematics, **II** 612b, 613a, 613b, 614a; **III** 171b–174a, 175a, 176a, 178a, 180a, 184a, 184b; **IV** 304a
  matter, **III** 188b, 193a, 195a
  medieval science, **II** 196b, 197b, 199a, 200a, 202b
  methodology, **III** 380b, 382a, 389b
  Monge, **IV** 304a
  music, **II** 313b, 390a; **III** 260b, 263b, 270b
  mythology, **III** 290b
  Nature, **III** 350b
  necessity, **III** 352a, 353b, 356a, 356b, 357a
  Newton, **III** 195a, 380b, 382a, 389b
  non-Euclidean, **IV** 304a

numbers, **III** 406a, 406b
  optics, **III** 410a, 412a, 416a, 416b–417b, 420b
  Plato, **I** 462b–463a; **III** 188b; **IV** 33b, 39a, 40a
  Poncelet, **IV** 304a
  pragmatism, **III** 557b, 559b
  probability, **III** 605b, 610b
  progress, **III** 642a
  projective, **IV** 304a
  Pythagoreans, **IV** 33b, 38a, 39a, 40a, 40b, 41b
  Rameau, **III** 263b
  Ramism, **IV** 42b
  rationalism, **IV** 47b
  relativity, **IV** 84b, 85a, 87a–88a, 89a, 89b, 90b, 91a, 91b
  Renaissance, **IV** 438b, 440a
  Riemann, **IV** 304a
  scientific classification, **I** 462b–463a, 464a
  space, **IV** 295a, 295b, 301b, 302a–305a
  Sumer, **III** 171a–172b
  symmetry, **IV** 346a, 349b, 351b
  Tartini, **III** 263b
  technology, **IV** 359b
  time, **IV** 349b, 399b, 400a, 403a, 403b
  unity of science, **IV** 431b, 434a, 435b
  universal man, **IV** 438b, 440a
  universe, **IV** 38a, 39a, 40a, 40b, 41b
  utility, **IV** 456a–456b
  Vico, **III** 357a

George, Stefan (1868–1933),
  classicism, **I** 451a, 455b
  literary criticism, **I** 606a
  Platonism, **III** 524b
  symbolism, **IV** 342b, 344b

George II, King (1683–1760),
  Enlightenment, **II** 89b
  periodization in literary history, **III** 483a

George III, King (1738–1820),
  loyalty, **III** 114a
  periodization in literary history, **III** 482b
  social contract, **IV** 260b

George IV, King (1762–1830),
  periodization in literary history, **III** 482b

Gerard (c. 1100), reformation, **IV** 65a

Gerard, Alexander (1728–1795)
  aesthetics, **I** 588a
  catharsis, **I** 265b
  empathy, **II** 87b
  genius, **II** 295a, 306b, 307a
  pity, **I** 265b

sympathy, **II** 87b
  taste, **IV** 355b–356a

Gerard of Borgo San Don-nino, prophecy, **III** 668a–668b

Gerard of Brussels, mechan-ical science, **II** 197b

Gerard of Cremona (1114?–1187), methodology, **III** 381a

Gerde, Daniel, Reformation, **IV** 68a

Geremia of Montagnone, humanism, **II** 517b

Gergonne, Joseph Diez (1771–1859), axiomatiza-tion, **I** 167b, 168a

Gerhard, Johann (1582–1637), hierarchy, **II** 435a

Geri of Arezzo, humanism, **II** 515b

Geriatrics, longevity, **III** 93a

Géricault, Jean Louis (1791–1824)
  David and, **III** 341a
  naturalism in art, **III** 341b
  romanticism, **IV** 208b

Germ theory
  disease, **II** 405a
  genetic continuity, **II** 284a

German language, **II** 667b, 669b, 670b–671b, 691b

Germanicus Caesar (15 B.C.–19 A.D.)
  neo-classicism in art, **III** 368b
  primitivism, **III** 579b

Germany
  absolutism, **I** 593b
  academic freedom, **I** 10b
  acquired characteristics, **II** 620b
  aesthetics, **II** 216a; **IV** 356a–356b
  agriculture, **III** 651b
  animals, **III** 651b
  apocalypse, **I** 391a
  architecture, **I** 398b
  art, **II** 305b, 306b, 307a
  balance of power, **I** 181b, 186a, 186b, 187b
  baroque, **I** 189a, 189b–190b, 191a, 191b, 192a, 194a, 194b, 195a; **III** 483b, 484a
  Biedermeier, **III** 483b
  Buddhism, **I** 256b
  capitalism, **I** 396a
  Capuchins, **I** 394b
  catastrophism, **IV** 418a
  Church, **I** 412b
  city, **I** 432a
  Civil Code (1900), **III** 29b

civil disobedience, I 435a, 438a

class, I 441b; IV 500a

classicism, I 450b–451a, 451b, 453a–454b, 455b; III 483b

common law, II 691a–691b, 692b–693a, 693b

communism, IV 268b, 273b

conservatism, I 479b, 480b, 481a, 481b, 482b, 483a–483b, 484b

Counter-Enlightenment, II 103b, 104b, 106a–106b, 107a, 108a–109b

crisis in history, I 591a, 591b, 592b, 593b, 595a

culture, I 613b–614a; III 250b, 252a; IV 165a, 165b

custom, II 692b, 693a

das junge Deutschland, III 483b

deism, I 649b, 651a

democracy, I 661a, 665b; IV 264b, 265b, 266b, 267a, 268b, 272b, 274a

despotism, II 12a

determinism, II 20a–20b, 25a, 30b

drama, II 206b, 208a–208b, 209a

dualism, II 39a

economic history, II 45a, 60b, 61a

education, I 388a; II 99b

empathy, II 85b–87a, 88a, 88b

Enlightenment, II 89a, 89b, 91b, 99b

environment, II 124b

equality, II 141a, 142a

evolution of literature, II 170b, 171a

evolutionism, II 181b

expressionism, II 206a–207a, 208b–209a; III 483b

fascism, III 331b–332a

Faust (legend), III 245a, 247a, 248a, 250b, 251a, 251b, 252a

folklore, II 265a

genius, II 295a, 295b–296a, 305b, 306b, 307a, 315b, 317b, 323a

Genossenschaft, III 651b

Gothic, II 367a–369a, 370b–371a, 371b–372a, 372b, 373a, 373b; III 484a

Great Britain, IV 106b

heresy, I 649b

historicism, II 456b–462b

historiography, II 20a–20b, 25a, 483b, 484a, 489b, 490b–491a, 491b, 493a,

493b–495b

history, II 20a–20b, 25a

holy, II 512a

humanism, II 515b, 520b

ideal, II 549a, 550a–551b

idealism, I 447a; III 494b; IV 200a, 220a

impressionism, II 583a; III 484a

individualism, II 305b, 306b, 307a, 595b–596a, 601a–601b

industry, III 653a

international peace, III 449a, 454a, 455a

intolerance, IV 117a

irony, II 629b, 633a

Judaism, III 488a

Jugendstil, III 484a

Julius Caesar, III 651b

law, II 673b–674a, 686a, 689b, 690b; III 3b, 5a, 7a, 11a–12a, 29b–30a, 653a

liberalism, III 676b

linguistics, II 670b–671b; IV 425a, 428b

literary criticism, I 596a–596b, 597b–298b, 600a, 606a

literature, III 82a, 83a, 84a–84b, 494b–495a

Machiavellism, III 120b, 125a

Magyars, I 381a

Man-Machine, III 142b–143a

mannerism, III 484a

Marxism, I 664a–664b; III 149a, 149b, 151a, 152a, 152b, 154a, 157a, 161a–166a; IV 264b–267b, 275a

materialism, IV 106b

mathematics, III 178a

millenarianism, III 225a

mimesis, III 227b, 228a

modernism, I 419b–420b, 424a–424b, 425b, 426b

music, II 315b, 317b, 323a; III 265a, 267a, 267b, 271a–271b

mythology, II 39a; III 292b, 293a, 304a, 304b–306b, 310a, 311a, 313b, 314a, 315b

nationalism, II 690b; III 250b, 319a, 320b, 321a, 326a–328b, 330a–331b, 335a–337b; III 304b; IV 125a, 493b

natural law, III 5a, 21a, 22a, 23a

natural liberty, II 69a

naturalism, III 483b

naturalism in art, III 339a,

341a, 345a

necessity, III 358b

neo-classicism in art, III 369b

nomads, III 651b

organicism, III 421b, 424b, 425a–425b, 426a

Orientalism, III 432a, 436a, 438a

peasantry, IV 500a

Peasants' Revolt, I 391a, 391b, 479b

perfectibility, III 475a

periodization in history, III 478a

periodization in literary history, III 482a–484a, 485b

philanthropy, III 488a

philosophy, IV 106b, 208a–211a

Pietism, I 403a, 595a; IV 493a–495b; IV 199b–200a

Platonism, III 506b, 514a, 519a–522a, 523b

poetry, III 529b

polygamy, I 391a

positivism, III 538a, 540b

pragmatism, III 557a, 557b, 560a, 565b, 567a

predestination, II 30b

primitivism, III 591b, 593a, 596b, 597a–597b, 602a

private property, III 651b, 653a, 653b, 655b

probability, III 605a

progress, III 647b

prophecy, III 666a–666b, 669b

protest movements, III 672b, 674a, 674b, 676a, 676b

psychology, IV 11b, 13a, 13b, 15b, 22b, 24a, 24b, 25a

Ramism, IV 44b

realism, III 483b

realism in literature, IV 51b, 52b–53a, 54b, 55a, 55b

Reformation, I 389a–391a, 394b, 395b; IV 66a–67a, 68a

religion, IV 97a, 106a, 106b, 107b, 108a, 116b

Renaissance, IV 121b, 123b, 124b, 125a

revisionism, IV 263b–276a

revolution, IV 156b, 158a–160b, 164a, 165a, 165b

rococo, III 484a

romanticism, I 453b–454a, 482b–483a, 595a; III 250b, 304a, 304b–306b, 483b, 519a–522a; IV 187b, 188b,

189b, 190a, 192a, 192b, 193b–195a, 196b–202a, 203a, 204a, 205a–205b, 206b, 207a–209b

Rome (ancient), III 591b

scientific method, IV 106b

Seven Years War, III 483a

skepticism, IV 248b–250a

social contract, IV 253a, 261a

Social Democratic Party (SPD), IV 264a–268b, 272a–273a

social welfare, IV 277b

socialism, III 651b, 676b; IV 264a, 264b, 266a–267b, 269b, 270b, 271b–272b, 273b–274b, 290a, 292a, 510a

society, II 692b, 693a

space, IV 298a, 300b, 303a

State, I 405b, 661a, 665b

Sturm und Drang, III 483b, 485b

symbolism, III 483b; IV 338a–338b, 341a, 342b–343a, 343b, 344b

taste, IV 356a–356b

technology, IV 360a, 360b, 361a, 362a, 364a

temperance, IV 371a

theology, II 30b

Thirty Years War, III 483a

thought, III 250b

tolerance, I 400b

totalitarianism, IV 406a, 408b, 410a

tribes, III 651b

truth, IV 106b

uniformitarianism, IV 418a, 425a, 428b

U.S.S.R., II 563a

utility, IV 453b

Utopia, IV 461b

Volksgeist, IV 491a, 491b–494b, 495a–496a

vox populi, IV 500a

war, III 455a; IV 503b, 504a, 504b, 505a, 505b

welfare state, IV 509a, 510a–510b, 512b, 514a

Weltschmerz, IV 204a

Wilson, Pres., I 665a

witchcraft, IV 521a

women, IV 528a

See also East Germany; Nazism; West Germany

Germplasm

   chromosomes, II 288b, 289a

   genetic continuity, II 288b, 289a

   pangenesis, II 624b–625a

Geroch of Reichersberg, prophecy, III 666a

Gerontology, apologism, III 89b–90a

Gerson, Jean de (1362–?1428)
double truth, II 34a
iconography, II 526b, 539a

Gerstenberg, Heinrich Wilhelm von (1737–1823)
Counter-Enlightenment, II 107a
romanticism, IV 187b

Gerville, Charles de, Gothic, II 373a

Gervinus, Georg Gottfried (1805–1871)
classicism, I 454a
historiography, II 494a
literature, III 83a

Gesner, Konrad von (1516–1565)
alchemy, I 31b
classification of the sciences, I 465b
linguistics, III 63b

Gestalt treatment
perception, IV 182b
pleasure, II 383a
psychology, IV 14a–14b, 15b, 28a

Gesualdo, Carlo
genius, II 320b
music, II 320b–321a, 321b

Geulincx, Arnold (1624–1669)
Cartesian, I 302b
teleology, I 302b

Geyl, Pieter
determinism, II 19a, 19b, 21b
historiography, II 19a, 19b, 21b
progress, III 647b

Gherardini, Giovanni, romanticism, IV 190b

Ghil, René (1862–1925), symbolism, IV 343a

Ghiberti, Lorenzo (1378–1455)
art, II 298a, 301a
genius, II 298a, 301a
mimesis, III 227b
mythology, III 280a
neo-classicism in art, III 370a

Ghirlandaio (1449–1494), Platonism, III 511b

Ghosts, mythology, III 309a, 309b, 315a

Ghyka, M., aesthetics, II 219a

Giarda, Christoforo, iconography, II 532b

Gibbon, Edward (1737–1794)
balance of power, I 186a
deism, I 651a
economic history, II 46b
Enlightenment, II 89b, 90a, 90b, 92a, 93a, 94b
historicism, II 458a
historiography, II 491a, 491b
liberty, II 94b
mathematics, III 181a–181b
mythology, III 303a
revolution, IV 155a

Gibbs, Josiah Willard (1839–1903)
entropy, II 113a–113b, 114b, 116a
determinism, II 24b
historiography, II 24b
probability, III 620a
space, IV 304b
technology, IV 363b

Gibb's Phase Rule, II 24b

Gibb's thermodynamic potential, II 114b

Gibraltar, positivism, III 537a

Giddings, Franklin Henry (1855–1931), classification of the sciences, I 465b

Giddon, Charles, attitude toward antiquity, I 80a

Gide, André (1869–1951), classicism, I 455a; IV 196b
evolutionism, II 183a
imagination, III 208a
motif, III 240b
romanticism, IV 196b
symbolism, IV 340b, 344b

Giehlow, K., iconography, II 537b

Gierke, Otto von (1841–1921)
individualism, II 597a, 600a
Volksgeist, IV 494a

Giesebrecht, Wilhelm von (1814–1889), historiography, II 494b

Gifts
Greece (ancient), II 676b, 677b, 678a
law, II 676b, 677b, 678a, 686b, 688b

Gilbert, Cass (1859–1934), Gothic, II 372b

Gilbert, Neal, methodology, III 382b

Gilbert, William (1540–1603), anthropomorphism, I 89a
atomism, I 135a, 136a
cosmic voyages, I 533b
economic history, II 45a
gravitation, III 194a

imagination, III 213a
magnetism, II 197a
matter, III 192b, 194a
methodology, III 387a
mountains, III 256b
Newton and, III 387a

Gildon, Charles, deism, I 650a

Giles, Herbert Allen (1845–1935), China, I 367a

Giles of Rome (d. 1262), Islam, II 649b
matter, III 192a

Gilgamesh, King (legend), III 275b, 279a, 279b
death, I 634b
freedom of speech, II 252b
longevity, III 89b

Gilliéron, Jules (1854–1926), language, II 671b
linguistics, III 70a

Gilly, Friedrich, neo-classicism in art, III 369b

Gilpin, William (1724–1804), Gothic, II 370a
ut pictura poesis, IV 473b

Gilson, Etienne
beauty, I 197b, 210a
Creation, I 574b
God, I 574b; II 363b

Ginsberg, Morris, individualism, II 600a, 601a

Ginsburg, Christian D. (1831–1914), iconography, II 539b

Giorgi-Bertòla, A. de, literature, III 82b

Giorgione (c. 1478–1511), iconography, II 529b
impressionism, II 577b
Nature, III 349b

Giotto (1276?–?1337)
Boccaccio and, IV 122a
Christianity, I 383a
genius, II 298b
mythology, III 289a, 291a
neo-classicism in art, III 369a, 370a
painting, IV 122a, 122b
temperance, IV 372a, 373a, 373b, 374b

Giovio, Paolo (1483–1552), genius, II 293b
iconography, II 530a

Girard, Abbé Gabriel (1677–1748), numbers, III 403a

Giraudoux, Jean (1882–1944), motif, III 241a

Girondins, democracy, I 661b

Gissing, George (1857–1903), realism in literature, IV 52b, 54a

Giustiniani, Bernardo (1408–1489), historiography, II 485a, 485b

Gjellerup, Karl (1857–1919), Buddhism, I 256b

Glaber, Radulphus (fl. 1059), macrocosm, IV 372a

Glacken, Clarence, conservation, I 471b, 472a, 472b

Gladden, Washington (1836–1918)
philanthropy, III 489a
reformation, IV 69a

Gladiators, law, II 687a

Gladstone, William Ewart (1809–1898)
constitutionalism, I 491a
rhetoric, IV 172a

Glanvil, Ranulf de (d. 1190), common law, II 694a, 694b

Glanville, Joseph (1636–1680)
causation, I 276b
demonology, I 670a
Cosmic Fall, I 510b
cosmic voyages, I 529b
certainty, I 304b, 308a, 310a
perennial philosophy, III 461a
skepticism, IV 245b

Glareanus, Henricus (1488–1563), genius in music, II 315b, 316a, 317b–318a, 319b, 320a, 325b

Glasenapp, Helmuth von, Buddhism, I 256b

Glauber, Johann Rudolf (1604–1668), alchemy, I 33a

Glaucera (myth), III 290b

Glisson, Francis (1597–1677), health, II 401a

Glorious Revolution, I 657b
conservatism, I 479b
Great Britain, II 369b

Glory
Boethius on, II 231b
fate, II 231b
fortune, II 231b
good, II 231b
humanism, II 522a
prophet, III 665a

Glossa ordinaria, II 685b

Glossators, II 691b, 692b, 694a

Glossology, linguistics, III 61b

Glottochronology, III 72a

Glover, Edward, war, IV 505b

Glover, Richard (1712–1785), Newton and, III 393a
optics, III 393a

Gluck, Christoph Willibald (1714–1787)
genius, II 324a
poetry, IV 472b

Gnomon, measurement of time, **IV** 400a
Gnosticism, **II** 326b–331b
  Adam (Bible), **II** 327a
  aeons, **II** 330b
  agnosticism, **I** 19a
  alienation, **I** 35b–36a
  angels, **II** 329a, 330b
  Aristotelianism, **II** 329b, 347a–347b
  asceticism, **II** 328a–328b
  astrology, **I** 125a–125b
  Basilides of Alexandria, **II** 329a–329b, 330b
  Bible, **II** 327b–330a, 337b, 341b, 342b, 349b, 353a
  Bogomils, **II** 327a
  Buddhism, **I** 255a
  Cathari, **II** 327a
  Celsus, **II** 330a
  Christianity, **I** 35a, 35b; **II** 42a–42b, 155b, 326b–331a; **IV** 229b
  cosmos, **II** 329b
  death, **I** 645a
  demiurge, **II** 327a
  demonology, **II** 327a, 328a
  dignity, **IV** 138b
  Doresse, **II** 327b
  dualism, **II** 38b, 42a–43a
  Egypt (ancient), **II** 327b, 330a
  Elohim, **II** 329a
  Epiphanes, **II** 328a
  eschatology, **II** 155a–155b, 157b
  ethics, **II** 328a–328b, 331a
  evil, **II** 327a, 328b, 329a
  faith, hope, and charity, **II** 210a
  Faust (legend), **III** 246a
  free will, **II** 244a
  freedom, **II** 328b
  God, **II** 328b, 329a, 331a, 339b
  good, **II** 329a
  Greece (ancient), **II** 327b, 328a, 329a, 330a
  harmony, **IV** 40b–41a
  Harnack, **II** 330b
  Hegesippus, **II** 327a
  Hekhaloth, **II** 330b
  Heracleon, **II** 330a
  heresy, **II** 330a, 331a
  hermeticism, **II** 431b
  Ialdabaoth (Bible), **II** 328b, 329a
  impiety, **II** 565a
  India (ancient), **II** 329a, 330a
  Iran (ancient), **II** 327b, 330a
  Islam, **II** 645b, 650a–652a
  Israel (ancient), **II** 565a
  Jesus Christ, **II** 327a, 327b, 328a, 329b, 330b
  Jonas, Hans, **II** 330a
  Judaic Christianity, **I** 375a
  Judaism, **II** 326b–329a, 330a, 330b, 331a, 565a
  Judas Iscariot (Bible), **II** 328a
  Justin, **II** 327a, 329a
  knowledge, **II** 326b, 327a–327b, 645b, 650a, 650b–651a, 651b, 652a
  Krause, M., **II** 327b
  law, **II** 328a
  love, **III** 96b, 107a
  magic, **II** 327a–328a, 329b
  Manicheism, **II** 42b, 327a
  Marcion of Pontus, **II** 327a, 330b
  Marcus, **II** 329b
  matter, **III** 190b
  Menander, **II** 327a
  Mesopotamia (ancient), **II** 330a
  metaphor, **III** 205b
  Mithraism, **II** 330a
  morality, **II** 328a
  Moses (Bible), **II** 328b–329a
  mythology, **II** 327a–329b
  Nag-Hammadi texts, **II** 327b
  Neo-Platonism, **III** 376b
  Ophites, **II** 330a
  Orientalism, **III** 438b
  origin of, **I** 375a; **II** 42b, 330a–330b
  paganism, **II** 42b, 330b
  perfectibility, **III** 468a
  Peterson, E., **II** 330b
  philosophy, **II** 329a–331a
  Platonism, **II** 327a, 329b, 330a
  Plotinus, **II** 330a
  psychology, **II** 327b
  Ptolemy, **II** 329b
  Puech, **II** 327b
  Pythagoreans, **IV** 40b–41a
  Quispel, **II** 330b
  reincarnation, **I** 645a
  religion, **III** 205b
  Renaissance, **IV** 138b
  Roman Catholic Church, **II** 42b, 327a–327b
  Rome (ancient), **II** 327a, 328a, 329a–330b
  Saint Augustine, **II** 43b
  Saint Ignatius of Antioch, **II** 330b
  Saint Irenaeus, **II** 327a–327b, 329b
  Saint James, **II** 327b
  Saint John, **II** 43a–43b, 327b, 328a, 328b, 329b
  Saint Paul, **II** 43a–43b, 327b, 330b–331a
  salvation, **II** 326b; **IV** 229a, 229b
  Satan, **II** 328a
  Saturninus, **II** 328a
  Scholem, **II** 330b
  sex, **II** 328a
  Simon Magus (Bible), **II** 327a, 328a, 330b
  sin, **II** 328a; **IV** 229a, 229b
  syncretistic aspect of, **II** 331a
  Syria (ancient), **II** 330a
  theodicy, **IV** 380b
  Theodosius II, **II** 329b
  Theodotus, **II** 329b
  theology, **II** 328b–330a
  tragic sense, **IV** 414b, 415a
  Trajan, **II** 330b
  transcendentalism, **II** 330a
  universe, **IV** 40b–41a
  Valentianism, **II** 327b, 329b–330a, 330b–331a
  wisdom, **II** 328b, 329b
  Wolfson, H. A., **II** 329b, 330b
  Zeus (myth), **II** 329a
Goals
  Aristotle, **IV** 175a–175b
  Bentham, **IV** 178b
  evolution, **IV** 180a, 181a
  good, **IV** 173b–175a, 176a–176b, 177a, 178b, 180a, 181a, 181b, 185b
  Marxism, **III** 146b–147a; **IV** 181a
  Plato, **IV** 175a
  pleasure, **IV** 178b
  progress, **III** 624a, 637b
  right, **IV** 173b–175a, 176a–176b, 177a, 178b, 180a, 181a, 181b, 185b
  Saint Augustine, **IV** 176a–176b
  Socrates, **IV** 174b–175a
  Stoicism, **IV** 176a
  Victorians, **IV** 218b
Gobineau, Joseph Arthur de (1816–1882)
  China, **I** 370b
  historiography, **II** 500a
  nationalism, **III** 330b
Goclenius (1547–1628), classification of the arts, **I** 459a
God, **I** 571a–577a; **II** 331b–366b
  Abelard, **I** 326a; **II** 343a
  Aeschylus, **III** 574b
  Alexander, S., **I** 576a
  Al-Ghazali, **I** 288b, 289a
  Allah, **II** 344b–345a
  Al-Nazzām, **I** 287a–287b
  ambivalent form, of, **II** 338b
  amorality, **II** 334b
  Anatolia (ancient), **II** 333b
  annihilation, **I** 571b
  Anselm, **I** 573a; **II** 343a
  apostasy, **II** 337a
  archeology, **II** 331b–333a, 343b
  Aristotelianism, **II** 363a
  Aristotle, **I** 272a, 572a, 672b; **II** 32a, 163a, 339a, 339b, 341a, 377b; **III** 273b, 465a; **IV** 6b, 50b, 530b
  Arius, **I** 377a–377b
  Arminius, **II** 28b
  art, **I** 597b; **II** 297b, 308a–308b, 340b, 574b, 582b; **III** 574b; **IV** 123a
  Assyria, **II** 335b–336a
  authority, **I** 146b, 147a, 147b, 148b, 150a; **II** 356a, 358b
  Averroës, **II** 32a
  Avicenna, **I** 288a–288b
  Babylonia, **II** 335b–336a
  Bach, **III** 267a–267b
  Bacon, Francis, **I** 294b, 301b; **II** 349a, 355b; **IV** 434a
  Barth, **II** 29a, 359b, 360a–360b, 363b; **III** 467a
  Bayle, **II** 355b; **IV** 119b, 120a
  beauty, **I** 197a–197b, 585b; **III** 368b
  Being, **II** 361b, 363a, 363b, 364b, 365b
  Bergson, **I** 576a; **II** 359a
  Berkeley, **I** 276b, 572b; **II** 246a, 352a–352b
  Bible, **I** 571a–571b; **II** 336a–337b, 358a, 359b, 360b, 361a, 363a, 365b, 366a
  biology, **II** 359a
  birth, **II** 332a–332b
  Blake, William, **II** 433b
  Blanshard, Brand, **II** 358a
  Boccaccio, **II** 233b–234a
  Bodin, **II** 355a
  Boethius of Dacia, **II** 33b
  Bosanquet, **II** 358a
  Bossuet, **I** 279b
  Bowne, **II** 358a
  Boyle, **I** 311a; **II** 352a, 355a
  Bradley, F. H., **II** 358a, 415b
  Brahmanism, **II** 344a
  Brightman, **I** 576b; **II** 359a
  Brunner, **II** 360a–360b
  Bruno, **I** 327b; **II** 347b–348b, 350b; **II** 443; **III** 194a, 510b
  Buddha, **II** 344a–344b

Buddhism, I 251a, 256b; II 344a–344b

Bultmann, II 360a–360b, 361a, 365b

Buridan, II 202a

Calvin, I 262a, 392a; II 142b, 349a; III 271a; IV 67a, 533a

Calvinism, I 572b; III 654a

Camus, II 364a

Canaan, II 336b, 337b

Carlyle, IV 200b

Cartesianism, III 461a

causation, I 272a, 273b, 274a, 274b–275a, 276b, 277a, 279b, 290a, 294b, 296b, 297b–299a, 299b, 301a–304a; II 341a, 352b, 357a, 358b

Chain of Being, I 326b

Chalcidius, III 381b

chance, I 336a, 336b; II 226b–231a, 232a–235a, 236a

chance images, I 342a

charity, II 209b–214b

Charron, I 301b

Chateaubriand, IV 201a

China (ancient), II 344b

Christianity, I 571a–571b, 572b; II 338a, 339b, 341b–343a, 345a, 349b, 354b–366b, 567a, 582b; III 588b, 589a, 590a, 590b, 592a

Church of England, II 361b

Cicero, II 340b, 438b–439a

city, I 427b, 428b–429a, 430b

civil disobedience, I 435b–437a

Clarke, Samuel, II 352a

class, I 446a

Cohen, Morris R., II 360a

common law, II 691b, 695b

communication, III 657a–661a

Comte, II 356a, 415b; III 642a

Confucianism, I 356a, 357a, 360a, 360b

conservatism, I 482a

Constantine, I 376b

Copernicus, II 347b

Cosmic Fall, I 505a–505b, 506a, 507a–508a, 509a, 510b, 511a, 512a, 512b

cosmic images, I 513a, 514b, 516a, 517a, 518a, 519a

cosmic voyages, I 526b, 532a

cosmology, I 543b, 549b; II 348a, 356a, 357a, 359a; IV 306a

cosmos, II 334a–336a, 338b, 340a–341a, 343b

Counter-Enlightenment, II 102a, 102b, 103b, 104a, 108b, 111b

creatio ex nihilo, I 571a–573a, 575b, 576a–576b, 577a

Creation, I 573a–577a; II 336a, 336b, 338b, 339a, 340a, 343b, 344a, 345a, 357a

creativity in art, I 577b–578a, 578b–579a, 580a, 585b, 586a–587b

Crete (ancient), II 333a, 333b

Critias, III 575a

Cullman, II 363a

culture, II 127b–129a, 132b, 356a, 358a, 359b, 364a, 364b, 365b–366b

cycles, I 623b, 624b

cynicism, III 585b

Cyprus, II 333b

Dalton, II 355a

damnation, II 345a, 359b, 361a

dance, II 333a

Dante, II 233a; III 511a

Darwin, II 356a

David (Bible), II 336b, 412b

death, I 635b, 640b, 644a; II 333a, 335a–335b, 336a, 337b, 338b, 340b, 341a, 343b, 353b

deism, I 646b, 647a, 647b, 648a, 648b, 650a, 650b

demonology, I 667b, 668a, 669a, 669b; II 336a, 337a, 342a

Derham, II 352a

Descartes, I 276a, 296b, 297b, 302a, 304b, 305a–306a, 575a, 639b; II 349b–350a, 350b, 351a, 355a, 444a; III 193a, 193b, 257a, 356a; IV 244b

design argument, I 672b, 673a–676a

destiny, II 336a

determinism, II 19b, 20a, 20b, 21a, 21b, 24b, 25b–31a, 237b–238a, 240b

Dewart, II 365b

Dewey, II 360a

Diderot, II 353a–353b

dignity, IV 136b–139a, 140b, 142a–143a, 144a, 145a–146a

Diopithes, II 566b

ditheism, II 342b

double truth, II 32a–37a

drama, II 340b

Drummond, III 474b

dualism, II 38a, 38b, 40b, 41a, 42a–42b, 43a, 335b, 337a, 338b, 339b, 344b; IV 393b

Duns Scotus, I 275a

Ebeling, II 365b

education, II 74b, 79a

Edwards, IV 109b, 110a

Egypt (ancient), II 331b, 333b–335b, 336b, 340a, 341b, 345a, 564b; III 11a; IV 225b

emanationism, I 572a

empiricism, II 351b–353a, 355b

Enlightenment, II 353a–354a, 355b–359a, 364a

environment, II 122b, 127b, 128a, 128b, 129a, 132b

Epicurus, III 274a

equality, II 138a–138b, 140a–141a, 142a, 142b, 143b

equity, II 151a

Erasmus, II 348b

Erigena, I 573–574a; II 210b

eschatology, II 154b–156a, 157a–161a, 337a–337b, 339a, 365b, 366a

ethics, II 334b, 347b, 348b, 351a; III 440b, 441a, 441b, 445b; IV 70b, 72a, 319a, 319b, 320a, 320b

Eudemus of Rhodes, II 339a

evil, II 161b, 162b–165a, 166a, 168a, 335a, 338a, 339a, 339b, 340b, 343b–344a, 353a; III 571b; IV 378b–382a

evolution, II 352a

evolutionism, II 176a, 178b, 179a, 180a, 183b, 184a, 185a, 186a, 359a

existence of, I 23b–24a; II 352b, 353b, 355b

existentialism, II 189b, 192a–193b, 359a, 360a, 362b

faith, II 209b–214b, 337b, 347a, 349a, 356a, 358b, 359b, 360b, 363a, 364a, 365a

Farrer, II 361b

fate, II 226b–231a, 232a–235a, 236a; III 571b

Faust (legend), III 246a, 247a, 248a, 248b, 251b

fear, III 575a

Feuerbach, II 356a

Ficino, II 347a, 442a; III 511a; IV 145a

fideism, II 355b, 356a

Figurism, I 359b, 360a, 360b

foreknowledge, II 229b, 230a–230b, 232b, 238a

fortune, II 226b, 227b–231a, 232a–235a, 236a

free will, I 586b; II 237b–238a, 240b, 242b, 243b, 244a, 244b, 245a, 246a–247a, 248b, 343a, 345a

freedom, I 571b, 575b, 576b, 577b, 586b; II 249b, 250a, 251a, 360b, 361b, 364a

freedom of speech, II 253a, 254b, 255a–255b, 256b, 258b, 262a

Galileo, I 301b; II 346b–347a, 352a; IV 393b

game theory, II 263b

Gassendi, I 303b

Gay, II 355b

general will, II 275b

genius, II 293b, 297b, 300a, 308a–308b, 313a, 319b–320a

geology, II 359a

Gilson, I 574b; II 363b

Gnosticism, II 328b, 329a, 331a, 339b

Goethe, II 350b

good, II 338b, 339a, 339b, 340b, 341a, 349a, 352b, 354a; III 571b; IV 174a, 176b–177b, 182b, 183a, 379a, 380a, 380b, 484b

grace, II 238a, 359b; III 466a, 466b

Greece (ancient), I 571a, 571b–572a, 645a; II 333a, 338a, 339b–341b, 343a, 357a, 357b, 360b, 363a, 565b, 566a, 566b, 674b, 678a, 678b, 681a, 682a, 682b, 684a; III 347a

Green, T. H., II 415a

Grotius, I 488b; II 355a

Hakewill, I 507b–508a, 512a

Hamann, II 103b, 104a, 354a

Hamilton, Wm., II 363b–364a

happiness, II 377b, 378b–379a, 380b

harmony, II 388a, 389b, 390a, 390b, 391a, 392a, 392b, 393b, 394a, 394b

Harnack, II 357b

Harris, W. T., II 358a

Hartshorne, I 576a; II 362a

health, II 395b, 396a, 396b,

397a, 397b, 399a, 403a, 403b
Hegel, II 16a, 24a, 158a, 348b, 357b–358a, 358b, 359a, 362b, 409b, 410a–411a, 412a, 412b; IV 290b, 291a, 318a, 493a
Heidegger, II 193b
henotheism, II 334a–334b
Herder, II 350b
heresy, II 339a, 416b–420b, 422a–427a
hermeticism, II 431a, 431b–432a, 432b, 433a
Herodotus, II 513a
Hesiod, II 513a; III 573b
hierarchy, II 438b–439b, 440b, 441a, 442a, 443a, 444a–446b
Higher Law doctrine, I 435b–437a
Hinduism, II 343a–344a, 345a
historicism, II 460b
historiography, II 19b–21b, 24b, 466a, 471a–472b, 474a, 488b, 489a, 490a; IV 149b
history, I 51b; II 19b, 20a, 20b, 21a, 21b, 24b, 337b–338a, 359b, 360b–361a, 363a, 364a–364b, 365b; III 471a–471b, 635a, 635b
Hobbes, I 303a; II 212b, 351b
Holbach, II 353a, 353b, 355b
holy, II 511b, 512b–513a, 514a
Homer, II 339b–340b; III 573b
Hooke, I 674a
hope, II 209b–214b
human nature, II 337b, 353a; III 571a–572b, 573b, 574b, 575a, 576a–577a
humanism, II 347a, 348b, 351a, 351b, 520a; IV 131a, 131b, 132a, 132b
Hume, I 312a, 313b, 675b–676a; II 352a–353a, 353b, 355b; IV 247b, 382b
hunting-ritual, II 333b
hymns, II 343b
iconography, II 340b, 343a, 343b–344a, 526a–526b, 527a, 527b
idea, II 331b–333b, 546a, 546b, 548a
ideal, II 549a, 549b, 550b, 551b
idealism, II 357b, 359a, 360a; III 368b
imagery, IV 138a–138b,

140b, 142b, 144a
immorality, II 334b, 357a
immortality, I 571b, 640b, 644a; II 335a–335b, 336a
impiety, II 564b, 565a, 565b, 566a, 566b, 567a
impressionism, II 574b, 582b
India (ancient), I 571a; II 338a, 340a
individualism, II 297b, 300a, 308a–308b, 337b, 340b, 356a, 597a, 598a, 598b, 602b, 603a
Indus Valley, II 333a, 343b
infinity, II 441a, 443a, 446b, 604b, 606b, 608a, 611b, 614b; IV 75b
instinct, II 349a
irony, II 630a, 631b, 632a, 632b, 634b
irrationalism, II 635b, 637a
Islam, I 495b, 496a, 571a, 571b; II 339b, 344b–345a, 639b, 641b, 642a, 642b, 643b, 645b
Israel, II 364a
Israel (ancient), II 336a–338a, 341b
James, William, II 359a, 362a
Jesus Christ, II 335a, 335b, 341a, 341b–343a, 344b, 348b, 357a, 360b, 363a, 365b
Job (Bible), II 337b
John of Jandun, II 35a
Judaism, I 571a–571b; II 29b–30a, 42a, 336a–337b, 339b, 341b, 342b, 345a, 363b–364a, 364b; III 636a
judgment, II 357a, 359b, 360b
justice, I 287a–287b; II 334b, 335a, 337b, 352b, 354a, 654a, 656a, 657a, 658b; III 572b, 573a; IV 378b, 379a, 381b, 382b, 383a
Justinian, III 17b
Kant, I 315b–316a, 330a, 521a, 641a, 676a; II 240b, 353a–354a, 355b, 356b–357a, 357b, 358a, 358b, 362b, 548a; IV 248b, 382b
Kepler, I 517a; III 271a
Keynes, III 611a
Kierkegaard, II 168a, 189b, 192a, 192b, 360a
knowledge, II 229b, 232b, 334a, 348a, 348b, 349a, 350a, 351b, 353a, 360b
Königsberger, II 354a
Koran, II 344b–345a

La Mettrie, I 334b
language, I 376b; II 352b
law, I 290a; II 249b, 250a, 251a, 344b, 352b–354a, 674b–688a, 689a; III 10b, 11a, 15a, 27b, 566b; IV 176b
Le Roy, I 422a
Leibniz, I 277a, 299b, 328a, 328b, 360b, 572b; II 166a, 346b–351b, 355a, 444a–444b, 446a–446b, 447b; III 131a, 458a, 461a; IV 378b, 379a, 382a, 435b
liberalism, II 356b, 357a, 358b, 359b, 360b, 361a; III 36a, 37a, 40a–40b, 41a, 41b, 42b, 43a
light, III 393b
linguistics, IV 424a, 424b, 426a
Lipsius, II 355a
literary paradox, III 80b
Locke, I 488b; II 351b–352a, 446b; IV 288a
Loisy, I 420b, 421a
Longfellow, II 434a
love, II 209b–210a, 237b, 244a, 351a, 360b, 361a; III 94a, 96a, 96b, 97a, 98a, 100b, 101a, 101b, 106b, 469a; IV 381a
loyalty, III 108b, 109a, 109b, 110b, 111b, 112a, 112b, 115a
Lucretius, I 573a
Lully, I 327a
Luther, II 212a, 348b–349a, 357a; III 11a, 270b; IV 381b, 532b–533a
Machiavelli, II 235b; IV 483a
Machiavellism, III 116a, 116b, 119a
Macrobius, II 440b
macrocosm and microcosm, III 127b, 128a, 128b, 131a
magic, II 334a, 335a
makom, IV 296b
Malebranche, I 276a, 297b–298b, 302b
Manichaeism, II 339b
Man-Machine, III 135a, 137a, 137b
Marcus Aurelius, II 340b
Maritain, I 585b; II 361b
Marx, II 159a, 356a
Marxism, II 213b; III 147a, 153a
materialism, II 355b
mathematics, II 346a–347a
matter, II 348a, 353a; III 186b, 190b, 191b–195a
Maupertuis, I 333a

mercy, II 352b, 353b
Merton, Thomas, II 79a
Mesopotamia (ancient), II 331b, 333b, 335a, 335b–336a, 337b, 564b; IV 226b
metaphor, III 199a, 202a, 202b, 204b, 205a, 206a, 206b, 207a
metaphysics, II 347b, 348a, 351a, 355b, 356b, 357a–357b, 358a, 360a, 361a, 362a, 363a, 365a, 366a; III 212b, 214b, 217b, 222a
Michelangelo, III 228a–228b; IV 443a
Middle Ages, II 343a; III 116b; IV 253b
Mill, J. S., II 359a
millenarianism, III 223b, 225a, 225b
mimesis, III 227a–228b
mind, II 344a
miracles, II 231a
Mithraism, II 339a–339b
modernism, I 420b–425b
monism, I 571a, 572a, 572b; II 344b, 348a
monotheism, II 336b, 341a, 342b
Montaigne, I 304a; II 349b; IV 243b
morality, II 334b, 337a, 347a–347b, 349a, 351a, 352b–357a, 358a
Moses (Bible), II 336a–336b
motion, III 461a; IV 390b, 392a
Mo-tzŭ, II 344b
mountains in literature, III 254b–258b
Mucammar, I 287b
Muhammad, II 345a
music, II 313a, 319b–320a, 343b, 388a–394b; III 265a, 265b–271a
mystery cults, II 341a
mythology, II 331b–341b; III 272b–295a, 296b, 298a, 299a, 300b, 302b, 303a, 305a–309b, 314a
nationalism, II 337a, 344b; III 318b, 320a, 321a, 322b, 324b, 325a
natural law, I 487b; II 356a; III 15a, 16b, 17b–18a, 18b, 19b, 20a
natural liberty, II 62a, 63a
naturalism, II 348b, 353b
Nature, I 376b, 572b, 574a, 574b–575a; II 340b, 350a–350b, 352b; III 20a, 346b, 347a–349b, 351a

Near East, II 332b, 333a–341b

necessity, III 352a, 355b, 356a, 356b, 357a; IV 484b

neo-classicism in art, III 368b

Neolithic period, II 332b, 333a

Neo-Platonism, II 244b, 347a; III 372b–377b

Newton, I 299b, 311a–311b, 401b, 519a, 674b; II 352a, 353a, 355a, 444a; III 194b, 195a; IV 75b, 177b

Nicholas of Cusa, II 346a–348b, 441a; III 510b

Niebuhr, II 360a–360b

Nietzsche, II 192b, 213a, 356a

Nygren, II 360a–360b

omnipotence, I 26a–26b, 28a; II 158a, 336b, 337a, 337b, 340a, 345a, 350b, 356a–356b, 361a

omniscience, II 345a; IV 381b

ontology, I 672b; II 356a, 357a, 361a, 363a

Orientalism, III 429b, 432b, 433b, 435a

Ott, II 365b

painting, II 574a, 582b; IV 467a, 471b, 474b

Paleolithic period, II 331b–333b

Paley, II 352a

pantheism, I 571a; II 350b

Pascal, II 168a, 349b, 355b; III 469a; IV 246a

peace, III 440b, 441a, 441b, 445b

Pelagius, III 466b

perennial philosophy, III 457b–461a

perfectibility, III 463b–472b, 474b

Persia (ancient), II 335b, 337a, 338a–339b, 340a, 343b

Petrarch, II 234a–234b; IV 192a

philanthropy, III 487b, 488a, 488b, 489a, 489b

Philo of Alexandria, I 571b, 586b; II 42a, 513a; III 127b, 465b–466a

Philo Judaeus, I 571b, 586b; II 42a, 513a; III 127b, 465b–466a

philosophy, II 339b, 341a, 343a, 343b, 344a, 347a, 348b–351b, 355a–550b, 551b; III 199a

physicotheologians, II 352a

physics, II 347a

Pico della Mirandola, II 349a; IV 145b

Pietism, III 495b

Plato, I 325b, 333a, 539b, 571b–572a, 578b–579a, 580a, 586b; II 162b–163a, 339b, 341a, 349a, 566a; III 465a, 497a–499b, 500b, 574b; IV 368b, 380b

Platonism, II 347b; III 496b, 497a–499b, 500b, 505b, 506a–506b, 510a–513a, 516a, 517a, 521b

pleasure, II 377b, 378b–379a, 380b; IV 235b

Plotinus, I 325b, 572a; II 163a, 341a, 439b

pluralism, II 353a

Plutarch, II 341a–341b; IV 380b

poetry, II 340b, 348b; III 526b, 527a, 530a, 530b; IV 467a, 471b, 474b

polytheism, II 333b–336a, 338a, 341b, 345a

Pomponazzi, II 36b, 37a

Pope, Alexander, I 554b

Posidonius, III 630b

power, II 349a, 353a, 353b; III 571b, 672a, 660b; IV 380a, 380b, 381b, 392a

pragmatism, III 554b–555a, 564b, 566b, 569b

predestination, II 19b, 25b–31a, 343a, 345a

Priestley, III 472a

primitivism, III 581b–584b, 585b, 588a–594b, 596b, 598a, 598b, 599a

Pringle-Pattison, II 358a

private property, III 654a

probability, III 611a

progress, III 624b, 625a, 626a, 626b, 630b, 634b, 635a, 635b, 636a, 642a

prophecy, II 336b, 337a, 345a, 357a; III 657a–661a, 664a–665b, 668b

prosperity, II 341a

Protagoras, III 574b, 576b

protest movements, III 675a

Protestantism, I 572b; II 355a–355b, 357a, 360b, 361b–362a, 363b, 365a, 365b

Proudhon, II 280b

Pseudo-Dionysius, II 210b, 439a–439b

psychology, IV 1b, 6b, 8a, 9a, 10a, 11b, 16a, 17a–18b, 19b, 20a, 21b, 23a, 23b

Pufendorf, I 488b

punishment, II 27b

Puritanism, IV 18a, 18b

Qumrân sectaries, II 39b

rationalism, II 347b, 349b–351b; IV 46a, 46b, 47a, 48b, 49b, 50b

reason, I 487b; II 211b

Réaumur, I 332a

reformation, IV 60a, 61b, 62a–62b, 63a, 65b, 66a, 66b, 67a, 69a, 69b

Reformation, II 359b–361a; IV 67a, 67b

relativism, IV 70b, 72a

relativity, IV 75b

revelation, II 360b, 361b, 362b, 363a, 365b, 366a

Renan, III 474b

resurrection, II 335a–335b, 337b, 341a, 342a

right, IV 174a, 176b–177a, 177b, 182b, 183a

Ritschl, II 357a–358a

Rodin, II 574b

Roman Catholic Church, II 342b–343a, 355a–355b, 356b, 361b, 362a, 363b, 364b, 365a, 365b; III 466b

romanticism, II 356b, 358b; IV 200b–202b, 204a

Rome (ancient), II 340b, 341a–341b, 566b, 687b, 688a, 689a

Rousseau, II 353b, 356b

Royce, II 358a

Ruskin, II 297b

Saint Ambrose, III 589b

Saint Anselm, I 672b

Saint Augustine, I 273b, 571b, 573a–573b, 575a, 586b, 587a; II 160b, 164b, 210a–210b, 230a–231a, 237b–238a, 244a, 244b, 245a, 687b; III 17b–18a, 191b, 469a, 505b, 635a; IV 9a, 138a–138b, 176b, 286b, 349a, 380b, 381a, 391b–392a

Saint Bernard, III 591a

Saint Paul, II 341b–342a, 343a; IV 517a

Saint Thomas Aquinas, I 260a, 274b–275a, 384b, 574a–574b, 585b, 669b, 673a–673b; II 210b, 211a, 232a–233a, 238a, 320a, 343a; III 466b–467a; IV 140b, 392a, 525a–525b

salvation, II 341a, 345a, 351a, 359b, 361a, 365b; IV 225a–231a, 232a

Santayana, II 360a

Sartre, II 168a, 192b, 246b–247a

Saul (Bible), II 336b

Schelling, II 362b; IV 202a

Schillebeecx, II 365b

Schleiermacher, II 356a, 358a–359a, 362b, 363a; IV 201a

science, II 352a, 353a, 355a, 355b, 357a, 358b, 359b; III 193a

Seneca, II 228a, 349a; III 588a

Sextus Empiricus, II 349a

Shaftesbury, III 599a

Shaw, II 186a

Siger of Brabant, II 32b–33b

sin, I 576a; II 358b, 360b; IV 225a–232a

Sinai Covenant, II 336a, 337a

skepticism, II 348b–349b, 352b, 356a; IV 236a, 237a, 243b, 244a, 244b, 246a, 247b, 248a, 248b, 250b

social contract, IV 252a–255b, 257b, 262a

socialism, IV 285a–291a

society, II 341a, 351b–353a, 355b, 356a

Socrates, II 40b; III 577a; IV 414b

Sophocles, III 15a, 626b

sorcery, II 333a

soul, I 571b; II 26a

space, III 195a; IV 296b, 298a, 301b, 306a

Spencer, I 319a

Spinoza, I 276b, 296b, 298b–299a, 301a, 303a, 572a; II 41a, 348a, 349a, 350a, 350b, 351a, 355a, 444b–445a; III 512a–512b, 554b–555a; IV 177b, 201a, 381b

spontaneous generation, IV 308a–308b, 310a

stars, III 287a–287b

state, IV 317a, 318a

Stoicism, II 340b, 347a–347b, 349a, 355a; IV 50b, 319a, 319b, 320a, 320b

Stoics, IV 8a

Suárez, III 461a

sublime in external nature, IV 335a, 336b, 337a

superstition, II 356a

Sydney, I 488b

symbolism, IV 341b, 345a

symmetry, IV 349a, 353b

syncretism, II 341b

Syria (ancient), II 333b, 335a–335b

Taoism, II 344b

technology, II 347a; IV 358b

teleology, II 338a
temperance, IV 366a, 366b, 368b, 371a, 372b
Tennant, I 574b–575b, 576a
theism, I 571a–576a; II 351a–355b, 363b
theodicy, IV 378b–383b
theology, II 25b–31a, 354b–366b
Thomism, I 572b, 574b–575b; II 356b, 361b, 362a, 363a, 363b, 365a, 365b
Thucydides, III 576a
Tillich, I 575b; II 362b–363a
time, I 576b–577a; II 338a, 338b, 339a–339b, 343b, 344a; IV 390b, 391b–392a, 393b, 402b
Tolstoy, I 438a
tradition, II 358b
tragic sense, IV 413a, 413b, 414b, 415a, 415b, 416a
transcendentalism, I 575b, 576a; II 356a–365b
Trinity, II 342b–343a
truth, II 334b, 344a, 351b, 355a
Tyrrell, I 423a
uniformitarianism, IV 424a, 424b, 426a
U.S., III 429b, 432b, 433b, 435a
U.S. Declaration of Independence, I 571a
unity of science, IV 434a, 434b, 435b, 436b
universal man, IV 443a
universe, II 335b, 336b, 338b, 340a, 340b, 343b, 344a, 344b, 347b, 348a, 348b; III 465b; IV 380b
utilitarianism, IV 444a, 445b, 447b, 449a, 449b
Utopia, IV 460a, 460b
Valla, IV 142b–143a
Vallisnieri, I 332a
Vasari, IV 123a
Venus of Laussel, II 331b–333a
Vico, II 102a; III 357a
Victorians, IV 217b, 218b, 222b
virtuoso, IV 490a
Volksgeist, IV 493a, 495b
Voltaire, I 329b, 330a; II 353a, 356b
vox populi, IV 497a, 498a, 498b
war, IV 502a
Whitehead, I 576a; II 359a, 360a, 362a
Will, II 230a, 230b, 234a
William of Ockham, I 275a–

275b, 384b; III 19b
wisdom, II 347a; IV 379a, 380b, 517a, 517b
wisdom of the fool, IV 516a, 517a, 517b, 518a
witchcraft, IV 521a, 521b, 522a, 522b, 523a
Wolff, II 353a
women, III 596b; IV 524a, 524b, 525a, 525b, 526b, 527b
work, IV 530b–533b
World Spirit, II 392b
Wycliffe, I 387a
Xenophanes, III 573a, 624b, 625a
Yahweh, II 336a–338a, 341b
Yin and Yang, II 344b
Zechariah (Bible), II 337a
Zeitgeist, IV 536b
Zeno of Citium, II 340b
Zoroaster, II 338a–339a
Zoroastrianism, II 335b, 339a, 339b
Zurvanism, II 339a
See also Religion
Goddard, Henry H. (1866–1957), psychology, IV 26b
Gödel, Kurt
axiomatization, I 170a–170b
empiricism, III 545b
game theory, II 263b
Godwin, Francis (1562–1633)
cosmic voyages, I 527a–528a, 530b, 531b, 532b
Kepler and, I 527b–528a
Godwin, Mary Wollstonecraft (1759–1797)
democracy, I 661b
women, IV 526a, 526b
Godwin, William (1756–1836)
anarchism, I 72b–73a
association of ideas, I 114a–114b
authority, I 160b
conservation, I 473b
cooperation, III 470b
education, III 643b
Enlightenment, II 98b, 99b
human nature, III 643b
idea, I 114a–114b
immortality, III 470b
longevity, III 92a
marriage, III 470b
perfectibility, III 470a–470b, 471a, 472a
private property, III 470b
progress, III 643b
psychology, IV 21a
revolution, III 471a

Shelley and, III 470b
social contract, IV 262b
State, III 470b
Stoicism, III 470b
utilitarianism, IV 444b–445a, 447b
Goebbels, Joseph P. (1897–1945), totalitarianism, IV 408a
Goering, Reinhard, expressionism, II 208a–208b, 209a
Goethe, Johann Wolfgang von (1749–1832)
aesthetics, IV 124b
architecture, II 371b
art, II 310b
art for art's sake, I 109a
attitude toward antiquity, I 84a
beauty, I 203b
Burckhardt and, IV 126a
Byron and, IV 192b
certainty, I 322a
China, I 365a, 368b
classicism, I 451a, 453a–455b; IV 197a
classification of the arts, I 460b
comedy, I 470a
conservation, I 473b
Counter-Enlightenment, II 104a, 107a, 108b
criticism, III 237a
death, I 646a
disease, II 403b
Enlightenment, III 343a
evil, II 165b
Faust (legend), III 248a–252b
genius, II 296a, 310b
God, II 350b
good, II 165b
Gothic, II 371b
Herder and, III 305a; IV 209a
hermeticism, II 433a
historicism, II 457b, 461b
idealism, I 237a, 237b
immortality, I 646a
impressionism, II 580b
irony, II 630a, 634a
Kant and, IV 202b
language, III 435a
light, II 580b
literary criticism, I 597b, 600b
literary paradox, III 79b
literature, III 84a, 84b
longevity, III 92b
Machiavellism, III 119a, 121b
metaphysical imagination, III 217b

motif, III 237a, 238a, 240b, 241a
mythology, III 305a, 306a, 316b
naturalism in art, III 343a
Nature, III 425a
neo-classicism in art, III 371a
Neo-Platonism, III 425a
organicism, III 423a, 424b, 425a
perfectibility, III 473b
periodization in literary history, III 486a
Pietism, III 494b
Platonism, III 519a, 521b
realism in literature, IV 51b, 52b
recapitulation, IV 56b
reincarnation, I 646a
romanticism, I 451a, 453b; IV 188a, 188b, 192b, 197a, 198a, 200a, 201a, 208a–208b, 209a, 209b
Rousseau and, IV 209b
Schelling and, IV 201a
Scherer and, III 237a
Schiller and, III 237a, 238a
Schlegel, August Wilhelm and, I 454a; IV 198b
Schlegel, Friedrich and, I 454a; IV 198a, 208b
Spinoza and, III 519a
Strauss and, II 413a
Sturm und Drang, IV 200a
symbolism, IV 338a, 338b, 339a, 341b, 343a, 343b
Tasso and, III 84b
truth, I 322a
ut pictura poesis, IV 468a, 472a, 473a
world literature, III 84b
Zeitgeist, IV 536a–536b
Gog (Bible), mythology, III 276b
Gogol, Nikolai Vasilievich (1809–1852)
naturalism, IV 53b
realism in literature, IV 53a, 53b, 55a
satire, IV 214b
Goguet, Antoine Yves, Enlightenment, II 93a
Gold
economic history, II 57b
Lucretius, III 587b
Gold standard, natural liberty, II 68b–69a
Gold, T., cosmology, I 567b–568a
Golden Age (myth)
Christianity, III 590a
cynicism, III 586a–586b
Great Britain, III 482a, 600a

Greece (ancient), III 591a
Hesiod, III 481b–482a
humanism, IV 131a
Montaigne, III 594a
Plato, IV 131a
Posidonius, III 630b
primitivism, III 578a–586a,
588a, 590a, 593b, 594a,
596b, 600a–603b
progress, III 624b, 630a–
632b
reformation, IV 60b, 62b
Renaissance, IV 131a
Seneca, III 588a, 632a
social contract, IV 252a
socialism, IV 285a–285b
Utopia, IV 459a, 460a
Vergil, III 631b
Golden Chain (myth), III 273b
Golden Rule, law, III 6b
Goldenweiser, Alexander A.
(1880–1940), Marxism, III
153b
Golding, William
Nature, III 349a
satire, IV 215a
Goldmann, Lucien, literary
criticism, I 606b
Goldschmidt, V., harmony, IV
42a
Goldsmith, Oliver (1728–
1774)
antiprimitivism, III 604a
attitude toward antiquity, I
86b
Gothic, II 368b
periodization in literary
history, III 483a
philanthropy, III 490a–
490b
primitivism, III 600b–601a,
604a
Goldstein, Kurt, psychology,
IV 14b
Golem, Man-Machine, III
146a
Golius, Jacobus (1596–
1667), language, I 358a
Goltz, Kolmar von der (1843–
1916), war, IV 504a, 505a
Gomarus, Franciscus (1563–
1641), predestination, II
28a
Gombrich, E. H., iconography,
II 538a
Gomez Pereira, Wenceslau,
Man-Machine, III 135b
Gompertz curve, longevity, III
89b
Gomulka, Wladyslaw, Marx-
ism, III 166a–166b
Goncourt, Edmond Louis
Antoine de (1822–1896),
China, I 369a

Japan, I 369a
realism in literature, IV 52a
vox populi, IV 499b
Goncourt, Jules Alfred Huot
de (1830–1870)
China, I 369a
Japan, I 369a
realism in literature, IV 52a
vox populi, IV 499b
Góngora, Luis de (1561–
1627)
baroque in literature, I 190a,
192a, 195a
symbolism, IV 342b
Gongorism, baroque in literature, I 190a, 195a
Gonseth, F., axiomatization, I
168a
Gontery, Jean, skepticism, IV
242b
Gonzaga, Federico (d. 1540),
mythology, III 291a
González, Joaquín V., positivism, III 543b
Gooch, George Peabody,
historiography, II 494b
Good, IV 173a–187a
Adam (Bible), III 582a,
583a
aesthetics, IV 182b, 184a,
354a, 355a, 356a, 356b
aggression, IV 174a
anarchy, III 470a; IV 180b
angels, II 232b
Aristotle, II 227b–228a,
377a–377b; III 354a, 465a;
IV 5a, 5b, 36a, 49b, 175a–
175b, 176b, 180a, 436a,
451b
Bentham, IV 177b, 178b,
179a, 181b–182a, 185a
Boccaccio, II 234a
Boethius, II 231b–232a
Bruno, III 513b
Calvin, IV 67a
Calvinism, IV 177a
chance, II 227b–229a,
231b–235b
charity, II 209b, 212a
Christianity, IV 174a–174b,
176a–177a
Cicero, IV 50a
Dante, II 233a–233b; IV
176b–177a
Darwin, IV 182a
decision, IV 175a
democracy, IV 175a, 175b
Democritus, III 576b
deontology, IV 184b
desire, IV 173a, 173b,
177a–179b, 182b, 186b
determinism, II 237a, 237b,
238a–238b; IV 177b
Dewey, IV 185b–186a

dignity, II 231b; IV 138b,
143a
distributive, IV 179a
divination, IV 179b, 180a
dualism, II 38a, 38b, 39a–
40a, 43a; IV 180a
duty, IV 173b, 176a, 179b,
180a, 182a, 183b, 186a
economics, IV 177a, 179a,
180b–182b
Edwards, J., IV 109b
egoism, IV 178a, 185a
emotion, IV 176a, 177b,
184a
empiricism, IV 178b, 179b,
184a
Epicureanism, II 378a; III
587b; IV 175b–176a
eschatology, II 154b, 155a–
155b
ethics, IV 70b, 71b, 72b,
173b–186b, 319b, 320a,
320b, 321a, 321b
evil, II 161b–169b; IV
174b, 177a, 180b
evolution, IV 179b–181b,
183a, 185b, 186b
experience, IV 177a, 177b
faith, II 209b, 212a
fate, II 227b–229a, 231b–
235b
Faust (legend), III 248b
fear, IV 174a, 181a
feeling, IV 174a
fortune, II 227b–235b
free will, II 237a, 237b,
238a–238b, 243a, 243b,
244b, 245a; IV 176b
freedom, IV 177b, 179b,
180a, 181a
Freudianism, IV 185a
general will, II 277a, 280a
glory, II 231b
Gnosticism, II 329a
goals, IV 173b–175a,
176a–176b, 177a, 178b,
180a, 181a, 181b, 185b
God, II 338b, 339a, 339b,
340b, 341a, 349a, 352b,
354a; III 571b; IV 174a,
176b–177a, 177b, 182b,
183a, 379a, 380a, 380b,
484b
Goethe, II 165b
Greece (ancient), II 677a;
IV 174b–176a
happiness, II 374b, 375b,
376b–381a
harmony, II 388a, 390b; IV
175a, 177b
Hartmann, IV 182a–182b
health, II 397a, 398a, 403a,
406a
heaven, IV 176b–177a

hedonism, IV 179a, 180a–
180b
Hegel, IV 180a, 180b, 181a,
291b
hell, IV 176b
hermeticism, II 432a, 433b
hierarchy, IV 173b
history, IV 173a, 174a,
175a, 179b–181b, 183a,
185b, 186a
Hobbes, II 380a; IV 177a–
177b, 178a, 182a
holy, II 512a, 514a
hope, II 209b, 212a; IV
174a
human nature, III 571b,
572a, 575a, 575b, 576b,
577a, 643b; IV 173b, 175a
humanism, II 519b; IV
133b, 180b
Hume, IV 178a, 382b
Hutcheson, III 231a
ideal, II 549a–549b, 550b
ignorance, IV 174b
individualism, IV 174b–
180b
infinity, II 614a
instinct, IV 180a, 185a
institutions, IV 178b, 179a,
180a, 180b, 181b, 186b
instrumentalism, IV 185b
intuition, IV 177b, 183a
irrationalism, II 635a, 637b
Jefferson, IV 21b
joy, IV 175b
Judaism, IV 174a, 176a
judgment, IV 178b, 181b,
182b, 183a, 185a, 186a
justice, II 655b; IV 175a,
175b, 178a, 179a, 180b,
181a, 183b, 186a
Justinian, III 17b
Kant, IV 179a–179b, 181a,
181b, 186b, 382b
knowledge, IV 173a–175b,
185b, 186b
Kropotkin, IV 180b
labor, IV 179a
language, IV 176b, 183b,
184a, 184b
law, II 677a; IV 173b–
185b, 186b
Leibniz, IV 379a, 382b
Locke, III 598b; IV 178a
love, IV 174a, 175a, 177a,
178a
Machiavelli, II 379b; III
116a–125a; IV 482a, 483a
Mandeville, IV 178b
Marcus Aurelius, IV 176a
Marx, IV 450b; IV 177a
Marxism, IV 180b–181a
materialism, II 450a; IV
175b, 180b

mathematics, IV 177a, 177b
matter, III 190b; IV 177a, 177b
measurement, IV 178b, 181b–182a
Mill, J. S., II 167b; IV 179a
millenarianism, III 223b
Milton, II 165a
mimesis, III 228a
mind, II 231b
Moore, G. E., III 234b; IV 183a
moral sense, III 231a, 234b
music, II 388a, 390b; III 264b, 265a, 265b, 554b; IV 176b
mythology, III 273a, 278b
nationalism, IV 174a
natural law, III 17b, 19a, 19b; IV 175b, 176a, 176b, 177a, 177b
naturalism, IV 181a, 182a, 184b–186b
Nature, III 347a, 350b, 351a; IV 174b, 175a, 176a, 177b, 178a, 179b
necessity, III 354a; IV 177b
Neo-Platonism, IV 176a
Newton, IV 177b
Nicholas of Cusa, IV 381b
Nietzsche, IV 180b
nomos, IV 174b
norms, IV 182b
obedience, IV 173b, 174a
obligation, IV 173b, 174a, 179b, 181b, 182a, 183a, 184b
oligarchy, IV 175a, 175b
open-question argument, IV 183a
pain, IV 174a, 175b, 178b, 179a, 185a
Palmieri, IV 478b–479a
passions, IV 178a
peace, IV 175b, 176a, 177b
Pelagius, III 466b
perception, IV 182b
perfectibility, III 465a, 466b, 467a, 469a, 470a, 643b
Petrarch, II 234a, 234b
philosophy, II 549a–549b, 550b; IV 173a, 174a, 174b, 175a–175b, 177a, 183a
physiology, IV 177a
Plato, II 162b–163a, 209b, 375b, 376b; III 273a, 465a, 496b–497a, 498a, 501a, 501b, 502a, 508b; IV 4a, 36a, 37a, 37b, 49b, 174b, 175a, 182b, 380b, 431b
Platonism, III 496b–497a, 498a, 501a, 501b, 502a,

508b, 509a, 511b, 513b, 514a, 517a; IV 181b
pleasure, II 374b, 375b–381a; IV 173b, 174a, 175b, 176b, 178b, 179a, 180a–180b, 181b, 183a, 185a, 185b
Plotinus, IV 8b
pluralism, IV 184b
Plutarch, IV 380b
positivism, IV 183b–184b
poverty, IV 65a, 175a
power, II 231b; IV 174b, 175b, 176a, 177a, 180b, 181a
pragmatism, III 553b, 554b, 568a, 568b, 569a; IV 184b–186b
primitivism, III 582a, 587b, 588a, 594b, 598a–599b
progress, III 626a, 634a, 635b, 642b, 643b, 648a, 648b, 649a; IV 178b
prophecy, III 664b
Protagoras, III 575b
protest movements, III 671a
Protestantism, IV 177a
providence, II 232a
psychology, IV 3b, 4a, 5a, 5b, 8b, 17b, 19a, 20a, 21b, 177a, 178a, 178b, 179a, 180b, 182b, 185a–186a
punishment, IV 174a, 176a, 179a
Pythagoreans, IV 36a, 37a, 37b
rationalism, IV 46a, 49b, 50a, 173b, 175a, 175b, 176a, 179b, 181b
reason, IV 174a, 175a–178b, 179b, 180a
reformation, IV 65a
Reformation, IV 67a
relativism, IV 70b, 71b, 72b
religion, IV 109b, 174a–174b, 177b, 182a–182b, 184a
Renaissance, IV 133b, 138b, 143a
responsibility, IV 176b, 184b
retaliation, IV 179a
revelation, IV 176b
reward, IV 174a, 179a
Rome (ancient), IV 176a
Rousseau, II 277a; III 598a, 599b
rules, IV 173a–177a, 180b, 181a, 181b, 183a–186b
Saint Augustine, II 210b; IV 138b, 176a–176b, 381a
Saint Thomas Aquinas, II 212a; IV 176b
salvation, IV 174b, 176a,

176b, 177a, 224b, 231a, 231b
Santayana, III 553b
satire, IV 212a
Sartre, II 168b
Schopenhauer, II 166b
science, III 642b, 648a; IV 173a, 175b, 176b, 177a, 179b–181b, 182a, 185b, 186a
secularism, IV 177a, 177b
self-love, IV 178a
self-realization, IV 181a–181b
sex, IV 174a, 185a
Shaftesbury, III 598a, 599a
shame, IV 173b
sin, IV 176b–177a, 180b, 224b, 231a, 231b
skepticism, IV 235a, 235b, 238a
slavery, IV 174b
socialism, IV 181a, 291b
society, IV 173a–179a, 180a, 180b, 181b
Socrates, II 375b; III 496b–497a, 577a; IV 3b, 174b–175a, 415a, 436a
Sophism, IV 174b
soul, IV 174a, 174b, 175a, 176b–177a
species, IV 175a, 182a
Speusippus, IV 36a
Spinoza, IV 177b, 182a, 381b
State, IV 180a
Stoicism, III 588a; IV 50a, 176a, 319b–321b
suffering, IV 175a, 178a
symmetry, IV 348a
sympathy, IV 178a, 178b, 182a
taste, IV 354a, 355a, 356a, 356b
technology, III 648a
teleology, IV 175a, 175b, 176b, 177a, 180a, 182a–182b, 184b
temperance, IV 174b, 371a
theodicy, IV 379a–383a
tragic sense, IV 413a, 414a–415b
tranquility, IV 176a
truth, IV 177a, 177b, 183b–184a
universality, IV 173b, 174a, 175b, 179b
utilitarianism, IV 178b–179a, 180a–180b, 183b, 185a, 185b, 444a, 446b–449b
utility, IV 450a, 451b
Utopia, IV 458b, 459b, 460a, 468b

value, IV 181b–183a, 185a, 450a, 451b
virtue, IV 173a–182b
wealth, II 231b; IV 175a, 177a
wisdom, IV 174b, 175b, 184b
witchcraft, IV 521a, 523a
work, IV 174a, 176a, 177a
Zeus (myth), III 571b
Zoroastrianism, IV 231a, 231b
See also Ethics, Right
Goodfield, J.
matter, III 190a–190b, 195a
Newton and, III 195a
Goodman, Bishop Godfrey, Chain of Being, I 511b
Cosmic Fall, I 505b, 506b–508b, 510a, 511b, 512a
Hakewill and, I 507b–508b, 510a
hierarchy, II 435b
Goodman, Leo, social welfare, IV 280b
Gordon, Thomas (d. 1750), deism, I 650b–651a, 651b
Gorgias (485?–?380 B.C.), cynicism, I 628a, 629a
justice, II 653b
literary paradox, III 77a
Plato and, III 496b–497a, 501b
poetry, III 526a
rhetoric, III 496b–497a
skepticism, IV 234b
Gorren, Aline, symbolism, IV 341a
Görres, J. J. von (1776–1848)
iconography, II 525a
mythology, III 305a, 306a
romanticism, IV 197a, 207a
Gorton, Samuel (1592?–1677), psychology, IV 18b
Gorton, William, Puritanism, IV 18b
Göschel, Karl Friedrich (1784–1862)
faith, II 412a
God, II 412a
Hegel and, II 412a–412b, 414a, 415b
knowledge, II 412a
Strauss and, II 413a
Gosse, Edmund William (1849–1928)
realism in art, IV 54a
symbolism, IV 340b
Gossen, Herman H. (1810–1858)
economic history, II 50b
social welfare, IV 277b

utility, IV 451a, 453b, 454b, 458a
Gothic, II 366b–374a
  Abraham, II 373a
  aesthetics, II 367a–374a
  Alberti, II 367b
  apotheosis of, II 371a–373a
  architecture, II 367a–374a
  Ariosto, II 368b
  aristocracy, II 369b
  art, II 367a–374a, 527a
  Arundel, II 369a
  Ascham, II 368a
  Avaux, II 372b–373a
  as bad taste, II 367b
  Baïf, II 368a
  baroque, II 368b, 373a
  beauty, II 370a
  Bede, II 367a
  Bible, II 369a
  Borromini, II 368b
  Carducho, II 369b
  Cassiodorus, II 367a
  Caumont, II 373a
  Cervantes, II 370a
  Christianity, II 371a–372a
  culture, II 367b–374a
  Delaunay, II 372b
  Dennis, II 368a
  dictionaries, II 369a
  Dryden, II 368a
  duelling, II 368b
  Eiffel, II 373a
  Enlightenment, II 371a
  ethics, II 372a–372b
  France, II 367a, 367b, 368a, 369b, 370a, 371b, 372b–373a
  Frankl, II 369a, 372b, 373b
  gardening, II 368b, 370a, 370b
  Germany, II 367a–373b; III 484a
  Goethe, II 371b
  Goldsmith, II 368b
  Great Britain, II 367a, 368a–373a
  Greenland, II 367a
  Gustavus Adolphus, II 367a
  handwriting, II 367b, 518a
  Heine, II 371b
  Hugo, II 369b, 370b
  humanism, II 367b, 518a
  hunting, II 368b
  Iceland, II 367a
  Italy, II 367a, 367b, 368b, 370b, 371a, 371b
  Jesus Christ, II 373b
  Jordanes, II 367a, 369b
  Junius, II 369a
  Klopstock, II 370b
  language, II 367a, 367b, 369a, 369b
  literature, II 367a, 368a–

368b, 370b, 371b, 372a, 372b, 373b; III 243a
  Lovejoy, II 368b
  Middle Ages, II 367a–367b, 371b
  Molière, II 368a
  Monet, II 372b
  motif, III 243a
  motion pictures, II 372b
  music, II 373b
  nationalism, II 369b–370a
  Nature, II 370a, 371a; III 350b
  Nazarenes, II 371a–371b
  neo-classicism in art, III 369b, 370a, 370b, 371a
  novel, II 370b
  opera, II 368b
  Orosius, II 367a
  Ossian, II 370b
  painting, II 370b, 371a, 372b
  Panofsky, II 373b
  periodization in literary history, III 484b
  Petrarch, II 367b
  philosophy, II 373b
  pluralism, II 370b
  poetry, II 368a, 368b, 370b, 371b, 373b
  Pound, Ezra, II 372b
  primitivism, II 370b, 371a
  pseudo-Raphael, II 370b
  Pugin, II 369a, 372a
  Rabelais, II 367b, 368a
  relativism, II 370a
  Renaissance, II 367b–368b, 371a, 373a, 373b
  Rodrigo of Toledo, II 369b
  Roman Catholic Church, II 371b, 372a
  Romanesque, II 373a
  romanticism, II 371a–371b; IV 187b, 201a, 208b
  Rome (ancient), II 368b–369a
  Ruskin, II 372b
  Scandinavia, II 367a, 369b
  Schlegel, F., II 372a
  Scott, II 372b
  sculpture, II 371b
  Sidney, II 369a
  society, II 367a, 369b
  space, IV 298b
  Spain, II 367a, 368b, 369b–370a, 372b
  Spengler, IV 298b
  Spenser, II 368b
  sublime in external nature, II 370a
  supernatural, II 370b
  Tacitus, II 368b
  Tasso, II 368b
  taste, II 368a, 368b, 370a

temperance, IV 373a, 377a
  tout court, II 367b
  Ulphilas, II 369a
  U.S., II 372b
  Valla, II 367b
  Vasari, II 367b–368a, 369b
  Villani, II 367b
  Viollet-le-Duc, II 373a
  virtue, IV 373a
  Vredeman de Vries, II 371a
  Walpole, II 370b
  Warburton, II 370b–371a
  Warton, II 370b
  Wetter, II 373a
  Wiene, II 372b
  Worringer, II 373b
  Wotton, II 368a
  Wren, II 369a
Goths
  Christianity, III 592a
  primitivism, III 592a
  Rome (ancient), III 592a
Gottschalk (805?–868)
  heresy, II 418a
  predestination, II 27b
Gottschall, Rudolf von (1823–1909), literature, III 83a
Gottsched, Johann Christoph (1700–1766)
  aesthetics, IV 356a
  Enlightenment, II 89b
  periodization in literary history, III 482a
  taste, IV 356a
Goujon, Jean (1510?–?1568), mythology, III 292b
Gourmont, Remy de (1858–1915)
  irony, II 633b
  style, IV 332a, 332b
  symbolism, IV 341a, 342b, 344b
Goya, Francisco José de (1746–1828)
  art, II 302a
  genius, II 302a
  iconography, II 532b
  romanticism, IV 202b
  witchcraft, IV 522b
Goyen, Jan van (1596–1656), impressionism, II 578a
Gozzi, Count Carlo (1720–1806), motif, III 238a
Gozzoli, Benozzo (1420–1498), mythology, III 280a
Grabar, A., iconography, II 537b
Grabbe, Christian Dietrich (1801–1836)
  Faust (legend), III 250a, 250b

irony, II 633b
Gracchi
  historiography, II 510a, 511a
  private property, III 652a
  revolution, IV 161a
  Rome (ancient), III 652a; IV 161a
Gracchus Tiberius (163–133 B.C.), conservatism, I 479b
Grace
  art, II 305a
  Barth, III 467a
  charity, II 211a
  Christianity, IV 370b
  Dante, II 233b
  determinism, II 27a, 238a
  dignity, IV 138a, 138b, 139a, 142a, 142b
  Dominicans, I 394a–394b
  Edwards, IV 110a, 111a
  fortune, II 233b
  free will, II 238a, 244b, 245a, 245b
  general will, II 275b
  God, II 238a, 359b; III 466a, 466b
  happiness, II 379a
  heresy, II 417a
  holy, II 512b–513a
  infinity, II 614a
  Jesuits, I 394a–394b
  millenarianism, III 224b
  natural law, III 17b
  Pelagius, III 466b
  perennial philosophy, III 459b
  perfectibility, III 466a, 466b, 467a
  Petrarch, IV 142a
  Philo Judaeus, III 466a
  prophecy, III 667a
  psychology, IV 17b
  reformation, IV 62b
  religion, IV 110a, 111a, 112a
  Renaissance, IV 138a, 138b, 139a, 142a, 142b
  Roman Catholic Church, III 466b
  Saint Augustine, II 238a, 244b; III 17b, 224b; IV 138a, 139a
  Saint Thomas Aquinas, III 466b
  temperance, IV 370b
  theodicy, IV 380b
  tragic sense, IV 415b
  vox populi, IV 498a
  work, IV 533a
Gracián, Baltasar (1601–1658)
  aesthetics, IV 354b

baroque in literature, I 189b, 190a
genius, II 293b–294a
literary criticism, I 596a
taste, IV 354b

Gradualism, Marxism and, III 149b, 164b

Graf, Arturo (1848–1913), literature, III 84b
motif, III 238b

Graham, Edward, conservation, I 471b, 472b, 474a

Graham, Howard Jay, constitutionalism, I 485b

Grammar
Aristotle, II 663a–663b
art, I 456b, 459a
Chomsky, II 672b–673a
genius, II 313b
Greece (ancient), III 62a, 528a
Grimm, III 67a
humanism, II 515a, 515b, 516a, 516b, 519a
Indian (American), II 661b
Islam, II 641a
knowledge, II 641a
language, II 659b–660b, 661b, 663a–670b, 671b–673b
Latin, II 661b
linguistics, III 62a–67a, 68a, 69a, 71b, 72a, 74a
literary crIcitism and, I 596b, 597a
literary paradox, III 76b, 77a
music, II 313b
Ramism, IV 42b, 45a
Renaissance, IV 123b, 438b, 439b
Rome (ancient), III 528a
Sanskrit, II 661b
science, II 666b
scientific classification, I 464b, 466b
structuralism, IV 323b, 324b
transformational, II 672a–673b
universal man, IV 438b, 439b

Gramsci, Antonio
Machiavellisrn, III 124b
pragmatism, III 564a

Grandmaison, Léonice de, modernism, I 425a

Grandville (1803–1847), chance images, I 350a

Granet, François Marius (1775–1849), literature, III 82a

Grant, Arthur James (1862–1948), creativity in art, I 585a

Grant, Ulysses S. (1822–1885), conservation, I 475a

Graphics, neo-classicism in art, III 366b

Grappin, genius, II 294a–295a

Grässe, Johann Georg, literature, III 85b

Grassmann, Hermann G. (1809–1877), Orientalism, III 436a

Gratian, philanthropy, III 489a

Gratianus (12th century), natural law, III 18a

Graunt, John (1620–1674), disease statistics, II 402a
probability, III 607a

Graves, Robert (1895–), motif, III 240a
mythology, III 240a, 279a, 280b

Gravesande, William Jakob (1688–1742)
metaphysics, III 217a
methodology, III 385a, 385b

Gravina, Gian Vincenzo (1664–1718)
general will, II 275b
romanticism, IV 190b

Gravitational mass, I 558a–558b

Gravitational red shift, IV 87a

Graviton, IV 91b

Gravity
Copernicus, III 194a
cosmology, I 547a, 547b–548b, 549b–550b, 554a–555a, 556a, 557b–559b, 560b, 561a, 564b, 570a
Einstein, I 557b–559b, 560b, 561a; IV 83b, 86a–87a, 88a, 89a, 89b, 91b
Gilbert, William, III 194a
Kepler, III 194a
Leibniz, I 229b–300a
matter, III 194a, 194b, 195a
medieval theories of, II 197b, 201b
methodology, III 379b, 389a, 393a
Newton, I 299a, 548a–548b, 549b–550a, 560b; III 194b, 195a, 379b, 389a, 393a; IV 290a, 302a
relativity, IV 75a, 77b, 83b, 86a–87a, 88a, 89a–91b
space, IV 296a, 297b, 300a, 301b, 302a
symmetry, IV 348a, 349a, 352b, 353a
time, IV 397b, 403a

Gray, Andrew, entropy, II 116a

Gray, Asa (1810–1888)

evolutionism, II 180b
religion, IV 108a

Gray, John Chipman, Orientalism, III 429a

Gray, John H. (1859–1946), economic history, II 60a
socialism, IV 292b

Gray, Thomas (1716–1771)
baroque in literature, I 193a, 195a
mythology, III 298b
periodization in literary history, III 485b
primitivism, III 601a
romanticism, IV 195a

Great Awakening
Edwards, IV 110a
illuminists, IV 109a
revivalism, IV 109a, 109b, 110a, 112a

Great Britain
academic freedom, I 10a, 14a
acquired characteristics, II 617b
aesthetics, II 219a, 221a; IV 355a, 355b–356a
agriculture, III 600a
American Revolution, I 658b–660b
art, II 297b, 298b, 300b, 303b, 305a, 305b, 306a, 308a, 310a
Augustan period, III 483a, 483b, 484b
balance of power, I 181a, 181b, 183a, 184a, 186a, 186b, 187a
baroque in literature, I 189b, 191a, 191b, 193a–195a
Buddhism, I 255a, 256b
capitalism, I 396a
catastrophism, IV 418a, 418b, 419b, 420a, 420b, 421b, 422a
charity, III 489b
China, I 367b
Christianity, III 671a
civil disobedience, I 435a
civil service, I 367b
Civil War, III 450a
class, I 441b, 449a; III 674b; IV 500a
classicism, I 450a–453a, 454a, 454b; III 483b
colonialism, III 537a
common law, II 686a, 691a, 692a, 693b–696a; III 30b–32b
conservation, I 472b, 473a–473b
conservatism, I 477a–478a, 479a–480a, 481b
Constitution, I 487b–488b,

490b–491b, 657b, 658b–659b; II 410a
constitutionalism, I 487b–488b, 490b–491a, 491b
cosmic images, I 516b, 517b–519b, 522b–523a
cosmic voyages, I 524a–530a, 532a–534b
Counter-Enlightenment, II 105a, 105b, 107a
criminology, I 71b
crisis in history, I 592b, 593a
deism, I 648b, 649a–652a
democracy, I 656a–663a
despotism, II 5b–8a
determinism, II 22a, 30b
drama, II 208b; III 482b, 483b, 530a, 531a
economic history, II 44b–46a, 47a, 60a, 60b
education, IV 510b, 511a
Elizabethan Age, III 482a, 482b, 483a, 484b
Elizabethan Statute of Charitable Uses, III 489b
empathy, II 86b, 88a
empiricism, II 351b–353a; III 550b; IV 199b
Enlightenment, III 89a–91b, 94b, 95a, 98b
environment, II 124a, 124b
equality, II 138b, 142a–143a, 144a, 145a; III 11a
equity, II 148a, 152a–154a
ethics, III 538a
evangelicalism, I 403a
evolution of literature, II 171a–171b, 173a
evolutionism, II 180b–181b
expressionism, II 208b
France, III 537a
freedom, II 44b, 250b–251a
game theory, II 264a
general will, II 275b
geology, III 256a–256b
Gibraltar, III 537a
Golden Age, III 482a
Golden Age (myth), III 600a
Gothic, II 367a, 368a, 369b–373a
Great Depression (1930s), IV 511b–512a
harmony, II 388b
heresy, I 649b
hermeticism, II 431b
historiography, II 22a, 483b, 484a, 486a, 487b; III 483b
House of Commons, IV 153b

Housing Act of 1919, IV 511b
Huguenots, IV 116b
humanism, II 520b; III 483b, 484b; IV 131a
idea, II 547b
ideal, II 549a, 550a
idealism, IV 220a
impressionism, II 567b, 570b, 575a, 578a, 579a–579b, 583a
India, I 664a; II 17a, 105b
Inns of Court, II 694b–695a
international peace, III 448b–450a, 451a, 453b, 454a, 455b, 456a
irony, II 628b
Jay Treaty, III 450a
Judicature Acts, III 31a
Labor Party, III 152a
language, II 661a, 666b, 670a; III 73a
law, I 292a–292b, 487b–488b; II 142b, 148a, 152a–154a, 250b–251a, 685b–686a, 687a, 689a, 690a; III 5a, 6b, 7b–8a, 11a, 12a, 28b, 29b, 30b–32b
League of Free Nations Society, III 454a
League of Nations Union, III 454a
liberty, I 392b
linguistics, II 247a; III 70b, 73a–75b; IV 425a
literary criticism, I 596a, 597a, 598a–600a, 601a–603a
literature, III 82a–83b
loyalty, III 114a
Machiavellism, III 117a, 118a–120a, 121a–121b
mammonism, I 396b
Man-Machine, III 143a
Marxism, III 151a, 152a, 154a, 157a, 162a, 165a
medieval scientists, II 196a–196b, 197b, 199b–201b
Methodism, III 674b
methodology, III 382a
Middle Ages, II 666b
millenarianism, III 225a
mimesis, III 227b
modernism, I 419a, 420a, 422b–423a, 424b, 426a; III 483b
monarchy, IV 154a
monasteries, III 489b
Moravians, I 403a
mountains in literature, III 256a–256b, 257a–259a
music, II 315b, 322a, 388b
mythology, III 291b, 293a, 294a–300b, 304a, 305b,

306b, 310b, 311b–312a
National Health Act of 1947, IV 513b
National Peace Council, III 448b–449a
nationalism, I 397a; II 690a; III 319a–319b, 320b, 321a, 322a, 322b, 323b, 326a, 327a, 330a, 330b, 331a, 333a
natural law, III 7b, 21a, 22a
natural liberty, II 63b, 69a
naturalism, III 483b
necessity, III 357b
neo-classicism, III 482b
neo-classicism in art, III 363a, 364a–364b, 369b
Noble Savage, III 601a
novel, III 600b
organicism, III 424b, 426a
Orientalism, III 428b, 429a, 429b, 432a, 435b, 437a, 438a
Oxford movement, I 405a, 405b, 406b
perfectibility, III 468a–468b, 470a
periodization in literary history, III 481b–483b, 484b, 485b
philanthropy, III 489b, 490a, 491a–492b
philosophy, III 73a–75b
Pietism, III 493b
Platonism, III 506a, 507b–508a, 514a–515b, 519a–519b, 521b, 522a, 523a–524a
poetry, III 482a, 483b, 485b, 529b, 530a, 531a, 600a, 601a; IV 467a, 469a
Poor Law of 1834, IV 509a, 510a, 511a
positivism, III 537a, 538a, 538b, 539a, 542b, 543b, 545b, 550b
pragmatism, III 554a, 557a, 560a, 565b, 567a
primitivism, III 593a, 600a, 600b–602b
private property, III 654b, 655a, 655b
progress, III 643a, 643b
protest movements, III 670b, 671a, 672a, 672b, 674b, 677a
psychology, IV 11b, 13b, 19a, 21a, 24b, 25a, 26b
Puritanism, IV 19a
Ramism, IV 42b, 44b
rationalism, IV 199b
realism, III 483b
realism in literature, IV 52b, 54a, 54b

Reform Bill (1832), IV 179a
Reform Bill (1833), I 406b
reformation, IV 68b
Reformation, III 483b; IV 68a
religion, III 489b, 674b; IV 92a, 106a, 106b, 107a, 107b, 108a, 116b, 120a
Renaissance, III 483b, 484b; IV 123b, 124a, 131a
Restoration, III 483a, 483b
revisionism, IV 269b, 272a
revolution, III 600b; IV 153b–154a, 154b, 155b, 156b, 159b, 160b, 162b
rhetoric, IV 172a–172b
romanticism, III 304a, 305b, 306b, 483b, 484b; IV 187a, 187b, 189a, 189b, 191a–197a, 198a, 199b, 201a, 203a, 205a, 208b
Royal Navy, III 490a
satire, IV 213a, 213b, 214b, 215a, 216b
science, III 602a, 602b; IV 153b
semantics, III 73a
skepticism, IV 245b–246a
slavery, IV 219b
social contract, IV 253b, 254a, 254b, 257b, 258a, 260b, 261a, 262b
social welfare, IV 277b, 282a
socialism, III 165a, 674b; IV 287a, 287b–288a, 289b, 290a, 293a, 510b–512a, 513b
sociology, III 537a
sovereignty, I 659a
State, I 397b, 656a–657b, 658b–663a; IV 153b, 315a
sublime in external nature, IV 333a–337b
suffrage, II 138b
symbolism, III 483b; IV 338b–339a, 340b–341a, 343b, 344b
syndicalism, III 677a
Tahiti, III 602a
taste, IV 355a, 355b–356a
technology, IV 360b, 361b, 362a–363a
temperance, IV 374b
theology, II 30b
tolerance, I 400b, 401a, 401b
treason, II 689a
trusts, III 492a
Tudor policy, III 489b
tyranny, IV 154a
unemployment, IV 511b–512a, 512b, 513a
Unemployment Insurance

Act of 1920, IV 511b
uniformitarianism, IV 418a, 418b, 419b, 420a, 420b, 421b, 422a, 425a
unions, III 537a
Unitarianism, III 429b
U.S., IV 155b
utilitarianism, III 538a; IV 444a, 444b
Utopia, IV 462a, 463a, 463b
Victorian period, III 482b–483a; IV 217a–224a
virtuoso, IV 486a–490a
Volksgeist, IV 494a–494b, 495b
vox populi, IV 499a, 500a
war, IV 503b, 504a, 505a, 505b, 507a
welfare state, III 492a; IV 509a–514a
witchcraft, IV 522b
women, IV 526a, 528a
Workingmen's Peace Association, III 448b
World War I, IV 511b
World War II, IV 512b
Year Books, II 694b, 695b; III 31a
Great Depression of the 1930's
economic history, II 58a, 58b
Great Britain, IV 511b–512a
Marxism, III 164a
natural liberty, II 70a–70b
New Zealand, IV 512a
Sweden, IV 512a
U.S., II 70a–70b; IV 511b, 512a–512b
welfare state, IV 511b–512b
Great Gloss of Accursius, II 691b–692b
Great Goddess (myth), II 333a–333b, 340a
Great Goddess of Fertility (myth), III 272b
Great Northern War, balance of power, I 186a
Great Schism (1378–1417), I 385a, 386a–386b, 387b; IV 65a
Great Year (myth)
Archytas of Tarentum, IV 400b
Aristotle, III 628b; IV 400b
cycles, IV 401a
Heraclitus, IV 401a
Plato, III 628b; IV 400b–401a
progress, III 628b, 631b
Stoics, IV 401a

155

time, IV 390a, 391a, 392a, 400b–401a
tragic sense, IV 415a
Greece
  archeology, III 336a
  biology, I 229b–236a
  international peace, III 454b
  nationalism, III 329b
  neo-classicism in art, III 363a, 363b, 364b
  revolution, IV 160b
  war, III 454b
Greece (ancient)
  adjudication, II 676b, 677a, 678b
  Aeolians, III 61b
  aesthetics, II 216b–218a, 219a, 220a, 222a–223a
  alchemy, I 28a–29a, 29b
  allegory, III 526b
  ambiguity, I 48b–52a
  analogy, I 68a–68b
  anthropology, IV 96b
  anthropomorphism, II 652b
  apeiron, II 604b, 605a, 607a–607b
  arbitration, III 449b
  architecture, I 428a; III 350b
  argumentation, III 7a
  aristocracy, II 675a
  art, II 297c, 299a, 299b, 459a; III 363a, 365a–365b
  artists, III 527a
  asceticism, I 631b–632a
  asebeia, II 565b–567a
  assemblies, II 256b–260b, 675b, 680a
  astrology, I 119a–122b, 123a, 124b, 125a, 125b
  atheism, II 565b
  athletes, II 683b
  atomism, I 126a–131a, 494b–497a
  Atticism, III 527b–528a
  authority, II 678b, 680a, 681a, 681b, 682b
  balance of power, I 180a
  barbarians, I 629a, 632a
  behaviorism, II 677b–678b, 682b
  Buddhism, I 254b
  canon of proportions, I 580a, 581b, 582a
  catharsis, I 264a–270a
  causation, I 271a–273a, 275b, 290b, 291b, 293b; II 18b
  certainty, I 304a
  chance, I 335b–336a; II 225b–228b
  chance images, I 340b–342b, 347a
  chaos, IV 296b, 297b

Christianity, I 375a; IV 228a
Church, I 412b, 416b
city, I 427b, 428a–428b, 432a
city state, I 653b–654b, 655b; II 46b, 236b–258a, 674a, 679b, 681b, 682b; III 37b, 449b; IV 228a, 313a–313b, 366b
civil disobedience, I 434b
claims, II 676a–677a, 678b, 679a
class, I 443a
classicism, I 451a, 453a
classification of the arts, I 456b–458b
classification of the sciences, I 462b–463b
colonialism, III 61b
comedy, I 467b, 468b 469a–469b; III 61b
community, II 675a, 677a, 677b, 678b, 679b, 681a, 681b, 683a–683b, 685a
conduct, II 674a, 681b–685a
conservation, I 471b–472a, 472b
conservatism, I 477b, 479b
constitutionalism, I 486b–487b, 488b
constitutions, II 675a, 675b, 677b
continuity, I 492b–503a
Cosmic Fall, I 505b, 512a
cosmic voyages, I 524a–525a, 527a
cosmology, I 538b, 539a–541a, 543a, 544b; II 117b, 674a
cosmos, III 94b
councils, II 258b
courts, II 676b, 679b
Creation, I 571a, 571b–572a
creativity in art, I 578a–585b, 586a
creditors, II 679a
culture, I 607b–613a; IV 367a
custom, III 347b
cycles, I 621b, 622a–623b, 624b–626a
cynicism, I 627b–633b; III 476b
dance, IV 96b
death, I 634b–639b, 642a, 643b–645b; II 674b, 676a, 678a; IV 228a
debts, II 679a, 684b
democracy, I 652b–655b, 657a–658b, 667a; II 257a, 259a, 682a, 685a; III 11a

demonology, I 667b–669a
design argument, I 670b–673b
despotism, II 1b, 2a–3a, 4a, 4b, 5a, 6a, 7b, 9a, 11b, 13a, 13b, 15b, 16a, 17a
determinism, II 18b, 19b, 22a, 22b, 24b
dialects, III 62b
dignity, IV 136a–136b, 137a–138a, 139a, 144a
dikē, II 674a–679b, 680a, 681b, 682a, 683a
discontinuity, I 495b–497a
disease, II 397a–399a
divination, II 675a–675b, 676a, 679b, 680a, 680b, 682b
divine, III 95a
Dorians, III 61b
double truth, II 31b–33a
drama, III 112a, 527a, 527b
dualism, II 39a, 40a–41a, 42a, 42b, 164a, 164b
economic history, II 44b, 45a, 45b, 46b
education, I 258a; II 74b, 75a–84b, 339b; IV 367a
Egypt (ancient), IV 228b
eighteenth-century attitudes toward, I 76b–87b
Eleusinian Mysteries, IV 102a
empathy, II 87b
environment, II 120b, 122b
Epicureanism, IV 7a
equality, II 138a, 138b, 140a, 140b, 144b; III 11a
equity, II 148a–151a, 153b
epics, II 466b
Epicureanism, II 135a
eschatology, II 155a–160a
ethics, III 353a, 440a, 440b, 585a; IV 319a, 320a–320b
Ethiopia, III 591a
etymology, II 675a, 676a, 679b–682a
eusebeia, II 565b
evil, II 162b–163b, 167b, 674b, 677a
evolution of literature, II 169b–170a, 171b
evolutionism, II 175a–176a
family, II 674b, 677b, 678a, 678b
fate, II 225b–228b
foreign literature, III 528a
foreigners, II 260a
Fortunate Islands (myth), III 591a
fortune, II 225b–228b
free will, II 135a, 245b
freedom, II 44b, 249b, 684b
freedom of speech, II 252a,

252b, 254b, 256b–260b, 261b
friendship, III 112a
general will, II 276a
genetic continuity, II 281b–282a
genius, II 297b, 299a, 299b, 312b–313a, 315b, 317b–318a, 318b
geometry, *See* Euclid
gifts, II 676b, 677b, 678a
glassology, III 61b
Gnosticism, II 327b, 328a, 329a, 330a
God, I 571a, 571b–572a, 645a; II 333a, 338a, 339b–341b, 343a, 357a, 357b, 360b, 363a, 565b, 566a, 566b, 674b, 678a, 678b, 681a, 682a, 682b, 684a; III 347a
Golden Age (myth), III 591a
good, II 677a; IV 174b–176a
grammar, III 62a, 528a
happiness, II 375a, 375b–378b, 379a, 380b
harmony, II 388b, 392a–392b; IV 38a–41a, 41b
heresy, II 565b, 566a, 566b
hermeticism, II 431b
heroes, IV 366b
hierarchy, II 442b, 444a
historians, III 353b, 356a, 476b
historicism, II 459a
historiography, II 18b, 19b, 22a, 22b, 24b, 466a–471a, 474b, 475a, 475b, 476b, 477a, 483a, 483b, 484b, 488a–511a; IV 147a
homicide, II 680b
hubris, IV 228a
human nature, III 570b–577b
humanism, II 515a, 516a–516b; IV 129b, 131a, 131b, 132b–133a
hylozoism, I 61b, 68a, 70a
iconography, II 525a–528b
ideal, II 550b
immortality, I 638b–639b, 642a–645b; III 347a; IV 228b
impiety, II 564a, 565b–566b
impressionism, II 582a–582b
indeterminacy, II 586b–587a
inequality, III 11a
infinity, II 604b–605b, 607a–611a, 614b

intolerance, II 565b–566a
Ionians, III 61b
irony, II 632a
irrationalism, IV 46a, 49a
Islam, II 639a, 639b, 644a, 647b, 650a, 651b
isonomos, II 682a
Isthmian Games, II 681a
Judaic Christianity, I 374a–374b, 375a
judges, II 675a, 676a, 678b, 680a, 681b
judgment, II 675b, 676b–677a, 682b–683a
jurisdiction, II 675b–676a
jurors, II 684a
justice, II 652b–656a, 656b, 659a, 675b–676a, 677a, 679a, 679b
kingship, II 675a–676a, 678a, 678b
knowledge, II 678b
language, II 661a, 661b–666a
law, I 290b, 291b, 293b, 486b–487b, 653b; II 148a–150b, 151a, 153b, 249b, 501b, 556b, 673b–685b; III 1a–1b, 7a, 11a; IV 252b
liberalism, III 36a, 36b
liberty, II 259a, 500b–501a
linguistics, II 661a, 661b–666a; III 61b
literary criticism, I 596b
literature, II 674a–679b, 682a, 683b–684a; III 81b, 82a, 527b; IV 228a, 330a, 330b, 331b
longevity, III 89b, 90a
love, III 94b–96a, 97a
loyalty, III 109b–111a, 112b
lyric poetry, III 527a
Machiavelli, III 356a
Machiavellism, III 116a
macrocosm and microcosm, III 126a, 126b, 127a, 128a, 129a, 129b, 130b
magic, IV 102a
Man-Machine, III 131b–134b
marriage, II 681a, 682b, 683b, 684a; III 94b
mathematics, I 497b–498a; III 171a–184b
matter, II 42a; III 186a, 186b–190b, 191a
metaphor, III 201b, 202b, 203a–204a, 204b–206a
metaphysics, III 210a–210b, 217b
method of exhaustion, II 609b, 610b
methodology, III 379b–

381b
migration, II 499a
mimesis, III 225b–227a, 229b, 230a, 526b
misogynism, IV 524a
moderation, IV 369a
morality, II 566a, 678a, 679b, 681a; III 353a; IV 229a
mores, II 683a–683b, 685a
mountains in literature, III 253a–253b, 255b
multi-lingualism, III 61b
murder, II 674b, 676a, 681a, 683a, 683b, 684b
music, II 312b–313a, 315b, 317b–318a, 318b, 388b, 392a–392b; III 260b–261b, 265a, 266b, 268b–269a
musicians, II 312b–313a
Mycenaean Age, II 466b, 467a
mysticism, IV 228a–228b
mythology, II 39a, 226b, 228a, 652b–653a, 656b; III 94b, 95a, 96a, 272a–274b, 275a, 275b, 278b, 279a, 279b, 281b, 284a, 286a–286b, 287a, 290a, 292b, 293a, 301a, 302a–309a, 311a, 314a, 571a–572b, 573a, 574b; IV 228a–229a, 367a
nationalism, III 324b, 325a, 335a
natural law, I 487a–487b; III 14b–16b
natural liberty, II 61b
naturalism, II 581b
naturalism in art, III 342a, 342b
Nature, I 127b–129b; III 347a, 347b, 350b; IV 229a
necessity, III 351b, 352b–354b, 356a, 361a
neo-classicism in art, III 363a, 364b, 365a, 365b, 366b, 367a, 367b, 368b, 369b, 370b
Neo-Platonism, III 371b, 372b, 373a, 373b, 377a, 377b
Noble Savage, III 591a–591b
nomos, II 681b–685a; III 1a
norms, II 677a–678a, 679a, 679b, 682a–683b, 685a
numbers, III 401b, 403a, 403b
nymphs, III 347a
oaths, II 675b, 676a, 681a, 684a
obligation, II 675a, 680b,

681b, 682b, 684a
oligarchy, II 683a
Olympic Games, II 681a
omens, III 347a
One, II 614b, 615a
opinion, II 565b, 566b
optics, III 407a–408b, 415b, 420b
oratory, II 150a–150b, 170a, 684a–684b; III 7a, 112a
order, II 442b, 444a, 674b, 675a, 676a, 676b, 677a, 681a–683a, 685a
organicism, III 421b
Orientalism, II 500b–501a
pangenesis, II 622b–623b, 624a, 626a
peace, III 440a, 440b; IV 366b
Peloponnesian War, II 468a, 501a
perception, II 607b
perfectibility, III 463b–465b, 468b, 473a
periodization in history, III 476b
persecution, II 565b–566b
Persia (ancient), IV 228b
Persian War, II 468a, 501b–502a
pessimism, II 566a
philanthropy, III 487a–487b, 488b
philology, II 516b
philosophy, II 674a; III 112a; IV 228a, 229a
Platonism, III 496a–502a
pleasure, II 375a, 375b–378b, 379a, 380b
poetry, II 679b, 680b, 683b; III 112a, 525b–528a, 529a, 530b, 531a, 531b; IV 469a, 470b
politics, I 60a–61b; II 256b–257b, 258b, 259a, 674a, 675b, 680a, 680b, 681a–685a; III 353a; IV 252b
power, I 613a; II 674b, 675a, 677a, 678b, 679a
pragmatism, III 554a–554b
prerogatives, II 675a–675b, 677b, 678b
primitivism, III 578a–581a, 583a, 583b, 585a, 591a, 592a, 597a, 603b
private property, III 654a
probability, III 605b, 613a
progress, II 623b–633a, 634a, 634b, 641a, 642a, 645a, 648a
prolongevity, III 90a
prophecy, III 657a–657b,
proportions, II 609b, 665b

681b, 682b, 684a
psychology, IV 1a–8b, 9a, 9b, 10a, 11a, 11b, 19b
punishment, II 565b–566b, 677a, 679b
puzzles, II 608b, 610a, 615a
race, II 500a–500b
rationalism, IV 46a–51b
reformation, IV 60b, 61b
reincarnation, I 644b, 645a; IV 228b
relativity, IV 74b, 75a, 87a
religion, II 565b–566b, 674a–679b, 681a–681b, 683a–684a, 685a; III 201b, 202b–206a, 572a; IV 92b–93b, 94a, 96b, 98a, 100a, 101b–102a, 228a, 228b, 366b
Renaissance, IV 122a, 123a, 124a–126a, 129b, 131a, 131b, 132b–133a, 136a–138a, 139a, 144a
retribution, II 677a, 679a, 679b
revival, III 365b
revolution, IV 152b
rhetoric, III 526a, 526b, 528a; IV 167a–169a, 169b
rhetra, II 680a
right, II 677a, 678a, 678b, 679b; IV 174b, 176a
rights, II 675a, 676a, 678b
ritual, II 675b, 681a, 683b–684a; IV 228a–228b
romanticism, IV 189b, 208a, 210a
Rome (ancient), IV 370a
rules, II 675b, 676a, 678b, 681a
sacrifice, II 675b, 677b
salvation, IV 228a–229a, 229b
satire, IV 211a, 211b, 212a, 212b, 214b
sculpture, II 170a–170b; III 342a, 363a
Scythia, III 591a–591b
self-sufficiency, III 585a
sex, II 677b, 678a, 681a, 682b; III 94b, 95a
skepticism, I 273a, 304b, 401b; IV 234a–240a, 241a, 242a
slavery, I 443a; II 1b, 2a, 2b–3a, 249b, 260a, 678a; IV 286a
social contract, IV 251b, 252a, 252b–253a
socialism, IV 285a–286a
society, I 60a–61b, 487a; II 674a–675b, 676a, 677b–679a, 680b, 681a, 682a, 683a–683b, 684b, 685a; III 353a; IV 252b, 366b

Sophism, IV 367a
soul, II 42a, 565b, 678a; IV 228b, 229a
space, IV 295a, 296b, 297a, 297b, 298a
spirit, IV 96b
spontaneous generation, IV 307a–308a
State, I 487a, 652b–655a, 655b, 657a, 657b, 658a, 658b, 667a; IV 228a, 252b, 312b–313b
statutes, II 680a, 681b–685a
Stoicism, IV 319a, 320a–320b
Stoics, IV 7a
style, IV 330a, 330b, 331b
suffrage, II 138b
symmetry, IV 346a–349a
taxonomy, III 61b
technology, I 60b, 62a; IV 358a
temperance, IV 365b–370a, 371a, 373b
themis, II 674a–679b, 683a
theodicy, IV 379b, 380a–380b, 381b
theology, II 516b
thesmos, II 680a, 680b–681a, 681b–682a, 685a
Thucydides, IV 367a
time, II 681b; IV 389a–391b, 392a, 393a–393b, 399b–401a, 402a
tragedy, II 228a, 652b; III 347a, 527a, 527b; IV 366b
tragic sense, IV 411b–416b
trials, II 676a, 679b
Trojan War, II 466b–467a, 675a
truth, II 677b
tyranny, II 680b, 681b, 682a, 683a, 684b, 685a
unity of science, IV 431a–432b
universal man, IV 438a, 441b
universe, II 675b, 677b, 681b, 682a; IV 38a–41b
utilitarianism, IV 444a
utility, IV 450b, 451a–452a
Utopia, IV 459a–460a
value, II 682b–683a; IV 450b, 451a–452a
vases, III 366b, 369a, 370b
verdicts, II 676a–677a, 679a, 680a
violence, II 677a, 679a, 683b
virtù IV 477a
vitalism, I 60b, 61b–62a
Volksgeist, IV 491a, 494a
vox populi, IV 497a–498a

war, II 678b, 683b; III 448a; IV 366b, 367b, 501a–502a
Winckelmann, III 367a
wisdom of the fool, IV 516b, 517a
witchcraft, IV 521a
women, IV 524a
work, IV 530a–531a
World Spirit, II 392a–392b
writing, III 180b
wrong, II 677a, 678a, 678b
Greed,
law, II 688a
progress, III 630a, 639b, 640a
Rome (ancient), II 688a
Greek language, II 660b, 661b–666a, 667a, 667b, 669b, 670a, 670b, 671a, 684b; III 61b, 65a, 66b–67a, 305b, 505b, 509b
dignity, IV 143b
linguistics, IV 425b, 427b
Renaissance, IV 123b, 143b
uniformitarianism, IV 425b, 427b
Greek Orthodox Church, millenarianism, III 224a–224b
Green, George (1793–1841), continuity, I 494a
Green, John Richard (1837–1883), Gothic, II 369b
Green, Nicholas St. John (1830–1876)
Peirce and, III 567a
pragmatism, III 553b, 558a 566a, 567a
Green, T. H. (1836–1882), general will, II 280a
God, II 415a
Hegel and, II 414a, 414b–415a
individualism, II 596b
liberalism, III 51a, 51b
Mill, J. S. and, II 414b
Platonism, III 522a
right and good, IV 181a
social contract, IV 236a
State, II 415a
war, IV 503b
welfare state, IV 509b
utilitarianism, IV 445a, 447b
Greene, J. C., linguistics, IV 427b
Greenlaw, Edwin, literature, III 85b
Gregorian chants, II 314b, 315a
Gregory of Nazianzus (329?–

?389 A.D.)
allegory; I 44a
humanism, II 520b
Gregory of Nyssa, Saint (331?–396 A.D.)
Adam (Bible), III 583a
allegory, I 44a
dignity, IV 137a–137b, 139b
primitivism, III 583a
soul, IV 137a
Gregory of Tours (538?–593 A.D.), historiography, II 472b
Gregory Thaumaturgus (213?–?270 A.D.), casuistry, I 258b
Gregory I (the Great), Pope (540–604)
Christianity, I 379b, 381b
demonology, I 669b
iconography, II 526b
mythology, III 288a
temperance, IV 371a
wisdom of the fool, IV 517b
Gregory VII, Pope (1020?–1085)
Christianity, I 381b, 382a–382b
love, III 97b
reformation, IV 64a
Gregory IX, Pope (1147?–1241)
double truth, II 31b
heresy, II 421a, 425a
Gregory XI, Pope (1331–1378), Christianity, I 385a
Gregory XIII, Pope (1502–1585)
China, I 354b
time, IV 399b
Gregory XIV, Pope (1535–1591), Platonism, III 514a
Grelling, Kurt, empiricism, III 546a
Grenier, Jean, skepticism, IV 250a, 250b
Gressmann, Hugo (1877–1927), mythology, III 311b
Greuze, Jean Baptiste (1725–1805), neo-classicism, III 366a
Greville, Fulke (1554–1628), aesthetics, I 512a
Chapman, George and, III 294b
Cosmic Fall, I 505b, 506b, 512a
historiography, IV 150a, 151a
mythology, III 294b
Grierson, Herbert (1866–1960), baroque in literature, I 193a

Grigoriev, Apollon, literary criticism, I 606b
Grillparzer, Franz (1791–1872), realism in literature, IV 55a
Grimaldi, Father Francesco Maria (1618?–1663), Newton and, III 418b
optics, III 418a, 418b, 419a
Grimm, Baron Friedrich Melchior von (1723–1807), China, I 365a
Grimm, Jacob (1785–1863), *ablaut*, III 67b
consonant shift, III 67a
dialects, III 67a
etymology, III 67a
evolution of literature, II 170b
folklore, III 236b, 239a
German dictionary, III 67a
grammar, III 67a
language, II 670b–671b; III 64b, 67a, 68a, 68b
linguistics, II 671a–671b; III 64b, 67a, 68a, 68b; IV 427b
motif, III 236b, 239a, 239b
mythology, III 306a
phonology, III 67a
Pott and, III 68a
sound law, II 671a– 672a; III 66b, 70a
Teutonism, III 67a
umlaut, III 67b
uniformitarianism, IV 427b
Volksgeist, IV 494a, 495a
Grimm, Wilhelm (1786–1859)
evolution of literature, II 170b
folklore, III 236b, 239a
motif, III 235b, 236b, 239a, 239b
mythology, III 306a
Grimme, Adolf, romanticism, IV 197b
Grimmelshausen, Hans Jakob (1620?–1676)
baroque in literature, I 195a
wisdom of the fool, IV 520a
Grisar, Hartmann (1845–1932)
heresy, II 428a, 430b
Luther, II 428a
Grisebach, Eduard (1845–1906), Buddhism, I 256b
Grocheo, Johannes (c. 1300) musical genius, II 314b
Grocyn, William (1446?–1519), Platonism, III 507b
Gronbech, W., mythology, III 311a

Groningen, B. A. van, progress, III 624a

Gross, Karl (1861–1946
art and play, I 106a–106b
empathy, II 88a

Gropius, Walter (1883–1969),
culture, IV 165a–165b
revolution, IV 165a–165b

Gross National Product,
natural liberty and, II 70b

Grosseteste, Robert (d. 1253),
aesthetics, II 218a, 224b
Aristotle and, II 196a–196b
beauty, II 218a
causation, I 274b
classification of the
sciences, I 464b
cosmology, III 191a
induction, II 196b
knowledge, I 4b, III 382a
matter, III 191a
mechanical sciences, II
196a–196b, 198b, 204a
mythology, III 191a
Newton and, III 382a–
382b, 385a
optics, III 410a
prophecy, III 668a

Grossi, Tommaso (1790–
1853), romanticism, IV
192b

Grote, George (1794–1871),
Platonism, III 522a

Grotius, Hugo (1583–1645),
balance of power, I 182a,
184a, 184b
constitutionalism, I 488b
deism, I 648b
despotism, II 1a, 4a, 4b–5b,
6a, 7a, 11a
Enlightenment, II 90a
ethics, III 441b–442a
freedom, II 250b
God, I 488b; II 355a
international peace, III
450b–451a, 451b
justice, I 654b, 657a
law, II 5a, 250b; III 19b–
20a, 442a
morality, III 441b
natural law, I 488b; III 19b–
20a, 21a
Nature, II 5a–5b; III 19b–
20a
norms, III 19b–20a
peace, III 441b–442a
reason, III 19b–20a, 442a
reunion of Protestants and
Catholics, I 398b
Rousseau and, IV 259b
Saint Thomas Aquinas and,
III 20a
slavery, II 5a–5b, 11a
social contract, IV 254b,

259b, 317a
society, III 19b–20a
State, IV 317a
Stoicism, III 441b
Thirty Years War, III 441b
war, II 6a; III 441b–442a

Grousset, René, China, I 368a

Grun, Karl
Marxism, III 158b
socialism, IV 290a

Grünbaum, Adolf, empiricism,
III 550a

Grünewald, Matthias (fl.
1500–1530), heresy, II
427a

Gryllus (myth), III 296a

Gryphius, Andreas (1616–
1664), baroque in literature,
I 195a

Guarini, Giovanni Battista
(1538–1612)
mimesis, III 228a
poetry, III 529b, 531a
universal man, IV 438b

Guarini, Guarino (1624–
1683), baroque in literature,
I 188b

Guarino of Verona (1370–
1400)
humanism, II 519a–519b;
IV 133a

Guedeville, primitivism, III
599a, 599b

Guelfism, humanism, II 522b

Guérard, Albert Leon (1880–
1959), literature, III 83a

Guericke, Otto van (1602–
1686), cosmic voyages, I
532a

Guerrilla warfare, revolution,
IV 166a, 166b

Guesde, Jules (1845–1922),
Marxism, III 165a
revisionism, IV 273b

Guettard, Jean Etienne, catastrophism, IV 420a

Guevara, Ernesto ("Che")
(1928–1967?)
revolution, IV 166a
U.S.S.R., IV 166a–166b

Guevara y de Noroña, Antonio
de (1480?–1545), baroque
in literature, I 190a, 195a

Guibert de Nogent (1053–
1124), historiography, II
473b

Guibertus the Venerable
Christianity, III 591a
primitivism, III 591a

Guicciardini, Francesco
(1483–1540)
balance of power, I 181a–
183a
cycles, I 626b; IV 150b

historiography, II 483a,
492a, 518b; IV 150b
humanism, II 518b
revolution, IV 152b

Guido of Arezzo (c. 995?–
?1050), music, II 313b,
314a; III 266b

Guigo the Carthusian
Christianity, III 590b
primitivism, III 590b

Guignes, Joseph de (1721–
1800), mythology, III 305b

Guilds
artists, II 300a–300b
education, II 300a
France, II 300b
Italy, II 300a–300b
law, II 687a

Guillaume de Conches, Pythagorean harmony, IV 41a

Guillaume de Machaut
(1305?–1377), music, II
315a

Guillén, Jorge, symbolism, IV
342a, 344b

Guilt
Freud, IV 96b
good, IV 173b
Israel (ancient), IV 226b
law, III 35b
love, III 100b
religion, IV 96b
right, IV 173b
sin, IV 226b
tragic sense, IV 415b
vox populi, IV 498a

Guimet, Émile E, (1836–
1018), China, I 369a

Guinea, nationalism, III 338a

Guiraudet, T., Machiavellism,
III 123a–123b

Guise, Duc de (1519–1563),
Machiavellism, III 120b

Guizot, Francois (1787–
1874)
Comte and, III 533b
French Revolution, IV 159b
historicism, II 458b
literature, IV 189b
periodization in history, III
477b
positivism, III 533b
revolution, IV 159b
romanticism, IV 189b

Gummere, Francis B. (1855–
1919), evolution of literature, II 171b

Gundolf, Friedrich (1880–
1931)
classicism, I 451a
Platonism, III 524b
symbolism, IV 342b

Gundulić, Ivan (1588–1678),
baroque in literature, I 193a

Gunkel, H., mythology, III
311b

Gunn, William, Gothic, II 373a

Gurewitch, Morton, irony, II
633b

Gurlitt, Cornelius (1850–
1938), baroque, I 189a

Gurvitch, George, individualism, II 601a

Gusdorf, Georges, mythology,
III 315b

Gusmão, Bartholomeu Lour-
encode (1675–1724), cos-
mic voyages, I 532b

Gustavus Adolphus, King
(1594–1632), Gothic, II
367a

Gutenberg, Johann (1400?–
?1468), Faust (legend), III
247a

Guthrie, E. R. behaviorism, I
225b–226a, 227b

Guthrie, Woody (1912–1967),
mythology, III 276b

Guyau, Marie Jean (1854–
1888)
beauty, I 213a
indeterminacy, II 587a

Guys, Constantin (1802–
1892), impressionism, II
573a

Gyarmathi, S. (1751–1830),
linguistics, III 64b–65a, 66a

Gymnastics, Plato, I 462b

Gymnosophists, I 631b–632a

Gyraldi, G. B., mythology,
III 292b–293a

H

Habakkuk (Bible)
loyalty, III 108b
prophecy, III 662b

Habermas, J., historicism, II
463b

Habit
imprinting, II 584b–585a
necessity, III 357b

Habsburgs
balance of power, I 181b,
182b, 183a, 186a
Counter-Reformation, I
394b
nationalism, III 332a
Richelieu and, I 399a
World War I, III 332a

Hadas, Moses (1900–1966),
education, II 71b

Hades (myth), III 272b
sin, IV 228a

Hadot, P., Neo-Platonism, III 376b

Hadrian (76–138 A.D.)
art as pastime, II 299b
equity, II 151a
neo-classicism in art, III 364a, 365a–365b

Haeckel, Ernst H. (1834–1919)
chromosomes, II 288a
Darwin and, IV 57b
evolutionism, II 181b–182b
genetic continuity, II 288a
pragmatism, III 556b
psychology, IV 12a
recapitulation, IV 56a, 56b, 57b–59a
religion, IV 108a
spontaneous generation, IV 312a
Wright and, III 556b

Haerten, Heinz, baroque in literature, I 191b

Hagdorn, C. W., China, I 364a

Hagedorn, Friedrich von (1708–1754), beauty, II 550b

Hägerström, Axel, agnosticism, I 26a

Haggai (Bible), metaphor, III 202b

Hagiography, evil, II 165a

Hague Peace Conferences, III 450a, 451a, 453b, 455a

Hahn, Hans, empiricism, III 545b, 548a, 548b

Haiti, natural liberty, II 70a

Hakewill, George (1578–1649)
Bacon, F., and, I 510a
Chain of Being, I 512a
Cosmic Fall, I 506b, 507b–508b, 510a, 512a
Goodman and, I 507b–508b, 510a

Haldane, John B. S. (1892–1964)
entropy, II 118b
evolutionism, II 186b, 187a
genetics, II 186b

Haldane, Richard B. (1856–1928), welfare state, IV 511b

Hale, Edward Everett (1822–1909), international peace, III 453a

Hales, John (1584–1656), deism, I 649b

Halévy, Élie (1799–1862), utility, IV 453b

Halifax, Marquis de (1633–1695)
deism, I 650a
Puritanism, I 650a

Hall, Charles Cuthbert (1852–1908), Orientalism, III 435b

Hall, G. Stanley (1846–1924), Freud and, III 562b
psychology, IV 12b, 26b, 28b

Hall, Joseph (1574–1656), satire, IV 213a

Hall, Marshall (1790–1857), behaviorism, I 218a
psychology, IV 24b

Haller, Albrecht von (1708–1777)
longevity, III 91b
Man-Machine, III 140a
positivism, III 534a
primitivism, III 600b
spontaneous generation, IV 310b

Haller, Karl Ludwig von, conservatism, I 482a–482b
romanticism, IV 205b

Hallet, George, social welfare, IV 282a, 282b

Halley, Edmund (1656–1742), Apollonius of Perga and, III 380b
cosmology, I 549a–549b
Newton and, III 380b, 392b, 393a
optics, III 392b, 393a
space, IV 303a

Halley, Edward, probability, III 607a

Halley's comet, cosmic images, I 523a

Hallucinations
Aristotle, IV 5b
psychology, IV 4b, 7b
Stoics, IV 7b

Hals, Frans (1580?–1666), illusionism, III 344b
Leibl and, III 344a
motif, III 344b
naturalism in art, III 341a, 344a–345a

Haly Rodohan, methodology, III 381a, 381b

Ham (Bible), mythology, III 277b, 280a

Hamann, Johann Georg (1730–1788)
aesthetics, IV 356b
Counter-Enlightenment, II 103b–105a, 108b, 109b
faith, II 104a
genius, II 295b
God, II 103b, 104a, 354a
history, II 104b
Hume and, II 103b–104a
irrationalism, II 635b, 638a
mythology, III 304a
Nature, II 105a
romanticism, IV 209b, 210b

skepticism, IV 249a–250b
Schelling and, IV 210b
taste, IV 356b

Hamann, Richard, periodization in literary history, III 484a

Hamerton, P. S., impressionism, II 573b

Hamilton Alexander (1755–1804)
conservatism, I 484a
Jefferson and, IV 21b
psychology, IV 21b, 22a, 22b

Hamilton, Alexander (1762–1824), linguistics, III 65b

Hamilton, Gavin, neo-classicism in art, III 364a, 369a

Hamilton, William (1788–1856)
agnosticism, I 17b, 18a
God, II 363b–364a

Hamilton, William (1730–1803), neo-classicism in art, III 366b

Hamilton, William Rowan (1805–1865)
cosmology, I 554b
infinity, II 613b
pragmatism, III 561a
quaternions, III 405b

Hamlet (fiction)
literary paradox, III 77a, 80b
motif, III 240b
tragic sense, IV 416b

Hamlet problem, I 54b–56a

Hammond, William A. (1828–1900), psychology, IV 28b

Hammurabi (c. 1955–1913 B.C.)
justice, II 655b
law, II 686b; III 11a, 28b
mathematics, III 179b, 180a
salvation, IV 226b

Hammurabic Code, philanthropy, III 487a

Han dynasty
historiography, II 480b
ut pictura poesis, IV 476a

Hananiah ben Azzur, prophecy, III 663a

Handel, George Frederick (1685–1759), Messiah, I 404b

Handwriting
Boccaccio, II 518a
Caroline minuscule, II 518a
cursive, II 518a
Gothic, II 367b, 518a
humanism, II 518a
Medici, II 518a
Niccoli, II 518a
Petrarch, II 518a
Poggio, II 518a

Salutati, II 518a

Hankel, Wilhelm G. (1814–1899)
continuity, I 498b
infinity, II 606b

Hannibal (247–183 B.C.)
neoclassism in art, III 368b
virtù IV 480a, 481b

Hansch, Michael, perennial philosophy, III 461b

Hansen, Alvin H., welfare state, IV 513a

Hansen, Joseph, witchcraft, IV 522b

Hanslick, Eduard (1825–1904), art for art's sake, I 110b

Hanson, N. R., empiricism, III 550b

Happiness, II 374b–387b
advertising, II 385a
aesthetics, II 374b, 380b, 386a
aggression, II 383b
Alberti, IV 478a
anthropology, II 384a
Antisthenes, II 375b
anxiety, II 383b, 384a
apparent, II 375a
architecture, II 374b
Aristippus, II 375b, 378a
Aristotle, II 227a, 228a, 375a, 377a–378a, 379a, 380b, 387a; III 465a; IV 175b, 176b, 530b
art, II 386a
art and play, II 374b
Bacon, II 379b
Beccaria, II 380b
behaviorism, II 382b
belief, II 387a
benevolence, II 380a
Bentham, II 380b, 381a–381b; IV 454a
Bible, II 375b, 378b
biology, II 375a, 382a–384b
biopsychological disciplines, II 382a–384b
birth, II 384a–384b
blessedness, II 378b, 379a
Bradley, II 381b
Butler, II 380a
Calicles, II 375b
Cartesianism, II 387a
catharsis, II 378b
causation, II 378a
chance, II 227a, 228a, 235a
Christianity, II 378b–379a
Cicero, IV 50a
city planning, II 374b
community, II 374b, 380b; IV 178b
Comte, III 637a, 644a

concept of, II 374b–375a, 379a–379b
Condillac, II 381a
consciousness, II 382b–383a
Counter-Enlightenment, II 101a, 102a, 108a
culture, II 384a
Cumberland, II 380b
cynicism, II 375b
damnation, II 374b, 379a
Dante, II 379a
death, II 378a, 383b, 384b
Democritus, II 378a; III 576b, 577a
Descartes, II 380b, 381a
desire, II 375a, 380a, 380b
determinism, II 378a
Dewey, II 381b, 382b
dignity, IV 143a
discipline, II 385b
dualism, II 381a, 382b, 387a
economy, II 374b, 379b, 381b, 384b–385a
education, II 374b, 380a, 382a, 385a, 385b
ego, II 383a, 383b
emotion, II 382b
employment, II 385a
Enlightenment, II 96b, 98a, 99a
Epicureanism, II 378a
Epicurus, II 378a; III 465a
epiphenomenalism, II 382b
ethics, II 374b–375a, 375b, 378a, 379a, 379b, 380a, 380b, 381b, 383a; IV 70b, 319b, 320b, 321a, 321b
evil, II 167a–167b, 374b, 375b, 376b, 379a
evolution, II 383a
failure, II 374b
faith, II 378b
false, II 387a
fate, II 227a, 228a, 235a
fear, II 378a, 384b
feelings, II 382b, 383a, 386b
fortune, II 227a, 228a, 235a
free will, II 238a
freedom, II 379b
Freud, II 383a–384a
friendship, II 377b, 378a
Fromm, II 384a
fun, II 385b
general will, II 277a
Gestalt treatment, II 383a
God, II 377b, 378b–379a, 380b
good, II 374b, 375b, 376b, 377a–377b, 378a, 379a, 379b–380a, 380b, 381a; IV 175b, 176b, 178b, 179a,

179b, 180a
grace, II 379a
Greece (ancient), II 375a, 375b–378b, 379a, 380b
guilt, II 383b, 385a
Hartley, II 380b, 381a
health, II 374b, 376a, 383a, 384a, 399a, 406b
hedonism, II 375b, 380a, 380b, 381a, 381b, 383b, 384b, 385a; III 576b, 577a
Hegel, II 409b; IV 180a
hell, II 379a
Helvétius, II 380b
Herder, III 639a–639b
Herodotus, II 375b
Hesiod, II 375b
hippies, II 385b
historiography, IV 152a
Hobbes, II 379b, 380a, 380b–381a
Holbach, II 380b
Homer, II 375b
honor, II 376a
hope, II 212a
human nature, II 377a, 379b; III 644a
humanism, II 519b; IV 132a
Hume, II 380a, 381a; III 232a, 232b
Hutcheson, II 380a, 380b; III 231b
id, II 383b
illusory, II 375a
immorality, II 375a, 376a
individualism, II 374b, 375b, 378a, 379a–379b, 382a, 384b
injustice, II 376a
instinct, II 383b, 385a
as intrinsic values, II 374b–375a
intuition, II 383a
Jefferson, II 379b
Jesus Christ, II 378b
Jevons, II 384b
Job (Bible), II 378b
joy, II 378a, 384a, 385b
Judaism, II 375b, 378b
judgment, II 379b
justice, II 375b–376a
Kant, II 375a, 380a, 385b; III 637a; IV 179b
knowledge, II 376a, 379a, 379b, 386b–387a
labor, II 379b, 384b
language, II 375a, 381b, 386a–387b
law, II 379b, 380b, 381b, 385a, 385b
Leibniz, II 381a
liberalism, II 379a, 379b
liberty, II 379a–379b, 381b

literature, II 385a
Locke, II 96b–97a, 379b, 380a, 381a
logic, II 375a, 386a
love, II 379a
Lucretius, II 378a
McDougall, II 382b
Machiavelli, II 379b; IV 481a
Marx, II 381b
masochism, II 383b
materialism, II 378a
maximization, II 374b
medicine, II 374b, 382a–384b
mental health, II 384a
metaphysics, II 375a, 376a–376b, 377a, 383b
Middle Ages, II 378b–379a
Mill, II 381b–382a; IV 179a
millenarianism, III 223b, 224b
mind, II 378a
money, II 384b
moral sense, III 231b, 232a, 232b
morality, II 374b, 375b–376a, 376b, 380a, 380b, 383a–385b, 387a
More, Thomas, II 379b
mysticism, II 378b–379a
nationalism, II 379b
natural selection, II 383a
Nature, II 377a, 378a, 381a
Neo-Platonism, II 378b
Owen, II 380a; III 469a
pain, II 374b–387a
Paley, II 380b
Pareto, II 384b
passions, II 381a
perfectibility, III 463b, 464a, 465a, 468b, 469a, 475a, 644a
phenomenological psychiatry, II 383a
philosophy, II 375a, 378a–379a, 381b, 386a–387b
physiology, II 383a
Pico della Mirandola, IV 132a
Plato, II 375b–377a, 383b
Platonism, II 380a; III 512b–513a
Plotinus, II 378b
poverty, II 374b
power, II 379a, 379b, 384b
prestige, II 376a, 379a
Priestley, II 380b
private property, II 379b, 381a
progress, II 379b, 380a; III 624a, 637a, 639a–639b, 644a, 644b, 648b
prophecy, III 665b

Protagoras, II 375b
Protestantism, II 378b–379a
psychiatry, II 383a
psychology, II 374b, 375a, 376a
punishment, II 381a, 385b
rationalism, II 375b, 380a; IV 50a
reinforcement theory, II 382b
relativism, IV 70b
religion, II 374b, 386a
Renaissance, IV 132a, 143a, 152a
repression, II 383b, 385b
revolution, II 379a
right, IV 175b, 176b, 178b, 179a, 179b, 180a
Roman Catholic Church, II 378b–379a
Rome (ancient), II 378b
Rousseau, II 277a; III 326a
Ryle, II 386b
sadism, II 383b
Saint Augustine, II 378b, 380b
Saint Bonaventura, II 379a
Saint Thomas Aquinas, II 212a, 238a
Saint-Simon, II 380a
salvation, II 374b, 379a
Schlick, II 385b
science, II 375a, 379a, 386a, 387a–387b
sex, II 374b, 385a
Shaftesbury, II 380a
skepticism, IV 238b
social contract, II 379b
society, II 374b, 379b–380a, 381b, 383b, 386a
Socrates, II 375b, 376a; III 576b
Solon, II 375b
Sophists, II 375b
soul, II 376a, 377a, 378a, 378b, 381a
Spencer, II 383a; III 637a
State, II 379b, 380a, 381b
Stoicism, II 378a; IV 50a, 319b, 320b, 321a, 321b
sublime in external nature, IV 335a
success, II 374b
superego, II 383a
sympathy, II 380a
teleology, II 378a, 381a
theriophily, IV 384a, 388a
Thrasymachus, II 375b
tradition, II 379a
tragedy, II 376b
tranquilizers, II 384b
truth, II 376b, 377a
tyranny, II 376a

utilitarianism, II 379a–383a, 384b; IV 178b, 179a, 444a–450a, 454a

utopianism, II 374b, 379b–380a; IV 460a, 463b

virtue, II 376b, 377a, 377b, 380b

wealth, II 376a, 377b, 379a, 381a

welfare, II 374b, 378a, 384b–385a; IV 509a

well-being, II 375a, 375b, 377b, 384b, 387b

will, II 379b, 380b, 381a

wisdom of the fool, IV 516a

work, II 374b, 385a, 385b; IV 530b

Wundt, II 382b

Harcourt, Lord, equity, II 153a

Hardenberg, Friedrich von, see Novalis

Harding, Francis, cosmic voyages, I 529b–530a

Harding, Stephen (1048?–?1134), reformation, IV 64b

Hardwicke, Lord, equity, II 153b

Hardy, Thomas (1840–1928), Cosmic Fall, I 511b
irony, II 632b, 633b
literature, III 84b
love, III 104b
nature, I 511b
tragic sense, IV 414a
ut pictura poesis, IV 466a, 467a

Hare, R. M.
good, IV 184b
individualism, II 603b
right, IV 184b

Harich, Wolfgang, Marxism, III 166b

Harington, John (1561–1612), literary paradox, III 78a

Hariot, Thomas (1560–1621), atomism, I 133a, 133b–134a, 134b
Kepler and, I 133b–134a
Percy and, I 133b
Raleigh and, I 133b

Harlan, John Marshall (1833–1911), law, III 10a

Harmhab, King, law, III 6b

Harmony, II 388a–395a
aesthetics, II 216b, 217a, 217b, 219a, 222a
Agrippa, II 389b, 393b, 394a
Alain de Lille, IV 41a
Alberti, II 390b; IV 41b

alchemy, II 392b

analogy, II 389a

Anaximander, IV 38b

angels, II 393b, 394a, 394b; IV 40b–41a

Anglicus, II 388a

Anselmi, IV 41a

Arabs, IV 41a

architecture, IV 41a–41b

Archytas, IV 38a

Aristides Quintilianus, IV 39a, 40a–40b

Aristotle, I 580b; II 389b, 390a, 392b; III 92a; IV 38a, 40a

arithmetic, II 390a; IV 38a, 39a, 40b, 42a

art, II 388b, 390a

astrology, II 392b; IV 40b

astronomy, II 389a–390a; IV 40b

Babylonia, IV 38b

Bacon, Francis, II 393a

Bardi, IV 41a

Bartas, II 391a, 391b, 392b

beauty, I 197a

Bible, II 394a; IV 38b, 40b

Bode, IV 42a

Bodin, II 390a–390b

Boethius, IV 40b, 41a

Cassiodorus, IV 41a

Chain of Being, II 389a

Chalcidius, IV 39b

Chaldeans, IV 38b

chaos, III 15b

Christianity, II 389a, 389b, 390b, 392b

Church of England, II 388b

Cicero, II 389b; IV 40a

color, III 395b

composers, II 388b

composition, II 388b

Comte, III 637a

Copernicus, II 389b

cosmos, II 388a, 389a, 389b; III 270b; IV 38a–39b, 40b–42a

Creation, IV 38b, 39a

creativity in art, I 579a–579b, 580b

cynicism, I 629b, 630a

Dante, IV 41a

defined, II 388a–388b

Demiurge, II 390b; IV 39a–39b

demonology, II 390b, 392b, 393b–394a

determinism, II 236b, 238a

dignity, IV 142b

Donne, II 394b

earth, II 389b–390a

Eddington, IV 42a

Edwards, IV 110a

Egypt (ancient), II 389a,

393b

Einstein, II 448b

elements, IV 40a

emotions, II 393a

Empedocles, II 390a

environment, II 128a, 128b

Er (myth), II 389b; IV 38b, 39b, 41a

ethics, II 390b

Euclid, IV 39b

evil, II 388a

Ficino, II 389a, 389b, 393a, 393b, 394a; IV 39b, 41a

Fludd, II 390a; IV 41b

France, II 388b

free will, II 236b

genius, II 313b, 314a, 315a, 315b, 322b, 323a, 324a

geocosm, II 389a

geometry, II 390a; IV 38a, 39a, 40a, 40b, 41b

Giorgio, IV 41b

Gnosticism, IV 40b–41a

God, II 388a, 389a, 390a, 390b, 391a, 392a, 392b, 393b, 394a, 394b

good, II 388a, 390b; IV 175a, 177b

Great Britain, II 388b

Greece (ancient), II 388b, 392a–392b; IV 38a–41b

Guillaume de Conches, IV 41a

health, II 122a–122b, 397b

Heraclitus, IV 38b

Herder, III 304b

Hermes Trismegistus, II 393b

hierarchy, II 446a–446b, 448b

Hippolytus, IV 39a

Hooker, II 391b, 392a

humanism, II 388b, 521a, 521b; IV 41a, 134b

Iamblichus, IV 39a

instinct, II 388a

Italy, II 388b

joy, II 388a

Judaism, II 392b; IV 38b

justice, II 654a; III 15b

Kepler, II 389b–390a; III 260b, 271a; IV 41b, 75a

Kircher, IV 41b

knowledge, II 388a

law, II 388a, 391a

Leibniz, II 445a–446b; III 193a; IV 41b, 382a

Leonardo da Vinci, IV 41a

literature, II 388b–389a

love, II 390b, 391a, 391b, 393a; III 94b–95a

Machiavelli, IV 480b

Macrobius, II 389b; IV 40a

macrocosm, II 389a, 390a

madrigals, II 388b

magic, II 392b–394a

Martianus Capella, IV 40a

materialism, II 392b

mathematics, II 388a, 389a, 390a–390b; III 387b; IV 38a–40a

matter, II 392a–392b; III 193a

Medici family, IV 41a

Mersenne, IV 41b

metaphysics, II 388b, 390b

microcosm, II 390a; IV 40a

Middle Ages, IV 39b, 41a

Milton, II 389b, 391b–392a, 393a, 394b

mind, II 388b

moon, II 389a–389b, 390a

motion, II 389a–390b, 393a; IV 39a, 40a

music, III 260b, 261a, 262b, 263a, 263b, 265b, 268b, 269a, 270b, 271a; IV 38a–42a

musicians, II 388b, 389a

mythology, II 389a, 389b, 393b; III 304b; IV 38b, 39b, 41a

natural law, III 15b, 20a

Nature, II 128a, 128b, 391a

Near East, IV 38b

necessity, IV 39b

Neo-Platonism, II 389a, 391b, 393a–393b; IV 39a, 39b, 41a

Neo-Pythagoreans, IV 39a, 39b, 42a

Newton, III 395b

numbers, III 261a, 269a; IV 38a–39b, 42a

Numenius, IV 40b

order, II 446a–446b, 448b; IV 38b

Orientalism, IV 38b

Orpheus (myth), II 393b

painting, III 350a; IV 466b, 467b, 471b, 472b, 473a

Palladio, IV 41b

Parmenides, IV 38b

perennial philosophy, III 458b, 460b, 462a

perfectibility, III 463b, 464b, 467a

Philo Judaeus, IV 38b, 40b

philosophy, II 388b–389a, 390b, 392b, 393b

pitch, II 389a

planets, II 389a–390a, 390b, 392b, 393b, 394b

Plato, I 579a–579b, 629b; II 236b, 389b, 390a–391b; III 500b; IV 38b–41b, 175a, 368b

Platonism, II 390b–391b, 392b; III 500b, 506a, 524a
Plotinus, II 391b, 393b; IV 380a
Plutarch, IV 38b
Pluto (myth), II 393b
poetry, II 388b, 391b, 394b–395a; IV 466b, 467b, 471b, 472b, 473a
poets, II 391b
Pontus de Tyard, IV 41a
power, II 388b, 391b, 392a, 393b, 394a–394b
pre-Socratics, IV 38b
Proclus, IV 39b
progress, III 635b, 637a
prophecy, II 394a
Protestantism, II 394a
Pseudo-Dionysius, IV 41a
psychology, II 393a
Ptolemy, II 389b; IV 39b, 40b, 41b
Puritanism, II 388b
Pythagoras, I 579b; II 390a; III 269a; IV 38a, 39a
Pythagorean scale, IV 39a–39b
Pythagoreans, II 217a, 389a, 389b; IV 38a–42a
rationalism, II 390b
reason, II 388a, 390b, 391a, 391b
Regino of Prum, IV 41a
relativity, IV 75a
religion, II 388a, 389a, 392a; IV 110a
Renaissance, II 389a, 389b, 390b–391a, 391b, 392a, 393a; IV 39b, 41a–41b, 134b, 142b, 439b, 440b
rhetoric, IV 168a, 169b
Riccioli, IV 41b
right, IV 175a, 177b
Roman Catholic Church, II 388b, 389a, 394a
Saint Jerome, IV 40b
Schopenhauer, IV 41b
science, II 388b, 448b
senses, II 388b
Shakespeare, II 388a, 388b, 391b, 394b
singers, II 393a, 393b
socialism, IV 285a
society, II 389a
soul, II 388a–392b, 394a
sound, II 389b, 391b–392a, 393a
space, IV 300a
Spinoza, IV 177b
spontaneous generation, IV 310a
stars, II 389a–389b, 390b, 392b, 393b, 394a
State, II 389a

Stoicism, II 392b
Sylvester, II 391b
Symmachus, IV 40b
symmetry, IV 353a
temperance, IV 369a
theodicy, IV 380a, 381a, 381b, 382a
time, IV 394b
tone, II 389a
unity of science, IV 431b, 436b
universal man, IV 439b, 440b
universe, II 388a–394b; III 260b, 268b, 270b; IV 38a–42a
Utopia, IV 458b, 460b, 464a
vibration, II 389a
virtue, II 388b, 391a–392a; IV 480b, 485a
visions, IV 40a
Whitehead, IV 42a
World Spirit, II 389a, 392a–395a
Harnack, Adolf von (1851–1930)
Gnostic, II 330b
God, II 357b
modernism, I 419b, 420b, 426b
Harnack, Otto (1857–1914), classicism, I 450b–451a
Harper, George McLean (1863–1947), appearance and reality, I 97a
Harrānians, astrology, I 119a, 125b
Harrington, James (1611–1677)
constitutionalism, I 488b
deism, I 649b
democracy, I 657a
Machiavellism, III 121a
socialism, IV 288a
State, I 657a
Utopia, IV 462a–462b
Harris, James (1709–1773), classification of the arts, I 460b
organicism, III 424b
Harris, Samuel (1814–1899), reformation, IV 69a
Harris, William T. (1835–1909)
God, II 358a
Hegel and, II 415a–415b
Orientalism, III 429a, 435b
pragmatism, III 556b, 567a
Spencer and, II 415a
State, II 415a
transcendentalism, III 429a
Harrison, Benjamin (1833–1901), conservation, I 475b

Harrison, E. R., cosmology, I 556a
Harrison, Frederick (1831–1923), positivism, II 415a; III 537b, 538b, 539a
Harrison, Jane (1850–1928), mythology, III 310b–312a
religion, IV 96b
tragic sense, IV 412b
Harrison, John (1693–1776), time, IV 404b
Harrod, R. F., utilitarianism, IV 448b
Harsanyi, J., social welfare, IV 280b
Harsnett, Bishop Samuel (1561–1631), witchcraft, IV 522b
Hart, B. H. Liddell, war, IV 502b
Hart, H. L. A.
Austin and, III 2b
causation, I 293a
duty, III 2b–3a
Kelsen and, III 3a
law, I 293a; III 1b, 2b–3b, 4b, 5a
positivism, III 1b, 2b–3a
power, III 2b–3a
rules, III 2b–3a, 4b–5a
Hartley, David (1705–1757), aesthetics, III 234b; IV 356a
association of ideas, I 111b, 113a–114a, 114b
behaviorism, I 220a
feeling, III 234b
Gay and, III 234a
happiness, II 380b, 381a
Hutcheson and, III 234b
idea, I 111b, 112a, 113a–114a, 114b, 116a, 116b
Man-Machine, III 141a
moral sense, III 234a–234b
pain, II 381a; III 234a–234b
perfectibility, III 469b, 471b
pleasure, II 380b, 381a; III 234a–234b
psychology, III 234a; IV 21b, 22b
sympathy, III 234b
taste, IV 356a
utilitarianism, IV 445b, 446a
Hartlib, Samuel (d. about 1670), Utopia, IV 462a
Hartmann, Eduard von (1842–1906)
Buddhism, I 255b
evil, II 166a, 166b–167a
irrationalism, II 636a
symbolism, IV 345a
unconscious, II 636a

Hartmann, Johann David, literature, III 84b–85a
Hartmann, Nicolai (1882–1950)
death, I 637b
good, IV 182a–182b
Nature, II 167a
perennial philosophy, III 463a
Platonism, III 522b
reason, I 93b
right, IV 182a–182b
Hartshorne, Charles
Creation, I 576a
design argument, I 677a
God, I 576a; II 362a
Haruspication, I 336a
Harvey, Gabriel (1545?–?1630), historiography, IV 149b, 150a–150b
Harvey, William (1578–1657), beauty, I 195a
behaviorism, I 217b
Descartes and, I 640a
health, II 400a, 400b, 401a
Hobbes and, I 216b
longevity, III 91b
Man-Machine, III 135b
methodology, III 387a
Newton and, III 387a; IV 56b
pangenesis, II 623b
pneuma concept, I 231a
recapitulation, IV 56b
socialism, IV 293b
spontaneous generation, IV 308b–309a
Haskins, Charles H. (1870–1937), periodization in history, III 480b
Hassan, Ihab, literature, III 88b
Hastings, Hester, theriophily, IV 388a
Hate
Empedocles, III 187a
Hutcheson, III 231a
matter, III 187a
moral sense, III 231a
Hathor (myth), II 333b
music, III 268a
Hattushilish I (c. 1650 B.C.), freedom of speech, II 253a–253b
Hatzfeld, Helmut, baroque in literature, I 190a–191a, 194a
Hauptmann, Gerhart (1862–1946)
naturalism in art, III 339a
symbolism, IV 344b
wisdom of the fool, IV 520a
Hauser, Arnold
creativity in art, I 582a

163

universal man, **IV** 442a
Haven, Joseph, psychology, **IV** 22b
Hawkesworth, John (1715?–1773)
  Diderot and, **III** 603a
  primitivism, **III** 602b, 603a
Hawthorne, Nathaniel (1804–1864)
  motif, **III** 242b
  plastic arts, **IV** 469a
  romanticism, **IV** 208b
  symbolism, **IV** 341b
Hawtrey, R. G., peace, **III** 445a–445b
Haydn, Franz Joseph (1732–1809)
  ambiguity, **I** 57a–58a
  determinism, **II** 20b
Haydn, Hiram, humanism, **IV** 130a, 135a
Haydocke, Richard, mythology, **III** 297b–298a
Hayes, Rutherford B. (1822–1893), conservation, **I** 475b
Hayek, F. A., individualism, **II** 597a, 601a, 602b
Haym, Rudolf (1821–1901),
  Hegel and, **II** 414a, 414b
  irony, **II** 633b
  romanticism, **IV** 189a, 197a
Haywood, Eliza (1693?–1756), virtuoso, **IV** 490a
Hazard, Paul (1878–1944),
  crisis in history, **I** 594b
  periodization in history, **III** 480a
Hazlitt, Nathan
  romanticism, **IV** 192a, 192b, 194a
  Schlegel and, **IV** 192a, 192b
Hazlitt, William (1778–1830),
  literary criticism, **I** 598b–599a
Head, Richard (1637?–?1686), deism, **I** 650a
Health, **II** 395b–407b
  Aeschylus, **II** 399a
  air pollution, **II** 397b
  alcoholism, **II** 402b
  anatomy, **II** 400b, 401a–401b, 404a
  antibiotics, **II** 406a
  anti-ontology, **II** 405a
  Apollo (myth), **II** 397b
  apothecary, **II** 401a
  Arabia, **II** 398b
  Aretaeus, **II** 398b
  Aristotelianism, **II** 398a, 399a, 400b
  art, **II** 396a, 399a
  asceticism, **II** 399a
  Asclepiades, **II** 398a
  Atharva-Veda, **II** 395b

atomism, **II** 398b
bacillus (tubercle), **II** 405a
bacteriology, **II** 405a, 405b
baroque, **II** 403b
Bayle, **II** 403b
beauty, **II** 399a
Bede, **II** 399a
Bentham, **II** 403a
Bernard, **II** 404a, 404b, 405a
Bible, **II** 396b, 399a, 403a
Bichat, **II** 404a
biochemistry, **II** 404b
biology, **II** 398a, 400b, 403b, 405b
biophysics, **II** 404b
Bismarck, **II** 406a
body, **II** 397a, 398a–406b
Boyle, **II** 400b
Broussais, **II** 404a
Buddhism, **II** 397a
Burton, **II** 399a
Cannon, **II** 404b
Celsus, **II** 397b
chemistry, **II** 400b, 401a
China (ancient), **II** 396b, 397a
Chopin, **II** 403b
Christianity, **II** 399a, 406a
Cicero, **II** 397b
colds, **II** 404b
Columbus, **II** 399b
crime, **II** 400b
DDT, **II** 406a
death, **II** 396a, 397a, 401a, 401b, 402a, 404a
defined, **II** 395b, 396a–396b, 397a, 405a
degeneration, **II** 404a
demonology, **II** 396a–396b, 397a
Descartes, **II** 400b
diagnosis, **II** 396a
Du Bois-Reymond, **II** 404b
Dürer, **II** 399a
Egypt (ancient), **II** 395b–396b
elements, **II** 398a
Elisha (Bible), **II** 396b
emotion, **II** 395b
empiricism, **II** 398b
endocrine glands, **II** 405a
Enlightenment, **II** 402b, 403a
environment, **II** 122a–122b, 124b–125a
epidemics, **II** 397b, 399b, 400a, 402a, 403a–403b, 405a
ethics, **IV** 321a, 321b
eugenics, **II** 620b
evil, **II** 395b, 396b
examinations, **II** 396a
faith, **II** 399a

fatigue, **II** 404b
four temperaments, **II** 398b, 399a
Fracastoro, **II** 399b
Galen, **II** 398a–398b, 400b, 402a; **III** 381b
Gehazi (Bible), **II** 396b
germ theory, **II** 405a
God, **II** 395b–397b, 399a, 403a, 403b
Goethe, **II** 403b
good, **II** 397a, 398a, 403a, 406a
Graunt, **II** 402a
Greece (ancient), **II** 397a–399a
happiness, **II** 374b, 376a, 383a, 384a, 399a, 406b
harmony, **II** 122a–122b, 397b
Harvey, **II** 400a–401a
Helmholtz, **II** 404b
Helmont, **II** 400a–401a
heresy, **II** 400b
Hesiod, **II** 395b
Hippocrates, **II** 396a, 397b, 398a–398b, 400a, 400b
homeostasis, **II** 404b
Homer, **II** 397b
hospitals, **II** 401b–402a, 406a
human nature, **III** 574a
humanism, **IV** 133b
humours, **II** 398a–398b, 400a, 400b
hunger, **II** 440b
hygiene, **II** 397a–397b
immortality, **II** 397a, 402b
immunology, **II** 405a, 406a
India (ancient), **II** 395b–397a
indolence, **II** 397b
Industrial Revolution, **II** 403a, 403b, 405b–406a
infection, **II** 399b, 405a, 405b, 406a
injury, **II** 396a
insurance, **II** 406a
intolerance, **IV** 116a
irritation, **II** 404a
Israel (ancient), **II** 396b
Jenner, **II** 403a
Jesus Christ, **II** 399a
joy, **II** 397a
Judea (ancient), **II** 398b
Justinian, **II** 399b
Keats, **II** 403b
kidneys, **II** 398b
knowledge, **II** 396a
Koch, **II** 405a, 405b
laboratory, **II** 402a–402b, 405a, 406a
Laennec, **II** 401b, 403b
League of Nations, **II** 406a

Linné, **II** 400a
liver, **II** 398a, 398b
luxury, **II** 397b
macrocosm and microcosm, **II** 397a
Magendie, **II** 404a
magic, **II** 396b, 397b
Mann, **II** 406b
Mark (Bible), **II** 399a
masturbation, **II** 403a
Mather, **II** 403a
Matthew (Bible), **II** 399a
Medicaid, **II** 406a
medicine, **II** 384a, 395b, 396a, 396b, 397a, 406a
Mesopotamia (ancient), **II** 396a–396b
methodology, **III** 381b
microbes, **II** 405a, 406a
Middle Ages, **II** 399b
mind, **II** 397a, 399a, 402b, 406b
Miriam (Bible), **II** 396b
morality, **II** 396b
Morgagni, **II** 401a–401b, 404a
music, **IV** 41a
mythology, **II** 395b, 397b
natural law, **II** 122b
Nature, **II** 397b, 398a, 400a, 400b, 402a, 402b, 403a, 403b, 404b, 406b
Nirvana, **II** 397a
nominalism, **II** 406b
nosology, **II** 400a, 401a, 404b
Novalis, **II** 403b
Oedipus (myth), **II** 397b
omens, **II** 396a
onanism, **II** 403a
ontology, **II** 399b–400a, 404a, 404b
Origen, **II** 399a
pain, **II** 396a, 398a
Papyrus, **II** 396a
Paracelsus, **II** 400a–401a
passions, **II** 397a, 398a
Pasteur, **II** 405a, 405b
pathology, **II** 400b, 405b
Persia (ancient), **II** 398b
philanthropy, **II** 406a; **III** 491b
philosophy, **II** 395b–399a
physicians, **II** 395b–405b
physics, **II** 400b
physiology, **II** 404a–404b, 406b
plague, **II** 399b
Plato, **II** 399a, 399b–400a; **III** 497a; **IV** 368b
Platonism, **II** 398a; **III** 497a
pleasure, **II** 374b, 376a, 383a, 384a
Poe, **II** 403b

poetry, II 399a
Polybius, III 574a
power, III 574a
primitivism, III 590b, 600b, 604b
private property, III 655a
punishment, II 396b
rationalism, II 395b, 396b; IV 48a
realism, II 406b
reductionism, II 404b
religion, II 396b, 397a, 406a; IV 116a
remedies, II 397a
Renaissance, II 399b, 403b; IV 133b
romanticism, II 403b
Rousseau, II 402b, 403b
Rufus of Ephesus, II 398b
Seneca, II 399a
sin, II 395b, 396b, 399a, 400b, 403a
society, II 396a, 403a, 403b, 406b
Sophocles, II 397b
sōphrosynē, II 398b–399a
sorcery, II 396b
prognosis, II 396a
prophecy, III 659a, 660b
pseudo-Aristotelianism, II 399a
psychology, II 397a, 398a
soul, II 397b, 398a, 400b, 401a
Stahl, II 400a
stars, II 399b
stethoscopes, II 401b
Stoicism, II 397b, 398a, 399a; IV 321a, 321b
sulfonamides, II 406a
sun, II 397b
superstition, II 396b
surgeons, II 401a, 401b
surgery, II 406a
Sutrasthana, II 397a
Sydenham, II 400a
symmetry, II 399a
Syria (ancient), II 398b
Taoism, II 397a
teleology, II 398a
temperance, II 398b–399a; IV 368b
Thebes, II 397b
Theognis, II 397a
thermometers, II 402a, 402b
thirst, II 404b
time, II 398b
Tissot, II 402b–403a
truth, II 397a
universe, II 396b
vaccination, II 403a
value, II 397b
variolation, II 403b
Varro, II 400a

Vesalius, II 400b, 401a, 402a
vice, II 402b
Virchow, II 403a–405b
virtue, II 397a, 397b, 399a; IV 478b
vox populi, IV 499b
wealth, II 397a
welfare state, IV 509b, 512a, 513b–515a
will, II 400b
wisdom, II 399a
Wordsworth, II 403b
work, II 395b, 403a
World Health Organization (U.N.), II 406a
yang and yin, II 397a
Hearn, Lafcadio (1850–1904), Buddhism, I 256b; III 437a–438b, 439a
Heat
catastrophism, IV 419a, 423a
symmetry, IV 349b
Heaven
Aristotle, III 273b
Christianity, III 670b; IV 230a
Dante, IV 176b–177a
dignity, IV 142b, 143a
good, IV 176b–177a
hermeticism, II 431a, 433a, 434a
hierarchy, II 440b
Islam, IV 230b
macrocosm and microcosm, III 128a, 128b, 129b, 130b
Middle Ages, IV 153b
millenarianism, III 223b, 224a, 224b
Milton, III 393b
music, III 265a, 269b, 271a, 271b
mythology, III 273b, 284b, 287b, 294a
primitivism, III 600a
progress, III 635a
prophecy, III 664a, 665a
protest movements, III 670b
reformation, IV 62b, 63b
Renaissance, IV 142b, 143a
revolution, IV 153b
salvation, IV 230a–231b
socialism, IV 291a
Zoroastrianism, IV 231b
Heavenly Muse, poetry, III 530b
Hebbel, Friedrich (1813–1863), symbolism, IV 338b
Hébert, Marcel, modernism, I 420a, 424a
Hebrew language, II 667a, 667b, 669a, 669b, 670a; III 62b, 63a, 65a

dignity, IV 143b
linguistics, III 62b; IV 426b, 427a
primitivism, III 584a
Renaissance, IV 143b
Hebrides Islands, primitivism, III 601a
Hecataeus of Miletus (c. 550–480 B.C.)
custom, III 575a
historiography, II 467a, 499b–500a
human nature, III 575a
progress, III 625b
Hecate (myth), III 272b
witchcraft, IV 521a
Hecker, Isaac Thomas (1819–1888), modernism, I 419b
Heckscher, W. S., iconography, II 537b
Hector (myth)
human nature, III 571b
metaphor, III 203b
neo-classicism in art, III 368a, 368b
peace, III 440a
Hecuba (myth), law, II 681b
Hederich, Benjamin, mythology, III 303a
Hedges, Frederick H., peace, III 444a
Hedonimeters, IV 454b, 457b
Hedonism
art, II 575b
Bentham, II 167b, 381a; IV 277b, 454b
cynicism, I 631b, 632a
Democritus, III 576b
Egypt (ancient), II 256b
Epicureanism, II 137b; III 587a
evil, II 167a–167b
evolution, IV 180a–180b
free will, II 137b
freedom of speech, II 256b
Gassendi, II 137b
good, IV 179a, 180a–180b
happiness and pleasure, II 375b, 380a–381b, 383b, 384b, 385a
human nature, III 576b
impressionism, II 575b
Kant, III 234a
Locke, II 239b, 380a, 380b
moral sense, III 234a
mythology, III 292a
Pater, II 575b
Platonism, III 513a, 514b, 516a
poetry, III 526b
primitivism, III 587a
right, IV 179a, 180a–180b
social welfare, IV 277b
Spencer, IV 180b

Tasso, III 514b
utilitarianism, IV 180a–180b; IV 445b–447a
utility, IV 454b
Heeren, Arnold (1760–1842), balance of power, I 186a
historiography, II 494b–495a
Heffner, H., indeterminacy, II 592a
Hegel, Georg Wilhelm Friedrich (1770–1831), II 407b–416b
absolutism, II 414a; III 556b
alienation, I 37a–41a
Altenstein and, II 411b
anarchy, I 74a
antinomy of pure reason, I 93a
appearance and reality, I 94b, 98a–98b
Aristotelianism, II 454a
Aristotle and, II 407b, 408a, 409b
art, II 408a
art for art's sake, I 108b
atheism, IV 291a
atomism, II 414b
authority, I 152b, 154b–155b
Bacon and, I 175b; II 412b
Bauer and, IV 291a
beauty, I 204a–205a
Bible, II 411a, 412a
Blake and, II 412b
Bosanquet and, II 414b–415a, 415b
Bradley and, II 414b–415a
Caird, Edward, and, II 414a, 414b
Caird, J. and, II 415a
categories, III 358b–359a
causation, I 277b, 280a–281a
certainty, I 319a–319b
China, I 366a–366b, 370a
Christianity, II 408b, 410a–411b, 414a
Cieszkowski and, II 414a–414b
civil service, II 409a
classification of the arts, I 461a
classification of the sciences, I 465b
colonialism, II 16b
communism, II 413b
Comte and, III 533b
Confucius and, I 366a
constitutions, II 410a
continuity, I 502a
cosmos, II 583a
Cotta and, II 411b

Counter-Enlightenment, II 108b

Cousin and, II 411b

culture, I 614b–615a, 619a, 619b; III 555b, 556b; IV 180a

cycles, I 627a

death, I 637b

despotism, II 2a, 4b, 13a, 15a–16b, 17a

determinism, II 20a–20b, 21a, 25a

Dewey and, III 556a–556b

dialectics, III 199b, 358b

dualism, II 41b; III 159b; IV 180a, 291a

duty, III 160a

Echtermeyer and, II 413a–413b

Eckhart and, II 412b

economic history, II 61a

economics, II 408b, 409a, 415b

empiricism, II 407b, 414b

Engels and, II 413b, 453b, 454a, 454b, 455a

Enlightenment, II 93b, 95a

Ense and, II 412a

epistemology, II 414b

eschatology, II 158a–158b, 159a

establishes *Jahrbücher* journal, II 411b–412a

ethics, II 408b; III 445a; IV 180a, 290b

evil, II 167a, 167b, 408a, 409b

evolution, II 583a

evolution of literature, II 170b–171a, 171b, 172a, 173b

evolutionism, II 184b

existentialism, II 191b

experience, III 556a, 556b

experiments, III 556b

faith, II 411a, 412a; IV 290b

family, II 408b–409a

Feuerbach and, I 38a; II 414a

Fichte and, II 279a, 407b

free will, II 246b, 408b, 409a, 414a

freedom, I 37b; II 16a, 407b–409b; IV 180a

French Revolution, II 409a–409b, 410a; IV 156b

Gans and, II 411b, 412a

general will, II 279a, 280a, 280b

God, II 16a, 24b, 158a, 348b, 357b–359a, 362b, 409a–415b; IV 290b, 291a, 318a, 493a

good, IV 180a, 180b, 181a, 291b

Göschel and, II 412a–412b, 414a, 415b

Green and, II 414a–415a

happiness, IV 180a, 409b

Harris and, II 415a–415b

Haym and, II 414a, 414b

Hengstenberg and, II 411b

heroes, III 556a

Hess and, II 414a

Hinrichs and, II 411b

historicism, II 460b, 463b

historiography, II 20a–20b, 21a, 25a, 488b, 492b, 494a

history, I 280a–281a, 402b, 409a, 614b–615a; II 15a–15b, 20a–20b, 21a, 25a, 158a–158b, 410b, 414b, 451b, 453a, 454a, 454b; III 22a, 358b, 462a, 473a–473b, 566a, 566b; IV 180a, 290b

Hölderlin and, IV 210a

Hugo and, II 411b

human nature, III 556b

idea, III 358b; IV 290b

idealism, I 277b; II 158a–158b, 407b, 453a, 583a; III 159a, 358b

impressionism, II 583a

individualism, II 415b, 600b, 601a, 601b; III 22a, 556a; IV 180a, 290b

irony, II 629b, 631a, 631b–632a, 633a

irrationalism, II 635b

Jacobi and, II 412a

Jesus Christ, II 410b, 411a, 414b; III 494b, 290b

Jowett and, II 414a

justice, II 653a

Kant and, II 407b, 410b, 414a; III 445a, 555b, 556b

Kierkegaard and, II 191b

knowledge, I 37a, 319a; II 412a, 414a

labor, II 409a

Lassalle and, II 414a

Lasson and, II 414a, 416a

law, II 407b–408a, 408b, 409b, 410a, 411b, 414a; IV 290b, 492a–492b

Leibniz and, II 414a

liberalism, II 409a; III 36b–37a, 48a, 48b, 49a

liberty, II 95a

linguistics, IV 427b, 428a

literary criticism, I 596b, 598a, 600b

literature, III 88b

Locke and, II 412b

logic, II 407b, 412a, 414b; III 358b; IV 556b

love, II 409a, 411a; III 160a

Machiavellism, III 119a

Marx and, II 413b, 451b, 452b, 453a, 454a; III 159b, 359a–359b; IV 161a, 290a–292a

Marxism, III 163a, 168b, 556a

materialism, II 407b, 414a, 451b, 452b–455a

mathematics, III 556b

matter, III 185b

metaphor, III 198a, 198b, 199b

metaphysics, II 414a, 414b, 454b, 583a; III 217b, 219b–220a, 222a

Michelet and, II 407b, 414a, 414b

mind, II 407b, 408a, 409b, 410a, 413b; III 22a; IV 290b

modernism, I 419b, 420a

monarchy, II 16a, 409a, 409b, 414b

money, II 409a

monism, III 556b

morality, II 408b, 410b; III 22a, 555b, 556a; IV 180a

motion, II 454a

mysticism, II 412b, 414a

mythology, II 410b, 414a

Napoleon I and, II 414a

nationalism, III 445a

natural law, III 22a

Nature, I 204a–204b; II 408a, 454a; III 358b

necessity, III 351b, 355b, 357a, 358a–359b, 360b, 361a; IV 534a

Neo-Platonism, II 414a, 454a

Newton and, II 412b

organicism, III 421b, 425b, 426a

paternalism, II 409b

peace, III 445a

Peirce and, III 556a–556b, 558a

penal institutions, II 408b

perennial philosophy, III 462a

perfectibility, III 473a–473b, 474a

periodization in history, III 478a

Persia, II 15b

philosophy, II 20a, 408a–411b, 412a, 413b, 414a; III 198a, 198b, 199b; 220a, 473a, 474a

physics, III 556b

Pietism, III 494b

Plato and, II 410b

Platonism, III 506b, 520a–520b, 521a, 521b, 522a, 522b

pluralism, II 409b, 414b

poetry, II 170b

power, II 411a

pragmatism, III 555b–556b, 558a, 561a, 567a

private property, II 408b–409a, 415a; III 653b

prophecy, II 20a

Protestantism, II 410a

psychology, IV 11b, 12a, 24a

Ranke and, II 412a

realism, II 407b; III 22a

realism in literature, IV 54b

reality, III 358b

reason, I 312a; II 408b, 409a–409b, 410a, 413b, 414a, 416a; III 556a; IV 180a

religion, II 408a, 410a–411b, 414a, 414b; IV 96a

republicanism, II 409b

revisionism, IV 270a

revolution, IV 156b, 161a

Ricardo and, II 409a

right, IV 180a, 180b, 181a

romanticism, IV 201b, 204a, 208a, 209b, 210a, 210b

Rosenkranz and, II 412b, 413a–413b, 414a

Rousseau and, II 407b; IV 209b

Royce and, II 415b; III 556b, 561a

Ruge and, II 413a–413b, 414a

Savigny and, II 411b, 412a; III 22a

Say and, II 409a

Schelling and, II 407b; IV 210b

Schleicher and, IV 428a

Schleiermacher and, II 411b; III 520a

skepticism, IV 241a, 249a, 249b

slavery, II 15b, 16a, 408a

Smith, Adam, and, II 409a

socialism, I 74b; II 415a; IV 290a–292a

society, I 614b–615a; II 408b, 409a–409b, 414a, 452b; III 556b; IV 180a, 290b, 291b

Socrates and, II 411a

sovereignty, II 16a

Spengler and, III 361a

Spinoza and, II 410b

spirit, I 37b

spiritualism, III 556b

spontaneity, **II** 407b, 409a
State, **II** 408b, 409a–409b, 415a, 415b, 452b; **III** 22a, 48b–49a, 473a, 556a; **IV** 180a, 290b, 291b, 318a, 492b–493a
Stirling and, **II** 414a, 414b
Strauss and, **II** 412b–413a, 414a
structuralism, **IV** 329b
suffrage, **II** 409b
symbolism, **IV** 338b
theodicy, **IV** 383a
theology, **III** 473b, 474a; **IV** 290b
thought, **III** 556a
time, **IV** 390a, 394a
totalitarianism, **IV** 408a, 408b
tradition, **II** 409a, 409b, 410a, 411b
tragedy, **II** 171a
tragic sense, **IV** 411b
transcendentalism, **IV** 24a
truth, **I** 37a, 319a–319b; **II** 410b
tyranny, **II** 409a–409b
uniformitarianism, **IV** 427b, 428a
unity, **III** 556a, 556b; **IV** 180a
universe, **I** 319a
utilitarianism, **II** 409b
Vico and, **III** 357a
virtue, **IV** 485a
Volksgeist, **IV** 492a–493b
voluntariness, **II** 280b
Vorstellung, **II** 410a–410b
Wallace and, **II** 414a, 414b
war, **II** 16a, 409b, 415b–416a; **III** 445a; **IV** 502a, 503a, 503b, 506a
Wolff and, **II** 414a
women, **IV** 526b
work, **IV** 534a, 534b
Wright and, **III** 556b
Zeitgeist **IV** 535b–536a
Zeller and, **II** 414a
Hegelianism, **II** 413a–416a
civilization, **III** 473b
determinism, **II** 24b
empathy, **II** 85b
historiography, **II** 24b
irony, **II** 634b
Left, **IV** 291a
liberalism, **III** 49b
logic, **III** 546a
Marx, **III** 473b
Marxism, **II** 24b
necessity, **III** 356b, 360b
progress, **III** 634a
revisionism, **IV** 270a, 272a
Right, **IV** 291a
socialism, **IV** 290b–292a

Hegemony, World War I, **III** 332a
Hegesias of Magnesia (4th century B.C.)
impiety, **II** 566a
pessimism, **II** 566a
Hegesippus (d. 180), Gnosticism, **II** 327a
Hegira, Islam, **II** 638b–639a
Heidegger, Martin (1889–)
Bacon and, **I** 179a
beauty, **I** 212a
Being, **II** 193b, 195a, 637b
death, **I** 634b, 642b; **II** 193b
eschatology, **II** 161a
existentialism, **II** 189a, 190a, 192b–195a
freedom, **II** 193b
God, **II** 193b
immortality, **I** 642b
irrationalism, **II** 637a, 637b
metaphor, **III** 207a
metaphysics, **III** 212b, 221a, 221b
morality, **II** 193a
perennial philosophy, **III** 462b
phenomenology, **II** 193b
poetry, **III** 221a
psychology, **IV** 14a
religion, **III** 207a
romanticism, **IV** 210b
Schelling and, **IV** 210b
time, **II** 193a; **IV** 396b
work, **IV** 535a
Zeitgeist, **IV** 536b
Heiler, Friedrich, theodicy, **IV** 379b
Heilsgeschichte, mythology, **III** 277a
Heimarmene (myth), fortune, fate, and chance, **II** 229a
Heindorf, Ludwig Friedrich, Platonism, **III** 519b
Heine, Heinrich (1797–1856), China, **I** 368b
classicism, **I** 450a
Faust (legend), **III** 252a
Gothic, **II** 371b
irony, **II** 629b, 632a, 632b, 633b
literature, **IV** 189a
naturalism, **IV** 53b
realism in literature, **IV** 53b
romanticism, **IV** 189a, 207b, 208a
symbolism, **IV** 338b, 344b
Heinroth, Oskar, imprinting, **II** 585a
Heinse, J. J. W., Counter-Enlightenment, **II** 107a–107b

Heinse, Wilhelm (1746–1803), Gothic, **II** 372a
Heinsius, Daniel (1580–1655)
classicism, **I** 453a
literary criticism, **I** 597a
organicism, **III** 424b
Heisenberg, Werner (1901–)
Bohr and, **II** 588b, 589a, 590a
causation, **I** 278a; **II** 589b, 590a
chance, **I** 339b
energy-time uncertainty relation, **II** 589a, 590b, 591a
entropy, **II** 116b
game theory, **II** 273b
gamma-ray microscopic experiment, **II** 588b–589a, 591b
Heisenberg position-momentum uncertainty relation, **II** 588b
indeterminacy, **II** 586b, 587b–589a, 590b, 591b
infinity, **II** 606b
irony, **II** 634a
Laûe and, **II** 590a
light, **II** 589a
matrix mechanics, **II** 588b
philosophy, **II** 589b–590a
Popper and, **II** 590a
Principle of Indeterminacy, **I** 278a
Schrödinger and, **II** 588b, 590a
time, **IV** 398a
Uncertainty Principle, **I** 323a, 324a–324b; **II** 586b, 587b, 588b, 589a–590a, 591a
variables, **II** 588b, 589b
Hekate (myth), law, **II** 676b
Hekhaloth, Gnosticism, **II** 330b
Held, J. S., iconography, **II** 538a
Helen of Troy (myth), **III** 272b
Faust (legend), **III** 246a, 247a–247b, 248a, 248b, 249a
human nature, **III** 571b
ideal, **II** 549b
literary paradox, **III** 79b
neo-classicism in art, **III** 368b
Helinandus
Christianity, **III** 591a
primitivism, **III** 591a
Heliocentric universe, **II** 442b
Hell
Christianity, **IV** 230a, 230b

death, **I** 635a, 643b
Faust (legend), **III** 247a, 247b, 248b
fear, **II** 62a
good, **IV** 176b
happiness, **II** 379a
hierarchy, **II** 435b
Islam, **IV** 230b, 231a
Milton, **III** 393b
music, **III** 265a–268b
mythology, **III** 281b, 282a, 288a
prophecy, **III** 664a
psychology, **IV** 1b
right, **IV** 176b
sin, **IV** 230a, 231a, 231b
witchcraft, **IV** 522a
Zoroastrianism, **IV** 231b
Heller, Joseph, satire, **IV** 213b, 216a
Helm, G., probability, **III** 616b
Helmer, Olaf, empiricism, **III** 546a
Helmholtz, Hermann Ludwig Ferdinand (1821–1894), anthropomorphism, **I** 89b
classification of the sciences, **I** 465b
continuity, **I** 494a–494b
empiricism, **III** 545b
entropy, **II** 113a, 114b, 115b, 116a, 117b
health, **II** 404b
impressionism, **II** 580b
light, **II** 580b
psychology, **IV** 12a, 24b
space, **IV** 303a
Spencer and, **II** 116a
symmetry, **IV** 352a
technology, **IV** 363b
time, **IV** 395b
universe, **II** 115b
Helmholtz free energy, **II** 114b
Helmont, Jean Baptiste van (1577?–?1644)
alchemy, **I** 32b, 33a
causation, **I** 301a
health, **II** 400a, 400b–401a
metaphysical imagination, **III** 212a
spontaneous generation, **IV** 308b
teleology, **I** 301a
Héloise (d. c. 1164) love, **III** 98a
Helphand, Alexander, *see* Parvus
Helvétius, Claude Adrien (1715–1771)
benevolent despots, **III** 470a
class, **I** 448a
Counter-Enlightenment, **II** 106a, 107b, 110a
democracy, **I** 661a

Descartes and, II 450a
education, III 407a
Enlightenment, II 94b
equality, II 143b
genius, II 294b
human nature, III 643a–643b
ideology, II 553a, 554b–554a
inequality, I 448a
Jefferson and, IV 21a
law, III 470a
liberty, II 94b
love, II 451a
Man-Machine, III 141a, 141b
materialism, II 450a, 451a
metaphysical imagination, III 216b
perfectibility, III 470a, 643a–643b
pleasure, II 380b
progress, III 643a–643b
psychology, IV 21a
State, I 661a
superstition, III 470a
utilitarianism, II 380b; IV 444a
Utopia, IV 462b
value, II 451a
virtue, III 470a
women, IV 526a
Hemingway, Ernest (1899–1961)
class, I 445b
death, I 637b
Hempel, Carl G.
causation, I 284b–285a
empiricism, III 546a, 550a
history, I 284b–285a
necessity, III 362a
Hemsterhuis, Frans (1721–1790), beauty, II 550a
Henderson, Lawrence J. (1878–1942)
entropy, II 114b
environment, II 121b–122a, 125b
fitness, II 121b–122a
milieu intérieur concept, II 125b
theodicy, IV 383b
Hengstenberg, Ernst W. (1802–1869), Hegel and, II 411b
Henkel, Arthur, iconography, II 538a
Henle, Friedrich G. J. (1809–1885), health, II 404b
Hennequin, Emile, literary criticism, I 600b
Hennequin, Phillipe A. (1763–1833), symbolism, IV 343b
Henotheism, II 334a–334b

theodicy, IV 379a
Henri II, King (1519–1559), mythology, III 292b
Henriot, Emile (1889–1961), classicism, I 455a
Henry, Emil, anarchy, I 72a
Henry II, King (1133–1189), common law, II 693b
love, III 102a
nationalism, III 319b
Henry III, Emperor (1017–1056), history, I 381b
Henry III, King (1207–1272), constitutionalism, I 488a
Henry IV, Emperor (1050–1106)
history, I 381b
burning of heretics, I 387a
Henry IV, King (1367–1413), alchemy, I 31a
historiography, II 498a
Henry IV, King (1553–1610), intolerance, IV 119a
religion, IV 119a
social contract, IV 254a
Henry VIII, King (1491–1547), authority, II 690a
balance of power, I 182a
Dissolution of the Monasteries, II 408b
history, I 395a
law, II 690a
nationalism, III 321a, 321b, 322a
politics, I 69a
Henry of Ghent (d. 1293), nationalism, III 323a
Henry of Lausanne (12th century), heresy, II 418b, 419a
Hephaestio of Thebes, astrology, I 119a, 121a, 124a
Hera (myth), II 340a; III 272b
fortune, fate, and chance, II 229a
human nature, III 571b
law, II 684b
Heracleodor, aesthetics, II 220a
Heracleon (2nd century), Gnosticism, II 330a
Heraclides of Pontus (4th century B.C.), cosmic images, I 515b
Heraclitus (6th–5th century B.C.)
allegory, I 42b, 44b, 61a–61b
atomism, I 127a–128a
Being, III 187a
causation, I 271a
constitutionalism, I 486b
cosmic images, I 514a, 516b, 517a
cosmos, III 573b; IV 297b

creativity in art, I 578b, 582a–582b
cycles, I 622b
death, I 637a
Democritus and, III 187b
design argument, I 671a, 671b
dualism, II 40b; IV 346b
ethics, IV 320b
Great Year (myth), IV 401a
harmony, IV 38b
human nature, III 571a, 572a, 573a, 573b
irrationalism, II 635a, 638a, 638b
justice, II 653a, 653b, 658b
law, I 486b; II 677a, 682b
love, III 94b
matter, III 186b–188a, 190a
measurement, IV 399b, 400b, 401a
metaphor, III 203b
motion, IV 390a
mythology, III 275b
natural law, III 14b, 16a
Nature, III 347a
Plato and, I 578b, 582a–582b; IV 34b
Platonism, III 496a
pluralism, III 187a
poetry, III 526a
primitivism, III 581a
psyche, IV 2a
psychology, IV 2a–2b
Pythagoreans, IV 34b, 38b
rationalism, IV 47a
religion, III 203b
sense objects, I 1a
senses, III 187a
skepticism, IV 234b, 235a, 239b
soul, III 573a
space, IV 297b
Stoicism, IV 320b
symmetry, IV 346b
theodicy, IV 380a
time, IV 390a, 390b, 394a, 398a, 399b, 400b, 401a
tragic sense, IV 413b
unity, III 187a
wisdom, III 14b
wisdom of the fool, IV 517a
Zeno of Citium and, IV 320b
Heraldry, mythology, III 296b
Herbart, Johann Friedrich (1776–1841)
aesthetics, II 218b, 223b
continuity, I 501a–501b
infinity, II 605b
psychology, IV 11b
time, IV 394b
Volksgeist, IV 495b
Herbartians, empathy, II 85b

Herbert, Auberon, individualism, II 596b
Herbert, George (1593–1633), Cosmic Fall, I 509a
harmony, II 392b–393a
ut pictura poesis, IV 469b, 470b, 471a
Herbert of Cherbury (1583–1648)
China, I 360a
deism, I 648b, 650a
idea, II 547a
Nature, III 348a
skepticism, IV 244b
Herbrand, Jacques (1908–1931), pragmatism, III 557b
Hercules (myth), III 273b, 274a, 274b, 275b, 282b, 287a, 288a, 290a, 292b, 308a
Christianity, III 590b
cynicism, I 628a, 630a, 630b, 632a–633a; III 590a
historiography, II 499b
human nature, III 572a
law, II 681a, 683b
primitivism, III 590b
Saint Basil, III 590b
virtue, IV 477b
Herder, Johann Gottfried von (1744–1803)
aesthetics, IV 356b
allegory, III 305a
art for art's sake, I 109a
art and play, I 103b, 105a
attitude toward antiquity, I 86b
beauty, II 551a
China, I 365b
climate, IV 492a
cosmopolitanism, III 326a
Counter-Enlightenment, II 103b, 104b, 105a–106b, 107a
culture, I 613b–614b, 616b, 617a, 618a–621a; II 105b–106a, 128a–128b; IV 203a
deism, I 651b
dualism, I 618b
Enlightenment, II 89b
environment, II 128a, 129b–130a; III 639a
evolution of literature, II 170b
evolutionism, II 178b
experience, IV 492a
folklore, IV 209a
freedom, I 614b
genius, II 295b, 306b, 324a–324b
geography, II 129b–130a
God, II 350b
Goethe, III 305a; IV 209a

happiness, III 639a–639b
harmony, III 304b
historicism, II 458b, 459a, 460b–461a
historiography, II 488b, 489a, 489b
history, III 473a, 638a, 639a–639b; IV 203b, 204a
humanism, III 326a
iconography, II 535a, 540a
ideal, II 551a
imagination, III 219b, 305a
justice, II 658b; III 639a
Kant and, II 324a; III 326a, 472b; IV 209a
language, III 305a; IV 203a
Lessing and, IV 209b
linguistics, III 64b; IV 426b
literary criticism, I 597b, 599a, 600a
literature, III 82a, 85b; IV 203a
mankind, III 326a
Mazzini and, IV 203b
Michelet and, IV 203b
music, II 324a–324b
mythology, III 304b–305a, 305b–306a, 306b
nationalism, III 305a, 325b, 326a, 327a, 330b; IV 203a, 203b
Nature, I 614b; II 129b–130a, 178b; IV 204a
organicism, III 424b
pacifism, III 326a
perfectibility, II 551a; III 472b–473a, 639a
periodization in literary history, III 482a
philosophy, II 551a
Platonism, III 519a
pluralism, I 619a; III 639a
poetry, II 170b; IV 209a, 472b
progress, III 638a, 639a–639b
reason, III 305a, 639a; IV 209a
religion, IV 203a, 209a
rights, III 326a
romanticism, III 326a, 327a; IV 187b, 190b, 199a, 200a, 201a, 201b, 203a, 203b, 204a, 209a
Rome (ancient), III 326a
Rousseau and, II 324a–324b; III 326a
Schelling and, IV 210b
society, III 473a
soul, IV 209a, 492a
Spinoza and, IV 201a, 209a
State, III 472b
symbolism, III 305a; IV 338a

taste, IV 356b
tradition, I 621a; III 327a
truth, III 305a
uniformitarianism, IV 426b
unity, III 304b
Volk, III 326a
Volksgeist, III 305a; IV 203a, 492a, 494a, 495a
Voltaire and, I 618a
vox populi, IV 499a
war, III 326a
wisdom, III 304b
Zeitgeist, IV 535b
Heredity
acquired characteristics, II 617a–619a, 620b, 621b, 622a
chromosomes, II 286b, 288a–288b
Darwin, II 285a
DNA, II 289b–292b
Egypt (ancient), III 10b
evolutionism, II 177a, 177b–178a, 186b
genetic continuity, II 281b–293a
Lamarck, II 623b, 624a
Maupertuis, II 284b–285a
pangenesis, II 623b, 624a, 626a
probability, III 616a, 616b, 617b, 620a
psychology, IV 25a, 26b, 27a, 28a
religion, IV 107b
Heresiography, II 648b
Heresy, II 416b–431a
Abelard, II 418a
absolution, II 420a
Albigensians (Cathars), II 423a
Anabaptists, II 425b, 426a, 427b
Andreas of Isernia, II 425a
Antichrist, II 418a, 419a, 421b
anti-Trinitarianism, II 426a
Apocalypse, II 420b, 421b
Arianism, II 417a
Aristotelianism, II 418a, 427a
Arnold of Brescia, II 418b, 419a, 430a
Arnoldists, II 418b
art, II 427a
asceticism, II 418b, 423b
Averroism, II 426b
Bacon, II 428a
Bayle, IV 120a
Beghards, II 423a
Beguines, II 423a
Berengarius, II 418a
Beza, II 424b, 425a
Bible, II 416b–420a, 421b,

422a, 425a–428b
blasphemy, II 425b
Bogomils, II 423a–423b
Boniface VIII (Pope), II 421b
Bossuet, II 428b
Bruno, III 193b, 194a, 513b
burning of heretics, I 387a
Cabbala, II 427a
Calvin, II 425a, 425b, 427b
Calvinism, II 424b, 427b, 428a
Castellio, II 426a, 430b
Cathars, II 417b, 423a–424a, 426b
Celsus, II 426a
Chain of Being, II 427a
Charles V (Emperor), II 425b
chastity, II 418b, 421a
Christianity, I 378b, 383a–383b, 386b–387a; II 42a–42b, 43a, 416b–430b, 566b, 567a; III 589a, 670b
Cochlaeus, II 428a
Code of Justinian, II 425a
common law, II 691a
confession, II 420a, 425b, 428a, 430b
Copernicus, II 428a
Council of Trent, II 425a, 427b–428a
Counter-Reformation, II 427a
Cromwell, II 428a
Dante, II 419a
Darwinism, II 429a
defined, II 416b, 424a
Denifle, II 428a, 430b
Descartes, III 136b
disease, II 400b
dogma, II 424b, 425b, 426a, 426b, 427b, 429a, 429b, 430b
Donation of Constantine, II 419a, 420b
Donatism, II 417a, 418b
double truth, II 31b
dualism, II 42a–42b, 43a
Duns Scotus, II 426a
Durandus of Huesca, II 419b
Eckhart, II 417b, 418a, 422b, 426b
Edict of Nantes, II 425b, 428a
Emerson, II 429b
Enlightenment, II 427a, 428b, 429a
Erasmus of Rotterdam, II 426a, 427b, 429a
eucharist, II 418a
evil, II 164b
evolution, II 429a, 430b

excommunication, I 416b; II 420a, 420b, 425b
faith, II 416b, 424a, 426a
Fathers, II 418b
Faust (legend), III 245b, 246b
Flagellants, II 427a
formal, II 424b
Fourth Lateran Council, II 425b
Franciscans, II 417b, 418b, 419a, 419b, 420b–422a
Frederick II, II 425b
Frederick III, II 421b
Free Spirits, II 417b, 422a–423a
free will, II 417a
freedom of speech, II 252b, 256a
fundamentalism, II 429b, 430a
Galileo, II 428a
Gallicanism, II 428b
Gassendi, II 428a
general categories of, II 424b
Germany, I 649b
Gnosticism, II 330a, 331a
God, II 339a, 416b–422b, 423b–427a
Gottschalk, II 418a
grace, II 417a
Greece (ancient), II 565b, 566a, 566b
Gregory IX (Pope), II 421a, 425a
Grisar, II 428a, 430b
Henry of Lausanne, II 418b, 419a
historiography, II 430a
Holy Roman Empire, II 425b
Huguenots, II 424b, 428a
humanism, II 419a, 425b–426a, 427b, 430b, 520b
Humbert, II 418b
Hus, II 419a, 426b
Hussites, II 420b, 421b, 422a, 428a
immortality, II 426b
impiety, II 564a, 565a, 565b, 566a–566b, 567a
Index, II 425a, 428a
Innocent III (Pope), II 419b, 423a
Innocent IV (Pope), II 425b
Innocent VIII (Pope), II 427a
Inquisition, II 417a, 425a, 427a, 430a
intolerance, IV 113b–117a, 119a, 120a, 120b
Israel (ancient), II 565a
Jansenism, II 428b

169

Jesus Christ, II 416b–421b, 422a, 422b, 423b, 426a, 426b, 427a, 428b–429b
Joachim of Floris, II 417b, 418a, 421a, 421b
John XXII (Pope), II 420a, 421a, 421b
Judaism, II 565a
Kepler, II 428a
Latitudinarianism, II 428b
law, II 425b, 686a, 689a
liberalism, III 42a, 42b
Locke, II 429a
Lollards, II 418b, 420b
love, III 97b–98a, 98b, 99b, 100a, 101b, 102b, 107a
Lucius II (Pope), II 419b
Luther, II 425b, 427b, 428a, 430a
Lutheranism, II 427b, 428a, 429b
Machiavelli, II 427a
Man-Machine, III 136b, 137a
Marian exiles, II 426a
Marsilius of Padua, II 418a, 419a, 422a
Mary Tudor, II 426a
material, II 424b
metaphysics, II 416b
Michael of Cesena, II 421a
Middle Ages, II 416a–424a
modernism, I 419a, 423b; II 429b
monasteries, II 418b
morality, II 416b, 418b
mysticism, II 422a, 422b, 424a, 426b
nationalism, II 428b
Neo-Platonism, II 422b, 427a–427b
Newman, II 429b
Newton, II 428a, 429a
nominalism, II 426b
obedience, II 418b, 421a
objective, II 424b
Orientalism, II 427a
orthodoxy, II 416b, 417a, 418a, 419b, 424a, 425b, 428a, 430a
Osiander, II 428a
pantheism, II 422b
Peace of Augsburg, II 428a
Peace of Westphalia, II
perennial philosophy, III 458b
perfectibility, III 467b, 468a–468b
Peter of Bruys, II 418b, 419a
Pico della Mirandola, II 427b
Pietism, II 429a; III 494a–494b

Pius IX (Pope), II 429b
Pius X (Pope), II 429b
Plato, II 427a, 566a
Platonism, II 427b; III 513b
Plotinus, II 427a
pluralism, II 424b, 428a, 428b, 430b
Porrée, II 418a
poverty, II 417b–422a, 424a
predestination, II 417a, 418a, 426b
primitivism, III 589a
prophecy, III 668b, 669b
protest movements, III 670b
Protestantism, II 424a–430b
reform, II 417b, 421b, 422a, 424a
reformation, IV 62b–63a, 65a
Reformation, II 424b–428a
religion, IV 96a, 112b, 113b, 114a–120b
Renaissance, II 424a–431a
Ritschl, II 429a
Roman Catholic Church, II 416b–430a
romanticism, II 428b
Rome (ancient), II 686a, 689a; IV 115a
Roscellin, II 418a
sacraments, II 417a, 418b, 426b, 427b
Saint Augustine, II 421b, 424b, 428b
Saint Bernard, II 417b
Saint Dominic, II 419b
Saint Francis of Assisi, II 418a, 419b–421b
Saint John, II 425a
Saint Thomas Aquinas, II 425a
Satan, II 423b
Schleiermacher, II 429a, 430b
scholarship, II 430a–430b
scholasticism, II 427a, 427b
science, II 428b–429a
Scopes trial, II 430b
sedition, II 425b
self-deification, II 417b
Servetus, II 424b, 426a
Simony, II 418b
sin, II 417a, 429a
Social Gospel Movement, II 429a
society, II 416b, 424b, 425b
Sophists, II 427a
soul, II 416b, 417b, 422a, 422b, 423b, 425a
spiritual renewal, II 417b
Spirituals, II 416b, 420a
Stoicism, II 427a
subjective, II 424b

superstition, II 426b
Sybillines, II 427a
Syllabus of Errors (1864), II 429b
Synod of Toulouse (1229), II 425a
Taborites, II 418b
Tanchelm, II 418b, 419a
theodicy, IV 379b, 380b
tolerance, II 426a
trials, II 430b
Trinity, II 417a, 418a, 425a, 426b, 427b
truth, II 416b, 417a
U.S., II 429a, 429b, 430b
universities, II 427a
Utopia, IV 461a
Valdes, II 419a, 419b
Vincent of Lérins, II 428b
Virgin Birth, II 429b
Waldensians, II 418b, 419a–420b, 421b, 422a, 423b, 426b
Weltanschauung, II 419a
William of Ockham, II 418a, 426a, 426b
witchcraft, II 426b–427a; IV 521a, 521b, 522a, 522b
women, IV 526a
work, II 420a
Wycliffe, II 417b, 418a, 419a, 421b–422a, 426b
Zwingli, II 425b, 427b
Hering, Ewald (1834–1918), genetic continuity, II 288a
Hermeren, G., iconography, II 539b
Hermes (myth), III 272b, 282b
   astrology, I 122b
   cosmic voyages, I 524a
   human nature, III 571a
   law, II 684a
   music, III 268b
Hermes Trismegistus
   alchemy, I 28b, 29b
   chance, II 232a
   cosmological principle, IV 306a
   dignity, IV 139a
   fate, II 232a
   harmony, III 393b
   hermeticism, II 431a–434a
   hierarchy, II 439a
   Islam, II 640a
   music, II 393b
   Neo-Platonism, III 510a
   skepticism, IV 242a
   space, IV 306a
Hermeticism, II 431a–434b
   Alberti, II 433b
   alchemy, II 431b, 432b, 433a
   art, II 431a–431b, 433a
   astrology, I 125a

Babylonia, II 431b
Blake, II 432b, 433a, 433b
Böhme, II 433a, 433b
Bruno, II 433a, 433b
chaos, II 431a–433a, 434a
Christianity, II 431a, 432a, 433a; IV 229b
cosmos, II 432a, 433a
Creation, II 431b–433b
earth, II 433a, 433b
education, II 432a
Egypt (ancient), II 431a, 431b
esotericism, II 431a, 431b, 434a
Eternal Connectedness, II 432b–433a
evil, II 431b, 432a, 432b, 433b
gnosticism, II 431b
God, II 431a–433a
Goethe, II 433a
Great Britain, II 431b
Greece (ancient), II 431b
heaven, II 431a, 433a, 434a
Hermetica, II 433a
Iamblichus, II 432b
Islam, II 639a, 642a, 646a, 646b, 651a
Italy, II 431b
Jesus Christ, II 432b
Jonson, II 432a
joy, II 431a
Lawrence, II 433a, 434a
light, II 432a, 433b
Longfellow, II 433a, 434a
love, II 432a
Lovejoy, II 433a
macrocosm and microcosm, II 433a
matter, II 431a, 433a
Mercury (myth), II 432b
metaphysical imagination, III 211b, 212b, 221b
Milton, II 433a, 433b–434a
monsters, II 431a
Moses (Bible), II 431b
mythology, II 431a–433b
Nature, II 432b, 433a, 433b
Near East, II 431a, 431b, 434a
Neo-Platonism, II 431b–434b
Nietzsche, II 433a, 434a
Persia, II 431b
Phoenicia (ancient), II 431b
physis, II 433b
Pico, II 432b
Platonism, II 431a, 433a; III 507b
Plotinus, II 432b
pluralism, II 433b
poetry, II 432a, 433b; III 530b

purification, II 432b
Renaissance, II 431a–434b
romanticism, II 431a
Saint Augustine, II 432a
salvation, IV 229a, 229b
serpents, II 431a, 431b
sex, II 432a, 432b, 433b
Shakespeare, II 432b, 433a
Silvestris, II 433a–433b
sin, IV 229a, 229b
Spenser, II 432b, 433a, 433b
Sterne, II 433a, 434a
Tat (myth), II 431b
Tertullian, II 432a
Thoth (myth), II 431a
truth, II 432a
unity, II 432a, 433a
universe, II 432a, 433a
unorthodox view, II 431a, 431b, 432b, 433b, 434a
Utopia, IV 461b
Valeriano, II 432b
Vaughan, II 433a
wisdom, II 431a, 431b
Wordsworth, II 433a
Hermogenes (late 2nd century A.D.)
rhetoric, IV 170a–171a
ut pictura poesis, IV 468b
Hero of Alexandria (3rd century A.D.)
atomism, I 134a, 134b
Man-Machine, III 134a–134b
mechanics, II 197b
technology, IV 358a
Herodotus (5th century B.C.),
atomism, I 132b
continuity, I 503b
culture, II 129a
custom, III 575a
cynicism, I 632a
democracy, I 653a–653b, 667a
despotism, II 2a
eighteenth century view of, I 78a
environment, II 129a
Epicurus, I 132b
equality, II 144b
freedom of speech, II 254b, 259a, 259b
God, II 513a
happiness, II 375b
historiography, I 503b; II 467a, 468a, 469a, 477a, 484b, 500b–501b, 507b, 508b
human nature, III 571a, 572a, 573a, 575a
humanism, II 516b
justice, II 653a
language, III 62b

law, II 680b, 681a, 682b, 683a, 683b, 684b
linguistics, III 62b
mathematics, III 180a
mimesis, III 497b
monarchy, I 653a
mythology, III 272b, 275b
necessity, III 353a, 353b
oligarchy, I 653a
philanthropy, III 487a
Platonism, III 497b
pleasure, II 375b
poetry, III 525b
primitivism, III 591b
progress, III 628a
psychology, IV 1b, 7b
rationalism, IV 48a
revolution, IV 152b
sacred, II 513a
soul, III 573a
State, I 653a, 667a
symmetry, IV 347a
truth, II 513a
Heroes
Aeschylus, IV 366b
Bible, III 276b, 279b, 280b, 281a, 281b–282a, 282b
Carlyle, IV 204a
demonology, I 669a
Euripides, IV 367a
Greece (ancient), IV 366b
Hegel, III 556a
human nature, III 572a, 573a
humanism, II 520a
liberalism, III 37b
mythology, III 276b, 279b–282b, 287a, 288a, 291a, 291b, 308a–309a, 311a, 312b
Plato, III 497a
pragmatism, III 556a
progress, III 634b, 625b, 626a
romanticism, IV 188b–189a, 200b, 204a, 209a
Rome (ancient), IV 370a
Sophocles, IV 367a
temperance, IV 365b, 366b, 367a, 367b, 370a
tragic sense, IV 411b–414a, 415b, 416a
virtue, IV 413a, 413b, 414a
Héroet, Antoine (d. 1568), Platonism, III 514a
Herrad of Landsberg, temperance, IV 372b
Herrera, genius, II 293b
Herrera y Reissig, Julio (1873–1909), symbolism, IV 342a
Herschel, J. F. W. (1792–1871)
cosmic images, I 521b
hierarchy, II 448a

natural selection, II 448a
optics, III 419b
Herschel, William (1738–1822)
cosmic images, I 519b
cosmology, I 550a–552a
Hersey, G., iconography, II 538b
Herskovits, Melville Jean (1895–1963), beauty, I 213b
Hertwig, Oscar (1849–1922), cell division, II 287a
chromosomes, II 287a, 289a
Hertz, G. W., Faust (legend), III 251a
Hertz, Heinrich (1857–1894), continuity, I 494a
empiricism, III 545b
relativity, IV 78b
Hertzka, Theodor (1845–1924), Utopia, IV 463b
Hervas, Lorenzo (1735–1809)
language, II 669b
linguistics, III 64b
Hervé, Julien Auguste, expressionism, II 208b
Hervet, Gentian, skepticism, IV 242b
Hervey de Saint-Denys, Marquis (1823–1892), China, I 367b
Herzen, A. I. (1812–1870), motif, III 243a
Volksgeist, IV 494b
Hesiod (8th century B.C.),
beauty, I 196b
catharsis, I 264b
chaos, IV 297a
Christianity, III 590a
cosmogony, II 432a
culture, I 607b–608b
death, I 644b
demonology, I 667b
disease, II 395b
freedom of speech, II 259a
God, II 513a; III 573b
happiness and pleasure, II 375b
historiography, II 506b
human nature, III 571b, 572b, 573a, 573b
immortality, I 644b
infinity, II 604b
justice, II 653a; III 572b, 573a
law, II 674a–674b, 675b–677a, 678b–682b, 684a
longevity, III 89b
Middle Ages, III 580a
mimesis, III 226a
motif, III 240b
mythology, III 273a, 278a

perfectibility, III 463b
periodization in literary history, III 481b–482a
philanthropy, III 487a
poetry, III 526a
primitivism, III 578a–581a, 581b, 590a
progress, III 624b, 626a, 629b
psyche, IV 32b
Pythagoras and, III 273a
Pythagoreans, IV 32b
rationalism, IV 46a, 46b
reformation, IV 60b
reincarnation, I 644b
sacred, II 513a
Saint Basil and, III 590a
space, IV 296b–297a
temperance, IV 366a
time, IV 399b
truth, II 513a
Utopia, IV 459a
vox populi, IV 498b
Xenophanes and, III 573b
Hess, J. J., eschatology, II 157b
Hess, Moses (1812–1875),
alienation, I 38a
Cieszkowski and, II 413b
Engels and, II 413b
Hegel and, II 414a
Marx and, II 413b
Marxism, III 158b
socialism, IV 290a, 291b
Hesse, Hermann (1877–1962)
art and play, I 106a
Buddhism, I 256b
Faust (legend), III 251a
Hessen, Philipp von, casuistry, I 262b
Heterodoxy
Galileo, III 356a
love, III 97b
religion, IV 113b
romanticism, IV 199b
Heterogeneity
hierarchy, II 442a
spontaneous generation, IV 307a, 308b, 310a, 310b, 311a, 311b, 312a
Hettner, Hermann (1821–1882)
classicism, I 450b
realism in literature, IV 52b
Heuser, F.
chromosomes, II 287b
genetic continuity, II 287b
Hevelius, Johannes (1611–1687), cosmology, I 549a
Heyden, Sebald, musical genius, III 315b
Heydenreich, Ludwig H., universal man, IV 440a

171

Heydon, John, harmony, II 394a

Heyl, Bernard, literary criticism, I 604a

Heyne, Christian Gottlob (1729–1812), mythology, III 302a, 304b

Heywood, Thomas (1574?–1641)
hermeticism, II 432a
mythology, III 299b
wisdom of the fool, IV 520a

Hezekiah (Bible), freedom of speech, II 255a

Hibbert, Samuel, witchcraft, IV 523a

Hick, John.
agnosticism, I 24a
theodicy, IV 381a

Hickman, Charles, harmony, II 394b

Hickok, Laurens P. (1798–1888), psychology, IV 24b

Hierarchy, II 434b–449b
Addison, II 446b, 447b
Agrippa, II 435b
angelology, II 435b, 439b, 441b
Apianus, II 436b, 437a
architecture, II 440b–441b
Aristotle, II 438a–438b, 443a–443b, 448a
art, II 436a, 436b
astronomy, II 443a, 448a
atheism, II 444b, 445a
Averroës, II 441a
Avicebron, II 441a
Avicenna, II 441a
Being, II 445a, 446a
Bible, II 435b, 440a
Brahe, II 442b
Brooke, II 446b
Bruno, II 442a–443a, 445b
Byzantine Empire, II 440b–441a
cabbalism, II 441a
Cartesianism, II 444a, 444b, 445b
causation, II 446b
Chain of Being, II 440b, 446b–448a
chaos, II 444b
Christianity, II 438a, 439a–439b, 440b, 441a
Cicero, II 438b–439a
Coleridge, II 441a
common law, III 31a, 31b
Copernicus, II 436b, 437b, 442a, 442b, 443b
cosmic images, I 514a
cosmos, II 436a, 436b, 439a, 439b, 442b, 443b, 445a, 445b, 446b, 447b
Creation, II 438a, 439b,

445a, 447b
Crooke, II 436a–436b, 439b
Cudworth, II 444a
Dante, II 440b; III 509b, 511a
Darwin, II 448a
Descartes, II 443b, 444a, 444b
Digges, II 436b, 437b, 442b
dignity, IV 139b, 145a, 145b, 146a
Donne, II 434b, 443b
Drummond of Hawthornden, II 436a
dualism, II 443b, 444a, 445b
economics, II 442a
Einstein, II 448b
Elyot, II 434b
Erigena, II 441a
ethics, II 444a
evolution, II 447b, 448a
Ficino, II 442a, 442b; III 511a
Fludd, II 437a
Francis I, II 436b
Galileo, II 436b, 443b
Gerhard, II 435a
God, II 438b–439b, 440b, 441a, 442a, 443a, 444a–446b
good, IV 173b
Greece (ancient), II 442b, 444a
harmony, II 446a–446b, 448b
heaven, II 440b
hell, II 435b
Hermes Trismegistus, II 439a
Herschel, II 448a
heterogeneity, II 442a
Hippocrates, II 446a
historiography, IV 147b
history, II 442a
Hobbes, II 443b–444b
Homer, II 440a, 440b
humanism, IV 131a
Iamblichus, II 439a
infinity, II 438b, 441a–441b, 442b–443a, 444b, 445a, 446a, 446b, 447b
Jacob (Bible), II 440a
Johnson, II 447a–447b
Judaism, II 441a
Kant, II 447b
Kepler, II 442b, 443a–443b
law, III 10b, 28b, 30b, 31a, 31b
Leibniz, II 444a–444b, 445b–447b, 448b
Leonardo da Vinci, II 437b
literature, II 440b
Locke, II 446a, 446b

logic, II 444b
love, II 439a, 442a
Lovejoy, II 438b
Luther, II 442a; IV 66b
Macrobius, II 440a–440b
macrocosm, II 436b
Marxism, III 156a
materialism, II 444a, 448a
mathematics, II 438a, 442b, 443b, 444b, 445a
matter, II 444a; III 190b, 192a, 192b, 193a
metaphysics, II 438b, 447a
microcosm, II 436a, 436b, 437a, 439b, 442b
Middle Ages, II 438a, 439b–440b, 442a
Milton, II 438a
Mohammedanism, II 441a
monads, II 445b–446a, 448b
morality, II 447a
More, II 444a, 444b
music, II 439b; III 266a
natural law, III 17b, 23b
Nature, II 435b, 436b, 438a, 438b, 440a, 442b, 443a, 444a–445a, 446a–448a
Neo-Platonism, II 438b, 439a–439b, 442a
Newton, II 443b, 444a
Nicholas of Cusa, II 441a–441b, 443b
numbers, II 438a
Order, II 434b–449b
Orosius, II 438a
Otto of Freising, II 438a
painting, II 436a; 436b
pantheism, II 443a, 445a
Pascal, II 444a
Peacham, II 435a
Perrière, II 435b
Person, II 438a
Pico della Mirandola, II 442a–442b
planets, II 442b
Plato, II 438a, 438b, 441a, 443a, 443b
Platonism, II 441a, 444a, 445a; III 509a, 509b, 511a, 513b
plentitude principle, II 442b
Plotinus, II 439a, 439b, 441a, 444a
pluralism, II 443a
Pont, II 438a
Pope, II 447a, 447b
Porphyry, II 439a
Proclus, II 439a, 441a
prophecy, III 659b, 660b, 661b
Protestantism, II 438a
Pseudo-Dionysius, II 435b, 439a–439b, 441a, 442a

psychology, II 436b
Ptolemy, II 436b, 437a
Purchas, II 436b
Puritanism, II 442a
race, IV 491b
Raleigh, II 436b
rationalism, II 445b
reason, II 446b, 447b
reformation, IV 64a, 65a, 66b
Reformation, II 442a
Renaissance, II 434b, 436b–438b, 440b, 442b–443a; IV 131a, 139b, 145a, 145b, 146a, 147b
revolution, II 441b
right, IV 173b
romanticism, IV 206a
Rome (ancient), II 444a
Saint Augustine, II 438a, 441a
Saint Bede, II 438a
Saint Francis, IV 65a
Saint Paul, II 439a
Saint Thomas Aquinas, II 440b
Satan, II 435b
science, II 448b
secularization, II 442a, 444a
Shakespeare, II 438a
socialism, IV 285a, 286b, 287a, 293b
society, II 442a
soul, II 442a
Spenser, II 434b
Spinoza, II 444b–445b
Sprat, II 444b
theater, II 436b
theodicy, IV 380a
Thomson, II 446b
tradition, II 441b, 442a
truth, II 439a, 443b, 446a
unity, II 442a, 444b, 445a, 445b, 446a, 448b
universe, II 434b, 436a–439b, 441a–448b; III 192a
utility, IV 451b, 454b, 457b
Vincent of Beauvais, II 438a
Vitruvius, II 437b
Volksgeist, IV 491b
Voltaire, II 446b
Ward, II 434b
welfare state, IV 510a
Wells, H. G., II 448a
Wesley, II 446b
Wilkins, II 443b
work, IV 534b
Young, Edward, II 446b–447a
Zeus (myth), II 440a

Hieroglyphics
art, II 529b–531a
iconography, II 529b, 530a,

530b, 531a, 537b, 538a
mythology, III 290a
numbers, III 401a, 401b
symbolism, II 529b, 530a
Hieron, literary criticism, I 596b
Higginson, Thomas Wentworth (1823–1911), Orientalism, III 429a, 431b, 434a–434b
transcendentalism, III 429a, 431b, 434a–434b
Higher Law doctrine, I 435b–437a
civil disobedience, I 435b–437a
transcendentalism, I 436a–436b
Highet, Gilbert, linguistics, IV 425b
Hilbert, David (1862–1943), axiomatization, I 168a, 170a, 170b
empiricism, III 545b, 547b
infinity, II 610b
mathematics, III 170b, 176b
pragmatism, III 557b
relativity, IV 89a
Hilbert space, II 590b, 591a
Hildebert (1055–1133)
Christianity, III 591a
primitivism, III 591a
Hildebrand, Adolf von (1847–1921), aesthetics, II 223b
Hildebrand, Bruno (1812–1878), economic history, II 60b
Hildebrandine Reform, IV 64a
Roman Catholic Church, IV 64a
Hill, Aaron (1685–1750), Newton and, III 394b
Hill, R. N., indeterminacy, II 591b–592a
Hillel (fl. 30 B.C.–9 A.D.), peace, III 440b
Hiller, Kurt, expressionism, II 206a, 208b
Hilliard, Nicholas (1537–1619), mythology, III 297b
Hīnayāna, the, I 247b–248a
Hinde, R. A., imprinting, II 585a
Hindemith, Paul (1895–1963)
creativity in art, I 579b
difference tones, III 263b
Pythagoras and, I 579b
Hindu language, II 660b
Hinduism
Bhagavadgītā, IV 232a
Brahman, III 430a, 431b
Buddhism, I 248a, 249a, 254a, 254b; IV 232b

cosmology, I 539a, 543b
culture, IV 231b
cycles, IV 232a
death, I 644b, 645a
destiny, IV 231b
existentialism, IV 232a
free will, IV 232b
God, II 343a–344a, 345a
holy men, III 487a
human nature, IV 231b
immortality, I 644b, 645a
India, I 248a, 249a
individualism, II 597a
karma, IV 231b–232b
law, III 7a
liberation, IV 232a
longevity, III 89b
love, III 95a
mythology, III 283a, 306a
numbers, III 402a, 403a
Orientalism, III 429a, 430a–434a, 436b, 439a
philanthropy, III 487a
reincarnation, I 644b, 645a
salvation, IV 231b–232b
saṃsāra, IV 231b–232b
scriptures, III 487a
sin, IV 231b–232b
soul, IV 231b
Upanishadic period, IV 231b–232a
U.S., III 429a, 430a–433b, 434a, 436b, 439a
Hinks, R., iconography, II 525a–525b
Hinrichs, H. F. W. (1794–1861), Hegel and, II 411b
Hipparchus (2nd century B.C.)
cosmology, I 541a
mathematics, III 182b
primitivism, III 579b
progress, III 630b, 633a
Hippasus of Metapontum, Pythagoreans, IV 32a
Hippias of Elis (5th century B.C.)
poetry, III 526a
progress, III 627b
Hippies
happiness, II 385b
love, III 107a, 107b
progress, III 628b
rationalism, IV 48b
Hippocrates (460?–?377 B.C.), analogy, I 61b–62a
axiomatization, I 164a
biology, I 230a
catharsis, I 264b, 267a, 269a
causation, I 271b
Darwin and, II 624a
environment, II 122b, 124a–124b, 125a, 125b, 129a

health and disease, II 396a, 397b, 398a–398b, 400a, 400b
hierarchy, II 446a
historiography, II 478a, 500a
human nature, III 574a
humanism, II 521b; IV 133a, 135a–135b
Islam, II 646a
Man-Machine, III 133a 133b, 134a, 134b
mimesis, III 227a, 497b
pangenesis, II 622b, 624a
Plato and, III 500a
Platonism, III 497b, 500a
psychology, IV 10b
rationalism, IV 47b–48a
skepticism, IV 234b, 236a
Hippodamus of Miletus (5th century B.C.)
Aristotle and, I 428a
city, I 428a–428b
culture, I 612b
progress, III 627b
Utopia, IV 459b
Hippolytus (3rd century A.D.), Pythagorean cosmos, IV 39a
Hiriyanna, M., Buddhism, I 254b
Hiroshima, international peace, III 455b
Hirsch, E. D., romanticism, IV 196a
Hirth, G., entropy, II 117b–118a
Hirzel, Hans Caspar, primitivism, III 600b
His, Wilhelm (1831–1904), recapitulation, IV 57b
Historians
art, II 297b
Bacon, III 356a
Descartes, III 356b
Greece (ancient), III 353b, 356a, 476b
historicism, II 459b–460a, 460b, 462a
Marxism-Leninism, III 478b–479a
necessity, III 353b, 354b, 356a, 356b, 357a, 358a, 359a, 360b, 361b
neo-classicism in art, III 363a
periodization in history, III 476a, 476b, 477b–480a
protest movements, III 676b
Renaissance, III 356a
revolution, IV 159b, 160a, 164a
Rome (ancient), III 356a, 476b; IV 370b

style, II 297b
temperance, IV 370b
women, IV 529a
Historicism, II 456b–463b
Adorno, II 463b
Antoni, II 456b, 458a
art, II 459a
Beard, II 462a
Becker, II 462a
Bloch, II 462b, 463a
Buckle, II 462a–462b
Burckhardt, II 460b
Burke, II 458b
Christianity, II 457a, 461a
Collingwood, II 461b–462a
crisis of, II 461a
Croce, II 457b, 461b, 462a
defined, II 456b–457a
determinism, II 20a–21a
development of, II 462a–463b
Droysen, II 461a
Dühring, II 457a
economic history, II 60b
empiricism, II 456b, 457a
Enlightenment, II 457a, 458b, 459a
Febvre, II 462b, 463a
Feuerbach, II 456b
Fichte, II 457a
freedom, II 458b
Germany, II 456b–462b
Gibbon, II 458a
God, II 460b
Goethe, II 457b, 461b
Greece (ancient), II 459a
Guizot, II 458b
Harkheimer, II 463b
Hegel, II 460b, 463b
Herder, II 458b, 459a, 460b–461a
historians, II 459b–460a, 460b, 462a
Historical School of economics, II 457a, 459b, 460b, 462b
Historical School of Law, II 457a, 459b, 460a, 460b, 463b
historiography, II 20a, 20b–21a, 462a, 489a, 496a
history, II 20a, 20b–21a, 459b–460a
Holy Roman Empire, II 459a
Humboldt, II 460a
individualism, II 457b
Italy, II 457b, 461b
Latin America, III 539b
Lessing, II 462a
logic, II 463a–463b
Lutheranism, II 458b
Mabillon, II 458a, 459a, 459b

173

Macaulay, II 458b
Mannheim, II 457a
Marcuse, II 463b
Marx, II 460b, 462b, 463a, 463b
Meinecke, II 456b, 457b, 458a, 461a, 461b; IV 203b
Menger, II 457a
Michelet, II 458b, 459a
Montesquieu, II 458a
Möser, II 459a
neo-Kantian philosophy, II 461a
Niebuhr, II 459a, 459b
origin of the term, II 456b–458a
Osnabrück, II 459a
perennial philosophy, III 457a
political, II 457b, 458b, 461a, 461b, 462a
Popper, II 457b, 462a
positivism, II 456b, 462b, 463a, 463b
Prantl, II 457a
Ranke, II 457b, 459a–462b
realism in literature, IV 54b, 56a
Reformation, II 457b
relativism, II 457a
Renaissance, II 458a, 459a
Schlegel, Friedrich, II 456b
scholarship, II 460a, 462b
science, II 462a–463a
Spengler, II 461b
Troeltsch, II 457a–457b, 458a, 458b, 461a, 461b
Vico, II 458b–459a
Voltaire, II 458a
Wagner, II 457a
Weber, II 462b, 463a, 463b
Winkelmann, II 459a
World War I, II 461a, 461b
World War II, II 462a
Historiography, II 464b–511b; IV 147a–152a
abstraction, II 18b–19a
academic history, II 491a, 492b, 496a
Achilles (myth), II 504b
Acton, II 496b
Adams, II 24a–24b
Aegyptus (myth), II 499b
Aemilius Paullus, II 508a
Africanus, II 471a
Agatharchides of Cnidus, II 509b
Agbar of Edessa, II 478b
Agesilaus, II 503a
Alexander the Great, II 469a, 504a, 504b–505b, 508b
alienation, II 25a
al-Tabari, II 474b
Alvarez, IV 148b

Anaximander, I 502b; II 499a
Anaximenes, I 502b
annals, II 465b–476b, 480a, 481b, 482a, 484a, 497b
Annius of Viterbo, II 485b
antiquity, II 476b, 482b, 485a, 487a
archives, II 475a, 476b, 479b–480a, 486b, 493a–493b, 494b, 496a, 496b
aristocracy, II 468b, 469b, 470a
Aristophanes, II 506a
Aristotelianism, II 468a, 471b, 488a, 509a
Aristotle, I 502b–503a, 503b; II 19b, 468a, 474b, 486a, 505b–506b, 507a, 507b, 508b
art, II 577b; IV 148b, 149a, 150a
Arthur (myth), II 483b
Ashley, II 495a
Assyria, II 465b–466a, 475a, 475b
astrology, II 479b–480a
Astruc, II 490b
Athenion, II 510b
atomism, II 18b
Aulard, II 496a
autobiographies, II 469b
Babylonia, II 465a, 469a, 472a, 474a, 476b
Bacon, Francis, I 503a; IV 148b, 151a
ballads, II 464b
Bancroft, II 493a
Baronius, II 484a, 486b
Beaufort, II 487a
Becket, II 484a
Bede, II 473a, 478b
behavior, IV 147b
belief, IV 147b
Benedictines, II 473b
Bible, I 503b; II 470b, 471a, 472a, 473b, 474b, 475b, 476a, 477b–478a, 479a, 484a, 488a, 489b, 490b, 499a
biology, II 24a
Biondo, II 484b–485a, 485b
Bismarck, II 493b–494a
Bodin, II 486a; IV 149b–150a
Bossuet, II 488b
boundary stones, II 465a
bourgeois, IV 147b
Bruni, II 482a
Bruno, II 488a
Buckle, II 22a, 495b
Buddhism, II 481b
Budé, II 486a
Burckhardt, II 495a

Burke, II 492a
Burnet, II 487b
Byzantine Empire, II 473a, 473b, 474b, 491a
calendar, II 468b, 472b
Callisthenes, II 504b–505a
capitalism, IV 147b, 151b
Cardan, IV 149a
Cartesianism, II 19b
Cato, II 469a, 469b
causation, II 18a–19b, 21b–22a, 480b, 489a, 501b–502a, 509b
Cerberus (myth), II 499b
Charlemagne, II 473a
Charles V, II 484a
Charron, IV 150b
China, II 22b, 479b–481b
China (ancient), II 467b, 479b–481b, 487a, 488b
Chou dynasty, II 480a
Christianity, I 503b; II 19b, 20a, 22a, 470b–472a, 473a, 474b, 477a, 478a, 483b, 488a, 491a
chronicle, II 465a, 472b, 473a, 475b, 478b, 479a, 481b, 482a, 484a, 484b
Cicero, II 469b, 470a
city state, II 482a, 482b, 483a
civilization, II 21a–21b, 22b–23b; IV 150a
class, II 25a
Cleon, II 502b
climate, IV 148a, 150a
Collingwood, II 23b
Comte, II 23b–24a, 24b, 25b, 495b
Condorcet, II 488b
Confucianism, II 480b
Constantine, II 471b
continuity, I 493b, 502b–504a
Copernicus, IV 148b
Cratippus, II 509a
Creation, II 471a–471b
criticism, II 476a–492a, 499a, 500a
Croesus, II 500b
cycles, IV 148a, 150a–150b, 151b
Danaos (myth), II 499b
Dante, II 482a
Danto, II 19b
Darwin, II 24a, 24b, 492b, 499b, 505b
date-lists, II 465a
Davies, IV 151a
defined, II 464b
degeneration, IV 148a, 150a, 150b–151a
Deioces, II 501a
Demaratus, II 501a

Democritus, I 502b, 503a; II 501b, 502a, 510b
Descartes, II 18b, 19b, 487b
determinism, II 18a–25b
Dicaearchus of Messene, II 506b–507a, 508b, 510b
Dilthey, II 496a
Diogenes Laërtius, I 503b
discovery, IV 148a, 148b, 149a, 149b
Donation of Constantine, II 485a
Droysen, II 494a–494b
Duhem, I 503b
Duris of Samos, II 507a–507b
Durkheim, II 497a
earth, II 19a
Easter, II 472b, 473a
ecclesiastical history, II 471b
economics, II 494b–495a, 495b, 497a; IV 147b, 148a, 151b
Eden, IV 149b
Egypt (ancient), II 465a, 465b–469a, 475a, 476b
Einard, II 473a
Eliot, T. S., IV 147a
Elizabeth I, II 484a
emotion, IV 147b
Empedocles, I 503a
Engel-Janosi, II 20b
Engels, II 24b, 25a, 25b
Enlightenment, II 23b–24a, 491a, 492a
environment, II 22a, 23a
Epaminondas, II 504b
Ephorus of Cumae, II 503b–504a, 507a–507b
epics, II 464b–465a, 465b, 466b, 472b, 476b, 491b, 504b, 507a
Euripides, II 506a
Eurystheus (myth), II 499b
Eusebius, II 471b, 472a, 473a, 474b, 478a–478b, 488b
evolution, II 24a, 505b–507a
evolution of literature, II 173a
faith, IV 147b
feeling, IV 147b
fifteenth century, II 484b–486a
first interpretation of history, II 465a
Flood, II 470b
forgeries, II 481b, 485a, 485b
fortune, II 470b
Foulcher of Chartres, II 473b

Foxe, II 484a; IV 149a–149b
France, II 485a–486a, 494b
Frederick I, II 474a
Frederick the Great, II 493b–494a, 495a, 496b
freedom, IV 147b, 152a
Galileo, II 18b
Geoffrey of Monmouth, II 483b
Germany, II 20a–20b, 25a, 483b, 484a, 489b, 490b–491b, 493a–495b
Gervinus, II 494a
Geyl, II 19a, 19b, 21b
Gibbon, II 491a, 491b
Gibbs phase rule, II 24b
Giustiniani, II 485a, 485b
Gobineau, II 500a
God, II 19b, 20a, 20b, 21a, 21b, 24b, 466a, 471a, 471b, 472a, 472b, 474a, 488b, 489a, 490a; IV 149b
Gooch, II 494b
Gothein, II 495a
Gracchi, II 510a, 511a
Great Britain, II 22a, 483b, 484a, 486a, 487b; III 483b
Greece (ancient), II 18b, 19b, 22a, 22b, 24b, 466a, 466b–468b, 469a, 469b, 471a, 474b, 475a, 475b, 476b, 477a, 483a, 483b, 484b, 488a, 489b, 499a–511a; IV 147a
Gregory of Tours, II 472b
Greville, IV 150a, 151a
Guibert of Nogent, II 473b
Guicciardini, II 483a, 492a, 518b; IV 150b
Han dynasty, II 480b
happiness, IV 152a
Harvey, IV 149b, 150a–150b
Hecataeus of Miletus, II 467a, 499b–500a
Heeren, II 494b–495a
Hegel, II 20a–20b, 21a, 25a, 488b, 492b, 494a
Hegelianism, II 24b
Henry IV, II 498a
Hercules (myth), II 499b
Herder, II 488b, 489a, 489b
heresy, II 430a
Herodotus, I 503b; II 467a, 468a, 469a, 477a, 484b, 500b, 504b, 506b
Hesiod, II 506b
hierarchy, IV 147b
Hippocrates, II 468a, 500a
historical evidence, II 476a, 486b–487a, 490b, 491b
historical methods, II 475a–479b

historicism, II 20a, 20b–21a, 462a, 489a, 496a
history, II 464b–498b; IV 147a, 147b, 150a, 151a, 151b
History Office, II 481a
Hittites, II 465a–465b, 475a
Homer, II 466b, 471a, 476b, 489a, 489b, 491b, 500b, 504b, 506b
Hugh of Saint Victor, II 473b
human nature, IV 150b
humanism, II 482a, 482b, 483a, 484b, 485b, 486a, 518a–518b; IV 130b, 131a, 134a, 148a–148b
Huxley, II 24a
Iason of Pherai, II 504a
Ibn Khaldūn, II 475a, 479a–479b, 485a
idea, II 499a–511a
idealism, II 20a–20b
impressionism, II 577b
India, II 488b
individualism, IV 147b
inevitability, II 20b–21a
International Congress of Historical Sciences, II 496a
interpretation, II 476a
invention, IV 148a–149b
investigation, II 476b, 478a
Ionia, II 466b–467a
Irenaeus, II 471b
irony, II 470b
Islam, II 474a–475a
Isocrates, II 467b, 503b, 504a
Italy, II 22a, 23a, 23b, 481b–483a, 484b–485b
Jerome, II 473a
Jerusalem, II 470b
Jesus Christ, II 470b, 471a–471b, 477b
Jews (ancient), II 465b–466b, 467b, 470b, 471a, 471b, 474b, 476a, 478a, 478b, 483b, 488a, 492b, 499a
John (King), II 484a
Joseph of Arimathea (Bible), II 483b
Josephus, II 466b, 476b, 476a, 478b
Judaism, I 503b; II 22a
judgment, IV 147b
Julius Caesar, II 469b, 481b, 482a
Kautsky, II 25a
King Arthur (legend), II 483b
knowledge, IV 149a, 149b
Koran, II 474b
Kronos (myth), II 506b

Labrousse, II 498a
Lamarck, II 24a
Lamprecht, II 495b
Laplace, II 18b, 19a
law, II 501b
Le Roy, IV 148b–149a, 149b, 150b
Lefebvre, II 498a
Leroy, IV 148b–149a, 149b, 150b
Leucippus, I 503a
liberty, II 500b–501b
linguistics, III 72b
Livy, II 469b, 470a, 477a, 487a, 491b
Lopez de Gomara, IV 149a
Louis XVI, II 498a
Luther, II 483b–484a
Lycortas, II 508a
Lycurgus, II 509a, 511a
Lysander, II 504a
Macaulay, II 494a
Maccabees, II 466b
Machiavelli, II 483a; IV 150a
Magna Carta, II 486a
Marius Victorinus, II 510a
Marsyas of Pella, II 505b
Marx, II 24b–25a, 492b, 495b, 496a, 499a
Marxism, II 24b–25a, 497a, 499a
Mazzini, II 492b
Medici, Lorenzo de', IV 149a
Meinecke, II 20b, 496a
Melanchthon, II 484a, 484b
Melissus, I 503a
Mesopotamia (ancient), II 465a–465b, 467b
metaphysics, II 24a
methodology, IV 147b–148a
Michelet, II 23b
Middle Ages, II 18a, 22b, 472b–481b, 489b, 491b, 493a, 518b; IV 147a, 147b, 148b, 151b
mimesis, II 507a, 507b
Mithridates VI of Pontus, II 410b
Mabillon, II 486b, 487a, 490b
modernism, I 425a–426b
Montaigne, IV 150b
Montesquieu, II 475a, 489a, 494b, 500a
morality, II 468b, 469b, 480a, 480b, 481a, 502b–503a; IV 147b
Möser, II 489b
Moses (Bible), II 470b–471a, 471b, 473b, 479a, 490b

Motley, II 493a
Muhammad, II 474b, 475a
Mycenaean Age, II 466b, 467a
mythology, II 465b, 470a, 480b, 483b, 489a, 491b, 499b–500a
Nain de Tillemont, II 478b
Napoleon I, II 493a, 496b
narratives, II 475a, 475b, 477a, 477b, 480b, 481a, 482a, 483a, 484b, 485b, 487a, 487b, 490b, 491a, 493b, 494b, 498a, 501a, 503a
nationalism, IV 151b
natural science, II 18b
Nature, II 18b, 20a, 510b–511a; IV 149b, 150b, 151a
Nearchus, II 505a
neo-classicism, IV 147a
Newton, I 503b; II 18b, 19a, 488a
Nicias, II 502b, 510b
Niebuhr, II 491b
nineteenth century, II 492a–498a
Norden, IV 151a
Nureddin, II 474a
oral transmission, II 464b–465a, 467a, 477b, 479a, 480a
Ordericus Vitalis, II 473b, 479a
Orientalism, II 500b–501a, 504b, 505a
Origen, II 478b
Orosius, II 472a–472b, 473b, 474b, 488b
Ossian, II 489b
Otto of Freising, II 473b–474a
Otto the Great, II 473a
painting, II 577b
Pallavicino, II 486b
Pan Ku, II 481a
pangenesis, II 624b
papacy, IV 149b
Papebrochin, II 486b
Paracelsus, IV 148b
Paris, II 474a
Parmenides, I 503a
Pasquier, IV 148b
Pausanias, II 501a
peasantry, II 479a
Pelopidas, II 504b
perfectibility, IV 148a, 149a, 150a, 151b
Pericles, II 501a–501b, 502a, 502b
periodization in literary history, III 483b
Perizonius, II 487a
pessimism, IV 148a, 151a

Philip of Macedonia, II 504a, 508b

Philip II, II 496b

philosophy, II 20a–20b, 23a–23b, 24a, 467b, 473b, 478b, 480a, 488b, 489b, 496a, 507b, 510b; IV 151a

Phoibidas, II 503a–503b

Phylarchus, II 507b

physics, II 18b

Pictor, II 469a

Plato, II 22a, 471a, 502b, 504b, 508b

poetry, II 464b–465a, 465b, 466b, 470a, 472b; IV 151a

politics, II 467b, 468a, 471a, 474a, 474b, 475a, 478b, 480a, 481a, 482a–483a, 487b, 492a, 492b, 493a, 494a, 499a, 500a, 502a–504b, 508a; IV 147a, 147b

Polybius of Megalopolis, II 467b, 468b, 469b, 477a, 482b, 507b–509b

Popelinière, II 485a, 485b

Popper, II 20b–21a

Posidonius of Apamea, II 509a–511a

positivism, III 532b–536b, 538a–539b, 545b, 546b, 550b

Postel, IV 148b

Pouilly, II 487a

power, IV 147b

pragmatic history, II 508a

pre-classical times, II 464b–466b

predestination, II 19b–20a, 21a

Price, II 483b

printing, II 482b

Proctor, IV 150a

progress, IV 148a–151b

Prometheus (myth), II 506b

Protestantism, II 20a

Ptolemy I, II 505a

Pythagoras, II 471a

race, II 22a, 500a–500b, 504b, 509b

Ramus, IV 148b

Ranke, II 20b, 475b, 485b, 488b–493b, 494a, 494b

Raoul of Caen, II 473b

rationalism, IV 48a–48b, 147b

reason, IV 149b, 151a

rebellion, II 500a

reconstructing the past, II 475b, 476a, 481b

Reformation, II 478b, 481b–484b; IV 68a, 149a

relativism, II 20b

relazioni, II 493a

religion, II 466a, 468b, 469b, 470b, 471a, 471b, 473a, 474a, 474b, 483b, 487b; IV 147a

Renaissance, II 474b, 476b, 479a, 481b–484b, 490b, 506a, 518a–518b; IV 130b, 131a, 134b, 147a–152a

revolution, II 23b; IV 147b

Rhenanus, II 485b

Rickert, II 496a

Robertson, II 492a

Robinson, II 497b

Roger of Wendover, II 474a

Roman Catholic Church, II 478a, 483b; IV 147a, 149b

romanticism, II 489b–492b, 494b; IV 147a, 200b

Rome (ancient), II 22a, 22b, 468a–473b, 477a, 483a, 483b, 484b, 486a, 489a, 491b

Roscher, II 495a

Roscoe, II 492a

Russia, II 496a

Saint Augustine, II 19b, 471b–474a, 488b

Saint Paul, II 477b

Saladin, II 474a

Sallust, II 469b

Sarpi, II 486b

Savigny, II 496a

Schlözer, II 491a

Schmaller, II 495a

scholarship, II 473a–473b, 474a, 477a, 480b, 481a, 482b, 486a–488a, 490a–493b, 496a, 496b, 497b

science, II 21b–22a, 24a–24b, 488a; IV 147b–150a, 151b, 152a

Shäfer, II 495a

Shakespeare, I 503b

Sigibert of Gembloux, II 473b

Simon, II 490b

Sismondi, II 492a

sixteenth century, II 484b–486a

skepticism, II 25b; IV 148a

Sleidanus, II 484a

Smith, II 494b

society, II 22b–23b, 25a; IV 147b, 148a

sociology, II 475a, 497a–498a, 499a, 504b, 510b

Socrates, II 502b, 503a

Solomon (Bible), II 479a

Solon, II 500b, 511a

Spain, II 22a

Spelman, II 486a

Spencer, II 24a, 505b, 506b

Spengler, I 503b; II 22a–22b, 23a, 23b, 506b

Spenser, IV 151a

Ssū-ma Ch'ien, II 480b–481a

State, II 20a, 22a; IV 147b

Stenzel, II 492a

Stoicism, II 469b, 470a, 471a, 509b, 510b

Stubbs, II 491b, 496a

style, IV 147a

Sumer, II 465a

supernatural, II 468a, 470b, 478b–488a, 488b

Surius, IV 148b

surveys, II 488b

Tacitus, II 470a–470b, 482b

Taine, II 495b

teleology, II 24a

Thales, I 502b

theology, II 21a, 24a, 473b; IV 151a

Theophrastus, II 507a

Theopompus of Chios, II 504a–404b, 507a–507b, 509a

Thucydides, I 502b; II 467a, 468a, 469a, 469b, 475b, 476b, 477a, 482b, 501a, 501b–503a, 504a, 509a, 509b, 510b

Thutmose III, II 475a

Tocqueville, II 494b

Toynbee, I 503b, 504a; II 21a–23b, 506b

tradition, IV 148b

Troeltsch, II 496a, 496b

Trojan War, II 466b–467a, 483a

truth, IV 149b

Tudors, II 483b

T'ung dynasty, II 481a

Turner, F. J., II 497b

twentieth century, II 492a–498a

typography, IV 149a–149b

uniformitarianism, IV 148a, 150b, 151b

unity, IV 148a

universal history, II 489a

universe, II 18a–19b

utopianism, IV 151b

Valla, II 485a, 485b, 487a

Vasari, IV 150a, 150b

Vergil, II 483b, 484b

Vespucci, IV 149a

Vico, II 22a, 23a, 23b, 475a, 489a, 489b

Villani, II 482a

virtue, IV 147b

Voltaire, II 487b, 488b, 489b, 495a

Waitz, II 494a

war, II 466b–469b, 472a, 473a, 474a, 480a, 482b,

492a, 496b, 498a, 500b, 501b, 503a

Weber, II 496a, 496b, 497a

William of Malmesbury, II 473b, 478b–479a

William of Tyre, II 474a

Winckelmann, II 489b

Windelband, II 496a

Wolf, F. A., II 491a–491b

Wu, II 480b

Xenophon, II 503a–503b, 509a

Xerxes, II 501a

Zeus (myth), II 506b

History

Aeschylus, III 625a

alienation, II 25a

Argentina, III 543b

Aristotle, I 500a; II 19b, 507a; III 354b

art, II 528a–529a, 576a–580b

Berlin, I., I 286a

biology, I 236b–239a; II 24a

Burke, Kenneth, II 634b

Bury, I 283b

Carlyle, I 283a

Carr, I 285b–286a

China, II 22b

Christianity, II 19b, 20a, 22a; III 626a; IV 60b, 61a

Church of England, I 401a

Collingwood, I 284b, 285a, II 23b

Comte, I 281a; II 23b–24a, 24b, 25b, 451b; III 640a

consciousness, IV 179b–181b

continuity, I 492b

Counter-Enlightenment, II 102b–103a, 104b, 109a, 110a–110b, 111b

Cournot, I 283b–284a

crucifixion, III 276a

Cuba, III 544b

cycles, I 52a; II 22a–23b, 154b, 518b; III 624b, 627b, 628a, 630b, 633a, 640b; IV 148a, 150a–150b, 151b, 156a

Dante, I 383a

Darwin, II 24a, 24b

deism, I 648b

Descartes, II 18b, 19b

dialects, II 660b

dignity, IV 138a, 141a, 141b, 142a, 144a, 145b

Dilthey, I 284a–284b, 285a

Dray, I 285a

earth, II 19a

education, II 79a–85a
Engels, I 282b; II 24b, 25a, 25b, 450a, 452a, 454a–454b; III 643a
Enlightenment, II 23b–24a
environment, II 22a, 23a
equality, II 146b
Erasmus, I 393a, 397b
eschatology, II 154b–161b
ethics, IV 320a–320b
euhemerism, III 286b–287a, 294a, 301b, 302b, 303a, 306b
Eusebius, I 378a
evangelicalism, I 403a, 406b
evolution, II 24a
evolution of literature, II 171a–174a
existentialism, III 159a, 159b–160a
expressionism, II 206a, 206b–207a
Faust (legend), III 249a, 251a, 252a
first interpretation of, II 465a
France, III 366a
Franciscans, I 383b
freedom, I 285b–286a
French Revolution (1789), III 671b
Galileo, II 18b
game theory, II 263b–265a
genius, II 297a–297b
Germany, II 20a–20b, 25a
Geyl, II 19a, 19b, 21b
Great Britain, II 22a
Greece (ancient), II 18b, 19b, 22a, 22b, 24b, 466b–467a
Hamann, II 104b
Handel, I 404b
Hegel, I 280a–281a, 402b, 409a, 614b–615a; II 15a–15b, 20a–20b, 21a, 25a, 158a–158b, 410b, 414b, 451b, 453a, 454a, 454b; III 22a, 358b, 462a, 473a–473b, 566a, 566b; IV 180a, 290b
Hegelianism, II 24b
Hempel, I 284b–285a
Henry III, I 381b
Henry IV, I 381b
Henry VIII, I 395a
Herder, III 473a, 638a, 639a–639b; IV 203b, 204a, 290b, 318a
hierarchy, II 442a
holy, II 513a, 513b
Hontheim, I 403b
Hügel, I 396b, 406b
human nature, III 576b
humanism, II 515b–517b,

518b; IV 129a, 132b, 135a
Hume, II 92a
Hus, I 387a
iconography, II 525a, 528a–529b, 532a, 539a–540b
idealism, II 20a–20b
impressionism, II 576a–580b
individualism, II 297a–297b, 594a–597a
inevitability, II 20b–21a
Innocent III (Pope), I 383a–383b, 386a
Inquisition, I 383b
international peace, III 448b
irony, II 634b
islam, II 650a
Italy, II 20b–21a
Ivan II, I 410b
James I, I 398b
Jesuits, I 406a
Jesus Christ, II 477b
Joachim of Floris, III 472a–472b
John XXIII (Pope), I 408b
Joseph, I 399a
Judaism, II 22a; IV 61a
Kant, I 280a, 280b, 615a; III 638a, 639b–640b, 649a
Lamarck, II 24a
language, II 660b, 661b, 670b–671b
Laplace, II 18b, 19a
law, I 291b–292a; III 3b, 12a, 12b, 23a; IV 493a–493b
Lenin, I 283b
Leo XIII (Pope), I 406a
Leopold II, I 404a
liberalism, III 37b–41b
linguistics, II 670b–671b; III 61a–72b; IV 426b, 428a
literature, III 82b, 85a, 85b; IV 332a
loyalty, III 108b, 112b
Machiavellism, III 124b
Man-Machine, III 131b, 134a, 135b, 138b, 142a
Manning, I 406b
Martin V (Pope), I 386b
Marx, I 282a–282b; II 24b–25a, 159a–159b, 450a, 451a, 451b, 452a, 452b–453a, 454a; III 167b; IV 161a, 161b, 162a, 290a, 293b, 534a
Mary, Queen, I 393b, 398a
Mary, Queen of Scots, I 397b
materialism, II 450a–456b
matter, III 186a–186b
measurement, IV 402a
Medici, I 398a
metaphor, III 199a

metaphysical imagination, I 279b–281a; II 24a; III 209a, 209b, 210a, 213a, 219b, 222a
Methodism, I 404b
Michael (Czar), I 410b
Michael VIII Paleologus, I 410a–410b
Michelet, II 23b
Middle Ages, II 18a, 22b
millenarianism, III 223b, 224a, 225a, 225b
Moghila, I 411a
monasticism, I 383b, 388a
morality, III 277b
Moravians, I 403a
motif, III 235a–236b, 238a
Münzer, I 390b–391a
music, III 264b
nationalism, III 324b, 326a, 328a, 329a, 330a, 334b, 335a, 337a, 338b
natural law, III 22a, 23a
natural science, II 18b
naturalism in art, III 339b, 341b
Nature, II 18b, 20a
necessity, III 351b–362a, 645b
neo-classicism in art, III 366a, 367a, 369a, 371a
Newton, II 18b, 19a
Niebuhr, I 280a; II 634b; III 635b
numbers, III 402b, 403a, 403b, 404b
organicism, III 422a, 426b
Orientalism, III 436b, 437a
original, III 556a
overall purpose in, I 279b
painting, II 576a–580b; IV 465b, 467a, 469b, 470a, 471a, 472a, 474a, 474b
peace, III 440a, 440b, 443b, 444a, 445a
Peirce, III 556b, 560b
periodization in literary history, III 482b, 483b–486a
philosophy, II 20a–20b, 23a–24a; III 199a, 556a
physics, II 18b
Pietism, I 406a; III 494a–494b
Plato, II 22a; III 354a, 629a–629b; IV 175a
Platonism, III 496a, 516b, 521a–521b, 523a, 523b
Plekhanov, I 283a
pluralism, I 282b–284b
predestination, II 19b–20a, 21a
primitivism, III 597b, 581a, 582b, 593a, 596a, 597b
private property, III 650a,

650b, 652a, 654a, 656b
progress, III 624b–649a
prophecy, III 666a–666b
protest movements, III 670a, 671b, 674a, 675a
Protestantism, I 386b–387a; II 20a
psychology, IV 1a, 9b
Puritanism, I 390b
race, II 22a
Ramism, IV 45b
Ranke, I 409a; II 20b
rationalism, III 301a–303b
realism in literature, IV 51b
recapitulation, IV 56a, 58a–58b
reflective, III 556a
reformation, IV 60b, 61a, 63a, 65a, 69a
Reformation, IV 68a
relativism, II 20b
religion, IV 93b, 100b, 105a, 106a, 107a, 107b, 108a, 111a, 112b, 117a
revisionism, IV 269b, 275a
revolution, II 23b; IV 154a, 155a, 159b, 161a, 162a, 163b, 167a
rhetoric, IV 171b
right, IV 173a, 174a, 175a, 179b–181b, 183a, 185b, 186a
romanticism, I 595a; IV 187a–201b, 203a–204a, 205a, 208a, 210b
Rome (ancient), II 22a, 22b; III 354b
Rousseau, I 409a
Russia, III 333b
Russian Revolution (October 1917), IV 163b
science, I 466a; II 21b–22a, 24a–24b; III 472a
skepticism, II 25b; IV 246b–247a, 247b, 248a, 249b
Spain, II 22a
Spencer, II 24a
Spengler, II 22a–23b; III 360b
State, II 20a, 22a
Stoicism, III 626a; IV 320a–320b
structuralism, IV 322b, 323a, 329b
style, IV 332a
symbolism, IV 337b–338a, 344a
Taine, II 171b
teleology, II 24a
temperance, IV 365b, 375a, 375b
theodicy, IV 383a
theology, I 279b–281a; II 21a, 24a

Thirty Years' War, I 400b
Thucydides, III 576b
time, IV 392a, 393b, 394a, 395b, 402a
totalitarianism, IV 408a–409b, 410b
tragic sense, IV 413a–413b, 415b
Turgot, III 638a, 638b–639a
U.S.S.R., III 333b
unity, III 648a
unity of science, IV 434a
universal, II 489a; III 638a–640a, 648a
universal man, IV 438b, 439a, 441a, 442b
universe, II 18a–19b
Utopia, IV 461b
war, IV 504a, 508a
witchcraft, IV 522b
work, IV 534a, 535a
world, II 459b–460a
See also Historians, Historicism, Historiography, Renaissance
Hitler, Adolf (1889–?1945), authority, I 159b–160a
Darwinism, III 125a
Faust (legend), III 251b
Machiavellism, III 125a
natural liberty, II 70b
progress, III 647b
relativism, IV 73a
revolution, IV 164b
Stalin and, II 563a
totalitarianism, IV 408b, 409a, 410a, 410b
war, IV 505a
Hittites
annals, II 465b
assemblies, II 252b
freedom of speech, II 235a–235b, 252a, 252b
historiography, II 465a–465b, 475a
Pankus, II 253a–253b
prophecy, III 659b
Hjelmslev, L., language, II 672a
Hlaváček, symbolism, IV 343b
Hobart, Alice Tisdale, China, I 372a
Hobbema, Meindert (1638–1709), impressionism, II 578a
Hobbes, Thomas (1588–1679)
absolutism, IV 256b, 257a
abstraction, I 4a
anarchy, I 656b
aristocracy, I 656b; II 6a
Aristotle and, III 20b, 75b
atheism, I 136b

atomism, I 134b, 135b, 136a–136b, 137b, 138a
authority, I 151b–152a, 657a; III 20b
Bacon and, I 216b
behaviorism, I 214a, 214b, 216a–217a, 219b, 220a, 224b
causation, I 276a, 290b, 294b, 295a–296a, 301b, 303a; IV 177a, 434a
certainty, I 306a
civil disobedience, I 437b
conservatism, IV 256b
Copernicus and, I 216b
death, III 20b
deism, I 648b, 650a
democracy, I 656a–656b, 657a–657b; II 6a
Descartes and, II 450a
desire, IV 177a–177b
despotism, II 1a, 4a, 4b, 5a, 5b–7a, 9b, 11a
Engels and, II 453b
Enlightenment, II 90a, 94a, 98a
Epicureanism, II 137b
equality, II 144a
Erastianism, IV 119a
eschatology, II 160a
ethics, III 441b, 442b, 443a, 443b, 445b, 446a; IV 72a, 72b, 177a–177b
evil, III 20b
experience, IV 177a, 177b
fear, II 9b; III 20b
force, IV 484a
fraud, IV 484a
free will, II 246a
freedom, II 250a; IV 256b
general will, II 276a–276b
God, I 303a; II 212b, 351b, 355b
good, II 380a; IV 177a–177b, 178a, 182a
happiness, II 379b, 380a, 380b–381a
Harvey and, I 216b
hierarchy, II 443b–444a, 444b
human nature, III 575b, 576a
idea, I 111b
individualism, II 600a, 600b, 601b; IV 177a–177b
infinity, II 606a
justice, II 654b, 657a; III 20b
Kant and, III 442a, 443a, 443b
knowledge, IV 434a
law, I 290b; 250a; III 1a; IV 177b, 257a, 316a
Leibniz and, II 444b; III

461a
liberalism, III 11a, 43b–44a
linguistics, III 75a, 75b
Locke and, III 21a
loyalty, III 112a
Machiavelli and, IV 484a
Man-Machine, III 138b
Marxism, I 216b
materialism, II 444a, 450a, 453b; IV 434a
mathematics, IV 177a
matter, III 185b, 195a
metaphysical imagination, III 211a
methodology, III 387b
mind, IV 434a
monarchy, I 656b; II 6a
morality, IV 177a, 484a
natural law, III 20b; IV 177b
natural liberty, II 61b, 62a
natural rights, I 437b
Nature, III 20b; IV 177b, 178a, 257a
necessity, IV 177b
Newton and, III 387b, 395b
obedience, IV 256b
obligation, III 20b
oligarchy, I 656b
optics, III 395b
pain, II 380b–381a
patriarchalism, I 479b
peace, III 441b, 442b, 443a, 443b, 445b, 446a; IV 177b, 484a
perennial philosophy, III 461a
philosophy, IV 434a
Platonism, III 506a
pleasure, II 379b, 380a, 380b–381a
politics, II 98a; III 11a; IV 153b, 434a, 484a
positivism, III 20b
power, II 7a, 240a; III 20b; IV 256b, 316a
pragmatism, III 566b
psychology, IV 11a, 12a, 19a, 20a, 22a
radicalism, IV 256b
rationalism, III 11a
reason, IV 177a
relativism, IV 72a, 72b
religion, IV 119a
revolution, IV 153b
right, IV 177a–177b, 178a, 182a
Rousseau and, IV 259b
Russell and, III 446a
science, IV 153b
self-interest, III 1a
senses, IV 434a
slavery, II 5b, 11a

social contract, III 20b, 575b, 576a; IV 252a, 256a–257b, 259a, 259b, 260a, 261b, 317a
social welfare, IV 276b
society, II 62a; III 20b; IV 177b, 256b, 316a
sovereignty, I 656b, 657a; IV 316a
Spinoza and, II 351b; IV 256b
state, I 70a, 656a–656b, 657a–657b; II 62a; III 20b; IV 259a, 315a, 315b–316a, 317a, 317b
suffering, III 20b; IV 178a
teleology, I 301b, 303a; IV 177a
Thucydides and, I 656a
truth, IV 177a
tyranny, I 656b
unity of science, IV 434a
universe, II 443b, 444b
utilitarianism, IV 445b, 446a
Utopia, IV 462a
virtù, IV 484a
virtue, II 212b
war, I 656a; II 6a; III 441b, 442b–443a; IV 484a
Hobhouse, Leonard T. (1864–1929)
Comte and, III 538b
individualism, II 596b
positivism, III 538b
progress, III 645a, 645b, 647a–647b
relativism, IV 71a
Hobson, John A. (1858–1940), welfare state, IV 511a
Hocart, A. M., mythology, III 311a
Hocking, William Ernest, Buddhism, I 256b
God, II 358a
immortality, I 642a
Hodge, Charles, heresy, II 429b
Hodgskin, Thomas, socialism, IV 292b
Hodgson, Brian (1800–1894), Orientalism, III 429b
transcendentalism, III 429b
Hodgson, John Evan (1831–1895), cosmic voyages, I 532a
Hoebel, E. A., law, III 27a–27b
Hoering, W., indeterminacy, II 592a
Hoffmann, E. T. A. (1776–1822)
disease, II 403b
genius, II 324b

motif, III 241b
music, II 324b; III 271b
romanticism, I 453b; IV 189a, 196b
Rousseau and, II 324b
symbolism, IV 344b
Hofhaimer, Paul (1459–1537), musical genius, II 321a
Hofmann, J. C. K. (1810–1877), eschatology, II 157b
Hofmann, Melchior, eschatology, II 157a
Hofmann, W., iconography, II 538b
Hofmannsthal, Hugo von (1874–1929)
classicism, I 455b
conservatism, I 480a
symbolism, IV 342b, 344b
Hofmeister, Wilhelm (1824–1877)
cell division, II 286a
genetic continuity, II 286a
Hofstadter, Albert, beauty, I 212a, 212b
Hogarth, William (1697–1764)
art, II 300b, 306a
beauty, I 202b, 210b
genius, II 300b, 306a
ut pictura poesis, IV 469b, 470b, 471a
Hogg, James (1770–1835), romanticism, IV 193a
Hohenzollern, nationalism, III 332a
Holbach, Paul Henri Dietrich d' (1723–1789)
causation, I 281a
certainty, I 318a
Counter-Enlightenment, II 106a, 107a, 110a
despotism, II 10b, 12a, 12b
God, II 353a, 353b
happiness and pleasure, II 380b
human nature, III 643a–643b
immortality, I 641a
Jefferson and, IV 21a
Kant and, IV 209a
love, II 451a
Man-Machine, III 141a, 141b
materialism, II 451a
mythology, III 302a, 303a
perfectibility, III 643a–643b
progress, III 643a–643b
psychology, IV 21a
romanticism, IV 209a
utilitarianism, II 380b
Utopia, IV 462b

value, II 451a
Holbein, Hans (1465?–1524),
iconography, II 529b
impressionism, II 571a
Leibl and, III 344a
mythology, III 292b
wisdom of the fool, IV 519b
Holbein, Hans the Younger (1497?–1543), naturalism in art, III 340b, 341b, 344a, 345a
Holberg, Ludwig (1684–1754), cosmic voyages, I 534b
Holborn, H., periodization in history, III 479a
Hölderlin, Friedrich (1770–1843)
beauty, III 524a
city, I 432a
death, I 636a
Hegel and, IV 210a
irrationalism, II 637b, 638a, 638b
metaphysical imagination, III 221b
mythology, III 305a, 305b
Pietism, III 495a
Platonism, III 524a
romanticism, IV 209a, 209b, 210a
Schelling and, IV 210a
Holland, Norman, irony, II 634a
Hollanda, Francisco de, genius, II 293b, 303a, 305a, 308b
Hollander, John, *ut pictura poesis,* IV 470b
Holmes, Oliver Wendell (1809–1894)
Buddhism, III 437a
Orientalism, III 429a, 437a
transcendentalism, III 429a
Holmes, Oliver Wendell, Jr. (1841–1935)
behaviorism, III 567a
censorship, III 567b
constitutions, III 567b
freedom of speech, III 567b
judges, III 567b
justice, III 568a
law, III 4a, 4b, 566a, 566b, 567a–567b, 568a
morality, III 567b
Peirce and, III 567a
pragmatism, III 551b, 553a, 553b, 558a, 566a, 566b, 567a–567b, 568a, 569a–569b
psychology, IV 26b, 28b
Vaihinger and, III 566a
Holmyard, E. J., alchemy, I 29b

Holofernes (Bible), temperance, IV 372b, 375b
Holst, Gustav (1874–1934),
creativity in art, I 579b
Pythagoras and, I 579b
Holt, E. B. (1873–1946),
behaviorism, I 223a
Holt, Hamilton (1872–1951),
international peace, III 453b
Holthusen, Hans Egon, literary criticism, I 606a
Holtzmann, H. J., modernism, I 419b
Holwell, J. Z., mythology, III 305b
Holy, II 511b–514b
archaeology, II 513b
authority, II 512a, 512b
Barth, II 513b, 514a
behaviorism, II 513b, 514a
Bible, II 512a–512b, 513b
China, II 513a
Christianity, II 511b–514b
community, II 512b
Constantine, II 512b
cults, II 512b
culture, II 513b, 514a–514b
Darwin, II 513b
discipline, II 512a
Durkheim, II 513b
emotion, II 513a
Enlightenment, II 512b
ethics, II 512a, 513a, 513b
evaluation of the term, II 411b–512a
evolution, II 513b
faith, II 513b
feeling, II 513a, 514a
France, II 512a
Franciscans, II 513a
Freud, II 513b
Germany, II 512a
God, II 511b, 512b–513a, 514a
good, II 512a, 514a
grace, II 512b–513a
Herodotus, II 513a
Hesiod, II 513a
history, II 513a, 513b
Holy Roman Empire, II 512a, 512b
honor, II 512a
humanism, II 513a
Hume, II 513a
inaccessibility, II 512a
Isaiah (Bible), II 512b
Islam, II 513a
Israel (ancient), II 512a–512b, 513b
Italy, II 512a
Jesuits, II 513a
Jesus Christ, II 513b
Judaism, II 512a–512b,

513b
judgment, II 512b
Kant, II 513a
knowledge, II 513a
law, II 512b
literature, II 513a
majesty, II 512b
Middle Ages, II 512a, 512b
morality, II 512a, 512b
Moses (Bible), II 512a–512b
music, II 512a
mythology, II 513a, 514a
nationalism, II 512b
Otto, Rudolf, II 512a, 514a; IV 97b
paganism, II 513a
persecution, II 512b
phenomenology, II 514a
Philo Judaeus, II 513a
philosophy, II 514a
pietism, II 512b–513a
pluralism, II 514a
power, II 512a, 512b, 514a
profane, II 511b, 512b
prophecy, II 665a
prophets, II 512b, 513b
Protestantism, II 512b, 513b, 514a
psychology, II 513b, 514a
reductionism, II 513b, 514a
Reformation, II 513a
religion, II 511b–514b; IV 97b
Renaissance, II 513a
revelation, II 514a
ritual, II 512b
Roman Catholic Church, II 512b
romanticism, II 513a
saints, II 512a, 512b
Schleiermacher, II 513a, 514a
science, II 513b
secularization, II 511b, 512b, 513a
Smith, W. Robertson, II 513b
society, II 512b
Söderblom, II 513b
taboo, II 513b, 514a
Tillich, II 514a
tradition, II 512b, 513a
truth, II 513a
Tylor, Edward, II 513b
van der Leeuw, II 514a
war, II 512b
Holy Alliance, III 453a
conservatism, I 482b
nationalism, III 328a
periodization in literary history, III 485b
Holy Roman Empire
Christianity, I 375a–378b

common law, II 691b–692a
despotism, II 3a
heresy, II 425b
historicism, II 459a
holy, II 512a, 512b
intolerance, IV 117a
Jews, I 375a
law, II 689b–690a
nationalism, III 320b, 321a, 323a
religion, IV 117a
Roman Catholic Church, I 375a–378b
romanticism, IV 206b
social contract, IV 253a
Holy Spirit
Arminius, II 28b
authority, I 148b, 150a
Edwards, Jonathan, IV 110a
filioque clause, I 410a
religion, IV 111a
See also God
Holz, Arno (1863–1929), naturalism in art, III 339a
Holze, Dick H., indeterminacy, II 592a
Homans, George, individualism, II 601b
Home, Henry, *see* Kames
Homeostasis
environment, II 125b–127a
health, II 404b
Homer (850? B.C.)
allegory, I 42b, 43a, 44b, 46a
ambiguity, I 49b
art and play, I 99b–100a
beauty, I 196a
catharsis, I 264b, 266b
classicism, I 452b
comedy, I 468b
continuity, I 493a
cosmos, IV 297b
Counter-Enlightenment, II 103a
culture, I 607b, 608a
demonology, I 667b
education, II 80a; III 496a, 497a
eighteenth century view of, I 76b–77a, 78b–79a, 80a, 81b–83b, 86b
empathy, II 87b
ethics, III 440b
evolution of literature, II 172b
freedom of speech, II 257a–257b, 259a
genius, II 294b, 317a, 318a
God, II 339b–340b; III 573b
happiness and pleasure, II 375b

health, II 397b
hierarchy, II 440a, 440b
historiography, II 466b, 471a, 476b, 489a, 489b, 491b, 500b, 504b, 506b
human nature, III 571a, 571b, 572a, 573b
humanism, II 516b, 517b
immorality, III 496a, 497a
impiety, II 566b
infinity, II 604b
justice, II 652b–653a
language, II 661b, 664a–664b, 669a
law, II 674a, 676a, 679a, 679b, 680b–681a, 683a; III 7a
literary criticism, I 597a
literary paradox, III 79a
literature, III 86a
mathematics, III 180a
metaphor, III 203a, 203b, 207a
mimesis, III 226a, 497b
motif, III 237a, 241b
music, II 318a; III 268b
mythology, III 272b, 273a, 274a, 274b, 295a, 295b, 298a, 299a, 302b, 304a, 304b
neo-classicism in art, III 370b
ouranos, IV 300b
peace, III 440b
perfectibility, III 463b
philanthropy, III 487a
Plato and, III 497a
Platonism, III 496a, 497a, 507a, 519a
poetry, III 525b, 526a, 526b, 527b; IV 471a
psyche, IV 32b
psychology, IV 1a–1b
Pythagoras and, III 273a
Pythagoreans, IV 32a, 32b
rationalism, IV 46a, 46b
realism in literature, IV 54b
reincarnation, I 644b
skepticism, IV 234b
slavery, II 259a
space, IV 297b, 300a, 300b
symmetry, IV 346a
temperance, IV 365b, 366a
time, I 493a; IV 399b
to pan, IV 300a
tragic sense, IV 413a, 413b
Xenophanes and, III 573b
Homicide, Greece (ancient), II 680b
Homology, *see* Biology,
Homoousion theory, I 377b
Homosexuality
ethics, IV 70a, 70b
love, III 95a

mythology, III 279a
Nature, III 350a
Plato, III 512b
Platonism, III 512b, 514b
Renaissance, III 512b, 514b
Winckelmann, III 368a
Homunculus (fiction), Faust (legend), III 249a, 250a
Honor
Gay, John, III 233b
happiness and pleasure, II 376a
holy, II 512a
human nature, III 576a
humanism, II 522a; IV 133b
Hutcheson, III 231b, 232b
moral sense, III 231b, 232b, 233b
Renaissance, IV 133b
romanticism, IV 205a
virtue, IV 483a
war, IV 505b
Honoré, A. M., causation, I 293a
Honorius of Autun, dignity, IV 140a
Hontheim, Nikolaus von (1701–1790), history, I 403b
Hoogewerff, G. J., iconography, II 536a–536b
Hook, Sidney, pragmatism, III 553a, 564a
Hooke, Robert (1635–1703), atomism, I 135a, 140a
certainty, I 308a
cosmic voyages, I 529b
cosmology, I 547a–547b, 548a
design argument, I 674a
God, I 674a
methodology, III 387a
Newton and, I 311a; III 387a
virtuoso, IV 487b, 488b
Hooke, S. H.
mythology, III 276b, 277a, 277b, 281a, 281b, 282b, 284a, 311b
religion, IV 104b
Hooker, Richard (1552–1600)
deism, I 648b, 649b
harmony, II 391b, 392a
social contract, IV 254a–254b, 255b
Hooker, Thomas (1586?–1647)
patriarchalism, I 479b
psychology, IV 18a
Puritanism, IV 18a
Hoover, Herbert (1874–1964), conservatism, I 484a
individualism, II 596b
Hope, II 209b–216a

agapē, II 209b, 210a
Aristotelianism, II 210b–211a, 211b
asceticism, II 212b
atheism, II 213a, 213b
Augustinianism, II 210b
authority, II 212a
Bible, II 209b, 210a
Camus, II 213b, 215a
charity, II 209b–216a
Christianity, II 209b–215b
egocentric aspect of, II 209b
Erigena, II 210b
eros, II 209b, 210a, 210b
eschatology, II 214b
ethics, II 212b, 215a
faith, II 209b–216a
Feuerbach, II 213b
Freud, II 213b
friendship, II 210b–211a
Gnosticism, II 210a
God, II 209b–211b
good, II 209b, 212a; IV 174a
grace, II 211a
Greece (ancient), II 209b
happiness, II 212a
Hobbes, II 212b
humanism, II 214a, 215a
Jesus Christ, II 211b, 214b
knowledge, II 210a, 211b
love, II 209b, 210a, 210b, 212a, 215a
Luther, II 212a–212b
Lutheranism, II 212b, 213a
Marxism, II 213b–214a; III 147a
Middle Ages, II 210a–212b
millenarianism, III 223b
monasticism, II 212b
morality, II 212b, 213a
Nietzsche, II 213a
Pannenberg, II 214b
Pietism, III 493b
Plato, II 209b
Platonism, II 210b
progress, III 632b, 647b
Protestantism, II 212a–213a, 215b
Pseudo-Dionysius, II 210b
reformation, IV 60a
Reformation, II 212a–213a, 215b
right, IV 174a
Roman Catholic Church, II 210a, 210b, 211a–211b, 212b, 213a, 215a–215b
Saint Augustine, II 210a–210b, 213a
Saint Bonaventure, II 210b
Saint John, II 210a
Saint Paul, II 210a, 211b
Saint Thomas Aquinas, II 210b–212a, 213a

salvation, II 210a, 212b
Sartre, II 213b
society, II 212b, 213a
soul, II 211a
Teilhard de Chardin, II 214a
temperance, IV 372b, 375b
Tillich, II 211a
tragic sense, IV 412b
transubstantiation, II 212b
Utopia, IV 458b
utopianism, II 214b, 215a
virtue, II 211a, 211b–212a, 212b
Hope, Thomas (1770?–1831), neo-classicism in art, III 365a
Hopkins, Edward Washburn (1857–1932), Orientalism, III 434b
Hopkins, Gerard Manley (1844–1889), hermeticism, II 433a, 434a
Hopkins, Johns (1795–1873), philanthropy, III 491b
Hopkins, Mark (1802–1887), education, II 72b
psychology, IV 22b
Hopkins, Samuel (1721–1803), religion, IV 110b, 111a
Horace (65–8 B.C.)
allegory, I 41b–42a
art and play, I 102b
beauty, I 200b, 201b
dignity, IV 141b
eighteenth century view of, I 79a, 82a
evolutionism, II 176a
freedom of speech, II 260b
mimesis, III 227a
morality, III 631b
mountains in literature, III 253b
mythology, III 298a
organicism, III 423a, 423b, 424a, 424b
poetics, III 526a–530a
primitivism, III 591a, 591b
progress, III 631b
rhetoric, IV 171b, 172a
satire, II 211a, 213a, 213b, 214b, 215a
style, IV 330b, 331a
unity, III 423b
ut pictura poesis, IV 467b, 468a, 469b
wisdom of the fool, IV 517a
Horapollo (4th century A.D.), temperance, IV 377b
Horatius Cocles (6th century B.C.), temperance, IV 377a
Horkheimer, Max, authority,

I 157b, 158a–158b; II 463b
Horn, Georg, China, I 359a
Horne, R. H. (1803–1884), romanticism, IV 195a
Horney, Karen (1885–1952), psychology, IV 14a, 29a
Hornstein, Ferdinand von, Buddhism, I 256b
Horology, measurement, IV 399a, 401a, 401b, 402b, 403a
Hort, H. F. D., modernism, I 424b
Horta, Baron Victor, Gothic, II 373a
Horus (myth), II 39a; III 289b, 290a
Horwicz, A., Man-Machine, III 143a
Hosea (Bible), metaphor, III 202a
Hospers, John, organicism, III 421b
Hospitals, disease, II 401b–402a, 406a
Hostos y Bonilla, Eugenio Maria de, positivism, III 544b
Hotelling, Harold, social welfare, IV 283a
Hotman, François (1524–1590), Machiavellism, III 118a
Hottentots, primitivism, III 604b, 605a
Hough, Graham, literary criticism, I 603a
Houghton, Walter E., Jr., virtuoso, IV 486a
Hours, measurement, IV 401a
House of Wisdom, Islam, II 640b
Housman, A. E. (1859–1936), irony, II 633b
Houthakker, H. S., utility, IV 457a
Houtin, Albert, modernism, I 424a
Howard, Ebenezer (1850–1928), city, I 432b
Howe. Samuel Gridley (1801–1876), phrenology, IV 23b
Howell, James (1594?–1666), mountains in literature, III 254a
Howells, W. D. (1837–1920), realism in literature, IV 52b
Howitt, Alfred William (1830–1908)
Lang and, III 309a
mythology, III 309a
Hoyle, F., cosmology, I 567b, 568a

Hubbard, Rev. William (1621?–1704)
psychology, IV 18a
Puritanism, IV 18a
Hubble, Edwin P. (1889–1953), cosmology, I 562a, 564b
Hubble's law, I 562a, 564a, 564b, 565a, 568a, 568b
space, IV 305b, 306a
Hubris
Apollo (myth), IV 366a
Aristotle, IV 413a
Greece (ancient), IV 228a
sin, IV 228a
temperance, IV 366a, 366b, 367b, 369a
tragic sense, IV 413a, 414b
Hübscher, Arthur, baroque in literature, I 190a
Huch, Ricarda (1864–1947), romanticism, IV 197a
Huet, Pierre-Daniel (1630–1721), skepticism, IV 245a, 246a, 246b
Hufeland, Christoph Wilhelm (1762–1836), longevity, III 91b, 92b
Hügel, Friedrich von (1852–1925)
history, I 396b, 406b
modernism, I 420a, 421a, 422b, 424a, 424b
Huggins, William (1824–1910), space, IV 305b
Hugh of St. Victor (1096?–1141)
analogy, I 65b
Christianity, III 592a
classification of the arts, I 458b–459a
classification of the sciences, I 464b
dignity, IV 140a
historiography, II 473b
iconography, II 526a
natural law, III 20a
primitivism, III 592a
temperance, IV 372b
Hughes, Charles Evans (1862–1948), constitutionalism, I 490a
Hughes, H. S., crisis in history, I 595a–595b
Hughes, John (1677–1720), Newton and, III 392b
optics, III 392b
Hughes, Merritt, theriophily, IV 387a
Hugo, G. von (1764–1844), Hegel and, II 411b
Hugo, Victor (1802–1885), art for art's sake, I 109b
chance images, I 350b

China, I 369a
Counter-Enlightenment, II 109a
evolution of literature, II 172a, 172b
genius, I 599b; II 310b
Gothic, II 369b, 370b
literary criticism, I 599b, 601a
motif, III 240b
mythology, III 306b
naturalism, IV 53b
periodization in literary history, III 486a
positivism, III 544b
realism in literature, IV 52a, 53b
romanticism, I 453b; IV 191a, 196b, 198a, 201b, 203b, 205a, 208b
style, IV 332b
symbolism, IV 344a
Huguenots
Augustinianism, IV 109a
balance of power, I 182b
Bayle, IV 119b
despotism, II 7b–8a
determinism, II 30b
Edict of Nantes, II 428a; IV 113a, 116a, 116b, 117b, 119b
France, IV 113a, 119b
Great Britain, IV 116b
heresy, II 424b, 428a
intolerance, IV 113a, 113b, 116b, 117a
liberalism, III 43b, 44a
Louis XIV, IV 113b
Machiavellism, III 117b
pluralism, II 428a
predestination, II 30b
religion, II 428a; IV 109a, 112b, 113b, 116b, 117a, 119b
Renaissance, II 424b, 428a
sin, IV 113b
social contract, IV 254a
war, IV 113a, 116a–116b
Huizinga, Johan (1872–1945)
crisis in history, I 594a–594b
periodization in history, III 476a–476b, 480a, 480b
Hull, Clark L.
behaviorism, I 214b, 217a, 223b, 224b–225b, 227a
empiricism, II 549a
psychology, IV 28b, 29a
Hulme, T. E. (1883–1917), classicism, I 450b, 452a, 455a–455b
expressionism, II 208b
organicism, III 427a

181

Human nature
  Achilles (myth), III 571b, 572a
  Aeschylus, III 571b, 573a, 574b
  Agamemnon (myth), III 571b, 573a
  Alcmaeon of Croton, III 574a
  altruism, III 644a
  ambition, III 576a
  Anaxagoras, III 573b, 574b, 575a, 575b
  Anaximander, III 573b
  Anaximenes, III 574a
  Anglicanism, IV 20a
  animals, III 573b, 574b
  Antiphon, III 575a, 575b–576a
  Aphrodite (myth), III 571b, 572b
  appearance, III 575b
  Archelaus, III 575a
  Aristophanes, III 574a, 575b, 576a
  Aristotle, II 377a; III 554b, 574b; IV 285b
  art, III 574b
  Athena (myth), III 571b, 572a
  atomism, III 577a
  belief, III 572a, 575b
  comedy, III 574a, 575b, 576a
  Comte, III 534b, 644a
  Condillac, III 643b
  Condorcet, III 644a
  consciousness, III 574a
  Cosmic Fall, I 504b, 507b
  cosmogony, III 574a
  cosmos, III 573b
  Counter-Enlightenment, II 101a, 108a, 111a
  courage, III 572a
  critics, III 575a, 576a
  cults, III 573a
  culture, III 574b–575a
  custom, III 574b, 575a, 575b
  cycles, III 572a
  death, III 571b, 572a
  Democritus, III 571a, 573b, 575b, 576b–577a
  desire, III 576b
  Dewey, John, III 554b, 556b, 569b
  dignity, III 572a; IV 142b–143a
  Diodorus of Sicily, III 573b, 574b
  Diogenes of Apollonia, III 574a
  Dionysus (myth), III 572b
  economics, III 576a, 644a

  education, III 643b
  emotion, III 572b
  Empedocles, III 573a, 574a–574b, 575b
  empiricism, III 643b
  Enlightenment, II 91b–92b, 93a, 96b–98a, 98b, 100a
  environment, III 643b
  epistemology, III 572a, 575b
  equality, III 644a
  ethics, III 442b, 443b, 446a, 577a, 644a; IV 72a, 72b
  Euripides, III 571a, 573a
  evil, II 162b; III 571b, 572a, 575a, 577a, 643b
  evolution, III 575b
  existentialism, III 159b
  fate, III 571b, 573a
  fear, III 575a, 576a, 576b
  feeling, III 643b
  force, III 573b
  fortune, III 572a
  Franklin, IV 22a
  freedom, III 644a
  God, II 337b, 353a; III 571a–572b, 573b, 574b, 575a, 576a, 576b, 577a
  Godwin, III 643b
  good, III 571b, 572a, 575a, 575b, 576b, 577a, 643b; IV 173b, 175a
  Greece (ancient), III 570b–577b
  happiness, II 377a, 379b; III 576b, 577a, 644a
  health, III 574a
  Hecataeus, III 575a
  Hector (myth), III 571b
  hedonism, III 576b
  Hegel, III 556b
  Helen of Troy (myth), III 571b
  Helvétius, III 643a–643b
  Hera (myth), III 571b
  Heracles (myth), III 572a
  Heraclitus, III 571a, 572a, 573a, 573b
  Hermes (myth), III 571a
  Herodotus, III 571a–572a, 573a, 575a
  heroes, III 572a, 573a
  Hesiod, III 571b, 572b, 573a, 573b
  Hinduism, IV 231b
  Hippocrates, III 574a
  historiography, IV 150b
  history, III 576b
  Hobbes, III 575b, 576a
  Holbach, III 643a–643b
  Hölderlin, III 524a
  Homer, III 571a, 571b, 572a, 574b
  honor, III 576a

  humanism, II 518b
  Hume, III 232a, 575b; IV 248a, 433a
  Hutcheson, III 231a
  ignorance, III 577a, 643b
  immortality, III 571b, 572a, 572b, 573a, 573b, 577a
  individualism, III 572a, 577a
  injustice, III 577a
  instinct, III 644a
  Iphigeneia (myth), III 573a
  Jefferson, IV 21b, 22a
  justice, III 572b, 573a, 575a–577a
  Kant, III 442b
  Keats, III 524a
  knowledge, III 572a, 577a, 644a
  labor, III 644a
  law, III 574b–576a
  Leibniz, III 643b
  literature, III 571a–572b
  Locke, III 643b
  Lucretius, III 574b
  Machiavelli, III 315a, 480b, 481a, 481b–482a, 483a
  magic, III 571a
  Marx, II 450b, 451a
  Marxism, III 159b
  materialism, II 450b, 451a; III 577a
  Mead, G. H., III 554b
  medicine, III 574a
  Mesopotamia (ancient), III 572a
  microcosm, III 573b
  mind, III 576b–577a
  moral sense, III 231a–232b
  morality, III 572a–572b, 575a, 575b–576a, 577a, 643b, 644a, 645a
  mortality, III 571b, 572a, 573a, 573b, 577a
  mythology, III 302a, 571a–572b, 573a, 574b
  natural law, III 14b, 15a, 18b, 23b
  Nature, III 348a, 348b, 350a, 571a, 573b, 575b, 644a
  necessity, III 571b
  Neo-Platonism, III 373a
  nobility, III 572a
  Odysseus (myth), III 571b, 572b
  Oedipus (myth), III 572a
  ontogeny, III 573b–574a
  pain, III 643b
  Paris (myth), III 571b
  Parmenides, III 572a, 573a, 574a, 575b
  passions, III 572b, 573a, 575b, 576b, 644a
  peace, III 442b, 443b, 446a
  perfectibility, III 643a–644a

  philosophy, III 571a, 572a, 573a–574b, 575a, 577a
  phrenology, IV 23b
  phylogeny, III 573b–574a
  Pindar, III 571a, 571b–572a, 572b, 575a
  Plato, III 500b, 554b, 571a, 573a, 574b, 575a, 575b, 576a, 577a
  Platonism, III 500b, 524a
  pleasure, II 377a, 379b; III 576a, 576b, 577a, 643b
  poetry, III 571a, 571b, 572a, 572b
  politics, III 572b, 575a, 575b, 576a, 576b, 644a
  Polybius, III 574a
  positivism, III 534b
  power, III 571b, 572a, 572b, 574a, 575b, 576a
  pragmatism, III 554b, 556b, 569b
  pre-Platonic theories of, III 570b–577b
  Priam (myth), III 571b
  primitivism, III 581b
  Prodicus of Ceos, III 575a
  progress, III 628a, 634a, 638b, 640a, 643a–644a, 645a, 648a–648b
  Prometheus (myth), III 574b
  Protagoras, III 571a, 574b, 575b, 576b
  psychological schools, IV 10a–15b
  psychology, in U.S., IV 16a–29a
  punishment, III 572b, 575a, 576a
  Puritanism, IV 16b, 17b, 18a, 18b, 19a, 19b
  Pythagoras, III 572b–573a
  Quakers, IV 20a
  reality, III 572a, 575b
  relativism, IV 72a, 72b
  religion, III 572a; IV 105a, 107b, 108a, 111a
  Renaissance, IV 142b–143a, 150b
  responsibility, III 572a
  revisionism, IV 270b, 272a
  right, III 575b; IV 173b, 175a
  Sarpedon (myth), III 571b
  science, III 571a, 644a
  sex, III 575b
  Shelley, III 524a
  sin, IV 231b, 233a
  skepticism, IV 248a
  slavery, III 572a
  social contract, III 575b, 576a

socialism, IV 285b, 289b, 291a
society, III 572b, 574b–575b, 644b
Socrates, III 570b–571a, 576b–577a
Solon, III 572b, 573a
Sophists, III 571a, 573b, 575a, 575b
Sophocles, III 571a, 572a, 573a, 574b–575a
soul, III 572b–573a, 574a, 576b–577a
State, IV 315a
Stoics, III 348a
suffering, III 572b
temperament, III 573a
temperance, III 576b
theater, III 572a, 573a, 574a, 575b, 576a
Theseus (myth), III 572a
thought, III 574a
Thucydides, III 571a, 573b, 575b, 576a, 576b
tragedy, III 572a, 573a
tragic sense, IV 414a, 416a
truth, III 572a, 575a
unity, III 648a–648b
unity of science, IV 433a
Utopia, IV 463a
Valla, IV 142b–143a
vice, III 571b
virtue, III 571b, 577a; IV 478a–478b, 480b, 481a, 481b–482a, 483a
war, IV 506a
wealth, III 575b
wisdom, III 572a, 576b, 577a, 643b
wisdom of the fool, IV 518b, 519a
work, IV 532b
Xenophanes, III 572a, 573a, 573b, 574b
Xenophon, III 577a
Zeus (myth), III 571b, 572b
Human sacrifice
  ethics, IV 71a
  progress, III 629b
Humane Societies, IV 388a
  longevity, III 92a, 92b
Humanism, II 515a–524a; IV 129a–136a
  agnosticism, II 520a
  Agricola, II 519a
  Albert of Saxony, IV 134a
  Alberti, II 522a; IV 437b–438a, 439a–442b
  allegory, II 520a
  angels, IV 132a
  aprioristic conceptions, II 520a
  archeology, II 516a
  Archimedes, IV 133a

architecture, II 521b; IV 133a
argumentation, IV 129a
aristocracy, II 519b
Aristotelianism, II 520a, 521a, 521b; IV 130a, 131b, 132a, 133a, 134a–135a
Aristotle, II 516b, 519b, 520a; IV 129b, 132b–133a, 134a, 135a
art, II 516a, 517a, 517b, 519b, 521b, 523a; IV 130b, 131a, 133a, 134b
asceticism, IV 133b
astrology, II 517b, 520a, 521a
astronomy, II 521a
atheism, II 520a; IV 128a
atomism, III 187b
Augustinianism, II 520b
Aurispa, II 516b
Avicenna, II 521b
Barlaam (monk), II 516b
Basil, II 520b
beauty, IV 129b
Bessarion, II 516b
Bible, II 517b, 520b; IV 135a
Boccaccio, II 518a
bourgeois, II 521b–522a; IV 131a
Bruni, II 517b, 518a, 519b, 522a, 522b, 523a; IV 129b, 132b–133a
Buridan, IV 134a
Calvin, II 520b
Caroline miniscule, II 518a
Celsus, IV 133a
chance, II 225b, 235a, 236a
Chapman, III 294b
charity, II 214a, 215a
Charlemagne, II 515a
Christianity, II 520a–520b; IV 129b, 130b, 131a, 132b, 134b, 135a
Chrysoloras, II 516b
Chrysostom, II 520b
Cicero, II 515a, 515b, 516a; IV 129b
Ciriaco of Ancona, II 516b
city-state, II 518b
class, II 521b
Columbus, IV 131a
Constantine, IV 130b
continuity, IV 134b
Copernicus, II 521a; IV 134a
copyists, II 516a, 516b
coronations, II 517a
cosmology, II 520a, 521a; IV 134a, 134b
Counter-Renaissance, IV 130a, 135a
craftsmanship, IV 133a,

134b
criticism, II 516a, 518b
culture, II 515b, 520a; IV 129b, 130a, 130b
Dante, II 517b; IV 132a
Decembrio, II 522b
defined, II 515a, 516a
deism, I 648b
Descartes, II 351a, 523a
despotism, II 4a
dialectics, II 520b, 521b
Diderot, III 141a
dignity, IV 136b, 137b, 141a–146a
Diogenes Laërtius, II 520a
discontinuity, IV 134b
dissonance, II 521b
drama, II 517b
Duhem, IV 130a
Eastern Orthodox Church, II 515a, 516b
eclogues, II 517b
economics, IV 129b
editors, II 516a
education, II 515a–515b, 516a, 519a–519b, 522a, 523a; IV 129b, 130b, 438b–440a, 440b, 441a
elegies, II 517b
eloquence, II 519a; IV 129b
empiricism, II 521a; IV 134a, 135a
Enlightenment, II 90a
epics, II 517b
Epictetus, II 520a
Epicureanism, II 520a
Epicurus, II 520a; IV 133b
epigrams, II 516a, 517b
epigraphy, II 516a
epistemology, II 515a, 515b
Erasmus, II 520a, 520b; III 514b; IV 135a
eschatology, II 158b, 159b
Euclid, IV 135a–135b
evolution, II 518b
existentialism, III 158a, 160a
experience, IV 134a
faith, II 214a, 215a; IV 134b, 135a
fate, II 225b, 235a, 236a
Faust (legend), III 246b
Feltre, II 519a–519b
Ficino, II 520a, 521b; IV 131b–132a, 144a–145a
Apuleius, III 292b
Filelfo, II 516b, 519b
fortune, II 225b, 235a, 236a, 519b
France, II 515a, 515b, 517b, 522b; IV 131a
Frederick II, II 515a
free will, II 245b; IV 131a–131b, 132a

freedom, IV 130a, 131a–131b, 135b
Galen, II 521b; IV 133a
Galileo, II 521a, 523a; IV 130a, 133a, 134a, 134b, 135b
Gandhi, III 446a
Gellius, IV 129b
genetics, II 518b
geography, II 521b
Geremia of Montagnone, II 517b
Geri of Arezzo, II 515b
Germany, II 515b, 520b
glory, II 522a
God, II 347a, 348b, 351a, 351b, 520a; IV 131a, 131b, 132a, 132b
Golden Age (myth), IV 131a
good, II 519b; IV 133b, 180b
Gothic, II 367b, 518a
grammar, II 515a, 515b, 516a, 516b, 519a
Great Britain, II 520b; III 483b, 484b; IV 131a
Greece (ancient), II 515a, 516a–516b; IV 129b, 131a, 131b, 132b–133a
Gregory of Nazianzus, II 520b
Guarino of Verona, II 519a–519b; IV 133a
Guelfism, II 522b
Guicciardini, II 518b
handwriting, II 518a
happiness, II 519b; IV 132a
harmony, II 388b, 521a, 521b; IV 41a, 134b
Haydn, IV 130a, 135a
health, IV 133b
Herder, III 326a
heresy, II 419a, 425b–426a, 427b, 430b, 520b
Herodotus, II 516b
heroes, II 520a
Heytesbury, IV 129a
hierarchy, IV 131a
Hippocrates, II 521b; IV 133a, 135a–135b
historiography, II 482a, 482b, 483a, 484b, 485b, 486a, 518a–518b; IV 130b, 131a, 134b, 148a–148b
history, II 515b–517b, 518b; IV 129a–132b, 135a
holy, II 513a
Homer, II 516b, 517b
honor, II 522a; IV 133a
hope, II 212b
human nature, II 518b
Humphrey, II 519a
iconography, II 521b, 528a,

529b, 530a, 531a, 532a, 532b, 533a, 539b
idealism, II 522a
imitation, II 518a
individualism, II 517a, 519b, 522a
infinity, IV 129a
instinct, IV 135a
irrationalism, II 637b
Islam, II 650a
Isocrates, II 516b
Italy, II 515a–524a; IV 129a–135b
Jaeger, IV 129b
James, III 568a
Jesuits, II 520b
Jesus Christ, II 517b; IV 132b
Judaism, IV 130b
justice, II 653b, 658b; IV 131a
Kepler, II 521a; IV 134a
knowledge, II 650a; IV 132a, 133a, 135b
language, II 515b, 516a–516b, 517b–518a, 520a, 667a; IV 130b, 131a, 135a
Latin language, IV 130b
law, II 515a, 519a, 521b; IV 130b, 132b, 135a
Leonardo da Vinci, IV 130a, 133a, 134a, 440b, 442a, 442b
letter-writing, II 515b–519a
liberalism, II 520a
liberty, II 522b
libraries, II 519a, 522a
literary criticism, I 603a
literary paradox, III 77b, 81a
literature, II 515b–522b, 523a; IV 124a, 130b, 131a, 134b
love, III 100a
Lucian, III 292b
Lucretius, II 516a, 520a
Luther, II 520a; IV 135a
Machiavelli, II 519b; IV 132b, 135a, 479a
magic, II 521a; IV 134a
Manetti, II 520b; IV 131a–131b
Manilius, II 516a
Man-Machine, III 141a
Manutius, II 516a, 518a
Marx, II 450b, 454b; III 168a
Marxism, III 158a, 160a, 168a, 169a
materialism, II 450b, 454b, 455a
mathematics, II 515b, 521a; IV 129a, 134a
matter, III 187b, 193b

Matthias Corvinus, II 519a
mechanics, II 200b, 203a–204a
Medici family, II 518a, 523a
medicine, II 515b, 519a, 521a; IV 132b, 135a
Melanchthon, II 520b
metaphysics, II 515b, 519a, 520a
methodology, II 519a
Middle Ages, II 515a–523a; IV 129b–135b, 153b
mimesis, III 227b
miracles, IV 133a
monarchy, II 519b, 522b–523a
Montaigne, IV 135a
morality, II 515b, 516a, 518a–519b, 522b–523a; IV 132a, 132b, 133b,
More, II 520b; III 514b; IV 461a
music, II 388b, 521b; III 260b, 261a–261b; IV 133b
Mussato, II 515b, 517a, 517b
mythology, II 516a, 516b, 517b, 518b; III 289b–293a, 293b, 294b
nationalism, III 323b, 327b
naturalism, IV 132b–134b
Nature, IV 129a, 131a, 133a, 133b, 134a, 134b
Neo-Platonism, II 519b; IV 131b, 132a–132b
Niccoli, II 518a, 522a
Nicolas of Oresme, IV 134a
Nietzsche, IV 180b
nominalism, II 520b
novella, II 517a
numbers, II 521a
odes, II 517b
oligarchy II 522a, 522b
oratory, II 515a, 515b, 516a, 517a
Orientalism, III 432b
origin of the term, II 515b
Ovid, II 516a, 517b
paganism, II 520a
pain, IV 133b
painting, II 521b; IV 133a, 469a, 474b
Palmieri, II 522a; IV 132b
pantheism, II 520a
papacy, II 522b
Patrizi, II 520a
peace, III 446a; IV 131a
perennial philosophy, III 459b
periodization in history, III 476b, 477a, 477b, 479b
periodization in literary history, III 483b, 484b
Petrarch, II 515b, 516b,

517a–518a, 520b; III 509b; IV 125b, 129a–129b, 141b–142a
philology, II 516b, 518b, 519a, 520a
philosophy, II 515a, 515b, 516a, 516b, 519a–520a, 521a, 522b–523a; IV 129a, 129b, 132a, 132b, 134b
physics, II 521a; IV 132b, 133a, 134b
Pico della Mirandola, II 520a; IV 131b, 132a, 134b
Pietism, II 520a
Pirandello, III 568a
Plato, II 516b, 519b, 520a, 521b; IV 129b, 131a, 131b
Platonism, II 520a, 521a; III 504b, 507b, 509b, 514a, 514b; IV 131b–132b, 134a, 134b
pleasure, IV 133b
Plotinus, II 520a
poetry, II 515b, 517a–517b; III 529a, 530b; IV 129b, 130b, 135a, 469a, 474b
Poggio, II 517b, 518a, 519b, 522a
politics, II 517a, 518b, 519a, 519b, 522a, 522b–523a; IV 129b, 130b, 131a, 132b
Poliziano, II 517b
Pontano, II 517b
positivism, III 535b, 536a, 538a
poverty, IV 132b
power, IV 133b
pragmatism, III 553a, 568a
pre-humanism, II 515b
printing, II 516a, 516b, 518a, 519a
progress, III 626a–626b
propaganda, II 517a, 522a, 522b
Propertius, II 517b
Protestantism, II 520a, 520b, 523a; IV 135
Protorenaissances, II 515a
psychology, IV 16b
Ptolemy, II 521b
Puritanism, IV 16b
Pythagoreans, II 521a; IV 41a
Raimondi, IV 133b
Ramism, IV 42b, 43a, 44b, 45a–45b
Ramus, IV 42b, 43a, 45a–45b, 135b
realism, II 520b
reason, II 519b; IV 134a, 134b, 135a
rebirth, IV 129a, 130b, 131a

reformation, IV 61b
Reformation, II 520b, 523a; IV 135a
religion, II 519b, 520b; IV 132a, 132b
research, IV 134b
revolution, IV 153b
rhetoric, II 515a–522b; IV 129a, 171a, 171b
Rolando of Piazzola, II 517b
Roman Catholic Church, II 516b, 520b, 523a
romanticism, IV 195a, 201b
Rome (ancient), II 515a, 516a, 517a; III 476b; IV 130b, 132b
Saint Augustine, II 520b
Saint Dominic, IV 132b
Saint Francis of Assisi, IV 132b
Saint Thomas Aquinas, II 515a; IV 129b, 134b
Salutati, II 515b, 517b–518a, 519b, 522a, 522b, 523a; IV 129b, 132b
salvation, II 518b
satire, II 517b; IV 214b
scholasticism, II 519b; IV 129b, 133b–134a, 134b
science, II 200b, 203a–204a, 516a, 517a, 517b, 519b, 520b–521a, 523a; IV 129b, 130a, 132a–134b
Seneca, II 516a
Sforza, II 518a
skepticism, II 520a–520b; IV 135a, 241b–242a, 243a
socialism, IV 292a, 294a
society, II 522a; IV 131b, 133a, 135a
sociology, II 521b–522a
soul, IV 131b–132b, 133b
Spain, II 520b; IV 131a
spelling, II 516a
State, II 519b, 522b; IV 129b, 132b
Stoicism, II 520a; IV 129a, 135a
Strabo, II 521b
structuralism, IV 328b–329a
Swineshead, IV 129a
Sylvester (Pope), IV 130b
symbolism, II 521a
Tacitus, II 516a
technology, II 521a
theodicy, IV 383b
theology, II 515a, 515b, 516b, 517b, 520b; IV 129b, 130a, 131b, 132a
Thomism, II 520b
Thucydides, II 516b
Tibullus, II 517b
Tolstoy, III 445b

Tortelli, II 516b
tradition, II 515a, 519b; IV 131b, 135a
Traversari, II 520b
truth, IV 129b, 130a, 135a, 135b
unity, IV 132a
universal man, IV 437b, 438b–443a
universe, IV 41a, 521a
Utopia, IV 461a
Valla, II 519a, 519b, 520a, 520b; IV 129b, 130b, 133b, 134a, 135a–135b
Vergil, II 516a
virtù, IV 477a, 478a–479a
Visconti, II 522b
wealth, IV 133b
wisdom, II 519a; IV 129b, 132a, 133b
wisdom of the fool, IV 518b, 519b
women, IV 526a
work, IV 134b, 135a, 532a
Xenophon, II 516b
See also Renaissance
Humanitarianism
Cuba, III 544b
equality, II 143b, 144a
Floresta, III 540a
Judaism, III 487b, 488a
Mussolini, III 597a
nationalism, III 331a
natural law, III 17a, 17b
peace, III 441a
philanthropy, III 486b, 487a, 487b, 488a, 490b, 491a–491b
Pietism, III 494b
positivism, III 544b
primitivism, III 597a
progress, III 636b, 647a
psychology, IV 19b, 23b, 24a, 27a
romanticism, IV 205a
Stoicism, III 17a, 17b
transcendentalism, IV 24a
Humason, M. L., cosmology, I 565a, 567b
Humboldt, Alexander von (1769–1859)
conservation, I 473a–473b
cosmic images, I 520a
environment, II 128b, 130a
Humboldt, Wilhelm von (1767–1835)
anarchism, I 71a
historicism, II 460a
individualism, II 595b, 598a
liberalism, III 49b, 51b
linguistics, III 67b, 70b, 71a, 71b; IV 427b
literary criticism, I 598a

structuralism, IV 324b, 325a
Volksgeist, IV 494a
Hume, David (1711–1776),
abstraction, I 6b, 7a–9a
aesthetics, III 232a, 232b–233a; IV 355b, 356a
agnosticism, I 19a, 20a, 23b
Al-Ghazali and, I 274a
anarchy, I 437b
art for art's sake, I 108b
art and play, I 103b
attitude toward antiquity, I 80a–80b
balance of power, I 180a–180b
beauty, I 201b, 202b; III 232b
behaviorism, I 219a, 219b–220a, 221b
benevolence, III 232a, 232b
Bentham and, I 317a, 317b–318a; III 234a
Berkeley and, I 312b
Burke and, IV 203b
catharsis, I 266a, 268a, 268b
causation, I 273a–277b, 290b, 291a, 294a, 295a–296b, 298b–300a, 339b, 674b–675a; II 238a; III 232b
certainty, I 304b, 312a–318a, 319b, 320a, 321b, 323b
chance, I 339b
change, IV 395a
civil disobedience, I 437b
classification of the arts, I 460b
commodities, III 232b
compulsion, II 238a, 240a
Cosmic Fall, I 511b
Counter-Enlightenment, II 101b, 103b–104a, 109b, 110a
creativity in art, I 588a
death, I 641a, 642a, 645a
deism, I 651b
Descartes and, III 357b
design argument, I 674b, 675a–676b
determinism, II 238a, 239a, 239b–240a; III 357b
economic history, II 45a–45b, 57b
empathy, II 88a
empiricism, I 291a, 296b, 319b; II 582a; III 231b, 233a, 545b, 546b, 547a, 550b; IV 203b
Enlightenment, II 89b, 91a, 92a–98a, 99a, 100a
environment, II 120b, 128b

eschatology, II 160a
ethics, III 231b, 232a, 233a, 233b, 235a; IV 70a–70b, 71b, 72a, 72b,
evil, IV 382b
free will, II 238a–240a, 246a
God, I 312a, 313b, 675b–676a; II 352a–353a, 353b, 355b; IV 247b, 382b
good, IV 178a, 382b
Hamann and, II 103a–104a
happiness, II 380a, 381a; III 232a, 232b
Herder and, IV 203b
as historian, III 358a
history, II 92a; IV 203b
human nature, III 232a, 575b; IV 248a
Hutcheson and, III 230a–230b, 231b, 232a, 232b
idea, I 113b, 116a; II 547b, 548a
immortality, I 641a, 642a, 645a
impressionism, II 582a
individualism, II 603a, 603b
justice, III 232a, 232b; IV 178a
Kames and, III 234b
Kant and, I 314a–316b; III 357b–358a; IV 209a
knowledge, I 313a–314a, 316a, 321b; II 103b–104a, 239b, 582a; III 233a
language, I 314a
law, I 291a
Leibniz and, I 312b; IV 382a
liberalism, III 44b, 46b, 47a
liberty, II 95a, 239b–240a
Lipps and, II 88a
Locke and, IV 261b
Machiavellism, III 121b
mathematics, I 312a–312b, 320a
metaphor, III 199b
metaphysical imagination, III 218b
mind, II 120b
money, II 45a–45b, 57b
moral sense, III 230a–230b, 231b–235a
morality, III 471b; IV 247b
mythology, III 302a, 303b
natural law, III 232b–233a
natural liberty, II 64a
Nature, I 277a, 312a, 511b, 641a; II 92a, 94a; IV 247b–248a
necessity, II 238a; III 357b–358a, 359b
Newton and, I 312a, 312b, 313b
pain, II 381a; III 232a

peace, III 444a
Peirce and, III 558a, 560b
perennial philosophy, III 462b
perfectibility, III 471b
pity, I 266a
pleasure, II 380a, 381a; III 232a–232b
positivism, III 359b, 545b, 546b, 547a, 550b
power, II 240a
pragmatism, III 558a, 560b, 563a
Price and, III 233a
pride, III 232b
probability, III 612a
psychology, III 239b; IV 11b, 20a, 22b
rationalism, III 232a, 232b–233a, 302a, 303a–303b; IV 247b
reason, I 312a–314a; II 96a; III 231b, 232a, 233a, 303a–303b, 471b; IV 247b
Reid and, III 234a
reincarnation, I 645a
relativism, IV 70a–70b, 71b, 72a, 72b
religion, IV 93a–93b
responsibility, II 240a
revolution, IV 154b, 155a
right, IV 178a
romanticism, IV 202a, 203b, 209a
rules, III 232b
sacred, II 513a
senses, II 582a
skepticism, I 277b, 278a; II 96a, 352b; IV 241a, 241b, 245b, 247b–248a, 248b, 249a, 250b
Smith, Adam and, III 233a
social contract, III 575b; IV 254a–254b
society, II 99a; IV 261b
sympathy, III 232a–232b; IV 178a
State, IV 261b
sublime in external nature, IV 336b
taste, III 232a; IV 355b
theodicy, IV 382a, 382b, 383b
time, IV 395a
tragedy, I 268a, 268b
truth, II 101b
unity of science, IV 432b
universe, I 314a
utilitarianism, II 97a, 380a; III 232a, 232b; IV 444b, 448b
Vico and, III 357b
violence, IV 261b
Volksgeist, IV 491b, 492a

work, IV 534b
Humors
  disease, II 398a–398b, 400a, 400b
  Man-Machine, III 133a–133b
  microcosm, III 128a
  Seneca, III 128a
Humphrey, Duke of Gloucester (1391–1447), humanism, II 519a
Hundred Years' War, papacy and, I 386a
Huneker, James (1860–(1921)
  irony, II 633b
  symbolism, IV 341a, 341b
  Wilson and, IV 341b
Hungary
  balance of power, I 181b
  baroque in literature, I 191a, 193a
  communism, III 334a
  Counter-Enlightenment, II 106a
  literary criticism, I 606b
  Magyars, I 381a
  Marxism, III 156a, 166a–166b, 167a
  nationalism, III 334a
  protest movements, III 673a
  realism in literature, IV 55b
  revolution, III 166b
  U.S.S.R., III 334a
Hunger, disease, II 404b
Hunt, Leigh (1784–1859), romanticism, IV 192a, 194a
Hunter, W. S. (1889–1954), behaviorism, I 223a, 223b
Hunting
  conservation, I 474a
  cosmology and, I 535b
  Gothic, II 368b
  as mechanical art, II 313b
  private property, III 650b, 651a
  religion, IV 100a
  scientific classification, I 464b
Huntington, Ellsworth (1876–1947) environment, II 131b
Huntington, S. P., war, IV 506a, 506b
Hurd, Bishop Richard (1719–1808)
  catharsis, I 265b
  Gothic, II 368b, 370a
  literature, IV 187b
  periodization in literary history, III 482a
  pity, I 265b
  romanticism, IV 187b
Hurwicz, L., game theory, II 272a

Hus, Jan (1369?–1415),
  heresy, II 419a, 426b
  history, I 387a
  reformation, IV 65b
Husserl, Edmund (1859–1938)
  abstraction, I 18a
  appearance and reality, I 98b
  Bacon and, I 178b
  certainty, I 322a
  empiricism, III 550a
  existentialism, II 192b, 193b, 194a
  irrationalism, II 636a, 637a
  metaphor, III 207a
  phenomenology, I 98b, 322a
  Platonism, III 522b
  psychology, IV 13b, 14a
  space, IV 305a
  structuralism, IV 329a
  time, IV 396b–397a
  truth, I 322a–322b
Hussites
  heresy, II 420b, 421b, 422a, 428a
  socialism, IV 287a
  Waldensians, II 420b
Hutcheson, Francis (1694–1746)
  aesthetics, I 588a; III 230b–231a; IV 355b
  association of ideas, I 112b
  Balguy and, III 233a
  beauty, I 198b–199b; III 231a, 231b
  benevolence, III 231a, 231b, 232a
  Bentham and, III 234a
  Butler (Bishop) and, III 231a
  classification of the arts, I 460b
  creativity in art, I 588a
  Diderot and, I 199b
  empiricism, III 231b
  Enlightenment, II 89b, 97b–98a, 100a
  ethics, III 231a–231b, 232a; IV 70b, 71b, 72a, 72b
  Gay and, III 233a
  happiness, II 380a, 380b; III 231b
  Hartley and, III 234b
  hatred, III 231a
  honor, III 231b, 232b
  Hume and, III 230a–230b, 231b, 232a, 232b
  illuminists, IV 109a
  Kames and, III 234b
  knowledge, III 231b
  love, III 231a, 231b
  malevolence, III 231a

Mandeville and, III 231a
  moral sense, III 230a–234b
  morality, II 380a
  pain, III 231b
  pleasure, II 380a, 380b; III 231b, 232b
  Price and, III 233a
  psychology, IV 22b
  rationalism, III 231b, 232a
  relativism, IV 70b, 71b, 72a, 72b
  religion, IV 109a, 111a
  self-love, III 231a
  senses, III 231b
  Smith, Adam, and, III 233b
  sympathy, III 232b
  taste, IV 355b
  utilitarianism, II 97b–98a, 380b; III 231a–231b, 234a; IV 444a–444b, 447a, 448b
Hutchins, R. M., education, II 73b, 83a
Hutten, Ulrich von (1488–1523), literary paradox, III 79a
Hutton, James (1726–1797),
  catastrophism, IV 419a, 419b, 420a, 420b
  continuity, I 499b
  uniformitarianism, I 499b; IV 419a, 419b, 420a, 420b
Huusman, Roelof, see Agricola, Rudolph
Huxley, Aldous (1894–1963),
  Buddhism, I 256a
  comedy, I 469b
  idea, I 111b
  longevity, III 89b
  perennial philosophy, III 458a, 462b
  perfectibility, III 474b
  satire, IV 214b, 215b
  Utopia, IV 464a
Huxley, Julian (1887–   ),
  Chain of Being, I 334a
  education, III 474a
  evolution, II 187b, 188a
  evolutionism, III 474a
  morality, III 474a
  natural selection, III 474a
  perfectibility, III 474a
  universe, III 474a
  Wallace and, III 474a
Huxley, Thomas Henry (1825–1895)
  agnosticism, I 17a–19a, 20a–21b, 22b–23a
  association of ideas, I 111b
  Bible, I 18a–18b, 21a
  certainty, I 318b
  Cosmic Fall, I 511b
  Darwin and, I 318b
  Darwinism of, I 17b; IV

107a
  determinism, II 24a
  evolution, III 474a, 647a
  evolutionism, II 180a–180b, 183b, 186b, 187a
  historiography, II 24a
  Jesus, I 18b
  linguistics, IV 424a, 424b, 425a, 427b, 428b
  Nature, I 511b; II 183b
  perfectibility, III 474a
  positivism, III 538b, 541b
  progress, III 647a
  religion, IV 107a, 108a
  social contract, IV 263a
  spontaneous generation, IV 311b
  uniformitarianism, IV 424a, 424b, 425a, 427b, 428b
Huygens, Christian (1629–1695)
  atomism, I 138a
  Bernoulli and, III 607a
  calculus, III 606b–607a
  Carcavi and, III 607a
  chance, I 337b
  color, III 418a
  cosmology, I 547b–548a, 548a, 550a
  eighteenth century view of, I 78b, 177a
  game theory, II 264a
  genius, II 294b
  light, III 418a
  mathematics, III 179a
  matter, III 194a
  metaphysical imagination, III 217a
  methodology, III 389a
  mind, III 418a
  Newton and, III 389a, 395a
  optics, III 395a, 418a
  perennial philosophy, III 461a
  poetry, III 395a
  probability, III 606b–607a
  relativity, IV 77a, 77b, 78a
  technology, IV 362a
  time, IV 403a
Huysmans, Joris-Karl (1848–1907)
  impressionism, II 575a
  symbolism, IV 340b
Hyacinthus (myth), III 272b
Hybridization, acquired characteristics, II 618a, 618b, 621a
Hybris, see Hubris
Hyde, Thomas (1636–1703), dualism, II 38a
Hygeia (goddess), environment, II 122b
Hygiene, II 397a–397b
  prolongivity, III 91b

Hyginus Gromaticus (2nd century A.D.), the city, I 428b

Hyginus, Gaius (1st century B.C.), mythology, III 299b

Hylomorphism
Aristotle, III 187a–187b, 189a, 194a
Bruno, III 194a
Islam, II 645a
matter, III 187a–187b, 189a, 194a
organicism, III 423b

Hylozoism, I 61b, 70b, 229b
biology, I 229b, 234b
Greece (ancient), I 61b, 68a, 70a
matter, III 187a

Hymns, III 266a, 269b
God, II 343b
impiety, II 564a
mimesis, II 226a
mythology, III 284b
Platonism, III 498a

Hyperboreans (myth)
Nature, III 348b
primitivism, III 591a
Utopia, IV 460a

Hypotheses
explanatory, III 199a
Galileo, III 356a
metaphor, III 197b–200a, 201a
methodology, III 379b, 383b, 385b
necessity, III 356a, 357a
Newton, III 184a, 379b, 383b, 385b
sources, III 197b–198a
unity of science, IV 431b, 435a
world, III 197b–198b, 200a

Hypsicles (fl. 200 B.C.), mathematics, III 182b

Hysteria, catharsis, I 269a

I

Ialdabaoth (Bible), Gnosticism, II 328b, 329a

Iamblichus (d. about 333 A.D.)
astrology, I 125a
catharsis, I 269a, 270a
classification of the sciences, I 462b
comedy, I 467b
dualism, IV 346b–347a
harmony, IV 39a
hermeticism, II 432b
hierarchy, II 439a
music, III 269a

mythology, III 292a
Neo-Platonism, III 376a, 376b, 377a
Porphyry and, III 376b
Pythagoreans, IV 32a, 35a, 35b, 39a
symmetry, IV 346b–347a
universe, IV 39a

Iambulus, progress, III 630a

Iason of Pherai, ideas, II 504a

Ibn al-Haytham (965?–?1039), see Alhazen

Ibn al-Shatir, cosmology, I 544a

Ibn 'Arabī (1165–1240)
Islam, II 648b, 650a, 650b–651a, 651b
love, III 99b, 101a

Ibn Bajjah (Avempace) (d. 1138), Islam, II 648b–649a

Ibn-Dawoud (1110?–1180), love, III 99b

Ibn Gabirol, see Avicebron

Ibn Hazm of Cordova (994–1064)
Islam, II 641a, 648b
love, II 648b; III 107b

Ibn Ishāq, Hunayn, II 640b

Ibn Khaldun (1332–1406), II 650a
class, I 442b
historiography, II 475a, 479a–479b, 485a

Ibn Masarrah (777–857)
cosmology, II 648b

Ibn Muqaffa', convert to Islam, II 640b

Ibn Qutaibah (828–?889), classification of the sciences, I 463b

Ibn Rushd, II 649a–649b; see also Averroës

Ibn Sab'in (1217?–1269), II 650a

Ibn-Tofail (Tufayl) (d. 1185), II 649a
causation, I 273b

Ibn Yusuf, Ahmad, medieval science, II 200a

Ibsen, Henrik (1828–1906)
Kierkegaard and, IV 416b
literature, III 84b
symbolism, IV 341a, 344b
tragic sense, IV 416b–417a
world literature, III 84b

Icarus (myth), cosmic voyages, I 524a, 529a

Iceland
Christianity, III 592b
Gothic, II 367a
Middle Ages, III 592b
primitivism, III 592b

Icelandic language, III 66b–67a

Iconography, II 524a–541b
abstraction, II 525b, 534a, 539a
Alain de Lille, II 526a–526b
Alberti, II 528a, 528b
Alciati, II 530b
Alföldi, II 537b
Algarotti, II 533a
allegory, II 525b–527b, 530b–534a, 540a
Alpatov, II 535b
Altdorfer, II 531b
archaeology, II 535a
Ariosto, II 531a
Aristotelianism, II 526b, 532b
Aristotle, II 525a
art, II 525b–528a, 530a–540b
Bauer, II 538b
Bayeux Tapestry, II 528a
Bellori, II 528b, 534b
Berliner, II 538b, 540b
Bernini, II 530a, 538a
Bible, II 527b, 528a, 539a
Blake, II 533b
Blunt, II 538a
Bober, II 538b
Borromeo, II 531a
Botticelli, II 529b
Braun, II 535b
Bréhier, II 535a
Bruegel, II 529b, 531b, 538a
Byzantine Empire, II 526a, 535b, 539b
Cassirer, II 536a
Caylus, II 533a, 534b
Cézanne, II 538b
Chantelou, II 528b
Chastel, II 538a
Chateaubriand, II 535a
Christianity, II 525b–526a, 533b
city, I 429b
classicism, II 539b
Clements, II 537b
Colonna, II 529b
Correggio, II 529a, 538a
Cossa, II 535b–536a
Council of Trent, II 531a
Counter-Reformation, II 526b, 532b, 535b
Creuzer, II 535a
criticism, II 534a–540b
Croce, II 540a
Crosnier, II 535a
Cubism, II 534a
Cumont, II 540a
David, II 533b
Delacroix, II 538b
Detzel, II 535b
didactic doctrine, II 526b–527a, 528a, 529b

Didron, II 535a
Dionysius of Fourna, II 526a
disguised symbolism, II 531b
Dobrzeniecki, II 538b
documentation, II 538b–539b
Dossi, II 529b
Durandus, II 527a
Dürer, II 529b, 530b
Egypt (ancient), II 526a
emblems, II 530a, 530b, 531a, 533b, 537b, 538a
Enlightenment, II 533a, 533b
Erasmus of Rotterdam, II 530a
Erffa, II 538a
Erigena, II 526a
Félibien, II 534b
Filla, II 534a
Fontainebleau, II 529b, 538a
Forssman, II 539b
François I, II 529b, 538a
Friedländer, II 538a
Gerson, H., II 539a
Gerson, Jean, II 526b
Giarda, II 532b
Giehlow, II 537b
Ginzburg, II 539b
Giorgione, II 529b
Giovio, II 530a
God, II 340b, 343a, 343b–344a, 526a–526b, 527a, 527b
Gombrich, II 538a
Görres, II 535a
Goya, II 533b, 538a
Grabar, II 537b
Greece (ancient), II 525a–528b
Gregory I (the Great), Pope, II 526b
Heckscher, II 537b
Held, II 538a
Henkel, II 538a
Herder, II 535a, 540a
Hermeren, II 539b
Hersey, II 538b
hieroglyphic signs, II 529b, 530a–531a, 537b, 538a
Hinks, II 525a–528b
history, II 525a, 526a, 528a–529b, 532a, 539a, 539b, 540a–540b
Hoffmann, II 538b
Holbein, II 529b
Hoogewerff, II 536a–536b
Hugh of St. Victor, II 526a
humanism, II 521b, 528a, 529b, 530a, 531a, 532a, 532b, 533a, 539b

Iconographic Index, II 539a–539b; *see* Iconology
imagery, II 526a, 526b, 527a, 530a–530b, 532b, 536a
imago, II 525b
implied, II 534a–540b
impressionism, II 534a
intrinsic meaning, II 536b–537a
Italy, II 529a–529b
Jerphanon, II 535a
Jesus Christ, II 525a, 526a, 527b, 528a, 530a, 539a
Jung, II 540a
Kalinowski, II 538b
Kant, II 536a
Kantorowicz, II 537b
Katzenellenbogen, II 538b
Lebrun, II 533a
Leclerq, II 535b
Leonardo da Vinci, II 529a
Leroquais, II 535a
Lessing, II 528b, 535a
Leszczyński, II 532a
literature, II 528a–529a, 530a, 531a, 537b
L'Orange, II 537b
Lotto, II 529b
Lucian, II 534a
Luther, II 530b
Mâle, II 530b, 535b, 537b, 538b
Mander, II 530a, 531a
Mantegna, II 529a
Manutius, II 529b
Marino, II 534b
Martin, II 538a
Master of the Housebook, II 531b
Maximilian I, II 530b
Medici family, II 529b
Michelangelo, II 529a, 529b, 530a, 538b, 540b
Middle Ages, II 526b–528a, 529a, 530b, 540b
Millet, II 535b
Molanus, II 524b, 531a, 534b
Molsdorf, II 535b
Monroy, II 537b
morality, II 533b
Morey, II 535b, 538b
Mrazek, II 538b
mythology, II 524b–525b, 528a, 529a–535a, 536b, 539a, 540a; III 286b, 288b, 290b, 292a, 293a, 298a, 299a
Neo-Platonism, II 526a, 526b, 527a, 527b, 530a, 535a, 538a
Netherlands, II 530b, 532a–532b

nude in, II 531a–531b
numbers, II 527b
origin of the term, II 524a–524b
Orthodox, II 535b
Ovid, II 529a, 531a, 534b
painted enigmas, II 533a
Paleotti, II 531a
Panofsky, D., II 529b
Panofsky, Erwin, II 529a, 529b, 531b, 536a–540a
Paulinus of Nola, II 526b
Perdrizet, II 535a
personification, II 525b
Philostratus, II 534a
Pisano, II 529a
poetry, II 529a–529b, 531a, 536a
Pokrovski, II 535b
politics, II 526a, 533b, 536b, 537b
Pope-Hennessy, II 538a
Poussin, II 528b, 534b, 538a
Praz, II 537b
Previtali, II 539b
Protestantism, II 530b
Pseudo-Bonaventure, II 528a
Pseudo-Dionysius, II 526a, 527a
pseudomorphosis, II 529a
psychology, II 540a–540b
Ramism, IV 44a–44b, 45b
Raphael, II 529a, 538a
realism, II 532a–532b, 534a
Réau, II 535b
religion, II 524b–525a, 526a, 530b, 531a–539b
Rembrandt, II 538a
Renaissance, II 528a–532a, 534a, 538a
research, II 540a–540b
Ripa, II 530a, 530b–531a, 532a, 532b, 533a
Rohault de Fleury, II 535a
Roman Catholic Church, II 532b
romanticism, II 533b–534a, 535a, 538b
Rome (ancient), II 525b
Rubens, II 531b, 533a
Ruthwell Cross, II 527a
saints, II 526a–528a
Saxl, II 529a, 536a, 537b
Schapiro, M., II 538b, 540b
Schlegel, F., II 535b
scholarship, II 534a–540b
Schöne, II 538a
Schramm, II 537b
sculpture, II 534a
Seznec, II 538b
Sistine Chapel, II 529b
Stanza della Segnatura, II

529b
Steen, II 532b
Strabo, II 527a
Suger, II 527a–527b
symbolism, II 525a–531b, 534a, 534b, 535a, 537b, 540a
Tasso, II 531a
temperance, IV 371a–378a
Teyssèdrey, II 539b
theater, II 538a
Thompson, II 539a
Timmers, II 535b
Titian, II 529a, 529b, 538a
tomb decorations, II 525b, 531b, 540a
Valerius Maximus, II 531a
van Gelder, II 538a
van Gogh, II 538b
van Marle, II 537b
van de Waal, II 532a, 538a, 539a–539b
Vasari, II 524b, 534b
Vergil, II 531a
Vico, II 538b
Vincent of Beauvais, II 527a
Virgin Mary, II 526a, 528a
virtue, IV 371a–378a
wall-paintings, II 529b
Warburg, II 535b, 536a
Wilbert, II 537b
William I, II 528a
Winckelmann, II 533a
Wind, II 538a
Wirth, II 537b
Wittkower, II 538b
Wormald, II 538b
Iconology, II 524b, 536a–540a
motif, III 236b
pleasure, II 383b
wisdom of the fool, IV 516a, 516b
Idea, II 542a–549a
abstraction, II 542a–542b, 546b, 599b–600b, 601b
adjectives, II 542a
Adam (Bible), II 546b
Aeschylus, II 545a
aesthetics, II 223a, 546a, 548b
anti-Platonism, II 547a
Aristotelianism, II 545a, 547a
Aristotle, I 111b; II 543a, 543b–545a, 546a, 663b; IV 34b, 35a
art, II 544a, 544b, 547a–547b
association of ideas, I 111a–118a
atomism, II 547b
autonomy, II 598a–598b, 602b, 603a

Bacon, II 547a
beauty, II 545b
Berkeley, II 547b
Boethius, II 546a
Brown, Thomas, I 116a
causation, II 544a–544b 548a–548b
Coleridge, I 117a
Comte, II 547b; III 535a, 535b
Condillac, I 113b; II 547b
Condorcet, I 114a, 114b
Cordemoy, II 548a
Darwin, Charles, I 115b, 116a
Darwin Erasmus, I 114b, 115a, 116a
deduction, II 543a
Democritus, II 547b
Descartes, I 111b–114a; III 561b
desire, II 548b
Dewey, I 116b; III 568b
dialectical method, II 543a–543b
dogma, II 546a–546b
Ebbinghaus, I 116b
Eliot, George, I 115a, 117a
empiricism, II 547a–547b
Epicureanism, IV 7b
epistemology, II 603b
eternal objects, II 542b
ethics, II 544b, 548b, 603a–603b
Euripides, II 545a
experience, II 547a–548a
Fichte, II 548a, 548b
Ficino, II 547a
freedom, II 548b
Freud, I 116b; II 544b, 548b
Gay, John, I 112a, 112b, 113a
God, II 331b–333b, 546a, 546b, 548a
Godwin, I 114a–114b
Great Britain, II 547b
Hartley, I 111b–116b
Hegel, III 358b; IV 290b
Herbert of Cherbury, II 547a
historiography, II 499a–511a
Hobbes, I 111b
Hume, I 113b, 116a; II 547b, 548a
Huxley, I 111b
ideal, II 543b–545b, 549b–551b
ideology, II 553a, 556a, 557b
immortality, II 548a
imprinting, II 584a
indeterminacy, II 586b
individualism, II 597a–603b

Ingres, II 546a
innate, II 543a
intelligible world, II 543a
international peace, III 448a–448b, 456a–456b
Jackson, I 116a, 116b
James, William, I 116b; III 552b, 564a
Jesus Christ, II 546b
justice, II 543b–544a, 544b, 652b–655a, 657b–659a
Kant, II 453a, 547b–548b, 551a–551b; III 219a, 358a, 518a, 518b
knowledge, II 542a, 547a, 547b, 548a
Lamarck, I 113b–115a
language, II 663b
law, II 685b–690b; III 27b
Law of Contradiction, II 547b
learning, II 584a
Leibniz, III 515b, 561b
Lewes, I 115a, 116a
Lewis, C. I., III 568b
liberalism, II 41b–55b
literary paradox, III 76a
literature, IV 332a
Locke, I 111b–114b, 116a; II 547a, 547b; III 598b
Lovejoy, III 552b
loyalty, III 108b
Mach, II 547b
macrocosm and microcosm, III 126a, 126b, 129a
Malebranche, II 548a
Malthus, I 114a–114b, 115b
Man-Machine, III 132b
Marx, II 544b
Marxism, III 146b
material objects, II 542b
mathematics, II 542b, 546a, 546b
matter, III 185a–196b
Mead, I 116b
methodology, II 600b–601b
Middle Ages, II 546a, 546b
Mill, James, I 116a
Mill, John Stuart, I 115a, 116a, 117a
mimesis, III 228b
moral sense, III 231b, 232a, 234a
morality, II 548a–548b
motif, III 237a, 243a
mythology, II 543a; III 317a
nationalism, III 324a–324b, 332a
natural law, III 15a, 25a
Nature, II 544a, 546a; III

346b–351b
Neo-Platonism, II 545a–546a, 547a; III 372b, 375a
Newton, I 112a, 112b, 113a, 113b; II 544a
Nietzsche, II 548b
nominalism, II 546a–547a
nouns, II 542a
numbers, II 546a; III 403b; IV 36b
Numenius, II 545a
organicism, III 422a
origin of the word, II 542a
painting, II 544a, 546a
Pavlov, I 116a
Peirce, III 558a
perennial philosophy, III 458b–463a
philanthropy, III 491b
Philo Judaeus, II 543a, 545a
philosophy, II 549b–551b
Pindar, II 542a
Plato, I 42b–43b, 111b, 325a–325b, 462b, 582a; II 223a, 542a–542b, 544b, 547b, 582b, 633b; III 15a, 188a, 353b, 508b, 517a; IV 34b, 35a, 35b
Platonism, I 375a; II 545a, 546a, 547a; III 95b–96a, 508b, 509a, 513b, 515b, 516b–518b, 524a, 524b
Plotinus, II 545a–546a
poetics, III 526b
politics, II 544b, 548b
Porphyry, II 545b, 546a
pragmatism, III 552b, 553a, 558a, 561b, 563b, 564a, 568b, 569a
pre-Socratics, II 547a
Priestley, I 114a, 116a, 116b
primitivism, III 584a, 598b
privacy, II 599a–599b, 602b
progress, III 634a
protest movements, III 671a–677a
psychology, IV 7b, 8b
Pythagoreans, II 546a; IV 34b, 35a, 35b, 36b
realism, II 546a–548b
reason, II 543b
religion, II 548a, 548b
Renaissance, II 543a, 545b, 546a; IV 121a–129a
Roman Catholic Church, II 546a–547a
romanticism, IV 197a
Roscellinus, II 546b
Rousseau, III 602b
Saint Anselm, II 546b

Saint Augustine, II 546a, 546b; III 584a
Saint Thomas Aquinas, II 546b
Schopenhauer, II 548b; III 524a
science, II 547a–547b
sculptor, II 544a
self-development, II 597b–598a
senses, II 543a
Sherrington, I 116a
Smith, Adam, I 114a
socialism, IV 290b
Socrates, II 543a; IV 34b
Solomon (Bible), II 546a
Sophocles, II 545a
soul, II 543a, 546a
space, II 547b, 548a
Spencer, I 115a–115b, 116a, 116b
Speusippus, IV 35a, 35b
Spinoza, III 561b
structuralism, IV 322b
style, IV 332a
symbolism, II 546a; IV 338a, 339b, 342b
symmetry, IV 348a
Telesio, II 547a
testing the value of, I 10a
time, II 547b, 548a; IV 390b, 391a
timeless objects, II 542b
Titchener, I 116b
tragedy, II 544b
traits, II 554b
Tree of Porphyry, II 545b
Trinity, II 546b
truth, II 548b
two aspects of, I 111a
U.S., III 329a
unity of science, IV 436b
Vaihinger, II 548b
Vives, I 111b
war, III 448a–448b
Watson, J. B., I 116b–117a
Wordsworth, II 543a
Wundt, I 116b
Xenocrates, IV 35a
Zeus (myth), II 545b
Ideal, II 549a–552b
abstraction, II 551a, 551b
aesthetics, II 549a–550a, 551a–551b
art, II 549a, 549b, 550a, 550b–551a, 551b
artists, II 550b, 551a, 551b
Batteux, II 550a
Bayle, II 549b
beauty, II 549a–551b
Bellori, II 549b, 550a
Bernini, II 549b
Bredvold, II 549b
Caravaggio, II 549b

Crousaz, II 549b
Diderot, II 549b–550a
Du Fresnoy, II 549b
empiricism, II 549a, 549b, 551a, 551b
ethics, II 549a, 550b, 551a
Feder, II 551a
feeling, II 550a
Félibien, II 549b
Ferber, II 551a
France, II 549a, 549b–550a
Fréart de Chambray, II 549b
Frommichen, II 551a
genius, II 551a
Germany, II 549a, 550a–551b
God, II 549a, 549b, 550b, 551b
good, II 549a–549b, 550b
Great Britain, II 549a, 550a
Greece (ancient), II 550b
Helen of Troy (myth), II 549b
Hemsterhuis, II 550a
Herder, II 551a
idea, II 543b, 544b, 545a, 545b, 549b–551b
imagination, II 550a, 551a
imitation, II 549b, 550b
individualism, II 550b, 551a
intuition, II 549b, 551b
Italy, II 549a, 549b, 550a
justice, II 654a, 658a
Kant, II 551a–551b
Kate, II 549b
Klopstock, II 550b
knowledge, II 551a
Lana Terzi, II 551a
language, II 551a, 662b
Lavater, II 551a
Leibniz, IV 436a
Lenz, II 551b
Lessing, II 551a
Lomazzo, II 550a
Lossius, II 551b
love, II 96a, 98b, 100b, 104a, 105a–105b, 107b
mannerism, II 549b
Mendelssohn, M., II 550b
Mengs, II 550a, 550b
Micraelius, II 549b
morality, II 550a, 551a
mythology, III 273a
naturalism, II 549b
Nature, II 549b, 551b
Neo-Platonism, II 549b
nonsensory origin of, I 1a
origin of the term, II 549a–549b
painting, II 549b
Panofsky, II 549b

perennial philosophy, III 457a–463a

perfectibility, II 549b, 551a, 551b; III 465a–564b

philosophy, II 549a–552b

Plato, II 662b; III 273a; IV 285b

Platonism, II 549a, 549b, 550a

poetry, II 551a

pragmatism, II 551b

primitivism, III 596b

Prinner, II 551b

psychology, II 551a

Racine, II 550a

Renaissance, IV 438b, 439a, 439b, 440b, 441b, 443a

Reynolds, II 550a

Riedel, II 550b–551a

Scheyb, II 551a

senses, II 549a, 551a

Shaftesbury, II 550a

Shelley, III 508a

socialism, IV 285a, 285b

Spain, II 549a

species, II 551b

Sulzer, II 550a, 551a

supranatural, II 549b, 550b, 551b

symmetry, IV 348a

technology, IV 361a

time, IV 395a

tragedy, II 551b

unity, II 550b, 551b

unity of science, IV 431a, 436a

universal man, IV 438b, 439a, 439b, 440b, 441b, 443a

universe, II 550b, 551a

utilitarianism, IV 446b, 447a

virtue, II 550b, 551a

von Hagedorn, II 550b

Webb, D., II 550a

Wieland, II 550b, 551a, 551b

Winckelmann, II 550a, 550b, 551a

Zeuxis, II 549b

Idealism

absolute, II 20a–20b, 407b

abstraction, I 8a

agnosticism, I 22b–23a

Anglicanism, IV 20a

art for art's sake, I 108b

beauty, I 203b, 207a

Berkeley, I 276b; III 561b

Bernstein, E., III 162b

biology, I 237a, 237b

Chain of Being, I 334a

Chapman, III 295a

Christianity, I 402b

determinism, II 20a–20b

economic history, II 46b

Enlightenment, II 96a

eschatology, II 157b–159b

existentialism, III 158a

Faust (legend), III 249b

Fichte, II 158a, 158b, 407b

Germany, I 447a; III 494b; IV 200a, 220a

God, II 357b, 359a, 360a; III 368b

Goethe, I 237a, 237b

Great Britain, IV 220a

Hegel, I 277b; II 158a–158b, 407b, 453a, 583a; III 159a, 358b

historiography, II 20a–20b

history, II 20a–20b

humanism, II 522a

impressionism, II 583a

international peace, III 448a, 450b

Italy, I 493a; IV 220a

Kant, II 407b

law, II 687b, 690b

Locke, II 96a

McTaggart, I 641b

Marxism, III 150a, 158a, 159a, 162b, 168a

materialism, II 453a

metaphysical imagination, III 209b

Michelet, II 407b

morality, III 645a

More, Thomas, IV 461a

mythology, III 295a, 305a, 305b, 312a

nationalism, III 330a

naturalism in art, III 341a, 341b, 342b, 343a, 345b

Nature, III 346b, 347a, 350b

neo-classicism in art, III 368a–368b, 370a, 371a

objective, II 407b

organicism, III 421b, 425b, 426b

Orientalism, III 429b, 430a, 430b, 432b, 439a

painting, III 341b

peace, III 443a, 443b, 444a, 445b

Peirce, III 552b, 568b

perfectibility, III 472b, 473a

Pietism, III 494b

Plato, III 347a

Platonism, I 237a, 237b; III 504b, 506b, 515b

Plotinus, III 159a

pragmatism, III 552b, 561a, 561b, 567a, 568b

progress, III 645a

prophecy, III 661a

psychology, IV 20a, 24a, 24b

realism in literature, IV 51b, 52b, 53a

religion, IV 106a

revisionism, IV 269b, 270a, 273a

revolution, IV 165a

romanticism, IV 200a, 202a, 208a, 209a

Rome (ancient), II 687b, 690b

Royce, III 561a

Russia, IV 220a

Sartre, III 158a

Schelling, II 407b

Schlegel, F., IV 209a

skepticism, IV 249b–250a

space, IV 298a

subjective, II 407b

symbolism, IV 343b

time, IV 393b

transcendentalism, IV 24a

U.S., I 408a; III 429b, 430a, 430b, 432b, 439a

Utopia, IV 458b, 461a, 463b

Venice, I 593a

Victorian, IV 219a, 219b, 220a, 222b, 223b

Ideograms, language, II 661a

Ideologues, ideology, II 553a–554a

Ideology, II 552b–564a

absolute materialism, II 561a–561b

acquired characteristics, II 620b

alienation, II 557b

anarchy, III 674a

anti-industrialism, III 676a

Antisthenes, I 632a–632b, 633a

art, II 555b, 582a, 583a

Bacon, II 553a

behaviorism, II 555b–556a, 557b–558a

Bell, II 556a–556b

Blanqui, II 559b

Brazil, III 543a

Bukharin, II 506a

Cabanis, II 553a, 553b, 554a

Cartesianism, II 553a

class, II 555b

communism, II 559a–563b

Comte, III 533b

concept, II 552b–553a, 554b–555a

Condillac, II 553a–553b

conservatism, I 480a

culture, II 555b, 557a, 557b, 558a–558b

cynicism, I 632a–633b

derivation, II 556a

Destutt de Tracy, II 553a, 553b, 554a

Dio Chrysostomus, I 632b–633b

Diogenes of Sinope, I 632b, 633a

Dion, II 558a

economics, II 554a–554b

Engels, II 554a–554b, 559b, 560b

Enlightenment, II 554a

epistemology, II 553a–554a, 554b, 555a

ethics, II 554a

fascism, III 674a

Faust (legend), III 252a

French Revolution (1789), III 671b

Freud, II 555b, 556b–557b

Geertz, II 558a

Helvétius, II 553a–554a

idea, II 553a, 556a, 557b

Ideologues, II 553a–554a

impiety, II 566b

impressionism, II 582a, 583a

international peace, III 448a, 451b, 453a, 456b

intolerance, IV 115b–116a

knowledge, II 553a

Latin America, III 545a

law, III 4a; 35b

Lenin, II 560a–563a

Leninism, II 562a–562b

Lerner, II 556b

liberalism, III 672b

Locke, II 553a

loyalty, III 108b, 113a, 115a

Man-Machine, III 135a

Mannheim, II 554b

Marx, II 553a, 554b–555a, 559a, 559b–562b; III 161b, 162b, 163a, 165a, 167a, 167b, 654a

Marxism-Leninism, II 562b, 563b

Mexico, III 544b

morality, II 553b, 554a; III 645a–645b

Mosca, II 555a–555b

Mussolini, II 563a

mythology, II 555b, 556a, 558b; III 307a, 315a

Napoleon, I, II 554a

nationalism, III 333b, 334a, 334b

natural rights, III 22a

naturalism in art, III 343a

Pareto, II 555a–556a

Parsons, II 556a–556b

physiology, II 553b, 554a

Plekhanov, II 559a
political, II 552b–559b
positivism, III 532b, 535a, 535b
private property, III 653b–655a
progress, III 642b, 645a–645b
prophecy, III 659b, 661a
protest movements, III 670a–677a
psychoculturism, II 558a–558b
psychology, II 553b, 556b–558a, 558b
radicalism, II 560a; III 672b, 673a
rationalism, II 553a
reformation, IV 60b–61a
religion, II 555b, 557a–557b; IV 115b–116a
revisionism, IV 264a–274a
Rome (ancient), II 566b
Rousseau, II 561b
Russia, II 559a, 559b
salvation, IV 227b, 227a
science, II 553a–555a
sensation, II 553a, 553b
social revolution, II 559b
socialism, III 673b; IV 291b
socioeconomics, II 554a, 554b
sociology, II 554a–558a
Sorel, II 555b
spontaneous generation, IV 310b, 311a
Stalinism, II 562b–563b
State, IV 316b–318a
structuralism, IV 327b, 329a–329b
Sutton, II 556b, 557b
symbolism, II 558a–558b
syndicalism, III 674a
totalitarianism, IV 406b–410b
truth, II 556b
U.S.S.R., II 559a–563b
Utopia, II 555a; IV 463b
Volksgeist, IV 493b–495a
war, III 448b; IV 506a
Weber, II 554b
Weltanschauung, II 555a
women, IV 527b, 528a
zoology, II 553b
Idioplasm
chromosomes, II 288a, 288b
Nägeli, II 288a
Weismann, II 288b
Idioscopy, scientific classification, I 466a
Ido language, II 669a
Idolatry
Bacon, Francis, III 212b–

213a, 215a, 218a
impiety, II 546b, 565a, 567a
Judaism, II 564b, 565a
mythology, III 301a–303b
prophecy, III 662a, 662b
sin, IV 226b, 227a
witchcraft, IV 521a
Idris, Islam, II 640a
Ignatius of Antioch, Saint (c. 110)
Gnosticism, II 330b
perfectibility, III 466a
Ignoble (Ugly) Savage, anti-primitivism, III 604a–605a
Ignorance
Aristotle, II 237a
determinism, II 236b, 237a 238b
Dewey, III 569a
free will, II 236b, 237a, 238b
good, IV 174b
human nature, III 577a, 643b
James, III 569a
knowledge, III 472a
language, II 662b
law, II 35b
Machiavellism, III 118a
morality, III 645b
mythology, III 301b, 302a, 303b
Nicholas of Cusa, III 510b
perfectibility, III 468a, 472a, 643b
Plato, II 236b, 662b
Platonism, III 496b–497a, 510b, 513b
pragmatism, III 569a
progress, III 643b, 645b
prophecy, III 658b, 662b
rationalism, IV 49a
right, IV 49a, 174b
Socrates, III 577a; IV 49a, 174b, 414b, 517a
Spinoza, II 238b
State, III 472a
tragic sense, IV 414b, 415b
Utopia, IV 463b
wisdom, IV 174b, 517a, 517b, 519b
wisdom of the fool, IV 517a, 517b, 519b
wrong, IV 49a
Ilithyia (myth), III 272b
Illuminists
Augustinianism, IV 109a
Campanella, IV 109a
Edwards, IV 109a, 109b–110a, 110b
Fénelon, IV 109a
Great Awakening, IV 109a
Hutcheson, IV 109a
love, IV 109a

Malebranche, IV 109a
Pascal, IV 109a
Pestalozzi, IV 109a
Pietism, IV 111a–112a
Vico, IV 109a
Illusion
Kant, III 218a
space, IV 302a
tragic sense, IV 414a
Illusionism
Hals, III 344b
impressionism, III 342a
naturalism, III 339b, 340a, 341a, 342a, 344b
Vermeer, III 341a
Imagery
art, II 526a, 526b, 527a, 530a, 530b
God, IV 138a–138b, 140b, 142b, 144a
iconography, II 526a–530b, 532b, 536a
literature, IV 331b, 333a
metaphor, III 201b–206a, 207a, 207b
mountains in literature, III 253b
optics, III 412a–413a, 416b–417b, 420b
Platonism, III 500a, 508a
Renaissance, IV 138a–138b, 140b, 142b–144a
Saint Augustine, IV 138a–138b
Shelley, III 508a
style, IV 331b, 333a
symbolism, IV 338a, 341b, 343b, 344a, 345a
ut pictura poesis, IV 470a, 471b, 472b, 475a
Imhotep (fl. c. 2950 B.C.), religion, IV 93a
Imitation
Aristotelianism, II 306a
Aristotle, IV 411b
art, II 298a, 306a–306b, 582b; III 497b–498a
artists, II 298a
genius, II 294a, 294b, 298a, 304b, 306a–307b, 317a, 322b–324a
humanism, II 518a
ideal, II 549b, 550b
Kant, II 324a
Leonardo da Vinci, II 298a
music, II 317a, 323b, 324a; III 264b, 267b
painting, II 582b
philosophy, II 549b, 550b
Plato, II 582b; III 497b–498a, 498b, 500a, 501a
pseudo-Aristotelianism, II 306a
religion, IV 100b–103a

technology, IV 358b, 364b
tragic sense, IV 411b
See also Mimesis
Immaculate Conception, Virgin Mary (Bible), III 98b
Immortality, I 638a–643b
Alexander of Aphrodisias, I 639b
Aristotle, I 639a–639b, 644a, 645b; IV 34a
art, II 582b
atomism, I 640a
Averroës, I 639b, 645b
Babylonia, I 644b
Bardo Tödol, I 644b
Bergson, I 641b
Bible, I 639b, 640b, 644a
biological, I 645b–646a
Brahmanism, I 644b
Bruno, I 645a, 644b
Buddhism, I 644b
cabalism, I 645a
Cabanis, I 641a
Christianity, I 639b, 640b, 643b–645a; IV 230b
Cicero, I 644b
Condorcet, I 646a
cosmology and, I 644b–645a
Creation, I 571b
creativity in art, I 584a
Crito, I 638b
dignity, IV 137a, 137b, 144b, 145a
Ducasse, I 645a
Egypt (ancient), I 644b
evil, II 167a
Feuerbach, I 646a
Ficino, IV 144b, 145a
Gnosticism, I 645a
God, I 571b, 640b, 644a; II 335a–335b, 336a, 357a
Godwin, III 470b
Goethe, I 642a, 642b, 646a
Greece (ancient), I 637b–638b, 641a, 642b, 643a–644b; IV 228b
health, II 397a, 402b
Heidegger, I 642b
heresy, II 426b
Hesiod, I 644b
Hinduism, I 644b, 645a
Hocking, I 642a
Holbach, I 641a
Homer, I 644b
human nature, III 571b–573b, 577a
Hume, I 641a, 642a, 645a
idea, II 548a
India, I 645a
India (ancient), I 644b
Irenaeus, I 643a

James, William, I 642a, 643a

Jaspers, I 642b

Jesus Christ, I 643b, 644a

Josephus Flavius, I 643b

Judaism, I 643b, 644b, 645a; III 223b

Kant, I 639a, 641a–641b; II 240b, 357a, 548a

Kardec, I 642b

La Mettrie, I 641a

Leibniz, I 645a; IV 382a

longevity, III 89a–89b, 90b

Longfellow, I 646a

Lucretius, I 640a

McTaggart, I 641b, 645a

Marcel, I 642a

Maritain, I 642a–642b

Mersenne, I 640b

Mesopotamia (ancient), IV 226a

metaphor, III 199a

metaphysics, III 217b

metempsychosis, I 644b

Michelangelo, I 646a

millenarianism, III 223b

mythology, III 273a, 278b, 279a, 284b, 288a, 291a, 309b

Nature, III 346b

Neo-Platonism, I 645a

Neo-Pythagoreans, III 505a

Omar Khayyam, I 642b

Orphism, I 644b

palingenesis, I 644b

Paul VI, Pope, I 643b

perfectibility, III 463b, 464a, 468a, 470b

Pherecydes of Syros, I 644b

philanthropy, III 487a

Plato, I 584a, 638b–639b, 643b, 644a, 645a; III 577a; IV 4a

Platonism, I 645a; III 509a, 516a

Plotinus, I 645a

Pomponazzi, I 640b

psychical research, I 642b–643b

psychology, IV 1b, 2b, 3b, 4a, 7a

Pythagoras, I 644b, 645a

Radhakrishnan, I 645a

reincarnation, I 644b–646a

religion, IV 93a, 98a, 98b

Renaissance, I 645a; IV 137a, 137b, 144b, 145a

resurrection, I 643b–644b

Rhine, I 643a

Roman Catholic Church, I 643b

romanticism, I 645b

Rome (ancient), I 646a

Saint Paul, I 644b–644a

Saint Thomas Aquinas, I 644a–644b

salvation, IV 226a, 228a, 228b, 230b

Santayana, I 646a

Scheler, I 641b

Siger of Brabant, I 639b, 640b

sin, IV 226a, 228a, 228b, 230b

skepticism, I 644a, 645a

Socrates, I 638b, 642a; III 577a

soul, I 634b, 635a, 637a–637b, 638b–644b

Spinoza, I 645b

spiritism, I 642b–643b

Staël, I 645b, 646a

Strato, IV 7a

substitute, I 645b–646a

Tatian, I 643a

theodicy, IV 380a, 380b, 382a

theriophily, IV 384b

Wordsworth, III 508a

Xenophanes, III 273a

Immortals, Greece (ancient), III 347a

Immunities, II 249a, 250b

Immunology, IV 311a

  disease, II 405a, 406a

Immutability

  of justice, II 653b

  Nature, III 346b, 347a, 347b, 351a

  perfectibility, III 463b, 464a

Impartial rule, morality, III 645a

Imperialism

  China (Communist), III 161b, 167a, 334a

  Cleon, II 260a

  despotism, II 1b

  Diodotus, II 260a

  freedom of speech, II 260a

  Lenin, II 561a

  Marxism, III 150b, 161b, 165b, 166b, 167a, 169a

  missionaries, I 407b–408a

  nationalism, III 333b, 334a

  peace, III 445a

  periodization in history, III 477a, 477b

  philanthropy, III 490b

  Platonism, III 503b

  pragmatism, III 565b

  progress, III 647a

  revolution, IV 166a

  Russia, III 333b

  Saint Augustine, II 260a

  Spain, III 539b

  Stalin, II 563b

  totalitarianism, IV 408b

  U.S.S.R., III 161b, 167a;

  IV 166a

Impiety, II 564a–567a

  Akhnaton, II 564a, 564b

  Akkadian, II 564a

  Anaxagoras, II 565b

  anomie, II 565a

  Antiochus VI, II 566a

  Aristotle, II 565b

  asebeia, II 565b–567a

  Aspasia, II 565b

  Assyria, II 564a

  atheism, II 565b

  Athens (ancient), II 565b, 566b

  Augustus, II 566b

  behaviorism, II 564b

  Bible, II 564a, 565a

  Christianity, II 564a–567a

  Cicero, II 566a

  culture, II 564b

  Dicaearchus, II 566a

  didacticism, II 564b

  Diopithes, II 565b–566b

  divination, II 564b

  Egypt (ancient), II 564a–564b, 566a

  Eleazar ben Arach, II 565a

  Elisha ben Abujah, II 565a

  eusebeia, II 565b

  freedom of speech, II 252b

  Gamliel II, II 565a

  Gnosticism, II 565a

  God, II 564b–567a

  Greece (ancient), II 564a, 565b–566b

  Hegesias, II 566a

  heresy, II 564a, 565a–567a

  Homer, II 566b

  hymns, II 564a

  ideology, II 566b

  idolatry, II 564b, 565a, 567a

  Israel (ancient), II 564b–565a

  Judaism, II 564a, 564b–565b

  Jumilhac Papyrus, II 564b

  Kyrnos, II 565b

  language, II 564a, 566b

  law, II 564a, 565b, 566b

  literature, II 564a

  Lysimachus, II 566a

  Manicheism, II 565a

  Mesopotamia (ancient), II 564a, 564b

  origin of the term, II 564a

  Pericles, II 565b

  persecution, II 565b–567a

  Persia (ancient), II 565a–565b

  Philip V, II 566a

  Pindar, II 565b

  Plato, II 566a

  Plutarch, II 565b

  politics, II 565b–566b

  propaganda, II 566b

  prophecy, II 564b

  Protagoras, II 565b

  purification, II 564b

  rationalism, IV 48b

  responsibility, II 564b

  rhetoric, II 565a

  Rome (ancient), II 564a, 566b–567a

  Saint Paul, II 565a

  Samuel the Little, II 565a

  secularism, II 564a

  sin, II 564b–565a

  skepticism, II 565a; IV 238b

  Socrates, II 565b, 566a

  Sophists, II 565b

  soul, II 565b

  Stilpo, II 565b

  suicide, II 566a

  Tacitus, II 566b

  Theodorus of Cyrene, II 565b

  Theognis, II 565b

  Theophrastus, II 565b

  treaties, II 566b

  Vergil, II 566b

  war, II 566b

  Yahweh, II 564b–565a

Impressionism, II 567b–583b

  abstraction, II 580b–581a

  academic painting, II 567b–570b, 581a

  Academy of Fine Arts, II 573a, 579b–580a, 583a

  aesthetics, II 219b, 575b, 576a, 583a, 584b

  architecture, II 578a

  aristocracy, II 570a, 578b, 581b

  Astruc, II 573a

  atomism, II 582a–582b

  authority, II 581b

  baroque, II 582b

  Baudelaire, II 571b, 573a, 574b, 578a, 581a

  beauty, II 580b, 581a, 583a

  Belgium, II 578a

  Bellini, II 577b

  Boucher, II 572b

  Bouguereau, II 580a

  bourgeois, II 570a, 580a

  Braque, II 577b

  Bruegel, II 578a

  Cabanel, II 580a

  Cartesianism, II 582a

  Castagnary, II 573a, 574b–574a, 581a

  Cézanne, II 567b, 573a

  chaos, II 582a

  characteristics, II 570a–570b, 574a–574b

Chardin, II 572b, 578b
Chevreul, II 580a, 580b
Christianity, II 582b
class, II 576b, 581b, 583a
clergy, II 570a
color, II 567b, 570a–574a, 574b, 577a, 577b, 578b, 579a–580b, 582b, 583a
composers, II 574b, 581a
composition, II 570a, 571a, 581b, 582b
Comte, II 582a, 583a
concept of, II 567b
conservatism, II 571a
Constable, II 578a, 579a–579b; III 342a
contribution of, II 567b, 583a–583b
Corot, II 572b, 578a, 578b; III 342a
cosmos, II 583a
Courbet, II 571a, 571b, 573a, 575b, 578a, 581b, 583a
criticism, II 572b–576a, 577a, 581a
Crome, II 579a
culture, II 567b, 577a, 580b, 581b, 582b, 583a
Currier, II 579b
Cuyp, II 578a
Daguerre, II 572a
Daubigny, II 577b, 578a
David, II 572b, 577a, 577b
Debussy, II 575a, 580b
decadence, II 575b, 582a
Degas, II 567b, 570b–571a, 571b, 572a, 573b, 574b, 580a
Delacroix, II 572b, 578b, 579b, 580a
democracy, II 583a
Democritus, II 582a–582b
Desnoyers, II 573a
Diderot, II 582a, 582b
divisionism, II 570b
drawing, II 580a
dualism, II 581b
Durand-Ruel, II 580a
Duranty, II 573b
education, II 583a
Egypt (ancient), II 582b
El Greco, II 577b
emotion, II 575a, 575b, 576b, 581a
emphasis of, II 567b
empiricism, II 576b, 580b, 581b, 582a, 583a
Epicureanism, II 576a, 581a, 581b, 582a
Epicurus, II 582a–582b
essential feature of, II 573a
evolution, II 581b, 583a
expressionism, II 206a–

207a
folklore, II 581a, 582b
France, II 567b–583b
France, Anatole, II 575b–576a
French Revolution, II 577a, 581b
Germany, II 583a; III 484a
Giorgione, II 577b
God, II 574b, 582b
Goethe, II 580b
Great Britain, II 567b, 570b, 575a, 578a, 579a–579b, 583a
Greece (ancient), II 582a–582b
hedonism, II 575b
Hegel, II 583a
Helmholtz, II 580b
Heraclitus, II 582a
history, II 576a–580b
Hobbema, II 578a
Holbein, II 571a
human figure, III 342a
Hume, II 582a
Huysmans, II 575a
iconography, II 534a
ideology, II 582a, 583a
illusionism, III 342a
imitation, II 582b
immortality, II 582b
individualism, II 567b, 570b, 572a, 574b, 577a, 577b, 581b, 582b
industry, II 580a
Ingres, II 570a, 572b, 577b, 579b, 580a
Ireland, II 575a
Italy, II 577b
Ives, II 579b
James, Henry, II 575a
joint stock company formed, II 573b
Jongkind, II 573a
Joyce, II 575a
Keats, II 581a
knowledge, II 582a, 582b, 583b
labor, II 576b
Lalande, II 582a
landscapes, II 567b, 571b, 572a, 573a, 574a, 577b–579a, 580a
Leibl, III 345a
Leroy, Louis, II 573b
liberalism, II 583a
light, II 567b, 570a–570b, 572a, 574a–574b, 578b; 579a, 580a–580b, 581b
line, II 570a, 581b
literature, II 567b, 574b–575b
Lorrain, II 577b–578a
Lowell, Amy, II 575a

Lumière, Auguste, II 572a
Lumière, Louis Jean, II 572a
Mallarmé, II 573b, 575a, 575b
Manet, II 567b, 568a–568b, 570a, 573a, 573b, 577b, 580a
Martinet, II 580a
Marx, II 583a
Maxwell, II 572a, 580b
Michelangelo, II 572b, 574b
Millet, II 578a
Monet, II 567b, 568a–568b, 570a–570b, 571a, 572b, 573b, 574b, 577b, 579a
morality, II 582b, 583a
Morisot, II 567b
motif, III 236b
motion, II 570b–571a, 572a, 572b, 583a
music, II 567b, 574b–575a
mutability, II 581a–581b
mysticism, II 575b, 581b, 582a
mythology, II 581a
Napoleon III, II 573a
nationalism, II 579b
natural science, II 576b
naturalism, II 571a, 573a, 575b–578b, 579b–583a; III 339b, 342a
Nature, II 570a, 571a, 574a–576a, 582b, 583a
Neo-Platonism, II 576b
Netherlands, II 578a
neuroses, II 575b
Newton, II 580b
Niepce, II 572a
nominalism, II 576b
origin of the term, II 582a
painting, II 206a, 207a, 567b–574b, 576a–582b; III 342a; IV 473b
Paris Salon, II 567b–570a, 571a, 573a, 580a, 581b, 583a
Pater, II 575b–576a
Patinir, II 578a
patrons, II 573a, 577a, 580a
periodization in literary history, III 484a
perspective, II 570a, 577a
perversion, II 575b
philosophy, II 575b, 576b, 580b–583b
photography, II 571b–572a
physics, II 580a–580b
Picasso, II 577b
Pissarro, II 567b, 573a, 573b, 579a, 580a–580b

Platonism, II 581b–582b
poetry, II 574b, 575a–575b, 578a, 580b–581a; IV 473b
politics, II 581b–583a
post-impressionism, II 567b
Poussin, II 570a, 577b–578a
power, II 576a–576b, 577a
prestige, II 572b, 573a
projection, III 342a
Proust, II 575a
psychology, II 575a, 580b, 583a
Raphael, II 570a, 573a
Ravel, II 575a
realism, II 570a, 571a, 576b, 578b–581b, 582b
realism in literature, IV 55a
reason, II 582a
religion, II 575b, 576a, 576b, 581b, 582b
Rembrandt, II 578a
Renaissance, II 577b, 582b
Renoir, Auguste, II 567b, 569a, 569b, 573b, 574a
Renoir, Edmond, II 573b
revolt, II 567b–570b, 577a, 581b
revolution, II 577a, 581b, 582b
Rewald, II 573a, 573b, 574a, 577b, 579a
Rimbaud, II 575a
Rodin, II 574a, 574b
romanticism, II 575b, 578a, 578b, 579a, 580a, 581a, 581b
Rood, II 580b
Rousseau, II 582b
Rubens, II 577b, 578a, 578b
Ruysdael, II 578a
Salon des Refusés, II 573a
Satanism, II 582a
science, II 575b, 580a–580b, 581b, 582b, 583a
sculpture, II 567b, 574b, 576a, 576b, 577b
senses, II 574b, 575b, 576b, 580b, 582a, 583a–583b
Seurat, II 567b, 580a, 580b
Shelley, II 581a
Signac, II 580b
sin, II 575b
Sisley, II 567b, 573b, 579a–579b
society, II 577a, 581b, 583a
space, III 342a
Spain, II 577b
State, II 570a, 576a, 582b
Strauss, II 575a

style, II 567b, 570a–570b, 572a, 572b, 574a, 574b, 576a, 576b–577b, 580a, 580b, 581b, 583a
suicide, II 575b
supernatural, II 575b, 576b, 580b
symbolism, II 570b, 575b, 576b, 580b–581a, 581b–582a
Taine, II 583a
technique, II 567b, 570a–570b, 574a, 580a, 581b, 583a
  as a term of ridicule, II 572b
Tiepolo, II 578b
Tintoretto, II 577b
Titian, II 577b
trade, II 580a
tradition, II 577a–577b, 579b, 581b
transitory phenomena, II 571a
truth, II 571a, 575b, 576a–576b, 582b
Turner, II 578a–579b
types of, II 570b–572b
ugliness, II 571a
U.S., II 567b, 570b, 573b, 575a, 579b
unity, II 576a
universe, II 582a
value, II 576b, 577b
Velázquez, II 577b, 578b
Verlaine, II 575a
Vermeer, II 578b
vibrism, II 570b
Wagner, II 575a
war, II 577a, 580a, 582b
wealth, II 570a, 577a, 580a
Whistler, II 567b, 569a, 569b, 570b, 573a, 579a–579b
Zola, II 573a, 575b, 581a, 581b
Imprinting, II 583b–586a
  aetiology, II 584b
  behaviorism, II 584a–586a
  Darwin, II 584b
  Descartes, II 584a
  early learning, II 584b–585b, 586a
  ethology, II 584a, 585a–585b
  Freud, II 584b, 585b
  Gassendi, II 584a
  Heinroth, II 585a
  instinct, II 584b–585a
  James, II 584b, 585a
  Locke, II 584a
  Lorenz, II 585a, 585b
  pathology, II 585b
  psychology, II 584b, 585b,

586a
  research, II 585b, 586a
  Rousseau, II 584a
  sensory experience, II 584a, 586a
  Saint Thomas Aquinas, II 584a
  Spalding, II 584b, 585a
  Thorndike, II 585a
Incarnation
  Buddhism, IV 233b
  Christianity, I 376a–376b, 377a; III 477a
  dignity, IV 137a, 138a, 140a, 142a, 146a
  Jesus Christ, II 472a, 472b, 473a; III 667b–668a
  Joachim of Floris, IV 286b
  mythology, III 276a, 277a
  Neo-Platonism, III 509b
  periodization in history, III 477a
  Platonism, III 505b, 509b
  prophecy, III 667b–668a
  Pythagoras, IV 31a
  Pythagoreans, IV 31a–32a
  reformation, IV 62b
  Roman Catholic Church, I 376a–376b, 377a
  Saint Augustine, III 505b, 509b
  salvation, IV 232b
  socialism, IV 286b
  time, IV 392a
Incest
  culture, IV 327a
  cynicism, III 586a
  Freud, IV 96b
  Lévi-Strauss, IV 327a
  mythology, III 279a, 312b
  primitivism, III 586a, 588a
  religion, IV 96b
  theriophily, IV 385a
Income
  class, III 151a
  discounting, II 53b
  economic history, II 46b, 49a–49b, 52b–53b, 55a
  equality, II 145b, 146a
  Marx, II 49b
  Marxism, III 151a
  natural liberty, II 62a, 63b, 65a–65b, 66b, 69b, 71a
  Smith, Adam, II 49a–49b
  socialism, II 146a
  utility, IV 451b–453b
  welfare state, IV 512a–512b, 514b, 515a
Incommensurability
  mathematics, III 172a
  Pythagoreans, IV 32a
Independence
  genius, II 295b
  India, III 337a

Machiavelli, IV 483a–483b
Mexico, III 544a
nationalism, III 330a, 334a, 335a, 337a, 338b
Nature, III 348a
U.S., III 348a
Indeterminacy, II 586a–594a
  absolute, II 587a
  acausal behavior, II 586a–586b, 587a, 588a, 589b
  Aristotle, II 228b, 587a
  atomism, II 586b–587a
  Augustinianism, II 230b
  behaviorism, II 586a–586b
  black-body radiation, II 590a
  Bohm, II 591a
  Bohr, II 588b–591a
  Boltzmann, II 587b–588a
  Born, II 592a–592b
  Boutroux, II 587a–587b
  Bradley, F. H., II 587b
  Brillouin, II 592a
  Broglie–Einstein equations, II 589a–589b
  Brownian motion, II 588a
  Cassirer, II 590a
  causation, II 586b–590a
  chance, II 225b, 226a–226b, 228b, 230b, 587b
  Cicero, II 587a
  Cohen, Leon, II 592a
  Compton effect, II 589a
  computers, II 592a
  contingency, II 587a–587b
  continuity, II 590a
  cosmos, II 586b
  Cournot, II 587a
  Darwin, C. G., II 588a
  Dear, II 592a
  Demiurge, II 586b
  Democritus, II 586b
  determinism, II 586b–590a
  Dirac-Jordan theory, II 588b
  Einstein, II 590a–592b
  Einthoven, II 588a
  Eisenmann, II 589a
  electrons, II 588a, 589a, 591b
  empiricism, II 587b, 591b
  energy-time uncertainty relation, II 589a, 590b, 591a
  Epicurus, II 586b–587a, 590a
  epistemology, II 589b, 590a
  error, II 587b, 592b
  evolution, II 587b
  Exner, II 588a
  experimentation, II 587b
  fate, II 225b, 226a–226b, 228b, 230b
  formalism, II 588b, 590b–591a, 592a

fortune, II 225b, 226a–226b, 228b, 230b
Fourier transformation, II 588b
free will, II 587a, 588a, 589b
Friedländer, II 586b
Galileo, II 587a
gamma-ray microscopic experiment, II 588b–589a, 591b
Gaussian distribution, II 588b
Greece (ancient), II 586b–587a
Guyau, II 587a
Heffner, II 592a
Heisenberg, II 586b, 587b, 588b–589a, 590b, 591b
Hilbert space, II 590b, 591a, 592a
imprecision, II 586b, 588a, 589b, 592b
infinity, II 588b
Krylov, II 591a
Landau, II 591a
Laplace, II 587a, 587b
Laúe, II 590a, 592a
law, II 586b, 587b–589a
Leucippus, II 587a
light, II 587a, 589a
Liouville theorem, II 592b
literary paradox, III 76b
Lucretius, II 587a, 590a
Margenau, II 591b–592a, 592b
mathematics, II 586b, 588b, 592a, 592b
matrix mechanics, II 588b
matter, II 588a
meanings of, II 586a–586b
measurement, II 586b, 587b–593a
metaphysics, II 586b
microphysics, II 586b, 589a, 589b
momentum distribution, II 588b
motion, II 587a, 588a, 591b, 592b
music, II 263b
Nature, II 586b–588a
necessity, II 587a
Newton, II 587a, 587b
noise, II 588a
observation, II 587b
optics, II 589a
Peirce, II 587b
photon–box thought experiment, II 590b
physics, II 586a–594a
Planck, II 590a
Plato, II 586b

Plutarch, II 587a
Podolsky, II 590b
Poincaré, II 588a
Popper, II 590a, 591b, 592a
precision, II 588a, 589a
predictions, II 586b, 589b, 592a
principle of, IV 398a
probability, II 588b, 590a, 591b, 592a
progress, III 643a
Prugovečki, II 592a
quantum mechanics, II 586a, 588a–593a
quantum-mechanical perturbation theory, II 591a
Renouvier, II 587a
Rosen, N., II 590b
Saint Augustine, II 230b
Schlick, II 589b
Schrödinger, II 588b, 690a
Sommerfeld, II 589a
space, II 587a, 588a, 590a, 590b
speed, II 587a
stars, II 586b
statistics, II 591a–592a
Stern-Gerlach experiment, II 588b
subatomic realm, II 586b
subject-object problem, II 590a
super-Hilbert space, II 591a
time, II 588a, 590a, 590b–591a; IV 396a
tychism, II 587b
uncertainty principle, II 586b–591b
unpredictable behavior, II 586b, 587a, 588a, 589b, 592a, 592b
value, II 587b, 589b, 591b, 592a–592b
variables, II 588b, 589b, 591b, 592a
wave mechanics, II 588b
weight, II 587a
Index, II 425a
India
  alchemy, I 27a, 29a
  All-India National Congress, III 338a
  analogy, I 68a
  autonomy, III 337a
  Buddhism, I 247b–248a, 248b, 249a, 252b, 254a, 254b
  caste, I 442a; II 141a
  civil disobedience, I 435a
  classification of the sciences, I 464a
  Constitution, I 491b; III 13b
  Counter-Enlightenment, II

105b
death, I 645a
Dravida Munnetra Karagam, III 337a
encyclopedias, I 464a
equality, II 141a; III 12a, 13b
Great Britain, I 663a; II 17a, 105b
Hinduism, I 248a, 249a
historiography, II 488b
immortality, I 644a
independence, III 337a
Islam, I 354a; III 337a
language, III 65a
law, III 12a, 13b
linguistics, III 65a
Mahabodhi Society, I 249a
Marx, II 17a
Mohammedanism, I 248a
mythology, III 272a
Nagas, III 337a
nationalism, III 332b, 337a, 338a
Orientalism, III 428a–431b, 433a, 433b, 434b, 436a
pan-Islamism, III 338a
Pakistan, III 338a
peace, III 446a
private property, III 654b
progress, III 638b, 648a
reincarnation, I 645a
religion, III 430a–430b
trade, III 428b
transcendentalism, I 368b
U.S., III 428a, 428b–436a
unity, III 338a
welfare state, IV 513b
India (ancient), I 354a
  asceticism, I 631b–632a
  astrology, I 119a–119b, 121b–125b
  atomism, I 496b
  balance of power, I 180a–180b
  Brahmanism, IV 104a
  Buddhism, I 247a–255a
  city, I 427b, 428a
  classification of the sciences, I 464a
  cosmology, I 539a
  cosmos, IV 104a
  Creation, I 571a
  cycles, I 621b, 622a
  death, I 644b
  despotism, II 13a–13b
  disease, II 395b–397a
  dualism, II 39a, 41b
  eighteenth century attitudes toward, I 80b, 83a
  evil, II 162a
  evolutionism, II 174b
  Gnosticism, II 327b, 329a, 330a

God, I 571a; II 338a, 340a
Gymnosophists, I 631b–632a
immortality, I 644b
Islam, II 639a, 639b, 640b, 650b
justice, III 7a
language, II 661b, 663a, 669b, 670a–670b, 671b, 673b
law, III 7a
linguistics, II 670a–670b
literature, II 670a
music, III 268b
mythology, II 39a; III 303a, 304a, 305b–306a, 308a
neo-classicism in art, III 365a
reincarnation, I 644b
religion, IV 94b, 98b, 104a
sacrificial ritual, IV 104a
salvation, IV 232b
symbolism, IV 338b
theodicy, IV 379b
writing, II 670a–670b
Indians (American)
  anarchism, I 71a
  conservation, I 471b, 474a
  dualism, II 38b
  environment, II 122b
  equality, II 143b, 145a
  language, II 660b, 661a, 661b, 669a–669b; III 63a, 71a; IV 325a
  linguistics, II 661a, 661b
  Montaigne, III 594a
  mythology, III 279b, 301a, 302a, 304a
  numbers, III 403b, 404a
  primitivism, III 594a–605a
  Protestantism, III 490b
  psychology, IV 18b
  Puritanism, IV 18b
  religion, IV 94a
  structuralism, IV 325a
  time, IV 399a–399b, 402a
  Voltaire, III 605a
Indians (pre-Columbian), time, IV 399a–399b, 402a
Indifference curve, IV 456b
Indifference principle, III 612a, 615a
Individualism, II 594a–604a
  abstraction, II 599b–600b, 601b
  academicians, II 303b–304a, 306b
  acquired characteristics, II 622a
  Acton, Lord, II 599a
  Adam, Robert, II 308a
  Addison, II 306b, 307b
  Alberti, II 301a, 308a, 309b
  Alexander the Great, II 299b

anarchy, I 71b; II 594b, 595a, 597b
anthropology, II 603b
Apelles, II 299a, 299b
Apuleius, II 310a
architecture, II 298a, 299a, 300a, 300b, 308a
Aretino, II 304b–305a, 308b
Ariosto, II 308b
Aristotle, II 299b, 309a, 309b, 598a; III 37a; IV 49b, 175a–175b
Armenini, II 303a
art, II 297a–299a, 299b, 304b–311a, 567b, 570b, 572a, 574b, 577a, 577b, 581b, 582b
artists, II 297a, 299a–304b
atomism, II 603b
authority, I 161a–162a; II 599b
autonomy, II 598a–598b, 602b, 603a
Balzac, II 308b
Baudelaire, II 310b
Bayle, IV 119b
Bell, II 298b
Benthamites, II 596b, 597b, 602a
Berlin, II 599a
Bernini, II 303a–303b, 309a
Bible, II 597a
Blake, II 304a, 306b, 307a, 308a
Blanqui, II 595a
Boccaccio, II 301a, 310a
Bodin, III 19b
Bohemians, II 303b–304a
Boileau, II 310a
Bonald, II 600b; III 534a
Boucher, II 310b
Bourget, II 310b
Bradley, F. H., II 600b
Brüggemann, II 595b
Brunelleschi, II 298a, 300b
Brunetière, II 595a
Bruno, II 306a
Bryce, II 596b
Buddhism, I 251b–252a
Burckhardt, II 300a–300b, 595b–596a, 596b, 597b; IV 485a
Burke, II 594a, 599a
Butler, Bishop, IV 178a
Byron, II 598a
Cabet, II 595a
Calvin, II 597a, 598b
Calvinism, II 602b, 603a
capitalism, II 595b–597a
Carnegie, II 596b
Cassirer, II 308b
Castiglione, II 305a

Catullus, II 310a
causation, II 598b
Cennini, II 298a, 300b–301a
Chagall, II 304b
Chapman, III 294b, 295a
Chardin, II 306a
Chevalier, II 596a
Christianity, I 400b; II 596b, 597a
Cicero, II 305a, 309b
city-state, II 300b–302b
Clews, II 596b
Clovio, II 301b
Colbert, II 303b
Coleridge, II 307b
Colman, II 307a–307b
Colonna, II 303a
common sense, II 309b
communism, II 596a, 598a, 599b
competition, II 300b, 384b, 596b
Comte, II 600b, 601a; III 534a
consciousness, I 215a–215b
Constant, II 599a
Cooley, II 601a
Cosimo, II 302b
Counter-Enlightenment, II 111b
Courbet, II 298b
craftsmanship, II 300a
creativity, II 297a, 297b, 307a–307b, 309a
culture, II 297b, 298b, 311a
d'Argenson, II 602a
defined, II 297a
Delacroix, II 305b
democracy, I 664a; II 595a, 599a, 602a
Dicey, II 596b, 602a
dichotomy, II 309b–311a
Diderot, II 310a–310b, 600a–600b, 601a, 601b; III 644b
Dolce, II 305a
drawing, II 305b
Dryden, II 307a, 308b
Dubos, II 309b
Duff, II 306b, 307a, 307b
Dürer, II 309a
Duris of Samos, II 299b
Durkheim, II 601a, 603b
economic history, II 45b, 46b, 47a, 59a
economics, II 602a–602b
education, II 299a–299b, 300a, 307b–308a
Egypt (ancient), II 298b
Emerson, II 596a
emotion, II 297b

emotivism, II 603a
empiricism, II 603b
Engels, III 643a
Enlightenment, II 89a, 90a, 594a, 595a, 595b, 598b, 600b
enterprise, II 300b
environment, II 125b–127a
Epicurus, II 594b
epistemology, II 603b
Erasmus, II 302a, 599a
Espinas, II 601a
ethics, II 603a–603b; IV 49b
evangelicalism, II 596a
evil, II 595a–595b
evolution, II 126b–127a, 297a; III 646b
existentialism, II 189b, 191a, 603a
fancy, II 307a–307b
Ferguson, Adam, II 307b
Ficino, II 309a, 310a, 597b; IV 209b
Filarete, II 298a
Fiorentino, II 302b
Flaubert, II 310b
Florence, II 300b–302b, 303b
Fourier, II 595a
France, II 297b, 298b, 300b, 305a, 594a–596a, 601a
Franciabigio, II 302a
free associations, III 45a–47a
freedom, II 297b, 298a, 300b, 304a–304b, 596a–596b, 598a, 598b
French Revolution, II 595a–595b
Freud, II 601b
general will, II 275b–280b
Gerard, II 306b, 307a
Germany, II 305b, 306b, 307a, 595b–596a, 601a–601b
Ghiberti, II 298a, 301a
Gierke, II 597a–600a
Ginsberg, M., II 600a, 601a
Giotto, II 298a, 298b
God, II 297b, 300a, 308a–308b, 337b, 340b, 356a, 597a, 598a, 598b, 602b, 603a
Goethe, II 310b, 595b, 598a
good, IV 174b–180b
Gothic, II 297b, 298a
Goya, II 302a
grace, II 305a
Great Britain, II 297b, 298b, 300b, 303b, 305a, 305b, 306a, 308a, 310a, 596b

Greece (ancient), II 297b, 299a, 299b, 582b, 675a, 677b, 679a, 680a, 682b
Green, T. H., II 596b
groupism, II 599b
guilds, II 300a–300b
Gurvitch, II 601a
Hadrian, II 299b
happiness, II 374b, 375b, 378a, 379a–379b, 382a, 384b
Hare, II 603b
Hayek, II 597a, 601a, 602b
Hegel, II 415b, 600b, 601a, 601b; III 22a, 556a; IV 180a, 290b
Herbert, II 596b
Herder, II 306b
Hinduism, II 597a
historicism, II 457b
historiography, IV 147b
history, II 297a–297b, 594a–597a
Hobbes, II 600a, 600b, 601b; IV 177a–177b
Hobhouse, II 596b
Hogarth, II 300b, 306a
Hollanda, II 303a, 305a, 308b
Homans, II 601b
Hoover, Herbert, II 596b
Hugo, II 310b
human nature, III 572a, 577a
humanism, II 517a, 519b, 522a
Humboldt, W. von, II 595b, 598a
Hume, II 603a, 603b
idea, II 597a–603b
ideal, II 550b, 551a
ideology, II 596a, 596b, 597a
idiosyncracies, II 297b, 301b–303a
imagination, II 304b, 307a–307b
imitation, II 298a, 306a–306b
impiety, II 564b, 565a, 567a
impressionism, II 567b, 570b, 572a, 574b, 577a, 577b, 581b, 582b
Industrial Revolution, II 595a
inspiration, II 307a–307b
invention, II 304b, 307a–307b
inviolability, II 298b
irrationalism, II 305a
isolationism, II 595a, 602b–603a
Israel (ancient), II 564b;

IV 227b
Italy, II 297b, 298b, 299a, 300b–303b, 308b
Jackson, William, II 305b
Jacone, II 302b
James, III 561a, 563a
Jaurès, II 595a
Jefferson, II 596a, 599a
Jeremiah (Bible), II 602b
Johnson, Samuel, II 307b
Judaism, II 564b, 597a
Kant, II 279b–280a, 307a, 597b, 598b, 600a, 603a; III 472b, 555b; IV 179b
Keble, II 310b
Klee, II 304b
laissez-faire, II 596a–596b, 597a, 602b
Lamb, II 309b
Lamennais, II 594b
Lanfrancus, II 300a
Lange-Eichbaum, II 308b
law, II 675a, 677b, 679a, 680a, 682b, 689b; III 27b, 28a, 33a, 35a–35b
Lebrun, II 303a
Leibniz, II 603b; IV 382a
Leonardo da Vinci, II 298a, 298b, 301b, 302a, 304a, 308a
Leroux, II 595a
liberalism, II 595a, 596b, 597a, 598a, 599a, 602a, 602b; III 36b, 37a, 39b, 43b–47a, 49b, 52a, 59a, 59b; III 36b, 39b, 43b–47a, 52a, 52b–53a, 53b–54a, 56a, 56b
liberty, II 300b
Lindsay, A. D., II 597a
List, II 596a
literary criticism, II 297a, 306a, 318b
literature, II 298a, 299a, 301a–301b, 306a–307b; IV 333a
Locke, II 599a, 600a, 601b, 603b; III 21a; IV 120a
Lomazzo, II 303a, 305a, 308a
Lombroso, II 308b
Longinus, II 304b
love, III 104a
Lowell, J. R., II 305b
Lucian, II 299b
Luther, II 597a, 598b
Lutheranism, II 603a
McCall, II 596b
McDougall, II 601a
Machiavelli, IV 480b–481a, 483a–483b
Macpherson, II 602a
macrocosm and microcosm, III 126a, 127a, 129a

McTaggart, II 597b
madness, II 308b–309b
Maistre, II 594b, 595a, 598b
Malinowski, II 601a
Manetti, II 597a–597b
Mao Tse-tung, II 599b
Marcus Aurelius, II 299b
Marshall, Alfred, II 602b
Marx, II 451a, 451b, 598a, 600b, 601a
Marxism, III 147b, 151a–151b, 154a, 167b, 168a, 168b, 645b, 646a
Masaccio, II 301b
materialism, II 451a, 451b
matter, II 298b; III 191b
Mayo, Elton, II 599b
Meinecke, II 597a; IV 203b
melancholy, II 308b–309b
Menger, Carl, II 601a
Mengs, A. R., II 306a
Michelangelo, II 298b, 302a–305a, 308b, 309a
Middle Ages, II 297b, 298a, 298b, 300a, 303b, 597a, 598a, 599a
Mill, J. S., II 596b, 598a, 599a, 599b, 601a
millenarianism, III 224a
mind, II 298b
Moebius, II 308b
Montesquieu, II 600b
morality, II 594b, 595b, 596a, 597a, 598b, 603a–603b; III 644b, 645a
music, II 314b, 315b, 316b, 318a, 319b, 320b
mysticism, II 602b
mythology, III 294b, 295a, 308b
Naples, II 297b
nationalism, III 336b
natural law, II 457a, 600a, 601b; III 14b, 15b, 17b, 19a–19b, 20b, 21a, 21b, 22a
naturalism in art, III 342b
Nature, II 307a; III 346b, 350a
negative liberty, II 599a–599b
Neo-Platonism, II 308b; III 516b
Nero, II 299b
Nietzsche, II 307b, 603a; IV 485a
non-finito, II 297b, 298b–299a
Northcote, II 303b, 309b
Occam, II 599a
originality, II 306a–306b
Ovid, II 310a
Owen, II 596b

Paine, II 599a
Pamphilos, II 299a–299b
pangenesis, II 623b
Panofsky, II 308a
Pareto, II 601a, 601b
Parrhasios, II 299b
Parsons, II 601a
passions, III 642b
Pausanias, II 299b
Pecqueur, II 595a
Peirce, III 561a
perfectibility, III 472b
periodization in history, III 476b, 478a, 480b
Petrarch, II 302a
Philostratus, II 299b
phrenology, IV 23b
Picasso, II 304b
Pico della Mirandola, II 597b
Piero di Cosimo, II 302b
Pietism, III 493b, 495a, 495b
Pini, II 309b
Pinkerton, II 306b
Piranesi, II 308a
Plato, II 299b, 308a, 309a, 309b; III 37a, 496a
Platonism, II 298b, 308b, 310a, 310b; III 496a, 516b
pleasure, II 374b, 375b, 378a, 379a–379b, 382a, 384b
Pliny, II 299a–299b, 305a, 310a
Plutarch, II 299b
poetry, II 299b, 302a–302b, 304b, 310b
politics, II 594b, 595b, 598b, 599a, 599b, 601b–602a, 602b, 603b
Pollock, II 304b
Pontormo, II 301b, 302b
Pope, II 305a, 306a–306b
Popper, II 600b, 601a
Portugal, II 303b
positivism, III 534a
power, IV 437b, 438a
pragmatism, III 551b, 552a, 553a, 555b, 556a, 558a, 561a, 563a
predestination, II 603a
prescriptivism, II 603a
press, III 45a–47a
privacy, II 599a–599b, 602b
pro-Bohemians, II 304a
progress, III 630a, 637a, 640b, 642b–647b
prophecy, III 659a
Protestantism, I 400b; II 596b, 602a, 602b
Proudhon, II 594b
psychology, II 297a, 304a–304b, 309b, 310b–311a,

603a–603b; IV 23b, 29a
Puritanism, II 596a, 603a
Quintilian, II 305a, 309b
Rainaldus, II 300a
Raphael, II 298a, 302b–303a, 309a, 309b
rationalism, IV 49b
recapitulation, IV 56a, 57a, 57b, 58b
reformation, IV 60a–65a, 65b, 68b, 69a
Reformation, I 395a–395b; II 89a, 594b, 595a, 597a, 602b, 603a; IV 67b–68a
religion, II 596a, 597b, 598b, 602b–603a; IV 118a, 119a, 119b, 120a, 120b
Rembrandt, II 309a
Renaissance, II 89a, 297b, 298a–310a, 595a–597b; IV 126b, 136b, 141a–142b, 147b, 437a, 438a, 439a
revisionism, IV 268b
Reynolds, II 300b, 303a–303b, 306a, 306b, 307b–308a, 309b
rhetoric, IV 141a
Riesman, II 598b, 599b
right, IV 174b–180b
Rimbaud, II 308b
Robbia, II 301b
Rodin, II 299a
Roman Catholic Church, I 400b; II 595a, 598b, 602b, 603a
romanticism, II 298b, 304a–304b, 595b, 597a, 598a, 600b; IV 198b, 199b, 200a, 201a, 202b, 203a, 203b, 205a, 205b, 209a, 209b, 210a, 210b
Rome (ancient), II 299b, 689b
Rousseau, II 275b–280b, 597b, 599b, 600a, 601b; III 21b
Royce, III 561a
Rubens, II 303a, 309a
rugged, II 596a, 596b
Ruskin, II 297b, 307a
Rustici, II 302a
Sacchetti, II 301a
Saint Antonio, II 305a
Saint Augustine, II 602b; IV 63a
Saint Francis of Assisi, IV 65a
Saint Thomas Aquinas, II 598a
Saint-Simon, II 600b, 601a
Saint-Simonians, II 594b, 595b
Sarto, II 302b
Sartre, II 603a–603b

Satan, II 603a
Scaliger, II 308a
Schelling, IV 210b
Schiller, II 307b
Schlegel, II 595b
Schleiermacher, II 595b, 597b; IV 201a
Schopenhauer, II 308b
selective interventionism, II 602b
self-development, II 597b–598a
self-direction, II 598a–598b
self-reliance, II 596a, 596b
Seneca, II 308b
Shaftesbury, II 308b
Shakespeare, II 306a–306b, 307a
Sidney, II 306a
Simmel, II 595b, 597a, 601a
Smith, Adam, II 602a
social contract, II 600a–600b, 601b; IV 254b, 255b, 257a, 259b, 260a, 263b
Social Darwinism, III 646b
socialism, II 595a–596b, 598a–601a, 602b, 603b; IV 285a, 287b, 288a, 289a, 290b, 291a
Société d'Individualistes, II 594b
society, II 597a, 599a–601b
sociological, II 600a–600b
sociology, II 297a
Socrates, III 577a; IV 174b
Sombart, II 602a
Spencer, II 596a, 596b; III 637a, 643a; IV 180b
Spinoza, II 598b
Stahl, II 309b
State, II 598a; IV 316a–318a
Stoicism, I 623b–624a; II 299b, 594b; IV 176a
structuralism, IV 326b
style, II 297b–298b; IV 333a
suffrage, III 45a–47a
Sumner, II 596a, 601a
supremacy, II 597a–597b
Taine, II 308b
talent, II 304b–306a
Tarde, II 601a, 601b
Tawney, II 596b
Temple, II 305b, 307b
theodicy, IV 379b, 382a, 383a
Theodorus of Samos, II 299a
Tintoretto, II 302a

197

Tocqueville, II 17b, 595a, 595b, 596a, 599a
Torri, II 301b
totalitarianism, IV 407a, 410b
tragic sense, IV 415b
transcendentalism, II 596a
Trilling, II 308b–309a
Troeltsch, II 596b
Turgot, II 600a–600b, 602a
types of, II 594a–604a
Uccello, II 301b
Ullmann, II 598a–598b
union in, II 309b–311a
uniqueness, II 298b
Unitarianism, II 596a
U.S., II 595a, 596a–596b
unit–ideas of, II 597a–603b
universal man, IV 437a, 438a, 439a
utility, IV 452a, 453b, 454a, 454b, 456b–457b
Utopia, IV 463b
Vasari, II 298a, 301b–303b, 305a–305b, 309b
Velázquez, II 309b
Venice, II 297b
Veuillot, II 595a
Vico, II 600b
Victorians, IV 217a–218b, 223a, 223b
Vinet, II 594b
virtù, IV 479b–485a
Volksgeist, IV 492b, 493a, 494a, 495b, 496a
Walpole, II 306a
Walras, II 602b
war, IV 503b
wealth, II 299b
Weber, II 596b, 602a, 602b–603a
welfare state, IV 509b–511a, 512b, 514b
Wellek, II 304b, 307a
Whitman, II 596a
will, II 598b, 600a
William of Ockham, III 19a–19b
Winckelmann, II 297b
Wittgenstein, II 603b
Wölfflin, II 297b
Young, II 306b, 307a, 307b
Zeitgeist, IV 536a
Zeuxis, II 299b
Indo-European languages, III 66a–71a
Indonesia, nationalism, III 337a, 338b
Indra (myth), II 343b
Induction
   Aristotle, III 380a
   Bacon, III 384a
   empiricism, III 550a

Grosseteste, II 196b
Newton, III 379b, 382a, 384a, 385b, 390b
Inductivism, I 503a
   Bacon, I 221b, 503a
   behaviorism, I 221b–222a
   continuity, I 503a
   Indulgences, I 386b, 388b, 389b
   Luther, I 389b
Indus Valley, God, II 333a, 343b
Industrial Revolution, I 70a
   class, I 441b
   crisis in history, I 590a
   disease, II 403a, 403b, 405b–406a
   environment and, II 124b
   individualism, II 595a
   periodization in history, III 480b
   private property, III 651a, 652b
   protest movements, III 672a
   romanticism, IV 203b
   utility, IV 453a, 453b
   war, IV 500b, 504a
Industry
   anarchy, III 673b
   art, II 580a
   capitalism, III 148b
   Christianity, I 405b
   civilization, III 182b
   Comte, III 642a–642b
   despotism and, II 12a
   economic industry, II 49a
   Engels, III 153b
   Enlightenment, II 90b
   existentialism, III 158b, 160b
   Gandhi, III 446a
   Germany, III 653a
   impressionism, II 580a
   John XXIII (Pope), III 654b
   labor, III 675b
   love, III 104a
Marx, I 39b–40b; III 479a
Marxism, III 147b, 148b, 149a, 150b, 153b, 154a, 155a, 158b, 160b, 654a
   nationalism, III 325a, 330b, 331b, 334a, 334b
   Nature, III 349b
   painting, II 580a; IV 475a
   peace, III 445a, 445b, 446a, 642a–642b
   philanthropy, III 490a
   private property, III 651a, 652a, 653a–655b, 656b
   progress, III 638b, 641b, 642a–642b
   protest movements, III 671b–676a

psychology, IV 24a, 26a, 28b
revisionism, IV 264a, 266a, 271b–272a
revolution, IV 160a, 160b, 162b
romanticism, IV 206b, 207b
Rumania, III 336b
science, III 150b
socialism, IV 289a, 289b–290a, 293a–293b, 294a
Spencer, III 642a
syndicalism, III 673b
technology, III 150b; IV 358b, 360a, 363a, 364a
Tolstoy, III 445b
totalitarianism, IV 406b, 409b
transcendentalism, IV 24a
U.S.S.R., III 150b, 153b–154a, 154b, 155a, 334a, 655a
Victorians, IV 217b, 218b
Vox populi, IV 499b
war, III 642a–642b; IV 503b, 504b, 506b
welfare state, IV 509a–510b, 511b, 512b, 514b
women, IV 529a
Inequality
   Aristotle, II 140a; III 11a; IV 318a
   Campanella, I 448a
   class, I 448a–448b
   common law, III 31b
   Condillac, I 448a
   Diderot, I 448a
   evolution, III 646b
   Galton, I 448a
   general will, II 277a, 277b, 278a, 278b
   Greece (ancient), III 11a
   Helvétius, I 448a
   law, III 11a, 11b, 28b, 31b
   Locke, I 448a
   Marxism, III 151b
   matter, II 186b
   Pearson, I 448a
   private property, I 448b
   progress, III 639a, 646b
   Rousseau, I 448a–448b; II 277a, 277b, 278a, 278b; IV 288a
   Social Darwinism, III 646b
   socialism, IV 284b–293b
   State, IV 318a
Inertia
   causation, I 276a
   cosmology, I 547a, 548a, 558b
   Descartes, III 193a
   Einstein, IV 84a, 86a, 86b, 89a, 89b
   matter, III 193a, 194b, 195a

medieval theories of, II 199b, 201b, 202a
Newton, III 194b, 195a; IV 89b–90a
relativity, IV 75a, 77a, 84a, 86a, 86b, 89a, 89b–90a
time, IV 397b, 404b
Inertial mass, I 558a–558b
Inevitability
   determinism, II 20b–21a
   historiography, II 20b–21a
   pragmatism, III 553a
Infallibility, criticized, III 553a
Infinite fields, III 620b–621a
Infinity, II 604–617a
   Abel, II 606b
   absolute, II 606a, 611b
   abstraction, II 609a
   Achilles (myth), II 608b
   aether, II 608a–608b, 612b
   Anaximander, II 604b, 605a, 608b, 609a
   apeiron, II 604b, 605a, 607a–607b, 608b, 609b; IV 298a
   Apollonius, II 611a
   Arabia, II 609b
   Archimedes, II 609a, 609b, 610a, 610b, 611a
   architecture, II 612b
   Aristotle, II 604b–605b, 607b, 608a–609a, 610a, 611a–612b, 614a–615a
   art, II 612b, 614a
   Being, II 614a, 615a
   Bentley, II 608a
   Berkeley, II 606a
   Bible, II 604b
   Bolzano, II 606b
   Born, II 606b
   Broglie, II 606b–607a
   Bruno, II 442b–443a, 605a, 607a, 608a; IV 298a, 298b
   Cantor, II 606b, 609b, 610a, 611a, 611b–612b
   Carlyle, IV 200b
   cartography, II 613a
   Cassirer, II 611b
   Cauchy, II 606b, 609b
   Cézanne, II 614a
   Christianity, II 615a
   completeness, II 614a–615b
   conception, II 607b
   conservation of energy, II 612b
   continuity, II 605b
   Copernicus, II 605a, 608a
   cosmology, II 605a, 605b, 606b, 607a, 612b, 615a
   cosmos, I 543b, 544b, 545a; IV 604b, 606b, 608a
   Creation, II 605b

Crescas, II 605a
Dedekind Cut, II 610b
Descartes, II 605b, 606a, 608a
Diogenes Laërtius, II 604b
divination, II 605a
Duhem, II 609b
Enlightenment, II 611a
eternity, II 604b
Euclid, II 610a, 611a, 612b–613a, 614a
Eudoxus of Cnidos, II 609b
Euler, II 611a
finite, II 614a–615b
Frege, II 611b
Gauss, II 611a, 613a–613b
God, II 441a, 443a, 446b, 604b, 606b, 608a, 611b, 614b; IV 75b
good, II 614a
grace, II 614a
Greece (ancient), II 604b–605b, 607a–611a, 614b
Hamilton, W. R., II 613b
Hankel, II 606b
Heisenberg, II 606b
Herbart, II 605b
Hesiod, II 604b
hierarchy, II 438b–447b
Hilbert, II 610b
Hobbes, II 606a
Homer, II 604b
humanism, IV 129a
indefinite, II 607a–608a
indeterminacy, II 588b
Ingres, II 614a
Islam, II 605b
Jenyns, II 447a
Johnson, Samuel, II 447a
Judaism, II 604b–605b
justice, II 614a
Kant, II 447b, 605b, 606a
Kepler, II 605a
Klein, Felix, II 613b
La Grange, II 611a
Leibniz, II 446a, 605b, 606a, 611a
linear continuum theory, II 610a
Locke, II 446b, 606a
Lucretius, II 612b
Maier, II 609b
mathematics, II 606a, 606b, 608a–614a, 615a, 615b; III 173b, 174b, 176a, 177a
matter, II 605b, 614a
method of exhaustion, II 609b, 610b
Middle Ages, II 605a, 605b, 608a, 609a–609b
More, Henry, II 608a
motion, II 605b
music, III 271b
mythology, III 305a, 305b,

306a
natural law, III 15a
Newton, II 605a, 608a, 611a; IV 75b
Nicholas of Cusa, II 441a–441b, 608a
nonscientific aspects, II 614a–614b
nuclear indefinite, II 607b
numbers, II 606b, 609b–613b
One, II 614b, 615a
ontology, II 615a
painting, II 614a
Parmenides, II 614b, 615a, 615b
Peirce, II 611b
perception, II 607b
perfectibility, II 614a–615b; III 464a
perspective, II 612b, 614a; IV 302a
Philo Judaeus, II 605b, 614b
philosophy, II 604b–606a, 607a–608b, 611a, 611b, 614a–614b, 615b
physics, II 605b, 606a–607b, 608b, 610b, 612a–612b
Pindar, II 604b
Plato, II 605a, 605b, 607a, 609b
Plotinus, II 605b, 614b
power, II 614a
pre-Socratics, II 604b, 605a, 607a
proportion, II 609b, 610a
Ptolemy, II 613a
puzzles, II 608b, 610a, 615a
Pythagoras, II 604b, 607a
quantum mechanics, II 607b
quaternion, II 613b
relativity, IV 75b, 87a
Renaissance, II 605a, 608a, 609a, 609b, 612b; IV 129a
Riemann, II 611b, 613b, 614a
Riemann-Darboux integral, II 610b
romanticism, IV 199b–202b, 204b, 210a
Russell, II 611b
Saint Augustine, II 611b
Saint Thomas Aquinas, II 605b, 614b
Schelling, IV 202a
Schleiermacher, IV 200b, 201a
science, II 609b, 611a
scientific revolution, II

609b, 611a
secularization, II 605b, 606a, 606b
solar system, II 608a
space, II 604b, 605a, 606a, 611a, 611b, 613b, 614a; IV 298a, 302a, 305a
Spengler, II 605a; IV 298b
Spinoza, II 444b, 445a, 606a, 614a
sublime in external nature, IV 336b
survey of, II 604b–607a
symbol for, II 609b, 611a, 613a–614b
Thales, II 604b
theology, II 605b, 606a, 608a, 611b, 614a, 614b, 615a
time, II 605b, 606a, 610a, 614a
universe, II 441a–443b, 608a, 612a, 615a, 615b
vanishing point, II 612b, 614a
Veronese, II 610b
Wallis, II 609b, 611a
Weierstrass, II 606b
Whitehead, II 611b
Xenophanes, II 605b, 607b
Zeno of Elea, II 607b, 608b, 610a, 610b
Inflation, economic history, II 57b
Infra-red rays, optics, III 419b
Ingalls, Daniel H. H., Buddhism, I 256b
Inge, William Ralph (1860–1954)
  Platonism, III 503a, 523a
  progress, III 635b
Ingenieros, José (1877–1925), positivism, III 543b
Ingpen, William
  harmony, II 394a
  hierarchy, II 438a
Ingram, James, literature, III 82a
Ingres, Jean A. D. (1870–1867)
  art, II 614a
  classic naturalism, III 345a
  David and, III 341a
  idea, II 546a
  impressionism, II 570a, 572b, 577b, 579b, 580a
  infinity, II 614a
  naturalism in art, III 341a, 345a
  neo-classicism in art, III 370b
Injury, II 396a
  ethics, IV 71a
  law, II 686b, 687b, 688b;

III 33a–33b
Rome (ancient), II 686b, 687b, 688b
Ink blots, chance images, I 340b, 349b–351a, 353a
Innina-Ishtar (myth), II 333b
Innocence
  law, II 688b–689a
  Lemoine, II 689a–689b
  mythology, III 278b, 305a
  primitivism, III 580a
  Rome (ancient), II 688b–689a
Innocent III, Pope (1161–1216)
  Christianity, III 591a
  common law, II 694b
  Crusades, I 383a
  dignity, IV 140a, 143a
  heresy, II 419b, 423a
  history, I 383a–383b, 386a
  jurisdictions, I 385b
  nationalism, III 320b–321a
  primitivism, III 591a
  reformation, IV 64a
  scholasticism, I 383a
  witchcraft, IV 522a
Innocent IV, Pope (d. 1254), heresy, II 425b
Innocent VIII, Pope (1432–1492), heresy, II 427a
Innocent X, Pope (1574–1655)
  China, I 357b
  Jansenism, I 400a
Innovation
  impressionism, II 577a, 579b
  music, II 315b
  perennial philosophy, III 458b
Inquisition
  Bruno, III 194a
  Galileo, III 356a
  heresy, II 417a, 425a, 427a, 430a
  history, I 383b
  intolerance, IV 117a
  law, II 686a, 689a; III 7b
  love, III 102b
  Middle Ages, II 417a, 425a, 427a
  Roman Catholic Church, I 383b, 546b; II 425a
  Spain, I 393b; IV 117a
  witchcraft, IV 521b, 522a, 522b
Inspiration
  art, II 307a–307b
  Blake, II 307a
  creativity in art, I 583b–584a
  genius, II 293b, 294a, 294b,

295a, 295b, 307a–307b, 316b, 318b, 323b–324a
Kant, II 323b–324a
music, II 316b, 318b, 323b–324a
Plato, I 583b–584a; III 499a–499b, 501b
Socrates, I 583b
unity of science, IV 435a
Instinct
Comte, III 644a, 648b–649a
evolution, IV 108a
general will, II 277a
genius, II 294a, 295a, 295b, 314a, 317a, 325a
God, II 349a
good, IV 180a, 185a
happiness, II 383b, 385a
harmony, II 388a
human nature, III 644a
humanism, IV 135a
Hutcheson, III 234b
imprinting, II 584b–585a
learning, II 584b–585a
love, III 94a
moral sense, III 234b
music, II 314a, 317a, 325a, 388a
mythology, III 315b
natural law, III 16a, 18a, 19b, 20a
Nature, II 227b; III 16a, 348b
perfectibility, III 644a
pleasure, II 383b, 385a
pragmatism, III 564b
progress, II 644a, 647a, 648b–649a
reason, II 227b
Renaissance, IV 135a
right, IV 180a, 185a
Rousseau, II 277a
Victorian, IV 217a, 222a, 222b, 223a
theriophily, IV 384b, 385a
wisdom of the fool, IV 516a, 518b
Institute of International Law, III 451a
Institutions
economic history, II 60b
law, III 11b, 13a, 27b
metaphor, III 198b
philanthropy, III 488a, 488b, 489b
reformation, IV 60a, 61b, 63b–66a
Instrumentalism
Dewey, III 552b, 566a, 569a; IV 185b
good, IV 185b
Lovejoy, III 552b
pragmatism, III 552b, 553b,

566a, 569a
right, IV 185b
Santayana, III 553b
Instruments, music, III 260b, 261a, 265a, 266a–266b, 268a–270b
Insufficient reason principle, III 615a
Insurance, II 406a
welfare state, IV 509b–514a
Interest, economic history, II 45b, 49b, 53b, 54a, 54b–58b
International Association of University Professors and Lecturers, I 14a
International Court of Justice, III 32b, 451a, 451b
International Labour Organisation, IV 513a, 513b–514a
International law, II 250b, 687b; III 18a, 32b, 34a
International Law Association, III 451a
International peace, III 448a–457a
advocates of, III 448b, 449b–453a
Alexander I, III 453a
alliances, III 448b, 452a
American Peace Society, III 448b, 453a
American Revolution, III 453a
appeasement, III 454b
arbitration, III 449b–454a
armament, III 448b, 449b, 455a–456b
arms control, III 456a, 456b
Arms Control and Disarmament Agency, III 455b
Atomic Energy Commission, III 455b
Austria, III 449a, 453b
autocracy, III 453a
balance of power, III 452a, 456a, 456b
Bartholdt, III 453b
Bentham, III 452b
Bethune, III 452b
biology, III 448b
Bluntschli, III 451a
Bridgman, III 453b
British Peace Society, III 448b
Bryan, III 450b
Burritt, III 453a
Carnegie, III 453a, 453b
Carnegie Endowment for International Peace, III 449a
Central American Court of International Justice, III

451a
Central Organization for a Durable Peace, III 454a
China (Communist), III 455b, 456a
Christianity, III 448a
Church Peace Union, III 449a
Civil War, III 450a
Clark, III 451b
commerce, III 451a
Commission for Conventional Armaments, III 455b
communications, III 451a, 453a, 456b
Concert of Europe, III 453a
conciliation, III 450b
Congo, III 454b
Congress of Vienna, III 453a
Constant, III 453b
"cooling off" principle, III 450b
Cremer, III 448b
Crucé, III 452b
Crusades, III 452b
culture, III 451b, 456b
Cyprus, III 454b
Davis, III 453b
defined, III 448a
democracy, III 449a, 451a
diplomacy, III 452a–452b, 454b, 456b
disarmament, III 449b, 454a, 455a, 455b, 456b, 456a, 456b
Disarmament Committee, III 455b
Dubois, Pierre, III 452b
economics, III 448b, 454a, 454b
education, III 448b, 449a
Enlightenment, III 452b
Ethiopia, III 454a
evolution, III 488b
Fabian Society, III 454a
Five Power Treaty, III 455b
France, III 449a, 453b, 455b, 456a
free will, III 452b
Fried, III 449a
Germany, III 449a, 454a, 455a
Great Britain, III 448b–449a, 449b, 450a, 451a, 453b, 454a, 455b, 456a
Greece, III 454b
Greece (ancient), III 448a, 449b
Grotius, III 450b–451b
Hague Peace Conferences, III 450a, 451a, 453b, 455a
Hale, III 453a

Hiroshima, III 455b
history, III 448b
Holt, III 453b
Holy Alliance, III 453a
idea, III 448a–448b, 456a–456b
idealism, III 448a, 450b
ideology, III 448b, 451b, 453a, 456b
Institute of International Law, III 451a
International Court of Justice, III 451a, 451b
International Law Association, III 451a
international organization, III 448b, 452b–455a
International Peace Bureau, III 449a
internationalism, III 453a, 455a
Interparliamentary Union, III 449a, 450b
isolationism, III 449b
Italy, III 454a, 455b
Japan, III 454a
Jay Treaty, III 450a
justice, III 450b, 451b, 452a, 453b
Kant, III 452b–453a
Kashmir, III 454b
Kennedy, J. F., III 456a
Korea, III 454b
law, III 449a, 450b–456b
League to Enforce Peace, III 454a
League of Free Nations Society, III 454a
League of Nations, III 449b, 451a, 451b, 454a–455b
League of Nations Union, III 454a
League of Peace, III 449a
Lebanon, III 454b
Locarno Pact, III 452b
Love, III 449a
Manchuria, III 454a
Middle Ages, III 448a
Middle East, III 454b
military, III 448a, 448b, 452a, 455a, 456b
millenarianism, III 456b
morality, III 448a, 450a, 453a
moratorium, III 450b
Nagasaki, III 455b
National Arbitration and Peace Congress, 449a
National Peace Council, III 448b–449a
nationalism, III 448b, 449b, 451b, 452a, 456b
nation-states, III 448a, 449a–456a

neutrality, III 454b
New York Peace Society, III 448b, 449a
Nicholas II, III 453b
nonproliferation pact, III 456a
North Atlantic Treaty Organization, III 456b
Novicow, III 453b
nuclear deterrence, III 456b
nuclear weapons, III 449b, 455a, 455b, 456a
Nuremberg Trials, III 452a
Organization of American States, III 456b
pacifism, III 448a, 448b, 449a, 450b, 452a, 455a, 455b
Pact of Paris, III 452a
Passy, III 449a
Pax Romana, III 448a
peace movement, III 448b–449b
Penn, III 452b
Permanent Court of Arbitration, III 450a, 451a, 453b
Permanent Court of International Justice, III 451a–451b, 452a
politics, III 448b, 451b–456b
propaganda, III 448b
racism, III 448b
religion, III 448a, 448b, 449b
Republican Party, III 455b
Roman Catholic Church, III 448a, 452b
Roosevelt, Theodore, III 450a, 453b
Root, III 450a
Rousseau, III 452b
Russia, III 453b
Saint-Pierre, III 452b
Salisbury, III 453b
society, III 451b, 453a
sociology, III 453a, 454b
sovereignty, III 452b, 453a, 456b
Suárez, III 451b
Sully, III 452b
Suttner, III 449a, 453b
Switzerland, III 451a
Taft, W. H., III 450a, 450b
treaties, III 448b, 449b, 450a, 451a, 452a, 452b, 455a, 455b
Truce of God, III 448a
Trueblood, III 453a, 453b
U.S.S.R., III 455b, 456a
U.N., III 449b, 451b, 452a, 454b–455a, 455b, 456b
U.N. Disarmament Commission, III 455b
U.S., III 449a, 449b, 450a, 451a, 451b, 453a, 453b, 454a, 455b, 456a
U.S. Senate, III 449b, 450a
unity, III 453a
Universal Peace Congress, III 449a
Universal Peace Union, III 449a
Vietnam War, III 449b
war, III 448a–456b
Warsaw Pact, III 456b
Washington Conference, III 455b
Workingmen's Peace Association, III 448b
World Court, III 449b
World Peace Foundation, III 449a
World War I, III 449a, 449b, 450a, 452b, 453b–454a, 455a
World War II, III 449b, 452a, 454a, 455b
World's Court League, III 454a
International Peace Bureau, III 449a, 450b
International Peace Congress (1899), IV 504b
International trade
  economic history, II 45b, 57a
  natural liberty, II 67a–68a
International Union for the Conservation of Nature, I 471a
International Union for the Conservation of Nature and Natural Resources, I 476b
International Working Men's Association, IV 293a
Internationalism
  nationalism, III 325a–334a
  peace, III 442a, 444b, 446a, 453a, 455a
  Russell, III 446b
  socialism, IV 293b
  war, III 447a; IV 502b
Intolerance
  Anabaptists, IV 117a, 117b
  anticlericalism, IV 120b
  anti-Semitism, IV 114a
  Antitrinitarians, IV 117a
  Arminians, IV 117b
  atheism, IV 120a
  Bayle, IV 119b–120a
  Charlemagne, IV 115b
  Christianity, IV 113b, 114a
  conformity, IV 114a
  conscience, IV 118a
  Council of Trent, IV 117a, 119a
crusade, IV 113b
dissent, IV 113b, 114a
Donatists, IV 114b
economics, IV 120a–120b
Edict of Nantes, IV 113a, 116a, 116b, 117b, 119a, 119b
Erasmus, IV 118b
Europe, IV 113a, 117a, 118a
excommunication, IV 117b
external, IV 113a
France, IV 113a, 119a
Germany, IV 117a
Greece (ancient), II 565b–566a
Henry IV, IV 119a
heresy, IV 113b, 114a, 114b, 115a, 115b, 116a, 117a, 119a, 120a, 120b
Holy Roman Empire, IV 117a
holy war, IV 113b
Huguenots, IV 113a, 113b, 116b, 117a
ideology, IV 115b–116a
impiety, II 565b–566a
Inquisition, IV 117a
Islam, IV 114a
Italy, IV 116a
Jesuits, IV 113a, 117a
Judaism, IV 113b, 114a
liberalism, III 40b, 42b
Locke, IV 119b, 120a
majorities, IV 116a
Manicheans, IV 115a, 115b
Marxism, IV 113a
medicine, IV 116a
Middle Ages, IV 115b
military, IV 113b
minorities, IV 112b, 116a
monotheism, IV 113b, 114a
mythology, III 301a
Netherlands, IV 117b, 120b
peace, III 446b
Peace of Augsburg, IV 118a
persecution, IV 112b–114a, 116a–118b, 119b–120a
Persia (ancient), IV 115a
Plato, II 566a
pluralism, IV 119a
politics, IV 113b, 116a, 120a
Protestantism, IV 113a
race, IV 116a
rationalism, III 301a
Reformation, IV 118a
Renaissance, IV 115b
Roman Catholic Church, IV 119a
Rome (ancient), IV 115a
Saint Augustine, IV 113b–114a, 116a
Saxons, IV 113b
schism, IV 113b, 117a, 117b
Servetus, IV 117a
Socinians, IV 117b
society, IV 114a
sociology, IV 116a
Spain, IV 113a, 117a, 120b
State, IV 116a
Sweden, IV 113a
Switzerland, IV 113a, 117a
totalitarianism, IV 408a
vice, IV 112b
  See also Religious Toleration
Intorcetta, Prospero, China, I 356a–356b
Intuition
  Bellori, II 549b
  Bergson, III 565a, 565b
  empiricism, III 547b
  Galileo, IV 361a
  genius, II 295b
  good, IV 177b, 183a
  happiness, II 383a
  ideal, II 549b, 551b
  James, III 565a
  Kant, II 551b
  mathematics, III 176b–177a
  medieval science, II 196b
  Mill, J. S., III 561a
  motion, IV 76b
  Peirce, III 558a
  perennial philosophy, III 458b
  Platonism, III 509a, 512a, 516b
  pragmatism, III 551b, 555a, 557a–557b, 558a, 561a, 565a, 565b
  primitivism, III 596b
  relativity, IV 76b
  Renaissance, IV 440b
  right, IV 177b, 183a
  skepticism, IV 245b, 250b
  Sorel, III 565b
  Spencer, II 383a
  Spinoza, IV 177b
  technology, IV 361a
  theriophily, IV 388b
  universal man, IV 440b
  utilitarianism, IV 445a, 445b
  wisdom of the fool, IV 516a
  women, III 596b
Invention
  art, II 304b, 307a–307b
  Bacon, IV 128a
  China (ancient), IV 358a
  culture and, I 608b, 609b
  genius, II 293a–295a, 304b, 307a–307b, 314b, 317b,

318a, 318b, 319b
historiography, **IV** 148a–149b
mimesis, **III** 228b
music, **II** 314b, 317b, 318a, 318b, 319b
progress, **III** 624b, 625a, 629a, 631a, 632b–633a, 636b
Ramus, **IV** 43a, 43b
Renaissance, **IV** 148a, 148b, 149a–149b
simultaneous, **IV** 359a
technology, **IV** 358a–364a, 364b
theriophily, **IV** 385a
Investment, economic history, **II** 51a, 51b, 53a–53b, 54a, 56a–56b
Io (myth), **III** 296b
Ionesco, Eugène (1912–)
  death, **I** 637b; **IV** 214b–215a, 215b
  satire, **IV** 214b–215a, 215b
Ionia
  Greece (ancient), **III** 61b
  historiography, **II** 466b–467a
  matter, **III** 186b, 187a
Ipu-Wer, freedom of speech, **II** 256a
Iran
  Buddhism, **I** 255a–255b
  dualism, **II** 155a
  eschatology, **II** 154b, 155a
  theodicy, **IV** 379b
Iran (ancient), *see* Persia (ancient)
Irānshahrī, **II** 643a
Iraq, Christian missionaries, **I** 376a
Ireland
  catastrophism, **IV** 420b
  equality, **II** 145a
  impressionism, **II** 575a
  music, **III** 269b–270a
  nationalism, **III** 330a, 334b
  Roman Catholic Church, **III** 334b
  satire, **IV** 211b, 212a–212b, 213b
  symbolism, **IV** 340b
  tolerance, **I** 401a
Ireland, John (1838–1918), modernism, **I** 419b
Irenaeus, Saint (2nd century A.D.)
  alienation, **I** 35b
  death, **I** 643a
  Gnosticism, **II** 327a–327b, 329b
  historiography, **II** 471b
  history, **I** 375b

immortality, **I** 643a
metaphor, **III** 205b
millenarianism, **III** 224a–224b
perfectibility, **III** 466a
theodicy, **IV** 381a, 383b
Irenicism, deism, **I** 649b
Iron Age (myth)
  primitivism, **III** 578a, 578b, 579b, 580a, 581b, 585b
  temperance, **IV** 366a
  Utopia, **IV** 459a
Irony, **II** 626b–634b
  abstract definition of, **II** 628b
  allegory, **II** 628b, 630b, 634a
  Aristotle, **II** 627b–628b
  Aristophanes, **II** 630b
  art, **II** 630b
  aspects of, **II** 627a
  audience, **II** 627a, 628a–628b, 630b, 634a
  Babbitt, **II** 633b
  Baudelaire, **II** 633b
  Beckett, **II** 633b
  blame, **II** 627b–630b
  Blok, **II** 632b
  Boileau, **II** 629a
  Bourne, **II** 633a
  Brooks, Cleanth, **II** 633a, 634a
  Brown, Norman, **II** 634a
  Büchner, **II** 633b
  Burke, Kenneth, **II** 633a–634b
  burlesque, **II** 629a, 629b, 630b
  Byron, **II** 633b
  Cambridge, **II** 629a, 629b
  Camus, **II** 633a
  Cervantes, **II** 629a, 629b, 630b, 632b
  Chantavoine, **II** 633a
  Chevalier, **II** 633a
  Christianity, **II** 630a, 632a
  Cicero, **II** 627b, 628a, 628b; **III** 77a
  comedy, **II** 627a, 628b, 630a, 631a–634b
  concrete universal, **II** 631b
  contradiction, **II** 630a–630b, 631b
  Crane, **II** 634a
  criticism, **II** 629a, 632b–633a, 633b, 634a–634b
  Dante, **II** 627a
  De Mott, **II** 633b
  defined, **II** 626b–627a, 627b–628a
  Defoe, **II** 629a
  Demosthenes, **II** 627a
  drama, **II** 627a, 629b, 631a, 631b, 633b–634a

eiron, **II** 627b
Eliot, George, **II** 633b
Empson, **II** 633a, 634a
enthusiasm, **II** 630b–631a
Erasmus, **II** 629a
evil, **IV** 411b
fate, **II** 627a, 632a
Fielding, **II** 629a
Fichte, **II** 630a
Flaubert, **II** 633b
Fowler, **II** 632b
France, Anatole, **II** 632b, 633a
Freud, **II** 634a
Frye, **II** 634b
Germany, **II** 629b, 633a
God, **II** 630a, 631b, 632a, 633b, 634b
Goethe, **II** 630a, 634a
Gourmont, **II** 633b
Grabbe, **II** 633b
Great Britain, **II** 628b
Greece (ancient), **II** 632a
Gurewitch, **II** 633b
Hardy, **II** 632b, 633b
Haym, **II** 633b
Hegel, **II** 629b, 631a, 631b–632a, 633a, 634b
Heine, **II** 629b, 632a, 632b, 633b
Heisenberg, **II** 634a
historiography, **II** 470b
history, **II** 626b–634b
Holland, **II** 634a
Housman, **II** 633b
Huneker, **II** 633b
ironic attitude, **II** 627a, 630a
ironic concession, **II** 629a, 629b
ironic defense, **II** 629a, 629b
ironic dilemma, **II** 632a–632b
James, **II** 633a, 633b–634a
Jankélévitch, **II** 634b
Kant, **II** 629b
Kierkegaard, **II** 629b, 632a, 633a
Laforgue, **II** 633b
Leopardi, **II** 633b
literary paradox, **III** 77a, 78a, 79b
Lucian, **II** 629a
Mann, **II** 633a, 634a
Melpomene (myth), **II** 632b
Miller, Arthur, **II** 634a
mock-gravity, **II** 629a
Muecke, **II** 634a
music, **II** 634a
mythology, **III** 272a
narrative, **II** 629b, 632a
negativism, **II** 631b
Neo-Platonism, **II** 629b

Niebuhr, R., **II** 634a, 634b
Nietzsche, **II** 633a
nihilism, **II** 627a, 627b, 630a, 632b, 633a–633b
Ortega y Gasset, **II** 634a
Palante, **II** 633b, 634a,
paradox, **II** 627a, 627b, 630b, 632b, 633a, 634a
pathos, **II** 633b
Paul, **II** 627b
Faulhan, **II** 633a
Pirandello, **II** 627b
Platonism, **II** 630a
Pope, **II** 628b, 629a
praise, **II** 627b–628a, 629b, 629a, 630b
Proudhon, **II** 634a
Quintilian, **II** 628a, 628b, 629a
Ransom, **II** 633a
realism, **II** 626b
religion, **II** 634b
Renan, **II** 633a
Richards, I. A., **II** 632b, 633a, 634a
romanticism, **II** 633b
Rome (ancient), **II** 632a
Sartre, Jean-Paul, **II** 633a
satire, **II** 627a–628b, 629b–632b, 633b–634b
schema, **II** 628b
Schiller, **II** 630a
Schlegel, August Wilhelm, **II** 629b–632a
Schlegel, Friedrich, **II** 629b–631b, 633a, 633b
science, **II** 634a
Sedgewick, **II** 633a
Shaftesbury, **II** 628a–628b, 629b, 630a
Shakespeare, **II** 630a, 630b, 631a, 632b
Socrates, **II** 627b, 628a, 628b, 629b, 630a, 631b, 632a
soft, **II** 628a
Solger, **II** 629b, 631b, 632a
Sophocles, **II** 632a; **IV** 367a
Sterne, **II** 630b
Swift, **II** 628b, 629a, 634a
Symons, **II** 633b
Theophrastus, **II** 627b
Thirlwall, **II** 629b, 632a, 632b, 634b
Tieck, **II** 629b, 630a, 630b, 632b
tragedy, **II** 627a, 627b, 628b, 630a, 631a–633b
tragic sense, **IV** 411b, 412b, 414b
trope, **II** 628b, 629a
understatement, **II** 628b
verbal, **II** 627a, 630b, 634a

victim, II 627a, 632a
visual arts, II 634a
Voltaire, II 629a
Warren, II 633a
wisdom of the fool, IV 518b, 519a
Irrational numbers, mathematics, III 174a
Irrationalism, II 634b–638b
  Absolute, II 637a
  aesthetics, IV 355a, 355b, 356b
  Aristotle, II 635a, 635b
  Artaud, II 638a
  atheism, II 637a
  atomism, II 638a
  Bachelard, II 636b, 638b
  Bataille, II 638a, 638b
  Being, II 637a, 637b
  Bergson, II 636b
  Blake, II 638a, 638b
  Breton, II 638a
  Cartesianism, II 635a, 638a
  concept of, II 634b–635a
  Damascius, II 635b
  Descartes, II 635b, 638a
  destiny, II 635a
  Dilthey, II 636b
  Enlightenment, II 635b
  Eternal Return, II 635a, 638a
  evil and, II 167b
  existentialism, II 635b
  Fechner, II 636b
  Fénelon, II 638a
  fictionalism, II 636a
  Foucault, II 637b
  Freud, II 636a, 637a
  Freudianism, II 637a–637b
  genius, II 293a–293b, 294b, 295a, 295b, 305a, 318b
  God, II 635b, 637a
  good, II 635a, 637b
  Greece (ancient), IV 46a, 49a
  Hamann, II 635b, 638a
  Hartmann, Edouard von, II 636a
  Hegel, II 635b
  Heidegger, II 637a, 637b
  Heraclitus, II 635a, 638a, 638b
  history, II 634b–638b
  Hölderlin, II 637b, 638a, 638b
  humanism, II 637b
  Husserl, II 636a, 637a
  Jacobi, II 635b, 636a
  James, II 636b
  Kant, II 635a–638a
  Keats, II 638a
  Kierkegaard, II 636b–637a, 637b

  Le Roy, II 636b
  Leibniz, II 638a
  literature, II 638a–638b
  Lukacs, II 637a
  Malebranche, II 635b
  Marcel, II 637a
  Marxism, II 637a, 637b
  matter, II 635a, 635b
  Merleau-Ponty, II 636b, 638a, 638b
  Michaux, II 638a
  Montaigne, II 635b
  music, II 318b
  mythology, II 635a; III 301a, 302a, 309b, 314a
  nationalism, III 331b
  Neo-Kantianism, II 636a
  Neo-Platonism, II 635a
  Newton, II 638a
  Nietzsche, II 635a, 636b, 637b, 638b
  non-reason, II 637b
  Novalis, II 638a, 638b
  numbers, II 635b
  One, II 635b
  Otto, II 638a
  Pascal, II 635b, 637a, 637b, 638a, 638b
  Péguy, II 637a
  periodization in history, III 479a
  pessimism and, II 167b
  Plato, II 635a, 635b, 637a, 637b, 638a; IV 368b
  Plotinus, II 635b
  poetry, II 638a–638b
  post-Nietzscheanism, II 635a
  pragmatism, II 636a
  Proclus, II 635b
  psychoanalysis, II 637a
  psychophysics, II 636b
  Pythagoreans, II 638a
  rationalism, II 634b–638b; III 301a, 302a, 309b; IV 46a, 49a
  religion, II 635b, 637a–637b
  Rimbaud, II 638b
  romanticism, II 638a–638b; IV 197a, 200a
  Rome (ancient), IV 46a
  Sartre, II 637a
  Schelling, II 636a
  Schopenhauer, II 636a, 636b
  science, II 635b, 636a, 636b, 637b–638a
  Shakespeare, II 635b
  Simmel, II 636a–636b
  skepticism, II 635b
  Socrates, II 635b
  Sophocles, II 637b
  Sorel, II 636b

  Stirner, II 638a
  subrational, II 638b
  super-rational, II 638b
  surrealism, II 638a
  taste, IV 355a, 355b, 356b
  temperance, IV 367b, 368b
  Thucydides, IV 367b
  tradition, II 635a
  tragic sense, IV 413b, 414a, 415a
  Vaihinger, II 636a
  vitalism, II 636b
  war, II 635a
  will, II 636a
  wisdom of the fool, IV 515b
  Xenophanes, II 635a
Irreversibility
  symmetry, IV 349b
  time, IV 390a
Isaac (Bible)
  loyalty, III 108b
  mythology, III 279a, 280b, 283a
  prophecy, III 666b
Isabella, Queen (1451–1504), Counter-Reformation, I 392b–395a
Isabella d'Este (1474–1539), mythology, III 290b
Isaeus (4th century B.C.), law, II 684b
  temperance, IV 368a
Isagoras (c. 500 B.C.), freedom of speech, II 259b
Isaiah (Bible)
  ambiguity, I 51b
  freedom of speech, II 255b–256a
  holy, II 512b
  music, III 269b
  mythology, III 283b
  philanthropy, III 487b
  prophecy, III 660b, 661b, 662b, 663b
Isherwood, Christopher (1904–   ), Buddhism, I 256a
Ishmael (Bible), mythology, III 279a, 280b
Ishtar (myth), II 335b
  love, III 94b
  Mesopotamia (ancient), IV 101b
  religion, IV 101b
  salvation, IV 226b
Isidore of Seville (560?–636)
  aesthetics, II 217b
  allegory, I 41a–41b
  law, III 18a
  mythology, III 286b, 288b
  natural law, III 18a

  poetry, III 528a
  temperance, IV 371a
  work, IV 531b
Ising, G., indeterminacy, II 588a
Isis (myth), II 39a, 333b, 341b
  Egypt (ancient), IV 100b
  religion, IV 93b, 100b
  salvation, IV 228b
Islam, II 638b–652a
  Abbasid period, II 640b, 641a
  Abū Ma'Shar, II 646b
  Adelard of Bath, II 64b
  al-'Amiri, II 645a
  al-Ash'ari, II 642a
  al-Bāqillāni, II 642a
  al-Birūni, II 647a
  alchemy, I 29a–30a; II 641a, 646a, 646b
  al-Din Shirāzi, II 651b
  Alexander of Aphrodisias, II 644a
  al-Fārābi, II 643a, 644a–644b, 645a, 649a, 649b
  al-Ghazzāli, II 642b, 648a, 648b, 649b, 650b
  al-Juwayni, II 642b
  al-Kindi, II 643a–643b, 644a
  al-Kūdat Hamadāni, II 650b
  'Allāf, II 641b
  al-Majriti, II 646b
  al-Ma'mūn, II 641b
  Almohads, II 648b
  al-Rāzi (Fakhr al-Din), II 642b, 643a, 647a, 648a–648b, 651b
  al-Rāzi (Muhammad ibn Zakariyā), II 646b–647a
  al-Sādiq, II 641a
  al-Shirāzi, II 651b
  al-Sijistāni, II 644b
  al-Tūsi, II 651a–651b
  Angelus Silesius, II 651a
  anthropology, II 651a
  anti-Aristotelianism, II 646b
  Arabic language, II 639a, 640a, 640b, 641a, 642a–642b, 643a, 644a, 644b
  Archimedes, II 640b
  Aristotelianism, II 641a, 642a, 643b, 646a, 646b, 647b, 650a
  Aristotle, II 639b, 640b, 643a, 644a, 644b, 645a, 645b, 647a, 649a, 649b, 650a, 650b
  art, II 640a
  Ash'arism, II 641b, 642a, 642b, 643a, 647b, 648b
  astrology, I 122b–125b; II 644a, 646b

astronomy, II 639a, 640b, 647a, 651b
atomism, I 287a, 289a, 495b–496b; II 641b, 642a, 642b, 643a
Averroës, II 642b, 644b, 645b, 646a, 648a, 649a–649b, 650a
Avicebron, II 648b
Avicenna, II 644b–651b
Babylonia, II 639a
Bacon, II 645b, 650b
Böhme, II 651b
Bradwardine, II 649a
Byzantium, II 639b
Cardanus, II 644a
Cassirer, II 647b
causation, I 273a–274a, 277a, 286b–289b, 495b; II 642b, 643a
Chaldea, II 639a
chance, I 336b
China, I 354a
China (ancient), II 640b
Christianity and, I 378b, 379a, 380b, 381a; II 639a, 639b, 640a, 640b, 641b, 646a, 650a, 651a; IV 230b
civilization, II 650a; III 181a
class, I 442a
classification of the sciences, I 463b
Copernicus, II 646a, 651b
cosmology, I 542b, 544a; II 640a, 644b, 646a, 646b, 648b, 651a
Creation, I 571a, 571b; II 345a
crisis in history, I 591a
Crusades, II 651a
Dante, II 644a, 649b, 651a
debates, II 640a–640b
deism, I 648a, 650b
Democritus, II 642b
Descartes, II 651b
determinism, II 29b, 30b
discontinuity, I 495b–496b
Divine Unity, II 641b
Divine Will, II 642b
double truth, II 35a
dualism, II 42b
Duns Scotus, II 645a, 645b–646a
Eastern Orthodox Church, I 417b
Eckhart, II 651a
economic history, II 46b
Enoch, II 640a
Epicurus, II 642b
eschatology, II 154b
esotericism, II 648b, 650b, 651a
Euclid, II 640b, 647b

Europe, II 648b
existentialism, II 651b, 652a
fatalism, II 29b
Fludd, II 646b
free will, II 29b, 245a, 345a, 641b; IV 230b
Galen, II 640b, 646a, 647a
Galileo, II 649a
geodesy, II 647a
geology, II 645b
Giles of Rome, II 649b
Gnosticism, II 645b, 650a, 650b–651a, 651b, 652a
God, I 286b, 287a–289a, 495b, 496a, 571a, 571b; II 339b, 344b–345a, 640b, 642b, 643a, 643b, 644b, 646b
grammar, II 641a
Greco-Alexandrian philosophy, II 639a, 642a
Greece (ancient), II 639a, 639b, 644a, 647b, 650a, 651b
Hadith, II 641a
heaven, IV 230b
Hegira, II 638b–639a
hell, IV 230b, 231a
heresiography, II 648b
Hermann the German, II 649b
Hermes Trismegistus, II 640a
Hermeticism, II 639a, 642a, 646a, 646b, 651a
Hippocrates, II 646a
historiography, II 474b–475a
history, II 650a
holy, II 513a
Holy Land, II 651a
House of Wisdom, II 640b
humanism, II 650a
Hume, II 642b
hylomorphism, II 645a
Ibn al-Haytham, II 647a–647b
Ibn 'Arabī, II 648b, 650a, 650b–651a, 651b
Ibn Bajjah (Avempace), II 648b–649a
Ibn Hazm of Cordova, II 641a, 648b
Ibn Ishāq, II 640b
Ibn Khaldūn, II 650a
Ibn Masarrah, II 648b
Ibn Muqaffa', II 640b
Ibn Sab'in, II 650a
Ibn Tufayl, II 649a
Idrīs, II 640a
India, I 354a; III 337a
India (ancient), II 639a, 639b, 640b, 650b

infinity, II 605b
inner light, II 649a
intolerance, IV 114a
Irānshahrī, II 643a
Ismā'ilis, II 646a
Jābir ibn Hayyān, II 641a, 646a
Jerusalem, II 651a
Jesus Christ, II 640a
John the Damascene, II 640b
John Philoponus, II 645a–645b, 649a
Judaism, II 639a, 640a, 651a
kadar, II 29b, 30b
Kalam, II 641b, 642a, 642b, 643a, 647b, 648b
Kepler, II 647a
Khawārij, II 641b
knowledge, II 639b, 642a, 646a
Koran, II 474b, 640a, 641a, 641b, 650b
law, II 641a; III 28b
Leibniz, II 644b, 649a, 651b
logic, II 640b, 644a, 645a, 648a
love, III 99b, 100a, 101a, 101b
Lucretius, II 642b
Lull, II 641a–641b, 646b, 651a
Maimonides, II 642b, 649a
mathematics, II 640b, 643b, 646b, 647a, 647b, 651b; III 181a
matter, III 190b
Māturidites, II 642a
Mecca, II 638b; IV 231a
medicine, II 639a, 645a, 645b, 646b
metallurgy, II 644a
metaphysics, II 641a, 643b, 644b, 645a, 648b, 651a, 651b
Meyerson, II 647b
Middle Ages, II 474b–475a, 640a, 644a, 646a, 646b
militancy, II 30b
minerology, II 645b
Mir Damād, II 651b
Monophysites, II 639a
Moses (Bible), II 640a
motion, II 651b
Muhammad, II 474b, 475a
Murji'ites, II 641b
Mu'tazilah, II 641b
Mu'tazilites, II 642a
mythology, III 275b, 276b, 279b, 283a
Nasir-e Khusraw, II 646a
nationalism, III 324b, 338a

Nature, II 639b, 643b
Nāzzām, II 641b
Neo-Platonism, I 287a, 288a; II 643a, 643b, 644b, 646b, 651a; III 377b
Neo-Pythagoreans, II 639a, 643b, 646a
Nestorians, II 639a
Newton, II 647a, 647b
Nicolas of Autrecourt, II 649a
nihilism, II 651b
Northrop, II 647b
Occasionalism, I 286b, 289a
occult science, II 640b, 644a, 646a, 646b
One, II 643b, 644b
optics, II 647a
Order of the Templars, II 651a
Oresme, II 649a
Orientalism, III 434b
Paracelsus, II 646b
paradise, IV 220b
people of the book, II 639a
perennial philosophy, II 650b
periodization in history, III 480a
Persia (ancient), II 639a
pharmacology, II 644a, 645b
phenomenology, II 652a
philanthropy, III 488a
Philo Judaeus, II 640a
philosophy, II 639a, 640a, 640b–652a
physics, II 643a, 645b, 646b, 647a, 647b, 649a
planets, II 651b
Plato, II 639b, 644b, 646b, 647b, 649b
Platonism, II 648b
Plotinus, II 643b
politics, II 644b, 645a, 647b, 649a
polytheism, IV 231a
predestination, II 29b, 30b, 345a, 641b; IV 230b
Proclus, II 643b
Prophet, II 641a
psychology, II 651a
Ptolemy, II 640b, 647b
Pythagoras, II 650a
Qadarites, II 641b
religion, II 639b, 640a, 641a, 644b, 646a, 647a, 648b, 649a, 650a; III 648b; IV 93b, 98a, 114a
Renaissance, II 640a, 640b, 644a, 646b, 649b, 650a
Roman Catholic Church, I

378b, 379a, 380b, 381a, 418a
Sabeans of Harran, II 639a, 639b
sacred, II 513a, 641a
Safavid period, II 651b
Saint Thomas Aquinas, II 644a, 645a, 645b, 649b, 651b
salvation, IV 224a, 230b–231a
Sassanid period, II 639a
scholasticism, II 639b, 640a, 645a
School of Illumination, II 650a–650b
science, II 639a–645a, 647a, 647b, 651a, 651b
Scot, Michael, II 649b
Shapur I, II 639a
Shi'ite Imans, II 640a
Sh'ism, II 641b–642a, 646a
Sicily, II 651a
Siger of Brabant, II 649b
sin, IV 224a, 230b–231a
skepticism, IV 245b, 250b
society, II 639b
solar system, II 647a
Spain, II 651a
Spengler, II 650a
spiritualism, II 650b
spread of, II 638b–639a
Steuchius, II 644b
Stoicism, II 641a, 646a
structuralism, II 652a
Sufism, II 648a, 648b, 650a, 650b–651a
Suhrawardī, II 645b, 650a–650b, 651b
theology, II 29b, 30b, 474b, 641a, 641b, 643b, 647a, 647b–648a, 648b
Theophrastus, II 645b
theosophy, II 643a, 645b, 650b
Thomism, II 646a
time, IV 391b, 402a
Toynbee, II 650a
translations, II 639b–641b, 643a, 649b, 650b
truth, II 643b
Umayyod era, II 641a
U.S., III 434b
unity, II 640a
university system, II 647b
utopianism, II 649a
Vico, II 650a
war, IV 502a
Wāsil ibn 'Atā', II 641b
William of Auvergne, II 646a
wisdom, II 650a–650b
Witelo, II 647a
Zoroastrianism, II 639a,

639b, 640b
Isle of Wight, catastrophism, IV 420b
Ismā'īlis, II 646a
Ismene (myth), law, II 683a
Isocrates (436–338 B.C.)
  education, II 81a–81b
  freedom of speech, II 260a, 262a
  historiography, II 467b, 503b, 504a
  humanism, II 516b
  literary paradox, III 77a, 79b
  Plato and, III 500a
  Pythagoreans, IV 31b
  rhetoric, IV 167b–169a
Isolationism
  individualism, II 595a, 602b–603a
  international peace, III 449b
  revisionism, IV 271a, 271b, 275a
  temperance, IV 367b
  U.S., III 449b
Isolde (fiction), love, III 96a, 98b, 102a, 104b, 105b, 106a
Isonomos, Greece (ancient), equality in law, II 682a
Israel
  constitutionalism, I 491a, 491b
  equity, II 152a
  eschatology, II 155a
  God, II 364a
  Judaism, III 488a
  law, II 256a
  philanthropy, III 488a
  principle of parliamentary supremacy, I 491a, 491b
  progress, III 634b, 638b
Israel (ancient)
  anomie, II 565a
  apocalyptic destiny of, I 413a
  Bible, IV 226b–227b
  Church, I 412b–414a, 414b, 415a–415b, 416a, 417a
  collective solidarity, II 564b
  cosmic voyages, I 524a
  deism, IV 226b
  disease, II 396b
  freedom of speech, II 253b–254a, 254b–256a
  Gnosticism, II 565a
  God, II 336a–338a, 341b
  guilt, IV 226b
  holy, II 512a–512b, 513b
  idolatry, II 564b, 565a
  individualism, II 564b; IV 227b
  Judaism, IV 226b–228a

justice, II 564b, 565a
millenarianism, III 223b–224a
morality, II 565a
mythology, III 281a, 282b, 301a, 303a, 311b; IV 226b
nationalism, II 337a; IV 227b
Near East, IV 227b, 228b
power, IV 227b
prophecy, II 564b; III 657a–664a
responsibility, II 564b
resurrection, IV 226b, 228a
Rome (ancient), I 413a, 415a–415b
sin, II 564b–565a; IV 226b–228a
skepticism, II 565a
Yahwism, IV 227b
Israeli, Isaac, macrocosm, III 129a
Isthmian Games, II 681a
Italy
  academicians, II 303b–304a
  aesthetics, II 216a, 218a–218b, 221b, 224a
  Arcadia, III 484a
  architecture, I 398b
  art, II 297b, 298b, 299a, 300b–303b, 308b
  balance of power, I 180b–181b, 187a
  baroque in literature, I 189a–189b, 191a, 191b–192a, 194a, 195a
  capitalism, I 396a
  Capuchins, I 394b
  Carbonari, III 674b
  catastrophism, IV 418b, 420b, 421b, 422a
  century labels, III 482b, 484a
  Christianity, III 674b
  city, I 429b–430b
  city-states, IV 438a, 477a
  classicism, I 450a, 451b, 452a, 453a, 454a
  common law, II 691b–693a
  conservatism, I 484b
  cosmic voyages, I 525a, 531b–532b
  Counter-Enlightenment, II 107a
  crisis in history, I 592a
  deism, I 648a, 649a
  democracy, I 665b; III 674b
  determinism, II 22a, 23a, 23b
  dignity, IV 136a–146a
  drama, III 531a
  Enlightenment, II 89b, 91b,

98b
evolution of literature, II 171b
genius, II 293b, 297b–303b, 308b, 315b, 323a–323b
Gothic, II 367a, 367b, 368b, 370b, 371a, 371b
guilds, II 300a–300b
harmony, II 388b
Hermeticism, II 431b
historicism, II 457b, 461b
historiography, II 22a, 23a, 23b, 481b–483a, 484b, 485a–485b
holy, II 512a
humanism, II 515a–524a; IV 129a–135b
iconography, II 529a–529b
ideal, II 549a, 549b, 550a
idealism, I 593a; IV 220a
impressionism, II 577b
individualism, II 297b, 298b–303b, 308b
international peace, III 454a, 455b
intolerance, IV 117a
Jansenism, I 400a–400b
Jesus Christ, III 674b
justice, III 674b
law, III 3b, 29b, 30a
Lazzarretti, III 674b
liberalism, III 674b
literary criticism, I 596a, 596b, 597a, 600a, 605b–606a
literature, III 82a, 84b, IV 331a
Machiavellism, III 117a, 117b–118a, 119b, 120b, 124a, 124b, 125a
Marxism, III 157b, 165a, 167b
mathematics, III 178a–178b
medieval sciences, II 203a–204a, 204b–205a
Middle Ages, III 528a
mimesis, III 227b–228a
modernism, I 419b, 422b, 423b, 424a, 424b, 425b, 426a
motif, III 235b–236a
music, II 315b, 323a–323b, 388b; III 267a, 271b
mythology, III 289a, 289b, 290a, 291a, 295a, 315b
nationalism, III 320a, 321a, 322b, 323b, 327a, 328a, 329b, 330a, 333a, 335a, 336a, 336b; IV 493b
naturalism, in art, III 339a
neo-classicism in art, III 364b, 366b, 368b, 369b
organicism, III 426a

peasantry, III 674b
periodization in history, III 479b, 480a
periodization in literary history, III 482a, 482b, 483a, 484a
plagues, I 394b
Platonism, III 506a–514a, 515a
poetry, III 528a, 529a–529b, 531a, 531b; IV 467a, 469a, 472b
pragmatism, III 552a–552b, 557a, 557b, 560a, 563a–564a, 565b
primitivism, III 593b, 597a
private property, III 654b
progress, III 647b
prophecy, III 667a, 667b, 668b–669a
protest movements, III 673a, 674b
radicalism, III 673a
realism in literature, IV 53a, 55a
Reformation, I 394b, 395b
religion, IV 117a
Renaissance, III 479b, 480a; IV 121a–146a, 437a–443a
rhetoric, IV 171a–171b
riots, III 674b
Roman Catholic Church, III 674b
romanticism, III 484a; IV 188a–194b, 198b, 203b, 205a
social contract, IV 253a
socialism, III 165a
Socialist Party, III 165a
space, IV 300b–301a
State, I 665b; IV 314a, 315a, 316b
Switzerland, III 328b
symbolism, III 484a; IV 341a, 342a, 343b
technology, IV 360b, 361a, 362a
temperance, IV 371b–373a–374b, 378a
time, IV 401b
totalitarianism, IV 406a, 407b, 408a, 409b, 410a
uniformitarianism, IV 418b, 420b, 421b, 422a
universal man, IV 437a–443a
Utopia, IV 461a, 461b
virtue, IV 374a–374b
virtù, IV 476b–483b
virtuoso, IV 486a
Volksgeist, IV 493b, 495a
war, III 454a; IV 505b
Italian language, III 298b

Ius civile, II 691a
Ius commune omnium hominum, II 691a, 692a, 694a, 696a
Ius gentium, II 691a
Ius singulare, II 691a
Iuvencus, poetry, III 528b
Ivan III, Grand Duke (1440–1505), history, I 410b
Ivanov, Vyacheslav (1866–1949)
classicism, I 455b
symbolism, IV 343a, 344b
Ives, James Merritt (1824–1895), impressionism, II 579b
Ivo of Chartres (d. 1117), reformation, IV 64b
Ixion (myth), temperance, IV 366a

J

Jabal (Bible), mythology, III 279b
Jabir ibn Hayyan (Geber) (721–776)
alchemy, I 29b, 30b; III 91a
Islam, II 641a, 646a
longevity, III 91a
Jack, Ian, romanticism, IV 195b
Jackson, John Hughlings (1859–1911)
behaviorism, I 218a
idea, I 116a, 116b
psychology, IV 13b
Jackson, Robert Houghwout (1892–1954)
academic freedom, I 13a–13b
constitutionalism, I 490a
loyalty, III 113b
Jackson, William (1730–1803)
art, II 305b
genius, II 305b
Jackson, William (fl. 1616), Scale of Nature, II 436b
Jacob (Bible)
hierarchy, II 440a
mythology, III 275b, 279a, 280b
prophecy, III 657b, 666b
Jacobi, Carl (1804–1851), space, IV 302b
Jacobi, Friedrich Heinrich (1743–1819)
Counter-Enlightenment, II 104b, 108b

fideism, II 412a
Hegel and, II 412a
irrationalism, II 635b, 636a
Kant and, IV 202a
literary criticism, I 596b
romanticism, IV 201a, 202a, 206a
Spinoza and, IV 201a
Jacobins
conservatism and, I 480a
democracy, I 661a, 661b–662a
despotism, II 15a
equality, II 143a
liberalism, III 54a
protest movements, III 673a
socialism, IV 288b
Jacobstahl, P., mythology, III 286b
Jacobus of Liège (c. 1330), music, II 315a; III 270b
Jacopo da Bergamo, mythology, III 290a
Jacopone da Todi (1230?–1306), wisdom of the fool, IV 517b
Jaeger, Werner (1888–1961), humanism, IV 129b
Jago, Richard (1715–1781), Newton and, III 395b
Jainism, I 251a
Gandhi, III 446a
peace, III 446a
Jakobson, Roman
pragmatism, III 557a
structuralism, IV 324a, 327b
Jamaica, primitivism, III 604a
James, Henry (1843–1916), class, I 445b
impressionism, II 575a
irony, II 633a–634a
literary criticism, I 601b
literature, IV 332b
Nature, III 349a
psychology, IV 25a
realism in literature, IV 52b
style, IV 332b
symbolism, IV 341a, 344b
ut pictura poesis, IV 466a, 469a
James, Jesse (1847–1882), mythology, III 276b
James, Saint
Church, I 413b, 415b
Gnosticism, II 327b
Judaic Christianity, I 374a
temperance, IV 375b
James, William (1842–1910), agnosticism, I 17a–17b; III 563a
appearance and reality, I 98a
association of ideas, I 116a

authority, III 565b
behaviorism, I 214b, 222a–222b; III 562b–563b
Bergson and, III 565a, 565b; IV 396a, 396b
Cannon and, III 562b
cash value, III 565b
causation, III 562a
chance, IV 395b
consciousness, III 562a, 562b, 563a, 565a
cynicism, III 563a
death, I 641a, 642a
democracy, III 554a, 563a
Descartes and, III 561b
determinism, III 562a, 569a; IV 395b–396a
Dewey and, III 569a
Edwards and, IV 112a
emotion, III 562b–565a
empiricism, III 546b, 552b, 559a, 561b, 562a
environment, II 125b
evolutionism, II 183a, 184b, 186a
experience, III 552b, 561b, 562a, 562b, 563a
faith, III 563b
fascism, III 565b
free will, III 562a, 563a, 563b; IV 395b–396a
Freud and, III 562b, 563a
God, II 359a, 362a
good, IV 185b
humanism, III 568a
idea, I 116b; III 552b, 564a
ignorance, III 569a
immortality, I 642a, 643a
imprinting, II 584b, 585a
individualism, III 561a, 563a
injustice, III 563a, 569a
intuition, III 565a
irrationalism, II 636b
judgment, III 556a, 562b
knowledge, III 561b, 562a, 568a
Lange and, III 562b
learning, II 584b, 585a
Leibniz and, III 561b
Lovejoy and, III 552b
Man-Machine, III 143b
Marxism, III 565b
meliorism, IV 396b
metaphor, III 197a
metaphysics, III 565b
milieu intérieur concept, II 125b
mind, III 561b, 562a, 566a
monopoly, III 563a, 565b
morality, III 565a
Mussolini and, III 563a
naturalism, III 554a
Nature, III 561b
nominalism, III 552b

Papini and, III 563a–563b

peace, III 447a; IV 507a–507b

Peirce and, III 546b, 551b, 552a–552b, 559a, 560a, 561a–563b

perennial philosophy, III 462b

Platonism, III 554a

pluralism, III 561b, 563a; IV 396a

poverty, III 569a

pragmatism, I 323b; II 184b; III 551b–554a, 559a, 560a, 561a–569a

probability, III 562a

psychology, III 554a, 563b, 565a; IV 12b, 23a, 25b, 26b, 27b, 28b

religion, III 561b, 563a, 565b, 568b; IV 112a

Renouvier and, IV 396a

rhetoric, III 565b

right, IV 185b

Royce and, III 561a

Santayana and, III 553b, 554a

science, III 561b, 562b

skepticism, III 561b; IV 250a

Socrates and, III 554a

Sorel and, III 564a, 565b

space, IV 303a

Spinoza and, III 561b

spiritualism, III 563a, 565a

State, III 565b

stream of consciousness, III 197a

supernatural, III 568a

theodicy, IV 383a–384a

theory of emotion, III 143b, 562b

time, IV 395b–396a, 396b

truth, III 562b, 563a, 563b

Vaihinger and, III 566a

Vailati and, III 560a

value, III 556a, 568a

war, III 447a; IV 507a–507b, 508a

Weismann and, III 565a

will to believe, III 552b, 561a–563a, 563b, 565b

Wright and, III 561a, 561b, 562a, 562b

James I, King (1566–1625),
constitutionalism, I 488a–488b

equity, II 152b, 153a

history, I 398b

mythology, III 297a

periodization in literary history, III 482b

social contract, IV 254a

virtuoso, IV 486a

James II, King (1633–1701),
genius, II 322a

music, II 322a

revolution, IV 154a

social contract, IV 258a

Jameson, Robert (1774–(1854), uniformitarianism, IV 419b

Jammer, Max, matter, III 188b–189a, 192a

Janes, Lewis George
Orientalism, III 429a, 434b

transcendentalism, III 429a, 434b

Janet, Pierre (1859–1947), psychology, IV 13b

Jankélévitch, Vladimir, irony, II 634a

Janowitz, M., war, IV 506b, 507a

Jansen, Cornelius (1585–1638), Saint Augustine and, I 400a

Jansenism, I 400a–400b
casuistry, I 262a–262b, 263a

Conciliar Movement, I 404a

Counter-Enlightenment, II 101b

determinism, II 30b

dualism, II 43b

France, I 400a

French Revolution, I 400a

Gallican Movement, I 404a

heresy, II 428b

Innocent X (Pope), I 400a

Italy, I 400a–400b

Louis XIV, I 400a

Man-Machine, III 137a–137b

Netherlands, I 400a

Pius VI (Pope), I 400a

Saint Augustine, I 394a

tragic sense, IV 415a

Japan
academic freedom, I 16b

Buddhism, I 248b–256b

chance images, I 353a

China, I 369a, 372a

Christianity, I 357a

culture, III 438a

Goncourt, Edmond, I 369a

Goncourt, Jules de, I 369a

international peace, III 454a

Jesuits, I 357a

linguistics, II 661b

nationalism, III 337a

opened to the West, I 369b

Orientalism, III 428a, 437b–438b

Russia, I 370b

U.S., III 428a, 437b–438b

war, III 454a; IV 505b

Japan (ancient)

Buddhism, I 247a, 248a–248b, 253b

game theory, II 264b

law, III 28b

Jarrell, Randall (1914–1965),
literary criticism, I 604a

Jason (myth), III 275b, 290a

law, II 683a

Jaspers, Karl (1883–1969),
Buddhism, I 256a

death, I 642b

faith, II 213a

metaphysical imagination, III 208b, 212b, 220b, 221a, 221b

perennial philosophy, III 462a, 462b

psychology, IV 14a

tragic sense, IV 416a

Zeitgeist, IV 536b

Jastrow, Joseph (1863–1944), psychology, IV 25a

Jaucourt, Chevalier Louis de (1704–1779)
despotism, II 10b

mountains in literature, III 259a

mythology, III 303a

socialism, IV 288a

Jaurès, Jean Lèon (1859–1914)
individualism, II 595a

Marxism, III 165a

revisionism, IV 273b

war, IV 506a–506b

Java, structuralism, IV 325a

Jay, H., literature, IV 190b

Jay, John (1745–1829)
psychology, IV 22a

vox populi, IV 499a

Jay Treaty, III 450a

Jaynes, E. T., entropy, II 116b

Jealousy
allegory, I 42b

Socrates, IV 414b

tragic sense, IV 413a, 414b

Jean de Blanot
nationalism, III 321a

Jeanneret, Charles, *see* Le Corbusier

Jeans, James Hopwood (1877–1946)
cosmic images, I 521b, 522a

cosmology, I 569b

Jefferson, Thomas (1743–1826)
Adams and, IV 21b

blacks, IV 21b

Cabanis and, IV 21a

class, IV 21b

conservatism, I 483b–484a

Cooper, IV 21a

culture, I 619b

Declaration of Independence, IV 21b

democracy, I 660a, 660b

Destutt de Tracy and, IV 21a

economic history, II 44b, 46a

education, IV 21b

Enlightenment, IV 22b

environment, IV 21b

equality, IV 317b

evil, IV 21b

Franklin and, IV 22a–22b

freedom, II 44b

good, IV 21b

Hamilton and, IV 21b

happiness and pleasure, II 379b

Helvétius and, IV 21a

Holbach and, IV 21a

human nature, IV 21b

individualism, II 596a, 599a

La Mettrie and, IV 21a

loyalty, III 114a

Marshall and, IV 21b

morality, IV 22b

nationalism, III 326b, 332b

pragmatism, III 553b

psychology, IV 21a–22a

rationalism, IV 21b

religion, IV 21a

slavery, IV 21b

State, IV 317b

Jeffrey, Lord (1773–1850), romanticism, IV 194a

Jeffreys, Harold, chance, I 338b

Jehoshaphat (Bible), prophecy, III 660b

Jehovah's Witnesses, eschatology, II 157a

Jenkin, Fleeming (1833–1885), utility, IV 452b

Jenkins, Thomas, neo-classicism in art, III 364a

Jenner, Edward (1749–1823), disease, II 403a

positivism, III 541a

Jennings, Richard, utility, IV 451b, 454b

Jensen, Adolf E., mythology, III 313b–314a

Jenyns, Soame (1704–1787),
hierarchy, II 447a

infinity, II 447a

Johnson, Samuel, and, II 447a

utilitarianism, IV 444b, 445b

Jephthah (Bible), freedom of speech, II 254b

Jeremiah (Bible)
  freedom of speech, II 255b–256a
  individualism, II 602b
  metaphor, III 202a, 204b
  mythology, III 277a, 281a, 283b, 284b
  prophecy, III 662a–663a
Jeremias, A., mythology, III 310a
Jeroboam (Bible)
  freedom of speech, II 255a
  prophecy, III 660b
  salvation, IV 226b–227a
Jerome, Saint (340?–420),
  allegory, I 46b
  Christianity, III 590a, 591b
  harmony, IV 40b
  historiography, II 473a
  history, I 378b
  metaphor, III 205b
  Neo-Platonism, III 373b
  primitivism, III 590a, 591b
  Pythagoreans, IV 40b
  reformation, IV 63a
  satire, IV 215a
  Seneca and, III 590a
  universe, IV 40b
  wisdom of the fool, IV 518a
Jerphanon, G. de, iconography, II 535a
Jerusalem
  Church, I 413a, 413b, 415a
  city, I 427b–429b
  evil, II 163b
  historiography, II 470b
  Islam, II 651a
  mythology, III 281a
Jespersen, Otto (1860–1943)
  language, II 672b
  linguistics, III 62a; IV 425b
Jessop, T. E., beauty, I 210a
Jesuits
  allegory, III 293a, 293b
  casuistry, I 262a, 262b
  Catherine II and, I 403b
  China, I 353b, 354b, 355b–365b, 367a
  deism, I 649a
  determinism, II 30b
  education, III 293a–293b
  Enlightenment, II 91a
  expelled from Bourbon courts, I 403b
  grace, I 394a–394b
  history, I 406a
  holy, II 513a
  humanism, II 520b
  intolerance, IV 113a, 117a
  Japan, I 357a
  liberalism, III 43b, 44a
  Machiavellism, III 117b,

118a
  Maria Theresa of Austria, I 403b
  modernism, I 425a
  mythology, III 293a–293b, 301a
  pleasure, III 293b
  primitivism, III 599a
  Prussia, I 403b
  religion, IV 109a, 113a, 117a
  Saint Augustine and, I 400a
  skepticism, IV 242b, 245a
  social contract, IV 254a
  Sweden, IV 113a
  Switzerland, IV 113a
  Ultramontanes, I 499b
  utilitarianism, III 293b
  women, IV 526a
Jesus Christ (8 B.C.?–?29 A.D.)
  ambiguity, I 51b
  apocalyptic program, I 413a
  Arminius, II 28b
  Ascension, II 411a
  authority, I 147a, 147b, 149a, 149b
  Barth, II 29a
  Blake, II 412b
  Blondel, I 421b, 422b
  Calvin, IV 67b
  charity, II 211b, 214b
  children, III 595b
  Christianity, III 589b, 670b; IV 102b
  chronology, IV 402a
  Church, I 413a–416a, 416b, 417a, 418a
  city, I 429a
  civil disobedience, I 434b–435a
  cosmic voyages, I 524a
  cosmology, I 624a
  Counter-Reformation, I 393a, 393b, 394b
  crucifixion of, II 42b, 470b, 477b; III 276a, 281b, 282a, 293a; IV 402a
  cycles, I 624a
  death, I 643b, 644a
  deism, I 651a
  despotism, II 3b
  determinism, II 26b, 27a, 28b, 29a
  dignity, IV 137a, 140a, 142b, 146a
  disciples of, I 373b–374b
  disease, II 399a
  equality, II 140b, 142a
  eschatology, II 155b, 156a, 156b, 157a, 157b, 159a, 160b, 161a
  evil, II 164a, 165a
  existentialism, II 190b, 192a

faith, II 211b, 214b
  Faust (legend), III 245a, 247b
  Frederick the Great and, I 403b
  freedom of speech, II 262a
  Gautama Siddhārtha, I 255a
  Gnosticism, II 327a, 327b, 328a, 329b, 330b
  God, II 335a, 335b, 341a, 341b–343a, 344b, 348b, 357a, 360b, 363a, 365b
  Gothic, II 373b
  happiness and pleasure, II 378b
  Hegel and, II 410b, 411a, 414b; III 494b; IV 290b
  heresy, II 416b–426a, 426b–429b
  Hermeticism, II 432b
  historiography, II 470b, 471a–471b, 477b
  holy, II 513b
  hope, II 211b, 214b
  humanism, II 517b; IV 132b
  Huxley, I 18b
  iconography, II 525a, 526a, 527b, 528a, 530a, 539a
  idea, II 546b
  immortality, I 643b, 644a
  Incarnation, II 411a, 472a, 472b, 473a; III 667b–668a
  Islam, II 640a
  justice, II 657a
  Laberthonnière, I 422b
  law, III 7a–7b, 13b
  Le Roy, I 422a
  literary paradox, III 80b
  Loisy, I 420b
  love, III 96a–96b, 97a
  Luther, III 267a
  Marx, III 147b
  metaphor, III 205b, 206b
  millenarianism, III 223a–223b, 224b, 225a
  modernism, I 419b, 420b, 421b, 422b, 425b
  motif, III 242b
  music, III 265a, 266a, 267a, 269b, 270a, 270b
  mythology, III 275b–284b
  Nature, III 347a, 349a
  necessity, III 355a
  optics, III 408b
  papacy, I 382b
  perennial philosophy, III 460a
  perfectibility, III 467a, 468a, 474b
  periodization in history, III 476b, 477a; IV 402a
  philanthropy, III 488b
  Pietism, III 493b, 494b,

495a
  Platonism, III 505a, 505b, 514b
  poverty, III 668b
  predestination, II 29b–30a
  primitivism, III 589b, 594b, 595a, 595b, 596b
  progress, III 634b–635b
  prophecy, III 664b–668b
  protest movements, III 670b, 674b
  reformation, IV 61a–69a
  Reformation, IV 67b
  religion, III 205b, 206b; IV 93b, 94a, 96a
  resurrection, I 21b–22b; II 155b, 335a, 335b, 342a, 411a, 413a, 470b; III 223a–223b, 277a, 282a, 283a, 284a
  revolution, IV 153a
  Saint Augustine, III 505b; IV 63a
  Saint Francis of Assisi, IV 65a
  Saint Paul, II 341b–342a, 343a
  salvation, IV 227b, 229a–230b
  Satan, III 281b, 665a
  sin, IV 227b, 229a–230b
  socialism, IV 286a, 287a, 287b, 290b, 291a
  Socrates, II 411a
  Strauss, David, II 412b–413a
  Symeon (Bible) and, I 413b
  temperance, IV 371a
  theodicy, IV 380b
  theology, II 26b, 29a
  time, IV 392a, 402a
  Tolstoy, I 438a
  tragic sense, IV 416a
  Tyrrell, I 422b
  Utopia, IV 460b
  wisdom of the fool, IV 517a–517b, 519a–519b
  witchcraft, IV 521b
  women, III 596b; IV 524b
  work, IV 531a–531b
  Wycliffe, I 387a
Jevons, William Stanley (1835–1882)
  economic history, II 47a, 50b, 52b
  labor, II 384b
  methodology, III 386b
  pain, II 384b
  pleasure, II 384b
  social welfare, IV 277b
  utility, IV 450a, 450b, 453b, 454b, 455a, 458a

Jewel, Archbishop (1522–1571), deism, I 649b
Jews (ancient)
   historiography, II 465b–466b, 467b, 470b, 471a, 471b, 474b, 476a, 478a, 478b, 483b, 488a, 492b, 499a
   holy, II 513a
   Holy Roman Empire, I 375a
   monotheism, II 466a
   Promised Land, II 466a
   release from slavery, II 466a
   religion, II 466a
Jezebel (Bible)
   freedom of speech, II 255b
   mythology, III 282a
   prophecy, III 661a
Jhering, Rudolf von (1818–1892), natural law, III 22a
Jiménez, Juan Ramón (1881–1958), symbolism, IV 342a
Joachim of Floris (1145?–?1202)
   allegory, I 47a
   eschatology, II 156b
   evolution, IV 286b
   heresy, II 417b, 418a, 421a, 421b
   incarnation, IV 286b
   history, III 472a–472b
   love, III 107b
   millenarianism, III 666b–669b
   Müntzer and, IV 287a
   perfectibility, III 472a–472b
   reformation, IV 65a
   revolution, IV 153a
   socialism, IV 286b, 287a, 290a
Joan of Arc, Saint (1412–1431), women, IV 525b
Joash (Bible)
   freedom of speech, II 255a
   prophecy, III 660b
Job (Bible)
   God, II 337b
   happiness and pleasure, II 378b
   loyalty, III 109a–109b
   mythology, III 277a, 278a, 281b
   salvation, IV 227b–228a
   sin, IV 227b–228a
   theodicy, IV 379b, 380b, 381b, 383a
   tragic sense, IV 416a, 416b
Joblot, Louis, spontaneous generation, II 282b–283a
Jodelle, Étienne (1532–1573), evolution of litera-

ture, II 172a
Joel (Bible), prophecy, III 663b
Johannes of Garlandia, music, II 314b
   mythology, III 288a
   poetry, III 528b
Johannes de Muris, music, II 315a
John, King (1167?–1216), Christianity, I 383a
   historiography, II 484a
John, Saint (470?–526), Christianity, III 592a
   Church, I 412b
   dualism, II 43a
   eschatology, II 156a, 156b
   Gnosticism, II 43a–43b, 327b, 328a, 328b, 329b
   heresy, II 425a
   iconography, II 528a
   mythology, III 278a, 283b, 284a
   primitivism, III 592a
   prophecy, III 664a
   religion, IV 103a
John the Baptist (Bible), prophecy, III 666b
John Cassian, Saint (360–435), I 47a
John Chrysostom, Saint (345?–407)
   freedom of speech, II 262a
   music, III 266a
   predestination, II 26b
John of the Cross, Saint (1542–1591), perfectibility, III 467b
John Damascene, Saint (700?–?754)
   analogy, I 65a
   demonology, I 668b
   dignity, IV 138a
   Islam, II 640b
John of Dumbleton (14th century), kinematics, II 200b
John the Evangelist (Bible), temperance, IV 375b
John of Holland (14th century), dynamics, II 201b
John of Jandun (d. 1328)
   Averroës and, I 35a
   double truth, II 34b
   reason, II 34b
   revelation, II 34b
John of Paris, authority, I 148b
John Philoponus (fl. 5th century A.D.)
   atomism, I 130b
   cosmology, I 543b
   Islam, II 645a–645b, 649a
   kinematics, II 201b
   Pythagoreans, IV 36b

space, IV 298a
John of Rupescissa
   alchemy, I 31a–31b
   prophecy, III 669b
John of Saint Thomas, abstraction, I 6b
John of Salisbury (d. 1180), abstraction, I 3a–3b
   analogy, I 69a
   body politic, III 130a
   class, I 445b
   constitutionalism, I 487b
   loyalty, III 112b
   macrocosm and microcosm, III 130a
   mimesis, III 227b
   nationalism, III 319b, 320a, 320b, 322a
   painting, III 227b
   revisionism, IV 267b, 269a
John of Segovia, reformation, IV 66a
John XIII, Pope (d. 972), Christianity, III 590b
John XXI, Pope (d. 1277), prophecy, III 668a
John XXII, Pope (1249–1334)
   alchemy, I 31a
   heresy, II 420a, 421a, 421b
   prophecy, III 668b
   reformation, IV 65b
John XXIII, Pope (1881–1963)
   history, I 408b
   industry, III 654b
   nationalism, III 334b
   primitivism, III 590b
   private property, III 654b
   Roman Catholic Church, III 334b, 654b; IV 527b
   women, IV 527b
Johnson, Samuel (1709–1784)
   aesthetics, IV 356a
   Anglicanism, IV 19b–20a
   antiprimitivism, III 604b
   art, II 307b
   Chain of Being, I 329b, 330a, 499a; II 447a–447b
   China, I 365a
   continuity, I 499a
   cosmic voyages, I 530a
   genius, II 307b
   Hermeticism, II 432a
   hierarchy, II 447a–447b
   infinity, II 447a
   Jenyns and, II 447a
   literary criticism, I 597a
   literature, III 81b–82a
   metaphysics, II 447a
   Milton and, III 300a
   morality, II 447a

mythology, III 300a
   nature, I 329b
   poetry, III 530b, 531b
   Pope and, II 447a
   primitivism, III 604b
   psychology, IV 17b, 19b–20a
   Puritanism, IV 17b
   romanticism, IV 194a
   taste, IV 356a
Johnson, Samuel (1696–1772)
   Clarke and, III 433a, 433b, 434a
   evolution, III 433b, 434a
   Orientalism, III 428b, 429a, 431b, 433a–434a, 434b, 435a, 439a
   Ramism, IV 44b
   transcendentalism, III 428b, 429a, 431b, 433a–434a, 434b, 435a, 439a
Johnson, Thomas T., Platonism, III 522b
Johnson, William E. (1862–1945), behaviorism, I 219b
Joly, Claude, Machiavellism, III 119b
Joly, Louis, nationalism, III 330b
Jomini, A. H. (1779–1869), war, IV 502b
Jommelli, Niccolò (1714–1774), music, II 323a, 324a
Jonah (Bible)
   mythology, III 281b
   prophecy, III 660b
Jonas, Hans, Gnosticism, II 330a
Jones, Inigo (1573–1652), mythology, III 297a
Jones, William (1746–1794)
   China, I 367a
   linguistics, III 65a–65b, 66b; IV 427b
   mythology, III 305b
   Orientalism, III 428a–429b
   transcendentalism, III 429b
   uniformitarianism, IV 427b
Jongkind, Johan Barthold (1819–1891), impressionism, II 573a
Jonson, Ben (1573?–1637)
   attitude toward antiquity, I 77b, 81a
   baroque in literature, I 191a
   Chapman and, III 294b
   classicism, I 453a
   comedy, I 469b
   cosmic voyages, I 528b
   literature, IV 331b, 332a

209

mythology, III 294b, 295b, 297a, 299b
neo-classicism, III 424b
organicism, III 424b
poetry, IV 471a
realism in literature, IV 54a
satire, IV 212b–215b
style, IV 331b, 332a
wisdom of the fool, IV 519b–520a
Joram (Bible), prophecy, III 660b
Jordan, Louis Henry, Orientalism, III 435b
Jordan, P., cosmology, I 568b
Jordanes (6th century), Gothic, II 367a, 369b
Jordanus Nemorarius (d. 1237?), science, II 197b, 203b
Joseph (Bible)
ambiguity, I 52a
metaphor, III 204b
mythology, III 275b, 279a
prophecy, III 657b
temperance, IV 371a, 375a
Joseph, Father (1577–1638), history, I 399a
Joseph of Arimathea (Bible), historiography, II 483b
Joseph II, Emperor (1741–1790)
Belgium revolt, I 404a
casuistry, I 263a
conservatism, I 480b
Enlightenment, II 90b
papacy and, I 403b, 404a
pietism, I 403b–404a
Josephus, Flavius (37–?100), Church, I 415b
death, I 642b
freedom of speech, II 262a
historiography, II 466b, 476b, 476a, 478b
immortality, I 643b–644a
predestination, II 29b
Pythagoreans, IV 40b
resurrection, I 643b
Joshua (Bible)
freedom of speech, II 255a
mythology, III 280b
salvation, IV 226b
Josiah (Bible)
freedom of speech, II 255a
mythology, III 282b, 283a
reformation, IV 61b
Jost, François, romanticism, IV 187a
Jouffroy, Théodore (1796–1842)
Nature, III 348a
positivism, III 538a
progress, III 642b
psychology, IV 11b

Joule, James P. (1818–1889)
entropy, II 113a
technology, IV 363b
Jouvenel, Henry de (1876–1935), natural law, III 23a
Jovellanos, Gaspar Melchor de (1744–1811), I 83b
Jowett, Benjamin (1817–1893)
Hegel and, II 414a
Platonism, III 521b–522a
Joy
Epicureanism, IV 175b
Fromm, II 384a
happiness, II 378a, 384a, 385b
harmony, II 388a
health, II 397a
Hermeticism, II 431a
music, II 392b
right and good, IV 175b
Saint Augustine, II 378b
Stoicism, II 378a; IV 321a
Joyce, James (1882–1941), impressionism, II 575a
literary paradox, III 77b
motif, III 236a–236b, 240a, 240b
mythology, III 240a
realism in literature, IV 55a
symbolism, IV 341a, 344a
Wagner and, III 236a
Juan de Palafox, primitivism, III 601b
Juárez, Benito (1806–1872), positivism, III 544a
Jubal (myth), III 276b
mythology, III 279b
Judah (Bible)
freedom of speech, II 254b, 255a
prophecy, III 661b
Judah Ha-Levi (1085?–?1140), skepticism, IV 241b
Judaic Christianity, I 373b–375a
Arabia, I 374b
baptism, I 413b
Church, I 412b–416a, 416b
Gnosticism, I 375a
Greece (ancient), I 374a–374b, 375a
missionaries, I 374a–374b
Palestine, I 373b–375a
Saint James, I 374a
Saint Paul, I 374a
Samaria, I 375a
Syria, I 375a
Transjordan, I 374b
Zealotism, I 415b
Judaism
agnosticism, I 17a–27a

alienation, I 34a–34b
allegory, I 43a–44a, 46a, 47a–48a
ambiguity, I 51a–52a
anomie, II 565a
anti-Semitism, IV 114a
apocalypse, III 223b–224a
astrology, I 119a
astronomy, I 536b
Babylonian Captivity, II 656a
Bible, IV 103b, 104a
Cabala, III 129a, 130a, 130b
casuistry, I 258a
causation, I 273a, 274a–274b, 290a
chance, I 336a
charity, III 487b, 488a
China, I 360b
Christianity, I 373b–375a; III 488a–488b, 591b; IV 114a
Church, I 412b, 413a, 413b, 417a
city, I 427b
class, I 442a
collective solidarity, II 564b
Commandments, II 656a
conformity, IV 114a
continuity, I 492b, 493a, 502b, 503b
Cosmic Fall, I 505a–505b
cosmic voyages, I 524a
cosmology, I 536b–537a, 538b, 539a, 543a, 543b, 622b
Counter-Enlightenment, II 102a
covenant, I 396a; II 656a, 656b, 657a
Creation, I 536b, 571a–571b
creativity in art, I 585b, 586b
culture, II 127b, 132a–132b
cycles, I 622b, 623a, 624b
Day of Atonement, IV 104a
Dead Sea Scrolls, I 413b, 415b
death, I 643b, 644b, 645a
deism, I 647b, 648a
demonology, I 667b–670a
despotism, II 5a
determinism, II 22a, 29a–30a
double truth, II 32b, 34b–35a, 35b, 37a, 37b
dualism, II 39a, 42a–42b; III 281b
duty, III 487b
Egypt (ancient), II 656a
environment, II 127b, 132a–132b
equality, II 138a–138b,

140a–140b
equity, II 151a–152a, 153a
eschatology, II 29b, 154b–155a
ethics, III 487b, 488a; IV 176a
evil, II 30a, 163b–165a
exodus from Egypt, II 656a
freedom, II 249a
freedom of speech, II 254b–256a, 256b, 262a
Germany, III 488a
Gnosticism, II 326b–329a, 330a, 330b, 331a, 565a
God, I 571a–571b; II 29b–30a, 42a, 336a–337b, 339b, 341b, 342b, 345a, 363b–364a, 364b; III 636a
good, IV 174a, 176a
happiness and pleasure, II 375b, 378b
harmony, II 392b; IV 38b
heresy, II 565a
hierarchy, II 441a
historiography, I 503b; II 22a
history, II 22a; IV 61a
holy, II 512a–512b, 513b
humanism, IV 130b
humanitarianism, III 487b, 488a
idolatry, II 564b, 565a
immortality, I 643b, 644b, 645a; III 223b
impiety, II 564a–565b
individualism, II 564b, 597a
infinity, II 604b–605b
intolerance, IV 113b, 114a
Islam, II 639a, 640a, 651a
Israel, III 488a
Israel (ancient), IV 226b–228a
justice, II 564b, 565a, 656a–656b, 657a, 658b; III 487b
law, I 290a, 376a; II 151a–152a, 153a, 249b, 686b; III 6b, 7a–7b, 11a, 28b, 636a
love, III 96a, 100b, 636a
loyalty, III 108b–109b, 111b, 112a, 112b
makom, IV 296a–296b
matter, III 186a–186b, 190b
Messiah, III 636a
metaphor, III 202b–206a
Middle Ages, III 487b, 488a; IV 153a
millenarianism, III 223b–224a
modern times, III 487b
monotheism, II 342b
morality, II 565a; III 6b, 636a

Mosaic law, II 656a
mountain-origin, III 254a–255a
mountains in literature, III 254a, 254b, 255a, 255b
music, II 392b; III 265a, 269b
mythology, III 276a–284b, 304a, 304b, 307a, 314a
nationalism, I 374b; III 324b
natural law, III 17b
necessity, III 355a
Neo-Platonism, III 371b, 372b, 375b, 377b
obligation, III 487b
Orientalism, III 432a–432b
pain, II 30a
Passover, IV 103b
peace, III 440b
perennial philosophy, III 459a
perfectibility, III 467b
persecutions, III 488a
philanthropy, III 487b–488a
Platonism, III 512a
poverty, III 487b, 488a
predestination, II 29b–30a
primitivism, III 591b, 603b
progress, III 634b, 635a, 635b–636a
prophecy, II 255b–256a, 564b; III 223b, 224a, 636a, 657a–664a, 664b, 665b, 666a
psychology, IV 16b
punishment, II 30a
Pythagoras, IV 40b
Pythagoreans, IV 38b, 40b–41a
Qumrân community, I 413b, 415b
rabbi, II 256a
rabbinical literature, III 487b–488a
reformation, IV 60a, 61a
reincarnation, I 644b, 645a
religion, III 202b, 203a, 204a–206a; IV 93b, 94b, 98a, 101a, 102b, 103a, 103b, 104a, 105b, 113a, 114a
Renaissance, IV 130b, 136b–137a, 139a, 143b, 145b
repentance, III 636a
responsibility, II 564b
resurrection, I 643b; II 337b
revolution, IV 153a
right, IV 174a, 176a
Russia, III 488a
Saint Paul, I 414b

salvation, III 487b; IV 226b–228a, 229a–230b
sin, II 564b–565a; III 636a; IV 226b–228a, 229a, 229b, 230b
skepticism, II 565a; IV 241b, 242a, 243a, 246b–247a, 250b
socialism, IV 290b
society, IV 114a
space, IV 296a–296b
stewardship, III 488a
Talmud, III 488a
theodicy, II 163b, 164a; IV 379b, 380b
theology, II 29b–30a
time, IV 391b, 392a, 402a
tithing, III 487b
tragic sense, IV 415b
U.S., III 432a–432b
universality, III 636a
universe, IV 38b
Utopia, IV 460a–460b
Volksgeist, IV 491a, 492b, 493a, 494b
witchcraft, IV 521a
women, IV 523b–524a
work, IV 531a
Judas Iscariot (Bible),
Gnosticism, II 328a
mythology, III 276b
Judea (ancient)
freedom of speech, II 252a
health, II 398b
Judges
common law, II 692a–695b; III 31a–32a
equity, II 149a–149b, 153b
Greece (ancient), II 675a, 676a, 678b, 680a, 681b
Holmes, Justice, III 567b
law, II 675a, 676a, 678b, 680a, 681b, 686a, 688b; III 2a, 2b, 4a, 4b, 6b, 7a, 13a, 15a, 15b, 23b, 24a–31b, 32a
Plato, II 149a–149b
pragmatism, III 567b
rhetoric, IV 168a
Rome (ancient), II 686a, 688b
Judgment
aesthetics, IV 354a, 354b, 355a, 355b, 356a, 356b
Aristotle, II 243a; IV 238a
Balguy, III 233a
common law, III 31a
Descartes, IV 244b
Dewey, III 556a, 568b–569a, 569b
ethics, IV 71b, 72a, 73a, 321a
existentialism, III 160a
free will, II 237b, 238a,

239a, 240a–240b, 243a
genius, II 294a, 294b, 295a, 296a, 297b, 313a, 314a, 317a, 318a, 318b, 322b–323a
God, II 357a, 359b, 360b
good, IV 178b, 181b, 182b, 183a, 185a, 186a
Greece (ancient), II 675b, 676b–677a, 682b–683a
happiness and pleasure, II 379b
historiography, IV 147b
holy, II 512b
Hume, II 240a; III 232a, 232b–233a
Hutcheson, III 231a–231b
James, III 556a, 562b
Kant, II 240a–240b; III 234a; IV 248b, 433a, 433b
language, II 667b
law, II 675b, 676b–677a, 682b–683a; III 28b, 31a, 33b
Lewis, C. I., III 568b–569a
Locke, II 239b
Lovejoy, III 552b
Marxism, III 153b, 160a, 168b
millenarianism, III 223a–223b
moral sense, III 230a–235a
motif, III 239b
music, II 313a, 314a, 317a, 318a, 318b, 322b–323a
mythology, III 283a
natural law, III 19a
Peirce, III 552b, 556a, 559a, 568b
perennial philosophy, III 459a
Plato, II 243a; III 497a–497b
Platonism, III 497a–497b, 504b
pragmatism, III 552a, 552b, 554a, 555b, 556a, 559a, 562b, 568a–569a, 569b
Price, Richard, III 233a
probability, III 614b
progress, III 624a, 648b
prophecy, III 664a, 664b
Ramism, IV 43a, 43b
rationalism, IV 47a
Reid, III 234a
relativism, IV 71b, 72a, 73a
religion, IV 106b, 108b, 110a, 111a
Renaissance, IV 147b
rhetoric, IV 167b, 168a, 172a
right, IV 178b, 181b, 182b, 183a, 185a, 186a

Saint Augustine, IV 286b
Shaftesbury, III 230b
skepticism, IV 235a–238a, 241a, 243a–244b, 248b
Smith, Adam, III 233b
socialism, IV 286b
Stoicism, IV 321a
taste, IV 354a, 354b, 355a, 355b, 356a, 356b
unity of science, IV 433a, 433b
value, III 552a, 552b, 554a, 555b, 556a, 559a, 562b, 568a–569a, 624a; IV 181b, 182b, 533b
Volksgeist, IV 491a
wisdom of the fool, IV 519a
work, IV 533b
Judith (Bible), temperance, IV 371a, 372b, 375a
Juglar, Clement, crisis in history, I 590b
Julian, Emperor (331–363),
mythology, III 288a
Neo-Platonism, III 373b
paganism, I 648a
Julian the Chaldaean, Neo-Platonism, III 376b
Julian the Theurgist, Neo-Platonism, III 376b
Julius Africanus (c. 3rd century), religion, IV 93b
Julius Caesar (100 B.C.–44 B.C.)
determinism, II 23b
Germany, III 651b
historiography, II 469b, 481b, 482a
justice, II 656b
language, II 664b
literature, III 81b
mythology, III 308b
primitivism, III 591b
private property, III 651b
universal man, IV 439a
Julius II, Pope (1443–1513),
dignity, IV 145b
Michelangelo and, II 302b
Platonism, II 513a
virtù, IV 481a
Julius III, Pope (1487–1555),
Counter-Reformation, I 393b
Jully, Lalive de, neo-classicism in art, III 365b
Jumilhac Papyrus, impiety, II 564b
Jung, Karl Gustav (1875–1961)
art and play, I 107a
aestheticism, III 597a
archetypes, III 597a
Bastian and, III 312b
Burckhardt and, III 312b

children, III 597a
collective unconscious, III 312b–313a, 348b
culture, III 313a
emotion, IV 97a
Faust (legend), III 251a
free will, II 246b
Freud and, III 312b–313a; IV 97a
iconography, II 540a
love, III 107a, 107b
metaphysical imagination, III 212b
mind, IV 97a
motif, III 240b, 242a
mythology, III 281a, 282b, 312b–313a, 314a; IV 97a
Nature, III 348b
primitivism, III 597a
psychology, IV 14a, 28b
race, IV 58b
recapitulation, IV 58b, 59a
redemption, IV 97a
religion, III 313a; IV 97a
repentance, IV 97a
sacrifice, IV 97a
symbolism, IV 341a
unconscious, IV 97a
Junius, Franciscus (1589–1677)
  Gothic, II 370a
  mythology, III 298a–299a
  ut pictura poesis, IV 467b
Juno (myth), III 289a, 290b
Jupiter (myth), III 289a, 290a, 291a, 296a, 296b, 299b, 305a
  primitivism, III 579b, 580a, 580b, 583b
Jupiter (planet), III 414b
  cosmology, I 538a, 539a, 540b, 541b–542a, 546b, 547a, 550a, 552a
  mythology, III 287b
Jurors
  common law, II 692a, 693a, 695a; III 31a
  Greece (ancient), II 684a
  law, II 685a, 685b, 686b, 687b, 689a, 689b, 690a; III 1b, 3b, 4a–4b, 5a, 17a, 17b, 22b, 24a, 24b, 27b, 28a, 28b, 29a–31a
  nationalism, III 319b, 320a, 321a, 321b, 322a, 323b
  necessity, III 358b
  reformation, IV 61b
  Rome (ancient), II 685b, 686a, 687b, 689a–690a
Jurieu, Pierre (1637–1713), despotism, II 8a
Justi, Johann H. G. von (1705?–1771), China, I 362b

Justice, II 652b–659b
  abolition of the punitive element, I 71b
  absolute, II 658a
  Aeschylus, II 653a; IV 366b
  Al-Nazzam, I 287a–287b
  Anaximander, I 290b; II 653a
  anthropomorphism, II 652b
  Antiphon, III 575b–576a
  approval, III 232a, 232b
  Aristotle, II 150a, 653a, 653b, 654a, 655a, 656a, 656b, 657a, 658b; III 1b, 15a–15b, 16b, 27b; IV 285b, 313a
  Austin, III 1b
  Austrian Civil Code, II 656a
  benevolence, III 232a
  Bentham, IV 279a
  Brecht, II 658b
  Brennan, II 657b
  Burke, II 654a–654b
  Cardozo, II 657b
  chaos, III 15b
  characteristics of, II 659a
  Christianity, II 656b, 657a; III 671a
  Cicero, II 658b
  Code of Hammurabi, II 655b
  Code Napoléon, II 656a
  commercial, II 655b
  common law, II 693b, 695a
  concept, II 652b
  contract theory, II 658b
  cosmology, IV 382b
  Covenant, II 656a–657a
  deliverance, II 656a
  Democritus, II 576b
  Dewey, John, III 569b
  Diderot, II 276a
  dignity, IV 138a
  distribution, IV 179a
  dualism, II 657b–658a
  due process of law, II 654b–655a
  Egypt (ancient), IV 224b, 225b
  Enlightenment, II 94a
  Epicurus, II 654b, 656b
  equality, II 141a, 147a–147b; III 15b, 27b, 28a
  equity, II 150a, 150b, 151b, 656a, 656b
  Euripides, III 573a
  evil, II 163b, 166b
  fortune, II 233b
  France, II 657b
  France, Anatole, II 655b
  free will, II 236b, 653a, 656a, 656b
  freedom, II 249a
  freedom of speech, II 252b,

253b, 255a
  general will, II 276a, 278a, 279b, 280b
  give and take form, II 656a–656b
  God, I 287a–287b; II 334b, 335a, 337b, 352b, 354a, 654a, 656a, 657a, 658b; III 572b, 573a; IV 378b, 379a, 381b, 382b, 383a
  good, II 655b; IV 175a, 175b, 178a, 179a, 180b, 181a, 183b, 186a
  Gorgias, II 653b
  Greece (ancient), II 652b–656a, 656b, 659a, 675b–676a, 677a, 679a, 679b
  Grotius, II 654b, 657a
  Hammurabi, II 655b
  happiness, II 375b–376a
  harmony, II 654a; III 15b
  Hegel, II 653a
  Herder, II 658b; III 639a
  Heraclitus, II 653a, 653b, 658b
  Herodotus, II 653a
  Hesiod, II 653a; III 572b, 573a
  history, II 652b–657b
  Hobbes, II 654b, 657a; III 20b
  Holmes, Justice, III 568a
  Homer, II 652b–653a
  human nature, III 572b, 573a, 575a, 575b–577a
  humanism, II 653b, 658b; IV 131a
  Hume, III 232a, 232b; IV 178a
  idea, II 543b–544a, 546b, 652b–655a, 657b–659a
  ideal, II 654a, 658a
  immutability of, II 653b
  impiety, II 564b, 565a
  independence on Man, II 657b–658a
  India (ancient), III 7a
  infinity, II 614a
  injustice, II 655a, 657a, 659a
  international peace, III 450b, 451b, 453b
  Israel, (ancient), II 564b, 565a
  Italian Civil Code, II 656a
  Italy, III 674b
  Jesus Christ, II 657a
  Judaism, II 564b, 565a, 656a–656b, 657a, 658b; III 487b
  Julius Caesar, II 656b
  Justinian, II 656b
  Kames, III 234b
  Kant, II 279b, 653a; III

639b, 640b; IV 382b
  Kelsen, III 2a
  Lao-Tzu, II 658a
  law, II 249a, 652b–658a, 675b–676a, 677a, 679a, 679b, 686a, 686b, 687b, 688b; III 1b, 2a, 5b, 7a, 11a, 16b, 23a, 24a, 27b–28a, 32b, 110a, 111a, 111b, 112a, 115a
  Leibniz, II 659a; IV 378b, 379a, 382a
  Leonidas, II 659a
  Lewis, III 568a
  liberalism, III 671a
  Locke, II 658b
  Lucretius, II 656b
  Luther, IV 381b
  Machiavelli, III 122a
  Magna Carta, II 657b
  Maine, II 658b
  man, II 657b–659a
  Marxism, IV 181a
  Mayflower Compact, II 658b
  Middle Ages, III 116a
  Mill, J. S., IV 179a
  millenarianism, III 224a, 224b–225a
  Montesquieu, III 21a
  moral sense, III 232a, 232b, 234b
  morality, II 656a, 656b
  Mosaic law, II 656a
  mythology, II 652b–653a, 656b
  natural law, II 653a, 654a, 654b, 656b, 657a; III 14a, 15a–15b, 16a, 16b, 17b, 19b, 20b, 21a, 22b, 23a, 24a, 25b
  Nature, III 15a, 15b, 16a
  negativism, II 659a
  obedience, II 659a
  Orientalism, III 431a
  Parmenides, II 653a, 653b
  peace, III 443a, 444b
  Peirce, III 552b
  Perelman, III 27b
  perfectibility, III 475a
  philanthropy, III 487b
  Plato, II 236b, 375b–376a, 653a, 655b, 656a, 656b, 658b; III 15a, 16b, 110a, 497a, 554a; IV 3b, 175a, 368b, 440b
  Platonism, II 653a, 653b–654b, 655a, 657a, 658a; III 497a
  pleasure, II 375b–376a
  Plotinus, II 657a
  politics, II 659a
  Pollock, Frederick, II 654b
  polytheism, II 652b

positive law, II 654b
in practice, II 655a–658a
pragmatism, II 658b
probability, III 612b
progress, III 634b, 636a, 637b, 638b, 639a, 639b, 640b, 647a, 648a, 649a
Protagoras, II 653b, 657a
protest movements, III 671a–672a, 674b, 676b
Proudhon, II 280b
psychology, IV 3b
punishment, II 653a; III 575a
Pythagoreans, II 653a, 655b, 656a
radicalism, III 671a
rationalism, IV 46a, 46b, 49a
reason, II 656b–657a, 658a
reformation, IV 64a, 69a
religion, II 652b, 656a, 657a
remedial, II 655a
Renaissance, IV 131a, 138a, 440b
retaliation, II 656a–656b
rhetoric, IV 167b
right, III 15a–15b; IV 175a, 175b, 178a, 179a, 180b, 181a, 183b, 186a
romanticism, IV 203a, 205b
Rome (ancient), II 653a, 656b, 686a, 686b, 687b, 688b
Romulus, II 656b
Rousseau, II 278a, 280b, 653b
rules, III 232b
Saint Augustine, II 657a, 658a
Saint Thomas Aquinas, II 655a, 656b–657a
salvation, IV 224b, 225b, 227b
satire, IV 212b
Savigny, II 658b
Schopenhauer, II 166b
Smith, Adam, II 59a
as a social ideal, II 655a–658a
social welfare, IV 279a, 280a–280b
socialism, III 671a; IV 285b
society, II 659a; III 475a
Socrates, II 659a; III 554a, 576b, 577a; IV 49a, 285b
Sophism, II 653a–653b
Sophists, II 653b
Sophocles, II 653a; III 573a
Spencer, IV 180b
Stammler, II 657b

State, IV 313a, 313b
Stoicism, II 653a, 656b, 658a; IV 320b
as a supramundane idea, II 652b–655a
temperance, IV 366b, 368b, 370a, 371a–375b
theodicy, IV 378b, 379a, 381b, 382a, 382b, 383a
theory, II 652b–655a
Thomism, II 656b–657a
Thoreau, IV 431a
Ti (myth), II 658a
tragic sense, IV 413a–414a
Ulpian, II 656b, 688b
United Nations, II 657b
U.S., II 654b–655a, 657b
U.S. Supreme Court, II 654b–655a
U.S.S.R., II 657b
universal man, IV 440b
utilitarianism, IV 179a, 448a, 449a
utility, IV 452a
Utopia, IV 459b
virtue, IV 366b, 368b, 370a, 371a, 371b–377b
war, III 441b
welfare state, IV 509b, 512a
William of Ockham, III 19b
witchcraft, IV 522b
World War II, II 659a
Yahweh, II 565a
Zeno of Elea, II 653b
Zeus (myth), II 652b, 653a; III 572b
Justin, Saint (100?–?165), demonology, I 668b
Gnosticism, II 327a, 329a
millenarianism, III 224a
peace, III 441a
primitivism, III 589b
Justinian I, Emperor (483–565)
authority, III 29b
common law, II 691a, 691b
disease, II 399b
law, II 685b, 686b, 687b, 688a, 689b; III 24b, 29b, 30a,
mathematics, III 181b
natural law, III 17b, 24b
Neo-Platonism, III 373b
Platonism, III 503b
Juvenal (60?–?140 A.D.), freedom of speech, II 261b
law, II 689a
longevity, III 89b
pragmatism, III 554a
primitivism, III 580b, 581a
progress, III 632a
satire, IV 211a–215b

K

Kac, M., probability, III 620a
Kadar, II 29b, 30b
Kadar, Jan, Marxism, III 156a
Kafka, Franz (1883–1924), allegory, I 47b–48a
Enlightenment, II 99a
metaphysical imagination, III 208a
motif, III 242b
symbolism, IV 345a
Kahn, Gustave (1859–1936), symbolism, IV 339b, 340a, 344a
Kainz, Friedrich, beauty, I 211a
Kaiser, Georg (1878–1945), expressionism, II 208a, 208b, 209a
Kaiser, Wilhelm, Pythagorean harmony, IV 42a
Kalam, Islam theology, II 641b, 642a–643a, 647b, 648b
Kāla-Rudra (myth), II 344a
Kālī (myth), II 344a
Kalinowski, L., iconography, II 538b
Kalista, Zdeněk, baroque in literature, I 193a
Kallen, Horace M., loyalty, III 113a
Kama-Sutra (myth), love, III 100b
Kames, Lord (1696–1782), aesthetics, II 221a; III 234b
catharsis, I 265b
creativity in art, I 587b–588a
empathy, II 87b
Hume and, III 234b
Hutcheson and, III 234b
literary criticism, I 597a
literature, IV 332a
moral sense, III 234a, 234b
pity, I 265b
Shaftesbury and, III 234b
style, IV 332a
sympathy, II 87b
ut pictura poesis, IV 472a
Kandinsky, Wassily (1866–1944)
aesthetics, II 221a
expressionism, II 208a
K'ang Yieu Wei (1858–1927), Utopia, IV 459a
K'ang-hsi dynasty, I 360b, 361a
Kant, Immanuel (1724–1804), aesthetics, I 588a; II 551a,

551b; II 216b, 218b, 221a, 223a–223b; IV 356a, 356b
agnosticism, I 18a, 19a, 23b; II 246b
appearance and reality, I 97b–98a
art, I 598a; II 307a
art for art's sake, I 108b, 109b
art and play, I 101b, 103b–105b
atheism, IV 209a
authority, I 153a
Bacon and, I 178a; III 218a
beauty, I 203a–203b; II 85b, 221a, 223a–223b
behaviorism, I 219b
Bentham and, III 444b
Bernstein and, III 163a
Bruno and, IV 298a
casuistry, I 263a
categorical imperative, III 443a
categories, III 357b
causation, I 277b, 280a, 280b, 291a, 676a; II 240a; IV 433b
certainty, I 314a–316a, 317b, 319a, 319b, 321b, 324b
Chain of Being, I 330a–331b, 332b, 334a
change, IV 395a
civilization, I 614a, 616a, 617b, 619b, III 443b
classification of the arts, I 460b–461a
cognition, I 103b–104a; III 218b
Coleridge and, I 617b; IV 199a, 200a, 202a
community, IV 179b
concept formation, I 7a–8b
consciousness, III 555b
conservation, I 473a
continuity, I 501a, 502a
cosmic images, I 513b, 519a, 519b, 521a–521b
cosmology, I 549b–550a; II 182a, 187b, 447b; IV 382b, 383b
Counter-Enlightenment, II 103b, 104a, 107b–108a, 109b
creativity in art, I 588a, 588b
culture, I 614a, 616a, 617b, 619b; II 128b
death, I 637b, 639a, 641a–641b
Demiurge, I 676a

design argument, I 675b, 676a, 676b

desire, II 240a, 240b

determinism, II 240a–240b, 241a, 141b, 242a

Dewey and, I 324b; III 555b

Diderot and, III 218b

diplomacy, III 443b

disteleology, IV 382b

dualism, II 41a–41b; III 436b

duty, III 472b; IV 179b

education, II 72a, 75a–75b, 80b, 82b, 83a, 83b, 84a

emotion, II 324a

empathy, II 85b–86a

empiricism, II 407b, 551b; III 233b, 358a, 547a, 547b, 556b, 562a; IV 248b–249a, 382b, 435b

Enlightenment, II 89b, 93a, 98b; III 326a, 343a, 479b; IV 209a

environment, II 120b, 128b

epistemology, III 218a, 218b, 219b, 233b

equality, II 279b

eschatology, II 159a

ethics, II 551a; III 233b, 555b–556a, 639b; IV 179a–179b, 181a, 322a

evil, III 472b; IV 382b

evolution, I 521a

evolutionism, II 176a, 178a, 182a, 187b

experience, III 555b, 556a; IV 248b–249a, 382b–383a, 433a

faith, I 316a; III 234a

formalism, I 104b

free will, II 240a–240b, 241a, 241b, 242a, 246a–246b, 247a; III 555b, 562a, 640b

freedom, I 104a, 588a, 641a; II 240a–240b, 242a, 279b, 407b, 548a; III 21b–22a, 47b–48a, 637a, 639b; IV 179b

general will, II 279b–280a

genius, I 588a; II 223b, 295b–296a, 307a, 317b, 323b–324a

God, I 315b–316a, 330a, 521a, 641a, 676a; II 240b, 353a–357b, 358a, 358b, 362b, 548a; IV 248b, 382b

Goethe and, IV 202b

good, IV 179a–179b, 181a, 181b, 186b, 382b

happiness, II 375a, 380a, 385b; III 637a, IV 179b

hedonism, III 234a

Hegel and, II 407b, 410b, 414a; III 445a, 555b, 556b

Herder and, II 324a; III 326a, 472b; IV 209b

hierarchy, II 447b

as historian, III 358a

history, I 280a, 280b, 616a; III 638a, 639b–640a, 640b, 649a

Hobbes and, III 442b, 443a, 443b

Holbach and, IV 209a

holy, II 513a

human nature, III 442b

Hume and, I 314a–316b; III 357b–358a; IV 209a

iconography, II 536a

idea, II 453a, 547b–548b, 551a–551b; III 219a, 358a, 518a, 518b

ideal, II 551a–551b

idealism, II 407b

illusion, III 218a

imagination, I 588a; III 215b, 217b–219b, 222a, 222b

immorality, II 240b

immortality, I 639a, 641a–641b; II 357a, 548a

inclination, II 240a, 240b

individualism, II 279b–280a, 307a, 597b, 598b, 600a, 603a; III 472b, 555b; IV 179b

infinity, II 447b, 605b, 606a

inspiration, II 323b–324a

international law, III 444a

international peace, III 452b–453a

intuition, II 551b

irony, II 629b

irrationalism, III 635a–638a

Jacobi and, IV 202a

judgment, II 240a–240b; III 234a; IV 248b, 433a, 433b

justice, II 279b, 653a; III 639b, 640b; IV 382b

law, I 291a; II 240a, 240b, 279b; III 472b, 649a; IV 179b

Leibniz and, III 443b; IV 382a

liberalism, III 37a, 47b–48a

liberty, II 240a

Lieber and, III 444a

Lincoln and, III 444a

literary criticism, I 596b, 597b–598a

literature, III 85a

logic, I 316a; III 547a, 547b, 562a; IV 433b

Marxism, III 163a, 164b, 168a

materialism, II 407b, 455a

mathematics, III 179a, 357b; IV 248b, 433a, 433b

matter, I 330a, 521a; III 185b

metaphor, III 199a, 199b

metaphysics, III 215b, 217b–219b, 222a, 222b, 472b; IV 433a–433b

millenarianism, II 159a

mind, II 120b, 324a; IV 502a

modernism, I 419b, 420a, 425b

moral sense, III 233b, 234a, 234b

morality, I 316b; II 107b, 240b, 247a, 279b, 353b–354a, 357a, 407b, 548a; III 442a–442b, 494b, 637a, 639b, 640b; IV 179b, 181a, 382b, 383a, 433b

music, II 317b, 323b–324a

nationalism, III 325b, 326a–326b

natural law, II 240a–240b; III 21b–22a, 22b

naturalism in art, III 343a

Nature, I 315a, 315b, 588a; III 555b, 640b; IV 433a, 433b

necessity, II 240b; III 351b, 357b–358a, 358b

Newton and, I 277b, 314a–315a, 316a

obligation, IV 179b

observation, III 555b

organicism, III 421b, 422a, 425a

Orientalism, III 436b

originality, II 323b, 324a

peace, III 442a–445b

Peirce and, III 555b–556a, 558a, 558b

perennial philosophy, III 457b, 462a, 462b

perfectibility, II 551b; III 472b; IV 382b

periodization in history, III 479b

periodization in literary history, III 484b

philosophy, II 551a–551b; III 199a, 199b; IV 436a

physics, IV 433b

Pietism, III 494b

Plato and, II 223a; III 518a–518b

Platonism, III 518a–518b, 520a, 522b

Poe and, I 519b

poetry, III 219b

politics, II 98b, 279b; III 443a, 444b, 640b

positivism, III 547a, 547b

post-Kantianism, IV 209a

power, II 247a

pragmatism, II 551b; III 553b, 555b–556a, 556b, 558a, 558b, 562a, 563b

pride, III 472b

progress, III 637a, 638a, 639b–640a, 640b, 649a

prudence, III 555b

psychology, II 240a; IV 11b, 24a, 24b, 433b

rationalism, I 104b; III 233b, 358a, 640b; IV 179b, 181b

realism in literature, IV 51b

reason, I 91a–93b, 315a–316a, 317b; II 240b, 280a; III 21b, 218b, 494b, 555b; IV 200a, 202a, 248b–249a, 382b, 383a

Reid and, III 233b

relativity, IV 87a

religion, II 548a

revisionism, IV 270a

right, IV 179a–179b, 181a, 181b, 186b

rights, III 326a

romanticism, III 555b; IV 189b, 209a, 210a

Rousseau and, II 107b; III 442a; IV 209b, 502a

rules, III 21b, 555b, 556a

Saint-Pierre and, III 442a

Scale of Creatures, I 331a–331b

Schelling and, III 555b; IV 210a

Schlegel and, IV 200a

Schleiermacher and, III 518b, 520a; IV 202b

Schopenhauer and, I 255b; III 555b

science, III 219b

senses, III 518a

skepticism, IV 209a, 241a 248b–249a, 249b, 250b

social contract, IV 261a, 263a

social welfare, IV 280a

socialism, IV 290b

society, I 616a; III 555b, 639b, 640b

sociology, III 443b

soul, I 639a, 641a–641b

space, II 547b, 548a; IV 295a, 298a, 303a, 305a

species, I 330b–331a; II 551b

spontaneity, II 407b

State, II 279b; III 472b, 639b
Stoicism, IV 322a
subjectivism, II 455a
sublime in external nature, IV 335a
suffering, IV 382b
symbolism, IV 338a
talent, II 323b–324a
taste, IV 356a, 356b
teleology, IV 382b, 383a
Tennemann and, III 518b, 522b
theodicy, IV 381b, 382a–383a, 383b
theology, IV 382b
time, II 240b, 547b, 548a; IV 393b–394a, 394b, 395a
transcendentalism, III 219a, 358b, 444a; IV 200a
translation, III 444a
truth, I 315b, 319a; III 518a–518b; IV 383a, 433a, 433b
understanding, IV 202a
unity, II 551b; III 639b
unity of science, IV 431b, 432b, 433a–433b, 436a, 436b
universality, IV 179b, 433b
universe, II 447b
Vattel and, III 442a
virtue, II 80b; IV 179b
Volksgeist, IV 491b–492a
war, III 442a–442b, 443a–444a; IV 502a
Weber and, I 260b
wisdom, IV 382b, 383a
Wright and, III 555b, 562a
Zeitgeist, IV 536a
Kantorowicz, E. H., iconography, II 537b
Kaplan, Abraham, Buddhism, I 256b
Karamazov family (fiction), tragic sense, IV 416b
Karcewski, S., structuralism, IV 324a
Kardec, Allan, Spiritism, I 642b
Kardelj, Edvard, Marxism, III 166a–166b
Kardiner, Abram, psychology, IV 29a
Karlstadt, Andreas (1480?–1541), history, I 390b
Karma, salvation, IV 231b–232b
Kashmir, international peace, III 454b
Kate, Lambert ten (1674–1731), ideal, II 549b
Katz, J., language, II 668b
Katzenellenbogen, A., iconog-

raphy, II 538b
Kauffmann, Angelica (1741–1807), neo-classicism in art, III 365b, 369a
Kauffmann, H., iconography, II 538b
Kautsky, Karl Johann (1854–1938)
acquired characteristics, II 620a, 620b
Bernstein and, III 164a
determinism, II 25a
evolution, II 454b
Luxemburg, III 164a
Marxism, III 148a, 150a, 164a, 165b
materialism, II 453a, 454b
production, II 25a
revisionism, IV 265a, 267b, 268b, 269a, 270a, 271a, 271b, 272b, 273a, 273b
Kavolis, Vytautas, beauty, I 213b
Kayser, Hans, Pythagorean harmony, IV 42a
Kayser, Wolfgang, symbolism, IV 343a
Keats, John (1795–1821), beauty, III 524a
death, I 636b
disease, II 403b
human nature, III 524a
impressionism, II 581a
irrationalism, II 638a
literature, III 86a
mythology, III 299b
Newton and, III 394b
periodization in literary history, III 485b
Platonism, III 524a
romanticism, IV 195a, 205a, 208b, 209b
ut pictura poesis, IV 471a
Keble, John (1792–1866)
art, II 310b
wish-fulfilment, II 310b
Kedrov, Bonifatii M., classification of the sciences, I 466a
Keep, John, civil disobedience, I 436b
Keil, John (1671–1721), Cosmic Fall, I 510b
Kellogg, Samuel Henry, Orientalism, III 435b
Kelly, J. L., indeterminacy, II 592a
Kelsen, Hans (1881–), Hart and, III 3a
law, III 1b–2b, 3a, 3b, 22b, 24a
natural law, III 22b, 23b, 24a
positivism, III 1b–2b

unity, III 2a–2b
Kelvin, Lord (1824–1907), axiomatization, I 171b
catastrophism, IV 423a
continuity, I 494a
entropy, II 113a, 113b, 115b, 116a, 116b, 117a
linguistics, IV 426b
religion, IV 108a
technology, IV 363a
time, IV 404b
uniformitarianism, IV 423a, 426b
Kennedy, John F. (1917–1963)
international peace, III 456a
loyalty, III 113b
Kenon, IV 298b, 299a
Kepler, Johannes (1571–1630)
alchemy, I 32b
beauty, IV 75a
Bruno and, II 443a
causation, I 281a
Copernicus and, I 545b–546a
cosmic images, I 515a, 515b, 516a, 516b, 517a
cosmic voyages, I 525a, 525b–533a, 546a
cosmology, I 545b–526a, 547a, 548a, 549a, 550b; II 443b; IV 306a
creativity in art, I 579b
design argument, I 673b–674a
determinism, II 23b
Galileo and, III 414b–415a
God, I 517a; III 271a
Godwin and, I 527b–528a
gravitation, III 194a
Hariot and, I 133b–134a
harmony, II 389b–390a; III 260b, 271a; IV 41b, 75a
heresy, II 428a
hierarchy, II 442b, 443a–443b
humanism, II 521a; IV 605a
infinity, II 605a
Islam, II 647a
lenses, III 413b, 414b–415a
light, IV 77b
mathematics, II 390a; III 178b, 182b
matter, III 189a, 192a, 192b, 194a, 194b
Maurolico and, III 412a
medieval science, II 197a
motion, III 260b
mountains in literature, III 256b

music, II 389b–390a; III 260b, 271a; IV 41b
Nature, I 281a
Newton and, III 194b
optics, III 409b, 411b, 412a–414a, 414b, 416a, 416b, 417a
planets, III 260b
Platonism, II 521a
progress, III 640b
Pythagoras and, I 579b
Pythagoreans, IV 41b, 42a
relativity, IV 74b–75a, 75b, 77b, 90a
skepticism, IV 242a
space, IV 302a, 306a
symmetry, IV 348b
time, IV 402b
universe, II 443a–443b; III 260b, 271a; IV 41b
Utopia, IV 462a
Kerameus, A. Papadopoulos, iconography, II 526a
Kerényi, C., mythology, III 281a, 282b, 313a–313b, 314a
Kermode, Frank, romanticism, IV 196a
Kerner, Justinus (1786–1862), chance images, I 350b–351a, 351b
Kerr, Alfred (1867–1948), literary criticism, I 606a
Kerr, Robert, catastrophism, IV 420a
Key, Ellen (1849–1926)
children, III 596b
music, III 262a, 262b, 263a
Nature, III 349a
primitivism, III 596a
Keyishian v. Board of Regents of New York, I 12a
Keynes, John Maynard (1883–1946)
behaviorism, I 219b
crisis in history, I 591a
economic history, II 58b
God, III 611a
militarism, IV 507a
natural liberty, II 62a, 70a, 70b–71a
probability, III 606b, 611a, 614a, 614b, 618b
Quételet and, III 614b
welfare state, IV 512a, 513a
Keyserling, Edward von (1855–1918), realism in literature, IV 55a
Keyserling, Count Hermann (1880–1946), Buddhism, I 256a
Khalid ibn Yazid, Prince (d. 704), alchemy, I 29b, 30a

Kharchev, A. G., beauty, I 211a

Khawārij, II 641b

Khepri (myth), II 334a

Khintchine, A., probability, III 608b–609a, 620a

Khnopff, Fernand, naturalism in art, III 341b

Khrushchev, Nikita (1894–1972)
Djilas and, III 166a
Marxism, III 153b, 155a, 157a–157b, 166a
nuclear power, III 157a
peaceful coexistence, III 157a
Stalin and, III 157b

Kidd, Benjamin (1858–1916), acquired characteristics, II 620a

Kierkegaard, Søren (1813–1855)
allegory, I 48a
atheism, II 192b
Being, II 192b, 193b
Counter-Enlightenment, II 109b
crisis in history, I 591a
Enlightenment, II 99a
eschatology, II 160b, 161a
evil, II 168a
existentialism, II 189a–193b
faith, II 192a, 192b
Faust (legend), III 250b
free will, II 246b
God, II 168a, 189b, 192a, 192b, 360a
Hegel and, II 191b
Ibsen and, IV 416b
irony, II 629b
irrationalism, II 636b–637a, 637b
knowledge, II 189b, 192a
law, II 191b–192a
love, III 104a
perennial philosophy, III 462a
realism in literature, IV 54b
skepticism, IV 249a–249b
time, II 189b
tragic sense, IV 416b
truth, II 189b
virtue, II 192a

Kindermann, Eberhard, cosmic voyages, I 532b

Kinematics
Galileo, III 383a
medieval development, II 197b, 199b–201b, 203b, 204a
methodology, III 378b
Newton, III 383a
time, IV 403a

Kinesis, Aristotle, IV 301a

King, Gregory, utility, IV 452b

King, Henry (1592–1669), association of ideas, I 112b

King, Martin Luther, Jr. (1929-1968)
civil disobedience, I 438a, 438b–439a
Fortas and, I 440a
Gandhi and, I 439a
love, I 438b–439a

King, Thomas Starr (1824–1864), Volksgeist, IV 495b

Kingship
Bible, III 277a, 281a
common law, II 693b–694a, 694b, 695a, 695b, 696a
despotism, II 1b, 2a, 3a, 3b, 4b, 5a, 8a, 8b, 13b–14a
equality, II 138b
equity, II 152a–153a
free will, II 242b
freedom of speech, II 252b, 253a–257b, 258a, 259a
Greece (ancient), II 675a–676a, 678a, 678b
law, II 675a–676a, 678a, 678b, 689b–690a
Middle Ages, III 319b–320a
mythology, III 277a, 281a, 287a
nationalism, III 319b–320a
Plato, III 498b–499a
prophecy, III 658b, 660b, 661a, 664b
Rome (ancient), II 689b–690a

Kingsley, Charles (1819–1875)
exchatology, II 159a
socialism, IV 290a

Kinsey, Alfred C. (1894–1956), psychology, IV 29a

Kircher, Athanasius (1601–1680)
chance images, I 343b
China, I 358a
cosmic voyages, I 526a
music, III 271a
Pythagoreans, IV 41b
ut pictura poesis, IV 473a

Kirchoff, Gustav (1829–1887)
continuity, I 494a
cosmology, I 553a

Kirk, Hyland, longevity, III 93a

Kirk, Geoffrey S., time, IV 390a

Kismet, II 30b

Klages, Ludwig, psychology,

IV 15a

Klaproth, Heinrich J. (1783–1835), China, I 367a

Klee, Paul (1879–1940)
art, II 304b; III 597a
primitivism, III 597a
ut pictura poesis, IV 469a

Klein, Carl August, symbolism, IV 342b

Klein, Felix (1849–1925)
cosmology, I 555a
infinity, II 613b
pragmatism, III 557b

Klein, R., iconography, II 539b

Kleiner, Julius, baroque in literature, I 193a

Kleinjogg, Jacob, primitivism, III 600b

Kleist, Ewald von (1715–1759), ut pictura poesis, IV 472a

Kleist, Heinrich von (1777–1811), romanticism, IV 207a, 209b

Klemperer, V., baroque in literature, I 190b

Klibansky, R., mythology, III 290b

Klingenstierna, S., optics, III 420a

Klinger, Friedrich Maximilian von (1752–1831)
Counter-Enlightenment, II 107a
Faust (legend), III 250a
periodization in literary history, III 483b
symbolism, IV 342b

Klopstock, Friedrich Gottlieb (1724–1803)
baroque in literature, I 195a
beauty, II 550b
classicism, I 453a
genius, II 295b
Gothic, II 370b
ideal, II 550b
Winckelmann and, II 550b

Kneller, Godfrey (1646–1723), mythology, III 298a–298b

Knies, Karl (1821–1898), economic history, II 60b

Knight, Richard Payne
mythology, III 303b
ut pictura poesis, IV 473b

Knipping, J. B., iconography, II 535b, 537b

Knolles, Richard (1550?–1610), despotism, II 5b

Knowledge
aesthetics, II 223a, 223b; IV 354a, 355a
agnosticism, I 17a–27a
angels, II 232b

Aristotle, I 128a, 456b, 625b; II 196b; III 190a, 380a; IV 6b, 49b, 175b, 431b, 436a, 530b
art, I 456b
Bacon, I 173a; III 559a; IV 361b, 434a, 462a
beauty, I 203a, 206a–206b
behavior, III 552a
Bentham, I 662b
Berkeley, IV 246a
Blasius of Parma, II 35b
Bridgman, III 561b
Bruno, II 348a
certainty, I 312a–325a
chance, II 232b
classification, I 462a–462b, 466a
Comte, II 25b
Condillac, I 318a
Condorcet, III 472a, 644a
Counter-Enlightenment, II 100b, 101b, 103b–104a, 104b, 108a
culture, I 620a
cynicism, I 629b
Dante, III 511a
Descartes, I 640a; IV 244b, 435b
Dewey, I 324b–325b; III 561b, 568a, 568b
Diderot, II 96b
dualism, II 38b
education, II 73b, 78b, 81b
empiricism, I 218b–219a; III 547b, 548a, 549b
Engels, II 25b
Enlightenment, II 90a, 96b
Epicureanism, IV 7b, 8a
eschatology, II 158a–158b
evil, II 162b, 167a, 168b, 169a
existentialism, II 189b, 192a
fate, II 229b
Ficino, III 511a, 513a
Forms, I 1a–1b; III 504b
free will, II 236b, 238b, 239a, 239b, 241a, 241b, 246b, 247b
genius, II 294b, 295b, 313a
Gnosticism, II 326b, 327a–327b, 645b, 650a, 650b–651a, 651b, 652a
God, II 229b, 232b, 334a, 348a, 348b, 349a, 350a, 351b, 353a, 360b
good, IV 173a, 173b, 174a, 174b, 175b, 185b, 186b
Göschel, II 412a
grammar, II 641a
Greece (ancient), II 678b
Grosseteste, III 382a
happiness, II 376a, 379a, 379b, 386b–387a

health, II 396a
Hegel, I 37a, 319a; II 158a–158b, 412a, 414a
historiography, IV 149a, 149b
Hobbes, IV 434a
holy, II 513a
human nature, III 572a, 577a, 644a
humanism, II 650a; IV 132a, 133a, 135b
Hume, I 313a–314a, 316a, 321b; II 103b–104a, 239b, 582a; III 233a
Hutcheson, III 231b
idea, II 542a, 547a, 547b, 548a
ideal, II 551a
ideology, II 553a
ignorance, III 472a
impressionism, II 582a, 582b, 583b
individualism, II 603b
Islam, II 639b, 642a, 646a
James, II 561b, 562a, 568a
Kant, I 315a–315b, 316a, 316b, 322a, 323b, 330b, 331a; II 223a, 223b, 376a, 379a, 379b, 386b–387a; III 218b, 219a, 222a, 556a; IV 248b–249a, 433b
Kierkegaard, II 189b, 192a
language, I 466b; II 662b, 663b, 668b, 672a
law, II 678b; III 28b–29a
Leibniz, II 350a, 668b; III 515b; IV 382a, 435a
Leonardo da Vinci, IV 442a–442b
Lewis, C. I., III 568a, 568b
literary criticism, I 597a, 606b
literary paradox, III 81a
Locke, I 218b; II 239a, 351a; III 216a
Lovejoy, III 552b, 553a
Lully, I 327a
Luther, II 349a
macrocosm and microcosm, III 129a, 131a
Marx, II 451a
materialism, II 451a
mathematics, III 179b–180a, 180b, 184b
matter, III 188b, 190a
Matthew of Aquasparta, I 4b–5a
metaphysical imagination, III 210b, 211b, 212b, 214a, 214b, 215b, 216a, 216b, 218a–222b
methodology, III 378b
mimesis, III 500a
Montaigne, IV 243b

moral sense, III 230b, 231b, 233a, 233b–234a, 234b
morality, I 316b; III 645a
music, I 457a; II 313a, 388a; III 269a
mythology, III 287b, 288b, 290b, 301b, 302b, 304b, 305b, 313b
Nature, III 348a, 348b
necessity, III 356b, 357a, 358b, 360a, 361b
neo-classicism in art, III 363a, 367b
Neo-Platonism, III 372b, 375a
Newton, III 378b
optics, III 408a, 408b
pain, II 386b–387a
Parmenides, III 572a
Peirce, III 556a, 561a, 561b, 568a
perennial philosophy, III 457a, 458b, 459b, 460a, 460b, 461a, 462a
perfectibility, III 464b–465a, 467b, 468b, 472a, 643b, 644a
philanthropy, III 491b
philology, III 520a
physics, III 387b
Pico della Mirandola, IV 132a
Pirandello, III 568a
Plato, I 584a; II 149a, 236b, 582b, 662b, 663b; III 188b, 211a–211b, 464b–465a, 496a–503b, 504b, 507a, 508b, 513a, 515b; IV 4a–4b, 33b, 34b, 49a, 49b, 368a, 431b
Platonism, I 1a–1b; III 496a–507a, 508b, 509a, 512a, 513a, 520a
pleasure, II 376a, 379a, 379b, 386b–387a
Plotinus, I 2b–3a; III 513a
poets, III 501a–501b
Popper, I 323b
positivism, III 533a, 545b, 547b, 548a, 549b
pragmatism, III 552a, 552b, 553a, 555b, 559a, 561a, 561b, 562a, 564b, 565a, 565b, 567b–568a, 568b, 569b
primitivism, III 582a, 582b, 588a, 589b, 591a, 595a, 595b, 602b
probability, III 614b
progress, III 632b, 634a, 638a, 641a, 643a, 644a, 645a, 648a, 648b, 649a, 649b
prophecy, III 662b, 667a

psychology, IV 2a, 3b, 4a–4b, 6b, 7b, 9a, 9b, 11a, 11b
Pythagoreans, IV 33b, 35b
Ramism, IV 42b, 44a–45a
rationalism, IV 49a, 49b
Reid, III 233b–234a
relativism, IV 71a
religion, IV 94a, 105a, 106a, 111b
reminiscence, I 1a
Renaissance, IV 132a, 133a, 135b, 139b, 149a, 149b, 437a, 440b, 441a–443a
rhetoric, IV 168a, 170a, 172b
right, IV 173a, 173b, 174a, 174b, 175b, 185b, 186b
Royce, III 561a
Russell, I 319b, 320a–321b
Saint Ambrose, III 589b
Saint Augustine, IV 9a
Saint Bernard, III 591a
Saint Thomas Aquinas, IV 432a
Saint-Simon, III 641a
Schiller, III 568a
Seneca, III 588a
Shaftesbury, III 230b
skepticism, IV 234b, 235b, 236b, 238b, 241a–246a, 247a, 248b–249b
social contract, IV 259a, 262b
Socrates, III 496a–497b, 499b, 504a, 577a; IV 49a, 49b, 174a, 415a
sophism, I 629a
Sorel, III 565b
space, IV 300a
Spencer, I 465b
Speusippus, IV 35b
Spinoza, II 238b; IV 246a, 434b
Stoics, IV 8a
structuralism, IV 329a
taste, IV 354a, 355a
technology, IV 360b, 361b
temperance, IV 368a, 369a
theodicy, IV 382a
theriophily, IV 387a
time, IV 390b, 391b
tragic sense, IV 415a
transformism, I 499b, 500b
translations, II 639b, 640a–640b, 641a, 641b, 643a, 649b, 650b
unity of science, IV 431a, 431b, 435b, 436a, 436b
universal man, IV 437a, 440b, 441a, 441b, 442a–442b, 443a
universality, IV 435a
university systems, II 647b

Utopia, IV 461b, 462a
value, III 567b–568a, 568b, 569b
virtue, III 472a, 508b; IV 49a
wisdom, II 650a–650b
wisdom of the fool, IV 515b, 517a, 517b, 519a
work, IV 530b, 531b, 533b, 534a
writing, III 180a
Knowles, David, history, I 381a
Ko Hung (c. 320 A.D.), alchemy, I 29a
longevity, III 91a
Koberstein, Karl August (1797–1870), literature, III 83a
Købke, Christen, naturalism in art, III 341a
Koch, J. A. (1768–1839), neo-classicism in art, III 370b
Koch, Max (1855–1931), literature, III 84a, 84b
Koch, Robert (1843–1910), disease, II 405a, 405b
Koestler, Arthur (1905–   ), cosmic images, I 513b, 514a, 515b–516a
Koffka, Kurt (1886–1941), beauty, I 213a
psychology, IV 14b
Kohlbrugge, J. H. F., recapitulation, IV 56b
Köhler, Wolfgang (1887–1967)
empiricism, III 549a
psychology, IV 14b
Kölliker, Rudolf Albert von (1817–1905), cell division, II 286a
Kolmogorov, A. N., probability, III 609a, 620a–622a, 623a
Kondakov, N. P., iconography, II 538b
König, Johann Friedrich, casuistry, I 262b
König, J. U., aesthetics, IV 356a
Koran
casuistry, I 258a
class, I 442a
cosmology, I 542b
God, II 344b–345a
historiography, II 474b
Islam, II 474b, 640a, 641a, 641b, 650b
longevity, III 90b
love, III 100a
philanthropy, III 488a
predestination, II 29b
salvation, IV 230b, 231a

217

sin, IV 230b, 231a
Korea
  Buddhism, I 248a, 248b, 249a, 251a–251b, 253a, 254a
  international peace, III 454b
  nationalism, III 337a
Korean War, III 114b
Korn, Alejandro, positivism, III 543b
Kornberg, Arthur, DNA, II 291a
Kosciuszko, Thaddeus (1746–1817)
  equality, II 144b
  revolution, IV 160b
Kosík, Karel, Marxism, III 168b, 169a, 169b
Kossuth, Louis (1802–1894), revolution, IV 160b
Koszul, André, baroque in literature, I 192a
Kotakowski, Leszek, Marxism, III 168a, 168b, 169a, 169b
Kraft, Victor, empiricism, III 545b–546a
Kramer, Heinrich, witchcraft, IV 521b
Kraus, Chr. J., linguistics, III 64a, 64b
Kraus, Karl (1874–1936), empiricism, III 546a
Krause, Karl Christian Friedrich (1781–1832), Buddhism, I 255b
Krause, M., Gnosticism, II 327b
Krell, Max, expressionism, II 206b
Kretschmer, Ernst (1888–1964), psychology, IV 15a
Krieger, Murray
  organicism, III 426b
  ut pictura poesis, IV 471a
Krishna, theodicy, IV 379b
Krochmal, Nachman, *Volksgeist*, IV 493a
Kronecker, Leopold (1823–1891), mathematics, III 176b
Kroner, Richard, Pietism, III 494b
Kronos, *see* Cronus (myth)
Kropotkin, Peter (1842–1921)
  anarchism, I 71b–72a, 74b–75a, 75b
  authority, I 160b
  evolutionism, II 181a
  good, IV 180b
  peace, III 445a
  perfectibility, III 470b
  philanthropy, III 486b
  Social Darwinism, II 181a

Krüger, G., eschatology, II 157b
Kruszewski, N., linguistics, III 71a; IV 425a
Krylov, N. S., indeterminacy, II 591a
Kubler, G., iconography, II 539b
Kugler, Franz (1808–1858), Burckhardt and, IV 125b–126a
Kuhn, A. (1812–1881), linguistics, III 69b
Kuhn, Richard, beauty, I 212a
Kuhn, Thomas S.
  empiricism, III 550b
  metaphor, III 200b
Kuhnau, Johann (1660–1722), music, III 267a
Kuiper, G. F., cosmology, I 570a
Külpe, Ostwald (1862–1915), psychology, IV 13a, 13b, 27a
Kummer, Frederic A. (1873–1943), periodization in literary history, III 485b
Küng, Hans, heresy, II 430a
Kunstle, K., iconography, II 535b
Kyōgoku, Itsuzō, Buddhism, I 257a

L

La Boétie, Étienne de (1530–1563), anarchy, I 72a
La Bruyère, Jean de (1645–1696), I 77b
  despotism, II 8a
  literary criticism, I 597a
  literature, IV 331b
  style, IV 332b
  taste, IV 355b
La Calprenède, Gautier (1610–1663), romanticism, IV 187a
La Dixmerie, Nicolas Bricaire de, primitivism, III 602b
La Fontaine, Jean de (1621–1695)
  aesthetics, IV 354b
  baroque in literature, I 190b
  classicism, I 452a
  theriophily, IV 384b
La Mettrie, Julien Offroy de (1709–1751)
  behaviorism, I 214a, 218b, 220a
  biology, I 242b
  causation, I 281b

Chain of Being, I 333b, 334b
  death, I 641a
  DNA, II 292a
  Enlightenment, II 96a
  genetic continuity, II 292a
  God, I 334b
  immortality, I 641a
  Jefferson and, IV 21a
  Man-Machine, III 131b, 134a, 135a, 137a, 138a, 138b–142a, 143b
  Nature, I 333b, 334b
  psychology, IV 11a, 21a, 28a
La Mothe Le Vayer, François de (1588–1672)
  certainty, I 304b
  China, I 360a
  deism, I 648b
  skepticism, IV 244a
La Motte, Abbé (1672–1731), attitude toward antiquity, I 81b, 82a–82b, 84b, 85b
La Peyrère, Isaac, skepticism, IV 246b–247a
La Placette, Jean, skepticism, IV 242b
La Rochelle, Drieu, pragmatism, III 564b–565a
La Rochefoucauld, François de (1613–1680)
  aesthetics, IV 354b
  theriophily, IV 388a
Laban (Bible), mythology, III 275b
Label space, III 621b, 622a
Laberthonnière, Lucien (1860–1932), modernism, I 422a–422b
Labor
  economic history, II 47b–54a, 57a, 59b–60a
  Enlightenment, II 90b, 99a
  equality, II 145b, 146a
  fascism, III 674a
  good, IV 179a
  happiness, II 379b, 384b
  Hegel, II 409a
  human nature, III 644a
  impressionism, II 576b
  industry, III 675b
  Jevons, II 384b
  liberalism, III 675b
  Malthus, II 49a
  Marx, II 49b, 60a, 69b; IV 292a, 292b
  Marxism, III 146b–170a
  materialism, III 676a
  monopoly, II 57a
  morality, III 675b
  natural liberty, II 65b, 69a–69b
  perfectibiliy, III 644a

power, IV 499b–500a
  primitivism, III 583a
  private property, III 653a, 653b, 654b, 655a, 656b
  progress, III 644a
  protest movements, III 672a, 672b, 674a, 674b, 675b, 677a
  radicalism, III 675b
  reformation, IV 60b, 61b
  revisionism, IV 264b, 270b, 272a
  revolution, IV 161a, 166a
  Ricardo, II 49b
  slavery, III 182b
  social contract, IV 259a
  socialism, III 675b, IV 289a, 289b, 291b, 292a, 292b
  Smith, II 47b, 48a–48b
  U.S., III 151a; IV 512a–512b
  utilitarianism, IV 447b
  utility, IV 453b
  Utopia, IV 459b, 462b
  utopianism, III 676a
  value, IV 292b, 453b
  vox populi, IV 497a–500a
  war, IV 501b
  welfare state, IV 510a, 510b, 512a–515a
  women, IV 529a
Laborde, Alexandre de (1774–1842), Gothic, II 373a
Labriola, Antonio
  Marxism, III 165a
  materialism, II 453a
Labrousse, Camille Ernest, historiography, II 498a
Lacan, Jacques, structuralism, IV 328a, 328b, 329b
Lachmann, Karl (1793–1851), Platonism, III 522a
Lacordaire, B. Henri (1802–1861), modernism, I 419b
Lacretelle, Jean (1766–1855), romanticism, IV 191a
Lactantius (c. 260–340)
  dignity, IV 138a, 139a, 140a
  millenarianism, III 224a
  mythology, III 299b
  natural law, III 17b
  primitivism, III 583b, 589a, 599a
  reformation, IV 62b
  skepticism, IV 236a
  spontaneous generation, IV 308a
  temperance, IV 370b
  theodicy, IV 380a–380b
Ladd, William (1778–1841), international peace, III 453a
Ladendorf, Heinz, chance images, I 341b, 343b, 345a

Ladner, Gerhart, reformation, IV 60a, 60b, 64a

Laënnec, René (1781–1826), disease, II 401b, 403b

Laffitte, Pierre (1823–1903), Pereira Barreto and, III 540b positivism, III 537b, 538a, 540a, 540b, 543a

Lafitau, Joseph François (1670–1740) mythology, III 301a primitivism, III 599a, 599b, 603b religion, IV 94a

Laforgue, Jules (1860–1887), cosmic images, I 522a irony, II 633b symbolism, IV 340b, 341a, 345a

Lagarde, Paul Anton de (1827–1891), conservatism, I 483a

Lagrange, Joseph Louis (1736–1813) axiomatization, I 166b Condorcet and, III 533a continuity, I 498b cosmology, I 554b entropy, II 117a geometry, IV 304a infinity, II 611a mathematics, III 179b positivism, III 533a probability, III 609b space, IV 302b, 304a

Lagrange, Marie-Joseph, modernism, I 421a

Laharpe, Jean François de (1739–1803), style, IV 332a

Lahontan, Louis Armand de (1666–1715) anarchy, I 71a deism, I 649a

Laird, John (1887–1946), war virtues, IV 484a

Laissez-faire Comte, III 540a economic history, II 47a, 55b, 58b–59a evolutionism, II 180b individualism, II 596a–596b, 597a, 602b natural liberty, II 61b, 69a philanthropy, III 490a positivism, III 542a private property, III 654a welfare state, IV 509b, 510a, 511a, 512a, 514b

Lalande, A. aesthetics, II 221b impressionism, II 582a

Lamaism, I 248a, 249a, 253a

Lamarck, Jean Baptiste Pierre

de Monet (1744–1829), acquired characteristics, II 618a–618b, 620a adaptation, II 618a association of ideas, I 113b, 114b Chain of Being, I 335a Comte and, II 620a continuity, I 499b Darwin and, II 618a–618b deism, II 179a determinism, II 24a Enlightenment, II 91b environment, II 618a, 623b–624a evolution, II 620a, 623b, 624a evolutionism, II 178a, 179a, 179b, 182a, 185b Faust (legend), III 248b historiography, II 24a idea, I 113b, 114b, 115a pangenesis, II 623b–624a, 626a pragmatism, III 565a psychology, IV 11b, 26a recapitulation, IV 58a species, II 179a, 618a Spencer and, II 620a spontaneous generation, IV 311b transformism, I 499b

Lamarckism, II 617a–622b evolutionism, II 185b Marxism, II 619b–620a mechanist versions of, II 619a–619b religion, IV 106a

Lamartine, A. M. L. de (1790–1869) French Revolution (1789), III 671b Platonism, III 524a protest movements, III 671b romanticism, IV 205a

Lamb, Charles (1775–1834), art, II 309b sanity of genius, II 309b virtuoso, IV 488a

Lambert, Johann Heinrich (1728–1777) cosmic images, I 519a space, IV 303b

Lamech (Bible), mythology, III 279a, 279b

Lamennais, Félicité Robert de (1782–1859) cosmic images, I 521b individualism, II 594b modernism, I 419b romanticism, IV 205a skepticism, IV 248a, 249a, 249b

Lamprecht, Karl (1856–1915),

historicism, II 461a historiography, II 495b

Lamy, Bernard (1640–1715), style, IV 331b, 332a, 332b rhetoric, IV 172a

Lamy, Guillaume (fl. 1678), Man-Machine, III 139a

Lana, Francesco, cosmic voyages, I 531b–532b

Lana Terzi, F. ideal, II 551a Lessing and, II 551a

Land economic history, II 48a–48b, 49a, 49b, 50a, 51a, 52b, 54a as fixed in supply, II 54a improvement of, II 49a Malthus, II 49b Mill, II 49b nationalism, III 334b private property, III 651b–653b, 654b, 655b, 656b Ricardo, II 49b Rome (ancient), III 652a scarcity of, II 48a–48b

Landau, L. D., indeterminacy, II 591a

Landauer, Carl, economic history, II 60a

Landé, Alfred, entropy, II 114b

Landi, Ortensio, theriophily, IV 386b

Landino, Christoforo, poetry, III 530b

Lando, Orenslo, literary paradox, III 78a, 78b, 80b

Landsberg, Paul death, I 634a entropy, II 114b

Landscapes impressionism, II 567b, 571b, 572a, 573a, 574a, 577b–579a, 580a Nature, III 349b, 350a

Lang, Andrew (1844–1912), Howitt and, III 309a Müller and, III 309a mythology, III 306b, 317a rationalism, III 309b religion, IV 96a Schmidt and, III 309b Tylor and, III 309a

Lang, Fritz, Gothic, II 372b

Langbehn, J., conservatism, I 483a

Lange, Carl Georg (1834–1900) emotion, III 562b James and, III 562b psychology, IV 23a pragmatism, III 562b

Lange, Friedrich Albert (1828–

1875) Marxism, III 163a metaphysical imagination, III 216a revisionism, IV 269b

Lange, Oscar, Marxism, III 154b

Lange-Eichbaum, W. art, II 308b genius, II 308b

Langer, Susanne metaphysical imagination, III 210a mythology, III 315a–315b

Langevin, Paul (1872–1946), time, IV 397b

Langfield, Herbert Sidney (1879–1958) beauty, I 213a empathy, II 88b

Langland, William (1332?–?1400), symbolism, IV 341b

Langley, Batty, Gothic, II 371a

Langley, Samuel P. (1834–1906), Peirce and, III 560b

Langley, Thomas, Gothic, II 371a

Language, II 659b–673a abstraction, II 665a Adam (Bible), II 669a Adelung, II 669b allegory, I 41a alphabet, II 661a, 666a analogy, II 664b, 665a, 671a anomalism, II 664b, 671b Apollonius Dyscolus, II 664b, 665a, 665b Arabic, II 668a; III 62b, 505b Aristarchus of Alexandria, II 664b Aristotelianism, II 666b Aristotle, II 661b, 663a–663b, 664a, 665a, 667b, 672b, 673a arithmetic, II 660a Armenian, III 62a Arnauld, II 667b ascertaining fitness, II 662a background, II 659b–661b Bacon, Francis, II 667b; III 62b–63a, 73a–74b Bacon, Roger, III 62b–63a barbarian, III 62a Basque, III 63a behaviorism, II 660b Belgium, II 660b Bentham, I 317b–318a Berkeley, II 352b Bible, II 669a bilingualism, II 660b, 661a biology, II 669b

Bloomfield, II 672a, 672b
Bopp, II 671a; III 67b, 68a
Breton, III 63a
British and Foreign Bible Society, III 63b
Catherine the Great, II 669b; III 64a
Celtic, III 66b
change, III 62a, 62b
chaos, II 664b
China, I 354a, 354b–355a, 355b, 358a–358b, 362a, 366b–367a, 369b, 372a; II 661a, 661b, 668a, 669b
Chomsky, II 672b–673a
Christianity, II 666a, 667a, 669a
classification, II 660a; III 64a
clergy, II 666a, 667a
common law, II 691b, 692a
communication, II 660b, 661a, 661b, 668a–668b; IV 325b–326a
community, II 660b
comparison, III 64a, 65b, 66a–68a, 70b–72b, 75a
computer, II 660a, 673a
Condillac, II 669a; IV 435b–436a
Condorcet, IV 436a
cosmogony, II 661b
Counter-Enlightenment, II 105a
Corce, I 588a–588b
Cruciger, II 671a
culture, I 610a, 611b, 615b; II 659b, 660a, 661a, 664b; IV 327a–327b
custom, II 662b, 664b
Dante, II 667a; III 62b–63a, 63b
Darwin, II 669b, 670b; III 68b–69a
Delbrück, II 672b
Denmark, II 671b, 672a, 672b
Descartes, II 667b, 669a
Dewey, II 381b
dialect, II 660a, 660b, 671b, 691b
dictionary, III 63a
dignity, IV 143b
Dionysius Thrax, II 664b–665a
Donatus, II 665a, 666b, 667a
Dutch, III 63a
Egypt (ancient), II 669b
eloquence, IV 168a
empiricism, II 667b, 669b, 672b; III 546a, 546b, 547a, 547b, 548a, 549b, 550b
English, II 661a, 670b

Enlightenment, II 667a–669b
environment, II 660a, 665a
epistemology, II 661a, 661b
Esperanto, II 669a
ethics, IV 72b, 319b, 321b
Etruscan, III 61b
etymology, II 662a–663a, 664b, 666a, 671b
everyday, III 86b, 87a, 87b
evolution, II 669b, 670b; III 68b; IV 323a–323b
evolutionism, II 175b
Finland, II 660b
Finno-Ugric, III 64b, 71a
Fodor, II 668b
foreign, II 660a, 660b, 661a
fossils, II 660b
France, II 670a, 671b
French Orientalists, III 65b
Gaelic, II 660b
Galileo, II 667b
genealogy, III 63a, 65b
genius, II 313b
German, II 667b, 691b
Germany, II 669b, 670b–671b
Gilliéron, II 671b
glottochronology, III 72a
God, I 376b; II 352b
Goethe, III 435a
Golius, I 358a
good, IV 176b, 183b, 184a, 184b
Gothic, II 367a, 367b, 369a, 369b
grammar, II 659b–670b, 671b, 672a–673b; III 62a, 62b–67a, 68a
Great Britain, II 661a, 666b, 670a; III 73a
Greece (ancient), II 661a, 661b–666a
Greek, II 660b, 661b–666a, 667a, 667b, 669b, 670a, 670b, 671a, 684b; III 61b, 65a, 66b–67a, 305b, 505b, 509b
Grimm, II 670b–671b; III 64b, 67a, 68a, 68b
happiness, II 375a, 381b, 386a–387b
Hebrew, II 667a, 667b, 669a, 669b, 670a; III 62b, 63a, 65a
Herder, III 305a; IV 203a
heritage, II 660b, 670a
Herodotus, III 62b
Hervas, II 669b
Hindu, II 660b
history, II 660b, 661b, 670b–671b
Hjelmslev, II 672a
Homer, II 661b, 664a–

664b, 669a
humanism, II 515b, 516a–516b, 517b–518a, 520a, 667a; IV 130b, 131a, 135a
Humboldt, W., III 67b, 70b
Hume, I 314a
Icelandic, III 66b–67a
idea, II 663b
ideal, II 551a, 662b
ideograms, II 661a
Ido, II 669a
ignorance, II 662b
impiety, II 564a, 566b
incentives, II 661a
India, II 661b, 663a, 669b, 670a–670b, 671b, 673b; III 65a
Indians (American), II 660b, 661a, 661b, 669a–669b; III 63a, 71a; IV 325a
Indo-European, III 66a, 66b, 67b–69b, 70b, 71a
innate, III 74b
inner fitness, II 662a
Japan, II 661b
Jespersen, II 672b
Jones, William, II 670a; III 65a–65b, 66b
judgment, II 667b
Julius Caesar, II 664b
just, III 69b
knowledge, I 466b; II 662b, 663b, 668b, 672a
Latin, II 661b, 662a, 664a, 665a, 665b, 666a, 667a, 667b, 669b, 670a, 691b, 692a; III 65a, 298b, 305b
Launcelot, II 667b
law, II 671a–671b
learning, II 661a
Leibniz, I 358b; II 668a, 668b–669a; III 471b–472a; IV 436a
lingua Adamica, III 62b
linguistic paleontology, IV 425a
literature, II 660b, 661a, 664b–665a, 665b, 666a, 667a, 670a; IV 330a, 330b, 331a, 332a, 332b, 333a
Lithuanian, III 68b
logic, II 661a, 663a, 663b, 666b, 668b; III 546a, 546b, 547a, 547b, 548a, 549b, 550b
logos, III 74b
Lord's Prayer, III 63b
mathematics, II 660a
matrix lingua, III 63b
metaphor, III 198b
metaphysical imagination, II 662b, 666a, 667a; III 222a

methodology, III 390b
Middle Ages, II 666a–667a, 669a
mixture, III 72a
modernism, I 420b
Modistae, II 666b–667b
Monboddo, II 669a–669b
Montaigne, II 266b
morphemes, II 663a, 665a, 666a, 670b, 672a, 672b
morphology, II 665a, 665b, 670b, 672b
Müller, Andreas, I 358a
multilingualism, II 660b
music, II 313b; III 268b
mythology, III 280b, 289b–290a, 298a, 298b, 299a, 304a–308b, 315b, 317a, 317b
nationalism, II 660b; III 324b, 325b, 333b, 335a, 337a
Nature, III 74b
nature of, II 660b, 661b, 672a
necessity, III 357a
Newton, II 667b; III 390b
nomadic peoples, II 660b
nominalism, II 667a
number of, II 660a–660b
numbers, III 399b, 400a, 403a, 403b, 404b
order, II 664b
organicism, III 423b, 426b
origin of, II 661b, 669a–669b, 670a; III 64b
Osthoff, II 671b
pain, II 387a
painting, IV 466a, 466b, 469a–475b
Pallas, II 669b; III 64a, 64b
Pānini, II 670a, 670b
perfectibility, III 471b–472a, 474b–475a
philology, II 661b, 664b
philosophy, II 551a, 661a–661b, 664a, 664b, 665a, 665b, 666b, 668b, 669a, 673a; III 198b
phonemes, II 665b–666a, 672a
phonemic innovation, III 69a
physics, II 666b
picture theory, I 90a
pidgin, II 660b–661a
Plato, II 661b–663a, 663b, 664a, 669a; III 62b, 65b, 554a–554b
Platonism, III 511b
pleasure, II 375a, 381b, 386a–387b

poetry, II 661b; III 87a–87b; IV 466a, 466b, 469a, 470a–475b
Polish, III 63a
polygenesis, III 65a–65b
positivism, II 672b; III 546a, 546b–549b, 550b
Pott, III 68a, 68b
practice, II 660b
pragmatism, III 552b, 554a–554b, 557a, 559a
printing, III 63a
Priscianus, II 661b, 665a, 665b, 666b–667a, 667b
progress, III 638a
pronunciation, II 664b, 665b–666a
psychology, IV 1a, 13b
Punic, III 61b
Pythagoras, III 65b
Ramism, IV 45a
Rask, II 671a; III 66b–67b, 68a
reading, II 666b, 668a
realism, II 667a
reality, II 661b, 662a
reason, II 667b
religion, II 661a, 661b, 670b; IV 94a–94b, 106a
Renaissance, II 667a–669b; IV 121b, 122a, 122b, 123b, 124b, 127b, 130b, 131a, 135a, 143b
research, III 64a
rhetoric, IV 167b–172a
right, IV 176b, 183b–184b
Ritschl, III 68a, 69a
ritual, II 670b
Roman Catholic Church, II 666a
Romance, II 667b, 669b
romanticism, II 670b–671a; IV 203a, 207a
Rome (ancient), II 566b, 661b, 663a, 664a, 665a–665b, 666a
Rousseau, II 669a
rules, II 660a, 664b
Russia, II 669b, 672a
Ryle, II 386b
Saint Augustine, IV 176a–176b
Sanskrit, II 661b, 663a, 669b–671b, 673b; III 65a, 66a, 70a, 70b, 268b, 305b, 306a, 308b
Sassetti, III 670a
Saussure, II 671b–672a; IV 323b
Scaliger, II 667a; III 63b
Schlegel, F., III 65b, 66a
Schleicher, III 68a–70b; IV 428a
scholasticism, II 661a–

661b, 666b
science, II 661b, 666b–667a, 673b; III 86b
scientific classification, I 465a, 466b
scientific vs. literary, III 86b
scribal error, III 69a
second, II 660b, 661a
senses, II 662b
shared error, III 68a–68b
signification, IV 324a
signs, IV 324a
skepticism, IV 250a
society, II 669a
Socrates, II 662a
sound, II 662b–663a, 664b, 665b–666a, 671a–671b, 672a, 672b
sound law, II 671a–671b, 672a; III 67a–69b, 70a
sound symbolism, III 87a
Spain, II 669b
species, II 660b, 669a, 669b
speech, II 659b–660a, 663a, 664a, 664b, 665b–666a, 667b–671b, 672a
Stoicism, II 664a; IV 319b, 321b
structuralism, IV 322b, 323a–329a
structure of, II 659b–673a; III 67b
study of, II 659b–673a
survey in Europe, III 64a
Swedish, II 660b
Switzerland, II 660b, 671b–672a
syllables, II 661a
symbolism, II 662b, 663a, 668b; IV 339b, 345a
synchronic view, II 672a
taxonomy, III 66b
techniques of, III 86b
textual criticism, III 68a
theory, II 660b
thought, II 661a, 661b, 665a, 668a
time, II 664a, 669a, 669b, 672a
trade names, II 662b
tradition, II 661a, 661b, 665a
traits, III 66a
transformation syntax, III 72a–72b
Troubetskoy, II 672a
truth, II 662b, 663a, 663b
uniformitarianism, IV 424b, 425a–430a
U.S.S.R., III 333b
U.S., II 660b, 661a, 661b, 669a–669b, 672a, 672b
unity, II 660b
unity of science, IV 435b–

436a
universal, II 668a–669a; IV 436a
utilitarianism, II 660a
Varro, II 665b
vernacular, II 63a, 63b
Vico, III 357a
vocabulary, II 659b, 668b; III 63b
Volapük, II 669a
Volksgeist, IV 491a, 492a, 493a, 493b, 494a, 496a
Voltaire, II 662a
Wallis, II 667a
Webb, I 358a
Webster, III 74b
Welsh, III 63a
Wilkins, I 327b; II 668a–669a
Wittgenstein, I 322a
words, II 662b–663a, 666a, 670b
Words-and-Things technique, III 69b
writing, II 661a, 663a, 666b, 670a–670b, 672a
See also Linguistics
Langue, IV 323b 324a
Languet, Hubert (1518–1581), social contract, IV 254a
Lankester, Edwin Ray (1847–1929), biology, I 237a–237b
Lanman, Charles Rockwell (1850–1941), Orientalism, III 434b–435a
Lanson, Gustave (1857–1934), classicism, I 450b
Laodamia (myth), love, III 96a
Laos, Buddhism, I 248b, 251b, 252b
Lao-Tzu (c. 604-531 B.C.)
China (ancient), I 355b
justice, II 658a
longevity, III 90b
Laplace, Guisbain, F. M. J. de, literature, III 83b
Laplace, Pierre Simon de (1749–1827)
Bayes and, III 612b
Bernoulli and, III 612a, 612b
biology, I 242b–243a
chance, I 337b, 339a; III 612a–612b
continuity, I 498b
cosmic images, I 519b–521b
cosmology, I 550a, 554b; II 182a, 187b
De Moivre and, III 609a–609b, 612b
determinism, II 18b, 19a,

587a
entropy, II 117a
evolutionism, II 176a, 182a, 187b
game theory, II 264a, 272a
Gauss and, III 613b
historiography, II 18b, 19a
indeterminacy, II 587a, 587b
mathematics, III 179b
methodology, III 378b
Newton and, III 378b
perfectibility, III 471b
probability, III 609a–615b, 618a–618b, 619b, 621b
reality, IV 393b
social welfare, IV 282a
time, IV 393b, 394a, 394b, 395b, 396a, 398a
universe, II 18b
Laplace's limit theorem, III 613a, 613b
Laplace's rule of succession, III 611a
Laplanders, primitivism, III 600b
Lerbaud, Valéry (1881–1957), symbolism, IV 340a
Larmor, Joseph (1857–1942), relativity, IV 79b, 80a, 83b
Lasarev, V., iconography, II 535b
Lashley, Karl S., behaviorism, I 223a–223b
Lasker, Emanuel (1868–1941), game theory, II 265a
Lassalle, Ferdinand (1825–1864)
class, I 443b
Hegel and, II 414a
revisionism, IV 264a–264b, 265a, 267a
socialism, IV 293a
time, IV 390a
totalitarianism, IV 408a
welfare state, IV 509a
Lasserre, Pierre
classicism, I 450b, 455a
romanticism, IV 196b
Lasso, Orlando di (1532?–1594), music, II 319a, 320b
Lasson, Georg, Hegel and, II 414a, 416a
Last Judgment
mythology, III 276a, 277a, 284a–284b
necessity, III 355a
prophecy, III 664a, 665a, 666b, 667b
theodicy, IV 380b
Lastarria, José Victoriano, (1817–1888), positivism, III 543b

Lateran Council of 1215, I 383a

Latin America
communism, III 335b
crisis in history, I 539a–593b
Darwinism, III 542b
dictatorship, III 540a
education, III 541a
France, III 539b
historicism, III 539b
ideology, III 545a
law, III 30b
liberalism, III 336a
medicine, III 544a
Mexican revolution, III 335b
nationalism, III 335a–336a, 336b, 337a, 338a, 338b
numbers, III 403b
politics, III 539b, 542a, 542b
positive neutralism, III 336b
positivism, III 336b, 537b, 539b–545a
primitivism, III 603a, 604a
proletariat, III 541b, 542a
racial prejudice, III 542b
religion, IV 94a
revisionism, IV 274b
revolution, III 335b; IV 160b, 166a
Roman Catholic Church, III 539b, 540a
socialism, III 336a–336b
society, III 539b, 542b
symbolism, IV 341b
totalitarianism, IV 409b
unification, III 335a–335b
U.S., III 563a, 565b
Utopia, IV 463b

Latin language, II 661b, 662a, 664a, 665a, 665b, 666a, 667a, 667b, 669b, 670a, 691b, 692a; III 65a, 298a, 298b, 305b
extensio, IV 301b
humanism, IV 130b
linguistics, IV 425b, 427b
literature, III 81b, 82a; IV 330a
motif, III 243a
mountains in literature, III 253b, 254a
poetry, III 525b, 528a, 528b, 529a, 530b, 531b; IV 466b, 468b
primitivism, III 579b, 584a, 591b
Renaissance, IV 121b, 122a, 122b, 123b, 124b, 127b, 130b, 143b
revolution, IV 152b
social contract, IV 252a
space, IV 296a, 300b, 301b

spatium, IV 300b
style, IV 330a
temperance, IV 365b, 370a
uniformitarianism, IV 425b, 427b

Latitudinarianism
deism, I 649b
heresy, II 428b

Lauderdale, Lord (1759–1839), utility, IV 453b

Laúe, Max von (1879–1960), Heisenberg and, II 590a
indeterminacy, II 590a, 592b

Laugier, Abbé Marc-Antoine (1713–1769), Gothic, II 370a, 371b

Launcelot, Claude, language, II 667b

Lavater, Johann Kaspar (1741–1801)
beauty, II 551b
Counter-Enlightenment, II 104a, 107a
genius, II 295b
ideal, II 551b
phrenology, II 551b

Lavisse, Ernest (1842–1922), China, I 370a

Lavoisier, Antoine Laurent (1743–1794)
empiricism, III 546b
genetic continuity, II 283a
matter, III 195b
methodology, III 386b
Newton and, III 386b
spontaneous generation, II 283a

Law, II 673b; III 36a
absolutism, II 686a
Accursius, II 685b
accusatorial proceedings, III 7b
Achilles (myth), II 675b, 676b, 677b
adjudication, II 676b, 677a, 678b
adultery, II 688b
adversary proceedings, III 7b, 10a
advice, II 675a; III 29a
Aegisthus (myth), II 683a
Aeschines, II 684b
Aeschylus, II 681a, 681b, 682a, 682b, 683a, 684a; III 625b
Agamemnon (myth), II 675a, 676b
Ajax (myth), II 681b
Alcibiades, II 684b
Alcinous (myth), II 684b
alcoholism, III 34b
Alexander the Great, II 674a
Allen, III 31a

American Revolution, III 7b
Amphinomus, II 676b
Anacreon, II 681a
analogy, III 29b
anarchy, II 688a; III 20a
Anaximander, II 677a
Andocides, II 680b
animals, II 677a, 682a, 682b; III 33a
anthropology, III 28b
Antigone (myth), II 683a
Antilochus (myth), II 676b
Aphrodite (myth), II 681a
Apollo (myth), II 675b, 682b
Archilochus, II 674b, 679a
architecture, II 687a
Areopagus, the (myth), II 681a, 681b, 684b
argumentation, III 7a, 25a, 28a, 31a
aristocracy, II 675a, 687b, 690a; III 28b–29a
Aristophanes, II 681a, 682b, 684b; III 576a
Aristotelianism, III 1b
Aristotle, I 290b, 487a; II 2a–2b, 149b–150b, 249b, 679b, 680b, 684b, 688a; III 11a, 15a–15b, 16b, 27b; IV 175b, 313a
assembly, II 675b, 680a
Athens (ancient), II 565b, 674a, 679b, 680a, 680b, 681b–685a; III 7a
Augustus, II 689b; III 29a
Austin, III 1b–2a, 2b, 31a
authority, I 141b–146b; II 249a, 249b–250a, 678b, 680a, 681a, 681b, 682b, 686a, 689b–690a; III 4b, 5b, 11a, 29a–29b, 31a, 31b, 32b, 33b, 34a
axiomatization, I 165a–165b
Babylonia, II 686b; III 6b
Bacon, I 290b; II 688b
Beaumanoir, III 28a
behaviorism, II 677b–678b, 682b; III 3a, 3b
Bellerophon (myth), II 681a
Bentham, I 291a; III 31a, 470a
Bible, I 290a; II 249b, 250a; III 6b, 7a, 35b
Black, Justice, III 9b
Blanot, III 690a
Boltzmann, II 587b–588a
Bonald, III 22a
Boniface VIII (Pope), II 689b
Borah, III 9a
Bracton, II 690a, III 30b–31a

Bradley, Justice, III 9a
Brandeis, Justice, III 9a–9b, 12b
Brazil, III 541a
bribes, II 688b
Canada, III 13b, 31b
canon, II 694a–695a
Cardozo, Justice, III 32a
cases, III 24b–25a
casuistry, III 30b, 31a, 34a, 34b
causation, I 289b–294a
Celts, III 7a
censorship, III 567b
Ceylon, III 31b
chance, II 226a–231b, 235b
charity, II 687a
Charles I, III 8a
children, II 686b, 688a
China (ancient), III 7a, 28b
Christianity, I 290b; II 250a, 251a–251b, 686b, 688a, 689a
Cicero, I 487b; II 150b–151a, 249b–250a; III 16b, 587b
city, II 687a
city-state, II 674a, 679b, 681b, 682b
civil, I 291a; II 691a, 692a, 692b–696a; III 17a, 18a–18b, 19b, 21a, 33b
civil disobedience, I 435a–435b
civilization, II 677a, 685b, 690b
claims, II 676a–679a
class, III 11a, 11b, 12b
classification, III 11b–13b
Cleisthenes, II 682a
Clytemnestra (myth), II 683b
code of Gortyn, II 680a, 680b
Codex, II 685b
coercion, III 2b, 3a, 5a
Coke, II 250b–251a; III 7b
commands, II 675b; III 1b, 2b
Common, I 291a–292a
community, II 675a, 677a, 677b, 678b, 679b, 681a, 681b, 683a–683b, 685a, 687a, 690a; III 3b, 5a
computers, III 32b
Comte, I 291a; III 22a, 360a, 640a, 640b–642b
concept of, III 1a–6a
conduct, II 674a, 681b–685a; III 27a, 33a–35b
Conrad II, III 7a
conscience, III 1a
Constant, II 279b

constitutionalism, I 485b–492a; II 686a

constitutions, I 486a–492a; II 675a, 675b, 677b; III 2a, 2b, 3a, 7b–10a, 11b, 12a, 32a

contracts, II 686b; III 2a

content of, III 1b

convention, III 1a

Coriolanus, II 690a–690b

corporations, II 686b–687a; III 1b, 13a

Corpus Iuris Civilis, II 685b–690b

cosmology, II 674a

counsel, II 675a, 675b, 676a

counterclaims, II 676b

Counter-Enlightenment, II 102a, 102b, 106b, 108a

courts, II 676b, 679b, 686a, 686b, 687b, 688b–689a; III 2a, 7a, 15a, 27b–28a, 30a, 30b, 31a, 32a, 32b, 33b

creditors, II 679a

Creon (myth), II 682b

Critias, III 575a

criticism, II 676b

Cronus (myth), II 674b, 675b, 677b

Cross, R., III 31b

Cujas, Jacques, III 3b

culture, II 677b; III 6a–6b, 12b, 35a

custom, II 681b–688a; III 3b, 6a–6b, 27b, 29b, 30b

Cyclopes (myth), II 674b, 678b, 683a

cynicism, I 629a, 629b

Darius, II 683a

Dark Ages, II 685b

Darwin, II 588a; III 11b

Dawson, III 28a, 29b–30a

death, II 674b, 676a, 678a

debts, II 679a, 684b

decision-making, III 4a–5a 5b, 6a

deism, I 648b

Delphi, II 681b

Demeter, II 681a

democracy, II 249b, 682a, 685a, 686a; III 2a, 11a

Democritus, II 681b, 683b

Demosthenes, II 684b; III 7a

Descartes, I 290b

desire, III 1a

despotism, II 1a, 2a–2b, 3b, 4a, 5a, 12a, 12b

determinism, II 237a, 240a, 240b, 241a

Devlin, II 251a–251b

dictatorship, III 5a

Digest, II 685b

dikē, II 674a–679b, 680a, 681b, 682a, 683a

Diogenes of Sinope, I 632a

divination, II 675a–675b, 676a, 679b, 680a, 680b, 682b; III 11a

Douglas, Justice, III 9a, 9b

dowries, II 686b

Draco, II 674a, 679a, 680b, 681a, 681b

drugs, III 34b

due process, III 6a–10b

duty, II 249a; III 1b, 2b–3a, 5a, 27b

easements, II 686b

economic history, II 51a, 59a

economics, II 250a; III 6b, 9a–9b, 10b, 11b, 13b, 28a, 30b, 32a

education, II 249b, 687a, 690a; III 3b, 4b, 5a, 12b, 13b, 32a

Edward III, III 7b

Egypt (ancient), II 249b, 686b; III 6b–7a, 10b, 11a, 249b; IV 226a

Ehrlich, III 3b–4a

Empedocles, II 683b

empiricism, I 291a; III 2a, 3a, 4a

Engels, III 22a, 28b

English Revolution, III 11a

Enlightenment, II 90b, 91b–92b, 93a; III 11a–11b

equality, II 140a, 140b, 142a, 144a, 145a, 145b, 687b, 688b; III 10b–13b, 15b, 27b, 28a

equity, II 148a–154a

ethics, III 1a, 2a, 6a, 440b, 441b–445b, 447a; IV 72b

etymology, II 675a, 676a, 679b–680a, 680b, 681a, 682a

Eumelus (myth), II 676b

Euripides, II 681a–684b

evil, II 674b, 677a

evolution, III 24b–25a, 26a, 35a, 566b; IV 180a

existentialism, II 191b–192a

Ezekiel (Bible), III 35b

faith, II 689a, 10b

family, II 674b, 677b, 678a, 678b, 686b

fate, II 226a–231b, 235b

fault, III 33a–35b

feudalism, II 250a–250b, 692a

force, III 2b

formulary system, III 29a

Fourier, III 22a

France, II 250b, 251a, 673b, 687b, 690a; III 3b, 5b,

7b, 11b, 12a, 28a, 30a–30b, 32b

France, Anatole, III 11b

Frank, Jerome, II 153b; III 4b, 31b

Frankfurter, Justice, III 12a

fraud, II 687b, 688b, 690a

Frederick I, II 689b

Frederick II, II 689b

free will, II 237a, 240a, 240b, 241a, 242b, 247a

freedom, II 248b–251b, 684b, 686a, 687b; III 1a 12a, 13b, 35b

freedom of speech, II 252b, 253a, 255a, 256a, 258b, 259a, 261a

freemen, II 249a

French Revolution (1789), II 250b

Fuller, III 5b

Gaius, III 17a

game theory, II 263b, 267a

Gauls, III 7a

general will, II 275b–279b

Germany, II 673b–674a, 686a, 689b, 690b; III 3b, 5a, 7a, 11a–11b, 12a, 29b–30a, 653a

gifts, II 676b, 677b, 678a, 686b, 688b

gladiators, II 687a

Glaucus, II 677a

Glossa ordinaria, II 685b

Gnosticism, II 328a

God, I 290a; II 249b, 250a, 251a, 344b, 352b–354a, 674b–678b, 681a–682b, 684a, 687b, 688a, 689a; III 10b, 11a, 15a, 27b, 566b; IV 176b

Golden Rule, III 6b

good, II 677a; IV 173b–181b, 185b, 186b

Great Britain, I 292a–292b, 487b–488b; II 142b, 148a, 152a–154a, 250b–251a, 685b–686a, 687a, 689a, 690a; III 5a, 6b, 7b–8a, 11a, 12a, 28b, 29b, 30b–31b, 32a, 32b

Greece (ancient), I 290b, 291b, 293b, 486b–487b, 653b; II 148a–150b, 151a, 153b, 249b, 501b, 565b, 673b–685b; III 1a–1b, 7a, 11a; IV 252b

greed, II 688a

Grotius, II 5a, 250b; III 19b–20a, 442a

guilds, II 687a

guilt, III 35b

Hammurabi, II 686b; III 11a, 28b

happiness, II 379b, 380b, 381b, 385a, 385b

Harlan, III 10a

Harmhab, III 6b

harmony, II 388a, 391a

Hart, I 293a; III 1b, 2b–3b, 4b, 5a

Hecuba (myth), II 681b

Hegel, II 407b–408a, 408b, 409b, 410a, 411b, 414a; IV 290b, 492a–492b

Hekate (myth), II 676b

Helvétius, III 470a

Henry VIII, II 690a

Hera of Argos (myth), II 684b

Heracles (myth), II 681a, 683b

Heraclitus, I 486b; II 677a, 682b

heresy, II 425b, 686a, 689a

Hermes (myth), II 684a

Herodotus, II 680b, 681a, 682b, 683a, 683b, 684a

Hesiod, II 674a–679b, 682a, 682b, 684a

hierarchy, III 10b, 28b, 30b, 31a, 31b

Higher Law doctrine, I 435b–437a

Hinduism, III 7a

historiography, II 501b

history, I 291b–292a; III 3b, 12a, 12b, 23a; IV 493a–493b

Hobbes, I 290b; II 250a; III 1a, 11a; IV 177b, 316a; IV 257a

Hoebel, III 27a–27b

Holmes, Justice, III 4a, 4b, 566a, 566b, 567a–567b, 568a

holy, II 512b

Holy Roman Empire, II 689b–690a

Homer, II 674a, 676a, 679a, 679b, 680b–681a, 683a; III 7a

homicide, II 680b

Honoré, I 293a

Hughes, Justice, III 9a

human nature, III 574b, 575a, 575b, 576a

humanism, II 515a, 519a, 521b; IV 130b, 132b, 135a

Hume, I 291a

idea, II 685b–690b; III 27b

idealism, II 687b, 690b

ideology, III 4a, 35b

ignorance, III 34b

immunities, II 249a, 250b

impiety, II 564a, 565b, 566b

indeterminacy, II 586b, 587b–588a, 588b–589a

India, III 12a, 13b
India (ancient), III 7a
individualism, II 675a, 677b, 679a, 680a, 682b, 689b; III 27b, 28a, 33a, 35a–35b
inequality, III 11a, 11b, 28b, 31b
inheritance, II 684b, 686b
injury, II 686b, 687b, 688b; III 33a–33b
innocence, II 688b–689a
Inquisition, II 686a, 689a; III 7b
Institutes, II 685b
institutions, III 11b, 13a, 27b
international, II 250b, 687b; III 18a, 32b, 34a
international peace, III 449a, 450b–454b, 456b
interpretation of, II 679b–680a; III 24b–25a, 29a, 29b
investigatory proceedings, III 7b
irrigation, II 686b
Isaeus, II 684b
Isidore of Seville, III 18a
Islam, III 28b
Ismene (myth), II 683a
isonomos, II 682a
Israel, II 256a
Italy, III 3b, 29b, 30a
Japan (ancient), III 28b
Jason (myth), II 683a
Jesus Christ, III 7a–7b, 13b
John of Salisbury, I 487b
Judaism, I 290a, 376a; II 151a–152a, 153a, 249b, 686b; III 6b, 7a–7b, 11a, 28b, 636a
judgment, II 675b, 676b–677a, 682b–683a; III 28b, 31a, 33b
jurisdiction, II 675b–676a
jurors, II 684a, 685b, 686a, 687b, 689a, 689b, 690a; III 1b, 3b, 4a–4b, 5a, 7a, 17a, 17b, 22b, 24a, 24b, 27b, 28a, 28b, 29a–29b, 30b, 31a
justice, II 249a, 652b–658a, 675b–676a, 678b, 680a, 681b, 686a, 686b, 687b, 688b; III 1b, 2a, 5b, 7a, 11a, 16b, 23a, 24a, 27b–28a, 32b; IV 212a, 212b, 215b
Justinian, II 685b, 686b, 687b, 688a, 689b; III 24b, 29b, 30a
Juvenal, II 689a
Kant, I 291a; II 240a, 240b, 279b; III 472b, 649a;

IV 179b
Kelsen, III 1b–2b, 3a, 3b, 22b, 24a
Kierkegaard, II 191b–192a
kingship, II 675a–676a, 678a, 678b, 689b–690a
knowledge, II 678b; III 28b–29a
language, II 671a–671b
Latin America, III 30b
lawgivers, II 682a
lawmakers, III 27b, 29a, 29b, 30a
lawmaking, III 2b, 3a
lawyers, II 688b, 689a; III 27a, 27b, 28a, 29b, 30b–31a, 32a
legal transactions, II 249a
Leibniz, I 290b; IV 378b, 382a
Lemoine, II 689a–689b
Lenin, III 156a
liability, III 33b–35b
liberalism, III 11a, 36a, 36b, 44b, 46b, 49b, 54b, 58a, 60a, 672b
liberty, II 248b–249a, 249b, 250b, 686a; III 8a
literature, II 674a–679b, 682a, 683b–684a, 690a
Llewellyn, III 4b, 27b
Locke, I 290b; III 11a
loyalty, III 109a, 110b, 111b, 112a, 112b, 113a, 114a, 114b, 115b
Luther, III 11a; IV 66b
Lycurgus, II 679b, 680a
McDougal, III 5a
Machiavelli, II 250a; III 116b, 119b; IV 315a–315b, 482b
Machiavellism, III 116b, 118a
Madison, III 7b, 8a
Magna Carta, II 689a; III 7b, 8b
Maimonides, II 151b
Maistre, III 22a
maritime, II 686a
marriage, II 681a, 682b, 683b, 684a, 686b, 688a
Marshall, Justice, III 8a
Marx, III 22a; IV 291a, 292a
Marxism, III 148b, 150a, 151b, 153a, 156a
Medea (myth), II 683a
medicine, II 687a
Megarian Decree, II 684b
mental illness, III 34b
merchants, II 687a
Mesopotamia (ancient), II 564a; III 7a, 11a; IV 226a, 226b

Middle Ages, II 685b–690b; IV 253a, 253b
Mill, I 291a; II 251a; III 470a, 567b
Minoan, II 675b
Minos (myth), II 676a, 677a
monarchy, II 686a
monopoly, III 28b–29a
Montesquieu, II 10a, 251a; III 21a, 640a–640b
morality, II 249a, 251a–251b, 678a, 679b, 681a, 687a, 688a; III 1a, 1b, 2a, 3b, 5a, 5b, 6a, 6b, 29a, 29b, 35b, 645a
mores, II 683a–683b, 685a; III 28a
motives, III 34b
murder, II 674b, 676a, 681a, 683a, 683b, 684b, 688b
music, II 388a, 391a
mythology, III 280a, 283a, 283b, 291a, 304a
nationalism, II 689b–690a, 690b; III 318b, 319a, 320a, 320b–323a, 326b
natural law, II 249a, 250a; III 13b, 14a, 15a, 16a, 16b–24a
natural liberty, II 63b
Nature, II 225b, 250a, 687b, 688a–688b; III 1a, 10b, 11b, 32b, 347a, 347b
Nazism, II 690b
Near East, II 686a–686b, 690b
necessity, III 353a, 354b, 356a, 358b, 360a
Neo-Thomism, III 5b
Nereus (myth), II 676a
Nessus (myth), II 681b
Nestor, II 674b, 678b
Netherlands, III 32b
Nicholas of Lire, II 688a
nomos, II 681b–685a; III 1a
as normative ought-propositions, III 2a
norms, II 677a, 677b–679b, 682a–683b, 685a; III 2a–4a, 23a–24b
notice and hearing, III 7a, 8b
oaths, II 675b, 676a, 681a, 684a, 688b; III 6b–7a, 10a
obedience, III 1b, 2b
obligations, III 675a, 680b, 681b, 682b, 684a, III 1a, 3a, 4a, 5a, 8a, 28b, 29a
Odysseus (myth), II 676b, 678a, 681a
Olbrechts-Tyteca, III 5b–6a
oligarchy, II 683a

Olivecrona, III 2b
oratory, II 684a–684b; III 7a
order, II 674b–683a, 685a, 688b; III 1b, 3a, 33a
Orestes (myth), II 682b, 683a, 683b
organization, III 1a
pain, II 385b
papacy, II 686a, 689a, 689b–690a
Papal Inquisition, II 686a, 689a
Park, III 31a
partnerships, II 686b
Patroclus (myth), II 675b, 676b
peace, III 1a
Peisistratus, II 680b
Penelope (myth), II 681a
Perelman, III 5b–6a, 27b
perennial philosophy, III 458b, 460b–461a
perfectibility, III 470a, 472a–473b
Pericles, II 684a–684b
periodization in history, III 477b, 480b
personal conduct, II 674a, 681b–685a
philanthropy, III 487a, 492a
Philippines, III 13b
philosophy, I 290a–291a; II 674a, 686a, 687b; III 1b, 3a–5b, 22b, 23a, 27a, 32a, 35b
Phoebus Apollo (myth), II 675b
Phoenicia (ancient), II 686a–686b
Pindar, II 681a, 682b–683b
Plato, I 487a, 654a; II 148a–149b, 249b, 679b, 683b, 684b; III 1b, 11a, 15a, 16b, 497a, 631a; IV 285b
Platonism, III 1b, 497a, 514b, 520b
pleasure, II 379b, 380b, 381b, 385a, 385b
Plutarch, II 679b, 680b
poetry, II 679b, 680b, 683b; III 528b
Poincaré, II 588a
politics, II 674a, 675b, 680a–685a, 688a; III 6b, 7a, 11a–11b, 13b, 16b, 23a, 640a–640b
Pollock, Frederick, I 293a; III 27b
Polyphemus (myth), II 675a
Polyxena (myth), II 681b
Poseidon (myth), II 677b, 681a

Posidonius, III 631a
positivism, III 1b–3a, 4a, 5a–6a, 533a, 541a
Pound, Roscoe, III 4b
poverty, II 686a
power, II 249a, 250a, 250b, 251a, 674b, 675a, 677a, 678b, 679a, 686a, 686b, 689b, 690b; III 1b, 2a, 2b–3a, 5a, 11a, 12a–13a, 15b, 24a, 25a, 28a, 30a
praetorian, II 150b–151a, 152a
praetors, III 7a, 16b, 28b, 29a
pragmatism, III 552b, 554a, 558a, 566a–567b, 568a
precedent, III 24a, 27a–33a
prejudgment, III 28a
prejudice, III 28a
prerogatives, II 675a–675b, 677b, 678b
prescriptive right, II 686b
prestige, III 29a
primitivism, III 579b, 580b, 587b, 588b, 600a, 603a
private, II 689b, 690a
private property, II 686b, 687b, 688a, 688b, 689b; III 6b, 9a, 11a, 11b, 650b, 651a–657a
privileges, III 5a
probability, III 613b, 614b
Proclus, II 675a
progress, III 625b, 631a, 632b, 636a, 636b, 638a, 638b, 640a–643a, 645a, 649a
prohibitions, II 675b
prophecy, III 660b, 662b, 667a
propriety, II 681a
prostitution, II 683b, 688a
protest movements, III 671a, 672a, 672b
Proudhon, III 22a
psychology, III 4a, 4b, 27a, 27b; IV 16b, 19a, 27b
punishment, II 677a, 679b, 686a, 687a, 688b; III 3a, 33b, 35a, 35b, 567a, 575a
Puritanism, IV 16b
Pythagoras, I 631a
Rabelais, III 11a
racial discrimination, III 12b–13a
Ramus, III 11a
rationalism, III 2a, 11a, 28b; IV 46a, 49a
realism, III 4b–5a
reason, II 250a, 686a, 687b, 688a–688b, 689a, 690a; III 1a, 1b, 5b
reciprocity, III 1a

reformation, IV 60a, 61b, 62b, 64a, 66a, 67a
Reformation, III 11a; IV 66a
reforms, II 677a
relativism, IV 72b
relativity, IV 75a–76a
religion, I 290a; II 674a–679b, 681a–681b, 683a–684a, 685a, 686b, 688a, 689a, 689b–690a; III 1a, 6b, 7a, 11a, 11b, 28b–29a; IV 113a, 115a, 115b, 119a
Renaissance, III 11a; IV 130b, 132b, 135a, 437b
responsibility, III 5a, 33a–36a
retribution, II 677a, 679a, 679b
revisionism, IV 264a, 265a, 269b
revolution, IV 155a, 157b, 158a
rhetoric, III 5b–6a; IV 168a, 168b, 169a, 170a, 170b, 171b
rhetra, II 680a
Rhodesia, III 13a
right, II 677a, 678a, 678b, 679b; III 5a, 6b, 7b–10a, 10b–13b; IV 173b–174a, 174b, 175b, 176a, 176b, 177b, 179a, 179b, 180a, 181a, 181b, 185b, 186b
rights, II 675a, 676a, 678b, 686a, 687a, 687b, 688b, 689b, 690b; III 27b
ritual, II 675b, 681a, 683b–684a
Roman Catholic Church, II 250a, 688a, 689a, 689b–690a
romanticism, IV 203a, 204a, 205b, 206a
Rome (ancient), I 141b–146b, 290b, 291a, 291b, 293a, 382a, 487b; II 4b, 10a, 102b, 150b–151a, 152a, 249b–250a, 261a, 411b, 412a, 515a, 521b, 566b, 673b, 685b–690b; III 3b, 6b, 7a, 11a, 16a, 16b–17a, 28a, 28b–30b, 354b, 441b, 632a, 652a, 655a–655b; IV 61b, 66a, 115a, 313b–314a, 314b, 315b, 492a–492b, 494a, 497b
Ross, III 4a
Rousseau, II 250b, 277a, 277b, 278a, 278b; III 21b
rules, II 675b, 676a, 678b, 681a, 691a; III 1a–6b, 20a, 23a, 24a, 24b, 26a, 28b,

30b, 31b, 33a–35a
sacrifice, II 675b, 677b
Saint Augustine, II 250a, 687b, 688a; III 11a
Saint Paul, II 250a, 686b, 688b; III 17b
Saint Thomas Aquinas, I 292a; III 11a, 19a
Saint-Simon, III 22a, 641a
salvation, IV 224a, 226a, 226b, 233a
sanctions, III 1b, 20a
Saul (Bible), II 249b
Savigny, IV 411b, 412a; III 3b, 22a
Scandinavia, III 2b, 4a
Schiller, IV 157a
scholasticism, III 3b
science, II 687b, 690a, 690b; III 11b, 35b
Scotland, III 31b
security, III 1a
self-discipline, II 251b
self-incrimination, II 689a
self-interest, III 1a
Seneca, III 588b
servitude, II 686b
sex, II 677b, 678a, 681a, 682b, 688a
Shakespeare, II 690a–690b
shipping, II 686a
sin, II 250a; IV 224a, 226a, 226b, 233a
skepticism, III 35b; IV 245b
slavery, II 249a, 249b, 250a, 250b, 678b, 686a, 687b, 688b, 689a; III 10b, 11a
Smith, II 63b; III 11b
social contract, III 11a, 566b; IV 252b, 253a, 253b, 254a, 257a, 261a, 263a
social security, II 687a
social welfare, IV 276b, 279a
socialism, IV 285b, 287a, 288a, 289a, 290b, 291a, 292a
society, II 249a, 249b, 674a–675b, 676a, 677b–679a, 680b, 681a, 682a, 683a–683b, 684b, 685a, 687b, 688a; III 1a–6b, 10b, 11a–11b, 28b, 29a, 29b, 30b, 32a, 35a, 567b
sociology, III 3b, 4b, 5a, 27a
Socrates, I 632a
Solon, II 249b, 676b, 677a, 679a, 679b, 680b, 681a, 684a, 684b
Sophists, III 1a–1b
Sophocles, II 681a–684a
soul, II 678a, 687a
sovereignty, II 250a–250b;

III 1b, 2b
Spain, II 686a, 690a; III 30b
Spanish Inquisition, II 686a
Sparta (ancient), II 679b, 680a
Spencer, I 291a
Spinoza, I 290b
State, II 44b, 686b–690a; III 10b–13b, 33b; IV 313a–317b
statutes, II 680a, 681b–685a; III 2a, 4a, 7b
Stoicism, I 290b; II 686a, 687a, 688a, 689a; IV 176a
Stoics, I 487a, 487b
Stone, III 28a
structure of, III 1b, 6a
Stubbs, II 686a
supernatural, III 10b, 27b, 29a
supremacy of, II 696a
ta eirêmena, II 680a
Tacitus, II 686a
Talleyrand, II 688b
Taney, III 8a
taxation, II 690a; III 1b
Telemachus, II 676a
Ten Commandments, III 6b, 7a, 11a
tetthmoi, II 681a–681b
theft, II 688b, 689a
themis, II 674a–679b, 683a
Themis (myth), II 674b, 675a, 675b, 679a
theodicy, IV 378b, 382a
Theognis, II 677a, 678b, 679a, 682a, 683a
theology, II 688a
theriophily, IV 385a, 385b
Theseus (myth), II 683a
thesmos, II 680a, 680b–681a, 681b–682a, 685a
Thirty Years War, II 250b
Thucydides, I 653b; II 682b, 683a, 684a–684b
Thutmose III, III 11a
time, II 681b; III 28a
titles, II 676a
Tolstoy, III 445b
torture, II 689a; III 567a
totalitarianism, II 690b; III 2a, 5a; IV 407a, 407b, 408b, 409b, 410a
trade, II 686a, 687b; III 3b
treason, II 686a, 689a
trials, II 676a, 679b, 686a, 687b, 688b–689a, 690b; III 7a–7b
Trojan War, II 675a
truth, II 677b; III 32b
tyranny, II 250a, 250b,

680b, 681b, 682a, 683a, 684b, 685a, 688b
Ulpian, II 687b, 688a, 688b, 689b
U.N., III 7b, 11b, 12a, 13a
U.S., I 292a–292b; II 148a, 152a, 153a, 251a, 686b, 689a, 690a; III 4a–5a, 5b, 7b–10a, 11b, 12a–13a, 29b, 31b–32a, 32b
unity, III 2b, 35a
universal man, IV 437b
universality, II 149b
universe, II 226a, 227a, 675b, 677b, 681b, 682a; III 19a
unrighteous, II 677a
unwritten, II 674a, 694b, 695b; III 14a, 15a, 24a
utilitarianism, III 1a; IV 445a, 448a, 448b
Utopia, IV 460a
validity, III 2a, 2b, 3a, 6a
value, II 682b–683a; III 5a, 5b
verdicts, II 676a–677a, 679a, 680a
Victorians, IV 218a, 218b, 219b, 222a, 222b
violence, II 677a, 679a, 683b, 688a
virtue, II 249b
virtù, IV 479a, 482b, 484b
Volksgeist, IV 491a, 491b, 492a–492b, 493a–493b, 494a, 494b, 495a, 495b
Voltaire, II 106b
vox populi, IV 497b
war, II 678b, 683b, 687b, 689b, 690a; III 10b, 33b, 451a, 451b, 452a; IV 502a, 502b, 504b
wealth, II 686a, 688b; III 11a, 11b
welfare, II 686b, 687a, 688a, 688b, 689b
welfare state, IV 509a, 510a, 511a, 512a, 514a
William of Ockham, III 19a–19b
Williams, II 152a–152b
wills, II 686b; III 2b
wisdom, III 27b
witchcraft, IV 531a, 522a
Wolff, I 290b; III 11b
women, II 686b; IV 524b, 526a, 528a, 528b, 529a
Wright, Chauncey, III 566b
written, II 674a, 679b–680b, 681b, 684a–684b; III 14a, 15a, 18b, 24a, 29a, 30a
wrong, II 677a, 678a, 678b
Zeus (myth), II 674b–677b,

678b, 679a, 682a, 682b, 684b
See also Judges, Judgment
Law, Edmund (1703–1787), association of ideas, I 112b
Law, John (1671–1729), utility, IV 452b
Law of Large Numbers, III 607a–609a, 611b, 612a, 614a, 615b, 618a
Law of Recapitulation, primitivism, III 597b
Law of Universal Gravitation, Newton, IV 75a, 77b, 78a, 83b
Lawrence, D. H. (1885–1930), Hermeticism, II 433a, 434a
literary criticism, I 602b
literature, III 88a
symbolism, IV 344b
Lawyers
common law, II 691a, 692a, 692b, 695a, 695b; III 30b–31a, 32a
law, II 688b, 689a; III 27a, 27b, 28a, 29b, 30b–31a, 32a
nationalism, III 320b, 323a, 323b
pragmatism, III 567b
Rome (ancient), II 688b, 689a
Lax, Gaspar, medieval science, II 204a
Laycock, T., Man-Machine, III 143a
Lazarus, Moritz (1824–1903), evolution of literature, II 171a
Volksgeist, IV 495b, 496a
Lazzarretti, protest movements, III 674b
Le Bossu, René (1631–1689), poetics, III 529b
Le Clerc, Jean (1657–1736), deism, I 650b
mythology, III 302b
Le Comte, Louis, China, I 357b
Le Corbusier (1887–1965), aesthetics, II 219a, 221a
canon of proportions, I 580a
city, I 432b, 433a–434a
creativity in art, I 580a
formalism, II 221a
hierarchy, I 433b
Le Dantec, Felix A. (1869–1917), spontaneous generation, IV 311b
Le Grand, Antoine, pangenesis, II 623b
Le Roy, Adrian, genius, II 318b–319a

Le Roy, Edouard (1870–1954)
environment, II 133a
irrationalism, II 636b
God, I 422a
Jesus Christ, I 422a
modernism, I 422a–422b, 423b
pragmatism, III 553b, 565a–565b
religion, III 565a–565b
Sorel and, III 565a–565b
Le Roy, Julien David (1686–1759), neo-classicism, in art, III 365a
Le Trosne, G. F., Machiavellism, III 123a
Lea, Henry Charles (1825–1909), witchcraft, IV 522a, 522b
Leadbetter, Charles, virtuoso, IV 489b
League to Enforce Peace, III 454a
League of Free Nations Society, III 454a
League of Nations
democracy, I 665a
fascism, III 332a
health, II 406a
international peace, III 449b, 451a, 451b, 454a, 454b, 455a, 455b
loyalty, III 113a
nationalism, III 328b, 332a
U.N., III 454b
League of Nations Association, III 449b
League of Nations Union, III 454a
League of Peace, III 449a
Lear, King (tragedy), tragic sense, IV 416b
Learning, II 583b–586a
aetiology, II 583b
Aristotle, IV 530b
Bacon, I 173a; IV 434a, 486b
behaviorism, II 584a, 584b, 585a, 585b, 586a
conditioning, II 585b
Darwin, II 584b
derivation from, II 584a, 585a
Descartes, II 584a
early, II 584b–585b, 586a
education, II 584a–586a
ethology, II 584a, 585a–585b
Freud, II 584b, 585b
Gassendi, II 584a
Guthrie, I 225b
habit, II 584b-585a

Heinroth, II 585a
Hinde, II 585a
ideas, II 584a
impressions, II 584a
instinct, II 584b–585a
James, II 584b, 585a
Locke, II 584a
Lorenz, II 585a, 585b
pathology, II 585b
Plato, I 1a–1b; IV 4a–4b
progress, III 624a, 632b
psychology, II 584b, 585b, 586a; IV 4a–4b
psychopathology, II 585b
psychosexuality, II 585b
reflection, II 584a
reminiscence, I 1a
research, II 585b, 586a
Rousseau, II 584a
Saint Thomas Aquinas, II 584a
sensory experience, II 584a, 586a
sex, II 585b
Spalding, II 584b, 585a
S–R (Stimulus-Response), theory of, I 215a
tabula rasa, II 584a
Thorndike, I 222a; II 585a
Thorpe, II 585a
unity of science, IV 434a, 435a
virtuoso, IV 486b
Watson, I 222a
wisdom of the fool, IV 515b, 517a, 518a, 519a, 520a
work, IV 530b, 531b, 632a, 532b
See also Education; Imprinting
Least squares method, III 613b
Leavis, F. R.
literary criticism, I 602b
romanticism, IV 195a
Lebanon conservation, I 472b
Eastern Orthodox Church, I 411a
international peace, III 454b
Lebesgue, Henri Leon (1875–1941), probability, III 622a, 622b, 623a
Lebesgue integrals, III 620b, 621a
Lebrun, Charles (1619–1690), aesthetics, II 221b
genius, II 303a
iconography, II 533a
Lecky, William (1838–1903)
democracy, I 655b–656a
ethics, IV 70b, 71b
State, I 655b–656a
war, I 655b–656a
witchcraft, IV 522b

Leclerq, H., iconography, II 535b

Ledoux, Claude Nicholas (1736–1806)
architecture, III 366a
city, I 432a–432b
neo–classicism, in art, III 366a, 369b
Rousseau and, I 432a

Lee, Nathaniel (1653?–1692), baroque in literature, I 191a

Lee, Vernon, see Paget, Violet

Leeuwenhoek, Anton van (1632–1723)
ambiguity, I 57a
genetic continuity, II 282b
microscope, III 415b–416a
spontaneous generation, II 282b; IV 309b–310a

Lefebvre, Georges, historiography, II 498a

Left
Hegelianism, IV 291a
liberalism, III 53a, 53b, 54a, 55b
Marxism, III 147b, 160b, 163a, 165b, 167a, 169a–169b
nationalism, III 336a
socialism, IV 291a
totalitarianism, IV 408a, 409b, 410a, 410b
Utopia, IV 463b

Legendre, Adrien M. (1752–1833), probability, III 613b

Legends
dualism, II 38b–40a, 43a
millenarianism, III 224a
motif, III 238b
music, III 265a, 266a, 267a, 270a
mythology, III 275a, 275b, 277a–277b, 279b–280a, 286a, 288a, 308a, 308b
prophecy, III 664b, 665b, 669a
theriophily, IV 384a

Legge, James (1815–1897), China, I 367b, 370a
Confucius and, I 369b–370a

Legman, G., motif, III 239b

Lehmann, Paul, equity, II 153b

Leibl, Wilhelm (1854–1900), composition, III 344b
detail, III 345a
Dürer and, III 345a
Hals and, III 344a
Holbein and, III 344a
human figure, III 344b
impressionism, III 345a
naturalism in art, III 341b, 344a–345a, 345b

Leibniz, Gottfried Wilhelm von (1646–1716)
absolute space, IV 302b
aesthetics, IV 356a
algebra of logic, IV 435b
allegory, I 47b
ancestor worship, I 360b
appearance and reality, I 95b
Aristotle and, IV 435a–435b
arithmetic, IV 435b
art and play, I 103a, 103b
atomism, III 193b
axiomatization, I 163a, 165a, 165b, 169b
Bacon and, I 172b, 177a
beauty, II 446a, 447b
Being, IV 434b
Bernoulli and, III 607a, 608b
Bruno and, II 445b
Burnet and, III 259a
calculus, II 668b
causation, I 276b–277a, 290b, 294b, 299a–300a, 300b, 302b, 303b–304a; II 446b; III 193a
certainty, I 312b, 314a, 315b
Chain of Being, I 326a, 327b–329a, 330a, 331b, 332a, 333a, 499a–499b
change, IV 394b, 395a
China, I 358b, 359b–360b, 361a, 362b
choice, II 239a
Christianity, III 471b–472a
Clarke, I 327b–328a
classification of language, III 64a
classification of the sciences, I 465a
compulsion, II 239a
conservation, I 473a
continuity, I 493b, 498a–499b, 501a–501b, 502b
cosmic images, I 515a
Counter–Enlightenment, II 103a
Creation, I 572b; II 166a
culture, II 128a, 130a
De Witt and, III 607a
death, I 637b, 645a
Descartes and, III 384b
determinism, II 239a
dualism, II 38a, 41a
emotions, II 239a
Enlightenment, II 89b, 90a; III 248a
environment, II 128a, 130a
ethics, III 442a, 443b
evil, I 329a; II 166a–166b;
IV 378b, 381b–382a
evolution of literature, II 170b
evolutionism, II 176b, 177a, 178a
extensio, IV 301b
Figurism, I 359b–360b
free will, II 239a
freedom, II 239a; IV 382a
game theory, II 264a–264b, 265a, 274b
God, I 277a, 299b, 328a, 328b, 360b, 572b; II 166a, 346b–347a, 349b, 350a, 351a–351b, 355a, 444a–444b, 446a–446b, 447b; III 131a, 458a, 461a; IV 378b, 379a, 382a, 435b
good, IV 379a, 382a
gravity, I 299b–300a
happiness, II 381a
harmony, II 446a–446b; III 193a; IV 41b, 382a
Hegel and, II 414a
hierarchy, II 444a–444b, 445b–447b, 448b
Hobbes and, II 444b; III 461a
human nature, III 643b
Hume and, I 312b; IV 382a
idea, III 515b, 561b
ideal, IV 436a
immortality, I 645a; IV 382a
individualism, II 603b; IV 382a
infinity, II 446a, 605b, 606a, 611a
irrationalism, II 638a
Islam, II 644b, 649a, 651b
James and, III 561b
justice, II 659a; IV 378b, 379a, 382a
Kant and, III 443b; IV 382a
knowledge, II 668b; III 515b; IV 382a, 435a
language, I 358b; II 668a, 668b–669a; III 471b–472a; IV 436a
law, I 290b; IV 378b, 382a
Law of Continuity, I 498a–498b, 501a, 501b
linguistics, III 64a, 64b, 65b; IV 423b, 426a, 426b
literary criticism, I 597b
literature, III 86b
Locke and, II 446a; III 195b–196a
logic, IV 382a, 435b
love, IV 382a
macrocosm and microcosm, III 130b–131a
Man–Machine, III 138a
materialism, II 450a; III 193a
mathematics, II 444b, 668b; III 173a, 174a, 174b, 179b
matter, III 185b, 193a, 195b–196a
metaphysics, II 414a, 450a; III 130b–131a, 214b, 472b; IV 432b–433a, 434b
methodology, IV 435a–435b, 436a
monads, I 299b, 360b, 493b; II 445a–446a, 448b; III 131a, 193b, 196a, 515b, 516b; IV 434b
morality, I 465a
motion, I 299a, 498a; III 461a
mountains in literature, III 259a
natural sciences, I 465a
Nature, I 328b, 332a; II 177a, 444b, 446a, 446b; IV 433a
necessity, II 239a; III 355a
Newton and, I 299a–299b; II 444a; IV 75b, 394b
optimism, I 329a
organicism, III 424b, 427a
Orientalism, III 428a, 458a
pain, II 381a
peace, III 442a, 443b
perennial philosophy, III 457b–458a, 460a, 460b, 461b
perfectibility, III 471b–472a, 472b
Peter the Great and, III 64a
physics, IV 434b
Platonism, III 193a, 515b–516a, 516b
pleasure, II 381a
pluralism, III 515b
post–Kantianism, IV 209a
power, IV 491a
pragmatism, III 557b, 558a, 561b
probability, III 607a, 608b
progress, III 643b
psychology, IV 11a, 11b, 20a
rationalism, II 445b; III 195b
reason, I 91b, 327b–328a, 334b; II 239a, 239b, 446b
reincarnation, I 645a
relativity, IV 75b
research, III 64a
reunion of Protestants and Catholics, I 398b
romanticism, IV 209a, 210b

Saint Augustine and, **III** 355a

Schelling and, **IV** 210b

science, **I** 465a

scholastics and, **II** 200b

signs, **II** 435a, 435b

sin, **IV** 382a

skepticism, **IV** 245a, 246a, 247a

space, **IV** 295b, 297b, 298a, 301b, 302b, 305a, 305b

suffering, **IV** 382a

symbolism, **IV** 338a

symmetry, **IV** 353a

taste, **IV** 356a

teleology, **I** 303b–304a

theodicy, **II** 166a–166b; **IV** 378b, 380b, 381b–383a

theology, **IV** 378b

time, **IV** 394a–394b, 395a, 404a

truth, **I** 315b; **II** 446a

uniformitarianism, **IV** 423b, 426a, 426b

unity of science, **IV** 432b–433a, 434a–435b, 436a

universal man, **IV** 443a

universe, **II** 445b–446a, 447b; **III** 131a; **IV** 41b, 382a

Volksgeist, **IV** 491a

Voltaire and, **II** 446b, 447a; **IV** 382b

war, **III** 442a

Wilkins and, **II** 668b–669a

wisdom, **IV** 379a, 382a

Leisewitz, J. A., Counter-Enlightenment, **II** 107a

Leisure

Aristotle, **I** 102a; **IV** 497b

as the basis of culture, **I** 102a

Plato, **IV** 497b

Renaissance, **IV** 438a, 439a

universal man, **IV** 438a, 439a

virtuoso, **IV** 464a

vox populi, **IV** 497b

work, **IV** 532b

Leitmotiv, **III** 236a

Lejewski, C., matter, **III** 186b

Lemaire de Belges, Jean (1470?—?1525), mythology, **III** 290a

Lemaître, Georges Edouard (1894–1966)

cosmology, **I** 562b, 565b, 567a

space, **IV** 305b

Lamaître, Jules (1853–1914), literary criticism, **I** 601b

Lemercier, Louis (1771–1840), evolution of literature, **II** 172a

Lemmi, Charles W., mythology, **III** 299a

Lemoine, Jean

innocence, **II** 689a–689b

law, **II** 689a–689b

Lemos, Miguel, positivism, **III** 539b, 541a, 532a, 543a

Lenau, Nikolaus (1802–1850), Faust (legend), **III** 250a, 250b

Lenin, Nicolai (1870–1924),

acquired characteristics, **II** 620b, 621b

atomism, **I** 497a–497b

authority, **I** 158b

capitalism, **III** 156b

causation, **I** 283b

China, **I** 372a, 372b

class, **II** 561b–562a; **III** 156a–156b; **IV** 163b

communism, **II** 560a–560b

crisis in history, **I** 590b

cult of personality, **IV** 562a

culture, **IV** 165b

democracy, **I** 665a–665b; **II** 563a

dictatorship, **II** 560b; **III** 156a

discontinuity, **I** 497a–497b

economics, **II** 562a; **III** 153b–154a

existentialism, **III** 158a

force, **III** 156a

history, **I** 283b

ideology, **II** 560a–563a

imperialism, **II** 561a

law, **III** 156a

Marxism, **II** 560b, 561b; **III** 150a, 152a–158a, 165a, 166b, 167b, 168a

materialism, **II** 454b–455a

mythology, **II** 562b

nationalism, **III** 333b, 335b

oligarchy, **II** 561a

peaceful coexistence, **III** 157a

Penal Code, **II** 561a

politics, **III** 154a; **IV** 163b

power, **III** 156a

proletarianism, **II** 560b, 562a

revisionism, **IV** 268b, 270a, 271b

revolution, **III** 156a–156b; **IV** 162a, 163b, 165a, 165b

rules, **III** 156a

Russian Revolution (October 1917), **I** 665b; **III** 150a, 150b

socialism, **I** 372a; **III** 153b–154a; **IV** 293a

Stalin and, **II** 562b

State, **II** 560b

technology, **III** 153b–154a

U.S.S.R., **II** 560a, 562a

voluntarism, **III** 152b–153a

Leninism

ideology, **II** 562a–562b

totalitarianism, **IV** 410a

U.S.S.R., **II** 562a–562b

Lennox, Charlotte (1720–1804), virtuoso, **IV** 490a

Lenoble, Robert, technology, **IV** 360a

Lenses

Kepler, **III** 413b, 414b–415a

optics, **III** 411a–412a, 413b, 414a–416a, 416b, 420a

science, **III** 411a–412a, 413b, 414a–415a

Lentils of glass, optics, **III** 411a

Lenz, Jakob M. R. (1751–1792)

beauty, **II** 551b

Counter-Enlightenment, **II** 107a

Leo, Leonardo (1694–1744) genius, **II** 323a

Leo III, Pope (750?–816), Charlemagne, **I** 418a

Leo X, Pope (1475–1521)

classicism, **I** 451b

dignity, **IV** 145b

Gothic, **II** 370b

periodization in literary history, **III** 481b, 482a

private property, **III** 654a

Roman Catholic Church, **III** 654b

Leo XIII, Pope (1810–1903)

history, **I** 406a

modernism, **I** 420a, 420b, 422b

women, **IV** 526b

Leo Oracles, **III** 669a

Leo the Wise (866–912), prophecy, **III** 669a

Leonardo da Vinci (1452–1519)

ambiguity, **I** 56a–56b

art, **II** 298a, 298b, 301b, 302a, 304a, 308a, 529a

atomism, **I** 133a

canon of proportions, **I** 580a

chance images, **I** 346b, 347b–349a, 349b–350a

city, **I** 430b–431a

cosmic voyages, **I** 524a

creativity in art, **I** 580a, 585b

death, **I** 636a

economic history, **II** 45a

education, **IV** 440b

empiricism, **IV** 440b–441a

ethics, **IV** 442a–442b

game theory, **II** 274b

genius, **II** 298a, 298b, 301b, 302a, 304a, 308a, 317b

harmony, **IV** 41a

hierarchy, **II** 437b

humanism, **IV** 130a, 133a, 134a, 440b, 442a, 442b

iconography, **II** 529a

imitation, **II** 298a

knowledge, **IV** 442a–442b

Machiavelli and, **IV** 442b

Man-Machine, **III** 135b

mathematics, **IV** 440a, 440b–441a

mechanics, **III** 555a–555b

medieval experiments, **II** 202b

mimesis, **III** 227b

mountains in literature, **III** 258b

music, **II** 317b

non finito, **II** 298b–299a

optics, **III** 408b–409a, 411a

painting, **III** 227b; **IV** 467a

pragmatism, **III** 555a–555b

reason, **IV** 134a

senses, **IV** 440a

symmetry, **IV** 351b

technology, **IV** 360a

universal man, **IV** 437a, 437b, 438a, 439b, 440a–441a, 442a–442b

Utopia, **IV** 461a

work, **IV** 532a, 533b, 534a

Leonardo of Pisa (1180?–?1250), mathematics, **III** 181b

Leonidas I (fl. early 5th century B.C.)

justice, **II** 659a

temperance, **IV** 377a

Leontius (fl. 2nd century B.C.), freedom of speech, **II** 257b

Leopardi, Giacomo (1798–1837)

Cosmic Fall, **I** 511b

cosmic images, **I** 520a

evil, **II** 166a

irony, **II** 633b

literature, **III** 85b

romanticism, **IV** 204a, 209b

Leopold, Aldo, conservation, **I** 472b, 476a

Leopold II, Grand Duke of Tuscany (1824–1859)

Enlightenment, **II** 90b

history, **I** 404a

Lermontov, Mikhail (1814–1841), romanticism, **IV** 209b

Lerner, Max (1902–), ideology, **II** 556b

Leroux, Pierre (1797–1871), individualism, **II** 595a

progress, III 635a
socialism, IV 290a
symbolism, IV 339a
Leroy, Louis
despotism, II 7b
historiography, IV 148b-
149a, 149b, 150b
Leroquais, V.
iconography, II 533a
impressionism, II 573b
Platonism, III 514a
Leskien, August (1840–1916),
linguistics, III 69b, 70a,
70b
Lessing, Gotthold E. (1729-
1781)
aesthetics, IV 124b, 356a
art and play, I 103b, 105a
catharsis, I 268a
classicism, I 453a
deism, I 651a, 651b
Enlightenment, II 89b; III
248a, 343a
eschatology, II 158b-159a
Faust (legend), III 248a
genius, II 295b
Herder and, IV 209b
iconography, II 528b, 535a
ideal, II 551a
Lana Terzi and, II 551a
literature, III 82a
Machiavellism, III 118b
naturalism in art, III 343a
painting, IV 468a, 469a,
469b, 471a, 474a, 474b
poetics, III 529b, 530a, 531b
poetry, III 529b, 530a, 531b;
IV 468a, 469a, 469b, 471a,
474a, 474b
primitivism, III 581b-582a,
604b
progress, III 639a
romanticism, IV 209b
symbolism, IV 338a
taste, IV 356a
Lessing, Theodor, historicism,
II 462a
Leszczyński, Stanislaw (1677–
1766), iconography, II 532a
Letelier, Valentín, positivism,
III 543b
Lethe (myth), III 274b
Letter-writing
Cicero, II 515b, 516a
Geri of Arezzo, II 515b
humanism, II 515b–519a
politics, II 517a
Salutati, II 515b
Leucippus (5th century B.C.),
Aristotle and, I 495a
atomism, I 26b, 132b, 494b,
495a; III 187b; IV 51a
causation, I 272a; II 587a
continuity, I 494b, 495a,

503a
creativity in art, I 583b
historiography, I 503a
matter, III 187b, 192b, 193b,
194a
motion, IV 51a
necessity, III 353a; IV 51a
Non-Being, IV 299a, 299b
optics, III 407a, 407b, 408a
Pythagoreans, IV 37a
rationalism, IV 51a
reason, IV 51a
space, IV 299a, 299b
Levellers
class, I 442b
deism, I 649b
democracy, I 656b
equality, II 142b, 143a,
144a
Leverrier, Urbain J. J. (1811–
1877)
cosmology, I 552b
determinism, II 23b
Levi, Adolfo, skepticism, IV
250a
Leviathan (myth), III 281b
Levin, Harry, literary criticism,
I 604a; III 235a–244b
Levinthal, Cyrus
DNA, II 291a
genetic continuity, II 291a
Levison, Salmon, international
peace, III 452a
Lévi-Strauss, Claude
axiomatization, I 171b
communication, IV 325b–
326a
incest, IV 327a
literature, IV 327b
motif, III 240a
mythology, III 307a, 316a–
317b
necessity, III 352b
Propp and, III 316a–316b
society, IV 325b
structuralism, IV 324a,
324b–328a, 329a, 329b
Lévy, Paul (1886–),
chance, I 336b; III 620a
Lévy-Bruhl, Lucien (1857–
1939), ethics, IV 70b, 71b
Lewes, George Henry (1817–
1878)
association of ideas, I 115a
idea, I 115a, 116a
literature, IV 332b
Man-Machine, III 143a
realism in literature, IV 52b
style, IV 332b
Lewin, Kurt (1890–1947)
behaviorism, I 224b
psychology, IV 28a
Lewis, Clarence I (1883–
1964)

behaviorism, III 568b
emotion, III 568b
ethics, III 568a
good, IV 185b–186a
idea, III 568b
judgment III 568b, 569a
knowledge, III 568a, 568b
metaphor, III 199a, 199b
pragmatism, III 553b, 553b,
567b, 568a, 568b, 569a
value, III 568a, 568b–569a
Lewis, Matthew Gregory
(1775–1818), romanticism,
IV 193a
Lewis, R. W., literary criticism,
I 604b
Lewis, Wyndham (1884–
1957), expressionism, II
208b
Lex communis, II 694b
Lex romana visigothorum, II
691b, 692b
Lexis, W., probability, III 614b
Leyden papyrus, I 28a; II
256a
Liapounov, Alexander (1857–
1918), probability, III 619a
Libavius, Andreas (d. 1616),
alchemy I 32b
Libel
freedom of speech, II 252a
satire, IV 212b
Liber (myth), III 274a, 287a
Liberalism, III 36a–61a
anarchy, I 71a; III 51b,
56b, 58a, 58b
Aristotle, III 36b–37a, 46a,
47a
association III 45a, 45b
atheism, III 42b
authority, I 154a–154b,
158a; III 39b, 673a
Bayle, III 42b, 43a
beliefs, III 45a
Bentham, III 45a–45b, 46b
Bible, III 40b, 42a
bourgeois, III 54a, 59a
Burke, III 44b, 45b
Calvin, III 42a–42b
Calvinism, III 40b
Castellion, III 42a 42b
causation, III 37b–41b
Christianity, III 36a, 36b,
37a, 40b, 41b, 42a
city-state, III 37b
class, III 672b
communism, III 59a, 59b
conscience, III 42a, 42b,
43a
conservatism, I 480a, 481a,
482b, 483b
Constant, III 45b, 46a, 58a
Cousin, III 533b
democracy, I 663a, 664a;

III 39b, 40a, 44b, 46a, 52b,
55a, 59a, 60b
economic history, II 47a,
47b
economics, III 672b
education, II 147a
elections, III 45a
equality, II 146a–147a, III
55b, 60b
evolution, III 672b
faith, III 41a, 42b
fascism, III 331b
Faust (legend), III 250b
Fourier, III 58a
France, III 45b, 52b
freedom, III 36a, 60b
general will, II 278b, 280b
Germany, III 676b
God, II 356b, 357a, 358b,
359b, 360b, 361a; III 36a,
37a, 40a–40b, 41a, 41b,
42b, 43a
government by consent, III
43b–47a
Greece (ancient), III 36a,
36b
Green, T. H., III 51a, 51b
happiness, II 379a, 379b
Hegel, II 409a, III 36b–
37a, 48a, 48b, 49a, 49b
heresy, III 42a, 42b
heroes, II 37b
history, III 37b–41b
Hobbes, III 11a, 43b–44a
Huguenots, III 43b, 44a
humanism, II 520a
Humboldt, III 49b, 51b
Hume, III 44b, 46b, 47a
idea, III 41b–55b
ideology, III 672b
impressionism, II 583a
individualism, II 595a, 596b,
597a, 598a, 599a, 602a,
602b; III 36b, 37a, 39b,
43b–47a, 49b–54a, 56a,
56b, 59a, 59b
intolerance, III 40b, 42b
Italy, III 674b
Jacobinism III 45b, 54a
Jesuits, III 43b, 44a
justice, III 671a
Kant, III 37a, 47b–48a
labor, III 675b
Latin America, III 336a
law, III 11a, 36a, 36b,
44b, 46b, 49b, 54b, 58a,
60a, 672b
Left, III 53a, 53b, 54a,
55b
liberal, III 36a, 36b, 50a,
51b, 56a, 58b
liberty, III 40a–41b, 45a
Locke, III 37a, 40a, 42b,

229

43a, 43b, 44a, 44b, 45a, 45b, 46a, 54b
Luther, III 40b–41b, 45a
Lutheranism, III 40b
Machiavelli, III 37a, 121a, 121b
Marx, II 450b–451a, 451b; III 59b, 60a
Marxism, III 40a, 46b, 54a, 58b, 59b, 60a
materialism, II 450b–451a, 451b
metaphysics, III 48a
Mexico, III 544a
Middle Ages, III 36b, 40a–40b, 41b, 49b–50a
Mill, III 37a, 43a, 49b, 51a, 51b
mobility, III 38a–38b, 50a
modern state, III 37b–40a
Mohammedanism, III 42a
Montesquieu, III 37a, 44b, 45a, 45b, 46a, 54b
morality, III 41a, 42b, 43b, 47b, 48a, 48b, 51a, 51b, 56b
Napoleon I III 45b, 51a
nationalism, III 329b, 330b, 331b, 335a, 336a, 673a
philosophy, III 36a, 36b, 37a, 40a, 57b, 60b
Pius IX (Pope), I 406a
Plato, III 37a
pleasure, II 379a, 379b
positivism, III 544a
pragmatism, III 569a
press, III 45a
private property, III 46a, 653a
progress, III 647b–648a, 671a
protest movements, III 670a, 671a–676b
Protestantism, I 408b; III 40b
radicalism, III 52b–55b
rationalism, II 450b–451a
reform, III 672b
Reformation, III 36a, 36b, 40b, 41b, 42a, 47a
religion, III 36a, 40a–40b, 42a, 42b, 43a, 43b, 45a; IV 109b, 110b, 111a, 112b, 117b
Renaissance, III 36a, 37a–37b
revisionism, IV 264a
revolution, III 673a; IV 160a, 160b, 162a
Right, III 54a–54b, 55b
rights, III 36b, 39b, 43b–47a, 52a, 52b–53a, 53b–54a, 56a, 56b
Ritschl, II 357a

Robespierre, III 45b
Roman Catholic Church, III 42b
romanticism, IV 196b, 198a, 202b, 203b, 205a, 206b, 207b, 208b
Rome (ancient), III 36a, 36b
Rousseau, III 37a, 45b, 46a, 47a, 47b, 48a
Saint Thomas Aquinas, III 37a
Saint-Simon, III 57b, 58b
Schlegel, IV 207b
self-improvement, III 49b, 50a–50b, 51b, 56b
self-realization, III 50a–51b, 56b
self-reliance, III 37a
Servetus, III 42b
social contract, III 43b–44a, 46b; IV 251b, 255a, 256a, 263b
Social Democrats, III 58b
socialism, III 51b, 57b, 58a, 58b, 673b; IV 293b, 294a
society, III 39a–39b, 43b, 47a–47b, 56a
sociology, III 37a, 40a, 46b, 47a, 48a, 49a, 50a, 53a, 56b, 58b, 60a
Socrates, III 41b–42a
speech, III 41a–41b
Spinoza, III 42b, 43a
State, I 10a; III 37b–40a, 43b–47a, 55b–60b, 672b
Tawney, III 56b
Tocqueville, III 49b, 50a, 57a
tolerance, III 40b–42b
Toynbee, III 647b–648a
utopianism, III 671a
violence, III 672b
Volksgeist, IV 494a
Voltaire, III 45a
war, IV 502b, 503b, 504b, 505a, 506b, 507a
welfare state, IV 510a
Liberation
Buddhism, IV 233a
Hinduism, IV 232a
salvation, IV 232a, 233a
Liberia
African personality, III 337b
Anglo-Saxon, III 337b
folklore, III 337b
nationalism, III 337b
Liberman, E. G.
Marxism, III 155a
natural liberty, II 70a
Liberty
Acton, III 328b
balance of power, I 185a–185b

Calvinism, I 392b
Comte, II 95a
Constant, II 95a
Daguesseau, II 95b
Delolme, II 94b
democracy, I 655b; II 260a
determinism, II 239b–240a, 241a
Diderot, II 95a
Diodorus Curtius, II 95b
Enlightenment, II 90a, 91a, 92a, 94a, 94b–95b
equality, II 140a, 146a, 147b
Filmer, II 95a
free will, II 239b–240a, 241a, 248a
freedom, II 248b–250b
freedom of speech, II 258b–259a, 260a, 262a
French Revolution (1789), II 94b
general will, II 276a, 277a, 279b
genius, II 300b
Gibbon, II 94b
Great Britain, I 392b
Greece (ancient), II 259a, 500b–501b
happiness, II 379a–379b, 381b
harmful aspect, II 249a
Hegel, II 95a
Helvétius, II 94b
historiography, II 500b–501b
humanism, II 522b
Hume, II 95a, 239b–240a
Kant, II 240a
law, II 248b–249a, 249b, 250b, 686a; III 8a
liberalism, III 40a–41b, 45a
Locke, II 95a, 239b; IV 154a
Macaulay, II 95a
Machiavelli, IV 316b
Machiavellism, III 121a, 121b
Mandeville, II 94b
Montesquieu, II 95a
nationalism, III 325b–329a, 329b, 331a, 332a
natural rights, III 23b
Netherlands, I 392b
Newton, I 518a
pleasure, II 379a–379b, 381b
Plutarch, II 95b
private property, III 656b
progress, III 636b
prophecy, III 667a
religion, IV 113b
Renaissance, IV 122b
revolution, IV 154a

Robertson, II 94b
Rollin, II 95b
romanticism, IV 203b, 205a, 206b, 207b
Rome (ancient), II 686a
Rousseau, II 94b, 98a, 277a
Schiller, II 94b
Sismondi, II 95a
Smith, Adam, II 94b
socialism, IV 288a, 289a
Spinoza, III 42b
State, IV 313b–314a, 316b, 317b
Thucydides, II 95a
totalitarianism, IV 407a
U. S., I 392b; III 329a
Volksgeist, IV 495a
Voltaire, II 94b, 95a
Xenophon, II 95a
Libri feudorum, II 692a
Lichtenberger, Johannes von, reformation, IV 65a
Lichtenthal, Peter, genius, II 324b
Lie, Jonas (1833–1909), literature, III 84b
Lieber, Francis (1800–1872), Kant and, III 444a
peace, III 444a
Volksgeist, IV 495a
Liebert, Arthur, perennial philosophy, III 462b
Liebig, Justus von (1803–1873)
Bacon and, I 178a
spontaneous generation, II 283a, 283b
Liebknecht, Karl (1871–1919)
Marxism, III 153a
war, IV 506a
Liebknecht, Wilhelm (1826–1900), revisionism, IV 264b
Lieh–Tzu (fl. 5th or 4th century B.C.), longevity, III 90b
Life
death, I 636a
longevity, III 89a–89b
metaphysical imagination, III 209a
Montaigne, I 636a
naturalism in art, III 343a
Nature, III 346b
Neo-Platonism, III 375a, 376a, 376b, 377a
Plato, I 639a
Renaissance, I 636a
Life expectancy, longevity, III 89a–89b
Light
aberration, IV 77b
aesthetics, II 218a; III 396b
art, II 567b, 570a–570b,

572a, 574a–574b, 578b, 579a, 580a–580b, 581b
Bradley, **IV** 77b
colorimetry, **III** 418a
cosmology, **I** 553b, 554b, 555a, 557a
Descartes, **III** 384a, 418a, 418b; **IV** 77b
Edwards, **IV** 110a
Einstein, **IV** 81a, 81b, 83b
Empedocles, **III** 407a
Galileo, **II** 587a; **IV** 77b
God, **III** 393b
Goethe, **II** 580b
Grimaldi, **III** 418a, 418b, 419a
Heisenberg, **II** 589a
Helmholtz, **II** 580b
hermeticism, **II** 432a, 433b
Huygens, **III** 418a
impressionism, **II** 567b, 570a–570b, 572a, 574a–574b, 578b, 579a, 580a–580b, 581b
indeterminacy, **II** 587a, 589a
Kepler, **IV** 77b
matter, **III** 191a, 195a
medieval science, **II** 196b, 198a–199a, 200b
methodology, **III** 386a, 387a, 389b, 390a
Milton, **III** 393b
motion, **III** 419b
naturalism in art, **III** 340a, 340b, 342b
Newton, **II** 580b; **III** 195a, 386a, 387a, 389b, 390a, 391b–398b, 418a; **IV** 77b, 78a, 80b, 86b–87a
optics, **III** 391b–398b, 407a, 410a, 410b, 417b–420b
particle-and-wave theory, **IV** 78a
photometry, **III** 418a
physics, **II** 580a–580b
Platonism, **III** 511b
poetry, **III** 391b–398b
Pope, **IV** 337a–337b
precious stones, **III** 394a
reason, **III** 396b
relativity, **IV** 77b–78b, 80b, 81b, 82a, 82b, 83b, 86b–87a, 91b
religion, **IV** 110a
Roemer, **III** 395a; **IV** 77b
speed of, **IV** 77b–78a, 79a, 81a, 82b, 83b, 91b
sublime in external nature, **IV** 335b, 336b, 337a–337b
symmetry, **IV** 349a
time, **IV** 404b, 405a, 405b
Light cones, **IV** 85a, 91b
Light waves, relativity, **IV** 77b–78b, 79a, 80b, 81a–

81b, 83b
Ligon, Richard, primitivism, **III** 602a
Lilburne, John (1614?–1657),
democracy, **I** 656b
equality, **II** 142b
social contract, **IV** 254b–255a
State, **I** 656b
Lilith (myth), **III** 282b
Lilley, Alfred, modernism, **I** 424b
Limayrac, Paulin, symbolism, **IV** 339a–339b
Limit theorems, **III** 612b, 613a, 613b
Linacre, Thomas (1460?–1524), Platonism, **III** 507b
Lincoln, Abraham (1809–1865)
economic history, **II** 44b
freedom, **II** 44b
Kant and, **III** 444a
peace, **III** 444a
pragmatism, **III** 553b
Lindahl, Erik, social welfare, **IV** 283a
Lindeberg, J. W., probability, **III** 619a
Lindenberger, H., symbolism, **IV** 342b
Lindsay, A. D., individualism, **II** 597a
Linear continuum theory, infinity, **II** 610a
Linear zigzag function, cosmology, **I** 537b, 538a
Linguet, Simon Nicolas (1736–1744)
Enlightenment, **II** 99b
socialism, **IV** 288b
Linguistic paleontology, **IV** 425a–425b
Linguistics, **III** 61a–76a; **IV** 423b–430b
Adam (Bible), **III** 65a–65b
Adamic language, **III** 74a, 74b, 75a
Adelung, **III** 63b
Agrippa, **III** 74b
Alexander of Villedieu, **III** 63a
alphabetic representation, **III** 70b, 71a
anatomy, **IV** 427b
animals, **IV** 426b, 427b
archeology, **III** 69a, 69b; **IV** 430a
Aristophanes of Byzantium, **III** 62b
Aristotle, **III** 62a, 75a, 75b
Ascoli, **III** 70a–70b, 71b
artificial language, **III** 75a
Bacon, **III** 62b–63a, 73a–

74a
Bible, **IV** 423b–424a, 426a, 427a, 427b
biology, **IV** 424a, 424b, 425b–427b, 428a, 429a
Bloomfield, **III** 71b
Boas, Franz, **III** 71a–71b
Boehme, **III** 74b
Bohtlingk, **III** 70b
Boltwood, **IV** 426b
Bopp, **III** 67b–68a; **IV** 427b
British and Foreign Bible Society, **III** 63b
Brooks, **IV** 425b
Brugmann, **IV** 425a
Buck, **III** 72b
calculus, **IV** 430a
Callimachus, **III** 62a
Cassirer, **IV** 428b
catastrophism, **IV** 423b, 425a
Catherine II, **III** 64a
chemistry, **IV** 424b
China, **II** 661a, 661b
Chomsky, **II** 672b–673a
climate, **III** 62a
Columbus, **IV** 427b
communication, **IV** 426a
Comparative Method, **III** 69b, 70a; **IV** 426b, 427a, 428a, 430a
consonant shift, **III** 67a–67b
conventionalist thesis, **III** 74b
Courtenay, **III** 71a
Creation, **IV** 423b, 424a, 426a
criticism, **III** 73a–74a, 74b–75a
Cuvier, **III** 65b; **IV** 427b
Dalgarno, **III** 75a
Dante, **III** 62b–63a, 63b, 65a
Darwin, **III** 68b–69a; **IV** 424a–425a, 428a–429b
Delbrück, **III** 71b
demography, **III** 70a
determinism, **IV** 429a
dialect, **III** 62b, 63b, 67a, 70a, 70b, 73b
Diaspora, **III** 63a
dictionary, **III** 63a, 67a
Dionysius of Halicarnassus, **III** 62a
Dionysius the Thracian, **III** 62a
Du Bois-Reymond, **IV** 428b
earth, **IV** 424a, 424b, 426b
education, **IV** 426a
Eisley, **IV** 424a
empiricism, **III** 73a–74a
Enlightenment, **III** 64b
epistemology, **III** 75a

ethnic substratum, **III** 70b
etymology, **III** 61b, 66a, 67a, 68a, 75a
evolution, **III** 68b; **IV** 424a, 424b, 429a
exceptionlessness, **III** 70a
extralinguistic exploitation, **III** 69a
Fall of Constantinople, **III** 63a
Fechner, **IV** 429b
Finck, **III** 71a
Flood, **IV** 423b, 424a, 426a
Fludd, **III** 74b
fossils, **IV** 425a, 425b
free will, **II** 247a–248b
French Linguistic Atlas, **III** 70a
French Revolution (1789), **III** 64b
French-Oriental scholars, **III** 65b
Greiger, **IV** 425a
genealogy, **III** 65b, 66b, 68b, 71b
geology, **IV** 423b–424b, 425a–427b, 429a
Germany, **II** 670b–671b; **IV** 425a, 428b
Gesner, **III** 63b
Gilliéron, **III** 70a
glossology, **III** 61b
glottochronology, **III** 72a; **IV** 429b–430a
God, **IV** 424a, 424b, 426a
grammar, **III** 62a–64a, 65b–67a, 68a, 69a, 71b, 72b, 74a
Great Britain, **II** 247a; **III** 70b, 73a–75b; **IV** 425a
Greece (ancient), **II** 661a, 661b–666a; **III** 61b
Greek language, **IV** 425b, 427b
Greene, **IV** 427b
Grimm, **II** 671a–671b; **III** 64b, 67a, 68a, 68b; **IV** 427b
Grimm's law, **III** 66b, 70a
Gyarmathi, **III** 64b–65a, 66a
Hamilton, **III** 65b
Hebrew language, **III** 62b; **IV** 426b, 427a
Hegel, **IV** 427b, 428a
Herder, **III** 64b; **IV** 426b
Herodotus, **III** 62b
Hervas, **III** 64b
Highet, **IV** 425b
historiography, **III** 72b
history, **II** 670b–671b; **III** 61a–72b; **IV** 426b, 428a
Hobbes, **III** 75a, 75b
Hoenigswald, **IV** 427b

231

Humboldt, III 67b, 70b, 71a, 71b; IV 427b
Huxley, IV 424a, 424b, 425a, 427b, 428b
India, II 670a–670b, III 65a
Indians (American), II 661a, 661b
indistinguishability, IV 429b
Indo-European family, IV 426b, 427b
innate language, III 74b
Japan, II 661b
Jespersen, III 72a; IV 425b
Jones, III 65a–65b, 66b; IV 427b
just languages, III 69b
Kelvin, IV 426b
Kraus, III 64a, 64b
Kruszewski, III 71a; IV 425a
Kuhn, III 69b
language mixture, III 72a
language of nature, III 74b
language reform, III 73b
language structure, III 67b
language survey, III 64a
langue, IV 323b–324a
Latin Language, IV 425b, 427b
Leibniz, III 64a, 64b, 65b; IV 423b, 426a, 426b
Leskien, III 69b, 70a, 70b
lingua Adamica, III 62b
linguistic paleontology, IV 425a
Linnaeus, III 66b
literature, IV 327b; IV 425b
Locke, III 73a, 75b
logic, III 72a; IV 425a
logos, III 74b
Lord's Prayer, III 63b
Ludolf, III 64b, 66a
Lyell, IV 423b–425a, 426a, 427a–428a, 429b
Malkiel, IV 425a
mathematics, III 72a; IV 426a, 429a, 430a
matrix lingua, III 63b
matter, IV 424a
Meillet, III 71b; IV 427b
metaphor, III 64a
methodology, III 70a, 71b, 72a
Middle Ages, III 62b–63a
missionary grammar, III 63a
Monboddo, III 65a
monogenesis, III 65b, 75a; IV 426b
Morhof, III 65a
Müller, IV 424b–425a, 426b
multilingualism, III 61a–61b
mutation, IV 424b
mythology, III 61a–61b, 69a, 304a, 316a, 316b,

317a
Napoleon I, III 64b
nationalism, III 328b, 329a, 336b
natural selection, IV 424a, 428a
Nature, III 73b; IV 424a, 427b–429a
necessity, III 352a
Nehring, IV 425a
neo-grammarianism, III 69b–71b; IV 428a–429b
Orientalism, III 435a
orthography, III 71a
paleontology, IV 425a, 427b
Pallas, III 64a, 64b, 68b
parole, IV 323b–324a, 324b
Paul, III 70b
Peirce, IV 429a
Peter the Great, III 64a
philosophy, II 661a–661b; III 61b, 71a, 71b, 72a
Philoxenus, III 62b
phonemic innovation, III 69a
phonemic theory, III 71a
phonetics, III 68b, 70b–71b
phonology, III 67a, 68b–69b
physics, IV 424b, 426b, 427a
Pictet, A., IV 425a
Pictet, F. J., IV 425a
plants, IV 425b, 427b
Plato, III 61b, 62b, 65b, 68a, 74b
Platonism, III 74b, 521a
polygenesis, III 65a–65b; IV 426b
Posidonius, III 62a
Pott, III 68a, 68b; IV 427b
pragmatism, III 553a
pre-Darwinism, III 68b
pre-Hegelianism, IV 428a
primordial unity, III 75a
printing, III 63a
probability, IV 424b, 426a
psychology, IV 428b, 429b
Pythagoras, III 65b
radioactivity, IV 426b, 430a
Rask, III 66b–67b, 68a; IV 427b
reason, IV 424a
religion, III 69a
revelation, IV 424a, 426b, 427b
Ritschl, III 68a, 69a
rocks, IV 424b, 427b
Romance languages, III 70a
romanticism, III 66a, 67a, 69a; IV 425b

Rosicrucianism. III 74b
Rousseau, III 64b
Sajnovics, III 64b
Sanskrit language, III 65a, 66a, 70a, 70b; IV 427b
Sapir, III 71b; IV 426b
Saussure, II 671b–672a; III 70a, 71a; IV 323b–324a, 425a
Scaliger, III 63b, 64b
Schildberger, III 63b
Schlegel, III 65b, 66a, 66b, 69a
Schleicher, III 68a–70b; IV 426b, 427b–428a
Schlözer, III 65a
Schmidt, III 70a; IV 428a
scholarship, III 65b
Schuchardt, III 70a
science, III 73b, 74b; IV 423b, 424a, 425a, 426a, 426b
science of grammar, III 74a
scribal error, III 69a
semantics, III 71a, 71b, 72b, 74a, 75a
sensory intuition, III 74a
Shankara, IV 429a
shared error, III 68a–68b
Sibscota, III 74b–75b
Sievers, III 70b
Smith, III 65b
Société de Linguistique of Paris, III 69b
society, IV 426a
sociolinguistics, III 71b–72a
sound-change, IV 428b
sound laws, III 67a, 67b, 68a, 69b, 70a, 72b; IV 428b
space, IV 428b
species, IV 424b, 428a
spirit, IV 428a
statistics, IV 426a
Stoicism, III 62a
Strahlenberg, III 64b
structuralism, II 671b–672a; III 71a; IV 323a–327a, 327b, 328a, 329a, 329b
substratum, IV 425a
Sumer, III 61a–61b
Swadesh, III 72a; IV 429b–430a
Sweet, III 70b
synchronic phonemic analysis, III 70a, 71a
taxonomy, III 66b
Techmer, IV 425a
Teutonism, III 67a
textual criticism, III 68a
theology, III 61a–61b
theory of, III 73a–77b

time, IV 427a, 428b
Tolomei, III 63b
Tower of Babel (Bible), III 61b; IV 426a–426b, 427a
traits, III 66a
transformational syntax, III 72a–72b
translations, III 61b, 62a, 72a
Trobetskoy, III 71a
typology, III 66b, 67b, 68b, 71a, 71b, 72a
U. S., II 247a
universality, III 67b, 75b
universe, IV 424a
Ussher, IV 426b, 427a
vernacular, III 63a, 63b
Verner, III 70a
Vico, III 64b
vocabulary, III 63b, 64b; IV 430a
Wachter, III 67a
Wackernagel, III 72b
Ward, III 74b
wave theory, III 70a
Webster, III 74b
Weinreich, III 72a
Whewell, IV 423b
Whitney, IV 425a, 426b, 427b
Whorf, III 71b
Wilkins, III 74b, 75a
Wimsatt, IV 425b
Winteler, III 70a, 70b
Words-and-Things technique, III 69b
Zeno of Citium, III 62a
See also Language

Linnaeus, Carolus (1707–1778)
Chain of Being, I 332a
conservation, I 473a
evolutionism, II 177a
linguistics, III 66b
socialism, IV 293b
species, I 233a, 332a

Linos (myth), music, III 268b
Liouville theorem, II 592b
Lippmann, Walter, psychology, IV 26b
Lipps, Theodor (1851–1914),
beauty, I 213a
empathy, II 86a, 86b, 87a, 88a, 88b
Hume and, II 88a
Lipset, Seymour Martin
class, I 449a
democracy, I 666b–667a
Lipsius, Richard A. (1830–1892), God, II 355a
List, Georg Friedrich (1789–1846)
nationalism, III 330a–330b
individualism, II 596a

Müller and, **IV** 207b
natural liberty, **II** 68b
romanticism, **IV** 207b
Volksgeist, **IV** 494b
Lister, Joseph (1786–1869),
religion, **IV** 108a
Liszt, Franz (1811–1886),
ut pictura poesis, **IV** 473a
Literary criticism, **I** 596a–607b
aesthetics, **I** 596a, 597b–
598a, 602a, 602b–603a,
603b, 606a, 606b
Aristarchos, **I** 596b
Aristotelianism, **I** 597b,
604a
Aristotle, **I** 596a, 596b,
602a, 604a
Arnold, **I** 599b–600a
art, **I** 599a, 605a, 606b;
II 297a, 306a, 318b
artists, **I** 598a
Auerbach, **I** 606a
authority, **I** 597a
autobiography, **I** 601b
Babbitt, **I** 603a
Balzac, **I** 601a
Barthes, **I** 605a–605b
Baudelaire, **I** 601a–601b,
605a
beauty, **I** 597b
Belinsky, **I** 606b
Bergson, **I** 604b
Bernard, **I** 601a
Bible, **I** 596b
Blok, **I** 606b
Boas, George, **I** 604a
Bouhours, **I** 597a
Brooks, **I** 603b
Brunetière, **I** 600b–601a,
601b
Burke, Kenneth, **I** 603b
Campistron, **I** 601a
Carlyle, **I** 599a
Casey, **I** 602b
Chateaubriand, **I** 599b
Coleridge, **I** 598a, 598b
communism, **I** 606b–607a
Crane, **I** 604a
Crates, **I** 596b
critics, **I** 596a–599b, 601a,
601b, 603b–605b
Croce, **I** 605b–606a
Curtius, **I** 606a
Dante, **I** 605b
De Sanctis, **I** 600a
Debordes-Valmore, **I** 601a
defined, **I** 596a
Dewey, **III** 569b
Dilthey, **I** 600a
Dryden, **I** 596a
Egypt (ancient), **I** 596b
Eliot, T. S., **I** 602a–603a,
604b
Emerson, **I** 599a

Erasmus, **I** 596b
existentialism, **I** 606a
Fabini, **I** 606a
feeling, **I** 597a, 598a
Fernandez, **I** 604b
Fichte, **I** 598a
Fioretti, **I** 597a
Foerster, **I** 603a
France, **I** 596b, 597a, 598b–
601a, 604b–606b
France, Anatole, **I** 597b,
600b, 605a
Frye, **I** 604a–604b
Fuller, **I** 599a
Galen, **I** 596b
Gardner, **I** 602b
Genet, **I** 605a
genius, **I** 599b, 600a; **II**
297a, 306a, 318b
Geoffroy, **I** 599a
George, Stefan, **I** 606a
Germany, **I** 596a–596b,
597b–598b, 600a, 606a
Goethe, **I** 597b, 600b
Goldmann, Lucien, **I** 606b
Gracián, **I** 596a
grammar, **I** 596b, 597a
Great Britain, **I** 596a, 597a,
598a–600a, 601a–603a
Greece (ancient), **I** 596a,
596b, 602a, 604a
Grigoriev, **I** 606b
Hazlitt, **I** 598b–599a
Hegel, **I** 596b, 598a, 600b
Heinsius, **I** 597a
Hennequin, **I** 600b
Herder, **I** 597b, 599a, 300a
Heyl, **I** 604a
Hieron, **I** 596b
Holthusen, **I** 606a
Homer, **I** 597a
Hough, **I** 603a
Hugo, **I** 599b, 601a
humanism, **I** 603a
Humboldt, **I** 598a
Hungary, **I** 606b
Italy, **I** 596a, 596b, 597a,
600a, 605b–606a
Jacobi, **I** 596b
James, **I** 601b
Jarrell, **I** 604a
Johnson, Samuel, **I** 597a
Kames, **I** 597a
Kant, **I** 596b, 597b–598a
Kerr, **I** 606a
knowledge, **I** 597a, 606b
La Bruyère, **I** 597a
Lawrence, D. H., **I** 602b
Leavis, **I** 602b
Leibniz, **I** 597b
Lemaître, **I** 601b
Levin, Harry, **I** 604a
Lewis, R. W., **I** 604b
Longinus, **I** 596b

Lukács, **I** 606b
Macaulay, **I** 599a
Manzoni, **I** 597b
Marxism, **I** 603b, 606a,
606b–607a
Matthiessen, **I** 604a
Maurras, **I** 604b
Mencken, **I** 603a
metaphor, **I** 598b–599a
Middle Ages, **I** 596b
Molière, **I** 601a
More, P. E., **I** 603a
Müller, Adam, **I** 598b
mythology, **III** 306b, 317a
Netherlands, **I** 597a
Nisard, **I** 599a–599b
Nisiely, **I** 597a
objectivity, **I** 598b, 599b,
600b, 601b
organicism, **III** 421b–423a,
424a, 424b, 425b–427a
origin of the term, **I** 596b
Osborne, **I** 602b–603a
Pater, **I** 601b
periodization in literary his-
tory, **III** 484b, 485a
Philitas, **I** 596b
Picard, **I** 605a–605b
Platonism, **I** 596a
pluralism, **I** 604a
Poe, **I** 599a
poetics, **I** 596a, 597a
Poliziano, **I** 596b
Pope, **I** 596a, 597a
Poulet, **I** 605b
pragmatism, **III** 569b
Proust, **I** 605a
psychology, **I** 597a, 600a,
600b, 602b, 603b, 605a
Ptolemy II, **I** 596b
Pushkin, **I** 606a
Quintilian, **I** 596b
Racine, **I** 600b, 601a
Ransom, **I** 603a
Read, **I** 602b
realism, **IV** 51b, 52b–54a
Renaissance, **I** 596b, 597a
rhetoric, **I** 596a, 597a
Richards, **I** 602a–603a
Righter, **I** 602b
Rivière, **I** 604b–605a
romanticism, **IV** 205b
Rousset, **I** 605b
Russia, **I** 606a–606b
Rymer, **I** 596a
Sainte-Beuve, **I** 599b,
601b, 602a, 602b, 605a
Sartre, **I** 605a
Scaliger, J. J., **I** 596b,
597a
Scaliger, J. C., **I** 596b
Schelling, **I** 596b, 598a
Schiller, Friedrich, **I** 598a
Schlegel, August Wilhelm

von, **I** 598a–598b, 599a,
605b
Schlegel, Friedrich, **I** 596b,
598a, 598b, 599a, 605b
Schoppe, **I** 596b
science, **I** 599b, 602a, 606a,
607a
sentiment, **I** 597a
Shakespeare, **I** 597a, 599a,
599b, 600b
Shapiro, Karl, **I** 604a
Shumaker, **I** 604a
skepticism, **I** 596a, 597a,
603a
Spain, **I** 596a, 596b
Sparshott, **I** 603a
Spingarn, **I** 603a
Staiger, **I** 606a
Stoicism, **I** 596a
structuralism, **I** 606a; **IV**
323a, 327a–328b
stylistics, **I** 606a
subjectivity, **I** 597a, 598b,
601b
sublime in external nature,
IV 333a, 334a
symbolism, **IV** 337b, 340b,
341b–342a, 344b
Symonds, **I** 601a
Taine, **I** 600a–600b
taste, **I** 597a, 597b–598a,
600a, 603a
Tate, **I** 603a–603b
Thibaudet, **I** 604b
tragedy, **I** 596a
Trilling, **I** 604a
U.S.S.R., **I** 606b
U.S., **I** 596a, 599a, 601b,
603a–604b; **IV** 341b–342a
ut pictura poesis, **IV** 465b,
466b, 467a, 467b, 469a,
469b, 471a, 473b, 475a
Valéry, **I** 605a
Vossius, **I** 597a
Watson, **I** 602b
Wilde, **I** 601b–602a, 605a,
606b
Wimsatt, **I** 603b
Winters, **I** 603a, 603b
Wittgenstein, **I** 602b
Literary paradox, **III** 76a–81b
Agrippa, **III** 79a
Alcibiades, **III** 78b
anti-idealism, **III** 78b
antiquity, **III** 77a–77b
atomism, **III** 76b
Belleau, **III** 77b
belles-lettres, **III** 76a, 76b
Bodin, **III** 78a
Borges, **III** 77b
Browne, Thomas, **III** 80a
Bruno, **III** 79a
Burton, **III** 80b
Carroll, Lewis, **III** 77b

233

Castiglione, III 80b
Chesterton, III 77b
Christianity, III 80a
Cicero, III 77a
commentary, III 78b
Copernicus paradox, III 77a
criticism, III 77b
defense of contraries, III 76b
dialectic, III 76a, 76b, 77a, 78a, 79b
Diderot, III 77b
Donne, III 77b, 78b, 79b, 80a, 80b
Eleaticism, III 76b
Epicureanism, III 79b
epigrams, III 79b
Epimenides the Cretan, III 76b
epistemology, III 77b, 81a
Erasmus, III 78a, 78b
Falstaff (fiction), III 78b
first vernacular collection of, III 78a
Freeling, III 77b
Freud, III 77b
God, III 80b
Goethe, III 79b
Gorgias, III 77a
grammar, III 76b, 77a
Hamlet (fiction), III 77a, 80b
Harington, III 78a
Helen of Troy (myth), III 79b
Heller, III 77b
Homer, III 79a
humanism, III 77b, 81a
Hutten, III 79a
idea, III 76a
indeterminacy, III 76b
irony, III 77a, 78a, 79b
Isocrates, III 77a, 79b
Jesus Christ, III 80b
Joyce, III 77b
knowledge, III 81a
Lando, III 78a, 78b, 80b
Lear (fiction), III 78b–79a
Lear's fool (fiction), III 78b, 79a
literary fool, III 78b
logic, III 76b–78a
love, III 80a
Lovelace, III 77b
Marlowe, III 79b
mathematical recreation, III 77b
mathematics, III 76b, 77b
Mandeville, III 77b
Marino, III 77b
metaphor, III 80a–80b
Middle Ages, III 79a
Milton, III 80a
Montaigne, III 76b, 78a,

79a, 79b, 80b
More, Thomas, III 79a–79b
Morgenstern, III 77b
multiple standard, III 79a
negativism, III 79a
Nero, III 80a
New Critics, III 77b
Nicholas of Cusa, III 78b, 79a
nonsense, III 77b
nowheres, III 79a–79b
oratory, III 77a, 79a, 79b
Ovid, III 77b
oxymoron, III 80a
paradoxical topics, III 77b, 78a, 78b, 81a
Pascal, III 79b
Passerat, III 77b, 79a
Petrarch, III 80a
Plato, III 77a
play on words, III 77b, 79b
poetics, III 77b
Pseudo-Dionysius, III 78b, 79a
psychology, III 77b
Pyrrhonism, III 79b
Pythagoreans, III 76b
Queneau, III 77b
Rabelais, III 78a–78b, 79b
religion, III 79b–80a
Renaissance, III 77a–79a
rhetoric, III 76a–77b
Rochefoucauld, III 79b
Ronsard, III 77b
Saint Augustine, III 80b
Saint Paul, III 76b, 78b, 80a
Saint Theresa, III 80a
Saint-Amant, III 77b
Sancho Panza (fiction), III 76b
Sartre, III 77b
satire, III 78b
self-criticism, III 76b
Seneca, III 80a
Shakespeare, III 78a, 78b–79a, 80a
Sidney, III 77b
Silesius, III 80a
skepticism, III 78a, 79b
sociology, III 78b
Socrates, III 78b
Sophism, III 79a
Sterne, III 77b
Stoicism, III 77a, 79b, 80a
suicide, III 80a–80b
Swift, III 77b
Synesius, III 77b
utopia, III 79a–79b, 81a
verbal paradoxy, III 80a
Vergil, III 77b
word-play, III 77b
Zen Buddhism, III 77b
Zeno, III 76b

Literary prophecy, III 661a–662b, 663b
Literature, III 81b–89a
Abrams, IV 196a
absurd, IV 414a–414b
adornment, IV 331a
aesthetics, II 216a, 219b–220b, 224a; III 82b, 85a, 85b, 86a, 87b, 88a–88b; IV 330b, 331b, 332b
Albalat, IV 332b
alliteration, III 86b
Almeida-Garrett, IV 191a
Ampère, III 84a
antiprimitivism, III 604a
Apocalypse, III 202b
Aristotelianism, IV 330b
Aristotle, IV 330b, 331a
Arnim, IV 189a, 190a, 196b
Arnold, III 83a
art, II 528a–529a, 530a, 531a; III 85a–85b, 87a
artists, II 298a, 299a, 301a
Ast, IV 189a
Auger, IV 191a
Babbitt, IV 195a, 196b
Bachelard, III 242b
Bacon, III 85a–85b
Bagehot, IV 193a
Balzac, III 86a, 87b
Baretti, III 81b
Barolo, IV 190b
baroque, IV 331b
Bayle, IV 124a
beauty, IV 330b, 332a
Beckett, III 88b
Beers, IV 193b
Béguin, IV 196b
belles-lettres, III 81b, 83a, 85a, 85b
Benz, IV 197a
Berchet, IV 190b
Berkenhout, III 82a
biography, IV 333a
Blackmur, III 88b
Blair, III 83a
Blanchot, III 88b
Bloom, IV 196a
Boccaccio, IV 189b
Boileau, IV 330b, 331b
Bossuet, III 86a
Boswell, III 81b
Bouterwek, IV 188a, 189a, 189b, 191b
Brandl, IV 193b
Breme, IV 190b
Brentano, IV 189a, 190a, 196b, 197a
Brodzinski, IV 191b
Brunetière, IV 196b; IV 332b
Brydges, IV 192a
Buffon, IV 330b, 331b, 332a

Bulwer-Lytton, IV 193a
Burke, Kenneth, III 88b
Burton, IV 331b
Carlyle, IV 192b, 194a–194b
Carriere, III 84a
Cassian, III 81b
Cassiodorus, III 82b
Castres, III 82a
censorship, III 497a–498a
Chambers, III 82b
Chapelain, III 81b
Chasles, III 82b, 84a
Chateaubriand, IV 189b, 195b, 332b
China, I 364a–364b, 366b–367b, 368b–369b, 372a
China (ancient), IV 466a
Chomsky, III 88a
Cicero, III 81b, 82b, 86a; IV 330a, 330b, 331a
clarity, IV 331a, 331b, 332a
class, I 445b
classicism, I 449b–456a; III 363b
cognates, III 81b–89a
Colbert, III 83a
Coleridge, IV 191b, 192b, 193a, 195a, 196b
Colman, III 82a
common law, II 694a
comparative, III 83a–84b, 85a, 237b, 238b
computers, IV 333a
concept of, III 85a, 88a–88b
content, IV 330b, 332a, 332b
correctness, IV 331a
Counter-Enlightenment, II 101b, 107a–107b
Crevier, IV 332a
criticism, III 82b, 83a, 84b, 86a; IV 332a, 333a
Croce, III 88a
cultural history, III 85b
Cuvier, III 83b
Dale, III 84b
Dalla, IV 190b
Dante, III 86a; IV 331a
De Quincey, III 83a; IV 332b
De Sanctis, III 84a
defined, III 81b–82a, 84b, 88a–88b
Degérando, III 83b
Demetrius, IV 330b, 331a
Denina, III 82b
derivation of term, III 81b–82b
Deutschbein, IV 197a
devotional, II 202b
Dewey, III 88a
didactic, IV 331a

dignity, **IV** 141a, 142a, 146a
Dionysius of Halicarnassus, **IV** 330b, 331a
distinguishing trait of, **III** 86a
Dostoevsky, **III** 86a
dramatic, **III** 87b
Du Bellay, **III** 82b
du Marsais, **IV** 332a
Eastlake, **IV** 193b
Eckermann, **IV** 188a
Edwards, **IV** 109b, 110b
Eggli, **IV** 190a
Eichhorn, **III** 84b; **IV** 187b
Eliot, T. S., **IV** 147a
elocution, **IV** 331a
Emerson, **III** 86a
Enlightenment, **II** 91a–91b, 96b, 98b–99a, 100a
epics, **III** 87b, 241b; **IV** 331b
Erasmus, **IV** 124a
erudition, **III** 81b, 82b
ethnology, **IV** 327b
evil, **II** 162a, 169a
expressionism, **II** 206a–209b
Faust (legend), **III** 244b–253a
Ferguson, **III** 82a
fictionality, **III** 82b, 86a, 87b
Flaubert, **IV** 332b
Foster, **IV** 191b
Fouqué, **IV** 189a
France, **III** 82a, 82b, 83b–84a; **IV** 331a, 331b, 332b
French Academy, **III** 83a
French Revolution (1789), **III** 671b
Freudianism, **III** 242a
function of, **III** 88b
Garland, **IV** 331a
general, **III** 83a, 84b–85a
Geoffroi de Vinsauf, **IV** 331a
Germany, **III** 82a, 83a, 83b, 84a–84b, 494b–495a
Gerstenberg, **IV** 187b
Gervinus, **III** 83a
Gherardini, **IV** 190b
Giorgi-Bertòla, **III** 82b
Goethe, **III** 84a, 84b
Gothic, **II** 367a, 368a–368b, 370b, 371b, 372a, 372b, 373b; **III** 243a
Gottschall, **III** 83a
Gourmont, **IV** 332a, 332b
Graf, **III** 84b
Granet, **III** 82a
Grässe, **III** 85a
Gravina, **IV** 190b
Great Britain, **III** 82a–82b, 83a, 83b

Greece (ancient), **II** 674a–679b, 682a, 683b–684a; **III** 81b, 82a, 527b; **IV** 228a, 330a, 330b, 331b
Greenlaw, **III** 85b
Grimme, **IV** 197b
Guérard, **III** 83a
Guizot, **IV** 189b
happiness and pleasure, **II** 385a
Hardy, **III** 84b
harmony, **II** 388b–389a
Hartmann, **III** 84b–85a
Hassan, **III** 88b
Haym, **IV** 189a, 197a
Hegel, **III** 88b
Heine, **IV** 189a
Herder, **III** 82a, 85b; **IV** 203a
hierarchy, **II** 440b
history, **III** 82b, 85a, 85b; **IV** 332a
holy, **II** 513a
Homer, **III** 86a
Horace, **IV** 330b, 331a
Huch, **IV** 197a
Hugo, **IV** 332b
human nature, **III** 571a, 571b, 572a, 572b
humanism, **II** 515b–517a, 518a–520a, 522a–523a; **IV** 124a, 130b, 131a, 134b
humanities, **III** 83a
Hurd, **IV** 187b
Ibsen, **III** 84b
iconography, **II** 528a–529a, 530a, 531a, 537b
idea, **IV** 332a
imagery, **IV** 331b, 333a
impiety, **II** 564a
impressionism, **II** 567b, 574b–575b
India, **II** 670a
individualism, **IV** 333a
Ingram, **III** 82a
irony, **II** 628a, 629a, 630b, 631a, 632b, 633a
irrationalism, **II** 638a–638b
Italy, **III** 82a, 84b; **IV** 331a
James, **IV** 332b
Jay, **IV** 190b
Johnson, Samuel, **III** 81b–82a
Jonson, Ben, **IV** 331b, 332a
Jost, **IV** 187a
Julius Caesar, **III** 81b
Kames, **IV** 332a
Kant, **III** 85a
Keats, **III** 86a
Kermode, **IV** 196a
knowledge, **III** 81b
Koberstein, **III** 83a

Koch, **III** 84a, 84b
La Bruyère, **IV** 331b
Laharpe, **IV** 332a
Lamy, **IV** 331b, 332a, 332b
language, **II** 660b, 661a, 664b–666a, 667a, 670a; **III** 86a–86b; **IV** 330a, 331a, 332a–333a
Laplace, **III** 83b
Lasserre, **IV** 196b
Latin language, **III** 81b, 82a; **IV** 330a
law, **II** 674a–679b, 682a, 683b–684a, 690a
Lawrence, **III** 88a
Leibniz, **III** 86b
Leopardi, **III** 85b
Lessing, **III** 82a
levels, **IV** 331a–332b
Lévi-Strauss, **IV** 327b
Lewes, **IV** 332b
Liberia, **III** 337b
Lie, **III** 85b
linguistics, **IV** 327b, 425b
Locke, **IV** 332a
Longinus, **IV** 330b, 331b, 332b
López Soler, **IV** 191a
love, **III** 94a, 98a, 101b, 102b, 103b, 104b, 105b, 106a
loyalty, **III** 112a
lyricism, **III** 87b, 88a
Machiavellism, **III** 118a–119a, 121b, 122b, 123b, 124a, 124b
McLuhan, **III** 88b
macrocosm, **III** 127b–128a
magic, **III** 246a
Mallarmé, **III** 88b
Man-Machine, **III** 143a, 146a
mannerism, **IV** 331b
Marmontel, **III** 81b; **IV** 332a
Marxism, **III** 149b
Mathieu of Vendôme, **IV** 331a
meanings of, **III** 85b
Medici family, **III** 506a
Meister, **III** 83a
Meltzl, **III** 84a–84b
metaphor, **III** 202b, 204b, 206b; **IV** 330b, 331b
metaphysical imagination, **III** 208b, 209b, 211b
meter, **III** 86b
Mickiewicz, **IV** 191b
Middle Ages, **III** 81b, 82b, 528a; **IV** 331a
Mignet, **IV** 190a
Mill, **III** 85b; **IV** 199a
Milton, **III** 82a
Moir, **IV** 193a

Montaigne, **III** 82b, 86a; **IV** 331b
Monteggio, **IV** 191a
Montgomery, **III** 84b
motif, **III** 236a–238a, 240b, 241b–242a, 244b–253b
movement, **IV** 332a
music, **II** 388b–389a; **III** 265a, 266b, 269b, 270a
mythology, **III** 272a, 274b, 275b, 288a–290a, 292b–293a, 294a–300b, 301b, 306b, 316b; **IV** 46a
Nadler, **IV** 197a
nationalism, **III** 83a–83b, 324b; **IV** 332a
naturalism in art, **III** 339a
Nature, **III** 82b; **IV** 332a
neo-classicism, **I** 455b
neo-classicism in art, **III** 362a, 363b, 367a, 370b, 371a
new concepts in, **III** 88a–88b
New French critics, **III** 86a
Newman, **IV** 332b
Newton, **III** 392a; **IV** 332a
Nisard, **IV** 196b
Noël, **III** 83b
Novalis, **IV** 188a–188b, 189a, 196b
novel, **III** 85b, 86a, 86b, 87a, 242b
Opitz, **IV** 331b
oral, **III** 86a, 88b, 237a
organicism, **III** 423a, 423b, 426a
Orientalism, **III** 428a, 428b, 429a, 429b–431b, 438b
pangenesis, **II** 622b
Parrington, **III** 83a
passions, **IV** 332a
pastoral, **IV** 331a
Pater, **IV** 193b
Pellegrini, **IV** 190a
perennial philosophy, **III** 459a–459b
periodization in history, **III** 477b, 479b
periodization in literary history, **III** 481b–486a
Perrault, **III** 83a
Petersen, **IV** 197a
Petherham, **III** 82a
Petrarch, **IV** 121b, 124a
Pezzi, **IV** 190b
Phelps, **IV** 193b
phenomenology, **III** 242b
philanthropy, **III** 487b
philosophy, **III** 82b, 85b–88b; **IV** 332a
physiology, **IV** 332b
Piciarelli, **IV** 190b
Pietism, **III** 493b–495a

235

Plato, III 86a, 495b–502a, 518b–519a, 571a; IV 330b, 332b
Platonism, III 495b–502a, 506a, 506b–508a, 510b, 511a, 512b, 518b–519a, 519b, 521b, 523b–525a; IV 330b, 331b
poetry, III 85a–88a, 525b, 526a, 530b, 531a, 531b; IV 330b, 331a, 466b, 476a
Pollock, III 86a–86b
Poulet, II 242b; IV 196b
primitivism, III 593b, 601a, 602a, 603b, 604a
progress, III 628a, 638a
prose, III 82b, 85a; IV 330b
protest movements, III 671a, 671b, 672a
Proust, IV 330b
psychology, IV 1a, 16a, 16b, 22b, 24a, 25a, 330b
Puibusque, III 84a
Quintilian, III 81b; IV 330b, 331a, 331b, 332a
Rabelais, III 82b
Raleigh, IV 332b
Rank, III 242a
Rapin, IV 331b
rationalism, IV 46a, 48b–49a, 332a
reason, IV 332a
recapitulation, IV 58a
re-defined, III 88a–88b
reformation, IV 60b, 61b
religion, III 202b, 204b, 206b; IV 94a, 109b, 110b
Remak, IV 196a
Renaissance, III 81b, 82b; IV 121b–124a, 125b, 126b, 127a, 127b, 130b, 131a, 134b, 141a, 142a, 146a, 147a–152a, 331a–331b, 437b, 439a, 439b, 440a, 441a, 441b, 442b, 443a
Renan, III 82b
revolution, IV 154a, 154b, 157b, 159b, 162a
rhetoric, III 87b; IV 171b, 172b, 330a–333a
Richards, III 88a; IV 332a
Robortello, IV 331a
Rollin, IV 332a
romanticism, IV 199a, 203a, 204a, 205a, 207a, 208a, 209b, 330b, 332a–332b
Rome (ancient), II 690a; III 528a; IV 330b, 331a, 370a
Ronsard, IV 331a, 331b
Roscoe, III 83a
Sainte-Beuve, III 84a

Sallust, IV 331b
salvation, IV 228a, 233a
Sanskrit, IV 331a
Sartre, III 88a
satire, IV 211a, 212b, 214a, 214b, 216a
Saussure, IV 189b, 333a
Scaliger, IV 331b
Schelling, IV 189a
Schlegel, August Wilhelm von, III 84a; IV 188a–190a, 191a–192b, 193b, 194a, 197a
Schlegel, Friedrich, III 84a, 519a, 519b; IV 188a, 188b, 192a, 192b, 195b, 197a, 208a
Schopenhauer, IV 332b
science, III 85b, 86b; IV 332a, 332b
Scott, III 85a
Scudéry, Georges de, IV 187a
Scudéry, Magdeleine de, IV 187a
sculpture, IV 331b
secular, III 82b
Selden, III 81b
Senancour, IV 190a
Seneca, III 331b
sermons, III 87b
Shakespeare, III 82a, 86a
Shaw, IV 193a
sin, IV 228a, 233a
Singer, IV 192a
Sismondi, IV 189b, 190b, 192a
social contract, IV 252a
Socrates, IV 330b
Sontag, III 88b
sound patterns, III 86b
Spain, III 601a–601b
Spencer, IV 332a
Staël, IV 189b, 190a, 190b, 192a, 193b
Stapfer, IV 189b
Steiner, III 88b
Stevenson, IV 332b
Strich, IV 197a
structuralism, IV 322b, 327b, 328b, 329b, 333a
style, III 88a; IV 147a, 330a–333a
sublime in external nature, IV 334b, 336b
surrealism, II 638a; III 242b
Swift, III 84b; IV 332a
symbolism, IV 337b–345b
syntax, IV 332a
Taine, IV 332a
Tasso, III 84b
technique, IV 330b
temperance, IV 366a, 368b, 369b, 370a, 372a, 377a

Tertullian, III 81b
Tesauro, IV 331b
theology, III 82b
Theophrastus, IV 331a
theriophily, IV 388b
thought, IV 332a
Tieck, IV 189a, 194b, 197a
Tieghen, IV 196b
time, IV 399b
Tiraboschi, III 82a
traditional genres of, III 87b
tragic sense, IV 414a–414b
transcendentalism, IV 24a
Trissino, IV 331a
Trublet, III 82a
truth, I 322a
Uhland, IV 189a
uniformitarianism, IV 425b
U.S., III 85a, 428a, 428b, 429a, 429b–431b, 438b
universal man, IV 437b, 439a–443a
Utopia, IV 458b, 459b, 460a, 462a, 462b, 463b, 464a, 464b
Van Tieghem, III 85a
Vergil, IV 331a
Veselovsky, II 173a–174b; III 84b
Victorians, IV 219b, 221a, 222a, 223a
Villemain, III 83b–84a; IV 191a
Villers, IV 189b
Vilmar, III 83a
virtue, IV 368b
Visconti, IV 190b
Vives, IV 331b
vocabulary, IV 331a
Volksgeist, IV 492a, 493b, 494a
Voltaire, III 81b, 82a; IV 332a
Voss, IV 189a
vox populi, IV 497b, 498b
Vyazemsky, IV 191b
Wachler, Ernst, III 83a
Wachler, Ludwig, III 85a
Wackernagel, IV 332b
war, IV 500b, 501a, 504a
Warton, IV 187b, 188a, 189b, 190b, 191b, 194a, 195a, 195b
Weisinger, IV 192a
Wellek, IV 195b–196a
Weltschmerz, IV 204a
wisdom of the fool, IV 515b, 516a, 517a, 517b–520a
witchcraft, IV 522b
women, IV 523a, 523b, 524a
words, III 241b; IV 330b, 332a
Wordsworth, IV 332b

Zeitgeist, IV 535b, 536b
Lithuania, nationalism, III 335a
Lithuanian language, III 68b
Littré, Maximilien Paul Émile (1801–1881)
classicism, I 450a
Comte and, III 536b, 537b, 642b
positivism, III 536b, 537b
progress, III 627b, 642b
Liturgical music, III 265b, 266a, 269b, 270a, 270b
Liu Hsi (2nd century B.C.), classification of the sciences, I 464a
Liu Shau-tze, nationalism, III 334a
Livy (59 B.C.–17 A.D.)
analogy, I 69b
constitutionalism, I 488b
dignity, IV 141b
historiography, II 469b–470a, 477a, 487a, 491b
necessity, III 356a
periodization in history, III 476b
reformation, IV 61b
temperance, IV 370b
virtù, IV 478a, 480a
vox populi, IV 497b
Llewellyn, Karl
law, III 4b, 27b
pragmatism, III 553b
Lloyd, W. F.
economic history, II 50b
utility, IV 450a, 454a
Lloyd George, David (1863–1945), welfare state, IV 511b
Lobachevsky, Nicolai Ivanovich (1793–1856)
cosmology, I 555a
relativity, IV 87a–87b
space, IV 302b, 304a
Lobeck, Christian August (1781–1860), mythology, III 306a
Loeb, Jacques (1859–1924), psychology, IV 14b
Locarno Pact, III 452b
Locke, John (1632–1704),
abstortion, I 7a
anthropology, III 598b
appearance and reality, I 95b, 97b
atheism, IV 120a
authority, I 152b–153a, 657a
Bayle and, IV 120a
beauty, I 198b
behaviorism, I 219a, 220a, 221b
Bible, IV 258a

Blake and, II 412b; III 398b
causation, I 276b, 290b, 296a
certainty, I 304b, 306a, 308a, 311b, 317b
Chain of Being, II 446b
change, IV 395a
children, III 469b
choice, II 239a
class, I 448a
classification of the sciences, I 465a
community, III 21a
conscience, III 42b, 43a
conservatism, I 483b, 484a
constitutionalism, I 488b
cosmos, II 446b
Counter-Enlightenment, II 108a
custom, III 598b
deism, I 650b
democracy, I 656a, 657a–657b, 669a
Descartes and, II 450a
despotism, II 4a–7b
determinism, II 239a–239b
economic history, II 45b, 57b
economics, IV 259a
education, III 469b
Edwards and, IV 109b
empiricism, III 195b, 546b; IV 199a
Enlightenment, II 89a–90a, 95a–96b; IV 120a
environment, II 120b
equality, I 448b; II 143a, 143b; III 11a, 21a
eschatology, II 160a
evil, III 469b
Filmer and, IV 258a
free will, II 239a–239b
freedom, II 239a; III 21a
French Revolution, IV 156b
general will, II 277a
genius, II 294b
God, I 488b; II 351b–352a, 446b; III 469a; IV 288a
good, III 598b; IV 178a
happiness, II 96b–97a, 379b, 380a, 381a
hedonism, II 239b, 380a, 380b
Hegel and, II 412b
heresy, II 429a
hierarchy, II 446a, 446b
Hobbes and, III 21a
human nature, III 643b
Hume and, IV 261b
idea, I 111b–113b, 114b, 116a; II 547a, 547b; III 598b
idealism, II 96a

ideology, II 553a
imprinting, II 584a
individualism, II 599a, 600a, 601b, 603b; III 21a; IV 120a
inequality, I 448a
infinity, II 446b, 606a
intolerance, IV 119b, 120a
judgment, II 239b
justice, II 658b
knowledge, I 218b; II 239a, 351b; III 216a
law, I 290b; III 11a
learning, II 584a
Leibniz and, II 446a; III 195b–196a
liberalism, III 37a, 40a, 42b–46a, 54b
liberty, II 95a, 239b; IV 154a
linguistics, III 73a, 75b
literature, IV 332a
Man-Machine, III 138b, 139a
materialism, II 450a
mathematics, III 183b
matter, III 195b–196a
memory, II 120b
metaphor, III 199b
metaphysical imagination, III 215b–216a, 516a
methodology, III 389a
mind, II 120b, 239a
monarchy, I 657b; IV 154a
money, II 57b
moral science, I 465a
moral sense, III 231b
morality, I 465a; III 469b; IV 178a
nationalism, III 326b
natural law, I 488b; III 21a, 21b
natural liberty, II 62a
natural rights, III 21a, 21b; IV 178a
natural sciences, I 465a
Nature, III 21a; IV 258b, 259a
necessity, II 239a; III 357b
Newton and, III 389a, 392a, 395b, 397a, 398b
oligarchy, I 657b
optics, III 392a, 395b, 397a, 398b
Orientalism, III 429a–429b
pain, II 381a
Paine and, IV 260b
patriarchalism, I 479b
perfectibility, III 469b
Platonism, III 506b, 516a
pleasure, II 379b, 380a, 381a
politics, II 6b–7a; III 21a; IV 120a, 258b, 262a

post-Kantianism, IV 209a
power, II 6b–7a, 239a, 239b; III 21a, IV 262a
pragmatism, III 553a, 566b
primitivism, III 598b
private property, II 62a, 379b; III 653b; IV 288a
probability, III 606b
progress, III 643b
psychology, II 239b; IV 11a, 11b, 19a, 19b, 20a, 21b, 22b
Pufendorf, IV 258b
radicalism, IV 258b
rationalism, II 553a; III 195b; IV 120a
reason, II 95b–96a, 96b–239b; III 21a; IV 258a
rebellion, IV 154a
religion, III 598b; IV 109b, 119b, 120a
revolution, IV 154a, 155b, 156b
right, IV 178a
rights, III 21a; IV 259a
Roman Catholic Church, IV 120a
romanticism, IV 199a, 202a, 209a
Rousseau and, IV 259a, 259b, 260a
science, I 465a
sensation, II 120b
sensationalism, II 96a
Shaftesbury and, III 598b
sin, III 469b
skepticism, IV 245b
slavery, II 6b–7b
social contract, III 21a; IV 252a, 253a, 255b, 257b–262a, 288a, 317a
socialism, IV 288a, 292a
society, II 62a; III 21a; IV 154a, 258a, 258b
sovereignty, I 657a
space, IV 295a, 303a
spiritualism, IV 120a
State, I 656a, 657a–657b, 659a; II 62a; IV 120a, 258b, 317a
style, IV 332a
tabula rasa, II 553a
temperament, III 469b
time, IV 394b, 395a, 397b, 404a
tribes, III 598b
trust, IV 258b, 259a
tyranny, III 21a; IV 259a
ut pictura poesis, IV 471a, 472a, 473b
utilitarianism, IV 120a
voluntariness, II 239a
wealth, IV 259a
wisdom, III 598b

Loeb, Jacques (1859–1924), association of ideas, I 115b–116a
behaviorism, I 221a
Löf, P. Martin, probability, III 623a
Logic
acquired characteristics, II 619b–620a, 622a
Agricola, II 519a
analogy, I 63a–63b
Aristotle, I 316a, 382b, 463a; II 663a, 663b, 666b; III 162b–173a, 176b, 380b, 381b–382a, 554a, 554b; IV 135a
art, I 459a
Avenarius, III 545b, 547b
Bacon, III 355b; IV 434a
Beckner, III 550b
behaviorism, III 549a, 549b
Bergmann, III 545b, 549a
Berlin Society of Scientific Empiricists, III 545b, 546a–550b
Bernays, III 547b
biology, III 548b, 549a, 550b
Boethius, I 381a
Boltzmann, III 545b
Bridgman, III 550b
Bühler, III 547a
Bunge, III 550a
Carnap, III 545b, 546a, 547b–550a
causation, III 546b
chemistry, III 548b
comedy, I 467b
communication, III 547a
Comte, III 535a
Counter-Enlightenment, II 101a
criticism, III 550b
deontic, I 172a; IV 183b
Descartes, III 356a, 384b; IV 435b
determinism, II 19b, 20a, 238b
Dewey, II 184b
Dingler, III 546a
Du Bois-Reymond, III 546a
dualism, III 549b
Dubislav, III 546a
education, III 550b
Einstein, III 545b, 546b, 549a
electrodynamic field theory, III 549a
electromagnetics, III 548b, 549a
emergentism, III 548b–549a
emotion, III 550a
Engels, II 454b, 455a

epistemology, III 547b, 548a
ethics, III 568b; IV 319a–320b, 322a
Feigl, III 546a, 550a, 550b
Feyerabend, III 550b
Fitzgerald, III 546b
Frank, III 546a, 548a
Frege, III 545b, 547b, 548a, 550a
Galen, III 381a
game theory, II 263b, 266b
geometry, III 547a
Gerbert, I 381a
Gödel, III 545b
good, IV 183b–184a, 185b, 186a
Grelling, III 546a
Grünbaum, III 550a
Hahn, III 545b, 548a, 548b
Hanson, III 550b
happiness, II 375a, 386a
health, II 396b
Hegel, II 407b, 412a, 414b; III 358b, 556b
Hegelianism, III 546a
Helmer, III 546a
Helmholtz, III 545b
Hempel, III 546a, 550a
Hertz, III 545b
hierarchy, II 444b
Hilbert, III 545b, 547b
historicism, II 463a–463b
Hobbes, IV 434a
holy, II 513a
Hull, III 549a
humanism, II 519a, 519b, 520b; IV 129a, 129b, 134b–135b
Hume, III 545b, 546b, 547a, 550b
Husserl, III 550a
idea, II 542a–543a
indeterminacy, II 592a
induction, III 550a
intuition, III 547b
Islam, II 640b, 644a, 645a, 648a
James, III 546b, 562a
Kant, I 316a; III 547a, 547b, 562a; IV 433b
knowledge, III 379b, 547b, 548a, 549b
Köhler, III 549a
Kraft, III 545b–546a
Kraus, III 546a
Kuhn, III 550b
language, II 661a, 663a, 663b, 666b, 668b; III 546a–548a, 549b, 550b
Lavoisier, III 546b
Leibniz, IV 382a; IV 435b
linguistics, III 72a; IV 425a
literary paradox, III 76b,

77a, 77b, 78a
Locke, III 546b
Lorentz, III 546b
Mach, III 545b, 546a, 547b, 550b
macrocosm and microcosm, III 127a, 129a
Marx, II 454a
materialism, II 453b, 454a, 454b, 455a
mathematics, III 172a, 172b, 175a–177a, 180a, 184a, 547b, 548a
matter, III 546b
medieval science, II 199a, 204b
Meehl, III 550b
Megaric-Stoic, I 164a–164b
Menger, III 545b
metaphor, III 198b, 201a
metaphysical imagination, III 209a, 213b–215a, 547a, 551a
methodology, III 379b–385a
Middle Ages, III 528a
Mill, I 318b; III 545b
Mises, III 546a
molecular biology, III 549a
monism, III 549b, 550a
Morris, III 547a
mythology, III 316b–317a, 317b
Nagel, III 550a
natural science, III 549b
Nature, III 348a, 547a, 548b, 549a
necessity, III 351b–352a, 353a, 356a, 356b, 357b, 358b, 359a, 359b, 361b
Neo-Platonism, III 377a
Neurath, III 545b, 548b
neurophysiology, III 549b, 550a
Newton, III 379b–385a, 546b, 549a
numbers, III 403b, 406a, 406b
operationalism, III 550b
optics, III 548b
organicism, III 422a, 425a, 427a
Parmenides, IV 400a
Peirce, III 546b, 552b, 553a, 555a, 556b, 558a, 559a–559b, 560a, 560b–561a, 567a, 568a, 568b
perennial philosophy, III 459a–462b
Petrarch, IV 129b
phenomenalism, III 548a, 548b, 549b, 550b
philosophy, III 198b, 201a,

546a, 547b, 548b, 549b, 550a, 550b, 551a
physics, III 547b, 548b–550b
Plato, III 499b, 546b, 554a
Platonism, III 499b, 503b
pleasure, II 375a, 386a
poetry, III 526a, 528a
Popper, I 323b; III 545b, 550b
positivism, III 535a, 538a, 545b–551a
pragmatism, III 546b, 549a, 551a, 552b, 553a, 554a–561a, 562a, 567a, 568a–568b
Pratt, III 550b
primitivism, III 585b
probability, III 550a, 606b, 608b, 611a, 612a, 615a, 617a, 618b, 623a
psychology, III 548a–549b, 550b; IV 27b
Putnam, III 550b
quantum mechanics, III 548b, 549a, 550b
quantum physics, III 549a
Quine, III 547a
Ramism, IV 42b–43b, 44a, 44b, 45a, 45b
rationalism, IV 46a
reductionism, III 547b–550a
Reichenbach, III 546a, 547b, 548a, 550a, 550b
Reidemeister, III 545b
Renaissance, IV 122a, 129a, 129b, 134b–135b, 438b
rhetoric, IV 168b, 169a, 169b, 170b
Riemann, III 545b
right, IV 183b–184a, 185b, 186a
romanticism, IV 210b
Russell, I 319b–320a, 320b–321b; III 545b, 547b, 548a, 549a
Ryle, III 549a, 549b
Saint Augustine, II 230a, 230b, 231a
satire, IV 216a
Schaffner, III 550b
Schlick, III 545b, 548a
science, III 546b, 547b–551a
scientific classification, I 463a, 464b–466b
Sellars, III 550a
Singer, III 549a
skepticism, IV 236a, 237a, 246a, 250b
Skinner, III 549a–549b

Smart, III 550a
social science, III 548b, 549a
space, III 546b, 550a; IV 295a
Spinoza, II 238b, 444b
Stegmüller, III 550a
Stevens, III 550b
Stoicism, IV 319a, 319b–320a, 320b, 322a
structuralism, IV 329b, 330a
symbolism, IV 337b, 338a
theodicy, IV 379a, 380a, 382a
thermodynamics, III 548b
thought, III 550a
time, III 546b, 550a; IV 394b, 400a
Toulmin, III 550b
tragedy, I 467b
uniformitarianism, IV 425a
unity, III 548a–549b
unity of science, IV 431a, 433a, 433b, 434a, 435b, 436a
universal man, IV 438b
Vailati, III 560a
Valla, II 519a; IV 135a–135b
Victorians, IV 218a, 219b
Vienna Circle of Logical Positivists, III 545b, 546a–550b
vitalism, III 548b–549a
Waismann, III 545b
Watson, J. B., III 549a
Watson, W. H., III 550b
Weiss, III 549a
Wertheimer, III 549a
Whewell, I 318b
Whitehead, III 545b, 547b, 548a
Wittgenstein, III 545b, 546a, 546b, 548a, 549b, 550b
Woodger, III 550b
Wright, III 562a
Zilsel, III 545b
Logical space, IV 304b–305b
Logos
astrology, III 74b
design argument, I 671a, 671b
Erigena, I 574a
metaphysics, III 213b
mythology, III 276b, 284a, 307b
natural law, III 14b, 16a, 19b
organic purpose, II 282a
peace, III 440b
Platonism, III 505b
poetics, III 526a

psychology, **IV** 1a, 2a, 2b, 10a

rationalism, **IV** 46a, 47a, 51a

rhetoric, **IV** 168a

Saint Augustine, **III** 505b

Stoicism, **I** 45b; **IV** 319a–321a

syncretism, **I** 45b–46a

Zeno of Citium, **IV** 320b

Loisy, Alfred Firmin (1857–1940)

excommunication of, **I** 423b

God, **I** 420b, 421a

Jesus Christ, **I** 420b

modernism, **I** 419b, 420b–421a, 422a–424a, 425b, 426b

Saint Paul, **I** 421a

Loki (myth), **III** 282b

Lollards

heresy, **II** 418b, 420b

Waldensians, **II** 420b

Lomazzo, G. P. (1538–1600), art, **II** 303a, 305a, 308a

beauty, **II** 550a

genius, **II** 303a, 305a, 308a

mythology, **III** 293a, 295b, 297b, 298a, 299a

Lombard, Peter (1100?–1160), dignity, **IV** 138b, 140a, 140b

Lombroso, Cesare (1836–1909)

art, **II** 308b

genius and insanity, **II** 308b

Lomonosov, Mikhail Vasilievich (1711–1765), **I** 78b

Long, Huey P. (1893–1935), Machiavellism, **III** 124b

Longevity, **III** 89a–93b

Adam (Bible), **III** 90a

aging, **III** 89b

alchemy, **III** 91a–91b

Alexander the Great, **III** 90a–90b

anabiosis, **III** 92a

antediluvian legend, **III** 90a

apologism, **III** 89a, 89b–90a, 92b

Aristotelianism, **III** 90a, 92a

Aristotle, **III** 89b–90a

Avicenna, **III** 89b–90a, 91b

Bacon, Francis, **III** 92a

Bacon, Roger, **III** 90a

Bernard, **III** 93a

Bible, **III** 90a

biomedicine, **III** 89a, 91a, 92b, 93a

Brown-Séquard, **III** 93a

Buddhism, **III** 90a

Celts, **III** 90a

China, **III** 90b, 91a

Christianity, **III** 90a, 91b, 92b

Chuang Tzu, **III** 90b

Cicero, **III** 91b

cognitive dissonance, **III** 89b

communism, **III** 93a

Comte, **III** 93a

Condorcet, **III** 92a, 92b

Cornaro, **III** 91b

cosmology, **III** 90a

cryonics, **III** 93a

Darwin, **III** 92b

death, **III** 89b

Descartes, **III** 91b–92a

dietary techniques, **III** 91a

disease, **III** 90a

endocrinology, **III** 93a

Enlightenment, **III** 91b, 92a

Epicureanism, **III** 89b

etiology, **III** 91b

Fountain of Youth, **III** 90a–90b

Franklin, **III** 92a

Frazer, **III** 89b

Freud, **III** 92b

Fyodorov, **III** 92b

Galen, **III** 89b–90a, 91b

geriatrics, **III** 93a

gerontology, **III** 89b, 93a

Gilgamesh (myth), **III** 89b

Godwin, **III** 92a

Goethe, **III** 92b

Gompertz curve, **III** 89b

Greece (ancient), **III** 89b, 90a

Gruman, **III** 89a

Haller, **III** 91b

Harvey, **III** 91b

Hesiod, **III** 89b

Hinduism, **III** 89b

Holy Grail, **III** 90a

Hufeland, **III** 91b, 92b

Humane Societies, **III** 92a

Huxley, **III** 89b

hygiene, **III** 91b

hyperborean legend, **III** 90a

immortality, **III** 89a–89b, 90b

Jabir, **III** 91a

Juvenal, **III** 89b

Kirk, Hyland, **III** 93a

Ko Hung, **III** 91a

Koran, **III** 90b

Lao Tzu, **III** 90b

Lieh Tzu, **III** 90b

life expectancy, **III** 89a–89b

Lucretius, **III** 89b

magic, **III** 90b

Malthus, **III** 92a–92b

Marcus Aurelius, **III** 89b

Marxism, **III** 93a

Medawar, **III** 93a

medicine, **III** 89a, 89b, 92b

meliorism, **III** 89a, 91b, 92b, 93a

Metchnikoff, **III** 92b–93a

mythology, **III** 89b, 90a–90b

Napoleon I, **III** 92b

Neo-Platonism, **III** 91a

Newton, **III** 92a

organ transplants, **III** 93a

overpopulation, **III** 92a

Pandora (myth), **III** 89b

pantheism, **III** 90b

Paracelsus, **III** 91b

philosophy, **III** 89b, 92a, 92b

physiology, **III** 90b

Ponce de León, **III** 90b

prolongevity, **III** 89a–93b

Prometheus (myth), **III** 89b

psychoanalysis, **III** 92b

religion, **III** 90a, 90b, 92a, 93a

Renaissance, **III** 89a, 91b

romanticism, **III** 92b

Rome (ancient), **III** 89b, 91b

Saint Augustine, **III** 90a

Saint Thomas Aquinas, **III** 90a

science, **III** 89a, 89b, 92b

senescence, **III** 92b

Shelley, **III** 92b

sociology, **III** 89a

Stephens, **III** 93a

Stoicism, **III** 89b

Sweetser, **III** 93a

Swift, **III** 89b

Tantrism, **III** 90a

Taoism, **III** 90a, 90b, 91a, 93a

Tennyson, **III** 89b

therapy, **III** 91b

Thoms, **III** 91b

Tithonus (myth), **III** 89b

transformation, **III** 90b, 91a

utopianism, **III** 92b

Vedanta, **III** 90a

Voronoff, **III** 93a

Weber, **III** 90b

Weismann, **III** 92b

Wilde, **III** 89b

Yoga, **III** 90a

Longfellow, Henry Wadsworth (1807–1882)

God, **II** 434a

Hermeticism, **II** 433a, 434a

immortality, **I** 646a

Orientalism, **III** 429a, 434a–434b

transcendentalism, **III** 429a, 434a–434b

Longfield, M., economic history, **II** 50b

Longinus (3rd century A.D.)

art, **II** 304b

imagination, **I** 586a

individualism, **II** 304b

literary criticism, **I** 596b

literature, **IV** 330b, 331b, 332b

organicism, **III** 423b, 424b

poetics, **III** 526a, 527a, 528a

rhetoric, **IV** 169b–170a

style, **IV** 330b, 331b, 332b

sublime in external nature, **IV** 333b

Longobardi, Father Nicolas China, **I** 357a

Confucianism, **I** 357a

Lopez de Gomara, Francisco (1510–?1560), historiography, **IV** 149a

Lopez Pinciano, poetics, **III** 529b

López Soler, romanticism, **IV** 191a

L'Orange, H. P., iconography, **II** 537b

Lorentz, Hendrik Antoon (1853–1928)

entropy, **II** 114b

Einstein and, **IV** 80a

empiricism, **III** 546b

relativity, **IV** 79a–79b, 80a, 83a, 83b, 89a

Lorentz transformation, relativity, **IV** 79b, 80a, 83a, 83b, 84b

Lorenz, Konrad

anarchy, **I** 74b

imprinting, **II** 585a, 585b

psychology, **IV** 15a

theriophily, **IV** 388b

war, **IV** 507b

Lorenzetti, Ambrogio (c. 1300–?1348), temperance, **IV** 374a

Lorrain, Claude (1600–1682), impressionism, **II** 577b–578a

ut pictura poesis, **IV** 469b

Loschi, Antonio, humanism, **II** 522b

Loschmidt, Josef, entropy, **II** 117a

Lossius, J. C. ideal, **II** 551b

Lost Paradise (myth), progress, **III** 624b, 625a, 629a, 629b, 631a

Lot (Bible), mythology, **III** 275b

Loti, Pierre (1850–1923), China, **I** 369a

Lotto, Lorenzo (c. 1480–c. 1556), iconography, **II** 529a

Lotze, Rudolph Hermann

(1817–1881), pragmatism, III 562a, 563a

Louis I, King of Bavaria (1786–1868), romanticism, IV 207b

Louis VII, King (1121?–1180), love, III 102a

Louis IX, King (1214–1270)
city, I 429a
nationalism, III 321a

Louis XIV, King (1638–1715), I 356b, 363b, 364a, 401b; II 221b, 303b
absolutism, II 8a
balance of power, I 183a–183b, 184a
conservation, I 473a
Counter-Enlightenment, II 106b, 111b
despotism, II 2a, 8a, 8b, 14a–14b
Gallicanism, I 399b
Huguenots, IV 113b
Jansenism, I 400a
love, III 103a
papacy, I 399b
periodization in literary history, III 483a
religion, IV 113b
tolerance, I 401a

Louis XV, King (1710–1774), balance of power, I 186a

Louis XVI, King (1754–1793), I 661b
Counter-Enlightenment, II 110b, 111b
historiography, II 498a

Louvois, Marquis de (1641–1691), despotism, II 8b

Lovati, Lovato, humanism, II 517b

Love, III 94a–108a
Abélard, III 98a, 98b, 103a, 107b
Admetus (myth), III 96a
agapē, III 94b, 96b, 97a, 107b
Albigensian Crusade, III 102b
Alcestis (myth), II 96a
Al-Hallaj of Bagdad, III 99b
Anabaptists, III 107b
angels, III 101b
Aphrodite (myth), III 94b, 95a
Arabia, III 99b, 100b
Arbrissel, III 98a, 99a, 99b, 100a
Aristippus of Cyrene, III 95b
Aristophanes, III 95a
Aristotle, II 210b; III 95a, 95b, 110b–111a

art, III 97b, 103b, 106a–106b, 107a
asceticism, III 96b, 99b
astronomy, III 106b
attraction, III 94b
Baudelaire, III 104a–104b
beauty, I 205a–205b; III 231a
Belle Époque, III 105b
Bembo, III 512b
Berdayev, III 97a
Béroul, III 98b
Bible, III 96a–96b, 97a, 98a, 100a, 101a
Boccaccio, II 234a
bourgeois, III 103b, 104a–104b, 105b, 106a
Brahminism, III 100a
Brontë sisters, III 104b
Bruno, III 513b
Buddhism, III 100a
Byron, III 507a
capitalism, III 104a, 107b
Castiglione, III 512b
catharis, III 98a, 98b, 99b, 100a, 107a
Catharism, III 98a, 98b, 99b, 100a, 107a
Catullus, III 104a
censorship, III 106a
charity, II 209b, 210a, 210b, 212a, 215a
chess, III 98b
chivalry, III 97a–100a, 101b, 102b
Chrétien de Troyes, III 102a
Christianity, III 94b, 96b, 97a, 97b, 100a–101b, 104a, 105b
communication, III 507a
cosmos, III 94a, 94b, 106b
conjugality, III 100b
cortezia, III 97b, 100a, 101b–103a, 104a, 107b
court of love, III 98b, 102a
courtesy, III 102b
courtly love, III 97b–100a, 101b–104a, 107b
courtship, III 95b, 99a, 100a
Creation, III 94a
Crusades, III 99b
culture, III 94a, 100b, 104a, 104b, 106b
Dante, III 102b, 105b, 511a; IV 177a
death, III 96a, 98b, 104b
defined, III 94a
Democritus, III 106b
determinism, II 237b, 238a, 238b
Diana (myth), III 95a
dignity, IV 138b, 142b–143a

divine, III 94a, 95a, 98b, 99b, 101b
Don Juan (fiction), III 103a
Durkheim, III 97b
economics, III 104a, 104b
education, III 106a
Edwards, IV 109b, 110a, 111a
Eleanor of Aquitaine, III 102a
Empedocles, III 94b, 95a, 187a; IV 2b
Engels, III 104b
Enlightenment, III 107b
Epicurus, III 95b
Erigena, II 210b
Eros, III 94b, 95a, 96b
eroticism, III 94a, 96b, 104a, 106a, 107a, 107b
Euripides, III 95a
Eurydice, III 96a
evangelicalism, III 96b
evil, III 104b
existentialism, III 160a
family, III 100b
femininity, III 107a
fertility, III 100b
Ficino, II 442a; III 410b, 473a, 511a, 511b, 512b
Fourier, III 104a
France, III 97b–100a, 102a, 103a
Franciscans, III 98b
free will, II 237b, 238a, 238b, 244a
Freud, II 104b–105b, 106a
friendship, III 94a, 94b
genital, III 105a
Gnosticism, III 96b, 107a
God, II 209b–210a, 237b, 244a, 351a, 360b, 361a; III 94a, 96a, 96b, 97a, 98a, 100b, 101a, 101b, 106b, 469a; IV 381a
good, IV 174a, 175a, 177a, 178a
Greece (ancient), III 94b–96a, 97a
Gregory VIII (Pope), III 97b
guilt, III 100b
happiness, II 379a
Hardy, III 104b
harmony, II 390b, 391a, 391b, 393a; III 94b–95a
Hegel, II 409a, 411a; III 160a
Héloise, III 98a
Helvétius, II 451a
Henry II, III 102a
Heraclitus, III 94b
heresy, III 97b–100a, 101b, 102b, 107a
Hermeticism, II 432a
heterodoxy, III 97b

hierarchy, II 439a, 442a
Hinduism, III 95a
hippies, III 107a, 107b
Holbach, II 451a
Holy Grail, III 102a
homosexuality, III 95a
humanism, III 100a
Hutcheson, III 231a, 231b
Ibn-Arabi of Murcia, III 99b, 101a
Ibn-Dawoud, III 99b
Ibn-Hazm, III 107b
ideal, III 96a, 98b, 100b, 104a, 105a–105b, 107b
illuminists, IV 109a
incontinence, III 96b
individualism, III 104a
industry, III 104a
Inquisition, III 102b
instinct, III 94a
Ishtar (myth), III 94b
Islam, III 99b, 100a, 101a, 101b
Isolde (fiction), III 96a, 98b, 102a, 104b, 105b, 106a
Jesus Christ, III 96a–97a
Joachim of Floris, III 107b
Judaism, III 96a, 100b, 636a
Jung, III 107a, 107b
Kama-Sutra (myth), III 100b
Kierkegaard, III 104a
King, Martin Luther, I 438b–439a
Koran, III 100a
Laodamia (myth), III 96a
Leibniz, IV 382a
lewdness, III 96b
literary paradox, III 80a
literature, III 94a, 98a, 101b, 102b, 103b, 104b, 105b, 106a
Louis VII, III 102a
Louis XIV, III 103a
loyalty, III 109b, 110b, 112a
love tribunals, III 103b
Luther, II 212a; IV 66b
lyricism, III 99a–99b
Machiavelli, IV 481b
magic, III 107a
Manicheism, III 97b, 98a, 99b, 100a, 102b, 107a
Marie de Champagne, III 102a, 103b
Marivaux, II 96b
marriage, III 95a–98b, 101a, 102b, 103b–105b, 107b
Marx, III 104b, 105a, 160a
Mary Magdalene (Bible), III 96b
masculinity, III 107a
materialism, II 451a

matter, III 187a
Medici, III 511a
metaphysics, III 95b, 99b
Methodius, III 97a
Middle Ages, III 96a, 103b
money, III 104a, 104b, 105a
Montaigne, III 103b
moral sense, III 231a, 231b
morality, III 95a, 97b, 99a, 100b–106b
motion pictures, III 106a
Mozart, III 103b
Muhammadanism, III 100b
music, II 390b, 391a, 391b, 393a; III 94a, 99a, 101a, 101b, 104b, 106a
Musil, III 106a
mysticism, III 99b, 100b, 101a, 101b, 102b, 104a
mythology, III 94a, 96a, 98b, 105b, 106a, 282b, 295b–296a, 297b, 304b
Nabokov, III 106a
Nature, III 100a–100b
Novalis, III 103b
novel, III 106a
nudity, III 106a
Oedipus complex, III 105a
Origen, II 210a
Orpheus (myth), III 96a
Ortega y Gasset, III 95b
paganism, III 96a
painting, III 106a
pan-sexuality, III 105b
passions, III 94a, 97b, 101b, 102a, 103a–104b, 105b–107a
Paulines, III 98a
peace, III 440b, 441a, 445b, 447a
Peirce, III 560b
perfectibility, III 463b, 468b, 469a, 473a, 474b
Petrarch, III 510a, 511a, 511b, 512b
Philippa of Aragon, III 99a, 99b
philosophy, III 94b, 95a
physics, III 106b
physiology, III 94a, 97a
Pico della Mirandola, III 512a
Plato, II 648b; III 94a, 95a, 95b, 96a, 499a, 507a, 508b; IV 175a
Platonism, II 648b; III 95b–96a, 499a, 506a, 507a–508b, 510a–514b, 516a, 523b
pleasure, II 379a
Plutarch, III 94b, 96a
poetry, III 94a, 97b–100a, 101a–102b, 104a, 107b,

530a
power, III 94a, 107b
pragmatism, III 560b
Prévost, II 96b
Proclus, II 439a
profane love, III 99a–99b
progress, III 636a
prohibitions, III 106a
Propertius, III 96a
prophecy, III 665b
Protesilaus (myth), III 96a
Proust, III 105b
pseudo-Manicheism, III 105b
psychology, III 94a, 97b, 104b; IV 2b, 19a, 20a
puberty, III 100b
Racine, III 103a
Reformation, III 107a
religion, III 98b, 100a–100b, 101b, 103a, 103b, 106a, 107a, 107b; IV 109a, 109b, 110a, 111a, 111b, 118b
Renaissance, III 95b, 508b, 510a–514b, 516a, 523b; IV 138b, 142b–143a
repulsion, III 94b
rhetoric, III 99a–99b, 100a
Richard the Lion-Hearted, III 102a
right, IV 174a, 175a, 177a, 178a
rights, III 104b
Rochefoucauld, III 103b
romanticism, III 98b, 100a–100b, 102b–103b, 104a, 105b; IV 195a, 203a, 204a, 206a
Round Table, III 98b, 101a, 102a
Rousseau, III 103a–103b
Rudel, III 102a
Ruzbehan of Shiraz, III 99b
Sacher-Masoch, III 105b
Sade, III 94a
Saint Augustine, II 237b, 238a; III 96b, 97a; IV 138b
Saint Bernard of Clairvaux, III 98b, 107b
Saint Francis of Assisi, III 98b; IV 65a
Saint Paul, III 96a–96b, 97a
Saint Theresa, III 101a
Satan, III 96b, 98a
science, III 94b, 105b, 106b, 107b
Seignobos, III 97b
self-control, III 102a
sentiment, III 103b–105b, 107b; IV 219b, 221a
sex, III 94a, 94b, 96b,

97a, 101b, 104a–106b, 107b
Shelley, III 508a
sin, III 96b, 97a, 107b
sociology, III 95b, 97a, 97b, 103a, 104a, 104b, 105b, 106b, 107a
Socrates, III 95a
soul, III 95b, 97b–99a, 101a, 101b, 104b, 106a–107b
Spain, III 99b
Spenser, III 514b
Spinoza, II 238b; III 512a–512b, 555a
spirituality, III 95a, 97b, 98a, 99a, 101a, 105b, 106b, 107a
Sufis, III 99b, 100a, 101a
Suhrawardī of Aleppo, III 99b
surrealism, III 107a, 107b
symbolism, III 104a
taboos, III 107b
Teilhard de Chardin, III 107a, 107b
temperance, IV 367b, 371a
Thanatos (myth), III 96a
theater, III 103a, 105b
theodicy, IV 381a, 382a
Tibullus, III 96a
Tolstoy, I 438a; III 445b
Tournament, III 102b–103a
tragic sense, IV 415b
Tristan (fiction), III 96a, 98b, 102a–103b, 104b, 105b, 106a
troubadours, III 95b, 97b–99b, 101a–102b, 103b, 104a, 105b, 106a, 107b
unconscious, III 107a
Upanishads, III 100b
utilitarianism, IV 446b
Valla, IV 142b–143a
Virgin Mary, III 98b, 107a
virtù, IV 481b
Voltaire, III 94a
Wagner, III 104b
war, III 101b, 102b–103a; IV 502a
William IX of Poitiers, III 98a, 99a–99b, 100a, 102a
wisdom of the fool, IV 519a
work, IV 531b
yin and yang, III 96a
Love, Alfred, international peace, III 449a
Lovejoy, Arthur O. (1873–1962)
academic freedom, I 11b
aesthetics, III 552b
belief, III 552b
Bergson and, III 552b
Chain of Being, I 325b,

326a, 327b, 329a, 330a, 333a
conservation, I 472a
cosmic images, I 513b
Dewey and, III 552b
dualism, II 41b
emotion, III 552b
ethics, III 552b
evolutionism, II 177a, 177b, 178a, 182b–183a
experience, III 552b
expressionism, II 206a
Gothic, II 368b
Hermeticism, II 433a
hierarchy, II 438b
idea, III 552b
instrumentalism, III 552b
James and, III 552b
judgment, III 552b
knowledge, III 552b, 553a
Mead and, III 552b
mythology, III 277a, 279a
Nature, III 346b, 350b
Peirce and, III 552b–553a
perception, III 552b
perennial philosophy, III 458b
personalism, III 552b, 553a
Platonism, III 508a
pragmatism, III 551a–551b, 552b–553a
progress, III 624a, 637a
psychology, III 552b
reason, I 329a
romanticism, IV 188a, 195b, 196a, 198a, 198b, 208a, 208b
Schiller and, III 552b, 553a
science, III 552b–553a
socialism, IV 285a–285b
society, III 552b
truth, III 552b–553a
utilitarianism, III 552b
value, III 552b
will to believe, III 552b
Lovelace, Richard (1618–1658), literary paradox, III 77b
Loveland, D. L., probability, III 623a
Lowell, Amy (1874–1925), China, I 369b
impressionism, II 575a
Lowell, James Russell (1819–1891)
art, II 305b
classicism, I 450a
genius, II 305b
Lowell, Percival (1855–1916), Buddhism, III 437a
Orientalism, III 437a
Lowie, Robert (1883–1957), Marxism, III 153b

Löwith, K.
  eschatology, II 157b
  Zeitgeist, IV 535b
Lowth, Robert (1710–1787),
  mythology, III 304a, 304b
Loyalty, III 108a–116a
  Abraham (Bible), III 108b
  absolutism, III 113a, 115a
  Akedah (Bible), III 109b
  Alexander the Great, III
    111a
  allegiance, III 113b
  Americanism, III 114a
  anarchy, III 112a
  Antigone (myth), III 110b
  Aristotle, III 110b–112a
  bad tendency doctrine, III
    114a
  Bible, III 108b–109b, 112a,
    115a
  blacklisting, III 114b
  blacks, III 113b
  Blackstone, III 113b, 114a
  brotherhood, III 111a,
    111b, 115b
  causation, III 115a
  censorship, III 113a
  Christianity, III 109a, 115a
  Cicero, III 112a
  city-state, III 110a, 111a,
    111b, 112a
  communism, III 113a, 114b
  conformism, III 108a
  Council of Europe, III 113a
  courage, III 110a, 110b
  culture, III 108b, 113a–
    113b
  covenant, III 112a, 112b
  David (Bible), III 108b
  defined, III 108a, 115a
  democracy, III 113a
  disloyalty, III 108b, 109a,
    110a, 111a, 113b–115a
  drama, III 112a
  environment, III 110b
  Epictetus, III 111a, 111b
  Ezra (Bible), III 108b
  fanaticism, III 113a
  fascism, III 112a
  fealty, III 112a
  feudalism, III 112a
  fidelity, III 111a, 111b, 115a
  friendship, III 110b, 111a,
    112b
  George III, III 114a
  God, III 108b, 109a, 109b,
    110b, 111b, 112a, 112b,
    115a
  government, III 108a, 110a,
    110b, 111a
  Great Britain, III 114a
  Greece (ancient), III 109b–
    111a, 112b
  Habakkuk (Bible), III 108b

  history, III 108b, 112b
  Hobbes, III 112a
  homage, III 112a
  idea, III 108b
  ideology, III 108b, 113a,
    115a
  Isaac (Bible), III 108b
  Jackson, Justice, III 113b
  Jefferson, III 114a
  Job (Bible), III 109a–109b
  John of Salisbury, III 112b
  Judaism, III 108b–109b,
    111b, 112a, 112b
  justice, III 110a, 111a,
    111b, 112a, 115a
  Kallen, III 113a
  Kennedy, J. F., III 113b
  Korean War, III 114b
  law, III 109a, 110b, 111b,
    112a, 112b, 113a, 114a,
    114b, 115b,
  League of Nations, III 113a
  literature, III 112a
  love, III 109b, 110b, 112a
  loyalty tests, III 114b
  McCarthy, Joseph, III 114b
  Machiavelli, III 113a; IV
    316b
  Magna Carta, III 112a–112b
  Marcus Aurelius, III 111b
  martyrdom, III 109a, 109b
  metaphysics, III 108b
  Middle Ages, III 112a
  militancy, III 113b
  morality, III 108b, 109b,
    110b, 111b, 112b, 113a,
    114a
  multiple, III 113a–113b
  nationalism, III 108a, 110a,
    110b, 111a, 113a, 113b,
    114b
  Nature, III 110b, 111b
  Nazism, III 113a
  Neo-Hegelianism, III 115a
  oratory, III 112a
  Organization of American
    States, III 113a
  Palmer, A. M., III 114a
  patriotism, III 108a–109b,
    114b
  personal, III 108a, 112a
  philosophy, III 108b, 109b,
    110a, 111b, 112a, 112b,
    113a, 115a–115b
  Plato, III 110a–112a
  pluralism, III 113a–113b,
    114b, 115a
  poetry, III 112a
  politics, III 108a, 110b,
    111b–113b, 115a
  polycentrism, III 114a
  psychology, III 108b
  religion, III 108b, 109a,
    112b, 113a, 113b, 115a

  resistance, III 112a, 112b
  romanticism, IV 205a, 206a
  Rome (ancient), III 109a
  Roosevelt, III 113a
  Royce, III 115a
  Saint Augustine, III 112b
  Saint Thomas Aquinas, III
    112b
  Saul (Bible), III 108b
  sedition, III 112b, 114a,
    114b
  self, III 108a, 111b
  self-control, III 110a
  socialism, III 114a
  society, III 108b, 110b,
    112a
  Socrates, III 109b–111b
  Solon, III 110a
  Sophocles, III 110a
  soul, III 110a, 110b, 111b,
    112b
  sovereign, III 112a–114a
  State, III 108a, 110a–112b,
    115b; IV 316b
  Stoicism, III 111a, 111b,
    112a, 115a–115b
  theodicy, III 379b
  Theophrastus, III 112a
  tradition, III 110
  treason, III 110a, 113b–
    114a, 114b
  truth, III 110a, 111b, 115a
  tyranny, III 112a, 112b
  U.S.S.R., III 114b
  U.N., III 113a
  U.S., III 113a–115a
  U.S. Supreme Court, III
    114b
  unity, III 115a
  universe, III 111b, 115a
  war, III 114a
  Wilson, III 113a
  wisdom, III 110a
  witch hunt, III 114b
  World War I, III 114a–114b
  World War II, III 114b
  Xenophon, III 112a
  Zeno of Citium, III 111a
Loyola, Saint Ignatius (1491–
  1556)
  Comte and, III 536b
  positivism, III 536b
LSD, death and, I 638a
Lubac, Henri de, God, II 361b
Lucanus (39–65 A.D.), magic,
  III 246a
Lucaris, Cyril (1572?–1638),
  history, I 411a
Lucas, W. F., game theory,
  II 271a
Lucian (2nd century A.D.), I
  44a
  art, II 299b
  art and play, I 102b

  cosmic voyages, I 524a
    524b, 530b
  cynicism, I 630b, 631b; III
    586a
  education, I 630b
  genius, II 299b
  humanism, III 292b
  iconography, II 534a
  irony, II 629a
  magic, III 246a
  mimesis, III 227a
  mythology, III 292b
  primitivism, III 580b, 586a
  progress, III 632a
  satire, IV 214a, 215a, 215b
  skepticism, IV 242a–242b
  ut pictura poesis, IV 469b
  Utopia, IV 460a
  wisdom of the fool, IV
    516b, 519b
Lucilius, Gaius (2nd century
  B.C.)
  primitivism, III 588a
  satire, IV 211a
Lucius Sicinnius, temperance,
  IV 377a
Lucius II, Pope (d. 1185),
  heresy, II 419b
Luck, II 225b, 227a–227b,
  234a–234b
  motif, III 239b
  Nature and, II 227b
  as a superrational impulse,
    II 227b
Lucretia, temperance, IV 370a
Lucretius (96?–55 B.C.)
  agriculture, III 587b
  appearance and reality, I
    94a
  art, III 587b
  atomism, I 130b, 132b–
    133a, 136b, 137a, 497a;
    II 137b, 237b; IV 51a
  biology, I 234a
  Bruno and, III 193b, 194a
  causation, I 273a, 301a–
    301b
  chance images, I 341b,
    343a
  civilization, III 587b
  classification of the arts, I
    458a
  Cosmic Fall, I 505b
  Creation, I 573a
  creativity in art, I 584b
  culture, I 610b, 611b
  death, I 635b, 640a
  determinism, II 237b
  discontinuity, I 497a
  education, III 57b
  eighteenth century view of,
    I 82a
  Epicureanism, III 587a–
    587b

evolution of literature, II 171b
evolutionism, II 176a
free will, II 237b
God, I 573a
gold, III 587b
happiness, II 378a
human nature, III 574b
humanism, II 516a, 520a
indeterminacy, II 587a, 590a
infinity, II 612b
Islam, II 642b
justice, II 656b
longevity, III 89b
Man-Machine, III 132a
materialism, III 631a
metaphor, III 197a
metaphysics, III 213b
mimesis, III 227a
Montaigne and, I 133a
morality, III 631a–631b
motion, IV 51a
mountains in literature III 253b, 258b, 259b
natural law, III 16b
Nature, III 351a, 631b
navigation, III 587a
necessity, III 631a
optics, III 408b, 409a
pacifism, III 587b
peace, III 587b
primitivism, III 587a–587b, 600a
progress, III 630a–633a
psychology, IV 8a
rationalism, IV 51a
religion, IV 93a
Rousseau and, III 587b
science, III 631b
skill, III 631a
society, III 631a–631b
Spenser and, I 133a
spontaneous generation, IV 308a
technology, III 631a–631b
teleology, I 301a–301b
time, IV 389b
trade, III 587a
wealth, III 587b
Luddism, protest movements, III 676a, 676b
Ludendorff, Erich Friedrich (1865–1937)
Nazism, III 597b
primitivism, III 597b
totalitarianism, IV 408a
Ludlow, John M. F., socialism, IV 290a
Ludolf, Job (1624–1704), linguistics, III 64b, 66a
Ludwig, Carl (1816–1895), reductionism, II 404b
Ludwig, Otto (1813–1865),

periodization in literary history, III 483b
realism in literature, IV 52b, 55a
Luethy, H., periodization in history, III 480b
Lukács, Georg (1885–1971),
alienation, III 168b
irrationalism, II 637a
literary criticism, I 606b
Marxism, III 165b, 168b, 169a
realism in literature, IV 55b
revisionism, IV 270a
Lukasiewicz, J., axiomatization, I 168b–169a
Luke, Saint
eschatology, II 157b
mythology, III 276b
socialism, IV 286a
Lully, Raymond (1235?–1315)
Chain of Being, I 327a
God, I 327a
Islam, II 641a–641b, 646b, 651a
knowledge, I 327a
perennial philosophy, III 460a
unity of science, IV 434b, 435a
wisdom of the fool, IV 517b
Lumen, optics, III 410a, 410b, 416a, 417b–419b
Lumière, Auguste (1862–1954), impressionism, II 572a
Lumière, Louis Jean (1864–1948), impressionism, II 572a
Lunn, Arnold, entropy, II 118b
Luscinius, Othmar, musical genius, II 315b–316a, 317b, 319a
Lüth, E. H., symbolism, IV 342b
Luther, Martin (1483–1546), I 389a–391a
alienation, I 36b
authority, I 149b–150a
Bible, I 390a–390b, 392a, 394a
Calvin and, II 142b; III 255a; IV 67b
canon law, I 396a
capitalism, I 396a
casuistry, I 262a, 262b
charity, II 212a–212b
city-state, I 395a
class, I 446a; III 11a
Cochlaeus and, II 428a
condemnation of, I 390b
conservatism, I 479b

Cosmic Fall, I 505b–506a
crisis in history, I 592b
demonology, III 267a
Denifle and, II 428a
dualism, II 43b
economic history, II 45a
end-of-the-world, III 255a
equality, II 141b–142a, 142b
Erasmus and, II 348b–349a
eschatology, II 156b, 157a, 160b, 161a; III 270b–271a
evil, IV 381b
failure to establish unity, I 395a
faith, II 160b, 212a–212b; IV 66b, 381b
Fall, IV 381b
Faust (legend), III 245a, 246b, 247a, 248a
fideism, IV 381b
free will, II 245a–245b
freedom, I 389b–390a
Gansfort and, IV 65b
God, II 212a, 348b–349a, 357a; III 11a, 270b; IV 381b, 532b–533a
Grisar and, II 428a
heresy, II 425b, 427b, 428a, 430a
hierarchy, II 442a; IV 66b
historiography, II 483b–484a
hope, II 212a–212b
humanism, II 520a; IV 135a
iconography, II 530b
individualism, II 597a, 598b
indulgences, I 389b
Jesus Christ, III 267a
justice, IV 381b
knowledge, II 349a
law, III 11a; IV 66b
liberalism, III 40b, 41b, 42a
love, II 212a; IV 66b
Melanchthon and, IV 67a
metaphor, III 206a–206b
mountain-origin, III 255a–255b
mountains in literature, III 255a–255b, 258a
Müntzer and, IV 287a
music, III 267a, 270b–271a
papacy, I 390a, 395a, 396a
peace, III 441b
Peasant Rebellion, II 142a
perfectibility, III 467b
pessimism, I 390b; III 255a–255b
piety, II 212a
power, II 142a; III 11a
predestination, II 27b
prophecy, IV 67a, 67b

reason, IV 381b
reformation, IV 65b–67b, 68b, 69b
Reformation, IV 65b–69b
religion, III 206a–206b
revolution, I 392b
Roman Catholic Church, II 430a
Saint Augustine and, I 389b
Saint Paul and, I 389b
salvation, II 212b, 245b
Satan, III 267a
scholasticism, III 357a
sin, III 255a; IV 381b
skepticism, IV 242a–242b
socialism, IV 287a
spiritualism, IV 66b
State, I 396a; III 11a
theodicy, IV 381b
usury, I 396a–395b
virtue, II 212a
voluntarism, IV 381b
wisdom of the fool, IV 518b
witchcraft, IV 522a–522b
women, IV 528a
work, IV 532b–533a
Lutheranism
Barth, I 408a
Calvinism, III 654a
casuistry, I 262b
Charles V, I 390a
Church, I 418a
class, I 446a
Counter-Enlightenment, II 103b, 105b
Counter-Reformation, I 393a–393b, 394a, 395a
creativity, I 406b
faith, hope, and charity, II 212b, 213a
heresy, II 427b, 428a, 429b
historicism, II 458b
history, I 392a
individualism, II 603a
liberalism, III 40b
Melanchthon, II 391b
missionaries, III 493b
natural ability, II 64a–64b
Pietism, I 403a; III 493b
private property, III 654a
Scandinavia, II 64b
as Teutonic, I 390b
U.S., II 64b
Lux, optics, III 417b
Luxemburg, Rosa (1870–1919)
Bernstein and, III 162b
economics, III 162b
Kautsky and, III 164a
Marxism, III 152b, 162b, 164a

revisionism, **IV** 267b, 269a, 270b, 272b
socialism, **III** 162b
Luxury
  cynicism, **III** 586a
  disease, **II** 397b
  millenarianism, **III** 224a
  primitivism, **III** 586a, 588b, 600a, 600b, 604b
  Rousseau, **III** 600a
  Seneca, **III** 588b
  utility, **IV** 453a, 458a
  Voltaire, **III** 604b
Luzi, Mario, symbolism, **IV** 342a
Lycaon (myth), **III** 296a
Lycortas, historiography, **II** 508a
Lycurgus (9th century B.C.),
  freedom of speech, **II** 257b
  general will, **II** 277a
  historiography, **II** 509a, 511a
  law, **II** 679b, 680a
  Utopia, **IV** 460a
Lydgate, John (1370?–?1451), wisdom of the fool, **IV** 518a
Lydus, John, astrology, **I** 119a
Lye, Len, *ut pictura poesis*, **IV** 475b
Lyell, Charles (1795–1875)
  association of ideas, **I** 115a
  catastrophism, **IV** 421b–423a
  continuity, **I** 499b, 500a–500b
  Darwin and, **II** 176b, 180a; **IV** 422b–423a, 424a
  environment, **II** 133a
  evolution, **IV** 424b
  evolutionism, **II** 176b, 180a, 180b
  linguistics, **IV** 423b–425a, 426a, 427a, 427b, 428a, 429b
  Schleicher and, **IV** 428a
  uniformitarianism, **I** 499b, 500a–500b; **II** 176b; **IV** 421b–425a, 426a, 427b, 428a, 429b
Lyly, John (1554?–1606), baroque in literature, **I** 195a
Lysander (d. 395 B.C.), historiography, **II** 504a
Lysenko, T. D. (1898–   ),
  acquired characteristics, **II** 619a–621b
  Darwinism, **II** 620b
  Engels and, **II** 620b
  Michurin and, **II** 621a
  pangenesis, **II** 626b
Lysias (450?–380 B.C.)
  Plato and, **III** 499a
Socrates and, **III** 499b
  temperance, **IV** 368a
Lysimachus (361?–281 B.C.), impiety, **II** 566a
Lysippus (4th century B.C.), creativity in art, **I** 582a

M

Maat (myth), **II** 334a, 334b
Mabbott, J. D., utilitarianism, **IV** 448b
Mabillon, Jean (1632–1707)
  historicism, **II** 458a–459b
  historiography, **II** 486b–487a, 490b
Mably, Gabriel Bonnet de (1709–1785)
  Counter-Enlightenment, **II** 102a
  despotism, **II** 12a, 15a
  Enlightenment, **II** 99b
  Platonism, **III** 520b
Macapagal, Diosdado, nationalism, **III** 338b
Macaulay, Thomas B. (1800–1859)
  Byron and, **IV** 194b
  classicism, **I** 452b
  Enlightenment, **II** 95b
  historiography, **II** 494a
  liberty, **II** 95b
  literary criticism, **I** 599a
  romanticism, **IV** 194b
  Wordsworth and, **IV** 194b
Maccabees, historiography, **II** 466b
McCall, William, individualism, **II** 596b
McCarthy, Eugene, women, **IV** 528b
McCarthy, Joseph R. (1909–1957), loyalty, **III** 114b
McCosh, James (1811–1894), eschatology, **II** 160a
McDougal, Myres, law, **III** 5a
McDougall, William (1871–1938)
  association of ideas, **I** 115b–116a
  behaviorism, **I** 220b, 221a, 224a; **II** 382b
  happiness, **II** 382b
  individualism, **II** 601a
  war, **IV** 507a
Mace, Thomas (fl. 1676)
  harmony, **II** 394b
  music, **II** 321b–322a, 394b
Macedonia
  freedom of speech, **II** 257b, 260a
Buddhism, **I** 247b
Mach, Ernst (1838–1916),
  Einstein and, **IV** 86a
  empiricism, **III** 545b, 546a, 547b, 550b
  idea, **II** 547b
  Newton and, **IV** 302b
  Peirce and, **III** 558a
  pragmatism, **III** 558a
  relativity, **IV** 86a, 89b
  space, **IV** 302b
Machado Dias, Antônio, positivism, **III** 539b
Machado, Antonio (1875–1939), symbolism, **IV** 342a, 344b
Mach's Principle, **IV** 89b
Machiavelli, Niccolò (1469–1527), **III** 116a–126a
  absolutism, **III** 113a
  animals, **IV** 480b, 481b–482a
  atheism, **III** 119b
  audacity, **IV** 480b, 482a
  authority, **I** 151a–151b
  Bacon and, **I** 173a
  balance of power, **I** 180a, 180b–181a, 182a–182b
  choice, **IV** 481b, 482a
  conduct, **III** 116a–125a
  cruelty, **IV** 480a
  cycles, **I** 626b; **IV** 150a
  democracy, **I** 652b, 656a
  Descartes and, **III** 356b
  despotism, **III** 116a–125a
  discipline, **IV** 316a
  drama, **III** 118a–119a, 121b
  evil, **III** 116a–125a; **IV** 482a, 483a
  fear, **IV** 481a, 481b
  Ferdinand II and, **IV** 502a
  force, **III** 116b, 122a; **IV** 315a
  foreign policy, **III** 117a, 122a, 122b–123a; **IV** 484a
  fortune, **II** 235b–236a; **IV** 479b–482b
  Frederick the Great and, **IV** 484a
  free will, **II** 236a
  freedom, **II** 250a; **III** 117a, 123b
  God, **IV** 483a
  good, **II** 235b, 379b; **III** 116a–125a; **IV** 482a, 483a
  Greece (ancient), **III** 356a
  happiness, **II** 379b; **IV** 481a
  harmony, **IV** 480b
  heresy, **II** 427a
  historiography, **II** 483a; **IV** 150a
  Hobbes and, **IV** 484a
  human action, **IV** 480a–482b, 484a
human nature, **IV** 480b, 481a, 481b–482a
  humanism, **II** 519b; **IV** 132b, 135a, 479a
  indecisiveness, **IV** 482a
  independence, **IV** 483a–483b
  individualism, **IV** 480b–481a, 483a–483b
  internal affairs, **III** 117a, 119b
  justice, **III** 122a
  law, **II** 250a; **III** 116b, 119b; **IV** 315a–315b, 482b
  Leonardo da Vinci and, **IV** 442b
  liberalism, **III** 37a
  liberty, **III** 121a, 121b; **IV** 316b
  literature, **III** 118a–119a, 121b
  love, **IV** 481b
  loyalty, **III** 113a; **IV** 316b
  metaphysics, **III** 213b
  military, **IV** 479b, 480a, 481b, 482a
  morality, **III** 116a–125a; **IV** 477a, 479a, 479b–480b, 482a, 482b
  murder, **III** 116b
  nationalism, **III** 123a, 124a, 322b, 323b
  Nature, **IV** 483a
  necessity, **III** 356a, 356b; **IV** 480b, 481b, 482a, 482b
  Nietzsche and, **IV** 484b–485b
  norms, **III** 116a–125a
  novel, **III** 118a–119a
  order, **IV** 480b, 482a–482b, 483b
  papacy, **III** 116b
  passions, **IV** 482a–482b
  patriotism, **IV** 315a, 316b
  peace, **III** 441b; **IV** 502a
  periodization in history, **III** 476b
  pessimism, **IV** 483a
  Plato and, **III** 514b
  politics, **II** 235b–236a, 519b; **III** 113a, 116a–125a, 514b; **IV** 123a, 127b, 314b–316b, 479a–483b, 502a
  poverty, **IV** 483a
  power, **II** 235b, 236a, 379b; **III** 116a–125a; **IV** 479a, 480b, 481a, 482b, 483b
  providence, **II** 235b
  psychology, **IV** 22a
  reason, **IV** 482a–482b
  Renaissance, **III** 356a
  republicanism, **III** 117a

revolution, IV 152b
Roman Catholic Church, III 116b
Rome (ancient), III 356a; IV 502b
Satan, III 117b
skepticism, IV 244a
society, III 116a–125a
soul, II 235b
State, I 652b–656a; II 235b; III 116a–125a; IV 132b, 314b–316b
universal man, IV 442b
vice, III 116b
violence, IV 502a
virtue, I 652b; II 235b, 236a; III 116b; IV 315a
virtù, IV 477a, 477b, 479a–485a
virtuoso, IV 482b
war, III 441b; IV 483a, 501a, 502a, 502b, 507b
wealth, IV 483a
Machiavellism, III 116a–126a
absolutism, III 17a, 119b, 120a, 120b, 122b
alliances, III 122b
amorality, III 118b, 120a, 120b, 121b, 124a
anti-Italianism, III 117b–118a
art, III 117b
Athens (ancient), III 116a
Bacon, III 121a–121b
Bismarck, III 124a
Boccalini, III 122b–123a
Bolingbroke, III 120a
Borgia, III 125a
Botero, III 122b
casuistry, I 260b
Charles I, III 119b
Choderlos de Laclos, III 119a
Cicero, III 116a
cleverness, III 124b
common law, III 116b
community, III 116b
competition, III 122b
conduct, III 116a–125a
constitutions, III 123b–124a
Cromwell, III 120a
d'Alençon, III 117b
Darwinism, III 125a
defined, III 116a
despotism, III 116a–125a
dictatorship, III 125a
Diderot, III 120a, 121b
divination, III 116b, 119a
drama, III 118a–119a, 121b
economics, III 117b, 123a, 124b
elite, III 125a
Euripides, III 116a

evil, III 116a–125a
fascism, III 125a
Fielding, III 119a
force, III 116b, 122a
foreign policy, III 117a, 122a, 122b–123a, 124a
France, III 117a, 117b, 118a, 119b, 120b, 123a–123b
Frederick the Great, III 120a, 121b–122a
freedom, III 117a, 120b–121a, 123b
French Revolution (1789), III 123a–123b
Froumenteau, III 117a
Gentili, III 121a
Gentillet, III 117b
Germany, III 120b, 125a
God, III 116a, 116b, 119a
Goethe, III 119a, 121b
good, III 116a–125a
Gramsci, III 124b
Great Britain, III 117a, 118a–119a, 119b, 120a, 121a–121b
Greece (ancient), III 116a
Guiraudet, III 123a–123b
Guise, III 120b
Harrington, III 121a
Hegel, III 119a
history, III 124b
Hitler, III 125a
Hotman, III 118a
Huguenots, III 117b
Hume, III 121b
ignorance, III 118a
internal affairs, III 117a, 119b
Italy, III 117a, 117b–118a, 119b, 120b, 124a, 124b, 125a
James IV, III 122a
Jesuits, III 117b, 118a
Joly, III 119b
justice, III 122a
law, III 116b, 118a
Le Trosne, III 123a
Lessing, III 118b
liberty, III 121a, 121b
literature, III 118a–119a, 121b, 122b, 123b, 124a, 124b
Long, III 124b
Machon, III 120b, 124a
Marlowe, III 118a, 121b
Mazarin, III 119b, 120b
Medici, III 117b, 118a
Meredith, III 119a
Metternich, III 124a
Middle Ages, III 116a–116b, 122b
Mirabeau, III 123a
monarchy, III 117a, 120a,

120b
Montesquieu, III 121b, 124b
Mosca, III 124b
murder, III 116b
Mussolini, III 125a
Nash, III 117a
nationalism, III 123a, 124a, 330a
natural law, III 116b
Nature, III 116b
Naudé, III 120b, 124a
Neville, III 121a
Nietzsche, III 125a
norms, III 116a–125a
papacy, III 116b, 117b, 118a, 120b
Paruta, III 123a
patriotism, III 120a
philosophy, III 120a, 123a, 125a
pietism, III 118b
Pole, III 117b
politics, III 116a–125a
power, III 116a–125a
Presbyterians, III 120a
prestige, III 120a
princes, III 116b, 120a, 122b, 123a
Protestantism, III 117b, 120a
Prussia, III 121b–122a
psychology, III 123b, 124b
radicalism, III 124a
Ranke, III 124a
reason, III 120a, 122b, 123a
religion, III 118a, 119b–120a, 122a–122b
Renaissance, III 116b–117a, 124b, 125a
republicanism, III 117a, 120b–121a
Richelieu, III 120b
rights, III 120b
Roman Catholic Church, III 116b–118a, 119b–120a
Rome (ancient), III 116a
Rousseau, III 121b
Saint Bartholomew, III 117b
scholarship, III 117b, 124b, 125a
Scotland, III 122a
selfishness, III 120a
Shakespeare, III 118a–118b
Sheridan, III 119a
Sienkiewicz, III 119a
sin, III 118a
society, III 116b–125a
Spain, III 117a
State, III 116b–125a
Stendhal, III 119a

Tacitus, III 116a
taxation, III 119b, 120a
technology, III 124b
Thucydides, III 116a
totalitarianism, III 125a
treaties, III 122b
tyranny, III 121a, 122b–123a, 123b
U.S., III 124a, 124b
Venice, III 120b
vice, III 116b, 119a
virtue, III 116b
virtù, IV 483b–484b
Voltaire, III 120a
Wallenstein, III 120b
war, III 120a
welfare, III 116a
will, III 119a
Williams, III 124a
Wilson, III 124a
Machon, Louis, Machiavellism, III 120b, 124a
McIlwain, Charles H., constitutionalism, I 485b, 486b, 488a
Mackail, John W. (1859–1945), mythology, III 295b
Mackenna, S., Platonism, III 525a
Mackenzie, A. S., evolution of literature, II 171b
MacKenzie, Gordon, organicism, III 425b
McKeon, Richard, rhetoric, IV 171a
Mackintosh, James (1765–1832), romanticism, IV 192a
Mackintosh, Robert, acquired characteristics, II 620a
Maclaurin, Colin (1698–1746), Newton and, III 378b, 393a
McLuhan, Marshall
Gothic, II 373b
literature, III 88b
McNeill, J. J., modernism, I 426a
McNeill, William, China, I 372a
Macpherson, C. B., individualism, II 602a
Macpherson, James (1736–1796), mythology, III 304b
MacQuarrie, John
Creation, I 575b–576a
God, I 575b–576a
Macrobius, Ambrosius Theodosius (4th and 5th century A.D.)
analogy, I 65b
Chain of Being, II 440b
city, I 428a
dignity, IV 139a

God, II 440b
harmony, II 389b; IV 40a
hierarchy, II 440a–440b
music, II 389b
mythology, III 287b, 291a, 299b
Pythagorean cosmos, IV 40a
temperance, IV 371a
Macrocosm and Microcosm, III 126a–131b
Adam (Bible), III 131a
alchemy, I 27b, 28a
Al-Kindi, III 129a
allegory, III 130a
analogy, I 27b, 28a, 29a
anatomy, III 126a, 128b
animals, III 126a, 127a, 128b
Aphrodite (myth), III 126b
architecture, III 130a
Ares (myth), III 126b
Aristotle, III 126b, 127a, 127b
astrology, I 119b–120a; III 128a–128b, 130b, 131a
Being, III 129a
Bible, III 127b, 129a, 130a
biological clock, III 126b
Burton, I 508b
causation, III 126a
Christianity, III 129b
Cosmic Fall, I 508b, 511a
cosmic images, I 513a
cosmos, III 126a–129b
creativity in art, I 586b
Demiurge, III 127a
earth, III 128a, 129b
Empedocles, III 126b
eternity, III 128a
genius, II 313b
God, III 127b, 128a, 128b, 131a
Greece (ancient), III 126a, 126b, 127a, 128a, 129a, 129b, 130b
harmony, II 389a, 390a
health, II 397a
heaven, III 128a, 128b, 129b, 130b
hermeticism, II 433a
history, III 126a
humors, III 128a
idea, III 126a, 126b, 129a
individualism, III 126a, 127a, 129a
Israeli, Isaac, III 129a
John of Salisbury, III 130a
Judaism, III 129a
knowledge, III 129a, 131a
Leibniz, III 130b–131a
literature, III 127b–128a
logic, III 127a, 129a
love, III 126b

magic, III 130a, 130b
man, III 126a–131a
matter, III 130b, 188a, 193a
memory, III 130b
metaphysical imagination, III 130b–131a, 212a
Middle Ages, III 127a, 129a
moon, III 128a, 130b
Moses (Bible), III 129b
music, II 313b, 389a, 390a; III 130b, 268b, 269a
mythology, III 126b
Nathan, III 129a
Nature, III 126a, 128a, 129a
Neo-Platonism, III 128b, 129a, 130b
One, III 128b
order, II 436a, 436b, 437a, 439b, 442b
parallelism, III 129b, 130a
pathetic fallacy, III 126a
perennial philosophy, III 458b
perfection, III 126b
Philo Judaeus, III 127b, 128a, 128b
Pico della Mirandola, III 130a–130b, 131a
planets, III 128a, 128b, 130b
plants, III 127a, 128b
Plato, III 126b, 127a–127b, 130a; IV 32b
Platonism, III 127b, 128b
Plotinus, III 127a, 128b, 130b
Porphyry, III 129a
pseudoscience, III 128a–128b
psychology, III 126a, 127a–128b, 130a
Pythagoreans, IV 32b, 33a, 36a
rationalism, III 127a
relativity, IV 91b, 92a
religion, III 128a
Reuchlin, III 130a–130b
Rome (ancient), III 126a
Saint Augustine, III 129b, 130a
Saint Victor, III 129b–130a
Scève, III 131a
science, III 126b, 127a, 131a
Seneca, III 128a
Socrates, III 126b, 127a
soul, III 127a, 127b, 128b, 129a, 130a, 130b, 131a
spirit, III 130a
State, III 127a–127b
Stobaeus, III 128a, 129a
Stoicism, III 127a

strife, III 126b
sun, III 128a, 130b
superstition, III 126a–126b
teleology, III 126a
temperance, IV 372a
Trinity, III 130a
universe, III 126a–127b, 128b, 129b, 130b–131a
vision, III 129a
wisdom, III 127a
zodiac, III 128a–129a, 131a
Macrophysics, indeterminacy, II 586b, 588a
McTaggart, John (1866–1925)
death, I 641b, 645a
immortality, I 641b, 645a
individualism, II 597b
organicism, III 426a
reincarnation, I 645a
time, IV 394a, 394b
Madero, Francisco (1873–1913), positivism, III 545a
Madison, James (1751–1836)
conservatism, I 484a
democracy, I 660b, 666a, 666b
law, III 7b, 8a
Magna Carta, III 7b
psychology, IV 22a
rights, III 7b
Madness
art, II 308b–309b
genius, II 294a, 308b–309b
music, III 265a
Maeterlinck, Maurice (1862–1949)
cosmic images, I 523b
Proust and, IV 340a
symbolism, IV 340a, 340b, 343a, 344b
Maffei, Giovanni Petri, China, I 354b
Magalhães, Celso, positivism, III 541b
Magendie, François (1783–1855)
association of ideas, I 116a
behaviorism, I 218a
disease, II 404a
Magi (Bible), III 282b
Magic
Bacon, I 174a–174b
Christianity, III 246a
Faust (legend), III 246a, 247a, 247b, 248b, 249b, 251a
Ficino, IV 145a
genius, II 313a
Gnosticism, II 327a–329b
God, II 334a, 335a
Greece (ancient), IV 102a
harmony, II 393b–394a

health, II 396b, 397b
human nature, III 571a
humanism, II 521a; IV 134a
literature, III 246a
longevity, III 90b
love, III 107a
Lucanus, III 246a
Lucian, III 246a
macrocosm and microcosm, III 130a, 130b
matter, III 186a
metaphysics, III 211b, 212a
motif, III 239a
music, II 313a, 392b–394a; III 264b, 265a, 267a, 268a, 268b, 269b, 271b
mythology, III 274a, 282b–283a, 287b, 290b, 311a
Pico della Mirandola, IV 145b
primitivism, III 582b
rationalism, IV 46a
religion, III 246a; IV 96a, 98b, 100a, 100b, 101a, 102a
Renaissance, IV 134a, 145a, 145b
satire, IV 211b, 212a, 216a
Seneca, III 246a
skepticism, IV 242a, 243a
superstition, III 246a
technology, IV 360a
theater, III 246a
Theocritus, III 246a
time, IV 402a, 402b
Vergil, III 246a
witchcraft, IV 521a
words, I 43b
Magna Carta
constitutionalism, I 487b–488a, 488b
historiography, II 486a
justice, II 657b
law, II 689a; III 7b, 8b
loyalty, III 112a–112b
Middle Ages, III 112a–112b; IV 253b
social contract, IV 253b, 261b
Magnetism
Newton, III 195a
relativity, IV 78b, 80a
symmetry, IV 353a–353b
Magnin, Charles (1793–1862), symbolism, IV 339a
Magog (Bible), mythology, III 284b
Magyars, I 381a
nationalism, III 330a
Mahan, Asa
civil disobedience, I 436b
Pietism, IV 111b
psychology, IV 22b
religion, IV 111b

Mahāyāna, I 247b- 248a

Mahood, M. M., baroque in literature, I 193a

Maier, Anneliese
mechanical sciences, II 202a
infinity, II 609b

Maigron, Louis, evolution of literature, II 172a–172b

Maigrot, Charles, China, I 357b

Mailla, Father Mauriac de, China, I 361a

Maillet, B. de (1656–1738), cosmic images, I 518a
evolutionism, II 176b
geology, II 176b

Maimbourg, Louis (1620?–1686), Reformation, IV 67a

Maimon, Solomon (1754–1800), skepticism, IV 249a

Maimonides (1135–1204),
abstraction, I 4b
atomism, I 495b, 496a
causation, I 289a
discontinuity, I 495b, 496a
equity, II 151b
Islam, II 642b, 649a
occasionalism, I 496a
philanthropy, III 487b–488a

Maine, Henry Sumner (1822–1888)
economic history, II 61a
equity, II 151a
evolutionism, II 187a
justice, II 658b
pragmatism, III 566b

Maine de Biran (1766–1824)
causation, I 278a
modernism, I 420a
psychology, IV 11b
romanticism, IV 201b

Mair, Jean, see Major, John

Mairet, Jean (1604–1686), genius, II 294a

Maistre, J. M. de (1753–1821)
Bacon and, I 178a
Bonald and, III 534a–534b
Comte and, III 533b–534b
conservatism, I 480a, 482a
Counter-Enlightenment, II 95b, 110a–111b
individualism, II 594b, 595a, 598b
natural law, III 22a
papacy, I 482a
positivism, III 533b–534b
reason, I 482a; II 95b
romanticism, IV 205b
skepticism, IV 248a
society, III 22a
war, IV 504a

Maitland, F. W. (1850–1906), common law, II 694b, 695a

Maitreyanātha (c. 270–350 A D), I 248a

Majer, Friedrich, mythology, III 306a

Major, H. D. A., modernism, I 424b

Major, John (1469–1550), Scottish nominalist, II 204a

Major, Thomas (fl. 1768), neo-classicism in art, III 365b

Majorities
democracy, I 666a
equality, II 139a
general will, II 278b, 280a
intolerance, IV 116a
nationalism, III 328b, 329a, 329b, 333b, 334a
religion, IV 116a
Switzerland, III 328b, 329a

Makom
Arabic language, IV 296b
Aramaic, IV 296b
Bible, IV 296a–296b
God, IV 296b
Judaism, IV 296a–296b

Malachi (Bible), metaphor, III 202b

Malatesta, Enrico (1850–1932), anarchism, I 74b–75a

Maldonado, Juan (1533–1583), skepticism, IV 242b

Mâle, Émile (1862–1954), iconography, II 530b, 535b, 537b, 538b

Malebranche, Nicolas de (1638–1715), I 77b, 85b
aesthetics, IV 355a
al-Ghazali and, I 2/4a
causation, I 274a, 276a, 296b, 297b–298b, 302b–303a; III 193a
China, I 360a
general will, II 275b
God, I 276a, 297b–298b, 302b
idea, II 548b
illuminists, IV 109a
Man-Machine, III 138a
matter, III 193a
metaphysical imagination, III 213b–214a, 214b
Newton and, III 392a
occasionalism, I 276a; III 193a
optics, III 392a
perennial philosophy, III 461a
rationalism, II 635b
religion, IV 109a

skepticism, IV 241b, 245a, 247a
taste, IV 355a
teleology, I 302b–303a

Malenkov, Georgi M. (1902–)
Marxism, III 157a
realism in literature, IV 55b

Malevitch, Kazimir (1878–1935), aesthetics, II 221a

Malevolence
Hutcheson, III 231a
moral sense, III 231a
tragic sense, IV 413a

Malherbe, François de (1555–1628), baroque in literature, I 192b

Malinowski, Bronislaw (1884–1942)
individualism, II 601a
mythology, III 314b
structuralism, IV 325b

Malkiel, Y., linguistics, IV 425a

Mallarmé, Stéphane (1842–1898)
art for art's sake, I 109b
impressionism, II 574b, 575a, 575b
literature, III 88b
Platonism, III 524b
romanticism, IV 196b
symbolism, IV 339a–341a, 342a, 343b, 344b, 345a
ut pictura poesis, IV 470b

Mallet, David (1705?–1765), baroque in literature, I 191a
Gothic, II 370b
mountains in literature, III 259a
Newton and, III 393b
sublime in external nature, IV 335a–335b

Mallet, Paul Henri, mythology, III 304a–304b

Malone, K., baroque in literature, I 193b

Malpighi, Marcello (1628–1694), spontaneous generation, II 282b; IV 309b

Malraux, André (1901–   ), death, I 637b
ut pictura poesis, IV 469a

Malthus, Thomas Robert (1766–1834)
association of ideas, I 114a–114b
capital, II 49a
China, I 365b–366a
class, I 441b
conservation, I 473b
crisis in history, I 590a
culture, II 128a, 130b
Darwin and, I 89a; II

180a
economic history, II 49a, 49b
environment, II 128a, 130b
evolutionism, II 180a, 180b
idea, I 114a–114b, 115b
labor, II 49a
land, II 49b
longevity, III 92a–92b
population theory, II 49a
Victorians, IV 218b, 221b–222a

Malus, Étienne-Louis (1775–1812), mathematics, III 179a

Mammonism, I 396b, 397a

Man, Henri de (1885–1953), Marxism, III 165b

Manadros, King (c. 2nd century B.C.), Buddhism, I 254b

Manchuria, international peace, III 454a

Mandelstam, L. I., indeterminacy, II 591a

Mandelstam, Osip, symbolism, IV 343a

Mander, Karel van (1548–1606), iconography, II 530a, 531a

Mandeville, Bernard (1670?–1733)
aesthetics, IV 356a
Enlightenment, II 94b
good, IV 178b
Hutcheson and, III 231a
liberty, II 94b
literary paradox, III 77b
moral sense, III 231a
primitivism, III 604b–605a
psychology, IV 22a
right, IV 178b
taste, IV 356a
Voltaire and, III 604b–605a

Manegold of Lautenbach (c. 11th century), social contract, IV 253a

Manet, Édouard (1832–1883), impressionism, II 567b, 568a–568b, 570a, 573a, 573b, 577b, 580a

Manetho (3rd century B.C.), astrology, I 124a

Manetti, Giannozzo (15th century)
classification of the arts, I 459b
dignity, IV 137b, 143a–143b
free will, IV 131a–131b
Gothic, II 367b
hierarchy, II 442b
humanism, II 520b; IV 131a–131b

individualism, II 597a–597b
work, IV 532a
Manget, Jean Jacques (c. 1700), alchemy, I 31b
Mani (216?–276), dualism, II 42b–43a
Manicheism
  alienation, I 35a, 35b
  Buddhism, I 255a; II 42b
  Christianity, I 35a, 35b; II 42b–43a
  dualism, II 38b, 42b–43a
  evil, II 164b
  Faust (legend), III 246a, 246b
  free will, II 244a
  Gnosticism, II 42b, 327a
  God, II 339b
  history, I 383a–383b
  impiety, II 565a
  intolerance, IV 115a, 115b
  love, III 97b, 98a, 99b, 100a, 102b, 107a
  matter, III 190b
  perfectibility, III 468a
  religion, IV 98a, 115a, 115b
  Rome (ancient), IV 115a
  Saint Augustine, II 43a, 244a; IV 380b
  theodicy, IV 380b
  Zoroastrianism, II 42b
Manilius, Gaius (1st century B.C.)
  humanism, II 516a
  mythology, III 291a
  progress, III 632b
Manly, John Matthews (1865–1940), evolution of literature, II 172b
Man-Machine, III 132a–146b
  anatomy, III 132b, 135a–135b
  animal soul, III 136b–138a
  Archimedes, III 134a–134b
  Aristotelianism, III 133b, 135a, 137a
  Aristotle, III 135a
  Arnauld, III 137a
  atheism, III 141a–142a
  atomism, III 132a, 132b, 133a, 134b, 139a
  automatic theater, III 134a
  automatism, III 134b–146a
  Bacon, III 135b
  Bain, III 143a
  beast-machine, III 135b–138a, 139b, 144a
  behaviorism, III 134a, 139b 140a, 143b–145a
  Bell, Charles, III 142b
  Bernard, III 142b
  bile, III 133a
  biology, III 131b, 134b,
136a, 136b, 139a–146a
  blood, III 132a, 133a, 135b, 138a
  body, III 132a–133b, 135b, 139b–140a, 143b, 144b, 145a
  Boerhaave, III 139b
  brain, III 132a, 133b, 138a–139b, 141a, 141b, 142b, 143b, 144a–145b
  Buffon, III 141b, 142a
  Cabanis, III 141b
  Carpenter, III 143a
  Cartesianism, III 135a, 136a–138b, 139b, 141b
  causation, III 137a, 139b, 143b
  character-traits, III 133a–133b
  chemistry, III 131b
  Christianity, III 133a, 135a
  circulatory system, III 135b
  computers, III 145b–146a
  Comte, III 142b
  Condillac, III 141b
  consciousness, III 140b, 143b
  craftmanship, III 134b
  Ctesibios, III 134a
  cybernetics, III 145b
  Darwinism, III 143b
  death, III 132b, 133a
  dehumanization, III 146a
  Democritus, III 132a
  Descartes, III 135b–138a
  determinism, III 139a, 144b
  Diderot, III 140b–142a
  dualism, III 138a, 138b, 143a, 145a, 145b
  electronics, III 145b
  Empedocles, III 132a, 133a
  empiricism, III 132a, 138b, 139a, 146a
  endocrinology, III 144b
  engineering, III 134a
  Enlightenment, III 135b, 138b–141b, 142a
  Epicureanism, III 132a, 132b, 133a, 134a, 138b, 139a
  Epicurus, III 132a
  epistemology, III 138b, 140a, 145a
  evolution, III 140b, 143b
  feeling, III 137b
  Flourens, III 142b
  four temperaments, III 133a–133b
  France, III 139a–139b
  free will, III 135a, 139a, 140b–141a
  Freudianism, III 144b
  Galen, III 133b–134b
  Gall, III 142b
  Gassendi, III 139a
  Germany, III 142b–143a
  God, III 135a, 137a, 137b
  golem, III 146a
  Gomez Pereira, III 135b
  Great Britain, III 143a
  Greece (ancient), III 131b–134b
  Haller, III 140a
  Hartley, III 141a
  Harvey, III 135b
  heart, III 132a
  Helvétius, III 141a, 141b
  heresy, III 136b, 137a
  Heron of Alexandria, III 134a, 134b
  Hippocrates, III 133a–134b
  history, III 131b, 134a, 134b, 135b, 138b, 142a
  Hobbes, III 138b
  Holbach, III 141a, 141b
  Horwicz, III 143a
  humanism, III 141a
  humors, III 133a–133b
  idea, III 132b
  ideology, III 135a
  James-Lange theory, III 143b
  Jansenists, III 137a–137b
  La Mettrie, III 131b, 134a, 135a, 137a, 138a–140b, 141b, 142a, 143b
  Lamy, III 139a
  Laycock, III 143a
  Leibniz, III 138a
  Leonardo da Vinci, III 135b
  Lewes, III 143a
  literature, III 143a, 146a
  Locke, III 138b, 139a
  Lotze, III 143a
  Lucretius, III 132a
  Malebranche, III 138a
  materialism, III 133a, 133b, 136b, 137a, 139a, 139b, 140b, 141a, 142a, 142b, 143a, 145a
  mathematics, III 134a, 134b, 142a, 145b
  Maudsley, III 143a–143b
  Maupertius, III 141b
  mechanism, III 134a–135b, 136b–145b, 146a
  medicine, III 131b–134a, 135a, 136a, 139b–141b
  memory, III 137b, 139b, 140b
  metaphysics, III 131b, 135a, 135b, 137a–139b
  morality, III 140b
  motion, III 135a
  Münsterberg, III 143a
  naturalism, III 135a
  Nature, III 135b
  Needham, III 144a
  nervous system, III 133b, 136b, 138a, 139b, 141a, 142b, 143a, 145a, 145b
  neurology, III 142b, 144b, 145a–146a
  Newton, III 141a
  organicism, III 138b, 139b, 140a–141b, 143b–145a
  paganism, III 133a
  passions, III 133b–134a, 139b, 140b
  Peripateticism, III 135a, 137a
  Philo of Byzantium, III 134a
  philosophy, III 131b, 132a, 133a–135b, 138a, 139a–146a
  phlegm, III 133a
  physico-mathematics, III 135a, 138b
  physics, III 131b–140a
  physiology, III 132b, 133a, 133b, 135a–136b, 138a, 139a, 140a, 141a–144b
  Platonism, III 133b, 134b
  Pomponazzi, III 135a, 137a
  psychodynamism, III 144b
  psychology, III 132b–146a
  psychophysiology, III 131b, 132a, 133a, 137a, 137b, 139b, 141a–145b, 146a
  Pythagoreans, III 132a, 134b
  reflection, III 140b
  reflex action, III 142b
  Régis, III 138a
  Regius, III 137b
  religion, III 132b, 133a, 137a, 140a
  Rignano, III 144a
  robot, III 136b, 146a
  romanticism, III 142a
  Ryle, III 145a
  Saint Thomas Aquinas, III 136a
  salvation, III 141b
  science, III 131b–135a, 138a–142a, 143b, 144b
  science-fiction, III 146a
  scientific revolution, III 135a
  senses, III 132a, 133b, 137b, 139b, 140b
  sociology, III 134b, 143a, 146a
  soul, III 132a–133b, 135a, 137a, 137b, 138a, 139a
  soul-atom, III 132a–132b
  Spinoza, III 138a, 139a
  supernatural, III 133a
  Taine, III 143a
  technology, III 131b, 134a–135b, 136b, 140a, 142a, 145b, 146a

theology, III 135a, 137b
thermodynamics, III 136b
universe, III 137b
Vaucanson, III 140a
Vesalius, III 135a–135b
vitalism, III 141b, 144a
volition, III 137b, 139b
war, III 135b
Watson, III 144a
Wittgenstein, III 145a
Zabarella, III 135a
Ziehen, III 143a
Zola, III 143a
Mann, Horace (1796–1859), psychology, IV 23b
Mann, Thomas (1875–1955)
creativity, III 252a
disease, II 406b; III 252a
Faust (legend), III 251a, 252a
irony, II 633a, 634a
leitmotiv, III 236a
mythology, III 252a
symbolism, IV 344b
Wagner and, III 236a
Mannerism
Germany, III 484a
ideal, II 549b
literature, IV 331b
neo-classicism in art, III 369a
periodization in literary history, III 484a
Manners
Nature, III 350a
primitivism, III 599a, 600a
realism in literature, IV 52a
Volksgeist, IV 491b
Mannheim, Karl (1867–1951)
historicism, II 457a
ideology, II 554b
Manning, Henry Edward (1808–1892), history, I 406b
Mans, Pelletier du, mimesis, III 228a
Mansel, Henry Longueville (1820–1871)
agnosticism, I 19b
evolutionism, II 182a
Mantegna, Andrea (1431–1506)
chance images, I 345b–347b
iconography, II 529a
mythology, III 290b, 292b
Mantell, Gideon (1790–1852), paleontology, IV 420a, 421b
Manuel, Frank, mythology, III 302a
Manufacturing
economic history, II 49a

Enlightenment, II 90b, 93b
national liberty, II 62b
utility, IV 453b
virtù, IV 477a
Manutius, Aldus (1450–1515)
humanism, II 516a, 518a
iconography, II 529b
mythology, III 289b
Manzoni, Alessandro (1785–1873)
literary criticism, I 597b
romanticism, IV 192b, 205a
Mao Tse-tung (1893–   ),
groupism, II 599b
individualism, II 599b
Marxism, III 161b, 166b
nationalism, III 334a–334b
natural liberty, II 70a
Stalin and, I 372b
totalitarianism, IV 409b
Maoris, art, III 597a
Marana, Giovanni, deism, I 649a
Marat, Jean Paul (1743–1793)
despotism, II 13b, 14a
freedom, II 14a
violence, II 14a
Marbe, Karl (1869–1953), psychology, IV 13a
Marbod of Rennes, chance images, I 343b
Marburg School
aesthetics, II 223a
Platonism, III 522b
Marc, Franz (1880–1916), expressionism, II 207b
Marcel, Gabriel (1889–   ),
existentialism, II 189b, 191b
immortality, I 642a
irrationalism, II 637a
Marche, François de la, time, IV 392a
Marcion of Pontus (2nd century), Gnosticism, II 327a, 329b, 330b
Marcionites, primitivism, III 589a
Marcus Aurelius, Emperor (121–180)
art, II 299b
death, I 635b
free will, II 243b
freedom of speech, II 260b
genius, II 299b
God, II 340b
good, IV 176a
longevity, III 89b
loyalty, III 111b
peace, III 440b
perfectibility, III 465b
progress, III 633a

rationalism, IV 50b
right, IV 176a
Stoicism, II 340b; IV 321b, 322a
Marcuse, Herbert
authority, I 158a, 160a, 160b, 161b
happiness, II 385a
historicism, II 463b
psychology, IV 14a
work, IV 535a
Mardonius (d. 479 B.C.), freedom of speech, II 254b
Marduk (myth), II 335b–336a; III 275b, 281a, 281b
freedom of speech, II 253a
religion, IV 104a
salvation, IV 226b
Maréchal, Sylvain, socialism, IV 288b
Marett, Robert R. (1866–1943), religion, IV 95b
Margarete (fiction), Faust (legend), III 248b, 249a, 249b, 250a, 251b
Margenau, Henry
indeterminacy, II 591b–592a, 592b
measurement, II 591b
Marguerite of Navarre (1492–1549), Platonism, III 507a–507b, 514a
Marheineke, Philipp (1780–1846), Strauss and, II 412b
Maria Theresa of Austria (1717–1780), Jesuits and, I 403b
Mariana, Juan de (1536–1624), social contract, IV 253b, 261b
Marino, Giambattista (1569–1625)
baroque in literature, I 190a, 194b, 195a
iconography, II 534b
literary paradox, III 77b
Mariology, Virgin Mary (Bible), III 107a, 107b
Maritain, Jacques (1882–   )
abstract art, I 585b
artist, I 585b
beauty, I 210a
classicism, I 455a
creativity in art, I 585b
death, I 642b
God, I 585b; II 361b
immortality, I 642a–642b
natural law, III 22b
peace, III 441b, 445b
Marius Victorinus (c. 465 A.D.)
dignity, IV 139a
historiography, II 510a

Neo-Platonism, III 376b, 377b
Plotinus and, III 377b
Porphyry and, III 376b, 377b
Marivaux, Pierre (1688–1763)
attitude toward antiquity, I 84a, 85b–86a
Enlightenment, II 96b
love, II 96b
Mark, Saint (1st century A.D.),
Church, I 416a, 416b
eschatology, I 416a
faith, II 399a
Markov, A. A., probability, III 608b, 614a, 620a
Markov chains, III 617b, 620a
Markowitz, Harry, social welfare, IV 280b
Marlowe, Christopher (1564–1593)
Chapman and, III 294b
drama, III 247b–248a
Faust (legend), III 247b–248a
literary paradox, III 79b
Machiavellism, III 118a, 121b
morality, III 247b–248a
motif, III 241a
mythology, III 294b
romanticism, IV 192a
tragic sense, IV 416a–416b
Marmion, Shakerley (1603–1639), mythology, III 295b
Marmontel, Jean-François (1723–1799), literature, III 81b; IV 332a
Marmur, J., DNA, II 291a
Marriage
Godwin, III 470b
Greece (ancient), II 681a, 682b, 683b, 684a; III 94b
law, II 681a, 682b, 683b, 684a, 686b, 688a
love, III 95a, 95b, 96a, 97a, 100b, 101b, 102b–104b, 105b, 107b
monogamy, II 251a–251b
natural law, III 17a, 18a, 26a–26b
perfectibility, III 470b, 471a
Plato, III 471a
primitivism, III 583a
religion, IV 94a
Rome (ancient), II 686b, 688a
women, IV 523b, 525b, 526b, 527b
Marrou, H. I., education, II 82b, 83a
Mars (myth), III 289a

249

Mars (planet)
  cosmology, I 538a, 539a, 540a–540b, 541b–542a, 544b, 545b, 550a, 552a
  mythology, III 287b
Marsh, Adam de (d. ?1257), prophecy, III 668a
Marsh, George Perkins (1801–1882)
  conservation, I 474b, 475b
  environment, II 128a, 132b–133b
  Nature, II 132b
Marsh, James, Pietism, IV 111b
Marshall, Alfred (1842–1924)
  economic history, II 48b, 50b, 53b–54b, 55a, 55b, 56b, 57a
  individualism, II 602b
  social welfare, IV 283a
Marshall, George (1880–1959), utility, IV 454a–454b
Marshall, Henry Rutgers (1852–1927), beauty, I 209a
Marshall, John (1755–1835), constitutionalism, I 489a–489b
  Jefferson and, IV 21b
  law, III 8a
  psychology, IV 21b
Marshall, T. H., welfare state, IV 513b
Marsilius of Padua (1290?–?1343)
  despotism, II 3a, 3b–4a
  heresy, II 418a, 419a, 422a
  nationalism, III 321b
  reformation, IV 65b
  social contract, IV 253a
Marston, John (1575?–1634)
  satire, IV 211b, 213a,
  wisdom of the fool, IV 520a
Marsyas (myth), III 292a
Marsyas of Pella, historiography, II 505b
Martello, Pier Jacopo (1665–1727), cosmic voyages, I 532b
Marten, Henry (1602–1680), deism, I 649b
Martí, José (1853–1895), positivism, III 544b
Martial (1st century A.D.), poetry, IV 469a
Martial, Saint, genius, II 315a
Martianus Capella (5th century A.D.), II 229a
  harmony, IV 40a

temperance, IV 371a
universe, II 229a; IV 40a
work, IV 531b
Martin, Alfred von, universal man, IV 442a
Martin, Benjamin, Newton and, III 393a
Martin, J. R., iconography, II 538a
Martin, Martin (d. 1719), primitivism, III 601a
Martin, Richard, theriophily, IV 388a
Martin of Braga, temperance, IV 371a, 375a
Martin V., Pope (1368–1431), history, I 386b
Martínez de la Rosa, Francisco (1789–1862), periodization in literary history, III 482a
Martini, Father Martin, China, I 356a, 358b–359a
Martino, Pierre
  naturalism, IV 54a
  realism in literature, Iv 54a
Martyr, Peter (1459–15.'6), primitivism, III 593b
Marvell, Andrew (16.'1–1678)
  Cosmic Fall, I 509b
  mountains in literature, III 253b, 254b, 259a
  mythology, III 295b, 297b
  ut pictura poesis, IV 471a
Marx, Karl (1818–1883),
  acquired characteristics, II 620a, 620b, 621b
  alienation, I 37a–41a, 620b; II 25a; III 158b–159b, 168b
  anarchy, I 72b, 74b, 409a; IV 162a
  anthropology, II 450a–450b, 451a, 454a
  atheism, IV 291a
  authority, I 152b, 153b, 155a, 158b; IV 534b
  Baader and, IV 207b
  Bacon and, I 179a
  Bakunin and, IV 166b
  Bauer and, IV 291a
  Bentham and, II 381b
  Bernstein and, III 161b, 162a, 162b, 163a, 163b
  bourgeois, II 25a, 451b, 452a, 452b, 453a; IV 161b, 163a, 292a, 293a, 316b
  Buber and, III 158a
  capital, I 39a–40b
  capitalism, I 590b–591b; II 146a, 452b, 453a; III 149a, 154a, 158b–159a, 160a, 161b, 167b, 168b;

IV 161b, 292a, 292b, 293a
  Cartesianism, II 450a–450b
  causation, I 282a–282b; II 452b
  China, I 366b, 369b, 372a
  class, I 442b, 444a, 445a–448b; II 25a, 159a, 451b, 554a, 583a; III 22a, 156a, 162a, 359a–359b; IV 161a, 162a, 265a, 291b, 292a, 292b, 534a, 534b
  collectivism, II 451a
  colonialism, II 16b–17a
  commodities, III 158b–159a
  Communism, II 450a, 450b, 451a; III 359b, 473b, 673b; IV 161b, 292a–292b
  Comte and, II 451b, 452a
  crisis in history, I 590b–591a, 593b–594a
  culture, I 619b, 620a–620b; II 451a, 583a
  Darwin and, II 620a, 626a–626b; III 146b
  democracy, I 664a
  despotism, II 2a, 4b, 13a, 16b–17a
  determinism, II 24b–25a; III 162b
  dignity, IV 534b
  dualism, III 159b
  duty, III 160a
  economic history, II 49b, 59b, 60a
  economics, II 451b, 452b, 453a, 453b; III 22a, 149a, 156a, 359b; IV 161b, 163a, 290a–290b, 292a, 534a
  Engels and, III 359a; IV 292a, 293a
  Enlightenment, II 99a
  environment, II 451a
  equality, II 145b–146a
  eschatology, II 159a–159b
  ethics, II 450b, 452a; III 159b, 160a, 445a
  evolution, II 180b, 454a, 583a
  existentialism, II 191b; III 157b–160a, 160b
  feudalism, IV 161b
  Feuerbach and, I 38a; II 450b, 451b
  freedom, II 159a; III 473b; IV 291a, 292a
  French Revolution (1789), IV 162a
  God, II 356a
  good, II 450b; IV 177a
  happiness, II 381b
  Hegel and, II 413b, 451b, 452b, 453a, 454a; III 159b,

359a–359b; IV 161a, 290a–292a
  Hegelianism, III 473b
  Hess and, II 413b
  historians, III 479a
  historicism, IV 460b, 462b, 463a, 463b
  historiography, II 24b–25a, 492b, 495b, 496a, 499a
  history, I 282a–282b; II 24b–25a, 159a–159b, 450a, 451a–453a, 454a; III 167b; IV 161a, 161b, 162a, 290a, 293b, 534a
  human nature, II 450b, 451a
  humanism, II 450b, 454b; III 168a
  ideology, II 553a, 554a–554b, 555a, 559b, 560b, 562b
  impressionism, II 583a
  income, II 49b
  India, II 17a
  individualism, II 451a, 451b, 598a, 600b, 601a
  industry, I 39b–40b; III 479a
  irrationalism, II 637a
  Jesus Christ, III 147b
  knowledge, II 451a
  labor, II 25a, 49b, 60a, 69b; IV 292a, 292b
  law, III 22a; IV 291a, 292a
  liberalism, II 450b–451a, 451b; III 59b, 60a
  logic, II 454a
  love, III 104b, 105a, 160a
  materialism, II 450a–455a; III 153a, 167b, 359a
  matter, III 195b
  millenarianism, IV 161b
  modernism, III 479a
  morality, II 450b, 451a
  motion, II 454a
  nationalism, III 332b, 334b
  natural law, I 620b; III 22a
  natural liberty, II 69b
  natural science, II 450a, 451b
  naturalism, II 451a–451b, 583a
  Nature, II 450a, 450b, 451a, 452b–453a, 454a; III 159a, 159b, 359a
  necessity, III 351b, 355b, 358a–359b; IV 534b
  Newton and, II 451b; III 146b
  overproduction, IV 292b
  pangenesis, II 626a–626b
  peace, III 445a

perennial philosophy, III 462a
perfectibility, III 473b, 474a
periodization in history, III 478a, 478b, 479a
philosophy, II 452b, 453b; III 334b, 359b
politics, II 16b–17a, 451b, 452b; IV 161a, 161b, 162a, 163a, 291a
positivism, II 451b; III 534b
power, IV 161b
pragmatism, III 553b
private property, II 17a, 25a; II 49b, 69b; III 654a; IV 292a, 292b, 316b, 534b
production, II 159a, 452b, 453a; III 158b–159a; IV 291a, 292a, 292b, 534a
profit, III 162a; IV 292b
progress, III 646a
proletariat, II 25a, 559b; IV 291b–293a
protest movements, III 673b
rationalism, II 450a–451a
realism, II 451a, 454a
realism in literature, IV 53a
religion, III 167b
revisionism, IV 264b–267a, 268b–270a, 272a, 274a, 274b
revolution, II 450b, 452a; III 162a; IV 161a–163b, 166b, 265a, 290a, 290b, 293a, 534a
Ricardo and, II 453a
right, IV 177a
romanticism, IV 207b, 208b, 210a
Ruge and, II 413b
Saint-Simon and, III 534b
salvation, III 334b
science, II 452b
self-determination, IV 291b
skepticism, IV 250a
slavery, II 25a
Smith and, II 451a, 453a
socialism, II 17a, 450a–451b; II 154a, 155b, 158a, 673b; IV 285a, 289b, 290a–294a
society, II 25a, 450b–453a, 454a; III 159a, 159b, 162a, 473b; IV 161a, 161b, 162a, 290a–290b, 291b, 292a, 534a, 534b
socioeconomic existence, II 554a
sociology, II 452a, 452b, 453b
State, II 59b; IV 161b, 162a, 316b
Stirner and, IV 291a
structuralism, IV 326a–

327b, 328b, 329a
technology, IV 292b
terror, IV 162a
theology, IV 291a
theory of base and super-structure, II 556a
Tillich and, III 158a
totalitarianism, IV 408a
truth, III 22a
Tucker and, III 158a
unemployment, IV 292b
universe, II 451a
utilitarianism, II 381b
Utopia, II 59b; III 160a
value, II 450b, 451a; IV 292b, 452a, 452b
wages, IV 292b
war, I 593b–594a; III 445a
Weber and, II 453a
women, IV 528a
work, IV 534a–534b
Zeitgeist, IV 536a
Marxism, III 146b–170a
acquired characteristics, II 619b–620b, 621a, 621b
Adler, Max, III 164b
agriculture, III 152b, 155a, 166a, 166b
Albania, III 169a
alienation, III 158b–159b, 168b
anarchism, III 160b
anthropology, III 153b, 168a
art, III 148a, 152b, 153b
atheism, II 213b
atomism, I 497a–497b
Austria, III 164b
authority, III 152b
Bakunin, III 152a
Beard, III 149b
Beria, III 157a
Bernstein, III 148a, 149a, 152b, 161a–166a, 167b, 168b, 169a, 169b; IV 266b–267b, 270a
biology, II 620a, 621a
Blanqui, III 152a
Boas, Franz, III 153b
Böhm-Bawerk, III 164b
Bolshevik Party, III 152b
Bolshevik-Leninism, III 148a, 150b, 152a–157b, 159b
bourgeois, III 156a, 161b, 164a, 165b, 166a, 168a, 169a; IV 181a
Brazil, III 540b
Brezhnev, III 167a
Browder, III 156b
Buber, III 158a
Bukharin, III 165b, 166a
Bulganin, III 157a

Bulgaria, III 157b
bureaucracy, III 168b, 169b
capitalism, III 147a–169a, 169b, 645b, 646a
Carlyle, III 158b
charity, II 213b–214a
China, III 154a
China (Communist), III 147b, 150b, 154b, 157a–157b, 161b, 166b, 167a, 167b, 169a
Christianity, II 213b–214a; III 146b, 160b
class, III 147a–148b, 150a–152a, 154a–155b, 156b, 160a, 162a, 162b, 164b, 166b, 645b
Cohen, Hermann, III 163a
collaborationism, III 166b
collectivism, III 151a–152b, 152b, 166a, 167a, 654a
commodities, III 158b–159a
communism, II 559a; III 147b, 148a, 151a, 152a–157b, 645b–646a; IV 181a
Communist Parties, III 153b, 154b, 156a–157b, 167b
community, III 148b, 154b
cooperatives, III 148b, 163b
criticism, III 146b, 147b, 168b, 169b
Croce, III 165a
culture, I 618b; III 146b, 148a, 149a, 150a, 150b; IV 165a, 165b
Czechoslovakia, III 167a–167b, 168b, 169a, 169b
De Leon, III 148a
democracy, I 664a–664b; III 147b, 148b, 152a, 153a, 155b, 156a, 156b
despotism, III 147b
determinism, II 24b–25a; III 149a–150a, 152b, 162b, 163b, 168a–168b, 569a
Dewey, III 153b, 565b
dictatorship, III 147b, 155b–156a, 158a, 166b
dignity, III 148b
discontinuity, I 497a–497b
Djilas, III 154b
dualism, III 159a, 159b
Dubcek, III 169b
Duclos, III 156b
duty, III 160a
East Germany, III 166b
economic history, II 49b, 55a, 59b
economics, III 146b–170a, 646a; IV 180b–181a
elite, III 154b
Emerson, III 158b

empircism, III 147a, 160b, 162a, 162b, 163a
employment, III 148a
Engels, III 147b, 148a, 148b, 149a, 150a, 152a, 153a, 153b, 154a, 155b, 156a, 159b, 162b, 167b, 168a
Epicurus, I 497a
equality, II 142a; III 148b
eschatology, II 160a
ethics, III 148a, 151b, 158a, 158b, 159b, 160a, 162b–163a, 163b, 164b, 167b, 168a–168b; IV 180b
eugenics, II 620b
evil, III 147a
evolution, III 149a, 149b, 153b, 161b, 162b, 163a, 163b, 167b, 169b; IV 180b–181a
evolution of literature, II 173b
existentialism, II 191a, 194a, 194b, 195a; III 147a, 148a, 157b–161a, 164b, 168a
faith, II 213b–214a
fascism, III 147a, 166a
Faust (legend), III 252a
force, III 155b, 156a, 169b
Foster, III 156b
France, I 664a–664b; III 150b–151a, 156b, 158b, 165a, 167a, 167b
free will, II 246b
freedom, III 147a, 148b–149a, 152a, 155b, 156a, 157b, 158a, 160a, 167b, 168a–168b, 645b–646a; IV 181a
Fromm, III 158a
fundamentalism, III 169a
Germany, I 664a–664b; III 149a, 149b, 151a, 152a, 152b, 154a, 157a, 161a–164b, 165a, 165b–166a; IV 264b–267b, 268b–272a, 273a–275a
goals, III 146b–147a; IV 181a
God, II 213b; III 147a, 153a
Goldenweiser, III 153b
Gomulka, III 166a–166b
good, IV 180b–181a
gradualism, III 149b, 164b
Great Britain, III 151a, 152a, 154a, 157a, 162a, 165a
Great Depression (1930s), III 164a
Guesde, III 165a
Hegel, III 162a, 168b, 556a

Hegelianism, II 24b
Hess, III 158b
hierarchy, III 156a
historiography, II 24b–25a, 497a, 499a
history, II 24b–25a, 453a; III 147a, 147b–148a, 149b–152a, 159a, 159b–160a, 162b, 167b, 225b, 645b; IV 180b–181a
Hobbes, I 216b
hope, II 213b–214a; III 147a
human nature, III 159b
humanism, III 158a, 160a, 168a, 169a
Hungary, III 156a, 166a–166b, 167a
idealism, III 150a, 158a, 159a, 162b, 168a
ideology, II 559a–562a; III 161b, 162b, 163a, 165a, 167a, 167b, 654a
immediatism, III 160b
imperialism, III 150b, 161b, 165b, 166b, 167a, 169a
income, III 151a
Independent Party, III 164a
individualism, III 147b, 151a–151b, 154a, 167b, 168a, 168b, 645b, 646a
industry, III 147b, 148b, 149a, 150b, 153b, 154a, 155a, 158b, 160b, 654a
inequality, III 151b
intolerance, IV 113a
irrationalism, II 637a, 637b
Italy, III 157b, 165a, 167b
James, III 565b
Jaurès, III 165a
judgment, III 153b, 160a, 168b
justice, IV 181a
Kadar, III 156a
Kant, III 163a, 164b, 168a
Kardelj, III 166a–166b
Kautsky, III 148a, 150a, 164a, 165b
Khrushchev, III 153b, 155a, 157a–157b, 166a
Kosík, III 168b, 169a, 169b
Kotakowski, III 168a–169b
labor, III 146b–170a
Labriola, III 165a
Lamarckism, II 619b–620a
Lange, F. A., III 163a
Lange, Oscar, III 154b
law, III 148b, 150a, 151b, 153a, 156a
Left, III 147b, 160b, 163a, 165b, 167a, 169a–169b
Lenin, II 560a–560b, 561b; III 150a, 152a–155a, 156a–

157a, 158a, 165a, 166b, 167b, 168a
liberalism, III 40a, 46b, 54a, 58b, 59b, 60a
Liebknecht, III 153a
literary criticism, I 603b, 606a, 606b–607a
literature, III 149b
longevity, III 93a
love, III 160a
Lowie, III 153b
Lukács, III 165b, 168b, 169a
Luxemburg, III 152b, 162b, 164a
Malenkov, III 157a
Mao Tse-tung, III 161b, 166b
Marković, III 169b
Marx, III 146b, 147b–148a, 149a, 152a, 154a, 154b, 155b, 156a, 157b–160a, 160b, 161b–163b, 167b–169b
Marxism-Leninism, III 153a, 154a–157b, 167a–168a
materialism, II 450a–456b; III 149b–150b, 153a, 153b–154a, 157a, 158a, 159b, 167b, 168a, 565a; IV 180b
Mead, III 565b
Merleau-Ponty, III 158a
Michels, III 151a
millenarianism, III 224a, 225b
Millerand, III 165a
minorities, III 148b, 155a
monism, III 147a, 150a
monopoly, III 150b, 162a, 654a
morality, III 153b, 160a, 163a, 168b; IV 181a
More, Thomas, III 654a
Morgan, Lewis, III 153b
Nagy, III 166a–166b, 167a
nationalism, III 148b, 150b–151a, 151b, 152b, 157b, 164b, 167b, 168b–169a, 333a–334b, 335b
natural liberty, II 69a–69b
natural science, III 149a
Nature, III 159a–159b, 167b, 168b, 645b
Nazism, III 164b
necessity, III 149a–149b, 356b, 359a–360b, 569a, 645b–646a
Neo-Kantianism, III 163a, 165a
norms, III 151b, 160a
nuclear power, III 155a, 157a
ontology, III 153a, 167b
opportunism, III 164a, 166a

overproduction, III 162a
ownership, III 645b, 646a
pangenesis, II 626b
Pareto, III 151a, 165a
peace, III 147a
peasantry, III 154a
Peirce, III 565b
Pejović, III 168b
pessimism, III 645b
Petrović, III 169b
philosophy, III 147b–149a, 153a, 157a–159b, 162b–163a, 164b–165a, 166b, 167b–169b
Plekhanov, III 148a, 150a
Poland, III 154b, 166a–166b, 167b, 168a, 169a
political parties, III 155b–156b
Ponomarev, III 166b, 167a
Popper, III 160a
positivism, III 153a, 169b, 540b
poverty, III 151b
power, III 148b, 149b–151b, 154b, 155b, 156a, 160a, 166a, 167b, 645b, 646a; IV 181a
pragmatism, III 556a, 565a, 565b, 566a, 569a
private property, III 148b, 154b, 158b, 159b, 645b, 646a, 652b, 653a, 654a
production, III 147a, 148a, 148b, 149a, 150a–151a, 155b, 158a–160a, 162b, 645b; IV 181a
profit, III 147a, 148a, 148b, 150b, 155a–155b, 162a
progress, III 634a, 645b–646a
proletariat, III 154b, 155b–156a, 162a, 164b, 166b, 654a
prosperity, III 147a, 151b
protest movements, III 671a, 675a
Prücha, III 168b
psychology, III 150a, 158b, 159a, 159b
race, III 148b
rationalism, III 149a, 152b, 645b
realism in literature, IV 53a, 55a, 55b, 56a
reform, III 149a, 149b
reformation, IV 69a
religion, III 147a, 148a, 148b–149a, 150b, 159a, 166b, 167b; IV 113a, 115b
Renner, III 164b
responsibility, III 149b, 167b, 168a, 646a

revisionism, III 161a–170a; IV 264b–267b, 268b–272a, 273a–275a
revolution, III 148b, 149a, 154a, 156b, 160b, 161b–163b, 165a, 166a, 167b, 169b, 645b; IV 161a, 162a–163b, 165a, 165b, 166a
rhetoric, III 149b, 152a
right, IV 180b–181a
Right, III 165b, 167a, 169a–169b
Roman Catholic Church, III 147a, 166b
Rousseau, III 156a
rules, III 151b, 156a
Russia, III 152a, 154a, 164b–165a
Russian Revolution (October 1917), III 148a, 150a, 150b, 152a–152b, 154a, 155b, 164a, 165a
Rykov, III 165b
Sartre, IV 194a, 194b, 195a; III 158a, 160b, 161a, 168a; IV 536a
Schaff, III 168a, 169a
Schmidt, III 163a
Schulze-Gävernitz, III 162a
science, III 146b–147a, 147b, 150b, 152b, 153a–154a, 159a, 160b, 162b, 163a, 168b; IV 180b–181a
Second International, III 149a, 152a, 152b, 161a, 164b, 165b
self-determination, III 148b
sensualism, III 160b
sex, III 148b
Sixth World Congress, III 165b
skepticism, III 163a
social science, III 149a
Social-Democratic Party (Germany), III 149a, 152a, 152b, 161b, 162b, 163a, 163b, 164a, 165a, 165b, 166b
Social-Democratic version, III 148a–152a, 152b, 153a, 155b, 159b, 161a, 161b, 164b, 165b, 169a
society, III 146b–170a, 645b, 646a, 654a; IV 180b–181a
sociology, II 620a, 621a; III 149a, 158a, 158b, 160b
Sorel, III 565a, 565b, 566a
Stalin, III 152b, 153a, 154b, 155a, 156b, 157a, 157b,

158a, 165b, 166a, 167b, 168a
Stalinism, III 167b, 168a, 168b, 169b
State, III 148b, 151b–152a, 153a, 154b, 155a, 162b, 167a, 646a; IV 316b, 318b
Stojanović, III 168a, 168b
strikes, III 149b, 150b–151a, 152a
structuralism, IV 326a, 327b
Struve, III 165a
subjectivism, III 153a
surplus value, III 148a, 150b, 162b
Sviták, III 169a, 169b
taxation, III 151b
technology, III 147a, 147b, 150a, 150b, 153b–154a, 155b, 157a, 168b
Teilhard de Chardin, II 214a
teleology, III 149b
Third Communist International, III 153b, 165a
Thomism, III 169a
Tillich, III 158a
time, III 149b
Titoism, III 166b
Tomsky, III 165b
totalitarianism, III 147b, 150b, 165b, 569a; IV 409b
Trotsky, III 153b–154a, 165b, 168b
truth, III 146b, 147b, 153a–153b, 160b, 161a
Tucker, III 158a, 159a–159b
Ulbricht, III 166b
unemployment, III 151b
U.S.S.R., III 147b, 150b, 151a, 152b–157b, 161b, 165a–165b, 166a–169b; III 645b
unions, III 148b, 154b, 163b
U.S., III 151a, 152a, 154a, 156b, 157a, 157b, 160b
Utopia, IV 463b
utopianism, III 160a
value, III 148a, 148b, 150b, 159a, 162b, 163b
Veblen, III 150a
violence, III 148b, 149b, 160b
Vollmar, III 166a
voluntarism, III 152a, 152b–153a, 153b, 158a
vox populi, IV 499a
wages, III 151b
war, III 149b, 150b–151a, 155a, 157a, 157b; IV 501a, 506a

Warsaw Pact, III 167a
wealth, III 151b
Webb, III 163b
Weber, III 149b
welfare, III 149b, 152a
West Germany, III 166b
Whitehead, III 150a
Wolf, III 162a
Woltmann, III 163a
World Communist Movement, III 161b, 165b
World War I, III 149b, 150b–151a, 152a, 152b, 164a
World War II, III 151a
Yugoslavia, III 154b, 157b, 166a–169b
Zeitgeist, IV 536a
See also Socialism
Marxism-Leninism
    capitalism, III 478b, 479a
    China (Communist), II 453b; III 334a, 334b
    class, III 154a–154b
    dictatorship, III 155b–156a
    feudalism, III 478b
    historians, III 478b–479a
    ideology, II 562b, 563b
    Marxism, III 153a, 154a–157b, 167a, 167b, 168a
    materialism, II 450a, 453b, 455a
    nationalism, III 334a, 334b
    periodization in history, III 478b
    progress, III 647b
    proletariat, III 155b–156a
    revolution, IV 166a
    Stalin, II 562b–563a; III 152b
    State, III 155a
    U.S.S.R., II 453b, 562b, 563b; IV 512b
    welfare state, IV 512b
Mary, *see* Virgin Mary (Bible)
Mary I, Queen (1516–1558), heresy, II 426a
    history, I 393b, 398a
Mary, Queen of Scots (1542–1587), history, I 397b
Mary Magdalene (Bible), love, III 96b
Masaccio (1401–1428)
    art, II 301b
    individualism, II 301b
Mascall, E. L., God, II 361b
Masculinity
    Aeschylus, IV 366b
    love, III 107a
    temperance, IV 366b
    women, IV 523b
Maslow, Abraham, happiness, II 385a
Masochism

Freud, II 383b
    pleasure, II 383b
Mason, William (1729–1797), mythology, III 298b
Masque
    mythology, III 297a
    ut pictura poesis, IV 470a, 472b
Mass
    Einstein, IV 84a, 86a, 86b
    matter, III 192a
    painting, II 570a
    relativity, IV 82b, 84a, 86a, 86b
Massis, Henri, natural law, III 22b
Masson, David (1822–1907), realism in literature, IV 52b
Masson-Oursel, Paul, Buddhism, I 256a
Massys, Quentin (1466?–1530), wisdom of the fool, IV 519b
Masturbation, health, II 403a
Materialism, II 450a–456b
    agnosticism, I 22b–23a
    analogy, I 70a
    anthropology, II 450a–450b, 451a, 454a
    Aristotelianism, II 464a
    atomism, II 245b
    Bacon, IV 432a
    bourgeois, II 451b, 452a, 452b, 453a
    capitalism, II 452b, 453a
    Cartesianism, II 450a, 450b, 453b
    Carus, II 454b
    causation, II 452b
    China (Communist), II 453b; III 334a, 453b
    class, II 451b, 452a, 454b
    collectivism, II 451a
    communism, II 450a, 450b, 451a
    Comte, II 451b, 452a, 454b
    Condillac, II 450a
    Darwinism, IV 107b
    deism, I 651b
    Democritus, III 577a
    Descartes, II 450a; III 193a
    determinism, II 237a, 454b
    dialectical, II 450a–456b
    Diderot, III 140b
    economic history, II 46b, 52b
    economics, II 451b, 452a, 452b, 453a, 453b
    Emerson, III 430a
    Engels, II 450a, 452a–455a; III 153a
    Enlightenment, II 450a, 450b
    environment, II 451a

Epicureanism, IV 7a, 8a, 175b
    ethics, II 450b, 452a
    evolution, II 177b, 180b, 188a, 454a, 454b; III 140b, 433b; IV 180b
    existentialism, III 158a, 159a
    Feuerbach, II 450b, 451b
    France, II 450a, 450b, 451a–451b
    free will, II 237a, 345b–246b
    Gassendi, II 450a
    God, II 355b
    good, II 450b; IV 175b, 180b
    happiness, II 378a
    harmony, II 392b
    Hegel, II 407b, 414a, 451b, 452b–455b
    Helvétius, II 450a, 451a
    hierarchy, II 444a, 448a
    history, II 450a–456b
    Hobbes, II 444a, 450a, 453b; IV 434a
    Holbach, II 451a
    human nature, II 450b, 451a; III 577a
    humanism, II 450b, 454b, 455a
    idealism, II 453a
    individualism, II 451a, 451b
    Kant, II 407b, 455a
    Kautsky, II 453a, 454b
    knowledge, II 451a
    labor, III 676a
    Labriola, II 453a
    Leibniz, II 450a; III 193a
    Lenin, II 454b–455a
    liberalism, II 450b–451b
    Locke, II 450a
    logic, II 453b–455a
    love, II 451a
    Lucretius, III 631a
    Man-Machine, III 133a, 133b–145a
    Marx, II 450a–455a; III 153a, 167b, 359a
    Marxism, II 450a–456b; III 149b–150b, 153a, 153b–154a, 157a, 158a, 159b, 167b, 168a; III 565a; IV 180b
    Marxism-Leninism, II 450a, 453b, 455a
    matter, II 455a; III 185b–186a, 193a–193b
    metaphysics, II 450a, 454a, 454b, 455a
    monasticism, IV 64a
    monism, II 455a
    morality, II 450b, 451a
    motion, II 454a, 454b

music, II 392b
nationalism, III 334a
natural science, II 450a, 451b, 453b, 455a
naturalism, II 451a–451b
Nature, II 450a, 450b, 451a, 452b–453a, 454a–454b
necessity, III 359a, 360a
Neo-Platonism, II 454a
Newton, II 451b
ontology, II 450a, 454b, 455a
Orientalism, III 429a–429b, 430a, 433b, 438a
perfectibility, III 473a
periodization in history, III 478a, 478b
Petrarch, IV 141b
philosophy, II 452b, 453b; IV 53b
Platonism, III 504a, 505b, 506a, 507b, 522b, 524a
pleasure, II 378a
Plekhanov, II 453a, 453b, 455a
Plotinus, III 505b
politics, II 451b, 452b, 454b
positivism, II 451b, 452a, 453b, 454b; III 545a
power, II 450b
pragmatism, III 565a, 565b, 569a
production, II 452a, 452b, 453a
progress, III 631a
protest movements, III 675b, 676a
psychology, IV 7a, 8a, 9b, 10b, 11a, 12a, 21a, 22b, 24a
rationalism, II 450a, 450b–451a
realism, II 451a, 454a
realism in literature, IV 51b, 53b, 54a
reformation, IV 64a, 69a
religion, IV 106b, 107b
Renaissance, IV 141b, 142a
revisionism, IV 269b, 270a
revolution, II 452a, 452b
Ricardo, II 453a
right, IV 175b, 180b
romanticism, IV 201a, 203b, 210a
Sartre, III 158a
satire, IV 214b
Schelling, II 454b
science, II 452a, 452b–455a
Shelley, III 524a
Smith, II 451a, 453a
socialism, II 450a, 451a, 451b, 452a, 454b

society, II 450b–454b
sociology, II 452a–453b
sophism, I 629a
Sorel, III 565b
Spencer, II 454b
Spinoza, II 450a; III 193a
spontaneous generation, IV 310b, 311a
Stalin, III 153a
State, II 452b
Stoicism, III 504a
Stoics, IV 7a, 8a
subjectivism, II 455a
transcendentalism, IV 24a
U.S.S.R., II 453b, 455a; III 153a
U.S., III 429a–429b, 430a, 433b, 438a
unity of science, IV 432a, 434a
universe, II 451a, 455a
value, II 450b, 451a
Weber, II 453a
Maternus, Firmicus, mythology, III 291a
Mathematical Proof Methods, assumption, III 172b
  axiom, III 172a, 174a, 174b, 175a, 176a, 176b, 177a
  deduction, III 171b–172a
  implication, III 172b–173a
  indirect form, III 172a, 172b
  logical deduction, III 172b, 175a
  postulate, III 172a
  superposition, III 171b–172a
  visual, III 171b–172a
Mathematics, III 170a–185a
  abstract, II 611b
  abstraction, III 184b
  acoustics, III 387b
  Aeschylus, III 180a
  Age of Eclosion, III 179b–180a
  Alembert, III 179b
  Alexander of Aphrodisias, I 580b
  algebra, III 173a, 174a, 175a, 175b, 178a, 178b, 179a, 183b, 184a
  alphabet, III 180b
  analysis, III 174b, 175a, 175b, 176a, 177a, 178b, 179a
  analytic geometry, III 173a, 174a
  Apollonius, III 178b, 182b, 183a
  Apollonius of Perga, III 380a
  Arabia, III 181a, 184b–185a
  archeology, III 181a

Archimedes, III 178b, 182b, 183a, 183b, 184a, 184b
Aristaeus the Elder, III 380a
Aristotelianism, III 174a
Aristotle, I 1b–2b, 463a; III 172a, 172b–173a, 173b, 180a, 184a, 380a, 380b, 554b; IV 38a, 400b
arithmetic, III 171b, 173a, 173b, 178a, 178b
art, I 456b, 457b, 459a; II 614a
astronomy, III 180a, 182b
axiomatization, III 172b, 174a, 174b, 175a, 176a, 176b, 177a, 180a
Babylonia, III 171a, 171b, 173a, 180b, 182b
Bacon, III 356a
Barrow, III 178b–179a, 388a–388b
Berkeley, III 173a
Bernoulli, Jacob, III 179b
Bernoulli, John, III 179b
Bible, III 180b
biology, III 178a
Brazil, III 543a
Briggs, III 178b
Brouwer, III 170b, 176b
Burckhardt, III 178a
Bürger, III 178b
Byzantine Empire, III 181a, 181b
calculus, II 610b; III 173a–173b, 174a, 177b, 178b, 182b
Cantor, III 175b
cardinal numbers, I 8b–9a
Cauchy, III 174a, 174b
Cavendish, III 179a
certainty, I 309a, 312a–312b, 314b
chance, I 337a–337b
chemistry, III 177a, 178a
China, I 355a
China (ancient), III 180b–181a
chora, IV 299b
Christianity, III 182a
civilization, III 177b, 180a, 181a–182b
Clairaut, III 179b
cognition, III 183b, 184a, 184b
collection, III 175a–175b
color, III 395b–396a
commerce, III 178b
completeness, II 614a–615b
complex numbers, III 173b, 174b
Comte, III 535a, 535b
concepts, III 171b, 172a,

173a, 173b, 175a, 175b, 176b, 183b, 184b, 185a
Condorcet, III 533a
Copernicus, II 442b, 443b; III 178a, 182b
Coulomb, III 179a
Counter-Enlightenment, II 101b, 103a
continuity, I 492b, 493b, 494a, 497b–498b, 500b–501a, 502b
creativity in art, I 580a–580b, 581a, 583b, 584a, 584b
criticism, III 179b
culture, III 171a, 171b, 173a, 177a, 185a
decimal system, III 171a, 173a
Dedekind, III 175b
Descartes, III 178b, 183a, 183b, 214b, 357a; IV 435b
Dioclos, III 182b
Dionysius Exiguus, III 182a
economics, III 178a, 178b
Egypt (ancient), III 180a, 180b, 182b
Einstein, IV 83a, 84a
Eleaticism, III 171b
electricity, III 179a
empiricism, III 547b, 548a
Enlightenment, III 179a–179b
equality, II 138b, 140b
equations, III 173b, 175a, 175b, 178a, 182b
Euclid, III 172b, 174a, 174b, 178b, 179a, 179b, 180a, 182b, 184b, 380a
Euclidean geometry, III 174a, 175b
Eudoxus, III 172b, 173b, 175a, 380a
Euler, III 179b
Eurytos, I 580a–580b
evolutionism, II 187b
formalism, II 588b
formism, III 176b
Fourier, III 174b, 175b
fractions, III 174a
France, III 178b
Fraunhofer, III 179a
free will, II 245b, 246b
Frege, III 175b, 176a
Fresnel, III 179a
functions, I 498a–498b
Galileo, III 193a, 356a, 383a, 385b, 388a; IV 134a, 361a
game theory, II 263b, 264a, 264b, 265a–265b, 266b, 271a, 273a, 274a
Gauss, III 179a
genius, II 313b, 325b

geology, III 178a
geometry, II 612b–614a;
III 171b–175a, 176a, 178b,
180a, 184a, 184b; IV 304a
Germany, III 178a
Gibbon, III 181a–181b
God, II 346a–347a
good, IV 177a, 177b
Greece (ancient), I 497b–
498a; III 171a–173a, 174b,
175a, 176a, 178b, 179b,
180a–184b
Hammurabi, III 179b, 180a
harmony, II 388a, 389a,
390a–390b; III 387b; IV
38a–40a
Hegel, III 556b
Herodotus, III 180a
hierarchy, II 438a, 442b,
443b, 444b, 445a
Hilbert, III 170b, 176b
Hipparchus, III 182b
Hobbes, IV 177a
Homer, III 180a
humanism, II 515b, 521a;
IV 129a, 134a
Hume, I 312a–312b, 320a
Huygens, III 179a
Hypsicles, III 182b
idea, II 542b, 546a, 546b
incommensurability, III
172a
indeterminacy, II 586b,
588b, 592a, 592b
infinity, II 606a, 606b,
608a–615b; III 173b, 174b,
176a, 177a
integers, III 175b, 179b
intuitionism, III 176b–177a
irrational numbers, III 174a
Islam, II 640b, 643b, 646b–
647b, 651b; III 181a
Italy, III 178a–178b
Justinian, III 181b
Kant, III 179a, 357b; IV
248b, 433a, 433b
Kepler, II 390a; III 178b,
182b
knowledge, III 179b–180a,
180b, 184b
Kronecker, III 176b
Lagrange, III 179b
language, II 660a
Laplace, III 179b
Leibniz, II 444b, 668b; III
173a, 174a, 174b, 179b
Leonardo da Vinci, IV 440a,
440b–441a
Leonardo of Pisa, III 181b
linguistics, III 72a; IV 426a,
429a, 430a
literary paradox, III 76b, 77b
Locke, III 183b
logarithms, III 178b

logic, III 172a, 172b, 175a,
175b, 176a, 176b, 177a,
180a, 184a, 547b, 548a
Malus, III 179a
Man-Machine, III 134a–
135b, 137b, 140a, 142b,
143b, 145b
matter, III 187a, 187b,
189b, 192b, 193a, 194b
Maupertuis, III 179b
measurements, III 177a; IV
400b, 402a, 403a, 403b
mechanism, III 179b, 183b,
184a, 387b
Mesopotamia (ancient), III
179b, 180a, 180b
metaphor, III 201a
metaphysics, III 179a, 214a,
214b, 215a
method of exhaustion, II
609b, 610b
method of proof, III 170b
methodology, III 379a,
379b, 380a, 380b, 382a,
383a, 386a, 387b–390b
Middle Ages, II 196b–198a,
200a–205a; III 178a, 178b
music, I 457a, 459a; II
313b, 325b, 388a, 389a,
390a–390b; III 260b, 263b,
387b
mythology, III 316b
Napier, III 178b
natural numbers, III 175b,
176b, 177a
natural science, III 177a,
177b
Nature, III 348a
necessity, III 352b–355a,
356a, 357a, 357b, 358a,
359b, 360b, 361b
negative numbers, III 173b,
174b
new, II 611a
Newton, III 173a, 174b,
178b–179a, 182b, 183a,
183b–184b, 194b, 379a,
379b, 380a, 380b, 382a,
383a, 386a, 387b–390b,
393b, 395b–396a, 398b
Nicomedes, III 182b
non-Euclidean geometry,
III 174a
nonsensory origin of, I 1a
numbers, III 171a, 174a,
174b, 175a, 175b, 177a,
400b, 403b, 404b, 405a
406a, 406b
optics, III 387b, 393b,
395b–396a, 398b, 407b–
408a, 410a, 410b, 411a,
416a, 416b–417b, 420a,
420b
ordinal numbers, I 9a

organicism, III 422a
organized, III 180a–180b
painting, I 580a
Pappus, III 178b, 380a–
380b
paradox, III 172b
Parmenides, III 171b, 172b;
IV 32a–32b
Peano, III 175b, 176a
Peirce, III .184a, 556b,
557b–558a, 559b–560a,
560b, 568a
perennial philosophy, III
457b, 460a, 461b
perfectibility, III 471b, 472a
philosophy, III 171b, 172a–
172b, 173a, 176b, 178a,
179b, 183a, 184b, 201a,
387b–388b, 416b; IV 33b
physics, III 174b, 175a,
177a, 178a, 179b, 387b–
388a, 388b
Pirenne, III 181a
Plato, I 581a, 583b, 584a,
584b; II 390a, 443b; III
172a, 180a, 308a, 503a;
IV 31a, 33a, 33b, 34b, 37b,
39a–39b
Platonism, III 177a–177b,
184b, 503a, 503b, 523b
Poincaré, III 176a
Pope, III 397a
Popper, I 323b
positivism, III 533a, 535a,
535b, 540b, 543a, 545b,
546a, 547b, 548a
pragmatism, III 552b, 553a,
558a, 558b, 560b, 561a,
563b, 564b, 565a, 565b,
567a
printing, III 178a
probability, III 605b–607a,
608a, 608b, 609b, 612a,
614a, 615b, 617a, 618b–
623a
progress, III 628a
proof, III 171b–177a
proportion, II 609b; III 175a
psychology, IV 11a, 11b,
12b, 29a
Ptolemy, III 182b
Pythagoras, III 390a; III
179b; IV 31a, 46b–47a
Pythagoreans, I 539b, 580a,
580b; III 171a–172a; IV
31a, 32a–40a
radical numbers, III 178a
Rameau, III 263b
Ramism, IV 42b, 43a, 43b,
45a
rationalism, IV 46b, 47b
real numbers, I 497b–499b
reasoning, III 178b
Regiomontanus, III 178b

relativity, IV 74b, 78b–80a,
83a, 84a, 85b, 89a
Renaissance, III 178a–
178b, 179a, 181b, 184b;
IV 129a, 134a, 437a,
438b, 439b–443a
Rheticus, III 178b
Riemann-Darbaux integral,
II 610b
right, IV 177a, 177b
rigor, III 170a–177b
Rome (ancient), III 181a,
181b
rules, II 660a
Russell, I 319b–320a, 321b;
III 176a, 176b
Sarton, III 178a
Saturn (myth), III 581a
scientific classification, I
463a–466a
science, II 640b, 643b,
646b, 647a, 647b, 651b;
III 178b–179a
sculpture, I 580a
set, III 175a–177a
skepticism, IV 236b, 246a,
248b
social sciences, III 177a
Socrates, III 172a
soul, IV 33a, 36b
space, IV 295a–297a,
299b–303a, 303b, 304b
Speusippus, IV 35b, 36a
Spinoza, II 273a, 445a; III
174a; IV 177b
Stoicism, III 184a
structuralism, IV 329b
study of, II 660a
Sumer, III 171a, 173a
symbolism, III 173a, 175b,
176a, 176b, 178a, 179a,
183b, 184b; IV 337b, 338b
symmetry, IV 346b, 348b,
349a, 349b, 351a, 351b,
352a–352b
Tartini, III 263b
technology, III 177a; IV
359b, 361a
theodicy, IV 381b, 382a
Theory of Sets, III 175b,
176a, 177a
Thucydides, III 180a
time, III 176b; IV 392b–
397b, 400b, 402a–403b
topos, IV 299b
translations, III 181b
trigonometry, III 178b
uniformitarianism, IV 426a,
429a, 430a
unity of science, IV 431b,
432b, 433a, 435b
universal man, IV 437b,
438b, 439b–443a

universe, II 442b; IV 38a–40a
utility, III 181b; IV 451a, 454a–456a, 458a
Vailati, III 560a
vanishing point, II 612b, 614a
Vico, II 102a
Viète, III 178b, 183b
Voltaire, III 179a
war, IV 502b
Werner, III 178b
Whewell, III 179a
Whitehead, III 176a, 176b
Wittgenstein, I 320a
Wollaston, III 179a
Wright, Chauncey, III 558a, 561a
writing, III 178a, 180a–181a
Young, Thomas, III 179a
Zeno of Citium, IV 32a–32b
Zeno of Elea, III 172b
Zermelo, III 176a
zoology, III 177a
Mather, Cotton (1663–1728), health, II 403a
philantropy, III 490b
psychology, IV 18a
Puritanism, IV 18a
Ramism, IV 44b
Mather, Increase (1639–1723), Ramism, IV 44b
Mather, Stephen Tyng (1867–1930), conservation, I 475a
Mathieu of Vendôme (d. 1286)
aesthetics, II 220a
style, IV 331a
Matronit (myth), III 282b
Matter, III 185a–196b
abstraction, III 187a, 190a
aesthetics, II 216a, 216b, 221b–222a, 222b
aether, IV 78a–78b
Albert of Saxony, III 192a
alchemy, III 190b–191a, 192a
analogy, III 189b
Anaxagoras, III 187a
Anaximander, III 186b
Anaximenes, III 186b
apeiron, IV 298a
appearance, III 187b, 188a, 188b, 190b, 192b
Archimedes, III 193b
Aristotelianism, III 190b, 191b, 192a, 192b, 194a, 194b, 196a
Aristotle, II 41a, 163a, 175b, 389b, 392b, 407b; III 187a–187b, 189a–190a, 190b, 191a, 192b, 195a; IV 4b, 5a
art, II 298b; III 189b

astronomy, III 192a, 194b
atomism, III 185a, 187a–193b, 194b, 195a
Augustinianism, III 191a–191b
Ayer, III 195b
Babylonia, III 186a
Bacon, III 187a; IV 434a
Being, III 185b, 187a, 188a, 188b, 189b
Berkeley, I 317a; II 120b; III 185b
Bible, III 186a–186b, 190b
biology, III 192a, 194a
Boscovich, III 185b
Boyle, III 190b, 194a, 194b
Bruno, II 348a; III 193b–194a
Büchner, III 185a
Buridan, III 192a
Butterfield, III 194b
causation, III 192b, 193a
Chain of Being, III 193b
chance, III 187b
change, III 185b, 186b, 187a, 187b, 188a, 189b, 190a
Christianity, III 190b
Chrysippus, III 190a
Copernicus, III 192b, 193b, 194a
cosmology, I 559b–560b, 561a, 562b; III 186b, 190a, 191a, 193b, 195b
craftsmanship, III 187a
Creation, III 186b, 190b, 193a
Darwin, II 588a
defined, III 185b–186a
Democritus, III 185b, 187a–189a, 192b, 195a, 196a
density, III 192a
Descartes, I 517a; II 41a; III 185b, 192b–195b
determinism, III 189b
divination, III 186a
dualism, II 38a, 38b, 41a, 43a
Duhem, III 192a
Einstein, I 559b–560b, 561a, 562b
Eleatics, III 187a
electricity, III 195a
emotion, III 187b
Empedocles, III 187a, 188b
empircism, III 188a, 189b, 190b, 195b, 546b
energy, III 185b
Engels, II 455a
Enlightenment, III 193b, 194a–195a
environment, III 191b
Epicureanism, III 187b, 190a

Epicurus, II 244a; III 187b
equality, II 138b
evil, II 43a, 163a, 163b, 164a, 164b
evolutionism, II 175b, 177b, 182b, 183a, 184a
fear, III 187b
Ficino, III 192b
flux, III 188a
force, III 192a, 194b, 195a, 196a
Galileo, III 193a, 194a
geometry, III 188b, 193a, 195a
Gilbert, Wm., III 192b, 194a
Giles of Rome, III 192a
Gnosticism, III 190b
God, II 348a, 353a; III 186b, 190b, 191b, 192b, 193a–195a
good, III 190b; IV 177a, 177b
Goodfield, III 190a–190b, 195a
gravity, III 194a–195a
Greece (ancient), II 42a; III 186a, 186b–190b, 191a
Grosseteste, III 191a
harmony, II 392a–392b; III 193a
hate, III 187a
Hegel, III 185b
Heraclitus, III 186b, 187a, 187b, 188a, 190a
hermeticism, II 431a, 433a
hierarchy, II 444a; III 190b, 192a, 192b, 193a
history, III 186a–186b
Hobbes, III 185b, 195a
humanism, III 187b, 193b
Huygens, III 194a
hylomorphism, III 187a–187b, 189a, 194a
hylozoism, III 187a
idea, III 188a
impenetrability of, III 187b
indeterminacy, II 588a
individualism, II 298b; III 191b
inequality, III 186b
inertia, III 193a, 194b, 195a
infinity, II 605b, 614a
Ionia, III 186b, 187a
irrationalism, II 635a, 635b
Islam, III 190b
Jammer, III 188b–189a, 192a
Judaism, III 186a–186b, 190b
Kant, I 330a, 521a; III 185b
Kepler, III 189a, 192a, 192b, 194a, 194b
knowledge, III 188b, 190a

Lavoisier, III 195b
Leibniz, III 185b, 193a, 195b–196a
Lejewski, III 186b
Leucippus, III 187b
light, III 191a, 195a
linguistics, IV 424a
Locke, III 195b–196a
love, III 187a
Lucretius, III 187b, 192b, 193b, 194a
macrocosm, III 130b, 188a, 193a
magic, III 186a
magnetism, III 195a
Malebranche, III 193a
Manicheism, III 190b
Marx, III 195b
mass, III 192a
materialism, II 455a; III 185b–186a, 193a–193b
mathematics, III 187a, 187b, 189b, 192b, 193a, 194b
mechanism, III 188a, 192b, 193a, 194b, 195a
Melissus, III 187a
Mesopotamia (ancient), III 186a
metaphysics, III 186b, 187a, 190b, 191a, 193b, 195a–196a
microcosm, III 130b
Middle Ages, II 196b, 201a–201b; III 190b–192b, 193b
mind, III 186b, 187a, 188a, 188b, 189b, 192b
miracles, III 186a
monads, III 193b, 196a
monism, III 187a, 193a
morality, III 186a–186b, 190a
motion, III 185a, 187b, 192a, 193a, 193b, 194b
music, II 392a–392b
mythology, III 186a, 191a
natural law, III 17b
Nature, III 186b, 189b, 193a, 194a, 194b
necessity, III 188a, 188b, 189b, 190a
Neo-Platonism, III 189a, 190b, 191a
Newton, I 548a; III 190b, 192a–196a, 418b, 419a
Nicolas of Autrecourt, III 192b
Nicolas of Cusa, III 192a, 192b, 193b
non-being, III 188a, 188b, 190b
occasionalism, III 193a
ontology, III 187b, 188b, 189a–189b

optics, III 195a, 418b, 419a
order, II 444a; III 186a–
186b, 190b
Oresme, III 192a
organicism, III 187a–187b
pain, III 187b
pantheism, III 194a
Parmenides, III 187a, 187b,
188a
Patrizi, III 193b
Philo Judaeus, II 42a
philosophy, III 185b, 187a,
187b, 188b, 189b–190a,
192b, 193a, 195b–196a
physics, III 187a, 190a
planets, III 194b
Plato, I 622b; III 185b,
187a–190b; IV 380b
Platonism, III 190b–193b,
196a, 509a, 513b
Plotinus, III 193b; IV 380a
pluralism, III 187a, 190a,
191a
positivism, III 195b, 546b
power, III 188a, 191b
pre-Socratics, III 186b–
187b
prophecy, III 186a
Protestantism, III 192b
psychology, IV 4b, 5a, 11a,
12a, 17a
Pythagoreans, III 187a,
188a
rationalism, III 195b
reality, III 187b, 188b
reason, III 187a
relativity, IV 78a–78b, 84a,
91b, 92a
religion, III 187b–188a
Renaissance, III 191b–
192a, 192b, 193b–194a;
IV 138b
revelation, III 186a, 190b
ritual, III 186a
Roman Catholic Church, III
192b
Saint Augustine, I 586b;
III 191b; IV 138b
Saint Bonaventura, III 191b
Saint Thomas Aquinas, III
191b
Scaliger, III 192a
science, III 186a–187b,
189b–190a, 191a, 192b,
193a, 193b, 194b
Sennert, III 192a
senses, III 185b, 187a,
187b, 188b, 189b, 190a
Socrates, III 187a
soul, III 191b, 194a
space, III 185b, 187b, 188a,
188b, 189a–189b, 194b–
195a, 196a; IV 296a, 296b,
297a, 298a, 301b, 302a

species, III 191a, 192b–
193a
Spinoza, III 193a, 194a
spontaneous generation, IV
307a, 308b, 312a
Stoicism, III 190a, 192b–
193a; IV 319a
superstition, III 187b
Swineshead, II 201a–201b;
III 192a
symmetry, IV 349a, 350a,
351a, 352b
technology, III 191a
teleology, III 188b, 192b–
193a
Telesio, III 193b
Thales, III 186a, 186b
Theaetetus, III 188b
theodicy, IV 380a, 380b
time, III 187b, 189a–189b,
194b–195a, 196a; IV 390a
Toulmin, III 190a–190b,
195a
truth, III 188b
unity, III 186b, 187a, 193b
universe, III 187b, 190a,
191a, 192a, 192b, 193a,
194a, 194b
velocity, III 187b
virtue, III 191a, 191b
vision, III 418b, 419a
vitalism, III 187a
void, III 186b, 187b, 195a
volume, III 192a
weight, III 192a
Whitehead, III 194a
William of Ockham, III 191b
Yahweh, III 186a–186b
Zeno of Citium, III 187a
Matthew, Saint
Church, I 413a, 414a
faith, II 399a
mythology, III 276a–276b
Matthew of Aquasparta
abstraction, I 4b–5a
knowledge, I 4b–5a
soul, I 5a
Matthias Corvinus, King
(1440–1490)
dignity, IV 144a
humanism, II 519a
Matthiessen, F. O.
literary criticism, I 604a
symbolism, IV 341b
Matthisson, Friedrich von
(1761–1831), symbolism,
IV 338a
Māturidites, II 642a
Maturin, Charles Robert
(1780–1824), love III 104b
Maudsley, Henry (1835–
1918)
Man-Machine, III 143a–
143b

progress, III 644b
Maui (myth), III 308a
Maupassant, Guy de (1850–
1893)
naturalism, IV 54a
realism in literature, IV 53b,
54a
Maupertuis, Pierre de (1698–
1759)
biology, II 177a–177b
Chain of Being, I 332b–
333a
deism, I 651a
evolutionism, II 177a–178a
genetic continuity, II 284b–
285a, 288a
God, I 333a
inheritance, II 623b
Man-Machine, III 141b
mathematics, III 179b
metaphysical imagination,
III 217a
Nature, I 332b–333a
pangenesis, II 623b
species, II 177a–177b
spontaneous generation, II
284b–285a
Maurice, Frederick Denison
(1805–1872)
eschatology, II 159a
modernism, I 424b
socialism, IV 290a
Maurolico, Francesco
Kepler and, III 412a
optics, III 409b, 412a
Maurras, Charles (1868–
1952)
authority, I 155b
classicism, I 450b, 454b–
455a
conservatism, I 483a
Eliot and, I 455a
literary criticism, I 604b
Maurus, Rabanus, mythology,
III 288b
Mauss, Marcel, structuralism,
IV 324a, 325b
Mauthner, Fritz (1849–1923),
Buddhism, I 256b
skepticism, IV 250a
Maximilian I, Emperor (1459–
1519)
disease, II 403a
iconography, II 530b
Maximus, Saint (580?–662),
astrology, I 124a
Neo-Platonism, III 378a
Maximus of Tyre (2nd cen-
tury A.D.)
cynicism, III 586a–586b
mimesis, III 227a
primitivism, III 586a–586b
theriophily, IV 386b
Maxwell, James Clerk (1831–

1879)
aether, IV 80b
axiomatization, I 166b
Berkeley and, IV 80b
continuity, I 494a
cosmology, I 554b, 555a
demonology, I 670a
entropy, II 114b, 115a,
116a–117a
Faraday and, I 89b
impressionism, II 572a,
580b
Newton and, IV 393a
optics, III 419b
photography, II 572a
probability, III 619b–620a
relativity, IV 78b, 79a, 80a,
80b, 83b, 87a, 91b
religion, IV 108a
space, IV 301b
symmetry, IV 353a
time, IV 393a
May, Kenneth, social welfare,
IV 284a
Mayakovsky, Vladimir V.
(1893–1930), revolution,
IV 165b
Mayall, N. V., cosmology,
I 565a, 567b
Mayer, Julius Robert von
(1814–1878)
entropy, II 113a
time, IV 395b
Mayflower Compact, justice,
II 658b
Mayo, Elton, individualism,
II 599b
Mazarin, Jules (1602–1661),
balance of power, I 182b–
183a
Machiavellism, III 119b,
120b
Mazzini, Giuseppe (1805–
1872)
authority, I 153a, 153b
French Revolution, I 408b–
409a
historiography, II 492b
Herder, IV 203b
history, I 409a
nationalism, III 328a, 336b
revolution, IV 160b
romanticism, IV 203b
work, IV 534b
Mead, George Herbert (1863–
1931)
Aristotle and, III 554b
association of ideas, I 116b
education, III 569b
evolutionism, II 184b
experience, III 569a
fascism, III 565b
human nature, III 554b
Lovejoy and, III 552b

Marxism, III 565b
mind, III 561b
Papini and, III 564a
Plato and, III 554b
pragmatism, III 551b, 552b, 553a, 554b, 564a, 565b, 568a, 569a
psychology, IV 23b
society, III 564a
value, III 568a
Mead, Margaret (1901–   ), women, IV 523b
Meadows, T. T., China, I 367b, 371a
Mean-speed Theorem, 200b, 202b, 204b
Measurement, IV 398b–406a
aborigines IV 399a
absolute space, IV 403b
absolute time, IV 403b
abstract, IV 400a
aether, IV 405a
agriculture, IV 402a
Archytas of Tarentum, IV 400b
Aristotle, IV 400a–400b, 451b–452a
astrology, IV 399a, 402b
astronomy, IV 399a, 399b, 401a, 402b, 403a, 405b
Australia, IV 399a
Barrow, IV 403a–403b, 405a
Bentham, IV 181b–182a, 453b
Bible, IV 402a
Boyle, IV 402b
calendar, IV 399b
China (ancient), IV 399a, 401a, 402a
Christianity, IV 402a
chronology, IV 400a
chronometry, IV 403a, 404b
class, IV 402a
clocks, IV 399a, 401a–401b, 402b, 403a, 404a
cosmic rays, IV 405b
cosmic time, IV 405b
cosmogony, IV 399b, 400a
cosmology, IV 400b, 405b
culture, IV 399a
cycles, IV 399b, 400b, 401a, 402a, 403a
Descartes, IV 402b
Dionysius Exiguus, IV 402a
Dondi, IV 402b
earth, IV 404a, 405a, 405b
economics, IV 402a
Egypt (ancient), IV 401a
Einstein, II 590a, 590b; IV 404b–405a
electromagnetics, IV 405a, 405b

electrons, II 589a
error, II 587b; III 613a
eternity, IV 400a
France, IV 401b
galaxies, IV 405b
Galileo, IV 402b–403a, 403b
geometry, IV 399b, 400a, 403a, 403b
gnomen, IV 400a
God, IV 402b
good, IV 178b, 181b–182a
gravity, IV 403a
Great Britain, IV 404b
Great Year (myth), IV 400b–401a
Greece (ancient), IV 399b–401a, 402a
Greenwich time, IV 404b
Gregory, XIII (Pope), IV 399b
Heraclitus, IV 399b, 400b, 401a
Hesiod, IV 399b
history, IV 402a
Homer, IV 399b
horology, IV 399a, 401a, 401b, 402b, 403a
hours, IV 401a
hubris, IV 399b
Huygens, IV 403a
imprecision, II 586b, 588a, 589b, 592b
indeterminacy, II 586b, 587b–593a
Indians (American), IV 399a–399b
inertia, IV 404b
instruments, II 588a
Islam, IV 402a
Italy, IV 401b
Jesus Christ, IV 402a
Judaism, IV 402a
Kelvin, IV 402b
Kepler, IV 402b
kinematics, IV 403a
leap year correction, IV 399b
Leibniz, IV 404a
light, IV 404b, 405a, 405b
literature, IV 399b
Locke, IV 404a
logic, IV 400a
magic, IV 402a, 402b
Margenau, II 591b
mathematics, III 177a; IV 400b, 402a, 403a, 403b
mechanism, IV 402b
mesons, IV 405b
methodology, III 379b, 390a–390b
Michelson-Morley experiment, IV 405a
Middle Ages, IV 399a,

401b, 402a
monasteries, IV 399a
moon, IV 400b, 404a
morality, IV 399a
motion, IV 400a, 400b, 403a, 403b
Mumford, IV 402b
music, III 260b; IV 399a, 399b, 402a
Nature, IV 399a, 399b, 402b, 404b, 405b
navigation, IV 403a
Newton, III 379b, 390a–390b; IV 403a, 403b, 404a
numbers, III 401b; IV 399b–400a, 400b
Oresme, IV 402b
Parmenides, IV 400a
philosophy, IV 399b, 402b
physics, IV 405a, 405b
planets, IV 400b
Plato, IV 400a, 400b–401a
pleasure, IV 178b
Plutarch, IV 399b
pragmatism, III 553a
precision, II 587b, 588a, 589a
probability, III 608a, 613a, 613b, 616b, 619a–621a, 622a, 623a
Pythagoreans, IV 399b, 400a, 400b
radar, IV 405b
rationalism, IV 51a
relativity, IV 78a, 82b, 91b, 405a, 405b
religion, IV 399a, 399b
Renaissance, IV 440a, 440b, 441a, 443a
rhythm, IV 399a
right, IV 178b, 181b–182a
Rome (ancient), IV 401a
Royal Observatory, IV 404b
seasons, IV 402a
science, IV 402a, 402b, 403a, 404a
Shakespeare, IV 399a
solar system, IV 400b, 405b
soul, IV 399b
space, IV 400a, 403b
Stoics, IV 401a
Su Sung, IV 401b
sun, IV 400b
sundial, IV 401a
Tait, IV 404b
technology, IV 361a–361b
teleology, IV 402a
theology, IV 399b
time, IV 389b, 392b, 398b–406a
Torricelli, IV 403a
uncertainty principle, IV 398a
universal man, IV 440a,

440b, 441a, 443a
universe, IV 399b, 400a, 402a, 402b, 404b, 405b
value, II 588b–589a; IV 450b, 451b–452a, 454a–454b, 455a, 456b–457b
velocity, IV 404b, 405a, 405b
Vitruvius, IV 401a–401b
wealth, IV 402a–402b
Zeno of Elea, IV 400a
zodiac, IV 402a
Zoroastrianism, IV 402a
Mecca
city, I 428a
Islam, II 638b; IV 231b
salvation, IV 231a
Mechanics in Middle Ages, II 196a–205b
Abū'l-Barakāt, II 201b, 202a
Ahmad ibn Yusuf, II 200a
Albert of Saxony, II 201b, 202a–202b, 203b
alchemy, II 197b
Alexander of Aphrodisias, II 203b
Alhazen, II 198b
al-Kindi, II 197b
Apollonius, II 203a
Arabs, II 196a, 197b, 198b, 200a, 201b, 203b
Archimedes, II 197b, 203a, 204b, 205a
Aristotelianism, II 196a, 199a, 199b, 201b, 203b, 205a
Aristotle, II 196a–204b
arithmetic, II 197b, 200a
Arnold of Villanova, II 197b
art, II 203b, 205b
astrology, II 202b
astronomy, II 199b
atomism, II 199b, 200a
Augustinianism, II 196a
Averroës, II 199a, 203b, 204a
Avicenna, II 201b
Bacon, Roger, II 197a
Benedetti, II 205a
Boethius, II 200a
Bradwardine, II 197b, 199b–202b, 204a
Bruno, II 203b
Buonamici, II 205a
Buridan, II 202a
Burley, II 197a
calculation, II 197a–197b, 204a
Calculatores, II 201a, 201b, 204b
calculus, II 200b
Cardano, II 205a
causation, II 199b, 201b
Celaya, II 204a–204b

Christianity, II 197a, 199b, 201b–202b
classification, II 197a
conjecture, II 196b
Copernicus, II 203b
cosmology, II 199a
Creation, II 196b
Crombie, II 197a
Dark Ages, II 196a
Democritus, II 199b
Descartes, II 199a, 202b
di Casali, II 202b
Dietrich von Freiberg, II 198a, 198b–199a
Diophantus, II 203a
Duhem, II 201b
Dullaert, II 204a
dynamics, II 201b–204a
encyclopedists, II 196a
Erasmus, II 203a
Euclid, II 198b, 200a, 203a
experimentation, II 196a–205b
Ficino, II 203a
France, II 196a, 197b, 201b–202b, 203b–204b
Franciscus de Marchia, II 201b–202a
Gaetano da Thiene, II 204a
Galileo, II 196b, 197b, 198a, 202a–205a
geometry, II 196b, 197b, 199a, 200a, 202b
Gerard of Brussels, II 197b
Gilbert, William, II 197a
God, II 199a, 199b, 202a
gravity, II 197b, 201b
Great Britain, II 196a–196b, 197b, 199b–201b
Greece (ancient), II 196a, 196b, 197a, 197b, 198b, 201b, 202a, 203a
Grosseteste, II 196a–196b, 198b, 204a
heat, II 200b, 202a
Hero, II 197b
humanism, II 200b, 203a–204a
impetus, II 201b–202b
induction, II 196b
inertia, II 199b, 201b, 202a
intuition, II 196b
Italy, II 203a–205a
John of Holland, II 201b
John Philoponus, II 201b
Jordanus Nemorarius, II 197b, 203b
Kepler, II 197a
kinematics, II 197b, 199b–201b, 203b, 204a
knowledge, II 196b
Koyré, II 203b
Lax, II 204a
Leibniz, II 200b

Leonardo da Vinci, II 202b, 203b
light, II 196b, 198a–199a, 200b
logic, II 199a, 204b
Maier, II 202a
Major, John, II 204a
Marsilius of Inghen, II 202a
mathematics, II 196b–198a, 200a–205a
matter, II 196b, 201a–201b
mean-speed theorem, II 200b, 202b, 204b
medicine, II 197b
Mertonians, II 197b, 199b–201b, 202b, 204a, 204b
Mill, J. S., II 197a
motion, II 197b, 199a–202b, 204a, 204b
Nature, II 197a, 202a, 204a
Near East, II 196a
Neo-Platonism, II 196a, 203b
Neo-Pythagoreans, II 196b–197a
Newton, II 198a, 199a, 200a, 201b, 202a, 205a
Nicholas of Autrecourt, II 199b
Nicholas of Cusa, II 203b
nominalism, II 199a–199b, 201b, 204a, 204b
observation, II 197a
optics, II 198a–199a, 202b
Oresme, II 202b–204a
Oxford school, II 196a–196b, 197b, 199b–201b, 202a, 203b, 204a
Pappus, II 203a
Paul of Venice, II 204a
Peregrinus, II 197a
pharmacy, II 197b
philology, II 203a
philosophy, II 199a, 204a, 204b
Plato, II 203a
Platonism, II 196a
pluralism, II 202b
positivism, II 199b
Ptolemy, II 197a, 198b, 203b
rationalism, II 196b–197a
reason, II 196b
relativity, II 199b
Renaissance, II 203a–204a
Roman Catholic Church, II 196a
Rome (ancient), II 201b
Saint Albertus Magnus, II 197a
Saint Thomas Aquinas, II 197a
scholasticism, II 200b, 201b, 203a

Silíceo, II 204b
skepticism, II 199b
Soto, II 204b, 205a
Spain, II 204a–204b
species, II 196b
Tartaglia, II 205a
Tempier, II 199a
terminism, II 199a, 201b, 203b
Thâbit, II 200a
theory, II 198a–199a
Thomaz, Alvaro, II 204a
Thomism, II 203b–204b
universe, II 196b, 197a, 203b
University of Paris, II 196a, 197b, 201b–202b, 203b, 204a–204b
William of Heytesbury, II 200b, 204a
William of Ockham, II 197a, 199a–199b
Zabarella, II 204a
Mechanism
Descartes, III 357a
Diderot, III 140b–141a
economic history, II 50a
Enlightenment, III 179b
inheritance, II 623a, 623b, 624b
Leonardo da Vinci, III 555a–555b
mathematics, III 179b, 183b, 184a, 387b
matter, III 188a, 192b, 193a, 194b, 195a
measurement, IV 402b
metaphysics, III 209b, 219a
methodology, III 378b, 387b, 389a, 390b
music, III 262b–263a
mythology, III 273b
necessity, III 355b, 357a, 357b, 360b, 361b, 362a
Newton, III 183b, 194b, 195a, 378b, 387b, 389a, 390b; IV 302a, 302b
numbers, III 406a–406b
optics, III 412a–413a, 418b
organicism, III 422b, 424b, 425a, 426b
pangenesis, II 623a, 623b, 624b
Peirce, III 558a
pragmatism, III 555b, 558a
psychology, IV 13b, 21a, 27b, 28a, 28b
religion, IV 115a
Renaissance, IV 440a, 441b
romanticism, IV 199a, 201b, 202b–203a, 209a
scientific classification, I 465b
space, IV 295b, 299b, 300a,

302a, 302b, 304b
Spinoza, IV 434b
symmetry, IV 348b, 349b, 350a
technology, IV 360a–364a
time, IV 402b
unity of science, IV 432b, 434b
universal man, IV 440a, 441b
vision, III 412a–413a, 418b
See also Man-Machine
Meckel, Johann Friedrich (1724–1774), recapitulation, IV 56b–57a
Medawar, P. B.
longevity, III 93a
perfectibility, III 471a
Médard, Saint (456?–?545), chance images, I 343b
Medea (myth), III 273b–274a
law, II 683a
temperance, IV 367b
Medicaid, II 406a
Medicare Act, III 114b
Medicean Planets, III 414b
Medici, Catherine de (1519–1589), I 398a
Machiavellism, III 117b, 118a
mythology, III 291b
Platonism, III 507b
politics, III 118a
Medici, Cosimo de (1389–1464)
balance of power, I 180b
dignity, IV 144a–144b
optics, III 414b
Medici, Lorenzo de (1449–1492)
balance of power, I 180b
historiography, IV 149a
love, III 511a–511b
periodization in literary history, III 481b
Platonism, III 510b, 511a–511b, 513a
universal man, IV 442a
Medici family
art, III 506a
handwriting, II 518a
humanism, II 518a, 523a
iconography, II 529b
literature, III 506a
Platonism, III 506a, 511b
universal man, IV 443a
virtù, IV 483a
Medicine
acquired characteristics, II 620b
alchemy, I 27b, 32a–32b, 33a
art, I 458a; II 313b
astrology, I 118b

259

Brazil, III 541a, 542a, 542b, 543a
catharsis, I 264b, 266b, 267a, 268b–269a, 269b
causation, I 271b
Comte, III 537a
crisis in history, I 589b–590a, 594a
culture, I 608b
Faust (legend), III 247a
Galen, III 133b, 381a–382a
happiness, II 374b, 382a–384b
health, II 384a, 395b–407b
human nature, III 574a
humanism, II 515b, 519a, 521b; IV 132b, 135a
intolerance, IV 116a
Islam, II 639a, 645a, 645b, 646b
Latin America, III 544a
law, II 687a
longevity, III 89a, 89b, 92b
Man-Machine, III 131b–141b
as mechanical art, II 313b
medieval, II 197b
methodology, III 381a–381b, 382a
Mexico, III 544a
mythology, III 287b, 290a
optics, III 414b
overpopulation, I 594a
pain, II 384a
Pereira Barreto, III 540b
philanthropy, III 492a
phrenology, IV 23b
Platonism, III 497a, 500a
pleasure, II 374b, 382a–384b
positivism, III 540a–543a
progress, III 625a, 627b, 629b, 632b, 635a
psychology, IV 7a, 10b, 13b, 23b
Ramism, IV 44b
rationalism, IV 47b–48a
religion, IV 116a
Renaissance, IV 132b, 135a
revolution, IV 163a
Rome (ancient), II 687a
Saint Augustine, III 635a
scientific classification, I 463b, 464b
science, II 639a, 645a, 646b
skepticism, IV 234a, 236a–236b, 237a, 239a, 240a
Spinoza, IV 434b
Strato, IV 7a
technology, IV 360a
unity of science, IV 432b, 433b, 434b

welfare state, IV 510b
Medicine men
music, III 264b, 268a
mythology, III 309a
Mediums, prophecy, III 657b
Meehl, P. E.
empiricism, III 550b
logic of psychology, III 550b
Megaric-Stoic logic, I 164a–164b
Megasthenes (fl. 3rd century B.C.)
Buddhism, I 255a
progress, III 630a
Mei, Girolamo, music, III 262b
Mei Ying-tsu, classification of the sciences, I 464a
Meier, G. F., aesthetics, IV 356a
Meillet, Antoine (1866–1936), linguistics, III 71b; IV 427b
Meinecke, Friedrich (1862–1954)
determinism, II 20b
historicism, II 456b, 457b, 458a, 461a, 461b; IV 203b
historiography, II 20b, 496a
individualism, II 597a; IV 203b
metaphysical imagination, III 219b
romanticism, IV 203b
virtue, IV 483b
Meiosis, pangenesis, II 624b
Meissner, Paul, baroque in literature, I 191a
Meister, Leonhard, literature, III 83a
Mela, Pomponius (1st century A.D.), primitivism, III 591a
Melancholy
Aristotle, II 309a, 320a
art, II 308b–309b, 581a
Burton, III 80b
Byron, IV 204a
catharsis, I 267a
genius, II 308b–309b, 320a–321b
impressionism, II 581a
individualism, II 308b–309b
Michelangelo, II 309a
music, II 320a–321b; III 265a, 267a
mythology, III 290b, 295b–296a, 304b
Plato, II 309a
Pseudo-Aristotle, II 320b
romanticism, IV 204a
virtuoso, IV 486b
Melanchthon, Philip (1497–1560)

education, IV 123b
Faust (legend), III 245a
historiography, II 484a, 484b
humanism, II 520b
Luther and, IV 67a
Lutheranism, I 391b
predestination, II 28a
Ramism, IV 43b
reformation, IV 66b, 67a
Melchizedek (Bible), mythology, III 283a
Melden, A. I., determinism, II 241b–242a
Meleager of Gadara (2nd century B.C.), cynicism, I 624a
Meletus
cycles, I 623b
Platonism, III 507a
Meliorism
Bacon, Roger, III 91b
Descartes, III 91b
James, IV 396b
longevity, III 89a, 91b, 92b, 93a
Metchnikoff, III 92b–93a
reformation, IV 62b
time, IV 396b
Melissus of Samos (fl. 440 B.C.)
causation, I 271b
continuity, I 503a
historiography, I 503a
matter, III 187a
space, IV 305a
Melkart (myth), III 281b
Melody, II 313a–315a, 317b, 318b, 323b; III 262a
Melpomene (myth), irony, II 632b
Meltzl, Hugo von, literature, III 84a–84b
Melville, Herman (1819–1891)
mythology, III 306b
symbolism, IV 341b
tragic sense, IV 416b
wisdom of the fool, IV 517b
witchcraft, IV 522b
Memory
Bacon, IV 434a
dignity, IV 138b
genius, II 293b, 294b
Locke, II 120b
macrocosm and microcosm, III 130b
Man-Machine, III 137b, 139b, 140b
mimetic arts, III 226a
Plotinus, IV 9a
psychology, IV 9a, 13a, 23a, 24b

Ramism, IV 43a, 44b, 45a
recapitulation, IV 59a
Renaissance, IV 138b
Saint Augustine, IV 138b
theriophily, IV 385b
time, IV 396a
unity of science, IV 434a
wisdom of the fool, IV 516a
Menabuoi, Giusto, temperance, IV 375b
Menander (343?–?291 B.C.), comedy, III 238a
freedom of speech, II 260a
Gnosticism, II 327a, 330a
motif, III 238a
theriophily, IV 386a
Mencius (372?–?289 B.C.), philanthropy, III 486b
Mencken, H. L., (1880–1956), literary criticism, I 603a
Mendel, Gregor Johann (1822–1884), II 617b–621a
adaptation, II 618b
chromosomes, II 286b, 288a, 289b
environment, II 126a
evolution, II 126a, 186b, 618b
genetic continuity, II 286b, 288a, 289b
pangenesis, II 626a, 626b
probability, III 616a, 616b, 617b, 620a
species, II 618b
Mendelssohn, Moses (1729–1786)
art, II 550b
beauty, II 550b
classification of the arts, I 460b
Enlightenment, II 89b
genius, II 295b
Platonism, III 516a–516b
taste, IV 356a
ut pictura poesis, IV 474a
virtue, II 550b
Mendes, Candido Antonio, nationalism, III 336b
Mendoza, Francesco de, cosmic voyages, I 532a
Mendoza, Juan González de (1540?–1617), China, I 354b, 355a, 355b
Menedemus (350?–?276 B.C.), cynicism, I 629a
Menelaus (myth), Faust (legend), III 249a
Menéndez y Pelayo, Marcelino (1856–1912), baroque in literature, I 188b–189a
Menenius Agrippa (c. 494 B.C.), penalogy, I 68b

Menger, Karl (1840–1921), economic history, II 47a, 50b, 52b, 60a, 61a
empiricism, III 545b
historicism, II 457a
individualism, II 601a
probability, II 622a
social welfare, IV 277b, 283a
utility, IV 450b, 453b, 454b–455a, 457b

Mengs, Anton Raphael (1728–1779)
art, II 306a
beauty, II 550b
genius, II 306a
ideal, II 550a, 550b
mimesis, III 229b
neo-classicism in art, III 364b, 368b, 369a
taste, IV 356a

Menippus, cynicism, I 628b, 630b, 631b

Menodotus of Nicomedia, skepticism, IV 234a

Mental health
anxiety, II 384a
law, III 34b
pleasure, II 384a

Menzel, Adolf Friedrich von (1815–1905), naturalism in art, III 341b

Merchants
common law, II 694b
Rome (ancient), II 687a

Mercier, Louis Sebastien (1740–1814)
Utopia, IV 462b
women, IV 526a

Mercury (myth), III 291a, 292a, 294a
hermeticism, II 432b
Ramism, IV 44a

Mercury (planet), cosmology, I 538a, 539a, 540b–541a, 542a, 542b, 544b, 555a, 561a

Meredith, George (1828–1909), Machiavellism, III 119a

Meredith, John, comedy, I 468a

Merezhkovsky, Dimitri (1865–1941), symbolism, IV 343a

Mérimée, Prosper (1803–1870)
evolution of literature, II 172b
realism in literature, IV 52a

Merleau-Ponty, Maurice, existentialism, II 189b; III 158a
Marxism, III 158a
psychology, IV 14a

Mersenne, Marin (1588–1648)
alchemy, I 32b
atomism, I 135b, 137b–138a
axiomatization, I 165b
Bacon and, I 176b
certainty, I 304b, 305a, 306a–306b, 310a, 310b, 311b
Charron and, I 301b
Descartes, I 640b
music, III 262b, 263a
Pythagorean cosmos, IV 41b
skepticism, I 306a–306b, 307a; IV 244b, 245a

Mertens, Franz, Gothic, II 373a

Merton, Thomas, education, II 79a

Mertonians, mechanical experiments, II 197b, 199b–201b, 202b, 204a, 204b

Meselson, M., DNA, II 291a–291b

Meslier, Jean
Enlightenment, II 99b
Man-Machine, III 139a
socialism, IV 288b

Mesmer, Franz (1734–1815), imagination, III 212a

Mesons, IV 405b

Mesopotamia (ancient)
assemblies, II 252b–253a
astrology, I 118b–120a, 122a–122b, 125a, 125b
Babylon, IV 104a
causation, I 270b
city, I 428a
continuity, I 504a
cosmology, I 536b–539a
Creation, I 536b
death, IV 226a
disease, II 396a–396b
Egypt (ancient), IV 226a
evil, IV 226a
freedom of speech, II 252a, 252b–253a
God, II 331b, 333b, 335a, 335b–336a, 337b, 564b; IV 226a, 226b
Hammurabi Code, IV 226b
healing ritual, IV 101b
historiography, II 465a–465b, 467b
human nature, III 572a
immortality, IV 226a
impiety, II 564a, 564b
Ishtar (myth), IV 101b
law, II 564a; III 7a, 11a; IV 226a, 226b
mathematics, III 179b, 180a, 180b
matter, III 186a
music, III 264b, 268a
mythology, III 280a, 310a–310b; IV 226a, 226b
polytheism, II 333b
religion, IV 93b, 94b, 101b, 104a, 105b, 226a
ritual, IV 226a
salvation, IV 226a–226b
sin, II 564b; IV 226a–226b
society, IV 226b
State, IV 226b
Tammuz (myth), IV 101b
theodicy, IV 379b
writing, III 180a–180b

Messer, August (1867–1937), psychology, IV 13a

Messiah
Judaism, III 636a
mythology, III 281a, 283a, 284a
progress, III 636a
prophecy, III 664a, 665b

Messinger, Philip (1583–1640), baroque in literature, I 191a

Metallurgy
Islam, II 644a
primitivism, III 588b, 599a, 599b
science, II 644a
Seneca, III 588b
Swift, III 599a
war, IV 501b

Metaphor, III 196b–208a
Absolute, III 199b
Achilles (myth), III 203b
aesthetics, III 196b–197a, 198b, 199a
allegory, I 42a; III 203b–204b, 205b–206b
Amos (Bible), III 202a
anagogical, III 205b
analogy, III 198b, 206b
Anaxagoras, III 203a, 203b
animals, III 198b
anthropomorphism, III 202b, 206a
archetypes, III 204b
Aristotelianism, III 198b
Aristotle, I 585a–585b; III 200a–205b, 206a, 207a
art, I 460a; III 198b
atomism, III 203b
Bacon, III 197a–197b, 199a
belief, III 203a
Bergson, III 197a, 207a
Bible, III 201b–202b, 204a–207b
Bultmann, III 207a
Cartesianism, III 198b
category, III 198a–200a

causation, III 199a
Christianity, III 205a, 205b, 206a, 207a
classification of the arts, I 460a
Clement of Alexandria, III 205b
cognition, III 197b–201a
consciousness, III 207a
contextualism, III 199b
cosmos, III 198b–199b
criticism, III 205b, 206b, 207a
culture, III 198b, 203a, 207a
Jesus Christ, III 205b, 206b
Daniel (Bible), III 202b
Democritus, III 199b, 203b
Descartes, III 199b
Deutero-Isaiah (Bible), III 202b
Dewey, III 198a, 207a
Diogenes of Apollonia, III 203b
Dionysius (myth), III 203b
discovery of, III 202b–204a
Eddington, III 198b
empiricism, III 201a
epistemology, III 206a
existentialism, III 207a
explanation of, III 196b–197a
Ezekiel (Bible), III 202b
facts, III 198a
fantasy, III 197b, 198b
formism, III 200a
freedom, III 199a
God, III 199a, 202a, 202b, 204b, 205a, 206a, 206b, 207a
Fundamentalism, III 206b–207a
Greece (ancient), III 201b, 202b–206a
Hegel, III 198a, 198b, 199b
Hector (myth), III 203b
Heraclitus, III 203b
Heidegger, III 207a
history, III 199a
hypotheses, III 197b–201a
immortality, III 199a
institutions, III 198b
Husserl, III 207a
Joseph (Bible), III 204b
Jeremiah (Bible), III 202a, 204b
James, III 197a
Irenaeus, III 205b
imagery, III 201b–207b
Judaism, III 202b–206a
Kant, III 199a, 199b
Kuhn, III 200b
language, III 198b

Lewis, III 199a, 199b
literalism, III 205b, 206b, 207a
Hume, III 199b
Hosea (Bible), III 202a
Haggai (Bible), III 202b
identification, III 197a
Gnosticism, III 205b
Homer, III 203a, 203b, 207a
literary criticism, I 598b–599a
literary paradox, III 80a–80b
literature, III 202b, 204b, 206b; IV 330b, 331b
Locke, III 199b
Lucretius, III 197a
Luther, III 206a–206b
Malachi, III 202b
mathematics, III 201a
Metrodorus of Lampsacus, III 203b
mimesis, III 228b
Modernism, III 206b
morality, III 199a, 204a, 205a, 205b
Moses (Bible), III 204b, 205a
motif, III 242a
mysticism, III 197a, 198a
mythology, III 197b, 198b, 203a, 203b, 205a, 282b, 295a, 308b
Nature, III 198b, 199a, 203a
Origen, III 205b
paradigm, III 200a–201a
perennial philosophy, III 458b
Philo Judaeus, III 204a–205a, 206b
philosophy, III 196b–201b
plagiarism, III 205a
Plato, III 200a, 203b–204a, 204b, 205a, 207a, 207b
Platonism, III 198b, 513b
poetry, III 196b, 204a, 204b, 205a; IV 465b, 466b, 468b, 469b, 470b, 471b, 473b
pragmatism, III 199b
prophecy, III 201b, 202b, 667a
Protestantism, III 206a, 206b, 207a
Pythagoreans, III 203b
rationalism, III 203a
Reformation, III 206a–206b
religion, III 201b–208a
Renaissance, IV 121b
revelation, III 205a
rhetoric, III 203b
Roman Catholic Church, III 205b, 206a, 206b, 207a

root, III 197a–198a, 198b, 200a–200b, 201a
Saint Augustine, III 205b
Saint Jerome, III 205b
Saint Paul, III 205a–205b
Saint Thomas Aquinas, III 200a, 205b–206a
science, III 197b, 198b, 199a, 200b, 201a, 206b, 207a
senses, III 198b, 205b
Socrates, III 203a–204a
space, III 199a
Spinoza, III 199b
Stoicism, III 204a, 204b
superficial, III 197a
symbolism, III 203b; IV 339a, 344a
Tertullian, III 205b
Thales, III 197a, 203a
Theagenes of Rhegium, III 203b
Theodore of Mopsuestia, III 205b
theology, III 204a–206a
time, III 199a
tradition, III 203b
tragic sense, IV 413b
truth, III 204a, 204b, 205a, 206a
universe, III 203a
ut pictura poesis, IV 465b, 466b, 468b, 469b, 470b, 471b, 473b
Vaihinger, III 199b
Weltanschauung, III 198a, 199a
Whitehead, III 207a
Wittgenstein, III 200a, 200b, 207a
Xenophanes, III 203b
Zechariah (Bible), III 202b
Zeus (myth), III 203b
Metaphysical imagination, III 218a–222a
Metaphysics, III 208a, 223a
Aeschylus, III 208b
aesthetics, III 218b
analogy, III 209a, 216b
anthropology, III 210a
antithesis, III 209a
Aristotelianism, III 211b, 215a
Aristotle, II 377a; III 209b, 210a, 210b, 354a, 355b; IV 4b, 6b
art, III 217a, 219b, 221b, 222a, 222b
artists, III 209a, 221b
atomism, III 213b
Augustinianism, III 214b
Bach, III 208a
Bachelard, III 209b, 210a, 212b

Bacon, I 294b; III 211b, 212b–214a, 215a–219a, 222a; IV 434a
Baudelaire, III 212a
Bergson, III 209a, 212b, 221a–221b, 222a, 565a
Blake, III 208a, 209a, 211a
body, III 212a, 214b
Böhme, III 212a
Braque, III 208a
Breton, III 209a
Bruno, III 79a, 193b, 211b, 212a, 212b
Buddhism, IV 232b
Buffon, III 217a
Burton, III 211b
Cabanis, III 216a
Carnap, III 220a–221a
Cartesianism, II 450a; III 217a
Cassirer, III 208b, 210a, 222a–222b
causation, I 279b–281a; III 213b
Christianity, III 211b
cognition, III 211a, 212a, 214b, 217b, 218b, 219a, 221b, 222b
coincidence, III 209a
Coleridge, III 222a
Collingwood, III 208b
Comte, III 534b, 535b, 536b, 641b, 642a
Condillac, III 215b, 216a, 216b, 516a
consciousness, III 208b, 209b, 210a
Copernicus, III 215a
criticism, III 210a, 216a, 219b, 220a, 221b
culture, III 210a, 212a, 222a, 222b
Dante, III 211b
death, III 209a
defined, III 208a, 209b
Democritus, III 213b
Descartes, II 450a; III 136a, 213b–214a, 215a, 216b; IV 432a
Destutt de Tracy, III 216a
Diderot, III 215b–218b
Digby, III 221a
Dilthey, III 208b, 209a, 219b, 220b, 222a
dualism, III 220b
empiricism, III 211b, 212b, 215a, 216b, 218a, 218b, 219a, 219b, 221a, 547a, 551a
Engels, II 455a
Enlightenment, III 215b, 216a
Euclideanism, III 214b
evil, II 162b, 166b–167a;

IV 382a
evolutionism, III 178b, 181b–185a, 187b
experience, III 209a
fantasy, III 220b, 221b
feeling, III 208b
Fludd, III 212a
France, II 575b
freedom, III 210b, 217b, 219a
Freud, III 216a, 221a
fusion, III 209a
Galileo, III 218a
Gide, III 208a
Gilbert, III 213a
God, II 347b, 348a, 351a–363a, 365a, 366a; III 212b, 214b, 217b, 222a
Goethe, III 217b
Gravesande, III 217a
Greece (ancient), III 210a–210b, 217b
happiness, II 375a, 376a–376b, 377a, 383b
harmony, II 388b, 390b
Hegel, II 414a, 414b, 454b, 583a; III 217b, 219b–220a, 222a
Heidegger, III 212b, 221a, 221b
Helmont, III 212a
Helvétius, III 216b
Heraclitus, III 213b
Herder, III 219b
heresy, II 416b
hermeticism, III 211b, 212b, 221b
hierarchy, II 438b, 447a
history, I 279b–281a; II 24a; III 209a, 209b, 210a, 213a, 219b, 221b, 222a
Hobbes, III 211a
Hölderlin, III 221b
humanism, II 515b, 519a, 520a
Hume, III 218b
Huygens, III 217a
ideal, II 549a
idealism, III 209b
imagination, III 208a–223a
immortality, III 217b
indeterminacy, II 586b
insight, III 211a
Islam, II 641a, 643b, 644b, 645a, 648b, 651a, 651b
James, III 565b
Jaspers, III 208b, 212b, 220b, 221a, 221b
Johnson, Samuel, II 447a
Jung, III 212b
Kafka, III 208a
Kant, III 215b, 217b–219b, 222a, 222b, 472b; IV 433a–433b

knowledge, III 210b, 211b, 212b, 214a–216b, 218a–221b, 222b
Lange, III 216a
Langer, III 210a
language, II 662b, 666a, 667a; III 222a
Leibniz, II 414a, 450a; III 130b–131a, 214b, 472b; IV 432b–433a, 434b
liberalism, III 48a
life, III 209a
literature, III 208b, 209b, 211b
Locke, III 516a
logic, III 209a, 213b, 214a, 214b, 215a, 547a, 551a
logos, III 213b
love, III 95b, 99b
loyalty, III 108b
Lucretius, III 213b
Machiavelli, III 213b
macrocosm and microcosm, III 130b–131a, 212a
magic, III 211b, 212a
Malebranche, III 213b–214b
Man-Machine, III 131b, 135a, 135b, 137a–139b
materialism, II 450a, 454a, 454b, 455a
mathematics, III 179a, 214a, 214b, 215a
matter, III 186b, 187a, 190b, 191a, 193b, 195a–196a
Maupertuis, III 217a
mechanism, III 209b, 219a
Meinecke, III 219b
Mesmer, III 212a
Middle Ages, III 190b, 191a, 211b
Mill, III 209b
mind, III 213a, 213b, 214a, 215a, 219a, 219b, 222a
monism, III 220b
Montaigne, III 213b
mountains in literature, III 256b
music, II 388b, 390b; III 208a, 220b, 261a, 267b, 268a, 271b
mythology, III 222a, 302b, 306b
natural science, III 212b–222b
Nature, III 212b, 213a, 215a, 216b, 218a, 219a, 221b, 222a
necessity, III 352a–360b
Neo-Platonism, III 211a–212b, 221b, 374a, 377a
Newton, III 216b, 219a, 396b

Nietzsche, III 216a
nihilism, III 209b
optics, III 396b, 410a
organicism, III 422a, 424b
painting, III 208a
Paracelsus, III 211b, 212a, 212b, 222a
paranoia, III 221a
Parmenides, III 208b
Pascal, III 214b
peace, III 440b, 444a
Peirce, III 558b, 560b, 561a, 567a
perennial philosophy, III 459a–463b
periodization in history, III 478a
personalism, III 131a
philosophy, II 549a; III 208b–222a
phrenology, IV 23a
physics, IV 432b, 433a
Pirandello, III 208b
Plato, II 376a–376b; III 208a, 210a–211b, 214a, 464b, 498a, 498b, 503b, 507a; IV 33b, 34b, 36b, 37a, 37b
Platonism, III 214b, 498a, 498b, 503b, 504a, 504b, 505a, 506b, 507a, 508a, 516a, 521b, 522b–524a
Plotinus, III 211b, 374a
poetry, III 210a, 212b, 220b, 221a
poets, III 208b, 210a, 212a, 217a, 219b
Pope, III 397a
positivism, III 534b, 535b, 536b, 546a, 547a, 551a
post-Kantianism, III 209b
power, III 210a
pragmatism, III 552b, 553a, 558a, 558b, 560b, 561a, 563b, 564b–567a
progress, III 628b, 641b, 642a
psychoanalysis, III 220b–221b
psychology, IV 1a, 4b, 6b, 10a, 10b, 11b, 12a, 16b, 17a, 17b, 21a, 23a
psychophysics, III 214a
Puritanism, IV 16b
Pythagoras, III 215a
Pythagoreans, III 215a, 505a; IV 33b, 34b, 36b, 37a, 37b
Ramism, IV 42b
Randall, J. H., III 210a
rationalism, III 214a, 217b
reason, III 210b, 212a, 214b, 215a, 217b, 218a, 218b, 219b

recapitulation, IV 56b
religion, III 212b, 216a, 219b, 222a
Renaissance, III 210a, 211b, 212b, 221b, 222a; IV 122a, 140b, 439b, 440b, 441a
rhetoric, IV 167b
Rimbaud, III 209a
Roman Catholic Church, III 210b
romanticism, III 211a, 212a, 212b, 221b; IV 199a, 209a
Saint Augustine, III 210a
Saint Thomas Aquinas, III 210a; IV 432a
Sartre, III 208b, 209b–210a, 212b, 221b
Schelling, III 222a
Schlegel, F., III 222a
scholasticism, III 208b, 210a, 210b, 211b, 212a, 214a
Schopenhauer, III 208a
science, II 641a, 643b, 644b, 645a, 648b, 651a, 651b
scientific classification, I 464b, 466a
sensation, III 210b
senses, III 212a, 214b, 222a
Shaftesbury, III 218b, 219b
Shelley, III 508a
skepticism, IV 241a–250b
sophism, III 210b
soul, III 211b, 212a
space, IV 295a, 295b, 297b, 299a, 302b, 304a, 305a, 305b
Spinoza, II 450a; III 214b
spontaneous generation, IV 310b
Spranger, III 208b
Stahl, III 212a, 218a
Stoicism, III 210b
structuralism, IV 330a
surrealism, III 212b
symbolism, III 212a, 222a, 222b
symmetry, IV 352a
teleology, III 219a
Telesio, III 213b
Tetens, III 218b
theodicy, IV 380a–382a
theology, III 211b
thought, III 208b, 210b, 211a, 214a, 216a, 216b
time, IV 389b, 390b, 396b
Torricelli, III 218a
tragic sense, IV 411b
transcendentalism, III 210a
truth, III 213b
universal man, IV 439b, 440b, 441a

universe, III 213a, 217b, 218b
unity of science, IV 432a–433a, 434a, 434b, 436a
van Gogh, III 209a
Vico, III 219b
Voltaire, III 216b
Wahl, III 209a, 209b
Webern, III 208a
Weltanschauung, III 209b, 219b
will, III 208b, 213b
Wisdom, John, III 220b
Wittgenstein, III 220b
Wolff, II 414a
Zeitgeist, IV 536b–537a
Metastasio (1698–1782), genius, II 323a, 323b
Metchnikoff, Élie (1845–1916), longevity, III 92b–93a
Metempsychosis, I 644b
time, IV 392a
Methodism
Enlightenment, II 91a
France, III 674b
history, I 404b
moderation of, I 402a
perfectibility, III 468a, 468b
Pietism, III 493b; IV 68b
protest movements, III 674b
reformation, IV 68b
skepticism, IV 240a
usury, I 396b-397a
Victorians, IV 217b, 220a
Methodius, Saint (827–869 A.D.)
history, I 409b
love, III 97a
Method, III 378b–391b
Abelard, III 382a
Alembert, III 378b
algebra, III 379b, 380b
analogy of nature, III 379b
analytic method, III 379a, 383b, 385b, 388b–389a, 390b
Anselm, III 381b–382a
Apollonius of Perga, III 380a
Arabs, III 381a
Aristaeus the Elder, III 380a
Aristotle, III 380a–381a, 382a, 387b, 554b; IV 434b
arithmetic, III 379b, 389b
Arnauld, III 384b
axiomatization, I 162b–172b
Babbage, III 559b
Bacon, Francis, III 383b–384a, 384b, 386b, 387a, 387b; IV 462a
Bacon, Roger, IV 434b

263

Barrow, III 380b, 387a–388b

Boyle, III 386b, 387a

Bridgman, III 559b

Cartesianism, III 385a

Cassirer, III 382b

causation, III 382a, 382b, 387a

Chalcidius, III 381b

color, III 386a–387a, 389a–390b

compositional method, III 379a

Condillac, III 378b; IV 435b–436a

Condorcet, IV 436a

Constantine the African, III 381a

Cotes, III 378b

deduction, III 386a, 388a, 390b

Descartes, III 384a–384b, 385b, 387b, 388a; IV 435b

diffraction, III 389b, 390a

disease, III 381b

Erigena, III 381b

Euclid, III 380a, 380b

Eudoxus, III 380a

experiments, III 379a, 382b–383b, 384a, 385b–387a, 389a–390b, 391b

France, III 382a

Galen, III 381a–382a

Galileo, III 382b–383b, 385b, 386a, 387a–388a

Gassendi, III 387b

generalization, III 390b

geometry, III 380b, 382a, 389b

Gerard of Cremona, III 381a

Gilbert, Neal, III 382b

Gilbert, William, III 387a

Gravesande, III 385a, 385b

gravity, III 379b, 389a, 393a

Great Britain, III 382a

Greece (ancient), III 379b–381b

Grosseteste, III 382a–382b, 385b

Halley, III 380b

Haly Rodohan, III 381a, 381b

Harvey, III 387a

historiography, IV 147b–148a

Hobbes, III 387b

Hooke, III 387a

humanism, II 519a

Huygens, III 389a

hypotheses, III 379b, 383b, 385b

idea, II 600b–601b

individualism, II 600b–601b

induction, III 379b, 382a, 384a, 385b, 390b

Jevons, III 386b

kinematics, III 383a

knowledge, III 378b

language, III 390b

Laplace, III 378b

Lavoisier, III 386b

Leibniz, IV 435a–436a

light, III 386a, 387a, 389b, 390a

linguistics, III 70a, 71b, 72a

Locke, III 389a

logic, III 379b–385a

Maclaurin, III 378b

mathematics, III 379a–380b, 382a, 383a, 386a, 387b–390b

measurement, III 379b, 390a–390b

mechanics, III 378b, 387b, 389a, 390b

medicine, III 381a–381b, 382a

Middle Ages, III 381b–382a

monism, I 23a–23b

motif, III 237b

motion, III 383a, 389a

Nature, III 378b, 387a, 387b, 388b–389a

Neo-Platonism, III 381b

Newton, III 378b–391a

Nicolle, III 384b

Nifo, III 382b, 385b

numbers, III 389b–390b

observation, III 379a, 379b, 381a, 382b, 385b, 389a, 389b–390b

optics, III 378b, 389b, 390b, 416b

Paracelsus, III 387b

Parker, III 386b

Pascal, III 387a, 387b

Peirce, III 554a, 558a–558b, 559b–560a

philosophy, III 378b–379b, 381b–382b, 384a, 385b–388b

physics, III 382a, 387b–389a

Plato, III 379b, 380a, 381b

Platonism, III 521a, 523b

Porrée, III 381b–382a

power, III 385b

pragmatism, III 552a, 544a, 554b, 558a–558b, 559b–560a, 561a

probability, III 383b

Ramism, IV 43b–44b

Randall, J. H., III 382b

rationalism, III 381b–382a; IV 47b–48a

reason, III 379a–379b, 601b

reflection, III 389b

refraction, III 389b, 390b

Régis, III 384b–385a

Renaissance, III 382b–383b; IV 147b–148a, 440a, 441a, 441b

Richard of St. Victor, III 381b–382a

rules, III 390b

Socrates, III 379b

Sprat, III 386b

Strong, E. W., III 390b

structuralism, IV 323a, 327a

synthetic method, III 379a

Torricelli, III 387b

truth, III 379a

unity of science, IV 431a, 434b–436a

universal man, IV 440a, 441a, 441b

Utopia, IV 462a

Volksgeist, IV 494a

Voltaire, III 378b

Wallis, III 389a

Wren, III 389a

Wright, Chauncey, III 561a

Zabarella, III 382b, 385b

Methuselah (Bible), mythology, III 277b

Metis (myth), III 299b

Metternich, K. W. N. L. von (1773–1859)

balance of power, I 187a

conservatism, I 480b

crisis in history, I 591a

cycles, IV 157b

Machiavellism, III 124a

revolution, IV 157b, 158b

romanticism, IV 207a

Metz, Johannes, hope, II 214b

Metzger, H., cosmic images, I 518b

Mexican War, I 436a–436b

Mexico

academic freedom, I 16b

aesthetics, III 544b

anticlericalism, III 544a

class, III 544a

Constitution, I 491b

education, III 544a

nationalism, III 332b, 335b

politics, III 544a, 544b

positivism, III 543b–544b

pragmatism, III 569a

primitivism, III 597a, 601a

private property, III 544a

revolution, III 544b, 545a

Roman Catholic Church, III 544a, 544b

Spain, III 601a

Thoreau, I 436a–436b

Meyen, J., cell division, II 285b

Meyer, Gerald Dennis, virtuoso, IV 489a, 490a

Meyer, Richard Moritz, periodization in literary history, III 482b

Meyerson, Emile (1859–1933)

Islam, II 647b

time, IV 397a

Micah (Bible)

philanthropy, III 487b

prophecy, III 661b, 662a

Micaihu ben Imlah, prophecy, III 663a

Michael (Bible), mythology, III 284b

Michael, Czar (1596–1645), history, I 410b

Michael of Cesena, heresy, II 421a

Michael VIII Paleologus, Emperor (1234–1282), history, I 410a–410b

Michaelis, Johann David (1717–1791), mythology, III 302b

Michaud, Guy, symbolism, IV 340a, 340b

Michaux, Henri, irrationalism, II 638a

Michelangelo (1475–1564), aesthetics, IV 354b

art, II 298b, 302a–302b, 303a, 304a, 305a, 308b, 309a; IV 443a

baroque in literature, I 189a

beauty, III 229a

Ficino and, III 513a

game theory, II 274b

genius, II 293b, 298b, 302a–302b, 303a, 304a, 305a, 308b, 309a, 320a

God, III 228a–228b; IV 443a

iconography, II 529a, 529b, 532a, 538b, 540b

immortality, I 646a

impressionism, II 572b, 574b

Julius II (Pope) and, II 302b

melancholy, II 309a

mimesis, III 228a–228b, 229a

music, II 320a

mythology, III 276b, 278a–278b, 280a–280b, 283b, 291b–292a

Nature, III 228a–228b, 229a

non finito, II 298b–299a

rationalism, IV 442b, 443a

Rodin and, II 574b

spiritualism, III 513a
taste, IV 354b
universal man, IV 439b, 442a, 442b–443a
ut pictura poesis, IV 469a
Michelet, Jules (1798–1874),
Counter-Enlightenment, II 103a
determinism, II 23b
French Revolution, IV 159b
Gothic, II 370b
Herder, IV 203b
historicism, II 458b, 459a
mythology, III 306b
nationalism, III 328a, 330b
Nature, III 349a
periodization in history, III 479a
Renaissance, III 479b; IV 124b–126b
revolution, IV 160a
romanticism, IV 201b, 203b, 204a, 205a
Michelet, Karl Ludwig (1801–1893)
Cieszkowski and, II 413b
freedom, II 414b
Hegel and, II 407b, 414a, 414b
idealism, II 407b
monarchy, II 414b
Napoleon III and, II 414a
realism, II 407b
Strauss and, II 412b
Volksgeist, IV 492b
Michels, Robert (1876–1936),
class, III 151a
democracy, I 664b, 665a
Marxism, III 151a
revisionism, IV 268a
Michels, Wilhelm, baroque in literature, I 190a
Michelson, Albert Abraham (1852–1931)
cosmology, I 555a, 557a
relativity, IV 79a–80b, 89a
Michelson-Morley experiment, IV 405a
Michurin, I. V. (1855–1935),
acquired characteristics, II 621a
Lysenko and, II 621a
pangenesis, II 626b
Mickiewicz, Adam (1798–1855)
nationalism, III 328a
romanticism, IV 191b
Volksgeist, IV 494b
Microcosm, III 126a–131b
dignity, IV 137b, 140a
human nature, III 573b
Renaissance, IV 137b, 140a
spirit, III 130a
See also Macrocosm and

Microcosm
Microphysics
indeterminacy, II 586b, 589a, 589b
probability, III 620a
Microscope
Amici, III 415b
Leeuwenhoek, III 415b–416a
sublime in external nature, IV 334b
Microstructure, naturalism in art, III 345a–345b
Middle Ages
abbesses, IV 525b
Abelard, I 65b–66a
Adam of Bremen, III 592b
aesthetics, II 217b–218a, 220a, 222a–223a, 224a
Albigensian crusade, II 423a
alchemy, III 190b–191a, 192a
analogy, I 65b–67a, 69a
animals, III 596a
anti-intellectualism, III 590b–591a, 595a
Aristotelianism, II 666b
Aristotle, IV 369a
art, II 297b, 298a, 298b, 300a, 303b, 527a–528a; III 82b; IV 123b, 133a
astrology, IV 153a
atomism, I 127a, 129b, 132b
authority, I 141b, 146b–148b, 150a; III 528b
barbarian invaders, I 378b–381a
Bayeux Tapestry, II 528a
beauty, I 197b; II 217b–218a; IV 123b
beginning of decline, I 384a–385a
Boethius, I 65a, 67a
Brahmins, III 592a–592b
capitalism, III 479a
casuistry, I 259b–260a
cathedrals, II 527a
causation, II 18a
chance, II 227b, 232a
chance images, I 342b–345a
charity, II 210a–212b
Charlemagne, III 477a
China (ancient), II 479b–481b
chivalry, II 530a
Christianity, I 378b–387b, 401a; III 584b–585a, 670b; IV 153a, 153b, 230a, 371a
Church, I 417b–418a
city, I 428b–429b
city-state, IV 253a, 314a

class, I 442b, 445b–446a, 447a
classicism, I 451a; III 528a, 528b
classification of the arts, I 457a, 458b–459a, 459b, 461a–461b
classification of the sciences, I 464a–464b
Conciliar Movement, I 385a–386b
continuity, I 500b
corporation, III 320a–320b
cosmos, IV 153a
covenant, III 112a
crisis in history, I 592b
Cross, II 527a
Crusades, II 423a, 473a; III 452b
culmination of, I 382b–384a
culture, I 609b; II 129a–129b, 132b
cycles, I 626a
Dante, I 65b
deism, I 648a
democracy, I 654b, 656a
demonology, I 668b, 669b
design argument, I 672b–673b
despotism, II 1b, 3a–4a
determinism, II 18a, 22b, 28a
didacticism, III 528b
dignity, IV 139a–141a, 142a
disease, II 399b
doctrine of the four empires, III 477a
Donation of Constantine, II 419a, 420b
Donatus, II 666b, 667a
double truth, II 31b–37b
dowry system, IV 525b
drama, III 528b
dualism, II 43a, 218a
Dubois, III 452b
Duns Scotus, I 67a
Earthly Paradise, III 592b
Eckhart, I 67a
economic history, II 45a, 45b, 46b
environment, II 129a–129b, 132b
equality, II 141a–141b; III 11a
establishment of order, I 381a–382b
eternity, III 477a
evil, II 165a
evolution of literature, II 172b
expressionism, II 207b
extensio, IV 301b
faith, II 210a–212b
fate, II 227b, 232a

Faust (legend), III 246b
fealty, III 112a
feudal contract, III 112a, 112b
feudalism, III 112a, 319a–319b, 321b, 322a, 322b; IV 253b
fortune, II 227b, 232a
freedom, IV 254a
freedom of speech, II 262a
genius, II 297b, 298a, 298b, 300a, 303b, 313a–314b, 315a, 316b, 317b, 320a, 325b
God, II 343a; III 116b; IV 253a, 253b
Gothic, II 367a–367b, 371b
graphic arts, II 528a
Great Britain, II 666b
happiness, II 378b–379a
heaven, IV 153b
heresy, II 416a–424a
Hesiod, III 580a
hierarchy, II 438a, 439b–440b, 442a
historiography, II 18a, 22b, 472b–481b, 489b, 491b, 493b, 518b; IV 147a, 147b, 148b, 151b
holy, II 512a, 512b
homage, III 112a
hope, II 210a–212b
humanism, II 515a–517b, 518b–521b, 522b, 523a; IV 129b–131a, 133a, 133b, 134b, 135a, 135b, 153b
Iceland, III 592b
iconography, II 526b–528a, 529a, 538b, 540b
idea, II 546a, 546b
individualism, II 297b, 298a, 298b, 300a, 303b, 597a, 598a, 599a
infinity, II 605a, 605b, 608a, 609a–609b
Inquisition, II 417a, 425a, 427a
international peace, III 448a
intolerance, IV 115b
Islam, II 474b–475a, 640a, 644a, 646a, 646b
Italy, III 528a
Judaism, III 487b, 488a; IV 153a
justice, III 116a
kingship, III 319b–320a
language, II 666a–667a, 669a
law, II 685b–690b; III 11a; IV 253a, 253b
liberalism, III 36b, 40a–40b, 41b, 49b–50a
linguistics, III 62b–63a
literary criticism, I 596b

literary paradox, III 79a
literature, III 81b, 82b, 528a; IV 331a
logic, III 528a
love, III 96a, 103b
loyalty, III 112a
Machiavellism, III 116a–116b, 122b
macrocosm and microcosm, III 127a, 129a
Magna Carta, III 112a–112b; IV 253b
mathematics, III 178a, 178b
matter, III 190b–192b, 193b
mechanical experiments, II 196a–205b
mentality of, II 212a
metaphysical imagination, III 190b, 191a, 211b
methodology, III 381b–382a
military, IV 153a
millenarianism, III 224b–225a, 664a, 665a, 666b–669b; IV 153a
mimesis, III 227a–227b
monarchy, IV 153a, 253a, 253b
monasteries, IV 525b
motif, III 243a
mountains in literature, III 253b, 255a
music, II 313a–314b, 315a, 316b, 317b, 320a, 325b; III 260b, 261a, 265a–266b, 269b–270b
musicians, II 313a–314b
mythology, III 277a, 277b, 279b, 280a, 286a–290a, 291a, 292b
nationalism, II 689b; III 324b
natural law, III 17b–19b
natural liberty, II 62a, 69b
naturalism in art, III 340b, 341a, 342a, 342b
Nature, III 116b, 351a
necessity, III 354b, 355a
negativism, III 79a
neo-classicism in art, III 363b, 368b–370a
Neo-Platonism, III 377b–378a
Nicholas of Cusa, I 67a
Noble Savage, III 592a–592b
non finito, II 298b
Norman Conquest, II 473a; III 319b
Novalis, IV 203b
numbers, III 399b, 403b
numerical subdivisions, III 477a

nunneries, IV 525b
obedience, IV 253a
optics, III 408b, 410a
organicism, III 424a
Otto the Great, III 477a
Ovid, III 580a
painting, IV 130b, 465b, 467a, 468b, 470a, 471a
peace, III 116a
perfectibility, III 473a
periodization in history, III 477a–480a, 480b
periodization in literary history, III 481b
philanthropy, III 487b, 488a, 489a, 489b
Platonism, III 504b, 505a–505b, 507b, 509b, 510a
poetry, II 220a; III 528a–531b; IV 465b, 467a, 468b, 470a, 471a
post-Kantianism, IV 209a
power, IV 153a
pragmatism, III 555a, 555b
predestination, II 28a
primitivism, III 580a, 584b, 590b, 592a–592b, 593a, 595a, 596a
Priscianus, II 666b–667a
private property, III 652a, 655b
progress, III 640b–641a
prophecy, III 664a–669b
protest movements, III 670b
Pseudo-Callisthenes, III 592a
psychology, IV 9b, 16b
Puritanism, IV 16b
Pythagorean cosmos, IV 39b, 41a
radicalism, IV 253a
Ramism, IV 43a, 44b, 45a
rebellion, IV 253a
reformation, IV 61a–61b, 63a–66a, 67a, 69a
Reformation, IV 153a
religion, II 473a; III 528b; IV 93b, 114b, 115b
Renaissance, III 355b, 480a; IV 123a, 124a, 126a, 126b, 127a–127b, 129b, 130a, 130b, 131a, 133a, 133b, 134b, 135a, 135b, 139a–141a, 142a, 147a, 147b, 148b, 151b, 438a, 438b, 440b, 443a
revolution, IV 152b–153a, 162b
rhetoric, III 528a, 528b; IV 170b–171a
Roman Catholic Church, I 378b–387b, 403b, 404a; III 40a–40b, 452b
romanticism, III 478a, 478b;

IV 187a–188b, 191b, 192a, 193a, 197a, 203b, 206b, 208b, 210a–210b
Rome (ancient), IV 253a
Saint Augustine, III 593a
Saint Bonaventure, I 66a–66b
Saint Thomas Aquinas, I 66a, 66b–67a, 69a
salvation, III 40a–40b; IV 230a
satire, IV 214b
Schelling, IV 210a–210b
sculpture, III 342a
sin, IV 230a, 253a
skepticism, IV 241b
social contract, IV 252a, 253a–255a
socialism, IV 286b
society, IV 153a
space, IV 298b, 301b
Spengler, IV 298b
spontaneous generation, IV 308b
State, III 116a, 319a–320b, 323b; IV 153b, 314a–314b, 315b, 317a, 317b
style, IV 331a
symbolism, II 580b; IV 341b
syncretism, I 44a
technology, IV 358a, 358b–360b
temperance, IV 369a, 370a, 371a, 375a, 377a
theater, III 528b
theriophily, IV 386a–386b
time, IV 391b–392a, 393a–393b, 399a, 401b, 402a
transition to a new order, I 386b–387b
Translatio Imperii, III 477a
trivium, III 82b
Truce of God, III 448a
universe, IV 39b, 41a
universities, I 9b
utility, IV 452a
unity of science, IV 432a, 436a
universal man, IV 438a, 438b, 440b, 443a
Utopia, IV 461a
virtue, IV 371a
virtù, IV 477a, 477b, 483a
Volksgeist, IV 493b
Voltaire, I 619b
vox populi, IV 498a–498b
war, III 448a; IV 502a–502b
wealth, IV 123b, 153a
wisdom of the fool, IV 516a, 516b, 517b–519b
witchcraft, IV 522b, 523a

women, IV 525a–526a
work, IV 531b
Middle East
academic freedom, I 10a
international peace, III 454b
neo-classicism in art, III 364b
technology, IV 358a
Middle Platonism
dignity, IV 136b, 144a
Neo-Platonism, III 372a–374b, 377b
Platonism, III 517b
Plotinus, III 374a
Renaissance, IV 136b, 144a
Middleton, Thomas (1570?–1627), wisdom of the fool, IV 520a
Middleton, Conyers (1683–1750), deism, I 650b–651a
Mignet, François Auguste (1796–1884)
French Revolution (1789), IV 159b
romanticism, IV 190a
Migrations
Bible, III 275b, 279a, 280b–281a
Blacks, I 594a
crisis in history, I 591a, 594a
environment, II 130b
Greece (ancient), II 499a
mythology, III 272b, 275b, 279a, 280b–281a, 313b
Ratzel, II 130b
Miles, Josephine, evolution of literature, II 173a
Milieu intérieur concept, II 125a–125b, 126a
Bernard, II 126a
Henderson, II 125b
James, William, II 125b
Wiener, II 126a
Milinda, King (fl. 150 B.C.) Buddhism, I 254b
Military, IV 500b–509a
art, I 458a
Brazil, III 540a, 540b, 543a, 543b, 545a
democracy, II 253a
freedom of speech, II 253a, 253b, 257b, 261a
game theory, II 263b, 266a, 272b
general will, II 278b
intolerance, IV 113b
Machiavelli, IV 479b, 480a, 481b, 482a
Middle Ages, IV 153a
nationalism, IV 501a, 503b, 504a, 505b, 506a, 507b
necessity, III 354a

Newton, **IV** 502a
nuclear power, **IV** 501a
peace, **III** 440a, 441a, 443b,
444a, 445a, 445b, 446b,
447a, 448a, 448b, 452a,
455a, 456b
periodization in history, **III**
478a
positivism, **III** 540a, 540b,
543a, 543b, 545a
progress, **III** 641b, 642a,
647a
prophecy, **III** 661a, 662a
psychology, **IV** 26b
religion, **IV** 113b
revolution, **IV** 153a, 156b,
157b, 163b, 166a
Rome (ancient), **III** 354b
Rousseau, **II** 278b
technology, **IV** 357b, 361b
Tolstoy, **III** 445b–446a
totalitarianism, **IV** 410b
U.S.S.R., **IV** 506a, 507a
U.S., **III** 444a; **IV** 504a,
505b–506a, 507a, 508a
Utopia, **IV** 507a
violence, **IV** 502a, 502b,
504b, 507a
virtù, **IV** 479b, 480a, 481b,
482a
vox populi, **IV** 497a
war, **III** 448a, 448b, 452a,
455a; **IV** 500b, 501a, 501b,
502b, 504a, 505b–506a,
506b, 507a, 508a, 508b
Xenophon, **IV** 504a
Milizia, Francesco, baroque in
literature, **I** 188b
Mill, James (1773–1836),
alienation, **I** 38b, 40a, 40b
association of ideas, **I** 114a,
116a
associationism, **I** 220a
behaviorism, **I** 219a, 220a
democracy, **I** 662a, 662b
idea, **I** 116a
State, **I** 662a, 662b
Mill, John Stuart (1806–
1873)
abstraction, **I** 8a
anarchism, **I** 71a
aristocracy, **I** 154a
association of ideas, **I** 114a
authority, **I** 152b, 153b–
154a, 155b, 156a
Bacon and, **I** 178a
behaviorism, **I** 219b
Bentham and, **I** 318a–318b;
III 470a; **IV** 278b, 279a
Bosanquet and, **II** 414b
Bradley, F. H., and, **II**
414b
Buckle and, **I** 282a
causation, **I** 272b, 291a,

295a, 295b
censorship, **III** 567b
certainty, **I** 318b
China, **I** 369b
classicism, **I** 449b
classification of the
sciences, **I** 465b
Coleridge and, **IV** 199a
Comte and, **I** 318b; **III**
536b, 537b, 641b, 642b
Cosmic Fall, **I** 511b
crisis in history, **I** 590a
culture, **I** 619a
democracy, **I** 154a, 663a,
664a
desire, **IV** 179a
determinism, **II** 241a
distribution, **IV** 179a
drama, **IV** 199a
economic history, **II** 48b,
49b–50a, 54a, 55a, 57a,
57b, 60a
education, **II** 76b, 82b; **III**
470a
Enlightenment, **IV** 199a,
200a
Epicureanism, **II** 137b
equality, **II** 146b
evil, **II** 167b
free will, **II** 241a; **III**
562a
freedom, **II** 251a
God, **II** 359a
good, **II** 167b; **IV** 179a
Green and, **II** 414b
happiness, **II** 381b–382a;
IV 179a
history, **IV** 199a
idea, **I** 115a, 116a, 117a
individualism, **II** 596b,
598a, 599a, 599b, 601a
intellect, **III** 642b
intuition, **III** 561a
justice, **IV** 179a
land, **II** 49b
law, **I** 291a; **II** 251a; **III**
470a, 567b
liberalism, **III** 37a, 43a, 49b,
51a, 51b
literature, **III** 85b; **IV** 199a
metaphysical imagination,
III 209b
morality, **III** 561b, 642b;
IV 179a
nationalism, **III** 331a
natural law, **III** 22a
natural liberty, **II** 69a
Nature, **I** 511b
necessity, **III** 360a
pain, **II** 167b
passions, **III** 642b
Peirce and, **III** 558a, 560b
perfectibility, **III** 470a
politics, **III** 642b; **IV** 199a

positivism, **III** 536b, 537b,
538a, 539a, 541b, 544b,
545b
power, **III** 642b
pragmatism, **III** 556b, 558a,
560b–562a, 567b
private property, **II** 49b
profit, **II** 55a
progress, **III** 640b, 641b,
642b
psychology, **IV** 11b
punishment, **IV** 179a
relativism, **III** 561b
religion, **III** 642b
rent, **II** 49b
revolution, **IV** 199a
reward, **IV** 179a
romanticism, **IV** 199a–200a
scientific method, **II** 197a
science, **IV** 199a
social welfare, **IV** 278b,
279a
society, **III** 642b; **IV** 179a
State, **I** 663a, 664a
theodicy, **IV** 383a–384a
utilitarianism, **II** 381b–382a;
III 561b; **IV** 179a, 444b,
445b, 446a, 446b, 448b,
449a, 449b
Victorians, **IV** 220a, 221a
virtue, **IV** 179a
welfare, **IV** 179a
women, **IV** 526b, 528a
Wright and, **III** 561a, 561b,
562a
Zeitgeist, **IV** 536b
Mill, Mrs. John Stuart, progress, **III** 644b
Millar, John
Enlightenment, **II** 93a, 93b,
94b, 98a, 99b
liberty, **II** 94b
society, **II** 99b
Millenarianism, **III** 223a–225b
allegory, **III** 224b
American Civil War, **III**
225b, 450a
Anabaptists, **III** 225a
angels, **III** 223b
Antichrist, **III** 224a, 224b,
225a
anti-Semitism, **III** 225a
apocalypse, **III** 223b–224a,
224b
Armageddon, **III** 223b
avarice, **III** 225a
Baptists, **III** 225a
benevolence, **III** 223b
Bible, **III** 223b, 225a
Cerinthus, **III** 224a
Christianity, **III** 223a–225b,
477a, 488b
class, **III** 224a
Commodianus, **III** 224a

cosmology, **III** 223b
Creation, **III** 224a, 224b,
225a
Daniel (Bible), **III** 223b,
225a
death, **III** 224a, 224b
dispensationalism, **III** 225a
Ebionites, **III** 224a
economics, **III** 225a
Eddy, **III** 225b
Edwards, **III** 225b
Egypt (ancient), **III** 224a
equality, **III** 225a
eschatology, **II** 158b, 159a;
III 225a
evil, **III** 223b, 224a
feudalism, **III** 225a
folklore, **III** 224b
Frederick Barbarossa, **III**
224b, 225a
Free Spirit, **III** 225a
Fundamentalists, **III** 225a
Germany, **III** 225a
God, **III** 223b, 225a, 225b
good, **III** 223b
grace, **III** 224b
Great Britain, **III** 225a
Greek Orthodox Church, **III**
224a–224b
happiness, **III** 223b, 224b
heaven, **III** 223b, 224a,
224b
history, **III** 223b, 224a,
225a, 225b
hope, **III** 223b
immortality, **III** 223b
individualism, **III** 224a
injustice, **III** 224a, 224b–
225a
Israel (ancient), **III** 223b–
224a
Jacquerie revolt (1358), **III**
225a
Jesus Christ, **III** 223a–223b,
224b, 225a
Joachim of Floris, **III** 666b–
669b
Judaism, **III** 223b–224a
judgment, **III** 223a–223b
justice, **III** 224a, 224be
225a
Kant, **II** 159a
King Arthur (legend), **III**
224b
Lactantius, **III** 224a
legends, **III** 224b, 225a
luxury, **III** 224a
Marx, **IV** 161b
Marxism, **III** 224a, 225b
Middle Ages, **III** 224b–
225a, 664a, 665a, 666b–
669b; **IV** 153a
Miller, **III** 225a
Mormons, **III** 225a

267

mythology, III 284a
nationalism, III 223b
papacy, III 225a
Papias, III 224a
Parousia, III 223b, 225a
peace, III 224b, 456b
Peasant revolt (1831), III 225a
periodization in history, III 477a
philanthropy, III 488b
politics, III 224a, 225a
post-, III 224b, 225a
poverty, III 224a, 225a
power, III 224a, 224b, 225b
pragmatism, III 560b
pre-, III 224b
pride, III 225a
primitivism, III 581b
progress, III 225b
prophecy, III 223b, 224a, 224b, 664a, 665a, 666b–669b
prosperity, III 223b
Protestantism, III 225a–225b
reformation, IV 60b, 61a, 62b
Reformation, III 225a
religion, IV 117b
resurrection, III 223a–223b
revolution, III 224a, 225a; IV 153a, 161b
Roman Catholic Church, III 224b, 225a
Saint Augustine, III 224b
Saint Irenaeus, III 224a–224b
Saint Justin Martyr, III 224a
saints, III 223a–223b, 225a
Satan, III 223b, 224b
science, III 225b
slavery, III 224a, 224b
socialism, IV 285a, 286a, 286b, 287a, 293b, 294a
society, III 224a, 224b–225a
technology, III 225b
totalitarianism, IV 407b, 408a, 410b
tyranny, III 224a
U.S., III 225b
Utopia, IV 460b, 461b, 462a
utopianism, III 224a, 224b, 225b; IV 61a
violence, III 224a
virtue, III 224a
war, III 223b, 224b, 225b
wealth, III 224a
wisdom, III 223b
Yahweh, III 223b
Miller, Arthur (1915–   ), irony, II 634a

tragic sense, IV 414a
Miller, Henry (1891–   ), beauty, I 208a
Miller, N. E., behaviorism, I 223a
Miller, Perry, psychology, IV 18b
Miller, William (1782–1849), eschatology, II 157a
millenarianism, III 225a
Millerand, Alexandre (1859–1943)
Marxism, III 165a
revisionism, IV 272a
Millet, Gabriel, iconography, II 535b
Millet, Jean François (1814–1875), impressionism, II 578a
Mills, Charles De Berard, Orientalism, III 429a
transcendentalism, III 429a
Milne, Edward Arthur (1896–1950)
Bruno and, IV 298b
cosmology, I 568b; IV 306a
space, IV 298b, 303b, 306a
Milner, John (1752–1826), Gothic, II 372a
Milnor, J., game theory, II 272a
Milton, John (1608–1674), 80a, 83b, 86b
Addison and, III 300a
aesthetics, IV 355b
analogy, I 69b
baroque in literature, I 191a, 192a, 193a, 193b, 194b, 195a
catharsis, I 267a
chaos, III 393b
civil disobedience, I 435a
classicism, I 452b
Cosmic Fall, I 509a–509b
cosmic images, I 518b
cosmic voyages, I 526a–526b, 531b
deism, I 649b
democracy, I 657a
evil, II 165a–165b
genius, II 295a
good, II 165a
harmony, II 389b, 391b–392a, 393a, 394b
hierarchy, II 438a
Johnson, III 300a
heaven, III 393b
hell, III 393b
Hermeticism, II 433a, 433b–434a
light, III 393b
literary paradox, III 80a
literature, III 82a
mountains in literature, III

253b, 254a, 256a, 256b
music, II 389b, 391b–392a, 393a, 394b
mythology, III 295a, 295b, 299a, 299b, 300a, 306b
nationalism, III 326a
neo-classiciam in art, III 371a
Newton and, III 393b, 394b
optics, III 393b, 394b
patriarchalism, I 479b
poetry, III 530a, 530b; IV 468b
primitivism, III 581b
religion, IV 119a
social contract, IV 255a
Spenser and, III 295a
State, I 657a
sublime in external nature, IV 334b, 337a
taste, IV 355b
tragedy, I 267a
tragic sense, IV 415b
Mimesis, III 225b–230a
Adam, III 229b
aesthetics, III 228a, 229b
Alain of Lille, III 227b
Alberti, III 227b, 228a
allegory, III 228b
antiquity, III 229a, 229b
archeology, III 229b
architecture, III 226a
Aristotelianism, III 227b–228a, 229a, 229b
Aristotle, II 507a, 507b; III 226a–227a, 227b, 228a; IV 411b
art, III 225b–230a, 497b
Averroës, III 227b
Baldinucci, III 229a
Batteux, III 229a–229b
beauty, III 226b–229a
Bembo, III 229a
Bernini, III 228b
Bonaventura, III 227b
Burke, III 229b
Callistratus, III 227a
Canova, III 229b
Capriano, III 229a
Champfleury, III 229b
Cicero, III 227a, 229a
Comanini, III 228a
Correa, III 228b
Cortesi, III 229a
Courbet, III 229b
craftsmanship, III 226a
cults, III 226a
dance, III 226a, 226b
Danti, III 228b
Del Bene, III 228b
Democritus, III 226a, 226b, 227a, 230a
Dio Chrysostomus, III 227a
Dionysians, III 226a

Dolce, III 229a
Dubos, III 229a
Dürer, III 228a, 228b
epics, III 226b
Erasmus, III 229a
etymology, III 226a
Ficino, III 229a
fiction, III 228b
Flaxman, III 229b
Fracastoro, III 227b, 228b
France, III 227b, 228a, 228b
Germany, III 227b, 228a
Ghiberti, III 227b
God, III 227a–227b, 228a–228b
good, III 228a
Great Britain, III 227b
Greece (ancient), III 225b–227a, 229b, 230a, 526b
Guarini, III 228a
Herodotus, III 497b
Hesiod, III 226a
Hippocrates, III 227a, 497b
historiography, II 507a, 507b
Homer, III 226a, 497b
Horatius, III 227a
humanism, III 227b
hymns, III 226a
idea, III 228b
industrial arts, III 226a
invention, III 228b
Italy, III 227b–228a
John of Salisbury, III 227b
knowledge, III 500a
Leonardo da Vinci, III 227b
Lucian, III 227a
Lucretius, III 227a
Mans, III 228a
Maximus Tyrius, III 227a
Mengs, III 229b
metaphor, III 228b
Michelangelo, III 228a–228b, 229a
Middle Ages, III 227a–227b
mimetic art, III 226a
Mondrian, III 230a
music, III 226a, 226b
naturalism, III 226b, 229b
naturalism in art, III 343b
Nature, III 226a–230a
painting, III 226a–227b, 228b–229b; IV 465b, 469b, 471b–472b, 474b
Patrizi, III 228b
Petrarch, III 228b
Philostratus Flavius, III 227a
Picasso, III 230a
Pico della Mirandola, III 229a
Piles, R. D., III 228b
Pindar, III 226a

Planche, **III** 229b
Plato, **III** 226a–227a, 228a, 230a, 343b, 497b, 498a, 500a
Platonism, **III** 229a, 497b, 498a, 500a
Plutarch, **III** 226a
poetics, **III** 526b, 527a, 527b, 528a, 531a, 531b
poetry, **III** 226b–229b, 526b, 528a, 531a, 531b; **IV** 465b, 469b, 471b–472b, 474b
Poliziano, **III** 229a
Poussin, **III** 228a
Pseudo-Dionysius, **III** 227a
Pseudo-Longinus, **III** 227a
realism, **III** 229b
reality, **III** 226a, 226b
Renaissance, **III** 227b–229a; **IV** 137a
ritual, **III** 226a, 226b
Robortello, **III** 228b
Rome (ancient), **III** 225b, 227a, 227b
Ronsard, **III** 228b
Saint Augustine, **III** 227a
Saint Thomas Aquinas, **III** 227b
Sarbiewski, **III** 228a
Sassetti, **III** 228a
Savonarola, **III** 230a
Scaliger, **III** 228a
scholasticism, **III** 227b
Schopenhauer, **III** 343b
sculpture, **III** 226a, 226b, 227b, 229a, 229b
Seneca, **III** 227a
Shakespeare, **III** 228a
singing, **III** 226a
Socrates, **III** 226a, 497b
Strabo, **III** 226a
symmetry, **IV** 347b
Tasso, **III** 228b
Tertullian, **III** 227a–227b
Tesauro, **III** 228b
theater, **III** 226a, 226b
Thorvaldsen, **III** 229b
tragedy, **III** 226b
tragic sense, **IV** 411b
truth, **III** 226b, 227a, 227b, 228b
Varchi, **III** 228a, 228b
Vasari, **III** 229a
Vico, **III** 228a
Winckelmann, **III** 229b
wisdom, **III** 227a
Xenophon, **III** 226a, 497b
Zola, **III** 229b
Mimetic art
    Aristotle, **I** 578b, 585a
    creativity in art, **I** 581a–585a, 586a
    Plato, **I** 578b, 581a–585a

Plotinus, **I** 586a
Mind
    aesthetics, **II** 216b, 223a–223b, 224b; **IV** 354a, 355b
    Anaxagoras, **IV** 50a
    angels, **II** 232b
    Aristotle, **II** 120b, 226a; **III** 189b; **IV** 5a–6b
    art, **II** 298b
    Bacon, **III** 212b–213a, 215a
    beauty, **I** 201b
    Boethius, **II** 231a, 231b
    chance, **II** 226a, 227a, 229a, 232a, 232b, 233a
    Cicero, **IV** 50a, 136a–136b
    classification, **I** 513b–514a
    cosmos, **IV** 50a
    Democritus, **III** 576b–577a
    Descartes, **II** 41a; **III** 418a
    design argument, **I** 671a
    determinism, **II** 238b, 239a
    Dewey, **III** 561b
    dignity, **IV** 136a–136b, 137a, 138b
    disease, **II** 397a, 399a, 402b, 406b
    dualism, **II** 38a, 41a
    environment, **II** 120b–121a, 122a, 123b, 129a
    Epicureanism, **IV** 7b, 8a
    evil, **II** 38a
    fate, **II** 226a, 227a, 229a, 232a, 232b, 233a
    fortune, **II** 226a, 227a, 229a, 232a, 232b, 233a
    free will, **II** 238b, 239a, 245a, 246a
    general will, **II** 276b
    genius, **II** 293b, 298b, 324a
    God, **II** 344a
    good, **II** 231b
    Grimaldi, **III** 418a
    happiness, **II** 378a
    harmony, **II** 388b
    Hegel, **II** 407b, 408a, 409b, 410a, 413b; **III** 22a; **IV** 290b
    Hobbes, **IV** 434a
    human nature, **III** 576b–577a
    Hume, **II** 120b
    Huygens, **III** 418a
    individualism, **II** 298b
    James, **III** 561b, 562a, 566a
    Jung, **IV** 97a
    Kant, **II** 120b, 324a
    Locke, **II** 120b, 239a
    matter, **III** 186b–192b
    Mead, **III** 561b
    metaphysical imagination, **III** 213a–215a, 219a, 219b, 222a

music, **II** 324a, 388b
mythology, **III** 317a
natural rights, **III** 17b, 19a, 22a
optics, **III** 407b–408a, 408b, 409b, 412a–413a, 416b, 418a, 420a
Peirce, **III** 561b, 565b
phrenology, **IV** 23b
Plato, **II** 223a; **III** 188a, 188b, 353b; **IV** 3a–3b
Platonism, **III** 517b
pragmatism, **III** 558a, 561b, 562a, 565b, 566a
progress, **III** 625b, 631a, 634a
psychology, **IV** 5a–9b, 10a, 15b, 17a, 17b, 19b, 21a, 21b–24b, 25a, 27a, 27b
Pythagorean cosmos, **IV** 31b, 32b, 37b
rationalism, **IV** 47a, 50a
recapitulation, **IV** 59a
religion, **IV** 94b, 95b, 97a, 98a, 98b, 120b
Renaissance, **IV** 136a–136b, 137a, 138b
revolution, **IV** 154b, 155a
romanticism, **IV** 202a, 206a
Rosenkranz, **II** 413b
Rousseau, **II** 276b
Saint Albertus Magnus, **II** 232a
Saint Augustine, **IV** 9a, 138b
Saint Thomas Aquinas, **II** 120b
science, **I** 465a, 465b
social contract, **IV** 254a
socialism, **IV** 290b
Spinoza, **II** 238b; **IV** 434b
Stoicism, **II** 378a; **IV** 50a
Strato, **IV** 7a
taste, **IV** 354a, 355b
temperance, **IV** 365b, 366a
time, **IV** 391b, 393b
unity of science, **IV** 432b, 434a, 434b
Utopia, **IV** 463a
William of Ockham, **III** 19a
work, **IV** 532a, 534a
Zeitgeist, **IV** 536b
Mineralogy
    Islam, **II** 645b
    mythology, **III** 287b
Minerva (myth), **III** 290a, 290b, 291b, 292a
Ming dynasty (1368–1644), **I** 356a
Mingard, Pierre, aesthetics, **IV** 355a
Minkowski, Hermann (1864–1909)

relativity, **IV** 84a, 85a, 85b, 90a, 91a
time, **IV** 397a
Minorities
    general will, **II** 278b
    intolerance, **IV** 112b, 116a
    Marxism, **III** 148b, 155a
    nationalism, **III** 328b, 329a, 329b, 333b, 334a, 337a
    social contract, **IV** 254b
    Switzerland, **III** 329a
    U.S.S.R., **III** 155a
Minos (myth), law, **II** 676a, 677a
Minturno, Antonio
    catharsis, **I** 267a
    poetics, **III** 529a, 531a
    ut pictura poesis, **IV** 467b
Mir Dāmād, **II** 651b
Mirabeau, Honoré Gabriel de (1749–1791), Machiavellism, **III** 123a
Mirabeau, Victor Riqueti de (1715–1789) primitivism, **III** 600b
Miracles
    deism, **I** 646b
    God, **II** 231a
    humanism, **IV** 133a
    matter, **III** 186a
    mythology, **III** 282b–283a
    Nature, **III** 350b
    Pomponazzi, **II** 36b
    prophecy, **III** 660a, 662b
    religion, **IV** 106b, 108a
Miriam (Bible), disease, **II** 396b
Miró, Joan (1893–   )
    art, **III** 597a
    primitivism, **III** 597a
Mirrors
    optics, **III** 410b, 413a, 415b–416a, 416b
    symmetry, **IV** 346a, 348b, 351a, 351b
Misch, Georg, Buddhism, **I** 256b
Mises, Ludwig von (1881–   ), individualism, **II** 597a
Mises, Richard von (1883–1953)
    positivism, **III** 546a
    probability, **III** 608b, 611b, 614a, 615b–618b, 619b, 621a–623a
Mises' first postulate, **III** 616a–616b
Mises' second postulate, **III** 617a
Misogynism, **IV** 524a
Missionaries
    Africa, **I** 376a

Buddhism, I 248a, 252a, 257a
China, I 383b
Christianity, I 255b, 353b, 354a, 354b, 355a–361b, 375a–376b, 383b
Church, I 413b
Eastern Orthodox Church, I 409b
imperialism, I 407b–408a
Iraq, I 376a
Judaic Christianity, I 374a–374b
Lutheranism, III 493b
Northumbria, I 380b
Orientalism, III 428b
Persia, I 376a
Pietism, III 493b
Protestantism, I 388a, 407a
reformation, IV 68b
Rome (ancient), I 375a–376b; II 470b
Russia, I 409b
U.S., I 407a–407b
Mitchell, S. Weir (1829–1914), psychology, IV 28b
Mitchell, Wesley C. (1874–1948)
economic history, II 60b
psychology, IV 23a
Mithra (myth), II 338b
religion, IV 94a
salvation, IV 228b
Mithraism
astrology, I 125a
Gnosticism, II 330a
God, II 339a–339b
Mithridates VI of Pontus, King (c. 132–63 B.C.), historiography, II 510b
Moab (Bible), prophecy, III 660b
Mobility
economic history, II 51a
liberalism, III 38a–38b, 50a
style, II 298a
Mob-rule Polybius, I 626a
Moderation
Aristotle, IV 369a
Greece (ancient), IV 369a
temperance, IV 365b, 366b, 367b, 369a, 370a
Thucydides, IV 367b
Modernism, I 418b–427a
Acton, I 419b
ambiguity, I 58a–60a
Aristotelianism, I 422b
Battifol, I 421a
Baudelaire, I 58b–59a
Benedict XV (Pope), I 423b
Bergson, I 420a
Bible, I 419a, 420b–421a, 422a

Bismarck, I 424b
Blondel, I 419a, 420a, 421b–422b, 423b, 425a, 426a
Bossuet, I 419b
Bourget, I 420a–420b
Boutroux, I 420a
Buonaiuti, I 424a
Caird, I 420a
Chardin, I 425a
Church, I 419b, 420b, 422b, 423b, 425a, 425b
Church of England, I 424b
condemnation of, I 423a–424b
criticism, I 420b–421a
Darwin, I 419b
defined, I 418b–419a
Delbos, I 420a
democracy, I 424b
dogma, I 420b–421a
Döllinger, I 419b
Duchesne, I 420b
ecumenicalism, I 425a, 426a
Enlightenment, I 423a–423b, 425b–426a
Eucken, I 420a
evolutionism, I 420a
excommunication, I 423b
Exegetes, I 421a
faith, I 421b–423a
Fichte, I 420a
Foggazzaro, I 424a
France, I 419b–424a, 426a
fundamentalism, I 419a
Germany, I 419b–420a, 420b, 424a–425b, 426b
God, I 420b, 421a, 422a, 423a, 423b, 425b
Grandmaison, I 425a
Great Britain, I 419a, 420a, 422b–423a, 424b, 426a; III 483b
Harnack, I 419b, 420b, 426b
Hébert, I 420a, 424a
Hecker, I 419b
Hegel, I 419b, 420a
heresy, I 419a, 423b; II 429b
historiography, I 425a–426b
Holtzmann, I 419b
Hort, I 424b
Houtin, I 424a
Hügel, I 420a, 421a, 422b, 424a, 424b
Integrists, I 423b, 424b, 426a
Ireland, I 419b
Italy, I 419b, 422b, 423b, 424a, 424b, 425b, 426a
Jesuits, I 425a

Jesus Christ, I 419b, 420b, 421b, 422b, 425b
Kant, I 419b, 420a, 425b
Laberthonnière, I 422a, 422b
Lacordaire, I 419b
Lagrange, I 421a
Lamennais, I 419b
language, I 420b
Le Roy, I 422a–422b, 423b
Leo XIII (Pope), I 420a, 420b, 422b
Lilley, I 424b
Loisy, I 419b, 420b–426b
McNeill, I 426a
Maine de Biran, I 420a
Major, H. D. A., I 424b
Marx, III 479a
Matthew, I 422b
Maurice, I 424b
metaphor, III 206b
Mohler, I 419a
Montalembert, I 419b
Murri, I 424a
neo-scholasticism, I 422b
nationalism, III 334b, 336a
Newman, I 419a, 419b, 420b, 425a
Nietzsche, I 420a
Ollé-Laprune, I 420a
periodization in history, III 477a, 478a, 479a, 480a, 480b
periodization in literary history, III 483b
Petre, I 424b
philanthropy, III 489a–491b
philosophy, I 421b–423a
Pius X (Pope), I 419a
Pius XII (Pope), I 425a
poetics, III 528b, 531a, 531b
positivism, I 426a
Poulat, I 425a, 426a
pragmatism, I 420a
protest movements, III 674a–676a
Protestantism, I 419a, 419b, 420b, 421a, 424a, 425b, 426a–426b
Ravaisson, I 420a
Reformation, I 423a–423b
religion, III 206b
Renaissance, III 480a
Renan, I 419b, 420b, 421b
Ritschl, I 419b
Rivière, I 425a
Roman Catholic Church, I 406a–406b, 418b–427a
romanticism, IV 208b
Sangnier, I 423b
Schell, I 424a–424b
Schelling, I 420a
Schleiermacher, I 420a

scholasticism, I 420a
Schopenhauer, I 420a
Schweitzer, I 419b
Semeria, I 422b
Simon, I 419b
Spinoza, I 420a
Strauss, I 419b
Sullivan, I 424b
symbolism, IV 344a
Thomism, I 420a, 422b
Tyrrell, I 419b, 422b–423a, 423b, 424b, 425b
U.S., I 419a, 419b, 423b, 424b
Ward, Wilfrid, I 425a
Weiss, J., I 419b, 420b
Wellhausen, I 419b
Modistae, language, II 666b–667b
Moebius, P. J., genius and madness, II 308b
Moffat, James (1870–1944), Buddhism, I 255a
Moghila, Peter (1596?–1647), history, I 411a
Mohammed (570–632 A.D.), free will, II 245a
God, II 345a
historiography, II 474b, 476a
Islam, II 474b, 475a
predestination, II 29b
salvation, IV 230b–231a
Mohammedanism
casuistry, I 258a
hierarchy, II 441a
India, I 248a
liberalism, III 42a
love, III 100b
necessity, III 355a
Spain, I 393a
Mohl, Hugo von (1805–1872), cell division, II 285b
Möhler, Johann Adam (1796–1938), modernism, I 419a
Moh's scale of hardness, III 559b
Moir, David Macbeth (1798–1851), romanticism, IV 193a
Molanus, Joannes, iconography, II 524b, 531a, 534b
Molecular biology, empiricism, III 549a
Molecular homology, I 239b–241b
Molière (1622–1673)
aesthetics, IV 354b
baroque in literature, I 190b
catharsis, I 269b
causation, III 195a
classicism, I 452a, 453a

comedy, I 468b–469a; III 238a
economic history, II 46a
ethics, II 153b
Gothic, II 368a
literary criticism, I 601a
motif, III 238a
Plautus and, I 86b
poetry, III 529b
religion, IV 119b
satire, IV 211b, 213b, 215a
taste, IV 354b
virtuoso, IV 488b
wisdom of the fool, IV 520a
women, IV 526a
Wycherley and, I 453a
Molina, E. C., probability, III 609b
Molina, Luis (1535–1600), social contract, IV 254a
Moloch, primitivism, III 581a
Molsdorf, W., iconography, II 535b
Moltmann, J., eschatology, II 157b, 365b
Molyneux, William (1656–1698), Newton and, III 395b
Momigliano, A., historiography, III 302a, 307a
Mommsen, Theodor (1817–1903)
authority, I 143a
revolution, IV 160b–161a
Monads
appearance and reality, I 95b
atomism, I 133a
Bruno, II 445b
continuity, I 493b
hierarchy, II 445b–446a, 448b
Leibniz, I 299b, 328b, 360b, 493b; II 445b–446a, 448b; III 131a, 193b, 196a, 515b, 516b; IV 382a, 434b
matter, III 193b, 196a
Platonism, III 515b, 516b
Pythagoreans, IV 37a
theodicy, IV 382a
time, IV 394a–394b
Xenocrates, IV 37a
Monarchy
Aristotle, I 625b
Bodin, II 4a–4b
Cicero, I 655a, 655b
democracy, I 653a, 655a, 656b, 657b, 659b
despotism, II 4a–4b, 6a, 8a, 9a, 10b–11a, 11b, 12a, 14a, 16a
Enlightenment, II 91a
Great Britain, IV 154a

Hegel, II 16a, 409a, 409b, 414b
Herodotus, I 653a
Hobbes, I 655b; II 6a
humanism, II 519b, 522b–523a
Locke, I 657b; IV 154a
Machiavellism, III 117a, 120a, 120b
Michelet, II 414b
Middle Ages, IV 153a, 253a, 253b
Montesquieu, II 9a, 11b
mythology, III 281a
natural liberty, II 62b
Paine, I 659b
Plato, I 654a
Polybius, I 625b, 626a
progress, III 630a
reformation, IV 65b
revolution, IV 152b, 153b, 154a, 154b, 157b, 164a
romanticism, IV 207a
Rome (ancient), II 686a; IV 154b
Salutati, II 523a
social contract, IV 253a, 253b–257b, 258a, 262a
totalitarianism, IV 410a
Utopia, IV 461a–462a
virtù, IV 483b
Voltaire, II 11a
vox populi, IV 497a
Monasteries
Christianity, I 377b–378a, 380b, 383b, 388a, 392b–393a; III 590a, 590b; IV 371a
heresy, II 418b
perfectibility, III 467b, 468b
primitivism, III 590a, 590b
prophecy, III 664b, 665b
Roman Catholic Church, II 418b
temperance, IV 371a
time, IV 399a
women, IV 525b
Monasticism
community, I 378a
culture, I 380b
development of, I 377b–378a
faith, hope, and charity, II 212b
history, I 383b, 388a
immorality, I 388a
materialism, IV 64a
Pythagoreans, IV 31a–31b
reform, I 392b–393a
reformation, IV 60a, 62b, 63a, 63b–65a
Saint Augustine, IV 63a
Monboddo, Lord James Barrett (1714–1799)

evolutionism, II 178a–178b
language, II 669a–669b
linguistics, III 64b, 65b
primitivism, III 599b, 603b
progress, II 178a
Rousseau and, II 669a; III 599b
ut pictura poesis, IV 472b
Mondolfo, Rudolfo
pragmatism, III 555a, 555b
work, IV 530b
Mondrian, Piet (1872–1944)
aesthetics, II 221a, 222b
mimesis, III 230a
Nature, III 230a
Monet, Claude (1840–1926)
aesthetics, II 220b
Gothic, II 372b
impressionism, II 567b, 568a–568b, 570a–570b, 571a, 572b, 573b, 574b, 577b, 579a
Money
Aristotle, I 396a–396b; IV 451b
economic history, II 45a–45b, 47b, 49a, 52b, 54b, 55a, 56a, 57a–58b
game theory, II 264b, 265a–265b
happiness, II 384b
Hegel, II 409a
Hume, II 45a–45b, 57b
Locke, II 57b
love, III 104a, 104b, 105a
natural liberty, II 67b, 69b
primitivism, III 599b
reformation, IV 65b
temperance, IV 371a
utility, IV 451b, 452b, 454a, 454b
Monge, Gaspar (1746–1818), geometry, IV 304a
Monimus of Syracuse, cynicism, I 628b
Monism
agnosticism, I 23b–24a
beauty, I 208b
Creation, I 571a, 572a, 572b
dualism, II 40a, 41a, 41b
Engels, II 455a
Epicureanism, II 41a
God, I 571a, 572a, 572b; II 344b, 348a
Hegel, III 556b
Marxism, III 147a, 150a
materialism, II 455a
matter, III 187a, 193a
metaphysical imagination, III 220b
methodology, I 23a–23b

Neo-Platonism, III 376b
Orientalism, III 430a, 436b, 438a–438b, 439a
Peirce, III 556b
Porphyry, III 376b
positivism, III 549b, 550a
pragmatism, III 556b
psychology, IV 19b, 21a
Pythagoreans, IV 32a
romanticism, IV 195a
Royce, III 556b
Spinoza, III 193a
Stoicism, II 41a
time, IV 393b, 394b
U.S., III 430a, 436b, 438a–438b, 439a
utility, IV 450b
Monnier, Marc (1829–1885), realism in literature, IV 52a
Monochord, III 271a
Pythagoras, IV 39a
Pythagoreans, IV 39a, 39b, 40b
Monod-Herzen, E., aesthetics, II 219a
Monogamy
Christianity, II 251a–251b
marriage, II 251a–251b
religion, IV 96a
Monophysites, Islam, II 639a
Monopoly
agriculture, II 57a
economic history, II 48b, 51b, 57a
James, III 563a, 565b
labor, II 57a
law, III 28b–29a
Marxism, III 150b, 162a, 654a
natural, II 57a
occurrence of, II 57a
private property, III 653a, 654a
totalitarianism, IV 407a, 407b, 410a
trade, II 57a
Monotheism
Christianity, II 342b
Comte, III 641b–642a
dualism, II 42a
equality, II 140b
evil, II 163b–165a
God, II 336b, 341b, 342b
intolerance, IV 113b, 114a
Jews (ancient), II 466a
Judaism, II 342b
mythology, III 281a, 281b, 301a, 301b, 303a, 309a
Neo-Platonism, III 372b
progress, III 641b–642a
prophecy, III 657b
religion, IV 94b, 95b, 96a, 113b, 114a
technology, IV 358b

271

theodicy, **IV** 379a
tragic sense, **IV** 415b
Volksgeist, **IV** 493a
witchcraft, **IV** 521a
Monroy, E. V. von, iconography, **II** 537b
Montagu, Ashley, war, **IV** 508a
Montaigne, Michel Eyquem de (1533–1592), **I** 77a, 79a, 79b
  ambiguity, **I** 54b
  animals, **III** 594b
  anti-intellectualism, **III** 595a
  baroque in literature, **I** 188b
  cannibalism, **III** 594a, 594b
  causation, **I** 301b
  certainty, **I** 304a–304b, 305a
  chance images, **I** 349a
  children, **III** 595b
  civilization, **III** 594a
  Counter-Enlightenment, **II** 101b
  cruelty, **III** 594b
  death, **I** 635b–636a, 637b
  deism, **I** 648b
  disloyalty, **III** 594b
  education, **III** 595a
  evil, **II** 167b–168a
  fideism, **IV** 243b
  God, **I** 304b; **II** 349b; **IV** 243b
  Golden Age (myth), **III** 594a
  historiography, **IV** 150b
  humanism, **IV** 135a
  Indians (American), **III** 594a
  knowledge, **IV** 243b
  language, **II** 266b
  life, **I** 636a
  literary paradox, **III** 76b, 78a, 79a, 79b, 80b
  literature, **III** 82b, 86a; **IV** 331b
  love, **III** 103b
  Lucretius, **I** 133a
  metaphysical imagination, **III** 213b
  morality, **III** 594a, 594b
  natural law, **II** 20b
  Nature, **I** 635b–636a; **III** 594a, 594b
  Platonism, **III** 507b
  primitivism, **III** 594a–594b, 595a, 595b, 599b
  Pyrrhonism, **I** 79b
  religion, **IV** 114b
  skepticism, **II** 167b–168a, 349b; **III** 78a; **IV** 241a, 241b, 243a–243b, 244a, 244b, 246b

style, **IV** 331b
teleology, **I** 301b
theriophily, **IV** 385b, 387a–387b
treason, **III** 594b
tyranny, **III** 594b
Vergil, **III** 594a
war, **III** 594b
wisdom of the fool, **IV** 517b, 519b
Montalembert, Marquis de, Marc-René (1714–1800), modernism, **I** 419b
Montanari, Geminiano, utility, **IV** 452b
Montanism, **I** 375a–375b
  eschatology, **II** 156b
  Roman Catholic Church, **I** 375a–375b
  socialism, **IV** 286b
Montanus, Arnoldus, China, **I** 356b–357a
Monteggio, Luigi, romanticism, **IV** 191a
Montesquieu (1689–1755), aesthetics, **IV** 355a
  Anquetil-Duperron and, **II** 13a
  Burke and, **IV** 203a
  China, **I** 361b–362a, 365a; **II** 10b
  climate, **III** 640a; **IV** 491a, 491b
  Comte and, **III** 533a, 640a
  Counter-Enlightenment, **II** 101b, 103a, 109b
  culture, **I** 616a, 616b; **II** 129b, 131b
  cycles, **III** 640b
  deism, **I** 651a
  democracy, **I** 656a, 657b, 659a, 660a
  despotism, **II** 1a, 1b, 2a, 4b, 6a, 8a–12b, 13a, 13b, 16a
  economic history, **II** 60b
  economics, **II** 9b
  education, **II** 9b
  Enlightenment, **II** 89b, 93a, 93b, 95a, 98a, 100a
  environment, **II** 129b, 131b
  equality, **II** 143b
  fear, **II** 9b, 13b
  freedom, **II** 9a–9b, 251a; **III** 21a
  general will, **II** 275b, 276a
  historicism, **II** 458a
  historiography, **II** 475a, 489a, 494b, 500a
  individualism, **II** 600b
  justice, **III** 21a
  law, **II** 10a, 251a; **III** 21a, 640a–640b
  liberalism, **III** 37a, 44b, 45a, 45b, 46a, 54b
  liberty, **II** 95a
  Machiavellism, **III** 121b, 124b
  monarchy, **II** 9a, 11b
  mythology, **III** 304a
  natural law, **III** 21a, 21b, 640a
  necessity, **III** 358a
  politics, **II** 9b, 98a; **III** 21a, 640a–640b
  positivism, **III** 533a, 534a
  power, **II** 9b; **III** 21a
  progress, **III** 640a–640b
  psychology, **II** 9b
  revolution, **IV** 154b, 155a
  Robespierre and, **II** 13b–14a
  romanticism, **IV** 203a
  Rousseau and, **II** 11b–12a, 275b, 276a
  slavery, **II** 9a–10b
  socialism, **IV** 288a
  society, **III** 21a, 640a
  State, **I** 656a, 657b, 659a, 660a; **III** 21a
  structuralism, **IV** 325a
  taste, **IV** 355a
  tyranny, **II** 11b
  virtue, **II** 13b
  Volksgeist, **IV** 491a–491b, 492a
  Voltaire and, **II** 10a, 10b–11a
  war, **II** 10a; **IV** 500b–501a, 501b
Monteverdi, Claudio (1567–1643), genius, **II** 321b
Montfaucon, Bernard de (1655–1741)
  mythology, **III** 302b
  neo-classicism in art, **III** 363b, 367a
Montgolfier, Jacques Étienne (1745–1799), cosmic voyages, **I** 532a
Montgolfier, Joseph Michel (1740–1810), cosmic voyages, **I** 532a
Montgomery, James (1771–1854)
  literature, **III** 84b
  romanticism, **IV** 194b
Montluisant, Gobineau de, Gothic, **II** 369b
Montmort, P. R. (1673–1719)
  De Moivre and, **III** 609a
  probability, **III** 609a
Moon
  cosmology, **I** 535b, 536b, 537a–540a, 542a, 546a–549b
  eclipses, **I** 537b–539b

  evolution, **I** 549b
  fortune, fate, and chance, **II** 233b
  harmony, **II** 389a–390a
  macrocosm, **III** 128a, 130b
  measurement, **IV** 400b, 404a
  motion, **I** 537b–538a; **IV** 50a
  music, **II** 389a–389b, 390a
  mythology, **III** 278a, 282a, 310a
  numerical tables, **I** 537b–538a
Moore, Charles A., Buddhism, **I** 256a
Moore, George (1852–1933), realism in literature, **IV** 52b
  symbolism, **IV** 340b
Moore, George Edward (1873–1958)
  appearance and reality, **I** 98a
  beauty, **I** 209b–210a, 210b
  behaviorism, **I** 219b
  certainty, **I** 319b
  common sense, **I** 319b
  cycles, **I** 623b
  good, **III** 234b; **IV** 183a
  moral sense, **III** 234b
  truth, **I** 319b
  utilitarianism, **IV** 446b
Moore, Thomas (1779–1852), romanticism, **IV** 194b
Moore, W. E., class, **I** 446a
Moors
  classification of the sciences, **I** 463b
  Spain, **I** 393a, 463b
Moraes, Wenceslau de (1854–1929), Buddhism, **I** 256b
Moral sense, **III** 230a–235a
  aesthetics, **III** 230b, 232a, 232b–233a, 234b–235a
  Ayer, **III** 234b–235a
  Balguy, **III** 233a
  beauty, **III** 230b, 231a, 231b, 232b, 233a
  benevolence, **III** 231a, 231b, 232a, 232b
  Bentham, **III** 233b, 234a
  Butler, **III** 230b, 231a
  Carritt, **III** 234b
  causation, **III** 232b
  Clarke, **III** 230b
  commodities, **III** 232b
  common sense, **III** 233b–234a
  conscience, **III** 230b, 233b
  dignity, **III** 231b
  duty, **III** 232b–234b
  empiricism, **III** 230b, 231b, 233a, 233b, 234b, 235a

epistemology, III 230b, 233b, 234b
Gay, III 233a–233b
Hartley, III 234a–234b
hedonism, III 234a
honor, III 231b, 232b, 233b
human nature, III 231a, 232a, 232b
Hume, III 230a–231b, 233a–235a
Hutcheson, III 230a–234b
idea, III 231b, 232a, 234a
imagination, III 231b, 233a
immorality, III 232a
judgment, III 230a–235a
justice, III 232a, 232b, 234b
Kames, III 234a, 234b
Kant, III 233b, 234a, 234b
knowledge, III 230b, 231b, 233a, 233b–234a, 234b
Locke, III 231b
Mandeville, III 231a
Moore, G. E., III 234b
motive, III 230b, 231a
natural law, III 232b–234b
obligation, III 234b
origin of the term, III 230a–230b
pain, III 231b, 232a, 232b, 234a–234b
philosophy, III 230b, 231b, 232a, 234b
Plato, III 230b, 234b
pleasure, III 231b–234b
positivism, III 235a
Price, III 233a, 234a, 234b
Prichard, III 234b
pride, III 232b
psychology, III 233a, 234a, 235a
rationalism, III 230b–234b
Reid, III 233b–234a
religion, III 234b
Ross, III 234b
rules, III 232b
self-love, III 231a
senses, III 231b, 234a
Shaftesbury, III 230b–231a, 232a, 233a, 234b
shame, III 231b
Smith, III 233a, 233b
sympathy, III 232a–232b, 233b, 234b
taste, III 232a
truth, III 233a
utilitarianism, III 231a–232b, 234a, 234b
Victorian sentiment, III 231b, 232a, 233b, 234b
Morality
  aesthetics, IV 354b, 355b, 356a, 356b
  anarchy, III 470a

Antiphon, I 629b
Antisthenes, I 629b
Apollo (myth), IV 365b–366a
Aristotle, III 365b–366a; IV 49b, 175a, 175b
asceticism, I 260a
Austin, III 1b
Bacon, IV 433b–434a
beauty, III 512a
Bergson, III 565a
Berkeley, II 352b
Bernstein, III 163a
Boethius, II 231b–232a
Brazil, III 540b, 542b
Butler, II 380a
Calvinism, I 262a; III 654a
Chapman, III 294b
children, III 596a
China, I 355a, 356b, 357b, 361a–363a, 365a, 366a
China (Communist), III 334a
Christianity, III 588b
Cicero, III 116a; IV 50a
common sense, III 645a
communism, III 22b
Comte, III 533b, 534a
Condorcet, III 533a, 644a
Counter-Enlightenment, II 101a, 105b, 107b, 108a, 110a
Cousin, III 533b
culture, III 575a
cynicism, I 633a, 633b; III 585b
Darwin, III 646a
deism, I 646b, 648b, 651a; III 301b–302a
Democritus, III 577a
Descartes, IV 432b
determinism, II 237a–237b, 238a, 240b, 241a–241b
Dewey, III 555b; IV 186a
Diderot, III 603a, 644b
dignity, IV 136a, 141a, 141b, 142a
dualism, II 40a, 41b
economic history, II 51a
economics, III 644b, 645a
education, II 73b, 74a, 75a, 75b, 76b–77a, 77b, 84a
Edwards, IV 110a
Egypt (ancient), IV 224b
Ehrlich, III 3b
Emerson, III 430b
Epicureanism, IV 7a
equality, II 144a
equity, II 151a
evil, II 165b, 166b, 168a; IV 382a
evolution, II 184a; III 646a, 647a
existentialism, II 190b,

193a, 194a, 195a; III 160a
faith, hope, and charity, II 212b, 213a
fascism, III 331b
Faust (legend), III 247b–248a
Ficino, III 511a
Fontenelle, III 644a–644b
fortune, fate, and chance, II 229b, 231b–232a, 234a, 234b–235a
Franklin, IV 22b
free will, II 237a–237b, 238a, 240b, 241a–241b, 242b, 247a
freedom, II 249a, 251a–251b; III 645a
Freud, III 312b
game theory, II 265b
Gandhi, III 446a
general will, II 276b, 278a, 279b
genetics, III 645a
genius, II 295b, 314b
Gnosticism, II 328a
God, II 334b, 337a, 347a–347b, 349a, 351a, 352b, 353b–354a, 355b, 356a, 357a, 358a
good, IV 173a–186b
Greece (ancient), II 566a, 678a, 679b, 681a; III 353a; IV 229a
Grotius, III 441b
happiness, II 374b, 375b–376a, 376b, 380a, 380b, 383a, 383b, 384b, 385a, 385b, 387a
health, II 396b
Hegel, II 408b, 410b; III 22a, 555b, 556a; IV 180a
Heidegger, II 193a
heresy, II 416b, 418b
hierarchy, II 447a
historiography, II 468b, 469b, 480a, 480b, 481a, 502b–503a; IV 147b
history, III 277b
Hobbes, IV 177a, 484a
Holmes, Justice, III 567b
holy, II 512a, 512b
Horace, III 631b
human nature, III 572a–572b, 575a, 575b–576a, 577a, 643b, 644a, 645a
humanism, II 515b, 516a, 518a–518b, 519a, 519b, 522b–523a; IV 132a, 132b, 133b
Hume, III 471b; IV 247b
Hutcheson, II 380a
Huxley, J., III 474a
Huxley, T. H., III 474a
iconography, II 533b

idea, II 548a–548b
ideal, II 550a, 551a
idealism, III 645a
ideology, II 553b, 554a; III 645a–645b
ignorance, III 645b
impartial rule, III 645a
impiety, II 565a, 566a
impressionism, II 582b, 583a
individualism, II 594b, 595b, 596a, 597b, 598b, 603a–603b; III 644b, 645a
international peace, III 448a, 450a, 453a
Israel (ancient), II 565a
James, III 565a
Jefferson, IV 22b
Johnson, Samuel, II 447a
Judaism, II 565a; III 6b, 636a
justice, II 657b
Kant, I 316b; II 107b, 204b, 247a, 279b, 353b–354a, 357a, 407b, 548a; III 442a–442b, 494b, 637a, 639b, 640b; IV 179b, 181a, 382b, 383a, 433b
Kelsen, III 2a
Khrushchev, III 153b
knowledge, I 316b; III 645a
labor, III 675b
law, II 249a, 251a–251b, 678a, 679b, 681a, 687a, 688a; III 1a, 1b, 2a, 3b, 5a, 5b, 6a, 6b, 29a, 29b, 35b, 645a
Leibniz, I 465a
liberalism, III 41a, 42b, 43b, 47b, 48a, 48b, 51a, 51b, 56b
Locke, I 465a; III 469b; IV 178a
love, III 95a, 99a, 100b, 101b, 102b, 103a, 103b, 104b, 105b, 106a, 106b
loyalty, III 108b, 109b, 110b, 111b, 112b, 113a, 114a
Lucretius, III 631a–631b
Machiavelli, III 116a–125a; IV 477a, 479a, 479b–480b, 482a, 482b
Machiavellism, III 116a–125a
macrocosm and microcosm, III 126a
Malinowski, III 314b
Man-Machine, III 140a
Marlowe, III 247b–248a
Marx, II 450b, 451a
Marxism, III 153b, 160a, 163a, 168b; IV 181a

materialism, II 450b, 451a
matter, III 186a–186b, 190a
meliorism, IV 62b
metaphor, III 199a, 204a, 205a, 205b
music, II 76b–77a, 314b
Montaigne, III 594a, 594b
Mill, III 561b, 642b; IV 179a
mythology, III 273b, 274a, 277b, 282b–283a, 288a–288b, 289a, 290a, 290b, 293b, 294b, 295b, 301a, 301b–302a, 309b, 312b, 314b, 316a
nationalism, III 325b, 327b, 329a–334b, 336b
natural law, III 15a, 15b, 16b, 17b, 18b, 19a, 21b, 22a, 22b, 23a, 23b, 26a
Nature, III 347a, 349b
necessity, III 353a, 355a, 355b, 358a, 360a
neo-classicism in art, III 365b, 366a, 368b
Neo-Platonism, III 373a, 374a, 376a
Nietzsche, IV 180b, 484b
Orientalism, III 428a–429a, 430b, 436b
Ovid, IV 122a
Owen, IV 289b
Pascal, II 168a
passions, III 644b
peace, III 440b, 441a–446a
Peirce, III 555b, 556b
Pelagius, III 466b
Pereira Barreto, III 540b
perennial philosophy, III 457b, 460b, 462a
perfectibility, III 643b, 644a
Peripatetics, IV 478a–478b
Petrarch, II 234a; IV 141b, 142a, 479b–480a
philanthropy, III 460a, 491a
philosophy, II 550a, 551a; III 199a
phrenology, IV 23b
Pietism, III 493b, 494b, 495a, 495b
Plato, II 231b–232a, 375b–376a, 376b, 566a; III 496a, 500b, 501a, 503b, 508b, 577a, 629a; IV 4a
Platonism, III 496a, 500b, 501a, 503b, 504a, 506b, 508a, 508b, 511a, 512a, 512b, 522b–523a
pleasure, II 374b, 375b–376a, 376b, 380a, 380b, 383a, 383b, 384b, 385a, 385b, 387a
Plotinus, IV 8b

poetics, III 529b
Polybius, III 630b
positivism, III 6a, 533a, 533b, 539b, 540b, 542b
pragmatism, III 555b, 556a, 558b, 561b, 562a, 562b, 565a, 565b, 567b, 568a
primitivism, III 578a, 578b, 579b, 581b, 583a, 583b, 588b, 594a, 594b, 596a, 598b, 599b, 601b, 603a
progress, III 624a, 624b, 626b–645b, 648a, 648b
prophecy, III 661a, 661b, 662a, 663a
protest movements, III 675a, 675b
Protestantism, I 262a–263b; III 23a
Proudhon, III 637b
psychiatry, I 439b
psychology, IV 3b, 4a, 7a, 8a, 16b, 17b, 20a, 21a, 21b, 22a, 23a
punishment, III 35b
Pythagoras, IV 31a, 37a
Pythagoreans, IV 31a, 37a
rationalism, III 301a, 301b–302a; IV 46a, 48b, 49b, 50a, 50b, 51a
reformation, IV 60a, 61b, 62b, 63a, 64a, 65a
relativism, IV 70a–73b
religion, III 204a, 205a, 205b; IV 96a, 101a, 106b, 107a, 108a, 110a, 110b, 111a, 116b, 118b
Renaissance, III 116b, 508b, 511a, 512a, 512b; IV 121b, 122a, 123a, 123b, 124a, 126b, 127b, 128a, 132a, 132b, 133b, 136a, 141a, 141b, 142a, 147b, 438b, 439a, 439b, 440a, 440b, 442a, 442b, 443a
responsibility, III 645a
revisionism, IV 269b, 270a
revolution, IV 154b
rhetoric, IV 141a, 167b, 168a, 168b, 170a, 170b
Riedel, II 551a
right, IV 173a–186b
Ritschl, II 357a
Roman Catholic Church, I 260b–261b, 262a–262b
romanticism, IV 195a, 205a, 205b, 207a
Rome (ancient), II 687a, 688a; IV 154b
Rousseau, II 276b; III 21b, 599b
Saint Augustine, II 238a; III 17b; IV 176b, 381a
Saint Thomas Aquinas, III

466b
Salutati, II 234b
salvation, IV 224b, 225a, 225b, 229a, 229b, 231a
Santayana, III 522b–523a
Sartre, II 190b, 194a, 195a
satire, IV 214a–214b
Schelling, III 555b
Schleiermacher, II 356a, 358a–359a
Schopenhauer, III 555b
science, I 465a; III 642b
scientists, III 645a–645b
Seneca, III 632b
Shaftesbury, II 380a
Shelley, IV 508a
sin, IV 224b, 225a, 225b, 229a, 229b, 231a
skepticism, IV 247b
social contract, IV 263a
socialism, IV 284b–285a, 285b, 286a, 287b, 289a–289b
society, III 644b, 645a
Socrates, III 577a; IV 3b, 48b, 174b
Sophists, IV 48b
Spencer, II 383a; IV 180b
Spinoza, IV 434b
Stoicism, III 15b, 16b, 190a; IV 50a, 50b, 176a, 319a–322a, 478a
Stoics, IV 7a, 8a
symbolism, IV 338a
symmetry, IV 347b
Tacitus, III 116a
taste, IV 354b, 355b, 356a, 356b
technology, III 624a, 631a–631b, 645a–645b
temperance, IV 366a, 368b, 369a, 369b, 370a, 371a
theodicy, IV 379a–383b
theriophily, IV 384a, 387b, 388a
totalitarianism, IV 410a
tragic sense, IV 415a
Trotsky, III 473b
U.S., III 428a–429a, 430b, 436b
unity of science, IV 432b, 433a–434b, 436b
universal man, IV 438b, 439b, 440a, 440b, 442a, 442b, 443a
universality, III 645a
ut pictura poesis, IV 465b, 469a, 469b, 470a, 471b
utilitarianism, IV 444a–448b
Utopia, IV 458b, 459a, 460a, 461a, 462b
Victorians, 218a, 219a–220b, 221b–223b

virtù, IV 476b–483b, 485b
Volksgeist, IV 491a, 491b, 493a, 495b
Wagner, III 330b
war, III 442a; IV 500b, 502a, 504b
welfare, II 385a
welfare state, IV 509b, 512a, 514b
wisdom, IV 383a
wisdom of the fool, IV 517a
women, IV 523b, 524a
work, IV 532b
Wright, III 561b, 562a, 562b
Xenocrates, IV 37a
Zeitgeist, IV 536a, 536b
Zoroastrianism, II 40a; IV 231a
See also Ethics
Morandi, Benedetto, dignity, IV 143b–144a
Moratorium, war, III 450b
Moravians
  communism, I 391a
  equality, II 142a
  Great Britain, I 403a
  Pietism, III 493b, 494a
  reformation, IV 68b
  U.S., I 403a
  Wesley, I 403a
More, Hannah (1745–1833), philanthropy, III 490a
More, Henry (1614–1687), atheism, I 137a
  Bruno and, IV 298a
  Cosmic Fall, I 510a, 510b
  cosmic images, I 518a
  Descartes and, I 297a–297b
  infinity, II 608a
  Neo-Platonism, III 506a
  Platonism, III 506b
  space, IV 298a
  Spinoza and, II 444b
More, Paul Elmer (1864–1937)
  classicism, I 455a
  literary criticism, I 603a
  Platonism, III 523a
More, Thomas (1478–1535)
  Campanella and, IV 461b
  commerce, IV 287b
  communism, IV 287b
  deism, I 648b
  Epicureanism, III 79b
  equity, II 153b
  Erasmus and, IV 526a
  happiness, II 379b
  hierarchy, II 444a, 444b
  humanism, II 520b; III 514b; IV 461a

literary paradox, III 79a–79b
Marxism, III 654a
perennial philosophy, III 461a
Plato and, IV 461a–461b
Platonism, III 507b, 514b
private property, III 654a; IV 287b
socialism, IV 287b
State, IV 461a
Stoicism, III 79b
theology, III 514b
utopianism, II 379b
Utopia, III 79a–79b; IV 461a–461b
wisdom of the fool, IV 516b, 519b
women, IV 526a
Moréas, Jean (1856–1910), symbolism, IV 339b, 340a
Moreau, J.
art, II 308b
genius, II 308b
Platonism, III 522b
Moreri, Louis (1643–1680), Enlightenment, II 91b
mythology, III 299a
Moret, André, baroque in literature, I 192a
Moreaux, Abbé Théophile (1867–1954), cosmic images, I 523b
Morey, C. R., iconography, II 535b, 538b
Morgagni, Giovanni (1682–1771), disease, II 401a–401b, 404a
Morgan, Conway Lloyd (1852–1936), I 115b–116a
behaviorism, I 221a
evolutionism, II 183b, 187a
God, II 359a
time, IV 396b
Morgan, Kenneth W., Buddhism, I 257a
Morgan, Lewis, Marxism, III 153b
Morgan, Lewis H. (1818–1881), structuralism, IV 325a
Morgenstern, Christian (1871–1914), literary paradox, III 77b
Morgenstern, Oskar
game theory, II 265a, 265b, 267a, 269a, 271a, 272b
social welfare, IV 278b, 280a, 280b, 283a
utility, IV 457a
Morhof, Daniel (1639–1691), linguistics, III 65a
Morice, Charles (1861–1919), symbolism, IV 340a, 343b

Morisot, Berthe (1841–1895), impressionism, II 567b
Moritz, Karl Philipp (1757–1793), mythology, III 305a
Morley, Edward Williams (1838–1923)
cosmology, I 555a, 557a
relativity, IV 79a, 79b, 80a, 80b, 89a
Morley, John (1838–1923), positivism, II 539a
Morphemes, language, II 663a, 665a, 666a, 670b, 672a, 672b
Morphology
language, II 665a, 665b, 670b, 672b
motif, III 240a
Spengler, III 251a
Morris, Charles
empiricism, III 547a
pragmatism, III 553a
Morris, William (1834–1896)
classification of the arts, I 461b
environment, II 133b
Gothic, II 372a
ut pictura poesis, IV 469a
Victorian sensibility, IV 223b
Morrison, Robert (1782–1834), China, I 367a
Morse, H. B., China, I 367b
Morsztyn, Andrzej, baroque in literature, I 189a
Mortality
dignity, IV 137a, 137b
Epicureanism, IV 176a
human nature, III 571b, 572a, 573a, 573b, 577a
probability, III 607a, 608b
Renaissance, IV 137a, 137b
Socrates, III 577a
Morton, Charles (1627?–1698)
psychology, IV 16b–17b
Puritanism, IV 16b–17b
Mosca, Gaetano (1858–1941)
class, I 449a
democracy, I 664b, 665a
ideology, II 555a–555b
Machiavellism, III 124b
Moschion (2nd century A.D.), progress, III 626b
Moser, Carl von, Volksgeist, IV 491b
Möser, Justus (1720–1794), conservatism, I 481b
Counter-Enlightenment, II 104b, 106b, 107a
Enlightenment, II 89b
historiography, II 489b

historicism, II 459a
revolution, I 481b
Volksgeist, IV 493b
Moses (Bible)
ambiguity, I 51b
catastrophism, IV 419b
Christianity, III 590a
freedom of speech, II 255a
Gnosticism, II 328b–329a
God, II 336a–336b
hermeticism, II 431b
historiography, II 470b–471a, 471b, 473b, 479a, 490b
holy, II 512a–512b
Islam, II 640a
macrocosm and microcosm, III 129b
materialism, III 634b
metaphor, III 204b, 205a
motif, III 240b
mountains in literature, III 255b, 256b
mythology, III 240b, 275b, 276b, 277a, 277b, 280b, 281a, 282b, 283a, 283b, 284b
perfectibility, III 466b
philanthropy, III 487b
Philo Judaeus, III 590a
Plato, III 512a; IV 40b
Platonism, III 505a, 511b
primitivism, III 590a
prophecy, III 658b–662a
religion, III 204b, 205a
Saint Thomas Aquinas, III 466b–467a
Mosheim, Johann Lorenz von (1694–1755)
heresy, II 430a
Platonism, III 517a
Reformation, IV 68a
Moslem thought, see Islam
Mossner, E. C., deism, I 652a
Motif, III 235a–253a
Aarne, III 238b, 239a
Aeschylus, III 240b
aestheticism, III 237a, 238a
Afanasyev, III 239a
animals, III 239a
anthropology, III 238a, 238b, 240a–240b
archetypes, III 242a
architecture, III 236b
art, III 235a, 236b, 241b
artists, III 236a
Bachelard, III 242b
Balzac, III 237b, 239b, 242b
bargains, III 239b
Bergson, III 241a–241b
Berlioz, III 236a
Bible, III 237a, 240b, 242b

Boccaccio, III 241a
Bodkin, III 242a
Cain (Bible), III 237a
Calderón, III 240b
Campbell, III 240a
captives, III 239b
Cervantes, III 240b
Cézanne, III 241b
character, III 239b
classification, III 237b
Coleridge, III 235b
comedy, III 238a
commedia dell'arte, III 238a
cosmos, III 239a
Creation, III 239a
Croce, III 238b, 241b
cruelty, III 239b
Curtius, III 241b, 243a
Darwinism, III 243a
dead, III 238a
deceptions, III 239b
Dickens, III 237b, 239b, 242b
Dilthey, III 237a–237b
Dionysos, III 240b
Don Juan (legend), III 241a
Dopelgänger, III 241b
Dostoevsky, III 241b
drama, III 238a
Eckermann, III 237a
Eliade, III 242b
Eliot, George, III 240a
Eliot, T. S, III 236a
Elmes, III 236b
eroticism, III 241a
ethics, III 235b, 237a
Fairholt, III 236b
Faust (legend), III 240b–241a
Faustianism, III 241a
folklore, III 235a–235b, 238a–240a, 240b, 241b
folly, III 239b
fortune, III 239b
Frazer, III 238b, 240a
Freud, III 240b, 242a
Freytag, III 235b
Frye, III 242a
fugitives, III 239b
Germany, III 236b–238a
Gide, III 240b
Giraudoux, III 241a
God, III 239a
Goethe, III 237a, 238a, 240b, 241a
Gothic, III 243a
Gozzi, III 238a
Graf, III 238b
Graves, III 240a
Grimm, Baron Melchior von, III 235b
Grimm, Jakob Ludwig Karl, III 236b, 239a, 239b

Grimm, Wilhelm Karl, III 236b, 239a, 239b
Hals, III 344b
Hamlet (fiction), III 240b
Hawthorne, III 242b
Herzen, III 243a
Hesiod, III 240b
history, III 235a–236b, 238a
Hoffmann, III 241b
Homer, III 237a, 241b
homiletics, III 239b
Hugo, III 240b
humor, III 239b
iconology, III 236b
idea, III 237a, 243a
imagination, III 237a–237b, 242a
impressionism, III 236b
Italy, III 235b–236a
Jesus Christ, III 242b
Joyce, III 236a–236b, 240a, 242b
judgment, III 239b
Jung, III 240b, 242a
Kafka, III 242b
King Arthur (legend), III 240b
Latin language, III 243a
legend, III 238b
Legman, III 239b
leitmotiv, III 236a, 242a
Levi-Strauss, III 240a
literature, III 236a, 236b, 237b, 238a, 240b, 241b, 242a, 242b
luck, III 239b
magic, III 239a
Mann, III 236a
Marlowe, III 241a
marvels, III 239a
Menander, III 238a
metaphor, III 242a
methodology, III 237b
Middle Ages, III 243a
Molière, III 238a
morphology, III 240a
Moses (Bible), III 240b
motive, III 235a–235b
Mozart, III 236a, 239b
music, II 235b–236a, 236b, 241b, 243a
mythology, III 237a, 238b, 240a–241b, 295a
narrative, III 236b, 237b, 238b, 241b, 242b
Neo-Platonism, III 243a
novel, III 242b
oaths, III 239b
Oedipus (myth), III 240b
ogres, III 239a
Orestes (myth), III 237a
Ovid, III 241a
painting, III 236b

phenomenology, III 242b
philology, III 236b, 238a, 238b, 239a
Plautus, III 238a
plot, III 238a
Poe, III 241b
poetry, III 236b–238a, 242a
Polti, III 238a
Poulet, III 242b
Praz, III 242b
Prometheus (myth), III 240b
promises, III 239b
Propp, III 239a, 239b
prose, III 242b
Proust, III 236b
psychoanalysis, III 242a
psychology, III 235b, 242a
punishment, III 239b
Raglan, III 240a–240b
Rank, III 242a
realism, III 237b
Reformation, III 241a
religion, III 238a, 239b
rewards, III 239b
Rochefoucauld, III 235b
romanticism, III 237b–238a, 241a
Roscher, III 241b
Ruskin, III 235a, 236b
Scherer, III 237a
Schiller, III 237b, 238a
scholasticism, III 238b
semantics, III 235a–236b
sex, III 239b
Shaftesbury, III 240b
Shakespeare, III 240b, 241a, 241b, 242a
Shelley, III 240b
social, III 239b
Souriau, III 238a
Spitzer, III 242a
Spurgeon, III 242a
Stevenson, III 241b
subject, III 237b, 238a
survey, III 237b
symbolism, III 242a–243a
tabu, III 239a
taxonomy, III 240a
Tennyson, III 241a
Terence, III 238a
Tertullian, III 240b
tests, III 239b
thematics, III 241b–243a
Theseus (myth), III 240b
Thompson, III 238b, 239a–239b, 241b
Tirso de Molina, III 241a
Tomashevsky, III 239a
topos, III 243a
Totemism, III 239a
UNESCO, III 243a
universality, III 240a, 240b
van Gogh, III 241b

Veselovsky, III 237b, 238a, 239a
Voltaire, III 240b
Wagner, III 236a, 236b
Wilde, III 238a
wisdom, III 239b
witchcraft, III 239a
Wolzogen, III 236a
words, III 241b
Zola, III 242b
Motion
accelerated, III 383a
Aristotle, I 463a, 498a; II 46a, 200a, 202a, 387a; III 273b; IV 34a, 50b, 76b, 390b, 391a
art, II 570b–571a, 572a, 572b, 583a
atomism, IV 51a
Bacon, F., I 294b–295a
Berkeley, IV 85b
Boltzmann, II 588a
Bradwardine, II 200a
Brownian movement, II 588a
Bruno, III 510b
Buridan, II 202a
Cartesianism, III 461a
chance, II 229b, 231b
change, IV 75a, 75b
color, III 419b
cosmology, I 535b, 536a, 537b–538a, 539b, 542a, 543a–544a, 545a–546b, 548a–550a, 551a, 556b, 557a, 557b, 558b, 559a, 560b; IV 50b
Democritus, IV 51a, 389b–390a
Descartes, I 297b; III 418a
earth, I 544a, 545a, 545b, 546b, 550b; IV 74a, 74b, 76a–76b, 78a–78b
Einstein, I 556b, 557a, 558b, 559a, 560b; IV 80a, 81a–81b, 91b
Engels, II 454b
Epicurus, IV 51a
equality, II 138b
evolutionism, II 181b
fate, II 229b, 231b
fortune, II 229b, 231b
Galileo, II 46a, 205a, 587a; III 383a
God, III 461a; IV 390b, 392a
good, IV 177a
harmony, II 389a–390b, 393a; IV 39a, 40a
Hegel, II 454a
Heraclitus, IV 390a
impressionism, II 570b–583a
indeterminacy, II 587a,

588a, 591b, 592b
inertia, III 193a
infinity, II 605b
intuition, IV 76b
Islam, II 651b
Kepler, III 260b
Leibniz, I 299a, 498a
Leucippus, IV 51a
light, III 419b
Man-Machine, III 135a
Marx, II 454a
materialism, II 454a, 454b
matter, III 185a, 187b, 192a, 193a, 193b, 194b
measurement, IV 400a, 400b, 403a, 403b
methodology, III 383a, **389a**
Middle Ages, II 197b, 199a–202b, 204a, 204b
moon, I 537b–538a; IV 50a
music, II 389a, 389b, 390a, 390b, 393a; III 260b, 262b
mythology, III 273b
Newton, I 299a, 517b–518a, 548a–549a; II 202a; III 194b, 383a, 389a; IV 75a–76a, 77a–77b, 80b, 90a
Nicholas of Cusa, III 510b
optics, III 418a, 419b
Oresme, II 202b, 203a
perennial philosophy, III 461a
planets, I 542a, 543a–543b, 545b, 546a, 547a–547b, 552a, 555a, 561a; II 651b; IV 50a, 74b, 78a
Plato, I 671b–672a; II 390b; IV 75a
Platonism, III 510b
Poincaré, IV 80a
Ptolemy, IV 76b
Pythagoras, IV 34a, 39a
Pythagoreans, I 539b; IV 32b, 34a, 36a, 39a, 40a, 390b
rationalism, IV 50a, 50b, 51a
relativity, IV 74a–81b, 83a–83b, 85b, 86a, 90a, 91b
right, IV 177a
science, II 651b
skepticism, IV 237a, 245b
Soto, II 204b
soul, IV 34a, 36a
Spencer, II 115b
stars, I 549a–549b; IV 50a, 77b
Suárez, III 461a
sun, I 536a, 551a; IV 50a
symmetry, IV 349a, 350a

technology, IV 359a, 360a, 361a, 361b
time, IV 389b–392b, 400a, 400b, 403a, 403b
Tressan, I 518a
uniform, III 383a
unity of science, IV 434a
William of Ockham, II 199b
Zeno of Citium, IV 389b
Motion pictures
  art, I 461b; II 572a, 572b
  Degas, II 572a
  Gothic, II 372b
  impressionism, II 572a, 572b
  love, II 106a
  ut pictura poesis, IV 470b, 475a, 475b
Motivation
  Epicureanism, IV 8a
  psychology, IV 8a, 29a
  Stoics, IV 8a
Motive
  Hutcheson, III 230b, 231a
  law, III 34b
  moral sense, III 230b, 231a
  motif, III 235a–235b
  perfectibility, III 463b
  Shaftesbury, III 230b
Motley, John L. (1814–1877), historiography, II 493a
Mott, John R. (1865–1955), reformation, IV 69a
Mo-tzŭ (fl. 400 B.C.), God, II 344b
Moulton, Richard Green (1849–1924), evolution of literature, II 171b
Mountague, Zacheus, hierarchy, II 434b
Mountains
  catastrophism, IV 417b–421a, 423a
  uniformitarianism, IV 417b–421a, 423a
Mountains in literature, III 253a–260b
  abstraction, III 253b
  Adam (Bible), III 254b, 255a, 257b
  Addison, III 259a
  aesthetics, III 256b, 258a
  Agricola, III 255b, 256a
  allegory, III 253b
  astronomy, III 255b, 256a, 257a
  Augustinianism, III 255a
  Bentley, III 258b–259a
  Bible, III 253a–257b
  Blackmore, III 259b
  Blancanus, III 256b, 257a
  Boulanger, III 259a
  Buffon, III 259a

Bunyan, III 253b
Burnet, III 257a–258b, 259a
Burton, III 255b–256a
Cain (Bible), III 254b, 255a
Calvin, III 255a
Cartesianism, III 257a
Catullus, III 253b
Christianity, III 254a–255a
Clarkson, III 253a
Coleridge, III 259a
Coryate, III 253b–254a, 258b
Cotton, III 254a
Creation, III 254a–254b, 256a
Dante, III 253b
Denis, III 259a
Descartes, III 257a, 259a
Diderot, III 259a
Donne, III 254b, 256a
dualism, III 253a, 255a
earth, III 254b–259b
Eve (Bible), III 254b, 255a, 257b
Evelyn, III 254a, 258b
Flood, III 255a, 255b, 256b, 257b
Fontenelle, III 258b
Formey, III 259a
fossils, III 255b
France, III 256a–256b
Frascastoro, III 255b
fundamentalism, III 255b
Galileo, III 256a, 256b
geology, III 255b–257a, 259b
Gilbert, III 256b
God, III 254b–258b
Great Britain, III 256a–256b, 257a–259a
Greece (ancient), III 253a–253b, 255b
Helicon, III 253a
Hill Difficulty (fiction), III 253b
Horace, III 253b
Howell, III 254a
imagery, III 253b
Jaucourt, III 259a
Judaism, III 254a, 254b, 255a, 255b
Kepler, III 256b
Latin language, III 253b, 254a
Leibniz, III 259a
Leonardo da Vinci, III 258b
Lucretius, III 253b, 258b, 259b
Luther, III 255a–255b, 258a
Mallett, III 259a
Marvell, III 253b, 254b, 259a
metaphysics, III 256b

Middle Ages, III 253b, 255a
Milton, III 253b, 254a, 256a, 256b
Moses (Bible), III 255b, 256b
Mount Ararat, III 255a, 257b
Mount Olympus, III 253a
Mount of Purgatorio (fiction), III 253b
mountain-origin, III 254a–255a, 255b, 257a, 257b; IV 333b
mountain-paradox, III 257b
Murray, III 253a–253b
Nature, III 253b, 254b, 255a, 257b, 258a, 259a, 259b, 260a
Newton, III 256b, 258b, 259a
Noah (Bible), III 255a, 257b
Pepys, III 258b
personification, III 253b
Petrarch, III 253b
philosophy, III 253a
physico-theology, III 256b, 258b
Plato, III 259a
poetry, III 259a
poets, III 253b, 256a
psychology, III 255a
Ray, III 258b
realism, III 253b
Reformation, III 255a
religion, III 254a, 257b, 258a
Renaissance, III 253b, 255a
Roman Catholic Church, III 254b
romanticism, III 253b
Saint Augustine, III 255a
science, III 254a, 255b, 257a, 257b, 258b
Shaftesbury, III 259a
Shakespeare, III 253b
sin, III 254b, 255a
Steele, III 259a
Steno, III 255b, 256a
sublime in external nature, III 258b; IV 333a–337b
Temple, III 258b
Tertullian, III 255b
theology, III 258b
Thomson, III 256b, 259a, 259b
universe, III 257a
Varenius, III 256b
Vaughn, III 254b
Vergil, III 253b
Voltaire, III 259a
Wiltshire, III 257b
Wordsworth, III 259a, 259b–260a

Mountford, Charles P., beauty, I 213b
Mourgues, Odette de, baroque in literature, I 193a
Mowinckel, S., mythology, III 311b
Mowrer, O. H., behaviorism, I 223a
Moyle, Walter, revolution, IV 154b
Mozart, Wolfgang Amadeus (1756–1791)
  genius, II 324a, 325a
  love, III 103a
  motif, III 236a, 239b
Mozley, James B. (1813–1878), religion, IV 106b
Mnemosyne (myth), music, III 268b
Mrazek, W., iconography, II 438b
Mu'ammar (d. c. 825), causation, I 287b
Much, Hans (1880–1932), Buddhism, I 256b
Mudt, Conrad, Faust (legend), III 245a
Muecke, D. C., irony, II 634a
Muhammad Ali Jinnah, nationalism, III 338a
Muhammad Iqbal, nationalism, III 338a
Muir, John (1838–1914), conservation, I 475a, 475b, 476a
Muirhead, John H. (1855–1940), war, IV 503a
Mukařovský, Jan, evolution of literature, II 173b
Mulcaster, Richard (1530?–1611), harmony, II 390a
Müller, Adam H. (1779–1829)
  Counter-Enlightenment, II 109b–110a
  List and, IV 207b
  literary criticism, I 598b
  Nazis, IV 207b
  romanticism, IV 206b, 207a, 207b
  sociology, IV 207b
  Spann and, IV 207b
  State, IV 206b
  totalitarianism, IV 408a
  Volksgeist, IV 493b
Müller, Andreas, language, I 358a
Müller, Friedrich Max (1823–1900)
  Buddhism, I 255b
  China, I 368a
  Faust (legend), III 250a
  linguistics, IV 424b–425a, 426b

mythology, III 307b–308a, 308b, 309a
Orientalism, III 434b, 436a
religion, IV 94b
Muller, Hermann J., perfectibility, III 471a
Müller, Karl O. (1797–1840), Lang and, III 309a
mythology, III 306a
Tylor and, III 308a, 308b
Müller-Freienfels, Richard (1882–1949), beauty, I 212b
Multilingualism, II 660b
Greece (ancient), III 61b
linguistics, III 61a–61b
Multiplication
numbers, III 404b, 405b
probability, III 607b, 612a, 618a–618b
Mumford, Lewis (1895–)
anarchy, I 75b
conservation, I 472b
time, IV 402b
Utopia, IV 459a
Münsterberg, Hugo (1863–1916)
classification of the sciences, I 465b
Man-Machine, III 143a
Münzer, Thomas (1489?–1525)
class, I 442b
communism, II 158b
equality, II 142a
eschatology, II 157a, 158b
history, I 390b–391a
Joachim of Floris and, IV 287a
Luther and, IV 287a
Peasants' Revolt, I 391a
prophecy, III 669b
socialism, IV 287a, 287b
Murakami, Yasusuke, social welfare, IV 284a
Muratori, Lodovico A. (1672–1750), aesthetics, IV 354b
Murchison, Roderick (1792–1871), uniformitarianism, IV 422a
Murder
ethics, IV 71a
Greece (ancient), II 674b, 676a, 681a, 683a, 683b, 684b
law, II 674b, 676a, 681a, 683a, 683b, 684b, 688b
Machiavelli, III 116b
mythology, III 279a–279b, 281b
prophecy, III 661a
Rome (ancient), II 688b
Murger, Henri (1822–1861),

realism in literature, IV 52a
Murji'ites, II 641b
Murner, Thomas (1475–1537), wisdom of the fool, IV 519b
Murray, Gilbert (1866–1957), mountains in literature, III 253a–253b
mythology, III 307a, 311a
tragic sense, IV 412b
Murri, Romolo (1870–1944), modernism, I 424a
Musaeus (5th century A.D.), mythology, III 297a
romanticism, IV 192a
Muses (myth), III 500b, 501b
poetry, III 526b, 528b, 530a
Music, II 388a–395a
Aaron (Bible), III 265a
acoustics, III 260b, 263a, 264a
aesthetics, II 216a, 216b, 219b, 220b, 224a, 315b, 316a, 316b, 318b, 322b–323a, 323b, 325b; III 267b, 271b
Affligemensis, II 314a
Agrippa, II 389b, 393b, 394a
air waves, III 262a–262b
Alberti, II 317b, 390b
alchemy, II 392b
Alembert, III 263b
allegory, III 266a, 270a, 271a
ambiguity, I 57a–58a
Amphion (myth), III 266a
analogy, II 389a
angelic, III 265a, 265b, 266a, 269a–270b
angels, II 393b–394b; III 265a–266a, 269a–270b; IV 40b–41a
Anglicus, II 388a
animals, III 265a, 266b, 268a–268b
Apollo (myth), III 268b
apotropaic rites, III 264b
Aquila, II 320a
architecture, III 265a, 266b, 270a
Aretino, II 317b, 320a
Aribo Scholasticus, II 314a, 317b
Arion, II 313a
Arion (myth), III 266a
Aristides Quintilianus, II 313a
Aristotelianism, II 389b
Aristotle, I 264b–265a, 266b, 578b, 584b; II 389b, 390a, 392b; III 226b, 260b, 261b, 263a
Aristoxenus, II 313a; III 261b, 262a, 262b
arithmetic, II 313b, 390a;

III 260b, 270b
Aron, II 314a, 317a
Artusi, III 262b
assonance, III 269a, 271a
Assyria, III 264b
astrology, II 392b; III 260b
astronomy, II 313b, 389a–390a; III 260b, 270b
atheism, III 267a
Babylonia, III 260b, 264b
Bacchius Senex, II 313a
Bach, II 321a, 324a; III 267a–267b, 271b
Bacon, II 393a; IV 466b
baroque, II 321a–323a; III 271a–271b
beauty, III 269a–269b
Beethoven, II 325a, 325b
Benedetti, III 262a–262b
Berthold of Regensburg, III 266a
Bible, II 316a, 394a; III 265a, 265b, 266a, 267a, 269b, 270a
Black spirituals, I 407a
Bodin, II 390a–390b
Boethius, II 313a, 313b, 314a, 317a, 324b; III 261a, 261b, 270b
Browne, II 388a
Bruno, II 317a–317b
cacophony, III 265a
Calvin, III 271a
Cartesianism, III 263a
Case, II 390b, 391a
Castiglione, II 317a
catharsis, I 264b–265a, 266b, 269a
cathedrals, III 265a, 266b, 270a
celestial, III 265a
censorship, III 499a
Chain of Being, II 389a
chance, III 263b
chants, III 265b, 266a, 269b, 270a
chaos, III 265b, 267a
Chapman, II 394b
China (ancient), III 268b
chords, III 263a, 263b
Christianity, I 404b, 407a; II 389a, 389b, 390b, 392b; III 265a–266b, 269a, 269b–271a
Church of England, II 388b
Cicero, II 314b, 389b
Clement of Alexandria, III 266a
Cleonides, III 261b
Coclico, II 316b, 319a
combination tones, III 263b
composers, II 313a, 388b; III 261b, 262a, 262b, 263b, 271b

composition, II 388b; III 261a, 262b, 263b–264a, 270b, 271a
computer, III 264a
concerts, II 316b
conductus, II 314b
consonance, III 260b, 261a–262b, 263a, 269a
continuity, III 269b
Copernicus, II 389b
cosmology, II 388a, 389a, 389b; III 260b, 265a, 268a, 268b, 269a, 270b, 271a, 271b
counterpoint, II 314b, 316b, 319a, 321a–321b, 322b
Gowley, II 390a, 391b
Craen, II 316a, 319a
craftsmanship, II 319b, 321b–322a, 323b
Creation, III 265a, 268b, 271a
creativity, II 319b–320a, 321a–321b, 323b, 326a
creativity in art, I 578b, 579b, 581a, 584b
criticism, II 316a–316b, 318a, 325a
cycles, III 262b
dance, III 264b, 265b–267a, 268a–270a
Dante, III 265a, 270a, 270b
David (Bible), III 265a, 267a, 270b
death, II 320b, 323a, 324b; III 265a, 265b, 268b–269a, 271b
deception, II 313b
defined, II 313a, 314a
Demiurge, II 390b
demonology, II 390b, 392b, 393b–394a; III 264a–268a
Deprès, II 319a, 320a–320b, 325b
Descartes, III 262b, 263a
determinism, III 262b
dialectics, II 313b
difference tone, III 263b
Diogenes Laërtius, IV 38a
Dionysos (myth), III 268b
discord, III 265b
disharmony, III 265a
dissonance, III 262b, 263b, 271a
divination, III 264b, 267b–272a
Doni, Antonfrancesco, II 321a
Doni, Giovanni Battista, II 321a–321b
Donne, II 394b
drama, II 323b
Du Bartas, II 391a, 391b, 392b

dualism, III 264b–265a, 270b

duration, III 260b

earth, II 389b–390a

education, II 76b–77b, 313b, 314a, 317a, 323b

Egypt (ancient), II 389a, 393b; III 260b, 268a

electronic, III 264a

Elisha (Bible), II 394a

eloquence, II 317b

emotion, II 313b, 316a, 316b, 318b–319b, 323a–324a, 393a; III 271b

empathy, II 323a, 323b

Empedocles, II 390a

empiricism, III 262a

engineering, III 264a

Enlightenment, III 263b, 271b

enthusiasm, II 318a–318b

entropy, III 263b

Ephraem Syrus, III 266a

Er (myth), II 389b

Erasmus, II 315b

Ercole of Ferrara, II 320a

eschatology, III 270b–271a, 271b

ethics, II 390b

Euclid, III 261b

Euler, III 263b

evil, II 388a; III 264b, 265a, 265b

exorcism, III 264b, 267a

experiments, III 262b

Ezekiel (Bible) III 269b

fairy tales, III 266a, 267a, 270a

Faust (legend), III 250b, 252a

feeling, III 267b

Ficino, II 320b, 389a, 389b, 393a, 393b, 394a, 521b

Finck, II 318a–318b

Fludd, II 390a; III 271a

Fogliano, III 261b

folk songs, II 317b, 323b

folklore, III 265a

Fontenelle, II 324a–324b

France, II 315b, 317b, 322b–323a, 388b; III 267a, 271b

Franco of Cologne, II 314b

freedom, II 313b, 316a, 316b, 320b

frescoes, III 270a

fugue, II 322b

fundamental bass, III 263a–263b

Gaffurio, III 261a, 261b

Galilei, Vincenzo, III 261a, 261b, 262a, 262b

Galileo, III 261a, 262b, 263a

Galuppi, II 324a

genius, II 312b–326b

geocosm, II 389a

geometry, II 313b, 390a; III 260b, 263b, 270b

Germany, II 315b, 317b, 323a; III 265a, 267a, 267b, 271a–271b

Gesualdo, II 320b–321a, 321b

Glareanus, II 315b, 316a, 317b–318a, 319b, 320a, 325b

Gluck, II 324a

good, II 388a, 390b; III 264b, 265a, 265b, 554b; IV 176b

Gothic, II 373b

grammar, II 313b

Great Britain, II 315b, 322a, 388b

Greece (ancient), II 312b–313a, 315b, 317b–318a, 318b, 388b, 392a–392b; III 260a–261a, 261b, 265a, 266b, 268b–269a

Gregorian chants, II 314b, 315a

Guido of Arezzo, II 313b, 314a; III 266b

Guillaume de Machaut, II 315a

harmony, II 313b, 314a, 315a, 315b, 322b, 323a, 324a; III 260b, 261a, 262b, 263a, 263b, 265b, 268b, 269a, 270b, 271a

Hathor (myth), III 268a

health, IV 41a

heaven, III 265a, 269b, 271a, 271b

hell, III 265a, 265b, 266a, 268b

Herbert, II 392b–393a

Herder, II 324a–324b

Hermes (myth), III 268b

Hermes Trismegistus, II 393b

Heyden, II 315b

Heydon, II 394a

Hickman, II 394b

hierarchy, II 439b; III 266a

Hindemith, III 263b

history, III 264b

Hoffmann, II 324b; III 271b

Hofhaimer, II 321a

Homer, II 318a; III 268b

Hooker, II 391b, 392a

humanism, II 388b, 521b; III 260b, 261a–261b; IV 133b

hymns, III 266a, 269b

Iamblichos, III 269a

imagination, II 322b–323a, 323b; III 208a, 220b

imitation, II 317a, 323b, 324a; III 264b, 267b

immutable properties of, II 388a

impressionism, II 567b, 574b–575a

inborn gift for, II 314a, 318b

inclination, II 318a–318b

indeterminacy, III 263b

India (ancient), III 268b

individualism, II 314b, 315b, 316b, 318a, 319b, 320b

infinity, III 271b

Ingpen, II 394a

innovation, II 315b

inspiration, I 457a; II 316b, 318b, 323b–324a

instinct, II 314a, 317a, 325a, 388a

instrumental, II 388b

instruments, II 313b, 314a; III 260b, 261a, 265a, 266a–266b, 268a, 269a, 269b, 270a–270b

intervals, II 314a

invention, II 314b, 317b, 318a, 318b, 319b

Ireland, III 269b–270a

irony, II 634a

irrationalism, II 318b

Isaiah (Bible), III 269b

Italy, II 315b, 323a–323b, 388b; III 267a, 271b

Jacobus of Liège, II 315a; III 270b

James II, II 322a

Jankélévitch, II 634a

Jesus Christ, III 265a, 266a, 267a, 269b, 270a, 270b

Johannes of Garlandia, II 314b

Johannes de Muris, II 315a

John Chrysostom, III 266a

Jommelli, II 323a, 324a

jongleurs, II 314a

joy, II 388a

Judaism, II 392b; III 265a, 269b

judgment, II 313a, 314a, 317a, 318a, 318b, 322b–323a

Kant, II 317b, 323b–324a

Kepler, II 389b–390a; III 260b, 271a, IV 41b

key, III 262a, 262b, 263a

Kircher, III 271a

knowledge, I 457a; II 313a, 388a; III 269a

Lampadius, II 318b

language, II 313b; III 268b

Lasso, II 319a, 320b

law, II 388a, 391a

Le Roy, II 318b–319a

legend, III 265a, 266a, 267a, 270a

Leo, II 323a

Leonardo da Vinci, II 317b

Linos (myth), III 268b

literature, II 388b–389a; III 265a, 266b, 269b, 270a

liturgical, III 265b, 266a, 269b, 270a, 270b

love, II 390b, 391a, 391b, 393a; III 94a, 99a, 101a, 101b, 104b, 106a

Luscinius, II 315b–316a, 317b, 319a

Luther, III 267a, 270b–271a

Mace, II 321b–322a, 394b

Macrobius, II 389b

macrocosm and microcosm, II 313b, 389a, 390a; III 130b, 268b, 269a

madness, III 265a

madrigal, II 388b

magic, II 313a, 392b–394a; III 264b, 265a, 267a, 268a, 268b, 269b, 271b

materialism, II 392b

mathematics, I 457a, 459a; II 313b, 325b, 388a, 389a, 390a–390b; III 260b, 263b, 387b

matter, II 392a–392b

measurement, III 260b; IV 399a, 399b, 402a

mechanism, III 262b–263a

medicine men, III 264b, 268a

Mei, III 262b

melancholy, II 320a–321b; III 265a, 267a

melody, II 313a–315a, 317b, 318b, 323b; III 262a

Mersenne, III 262b, 263a

Mesopotamia (ancient), III 264b, 268a

metaphysics, II 388b, 390b; III 208a, 220b, 261a, 267b, 268a, 271b

Metastasio, II 323a, 323b

Michelangelo, II 320a

Middle Ages, II 313a–320a, 325b; III 260b, 261a, 265a–266b, 269b–270b

Milton, III 389b, 391b–392a, 393a, 394b

mimesis, III 226a, 226b

mind, II 324a, 388b

minstrels, III 266a–266b, 267a, 270a

Mnemosyne (myth), III 268b

modes, II 314a

modulation, III 262b

monochord, III 271a

Monteverdi, II 321b

moon, II 389a–390a
morality, II 76b–77a, 314b
morality plays, III 265a, 265b, 270a
mosaics, III 270a
motif, III 235b–236a, 236b, 241b, 243a
motion, II 389a–393a; III 260b, 262b
Mozart, II 324a, 325a
Muecke, II 634a
Mulcaster, II 390a
musicians, II 388b, 389a
mysticism, III 260b
mythology, II 389a, 389b, 393b; III 264b, 268a, 276b, 279b, 284b, 296b, 306b, 317a
Nature, II 318a, 321a, 324a, 391a; III 263a, 263b, 264b, 268a, 271b, 350a
Neo-Platonism, II 389a, 391b, 393a–393b; III 269a
Neo-Pythagoreans, III 269a
Nietzsche, II 318b, 325a–325b
Noble, III 263a
North, II 318b, 322a
Nottebohm, II 325b
novelty, II 315a–315b
numbers, III 260b–263b, 269a, 270b, 271a
numero senario, III 262a, 262b
octaves, III 260b–263a
Odo of Cluny, II 314b
opera, II 323a–325a
optics, III 263a
order, II 439b; III 265b, 271a
originality, II 317b, 318a, 320b, 321a, 323b, 324a
Orpheus (myth), II 313a, 316a, 393b; III 266a, 268b
Ortega y Gasset, II 634a
Osiris (myth), III 268a
Palestrina, II 321b
Pan (myth), III 268b
pandemonium, III 265a
patrons, II 320b
Pepys, II 322a
perfectibility, III 470b
performers, II 313a, 313b, 314a, 316a
Persia (ancient), III 264b–265a
philosophy, II 313a, 313b, 388b–389a, 390b, 392b, 393b; III 263b, 264b, 268a, 268b, 269a, 270b, 271b
physics, III 263b
pitch, II 389a; III 260b, 262a, 263a, 263b

plagues, III 269b
planets, II 389a–390a, 390b, 392b, 393b, 394b; III 260b, 269a, 271a
Plato, I 462b, 463a, 579b, 581a; II 299b, 317b–318b, 320b, 389b–391b; III 226b, 260b, 265b, 269a, 497b, 498b–500b; IV 38b–40a
Platonism, II 390b–391b, 392b; III 497b, 498b, 499a, 500a, 500b, 503b
Plotinus, II 391b, 393b
Pluto (myth), II 393b
poetic license, II 319a
poetry, II 313b–314a, 316a, 317b–319a, 320a, 321a, 323b, 388b, 391b, 394b–395a; IV 466b, 467b, 472a, 472b, 473a, 474a, 475a
poets, II 391b
polyphony, II 314b–316a; III 261a, 269b
Pontus de Tyard, II 318a
power, II 388b, 391b, 392a, 393b, 394a–394b; III 264a–272a
practical, III 260b
practical lessons from, II 388b
Praetorius, III 267a, 271a
Pragápati (myth), III 268b
pragmatism, III 266b
probability, III 263b
prophecy, II 394a; III 658b, 659a
Protestantism, II 394a; III 267a, 270b–271b
Proust, III 236b
psalms, III 266a, 269b
psychology, II 320a, 320b–321a, 393a
Ptolemy, II 389b; III 261a, 261b, 262a
punishment, III 266b
Puritanism, II 388b
Pythagoras, I 579b, 580a; II 390a; III 260b–261a, 261b, 269a, 271a; IV 38a, 39a, 399b
Pythagorean scale, IV 39a–39b
Pythagoreans, I 269a; II 389b; III 260b, 261b, 262a; IV 38a–42a
quadrivium, III 260b, 270b, 271b
Rameau, II 322b–323b; III 263a–263b
Ramos de Pareja, III 261b
ratio, III 260b–263a
rationalism, II 318b, 390b; III 262a, 264b, 266b, 268a
realism, III 270a

reason, II 388a, 390b, 391a, 391b
Reformation, III 270b–271a
Regino of Prüm, II 314a
religion, II 388a, 389a, 392a; III 264b–266b, 268b–271b
Rembrandt, III 267a
Renaissance, II 314a, 315a–321a, 325b, 389a–393a; III 260b–263a, 270a; IV 133b, 437b, 438b, 439a
resonance, III 263b
rhetoric, II 313b
rhythm, II 313a, 313b, 315a; III 261a, 268b
right, IV 176b
ritual, III 268a, 268b
Roman Catholic Church, II 388b, 389a, 394a
romanticism, I 595a; II 322a, 323a–326a; III 268a, 271b; IV 197a, 209a
Rore, III 262a
Rousseau, II 322a–324b
rules, II 317a, 319a, 319b, 323b, 325b
Sachs, II 325a
Saint Augustine, IV 176b
Saint Martial, II 315a
Salinas, III 261b
Satan, III 265b–265b, 266a, 266b, 267a
Saul (Bible), III 265a, 267a
Sauveur, III 263a
Scaliger, II 320a
Schopenhauer, III 271b
Schubart, II 324a
science, II 313a, 313b, 314a, 388b
scientific classification, I 464a
sculpture, III 265a, 270a
self-imposed limitations, II 575a
semitone, III 261a, 262a, 262b
senses, II 313b, 388b
Shaftesbury, II 320a
Shakespeare, II 388a, 388b, 391b, 394b
shamans, III 264b, 268a
Shiva (myth), III 268b
sin, II 391a; III 266b
singers, II 313b–317b, 393a, 393b
singing, III 260b, 268a–271a
skepticism, III 264b, 268a
society, II 389a; III 266a, 271b
sociology, III 271b
Socrates, II 317b–318a
soul, II 388a–392b, 394a;

III 268a–270b
sound, II 389b, 391b–392a, 393a; III 260b, 262a–263a, 268a, 268b, 269a, 271a
Spataro, II 316b, 318a
speculative ideas of, II 388b–389a
spontaneity, II 320b
stained glass, III 270a
stars, II 389a–389b, 390b, 392b, 393b, 394a; III 269a
State, II 389a
stochastic process, III 263b
Stoicism, II 392b
strings, III 260b, 261a, 262a, 263a, 268a, 269a
structure, III 261a, 263b
style, II 316a, 321a, 321b; III 263b, 270a
superparticular, III 262a
Switzerland, III 267a
symbolism, III 266b, 268b–271b; IV 342b
talent, II 314a, 316b, 318a–318b, 319b, 320a, 320b, 323b–324a, 325a
taste, II 323b
technique, III 263b
technology, III 264a
temperament, III 262b
tetrachord, III 261a
theater, III 265a, 265b, 270a
theology, III 264b, 266b, 268a, 270a–271b
Theon of Smyrna, III 261a
theoretical, III 260b
thermodynamics, III 263b
Thoth (myth), III 268a
time, IV 399a, 399b, 402a
Timotheus, II 313a, 316b
Tinctoris, II 315a–316b
tone, II 314a, 315b, 323b, 389a; III 261a, 262a, 263b, 268b
torture, III 266a–266b
troubadour songs, II 315a
trouvère songs, II 315a
truth, II 313b
tuning, III 261a–263a
uncertainty, II 313b
unity, III 269a
unity of science, IV 433b
universal man, IV 437b, 438b, 439a
universality, II 388b
universe, II 388a–394b; III 260b, 268b, 270a, 271a; IV 38a–42a
Vadian, II 321a
vibration, II 389a; III 262a–263a

virtue, II 388b, 391a–392a
vox populi, IV 498b–499b
Wagner, II 325a; III 271b
Weber, III 264b
witchcraft, III 264b, 265a, 267a
Wither, II 388b, 392a, 394a
World Spirit, II 389a, 392a–395a
Yahweh, III 265a, 269b
Zarlino, II 319a, 319b; III 261b–262a, 262b
Zeus (myth), III 268b
See also Art
Musicians
  beauty, III 269a–269b
  composers, II 313a, 314a–321a, 322a–323a, 325b
  defined, II 313a
  demonology, III 264b, 266a
  Greece (ancient), II 313a–313b
  harmony, II 388b, 389a
  instruments, III 260b
  Middle Ages, II 313a–314b
  music, II 388b, 389a
  natural, II 314a
  octaves, III 261a
  performers, II 313a, 313b, 316b
  professional, II 314a
  ratio, III 261a
  Renaissance, II 314a, 315a–321a
  temperament, III 262b
  tuning, III 262a
Musil, Robert, love, III 106a
Mussato, Albertino (c. 14th century A.D.)
  coronation of, II 517a
  humanism, II 515b, 517a, 517b
  poetics, III 529b
Musset, Alfred de (1810–1857)
  Byron and, IV 204a
  romanticism, IV 204a, 208b
  Weltschmerz, IV 204a
Mussolini, Benito (1883–1945)
  anarchy, III 597a
  animal, III 597a
  authority, I 159a–159b
  Darwinism, III 125a
  fascism, III 597a
  humanitarianism, III 597a
  ideology, II 563a
  James and, III 563a
  Machiavellism, III 125a
  neo-Darwinism, III 597a
  pragmatism, III 563a, 565b
  primitivism, III 597a
  progress, III 647b

revolution, IV 164b
  Sorel and, III 565b
  totalitarianism, IV 407b, 408a, 409a, 409b, 410a
Muste, A. J., peace, III 441a, 445b
Mutability
  impressionism, II 581a–581b
  Nature, III 350b, 351a
  Plato, III 350b–351a
Mutations, II 125a
  evolutionism, II 177b
  linguistics, IV 424b
  recapitulation, IV 58a
Mu'tazilites
  causation, I 287a–288a
  Islam, II 642a
Mycenaean Age
  Greece (ancient), II 466b, 467a
  historiography, II 466b, 467a
Mylius, Christlob, deism, I 651a
Myopia, optics, III 411a, 413b
Myrdal, Gunnar, welfare state, IV 512a
Mysticism
  art, II 575b, 581b, 582a
  Bergson, III 563a, 564b, 565b
  dignity, IV 137a, 138a, 138b
  Emerson, III 430a, 430b
  Empedocles, IV 2b
  Epicureanism, II 581b
  Erastianism, IV 119a
  Foggazzaro, I 424a
  Free Spirit, II 422b
  Germany, I 391a
  Greece (ancient), IV 228a–228b
  happiness, II 378b–379a
  Hegel, II 412b, 414a
  heresy, II 422a, 422b, 424a, 426b
  impressionism, II 575b, 581b, 582a
  individualism, II 602b
  love, III 99b, 100b, 101a, 101b, 102b, 104a
  metaphor, III 197a
  music, III 260b
  Nature, III 351a
  necessity, III 355b
  Neo-Platonism, III 375a, 377a
  numbers, III 260b, 262a
  Orientalism, III 429b, 430a, 430b, 431a
  Palamas, I 401b
  perennial philosophy, III 458b, 459a
  perfectibility, III 466a, 467b,

468b–469b, 474a–475a
  philosophy, III 197a
  Platonism, III 503a, 505b, 506a, 505b
  pleasure, II 378b–379a
  Plotinus, III 505b
  pragmatism, III 563a, 564a, 564b, 565b
  progress, III 632a
  psychology, IV 2b, 16b, 20b, 24a
  Puritanism, IV 16b
  Pythagoreans, IV 32a, 35b
  religion, IV 109a, 110a, 119a
  Renaissance, IV 126b, 137a, 138a, 138b
  romanticism, IV 205a, 206a, 209a
  Rosenkranz, II 412b
  salvation, IV 228a–228b, 229a
  skepticism, IV 241b, 246a
  socialism, IV 287b
  Sorel, III 565b
  Strauss, II 412b
  symbolism, IV 343a
  theodicy, IV 379b, 381b
  Thoreau, III 431a
  transcendentalism, IV 24a
  U.S., III 429b–431a
  wisdom of the fool, IV 517b
Myth and Ritual School, III 311b–312a
Myth, III 272a–318a
  abstraction, III 273a, 293a, 298b, 316b
  absurdity, III 299b
  acedia, III 290b
  adultery, III 273a
  advertising, III 276b
  Aeneas, III 287a
  Aesculapius, III 274a, 287a
  Aesop, III 275a, 275b
  aesthetics, III 289b, 292a, 305a
  agriculture, III 312a
  Aknahton, III 281a
  Alciati, III 290a, 296a
  Aldus, III 289b
  allegory, III 274a, 282b, 288a–288b, 290b, 293a, 294a, 295a, 295b, 298b, 299a, 299b, 301b, 303b
  allusions, III 300a
  alphabet, III 290a
  American Indian, III 279b, 301a, 302a
  amulets, III 287b
  analogy, III 273a, 273b, 301a
  Ananke (myth), III 272b
  ancestry, III 275a, 275b,

309a, 310a
  anecdotes, III 288b
  Anglicanism, III 300a
  animals, III 275a, 280a, 298a, 303b, 315a
  animism, III 308b–310b, 315a, 317b
  Anthology, Greek, III 290a
  anthropocentrism, III 274a, 278a
  anthropology, III 310b, 316a–318a
  anthropomorphism, III 273a, 309a
  Antichrist, III 276b
  Antinomy, III 277b
  antiquarianism, III 302b, 306b
  anxiety, III 287b, 314a
  Aphrodite (god), III 272b
  Apocrypha, III 282b
  Apollo (god), III 272b, 274a, 282b, 289a, 291a, 294a
  apotheosis, III 287a, 291a, 306b
  Apuleius, III 291a, 292b
  Aquinas, III 288a
  archaeology, III 274b, 289b, 291b
  archetypes, III 277a, 277b, 312b–313a
  architecture, III 296b, 297a, 299a
  Argonauts (myth), III 275b
  Ariadne (myth), III 272b
  Ariosto, III 298a
  Aristophanes, III 275b
  Aristotle, III 273b
  Ark of the Covenant, III 277a, 277b, 283a
  Armageddon, III 276b, 282a
  Armenini, III 293a, 295b, 299a
  Artemis (god), III 272b
  Arthur, King, III 308a
  the arts, III 272a, 274b, 290a, 291a–293b, 294b, 295b, 296b–298a, 301a, 304a, 304b, 305a, 306b, 309a, 312b
  astral-mythological school, III 310a–310b
  astrology, III 287b–288a, 288b, 290a, 291a
  astronomy, III 287b, 310b
  Athena (god), III 272b
  Atkinson, III 312a
  Atonement, III 277a, 279a, 281b
  attitudes, III 290b, 295a
  Atum, III 278a
  Augustine, III 276b, 277a, 283a, 287b, 299b

exaggeration, III 312a
exegesis, III 302b, 313b
exile, III 280a, 280b, 315b
Exodus, III 276b
experience, III 278b, 313b
explanations, III 272b–273a, 301b, 303b
fables, III 286b, 288a, 289b, 290a, 291a, 292b–294a, 299b, 300a, 307a, 307b, 315a, 316a
fairy tales, III 275b, 315a–315b
faith, III 276a, 282b, 293a, 294b, 310b, 313b, 314b
Fall, III 277a–280b, 288a, 315b
fancy, III 309b, 317b
fantasy, III 312b–313a, 315a, 315b, 317b
fatalism, III 306a
Fates (myth), III 274a, 274b, 292a
Faulkner, III 277a
fear, III 290b, 302a, 302b, 303a
feeling, III 303b, 315a
fertility, III 272b, 303b
festivals, III 281a, 281b, 292b, 311a–312a
fetishism, III 301a, 303b, 309b
Ficino, III 290b, 295a
fiction, III 274a, 275a, 275b, 293a, 307a, 307b, 308b
finite, III 305a, 305b
Flood, III 277a, 278b–280b, 305b
folklore, III 306a, 307a, 307b, 308a, 312b, 316a–316b
folktales, III 275a–275b, 279a, 304a, 307a, 314b, 315b, 316a–316b
Fontenelle, III 301a, 301b, 302a, 302b
formalism, III 316a–316b
forms, III 313b
fratricide, III 279a
Frazer, III 277a, 278b–281a, 282b
Fréart, III 298a, 298b, 299a
freedom, III 305a, 315b
French language, III 298b
frenzy, III 292a
frescoes, III 276b, 289a, 291a
Freud, III 281a, 307a, 309b, 312a–312b, 313a
Frobenius, III 307a, 313a–314b
fulfillment, III 313a
function, III 279a, 307b, 311a–312a, 313a, 314a–315a

Gaia (myth), III 273b, 274a
Galileo, III 299b
Gaster, III 281b, 307a, 312a
gems, III 287b
genealogy, III 272b
genius, III 293b, 299a, 304a, 313b
geometry, III 290b
gestures, III 272b
Ghiberti, III 280a
ghosts, III 309a, 309b, 315a
Gibbon, III 303a
Gilgamesh, III 275a, 279a
Giotto, III 289a, 291a
gods, III 273a, 273b, 275b, 278a, 281b–283a, 286b–289a; 290a–291b, 292b–293b, 295a, 296b, 298a, 300a–300b, 301b, 302b, 303a, 305b, 306b, 307b–308b
Goethe, III 305a, 306a, 316b
Golden Calf, III 280b
Golden Chain (myth), III 273b
Golden Fleece (myth), III 290a
good, III 278b
gospel, III 276a, 283a, 283b, 284a, 291b
grammar, III 306a, 307b
Graves, III 279a, 280b
Greece (ancient), III 272a–275a, 301a, 302a, 309a
Greek language, III 305b
Gregory the Great, III 288a
Grimm, Jacob, III 301a
Grimm, Wilhelm, III 306a
growth, III 310a
gullibility, III 301b
Gunkel, III 275a, 275b, 311b
Hades (myth), III 272b
Hamann, III 304a
harmony, III 304b
Harrison, Jane, III 310b–311a, 312a
heathenism, III 300a–301a
heaven, III 273b, 291a, 294a
Hebraism, III 282a–282b
Hebrew language, III 280a
Hecate (god), III 272b
hedonism, III 292b
Heilsgeschichte, III 277a
Helen, III 272b
Hell, III 273a, 281b, 282a, 288a
Hellenism, III 304b
Hera (god), III 272b
Heracles (myth), III 273b, 274b, 282b, 308a
Heraclitus, III 275b
heraldry, III 296b

Hercules (god), III 274a, 275b, 287a, 288a, 290a, 292b
Herder, III 304b–306b
heritage, III 308b
Hermes (god), III 272b, 282b
Herodotus, III 272b, 275b
heroes, III 276b, 280b–282b, 287a, 288b, 308a, 308b, 312b
Hesiod, III 272b, 273a, 278a
Heywood, III 299b
hieroglyphs, III 289b, 290a
Hinduism, III 283a, 306a
historiography, III 302b
history, III 276b–278b, 280a, 283b, 284a, 286b, 288b, 294a, 295a, 299a, 299b, 301a–301b, 302b–305a, 306a–307b, 308b, 313a, 313b, 314b, 315a, 316a, 317b
Hocart, III 311a
Holbach, III 302a
Holbein, III 292b
Hölderlin, III 305a, 305b
holism, III 276b
Homer, III 272b, 273a, 274a, 274b, 295b, 298a, 299a, 302b, 304a, 304b
homonymy, III 307b
homosexuality, III 279a
Horace, III 298a
horoscopes, III 290a
Hugo, III 306b
humanism, III 289b–290b, 291b, 292b, 294b
Hume, III 302a, 303a–303b
humors, III 287b
Hyacinthus (myth), III 272b
Hyginus, III 299b
hymns, III 308b
iconography, III 286b, 288b, 290b, 292a, 293a, 298a
idealism, III 304b, 305a, 305b, 312a
ideas, III 274b, 286b, 288b, 295b, 297b, 298a, 309a, 310b, 312a, 313b, 317a
identification, III 312a
ideology, III 315a
idolatry, III 301a–303b
ignorance, III 301b, 302a, 303b
Ilithyia (god), III 272b
illusion, III 307b
illustrations, III 289a, 289b, 293a
imagery, III 273b, 276b, 282a, 286b, 287b, 289b–291a, 293a, 293b, 295a, 304b–306a, 310a, 312b–

313a, 314b, 317a
imagination, III 272a, 273a, 274b, 276b, 286b, 289b, 297a, 302a, 305a, 315a, 315b
immorality, III 273a, 288a, 309b
immortality, III 278b, 279a, 284b, 291a
imperialism, III 291a
impersonation, III 308a, 311a
incantation, III 273a
Incarnation, III 276a, 277a
incest, III 279a, 312b
independence, III 304a
individualism, III 308b
indulgence, III 295a
infinite, III 305a, 305b, 306a
innocence, III 278b, 305a, 306a
instinct, III 315b
institutions, III 309a, 309b, 313b, 314b
intelligentsia, III 272a, 274b, 290a, 308a, 309b, 310a
interpretation, III 273a–274a, 277b, 286b, 288a, 288b, 290a, 292a, 294a–294b, 299b, 302a, 308a, 309a, 310a, 311b–313b, 315a, 316b–317b
intolerance, III 301a
invention, III 307a, 311a
irony, III 272a
irrationalism, III 301a, 302a, 309b, 314a
Isidore of Seville, III 286b, 288b
Islam, III 276b, 283a
Italian language, III 298b
Jamblichus, III 292a
James, Jesse, III 276b
James, M. R., III 281b, 282a
James I, III 296a, 297a
Jason (myth), III 275b, 290a
jests, III 275a, 275b
Jesuits, III 293a–293b
Jews, III 276a, 277a, 280b–281a, 282b, 283b, 284a, 293a
John of Garland, III 288a
Jonson, III 294b, 295b, 297a, 299b
Judaism, III 276b, 281a, 281b, 284a, 307a, 314a
Julius Caesar, III 308b
Jung, III 281a, 282b, 312b–313a
Junius, III 298a, 299a
Jupiter (god), III 299b, 305a

Keats, III 299b, 306b
kerygma, III 276a
kingship, III 281a–281b
knowledge, III 287b, 288b, 290b, 293a, 302b, 303b, 304b, 305b, 313b, 314b
Kronos (myth), III 274a, 274b, 308a, 309a
Lactantius Placidus, III 291a, 299b
language, III 273b, 280a, 280b, 302b, 304a, 304b, 305a, 307b, 308a, 308b, 315b, 317a, 317b
lapidaries, III 287b
Last Judgment, III 276a, 284a–284b
Latin language, III 298a, 298b, 305b
law, III 277a, 281a, 283a, 291a, 304a
learning, III 291a, 299a
legends, III 275a, 275b, 277a, 277b, 279b, 280a, 280b, 286a, 308b
Lethe (myth), III 274b
Lévi-Strauss, III 272a, 307a, 316a–317b
Lévy-Bruhl, III 272a
lexicons, III 299a
Liber (god), III 273b, 274a
liberal arts, III 287b, 288b, 290b, 291a
libido, III 313a
lies, III 274a
life, III 274a, 291b, 305b, 307b, 309b, 313a, 314b–315b, 317b
linguistics, III 316a–317a
literature, III 272a, 274b, 288a–290a, 293a, 294a–300b, 306b, 311a
logic, III 316b–317b
Logos, III 276b, 284a, 307b
Lomazzo, III 293a, 295b, 297b, 298a, 299a
Lot (Bible), III 275b
love, III 295b–296a, 297a, 304b
Lovejoy, III 277a, 279a
Lowth, III 304a, 304b
Lucian (Emperor), III 292b
lust, III 309a
Macpherson, III 304b
Macrobius, III 274a, 287b, 291a, 299b
Magi, III 282b
magic, III 282a–283a, 287b, 290b, 311a
Malinowski, III 314b
man, III 274b, 275b, 279a
mana, III 282b
Manilius, III 291a
manners, III 309a

Mantegna, III 290b, 292b
Mantua, Duke of, III 297b
manuscripts, III 288b, 289a, 289b, 296b, 298a
Märchen, III 275b
Marcion, III 283a
Marduk (god), III 275b, 281a, 281b
Marlowe, III 294b
marriage, III 282a–282b
Marvell, III 295b, 297b
mathematics, III 316b
matriarchy, III 313b
Maui, III 308a
meaning, III 272b, 274a, 275a, 275b, 288b, 291a, 291b, 295a, 300b, 304b, 305b, 307a, 307b, 308a, 310b, 311b, 313a, 313b, 314a, 315b, 316b, 317a
Medea (myth), III 273b–274a
Medici, Catherine de, III 291b
medicine, III 287b, 309a
meekness, III 282a
melancholy, III 290b, 304b
Melchizedek, III 283a
Melville, III 306b
mercy, III 282a
Messiah, III 281a, 283a, 284a
metaphor, III 282b, 295a, 308b
metaphysics, III 295b, 306a
meteorology, III 273a, 308a
methodology, III 311b
Methuselah, III 277b
Metis (myth), III 299b
Michelangelo, III 276b, 280a, 291b
Michelet, III 306b
microcosm, III 290a
Micyllus, III 299b
Middle Ages, III 280a, 286a–294a
migration, III 272b, 275b, 280b–281a, 306a, 313b
millenarianism, III 284a
Milton, III 295a, 295b, 299a, 299b, 300a, 306b
mind, III 286b, 290b, 302a, 303b, 308b, 310b, 314a, 317a, 317b
mineralogy, III 287b
miniatures, III 288b, 289a, 290b, 297b
Minotaur (myth), III 272b, 275b
miracles, III 282a–283a
mischief, III 309b
moderation, III 292a
monarchy, III 281a
monotheism, III 281a,

281b, 301a, 301b, 303a, 309a
monsters, III 281b, 282a
Montesquieu, III 304a
Montfaucon, III 302b
morality, III 273b, 274a, 282b–283a, 288a, 289a, 290a, 290b, 293b, 294b, 301a, 301b, 312b, 314b, 316a
morphology, III 313a–314a, 316a–316b
mosaics, III 276b, 289a
Moses (Bible), III 275b, 277a, 277b, 280b, 281a, 282b, 283a, 284b
motion, III 273b
mottoes, III 296a
Mowinckel, III 275b, 281b, 311b
Muller, Max, III 307b–309a
murder, III 279a–279b, 281b
Murray, III 307a, 311a
muses, III 291a, 295b
music, III 276b, 294a, 296b, 306b, 317a
mystery, III 272b, 277b, 282b, 283a, 284a, 292a, 299b, 301b, 307a, 310a
mythography, III 289a, 294b, 298a, 299a
mythology, III 272a, 274b, 296b, 300a–305a, 306b, 307b, 308a
mythopoesis, III 305a, 305b, 306b, 308a, 308b, 309a, 312a
Narcissus (myth), III 274b, 288b
narratives, III 316a–316b
nationalism, III 304a, 304b, 305a, 306a, 308b, 313b
Nature, III 274a, 302a, 303a, 304b, 305a, 305b, 307b–308a, 309a, 313b, 315a, 315b, 317a
necessity, III 272b, 305a
neo-classicism, III 295b
Neo-Platonism, III 288a, 292a, 292b
New Testament, III 277a, 282a
Newton, Isaac, III 301b
Nicodemus (Bible), III 282a
nightmares, III 310a
nostalgia, III 314b
Novalis, III 305a–306a
novella, III 275a, 275b
obscenity, III 309b
obscurity, III 294b, 295b
Odysseus (myth), III 308a
Oedipus (myth), III 275b, 312b

Old Testament, III 275b, 277a, 281b, 282a, 282b, 284a, 288a, 304a, 310b, 311b
Olympus, III 272b
One, III 277a, 292a
opera, III 293b, 306b
opinion, III 273b, 274a
order, III 273b, 288a, 291b, 313b, 317a
Orientalism, III 272b, 287b, 306a
origin, III 276b, 277a, 277b, 286b, 292b, 301a–303a, 304a, 307a, 307b, 310a–312b, 314a–315a, 316a
ornamentation, III 290a
Orosius, III 286b
Ossian, III 304b
Otto, III 313a, 314a, 314b
Ovid, III 278a, 283a, 286b, 288a, 293a, 296a, 298a, 299a, 299b
paganism, III 277a, 286a, 286b, 287b, 288a, 290a, 291b, 292a, 293a, 293b, 300a, 301a, 301b, 303a, 305b
pain, III 278b
painting, III 276b, 286a–286b, 291b, 293a, 294b, 296b, 297a, 298a–299a
Pan-Babyloniamism, III 310a–310b
Pandora (myth), III 274b
Pan-Egyptianism, III 310b
pan-lunarism, III 310a
Panofsky, III 290a, 292a
parables, III 275b, 282b, 296a, 299b
paradox, III 273a
paranoia, III 312b
Paris (myth), III 308a
parricide, III 312b, 313a, 317b
Passion, III 277a, 281b
passions, III 288a, 292a
Passover, III 276b
pasturage, III 294a
patriotism, III 306b
patternism, III 311b
Paul, III 276b, 283a
Paulinus of Nola, III 281b–282a
Pausanias, III 295a, 299a
peace, III 291b, 292a
pedanticism, III 292b
Pepys, Mrs. Samuel, III 297b
perfectibility, III 303b
Persius, III 274a
personification, III 288a, 308b
Perugino, III 290b

Petrarch, III 289b, 296a
Petrus Comestus, III 286b
phallus, III 312b
Philo Judaeus, III 283a
Philodemus, III 274a
philology, III 274b, 291b, 304b, 305b, 306a
philosophy, III 272a–274b, 277a, 288b, 290a, 291a, 292a, 300a, 302a, 302b, 304b–307a, 308b, 309a, 311a, 315a–316a
Philostratus, III 299a
phonology, III 316a, 316b
physics, III 274a, 297b, 301a
physiology, III 287b
pietism, III 274a, 291b, 304b
plagiarism, III 297b
planets, III 291b, 310a
Plato, III 272a–274b, 292a, 292b, 299b
Platonism, III 291b, 295a
pleasure, III 273b, 278b, 292a, 299b
plenitude, III 277b
Plotinus, III 274b, 292a
pluralism, III 301a, 303a
Plutarch, III 292a, 295a, 299a, 299b
poesy, III 294b
poetry, III 272b, 273a, 277a, 282b, 291a, 291b, 293b, 294b, 295a, 295b, 296b, 297a, 300a, 304a–305b, 306b, 307a, 308b
polynomy, III 307b
polytheism, III 274a, 279b, 303a, 309a
Porphyry, III 292a
Poseidon (god), III 272b
Poussin, III 280a, 293b
power, III 305b, 310a, 314b, 315a
pragmatism, III 314b
Praxiteles, III 274b
Praz, III 296a
prediction, III 283b
prefiguration, III 277b, 283a
prejudice, III 303b
preromanticism, III 304b
pre-Socratics, III 317b
prestige, III 286b, 293a, 293b
Priapus (god), III 291b
pride, III 287a, 288a
priests, III 276a, 281a, 282a, 283a–284a, 301b, 302a, 306a
primitive ages, III 299b, 304b, 307b–309a, 310b, 313a, 314b, 315b, 316b–317b

primordiality, III 309b, 313a, 313b, 314b, 315b, 316a
printing, III 289a
Pritchard, III 275a, 279a, 280a, 281a, 281b, 282b
Proclus, III 274a, 292a
Prometheus (myth), III 274b, 278b, 279b
Promised Land, III 277a, 280b
propaganda, III 291b
prophecy, III 277b, 281a, 282b–284b, 288a, 291a
proportions, III 273b
prose, III 294b, 295b, 296a
proverbs, III 275a
providence, III 302b
psalms, III 275b, 311b
pseudepigrapha, III 275b, 282b
psyche, III 276a
psychology, III 274a, 274b, 301b, 302a, 313a, 313b
punishment, III 273a, 279b
purification, III 292a
Puritanism, III 300a
purpose, III 285b
Pythagoras, III 273a
race, III 280b, 287a, 308b
Rahner, H., III 276b, 282b
Ramnoux, III 272a
Raphael, III 290a, 291a
rationalism, III 287b, 300a, 302a–304a, 309b, 314a, 315a
reading, III 299a
reality, III 274a, 274b, 300b, 312a, 313b, 314b–315b
reason, III 295a, 300b, 303a–303b, 305a, 315a
rebellion, III 288a, 291a
rebirth, III 315a
redemption, III 277a, 288a, 292a
reductionism, III 276b, 277a
refinement, III 304b
Reformation, III 293a
reliefs, III 289a, 291b
religion, III 272a, 274b, 275b, 276a, 277a, 281a, 282a–283b, 287b, 291b, 301a–304b, 305b, 306b, 307b, 308b, 309a–310a, 311a–312b, 313b–315b, 316b
Renaissance, III 286a–294a, 295a–296b, 299a
representation, III 272b, 273a, 292b, 295b
republicanism, III 291a
research, III 272b, 274b, 292a, 295a, 306a, 316b
respect, III 276a
resurrection, III 277a, 282a,

284a, 293b, 310a
revelation, III 302a, 302b, 304b, 306b, 307b, 313b
Rhampsinitus, III 275b
rhetoric, III 293a
riddles, III 275a, 291b
ritual, III 272b, 275b, 276b, 277a, 278a, 279a, 279b, 281b–282a, 282b, 284a, 284b, 291b, 292a, 301a, 302a, 308b, 310b–312a, 313a, 314a–315a, 316a
Robertson-Smith, III 310a–311a, 312a, 315a
Robinson, T. H., III 277a, 281b
romanticism, III 303b–307a
Ronsard, III 290a
Rousseau, III 278b
Rowley, III 275b, 281a
Roydon, III 294b
Rubens, III 293b
Rye, III 297a
Sabbath, III 277b, 278a, 282b
sagas, III 275a, 276a, 315b
saints, III 275a, 275b, 284b
Salisbury, III 297a
salvation, III 276b, 277a, 283b, 284b
Sanskrit, III 305b, 306a, 308b
Satan, III 278b, 281b, 282a, 284b
satires, III 300a
Saturn (god), III 287a, 287b
scholasticism, III 275b, 288b
Schopenhauer, III 306b
Schuhl, III 273a, 273b, 274b
Scriptures, III 291a
sculpture, III 289a, 291b, 296b, 305a
seasons, III 279b, 281b, 287b
semantics, III 307b
senses, III 273a, 292a
Sermon on the Mount, III 283a
Seth (Bible), III 277b
Shakespeare, III 299a–299b
Sheba, III 275b, 277b
Shere, III 299a
Sinai, III 280b–282a
skepticism, III 274b
Skinner, John, III 278a
sky-gods, III 276b, 279b
society, III 272b, 276b, 289b, 307a, 307b, 312a–312b, 315a, 315b
sociology, III 274b
Socrates, III 273b, 274a
Solomon, III 275b, 277b, 281a, 283a

Son of Man, III 277a
Song of Songs, III 282b
soothsayers, III 287b
sorcerers, III 282b, 287b–288a
soul, III 273b, 274b, 288a, 290b, 291a, 293b, 305b
speculation, III 278b, 284a
Speiser, III 278a
Spence, III 302b
Spenser, III 294b–296b, 298a, 299a
Sphinx, III 275b
stars, III 288a, 288b, 290a, 290b
Stoicism, III 274a–274b, 287b, 288a
Strauss, D. F., III 304b
structuralism, III 316b–318a
Sturm und Drang, III 304b
Sumerian Dispute, III 279a
sun, III 278a, 280b, 281b, 287b, 291a, 308a
supernatural, III 313b, 314b
superstition, III 287a, 302a
Supreme Being, III 309b, 310a
Swinburne, III 294b
Sybils, III 291a
Sydow, III 316a
symbolism, III 273b, 274a, 274b, 291b, 292a, 293a, 295a, 299a, 305a, 305b, 306b, 313b, 315b
syncretism, III 291b
talismans, III 287b
Tanaquil (myth), III 313b
tapestries, III 289a, 290a, 297a
Tasso, III 299a
tautegory, III 306b
Tefnut (myth), III 278a
Tehom (myth), III 281b
temperaments, III 288b, 290b
theogony, III 306b
theology, III 274a, 290b–292a, 293a, 300a, 305a
theories, III 276b, 307a, 308a–309b
Theseus (myth), III 272b, 275b, 288a
Thoreau, III 306b
thought, III 272a, 288b, 292b, 295a, 301a, 304b, 305a, 315a, 317a
Throckmorton, III 276a, 277b, 281b, 282a, 284a
Tiamat (myth), III 278a, 281b
time, III 306b
Titans (myth), III 274a
Torah, III 277a, 281a, 283a
Tory, III 292b

totem meal, III 312a–312b
Tower of Babel, III 275b, 280a
tradition, III 272b, 275b–276a, 286a–287a, 288b–290a, 291a, 293a, 295a, 298b, 308a
transcendentalism, III 275a, 276b
transfiguration, III 308b
transmutation, III 292a
Tree of Life, III 277b, 279a
tribes, III 280a, 280b
truth, III 273b, 274b, 276b, 290b, 300a, 305a
Tsui-goab (god), III 308a
Tubal (myth), III 276b, 294a
Tubal-Cain (myth), III 294a
typology, III 277b
tyranny, I 281a
Ulysses (myth), III 273b
unconscious, III 312b–313a
universe, III 276b, 277a, 278a, 290a
Uranus (god), III 273b, 274b
Utley, III 277a, 279b, 280a, 282b
Utnapishtim, III 279a
Vedas, III 305b
Venus (god), III 287b, 290b, 297a, 297b
Vico, III 302a, 302b, 304a, 304b, 306b
Virgin (Bible), III 276a, 282a, 282b, 291b
virtue, III 286b, 287b, 288a, 288b, 291a, 294b
visions, III 283b, 284a
Viterbo, III 291b
Volksgeist, III 304a
Voltaire, III 302b, 303a
Vries, Jan de, III 315b
Wandering Jew, III 280b–281a
Warburton, III 302a
Whore of Babylon, III 282a
Widengren, III 311b
Wilford, III 306b
Wilkins, III 305b
Wilson, III 306a
Winckelmann, III 304a, 304b
wisdom, III 286b, 290b, 299b, 304b
women, III 278a, 278b, 290a
Word, III 278a, 283a, 284a
Wordsworth, III 306b
World War II, III 314b
Xenophanes, III 273a
Xenophon, III 274a
Xylander, III 295a
Yahweh, III 277a, 278a,
278b, 280b–282a, 283a, 311b
Zeno, III 274a
Zeus (god), III 272b, 273a, 273b, 274b, 282b, 309a
zodiac, III 287b, 288b, 291a
zoology, III 287b
Zoroastrianism, III 281b

N

Naamah (Bible)
    mythology, III 279b
    prophecy, III 660b
Nabi, III 657b–660a
Nabokov, Vladimir (1899–), love, III 106a
Naboth (Bible)
    freedom of speech, II 255b
    prophecy, III 661a
Nadler, Joseph, romanticism, IV 197a
Naevius, Gnaeus (3rd century B.C.), freedom of speech, II 261a
Nāgārjuna (fl. latter part of 2nd century A.D.), Buddhism, I 248a
Nagasaki, international peace, III 455b
Nagel, Ernest
    empiricism, III 550a
    pragmatism, III 553a
Nägeli, Karl Wilhelm von (1817–1891), genetic continuity, II 286a, 287b–288a, 288b, 289a
Nag-Hammadi texts, II 327b
Nagl, J. W., baroque in literature, I 189b
Nagley, Winfield E., Orientalism, III 431b
Nagy, Imre, Marxism, III 166a–166b, 167a
Nain de Tillemont, Louis-Sébastien le (1637–1698), historiography, II 478b
Nanson, E. J., social welfare, IV 282a, 282b
Napier, John (1550–1617), mathematics, III 178b
Naples
    art, II 297b
    balance of power, I 181a–181b
    individualism, II 297b
Napoleon I, Emperor (1769–1821)
    causation, I 283b
    balance of power, I 186a, 186b
classicism, I 454b
Comte and, III 540a
Concordat of 1801, I 404b
conservatism, I 477b
deism, I 651b
despotism, II 13b–14b, 15a
Floresta and, III 540a
Hegel and, II 414a
historiography, II 493a, 496b
ideology, II 554a
liberalism, III 45b, 51a
linguistics, III 64b
longevity, III 92b
militarism, IV 502b, 503a, 504a, 505a
neo-classicism in art, III 364b, 370b
papacy and, I 404b
periodization in literary history, III 483a
positivism, III 540a
romanticism, IV 206b, 207a
Russia, II 14b
77 Organic Articles, I 404b
vox populi, IV 499a
Napoleon III, Emperor (1808–1873)
    impressionism, II 573a
    Michelet and, II 414a
    militarism, IV 503b
    nationalism, III 338b
    positivism, III 537a, 540a, 544a
    revolution, IV 157b, 158a, 158b, 160b
Napoleonic Code, women, IV 526a
Narcissus (myth), III 274b, 288b
Narrative
    historiography, II 475a, 475b, 477a, 477b, 480b–485b, 487a, 487b, 490b, 491a, 493b, 494b, 498a, 501a, 503a
    irony, II 629b, 632a
    motif, III 236b, 237b, 238b, 241b, 242b
Nash, Roderick, environment, II 133b
Nash, Thomas (1567–1601), Machiavellism, III 117a
    wisdom of the fool, IV 519b
Nasir-e Khusraw, II 646a
Nataraja (myth), II 343b–344a
Nathan (Bible), prophecy, III 659a, 660b, 661a
Nathan, R. (8th–9th century A.D.), macrocosm, III 129a
National Arbitration and Peace Congress, III 449a
National Association of Student Personnel Administrators, I 11a
National Association of Women Deans and Counselors, I 11a
National Council for the Prevention of War, III 449b
National Educational Association, I 13b
National Organization for Women, IV 528b–529b
National Peace Council, III 448b–449a
Nationalism, III 318b–339a
    absolutism, III 325a, 329b, 332a, 332b
    Abu'l Kalam Azad, III 338a
    activism, III 331b
    Acton, III 328b, 329b
    aesthetics, III 336b
    Africa, III 335a–338b
    agriculture, III 334b
    Alan the Englishman, III 320b
    Albania, III 334a
    Alfieri, III 336b
    Algeria, III 338a
    anti-communism, III 338a, 338b
    Arabs, I 411b; III 335a, 337b, 338a
    Argentina, III 335b
    Aristotle, III 324b
    art, II 579b; III 326a
    Atatürk, III 337a
    Austria, III 329b, 332a, 333a, 338b
    Austria-Hungary, III 328b
    authority, III 331b
    autonomy, III 329a, 337a, 338b
    Balkans, III 329b, 330a, 336a
    Bartolus of Sassoferrata, III 321b
    Beaumanoir, III 321a, 322b
    Becket, III 319b
    Beveridge, III 331a
    Bible, III 325a
    biology, III 330a, 330b
    Blacks, III 328b–329a
    Blyden, III 337b
    Bohemia, III 328b
    Bolívar, III 335a, 335b
    Boniface VIII (Pope), III 320b, 321a
    Bracton, III 319b, 321a, 322a
    Brazil, III 335b, 336b
    Buddhism, III 324b
    Burma, III 337a, 338a
    Cambodia, III 333a
    Canada, III 334b, 338b

capitalism, III 331b, 336b
Carbonari, III 328a
Cato the Censor, III 323b
Cattaneo, III 329b
Central America, III 335b
Ceylon, III 337a, 338a
chauvinism, III 333b
China, III 332b, 333a, 334a
China (Communist), III 334a–334b
Christianity, I 385a, 386b, 395a–397b, 399b–400a; III 319b, 320b, 321a, 332b
Church, I 412b
Cicero, III 323a
city-state, III 321a, 321b, 323b, 325a
civilization, III 326a, 327b, 330a, 332a, 332b, 335b, 336b, 337a, 338b
class, III 150b–151a, 673a
classicism, III 325a, 332b
colonialism, III 329a, 673a
common law, II 695a
communications, III 325a, 328a, 332b
communism, III 333a–334b, 335b, 336b, 338a, 338b
conservatism, I 482b–483a; III 328a
constitutionalism, III 332a
corporation, III 320a–320b
cosmopolitanism, III 325a, 325b, 326b, 329b, 331a
Counter-Enlightenment, II 105b–106a, 109a
Cruz Costa, III 335b
culture, II 106a; III 324a, 324b, 325a, 327a, 328a, 330a, 330b, 333a, 334a, 334b, 336b, 337a
Czechoslovakia, III 328b
da Cunha, 335b
Dante, III 320b
Darwin, III 330a
de Gaulle, III 337a, 338b
Decembrists, III 328a
Declaration of Independence, III 332b
democracy, III 325b, 326b, 328a, 329a, 329b, 330a, 331b, 333a, 334a, 335a, 335b
dictatorship, III 325a
dynasties, III 332a
Eastern Orthodox Church, I 411a–411b; III 324b
economic history, II 47a
economics, III 324a, 330a, 330b, 333a, 334b–337a
education, III 324b, 326b, 327b, 329a, 331b, 332a
Edward I, III 321a
Edward III, III 323b

egoism, III 329b
Egypt, III 332b, 337b, 338a
Egyptian-Pharaonic, III 337b
emancipation, III 326a
Enlightenment, III 324b, 326b, 327b, 329a, 331b, 332a
equality, III 326b, 327a, 328b–329b, 331b, 332a
evil, II 169a
expansion, III 327b
extremism, III 331a, 332a
fascism, III 331a, 674a
fatherland, III 326b–327b
Faust (legend), III 251b, 252a
federalism, III 329b
feudalism, III 319a–319b, 321b, 322a, 322b, 333a
Finland, III 328b
folklore, III 337b
France, II 690a; III 319a–328a, 330b, 333b, 334a, 335b–338b; IV 125a, 493b
Franklin, III 325b
free trade, III 330a
Frederick Barbarossa, III 320b
French Revolution, III 323b, 325a–327a, 331a
Gardiner, III 331a
general will, II 278b–279a
genius, II 295b; IV 125a
Germany, II 690b; III 250b, 304b, 319a, 320b, 321a, 326a–328b, 330a–331b, 335a–337b; IV 125a, 493b
Gobineau, III 330b
God, II 337a, 344b; III 318b, 320a, 320b, 321a, 322b, 324b, 325a
good, IV 174a
Gothic, II 369b–370a
Great Britain, I 397a; II 690a; III 319a–319b, 320b, 321a–323b, 326a, 327a, 330a, 330b, 331a, 333a
Greece, III 329b
Greece (ancient), III 324b, 325a, 335a
Guinea, III 338a
Habsburgs, III 332a
Hegel, III 445a
Henry of Ghent, III 323a
Henry II, III 319b
Herder, III 305a, 325b, 326a, 327a, 330b; IV 203a, 203b
heresy, II 428b
historiography, IV 151b
history, III 324b, 326a, 328a, 329a, 330a, 334b, 335a, 337a, 338b

Hohenzollern, III 332a
holy, II 512b
Holy Alliance, III 328a
Holy Roman Empire, III 320b, 321a, 323a
humanism, III 323b, 327b
humanitarianism, III 331a
Hungary, III 334a
idea, III 324a–324b, 332a
idealism, III 330a
ideology, III 333b–334b
imperialism, III 333b, 334a
impressionism, II 579b
independence, III 330a, 334a, 335a, 337a, 338b
India, III 332b, 337a, 338a
individualism, III 336b
indoctrination, III 325a
Indonesia, III 337a, 338b
industrialization, III 325a, 330b, 331b, 334a, 334b
industry, III 325a, 330b, 331b, 334a, 334b
Innocent III (Pope), III 320b–321a
integration, III 326b, 333b, 336b, 337a
internationalism, III 325a–329b, 331b–334a
Iraq, III 338a
Ireland, III 330a, 334b
irrationalism, III 331b
Islam, III 324b, 338a
Israel (ancient), II 337a; IV 227b
Italy, III 320a–330a, 333a, 335a, 336a, 336b; IV 493b
Japan, III 337a
Jean de Blanot, III 321a
Jefferson, III 326b, 332b
John of Salisbury, III 319b, 320a, 320b, 322a
John XXIII (Pope), III 334b
Joly, III 330b
Judaism, I 374b; III 324b
jurors, III 319b–322b
Kant, III 325b, 326a–326b
kingship, III 319b–320a
Korea, III 337a
land, III 334b
language, II 660b; III 324b, 325b, 333b, 335a
Latin America, III 335a–337a, 338a, 338b
law, II 689b–690a, 690b; III 318b, 319a, 320a–323a, 326b
lawyers, III 320b–323b
League of Nations, III 328b, 332a
Left, III 336a
Lenin, III 333b, 335b
liberalism, III 329b, 330b, 331b, 335a, 336a, 673a

Liberia, III 337b
liberty, III 325b, 326b–329b, 331a, 332a
linguistics, III 328b, 329a, 336b
List, III 330a–330b
literature, III 83a–83b, 324b; IV 332a
Lithuania, III 335a
Liu Shau-tze, III 334a
Locke, III 326b
Louis IX, III 321a
loyalty, III 108a, 110a, 110b, 111a, 113a, 113b, 114b
Macapagal, III 338b
Machiavelli, III 122a, 124a, 322b, 323b
Machiavellism, III 123a, 124a, 330a
Magyars, III 330a
majority groups, III 328b, 329a, 329b, 333b, 334a
Malaya, III 337a, 338b
Mao Tse-tung, III 334a–334b
Marsilius of Padua, III 321b
Marx, III 332b, 334b
Marxism, III 148b, 150b–157b, 164b, 167b, 168b–169a, 333a–335b
Marxism-Leninism, III 334a, 334b
materialism, III 334b
Mazzini, III 328a, 336b
Mendes, III 336b
Mexico, III 332b, 335b
Michelet, III 328a, 330b
Mickiewicz, III 328a
Middle Ages, II 689b; III 318b–324b
militancy, III 326b
military, IV 501a, 503b, 504a, 505b, 506a, 507a
Mill, J. S., III 331a
millenarianism, III 223b
Milton, III 336b
minority groups, III 328b, 329a, 329b, 333b, 334a, 337a
modernization, III 334b, 336a
morality, III 325b, 327b, 329a, 330b, 331b, 332a, 334a, 334b, 336b
Muhammad Ali Jinnah, III 338a
Muhammad Iqbal, III 338a
mythology, III 287a, 304a–305a, 308b, 313b, 327b
Napoleon III, III 338b
nation-state, III 318b, 323a, 323b–325a, 326b, 327a, 329b, 335a, 336b, 338b
Nature, III 324b

Ne Win, III 338a
necessity, III 355b, 357a, 358b, 360b
Neo-Colonialism, III 330a
Neo-Traditionalism, III 333a
Netherlands, III 326a, 327a, 330b
Ottoman Empire, III 332a
Paine, III 325b
painting, II 579b
Pakistan, III 338a
pan-nationalism, III 324b, 338b
papacy, I 385a, 386b; III 319b, 320a, 321a, 321b, 322a
patriotism, III 318b, 323a–324a, 325b, 328a, 328b, 333a, 333b, 334a–673a
peace, III 332a, 445a, 446b, 448b, 449b, 451b, 452a, 456b
Pearson, III 331a
periodization in history, III 476b
philanthropy, III 490a
Philip IV (the Fair), III 320b, 321a
Philippines, III 331a, 338b
philosophy, III 323a, 334a, 334b, 337b
Plato, III 325b
plutocracy, III 331b
poetry, III 333b, 531a
poets, III 319b
Pokrovsky, III 333b
Poland, III 328a, 328b, 334a, 335a; IV 493b
population explosion, III 336a
populism, III 333a, 335b
positive neutralism, III 336b
positivism, III 336b
post-Christian, III 332b
post-classicism, III 332b
post-Stalinism, III 333b, 334a
power, III 327b, 329b, 330a, 330b, 331a, 332a, 336b
progress, III 642a, 647a, 648b
prophecy, III 659b, 661a, 662a, 662b
protest movements, III 672a, 672b, 673a, 674a
psychology, III 328b
race, III 328b–331a, 336b, 337a, 337b
Ramos, III 335b
rationalism, III 327b, 329b, 331b, 332b, 336b
recapitulation, IV 58b
Reformation, I 395a–397a; IV 68a

religion, III 321b–326b, 328b, 334b–338a
Renaissance, III 318b–324a; IV 123b–124b, 151b
Renan, III 330b
republics, III 332a
revolution, III 328a, 329a, 329b, 330a, 331b, 332b, 335b, 338a, 338b, 673a; IV 158b, 160a, 160b
Right, III 331b
rights, III 322b, 326a, 326b, 327a, 331a, 331b, 336b
Roman Catholic Church, III 319b, 320a, 321a, 322a, 324b, 333a, 334b, 336b
Romanovs, III 332a
romanticism, III 326a, 327a, 327b, 328a, 336b; IV 197a, 203a–205a, 207a, 208b
Rome (ancient), II 689b; III 319a, 320a, 320b, 321b, 322a, 323a, 326a
Rousseau, III 325a–326a
Rumania, III 334a, 336b
Russia, I 482b–483a; III 327b, 328b, 332a, 333b, 336a, 337b
Russian Revolution (1917), III 332a, 333b
Saint Thomas Aquinas, III 323a
Saint-Just, III 326b
salvation, III 324a; IV 227b
San Martín, III 335a
Sayyah Ahmad Khan, III 338a
Scandinavia, III 326a, 333a
scholasticism, III 323a
science, III 324b, 334b
Scotland, I 397a
self-determination, III 324b
Shaikh Sa'di Shirazi, III 338a
Shestakov, III 333b
Shils, III 336a
Sieyès, III 326b
Sihanouk, III 333a
Sikkim, III 333a
Slavophilism, III 327b, 336b
socialism, III 325a, 327b, 330a, 331b–338a; IV 293b
society, III 324a, 325b, 327a, 327b, 328a, 330a, 331b, 333a, 334b, 338b
Sodré, III 335a
Solovyov, III 333b
Spain, III 319a, 319b, 320b, 335b, 336a
Stalin, III 333b
Stankević, I 482b–483a
State, III 318b–325b, 326b; IV 332a
style, II 297b; IV 332a

sub-nationalism, III 338a
Sun Yat-sen, III 333a, 334a
Sung Wu, III 334a
supranationalism, III 332b, 333a, 334b
Switzerland, III 328b, 329a, 329b, 330b, 338b
symbolism, IV 343a, 344b
Syria, III 338a
Tartars, III 333b
technology, III 324b, 325a, 332b, 334b, 336a
territorialism, III 328a, 328b
Thorez, III 334a
Tocqueville, III 330b
tolerance, III 325a
Tönnies, III 326b, 327a
totalitarianism, IV 407a, 410a, 410b
trade, III 330a
tradition, III 324b, 325a, 325b, 327a, 327b, 331b–335a, 337b
tribalism, III 325a
Trotsky, III 335b
Tunis, III 337b
Turkey, III 332b, 337a, 338a
Turner, F. J., III 335b
underdeveloped countries, III 332b, 335a, 336a–338b
U.S.S.R., III 167b, 333b–334a, 336b
U.N., III 332a
U.S., III 328b–332a, 337a
unity, III 329b, 330a, 335b, 336b, 338a
universality, III 329a, 332b
urbanization, III 325a, 331a, 334a
utilitarianism, III 336b
Vargas, III 335b
Vincent of Beauvais, III 319b
Vincent of Spain, III 320b
violence, III 673a
Volfius, III 326b
Volksgeist, IV 491b, 493b, 494a, 495a
Wagner, III 330b
war, III 322b, 324a, 326a, 329b, 330a, 673a; IV 501a, 503b–505b, 506a, 507a
welfare, III 318b, 319a, 320a–325a, 333a
Whitman, III 329a
William the Conqueror, III 319b
William of Ockham, III 323b
William I, III 319b
World War I, III 332a
World War II, III 328b
writers, III 319b, 327b
Young Europe, III 328a
Yugoslavia, III 328b, 334a,

335a
Nationality
literature, III 83a–83b
State, IV 315a
Natorp, Paul Gerhard (1854–1924), Platonism, III 522b
Natura (myth), III 351a
Natural law, III 13b–27a
absolutism, III 19b, 21b
abstraction, III 20a, 22a
Albert the Great, III 18b
ambiguity, III 14a
Anaxagoras, III 15a
animals, III 14b, 18b, 19b
Archelaus, III 16a
aristocracy, III 16b
Aristotelianism, III 14a, 17a, 19b, 20a, 23a
Aristotle, I 487a; III 15a–15b, 16b, 17a, 19a, 20b, 23a; IV 175b
Augustinianism, III 19a
Austin, III 1b
authority, III 20b, 23b, 24b, 25b
Barbeyrac, III 20b
Battifol, III 23a
behaviorism, III 15a, 20b
Bentham, III 22a, 234a
Beudant, III 22b
Bible, III 17b, 18b
Bobbio, III 23b
Bodin, III 19b
Bonald, III 22a
Brunner, III 23a
Burlamaqui, III 20b
casuistry, III 15b, 17a, 23a
causation, III 16a
Celsus, III 16b, 17b
chaos, III 14b, 15b
characteristics, III 18b
Charmont, III 22b
Christianity, III 17b–18b, 19a
Chrysippus, III 16a
Cicero, I 487b; III 16b
class, III 22a
classification, III 18a
Coïng, III 23a
communism, III 22b
community, III 19a, 21a
Comte, III 22a
constitutionalism, I 487a–487b
constitutions, III 21b
contracts, III 17a, 22b
cosmos, III 14b, 15a
Counter-Enlightenment, II 101a, 102a, 102b, 105a, 107b–108a
culture, I 617a, 620b
Cumberland, III 20b
custom, III 14b, 15a, 16a, 18a, 18b, 22a

cycles, III 14b
De Jouvenel, III 23a
De Page, III 23b, 24b
death, III 20b
defined, III 13b–14b
deism, I 646b, 648a, 648b, 651a
Del Vecchio, III 23a
d'Entrèves, III 23a
determinism, II 240a–240b
Dewey, I 324b
dictatorship, III 5a
divination, III 15a, 18a, 19a
duty, III 22b
economics, III 22a
education, III 15a
Eisemann, III 23b
empiricism, III 15a, 20a
Engels, III 22a
environment, II 122b; III 14a
Epicureanism, III 16a–16b
equality, II 140a, 142b; III 15b, 21a, 21b, 25b
ethics, III 16a–16b, 22b, 23a
Etienne de Tournai, III 18b
evil, III 17b, 20b
evolution, III 19a, 24b–25a, 26a, 646b
fear, III 20b
Fichte, III 22a
first use of the term, I 129a
Fourier, III 22a
France, III 21a, 21b, 22a
free will, II 240a–240b; III 14b, 15a
freedom, II 249a, 250a; III 17a, 21a, 21b–22a, 23a, 25b
Fuller, III 26a
Gaius, III 17a, 19b
genius, II 294a
Geny, III 22b
Germany, III 5a, 21a, 22a, 23a
God, I 487b; II 356a; III 15a, 16b, 17b–18a, 18b, 19b, 20a
good, III 17b, 19a, 19b; IV 175b–177b
grace, III 17b
Gratianus, III 18a
Great Britain, III 7b, 21a, 22a
Greece (ancient), I 487a–487b; III 14b–16b
Grotius, I 488b; III 19b–20a, 21a
harmony, III 15b, 20a
Hauriou, III 23a
health, II 122b
Hegel, III 22a

Heraclitus, III 14b, 16a
hierarchy, III 17b, 23b
history, III 22a, 23a
Hobbes, III 20b; IV 177b
Hugh of Saint Victor, III 20a
human nature, III 14b, 15a, 18b, 23b
humanitarianism, III 17a, 17b
Hume, III 232b–233a
idea, III 15a, 25a
ideology, III 22a
individualism, II 597a, 600a, 601b; III 14b, 15b, 17b, 19a–19b, 20b–22a
infinity, III 15a
instinct, III 16a, 18a, 19b, 20a
intellectualism, III 16b
Isidore of Seville, III 18a
Jhering, III 22a
Judaism, III 17b
judgment, III 19a
justice, II 653a, 654a, 654b, 656b, 657a; III 14a, 15a–17b, 19b, 20b, 21a, 22b, 23a, 24a, 25b
Justinian, III 17b, 24b
Kames, III 234b
Kant, II 240a–240b; III 21b–22b
Kelsen, III 22b, 23b, 24a
Kohler, III 22a
Lactantius, III 17b
law, II 249a, 250a; III 13b, 14a, 15a, 16a–19a, 21a, 22a–24a
liberty, III 23b
Locke, I 488b; III 21a, 21b
logos, III 14b, 15a, 16a, 19b
Lucretius, III 16b
Machiavellism, III 116b
Maistre, III 22a
Maritain, III 22b
marriage, III 17a, 18a, 26a–26b
Marx, I 620b; III 22a
Massis, III 22b
matter, III 17b
Middle Ages, III 17b–19b
Mill, III 22a
mind, III 17b, 19a, 22a
Montaigne, III 20b
Montesquieu, III 21a, 21b, 640a
moral sense, III 232b–233a, 234a, 234b
morality, III 15a, 15b, 16b, 17b, 18b, 19a, 21b, 22a, 22b, 23a, 23b, 26a
natural liberty, II 62a, 63a
Nature, III 13b–21b
Nazis, III 5a, 22a

Neo-Platonism, III 14b
nominalism, III 19a
norms, III 14a, 14b, 16a, 19b–20a, 23a, 23b, 24b
obligation, III 17a, 17b, 20b, 22b, 25a
ontology, III 18a
oppression, III 25b
order, III 14b, 15a, 15b, 19a, 19b, 25a
Panaetius, III 16b
Pascal, III 20b
perennial philosophy, III 459b, 460b
personal conduct, III 15a
philosophy, III 16a–16b, 20b–21a, 23a
Pietism, III 15a
Plato, I 487a; III 15a, 16b
Polybius, I 626a
Posidonius, III 16b
positivism, III 5a–6a, 16a–16b, 20b, 22b, 23b, 24a
power, III 15b, 16b, 20b–21b, 24a, 25a–26b
predictions, III 14b
private property, III 25b
progress, III 640a, 646b
protection, III 14a
Protestantism, III 14a, 19b–20b, 23a
Proudhon, III 22a
Pufendorf, I 488b; III 20a, 21a
Pyrrhonism, III 16a–16b
race, III 25b
rationalism, II 693a
realism, III 16a, 19a, 22a
reason, III 14b, 15b–21b
religion, III 20b, 22b, 25b
Renaissance, III 19b
right, III 15a–15b, 16a, 23a; IV 175b, 176a, 176b, 177a, 177b
rights, III 14a–14b, 17b, 21a, 21b, 25b
Ripert, III 23b
Roman Catholic Church, III 17b–18b
Rome (ancient), III 16a, 16b–17a, 17b, 18a
Roubier, III 23a
Rousseau, III 21a–21b
Rufinus, III 18b
rules, III 20b, 21b, 23a, 23b, 24b, 26a
Saint Ambrose, III 17b
Saint Augustine, III 17b–18a
Saint Paul, III 17b
Saint Thomas Aquinas, I 487b; III 19a, 20a, 23a
Saint-Simon, III 22a

Saleilles, III 22b
Savigny, III 22a
Scelle, III 23a
scholasticism, III 20a
school of, III 19b–20a
senses, III 17b
sex, III 25b
slavery, III 17a
social contract, III 20b–21b
Social Darwinism, III 646b
socialism, III 22a, 23b; IV 288a
society, III 14b, 16b, 19a–26b
Socrates, III 15a, 16a
Sophocles, III 15a
Spencer, III 22a
Spinoza, III 20a
State, III 14a, 15a, 19b, 20b–22b; IV 313b
Stoicism, III 14a–18a, 19b; IV 176a
Stoics, I 129a
Suarez, III 20a
suffering, III 20b
supernatural, III 15a, 19a
Sydney, I 488b
teleology, III 22a
theology, III 18b
Thomism, III 14a, 19b, 20a, 23a
thought, III 15a
time, III 15a, 15b
truth, III 15a, 19a, 22a, 22b
tyranny, III 21a
Ulpian, III 16b, 17a, 17b, 18a, 19b
U.N., III 26a
U.S., III 5a, 21b
universe, III 14b, 15a, 19a
utilitarianism, III 15b, 22a; IV 444b, 445b
utopianism, III 22a
value, III 14a, 18b, 19b, 23a
Villey, III 16a, 23a
virtue, III 15a, 16a, 17b
Voilquin, III 14b, 15a
Volksgeist, IV 494a–495b
voluntarism, III 22b
war, III 18a, 24b
Wiederkehr, III 23a
will, III 18a
William of Auxerre, III 18b
William of Ockham, III 19a–19b
wisdom, III 14b, 15a
Wolf, III 14a
Wolff, III 20b
Zeno of Citium, III 17b
Natural liberty (economic theory of), II 61b–71b
advertising, II 67a
agriculture, II 62b, 69a

balance of payments, II 67a–68a, 70b
banking, II 64b, 68a, 70b
Bastiat, II 69a
Boulding, II 65a
capitalism, II 69b, 70a, 70b
China (Communist), II 70a
Christianity, II 62a, 64a–64b
communism, II 69b
competition, II 64a, 66b
demand, II 63a
democracy, II 67a, 70a
ecology, II 64b
education, II 63b–64a, 64b, 71a
feedback principle, II 63b
Ford, II 66b
France, II 62a, 69a
free trade, II 67a–68a
Friedman, II 68a
Galbraith, II 66b–67a, 70a
Galton, II 65b
Germany, II 69a
God, II 62a, 63a
gold standard, II 68b–69a
Great Britain, II 63b, 69a
Great Depression of the 1930's, II 70a–70b
Greece (ancient), II 61b
Gross National Product, II 70b
Haiti, II 70a
Hitler, II 70b
Hobbes, II 61b, 62a
Hume, II 64a
income, II 62a, 63b, 65a–65b, 66b, 69b, 71a
international trade, II 67a–68a
Keynes, II 62a, 70a, 70b–71a
labor, II 65b, 69a–69b
laissez-faire, II 61b, 69a
law, II 63b
Liberman, II 70a
licensing, II 67a
List, II 68b
Locke, II 62a
Lutheran Church, II 64a–64b
manufacturing, II 62b
Mao Tse-tung, II 70a
Marx, II 69b
Marxism, II 69a–69b
Middle Ages, II 62a, 69b
Mill, II 69a
monarchy, II 62b
money, II 67b, 69b
natural law, II 62a, 63a
natural rights, II 62a, 63a
Nazis, II 70a, 70b
Newton, II 62a
Physiocrats, II 62a–62b

Plato, II 61b
pollution, II 64b
power, II 65a–67a
prices, II 62b–63b, 68b–70a
private property, II 62a, 65b, 69b
production, II 62b–63a, 64b, 65b, 67a, 69a–69b
profit, II 63b
public works, II 65a, 71a
Quesnay, II 62a
quotas, II 67a
religion, II 63b, 64a–64b
revised sequence, II 66b–67a, 70a
Ricardo, II 67b–69a
Rousseau, II 62a
savings, II 65b
Scandinavia, II 64a–64b
Senior, II 69a
slavery, II 65b
Smith, II 61b–69a
socialism, II 69a–70a
society, II 61b–71a
Stalin, II 70a
State, II 62a, 64a, 67a, 68b–69a, 71a
suffrage, II 70a
tariffs, II 67a, 68a, 69a
technology, II 63b
trade, II 67a–68a
Turgot, II 62b
tyranny, II 70a
unemployment, II 70a–71a
U.S.S.R., II 70a
U.S., II 63b–64a, 66b, 67a, 69a, 70a–70b
Vietnam War, II 67a
wealth, II 65a–65b, 66b
World War II, II 70b
Yugoslavia, II 70a
Natural resources
China, I 370a
defined, I 471a
economic history, II 51b
pollution, II 122a
private property, III 650b
progress, III 635b
utility, IV 453a
See also Conservation
Natural rights
civil disobedience, I 435b, 437a–438a
concept of, I 437a
conduct, III 15a
Thoreau, I 437a, 437b
Verdross, III 25b
See also Natural Law
Natural science
Aristotle, I 382b–383a
certainty, I 318a
Christianity, I 405b
Comte, III 534a–534b, 535b

Condorcet, III 533a
Counter-Enlightenment, II 101b, 103a, 105a, 110a
Cousin, III 534a
Defoe, III 601b
Descartes, III 357a
design argument, I 673b–675a
determinism, II 18b
empiricism, III 549b, 550a
Engels, II 455a
evolutionism, II 176a
Faust (legend), III 246a
imagination, III 212b–222b
Leibniz, I 465a
Locke, I 465a
Marx, II 450a, 451b
Marxism, III 149a
materialism, II 450a, 451b, 453b, 455a
necessity, III 354a, 355a, 356a, 357a, 358a, 360a, 360b, 361b, 362a
numbers, III 406b
painting, II 576b
periodization in history, III 478a
positivism, III 532b, 533a, 534a–534b, 549b, 550a
primitivism, III 601b
Natural selection
acquired characteristics, II 618b, 620a
catastrophism, IV 422b, 423a
Darwin, II 180a, 180b, 181a, 182a, 184a, 185a, 185b, 186b, 448a, 618b; III 473b, 561a, 646a; IV 107b, 422b, 423a
environment, II 125a
evolution, II 24a; III 646a, 646b
evolutionism, II 177b, 180a, 180b, 181a, 182a, 184a, 185a, 185b, 186b, 187b
Herschel, II 448a
Huxley, J., III 474a
Huxley, T. H., III 474a
inheritance, II 618b, 620a, 626a
linguistics, IV 424a, 428a
pangenesis, II 626a
perfectibility, III 473b
pleasure, II 383a
pragmatism, III 561a
progress, III 646a, 646b
race, III 646a
recapitulation, IV 58a
Social Darwinism, III 646b
Spencer, II 383a; III 473b
uniformitarianism, IV 422b, 423a, 424a, 428a
Wallace, III 473b

Naturalism
antinomy of pure reason, I 91b
Balzac, IV 53b
Baudelaire, IV 53b
Belinsky, IV 53b
Brunetière, IV 54a
Champfleury, III 229b
Comte, II 582a
Courbet, II 583a; III 229b
culture, I 609b–610a
Daudet, IV 54a
deism, I 648a
Dewey, III 554a
Diderot, II 582a
dualism, II 581b
Eliot, IV 54a
Epicureanism, II 581b
evil, II 161b, 162b
evolution, IV 181a, 182a
expressionism, II 206a, 207a
Flaubert, IV 54a
France, IV 53b, 54a
Germany, III 483b
God, II 348b, 353b
Gogol, IV 53b
good, IV 181a, 182a, 184b–186b
Great Britain, III 483b
Greece (ancient), II 581b
Heine, IV 53b
Hugo, IV 53b
humanism, IV 132b–134b
Italy, III 484a
James, III 554a
Man-Machine, III 135a
Martino, IV 54a
Marx, II 451b–451b, 583a
materialism, II 451a–451b
Maupassant, IV 54a
mythology, III 301b, 308b, 310a
Nature, IV 53b
necessity, III 351b–353a, 360a, 361b, 362a
Pater, II 576a
periodization in literary history, III 483b, 484a
philosophy, II 581b; IV 53b
Plato, III 226b
Platonism, II 581b
poetry, IV 53b, 471b
pragmatism, III 552a, 553b, 554a
psychology, IV 23b
realism in literature, IV 53a, 53b–54a, 55b
Renaissance, IV 132b–134b
revisionism, IV 270a
revolution, IV 165a
rhetoric, IV 53b
right, IV 181a, 182a, 184b–186b
Rome (ancient), II 581b

Ruskin, IV 339a
Russia, IV 53b
Santayana, III 553b, 554a
Schiller, IV 53b
spontaneous generation, IV 310b, 312a
supernatural, IV 53b
symbolism, IV 339a, 342b
Taine, IV 53b
U.S., III 483b; IV 54b
utilitarianism, IV 445a
Utopia, IV 462a, 463a
Zola, II 575b; III 229b; IV 53b–54a
Naturalism in art, III 339a–346b
abstraction, III 344a
accuracy, III 344b
aestheticism, III 343a, 343b
Alt, III 341a
anatomy, III 340a–340b
antinomy, III 343b
antique art, III 342a
appreciation, III 344a
arid naturalism, III 339b
art history, III 339a, 339b, 342b, 343a, 345a
Art Nouveau, III 341a
Assyria, III 340a, 340b
Austria, III 341a
autonomy, III 343a
baroque, III 340b, 341a, 342a
Bellori, III 339a–339b
Biedermeier period, III 341a, 341b
Brueghel, III 346a
Caravaggio, III 339b, 340b
Castagnary, III 339b
Christianity, III 342b
city scapes, III 341a
clarity, III 345a
classicism, III 341a, 342a, 345a
color, III 346a
comparison, III 339b–340a
composition, III 340b, 341a, 341b, 344b, 346a
conception, III 343b
Constable, III 342a
content, III 346a
conventionalism, III 341b
Corot, III 342a
cosmos, III 342b
Courbet, III 343a
creativity, III 341a, 342b, 343a, 343b, 345b
criteria, III 346a
criticism, III 339b, 343b, 346a
dark, III 340b
David, III 341a, 345a
Degas, III 341b
Denmark, III 341a

description, III 339a
designation, III 340a, 340b
detail, III 339a, 340b, 341a
distortion, III 344b, 345a
divine, III 342b
dualism, III 342a
drawing, III 342a
Dürer, III 345a
Dvořák, III 339b
Eckersberg, III 341a
Egypt (ancient), III 340a, 340b
Enlightenment, III 343a, 343b
epistemology, III 339b
essence, III 342b
extra-naturalism, III 341b
fantasy, III 342b, 344a
Feuerbach, III 341b
formalism, III 341a, 341b
France, III 339a, 341a
Gärtner, III 341a
Gautier, III 343b
genre, III 340b, 341a–341b
Géricault, III 341b
Germany, III 339a, 341a, 345a
Goethe, III 343a
Greece (ancient), III 342a, 342b
Hals, III 341a, 344a–345a
Hauptmann, III 339a
history, III 339b, 341b
Holbein, III 340b, 341b, 344a, 345a
Holz, III 339a
human figure, III 340b, 341a, 344a–344b
idealism, III 341a, 341b, 342b, 343a, 345b
ideology, III 343a
illusionism, III 339b, 340a, 341a, 342a, 344b
imagination, III 343b, 346a
imitative naturalism, III 339b
impressionism, II 571a, 573a, 575b, 576a, 576b, 578a, 578b, 579b, 580b, 581b, 582a, 582b, 583a; III 339b, 342a
indirect naturalism, III 344b
individualism, III 342b
Ingres, III 341a, 345a
Italy, III 339a
Kant, III 343a
Kunstwollen, III 343b
landscape, III 341a, 346a
Leibl, III 341b, 344a–345b
Lessing, III 343a
life, III 343a
light, III 340a, 340b, 342b
literalness, III 344a
literature, III 339a

manuscripts, III 340b
masterpiece, III 343b
microstructure, III 345a–345b
Middle Ages, III 340b, 341a, 342a, 342b
mimesis, III 343b
mood, III 345b
naturalists, III 339b, 343a
Nature, III 339a–343b, 345b
neo-classicism, III 342a, 343a
Netherlands, III 341a, 344a, 345b
Panofsky, III 339b, 343b
partial naturalism, III 340a, 340b, 341a, 342a, 342b
perception, III 340b, 345b
period, III 340b
perspective, III 340a, 340b, 341a, 344b
philosophy, III 343b
photography, III 345a
physiognomy, III 340a–340b
pictorial naturalism, III 344a, 344b, 345a
Plato, III 343b
portraiture, III 340b
Pre-Raphaelites, III 341b
primitivism, III 341a
profane, III 342b
projection, III 342a
psychology, III 339b
quality, III 343b–344a
realism, III 339a, 341b, 342b, 343a
reliefs, III 340a, 343a
religion, III 342a
Renaissance, III 340b, 342a, 343a, 345a
representation, III 340a, 340b, 341b, 342b, 343a
Riegl, III 339b, 343b
romanticism, III 341a, 343a
Rome (ancient), III 339b, 342a
Russia, III 339a
Scandinavia, III 339a
Schiller, III 343a
Schopenhauer, III 343b
sculpture, III 342a 342b
Slive, III 345b
space, III 340a, 342a
spiritualism, III 346a
structure, III 340b, 341a, 343b
style, III 339a, 339b, 340b
supra-individual, III 342b
surface, III 340b, 344a
surrealism, III 342b
survey, III 342b
symbolism, III 341b, 345b
symmetry, III 340b

synthesis, III 341a
texture, III 340a
theory, III 342b, 343a, 343b, 344a
total naturalism, III 340a, 340b, 341a, 342a, 342b
townscapes, III 341a
tradition, III 340b
unity, III 341b
Van Eyck, III 340a, 340b
Velázquez, III 341a, 343b
Vermeer van Delft, III 340b, 341a
vision, III 345b
visual arts, III 339a, 343b
visual reality, III 340a
Waldmüller, III 339b, 341a
Wickhoff, III 339b
Winckelmann, III 343a
Wölfflin, III 339b
writing, III 339a–339b
Zola, III 339a, 339b
Nature, III 346b–351b
abnormal, III 350b–351a
Adam (Bible), III 350a
aesthetics, III 347a, 350a, 350b; IV 355b
Alain of Lille, III 590b
alchemy, I 27b, 28a
anarchy, III 348b
angels, III 346b, 347b
animals, III 347b, 348b, 349a, 596a
Apostles, III 347a
architecture, III 350b
Aristotle, I 128b, 234a–234b, 382b, 672b, 673a; II 167b, 175b, 202a, 226a, 377a, 438b; III 15b, 189b, 226b, 273b, 350b, 355a, 380a, 424a; IV 4b, 50b, 175a, 629a, 629b, 436a
art, II 230a, 307a, 570a, 571a, 574a 576b, 582a, 583a; III 226a 230a, 346b, 348b, 349a 350b
artistry, III 347a
astrology, III 347b, 350b
astronomy, III 348b
atomism, I 543b
Bacon, I 173a, 175b–176a, 219a; III 383b; IV 361b, 432a, 434a
Bayle, II 94a
Beattie, I 317a
beauty, I 200a–200b; II 549b; III 347a, 350b
Berkeley, II 352b
Bible, III 349a
Boethius, II 231a
Boltzmann, II 588a
bravery, III 347a
Bruno, I 517a; II 433b, 443a; III 194a, 351a

Bryant, III 349b
Buddhism, IV 232b
Buffon, II 132b, 177a
Burke, IV 203a, 204a
Byron, III 350b
Calvin, III 255a
catastrophism, IV 418a, 419b, 422b
Chain of Being, I 326b–327b, 332a–334a
Chambers, I 364a
chance, I 336a, 336b; II 225b 227b, 228b, 229a, 230a, 231a, 233a, 233b; III 263b
chance images, I 340b, 341a, 341b, 343a
Chateaubriand, IV 201a
children, III 349a, 350a
Christianity, I 129b–130a; III 347a, 347b, 351a, 589a, 589b
Cicero, III 349a, 587b
civilization, III 347b, 348b
Claude, III 349b
Comte, III 642a
Condorcet, III 644a
constitution, III 350a
continuity, I 500b–501a
convention, *see Nomos*
Cosmic Fall, I 504b–513a
cosmology, I 542b, 543b, 556b, 558b; III 347b, 351a
Counter-Enlightenment, II 101a, 102a–102b, 105a, 108b, 110a–110b
Creation, I 572b, 574a, 574b–575a
creativity, III 350a
Cudworth, II 444a
custom, III 346b, 347b
cynicism, I 629a 630a; III 349a, 350a, 585a, 586a
cynics, III 347b
Dante, II 233a, 233b
Darwin, II 448a
death, I 635b–636a
deism, III 302a
Democritus, I 613a; III 226a
Dennis, III 350b
Descartes, II 350b, 381a; III 348a
design argument, I 672b, 673a
determinism, II 18b, 20a, 237a, 237b, 238b
Dickens, III 349a
Diderot, I 333b; III 603a
dignity, IV 140b
Diogenes of Sinope, I 632a; III 347b, 348a, 348b
disease, II 397b, 398a, 400a, 400b, 402a 403b, 404b,

406b
disposition, III 350a
divinity, III 347a, 347b, 351a
Dolce, III 229a
double truth, II 33a, 34b
dualism, II 38b, 43b; III 350b–351a
education, III 348b, 350a
Einstein, I 556b, 558b
Emerson, III 349b
empathy, II 86a
Empedocles, III 347a
empiricism, III 547a, 548b, 549a
Engels, II 450a, 454a–454b
Enlightenment, II 90a, 92a, 94a–94b
environment, II 127b–128b, 130a, 132a, 132b, 133b
Epicurus, II 136a, 137a
equality, II 144a
equity, II 150b
Erigena, I 574a; III 351a
ethics, III 348a, 348b, 349b, 350b, 440b, 442a, 444a, 446b; IV 72b, 319a, 319b, 320a, 320b, 321a
evil, I 575a; II 161b 163b, 164b, 166b 167b; IV 383b
evolutionism, II 174b 185a
existentialism, III 159a 159b
exoticism, III 348b
experiments, III 349b
Fall, III 347b
fate, II 225b 233b
Faust (legend), III 248b, 347a
Ficino, III 229a
fiction, III 348a
Fontenelle, I 332a
free will, II 237a, 237b, 238b, 245b, 246a, 246b
freedom, II 250a
Fux, III 350a
Gainsborough, III 349b
Galileo, I 281a; III 349b; IV 361a
general will, II 276b
genius, II 294a, 294b, 295a, 295b, 307a, 318b, 321a, 324a
geometry, III 350b
Giorgione, III 349b
God, I 376b, 572b, 574a, 574b–575a; II 340b, 350a–350b, 352b, 353a; III 20a, 346b-349b, 351a
Goethe, I 322a; III 425a
Golding, III 349a
good, III 347a, 350b, 351a; IV 174b, 175a, 176a, 177b, 178a, 179b
Goodman, I 506b–507b,

511b
Gothic, II 370a, 371a; III 350b
Greece (ancient), I 127b–129b; III 347a, 347b, 350b; IV 229a
Grotius, II 5a–5b; III 19b–20a
Hamann, II 105a
happiness, II 377a, 378a, 381a
Hardy, I 511b
harmony, II 128a, 128b, 391a; IV 38a
Hartmann, II 167a
Harvey, IV 56b
Hegel, I 204a–204b; II 408a, 454a; III 358b
Heraclitus, III 347a
Herbert of Cherbury, III 348a
Herder, I 615b; II 129b–130a, 178b; IV 204a
hermeticism, II 432b, 433a, 433b
hierarchy, II 435b, 436b, 438a, 438b, 440a, 442b 445a, 446a, 446b, 448a
historiography, II 18b, 20a, 510b–511a; IV 149b, 150b, 151a
history, II 18b, 20a
Hobbes, III 20b; IV 177b, 178a, 257a
homosexuality, III 350a
human nature, III 348a, 348b, 350a, 571a, 573b, 575b, 644a
humanism, IV 129a, 131a, 133a, 133b, 134a, 134b
Hume, I 277a, 312a, 511b, 641a; II 92a, 94a; IV 247b–248a
Huxley, T. H., I 511b; II 183b
Hyperboreans (myth), III 348b
idea, II 544a, 546a, 547a–547b
idealism, III 346b, 347a, 350b
imagists, III 349b
immortality, III 346b
immutability, III 346b, 347a, 347b, 351a
impressionism, II 570a, 571a, 574a–574b, 575a, 575b, 576a, 582b, 583a
independence, III 348a
indeterminacy, II 586b, 587a–587b, 588a
individualism, II 307a; III 346b, 350a
industrialism, III 349b

industry, III 349b
instinct, II 227b; III 16a, 348b
irregularity, III 350a 350b
Islam, II 639b, 643b
James, H., III 349a, 561b
Jesus Christ, III 347a, 349a
Johnson, I 329b
Jouffroy, III 348a
Jung, III 348b
justice, III 15a, 15b, 16a
Kant, I 315a, 315b, 588a; III 555b, 640b; IV 433a, 433b
Kepler, I 281a
Key, III 349a
knowledge, III 348a, 348b
La Mettrie, I 333b, 334b
landscape, III 349b, 350a
law, II 225b, 250a, 687b, 688a–688b; III 1a, 10b, 11b, 32b, 347a, 347b
Leibniz, I 328b, 332a; II 177a, 444b, 446a, 446b; IV 433a
Leopardi, I 511b
life, III 346b
linguistics, III 73b; IV 424a, 427b, 428a, 428b, 429a
literature, III 82b; IV 332a
Locke, III 21a; IV 258b, 259a
love, III 100a–100b
Lovejoy, III 346b, 350b
loyalty, III 110b, 111b
luck, II 227b
Lucretius, III 351a, 631b
Machiavelli, IV 483a
Machiavellism, III 116b
macrocosm and microcosm, III 126a, 128a, 129a
Man-Machine, II 135b
manners, III 350a
Marx, II 450a, 450b, 451a, 452b–453a, 454a; III 159a, 159b, 359a
Marxism, III 159a–159b, 167b, 168b, 645b
materialism, II 450a, 450b, 451a, 452b–453a, 454a–454b
mathematics, III 348a
matter, III 186b, 189b, 193a, 194a, 194b
Maupertuis, I 332b 333a
measurement, IV 399a, 399b, 402b, 404b, 405b
metaphor, III 198b, 199a, 203a
metaphysical imagination, III 212b, 213a, 215a, 216b, 218a, 219a, 221b, 222a
methodology, III 378b, 387a, 387b, 388b–389a

Michelangelo, III 228a–228b, 229a
Michelet, III 349a
Middle Ages, III 116b, 351a
Mill, I 511b
mimesis, III 226a, 226b, 227b, 228a 230a
miracles, III 350b
Mondrian, III 230a
Montaigne, I 635b–636a; III 594a, 594b
Montesquieu, III 21a
morality, III 347a, 349b
mountains in literature, III 253b 255a, 257b 260a
music, II 318b, 321a, 324a, 391a; III 263a, 263b, 264b, 268a, 271b, 350a
mutability, III 350b, 351a
mysticism, III 351a
mythology, III 273b, 274a, 302a, 303a, 304b, 305b, 307b 309a, 313b, 315b, 317a
nationalism, III 324b
Natura (myth), III 351a
natural, III 346b, 347a, 351b
natural law, III 13b 20b, 21a, 21b
natural light, III 348a
nature-worship, III 351a
necessity, III 353a, 353b, 355a, 356a, 357a, 357b, 358a, 359a, 360a, 360b, 362a
Needham, I 333b
neo-classicism in art, III 368a
Neo-Platonism, III 375b
Newton, I 281a, 311a–311b; II 444a; III 194b, 347b, 349b, 378b, 387a, 387b, 388b–389a, 392a
Nicholas of Cusa, III 351a
normal, III 350b–351a
numbers, III 406a
omens, III 347a
optics, III 416a–416b, 417b
order, II 128a, 435b, 436b, 438a, 438b, 440a, 442b, 443a, 444a, 444b–445a, 446a, 446b, 448a; III 350b
organicism, III 424a, 425a
Orientalism, III 433b
painting, II 570a, 571a, 574a 574b, 575a, 575b, 576a, 576b, 582b, 583a; III 349b, 350a; IV 466a, 467b, 469b, 470a, 471b, 472a, 473b, 476a
pangenesis, II 623b
Parmenides, I 127a–127b
Pascal, III 348a

Pater, III 349b
pathetic fallacy, III 351a
peace, III 440b, 442a, 444a, 446b
peasantry, III 349a–349b, 594b, 595b
Peirce, III 559a
perennial philosophy, III 459b, 460a, 460b, 462a
perfectibility, III 465b, 470b, 475a, 644a
philosophy, III 198b, 199a, 347a, 348a
Picasso, III 230a
Pico della Mirandola, II 442b; III 347b
Plato, I 127b–128a, 487a; II 438b; III 15a, 226a, 347a, 350b–351a; IV 380b, 390b
pleasure, II 377a, 378a, 381a
Plotinus, II 163a–163b; III 375b
Plutarch, IV 380b
poetry, III 349a, 349b, 525b, 527a; IV 466a, 467b, 469b 472a, 473b, 476a
poets, III 350b
Pope, III 348a
portraiture, III 350a
positivism, III 533a, 547a, 548b, 549a
post-primitive, III 346b
pragmatism, III 555a, 555b, 559a, 561b
pre-Socratics, III 350b
primitivism, III 346b, 348b 349b, 577b, 581b, 585b 586b, 587b 590b, 594a, 594b, 598a, 600a 604a, 605a
progress, III 624a, 629a, 629b, 631b, 632b, 634a, 635a, 636b, 637a, 640a, 640b, 641b, 642a, 642b, 643a, 644a, 645b, 648b
Protestantism, III 349a
psychology, IV 4b, 10b, 11a, 16a, 19a, 21a, 24a, 26b, 27a, 28a
Ptolemy, I 542b
punishment, III 35a
Pythagoras, I 632a
Pythagoreans, III 347a; IV 31b, 32a, 38a
rationalism, III 302a; IV 46a, 47a, 48b, 49b 50b
realism in literature, IV 53b, 55a
reality, III 347a, 347b
reason, III 350a
recapitulation, IV 56b
Reformation, III 348a

regular, III 350a 350b
Reid, III 348a
relativism, IV 72b
religion, III 203a, 348a, 351a; IV 93a, 95a, 95b, 96a, 104a–104b, 106b, 108b, 115a
Renaissance, III 347b, 349a; IV 140b, 149b, 150b, 151a, 441a
Renoir, III 350b
resignation, II 237b
revelation, III 348a
revolution, IV 152b, 155a
right, III 348a; IV 174b, 175a, 176a, 177b, 178a, 179b
Ritter, II 130a
Robinet, I 331b–332a, 332b
romanticism, III 350a, 351a; IV 187a, 195a 196b, 199a 202a, 203a, 204a, 206a, 206b, 208a, 208b, 209a, 210b
Rome (ancient), II 687b, 688a–688b; III 347a
Rosa, III 349b
Rousseau, I 616b–617a; II 144a; III 21b, 348a, 348b, 600a
Royen-Collard, III 348a
Russell, III 446b
Saint Albertus Magnus, II 197a
Saint Ambrose, III 589b
Saint Augustine, II 137a; 164b; III 17b, 635a
Saint Basil, III 590b
Saint Francis of Assisi, IV 127b
Saint Paul, III 17b
Saint Thomas Aquinas, I 673a; III 227b
salvation, IV 229a, 231b, 232b
Sarbiewski, III 228a
Schelling, IV 204a
Schlegel, IV 209a
Schopenhauer, II 182b–183a
science, III 347a, 349a
Scythia, III 348b
Senault, I 509a
Seneca, II 228a; III 348b, 588b
Shaftesbury, I 205b; III 348a
Shakespeare, III 228a, 351a
Siger of Brabant, II 33a
sin, III 350a; IV 229a, 231b, 232b
skepticism, IV 247b–248a
Skinner, I 226b–227a
social contract, IV 251b,

254a, 255a, 255b, 256b, 257a, 257b, 258b, 259a, 261b, 262a
social welfare, IV 277b
socialism, IV 285b
society, I 68a; III 346b, 347b, 348a
Socrates, I 632a; III 348b
Sophists, III 1a
soul, III 349a, 350b
Sparta (ancient), III 348b
Spengler, III 360b
Spinoza, II 238b, 350b, 444b–445a; III 20a, 351a; IV 434b
spirituality, III 346b, 347b
spontaneous generation, IV 307b, 310a, 311b
Stoicism, II 378a; III 15b, 588a; IV 49b–50a, 50b, 176a, 285b, 319a, 319b, 320a, 320b, 321a
Stoics, III 348a
style, IV 332a
sublime in external nature, IV 333b 336b
subordination, II 237b
supernatural, I 129b; III 346b, 347a, 347b
Sybarite, III 348b
symbolism, IV 338a, 338b, 339a, 345a
symmetry, IV 347b, 348a
taste, IV 355b
technology, IV 357b 361b
temperament, III 350a
Tennant, I 574b–575a, 677a
theodicy, IV 380b, 381b, 383a, 383b
theology, III 349b
theriophily, IV 384a 387a
Thoreau, III 347b–348a
time, IV 390b, 393b, 396b, 398a, 399a, 399b, 402b, 404b, 405b
Toland, III 348a
Toynbee, II 21b
tradition, III 347b, 348a, 350b
tragic sense, IV 414a
transformism, I 499b, 500b
transcendentalism, IV 24a
Ulpian, III 17a
uniformitarianism, IV 418a, 419b, 422b, 424a, 427b, 428a, 428b, 429a
U.S., III 347b–348b
unity, II 128a, 128b
unity of science, IV 432a, 433a 436b
universal man, IV 441a
universality, III 348a
unnatural, III 350b–351b
utilitarianism, IV 445b, 448a

utility, IV 451a
Utopia, IV 459a
Vasari, III 229a
Venus (myth), III 351a
Vico, II 102a–102b; III 357a
Victorian sensibility, IV 221b 223a
virtue, III 16a, 351a
Volksgeist, IV 491b
Voltaire, I 330a, 616a; II 176b; III 348a, 605a
vox populi, IV 499a
Watteau, III 349b
Wieland, II 551b
Windelband, III 351a
wisdom, III 347a, 349a
witchcraft, IV 522a, 522b
Wolff, III 11b
Wordsworth, III 259b, 260a, 349a–349b, 351a
work, IV 532a, 533b, 534b
world, III 350a–350b
wrong, III 348a
Zeitgeist, IV 536b
Zola, III 349a
Nature-worship, III 351a
Naudé, Gabriel (1600–1653), deism, I 648b
Machiavellism, III 120b, 124a
skepticism, IV 244a
Nausiphanes of Teos, skepticism, IV 234a, 240a
Navarrete, Domingo Fernández (1610–?1689), China, I 357b
Navigation
art, II 313b
Lucretius, III 587a
measurement, IV 403a
peace, III 442b
primitivism, III 587a
progress, III 635a
Saint Augustine, III 635a
scientific classification, I 464b
time, IV 403a
Utopia, IV 461a
Naville, Adrien, classification of the sciences, I 466a
Nazism
acquired characteristics, II 620b
animals, III 597a
anti-industrialism, III 676a
authority, I 159b–160a
Christianity, I 407b
civil disobedience, I 435a, 438a
civilization, III 597b
crisis in history, I 593b
democracy, I 667b
fascism, III 674a

Faust (legend), III 251b, 252a
law, II 690b
loyalty, III 113a
Ludendorff, III 597b
Marxism, III 164b
Müller, Adam, IV 207b
natural law, III 5a, 22a
natural liberty, II 70a, 70b
Nordics, III 597b
Odin (myth), III 597b
perfectibility, III 475a
philanthropy, III 488a
primitivism, III 597a–597b
progress, III 647b
protest movements, III 674a, 676a
religion, III 597b
revolution, IV 164a, 164b
romanticism, IV 197a, 207a
Rosenberg, III 597b
Thor (myth), III 597b
totalitarianism, IV 406a, 407a, 407b, 408b
Volksgeist, IV 494a
war, III 597b
Nãzzãm, Islam, II 641b
Ne Win, General, nationalism, III 338a
Near East
alchemy, I 27a 29a
astrology, I 119a
city, I 427b 428a, 429a
freedom of speech, II 252a, 252b, 253a, 254a, 255a
God, II 332b, 333a–341b
Hermeticism, II 431a, 431b, 434a
Israel (ancient), IV 227b, 228b
law, II 686a–686b, 690b
mechanical sciences, II 196a
Novalis, III 311b 312a, 315b
prophecy, III 657b, 659b
Pythagorean cosmos, IV 38b
rationalism, IV 46a
religion, IV 98b, 104b
salvation, IV 227b, 228b
Nearchus (fl. 4th century B.C.), historiography, II 505a
Nebat (Bible), IV 226b
Nebuchadnezzar (Bible), prophecy, III 657b
Necessity, III 351b–362b
Abel (Bible), III 355b
Absolute, III 357a
abstraction, III 360a
algebra, III 355b
analogy, III 361a, 361b
anthropology, III 352b, 354a, 357a, 362a
aristocracy, III 353b, 356a
Aristotelianism, III 354b,

355a, 355b
Aristotle, III 189b, 351b, 353a 355b; IV 50b, 411b 412a
art, III 360a, 362a
astrology, III 354a
astronomy, III 353b, 356a
atomism, III 353a
Augustinianism, III 357a
axiomatization, I 163a
Bacon, III 355b–356a, 358a
Being, III 359a
Bellarmine, III 356a
Berkeley, III 357b
Bible, III 354b, 355b
biology, III 354a, 355a, 360a, 360b
Buckle, III 360a
Burke, Edmund, III 358b
Cain (Bible), III 355b
calculus, III 361b
Cartesianism, III 356b, 357a, 359a
categories, III 357b 359a
causation, II 232b; III 352b, 357b, 360b
chance, II 225b, 226b, 228a, 229b 230b, 232a, 234a
change, III 353b, 354a
Christianity, III 354b–355b, 360b
city-community, III 353b
civilization, III 360b 361b
class, III 359a
classicism, III 355b
Collingwood, III 354b, 360b
communism, III 359b, 645b–646a
Comte, III 359b–360a, 643a
conception, III 352a, 352b, 353a, 357b, 358a, 361b
conceptualism, III 352a, 352b, 357b, 360b
Copernicus, III 356a
criticism, III 353a
culture, III 354b, 360b–361a
Darwin, III 360a, 360b
deduction, III 356a, 356b
Democritus, III 353a
Descartes, III 355b, 356a–357a, 357b, 362b
destiny, III 360b
determinism, II 237b, 238a, 239a, 240b; III 361a
dialectics, III 355b, 356b, 358b, 359a, 360b
Dilthey, III 354b, 360a, 360b, 361a
dogma, III 354b, 357a, 359b
economics, III 359b
empathy, III 351b, 359b–360b
empiricism, III 351b, 356b,

357b–358a, 359b, 360a
Engels, III 149a, 359a
epistemology, III 351b, 356a–357a
ethics, III 353a, 354a
Euclidean, I 163b, III 356a
evil, IV 381a
evolution, III 360a, 360b
explanation and, III 351b 352b
fate, II 225b, 226b, 228a, 229b 230b, 232a, 234a
Fichte, III 358b
fortune, II 225b, 226b, 228a, 229b 230b, 232a, 234a; IV 481b
free will, II 237b, 238a, 239a, 243a, 243b
freedom, II 237b; III 305a
Galileo, III 353b, 354a, 355b, 356a, 357a 358a
general will, II 277a
geometry, I 163b, III 353a 357a
Germany, III 358b
God, III 352a, 355a 357a; IV 484b
good, III 354a; IV 177b
Great Britain, III 357b
Greece (ancient), III 351b, 352b–354b, 356a, 361a
habit, III 357b
harmony, IV 39b
Hegel, III 351b, 355b, 357a, 358a–359b, 361a; IV 534a
Hegelianism, III 356b, 360b
Hempel, III 362a
Herodotus, III 353a, 353b
historians, III 353b, 354b, 356a, 356b, 357a, 358a, 359a, 360b, 361b
history, III 351b 362a, 645b
Hobbes, IV 177b
human nature, III 571b
Hume, II 238a; III 357b–358a, 359b
hypotheses, III 356a, 357a
idea, III 353b, 358a, 358b, 359a, 361a
idealism, III 359a
indeterminacy, II 587a
India, III 361a
induction, III 356b
Inquisition, III 356a
Jesus Christ, III 355a
Judaism, III 355a
jurists, III 358b
Kant, II 240b; III 351b, 357b 358b
knowledge, III 356b, 357a, 358b, 360a, 361b
language, III 357a
Last Judgment, III 355a

law, III 353a, 354b, 356a, 358b, 260a
Leibniz, II 239a; III 355a
Leucippus, III 353a; IV 51a
Lévi-Strauss, III 352b
linguistics, III 352a
Livy, III 356a
Locke, II 239a; III 357b
Lucretius, III 631a
Machiavelli, III 356a, 356b; IV 480b, 481b, 482a, 482b
Marx, III 351b, 355b, 358a–359b; IV 534b
Marxism, III 149a–149b, 356b–359b, 360a, 360b, 569a, 645b 646a
materialism, III 359a, 360a
mathematics, III 352b 358a, 359b, 360b, 361b
matter, III 188a, 188b 190a
mechanism, III 355b, 357a, 357b, 360b, 361b, 362a
metaphysics, III 352a 361b
Middle Ages, III 354b, 355a
military, III 354a
Mill, III 360a
Montesquieu, III 358a
morality, III 353a, 355a, 355b, 358a, 360a
Muhammadanism, III 355a
mysticism, III 355b
mythology, III 305a, 352b, 353a 355a, 357a
nationalism, III 355b, 357a, 358b, 360b
natural science, III 354a, 355a, 356a, 357a, 358a, 360a, 360b, 361b, 362a
naturalism, III 351b, 352a, 352b, 353a, 360a, 361b, 362a
Nature, III 353a, 353b, 355a, 356a, 357a 360b, 362a
Neo-Platonism, III 356a
Newton, III 358a, 360a
Nicholas of Cusa, III 361a
Nothing, III 359a
order, IV 482b
Orphism, III 361a
perennial philosophy, III 462a
phenomena, III 352a–356a, 356b, 357b, 360a
Plato, II 243a; III 188a, 188b, 351b, 352b, 353a–354b, 355a, 357a; IV 50a
Platonism III 354b–356a
poetry, III 354b
Polybius, III 354b–356b
Popper, III 358b, 361b
positivism, III 351b, 359b–360b

power, IV 482b
pragmatism, III 355b, 356a, 553a, 569a
prediction, III 362a
pre-Socratics, III 353a
progress, III 626b, 631a, 637b, 643a, 645b–646a
providence, III 355a, 355b, 357a, 358a
psychology, III 354a, 356b, 357b, 358a
Pythagoras, III 353a, 356a
Pythagoreans, III 353a; IV 39b
Ramism, IV 43a
rationalism, III 351b, 356a–357a; IV 50a, 50b, 51a
reality, III 352a, 352b, 353b, 356a, 356b, 358b
relativism, III 353a
religion, III 352a, 354a, 355a
Renaissance, II 355a, 355b–356a
revisionism, IV 269b
right, IV 177b
romanticism, III 358a, 358b
Rome (ancient), III 354b, 355a, 356a, 361a
Rousseau, II 277a; III 358b
Saint Augustine, III 355a, 355b, 356a, 361a; IV 381a
Saint Thomas Aquinas, II 238a
Satan, III 355b
Savigny, III 358b
Schelling, III 358b
science, III 351b, 353a–358b, 360a, 361b, 362a
secularism, III 356a
society, III 352a, 353a, 353b, 356a, 358b, 359b, 360a, 360b, 362a
sociology, III 353a, 353b, 355b, 356b, 358a, 358b, 359a, 359b, 362a
Socrates, III 353a, 353b
Spencer, III 643a
Spengler, III 360b–361a
Spinoza, IV 177b
spiritualism, III 360a
Stoicism, III 190a
supernatural, III 352b, 360a
syllogism, I 164a; III 356b
symbolism, III 361a
synthesis, III 358a–359b
Tacitus, III 356a
technology, III 355b
teleology, III 352b, 354a, 354b
Thales, III 352b
theodicy, III 355a; IV 381a
theology, III 351b, 354b–355b, 357a, 360a, 360b

Thomism, III 355b
Thucydides, III 353a, 353b, 356a
time, III 361a
Toynbee, III 360b–361b
tragic sense, IV 411b–413a
transcendentalism, III 358b
tyranny, III 354a
universe, III 353a, 354a, 356a, 360a, 361b; IV 39b
Upanishads, III 361a
Vico, III 355b, 356a, 357a, 357b, 358a, 360a–362a
virtù, IV 480b, 481b, 482a, 482b, 484b
Volksgeist, III 359a
Voltaire, III 358a
work, IV 534a, 534b
world, III 355b, 357a, 357b, 358a, 360b
Nechepso, King (c. 2nd century B.C.), astrology, I 119a
Necioni, Enrico, baroque in literature, I 189a–189b
Necker de Saussure, Albertine (1766–1841), classicism, I 451b
Neckham, Alexander (1157–1217), mythology, III 289a
Necromancy
  Faust (legend), III 247b
  prophecy, III 657b
Needham, John Turberville (1713–1781)
  Chain of Being, I 333b
  Man-Machine, III 144a
  nature, I 333b
  spontaneous generation, IV 310a–310b
Needham, Joseph
  progress, III 646b
  science in China, I 373b
Needler, Henry, Newton and, III 396a
Negativism
  Bruno, III 79a
  individualism, II 599a–599b
  irony, II 631b
  justice, II 659a
  literary paradox, III 79a
  Middle Ages, III 79a
Nelson, Lowry, Jr., baroque in literature, I 193b
Nemesis (myth)
  chance, II 229a
  fate, II 229a
Nemesius of Emesa (late 4th century A.D.), dignity, IV 137b, 138a
Neo-Aristotelianism
  free will, II 245a
  organicism, III 426b
  Platonism, III 514b
  poetics, III 529a–529b,

530b, 531a
Neo-classicism
  Coleridge, III 425b
  Great Britain, III 482b
  historiography, IV 147a
  Italy, III 484a
  Jonson, III 424b
  literature, I 455b
  mythology, III 295b
  naturalism in art, III 343a, 343b
  organicism, III 424b, 425b
  periodization in literary history, III 482b, 484a
  Pope, III 424b
  Renaissance, IV 147a
  romanticism, IV 189a, 191a, 193b, 194a, 195a, 195b, 196a, 199a, 208a
Neo-classicism in art, III 362a–371b
  Achilles (myth), III 368a
  Adam, R., III 365a, 365b, 366b, 369a
  Albani, III 366b
  Alfieri, III 370b
  Andromache (myth), III 368a, 368b
  antiquity, III 363a, 363b, 365a, 366a, 366b, 368b, 370b, 371a
  Apelles, III 365b
  archeology, III 363a, 363b, 364a, 364b, 367a, 368b
  architects, III 363a, 363b, 365a, 366a
  architecture, III 362b, 363a, 363b, 365a, 365b, 366b, 367b, 368b, 369b–370b
  Aristotle, III 365b
  artists, III 363a–371a
  Asia Minor, III 363a
  Bacchus (myth), III 365a
  Banks, III 370b
  baroque, III 363a, 365b, 366b, 368a, 369a, 370b
  Barry, III 364a
  Bartoli, III 363b
  Batoni, III 369a
  beauty, III 367b–368b
  Beger, III 363b
  Bernini, III 369b
  Bible, III 370b
  Blake, III 370b, 371a
  Boucher, III 369a
  Boullée, III 366a, 369b
  Canova, III 369a, 370a, 370b, 371a
  Caracalla, III 366a
  Ceres (myth), III 365a
  chinaware, III 366b
  classicism, III 363b–364b, 366a, 366b, 368b–371a
  controversy, III 365a–365b

Corneille, III 366a
costumes, III 368b
Cupid (myth), III 370b
Cyclades, III 363a
Dante, III 370a, 371a
David, III 366a, 367a, 370b, 371a
decorative art, III 362b, 366b, 369b, 370a
decorum, III 368b, 371a
defined, III 363a
designers, III 363a
Diderot, III 366a, 368b
Dryden, III 362b, 369b
Du Fresnoy, III 369b
dualism, III 371a
Egypt (ancient), III 363a, 364b, 365a, 368b
Elgin Marbles, III 363a–363b
eroticism, III 365b
Etruria, III 363a, 365a, 366b, 369a
Falconet, III 369a
Félibien, III 368a
Flaxman, III 369a, 370a, 370b, 371a
Fontaine, III 365b
Fra Angelico, III 370a
France, III 366a, 368b
French Revolution (1789), III 366a
frescoes, III 364b
furniture, III 364b–365a, 368b
Fuseli, III 371a
Germanicus Caesar, III 368b
Germany, III 369b
Ghiberti, III 370a
Giotto, III 369a, 370a
God, III 368b
Goethe, III 371a
Gothic, III 369b–371a
graphics, III 366b
Great Britain, III 363a, 364a–364b, 369b
Greece, III 363a, 363b, 364b
Greece (ancient), III 363a, 364b, 365a, 365b, 366b, 367a, 367b, 368b, 369b, 370b
Greuze, III 366a
Hadrian, III 364a, 365a–365b
Hamilton, Gavin, III 364a, 369a
Hamilton, William, III 366b
Hannibal, III 368b
Hector (myth), III 368a, 368b
Helen of Troy (myth), III 368b
historians, III 363a
history, III 366a, 367a, 369a, 371a

Homer, III 370b
Hope, Thomas, III 365a
idealism, III 368a–368b, 370a, 371a
illustrations, III 363b
imagination, III 371a
India (ancient), III 365b
Ingres, III 370b
Italy, III 364b, 366b, 368b, 369b
Jenkins, III 364a
jewelry, III 363b, 367a
Kauffmann, III 365b, 369a
knowledge, III 363a, 367b
Koch, III 370b
Le Roy, III 365a
Ledoux, III 366a, 369b
literature, III 362b, 363b, 367a, 370b, 371a
Major, III 365b
mannerism, III 369a
meaning of, III 362b–363a
Mengs, III 364b, 368b, 369a
Middle Ages, III 363b, 368b, 369a, 369b, 370a
Middle East, III 364b
Milton, III 371a
Montfaucon, III 363b, 367a
morality, III 365b, 366a, 368b
Mycenae, III 363a
Napoleon I, III 364b, 370b
Nature, III 368a
Nazarenes, III 369a–369b
Neo-Platonism, III 368b
Neo-Poussinism, III 368b
Netherlands, III 368a
Ossian, III 370b
painting, III 362b, 364a, 365b, 366b, 368a–370b
Palladio, III 365a
Percier, III 365b
Perugino, III 370b
Phidias, III 363b, 369a
Phigaleian Marbles, III 363b
philosophy, III 366a
Picart, III 363b
Piranesi, III 364b, 365a–365b
Plutarch, III 371a
Polygnotus, III 370b
Pope, III 362b
post-Raphaelism, III 369b
Poussin, III 362b, 365b, 368b, 369a
pre-Raphaelites, III 369a–369b
primitivism, III 369b, 370b
Psyche (myth), III 370b
Ramsay, III 365a
Raphael, III 365b, 368b
reason, III 371a
reliefs, III 363b, 366b

Renaissance, III 363b, 364b, 368a, 369a, 370a, 370b
Revett, III 363a, 365b
Reynolds, III 364b
Richardson, III 367b, 370a
Robespierre, III 366a
rococo, III 363a, 365b, 369a
romanticism, III 369a
Rome (ancient), III 363a, 364b, 365a, 366b, 369b, 370a
romanticism, III 369a
Rubens, III 368a
Rushton, III 362b
Schinkel, III 369b
Schliemann, III 363a
sculpture, III 342a, 362b, 363a, 363b, 364b, 365b, 366b, 368a, 369a, 370a, 370b
Shaftesbury, III 365b, 367b, 369b
Shakespeare, III 371a
Sicily, III 365b, 370b
simplicity, III 369a–370b
Soane, III 366a
Soufflot, III 369b
Stoicism, III 365b, 366a
Stosch, III 363b, 367b
Stuart, III 363a, 365b
styles, III 363b, 368b–369a, 369b, 371a
taste, III 370a
theory, III 366b, 367b, 368a
Turkey, III 365a
Turnbull, III 365b
Vien, III 364a, 369a
Voltaire, III 366a
Wedgewood, III 366b
West, III 368b, 369a
Winckelmann, III 365b, 366a, 366b–368a, 368b
writing, III 368b–369b
Zeuxis, III 368b
Neo-Darwinism
acquired characteristics, II 619a
environment, II 126a
evolution, II 126a
Mussolini, III 597a
primitivism, III 597a
Neo-Platonism, III 371b–378a
agapē, III 377a
agnosticism, III 373a
alchemy, I 28a; III 91a
alienation, I 34b
al-Kindi, III 377b
analogy, I 65a–65b, 67a
Antiochus of Ascalon, III 372a
Arabs, III 371b, 377b
Aristotle, III 372a, 374a, 377a
art, II 308b, 576b

asceticism, III 373a, 373b, 511a
astrology, I 119b, 123a, 125a
Atticus, III 372a, 372b
Augustinianism, IV 109a
Averroës, III 377b
Being, III 375a, 376a–377b
biology, I 235b
Boethius, III 377b, 378a
Botticelli, III 511b
Buddhism, I 255a
Byzantine Empire, III 377b
causation, I 273a–273b, 275b, 303b
Chain of Being, I 326a
Christianity, III 371b, 372b–373b, 375b–378a; IV 371a
Cicero, III 372a
Coleridge, III 507b
cosmic images, I 515a, 516a
cosmology, I 543a
Cudworth, III 506a
Dante, III 509b, 511a
deism, II 244b
deity, II 244b
demonology, I 667b–670a
described, III 371b–372a
design argument, I 674a
dignity, IV 137a, 139a–140b, 144a, 144b, 145b
Dodds, III 373a
dogma, III 372a, 373a
double truth, II 32a
dualism, III 373a, 375a
Egypt, III 373b, 377a
Emerson, III 430a
Enlightenment, II 97b
Epicureanism, III 373a
Erigena, III 378a
eros, III 377a
eschatology, II 155b
evil, II 163a–163b; III 373a
evolutionism, II 178a, 178b
Faust (legend), III 246b
Ficino, III 510b, 511a, 511b, 516a; IV 144b, 145b
Forms, III 372b, 374a–375b
free will, II 244a–245a
genius, II 308b
Gnosticism, III 376b
God, II 244b, 347a; III 372b–377a, 377b
Goethe, III 425a
good, IV 176a
Greece (ancient), III 371b, 372b–374a, 377b
Hadot, III 376b
happiness, II 378b
harmony, II 389a, 391b, 393a–393b; IV 39a, 39b, 41a
Hegel, II 414a, 454a
heresy, II 422b, 427a–427b

Hermes Trismegistus, III 510a
Hermeticism, II 431b
hierarchy, II 438b, 439a–439b, 442a
human nature, III 373a
humanism, II 519b; IV 131b, 132a–132b
Iamblichus, III 376a–377a
idea, II 545a–546a, 547a; III 373b, 375a
imagination, III 211a, 211b–212a, 212b, 221b
immortality, I 645a
impressionism, II 576b
Incarnation, III 509b
individualism, II 308b; III 516b
irony, II 629b
irrationalism, II 635a
Islam, II 643a, 643b, 644b, 646b, 651a; III 377b
Judaism, III 371b, 372b, 375b, 377b
Julian, III 373b
Julian the Chaldaean, III 376b
Julian the Theurgist, III 376b
Justinian, III 373b
knowledge, III 372b, 375a
life, III 375a, 376b, 377a
logic, III 377a
longevity, III 91a
macrocosm and microcosm, III 128b, 129a, 130b
Marius Victorinus, III 376b, 377b
materialism, II 454a
matter, III 189a, 190b, 191a
medieval sciences, II 196a, 203b
methodology, III 381b
Middle Ages, III 377b–378a
Middle Platonism, III 372a–373a, 374a, 374b, 377b
monism, III 376b
monotheism, III 372b
morality, III 373a, 374a, 376a
More, Henry, III 506b
motif, III 243a
music, II 389a, 391b, 393a–393b; III 269a
mysticism, III 375a, 377a
mythology, III 288a, 291a, 292a, 292b, 306a
natural law, III 14b
Nature, III 375b
necessity, III 356a
neo-classicism in art, III 368b
Neo-Pythagoreans, III

372b, 374a, 377a
Nicholas of Cusa, III 510b
Numenius, III 372b
One, III 372a, 372b, 374a–377a
organicism, III 425a
Orientalism, III 429b, 430a
Origen, III 377b
paganism, III 372b, 373b, 376a, 377b
painting, II 576b; III 511b; IV 466a
perennial philosophy, III 459a, 460b
perfectibility, III 465b, 466a, 467b
Peripateticism, III 374a
Philo Judaeus, III 372b
philosophy, II 549b, 643a, 643b, 644b, 646b, 651a; III 371b, 372a, 382b, 373a, 373b, 374a, 376a–378a
Pico della Mirandola, IV 145b
Plato, III 372a, 372b, 373a, 374a–377a
Platonism, III 371b, 372b, 374a, 375a–377b, 378a, 504a, 505a–506b, 508b–512a, 513a, 515b–517b, 519a–522a, 524b, 525a
pleasure, II 378b
Pletho, III 510a
Plotinus, III 128b, 372a, 372b, 373b–376a, 376b, 377a, 377b; IV 8b
Plutarch, III 372b, 505a
poetry, III 526b; IV 466a
Porphyry, III 373b, 374a, 374b, 376a, 376b–377b
post-Kantianism, IV 209a
post-Plotinian Platonism, III 374a
Proclus, III 376b
prolongevity, III 91a
Pseudo-Dionysius, III 377b–378a
psychology, IV 8b, 24a
Pythagoras, III 372a, 510a
Pythagoreans, III 372a, 376b; IV 32b, 39a, 39b, 41a
realism, III 374b, 375b, 376a, 376b
reincarnation, I 645a
religion, III 373a, 373b, 376a, 377a, 377b; IV 427a
Renaissance, II 427a; III 377b; IV 131b, 132a–132b, 137a, 139a–140b, 143b–144b, 145b, 442a, 442b
right, IV 176a
romanticism, IV 209a, 210a

Rome (ancient), III 371b, 372a, 373a, 373b, 377b
Saint Augustine, III 373b, 377b, 378a, 505b; IV 139a, 139b, 380b
Saint Basil, III 373b
Saint Jerome, III 373b
Saint Maximus, III 378a
Saint Paul, III 372b
salvation, IV 229a
Schelling, IV 210a
scholasticism, III 374b
Smith, John, III 506b
society, III 373b
soul, III 375a–377a
species, I 233a
Speusippus, III 372a
Stoicism, III 372a, 373a, 374a, 376b
Synesius, III 376b
Syria (ancient), III 373b
teleology, I 235b, 303b
temperance, IV 371a, 377a
theodicy, IV 380b, 381b, 383a
theology, III 372b, 376b, 377b, 378a
theurgy, III 376a, 377a
time, IV 392a
tragic sense, IV 415a
transcendentalism, III 372a, 372b, 374a, 374b, 375a, 376a; IV 24a
translations, III 377b
truth, III 509b
universal man, IV 442a, 442b
universe, IV 39a, 39b, 41a
virtù, IV 481b
Whichcote, III 506a
world, III 373a, 373b, 374a, 375b, 376a, 377a
World-Soul, III 372b, 375b
Xenocrates, III 372a
Zoroaster, III 510a
Neo-Pythagoreans
harmony, IV 39a, 39b, 42a
immortality, III 505a
Islam, II 639a, 643b, 646a
medieval science, II 196b–197a
music, III 269a
Neo-Platonism, III 372b, 374a, 377a
philosophy, II 639a, 643b, 646a
Platonism, III 505a
Plotinus, III 374a
Pythagoreans, IV 31b, 32a, 35b, 39a, 39b, 40a, 42a
reformation, IV 60b
soul, III 505a
temperance, IV 372b
Nepal, Buddhism, I 248b,

249a, 251a, 253b
Nephthys (myth)
Egypt (ancient), IV 100b
religion, IV 100b
Neptune (myth), III 298b
cosmology, I 552b
Nereus (myth), law, II 676a
Nergal (myth), II 335b
Nero, Claudius Caesar (37–68 A.D.)
art, II 299b
Christianity, I 416a
individualism, II 299b
literary paradox, III 80a
temperance (sōphrosynē), IV 375b
Nerval, Gérard de (1808–1855)
mythology, III 306b
romanticism, IV 196b
symbolism, IV 340b, 344a
Nessus (myth), law, II 681b
Nestorians, Islam, II 639a
Netherlands
art, II 532a–532b
balance of power, I 181b, 183a, 187a
baroque in literature, I 191b
capitalism, I 396a, 396b
China, I 356b–357a
classicism, I 453a
conservatism, I 484b
cosmic voyages, I 525a
criminology, I 71b
crisis in history, I 593a
deism, I 649a
despotism, II 7b–8a
education, I 388a
environment, II 124a
equality, II 142a
genius, II 295a–295b
impressionism, II 578a
intolerance, IV 117b, 120b
Jansenism, I 400a
law, III 35a
liberty, I 392b
literary criticism, I 597a
nationalism, III 326a, 327a, 330b
naturalism in art, III 341a, 344a, 345b
neo-classicism in art, III 368a
Pietism, I 403a
predestination, II 28a–28b, 30b
psychology, IV 15a
religion, IV 109a, 110b
revolution, IV 154a, 162a
Roman Catholic Church, IV 113a
symbolism, IV 340b, 344a
technology, IV 362a
Taiwan, I 357a

temperance, **IV** 371a, 374b

Nettesheim, Agrippa von, *see* Agrippa, Cornelius

Neubert, F., baroque in literature, **I** 190b

Neumann, Carl Gottfried (1832–1925), cosmology, **I** 556a

Neumann, Franz E. (1798–1895), progress, **III** 640b

Neumann, Franz L., totalitarianism, **IV** 409b

Neumann, John von
social welfare, **IV** 278b, 280a, 280b, 283a
utility and game theory, **II** 265a; **IV** 457a

Neurath, Otto, empiricism, **III** 545b, 548b

Neurone theory, **I** 116a–116b

Neurophysiology
empiricism, **III** 549b, 550a
Man-Machine, **III** 145b, 146a

Neuroses
art, **II** 575b
Freud, **IV** 96b
religion, **IV** 96b

Neville, Henry
deism, **I** 649b
Machiavellism, **III** 121a

New Left
anarchism, **I** 160a–161a
authority, **I** 160a–161a
fascism and, **I** 160a
U.S., **IV** 529b
women, **IV** 529b

New Models Union, **III** 672a

New York Peace Society, **III** 448b, 449a

New Zealand
common law, **II** 696a
philanthropy, **III** 490b
welfare state, **IV** 510b, 512a, 512b

Newbery, John (1713–1767), virtuoso, **IV** 489b

Newbigin, Marion, evolution, **II** 130b

Newcastle, Duchess of (1624?–1674)
atomism, **I** 135b, 136b
See also Cavendish, Margaret

Newcomen, Thomas (1663–1729), technology, **IV** 362a, 362b

Newman, Cardinal John Henry (1801–1890)
academic freedom, **I** 11a–11b
agnosticism, **I** 19b
Christianity, **I** 406b
democracy, **I** 663a

education, **II** 79a
heresy, **II** 429b
literature, **IV** 332b
modernism, **I** 419a, 419b, 420b, 425a
style, **IV** 332b
totalitarianism, **IV** 409b

Newton, Isaac (1642–1727), **III** 378b–399a
absolute space, **III** 183b; **IV** 302b
abstraction, **III** 398a
achievements of, **III** 194a–194b
Addison and, **III** 392a, 396b, 397b–398a, 398b
aesthetics, **III** 396b
Akenside and, **III** 395a, 396b, 398a
alchemy, **I** 33a; **III** 190b
Alembert and, **III** 378b
algebra, **III** 379b, 380b
ambiguity, **I** 58b
analogy, **III** 379b
analytic method, **III** 379a, 383b, 385b, 388b–389a, 390b
André and, **I** 198a
anthropomorphism, **I** 89a–89b
Aristotelianism, **III** 194b
Aristotle and, **III** 380a, 381a, 382a, 387b
arithmetic, **III** 379b, 389b
astronomy, **III** 194b
atomism, **I** 137a, 138a, 139a–140b, 518a; **II** 137b; **III** 194b, 195a
axiomatization, **I** 164b–165a, 166a, 166b
Bacon and, **I** 172b, 177a; **III** 383b–384a, 384b, 385b, 386b, 387a, 397a, 398b
Barrow and, **III** 380b, 387a–387b, 388a–388b
beauty, **III** 393a–394b, 398b
Bentley and, **I** 311a; **IV** 75b
Berkeley and, **III** 395b, 396a
Blackmore and, **III** 392a
Blake and, **II** 412b; **III** 398b; **IV** 199b, 201a
Born and, **IV** 302b
Boyle and, **III** 386b, 387a
Brooke and, **III** 395a
Browne and, **III** 395a
Burtt and, **III** 397b, 398a
Byron and, **IV** 201a
Cartesianism, **III** 385a, 397a, 397b
Cassirer and, **III** 382b
causation, **I** 281a, 294b,

299a–299b; **III** 193a, 382a, 382b, 387a
certainty, **I** 304b, 310b–311b
Chain of Being, **I** 330a
color, **I** 140a; **III** 386a–387a, 389a–390b, 392a–398b, 418a–419a
comets, **I** 674a
compositional method, **III** 379a
Condillac and, **III** 378b
continuism, **I** 503b
continuity, **I** 492b, 493a, 503b
Cosmic Fall, **I** 511b
cosmic images, **I** 515a, 517a, 517b–519b, 520b
cosmic voyages, **I** 528b, 529a, 533b
cosmology, **I** 548a–550b, 553b, 554b–558b, 560b
Cotes and, **III** 378b
Counter-Enlightenment, **II** 101a, 108a
deduction, **III** 386a, 388a, 390b, 392a
Derham and, **III** 393a
Desaguliers and, **III** 393a
Descartes and, **I** 518a; **III** 384a–384b, 385a, 387b, 388a, 395b, 398b
design argument, **I** 674a–674b, 675a, 676b
determinism, **II** 18b, 19a
diffraction, **III** 389b, 390a
disease, **III** 396a
dispersion, **III** 418b–419a
economic history, **II** 45a
Einstein and, **I** 557a
electricity, **III** 195a
empiricism, **III** 546b, 549a
Enlightenment, **II** 90a, 96b, 100a
entropy, **II** 117a
Euclid and, **III** 380b; **IV** 302b
evolutionism, **II** 176a–176b
experimental philosophy, **III** 378b–379b, 384a, 385b–386a, 386b, 387b–388b
experiments, **III** 379a, 382b–383b, 384a, 385b–387a, 389a–390b, 391b
First Law of Motion, **IV** 75a, 75b, 90a
force, **III** 194b, 195a
free will, **II** 246a
functions, **III** 184a
Galen and, **III** 381a–382a
Galileo and, **III** 382b–383b, 385b, 386a, 387a–388a
Gassendi and, **III** 387b; **IV** 393a

generalization, **III** 390b
geometry, **III** 195a, 380b, 382a, 389b
Gilbert and, **III** 387a
Glover and, **III** 393a
God, **I** 299b, 311a–311b, 401b, 519a, 674b; **II** 352a, 353a, 355a, 444a; **III** 194b, 195a; **IV** 75b, 177b
good, **IV** 177b
Goodfield and, **III** 195a
Gravesande and, **III** 385a, 385b
gravity, **I** 299a, 548a–548b, 549b–550a, 560b; **III** 194b, 195a, 379b, 389a, 393a; **IV** 290a, 302a
Grimaldi and, **III** 418b
Grosseteste and, **III** 382a–382b, 385b
Halley and, **III** 380b, 392b, 393a
harmony, **III** 395b
Harvey and, **III** 387a
Hegel and, **II** 412b
heresy, **II** 428a, 429a
hierarchy, **II** 443b, 444a
Hill and, **III** 394b
historiography, **I** 503b; **II** 18b, 19a, 488a
history, **II** 18b, 19a
Hobbes and, **III** 387b, 395b
Hooke and, **I** 311a; **III** 387a
Hughes and, **III** 392b
Hume and, **I** 312a, 312b, 313b
Huygens and, **III** 389a, 395a
hypotheses, **III** 184a, 379b, 383b, 385b
idea, **I** 112a, 113a, 113b; **II** 544a
impressionism, **II** 580b
indeterminacy, **II** 587a, 587b
induction, **III** 379b, 382a, 384a, 385b, 390b
inertia, **III** 194b, 195a; **IV** 89b–90a
infinity, **II** 605a, 608a, 611a; **IV** 75b
irrationalism, **II** 638a
Islam, **II** 647a, 647b
Jago and, **III** 395b
Kant and, **I** 277b, 314a–315a, 316a
Keats and, **III** 394b
Kepler and, **III** 194b
kinematics, **III** 383a
knowledge, **III** 378b
language, **II** 667b; **III** 390b
Laplace and, **III** 378b
Lavoisier and, **III** 386b

Law of Universal Gravitation, **IV** 75a, 77b, 78a, 83b
Leibniz and, **I** 299a–299b; **II** 444a; **IV** 75b, 394b
liberty, **I** 518a
light, **II** 580b; **III** 195a, 386a, 387a, 389b, 390a, 391b–398b, 418a; **IV** 77b, 78a, 80b, 86b–87a
literature, **III** 392a; **IV** 332a
Locke and, **III** 389a, 392a, 395b, 397a, 398b
logic, **III** 379b–385a, 546b, 549a
longevity, **III** 92a
Mach and, **IV** 302b
Maclaurin and, **III** 378b, 393a
magnetism, **III** 195a
Malebranche and, **III** 392a
Mallett and, **III** 393b
Man-Machine, **III** 141a
Martin and, **III** 393a
Marx and, **II** 451b; **III** 146b
materialism, **II** 451b
mathematics, **III** 173a, 174b, 178b–179a, 182b–184b, 194b, 379a–380b, 382a, 383a, 386a, 387b–390b, 393b, 395b–396a, 398b
matter, **I** 548a; **III** 190b, 192a, 192b, 193b–196a, 418b, 419a
Maxwell and, **IV** 393a
measurement, **III** 379b, 390a–390b; **IV** 403a–404a
mechanism, **III** 183b, 194b, 195a, 378b, 387b, 389a, 390b; **IV** 302a, 302b
metaphysical imagination, **III** 216b, 219a, 396b
methodology, **III** 378b–391a
military, **IV** 502a
Milton and, **III** 393b, 394b
mind, **III** 418a
Molyneux and, **III** 395b
motion, **I** 299a, 517b–518a, 548a–549a; **II** 202a; **III** 194b, 383a, 389a; **IV** 75a–76a, 77a–77b, 80b, 90a
mountains in literature, **III** 256b, 258b, 259a
mythology, **III** 301b
natural liberty, **II** 62a
Nature, **I** 281a, 311a–311b; **II** 444a; **III** 194b, 347b, 349b, 378b, 387a, 387b, 388b–389a, 392a
necessity, **III** 358a, 360a
Needler and, **III** 396a
Nifo and, **III** 382b, 385b
numbers, **III** 389b–390b

observation, **III** 379a, 379b, 381a, 382b, 385b, 389a, 389b–390b
Oldenburg and, **III** 392a
optics, **III** 195a, 378a, 389b, 390b, 391b–399a, 418a, 418b–419b; **IV** 78a
order, **II** 443b, 444a
Parker and, **III** 386b
parsimony, law of, **III** 379b
Pascal and, **III** 387a, 387b
Pemberton and, **III** 393a
perennial philosophy, **III** 461b
perfectibility, **III** 471b
philosophy, **III** 378b–379b, 381b–382a, 382b, 384a, 385b–386a, 386b, 387b–388b, 497a–398b, 419a
physics, **III** 382a, 387b–389a
planets, **I** 674a; **III** 194b
Plato and, **I** 676b; **III** 379b, 380a, 397a
Pluche and, **III** 393a
poetry, **III** 392a–398b; **IV** 473a
Pope and, **III** 392a–392b, 390b–397a, 398a; **IV** 199b
post-Kantianism, **IV** 209a
Power and, **III** 385b, 386b
pragmatism, **III** 557a
probability, **III** 383b
progress, **III** 640b
psychology, **IV** 12a, 19b
rainbows, **III** 394a–394b
Ramsay and, **III** 394b
Randall, J. H., **III** 382b
rationalism, **III** 381b–382a
reason, **II** 96b; **III** 379a–379b, 384a–384b; **IV** 199b
reflection, **III** 389b
refraction, **III** 389b, 390b, 418b, 419a
Régis and, **III** 384b–385a
relativity, **IV** 74a, 75a–78b, 80b–90a, 91b
revolution, **IV** 162b
Reynolds and, **III** 395a
right, **IV** 177b
Roemer and, **III** 395a
romanticism, **IV** 199b, 201a, 209a
rotation, **IV** 75b, 76a
rules, **III** 390b
Saint-Simon and, **IV** 199b
Savage and, **III** 393b
science, **III** 194b
scientific revolution, **I** 401a–402a
skepticism, **I** 304b, 310b, 311a–311b; **IV** 247b, 248a
Smart and, **III** 393b, 394b
socialism, **IV** 290a, 293b

Socrates and, **III** 379b
space, **I** 517b–518a, 520b, 554a–554b, 555a, 557a, 674b; **III** 194b–195a, 557a; **IV** 75b, 76a, 77a, 86a, 295b, 299b, 300a, 300b, 302a–302b, 303a
Sprat and, **III** 386b
stars, **I** 674b
Strong, E. W., **III** 390b
style, **IV** 332a
sun, **I** 674a
symmetry, **IV** 348b, 352b
synthetic method, **III** 379a
tangent concept, **III** 184a–184b
technology, **IV** 359b, 361b, 362a, 363b, 364a
theodicy, **IV** 382b
Thomson and, **III** 392b–396b, 398a–398b
time, **I** 492b, 493a, 549a, 554a–554b, 555a, 557a; **III** 194b–195a, 557a; **IV** 75b, 76a, 77a, 84b, 86a, 391a, 392b, 393a, 394b, 395a, 397a, 397b, 403a–404a
Torricelli and, **III** 387b
Toulmin and, **III** 195a
translational momentum, **III** 184a
truth, **III** 379a, 394b, 398b
uniformitarianism, **III** 379b
unity, **III** 390a
unity of science, **IV** 433a
universe, **III** 194b, 195a, 557a
Vigny and, **IV** 201a
virtuoso, **IV** 489a
void, **III** 195a
Voltaire and, **III** 378b
Wallis and, **III** 389a
war, **IV** 502a
Whitehead and, **III** 397b, 398a
Wren and, **III** 389a
Young and, **III** 395a, 395b, 398a
Zabarella and, **III** 382b, 385b
Neyman, J., probability, **III** 618b
Niccoli, Niccolò
  handwriting, **II** 518a
  humanism, **II** 518a, 522a
Nichol, John Pringle (1804–1859), cosmic images, **I** 523a
Nicholas of Autrecourt (fl. 1340)
  causation, **I** 275b, 277a
  Islam, **II** 649a
  matter, **III** 192b
  a medieval Hume, **II** 199b

Nicholas of Cusa (1401–1464)
  aesthetics, **II** 223a
  analogy, **I** 67a
  Bruno and, **II** 203b; **III** 193b, 510b
  chora, **IV** 300a–300b
  cosmological principle, **IV** 306a
  cosmology, **I** 545a; **IV** 306a
  dignity, **IV** 144b
  Ficino and, **III** 510b
  God, **II** 346–348b, 441a; **III** 510b
  good, **IV** 381b
  hierarchy, **II** 441a–441b, 443b
  ignorance, **III** 510b
  infinity, **II** 441a–441b, 608a
  literary paradox, **III** 78b, 79a
  matter, **III** 192a, 192b, 193b
  Middle Ages, **I** 67a; **II** 203b
  motion, **III** 510b
  Nature, **III** 351a
  necessity, **III** 361a
  Neo-Platonism, **III** 510b
  perennial philosophy, **III** 459b, 460b
  Platonism, **III** 510b
  plurality, **III** 510b
  Proclus and, **II** 441a
  Pseudo-Dionysius and, **II** 441a
  Saint Augustine and, **II** 441a
  social contract, **IV** 253b
  space, **IV** 295b, 300a–300b, 306a
  symmetry, **IV** 352a
  theodicy, **IV** 381b
  topos, **IV** 300a–300b
  universe, **II** 441a–441b; **III** 510b
  Utopia, **IV** 461a
  wisdom, **III** 510b
  wisdom of the fool, **IV** 517b, 518b, 519a
Nicholas of Lyra (1270?–?1340)
  eschatology, **II** 156b
  law, **II** 688a
Nicholas II, Czar (1868–1918)
  China, **I** 370b
  international peace, **III** 453b
  militarism, **IV** 504b
  periodization in literary history, **III** 483a
Nicholas V, Pope (1397?–1455)
  city, **I** 430b
  dignity, **IV** 143a
  free will, **II** 137b

Nicholson, Ben, aesthetics, **II** 222b

Nicholson, Francis (Governor) (1655–1728), slavery, **II** 7b

Nicias (4th century B.C.), historiography, **II** 502b, 510b

Nicodemus (Bible), mythology, **III** 282a

Nicolas of Oresme, humanism, **IV** 134a

Nicole, Pierre (1625?–1695), perfectibility, **III** 469a

probability, **III** 606b

Nicoletti, Paolo, *see* Paul of Venice

Nicolson, Mayorie, H., cosmic images, **I** 413b, 515b

Nicomachus (2nd century A.D.)

catharsis, **I** 269a

Pythagoreans, **IV** 35b

Niebuhr, Barthold Georg (1776–1831)

God, **II** 360a–360b

historiography, **II** 491b

revolution, **IV** 158b

Niebuhr, Reinhold (1892–1971)

anxiety, **III** 467a

historicism, **II** 459a, 459b

causation, **I** 280a

Enlightenment, **II** 93b

God, **II** 360a–360b

history, **I** 280a; **II** 364b; **III** 365b

irony, **II** 634a, 634b

perfectibility, **III** 467a

philanthropy, **III** 492b

politics, **II** 634a

predestination, **II** 29a, 30b

pride, **III** 467a

progress, **III** 635b

sin, **II** 29a; **III** 467a

Niepce, Joseph Nicéphore (1765–1833)

impressionism, **II** 572a

photography, **II** 572a

Nietzsche, Friedrich Wilhelm (1844–1900)

anarchy, **IV** 485a

anti-industrialism, **III** 676a

art, **II** 307b

baroque in literature, **I** 189a

beauty, **I** 200b

Burckhardt and, **IV** 485a

catharsis, **I** 268a

Christianity, **II** 213a

conformity, **I** 468a

conservatism, **I** 483a

Counter-Enlightenment, **II** 109b

creativity in art, **I** 588b

crisis in history, **I** 591a

criticism, **I** 588b

cycles, **I** 622a, 624a–624b, 626b

Darwin and, **II** 185b

death, **I** 637b

empathy, **II** 88b

Enlightenment, **II** 99a

entropy, **II** 117b

eschatology, **II** 159a, 160a, 160b

evil, **IV** 180b

evolution, **III** 474a

evolutionism, **II** 185b–186a

existentialism, **II** 192b

faith, hope, and charity, **II** 213a

Faust (legend), **III** 251a

genius, **II** 307b, 318b, 325a–325b

God, **II** 192b, 213a, 356a

good, **IV** 180b

Hermeticism, **II** 433a, 434a

humanism, **IV** 180b

idea, **II** 548b

individualism, **II** 307b, 603a; **IV** 485a

injustice, **IV** 180b

irony, **II** 633a

irrationalism, **II** 635a, 636b, 637b, 638b

Machiavelli and, **IV** 484b–485b

Machiavellism, **III** 125a

metaphysical imagination, **III** 216a

military, **IV** 503a

modernism, **I** 420a

morality, **IV** 180b, 484b

music, **II** 318b, 325a–325b

Nottebohm and, **II** 325b

perfectibility, **III** 474a

Platonism, **II** 520b

power, will to, **IV** 180b, 484b, 485a

protest movements, III 676a

right, **IV** 180b

romanticism, **IV** 204b, 209b, 210b

Rousseau and, **IV** 209b

Schiller and, **I** 106a

self-realization, **IV** 485a

sin, **IV** 180b

skepticism, **IV** 250a, 250b

Spengler and, **III** 251a

State, **IV** 485a

structuralism, **IV** 329a

superman, **III** 474a

symbolism, **IV** 342b, 345a

time, **IV** 395b

tragedy, **I** 626b

tragic sense, **IV** 414a, 415a

transcendentalism, **III** 520b

value, **IV** 250a

virtù, **IV** 484b–485b

war, **IV** 503a

Nieuhoff, John, **I** 80b, 356b

Nifo, Agostino (1473?–?1538)

atomism, **I** 130b, 131a

causation, **III** 382b

methodology and, **III** 382b, 385b

Newton and, **III** 382b, 385b

Nigel, Bishop of Ely (d. 1169), nationalism, **III** 319b

Nigel Wireker (fl. 1190), wisdom of the fool, **IV** 518a

Nihilism

eschatology, **II** 160b

Faust (legend), **III** 251b, 252a

irony, **II** 627a, 627b, 630a, 632b, 633a–633b

Islam, **II** 651b

metaphysical imagination, **III** 209b

pragmatism, **III** 561b

romanticism, **IV** 196a

Sartre, **III** 209b

Wright, **III** 561b

Nikon, Patriarch of Moscow (1605–1681), Christianity, **I** 411a

Nimrod (Bible)

despotism, **II** 4b

mythology, **III** 277b, 281a, 294a

Nirvāna, **II** 344a

Buddhism, **IV** 232b–233a

health, **II** 397a

salvation, **IV** 232b–233a

Nisard, Désiré (1806–1888), classicism, **I** 452a

literary criticism, **I** 599a–599b

romanticism, **IV** 196b

Nisiely, Udeno, literary criticism, **I** 597a

Noah (Bible)

mountains in literature, **III** 255a, 257b

mythology, **III** 275a, 277a, 277b, 279b, 280a, 280b, 281b, 283a, 284a

primitivism, **III** 582b, 593a

rainbows, **III** 394b

religion, **IV** 106a

social contract, **IV** 252a

Nobility

equality, **II** 138b, 144a

human nature, **III** 572a

Noble, John W. (1831–1912), conservation, **I** 475b

Noble, William, music, **III** 263a

Noble Savage

Christianity, **III** 591b–592b

Defoe, **III** 601b–602a

Great Britain, **III** 601a

Greece (ancient), **III** 591a–591b

Middle Ages, **III** 592a–592b

peasantry, **III** 594b, 595b

Plato, **III** 629a–629b

primitivism, **III** 591a–592b, 594b, 596b, 601a, 602a, 604a

progress, **III** 627a, 629a–629b

Rome (ancient), **III** 591b

skepticism, **IV** 241b

Noël, Francisco, China, **I** 356b

Noël, F. J. M., literature, **III** 83b

Nomads

Germany, **III** 651b

language, **II** 660b

mythology, **III** 279a, 281a

private property, **III** 651a, 651b

Nominalism

abstraction, **I** 4a, 4b

art, **II** 576b

evolutionism, **II** 176b–177a

health, **II** 406b

heresy, **II** 426b

humanism, **II** 520b

idea, **II** 546a–546b, 547a

impressionism, **II** 576b

James, **III** 552b

language, **II** 667a

medieval science, **II** 199a–199b, 201b, 204a, 204b

natural law, **III** 19a

Peirce, **III** 563b

perennial philosophy, **III** 462a

pragmatism, **III** 552b, 559a, 563b

realism in literature, **IV** 51b

Stoics, **I** 2b

William of Ockham, **III** 19a

Nomos

Babylonia, **II** 683b

Greece (ancient), **II** 681b–685a; **III** 1a

law, **II** 681b–685a; **III** 1a

Persia (ancient), **II** 683b

right and good, **IV** 174b

Sophists, **III** 1a

Non finito, **II** 298b–299a

art, **II** 297b, 298b–299a

Egypt (ancient), **II** 298b

genius, **II** 297b, 298b–299a

Leonardo da Vinci, **II** 298b–299a

Michelangelo, **II** 298b–299a

Middle Ages, II 298b
Rodin, II 299a
Non-Being
  atomism, IV 299a
  Being, IV 299a
  Democritus, IV 299a, 299b
  kenon, IV 299a
  Leucippus, IV 299a, 299b
  matter, III 188a, 188b, 190b
  Parmenides, IV 298b–299a
  Plato, III 188a, 188b
  space, IV 301a, 304b
  time, IV 390a
  void, IV 299a
Non-Euclidean geometries
  axiomatization, I 166a
  cosmology, I 555a–555b,
    559a–559b, 563a
  mathematics, III 175b,
    176b, 177a
Nonproliferation pact
  international peace, III 456a
  U.S.S.R., III 456a
  U.S., III 456a
Nordau, Max (1849–1923),
  symbolism, IV 341a, 343b
Norden, John, historiography,
  IV 151a
Nordenfalk, C., iconography,
  II 538b
Normal distribution function,
  III 612b
Normative science, I 466a
Norms
  behaviorism, II 677b–678b
  Ehrlich, Eugen, III 3b–4a
  existentialism, III 160a
  good, IV 182b
  Greece (ancient), II 677a–
    678a, 679a, 679b, 682a–
    683b, 685a
  Grotius, III 19b–20a
  Kelsen, III 2a, 2b
  law, II 677a–678a, 679a,
    679b, 682a–683b, 685a; III
    2a, 2b, 3b–4a, 23a–24b
  Machiavelli, III 116a–125a
  Machiavellism, III 116a–
    125a
  Marxism, III 151b, 160a
  natural law, III 14a, 14b,
    16a, 17a, 19b–20a, 23a,
    23b, 24b
  pragmatism, III 552a
  reformation, IV 62a
  right, IV 182b
  society, II 677b–678b
  Stoicism, III 17a
  Volksgeist, IV 491b
North, Dudley (1641–1691),
  economic history, II 45b
North, Roger (1653–1734),
  music, II 318b, 322a
North Atlantic Treaty Or-

ganization, international
  peace, III 456b
Northcote, James (1746–
  1831)
  art, II 303b, 309b
  genius, II 309b
  individualism, II 303b
Northrop, Filmer S. C.
  Buddhism, I 256b
  Islam, II 647b
Northumbria, missionaries, I
  380b
Norton, Thomas, alchemy, I
  31a
Norway
  civil disobedience, I 438a
  mythology, III 279a, 282b
  uniformitarianism, IV 421a
Nottebohm, Martin Gustav
  (1817–1882)
  musical genius, II 325b
  Nietzsche and, II 325b
Nottingham, Lord Chancellor,
  equity, II 152b, 153a–153b
Nous
  Anaxagoras, IV 3a
  Aristotle, IV 5a
  Parmenides, IV 3a
  Plato, IV 3b, 32b, 34a, 37a
  psychology, IV 1a, 3a, 3b
  Pythagoreans, IV 32b, 34a,
    37a
  Xenocrates, IV 37a
Novák, Arne, baroque in
  literature, I 193a
Novalis (1772–1801)
  Christianity, IV 207a
  Counter-Enlightenment, II
    109b
  disease, II 403b
  irrationalism, II 638a, 638b
  love, III 103b
  Middle Ages, IV 203b
  mythology, III 305a, 305b,
    306a
  Pietism, IV 206b
  romanticism, IV 188a–
    188b, 189a, 196b, 201b,
    203b, 205b, 206a, 207a,
    208a, 209b
  Schelling and, IV 206b
  Schlegels and, IV 208a
  State, IV 206a, 206b
  symbolism, IV 338a, 344b,
    345a
  Weltschmerz, IV 209b
Novel, II 172b
  Faust (legend), III 250a
  Gothic, II 370b
  Great Britain, III 600b
  literature, III 242b
  Machiavelli, III 118a–119a
  Machiavellism, III 118a–
    119a

motif, III 242b
  poetics, III 525b, 531b
  realism in literature, IV 51b,
    52a, 52b, 53a, 54a, 54b
  ut pictura poesis, IV 466a,
    472a, 473b, 474b, 475a
Novelists, painting, IV 469a
  romanticism, IV 208b
Novella
  humanism, II 517a
  mythology, III 275a, 275b
Novicow, Jacques, inter-
  national peace, III 453b
Nowell-Smith, P. H., determinism, II 241b
Noyes, John Humphrey
  (1811–1886), perfectibility,
  III 468b
Nuclear power
  Einstein, III 446b
  eschatology, II 160a
  evil and, II 169a
  Khrushchev, III 157a
  Marxism, III 155a, 157a
  military, IV 501a
  peace, III 446b
  progress, III 632a, 648a
  relativity, IV 91a
  Russell, III 446b
  Stalin, III 157a
  U.S.S.R., III 155a, 157a,
    455b
  U.S., III 455b
  war, III 456b; IV 501a
Nuclear weapons
  balance of power, I 187b
  international peace, III
    449b, 455a, 455b, 456a
  perfectibility, III 475a
  war, III 449b, 455a, 455b
Nuffield Foundation, philanthropy, III 492a
Numa Pompilius (715–673
  B.C.), temperance, IV 377a
Numbers, III 399a–407a
  abstraction, III 403b, 406a,
    406b
  addition, III 404b, 405b
  Africa, III 399b
  Alexandrian system, III
    401b–402a
  algebra, III 403a, 404b,
    405a, 406a
  alphabet, III 401b, 402a
  Arabs, III 399b, 402a, 403a
  Argand, III 405b
  Aristotelianism, III 406a
  Aristotle, IV 33a, 34a, 36a,
    36b
  astronomy, III 403a
  auxiliary sets, III 400b, 402a,
    404a
  base, III 401b–403a
  Bede, III 399b

body, III 404a
  calculus, III 406a, 406b
  Cantor, III 405b, 406a
  cardinal, I 8b–9a; II 611b
  Ceylon, III 400b
  character, III 402a
  China, III 402b
  cipher, III 403a
  code system, III 402a, 402b
  coefficients, III 404b
  collective unit, III 401a,
    401b, 402a, 402b
  commerce, III 399b, 400a
  communications, III 400a
  complex, II 613a, 613b;
    III 405a–405b
  computers, III 400a, 506b
  consonance, III 269a
  continuum, III 406a
  cosmology, I 537b–538a;
    III 269a
  counting, III 400b–401b,
    402a, 403b, 405b
  culture, III 399a, 404a,
    406a, 406b
  decimal system, III 402b,
    404a
  denumerable, III 406a
  Descartes, III 403a, 403b,
    406a
  differential equations, III
    406b
  division, III 403a, 404b,
    405b
  Egypt, III 401a
  equations, III 404b, 405a
  finger, III 399b, 400a, 403b,
    404a, 406b
  finite, II 612a
  fractions, III 403a, 404b,
    405a, 406a
  France, III 404a
  Galileo, III 405b, 406a
  Gauss, III 405b
  geometry, III 406a, 406b
  gestures, III 399b, 400a,
    406b
  Girard, III 403a
  Greece (ancient), III 401b,
    403a, 403b
  Hamilton, III 405b
  harmony, III 261a, 269a;
    IV 38a–39b, 42a
  hierarchy, II 438a
  hieroglyphics, III 401a,
    401b
  Hindu-Arabic system, III
    402a, 403a
  Hinduism, III 402a, 403a
  history, III 402b–404b
  humanism, II 521a
  idea, II 546a; III 403b,
    406b; IV 36b
  imaginary, III 405a

Indians (American), III 403b, 404a

infinite set, III 405b, 406a

infinity, II 606b–612a, 613a–613b; III 406a

integers, III 403b–406a

irrational, III 405a, 406a

irrationalism, II 635b

labels, III 402b

language, III 399b, 400a, 403a, 403b, 404b

Law of Large Numbers, III 607a–609a

linear equation, III 404b

logic, III 403b, 406a, 406b

mathematics, III 171a, 174a–175b, 177a, 400b, 403b, 404b, 405a, 406a, 406b

measurement, III 401b; IV 399b–400a, 400b

mechanism, III 406a–406b

methodology, III 389b–390b

Middle Ages, III 399b, 403b

multiplication, III 404b, 405b

music, III 260b–263b, 269a, 270b, 271a

mysticism, III 260b, 262a

names, III 399b, 400a, 400b, 402a, 403b, 404a

natural, II 611b; III 389b

natural science, III 406b

Nature, III 406a

negative, III 404b, 405a

Newton, III 389b–390b

objects, III 400b, 401a, 402a, 403b

one-to-one correspondence, III 400b, 402a, 405b, 406a

order, II 438a; III 403b

ordinal, I 9a; II 611b, 612a

Pacioli, III 400a

Papua, III 404a–404b

Philolaus, III 403a

philosophy, III 403a, 406a

physics, III 406b

placeholder, III 402b, 403a

planets, III 269a

Plato, IV 33b, 34b, 37b, 39a–39b

position, III 401a–402b

positional system, III 402b

positive, II 610a; III 404b

power, III 405b, 406a

pragmatism, III 557b, 566a

primitivism, III 400a, 400b, 403b, 406a, 406b

probability, III 406a

Pythagoras, III 269a; IV 31a, 32a, 37a, 39a, 46b–47a, 399b

Pythagoreans, III 399a, 403a, 405a; IV 31a, 32a, 33a–42a

quadratic equation, III 405a

quantity, III 403b

ratio, III 405a

rational, III 405a, 406a

rationalism, IV 46b–47a

real, II 610a; III 403a, 405a, 405b, 406a

recording, III 400a

reformation, IV 63a

Renaissance, III 406a

repetition, III 401b

Roman, III 401b–402a

roots, III 404b, 405a

Saint Augustine, IV 63a

scholasticism, III 403b

science, III 399b, 406a, 406b

second degree equations, III 405a

sequence, III 399b

skepticism, IV 242a

sociology, III 406b

sound, III 269a

Speusippus, IV 35a–36b

square root, III 405a

squares, III 405b

statistics, III 406a

strings, III 269a

subtraction, III 404b, 405b

Sumer-Babylonia, III 173a

symbolism, II 527b, 546a

symbols, III 399b, 400b, 401a, 402a, 402b, 406b

system, III 399a, 399b, 400b–402b, 406b

tallying, III 401a–402a

technology, III 406a, 406b

teleology, III 406a

time, III 401b; IV 390b, 391a, 399b–400a, 400b

transfinite, II 611a, 612a; III 406a

unity, III 403a, 403b

value, III 401a, 402b

virtue, IV 372a–372b

Wessel, III 405b

words, III 399b, 400a, 402a, 403a–404b, 406b

world, III 400a

writing, III 400b, 406b

Xenocrates, IV 36b

zero, III 402b–403b, 404b

Numenius (late 2nd century A.D.)

idea, II 545a

Neo-Platonism, III 372b

Platonism, III 505a

Pythagorean cosmos, IV 40b

Numero senario, III 262a, 262b

Numinous, Otto, IV 97a–97b

Nureddin (1118?–1174), historiography, II 474a

Nuremberg Trials, III 452a

Nygren, Anders, God, II 360a–360b

O

Oakeshott, Michael, Volksgeist, IV 496a

Oastler, Richard (1789–1861), welfare state, IV 509a–509b, 510a, 511a

Obedience

good, IV 173b, 174a

heresy, II 418b, 421a

Hobbes, IV 256b

justice, II 659a

law, III 1b, 2b

Middle Ages, IV 253a

perennial philosophy, III 459b, 460b–461a

perfectibility, III 467a, 468b

reformation, IV 65a

right, IV 173b, 174a

romanticism, IV 206a

Saint Francis of Assisi, IV 65a

social contract, IV 253a, 254a, 255a–257a, 262a

socialism, IV 286b

State, IV 316b, 317b

temperance, IV 367a, 368b, 369a, 373a

theodicy, IV 380b

tragic sense, IV 413a, 413b

utilitarianism, IV 449a

Obligation

good, IV 173b, 174a, 179b, 181b, 182a, 183a, 184b

Greece (ancient), II 675a, 680b, 681b, 682b, 684a

Hobbes, III 20b

Judaism, III 487b

Kames, III 234b

Kant, IV 179b

law, II 675a, 680b, 681b, 682b, 684a; III 1a, 3a, 4a, 5a, 8a, 28b, 29a

moral sense, III 234b

natural law, III 17a, 17b, 20b, 22b, 25a

philanthropy, III 487b

progress, III 645a

right, IV 173b, 174a, 179b, 181b, 182a, 183a, 184b

Saint Augustine, III 17b

society, III 3a, 22b

State, IV 313a, 316a–316b, 317a, 318a

value, IV 183a

virtue, IV 179b

welfare state, IV 511a

Obscenity, freedom of speech, II 252a

Observation

fate, II 226a

Fermat, III 606a

Galen, III 381a

Galileo, III 382b, 385b

indeterminacy, II 587b

Kant, III 555b

mechanical experiments, II 197a

methodology, employed by Newton, III 379a, 379b, 381a, 382b, 385b, 389a, 389b–390b

optics, III 415a, 416a–417a

Pascal, III 606a

Peirce, III 559a

Posidonius, III 630b, 631a

pragmatism, III 553a, 555a, 555b, 559a

probability, III 605b, 606a, 606b, 607b, 608b, 611a, 614a–616b, 619a

progress, III 630b, 631a, 634a

Ramism, IV 45a

rationalism, IV 47a, 48a

rhetoric, IV 168a

skepticism, IV 238b

Occasionalism

atomism and, I 496a

Averroës, I 496a

causation, I 274a, 276a, 277a, 296b, 302b

Cordemoy, I 276a

Descartes, I 276a, 296b

discontinuity and, I 496a

LaForge, I 276a

Maimonides, I 496a

Malebranche, I 276a; III 193a

matter, III 193a

Saint Thomas Aquinas, I 496a

teleology, I 302b

Occult

Islam, II 640b, 644a, 646a, 646b

prophecy, III 657b–659b

science, II 640b, 644a, 646a, 646b

symbolism, IV 345a

Oceanus (myth), temperance, IV 367a

Ockeghem, Jean d' (1430?–1495), musical genius, II 316a

Ockham, William of (1300?–?1349)

abstraction, I 6a

aesthetics, II 218a

allegory, I 46b

Aristotle and, III 19a

causation, I 275a–275b

classification, I 330b

common nature, I 4a, 6a–6b

despotism, II 3a–3b

God, I 275a–275b, 384b; III 19b

heresy, II 418a, 426a, 426b

individualism, II 599a; III 19a–19b

justice, III 19b

law, III 19a–19b

matter, III 191b

mechanical science, II 197a, 199a–199b

mind, III 19a

motion, II 199b

nationalism, III 323b

natural law, III 19a–19b

nominalism, III 19a

order, III 19b

papacy, II 3a–3b, 4a

poverty, IV 65b

Pythagoreans, IV 35b

reason, III 19b

reformation, IV 65b

scholasticism, I 384b

theodicy, IV 381a

time, IV 392a

wealth, IV 65b

Octaves, III 260b–261a, 261b, 262a, 262b, 263a

Odes, humanism, II 517b

Odin (myth), III 304a

  Nazis, III 597b

  primitivism, III 597b

Odo of Cluny, rules in music, II 314b

Odoric of Pordenone (1286–1331), China, I 354a

Odysseus (myth), III 308a

  cynicism, I 628a, 633a, 633b

  human nature, III 571b, 572b

  law, II 676b, 678a, 681a

  temperance, IV 365b

Oedipus (myth), III 275b

  disease, II 397b

  human nature, III 572a

  motif, III 240b

  mythology, III 240b

  sin, IV 228a

  Sophocles, IV 367a

  temperance, IV 367a

Oedipus complex

  Freud, III 312b; IV 96b

  love, III 105a

  mythology, III 312b

  religion, IV 96b

Oetinger, Friedrich Christoph

(1702–1782), eschatology, II 157a, 159b

Ogden, Charles Kay (1889–1957), beauty, I 208a, 209a

Oglethorpe, James Edward (1696–1785), philanthropy, III 490b

Ohrmazd (God of Light), II 39a–40a, 339a, 339b

  See also Ahura Mazdā

Oken, Lorenz (1779–1851), evolutionism, II 178b

  spontaneous generation, IV 311b

Olbers, Heinrich W. (1758–1840)

  space, I 555b–556a; IV 303a

  time, I 555b–556a

Olbers paradox, I 555b–556a; IV 303b

Olbrechts-Tyteca, L., law, III 5b–6a

Oldenberg, Hermann (1854–1920), Orientalism, III 434b, 436a

Oldenburg, Henry, Newton and, III 392a

Olds, James, pleasure, II 384a

Olearius, Johannes, casuistry, I 262b

Oligarchy

  Aristotle, I 625b, 654b; IV 175b

  democracy, I 653a–654b, 656b, 657b, 664b, 665a

  freedom of speech, II 260b

  good, IV 175a, 175b

  Greece (ancient), II 683a

  Herodotus, I 653a

  Hobbes, I 656b

  humanism, II 522a, 522b

  law, II 683a

  Lenin, II 561a

  Locke, I 657b

  Plato, I 653a; II 22a; IV 175a

  Polybius, I 625b–626a

  revolution, IV 152b

  temperance, IV 367b, 368a

  totalitarianism, IV 408a

  U.S.S.R., II 560b, 561a, 562b

Oliphant, Margaret (1828–1897), romanticism, IV 193a

Olivecrona, Karl, law, III 2b

Oliveira Lima, Manoel de Floresta and, III 539b

  positivism, III 539b

Olivetan, Pierre (d. 1538), Calvin and, IV 67a

  Reformation, IV 67a

Olivi, Peter John, prophecy,

III 668b

Olivier, Ferdinand, naturalism in art, III 341a

Olmsted, Frederick Law (1822–1903), conservation, I 474b

Olschki, Leonardo, technology, IV 360b

Olsen, Regina, existentialism, II 190a, 192a

Olympic Games, II 681a

Omar Khayyam (d. about 1123)

  death, I 642b

  immortality, I 642b

Omens

  disease, II 396a

  Greece (ancient), III 347a

  Nature, III 347a

  prophecy, III 659b

  Rome (ancient), III 347a

Omnipotence

  God, II 336b, 337a, 337b, 340a, 345a, 350a, 356a–356b, 361a

  perfectibility, III 464a, 469b

  religion, IV 93a

Onanism, health, II 403a

One

  Greece (ancient), II 614b, 615a

  infinity, II 614b, 615a

  irrationalism, II 635b

  Islam, II 643b, 644b

  macrocosm and microcosm, III 128b

  Neo-Platonism, III 372a, 372b, 374a, 374b–375a, 376b, 377a

  organicism, III 422a

  Plotinus, III 128b, 374b–375a; IV 8b

  Porphyry, III 376b

  psychology, IV 8b

  time, IV 390b, 393b, 394a

Oneida community, perfectibility, III 468b

O'Neill, Eugene (1888–1953), expressionism, II 208b

  symbolism, IV 341a, 344b

Onesicritus

  asceticism, I 631b–632a

  cynicism, I 628a, 628b, 631b–632a

  progress, III 630a

Onofri, Arturo, symbolism, IV 342a

Ontogeny

  evolutionism, II 178a

  human nature, III 573b–574a

  pangenesis, II 623b

  recapitulation, IV 56a, 57a, 57b, 58a

Ontology

  Bruno, III 79a

  disease, II 399b–400a, 404a, 404b

  Engels, II 450a, 454b, 455a

  God, I 671b; II 356a, 357a, 361a, 363a

  infinity, II 615a

  Marxism, III 153a, 167b

  materialism, II 450a, 454b, 455a

  matter, III 187b, 188b, 189a–189b

  natural law, III 18a

  Platonism, III 506b, 513b, 517a, 523a

  pragmatism, III 557b, 561b, 563b

  romanticism, IV 200a

  space, IV 299a, 305a

  structuralism, IV 326b

  symmetry, IV 348b, 351a

  time, IV 395b

  unity of science, IV 432a

Op art, repudiation of beauty, I 208a

Oparin, A. I., evolutionism, II 187a

Open future, IV 390b

Open world, IV 398a

Opera, II 323b, 324a–325a

  Gothic, II 368b

  mythology, III 293b, 306b

  ut pictura poesis, IV 470a, 472b, 475a

Operationalism, I 226a–226b; III 550b

Opinion

  Greece (ancient), II 565b, 566b

  impiety, II 565b, 566b

  mythology, III 274a

  skepticism, IV 238b

Opitz, Martin (1597–1639), poetics, III 529b

  style, IV 331b

Oppenheimer, J. Robert (1904–1967), ambiguity, I 59a

Opportunism

  Bernstein, III 164a

  Marxism, III 164a, 166a

  revisionism, IV 270b

Oppression

  natural rights, III 25b

  revolution, IV 160b

  women, IV 526a

Optics, III 391b–399a, 407a–421a

  abstraction, III 398a

  Addison, III 392a, 396b, 397b–398a, 398b

  aesthetics, III 396b

  after-images, III 409a

Alhazen, III 409a–410a
Al-Kindī, III 409a
Amici, III 415b
Apuleius, III 407a–407b
Arabs, III 409a–410b
Archytas of Tarentum, III 407a–407b
Aristotelianism, III 418a
art, III 408b–409a
astrology, III 414b
astronomy, III 414b, 416a
atomism, III 407a, 418a
as an autonomous science, III 419b–420a
Bacon, Francis, III 397a, 398b
Bacon, Roger, III 410a
Bartolinus, III 419a
beauty, III 393a–394b, 398b
Berkeley, III 395b, 396a
Blackmore, III 392a
calculus, III 420a
Cartesianism, III 397a, 397b
color, III 392a–398b, 407b, 410b, 416a, 417b–420b
colorimetry, III 418a
cosmology, I 554b, 556b, 557a, 557b
craftsmanship, III 411a–411b, 420a
deduction, III 392a
Democritus, III 407a
Descartes, III 395b, 398b, 418a
Diderot, III 420b
diffraction, III 418b, 419a
dispersion, III 418b–419a, 420b
Divini, III 420a
Dollond, III 420a
electromagnetic waves, III 419b, 420a
electromagnetism, III 419b
Empedocles, III 407a
Enlightenment, III 179a
Epicureanism, III 408a, 408b
Euclid, III 408a, 410a, 415b
experiments, III 410b–417a
eye, III 407b–410b, 412a–413b, 416b–417b, 418b, 419b, 420a
Fontana, III 420a
Fresnel, III 419a–419b
Galileo, III 411b, 414a–415b, 420a
geometry, III 410a, 412a, 416a, 416b–417b, 420b
Glover, III 393a
Greece (ancient), III 407a–408b, 415b, 420b
Grimaldi, III 418a, 418b,

419a
Grosseteste, III 410a
Halley, III 392b, 393a
Herschel, III 419b
Hobbes, III 395b
Hughes, III 392b
Huygens, III 395a, 418a
image, III 412a–413a, 416b–417b, 420b
indeterminacy, II 589a
infra-red rays, III 419b
Islam, II 647a
Jesus Christ, III 408b
Kepler, III 409b, 411b–414b, 416a, 416b, 417a
Klingenstierna, III 420a
knowledge, III 408a, 408b
Leeuwenhoek, III 415b–416a
lenses, III 411a–412a, 413b, 414–416a, 416b, 420a
lentils of glass, III 411a
Leonardo da Vinci, III 408b–409a, 411a
Leucippus of Miletus, III 407a, 407b, 408a
light, III 391b–398b, 407a, 410a, 410b, 417b, 418a–418b, 419b, 420b
Locke, III 392a, 395b, 397a, 398b
logic, III 548b
Lucretius, III 408b, 409a
lumen, III 410a, 410b, 416a, 417b, 418a–419b
luminous points, III 412b–413a
lux, III 417b
Malebranche, III 392a
Marcus Marci of Kronland, III 418b–419a
Mariani, III 420a
mathematics, III 387b, 393b, 395b–396a, 398b, 407b–408a, 410a–411a, 416a–417b, 420a, 420b
matter, III 195a, 418b, 419a
Maurolico, III 409b, 412a
Maxwell, III 419b
medieval theories of, II 198a–199a, 202b
Medici, III 414b
medicine, III 414b
metaphysics, III 396b, 410a
methodology, III 378b, 389b, 390b, 416b
microscope, III 415b–416a, 420a
Middle Ages, III 408b, 410a
Milton, III 393b, 394b
mind, III 407b–408a, 408b, 409b, 412a–413a, 416b, 418a, 420a
mirrors, III 410b, 413a,

415b–416a, 416b
motion, III 418a, 419b
music, III 263a
myopia, III 411a, 413b
Nature, III 416a–416b, 417b
Newton, II 391b–399a; III 195a, 378b, 389b, 390b, 418a, 418b–419b; IV 78a
observation, III 415a, 416a–417a
optical glass, III 420b
painting, III 408b–409a
Peckham, III 410a
Pemberton, III 393a
perspective, III 408a, 410a
philosophy, III 397a–398b, 407a–408b, 410a, 414b, 415a, 416a, 416b, 417b–419a, 420b
photometry, III 418a
physics, III 417b–418a, 419b, 420a, 420b
physiology, III 409b–410a, 420a
Plato, III 408a–408b
Platonism, III 415a
poetry, III 392a–398b
Pope, III 392a–392b, 396b–397a, 398a
Porta, III 411b–412a
positivism, III 416b, 417b, 419b, 548b
presbyopia, III 411a, 413b
psychology, III 409b–410a, 420a; IV 12a
Ptolemy, III 408a, 410a, 415b
radiation, III 420b
rainbows, III 418a
rays, III 410a–413a, 417a, 418b, 419a, 419b
refraction, III 411a, 411b–412b, 413a, 416a, 418a, 418b, 419a, 420b
relativity, IV 74b, 78a, 80b
Renaissance, IV 440a
replicas, III 407b–410a
retinal images, III 409a–409b, 412a–413b
Ritter, III 419b
Roemer, III 395a
Rucellai, III 415b–416a
Saint Bonaventura, III 410a
Saint Thomas Aquinas, III 408b, 410a
science, II 647a; III 408b, 411a–420b
scientific classification, I 465b
senses, III 407b, 408a, 415a
shape, III 407b
Snell, III 418a
solar rays, III 410a, 416a
spin, III 418a

spyglasses, III 414a, 415a
stars, III 410b, 414b
telemetric triangles, III 416b–417a
telescopes, III 414a–415a, 420a
theology, III 410a, 418a
Theophrastus, III 407a
Thomson, III 392b–395a, 396a–396b, 398a–398b
Torricelli, III 420a
touch, III 407b, 408a, 408b, 411a, 416a
truth, III 408a, 416b
ultra-violet rays, III 419b
unity of science, IV 433b
universal man, IV 440a
vibration, III 418b, 419a
vision, III 396a–396b, 398b
visual rays, III 407b–408a, 409a, 410a, 416a
Vitellius, III 409b
waves, III 418a, 418b, 419b, 420b
Wollaston, III 419b
Young, III 419a–419b
Optimism
deism, I 647b
Faust (legend), III 249b
Leibniz, I 329a
rationalism, II 167b
romanticism, IV 204a, 204b
social welfare, IV 277a
Utopia, IV 458b, 461a
Voltaire, I 329a
Oracles, prophecy, III 657b, 658a–663a, 665b, 669a
Orators
Christianity, III 590b
primitivism, III 590b
temperance, IV 379a
Oratory
aesthetics, II 220a
Aristotle, III 554b
art, I 460b
Cicero, II 170a; IV 169a–169b
Demosthenes, II 170a
Dionysius of Halicarnassus, II 170a
equity, II 150a–150b
evolution of literature, II 170a, 172a
five faculties, IV 168b
France, II 172a
Greece (ancient), II 170a, 684a–684b; III 7a, 112a
humanism, II 515a, 515b, 516a, 517a
law, II 684a–684b; III 7a
literary paradox, III 77a, 78a, 79b
loyalty, III 112a

Plato, III 496b, 499a, 500a, 500b, 501b
poetics, III 525b
politics, IV 167b
pragmatism, III 554a, 555a
progress, III 628a
Quintilian, II 170a
Ramism, IV 42b, 43b–44a
rationalism, IV 48b, 49a
Renaissance, IV 439a
rhetoric, IV 167b–170b, 171b, 172a
scientific classification, I 463b
temperance, IV 367b, 368a
universal man, IV 439a
ut pictura poesis, IV 465b, 469a
Velleius Paterculus, II 170a
Orbits
earth, I 544a, 544b, 545b, 550b; IV 74b, 79a
planets, I 540b, 545b–546a; IV 74b, 75a
relativity, IV 74b, 75a, 79a
sun, I 540a, 541a
symmetry, IV 348b
Order, II 434b–449b
Addison, II 446b, 447b
aesthetics, II 216a, 216b–219b
Agrippa, II 435b
angels, II 435b, 439b, 441b
Apianus, II 436b, 437a
architecture, II 440b–441b
Aristotle, II 438a–438b, 443a–443b, 448a; III 1b, 15b
art, II 436a, 436b
astronomy, II 443a, 448a
atheism, II 444b, 445a
Averroës, II 441a
Avicebron, II 441a
Avicenna, II 441a
Bamborough, II 436b
Barckley, II 435b
Being, II 445a, 446a
Bellers, II 436b
Benesch, II 436b
Bible, II 435b, 440a
Brahe, II 442b
Brooke, II 446b
Bruno, II 442a–443a, 445b
Byzantine Empire, II 440b–441a
cabbalism, II 441a
Camillo, II 436b
Campbell, II 436b
Carion, II 438a
Cartesianism, II 444a, 444b, 445b
causation, II 446b
Chain of Being, II 440b, 446b–448a

chaos, II 444b
Christianity, II 438a, 439a–439b, 440b, 441a
Cicero, II 438b–439a
Coleridge, II 441a
Comte, III 642a
Copernicus, II 436b, 437b, 442a, 442b, 443b
cosmos, II 436a, 436b, 439a, 439b, 442b, 443b, 445a, 445b, 446b, 447b; IV 297b
Creation, II 438a, 439b, 445a, 447b
Crollius, II 435b
Crooke, II 436a, 436b, 439b
Cudworth, II 444a
culture, II 128a
Dante, II 440b
Darwin, II 448a
Descartes, II 443b, 444a, 444b; III 561b; IV 435b
Digges, II 436b, 437b, 442b
Donne, II 434b, 443b
Drummond of Hawthornden, II 436a
dualism, II 443b, 444a, 445b
economics, II 442a
Einstein, II 448b
Elyot, II 434b
environment, II 128a
Erigena, II 441a
evolution, II 447b, 448a
Feyerabend, II 435b
Ficino, II 442a, 442b
Fludd, II 437a
Francis I, II 436b
Galileo, II 436b, 443b; IV 361a
Gerhard, II 435a
God, II 334b, 438b–439b, 440b, 441a, 442a, 443a, 444a–446b; IV 131b
good, IV 174b, 175a, 176a
Goodman, II 435b
Greece (ancient), II 442b, 444a, 652a, 674b, 675a, 676a, 676b, 677a, 681a, 681b–683a, 685a
harmony, II 446a–446b, 448b; IV 38b
heaven, II 440b
hell, II 435b
Hermes Trismegistus, II 439a
Hermeticism, II 432a, 433a
Herschel, II 448a
heterogeneity, II 442a
Hippocrates, II 446a
history, II 442a
Hobbes, II 443b–444a, 444b
Homer, II 440a, 440b
humanism, IV 131b, 133a,

133b, 134a
Iamblichus, II 439a
impressionism, II 582a
infinity, II 438b, 441a–441b, 442b–443a, 444b, 445a, 446a, 446b, 447b
Ingpen, II 438a
Jacob (Bible), II 440a
Jenyns, II 447a
Judaism, II 441a
justice, II 652b
Kant, II 447b
Kepler, II 442b, 443a–443b
language, II 664b
law, II 674b–677a, 681a–683a, 685a, 688b; III 1b, 3a, 33a
Leibniz, II 444a–444b, 445b–447b, 448b; III 561b
Leonardo da Vinci, II 437b
literature, II 440b
Locke, II 446a, 446b
logic, II 444b
love, II 439a, 442a
Lovejoy, II 438b
Luther, II 442a
Machiavelli, IV 480b, 482a–482b, 483b
Macrobius, II 440a–440b
macrocosm, II 436b
Manetti, II 442b
materialism, II 444a, 448a
mathematics, II 438a, 442b, 443b, 444b, 445a
matter, II 444a; III 186a, 186b, 190b
metaphysics, II 438b, 447a
microcosm, II 436a, 436b, 437a, 439b, 442b
Middle Ages, II 438a, 439b–440b, 442a
Milton, II 438a
morality, II 447a
Mohammedanism, II 441a
monads, II 445b–446a, 448b
morality, II 447a
More, Henry, II 444a, 444b
Mountague, II 434b
music, II 439b; III 265b, 271a
mythology, III 281b, 291b
natural law, III 14b, 15a, 15b, 19a, 19b, 25a
Nature, II 128a, 435b, 436b, 438a, 438b, 440a, 442b, 443a, 444a, 444b–445a, 446a, 446b, 448a; III 350b
necessity, IV 482b
Neo-Platonism, II 438b, 439a–439b, 442a
Newton, II 443b, 444a
Nicholas of Cusa, II 441a–441b, 443b

numbers, II 438a; III 403b
Orosius, II 438a
Otto of Freising, II 438a
painting, II 436a, 436b
pantheism, II 443a, 445a
Pascal, II 444a
Peacham, II 435a
perfectibility, III 463b, 464b, 475a
Perrière, II 435b
Person, II 438a
Philippson, II 438a
Pico della Mirandola, II 442a–442b
planets, II 442b
Plato, II 438a, 438b, 441a, 443a, 443b; IV 50a, 175a
Platonism, II 441a, 444a, 445a
plentitude principle, II 442b
Plotinus, II 439a, 439b, 441a, 444a
pluralism, II 443a
Pont, II 438a
Pope, II 447a, 447b
Porphyry, II 439a
Postel, II 438a
Powel, II 435a
pragmatism, III 560b, 561b
Proclus, II 439a, 441a
progress, III 638a, 638b, 642a
prophecy, III 664a, 666a, 667a
Protestantism, II 438a
Pseudo-Dionysius, II 435b, 439a–439b, 441a, 442a
psychology, II 436b
Ptolemy, II 436b, 437a
Purchas, II 436b
Puritanism, II 442a
Pythagoras, IV 50a
Pythagoreans, IV 38b
Raleigh, II 436b
rationalism, II 445b; IV 47a, 50a
reason, II 446b, 447b
reformation, IV 63a, 66a
Reformation, II 442a
Renaissance, II 434b, 436b–438b, 440b, 442b–443a; IV 131b, 133a, 133b, 134a
revolution, II 441b
right, IV 174b, 175a, 176a
romanticism, IV 205a
Rome (ancient), II 444a, 688b
Saint Augustine, II 438a, 441a; IV 63a
Saint Bede, II 438a
Saint Paul, II 439a
Saint Thomas Aquinas, II 440b
Satan, II 435b

science, II 448b
secularization, II 442a, 444a
Selden, II 438a
Sendivogius, II 435b
Shakespeare, II 438a
socialism, IV 285a
society, II 442a
soul, II 442a
space, IV 297b
Spenser, II 434b
Spinoza, II 444b–445b; III 561b
Sprat, II 444b
Sterry, II 435a
Stoicism, IV 176a
Stow, II 443b
symmetry, IV 350a
technology, IV 361a
Teilhard de Chardin, II 448b
temperance, IV 370a
theater, II 436b
theodicy, IV 380a, 380b
Thomson, II 446b
time, IV 393b
tradition, II 441b, 442a
tragic sense, IV 412a, 414a
Traherne, II 443b
truth, II 439a, 443b, 446a
Tymme, II 438a
unity, II 442a, 444b, 445a, 445b, 446a, 448b
unity of science, IV 435b
universe, II 434b, 436a–439b, 441a–448b; IV 38b
Utopia, IV 458b, 459b, 462b, 464a
Valades, II 436a, 436b
Vincent of Beauvais, II 438a
virtù, IV 480b, 482a–482b, 483b, 484b
Vitruvius, II 437b
Voltaire, II 446b; III 638b
Ward, II 434b
welfare state, IV 510a
Wells, H. G., II 448a
Wesley, II 446b
Wilkins, II 443b
William of Ockham, III 19b
Young, II 446b–447a
Zeitgeist, IV 536b
Zeus (myth), II 440a
See also Chain of Being; Hierarchy
Ore, Oystein, chance images, I 337a
Oresme, Nicole (1330?–1382)
cosmology, I 544a
despotism, II 4a, 7b
Islam, II 649a
matter, III 192a
measurement, IV 402b
mechanical science, II 202b, 203a, 204a
motion, II 202b, 203a
time, IV 402b
Orestes (myth)
law, II 682b, 683a, 683b
motif, III 237a
tragic sense, IV 413b
Organicism, III 421a–427b
Abrams, III 426b
aesthetics, III 421a–422b, 425a–426b
analysis, III 422b, 423a
Aristotelianism, III 422a, 422b, 424b, 425a, 426b
Aristotle, III 421b–424b
art, III 421a, 422a–425b, 426b, 427a
atomism, III 425a
biology, III 427a
Blake, III 425b
Boileau, III 424b
Bosanquet, III 426a
Bradley, A. C., III 422b
Broad, C. D., III 426a
Brooks, III 426b
Cicero, III 423b
Clark, H. H., III 426b
classicism, III 421b
Coleridge, III 421b, 422b, 425b, 426b, 427a
concept of, III 421a–421b
content, III 423b, 424a, 426b
creativity, III 421b, 422b
Croce, III 425b, 426a
Dante, III 424a
De Sanctis, III 426a
described, III 421a–422a
Dewey, III 421a
Don Quixote (fiction), III 422a
Emerson, III 426b
empiricism, III 422a, 425a
environment, II 120b–123a
epics, III 424a
evolutionism, II 174b, 175a, 177a–178a, 179a–183a, 184a, 187a–188a
Fogle, R. H., III 426b
Formalism, III 424a
forms, III 421a, 421b, 424a, 424b, 425b, 426b
France, III 424b
game theory, II 263b–264a
genius, III 422b
Germany, III 421b, 424b–426a
Goethe, III 423a, 424b, 425a
Great Britain, III 424b, 426a
Greece (ancient), III 421b
Harris, III 424b
Hegel, III 421b, 425b, 426a
Heinsius, III 424b
Herder, III 424b
history, III 422a, 426b
Horace, III 423a, 423b, 424a, 424b
Hospers, III 421b
Hulme, III 427a
hylomorphism, III 423b
idealism, III 421b, 425b, 426b
imagination, III 422a, 425b, 426a
Jonson, Ben, III 424b
Kant, III 421b, 422a, 425a
Krieger, M., III 426b
language, III 422b, 426b
Leibniz, III 424b, 427a
literary criticism, III 421b–423a, 424a, 424b, 425b, 426a–427a
literature, III 423a, 423b, 426a
logic, III 422a, 425a, 427a
Longinus, III 423b, 424b
MacKenzie, III 425b
McTaggart, III 426a
Man-Machine, III 138b, 139b–141b, 143b–145a
mathematics, III 422a
matter, III 187a–187b
mechanism, III 422b, 424b, 425a, 426b
Middle Ages, III 424b
Nature, III 424a, 425a
Neo-Aristotelianism, III 426b
neo-classicism, III 424b, 425b
Neo-Platonism, III 425a
One, III 422a
Osborne, III 426a, 427a
Pater, III 426a
Pepper, III 198a, 426b
Perrault, III 424b
Philodemus, III 423b
philosophy, III 421b, 422a, 422b, 424b, 425a, 426a, 426b, 427a
Plato, III 421b, 422a, 423a, 424a
Platonism, III 422a, 423b, 424a
Plotinus, III 423a, 424b, 425b
Poe, III 426b
poetry, III 422a, 423a, 423b–425b, 426b, 427a
poets, III 421b, 426a
Pope, III 424b
reality, III 422a
reason, III 425a
Renaissance, III 424a
rhetoric, III 423a, 424a, 426a, 426b
romanticism, III 421b, 424a; IV 206a, 207b
Sancho Panza (fiction), III 422a
Sappho, III 423b
Schelling, III 421b, 425a, 425b
Schiller, III 424a
Schlegel, August Wilhelm von, III 421b, 422b, 425b
Schlegel, Friedrich von, III 421b, 425b
Schleicher, III 426a
scholasticism, III 424a
science, III 424b, 425a
Shaftesbury, III 424a
Shakespeare, III 424b, 425b
Socrates, III 422a, 423a
Stallman, III 426b
State, III 422b
style, III 422b
teleology, III 425a
theater, III 423a, 424b, 425b
Thoreau, III 426b
thought, III 423b
totality, III 422a
tragedy, III 423a, 424a, 425b
U.S., III 426b
unity, III 421a–427a
universe, III 424a
Warren, R. P., III 426b
West, R. B., III 426b
Whitman, III 426b
Wilde, III 424a
writing, III 421b
Organization
anarchy, III 673b
anti-industrialism, III 676a
fascism, III 674a
law, III 1a
protest movements, III 671a, 672a–675b, 676a
socialism, III 673b
syndicalism, III 673b
totalitarianism, IV 408b, 409a
Organization of American States
peace, III 456b
loyalty, III 113a
Oriental ideas in America, III 427b–439b
Abbot, III 429a, 434b
abstraction, III 436b
activism, III 430a, 431a
Adams, III 437a
agnosticism, III 438b
ancestor worship, III 434a
anthropology, III 435a
archaeology, III 435a
Arnold, III 437a, 437b
art, III 428a, 428b
asceticism, III 431a
authority, III 436b
Barrows, III 435b

Bible, III 434b
Bigelow, III 437a
Bramo Samaj, III 429b
Buckley, III 435b
Buddhism, III 429a, 430b, 431a, 432b, 434b, 436a, 436b–438b, 439a
Calvinism, III 429a
Carus, III 435b–437a, 438a, 439a
caste, III 434a
Chadwick, III 429a
Channing, Edward Tyrrel, III 429a
Channing, William Henry, III 429a, 434b
Child, III 429a
China, III 428a, 428b, 430a–431a, 433a–434b, 436a
Cholmondeley, III 431a
Christianity, III 428b, 429a, 432a–434a, 436a, 436b
Christy, III 431a
Clarke, J. F., III 429a, 431b–434a, 435a–435b, 439a
climate, III 433b
common sense, III 430a
Confucianism, III 429a, 433b
Confucius, III 430a, 430b, 431a
Conway, III 429a, 431b, 434a–434b
culture, III 427b–439a
custom, III 428b
Davids, III 434b
despotism, II 1a–3a, 4b–5b, 6a, 7b–8a, 11a, 12a, 13a–13b, 14b, 15a–17a
Deussen, III 434b
dualism, III 436b
Duperron, III 428a, 429a
eclecticism, III 429b, 431a
economics, III 428a, 428b, 434a
Ellinwood, III 435b
Emerson, Mary Moody, III 429b
Emerson, Ralph Waldo, III 429a–430b, 431b, 432a, 433a, 433b, 439a
empiricism, III 436b
ethics, III 430a–430b, 436b
Everett, Alexander Hill, III 429a
Everett, Charles Carroll, III 435b
Everett, Edward, III 429a
evolution, III 433b, 434a, 435a, 438a–438b, 439a
Fenollosa, III 428b, 437a
Formalism, III 430b
France, III 429a, 432a
Free Religious Association,

III 434a–434b, 436a
freedom, III 430b
Frothingham, III 429a, 433a, 434b
Garbe, III 436a
Germany, III 432a, 436a, 438a
Gnosticism, III 438b
God, III 429b, 432b, 433b, 435a
Grassman, III 436a
Gray, III 429a
Great Britain, III 428b, 429a, 429b, 432a, 435b, 437a, 438a
Greece (ancient), II 500b–501a
Hafiz, III 430a
Hall, III 435b
harmony, IV 38b
Harris, Townsend, III 429a, 435b
Hearn, III 437a–438b, 439a
heresy, II 427a
Higginson, III 429a, 431b, 435a–437b
Hinduism, III 429a, 430a–431b, 432b, 433b, 434a, 436b, 439a
historiography, II 500b–501a, 504b, 505a
history, III 436b, 437a
Hodgson, III 429b
Holmes, O. W., III 429a, 437a
Hopkins, III 434b
humanism, III 432b
idealism, III 429b, 430a, 430b, 432b, 439a
India, III 428a, 428b, 429b, 430a, 431a, 431b, 433a, 433b, 434b, 436a
Islam, III 434b
Janes, L. G., III 429a, 434b
Japan, III 428a, 437b–438b
Johnson, III 428b, 429a, 431b, 433a–434a, 434b, 435a, 439a
Jones, William, III 428a, 429a, 429b
Jordan, III 435b
journals, III 435b, 436a
Judaism, III 432a–432b
justice, III 431a
Kant, III 436b
Kellogg, III 435b
Lanman, III 434b–435a
Leibniz, III 428a, 458a
linguistics, III 435a
literature, III 428a–431b, 438b
Locke, III 429a–429b
Longfellow, III 429a, 434a–

434b
Lowell, Percival, III 437a
materialism, III 429a–429b, 430a, 433b, 438a
Mills, Charles De B., III 429a, 434a–434b
missionaries, III 428b
monism, III 430a, 436b, 438a–438b, 439a
morality, III 428a–429a, 430b, 436b
Müller, III 434b, 436a
mysticism, III 429b, 430a, 430b, 431a
mythology, III 272b, 278b, 287b, 289a, 293a, 306a, 436a
Nagley, III 431b
Nature, III 433b
Neo-Platonism, III 429b, 430a
Oldenberg, III 434b, 436a
pantheism, III 432b
Parsons, Theophilus, III 429a
perennial philosophy, III 458a
periodicals, III 428b–429a, 429b
periodization in history, III 480a
Persia, III 430a, 430b, 431a, 433a, 434a
pessimism, III 430b
philosophy, III 428a, 429a–434b, 436a, 436b–437a, 438a–438b, 439a
Plato, III 430a
poetry, III 430a–430b
politics, III 428a, 434a
polytheism, III 434a
Potter, William James, III 434b
primitivism, III 430b
progress, III 624b, 628b, 632a, 638b
Protap Chunder Mozoomdar, III 429b
Protestantism, III 432b
psychology, III 435a; IV 24a
Pythagoreans, IV 38b
Quesnay, III 428a
quietism, III 430b
race, III 433b
rationalism, III 429a, 429b, 432b
religion, III 100a–100b, 101b, 428a–439a
revolution, III 428b
Ripley, III 437a
Roman Catholic Church, III 432b
Roy, III 429b
Saadi, III 430a

Sanborn, III 437a
Sarma, III 431b
science, III 432b–437a, 439a
self-discipline, III 431a, 431b
Sen, III 429b
society, III 428a, 428b, 429b, 434a
soul, III 436b
Spencer, III 438b, 439a
Suzuki, III 436a
Stein, III 431b
symbolism, III 431a
Taoism, III 430a, 434a
theology, III 432b, 435a
Thoreau, III 429a, 430a–431b, 433a, 433b, 439a
Tiele, III 434b
tolerance, III 432b
Toy, III 435b
trade, III 428b, 439a
transcendentalism, III 429a–434b, 439a; IV 24a
Tudor, III 429a
Underwood, III 434b
Unitarianism, III 429a, 429b, 432a, 433a, 434a
U.S., III 427b–439b
universality, III 437a
universe, III 438a; IV 38b
utilitarianism, III 433b
Voltaire, III 428a, 638b
war, III 428b
Warren, Henry Clarke, III 434b–435a
Warren, William Fairfield, III 435b
Whitney, W. D., III 434b
widow-burning, III 434a
Wilkins, III 429b
Wilson, Horace, III 429b
Wolff, Christian, III 428a
yoga, III 428a, 431a, 431b, 439a
Zen Buddhism, III 428a, 436a
Origen (185?–?254 A.D.)
allegory, I 44a, 46b
analogy, I 64a
Buddhism, I 255a
cycles, I 623b
dignity, IV 137a
disease, II 399a
eschatology, II 157b, 158a
historiography, II 478b
love, II 210a
metaphor, III 205b
Neo-Platonism, II 377b
patristic period, I 64a
peace, III 441a
perfectibility, III 466a
Philo Judaeus and, III 466a
Platonism, III 516b

religion, III 205b
syncretism, I 44b–45a
temperance, IV 370b
time, IV 392a
Originality
art, II 306a–306b
Daubigny, II 577b
genius, II 295b, 306a–306b, 317b, 318a, 320b, 321a, 323b, 324a
Kant, II 323b, 324a
Manet, II 577b
Monet, II 577b
music, II 317b, 318a, 320b, 321a, 323b, 324a
Orosius, Paulus (5th century A.D.)
Gothic, II 367a
hierarchy, II 438a
historiography, II 472a–477b, 473b, 474b, 488b
mythology, III 286b
Orpheus (myth), III 96a, 284a
Empedocles, IV 2b
genius, II 313a
Greece (ancient), III 96a
harmony, II 393b
love, III 96a
music, II 313a, 316b, 393b; III 266a, 278b
psychology, IV 1b, 2b
sin, IV 228b
symbolism, IV 345a
Orphic tragic sense, IV 411b, 414b–415b
Orphism
fate, II 226b
necessity, III 361a
psychology, IV 1b, 2b
Pythagoreans, IV 31a, 31b, 32a, 33a
reincarnation, I 644b; II 226b
Orr, H. B., chromosomes, II 288a
Ortega y Gasset, José (1883–1955)
baroque in literature, I 192a
irony, II 634a
love, III 95b
music, II 634a
symbolism, IV 342b
Orthodoxy
heresy, II 416b, 417a, 418a, 419b, 424a, 425b, 428a, 430a
religion, IV 113b, 115b, 116a, 118b
romanticism, IV 200b, 204a
Orthogonal transformation, IV 351b, 352a
Orwell, George (1903–1950),
perfectibility, III 474b
satire, IV 214b, 215a, 215b

Utopia, IV 464a
Osborn, Fairfield, conservation, I 471a, 476a
Osborne, Harold
beauty, I 208b
literary criticism, I 602b–603a
organicism, III 426a, 427a
Osiander, Andrew (1498–1552)
axiomatization, I 166b
Copernican heresy, II 428a
Osiris (myth), II 39a, 334b–335b, 341a; III 281a
Egypt (ancient), IV 100b–102b
music, III 268a
religion, IV 94a, 96a, 98a, 100b–102b, 104b, 225a, 225b, 228b
Ossian (legend)
Gothic, II 370b
historiography, II 489b
neo-classicism in art, III 370b
vox populi, IV 499a
Ossowski, Stanislaw, class, I 444b
Osten, G. von der, iconography, II 538b
Osthoff, Hermann (1847–1907), language, II 671b
Ostwald, Wilhelm (1853–1932)
classification of the sciences, I 465b
Peirce and, III 558a
pragmatism, III 558a
time, IV 395b
Ott, Heinrich, God, II 365b
Otto, Rudolf (1869–1937),
Buddhism, I 256a
demonology, IV 97b
holy, II 512a, 514a; IV 97b
irrationalism, II 638a
numinous, IV 97a–97b
primitivism, IV 97b
supernatural, IV 97a
taboos, IV 97b
totemism, IV 97b
Otto, Walter (1878–1941),
mythology, III 313a, 314a, 314b
Otto of Freising (1114?–1158)
hierarchy, II 438a
historiography, II 473b–474a
prophecy, III 666a
Otto I, Emperor (912–973)
historiography, II 473a
Middle Ages, III 477a
Ottoman Empire

balance of power, I 186b
crisis in history, I 591a
despotism, II 7b–8a
nationalism, III 332a
World War I, III 332a
Otway, Thomas (1652–1685),
baroque in literature, I 191a
Oudry, Jean Baptiste (1686–1755), iconography, II 532a
Ouranos
Aristotle, IV 300b
etymology, IV 300b
Homer, IV 300b
Overpopulation
longevity, III 92a
medicine and, I 594a
peace, III 446b, 447b
perfectibility, III 475a
Russell, III 446b
war, III 446b
Overproduction
Marx, III 162a; IV 292b
Marxism, III 162a
socialism, IV 289b, 292b
Ovid (43 B.C.–?17 A.D.)
amoral artist, II 310a
chaos, IV 297a
cycles, I 625a
humanism, II 516a, 517b
iconography, II 529a, 531a, 534b
literary paradox, III 77b
Middle Ages, III 580a
morality, II 310a; IV 122a
motif, III 241a
mythology, III 278a, 283a, 286b, 288a, 293a, 296b, 298a, 299a, 299b
periodization in literary history, III 482a
poetry, III 528b
primitivism, III 579b, 580a, 580b, 581b, 591b
reformation, IV 61b
social contract, IV 252a
space, IV 297a
Utopia, IV 460a
ut pictura poesis, IV 468b, 469a
Ovington, John, antiprimitivism, III 604b
Owen, Robert (1771–1858),
anarchism, I 73a
biology, I 237a, 237b
economic history, II 59b, 60a
environment, IV 289b
happiness, II 380a; III 469a
individualism, II 596b
morality, IV 289b
perfectibility, III 469a
revolution, IV 160a
socialism, IV 288b, 289b, 293a

Utopia, IV 463a
utopianism, II 380a
Owenites, protest movements, III 672b
Oxymoron, IV 517a, 518b

P

Pachomius, Saint (c. 318 A.D.), community principle, I 378a
Pacifism
Antisthenes, I 630b–631a
Buddhism, I 253a–253b, 257a
Crates, I 630b–631a
cynicism, I 630b–631a
Einstein, III 447a
eschatology, II 158b
ethics, III 441a, 441b, 445a, 445b, 447a
Herder, III 326a
international peace, III 448a–450b, 452a, 455a, 455b
Kant, III 442a–445a
Lucretius, III 587b
primitivism, III 579a, 580a, 580b, 587b
Reformation, IV 67b
revisionism, IV 271a
socialism, IV 287b
Tolstoy, III 445b
war, IV 502a
Pacioli, Luca (1450?–?1520),
numbers, III 400a
probability, III 605b
Pact of Paris, international peace, III 452a
Paganism
Arius, I 377a–377b
Celsus, I 647b
Christianity, I 376a–379a, 380a, 388b; II 341a; III 286b, 588b–590b, 591b
Church, I 417a
double truth, II 31b, 32a, 33a, 34a
faith, II 34a
Faust (legend), III 246b
Gnosticism, II 42b, 330b
holy, II 513a
humanism, II 520a
Julian, I 648a
love, III 96a
Man-Machine, III 133a
Neo-Platonism, III 372b, 373b, 376a, 377b
Plotinus, IV 9a
Plutarch, I 647b
primitivism, III 588b–591b

psychology, IV 8b, 9a
religion, IV 93b, 94a, 98a, 113b, 114a, 117b
Roman Catholic Church, I 376a–380a, 388b
Saint Augustine, I 378b
Saint Thomas Aquinas, IV 114a
Theodosius I, I 378b
witchcraft, IV 521b
Paget, Violet (1856–1935), beauty, I 213a
empathy, II 86b
Pain
Antisthenes, I 632a–632b
Aristotle, II 377a; IV 5a
atomism, III 187b
Bentham, II 167b, 381a–381b; III 470a; IV 178b, 277b, 451a, 451b
Bible, III 278b, 284a
birth, II 384a–384b
Condillac, II 381a
cynicism, I 632a–632b
death, I 635a, 638a
Descartes, II 381a
Dewey, II 382b
disease, II 396a, 398a
education, II 385b
Epicureanism, II 137b, 378a; IV 8a, 175b
Epicurus, II 137b, 378a; III 465a
ethics, IV 320a, 321a
evil, II 163a, 167a–167b
free will, II 137b
good, IV 174a, 175b, 178b, 179a, 185a
happiness, II 374b–387a
Hartley, II 381a; III 234a–234b
Hobbes, II 380b–381a
human nature, III 643b
humanism, IV 133b
Hume, II 381a; III 232a, 232b
Hutcheson, III 231b
Jevons, II 384b
Judaism, II 30a
knowledge, II 386b–387a
language, II 387a
law, II 385b
Leibniz, II 381a
Locke, II 381a
matter, III 187b
medicine, II 384a
Mill, J. S., II 167b
moral sense, III 231b, 232a, 232b, 234a–234b
mythology, III 278b, 284a
perfectibility, III 465a, 468a, 470a, 643b
Plato, II 376a–376b; IV 451a–451b

pleasure, II 374b–387a
primitivism, III 584b
progress, III 643b
psychology, IV 5a, 8a, 23a
punishment, II 385b
religion, IV 107b
Renaissance, IV 133b
right, IV 174a, 175b, 178b, 179a, 185a
Ryle, II 386b
social welfare, IV 277b
Stoicism, IV 320a, 321a
sublime in external nature, IV 336b, 337a
universe, III 187b
utilitarianism, IV 445b–447b
utility, IV 450a, 451a–451b
Victorian sensibility, IV 218a, 221a
Wesley, III 468a
Wolff, II 381a
Paine, Thomas (1737–1809), aristocracy, I 659b
attitude toward antiquity, I 77b, 86a
civilization, I 619b
Constitution (U.S.), IV 261a
constitutionalism, I 486b
crisis in history, I 590a
culture, I 619b
deism, I 651b, 652a
democracy, I 659a–659b, 661b
Enlightenment, II 99b
equality, II 140a
individualism, II 599a
Locke and, IV 260b
monarchy, I 659b
nationalism, III 325b
pragmatism, III 553b
revolution, IV 156a
Rousseau and, IV 260b
social contract, IV 260b–261a
society, IV 260b
sovereignty, I 659b
State, I 659a–659b; IV 260b
trust, IV 260b
Painters
mythology, III 297b, 298a, 299a
Nature, III 350b
painting, IV 465b–475a
Plato, III 498b–499a, 500a
poetry, IV 465b, 466a, 467a, 469b, 471a, 473a, 475a
poets, III 297b, 298a
Renaissance, IV 439b
romanticism, IV 208b
Socrates, III 498b, 499a
universal man, IV 439b
Painting, IV 465b–476b

abstraction, IV 470a, 474a
academic, II 567b–570b, 581a
Addison, IV 471a, 471b
Aelius Theon, IV 468b
aesthetics, II 217a, 219b, 220b, 221b, 224a, 575b, 576a, 583a, 583b; IV 465b, 466b, 467a, 469a, 471b, 472a, 473a, 474a
Alberti, IV 467b–469b
Alembert, IV 472b
Algarotti, IV 472b
allegory, IV 469a, 470a, 471a, 473b
ambiguity, I 56a–57a
Aphtonius, IV 468b
Apollinaire, IV 470b
Apuleius, IV 469a
Arabia, IV 473a
architects, IV 466b
Ariosto, IV 468b, 469a
aristocracy, II 570a, 578a, 581b
Aristotle, IV 467b, 468a, 469b, 473a
art, I 456a–461b; II 298a–301b, 304a, 305a–308a, 313b, 567a–574b, 576a–581b, 582b; IV 465a–467b, 469a, 470a–475b
Art Nouveau, III 341b
astronomers, IV 466b
Auden, IV 469b
Austen, Jane, IV 475a
Avison, IV 472b
Babbitt, Irving, IV 474b
Bacon, IV 466b, 467b
Balla, IV 475b
Balzac, IV 467a, 469a, 474b
Batteaux, IV 468a, 471b, 472b
Baudelaire, IV 469a, 473a
Bauhaus, IV 475a
Baumgarten, IV 471b
beauty, IV 467a, 468b, 471b, 473b, 474b
Bellori, IV 466a–466b, 469a
Berlioz, IV 473a
Bernini, III 228b
Bible, IV 465b
biography, IV 471a
Blake, IV 470b
Bosch, IV 467a
bourgeois, II 570a, 580a
Brazil, IV 470b
Breughel (the Elder), IV 467a, 469b
Breughel (the Younger), IV 467a
Brönte, Anne, IV 467a
Brönte, Charlotte, IV 467a
Brönte, Emily, IV 467a

Browning, IV 469a, 471a
Buddhism, IV 476a
Burke, Edmund, IV 471b
Calder, IV 475b
Callistratus, IV 468b, 469a
Carroll, IV 470b
cartoon, IV 470b, 475a
Castel, color symphony, IV 473a
Castelvetro, IV 467b
Caylus, Comte de, IV 467a
censorship, III 499a
Cézanne, IV 467a, 475b
chance images, I 341a–353b
Chapman, III 294b
Chaucer, IV 469a
China, I 353b–354a, 363b–364a, 369a
China (ancient), IV 470b, 473a, 475b–476a
Christianity, IV 471b
Cicero, IV 468a, 468b
class, II 576b, 581b, 583a
Claudian, IV 469a
Coleridge, IV 471a
color, II 567b, 570a–572b, 574a, 574b, 577a–580b, 582b, 583a; III 350a; IV 473a
comedy, IV 468b
composition, II 570a, 571a, 581b, 582b
conservatism, II 571a
Constable, IV 467a, 473b
content, IV 466b, 470b, 471a
Courbet, III 343a
creativity in art, I 580b, 581a–581b, 582a
criticism, II 572b–577a, 581a
Croce, IV 471a
Cubism, I 352a; IV 470b, 475b
culture, II 567b, 577a, 580b, 581b, 582b, 583a; IV 474a
Cummings, IV 470b
Dada, I 352b
dance, IV 467b, 470a, 475a
Daniello, IV 467b, 468a
Darwin, IV 473a
De Quincey, IV 475a
De Stilj, IV 475a
decadence, II 575b, 582a
decorum, IV 466b
deism, IV 471b, 472a
democracy, II 583a
Diderot, IV 469a, 470a, 472b, 478a
Disney, IV 473a
divisionism, II 570b
Dolce, IV 467b

drama, IV 467a, 467b, 468a, 472b, 475a
drawing, II 580a
Dryden, IV 468a, 472b
Du Fresnoy, IV 468a
dualism, II 581b
Dubos, IV 471b
Duchamp, IV 475b
Dufresnoy, IV 468a
education, II 583a
Egypt (ancient), I 581a; IV 470a
ekphrasis, IV 466a–469b
emblem books, IV 470a–470b, 472b
emotion, II 575a, 575b, 576b, 581a; IV 466a, 466b, 472a, 472b, 474b
empiricism, II 576b, 580b, 581b, 582a, 583a
English language, IV 466b
Enlightenment, IV 465b
environment, II 583a
epics, IV 465b, 469b, 473b
Epicureanism, II 576a, 581a, 581b, 582a
ethics, II 576a; IV 473b
evolution, II 581b, 583a
evolution of literature, II 171b
experiments, II 567b
expressionism, II 206a, 207a, 207b, 208a, 208b
fables, IV 468b, 469b
feeling, II 575b, 576b
Félibien, IV 470a
Ficino, IV 470b
figure poems, IV 470a, 470b, 476a
folklore, II 581a, 582b
Frascatoro, IV 467b
France, III 366a; IV 467a, 468b, 471b, 473b, 475a; III 342a; IV 473b
futurism, IV 475b
genius, II 317b–318a, 321a
Germany, IV 471a, 474a
Gesamtkunstwerk, IV 472b
Gilpin, IV 473b
Giotto, IV 122a, 122b
Gluck, IV 472b
God, II 574b, 582b; IV 467a, 471b, 474b
Goethe, IV 469a, 472a, 473a
good, IV 467a
Gothic, II 370b, 371a, 372b
Great Britain, IV 467a, 469a
Greece (ancient), IV 469a, 470b
Gregory I (the Great), Pope, IV 466a
Han dynasty, IV 476a
Hardy, IV 466a, 467a

harmony, III 350a; IV 466b, 467b, 471b, 472b, 473a
Hawthorne, IV 469a
hedonism, II 575b
Herbert, IV 470b
Herder, IV 472b
Hermogenes, IV 468b
hierarchy, II 436a, 436b
hieroglyphics, IV 466b, 470a
highlight, IV 466b
historians, IV 465b
historical, III 350a
historigraphy, II 577b
history, II 576a–580b; IV 465b, 467a, 469b, 470a, 471a, 472a, 474a, 474b
Hobbes, IV 471a
Hogarth, IV 469b, 470b, 471a
Hollander, IV 470b
Homer, IV 471a
Horace, IV 467b, 468a, 469b
human figure, III 349b
humanism, II 521b; IV 133a, 469a, 474b
Hume, IV 471b
Huxley, Aldous, IV 475b
iconography, IV 468b, 470a
idea, II 544a, 546a
ideal, II 549b
idealism, III 341b
ideology, II 582a, 583a
imagery, IV 470a, 471b, 472b, 474a
imagination, III 208a; IV 467a, 469b, 471a–474b
imitation, II 582b
immutability, II 582b
impressionism, II 206a, 207a, 567b–574b, 576a–582b; III 342a; IV 473b
India (ancient), IV 473a
individualism, II 567b, 570b, 572a, 574b, 577a, 577b, 581b, 582b
industry, II 580a; IV 475a
infinity, II 614a
innovation, II 577a, 579b
insanity, II 575b
Italy, IV 467a, 469a, 472b
James, Henry, IV 466a, 469a
Jesus Christ, IV 466a
John of Salisbury, III 227b
Jonson, IV 471a
Joyce, IV 470b
Junius, IV 467b
Kames, IV 472a
Keats, IV 471a
Kircher, IV 473a
Klee, IV 469a

Kleist, IV 472a
Knight, IV 473b
Krieger, Murray, IV 471a
landscapes, II 567b, 571b, 572a, 573a, 574a, 577b–579a, 580a; III 349b, 350a
language, IV 466a–475a
Latin language, IV 466b, 468b
Leonardo da Vinci, III 227b; IV 467a
Lessing, IV 468a, 469a, 469b, 471a, 474a, 474b
light, II 567b, 570a–574b, 578b, 579a, 580a–580b, 581b
line, II 570a, 581b
Liszt, IV 473a
literary criticism, IV 465b–469b, 471a, 473b, 475a
literature, IV 466b, 476a
Locke, IV 471a, 472a, 473b
Lorrain, IV 469b
love, III 106a
Lucian, IV 469a
Lye, IV 475b
Mallarmé, IV 470b
Malraux, IV 469a
Martial, IV 469a
Marvell, IV 471a
masque, IV 470a, 472b
mass, II 570a
mathematics, I 580a
meaning, IV 467b
mechanical art, II 313b
melancholy, II 581a
Mendelssohn, IV 474a
metaphor, IV 465b–473b
Michelangelo, IV 469a
Middle Ages, IV 130b, 465b, 467a, 468b, 470a, 471a
Mili, IV 475b
military, IV 475a
Milton, IV 468b
mimesis, III 226a–229b; IV 465b, 469b, 471b, 472a, 472b, 474b
Minturno, IV 467b
Monboddo, IV 472b
morality, IV 465b, 469a, 469b, 470a, 471b
Morris, William, IV 469a
motif, III 236b
motion pictures, II 572a, 572b; IV 470b, 475a, 475b
music, III 270a; IV 466b, 467b, 472a–475a
musicians, IV 466b
mutability, II 581a–581b
mysticism, II 575b, 581b, 582a
mythology, II 581a; III

276b, 286a–286b, 288b–294b, 296b–298b; IV 467b, 469b, 470a
nationalism, II 579b
natural science, II 576b
naturalism, II 571a, 573a, 575b–583a; IV 471b
naturalism in art, III 340a, 341b, 342a, 342b, 343a
Nature, II 570a, 571a, 574a–576a, 579b–583a; III 349b, 350a; IV 466a, 467b, 469b, 470a–473b, 476a
neo-classicism in art, III 362b, 364a, 365b, 366b, 368a–370b
Neo-Platonism, II 576b; III 511b; IV 466b
neuroses, II 575b
Newton, IV 473a
nominalism, II 576b
the novel, IV 466a, 472a, 473b, 474b, 475a
novelists, IV 469a
opera, IV 470a, 472b, 475a
optics, III 408b–409a
oratory, IV 465b, 469a
Ovid, IV 468b, 469a
Palmieri, IV 122b
parallelism, IV 465b, 466a–467b, 472a, 472b, 473b
Pater, IV 469a, 472b
patrons, II 573a, 577a, 580a
Persia (ancient), IV 470b, 473a
perspective, II 570a, 577a; III 350a; IV 302a
perversion, II 575b
philosophers, IV 465b
philosophy, II 549b
Philostratus, IV 468b, 469a
photography, II 571b–572b
phrenology, IV 475a
physics, II 580a–580b
physiognomy, IV 475a
Picasso, IV 475b
Pico della Mirandola, IV 466a
pictorialism, IV 471b, 472a
Plato, I 457b, 581a–581b, 582a; III 226b, 497b, 498b–499a; IV 467b
Platonism, III 497b, 498b–499a, 501a, 511b, 512b
playwrights, IV 469a
Pliny, I 580b
Plutarch, IV 467b, 468a
Poe, IV 469a, 472b
poetry, III 526b, 527b
poets, IV 465b–474b
pointillism, II 567b
politics, IV 470a–471a

Pope, **IV** 467a
portraits, **III** 350a
post-impressionism, **II** 567b
Pound, Ezra, **IV** 470b
Poussin, **IV** 469b
power, **II** 576a–576b, 577a
pre-Raphaelites, **III** 341b; **IV** 475a
prestige, **II** 572b, 573a
Price, Uvedale, **IV** 473b
primitivism, **III** 597a, 602b
proportion, **IV** 466b, 467b, 472b
Proust, **III** 236b
psychology, **II** 575a, 580b, 583a; **IV** 465b, 471b–473b
Quintilian, **IV** 468a
realism, **II** 570a, 571a, 576b, 578b, 579a, 580a, 581b, 582b; **IV** 471b, 472a
realism in literature, **IV** 52a
reason, **IV** 466a, 467a
religion, **II** 575b, 576a, 576b, 581b, 582b; **IV** 476a
Renaissance, **II** 571b–572b; **IV** 122a, 122b, 123a, 124a, 130b, 133a, 439a, 439b, 440a, 441b, 466a, 467a–471b, 472b, 473b
revolt, **II** 567b–570b, 577a, 581b
revolution, **II** 577a, 581b
Reynolds, **IV** 467a, 468a, 470a
rhetoric, **IV** 466a, 468a, 469b–471b
Rimbaud, **IV** 475a
Ripa, **IV** 470a
Robortello, **IV** 467b
Romance languages, **IV** 466b
Romano, **IV** 466a
romanticism, **I** 595a; **II** 575b, 578a, 578b, 579a, 580a, 581a, 581b; **IV** 201a, 201b, 202b, 204a, 465b, 468b, 469b, 471b, 473a
Rossetti, **IV** 470b, 475a
Rousseau, **IV** 467b, 472b, 473a
Ruskin, **IV** 469a
Saint Bonaventura, **III** 227b
Sannazaro, **IV** 468b
Savonarola, **IV** 466a
Scaliger, **IV** 467b
Schiller, **IV** 474a
scholasticism, **IV** 467a
science, **II** 575b, 580a–583a; **IV** 466b, 467b, 471b–475a
Scott, **IV** 474b
Scriabin, **IV** 473a

sculpture, **IV** 466b, 469a, 471a, 473b–475b
senses, **II** 574b, 575b, 576b, 580b, 582a, 583a–593b; **IV** 466a–468b, 472a, 472b, 474b
sentio, **IV** 466b
Shakespeare, **IV** 471a
Sidney, **IV** 467b
Simias of Rhodes, **IV** 470b
Simonides of Ceos, **IV** 467b
skepticism, **II** 575b; **IV** 236b
society, **IV** 466b, 467a
Socrates, **III** 226a
sophism, **IV** 468b, 470a
space, **IV** 302a, 465b, 466a, 469b, 471a, 474a–475b
Spenser, **IV** 468b, 469a, 471a
Spitzer, **IV** 471a
State, **II** 570a, 576a, 582b
Statius, **IV** 469a
Stendhal, **IV** 469a, 475a
Strauss, **IV** 473a
structure, **IV** 472a
style, **II** 567b, 570a–570b, 572a, 572b, 574a, 574b, 576a, 576b–577b, 580a, 580b, 581b, 583a; **IV** 467a
Su Shih, **IV** 475b
sublime in external nature, **IV** 472a, 473b
Sung dynasty, **IV** 475b
sunlight, **II** 567b, 570a–570b, 571a, 579a, 581a
supernatural, **II** 575b, 576b, 580b
Surrealism, **I** 352b
symbolism, **II** 570b, 575b, 576b, 580b–581a, 581b–582a; **IV** 468b, 474b
symmetry, **IV** 34ba, 467b
synaesthesia, **IV** 471b, 473a
Taoism, **IV** 476a
Tasso, **IV** 467b, 468b, 469b
taste, **II** 572b, 573a; **IV** 471b, 472a, 473b, 474a
technology, **IV** 359b
television, **IV** 475a
Thomas, Dylan, **IV** 470b
Thomson, James, **IV** 471b
time, **IV** 465b, 469b, 471a, 474a, 474b, 475a, 475b
Tinguely, **IV** 475b
Titian, **IV** 469a, 471a
tradition, **II** 577a–577b, 579b, 581b
Trajan Column, **IV** 471a
Trapp, **IV** 466b
truth, **I** 322a; **II** 571a, 575b, 576a–576b, 582b; **IV** 465a,

466a, 475a
Turner, **IV** 467a, 467b, 470b, 473b
ugliness, **II** 571a; **IV** 468b
understanding, **IV** 466b
U.S., **IV** 469b
unity, **II** 576a
universal man, **IV** 439a, 439b, 440a, 441b
ut pictura poesis, **IV** 465b–476b
value, **II** 576b, 577b
Vasari, **IV** 469a
Vendôme, **IV** 468b
Venus (myth), **IV** 474a
Vergil, **IV** 468b, 469a
Verlaine, **IV** 472b, 473a
vibrism, **II** 570b
vice, **IV** 470a, 473b
Vida, **IV** 467b
Vinsauf, **IV** 468b
virtue, **IV** 470a, 473b
virtuoso, **IV** 486b
Vossius, **IV** 467b
Wagner, **IV** 472b
war, **II** 577a, 580a
Warton, Joseph, **IV** 471b
Warton, Thomas, **IV** 471b
Watteau, **IV** 467a
wealth, **II** 570a, 577a
Webb, **IV** 472a
Williams, W. C., **IV** 469b
Winckelmann, **IV** 469b, 474a
wisdom of the fool, **IV** 519b
writers, **IV** 469a
Zola, **IV** 467a
See also Painters
Pakistan, nationalism, **III** 338a
Palamas, Gregory (1296?–1359), mysticism, **I** 410b
Palante, Georges
irony, **II** 633b, 634a
politics, **II** 634a
Paleography, aesthetics, **II** 219b
Paleontology
evolutionism, **II** 176b, 179b
linguistics, **IV** 425a, 427b
uniformitarianism, **IV** 420a, 421b, 425a, 427b
Paleotti, Gabrielle, iconography, **II** 531a
Palestine
assemblies, **II** 253b–256a
Counter-Enlightenment, **II** 106b
Judaic-Christianity, **I** 373b–375a
Palestine (ancient), freedom of speech, **II** 253b–256a
Palestrina (1526?–1594), musical genius, **II** 321b

Paley, William (1743–1805),
association of ideas, **I** 114a
culture, **II** 127b
design argument, **I** 674b–675a, 676b
environment, **II** 127b
evolutionism, **II** 180a, 180b
God, **II** 352a
happiness, **II** 380b
utilitarianism, **II** 380b; **IV** 444b, 445b
Palingenesis, **I** 644b
Palladio, Andrea (1518–1580)
aesthetics, **II** 218b
architecture, **II** 218b
harmony, **IV** 41b
neo-classicism in art, **III** 365a
Pythagoreans, **IV** 41b
Pallas (myth), **III** 290b
Pallas, Peter Simon (1741–1811)
geology, **IV** 418b
language, **II** 669; **III** 64a, 64b
linguistics, **III** 64a, 64b, 68b
Pallavicino, Sforza (1607–1667), historiography, **II** 468b
Palmer, Alexander Mitchell (1872–1936), loyalty, **III** 114a
Palmer, Elihu, deism, **I** 651b, 652a
Palmieri, Matteo (1406–1475)
good, **IV** 478b–479a
humanism, **II** 522a; **IV** 132b
painting, **IV** 122b
utilitarianism, **IV** 478b–479a
virtue, **IV** 478b–479a
work, **IV** 532a
Pamphilos (4th century B.C.),
art, **II** 299a–299b
genius, **II** 299a–299b
Pan (myth), **III** 292a
music, **III** 268b
Pan Ku (32–92 A.D.), historiography, **II** 481a
Panaetius (2nd century B.C.),
cycles, **I** 623a
dignity, **IV** 136a
ethics, **IV** 321b
natural law, **III** 16b
Platonism, **III** 504a
progress, **III** 631a
Stoicism, **IV** 321b
temperance, **IV** 369b–370a

Pan-Babylonianism, III 310a–310b
Pandora (myth), III 274b, 279a
longevity, III 89b
Pan-Egyptianism, III 310b
Pangenesis, II 622b–626b
acquired characteristics, II 623b
Anaxagoras, II 622b
Aristotle, II 623a–623b
atomism, II 622b, 623a
biology, I 231b; II 623a, 623b, 624b 626b
Buffon, II 623b
Darwin, II 624a–624b, 626a–626b
defined, II 622b
Digby, II 623b
empiricism, II 623a
environment, II 623b–624a, 625b
epigenesis, II 623a, 623b
evolution, II 623b, 624a, 626a
genetics, II 624b–626a
germinal link, II 623a, 623b
germplasm theory, II 624b–625a
Greece (ancient), II 622b–623b, 624a, 626a
Harvey, II 623b
heredity, II 623b, 624a, 626a
Hippocrates, II 622b, 624a
historiography, II 624b
individualism, II 623b
Lamarck, II 623b–624a, 626a
Le Grand, II 623b
literature, II 622b
Lysenko, II 626b
Marx, II 626a–626b
Marxism, II 626b
Maupertuis, II 623b
mechanism, II 623a, 623b, 624b
meiosis, II 624b
Mendel, II 626a, 626b
Michurin, II 626b
mitosis, II 624b
modes of acquisition, II 623b
natural selection, II 626a
Nature, II 623b
ontogeny, II 623b
panmixis, II 624b
philosophy, II 623a–623b, 626a
position effects, II 624b
Pre-Socratics, II 622b
race, II 626a
reductionism, II 623b
reproduction, II 622b

science, II 622b–626b
society, II 626a
somatoplasm, II 624b–625a
species, II 626a
Spencer, II 626a
Stalin, II 626b
teleology, II 623a
U.S.S.R., II 626b
unity, II 623a
variation, II 624a
vitalism, II 623b
Weismann, II 624b–626b
Pāṇini (fl. 350 B.C.?), language, II 670a, 670b
Pankus, Hittites, II 253a–253b
Pannenberg, Wolfgang, eschatology, II 157b
faith, hope, and charity, II 214b
God, II 365b
Pannwitz, Rudolf (1881–), crisis in history, I 594b
Panofsky, D., iconography, II 529b
Panofsky, Erwin (1892–1968)
ambiguity, I 52a–52b
art, II 308a
genius, II 308a
Gothic, II 373b
iconography, II 529a, 529b, 531b, 536a–540a
ideal, II 549b
mythology, III 290b, 292a
naturalism in art, III 339b, 343b
philosophy, II 549b
Platonism, III 513a
universal man, IV 440a
Panspermist theory, IV 311a
Pantaenus (c. 180–200), Buddhism, I 255a
Pantheism
Bruno, II 443a; III 194a
Confucianism and, I 360a
Creation, I 571a
deism and, I 649b
evil, II 162a
God, I 571a; II 350b
heresy, II 422b
hierarchy, II 443a, 445a
humanism, II 520a
longevity, III 90b
matter, III 194a
Orientalism, III 432b
Platonism, III 515b, 522a
religion, IV 108a
romanticism, IV 196b, 201b
Spinoza, I 360a; II 445a
theodicy, IV 379a, 379b
time, IV 393b
U.S., III 432b
Papacy

Antichrist, I 390a; III 225a
authority, I 149a–150a; II 689b
Avignon papacy (1309–1377), II 3a; IV 64a, 65a
caesaropapism, I 380b
Church, I 417b, 418a
Counter-Reformation, I 394b 395a
despotism, II 3a–4a
Enlightenment, II 91a
equality, II 414a, 141b
eschatology, II 156b
feudalism, III 225a
Free Spirit, II 422b–423a
French Revolution (1789), I 404a–404b
Great Schism (1378–1417), I 385a, 386a–386b, 387b; IV 65a, 65b
historiography, IV 149b
humanism, II 522b
Hundred Years' War, I 386a
Jesus Christ, I 382b
Joseph II, I 403b, 404a
law, II 686a, 689a 690a
Louis XIV, I 399b
Luther, I 390a, 395a, 396a
Machiavellism, III 116b, 117b, 118a, 120b
Maistre, I 482a
millenarianism, III 225a
Napoleon I, I 404b
nationalism, I 385a, 386b; III 319b, 320a, 321a 322a
power, III 116b
power of self-rectification, I 386a
prophecy, III 665b–669b
reformation, IV 60a, 64a–65b
Reformation, I 388b, 394b–395a
Renaissance, IV 123a, 149b
Roman Catholic Church, II 419b–425b, 426b, 429b
socialism, IV 286b
virtù, IV 477a
William of Ockham, II 3a–3b, 4a
Papebrochin, Daniel, historiography, II 486b
Papias (2nd century A.D.), millenarianism, III 224a
Papin, Denis (1647–?1712), technology, IV 362a
Papini, Giovanni (1881–1956)
experience, III 563b
free will, III 563b
Hook and, III 564a
imagination, III 563b
James and, III 563a–563b
Mead and, III 564a

politics, III 564a
pragmatism, III 551b, 552a–552b, 563a–564a
progress, III 632b
will to believe, III 563b
Pappus (c. 3rd–4th century A.D.)
Commandino and, III 380b
mathematics, III 178b, 380a–380b
science, II 203a
Papyrus, Edwin Smith, disease, II 396a
Parables
mythology, III 275b, 282b
progress, III 635a
theriophily, IV 384b
Paracelsus, Philippus (1493–1541)
alchemy, I 28b, 31b–32a, 33b; III 91b
Bacon, F., I 173b, 174b
disease, II 400a, 400b, 401a
historiography, IV 148b
Islam, II 646b
longevity, III 91b
metaphysics, III 211b, 212a, 212b, 222a
methodology, III 387b
post-Kantians on, IV 209a
Renaissance, IV 148b
romanticism, IV 209a
skepticism, IV 242a
spontaneous generation, IV 308b
Paradise
Islam, IV 230b
salvation, IV 230b
Paradox
Faust (legend), III 252b
irony, II 627a, 627b, 630b, 632b, 633a, 634a
mathematics, III 172b
social welfare, IV 281b
Parallelism
macrocosm and microcosm, III 129b, 130a
painting and poetry, IV 465b–467b, 472a, 472b, 473b
recapitulation, IV 56b, 57a
Paranoia
imagination, III 221a
mythology, III 312b
Paré, Ambroise (1510?–1590), spontaneous generation, IV 308b
Parent, Antoine, technology, IV 361b
Pareto, Vilfredo (1848–1923), authority, I 155b, 157b–158a
class, I 448a; III 151a
democracy, I 664b, 665a

game theory, II 271a
happiness and pleasure, iI 384b
ideology, II 555a–556a
individualism, II 601a, 601b
inequality, I 448a
Marxism, III 151a, 165a
social welfare, IV 277b, 279a–280a, 283a
utility, IV 450a, 456b, 457a
Paris (myth), III 288a, 292a, 308a
human nature, III 571b
Paris, Matthew (1200?–1259), historiography, II 474a
Park, Chief Justice, common law, III 31a
Park, James L., indeterminacy, II 592a
Parker, Samuel (1640–1688), atomism, I 138b
methodology, III 386b
Newton and, III 386b
Parker Theodore (1810–1860)
civil disobedience, I 436a
Pietism, IV 111b
transcendentalism, I 436a
Volksgeist, IV 495b
Parkinson, James (1755–1824), Chain of Being, I 334b–335a
Parmenides (5th century B.C.), analogy, I 60b
appearance and reality, I 94a, 96a, 99a
Aristotle and, IV 3a
atomism, I 127a–128a
Being, I 493b, 495a; III 187a
causation, I 271a
continuity, I 493b, 503a
cosmic images, I 513b 517a, 519b, 520b–522b
cosmology, III 179b
custom, III 575b
Democritus and, III 187b
dualism, II 40b; IV 346b
Empedocles and, IV 3a
harmony, IV 38b
historiography, I 503a
human nature, III 572a, 573a, 574a, 575b
infinity, II 614b, 615a, 615b
justice, II 653a, 653b
knowledge, III 572a
logic, IV 400a
mathematics, III 171b, 172b; IV 32a–32b
matter, III 187a, 187b, 188a
measurement, IV 399b
metaphysics, III 208b
Nature, I 127a–127b

Non-Being, IV 298b–299a
nous, IV 3a
perfectibility, III 464a
Plato and, IV 3a, 400a
pluralism, III 187a
psychology, IV 3a
Pythagoreans, IV 32a–32b, 37a, 38b, 400a
rationalism, IV 47a–47b
reality, III 572a
senses, III 187a; IV 47b
skepticism, IV 234b
soul, III 573a
space, IV 296a, 296b, 298b–299a, 305a
symmetry, IV 346b
time, IV 389b, 390b, 398a, 399b
truth, IV 47a
unity, III 187a
universe, IV 38b
Xenophanes and, III 464a
Zeno of Citium and, IV 47b
Zeno of Elea and, IV 400a
Parochialism, anthropomorphism, I 88b, 90a
Parole, IV 323b–324a, 324b
Parrhasios (5th century B.C.), art, II 299b
Parrington, Vernon Louis (1871–1929)
literature, III 83a
periodization in literary history, III 485a
realism in literature, IV 54b
Parsons, Talcott
ideology, II 556a–556b
individualism, II 601a
Parsons, Theophilus (1750–1813), Orientalism, III 429a
Parsons, William (Earl of Rosse) (1800–1867), cosmic images, I 521b
Particle-and-wave theory of light, IV 78a
Paruta, Paolo (1540–1598), Machiavellism, III 123a
Pascal, Blaise (1623–1662), authority, IV 118b
axiomatization, I 165b–166a
Bacon and, I 176b
casuistry, I 262b
chance, I 337b
China, I 360a
classicism, I 452a
death, I 637b
existentialism, II 189b
evil, II 168a; IV 381b
faith, IV 381b
Fermat and, III 606a–606b
frequency, III 606a
gambling, III 606a–606b
game theory, II 264a

God, II 168a, 349b, 355b; IV 246a
hierarchy, II 444a
illuminists, IV 109a
imagination, III 214b
irrationalism, II 635b, 637a, 637b, 638a, 638b
literary criticism, I 600b
literary paradox, III 79b
love, III 469a
methodology, III 387a, 387b
morality, II 168a
natural law, III 20b
Nature, III 348a
Newton and, III 387a, 387b
observation, III 606a
perennial philosophy, III 461a
perfectibility, III 469a, 469b
periodization in literary history, III 483a
pragmatism, III 563b
probability, III 606a–607b
progress, III 638b
reason, II 168a; IV 118b
religion, IV 109a, 109b, 118a–118b
responsibility, II 189b
rhetoric, IV 172b
romanticism, IV 209a
science, IV 118b
sin, IV 381b
skepticism, II 349b; IV 245b–246a, 248a, 250b
space, IV 302a
sublime in external nature, IV 334a
theodicy, IV 381b
tragic sense, IV 416b
Pasch, Moritz (1843–?1933), axiomatization, I 167a–167b, 168a
Pascoli, Giovanni (1855–1912), symbolism, IV 342a
Pasquier, Étienne (1529–1615), historiography, IV 148b
Passerat, Jean, (1537–1602), satire, III 77b, 79a
Passions
Butler, IV 178a
Comte, III 641b, 644a
Democritus, III 576b
Descartes, II 381a
determinism, II 236b
dignity, IV 138b, 142b
disease, III 397a, 398a
Enlightenment, III 248a
Euripides, III 573a
evil, II 163a
Fontenelle. III 644b
fortune, fate, and chance, II 233b

free will, II 236b, 242b
general will, II 276b
genius, II 294a
good, IV 178a
happiness, III 381a
human nature, III 572b, 573a, 575b, 576b, 644a
individualism, III 642b
literature, IV 332a
love, III 94a, 97b, 101b, 102a–107a
Machiavelli, IV 482a–482b
Man-Machine, III 133b–134a, 139b, 140b
Mill, J. S., III 642b
morality, III 644b
mythology, III 277a, 288a
perfectibility, III 644a
Plato, II 236b, 243a; III 498a, 499b, 501b; IV 3b, 4a
Platonism, III 498a, 499b, 501b
pleasure, II 381a
power, III 572b; IV 482b
progress, III 640b, 641b, 642b, 644a, 644b, 648b
psychology, IV 3b, 4a
Renaissance, IV 138b, 142b
rhetoric, IV 167b, 168b, 172a
right, IV 178a
romanticism, IV 195a
Saint Augustine, IV 138b
style, IV 332a
temperance, IV 367b
tragic sense, IV 413b, 415a
unity of science, IV 432b
virtù, IV 482a–482b
wisdom of the fool, IV 519a
Passover, mythology, III 276b, 282b
Passy, Frédéric (1822–1912), international peace, III 449a
Pasteur, Louis (1822–1895), biology, I 232a
disease, II 405a, 405b
genetic continuity, II 282a, 283b
spontaneous generation, II 282a, 283b; IV 309b, 310a, 310b
Patagonians, primitivism, III 596b
Pater, Walter (1839–1894), art for art's sake, I 109b
aesthetics, II 576a
classicism, I 450a
criticism, II 575b, 576a
Epicureanism, II 137b, 576a
ethics, II 576a
hedonism, II 575b

impressionism, **II** 575b–576a
literary criticism, **I** 601b
literature, **IV** 193b
naturalism, **II** 576a
Nature, **III** 349b
organicism, **III** 426a
Platonism, **III** 502b–503a, 522b, 524a
skepticism, **II** 575b
realism in literature, **IV** 55a
romanticism, **IV** 193b
ut pictura poesis, **IV** 469a, 472b

Pathetic fallacy
macrocosm microcosm, **III** 126a
Nature, **III** 351a

Pathology
disease, **II** 400b, 405b
imprinting, **II** 585b
learning, **II** 585b
psychology, **IV** 13b
rationalism, **IV** 48a

Patin, Guy (1601–1672), **IV** 244a

Patinir, Joachim de (1485?–1524), impressionism, **II** 578a

Patot, Simon Tyssot de
deism, **I** 649a
Utopia, **IV** 462b

Patrick, Simon, atomism, **I** 132a–132b

Patriotism
ethics, **III** 445a, 445b
general will, **II** 278a
loyalty, **III** 108a–108b, 114b
Machiavelli, **IV** 315a, 316b
Machiavellism, **III** 120a
nationalism, **III** 318b, 323a, 323b–325b, 328a, 328b, 333a, 333b, 334a, 673a
peace, **III** 445a, 445b
protest movements, **III** 673a
romanticism, **IV** 207a
Rousseau, **II** 278a; **III** 325b
State, **IV** 315a, 316b, 318b
Tolstoy, **III** 445b
Volksgeist, **IV** 491b
war, **III** 445a; **IV** 503b
welfare state, **IV** 510a

Patristic period
Clement of Alexandria, **I** 64a
Denis, **I** 64b, 65b
Origen, **I** 64a
Saint Augustine, **I** 64b–65a, 68b–69a

Patrizi, Francesco (1529–1597)
cosmology, **I** 545a
humanism, **II** 520a
matter, **III** 193b

mimesis, **III** 228b
Platonism, **III** 512a–514b
poetics, **III** 529a

Patroclus (myth), **II** 340a
law, **II** 676b

Patrons
art, **II** 573a, 577a, 580a; **IV** 437b
music, **II** 320b

Paul, Hermann (1846–1921), linguistics, **III** 70b

Paul, Jean (1763–1825),
genius, **II** 324b, 325a
irony, **II** 627b
romanticism, **IV** 188b, 189a, 196b

Paul, Saint
alienation, **I** 35a–35b, 36a
analogy, **I** 68b, 69a
baptism, **I** 416a
Christianity, **I** 375a, 375b, 414a–415b; **III** 589a–590a; **IV** 102b, 103a
Church, **I** 413b, 414b–417b
circumcision, **I** 414a, 415a
class, **I** 446a
Cosmic Fall, **I** 505a
death, **I** 643b–644a
deism, **I** 647b
Diderot and, **III** 603a
Donne, **III** 80a
dualism, **II** 43a
demonology, **II** 342a
equality, **II** 140b, 144b
eschatology, **II** 156a
evil, **II** 164a
faith, hope, and charity, **II** 210a, 211b
free will, **II** 245a
freedom, **II** 250a
freedom of speech, **II** 262a
Gnosticism, **II** 43a–43b, 327b, 330b–331a
God, **II** 341b–342a, 343a; **IV** 517a
hierarchy, **II** 439a
historiography, **II** 477b
immortality, **I** 643b–644a
impiety, **II** 565a
incontinence, **III** 96b
Jesus Christ, **II** 341b–342a, 343a
Judaic-Christianity, **I** 374b
Judaism, **I** 414b
law, **II** 250a, 686b, 688b; **III** 17b
lewdness, **III** 96b
literary paradox, **III** 76b, 78b, 80a
Loisy, **I** 421a
love, **III** 96a–96b, 97a
Luther and, **I** 389b
metaphor, **III** 205a–205b
mythology, **III** 276b, 283a,

284a
natural law, **III** 17b
Nature, **III** 17b
Neo-Platonism, **III** 372b
peace, **III** 440b
perfectibility, **III** 466b
philanthropy, **III** 488a
Platonism, **III** 509a
positivism, **III** 538b
primitivism, **III** 589a, 589b, 590a, 590b, 591b, 599a
reason, **III** 17b
reformation, **IV** 61b, 62a
religion, **III** 205a–205b; **IV** 102b, 103a
resurrection, **I** 643b–644a
rights, **II** 688b
Saint Thomas Aquinas and, **III** 466b–467a; **IV** 525b
salvation, **IV** 229b–230a
Seneca and, **III** 588b
sexual taboos, **III** 96b
Shakespeare, **III** 80a
sin, **II** 164a; **IV** 229b–230a
skepticism, **IV** 243b
slavery, **II** 250a
socialism, **IV** 286a
theodicy, **IV** 380b
tragic sense, **IV** 415a, 416a
Volksgeist, **IV** 491a
wisdom, **IV** 416a, 517a
wisdom of the fool, **IV** 517a, 518a, 519a
women, **IV** 524a–525b
work, **IV** 531a–531b

Paul of Alexandria, astrology, **I** 121a

Paul of Venice, medieval science, **II** 204a

Paul III, Pope (1468–1549),
Christianity, **I** 393a
Copernicus and, **IV** 74b
perennial philosophy, **III** 457b

Paul IV, Pope (1476–1559), Counter-Reformation, **I** 393b

Paul VI, Pope (1897–   )
private property, **III** 654b
resurrection, **I** 643b
Roman Catholic Church, **III** 654b

Paulhan, F., irony, **II** 633a

Pauli, Alfred, baroque in literature, **I** 191b

Pauli, Wolfgang (1900–1958), entropy, **II** 118a

Paulinus of Nola, Saint (353–431)
iconography, **II** 526b
mythology, **III** 281b–282a

Paulsen, Wolfgang, expressionism, **II** 206b

Pausanias (2nd century A.D.),

art, **II** 299b
genius, **II** 299b
historiography, **II** 501a
mythology, **III** 295a, 299a

Pauthier, G., China, **I** 369a

Pavlov, Ivan (1849–1936),
behaviorism, **I** 218a–218b, 222a, 224b
idea, **I** 116a
psychology, **IV** 14a, 14b, 28a

Pax Romana
peace, **III** 440b, 441b, 448a
Rome (ancient), **II** 656b; **III** 440b, 441b
Utopia, **IV** 459b

Pazmány, Peter, Cardinal (1570–1637), baroque in literature, **I** 193a

Pazzi, Alessandro de'
balance of power, **I** 180b
poetics, **III** 529a

Peabody, Elizabeth (1804–1894), transcendentalism, **IV** 24a

Peace, **III** 440a–457a
aggression, **III** 446b, 447a
agriculture, **III** 442b
anarchy, **III** 445a, 446a
anthropology, **III** 443a
Aristophanes, **III** 440a
Aristotle, **III** 440a
Bellarmine, **III** 441b
Bentham, **III** 444a–444b
Bible, **III** 440b, 441a, 445b
Buddhism, **III** 446a
Calvin, **III** 441b
Christianity, **III** 440b, 441a, 441b, 445b, 446a; **IV** 502a
Clement of Alexandria, **III** 441a
comedy, **III** 440a
commerce, **III** 443b
Comte, **III** 642a–642b
Cudworth, **III** 441a–441b
culture, **III** 442b, 443b, 444a, 447a
destiny, **III** 442a
Dewey, John, **III** 446b, 447a, 569a
diplomacy, **III** 443b
disarmament, **III** 444b
Doukhobors, **III** 441a
drama, **III** 440a
economics, **III** 442a, 444a, 445b, 446b
education, **III** 440a; **IV** 500b
Einstein, **III** 445b, 446b–447a
emancipation, **III** 444b
empiricism, **III** 443b
Enlightenment, **III** 446a
Epicureanism, **IV** 175b

Euripides, III 440a
Fox, III 441a
France, III 444b
Freud, III 445b, 446b, 447a
Ghandi, III 445b, 446a
God, III 440b, 441a, 441b, 445b
good, IV 175b, 176a, 177b
Greece (ancient), III 440a, 440b; IV 366b
Grotius, III 441b–442a
Hawtrey, III 445a–445b
Hector (myth), III 440a
Hedges, III 444a
Hegel, III 445a
Hillel, III 440b
history, III 440a, 440b, 443b, 444a, 445a
Hobbes, III 441b, 442b, 443a, 443b, 445b, 446a; IV 177b, 484a
Homer, III 440b
human nature, III 442b, 443b, 446a
humanism, III 446a; IV 131a
humanitarianism, III 441a
Hume, III 444a
idealism, III 443a–445b
imperialism, III 445a
India, III 446a
industry, III 445a, 445b, 446a, 642a–642b
internationalism, III 442a, 444b, 446a
intolerance, III 446b
Jainism, III 446a
James, William, III 447a; IV 507a–507b
Judaism, III 440b
justice, III 443a, 444b
Kant, III 442a–445b
Kropotkin, III 445a
law, III 1a, 440b–447a
Leibniz, III 442a, 443b
Lieber, III 444a
Lincoln, III 444a
logos, III 440b
love, III 440b, 441a, 445b, 447a
Lucretius, III 587b
Luther, III 441b
Machiavelli, III 441b; IV 502a
Marcus Aurelius, III 440b
Maritain, III 441a, 445b
Marx, III 445a
Marxism, III 147a
metaphysics, III 440b, 444a
Middle Ages, III 116a
military, III 440a, 441a, 443b, 444a, 445a, 445b, 446b, 447a
millenarianism, III 224b

morality, III 440b–446a
Muste, III 441a, 445b
mythology, III 291b
nationalism, III 332a, 445a, 446b
nation-state, III 441b–445b
Nature, III 440b, 442a, 444a, 446b
navigation, III 442b
nuclear power, III 446b
Origen, III 441a
over-population, III 446b, 447b
pacifism, III 441a, 441b, 445a, 445b, 447a; IV 502a
patriotism, III 445a, 445b
Pax Romana, III 440b, 441b
philosophy, III 442a 444a
Plato, III 440a
Platonism, III 441a
politics, III 441a, 443a, 444a, 445a, 446a, 446b
pollution, III 447b
poverty, III 447b
power, III 445a, 446a
pragmatism, III 569a
primitivism, III 580a, 581a, 587b
prisoners of war, III 441b
progress, III 634b, 636a, 642a–642b, 647a, 648a
prophecy, III 662b, 664a, 665b
Protestantism, III 441b
psychology, III 447a
Quakers, III 441a
race, III 446b
rationalism, IV 46a
reason, III 442a, 442b, 443a, 443b, 444b, 446a
reformation, IV 69a
religion, III 444a, 445b, 446b
Renaissance, IV 131a
republicanism, III 443a–443b
right, IV 175b, 176a, 177b
Rome (ancient), III 440b, 441b
Rousseau, III 442a, 445b
Russell, Bertrand, III 445b–446b
Saint Augustine, III 441b
Saint Justin, III 441a
Saint Paul, III 440b
Saint Thomas Aquinas, III 441a, 441b
Saint-Pierre, III 442a
Schwenkfelders, III 441a
science, III 442b, 443b, 444a, 446b, 447b, 642b
security, III 445a
Sermon on the Mount, III 441a, 441b, 445b, 446a

slavery, III 441a
Smith, Adam, III 444a
socialism, III 445a; IV 285a
society, III 440a–443b, 445b, 446b, 447a
sociology, III 445a–447b
soul, III 441a
Spencer, III 445a, 642a; IV 503b, 506b
State, III 441a, 441b, 443a, 446b
Stoicism, III 440b, 441a, 441b; IV 176a
taxation, III 441a
technology, III 445a, 445b, 446b; IV 504b
temperance, IV 366b
Thirty Years War, III 441b
Thoreau, III 446a
Tocqueville, IV 503a
Tolstoy, III 441a, 445b–446a
Toynbee, IV 508a
tragedy, III 440a
transcendentalism, III 444a
treaties, III 444b
Trojan War, III 440a
U.S.S.R., IV 506a
U.S., III 444a, 444b, 446b, 447a; IV 505b–506a
unity, III 441b
utilitarianism, III 441a
Utopia, IV 459a, 459b, 460b
Vattel, III 442a
virtù, IV 483b, 484a
war, III 440a–447b; IV 502a, 503a, 503b, 504b, 507b, 508a
Wilson, III 444b
Zeno of Citium, III 440b
Peace of Augsburg (1555), heresy, II 428a
toleration, IV 118a
Peace of Westphalia (1648), equality, II 138b
heresy, II 428a
Peacham, Henry (1576?–?1643)
hierarchy, II 435a
mythology, III 296a–296b
Scaliger and, III 296b
virtuoso, IV 486a
Peacock, Thomas Love (1785–1866), periodization in literary history, III 482a–482b
Peano, Giuseppe (1858–1932)
axiomatization, I 168a, 169b
mathematics, III 175b, 176a
pragmatism, III 557b, 560a
Pearson, Charles Henry,

China, I 370b
nationalism, III 331a
Pearson, E., probability, III 618b
Pearson, Karl (1857–1936), class, I 448a
classification of the sciences, I 465b
evolution, III 646a
inequality, I 448a
probability, III 615b
progress, III 646a
psychology, IV 26b
religion, IV 108a
Peasants' Revolt, I 391a, 391b
equality, II 142a
Luther, II 142a
millenarianism, III 225a
Peasantry
acquired characteristics, II 617b, 620b, 621b
agriculture, II 595a
antipeasantry, III 595a–595b
arts, III 595a
Austria, II 144a
China, I 371a, 372a–372b
China (Communist), III 154b
Christianity, III 670b
Egypt (ancient), II 256a
evil, III 595b
France, IV 500a
Germany, IV 500a
historiography, II 479a
Italy, III 674b
Marxism, III 154b
Nature, III 349a–349b, 594b, 595b
Noble Savage, III 594b, 595b
Poland, II 144b
primitivism, III 594b–595a, 600b
private property, III 650b, 651b, 652b
prophecy, III 666a
protest movements, III 670a, 672b, 674a, 674b
Prussia, II 144a
revisionism, IV 265b, 266b
Rousseau, III 594b; IV 259b
Russia, III 674b
science, III 595a
social contract, IV 259b
socialism, IV 287a
songs, IV 498b–499a
Spain, III 674b
theriophily, IV 386b
U.S.S.R., II 620b
war, IV 502a, 506b
Wordsworth, III 595a
vox populi, IV 498a, 498b–499a, 500a

Peckham, John (d. 1292),
  optics, III 410a
  prophecy, III 668a
Peckham, Morris, romanticism,
  IV 196a
Pecqueur, Constantin (1801–
  1887)
  individualism, II 595a
  socialism, IV 290a
Pedagogy
  children, III 595b
  phrenology, IV 23b
  primitivism, III 595b, 597b
  psychology, IV 23b
Pedro II, Emperor (1825–
  1891), positivism, III 539b,
  540a, 542b, 543a
Peebles, P. J. E., cosmology,
  I 567a
Peel, Robert (1788–1850),
  conservatism, I 481a
Péguy, Charles (1873–1914),
  irrationalism, II 636b
  Proust and, IV 340a
  symbolism, IV 340a
Peierls, R., indeterminacy, II
  591a
Peirce, Benjamin (1809–
  1880)
  classification of the
    sciences, I 465a
  cosmology, I 552b; III
    558b, 559b, 561a, 562a
Peirce, Charles S. (1839–
  1914)
  aesthetics, III 568b, 569b
  Aristotle and, III 555a, 567a
  art, III 569b
  authority, III 555a
  Bacon and, III 558b–559a
  Bain and, III 558a
  behaviorism, I 214b
  Bentham and, III 558a
  Cantor and, III 558a
  causation, II 587b
  chance, II 587b; III 560b
  classification of the
    sciences, I 465b–466a
  Comte and, III 558a
  conception, III 558a, 559b
  continuity, I 501b, 502a–
    502b; III 560b
  culture, III 555b, 556b
  Darwin and, III 518a, 560b
  Darwinism, III 558a, 560b
  Dedekind and, III 558a
  determinism, II 587b
  Duns Scotus and, III 555a
  empiricism, III 546b, 559a,
    559b
  ethics, III 556a, 568b
  evolution, II 181a, 184b,
    185a; III 562a
  experience, III 556b, 559a

experiments, III 554a, 555a,
  558a, 559a, 559b, 560b,
  561a
God, III 569b
Green and, III 567a
Hegel and, III 556a–556b,
  558a
history, III 556b, 560b
Holmes and, III 567a
Hume and, III 558a, 560b
idealism, III 552b, 568b
indeterminacy, II 587b
individualism, III 561a
infinity, II 611b
intuition, III 558a
James and, III 546b, 551b,
  552a–552b, 559a, 560a,
  561a–562a, 562b, 563b
judgment, III 552b, 556a,
  559a, 568b
justice, III 552b
Kant and, III 555b–556b,
  558a, 558b
knowledge, III 556a, 561a,
  561b, 568a
Langley and, III 560b
linguistics, IV 429a
logic, III 546b, 552b, 553a,
  555a, 556b, 558a, 559a–
  561a, 567a, 568a, 568b
love, III 560b
Lovejoy and, III 552b–553a
Mach and, III 558a
Marxism, III 565b
mathematics, III 184a,
  556b, 557b–558a, 559b–
  560a, 560b, 568a
mechanism, III 558a
metaphysics, III 558b,
  560b, 561a, 567a
methodology, III 554a,
  558a–558b, 559b–560a
Mill and, III 558a, 560b
mind, III 561b, 565b
monism, III 556b
morality, III 555b, 558b,
  565a
Nature, III 559a
nominalism, III 563b
observation, III 559a
Ostwald and, III 558a
perception, III 559a
perennial philosophy, III
  457a–457b
physics, III 556b, 558b,
  559b, 567a
Platonism, III 560b
positivism, III 546b, 558b
pragmatism, I 323b, 465b;
  II 184b, 185a; III 532b,
  551b, 552a–569b
probability, III 559a, 560b,
  561a, 615a–615b, 616b
psychology, IV 25a

Ramsey and, III 561a
realism, III 552b, 555a,
  560b, 561b
reality, III 560b
reason, III 558a, 559a,
  568a, 568b
religion, III 555a, 565a,
  569b
romanticism, III 568b; IV
  210b
Royce and, III 561a
Russell and, III 561a
Schelling and, II 185a; III
  568b; IV 210b
Schiller and, III 552b, 553a,
  559a, 568b, 569b
science, III 552b–553a,
  555a, 557b–559a, 559b,
  560b, 561a
signs, III 557a, 559a–560b
Social Darwinism, II 181a
Socrates and, III 554a
Sorel and, III 565a
Spencer and, III 558a, 560b
spiritualism, III 556b
structuralism, IV 327a,
  328a
thought, III 558a, 560b
time, IV 395b, 396a, 396b,
  398a
truth, III 552b–553a, 559a,
  561a, 568b
Turquette and, III 560b–
  561a
tychism, II 587b; IV 396a
uniformitarianism, IV 429a
unity, III 556b
Vailati and, III 560a
value, III 552b, 556a, 568a
Whitehead and, III 561a
will to believe, III 562b
Wright and, III 555b, 558a,
  561a
Peiresc, Bacon and, I 176b
Pejović, Danilo, Marxism, III
  168b
Pelagianism
  Augustinianism, III 466a–
    467a
  dignity, IV 138b
  evil, II 164b
  free will, II 245a
  perfectibility, III 466a–467a
  reformation, IV 63a
  Renaissance, IV 138b
  Roman Catholic Church
    and, I 394a; III 466b
  Saint Augustine, II 245a
  Tennant, III 467a
Pelagius (360?–?420)
  determinism, II 26b–27a
  evil, II 26b
  free will, II 244b; III
    469a

God, III 466b
good, III 466b
grace, III 466b
morality, III 466b
perfectibility, III 466b, 469a
predestination, II 26b–27a
Saint Augustine, II 26b–27a
theology, II 26b–27a
Peletier, Jacques (1517–
  1582)
  poetics, III 529b
  rhetoric, IV 171a
Peleus (myth), temperance, IV
  366b
Pell, John (1610–1685),
  atomism, I 135b
Pellegrini, Pellegrino (1527–
  1596)
  genius, II 293b
  romanticism, IV 190a
Pellico, Silvio (1789–1854),
  romanticism, IV 205a
Pelliot, Paul (1878–1945),
  China, I 368a
Pellisier, Georges Jacques
  Marie (1852–1918), classicism, I 450b
Pelopidas (fl. 4th century B.C.),
  historiography, II 504b
Pemberton, Henry (1694–
  1771)
  Newton and, III 393a
  optics, III 393a
Pende, Nicola, psychology, IV
  15a
Penelope (myth)
  law, II 681a
  temperance, IV 365b
Penn, William (1644–1718),
  conservation, I 474a
  international peace, III
    452b
Pennaforte, Raimundus de
  (fl. 13th century A.D.),
  casuistry, I 259a
Pensions, IV 510b, 511a
Penzer, N. M., baroque in
  literature, I 192a
Penzias, A. A., cosmology, I
  567a
People, see Vox populi
People of the book, II 639a
People's Crusade, III 666a
Pepper, Stephen C.
  beauty, I 208b, 209a
  organicism, III 426b
  pragmatism, III 553a, 569b
  right and good, IV 185a
Pepys, Samuel (1633–1703),
  mountains in literature, III
    258b
  musical genius, II 322a
  virtuoso, IV 486b, 487a,
    487b, 488a–488b

Pepys, Mrs. Samuel, virtuosa, **IV** 488b

Peraldus, Guielmus, casuistry, **I** 259a

Perception
Aristotle, **I** 1b–2a; **IV** 5a, 5b–6a
environment, **II** 123a–123b
Epicureanism, **IV** 7b, 8a
Epicurus, **I** 2b
extensio, **IV** 301b
Gestalt psychology, **IV** 182b
good, **IV** 182b
Greece (ancient), **II** 607b
humanism, **IV** 130b
infinity, **II** 607b
Lovejoy, **III** 552b
naturalism in art, **III** 340b, 345b
Peirce, **III** 559a
Plato, **IV** 4a, 34a
Plotinus, **IV** 9a
pragmatism, **III** 552b, 559a
psychology, **IV** 4a–9a, 23a
Pythagoreans, **IV** 34a, 35b
rationalism, **IV** 47b
Renaissance, **IV** 130b
right, **IV** 182b
Saint Augustine, **I** 3a
skepticism, **IV** 234b, 235b, 236a, 237a
space, **IV** 301b, 303a
Speusippus, **IV** 35b
Stoics, **I** 2b; **IV** 8a
Strato, **IV** 7a
symmetry, **IV** 347b
Theophrastus, **IV** 6b
tragic sense, **IV** 411b

Percier, Charles (1764–1838), neo-classicism in art, **III** 365b

Percy, Henry (1567–1632), Hariot and, **I** 133b

Percy, Thomas (Bishop) (1729–1811)
romanticism, **IV** 194a, 194b, 195a
vox populi, **IV** 498b–499a

Perdrizet, P., iconography, **II** 525a

Peregrinus, Peter (fl. 13th century A.D.), experiments on magnets, **II** 197a

Pereira Barreto, Luis
Brandão Júnior and, **III** 541b
Comte and, **III** 540b
education, **III** 541a
engineering, **III** 540b
Finlay and, **III** 541a
Laffitte and, **III** 540b
Lemos and, **III** 541a
medicine, **III** 540b
morality, **III** 540b

politics, **III** 540b
positivism, **III** 540b 541b
proletariat, **III** 541b
Ribbentrop, Marie de, and, **III** 540b
Roman Catholic Church, **III** 540b
science, **III** 540b
slavery, **III** 541b

Perelman, Chaim
justice, **III** 27b
natural law, **III** 5b–6a, 27b
positivism, **III** 5b–6a

Perennial philosophy, **III** 457a–463a
abstraction, **III** 462b
Alsted, **III** 460a
Aristotelianism, **III** 458b, 459b
Aristotle, **III** 459a–462b
Augustinianism, **III** 461a
authority, **III** 459a
Ayer, **III** 462b
Bacon, **III** 459b, 460a, 461a
Bayle, **III** 461b
Berkeley, **III** 457a
Bisterfeld, **III** 460a
Bouvet, **III** 461b
Boyle, **III** 461a
Brucker, **III** 460a
Bruno, **III** 460b
Cartesianism, **III** 461a
casuistry, **III** 459a
causation, **III** 459b
Christianity, **III** 457b, 458a, 459a, 459b, 461a
civil law, **III** 460b
Comenius, **III** 460a
common sense, **III** 459b
Comte, **III** 462b
cosmology, **III** 459b
Counter-Reformation, **III** 457b
Creation, **III** 459b, 460b
Croce, **III** 462a, 462b
De Volder, **III** 461b
defined, **III** 457a
Descartes, **III** 460b, 461a
Dewey, **III** 462a
Dilthey, **III** 462a, 462b
dualism, **III** 458b, 460b
eclecticism, **III** 458b–459a, 459b, 460a–461a, 461b, 462b
Egypt (ancient), **III** 459a
empiricism, **III** 457a, 460a, 462b
encyclopedism, **III** 459b, 460a
Enlightenment, **III** 459b–461b
error, **III** 458b, 459a
eschatology, **III** 458b, 459b,

461a
ethics, **III** 460a
Euclid, **III** 461a
evil, **III** 458b, 459a
existentialism, **III** 462b
faith, **III** 458b, 459a, 461b
Fall, **III** 459b
Ficino, **III** 459b
fideism, **III** 459a
Forms, **III** 458b
Foucher, **III** 458a, 461a
freedom, **III** 459b
Galen, **III** 461a
Glanvill, **III** 461a
God, **III** 457b, 458a, 459a, 459b, 460a, 460b, 461a
good, **III** 459a, 460b–461a
grace, **III** 459b
Greece (ancient), **III** 458b–459a, 460b
Hansch, **III** 461b
harmony, **III** 458b, 460b, 462a
Hartmann, **III** 463a
Hegel, **III** 462a
Heidegger, **III** 462b
heresy, **III** 458b
Hirschberger, **III** 462a
historicism, **III** 457a
history, **III** 457b, 458b, 459a, 459b, 462a, 462b
Hobbes, **III** 461a
humanism, **III** 459b
Hume, **III** 462b
Huxley, A., **III** 458a, 462b
Huygens, **III** 461a
idea, **III** 458b–463a
ideal, **III** 457a–463a
innovation, **III** 458b
intuition, **III** 458b
Islam, **II** 650b
James, **III** 462b
Jaspers, **III** 462a, 462b
Jesus Christ, **III** 460a
Judaism, **III** 459a
judgment, **III** 459a
Kant, **III** 457b, 462a, 462b
Kierkegaard, **III** 462a
knowledge, **III** 457a, 458b, 459b 461a, 462a
Korthold, **III** 461b
law, **III** 458b, 460b–461a
Leibniz, **III** 457b–458a, 460a, 460b–461b
Liebert, **III** 462b
literature, **III** 459a–459b
logic, **III** 459a–462b
Lovejoy, **III** 458b
Lully, **III** 460a
macrocosm and microcosm, **III** 458b
Malebranche, **III** 461a
Marx, **III** 462a
mathematics, **III** 457b,

460a, 461b
metaphor, **III** 458b
metaphysics, **III** 459a, 459b, 460a, 461a–463a
morality, **III** 457b, 460b, 462a
mysticism, **III** 458b, 459a
natural law, **III** 459b, 460b
Nature, **III** 459b, 460a, 460b, 462a
necessity, **III** 462a
Neo-Platonism, **III** 459a, 460b
Neo-Scholasticism, **III** 462a–462b
Newton, **III** 461b
Nicholas of Cusa, **III** 459b, 460b
nominalism, **III** 462a
obedience, **III** 459b, 460b–461a
Orientalism, **III** 458a
Pascal, **III** 461a
Paul III (Pope), **III** 457b
Peirce, **III** 457a–457b
Petrarch, **III** 459b
physics, **III** 459b–461b
Pico della Mirandola, **III** 459b
piety, **III** 457a
Plato, **III** 458b–463a
Platonism, **III** 457b–461b
Plotinus, **III** 458b, 459a
pluralism, **III** 457a, 458b, 461b
positivism, **III** 462b
power, **III** 459b
pragmatism, **III** 462b
psychology, **III** 457b, 459a, 463a
Pythagoreans, **III** 459a
rationalism, **III** 460a
realism, **III** 458b
reason, **III** 457a–461b
redemption, **III** 459a, 459b, 462b
religion, **III** 457b–459b
Remond de Montmort, **III** 458a, 461a
Renaissance, **III** 457b, 459a–459b
revelation, **III** 457b, 458b, 459a, 459b
right, **III** 462a
Rintelen, **III** 458a, 462a
Roman Catholic Church, **III** 457b
Rothacker, **III** 463a
Saint Augustine, **III** 458b, 459a, 459b
Santayana, **III** 462b
Schelling, **III** 463a
scholasticism, **III** 457b,

458a, 459a, 459b, 461a, 461b
science, III 457b, 459b, 460a, 461a, 462a, 462b
sectarianism, III 457a
sin, III 459a
skepticism, III 457a, 458a, 459a, 459b, 462a
Spencer, III 462b
Spranger, III 462b
Steuchius, III 457b–458a, 459a–459b, 460a
Stoicism, III 457b, 459b
Suárez, III 461a
subjectivity, III 462a
symbolism, III 460a, 461a
theism, III 458b
theology, III 458b, 459a, 459b, 460a, 461a
Thomasius, III 460b
Tillich, III 463a
time, III 459a
tradition, III 458a, 458b, 459b, 461b
Trendelenberg, III 462a–462b
truth, III 457b, 458a, 458b, 459b–462b
unity, III 457b, 458a, 458b, 460a, 460b, 462b
universality, III 458b, 460b, 462a, 462b
utopianism, III 458b
Voss, III 460b
Wagner, III 461b
Whitehead, III 463a
wisdom, III 457a, 457b, 459a, 459b, 460a
Wolff, III 461b
Perfectibility, III 463b–476a
aesthetics, III 463b, 467b; IV 356a, 356b
Albigensians, III 468a
altruism, III 644a
American Revolution, III 472a
anarchy, III 470a–471a
Anaximander, III 464a
anthropomorphism, III 464a
anxiety, III 465a, 467a
Aristotle, III 464a, 465a, 473b
artists, I 205b
asceticism, III 467b
association, III 470b
Augustinianism, III 466a–467a, 469a, 469b
Bacon, III 471b
Bakunin, III 471a
Barth, III 467a
beauty, II 549b; III 465a
Being, III 464a–464b, 467b
benevolent despots, III

470a, 475a
Bergson, III 474a
Bible, III 465b, 466a, 466b, 468b, 472a
biology, III 471a, 475a
breeding, III 471a
Brown, Norman, III 475a
Buddhism, III 464b, 465b, 466a
Butler, Bishop, III 469a
calculus, III 471b
Calvin, III 467a, 468b–469a
Catherine the Great, III 470a
chance, III 470a
Charron, III 468b
chastity, III 467a
children, III 469b–470a, 471a
Christianity, III 464a, 464b, 465b–469b, 471b–472a, 474b
classification of the arts, I 457a
Clement, III 466a
communism, III 473b
Condorcet, III 471b, 472a, 643b–644a
conduct, III 463b
consciousness, IV 112a
contemplation, III 464b, 465a
cooperation, III 470b
cosmology, III 464a
cults, III 464b
Darwin, III 473b, 474a
de Moivre, III 471b
Descartes, III 471b
desire, III 465b, 472a
dignity, IV 144a
Dionysius (myth), III 464b
drugs, III 475a
Drummond, III 474b
Dühring, III 474a
duty, III 472b
dystopias, III 474b
Eckhart, III 467b
economics, III 472a, 473b, 644a
education, III 465a, 466b, 469a–470a, 470b, 472a, 474a, 474b
elite, III 465a
Empedocles, III 464b
empiricism, III 471a–471b, 643b
Engels, III 473b
Enlightenment, II 92b–93a; III 469a–469b, 471b–472a, 473a–473b, 474b
environment, III 469b–470a, 473a, 473b, 643b
Epicurus, III 465a–465b,

468b
equality, III 644a
ethics, III 644a
evil, III 469b, 470a, 470b, 472b, 474a, 475a, 643b
evolution, III 473b–474b
Fabians, III 470a
faith, III 465b–466a
Fall, III 466a–466b
fear, III 465a
feeling, III 643b
Fichte, III 473a, 475a
flaws, III 463b
Forms, III 464b–465a
Fourier, III 470b
Frederick the Great, III 470a
free will, III 467a, 469a
freedom, III 470a, 472b, 473a, 473b, 475a, 644a
Fromm, III 475a
Galton, III 471a
genes, III 471a
genetics, III 471a, 474b
Germany, III 475a
Gnosticism, III 468a
God, III 463b–467b, 468b, 469a–472b, 474b
Godwin, III 470a–472a
Goethe, III 473b
good, III 465a, 466b, 467a, 469a, 470a, 643b
grace, III 466a, 466b, 467a
Great Britain, III 468a–468b, 470a
Greece (ancient), III 463b–465b, 468b, 473a
happiness, III 463b, 464a, 465a, 468b, 469a, 473b, 475a, 644a
harmony, III 463b, 464b, 467a
Hartley, III 469b, 471b
Hegel, III 473a–473b, 474a
Helvétius, III 470a, 643a–643b
Herder, II 551a; III 472b–473a, 639a
heresy, III 467b–468b
hermitages, III 467b
Hesiod, III 463b
historiography, IV 148a, 149a, 150a, 151b
history, III 471a–474b
Holbach, III 643a–643b
Homer, III 463b
human nature, III 643a–644a
Hume, III 471b
Huxley, Aldous, III 474b
Huxley, Julian, III 474a
Huxley, T. H., III 474a
ideal, II 549b, 551a–551b; III 465a–465b
idealism, III 472b, 473a

Ignatius, III 466a
ignorance, III 468a, 472a, 643b
imagination, III 465b
immortality, II 463b, 464a, 468a, 470b
immutability, III 463b, 464a
individualism, III 472b
infinity, II 614a–615b; III 464a
inheritance, III 471a, 473b
instinct, III 644a
Irenaeus, III 466a
Jesus Christ, III 467a, 468a, 474b
Joachim of Floris, III 472a–472b
Judaism, III 467b
justice, III 475a
Kant, II 551b; III 472b; IV 382b
knowledge, III 464b–465a, 467b, 468b, 472a, 643b, 644a
Kropotkin, III 470b
labor, III 644a
language, III 471b–472a, 474b–475a
Laplace, III 471b
law, III 470a, 472a–473b
Leibniz, III 471b–472b
Locke, III 469b
love, III 463b, 468b, 469a, 473a, 474b
Luther, III 467b
macrocosm, III 126b
Manicheism, III 468a
Marcus Aurelius, III 465b
marriage, III 470b, 471a
Marx, III 473b, 474a
materialism, III 473a
mathematics, III 471b, 472a
Medawar, III 471a
metaphysics, III 463b, 464a, 465a, 465b, 468b, 470b, 472b, 474a, 474b
Methodism, III 468a, 468b
Middle Ages, III 473a
Mill, III 470a
monasteries, III 467b, 468b
morality, III 463b, 464a, 466b, 468b–471b, 473b, 474a, 643b, 644a
Moses (Bible), III 466b
motive, III 463b
Muller, H. J., III 471a
music, III 470b
mysticism, III 466a, 467b, 468b–469b, 474a–475a
mythology, III 463b–464b
natural selection, III 473b
Nature, III 465b, 470b, 475a, 644a
Nazism, III 475a

Neo-Platonism, III 465b–466a, 467b
Newton, III 471b
Nicole, III 469a
Niebuhr, III 467a
Nietzsche, III 474a
Noyes, III 468b
nuclear weapons, III 475a
obedience, III 467a, 468b
omnipotence, III 464a, 469b
Oneida community, III 468b
order, III 463b, 464b, 475a
Origen, III 466a
Orwell, III 474b
overpopulation, III 475a
Owen, III 469a
pain, III 465a, 468a, 470a, 643b
Parmenides, III 464a
Pascal, III 469a, 469b
passions, III 644a
Pelagianism, III 466a–467a
Pelagius, III 466b, 469a
Philo Judaeus, III 465b–466a, 466b
philosophy, II 549b, 551a, 551b; III 464b, 465a, 473a–473b, 474a
Plato, III 464b 466b, 468b 469b, 471a; IV 285b
Platonism, III 466a, 466b, 468b, 469a, 471a
pleasure, III 643b
Plotinus, III 466a
politics, III 471b, 473b, 475a, 644a
pollution, III 475a
Pomponazzi, III 468b
poverty, III 467a
power, III 463b
pre-Socratics, III 463b–464b
pride, III 464a, 467a, 468b–469a, 472b
Priestley, III 472a
private property, III 468b, 470b
probability, III 471b
progress, III 471a–472b, 628b–629b, 635b, 639a, 643a–644a, 648b
prophecy, III 474b
Protestantism, III 467a, 467b–468a
Proudhon, III 470b–471a
Prussia, III 473a, 473b
Pseudo-Dionysius, III 467b
psychology, III 469b, 474b, 475a; IV 20b–21a
public esteem, III 469b
public reprobation, III 469b

punishment, III 465a
purification, III 464b
Pythagoras, III 464b
Quakers, III 467b–468b
race, III 471a
Reade, III 474b, 475a
reason, III 464b–465a, 465b, 471b, 472a
reformation, IV 61a, 62b
reincarnation, III 464b
Renaissance, III 468b; IV 123b, 144a, 148a, 149a, 150a, 151b
Renan, III 474b
revelation, III 465b–466a, 468a
revisionism, IV 269b, 270b
revolution, III 471a, 472a
ritual, III 464b
Roman Catholic Church, III 466b–467b
Rome (ancient), III 473a
Rousseau, III 469b, 470a
Saint Ambrose, III 467a
Saint Augustine, III 466a–466b, 468b–469a, 475a; IV 381a
Saint John of the Cross, III 467b
Saint Paul, III 466b
Saint Teresa, III 467b
Saint Thomas Aquinas, III 466b–467a, 467b
sanctification, III 468a
science, III 471a–472a, 474a, 644a
secularism, III 465b 469a
self-denial, III 468a
selfishness, III 468b, 469a
self-love, III 468b–469a
self-sufficiency, III 463b, 464a, 468b
Seneca, III 465b
senses, III 466a
Shakespeare, III 473a
Shelley, III 470b
sin, III 463b, 466a–469b
Skinner, III 469b
socialism, III 470a, 470b; IV 285a, 285b, 286b
society, III 465a, 467b, 468b, 469a, 470a–475a, 644a
Socrates, III 465b, 472a
soul, III 464b, 465a, 466a, 469a
Spain, III 467b
Spencer, III 473b–474a
spiritualism, III 468a–468b
State, III 463b, 469b–473b; IV 313a, 314b
Stoicism, III 465b, 466a, 468b, 469a, 470b
suffering, III 466a, 467b

superman, III 474a
superstition, III 465a, 470a, 470b
survival of the fittest, III 473b
Suso, III 467b
systematism, III 463b
taste, IV 356a, 356b
Tauler, III 467b
technology, III 475a
Teilhard de Chardin, III 474b
teleology, III 463b
temperament, III 469b
temptation, III 468a
Tennant, III 467a
theater, III 470b, 473a
theodicy, IV 381a, 382b
theology, III 463b, 464a, 464b, 468b–469a, 469b, 470b, 473b, 474a, 475a
timelessness, III 463b
totalitarianism, IV 407b
transcendentalism, III 463b
Trotsky, III 473b
U.S.S.R., III 475a
unity, III 473a
universe, III 464b, 465b, 473b–474a
Utopia, IV 458b, 463a, 464b
utopianism, III 469a, 470b
virtue, III 464b, 465b, 466a, 466b, 467a, 470a, 472a
Wallace, Wm., III 473b
Watson, J. B., III 469b
Wells, H. G., III 474b, 475a
Wesley, III 468a
wisdom, III 643b
Xenophanes, III 464a
Yahweh, III 465b
Zamyatin, III 474b
Zeno of Citium, III 465b
Zeus (myth), III 464a
Pergolesi, Giovanni Battista (1710–1736), musical genius, II 323a
Peri, Jacopo (1561–1633), music, II 321b
Periander of Corinth (d. 585 B.C.), despotism, II 2b
Pericles (d. 429 B.C.)
cynicism, I 629b
democracy, I 653b, 654a, 658b
freedom of speech, II 259a, 260a
historiography, II 501a 502b
impiety, II 565b
law, II 684a–684b
periodization in literary history, III 481b
Plato and, III 500a

politics, II 565b
State, I 653b–654b
temperance, IV 367b, 377a
Thucydides and, IV 367b
Periodization in history, III 476a–481b
Abelard, III 480a
absolutism, III 499a
Age of Reason, III 479b
annalists, III 476b, 477a
antiquity, III 477a, 477b, 479b, 480a
Aristotelianism, III 480b
art, III 477b, 479b
Baron, Hans, III 480a
baroque, III 479a
Barraclough, III 479a
Bayle, III 479a
Bible, III 476b, 477a
Bossuet, III 477b
Braudel, III 480b
Brunner, III 478b
Burckhardt, III 479a
Byzantine Empire, III 480a
capitalism, III 478b, 479a, 480b
Cellarius, III 477b, 478a, 480a
centuries, III 477a, 478a
Charlemagne, III 477a, 477b, 480a
Christianity, III 476b, 477a, 477b, 478a, 478b
chronicles, III 477a
chronology, III 476b
civilization, III 476b, 478b, 480a, 480b
commerce, III 480a
Comte, III 478a
cosmology, III 476b
Counter-Reformation, III 480b
Creation, III 476b, 477a
cynicism, III 476b
Dark Ages, III 478b, 480a
Dawson, III 480a
democracy, III 479a
dialectics, III 478a
economics, III 478a, 478b, 479a
education, III 480b
Engels, III 478b
Enlightenment, III 477b, 478a, 478b, 479b
eschatology, III 477b
eternity, III 477a
evolution, III 476b, 478a, 479a, 480b
Ferguson, W. K., III 479b
feudalism, III 478b
Fischer, E., III 479a
four empires doctrine, III 477a
France, III 478a, 479b

PERIODIZATION IN HISTORY; IN LITERARY HISTORY

French Revolution (1789), III 478a, 479a, 480a
Friedrich, C. J., III 479b
Germany, III 478a
God, III 477a
Greece (ancient), III 476b
Guizot, III 477b
Haskins, III 480b
Hazard, III 480a
Hegel, III 478a
historians, III 476a–480a
Holborn, III 479a
Hornius, III 477b, 478a
Huizinga, III 476a–476b, 480a, 480b
humanism, III 476b, 477a, 477b, 479b
imperialism, III 477a, 477b
Incarnation, III 477a
individualism, III 476b, 478a, 480b
Industrial Revolution, III 480b
industry, III 478a, 479a
International Historical Congress, III 479a
irrationalism, III 479a
Islam, III 480a
Italy, III 479b, 480a
Jesus Christ, III 476b, 477a
Kant, III 479b
law, III 477b, 480b
literature, III 477b, 479b
Livy, III 476b
Luethy, III 480b
Machiavelli, III 476b
Machine Age, III 479a
Marx, III 478a, 478b, 479a
Marxism-Leninism, III 478b
materialism, III 478a, 478b
mercantilism, III 479a
metaphysics, III 478a
Michelet, III 479a
Middle Ages, III 477a, 478a, 478b, 479a, 480a, 480b
military, III 478a
millenarianism, III 477a
modernism, III 477a, 477b, 478a, 479a, 480a, 480b
nationalism, III 476b
natural science, III 478a
numerical subdivisions, III 477a
Orientalism, III 480a
Otto the Great, III 477a
Petrarch, III 477b
philosophy, III 476b, 478a, 479b, 480b
Pirenne, III 480a
politics, III 476b–480b
positivism, III 478a
Protestantism, III 477b, 480b
Ranke, III 477b

realism, III 476b, 480b
religion, III 479b, 480b
Renaissance, III 477a–477b, 479b–480b
romanticism, III 478a, 478b, 479b
Rome (ancient), III 476b, 477a, 477b
Saint-Simon, III 478a
scholasticism, III 476b, 477a, 478b, 480a, 480b
science, III 478a
secularism, III 477a 478a
slavery, III 478b
Smith, Adam, III 479a
socialism, III 478b
society, III 477b, 478a, 478b, 480b
sociology, III 478a, 478b, 479a, 480b
Sombart, III 478b
Southern, W. E., III 480a–480b
Spencer, III 478a
State, III 477b
technology, III 479a
theology, III 476b, 478a
time, III 476b
Tocqueville, III 479a
tolerance, III 479b
Trevor-Roper, III 480b
U.S.S.R., III 479a
U.S., III 479a
Universal Spirit, III 478a
Vasari, III 479b
Voltaire, III 477a, 477b
Weber, III 480b
Wolff, III 480a
Wölfflin, III 479b
world periods, III 476b–477a
World War I, III 479a
Zhukov, III 479a
Periodization in literary history, III 481b–486a
Ainsworth, III 482a
Alexander the Great, III 481b
Algarotti, III 482a
annals, III 482b
Anne, Queen, III 483a
antiquity, III 481b, 482b
Arcadia, III 484a
Aristophanes, III 481b
art, III 482b, 483b 485b
Atterbury, III 483a
Augustus, III 481b, 483a, 483b, 484b
baroque, III 483b, 484a
Berkeley, III 482a
Besser, III 482a
Biedermeier, III 483b
biology, III 485b
Brandes, III 485a

Brie, III 484a
Byron, III 485b
Calderón de la Barca, III 482a
Catherine the Great, III 483a
Cellarius, III 481b
centuries, III 482b
Charles I, III 482b
Chaucer, III 485b
classicism, III 483a, 483b
Coleridge, III 488b
concepts, III 484b–486b
Cournot, III 485b
currents, III 485a
Curtius, III 484a
Daniells, III 484a
Dante, III 485b
das junge Deutschland, III 483b
Donne, III 485b
drama, III 482b, 483a
Dryden, III 481b, 482a
Dvořák, III 484a
education, III 485a–485b
Eichrodt, III 483b
Elizabeth I, III 482a–483a
Elizabethan Age, III 482a, 482b, 483a, 484b
Erasmus, III 482a
Euripides, III 481b
evolution, III 482b, 484b
expressionism, III 483b
Fénelon, III 483a
Ficino, III 482a
France, III 481b, 482a, 483a, 483b, 485b
Frederick the Great, III 482a, 483a
French Revolution (1789), III 483a, 485b
Garcilaso, III 482a
generation concept, III 485b–486a
George II, III 483a
George III, III 482b
George IV, III 482b
Germany, III 482a–485b
Goethe, III 486a
Golden Age, III 481b–482a
Goldsmith, III 483a
Gothic, III 484a
Gottsched, III 482a
Gray, III 485b
Great Britain, III 481b–483b, 484b, 485b
Hamann, III 484a
Herder, III 482a
Hesiod, III 481b–482a
historiography, III 483b
history, III 482b 486a
Holy Alliance, III 485b
Hugo, III 486a
humanism, III 483b, 484b

Hurd, III 482a
impressionism, III 484a
Italy, III 482a, 482b, 483a, 484a
James I, III 482b
Jugendstil, III 484a
Kant, III 484b
Keats, III 485b
Klinger, III 483b
Kummer, III 485b
Leo X (Pope), III 481b, 482a
literary criticism, III 484b, 485a
Louis XIV, III 483a
Ludwig, III 483b
mannerism, III 484a
Martínez de la Rosa, III 482a
Medici, III 481b
Meyer, R. M., III 482b
Middle Ages, III 481b
modernism, III 483b
movements, III 485a
mythology, III 481b
Napoleon I, III 483a
naturalism, III 483b, 484a
neo-classicism, III 482b, 484a
Neukirch, III 482a
Nicholas I, III 483a
Nicholas II, III 483a
Ovid, III 482a
Parrington, III 485a
Pascal, III 483a
Peacock, III 482a–482b
Pericles, III 481b
periods, III 484b, 485a
Peter the Great, III 483a
Petersen, III 485b
Petrarch, III 481b, 485b
Peyre, III 485b
Pietsch, III 482a
Platonism, III 484b
Pliny, III 482a
poetry, III 482a, 483a, 484b, 485b
politics, III 481b–485b
Pope, III 483a, 484a, 485b
Proust, III 486a
Puritanism, III 483b
realism, III 483b
Reformation, III 483b
Renaissance, III 481b, 482a, 483b, 484b
Restoration, III 483a, 483b
rococo, III 484a
romanticism, III 482a, 483b, 484a, 484b, 485a, 485b
Rubens, III 485b
Russia, III 483a
Schalk, III 482a
Schiller, III 481b
Schlegel, August Wilhelm

von, III 481b
Schlegel, Friedrich von, III 481b, 482a, 485b
Seven Years War, III 483a
Seward, III 483a
Shelley, III 482b, 485b
Silver Age, III 482a–482b
sociology, III 482b, 483b, 485b
Sophocles, III 481b
Spain, III 482a
Spence, III 483a
Spengler, III 485a
Spenser, III 485b
Stendahl, III 486a
Sturm und Drang, III 483b, 485b
Suetonius, III 482a
symbolism, III 483b, 484a
Sypher, III 484a
Tacitus, III 482a
Thibaudet, III 485b, 486a
Thirty Years War, III 483a
Tiraboschi, III 482a
Titian, III 485b
transcendentalism, III 483b
U.S., III 483b
Victoria, III 482b–483a
Victorian period, III 482b–483a
Voltaire, III 481b
Waller, III 483a, 485b
Walzel, III 484a
Waterloo, III 485b
Wechssler, III 485b
Welsted, III 483a
Wharton, III 482a
Wilde, III 483a
Wilhelm I, III 483a
William IV, III 482b
Wolf, F. A., III 482a
Wordsworth, III 485b
World War I, III 485b
Zeitgeist, III 484a
Peripatetic School of Islam, II 643a 650a
Peripateticism
  dignity, IV 137a, 137b
  Man-Machine, III 135a, 137a
  morality, IV 478a–478b
  Neo-Platonism, III 374a
  psychology, IV 7a
  Renaissance, IV 137a, 137b
  virtue, IV 478a–478b
Perizonius, Jakob (Voorbroek) (1651–1715), historiography, II 487a
Perkins, William (1558–1602), casuistry, I 262b–263a
Permanent Court of Arbitration, III 450a, 451a, 453b

Permanent Court of International Justice, III 451a–451b, 452a
Perotinus (fl. 13th century), music, II 315a
Perrault, Charles (1628–1703)
  attitude toward antiquity, I 78b 80b, 85a, 85b
  genius, II 294a
  literature, III 83a
  organicism, III 424b
  poetics, III 531b
Perrière, Guillaume de la, hierarchy, II 435b
Perry, Ralph Barton (1876-1957)
  good, IV 185a
  romanticism, IV 210b
Perry, Thomas Sergeant, classicism, I 450a
  symbolism, IV 341a
Persecution
  Bayle, IV 119b
  Christianity, I 377a
  Erasmus, IV 118b
  Greece (ancient), II 565b–566b
  holy, II 512b
  Huguenots, IV 113a, 116a–116b
  impiety, II 565b–567a
  intolerance, IV 112b 114a, 116a 120a
  philosophers, II 565b–566b
  prophecy, III 664a, 664b, 667b, 668a
  reformation, IV 62b
  Reformation, IV 68a
  religion, IV 112b 114a, 116a 119b
  Roman Catholic Church, I 377a
  Rome (ancient), II 566b–567a
  totalitarianism, IV 409a
Persephone (myth), II 340b
  Greece (ancient), IV 102a
  religion, IV 102a
  salvation, IV 228b
Perseus (myth), III 275b
Persia
  biology, I 231b
  Christianity, I 376a
  despotism, II 13a, 13b, 15b, 252b, 259a
  Hegel, II 15b
  Hermeticism, II 431b
  missionaries, I 376a
  mythology, IV 43a
  Orientalism, III 430a, 430b, 431a, 433a, 434a
  poetry, III 430a, 430b
  progress, III 638b
  salvation, IV 228b, 231a

U.S., III 430a, 430b
Persia (ancient)
  astrology, I 122a 122b, 125b
  Bible, I 359a 359b
  Buddhism, I 248a
  cosmic voyages, I 527a
  cosmology, I 536b
  despotism, II 2a
  disease, II 398b
  dualism, II 38a, 39a–40a, 42a, 42b–43a
  evil, II 162b
  freedom of speech, II 252a, 252b, 254a–254b, 259a, 259b
  God, II 335b, 337a, 338a–339b, 340a, 343b
  Greece (ancient), IV 228b
  health, II 398b
  impiety, II 565a–565b
  intolerance, IV 115a
  Islam, II 639a, 649b
  music, III 264b–265a
  nomos, II 683b
  prophecy, III 663b
  religion, IV 115a, *see* Zoroaster
  Rome (ancient), IV 115a
  temperance, IV 366b
  ut pictura poesis, IV 470b, 473a
Persian War, Greece (ancient), II 468a, 501b–502a
Persius (34 62 A.D.)
  freedom of speech, II 261b
  mythology, III 274a
  satire, IV 211a
Person, David, hierarchy, II 438a
Personalism
  Lovejoy, III 552b, 553a
  pragmatism, III 552b, 553a
  Schiller, F. C. S., III 552b, 553a
Perspective
  art, II 570a, 577a, 612b, 614a; IV 302a
  Cézanne, IV 302a
  creativity in art, I 580a, 582a, 582b
  cubism, IV 302a
  infinity, II 612b, 614a; IV 302a
  naturalism in art, III 340a, 340b, 341a, 344b
  optics, III 408a, 410a
  painting, II 570a, 577a; III 350a; IV 302a
  Renaissance, II 612b; IV 440b
  space, IV 302a
  universal man, IV 440a
  vanishing point, IV 302a

Peru, primitivism, III 601a
Perugino (1445 1531)
  mythology, III 290b
  neo-classicism in art, III 370b
  temperance, IV 377a
Perversion, art, II 575b
Pesellino, II (c. 1422 1457), temperance, IV 375b
Pessimism
  acquired characteristics, II 620b
  Bonald, III 534a
  Byron, IV 204a
  capitalism, III 645b
  death, I 635b
  evil, II 163b, 166b–167b, 169a
  Greece (ancient), II 566a
  Hegesias, II 566a
  historiography, IV 148a, 151a
  impiety, II 566a
  irrationalism, II 167b
  Luther, I 390b; III 255a–255b
  Machiavelli, IV 483a
  Marxism, III 645b
  Orientalism, III 430b
  Plato, III 440a
  Platonism, III 518b
  progress, III 624b, 645b
  Renaissance, IV 148a, 151a
  romanticism, IV 202b, 204a, 209b
  Schopenhauer, IV 202b
  skepticism, II 167b
  symbolism, IV 345a
  virtù, IV 483a
Pestalozzi, Johann Heinrich (1746 1827)
  education, II 99b
  Enlightenment, II 99b
  illuminists, IV 109a
  Pietism, III 495a
Peter Saint
  authority, I 149a
  baptism, I 414a
  Christianity, I 375b, 385a, 385b; III 590a, 590b
  Church, I 413b, 414a
  Faust (legend), III 246a
  mythology, III 281b
  primitivism, III 582a, 590a, 590b
  temperance, IV 375b, 377b
  Utopia, IV 460b
Peter of Bruys (d. about 1126), heresy, II 418b, 419a
Peter the Lombard (1100?–1160), women, IV 525a
Peter I (the Great) (1672 1725)

321

Counter-Enlightenment, II 110b

Eastern Orthodox Church, I 411a

Leibniz and, III 64a

linguistics, III 64a

periodization in literary history, III 483a

Peters, R. S., education, II 73a, 73b–74a, 82a

Petersen, Julius (1878–1941)

periodization in literary history, III 485b

romanticism, IV 197a

Peterson, E., Gnosticism, II 330b

Petherham, John, literature, III 82a

Petrarch (1304–1374)

Aristotle and, IV 141b

art, II 302a

Bembo and, III 512b

causation, II 234b

chance, II 234a–235a

coronation of, II 517a

determinism, II 234b

dignity, IV 136b, 141b–142a, 142b, 143b

education, IV 124b

faith, IV 142a

fate, II 234a–235a

fortune, II 234a–235a; IV 478a

genius, II 293b, 316a, 317a

God, II 234a–234b; IV 142a

good, II 234a, 234b

Gothic, II 367b

grace, IV 142a

handwriting, II 518a

humanism, II 515b, 516b, 517a, 517b, 518a, 520b; III 509b; IV 125b, 129a–129b, 141b–142a

individualism, II 302a

literary paradox, III 80a

literature, IV 121b, 124a

logic, IV 129b

love, III 510a, 511a, 511b, 512b

materialism, IV 141b

mimesis, III 228b

morality, II 234a; IV 141b, 142a, 479b–480a

mountains in literature, III 253b

mythology, III 289b, 296a

perennial philosophy, III 459b

periodization in history, III 477b

periodization in literary history, III 481b, 485b

Plato and, III 509b–510a

Platonism, III 509b–510a, 511a, 512b, 514a

poetry, III 530a, 531b

responsibility, IV 142a

rhetoric, IV 171a

romanticism, IV 188b

Saint Augustine and, III 509b; IV 141b–142a

salvation, IV 142a, 142b

sin, IV 142a

Stoicism, II 234b

temperance, IV 371b

virtù, IV 477b, 478a, 478b, 479b–480a

wisdom of the fool, IV 519b

Petre, Maud, modernism, I 424b

Petronius, Gaius (1st century A.D.)

realism in literature, IV 54a

satire, IV 214a, 215b

Petrus Bonus of Ferrara (c. 1330), alchemy, I 30b

Petrusevski, M. D.

catharsis, I 269b–270a

tragedy, I 269b–270a

Pettazzoni, Raffaele, mythology, III 307b, 314b

Pettenkoffer, Max von (1818–1901), environment, II 124b

Petty, William (1623–1687), atomism, I 135b, 136b, antiprimitivism, III 604b

economic history, II 45b

Peuckert, W. E., mythology, III 316a

Peutinger, Konrad (1465–1547)

musical genius, II 315b

mythology, III 292b

Peyre, Henri

baroque in literature, I 192a–192b

classicism, I 454b

periodization in literary history, III 485b

Peyrère, Isaac de la, deism, I 649a, 649b

Pezzi, Francesco, romanticism, IV 190b

Pfandl, Ludwig, baroque in literature, I 190b

Pfemfert, Franz, expressionism, II 206a

Pfleiderer, Otto (1839–1908), religion, IV 108a

Pflüger, Eduard (1829–1910), spontaneous generation, IV 311b

Phaedra (myth), III 496b

temperance, IV 367b

Phaedrus (5th century B.C.),

freedom of speech, II 261b

theriophily, IV 384b

Phalaris (6th century B.C.), Eighteenth Century view of, I 81a, 82a

Phaleas of Chalcedon, Utopia, IV 459b

Pharmacology

Islam, II 644a, 645b

medieval, II 197b

Phelps, William Lyon (1865–1943), romanticism, IV 193b

Phenix, P. H., education, II 83a

Phenomena

Aristotle, III 354a

Bacon, Francis, III 355b–356a

Comte, III 360a

metaphor in philosophy, III 199a

necessity, III 352a–354a, 355a, 356a, 356b, 357b, 360a

Plato, III 353a, 353b, 354a

Phenomenalism, positivism, III 548a–550b

Phenomenology

beauty, I 212a–212b

existentialism, II 192b 193b

Heidegger, II 193b

holy, II 514a

Husserl, I 98b, 322b

Islam, II 652a

literature, III 242b

motif, III 242b

pleasure, II 383a

Sartre, III 209b

scientific classification, I 466a

structuralism, IV 329a

time, IV 395a, 396b–397a

Phenotype, acquired characteristics, II 618a, 619a

Pherecydes of Syros (6th century B.C.)

death, I 644b

reincarnation, I 644b

Phidias (5th century B.C.), classicism, I 455b

creativity in art, I 581b, 582a, 586a

neo-classicism in art, III 369a

Philanthropy, III 486b–493a

Aeschylus, III 487a

aesthetics, III 491b, 492a

Alexander the Great, III 487a

Amos (Bible), III 487b

animals, III 491a

art museums, III 491b

Asia, III 492b

Aśoka, III 487a

Baron de Hirsch Fund, III 488a

Bible, III 487b, 488a–488b, 489a

Blake, III 490b

brotherhood, III 488b

Buddhism, III 487a

Calvin, III 489b

capital punishment, III 491a

Carnegie, III 491b–492a

casuistry, III 489a

charity, III 486b, 492b

children, III 491a

China (ancient), III 486b

Christianity, III 487b, 488a–489a, 490a, 490b, 492a

Chuang-Tzú, III 486b

civilization, III 486b, 488a, 491b

class, III 489b, 490a, 491a

colonialism, III 490b

communications, III 490b

Confucius, III 486b

conservatism, III 490a, 492a

Constantine, III 488b

Cornell, III 491b

creativity, III 488a

culture, III 487a, 492b

democracy, III 487a, 490b

Demosthenes, III 487a

disease, II 406a

doles, III 487a

donations, III 489b, 491b

duty, III 487b

Eastern Orthodox Church, III 488b

Eastman, III 491b

economics, III 489b, 490a

Eden, III 490a

education, III 488b, 490a, 491a, 491b, 492a, 492b

Egypt (ancient), III 487a

Elizabethan Statute of ethics, III 486b, 487b, 488a, 489a

evangelicalism, I 403a

feudalism, III 488b, 489b

Ford Foundation, III 492a

foundations, III 489b, 492a–492b

France, III 489b

Franklin, III 490b–491a

French Revolution (1789), III 490a

Fuller, Thomas, III 489b

fund-raising, III 490b–491a

Gautama, III 487a

Germany, III 488a

gifts, III 489b, 490a, 492a

Gladden, III 489a
God, III 487b–489b
Goldsmith, III 490a–490b
Gratian, III 489a
Great Britain, III 489b–492b
Greece (ancient), III 487a–487b, 488b
Hammurabic Code, III 487a
health, II 406a; III 491b
Herodotus, III 487a
Hesiod, III 487a
Hinduism, III 487a
holiness, III 487a
Homer, III 487a
Hopkins, III 491b
hospitals, III 488b, 490a
hostels, 488b
Hsüntze, III 486b
humanitarianism, III 486b, 487a–491b
idea, III 491b
immortality, III 487a
imperialism, III 490b
industry, III 490a
institutions, III 488a, 488b, 489b
Isaiah (Bible), III 487b
Islam, III 488a
Israel, III 488a
Jesus Christ, III 488b
Judaism, III 487b–488a
justice, III 487b
knowledge, III 491b
Koran, III 488a
Kropotkin, III 486b
laissez-faire, III 490a
large-scale giving, III 491b–492b
Latin America, III 492b
law, III 487a, 492a
literature, III 487b
McCarthyism, III 492a
Maimonides, III 487b–488a
Mather, III 490b
meaning, III 486b
medicine, III 492a
Mencius, III 486b
Micah (Bible), III 487b
Middle Ages, III 487b, 488a, 489a, 489b
millenarianism, III 488b
modernism, III 489a–491b
monasteries, III 488b, 489b
morality, III 490a, 491a
More, Hannah, III 490a
Moses (Bible), III 487b
nationalism, III 490a
nation-state, III 489b
Nazism, III 488a
New Zealand, III 490b
Niebuhr, Reinhold, III 492b
Nuffield Foundation, III 492a

obligation, III 487b
Oglethorpe, III 490b
orchestras, III 491b
orphanages, III 490a
overseas expansion, III 490b
penal code, III 491a
politics, III 487b, 489b
population dislocation, III 489b
poverty, III 487a–491a
preventive, III 488a
private, III 487a–489b
Protestantism, I 403a; III 489a, 489b, 490b
Raikes, III 490a
rationale, III 491b–492a
recreational facilities, III 491b
reform, III 490a, 491a
Reformation, III 489a, 489b
refugees, III 488a, 489b
relief projects, III 487a, 489b, 490a, 491a
religion, III 486b–491b
Renaissance, III 491b
research, III 491b, 492a
Rockefeller Foundation, III 489a, 491b, 492b
Roman Catholic Church, III 488b, 489a, 489b, 490b
Rome (ancient), III 487a–487b, 488b
Russia, III 488a
sacrifice, III 489a
Saint Ambrose, III 489a
Saint Augustine, III 489a
Saint Francis of Assisi, III 489a
Saint Paul, III 488a
salvation, III 489b
science, III 491b, 492a
secularism, III 489a–490b
self-interest, III 487b, 488b, 489a
slavery, III 490a, 491a
social reform, III 486b, 489b, 490a, 491a
social settlements, III 491b
social welfare, III 492a, 492b
Society for the Promotion of Christian Knowledge, III 490a
Society for the Propagation of the Gospel in Foreign Parts, III 490a
Socrates, III 487a
Stanford, III 491b
State, III 488b, 492b
stewardship, III 488a, 489b, 490b, 492a
Stoicism, III 487a
Talmud, III 488a
Taoism, III 486b

taxes, III 490a, 492a
theology, III 489a
Thucydides, III 487a
tithing, III 487b
trusts, III 489b, 492a
Uhlhorn, III 487b
U.S., III 490b–492b
utilitarianism, III 488a
Vanderbilt, III 491b
Vassar, III 491b
Victorian sensibility, IV 218a, 218b, 219b
voluntary, III 490a, 491a, 492b
war, III 491a
wealth, III 491b
welfare state, III 492a–492b; IV 510b
Wellcome, III 492a
women's rights, III 491a
Xenophon, III 487a
Philemon (myth), III 283a
Philemon (ca. 361?–?263 B.C.), theriophily, IV 386a
Philip II, King of Macedon (382–336 B.C.)
  analogy, I 68b
  Christianity, I 397b, 398a
  freedom of speech, II 257b
  historiography, II 504a, 508b
  vox populi, IV 497a
Philip II (Augustus), King of France (1165–1223), Christianity, I 383a
Philip II, King of Spain (1527–1598)
  Counter-Reformation, I 383b
  historiography, II 496b
Philip III, King of France (1245–1285), temperance, IV 372b
Philip IV (the Fair), King of France (1268–1314), nationalism, III 320b, 321a
Philip V, King of Macedon (237–179 B.C.)
  freedom of speech, II 257b
  impiety, II 566a
Philip of Opus
  astrology, I 125a
  culture, I 611a, 611b
Philippa of Aragon, love, III 99a, 99b
Philippe de Vitry, musical genius, II 315a
Philippines
  China, I 355a
  equality, III 13b
  Indonesia, III 338b
  law, III 13b
  Malaya, III 338b
  nationalism, III 331a, 338b

Pan-Malaysia, III 338b
  U.S., III 331a, 563a, 565b
Philippson, Johann, hierarchy, II 438a
Philips, Ambrose (1675?–1749), virtuoso, IV 489a
Philips, John (1675?–1749), primitivism, III 600a
Philipson, Morris, universal man, IV 437a
Philiscus of Aegina, cynicism, I 628b
Philitas (4th century B.C.), literary criticism, I 596b
Philo of Byzantium, Man-Machine, III 134a
Philo Judaeus (fl. 1st century B.C.–1st century A.D.), allegory, I 42a, 45a–45b, 46a
  ambiguity, I 51a, 52a, 54a
  analogy, I 64a, 68b
  Christianity, III 590a
  Clement and, III 466a
  Creation, I 571b
  creativity in art, I 578a, 586b
  demonology, I 668b
  dignity, IV 137a
  dualism, II 42a
  environment, II 132a
  faith, II 465b–466a
  free will, I 586b
  freedom of speech, II 260b, 261b, 262a
  God, I 571b, 586b; II 42a, 513a; III 127b, 465b–466a
  grace, III 466a
  holy, II 513a
  idea, II 543a, 545a
  infinity, II 605b, 614b
  Islam, II 640a
  macrocosm, III 127b, 128a, 128b
  matter, II 42a
  metaphor, III 204a–205a, 206b
  Moses (Bible) and, III 590a
  mythology, III 283a
  Neo-Platonism, III 372b
  Origen and, III 466a
  perfectibility, III 465b–466a, 466b
  Plato and, III 465b–466a, 590a
  Platonism, III 505a
  primitivism, III 590a
  Pythagorean cosmos, IV 38b, 40b
  religion, III 204a–205a, 206b
  revelation, III 465b–466a
  Saint Augustine and, III 466a–466b

skepticism, **IV** 240a
soul, **III** 127b
syncretism, **I** 44a
temperance, **IV** 372b, 375a
truth, **II** 513a
Philo of Larissa, skepticism, **IV** 234a
Philodemus (1st century B.C.),
aesthetics, **II** 219b
freedom of speech, **II** 260b
mythology, **III** 274a
organicism, **III** 423b
poetry, **III** 526a
Philolaus (5th century B.C.),
cosmology, **I** 539b
creativity in art, **I** 580a
numbers, **III** 403a
Pythagoreans, **IV** 32b, 37a–37b
Philology
Greece (ancient), **II** 516b
humanism, **II** 516b, 518b, 519a, 520a
knowledge, **III** 520a
language, **II** 661b, 664b
medieval, **II** 203a
motif, **III** 236b, 238a, 238b, 239a
mythology, **III** 274b, 291b, 304b, 305b, 306a, 312a
necessity, **III** 357a, 360a
Platonism, **III** 519b–521b, 522a, 522b
religion, **IV** 94b
Renaissance, **IV** 124a, 127b, 440a
rhetoric, **IV** 169b, 172a
universal man, **IV** 440a
Vico, **III** 357a
See also Language
Philosophers
Christianity, **III** 590b
painting, **IV** 465b
persecution, **II** 565b–566b
Plato, **III** 498b–499a, 500b, 501a, 501b, 502a, 523b
Platonism, **III** 498b–499a, 500b–503b, 510a, 523b, 524b
poetry, **III** 526a, 528b, 529b; **IV** 465b
positivism, **III** 532b, 533a, 545b, 546a, 550b
primitivism, **III** 579a, 580b, 585a, 590b, 598b
realism in literature, **IV** 53b
Schelling, **IV** 210b
temperance, **IV** 368a, 368b
Utopia, **IV** 459b
vox populi, **IV** 497a
war, **IV** 503a
women, **IV** 526b, 528a
Philosophy
Absolute, **II** 637a; **III** 199b

abstraction, **II** 551a, 551b
acquired characteristics, **II** 617a, 617b, 620b
aesthetics, **II** 549a–550a, 551a–551b; **III** 196b–197a, 198b, 199a; **IV** 356a, 356b
agnosticism, **I** 17a–27a
analogy, **III** 198b
analytical, **II** 611a
animals, **III** 198b
Aristotelianism, **II** 641a, 642b, 643b, 646a, 646b, 647b, 650a; **III** 198b
Aristotle, **I** 463a; **II** 408a, 661b, 666b; **III** 189b–190a, 200a, 273b, 380a, 628b, 629b; **IV** 4b, 436a
art, **II** 549a, 549b, 550a, 550b–551a, 551b; **III** 198b
artists, **II** 550b, 551a, 551b
Bacon, **III** 197a–197b, 199a; **IV** 432a–432b, 433b–434a, 462a
Batteux, **II** 550a
Bayle, **II** 549b
beauty, **II** 549a–551b
Being, **II** 637a, 637b
Bellori, **II** 549b, 550a
Bergson, **III** 197a
Bernini, **II** 549b
Bernstein, **III** 149a, 162b–163a, 164b, 167b
Boethius of Dacia, **II** 33b
Bonald, **III** 534b
Brazil, **III** 545a
Brevold, **II** 549b
Bruno, **IV** 298a
Caravaggio, **II** 549b
Cartesianism, **III** 198b
categorial set, **III** 198a, 198b–200a
category, **III** 198a, 198b–200a
causation, **I** 290a–291a; **III** 199a; **IV** 434a
chance, **III** 612a
Christianity, **III** 588b, 591a
Cicero, **III** 116a
common law, **III** 32a, 116b
Comte, **III** 534b, 535b, 536b
contextualism, **III** 199b
continuity, **I** 493b, 494b, 500b–502b
cosmology, **II** 640a, 644b, 646a, 646b; **III** 198b–199b
Counter-Enlightenment, **II** 103a, 111a
Cousin, **III** 533b
crisis in history, **I** 592a
Crousaz, **II** 549b
culture, **I** 608b, 612a, 612b, 613a, 615b, 617a, 619b,

620a; **II** 127b; **III** 198b
cycles, **I** 622a–622b
cynicism, **III** 586b
death, **I** 637a–637b
deism, **I** 647b, 648b, 649a
Democritus, **III** 199b
Descartes, **III** 199b; **IV** 432b
determinism, **II** 20a–20b, 23a–23b, 24a
Dewey, **III** 198a
Diderot, **II** 549b–550a; **IV** 154b–155a
dignity, **IV** 138a, 140b–145a, 146a
disease, **II** 395b, 396b, 397a, 397b, 398b, 399a
double truth, **II** 31a–37b
Du Fresnoy, **II** 549b
dualism, **II** 38a–38b, 40a–42a
Eddington, **III** 198b
education, **II** 71b, 74b, 76a, 76b, 78a, 78b, 81a–81b, 82b, 83a
Edwards, Jonathan, **IV** 110a
empathy, **II** 85b–86a
empiricism, **II** 549a, 549b, 551a; **III** 201a, 546a, 547b, 548b, 549b–551a
Engels, **II** 452b, 453b
Enlightenment, **II** 89b, 90a, 91a, 93a, 97a–97b
environment, **II** 127b
Epicureanism, **IV** 7a, 53b
equality, **II** 139b, 143b–144a
equity, **II** 151a
eschatology, **II** 155b, 158b, 159b, 160a
Eternal Return, **II** 635a, 638a
ethics, **II** 549a, 550b, 551a; **III** 442a, 443a, 443b, 444a; **IV** 70a, 71b, 319a
evil, **II** 162a, 163a, 165b, 169a
evolution of literature, **II** 172b
evolutionism, **II** 176b–177a, 179a, 181a, 181b, 182b, 184a–185a, 186b, 187b
existentialism, **II** 606a, 635b, 651b, 652a; **III** 157b, 158b–159a, 159b
experimental, **III** 378b–379b, 384a, 385b–386a, 386b, 387b–388b
explanation of, **III** 196b–197a
expressionism, **II** 206a
facts, **III** 198a

fantasy, **III** 197b, 198b
Faust (legend), **III** 246b, 249a, 250a, 252a
Feder, J. G., **II** 551a
feeling, **II** 550a
Félibien, **II** 549b
Ferber, J. C. C., **II** 551a
formism, **III** 200a
Forms, **III** 629b
France, **III** 366a
Fréart de Chambray, **II** 549b
freedom, **III** 199a
freedom of speech, **II** 260b
Frommichen, **II** 551a
Galileo, **III** 382b, 388a
game theory, **II** 264a, 265a, 265b, 266a, 267a, 273b–274b
genius, **II** 294b, 313a, 313b, 551a
Gnosticism, **II** 329a–331a
God, **II** 339b, 341a, 343a, 343b, 344a, 347a, 348b–351b, 355a–359a, 360a, 361a, 362a, 363a, 363b, 365a, 366a, 549a, 549b, 550b, 551b; **III** 199a
good, **II** 549a–549b, 550b, 635a, 637b; **IV** 173a, 174a–175b, 177a, 183a
Gothic, **II** 373b
Greece (ancient), **II** 674a; **III** 112a; **IV** 228a, 229a
happiness, **II** 375a, 378a–381b, 386a–387b
harmony, **II** 388b–389a, 390b, 392b, 393b
health, **II** 395b, 396b, 397a, 397b, 398b, 399a
Hegel, **II** 20a, 408a–411b, 412a, 413b, 414a; **III** 198a, 198b, 199b, 220a, 473a, 474a
Heisenberg, **II** 589b–590a
Helen of Troy (myth), **II** 549b
Hemsterhuis, **II** 550a
Herder, **II** 551a
historicism, **II** 606a
historiography, **II** 20a–20b, 23a–23b, 24a, 467b, 473b, 478b, 480a, 488b, 489b, 492b, 496a, 507b, 510b; **IV** 151a
history, **II** 20a–20b, 23a–23b, 24a; **III** 199a
holy, **II** 514a
human nature, **III** 571a, 572a, 573a–574b, 575a, 577a
humanism, **II** 515a, 515b, 516a, 516b, 519a–520a, 521a, 522b–523a; **IV** 129a, 129b, 132a, 132b, 134b

Hume, III 199b; IV 155a
hypotheses, III 197b–201a
idea, II 549b–551b
ideal, II 549a–552b
idealism, II 606a
identification, III 197a
illuminists, IV 109a
imagination, II 550a, 551a; III 208b–215b, 217a, 218a–222a
imitation, II 549b, 550b
immortality, III 199a
impiety, II 565b–566a
impressionism, II 575b, 576b, 580b–583b
indeterminacy, II 587a–587b, 589b–590a
individualism, II 550b, 551a, 594b
infinity, II 604b–606a, 607a–609b, 611a, 611b, 614a–614b, 615b
institutions, III 198b
international peace, III 448a, 448b, 450b, 451b, 456a
intuition, II 549b, 551b
irony, II 629b
irrationalism, II 634b–638b
Islam, II 639a–652a
James, William, III 197a
John of Jandun, II 34b
justice, II 653a–653b, 655b, 658a–658b
Kant, II 551a–551b; III 199a, 199b; IV 436a
Kate, II 549b
Klopstock, II 550b
knowledge, II 551a
Kuhn, III 200b
Lana Terzi, II 551a
language, II 551a, 661a–661b, 664a–665b, 666b, 668b, 669a, 673a; III 198b
Latin America, III 540a, 542a, 544a
Lavater, II 551b
law, I 290a–291a; II 674a, 686a, 687b; III 1b, 3a–5b, 22b, 23a, 27a, 32a, 35b
Leibniz, II 668b
Lenz, II 551b
Lessing, II 551a
Lewis, C. I., III 199a, 199b
liberalism, III 36a, 36b, 37a, 40a, 57b, 60b
linguistics, II 661a–661b; III 61b, 71a, 71b, 72a
literary paradox, III 79a
literature, III 82a, 85b, 86a, 86b, 87a, 87b, 88b; IV 332a
Locke, III 199b
logic, III 198b, 201a, 546a, 547b–551a

Lomazzo, II 550a
longevity, III 89b, 92a, 92b
Lossius, II 551b
love, III 94b, 95a
loyalty, III 108b, 109b, 110a, 111b, 112a, 112b, 113a, 115a–115b
Lucretius, III 197a
Machiavellism, III 120a, 123a, 125a
macrocosm and microcosm, III 126b, 127a, 128a, 129a, 129b, 131a
Man-Machine, III 131b–146a
mannerism, II 549b
Marx, II 452b, 453b; III 334b, 359b
Marxism, III 147b–149a, 153a, 157b–159b, 162b–169b
materialism, II 452b, 453b; IV 53b
mathematics, III 171b, 172a–172b, 173a, 176b, 178a, 179b, 183a, 184b, 201a, 387b–388b, 416b; IV 33b
matter, III 185b, 187a, 187b, 188b, 189b–190a, 192b, 139a, 195b–196a
measurement, IV 399b, 402b
medieval experimental, II 199a, 204a, 204b
Mendelssohn, II 550b
Mengs, II 550a, 550b
metaphor, III 196b–201b, 203a, 204a–207a
metaphysics, II 549a; III 208b–222a
methodology, III 378b–379b, 381b–382b, 384a, 385b–388b
Mexico, III 544a, 544b
Micraelius, II 549b
Middle Ages, IV 253a
Mill, IV 199a
mimesis, III 226a
Montesquieu, IV 155a
moral sense, III 230b, 231b, 232a, 234b
morality, II 550a, 551a; III 199a
mountains in literature, III 253a
music, II 313a, 313b, 388b–389a, 390b, 392b, 393b; III 263b, 264b, 268a, 268b, 269a, 270b, 271b
mysticism, III 197a, 198b
mythology, I 42b; III 197b, 198b, 272a–272b, 273a, 273b, 274b, 277a, 278a,

288a, 288b, 290a, 291a, 292a, 300a, 301a, 302a, 302b, 304b, 305a, 306a–306b, 307a, 309a, 315a–315b, 316a, 317a
nationalism, III 323a, 334a, 334b, 337b
natural, II 607a–608b
natural law, III 16a–16b, 20b–21a, 23a
naturalism, II 549b, 581b; IV 53b
naturalism in art, III 343b
Nature, II 549b, 551b; III 198b, 199a, 347a, 348a
necessity, II 587b; III 351b–362a
neo-classicism in art, III 366a
Neo-Platonism, II 549b, 643a, 643b, 644b, 646b, 651a; III 371b–378a
Neo-Pythagoreans, II 639a, 643b, 646a
Newton, III 378b–379b, 381b–382b, 384a, 385b–388b, 397a–398b, 419a
nihilism, II 651b
numbers, III 403a, 406a
optics, III 397a–398b, 407a–408b, 410a, 414b, 415a, 416a–419a, 420b
organicism, III 421b, 422a, 422b, 424b–427a
Orientalism, III 428a, 429a–434b, 436a–439a
painting, II 549b
pangenesis, II 623a–623b, 626a
Panofsky, II 549b
paradigm, III 200a–201a
peace, III 442a, 443a, 443b, 444a
Pereira Barreto, III 540b
perfectibility, II 549b, 551a, 551b; III 464b, 465a, 473a–473b, 474a
Peripatetic School of Islam, II 643a–650a
permeating, III 197a
phenomena, III 199a
physics, III 387b–388a
Pietism, III 494a, 494b
Plato, II 661b; III 188b, 200a, 210a, 465a, 502a, 508a, 515b
Platonism, II 549a, 549b, 550a; III 198b, 502a–508b, 510a, 515b, 516b, 517a–523b
pleasure, II 375a, 378a–378b, 379a, 381b, 386a–387b
Plotinus, III 373b–376a

poetry; II 551a; IV 196b, 507a 508a, 525b, 526a, 527b, 528a, 528b, 530a
Pomponazzi, II 36b–37a
Pope, III 397a
Porphyry, III 376b–377b
positivism, II 606a; III 533b, 534a 536b, 540a, 540b, 542a, 544a–551a
pragmatism, II 551b; III 199b
primitivism, III 581a, 586b–589a, 591a, 600b
Prinner, II 551b
private property, III 653b, 654a, 654b, 655a, 656b
progress, III 628a–633a, 634a, 636b, 641a, 642a, 644b
protest movements, III 676a
psychology, II 551a; IV 1a, 1b, 2a, 3a, 4a, 4b, 6b, 7a, 8b, 11b, 12a, 15a, 16a, 17b, 19b, 20a, 22b, 23a, 24a, 24b
Pythagoreans, IV 31b–33a
Ramism, IV 42b, 45a
rationalism, II 634b–652a; IV 46b 47b, 48a, 50a
Raynal, IV 155a
realism in literature, IV 51b, 53b, 54a
relativism, IV 70a, 71b
relativity, IV 82b
religion, III 203a–207a; IV 93a, 93b, 97a, 97b, 106a, 106b, 107b–110a, 111b
Renaissance, IV 121b–124a, 129a, 129b, 132a, 132b, 134b, 138a, 140b–146a, 151a, 438b–441a, 443a
revelation, III 205a
revolution, IV 154b, 155b
Reynolds, II 550a
rhetoric, IV 167b–172b
Riedel, II 550b–551a
right, IV 173a, 174a, 174b, 175a–175b, 177a, 183a
Roman Catholic Church, III 654a
romanticism, I 594b–595a; II 638a–638b; IV 195a, 199a, 200a, 201a–202b, 204a, 205a, 205b, 206b, 207b–211a
Rome (ancient), II 686a, 687b; IV 370a
root metaphor, III 197a–198b, 200a–201a
Rousseau, IV 155a
Saint Augustine, III 355a

325

Saint Thomas Aquinas, III 200a
Saint-Simon, III 641a
salvation, IV 228a, 229a
Saturn (myth), III 581a
Scheyb, II 551a
Schopenhauer, IV 202b
science, III 197b, 198b, 199a, 200b, 201a
Seneca, III 588a, 632b
senses, II 549a, 551a; III 198b
Shaftesbury, II 550a
Siger of Brabant, II 32b–33b
sin, IV 228a, 229a
social contract, IV 253a, 255a, 256a, 261a, 261b
social welfare, IV 277b
socialism, IV 290b
Socrates, III 498b–499a, 577a; IV 431b
space, III 199a; IV 295a–297a, 298a, 298b, 299a, 301b, 303a 306a
species, II 551b
speculative, II 604b
Spinoza, II 199b; IV 434b
State, III 153a
Stein, K. H. von, II 551a
Stoicism, II 641a, 646a; III 588a; IV 319a
Stoics, IV 7a
Strato, IV 7a
structuralism, II 652a; IV 322b, 323a, 328b–330a
Sulzer, II 550a, 551a
superficial, III 197a
supranatural, II 549b–551b
symmetry, IV 346a–346b
taste, IV 356a, 356b
technology, IV 359b, 360b, 361b
temperance, IV 370a, 371a
Thales, III 197a
theodicy, IV 379a, 380a–383b
Theophrastus, IV 6b
theriophily, IV 388a–388b
time, III 199a; IV 390b, 391a, 391b, 399b, 402b
totalitarianism, IV 408a, 408b, 409a
Toynbee, III 361a–361b
tragedy, II 551b
tragic sense, IV 414b–415a
transcendentalism, II 629b
uncertainty principle, II 589b–590a
U.S., III 428a, 429a–434b, 436a–439a
unity, II 550b, 551b
unity of science, IV 431a–

434b, 436a
universe, II 550b, 551a
universal man, IV 438b–440a, 441a, 443a
utilitarianism, IV 446b
Utopia, IV 462b, 464a
utopianism, II 649a
Vaihinger, III 199b
virtue, II 550b, 551a; IV 477a, 477b, 478b
vision, III 407a 408b, 410a, 414b–420b
Volksgeist, IV 492a–494b
Voltaire, IV 155a
von Hagedorn, II 550b
war, IV 500b, 501a, 502a, 504a, 508b
Webb, D., II 550a
Weltanschauung, III 198a, 199a
Weltschmerz, IV 204a
Wieland, II 550b, 551a, 551b
Winckelmann, II 550a, 550b, 551a
wisdom, II 32b
Wittgenstein, III 200a, 200b
work, IV 531b, 533a–533b
Zeitgeist, IV 535b–536b
Zeuxis, II 549b
See also Perennial philosophy
Philostratus (170?–245 A.D.), art, II 299b
Buddhism, I 255a
chance images, I 342a–342b
creativity in art, I 578a, 586a
genius, II 299b
iconography, II 534a
imagination, I 586a
mimesis, III 227a
mythology, III 299a
poetics, III 527a
ut pictura poesis, IV 468b, 469a
Philoxenus (fl. 1st century B.C.), linguistics, III 62b
Phoebus Apollo (myth), law, II 675b
Phoenicia (ancient)
freedom of speech, II 252a, 254a, 257a
hermeticism, II 431b
law, II 686a–686b
Phoenix (myth), III 284a
Phonetics
linguistics, III 68b, 70b, 71a, 71b
structuralism, IV 324b, 327b
Phonology
linguistics, III 67a, 68b, 69a

69b
mythology, III 316a, 316b
structuralism, IV 324a–324b, 327b
Photius (820?–891)
Christianity, I 409b
skepticism, IV 237a
Photoelectric cells, III 419b
optics, III 419b
Photography
art, I 461b; II 571b–572b
Baudelaire, II 571b
color, II 572a–572b
cosmology, I 552b
Daguerre, II 572a
Degas, II 571b, 572a
Maxwell, II 572a
naturalism in art, III 345a
painting, II 571b–572b
Photometry, III 418a
Photon-box thought-experiment, II 590b
Photosensitive, emulsions, III 419b
Phrenology
Austria, IV 23a
Beecher, H. W., IV 23b
Bible, IV 23b
brain, IV 23b
Calvinism, IV 23b
Combe, IV 23b
criminology, IV 23b
cults, IV 23b
Emerson, IV 23b
four temperaments, IV 23b
Fowler, O. S., IV 23b
Gall, IV 23a
Howe, S. G., IV 23b
human nature, IV 23b
individualism, IV 23b
Mann, IV 23b
mind, IV 23b
medicine, IV 23b
morality, IV 23b
pedagogy, IV 23b
physiology, IV 23b
Poe, IV 23b
positivism, III 534a, 539b
psychiatry, IV 23b
psychology, IV 23a–23b
Silliman, IV 23b
Spurzheim, IV 23a, 23b
U.S., IV 23a–23b
ut pictura poesis, IV 475a
Wells, S. R., IV 23b
Whitman, IV 23b
Phylarchus (late 3rd century B.C.), historiography, II 507b
Physicalism
Empedocles, IV 2b
free will, II 245b–246b
positivism, III 549a

psychology, IV 1a, 2b, 3a
Physics, II 586a–594b
Archimedes, III 134a
Aristotle, I 463a; II 666b; III 354a, 355a
Bacon, III 356a; IV 434a
behaviorism, II 586a–586b
Cartesianism, II 450b
catastrophism, IV 419a, 423a
causation, III 382a
chora, IV 299b
color, II 580a–580b
Comte, II 451b; III 360a, 535b
continuity, I 493b, 494a
cosmology, I 554a–554b, 555a, 556a–561b
Descartes, III 388a; IV 432b
determinism, II 18b
empiricism, III 547b–550b
Enlightenment, III 179b
Galileo, II 521a
game theory, II 264a, 271b, 273a
God, II 347a
happiness, II 387a
health, II 400b
Hegel, III 556b
hermeticism, II 433b
historiography, II 18b
history, II 18b
humanism, II 521a; IV 132b, 133a, 134b
hypothetical, I 137b–140a
indeterminacy, II 586a–594a
infinity, II 605b–608b, 610b, 612a–612b
Islam, II 643a, 645b, 646b, 647a, 647b, 649a
Kant, IV 433b
kenon, IV 298b
knowledge, III 387b
language, II 666b
Leibniz, IV 434b
light, II 580a–580b
linguistics, IV 424b, 426b, 427a
logic, III 547b, 548b–550b
love, III 106b,
Man-Machine, III 131b, 132a, 133a, 134a, 135a, 136a, 137b, 138b, 140a
mathematics, III 174b, 175a, 177a, 178a, 179b, 387b–388a, 388b
matter, III 187a, 190a
measurement, IV 405a, 405b
metaphysics, IV 432b, 433a
methodology, III 382a,

387b–388a, 388b, 389a
music, III 263b
mythology, III 274a
necessity, III 352b–362a
Newton, III 382a, 387b–
388a, 388b, 389a
numbers, III 406b
optics, III 417b–420b
painting, II 580a–580b
Peirce, III 556b, 558b,
559b, 567a
perennial philosophy, III
459b, 460a, 461a, 461b
philosophy, III 387b–388a
Plato, IV 368b
Platonism, III 510a
positivism, III 535b, 547b,
548b, 549a, 549b, 550a
pragmatism, III 556b, 558b,
559b, 564b, 567a
probability, II 264a; III
612a, 613b, 615b, 616b,
618a, 620a
psychology, IV 11a, 12a,
12b, 16b, 17a, 24b
Ramism, IV 42b, 45a
rationalism, III 301a
Renaissance, IV 132b,
133a, 134b, 437b
revolution, IV 163a
Rohault, III 388a
romanticism, IV 210b
science, II 643a, 645b,
646b 647a, 647b, 649a
scientific classification, I
463a, 464b–466a
skepticism, IV 236a, 244b
space, IV 295a, 295b, 298b,
299b–305b
Spengler, III 361a
Spinoza, IV 434b
Stoicism, IV 319a–322a
symmetry, IV 349a–353b
temperance, IV 368b
time, IV 393a, 393b, 395b,
396a, 397a–398a, 405a,
405b
topos, IV 299b
uniformitarianism, IV 419a,
423a, 424b, 426b, 427a
unity of science, IV 432b
433a–434b, 436b
universal man, IV 437b
Physiocrats
China, I 362b–363a
despotism, II 11a, 12a–
12b
economic history, II 49b
natural liberty, II 62a–62b
primitivism, III 600b
socialism, IV 288a
society, II 62a–62b
Physiognomy
naturalism in art, III 340a–

340b
painting, IV 475a
Physiology
Aristotle, IV 5b
Brazil, III 539b
disease, II 404a–404b,
406b
health, II 404a–404b, 406b
ideology, II 553b, 554a
literature, IV 332b
longevity, III 91b
love, II 94a, 97a
Man-Machine, III 132b,
133a, 133b, 135a–144b
mythology, III 287b
necessity, III 360a
optics, IV 409b–410a, 420a
phrenology, IV 23b
pleasure, II 383a
positivism, III 534a, 539b
primitivism, III 578b, 579a
psychology, IV 3a, 5b, 7a,
11a–14a, 21a, 23b, 24b
Pythagoreans, IV 32b
rationalism, IV 48a
recapitulation, IV 58a
right, IV 177a
space, IV 303a
spontaneous generation, IV
309a
Strato, IV 7a
vision, III 409b–410a, 420a
Piaget, Jean (1896–   )
behaviorism, I 229a
classification of the
sciences, I 466a–466b
psychology, IV 13b
Pica, Vittorio, symbolism, IV
342a
Picard, Raymond
literary criticism, I 605a–
605b
structuralism, IV 327b–
328a
Picart, Bernard, neo-classicism in art, III 363b
Picasso, Pablo (1881–1973),
art, II 304b;
III 230a, 597a
biology, I 239a
chance images, I 352a–
352b
culture, IV 165b
genius, II 304b
impressionism, II 577b
Nature, III 230a, 347b
painting, IV 475b
primitivism, III 597a
revolution, IV 165b
Piccolomini, Alessandro
(1508–1578)
genius, II 293b
poetics, III 529a
Piciarelli, Camillo, romantic-

ism, IV 190b
Picq, Ardant du, war, IV 504a
Pico della Mirandola (1463–
1494)
aesthetics, II 218a
Cabala, III 130b
cosmic images, I 516a
cosmology, IV 145b
Creation, IV 145b
dignity, IV 139a, 145b
four worlds, III 130b
free will, IV 131b
genius, II 293b
God, II 349a;
IV 145b
happiness, IV 132a
heresy, II 427b
Hermeticism, II 432b
hierarchy, II 442a–442b
humanism, II 520a; IV
131b
individualism, II 597b
knowledge, IV 132a
love, III 512a
magic, IV 145b
microcosm, II 442b; III
130a–131a
mimesis, III 229a
Nature, II 442b
Neo-Platonism, IV 145b
perennial philosophy, III
459b
Platonism, III 506b, 507b,
510a, 511b, 512a, 514b
poetry, IV 466a
skepticism, IV 242a, 243a
soul, III 512a
syncretism, IV 126b
Tree of Sephirot, III 130b
universality, IV 145b
ut pictura poesis, IV 466a
wisdom, IV 132a
work, IV 532a
Pictet, A. (1799–1875)
linguistics, IV 425a
uniformitarianism, IV 425a
Pictet, F. J. (1809–1872),
linguistics, IV 425a
uniformitarianism, IV 425a
Pictor, Fabius, historiography,
II 469a
Pieri, M., axiomatization, I
167a
Piero della Francesca (1420?–
1492), mythology, III 276a,
276b
Piero di Cosimo (1462–1521),
art, II 302b
chance images, I 348a–
348b, 349b
individualism, II 302b
mythology, III 291b–292a
Pietism, III 493a–495b
aims, III 493b

Amana Community, III
493b
Arnold, III 494a–494b
Basedow, III 495a
Bergstraesser, III 494b
Bible, III 493b
Channing, IV 111a
Church of the Brethren, III
493b
Coleridge, IV 111b
Comenius, III 493b, 495a
Counter-Enlightenment, II
103b, 105a
education, III 493b, 494a,
495a
Edwards, Jonathan, IV
110b
Enlightenment, II 91a, 97b;
III 494a, 495a
eschatology, II 157a
ethics, III 493b, 495a
evangelicalism, III 493b,
494b
evil, II 165a
faith, hope, and charity,
III 493b
feeling, IV 68b
Finney, IV 111b
Francke, III 493b, 494a,
495a
Frederick William I, I 361b
Germany, I 403a, 595a; III
493a–495b; IV 199b–200a
God, III 495b
Goethe, III 494b
Great Britain, III 493b
Hegel, III 494b
heresy, II 429a; III 494a
history, I 406a; III 494a–
494b
Hölderlin, III 495a
holy, II 512b–513a
humanism, II 520a
humanitarianism, III 494b
idealism, III 494b
illuminists, IV 111a–112a
individualism, III 493b,
495a, 495b
Jesus Christ, III 493b, 494b,
495a
Joseph II, I 403b–404a
Kant, III 494b
Kroner, III 494b
literature, III 493b–495a
Lutheranism, I 403a; III
493b
Machiavellism, III 118b
Mahan, IV 111b
Marsh, James, IV 111b
Methodism, III 493b; IV
68b
missionaries, III 493b
morality, III 493b, 494b,
495a, 495b

Moravians, III 493b, 494a
mythology, III 288a, 291b, 304b
natural law, III 15a
Nazarenes, III 493b
Netherlands, I 403a
Novalis, IV 206b
Parker, IV 111b
Pestalozzi, III 495a
philosophy, III 494a, 494b
piety, III 493b
poetry, III 495a
practicality, III 493b
Protestantism, II 429a; III 493a–495b
Rappites, III 493b
rationalism, III 494a
reformation, IV 68b
religion, IV 109b–111b
Roman Catholic Church, III 493b
romanticism, I 595a; IV 199b–200a, 206b, 210a
Royce, IV 111b
Schleiermacher, III 494a; IV 210a
society, III 494b
Spener, III 493b, 494a, 495a
temperance, III 495a
theology, III 493b–495a
tolerance, III 494b
transcendentalism, IV 111b
uniformitarianism, IV 111a
Unitarianism, IV 111a
U.S., III 493b, 495a
Wesley, III 493b
Wolff, I 361b
Zinzendorf, III 493b, 495a
Piety
Aeschylus, IV 366b
Cicero, III 16b
dignity, IV 144b, 145b
Ficino, IV 144b, 145b
Luther, II 212a
mythology, III 274a
perennial philosophy, III 457a
Pietism, III 493b
Plato, III 554a
Platonism, III 503b
progress, III 626a
Renaissance, IV 144b, 145b
skepticism, IV 238b
socialism, IV 287b
Socrates, III 554a
syncretism, I 44a–44b
temperance, IV 366b, 368b
tragic sense, IV 414a
Victorian sentiment, IV 219a, 222b
virtue, IV 366b, 368b

wisdom of the fool, IV 518b
Pigler, A., iconography, II 539a
Pigot, Thomas, music, III 263a
Piles, Roger de
  aesthetics, II 222a
  iconography, II 533a
  mimesis, III 228b
  mythology, III 298b–299a
Pillement, Jean-Baptiste, China, I 364a
Pillsbury, Walter (1872–1960), behaviorism, I 220b, 221a
Pinchot, Gifford (1865–1946), conservation, I 471a, 475b–476a
Pindar (522?–443 B.C.)
  ambiguity, I 49a–50a
  baroque in literature, I 192a
  education, II 75b
  freedom of speech, II 259b
  human nature, III 571a, 571b–572a, 572b, 575a
  idea, II 542a
  impiety, II 565b
  infinity, II 604b
  law, II 681a, 682b–683b
  mimesis, III 226a
  poetics, III 527a, 530b
  Pythagoreans, IV 32a
  soul, II 572b
  temperance, IV 366a–366b, 368b
  utility, IV 450b
  virtue, IV 365a–365b, 368b
Pinel, Philippe (1745–1826), nosology, II 400a
Pinkerton, John
  art, II 306b
  individualism, II 306b
Pino, Paolo
  aesthetics, II 221b
  art, II 309b
  genius, II 309b
Pinthus, Kurt, expressionism, II 206b, 209a
Piper, F., iconography, II 535b
Pirandello, Luigi (1867–1936)
  humanism, III 568a
  irony, II 627b
  metaphysical imagination, III 208b
  pragmatism, III 551b, 553b, 564a, 568a
  relativism, III 564a, 568a
  truth, III 564a
  value, III 564a, 568a
Piranesi, Giovanni Battista (1720–1778)
  art, II 308a
  imagination, II 308a
  neo-classicism in art, III

364b, 365a 365b
Pirenne, Henri (1862–1935), Islam, III 181a
  periodization in history, III 480a
Pirkheimer, Willibald (1470–1530), mythology, III 292b
Pisano, Giovanni (1245–1314)
  iconography, II 529a
  temperance, IV 375a
  virtue, IV 375a, 477b
Pisano, Nicola (c. 1220–1287), art, IV 123a
Pisarev, Dimitri, realism in literature, IV 53a
Piscator, Johannes (1546–1625), Ramism, IV 45a
Pisistratus (d. 527 B.C.)
  freedom of speech, II 260a
  law, II 680b
Piso Frugi (fl. 150 B.C.), temperance, IV 370a
Pissarro, Camille (1830–1903), impressionism, II 567b, 573a, 573b, 579a, 580a–580b
Pitch, III 260b, 262a–263b
  music, II 389a
Pitt, William (1759–1806), balance of power, I 187a
  rhetoric, IV 172a
Pittacus (650?–?570 B.C.), temperance, IV 366a, 377a
Pity
  Aristotle, IV 411b, 412a
  Blair, I 265b
  Burke, I 265b
  Campbell, I 265b
  catharsis, I 102a, 264b–267b, 268b
  Gerard, I 265b
  Hume, I 266a
  Hurd, I 265b
  Kames, I 265b
  progress, III 638b
  romanticism, IV 203a
  Smith, Adam, I 265b
  tragic sense, IV 411b, 412a
  vox populi, IV 499b
Pius II, Pope (1405–1464), city, I 430b
  temperance, 375a, 375b
Pius VI, Pope (1717–1799), civil disobedience, I 404b
  Jansenism, I 400a
Pius VII, Pope (1472–1823), Christianity, I 404b
Pius IX, Pope (1792–1878), heresy, II 429b
  liberalism, I 406a
  religion, IV 107a, 114b
Pius X, Pope (1835–1914), heresy, II 429b

modernism, I 419a
  reformation, IV 68b
Pius XI, Pope (1857–1934), women, IV 527a
Pius XII, Pope (1876–1958), modernism, I 425a
  women, IV 527a–527b
Placidus, Lactantius, mythology, III 291a
Plagiarism, metaphor, III 205a
Plague
  disease, II 399b
  music, III 269b
Planche, Gustave
  mimesis, III 229b
  naturalism, III 229b
  realism in literature, IV 51b, 52a
Planck, Max (1858–1947), entropy, II 113a, 113b
  indeterminacy, II 590a
  probability, III 620a
  revolution, IV 163a
Planck's constant, IV 91b, 92a
  time, IV 397b–398a
Planets
  Aristotle, I 540a 541a, 668a
  Blasius of Parma, II 35b 36a
  cosmology, I 538a–547b, 552a, 555a, 561a, 570a
  demonology, I 669b
  Descartes, III 257a
  determinism, II 18b–19a
  distance from the sun, I 552a
  epicycles, I 541a, 541b, 542a, 544a
  harmony, II 389a–390a, 390b, 392b, 393b, 394b
  hierarchy, II 442b
  Islam, II 651b
  Kepler, III 260b
  macrocosm, III 128a, 128b, 130b
  matter, III 194b
  measurement, IV 400b
  Medicean, III 414b
  motion, I 542a, 543a–543b, 545b, 546a, 547a–547b, 552a, 555a, 561a; II 651b; IV 50a, 74b, 78a
  music, II 389a–390a, 390b, 392b, 393b, 394b; III 260b, 269a, 271a
  mythology, III 287b, 288b, 290a, 291a, 310a
  Newton, I 674a; III 194b
  numbers, III 269a
  numerical tables, I 538a, 539a
  orbits, I 540b, 545b–546a; IV 74b, 75a
  Plato, I 539b

PLANETS to PLATO

relativity, **IV** 74b, 76a
science, **II** 651b
shape of, **I** 547b
space, **IV** 299b, 300b, 304a
sublime in external nature, **IV** 336b
time, **IV** 400b
velocity, **I** 538a, 539b, 545b
World Spirit, **II** 392b
zodiacal signs, **I** 538b–539a
Plantinga, Alvin, agnosticism, **I** 23b–24a
Plants
catastrophism, **IV** 421b
linguistics, **IV** 425b, 427b
macrocosm, **III** 127a, 128b
uniformitarianism, **IV** 420a, 421b, 425b, 427b
Plato (427?–347 B.C.)
abstraction, **I** 1a–1b, 3a, 3b; **III** 273a
aesthetics, **II** 217a, 221a, 223a; **III** 502a
alchemy, **I** 28a
allegory, **I** 42a–43b, 46b
analogy, **I** 61a, 62a, 62b, 63a, 63b, 68a; **III** 273b
anarchy, **I** 71a
Anaxagoras and, **IV** 34a
anger, **IV** 3b
antimony of pure reason, **I** 91b
Antisthenes and, **I** 630a; **III** 518a
appearance and reality, **I** 94a–95a, 97a–97b; **III** 188b
architecture, **I** 457b, 581a; **III** 497b, 498b, 499a; **IV** 41b.
Archytas of Tarentum and, **III** 516a; **IV** 32b–33a
Aristippus and, **III** 516a, 518a
aristocracy, **IV** 175a
Aristotle and, **II** 390a, 663a, 663b; **III** 189a, 459b, 461a, 500b, 503a, 509a, 509b, 510b, 512a, 514b, 516b, 554a; **IV** 4b, 5a, 6b, 33a, 33b, 34a–34b, 49b, 50b, 175b, 369a, 400b
arithmetic, **I** 462b–463a; **IV** 39a
art, **II** 299b, 308a, 309a, 309b, 582b; **III** 226b, 227a, 497a–502a
art and play, **I** 100a–101b
artists, **I** 578b–579a
astronomy, **I** 462b–463a, 539b
atomism, **I** 127b–128a, 539b; **II** 586b; **III** 188b;

IV 34a
Bacon and, **I** 173b
beauty, **I** 196a–197b, 198a, 205a–205b, 578b, 579a, 581a, 581b, 583a–584b; **II** 217a, 221a; **III** 465a, 500b, 501a, 502a, 507a, 508b
Being, **II** 40b; **III** 188a, 188b; **IV** 431b
belief, **IV** 33b, 35b
Bible, **IV** 369a
biology, **I** 232a, 233a–235a; **III** 354a
Bodin and, **II** 390a–390b
body, **IV** 3b, 4a, 4b
Bruni and, **III** 509b
Castiglione and, **III** 512b
catastrophes, **III** 628b, 630b
catharsis, **I** 264b, 266a, 268a, 268b–269a; **III** 500b
causation, **I** 271b–272a, 273b, 303b
censorship, **III** 497a–498a, 499a, 501b, 554b
certainty, **I** 316b
Chain of Being, **I** 325a–325b, 326b, 330a, 333a
Chalcidius and, **III** 509b
chance, **II** 226b, 231b–232a; **III** 629a–629b
change, **III** 354a; **IV** 390b, 391b
chaos, **IV** 296b–297a
children, **III** 471a, 501a
chora, **IV** 299b
Christianity, **III** 505b, 506a, 509b, 590a
Church, **I** 417a
Cicero and, **III** 509b; **IV** 40a
city, **I** 427b
civilization, **III** 629a
class, **I** 443a; **III** 508b; **IV** 3b
classification, **I** 233a–233b
classification of the arts, **I** 456b–459b, 460b, 583a
classification of the sciences, **I** 462b–463a
cognition, **I** 1a
comedy, **I** 467b; **III** 498a, 501a
communism, **III** 520b; **IV** 285b
conflict, **IV** 3b
conservation, **I** 471b–472a
conservatism, **I** 582a
constitutionalism, **I** 487a, 488b
continuity, **I** 500b
Cosmic Fall, **I** 505b, 512a
cosmic images, **I** 514b
cosmic voyages, **I** 524a

cosmology, **I** 539a, 543a, 552b, 578b–579a, 586b, 624b; **II** 162b–163a; **III** 512a; **IV** 34a, 35b, 37b, 39a–39b, 41b, 50a, 50b, 368b
courage, **III** 110a
Creation, **I** 539b, 571b–572a, 622b; **IV** 39a
creativity in art, **I** 578a–586b, 587b, 588a
criticism, **III** 499a, 507a
critics, **III** 501a
culture, **I** 608b–609a, 611a, 611b–612b; **II** 127b, 129b
custom, **II** 662b; **III** 15a
cycles, **I** 621b–625a
cynicism, **I** 627b, 629a, 632a, 633b
dance, **III** 226b, 500b
death, **I** 635b–639b, 643b, 644a, 645a; **III** 273b
degeneration, **III** 629b
deism, **I** 647b
Demiurge, **I** 325b, 333a, 571b–572a, 579a, 672a, 673b; **II** 40b, 390b, 586b; **III** 127a, 505a; **IV** 39a–39b, 50a, 415a
democracy, **I** 653a, 653b–654a, 655a, 658a; **II** 22a; **III** 554a, 629a; **IV** 175a, 497a
Democritus and, **III** 188a, 188b
demonology, **I** 668a–669a
design argument, **I** 671a–673b, 674a, 674b, 676b
desire, **III** 498a, 499b
despotism, **II** 2a
determinism, **II** 22a, 135a, 236b, 237a
Dewey and, **III** 554b
dignity, **IV** 139a, 144a–144b
doctrine of divine enthusiasm, **II** 299b
drama, **III** 497b–498a
dramatists, **III** 500a
dualism, **II** 40a–41a; **III** 507a, 508b; **IV** 3b, 4a, 4b, 34b
dyad, **IV** 34a, 34b
education, **II** 74b, 75a–83a, 99b; **III** 465a, 466b, 469a–501a, 502a; **IV** 49b, 368b
elite, **III** 465a; **IV** 175a
Emerson and, **III** 430a, 502b
emotion, **III** 496b–501b; **IV** 4b
empathy, **II** 87b
Empedocles and, **III** 188b

empiricism, **III** 15a, 497a, 500b, 546b
Enlightenment, **II** 90a, 99b
entropy, **II** 117b
environment, **II** 127b, 129b
epics, **III** 226b, 497b, 501a
Epicureanism, **II** 135a, 135b; **III** 504a; **IV** 7a
Epicurus and, **III** 274a
equality, **I** 449a; **II** 140a
equity, **II** 148a–150b
Eros, **III** 95a
ethics, **II** 148a–149b, 375b; **III** 440a; **IV** 33b, 49a–49b, 175a, 320a, 320b, 321a
etymology, **II** 662a–662b
Euripides and, **III** 500a
evil, **II** 40b–41a, 162b–163a, 376b; **III** 496b–497a, 498a, 500b, 501b; **IV** 380b
evolutionism, **II** 175b
faith, hope, and charity, **II** 209b
fate, **II** 226b, 231b–232a; **IV** 415a
Faust (legend), **III** 245a
Ficino and, **III** 506a, 509b, 510b, 515b–516a; **IV** 144a–144b
Flood, **I** 625a
Forms, **I** 271b, 505b, 571b–572a, 639a, 672a–672b; **II** 175b; **III** 188a–188b, 211a, 353b, 354a, 464b–465a, 498b–502a, 504b, 507a, 508a, 577a, 628b; **IV** 3b, 4a, 6a, 47a–47b, 49b, 369a, 431b
fortune, **II** 226b, 231b–232a
four elements, **III** 126b, 130a
free will, **I** 586b; **II** 135a, 135b, 236b, 237a, 242b–243b
freedom, **I** 578b, 583a, 584a; **II** 243a, 249b
freedom of speech, **II** 258b, 260a
Freud and, **II** 383b
friendship, **III** 112a, 554a; **IV** 285b
Galileo and, **III** 353b
genius, **I** 578a; **II** 293b, 295a, 299b, 308a, 309a, 309b, 317b–318b, 320b
geometry, **I** 462b–463a; **III** 188b; **IV** 33b, 39a, 40a
goals, **IV** 175a
God, **I** 325a, 333a, 539b, 571b–572a, 578b–579a, 580a, 586b; **II** 162b–163a, 339b, 341a, 349a, 566a;

329

III 465a, 497a–499b, 500b, 574b; IV 368b, 380b
Goethe and, III 519a
Golden Age (myth), IV 131a
good, II 162b–163a, 209b, 375b, 376b; III 273a, 465a, 496b–497a, 498a, 501a, 501b, 502a, 508b; IV 4a, 36a, 37a, 37b, 49b, 174b, 175a, 182b, 380b, 431b
Gorgias and, III 496b–497a, 501b
Great Year (myth), III 628b; IV 400b–401a
gymnastics, I 462b
happiness, II 375b–377a, 383b
harmony, I 579a–579b, 629b; II 236b, 389b, 390a–391b; III 500b; IV 38b, 39a–41b, 175a, 368b
health, II 399a, 399b–400a; III 497a; IV 368b
Hegel and, II 410b
Heraclitus and, I 578b, 582a–582b; IV 34b
heresy, II 427a, 566a
heroes, III 497a
hierarchy, II 438a, 438b, 441a, 443a, 443b
Hippocrates and, III 500a
historiography, II 22a, 471a, 502b, 504b, 508b
history, II 22a; III 354a, 629a–629b; IV 175a
Homer and, III 497a
homosexuality, III 512b
human nature, III 500b, 554b, 570b–577b
humanism, II 516b, 519b, 520a, 521b; IV 129b, 131a, 131b
hymns, III 498a
idea, I 42b–43b, 325a–325b, 462b, 582a; II 223a, 542a–542b, 544b, 547b, 582b, 633b; III 15a, 188a, 353b, 508b, 517a; IV 34b, 35a, 35b
ideal, II 662b; III 273a; IV 285b
idealism, I 582a; III 347a
ignorance, II 236b, 662b
image, III 500a
imagination, III 208a, 210a–211b, 214a
imitation, II 582b; III 497b–498a, 498b, 500a, 501a
immorality, II 376a; III 497a
immortality, I 584a, 638b–639b, 643b, 644b, 645a; III 577a; IV 4a
impiety, II 566a

impressionism, II 582b
indeterminacy, II 586b
individualism, II 299b, 308a, 309a, 309b; III 37a, 496a
infinity, II 605a, 605b, 607a, 609b
injustice, II 376a
inspiration, I 583b–584a; III 499a–499b, 501b
intolerance, II 566a
irrationalism, II 635a, 635b, 637a, 637b, 638a; IV 368b
Islam, II 639b, 644b, 646b, 647b, 649b
Isocrates and, III 500a
judges, II 149a–149b
judgment, II 243a; III 497a–497b
justice, II 236b, 375b–376a, 653a, 655b, 656a, 656b, 658b; III 15a, 16b, 110a, 497a, 554a; IV 3b, 175a, 368b, 440b
Kant and, II 223a; III 518a–518b
kingship, III 498b–499a
knowledge, I 584a; II 149a, 236b, 582b, 662b, 663b; III 188b, 211a–211b, 464b–465a, 496a–503b, 504b, 507a, 508b, 513a, 515b; IV 4a–4b, 33b, 34a, 49a, 49b, 368a, 431b
language, II 661b–663a, 663b, 664a, 669a; III 62b
law, I 487a, 654a; II 148a–149b, 249b, 679b, 683b, 684b; III 1b, 11a, 15a, 16b, 497a, 631a; IV 285b
learning, I 1a–1b; IV 4a–4b
Leibniz and, III 515b–516a
leisure, IV 497b
liberalism, III 37a
limbo, I 417a
linguistics, III 61b, 62b, 65b, 68a, 74b
literary paradox, III 77a
literature, III 86a, 495a–502a, 518b–519a, 571a; IV 330b, 332b
logic, III 499b, 546b, 554a
Lost Paradise (myth), III 629a
love, II 648b; III 94a, 95a, 95b, 96a, 499a, 507a, 508b; IV 175a
loyalty, III 110a–112a
Lysias and, III 499a
Machiavelli and, III 514b
macrocosm and microcosm, III 126b, 127a–127b, 130a; IV 32b
marriage, III 471a

mathematics, I 581a, 583b, 584a, 584b; II 390a, 443b; III 172a, 180a, 308a, 503a; IV 31a, 33a, 33b, 34b, 37b, 39a–39b
matter, I 622b; III 185b, 187a–187b, 188a–189a, 190b; IV 380b
Mead and, III 554b
measurement, IV 400a, 400b–401a
medicine, III 497a, 500a
melancholy, II 309a
metaphor, III 200a, 203b–205a, 207a, 207b
metaphysics, II 376a–376b; III 208a, 210a–210b, 211a–211b, 214a, 464b, 498a, 498b, 503a, 507a; IV 33a, 34b, 36a, 37a, 37b
methodology, III 379b, 380a, 381b
mimesis, III 226a–226b, 227a, 228a, 230a, 343b, 497b, 498a, 500a
mimetic art, I 578b, 581a–585a
mind, II 223a; III 188a, 188b, 353b; IV 50a
monarchy, I 654a
moral sense, III 230b, 234b
morality, II 231b–232a, 375b–376a, 376b, 566a; III 496a, 500b, 501a, 503b, 508b, 577a, 629a; IV 4a
More, Thomas and, IV 461a–461b
Moses (Bible), III 512a; IV 40b
motion, I 671b–672a; II 390b; IV 75a
mountains, III 259a
music, I 462b, 463a, 579b, 581a; II 299b, 317b–318a, 318b, 320b, 389b, 390a–391b; III 226b, 260b, 265b, 269a, 497b, 498b, 499a, 500a, 500b; IV 38b, 39a–40a
mutability, III 350b–351a
mythology, I 624b; II 226b, 410b; III 272a, 272b, 273a–273b, 274b, 292a, 292b, 299b, 354a, 497b, 499b; IV 4a, 38b, 39b, 41a
nationalism, III 325b
natural law, I 487a; III 15a, 16b
natural liberty, II 61b
naturalism, III 226b
naturalism in art, III 343b
Nature, I 127b–128a, 487a; II 438b; III 15a, 226a, 347a, 350b–351a; IV 380b, 390b

necessity, II 243a; III 188a, 188b, 351b, 352b, 353a–354a, 355a, 357a; IV 50a
Neo-Platonism, III 372a, 372b, 373a, 374a, 375a, 375b, 376b, 377a
Newton and, I 676b; III 379b, 380a, 397a
Noble Savage, III 629a–629b
non-being, III 188a, 188b
nous, IV 3b, 32b, 34a, 37a, numbers, IV 33b, 34b, 37b, 39a–39b
oligarchy, I 654a; II 22a; IV 175a
optics, III 408a–408b
oratory, III 496b, 499a, 500a, 500b, 501b
organicism, III 421b, 422a, 423a, 424a
Orientalism, III 430a
origin of Greek language, III 61b, 68a
pain, II 376a–376b; IV 451a–451b
painting, I 457b, 581a–581b, 582a; III 226b, 497b, 498b–499a, 501a; IV 467b
Parmenides and, IV 3a, 400a
passions, II 236b, 243a; III 498a, 499b, 501b; IV 3b, 4a
peace, III 440a
perception, IV 4a, 34a
perennial philosophy, III 458b–463a
perfectibility, III 464b–466b, 468b 469b 471a; IV 285b
Pericles and, III 500a
pessimism, III 440a
Petrarch and, III 509b–510a
phenomena, III 353a, 353b, 354a
Philo Judaeus and, III 465b–466a, 590a
philosophers, III 498b 502a, 523b
philosophy, II 661b; III 188b, 200a, 210a, 465a, 502a, 508a, 515b
physics, IV 368b
piety, III 554a
planets, I 539b
pleasure, II 375b–377a, 383b; III 497a, 500b, 501a; IV 4b, 451a–451b
plentitude principle, I 42b–43a; II 438b
Plotinus and, III 274b, 374a, 466a, 509a, 516b; IV 8b

Plutarch and, II 341a–341b; III 502b

poets, III 495b–501b, 523b

poetry, I 457a; III 226b, 495b–502a, 525b–527b, 529b, 530a, 531a; IV 467b

politics, III 353b, 499a, 502b, 507a, 520b, 554b, 629b

Polybius and, III 630b

Popper and, III 502b

positivism, III 546b

poverty, I 654a; III 629a; IV 175a

power, III 1b, 188a; IV 380b

pragmatism, III 554a–555b

primitivism, III 586a, 590a

probability, III 500b

progress, III 626b–633a

Protagoras and, III 574b

psyche, IV 34a, 37a, 49b

psychology, II 135b, 376a, 376b; III 354a, 498a, 500b, 505a; IV 2a–4b, 6a–7a, 8b, 9b, 10b, 16b, 17b

punishment, II 135a, 566a

puppet shows, III 501a

Puritanism, IV 16b

Pythagoras and, III 523b; IV 3b, 31a–41b, 46b

Pythagoreans, I 578b, 579a–581a; III 353a–353b, 503a; IV 31a–41b

rationalism, IV 46b, 47a 50b, 175a

realism in literature, IV 51b

reality, III 273a, 274b, 347a, 353b, 498b, 501b, 502a, 508b; IV 390b

reason, I 236b, 243a, 390b; III 1b, 210b, 464b–465a, 496a, 496b, 499b, 500b, 501b, 508b, 586a; IV 3b, 4a, 4b, 50a, 175a

recreation, III 500b

reincarnation, I 645a; II 226b; III 505a

relativism, III 77a

relativity, IV 75a

religion, II 566a; III 203b–207b

reminiscence, I 1a–1b

Renaissance, III 95b

responsibility, III 501b

revolution, IV 152b

rhetoric, III 495b–502a; IV 167b, 171b

rhythm, III 500b

right, IV 174b, 175a, 182b

Rousseau and, III 325b

Ryle and, III 502b

Saint Augustine and, III 355b, 509b

Saint Thomas Aquinas and, I 259b, 673a

salvation, IV 228a

Santayana and, III 554b

Schleiermacher and, III 516a, 518b, 519a–522a

Schopenhauer and, I 255b

science, III 353a, 503a

sculptors, III 500a

sculpture, I 581a–582a; III 226b, 497b, 501a

self-control, III 110a

senses, I 1a–1b; II 662b; III 188b, 273a, 503a, 504b, 508b; IV 3b, 4a, 4b, 33b, 35b

sin, II 236b; IV 228a

skepticism, III 503a, 504a–504b; IV 234b, 235a, 235b, 238b

skill, III 629a

social contract, IV 252b

socialism, IV 285b

society, I 654a; II 149a; III 354a, 497a, 629a, 629b; IV 175a

Socrates and, I 578b, 581b–582a, 583b; III 226a–226b, 496a–497a, 498b–499a, 554a, 571a, 577a, 627b; IV 3b, 34a, 34b, 48b, 49a–49b, 175a, 368a, 415a

Sophists, I 578b, 582a–582b; III 77a, 496a, 496b–497a, 499a, 500a

Sophocles and, III 500a; IV 367a

soul, I 196a–196b, 234b, 637a–639b, 668a, 671b 673b; II 40b–41a, 236b, 243a, 243b, 390b–391b; III 273b, 464b, 465a, 496a, 497a, 498a, 499a, 508b, 573a; IV 3a–4b, 31a, 32b–37b, 175a, 368a, 368b

space, III 188a, 188b, 189a; IV 295a, 296b, 297a, 299b

Spencer and, III 502b

Speusippus, IV 34b–36b

State, I 630a, 651a, 653b–654a, 655a, 658a; III 440a, 471a, 508b, 554b, 629a; IV 3b, 49, 285b, 313b, 368b, 497a–497b

Stoicism, IV 7a, 320a, 320b, 321a

style, IV 330b, 332b

subatomic realm, II 586b

suffering, III 498a

symmetry, IV 346b, 347a, 348a, 348b, 350b

technology, I 612a; III 499b–500a, 629a

teleology, I 234a, 234b, 235a, 271b, 272a, 303b

temperance, IV 367a–369b

Tennemann and, III 518b, 522b

theater, III 496b, 497b–498a, 500a, 501a

theodicy, II 162b; IV 380a, 380b

theology, III 510a

time, IV 390b, 391a, 391b, 400a, 400b–401a

timocracy, II 22a

topos, IV 299b

totalitarianism, III 554b; IV 406b

trade, III 629a

tragedy, II 376b; III 226b, 498a, 501a

tragic sense, IV 414b, 415a

transcendentalism, I 578b, 583b, 584a–584b

truth, II 582b, 662b; III 188b, 273a, 273b, 408a, 496a, 498b, 499b, 501b, 502a, 507a; IV 431b

tyranny, I 654a; II 22a; III 498a; IV 175a

ugliness, I 585a, 586b; II 217a

unity, III 503b; IV 34a

unity of science, IV 431a–431b, 432b, 436a

universal man, IV 440b

universality, IV 34b, 35b

universe, I 579a, 580a, 671b–672a; II 390a; III 353a; IV 34a, 38b, 39a–40a, 40b, 41a, 41b

utility, IV 450b–452b

Utopia, IV 459b–460a, 461a–461b

utopianism, III 554b

virtue, I 612a; II 80b, 376b; III 465b, 508b; IV 49a, 49b, 175a, 368a–368b, 378a, 415a

vocabulary, III 211a

vox populi, IV 497a–497b

wealth, I 654a; III 629a; IV 175a

Whitehead and, III 502b, 515a, 522b

wisdom, I 612a; III 110a, 501b; IV 4a, 368b

women, III 501a

work, IV 530b

Xenocrates and, IV 34b–35a, 36b–37a

Xenophon and, III 577a

Zeno of Citium and, IV 320b

Plato (comic poet), (5th–4th century B.C.), progress, III

625b–626a

Platonism, III 495b–525b

Abarbanel, III 509a, 510b, 512a–512b, 514a

aesthetics, II 218a; III 496a, 502a, 514b, 516b, 518b, 523b, 524a, 524b

Alcott, III 522b

allegory, III 505a, 513b, 514b

animals, III 510a

anthropocentrism, III 510a

Arabs, III 505b

Arcesilaus, III 504a, 504b

architecture, III 497b, 498b, 499a

Ariosto, III 514b

aristocracy, III 505b, 520b

Aristophanes, III 496a, 497b, 512a, 524a

Aristotelianism, III 500b, 510a, 513a, 514a, 520a

Aristotle, III 500b, 503a, 504a, 505a, 509a, 509b, 510b, 512a, 513b, 514a, 514b, 516b, 519a, 519b, 530b 531a

Arnold, III 507b

art, II 298b, 308b, 310a, 310b; III 497a–502a, 506a, 510a–513a, 524a

asceticism, III 509a, 511a

Ascham, III 507b

astrology, III 506a, 507b

Augustinianism, III 505b, 509a, 521b

authority, III 513b

Babeuf, III 520b

Bacon, III 510b

beauty, II 550a; III 500b 514a, 524a, 524b

Being, III 509a

Bellarmino, III 513b–514a

Bembo, III 510a, 511a, 512a, 512b, 514a

Benivieni, III 511a–512a

Bergson, III 523a

Berkeley, III 506b, 523b

Berni, III 513a

Bible, III 505a, 512a, 519a

biology, I 237a, 237b

Blake, III 523b, 524b

Boccaccio, III 512b

Boeckh, III 519b, 520a, 521a

Bosanquet, III 522a

Botticelli, III 511b

Bradley, III 506b, 522a

Brandis, III 521b

Brucker, III 517a–518a

Bruni, III 509b

Bruno, III 510a, 510b, 513b

Byron, III 507a

cabbalism, III 507b

Campanella, III 510a–510b
Carneades, III 504b
Castiglione, III 507b, 512b
catharsis, III 500b
Cattaneo, III 511b
censorship, III 497a–498a, 499a, 501b
Chalcidius, III 509b
Champier, III 507b
Chapman, III 295a
Chaucer, III 507b
children, III 501a
Christianity, I 375a; III 505a–506b, 509a–514b, 516a, 517a, 519a, 523a, 589a; IV 371a
Chrysippus, III 504a
Cicero, III 509b, 512b
city, I 427b
city-state, III 503b
class, III 508b, 520b
Clement VIII (Pope), III 513b
Cohen, Hermann, III 522b
Coleridge, III 507b, 523b–524a
Colet, III 507b, 514a–514b
color, III 511b, 519a
comedy, III 498a, 501a
common sense, III 516a
communication, III 507a
communism, III 520b
Condillac, III 516a
constructivism, III 521a–521b
cosmology, III 510a–512a
courtship, III 95b
Cousin, III 521b, 522a
Creation, III 512a
creativity, III 507a, 524b
Creuzer, III 521b
criticism, III 496a, 499a, 507a, 521b, 523a
critics, III 501a
Crombie, III 523a
Cudworth, III 506b, 517a
cults, III 505a
culture, I 610b; II 127b
cynicism, III 585b
Cynics, III 503b–504a
dance, III 500b
Dante, III 507a, 507b, 509b, 511a, 512a, 512b, 513a
death, I 645a
deism, I 649b
Demiurge, III 505a
demonology, I 668b; III 506a, 510b
Descartes, III 193a
design argument, I 674a
desire, III 498a, 499b, 512a
Dewey, III 554a
Diacceto, III 512b–513a
Diderot, III 518a

dignity, IV 137a–140a, 142a, 143b, 144a–146a
Diogenes Laërtius, III 516b
Diogenes of Sinope, III 503b
drama, III 497b–498a
dramatists, III 500a
Du Bellay, III 507b, 514a
dualism, II 41b, 42a, 42b; III 504a, 505a, 507a–509a
Eastern Orthodox Church, III 510a
eclecticism, III 516b–517b, 521b, 522a
education, III 496a, 497a, 498b, 500b–522b
emanation, III 505b
Emerson, III 502b, 522a–522b
emotion, III 496b–501b
empiricism, III 497a, 500b, 506b
Enlightenment, III 516a
environment, II 127b
epics, III 496a, 497b, 501a, 513b
Epicureanism, III 504a, 524a
epistemology, III 505b
Equicola, III 514a
Erasmus, III 514b
Erdmann, III 522a
error, III 506a
eschatology, II 157b
ethics, III 441a, 503b, 504a, 505b, 506a, 507b, 523a; IV 319b, 320b
Euripides, III 500a
evil, II 162b, III 496b–497a, 498a, 500b, 501b, 513a
evolutionism, II 175b, 177a, 178a, 181a
expressionism, II 207a
faith, hope, and charity, II 210b
fascism, III 520b
feeling, III 498a
festivals, III 500b
Ficino, III 506a–516a; IV 131b–132a, 144a–145b
Florence, III 506a–515b
Formalism, III 518b
Forms, I 427b; II 218a; III 498b–507a, 508b, 513b
France, III 506a, 507a–507b, 514a, 520b, 521b
Francis I, III 507a–507b
French Revolution (1789), III 520b
friendship, III 507a, 511a
Galileo, II 521a; III 356a, 510b; IV 361a
genius, II 293a–293b, 298b, 308b, 310a, 310b

Gentile, III 510a
George, III 524b
Germany, III 506b, 514a, 519a–522a, 523b
Ghirlandaio, III 511b
Gnosticism, II 327a, 329b, 330a
God, II 347b; III 496b–506b, 510a–513a, 516a, 517a, 521b
Goethe, III 519a, 521b
good, III 496b–502a, 508b, 509a, 511b, 513b, 514a, 517a; IV 181b
Gorgias, III 496b–497a, 501b
Great Britain, III 506a, 507b–508a, 514a–515b, 519a–519b, 521b, 522a–524a
Greece (ancient), III 496a–502a
Green, T. H., III 522a
Gregory XIV (Pope), III 514a
Grocyn, III 507b
Grote, III 522a
Gundolf, III 524b
happiness, II 380a;, III 512b–513a
harmony, II 390b–391b, 392b; III 500b, 506a, 524a
Hartmann, III 522b
health, II 398a; III 497a
hedonism, III 513a, 514b, 516a
Hegel, III 506b, 520a–522b
Heindorf, III 519b
Heraclitus, III 496a
Herder, III 519a
heresy, III 513b
Hermann, III 521a
hermeneutics, III 519b
hermeticism, II 431a, 433a; III 507b
Herodotus, III 497b
heroes, III 497a
Héroet, III 514a
hierarchy, II 441a, 444a, 445a; III 509a, 509b, 511a, 513b
Hippocrates, III 497b, 500a
history, III 496a, 516b, 521a–521b, 523a, 523b
Hobbes, III 506a
Hölderlin, III 524a
Homer, III 496a, 497a, 507a, 519a
homosexuality, III 512b, 514b
human nature, III 500b, 524a
humanism, II 520a, 521a;

III 504b, 507b, 509b, 514a, 514b; IV 131b–132b, 134a, 134b
Husserl, III 522b
hymns, III 498a
idea, I 375a; II 545a, 546a, 547a; III 95b–96a, 508b, 509a, 513b, 515b, 516b–518b, 524a, 524b
ideal, II 549a, 549b, 550a
idealism, I 237a, 237b; III 504b, 506b, 515b
ignorance, III 496b–497a, 510b, 513b
image, III 500a, 508a
imagination, III 211b, 214b, 523b, 524b
imitation, III 497b–498a, 498b, 500a, 501a
immorality, III 496a, 497a, 504a, 505a, 508a, 509a, 516a
imperialism, III 503b
impersonation, III 497b–498a
impressionism, II 581b, 582a, 582b
Incarnation, III 505b, 509b
individualism, II 298b, 308b, 310a, 310b; III 496a, 516b
Inge, III 503a, 523a
inspiration, III 499a–499b, 501b, 507a
intuition, III 509a, 512a, 516b
irony, II 630a
Islam, II 648b
Isocrates, III 500a
Italy, III 506a 514a, 515a
James, William, III 554a
Jesus Christ, III 505a, 505b, 514b
Johnson, T. J., III 522b
Jowett, III 521b–522a
Judaism, III 512a
judgment, III 497a–497b, 504b
Julius II (Pope), III 513a
justice, II 653a, 653b–654b, 655a, 657a, 658a; III 497a
Justinian, III 503b
Kant, III 518a–518b, 520a, 522b
Keats, III 524a
Kepler, II 521a
kingship, III 498b–499a
knowledge, I 1a–1b; III 496a–515b, 520a
Lachmann, III 522a
Lamartine, III 524a
language, III 511b
law, III 1b, 497a, 514b, 520b

332

Le Roy, III 514a

Leibniz, III 193a, 515b–516b

light, III 511b

Linacre, III 507b

linguistics, III 74b, 521a

literary criticism, I 596a

literature, III 495b–502a, 506a, 506b–508a, 510b, 511a, 512b, 518b–519a, 519b, 521b, 523b–525a; IV 330b, 331b

Locke, III 506b, 516a

logic, III 499b, 503b

logos, III 505b

love, II 648b; III 95b–96a, 499a, 506a, 507a–516a, 523b

Lovejoy, III 508a

Lysias, III 499a, 499b

Mably, III 520b

Machiavelli, III 514b

Mackenna, III 525a

macrocosm, III 127b, 128b

Mallarmé, III 524b

Man-Machine, III 133b, 134b

Marburg school, III 522b

Marguerite of Navarre, III 507a–507b, 514a

materialism, III 504a, 505b, 506a, 507b, 522b, 524a

mathematics, III 177a–177b, 184b, 503a, 503b, 523b

matter, III 190b, 191a–193b, 196a, 509a, 513b

Medici family, III 506a–511b, 513a

medicine, III 497a, 500a

Meletus, III 507a

Mendelssohn, Moses, III 516a–516b

metaphor, III 198b, 513b

metaphysics, III 214b, 498a, 498b, 503b–508a, 516a, 521b–524a

methodology, III 521a, 523b

Michelangelo, III 511a, 513a

microcosm, III 127b, 128b, 510a, 513b

Middle Ages, III 504a, 505b, 506a, 507b, 522b, 524a

Middle-Platonism, III 517b

mimesis, III 229a, 497b, 498a, 500a

mind, III 517b

monads, III 515b, 516b

Montaigne, III 507b

morality, III 496b, 500b, 501a, 503b, 504a, 506b,

508a, 508b, 511a, 512a, 512b, 522b–523a

More, Henry, III 506b, 507b

More, Paul Elmer, III 523a

More, Thomas, III 514b

Moreau, III 522b

Moses (Bible), III 505a, 512a

Mosheim, III 517a

motion, III 510b

music, II 390b–391a, 392b; III 497b, 498b–503b

mysticism, III 503a, 505b, 506a, 515b

mythology, III 291b, 295a, 496b, 497b, 499b, 510b, 524b

Natorp, III 522b

naturalism, II 581b

necessity, III 354b, 355a, 356a

Neo-Aristotelianism, III 514b

Neo-Pythagoreans, III 505a

Nicholas of Cusa, III 510b

Nietzsche, III 520b

Numenius, III 505a

ontology, III 506b, 513b, 517a, 523a

optics, III 415a

oratory, III 496b, 499a, 500a, 500b, 501b

organicism, III 422a–424a

Origen, III 516b

painting, III 497b, 498b–499a, 501a, 511b, 512b

Panaetius, III 504a

Panofsky, III 513a

pantheism, III 515b, 522a

passions, III 498a, 499b, 501b

Pater, III 502b–503a, 522b, 524a

Patrizi, III 512a, 513b–514a, 514b

peace, III 441a

Peirce, III 560b

perennial philosophy, III 457b, 458b–459b, 460b

perfectibility, III 466a, 466b, 468b, 469a, 471a

Pericles, III 500a

periodization in literary history, III 484b

pessimism, III 518b

Petrarch, III 509b–510a, 511a, 512b, 514a

Philo Judaeus, III 505a

philology, III 519b–522b

philosophers, III 498b–503b, 510a, 523b, 524b

philosophy, II 549a, 549b, 550a; III 198b, 502a–508b, 510a, 515b, 516b–523b

physics, III 510a

Pico della Mirandola, III 506b, 507b, 510a, 511b, 512a, 514b

piety, III 503b

pleasure, II 380a; III 497a, 500b, 501a

Plotinus, III 505a–505b, 508b–513a, 516b, 517b, 519a, 523a, 525a

pluralism, III 510b, 515b

Plutarch, III 502b, 505a, 517b

poetics, III 526b, 527a, 528b, 530b

poetry, III 495b–513a, 523b–524a, 524b, 526b, 527a, 528b, 530b

poets, III 495b–501b, 507a, 510a, 511a, 523b, 524b

Polemo, III 504a

politics, III 499a, 502b, 503b, 505b, 507a, 507b, 514b, 520b

Poliziano, III 511a, 511b

Pollaiuolo, III 511b

polytheism, III 519a

Popper, III 502b

populism, III 505b

Posidonius, III 504a

positivism, III 532b

post-Kantianism, IV 209a

Potamon of Alexandria, III 516b, 517b

power, III 517a

pragmatism, III 503b, 504b, 551b, 553b, 554a, 560b

priesthood, III 513b

primitivism, III 585a, 585b, 589a

probability, III 500b, 504b

Proclus, III 508b, 519b, 521b

progress, III 633a

Protestantism, III 514a, 516a

Pseudo-Dionysius, III 514b

psychology, III 498a, 500b, 505a, 505b; IV 6b, 16b, 19a, 24a

puppet shows, III 501a

Puritanism, IV 16b, 19a

Pyrrhonism, III 504b

Pythagoras, III 523b

Pythagoreans, III 503a, 505a; IV 34b, 35a, 36b, 37a

Rabelais, III 507b

rationalism, III 516a, 522a; IV 51a

reality, III 498b, 501b, 502a, 505a, 508b

reason, III 496a, 496b, 499b, 500a, 501b, 508b, 516a

recreation, III 500b

reformation, IV 60b

reincarnation, I 645a; III 505a

relativism, III 523a

relativity, IV 77a

Renaissance, III 504b, 506b–516a, 523b; IV 126b, 131b–146a, 440a

responsibility, III 501b

revolution, III 520b

rhetoric, III 495b–502a, 506a, 507a, 518b

rhythm, III 500b

right, III 496b; IV 181b

Robespierre, III 520b

Roman Catholic Church, I 375a; III 512a, 513b–514a, 516a, 517a

romanticism, III 519a–524b; IV 209a

Ronsard, III 507b, 514a

Rousseau, III 518a, 518b, 520b

Royce, III 506b

Ryle, III 502b

Saccas, III 516b–517b

Saint Augustine, III 505b, 509b; IV 139a

Saint Just, III 520b

Saint Paul, III 509a

Saint Thomas Aquinas, II 210b

salvation, III 509a

Sansovino, III 514b

Santayana, III 503a, 522b–523a, 553b, 554a

Scève, III 514a

Schelling, III 516a, 520a, 521b

Schlegel, F., III 519a

Schleiermacher, III 516a, 518b–522a

Schopenhauer, III 524a

science, III 503a, 510a

sculptors, III 500a, 519a

sculpture, III 497b, 501a

self-sufficiency, III 585a

senses, III 503a, 503b, 504b, 505a, 508b, 511a, 518a

Sextus Empiricus, III 504b

Shaftesbury, III 516b, 518b, 523b

Shakespeare, III 519a

Shelley, Mary, III 508a

Shelley, Percy Bysshe, III 508a, 524a

Shorey, III 522a

skepticism, III 503a, 504a–504b; IV 236a, 243b, 250b

Smith, Adam, III 506b

socialism, III 520b

society, III 497a, 503b

Socrates, III 496a–499b, 500a, 503a, 504a, 504b, 507a, 508b, 510b, 512a, 513b, 514b, 517b, 524b

Sophists, III 496a, 496b–497a, 499a, 500a

Sophocles, III 500a

soul, III 95b, 496a, 497a, 498a, 499a, 504a, 505a, 508a, 508b, 509a, 511a, 512a–513b, 516a, 516b

Souverain, III 517a

Spencer, III 502b, 507b, 514b

Speroni, III 514a

Speusippus, III 504a

Spinoza, III 193a, 512a–512b, 519a, 520a

spiritualism, III 505b, 509a, 513a, 521b, 524a

Stanley, III 516b–517a, 517b

Stoicism, III 504a, 504b; IV 319b, 320b

Strato, IV 6b–7a

style, IV 330b, 331b

suffering, III 498a

Sydenham, III 518a

symbolism, III 508a, 511a, 523b, 524b; IV 341b

symmetry, IV 348a

Tasso, III 513a–513b, 514b

Taylor, III 519a–519b, 522a–524b

technology, III 499b–500a; IV 359b, 361a

teleology, III 522b

Telesio, III 510a–510b

temperance, IV 369a, 369b, 370a, 371a, 378a

Tennemann, III 518b, 522b

theater, III 496b, 497b–498a, 500a, 501a

theodicy, IV 380b, 381a

theology, III 504b, 505a, 505b, 506a–506b, 507b, 509a, 510a, 511a, 512a, 514b, 516b, 517a, 522b

Thomism, III 514a

Tiedemann, III 518a

time, III 508a, 513a

Timon, III 504b

totalitarianism, III 520b

trade, III 506a, 507a

tradition, III 496a

tragedy, III 498a, 501a, 520a

transcendentalism, III 503a, 519b, 520b, 522a–522b, 523b–524a; IV 24a

troubadours, III 95b

truth, III 496a, 498b, 499b, 501b, 502a, 504b, 507a, 509b, 511b, 517a, 518a–518b

Turkey, III 505b, 506a

tyranny, III 498a

U.S., III 519b, 522a–522b

unity, III 503b, 519b

universal man, IV 440a

universe, III 503b, 510a, 510b, 513a

Valéry, III 524b

value, III 503a

virtue, III 508b, 512a; IV 378a

Voltaire, III 516a

vox populi, IV 497b

Whichcote, III 506b, 515a

Whitehead, III 502b, 515a, 522b

Wieland, III 516a, 523b

Winckelmann, III 519a

wisdom, III 501b, 506a, 510b, 512a, 517a, 524b

wisdom of the fool, IV 516b

witchcraft, III 506a

Wolff, III 504a–504b

women, III 501a, 510a

Wordsworth, III 507b–508a, 524a

Xenocrates, III 504a

Xenophanes, III 496a

Xenophon, III 497b, 517b, 519a

Yeats, III 524b–525a

Zeller, III 521a

See also. Neo-Platonism

Plautus (254?–184 B.C.), Eighteenth Century view of, I 86b

Molière and, I 86b

motif, III 238a

Playne, Carolyn E., war, IV 505b

Pleasure, II 374b–387b

advertising, II 385a

aesthetics, II 374b, 380b, 386a; IV 354a, 354b

aggression, II 383b

Allport, II 385a

anthropology, II 384a

Antisthenes, II 375b

anxiety, II 383b, 384a

apparent, II 375a

architecture, II 374b

Aristippus, II 375b, 378a

Aristotle, II 375a, 377a–378a, 379a, 380b, 387a; IV 5a, 369a, 412a

art, II 386a, 582b

art and play, II 374b

Bacon, II 379b

Beccaria, II 380b

behaviorism, II 382b

belief, II 387a

benevolence, II 380a

Bentham, II 380b, 381a–

381b; IV 178b, 181b, 277b, 451a, 451b, 454a

Bible, II 375b, 378b; III 278b

biology, II 375a, 382a–384b

biopsychological disciplines, II 382a–384b

birth, II 384a–384b

blessedness, II 378b, 379a

Boccaccio, II 234a

Bradley, F. H., II 381b

Butler, Bishop, II 380a

Calicles, II 375a

Cartesianism, II 387a

catharsis, II 378b

causation, II 378a

Christianity, II 378b–379a

Cicero, IV 136b

city planning, II 374b

comedy, I 467b, 468a

community, II 374b, 380b

concept, II 374b–375a, 379a–379b

Condillac, II 381a

consciousness, II 382b–383a

creativity in art, I 585a

culture, II 384a

Cumberland, II 380b

cynicism, II 375b

damnation, II 374b, 379a

Dante, II 379a

death, II 378a, 383b, 384b

Democritus, II 378a; III 576b

Descartes, II 380b, 381a

desire, II 375a, 380a, 380b

determinism, II 238b, 378a

Dewey, II 381b, 382b

dignity, IV 136b, 142b, 143a

discipline, II 385b

dualism, II 381a, 382b, 387a

economics, II 374b, 379b, 381b, 384b–385a

education, II 374b, 380a, 382a, 385a, 385b

ego, II 383a, 383b

emotion, II 382b

empathy, II 86b

employment, II 385a

Epicureanism, II 137b, 378a; III 587a; IV 8a, 175b

Epicurus, II 137b, 378a

epiphenomenalism, II 382b

ethics, II 374b–375a, 375b, 378a, 379a, 379b, 380a, 381b, 383a; IV 320a, 321a

evil, II 163a, 167a–167b, 374b, 375b, 376b, 379a

evolution, II 383a; IV 180a–180b

failure, II 374b

faith, II 378b

false, II 387a

fear, II 378a, 384b

feeling, II 382b, 383a, 386b

Fourier, II 380a

free will, II 137b, 238b

freedom, II 379b

freedom of speech, II 256b

Freud, II 383a–384a

friendship, II 377b, 378a

Fromm, II 384a

fun, II 385b

Gay, II 380b; III 233a–233b

Gestalt treatment, II 383a

goals, IV 178b

God, II 377b, 378b–379a, 380b

good, II 374b, 375b–381a; IV 173b–180b, 181b, 183a, 185a, 185b, 235b

grace, II 379a

Greece (ancient), II 375a, 375b–378b, 379a, 380b

guilt, II 383b, 385a

Hartley, II 380b, 381a; III 234a–234b

health, II 374b, 376a, 383a, 384a

hedonism, II 375b, 380a 381b, 383b, 384b, 385a

hell, II 379a

Helvétius, II 380b

Herodotus, II 375b

Hesiod, II 375b

hippies, II 385b

Hobbes, II 379b–381a

Holbach, II 380b

Homer, II 375b

honor, II 376a

human nature, II 377a, 379b; III 576b, 576b, 577a, 643b

humanism, IV 133b

Hume, II 380a, 381a; III 232a–232b

Hutcheson, II 380a, 380b; III 231b, 232b

id, II 383b

illusory, II 375a

imagination, IV 334b

immorality, II 375a, 376a

impressionism, II 582b

individualism, II 374b, 375b, 378a, 379a–379b, 382a, 384b

injustice, II 376a

instinct, II 383b, 385a

intuition, II 383a

Jefferson, II 379b

Jesuits, III 293b

Jesus Christ, II 378b

Jevons, II 384b

Job (Bible), II 378b

joy, II 378a, 384a, 385b
Judaism, II 375b, 378b
judgment, II 379b
justice, II 375b–376a
Kant, II 375a, 380a, 385b
knowledge, II 376a, 379a, 379b, 386b–387a
labor, II 379b, 384b
language, II 375a, 381b, 386a–387b
law, II 379b, 380b, 381b, 385a, 385b
Leibniz, II 381a
liberalism, II 379a, 379b
liberty, II 379a–379b, 381b
literature, II 385a
Locke, II 379b, 380a, 381a
logic, II 375a, 386a
love, II 379a
Lucretius, II 378a
McDougall, II 382b
Machiavelli, II 379b
Marcuse, II 385a
Marx, II 381b
Maslow II 385a
masochism, II 383b
materialism, II 378a
maximization, II 374b
measurement, IV 178b
medicine, II 374b, 382a–384b
mental health, II 384a
metaphysics, II 375a, 376a–376b, 377a, 383b
Middle Ages, II 378b–379a
Mill, II 167b, 381b–382a
mind, II 78a
money, II 384b
moral sense, III 231b–234b
morality, II 374b–380b, 383a–387a
More, II 379b
mysticism, II 378b–379a
mythology, III 278b, 292a, 293b
nationalism, II 379b
natural selection, II 383a
Nature, II 377a, 378a, 381a
Neo-Platonism, II 378b
Olds, II 384a
Owen, II 380a
pain, II 374b, 387a
Paley, II 380b
Pareto, II 384b
passions, II 381a
perfectibility, III 643b
phenomenological psychiatry, II 383a
philosophy, II 375a, 378a–379a, 381b, 386a–387b
physics, II 387a
physiology, II 383a
Plato, II 375b–377a, 383b; III 497a, 500b, 501a; IV 4b,

451a 451b
Platonism, II 380a; III 497a, 500b, 501a
Plotinus, II 378b
politics, II 374b, 377b, 381b, 384b 385a
poverty, II 374b
power, II 379a, 379b, 384b
prestige, II 376a, 379a
Priestley, II 380b
primitivism, III 587a, 590b
private property, II 379b, 381a
progress, II 379b, 380a; III 638a, 643b
Protagoras, II 375b
Protestantism, II 378b 379a
psychiatry, II 383a
psychology, II 374b, 375a, 376a; IV 4b, 5a, 8a, 23a
punishment, II 381a, 385b
rationalism, II 375b, 380a
real, II 375a
reality, II 383b
reinforcement theory, II 382b
religion, II 374b, 386a
Renaissance, IV 133b, 136b, 142b, 143a
repression, II 383b, 385b
revolution, II 379a
rhetoric, IV 171b 172a
right, IV 173b, 174a, 175b, 176b, 178b 185b
Roman Catholic Church, II 378b 379a
Rome (ancient), II 378b
Ryle, II 386b
sadism, II 383b
Saint Augustine, II 378b, 380b; IV 176b
Saint Basil, III 590a 590b
Saint Bonaventura, II 379a
Saint-Simon, II 380a
salvation, II 374b, 379a
Schlick, II 385b
science, II 375a, 379a, 386a, 387a 387b
sex, II 374b, 385a
Shaftesbury, II 380a
sin, II 379a, 379b
skepticism, IV 235b
Smith, Adam, II 380a
social contract, II 379b
social welfare, IV 277b
society, II 374b, 379b 380a, 381b, 383b, 386a
sociology, II 374b, 383a, 385a 385b
Socrates, II 375b, 376a
Solon, II 375b
Sophists, II 375b
soul, II 376a, 377a, 378a,

378b, 381a
Spencer, II 383a; IV 180b
Spinoza, II 238b
State, II 379b 381b
Stoicism, II 378a; IV 320a, 321a
sublime in external nature, IV 334b, 336b
success, II 374b
superego, II 383a
superstition, II 378a
sympathy, II 380a
taste, IV 354a, 354b
teleology, II 378a, 381a
temperance, IV 369a, 369b
Thrasymachus, II 375b
tradition, II 379a
tragedy, II 376b
tragic sense, IV 412a
tranquilizers, II 384b
truth, II 376b, 377a
tyranny, II 376a
utilitarianism, II 379a 382a, 382b, 383a, 384b; IV 178b, 179a, 185a, 444b, 445b 447a, 448a
utopianism, II 374b, 379b 380a
Valla, IV 133b
value, II 373b 375a, 386a; IV 450a 451b, 454a, 454b
virtue, II 376b 377b, 380b
virtuoso, IV 486b
vox populi, IV 499b
Watson, II 382b
wealth, II 376a, 377b, 379a, 381a
welfare, II 374b, 378a, 384b 385a
well-being, II 375a, 375b, 377b, 384b, 387b
will, II 379b, 380b, 381a
wisdom, II 378b
wisdom of the fool, IV 516a, 518a, 518b, 519a
Wolfenstein, II 385b
Wolff, II 381a
work, II 374b, 385a, 385b; IV 533b
Wundt, II 382b
Pleiades (myth), III 310b
Plekhanov, Georgi (1857–1918)
acquired characteristics, II 620b
causation, I 283a
communism, II 559a
Engels and, II 455a
history, I 283a
ideology, II 559a
Marxism, III 148a, 150a
materialism, II 453a, 453b, 455a
revisionism, IV 273b

Pletho, George Gemisthus (1355?–1450)
Neo-Platonism, III 510a
dignity, IV 144b
Plenitude, I 42b–43a
hierarchy, II 442b
Plato, I 42b 43a; II 438b
Pliny the Elder (23–79 A.D.),
alchemy, I 29a
art, II 299a 299b, 305a, 310a
art and play, I 102b
chance images, I 340b 341b, 342b, 345b
city, I 428b
classification of the sciences, I 463b
conservation, I 472a, 472b
cosmology, I 541a
creativity in art, I 580b
cycles, I 623a
genius, II 299a 299b, 305a, 310a
painting, I 580b
periodization in literary history, III 482a
progress, III 632b, 633a
reformation, IV 61b
temperance, IV 377a
theriophily, IV 384b, 386a, 386b, 387b, 388b
sculpture, I 580b
spontaneous generation, IV 307b
symmetry, IV 345b, 346a
universal man, IV 437b
Plotinus (205?–270 A.D.)
abstraction, I 3b
aesthetics, II 217a 217b, 218a
allegory, I 43b, 46b
analogy, I 64b
Aristotelianism, III 423b
Aristotle and, III 372a, 374a
beauty, I 197a, 586a; II 217a 217b; III 423b; IV 347a
body, IV 8b, 9a
Bruno and, III 193b
Buddhism, I 255a
Chain of Being, I 325b
change, IV 391b
Christianity, III 505a 505b
classification of the arts, I 458a 458b
Coleridge and, III 425b
consciousness, IV 9a
cosmos, II 163a 163b
Creation, I 572a
creativity in art, I 586a, 586b
death, I 645a
demonology, I 669a
desire, IV 9a

dualism, **IV** 8b
emanation, **III** 211a
epistemology, **III** 505b
ethics, **IV** 322a
evil, **II** 163a–163b; **IV** 380a
Ficino and, **III** 510b, 511a
Forms, **III** 423b; **IV** 8b
Gnosticism, **II** 330a
God, **I** 325b, 572a; **II** 163a, 341a, 439b
Goethe and, **III** 519a
good, **IV** 8b
happiness, **II** 378b
harmony, **II** 391b, 393b; **IV** 380a
heresy, **II** 427a
Hermeticism, **II** 432b
hierarchy, **II** 439a, 439b, 441a, 444a
humanism, **I** 520a
idea, **II** 545a–546a
idealism, **III** 159a
imagination, **III** 211b
immortality, **I** 645a
infinity, **II** 605b, 614b
irrationalism, **II** 635b
Islam, **II** 643b
justice, **II** 657a
knowledge, **I** 2b–3a; **III** 513a
macrocosm and microcosm, **III** 127a, 128b, 130b
Marius Victorinus and, **III** 377b
materialism, **III** 505b
matter, **II** 163b; **III** 193b; **IV** 380a
memory, **IV** 9a
metaphysics, **III** 211b, 374a
Metatron, **III** 130b
Middle Platonism, **III** 374a
mimetic art, **I** 586a
morality, **IV** 8b
music, **II** 391b, 393b
mysticism, **III** 505b
mythology, **III** 274b, 292a
Nature, **II** 163a–163b; **III** 375b
Neo-Platonism, **III** 128b, 372a–377b; **IV** 8b
Neo-Pythagoreans, **III** 374a
One, **III** 128b, 374b–375a; **IV** 8b
organicism, **III** 423a, 424b, 425b
paganism, **IV** 9a
perception, **IV** 9a
perennial philosophy, **III** 458b, 459a
perfectibility, **III** 466a
pleasure, **II** 378b
philosophy, **III** 373b–376b
Plato and, **III** 274b, 374a, 466a, 509a, 516b; **IV** 8b

Platonism, **III** 505a–505b, 508b–513a, 516b, 517b, 519a, 523a, 525a
poetics, **III** 527a
Porphyry and, **III** 373b, 374a, 374b, 376a, 376b
progress, **III** 632b–633a
psychology, **IV** 8b–9a, 9b
Pythagoreans, **IV** 36b
realism, **III** 374b, 375b
reason, **II** 163b; **IV** 9a
reincarnation, **I** 645a
religion, **III** 376a
romanticism, **IV** 347a–347b
Saint Augustine and, **III** 377b, 378a; **IV** 9a
Shaftesbury and, **III** 424b
sin, **III** 466a
soul, **I** 586a; **II** 163b, 341a; **III** 375a–376a, 466a; **IV** 8b, 9a
space, **IV** 296b
spiritualism, **III** 505b
Stoicism, **III** 374a; **IV** 8b, 322a
suffering, **III** 466a
symmetry, **IV** 347a–348a
theodicy, **II** 163a–163b; **IV** 380a, 380b
thought, **IV** 9a
time, **IV** 391b, 393b
ugliness, **I** 586b
universe, **II** 439a
virtue, **III** 466a
World-Soul, **III** 375b
Pluche, Abbé Noël-Antoine, deism, **I** 651b; **III** 302a
Newton and, **III** 393a
Pluralism
aesthetics, **II** 223b
Aristotle, **III** 190a, 190b, 554b
beauty, **I** 208b
Bruno, **II** 443a; **III** 510b
causation, **I** 282b–284a
Chain of Being, **I** 327b
Counter-Enlightenment, **II** 103a, 106a, 108b
culture, **III** 113a–113b
deism, **I** 651b
Descartes, **I** 517b; **IV** 435b
God, **II** 353a
good, **IV** 184b
Gothic, **II** 370b
Hegel, **II** 409b, 414b
Heraclitus, **III** 187a
Herder, **I** 618a; **III** 639a
heresy, **II** 424b, 428a, 428b, 430b
Hermeticism, **II** 433b
hierarchy, **II** 443a
history, **I** 282b–284a
holy, **II** 514a
Huguenots, **II** 428a

intolerance, **IV** 119a
James, William, **III** 561b, 563a; **IV** 396a
Leibniz, **III** 515b
literary criticism, **I** 604a
loyalty, **III** 113a–113b, 114b, 115a
matter, **III** 187a, 190a, 191a
medieval science, **II** 202b
mythology, **III** 301a, 303a
Nicholas of Cusa, **III** 510b
order, **II** 443a
Parmenides, **III** 187a
perennial philosophy, **III** 457a, 458b, 461b
Platonism, **III** 510b, 515b
pragmatism, **III** 552a, 553a, 554b, 561b, 563a
progress, **III** 639a
Pythagoreans, **IV** 35b, 36a
rationalism, **IV** 47b
religion, **IV** 113a, 119a
right, **IV** 184b
romanticism, **IV** 198b, 204a
society, **IV** 316a
Speusippus, **IV** 35b, 36a
State, **IV** 314b, 316a
theodicy, **IV** 379b
time, **IV** 394a, 394b, 396a
unity of science, **IV** 435b
Vico, **II** 103a
Volksgeist, **IV** 493a, 496a
Voltaire, **III** 303a
Plutarch (46?–?120 A.D.)
allegory, **I** 42a, 43a, 44a
analogy, **I** 69a
art, **II** 299b
art and play, **I** 102b
atomism, **I** 497a
Bacon on, **I** 173b
Buddhism, **I** 254b
causation, **I** 272b
classification of the arts, **I** 457a–457b
cosmic voyages, **I** 524a, 524b–525a
cosmos, **IV** 38b
cycles, **I** 623a
demonology, **I** 668b
discontinuity, **I** 497a
Enlightenment, **II** 90a, 95b
ethics, **IV** 321b
evil, **IV** 380b
freedom of speech, **II** 257b, 258a, 260b, 261b
genius, **II** 299b
God, **II** 341a–341b; **IV** 380b
good, **IV** 380b
harmony, **IV** 38b
impiety, **II** 565b
indeterminacy, **II** 587a
individualism, **II** 299b
law, **II** 679b, 680b

liberty, **II** 95b
love, **III** 94b, 96a
matter, **IV** 380b
measurement, **IV** 399b
mimesis, **III** 226a
mythology, **III** 292a, 295a, 299a, 299b
Nature, **IV** 380b
neo-classicism in art, **III** 371a
Neo-Platonism, **III** 372b, 505a
paganism, **I** 647b
Plato and, **II** 341a–341b; **III** 502b
Platonism, **III** 502b, 505a, 517b
power, **IV** 380b
Pythagoreans, **III** 505a; **IV** 36b, 38b
skepticism, **IV** 234b, 235a, 237b, 239b, 240a
Stoicism, **IV** 321b
temperance, **IV** 377a
theriophily, **IV** 385a–385b, 386a, 386b, 387b, 388b
theodicy, **IV** 380b
time, **IV** 391b, 399b
universal man, **IV** 439a
Utopia, **IV** 459b, 460a
Pluto (myth), **II** 340b
music, **II** 393b
Pneuma, **I** 231a, 232a
Stoicism, **IV** 319a, 320a
Podolsky, B., indeterminacy, **II** 590b
Poe, Edgar Allan (1809–1849)
cosmic images, **I** 519b, 523a
cosmic voyages, **I** 527a, 528a
disease, **II** 403b
literary criticism, **I** 599a
Kant and, **I** 519b
motif, **III** 241b
organicism, **III** 426b
phrenology, **IV** 23b
psychology, **IV** 23b, 24a
romanticism, **IV** 208b, 210b
Schelling and, **IV** 210b
symbolism, **IV** 341a, 345a
transcendentalism, **IV** 24a
ut pictura poesis, **IV** 469a, 472b
Poetics, **III** 525b–532b
Abu Bišr, **III** 528a–528b
aesthetics, **III** 525b, 527b, 531a
allegory, **III** 526b, 528b, 529b
Anselm of Canterbury, **III** 528a
Apollo (myth), **III** 530a

Arator, III 528b
Aretino, III 530b
Ariosto, III 531a
Aristotle, III 526a–531a
art, II 304b; III 525b, 527a, 527b
artists, III 530b
Ascham, III 529b
Atticism, III 527b–528a
Averroës, III 528a, 528b
Avienus, III 528b
baroque, III 529b
Battle of the Books, III 531b
beauty, III 525b, 526a
belles lettres, III 525b
Bembo, III 531b
Beni, III 529a, 531a
Bentley, III 531b
Bernard of Chartres, III 528b
Bible, III 528b
Blackwell, III 530a
Boccaccio, III 529b, 531b
Boiardo, III 531a
Boileau, III 529b–530b
Bruno, III 530b
Byzantine Empire, III 527b
Callimachus, III 527b
Callistratus, III 527a
Calvinism, III 530a
Cartesianism, III 530a
Castelvetro, III 529a–531a
Cato, III 528b
Christianity, III 526b, 528b, 530a, 530b, 531a
Cicero, III 526a, 527a, 528b, 529a
Cinthio, III 529a, 531a
classicism, III 528a–531b
comedy, III 527a, 528a, 531a
condemnation of, III 526a–526b, 528b, 530a
Corneille, III 529b, 530a
Counter-Reformation, III 529b, 530b
creativity, III 526b, 528a, 530b, 531b
criticism, III 527b, 529a, 530b, 531a, 531b
culture, III 526a, 526b, 528a, 531b
Daniello, III 529a, 531a
Dante, III 529a–531b
d'Aubignac, III 529b
defined, III 525b
Democritus, III 526a
dialect, III 527b
Diomedes, III 526a
Dionysius of Halicarnassus, III 526a
divinization, III 530b
Donatus, III 528b
drama, III 527a, 527b,

528b, 529b, 530a, 531a
Du Bos, III 530b
education, III 525b, 526a, 527b, 528b
epics, III 527a, 527b, 530b, 531a
Epicureanism, III 526a, 526b
ethics, III 527b, 531a
Ficino, III 529b, 530a
fiction, III 525b, 531a
Fonte, III 529a
Fontenelle, III 530a
France, III 529b, 530a, 531a
genius, II 293a–293b, 304b
genres, III 527a–527b, 528b, 530b, 531a, 531b
Geoffroy de Vinsauf, III 528b
Germany, III 529b
God, III 526b, 527a, 530a, 530b
Gorgias, III 526a
grammar, III 528a
Great Britain, III 529b, 530a, 531a
Greece (ancient), III 525b–528a, 529a, 530b, 531a, 531b
Guarini, III 529b, 531a
Heavenly Muse, III 530b
hedonism, III 526b
Heraclitus, III 526a
Hermeticism, III 530b
Herodotus, III 525b
heroic, III 531a
Herrmannus Alemannus, III 528a
Hesiod, III 526a
Hippias, III 526a
history, III 525b
Homer, III 525b, 526a, 526b, 527b
Horace, III 526a–530a
humanism, III 529a, 530b
humours, III 527a
idea, III 526b
individualism, II 304b
inspiration, III 527a, 528b, 530a–530b
Isidor of Seville, III 528a
Italy, III 528a, 529a–529b, 531a, 531b
Iuvencus, III 528b
Johannes de Garlandia, III 528b
Johnson, S. III 530b, 531b
Landino, III 530b
Latin language, III 525b, 528a–530b, 531b
law, III 528b
Le Bossu, III 529b
Lessing, III 529b, 530a, 531b

literary criticism, I 596a, 597a
literary paradox, III 77b
literature, III 525b–531b
logic, III 526a, 528a
logos, III 526a
Longinus, III 526a, 527a, 528a
Lope de Vega, III 529b
Lopez Pinciano, III 529b
love, III 530a
lyric poetry, III 527a, 527b, 531a
Maggi, III 529a
Middle Ages, III 528a–531b
Milton, III 530a, 530b
mimesis, III 526b, 527a, 527b, 528a, 531a, 531b
Minturno, III 529a, 531a
modernism, III 528b, 531a, 531b
Molière, III 529b
morality, III 529b
Muses (myth), III 526b, 528b, 530a
Mussato, III 529b
mythology, III 530a
nationalism, III 531a
Nature, III 525b, 527a
Neo-Aristotelianism, III 529a–529b, 530b, 531a
Neo-Platonism, III 526b
novel, III 525b, 531b
Opitz, III 529b
oratory, III 525b
Ovid, III 528b
painting, III 526b, 527b
pastoral drama, III 531a
Patrizzi, III 529a
Pazzi, III 529a
Peletier du Mans, III 529b
Perrault, III 531b
Petrarch, III 530a, 531b
Philodemus of Gadara, III 526a
philosophers, III 526a, 528b, 529b
philosophy, III 525b–530a
Philostratus, III 527a
Piccolomini, III 529a
Pindar, III 527a, 530b
Plato, III 525b–527b, 529b, 530a, 531a
Platonism, III 526b, 527a, 528b, 530b
Plotinus, III 527a
poetical ecstasy, III 530a–530b
poets, III 526a–531b
Pontanus, III 529b
Pope, III 531b
post-Aristotelianism, III 526a

pre-humanists, III 529a
Prodicus, III 526a
propaganda, III 526b
Protagoras, III 526a
Prudentius, III 528b
Puritanism, III 530a
Puttenham, III 529b, 530a
Quintilian, III 526a, 526b, 529a
Racine, III 529b
Reformation, III 529b, 530b
religion, III 528b
Renaissance, III 530a, 530b, 531a
rhetoric, III 525b–530b
Robortello, III 529a
romanticism, III 525b, 527b, 530a, 530b
Rome (ancient), III 526b, 527a–531b
Ronsard, III 529b, 530a
Salutati, III 529b
Sanskrit language, III 527b
satire, III 527a
Scaliger, III 529a, 530a, 530b
scholasticism, III 528a
science, III 530a, 531b
sculpture, III 526b, 527b
Servius, III 528b
Shaftesbury, III 530b
short story, III 525b
Sidney, III 529b, 530a, 530b
society, III 528b, 531a
Sophists, III 526a
soul, III 527a
Spain, III 529b, 531a
Stoics, III 526b
supernatural, III 531a
Tasso, III 529a–529b, 530b
Terrasson, III 530a
Tertullian, III 525b
theater, III 528b, 530a
theology, III 528b, 529b, 530a, 530b
Theophrastus, III 526a
tragedy, III 526b, 527a, 527b, 531a
tragicomedy, III 531a
Trissino, III 529a
troubadours, III 530a
truth, III 529b, 530a
Tuscan language, III 531b
unity, III 527a, 527b, 531a
Valla, III 529a
Vauquelin de la Fresnaye, III 529b
Vedas, III 527b
Velleius Paterculus, III 528a
Vergil, III 526b, 528b, 531a, 531b
vernacular, III 528a, 528b, 531a, 531b

verse, III 531a
Vettori, III 529a
Vico, III 530a
Vida, III 529a
Voltaire, III 530a
William of Moerbeke, III 528a
Wotton, III 531b
Xenophanes, III 526a
Poetry, III 525b–532b; IV 465b–476b
abstraction, II 580b–581a; IV 470a, 474a
Addison, IV 471a, 471b
Aelius Theon, IV 468b
aesthetics, II 216a, 219b–220a, 224a; III 525b, 527b, 531a; IV 465b, 466b, 467a, 469a, 471b 472a, 473b, 474a
Alberti, IV 467b, 468a, 469a, 469b
Alembert, IV 472b
Algarotti, IV 472b
allegory, III 526b, 528b, 529b; IV 469a, 470a, 471a, 473b
ambiguity, I 49a–50a, 54b–56a, 58a–58b
Anacreontea, IV 471a
animals, II 87b
Anselm of Canterbury, III 528a
Aphtonius, IV 468b
Apollinaire, IV 470b
Apollo (myth), III 530a
Apuleius, IV 469a
Arabia, IV 473a
Arator, III 528b
architects, IV 466b
Aretino, III 530b
Ariosto, III 531a; IV 468b, 469a
Aristotelianism, III 529a–529b, 530a, 531a
Aristotle, I 265a, 457a; II 299b, 507a; III 226b, 354b, 526a–529b; IV 467b–473a
art, I 456b–461a; III 525b–527b; IV 465b, 466a, 467a, 467b, 469a, 470a, 470b, 471b, 472a, 473b, 475a, 475b
artists, III 530b
Ascham, III 529b
astronomers, IV 466b
Atticism, III 527b–528a
Auden, IV 469b
Austen, IV 475a
Averroës, III 528a, 528b
Avienus, III 528b
Avison, IV 472b
Babbitt, IV 474b

Bacon, IV 434a, 466b, 467b
Balla, IV 475b
Balzac, IV 467a, 469a, 474b
baroque, III 529b
Batteux, IV 468a, 471b, 472b
Battle of the Books, III 531b
Baudelaire, IV 469a, 473a
Bauhaus, IV 475a
Baumgarten, IV 471b
beauty, III 394b, 525b, 526a; IV 467a, 468a, 471b, 473b, 474b
belles lettres, III 525b
Bellori, IV 466a–466b, 469a
Bembo, III 531b
Beni, III 529a, 531a
Bentley, III 531b
Berlioz, IV 473a
Bernard of Chartres, III 528b
Bible, III 528b; IV 465b
biography, IV 471a
Blackwell, III 530a
Blake, IV 470b
Boccaccio, III 529b, 531b
Boiardo, III 531a
Boileau, III 529b, 530a, 530b
Bosch, IV 467a
Brazil, IV 470b
Breughel (the Elder), IV 467a, 469b
Breughel (the Younger), IV 467a
Brönte, Anne, IV 467a
Brönte, Charlotte, IV 467a
Brönte, Emily, IV 467a
Browning, IV 469a, 471a
Bruno, III 530b
Buddhism, IV 476a
Burke, IV 471b, 472a
Byron, IV 192b
Byzantine Empire, III 527b
Calder, I 635b, 636a
Callimachus, III 527b
Callistratus, III 527a; IV 468b, 469a
Calvinism, III 530a
Carroll, IV 470b
Cartesianism, III 530a
cartoon, IV 470b, 475a
Castel, IV 473a
Castelvetro, III 529a, 529b–530a, 530b, 531a; IV 467b
catharsis, I 265a, 269a
Cato, III 528b
Caylus, IV 467a
censorship, III 499a, 501b
Cézanne, IV 47b, 475b

Chapman, III 294b–295a
Chaucer, IV 469a
China, I 354a, 367a, 368b–369b
China (ancient), IV 470b 473a, 475b–476a
Christianity, III 526b, 528b, 530a, 530b, 531a; IV 471b
Cicero, III 526a, 527a, 528b, 529a; IV 468a, 468b
Cinthio, III 529a, 531a
civilization, III 526b
classicism, III 528a, 528b, 529a–531b
Claudian, IV 469a
Coleridge, IV 471a
color, III 392a 398b; IV 473a
comedy, III 527a, 528a, 531a; IV 468b
condemnation of, III 526a–526b, 528b, 530a
Constable, IV 467a, 473b
content, IV 466b, 470b, 471a
Corneille, III 529b, 530a
Counter-Enlightenment, II 102b, 103a, 104b
Counter-Reformation, III 529b, 530b
creativity, III 526b, 528a, 530b, 531b
criticism, III 527b, 529a, 530b, 531a, 531b
Croce, IV 471a
cubism, IV 470b, 475b
culture, III 526a, 526b, 528a, 531b; IV 474a
Cummings, IV 470b
dance, IV 467b, 470a, 475a
Daniello, III 529a, 531a; IV 467b, 468a
Dante, III 529a, 529b, 530a, 530b, 531a, 531b
Darwin, IV 473a
d'Aubignac, III 529b
De Quincey, IV 475a
De Stilj, IV 475a
death, I 635b, 636a
Debussy, II 575a
decorum, IV 466b
defined, III 525b
deism, IV 471b, 472a
Democritus, III 526a
dialect, III 527b
Diderot, IV 469a, 470a, 472b, 473a
dignity, IV 141a, 141b
Diomedes, III 526a
Dionysius of Halicarnassus, III 526a
disease, II 399a
Disney, IV 473a
divinization, III 530b

Dolce, IV 467b
Donatus, III 528b
drama, III 527a–531a; IV 467a–468a, 472b, 475a
Dryden, IV 468a, 472b
Du Bos, III 530b; IV 471b
Du Fresnoy, IV 468a
Duchamp, IV 475b
Dufresnoy, IV 468a
education, III 496a, 497a, 525b, 526a, 527b, 528b
Egypt (ancient), IV 470a
ekphrasis, IV 466a, 467a, 468b, 469a, 469b
emblem books, IV 470a–470b, 472b
emotion, II 575b; III 501b, 572b; IV 466a, 466b, 472a, 472b, 474b
empathy, II 87b
Empedocles, IV 2b
English language, IV 466b
Enlightenment, IV 465b
epics, III 527a, 527b, 530b, 531a; IV 465b, 469b, 473b
Epicureanism, III 526a, 526b
ethics, III 527a, 531a; IV 473b
evil, II 165a–166a
evolution of literature, II 170a–172a, 173a
expressionism, II 206b, 208a, 208b, 209a
external factors, II 220a
fables, IV 468b, 469b
Faust (legend), III 248b, 250a
Félibien, IV 470a
Ficino, III 529b, 530a; IV 470b
fiction, III 525b, 531a
figure poems, IV 470a, 470b, 476a
fine arts, III 525b, 527b
Fonte, III 529a
Fontenelle, III 530a
Fracastoro, IV 467b
France, III 529b, 530a, 531a; IV 467a, 468b, 471b, 473b, 475a
freedom of speech, II 252b, 259a
futurism, IV 475b
genius, II 294a–295b, 312b–313a, 314a, 316a, 317b–321a, 323b
genres, III 527a–531b
Geoffroy de Vinsauf, III 528b
Germany, III 529b; IV 471a, 474a
gesamtkunstwerk, IV 472b
Gilpin, IV 473b

Gluck, IV 472b
God, II 340b, 348b; III 526b, 527a, 530a, 530b; IV 467a, 471b, 474b
Goethe, IV 469a, 472a, 473a
good, IV 467a
Gorgias, III 526a
Gothic, II 368a, 368b, 370b, 371b, 373b
grammar, III 528a
Great Britain, III 482a, 483b, 485b, 529b, 530a, 531a, 600a, 601a; IV 467a, 469a
Greece (ancient), II 679b, 680b, 683b; III 112a, 525b–528a, 529a, 530b, 531a, 531b; IV 469a, 470b
Gregory I (the Great), Pope, IV 466a
Guarini, III 529b, 531a
Han dynasty, IV 476a
Hardy, IV 466a, 467a
harmony, II 388b, 391b, 394b–395a; IV 466b, 467b, 471b, 472b, 473a
Hawthorne, IV 469a
Heavenly Muse, III 530b
hedonism, III 526b
Hegel, II 170b
Heidegger, III 221a
Heraclitus, III 526a
Herbert, IV 470b
Herder, II 170b; IV 209a, 471b
hermeticism, II 432a, 433b; III 530b
Hermogenes, IV 468b
Herodotus, III 525b
heroic, III 531a
Hesiod, III 526a
hieroglyphics, IV 466b, 470a
Hippias, III 526a
historians, IV 465b
historiography, II 464b–465a, 465b, 466b, 470a, 472b; IV 151a
history, III 525b; IV 465b, 467a, 469b, 470a, 471a, 472a, 474a, 474b
Hobbes, IV 471a
Hogarth, IV 469b, 470b, 471a
Hollander, IV 470b
Homer, III 525b, 526a, 526b, 527b; IV 471a
Horace, III 423b, 526a, 527a–530a; IV 467b–469b
human nature, III 571a, 571b, 572a, 572b
humanism, II 515b, 517a–517b; III 529a, 530b; IV

129b, 130b, 135a, 469a, 474b
Hume, IV 471b
humours, III 527a
Huxley, Aldous, IV 475b
Huygens, III 395a
iconography, II 529a–529b, 531a, 536a; IV 468b, 470a
idea, III 526b
ideal, II 551a
imagery, IV 470a, 471b, 472b, 475a
imagination, III 210a, 212b, 220b, 221a; IV 467a, 469b, 471a–473b, 474b
impressionism, II 574b, 575a–575b, 578a, 580b–581a; IV 473b
India (ancient), IV 473a
industry, IV 475a
inspiration, III 527a, 528b, 530a–530b
internal factors, II 220a
irrationalism, II 638a–638b
Isidor of Seville, 528a
Italy, III 528a, 529a–529b, 531a, 531b; IV 467a, 469a, 472b
Iuvencus, III 528b
James, Henry, IV 466a, 469a
Jesus Christ, IV 466a
Johannes de Garlandia, III 528b
Johnson, Samuel, III 530b, 531b
Jonson, IV 471a
Joyce, IV 470b
Junius, IV 467b
Kames, IV 472a
Kant, III 219b
Keats, IV 471a
Kircher, IV 473a
Klee, IV 469a
Kleist, IV 472a
Knight, R. P., IV 473b
Krieger, M., IV 471a
Landino, III 530b
language, II 661b; IV 466a, 466b, 469a, 470a–475b
Latin language, III 525b, 528a, 528b, 529a, 530b, 531b; IV 466b, 468b
law, II 679b, 680b, 683b; III 528b
Le Bossu, III 529b
Leonardo da Vinci, IV 467a
Lessing, III 529b, 530a, 531b; IV 468a, 469a, 469b, 471a, 474a, 474b
light, III 391b–398b
Liszt, IV 473a
literary criticism, IV 465b, 466b, 467a, 467b, 469a,

469b, 471a, 473b, 475a
literature, III 85a–88a, 525b, 526a–531b; IV 330b, 331a, 466b, 476a
Locke, IV 471a, 472a, 473b
logic, III 526a, 528a
logos, III 526a
Longinus, III 526a, 527a, 528a
Lope de Vega, III 529b
Lopez Pinciano, III 529b
Lorrain, IV 469b
love, III 94a, 97b–104a, 107b, 530a
loyalty, III 112a
Lucian, IV 469a
lyric, III 527a, 527b, 531a
Maggi, III 529a
Mallarmé, IV 470b
Malraux, IV 469a
manuscripts, IV 470a
Martial, IV 469a
Marvell, IV 471a
masque, IV 470a, 472b
meaning, IV 467b
Mendelssohn, Moses, IV 474a
metaphor, III 196b, 204a, 204b, 205a; IV 465b, 466b, 468b, 469a, 470b, 471b, 473b
metaphysics, III 210a, 212b, 220b, 221a
Michelangelo, IV 469a
Middle Ages, II 220a; III 528a–531b; IV 465b, 467a, 468b, 470a, 471a
Mili, IV 475b
military, IV 475a
Mill, J. S., IV 199a
Milton, III 530a, 530b; IV 468b
mimesis, III 226b–229b, 526b, 527a, 527b, 528a, 531a, 531b; IV 465b, 469b, 471b, 472a, 472b, 474b
Minturno, III 529a, 531a; IV 467b
Molière, III 529b
Monboddo, IV 472b
morality, III 529b; IV 465b, 469a, 469b, 470a, 471b
Morris, IV 469a
motif, III 236b–238a, 242a
motion pictures, IV 470b, 475a, 475b
mountains in literature, III 259a
Muses (myth), III 526b, 528b, 530a
music, II 313a–313b, 314a, 316a–320a, 321a, 323b, 388b, 391b, 394b–395a; IV 466b, 467b, 472a–475a

musicians, IV 466b
Mussato, III 529b
mythology, III 276a, 282b, 291a, 291b, 293b–300b, 302b, 304a–307a, 309a, 530a; IV 467b, 469b, 470a
nationalism, III 333b, 531a
naturalism, IV 53b, 471b
Nature, III 349a, 349b, 525b, 527a; IV 466a, 467b, 469b, 470a, 471b, 472a, 473b, 476a
necessity, III 354b
Neo-Aristotelianism, III 529a–529b, 530b, 531a
Neo-Platonism, III 526b; IV 466a
Newton, III 392a–398b; IV 473a
novel, III 525b, 531b; IV 466a, 472a, 473b, 474b, 475a
novelists, IV 469a
odes, III 531a
opera, IV 470a, 472b, 475a
Opitz, III 529b
optics, III 392a–398b
oratory, III 525b; IV 465b, 469a
organicism, III 422a, 423a–425b, 426b, 427a
Orientalism, III 430a–430b
Ovid, III 528b; IV 468b, 469a
painting, III 526b, 527b
painters, IV 465b–476b
pastoral drama, III 531a
Pater, IV 469a, 472b
Patrizzi, III 529a
Pazzi, III 529a
Peletier du Mans, III 529b
periodization in literary history, III 482a, 483a, 484b, 485b
Perrault, III 531b
Persia, III 430a, 430b
Persia (ancient), IV 470b, 473a
Petrarch, III 530a, 531b
Philodemus of Gadara, III 526a
philosophers, III 526a, 528b, 529b; IV 465b
philosophy, II 551a; III 196b, 507a–508a, 525b, 526a, 526b, 527b, 528a, 528b, 530a
Philostratus, III 527a; IV 468b, 469a
phrenology, IV 475a
physiognomy, IV 475a
Picasso, IV 475b
Piccolomini, III 529a

Pico della Mirandola, IV 466a

pictorialism, IV 465a–476b

Pietism, III 495a

Pindar, III 527a, 530b

Plato, I 457a; III 226b, 495b–502a–, 525b–531a; IV 467b

Platonism, III 495b–527a, 528b, 530b

playwrights, IV 469a

Plotinus, III 527a

Plutarch, IV 467b, 468a

Poe, IV 469a, 472b

poetical ecstasy, III 530a–530b

poets, III 526a–531b; IV 465b–471a, 473b–474b

politics, IV 470a–471a

Pontanus, III 529b

Pope, III 531b; IV 467a

post-Aristotelianism, III 526a

Pound, IV 470b

Poussin, IV 469b

power, I 201b

pre-humanists, III 529a

Pre-Raphaelites, IV 475a

Price, Uvedale, IV 473b

primitivism, III 602a, 602b, 604a

probability, III 605b

Prodicus, III 526a

progress, III 624b, 631b

propaganda, III 526b

prophecy, I 456b, 457a, 459a; III 659a

proportion, IV 466b, 467b, 472b

Protagoras, III 526a

Prudentius, III 528b

psychology, IV 2b, 17b, 24a, 465b, 471b–473b

Puritanism, III 530a

Puttenham, III 529b, 530a

Pythagoreans, IV 31b, 32a, 40a, 41a

Quintilian, III 526a, 526b, 529a; IV 468a

Racine, III 529b

Ramism, IV 43a, 43b, 45b

rationalism, IV 46a, 46b, 47a

realism, IV 51b, 53a, 53b, 471b, 472a

reason, IV 466a, 467a

reformation, IV 66a

Reformation, III 529b, 530b

religion, III 204a, 204b, 205a, 528b; IV 476a

Renaissance, II 220a; III 530a, 530b, 531a; IV 122a, 123b, 124a, 129b, 130b, 135a, 141a, 141b, 151a,

438b, 439a, 466a–473b

Reynolds, IV 467a, 468a, 470a

rhetoric, III 525b, 526a, 526b, 527b, 528a, 528b, 529a, 530b; IV 170b, 171a–171b, 172b, 466a, 468a, 468b, 469b, 471b

Rimbaud, IV 475a

Ripa, IV 470a

Robortello, III 529a; IV 467b

Roemer, III 395a

Romance languages, IV 466b

Romano, IV 466a

romanticism, I 594b–595a; II 638a–638b; III 525b, 527b, 530a, 530b; IV 187b, 188a, 188b–189a, 189b, 191b, 192a, 194a, 194b, 199a, 200a, 201a, 201b, 205a, 206a, 207a, 209a, 209b, 465b, 468b, 469b, 471b, 473a

Rome (ancient), III 526b, 527a, 527b, 528a, 528b, 529a, 530b, 531a, 531b

Ronsard, III 529b, 530a

Rossetti, IV 470b, 475a

Rousseau, IV 467b, 472b, 473a

Ruskin, IV 469a

Salutati, III 529b

salvation, IV 228a

Sannazaro, IV 468b

Sanskrit language, III 527b

Sassetti, III 228a

satire, III 527a; IV 211a, 213a

Savonarola, IV 466a

Scaliger, III 529a, 530a, 530b; IV 467b

Schiller, IV 474a

Schlegel, II 170b

scholasticism, III 528a; IV 467a

science, III 392a–398b, 530a, 531b; IV 466b, 467b, 471b, 472a, 473a, 474b, 475a

scientific classification, I 463b, 464b

Scott, IV 474b

Scriabin, IV 473a

sculpture, III 526b, 527b; IV 466b, 469a, 471a, 473b, 474a, 474b, 475b

senses, II 575b; IV 466a–468b, 472a, 472b, 474b

sentio, IV 466b

Servius, III 528b

Shaftesbury, III 530b

Shakespeare, IV 471a

short story, III 525b

Sidney, III 529b, 530a, 530b; IV 467b

Simias of Rhodes, IV 470b

Simonides of Ceos, IV 467b

socialism, IV 285a

society, III 528b, 531a; IV 466b, 467a

Socrates, III 499b

sophism, IV 468b, 470a

Sophists, III 526a

soul, III 527a

space, IV 300b, 465b, 466a, 469b, 471a, 474a, 475a, 475b

Spain, III 529b, 531a

Spenser, IV 468b, 469a, 471a

Spitzer, IV 471a

Statius, IV 469a

Stendhal, IV 469a, 475a

Stoics, III 526b

Strauss, Richard, IV 473a

structure, IV 472a

style, IV 467a

Su Shih, IV 475b

sublime in external nature, IV 335a–337b, 472a, 473b

Sung dynasty, IV 475b

supernatural, III 531a

symbolism, IV 338a–344a, 468b, 474b

symmetry, IV 467b

synaesthesia, IV 471b, 473a

Taoism, IV 476a

Tasso, III 228b, 529a–529b, 530b; IV 467b, 468b, 469b

Tassoni, I 78a

taste, IV 471b–474a

television, IV 475a

temperance, IV 365b, 366a, 366b, 368a, 369a, 371b, 372a

Terrasson, III 530a

Tertullian, III 525b

theater, III 528b, 530a

theology, III 528b, 529b, 530a, 530b

Theophrastus, III 526a

Thomas, IV 470b

Thomson, IV 471b

time, IV 465b, 469b, 471a, 474a, 474b, 475a, 475b

Tinguely, IV 475b

Titian, IV 469a, 471a

tragedy, III 526b, 527a, 527b, 531a

tragicomedy, III 531a

Trajan Column, IV 471a

transcendentalism, IV 24a

Trapp, IV 466b

Trissino, III 529a

troubadours, III 530a

truth, III 302b, 529b, 530a; IV 465b, 466a, 475a

Turner, J. M. W., IV 467a, 467b, 470b, 473b

Tuscan language, III 531b

ugliness, IV 468b

understanding, IV 466b

U.S.S.R., III 333b

U.S., IV 469b

unity, III 527a, 527b, 531a

unity of science, IV 434a

universal man, IV 438b, 439a

ut pictura poesis, IV 465b–476b

Valla, III 529a

Vasari, IV 469a

Vauquelin de La Fresnaye, III 529b

Vedas, III 527b

Velleius Paterculus, III 528a

Vendôme, IV 468b

Venus (myth), IV 474a

Vergil, III 526b, 528b, 531a, 531b; IV 468b, 469a

Verlaine, IV 472b, 473a

vernacular, III 528a, 528b, 531a, 531b

verse, III 531a

Vettori, III 529a

vice, IV 470a, 473b

Vico, II 102b; III 228a, 530a

Vida, III 529a; IV 467b

Vinsauf, IV 468b

virtue, IV 470a, 473b

Volksgeist, IV 492a, 494a, 495a

Voltaire, III 530a

Vossius, IV 467b

vox populi, IV 498b–499a

Wagner, Richard, IV 472b

Warton, Joseph, IV 471b

Warton, Thomas, IV 471b

Watteau, IV 467a

Webb, IV 472a

Wieland, II 551a

William of Moerbeke, III 528a

Williams, IV 469b

Winckelmann, IV 469b, 474a

Wotton, III 531b

writers, IV 469a

Xenophanes, III 526a

Zola, IV 467a

Poets

abstraction, III 398a

coronations, II 517a

harmony, II 391b

inspiration, III 499a–499b, 501b

knowledge, III 501a–501b

metaphysical imagination, III 208b, 210a, 212a, 217a, 219b

Middle Ages, III 528a

mountains in literature, III 253b, 256a

music, II 391b

mythology, III 272b, 273a, 292b, 293a, 297b, 298a, 299b, 305a

nationalism, III 319b

Nature, III 350b

organicism, III 421b, 426a

painters, III 297b, 298a

painting, IV 465b–474b

primitivism, III 579a, 579b, 580a, 583b, 594a, 600a

psychology, IV 1b, 16b

realism in literature, IV 51b, 53b

revolution, IV 165a

romanticism, IV 202a, 205b, 207b, 208b, 210a, 210b

Schelling, IV 210b

Socrates, III 496a–496b

temperance, IV 368a

tragic sense, IV 412b

virtue, IV 477a

See also Plato, Platonism, Poetics

Poggio Bracciolini, Giovanni (1380–1459)

atomism, I 132b

fortune, fate, and chance, II 235a

handwriting, II 518a

humanism, II 517b, 518a, 519b, 522a

virtù, IV 479a

Poincaré, Jules Henri (1854–1912)

aether, IV 80a, 80b

axiomatization, I 166b

cosmic images, I 523b

Einstein and, IV 79b–81a

entropy, II 117a–117b

indeterminacy, II 588a

law, II 588a

mathematics, III 176a

motion, IV 80a

positivism, III 545b, 547a

pragmatism, III 551b, 553b, 557b

relativity, IV 79b–81a, 83b, 84a

simultaneity, IV 81b–82a

time, IV 394b, 397b

Poincaré cycle, II 117b

Pointillism, Seurat, II 567b

Poisson, Siméon Denis (1781–1840)

continuity, I 494a

entropy, II 117a

probability, III 606a, 608b, 613b, 614a–616a

Poisson's Law, III 615b, 618a–618b

Poker, game theory, II 266a

Pokrovski, Mikhail N. (1868–1932)

iconography, II 535b

nationalism, III 333b

Poland

aesthetics, II 216a, 219a, 221a, 222a

agriculture, III 166b

architecture, I 398b

balance of power, I 186a, 186b

baroque in literature, I 189a, 191a, 192b

communism, III 334a

Eastern Orthodox Church, I 411a

equality, II 139a, 144a, 144b

language, III 63a

Magyars, I 381a

Marxism, III 154b, 166a–166b, 167b, 168a, 169a

nationalism, III 328a, 328b, 334a, 335a; IV 493b

partition of, I 186a, 186b

partition of (first), I 403b

peasantry, II 144b

pragmatism, III 557a

protest movements, III 673a

religion, IV 113a

revisionism, IV 274a

revolution, IV 160b

romanticism, IV 191b

Socinians, I 398a–398b

symbolism, IV 343b

technology, IV 360b

U.S.S.R., III 334a

Volksgeist, IV 493b, 494b

Polanyi, Michael

ambiguity, I 59b

environment, II 121a

sensation, II 121a

Pole, Reginald (Cardinal) (1500–1558)

Christianity, I 393a, 393b

Machiavellism, III 117b

Poliziano, Angelo (1454–1494)

classification of the arts, I 459b

humanism, II 517b

literary criticism, I 596b

mimesis, III 229a

Platonism, III 511a, 511b

Pollaiuolo, Antonio (1429–1498)

Platonism, III 511b

temperance, IV 373b

virtue, IV 373b

Pollock, Frederick (1845–1937)

causation, I 293a

common law, II 694b, 696a

justice, II 654b

law, I 293a; III 27b

Pollock, Jackson (1912–1956)

art, II 304b

individualism, II 304b

Pollock, Thomas Clark, literature, III 86a–86b

Pollution

environment, II 122a

ethics, III 447b

natural liberty, II 64b

natural resources, II 122a

perfectibility, III 475a

technology, IV 364b

Polo, Marco (1254?–?1324), China, I 354a, 365b

cosmic voyages, I 527a

Polonsky, Yakov (1820–1898), symbolism, IV 343a

Polti, Georges, motif, III 238a

Polyarchy, democracy, I 666a

Polybius (205?–?125 B.C.),

aristocracy, I 625b, 626a

balance of power, I 180a–180b

catastrophism, III 630b

city, I 428b

culture, I 610b; II 129a

cycles, I 625b–626b

democracy, I 626a, 655a, 655b, 657b

Descartes and, III 356b

environment, II 129a

freedom of speech, II 257b, 260b

health, III 574a

historiography, II 467b, 468b, 469b, 477a, 482b, 507b–508b, 509a, 509b

history, IV 508a

human nature, III 574a

mob-rule, I 626a

monarchy, I 625b, 626a

morality, III 630b

natural law, I 626a

necessity, III 354b, 356a, 356b

oligarchy, I 625b–626a

Plato and, III 630b

progress, III 630b

revolution, IV 152b, 154b

State, I 625b–626a, 655a, 655b, 657b

tyranny, I 625b, 626a

war, IV 501b, 508a

Polycentrism

communism, III 157a–157b

loyalty, III 114a

U.S.S.R., III 114b

Polycleitus (5th century B.C.),

beauty, I 196b

Canon, I 580a, 581a

creativity in art, I 581b

Polygamy

Anabaptists, IV 287a

Germany, I 391a

Reformation, I 391a

religion, IV 96a

theriophily, IV 385a

Polygenesis, language, III 65a 65b

Polygnotus (5th century B.C.), neo-classicism, III 370b

Polynesia

mythology, III 308a

primitivism, III 596b

Polyphemus (myth)

antiprimitivism, III 604a

lawlessness, II 675a

Polyphony, II 314b–316a; III 261a, 269b

Polytheism

cynicism and, I 629b

Egypt (ancient), II 333b

God, II 333b–336a, 338a, 341b, 345b

Islam, IV 231a

justice, II 652b

Mesopotamia (ancient), II 333b

mythology, III 274a, 279b, 303a, 309a

Orientalism, III 434a

Platonism, III 519a

progress, III 641a, 642a

religion, IV 94b, 95b, 96a, 113b

Rome (ancient), IV 113b

Saint-Simon, III 641a

sin, IV 231a

theodicy, IV 379a, 379b

U.S., III 434a

witchcraft, IV 521a

Polyxena (myth), law, II 681b

Pomey, F. A., mythology, III 303a

Pomfret, John (1667–1702), primitivism, III 600a

Pompeius Trogus (fl. 1st century B.C.–1st century A.D.), progress, III 631b

Pompey the Great (106–48 B.C.), temperance, IV 370b

Pomponazzi, Pietro (1462–1525)

angels, II 36b, 37a

death, I 640b

demons, II 36b, 37a

dignity, IV 146a

double truth, II 36b–37a

God, II 36b, 37a, 347a–347b

341

immortality, I 640b
Man-Machine, III 135a, 137a
miracles, II 36b
perfectibility, III 468b
philosophy, II 36b–37a
reason, II 36b
Ponce de León, Juan (1460?–1521), longevity, III 90b
Poncelet, Jean Victor (1788–1867)
  axiomatization, I 168a
  geometry, IV 304a
  space, IV 304a
Ponomarev, Boris, Marxism, III 166b, 167a
Pons, Abbé (1761–1831), astronomy, I 76b
Ponsard, François (1814–1867), classicism, I 452a–b
Pont, Robert, hierarchy, II 438a
Pontano, Giovanni (1426–1503)
  chance, II 235a
  fate, II 235a
  genius, II 317b
  humanism, II 517b
  music, II 317b
  mythology, III 290a
  poetry, III 529b
  virtue, IV 479a
Pontormo, Jacopo da (1494–1557)
  art, II 301b, 302b
  genius, II 301b, 302b
Pontus de Tyard (1521–1605)
  musical genius, II 318a
  Pythagorean cosmos, IV 41a
Poor Men of Lyons, see Waldensians
Pope, Alexander (1688–1744)
  abstraction, III 398a
  aesthetics, I 588a
  art, III 305a, 306a–306b
  art and play, I 103b
  attitude toward antiquity, I 78b, 82a, 83b
  baroque in literature, I 191a
  Boileau and, I 453a
  Byron and, IV 192b
  Chain of Being, I 329a; II 447a
  classicism, I 450a, 455a
  creativity in art, I 588a
  ethics, III 397a
  evil, II 165b
  genius, II 305a, 306a–306b
  God, I 554b
  hierarchy, II 447a, 447b
  irony, II 628b, 629a

Johnson and, II 447a
light, IV 337a–337b
literary criticism, I 596a, 597a
mathematics, III 397a
metaphysics, III 397a
Nature, III 348b
neo-classicism, III 362b, 424b
392b, 396b–397a, 398a; IV 199b
optics, III 392a–392b, 396b–397a, 398a
organicism, III 424b
periodization in literary history, III 483a, 484a, 485b
philosophy, III 397a
poetry, III 531b; IV 467a
primitivism, III 579b, 600a
religion, III 397a
romanticism, IV 192b, 193a, 194a, 195a, 199b
satire, IV 211b, 212b, 213b, 214a, 214b, 215b
science, III 397a
sublime in external nature, IV 333b, 337a–337b
theodicy, IV 382b
truth, III 397a
virtuoso, IV 489b
Popelinière, L. V. de la, historiography, II 485a, 485b
Popkin, Richard H., certainty, I 305b
Popper, Karl
  agnosticism, I 23a
  causation, I 281b
  certainty, I 323a–323b
  determinism, II 20b–21a
  empiricism, II 545b, 550b
  Enlightenment, II 94a
  historiography, II 20b–21a
  Heisenberg and, II 590a
  historicism, II 457b, 462a
  history, II 20b–21a
  indeterminacy, II 590a, 591b, 592a
  individualism, II 600b, 601a
  knowledge, I 323b
  logic, I 323b; III 545b, 550b
  Marxism, III 160a
  mathematics, I 323b
  necessity, III 358b, 361b
  Plato and, III 502b
  positivism, III 545b, 550b
  skepticism, IV 250a, 250b
  truth, I 323a–323b
  uncertainty principle, II 591b
Population explosion
  conservation, I 471a, 473b, 475b, 476b
  evil, II 169a
  evolutionism, II 180b

nationalism, III 336a
probability, III 607a
progress, III 636b, 637b
Victorian sentiment, IV 217b, 218b, 221b–222a
war, IV 507b
Population theory
  economic history, II 49a
  Malthus, II 49a
Populism
  Christianity, III 505b
  nationalism, III 333a, 335b
  Platonism, III 505b
  Russia, III 676b
Porcelain
  aesthetics, II 224a
  China, I 363a
Porebowicz, Edward, baroque in literature, I 189a
Porphyry (232?–?304)
  Aristotle and, III 377a
  astrology, I 121a, 125a
  classification of the sciences, I 462a
  cosmos, III 129a
  criticism, III 376b
  evil, III 265a
  good, III 265a
  hierarchy, II 439a
  Iamblichus and, III 376b
  idea, II 545b, 546a
  Marius Victorinus and, III 376b, 377b
  microcosm, III 129a
  monism, III 376b
  music, III 265a
  mythology, III 292a
  Neo-Platonism, III 373b, 374a, 374b, 376a, 376b–377b
  One, III 376b
  philosophy, III 376b–377b
  Plotinus and, III 373b, 374a, 374b, 376a, 376b
  Pythagoreans, IV 35a
  Saint Augustine and, III 377b, 378a
  self-knowledge, III 129a
  soul, III 376b
  Synesius and, III 376b
Porrée, Gilbert de la (1070–1154)
  aesthetics, II 217b, 224a–224b
  heresy, II 418a
  methodology, III 381b–382a
Porta, Giambattista della (1535?–1615)
  Bacon and, I 174b
  optics, III 411b–412a
  refraction, III 411b
  spontaneous generation, IV 308b

Portraiture, II 532a
  naturalism in art, III 340b
  Nature, III 350a
Portugal
  academic freedom, I 10a
  architecture, I 398b
  art, II 303a
  balance of power, I 181a
  Buddhism, I 256b
  Cosmic Voyages, I 532b
  China, I 354a–354b
  culture, III 539b
  genius, II 293b, 308a
  Jesuits expelled, I 403b
  primitivism, III 594a
  revolution, IV 154a
  romanticism, IV 191a
  symbolism, IV 340b
  technology, IV 360b
Poseidon (myth), II 340a; III 272b
  law, II 677b, 681a
Posidonius (c. 135–51 B.C.),
  aesthetics, II 219b
  anthropology, III 630b
  classification of the sciences, I 463b
  culture, I 611a; III 630b
  dignity, IV 136b, 137b
  ethics, IV 321b
  God, III 630b
  Golden Age (myth), III 630b
  historiography, II 509–511a
  law, III 631a
  natural law, III 16b
  observation, III 630b, 631a
  Platonism, III 504a
  primitivism, III 588b
  progress, III 630b–631a, 631b, 633a
  Seneca and, III 588b
  skill, III 631a
  Stoicism, III 588b; IV 321b
  technology, III 631a
Positivism, III 532b–551a
  aesthetics, III 538a
  Alembert, III 532b, 533a
  algebra, III 549a
  anticlericalism, III 536a, 538a, 544a
  Argentina, III 543b–544a
  Aristotle, III 538b
  art, III 538a
  artists, III 538a
  astronomy, III 535b
  atheism, III 540b
  atomic theory, III 548b
  Austin, III 1b
  Australia, III 550a
  authority, I 155b–156a, 156b; III 544a
  Avenarius, III 545b, 547b

Bacon, I 173b; III 534a
Barredo, III 544a
Batista, III 544b
beauty, I 196a
Beckner, III 550b
behaviorism, III 549a–549b
Bergmann, III 545b, 549a
Bergson, III 545a
Berlin Society of Scientific Empiricists, III 545b–550b
Bernays, III 547b
Bevilaqua, III 541b
Bichat, III 534a
Bilbao, III 543b
biology, III 534a, 535b, 548b, 549a, 550b
blacks, III 540a, 541b, 542b
Boltzmann, III 545b
Bonald, III 533b–534b
Borges de Medeiros, III 542a, 542b, 543a
bourgeois, III 537a
Brandão Júnior, III 541b
Brazil, III 537a, 539b–545a
Bridgman, III 550b
Broussais, III 534a
Bühler, III 547a
Bulnes, III 544a, 544b
Bunge, Carlos Octavio, III 543b
Bunge, Mario, III 550a
Cabanis, III 533a
Cabral, III 541b
Camargo, III 542a
Carnap, III 545b–550a
Cartesianism, III 535a
Caso, III 544b
Castilhos, III 542a
Castro, III 544b
causation, III 546b
certainty, I 318b, 321b–322a
Charles X, III 533b
chemistry, III 535b, 548b
Chile, III 544a
Christianity, III 534b, 538b, 543b
class, III 544a
classification of the sciences, III 533a, 535b
colonialism, III 537a
common law, II 693b
communication, III 547a
Comte, I 318b; II 415b, 452a; III 359b–360a, 478a, 532b–545b
Condillac, III 533a, 534a
Condorcet, III 532b, 533a
Congreve, III 537a
conservatism, III 537a
Constant, III 543a
Counter-Enlightenment, II 107b
Cousin, III 533b–534a,

534b, 538a, 538b
criticism, III 550b
Cuba, III 544b
culture, III 533b, 539b, 542b, 543b, 544b
Darwinism, III 542b
Descartes, III 532b
Destutt de Tracy, III 533a
determinism, II 241a
Díaz, III 544a, 544b
dictatorship, III 540a, 542a, 543a, 544a, 545a
Diderot, III 533a
Dingler, III 546a
Du Bois-Reymond, III 546a
dualism, III 549b
Dubislav, III 546a
Ducasse, III 532a
Durkheim, III 538b
economics, III 542b
education, III 533a, 538a, 540a–544a, 550b
Einstein, III 545b, 546b, 549a
electrodynamic field theory, III 549a
electromagnetics, III 548b, 549a
Eliot, George, III 539a
emergentism, III 548b–549a
emotion, III 538a, 540b, 550a
Engels, II 454b
engineering, III 533b, 540b
Enlightenment, III 532b–534a, 536a, 538a–545b
epistemology, III 547b, 548a
ethics, III 538a, 540b; IV 183b–184a
existentialism, III 546a
expressionism, II 206b–207a
Feigl, III 546a, 550a, 550b
Feyerabend, III 550b
Finlay, III 541a
Fitzgerald, III 546b
Floresta, III 539b–540a
Fonseca, III 542a
Fontenelle, III 536b
France, III 532b, 533b, 534b, 537a, 538a, 539b, 542b, 543b
Frank, III 546a, 548a
free will, II 241a
freedom, III 544b
Frege, III 545b, 547b, 548a, 550a
French Revolution (1789), III 533a, 533b, 534a, 534b, 537a, 538a, 538b
Gall, III 534a, 537a
geometry, III 547a

Germany, III 538a, 540b
Gibraltar, III 537a
Gödel, III 545b
González, III 543b
good, IV 183b–184b
Great Britain, III 537a, 538a, 538b, 539a, 542b, 543b, 545b, 550b
Grelling, III 546a
Grünbaum, III 550a
Guizot, III 533b
Hahn, III 545b, 548a, 548b
Haller, III 534a
Hanson, III 550b
Harrison, II 415a; III 537b, 538b
Hart, III 1b, 2b–3a
Hegel, III 533a
Hegelianism, III 546a
Helmer, III 546a
Helmholtz, III 545b
Hempel, III 546a, 550a
Hertz, III 545b
Hilbert, III 545b, 547b
historicism, II 456b, 462b, 463a, 463b
historiography, III 532b–536b, 538a–539b, 545b, 546b, 550b
history, III 533a, 534b, 538a, 539a, 543b, 544b
Hobbes, III 20b
Hobhouse, III 538b
Hostos y Bonilla, III 544b
Hugo, III 544b
Hull, III 549a
human nature, III 534b
humanism, III 535b, 536a, 538a
humanitarianism, III 544b
Hume, III 359b, 545b, 546b, 547a, 550b
Huxley, T. H., III 538b, 541b
idea, III 532b, 535a, 535b
ideology, III 533b, 543a, 544b, 545a
individualism, III 534a
induction, III 550b
Industrial Revolution, III 538a
Ingenieros, III 543b
intuition, III 547b
James, III 546b, 556b
Jenner, III 541a
Jouffroy, III 538b
Juárez, III 544a
Kant, III 547a, 547b
Kelsen, III 1b–2b
knowledge, III 533a, 545b, 547b, 548a, 549b
Köhler, III 549a
Korn, III 543b
Kraft, III 545b–546a
Kraus, III 546a

Kuhn, III 550b
Laffitte, III 537b, 538a, 540a, 540b, 543a
Lagrange, III 533a
laissez-faire, III 542a
language, II 672b; III 546a–548a, 549b, 550b
Lastarria, III 543b
Latin America, III 336b, 537b, 539b–545a
Lavoisier, III 546b
law, III 1b–3a, 4a, 5a–6a, 533a, 541a
Law of the Three Stages, III 533a, 534b, 535b
Lemos, III 539b, 541a, 542a, 543a
Letelier, III 543b
Littré, III 536b, 537b
Locke, III 546b
logic, III 535a, 538a, 545b–551a
Lorentz, III 546b
Loyola, III 536b
Mach, III 538a, 545b, 546a, 547b, 550b
Machado Dias, III 539b
Madero, III 545a
Magalhães, III 541b
Maistre, III 533b, 534a–534b
Martí, III 544b
Marx, II 451b; 534b
Marxism, III 153a, 169b, 540b
materialism, II 451b, 452a, 453b, 454b; III 545a
mathematics, III 533a, 535a, 535b, 540b, 543a, 545b, 546a, 547b, 548a
matter, III 195b, 546b
medicine, III 540a–543a
Meehl, III 550b
Menger, III 545b
metaphysics, III 534b, 535b, 536b, 546a, 547a, 551a
Mexico, III 543b, 544a–544b
military, III 540a, 540b, 543a, 543b, 545a
Mill, J. S., III 536b, 537b, 538a, 539a, 541b, 544b, 545b
Mises, R. von, III 546a
modernism, I 426a
molecular biology, III 549a
monism, III 549b, 550a
Montesquieu, III 533a, 534a
moral sense, III 235a
morality, III 6a, 533a, 533b, 539b, 540b, 542b
Morley, III 539a

Morris, Charles, III 547a
mythology, III 306b
Nagel, Ernest, III 550a
Napoleon I, III 540a
Napoleon III, III 537a, 540a, 544a
nationalism, III 336b
natural law, III 5a–5b, 6a, 16a–16b, 20b, 22b, 23b, 24a
natural science, III 532b, 533a, 534a–534b, 549b, 550a
Nature, III 533a, 547a, 548b, 549a
necessity, III 351b, 359b–360b
Neurath, III 545b, 548b
neurophysiology, III 549b, 550a
Newton, III 546b, 549a
Olbrechts-Tyteca, III 6a
Oliveira Lima, III 539b
operationalism, III 550b
optics, III 416b, 417b, 419b, 548b
Pedro II, III 539b, 540a, 542b, 543a
Peirce, III 546b, 558b
Pereira Barreto, III 540b–541b
Perelman, III 5b–6a
perennial philosophy, III 462b
periodization in history, III 478a
phenomenalism, III 548a, 548b, 549b, 550b
philosophers, III 532b, 533a, 545b, 546a, 550b
philosophy, III 533b–536b, 540a, 540b, 542a, 544a, 544b–551a
phrenology, III 534a, 537a
physicalism, III 549a
physics, III 535b, 547b, 548b, 549a, 549b, 550a
physiology, III 534a, 539b
Plato, III 546b
Platonism, III 532b
Poincaré, III 545b, 547a
politics, III 533b, 534a, 534b, 536a, 537a, 538a, 539b, 540b, 542a, 542b, 543b, 544a, 544b, 545a
Popper, III 545b, 550b
pragmatism, III 546b, 549a, 551a, 556b, 557a, 558a, 558b, 561b 563b, 564b
Pratt, III 550b
private property, III 544a
probability, III 550a
progressivism, III 538a, 539b, 544b

proletariat, III 537a, 541b, 542a
propaganda, III 537a
psychoanalysis, III 546a
psychology, III 533b, 534a, 537a, 538a, 548a, 549a, 549b, 550b; IV 12a
psychopathology, III 537a
Puerto Rico, III 544b
Putnam, III 550b
quantum mechanics, III 548b, 549a, 550b
quantum physics, III 549a
Quine, III 547a, 550b
racial prejudice, III 542b
realism, III 548a–548b, 550b
reason, III 547a–547b
reductionism, III 547b–550a
Reichenbach, III 546a, 547b, 548a, 550a, 550b
religion, III 533b, 534a, 534b, 537a, 538b, 540a, 541b, 543a–545a
Religion of Humanity, III 536a, 536b, 538b, 539a, 540a, 544a, 545a
republicanism, III 539b, 540b, 541b–543b, 545a
revisionism, IV 270a, 271b
revolution, III 542a, 543a, 544b
Ribbentrop, III 540b
Riemann, III 545b
Reidemeister, III 545b
Rocha Lima, III 541b
Rodó, III 545a
Roman Catholic Church, III 538b, 539b, 540a, 540b, 541b, 542b, 544a, 544b
romanticism, IV 196a
Rondon, III 543b, 545a
Russell, III 545b, 547b, 548a, 549a
Ryle, III 549a, 549b
Saint Paul, III 538b
Saint-Simon, III 533b–535b
Salmon, III 550a
Sarmiento, III 543b
Sarton, III 538a
Schaffner, III 550b
Schlick, III 545b, 548a
science, III 532b–551a
sectarianism, III 537b
Segond, III 540a
Segundo Flores, III 541b
Sellars, III 550a
Sierra, III 544b
Silva Gomes, III 540a
Singer, E. A., III 549a
skepticism, IV 244b, 249b–250a, 250b

Skinner, III 549a–549b
slavery, III 541b–543a
Smart, III 550a
social science, III 533a, 533b, 535b, 540b, 548b, 549a
socialism, III 534b
sociology, III 533a–540b, 543b, 548b, 549a
space, III 546b, 550a; IV 302a
Spencer, III 539b, 543b, 544b
spiritualism, III 536a, 543b
Stegmüller, III 550a
Stevens, III 550b
structuralism, III 329b
symbolism, IV 345a
Tarski, III 547b
technology, III 534b, 540b
Teixeira Mendes, III 539b, 543a
theocracy, III 534b
theology, III 533a, 535b, 536a, 539b
thermodynamics, III 548b
thought, III 550a
time, III 546b, 550a
Toulmin, III 550b
truth, III 535b
Tunisia, III 537a
Turgot, III 533a
unions, III 537a
U.S., III 5b, 537a, 542b, 544a, 545a, 546b, 547a, 549a, 549b
unity, III 548a–549b
Uruguay, III 543b, 545a
utilitarianism, III 538a
vaccination, III 541a
Vargas, III 542a
Varona y Pera, III 544b
Vasconcelos, III 545a
Vaux, III 536a, 536b, 537b
Vienna Circle of Logical Positivists, III 545b, 546a–550b, 556b
vitalism, III 548b–549a
Voltaire, III 532b
voluntarism, III 22b
Waismann, III 545b
war, III 544b; IV 500b, 501a
Watson, John B., III 549a
Watson, W. H., III 550b
Webb, III 538b
Weimar Republic, III 534b
Weiss, III 549a
Wertheimer, III 549a
Whitehead, III 545b, 547b, 548a
Wittgenstein, III 545b, 546b, 548a, 549b, 550b

Woodger, III 550b
Wright, III 561b
Zilsel, III 545b
Posnett, Hutchinson Macaulay
  evolution of literature, II 171b; III 83b
Post, E. L., axiomatization, I 169a
Postel, Guillaume
  hierarchy, II 438a
  historiography, IV 148b
  Renaissance, IV 148b
Post-impressionism, II 567b
Post-Kantian philosophy
  Boehme, IV 209a
  Kant, IV 209a
  Leibniz, IV 209a
  Locke, IV 209a
  Middle Ages, IV 209a
  Neo-Platonism, IV 209a
  Newton, IV 209a
  Paracelsus, IV 209a
  Platonism, IV 209a
  romanticism, IV 208a–211a
  Rousseau, IV 209b
  Schelling, IV 210a
  Spinoza, IV 209a
  Weltanschauung, IV 209a
Potamon of Alexandria, Platonism, III 516b, 517b
Potiphar (Bible), mythology, III 275b
Pott, August F. (1802–1887)
  Grimm, Jacob, and, III 68a
  linguistics, III 68a, 68b; IV 427b
  uniformitarianism, IV 427b
Potter, William James
  Orientalism, III 434b
  transcendentalism, III 434b
Pouchet, Felix A. (1800–1872)
  spontaneous generation, II 283b; IV 311a
Poulain de la Barre, women, IV 526a
Poulat, Émile, modernism, I 425a, 426a
Poulet, Georges
  literary criticism, I 605b
  motif, III 242b
  romanticism, IV 196b
Pound, Ezra (1885–1972)
  China, I 369b
  expressionism, II 208a
  Gothic, II 372b
  mythology, III 276b
  symbolism, IV 341a
  ut pictura poesis, IV 470b
Pound, Roscoe (1870–1964), law, III 4b
Poussin, Nicolas (1594–1665)
  aesthetics, II 218b

Aristotle and, III 365b
iconography, II 528b, 534b, 538a
impressionism, II 570a, 577b–578a
mimesis, III 228a
mythology, III 280a, 293b
neo-classicism in art, III 362b, 365b, 368b, 369a
romanticism, IV 200a
ut pictura poesis, IV 469b

Poverty
Calvinism, III 654a
capitalism, III 151b
Christianity, III 590a, 590b
Dewey, III 569a
dignity, IV 141a, 141b
equality, II 145a
ethics, III 447b; IV 70a, 70b, 321a
Franciscans, II 420b–421b
general will, II 276b, 277a, 277b, 279a
good, IV 65a, 175a
happiness and pleasure, II 374b
heresy, II 417b–422a, 424a
humanism, IV 132b
James, III 569a
Jesus Christ, III 668b
Judaism, III 487b, 488a
law, II 686a
Machiavelli, IV 483a
Marxism, III 151b
millenarianism, III 224a, 225a
peace, III 447b
perfectibility, III 467a
philanthropy, III 487a–491a
Plato, I 654a; III 629a; IV 175a
pragmatism, III 569a
primitivism, III 590a, 590b
private property, III 654a, 655a
progress, III 629a, 630a, 649a–649b
prophecy, III 668a, 668b
reformation, IV 63b–65b
relativism, IV 70a, 70b
Renaissance, IV 122b, 132b, 141a, 141b
right, IV 175a
Rousseau, IV 288a
Saint Francis of Assisi, III 668a, 668b; IV 64b
social welfare, IV 279b
socialism, IV 288a, 289a, 289b, 293a
Stoicism, IV 321a
U.S., I 440b
Utopia, IV 461a, 463b
Victorian sentiment, IV 218a, 218b, 219b, 220a

virtù, IV 483a
Voltaire, IV 288a
vox populi, IV 497a
Waldensians, II 419b–420a
war, IV 507b
welfare state, IV 509a, 509b, 510b, 512b, 513a, 514a
William of Ockham, IV 65b
work, IV 531b
Powel, Gabriel, hierarchy, II 435a
Powell, John Wesley (1834–1902), conservation, I 475a–475b, 476a
Power
Acton, I 626a
Aristotle, III 15b; IV 175b, 313a
art, II 576a–576b, 577a
balance of, I 179b–187a
Borgia, IV 316b
Burke, I 154b
capitalism, III 160a
causation, II 231a
balance of, I 179b–187a
chance, II 228a–231b, 233b, 235a–236a
communism, III 646a
Dante, II 233b
dead, IV 491a
despotism, II 1a–17b
determinism, II 239a, 239b, 240a, 241b
Diderot, III 644b
dignity, IV 137b, 138b, 139a, 140b, 143a
directive, IV 491a
disease, III 574a
economics, III 151b
equality, II 141b, 142a
ethics, III 444a, 446a
existentialism, III 160a
fascism, III 674a
fate, II 228a–233b, 235a–236a; IV 413a
fortune, II 228a–231b, 233b, 235a–236a; IV 480b
free will, II 239a, 239b, 240a, 241b, 244a, 246a, 247a
freedom, I 577b; II 249a, 250a, 250b, 251a, 252b
French Revolution (1789), IV 157a
Galbraith, II 66b
Gandhi, III 446a
general will, II 276b, 278a
genius, II 294a–295b
God, II 349a, 353a, 353b; III 571b, 572a, 660b; IV 380a, 380b, 381b, 392a
good, II 231b; IV 174b, 175b, 176a, 177a, 180b,

181a
Greece (ancient), I 613a; II 674b, 675a, 677a, 678b, 679a
happiness, II 379a, 379b, 384b
harmony, II 388b, 391b, 392a, 393b, 394a–394b
Hart, III 2b–3a
health, III 574a
Hegel, II 411a
historiography, IV 147b
Hobbes, II 7a, 240a; III 20b; IV 256b, 316a
holy, II 512a, 512b, 514a
human nature, III 571b, 572a, 572b, 574a, 575b, 576a
humanism, IV 133b
Hume, II 240a
impressionism, II 576a–576b, 577a
individualism, IV 437b, 438a
infinity, II 614a
Israel (ancient), IV 226b
Kant, II 247a
labor, IV 499b–500a
law, II 249a, 250a, 250b, 251a, 674b, 675a, 677a, 678b, 679a, 686a, 686b, 689b, 690a; III 1b, 2a, 2b–3a, 5a, 11a, 12a–13a, 15b, 24a, 25a, 28a, 30a
Leibniz, IV 491a
Lenin, III 156a
Locke, I 6b–7a, 239a, 239b; III 21a; IV 262a
love, III 94a, 107b
Luther, II 142a; III 11a
Machiavelli, II 235b, 236a, 379b; III 116a–125a; IV 479a, 480b, 481a, 482b, 483b
Machiavellism, III 116a–125a
Marx, IV 161b
Marxism, III 148b–151b, 154b, 155b, 156a, 160a, 166a, 167b, 645b, 646a; IV 181a
materialism, II 450b
matter, III 188a, 191b
Middle Ages, IV 153a
Mill, III 642b
millenarianism, III 224a, 224b, 225b
Montesquieu, II 9b; III 21a
music, II 388b, 391b, 392a, 393b, 394a–394b; III 264a–272a
mythology, III 287a, 287b, 303b, 305b, 310a, 314b

nationalism, III 327b, 329b, 330a, 330b, 331a, 332a, 336b
natural law, III 15b, 16b, 20b–21b, 24a, 25a–26b
natural liberty, II 65a–65b, 66b–67a
necessity, IV 482b
Nietzsche, IV 180b, 484b, 485a
numbers, III 405b, 406a
papacy, III 116b
passions, III 572b; IV 482b
peace, III 445a, 446a
perennial philosophy, III 459b
perfectibility, III 463b
Plato, III 1b, 188a; IV 380b
Platonism, III 517a
pleasure, II 379a, 379b, 384b
plenary, I 148b–149b
Plutarch, IV 380b
poetry, I 201b
politics, III 116a–125a; IV 509b, 514b, 531b
private property, III 650b, 651a, 652b, 653a, 653b, 655a, 655b, 656b, 657a
progress, III 624a, 630b, 634a, 639b, 640a, 641b, 642b, 643a, 644b, 645b, 646a, 648b, 649a
prophecy, III 660b, 662a, 662b, 663b, 664b, 665b
protest movements, III 670a, 671a, 673b, 674a
reformation, IV 64a, 65b, 68b
religion, IV 95b
Renaissance, IV 133b, 137b, 138b, 139a, 140b, 143a, 147b, 437b, 438a, 441b
revolution, IV 153a, 154b, 157a, 161b, 163b, 164b, 166a
right, IV 174b, 175b, 176a, 177a, 180b, 181a
Roman Catholic Church, II 212b; IV 64a, 314a
romanticism, III 303b, 305b; IV 205a
Rome (ancient), I 142b–144b, 146a–146b; II 686a, 686b, 689b, 690a; IV 154b
Rousseau, II 11a–11b, 276b, 278a; III 21b; IV 259b
Russian Revolution (October 1917), IV 164a
salvation, IV 227b

Satan, III 224b
satire, IV 212a
sin, IV 227b
skepticism, IV 236a
social contract, IV 256b, 259b, 260b, 262a
Spinoza, II 240a; IV 434b
stars, III 288a
State, III 12b, 151b; IV 313a–318b
Swift, III 599b
technology, IV 357b, 362a–363b
theodicy, IV 379b, 380a, 380b, 381b, 383a
time, IV 392a
totalitarianism, IV 407a–410b
tragic sense, IV 412a, 413a, 414a, 414b, 417a
U.S.S.R., III 154b, 155b; IV 166a
U.N., III 455a
U.S., III 12a–13a
unity of science, IV 434b
universal man, IV 437b, 438a, 441b
Utopia, IV 459a
virtù, IV 477a–485a
Volksgeist, IV 491a
vox populi, IV 499b–500a
war, III 445a; IV 504b, 508a
Weber, I 445a
welfare state, IV 509b, 510a, 513b, 514b
witchcraft, IV 521a–522b
work, IV 531b, 533a–533b
Zeitgeist, IV 536a
Power, Henry
  Cosmic Fall, I 510b
  Newton and, III 385b, 386b
Praetorian law, II 150b–151a, 152a
Praetorius, Michael (1571–1621), music, III 267a, 271a
Pragápati (myth), music, III 268b
Pragmaticism, pragmatism, III 552b, 558b, 559a
Pragmatism, III 551a–570b
  Abbott, III 556b, 558a
  absolutism, III 556b
  adaptation, III 552a
  aesthetics, III 552b, 568b, 569b
  agapē, III 560b
  agnosticism, III 561b, 563a
  Archimedes, III 555b
  aristocracy, III 553b–554a
  Aristotelianism, III 554b, 567a
  Aristotle, III 554a, 554b–

555a, 555b
  arithmetic, III 560a
  art, III 555a, 568b, 569b
  authority, III 552a, 553a, 555a, 565b, 568a
  Averroës, III 555b
  Ayer, III 568a
  Babbage, III 559b
  Bacon, Francis, III 355b, 356a, 558b–559a
  Bacon, Roger, III 555b
  Bain, III 558a, 566a
  Bar-Hillel, III 553a, 557a
  Beard, III 553b, 569a–569b
  Becker, III 553b
  behaviorism, I 226b; III 552a, 557a, 562b–563a, 567a, 568b
  Being, III 555a
  belief, III 552b, 558a, 562b
  Bentham, III 558a
  Bergson, III 552b, 563a, 564b, 565a, 565b
  Berkeley, III 561b
  biology, III 552a, 553a
  Boole, III 555a
  bourgeois, III 565b
  Bridgman, III 551b, 553b, 557b, 559b, 561b
  calculus, III 561a
  Calderoni, III 551b, 564a
  Cannon, III 562b
  Cantor, III 557b, 558a
  capitalism, III 564b, 565b
  Carnap, III 557a, 568a
  Cartesianism, III 558a
  cash value, III 565b
  casuistry, III 555a
  causation, III 553a, 562a, 567a
  censorship, III 554b, 567b
  certainty, III 553a
  chance, III 560b
  chaos, III 560b
  China, III 569a
  China (Communist), III 565b
  Cicero, III 554a
  civilization, III 554a, 560b, 569b
  class, III 565a
  Clifford, III 560a, 562b
  communism, III 564b, 565b–566a, 569a
  Comte, III 556b, 558a, 566b
  conception, III 558a, 559b
  consciousness, III 553a, 553b, 555b, 562a, 562b, 563a, 565a
  constitutions, III 567b
  continuity, III 560b
  control, III 552a

corporations, III 566a
  cosmology, III 558b, 559b, 561a, 562a
  Couturat, III 557b
  creativity, III 569b
  Croce, III 564a
  culture, III 552a, 552b, 556b, 566b
  cynicism, III 563a
  Darwin, III 556b, 558a, 561a–561b
  Darwinism, III 558a, 560b
  De Morgan, III 555a
  Dedekind, III 557b, 558a
  defined, III 551a–554a
  demagoguery, III 554a
  democracy, III 554a, 563a, 555a
  Descartes, III 557a, 561b
  determinism, III 553a, 562a, 569a
  Dewey, II 184b–185a; III 551b–556b, 564a, 565b, 566a, 568a, 568b–569b
  Duhem, III 553b, 555a, 564b
  Duns Scotus, III 555a
  economics, III 569a, 569b
  Edman, III 553b
  education, III 569a, 569b
  Emerson, III 553b
  emotion, III 552b, 562b–563a, 565a, 568a, 568b
  empiricism, III 546b, 549a, 551a–562a, 567a–568b
  Enlightenment, III 553a, 554a
  environment, III 558a, 562a
  Epicureanism, III 555b
  epistemology, III 565a, 565b
  ethics, III 552b, 554b, 555b–556a, 558a, 564b, 567a, 568a, 568b
  Euclid, III 557b, 559b
  evidence, III 562b
  evolution, II 184a–185a; III 556b, 559a, 560b–566b
  evolutionism, II 184a–185a
  existentialism, III 565a
  experience, III 551b–552b, 554a–557a, 559a, 561b–565a, 568a, 568b, 569a
  experiments, III 553a–569b
  faith, III 563b
  fallibilism, III 569a
  feudalism, III 566b
  Ficino, III 555a
  fideism, III 563b
  Fiske, III 558a, 566b
  France, III 557a, 557b, 560a, 564a–566a
  Frank, Jerome, III 553b
  Franklin, III 553b; IV 22a

free speech, III 567b
  free will, III 555b, 562a, 563a, 563b
  freedom, III 553a, 567b, 569b
  freedom of speech, III 566b
  Frege, III 557b
  Freud, III 562b, 563a
  Fuller, Lon L., III 566a
  Galileo, III 555a, 557b
  geometry, III 557b, 559b
  Germany, III 557a, 557b, 560a, 565b, 566a, 567a
  God, III 554b–555a, 564b, 566b, 569b
  good, III 553b, 554b, 568a, 568b; IV 184b–186b
  Gramsci, III 564a
  Great Britain, III 554a, 557a, 560a, 565b, 567a
  Greece (ancient), III 554a–554b
  Green, N. St. John, III 553b, 558a, 566a, 567a
  Haeckel, III 556b
  Hamilton, III 561a
  Harris, W. T., III 556b, 567a
  Hegel, III 555b–556b, 558a, 561a, 567a
  Herbrand, III 557b
  heroes, III 556a
  Hilbert, III 557b
  history, III 552b, 553a, 556a, 556b, 558a, 560b, 567a
  Hobbes, III 566b
  Holmes, III 551b, 553a, 553b, 558a, 566a–569b
  Hook, III 553a, 564a
  human nature, III 554b, 556b, 569b
  humanism, III 553a, 568a
  Hume, III 558a, 560b, 563a
  idea, III 552b, 553a, 558a, 561b, 563b, 564a, 568b, 569a
  ideal, II 551b
  idealism, III 552b, 561a, 561b, 567a, 568b
  ignorance, III 569a
  imagination, III 563b
  imperialism, III 565b
  individualism, III 551b, 552a, 553a, 555b, 556a, 558a, 561a, 563a
  inevitability, III 553a
  infallibility, III 553a
  inheritance, III 565a
  injustice, III 563a, 569a
  instinct, III 564b
  instrumentalism, III 552b, 553b, 566a, 569a

intuition, III 551b, 555a, 557a–557b, 558a, 561a, 565a, 565b
irrationalism, II 636a
Italy, III 552a–552b, 557a, 557b, 560a, 563a–564a, 565b
Jakobson, III 557a
James, I 323b; II 184b; III 551b–554a, 559a, 560a, 561a–566a, 568a–569a
Jefferson, III 553b
judges, III 567b
judgment, III 552a, 552b, 554a, 555b, 556a, 559a, 562b, 568a–569a, 569b
justice, II 658b; III 552b, 568a, 569b
Juvenal, III 554a
Kant, II 551b; III 553b, 555b–556a, 556b, 558a, 558b, 562a, 563b
Klein, III 557b
knowledge, III 552a, 552b–553a, 555b, 559a, 561a, 561b, 562a, 564b, 565a, 565b, 567b–569b
La Rochelle, III 564b–565a
Lamarck, III 565a
Lange, III 562b
Langley, III 560b
language, III 552b, 554a–554b, 557a, 559a
law, III 552b, 554a, 558a, 556a–567b, 568a
lawyers, III 567b
Le Roy, III 553b, 565a–565b
Leibniz, III 557b, 558a, 561b
Leonardo da Vinci, III 555a–555b
Lequier, III 562a, 563a
Lewis, III 553a, 553b, 567b, 568a, 568b–569a
liberalism, III 569a
Lincoln, III 553b
linguistics, III 553a
literary criticism, III 569b
Llewellyn, III 553b
Locke, III 553a, 566b
logic, III 546b, 549a, 551a, 552b–562a, 567a, 568a–568b
Lotze, III 562a, 563a
love, III 560b
Lovejoy, III 551a–553a
Mach, III 558a
Maine, III 566b
Marx, III 553b
Marxism, III 556a, 565a, 565b, 566a, 569a
materialism, III 565a, 565b, 569a

mathematics, III 552b, 554b–561a, 566a, 568a
Mead, III 551b, 552b, 553a, 554b, 564a, 565b, 568a, 569a
measurement, III 553a
mechanism, III 555b, 558a
metaphor, III 199b
metaphysics, III 552b, 553a, 558a, 558b, 560b, 561a, 563b, 564b, 565a, 565b, 567a
methodology, III 552a, 554a, 554b, 558a–558b, 559b–560a, 561a
Mexico, III 569a
Middle Ages, III 555a, 555b
Mill, III 556b, 558a, 560b, 561a, 561b, 562a, 567b
millenarianism, III 560b
mind, III 558a, 561b, 562a, 565b, 566a
modernism, I 420a
Mondolfo, III 555a, 555b
monism, III 556b
morality, III 555b, 556a, 558b, 561b, 562a, 562b, 565a, 565b, 567b, 568a
Morris, Charles, III 553a
music, III 266b
Mussolini, III 563a, 565b
mysticism, III 563a, 564a, 564b, 565b
Nagel, III 553a
natural selection, III 561a
naturalism, III 552a, 553b, 554a
Nature, III 555a, 555b, 559a, 561b
necessity, III 355b, 356a, 553a, 569a
Neo-Thomism, III 564b
Newton, III 557a
nihilism, III 561b
nominalism, III 552b, 559a, 563b
norms, III 552a
numbers, III 557b, 566a
observation, III 553a, 555a, 555b, 559a
ontology, III 557b, 561b, 563b
opportunism, III 555a, 566a
oratory, III 554a, 555a
order, III 560b, 561b
Ostwald, III 558a
Paine, III 553b
Papini, III 551b, 552a–552b, 563a–564a
Pascal, III 563b
peace, III 569a
Peano, III 557b, 560a
Peirce, I 323b, 465b; II 184b, 185a; III 532b, 551b,

552a–569b
Pepper, III 553a, 569b
perception, III 552b, 559a
perennial philosophy, III 462b
personalism, III 552b, 553a
philosophy, II 551b; III 199b
physics, III 556b, 558b, 559b, 564b, 567a
Pirandello, III 551b, 553b, 564a, 568a
Plato, III 554a–554b, 555b
Platonism, III 503b, 504b, 551b, 553b, 554a, 560b
pluralism, III 552a, 553a, 554b, 560b
Poincaré, III 551b, 553b, 557b
Poland, III 557a
politics, III 552b–556a, 563a, 564a, 566a–569b
positivism, III 546b, 549a, 551a, 556b, 557a, 558a, 558b, 561b, 563b, 564b
poverty, III 569a
practical, III 553b, 554a, 563b, 565b
pragmatism, III 552b, 558b, 559a
pragmatics, III 557a
pre-Socratics, III 555b
private property, III 655b
probability, III 553a, 559a, 560b, 561a, 562a
profit, III 553b
proletariat, III 564b
Protagoras, III 554b
protest movements, III 673b
Protestantism, III 565a
prudence, III 555b
psychology, III 552b, 553a, 554a, 557a, 559a, 563b, 565a, 569a; IV 22a
punishment, III 567a
Quine, III 553b
Quintilian, III 554a
Ramsey, III 553a, 561a
Randall, III 553a, 554b
rationalism, III 555b, 561b
realism, III 552b, 555a, 560b, 561b, 563b, 565a, 566a
reality, III 552a, 552b, 553a, 560b, 561a, 564b, 566a
reason, III 555b, 556a, 558a, 559a, 563b, 568a, 568b
reformation, IV 69a
Reichenbach, III 553a
relativism, III 552a, 553a, 554b, 561b, 564a, 568a
religion, III 552b, 554b, 555a, 558a, 561b, 563a,

563b, 565a–565b, 568b, 569b
Renaissance, III 555a–555b
Renouvier, III 562a, 563a
responsibility, III 562a
revelation, III 551b, 553a
revolution, III 564a–564b, 565b, 569a
Rey, III 564b
rhetoric, III 565b
right, III 568b; IV 184b–186b
Robinson, III 569a–569b
Roman Catholic Church, III 555a, 564a, 565a
romanticism, III 555b, 563b, 565a, 567a, 568b; IV 210b
Rome (ancient), III 554a
Royce, III 556b, 561a
rules, III 555b, 556a
Russell, III 561a
Russia, III 569a
Santayana, III 553b–554a, 554b
Schelling, III 555b, 568b; IV 210b
Schiller, III 551b, 552b, 553a, 559a, 568a–569b
Schlick, III 568a
Schopenhauer, III 555b, 563b
science, III 551b, 552a, 552b–553a, 555a–555b, 557b–564b, 565b, 566a
self-evidence, III 557a–557b
semantics, III 554a–554b, 557a
senses, III 555b
Sextus Empiricus, III 554b
signs, III 557a, 559a–559b, 560b
skepticism, III 561b, 568a; IV 244b, 249b–250a
slavery, III 566b
Snyder, III 556b
social contract, III 566b
socialism, III 563a, 564b
society, III 552a, 552b, 553a, 555b, 556b, 564a, 566a, 566b, 567b 569a, 569b
Socrates, III 554a, 559a
Sophists, III 554b
Sorel, III 551b, 553b, 555b, 564a–566a
Soucy, III 565a
soul, III 567a
space, III 553a, 557a
Spencer, III 558a, 560b, 566b
Spinoza, III 554b–555a, 561b

spiritualism, III 556b, 563a, 565a, 565b
Stallo, III 556b
State, III 554b, 556a, 565b
strikes, III 564a–564b
supernatural, III 552a, 553a, 554b, 564b, 568a
synechism, III 560b
syntactics, III 557a
temporalism, III 552a, 553a
testing, III 553a, 553b, 557b, 561b, 569a
Thayer, H. S., III 552a
theater, III 564a
theology, III 553a, 564b, 567a, 568a
Thoreau, III 553b
thought, III 552a, 553b–554a, 555b, 556a, 558a, 560b, 566a, 568a, 568b
Tilgher, III 564a
time, III 553a, 557a
timocracy, III 554a
torture, III 567a
totalitarianism, III 553a, 554b, 569a
transcendentalism, III 568a
truth, III 551b, 552b–553a, 557a, 557b, 559a, 561a–566a, 568b
tychism, III 560b, 561a, 569a
Ulpian, III 554a
U.S.S.R., III 565b–566a
U.S., III 551b–554a, 557a–563a, 564a, 565b, 566a–569b; IV 69a
unity, III 556a, 556b
utilitarianism, III 552b, 560b, 561b, 563b, 567a
utopianism, III 554b
Vacca, III 557b, 560a
Vaihinger, III 551b, 566a
Vailati, III 551b, 553b, 557b, 560a
value, III 552a, 552b, 553a–556a, 564a, 566a, 567b–569b
Veblen, III 569a–569b
violence, III 555a, 564b, 565a
vitalism, III 565b
voluntarism, III 563b
war, III 569a
Warner, Jos. B., III 558a, 566a–566b
Weismann, III 565a
Whitehead, III 561a
Whitman, III 553b
will to believe, III 552b, 561a–563a, 563b, 565b
Woolman, III 553b
Wright, III 553a, 553b, 555b, 556b, 561a–568a

Yugoslavia, III 565b
Prah-hotep, Vizier, freedom of speech, II 256a
Prantl, Carl, historicism, II 457a
Pratt, C. C.
behaviorism, I 219b
positivism, III 550b
Praxiteles (4th century B.C.)
creativity in art, I 586a
freedom of speech, II 253a
mythology, III 274b
theodicy, IV 379b
Victorians, IV 219a
Praz, Mario
baroque in literature, I 191b, 193a, 193b
iconography, II 537b
motif, III 242b
mythology, III 296a
Predestination, II 25b–31a
Arminianism, I 397b
Arminius, II 28b
Augustinianism, II 27b
Barth, II 29a, 30b
Bible, II 26b
caesaropapism, II 30a
Calvin, II 27b–29a, 30b, 142b, 245b; IV 67a, 533a
Calvinism, I 397b; II 28b–29a, 30a–30b
Christianity, I 394a; II 26a–31a
Counter-Reformation, II 30b
death, II 27a
determinism, II 19b–21a
double, II 27b, 29a
Eastern Orthodox Church, II 30a
equality, II 140b–142b
evil, II 26b, 27a
fatalism, II 29b, 30a
fortune, fate, and chance, II 225b
France, II 30b
free will, II 26b, 27a, 29b, 30a, 245a, 245b
freedom, II 25b–26a, 26b
Germany, II 30b
God, II 19b, 25b–31a, 343a, 345a
Gomarus, II 28a
Gottschalk of Orbias, II 27b
grace, II 27a
Great Britain, II 30b
heresy, II 417a, 418a, 426b
historiography, II 19b–20a, 21a
history, II 19b–20a, 21a
Huguenots, II 30b
individualism, II 603a
Islam, II 29b, 30b, 345a,

641b; IV 230b
Jesus Christ, II 26b, 27a, 28b, 29a
Josephus, II 29b
Judaism, II 29b–30a
Koran, II 29b
Luther, II 27b
Melanchthon, II 28a
Middle Ages, II 28a
Muhammad, II 29b
Netherlands, II 28a–28b, 30b
Niebuhr, II 29a, 30b
Pelagius, II 26b–27a
Protestantism, II 27b–30b
Puritanism, II 30b
reason, II 26b
Reformation, II 28a, 30b; IV 67a, 67b
Roman Catholic Church, I 394a; II 30a, 30b
Saint Ambrose, II 26b
Saint Augustine, I 573a; II 26a–27b, 28a, 29a
Saint John Chrysostom, II 26b
Saint Thomas Aquinas, IV 392a
salvation, IV 230b
science, II 29a
sin, II 26a, 26b–27b, 29a; IV 230b
socialism, II 30b; IV 287b
soul, II 26a, 26b
synergism, II 28a
time, IV 391b, 392a
work, IV 533a
Zwingli, II 30b
Predictions
indeterminacy, II 586b, 589b, 592a
natural law, III 14b
necessity, III 362a
probability, III 608b
Preformationism
biology, I 231b
evolutionism, II 178a
genetic continuity, II 284a
spontaneous generation, IV 309b, 310a, 310b
Prejudice
Bentham, III 233b
Cicero, III 587b
law, III 28a
primitivism, III 587b
utilitarianism, IV 445a
Pre-Raphaelites
naturalism in art, III 341b
neo-classicism in art, III 369a–369b
ut pictura poesis, IV 475a
Presbyopia (farsightedness)
optics, III 411a, 413b
Presbyterians

Augustinianism, IV 109a
Church, I 418a
Machiavellism, III 120a
religion, IV 109a, 111a, 111b
tolerance, I 401b
Prescott, Harriet, realism in literature, IV 52b
Present
progress, III 624b, 625a, 625b, 628b, 630a, 631b, 637a
tragic sense, IV 411b–412a
Pre-Socratics
beauty, I 196b
Bruno, III 513b
causation, I 290b
culture, I 609a, 610b
deism, I 647b
design argument, I 670b
Epicureanism, IV 7b
Euripides, IV 367b
evolutionism, II 175a
idea, II 547a
infinity, II 604b, 605a, 607a
matter, III 186b–187b
mythology, III 273a, 273b, 317b
Nature, III 350b
necessity, III 353a
pangenesis, II 622b
perfectibility, III 463b–464b
pragmatism, III 555b
progress, III 627a, 641a
psychology, IV 2a–3a, 6b, 7b
Pythagorean cosmos, IV 38b
rationalism, IV 46b–47a
skepticism, IV 234b, 237a
Stoics, IV 7b
symmetry, IV 350b
temperance, IV 367b, 369a
Theophrastus, IV 6b
time, IV 390a
Press
freedom of, III 45a–47a
individualism, III 45a–47a
liberalism, III 45a
rights, III 45a–47a
Utopia, IV 463b
Prester John (legend), Utopia, IV 461a
Prestige
art, II 572b, 573a
happiness and pleasure, II 376a, 379a
law, III 29a
Machiavellism, III 120a
mythology, III 276b, 286b, 293a
painting, II 572b, 573a

Previtali, G., iconography, II 539b

Prévost, Abbé (1697–1763)
Enlightenment, II 96b
love, II 96b

Preyer, Wilhelm T. (1841–1897), recapitulation, IV 59a

Priam (myth), human nature, III 571b

Priapus (myth), III 291b

Price
demand, IV 452b
economic history, II 46a–46b, 48a, 48b, 49a, 51b, 57b–58a
natural, II 48b, 63a
natural liberty, II 62b–63b, 68b, 69a, 69b, 70a
Smith, II 49a, 62b–63b
supply, IV 452b
utility, IV 452b

Price, H. H.
agnosticism, I 24a, 24b–25a
appearance and reality, I 98a

Price, John, historiography, II 483b

Price, Richard (1723–1791)
aesthetics, III 233a
democracy, I 661b
French Revolution, IV 156b
Hume and, III 233a
Hutcheson and, III 233a
moral sense, III 233a, 234a, 234b
revolution, IV 156a, 156b
social contract, IV 261a
Utopia, IV 463a

Price, Uvedale, ut pictura poesis, IV 473b

Prichard, H. A.
good, IV 183a
moral sense, III 234b

Pride
Hume, III 232b
Kant, III 472b
millenarianism, III 225a
moral sense, III 232b
mythology, III 287a, 288a
Niebuhr, III 467a
perfectibility, III 464a, 467a, 468b–469a, 472b
Saint Augustine, III 468b–469a
theodicy, IV 379b
tragic sense, IV 413a

Prierias, Silvester, casuistry, I 259a

Priesthood
Church, I 416a
deism, I 649b
mythology, III 283a–284a, 301b–302a
Platonism, III 513b
prophecy, III 658a, 660a, 665a
Roman Catholic Church, I 261a, 648b

Priestley, Joseph (1733–1804)
aesthetics, IV 356a
education, III 472a
Enlightenment, II 93a
God, III 472a
happiness and pleasure, II 380b
idea, I 114a, 116a, 116b
perfectibility, III 472a
politics, III 472a
psychology, IV 21a
revolution, III 472a
science, III 472a
society, III 472a
taste, IV 356a
utilitarianism, II 380b

Primitivism, III 577b–605a
Achilles Tatius, III 579b
Adam (Bible), III 581b–584a, 589b, 590b, 593a, 595b, 596b
Adam of Bremen, III 592b
Adamites, III 593b
Adanson, III 603b
adultery, III 580b
aesthetics, III 596b–597a
Africa, III 596b, 597a, 598b, 599a, 603b, 604a, 604b
Age of Heroes (myth), III 578a, 578b, 579a, 580a
agriculture, III 579a, 580a, 580b, 583a, 584b, 587b, 595a, 600a, 600b
Agrippa, III 591a, 595a
Alain of Lille, III 590b
Alexander the Great, III 592a, 592b
Anacharsis, III 591b, 592a
anarchy, III 597a, 597b
Andersen, III 596a
angels, III 582b, 595b
animals, III 578a, 580b, 581b, 583b, 585b, 594b, 596a, 597a, 597b, 599b, 604a, 605a
anthropology, III 598b
anti-intellectualism, III 582b, 587a, 590b, 595a, 595b, 597a, 599b, 604a
antipeasantry, III 595a
antiprimitivism, III 604a–605a
anti-rationalism, III 586a
Antisthenes, III 585a, 590b
Aphrodite (myth), III 585b

Apostles, III 591b, 595a
Aratus, III 579a–580a, 585b
archetypes, III 597a
architecture, III 588b
Aristotelianism, III 585a, 585b
Aristotle, III 586a
art, III 577b, 578a, 580b, 582b, 585b, 587b, 588a, 588b, 591a, 593b, 595a, 596a–597b, 599b
artists, III 597a
Astourou, III 602b
astrology, III 579b
astronomy, III 579b
Autolycus, III 581b
Banks, III 602a, 602b
Bantus, III 596b
behavior, III 596b
Behn, III 601b, 603a
belles lettres, III 593b, 599b
Bible, III 582b, 583a, 583b, 588b–590b, 591a, 593a, 595a, 595b, 600a
biology, III 596a, 604a
blacks, III 600b, 603b, 604a
Bosman, III 604a
Boswell, III 604b
Bougainville, III 602a, 602b, 603b
Brahmins, III 592a–592b
Brazil, III 599a, 599b
Bronze Age (myth), III 578a, 578b, 579a, 580a
Burnet, III 593a
Burns, III 600b
Camerini (legend), III 592a
cannibalism, III 586a, 588a, 594a, 594b, 599b
Cantor, III 590b
Carpocratians, III 589a
Cartesianism, III 596a
Chateaubriand, III 598b, 601b, 603b
children, III 595b–597b
Chinard, III 593b–594a
Christianity, III 577b, 578a, 581b–585a, 586b, 587a, 588b–591a, 592a, 593a, 593b, 595b, 598b, 603a
chronological, III 577b, 578a–585a, 585b, 587b, 595b, 596b, 603b, 605a
Chrysippus, III 587b
Cicero, III 579b, 587b, 589b, 591b, 595b, 599a
civilization, III 583a, 585b, 586b, 587b, 594a, 597a, 597b, 598a, 603a, 603b
class, III 595b
Cleanthes, III 587b, 588a
Clement of Alexandria, III

582b, 592a
climate, III 604a
Collins, III 601a
Columbus, III 592b, 593b, 601a
comedy, III 579b
commerce, III 599a
communism, III 589b, 590b
conquistadores, III 601b
Constantine, J. R., III 604a
Constantine I, III 581b, 589b
Cook, III 598b, 602a, 602b, 603b, 604a
Cooper, III 603b
cosmopolitanism, III 586b
cosmos, III 588a, 588b
Creation, III 593a
Cronus (myth), III 578a–580a, 581a
cruelty, III 594b
Cuba, III 593b
cultural, III 577b, 580b, 585a–591a, 592a, 592b, 593b, 595b, 596a, 597a, 603b, 605a
custom, III 598b, 599a, 603a
cynicism, III 583a, 583b, 585a, 585b, 586a, 587a, 588a, 590a, 591a, 592b
Day, III 600b
death, III 582a, 583a
Deerfield Massacre, III 594b
defined, III 577b
Defoe, III 601b
degeneration, III 595b–596a
deism, III 598a
Delille, III 602b
Demeter (myth), III 585b
despotism, III 588a–588b
Deucalion (myth), III 579b
Diderot, III 602a–603b
Dio Chrysostom, III 586a
Diogenes of Sinope, III 585a–585b, 586a, 586b, 589b, 590a, 592b, 596a
disease, III 583a
disloyalty, III 594b
diversitarianism, III 599a
domestic, III 600a, 601a, 604a
drama, III 601b–602b
Dryden, III 601a
Duck, III 600b
Dutch Guiana, III 601b
Dyer, III 600b
Earle, III 595b
Earthly Paradise, III 592b
economics, III 578b, 586a, 596b, 599b
education, III 585b, 587b,

591a, 595a, 595b, 596a, 597b, 598a, 600a
emancipation, III 596b
embryology, III 597b
Empedocles, III 579a, 579b, 581a
envy, III 583a
Epictetus, III 590a
Epicureanism, III 585a, 586a–587b, 590a
epistemology, III 589a, 595a, 596a
equalitarianism, III 589a
Erasmus, III 595a
eroticism, III 603a
Eskimos, III 596b
Essenes, III 590a
ethics, III 585a, 586a, 597a
Ethiopians, III 590a
Eve (Bible), III 581b–583b, 584b, 591a, 596b
evolution, III 596a, 596b
exotic, III 601a, 601b, 602a, 604a
Falconer, III 604a
Fall, III 578a, 581b, 595b, 596a
fascism, III 597a
Festus Avienus, III 579b
forms of, III 577b–578a
Fortunate Islands (myth), III 591a
France, III 593a, 597a, 601b, 602a, 602b
Franklin, III 598b, 600b, 603b
Freud, III 597a; IV 96b
Fréville, III 602b
Germanicus Caesar, III 579b
Germany, III 591b, 593a, 596b, 597a–597b, 602a
God, III 581b–585b, 588a–599a
gold, III 587b
Golden Age (myth), III 578a–582b, 586a, 588a, 590a, 593b, 594a, 596b, 600a, 600b, 602b, 603b
Goldsmith, III 600b–601a, 604a
good, III 582a, 587b, 588a, 594b, 598a–599b
Gothic, II 370b, 371a
Goths, III 592a
Gray, III 601a
Great Britain, III 593a, 600a, 600b–602b
Greece (ancient), III 578a–581a, 583a, 583b, 585b, 591a, 592a, 597a, 603b
Gregory of Nyssa, III 583a
Guedeville, III 599a, 599b
Guibertus the Venerable, III

591a
Guigo the Carthusian, III 590b
Haller, III 600b
hard, III 578a, 579b–581b, 587a, 590b, 601a
Hawkesworth, III 602b, 603a
health, III 590b, 600b, 604b
heaven, III 600a
Hebrew language, III 584a
Hebrides Islands, III 601a
hedonism, III 587a
Helinandus, III 591a
Heraclitus, III 581a
Hercules (myth), III 590b
heresy, III 589a
Herodotus, III 591b
Hesiod, III 578a–581b, 590a
Hildebert, III 591a
Hipparchus, III 579b
Hirzel, III 600b
Hispaniola, III 593b
history, III 579b, 581a, 582b, 593a, 596a, 597b
Horace, III 591a, 591b
Hottentots, III 604b, 605a
Hugh of Saint Victor, III 592a
human nature, III 581b
humanitarianism, III 597a
Hyperboreans (myth), III 591a
Iceland, III 592b
idea, III 584a, 598b
ideal, III 596b
Ignoble Savage, III 604a–605b
incest, III 586a, 588a
Indians (American), III 594a–605a
innocence, III 580a
Innocent III (Pope), III 591a
intuition, III 596b
Iron Age (myth), III 578a, 578b, 579b, 580a, 581b, 585b
Italy, III 593b, 597a
Jamaica, III 604a
Jesuits, III 599a
Jesus Christ, III 589b, 594b, 595a, 595b, 596b
John XIII (Pope), III 590b
Johnson, III 604b
Juan de Palafox, III 601b
Judaism, III 591b, 603b
Julius Caesar, III 591b
Jung, III 597a
Jupiter (myth), III 579b, 580a, 580b, 583b
Juvenal, III 580b, 581a

Key, III 596a
Klee, III 597a
Kleinjogg, III 600b
knowledge, III 582a, 582b, 588a, 589b, 591a, 595a, 595b, 602b
La Dixmerie, III 602b
labor, III 583a
Lactantius, III 583b, 589a, 599a
Lafitau, III 599a, 599b, 603b
Land of Cockaigne (legend), III 579b, 580a
Laplanders, III 600b
Latin America, III 603a, 604a
Latin language, III 579b, 584a, 591b
law, III 579b, 580b, 587b, 588b, 600a, 603a
Law of Recapitulation, III 597b
Lessing, III 581b–582a, 604b
Ligon, III 602a
literature, III 593b, 601a, 602a, 603b, 604a
Locke, III 598b
logic, III 585b
Lucian, III 580b, 586a
Lucilius, III 588a
Lucretius, III 587a–587b, 600a
Ludendorff, III 597b
luxury, III 586a, 588b, 600a, 600b, 604b
magic, III 582b
Mandeville, III 604b–605a
manners, III 599a, 600a
Maoris, III 597a
Marcionites, III 589a
marriage, III 583a
Martin, III 601a
Martyr, Justin, III 589b
Martyr, Peter, III 593b
Maximus of Tyre, III 586a–586b
Mela, III 591a
metallurgy, III 588b, 599a, 599b
Mexico, III 597a, 601a
Middle Ages, III 580a, 584b, 590b, 592a–592b, 593a, 595a, 596a
millenarianism, III 581b
Milton, III 581b
mining, III 580a
Mirabeau, III 600b
Miró, III 597a
Moloch, III 581a
monasteries, III 590a, 590b
Monboddo, III 599b, 603b
money, III 599b

Montaigne, III 594a–594b, 595a, 595b, 599b
morality, III 578a, 578b, 579b, 581b, 583a, 584b, 588b, 594a, 594b, 598b, 599b, 601b, 603a
Moses (Bible), III 590a
Mussolini, III 597a
mythology, III 301a, 302a, 303b, 304a, 304b–310b, 313a, 314b, 316b, 317a–317b, 578b, 579b, 580b, 594a, 597a, 600a, 604a
natural science, III 601b
naturalism in art, III 341a
Nature, III 346b, 348b–349b, 577b, 581b, 585b–590b, 594a, 594b, 600a–604a, 605a
navigation, III 587a
Nazis, III 597a–597b
neo-classicism in art, III 369b, 370b
neo-Darwinism, III 597a
Noah (Bible), III 582b, 593a
Noble Savage, III 591a–592b, 594b, 596b, 601a, 602a, 604a
Nordics, III 597b
numbers, III 400a, 400b, 403b, 406a, 406b
Odin, (myth), III 597b
Omai, III 602b
orators, III 590b
Orientalism, III 430b
Otto, Rudolf, IV 97a, 97b
Ovid, III 579b–581b, 591b
Ovington, III 604b
pacifism, III 579a, 580a, 580b, 587b
paganism, III 584b–591b
pain, III 584b
painting, III 597a, 602b
Patagonians, III 596b
peace, III 580a, 581a, 587b
peasantry, III 594b–595a, 600b
pedagogy, III 595b, 597b
Peru, III 601a
Petty, III 604b
Philips, III 600a
Philo Judaeus, III 590a
philoprogenitiveness, III 603b
philosophers, III 579a, 580b, 585a, 590b, 598b
philosophy, III 581a, 586b–589a, 591a, 600b
physiocracy, III 600b
physiology, III 578b, 579a
Picasso, III 597a
Plato, III 586a, 590a

Platonism, III 585a, 585b, 589a

pleasure, III 587a, 590b

poetry, III 602a, 602b, 604a

poets, III 579a, 579b, 580a, 583b, 594a, 600a

Polynesians, III 596b

Polyphemus (myth), III 604a

Pomfret, III 600a

Pope, III 579b, 600a

Portugal, III 594a

Posidonius, III 588b

Poutaveri, III 602b

poverty, III 590a, 590b

prejudice, III 587b

private property, III 579b, 580a, 580b, 588a, 589a, 599b, 603a, 605a

progress, III 624a, 627a, 628a–628b, 630b, 638a

Prometheus (myth), III 586b

prophecy, III 582a

Protestantism, III 593a, 595a

Pseudo-Callisthenes, III 592a

Pseudo-Clementine, III 582a

Pseudo-Scymnus, III 591b

psychology, IV 24a

Pyrrha (myth), III 579b

Pythagoras, III 580b

race, III 604a

rationalism, III 598a

reason, III 585b–586a, 588a, 589b, 598a, 600a

religion, III 582a, 586b, 588a, 593b, 597b, 598b, 599a, 602a, 603a, 603b; IV 95a, 96b, 97b, 99a, 107b

Renaissance, III 592b, 596a

revolution, III 600b

rights, III 596a

Roman Catholic Church, III 594b, 595a

romanticism, III 596a–596b

Rome (ancient), III 579b–581a, 599a

Rosenberg, III 597b

Rousseau, III 587b, 588b, 594b, 595b, 597b–603b, 605a

Russia, III 605a

Saint Ambrose, III 583b, 584a, 589a–589b

Saint Anselm, III 591a

Saint Augustine, III 582b, 584a–584b, 589b, 593a

Saint Basil, III 583a–583b, 589b, 590a–590b

Saint Bernard, III 591a

Saint Jerome, III 590a, 591b

Saint John, III 592a

Saint Justin, III 589b

Saint Paul, III 589a, 589b, 590a, 595a, 603a

Saint Peter, III 582a, 590a, 590b

Salvianus, III 592a

Sannazaro, III 593b

Satan, III 583b

Saturn (myth), III 579b, 580a–580b, 581a, 583b

science, III 578a, 586a, 588b, 591a, 595a, 597b, 598a, 599b, 600a

Scythia, III 591a–591b, 592a, 595b

self-sufficiency, III 585a, 587a, 590b

Seneca, III 588a–588b, 590a, 590b, 591b, 599a

sex, III 582a, 582b, 596a, 602a, 603a, 605b

Shaftesbury, III 598a, 598b, 599a, 603a

Shakespeare, III 604a

Shelley, III 587b

shipping, III 580a, 580b

Sicily, III 579a

Silver Age (myth), III 578a, 578b, 579a, 580a

sin, III 584a, 584b, 591a, 596b

slavery, III 580a, 604a

socialism, IV 285a

society, III 580b, 585a, 593a, 595b, 597b–602b

sociology, III 597b, 598b

Socrates, III 585a, 586a

soft, III 578a, 579b, 580a, 581b, 583b, 596b

Solander, III 602a, 602b

soul, III 582a, 596a

South Seas, III 578a, 596b, 603b

Spain, III 597a, 601a–601b

Spencer, III 596b

Spengler, III 593a, 597b

spiritualism, III 603a

State, III 593b, 595a

Steele, III 598a, 602a

Stoicism, III 585a–588b

Stoics, III 581a, 583a, 585b, 586a, 600b

Strabo, III 591b

structuralism, IV 326a

supernatural, III 587b

Swift, III 599a–599b

Switzerland, III 600b

Tacitus, III 591b

Tahiti, III 602a–603b

technology, III 580a, 597b

temptation, III 583a

territorial imperative, III 597b

Tertullian, III 582a, 583a, 589a, 590b, 595a

Theocritus, III 593b

Theognis, III 579a

Theophilus, III 581b, 582a

theriophily, IV 387a

Thicknesse, III 604a

Thomson, III 600a

Thor (myth), III 597b

Tibullus, III 579b, 580b

Toynbee, III 593a

trade, III 579b, 580a, 580b, 587a

transcendentalism, IV 24a

travel, III 598b, 599a

treason, III 594b

tribes, III 598b, 599a, 602a

Trojan War, III 578b

truth, III 587b, 595b, 596b, 599a, 599b

Tyler, III 593a

tyranny, III 594b

uniformitarianism, III 599a

U.S., III 591b, 597b, 598a, 598b, 599a, 603b, 604a

Vaughn, III 600b

vegetarianism, III 579a, 579b, 580a, 582a–583b

Vergil, III 580b, 581a–581b, 589b, 591b, 593b, 594a

vice, III 588b, 589b, 598a, 599b, 603a

Vico, III 599a

Virgin Mary, III 596b

Virgo, III 579a

virtue, III 600b, 603a

Voltaire, III 604b–605a

war, III 578a–581a, 582a, 587b, 594b–597b

Warton, III 600a, 601a

wealth, III 587b–589a, 600b

wisdom, III 598b

wisdom of the fool, IV 515b

women, III 596a–596b

Wordsworth, III 595a, 596a

Zeno, III 587b

Zeus (myth), III 578b, 579a, 580a

Prince, Morton (1854–1929), psychology, IV 28b

Principle of Decreasing Marginal Rate of Substitution, IV 457a

Principle of Decreasing Marginal Utility, IV 454a, 454b–455a, 455b, 456a

Principle of general covariance, IV 88b, 89b

Principle of equivalence, IV 86b, 89a, 90a

Einstein, I 558a–558b; IV 86b, 89a, 90a

Pringle-Pattison, Andrew Seth (1856–1931), God, II 358a

Prinner, F., ideal, II 551b

Printing

Faust (legend), III 247a

historiography, II 482b

humanism, II 516a, 516b, 518a, 519a

linguistics, III 63a

mathematics, III 178a

mythology, III 289a–290a

Reformation, I 390a

Renaissance, II 482b

Priscianus (fl. 500 A.D.)

language, II 661b, 665a, 665b, 666b–667a, 667b

Pritchard, J. B., mythology, III 275a, 275b, 278a–281b

Private property, III 650a–657a

agriculture, III 650b–656a

American Revolution, III 653b

animals, III 650b, 651a, 651b, 655a

anti-trust laws, III 655a

Aristotle, IV 285b

Arnold, III 654b

Austria, III 655b

Bentham, II 381a

bonitarian, III 652a

Calvin, II 142a

Calvinism, III 654a

capitalism, III 148b, 653a, 654b

charity, III 654a

China, III 651a

Christian Socialists, III 654a

Christianity, III 589a–589b, 654a

civil codes, III 655b, 656a

civilization, I 617a; III 650b, 651a

class, I 448b; III 651a, 651b, 652a, 652b, 653b

collective bargaining, III 656b

collective ownership, III 650b

collectivism, III 654a

commodities, III 651b

communism, III 653a

continental civil codes, III 655b, 656a

control of, III 654b, 655a, 655b

corporations, III 653a, 654b, 655a, 655b, 656a

craftsmanship, III 652a

culture, I 617a; III 656b

democracy, I 656b

despotism, II 1a, 13a–13b, 17a

Diderot, III 603a
economic history, II 51a, 60a
economics, III 650b–657a
Egypt (ancient), II 686b
eminent domain, III 656a
Engels, IV 316b
equality, II 142a, 144a, 145a; III 650b, 653b, 654a, 657a
evil, III 653b
existentialism, III 158b, 159b
expropriation, III 656b
family, III 656b
feudalism, III 650b, 652a
France, III 654b, 655b, 656a
free enterprise, III 654b, 656b
freedom, III 653b, 654b, 656b
French Civil Code, III 655b, 656a
Genossenschaft, III 651b
Germany, III 651b, 653a, 653b, 655b
God, III 654a
Godwin, III 470b
good, IV 174a
Gracchi, III 652a
Great Britain, III 654b–655b
Greece (ancient), III 654a
happiness, II 379b, 381a
health, III 655a
Hegel, II 408b–409a, 415a; III 653b
history, III 650a, 650b, 652a, 654a, 656b
hunting, III 650b, 651a
ideology, III 653b–655a
India, III 654b
Industrial Revolution, III 651a, 652b
industry, III 651a, 652a, 653a–655b, 656b
inequality, I 448b
intangible rights, III 655a
Italy, III 654b
Julius Caesar, III 651b
labor, III 653a–655a, 656b
laissez-faire, III 654a
land, III 651b–656b
law, II 686b, 687b, 688a, 688b, 689b; III 5a, 6b, 9a, 11a, 11b, 650b–657a
Leo X (Pope), III 654b
liberalism, III 46a, 653a
liberty, III 656b
Locke, II 62a, 379b; III 653b; IV 288a
Lutheranism, III 654a
management, III 653a
managerial society, III 655b

Marx, II 17a, 25a, 49b, 69b; III 654a; IV 292a, 292b, 316b, 534b
Marxism, III 148b, 154b, 158b, 159b, 645b, 646a, 652b, 653a, 654a
Mexico, III 544a
Middle Ages, III 652a, 655b
Mill, II 49b
Mir, III 651b
monopoly, III 653a, 654a
morality, III 654a
More, Thomas, III 654a; IV 287b
natural law, III 25b
natural liberty, II 62a, 65b, 69b
natural resources, III 650b
nomads, III 651a, 651b
Paul VI (Pope), III 654b
peasantry, III 650b, 651b, 652b
perfectibility, III 468b, 470b
philosophy, III 653b–656b
pleasure, II 379b, 381a
politics, III 646a, 651a, 652a–653a, 655a, 656a
positivism, III 544a
poverty, III 654a, 655a
power, III 650b–653b, 655a, 655b, 656b, 657a
pragmatism, III 655b
primitivism, III 579b, 580a, 580b, 588a, 589a, 599b, 603a, 605a
progress, III 645b, 646a
proletariat, III 654a
Protestantism, III 654a
Proudhon, II 49b
psychology, IV 21a, 23a
public ownership, III 654b, 655a–657a
public utilities, III 656a
Quirites, III 652a
regulations, III 656b, 657a
religion, III 654a
Renner, III 655b
restrictions, III 656b
revolution, III 651a; IV 154b, 157b, 160a
right, III 653b–657a; IV 174a
Roman Catholic Church, III 653b, 654a, 654b
Roman law, III 655a–655b
Rome (ancient), II 686b, 687b, 688a, 688b, 689b; III 651b–652a; IV 154b
Rousseau, III 599b; IV 288a
Russia, III 651b
Saint Augustine, III 11a
Saint Thomas Aquinas, III 654a

Seneca, III 588a
shipping, III 652a, 652b
social reform, III 651a
social welfare, III 653a, 654b
socialism, III 651a, 653a–654b; IV 285a, 285b, 287b, 288a–293b
socialization, III 651a, 653a, 653b, 656b
society, III 650b–655b, 656b
sociology, III 654b, 655b
sovereignty, III 652b
State, III 650b, 652a–655b, 656a; IV 316b
Switzerland, III 655b
Tacitus, III 651b
taxation, III 653a–655a
titular ownership, III 655a, 655b, 656a
trade, III 652a–653b, 656b
transfer of, III 655a, 656b
tribes, III 650b
trust, III 655b
U.S.S.R., IV 154b, 651b, 653b, 655a
U.S., III 654b, 655b
U.S. Constitution, III 654b
U.S. Supreme Court, III 654b
urbanization, III 652b, 654a
Utopia, III 654a; IV 459a
Voltaire, III 605a
vox populi, IV 499a
war, III 652a
wealth, III 650b, 651a, 653b, 654a, 655a
welfare state, IV 511a, 514b
will, III 654a
work, IV 534a, 534b
Probability, III 605a–623b
accidental forces, III 612a
addition, III 607b, 612a
addition theorem, III 617b
Alembert, III 606b
algebra, III 609a, 614a
annuities, III 607a
Aristotle, III 500b, 614b
arithmetic, III 606a, 617a
Arnauld, III 606b
astronomy, III 611b, 613b, 619a
Bayes, III 608b, 609b–611b, 612b, 613a, 615a
Bernoulli, III 607a–609a, 610a, 612a, 614a
Bernoulli Theorem, III 608a, 609a, 611a, 612b, 614a, 618a–618b, 619a
Bernoulli-de Moivre-Laplace theorem, III 611b
Bernoulli-Poisson theorem, III 614a, 615b

betting, III 605b
biology, III 612a, 613b, 615b, 618a
binary expansion, III 619b
Boltzmann, III 620a
Boole, III 610b
Borel, III 608b–609a, 619b
Brownian motion, III 620a
Bruns, III 616b
calculus, III 606a–609b, 612a, 612b, 621a, 623a
Cantelli, III 608b–609a
Carcavi, III 607a
Cardano, III 605b
Carnap, III 618b
Cauchy integrals, III 620b
Central Limit Theorem, III 609a–609b, 619a
certainty, III 608a–608b
Chaitin, III 623a
chance, I 337b–340a; II 226a; III 605a, 607a, 612a–612b, 614b, 615a, 616a
Chebychev, III 620a
Clausius, III 619b–620a
climate, III 608b
collective, III 617b, 622a
combination doctrine, III 608a
compound, III 610a
conditional, III 609b–610a
Condorcet, I 318a; III 609b, 614a
continuity, I 494a; III 620a
contradiction, III 608a
Cournot, III 614b–615b
Cramér, III 618b
De Finetti, III 620
de Méré, III 606a, 622a
de Moivre, III 609a–609b
de Moivre-Laplace formula, III 609a–609b, 612b, 613b, 619a
de Witt, III 607a
decimal fractions, III 619b
defined, III 612a
Denning, III 609b
density, III 621a
Descartes, I 305a
determinism, III 620a
differential equations, III 620a
direct problem, III 608b
discontinuity, III 620a
distributions, III 610b, 612b–613a, 616b, 619a, 620a
division, III 612a
double truth, II 33b–34b
duality, III 614a, 621b
Einstein, III 620a
elementary error theory, III 613b, 619a
Ellis, III 615a–616b

empiricism, III 550a, 606b, 612a, 613a, 614a, 615a, 615b
entropy, III 620a
error, III 613a–613b, 619a, 619b
Euclid, III 605b
Euler, III 609b
fate, II 226a
Fechner, III 616b
Fermat, III 606a–607b
Fisher, R. A., III 610b, 618b
fortune, II 226a
France, III 620a
Frederick the Great, III 609b
frequency, III 606a, 606b, 607b, 611a, 614a, 615a, 618b, 621a, 622a, 623a
Galileo, III 383b, 605b, 606a, 606b
gambling, III 605a–607a, 609a, 617a
game theory, II 264a, 265b, 269b–270a
games, III 605a–607a, 608b–610a, 612a, 615b
Gauss, III 613b, 619a, 619b
Gauss integral, III 612b
Gaussian law, III 613b
Geiringer, III 622a, 622b
genetics, III 616a, 616b, 617b, 620a
geometry, III 605b, 610b
Germany, III 605a
Gibbs, III 620a
God, III 611a
Graunt, III 607a
Greece (ancient), III 605b, 613a
Halley, III 607a
Hausdorff, III 608b–609a
Helm, III 616b
heredity, III 616a, 616b, 617b
Hume, III 612a
Huygens, III 606b–607a
indecision, III 612a
independence, III 619a–619b
indeterminacy, II 588b, 590a, 591b, 592a
indifference principle, III 612a, 615a
inference, III 610b–611b, 615a–615b
infinite fields, III 620b–621a
infinitely-dimensional spaces, III 621a
insufficient reason principle, III 615a
inverse problem, III 608b, 609b–611b

James, William, III 562a
judgment, III 614b
justice, III 612b
Kac, III 620a
Keynes, III 606b, 611a, 614a, 614b, 618b
Khintchine, III 608b–609a, 620a
knowledge, III 614b
Kolmogorov, III 609a, 620a–622a, 623a
label space, III 621b, 622a
labels, III 616a, 617a, 621b, 622a
Lagrange, III 609b
Laplace, III 609a–609b, 610b, 611a–613b, 614b, 615a, 615b, 618a–618b, 619b, 621b
Laplace's limit theorem, III 613a, 613b
Laplace's rule of succession, III 611a
law, III 613b, 614b
Law of Large Numbers, III 607a–609a, 611b, 612a, 614a, 615b, 618a
least squares method, III 613b
Lebesgue, III 622a, 622b, 623a
Lebesque integrals, III 620b, 621a
Legendre, III 613b
Leibniz, III 607a, 608b
Lévy, III 620a
Lexis, III 614b
Liapounov, III 619a
limit theorems, III 612b, 613a, 613b
Lindeberg, III 619a
linguistics, IV 424b, 426a
Locke, III 606b
Löf, III 623a
logic, III 550a, 606b, 608a, 611a, 612a, 615a, 617a, 618b, 623a
long-run, III 605b
Loveland, III 623a
Markov, III 608b, 614a, 620a
Markov chains, III 617b, 620a
Maxwell, III 619b–620a
measure of point-sets, III 620b
measure of precision, III 613b
measurement, III 608a, 613a, 613b, 616b, 619a–622a, 623a
Mendel, III 616a, 616b, 617b, 620a
Menger, III 622a

methodology, III 383b
microphysics, III 620a
Mises, III 608b, 611b, 614a, 615b–618b, 619b, 621a–623a
Mises' first postulate, III 616a–616b
Mises' second postulate, III 617a
mode, III 607b
Molina, III 609b
Montmort, III 609a
mortality, III 607a, 608b
multiplication, III 607b, 612a, 618a–618b
music, III 263b
Newton, III 383b
Neyman, III 618b
Nicole, III 606b
normal distribution function, III 612b
numbers, III 406a
objective theory, III 605a–623b
observation, III 605b, 606a, 606b, 607b, 608b, 611a, 614a–616b, 619a
occurrence, III 618a
Pacioli, III 605b
Pascal, III 606a–607b
Pearson, E., III 618b
Pearson, Karl, III 615b
Peirce, C. S., III 559a, 560b, 561a, 615a–615b, 616b
perfectibility, III 471a–472b
philosophy, III 605b, 606b, 612a
physics, II 264a; III 612a, 613b, 615b, 616b, 618a, 620a
place selection, III 617a
Planck, III 620a
Plato, III 500b
Platonism, III 500b, 504b
poetry, III 605b
point sets, III 607a, 621b
Poisson, III 606a, 608b, 613b–616a
Poisson's Law, III 615b, 618a–618b
polynomials, III 608a
population trends, III 607a
positivism, III 550a
pragmatism, III 553a, 559a, 560b, 561a, 562a
prediction, III 608b
quantum theory, III 620a
Quételet, III 614b
Ramism, IV 43a–43b
random deviations, III 613a
random sequence, III 617a, 617b, 623a
random variables, III 610b

rational numbers, III 622a–622b
rationalism, IV 49a
reason, III 607a, 612a, 613b–614a, 615a
rhetoric, IV 170b
Riemann integrals, III 620b
Roberval, III 606b
Rome (ancient), III 605b
Russia, III 620a
Schiller, III 605b
Schnorr, III 623a
science, III 605b, 613a, 615b
sets, III 621a–623a
Siger of Brabant, II 33b
skepticism, IV 236a, 238b–239a, 241a
Smoluchovski, III 620a
social welfare, IV 277a, 281a, 282a
Solomonov, III 623a
space, IV 304b
statistics, III 607a, 608b, 611b, 613b, 614b, 618b, 619b–620a
Stirling formula, III 609a
subjective, III 608b, 614a–614b, 620
symmetry, IV 350a
Tchebychev, III 608b
testimony, III 609b, 614b
theorems, III 607b
Todhunter, III 605b, 609b, 612b
Tornier, III 622a, 622b
tragic sense, IV 411b–412a
transition, III 617b
truth, III 606b
uncertainty, III 605b, 608a
uniformitarianism, IV 424b, 426a
unity, III 618a
Venn, III 615a–616b
Wald, III 617a, 622a
weather, III 608b
Procházka, Arnošt, symbolism, IV 343b
Proclus (410?–485)
    abstraction, I 3b
    analogy, I 64b
    catharsis, I 269a, 270a
    classification of the sciences, I 462b
    comedy, I 467b
    demonology, I 669a
    Euclid and, I 163b
    fortune, fate, and chance, II 228b
    hierarchy, II 439a, 441a
    irrationalism, II 635b
    Islam, II 643b
    law, II 675a
    love, II 439a

mythology, III 274a, 292a
Neo-Platonism, III 376b
Nicholas of Cusa and, II 441a
Platonism, III 508b, 519b, 521b
Pythagoreans, IV 33b, 36a, 36b, 39b
Speusippus and, IV 36a
universe, II 441a; IV 39b
Proctor, Thomas, historiography, IV 150a
Prodicus (5th century B.C.)
culture, I 609b
cynicism, I 630a, 632a
human nature, III 575a
poetics, III 526a
progress, III 626a
rationalism, IV 48b
work, IV 530b
Production
Bernstein, Eduard, III 162b
capitalism, III 148a, 148b
class, III 148a
Comte, II 25b
economic history, II 48b, 49a–53a, 54b, 58a
Engels, II 25b, 452b
Enlightenment, II 90b
existentialism, III 158a–160a
good, IV 181a
improvement of, II 49a
Kautsky, II 25a
Marx, II 159a, 452b, 453a; III 158b–159a; IV 291a, 292a, 292b, 534a
Marxism, III 147a, 148a–151a, 155b, 158a–160a, 162b, 645b; IV 181a
materialism, II 452a–453a
natural liberty, II 62b–63a, 64b, 65b, 67a, 69a–69b
progress, III 645b
revisionism, IV 266b, 269b
right, IV 181a
socialism, IV 289b–293a
U.S.S.R., III 157b
utility, IV 452b
work, IV 533a, 534a, 535a
Profane
holy, II 511b, 512b
love, III 99a–99b
naturalism in art, III 342b
Profit
capitalism, III 148a
economic history, II 46b, 48b–50a, 54b–58a, 60a
Marx, III 162a; IV 292b
Marxism, III 147a, 148a, 150b, 155a–155b, 162a
natural liberty, II 63b
pragmatism, III 553b

Santayana, III 553b
socialism, IV 292b
U.S.S.R., III 155a–155b
Progress, III 623b–650a
Acton, III 636a
Aeschylus, III 625a–626a
agapē, III 635b
Agatharchides, III 630a
agriculture, III 625a, 631b, 635a
allegory, III 626b
altruism, III 644a, 647a, 648b–649a
ambition, III 631a, 639b
Anabaptists, III 635b
anarchy, III 638a, 641a
Anaxagoras, III 626b, 627a
animals, III 627a, 627b
anthropology, III 625a–627b, 629a, 629b, 630b
anti-progressive sentiment, III 631b–632a
anxiety, III 630a
Arabs, III 638b, 642a
Aratus, III 630a
Archelaus, III 626b
archeology, III 648a
Archimedes, III 630a–630b, 633a
architecture, III 632b
Aristeas, III 625b
Aristotelianism, III 633a
Aristotle, III 627a–630a
arithmetic, III 625a
art, III 625b, 626a, 628a, 630b, 631b, 632b, 635a, 637b, 638b, 639a, 642a, 642b, 644a, 644b
astrology, III 628b, 631b
astronomy, III 625a, 628a, 630b, 632b, 642a
atheism, III 625a
Athena (myth), III 625b
authority, III 646b–647a
autocracy, III 647b
autonomy, III 629a
Babylonia, III 628b
Bacon, IV 433b
Bagehot, III 623b, 624a, 643a
Baillie, III 636b
Bateson, III 646b
Bazard, III 641a–641b
beatniks, III 628b
belief, III 625a, 632a, 635a, 636a–637b, 641a–642b
Bible, III 634b–636a
biology, III 629a, 646a, 646b
blacks, III 639b
Boas, George, III 624a, 637a
Bossuet, III 638b
Bouillier, III 643a, 644b

Buckle, III 640b, 644b
bureaucracy, III 630a
Bury, III 634a, 636a, 636b–637a, 640a, 641b, 649a
Calvinism, III 643a
Campanella, IV 461b
cannibalism, III 626b
capitalism, III 643a, 645b, 646a
Carr, E. H., III 637b–638a
Cartesianism, III 640a
caste system, III 647a
catastrophism, III 628a, 628b, 630b
causation, III 624a, 638b, 643a
Chaeremon, III 626b
chance, III 629a–629b
chaos, III 641a
China, III 638b, 639b, 648a
Christianity, III 626a, 634b–635b, 638b, 641a
Cicero, III 629b, 631b, 632a
city-state, III 629b, 630a
civilization, III 626b, 628b, 629a, 630b, 631a, 631b, 636b, 638a, 639a, 644b, 646a, 647b
class, III 645b, 648a
cleverness, III 626b
climate, III 640a
collectivism, III 646b
comedy, III 628a
common sense, III 645a
communication, III 635a
communism, III 629a, 645b–646a, 647b–648a
community, III 625a, 627a
competition, III 646b
Comte, III 634a, 637a, 640a–643a, 644b, 648a–649a
Condillac, III 643b; IV 435b
Condorcet, III 640b–641a, 643b–644a, 644b, 648b
corruption, III 631a, 631b
cosmogony, III 627a
Cournot, III 643a
Cratinus, III 627b
Critias, III 626b
Croce, III 638a
Cronus (myth), III 624b, 627b
Ctesias, III 628a
culture, III 624b, 625a, 625b, 626a, 629b, 630a, 630b, 633a, 636b, 649a
custom, III 624a, 629b, 639a
cycles, III 624b, 627b, 628a, 630b, 633a, 634a, 634b, 638a, 640b
Cynics, III 628b, 630a, 633a

Darwin, III 646a
defined, III 636b–638a
degeneration, III 624a, 624b, 625b, 629b, 631a–634b, 637b, 639a, 646b, 647a–647b
deism, III 641a
Delvaille, III 634a–635a
democracy, III 629a, 636b, 647b
Democritus, III 626b, 627a, 627b, 631a, 631b
determinism, III 630a, 643a
Dicaearchus, III 629b–630a
dictatorship, III 647b
Diderot, III 644b
dignity, IV 144a
Dio Chrysostom, III 631b
Diodorus, III 627a–627b, 631b
Diogenes Laërtius, III 630a
discoveries, III 624b, 627b
disease, III 649a
divination, III 625a–626a
duty, III 630b, 644b, 649a
economics, III 624a, 625b, 629a, 630a, 638b, 639a, 644a–647b
Edelstein, III 623b, 628a, 629a–632b, 634b
education, III 627a, 630a, 636b, 639a, 643b, 646a
Egypt (ancient), III 648a
emotion, III 648b–649a
Empedocles, III 627b
empiricism, III 631a, 643b
Engels, III 629a, 643a
Enlightenment, II 92b–93a; III 634a, 643a
environment, III 637a, 639a, 640a, 643b, 646b
Ephorus, III 628a
epics, III 624b
Epicureanism, III 630a, 630b, 633a
Epicurus, III 630a–631b
equality, III 637b, 644a, 648b
error, III 635b, 636b
eschatology, III 634b–635a
Eternal Return (myth), III 624b, 628b
ethics, III 636a, 639b, 644a, 645a, 646b, 647a, 648a–648b
Euripides, III 626a
evil, III 626a, 632a, 635b, 636a, 639a, 642b, 643b, 648a, 648b
evolution, II 178a–179b, 182a, 182b; III 625a, 629a, 634a, 637a, 641b, 643a, 646a–647a
experience, III 626b

faith, III 632a, 633a, 634a, 636a

Fall, III 634b

feeling, III 638a, 642b, 643b, 648b

fetishism, III 641a

feudalism, III 641a

Flint, III 634b

Fontenelle, III 644a–644b

force, III 641b, 642b

Forms, III 628b–629a, 629b

Fourier, III 640b–641a

France, III 538a, 634a, 639b, 642b, 643a, 643b, 644b

free will, III 628b, 637b, 640b, 649a

freedom, III 635b, 637a, 637b, 639b, 644a, 645a, 645b–646a, 647b, 649a

French Revolution, III 634a, 639b, 642b; IV 156b

future, III 624b–625b, 628a–639b, 641b, 643a, 648b–649b

Galen, III 632b

genetics, III 645a, 646b

geography, III 632b

geometry, III 642a

Germany, III 647b

Geyl, III 647b

goals, III 624a, 637b

God, III 624b, 625a, 626a, 626b, 630b, 634b, 635a, 635b, 636a, 642a

Godwin, III 643b

Golden Age (myth), III 624b, 630a–632b

good, III 626a, 634a, 635b, 642b, 643b, 648a, 648b, 649a; IV 178b

Great Britain, III 643a, 643b

Great Year (myth), III 628b, 631b

Greece (ancient), III 623b–634b, 641a, 642a, 645a, 648a

greed, III 630a, 639b, 640a

Groningen, III 624a

happiness, II 379b, 380a; III 624a, 637a, 639a–639b, 644a, 644b, 648b

harmony, III 635b, 637a

heaven, III 635a

Hecataeus, III 625b

Hegelianism, III 634a

Helvétius, III 643a–643b

Herder, III 638a–639b

Herodotus, III 628a

heroes, III 624b–626a

Hesiod, III 624b, 626a, 629b

Hipparchus, III 630b, 633a

Hippias, III 627b

hippies, III 628b

Hippodamus of Miletus, III 627b

historiography, IV 148a–151b

history, III 624b, 625a, 626a–630b, 633a–636a, 638a–643a, 645b, 648a, 648b, 649a

Hitler, III 647b

Hobhouse, III 645a, 645b, 647a–647b

Holbach, III 643a–643b

hope, III 632b, 647b

Horace, III 631b

human nature, III 628a, 634a, 638b, 640a, 643a–644a, 645a, 648a–648b

human sacrifice, III 629b

humanism, III 626a–626b

humanitarianism, III 636b, 647a

Huxley, III 647a

Iambulus, III 630a

idea, III 634a

idealism, III 645a

ideology, III 642b, 645a–645b

ignorance, III 643b, 645b

imagination, III 638a

impartial rule, III 645a

imperialism, III 647a

indeterminacy, III 643a

India, III 638b, 648a

individualism, III 630a, 637a, 640b, 642b, 643a, 644b, 645a–647a

industry, III 638b–642b

inequality, III 639a, 646b

Inge, III 635b

initiative, III 630a

injustice, III 644b

instinct, III 644a, 647a, 648b–649a

invention, III 624b, 625a, 629a, 631a, 632b–633a, 636b

Israel, III 634b, 638b

Italy, III 647b

Jesus Christ, III 634b, 635a, 635b

Jouffroy, III 642b

Judaism, III 634b, 635a, 635b–636a

judgment, III 624a, 648b

justice, III 634b, 636a, 637b, 638b, 639a, 639b, 640b, 647a, 648a, 649a

Juvenal, III 632a

Kant, III 637a, 638a, 639b–640a, 640b, 649a

Kepler, III 640b

knowledge, III 632b, 634a, 638a, 641a, 643a, 644a,

645a, 648a, 648b, 649a, 649b

labor, III 644a

language, III 638a

law, III 625b, 631a, 632b, 636a, 636b, 638a, 638b, 640a–643a, 645a, 649a

learning, III 624a, 632b

Leibniz, III 643b

Leroux, III 635a

Lessing, III 639a

liberalism, III 647b–648a, 671a

liberty, III 636b

limitations, III 628a, 629b, 635b

literature, III 628a, 638a

Littré, III 627b, 642b

Locke, III 643b

Lost Paradise (myth), III 624b, 625a, 629a, 629b, 631a

love, III 636a

Lovejoy, III 624a, 637a

Lucian, III 632a

Lucretius, III 630a–633a

Manilius, III 632b

Marcus Aurelius, III 633a

Marx, III 646a

Marxism, III 634a, 645b–646a

Marxism-Leninism, III 647b

materialism, III 631a

mathematics, III 628a

Maudsley, III 644b

medicine, III 625a, 627b, 629b, 632b, 635a

Megasthenes, III 630a

Messiah, III 636a

metaphysics, III 628b, 641b, 642a

Mexico, III 544b

Middle Ages, III 640b–641a

military, III 641b, 642a, 647a

Mill, John Stuart, III 640b, 641b, 642b

Mill, Mrs. John Stuart, III 644b

millenarianism, III 225b, 635b

mind, III 625b, 627b, 629b, 632b, 635a

monarchy, III 630a

Monboddo, II 178a

monotheism, III 641b–642a

Montesquieu, III 640a–640b

morality, III 624a, 624b, 626b, 629a, 630b–648b

mortality, III 632a

Moschion, III 626b

Moses (Bible), III 634b

Mussolini, III 647b

mysticism, III 632a

mythology, III 624b–632a

nationalism, III 642a, 647a, 648b

natural law, III 640a, 646b

natural resources, III 635b

natural selection, III 646a, 646b

Nature, III 624a, 629a, 629b, 631b, 632b, 634a, 635a, 636b, 637a, 640a–644a, 645b, 648b

navigation, III 635a

Nazis, III 647b

necessity, III 626b, 631a, 637b, 643a, 645b–646a

Needham, III 646b

Neumann, III 640b

Newton, III 640b

Niebuhr, III 635b

Noble Savage, III 627a, 629a–629b

nuclear power, III 632a, 648a

obligation, III 645a

observation, III 630b, 631a, 634a

Onesicritus, III 630a

oratory, III 628a

Orientalism, III 624b, 628b, 632a, 638b

ownership, III 645b, 646a

pain, III 643b

Panaetius, III 631a

Papinian, III 632b

parables, III 635a

Pascal, III 638b

passions, III 640b, 641b, 642b, 644a, 644b, 648b

past, III 624a–625b, 627b–633a, 637a

peace, III 634b, 636a, 642a–642b, 647a, 648a

Pearson, III 646a

perfectibility, III 471a–472a, 472b, 628b–629a, 629b, 635b, 639a, 643a–644a, 648b

Persia, III 638b

pessimism, III 624b, 645b

philosophy, III 628a, 628b, 629b–634a, 636b, 641a, 642a, 644b

piety, III 626a

pity, III 638b

Plato, III 626b–629b, 630b, 631a, 633a

Plato (playwright), III 625b–626a

Platonism, III 633a

pleasure, II 379b, 380a; III 638a, 643b

Pliny the Elder, III 632b, 633a

Plotinus, III 632b–633a

pluralism, III 639a

poetry, III 624b, 631b

politics, III 625b, 627b, 629a, 630a, 636a, 636b, 637b, 639a, 640a–648b

Polybius, III 630b

polytheism, III 641a, 642a

Pompeius Trogus, III 631b

population, III 636b, 637b

Posidonius, III 630b–631a, 631b, 633a

positivism, III 538a, 539b, 544b

poverty, III 629a, 630a, 649a–649b

power, III 624a, 630b, 634a, 639b–646a, 648b, 649a

present, III 624b, 625a, 625b, 628b, 630a, 631b, 637a

pre-Socratics, III 627a, 641a

primitivism, III 624a, 627a, 628a–628b, 630b, 638a

private property, III 645b, 646a

Prodicus, III 626a

production, III 645b

professions, III 627b, 629a

Prometheus (myth), III 625a–626b, 631b

prophecy, III 634b–636a

Protagoras, III 625b–627a

protest movements, III 671a, 673b, 674b

Protestantism, III 634b, 635b

Proudhon, III 637b, 643a

psychology, III 628a, 630a, 640a

Ptolemy, III 632b

Pythagoreans, III 628b

Quételet, III 640b

Quinet, III 637a–637b

race, III 639a, 646a, 648a

racial prejudice, III 648b

radicalism, III 625a, 671a

rationalism, III 626b, 627a, 627b, 634b, 636b, 640b, 643a, 645b, 646b, 649a

reason, III 625b, 632b, 637b, 638b, 639a, 644b, 647a, 648b, 649a

Reclus, III 637a, 644b

Reformation, III 641a, 642b, 643a

Reinhardt, III 627a

religion, III 625a, 626a, 628a, 630a, 631a, 636a–

639a, 641a–644b, 645a

Renaissance, III 630a; IV 144a, 148a–151b

Renan, III 634b

Renouvier, III 634b, 635a–637b, 643a, 644b

repentance, III 636a

research, III 627b

resignation, III 630a

responsibility, III 645a, 646a

revolution, III 634a, 637b, 645b, 647b; IV 156b

right, III 630b; IV 178b

rights, III 627a

Robertson, III 638a, 644b

Roman Catholic Church, III 634b, 635a, 635b, 642a

romanticism, IV 205a

Rome (ancient), III 624b, 630b, 631b–634b, 640a

Rousseau, II 178a

Russian Revolution (October 1917), III 647b

Rutilius Namatianus, III 632a

Saint Augustine, III 635a

Saint-Simon, III 640b–641b

salvation, III 630a, 635a

Schmid, III 625a

science, III 625a, 625b, 629b–634b, 636a–644b, 648a, 648b; IV 148b–149b

scientists, III 645a–645b

self-destruction, III 648a

self-determination, III 635b, 649a, 649b

self-love, III 635b, 641b, 644a

self-preservation, III 630b

self-sufficiency, III 628b

Seneca, III 630b–633a

Sextus Empiricus, III 631a

Simonides, III 624a

Simpson, III 646b–647a

sin, III 634b–638b

skepticism, III 634a, 647b

skill, III 628b, 629a, 629b, 631a, 635a, 638a

slavery, III 636b

social contract, IV 263a

Social Darwinism, III 646a–646b

social welfare, III 648a

socialism, III 645b, 646b, 647a, 671a, 673b; IV 289a

society, III 624a–624b, 625b, 627a, 628b, 629a, 629b, 631a–631b, 634a, 636b, 637a, 638a–648b

Socrates, III 626a, 627b, 628b

Sophists, III 625a–627b

Sophocles, III 626a–628a

species, III 640b

Spencer, III 637a, 642a, 642b, 643a, 647a

State, III 627b, 629a, 637a, 639b, 640a, 641b, 642a, 646a

statistics, III 640b

Stoicism, III 626a, 630a, 630b–633a

supernatural, III 635b

superstition, III 635b, 644b

symbolism, III 626a

Talmud, III 636a

technology, III 624a, 625a–625b, 629a, 630b–634a, 642a, 645a–645b, 648a; IV 357b, 360b, 364b

teleology, III 626a, 629b, 635b, 639b

Thales, III 625a

theater, III 625a–626b, 629a

Theocritus, III 630a

theodicy, IV 383b

theology, III 634b, 635a, 635b–636b, 641b, 642a

Theophrastus, III 629b–630a

Theseus (myth), III 626a

thought, III 624a, 625a, 638a, 641b

Thucydides, III 627b, 628a

totalitarianism, III 646b–647a; IV 409b, 410a

Toynbee, III 647b–648a

trade, III 629a, 630a, 642a

tradition, III 646a, 646b

tragedy, III 629a

transformism, II 179a

truth, III 636b

Turgot, III 637a, 638a, 638b–639a, 644b

tyranny, III 631a, 638b, 647a, 647b

Ulpian, III 632b

uncertainty, III 624a

uniformitarianism, IV 150b

U.S.S.R., III 645b, 647b

unions, III 646a

unity, III 638a–640a, 641a, 641b–642a, 648a–648b

unity of science, IV 433b, 435b

universality, III 636a, 637b, 645a, 648b

urbanization, III 630a, 636b

Utopia, IV 461b–464b

utopianism, III 628a–630a

Vacherot, III 636b

value, III 624a, 637b, 647a

vegetarianism, III 629b

Vergil, III 624b, 631b, 632a

Vico, III 638a–638b

violence, III 647a, 649a

virtue, III 627a, 638a, 648b

Vitruvius, III 631a, 632b

Voltaire, III 638a, 638b

war, III 629b, 631b, 632a, 638b, 639a, 642a–642b, 647a, 648a, 648b, 649a

wealth, III 629a, 630a, 636b, 637b

Westermarck, III 645a, 645b

wisdom, III 632b, 638a, 643b

women, III 636b

work, IV 532a, 532b, 534a

World War I, III 647a

Xenophanes, III 624b–625b, 626b

Xenophon, III 626a, 627a, 628a

Zoogony, III 627a

Proletariat

acquired characteristics, II 620b

Brazil, III 542a

China (Communist), III 154b

civilization, III 183a

communism, II 559a–559b; III 673b

Comte, III 537a

dictatorship, III 155b–156a, 166b

Engels, II 559b; III 155b

equality, II 146a

France, III 537a

Great Britain, III 537a

Latin America, III 541b, 542a

Lenin, II 560b, 562a

Marx, II 25a, 559b; IV 291b, 292a, 292b, 293a

Marxism, III 154b, 155b–156a, 162a, 164b, 166b, 654a

Marxism-Leninism, III 155b–156a

Pereira Barreto, III 541b

positivism, III 537a, 541b, 542a

pragmatism, III 564b

private property, III 654a

protest movements, III 673b

realism in literature, IV 55a

revisionism, IV 269a–269b

socialism, III 673b; IV 291b, 292a, 292b, 293a

Sorel, III 564b

totaliarianism, IV 409a

U.S.S.R., II 560a, 620b; III 154b

Prolongevity

alchemy, III 91a–91b

Alexander the Great, III 90b

anabiosis, III 92a

antediluvian legend, III 90a
Celts, III 90a
China, III 90b
Coronaro, III 91b
etiology, III 91b
fountain legend, III 90a–90b
Fountain of Youth, III 90a–90b
Greece (ancient), III 90a
Holy Grail, III 90a
hygiene, III 91b
hyperborean legend, III 90a
Ko Hung, III 91a
Koran, III 90b
Jabir, III 91a
longevity, III 89a–93b
magic, III 90b
Marxism, III 93a
mythology, III 90a–90b
Neo-Platonism, III 91a
Newton, III 92a
organ transplants, III 93a
pantheism, III 90b
physiology, III 90b
Ponce de León, III 90b
religion, III 90b
romanticism, III 92b
Saint Augustine, III 90a
Tantrism, III 90a
Taoism, III 90a, 90b, 91a, 93b
therapy, III 91b
transformation, III 90b, 91a
utopianism, III 92b
Western Civilization, III 89b, 90b, 91a, 91b
Prometheus (myth), III 274b, 278b, 279b
culture, I 608h
Faust (legend), III 251a
freedom of speech, II 259a
historiography, II 506b
human nature, III 574b
longevity, III 89b
motif, III 240b
primitivism, III 586b
progress, III 625a, 625b, 626a, 626b, 631b
tragic sense, IV 413b
Pronunciation, II 664b–666a
Propaganda
freedom of speech, II 254a
humanism, II 517a, 522a, 522b
impiety, II 566b
international peace, III 448b
mythology, III 291b
poetry, III 526b
positivism, III 537a
protest movements, III 672a
Rome (ancient), II 566b
totalitarianism, IV 406b, 410b

Utopia, IV 464a
war, IV 503a
Propertius (50?–?15 B.C.)
humanism, II 517b
love, III 96a
Prophecy, III 657a–669b
Abraham (Bible), III 659a, 666b
Adso, III 666a
adultery, III 661a
Ahab (Bible), III 660b, 661a
allegory, I 45a–45b; III 657b, 666b
Amos (Bible), III 661b, 663a
Angelo of Clareno, III 668b, 669a
angels, III 657b, 658a, 666b, 668b
animals, III 665a
Anselm of Havelberg, III 666a
Antichrist, III 664b–669b
apocalypse, III 664a–669b
apostasy, III 661a–662b
art, III 658a
Assyria, I 538b
augury, III 657b
authority, III 660b, 661a, 668a
Bathsheba (Bible), III 661a
Berak (Bible), III 660b
Bible, III 657a–664b, 666a–668a, 669b
Boniface VIII (Pope), III 668b
Byzantine Empire, III 669a
Catherine of Siena, III 669b
Celestine V (Pope), III 668b
Christianity, III 663b, 664a–669b
clairvoyance, III 658a
communication, III 657a–664a
community, III 659a, 662a, 663b
continuity, III 667b
cosmology, I 538a
cosmos, III 664b, 665a–665b, 668a, 668b
crusades, III 666a
Czechoslovakia, III 669b
Daniel (Bible), III 657b, 664b, 666b
David (Bible), III 658a, 659a, 661a
death, III 661a–664a
Deborah (Bible), III 660b
desire, III 664b
discontinuity, III 667b
disease, III 659a, 660b
disloyalty, III 661a
divination, III 657b, 658a,

663a
dreamer-prophets, III 657b
dreams, III 657b, 659b, 664b
dualism, III 665b, 667a–667b
ecstasy, III 658b
Egypt (ancient), III 660a
Elijah (Bible), III 658b, 660b, 661a
Elisha (Bible), II 394a; III 658a–658b, 660b, 661a
eminence, III 658b
error, III 658b
eschatology, III 663b, 664a, 666a
Eve (Bible), III 582a
evil, III 664b, 665b
faith, III 665a
false, III 662b–663a
France, III 667a, 668a
Franciscans, III 667a, 667b, 668a–669b
Fraticelli, III 669b
Frederick II, III 668b, 669a
Frederick III, III 668b, 669a
freedom of speech, II 255a–256a
future, III 657a–669b
Gad (prophet), III 659a
Gerard of Borgo San Donnino, III 668a–668b
Germany, III 666a–666b, 669b
Geroch of Reichersberg, III 666a
glory, III 665a
God, II 336b, 337a, 345a, 357a; III 657a–661a, 664a, 664b, 665a, 665b, 668b
good, III 664b
grace, III 667a
Greece (ancient), III 657a–657b, 665b
Grosseteste, III 668a
Habakkuk (Bible), III 662b
Hananiah ben Azzur, III 663a
happiness, III 665b
harmony, II 394a
health, III 659a, 660b
heaven, III 664a, 665a
Hegel, II 20a
hell, III 664a
heresy, III 668b, 669b
history, III 666a–666b
Hittites, III 659b
holy, III 665a
idealism, III 661a
ideology, III 659b, 661a
idolatry, III 662a, 662b
ignorance, III 658b, 662b
imagination, III 665b
impiety, II 564b

imprisonment, III 663b
Incarnation, III 667b–668a
individualism, III 659a
Isaac (Bible), III 666b
Isaiah (Bible), III 660b, 661b, 662b
Isaiah (the second—Bible), III 662b, 663b
Israel (ancient), II 564b; III 657a–664a
Italy, III 667a, 667b, 668b–669a
Jacob (Bible), III 657b, 666b
Jehoshaphat, III 660b
Jeremiah (Bible), III 662a, 662b, 663a
Jeroboam (Bible), III 660b
Jesus Christ, III 664b, 665a, 665b, 666b, 667b–668a, 668b
Jezebel (Bible), III 661a
Joachim of Floris, III 666b–669b
Joash (Bible), III 660b
Joel (Bible), III 663b
John the Baptist (Bible), III 666b
John of Rupescissa, III 669b
John XXI (Pope), III 668a
John XXII (Pope), III 668b
Jonah (Bible), III 660b
Joram (Bible), III 660b
Joseph (Bible), III 657b
Judah (Bible), III 661b
Judaism, II 255b–256a, 564b; III 223a, 224a, 636a, 657a–665b, 666a
judgment, III 664a, 664b
kingship, III 658b, 660b, 661a, 664b
knowledge, III 662b, 667a
Last Judgment, III 664a, 665a, 666b, 667b
law, III 660b, 662b, 667a
legends, III 664b, 665b, 669a
Leo Oracles, III 669a
Leo the Wise, III 669a
liberty, III 667a
literary, III 661a–663b
love, III 665b
Luther, IV 67a, 67b
Marsh, Adam, III 668a
martyrs, III 661a, 668a
matter, III 186a
mediums, III 657b
Messiah, III 664a, 665b
metaphor, III 201b–202b, 667a
Micah (Bible), III 661b, 662a
Micaihu ben Imlah, III 663a

Middle Ages, III 664a–669b
military, III 661a, 662a
millenarianism, III 223b, 224a, 224b, 664a, 665a, 666b–669b
miracles, III 660a, 662b
Moab (Bible), III 660b
monasteries, III 666b, 667a
monotheism, III 657b
morality, III 661a, 661b, 662a, 663a
Moses (Bible), III 658b, 659a, 660a, 660b, 661a, 661b, 662a
Münzer, III 669b
murder, III 661a
music, II 394a; III 658b, 659a
mythology, III 664b, 665b
Naaman (Bible), III 660b
nabi, III 657b, 658a–659b, 660a
Naboth (Bible), III 661a
Nathan (Bible), III 659a, 660b, 661a
nationalism, III 659b–662b
Near East, III 657b, 659b
Nebuchadnezzar (Bible), III 657b
necromancy, III 657b
occult, III 657b–659b
Olivi, III 668b
omens, III 659b
oracles, III 657b, 658a, 659a–663b, 665b, 669a
Otto of Freising, III 666a
papacy, III 665b–669b
payments for, III 659a, 660a
peace, III 662b, 664a, 665b
peasantry, III 666a
Pecham, III 668a
People's Crusade, III 666a
perfectibility, III 471b
persecution, III 664a, 664b, 667b, 668a
Persia (ancient), III 663b
poetry, I 456b, 457a, 459a; III 659a
politics, III 660b, 661a, 662a, 663a–663b, 669a
poverty, III 668a, 668b
power, III 660b, 662a, 662b, 663b, 664b, 665b
priesthood, III 658a, 660a, 665a
primitivism, III 582a
progress, III 634b–636a
prophets, III 657b–663b
psalms, III 659b
Pseudo-Methodius, III 665b
punishment, III 661a, 662a, 663a, 664a, 665b
quietism, III 662a–662b

radicalism, III 661a
reason, III 665b
redemption, III 665a
reformation, IV 61a, 61b, 67a, 67b
religion, III 201b–202b, 659a–661b
resurrection, III 665a
revelation, III 664b–666b
Roman Catholic Church, III 666b–669b
Rome (ancient), III 665a, 665b
Rupert of Deutz, III 666a, 666b
Saint Augustine, III 665b, 666a, 666b
Saint Benedict, III 667a
Saint Bonaventure, III 668a
Saint Francis of Assisi, III 668a, 668b
Saint John, III 664a
saints, III 664b, 665a
Samuel (Bible), III 658b, 659a, 660a–660b, 661a
Satan, III 665a, 665b
Saul (Bible), III 658a, 658b, 660a–660b
science, III 658a
seers, III 658a, 659a
Sennacherib (Bible), III 660b
Sibylline writings, III 665b, 668b–669a
sin, III 659a, 662a, 662b, 663b, 665a, 665b
singers, III 659a
socialism, IV 286b–287a, 288a, 293b, 294a
society, III 658b, 661b, 662a, 669a
spirit, III 658b, 663b, 665b, 667a
State, III 658a–662b
suffering, III 664a, 665a, 669b
symbolism, III 657b–658a
symmetry, IV 348a
theology, III 665b
thummim, III 658a–659b
Tiburtina, III 665b
tyranny, III 664b
Ubertino of Casale, III 668b
Urim, III 657b–659a
violence, III 661a, 662b, 664a, 665b, 667b
visions, III 657b–658a, 662b, 663a, 664a, 668a
war, III 659a, 660b, 662b, 663a, 664b, 665a, 667b
William of St. Amour, III 668a
wisdom, III 667a
wizards, III 657b

work, IV 531a
YHWH, III 658a–662b
Zachariah (Bible), III 666b
Zephaniah (Bible), III 662b
Prophetic companies, III 658b
Prophets
  holy, II 512b, 513b
  ideology, III 659b
  Islam, II 641a
  mythology, III 281a, 282a, 282b–284b, 288a, 291a
  prophecy, III 657b–663b
Proportion
  aesthetics, II 217b, 218a, 222b
  infinity, II 609b, 610a
  mathematics, II 609b; III 175a
  temperance, IV 369a
  ut pictura poesis, IV 466b, 467b, 472b
Propp, Vladimir
  folklore, III 239a
  Lévi-Strauss and, III 316a–316b
  motif, III 239a, 239b
  mythology, III 316a–316b
Prose
  fiction, III 82b
  literature, III 82b, 85a; IV 330b
  motif, III 242b
  symbolism, IV 340b, 344b
Proserpina (myth), III 289b
Prosperity
  capitalism, III 151b
  God, II 341a
  Marxism, III 147a, 151b
  millenarianism, III 223b
  war, IV 504b
  welfare state, IV 509a, 514a
Prostitution
  Babylonia, II 683b
  law, II 683b, 688a
Protagoras (5th century B.C.)
  community, III 627a
  Counter-Enlightenment, II 101a
  culture, I 608b–609a, 609b
  cynicism, I 629a
  education, II 80b–81b
  freedom of speech, II 258b
  God, III 574b, 576b
  good, III 575b
  happiness, II 375b
  human nature, III 571a, 574b, 575b, 576b
  impiety, II 565b
  justice II 653b, 657a
  Plato and, III 574b
  pleasure, II 375b
  poetics, III 526a
  pragmatism, III 554b

progress, III 625b–627a
psychology, IV 10a
rationalism, IV 48b
relativism, III 575b
rights, III 672a
skepticism, IV 235a
society, III 575b, 627a
virtue, III 627a
Protap Chunder Mozoomdar
  Orientalism, III 429b
  transcendentalism, III 429b
Protesilaus (myth), love, III 96a
Protest movements, III 670a–677b
  agriculture, III 672b, 674a
  Albigensian crusade, III 670b
  Anabaptists, III 670b
  anarchy, III 673a–674b
  anti-Christianity, III 671a
  anticlericalism, III 670b
  anti-industrialism, III 676a
  anti-Semitism, III 672a, 674a
  assassination, III 673b
  Austria, III 672a, 674a
  authority, III 673a–675a
  Balkans, III 672a
  banditry, III 672a
  Belgium, III 673a
  Bible, III 670b, 674b
  Blanc, III 672b
  Blanqui, III 671b
  Buonarroti, III 671b
  bureaucracy, III 673b, 675b
  cadres, III 672a
  capitalism, III 674a
  Carbonari, III 674b
  causation, III 676b
  censorship, III 672a
  Christianity, III 670a–671a, 672a, 674a–675b, 676a
  civil rights, III 672a
  class, III 670a–676b
  clergy, III 671a
  communism, III 673a–675b
  craftsmanship, III 672b, 674b
  culture, III 671a
  democracy, III 673a, 674b
  demonstrations, III 673a
  disorder, III 672b
  dissent, III 671b
  economics, III 672b–676b
  education, III 670b, 672a, 675b, 676a
  Enlightenment, III 671a, 672b, 675b
  equality, III 670b
  ethics, III 672a, 674a
  evolution, III 672b, 673b
  fascism, III 673a, 673b, 674a, 675b

France, III 671b, 672a, 672b, 673a, 676b
freedom, III 672a
French Revolution (1789), III 671b, 672b
French Revolution (1830), III 671b, 672a
French Revolution (1848), III 671b, 672a
Germany, III 672b, 674a, 674b, 676a, 676b
God, III 675a
good, III 671a
Great Britain, III 670b, 671a, 672a, 672b, 674b, 677a
heaven, III 670b
heresy, III 670b
historians, III 676b
history, III 670a, 671b, 674a, 675a
Hungary, III 673a
idea, III 671a–677a
ideology, III 670a–677a
Industrial Revolution, III 672a
industry, III 671b–676a
Italy, III 673a, 674a
Jacobins, III 673a
Jesus Christ, III 670b, 674b
justice, III 671a, 671b, 672a, 674b, 676b
labor, III 672a, 672b, 674a, 674b, 675b, 677a
Lamartine, III 671b
law, III 671a, 672a, 672b
Lazzarretti, III 674b
leadership, III 671a–676b
liberalism, III 670a–676b
literacy, III 672a
literature, III 671a–672a
Luddism, III 676a, 676b
Marx, III 673b
Marxism, III 671a, 675a
Masons, III 672a
materialism, III 675b, 676a
Methodism, III 674b
Middle Ages, III 670b
modernism, III 674a–676a
morality, III 675a, 675b
nationalism, III 672a–674a
Nazism, III 674a, 676a
New Models Union, III 672a
Nietzsche, III 676a
Old Believers, III 674b
organization, III 671a–676a
Owenites, III 672b
Paris Commune, III 671b
patriotism, III 673a
peasantry, III 670a, 672b, 674a, 674b
philosophy, III 676a
Poland, III 673a
politics, III 670a–676b

population explosion, III 671b
Populists, III 676b
power, III 670a, 671a, 673b, 674a
pragmatism, III 673b
professional revolutionary, III 671b
progress, III 671a, 673b, 674b
proletariat, III 673b
propaganda, III 672a
protest voting, III 672a, 673a, 673b, 674a
Protestantism, III 670b, 671a
racism, III 674a
radicalism, III 671a–675b
rationalism, III 673b, 676a
rebellion, III 670a, 670b, 671a, 673b, 675a, 676a
reform, III 672b, 673a, 673b, 675a
Reformation, III 670b
religion, III 670a, 671a, 674b, 675a
repression, III 673b
revolution, III 670b–673b, 675a
rights, III 670a, 674b
riots, III 671b–676a
Roman Catholic Church, III 670b, 674b
romanticism, III 676a
Russia, III 674b, 676b
secularism, III 671a, 671b, 674b, 675a
skepticism, III 670a, 677a
socialism, III 670a–676b
society, III 670b–676b
Spain, III 674a, 674b, 676b
State, III 671a–676a
status, III 670a, 671a, 676b
strikes, III 672a–676b
student revolutionary, III 672a
student unrest, III 675b, 676a
syndicalism, III 671a–677a
tactics, III 671a–674b, 676b
technology, III 675b
Thiers, III 671b
tradition, III 675a
urbanization, III 672a
utopianism, III 670b, 671a, 672b, 674b, 675a, 676a
violence, III 670b–676a
war, III 673a, 675b
wealth, III 670b, 672a
World War I, III 674a
Protestantism
Africa, III 490b
authority, I 146b–147a, 149b–150b, 401b

balance of power, I 182b
Bible, I 394a, 395b–396a, 406a–406b
capitalism, I 396a–397a
casuistry, I 262a–263b
causation, I 302b
certainty, I 304a, 305a, 307a–308a
charity, II 212a–213a, 215b
China, I 360a, 360b, 366a, 367a, 368a, 369b–370a
Christianity, III 670b, 671a; IV 230a–230b
Church, I 418a
civil disobedience, I 436a–437a
colonialism, III 490b
conservatism, I 408b
Counter-Enlightenment, II 101b, 102a, 103b
Creation, I 572b
crisis in history, I 519b, 592b
deism, I 648a, 648b, 649b
despotism, II 14a–14b
dignity, IV 146a
economic history, II 46b–47a
Ecumenical Movement, IV 68b
Eighteenth Century, I 402a–403a
equality, II 138a, 138b, 141b–143a
eschatology, II 156b, 160b; III 270b–271a, 271b
Enlightenment, II 429a
ethics, III 441b; IV 177a
evangelicalism, I 403a, 406b
evil, II 164b
faith, II 212a–213a, 215b
Faust (legend), III 246b–247a
free will, II 245a–245b
freedom, II 409b; III 23a
God, I 572b; II 355a–355b, 357a, 360b, 361b–362a, 363b, 365a, 365b
good, IV 177a
happiness and pleasure, II 378b–379a
harmony, II 394a
Hegel, II 410a
heresy, II 424a–430b
hierarchy, II 438a
historiography, II 20a
history, I 386b–387a; II 20a
hope, II 212a–213a, 215b
Huguenots, IV 113a
humanism, II 520a, 520b, 523a; IV 135a
iconography, II 530b

Indians (American), III 490b
individualism, I 400b; II 596b, 602a, 602b
intolerance, IV 113a
liberalism, I 408b; II 429a; III 40b
Machiavellism, III 117b, 120a
matter, III 192b
metaphor, III 206a, 206b, 207a
millenarianism, III 225a–225b
missionaries, I 388a, 407a
modernism, I 419a, 419b, 420b, 421a, 424a–426b
morality, I 262a–263b; III 23a
music, II 394a; III 267a, 270b–271b
natural law, III 14a, 19b–20b, 23a
Nature, III 349a
Orientalism, III 432b
peace, III 441b
perfectibility, III 467a, 467b–468a
periodization in history, III 477b, 480b
philanthropy, I 403a; III 489a, 489b, 490b
Pietism, II 429a; III 493a–495b
Platonism, III 514a, 516a
predestination, III 27b–30b
primitivism, III 593a, 595a
private property, III 654a
progress, III 634b, 635b
protest movements, III 670b, 671a
Ramism, IV 42b, 44b
reformers, II 427b
religion, III 206a, 206b, 207a; IV 108b, 112b, 113a, 116b, 117a, 117b
Renaissance, IV 124a, 128a, 135a, 146a
reunion to Roman Catholic Church, I 398b
revolution, IV 162a
right, IV 177a
romanticism, IV 198b, 201a
Rule of Faith controversy, I 307a–308a
sacred, II 512b, 513b, 514a
salvation, IV 230a
Schleiermacher, IV 201a
Seven Years' War, I 402b
sin, IV 230a
skepticism, IV 242a–242b, 243b, 247a
social contract, IV 253a, 254a

socialism, **IV** 285a, 287a–287b
society, **III** 23a
Spain, **IV** 113a
State, **I** 405a
symbolism, **IV** 341b
time, **IV** 392a
tolerance, **I** 400b–401a
U.S., **III** 432b
Volksgeist, **IV** 494b
Weber, **I** 396a
witchcraft, **IV** 521b
women, **IV** 528a
work, **IV** 532b–533a
Proteus (myth), **III** 292a
Protogenes (4th century B.C.), chance images, **I** 341a, 349a, 350b, 352b
Proudhon, Pierre-Joseph (1809–1865)
anarchism, **I** 73a–73b, 74a; **II** 280b
authority, **I** 160b
democracy, **I** 664b
economic history, **II** 49b
free will, **III** 637b
God, **II** 280b
individualism, **II** 594b
irony, **II** 634a
justice, **II** 280b
law, **III** 22a
morality, **III** 637b
natural law, **III** 22a
perfectibility, **III** 470b–471a
private property, **II** 49b
progress, **III** 637b, 643a
revolution, **III** 471a; **IV** 160a
Rousseau and, **II** 280b
socialism, **II** 280b; **IV** 289b, 290a, 293a
society, **II** 280b; **III** 22a, 470b–471a
State, **II** 280b; **III** 470b
voluntariness, **II** 280b
Proust, Marcel (1871–1922)
Claudel and, **IV** 340a
evolutionism, **II** 183a
impressionism, **II** 575a
literary criticism, **I** 605a
literature, **IV** 330b
love, **III** 105b
Maeterlinck and, **IV** 340a
motif, **III** 236b
music, **III** 236b
painting, **III** 236b
Péguy and, **IV** 340a
periodization in literary history, **III** 486a
realism in literature, **IV** 54b, 55a
romanticism, **IV** 196b
surrealism, **IV** 340a
style, **IV** 330b

symbolism, **IV** 340a, 340b, 341a, 343a, 344b
Wagner and, **III** 236b
Providence
Boccaccio, **II** 234a
Boethius, **II** 231b
chance, **II** 225b, 227a–236a
Cleanthes, **II** 237b
Dante, **II** 233a, 233b
determinism, **II** 237a–237b
ethics, **IV** 319a
fate, **II** 225b, 227a–236a
fortune, **II** 225b, 227a–236a
free will, **II** 237a–237b, 243b
good, **II** 232a
Machiavelli, **II** 235b
necessity, **III** 355a, 355b, 357a, 358a
Saint Albertus Magnus, **II** 232a
Saint Augustine, **II** 230a–231a
Saint Thomas Aquinas, **II** 232a, 232b
Stoicism, **IV** 319a
Vico, **III** 357a
Prŭcha, Milan, Marxism, **III** 168b
Prudence
chance, **II** 235a
fate, **II** 235a
general will, **II** 278a
Kant, **III** 555b
pragmatism, **III** 555b
temperance, **IV** 371a–377b
Prudentius (348–?410)
allegory, **I** 47a
poetry, **III** 528b
temperance, **IV** 371a, 371b
Prugovečki, E., indeterminacy, **II** 592a
Prussia
balance of power, **I** 186a, 186b
conservatism, **I** 482b
Counter-Enlightenment, **II** 103b, 104b
crisis in history, **I** 593b
equality, **II** 144a
Jesuits, **I** 403b
Machiavellism, **III** 121b–122a
peasantry, **II** 144a
perfectibility, **III** 473a, 473b
war, **IV** 500b, 501a, 503a, 503b, 504b–505a, 507a
Przesmycki, Zenon (1861–1944), symbolism, **IV** 343b
Psalms (Bible)
metaphor, **III** 202b
music, **III** 266a, 269b

prophecy, **III** 659b
Psellus, Michael (11th century), chance images, **I** 342b–343a
Pseudo-Aristotelianism
disease, **II** 399a
imitation, **II** 306a
Pseudo-Aristotle, melancholy, **II** 320b
Pseudo-Bonaventure, iconography, **II** 528a
Pseudo-Callisthenes
Christianity, **III** 592a
primitivism, **III** 592a
Pseudo-Clementine, primitivism, **III** 582a
Pseudo-Dionysius (c. 500 A.D.)
aesthetics, **II** 218a, 222b
angels, **I** 669a–669b
art, **III** 227a
beauty, **II** 218a, 222b; **III** 227a
dignity, **IV** 139b
faith, hope and charity, **II** 210b
God, **II** 210b, 439a–439b
hierarchy, **II** 439a–439b, 441a, 442a
iconography, **II** 526a, 527a
literary paradox, **III** 78b, 79a
mimesis, **III** 227a
Nicholas of Cusa and, **II** 441a
perfectibility, **III** 467b
Platonism, **III** 514b
Saint Thomas Aquinas and, **III** 467b
universe, **II** 441a; **IV** 41a
virtue, **II** 210a
Pseudo-Longinus, mimesis, **III** 227a
Pseudo-Manichaeism, love, **III** 105b
Pseudo-Palchus, astrology, **I** 124a
Pseudo-Platonism, demonology, **I** 668a
Pseudo Raphael, Gothic, **II** 370b
Pseudo-Scymnus, primitivism, **III** 591b
Pseudo-Vincent of Beauvais, temperance, **IV** 372b
Pseudo-Xenophon, freedom of speech, **II** 259b
Psyche (myth), **III** 276a, 284a, 291a, 292a
Anaximenes, **IV** 2a
asymmetry, **IV** 349a
Empedocles, **IV** 2b
Heraclitus, **IV** 2a
Hesiod, **IV** 32b
Homer, **IV** 32b
neo-classicism in art, **III**

370b
Parmenides, **IV** 32b, 34a, 37a
Plato, **IV** 34a, 37a, 49b
psychology, **IV** 1a, 1b, 2a, 2b, 10a, 14a
Pythagoras, **IV** 32b
rationalism, **IV** 47a, 49b
recapitulation, **IV** 59a
religion, **IV** 108a
symmetry, **IV** 349a
Thales, **IV** 2a
tragic sense, **IV** 414b
Volksgeist, **IV** 495b, 496a
Psychiatry
happiness and pleasure, **II** 383a
morality, **I** 439b
phrenology, **IV** 23b
psychology, **IV** 23b, 28b, 29a
war, **IV** 505b
Psychical science
classification of the sciences, **I** 466a
death, **I** 642b–643b
immortality, **I** 642b–643b
Psychoanalysis
existentialism, **II** 194a
Freud, **IV** 96b
irrationalism, **II** 637a
longevity, **III** 92b
metaphysical imagination, **III** 220b–221b
motif, **III** 242a
mythology, **III** 312a–312b
positivism, **III** 546a
psychology, **IV** 14a, 14b, 15a, 15b, 28b, 29a
religion, **IV** 96b
Sartre, **II** 194a
structuralism, **IV** 326a–328b
Psychogalvanometers, **IV** 457b
Psychology, **IV** 1a–30b
Ach, **IV** 13a
acoustics, **IV** 12a
acquired characteristics, **II** 620b
Adam, **IV** 21b, 22a
Adam (Bible), **IV** 16b, 17a
Adams, John, **IV** 21b, 22a
Addams, Jane, **IV** 27a
Adler, **IV** 14a
aesthetics, **IV** 24a, 27b
air, **IV** 2a
Alcmaeon, **IV** 2b
Alcott, **IV** 24a
Alexander, Franz, **IV** 29a
Alexander the Great, **IV** 7a
Allport, **IV** 15a
anatomy, **IV** 23b
Anaxagoras, **IV** 3a

Anaximenes, **IV** 2a
Angell, **IV** 27b
angels, **IV** 16a
anger, **IV** 3b
Anglicanism, **IV** 16b, 19b–20a
animals, **I** 220b–221b; **IV** 5a, 6b, 10a, 11a, 14b–15a, 17a, 17b, 20a, 25a, 25b, 28a
anthropology, **IV** 14a, 15b, 29a
anthropomorphism, **IV** 14b
Aristotelianism, **IV** 6b, 16b
Aristotle, **I** 499a; **II** 135b, 236b–237a, 377a; **IV** 2a, 2b, 4b–6b, 7a, 8a, 9b, 10b, 16b, 17b
Arminianism, **IV** 19b, 20a
art, **II** 297a, 304a–304b, 309b, 310b–311a, 575a, 580b, 583a
astronomy, **IV** 12a
atomism, **IV** 3a, 6a–7b, 8a, 22b, 27b, 28a, 28b
Austria, **IV** 23a
authority, **I** 161a–162a; **IV** 18a–18b
automatism, **IV** 11a
Avicenna, **I** 3b, 4b
Bacon, **IV** 19b, 23a
Bancroft, **IV** 24a
Barlow, **IV** 21a
Bascom, **IV** 24b
Beard, **IV** 28b
Beauty, **I** 212a–213a
Bechterer, **IV** 14a, 28a
Beecher, **IV** 23b, 25b
Bell, **IV** 24b
Bentham, **IV** 23a
Berger, **IV** 15a
Bergson, **III** 565a; **IV** 12b
Berkeley, **IV** 19b, 20a
Bible, **IV** 9a, 10a, 17b, 18b, 19a, 23b
Binet, **IV** 13a
biology, **IV** 4b, 7a, 11a, 12a, 12b, 16a, 26a, 29a
blacks, **IV** 20b, 21b, 27a
body, **IV** 1a–10b, 16b–17b, 19b, 24a–25a
Bovet, **IV** 13b
Bowen, **IV** 22b, 23a
Boyle, **IV** 16b
Bradford, **IV** 17b–18a
brain, **IV** 23b
Brattle, **IV** 18b
Brentano, **IV** 13b
Brill, **IV** 28b
Broussais, **IV** 21a
Brown, C. B., **IV** 21a
Bruno, **IV** 10b
Buchanan, Joseph, **IV** 21a
Büchner, **IV** 12a

Buffon, **IV** 21b
Bühler, **IV** 13a
Burton, Asa, **IV** 22b
Buytendijk, **IV** 15a
Cabanis, **IV** 21a
Calhoun, **IV** 22a
Calvinism, **IV** 16b, 19a, 19b, 20a, 22a, 23b
capitalism, **IV** 28a
Cartesianism, **IV** 11a, 12b, 18b
catharsis, **I** 268a, 269a
Cattell, **IV** 12b, 25a–25b
Chain of Being, **IV** 22a
chance, **II** 227b
character, **IV** 15a, 15b, 16a
Christianity, **IV** 8b, 9a, 10b, 16b, 18b, 19b, 20b, 24a
Cicero, **IV** 7b, 8a
civilization, **IV** 18b, 24a, 26a
Claparède, **IV** 13a, 27a
class, **IV** 3b, 16a, 18a, 21b, 22a, 26b, 27a
Combe, **IV** 23b
common sense, **IV** 6a
communitarianism, **IV** 21a
computers, **IV** 29a
Comte, **III** 142b, 534a, 537a; **IV** 12a
Condillac, **IV** 11a, 13a, 28a
consciousness, **IV** 3a, 7a, 9a, 27b, 28a, 28b
continuity, **I** 498b–499a
Cooley, **IV** 26b
Cooper, James Fenimore, **IV** 24a
Cooper, Thomas, **IV** 21a
Corman, **IV** 15a
cosmic images, **I** 515b, 522b
cosmos, **IV** 2a, 2b, 3a
Cotton, **IV** 18a
Cousin, **III** 533b; **IV** 11b
criminology, **IV** 23b
crisis in history, **I** 592a
cults, **IV** 23b
culture, **IV** 14a, 15b, 24a, 28a, 29b
Darwin, **IV** 11b–12a, 13b, 25a, 25b, 26b
death, **I** 634b, 637b–638a
deism, **IV** 20a, 22b
democracy, **IV** 18a, 19b, 24a, 26b, 29a
Democritus, **IV** 3a, 7a, 9b, 28a
Descartes, **IV** 9b, 11a, 16b, 17a
desire, **IV** 3b, 4a, 5a, 5b, 8a, 9a
despotism, **II** 9b
Destutt de Tracy, **IV** 21a
determinism, **II** 236b–237a,

238b–240a; **IV** 12a
Dewey, **IV** 27a–28a
Dilthey, **IV** 13b–14a
Diogenes Laërtius, **IV** 7b
disease, **II** 397a, 398a
double truth, **II** 32a–32b
dualism, **IV** 3b, 4a, 4b, 8b, 11a, 16b, 21a, 25a, 27b
Dugdale, **IV** 26b
earth, **IV** 2b, 7b
Ebbinghaus, **IV** 13a
economics, **IV** 16a, 16b, 17b, 23a
education, **II** 71b, 83a; **IV** 18b–19b, 20b, 21a, 21b, 22b, 23a, 24a, 25a, 27b
Edwards, **IV** 16b, 19a–19b, 22b, 24b, 110b, 112a
Eliot, Charles W., **IV** 26b
Eliot, John, **IV** 18a
Emerson, **IV** 23b, 24a
emotion, **IV** 1a, 1b, 2b, 3a, 4b, 5a, 7a, 8a, 22b, 23a, 23b, 27a, 27b
empathy, **II** 87b, 88b
Empedocles, **IV** 2b–3a
empiricism, **III** 548a, 548b, 549a, 549b, 550b; **IV** 2b, 3b, 11a, 11b, 13a, 24b
Enlightenment, **IV** 20b, 21b, 22a, 22b, 23b
environment, **IV** 21b, 23b, 24b, 25a, 26a–28b
Epicureanism, **IV** 7a–8b
Epicurus, **IV** 7a, 10b
epistemology, **IV** 4b, 11b, 24b
equality, **IV** 22a
Erikson, **IV** 29a
ethics, **III** 447a; **IV** 1a, 1b, 4b, 6b, 8a, 15a, 23a, 23b, 27b
ethnology, **IV** 22b
eugenics, **IV** 26b
Eve (Bible), **IV** 17a
evil, **IV** 17b, 19a, 20a, 21b
evolution, **IV** 12a, 13b, 25a, 25b, 26a, 27a
existentialism, **III** 158b, 159a, 159b; **IV** 14a
experience, **IV** 27b
extroversion, **IV** 23a
fate, **II** 227b
Faust (legend), **III** 252a
fear, **IV** 3b
Fechner, **IV** 12b, 13a, 24b
Fichte, **IV** 11b
Finney, **IV** 24a
Fiske, **IV** 26a
Flournoy, **IV** 12b–13a
fortune, **II** 227b
Fowler, **IV** 23b
France, **IV** 11a, 12a, 12b, 13a, 21b, 22b

Franklin, **IV** 20a, 22a–22b
free will, **II** 236b–237a, 238b, 239a, 239b, 240a, 243a, 244a, 246a, 246b
Freneau, **IV** 21a
Freud, **IV** 13b, 14a, 28b, 96b
Freudianism, **IV** 14a, 28b–29a
Fromm, **IV** 14a, 29a
Fuller, **IV** 24a
functionalism, **IV** 27a–28b
Galen, **IV** 8b
Galileo, **IV** 11a
Gall, **IV** 23a
Galton, **IV** 13b, 25a, 26b
general will, **II** 276b, 277a, 279b
genius, **II** 294a, 295a, 297a, 304a–304b, 309b, 310b–311a, 320a–321a
Germany, **IV** 11b, 13a, 13b, 15b, 22b, 24a, 24b, 25a
Gestalt treatment, **IV** 14a–14b, 15b, 28a
Glocenius, **IV** 10a
Gnosticism, **II** 327b
God, **IV** 1b, 6b, 8a, 9a, 10a, 11b, 16a, 17a, 17b, 18a–20a, 21b, 23a, 23b
Goddard, **IV** 26b
Godwin, **IV** 21a
Goldstein, Kurt, **IV** 14b
good, **IV** 3b, 4a, 5a, 5b, 8b, 17b, 19a, 20a, 21b, 177a, 178a, 178b, 179a, 180b, 182b, 185a–186a
Gorgias, **IV** 10a
Gorton, **IV** 18b
grace, **IV** 17b
Great Britain, **IV** 11b, 13b, 19a, 21a, 24b, 25a, 26b
Greece (ancient), **IV** 1a–8b, 9a, 9b, 10a, 11a, 11b, 19b
Haeckel, **IV** 12a
Hall, G Stanley, **IV** 12b, 26b, 28b
Hall, Marshall, **IV** 24b
hallucination, **IV** 5b, 7b
Hamilton, **IV** 21b, 22a, 22b
Hammond, **IV** 28b
happiness, **II** 374b–376a
harmony, **II** 393a
Hartley, **III** 234a; **IV** 21b, 22b
Haven, **IV** 22b
Hegel, **IV** 11b, 12a, 24a
Heidegger, **IV** 14a
hell, **IV** 1b
Helmholtz, **IV** 12a, 24b
Helvétius, **IV** 21a
Heraclitus, **IV** 2a–2b
Herbert, **IV** 11b

heredity, **IV** 25a, 26a–28a
Herodotus, **IV** 1b, 7b
Heymans, **IV** 15a
Hickok, **IV** 24b
hierarchy, **II** 436b
Hippocrates, **IV** 10b
history, **IV** 1a, 9b
Hobbes, **IV** 11a, 12a, 19a, 20a, 22a
Holbach, **IV** 21a
Holmes, **IV** 26b, 28b
holy, **II** 513b, 514a
Homer, **IV** 1a–1b
Hooker, **IV** 18a
Hopkins, **IV** 22b
hormic, **I** 216a
Horney, **IV** 14a, 29a
Howe, **IV** 23b
Hubbard, **IV** 18a
Hull, **IV** 28b, 29a
human nature, **IV** 16a, 16b, 17b–29a
humanism, **IV** 16b
humanitarianism, **IV** 19b, 23b, 24a, 27a
Hume, **II** 239b; **IV** 11b, 20a, 22b
Husserl, **IV** 13b, 14a
Hutcheson, **IV** 22b
iconography, **II** 540a–540b
idea, **IV** 5a, 6a, 6b
ideal, **II** 551a
idealism, **IV** 20a, 24a, 24b
ideology, **II** 553b, 556b–558a, 558b
immortality, **IV** 1b, 2b, 3b, 4a, 7a
impressionism, **II** 575a, 580b, 583a
imprinting, **II** 584b, 585b, 586a
Indians (American), **IV** 18b
individualism, **II** 297a, 304a–304b, 309b, 310b–311a, 603a–603b; **IV** 23b, 29a
industry, **IV** 24a, 26a, 28b
insanity, **IV** 21a
introspection, **IV** 28a, 28b
introversion, **IV** 23a
irony, **IV** 10a
Islam, **II** 651a
Jackson, J. H., **IV** 13b
James, Henry, **IV** 28b
James, William, **III** 554a, 563b, 565a; **IV** 12b, 23a, 25b, 26b, 27b, 28b
Janet, **IV** 13b
Jaspers, **IV** 14a
Jastrow, **IV** 25a
Jay, **IV** 22a
Jefferson, **IV** 21a–22a
Johnson, Samuel, **IV** 17b, 19b–20a

Jouffroy, **IV** 11b
Judaism, **IV** 16b
Jung, **IV** 14a, 28b
justice, **IV** 3b
Kant, **II** 240a; **IV** 11b, 24a, 24b, 433b
Kardiner, **IV** 29a
Kinsey, **IV** 29a
Klages, **IV** 15a
knowledge, **IV** 2a, 3b, 4a–4b, 6b, 7b, 9a, 9b, 11a, 11b
Koffka, **IV** 14b
Köhler, **IV** 14b
Kretschmer, **IV** 15a
Külpe, **IV** 13a, 13b, 27a
La Mettrie, **IV** 11a, 21a, 28a
Lamarck, **IV** 11b, 26a
Lange, **IV** 23a
language, **IV** 1a, 13b
law, **III** 4a, 4b, 27a, 27b; **IV** 16b, 19a, 27b
Le Senne, **IV** 15a
learning, **II** 584b, 585b, 586a; **IV** 4a–4b
Leibniz, **IV** 11a, 11b, 20a
Lewin, **IV** 28a
libido, **IV** 14a
linguistics, **IV** 428b, 429b
Lippmann, **IV** 26b
literary criticism, **I** 597a, 600a, 600b, 602b, 603b, 605a
literary paradox, **III** 77b
literature, **IV** 1a, 16a, 16b, 22b, 24a, 25a, 330b
Locke, **II** 239b; **IV** 11a, 11b, 19a, 19b, 20a, 21b, 22b
Loeb, **IV** 14b
logic, **III** 548a–550b; **IV** 27b
logos, **IV** 1a, 2a, 2b, 10a
Lorenz, **IV** 15a
love, **III** 94a, 97b, 104b; **IV** 2b, 19a, 20a
Lovejoy, **III** 552b
loyalty, **III** 108b
Lucretius, **IV** 8a
MacAuliffe, **IV** 15a
Machiavelli, **IV** 22a
Machiavellism, **III** 123b, 124b
macrocosm and microcosm, **III** 126a, 127a, 127b, 128a, 128b, 130a
Madison, **IV** 22a
Mahan, **IV** 22b
Maine de Biran, **IV** 11b
Mandeville, **IV** 22a
Man-Machine, **III** 132b, 133b–146a
Mann, **IV** 23b
Marbe, **IV** 13a
Marcuse, **IV** 14a

Marshall, **IV** 21b
Marxism, **III** 150a, 158b, 159a, 159b
materialism, **IV** 7a, 8a, 9b, 10b, 11a, 12a, 21a, 22b, 24a
mathematics, **IV** 11a, 11b, 12b, 29a
Mather, Cotton, **IV** 18a
matter, **IV** 4b, 5a, 11a, 12a, 17a
Mead, George H., **IV** 27b
mechanism, **IV** 13b, 21a, 27b, 28a, 28b
medicine, **IV** 7a, 10b, 13b, 23b
memory, **IV** 9a, 13a, 23a, 24b
mental set, **IV** 23a
Merleau-Ponty, **IV** 14a
Messer, **IV** 13a
metaphysics, **III** 208b, 212b, 213b, 215b, 216a, 220b, 221a; **IV** 1a, 4b, 6b, 10a, 10b, 11b, 12a, 16b, 17a, 17b, 21a, 23a
Middle Ages, **IV** 9b, 16b
military, **IV** 26b
Mill, **IV** 11b
Miller, **IV** 18b
mind, **IV** 5a–10a, 15b, 17a–25a, 27a, 27b
Mitchell, S. Weir, **IV** 28b
Mitchell, Wesley C., **IV** 23a
monism, **IV** 19b, 21a
Montesquieu, **II** 9b
moral sense, **III** 233a, 234a, 235a
morality, **IV** 3b, 4a, 7a, 8a, 16b, 17b, 20a–23b
Morton, **IV** 16b–17b
motif, **III** 235b, 242a
motivation, **IV** 8a, 29a
mountains in literature, **III** 255a
music, **II** 320a–321a, 393a
mysticism, **IV** 2b, 16b, 20b, 24a
mythology, **III** 273a, 274a, 274b, 301b, 302a, 312a–314a; **IV** 4a
nationalism, **III** 328b
naturalism, **IV** 23b
naturalism in art, **III** 339b
Nature, **IV** 4b, 10b, 11a, 16a, 19a, 21a, 24a, 26b–28a
necessity, **III** 354a, 356b, 357b, 358a
Neo-Freudianism, **IV** 29a
Neo-Platonism, **IV** 8b, 24a
Netherlands, **IV** 15a
neurology, **IV** 13b, 14a, 14b
Newton, **IV** 12a, 19a

nous, **IV** 1a, 3a, 3b
One, **IV** 8b
optics, **III** 409b–410a, 420a; **IV** 12a
Orientalism, **III** 435a; **IV** 24a
Orpheus (myth), **IV** 1b, 2b
Orphism, **IV** 1b, 2b
paganism, **IV** 8b, 9a
pain, **IV** 5a, 8a, 23a
painting, **II** 575a, 580b, 583a; **IV** 465b, 471b, 472a, 472b, 473b
Parmenides, **IV** 3a
passions, **IV** 3b, 4a
pathology, **IV** 13b, 14a, 28b
Pavlov, **IV** 14a, 14b, 28a
Peabody, **IV** 24a
peace, **III** 447a
Pearson, **IV** 26b
pedagogy, **IV** 23b
Peirce, **IV** 25a
Pende, **IV** 15a
perception, **IV** 4a–9a, 23a
perennial philosophy, **III** 457b, 459a, 463a
perfectibility, **III** 469b, 474b, 475a; **IV** 20b–21a
peripatetics, **IV** 7a
personality, **IV** 15a, 15b
philosophy, **II** 551a; **IV** 1a, 1b, 2a, 3a, 4a, 4b, 6b, 7a, 8b, 11b, 12a, 15a, 16a, 17b, 19b, 20a, 22b, 23a, 24a, 24b
phrenology, **IV** 23a–23b
physicalism, **IV** 1a, 2b, 3a
physics, **IV** 11a, 12a, 12b, 16b, 17a, 24b
physiology, **IV** 3a, 5b, 7a, 11a–14a, 21a, 23b, 24b
Piaget, **IV** 13b
Plato, **II** 135b, 376a, 376b; **III** 354a,, 498a, 500b, 505a; **IV** 2a, 2b, 3a–4b, 6a, 6b, 7a, 8b, 9b, 10b, 16b, 17b
Platonism, **III** 498a, 500b, 505a, 505b; **IV** 6b, 16b, 19a, 24a
pleasure, **II** 374b, 375a, 376a, 383a; **IV** 4b, 5a, 8a, 23a
Plotinus, **IV** 8b–9a, 9b
Poe, **IV** 23b, 24a
poetry, **IV** 2b, 17b, 24a, 465b, 471b–473b
poets, **IV** 1b, 16b
politics, **IV** 16a, 16b, 18a, 22a, 23a
positivism, **III** 533b, 534a, 537a, 538a, 548a–550b; **IV** 12a
potentiality, **IV** 6a
pragmatism, **III** 552b, 553a,

554a, 557a, 559a, 563b, 565a, 569a; IV 22a
pre-Socratics, IV 2a–3a, 6b, 7b
Priestley, IV 21a
primitivism, IV 24a
Prince, IV 28b
private property, IV 21a, 23a
progress, III 628a, 630a, 640a
Protagoras, IV 10a
psyche, IV 1a–2b, 10a, 14a
psychiatry, IV 23b, 28b, 29a
psychoanalysis, IV 14a, 14b, 15a, 15b, 28b, 29a
psychosomatics, IV 8a, 13b
psychotherapy, IV 10b
Ptolemy, IV 8b
Pufendorf, IV 19a
Puritanism, IV 16b–19b
Putnam, IV 28b
Pythagoras, IV 1b, 2b, 3b
Pythagoreans, IV 2b
Quakers, IV 16b, 20a–20b
race, IV 21b, 24b, 26a, 26b, 27a
Ramism, IV 17b, 45b
Ramus, IV 16b
rationalism, IV 8a, 11a, 16b, 17b, 18b–23b
Rauch, IV 24a–24b
Ray, IV 28b
realism, IV 4a, 22b
reason, IV 3b, 4a, 4b, 7a, 8a, 9a, 11a, 13a, 16b, 17a, 17b, 18b, 19a, 20a, 20b, 23a, 23b, 24b
recapitulation, IV 58a–59a
Reid, IV 22b
religion, IV 1b, 2a, 8b, 10a, 17a, 19a, 19b, 21a, 23b, 96b, 97a, 110b, 112b, 118a, 119b
Renaissance, IV 10b, 16b
Renan, IV 12a
revolution, IV 163a
Reynolds, IV 21a
Ribot, IV 12b, 13b
right, IV 177a, 178a, 178b, 179a, 180b, 182b, 185a–185b, 186a
Roman Catholic Church, IV 25b
romanticism, IV 24a, 199a, 201b, 209b
Rome (ancient), IV 1b, 8b
Rousseau, II 276b, 277a
Royer-Collard, IV 11b
Rush, Benjamin, IV 21a
Rush, James, IV 21a–21b
Russia, IV 14a, 28a
Ryle, IV 9b

Saint-Augustine, IV 8b–9b
Saint Thomas Aquinas, IV 16b, 17b, 18a
Sartre, IV 14a
Satan, IV 16b, 18b
Schelling, IV 11b
scholasticism, IV 16b, 17a, 17b, 19b
Schopenhauer, IV 11b
science, IV 2b, 4b, 6b, 7a, 7b, 8b, 10a, 11b, 12a, 13b, 14b, 15a, 23a
scientific classification, I 465b, 466a
Scotland, IV 22b, 23b
Scythians, IV 19b
senses, IV 2a–7b, 9a, 11b–13a, 17a, 17b, 18b, 20a, 21b, 22b, 23a, 24b, 27a, 27b
sex, IV 14a, 24b, 28b, 29a
Sextus Empiricus, IV 7b
Shaftesbury, IV 22b
Sigaud, IV 15a
Silliman, IV 23b
sin, IV 17a, 22a, 23b
skepticism, IV 22b, 29a, 243a–243b, 246b, 247b, 248a, 250a
Skinner, IV 28b
slavery, IV 21b, 22a, 22b
Smith, IV 21b
Snell, IV 1b
social welfare, IV 26a
socialism, IV 25b
society, IV 14a, 15b, 17b, 19a, 20b, 21a, 25b, 27a, 27b, 29a
sociology, IV 14a, 16a, 26a, 27b, 29a
Socrates, IV 3b, 6a, 10a, 10b
Sophists, IV 10a
soul, IV 1b–5b, 6b–11a, 16b, 17a, 17b, 22b
space, IV 295a, 303a
Spencer, IV 12a, 13b, 25a, 25b, 26b
Spinoza, II 238b
spiritualism, IV 9b, 10a, 12a, 14a
Spurzheim, IV 23a, 23b
State, IV 3b, 18a, 19a, 22a
Stewart, IV 22b
Stoics, IV 7a–8b, 10b, 22b
Strato, IV 6b–7a, 8a
strife, IV 2b
structuralism, IV 324a, 326a
sublime in external nature, IV 335a
Sullivan, IV 14a, 28a
Sumner, IV 25b
Switzerland, IV 12b–13b
symbolism, IV 338b

Taine, IV 12a
Taylor, Edward, IV 16b
Thales, IV 2a
Terman, IV 26b
theodicy, IV 379a
theology, IV 11b, 16a, 16b
Theophrastus, IV 6b–7a
theriophily, IV 384b, 388a
Thoreau, IV 24a
Thorndike, IV 26b, 28a
thought, IV 1a, 1b, 2a, 2b, 3a, 6a–6b, 7a, 7b, 9a, 11a, 13a, 13b, 15a, 19a
time, IV 391b, 395a–398a
Titchener, IV 27b
Tolman, IV 28b
transcendentalism, IV 23b–24a
truth, IV 9a, 17a, 18b, 19b, 20a, 24a
unconscious, IV 11b, 14a, 28b
uniformitarianism, IV 428b, 429b
U.S.S.R., IV 14a
Unitarianism, IV 23b
U.S., IV 12b, 14a, 15a, 16a–30b
U.S. Supreme Court, IV 26b
unity of science, IV 433a, 433b, 436b
Upham, IV 22b–23a
utilitarianism, IV 445a, 445b
Utopia, IV 464a
Victorian sensibility, IV 218a, 222b
Viola, IV 15a
Volksgeist, IV 491b, 495b–496a
war, III 447a; IV 18b, 22b, 24b, 25b, 28a, 507a–508b
Ward, Lester F., IV 26a
Warner, Amos, IV 26a
Watson, John B., IV 14a, 28a
Wayland, IV 22b
wealth, IV 18a, 23a
Weber, IV 12a, 12b, 24b
Weismann, IV 26a
Wells, S. R., IV 23b
Wertheimer, IV 14b
Whitman, IV 23b, 24a
Wiersma, IV 15a
will, IV 8a, 10b, 17a, 19b, 20a, 22b, 23a, 24b, 27b
Williams, Roger, IV 18b
Winthrop, IV 16b, 18b
wisdom, IV 4a
wisdom of the fool, IV 516a
Wise, IV 19a
witchcraft, IV 18b

Wolff, IV 11b, 20a
women, IV 523b
Woolman, IV 20a–20b
work, IV 533a
World War I, IV 14b, 26b
Wortman, IV 20b
Wright, Chauncey, IV 26b
Wundt, IV 12b, 13a, 13b, 24b, 25a, 27a, 27b
Youmans, IV 25a
Zeno of Citium, IV 7a
Zeus (myth), IV 1b
See also Behaviorism
Psychopathology
  France, II 537a
  imprinting, II 585b
  positivism, III 537a
  time, IV 395a
Psychophysics
  Fechner, II 636b
  imagination, III 214a
  irrationalism, II 636b
Ptolemy, Claudius (2nd century A.D.)
  alchemy, I 29b
  allegory, I 47b
  astrology, I 119a, 121a, 515b
  astronomy, I 515b; III 77a
  axiomatization, I 166a
  cosmic images, I 515b, 516a
  cosmic voyages, I 524b
  cosmology, I 541a–542b, 543a, 544a–544b, 546a
  equality, II 138b
  game theory, II 272a
  Gnosticism, II 329b
  harmony, II 389b; IV 39b, 40b, 41b
  hierarchy, II 436b, 437a
  humanism, II 521b
  infinity, II 613a
  Islam, II 640b, 647b
  mathematics, III 182b
  medieval science, II 197a, 198b, 203b
  motion, IV 76b
  music, II 389b; III 261a, 261b, 262a
  Nature, I 542b
  optics, III 408a, 410a, 415b
  progress, III 632b
  psychology, IV 8b
  Pythagoreans, IV 39b, 40b, 41b
  relativity, IV 74b, 76b
  space, IV 295a–295b
  symmetry, IV 349a
  technology, IV 358b
  tuning, III 261a
  universal man, IV 439b
  visual rays, III 408a
  Zarlino and, III 262a

Ptolemy I, King (367?–283 B.C.), historiography, II 505a

Ptolemy II, King (309–246 B.C.), literary criticism, I 596b

Puchta, Georg Friedrich (1798–1846), *Volksgeist,* IV 493a

Puech, H. C., Gnosticism, II 327b

Puerto Rico, positivism, III 544b

Pufendorf, Samuel von (1632–1694)
authority, I 152a
axiomatization, I 165a–165b
constitutionalism, I 488b
despotism, II 1a, 4a, 4b–5b, 6a, 7a, 11a
general will, II 276a–276b
God, I 488b
Locke and, IV 258b
natural law, I 488b
natural rights, II 20a, 21a
Puritanism, IV 19a
psychology, IV 19a
reason, III 20a
slavery, II 5b, 11a
social contract, IV 258b
society, III 20a
State, II 276b
war, II 6a

Puffer, Ethel, beauty, I 209a

Pugin, Augustus Welby Northmore (1812–1852), Gothic, II 369a, 372a

Puibusque, Adolphe-Louis de, literature, III 84a

Pulsars, I 570a

Punic language, III 61b

Punishment
Aristotle, II 135a
Bible, III 283a
casuistry, I 258b
Christianity, I 258b
determinism, II 241a
disease, II 396b
Epicureanism, II 135a; IV 176a
Epicurus, II 135a
fortune, fate, and chance, II 229b
free will, II 135a; II 241a
God, II 27b
good, IV 174a, 176a, 179a
Greece (ancient), II 565b–566b, 677a, 679b
happiness, II 381a, 385b
human nature, III 572b, 575a, 576a
impiety, II 565b–566b
Judaism, II 30a
justice, II 653a; III 575a

law, II 677a, 679b, 686a, 687a, 688b; III 3a, 33b, 35a, 35b, 567a, 575a
Mill, IV 179a
morality, III 35b
motif, III 239b
music, III 266b
mythology, III 283a
Nature, III 35a
pain, II 385b
perfectiblity, III 465a
Plato, II 135a, 566a
pleasure, II 381a, 385b
pragmatism, III 565a
psychology, IV 16b–19b
Pythagoras, IV 31a
Pythagoreans, IV 31a, 31b
right, IV 174a, 176a, 179a
Roman Catholic Church, I 258b
Rome (ancient), II 686a, 687a, 688b
theodicy, IV 379b, 380b

Puppet shows, III 501a

Purchas, Samuel (1575?–1626)
Cosmic Fall, I 506b
hierarchy, II 436b

Purgation, catharsis, I 264b

Purgatory, eschatology, II 156a

Purification
hermeticism, II 432b
impiety, II 564b
mythology, III 292a
Parmenides, III 464b
Pythagoreans, IV 31b–32a

Puritanism
Anglicanism, IV 19b
Aristotelianism, IV 16b
Aristotle, IV 16b
Augustinianism, IV 109a
authority, IV 18a–18b
Bradford, IV 17b–18a
Brattle, IV 18b
Buckingham, Duke of, I 650a
Calvinism, IV 16b
capitalism, I 396a–397a, 656a
Cartesianism, IV 18b
Christianity, IV 16b
class, IV 18a
Cotton, IV 18a
covenant, I 396a
deism, I 649b, 650a
democracy, I 656a–657a
Dryden, I 650a
dualism, IV 16b
education, IV 18b–19b
Edwards, IV 16b, 19a–19b, 109b
Eliot, John, IV 18a
Enlightenment, II 94a; IV

20b
equality, II 142b–143a
equity, II 152b–153a
Etherege, I 650a
God, IV 18a, 18b
Gorton, IV 18b
Great Britain, IV 19a
Halifax, Duke of, I 650a
harmony, II 388b
hierarchy, II 442a
history, I 390b
Hooker, IV 18a
Hubbard, IV 18a
human nature, IV 16b, 17b, 18a, 18b, 19a, 19b
humanism, IV 16b
Indians (American), IV 18b
individualism, II 596a, 603a
Johnson, Samuel, IV 17b
law, IV 16b
mammonism, I 396b, 397a
Mather, IV 18a
metaphysics, IV 16b
Middle Ages, IV 16b
Morton, IV 16b–17b
music, II 388b
mysticism, IV 16b
mythology, III 300a
periodization in literary history, III 483b
Plato, IV 16b
Platonism, IV 16b, 19a
poetry, III 530a
political theory, IV 18a
predestination, II 30b
Pufendorf, IV 19a
Ramism, IV 17b
Ramus, IV 16b
rationalism, IV 16b, 18b
religion, IV 109a, 109b, 111a
Renaissance, IV 16b
Saint Thomas Aquinas, IV 16b, 18a
scholasticism, IV 16b
Sedley, I 650a
Shadwell, I 650a
social contract, IV 254b, 256a
socialism, IV 287b
soul, IV 16b
symbolism, IV 341b
Taylor, IV 16b
thought, IV 19a
tragic sense, IV 415a, 415b
U.S., II 596a; III 483b
Victorians, IV 217b, 219a
wealth, IV 18a
Williams, Roger, IV 18b
Winthrop, IV 16b, 18b
Wise, IV 19a
witchcraft, IV 18b

Pushkin, Alexander (1799–1837)

Faust (legend), III 250a
literary criticism, I 606a
realism in literature, IV 55a
romanticism, IV 191b

Putman, Hilary, positivism, III 550b

Putnam, James J. (1846–1918), psychology, IV 28b

Puttenham, George (d. 1590)
creativity in art, I 587a–587b
God, I 587b
poetry, III 529b, 530a

Pyrrha (myth), primitivism, III 579b

Pyrrho of Elis (365?–?275 B.C.)
Buddhism, I 254b
Platonism, III 504b
skepticism, IV 234a, 235a, 236a, 237b, 238b, 239b–240a, 241a

Pyrrhonism
beauty, I 198a, 198b
Chain of Being, I 331b
literary paradox, III 79b
Montaigne, III 79b
mythology, III 302a–302b
natural law, III 16a–16b
Platonism, III 504b
rationalism, III 302a–302b
skepticism, IV 234a, 234b, 237b, 239a, 240a, 241a, 242b, 243a, 243b, 245a, 247a, 248b

Pyrrhus (318?–272 B.C.), chance images, I 340b–341a, 341b, 345a, 346a, 349a

Pythagoras (6th century B.C.)
acoustics, III 260b–261a
allegory, I 42b
Apollo (myth), IV 31a, 35a
Aristotle and, IV 31a
arithmetic, I 462b; IV 31a
asceticism, I 632a
askesis, IV 31b
astrology, I 120a
axiomatization, I 163b
Blake and, I 579b
body, IV 34a
classification of the sciences, I 462b
consonance, III 261a, 261b
cosmos, I 579b; IV 39a, 47a, 50a
creativity in art, I 578b, 579a–581a
cycles, I 623b
Diogenes Laërtius and, IV 38a
divination, IV 31a
dualism, II 40a–40b

Eighteenth Century view of, I 86a

Empedocles and, IV 2b, 31b–32a

ethics, IV 37a

fate, IV 31a

geometry, I 462b

harmony, I 579b;
II 390a

III269a; IV 38a, 39a

Hesiod and, III 273a

Hindemith and, I 579b

Hippolytus and, IV 39a

historiography, II 471a

Holst and, I 579b

Homer and, III 273a

human nature, III 572b–573a

imagination, III 215a

Incarnation, IV 31a

infinity, II 604b, 607a

Islam, II 650a

Judaism, IV 40b

Kepler and, I 579b

language, III 65b

law, I 632a

linguistics, III 65b

mathematics, II 390a; III 179b; IV 31a, 46b–47a

measurement, IV 399b

metaphysics, III 215a; IV 33b, 34b, 36b, 37a, 37b

microcosm, IV 32b, 33a, 36a, 40a

monochords, IV 39a

morality, IV 31a, 37a

motion, IV 32b, 34a, 36a, 39a, 40a

music, I 462b, 579b, 580a; II 390a; III 260b–261a, 261b, 269a, 271a; IV 38a–38b, 39a–42a

mythology, III 273a

Nature, I 632a

necessity, III 353a, 356a

Neo-Platonism, III 372a, 510a

numbers, III 269a; IV 31a, 32a, 37a, 39a, 46b–47a, 399b

order, IV 50a

perfectibility, III 464b

Plato and, III 523b; IV 3b, 31a–37b, 38b–41b, 46b

Platonism, III 523b

primitivism, III 580b

psyche, IV 32b

psychology, IV 1b, 2b, 3b

punishment, IV 31a

Pythagoreans, IV 30b–33a, 35a, 36b, 37a–39a

ratio, III 260b–261a

rationalism, IV 46b–47a, 50a

reincarnation, I 644b, 645a

relativity, IV 83a, 87b

reward, IV 31a

soul, III 572b–573a; IV 31a–32b, 34a, 36b, 37a

space, IV 399b–400a

time, IV 399b

tuning, III 261a, 261b

universe, II 390a; IV 32a, 37a, 39a

Yeats and, I 579b

Pythagorean scale, IV 39a–39b

Pythagoreans, IV 30b–42a

acquired characteristics, II 617b

aesthetics, I 514a; II 217a, 219a

Alain of Lille, IV 41a

Alcmaeon, IV 34a

Anaximander, IV 38b

angels, IV 40b–41a

animals, IV 31a, 31b, 33a

Anselmi, Giorgio, IV 41a

Apollo (myth), IV 31a, 35a

Arabs, IV 41a

Arcesilaus, IV 37b

architecture, IV 41b

Archytas, IV 32b–33a, 37a–37b, 38a

Aristides Quintilianus, IV 39a, 40a–40b

Aristotle, I 578b, 580a–580b; IV 31a, 31b, 33a, 33b–38a, 40a, 41a, 400b

arithmetic, IV 31a, 32a, 33a, 38a, 39a, 40b, 42a

asceticism, IV 31b

askesis, IV 31b, 32a

astrology, IV 40b

astronomy, IV 32b, 40b

atomism, IV 32a, 34a

Babylonia, IV 38b

Bardi, IV 41a

beauty, I 196b; II 217a

Being, I 580a–580b

belief, IV 33b, 35b

Bettini, IV 41b

Bible, IV 38b, 40b

biology, IV 35b

Bode, IV 42a

body, IV 31b, 34a

Boethius, IV 40b, 41a

Burkert, IV 32b

Cassiodorus, IV 41a

catharsis, I 269a

causation, IV 34a

Chalcidius, IV 39b

Chaldeans, IV 38b

Christianity, IV 40b–41a

Cicero, IV 40a

classification of the arts, I 457a

Clement of Alexandria, IV 40b

clothing, IV 31b

continuity, I 493b, 498b

Cornford, F. M., IV 32a

cosmic images, I 514a, 515b, 517a

cosmos, IV 34a, 35a, 35b, 37b, 38a–42a

Creation, IV 38b, 39a

cults, III 505a

cycles, I 621b, 623b; IV 31b

Dante, IV 41a

Demiurge, IV 39a–39b

Democritus, IV 34a

demonology, I 668a, 670a

diet, IV 31b, 32a

Diogenes Laërtius, IV 35a, 36a, 38a

Dionysus (myth), IV 31a

divination, IV 31a, 32a

Dodds, IV 31a

dualism, IV 34a–34b, 346b

dyad, IV 34a, 34b, 35b

Eddington, IV 42a

dialectic, III 171b

elements, IV 40a

Empedocles, IV 31b–32a, 37a

entropy, II 117b

Er (myth), IV 38b, 39b, 41a

ethics, IV 32a, 32b, 37a

Euclid, IV 39b

evil, IV 36b

fate, IV 31a

Ficino, IV 39b, 41a

Fludd, IV 41b

Frank, Erich, IV 36a

Gafori, IV 41a

geometry, IV 33b, 38a, 39a, 40a, 40b, 41b

Gnosticism, IV 40b–41a

Goldschmidt, V., IV 42a

good, IV 36a, 37a, 37b

Greece (ancient), IV 30b–37b, 38a–41a, 41b

Guillaume de Conches, IV 41a

harmony, I 579a–579b, 580b; II 217a, 389a, 389b; IV 38a–42a

Heraclitus, IV 34b, 38b

Hesiod, IV 32b

Hippasus of Metapontum, IV 32a

Homer, IV 32a, 32b

humanism, II 521a; IV 41a

Iamblichus, IV 32a, 35a, 35b, 39a

idea, II 546a; IV 34b, 35a, 35b, 36b

immortality, I 645a; IV 34a

Incarnation, IV 31a–32a

incommensurability, IV 32a

irrationalism, II 638a

Isocrates, IV 31b

John Philoponus, IV 36b

Josephus, IV 40b

Judaism, IV 38b, 40b–41a

justice, II 653a, 655b, 656a

Kaiser, Wilhelm, IV 42a

Kayser, Hans, IV 42a

kenon, IV 298b

Kepler, IV 41b, 42a

Kircher, IV 41a

knowledge, IV 33b, 35b

Leibniz, IV 41b

Leonardo da Vinci, IV 41a

Leucippus, IV 37a

literary paradox, III 76b

Macrobius, IV 40a

macrocosm, IV 32b, 33a, 36a

Man-Machine, III 132a, 134b

mathematics, I 539b, 580a, 580b; III 171a, 171b, 172a; IV 31a, 32a–40a

matter, III 187a, 188a

measurement, IV 399b, 400a, 400b

Medici family, IV 41a

Mersenne, IV 41b

metaphor, III 203b

metaphysics, III 215a, 505a; IV 33b, 34b, 36b, 37a, 37b

Middle Ages, IV 39b, 41a

mind, IV 31b, 32b, 37b

monads, IV 37a

monasticism, IV 31a–31b

monism, IV 32a

monochords, IV 39a, 39b, 40b

morality, IV 31a, 37a

motion, I 539b; IV 390b

music, I 269a; II 389a, 389b; III 260b, 261b, 262a

mysticism, IV 32a, 35b

mythology, IV 37a, 38b, 39b, 41a

Nature, III 347a; IV 31b, 32a, 38a

Near East, IV 38b

necessity, III 353a; IV 39b

Neo-Platonism, III 372a, 376b; IV 32b, 39a, 39b, 41a

Neo-Pythagoreans, IV 31b, 32a, 35b, 39a, 39b, 40a, 42a

Nicomachus, IV 35b

nous, IV 32b, 34a, 37a

numbers, III 399a, 403a, 405a; IV 31a, 32a, 33a–39b, 42a

Numenius, **IV** 40b
Orientalism, **IV** 38b
Orphism, **IV** 31a, 31b, 32a, 33a
Palladio, **IV** 41b
Parmenides, **IV** 32a–32b, 37a, 38b, 400a
perception, **IV** 34a, 35b
perennial philosophy, **III** 459a
Philo Judaeus, **IV** 38b, 40b
Philolaus, **IV** 32b, 37a–37b
philosophy, **IV** 31b–32b
physiology, **IV** 32b
Pindar, **IV** 32a
Plato, **I** 578b, 579a–581a; **III** 353a–353b, 503a; **IV** 31a–37b, 38b–41b
Platonism, **III** 503a, 505a; **IV** 34b, 35a, 36b, 37a
Plotinus, **IV** 36b
pluralism, **IV** 35b, 36a
Plutarch, **III** 505a; **IV** 36b, 38b
poetry, **IV** 31b, 32a, 40a, 41a
Pontus de Tyard, **IV** 41a
Porphyry, **IV** 35a
pre-Socratics, **IV** 38b
Proclus, **IV** 33b, 36a, 36b, 39b
progress, **III** 628b
Pseudo-Dionysius, **IV** 41a
psyche, **IV** 32b, 34a, 37a
psychology, **IV** 2b
Ptolemy, **IV** 39b, 40b, 41b
punishment, **IV** 31a, 31b
purification, **IV** 31b–32a
Pythagoras, **IV** 30b–33a, 35a–38a, 39a
rationalism, **IV** 41b
reality, **IV** 35b
Regino of Prüm, **IV** 41a
reincarnation, **I** 645a
religion, **III** 203b; **IV** 31a
Renaissance, **IV** 39b–41b
reward, **IV** 31a, 31b
Riccioni, **IV** 41b
Rohde, **IV** 31a
Sachs, **IV** 35a
Saint Jerome, **IV** 40b
Schopenhauer, **IV** 41b
science, **IV** 32a, 35b
senses, **IV** 33b, 34b, 35b
skepticism, **IV** 37b, 41a
Socrates, **IV** 31b, 34a, 34b
soul, **IV** 31a–37b
space, **IV** 298b
Speusippus, **IV** 33b, 34b–36b
Sumer-Babylonia, **III** 171a
superstition, **IV** 31b
Symmachus, **IV** 40b

symmetry, **IV** 346b
Tannery, **IV** 32a
Theaetetus, **IV** 35a
theodicy, **IV** 380a
Theophrastus, **IV** 36a
Thimus, **IV** 41b
time, **IV** 389a–390b, 399b, 400a, 400b
unity, **IV** 34a, 35b
universality, **IV** 34b, 35b
universe, **IV** 31b, 32a, 33a, 34a, 37a, 37b, 38a–42a
visible numbers, **I** 580b
visions, **IV** 40a
Von Fritz, **IV** 32a
Whitehead, **IV** 42a
William of Ockham, **IV** 35b
Xenocrates, **IV** 33b, 34b–35a, 36b–37a
Xenophanes, **IV** 31a, 32b
Zeno of Citium, **IV** 32a–32b, 37a
Zeus (myth), **IV** 37a

Q

Qadarites, Islam, **II** 641b
Quadrivium, music, **III** 260b, 270b, 271b
Quakers
  Augustinianism, **IV** 109a
  deism, **I** 649b
  Enlightenement, **IV** 20b
  ethics, **III** 441a
  human nature, **IV** 20a
  peace, **III** 441a
  perfectibility, **III** 467b–468b
  psychology, **IV** 16b, 20a–20b
  reformation, **IV** 68b
  Woolman, **IV** 20a–20b
Quantum mechanics
  Copenhagen interpretation, **II** 589a, 590b
  indeterminacy, **II** 586a, 588a, 588b–591a, 592b–593a
  infinity, **II** 607a
  mathematical formalism, **II** 588b
  nuclear indefinite, **II** 607b
  perturbation theory, **II** 591a
  positivism, **III** 548b, 549a, 550b
  space, **IV** 300a, 304b
  statistics, **II** 591a–592a
Quantum theory, **III** 620a
  cosmology, **I** 555a, 568a
  relativity, **IV** 85b, 91b
  space, **IV** 296a, 300a

time, **IV** 397b
truth, **I** 322b–323a
Quarles, Francis (1592–1644), mythology, **III** 296a
Quasars, cosmology, **I** 568a
Quesnay, François (1694–1774)
  China, **I** 362b–363a
  natural liberty, **II** 62a
  Orientalism, **III** 428a
  socialism, **IV** 292b
  utility, **IV** 453a
Quételet, Lambert Adolphe (1796–1874)
  chance, **I** 338a
  Keynes and, **III** 614b
  probability, **III** 614b
  progress, **III** 640b
Quevedo, Francisco (1580–1645), baroque in literature, **I** 190a, 192a, 195a
Quietism
  democracy, **I** 655b
  France, **I** 595a
  Orientalism, **III** 430b
  prophecy, **III** 662a–662b
  romanticism, **I** 595a
  socialism, **IV** 287a
  Spain, **I** 595a
  State, **I** 655b
Quincy, Quatremère de baroque in literature, **I** 188b
Quine, Willard van Orman
  antinomy of pure reason, **I** 93a
  positivism, **III** 547a, 550b
  pragmatism, **III** 553b
Quinet, Edgar (1803–1875)
  mythology, **III** 306b
  progress, **III** 637a–637b
  symbolism, **IV** 344b
Quintana, Ricardo, satire, **IV** 213b
Quintilian (1st century A.D.)
  aesthetics, **II** 219b
  allegory, **I** 41b
  art, **III** 305a, 309b
  classification of the arts, **I** 456b, 457b–459a
  education, **II** 81a–81b
  equity, **II** 151a
  evolution of literature, **II** 170a
  freedom of speech, **II** 261b
  irony, **II** 628a, 628b, 629a
  literary criticism, **I** 596b
  oratory, **II** 170a
  painting, **IV** 468a
  poetics, **III** 526a, 526b, 529a
  pragmatism, **III** 554a
  rhetoric, **IV** 169b–172a
  satire, **IV** 211a
  style, **IV** 330b–332a

Quintus Fabius Maximus (d. about 290 B.C.), temperance, **IV** 377a
Quispel, G., Gnosticism, **II** 330b
Qumrān, **II** 42a, 339b

R

Rabanus Maurus (776?–856), mythology, **III** 288b
  work, **IV** 531b
Rabelais, François (1494?–1553)
  ambiguity, **I** 54a, 54b
  baroque in literature, **I** 190b, 195a
  comedy, **I** 469b
  cosmic voyages, **I** 530b
  education, **I** 54a
  Gothic, **II** 367b, 368a
  law, **III** 11a
  literary paradox, **III** 78a–78b, 79b
  literature, **III** 82b
  Platonism, **III** 507b
  realism in literature, **IV** 54a
  wisdom of the fool, **IV** 519b
Race
  acquired characteristics, **II** 618a, 620b, 622a
  Acton, **III** 328b
  antiprimitivism, **III** 604a
  determinism, **II** 22a
  dignity, **IV** 136a–136b
  equality, **II** 139a–139b, 144b
  ethics, **III** 446b; **IV** 70b
  evolution, **III** 646a
  fascism, **III** 674a
  Greece (ancient), **II** 500a–500b
  hierarchy, **IV** 491b
  historiography, **II** 22a, 500a–500b, 504b, 509b
  history, **II** 22a
  inheritance, **II** 618a, 620b, 622a, 626a
  international peace, **III** 448b
  intolerance, **IV** 116a
  Jung, **IV** 58b
  Marxism, **III** 148b
  mythology, **III** 280b, 287a, 308b, 315b
  nationalism, **III** 328b–329a, 330b, 331a, 336b, 337a, 337b
  natural law, **III** 25b
  natural selection, **III** 646a
  Orientalism, **III** 433b
  pangenesis, **II** 626a
  peace, **III** 446b

perfectibility, **III** 471a
primitivism, **III** 604a
progress, **III** 639a, 646a, 648a
protest movements, **III** 674a
psychology, **IV** 21b, 24b, 26a, 26b, 27a
recapitulation, **IV** 58b, 59a
relativism, **IV** 70b
religion, **IV** 116a
Renaissance, **IV** 136a–136b
revolution, **IV** 164b, 166a
romanticism, **IV** 197a, 203a
Russian Revolution (October 1917), **IV** 164b
Social Darwinism, **III** 646a
State, **IV** 318a
Switzerland, **III** 328b, 329a
totalitarianism, **IV** 408b, 410a
Volksgeist, **IV** 491b, 494a, 495a
vox populi, **IV** 496b
war, **III** 448b
women, **IV** 529a–529b
Rachel, Mlle (1820–1858), classicism, **I** 452a
Racial discrimination, blacks, **I** 439a, 440a–440b; **III** 12b, 13a
Racial prejudice
blacks, **I** 439a, 440a–440b
Brazil, **III** 542b
Buddhism, **I** 252b
Ceylon, **III** 337a
evil, **II** 169a
Latin America, **III** 542b
law, **III** 12b–13a
nationalism, **III** 328b–329a, 330b, 331a, 337a, 337b
positivism, **III** 542b
progress, **III** 648b
U.S., **I** 16a–16b; **II** 139a–139b, 251a; **III** 9b
Wagner, Richard, **III** 330b
Racine, Jean Baptiste (1639–1699)
baroque in literature, 190b, 192b, 193b, 195a
catharsis, **I** 268a
classicism, **I** 452a, 455b
evolution of literature, **II** 172a
genius, **II** 294b
literary criticism, **I** 600b, 601a
love, **III** 103a
poetics, **III** 529b
structuralism, **IV** 327b
tragic sense, **IV** 415a
Racine, Louis (1692–1763), ideal, **II** 550a
Rackham, H., **III** 287a
Radar measurement, **IV** 405b

time, **IV** 405b
Radcliffe-Brown, A. R., structuralism, **IV** 325b
Radhakrishnan, Sarvepalli
immortality, **I** 645a
reincarnation, **I** 645a
Radiation cosmology, **I** 550b, 553a–553b, 555a, 556a, 567a, 567b, 568a, 569b
optics, **III** 420b
relativity, **IV** 84a
space, **IV** 303a, 303b, 304a
Radicalism
class, **III** 672b, 673a
conservatism, **I** 479b–480a
cycles, **I** 627a
deism, **I** 651b
democracy, **III** 673a
democrats of 1848, **III** 673a
demonstrations, **III** 673a
France, **III** 52b, 673a
Hobbes, **IV** 256b
ideology, **II** 560a; **III** 672b, 673a
Italy, **III** 673a
Jacobins, **III** 673a
justice, **III** 671a
labor, **III** 675b
liberalism, **III** 52b–55b
Locke, **IV** 258b
Machiavellism, **III** 124a
Middle Ages, **IV** 253a
progress, **III** 625a, 671a
prophecy, **III** 661a
protest movements, **III** 671a–674b, 675b
reform, **III** 673a
revisionism, **IV** 267a
revolution, **III** 673a; **IV** 165a
riots, **III** 673a
Saint-Simon, **III** 534b
social contract, **IV** 253a, 256b, 258b, 262a, 262b
socialism, **III** 673a, 673b
society, **III** 673a
totalitarianism, **IV** 408a, 408b, 409b
utopianism, **III** 671a
Victorian sentiment, **IV** 220a, 223b
war, **IV** 505b
Winstanley, **I** 479b
women, **IV** 529b
Radin, Paul, religion, **IV** 96a
Radio, **III** 419b
optics, **III** 419b
Radioactivity
catastrophism, **IV** 423a
chance, **I** 339b
linguistics, **IV** 426b, 430a
uniformitarianism, **IV** 423a, 426b, 430a

Raei, Jan de
causation, **I** 302a–302b
teleology, **I** 302a–302b
Raffaelli, Giuseppe, temperance, **IV** 377b
Raglan, Lord (1788–1855), motif, **III** 240a–240b
mythology, **III** 240a–240b, 281a–282b, 311a
Rahab (myth), **III** 281b
Rahner, Karl
God, **II** 365b
heresy, **II** 430a
Raikes, Robert (1735–1811), philanthropy, **III** 490a
Raimondi, Cosma, humanism, **IV** 133b
Rainaldus (c. 1063 A.D.)
art, **II** 300a
genius, **II** 300a
Rainborough, Colonel
equality, **II** 142b, 143a, 144a
social contract, **IV** 256a
Rainbows
mythology, **III** 279b, 280a
Newton, **III** 394a–394b
Noah (Bible), **III** 394b
optics, **III** 418a
Raleigh, Walter (1552?–1618)
Cosmic Fall, **I** 506b
Hariot and, **I** 133b
hierarchy, **II** 436b
literature, **IV** 332b
mythology, **III** 294a
style, **IV** 332b
Rameau, Jean Philippe (1683–1764)
genius, **II** 322b–323b
geometry, **III** 263b
music, **II** 322b–323a, 323b; **III** 263a–263b
Ramée, Pierre de la, *see* Ramus, Petrus
Ramism, **IV** 42b–45b
Agricola, **IV** 43a
algebra, **IV** 42b
allegory, **IV** 44a
anthropology, **IV** 45b
argumentation, **IV** 43a–43b
Aristotelianism, **IV** 42b, 43a, 44b, 45b
Aristotle, **IV** 43b
arithmetic, **IV** 42b
art, **IV** 44a, 45a, 45b
Athena (myth), **IV** 44a, 44b
Bible, **IV** 45a
Boethius, **IV** 43b
bourgeois, **IV** 44b, 45a
Bruno, **IV** 44b
Calvinism, **IV** 44b
Cartesianism, **IV** 42b

Christianity, **IV** 42b, 44b, 45a
Cicero, **IV** 43a, 44a, 44b
Colleoni, **IV** 44a
common sense, **IV** 43a
computers, **IV** 44b
craftsmanship, **IV** 45a, 45b
Descartes, **IV** 43b
diagrams, **IV** 44a
education, **IV** 42b, 43b, 44a, 44b, 45a, 45b
Eliot, John, **IV** 44b
empiricism, **IV** 45a
encyclopedias, **IV** 44a, 45b
experiments, **IV** 45a
France, **IV** 44b, 45a
Freige, **IV** 44a
Galen, **IV** 43b
geometry, **IV** 42b
Germany, **IV** 44b
grammar, **IV** 42b, 45a
Great Britain, **IV** 42b, 44b
history, **IV** 45b
humanism, **IV** 42b, 43a, 44b, 45a–45b
iconography, **IV** 44a–44b, 45b
imagination, **IV** 44b
invention, **IV** 43a, 43b
Johnson, Samuel, **IV** 44b
judgment, **IV** 43a, 43b
knowledge, **IV** 42b, 44a–45a
language, **IV** 45a
logic, **IV** 42b–45b
mathematics, **IV** 42b, 43a, 43b, 45a
Mather, Cotton, **IV** 44b
Mather, Increase, **IV** 44b
medicine, **IV** 44b
Melanchthon, **IV** 43b
memory, **IV** 43a, 44a–44b
Mercury (myth), **IV** 44a
metaphysics, **IV** 42b
methodology, **IV** 43b–44b
Middle Ages, **IV** 43a, 44b, 45a
mythology, **IV** 44a–44b
necessity, **IV** 43a
observation, **IV** 45a
oratory, **IV** 42b, 43b–44a
philosophy, **IV** 42b, 45a
physics, **IV** 42b, 45a
Piscator, **IV** 45a
poetry, **IV** 43a, 43b, 45b
probability, **IV** 43a–43b
Protestantism, **IV** 42b, 44b
psychology, **IV** 17b, 45b
Puritanism, **IV** 17b
Ramus, **IV** 42b–45b
rationalism, **IV** 42b
Reformation, **IV** 42b, 44b
Renaissance, **IV** 43a, 44a, 45a–45b

rhetoric, **IV** 42b, 43a, 45a
Scandinavia, **IV** 44b
scholasticism, **IV** 42b
science, **IV** 42b–43a, 45a
sculpture, **IV** 44a
sociology, **IV** 45b
Sprat, **IV** 45a
Sturm, **IV** 43b
Switzerland, **IV** 44b
syllogism, **IV** 43b
symbolism, **IV** 44a
Talon, **IV** 42b
theology, **IV** 45a
truth, **IV** 43a
typography, **IV** 42b, 44a, 44b, 45b
U.S., **IV** 42b, 44b
universe, **IV** 44a, 45a
Verrocchio, **IV** 44a
Yates, **IV** 44b
Zeus (myth), **IV** 44a, 44b
Zwinger, **IV** 44a
Ramos, Jorge Abelardo, nationalism, **III** 335b
Ramos de Pareja, Bartolomé, music, **III** 261b
Ramsay, Allan (1686–1758)
Newton and, **III** 394b
Ramsay, Allan (1713–1784)
neo-classicism in art, **III** 365a
Ramsay, André-Michel (1686–1743), Figurism, **I** 359b, 360a, 360b
Ramsay, David, revolution, **IV** 156a
Ramsey, Frank P.
game theory, **II** 265b
Peirce and, **III** 561a
pragmatism, **III** 553a, 561a
social welfare, **IV** 278b
utility, **IV** 457a–457b
Ramus, Petrus (1515–1572),
Agricola and, **IV** 43a
argumentation, **IV** 43a–43b
Aristotelianism, **IV** 42b, 43a, 44b
Bacon and, **I** 173b, 175b, 176a
classification of the arts, **I** 459a
education, **IV** 42b, 43b, 44a
historiography, **IV** 148b
humanism, **IV** 42b, 43a, 45a–45b, 135b
invention, **IV** 43a, 43b
judgment, **IV** 43a, 43b
knowledge, **IV** 42b
language, **IV** 45a
law, **III** 11a
logic, **IV** 42b–43b
mathematics, **IV** 42b, 43a, 43b

memory, **IV** 43a
necessity, **IV** 43a
philosophy, **IV** 42b
probability, **IV** 43a–43b
Protestantism, **IV** 42b, 44b
psychology, **IV** 16b
Puritanism, **IV** 16b
Ramism, **IV** 42b–45b
rationalism, **IV** 42b
rhetoric, **IV** 42b, 43a, 171b
scholasticism, **IV** 42b
Rand, Ayn, individualism, **II** 579a
Randall, Francis B., Romanticism, **IV** 208b
Randall, Hastings, utilitarianism, **IV** 446b
Randall, John Hermann (1899–   )
imagination, **III** 210a
methodology, **III** 382b
Newton and, **III** 382b
pragmatism, **III** 553a, 554b
romanticism, **IV** 209a
Rank, Otto (1884–1939)
art and play, **I** 107a
literature, **III** 242a
motif, **III** 242a
mythology, **III** 281a–282b, 312b
Ranke, Leopold von (1795–1886)
balance of power, **I** 186b
China, **I** 370a
conservatism, **I** 479b
determinism, **II** 20b
Hegel, **II** 412a
historicism, **II** 457b, 459a–462b
historiography, **II** 20b, 475b, 485b, 488b–489a, 490a, 491a, 491b, 492a, 492b, **493a, 493b, 494a, 494b**
history, **I** 409a, **II** 20b
Machiavellism, **III** 124a
periodization in history, **III** 477b
Volksgeist, **IV** 493b
Ransom, John Crowe (1888–   )
irony, **II** 633a
literary criticism, **I** 603a
Raoul of Caen, historiography, **II** 473b
Raphael (1483–1520)
art, **II** 298a, 302b–303a, 309a, 309b
chance images, **I** 347a
classicism, **I** 455b
genius, **II** 298a, 302b–303a, 309a, 309b
iconography, **II** 529a, 538a
impressionism, **II** 570a,

573a
mythology, **III** 290a, 291a
neo-classicism in art, **III** 365b, 368b
sculptural style, **II** 570a
temperance, **IV** 372a
Rapin, René
genius, **II** 294a
rhetoric, **IV** 171b–172a
style, **IV** 331b
taste, **IV** 355a
Rashnu (myth), salvation, **IV** 231b
Rask, Rasmus (1787–1832)
language, **II** 671a
linguistics, **III** 66b–67b, 68a; **IV** 427b
uniformitarianism, **IV** 427b
Ratio
Galileo, **III** 263a
music, **III** 260b–261a, 262a, 262b, 263a
Pythagoras, **III** 260b–261a
Rationalism, **IV** 46a–51b
Abelard, **III** 382a
acquired characteristics, **II** 617a
aesthetics, **IV** 355b, 356a
analogy, **IV** 46b
anatomy, **IV** 48a
Anaxagoras, **IV** 48b, 50a
Anaximander, **IV** 46b
Anaximenes, **IV** 46b, 47a
Antiphon, **IV** 48b
architecture, **IV** 46a
argumentation, **IV** 49a
Aristophanes, **IV** 48b
Aristotelianism, **IV** 51a
Aristotle, **IV** 48a, 49a, 49b, 50b, 51a, 122a, 175b
art, **IV** 46a, 46b, 49a, 50b
atomism, **IV** 51a
Bayle, **III** 301b
behavior, **IV** 49b
Bentham, **III** 233b, 234a
Blount, **III** 301a
Burke, **IV** 205b
catastrophism, **IV** 419b
causation, **III** 302a, 302b; **IV** 48a–48b, 50a, 50b
change, **IV** 47a, 49a, 50b
Christianity, **III** 301a–303b
Cicero, **IV** 50a, 50b
climate, **IV** 48a
comedy, **IV** 48b
communism, **III** 645b
Comte, **III** 303b
Cornford, **IV** 48a
cosmos, **IV** 46a, 47a, 50a–51a
craftsmanship, **IV** 46b, 49a, 50b
Creation, **IV** 46b
culture, **IV** 48a–48b

custom, **IV** 48b
de Brosses, **III** 302a, 302b, 303a, 303b
deism, **III** 301a–303a
Demiurge, **IV** 50a
democracy, **I** 656a
Democritus, **IV** 51a
Descartes, **I** 296b
desire, **IV** 50a
dignity, **IV** 136b, 142b
disease, **II** 395b, 396b; **IV** 48a
Dodds, **IV** 46a
Dupuis, **III** 302a, 303b
duty, **IV** 50a
education, **IV** 48b, 49b
Eleatics, **IV** 47b
emotion, **IV** 50a
empiricism, **I** 218b; **III** 302b; **IV** 48a
Enlightenment, **III** 494a
environment, **IV** 48a
Epicurus, **IV** 51a
Erasistratus, **IV** 48a
error, **IV** 48a, 51a
ethics, **III** 233a; **IV** 49a–50a, 319a, 320a, 320b, 321a
Euclid, **IV** 47b
Euripides, **IV** 49a, 367a
evil, **II** 162b, 163a, 166b, 167a, 167b
evolution, **III** 646b
experiments, **IV** 48a
Fontenelle, **III** 301a, 301b, 302a, 302b
Forms, **IV** 47a–47b, 49b
freedom, **IV** 50a
genius, **II** 318b
geometry, **IV** 47b
God, **II** 357b, 349b–351b; **IV** 46a, 46b, 47a, 48b, 49b, 50b
good, **IV** 46a, 49b, 50a, 173b, 175a, 175b, 176a, 179b, 181b
Great Britain, **IV** 199b
Greece (ancient), **IV** 46a–51b
happiness, **II** 375b, 380a; **IV** 50a
harmony, **II** 390b
health, **II** 395b, 396b; **IV** 48a
Hegelian, *see* Hegel
Heraclitus, **IV** 47a
Hesiod, **IV** 46a, 46b
hierarchy, **II** 445b
hippies, **IV** 48b
Hippocrates, **IV** 47b–48a
historiography, **IV** 48a–48b, 147b
history, **III** 301a–303b
Hobbes, **III** 11a

Homer, IV 46a, 46b
Hume, III 232a, 232b–233a, 302a, 303a–303b; IV 247b
Hutcheson, III 231b, 232a
ideology, II 553a
ignorance, IV 49a
imagination, III 214a, 217b
impiety, IV 48b
individualism, IV 49b
intolerance, III 301a
irrationalism, II 634b–635a, 635b, 636b, 637a, 637b, 638a, 638b; III 301a, 302a, 309b; IV 46a, 49a
James, William, III 561b
Jefferson, IV 21b
judgment, IV 46a, 46b, 49a
justice, IV 46a, 46b, 49a
Kames, III 234b
Kant, I 104b; III 233b, 358a, 640b; IV 179b, 181b
knowledge, IV 49a, 49b
Lang, III 309b
law, III 2a, 11a, 28b–29a; IV 46a, 49a
Leibniz, II 445b; III 195b
Leucippus, IV 51a
liberalism, II 450b–451a
literature, IV 46a, 48b–49a, 332a
Locke, II 553a; III 195b; IV 120a
logic, IV 46a
logos, IV 46a, 47a, 51a
Lucretius, IV 51a
macrocosm, III 124a
magic, IV 46a
Marcus Aurelius, IV 50b
Marx, II 450a, 450b–451a
Marxism, III 149a, 152b, 645b
materialism, II 450a, 450b–451a
mathematics, IV 46b, 47b
medicine, IV 47b–48a
metaphor, III 203a
metaphysics, III 214a, 217b
methodology, III 381b–382a; IV 47b–48a
Michelangelo, IV 442b, 443a
microcosm, III 127a
Milesians, IV 46b, 47a
mind, IV 47a, 50a
moral sense, III 230b–234b
morality, III 301a, 301b–302a; IV 46a, 48b, 49b, 50a, 50b, 51a
motion, IV 50a, 50b, 51a
music, II 318b, 390b; III 262a, 264b, 266b, 268a
mythology, III 287b, 300a, 301a–303b, 304a, 309b, 310a, 314a, 315a; IV 46a–

49a, 50b
nationalism, III 327b, 329b, 331b, 331b, 332b, 334b
natural law, II 693a
Nature, III 302a; IV 46a, 47a, 48b, 49b–50a, 50b
Near East, IV 46a
necessity, III 351b, 356a–357a; IV 50a, 50b, 51a
Newton, III 381b–382a
numbers, IV 46b–47a
observation, IV 47a, 48a
optimism, II 167b
oratory, IV 48b, 49a
order, II 445b; IV 47a, 50a
Orientalism, III 429a, 429b, 432b
Parmenides, IV 47a–47b
pathology, IV 48a
peace, IV 46a
perception, IV 47b
perennial philosophy, III 460a
philosophy, II 652a; IV 46b–47b, 48a, 50a
physics, III 301a
physiology, IV 48a
Pietism, III 494a
Plato, IV 46b–50b, 175a
Platonism, III 516a, 522a; IV 51a
pleasure, II 375b, 380a
pluralism, IV 47b
poetry, IV 46a, 46b, 47a
pragmatism, III 555b, 561b
pre-Socratics, IV 46b–47a
primitivism, III 598a
probability, IV 49a
Prodicus, IV 48b
progress, III 626b, 627a, 627b, 634b, 636b, 640b, 643a, 645b, 646b, 649a
Protagoras, IV 48b
protest movements, III 673b, 676a
matter, III 195b
measurement, IV 51a
medieval science, II 196b–197a
psyche, IV 47a, 49b
psychology, IV 8a, 11a, 16b, 17b, 18b, 19a, 20a, 21a, 21b, 22a, 23a, 23b
Puritanism, IV 16b, 18b
Pyrrhonism, III 302a–302b
Pythagoras, IV 46b–47a, 50a
Pythagoreans, IV 41b
Ramism, IV 42b
Ramus, IV 42b
reality, IV 47a
reason, IV 46a, 46b, 47a, 47b, 49b, 50a, 51a

Reid, Thomas, III 233b, 234a
religion, III 203a, 301a–303b; IV 48b, 93b, 94a, 96a, 97b, 98a, 105a, 109a, 118a, 120a
Renaissance, IV 122a, 136b, 142b, 147b, 438a, 440a, 441b, 442b, 443a
research, IV 48a
revolution, IV 155b
right, IV 46a, 49a, 173b, 175a, 175b, 176a, 179b, 181b
romanticism, IV 197a, 199b, 201a, 202b, 205a, 205b, 208a, 208b, 209a
Rome (ancient), IV 46a, 49b, 50a
rules, IV 48b
Schleiermacher, IV 201a
science, IV 47b–48a
seasons, IV 50a
senses, IV 36b, 47b
skepticism, IV 48a, 243a, 246a, 247a, 247b, 250b, 251a
slavery, IV 49a
Social Darwinism, III 646b
social welfare, IV 277a
socialism, III 673b; IV 286a
society, IV 46a, 46b, 48b
Socrates, IV 48b, 49a–49b
Sophists, IV 48b–49a
soul, IV 49b, 50a
State, IV 48b, 49b, 312b, 314b
Stoicism, IV 49b–50a, 50b, 51a, 176a, 319a, 320a, 321a
Stoics, IV 8a
style, IV 331a–331b, 332a
supernatural, IV 46a
superstition, IV 48a
symbolism, IV 345a
symmetry, IV 346b
taste, IV 355b, 356a
teleology, IV 51a
temperance, IV 367a–367b
Thales, IV 46b
theater, IV 48b, 49a
theology, IV 46b
theriophily, IV 384a, 385a, 385b, 388a, 388b
thought, IV 47b, 49b
Thrasymachus, IV 48b
Thucydides, IV 48a–48b, 367b
time, IV 47a
Toland, III 301b–302a
tradition, IV 48a, 48b

tragedy, IV 49a
tragic sense, IV 414a
truth, IV 47a
Turgot, III 303a, 303b
uniformitarianism, IV 419b
U.S., III 429a, 429b, 432b
unity, IV 46b
universal man, IV 438a, 440a, 441b, 442b, 443a
universality, IV 49b, 50a
universe, IV 46a, 50a
Utopia, IV 458b, 459a, 462b, 463a, 464a
vice, IV 50a
Vico, III 302a, 302b
Victorians, IV 218a, 219b, 222b
virtue, IV 46a, 49a–50a
Volksgeist, IV 496a
Voltaire, III 302b, 303a
war, IV 46b
wisdom, IV 46a, 49b
wisdom of the fool, IV 515b, 516a–516b
witchcraft, IV 522b, 523a
wrong, IV 49a
Xenophanes, IV 46b
Zeno of Citium, IV 47b
Zeus (myth), IV 48b
Ratzel, Friedrich (1844–1904)
   culture, II 128a, 130b–131a, 131b
   Darwin, II 130b
   environment, II 128a, 130b–131a, 131b
   migrations, II 130b
   Semple and, II 131a
Rauch, Frederic (1806–1841), psychology, IV 24a–24b
Rauschenbusch, Walter (1861–1918), reformation, IV 69a
Ravel, Maurice (1875–1937), impressionism, II 575a
Rawls, John
   social welfare, IV 280b
   utilitarianism, IV 448b
Ray, Isaac (1807–1881), psychology, IV 28b
Ray, John (1627?–1705), catastrophism, IV 418b
   Cosmic Fall, I 510b
   cosmic images, I 523a
   culture, II 127b, 128a, 130a
   design argument, I 674a
   environment, II 127b, 128a, 130a
   God, II 355a
   mountains in literature, III 258b

Raymond, Marcel, baroque in literature, I 192b

Raynal, Guillaume (Abbé) (1713–1796)
despotism, II 12a
revolution, IV 155a

Raynal, Thomas, socialism, IV 288a–288b

Rē (myth), II 38b, 39a, 334a, 334b–335a; IV 98a
salvation IV 224b–225a

Read, Herbert (1893–   ),
beauty, I 213b
expressionism, II 207a
literary criticism, I 602b

Reade, Wynnewood
longevity, III 93a
perfectibility, III 474b, 475a

Real numbers, I 497b–498a, 499a–499b
symmetry, IV 348a

Realism
Anaxagoras, IV 3a
Aristotle, III 19a
classicism, I 454b
culture, IV 165b
empiricism, III 548a–548b, 550b
expressionism, II 207a
France, III 483b
Germany, III 483b
Great Britain, III 483b
Hegel, II 407b; III 22a
humanism, II 520b
iconography, II 532a–532b, 534a
idea, II 546a–546b, 547a, 548b
impressionism, II 570a, 571a, 576b, 578b, 579a, 581b, 582b
irony, II 626b
James, William, III 561b
language, II 667a
law, III 5b
logic, III 548a–548b, 550b
Marx, II 451a, 454a
materialism, II 451a, 454a
Michelet, II 407b
mimesis, III 229b
motif, III 237b
mountains in literature, III 253b
music, III 270a
mythology, III 300b
natural law, III 16a, 19a, 22a
naturalism in art, III 339a, 342b, 343a
Neo-Platonism, III 374b, 375b, 376a, 376b
Peirce, III 552b, 555a, 560b
perennial philosophy, III 458b
periodization in history, III 476b, 480b
periodization in literary history, III 483b
Plotinus, III 374b, 375b
positivism, III 548a–548b, 550b
pragmatism, III 552b, 555a, 560b, 561b, 563b, 565a, 566a
psychology, IV 3a, 22b
realism in literature, IV 52b, 53a, 54a
revolution, IV 165a, 165b
symbolism, IV 344b
U.S., III 483b
ut pictura poesis, IV 471b, 472a
Utopia, IV 462a, 464a

Realism in literature, IV 51b–56a
aesthetics, IV 51b, 55b
art, IV 52a, 55b, 56a
Auerbach, IV 54b–55a
Balzac, IV 52a, 52b, 53b, 55a
Baudelaire, IV 53b
Belinsky, IV 53a, 53b
Bergson, IV 55a
Bernard, IV 52a
Bible, IV 55a
botany, IV 53b
Brinkmann, IV 55a
Brunetière, IV 54a
Capuana, IV 53a
Champfleury, IV 52a
classicism, IV 56a
communism, IV 55b
Comte, IV 55a
Courbet, IV 52a
Croce, IV 55a
Cuvier, IV 53b
Dante, IV 55a
Daudet, IV 54a
De Sanctis, IV 52b
Demetz, IV 55b
democracy, IV 55a
Dickens, IV 52a
Dostoevsky, IV 53a
drama, IV 54b
Dumas, IV 52a
Duranty, IV 52a
Eliot, IV 54a
emotion, IV 53b
Engels, IV 53a
Epicureanism, IV 53b
existentialism, IV 54b, 55a, 56a
Faulkner, IV 55a
Feydeau, IV 52a
Flaubert, IV 52a, 52b, 54a, 55a
Foerster, IV 54a
Fortoul, IV 52a
France, IV 51b–52b, 53b, 54a
Garnett, IV 54a
Germany, IV 51b, 52b–53a, 54b, 55a, 55b
Gissing, IV 52b, 54a
Goethe, IV 51b, 52b
Gogol, IV 53a, 53b, 55a
Goncourt, Edmond, IV 52a
Goncourt, Jules, IV 52a
Gosse, IV 54a
Great Britain, IV 52b, 54a, 54b
Grillparzer, IV 55a
Hegel, IV 54b
Heine, IV 53b
Hettner, IV 52b
historicism, IV 54b, 56a
history, IV 51b
Homer, IV 54b
Howells, IV 52b
Hugo, IV 52a, 53b
Hungary, IV 55a
idealism, IV 51b, 52b, 53a
impressionism, IV 55a
Italy, IV 53a, 55a
James, Henry, IV 52b
Jonson, Ben, IV 54a
Joyce, IV 55a
Kant, IV 51b
Keyserling, IV 55a
Kierkegaard, IV 54b
Lewes, IV 52b
literary criticism, IV 51b, 52b, 53a, 53b, 54a
Ludwig, IV 52b, 55a
Lukács, IV 55b
Malenkov, IV 55b
manners, IV 52a
Marino, IV 54a
Marx, IV 53a
Marxism, IV 53a, 55a, 55b, 56a
Masson, IV 52b
materialism, IV 51b, 53b, 54a
Maupassant, IV 53b, 54a
Mérimée, IV 52a
Monnier, IV 52a
Moore, George, IV 52b
Murger, IV 52a
naturalism, IV 53a, 53b–54a, 55b
Nature, IV 53b, 55a
nominalism, IV 51b
novel, IV 51b, 52a, 52b, 53a, 54a, 54b
painting, IV 52a
Parrington, IV 54b
Pater, IV 55a
Petronius, IV 54a
philosophers, IV 53b
philosophy, IV 51b, 53b, 54a
Pisarev, IV 53a
Planche, IV 51b, 52a
Plato, IV 51b
poetry, IV 51b, 53a, 53b
poets, IV 51b, 53b
Prescott, IV 52b
proletariat, IV 55a
Proust, IV 54b, 55a
Pushkin, IV 55a
Rabelais, IV 54a
realist, IV 52b, 53a, 54a
Reid, IV 51b
religion, IV 53b
Reynier, IV 54a
rhetoric, IV 53b, 55a
romanticism, IV 51b, 52a, 52b, 55a, 56a
Russia, IV 53a–53b, 54b, 55a–55b
Schelling, IV 51b
Schiller, IV 51b, 53b
Schlegel, IV 51b, 53a
Schmidt, IV 52b
Schnitzler, IV 55a
science, IV 54b
scientists, IV 54a
Scott, IV 52a, 53b
secularism, IV 53b
Shakespeare, IV 52b, 53a
socialism, IV 55a–55b
society, IV 55b
solipsism, IV 55a
Spain, IV 54a
Stendhal, IV 52a, 55a
Strakhov, IV 53a
stream of consciousness, IV 55a
supernatural, IV 53b
symbolism, IV 56a
Taine, IV 53b, 55a
Thackeray, IV 52b
Tolstoy, IV 53b
truth, IV 53b
U.S., IV 52b, 54a–54b
Victorianism, IV 52b, 54a
Woolf, IV 55a
Zola, IV 52a, 53b–54a, 55a
zoology, IV 53b

Reality
Aristotle, III 226b
Bruno, IV 393b
Democritus, III 187b
good, IV 177b, 182a
Hegel, III 358b
human nature, III 572a, 575b
language, II 661b, 662a
Laplace, IV 393b
matter, III 187b, 188b
mimesis, III 226a, 226b
mythology, III 273a, 274a, 274b

Nature, III 347a, 347b
necessity, III 352a, 352b, 353b, 356a, 356b, 358b
organicism, III 422a
Parmenides, III 572a
Peirce, III 560b
Plato, III 188b, 273a, 274b, 347a, 353b, 498b, 501b, 502a, 508b; IV 390b
Platonism, III 498b, 501b, 502a, 505a, 508b
pleasure, II 383b
pragmatism, III 552a, 552b, 553a, 560b, 561a, 564b, 566a
Pythagoreans, IV 35b
rationalism, IV 47a
Renaissance, IV 440a
right, IV 177b, 182a
Royce, III 561a
Saint Augustine, IV 391b
Spinoza, IV 177b, 393b
symbolism, IV 338a
time, IV 390b, 391a, 391b, 393b, 394b, 395b
universal man, IV 440a
Zeitgeist, IV 536a
Reason
Aeschylus, III 625b
aesthetics, IV 353b–356b
Alembert, II 96a–96b
Aristotle, II 196b; III 1b, 380a, 381b, 440a, 586a; IV 49b, 175b
art, I 458b; II 307b
asymmetry, IV 349a
Bacon, Francis, IV 434a
Bacon, Roger, IV 434b–435a
Bayle, IV 119b
Boccaccio, II 234a
Buddhism, I 249b
Buffon, I 334b
Buridan, II 34a
Burke, Edmund, IV 203a
catharsis, I 267b–268a
Cicero, III 16b
Coke, II 695b
common law, II 691a, 692a, 693a, 695b
Comte, III 649a
Condillac, II 96a
Condorcet, III 614a
Counter-Enlightenment, II 100b, 104b, 106b, 107b, 110b
cynicism, III 585b
Dante, II 233a
deism, I 645b–650b
Descartes, II 96a; III 384a–384b; IV 435b
determinism, II 26b, 236b, 237b, 238a, 238b, 239a, 240b

Diderot, II 96b; III 644b
dignity, IV 144b–145a
double truth, II 33a–36b
emotion, IV 50a
empiricism, I 91b; III 547a–547b
Enlightenment, II 94a, 95b–96b
Epicureanism, I 91b; III 586a
Epicurus, II 244a
equity, II 150b
eschatology, II 158a, 158b
ethics, III 442a, 442b, 443a, 443b, 444b, 446a, 586a; IV 319a–321b
evil, II 162b–164b, 168a
expressionism, II 208a
faith, I 384b–385a; III 458b
Ficino, IV 144b–145a
fortune, fate, and chance, II 225b–226a, 226b, 227b, 233a, 234a
free will, II 236b, 237b, 238a, 238b, 239a, 240b, 242b, 243a, 243b, 244a
freedom, II 250a
freedom of speech, II 260a
French Revolution (1789), II 409a–409b
game theory, II 267a–268a, 273b–274a
general will, II 280a
genius, II 294a, 294b, 295a, 295b, 296a, 307b
God, I 487b; II 211b
good, IV 174a, 175a–180a
Hartmann, I 93b
Hegel, I 312a; II 408b, 409a–409b, 410a, 413b, 414a, 416a; III 556a; IV 180a
Herder, III 305a, 639a; IV 209a
hierarchy, II 446b, 447b
historiography, IV 149b, 151a
Hobbes, IV 177a
humanism, II 519b; IV 134a, 134b, 135a
Hume, I 312a–314a; II 96a; III 231b, 232a, 233a, 303a–303b; IV 247b
idea, II 543b
impressionism, II 582a
individualism, II 307b
instinct, II 227b
irrationalism, II 635a–638b
John of Jandun, II 34b
justice, II 656b–657a, 658a
Kant, I 91a–93b, 315a–316a, 317b; II 240b, 280a; III 21b, 218b, 494b, 555b; IV 200a, 202a, 248b–

249a, 382b, 383a
La Mettrie, II 96a
language, II 667b
law, II 250a, 686a, 687b, 688a–688b, 689a, 690a; III 1a, 1b, 5b
Leibniz, I 91b, 327b–328b, 334b; II 239a, 239b, 446b
Leonardo da Vinci, IV 134a
Leucippus, IV 51a
light, III 396b
linguistics, IV 424a
literature, IV 332a
Locke, II 95b–96a, 96b, 239b; III 21a; IV 258a
logic, III 547a–547b, 585b
Lovejoy, I 329a
Luther, IV 381b
Machiavelli, IV 482a–482b
Machiavellism, III 120a, 122b, 123a
Maistre, I 482a; II 95b
mathematics, III 178b
matter, III 187a
medieval science, II 196b
metaphysical imagination, III 210b, 212a, 214b, 215a, 217b–219b
methodology, III 379a–379b, 384a–384b
moral sense, III 230b, 231b, 232a, 233a, 234b
music, II 388a, 390b–391b
mythology, III 300b, 302a, 303a–303b, 305a
natural law, III 14b, 15b, 16a–21a
Nature, III 350a
neo-classicism in art, III 371a
Newton, II 96b; III 379a–379b, 384a–384b; IV 199b
organicism, III 425a
Pascal, II 168a; IV 118b
peace, III 442a, 443a, 443b, 444b, 446a
Peirce, III 558a, 559a, 568a, 568b
perennial philosophy, III 457a, 457b, 458b, 459a, 460a, 461b
perfectibility, III 464b–465a, 465b, 471b, 472a
Pietism, III 494b
Plato, II 236b, 243a, 390b; III 1b, 210b, 464b–465a, 496a, 496b, 499b, 500b, 501b, 508b, 586a; IV 3b, 4a, 4b, 50a, 175a
Platonism, III 496a, 496b, 499b, 500b, 501b, 508b, 516a
Plotinus, II 163b; IV 9a
Pomponazzi, II 36b

positivism, III 547a–547b
pragmatism, III 555b, 561b
primitivism, III 585b–586a, 588a, 589b, 598a, 600a
probability, III 607a, 612a, 613b–614a, 615a
progress, III 625b, 632b, 637b, 638b, 639a, 644b, 647a, 648b, 649a
prophecy, III 665b
psychology, IV 3b, 4a, 4b, 7a, 8a, 9a, 11a, 13a, 16b, 17a, 17b, 18b, 19a, 20a, 20b, 23a, 23b, 24b
Pufendorf, III 20a
rationalism, IV 46a, 46b, 47a, 47b, 49b, 50a, 51a
Reformation, II 28a, 30b
religion, IV 107a, 118a, 119a, 119b
Renaissance, IV 134a, 134b, 135a, 144b–145b, 149b, 151a, 439a, 441a, 443a
revolution, IV 155b
rhetoric, IV 172a
right, IV 174a, 175a–177b, 178b, 179b, 180a
Roman Catholic Church, II 30a, 30b
romanticism, IV 196b, 199a, 199b, 200a, 200b, 202a, 202b, 203a, 205b, 209a
Rome (ancient), I 144b; II 686a, 687b, 688a–688b, 689a, 690a
Rosenkranz, II 413b
Saint Augustine, II 687b; 18a; IV 9a
Saint Paul, III 17b
Saint Thomas Aquinas, III 19a; IV 134b
Schleiermacher, IV 202b
science, III 586a
Seneca, III 465b
Shaftesbury, II 96b; III 230b
Siger of Brabant, I 639b; II 33a, 33b
social contract, IV 257a, 258a, 261a
socialism, IV 285b
Socrates, III 496a
Spinoza, II 238b; IV 177b, 257a
Stoicism, III 17a, 586a, 588a; IV 50a, 176a, 285a, 319a–321b
Stoics, I 2b; IV 8a
Strato, IV 7a
style, IV 332a
Swift, III 599b
symmetry, IV 349a–349b

371

taste, **IV** 353b, 354b–356b
temperance, **IV** 367b
theodicy, **IV** 380b, 381b, 382b, 383a
theriophily, **IV** 384a–388a
Turgot, **III** 303a, 303b
uniformitarianism, **IV** 424a
unity of science, **IV** 434a, 434b, 435b, 436a, 436b
universal man, **IV** 439a, 441a, 443a
ut pictura poesis, **IV** 466a, 467a
utilitarianism, **IV** 448b
Victorian sensibility, **IV** 217a, 221a, 221b, 222b
virtù, **IV** 482a–482b
Voltaire, **II** 11a
vox populi, **IV** 497b
William of Ockham, **III** 19b
wisdom of the fool, **IV** 515b, 517b, 519a
witchcraft, **IV** 522b
work, **IV** 531b, 532a
Zeno of Citium, **III** 17b
Réaumur, René de (1683–1757)
  Chain of Being, **I** 332a
  God, **I** 332a
  spontaneous generation, **IV** 310b
  theriophily, **IV** 388b
Rebellion
  Byron, **IV** 204a
  communism, **III** 673b
  freedom of speech, **II** 254b
  historiography, **II** 500a
  Locke, **IV** 154a
  Middle Ages, **IV** 253a
  protest movements, **III** 670a, 670b, 671a, 673b, 675a, 676a
  revolution, **IV** 154a, 154b
  romanticism, **IV** 204a, 205a
  social contract, **IV** 253a, 260b
  socialism, **III** 673b
Rebirth, **I** 644b
  evolutionism, **II** 176a–176b
  humanism, **IV** 129b, 130b, 131a
  reformation, **IV** 60b–61a, 61b
  Renaissance, **IV** 129b, 130b, 131a
Recapitulation, **IV** 56a–59b
  anatomy, **IV** 56b–57a
  animals, **IV** 56b–57a, 59a
  anthropology, **IV** 58a
  Aristotle, **IV** 56b
  Baer, **IV** 57a, 58a
  Biogenetic Law, **IV** 56a, 57b–58a

biology, **I** 239b; **IV** 56a, 56b–57a, 58a, 59a
  Blake, **IV** 56b
  causation, **IV** 57b
  children, **IV** 58b, 59a
  coenogenetic embryos, **IV** 57b, 58a
  criminology, **IV** 58a
  Darwin, **IV** 56a, 56b, 57a–57b, 58a
  Draper, **IV** 58b
  embryology, **IV** 56a–56b, 57a, 58a, 59a
  evolution, **IV** 56a–56b, 57a–57b, 58a
  experiments, **IV** 58a, 59a
  genes, **IV** 58a
  genetics, **IV** 56a–56b, 58a
  Goethe, **IV** 56b
  Haeckel, **IV** 56a, 56b, 57b–59a
  Harvey, **IV** 56b
  history, **IV** 56a, 58a–58b
  individualism, **IV** 56a, 57a, 57b, 58b
  inheritance, **IV** 59a
  Jung, **IV** 58b, 59a
  Lamarck, **IV** 58a
  literature, **IV** 58
  memory, **IV** 59a
  metaphysics, **IV** 56b
  mind, **IV** 59a
  mutation, **IV** 58a
  nationalism, **IV** 58b
  natural selection, **IV** 58a
  Nature, **IV** 56b
  ontogeny, **IV** 56a, 57a, 57b, 58a
  palingenetic embryos, **IV** 57b
  parallelism, **IV** 56b, 57a
  philosophy, **IV** 56b
  phylogeny, **IV** 56a, 57b, 58a
  physiology, **IV** 58a
  Preyer, **IV** 59a
  psyche, **IV** 59a
  psychology, **IV** 58a, 58b–59a
  race, **IV** 58b, 59a
  Scale of Beings, **IV** 56b
  science, **IV** 56a, 56b, 57a
  soul, **IV** 56b
  species, **IV** 58a
  Spemann, **IV** 59a
  Spock, **IV** 58b
Reclus, E., progress, **III** 637a, 644b
Recreation
  mythology, **III** 286b
  Plato, **III** 500b
Redemption
  mythology, **III** 277a, 288a
  perennial philosophy, **III**

459a, 459b, 462b
  prophecy, **III** 665a
  religion, **IV** 97a
  Saint Augustine, **III** 459a
  socialism, **IV** 287b
Redi, Francesco (1626?–1697 or 1698)
  genetic continuity, **II** 282a, 282b
  spontaneous generation, **II** 282a; **IV** 309a–309b
Reductionism
  disease, **II** 404b
  holy, **II** 513b, 514a
  mythology, **III** 277a
  pangenesis, **II** 623b
  positivism, **III** 547b–550a
Reeves, W. Pember (1857–1932), welfare state, **IV** 510b
Reflection
  imprinting, **II** 584a
  learning, **II** 584a
  Man-Machine, **III** 140b
  methodology, **III** 389b
  Newton, **III** 389b
  symmetry, **IV** 348b, 351a, 351b
Reform
  communism, **III** 673b
  Enlightenment, **II** 89b, 90a–91a, 98b
  heresy, **II** 417b, 421b, 422a, 424a
  law, **II** 677a
  liberalism, **III** 672b
  Marxism, **III** 149a, 149b
  philanthropy, **III** 490a, 491a
  protest movements, **III** 672b, 673a, 673b, 675a
  radicalism, **III** 673a
  revolution, **IV** 160a
  socialism, **III** 673b
Reformation (concept), **IV** 60a–69b
  Abel (Bible), **IV** 63a
  Adam (Bible), **IV** 63a
  apocalypse, **IV** 61a, 65a, 66a
  Arnobius, **IV** 62b
  asceticism, **IV** 63b
  astrology, **IV** 65a
  baptism, **IV** 61a, 61b, 62a
  Benedict of Aniane, **IV** 63b–64a
  Benedictines, **IV** 63b–64a
  Bernard of Clairvaux, **IV** 64b
  Bible, **IV** 61a–63a, 64b
  Boniface VIII (Pope), **IV** 64a
  Bruno of Cologne, **IV** 64b
  bureaucracy, **IV** 64b
  Bushnell, **IV** 69a

Cain (Bible), **IV** 63a
  Calvin, **IV** 67a–67b
  Camaldulians, **IV** 64b
  Carthusians, **IV** 64b
  child labor, **IV** 68b
  Christianity, **IV** 60a–69b
  Cicero, **IV** 61b
  Cistercians, **IV** 64b
  civil rights, **IV** 69a
  community, **IV** 60a, 64b, 69a–69b
  conversion, **IV** 60b, 61a, 63a, 65a
  cosmology, **IV** 60b, 61a
  culture, **IV** 60b–61a
  custom, **IV** 66a
  cycles, **IV** 60b, 61a
  Cyprian, **IV** 62b
  Daniel (Bible), **IV** 61a
  death, **IV** 60b
  democracy, **IV** 65b
  determinism, **IV** 60b, 61a
  Dietrich of Niem, **IV** 65b
  Dilthey, **IV** 69b
  discipline, **IV** 64a
  Donatists, **IV** 62b–63a
  Durand, **IV** 65a
  Eastern Orthodox Church, **IV** 62b
  economics, **IV** 63b, 65b
  Ecumenical Movement, **IV** 68b
  education, **IV** 61b, 69a
  Enlightenment, **IV** 68b
  entropy, **IV** 60b
  Erasmus, **IV** 63a
  eschatology, **IV** 60a, 61a, 61b, 65a
  Eternal Return, **IV** 60b
  Eugene III (Pope). **IV** 64b
  evil, **IV** 65b
  evolution, **IV** 60b–61a
  faith, **IV** 61b, 62a, 62b, 66b, 68a, 68b, 69b
  feeling, **IV** 68b
  fiscalism, **IV** 64b
  Fiske, **IV** 69a
  Flacius Illyricus, **IV** 67a
  folklore, **IV** 60b
  Franciscans, **IV** 65a, 65b
  Frederick III, **IV** 66a
  freedom, **IV** 60b, 61a
  Froude, **IV** 60a
  Gerard, **IV** 65b
  God, **IV** 60a, 61b, 62a–62b, 63a, 65b, 66a, 66b, 67a, 69a, 69b
  Golden Age (myth), **IV** 60b, 62b
  good, **IV** 65a
  grace, **IV** 62b
  Great Britain, **IV** 68b
  Greece (ancient), **IV** 60b, 61b

Gregory VII (Pope), IV 64a
heaven, IV 62b, 63b
heresy, IV 62b–63a, 65a
Hesiod, IV 60b
hierarchy, IV 64a, 65a, 66b
Hildebrandine Reform, IV 64a
history, IV 60b, 61a, 63a, 65a, 69a
Holy Ghost, IV 61a
humanism, IV 61b
humility, IV 64b
Hus, IV 65b
ideology, IV 60b–61a
individualism, IV 60a, 60b, 61b, 62a–63b, 64b, 65a, 65b, 68b, 69a
Innocent III (Pope), IV 64a
institutions, IV 60a, 61b, 63b–66a
Ivo of Chartres, IV 64b
Jesus Christ, IV 61a, 61b, 62a–62b, 63a, 64b, 65a, 65b, 66b, 67a, 69a
Joachim of Floris, IV 65a
John of Segovia, IV 66a
John XXII (Pope), IV 65b
Josiah (Bible), IV 61b
Judaism, IV 60a, 61a
juries, IV 61b
justice, IV 64a, 69a
labor, IV 69a
Lactantius, IV 62b
Ladner, IV 60a, 60b, 64a
law, IV 60a, 61b, 62b, 64a, 66a, 67a
Lichtenberger, IV 65a
literature, IV 60b, 61b
Livy, IV 61b
love, IV 65a, 66b, 69a
Luther, IV 65b, 66a–66b, 67a, 67b, 68b, 69b
Marxism, IV 69a
materialism, IV 64a, 69a
Melanchthon, IV 66b, 67a
meliorism, IV 62b
Methodism, IV 68b
Middle Ages, IV 61a–61b, 63a–66a, 67a, 69a
millenarianism, IV 60b–62b
missionaries, IV 68b
monarchy, IV 65b
monasticism, IV 60a, 62b, 63a, 63b–65a
money, IV 65b
morality, IV 60a, 61b, 62b, 63a, 64a, 65a
Moravian Brotherhood, IV 68b
Mott, John R., IV 69a
mythology, IV 60b
Neo-Pythagoreans, IV 60b
New Year celebrations, IV

60b
norms, IV 62a
numbers, IV 63a
obedience, IV 65a
order, IV 63a, 66a
Ovid, IV 61b
ownership, IV 64a
pamphlets, IV 66a
papacy, IV 60a, 64a, 64b, 65a, 65b
peace, IV 69a
Pelagians, IV 63a
penitence, IV 64b
perfectibility, IV 61a, 62b
persecution, IV 62b
Pfeffinger, IV 67a
Pietism, IV 68b
Pius X (Pope), IV 68b
Platonism, IV 60b
Pliny, IV 61b
poetry, IV 66a
political, IV 60a, 61b, 64a
poverty, IV 63b, 64b–65b
power, IV 64a, 65b, 68b
pragmatism, IV 69a
prophecy, IV 61a, 61b, 67a, 67b
Quakers, IV 68b
race, IV 69a
Rauschenbusch, IV 69a
rebirth, IV 60b–61a, 61b
regeneration, IV 60a, 60b, 61a, 61b, 62a
renaissance, IV 60a, 60b–61a, 61b, 67a, 67b
Renaissance, IV 61b, 67a
renewal, IV 60b–61a, 61b–62a, 63b
repentance, IV 61b
Roman Catholic Church, IV 60a, 61a, 62b–66a, 66b, 68b
romanticism, IV 62b
Rome (ancient), IV 60b, 61b, 66a
Romuald of Ravenna, IV 64b
Saint Augustine, IV 63a–63b, 64b
Saint Benedict, IV 63b, 64a, 64b
Saint Jerome, IV 63a
Saint Paul, IV 61b, 62a
saints, IV 61a
sanctification, IV 62a
Seneca, IV 61b
Sigismund, IV 66a
sin, IV 62a
slavery, IV 68b
society, IV 60b–61a, 63a, 63b, 68a, 68b–69a, 69b
spiritualism, IV 62b, 64a–66b
State, IV 64a

Stoicism, IV 60b
Strong, Josiah, IV 69a
terminology, IV 61a–62a
Tertullian, IV 62b
theology, IV 60a, 63a, 63b, 64a, 67a, 68b, 69a
time, IV 60b, 61a, 63a
truth, IV 64a, 67a
U.S., IV 68b, 69a
universe, IV 62b
utopianism, IV 61a, 65a, 66a
Valla, IV 63a
Vallombrosians, IV 64b
virtue, IV 63a
vitalism, IV 60b–61a
wealth, IV 63b, 65a, 65b
Wesley, IV 68b
William of Ockham, IV 65b
William IX, IV 63b–64a
work, IV 63b, 532b–533a
Wycliffe, IV 65b
Reformation (Period), IV 61b, 65b, 66a–68a, 69a
Anabaptists, IV 67b
apostasy, IV 67b
Austria, I 390a, 394b
authority, I 146b, 147a, 149b–150b
Bavaria, I 390a, 395a
Beza, IV 67b
Bible, IV 67a–68a
Bohemia, I 395a
Calvin, IV 67a–67b
capitalism, I 396a–397a
casuistry, I 262a
Cellarius, IV 67a
certainty, I 304a, 305b
Christianity, I 382a; III 670b
Church, I 418a
Church of England, IV 68b
city-state, I 391a–392b
crisis in history, I 591b, 592b
Counter-Reformation, IV 66a
culture, IV 68a
determinism, II 28a
Diet of Augsburg (1548), IV 66b–67a
dignity, IV 146a
economic history, II 46b–47a
Enlightenment, II 89a, 90a; IV 68a
equality, II 138a
eschatology, II 156b, 157a
Evangelical Rationalists, IV 67b
evangelicalism, IV 68b, 69a
faith, hope, and charity, II 212a–213a, 215b
Faust (legend), III 245a, 246a, 246b

France, I 394b, 395b; IV 68a
free will, II 245a–245b
freedom, I 648b
Germany, I 389a–391a, 394b, 395b; IV 66a–67a, 68a
God, II 359b–361a; IV 67a, 67b
good, IV 67a
Great Britain, I 395a, 395b, 396a; III 483b; IV 68a
heresy, II 424b–428a
hierarchy, II 442a
historicism, II 457b
historiography, II 478b, 481b–484b; IV 68a, 149a
history, IV 68a
holy, II 513a
humanism, II 520b, 523a; IV 135a
Incarnation, IV 62b
individualism, I 395a–395b; II 89a, 594b, 595a, 597a, 602b, 603a; IV 67b–68a
intolerance, IV 118a
Italy, I 394b, 395b
Jesus Christ, IV 67b
law, III 11a; IV 66a
liberalism, III 36a, 36b, 40b, 41b, 42a, 47a
love, III 107a
Luther, IV 65b, 66a–66b, 67a, 67b, 68b, 69b
Lutheran Church, IV 66b, 67a, 68a
Marsilius of Padua, IV 65b
monasticism, I 392b–393a
metaphor, III 206a–206b
Middle Ages, IV 153a
millenarianism, III 225a
modernism, I 423a–423b
Moravians, IV 68b
motif, III 241a
mountains in literature, III 255a
music, III 270b–271a
mythology, III 293a
nationalism, I 395a–397a; IV 68a
Nature, III 348a
pacifism, IV 67b
papacy, I 388b, 394b–395a
Peasants' Revolt, I 391a, 391b
periodization in literary history III 483b
persecution, IV 68a
philanthropy, III 489a, 489b, 490a, 491a
poetry, III 529b, 530b
politics, IV 68a
polygamy, I 391a
predestination, II 28a, 30b;

IV 67a, 67b
printing press, I 390a
progress, III 641a, 642b, 643a
protest movements, III 670b
Ramism, IV 42b, 44b
reasons for success, I 388b
Renaissance, IV 124a, 126a, 127b, 128a, 135a, 146a, 149a
results, I 395a–397a
revolution, IV 153a
romanticism, IV 198b, 206b
Rule of Faith controversy, I 307a–308a
sacraments, I 390a, 391b–392a
Saint Francis of Assisi, IV 64b–65a
saints, IV 67b, 68a
salvation, IV 67b
sanctification, IV 68a
Scandinavia, I 390b
Schmalkald Diet (1537), IV 66b
sin, IV 67b
social contract, IV 253b
socialism, IV 285a, 287a–287b
society, IV 68a
Spain, I 394b, 395b
Spiritualists, IV 67b
State, IV 67b
Switzerland, I 391a–392b; IV 67b
theodicy, IV 381b–382a
theology, II 28a, 30b
U.S., I 396a
Utopia, IV 460b, 461a
Wittenberger Reformation (1545), IV 66b
Zwingli, IV 67b, 68a
Refraction
  Descartes, III 384a, 418a
  methodology, III 389b, 390b
  Newton, III 389b, 390b, 418b, 419a
  optics, III 411a, 411b–412b, 413a, 416a, 418a, 418b, 419a, 420b
  Porta, III 411b
Regamee, Constantin, Buddhism, I 256b
Regino of Prüm (d. 915)
  musical genius, II 314a
  Pythagorean cosmos, IV 41a
  witchcraft, IV 521a–521b
Regiomontanus (1436–1476), mathematics, III 178b
Régis, Pierre Sylvain

Man-Machine, III 138a
methodology, III 384b–385a
Newton and, III 384b–385a
Regius, Henricus (1598–1679)
  causation, I 302b
  Man-Machine, III 137b
  teleology, I 302b
Regnault, Father Noël, attitude toward antiquity, I 85a
Régnier, Henri de (1864–1936), symbolism, IV 340a
Régnier, Jean (1390?–1468), symbolism, IV 342b
Rehberg, A. W.
  conservatism, I 481b
  revolution, I 481b
Rehoboam (Bible), freedom of speech, II 255b
Reichenbach, Hans (1890–1953)
  good, IV 184a
  positivism, III 546a, 547b, 548a, 550a, 550b
  pragmatism, III 553a
  right, IV 184a
  time, IV 397a
Reid, Thomas (1710–1796),
  certainty, I 317a
  common sense, III 233b–234a
  epistemology, III 233b
  Hume and, III 234a
  Kant and, III 233b
  knowledge, III 233b–234a
  moral sense, III 233b–234a
  Nature, III 348a
  psychology, IV 22b
  realism in literature, IV 51b
  senses, III 234a
  skepticism, IV 248a–248b
  truth, I 317a
Reidemeister, Kurt, positivism, III 545b
Reik, Theodore, women, IV 524a
Reimarus, Hermann (1694–1768), deism, I 651a
Reincarnation
  Aristotle, I 645b
  Averroës, I 645b
  Bible, I 644a
  Babylonia, I 644b
  Buddhism, I 644b
  Brahmanism, I 64b
  Bruno, I 645a, 645b
  cabalism, I 645a
  Cathars, I 645a
  Christianity, I 645a
  Cicero, I 644b
  cosmology, I 644b–645a

death, I 644b–646a
déjà vu, I 645b
Ducasse, I 645a
Egypt (ancient), I 644b
eschatology, II 160a–160b
evil, II 162a
fortune, fate, and chance, II 226b, 227a
genius, I 645b
Gnosticism, I 645a
Goethe, I 646a
Greece (ancient), I 644b, 645a; IV 228b
Hesiod, I 644b
Hinduism, I 644b, 645a
Homer, I 644b
Hume, I 645a
immortality, I 644b–646a
India, I 645a
India (ancient), I 644b
Judaism, I 644b, 645a
Leibniz, I 645a
Longfellow, I 646a
McTaggart, I 645a
Michelangelo, I 646a
Neo-Platonism, I 645a
Orphism, I 644b; II 226b
perfectibility, III 464b
Pherecydes of Syros, I 644b
Plato, I 645a; II 226b; III 505a
Platonism, I 645a; III 505a
Plotinus, I 645a
Pythagoras, I 644b, 645a
Pythagoreans, I 645a
Radhakrishnan, I 645a
Renaissance, I 645a
romanticism, I 645b
Rome (ancient), I 646a
Santayana, I 646a
sin, IV 228b
skepticism, I 645a
soul, I 644b–646a
Spinoza, I 645b
Staël, I 645b, 646a
Reinforcement theory
  pleasure, II 382b
Reinhardt, K., progress, III 627a
Reiss, M., game theory, II 264b–265a
Relational theory of time, IV 389b, 390b, 392b, 393a, 394b, 397b
Relativism, IV 70a–74a
  abortion, IV 70a
  aesthetics, IV 356a
  anthropology, IV 70b, 71a
  behaviorism, IV 72b, 73a
  capitalism, IV 70a
  color, IV 71b
  communism, IV 70a
  conscience, IV 70a, 71a

crime, IV 70a
cruelty, IV 72a
culture, IV 70a, 71a, 71b, 73a, 73b
death, IV 70b, 71b
desire, IV 72a
determinism, II 20b
dueling, IV 70a
duty, IV 71a
education, II 82b–83b, 84a
emotion, IV 72a
ethics, IV 70a–74a
evil, IV 70b, 71a, 72b
evolution, IV 71a
fear, IV 71b
Firth, IV 71a
Gandhi, IV 73a
Genghis Khan, IV 73a
God, IV 70b, 72a
good, IV 70b, 71b, 72b
Gothic, II 370a
happiness, IV 70b
historicism, II 457a
historiography, II 20b
Hitler, IV 73a
Hobbes, IV 72a, 72b
Hobhouse, IV 71a
homosexuality, IV 70a, 70b
human nature, IV 72a, 72b
human sacrifice, IV 71a
Hume, IV 70a–72b
Hutcheson, IV 70b–72b
infanticide, IV 70a
injury, IV 71a
judgment, IV 71b, 72a, 73a
kindness, IV 72a
knowledge, IV 71a
language, IV 72b
law, IV 72b
Lecky, IV 70b, 71b
Lévy-Bruhl, IV 70b–71a
Lewis, C. I., III 568a
lying, IV 71a, 72b
Mill, J. S., III 561b
murder, IV 71a
Nature, IV 72b
necessity, III 353a
Pirandello, III 564a, 568a
Plato, III 77a
Platonism, III 523a
poverty, IV 70a, 70b
pragmatism, III 552a, 553a, 554b, 561b, 564a, 568a
race, IV 70b
religion, IV 70b, 71a, 114a
right, IV 70b, 71a, 72a, 73a, 73b
Rome (ancient), IV 71b
Russell, IV 70a
Saint Francis of Assisi, IV 73a
Schiller, III 568a
science, IV 70b

senses, IV 72a
sex, IV 71a
sin, IV 70a
society, IV 70b, 71a, 72a, 72b
sociology, IV 72a
suicide, IV 70a
superstition, IV 71a
taste, IV 356a
theft, IV 71a
tribes, IV 71a, 72b
truth, IV 72b
value, III 568a
violence, IV 71a
war, IV 70a
Westermarck, IV 71a
wife-lending, IV 70a
Winch, IV 72b
Wright, Chauncey, III 561b
wrong, IV 71a, 72a–73b
Relativity, IV 74a–92b
  absolute location, IV 76a
  absolute rest, IV 76a, 78a, 80a, 85b
  absolute velocity, IV 75b, 76a, 78a, 79a
  acceleration, IV 75b–76a, 76b, 77a, 82b, 86a–86b, 89a, 89b
  aesthetics, IV 75a, 80a, 88b, 89a
  aether, IV 78a–81b, 83a, 89b
  aether drag, IV 78b, 79a, 83b
  Aristotle, IV 74b, 76b
  art, IV 75a, 83b–84a, 92a
  astronauts, IV 90a–90b
  astronomy, IV 74a, 77b–78a
  beauty, IV 75a, 86a, 88b, 91a
  Berkeley, IV 75b, 80b, 85b–86a, 89b
  Bohr, IV 91b
  Bolyai, IV 87a–87b
  Bradley, IV 77b
  Cartesianism, IV 87b, 88a
  center of mass, IV 76a
  Clifford, IV 88a
  Copernicus, IV 74b, 75a, 76b
  cosmology, I 555a, 556a–559b; IV 89b
  Descartes, IV 75a, 77b
  Dirac, IV 91a
  earth, IV 74a–76b, 78a–78b, 79a, 90a–90b
  Einstein, I 555a, 556a–559b; IV 74a, 74b, 79b–84a, 85b–87a, 88a–92a
  electromagnetics, IV 74b, 78b, 79a, 79b, 80a–80b,

84a, 91a
  energy, IV 82b, 84a, 85b, 86b, 91a, 91b
  epicycles, IV 74b
  Euclid, IV 87a
  experience, IV 75b
  experiments, IV 75b, 78a–81a, 86a, 88a
  Faraday, IV 78b
  Fitzgerald, IV 79a, 83a
  force, IV 82b, 90a
  Foucault, IV 80b
  fourth dimension, IV 84b, 85b, 88b, 91a
  Frank, IV 79b
  Fresnel, IV 78a–78b, 79a, 80a, 83b
  Galilean transformation, IV 79b, 84b
  Galileo, IV 74a, 75a, 76b–77a, 77b, 86a
  Gauss, IV 87a–87b, 88a, 88b
  general theory, IV 85b–87a, 88a–88b, 89b–90a, 91a, 91b, 92a, 405a
  geodesic hypothesis, IV 90a, 91b
  geometry, IV 84b, 85a, 87a–88a, 89a, 89b, 90b, 91a, 91b
  God, IV 75b
  gravitational red shift, IV 87a
  gravitation, IV 91b
  gravity, IV 75a, 77b, 83b, 86a, 86b–87a, 88a, 89a, 90a–90b, 91a, 91b
  Greece (ancient), IV 74b, 75a, 87a
  harmony, IV 75a
  Hertz, IV 78b
  Hilbert, IV 89a
  Huygens, IV 77a, 77b, 78a
  inertia, IV 75a, 77a, 84a, 86a, 86b, 89a, 89b–90a
  infinity, IV 75b, 87a
  intuition, IV 76b
  Kant, IV 87a
  Kepler, IV 74b–75a, 75b, 77b, 90a
  Larmor, IV 79b, 80a, 83b
  law, IV 75a–76a
  Leibniz, IV 75b
  light, IV 77b–78b, 80b, 81b, 82a, 82b, 83b, 86b–87a, 91b
  light cones, IV 85a, 91b
  light waves, IV 77b–78b, 79a, 80b, 81a–81b, 83b
  Lobachevsky, IV 87a–87b
  Lorentz, IV 79a–79b, 80a, 83a, 83b, 89a

Lorentz transformation, IV 79b, 80a, 83a, 83b, 84b
  Mach, IV 86a, 89b
  Mach's Principle, IV 89b
  macrocosm, IV 91b, 92a
  magnetism, IV 78b, 80a
  mass, IV 82b, 84a, 86a, 86b
  mathematics, IV 74b, 78b–79a, 79b, 80a, 83a, 84a, 85b, 89a
  matter, IV 78a–78b, 84a, 91b, 92a
  Maxwell, IV 78b, 79a, 80a, 80b, 83b, 87a, 91b
  Maxwell's equations, IV 78b, 79a–79b, 80a, 82a, 83b, 85b, 90b, 91a
  measurement, IV 78a, 82b, 91b, 405a, 405b
  Michelson, IV 79a–80b, 89a
  Minkowski, IV 84a, 85a, 85b, 90a, 91a
  momentum, IV 85b
  Morley, IV 79a, 79b, 80a, 80b, 89a
  motion, IV 74a–81b, 83a–83b, 85b, 86a, 90a, 91b
  Newton, IV 74a, 75a–78b, 80b, 81b, 82b, 83b–87a, 89a, 89b–90a, 91b
  nuclear power, IV 91a
  optics, IV 74b, 78a, 80b
  orbits, IV 74b, 75a, 79a
  Paul III (Pope), IV 74b
  philosophy, IV 82b
  Planck's constant, IV 91b, 92a
  planets, IV 74b, 76a
  Plato, IV 75a
  Platonism, IV 77a
  Poincaré, IV 79b–81a, 83b, 84a
  polarization, IV 78a
  principle of, IV 74a–74b, 76a–78a, 80a–81a
  principle of equivalence, IV 86b, 89a, 90a
  principle of general covariance, IV 88b, 89b
  Ptolemy, IV 74b, 76b
  Pythagoras, IV 83a, 87b
  quantum theory, IV 85b, 91b
  radiation, IV 84a
  relativistic kinematics, IV 84a
  Ricci, IV 89a
  Riemann, IV 87b–88a
  Riemann-Christoffel curvature tensor, IV 88a, 89a
  Roemer, IV 77b
  Roman Catholic Church, IV

74b
  rotation, IV 75b, 76a, 76b, 80b, 86a
  Saccheri, IV 87a
  science, IV 74b, 75a, 82b, 83b–84a
  simultaneity, IV 81b–83a, 83b
  solar system, IV 75a, 76a
  space, IV 74b, 75b, 76a, 77a, 80b, 83b–91a, 91b, 92a, 295b–296a, 297b, 298b, 300a, 300b
  spaceships, IV 81a–81b, 82b–83a, 84b, 90a–90b
  speed, IV 79a, 81a, 82b, 83b, 84a, 89b–90a, 91b
  stars, IV 76a, 76b, 77b, 86a
  sun, IV 74b, 76a
  symmetry, IV 352b–353a
  synchronization, IV 82a–82b, 84a
  tachyons, IV 83b, 84a
  tensors, IV 89a, 89b
  theory of, I 555a, 556a–559b; IV 79b–83b, 85b–87a, 88a, 88b, 89b–90a, 405b
  time, IV 74b, 75b, 76a, 77a, 79b, 81b–92a, 397a–397b, 405a, 405b
  universe, IV 74a, 74b
  velocity, IV 75b, 76b, 78a, 79a–79b
  Weber, IV 90a
  weightlessness, IV 90a–90b
  Weyl, IV 90b–91a
  Wheeler, IV 92a
  Whittaker, IV 79b–80a
  work, IV 82b
  world lines, IV 90b
  Young, IV 78a
Releus (myth), virtue, IV 366b
Religion, IV 92b–121a
  Abbey of Saint-Victor, III 205b
  aborigines, IV 100a
  Achilles (myth), III 203b
  Adam (Bible), IV 119a
  Adonis (myth), IV 96a, 104b
  aesthetics, IV 106b, 108b
  Africa, IV 94a
  agnosticism, IV 106b, 107b, 120b
  agriculture, IV 96a, 104b
  allegory, III 203b, 204a, 204b, 205b, 206a, 206b; IV 94a
  Amos (Bible), III 202a
  Anabaptists, IV 117a, 117b

anagogicalism, III 205b
analogy, III 206a
Anaxagoras, III 203a, 203b; IV 93a
ancestor worship, IV 93a
animals, IV 95a–95b, 96a, 100a, 107b
Animatism, IV 95b
anthropology, IV 95a, 95b, 96a, 96b, 97a, 107b
anthropomorphism, III 202b, 206a; IV 92b
anticlericalism, IV 120b
anti-Semitism, IV 114a
Antitrinitarians, IV 117a
Anubis (myth), IV 101b
Aphrodite (myth), IV 93a
Apollo (myth), III 203b
Apuleius, IV 93b
archeology, IV 97a, 98a–98b, 99b, 100a
archetypes, III 204b
Argyll (Duke of), IV 106b
Aristophanes, IV 100a
Aristotelianism, IV 109a
Aristotle, III 205b, 206a, 207a
Arminians, IV 117b
art, II 575b, 576b, 581b, 582b; IV 96b
artists, IV 94a
Asia, IV 93b, 94a
astrology, I 125a–126a
atheism, IV 116b, 120a
atomism, III 187b–188a, 203b
Attis (myth), IV 96a, 104b
Atum-Rē (myth), IV 100b
Augustinianism, IV 109a
Australasia, IV 94a
Australia, IV 97a, 100a
authority, IV 118a, 118b
Baal (myth), IV 104b
Babylonia, IV 104a
Bacchus (myth), IV 94a
baptism, IV 102b–103a, 113b, 114a–114b
Bayle, IV 119b–120b
beauty, IV 110a
Béguines, IV 109a
behaviorism, IV 92b, 97a, 99b
Being, IV 109a, 109b, 110b
belief, III 203a; IV 105a
Bellamy, IV 110b
benevolence, IV 111a, 111b
Bergson, III 207a, 565b; IV 119b
Bible, III 201b–202b, 204a–206b, 207b; IV 102b–104a, 106a, 106b, 107b, 111b, 114a, 115a, 118b
birth, IV 94a, 98b, 104b

body, IV 95a
Book of the Dead, IV 101a
Bossuet, IV 109b, 112a
Brahminism, IV 104a
brain, IV 106b, 108a
Brazil, III 541b, 543a, 543b, 545a
Brethren of the Free Spirit, IV 109a
Buddhism, IV 93b, 98a
Bultmann, III 207a
Burnet, III 258a
Burton, IV 112a
Calvin, IV 115a
Calvinism, IV 109b, 110b
Campanella, IV 109a
Campbell, IV 108a
capitalism, IV 115a
Carlyle, IV 200b
casuistry, IV 113a
catastrophism, IV 419b, 420a
Cave of the Trois Frères, IV 100a
cave-art, IV 100b
Chambers, Robert, IV 106a
Channing, IV 111a, 111b
Charlemagne, IV 113b
Chateaubriand, IV 201a
China, I 354a, 354b, 355a, 368a
China (ancient), IV 104a, 105a
Christian Brotherhoods, IV 109a
Christian Commonwealth Men, IV 109a
Christian Perfectionism, IV 111b
Christianity, III 205a, 205b, 206a, 207a; IV 93b, 94a, 96a, 98a, 102a–103a, 105a, 106a, 106b, 107b, 108a–108b, 110b, 113b, 114a, 114b, 115a, 115b, 117a, 118b, 119a
Cicero, III 16b
city-state, IV 99a
civilization, I 614a, 618b, 619b, 620a; IV 94a, 115a
class, I 422a; IV 112b, 114b
Clement of Alexandria, III 205b
Coleridge, IV 111b
colonialism, IV 94b, 95a, 113b
commemoration, IV 103b
communism, III 22b, 675a; IV 111a, 115b
competition, II 64a
Comte, III 534a, 534b, 535a, 536a, 538b, 540a; IV 106b

conformity, IV 114a
Confucius, IV 105a
conscience, IV 106b, 117b, 118a, 119a, 120a
consciousness, III 207a; IV 96b–98a, 112a
conservatism, IV 106a, 106b–107a, 115b, 117a
cosmogony, IV 93b
cosmos, IV 104a
Council of Trent, IV 116b, 119a
Counter-Enlightenment, II 100b, 101b, 102a, 102b, 105b, 106b–107a
Counter-Reformation, IV 116b
Covenanters, IV 109a
Creation, IV 93b, 104b
criticism, III 205b, 206b, 207a; IV 107a, 107b, 111b
Cronus (myth), IV 93a
crusades, IV 113b
culture, I 614a, 618b, 619b, 620a; II 127b, 128b; III 203a, 207a; IV 94a, 95a, 95b, 98a, 98b, 99b, 100a, 103b, 104a, 104b, 111a, 115a, 116b, 118b, 120b
cynicism, I 629a
dance, IV 96b, 100a
Daniel (Bible), III 202b
Darwin, IV 107a–107b
Darwinism, IV 107a
death, I 637a; IV 94a, 98a, 98b, 100b, 101b, 102b, 104b, 113b
defined, IV 99b, 112b
deism, IV 92b, 93a, 94b, 96a, 96b, 98b, 119a
Demeter (myth), III 203b; IV 102a
democracy, IV 114b
Democritus, III 203b
demonology, IV 97b
Descartes, IV 118a
desire, IV 99b
determinism, IV 107b
Deutero-Isaiah (Bible), III 202b
Dewey, John, III 207a
dignity, IV 136a–146a
Diogenes of Apollonia, III 203b
Dionysus (myth), IV 96b
disease, II 396b, 397a, 406a
dissent, IV 113b, 114a
dogma, IV 107a, 107b–108a, 116a, 117a, 118b, 119a, 120b
Donatists, IV 113b
drama, IV 100a
Draper, IV 107a
dualism, II 38a–40a, 42a–

43b
Dumézil, IV 94b–95a
Dupuis, IV 94a
Durkheim, IV 96b
Eastern Orthodox Church, IV 103a
economics, IV 96a, 100a, 115a, 115b, 120a–120b
Edict of Nantes, IV 113a, 116a, 116b, 117b, 119a, 119b
education, II 74b, 78b–79a, 80b
Edwards, Jonathan, IV 109a, 109b–110b, 111a, 111b
Egypt (ancient), II 582b; IV 93a, 93b, 94b, 98a, 100b–101b, 102a, 102b, 104b, 105a
Eleusinian Mysteries, IV 102a
embalmment, IV 100b
emotion, IV 97a, 98b, 99b, 105a, 110a, 112a
empiricism, IV 106a
Enlightenment, II 90a, 91a, 100a; IV 120a
environment, II 127b, 128b; IV 107b
Epicurus, IV 93a
epistemology, III 206a
Erasmus, IV 118b
Erastianism, IV 117b–118a, 119a
ethics, III 444a, 445b, 446b; IV 70b, 71a, 96b, 111b, 117a, 118b, 119a
ethnology, IV 95a, 96b–97a
Euhemerus of Messene, IV 93a
Eusebius of Caesarea, IV 93b
evangelicalism, IV 109a, 111a
evil, II 161b–162a, 162b, 163a, 165a, 168b, 169a–169b; IV 112b
evolution, III 435a; IV 95a, 95b, 96a, 106a, 107b, 108a
excommunication, IV 117b
existentialism, III 159a, 207a
exogamy, IV 96b
experience, IV 97b, 98a
exploration, IV 93b, 94a, 95a
Ezekiel (Bible), III 202b
faith, IV 103a, 106b, 113b, 114b, 116b, 119a
Faithful in Love, III 102b, 103a, 103b
Faraday, IV 108a
fascination, IV 97b

Faust (legend), III 249b, 250b

fear, IV 93b

Federalists, IV 109a

Fénelon, IV 109a, 109b

fertility, IV 98b, 100a, 104b

fetishism, IV 94a

Finney, IV 111b

Floresta, III 540a

food, IV 98b

France, I 397b–398a; III 543b; IV 100a, 106b, 107b, 109a, 113a, 116b, 119a

Franklin, III 603b

Frazer, IV 95b–96a

freedom, II 44b, 64a; III 40a–40b; IV 113a, 119a

freedom of speech, II 252a, 252b, 253b, 254b, 256b, 262a

Freud, II 556b–557b; III 216a, 312a–312b; IV 96b–97a

Friends of God, IV 109a

Fundamentalism, III 206b–207a

funerary ritual, IV 104b

geology, IV 106a

Germany, IV 97a, 106a, 106b, 107b, 108a, 116b

Gnosticism, III 205b

God, III 202a, 202b, 204b, 205a, 206a, 206b, 207a; IV 93a, 93b, 94a, 94b, 95b, 96a, 98b, 100b, 101a, 104a, 104b, 105a, 106a, 108a, 108b, 109b, 110a, 110b, 111a, 111b, 113b, 115b, 117b, 119b

good, IV 109b, 174a–174b, 177b, 182a–182b, 184a

grace, IV 110a, 111a, 112a

Great Awakening, IV 109a, 109b, 110a, 112a

Great Britain, III 489b, 674b; IV 95a, 106a, 106b, 107a, 107b, 108a, 116b, 120a

Greece (ancient), II 565b–566b, 674a–679b, 681a–681b, 683a–684a, 685a; III 201b, 202b, 203a, 203b–204a, 204b–206a, 572a; IV 92b–93b, 94a, 96b, 98a, 100a, 101b–102a, 228a, 228b, 336b

guilt, IV 96b

Haeckel, IV 108a

Haggai (Bible), III 202b

happiness, II 374b, 386a

harmony, II 388a, 389a, 392a; IV 110a

Harrison, Jane, IV 96b

Hartley, III 234b

healing ritual, IV 101b

health, II 396b, 397a, 406a; IV 116a

Hector (myth), III 203b

Hegel, II 408a, 410a–411b, 414a, 414b; IV 96a

Heidegger, III 207a

Heraclitus, III 203b

Herder, IV 203a, 209a

heredity, IV 107b

heresy, IV 93b, 112b, 113b–116a, 117a, 119a, 120a, 120b

heterodoxy, IV 113b

historiography, II 466a, 468b, 469b, 470b, 471a, 471b, 473a, 474a, 474b, 483b 487b; IV 147a

history, IV 93b, 100b, 105a 106a, 107a, 107b, 108a, 111a, 112b, 117a

Hobbes, IV 119a

holy, II 511b–514b; IV 97b

Holy Roman Empire, IV 117a

Holy Spirit, IV 111a

holy war, IV 113b

Homer, III 203a, 203b, 207a

Hooke, IV 104b

Hopkins, IV 110b, 111a

Hosea (Bible), III 202a

Huguenots, II 428a; IV 109a, 112b, 113b, 116b, 117a, 119b

human nature, III 572a; IV 105a, 107b, 108a, 111a

humanism, II 519b, 520b; IV 132a, 132b

Hume, IV 93a–93b

hunting, IV 100a

Husserl, III 207a

Hutcheson, IV 109a, 111a

Huxley, IV 107a, 108a

iconography, II 524b–525a, 526a, 530b–533b, 536a, 537b, 538b, 539b

idea, II 548a, 548b

idealism, IV 106a, 111b

ideology, II 555b, 557a–557b; IV 109a, 115b–116a

illuminism, IV 109a, 109b–112a

imagery, III 201b–202b, 203a, 203b, 204a, 206a, 207a, 207b

imagination, III 212b, 216a, 219b, 222a

Imhotep, IV 93a

imitation, IV 100b–103a

immanence, IV 108a, 108b

immortality, IV 93a, 98a, 98b

impiety, II 564a, 564b–565b, 566a

impressionism, II 575b, 576a, 576b, 581b, 582b

incest, IV 96b

India, III 430a–430b

India (ancient), IV 94b, 98b, 104a

Indians (American), IV 94a

individualism, II 596a, 597b, 598b, 602b–603a; IV 118a, 119a–120b

Inquisition, IV 117a

international peace, III 448a, 448b, 449b

Irenaeus, III 205b

irony, II 634b

irrationalism, II 635b, 637a–637b

Ishtar (myth), IV 101b

Isis (myth), IV 93b, 100b

Islam, II 639b, 640a, 641a, 644b, 646a, 647a, 648b, 649a, 650a; III 648b; IV 93b, 98a, 114a

Italy, IV 117a

James, Wm., III 561b, 563a, 565b, 568b; IV 112a

Jefferson, IV 21a

Jeremiah (Bible), III 202a, 204b

Jesuits, IV 94a, 109a, 113a, 117a

Jesus Christ, III 205b, 206b; IV 93b, 94a, 96a, 102b, 103a

Jews (ancient), II 466a

Joseph (Bible), III 204b

Judaism, III 202b, 203a, 204a–206a; IV 93b, 94b, 98a, 103b, 104a, 105b, 113a, 114a

judgment, IV 101a, 106b, 108b, 110a, 111a

Julius Africanus, IV 93b

Jung, III 313a; IV 97a

justice, II 652b, 656a, 657a

Kant, II 548a

Kelvin, IV 108a

knowledge, IV 94a, 105a, 106a, 111b

Lafitau, IV 94a

Lamarckism, IV 106a

Lang, IV 96a

language, II 661a, 661b, 670b; IV 94a–94b, 106a

Latin America, IV 94a

law, I 290a; II 674a–679b, 681a–681b, 683a–684a, 685a, 686b, 688a, 689a, 689b–690a; III 1a, 6b, 7a, 11a, 11b, 28b–29a; IV 113a, 115a, 115b, 119a

Le Roy, III 565a–565b

liberalism, III 36a, 40a–40b,

42a, 42b, 43a, 43b, 45a; IV 109b, 110b, 111a, 112b, 117b

liberty, IV 113b

light, IV 110a

linguistics, III 69a

Lister, IV 108a

literalism, III 205b, 206b, 207a

literary paradox, III 79b–80a

literature, III 202b, 204b, 206b; IV 94a, 109b, 110b

Locke, III 598b; IV 109b, 119b, 120a

logic, IV 102a

longevity, III 90a, 90b, 92a, 93a

Louis XIV, IV 113b

love, III 98b, 100a–100b, 101b, 103a, 103b, 106a, 107a, 107b; IV 109a, 109b, 110a, 111a, 111b, 118b

loyalty, III 108b, 109a, 112b, 113a, 113b, 115a

Lucretius, IV 93a

Luther, III 206a–206b

Machiavellism, III 118a, 119b–120a, 122a–122b

macrocosm and microcosm, III 128a

magic, III 246a; IV 96a, 98b, 100a, 100b, 101a, 102a

majorities, IV 116a

Malebranche, IV 109a

Manicheism, IV 98a, 115a, 115b

Man-Machine, III 132b, 133a, 137a, 140a

Marduk (myth), IV 104a

marriage, IV 94a

Marx, III 167b

Marxism, III 147a, 148a, 148b–149a, 150b, 159a, 166b, 167b; IV 113a, 115b

Mass, IV 103a

materialism, IV 106b, 107b

matter, III 187b–188a

Maxwell, IV 108a

measurement, IV 399a, 399b

mechanism, IV 115a

medicine, IV 116a

Mesopotamia (ancient), IV 93b, 94b, 101b, 104a, 105b, 226a

metaphor, III 201b–208a

metaphysics, III 212b, 216a, 219b, 222a

Metrodorus of Lampsacus, III 203b

Middle Ages, II 473a; III 528b; IV 93b, 114b, 115b

the military, IV 113b
Mill, J. S., III 642b
millenarianism, IV 117b
Milton, IV 119a
mind, IV 94b, 95b, 97a, 98a, 98b, 120b
minorities, IV 112b, 116a
miracles, IV 106b, 108a
Mithra (myth), IV 94a
Modernism, III 206b
Molière, IV 119b
monogamy, IV 96a
monotheism, IV 94b, 95b, 96a, 113b, 114a
Montaigne, IV 114b
moral sense, III 234b
morality, III 204a, 205a, 205b; IV 96a, 101a, 106b, 107a, 108b, 110a, 110b, 111a, 116b, 118b
mortuary ritual, IV 101a, 101b, 102a, 102b
Moses (Bible), III 204b, 205a
motif, III 238a, 239b
mountains in literature, III 254a, 257b, 258a
Müller, Max, IV 94b
music, II 388a, 389a, 392a; III 264b–266b, 268b, 269a, 269b–271a, 271b
mysticism, IV 109a, 110a, 119a
mythology, III 203a, 203b, 205a, 272a, 274b, 275a–294a, 295a, 301a–304b, 305b, 306a, 307a–309b, 311a–315a, 316b, 317b; IV 94b, 95b, 96a, 97a, 101a, 101b, 105b
nationalism, III 321b, 324b, 325a, 326b, 328b, 334b, 335a, 336b–338a
naturalism in art, III 342a
natural law, III 20b, 22b, 25b
natural liberty, II 63b, 64a–64b
Nature, III 203a, 348a, 351a; IV 93a, 95a, 95b, 96a, 104a–104b, 106b, 108b, 115a
Nazism, III 597b
Neanderthal Man, IV 98b
Near East, IV 98b, 104b
necessity, III 352a, 354a, 355a
need, IV 93b, 99a, 105a
Neolithic era, IV 98b
Neo-Platonism, III 373a, 373b, 376a, 377a, 377b; IV 109a
Nephthys (myth), IV 100b
Netherlands, IV 109a,

110b, 112b, 113a, 117b, 119b, 120b
neurosis, IV 96b
Noah (Bible), IV 106a
numinous, IV 97a–97b
obscurantism, IV 107a
Oedipus complex, IV 96b
omnipotence, IV 93a
Orientalism, III 100a–100b, 101b, 428a–439a
Origen, III 205b
origins of, IV 92b–99a
orthodoxy, IV 113b, 115b, 116a, 118b
Osiris (myth), IV 94a, 96a, 98a, 100b–102b, 104b
Otto, Rudolf, IV 97a–97b
paganism, IV 93b, 94a, 98a, 113a, 114a, 117b
pain, IV 107b
Palaeolithic era, IV 98b, 100a, 101b, 103b
pantheism, IV 108a
Parker, Theodore, IV 111b
parricide, IV 96b
Pascal, IV 109a, 109b, 118a–118b
peace, III 444a, 445b, 446b
Peace of Augsburg, IV 118a
Peirce, III 555a, 565a, 569b
periodization in history, III 479b, 480b
perennial philosophy, III 457b–459b
persecution, IV 112b–114a, 116a–118b, 119b
Persephone (myth), IV 102a
Persia (ancient), IV 115a
Pestalozzi, IV 109a
philanthropy, III 486b, 487b, 488a, 489b, 490a, 490b, 491b
Philo Judaeus, III 204a–205a, 206b
philology, IV 94b
philosophers, IV 106a, 108a
philosophy, III 203a, 204a, 204b, 205a, 205b, 206a, 207a; IV 93a, 93b, 97a, 97b, 106a, 106b, 107b–110a, 111b
Pietism, IV 109b–111b
Pius IV (Pope), IV 107a, 114b
plagiarism, III 205a
Plato, II 566a; III 203b–204a, 204b, 205a, 207a
pleasure, II 374b, 386a
Plotinus, III 376a
pluralism, IV 113a, 119a

poetry, III 204a, 204b, 205a, 528b
Poland, IV 113a
politics, IV 113b, 115a, 116a, 116b, 117a, 117b, 118b, 119a, 120a
polygamy, IV 96a
polytheism, IV 94b, 95b, 96a, 113b
Pope, III 397a
positivism, III 533b, 534a, 534b, 537a, 538b, 540a, 541b, 543a, 543b, 544a, 545a
power, IV 95b
pragmatism, III 552b, 554b, 555a, 558a, 561b, 563a, 563b, 565a–565b, 568b, 569b
Presbyterians, IV 109a, 111a, 111b
primitivism, III 582a, 586b, 588a, 593b, 597b, 598b, 599a, 602a, 603a, 603b; IV 95a, 96b, 97b, 99a, 107b
private property, III 654a
progress, III 625a, 626a, 628a, 630a, 631a, 636a, 636b, 637b, 638b, 639a, 641a, 642a, 642b, 643b, 644b, 645a
prophecy, III 201b–202b, 659a–659b, 606b, 661a, 661b
protest movements, III 670a, 671a, 674b, 675a
Protestantism, III 206a, 206b, 207a; IV 108b, 112b, 113a, 116b, 117a, 117b
Psalms (Bible), III 202b
psyche, IV 108a
psychoanalysis, IV 96b
psychology, IV 1b, 2a, 2b, 8b, 10a, 17a, 19a, 19b, 21a, 23b, 96b, 97a, 110b, 112b, 118a, 119b
puberty ritual, IV 105a
Puritanism, IV 109a, 109b, 111a
Pyramid Texts, IV 100b–101a, 105b
Pythagoreans, III 203b; IV 31a
Quakers, IV 109a
Radin, IV 96a
rationalism, III 203a, 301a–303b; IV 48b, 93b, 94a, 96a, 97b, 98a, 105a, 109a, 118a, 120a
Rē (myth), IV 98a
realism in literature, IV 53b
reason, IV 107a, 118a, 119a, 119b

redemption, IV 97a
Reformation, III 206a–206b; IV 118a, 119a
relativism, IV 70b, 71a, 114a
Renaissance, IV 93b–94a, 98a, 115a, 115b, 124a, 126b, 127b, 132a, 132b, 136a–146a, 147a
repentance, IV 97a
resurrection, IV 101a, 102b, 104b
revelation, III 205a; IV 108b
revivalism, IV 111a
revolution, IV 117a, 153a
rhetoric, III 203b
right, IV 174a–174b, 177b, 182a–182b, 184a
ritual, II 675b; IV 99a–105b, 113b
Roman Catholic Church, III 205b, 206a, 206b, 207a; IV 94a, 99a, 103a, 107a, 107b, 108b, 112b, 113a, 114b, 115a, 116b, 117a, 117b, 119a, 120a
romanticism, IV 111b, 196b, 199b, 200a, 200b, 201a, 202a, 203a, 203b, 205a, 205b, 206b, 209a, 210a
Rome (ancient), III 373b; IV 93a–93b, 94a, 98a, 103b–104a, 113b, 115a, 117b
Royce, IV 111b
Russia, III 674b
sacraments, IV 113b
sacrifice, II 675b; IV 97a
sacrificial ritual, IV 103b–104a
Saint Augustine, III 205b; IV 93b, 109a, 113b–114a, 115a, 119b
Saint Cyprian, IV 115b
Saint Jerome, III 205b
Saint John, IV 103a
Saint Paul, III 205a–205b; IV 102b, 103a
Saint-Simon, III 641a
Saint Thomas Aquinas, III 205b–206a; IV 114a, 116a
saints, IV 111a
salvation, IV 101a, 111a, 224a, 225a, 226a, 227a, 228a, 233a
sanctification, IV 111b
Sanskrit language, IV 94b
Satan, IV 93b, 94a, 103a
Saxons, IV 113b
schism, IV 113b, 117a, 117b

Schleiermacher, II 411b; IV 108b, 200b, 201a, 210a
Schmidt, IV 96a
scholasticism, IV 94b, 109a
science, III 206b, 207a, 432b–437a, 439a; IV 97a, 106a–108b, 115a, 118b
scientific method, IV 106a–106b, 108a
scientists, IV 106a, 106b, 107a, 108a
Scotland, IV 106a, 109a, 110a, 110b, 111a
sculpture, IV 94a
sects, III 648b
secularism, IV 105a, 112b, 113b, 116a, 117a, 117b, 120b
senses, III 205b
Set (myth), IV 100b
sex, IV 97a
Shang Ti (myth), IV 104a, 105a
sin, IV 93b, 102b, 103a, 107b, 110a, 113b, 116b, 224a, 225a, 226a, 227a, 228a, 233a
skepticism, IV 117a
slavery, IV 111b–112b
Smith, Adam, II 63b, 64a–64b
Smith, John, IV 109b
social contract, IV 254a, 254b, 255b, 256a
socialism, III 675a
society, IV 93b, 96b, 97a, 97b, 99a, 105a, 112b, 114a, 114b–115b, 117b, 120b
Socinians, IV 117a
sociology, IV 96b, 116a
Socrates, III 203a–204a
Sorel, III 565a, 565b
soteriology, IV 93b, 102a, 103b
soul, IV 95a, 109b, 111a, 115b
Spain, IV 113a, 117a, 120b
Spencer, II 182a; IV 93a, 106b, 107b
Spinoza, IV 108a, 119a
spirit, IV 95a, 96b, 110a, 111b
spiritualism, IV 102a
State, IV 112b, 115a, 116a, 117b, 119a, 120a
Stoicism, III 204a, 204b, 588a
supernatural, IV 95b, 97a, 99b, 106b, 111a
superstition, IV 107a
Sweden, IV 113a
Switzerland, IV 109a, 113a, 117a
symbolism, II 581a; III

203b; IV 99b, 341b
symmetry, IV 347b, 348a
syncretism, IV 93b
taboos, IV 96b, 97b
Tammuz (myth), IV 101b, 104b
technology, IV 364b
temperance, IV 366b, 373b, 378a
terror, IV 97a
Tertullian, III 205b
Thales, III 203a
Theagenes of Rhegium, III 203b
theater, II 538a
theodicy, IV 379a–381b
Theodore of Mopsuestia, III 205b
theologians, IV 108a
theology, IV 97a, 101a, 108a–108b, 110b, 111a, 111b, 114a, 116a, 117b, 118b
theophilanthropy, IV 109a
Thomism, IV 108b
thought, IV 97a, 106b
time, IV 97b–98a, 399a, 399b
toleration, IV 112b–121a
totemism, IV 96b, 97b
totalitarianism, IV 407a, 410b
trade, IV 94a
tradition, III 203b
tragic sense, IV 413a–413b, 414b
transcendentalism, IV 111b
Transylvania, IV 113a
tribes, IV 97b
Trinity, IV 103a
truth, III 204a, 204b, 205a, 206a; IV 106b, 113b, 114a, 118b, 119a, 120b, 177b
Tylor, IV 95a, 111a
Tyndall, IV 107a
uniformitarianism, IV 419b, 420a
U.S.S.R., II 562a
Unitarianism, IV 111a
U.S., II 64a–64b; III 428a–439a; IV 106b, 107a, 108a, 109a–112a
unity of science, IV 433a
universe, III 203a; IV 97b
Upper Palaeolitic era, IV 98b, 100a
Uranos (myth), IV 93a
ut pictura poesis, IV 476a
utilitarianism, IV 111b, 120a
Utopia, IV 459a, 461a, 461b, 462a, 463b, 464a
Vico, IV 94a, 109a
Victorian sentiment, IV

217b–219b, 221a, 222a, 222b
violence, IV 118b
virtue, IV 109a, 110a, 111a, 112b, 373a, 477b
Volksgeist, IV 491a, 491b, 492b, 494b
Voltaire, IV 118b, 124a
vox populi, IV 496b
Walloon Synod, IV 112b
war, III 444a, 448b; IV 113a, 113b, 118b
Weltanschauung, IV 93b
Whigs, IV 119b
Whitehead, III 207a; IV 97b, 105a
Wilberforce, IV 107a
will, IV 109b, 110a, 112b
witchcraft, IV 521a, 522b
Wittgenstein, III 207a
women, IV 526b–528a, 529a
Wright, III 561b
Xenophanes, III 203b; IV 92b–93a
Zechariah (Bible), III 202b
Zeus (myth), III 203b; IV 93a
Zoroastrianism, IV 98a
Remak, H. H. H., romanticism, IV 196a
Remak, Robert (1815–1865), cell division, II 286a–287a
Rembrandt (1606–1669)
  art, II 309a
  baroque in literature, I 191b
  genius, II 309a
  iconography, II 538a
  impressionism, II 578a
  music, III 267a
Rémi d'Auxerre, mythology, III 289a
Remond, Pierre, game theory, II 264b
Remond de Montmort, perennial philosophy, III 458a, 461a
Rémusat, Jean Pierre Abel (1788–1832), China, I 367a
Remy, Nicholas (c. 16th century A.D.), witchcraft, IV 522a
Renaissance, IV 121a–152a
  aesthetics, II 218a–218b, 220a, 221b, 222a, 223a; IV 124b, 128a, 354a–354b, 439b–440a, 442b
  alchemy, I 28b, 31b–32b
  algebra, III 178a
  allegory, I 46b, 47a–47b
  ambiguity, I 54b–56a, 58a–58b
  anatomy, IV 440a
  angels, IV 132a, 138b,

140b, 141a, 146a
  animals, III 596a
  anthropology, IV 138b, 139b, 145a, 145b
  Arabs, IV 139a, 139b
  architecture, IV 122b, 123a, 124a, 127a, 133a, 439b, 440a
  argumentation, IV 129a
  aristocracy, IV 441b
  Aristotelianism, IV 130a, 131b, 132a, 133a, 134a, 134b, 135a, 139a, 140b, 141b, 146a
  Aristotle, IV 369a
  arithmetic, III 178a; IV 438b
  art, II 297b–309a, 310a; III 510a, 511b, 512b, 513a; IV 121b–127b, 130b, 131a, 133a, 134b, 136a, 141a, 148b, 149b, 150a, 437a–441b, 442a, 443a
  artists, IV 123a, 437b, 439b
  asceticism, IV 133b, 141a
  astronomy, IV 438b, 440a, 441a
  atheism, IV 128a
  atomism, I 132b–138b
  atonement, IV 138a, 138b, 140a
  authority, III 11a
  balance of power, I 180b–181b
  beauty, I 197b, 198a, 200b; II 218a–218b; III 508b, 510a–514a; IV 122b, 126b, 129b, 136a, 139a, 440b
  behavior, IV 147b
  belief, IV 147b
  Bible, IV 121b, 124a, 135a, 136b–137a, 138a, 139b, 144a, 145b
  body, IV 439a
  bourgeois, IV 125a, 131a, 147b
  Buddhism, I 255b
  Burckhardt, III 479b, 480a; IV 124b, 125b–128a, 437a–440a, 441a, 485a
  capitalism, IV 147b, 151b, 442a
  Carolingian, IV 127b
  catastrophism, IV 142b
  catharsis, I 269a–269b
  causation, I 275b–276a
  Chain of Being, I 326b–327a, 327b; IV 139b
  chance images, I 342b, 345a–349a
  chaos, IV 138a, 141b, 142a
  Christianity, III 509a–514b; IV 121b, 122a, 123a, 125b, 126b, 128a, 129b, 130b,

131a, 132b, 134b, 135a, 136a–146a
city, I 429b–431b
city planning, I 429b–431b
city state, III 321a, 321b, 323b; IV 122b, 123a–123b, 438a, 441b
civil service, IV 123b
civilization, IV 130a, 142a, 150a
class, IV 438a, 441b
classicism, I 451a, 452a; III 355b
classification of the arts, I 457a, 459a–460b, 461b
classification of the sciences, I 464b
Clement of Alexandria, IV 137a
climate, IV 148a, 150a
community, IV 132b
continuity, IV 134b
cosmic images, I 515a
cosmic voyages, I 524a, 527a
cosmology, IV 131a, 134a, 134b, 136b, 139a, 139b, 143a, 145b, 440b, 442b
Counter-Reformation, IV 126a
Counter-Renaissance, IV 130a, 135a
craftsmanship, IV 133a, 134b, 437b, 441b
Creation, IV 137a–140b, 142a, 144a, 145b
creativity, IV 437a
creativity in art, I 585b
cryptography, IV 441b
culture, II 129a–129b; IV 129b, 130a, 130b, 141a–142a, 143b, 437a, 443a
cycles, I 626a–626b; IV 138a, 148a, 150a–150b, 151b
dancing, IV 439a
death, I 636a, 645a; IV 439b
degeneration, IV 148a, 150a, 150b–151a
deism, I 648a, 649a
demonology, I 668b, 669b, 670a
despotism, II 4a
determinism, IV 144b–145a
dialectics, IV 438b, 441a
dignity, IV 136a–147a, 439a, 441b
discontinuity, IV 134b
discovery, IV 148a, 148b, 149a, 149b
disease, II 399b, 403b
divination, IV 144b, 145a, 145b

dualism, II 41a, 218a; IV 138b
economic history, II 45a, 45b, 46b
economics, IV 122b, 129b, 141a, 147a, 148a, 151b, 438a, 439b, 442a
Edict of Nantes, II 424b, 428a
education, IV 121b, 122a, 123b, 124a, 127a, 127b, 128a, 129b, 130b, 437a, 437b, 438b–441b
Egypt (ancient), IV 139a
elite, IV 123b
eloquence, IV 129b; IV 438b–439a
emotion, IV 142b, 147b, 437b
empiricism, IV 134a, 135a, 440b–441a, 442b, 443a
Enlightenment, II 89a, 90a; IV 124a
entropy, II 116a
environment, II 129a–129b
Epicureanism, II 137b; IV 142b, 143a
epistemology, IV 139b
equality, IV 438a
eschatology, IV 137b, 138a
ethics, IV 129b, 440a, 441a, 442a–442b
evil, IV 133b, 138b
evolution of literature, II 170a, 172a
existentialism, IV 142a
experience, IV 134a, 440a, 440b, 441a, 443a
faith, IV 134b, 135a, 142a, 142b, 143a, 147b
Fall, IV 137a, 138a, 138b, 140a, 143a
fate, II 232a; IV 143a, 145a
Faust (legend), III 245b, 247b
feeling, IV 147b
Florence, IV 122a–124a
fortune, II 232a; IV 142a, 143a
France, II 294a–294b; III 479b, 483b; IV 121b, 124a, 124b–125b, 131a
free will, II 137b; IV 131a–131b, 132a, 142b, 143a
freedom, IV 130a, 131a–131b, 135b, 141a, 142a, 145a, 145b, 146a, 147b, 152a, 438a
French Revolution, IV 124b
genius, II 293a, 293b, 294a–294b, 297b, 298a, 298b, 300a–302b, 303b–304a, 304b, 305a, 306a, 307b, 308a, 308b, 309a, 310a,

314a, 315a–321a, 325b; IV 125a, 128a
geography, IV 440a
geometry, IV 438b, 440a
Germany, IV 121b, 123b, 124b, 125a
Gnosticism, IV 138b
God, II 347a–348b; IV 123a, 131a–132b, 136b–139a, 140b, 142a–143a, 144a, 145a–146a, 149b
Golden Age, III 481b–482a
Golden Age (myth), IV 131a
good, IV 133b, 138b, 143a
Gothic, II 367b–368b, 371a, 373a, 373b
grace, IV 138a, 138b, 139a, 142a, 142b
grammar, IV 123b, 438b, 439b
Great Britain, III 483b, 484b; IV 123b, 124a, 131a
Greece (ancient), IV 122a, 123a, 124a–126a, 129b–133a, 136a–138a, 139a, 144a, 147a
Greek language, IV 123b, 143b
happiness, IV 132a, 143a, 152a
harmony, II 389a, 389b, 390b–391a, 391b, 392a, 393a; IV 39b, 41a–41b, 134b, 142b, 439b, 440b
health, II 399b, 403b; IV 133b
heaven, IV 142b, 143a
Hebrew language, IV 143b
heresy, II 424a–431a
Hermeticism, II 431a, 432a, 433a, 433b
heroes, IV 136b
hierarchy, II 434b, 436b–438b, 440b, 442b–443a; IV 131a, 139b, 145a, 145b, 146a, 147b
historians, III 356a
historicism, II 458a, 459a
historiography, II 474b, 476b, 479a, 481b–484b, 490b, 506a, 518a–518b; IV 130b, 131a, 134b, 147a–152a
history, IV 123b, 125b, 126b, 127a, 129a, 129b–132b, 135a, 138a, 141a, 141b, 142a, 144a, 145b, 147a, 147b, 150a, 151a, 151b, 438b, 439a, 441a, 442b
holy, II 513a
homosexuality, II 512b, 514b

honor, IV 133b
Huguenots, II 424b, 428a
human nature, IV 142b–143a, 150b
humanism, II 425b–426a, 427b, 515a, 515b, 516a–516b, 518a–518b, 519a, 520a, 521a–521b, 523a; III 323b; IV 122a–122b, 124a, 124b, 125b, 126b, 128a, 129a–136a, 136b, 137b, 141a–146a, 148a–148b, 171a, 171b, 437b, 438b–443a
iconography, II 528a–532a, 534a, 538a
idea, II 543a, 545b, 546a; IV 121a–129a
ideal, IV 438b–439b; 440b, 441b, 443a
image, IV 138a–138b, 140b, 142b, 143a, 144a
imagination, III 210a, 211b, 212b, 221b, 222a; IV 145a
immortality, I 645a; IV 137a, 137b, 144b, 145a
impressionism, II 577b, 582b
incarnation, IV 137a, 138a, 140a, 142a, 146a
individualism, II 89a, 297b, 298a, 298b, 300a–302b, 303b–306a, 307b–309a, 310a, 595a–597b; IV 126b, 136b, 141a, 142a, 142b, 147b, 437a, 438a, 439a
infinity, II 605a, 608a, 609a, 609b, 612b; IV 129a
instinct, IV 135a
intolerance, IV 115b
invention, IV 148a, 148b, 149a–149b
Islam, II 640a, 640b, 644a, 646b, 649b, 650a
Italy, III 479b, 480a; IV 121a–146a, 437a–443a
Judaism, IV 130b, 136b 137a, 139a, 143b, 145b
judgment, IV 147b
justice, IV 131a, 138a, 440b
knowledge, IV 132a, 133a, 135b, 139b, 149a, 149b, 437a, 440b–443a
language, II 667a–669b; IV 121b, 122a, 122b, 123b, 124b, 127b, 130b, 131a, 135a, 143b
Latin language, IV 121b, 122a, 122b, 123b, 124b, 127b, 130b, 143b
law, III 11a; IV 130b, 132b, 135a, 437b
leisure, IV 438a, 439a

liberalism, III 36a, 37a–37b
liberty, IV 122b
life, I 636a
literary criticism, I 596b, 597a
literary paradox, III 77a–77b, 78a, 78b, 79a
literature, III 81b, 82b; IV 121b–127b, 130b, 131a, 134b, 141a, 142a, 146a, 147a–152a, 331a–331b, 437b, 439a–443a
logarithms, III 178b
logic, IV 122a, 129a, 129b, 134b–135b, 438b
longevity, III 89a, 91b
love, III 95b, 508b, 510a, 511a–513b, 514a, 514b, 516a, 523b; IV 138b, 142b–143a
Machiavelli, III 356a
Machiavellism, III 116b–117a, 124b, 125a
magic, IV 134a, 145a, 145b
materialism, IV 141b, 142a
mathematics, III 178a–178b, 179a, 181b, 184b; IV 129a, 134a, 437b, 438b, 439b–443a
matter, III 191b–192a, 192b, 193b–194a; IV 138b
measurement, IV 440a, 440b, 441a, 443a
mechanism, IV 440a, 441b
medieval science, II 203a–204a
medicine, IV 132b, 135a
memory, IV 138b
metaphor, IV 121b
metaphysics, III 210a, 211b, 212b, 221b, 222a; IV 122a, 140b, 439b, 440b, 441a
methodology, III 382b–383b; IV 147b–148a, 440a, 441a, 441b
Michelet, IV 124b, 125a–125b, 126b, 479b
microcosm, IV 137b, 140a
Middle Ages, III 355b, 480a; IV 123b, 124a, 126a–127b, 129b–131a, 133a, 133b, 134b, 135a, 135b, 139a–141a, 142a, 147a, 147b, 148b, 151b, 438a, 438b, 440b, 443a
Middle Platonism, IV 136b, 144a
mimesis, III 227b–229a; IV 137a
mind, IV 136a–136b, 137a, 138b
miracles, IV 133a
modernity, III 480a

morality, III 116b, 508b, 511a, 512a, 512b; IV 121b, 122a, 123a, 123b, 124a, 126b, 127b, 128a, 132a, 132b, 133b, 136a, 141a, 141b, 142a, 147b, 438b–440b, 442a–443a
mortality, IV 137a, 137b
mountains in literature, III 253b, 255a
music, II 314a, 315a, 321a, 325b, 389a, 389b, 390b–393a; III 261a–263a, 270a; IV 133b, 437b, 438b, 439a
musicians, II 314a, 315a–321a
mysticism, IV 126b, 137a, 138a, 138b
mythology, III 288b–293b, 295a, 296a, 299a; IV 137a, 139a
nationalism, IV 123b, 124b, 125a, 151b
natural law, III 19b
naturalism in art, III 340b, 342a, 343a, 345a; IV 132b–134b
Nature, III 347b, 349a; IV 129a, 131a, 133a, 133b, 134a, 134b, 140b, 149b, 150b, 151a, 441a
necessity, III 355a, 355b–356a
neo-classicism, IV 147a
neo-classicism in art, III 363b, 364b, 368a, 369a, 370a, 370b
Neo-Platonism, II 427a; III 377b; IV 131b, 132a–132b, 137a, 139a, 139b, 140a, 140b, 144a, 144a, 144b, 145b, 442a, 442b
numbers, III 406a
optics, IV 440a
oratory, IV 439a
order, II 434b, 436b–438b, 440b, 442b–443a; IV 131b, 133a, 133b, 134a
organicism, III 424a
origin of the term, IV 121a–121b, 123a
pain, IV 133b
painting, II 571b–672b; IV 122a, 122b, 123a, 124a, 130b, 133a, 439a, 439b, 440a, 441b, 466a, 467a, 467b, 468a, 468b, 469a, 469b, 471b, 472b, 473b
papacy, IV 123a, 149b
passions, IV 138b, 142b
peace, IV 131a
Pelagianism, IV 138b
perception, IV 129b, 131a, 131b

perennial philosophy, III 457b, 459a–459b
perfectibility, III 468b; IV 123b, 144a, 148a, 149a, 150a, 151b
periodization in history, III 477a–477b, 479b–480b
periodization in literary history, III 481b, 482a, 483b, 484b
Peripateticism, IV 137a, 137b
perspective, II 612b; IV 440a
pessimism, IV 148a, 151a
philanthropy, III 491b
philology, IV 124a, 127b, 440a
philosophy, IV 121b, 122a, 123b, 124a, 129a, 129b, 132a, 132b, 134b, 138a, 140b, 141a, 141b, 142a, 143b, 144a–144b, 145a, 146a, 151a, 438b, 439a, 439b, 440a, 441a, 443a
physics, IV 132b, 133a, 134b, 437b
piety, IV 144b, 145b
Plato, III 95b
Platonism, III 504b, 506b–507b, 508b–515a, 516a, 523b; IV 126b, 131b–132b, 134a, 134b, 137a–140a, 142a, 143b, 144a–145b, 146a, 440a
pleasure, IV 133b, 136b, 142b, 143a
poetry, II 220a; III 530a, 530b, 531a; IV 122a, 123b, 124a, 129b, 130b, 135a, 141a, 141b, 151a, 438b, 439a, 466a, 467a–473b
politics, III 117b–118a, 323b; IV 122b, 123a, 124a, 124b, 125a, 127b, 129b, 130b, 131a, 132b, 136a, 141a, 141b, 147a, 147b, 438a, 439a, 441b, 442a
poverty, IV 122b, 132b, 141a, 141b
power, IV 133b, 137b, 138b, 139a, 140b, 143a, 147a, 437b, 438a, 441b
pragmatism, III 555a–555b
primitivism, III 592b, 596a
printing, II 482b
professions, IV 437a
progress, III 630a; IV 144a, 148a, 148b–149a, 149b, 150b, 151a, 151b
Protestantism, IV 124a, 128a, 135a, 146a
psychology, IV 10b, 16b
Puritanism, IV 16b

Pythagoreans, IV 39b, 41a–41b
race, IV 136a–136b
radical numbers, III 178a
Ramism, IV 43a, 44a, 45a–45b
rationalism, IV 122a, 136b, 142a, 147b, 438a, 440a, 441b, 442b, 443a
reality, IV 440a
reason, IV 134a, 134b, 135a, 144b–145a, 149b, 151a, 439a, 441a, 443a
rebirth, IV 121a–124a, 128a, 129b, 130b, 131a
reformation, IV 60a, 60b–61a, 61b, 67a, 67b
Reformation, IV 124a, 126a, 127b, 128a, 135a, 146a, 149a
reincarnation, I 645a
religion, IV 93b–94a, 98a, 115a, 115b, 124a, 126b, 127b, 132a, 132b, 136a–146a, 147a
republicanism, IV 123a–123b, 126b
research, IV 134b
responsibility, IV 142a
revolution, IV 124a–124b, 147b, 152a, 152b
rhetoric, IV 123b, 129b, 136a, 138a, 138b, 139a, 141a, 141b, 142a, 142b, 144a, 170b, 171a–171b, 172a, 438b, 439a, 441b
Roman Catholic Church, IV 121b, 124a, 125b, 128a, 147a, 149b, 442a, 442b
romanticism, II 431a; IV 125a, 126a, 147a, 187b, 188a, 188b, 193b, 198b, 199a
Rome (ancient), IV 115a, 121b–124a, 125b, 130b, 132b, 136b, 139a, 141b, 144a
salvation, IV 142a, 142b
sanctification, IV 140a
satire, IV 213a, 214b
scholarship, IV 121b, 122a, 122b–125a, 126b, 128a
scholasticism, II 427a; IV 121b–125a, 126b, 128a, 129b, 133b–134a, 134b, 140a–140b, 141b, 437b, 441a
science, III 355b; IV 126b, 127b, 128a, 129b, 130a, 132a–134b, 140b, 146a, 147b–150a, 151b, 152a, 437a, 439b, 440a–443a
sculpture, III 342a; IV 122b, 123a, 124a, 439b

381

secular literature, III 82b
secularism, I 387b; IV 141a, 142a, 145b
self-realization, IV 438a
senses, IV 136b, 145a, 440a
sin, IV 138b, 142a
skepticism, IV 135a, 140b–141a, 148a
society, IV 123b, 124b, 126b, 127a, 128a, 131b, 133a, 135a, 136a, 141a, 142a, 147b, 148a, 439b, 441a–443a
soul, IV 131b–132a, 132b, 133b, 137a, 138b, 140a, 140b, 143a, 439a
space, IV 300b, 305a, 306a
Spain, I 393a; IV 123b, 124a, 131a
spiritualism, IV 142a
spontaneous generation, IV 308b
State, IV 126b, 127a, 127b, 129b, 132b, 147b
status, IV 141a, 438a
Stendhal, IV 124b, 125a, 128a
Stoicism, IV 129a, 135a, 136b, 137a, 137b, 138a, 139a, 142b, 143a, 144a, 146a
style, IV 147a
supernatural, IV 142b, 145a
Symonds, IV 128a
syncretism, I 43b, 44a; IV 126b, 144a
taste, IV 354a–354b
technology, IV 358a, 360a, 360b, 441b, 442a–442b
temperance, IV 369a, 370a, 371a, 374a–374b
theological literature, III 82b
theology, IV 121b, 122a, 129b, 130a, 131b, 132a, 137b, 138a, 138b, 139b, 140b–145a, 151a, 441a, 443a
Thorndike, IV 128a
time, IV 439b
tourism, IV 128b
tradition, IV 131b, 135a, 144a, 145b, 148b, 438b–439a
translations, III 181b
trigonometry, III 178b
trinity, IV 138b, 140b, 141a
truth, IV 129b, 130a, 135a, 135b, 149b, 441a
typography, IV 149a–149b
tyranny, IV 126b
uniformitarianism, IV 148a, 150b, 151b
unity, IV 132a, 148a,

437a, 440a, 441a
universality, IV 145a, 145b
universe, IV 39b, 41a–41b, 136b, 137a, 138a, 138b, 139a, 140b, 142a, 145a, 146a
urbanization, I 429b–430a, 431a; IV 438a, 439b, 441b
U.S., IV 125b
utilitarianism, IV 143a
Utopia, IV 461a
utopianism, IV 151b
vanity, IV 141b
versatility, IV 437a
virtù, IV 476b–486a
virtue, IV 132b, 136a, 137a, 138b, 141a, 143a, 147b, 374a–374b, 439a
vox populi, IV 497b, 498b
wealth, IV 122b, 133b, 438a, 441b
wisdom, IV 122a, 127b, 129b, 132a, 133b
wisdom of the fool, IV 515b, 516b, 518a–520a
witchcraft, II 426b–427a
women, IV 526a
work, IV 134b, 136b, 532a–532b, 533a–534a
See also Universal man
Renaissance of the Twelfth Century, IV 127b
Renan, Ernest (1823–1892)
conservatism, I 483a
crisis in history, I 592a
God, III 474b
irony, II 633a
literature, III 82b
modernism, I 419b, 420b 421b
nationalism, III 330b
perfectibility, III 474b
progress, III 634b
psychology, IV 12a
scientism, I 421b
Rengifo (c. 16th century A.D.), genius, II 293b
Renner, Karl (1870–1950)
Marxism, III 164b
private property, III 655b
Renoir, Auguste (1841–1919)
impressionism, II 567b, 569a, 569b, 573b, 574a
Nature, III 350b
Renoir, Edmond, impressionism, II 573b
Renouvier, Charles Bernard (1815–1903)
antinomy of pure reason, I 93b
evil, II 162a
indeterminacy, II 587a
James and, IV 396a
pragmatism, III 562a, 563a

progress, III 634b, 635b, 636a, 637b, 643a, 644b
time, IV 395b, 396a
Repentance
Judaism, III 636a
Jung, IV 97a
progress, III 636a
reformation, IV 61b
religion, IV 97a
Repression
pleasure, II 383b, 385b
protest movements, III 673b
Reproduction
acquired characteristics, II 617b
Saint Thomas Aquinas, IV 525a
women, IV 525a
Republicanism
Brazil, III 539b, 541b–543b, 545a
deism, I 647b, 649b
democracy, I 657a
French Revolution, IV 156b
Hegel, II 409b
Machiavellism, III 117a, 120b–121a
peace, III 443a–443b
positivism, III 539b, 540b, 541b–543b, 545a
Renaissance, IV 123a–123b, 126b
revolution, IV 156a, 156b, 164a
Rome (ancient), III 476b
Utopia, IV 462b
war, III 443a–443b
World War I, III 332a
Research
freedom, I 10b
humanism, IV 134b
iconography, II 540a–540b
imprinting, II 585b, 586a
learning, II 585b, 586a
philanthropy, III 491b, 492a
progress, III 627b
rationalism, IV 48a
Renaissance, IV 134b
Responsibility
Aristotle, II 236b–237a
capitalism, III 646a
communism, III 646a
determinism, II 236b–237a, 237b–238a, 240a, 241a
dignity, IV 142a
free will, II 236b–238a, 240a, 241a, 244b, 245a
good, IV 184b
human nature, III 572a
Hume, II 240a
impiety, II 564b
Israel (ancient), II 564b
Judaism, II 564b
law, III 5a, 33a–36a

Marxism, III 149b, 167b, 168a, 646a
morality, III 645a
Pascal, II 189b
Petrarch, IV 142a
Plato, III 501b
Platonism, III 501b
pragmatism, III 562a
progress, III 645a, 646a
Renaissance, IV 142a
right, IV 176b
Saint Augustine, II 189b, 237b–238a, 244b, 245a; IV 176b
satire, IV 214a
theodicy, IV 383a
welfare state, IV 513a
wisdom of the fool, IV 516a
Wright, III 562a
Restif de la Bretonne (1734–1806), cosmic images, I 519b, 522b–523a
Restoration
deism, I 650a
equality, II 143a
Great Britain, III 483a, 483b
periodization in literary history, III 483a, 483b
Resurrection, I 643b–644b
Christianity, I 21b–22b; IV 102b, 230b
God, II 335a–335b, 337b, 341a, 342a
immortality, I 643b–644b
Israel (ancient), IV 226b, 228a
Jesus Christ, I 21b–22b; II 155b, 335a, 335b, 342a, 411a, 413a, 470b; III 223a–223b, 277a, 282a, 283a, 284a
Josephus Flavius, I 643b
Judaism, I 643b; II 337b
man, III 224a
millenarianism, III 223a–223b
mythology, III 277a, 281a, 282a, 283a, 284a, 310a
Paul VI (Pope), I 643b
prophecy, III 665a
religion, IV 101a, 102b, 104b
Saint Paul, I 643b–644a
Saint Thomas Aquinas, I 644a–644b
saints, III 223a–223b
salvation, IV 226b, 228a, 228b, 230b, 231b
sin, IV 226b, 228a, 228b, 230b, 231b
skepticism, I 644a
soul, I 643b–644b
Zoroastrianism, IV 231b

Retinal images, III 409a–409b, 412a–413b

Retribution
  Greece (ancient), II 677a, 679a, 679b
  law, II 677a, 679a, 679b
  suffering, IV 379b, 380b, 382a
  theodicy, IV 379b, 380b, 382a

Retza, Franciscus de (c. 15th century A.D.), chance images, I 343a

Reuchlin, Johann (1455–1522)
  microcosm, III 130a–130b
  skepticism, IV 242a

Revelation
  double truth, II 34a, 34b
  God, II 360b, 361b–363a, 365b, 366a
  good, IV 176b
  holy, II 514a
  linguistics, IV 424a, 426b, 427b
  matter, III 186a, 190b
  metaphor, III 205a
  mythology, III 301b, 302a, 302b, 306b, 307b, 313b
  Nature, III 348a
  perfectibility, III 465b–466a, 468a
  Philo Judaeus, III 465b–466a
  philosophy, III 205a
  pragmatism, III 551b, 553a
  prophecy, III 664b–666b
  religion, III 205a; IV 108b
  right, IV 176b
  skepticism, IV 244a, 246b, 247a
  theodicy, IV 381b
  uniformitarianism, IV 424a, 426b, 427b

Revett, Nicholas, neo-classicism in art, III 363a, 365b

Revisionism, IV 263b–276a
  abstentionism, IV 272b, 273a, 273b
  activism, IV 271b–273b
  anarchy, IV 271a
  Austria, IV 274a
  Bebel, IV 264b, 265a
  Belgium, IV 274a
  Bernstein, IV 266b–273a, 275a
  bourgeois, IV 264b, 266b, 270b, 272a, 274b
  bureaucracy, IV 268a
  capitalism, IV 264b, 265a, 266b, 267a, 271b
  China, IV 275a
  class, IV 264a, 264b, 265a, 266b, 270b, 271b, 272a

collectivism, IV 264a
communism, IV 268b, 273b, 274a–275a
culture, IV 269b
Czechoslovakia, IV 274b
democracy, IV 264b, 265b, 266b, 267a, 268b, 272b, 274a
determinism, IV 270a, 271b–273b
eclecticism, IV 269b, 270b
economics, IV 264a, 266a, 266b, 269a, 269b, 270a, 271b–272a
empiricism, IV 269b, 270b
Engels, IV 265a–270a
Erfurt program, IV 265a–265b
ethics, IV 269b, 273a
evolution, IV 266b, 269b, 270b
Fabians, IV 269b, 272a
Feuerbach, IV 270a
France, IV 272a, 273b, 274a
Germany, IV 263b–276a
Great Britain, IV 269b, 272a
Guesde, IV 273b
Hegel, IV 270a
Hegelianism, IV 270a, 272a
history, IV 269b, 275a
human nature, IV 270b, 272a
idealism, IV 269b, 270a, 273a
ideology, IV 264a–274b
individualism, IV 268b
industry, IV 264a, 266a, 271b–272a
isolationism, IV 271a, 271b, 275a
Jaurès, IV 273b
John of Salisbury, IV 267b, 269a
Kant, IV 270a
Kautsky, IV 265a, 267b, 268b, 269a, 270a, 271a, 271b, 272b, 273a, 273b
labor, IV 264b, 270b, 272a
Lange, IV 269b
Lassalle, IV 264a–264b, 265a, 267a
Latin America, IV 274b
law, IV 264a, 265a, 269b, 270a, 271b
Lenin, IV 268b, 270a, 271b
Left, IV 271b, 272a, 273a, 273b, 274a–274b
liberalism, IV 264a
Liebknecht, IV 264b
Lukacs, IV 270a
Luxemburg, IV 267b, 269a, 270b, 272b
Marx, IV 264b, 265a, 265b, 266a, 266b, 267a, 268b,

269a, 269b, 270a, 272a, 274a, 274b
Marxism, III 161a–170a; IV 264b, 265a, 265b, 266a, 266b–267b, 268b, 269a–271b, 272a, 273a, 273b, 274a–274b, 275a
materialism, IV 269b, 270a
Michels, IV 268a
Millerand, IV 272a
morality, IV 269b, 270a
naturalism, IV 270a
necessity, IV 269b
opportunism, IV 270b
pacifism, IV 271a
peasantry, IV 265b, 266b
perfectibility, IV 269b, 270b
Plekhanov, IV 273b
Poland, IV 274a
positivism, IV 270a, 271b
production, IV 266b, 269b
proletariat, IV 269a–269b
radicalism, IV 267a
revolution, IV 163a, 163b, 166a, 264b, 265a, 267a, 267b, 268a, 269a–275a
Right, IV 271b, 273b, 274a
Russia, IV 268b, 271a, 273a, 274a
Social Democratic Party (SPD), IV 264a–268b, 272a–273a
socialism, IV 264a–274b
Stalin, IV 274a–274b
Sturm und Drang, IV 266a
tradition, IV 264b
unions, IV 267b, 268a, 271b–272a
urbanization, IV 264a
U.S.S.R., IV 274b–275a
wages, IV 264b
World War I, IV 268a, 271a, 271b, 272b–273a
Yugoslavia, IV 274b

Revolution, IV 152a–167b
  absolutism, IV 157b, 150a
  acquired characteristics, II 619b–620a, 621b
  agriculture, IV 161a, 162b
  Alembert, IV 154b
  American Revolution, IV 155b–156a, 156b, 160b
  anarchy, IV 152b, 157b, 158b, 162a, 165a, 166b
  anatomy, IV 155b
  architecture, IV 165a, 165b
  aristocracy, IV 152b, 154b, 161a
  Aristotle, IV 152b
  art, II 577a, 581b; IV 155b, 165a, 165b
  artists, IV 165a
  astrology, IV 155b
  astronomy, IV 153a

Bakunin, IV 166b
Bernstein, III 161b, 162b, 163a, 163b
Bismarck, IV 157b, 160b
blacks, IV 166b
Blanc, IV 160a
Blanqui, IV 160a
Bolívar, IV 160b
Bolshevism, IV 163b, 164a, 164b, 165b, 166a
bourgeois, IV 161a, 161b, 162a, 163a, 163b, 164b
Brandes, I 481b
Brecht, IV 165b
Brinton, IV 158a
Burckhardt, I 591b–592a; IV 159a
bureaucracy, IV 158a
Burke, I 481a–481b; IV 157b, 158b, 203a
Calvin, I 392b
capitalism, IV 161a–163a, 164a, 166a
Carlyle, IV 160a
Castro, IV 165a
Charles I, IV 153b
Charles II, IV 153b
China (Communist), IV 166a, 166b
Christianity, IV 153a, 153b
Cicero, IV 152b
civilization, IV 158b, 165b, 166b
class, IV 158a, 159b, 160a, 160b, 161a, 162a, 163b, 165a, 166a
colonialism, IV 166a
communism, III 673b; IV 157b, 161b, 164b, 165a, 165b, 166a
Condorcet, IV 156a–157b
conservatism, I 480a–482b; IV 157b, 158b, 160a
conspiracy, IV 154b, 162a
Copernicus, IV 153a, 162b
cosmos, IV 153a
crisis in history, I 590a, 591b–592a, 593a–593b
Cromwell, IV 153b
Cuba, IV 165a
culture, IV 165a–166a
cycles, IV 152b–158a
defined, IV 152a, 158a
Delacroix, IV 156b
democracy, IV 152b, 154b, 156b, 162a, 164a
despotism, IV 156b, 157b, 160a, 160b
determinism, II 23b
Dewey, III 569a
dictatorship, IV 157b
Diderot, IV 155a
economics, IV 160a, 161a–162b, 163a, 165a–166b

education, **IV** 165b–166a
Engels, **II** 452b; **IV** 163b, 293b
Enlightenment, **IV** 154b, 155b
evil, **IV** 159b, 166b
evolution, **IV** 160a
existentialism, **III** 160b
fascism, **IV** 164a–165a
fear, **IV** 157a, 157b, 159b, 162a
feudalism, **IV** 161b, 163a
Forster, **IV** 158b
Fox, **IV** 156a–156b
France, **IV** 155a, 156a, 156b, 158a, 159b, 160a, 164a
Franco-Prussian War (1870), **IV** 159a
freedom, **IV** 157b, 158a
French Revolution, **IV** 152a, 156a–158a, 159b, 160a, 160b, 162a, 164b, 165a
Freud, **IV** 163a
Futurism, **IV** 165a
Galileo, **IV** 162b
Garibaldi, **IV** 160b
general will, **II** 278b–279a
Germany, **IV** 156b, 158a, 158b, 159b, 160b, 164a, 165a, 165b
Gibbon, **IV** 155a
Godwin, **III** 471a
Gracchi, **IV** 161a
Great Britain, **III** 600b; **IV** 153b–154a, 154b, 155b, 156b, 159b, 160b, 162b
Greece, **IV** 160b
Greece (ancient), **IV** 152b
Gropius, **IV** 165a–165b
guerrilla warfare, **IV** 166a, 166b
Guevara, **IV** 166a
Guicciardini, **IV** 152b
Guizot, **IV** 159b
happiness, **II** 379a
heaven, **IV** 153b
Hegel, **IV** 156b, 161a
Herodotus, **IV** 152b
hierarchy, **II** 441b
historians, **IV** 159b, 160a, 164a
historiography, **II** 23b; **IV** 147b
history, **II** 23b; **IV** 154a, 155a, 159b, 161a, 162a, 163b, 167a
Hitler, **IV** 164b
Hobbes, **IV** 153b
humanism, **IV** 153b
Hume, **IV** 154b, 155a
Hungary, **III** 166b
idealism, **IV** 165a
imperialism, **IV** 166a

impressionism, **II** 577a, 581b, 582b
industry, **IV** 160a, 160b, 162b
James II, **IV** 154a
Jesus Christ, **IV** 153a
Joachim of Floris, **IV** 153a
Judaism, **IV** 153a
Kosciusko, **IV** 160b
Kossuth, **IV** 160b
labor, **IV** 161a, 166a
Latin America, **III** 335b; **IV** 160b, 166a
Latin language, **IV** 152b
law, **IV** 155a, 157b, 158a
Lenin, **III** 156a–156b; **IV** 162a, 163b, 165a, 165b
liberalism, **III** 673a; **IV** 160a, 160b, 162a
liberty, **IV** 154a
literature, **IV** 154a, 154b, 157b, 159b, 162a
Locke, **IV** 154a, 155b, 156b
Luther, **I** 392b
Machiavelli, **IV** 152b
Marx, **II** 452a; **III** 162a; **IV** 161a–163b, 166b, 265a, 290a, 290b, 293a, 534b
Marxism, **III** 148b, 149a, 154a, 156b, 160b–163b, 165a, 166a, 167b, 169b, 645b; **IV** 161a, 162a–163b, 165a, 165b, 166a
Marxism-Leninism, **IV** 166a
materialism, **II** 452a, 452b
Mayakovsky, **IV** 165a
Mazzini, **IV** 160b
medicine, **IV** 163a
Metternich, **IV** 157b, 158b
Mexico, **III** 544b, 545a
Michelet, **IV** 160a
Middle Ages, **IV** 152b–153a, 162b
military, **IV** 153a, 156b, 157b, 163b, 166a
Mill, **IV** 199a
millenarianism, **III** 224a, 225a; **IV** 153a, 161b
mind, **IV** 155b
Mommsen, **IV** 160b–161a
monarchy, **IV** 152b, 153b, 154a, 154b, 157b, 164a
Montesquieu, **IV** 154b, 155a
morality, **IV** 154b
Mussolini, **IV** 164b
mythology, **III** 288a
Napoleon III, **IV** 157b, 158a, 158b, 160b
nationalism, **III** 328a–335b, 338a, 338b, 673a; **IV** 158b, 160a, 160b
naturalism, **IV** 165a
Nature, **IV** 152b, 155a

Nazism, **IV** 164a, 164b
Netherlands, **IV** 154a, 162a
Newton, **IV** 162b
Niebuhr, **IV** 158b
oligarchy, **IV** 152b
oppression, **IV** 160b
Orientalism, **III** 428b
Owen, **IV** 160a
Paine, **IV** 156a
painting, **II** 577a, 581b
perfectibility, **III** 471a, 472a
philosophy, **IV** 154b, 155b
physics, **IV** 163a
Picasso, **IV** 165b
Planck, **IV** 163a
Plato, **IV** 152b
Platonism, **III** 520b
pleasure, **II** 379a
poets, **IV** 165a
Poland, **IV** 160b
politics, **IV** 152b, 153a, 154a, 154b, 155a, 156a, 157b, 158a, 161a–167a
Polybius, **IV** 152b, 154b
Portugal, **IV** 154a
positivism, **III** 542a, 543a, 544b
power, **IV** 153a, 154b, 157a, 161b, 163b, 164b, 166a
pragmatism, **III** 564a–564b, 565b, 569a
Priestley, **III** 472a
primitivism, **III** 600b
private property, **III** 651a; **IV** 154b, 157b, 160a
progress, **III** 634a, 637b, 645b, 647b; **IV** 156b
protest movements, **III** 670b–673b, 675a
Protestantism, **IV** 162a
Proudhon, **III** 471a; **IV** 160a
psychology, **IV** 163a
race, **IV** 164b, 166a
radicalism, **III** 673a; **IV** 165a
Ramsay, **IV** 156a
rationalism, **IV** 155b
realism, **IV** 165a, 165b
reason, **IV** 155b
rebellion, **IV** 154a, 154b
reform, **IV** 160a
Reformation, **IV** 153a
regime, **IV** 157a–157b
religion, **IV** 117a, 153a
Renaissance, **IV** 124a–124b, 147b, 152a, 152b
republicanism, **IV** 156a, 156b, 164a
resistance, **IV** 156b, 157a
revisionism, **IV** 163a, 163b, 166a, 264b, 265a, 267a–270a, 271b, 273a, 274b,

275a
Robespierre, **IV** 157a, 157b
Roentgen, **IV** 163a
romanticism, **IV** 199b, 203a, 204a, 205a–207b
Rome (ancient), **IV** 152b, 154b, 161a
Rousseau, **IV** 155a–155b
Russia, **IV** 158a, 160b, 162a, 163b–165a
Russian Revolution (October 1917), **IV** 158a, 163b, 164a, 165a, 166b
Saint Augustine, **IV** 152b
Satan, **IV** 153a
Schiller, **IV** 156b–157a
scholasticism, **IV** 155b, 158a, 166b
science, **IV** 153b, 155b, 162b
security, **IV** 157b
social contract, **IV** 317a
socialism, **III** 645b, 673b; **IV** 160a, 161a, 162a–166b, 285a–291b, 293a–294a
society, **IV** 152b, 153b, 154a, 155a, 156a, 158b, 160a–163b, 165a–166b
sociology, **IV** 166b
Sorel, **III** 564a–564b, 565b; **IV** 163b
Spain, **IV** 154a, 164a
Stalin, **IV** 158a
State, **IV** 153b, 154b, 155a, 155b, 156a, 157a, 158a, 161b, 162a
Stendhal, **IV** 157b
Stuart dynasty, **IV** 153b–154a
terror, **IV** 157b, 159b, 160a, 162a, 164a
Thermidor, **IV** 157a, 157b–158a
Thiers, **IV** 159b
Thucydides, **IV** 152b
Tocqueville, **IV** 158b–159a
totalitarianism, **IV** 407a, 408a, 408b, 409b
Toynbee, **IV** 162b
Trotsky, **IV** 158a, 163b, 165b
Turgot, **IV** 155a
Turkey, **IV** 160b, 162a
tyranny, **IV** 152b, 154a, 155b
U.S.S.R., **IV** 158a, 163b, 164a, 165a–166b
U.S., **III** 329a, 428b; **IV** 155b–156a, 160b, 164a
urbanization, **IV** 166a
Utopia, **IV** 463a
utopianism, **IV** 167a
vice, **IV** 152b, 154b

Victorian sentiment, **IV** 220a, 222a

violence, **IV** 156b, 157a, 157b, 158a, 158b, 159b, 160a, 164a

virtue, **IV** 152b

Voltaire, **IV** 155a, 155b

war, **IV** 155b, 166b, 503b, 504a, 505a, 506a

wealth, **IV** 153a

women, **IV** 529b

World War I, **IV** 164a, 165a, 166a

World War II, **IV** 166a

writers, **IV** 154a, 154b, 157b, 159b, 162a, 165a

Rewald, J.
impressionism, **II** 573a, 573b, 574a, 577b, 579a

naturalism in art, **III** 339b

Reward
determinism, **II** 241a

fortune, fate, and chance, **II** 229b

free will, **II** 241a

good, **IV** 174a, 179a

Mill, **IV** 179a

motif, **III** 239b

Pythagoreans, **IV** 31a, 31b

theodicy, **IV** 379b, 380b

work, **IV** 531a

Rey, Abel (1873–1940)
entropy, **II** 118b

pragmatism, **III** 564b

Reyes, Alfonso, symbolism, **IV** 342b

Reynaud, Jean (1806–1863), cosmic images, **I** 520a

Reynier, Gustave, realism in literature, **IV** 54a

Reynold de Cressier, Frédéric Gonzague, baroque in literature, **I** 192a

Reynolds, James, psychology, **IV** 21a

Reynolds, John, Newton and, **III** 395a

Reynolds, Joshua (1723–1792)
beauty, **II** 550a

Counter-Enlightenment, **II** 108b–109a

creativity in art, **II** 108b–109a

genius, **II** 300b, 303a–303b, 306a, 306b, 307b–308a, 309b

ideal, **II** 550a

mythology, **III** 298b

neo-classicism in art, **III** 364b

ut pictura poesis, **IV** 467a, 468a, 470a

Rhadamanthys (myth), tem-

perance, **IV** 366a

Rhazes, al-Razi (860–925), **I** 30a

Rhenanus, Beatus (1486–1547), historiography, **II** 485b

Rheticus (1514–1576), mathematics, **III** 178b

Rhetoric, **IV** 167a–173a
Alembert, **IV** 172a

allegory, **IV** 170b

argumentation, **IV** 167b–170b, 172b

Aristotle, **III** 500b; **IV** 168a–171b, 369a

art, **I** 458a, 458b, 459a; **IV** 168a, 168b, 171b, 172a

Augustinianism, **IV** 170b

Bacon, **III** 383b; **IV** 172a

Bayle, **IV** 172b

Burke, **IV** 172a

Cicero, **IV** 169a–172a

cynicism, **I** 632b

deliberative, **IV** 168b

Demetrius, **IV** 169b, 170a, 171a

Demosthenes, **IV** 171b

Descartes, **IV** 172b

Diderot, **IV** 172a

dignity, **IV** 136a, 138a, 138b, 139a, 141a, 141b, 142a, 142b, 144a

Dionysius of Halicarnassus, **IV** 169b

education, **IV** 168b, 169a, 170a, 172a–172b

eloquence, **IV** 168a, 169b, 171b–172a

emotion, **IV** 168a, 169b

enthymeme, **IV** 168b

epideictic, **IV** 168a, 168b, 171b

ethics, **IV** 168a–168b, 169a, 170a

forensic, **IV** 168b

France, **IV** 171b–172b

genius, **II** 313b

Gladstone, **IV** 172a

Gorgias, **III** 496b–497a

Great Britain, **IV** 172a–172b

Greece (ancient), **III** 526a, 526b, 528a, **IV** 167b–169a, 169b

harmony, **IV** 168a, 169b

Hermogenes, **IV** 170a–170b, 171a

history, **IV** 171b

Horace, **IV** 171b, 172a

humanism, **II** 515a, 515b, 516a, 516b, 517a, 518b, 519a, 519b, 520a, 522a, 522b; **IV** 129b, 171a, 171b

imagination, **IV** 172a

impiety, **II** 565a

individualism, **IV** 141a

Isocrates, **IV** 167b–169a

Italy, **IV** 171a–171b

James, William, **III** 565b

judges, **IV** 168a

judgment, **IV** 167b, 168a, 172a

justice, **IV** 167b

knowledge, **IV** 168a, 170a, 172b

language, **IV** 167b, 168a, 168b, 169b, 170b, 171a, 172a

law, **III** 5b–6a; **IV** 168a, 168b, 169a, 170a, 170b, 171b

literary criticism, **I** 596a, 597a

literary paradox, **III** 76a, 76b, 77a, 77b

literature, **III** 87b; **IV** 171b, 172b, 330a–333a

logic, **IV** 168b–169b, 170b

logos, **IV** 168a

Longinus, **IV** 169b–170a

love, **III** 99a–100a

Marxism, **III** 149b, 152a

metaphor, **III** 203b

metaphysics, **IV** 167b

Middle Ages, **III** 528a, 528b; **IV** 170b–171a

morality, **IV** 141a, 167b, 168a, 168b, 170a, 170b

music, **II** 313b

mythology, **III** 293a

naturalism, **IV** 53b

observation, **IV** 168a

oratory, **IV** 167b–170b, 171b, 172a

organicism, **III** 423a, 424a, 426a, 426b

Pascal, **IV** 172b

passions, **IV** 167b, 168b, 172a

Peletier, **IV** 171a

persuasion, **IV** 168a, 170a, 172b

Petrarch, **IV** 171a

philology, **IV** 169b, 172a

philosophy, **IV** 167b–171b, 172b

Pitt, **IV** 172a

Plato, **III** 495b–502a; **IV** 167b, 171b

Platonism, **III** 495b–502a, 506a, 507a, 518b

pleasure, **IV** 171b–172a

poetry, **III** 525b, 526a, 526b, 527b, 528a, 528b, 529a, 530b; **IV** 170b, 171a–171b, 172b; **IV** 466a, 468a, 468b, 469b, 471b

politics, **IV** 167b, 168a,

168b, 169a, 170a, 172b

pragmatism, **III** 565b

probability, **IV** 170b

Quintilian, **IV** 169b, 170a, 170b, 171b, 172a

Ramism, **IV** 42b, 43a, 45a

Ramus, **IV** 42b, 43a, 171b

Rapin, **IV** 171b–172a

realism in literature, **IV** 53b, 55a

reason, **IV** 172a

religion, **III** 203b

Renaissance, **IV** 123b, 129b, 136a, 138a, 138b, 139a, 141a–142b, 144a, 170b–172a, 438b, 439a, 441b

rhythm, **IV** 168a, 169b

Rome (ancient), **III** 528a; **IV** 167b, 168a, 169a–170b, 370a

Ronsard, **IV** 171a–171b, 172b

rules, **IV** 168a, 172a

Salutati, **II** 522b

scholasticism, **IV** 171a

science, **IV** 169a, 171a, 172a

scientific classification, **I** 464b

Sebillet, **IV** 171a

Socrates, **III** 379b, 496b–497a

sublime in external nature, **IV** 333a–333b, 334b

style, **IV** 167b, 168b–171a, 330a–333a

symbolism, **IV** 339a, 344a

taste, **IV** 172a, 172b

temperance, **IV** 369a, 370a, 371a

theology, **IV** 170b

totalitarianism, **IV** 408b

truth, **IV** 167b

U.S., **IV** 172b

universal man, **IV** 438b, 439a, 441b

Vellutello, **IV** 171a

virtù, **IV** 477a, 479a

virtue, **IV** 170a

Rhetorius of Egypt, astrology, **I** 121a, 124a

Rhetra, law, **II** 680a

Rhine, Joseph Banks
immortality, **I** 643a

spiritism, **I** 643a

Rhodesia, equality, **III** 13a

Rhythm, **II** 313a, 313b, 315a; **III** 261a, 268b

Plato, **III** 500b

time, **IV** 399a

Ribbentrop, Marie de
Pereira Barreto and, III 540b

positivism, III 540b

Ribot, Théodule (1839–1916), psychology, IV 12b, 13b

Ricardo, David (1772–1823),
capital, II 49b
class, I 441b
economic history, II 48a, 48b, 49b, 50a, 54a, 57a, 59a
economics, II 453a
Hegel and, II 409a
labor, II 49b
land, II 49b
Marx and, II 453a
materialism, II 453a
natural liberty, II 67b–69a
socialism, IV 292b
society, II 453a
utility, IV 453b
Victorians, III 218b, 222b

Ricci, Corrado (1858–1934), baroque in literature, I 189a

Ricci, Matteo (1552–1610),
China, I 355b–356a, 357a
Confucianism, I 355b–356a, 357a

Riccioli, Giambattista (1598–1671), Pythagorean cosmos, IV 41b

Rice, Elmer (1892–1967), expressionism, II 208b

Richard of Campsall, on common nature, I 4a

Richard of St. Victor, methodology, III 381b–382a

Richard I, King (the Lion-Hearted) (1157–1199), love, III 202a

Richards I. A. (1893–   ),
beauty, I 208a, 209a
irony, II 632b, 633a, 634a
literary criticism, I 602a–602b, 603a
literature, III 88a; IV 332a
style, IV 332a

Richardson, Benjamin Ward (1828–1896), environment, II 124b

Richardson, Jonathan
art, II 310a
genius, II 310a
neo-classicism in art, III 367b, 370a

Richelieu, Cardinal (1585–1642)
balance of power, I 182b, 185a
crisis in history, I 593b
Habsburgs and, I 399a
Machiavellism, III 120b
State, I 399a

Richter, Kurt, macrocosm and microcosm, III 126b

Richthofen, Baron Ferdinand

von (1833–1905), China, I 370a, 371a

Rickman, Thomas (1776–1841), Gothic, II 372a

Ricoeur, Paul, mythology, III 315b

Ridewall, John, mythology, III 288b, 289a

Riedel, F. J.
genius, II 295b
ideal, II 550b–551a
morality, II 551a
taste, IV 356b

Riegl, Alois (1858–1905)
art, II 297b
baroque in literature, I 189a
genius, II 297b
iconography, II 537a
naturalism in art, III 339b, 343b

Riehl, Alois (1844–1924), aesthetics, II 223b

Riemann, Georg Friedrich Bernhard (1826–1866)
axiomatization, I 167a
continuity, I 498b
cosmology, I 555a
geometry, IV 304a
infinity, II 611b, 613b, 614a
positivism, III 545b
relativity, IV 87b–88a
space, IV 302b–303a, 304a–304b

Riemann integrals, III 620b

Riemann-Christoffel curvature tensor, IV 88a, 89a

Riemann-Darbaux integral mathematics, II 610b

Rienzo, Cola di (1313–1354), conservatism, I 479b

Riepe, Dale, Buddhism, I 256b

Riesman, David
authority, I 161a
individualism, II 598b, 599b

Right, IV 173a–187a
aesthetics, IV 182b, 184a
aggression, IV 174a
anarchy, IV 180b
antipathy, IV 178b
aristocracy, IV 175a, 180b
Aristotelianism, IV 176b
Aristotle, III 15a–15b; IV 175a–175b, 176b, 180a
aspiration, IV 173a, 173b, 174a, 177a, 185a–185b, 186b
atomism, IV 175b
attitude, IV 174a
Austin, IV 184b
awe, IV 174a
Ayer, IV 184a
behavior, IV 180a, 185a–185b

benevolence, IV 178a
Bentham, IV 177b, 178b, 179a, 181b–182a, 185a
bourgeois, IV 177a, 181a
Bradley, F. H., IV 181a
Butler, Bishop, IV 178a
Calvinism, IV 177a
causation, IV 177a
Christianity, IV 174a–174b, 176a–177a
class, IV 174b, 177a
common sense, IV 183a, 183b
communism, IV 181a
community, IV 175a, 176a, 178b, 179b
conscience, IV 178a
consciousness, IV 173a, 178b, 179b–181b
contextualism, IV 184b
cosmos, IV 176a, 181a
courage, IV 174b
Creation, IV 176b
culture, IV 173a, 174a, 174b, 180a, 180b
damnation, IV 174b, 176b
Dante, IV 176b–177a
Darwin, IV 182a
decision, IV 175b
democracy, IV 175a, 175b
deontology, IV 184b
desire, IV 173a, 173b, 177a–179a, 181a, 182b, 186b
determinism, IV 177b
Dewey, IV 185b–186b
distribution, IV 179a
divination, IV 179b, 180a
dualism, IV 180a
duty, IV 173b, 176a, 179b, 180a, 182a, 183b, 186a
economics, IV 177a, 179a, 180b–182b
egoism, IV 178a, 185a
elite, IV 175a
emotion, IV 176a, 177b, 184a
empiricism, IV 178b, 179b, 184a
Epicureanism, IV 175b–176a
evil, IV 174b, 177a, 180b
evolution, IV 179b–181b, 183a, 185b, 186b
experience, IV 177a, 177b
fear, IV 174a, 181a
feeling, IV 174a
free will, IV 176b
freedom, IV 177b, 179b, 180a, 181a
Freudianism, IV 185b
goals, IV 173b–175a,

176a–176b, 177a, 178b, 180a, 181a, 181b, 185b
God, IV 174a, 176b–177a, 177b, 182b, 183a
Greece (ancient), II 677a, 678a, 678b, 679b; IV 174b–176a
Green, T. H., IV 181a
guilt, IV 173b
happiness, IV 175b, 176b, 178b, 179a, 179b, 180a
Hare, IV 184b
harmony, IV 175a, 177b
Hartmann, IV 182a–182b
heaven, IV 176b–177a
hedonism, IV 179a, 180a–180b
Hegel, IV 180a, 181a
hell, IV 176b
hierarchy, IV 173b
history, IV 173a, 174a, 175a, 179b–181b, 183a, 185b, 186a
Hobbes, IV 177a–177b, 178a, 182a
hope, IV 174a
human nature, III 575b; IV 173b, 175a
humanism, IV 180b
Hume, IV 178a
ignorance, IV 49a, 174b
individualism, IV 174b–180b
injustice, IV 175a, 180b
instinct, IV 180a, 185a
institutions, IV 178b, 179a, 180a, 180b, 181b, 186b
instrumentalism, IV 185b
intuition, IV 177b, 183a
James, IV 185b
joy, IV 175b
Judaism, IV 174a, 176a
judgment, IV 178b, 181b, 182b, 183a, 185a, 186a
justice, III 15a–15b; IV 175a, 175b, 178a, 179a, 180b, 181a, 183b, 186a
Kant, IV 179a–179b, 181a, 181b, 186b
knowledge, IV 173a–174b, 175b, 185b, 186b
Kropotkin, IV 180b
labor, IV 179a
language, IV 176b, 183b, 184a, 184b
law, II 677a–678b, 679b; IV 173b–176b, 177b, 179a–181b, 186b
Lewis, C. I., IV 185b–186a
Locke, IV 178a
logic, IV 183b–184a, 185b, 186a
love, IV 174a, 175a, 177a, 178a

Mandeville, IV 178b
Marcus Aurelius, IV 176a
Marx, IV 177a
Marxism, IV 180b–181a
materialism, IV 175b, 180b
mathematics, IV 177a, 177b
matter, IV 177a, 177b
measurement, IV 178b, 181b–182a
Mill, IV 179a
Moore, G. E., IV 183a
moral sense, III 230b, 233a
morality, IV 173a–186b
motion, IV 177a
music, IV 176b
nationalism, IV 174a
natural law, III 15a–15b, 16a, 23a; IV 175b–177b
naturalism, IV 181a, 182a, 184b–186b
Nature, III 348a; IV 174b, 175a, 176a, 177b, 178a, 179b
necessity, IV 177b
Neo-Platonism, IV 176a
Newton, IV 177b
Nietzsche, IV 180b
nomos, IV 174b
norms, IV 182b
obedience, IV 173b, 174a
obligation, IV 173b, 174a, 179b, 181b, 182a, 183a, 184b
oligarchy, IV 175a, 176b
open-question argument, IV 183a
order, IV 174b, 175a, 176a
pain, IV 174a, 175b, 178b, 179a, 185a
passions, IV 178a
peace, IV 175b, 176a, 177b
Pepper, Stephen, IV 185a
perception, IV 182b
perennial philosophy, III 462a
Perry, R. B., IV 185a
philosophy, IV 173a, 174a–175b, 177a, 183a
physiology, IV 177a
Plato, IV 174b, 175a, 182b
Platonism, III 496b; IV 181b
pleasure, IV 173b, 174a, 175b, 176b, 178b, 179a, 180a–180b, 181b, 183a, 185a, 185b
pluralism, IV 184b
politics, IV 175b, 176b, 177a, 177b, 179a
positivism, IV 183b–184b
poverty, IV 175a
power, IV 174b, 175b, 176a, 177a, 180b, 181a

pragmatism, III 568b; IV 184b–186b
Price, Richard, III 233a
private property, III 653b, 654a, 654b, 655a, 656a, 656b, 657a; IV 174a
production, IV 181a
progress, III 630b; IV 178b
Protagoras, III 575b
Protestantism, IV 177a
psychology, IV 177a, 178a, 178b, 179a, 180b, 182b, 185a–185b, 186a
punishment, IV 174a, 176a, 179a
rationalism, IV 46a, 49a, 173b, 175a, 175b, 176a, 179b, 181b
reality, IV 177b, 181a, 182a
reason, IV 174a, 175b, 176a–178b, 179b, 180a
Reichenbach, IV 184a
relativism, IV 70b, 71a, 72a, 73a, 73b
religion, IV 174a–174b, 177b, 182a–182b, 184a
responsibility, IV 176b, 184b
retaliation, IV 179a
revelation, IV 176b
reward, IV 174a, 179a
Roman Catholic Church, III 654a, 654b
Rome (ancient), IV 176a
rules, IV 173a, 173b, 174a, 174b, 175b, 177a, 180b, 181a, 181b, 183a, 184b, 185b, 186a, 186b
Russell, Bertrand, IV 184a
Saint Augustine, IV 176a–176b
Saint Thomas Aquinas, IV 176b
salvation, IV 174b, 176a, 176b, 177a
satisfaction, IV 173b, 174a
science, IV 173a, 175b, 176b, 177a, 179b–181b, 182a, 185b, 186a
secularism, IV 177a, 177b
self-love, IV 178a
self-preservation, III 630b
self-realization, IV 181a–181b
sex, IV 174a, 185a
Shaftesbury, III 230b
shame, IV 173b
sin, IV 176b–177a, 180b
slavery, IV 174b
Smith, Adam, IV 178a, 179a
socialism, IV 181a
society, IV 173a, 174a–179a, 180a, 180b, 181b

Socrates, III 496b; IV 49a, 174b–175a
Sophism, IV 174b
soul, IV 174a, 174b, 175a, 176b–177a
species, IV 175a, 182a
Spencer, IV 180b
Spinoza, IV 177b, 182a
State, IV 180a, 313b
status, IV 174a
Stevenson, C. L., IV 184a
Stoicism, IV 176a
Stoics, III 348a
success, IV 174a
suffering, IV 175a, 178a
superstition, IV 176a
sympathy, IV 178a, 178b, 182a
Tawney, IV 177a
teleology, IV 175a, 175b, 176b, 177a, 180a, 182a–182b, 184b
temperance, IV 174b
Tolman, E. C., IV 185a
tranquility, IV 176a
truth, IV 177a, 177b, 183b–184a
Tufts, IV 186b
unity, IV 176a, 176b, 180a, 184a
universality, IV 173b, 174a, 175b, 179b
Urmson, IV 184b
utilitarianism, IV 178b–179a, 180a–180b, 183b, 185a, 185b, 447a–449b
value, IV 181b–183a, 185a
vice, IV 178b
virtue, IV 173a–179b, 180b, 181a, 182b
wealth, IV 175a, 177a
welfare, IV 178b, 179a
Westermarck, IV 184a
wisdom, IV 174b, 175b, 184b
Wittgenstein, IV 184a
work, IV 174a, 176a, 177a
Wright, G. H. von, IV 184b
wrong, IV 174a, 176b, 177a, 179a, 184a, 185a
Right (political)
Hegelianism, IV 291a
liberalism, III 54a–54b, 55b
Marxism, III 165b, 167a, 169a–169b
nationalism, III 331b
revisionism, IV 271b, 273b, 274a
socialism, IV 291a
totalitarianism, IV 408a, 409b, 410a, 410b
Utopia, IV 463b
Righter, William, literary criticism, I 602b

Rights
animals, III 596a
Bentham, I 437b–438a
children, III 596a
civil disobedience, I 435b, 437a–438a
concept of, I 437a
free association, III 45a–47a
good, IV 178a
Greece (ancient), II 675a, 676a, 678b
Herder, III 326a
Kant, III 326a
law, II 675a, 676a, 678b, 686a, 686b, 687a, 687b, 688b, 689b, 690b; III 5a, 6b, 7b–10a, 10b–13b, 27b
liberalism, III 36b, 39b, 43b–47a, 52a, 52b–53a, 53b–54a, 56a, 56b
Locke, III 21a; IV 259a
love, III 104b
Machiavellism, III 120b
Madison, III 7b
nationalism, III 322b, 326a, 326b, 327a, 331a, 331b, 336b
natural law, III 14a–14b, 17b, 21a, 21b, 25b
press, III 45a–47a
primitivism, III 596a
progress, III 627a
Protagoras, III 627a
protest movements, III 670a, 674b
right, IV 178a
Rome (ancient), II 686a–689b, 690b
Rousseau, III 21b, 326a; IV 259b
Saint Paul, II 688b
social contract, III 43b–44a; IV 253b, 254a, 255b, 256a, 256b, 257b, 259a, 259b, 260b, 261a, 263b
socialism, IV 289a
State, IV 317a, 317b, 318b
suffrage, III 45a–47a
Thoreau, I 437a, 437b
U.N., III 12a, 13a, 26a
U.S., III 7b–10a
welfare state, IV 510a, 512a
women, IV 526b, 527b, 528b
Rignano, E., Man-Machine, III 144a
Rilke, Rainer Maria (1875–1926)
expressionism, II 206b, 208a
symbolism, IV 342b, 344b
Rimbaud, Arthur (1854–1891)
baroque in literature, I 195a

genius, II 308b
imagination, III 209a
impressionism, II 575a
irrationalism, II 638b
romanticism, IV 196b
symbolism, IV 340b, 342a, 342b
ut pictura poesis, IV 475a
Ringbom, S., iconography, II 538b
Rintelen, Fritz-Joachim von, perennial philosophy, III 458a, 462a
Rinuccini, Ottavio (1562–1621), aesthetics, IV 354b
Riots
anti-industrialism, III 676a
Italy, III 674b
protest movements, III 671b, 672a, 673a, 674a, 674b, 675a, 676a
radicalism, III 673a
Spain, III 674b
Ripa, Cesare (1560?–?1623)
iconography, II 530a–533a
mythology, III 293a
temperance, IV 377b
ut pictura poesis, IV 470a
Ripley, George (1802–1880)
Buddhism, III 437a
Orientalism, III 437a
Ritschl, Albrecht (1822–1889)
eschatology, II 158b
God, II 357a–357b, 358a
heresy, II 429a
liberalism, II 357a
modernism, I 419b
morality, II 357a
Ritschl, Friedrich W. (1806–1876), linguistics, III 68a, 69a
Ritter, Karl (1779–1859)
culture, II 128a, 130a
environment, II 128a, 130a
Ritter, Johann W. (1776–1810), optics, III 419b
Ritual
Aristotle, III 226b
Bible, III 275b, 276b, 277a, 278a, 279b, 281a–282b, 284a, 284b
Christianity, IV 229b, 230a
culture, III 311a
Durkheim, III 311b
Egypt (ancient), IV 225a–225b, 226a
Greece (ancient), II 675b, 681a, 683b–684a; IV 228a–228b
holy, II 512b
language, II 670b
law, II 675b, 681a, 683b–684a
Malinowski, III 314b

matter, III 186a
Mesopotamia (ancient), IV 226a
mimesis, III 226a, 226b
music, III 268a, 268b
mythology, III 272b, 275b, 276b, 277a, 278a, 279b, 281a, 281b–282a, 282b, 284a, 284b, 291b, 292a, 301a, 302a, 308b, 310b–312a, 313a, 314a, 314b–315a, 315b, 316a, 317b
perfectibility, III 464b
religion, II 675b; IV 113b
sacred, II 512b
salvation, IV 225a–225b, 226a, 228a–228b, 229b, 230a, 231a, 233a
Smith, W. R., III 310b
tragic sense, IV 413a
Zoroastrianism, IV 231a
Rivail, Léon, *see* Kardec, Allan
Rivière, Jacques (1886–1925)
classicism, I 455a
literary criticism, I 604b–605a
modernism, I 425a
RNA, II 289a
Robault, Jacques, cosmic voyages, I 530a
Robb, A. A., time, IV 397a
Robbe-Grillet, Alain (1922–), tragic sense, IV 414b
Robbia, Luca della (1400?–1482), genius, II 301b
Robert, Carl (1850–1922), mythology, III 286a–286b
Robert, P. aesthetics, II 221b
Robert of Champagne, reformation, IV 64b
Robert of Chester, alchemy, I 30a–30b
Robert of Melun, reformation, IV 63a
Roberts, Richard, technology, IV 362b–363a
Robertson, D. W., symbolism, IV 341b
Robertson, John M. (1856–1933), progress, III 638a, 644b
Robertson, William (1721–1793), Enlightenment, II 89b, 93b, 94b
Roberval, Gilles Personne de (1602–1675)
atomism, I 135b
cosmology, I 546a, 548a
probability, III 606b
Robespierre, Maximilien François de (1758–1794), authority, I 153b

Counter-Enlightenment, II 111a–111b
deism, I 651b
democracy, I 661b–662a
despotism, II 2a, 8b, 13b–14a
equality, II 144b, 145a
fear, II 13b–14a
French Revolution, IV 157a, 157b
liberalism, III 45b
Montesquieu and, II 13b–14a
neo-classicism in art, III 366a
Platonism, III 520b
revolution, IV 157a, 157b
Rousseau and, IV 260a
social contract, IV 260a
State, I 661b–662a
totalitarianism, IV 408a
virtue, II 13b
Robin, Léon (1866–1956), Platonism, III 523a
Robinson, Henry Crabb (1775–1867), Hegel and, II 412b
Robinson, James Harvey (1863–1936), pragmatism, III 569a–569b
Robinson, Bishop John A. T., equity, II 153b
Robortello, Francesco
aesthetics, II 220a
mimesis, III 228b
poetics, III 529a
ut pictura poesis, IV 467b
Rochefoucauld, François de La (1613–1680)
literary paradox, III 79b
love, III 103b
motif, III 235b
Rockefeller, John D. (1839–1937)
evolutionism, II 181a
Social Darwinism, II 181a
Rockefeller Foundation
philanthropy, III 489a, 491b, 492b
Rocks
catastrophism, IV 418b, 419a, 420b, 421b, 423a
linguistics, IV 424b, 427b
uniformitarianism, IV 418b, 419a, 420b, 421b, 423a, 424b, 427b
Rococo
classicism, I 454b
Germany, III 484a
neo-classicism in art, III 363a, 365b, 369a
periodization in literary history, III 484a
Rodin, François Auguste René

(1840–1917)
Degas and, II 574b
genius, II 299a
God, II 574b
impressionism, II 574a, 574b
Michelangelo and, II 574b
non finito, II 299a
Rodó, José Enrique (1872–1917), positivism, III 545a
Rodrigo of Toledo, Archbishop, Gothic, II 369b
Rodrigues, Olinde, socialism, IV 290a
Roemer, Olaus (1644–1710)
cosmology, I 551b
light, III 395a; IV 77b
Newton and, III 395a
optics, III 395a
poetry, III 395a
relativity, IV 77b
Roentgen, Wilhelm Conrad (1845–1923), revolution, IV 163a
Roger of Wendover (d. 1236), historiography, II 474a
Rohault, Jacques (1620–1675), physics, III 388a
Rohault de Fleury, C., iconography, II 535a
Rohde, Erwin (1845–1898), Pythagoreans, IV 31a
Rolando of Piazzola, humanism, II 517b
Roll, P. G., cosmology, I 567a
Rolle de Hampole, Richard (1290–1349), continuity, I 493a–493b
Rollin, Charles (1661–1741)
Enlightenment, II 95b
liberty, II 95b
style, IV 332a
taste, IV 355a
Roman Catholic Church
absolution, II 420a
Age of Reason, I 400b–401b
Albigensian crusade, II 423a
Anti-Modernist Oath, II 215b
apostolic succession, II 141a
architecture, I 398b
Athanasian Creed, II 342b–343a
auricular confession, I 258b–259b, 261a, 262a
authority, I 146b–150b; II 212a, 689b
Avignon papacy (1309–1377), IV 64a, 65a, 477a
balance of power, I 182b

Bayle, **IV** 120a
Benedict XV (Pope), **IV** 526b–527a
Bible, **I** 394a
bishops, **I** 377a, 378b, 381b, 394b, 395a, 399b, 404a, 410a
Brazil, **III** 540b, 541b, 542b
Brief of Suppression, **I** 403b
Buddhism, **I** 255b
caesaropapism, **I** 379b, 380b
Canada, **III** 334b
Carolingian Renaissance, **I** 380b
casuistry, **I** 258b–264a
Cathars, **II** 423a–423b
cathedral building, **I** 382b, 417b
certainty, **I** 304a, 307a–308a
chance, **I** 336b–337a
charity, **III** 488b, 654a
Chateaubriand, **IV** 200b
China, **I** 353b, 354b, 355a–361b
Christianity, **IV** 230a–230b
colleges, **III** 488b
colonialism, **III** 490b
communism, **I** 379b; **III** 334b
Conciliar Movement, **I** 385a–386b, 403b, 404a
Confucianism, **I** 355b–356a, 357a–358a
conservatism, **I** 482a, 483a, 484a
Constantine grants freedom to, **I** 376b
Constantinopolitan Creed (c. 381), **II** 342b
cosmic voyages, **I** 526a, 532a
Council of Aachen, **IV** 63b
Council of Basel (1431–1449), **I** 386b, **IV** 66a
Council of Carthage (417), **III** 466b
Council of Chalcedon, **I** 416b
Council of Constance, **I** 386a–386b, 387a, 410b
Council of Ferrara, **I** 386b
Council of 1545, **I** 394a–394b
Council of Florence, **I** 410b
Council of Nicaea (325), **I** 377a, 377b, 416b; **II** 342b
Council of Pisa, **I** 386b
Council of Trent (1545–1563), **II** 245b
Counter-Enlightenment, **II** 101b, 102a, 110a–112a
Crusades, **I** 383a, 418a

death, **I** 643b
Decretal of 1140, **III** 18a, 18b
defined, **I** 373b
deism, **I** 648b, 649a, 649b
democracy, **I** 661b
despotism, **II** 8a, 10b
determinism, **II** 30a, 30b
doctrine of Immaculate Conception (1854), **II** 429b
dogmatism, **I** 405b–406a
Donation of Constantine, **II** 419b, 420b, 520b
double truth, **II** 31a–31b, 36a–37a
dualism, **II** 42b
Eastern Orthodox Church, **I** 409a–411b
economic history, **II** 45a, 46b–47a
Ecumenical Council of Florence (1438–1439), **II** 516b
Ecumenical Movement, **IV** 68b
education, **I** 379b, 388a
Encyclicals, **III** 654a
Enlightenment, **II** 91a
equality, **II** 138b, 141a–141b, 142a
equity, **II** 152a
eschatology, **II** 156a–157b, 160b
evolutionism, **II** 177a, 180b
excommunication, **II** 420a, 420b
faith, hope, and charity, **II** 210a–211b, 212b, 213a, 215a–215b
Faust (legend), **III** 246a, 249a
Fifth Lateran Council of 1513, **II** 36a
filioque clause, **I** 410a
First Crusade, **I** 410a
First Lateran Council, **II** 418b
First Vatican Council (1864), **I** 406a; **II** 429b
Fourth Crusade, **I** 410a
Fourth Lateran Council (1215), **I** 259a; **IV** 64a
Franciscans, **II** 421a–421b
free will, **I** 394b; **II** 245a, 245b
freedom, **II** 250a
French Civil Constitution of July 1790, **I** 404a–404b
French Revolution (1789), **I** 404a–404b
gifts, **III** 488b
Gnosticism, **II** 42b, 327a–327b
God, **II** 342b–343a, 355a–

355b, 356b, 361b, 362a, 363b, 364b–365b; **III** 466b
Gothic, **II** 371b, 372a
grace, **III** 466b
Great Schism (1378–1417), **I** 385a, 386a–386b, 387b; **III** 669a–669b; **IV** 65a, 65b, 477a
great stabilizing feature of, **I** 394a
happiness and pleasure, **II** 378b–379a
harmony, **II** 388b, 389a, 394a
Hellenization, **I** 374a–374b, 375a
heresy, **II** 416b–430a
heretics, **II** 427a
Hildebrandine Reform, **IV** 64a
historiography, **II** 478a, 483b; **IV** 147a, 149b
holy, **II** 512b, 513a
Holy Roman Empire, **I** 375a–378b
homoousion theory, **I** 377b
hospitals, **III** 488b
Huguenots, **IV** 113b
humanism, **II** 516b, 520b, 523a
iconography, **II** 532b
idea, **II** 546a–547a
imagination, **III** 210b
immortality, **I** 643b
Incarnation, **I** 376a–376b, 377a
Index, **II** 425a; **III** 117a, 514a
individualism, **I** 400b; **II** 595a, 598b, 602b, 603a
Infallibility Decree, **I** 406a
Inquisition, **I** 383b, 546b; **II** 425a
inter-marriage, **II** 141a
international peace, **III** 448a, 452b
intolerance, **IV** 119a
Ireland, **III** 334b
Islam, **I** 378b, 379a, 380b, 381a, 418a
Italy, **III** 674b
Jansenism, **I** 400a
John XXIII (Pope), **III** 334b, 654b; **IV** 527b
Judaic, **I** 373b–375a
language, **II** 666a
Lateran Council of 1215, **I** 383a
Latin America, **III** 539b, 540a
law, **II** 250a, 688a, 689a, 689b–690a
Leo X (Pope), **III** 654b
Leo XIII (Pope), **IV** 526b

liberalism, **III** 42b
Locke, **IV** 120a
love, **III** 98b, 100a, 101b, 102b, 105b, 107a
Luther, **II** 430a
Machiavellism, **III** 116b, 117a, 117b, 118a, 119b–120a
Marxism, **III** 147a, 166b
Mass, **IV** 103a
matter, **III** 192b
medieval sciences, **II** 196a
metaphor, **III** 105b, 206a, 206b, 207a
Mexico, **III** 544a, 544b
Middle Ages, **I** 378b–387b, 403b, 404a; **III** 40a–40b, 452b 225a
modernism, **I** 406a–406b, 418b–427a
monasteries, **II** 418b; **III** 488b
Montanism, **I** 375a–375b
morality, **I** 260b–262b
mountains in literature, **III** 254b
music, **II** 388b, 389a, 394a
mythology, **III** 302a
nationalism, **III** 319b, 320a, 321a, 322a, 324b, 333a, 334b, 336b
nationalization of property, **I** 404a
natural law, **III** 17b–18b
Netherlands, **IV** 113b
Orientalism, **III** 432b
paganism, **I** 376a–376b, 377a–377b, 378b, 379a, 380a, 388b
papacy, **II** 419b–423a, 425b, 426b, 429b
Papal Inquisition, **II** 689a
Paul, VI (Pope), **III** 654b
Pelagianism, **I** 394a; **III** 466b
Pereira Barreto, **III** 540b
perfectibiliy, **III** 466b–467b
persecutions, **I** 377a
Person of Christ, **I** 376a
philanthropy, **III** 488b, 489a, 489b, 490b
philosophy, **III** 654a
Pietism, **III** 493b
Pius XI (Pope), **IV** 527a
Pius XII (Pope), **IV** 527a
Platonism, **I** 375a; **III** 512a, 513b–514a, 516a, 517a
positivism, **III** 538b, 539b–541b, 542b, 544a, 544b
power, **II** 212b; **IV** 64a, 314a

pragmatism, III 555a, 564a, 565a
predestination, I 394a; II 30a, 30b
priesthood, I 261a, 649b
primitivism, III 594b, 595a
private property, III 653b, 654a, 654b
progress, III 634b, 635a, 635b, 642a
prophecy, III 666b–669b
protest movements, III 670b, 674b
psychology, IV 25b
Punctuation of Ems, I 404a
punishment, I 258b
purgatory, II 156a
reformation, IV 60a, 61a, 62b–66a, 66b, 68b
relativity, IV 74b
religion, III 205b, 206a, 206b, 207a; IV 94a, 99a, 103a, 107a, 107b, 108b, 113b, 114b, 115b, 116b, 117a, 117b, 119a, 120a
Renaissance, IV 121b, 124a, 125b, 128a, 147a, 149b, 422a, 422b
reunion of Protestants with, I 398b
right, III 654a, 654b
Rites Controversy, II 513a
Roman Index of Forbidden Books, II 215b
romanticism, IV 189a, 200b, 205a, 206b, 207a, 207b
Rule of Faith controversy, I 307a–308a
Saint Cyprian, IV 115b
Saint Joan's International Alliance, IV 528a
Saint Thomas Aquinas, III 654a, 654b; IV 525b
salvation, IV 230a
scholarship, II 430a–430b
scholasticism, I 382b–383a, 383b, 384b
science, I 401b, 402a
Second Vatican Council, I 408b; IV 68b
self-rectification, I 386a
sin, I 512b; IV 230a
skepticism, IV 242a–243a, 244a, 246b
social contract, IV 253b, 254a
socialism, IV 286a–287a
Spain, III 539b, 674b
State, I 403a–406a, 426a, 505a–506a; IV 314a
supranational, III 334b
Syllabus of Errors, I 406a; 215b, 259b

temperance, IV 368b, 369b, 370b
theology, II 30a, 30b
Thirty Years' War, I 398b
tolerance, I 400b
totalitarianism, IV 410a
transubstantiation, I 394b
Trinity, I 376a
Unam Sanctam, I 385a
U.S., III 432b
U.S. Supreme Court, III 654b
universal man, IV 441b
universities, development of, I 382b
urbanization, I 376a
Vatican II, IV 114b, 527b
virtù, IV 477a, 479a, 483b
Volksgeist, IV 491b
vox populi, IV 498b
Waldensians, II 420a
war, III 452b; IV 502a
welfare, III 654b
witchcraft, IV 521a–522a
women, IV 524b–528a
Roman numbers, III 401b–402a
Romance language, II 667b, 669b
linguistics, III 70a
ut pictura poesis, IV 466b
Romanes, George John (1848–1894)
association of ideas, I 115b–116a
behaviorism, I 221a
evolutionism, II 180b
theriophily, IV 388a
Romano, Giulio (1499–1546), mythology, III 291a
ut pictura poesis, IV 466a
Romanovs, III 332a
Romanticism, IV 187a–211a
absolutism, IV 207b
aesthetics, II 224a
Alexander, IV 210b
alienation, I 36b, 620b
Ampère, I 207b
anarchy, IV 202b
anthropology, IV 201b, 202b
anticlassicism, IV 198b
anti-industrialism, III 676a
antiromanticism, IV 195a, 196b
architecture, IV 201a
Ariosto, IV 187a, 187b, 188a, 190b, 192a, 193b
aristocracy, IV 207a
Arndt, IV 207a
Arnim, IV 189a, 190a, 196b
art, II 298b, 304a–304b, 533b–534a, 575b, 578a, 578b, 579a, 580a, 581a,

581b; IV 196b, 199b, 200a, 201b, 202a, 202b, 208a, 209a
artists, II 298b; IV 199b, 200a, 201b, 208b, 210b
atheism, IV 208b, 209a
Austria, IV 207a, 207b
Babbitt, IV 195a, 196b
Bach, IV 209b
Bagehot, IV 193a
Balzac, IV 201b
Baudelaire, IV 196b, 209b
beauty, I 203b, 207b
Being, IV 204a
Bentham, IV 277b
Benz, IV 197a
Bergson, IV 210b
Berlioz, IV 208b
Bible, IV 198b, 200b
biology, II 178b–179a; IV 196a, 201b
Blake, I 304a; IV 199b, 200b, 201a, 202a
Boccaccio, IV 188b
Boehme, IV 209a, 209b, 210b
Bohemia, IV 191a
Bonald, IV 205b
Bouterwek, IV 188a, 189a, 189b, 191b
Brentano, IV 189a, 190a, 196b, 197a
Browning, IV 193a
Brunetière, IV 196b
Bruno, IV 210b
Bulwer-Lytton, IV 193a
Burke, IV 194a, 203a, 203b, 204a, 205b
Burns, IV 195a
Byron, IV 192b, 193a, 194b, 195a, 196a, 201a, 204a, 205a, 208a, 209b
Calderón de la Barca, IV 188a, 188b, 189a
Carlyle, IV 192b, 194a–194b, 199a, 200b, 201a, 204a, 210b
Carus, IV 201b
Cassirer, IV 209b
Cervantes, IV 188a, 188b
Chambers, IV 195a
Chateaubriand, I 404b–405a; IV 189b, 195b, 205a, 208b
Chatterton, IV 194b, 195a
Chaucer, IV 194b
chivalry, IV 187b, 206b
Chopin, IV 208b
Christianity, IV 188b, 192a, 195a, 201a, 206b–207b
civilization, IV 204a, 206b, 207b, 208a
class, IV 199b, 207a

classicism, I 449b, 451a, 453b–454a, 455a; IV 187b, 188a–193b, 195b–197a, 202b, 205a, 209a, 209b
Coleridge, IV 191b, 192b, 193a, 195a, 196b, 198a, 199a, 200a, 201a, 202a, 202b, 203a
common law, II 693b
composers, IV 208b
Condillac, IV 202a
consciousness, IV 202a, 208a, 208b
conservatism, I 482b–483a; IV 196b, 198a, 199a, 200a, 200b, 203a, 207b
Constable, IV 201a
Constant, IV 190a
corporation, IV 206b
cosmic images, I 520a
cosmos, IV 201b
Counter-Enlightenment, II 108b–110a
Cowper, IV 194b, 195a
Crane, IV 195b
creativity, IV 210b
crisis in history, I 594b–595a
criticism, IV 208a
Crusades, IV 203b
culture, IV 198b, 201b, 203a, 205a, 208a, 208b, 209a, 210a
cycles, I 627a
Czechoslovakia, IV 191a–191b
Dante, IV 187b, 188b, 189b
Darwin, Charles, IV 204b
Darwin, Erasmus, IV 201b
De Quincey, IV 192a, 195a
death, I 645b; IV 192a
deism, IV 208b
Delacroix, IV 204a, 208b
Demiurge, IV 204a, 208b
Denham, IV 194a
Descartes, IV 201a
Deutschbein, IV 197a
Dewey, IV 210b
Diderot, IV 199a, 199b
disease, II 403b
Drake, IV 192a
drama, IV 189a, 189b, 190a, 199a
dreams, IV 196b, 201b, 202a
Dreyfus, IV 196b
Dryden, IV 193a, 194a, 195a
dualism, IV 201a, 204a, 207a
dynamism, IV 196a, 197a
Eastlake, IV 193b
Eberhard, IV 191b

Eckermann, IV 188a
economics, IV 206a, 206b, 207b
Eggli, IV 190a
egoism, IV 209b
Eichendorff, IV 205b, 207b
Eichhorn, IV 187b
Eliot, IV 195a
Emerson, IV 210b
emotion, IV 208a
empiricism, IV 199a, 199b, 203b, 209a
Enlightenment, III 479b; IV 198b–204a, 206a, 206b, 207b–209a
epics, IV 188b–189a
equality, IV 205a, 206a
eternity, IV 196a, 202a
ethics, IV 195b, 209b
evil, IV 209b, 210b
evolutionism, II 178b–179a, 182b, 183b
existentialism, IV 210b
expressionsim, II 206a, 207b–308a
faith, IV 200b, 206a
fascism, IV 203a
Faust (legend), III 249b, 250a, 250b
fear, IV 206a
feudalism, IV 206b, 207a
Fichte, IV 202b, 205b, 208a, 210a
fiction, IV 187b, 188b, 191b, 208b
folklore, IV 207a, 208b, 209a
Foster, IV 191b
Fouqué, IV 189a
Fourier, IV 203b
France, IV 304a, 305b, 306b, 483b, 485b; IV 187a, 187b, 189b, 190a, 191a, 192a, 193a, 193b, 194a, 196a, 196b, 198a–204a, 205a, 206b, 207a
free will, II 247a
freedom, IV 203a, 205a, 209a, 209b, 210a, 210b
French Revolution (1789), I 450b; IV 195a, 196b, 199b, 203a, 204a, 205a, 206b
Freud, IV 204b
Friedrich, IV 201a
genius, II 298b, 304a–304b, 322a, 323a–326a; IV 201b, 202a, 202b, 205b
Gentz, IV 207a
Gericault, IV 208b
Germany, I 453b–454a, 482b–483a, 595a; III 250b, 304a, 304b–306b, 483b, 519a–522a; IV 187b, 188b,

189b, 190a, 192a, 192b, 193b, 194a, 194b, 195a, 196b, 197a, 198a–200a, 201a–202a, 203a, 204a, 205a–209b
Gherardini, IV 190b
Gide, IV 196b
God, II 356b, 358b; IV 200b, 201a, 201b, 202b, 204a
Goethe, I 451a, 453b; IV 188a, 188b, 192b, 197a, 198a, 200a, 201a, 208a–208b, 209a, 210a
Görres, IV 197a, 207a
Gothic, II 371a–371b; IV 187b, 201a, 208b
Goya, IV 202b
Great Britain, III 304a, 305b, 306b, 483b, 484b; IV 187a, 187b, 189a, 189b, 191a–197a, 198a, 199b, 201a, 203a, 205a, 208b
Greece (ancient), IV 189b, 208a, 210a
Guizot, IV 189b
Haller, IV 205b
Hamann, IV 209b, 210b
Hardenberg, IV 207a
Hawthorne, IV 208b
Haym, IV 189a, 197a
Hazlitt, IV 192a, 192b, 194a
health, II 403b
Hegel, IV 201b, 204a, 208a, 209b, 210a, 210b
Heidegger, IV 210b
Heine, IV 189a, 207b, 208a
Herder, III 326a, 327a; IV 187b, 190b, 199a, 200a, 201a, 201b, 203a, 203b, 204a, 209a, 209b, 210b
heresy, II 428b
heroes, IV 188b–189a, 200b, 204a, 209a
heterodoxy, IV 199b
hierarchy, IV 206a
historicism, IV 203b, 204a
historiography, II 489b–490a, 491a, 491b, 492a–492b, 494b; IV 147b, 200b
history, I 595a; IV 187a, 187b, 188a, 189a, 191a, 193b, 197a, 198b, 199a, 200a, 201b, 203a, 203b, 204a, 205a, 208a, 210b
Hoffmann, I 453b; IV 189a, 196b
Holbach, IV 209a
Hölderlin, IV 209a, 209b, 210a
holy, II 513a
Holy Roman Empire, IV 206b

honor, IV 205a
Hugo, I 453b; IV 191a, 196b, 198a, 201b, 203b, 205a, 208b
humanism, IV 195a, 201b
humanitarianism, IV 205a
Hume, IV 202a, 203b, 209a
iconography, II 533b–534a, 535a, 538b
idea, IV 197a
idealism, IV 200a, 202a, 208a, 209a
imagination, III 211a, 212a, 221b; IV 195b, 196a, 196b, 197a, 197b, 200b, 202a, 209a, 210a, 210b
immortality, I 645b
impressionism, II 575b, 578a–580a, 581a, 581b
individualism, II 298b, 304a–304b, 595b, 597a, 598a, 600b; IV 198b, 199b, 200a, 201a, 202b–203b, 205a, 205b, 209a–210b
Industrial Revolution, IV 203b
industry, IV 206b, 207b
infinity, IV 199b–202b, 204b, 210a
intrinsic, I 595a
irony, II 633b
irrationalism, II 638a–638b; IV 197a, 200a
Italy, III 484a; IV 188a, 188b, 189b, 190b, 191a, 192b, 194b, 198b, 203b, 205a
Jacobi, IV 201a, 202a, 206a
Jahn, IV 206a
justice, IV 203a, 205a
Kant, III 555b; IV 189b, 199a, 200a, 202a, 202b, 209a, 210a
Keats, IV 195a, 205a, 208b, 209b
Kermode, IV 196a
Kleist, IV 207a, 209b
knowledge, IV 199b, 202a, 204b
Lamartine, IV 205a
Lamennais, IV 205a
language, II 670b–671a; IV 203a, 207a
law, IV 203a, 205b, 206a
Leavis, IV 195a
Leibniz, IV 209a, 210b
Leopardi, IV 204a, 209b
Lermontov, IV 209b
Lessing, IV 209b
liberalism, IV 196b, 198a, 202b, 203b, 205a, 206b, 207b, 208b
liberty, IV 203b

linguistics, III 66a, 67a, 69a; IV 425b
List, IV 207b
literary criticism, IV 205b
literature, IV 199a, 203a, 204a, 205a, 207a, 208a, 209b, 330b, 332a–332b
Locke, IV 199a, 202a, 209a
logic, IV 210b
longevity, III 92b
López Soler, IV 191a
Louis I, IV 207b
love, III 98b, 100a–100b, 102b–103b, 104a, 105b; IV 195a, 203a, 204a, 206a
Lovejoy, IV 188a, 195b, 196a, 198a, 198b, 208a, 208b
loyalty, IV 205a, 206a
Macaulay, IV 194b
Mackintosh, IV 192a
Maine de Biran, IV 201b
Maistre, IV 205b
Mallarmé, IV 196b
Man-Machine, III 142a
Manzoni, IV 192b, 205a
Marlowe, IV 192a
Marx, IV 207b, 208b, 210a
materialism, IV 201a, 203b, 210a
Mazzini, IV 203b
mechanism, IV 199a, 201b, 202b–203a, 209a
Meinecke, IV 203b
melancholy, IV 204a
melodrama, IV 190a
Metternich, IV 207a
Michaud, IV 203b
Michelet, IV 201b, 203b, 204a, 205a
Mickiewicz, IV 191b
Middle Ages, III 478a, 478b; IV 187a, 187b, 188a, 188b, 191b, 192a, 193b, 197a, 203b, 206b, 208b, 210a–210b
Mill, IV 199a, 199b, 200a
mind, IV 202a, 206a
modernism, IV 208b
monarchy, IV 207a
monism, IV 195a
Monteggia, IV 191a
Montesquieu, IV 203a
morality, IV 195a, 205a, 205b, 207a
motif, III 237b–238b, 241a
mountains in literature, III 253b
Müller, IV 206b–207b
Musaeus, IV 192a
music, I 595a; II 322a, 323a–326a; III 268a, 271b; IV 197a, 209a
Musset, IV 204a, 208b

mysticism, **IV** 205a, 206a, 209a
mythology, **III** 300b, 301a, 302a, 302b, 303b–306b; **IV** 187b, 188b, 195b, 196a, 196b, 200b
Napoleon I, **IV** 206b, 207a
nationalism, **III** 326a, 327a, 327b, 328a, 336b; **IV** 197a, 203a, 203b, 204a, 205a, 207a, 208b
naturalism in art, **III** 341a, 343a
Nature, **III** 350a, 351a; **IV** 187a, 195a–196b, 199a–206b, 208a–209a, 210b
Nazism, **IV** 197a, 207a
necessity, **III** 358a, 358b
neo-classicism, **IV** 189a, 191a, 193b, 194a, 195a, 195b, 196a, 199a, 208a
neo-classicism in art, **III** 369a
neo-humanism, **IV** 195a
Neo-Platonism, **IV** 209a, 210a
neo-romanticism, **IV** 197a
Nerval, **IV** 196b
Newton, **IV** 199b, 201a, 209a
Nietzsche, **IV** 204b, 209b, 210b
nihilistic romanticism, **IV** 196a
Novalis, **IV** 188a–188b, 189a, 196b, 201b, 203b, 205b, 206a, 207a, 208a, 209b
novelists, **IV** 208b
obedience, **IV** 206a
ontology, **IV** 200a
optimism, **IV** 204a, 204b
order, **IV** 205a
organicism, **III** 421b, 424a; **IV** 206a, 207b
orthodoxy, **IV** 200b, 204a
painters, **IV** 208b
painting, **I** 595a; **II** 575b, 578a, 578b, 579a, 580a, 581a, 581b; **IV** 201a, 201b, 202b, 204a, 465b, 468b, 469b, 471b, 473a
pan-romanticism, **IV** 208b
pantheism, **IV** 196b, 201b
Paracelsus, **IV** 209a
Pascal, **IV** 209a
passions, **IV** 195a
Pater, **IV** 193b
patriotism, **IV** 207a
Paul, **IV** 188b, 189a, 196b
Peckham, **IV** 196a
Peirce, **III** 568b; **IV** 210b
Pellegrini, **IV** 190a
Pellico, **IV** 205a

Percy, **IV** 194a, 194b, 195a
periodization in history, **III** 478a, 478b, 479b
periodization in literary history, **III** 482a, 483b–485b
pessimism, **IV** 202b, 204a, 209b
Petrarch, **IV** 188b
Phelps, **IV** 193b
philosophy, **I** 594b–595a; **II** 638a–638b; **IV** 195a, 199a, 200a–204a, 205a–206b, 207b–211a
physics, **IV** 210b
Pietism, **I** 595a; **IV** 199b–200a, 206b, 210a
pity, **IV** 203a
Platonism, **III** 519a–522a, 523b, 524a, 524b; **IV** 209a
Plotinus, **IV** 347a–347b
pluralism, **IV** 198b, 204a
Poe, **IV** 208b, 210b
poetry, **I** 594b–595a; **II** 638a–638b; **III** 525b, 527b, 530a, 530b; **IV** 187b–191b, 192a, 194a, 194b, 199a, 200a, 201a, 201b, 205a, 206a, 207a, 209a, 209b, 465b, 468b, 469b, 471b, 473a
poets, **IV** 202a, 205b, 207b, 208b, 210a, 210b
Poland, **IV** 191b
politics, **IV** 195a, 195b, 196a, 198a, 199a, 199b, 202b, 203a, 203b, 205a–208a
Pope, **IV** 192b, 193a, 194a, 195a, 199b
Portugal, **IV** 191a
positivism, **IV** 196a
post-Kantianism, **IV** 208a–211a
Poulet, **IV** 196b
Poussin, **IV** 200a
power, **III** 303b, 305b; **IV** 205a
pragmatism, **III** 555b, 563b, 565a, 567a, 568b; **IV** 210b
primitivism, **III** 596a–596b
progress, **IV** 205a
protest movements, **III** 676a
Protestantism, **IV** 198b, 201a
Proust, **IV** 196b
psychology, **IV** 24a, 199a, 201b, 209b
Pushkin, **IV** 191b
Quietism, **I** 595a
race, **IV** 197a, 203a
Randall, Francis B., **IV** 208b
Randall, J. H., **IV** 209a
rationalism, **IV** 197a, 199b, 201a, 202b, 205a, 205b,

208a, 208b, 209a
realism in literature, **IV** 51b, 52a, 52b, 55a, 56a
reason, **IV** 196b, 199a, 199b, 200a, 200b, 202a, 202b, 203a, 205b, 209a
rebellion, **IV** 204a, 205a
reformation, **IV** 62b
Reformation, **IV** 198b, 206b
reincarnation, **I** 645b
religion, **IV** 111b, 196b, 199b, 200a, 200b, 201a, 202a, 203a, 203b, 205a, 205b, 206b, 209a, 210a
Renaissance, **II** 431a; **IV** 125a, 126a, 147a, 187b–188b, 193b, 198b, 199a
revolution, **IV** 199b, 203a, 204a, 205a–207b
Rimbaud, **IV** 196b
Roman Catholic Church, **IV** 189a, 200b, 205a–207b
Rome (ancient), **IV** 203b
Rousseau, **I** 404b; **IV** 196b, 199a, 200a, 200b–201a, 203a, 209b
Royce, **IV** 210a
Rubens, **IV** 200a
Russia, **IV** 191b, 193a
Saint-Simon, **IV** 199b, 203b
Santayana, **IV** 209b
Sartre, **IV** 204b
Saussure, **IV** 189b
Schelling, **IV** 189a, 201a, 201b, 202a, 204a, 206b, 208a, 209a, 209b, 210a
Schiller, **I** 451a; **IV** 188a, 193a, 197a, 209a
Schlegel, August Wilhelm von, **IV** 188a, 188b, 189b, 190a, 191a, 191b, 192a, 192b, 193b, 194a, 197a, 206b, 208a
Schlegel, Friedrich, **III** 66a; **IV** 188a, 188b, 192a, 192b, 195b, 197a, 198a, 200a, 206a–208b
Schleiermacher, **IV** 199b, 200b, 201a, 202b, 206b, 208a, 209b–210a
scholasticism, **IV** 195a, 196b, 197a–197b
Schopenhauer, **IV** 202a, 202b, 204a, 204b, 209b, 210b
Schubert, **IV** 201b, 208b
Schumann, **IV** 208b
science, **IV** 199a, 200a, 201b, 204a, 209a
Scotland, **IV** 188b
Scott, **IV** 191b, 192a, 193a, 194a, 194b, 199a, 203a
Scudéry, Georges de, **IV**

187a
Scudéry, Magdeleine de, **IV** 187a
secularism, **IV** 200b
Sénancour, **IV** 190a
senses, **IV** 196b, 199b
Shakespeare, **IV** 187b–189b, 192a, 194b
Shaw, **IV** 193a
Shelley, **IV** 193a, 195a–195b, 196b, 202a, 205a, 208b
Sismondi, **IV** 189b, 190a, 190b, 192a
skepticism, **IV** 199b, 200b, 208b, 209a
social welfare, **IV** 277b
socialism, **IV** 202b, 203a, 205a, 206a, 206b
society, **IV** 199b, 200a, 202b, 203a, 203b, 204a, 205a, 206a, 207b
sociology, **IV** 207b, 209b
soul, **IV** 197b, 209a
Southey, **IV** 193a, 194a, 195a
Spain, **IV** 188a, 188b, 189a, 189b, 191a, 194b
Spann, **IV** 207b
Spengler, **III** 251a
Spenser, **IV** 187b, 193a
Spinoza, **IV** 201a, 209a, 210b
spiritualism, **IV** 202a, 203b, 208b
Staël, **IV** 189b, 190a, 190b, 192a, 193b
State, **IV** 202b, 203a, 203b, 205b, 206a, 206b
Stendhal, **IV** 190a–190b, 191a, 192b, 198a
Sturm und Drang, **IV** 200a, 208a–208b
supernatural, **IV** 198a, 201a, 207a
Switzerland, **IV** 205b
symbolism, **IV** 195b, 196a, 197a, 338a, 338b, 341b, 343a, 344b, 345a
symmetry, **IV** 347a–347b
Tasso, **IV** 187a, 187b, 188a, 190b, 192a, 193b
Tennyson, **IV** 193a
theater, **IV** 207a
theology, **IV** 201a, 209b
Thomson, **IV** 194a, 195a
Tieck, **IV** 189a, 194b, 197a, 208a, 209b
Tillich, **IV** 210b
time, **IV** 196a
titanism, **IV** 202b
tradition, **IV** 205a, 207a
tragedy, **IV** 187b, 190b

transcendentalism, IV 24a, 200a, 202a, 202b
truth, III 303b, 304a, 304b, 305a
typology, IV 188a, 189a, 191a
Uhland, IV 189a
unconscious, IV 196b
understanding, IV 202a
uniformitarianism, IV 425b
U.S., III 306b, 483b; IV 189b, 195a, 195b, 196b, 210b
unity, III 303b, 304b, 305a
universality, IV 206b
universe, IV 200b, 204a, 204b, 205b, 206a
Utopia, IV 464b
utopianism, IV 203a
Valéry, IV 196b
Victorian sentiment, IV 221b, 223b
Vigny, IV 201a, 204a, 205a, 208b
Villemain, IV 191a
virtue, IV 485a
Visconti, IV 190b
Volksgeist, IV 203a, 494a
Voltaire, IV 200b
Voss, IV 189a
vox populi, IV 498b
Warton, Joseph, IV 194a, 195a
Warton, Thomas, IV 187b, 188a, 189b, 190b, 191b, 194a, 195a, 195b
wealth, IV 207b
Weisinger, IV 192a
Wellek, IV 195b–196a, 198b, 208b
Weltanschauung, IV 198b, 208a, 209a
Weltschmerz, IV 204a, 209b
Werner, IV 189a
Whitman, IV 208b
will, IV 202b, 204b
wisdom, III 303b, 304b
witchcraft, IV 522b
Wölfflin, IV 197a
women, III 596a–596b
Wordsworth, III 508a; IV 193a, 194a, 194b, 195a, 198b, 200a, 201a, 201b, 208b
World War II, IV 197a
writers, IV 200a, 205a, 205b, 207b
Rome (ancient)
adultery, II 688b
aesthetics, II 216a, 219b–220a
agriculture, III 651b, 652a
alchemy, III 91b
ambiguity, I 50b–51a, 51b

anarchy, II 688a
annals, II 468b
aristocracy, II 260b–261a; 468b, 687b, 690a; IV 154b
Aristotle, IV 369a
art, II 299b; III 365a–365b
assemblies, II 261a–261b
astrology, I 121b, 123a
authority, I 141b–146b; II 686a, 689b–690a
balance of power, I 180a
biography, II 469a
bonitarian property, III 652a
bribes, II 688b
Buddhism, I 247b, 255a
casuistry, I 258b
causation, I 290b, 291a, 291b, 293a
chance, I 335b–336a; II 226a
charity, II 687a
children, II 686b, 688b
China (ancient), I 354a
Church, I 417b
city, I 428a–429a; II 687a
city-state, III 37b; IV 313b–314a
civilization, I 613b; III 181a, 181b, 182a
class, III 652a
classicism, I 451a
classification of the arts, I 456b–458b
classification of the sciences, I 463b
colonialism, IV 113b
comedy, III 61b
common law, II 685b–691b
community, II 687a, 690a
conservation, I 471b–472b
conservatism, I 477b, 479b
constitutionalism, I 487b, 488b
contracts, II 686b
corporations, II 686b–687a
cosmic voyages, I 524b
cosmology, I 544b
Counter-Enlightenment, II 101b, 102b, 105b, 111a
courts, II 686a, 686b, 687b, 688b–689a
crisis in history, I 591a, 591b, 592a
culture, I 609a, 612b, 613a
custom, II 686a, 686b, 687b, 688a
cycles, I 622a–623b, 626a
death, I 635b, 646a
deism, I 647b
democracy, I 652b, 653a, 655a–655b, 657a, 658a; II 686a; IV 154b
despotism, II 4b, 10a, 11b,

13b
determinism, II 22a, 22b
dignity, IV 136b, 139a, 141b, 144a
economic history, II 44b, 45b, 46b
education, II 84b, 687a, 690a
eighteenth century attitudes toward, I 76b–87b
eloquence, II 262a
Enlightenment, II 90a
Epicureanism, II 134b–137b
equality, II 687b, 688b; III 11a, 140a, 140b
equity, II 150b–151a, 152a
ethics, III 440b, 441b, 585a; IV 71b, 176a, 321b–322a
evil, II 163a
evolution of literature, II 170a, 171b–172a
foreigners, II 261a
founding of, III 476b
fraud, II 688b
free will, II 134b–137b
freedom, II 44b, 249b–250a, 686a, 687a
freedom of speech, II 252a, 252b, 260b–262a
games, II 264a
general will, II 275b
Germany, III 591b
gladiators, II 687a
Gnosticism, II 327a, 328a, 329a, 329b, 330a, 330b
God, II 340b, 341a–341b, 566b, 687b, 688a, 689a
Gothic, II 368b–369a
Goths, III 592a
Gracchi, III 652a; IV 161a
grammar, II 528a
Greece (ancient), IV 370a
greed, II 688a
Greeks, II 469a
happiness and pleasure, II 378b
Herder, III 326a
heresy, II 686a, 689a; IV 115a
heroes, IV 370a
hierarchy, II 444a
historians, III 356a, 476b; IV 370b
historiography, II 22a, 22b, 468a–472a, 473b, 477a, 483a, 483b
humanism, II 515a, 516a, 517a; III 476b; IV 130b, 132b
iconography, II 525b
idea, II 685b–690b
idealism, II 687b, 690b
ideology, II 566b

immortality, I 646a
impiety, II 564a, 566b–567a
individualism, II 299b, 689b
injury, II 686b, 687b, 688b
innocence, II 688b–689a
international peace, III 448a
intolerance, IV 115a
irony, II 632a
irrationalism, IV 46a
Israel (ancient), I 413a, 415a–415b
judges, II 686a, 688b
jurisprudence, II 656b
jurors, II 685b, 686a, 687b, 689a, 689b, 690a
justice, II 653a, 656b, 686a, 686b, 687b, 688b
kingship, II 689b–690a
land, II 652a
language, II 566b, 661b, 663a, 664a, 665a–666a
law, I 141b–146b, 290b, 291a, 291b, 293a, 382a, 487b; II 4b, 10a, 102b, 150b–151a, 152a, 249b–250a, 261a, 411b, 412a, 515a, 521b, 566b, 673b, 685b–690b; III 3b, 6b, 7a, 11a, 16a, 16b–17a, 28a, 28b–30b, 354b, 441b, 632a, 652a, 655a–655b; IV 61b, 66a, 115a, 313b–314a, 314b, 315b, 492a–492b, 494a, 497b
law of nations, II 656b
law and order, II 656b
Law of the Twelve Tables, III 6b, 7a
lawyers, II 688b, 689a
liberalism, III 36a, 36b
liberty, II 686a
literature, II 690a; III 528a; IV 330b, 331a, 370a
longevity, III 89b, 91b
loyalty, III 109a
Machiavelli, III 356a; IV 502b
Machiavellism, III 116a
Manicheans, IV 115a
marriage, II 686b, 688a
mathematics, III 181a, 181b
medicine, II 687a
merchants, II 687a
Middle Ages, IV 253a
military, III 354b
mimesis, III 225b, 227a, 227b
missionaries, I 375a–376b; II 470b
monarchy, II 686a; IV 154b
morality, II 687a, 688a; IV 154b
murder, II 688b

mythology, II 656b; III 287a, 292a, 293a, 303a, 313b

nationalism, II 689b–690a, 690b; III 319a, 320a, 320b, 321b, 322a, 323a, 326a

natural law, III 16a, 16b–17a, 17b, 18a

naturalism, II 581b

naturalism in art, III 339b, 342a

Nature, II 687b, 688a–688b; III 347a

necessity, III 354b, 355a, 356a, 361a

neo-classicism in art, III 363a, 364b, 365a, 366b, 369b, 370a

Neo-Platonism, III 371b, 372a, 373a, 373b, 377b

Noble Savage, III 591b

oaths, II 688b

omens, III 347a

partnerships, II 686b

patricians, III 652a

Pax Romana, II 656b; III 440b, 441b, 448a

peace, III 440b, 441b

perfectibility, III 473a

periodization in history, III 476b, 477a, 477b

persecution, II 566b–567a

Persia (ancient), IV 115a

philanthropy, III 487a–487b, 488b

philosophy, II 686a, 687b; IV 370a

plebeians, III 652a

poetry, III 526b–529a, 530b, 531a, 531b

politics, II 566b, 688a; III 354b, 652a, 370b

polytheism, IV 113b

power, I 142b–144b, 146a–146b; II 686a, 686b, 689b, 690a; IV 154b

pragmatism, III 554a

primitivism, III 579b–581a, 599a

private property, II 686b, 687b, 688a, 688b, 689b; III 651b–652a; IV 154b

probability, III 605b

progress, III 624b, 630b, 631b, 632a–632b, 633a, 634b, 640a, 641a

propaganda, II 566b

prophecy, III 665a, 665b

psychology, IV 1b, 8b

punishment, II 686a, 687a, 688b

Quirites, III 652a

rationalism, IV 46a, 49b, 50a

reason, I 144b; II 686a, 687b, 688a–689a, 690a

reformation, IV 60b, 61b, 66a

reincarnation, I 646a

relativism, IV 71b

religion, III 373b; IV 93a–93b, 94a, 98a, 113b, 115a, 117b

Renaissance, IV 115a, 121b–124b, 125b, 130b, 132b, 136b, 139a, 141b, 144a

republicanism, III 476b

revival, III 369b

revolution, IV 152b, 154b, 161a

rhetoric, III 528a; IV 167b, 168a, 169a–170b, 370a

right and good, IV 176a

rights, II 686a, 686b, 687a, 687b, 688b, 689b, 690b

romanticism, IV 203b

Romulus, II 656b

sack of, II 468b

salvation, IV 227b–230a

satire, IV 211a, 212b, 213a, 214b, 215a, 216b

Saturnalia, IV 516b

Savigny, II 411b, 412a

scholarship, III 476b

sculpture, III 342a

self-sufficiency, III 585a

servitude, II 686b

sex, II 688a

shipping, II 686a

sin, IV 227b–230a

slavery, II 4b, 249b, 250a, 686a, 687b, 688b, 689a; IV 286a

social contract, IV 252b–253a

socialism, IV 285b, 286a

society, II 687b, 688a; III 373a, 373b, 651b, 652a; IV 252b

soul, II 687a

spontaneous generation, IV 307b

State, I 652b, 653a, 655a–655b, 657a, 658a; II 686b–690a; IV 252b, 313b–315a

Stoicism, IV 321b–322a

style, IV 330b, 331a

suffrage, II 261a

symmetry, IV 345b–346a

taxes, II 690a

technology, IV 358a, 358b

temperance, IV 369a–371a

theater, IV 370a

theft, II 688b, 689a

time, IV 401a

torture, II 689a

trade, II 686a, 687b; III 652a

treason, II 686a, 689a

trials, II 686a, 687b, 688b–689a, 690b

tyranny, II 688b

unity of science, IV 431a

universal man, IV 441b

vice, IV 154b

violence, II 688a

virtù, IV 477a, 478a, 479b, 481a, 482b, 483a

virtue, I 655b

Volksgeist, IV 491a, 492a–492b, 494a

vox populi, IV 497b, 498a

war, II 687b, 689b, 690a; III 448a, 652a; IV 501a–502a, 502b

wealth, II 686a, 688b

welfare, II 686b, 688a, 688b, 689b

wills, II 686b

wisdom of the fool, IV 516b, 517a

witchcraft, IV 521a

women, II 686b

writers, III 528a

Romuald of Ravenna (d. 1027), reformation, IV 64b

Romulus (c. 753–716 B.C.)
justice, II 656b

Rondon, Cândido Mariano, positivism, III 543b, 545a

Ronsard, Pierre de (1524–1585)
baroque in literature, I 192b, 195a

literary paradox, III 77b

mimesis, III 228b

mythology, III 290a

Platonism, III 507b, 514a

poetics, III 529b, 530a

rhetoric, IV 171a–171b, 172b

style, IV 331a, 331b

Rood, Ogden Nicholas (1831–1902), impressionism, II 580b

Roosevelt, Franklin D. (1882–1945), welfare state, IV 512a–512b

Roosevelt, Theodore (1858–1919)
conservation, I 471a, 475b, 476a

international peace, III 450a

loyalty, III 113a

Root, Elihu (1845–1937), international peace, III 450a

Root metaphor
contextualism, III 198a

formism, III 198a

mechanism, III 198a

organicism, III 198a

paradigm case, III 200a

philosophy, III 197a–198a, 198b, 200a–200b, 201a

Rore, Cipriano da (1516–1565), music, III 262a

Rorschach, Hermann (1884–1922), chance images, I 340b, 350b, 351a

Rosa, Salvator (1615–1673), Nature, III 349b

Roscellinus (d. after 1120)
heresy, II 418a

idea, II 546b

Roscher, Wilhelm (1817–1894), economic history, II 60b

Roscher, Wilhelm Heinrich (1845–1923), motif, III 241b

Roscoe, William (1753–1831), literature, III 83a

Rosen, N., indeterminacy, II 590b

Rosenberg, Alfred (1893–1946)
Faust (legend), III 251b

Nazis, III 597b

Rosenberg, B. G., beauty, I 213b

Rosenblum, R., iconography, II 538b

Rosenkranz, Karl (1805–1879)
freedom, II 413b

Hegel and, II 412b, 413a–413b, 414a

mind, II 413b

mysticism, II 412b

reason, II 413b

Strauss and, II 412b

Rosenstock-Huessy, E., crisis in history, I 593a

Rosicrucians, I 32b, 33a
linguistics, III 74b

Ross, Alf, law, III 4a

Ross, David
good, IV 183a–183b

moral sense, III 234b

right, IV 183a–183b

Rossetti, Dante Gabriel (1828–1882), *ut pictura poesis,* IV 470b, 475a

Rosshirt, Christoph, Faust legend, III 245b

Rossi, Alice, women, IV 529a, 529b

Rostand, Edmond (1868–1918), theriophily, IV 387a

Rotation
Berkeley, IV 86a

Newton, IV 75b, 76a

relativity, IV 75b, 76a, 76b, 80b, 86a
space, IV 75b
time, IV 389b, 392a
Rotermund, H. M., iconography, II 538a
Rothacker, Erich, perennial philosophy, III 463a
Rothe, Richard (1799–1867), eschatology, II 158b
Rothko, Mark, individualism, II 304b
Rottmann, Bernard, eschatology, II 157a
Rouault, Georges (1871–1958), comedy, I 470a
Rousseau, Henri (1844–1910), *ut pictura poesis*, IV 467b, 472b, 473a
Rousseau, Jean Jacques (1712–1778)
absolutism, III 21b
animal, III 599b
anti-intellectualism, III 595b, 599b
aristocracy, II 11a–11b, 276a
art, III 599b
art and play, I 105a
authority, I 152b–153b
Bacon and, I 179a
baroque in literature, I 188b
belles lettres, III 599b
Burke and, I 481b; IV 203a
Chateaubriand and, III 603b; IV 201a
children, III 469b, 595b
China, I 362a, 365a
citizenship, I 658a
civilization, I 616b–617a, 617b; III 598a
class, I 448a–448b
Constant and, II 279a–279b
cosmopolitanism, II 276a
Counter-Enlightenment, II 102a, 104b–105a, 107b, 109b, 110a, 111a
culture, I 616b–617a, 617b
Defoe and, III 601b
deism, I 651b
democracy, I 656a, 657b–658a, 661a, 661b; II 323b
despotism, II 4a, 4b–5a, 8b, 10a, 11a–12b, 15a
destiny, III 326a
Diderot and, III 603a
Dixmerie and, III 602b
economic history, II 44b
education, II 73a, 74a–74b, 75a, 80b, 83a, 99b, 276b, 277a, 278a, 278b, 279a; III 469b, 595b, 600a
Enlightenment, II 89b, 91a,

93a, 93b, 94b, 98a, 99b
equality, I 448b, 658a; II 143b–144a, 277a, 277b, 278b; III 21b
ethics, III 442a, 445b
evil, II 168b; III 599b
evolution of literature, II 170a
evolutionism, II 178a–178b
Fichte and, II 279a
freedom, II 44b, 250b, 276b, 277a, 278b, 279a; III 21b, 156a; IV 260a
French Revolution, III 326a
general will, II 275b–280b
God, II 353b, 356b
Goethe and, IV 209b
good, II 277a; III 598a, 599b
greatness, III 326a
Grotius and, IV 259b
happiness, II 277a; III 326a
health, II 402b, 403b
Hegel and, II 407b; IV 209b
Herder and, II 324a–324b; III 326a
history, I 409a
Hobbes and, IV 259b
Hoffmann and, II 324b
ideas, III 602b
ideology, II 561b
impressionism, II 582b
imprinting, II 584a
individualism, II 275b–280b, 597b, 599b, 600a, 601b; III 21b
inequality, I 448a–448b; II 277a–278b; IV 288a
instinct, II 277a
international peace, III 452b
justice, II 278a, 280b, 653b
Kant and, II 107b; III 442a; IV 209b, 502a
language, II 669a
law, II 250b, 277a–278b; III 21b
learning, II 584a
Ledoux and, I 432a
liberalism, III 37a, 45b, 46a, 47a, 47b, 48a
liberty, II 94b, 98a, 277a
linguistics, III 64b
Locke and, IV 259a, 259b, 260a
love, III 103a–103b
Lucretius and, III 587b
luxury, III 600a
Machiavellism, III 121b
mankind, III 325b, 326a
Marxism, III 156a
military, II 278b
mind, II 276b
Monboddo and, II 669a;

III 599b
Montesquieu and, II 11b–12a, 275b, 276a
moral freedom, III 47b
morality, II 276b; III 21b, 599b
musical genius, II 322a–324b
mythology, III 278b
nationalism, III 325a–326a
natural law, III 21a–21b
natural liberty, II 62a
Nature, I 616b–617a; II 144a; III 21b, 348a, 348b, 600a
necessity, II 277a; III 358a
Nietzsche and, IV 209b
Paine and, IV 260b
patriotism, II 278a; III 325b
peace, III 442a, 445b
peasantry, III 594b; IV 259b
perfectibility, III 469b, 470a
philosophy, IV 155a
Plato and, III 325b
Platonism, III 518a, 518b, 520b
politics, III 121b, 326a; IV 259b, 260a
post-Kantianism, IV 209b
poverty, IV 288a
power, II 11a–11b, 276b, 278a; III 21b; IV 259b
primitivism, III 587b, 588b, 594b, 595b, 597b, 598a, 599b, 600a, 600b, 602b, 603a, 603b, 605a
private property, III 599b; IV 288a
progress, II 178a
Proudhon and, II 280b
psychology, II 276b, 277a
revolution, IV 155a–155b
rights, III 21b, 326a; IV 259b
Robespierre and, IV 260a
romanticism, I 404b; IV 196b, 199a, 200a, 200b–201a, 203a, 209b
Saint-Just and, IV 260a
Schubart and, II 324a
science, III 598a, 599b, 600a
Seneca and, III 588b
slavery, II 11a, 11b
social contract, III 21a–21b; IV 252a, 259a–260a, 261a, 262a, 262b, 317a
socialism, IV 288a, 289b
society, II 99b, 276b–277b, 669a; III 600a; IV 259a, 260a
sovereignty, I 658a; II 11a–11b, 250b, 276b, 278a

the State, I 656a, 657b–658a, 661a, 661b; II 276a–276b, 277b, 278a, 279b, 407b; III 21b; IV 259a, 317a
structuralism, IV 323a
symbolism, IV 345a
Tolstoy and, III 445b
truth, III 595b
tyranny, II 11b–12a
utopianism, II 12b
vice, III 599b
Voltaire and, III 605a
will, IV 259b, 260a
Rousset, Jean
baroque in literature, I 192b
cosmic images, I 513b
literary criticism, I 605b
Roux, Wilhelm (1850–1924), chromosomes, II 287b
Roy, Rammohun
Orientalism, III 429b
transcendentalism, III 429b
Royal Observatory, IV 404b
Royal Society of London, IV 462a
Royal Society for the Prevention of Cruelty to Animals, IV 388a
Royce, Josiah (1855–1916)
empiricism, III 561a
God, II 358a
Hegel and, II 415b; III 556b, 561a
idealism, III 561a
individualism, III 561a
James and, III 561a
knowledge, III 561a
loyalty, III 115a
monism, III 556b
Peirce and, III 561a
Pietism, IV 111b
Platonism, III 506b
pragmatism, III 556b, 561a
reality, III 561a
religion, IV 111b
romanticism, IV 210a
spiritualism, III 556b
theodicy, IV 383a
time, IV 396b
truth, III 561a
Roydon, Matthew
Chapman and, III 294b
mythology, III 294b
Royer-Collard, Pierre Paul (1763–1845)
Nature, III 348a
psychology, IV 11b
Ruben, Walter, Buddhism, I 256b
Rubenists, aesthetics, II 222a
Rubens, Peter Paul (1577–1640)

compared to poetic styles,
I 189b
genius, II 303a, 309a
iconography, II 531b, 533a
impressionism, II 577b,
578a, 578b
mythology, III 293b
neo-classicism in art, III
368a
periodization in literary history, III 485b
romanticism, IV 200a
Rubenstein, Rabbi Richard,
God, II 363b–364a
Rucellai, Bernardo (1449–
1514), balance of power,
I 180b
Rucellai, Giovanni (1475–
1525), optics, III 415b–
416a
Rückert, Friedrich (1788–
1866), China, I 368b
Rudel, Jauffré, love, III 102a
Rudra (myth), II 343b
Rufus of Ephesus (fl. early
part 2nd century A.D.),
disease, II 398b
Ruge, Arnold (1803–1880),
Engels and, II 413b
Hegel and, II 413a–414a
Marx and, II 413b
work, IV 535b
Rule of Faith controversy, I
307a–308a
Rules
Aristotle, IV 175b
arithmetic, II 660a
common law, II 691a, 692b,
693a, 694a, 695a, 696a;
III 31b
Descartes, III 384b
genius, II 317a, 319a, 319b,
323b, 325b
good, IV 173a–177a, 180b,
181a, 181b, 183a, 184b,
185b, 186a, 186b
Greece (ancient), II 675b,
676a, 678b, 681a
Hart, III 2b–3a, 4b–5a
Hume, III 232b
justice, III 232b
Kant, III 21b, 555b, 556a
law, II 675b, 676a, 678b,
681a, 691a; III 1a–5b,
6a, 6b, 20a, 23a, 24a,
24b, 26a, 28b, 30b, 31b,
33a, 33b, 34a, 34b, 35a
Lenin, III 156a
Marxism, III 151b, 156a
mathematics, II 660a
methodology, III 390b
moral sense, III 232b
music, II 317a, 319a, 319b,
323b, 325b

mythology, III 314b
natural law, III 20b, 21b,
23a, 23b, 24b, 26a
Newton, III 390b
pragmatism, III 555b,
556a
rationalism, IV 48b
rhetoric, IV 168a, 172a
right, IV 173a–174b, 175b,
177a, 180b, 181a, 181b,
183a, 184b, 185b, 186a,
186b
Ross, III 4a
society, III 5b
Spencer, IV 180b
State, IV 313a, 313b
totalitarianism, III 232b
Rumania
communism, III 334a
industry, III 336b
nationalism, III 334a, 336b
U.S.S.R., III 334a, 336b
Rund, M. B., baroque in
literature, I 193b
Rupert of Deutz, prophecy,
III 666a, 666b
Rush, Benjamin (1745?–
1813)
democracy, I 660a
psychology, IV 21a
Rush, James (1786–1869),
psychology, IV 21a–21b
Rushton, William, neo-
classicism in art, III 362b
Ruska, J., alchemy, I 29b
Ruskin, John (1819–1900)
art, II 297b, 307a; IV 125b
baroque in literature, I
194a–194b
beauty, I 209a; IV 339a
classicism, I 450a
culture, II 127b, 133b
empathy, II 88a
environment, II 127b, 133b
genius, II 297b, 307a
God, II 297b
Gothic, II 372b
individualism, II 297b,
307a
motif, III 235a, 236b
naturalism, IV 339a
ut pictura poesis, IV 469a
Victorian sensibility, IV
221a
symbolism, IV 339a
welfare state, IV 509b
Russell, Bertrand (1872–
1969)
abstraction, I 8b–9a
agnosticism, I 22b
appearance and reality, I
98a
atomism, IV 394b
axiomatization, I 168b,

169b
behaviorism, I 219b
certainty, I 319b–321b,
323b
China, I 371a–371b
common sense, I 319b,
320a–320b
continuity, I 502b
Counter-Enlightenment, II
103a
data, I 320a–320b
Dewey and, III 446b
empiricism, I 319b; III
545b, 547b, 548a, 549a
Einstein and, III 446b
Enlightenment, III 446a,
446b; IV 70a
ethics, III 445b, 446a–
446b; IV 70a
Freud and, III 446b
good, IV 184a
Hobbes and, III 446a
infinity, II 611b
internationalism, III 446b
knowledge, I 319b, 320a–
320b, 321b
logic, I 319b–320a, 320b–
321b; III 545b, 547b, 548a,
549a
mathematics, I 319b–320a,
321b; III 176a, 176b
methodological-monism, I
23a
Nature, III 446b
nuclear power, III 446b
over-population, III 446b
peace, III 445b–446b
Peirce and, III 561a
positivism, III 545b, 547b,
548a, 549a
pragmatism, III 561a
relativism, IV 70a
space, IV 304a
technology, III 446b
time, IV 394b, 396b
truth, I 319b–321b,
323b
universals, I 320b
war, III 446b
Wittgenstein and, I 320a,
321b–322a
Russell, Charles T. (1852–
1916), eschatology, II 157a
Russell, F. T., Utopia, IV
463b
Russia
absolutism, I 593b
aesthetics, II 216a, 221a
balance of power, I 186a,
186b, 187a–187b
Bolsheviks, III 152a
capitalism, III 164a
China and, I 371a
classicism, I 454b, 455b
communism, II 559a

conservatism, I 482b–483a
Counter-Enlightenment, II
106a
crisis in history, I 593a,
593b
Decembrist revolution
(1825), IV 158a
democracy, I 665a–665b
Eastern Orthodox Church, I
409b, 410b–411a, 417b
economics, III 154a
evolution of literature, II
173a–173b
history, III 333b
idealism, IV 220a
ideology, II 559a, 559b
imperialism, III 333b
international peace, III
453b
Japan, I 370b
Jesuits, I 403b
Judaism, III 488a
language, II 669b, 672a
literary criticism, I 606a–
606b
Marxism, III 152a, 154a,
164b–165a
missionaries, I 409b
Napoleon I, II 14b
nationalism, I 482b–483a;
III 327b, 328b, 332a, 333b,
336a, 337b
naturalism, IV 53b
naturalism in art, III
339a
Old Believers, III 674b
peasantry, III 674b
periodization in literary history, III 483a
philanthropy, III 488a
Populists, III 676b
pragmatism, III 569a
primitivism, III 605a
private property, III 651b
probability, III 620a
protest movements, III
674b, 676b
psychology, IV 14a, 28a
realism in literature, IV 53a–
53b, 54b, 55a–55b
religion, III 674b
revisionism, IV 268b, 271a,
273a, 274a
revolution, IV 158a, 160b,
162a, 163b, 164a, 164b,
165a
revolution of 1905, IV 273a
romanticism, IV 191b, 193b
Russian Revolution, III
647b
satire, IV 214b
socialism, III 154a, 156b;
IV 293a
State, I 665a–665b

Tartars, III 333b
Treaty of Nerchinsk, I 360b
Tsarism, III 333b
Volksgeist, IV 494b
war, IV 504a
Russian Revolution (October 1917)
anarchism, I 75a
Bolshevism, IV 164a, 164b
capitalism, IV 164a, 164b
communism, IV 164b
Communist International, IV 164b
crisis in history, I 593a, 593b
democracy, I 665b
history, IV 163b
influence, IV 165a
Lenin, III 150a, 150b
Marxism, III 148a, 150a, 150b, 152a–152b, 154a, 155b, 164a, 165a
nationalism, III 332a, 333b
power, IV 164a
progress, III 647b
race, IV 164b
revolution, IV 158a, 163b, 164a, 165a, 166b
socialism, IV 164b
society, IV 163b, 164a
terror, IV 164a
U.S.S.R., IV 158a, 163b, 164a, 165a
World War I, III 332a
Rustici, Giovan Francesco
art, II 302a
individualism, II 302a
Rutherford, Ernest (1871–1937)
uniformitarianism and catastrophism, IV 423a
Ruthwell Cross, iconography, II 527a
Rutilius Namatianus, Claudius (early 5th century B.C.), progress, III 632a
Ruysdael, Jacob van (1628?–1682); impressionism, II 578a
Ruzbehan of Shiraz, love, III 99b
Rykov, Aleksei I. (1881–1938), Marxism, III 165b
Ryle, Gilbert (1900–   )
empiricism, III 549a, 549b
language, II 386b
Man-Machine, III 145a
pain, II 386b
Plato and, III 502b
Platonism, III 502b
pleasure, II 386b
positivism, III 549a, 549b

psychology, IV 9b
Rymer, Thomas (1641–1713)
genius, II 294b
literary criticism, I 596a

S

Saadi (1184?–1291)
Orientalism, III 430a
transcendentalism, III 430a
Sabeans of Harran, Islam, II 639a, 639b
Sabellicus, Georg, Faust legend, III 244b–245a
Saccas, Ammonius, Platonism, III 516b, 517a, 517b
Sacchetti, Franco (1335?–1400), genius in art, II 301a
Sacchi, Bartolommeo de' (1421–1481), humanism, IV 132b
Sacher-Masoch, Leopold von (1836–1895), love, III 105b
Sachs, Eva, Pythagoreans, IV 35a
Sachs, Hans (1494–1576), musical genius, II 325a
wisdom of the fool, IV 519b
Sackur, O., indeterminacy, II 589a
Sacraments
Calvin, I 392a
Christianity, I 390a, 391b–392a
Church, I 416a–416b
heresy, II 417a, 418b, 426b, 427b
Luther, I 390a
religion, IV 113b
Reformation, I 390a, 391b–392a
Saint Francis of Assisi, IV 65a
temperance, IV 372b
Zwingli, I 391b–392a
Sacred, *see* Holy
Sacrifice
Bible, III 279a, 279b, 280a, 281b
Greece (ancient), II 675b, 677b
Jung, IV 97a
law, II 675b, 677b
mythology, III 279a, 279b, 280a, 281b, 291b
philanthropy, III 489a
religion, II 675b; IV 97a
Sade, Marquis de (1740–1814)

Counter-Enlightenment, II 107b
Enlightenment, II 94b
love, III 94a
Sadism
Freud, II 383b
pleasure, II 383b
Sagas, mythology, III 275a, 275b, 276a, 308b–309a, 311a, 315b, 316b
Saint Antoine, symbolism, IV 340a
St. Germain, Christopher, (c. 16th century), common law, II 695a–695b
Saint Joan's International Alliance, IV 528a
St. Just, Louis (1769–1794), despotism, II 2a, 8b, 13b, 14a
Saint Victor, Godefroy de, microcosm, III 129b–130a
Saint-Amant, Marc Antoine de (1594–1661), literary paradox, III 77b
Saint-Evremond, Charles de (1610?–1703)
catharsis, I 266b
deism, I 649a
Epicureanism, II 137b
genius, II 294a
taste, IV 354b–355a
tragedy, I 266b
Saint-Just, Louis Antoine de (1767–1744)
nationalism, III 326b
Platonism, III 520b
Rousseau and, IV 260a
social contract, IV 260a
Saint-Lambert, Jean François de (1716–1803)
general will, II 276a
genius, II 294b
Saint-Pierre, Abbé de (1658–1743)
aristocracy, II 11a
deism, I 651a
despotism, II 8b, 11a, 12b
Enlightenment, II 90b
Kant and, III 442a
peace, II 442a, 452b
Saint-Simon, Claude Henri de (1760–1825)
causation, I 281a
chaos, III 641a
class, I 443b, 448b
Comte and, III 533b, 534b–535a, 535b
Condorcet and, III 640b
cosmic images, I 520a
crisis in history, I 590a
deism, III 641a
equality, I 448b, 449a
fetishism, III 641a

French Revolution, III 534b
happiness, II 380a
history, I 281a
individualism, II 594b, 595b, 600b, 601a
knowledge, III 641a
law, III 22a, 641a
liberalism, III 57b, 58b
Marx and, III 534b
natural law, III 22a
Newton and, IV 199b
periodization in history, III 478a
philosophy, III 641a
polytheism, III 641a
positivism, III 533b, 534b–535a, 535b
progress, III 640b–641b
radicalism, III 534b
religion, III 641a
romanticism, IV 199b, 203b
science, III 641a
socialism, III 534b; IV 288b, 289b, 290a, 293a, 293b
society, III 22a, 641a
species, III 640b
utopianism, II 380a
Saint-Simon, Louis de (1675–1755), despotism, II 8b
Sainte-Beuve, Charles Augustin (1804–1869),
classicism, I 450a, 452b
evolution of literature, II 170a
literary criticism, I 599b, 601b, 602a, 602b, 605a
literature, III 84a
Saints
Christianity, III 589b, 590a
holy, II 512a, 512b
humanism, II 517b
iconography, II 526a
millenarianism, III 223a–223b, 225a
mythology, III 275b, 284a, 284b
primitivism, III 589b, 590a
prophecy, III 664b, 665a
reformation, IV 61a
Reformation, IV 67b, 68a
religion, IV 111a
resurrection, III 223a–223b
virtue, IV 477a
women, IV 525b
Saintyves, P., mythology, III 316a
Sajnovics, J., linguistics, III 64b
Saladin (1138–1193), historiography, II 474a
Salazar y Frias, Alonso de, witchcraft, IV 522b

Šalda, F. X.
 baroque in literature, I 193a
 symbolism, IV 343b
Salem East India Marine
 Society, III 428b
Sales, Delisle de, cosmic
 images, I 519b, 523a
Salinas, Francisco de, music,
 III 261b
Salisbury, Lord (1830–1903)
 international peace, III 453b
Sallust (86–34 B.C.)
 God, II 341b
 historiography, II 469b
 style, IV 331b
 temperance, IV 370b
Salmon, Wesley
 empiricism, III 550a
 logic, III 550a
Salmon, William, mythology,
 III 298a–298b
Salutati, Coluccio (c. 14th
 century)
 chancellor, IV 122b
 determinism, II 234b
 dignity, IV 142b, 143b
 fortune, fate, and chance, II
 234b
 handwriting, II 518a
 humanism, II 515b, 517b–
 518a, 519b, 522a, 522b,
 523a; IV 129b, 132b
 letter-writing, II 515b
 monarchy, II 523a
 morality, II 234b
 poetics, III 529b
 rhetoric, II 522b
 salvation, IV 142b
 virtue, II 234b
Salvation, IV 224a–234a
 Achan (Bible), IV 226b
 Adam (Bible), IV 227a,
 230a
 Adonis (myth), IV 228b
 Advaita Uedanta, IV 232a
 Agamemnon (myth), IV
 228a
 Ahriman (myth), IV 228b,
 231b
 Ahura Mazdā (myth), IV
 231a, 231b
 Am-mut (myth), IV 225b
 Anubis (myth), IV 225b
 Apollo (myth), IV 228a
 Arabs, IV 230b
 art, IV 233a
 Attis (myth), IV 228b
 baptism, IV 230a
 Bhagavadgītā, IV 232a
 bhaktimarga, IV 232a
 Bible, IV 226b–227b, 229a–
 230b
 birth, IV 231b
 bodhisattvas, IV 233a

Book of the Dead, IV
 225a, 225b
Buddha, IV 232b, 233a
Buddhism, IV 232b–233a
Calvin, II 245a; IV 67b
Calvinism, IV 177a
causation, IV 232b
Christianity, IV 224a, 226a
 228a, 229a–230b, 231b
Church of England, IV 224a
city-state, IV 228a
Code of Hammurabi, IV
 226b
conscience, IV 225a, 226a
cosmos, IV 224b
crime, IV 225b
culture, IV 231b, 232b,
 233a
cycles, IV 232a
death, IV 224b–226a, 227b,
 228a, 228b, 229b, 230a,
 231a, 231b, 232b
deism, IV 224a, 226b
Demeter (myth), IV 228b
dignity, IV 142a, 142b
Dionysius the Areopagite,
 IV 228b
dualism, IV 229a, 231a
Egypt (ancient), IV 224b–
 226a, 228b
Eightfold Path, IV 232b
Eleusinian Mysteries, IV
 228a–228b, 229a
eschatology, IV 226a, 229a,
 230a, 231b
ethics, IV 225a, 225b, 227a
Eve (Bible), IV 227a
evil, IV 224a, 226a, 228b,
 229b, 231a, 231b, 233a
existentialism, IV 232a
faith, hope, and charity,
 210a, 212b
Faust (legend), III 250a
free will, II 244b–245b; IV
 230b, 231a, 232b
Gnosticism, II 326b; IV
 229a, 229b
God, II 341a, 345a, 351a,
 359b, 361a, 365b; IV 225a–
 231a, 232a
good, IV 174b, 176a,
 176b, 177a, 224b, 231a,
 231b
Greece (ancient), IV 228a–
 229b
guilt, IV 226b
Hades (myth), IV 228a
Hammurabi, IV 226b
happiness and pleasure, II
 374b, 379a
health, II 379a, 399a,
 406b
heaven, IV 230a, 230b,
 231b

hell, IV 230a, 231a, 231b
heresy, II 420a, 426a
Hermeticism, IV 229a, 229b
Hinduism, IV 231b–232b
history, II 518b; IV 224a
Homer, IV 228a
hubris, IV 228a
human nature, IV 231b,
 233a
humanism, II 518b
idolatry, IV 226b, 227a
immortality, IV 226a, 228a,
 228b, 230b
Incarnation, IV 232b
India (ancient), IV 232b
individualism, IV 227b
Ishtar (myth), IV 226b
Isis (myth), IV 228b
Islam, IV 224a, 230b–231a
Israel (ancient), IV 226b–
 228a
Jeroboam (Bible), IV
 226b–227a
Jesus Christ, IV 227b,
 229a–230b
Job (Bible), IV 227b–228a
Joshua (Bible), IV 226b
Judaism, III 487b; IV
 226b–229b, 230b
justice, IV 224b, 225b,
 227b
karma, IV 231b–232a, 232b
Koran, IV 230b, 231a
law, IV 224a, 226a, 226b,
 233a
liberation, IV 232a, 233a
literature, IV 228a, 233a
Luther, II 212b, 245a
Man-Machine, III 141b
Marduk (myth), IV 226b
Marx, III 334b
Mecca, IV 231a
Mesopotamia (ancient), IV
 226a–226b
metaphysics, IV 232b
Middle Ages, III 40a–40b;
 IV 230a
Mithra (myth), IV 228b
morality, IV 224b, 225a,
 225b, 229a, 229b, 231a
Muhammad, IV 230b–231a
mysticism, IV 228a–229a
mythology, III 277a–277b,
 284b; IV 224b, 226a,
 226b, 228a–229a
nationalism, III 324a; IV
 227b
Nature, IV 229a, 231b,
 232b
Near East, IV 227b, 228b
Nebot (Bible), IV 226b–
 227a
Neo-Platonism, IV 229a
Nirvāna, IV 232b–233a

Oedipus (myth), IV 228a
Orpheus (myth), IV 228b
Orphism, IV 228a–229a
Osiris (myth), IV 225a,
 225b, 228b
paradise, IV 230b
Persephone, IV 228b
Persia, IV 228b, 231a
Petrarch, IV 142a, 142b
philanthropy, III 489b
philosophy, IV 228a, 229a
Plato, IV 228a
Platonism, III 509a
polytheism, IV 231a
power, IV 227b
predestination, IV 230b
progress, III 630a, 635a
Protestantism, IV 230a
Pseudo-Dionysius, IV 228b
Pyramid Texts, IV 224b–
 225a
Rashnu (myth), IV 231b
Rē (myth), IV 224b–225a
Reformation, IV 67b
reincarnation, IV 228b
religion, IV 101a, 111a,
 224a, 225a, 226a, 227a,
 228a, 233a
Renaissance, IV 142a
resurrection, IV 226b, 228a,
 228b, 230b, 231b
right, IV 174b, 176a–177a
ritual, IV 225a–225b, 226a,
 228a–228b, 229b, 230a,
 231a, 233a
Roman Catholic Church, IV
 230a
Rome (ancient), IV 227b,
 228a–229a, 229b, 230a
Saint Augustine, II 244b–
 245a; III 635a; IV 176b,
 230a
Saint Paul, IV 229b–230a
Salutati, IV 142b
Samkhya-Yoga, IV 232a
Samsāra, IV 231b–232a,
 232b
Sankara, IV 232a
Saoshyans (myth), IV 231b
Satan, IV 229b, 230a
Set (myth), IV 225a
Shamash (myth), IV 226b
Sheol (myth), IV 227b,
 228a
Shiva (myth), IV 232a
skepticism, IV 248a
soteriology, IV 225b, 228a,
 229b
society, IV 224a, 224b,
 226b, 233a
Sophocles, IV 229a
soul, IV 228b, 229a, 230a,
 231b, 232b, 233a
State, IV 226b, 228a

Ten Commandments, **IV** 227a

Thoth (myth), **IV** 225b

transcendentalism, **IV** 224b, 233a

Troy, **IV** 228a

truth, **IV** 224b

universe, **IV** 224a

Upanishadic period, **IV** 231b–233a, 232b

virtue, **IV** 225b

Vishnu (myth), **IV** 232a

Weber, Max, **II** 212b

wisdom of the fool, **IV** 518a

work, **IV** 531a

Yahweh, **IV** 226b–227a

Yahwism, **IV** 227a, 227b

Zealots, **IV** 227b

Zoroaster, **IV** 231a–231b

Salvianus (c. 428 A.D.)
  Christianity, **III** 592a
  primitivism, **III** 592a

Samson (Bible)
  genetic continuity, **III** 281b
  mythology, **III** 275b, 276b, 282b
  temperance, **IV** 375a, 377a

Samuel (Bible)
  freedom of speech, **II** 254b, 255a
  prophecy, **III** 658b, 659a, 660a–660b, 661a
  vox populi, **IV** 498b

Samuel the Little, Rabbi, impiety, **II** 565a

Samuelson, Paul A. utility, **IV** 456b–457a

San Martín, José de (1778–1850), nationalism, **III** 335a

Sanborn, Franklin B. (1831–1917)
  Buddhism, **III** 437a
  Orientalism, **III** 437a

Sanchez, Francisco (1550–1623), skepticism, **IV** 243b–244a

Sanchez, Francisco (1523–1601), wisdom of the fool, **IV** 519b

Sancho Panza (fiction)
  literary paradox, **III** 76b
  organicism, **III** 422a

Sanctification
  dignity, **IV** 140a
  perfectibility, **III** 468a
  reformation, **IV** 62a
  religion, **IV** 111b
  Renaissance, **IV** 140a

Sand, George (1804–1876), Counter-Enlightenment, **II** 110a

Sandage, A., cosmology, **I** 565a, 567b

Sanderson, William, mythology, **III** 298a

Sandrart, Joachim von (1606–1688), Gothic, **II** 368a

Sandys, George (1578–1644), mythology, **III** 299b, 300a

Sanghabhadra, Buddhism, **I** 247a

Sangnier, Marc, modernism, **I** 423b

Sanity
  genius, **II** 309b
  temperance, **IV** 366a, 367b

Sankara (c. 788–820 A.D.)
  sin, **IV** 232a

Sannazaro, Jacopo (1458–1530)
  primitivism, **III** 593b
  ut pictura poesis, **IV** 468b

Sanskrit language, **II** 661b, 663a, 669b, 670a–670b, 671b, 673b; **III** 65a, 66a, 70a, 70b, 268b, 305b, 306a, 308b
  linguistics, **IV** 427b
  poetry, **III** 527b
  religion, **IV** 94b
  Schlegel, Friedrich, **III** 66a
  structuralism, **IV** 323a
  style, **IV** 331a

Sansovino, Francesco (1521–1586), Platonism, **III** 514b

Santayana, George (1863–1952)
  abstraction, **I** 8a
  aristocracy, **III** 553b–554a
  Aristotle and, **III** 554a
  beauty, **I** 209a; **II** 88b
  Being, **III** 555a
  consciousness, **III** 553b
  death, **I** 646a
  demagoguery, **III** 554a
  democracy, **III** 554a
  Dewey and, **III** 553b, 554a
  empathy, **II** 88b
  experience, **III** 554a
  Faust (legend), **III** 250b
  God, **II** 360a
  good, **III** 553b
  immortality, **I** 646a
  instrumentalism, **III** 553b
  James and, **III** 553b, 554a
  morality, **III** 522b–523a
  naturalism, **III** 553b, 554a
  perennial philosophy, **III** 462b
  Plato and, **III** 554a
  Platonism, **III** 503a, 522b–523a, 553b, 554a
  pragmatism, **III** 553b–554b
  profit, **III** 553b
  reincarnation, **I** 646a
  romanticism, **IV** 209b
  skepticism, **IV** 250a–250b

thought, **III** 553b–554a
timocracy, **III** 554a
value, **III** 553b

Sant' Elia, Antonio (1880–1916), the city, **I** 433a

Santorio, Santorio (1561–1636), disease, **II** 402a

Saoshyans (myth), salvation, **IV** 231b

Sapir, Edward (1884–1939), linguistics, **III** 71b; **IV** 426b

Sappho (fl. about 600 B.C.), organicism, **III** 423b

Sarbiewski, Maciej K. (1595–? 1640), mimesis, **III** 228a

Sarcophagi, mythology, **III** 292a

Sardanapalus (c. 822 B.C.), temperance, **IV** 375b

Sarma, Sreekrishna, Orientalism, **III** 431b

Sarmiento, Domingo Faustino (1811–1888), positivism, **III** 543b

Sarpedon (myth), **II** 340a
  human nature, **III** 571b

Sarpi, Paolo (1552–1623)
  Machiavellism, **III** 120b
  historiography, **II** 486b

Sarto, Andrea del (1486–1531), genius, **II** 302a

Sarton, George (1884–1956), mathematics, **III** 178a
  positivism, **III** 538a

Sartre, Jean-Paul (1905–)
  appearance and reality, **I** 98b
  atheism, **II** 192b, 673a
  Being, **II** 637a
  Christianity, **II** 213b
  consciousness, **III** 209b
  environment, **II** 194b
  evil, **II** 168a–168b
  existentialism, **II** 189a–195a; **III** 158a, 160b, 161a
  faith, **II** 194a, 194b, 213b
  free will, **II** 246b–247a
  freedom, **II** 193b, 194a, 194b; **III** 210a
  God, **II** 168a, 192b, 246b–247a
  good, **II** 168b
  idealism, **III** 158a
  imagination, **III** 208b, 209b–210a, 212b, 221b
  individualism, **II** 603a–603b
  irony, **II** 633a
  irrationalism, **II** 637a
  literary criticism, **I** 605a
  literary paradox, **III** 77b
  literature, **III** 88a
  Marxism, **II** 194a, 194b,

195a; **III** 158a, 160b, 161a, 168a; **IV** 536a
  materialism, **III** 158a
  morality, **II** 190b, 194a–195a
  nihilism, **III** 209b
  phenomenology, **III** 209b
  poetry, **III** 88a
  psychoanalysis, **II** 194a
  psychology, **IV** 14a
  romanticism, **IV** 204b
  voluntarism, **III** 158a
  Zeitgeist, **IV** 536a

Sasaki, Mrs. Ruth, Buddhism, **I** 256b

Sasaki, Shigatsu, Buddhism, **I** 256b

Sassanid period, **II** 639a

Sassetti, Filippo
  iconography, **II** 529b
  language, **II** 670a
  mimesis, **III** 228a
  poetry, **III** 228a

Satan
  cosmic voyages, **I** 526b
  death, **III** 265b
  demonology, **I** 668a, 668b, 670a
  dualism, **II** 38a
  eschatology, **II** 155b, 155b
  evil, **II** 163b, 165a–165b
  Faust (legend), **III** 245a, 247a, 247b, 248b, 249a, 249b, 250a, 251b, 252a
  Gnosticism, **II** 328a
  heresy, **II** 423b
  hierarchy, **II** 435b
  impressionism, **II** 582a
  individualism, **II** 603a
  Jesus Christ, **III** 281b, 665a
  love, **III** 96b, 98a
  Luther, **III** 267a
  Machiavelli, **III** 117b
  millenarianism, **III** 223b, 224b
  minstrel, **III** 266a–266b
  music, **III** 265b–267a
  mythology, **III** 288a, 279a, 280a, 281b, 282a, 284b
  necessity, **III** 355b
  power, **III** 224b
  primitivism, **III** 583b
  prophecy, **III** 665a, 665b
  psychology, **IV** 16b, 18b
  religion, **IV** 93b, 94a, 103a
  revolution, **IV** 153a
  Saint Augustine, **III** 224b
  sin, **IV** 229b, 230a
  tragic sense, **IV** 415b, 416a
  virtù, **IV** 477a, 477b
  witchcraft, **IV** 521a–522b

Satire, **IV** 211a–217a
  anthropology, **IV** 212a
  Arabs, **IV** 211b

Archilochus, **IV** 212a
Aristophanes, **IV** 212b, 214a, 214b, 215b
Aristotle, **IV** 211a, 216a
authority, **IV** 212a
Brecht, **IV** 214b, 215a
Byron, **IV** 212b, 214a–214b, 215b
Casaubon, **IV** 213a
censorship, **IV** 214b
comedy, **IV** 211a, 212b, 215b, 216a
community, **IV** 211b
Daumier, **IV** 215b
DeMott, **IV** 212a
drama, **III** 527a
Dryden, **IV** 214a, 214b
epics, **IV** 211a, 214b
Erasmus, **IV** 213b
ethics, **IV** 214b
Euripides, **IV** 212b
evil, **IV** 211b, 214a
Fielding, **IV** 215a
France, **IV** 214b
Freud, **IV** 214a
Gay, **IV** 215a
Gogol, **IV** 214b
Golding, **IV** 215a
good, **IV** 212a
Great Britain, **IV** 213a, 213b, 214b, 215a, 216b
Greece (ancient), **IV** 211a, 211b, 212a, 212b, 214b
Hall, **IV** 213a
Heller, **IV** 213b, 216a
Horace, **IV** 211a, 213a, 213b, 214b, 215a
hostility, **IV** 211a, 211b, 212b, 213a, 214a, 214b, 216b
humanism, **II** 517b; **IV** 214b
Huxley, **IV** 214b, 215b
Ionesco, **IV** 214b–215b
Ireland, **IV** 211b, 212a–212b, 213b
irony, **II** 627a–634b
Jerome, **IV** 215a
Jonson, **IV** 212b–215b
justice, **IV** 212b
Juvenal, **IV** 211a–215b
law, **IV** 212a, 212b, 215b
libel, **IV** 212b
literary paradox, **III** 78b
literature, **IV** 211a, 212b, 214a, 214b, 216a
logic, **IV** 216a
Lucian, **IV** 214a, 215a, 215b
Lucilius, **IV** 211a
magic, **IV** 211b, 212a, 216a
Marston, **IV** 211b, 213a
materialism, **IV** 214b
Menippean, **IV** 213b
Middle Ages, **IV** 214b

Molière, **IV** 211b, 213b, 215a
morality, **IV** 214a–214b
Orwell, **IV** 214b, 215a, 215b
Persius, **IV** 211a
Petronius, **IV** 214a, 215b
poetry, **III** 527a; **IV** 211a, 213a
political, **IV** 214b
Pope, **IV** 211b, 212b, 213b, 214a, 214b, 215b
power, **IV** 212a
Quintana, **IV** 213b
Quintilian, **IV** 211a
Renaissance, **IV** 213a, 214b
responsibility, **IV** 214a
Rome (ancient), **IV** 211a, 212b, 213a, 214b, 215a, 216b
Russia, **IV** 214b
Shakespeare, **IV** 211b, 213b
situational, **IV** 213b
society, **IV** 212a–214b
Socrates, **IV** 212b, 215b
Swift, **IV** 211b, 213b, 214b, 215a, 215b
temperance, **IV** 369b
theater, **IV** 211a, 212b, 215b, 216a
theriophily, **IV** 386b
Thomson, **IV** 215a
tragedy, **IV** 211a, 215b, 216a
truth, **IV** 212b–213a
U.S., **IV** 212a
Utopia, **IV** 464a
Varronism, **IV** 213b
virtuoso, **IV** 487b–488a
Voltaire, **IV** 213b, 214b, 215a, 215b
Waugh, **IV** 214a–215b
West, **IV** 211b, 215a
Wycherly, **IV** 215b
Saturn (myth)
   mathematics, **III** 581a
   philosophy, **III** 581a
   primitivism, **III** 579b, 580a–580b, 581a, 583b
Saturn (planet)
   cosmology, **I** 538a, 539a, 540b, 541b–542a, 544b, 546b, 547b, 550a
   mythology, **III** 287b
Saturninus (d. 100 B.C.)
   Gnosticism, **II** 328a
   skepticism, **IV** 234a
Satyagraha, doctrine of, **I** 438b
Sauer, Carl
   conservation, **I** 471b
   culture, **II** 131a, 133a
Sauer, J., iconography, **II** 535b
Saul (Bible)

freedom, **II** 249b
God, **II** 336b
law, **II** 249b
loyalty, **III** 108b
music, **III** 265a, 267a
mythology, **III** 281a
prophecy, **III** 658a, 658b, 660a–660b
Saussure, Ferdinand de (1857–1913)
   anthropology, **IV** 324a
   linguistics, **II** 671b–672a; **III** 70a, 71a; **IV** 323b–324a
   structuralism, **IV** 322b–324a, 328a
   style, **IV** 333a
Saussure, Horace Bénédict de (1740–1799), geology, **IV** 418b
Saussure, Madame Necker de (1766–1841), romanticism, **IV** 189b
Sauveur, Joseph (1653–1716), music, **III** 263a
Savage, L. J.
   chance, **I** 338a
   game theory, **II** 272a
Savage, Minot J., eschatology, **II** 160a
Savage, Richard (1697?–1743), Newton and, **III** 393b
Savigny, Friedrich Karl von (1779–1861)
   custom, **III** 22a
   economic history, **II** 60b
   Hegel and, **II** 411b, 412a; **III** 22a
   historiography, **II** 496a
   justice, **II** 658b
   law, **II** 411b, 412a; **III** 3b, 22a
   natural law, **III** 22a
   necessity, **III** 358b
   Rome (ancient), **II** 411b, 412a
   Volksgeist, **IV** 493a–494a
Savings
   economic history, **II** 49a, 53a
   natural liberty, **II** 65b
   welfare state, **IV** 509b
Savonarola, Girolamo (1452–1498)
   Christianity, **I** 388a
   mimesis, **III** 230a
   universal man, **IV** 442b
   ut pictura poesis, **IV** 466a
   virtù, **IV** 477a–477b, 479b, 483a
Savonarola, Michael (15th century), alchemy, **I** 31a
Saxe, Marshal de (1696–

1750), war, **IV** 504a
Saxl, Fritz
   iconography, **II** 529a, 536a, 537b
   mythology, **III** 290b
Saxons
   baptism, **IV** 113b
   Charlemagne, **IV** 113b
   death, **IV** 113b
   intolerance, **IV** 113b
Say, Jean Baptiste, (1767–1832)
   crisis in history, **I** 590a
   Hegel and, **II** 409a
   socialism, **IV** 292b
   utility, **IV** 450b, 452b
Sayers, Dorothy (1893–1957), Faust (legend), **III** 251b
Sayyah Ahmad Khan, Sir (1817–1898), nationalism, **III** 338a
Scacchi, Marco, music, **III** 271b
Scale of Beings, **IV** 56b
Scaliger, Joseph Justus (1540–1609)
   language, **II** 667a; **III** 63b
   literary criticism, **I** 596b, 597a
   mimesis, **III** 228a
   mythology, **III** 296b
   Peacham and, **III** 296b
   poetics, **III** 529a, 530a, 530b
   style, **IV** 331b
   ut pictura poesis, **IV** 467b
Scaliger, Julius Caesar (1484–1558)
   atomism, **I** 131a
   classicism, **I** 453a
   genius, **II** 308a, 320a
   literary criticism, **I** 596b
   matter, **III** 192a
   mythology, **III** 296b
   tragic sense, **IV** 412b
Scandinavia
   academic freedom, **I** 14a
   common law, **II** 692a
   conservatism, **I** 477a, 484b
   Council of Basel (1431–1449), **II** 369b
   Gothic, **II** 367a, 369b
   law, **III** 2b, 4a
   Lutheranism, **II** 64b
   Magyars, **I** 381a
   mythology, **III** 304a, 311b–312a
   nationalism, **III** 326a, 333a
   natural liberty, **II** 64a–64b
   naturalism in art, **III** 339a
   Ramism, **IV** 44b
   Reformation, **I** 390b
   technology, **IV** 360b

welfare state, **IV** 512a, 514a

Scanlan, J. F., beauty, **I** 210a

Scelle, Georges, natural law, **III** 23a

Scève, Maurice (16th century)
macrocosm, **III** 131a
Platonism, **III** 514a

Schaeffer, Albrech, Buddhism, **I** 256b

Schaff, Adam, Marxism, **III** 168a, 169a

Schaff, Philip (1819–1893), *Volksgeist*, **IV** 495a–495b

Schaffner, Kenneth, positivism, **III** 550b

Schalk, Fritz, periodization in literary history, **III** 482a

Schapiro, Leonard, totalitarianism, **IV** 409b

Schapiro, Meyer (1904–   )
iconography, **II** 527a, 538b, 540b

Scharnhorst, G. J. D. von (1755–1813), war, **IV** 504a, 505a

Scheffler, Karl, expressionism, **II** 208b

Scheler, Max (1874–1928)
death, **I** 634a, 641b
immortality, **I** 641b
work, **IV** 534b

Schell, Hermann, modernism, **I** 424a–424b

Schelling, Friedrich (1775–1854)
Alexander and, **IV** 210b
art for art's sake, **I** 108b, 109b
beauty, **I** 203b, 204b
Bergson and, **IV** 210b
Boehme and, **IV** 210b
Bruno and, **IV** 210b
Carlyle and, **IV** 210b
Chain of Being, **I** 334b
Coleridge and, **IV** 210b
conservatism, **I** 482b
Constable and, **IV** 201a
Counter-Enlightenment, **II** 104b, 108b, 109b
Creation, **IV** 202a
creativity, **IV** 210b
culture, **III** 555b
Dewey and, **IV** 210b
Emerson and, **IV** 210b
eschatology, **II** 159b
evolutionism, **II** 178b, 185a
existentialism, **II** 191b; **IV** 210b
Faust (legend), **III** 250a
Fichte and, **IV** 210a
free will, **II** 246b
freedom, **IV** 210b

God, **II** 362b; **IV** 204a
Goethe and, **IV** 201a
Hamann and, **IV** 210b
Hegel and, **II** 407b; **IV** 210b
Heidegger and, **IV** 210b
Herder and, **IV** 210b
Hölderlin and, **IV** 210a
idealism, **II** 407b
imagination, **III** 222a; **IV** 210b
individualism, **IV** 210b
infinity, **IV** 202a
irrationalism, **II** 636a
Kant and, **III** 555b; **IV** 210a
Leibniz and, **IV** 210b
literary criticism, **I** 596b, 598a
literature, **IV** 189a
materialism, **II** 454a
Middle Ages, **IV** 210a–210b
modernism, **I** 420a
morality, **III** 555b
mythology, **III** 305a–306b
Nature, **IV** 204a
necessity, **III** 358b
Neo-Platonism, **IV** 210a
Novalis and, **IV** 206b
organicism, **III** 421b, 425a, 425b
Peirce and, **II** 185a; **III** 568b; **IV** 210b
perennial philosophy, **III** 463a
philosophers, **IV** 210b
Platonism, **III** 516a, 520a, 521b
Poe and, **IV** 210b
poets, **IV** 210b
post-Kantianism, **IV** 210a
pragmatism, **III** 555b, 568b; **IV** 210b
psychology, **IV** 11b
realism in literature, **IV** 51b
romanticism, **IV** 189a, 201a, 201b, 202a, 204a, 206b, 208a, 209a, 209b, 210a
Schlegel and, **IV** 208a
Schleiermacher and, **III** 520a
Spinoza and, **IV** 210b
symbolism, **IV** 338a–338b, 343b
Tillich and, **IV** 210b
time, **IV** 394a
universe, **II** 108b
Wordsworth and, **IV** 201a

Scherer, Wilhelm (1841–1886)
classicism, **I** 450b
evolution of literature, **II** 171a
Goethe and, **III** 237a

motif, **III** 237a

Scheyb, F. C. von, ideal, **II** 551a

Schillebeecx, Edward, God, **II** 365b

Schiller, Ferdinand Canning Scott (1864–1937)
humanism, **III** 553a, 568a
knowledge, **III** 568a
Lovejoy and, **III** 552b, 553a
Peirce and, **III** 552b, 553a, 559a, 568b, 569b
personalism, **III** 552b, 553a
pragmatism, **III** 551b, 552b, 553a, 559a, 568a, 568b, 569b
relativism, **III** 568a
value, **III** 568a

Schiller, Johann Christoph Friedrich von (1759–1805)
aesthetics, **III** 569b
appearance and reality, **I** 97b
art for art's sake, **I** 108b
art and play, **I** 103b, 105a–106a, 107b, 203b–204a
attitude toward antiquity, **I** 87b
beauty, **I** 203b–204a
Chain of Being, **I** 334b
chance, **III** 605b
city, **I** 432a
classicism, **I** 449b, 451a, 453a, 453b; **IV** 197a
Counter-Enlightenment, **II** 107a, 108a–108b
creativity in art, **I** 578a
disease, **II** 403b
education, **III** 569b
empathy, **II** 85b
Enlightenment, **II** 94b; **III** 343a
Faust (legend), **III** 249a
freedom, **I** 578a
Freud and, **I** 105a
genius, **II** 307b
Goethe and, **III** 237a, 238a
irony, **II** 630a
law, **IV** 157a
liberty, **II** 94b
literary criticism, **I** 598a
motif, **III** 237a, 238a
mythology, **III** 305b
naturalism, **IV** 53b
naturalism in art, **III** 343a
Nietzsche and, **I** 106a
organicism, **III** 424a
periodization in literary history, **III** 481b
realism in literature, **IV** 51b, 53b
resistance, **IV** 157a
revolution, **IV** 156b–157a

romanticism, **I** 451a; **IV** 188a, 193a, 197a, 209a
Schopenhauer and, **I** 106a
symbolism, **IV** 338a
tyranny, **IV** 157a
ut pictura poesis, **IV** 474a
Zeitgeist, **IV** 536a

Schink, J. F., Faust (legend), **III** 250a

Schinkel, Karl Friedrich (1781–1841)
Gothic, **II** 369a
neo-classicism in art, **III** 369b

Schirmer, F. W., baroque in literature, **I** 191a

Schlaf, Johannes (1862–1941), naturalism in art, **III** 339a

Schlegel, August Wilhelm von (1767–1845)
art for art's sake, **I** 109a
Bouterwerk and, **IV** 189b
Byron and, **IV** 192b
Campbell and, **IV** 192a
classicism, **I** 451b, 453b, 454a
Coleridge and, **IV** 191b
Drake and, **IV** 192a
evolution of literature, **II** 171a
Faust (legend), **III** 250b
France and, **IV** 190a, 192a
Goethe and, **I** 454a; **IV** 189b
Hazlitt and, **IV** 192a, 192b
irony, **II** 629b–631b, 633a, 633b
Kant and, **IV** 200a
literary criticism, **I** 598a–598b, 599a, 605b
literature, **III** 84a; **IV** 188a–194a, 197a
mythology, **III** 305a, 306a
organicism, **III** 421b, 422b, 425b
periodization in literary history, **III** 481b
romanticism, **IV** 188a–194a, 197a, 206a–208a
Scott and, **IV** 192a, 194a
Shakespeare and, **IV** 192a
Sismondi and, **IV** 189b, 190a
Staël and, **IV** 189b, 190a, 192a, 193b
Stendhal and, **IV** 190a
symbolism, **IV** 338a, 339a, 345a

Schlegel, Friedrich von (1772–1829)
absolutism, **IV** 207b
art, **IV** 208a
Christianity, **IV** 207b

classicism, I 450b, 451b, 453b, 454a, 454b
comparative grammar, III 65b, 66a–66b
Counter-Enlightenment, II 109b–110a
criticism, IV 208a
culture, I 619a
dualism, III 306a
evolution of literature, II 170b, 171a
fatalism, III 306a
Fichte and, IV 208a
freedom, IV 209a
Goethe and, I 454a; IV 198a, 208b
Gothic, II 372a
historicism, II 456b
iconography, II 535a
idealism, IV 209a
imagination, III 222a
individualism, II 595b
irony, II 629b–631b, 633a, 633b
language, III 65b, 66a
liberalism, IV 207b
linguistics, III 65b, 66a, 66b, 69a
literary criticism, I 596b, 598a, 598b, 599a, 605b
literature, III 84a, 188a, 188b, 192a, 192b, 195b, 197a, 208a
mythology, III 305a–306a
Nature, IV 209a
Novalis and, IV 208a
organicism, III 421b, 425b
periodization in literary history, III 481b, 482a, 485b
Platonism, III 519a, 519b
poetry, II 170b
realism in literature, IV 51b, 53a
romanticism, III 66a; IV 188a, 188b, 192a, 192b, 198a, 200a, 208a–209a
Sanskrit, III 66a
Schelling and, IV 208a
Schleiermacher and, III 519a
science, IV 209a
symbolism, IV 338a, 339a
Tieck and, IV 208a
Schlegel, J. A. (1719–1749), genius, II 295a
Schleicher, August (1821–1868)
Darwin and, IV 428a
Hegel and, IV 428a
linguistics, III 68a–70b; IV 426b–428a
Lyell and, IV 428a
organicism, III 426a
Schleicher, W., chromosomes,

II 287b
Schleiden, Matthias J. (1804–1881), cell theory, II 285b, 286a
Schleiermacher, Friedrich Ernst (1768–1834)
causation, II 358b
Christianity, IV 201a
eschatology, II 158b
faith, II 358b
Fichte and, IV 202b
freedom, IV 210a
God, II 356a, 358a–359a, 362b, 363a; IV 201a
Hegel and, II 411b; III 520a
heresy, II 429a, 430b
holy, II 513a, 514a
individualism, II 595b, 597b; IV 201a, 210a
infinity, IV 200b, 201a, 210a
Kant and, III 518b, 520a; IV 202b
modernism, I 420a
morality, II 358a
Pietism, III 494a; IV 201a
Plato and, III 516a, 518b–522a
Protestantism, IV 201a
rationalism, IV 201a
reason, IV 202b
religion, II 411b; IV 108b, 200b, 201a, 210a
romanticism, IV 199b, 200b, 201a, 202b, 206b, 208a, 209b–210a
Schelling and, III 520a
Schlegel and, III 519a
scholasticism, IV 210a
Spinoza and, III 520a
Strauss and, II 412b
theodicy, IV 381b
time, IV 390a
Schlick, Moritz
causation, II 589b
determinism, II 239a, 241a
happiness, II 385b
indeterminacy, II 589b
positivism, III 545b, 548a
pragmatism, III 568a
uncertainty principle, II 589b
Schliemann, Heinrich (1822–1890), neo-classicism in art, III 363a
Schlosser, J., aesthetics, II 223b
Schlözer, August L. von (1735–1809)
historicism, II 458a
historiography, II 491a
linguistics, III 65a
Schmaller, Gustav

historicism, II 457a
historiography, II 495a
Schmid, Wilhelm, progress, III 625a
Schmidt, Conrad, Marxism, III 163a
Schmidt, Johannes (1843–1901), linguistics, III 70a; IV 428a
Schmidt, Julian (1818–1886), realism in literature, IV 52b
Schmidt, Wilhelm (1868–1954)
Lang and, III 309b
mythology, III 309b, 310b
religion, IV 96a
Schmitt, Carl
totalitarianism, IV 408b
Schmoller, Gustav (1838–1917), economic history, II 60b, 61a
Schneider, Anton
cell division, II 287a
chromosomes, II 287a
Schnitzler, Arthur (1862–1931), realism in literature, IV 55a
Schnorr, C. P., probability, III 623a
Schoell, Franck L., mythology, III 295a, 299a
Schoenlein, Johann Lucas (1793–1864), disease, II 400a
Scholarship
heresy, II 430a–430b
historicism, II 460a, 462b
historiography, II 473a–473b, 474a, 477a, 480b, 481a, 482b, 486a–497b
iconography, II 534a–540b
Islam, II 639b, 640a
linguistics, III 65b
Machiavellism, III 117b, 124b, 125a
Roman Catholic Church, II 430a–430b
Scholasticism
aesthetics, II 217b, 219a, 220a, 222b
alienation, I 36a–36b
art, I 459a
Avicenna, I 3b
beauty, II 217b
causation, I 300b–301a, 303b
chance, II 227b, 230a
Christianity, I 36a–36b, 382b–383a, 383b, 384b
common nature, I 4a
Comte, III 535a
cosmic images, I 515a
dignity, IV 140a–140b, 141b

Dominicans, I 383b
fate, II 227b, 230a
free will, II 245a
heresy, II 427a, 427b
humanism, II 519b; IV 129b, 133b–134a, 134b
imagination, III 208b, 210a, 210b, 211b, 212a, 214a
Innocent III (Pope), I 383a
Islam, II 639b, 640a, 645a
language, II 661a–661b, 666b
law, III 3b
Luther, II 357a
medieval sciences, II 200b, 201b, 203a
mimesis, III 227b
modernism, I 420a
motif, III 238b
mythology, III 290b
nationalism, III 323a
natural law, III 20a
Neo-Platonism, III 374b
numbers, III 403b
organicism, III 424a
perennial philosophy, III 457b, 458a, 459a, 459b, 461a, 461b
periodization in history, III 476b, 477a, 478a, 480a, 480b
poetics, III 528a
psychology, IV 16b, 17a, 17b, 19b
Puritanism, IV 16b
Ramism, IV 42b
religion, IV 94b, 109a
Renaissance, II 427a; IV 121b–134b, 140a–140b, 141b, 437b, 441a
revolution, IV 155b, 158a, 166b
rhetoric, IV 171a
Roman Catholic Church, I 382b–384b
romanticism, IV 195a–197b
Rome (ancient), III 476b
Saint Thomas Aquinas, I 383a, 384b
Schleiermacher, IV 210a
skepticism, IV 241b, 242a, 250b
structuralism, IV 329b
teleology, I 300b–301a, 303b
theodicy, IV 380b, 381a
unity of science, IV 432a, 432b, 433a, 436a
universal man, IV 437b, 441a
ut pictura poesis, IV 467a
utility, IV 452a
William of Ockham, I 384b
witchcraft, IV 521a, 521b

Scholem, G. G., Gnosticism, II 330b
Schöne, Albrecht, iconography, II 538a
Schoock, Martin, skepticism, IV 245a
Schopenhauer, Arthur (1788–1860)
  art for art's sake, I 108b
  Buddhism, I 255b
  catharsis, I 268a
  Chambers and, II 182b
  classification of the sciences, I 465b
  cosmic images, I 520b
  Counter-Enlightenment, II 108b, 109b
  culture, III 555b
  death, I 634b, 637a, 637b
  evolutionism, II 182b–183b
  free will, II 246b
  genius, II 308b
  good, II 166b
  harmony, IV 41b
  idea, II 548b; III 524a
  imagination, III 208a
  irrationalism, II 636a, 636b
  justice, II 166b
  Kant and, I 255b; III 555b
  literature, IV 332b
  macrocosm, III 129a–129b
  mimesis, III 343b
  modernism, I 420a
  morality, III 555b
  music, III 271b
  mythology, III 306a
  naturalism in art, III 343b
  Nature, II 182b–183a
  pessimism, IV 202b
  philosophy, IV 202b
  Plato and, I 255b
  Platonism, III 524a
  pragmatism, III 555b, 563b
  psychology, IV 11b
  Pythagoreans, IV 41b
  romanticism, IV 202a, 202b, 204a, 204b, 209b, 210b
  Schiller and, I 106a
  style, IV 332b
  symbolism, IV 345a
  time, IV 394a, 395b
  universe, IV 41b
  Upanisads and, I 255b
  virtue, II 166b
  Weltschmerz, IV 204a, 209b
  will, II 182b; IV 202b
Schoppe, Karl (1576–1649), literary criticism, I 596b
Schott, Gaspar, cosmic voyages, I 532a
Schramm, G. H. aesthetics, IV 356a
Schröder, H. G. F., spon-

taneous generation, II 283b; IV 310b
Schrödinger, Erwin (1887–1961)
  Bohr and, II 588b
  causation, II 588b
  Heisenberg and, II 588b, 590a
  indeterminacy, II 588b, 590a
  wave mechanics, II 588b
Schubart, Christian F. D. (1739–1791)
  Counter-Enlightenment, II 107a
  musical genius, II 324a
  Rousseau and, II 324a
Schubert, Gottfried-Heinrich von (1780–1860), romanticism, IV 201b, 208b
Schuchardt, Hugo (1842–1927), linguistics, III 70a
Schuetz, L. entropy, II 117b
Schulze, F. F., spontaneous generation, II 283b
Schulze-Gävernitz, F. G., economics, III 162a
Schulze, Gottlob Ernst (1761–1833), skepticism, IV 249a
Schumann, Robert (1810–1856), romanticism, IV 208b
Schumpeter, Joseph (1883–1950)
  crisis in history, I 590b
  democracy, I 665b–666a
  social welfare, IV 283a
Schur, Friedrich Heinrich (1852–1932), symmetry, IV 352a
Schürr, Friedrich, baroque in literature, I 190b
Schwann, Theodor (1810–1882), genetic continuity, II 283a–283b, 285b, 286a
Schweitzer, Albert (1875–1965)
  Buddhism, I 256a
  eschatology, II 160b–161a
  modernism, I 419b
Schwenkfelders
  ethics, III 441a
  heresy, II 427b
Science
  abstract, I 465b
  acquired characteristics, II 617a–622a
  Aeschylus, III 625a, 625b
  aesthetics, IV 354a, 356a
  Age of Reason, I 401a–402a
  agnosticism, I 17a–27a
  alchemy, II 641a, 646a, 646b

ambiguity, I 54a–54b, 58a
anthropology, II 651a
anthropomorphism, I 87b–91a
Aristotle, I 463a; III 189b–190a, 503a, 629b; IV 4b, 6b, 175b
art, I 456b, 457a, 457b, 458a, 459a, 461b; II 575b, 580a–580b, 581b, 582b, 583a; III 262b; IV 83b–84a
astrology, II 644a, 646b
astronomy, II 639a, 640b, 647a, 651b
Bacon, I 173b–174b; IV 462a
Bergson, II 636b
calculus, III 178b
catastrophism, IV 417b, 419b, 420a, 422a, 423a
certainty, I 312a–325a
Chain of Being, I 326b–327b
China, I 355a
chora, IV 299b
Christianity, I 401b, 402a; III 591a
common law, II 695a
Comte, III 641b–642a, 644b
concrete, I 465b
Condorcet, III 644a
continuity, I 492b–495b
cosmological, I 465a
Counter-Enlightenment, II 101a, 101b–102a, 104a, 104b, 106b
culture, I 608b, 620a, 621a
cynicism, I 631a–631b; III 585b
death, I 637b
deism, I 648a, 648b, 649a, 650a, 651b
determinism, II 21b–22a, 24a–24b, 29a
Diderot, III 216b
dignity, IV 140b, 146a
Duhem, III 555a
economics, II 50a–51a
Empedocles, IV 2b
empiricism, I 465b; III 546b, 547b–551a
Engels, II 455a
Epicureanism, IV 7b
Epicurus, III 630a
equality, II 140b
ethics, III 442b, 443b, 444a, 446b, 447b; IV 70b
evil, III 642b, 648a
evolution, II 196a
existentialism, III 159a, 160b

Faust (legend), III 249a, 250b, 251a, 252a
first order, I 465a
formal, I 465b
fortune, fate, and chance, II 225b
free will, II 245b–246b
freedom of inquiry, I 10a
Galileo as the modern founder of, III 415b
game theory, II 263b, 264a, 266a–268a
genius, II 293b–295b, 313a–314a
geodesy, II 647a
geology, II 645b
God, II 352a, 353a, 355a, 355b, 357a, 358b, 359b; III 193a
good, III 642b, 648a; IV 173a, 175b, 176b, 177a, 179a–182a, 185b, 186a
grammar, II 666b
Great Britain, III 602a, 602b; IV 153b
happiness, II 375a, 379a; 386a, 387a–387b
harmony, II 388b, 448b
heresy, II 428b–429a
hierarchy, II 448b
historicism, II 462a–463a
historiography, II 21b–22a, 24a–24b; IV 147b–152a
history, I 466a; II 21b–22a, 24a–24b; III 472a
Hobbes, IV 153b
human nature, III 571a, 644a
humanism, II 516a–521a, 523a; IV 129a, 130a, 132a, 132b–134b
idea, II 547a–547b
ideology, II 553a–555a
impressionism, II 575b, 580a–583a
industry, III 150b
infinity, II 609b, 611a
irony, II 634a
irrationalism, II 635b–638a
Islam, II 639a–645a, 647a, 647b, 651a, 651b
James, III 561b, 562b
Kant, III 219b
language, II 661b, 666b–667a, 673b; III 86b
law, II 687b, 690a, 690b; III 11b, 35b
Leibniz, I 465a
lenses, III 411a–415a
linguistics, III 73b, 74b; IV 423b, 424a, 425a, 426b
literary criticism, I 599b, 602a, 606a, 607a
literature, III 85b, 86b; IV

332a, 332b

Locke, I 465a

longevity, III 89a, 89b, 92b

love, III 94b, 105b, 106b, 107b

Lovejoy, III 552b–553a

Lucretius, III 631b

macrocosm and microcosm, III 126b, 127a, 131a

Man-Machine, III 131b–143b, 144b

Marx, II 452b

Marxism, III 146b–147a, 147b 150b, 152b, 153a–154a, 159a, 160b, 162b, 163a, 168b; IV 180b–181a

materialism, II 452b, 454b–455a

mathematics, II 640b, 643b, 646b, 647a, 647b, 651b; III 178b–179a

matter, III 186a–194b

measurement, IV 402a, 402b, 403a, 404a

medicine, II 639a, 645a, 645b, 646b

metallurgy, II 644a

metaphor, III 197b, 198b, 199a, 200b, 201a, 206b, 207a

metaphysics, II 641a, 643b, 644b, 645a, 648b, 651a, 651b

Mexico, III 544b

Mill, J. S., IV 199a

millenarianism, III 225b

mind, I 465a, 465b

mineralogy, II 645b

Moors, I 463b

morality, I 465a; III 642b

motion, II 651b

mountains in literature, III 254a, 255b, 257a, 257b, 258b

mythology, III 287b, 293b, 305b, 306a, 307a, 308b, 309a, 310b, 314a, 316b, 317a

nationalism, III 324b, 334b

natural, I 465a

music, II 313a, 313b, 314a, 388b

Nature, III 347a, 349b

necessity, III 351b, 353a–362a

Newton, III 194b

normative, I 466a

numbers, III 399b, 406a, 406b

occult, II 640b, 644a, 646a, 646b

optics, II 647a; III 408b, 411a–420b

organicism, III 424b, 425a

Orientalism, III 432b–437a, 439a

painting, II 575b, 580a, 580b, 581b, 582b, 583a

pangenesis, II 622b, 623b, 624a, 625a, 626a, 626b

Pascal, IV 118b

peace, III 442b, 443b, 444a, 446b, 447b, 642b

peasantry, III 595a

Peirce, III 552b, 553a, 555a, 557b, 561a

Pereira Barreto, III 540b

perennial philosophy, III 457b, 459b, 460a, 461a, 462a, 462b

perfectibility, III 471a–472a, 474a, 644a

periodization in history, III 478a

pharmacology, II 644a, 645b

philanthropy, III 491b, 492a

philosophy, III 197b, 198b, 199a, 200b, 201a

physical, I 465b, 466a

physics, II 643a, 645b, 646b, 647a, 647b, 649a

planets, II 651b

Plato, III 353b, 503a

Platonism, III 503a, 510a

pleasure, II 375a, 379a, 386a, 387a, 387b

poetry, III 392a, 398b, 530a, 531b

Pope, III 397a

positivism, III 532b–551a

practical, I 466a

pragmatism, III 551b–566a

predestination, II 29a

Priestley, III 472a

primitivism, III 578a, 585a, 586a, 588b, 591a, 595a, 597a, 598a, 599b, 600a

probability, III 605b, 613a, 615b

progress, III 625a–648b; IV 148b–149b

prophecy, III 658a

psychical, I 466a

psychology, IV 2b, 4b, 6b, 7a, 7b, 8b, 10a, 11b, 12a, 13b, 14b, 15a, 23a

pure, I 465b

Pythagoreans, IV 32a, 35b

Ramism, IV 42b, 43a, 45a

rationalism, IV 47b, 48a

real, I 465b

realism in literature, IV 54b

reason, III 586a

recapitulation, IV 56a, 56b, 57a

refutation, I 323a, 323b

relativism, IV 70b

relativity, IV 74b, 75a, 82b, 83b, 84a

religion, III 206b, 207a, 432b–437a, 439a; IV 97a, 106a–108b, 115a, 118b

Renaissance, III 355b; IV 126b, 127b, 128a, 129b, 130a, 132a–134b, 140b, 146a, 147b–150a, 151b, 152a, 437a, 439b–443a

revolution, IV 153b, 155b, 162b

rhetoric, IV 169a, 171a, 172a

right, IV 173a, 175b, 176b, 177a, 179b–181b, 182a, 185b, 186a

Roman Catholic Church, I 401b, 402a

romanticism, IV 199a, 200a, 201b, 204a, 209a

Rousseau, III 598a, 599b, 600a

Saint-Simon, III 641a

Schlegel, IV 209a

second order, I 465a

self-destruction, III 648a

Seneca, III 632a

signs, III 86b

skepticism, IV 236a, 236b, 242a, 243a, 243b, 244a, 244b, 245b, 246a, 247b, 248a, 248b, 249b, 250b, 251a

socialism, II 452a; IV 289b, 291b, 293b, 294a

solar system, II 647a

Sorel, III 564b, 565b

space, IV 295b, 299b, 300a, 304b

Spencer, II 182a

spontaneous generation, IV 307a–308b, 310a–311b

Stalin, III 152b

structuralism, IV 323a, 324a, 326b, 328a, 329b

style, IV 332a, 332b

Swineshead, II 200b, 201a, 204a, 204b

symbolic, I 465a

symmetry, IV 348b, 349a, 349b, 352b

taste, IV 354a, 356a

technology, IV 357b–364b

theology, II 29a

theophrastus, IV 6b

theorematics, I 466a

theriophily, IV 384b, 386a, 388a

third order, I 465a

thought, I 465b

time, IV 392a–393a, 395b–398a, 402a–403a, 404a

topos, IV 299b

tragic sense, IV 414a, 414b

truth, I 312a–325a

uniformitarianism, IV 417b, 419b, 420a, 422a, 423a, 423b, 424a, 425a–426b

U.S., III 432b–437a, 439a

unity, III 548a, 548b, 549b

universal man, IV 437a, 439b, 440a, 440b, 441a, 441b, 442a, 442b, 443a

ut pictura poesis, IV 466b, 467b, 471b, 472a, 473a, 474b, 475a

utility and value, IV 450b

Utopia, IV 461a, 462a, 462b, 463b, 464a

Vailati, III 560a

Victorian sentiment, IV 221a–222a

virtuoso, IV 487a–487b, 489b

vision, III 408b, 411a–420b

Volksgeist, IV 491a

war, III 642b; IV 504a, 504b, 507b, 508a, 508b

Watson, I 214b

witchcraft, IV 522b

women, IV 525b, 528a

work, IV 532b, 533a–534a

Wright, III 561b, 562b

Zeitgeist, IV 536b, 537a

Zola, II 575b

Science in Middle Ages, II 196a–205b

Abū'l-Barakāt, II 201b, 202a

Ahmad ibn Yusuf, II 200a

Albert of Saxony, II 201b, 202a, 202b, 203b

alchemy, II 197b

Alexander of Aphrodisias, II 203b

Alhazen, II 198b

al-Kindī, II 197b

Apollonius, II 203a

Arabs, II 196a, 197b, 198b, 200a, 201b, 203b

Archimedes, II 197b, 203a, 204b, 205a

Aristotelianism, II 196a, 199a, 199b, 201b, 203b, 205a

Aristotle, II 196a–197b, 199a, 200a, 201b, 202a, 203a–204b

arithmetic, II 197b, 200a

Arnold of Villanova, II 197b

art, I 456b, 458a, 459a–461b; II 534a
baroque, III 342a
blacks, II 577b
chance images, I 340b–341b, 345a–346a, 351a–353b
China, I 369a
classicism, III 363b
creativity in art, I 580b, 581a–582a
Egypt (ancient), I 580a, 581a
genius, II 317b–318a, 321a
Gothic, II 371b
Greece (ancient), II 170a–170b; III 342a, 363a
iconography, II 534a
literature, IV 331b
mathematics, I 580a
as mechanical art, II 313b
Middle Ages, III 342a
mimesis, III 226a, 226b, 227b, 229a, 229b
music, III 265a, 270a
mythology, III 274b, 289a, 291b, 292a, 296b, 314a
naturalism in art, III 342a–342b
neo-classicism, III 342a, 362b, 363a, 363b, 364b, 365b, 366b, 368a, 369a, 370a, 370b
Plato, I 581a–582a; III 226b, 497b, 501a
Platonism, III 497b, 501a
Pliny, I 580b
poetry, III 526b, 527b
Ramism, IV 44a
religion, IV 94a
Renaissance, III 342a; IV 122b, 123a, 124a, 439b
Rome (ancient), III 342a
Saint Bonaventure, III 227b
skepticism, IV 236b
space, III 342b
style, IV 331b
universal man, IV 439b
ut pictura poesis, IV 466b, 469a, 471a, 473b, 474a, 474b, 475b
virtuoso, IV 486b
Scythia
Nature, III 348b
primitivism, III 591a–591b, 592a, 595b
psychology, IV 19b
Sears, F. W., entropy, II 114b
Seasons
cosmology, I 535b–536a,

540a, 544a
measurement, IV 402a
mythology, III 281b, 287b
rationalism, IV 50a
time, IV 401a
tragic sense, IV 413a
Sebillet, Thomas
classicism, I 451a
rhetoric, IV 171a
Seckendorf, Veit Ludwig von (1626–1692), Reformation, IV 67a
Sectarianism
perennial philosophy, III 457a, 458a, 459a, 459b, 462a
positivism, III 537b
Secularism
dignity, IV 141a, 142a, 145b
eschatology, II 158b–159b, 160a
hierarchy, II 442a, 444a
holy, II 511b, 512b, 513a
impiety, II 564a
infinity, II 605b, 606a, 606b
moral theory, IV 177a, 177b
necessity, III 356a
perfectibility, III 465b, 468b–469a
periodization in history, III 477a, 477b, 478a
philanthropy, III 489a–489b, 490b
protest movements, III 671a, 671b, 674b, 675a
realism in literature, IV 53a
religion, IV 105a, 112b, 113b, 116a, 117a, 117b, 120b
Renaissance, IV 141a, 142a, 145b
romanticism, IV 200b
State, IV 317a
temperance, IV 373b
time, IV 393b
Utopia, IV 461a, 462a
virtue, IV 373b, 477a, 483a
Security
law, III 1a
peace, III 445a
revolution, IV 157b
totalitarianism, IV 410b
Sedgewick, G. G., irony, II 633a
Sedition
freedom of speech, II 252a
heresy, II 425a
loyalty, III 112b, 114a, 114b
Sedley, Charles (1639?–1701)
deism, I 650a

Puritanism, I 650a
Seers, III 658a, 659a
Segond, Louis Auguste
Comte and, III 540a
positivism, III 540a
Segregation, United States Supreme Court, I 440a
Segundo Flores, José, positivism, III 541b
Seignobos, Charles (1854–1942), love, III 97b
Seillière, Baron (1866–1955), classicism, I 450b
Selden, John (1584–1654), equity, II 152b
hierarchy, II 438a
literature, III 81b
Self-control
love, III 102a
loyalty, III 110a
Plato, III 110a
Stoicism, IV 320b
Self-deification, heresy, II 417b
Self-denial
Christianity, IV 370b
perfectibility, II 467b
Self-destruction, III 648a
Self-determination
democratic, III 147b
Marx, IV 291a
Marxism, III 148b
nationalism, III 324b
progress, III 635b, 649a, 649b
social contract, IV 255b
socialism, IV 291b
Self-discipline
freedom, II 251b
law, II 251b
Orientalism, II 431a, 431b
Victorian sensibility, IV 217b, 219a
Self-education, II 72a, 72b
Self-evidence, pragmatism, III 557a–557b
Self-help, welfare state, IV 509b, 510b
Self-improvement
liberalism, III 49b, 50a–50b, 51b, 56b
Victorian sensibility, IV 219a
Self-incrimination, law, II 689a
Self-interest
Hobbes, III 1a
law, III 1a
Sophists, III 1a
utilitarianism, III 1a
Selfishness
Machiavellism, III 120a
perfectibility, III 468b, 469a
Self-Knowledge

Prophyry, III 129a
temperance, IV 365b, 366b, 367a, 368a
virtue, IV 485a
Self-love
Butler, IV 178a
good, IV 178a
Hutcheson, III 231a
moral sense, III 231a
perfectibility, III 468b–469a
progress, III 635b, 641b, 644a
right, IV 178a
wisdom of the fool, IV 519a
Self-preservation
progress, III 630b
right, III 630b
war, IV 507b
Self-realization
good, IV 181a–181b
liberalism, III 50a–51b, 56b
Nietzsche, IV 485a
Renaissance, IV 438a
right, IV 181a–181b
tragic sense, IV 411b
universal man, IV 438a
Self-regeneration, Faust (legend), III 250a, 251b
Self-reliance
individualism, II 596a, 596b
liberalism, III 37a
Self-restraint
Euripides, IV 367b
temperance, IV 365b, 366b, 367b, 369b, 370b
Self-sufficiency
Aristotelianism, III 585a
Christianity, III 590b
Epicureanism, III 585a, 587a
Greece (ancient), III 585a
perfectibility, III 463b, 464a, 468b
Platonism, III 585a
primitivism, III 585a, 586b, 587a, 587b–588b
progress, III 628b
Rome (ancient), III 585a
State, IV 314b
Stoicism, III 585a
Sellars, Wilfrid
empiricism, III 550a
logic, III 550a
Semantics
linguistics, III 71a, 71b, 72b, 74a, 75a
motif, III 235a–236b
pragmatism, III 554a–554b, 557a
structuralism, IV 327b
Semedo, Alvaro, China, I 356a
Semeria, J., modernism, I 422b

Semiology, IV 324a
Semon, R. chromosomes, II 288a
Semple, Ellen Churchill (1863–1932)
  culture, II 131a
  Ratzel and, II 131a
Sen, Amartyn, social welfare, IV 283b
Sen, Keshub Chunder
  Orientalism, III 429b
  transcendentalism, III 429a
Sénancour, Étienne Pivert de (1770–1846), romanticism, IV 190a
Senault, Jean F. Cosmic Fall, I 509a
Sendivogius, Michael, hierarchy, II 435b
Seneca (54 B.C.?–39 A.D.), I 85b
  Alain of Lille and, III 590b
  analogy, I 68b
  Bacon on, I 173b
  Christianity, III 590a, 590b
  classification of the arts, I 457b, 459a–459b
  cosmology, I 545a
  cycles, I 623a
  death, I 635b
  dignity, IV 141b, 142b
  disease, II 399a
  Enlightenment, II 90a
  equality, II 140a
  fortune, II 228a; IV 478a
  genius, II 308b
  God, II 228a, 349a; III 588a
  Golden Age (myth), III 588a, 632a
  humors, III 128a
  humanism, II 516a
  literary paradox, III 80a
  literature, IV 331b
  magic, III 246a
  microcosm, III 128a
  mimesis, III 227a
  morality, III 632b
  Nature, II 228a; III 348b, 588b
  perfectibility, III 465b
  Posidonius and, III 588b
  primitivism, III 588a–588b, 590a, 590b, 591b, 599a
  private property, III 588a
  progress, III 630b–633a
  reason, III 465b
  reformation, IV 61b
  Rousseau and, III 588b
  Saint Jerome and, III 590a
  Saint Paul and, III 588b
  socialism, IV 286a
  Stoicism, III 588a–588b
  style, IV 331b
  temperance, IV 371a
  virtue, IV 478a
Senior, Nassau William (1790–1864)
  economic history, II 48b, 50b
  natural liberty, II 69a
  welfare state, IV 509a–509b
Sennacherib (705–681 B.C.)
  conservation, I 472b
  prophecy, III 660b
Sennert, Daniel (1572–1657)
  alchemy, I 32b
  atomism, I 131a–131b
  matter, III 192a
Sensation
  Berkeley, II 120b
  Enlightenment, II 96a
  Epicureans, IV 7b
  ideology, II 553a, 553b
  imagination, III 210b
  Locke, II 96a, 120b
  Polanyi, II 121a
  Saint Augustine, IV 9a
  Saint Thomas Aquinas, II 120b
  Strato, IV 7a
  Theophrastus, IV 6b
Senses
  aesthetics, II 216a–216b, 219b–221b; IV 355a, 355b
  Aristotle, I 1a–1b; III 189b, 190a; IV 5a, 5b–6a, 34b, 530b
  art, II 574b, 575b, 576b, 580b, 582a, 583a–583b
  Bacon, IV 466b
  Baudelaire, II 574b
  Dante, III 511a
  Democritus, III 188b
  Descartes, IV 244b
  dignity, IV 136b, 145a
  ethics, IV 72a
  experience, IV 435a
  Ficino, III 511a
  genius, II 294a, 313b
  harmony, II 388b
  Heraclitus, III 187a
  Hobbes, IV 434a
  Hume, II 582a
  Hutcheson, III 231b
  idea, II 543a
  ideal, II 549a, 551a
  imagination, III 212a, 214b, 222a
  impressionism, II 574b, 575b, 576b, 580b, 582a, 583a–583b
  Kant, III 518a
  language, II 662b
  Leonardo da Vinci, IV 440a, 440b–441a
  Man-Machine, III 132a,

132b, 137b, 139b
  Marxism, III 160b
  matter, III 185b, 187a, 187b, 188b, 189b, 190a
  metaphor, III 198b, 205b
  moral sense, III 231b, 234a
  music, II 313b, 388b
  mythology, III 273a, 317a
  natural law, III 17a
  optics, III 407b, 408a, 415a
  Parmenides, III 187a; IV 47b
  perfectibility, III 466a
  Plato, I 1a–1b; II 662b; III 188b, 273a, 503a–504b, 508b; IV 3b, 4a, 4b, 33b, 35b
  pragmatism, III 555b
  psychology, IV 2a–7b, 9a, 11b–13a, 17a–24b, 27a, 27b
  Pythagoreans, IV 33b–35b
  rationalism, IV 46b, 47b
  Reid, III 234a
  relativism, IV 72a
  religion, III 205b
  Renaissance, IV 136b, 145a, 440a
  romanticism, IV 196b, 199b
  skepticism, IV 234b, 235b, 236a, 237a, 244b, 248b
  Speusippus, IV 35b
  Strato, IV 7a
  sublime in external nature, IV 333a–337b
  taste, IV 355a, 355b
  theriophily, IV 384a
  unity of science, IV 434a, 435a
  universal man, IV 440a
  ut pictura poesis, IV 466a–467b, 468b, 472a, 472b, 474b
  Victorians, IV 217a, 218a, 218b
  wisdom of the fool, IV 516a
  women, IV 525a
  work, IV 530b
Senzaki, Nyogen, Buddhism, I 256b
Septuagint, I 412b, 417a
Serapion (4th century A.D.), astrology, I 124a
Sermons, literature, III 87b
Servetus, Michael (1511–1553)
  heresy, II 424b, 426a
  intolerance, IV 117a
  liberalism, III 4ab
  skepticism, IV 242a

Servius (4th–5th century A.D.), poetry, III 528b
Set (myth), II 334b, 335a, 335b; IV 100b, 225a
  dualism, II 39a
Set theory, space, IV 304b
Seth (Bible), mythology, III 277b
Settle, Elkanah (1648–1724), cosmic voyages, I 528a
Seurat, Georges (1859–1891), impressionism, II 567b, 580a, 580b
  pointillism, II 567b
Seven Wonders of the World
  sublime in external nature, IV 336a
  technology, IV 358a
Seven Years' War
  balance of power, I 186a
  Germany, III 483a
  periodization in literary history, III 483a
  Protestantism, I 402b
  U.S., I 402b
Serverus, Emperor (d. 307), virtù, IV 479b
Seward, Anna (1742–1809), periodization in literary history, III 483a
Sewell, Elizabeth, ambiguity, I 59b
Sewell, George, classicism, I 451a–451b
Sex
  animals, III 596a
  deviation, II 585b
  Diderot, III 603a, 603b
  equality, II 139a, 140a, 144b
  Freud, IV 97a
  Gnosticism, II 328a
  Greece (ancient), II 677b, 678a, 681a, 682b; III 94b, 95a
  happiness, II 374b, 383a
  Hermeticism, II 432a, 432b, 433b
  human nature, III 575b
  imprinting, II 585b
  law, II 677b, 678a, 681a, 682b, 688a
  learning, II 585b
  love, III 94a, 94b, 96b, 97a, 101b, 104a–107b
  Marxism, III 148b
  motif, III 239b
  natural law, III 25b
  primitivism, III 582a, 596a, 602a, 603a, 605b
  psychology, IV 14a, 24b, 28b, 29a
  relativism in ethics, IV 71a
  religion, IV 97a
  right, IV 174a, 185a

Rome (ancient), II 688a
Saint Augustine, III 584a
Saint Paul, III 96b
spontaneous generation, IV 307a–307b
Victorian sensibility, IV 219a, 219b, 222b
war, IV 507b
women, IV 524a, 527b
Sextus Empiricus (2nd and 3rd centuries A.D.)
certainty, I 304a
ethics, IV 320a
God, II 349a
mythology, III 274b
Platonism, III 504b
pragmatism, III 554b
progress, III 631a
psychology, IV 7b
skepticism, II 349a; IV 234a, 235a–243a, 245b
Stoicism, IV 320a
time, IV 389b
Sexual reproduction
acquired characteristics, II 619a
pangenesis, II 622b
Weismann, II 619a
Seznec, Jean
iconography, II 538b
mythology, III 295b, 298a
Sforza, Francesco (1401–1466), humanism, II 518a
Sforza, Ludovico (1451–1508), universal man, IV 442a
Shadow clocks, I 536a
Shadwell, Thomas (1642?–1692)
deism, I 650a
Puritanism, I 650a
virtuoso, IV 487b
Shäfer, Dietrich, historiography, II 495a
Shaftesbury, Third Earl of (1621–1683)
aesthetics, I 588a; IV 355b, 356a
Aristotle, III 365b
Balguy and, III 233a
beauty, I 201a, 205b
Clarke and, III 230b
Counter-Enlightenment, II 104b
creativity in art, I 588a
deism, I 650b–651a
Diderot and, III 603a
Enlightenment, II 89b, 96b, 97b
evil, II 166a
genius, II 294b, 308b, 320a
happiness and pleasure, II 380a
ideal, II 550a
imagination, III 218b, 219b
irony, II 628a–628b, 629b, 630a
Kames and, III 234b
Locke and, III 598b
moral sense, III 230b–231a, 232a, 233a, 234b
morality, II 380a
motif, III 240b
mountains in literature, III 259a
music, II 320a
Nature, I 205b; III 348a
neo-classicism in art, III 365b, 367b, 369b
organicism, III 424a
Platonism, III 516b, 518b, 523b
Plotinus and, III 424b
poetry, III 530b
primitivism, III 598a, 598b, 599a, 603a
psychology, IV 22b
reason, II 96b; III 230b
sublime in external nature, IV 334a, 335b, 336b
taste, IV 355b, 356a
utilitarianism, II 97b, IV 444b
Shaikh Sa'di Shirazi, nationalism, III 338a
Shakespeare, William (1564–1616), I 80a
acquired characteristics, II 617a, 617b
ambiguity, I 54b–56a
analogy, I 69b
antiprimitivism, III 604a
baroque in literature, I 189b, 190a, 191a
classicism, I 451b, 452b, 454a
comedy, I 468b, 469a, 470a
continuism, I 503b
continuity, I 503b
Counter-Enlightenment, II 104b
Faust (legend), III 248a, 251b
genius, II 294b, 306a–307a
harmony, II 388a, 388b, 391b, 394b
Hermeticism, II 432b, 433a
hierarchy, II 438a
historiography, I 503b
irony, II 630a, 630b, 631a, 632b
irrationalism, II 635b
law, II 690a–690b
literary criticism, I 597a, 599a, 599b, 600b
literary paradox, III 78a, 78b–79a, 80a
literature, III 82a, 86a
Machiavellism, III 118a–118b
mimesis, III 228a
motif, III 240b–242a
mountains in literature, III 253b
music, II 388a, 388b, 391b, 394b
mythology, III 299a–299b
Nature, III 228a, 351a
neo-classicism in art, III 371a
organicism, III 424b, 425b
perfectibility, III 473a
Platonism, III 519a
primitivism, III 604a
realism in literature, IV 52b, 53a
romanticism, IV 187b–189b, 192a, 194b
Saint Paul, III 80a
satire, IV 211b, 213b
Schlegel, IV 192a
symbolism, IV 338a
time, IV 399a
tragic sense, IV 416b
ut pictura poesis, IV 471a
vox populi, IV 497b
wisdom of the fool, IV 519b, 520a
words, III 241b
Shamash (myth), II 335b
sin, IV 226b
Shame
moral sense, III 231b
right, IV 173b
Shang Ti (myth), II 344b
religion, IV 104a
Shankara (fl. 800 A.D.) linguistics, IV 429a
Shannon, Claude, entropy, II 116b
Shapiro, Karl (1913–), literary criticism, I 604a
Shapley. Harlow (1885–), cosmology, I 562a
Shapur I, King (241–272), II 639a
Sharpe, William, genius, II 307a
Shaughnessy v. United States ex rel, Mezei, I 13a–13b
Shaw, George Bernard (1856–1950)
Darwin and, II 185b
evolutionism, II 181b, 183a, 185b–186a
God, II 186a
life force, II 186a
tragic sense, IV 415b
Shaw, Thomas, romanticism, IV 193a
She, C. Y., indeterminacy, II 592a
Sheba (Bible)
cosmic voyages, I 524a
mythology, III 275b, 277b
Shekhina (myth), III 282b
Shelley, Mary (1792–1851), Platonism, III 508a
Shelley, Percy Bysshe (1792–1822), I 84b, 109a
allegory, I 47a
anarchism, I 73a
beauty, III 524a
class, I 442b–443a
Counter-Enlightenment, II 110a
cycles, I 623a
dualism, III 508a
Eliot and, IV 195a–195b
Faust (legend), III 250b
Godwin and, III 470b
human nature, III 524a
ideal, III 508a
image, III 508a
impressionism, II 581a
longevity, III 92b
love, III 508a
materialism, III 524a
metaphysics, III 508a
morality, III 508a
motif, III 240b
perfectibility, III 470b
periodization in literary history, III 482b, 485b
Platonism, III 508a, 524a
primitivism, III 587b
romanticism, IV 193a, 195a–195b, 196b, 202a, 205a, 208b
soul, III 508a
symbolism, II 581a; III 508a
time, III 508a
Sheol (myth), IV 227b, 228a
Sherburn, George, romanticism, IV 195b, 196a
Shere, Henry, mythology, III 299a
Sheridan, Richard Brinsley (1751–1816), Machiavellism, III 119a
Sherrington, C. S. (1857–1952), ideas and reflexes, I 116a–116b
Shestakov, A. V., nationalism, III 333b
Shestov, Lev, skepticism, IV 250a, 250b
Shicism, Islam, II 641b–642a, 646a
Shisite Imams, II 640a
Shils, Edward, nationalism, III 336a
Shipping law, II 686a
primitivism, III 580a, 580b

private property, III 652a, 652b
Rome (ancient), II 686a
Shiva (myth)
music, III 268b
salvation, IV 232a
Shorey, Paul (1857–1934),
creativity in art, I 586b
Platonism, III 522a
Shōtoku, Prince, Buddhism, I 252b
Shu (myth), II 334a
Shuckford, Samuel, mythology, III 301b
Shumaker, Wayne, literary criticism, I 604a; III 311a
Shun, Emperor, cosmic voyages, I 524a
Shuppiluliumash I (fl. 1400 B.C.), freedom of speech, II 253b
Sibley, Frank, beauty, I 207a–207b
Sibscota, George, linguistics, III 74b–75b
Sicily
catastrophism, IV 421a–422a
freedom of speech, II 254a
neo-classicism in art, III 365b, 370b
primitivism, III 579a
uniformitarianism, IV 421a, 421b, 422a
Sickness, *see* Disease
Siddartha, Prince, *see* Buddha
Sidgwick, Henry (1838–1900)
social welfare, IV 279a
utilitarianism, IV 445a, 446b–447a
Sidney, Algernon (1622–1683)
democracy, I 657a
despotism, II 1b, 7b
Gothic, II 369a
slavery, II 7b
See also Sydney
Sidney, Philip (1554–1586)
genius, II 306a
literary paradox, III 77b
mythology, III 298a
poetics, III 77b, 529b, 530a
ut pictura poesis, IV 467b
Siecke, E., mythology, III 310a
Sienkiewicz, Henryk (1846–1916), Machiavellism, III 119a
Sierra, Justo, positivism, III 544b
Sievers, Eduard (1850–1932), linguistics, III 70b

Sieyès, Emmanuel J. (1748–1836)
democracy, I 661a
general will, II 279a
nationalism, III 326b
Siger of Brabant (1235?–1281)
double truth, II 31b, 32b–34a, 34b, 36a, 36b, 37b
faith, I 639b; II 33a, 33b
immortality, I 639b, 640b
Islam, II 649b
reason, I 639b
truth, II 32b–33b
Sigibert of Gembloux (ca. 1030–1112), historiography, II 473b
Sigismund, Emperor (1368–1437)
Council of Constance, I 386a–386b
reformation, IV 66a
Signac, Paul (1863–1935), impressionism, II 580b
Signs
Condillac, IV 435b
Leibniz, IV 435a, 435b
mythology, III 317a
Peirce, III 557a, 559a–559b, 560b
pragmatism, III 557a
science, III 86b
skepticism, IV 236b–237a
Stoicism, IV 237a
structuralism, IV 324a, 325b–326a, 328a
unity of science, IV 435a, 435b
Sihanouk, Prince Norodom (1922–   ), nationalism, III 333a
Sikkim
Buddhism, I 248b, 249a
nationalism, III 333a
Silesius, Angelus
expressionism, II 208a
literary paradox, III 80a
Silhon, Jean de, skepticism, IV 244b
Silhouette, Étienne de (1709–1767), China, I 358a
Silíceo, Jean Martinex, medieval science, II 204b
Sillman, Benjamin
phrenology, IV 23b
psychology, IV 23b
Silone, Ignazio (1900–   ), class, I 442b
Silva Gomes, Justiniano de
Comte and, III 539b
positivism, III 539b
Silver Age (myth), primitivism, III 578a–580a

Silvester, Bernard,
dignity, IV 140a
Hermeticism, II 433a–433b
Silvio, Enea, genius, II 293b
Simias of Rhodes (ca. 300 B.C.), *ut pictura poesis,* IV 470b
Simmel, Georg (1858–1918),
individualism, II 595b, 597a, 601a
irrationalism, II 636a–636b
Simon, Eugène, China, I 371a
Simon, Richard (1638–1712),
deism, I 650b
historiography, II 490b
modernism, I 419b
skepticism, IV 246b, 247a
Simon Magus (Bible)
ethics, II 328a
Faust (legend), III 246a
Gnosticism, II 327a, 328a, 330b
Simone, Franco, Renaissance, IV 126b
Simonides of Ceos (c. 556–467 B.C.)
progress, III 624a
ut pictura poesis IV 467b
Simplicius (6th century A.D.)
fortune, II 228b, 233a
time, IV 390a
Simpson, G. G.
biology, I 236b–238a
evolutionism, II 188a
progress, III 646b–647a
Simultaneity
Einstein, IV 81b–82b
Poincaré, IV 81b–82a
relativity, IV 81b–83b
Sin (myth), II 335b
Sin, IV 224a–234a
Achan (Bible), IV 226b
acquired characteristics, II 617b
Adam (Bible), IV 227a, 230a
Adonis (myth), IV 228b
Advaita Uēdanta, IV 232a
Agamemnon (myth), IV 228a
Ahriman (myth), IV 228b, 231b
Ahura Mazdā (myth), IV 231a, 231b
Am-mut (myth), IV 225b
Anubis (myth), IV 225b
Apollo (myth), IV 228a
Arabs, IV 230b
art, IV 233a
Attis (myth), IV 228b
baptism, IV 230a
Barth, II 29a; III 467a
Bhagavadgītā, IV 232a
bhaktimarga, IV 232a

Bible, IV 226b–227b, 229a–230b
birth, IV 231b
bodhisattvas, IV 233a
Book of the Dead, IV 225a, 225b
Brensted, IV 225a
Buddha, IV 232b, 233a
Buddhism, IV 232b–233a
Calvin, I 506a; III 467a; IV 381b
catharsis, I 264b
causation, IV 232b
Christianity, III 591a; IV 102b, 224a, 226a, 228a, 229a–230b, 231b
Church of England, IV 224a
city-state, IV 228a
Code of Hammurabi, IV 226b
conscience, IV 225a, 226a
Cosmic Fall, I 505a, 506a, 506b, 507a, 507b, 508b
cosmos, IV 224b
Counter-Enlightenment, II 110a
crime, IV 225b
culture, IV 231b, 232b, 233a
cycles, IV 232a
Dante, IV 176b–177a
death, IV 224b–226a, 227b, 228a, 228b, 229b, 230a, 231a, 231b, 232b
deism, IV 224a, 226b
Demeter (myth), IV 228b
determinism, II 26a, 26b–27b, 29a, 236b
dignity, IV 138b, 142a
Dionysius the Areopagite, IV 228b
disease, II 395b, 396b, 399a, 400b, 403a
dualism, IV 229a, 231a
Edwards, IV 110b
Egypt (ancient), II 564b; IV 224b–226a, 228b
Eightfold Path, IV 232b
Eleusinian Mysteries, IV 228a–228b, 229a
eschatology, IV 226a, 229a, 230a–231b
ethics, IV 70a, 225a, 225b, 227a
Eve (Bible), IV 227a
evil, II 164a, 164b, 165a, 165b, 166a; IV 224a, 226a, 228b, 229b, 231a, 231b, 233a
existentialism, IV 232a
Franklin, IV 22a
free will, II 236b, 243b; IV 230b, 231a, 232b
freedom, II 250a

Gnosticism, II 328a; IV 229a, 229b
God, I 576a; II 358b, 360b; IV 225a–232a
good, IV 176b–177a, 180b, 224b, 231a, 231b
Goodman, I 507a
Greece (ancient), IV 228a–229b
guilt, IV 226b
Hades (myth), IV 228a
Hakewill, I 507b, 508b
Hammurabi, IV 226b
happiness and pleasure, II 379a, 379b
harmony, II 391a
health, II 395b, 396b, 399a, 400b, 403a
heaven, IV 230a, 230b, 231b
hell, IV 230a, 231a, 231b
heresy, II 417a, 429a
hermeticism, IV 229a, 229b
Hinduism, IV 231b–232b
history, IV 224a
Homer, IV 228a
hubris, IV 228a
Huguenots, IV 113b
human nature, IV 231b, 233a
idolatry, IV 226b, 227a
immortality, IV 226a, 228a, 228b, 230b
impiety, II 564b–565a
impressionism, II 575b
Incarnation, IV 232b
India (ancient), IV 232b
individualism, IV 227b
inheritance, II 617b
Ishtar (myth), IV 226b
Isis (myth), IV 228b
Islam, IV 224a, 230b–231a
Israel (ancient), II 564b–565a; IV 226b–228a
Jeroboam (Bible), IV 226b–227a
Jesus Christ, IV 227b, 229a–230b
Job (Bible), IV 227b–228a
Joshua (Bible), IV 226b
Judaism, II 564b–565a; III 636a; IV 226b–228a, 229a, 229b, 230b
justice, IV 224b, 225b, 227b
karma, IV 231b–232a, 232b
Koran, IV 230b, 231a
law, II 250a; IV 224a, 226a, 226b, 233a
Leibniz, II 166a; IV 382a
liberation, IV 232a, 233a
literature, IV 228a, 233a
Locke, III 469b

love, III 96b, 97a, 107b
Luther, III 255a; IV 381b
Machiavellism, III 118a
Marduk (myth), IV 226b
Mecca, IV 231a
Mesopotamia (ancient), II 564b; IV 226a–226b
metaphysics, IV 232b
Middle Ages, IV 230a, 253a
Mithra (myth), IV 228b
morality, IV 224b, 225a, 225b, 229a, 229b, 231a
mountains in literature, III 254b, 255a
Muhammad, IV 230b–231a
music, II 391a; III 266b
mysticism, IV 288a–229a
mythology, III 279a, 284a, 315b; IV 224b, 226a, 226b, 228a–229a
nationalism, IV 227b
Nature, III 350a; IV 229a, 231b, 232b
Near East, IV 227b, 228b
Nebot (Bible), IV 226b–227a
Neo-Platonism, IV 227b
Niebuhr, II 29a; III 467a
Nietzsche, IV 180b
Nirvāna, IV 232b–233a
Oedipus (myth), IV 228a
original, II 26a–27b, 29a
Orpheus (myth), IV 228b
Orphism, IV 228a–229a
Osiris (myth), IV 225a, 225b, 228b
paradise, IV 230b
Pascal, IV 381b
perennial philosophy, III 459a
perfectibility, III 463b, 466a–468b, 469b
Persephone, IV 228b
Persia, IV 228b, 231a
Petrarch, IV 142a
philosophy, IV 228a, 229a
Pietism, III 494b
Plato, II 236b; IV 228a
Platonism, III 506b
poetry, IV 228a
polytheism, IV 231a
power, IV 227b
pragmatism, III 567a
predestination, II 26a, 26b–27b, 29a; IV 230b
primitivism, III 584a, 584b, 591a, 596b
progress, III 634b, 635a, 635b, 636a, 638b
prophecy, III 659a, 662a, 662b, 663b, 665a, 665b
Protestantism, IV 230a
Pseudo-Dionysius, IV 228b

psychology, IV 17a, 22a, 23b
Purchas, I 506b
Pyramid Texts, IV 224b–225a
Rashnu (myth), IV 231b
Rē (myth), IV 224b–225a
reformation, IV 62a
Reformation, IV 68a
reincarnation, IV 228b
relativism, IV 70a
religion, IV 93b, 102b, 103a, 107b, 110a, 113b, 116b, 224a, 225a, 226a, 227a, 228a, 233a
Renaissance, IV 138b, 142a
resurrection, IV 226b, 228a, 228b, 230b, 231b
right, IV 176b–177a, 180b
ritual, IV 225a–225b, 226a, 228a–228b, 229b, 230a, 231a, 233a
Roman Catholic Church, I 512b; IV 230a
Rome (ancient), IV 227b, 228a–229a, 229b, 230a
Saint Augustine, II 26a–27b; II 459a, IV 138b, 176b, 230a, 286b, 379b, 381a
Saint Bernard, III 591a
Saint Paul, II 164a; IV 229b–230a
Saint Thomas Aquinas, I 669b; III 466b
Samkhya-Yoga, IV 232a
Samsāra, IV 231b–232b
Sankara, IV 232a
Saoshyans (myth), IV 231b
Satan, IV 229b, 230a
Set (myth), IV 225a
Shamash (myth), IV 226b
Sheol (myth), IV 227b, 228a
Shiva (myth), IV 232a
slavery, II 250a
social contract, IV 253a
socialism, IV 286b
society, IV 224a, 224b, 226b, 233a
Sophocles, IV 229a
soteriology, IV 225b, 228a, 229b
soul, IV 228b, 229a, 230a, 231b, 232b, 233a
State, IV 226b, 228a, 314a, 317a
temperance, IV 372b, 378a
Ten Commandments, IV 227a
theodicy, IV 379b–382a
theology, II 26a–27b, 29a
theriophily, IV 386b

Thoth (myth), IV 225b
tragic sense, IV 413a, 416a
transcendentalism, IV 224b, 233a
Troy, IV 228a
truth, IV 224b
universe, IV 224a
Upanishadic period, IV 231b–232a, 232b
Utopia, IV 460b, 461a
virtue, IV 225a
Vishnu (myth), IV 232a
war, IV 508a
Wesley, III 468a
wisdom of the fool, IV 518a
work, IV 531a, 532b
Yahweh, IV 226b–227a
Yahwism, IV 227a, 227b
Zealots, IV 227b
Zoroaster, IV 231a–231b
Zoroastrianism IV 231a–231b
Sinclair, John, (1754–1835), Enlightenment, II 98b
Singer, Edgar A.
  empiricism, III 549a
  logic, III 549a
Singer, Samuel, romanticism, IV 192a
Singers
  harmony, II 393a, 393b
  musical genius, II 313b–315a, 316a, 316b, 317b, 393a, 393b
Singing, III 260b, 268a–271a
  mimesis, III 226a
  mythology, III 272b, 279b
  prophecy, III 659a
Sinology, I 354a
Siroto, Leon, beauty, I 214a
Sisley, Alfred (1839–1899),
  financial status, II 573b
  impressionism, II 567b, 573b, 579a–579b
Sismondi, Jean Charles Léonard de (1773–1842),
  crisis in history, I 590a
  economic history, II 58b–59a
  Enlightenment, II 95a, 98b–99a
  historiography, II 492a
  liberty, II 95a
  romanticism, IV 189b, 190a, 190b, 192a
  Schlegel, A. W. and, IV 189b, 190a
  socialism, IV 289b, 292b
Sitter, Willem de (1872–1934)
  cosmology, I 561b–562b
  Einstein and, I 561b–562b

Siva (myth), II 343b–344a

Skelton, John (1460?–1529), wisdom of the fool, IV 519b

Skepticism, IV 234a–251b
academic, I 647a
Aenesidemus of Crete, IV 234a, 235a, 236b–237a, 237b, 238b, 240a, 241a
Agrippa, IV 234a, 238a, 242a, 243a
Alain, IV 250a
alchemy, IV 242a
Al-Ghazali, IV 241b
Anaxagoras, IV 234b
Anaxarchus, IV 234a, 234b
Antiochus of Ascalon, IV 234a
Antipater, IV 239b
appearance, IV 236a–236b, 238b–239a, 246a
Arcesilaus of Pitane, IV 234a–235b, 238b–240a, 241a
Archilochus, IV 234b
argumentation, IV 235a–237a, 239b, 245a
Aristocles, IV 238a
Aristotelianism, IV 243b, 244a, 244b
Aristotle, III 503a; IV 234b, 238a, 239b, 244b
Arnauld, IV 245a
art, II 575b; IV 236a–236b
astrology, IV 242a
atheism, IV 244a
atomism, IV 234b
Atticus, IV 238b
Bacon, I 311b; IV 244b
Bayle, IV 241a, 245b–248a, 250b
Bellarmine, IV 242b
Berkeley, IV 245b, 246a, 248b
Bernstein, Eduard, III 163a
Bible, IV 242b, 246b–247a
Bodin, IV 242a, 246b
Boyle, I 304b, 306b, 308a, 310a–311a
Brahe, IV 242a
Brochard, IV 234b
Bryson, IV 234a, 234b
cabbala, IV 242a, 243a
Calvin, II 349a; IV 242a–242b
Calvinism, IV 242b, 244a
Camus, Albert (1913–1960), IV 250a, 250b
Camus, Jean-Pierre, IV 243b, 244a
Carneades of Cyrene, IV 234a, 235a, 235b–236a, 237a, 238b–239b, 241a
Cartesianism, IV 244b–245b
causation, I 273a, 277b; IV 237a, 247b
certainty, I 304a–311b
Charron, II 349b; IV 243b, 244a, 244b
Chillingworth, I 306a, 307a–308a, 308b, 309a, 310a, 311a, 311b; IV 245b
Christianity, I 401b; IV 241b, 242a–244b, 245b, 246b–247a, 250b
Cicero, IV 234a, 234b, 235b, 236a, 236b, 238b, 239a, 239b, 241a, 243a
Clitomachus of Carthage, IV 234a
Colotes, IV 239b, 240a
Columbus, IV 241b
common sense, IV 245b, 248b
constructive, I 306a–311b
Copernicus, IV 242a
Counter-Enlightenment, II 101a–101b
Counter-Reformation, IV 244a
culture, I 617b, 620a; IV 243a–243b, 250a
custom, IV 238b, 243b, 247b, 248a
cycles, I 627a
Da Costa, IV 246b
death, I 644a, 645a
deism, I 647a, 648b
Democritus, IV 234b, 235a, 239b
Descartes, I 304b, 305a–306a, 308b, 311b; IV 241a, 244b–245a, 245b, 247a, 248b, 249b
determinism, II 25b
dignity, IV 140b–141a
Diogenes Laërtius, IV 234b, 237b, 238a, 243a
Diogenes of Oenoanda, IV 234b
divination, IV 235b–236a
dogmatism, IV 235a–236a, 237a, 238b, 239b, 240a, 244a, 245a
Du Perron, IV 242b
economics, IV 250a
Eleatics, IV 234b
Empedocles, IV 234b
empiricism, IV 234a, 236b, 240a, 244a, 247b, 248b–250a
Enlightenment, II 96a
Epicureanism, IV 236a, 239b–240a, 241a
Epicurus, IV 234a, 234b, 236a, 240a
epistemology, IV 236b,

237a, 240a, 243b, 246a
equality, II 140b
Erasmus, IV 241b–242a
ethics, IV 236a, 237a, 241a
Euripides, IV 234b
Eusebius, IV 234b
evil, II 164a, 167b–168a; IV 235b
existentialism, IV 250a
experience, IV 242b, 247b, 248b–249a, 250b
experiments, IV 247b
faith, IV 243a, 243b, 244a, 248a, 250a, 250b, 251a
fate, IV 236a
Favorinus of Arles, IV 240a
Fichte, IV 249a, 249b
Ficino, IV 242a
fideism, IV 243b, 244a, 246b, 248a, 249a, 250b
Fontenelle, I 401b
Foucher, IV 245a–246a
France, IV 242b–245b, 248a
France, Anatole, II 575b
freedom of speech, II 256b
Freud, IV 250a
Galen, IV 236a, 237a, 239a, 240a
Gassendi, I 306a, 306b–307a; IV 244a, 244b, 245a, 250b
Germany, IV 248b–250a
Glanvill, IV 245b
God, II 348b–349b, 352b, 356a; IV 236a, 237a, 243b, 244a, 244b, 246a, 247b, 248a, 248b, 250b
good, IV 235a, 235b, 238a
Gorgias, IV 234b
Great Britain, IV 245b–246a
Greece (ancient), I 273a, 304b, 401b; IV 234a–240a, 241a, 242a
Grenier, IV 250a, 250b
Hamann, IV 249a–250b
happiness, IV 238b
Hegel, IV 241a, 249a, 249b
Heraclitus, IV 234b, 235a, 239b
Herbert of Cherbury, IV 244b
Hermes Trismegistus, IV 242a
Hervet, IV 242a
Hippocrates, IV 234b, 236a
historiography, II 25b; IV 148a
history, II 25b; IV 246b–247a, 247b, 248a, 249b
Hobbes, IV 245b
Homer, IV 234b
Huet, IV 245a, 246a, 246b
human nature, IV 248a

humanism, II 520a–520b; IV 135a, 241b–242a, 243a
Hume, I 277b, 278a; II 96a, 352b; IV 241a, 241b, 245b, 247b–249a, 250b
idealism, IV 249b–250a
immortality, I 644a, 645a
impiety, II 565a; IV 238b
impressionism, II 575b
intuition, IV 245b, 250b
irrationalism, II 635b
Islam, IV 241b, 242a
Israel (ancient), II 565a
James, III 561b; IV 250a
Jesuits, IV 242b, 245a
Judah Ha-Levy, IV 241b
Judaism, II 565a; IV 241b, 242a, 243b, 246b–247a, 250b
judgment, IV 235a–238b, 241a, 243a, 243b, 244b, 248b
Kant, IV 209a, 241a, 248b–249a, 249b, 250b
Kepler, IV 242a
Kierkegaard, IV 249a–249b
knowledge, IV 234b, 235b, 236b, 238b, 241a–246a, 247a, 248b–249b
La Mothe Le Vayer, IV 244a
La Peyrère, IV 246b–247a
La Placette, IV 242b
Lactantius, IV 236a
Lamennais, IV 248a, 249a, 249b
language, IV 250a
law, III 35b; IV 245b
Leibniz, IV 245a, 246a, 247a
Levi, Adolfo, IV 250a
literary criticism, I 596a, 597a, 603a
literary paradox, III 78a, 79b
Locke, IV 245b, 247a, 248b
logic, IV 236a, 237a, 246a, 250b
Lucian, IV 240a
Luther, IV 242a–242b
Machiavellism, IV 244a
magic, IV 242a, 243a
Maimon, IV 249a
Maistre, IV 248a
Malebranche, IV 241b, 245a, 247a
Marx, IV 250a
Marxism, III 163a
mathematics, IV 236b, 246a, 248b, 250a, 250b
Mauthner, IV 250a
medicine, IV 234a, 236a–236b, 237a, 239a, 240a
Menodotus of Nicomedia, IV 234a, 250a, 250b

411

Mersenne, I 306a–306b, 307a; IV 244b, 245a
metaphysics, IV 241a, 241b, 245b, 246a–246b, 247b, 248b–250b
Methodism, IV 240a
Metrodorus of Chios, IV 234b, 239a
Middle Ages, IV 241b
Montaigne, II 167b–168a, 349b; III 78a; IV 241a, 241b, 243a–243b
morality, IV 247b
motion, IV 237a, 245b
music, III 264b, 268a
mysticism, IV 241b, 246
mythology, III 274b, 300a, 302a–302b
Nature, IV 247b–248a
Naudé, IV 224a
Nausiphanes, IV 234a, 240a
Newton, I 304b, 310b, 311a–311b; IV 247b, 248a
Noble Savage, IV 241b
numbers, IV 242a
observation, IV 238b
opinion, IV 235a
painting, II 575b; IV 236b
Paracelsus, IV 242a
Parmenides, IV 234b
Pascal, II 349b; IV 245b–246a, 248a, 250b
Pater, II 575b
Patin, IV 244a
perception, IV 234b, 235b, 236a, 237a
perennial philosophy, III 457a, 458a, 459a, 459b, 462a
pessimism, II 167b
Philinus, IV 236a
Philo Judaeus, IV 240a
Philo of Larissa, IV 234a
Photius, IV 237a
physics, IV 236a, 244b
Pico della Mirandola, IV 242a, 243a
piety, IV 238b
Plato, III 503a, 504a–504b; IV 234b, 235a, 235b, 238b
Platonism, III 503a, 504a–504b; IV 236a, 243b, 250b
pleasure, IV 235b
Plutarch, IV 234b, 235a, 237b, 239b, 240a
Popper, IV 236a
positivism, IV 244b, 249b–250a, 250b
power, IV 236a
pragmatism, III 561b, 568a; IV 244b, 249b–250a
pre-Socratics, IV 234b,

237a
probability, IV 236a, 238b–239a, 241a
progress, III 634a, 647b
Protagoras, IV 235a
protest movements, III 670a, 677a
Protestantism, IV 242a–242b, 243b, 247a
psychology, IV 22b, 29a, 243a–243b, 246b, 247b, 248a, 250a
Pyrrho of Elis, IV 234a, 235a, 236a, 237b, 238b, 239b–240a, 241a
Pyrrhonism, IV 234a, 234b, 237b, 239a, 240a, 241a, 242b–243b, 245a, 247a, 248b
Pythagoreans, IV 37b, 41a
rationalism, IV 48a, 243a, 246a, 247a, 247b, 250b, 251a
reason, IV 236a, 243a, 247b, 248b–249a
Reformation, IV 242a–242b
Reid, IV 248a–248b
reincarnation, I 645a
religion, IV 117a
Renaissance, IV 135a, 140b–141a, 148a, 242a, 250b
resurrection, I 644a
Reuchlin, IV 242a
revelation, IV 244a, 246b, 247a
rhetoric, IV 237a
Roman Catholic Church, IV 242a–243a, 244a, 246b
romanticism, IV 199b, 200b, 208b, 209a
Rome (ancient), IV 235b–236a, 238b
Rousseau, IV 241b
Saint Augustine, IV 241a–241b, 244b
Saint Paul, IV 243b
salvation, IV 248a
Sanchez, IV 243b–244a
Santayana, IV 250a–250b
Saturninus, IV 234a
scholasticism, IV 241b, 242a, 250b
Schoock, IV 245a
Schulze, IV 249a
science, IV 236a–236b, 242a, 243a–251a
sculpture, IV 236b
senses, IV 234b, 235b, 236a, 237a, 244b, 248b
Servetus, IV 242a
Sextus Empiricus, II 349a; IV 234a, 235a–243a, 245b

Shestov, IV 250a, 250b
signs, IV 236b–237a
Simon, IV 246b, 247a
socialism, IV 288b
society, IV 241b, 246b, 250a
Socrates, III 504a; IV 234b, 235a, 239a–239b
Sophism, IV 234b, 235a
soul, IV 246b
Spinoza, IV 241a, 246a, 246b–247a
Stillingfleet, IV 245b
Stoicism, IV 234b–237b, 239b, 240a, 241a, 244b
theodicy, IV 380b, 381b, 383b
theology, IV 235b, 240b, 241b, 243a, 243b, 244a, 247a, 247b
theriophily, IV 386b
time, IV 235a
Timon of Phlius, IV 234a, 234b–235a, 236a–236b, 237b, 238b
tropes, IV 236b–237a, 237b–238a, 240a, 241a
truth, IV 235b, 237a, 242a, 243a, 244b, 245a, 246a, 246b, 250b, 251a
universe, IV 237a, 247b, 249b, 250b
Vaihinger, IV 250a
value, IV 250a
Vesalius, IV 242a
Vespucci, IV 241b
virtue, IV 237a
Vives, IV 241b
Voetius, IV 245a
Voltaire, IV 241b, 247b
Wilkins, I 308a–310a, 311a; IV 245b
wisdom, IV 238b
witchcraft, IV 522b
Wright, III 561b
Xenophanes, IV 234b, 235a
Zeno of Citium, IV 234b
Zwingli, IV 242b
Skill
Aristotle, III 628b, 629b
genius, II 295b
Lucretius, III 631a
Plato, III 629a
Posidonius, III 631a
progress, III 628b, 629a, 629b, 631a, 635a, 638a
Saint Augustine, III 635a
Socrates, III 496b
Skinner, B. F. (1904–   )
behaviorism, I 219b, 226a–228a
perfectibility, III 469b
positivism, III 549a–549b

psychology, IV 28b
Utopia, IV 464a
Slater, John, entropy, II 116b
Slater, Robert H. L., Buddhism, I 257a
Slavery
antiprimitivism, III 604a
Aristotle, I 443a; II 2a, 2b–3a, 5a, 5b, 259a; III 440a; IV 530b
blacks, III 280b
Bossuet, II 5a
Brazil, III 541b, 542a, 543a
charity and, II 213a
China, I 354b, 363a
Christianity and, II 250a
civilization, III 182b
class, I 443a
cynicism, I 630a–630b, 633b
democracy, I 652b
despotism, II 1b–3a, 4b–7b, 9a–11b, 13b, 15b, 16a
economic history, II 53a
Egypt (ancient), II 466a
Enlightenment, II 95a
equality, II 140a, 140b, 141a, 144b
France, II 144b
freedom, II 242b, 249a–250b
freedom of speech, II 256a, 259a, 260a
Garrison, I 436b
good, IV 174b
Great Britain, IV 219b
Greece (ancient), I 443a; II 1b, 2a, 2b–3a, 249b, 260a, 678a; IV 286a
Grotius, II 5a–5b, 11a
Hegel, II 15b, 16a, 408b
Hobbes, II 5b
Homer, II 259a
human nature, III 572a
Jefferson, IV 21b
labor, III 182b
law, II 249a, 249b, 250a, 250b, 678a, 686a, 687b, 688b, 689a; III 10b, 11a
Locke, I 6b–7b
Marx, II 25a
millenarianism, III 224a, 224b
Montesquieu, II 9a, 9b–10b
mythology, III 280b
natural, II 1b, 5b
natural law, III 17a
natural liberty, II 65b
peace, III 441a
Pereira Barreto, III 541b
periodization in history, III 478b
philanthropy, III 490a, 491a

positivism, III 541b, 542a, 543a
pragmatism, III 566b
primitivism, III 580a, 604a
progress, III 636b
psychology, IV 21b, 22a, 22b
Pufendorf, II 5b, 11a
rationalism, IV 49a
reformation, IV 68b
religion, IV 111b–112b
right, IV 174b
Rome (ancient), II 4b, 686a, 687b, 688b, 689a; IV 286a
Rousseau, II 11a, 11b
Saint Augustine, II 213a, 250a; III 11a
Saint Paul, II 250a
Saint Thomas Aquinas, II 213a
Sidney, II 7b
sin, II 250a
Smith, Adam, II 65b
socialism, IV 286a
Stoicism, III 17a
technology, IV 358a
Thoreau, I 436a
U.S., I 435a, 436a–437a, 437b; II 7a–7b
vox populi, IV 497a
war, III 441a
women, IV 523b
work, IV 530b, 532a
Sleidanus, Johannes (1506–1556), historiography, II 484a
Slipher, Vesto Melvin, cosmology, I 562a
Slive, Seymour, naturalism in art, III 345b
Smart, Christopher (1722–1771), Newton and, III 393b, 394b
Smart, J. J. C., positivism, III 550a
Smart, Ninian, agnosticism, I 22b, 23a–23b
Smeaton, John (1724–1792), technology, IV 362a
Smiles, Samuel (1812–1904), individualism, II 596b
Smith, Adam (1723–1790)
association of ideas, I 114a
capital, II 47b, 49a
catharsis, I 265b
China, I 365a–365b
class, I 444a, 446b–447b
competition, III 11b
deism, I 651a–651b
distribution, II 49b
economic history, II 45b–50a, 53a, 55a, 57a–59a
economics, II 453a; III 11b

education, II 63b–64a, 64b
Enlightenment, II 89b, 91b, 92b, 93a–93b, 94b, 95a, 97a, 98a, 99a–99b
equality, III 11b
exchange, II 62b–66a
freedom, II 58b–59a
good, IV 178a, 179a
happiness, II 380a
Hegel and, II 409a
historiography, II 494b
Hume and, III 233a, 233b
Hutcheson and, III 233b
idea, I 114a
income, II 49a–49b
individualism, II 602a
justice, II 59a
labor, II 47b, 48a–48b
law, II 63b; III 11b
liberty, II 94b
linguistics, III 65b
Marx and, II 451a, 453a
materialism, II 451a, 453a
moral sense, III 233a, 233b
natural liberty, II 61b–69a
Navigation Acts, II 68a
peace, III 444a
periodization in history, III 479a
pity, I 265b
prices, II 49a, 62b–63b
public works, II 65a
religion, II 63b, 64a–64b
rent, II 57b
slavery, II 65b
social welfare, IV 277a, 277b
socialism, IV 292b
State, II 64a
sympathy, III 233b; IV 178a
Turgot and, II 62b
uniformitarianism, IV 419b
utilitarianism, II 97a, 380a
utility, IV 452b, 453b
work, IV 534b
Smith, Adrian, the city, I 432a
Smith, G. Elliot, mythology, III 310b, 311a, 312a, 315a
Smith, John (17th century)
atomism, I 137a
Neo-Platonism, III 506b
Smith, Logan Pearsall (1865–1946), mythology, III 297a
Smith, Marian W., beauty, I 213b
Smith, Samuel Stanhope (1750–1819), psychology, IV 21b
Smith, W. Robertson (1846–1894)
holy, II 513b
mythology, III 310b, 311a, 312a, 315a
Smith, William S. (1755–

1816), revolution, IV 155b
Smits, C., iconography, II 535b
Snell, Bruno, psychology, IV 1b
Snell, Willebrord, optics, III 418a
Snow, C. P.
culture, I 617b
education, II 81b
Snyder, Denton J., pragmatism, III 556b
Soane, John (1753–1837), neo-classicism in art, III 366a
Sobriety, temperance, IV 366a, 367b, 370b, 371b
Social contract, IV 251b–263b
Abraham (Bible), IV 252a
absolutism, IV 256b, 257a
Adam (Bible), IV 257b
Adams, John Quincy, IV 262b–263a
Adams, Samuel, IV 260b
Althusius, IV 254b
American Revolution, IV 255a, 260b
Aristotle, IV 252b
atheism, IV 255b
Bartolus of Sassoferrato, IV 253a
Bible, IV 252a–252b, 258a
Bourgeois, IV 263a
Burke, IV 262a–262b
Charles, I, IV 255a
Christianity, IV 252b
city-state, IV 253a
class, IV 251b, 253b, 256a
Coleridge, IV 263a
conservatism, IV 256b, 257b, 262b
covenant, I 396a; IV 251b, 252a, 252b, 254b
criticism, IV 254a–254b, 261b
Cromwell, IV 255a
culture, IV 259a
David (Bible), IV 252a–252b
democracy, IV 251b, 253b, 255a, 256a, 257a, 257b, 263b
determinism, IV 263a
Diogenes of Sinope, IV 252b
Duplessis-Mornay, IV 254a
economics, IV 259a, 263a
Engelbert of Volkersdorf, IV 253b
English Civil War, IV 254b–255a
Epicurus, IV 252b

equality, IV 251b, 255b
feudalism, IV 253b
Fichte, IV 261a
Filmer, IV 257b, 258a
France, IV 253b, 254a, 261a, 263a
free will, IV 255b
freedom, IV 254a, 255b, 256b, 257b, 260a
French Revolution (1789), IV 255a, 260a, 261a, 262a, 262b
George III, IV 260b
Germany, IV 253a, 261a
God, IV 252a–254b, 255b, 257b, 262a
Godwin, IV 262b
Golden Age (myth), IV 252a
Great Britain, IV 253b, 254a, 254b, 257b, 258a, 260b, 261a, 262b
Greece (ancient), IV 251b, 252a, 252b–253a
Green, IV 263a
Grotius, IV 254b, 259b, 317a
happiness, II 379b
Henry IV, IV 254a
Hobbes, III 20b, 575b, 576a; IV 252a, 256a–257b, 259a–260a, 261b
Holy Roman Empire, IV 253a
Hooker, IV 254a–254b, 255b
Huguenots, IV 254a
human nature, III 575b, 576a
Hume, III 575b; IV 261b
Huxley, IV 263a
individualism, II 600a–600b, 601b; IV 254b, 255b, 257a, 259b, 260a, 263b
Italy, IV 253a
James I, IV 257b
James II, IV 258a
Jesuits, IV 254a
Kant, IV 261a, 263a
knowledge, IV 259a, 262b
labor, IV 259a
Languet, IV 254a
Latin language, IV 252a
law, III 11a, 566b; IV 252b, 253a, 253b, 254a, 257a, 261a, 263a
liberalism, III 43b–44a, 46b; IV 251b, 255a, 256a, 263b
Lillburne, IV 254b–255a
literature, IV 252a
Locke, III 21a; IV 252a,

253a, 255b, 257b, 258a–262a, 288a, 317a
Magna Carta, IV 253b, 261b
Manegold of Lautenbach, IV 253a
Mariana, IV 254a
Marsilius of Padua, IV 253a
Middle Ages, IV 252a, 253a–255a
Milton, IV 255a
mind, IV 254a
minorities, IV 254b
Molina, IV 254a
monarchy, IV 253a–255a, 256a, 257b, 258a, 262a
morality, IV 263a
mythology, IV 252a
natural law, III 20b, 21a–21b
Nature, IV 251b, 254a, 255a, 255b, 256b, 257a, 257b, 258a, 259a, 261b, 262a
Nicolas of Cusa, IV 253b
Noah (Bible), IV 425a
obedience, IV 253a, 254a, 255a, 256b, 257a, 262a
Ovid, IV 252a
Paine, IV 260b–261a
peasantry, IV 259b
philosophy, IV 253a, 255a, 256a, 261a, 261b
Plato, IV 252b
politics, IV 252b, 253b, 254b, 255a, 256a, 258b, 259b, 260a, 260b, 261b, 262a, 263a
power, IV 256b, 258b, 259b, 260b, 262a
pragmatism, III 566b
Price, IV 261a
progress, IV 263a
Protestantism, IV 253b, 254a
Pufendorf, IV 258b
Puritanism, IV 254b, 256a
radicalism, IV 253a, 256b, 258b, 262a, 262b
Rainborough, IV 256a
reason, IV 257a, 258a, 261a
rebellion, IV 253a, 260b
Reformation, IV 253b
religion, IV 254a, 254b, 255b, 256a
revolution, IV 317a
rights, III 43b–44a; IV 253b, 254a, 255b, 256a, 256b, 257b, 259a, 259b, 260b, 261a, 263b
Robespierre, IV 260a
Roman Catholic Church, IV 253b, 254a

Rome (ancient), IV 252b–253a
Rousseau, III 21a–21b; IV 252a, 259a–260a, 261a, 262a, 262b, 317a
Saint Thomas Aquinas, IV 253a
Saint-Just, IV 260a
self-determinism, IV 255b
sin, IV 253a
socialism, IV 288a
society, IV 251b–263a
Socrates, IV 252b
Sophists, IV 252b
Spinoza, IV 256b–257b
State, IV 251b–263b, 317a–317b
Stoics, IV 252a
Suárez, IV 254a
superstition, IV 261a
Switzerland, IV 259b
totalitarianism, IV 255b, 257b
trade, IV 259a
trust, IV 258b, 259a, 260b, 261a
Tucker, IV 263a
tyranny, IV 253a, 254a, 255a, 259a
U.S., IV 254b, 255a, 260b–261a, 262b–263a
utilitarianism, IV 261b, 262b
violence, IV 261a, 261b
wealth, IV 256a, 259a
will, IV 259b, 260a
William III, IV 258a
Xenophon, IV 252b
Social Darwinism
anarchy, I 70a–70b
environment, II 130b
evolution, III 646a–646b
evolutionism, II 181a
Kropotkin, II 181a
Peirce, II 181a
progress, III 646a–646b
race, III 646a
Rockefeller, II 181a
socialism, III 646b
Spencer, II 181a
Sumner, W. G., II 181a
Social Democratic Party (SPD), IV 264a–268b, 272a–273a
Erfurt Program, III 161b, 162a
liberalism, III 58b
Marxism, III 149a, 152a, 152b, 161b, 162b, 163a, 163b, 164a, 165a, 165b, 166b
revisionism, IV 264a–268b, 272a–273a
Social security, law, II 687a

Social welfare, IV 267a–284b
Aristotle, IV 285b
Armstrong, IV 280b
Arrow, IV 282b–284a
Australia, IV 282a
Austria, IV 277b, 283a
Bentham, IV 277a–277b, 278b–279a, 280a, 280b, 283a
Bergson, IV 279b, 280a, 283a, 283b
Bernoulli, IV 277a, 278a, 282a
Black, IV 282b–283a, 283b
Böhm-Bawerk, IV 283a
Borda, IV 281a–282b
cardinal utility, IV 276b, 278a, 278b, 279a, 280a, 281a
Condillac, IV 277a
Condorcet, IV 281a–282b, 283b, 284a
Dodgson, IV 282b
economics, IV 276a, 276b, 277a, 279a, 279b, 281a, 283a
Edgeworth, IV 279a, 283a
Enlightenment, IV 277a
epistemology, IV 277a, 278a
equality, IV 279a
Fisher, Irving, IV 277b
Fleming, IV 280a, 280b
France, IV 277b
Galiani, IV 277a
games, IV 278b, 283a
Germany, IV 277b
Gossen, IV 277b
Great Britain, IV 277b, 282a
Harsanyi, IV 280b
hedonism, IV 277b
history, IV 276b
Hobbes, IV 276b
Hotelling, IV 283a
Jevons, IV 277b
justice, IV 279a, 280a–280b
Kant, IV 280a
Laplace, IV 282a
law, IV 276b, 279a
marginal utility, IV 277a, 277b, 278a, 279a, 283a
Marshall, IV 283a
May, IV 284a
Menger, IV 277b, 283a
Mill, IV 278b, 279a
Morgenstern, IV 278b, 280a, 280b, 283a
Murakami, IV 284a
Nature, IV 277b
neo-positivism, IV 278a
Neumann, IV 278b, 280a, 280b, 283a

opportunity set, IV 276a, 276b
optimism, IV 277a
ordinal utility, IV 276b, 278a, 279a–280a, 281a, 281b
pain, IV 277b
paradox of voting, IV 281b
Pareto, IV 277b, 279a–280a, 283a
philanthropy, III 492a, 492b
pleasure, IV 277b
poverty, IV 279b
private property, III 653a, 654b
probability, IV 277a, 281a, 282a
progress, III 648a
psychology, IV 26a
Ramsey, IV 278b
rationalism, IV 277a
Rawls, IV 280b
romanticism, IV 277b
Schumpeter, IV 283a
Sen, IV 283b
Sidgwick, IV 279a
Smith, Adam, IV 277a, 277b
socialism, IV 285b
society, IV 276b, 277b, 278b, 280a, 280b, 283b
State, IV 279b, 280a
suffrage, IV 280b–284a
taxation, IV 279a, 283a
technology, IV 276a
Todhunter, IV 282a, 282b
Turgot, IV 277a
U.S., IV 277b, 282a
utilitarianism, IV 278b–280a
utility, IV 277a–280b
utility function, IV 276b, 280a
Vickrey, IV 280a, 280b
Walras, IV 277b
wealth, IV 276a, 277b, 279a, 279b
women, IV 529a
Socialism, IV 284b–294b
absolutism, IV 291b
alienation, III 168b
Anabaptists, IV 287a
anarchy, I 72a–72b; IV 290a
Antichrist, IV 286b
anti-industrialism, III 676a
apocalypse, IV 286a, 288a, 293b
aristocracy, IV 289b
Aristotle, IV 285b, 292b
asceticism, IV 286b
atheism, IV 291a
Babeuf, IV 288b
Bacon, IV 287b–288a

Bakunin, IV 293a
Bauer, IV 291a
Bernstein, I 664b; III 162b, 163a–163b, 164a, 164b
Bible, IV 286a, 287a, 291a
Blanc, IV 289b–290a
Blanqui, IV 293a
Boas, George, IV 285a–285b
Bonnot de Mably, IV 288b
bourgeois, IV 291b, 292a, 293a
bureaucracy, IV 293b
Burma, III 338a
Campanella, IV 287b–288a
capitalism, I 666a; III 148b; IV 292a, 292b, 293b
Cathars, IV 286b
chaos, IV 285a
China, III 154a
Christianity, III 670b, 674b; IV 285a, 286a–287b, 290a–290b, 291a
Cicero, IV 286a
class, III 673b; IV 285a, 286a, 286b, 288a, 288b, 291b, 292a, 292b, 293b
Cole, IV 289a
commerce, IV 286b, 287b, 290a
communism, III 673b; IV 285b
community, IV 285a, 287b, 289b, 294a
compromises, III 673b
Condorcet, IV 288b
conservatism, I 483b
Copernicus, IV 293b
cosmic images, I 520a
cosmos, IV 286b
Creation, IV 287b
Cynics, IV 285b
Czechoslovakia, IV 287a
Daniel (Bible), IV 287a
Darwinism, IV 293b
decline of, III 673b
democracy, I 664b, 666a; III 155b; IV 285b, 291b, 293b, 294a
despotism, II 17a
determinism, II 30b
discipline, IV 286b
discovery, IV 293b
dualism, IV 291a
economic history, II 59b–60b
economics, III 673b; IV 286b–292b
Enfantin, IV 290a
Engels, II 452a, 454b; III 154a, 155b; IV 292a, 293a
Enlightenment, IV 285a, 288a–288b, 290b
environment, IV 289b

equality, II 143a, 145b–146a, 147a; IV 285a, 285b, 288a, 288b, 293b, 294a
eschatology, II 159b
ethics, III 445a; IV 287a, 287b, 290b, 291b
evolution, III 646b, 673b; IV 286b, 293b, 294a
evolutionism, II 181a
existentialism, III 158a–160a
Fabianism, I 664b
faith, IV 286b, 290b
festivals, IV 286a
Feuerbach, IV 291a
Fourier, IV 289b, 290a, 293a, 293b
France, III 165a; IV 272a, 273b, 274a, 285a, 288a–289a, 291b, 292a, 293b
Franciscans, IV 286b, 287a
Frederick, II, IV 286b
Free Spirits, IV 286b
freedom, IV 289a, 290b, 291a, 292a
French Revolution (1789), III 671b; IV 288a, 288b, 293b
friendship, IV 285b
Fromm, III 158a
general will, II 278b, 280b
Germany, III 651b, 676b; IV 264a, 264b, 266a, 266b–267a, 267b, 269b, 270b, 271b, 272a–272b, 273b, 274a, 274b, 290a, 292a, 510a
God, IV 285a–285b, 286a, 287a, 288a, 290b, 291a
Golden Age (myth), IV 285a–285b
good, IV 181a, 291b
Gray, IV 292b
Great Britain, III 165a, 674b; IV 287a, 287b–288a, 289b, 290a, 293a, 510b–512a, 513b
Greece (ancient), IV 285a–286a
Grün, IV 290a
harmony, IV 285a
Harrington, IV 288a
Harvey, IV 293b
heaven, IV 291a
Hegel, I 74a; II 415a; IV 290a–292a
Hegelianism, IV 290b–292a
Hess, IV 290a, 291b
hierarchy, IV 285a, 286b, 287a, 293b
history, IV 285a, 290a, 290b, 293b, 294a
Hodgskin, IV 292b
human nature, IV 285b,

289b, 291a
humanism, IV 292a, 294a
Hussites, IV 287a
idea, IV 290b
ideal, IV 285a, 285b
ideology, III 673b; IV 291b
Incarnation, IV 286b
income, II 146a
individualism, II 595a–596b, 598a–599b, 600b, 601a, 602b, 603b; IV 285a, 287b, 288a, 289a, 290b, 291a
industry, IV 289a, 289b–290a, 293a–293b, 294a
inequality, IV 284b–285a, 285b, 286b, 287b, 288a, 289a–289b, 293b
injustice, IV 286b
institutional, III 675a
internationalism, IV 293b
Italy, III 165a
Jacobins, IV 288b
Jaucourt, IV 288a
Jesus Christ, IV 286a, 287a, 287b, 290b, 291a
Joachim of Floris, IV 286b, 287a, 290a
Judaism, IV 290b
judgment, IV 286b
justice, III 671a; IV 285b
Kant, IV 290b
Kingsley, IV 290a
labor, III 675b; IV 289a–289b, 291b, 292a, 292b
Lasalle, IV 293a
Latin America, III 336a–336b
law, IV 285b, 287a, 288a, 289a, 290b, 291a, 292a
Left, IV 291a
Lenin, I 372a; III 153b–154a; IV 293a
Leroux, IV 290a
liberalism, III 51b, 57b, 58a, 58b, 673b; IV 293b, 294a
liberty, IV 288a, 289a
Linguet, IV 288b
Linnaeus, IV 293b
Locke, IV 288a, 292b
Lovejoy, IV 285a–285b
loyalty, III 114a
Luther, IV 287a
Luxemburg, III 162b
Maréchal, IV 288b
Marx, II 17a, 450a, 450b, 451a, 451b; III 154a, 155b, 158a, 673b; IV 285a, 289b, 290a–294a
Marxism, II 559a; III 147b, 149b, 152a–160a, 162b–169b, 645b, 654a, 671a; IV 181a, 290b, 292b
materialism, II 450a, 451a,

451b, 452a, 454b
Maurice, IV 290a
Meslier, IV 288b
Middle Ages, IV 286b
millenarianism, IV 285a, 286a, 286b, 287a, 293b, 294a
mind, IV 290b
miners, III 676b
Montanism, IV 286b
Montesquieu, IV 288a
morality, IV 284b–286a, 287b, 289a–289b
More, Thomas, IV 287b
Müntzer, IV 287a, 287b
mutualism, IV 290a
mysticism, IV 287b
mythology, IV 285a, 291a, 294a
nationalism, III 325a, 327b, 330a, 331b, 332a–338a; IV 293b
natural law, III 22a, 23a; IV 288a
natural liberty, II 69a–70a
Nature, IV 285b
Newton, IV 290a, 293b
obedience, IV 286b
order, IV 285a
organization, III 673b
overproduction, IV 289b, 292b
Owen, IV 288b, 289b, 293a
pacifism, IV 287b
papacy, IV 286b
patience, IV 286a–286b
peace, III 445a; IV 285a
peasantry, IV 287a
Pecqueur, IV 290a
perfectibility, IV 285a, 285b, 286b
periodization in history, III 478b
philosophy, IV 290b
Physiocrats, IV 288a
piety, IV 287b
Plato, IV 285b
Platonism, III 520b
poetry, IV 285a
politics, III 671a, 673b; IV 289a, 291a, 291b, 293a
positivism, III 534b
poverty, IV 288a, 289a, 289b, 293a
pragmatism, III 563a, 564b
predestination, II 30b; IV 287b
primitivism, IV 285a
private property, III 651a, 653a–654b; IV 285a, 285b, 287b–289b, 292a, 292b, 293b

415

production, **IV** 289b, 291a, 292a, 292b, 293a
profit, **IV** 292b
progress, **III** 645b, 646b, 647a, 671a, 673b; **IV** 289a
proletariat, **III** 673b; **IV** 291b, 292a, 292b, 293a
prophecy, **IV** 286b–287a, 288a, 293b, 294a
protest movements, **III** 670a, 670b–676b
Protestantism, **IV** 285a, 287a–287b
Proudhon, **II** 280b; **IV** 289b, 290a, 293a
psychology, **IV** 25b
Puritanism, **IV** 287b
Quesnay, **IV** 292b
quietism, **IV** 287a
radicalism, **III** 673a, 673b
rationalism, **III** 673b; **IV** 286a
Raynal, **IV** 288a–288b
realism in literature, **IV** 55a–55b
reason, **IV** 285b
rebellion, **III** 673b
redemption, **IV** 287b
reform, **III** 673b
Reformation, **IV** 285a, 287a–287b
religion, **III** 675a
revolution, **III** 645b, 673b; **IV** 160a, 161a, 162a, 163a, 163b, 164b, 165a, 166b, 285a–293b, 294a
Ricardo, **IV** 292b
Right, **IV** 291a
rights, **IV** 289a
Rodrigues, **IV** 290a
Roman Catholic Church, **IV** 286a–287a
romanticism, **IV** 202b, 203a, 205a, 206a, 206b
Rome (ancient), **IV** 285b, 286a
Rousseau, **IV** 288a, 289b
Russia, **III** 154a, 156b; **IV** 293a
Russian Revolution (October 1917), **IV** 164b
Saint Ambrose, **IV** 286a
Saint Augustine, **IV** 286b
Saint Cyprian, **IV** 286a
Saint Luke, **IV** 286a
Saint Paul, **IV** 286a
Saint Zeno of Verona, **IV** 286a
Saint-Simon, **III** 534b; **IV** 288b, 289b, 290a, 293a, 293b
Saturnalia, **IV** 286a
Say, **IV** 292b

science, **II** 452a; **IV** 289b, 291b, 293b, 294a
self-determination, **IV** 291b
Seneca, **IV** 286a
sin, **IV** 286b
Sismondi, **IV** 289b, 292b
skepticism, **IV** 288b
slavery, **IV** 286a
Smith, Adam, **IV** 292b
social contract, **IV** 288a
Social Darwinism, **III** 646b
social welfare, **IV** 285b
Socrates, **IV** 285b
Sorel, **III** 564b
soul, **IV** 286a, 286b
Stalin, **II** 562b–563a; **III** 155a, 156b
State, **IV** 285b, 288a, 289a–291b, 293b, 316b–317a
Stein, Lorenz von, **IV** 291b
Stirner, **IV** 291a
Stoicism, **IV** 285b–286a, 288a
Strauss, **IV** 291a
symbolism, **IV** 339a–339b
Taborites, **IV** 287a
technology, **IV** 292b
textile workers, **III** 676b
theology, **II** 30b; **IV** 285a, 287b, 290b, 291a
totalitarianism, **IV** 407b
Trotsky, **III** 153b–154a
unemployment, **IV** 292b
U.S.S.R., **II** 561b; **III** 152b, 153b, 155a
U.S., **IV** 289b
universality, **IV** 285b
Utopia, **IV** 463a, 463b
utopianism, **III** 671a; **IV** 285a, 287b–288a, 289b, 294a
value, **IV** 292b
Voltaire, **IV** 288a
wages, **IV** 292b, 293a
Waldenses, **IV** 286b
war, **III** 445a; **IV** 502b, 504b, 505a, 507a
wealth, **IV** 288a–289b
Weber, **IV** 287b
welfare state, **IV** 510a, 510b–512a, 513b, 515a
Winstanley, **IV** 287a, 287b
work, **IV** 285a, 287b, 291b, 293a, 534b
Wycliffe, **IV** 287a
Société d'Individualistes, **II** 594b
Sociétés Joyeuses, **IV** 516b
Society
acquired characteristics, **II** 619b–620a, 621b–622a
Aeschylus, **III** 625b
Alembert, **II** 99b
anarchy, **III** 470a, 470b–

471a, 673b
Argentina, **III** 543b
Aristotle, **III** 20b, 629b
Baader, **IV** 207b
Bacon, **IV** 361b, 462a
Bakunin, **III** 471a
Bernstein, **III** 161b, 162a
biology, **II** 619b
Bonald, **III** 22a
Brazil, **III** 540a, 542b
Byron, **IV** 204a
capitalism, **III** 148a
Christianity, **III** 670b, 671a
class, **III** 150b
coercion, **III** 3a
common law, **II** 692b, 693a, 696a; **III** 32a
communism, **III** 646a
Comte, **III** 22a, 640a, 641b–643a, 644a, 644b
Condillac, **II** 669a
Counter-Enlightenment, **II** 101a, 102a, 102b–103a, 105a, 110a, 111a–112a
culture, **I** 609b–610b, 612a, 612b, 615b–616a, 616b, 620a, 620b; **IV** 165a, 165b
cynicism, **III** 585b
determinism, **II** 22b–23b, 25a, 30a–31a
Dewey, **III** 556b, 564a
Diderot, **III** 644b
dignity, **IV** 136a, 141a, 142a
Djilas, **III** 154b
economic history, **II** 44a–44b, 53a, 53b–54b
education, **II** 82a, 83a
Einstein, **III** 446b
Engels, **II** 452a, 452b, 454b
Enlightenment, **II** 90a–90b, 91a, 92a, 93b, 99a–100a
Epicurus, **III** 468b
equality, **II** 138b, 141a–141b, 145a, 146a–146b
equity, **II** 149a
ethics, **III** 440a, 440b, 442a, 442b, 443a, 443b, 445b, 446b, 447a; **IV** 70b, 71a, 72a, 72b, 320a, 320b, 322a
evil, **III** 147a
evolution, **II** 454a; **III** 153b, 566b, 646b–647a; **IV** 180b–181a
evolution of literature, **II** 171b
existentialism, **III** 157b, 158b, 159b, 160a
faith, hope and charity, **II** 212b, 213a
fascism, **III** 674a
Ferguson, **II** 99b
Fichte, **III** 473a

Fourier, **III** 22a
free will, **II** 242b
freedom, **II** 249a, 249b; **III** 475a
freedom of speech, **II** 252a, 252b, 253a, 253b, 261a
French Revolution (1789), **IV** 156a
Freud, **III** 312a–312b; **IV** 96b
game theory, **II** 264a, 266b, 267a, 268a–272a, 274a, 274b
general will, **II** 276a–281a
genetics, **II** 619b–620a
Germany, **II** 692b, 693a
God, **II** 341a, 351b–353a, 355b, 356a
good, **IV** 173a, 174a–175b, 177a–179a, 180a, 180b, 181b
Gothic, **II** 367a, 369b
Greece (ancient), **I** 60a–61b; 487a; **II** 674a–675b, 676a, 677b–679a, 680b, 681a, 682a, 683a–683b, 684b, 685a; **III** 353a; **IV** 252b, 366b
Grotius, **III** 19b–20a
happiness, **II** 374b, 379b–380a, 381b, 383b, 386a
harmony, **II** 389a
health, **II** 396a, 403a, 403b, 406b
Hegel, **I** 615b–616a; **II** 408b, 409a–409b, 414a, 452b; **III** 556b; **IV** 180a, 290b, 291b
Herder, **III** 473a
heresy, **II** 416b, 424b, 425b
hierarchy, **II** 442a
historiography, **II** 22b–23b, 25a; **IV** 147b, 148a
history, **II** 22b–23b, 25a
Hobbes, **II** 62a; **III** 20b; **IV** 177b, 256b, 316a
holy, **II** 512b
Hook, S., **III** 564a
human nature, **III** 572b, 574b–575b, 644a
humanism, **II** 522a; **IV** 131b, 133a, 135a
Hume, **II** 99a; **IV** 261b
impressionism, **II** 577a, 581b, 583a
individualism, **II** 597a, 599a, 599b–601b
international peace, **III** 451b, 453a
intolerance, **IV** 114a
Judaism, **IV** 114a
justice, **II** 659a; **III** 475a

Kant, I 616a; III 555b, 639b, 640b

language, II 669a

Latin America, III 539b, 542b

law, II 249a, 249b, 674a–675b, 676a, 677b–679a, 680b, 681a, 682a, 683a–683b, 684b, 685a, 687b, 688a; III 1a, 1b, 2a, 3a, 3b, 4a, 5a–5b, 6b, 10b, 11a–11b, 28b, 29a, 29b, 30b, 32a, 35a, 567b

Lévi–Strauss, IV 325b

liberalism, III 39a–39b, 43b, 47a–47b, 56a

linguistics, IV 426a

Locke, II 62a; III 21a; IV 21a, 154a, 258a, 258b

Lovejoy, III 552b

loyalty, III 108b, 110b, 112a

Lucretius, III 631b

Machiavellism, III 116b–125a

Maistre, III 22a

Marx, II 25a, 450b–453a, 454a; III 159a, 159b, 162a, 473b; IV 161a–162a, 290a–292a, 534a, 534b

Marxism, III 146b–170a, 645b, 646a, 654a; IV 180b–181a

materialism, II 450b–454b

Mead, G. H., III 564a

Mesopotamia (ancient), IV 226b

Middle Ages, IV 153a

Mill, J. S., III 642b; IV 179a

millenarianism, III 224a–225a

Montesquieu, III 21a, 640a

morality, III 644b, 645a

More, Thomas, IV 461a

music, II 389a; III 266a, 271b

mythology, III 272b, 275b, 276a, 280b, 289b, 302a, 304b, 307a, 307b, 309b, 310b, 312a–312b, 313b, 314b, 315a

nationalism, III 324a, 325b, 327a, 327b, 328a, 330a, 331b, 333a, 334b, 338b

natural law, III 14b, 16b, 19a–20a, 20b, 21a, 22a, 22b, 23a, 24b, 25a–26b

natural liberty, II 61b–71a

Nature, I 68a; III 346b, 347b, 348a

necessity, III 352a, 353a, 353b, 356a, 358b, 359b, 360a, 360b, 362a

Neo-Platonism, III 373b

norms, II 677b–678b

obligation, III 3a, 22b

Orientalism, III 428a, 428b, 429b, 434a

Paine, IV 260b

pangenesis, II 626a

peace, III 440a, 440b, 442a, 442b, 443a, 443b, 445b, 446b, 447a

perfectibility, III 465a, 467b, 468b, 469a, 470a, 470b–471a, 472a–472b, 473a, 473b, 474b–475a, 644a

periodization in history, III 477b, 478a, 480b

philanthropy, III 486b, 487b, 488b, 489b, 490a, 491a

Physiocrats, II 62a–62b

Plato, I 654a; II 149a; III 354a, 497a, 629a, 629b; IV 175a

Platonism, III 497a, 503b

pluralism, IV 316a

poetics, III 528b, 531a

politics, III 116a–125a

positivism, III 532b–540a, 542b, 543b

pragmatism, III 552a, 552b, 553a, 555b, 556b, 564a, 564b, 566a, 566b, 567b, 569a, 569b

Priestley, III 472a

primitivism, III 580b, 585a, 593a, 595b, 597b, 598a, 600a, 600b, 602b

private property, III 650b–655b, 656b

progress, III 624a–624b, 625b, 627a, 628b, 629a, 629b, 631a–631b, 634a, 636b, 637a, 638a–648b

prophecy, III 658b, 661b, 662a, 669a

Protagoras, III 575b, 627a

protest movements, III 670b, 671a, 672b–676b

Protestantism, III 23a

Proudhon, II 280b, III 22a, 470b–471a

psychology, IV 14a, 15b, 17b, 19a, 20b, 21a, 25b, 27a, 27b, 29a

Pufendorf, III 20a

radicalism, III 673a

rationalism, IV 46a, 46b, 48b

realism in literature, IV 55b

reformation, IV 60b–61a, 63a, 63b, 68a–69b

Reformation, IV 68a

relativism, IV 70b, 71a, 72a, 72b

religion, IV 93b, 96b, 97a, 97b, 99a, 105a, 112b, 114a–115b, 117b, 120b

Renaissance, IV 123b, 124b, 126b, 127a, 128a, 131b, 133a, 135a, 136a, 141a, 142a, 147b, 148a, 437a, 437b, 438a, 439a, 439b, 441a–443a

revolution, IV 152b–166b

Ricardo, II 453a

romanticism, IV 199b, 200a, 202b, 203a, 203b, 204a, 205b, 206a, 207b

Rome (ancient), II 687b, 688a; III 373a, 373b, 651b, 652a; IV 252b

Rousseau, II 99b, 276b–277b, 669a; III 600a; IV 259a, 260a

rules, III 5b

Russian Revolution (October 1917), IV 163b

Saint Augustine, IV 63a

Saint Thomas Aquinas, III 11a, 19a

Saint-Simon, III 22a, 641a

satire, IV 212a–214b

skepticism, IV 241b, 246b, 250a

Smith, II 62a, 62b–66a, 99a–99b, 453a

social welfare, IV 276b, 277b, 278b, 280a, 280b, 283b

socialism, IV 284b–286b, 288a–290b, 291b, 292a, 293b

Spencer, III 637a, 643a; IV 180b

State, IV 312b, 313a, 316a, 316b

Stewart, II 99b

Stoicism, IV 320a, 320b, 322a

structuralism, IV 325a, 325b

syndicalism, III 673b

Taine, II 171b

technology, IV 357b–358a, 358b, 361a–362a, 364a

temperance, IV 366a, 366b, 368b, 378a

theodicy, 379b, 383a

theriophily, IV 385a, 387a

Tolstoy, III 445b, 446a

totalitarianism, IV 406b–410b

tribal, II 252b

Trotsky, III 473b

uniformitarianism, IV 426a

U.S.S.R., III 154b, 155a, 653b

U.S., III 428a, 428b, 439a

universal man, IV 437a, 437b, 438a, 439a, 439b,

441a–443a

utilitarianism, IV 444b, 445b, 446a, 447b

utility, IV 452a–453b

Utopia, IV 458b, 459a, 459b, 461a, 461b, 462a, 463a, 463b, 464a

Victorian sentiment, IV 217a–219a, 220a, 222a, 222b, 223b

virtue, IV 484b

Volksgeist, IV 491b, 495b–496a

Voltaire, IV 288a

vox populi, IV 496b–500a

war, III 445b; IV 500b, 501b, 502a, 503b, 504a, 504b, 506a, 507a

welfare state, IV 509a–510b, 512a–515a

Wells, H. G., II 621b

Whitney, Lois, II 99a

wisdom of the fool, IV 515b, 516a–516b, 518a

witchcraft, IV 521a

women, IV 523a–529b

work, IV 530a, 530b, 532b, 533a, 534a, 534b, 535a

Zeitgeist, IV 535b, 536a, 536b

See also Social Contract

Society of Friends, see Quakers

Society of Jesus, see Jesuits

Socinians

deism, I 648a

Poland, I 398a–398b

Sociology

acquired characteristics, II 620a, 621a, 622a

Argentina, III 543b

authority, I 156b–158b

beauty, I 212a, 213a–213b

Bonald, III 534a

Buddhism, I 256a

Comte, III 534a, 534b, 535a, 535b, 536a, 538a

Counter-Enlightenment, II 106b

culture, I 619a

Enlightenment, II 98b

ethics, III 445a, 445b, 446a, 447a, 447b; IV 72a

existentialism, III 158a, 158b, 160b

Fichte, IV 209b

game theory, II 272b

genius in art, II 297a

Great Britain, III 537a

happiness, II 374b, 383a, 385a–385b

historiography, II 475a,

497a–498a, 499a, 504b, 510b
humanism, II 521b–522a
ideology, II 554a–558a
individualism, II 297a
international peace, III 453a, 454b
intolerance, IV 116a
Kant, III 443b
law, III 3b, 4b, 5a, 27a
liberalism, III 37a, 40a, 46b, 47a, 48a, 49a, 50a, 52a, 53a, 56b, 58b, 60a
literary paradox, III 78b
longevity, III 89a
love, III 95b, 97a, 97b, 103a, 104a, 104b, 105b, 106b, 107a
Man-Machine, III 134b, 143a, 146a
Marx, II 452a, 452b, 453b
Marxism, II 620a, 621a; III 149a, 158a, 158b, 160b
materialism, II 452a, 452b, 453b
mathematics, III 177a
Müller, Max, IV 207b
music, III 271b
mythology, III 274b, 311a, 313b
necessity, III 353a, 353b, 355b, 356b, 358a, 358b, 359a, 359b, 362a
numbers, III 406b
peace, III 445a–447b
perennial philosophy, III 457b
periodization in history, III 478a, 478b, 479a, 480b
periodization in literary history, III 482b, 483b, 485b
positivism, III 533a–549a
primitivism, III 597b, 598b
private property, III 654b, 655b
psychology, IV 14a, 16a, 26a, 27a, 27b, 29a
Ramism, IV 45b
relativism, IV 72a
religion, IV 96b, 116a, 117a
revolution, IV 166b
romanticism, IV 207b, 209b
scientific classification, I 465a, 466a
U.S.S.R., II 620a, 621a
war, IV 507a
work, IV 535a
Socrates (470?–399 B.C.) I 9b, 79b
analogy, I 68b
Anaxagoras and, I 671a
appearance and reality, I 94b
Aristophanes and, IV 48b

Aristotle and, III 226a–226b; IV 49a
art, III 226a
asceticism, I 632a
body, IV 3b
Church, I 417a
comedy, I 467b, 468b, 469a–469b
communism, IV 285b
creativity in art, I 578b, 581b–582a, 583b
cycles, I 623b
cynicism, I 627b, 629a, 632a, 633b; III 585a, 586a
death, I 636b, 638b, 642a; IV 415a
democracy, IV 285b
Democritus and, III 576b–577a
design argument, I 671a, 671b
dualism, II 40b
education, II 75b, 79b, 80a–80b, 81a–81b; III 496a
equality, IV 285b
ethics, III 577a; IV 49a–49b, 320b
evil, II 162b, 167b; III 496b–497a, 577a; IV 174b
Forms, III 499a; IV 436a
free will, II 242b
freedom of speech, II 258b
friendship, III 554a
genius, II 293b, 317b–318a
goals, IV 174a–175a
God, II 40b; III 577a; IV 414b
good, II 375b; III 496b–497a, 577a; IV 3b, 174b–175a, 415a, 436a
happiness, II 375b, 376a; III 576b
Hegel and, II 411a
historiography, II 502b, 503a
human nature, III 570b–571a, 576b–577a
idea, II 543a; IV 34b
ignorance, III 577a; IV 49a, 174b, 414b, 517a
immortality, I 638b, 642a; III 577a
impiety, II 565b, 566a
individualism, III 577a; IV 174a
injustice, III 577a; IV 414b
inspiration, I 583b
irony, II 627b, 628a, 628b, 629b, 630a, 631b, 632a
irrationalism, II 635b
James and, III 554a
jealousy, IV 414b
Jesus Christ and, II 411a
justice, II 659a; III 554a,

576b, 577a; IV 49a, 285b
knowledge, III 496a–497a, 499b, 504a, 577a; IV 49a, 49b, 174b, 415a
language, II 662a
law, I 632a
liberalism, III 41b–42a
limbo, I 417a
literary paradox, III 78b
literature, IV 330b
love, III 95a
loyalty, III 109b–111b
Lysias and, III 499b
mathematics, III 172a
matter, III 187a
metaphor, III 203a, 204a
methodology, III 379b
microcosm, III 126b, 127a
mimesis, III 226a, 497b
mortality, III 577a
music, II 317b–318a
mythology, III 273b, 274a
natural law, III 15a, 16a
Nature, I 632a; III 348b
necessity, III 353a, 353b
Newton and, III 379b
organicism, III 422a, 423a
painters, III 498b, 499a
painting, III 226a
Peirce and, III 554a
perfectibility, III 465b, 472a
philanthropy, III 487a
philosophers, III 498b–499a
philosophy, III 498b–499a, 577a; IV 31b
piety, III 554a
Plato and, I 578b, 581b–582a, 583b; III 226a–226b, 496a–497a, 498b–499a, 554a, 571a, 577a, 627b; IV 3b, 34a, 34b, 48b, 49a–49b, 175a, 368a, 415a
Platonism, III 496a–497a, 497b, 498b–499a, 499b, 500a, 503a, 504a, 504b, 507a, 508b, 510b, 512a, 513b, 514b, 517b, 524b
poetry, III 499b
poets, III 496a–496b
politics, II 565b, 566a; III 576b
pragmatism, III 554a, 559a
primitivism, III 585a, 586a
progress, III 626a, 627b, 628b
psychology, IV 3b, 6a, 10a, 10b
Pythagoreans, IV 31b, 34a, 34b
rationalism, IV 48b, 49a–49b

reason, III 496a
religion, III 203a–204a
rhetoric, III 379b, 496b–497a
right, III 496b; IV 49a, 174b–175a
rulers, III 498b–499a
satire, IV 212b, 215b
skepticism, III 504a; IV 234b, 235a, 239a–239b
skill, III 496b
social contract, IV 252b
socialism, IV 285b
Sophists, III 379b
soul, III 497a, 577a; IV 3b, 174b, 415a
Stoicism, IV 320b
style, IV 330b
symmetry, IV 347b
teaching, II 80a–80b
temperance, III 576b; IV 368a, 377a
theriophily, IV 385b
time, III 391a
tradition, IV 48b
tragic sense, IV 414b–415a
truth, III 496a, 499b
tyranny, II 376a
unity of science, IV 436a
universality, IV 34b
virtue, II 80b; III 508b, 577a; IV 49a, 174b, 414b, 415b
wisdom, III 577a; IV 174b, 517a
wisdom of the fool, IV 517a, 517b
wrong, III 496b; IV 49a
Xenophon and, III 577a
Zeno of Citium and, IV 320b
Soden, J. H. von, Faust (legend), III 250a
Söderblom, Nathan (1866–1931), holy, II 513b
Soderini, Piero (1450–1513)
universal man, IV 442a
virtù, IV 480b, 481a
Sodre, Nelson Wernecke, nationalism, III 335b
Sohn, Louis B., international peace, III 451b
Solander, Daniel Carl (1736–1782), primitivism, III 602a, 602b
Solar mythology, III 307b–308a, 308b
Solar rays, vision, III 410a, 416a
Solar system
determinism, II 18b–19a
evolutionism, II 174b, 176a, 182a
infinity, II 608a

Islam, II 647a
relativity, IV 75a, 76a
science, II 647a
time, IV 400b, 405b
Solger, Karl Wilhelm Ferdinand (1780–1819)
irony, II 629b, 631b, 632a
symbolism, IV 338a
Solomon, King (c. 973–c. 933 B.C.)
ambiguity, I 52a
historiography, II 479a
idea, II 546a
mythology, III 275b, 277b, 281a, 282b, 283a
temperance, IV 377a
Solomov, R. I., probability, III 632a
Solon (638?–?559 B.C.)
freedom of speech, II 258a, 259a
happiness, II 375b
historiography, II 500b, 511a
human nature, III 572b, 573a
justice, III 573a
law, II 249b, 676b, 677a, 679a, 679b, 680b, 681a, 684a, 684b
loyalty, III 110a
temperance, IV 366a, 377a
vox populi, IV 497a
Solovëv, Vladimir S. (1853–1900), symbolism, IV 343a
Somadeva (fl. 11th century A.D.), classification of the sciences, I 404a
Sombart, Werner (1863–1941)
individualism, II 602a
periodization in history, III 478b
Somerset, Earl of (1577–1646), mythology, III 294b, 297a
Sommerfeld, Arnold (1868–1951), indeterminacy, II 589a
Somner, William, Gothic, II 367a
Songs
mythology, III 304a
vox populi, IV 498b–499a
Sontag, Susan, literature, III 88b
Sophism
aesthetics, II 219b
culture, I 608b, 609b
cynicism, I 628a, 629a, 630a, 631a, 632a–633b
Greece (ancient), IV 367a
imagination, III 210b

justice, II 653a–653b
literary paradox, III 79a
nomos, IV, 174b
skepticism, IV 234b, 235a
State, IV 313b
ut pictura poesis, IV 468b, 470a
Sophists
ambiguity, I 50b
argumentation, IV 49a
causation, I 271b
classification of the arts, I 457a–459a
conservatism, I 479b
Counter-Enlightenment, II 101a, 110b
creativity in art, I 578b, 582a–582b
dualism, IV 346b
education, I 629a; II 75b, 81a–81b; IV 84b
Euripides, IV 367b
free will, II 242b
freedom, I 582b, 583a
happiness, II 375b
heresy, II 427a
human nature, III 571a, 573b, 575a, 575b
impiety, II 565b
justice, II 653b
law, III 1a–1b
morality, IV 48b
Nature, III 1a
nomos, III 1a
Plato, I 578b, 582a–582b; III 77a, 496a, 496b–497a, 499a, 500a
Platonism, III 496a, 496b–497a, 499a, 500a
poetics, III 526a
pragmatism, III 554b
progress, III 625a, 626a, 626b, 627b
psychology, IV 10a
rationalism, IV 48b–49a
self-interest, III 1a
social contract, IV 252b
Socrates, III 379b
symmetry, IV 346b
temperance, IV 367a, 367b
tragic sense, IV 413b
work, IV 530b
Sophocles (496?–406 B.C.)
Antigone (myth), IV 367a
Ajax (myth), IV 367a
catharsis, I 264b, 269a
culture, I 613a
Deianeira (myth), IV 367a
dignity, IV 137b
disease, II 397b
Electra (myth), IV 367a
freedom of speech, II 259b
God, III 15a, 626b
heroes, IV 367a

human nature, III 571a, 572a, 573a, 574b–575a
idea, II 545a
irony, II 632a; IV 367a
irrationalism, II 637b
justice, II 653a; III 573a
law, II 681a–684a
loyalty, III 110a
natural law, III 15a
Oceanus (myth), IV 367a
Oedipus (myth), IV 367a
periodization in literary history, III 481b
Plato and, III 500a; IV 367a
progress, III 626a–626b, 627b, 628a
salvation, IV 229a
temperance, IV 367a
tragedy, I 264b; IV 367a
tragic sense, IV 412a–412b, 413b
wisdom of the fool, IV 519a
Sōphrosynē, see Temperance
Sorcery
disease, II 396b
God, II 333a
mythology, III 282b
witchcraft, IV 521a–522a
Sorel, Charles (1597?–1674)
classicism, I 455a
conservatism, I 483a
Sorel, Georges (1847–1922)
Bergson and, III 564b, 565b
capitalism, III 564b
cash value, III 565b
democracy, I 664b
ethics, III 564b
fascism, III 565b
ideology, II 555b
intuition, III 565b
irrationalism, II 636b
James and, III 564a, 565b
knowledge, III 565b
Le Roy and, III 565a–565b
Marxism, III 565a–566a
materialism, III 565b
Mussolini and, III 565b
mysticism, III 565b
Peirce and, III 565a
pragmatism, III 551b, 553b, 555a, 564a–566a
proletariat, III 564b
religion, III 565a, 565b
revolution, III 564a–564b, 565b; IV 163b
science, III 564b, 565b
socialism, III 564b
strikes, III 564a–564b
truth, III 565b
violence, III 555a, 564b, 565a
vitalism, III 565b
will to believe, III 565b

Sorge, Georg Andreas
difference tone, III 263b
music, III 263b
Soriano, Francesco (1549–? 1621), musical genius, II 321b
Soteriology, IV 93b, 225b, 228a, 229b
Christianity, II 343a; IV 229b, 230a
religion, IV 102a, 103b
Soto, Domingo de (fl. 1550)
motion, II 204b
thought experiments, II 204b, 205a
Soucy, Robert, pragmatism, III 565a
Soufflot, Jacques-Germain (1713–1780), neo-classicism in art, III 369b
Soul
Alexander of Aphrodisias, II 36b
animals, II 390b, 391a; III 596a
Aristotle, I 2a, 2b, 61b, 215b, 231b, 234b, 639a–639b; II 36b, 41a, 243a, 377a, 392b; IV 4b–5b, 6b, 33a, 34a, 36b, 49b, 56b, 301a
artists, II 551b
Averroës, II 32b
Avicenna, I 3b
Blasius of Parma, II 35a, 35b
Bruno, III 194a
Buddha, III 436b
Buddhism, IV 232b, 233a
Buridan, II 34a, 34b
Case, II 390b
Christianity, IV 230a
confessional, I 261a
Counter-Enlightenment, II 103b
Creation, I 571b
creativity in art, I 586a
Dante, II 233a–233b; III 511a; IV 176b–177a
death, I 634b, 635a, 637a–637b
deism, I 646b
Democritus, I 215b; II 135b; III 576b–577a
Descartes, I 639b–641a; II 381a; III 137b, 138a
determinism, II 26a, 26b, 236b
dignity, IV 137a, 138b, 140a, 140b, 143a
double truth, II 32b, 34a, 34b, 35a, 35b
dualism, II 38a, 40b–41a
Duns Scotus, II 36b

Edwards, **IV** 109b
Empedocles, **I** 215b, 622a; **III** 573a; **IV** 2b, 31b–32a
Epicureanism, **IV** 7a
Epicurus, **I** 231a, 244a; **III** 274a
equality, **II** 141a
eschatology, **II** 156a, 157b
ethics, **III** 441a
Euripides, **III** 573a
evil, **II** 162a, 163b, 164a; **IV** 414b
evolutionism, **II** 174b
Faust (legend), **III** 252a
Ficino, **II** 442a, 442b; **III** 511a
fortune, fate, and chance, **II** 226b–230a, 233a–233b, 235b
four elements, **I** 230a
free will, **II** 236b, 243a, 243b, 244b
God, **I** 571b; **II** 26a
good, **IV** 174a, 174b, 175a, 176b–177a
Greece (ancient), **II** 42a, 565b, 678a; **IV** 228b, 229a
Gregory of Nyssa, **IV** 137a
happiness, **II** 376a, 377a, 378a, 378b, 381a
harmony, **II** 388a–392b, 394a
health, **II** 397b, 398a, 400b, 401a
Heraclitus, **III** 573a
Herder, **IV** 209a, 492a
heresy, **II** 416b, 417b, 422a, 422b, 423b, 425a
Herodotus, **III** 573a
hierarchy, **II** 442a
Hinduism, **IV** 231b
human nature, **III** 572b–573a, 574a, 576b–577a
humanism, **IV** 131b–132a, 132b, 133b
idea, **II** 543a, 546a
ideal in philosophy, **II** 551b
imagination, **III** 211b, 212a
immortality, **I** 635a
impiety, **II** 565b
John of Jandun, **II** 34b
Kant, **I** 639a, 641a–641b
law, **II** 678a, 687a
love, **III** 95b, 97b, 98a, 98b, 99a, 101a, 101b, 104b, 106a, 106b, 107a, 107b
loyalty, **III** 110a, 110b, 111b, 112b
Machiavelli, **II** 235b
Man-Machine, **III** 132a–132b, 133a, 133b, 135a, 135b, 137a, 137b, 138a, 139a

mathematics, **IV** 33a, 36b
matter, **III** 191b, 194a
Matthew of Aquasparta, **I** 5a
microcosm, **III** 127a, 127b, 128b, 129a, 130a–131a
motion, **IV** 34a, 36a
music, **II** 388a–392b, 394a; **III** 268a–270a
mythology, **III** 273b, 274a, 274b, 288a, 290b, 291a, 305b, 310a
Nature, **III** 349a, 350b
Neo-Platonism, **III** 375a–376a, 376b, 377a
Neo-Pythagoreans, **III** 505a
Orientalism, **III** 436b
Parmenides, **III** 573a
peace, **III** 441a
perfectibility, **III** 464b, 465a, 466a, 469a
philanthropy, **III** 488b
Philo Judaeus, **III** 127b
Pico della Mirandola, **III** 512a
Pindar, **III** 572b
Plato, **I** 196a–196b, 234b, 637a–637b, 638b–639b, 668a, 671a, 672a, 673b; **II** 40b–41a, 236b, 243a, 243b, 390b–391b; **III** 273b, 464b, 465a, 496a, 497a, 498a, 499a, 508b, 573a; **IV** 3a, 4a, 4b, 31a, 32b, 33a, 34a, 35b, 36a, 36b, 37b, 175a, 368a, 368b
Platonism, **III** 95b, 496a, 497a, 498a, 499a, 504a, 505a, 508a, 508b, 509a, 511a, 512a, 512b–513a, 513b, 516a, 516b
pleasure, **II** 376a, 377a, 378a, 378b, 381a
Plotinus, **I** 586a; **II** 163b, 341a; **III** 375a–376a, 466a; **IV** 8b, 9a
poetry, **III** 527a
Porphyry, **III** 376b
pragmatism, **III** 567a
predestination, **II** 26a, 26b
primitivism, **III** 582a, 596a
psychology, **IV** 1b–17b, 22b
Puritanism, **IV** 16b
Pythagoras, **III** 572b–573a; **IV** 31a–32b, 34a, 36b, 37a
Pythagoreans, **IV** 31a–37b
rationalism, **IV** 49b, 50a
recapitulation, **IV** 56b
reincarnation, **I** 644b–646a; **IV** 231b
Renaissance, **IV** 131b–132a, 132b, 133b, 137a, 138b, 140a, 140b, 143a, 439a
resurrection, **I** 643b–644b

right, **IV** 174a, 174b, 175a, 176b–177a
romanticism, **IV** 197b, 209a
Rome (ancient), **II** 687a
Saint Augustine, **I** 3a, 197b; **II** 210a, 244b; **IV** 9a, 138b, 176b, 391b
Saint Thomas Aquinas, **I** 644a–644b; **II** 36b, 211a; **III** 191b
salvation, **IV** 229a
Shelley, **III** 508a
sin, **IV** 228b, 229a, 230a
skepticism, **IV** 246b
socialism, **IV** 286a, 286b
Socrates, **III** 577a; **IV** 3b, 174b, 415a
Speusippus, **IV** 35b–36a
Stoicism, **II** 378a; **IV** 50a
Stoics, **IV** 8a
Strato, **IV** 7a
symbolism, **IV** 338b
temperance, **IV** 368a
theology, **II** 26a, 26b
theriophily, **IV** 384b, 386a, 388a
time, **IV** 391b, 392a, 399b
tragic sense, **IV** 414b, 415a
transmigration, **I** 250b, 255a, 644b, 645a; **II** 243b; **III** 573a
universal man, **IV** 439a
utilitarianism, **IV** 444a
Victorian sentiment, **IV** 217b, 218b, 221a
Volksgeist, **IV** 492a, 495b–496a
vox populi, **IV** 499a
witchcraft, **IV** 522a
Wither, **II** 392a
women, **IV** 525b
World Spirit, **II** 392a–392b, 394a
Xenocrates, **IV** 36b
Xenophanes, **III** 573a
Zoroastrianism, **IV** 231b
Soul-atom, Man-Machine, **III** 132a–132b
Sound
Aristotle, **II** 389b
harmony, **II** 389b, 391b–392a, 393a
language, **II** 662b–663a, 664b, 665b–666a, 671a–671b, 672a, 672b
Macrobius, **II** 389b
music, **II** 389b, 391b–392a, 393a; **III** 260b, 262a–263a, 268a, 268b, 269a, 271a
numbers, **III** 269a
symbolism, **II** 662b
Sound law, **II** 671a–672a
Souriau, Etienne, motif, **III**

238a
South America, *see* Latin America
Southern, R. W., periodization in history, **III** 480a–480b
Southey, Robert (1774–1843), romanticism, **IV** 193a, 194a, 195a
Soutine, Chaim (1894–1944), Gothic, **II** 372b
Souverain, N., Platonism, **III** 517a
Souza, Robert de, symbolism, **IV** 340a
Sova, Antonin (1864–1928), symbolism, **IV** 343b
Sovereignty
Blackstone, **I** 659a
Bodin, **IV** 315b, 316a
democracy, **I** 656b, 657a, 659a–661a
despotism and, **II** 1a–17b
Fichte, **II** 279a
free will, **II** 242b–243a, 244b, 245a, 248b
freedom, **II** 250a–250b
general will, **II** 276b, 278a, 279a
Great Britain, **I** 659a
Hegel, **II** 16a
Hobbes, **I** 656b, 657a; **IV** 316a
international peace, **III** 452b, 453a, 456b
law, **II** 250a–250b; **III** 1b, 2b
Locke, **I** 657a
loyalty, **III** 112a–114a
Paine, **I** 659b
private property, **III** 652b
Rousseau, **I** 658a; **II** 11a–11b, 250b, 276b, 278a
the State, **I** 656b, 657a, 659a–661a; **IV** 314b, 315b, 316a, 318b
Tocqueville, **II** 17b
U.S., **I** 659a–660b
Space, **IV** 295a–307a
absolute space, **IV** 302a–303a
Aeschylus, **IV** 296a
aesthetics, **II** 223a
Alembert, **IV** 302b
Anaxagoras of Clazomenae, **IV** 297a
Anaximander of Miletus, **IV** 297a, 298a
antimatter, **IV** 297a
apeiron, **IV** 298a–298b
Apollonius, **IV** 295a
Arabic language, **IV** 296b
Archimedes, **IV** 295a, 295b
architecture, **IV** 298b
Aristotelianism, **IV** 304b

Aristotle, III 189a–189b; IV 295a, 296b, 301b, 305b
art, IV 298b, 302a
astronomy, IV 295b, 299b, 303a, 304b, 306a
atomism, IV 299a
Bergson, IV 301a
Berkeley, IV 85b, 301b
Bible, IV 296a–297a
Boccaccio, IV 301a
Bolyai, IV 302b, 304a
Bondi, IV 303b, 304a
Born, IV 302b
Bridgman, IV 304b
Bruno, IV 298a, 298b, 303b, 305a
Cantor, IV 301a, 304b
Cartesianism, IV 304a
Cézanne, IV 302a
chaos, IV 296b–297b
chora, IV 299b–300a
Cicero, IV 301a
civilization, IV 298b, 301a
Clarke, IV 295b, 302b
Clifford, IV 304a
Comte, IV 303b
consciousness, IV 301a
Copernicus, IV 295b, 300b
cosmogony, IV 299b
cosmology, I 543b, 548a, 548b, 554a–560b, 561b, 565a; IV 295a, 296b–300b, 303b, 304a, 305a–306b
cosmos, IV 297b–298a
cubism, IV 302a
Dante, IV 301a
Darwin, II 588a
de Broglie, IV 296a
de Broglie waves, IV 302a
Dedekind, IV 301a
Democritus, III 188a, 189a; IV 299a, 299b
Desargues, IV 302a
Descartes, IV 295b, 301b, 304a
Diderot, IV 302b
Doppler effect, IV 305b
dualism, IV 295b, 296a, 299a, 304a
Duns Scotus, IV 301b
Eddington, IV 297a, 305b
Einstein, I 556b, 557a–560b, 561b; II 590a, 590b; IV 80b, 88b–89a, 89b, 90a, 90b, 92a, 297b, 301b, 306a
electromagnetism, IV 302a
empiricism, III 546b, 550a
energy, IV 296b, 297a, 302a, 303a, 303b
ether, IV 301b
etymology, IV 296b, 300b
Euclid, IV 295a, 298a, 299b–300a, 302a–304a
evolution, IV 297a

extensio, IV 301a–302a
Ficino, IV 306a
fields, IV 301b–302a
fortune, II 231b
France, IV 300b–301a, 302a
galaxies, IV 303b, 305b
Galileo, IV 302a
General Theory of Relativity, IV 295b–296a, 297b, 304b
geometry, IV 295a, 295b, 301b, 302a, 302b, 303a, 304a–304b, 305a
Germany, IV 298a, 300b, 303a
Gibbs, IV 304b
God, III 195a; IV 75b, 296b, 298a, 301b, 306a
Gothic, IV 298b
gravity, IV 296a, 297b, 300b, 301b, 302a
Great Britain, IV 298a, 300b–301a, 303a, 306a
Greece (ancient), IV 295a, 296b, 297a, 297b, 298a
Halley, IV 303a
harmony, IV 300a
Helmholtz, IV 303a
Heraclitus, IV 297b
Hermes Trismegistus, IV 306a
Hesiod, IV 296b–297a
Homer, IV 297b, 300a, 300b
Hubble, IV 305b
Hubble's Law, IV 305b, 306a
Husserl, IV 305a
idea, II 547b, 548a
idealism, IV 298a
illusion, IV 302a
impressionism, III 342a
indeterminacy, II 587a, 588a, 590a, 590b
infinity, II 604b, 605a, 606a, 611a, 611b, 613b, 614a; IV 298a, 302a, 305a
Italy, IV 300b–301a
Jacobi, IV 302b
James, William, IV 303a
John Philoponus, IV 298a
Judaism, IV 296a, 296b
Kant, II 547b, 548a; IV 295a, 298a, 303a, 305a
kenon (void), IV 298b, 299a
Kepler, IV 302a, 306a
kinesis, IV 301a
knowledge, IV 300a
Lagrange, IV 302b, 304a
Lambert, IV 303b
Latin language, IV 296a, 300b, 301b
Leibniz, IV 295b, 297b, 298a, 301b, 302b, 305a,

305b
Lemaitre, IV 305b
Leucippus, IV 299a, 299b
linguistics, IV 428b
Lobachevsky, IV 302b, 304a
Locke, IV 295a, 303a
logic, III 546b, 550a; IV 295a, 304b–305b
Mach, IV 302b
makom, IV 296a–296b
mathematics, IV 295a, 295b, 296a, 297a, 299b, 300a, 300b, 301a, 301b, 303a, 303b, 304b
matter, III 185b, 187b, 188a, 188b, 189a–189b, 194b–195a, 196a; IV 296a, 296b, 297a, 298a, 301b, 302a
Maxwell, IV 301b
mechanism, IV 295b, 299b, 300a, 302a, 302b, 304b
Melissus of Samos, IV 305a
metaphor, III 199a
metaphysics, IV 295a, 295b, 297b, 299a, 302b, 304a, 305a, 305b
Middle Ages, IV 298b, 301b
Milne, IV 298b, 303b, 306a
Monge, IV 304a
More, Henry, IV 298a
mythology, IV 296b
naturalism in art, III 340a, 342b
Nature, IV 301a, 304b
Neo-Hegelianism, IV 305a
Newton, I 517b–518a, 520b, 554a–554b, 555a, 557a, 674b; III 194b–195a, 557a; IV 75b, 76a, 77a, 86a, 295a, 299b, 300a, 300b, 302a–303a
Nicholas of Cusa, IV 295b, 300a–300b, 306a
night-sky, IV 303a–304a
non-being, IV 298b–299b
Olbers, I 555b–556a; IV 303a
Olbers paradox, IV 303b
ontology, IV 299a, 305a
order, IV 297b
ouranos, IV 300b
Ovid, IV 297a
painting, IV 302a, 465b, 466a, 468b, 471a, 474a, 475a, 475b
Parmenides, IV 296a, 296b, 298b–299a, 305a
Pascal, IV 302a
penetrability, III 187b

perception, IV 301b, 303a
perspective, IV 302a
philosophy, III 199a; IV 295a–299a, 301b, 303a–305b, 306a
physics, IV 295a, 295b, 298b–305b
physiology, IV 303a
planets, IV 299b, 300b, 304a
Plato, III 188a, 188b, 189a; IV 295a, 296b, 297a, 299b
Plotinus, IV 296b
poetry, IV 300b, 471a
Poncelet, IV 304a
pragmatism, III 553a, 557a
probability, IV 304b
psychology, IV 295a, 303a
Ptolemy, IV 295a–295b
Pythagoras, IV 399b–400a
Pythagoreans, IV 298b
quantum mechanics, IV 300a, 304b
quantum theory, IV 296a, 300a
radiation, IV 303a–304a
red-shift, IV 305b
relativity, IV 74b, 75b, 76a, 77a, 80b, 83b–92a, 295b–297b, 298b, 300a, 300b
Renaissance, IV 300b, 305a, 306a
Riemann, IV 302b–303a, 304a–304b
rotating, IV 75b
Russell, IV 304a
sculpture, III 342b
set theory, IV 304b
Spain, IV 300b–301a
Spengler, IV 298a–298b
Spinoza, IV 298a, 301b
Stallo, IV 304a, 304b
statistics, IV 304b
sublime in external nature, IV 336a, 336b
Switzerland, IV 303a
symmetry, IV 346b, 351a–351b, 352a, 352b, 353a
technology, IV 359b
Thales, IV 295b, 298a
theology, IV 295a, 302b
time, IV 301a, 303b, 389a, 389b, 393a, 394b, 397a–397b, 400a, 403b
to pan, IV 300a–300b
topos, IV 299b–300a, 300b, 301b
truth, IV 305a
uniformitarianism, IV 417b, 428b
U.S., IV 305b
unity, IV 300a
universe, IV 295a–306b
void, IV 298a, 298b, 299a

421

Wittgenstein, **IV** 304b–305a

Wright, **I** 519a

Zeno of Citium, **IV** 301a

Spain

academic freedom, **I** 10a

aesthetics, **II** 216a; **IV** 354b

anarchy, **III** 674a, 676b

architecture, **I** 398b

balance of power, **I** 181a, 181b, 182b, 183a

baroque in literature, **I** 188b–191a, 192a, 193b, 194a, 195a

capitalism, **I** 396a

cave art, **I** 351a

Christianity, **III** 674b

classicism, **I** 451b

classification of the sciences, **I** 463b

conquistadores, **III** 601b

cosmic voyages, **I** 525a

Council of Basel (1431–1449), **II** 369b

Counter-Reformation, **I** 392b–395a

crisis in history, **I** 593b, 595a

culture, **III** 539b, 544b

determinism, **II** 22a

drama, **III** 531a, 601b

genius, **II** 293b–294a

Golden Age, **III** 482a

Gothic, **II** 367a, 368b, 369b–370a, 372b

historiography, **II** 22a

humanism, **II** 520b; **IV** 131a

ideal, **II** 549a

imperialism, **III** 539b

impressionism, **II** 577b

injustice, **III** 674b

Inquisition, **I** 393b; **IV** 117a

intolerance, **IV** 113a, 117a, 120b

Islam, **II** 651a

Jesuits expelled, **I** 403b

language, **II** 669b

law, **II** 690a; **III** 30b

literary criticism, **I** 596a, 596b

literature, **III** 601a–601b

love, **III** 99b

Machiavellism, **III** 117a

medieval sciences, **II** 204a–204b

Mexico, **III** 601a

Mohammedanism, **I** 393a

Moors, **I** 393a, 463b

mythology, **III** 287b

nationalism, **III** 319a, 319b, 320b, 335b, 336a

peasantry, **III** 674b

perfectibility, **III** 467b

periodization in literary history, **III** 482a

Peru, **III** 601a

poetry, **III** 529b, 531a

primitivism, **III** 597a, 601a–601b

protest movements, **III** 674a, 674b, 676b

Protestantism, **IV** 113a

Quietism, **I** 595a

realism in literature, **IV** 54a

Reformation, **I** 394b, 395b

religion, **IV** 113a, 117a, 120b

Renaissance, **I** 393a; **IV** 123b, 124a, 131a

revolution, **IV** 154a, 164a

riots, **III** 674b

Roman Catholic Church, **III** 539b, 674b

romanticism, **IV** 188a–189b, 191a, 194b

space, **IV** 300b–301a

symbolism, **IV** 341a, 342a–342b, 343b, 344b

syndicalism, **III** 674a

taste, **IV** 354b

technology, **IV** 360b

totalitarianism, **IV** 409b

universal man, **IV** 442a, 442b, 443a

Visigoths, **I** 379a

vox populi, **IV** 500a

witchcraft, **IV** 522b

Spalding, D. A.

imprinting, **II** 584b, 585a

learning, **II** 584b, 585a

Spalding, Johann, deism, **I** 651a

Spallanzani, Lazaro (1729–1799)

evolutionism, **II** 178a

genetic continuity, **II** 283a

spontaneous generation, **II** 283a; **IV** 310b

Spanheim, Ezechiel von (1629–1710), mythology, **III** 302b

Spanish Civil War

anarchism, **I** 75a–75b

communism, **I** 75a–75b

Spann, Othmar (1878–1950)

economic history, **II** 60b

Müller and, **IV** 207b

romanticism, **IV** 207b

Sparshott, F. E., literary criticism, **I** 603a

Sparta (ancient)

assemblies, **II** 256b, 257a, 258a

balance of power, **I** 180a

constitutions, **II** 254a

freedom of speech, **II** 254a,

256b, 257a, 257b

general will, **II** 276a, 279a

law, **II** 679b, 680a

Nature, **III** 348b

Utopia, **IV** 460a

Spataro, Giovanni, musical genius, **II** 316b, 318a

Spate, O. H. K., environment, **II** 131b

Spear, R. E., iconography, **II** 534b

Species

acquired characteristics, **II** 617a–622b

Agassiz, **II** 179b

Aristotle, **I** 232b–233a, 463a; **IV** 175a

Baer, **II** 179b

Buffon, **II** 177a

Butler, **II** 185b

Chain of Being, **I** 330b–333b

Comte, **III** 640b

Cuvier, **II** 179b

Darwin, Charles, **II** 180a

Darwin, Erasmus, **II** 179a

Diderot, **II** 177b–178a, 618a

diversification of, **II** 177a

evolutionism, **II** 174b, 175b, 177a–180a, 182a

fossils, **II** 618a, 660b

genetic continuity, **II** 281b, 282a, 285b

ideal, **II** 551b

inheritance, **II** 618a, 618b, 626a

Kant, **I** 330b–331a; **II** 551b

Lamarck, **II** 179a, 618a

language, **II** 660b, 669a, 669b

linguistics, **IV** 424b, 428a

Linnaeus, **I** 332a

matter, **III** 191a, 192b–193a

Maupertuis, **II** 177a–177b

Mendel, **II** 618b

Neo-Platonism, **I** 233a

pangenesis, **II** 626a

progress, **III** 640b

recapitulation, **IV** 58a

right and good, **IV** 175a, 182a

Saint Thomas Aquinas, **I** 574a

Saint-Simon, **III** 640b

Spencer, **II** 182a

spontaneous generation, **IV** 307a–308b, 311b

Stoics, **I** 233a

transmutation, **II** 180a

uniformitarianism, **IV** 424b

428a

Specific heat, **IV** 419a

Spee, Friedrich von, witchcraft, **IV** 522b

Speech

Aristotle, **II** 663a

development, **II** 660a

language, **II** 659b–660a, 663a, 664a, 664b, 665b–666a, 667b, 668a, 669a, 670b, 671a–671b, 672a

liberalism, **III** 41a–41b

Speed

Galileo, **II** 587a

indeterminacy, **II** 587a

light, **IV** 79a, 81a, 82b, 83b, 91b

relativity, **IV** 79a, 81a, 82b, 83b, 84a, 89b–90a, 91b

Spelman, Henry (1564?–1641), historiography, **II** 486a

Spemann, Hans (1869–1941), recapitulation, **IV** 59a

Spence, Joseph (1699–1768)

iconography, **II** 535a

mythology, **III** 302b

periodization in literary history, **III** 483a

Spencer, Herbert (1820–1903)

acquired characteristics, **II** 620a

agnosticism, **I** 25b; **III** 438b

anarchy, **I** 70a–70b

art and play, **I** 106a, 106b

beauty, **I** 204a

behaviorism, **I** 218a

causation, **I** 291a

certainty, **I** 319a

chromosomes, **II** 288b

classification of the sciences, **I** 465b, 466a

Comte and, **III** 642a, 642b

culture, **IV** 180b

Darwin and, **III** 194a, **IV** 107b

determinism, **II** 24a

education, **II** 81b

entropy, **II** 115b–116a

ethics, **I** 383a; **III** 445a; **IV** 180b

evil, **III** 474a

evolution, **I** 319a; 177b, 181a, 182a–183a; **II** 383a, 454b, 620a; **III** 473b–474a, 637a, 643a; **IV** 180b, 395a, 395b

evolution of literature, **II** 171a, 171b, 172b

genetic continuity, **II** 288b

God, **I** 319a

Great Britain, **IV** 106b

happiness, II 383a; III 637a
Harris and, II 415a
health, II 383a
hedonism, IV 180b
Helmholtz and, II 116a
historiography, II 24a, 505b, 506b
idea, I 115a–116b
individualism, II 596a, 596b; III 637a, 643a; IV 180b
industry, III 642a
intuition, II 383a
justice, IV 180b
knowledge, I 465b
Lamarck and, II 620a
law, I 291a
literature, IV 332b
materialism, II 454b
morality, II 383a; IV 180b
motion, II 115b
natural law, III 22a
natural selection, II 383a; III 473b
necessity, III 643a
Orientalism, III 438b, 439a
pangenesis, II 626a
peace, III 445a, 642a, IV 503b, 506b
Peirce and, III 558a, 560b
perennial philosophy, III 462b
perfectibility, III 473b–474a
Platonism, III 502b
pleasure, II 383a; IV 180b
positivism, III 539b, 543b, 544b
pragmatism, III 558a, 560b, 566b
primitivism, III 596b
progress, III 637a, 642a, 642b, 643a, 647a
psychology, IV 12a, 13b, 25a, 25b, 26b
religion, II 182a; IV 93a, 106b, 107b
rules, IV 180b
science, II 182a
Social Darwinism, II 181a
society, III 637a, 643a; IV 180b
species, II 182a
style, IV 332b
survival of the fittest, III 473b
time, IV 395a, 395b
utilitarianism, II 383a; IV 180b
virtue, IV 180b
war, III 642a; IV 500b, 503b, 504a, 506b
Spencer, John (17th century),

Cosmic Fall, I 510b
Spener, Philipp Jacob (1635–1705)
eschatology, II 157a
Pietism, III 493b, 494a, 495a
Spengler, Oswald (1880–1936)
analogy, III 361a
Apollonian-soul, III 251a
architecture, IV 298b
art, IV 298b
China, I 371b
continuity, I 498a, 503b
crisis in history, I 595a
culture, I 616b, 617a–617b, 619a; II 22a–22b, 131b; III 251a, 360b–361a
culture-soul, III 251a
cycles, I 626b–627a
destiny, III 360b–361a
determinism, II 22a–23b
environment, II 131b
Europe, IV 298b
Faust (legend), III 251a
Gothic, IV 298b
Hegel and, III 361a
historicism, II 461b
historiography, I 503b; II 22a–23b, 506b
infinity, II 605a; IV 298b
Islam, II 650a
Middle Ages, IV 298b
morphology, III 251a
Nature, III 360b
necessity, III 360b–361a
Nietzsche and, III 251a
periodization in literary history, III 485a
physics, III 361a
primitivism, III 593a, 597b
romanticism, III 251a
Saint Augustine and, III 361a
space, IV 298a–298b
time, III 361a
Toynbee and, III 361a
Vico and, III 361a
Spenser, Edmund (1552?–1599)
allegory, I 41b
Chapman and, III 294b
Cosmic Fall, I 506a
Gothic, II 368b
Hermeticism, II 432a, 432b, 433b
hierarchy, II 434b
historiography, IV 151a
love, III 514b
Lucretius and, I 133a
Milton and, III 295a
mythology, III 294b 296b, 298a, 299a
periodization in literary his-

tory, III 485b
Platonism, III 507b, 514b
romanticism, IV 187b, 193a
syncretism, I 44a
theriophily, IV 387a
ut pictura poesis, IV 468b, 469a, 471a
Speroni, Sperone, Platonism, III 514a
Speusippus (c. 395–339 B.C.)
Aristotle and, IV 35a–36b
belief, IV 35b
dyad, IV 35b
evil, IV 36a
good, IV 36a
idea, IV 35a, 35b
knowledge, IV 35b
mathematics, IV 35b, 36a
Neo-Platonism, III 372a
numbers, IV 35a, 35b, 36a, 36b
perception, IV 35b
Plato and, IV 34b–36b
Platonism, III 504a
pluralism, IV 35b, 36a
Proclus and, IV 36a
Pythagoreans, IV 33b, 34b–36b
senses, IV 35b
soul, IV 35b–36a
unity, IV 35b
universality, IV 35b
Spingarn, Joel Elias (1875–1939)
creativity in art, I 588b
literary criticism, I 603a
Spinoza, Baruch (1632–1677)
appearance and reality, I 94a–98a
atheism, II 444b, 445a
axiomatization, I 165a
Being, II 445a; IV 434b
Bruno and, II 350b, 445b; III 194a
Cartesianism, II 444b, 445b
causation, I 276b, 290b, 296b, 298b–299a, 301a, 301b, 303a–303b; II 238b; III 193a; IV 434b
Chain of Being, I 326a, 329a
chance, I 336b
China, I 360a
choice, II 238b
conscience, III 42b
cosmos, II 445a, 445b
Counter-Enlightenment, II 108b
Creation, I 572a; II 445a
culture, II 128b
death, I 636a–636b, 637b, 645a
deism, I 649a, 650a, 650b
Descartes and, II 349b,

350a
design argument, I 675b
determinism, I 329a; II 237b, 238b–239a; IV 177b
dualism, II 41a, 445b; IV 393b
education, IV 434b
emotion, II 238b–239a; IV 177b, 381b, 434b
environment, II 128b
Erastianism, IV 119a
ethics, II 273a; IV 177b
evil, IV 381b
excommunication of, II 444b
extensio, IV 301b
free will, II 237b, 238b–239a, 246a
freedom, II 238b–239a; IV 177b
friendship, II 238b
game theory, II 273a
God, I 276b, 296b, 298b–299a, 301a, 303a, 572a; II 41a, 348a, 349b, 350a, 350b, 351a, 355a, 444b–445b; III 512a–512b, 554b–555a; IV 177b, 201a, 381b
Goethe and, III 519a
good, IV 177b, 182a, 381b
harmony, IV 177b
hate, II 238b
Hegel and, II 410b
Herder and, IV 201a, 209a
hierarchy, II 444b–445b
Hobbes and, II 351b; IV 256b
idea, III 561b
ignorance, II 238b
imagination, III 214b
immortality, I 645b
individualism, II 598b
infinity, II 444b, 445a, 606a, 614a
intuition, IV 177b
Jacobi and, IV 201a
James and, III 561b
knowledge, II 238b; IV 246a, 434a
law, I 290b
liberalism, III 42b, 43a
liberty, III 42b
life-force, IV 201a
logic, II 238b, 444b
love, II 238b; III 512a–512b, 555a
Man-Machine, III 138a, 139a
materialism, II 450a; III 193a
mathematics, II 273a, 445a; III 174a; IV 177b
matter, III 193a, 194a
mechanism, IV 434b

medicine, IV 434b
metaphor, III 199b
mind, II 238b; IV 434b
modernism, I 420a
monism, III 193a
morality, IV 434b
More, Henry, and, II 444b
natural law, III 20a
Nature, II 238b, 350b, 444b–445a; III 20a, 351a; IV 434b
necessity, IV 177b
periodization in history, III 478a
philosophy, III 199b; IV 434b
physics, IV 434b
Platonism, III 193a, 512a–512b, 519a, 520a
pleasure, II 238b
political ideas, IV 177a
post-Kantianism, IV 209a
power, II 240a; IV 434b
pragmatism, III 554b–555a, 561b
psychology, II 238b
reality, IV 177b, 393b
reason, II 238b; IV 177b, 257a
religion, IV 108a, 119a
right, IV 177b, 182a
romanticism, IV 201a, 209a, 210b
Schelling and, IV 210b
Schleiermacher and, III 520a
skepticism, IV 241a, 246a, 246b–247a
social contract, IV 256b–257b
space, IV 298a, 301b
Stoicism, II 238b
teleology, I 301a, 301b, 303a–303b; IV 177b
theodicy, IV 381b
theory of attributes, III 199b
thought, IV 434b
time, IV 393b, 394a, 395b
truth, IV 246a
unity, II 444b, 445a, 445b
unity of science, IV 434a–434b
universe, II 445a
virtue, IV 177b
vitalism, II 238b
wisdom, I 636b
Spiritualism
Bergson, III 563a, 565a, 565b
Brazil, III 543b
Cousin, III 534a
death, I 642b–643b
Diderot, III 603a
dignity, IV 142a

dualism, II 38b
environment, II 123b
Faust (legend), III 247a, 250b
Hegel, III 556b
immortality, I 642b–643b
Islam, II 650a
James, III 563a, 565a
Locke, IV 120a
love, III 95a, 97b, 98a, 99a, 101a, 105b, 106b, 107a
Luther, IV 66b
Michelangelo, III 513a
mythology, III 303b, 305a, 313b, 314a
naturalism in art, III 346a
Nature, III 346b, 347b
necessity, III 360a
Peirce, III 556b
perfectibility, III 468a–468b
Platonism, III 505b, 509a, 513a, 521b, 524a
Plotinus, III 505b
positivism, III 536a, 543b
pragmatism, III 556b, 563a, 565a, 565b
primitivism, III 603a
psychology, IV 9b, 10a, 12a, 14a
reformation, IV 62b, 64a–66b
Reformation, IV 67b
religion, IV 102a
Renaissance, IV 142a
Rhine, I 643a
romanticism, IV 202a, 203b, 208b
Royce, III 556b
Saint Francis of Assisi, IV 64b–65a
Spitzer, Leo (1887–1960)
baroque in literature, I 190b
classicism, I 454b
motif, III 242a
ut pictura poesis, IV 471a
Spock, Benjamin (1903–), recapitulation, IV 58b
Spoerri, Theophil, baroque in literature, I 190a, 191b
Spon, Jacques, iconography, II 534b
Sponde, Jean de, baroque in literature, I 192b
Spontaneity
Blake, II 307a
genius, II 293a, 294a, 295a, 307a–307b, 320b
Hegel, II 407a, 409a
Kant, II 407b
Spontaneous generation, IV 307a–312b
abiogenesis, IV 307a, 308b,

312a
Anaximander, IV 307b
Anaximenes, IV 307b
archebiosis, IV 311a, 311b
Aristotle, II 281b–282a; IV 307b
atheism, IV 310b
Bacon, IV 308b
bacteriology, IV 311a
Bastian, IV 311a
Berzelius, II 283a, 283b
Bible, IV 308b
biogenesis, IV 311a, 312a
biology, IV 310a–310b, 312a
Bonnet, II 284a–284b, 285a; IV 310b
Büchner, IV 311b–312a
Buffon, IV 310b
Cagniard de la Tour, II 283a–283b
Cardano, IV 308b
causation, IV 307b
Cesalpino, IV 308b
Christianity, IV 308a–308b
Cohn, II 284a
cosmogony, IV 307b
cosmos, IV 310a
Creation, IV 308b, 310a
Darwin, IV 311a–311b
Darwinism, IV 311b, 312a
determinism, IV 310a
Diderot, IV 310b
Empedocles, IV 307b
empiricism, IV 309a–309b, 310b
Enlightenment, IV 308b, 310a, 310b
Epicureanism, IV 308a
evolution, IV 310b, 311b, 312a
evolutionism, II 178a
experiments, IV 309a–309b, 310b, 311a
Flood, IV 308a
genetic continuity, II 281b–285b
genetics, IV 307a
God, IV 308a–308b, 310a
Greece (ancient), IV 307a–308a
Haeckel, IV 312a
Haller, IV 310b
harmony, IV 310a
Harvey, IV 308b–309a
Helmont, IV 308b
heterogenesis, IV 307a, 308b, 310a–312a
Huxley, IV 311b
ideology, IV 310b, 311a
immunology, IV 311a
Lactantius, IV 308a
Lamarck, IV 311b
Lavoisier, II 283a

Le Dantec, IV 311b
Leduc, IV 311b
Leeuwenhoek, II 282b; IV 309b–310a
Liebig, II 283a, 283b
Lucretius, IV 308a
Malpighi, II 282b; IV 309b
materialism, IV 310b, 311a
matter, IV 307a, 308b, 312a
Maupertuis, II 284b–285a
metaphysics, IV 310b
Middle Ages, IV 308b
naturalism, IV 310b, 312a
Nature, IV 307b, 310a, 311b
Needham, IV 310a–310b
Oken, IV 311b
panspermist theory, IV 311a
Paracelsus, IV 308b
Paré, IV 308b
Pasteur, II 282a, 283b; IV 310b–311a, 311b
Pflüger, IV 311b
physiology, IV 309a
Pliny, IV 307b
Porta, IV 308b
Pouchet, II 283b; IV 311a
preformationism, IV 309b, 310a, 310b
Réaumur, IV 310b
Redi, II 282a; IV 309a 309b
Renaissance, IV 308b
Rome (ancient), IV 307b
Saint Augustine, IV 308a–308b
Saint Thomas Aquinas, IV 308b
Schröder, II 283b; IV 310b
Schulze, II 283b
Schwann, II 283a–283b, 285b, 286a
science, IV 307a–308b, 311b
sex, IV 307a–307b
Spallanzani, IV 310b
species, IV 307a–308b, 311b
Swammerdam, IV 309b
theology, IV 308a–308b, 310a, 310b
Trembley, II 284a–284b
Turberville, II 283a
Tyndall, II 283b–284a; IV 311a
Vallisnieri, II 282b
Verworn, IV 311b
viruses, II 285a–285b; IV 312a
Voltaire, IV 310b
Wöhler, II 283b
Spranger, Eduard
imagination, III 208b

perennial philosophy, III 462b
Sprat, Thomas (1635–1713)
  Chain of Being, I 327a
  hierarchy, II 444b
  methodology, III 386b
  Newton and, III 386b
  Ramism, IV 45a
Sprengel, K. (1750–1816)
  cells, II 285b
  genetic continuity, II 285b
Sprenger, Jacob, witchcraft, IV 521b
Springer, A., iconography, II 535b
Spurgeon, Caroline (1869–1942), motif, III 242a
Spurzheim, Johann Christoph (1776–1832)
  phrenology, IV 23a, 23b
  psychology, IV 23a, 23b
Ssŭ-ma Ch'ien (ca. 145–87 B.C.), historiography, II 480b–481a
Stace, W. T., beauty, I 211a
Stadler, Ernst, expressionism, II 208a
Staël, Madame de (1766–1817)
  aristocracy, II 14a–14b
  attitude toward antiquity, I 84a
  Byron and, IV 192b
  classicism, I 451b
  conservatism, I 477b
  despotism, II 2a, 13b–14b
  Enlightenment, II 100a
  Faust (legend), III 250b
  freedom, II 14b
  immortality, I 645b, 646a
  romanticism, IV 189b, 190a, 190b, 192a, 193b
  Schlegel and, IV 189b, 190a, 192a, 193b
  symbolism, IV 339a
  tyranny, II 14b
  Volksgeist, IV 493b, 494a
Stahl, F. W.
  DNA, II 291a–291b
  genetic continuity, II 291a–291b
Stahl, Friedrich Julius (1802–1861), conservatism, I 481a
Stahl, Georg Ernst (1660–1734)
  art, II 309b
  genius, II 309b
  health, II 401a
  imagination, III 212a, 218a
Staiger, Emil, literary criticism, I 606a
Stair, Lord, common law, II 693a
Stalin, Joseph (1879–1953)

acquired characteristics, II 620b, 621b
agriculture, II 621b
anarchy, I 75a
art, III 152b
authority, I 158b; III 152b
capitalism, III 156b–157a
China (communist), I 372b
class, III 154b
constitutionalism, I 486a
democracy, I 665b
existentialism, III 158a
Hitler and, II 563a
ideology, II 562a, 562b, 563a, 563b
imperialism, II 563b
Khrushchev and, III 157b
Mao Tse-tung and, I 372b
Marxism, III 152b, 153a, 154b, 155a, 156b, 157a, 158a, 165b, 166a, 167b, 168a, 168b
Marxism-Leninism, II 562b–563a; III 153a
materialism, III 153a
national oppression, II 562b
nationalism, III 333b
natural liberty, II 70a
nuclear power, III 157a
pangenesis, II 626b
politics, III 152b
revisionism, IV 274a–274b
revolution, IV 158a
science, III 152b
socialism, II 562b–563a; III 155a, 156b
Stalin Constitution, I 486a
terror, III 157b
totalitarianism, II 563a; IV 406a, 406b, 407b, 409a, 409b, 410a, 410b
U.N., II 653b
war, III 157a
World War II, II 563a–563b
Stallman, R. W., organicism, III 426b
Stallo, J. B. (1823–1900)
  positivism, III 556b
  space IV 307a, 307b
Stammler, Rudolf (1856–1938), justice, II 657b
Stanford, Leland (1824–1893), philanthropy, III 491b
Stankevič, N. V.
  conservatism, I 482b–483a
  nationalism, I 482b–483a
Stanley, Thomas (1625–1678)
  eclecticism, III 516b–517a
  harmony, II 394b
  Platonism, III 516b–517b
Stanton, Elizabeth Cady (1815–1902), women, IV 526b

Stapfer, Philippe-Albert, romanticism, IV 189b
Star clocks, I 536a
Starkey, Thomas, analogy, I 69b
Starnes, De Witt T., mythology, III 299a
Staunton, George, China, I 365b
Stars
  Aristotle, I 668a
  binary, I 550b
  cosmology, I 535b, 536a, 537a–537b, 541a–541b, 542b, 543a, 544b–545a, 546a, 549a–549b, 550a–552a, 553b, 555b–556a, 566b, 569b–570a
  demonology, I 669a, 669b
  disease, II 399b
  evolution, I 553b
  fortune, fate, and chance, II 227a, 229b, 235a
  free will, II 245b
  God, III 287a–287b
  harmony, II 389a–389b, 390b, 392b, 393b, 394a
  indeterminacy, II 586b
  motion, I 549a–549b; IV 50a, 77b
  music, II 389a–389b, 390b, 392b, 393b, 394a; III 269a
  mythology, III 278a, 282a, 287a–287b, 288a, 288b, 290a–290b, 308b, 310a–310b
  Newton, I 674b
  Olbers paradox, I 555b–556a
  optics, III 410b, 414b
  power, III 288a
  relativity, IV 76a, 76b, 77b, 86a
  Saint Thomas Aquinas, III 288a
  sublime in external nature, IV 336b
  temperament, III 288b
  time, IV 392a, 392b, 393a
  World Spirit, II 392b
State, IV 312b–318b
  academic freedom, I 10a
  Adams, I 660a
  analogy, I 67b–70b
  anarchy, III 470a–470b, 673b
  anti-industrialism, III 676a
  Aristotle, I 625b, 653a, 653b–654b, 655a, 655b, 657a, 657b, 658a, 667a; IV 313a, 313b, 314b, 318a, 497a–497b
  art, II 570a, 576a, 582b
  authority, III 37b–38a; IV

313a, 314a, 314b, 315a, 316a, 318a
Bentham, I 657b, 662a–663a
Bernstein, Eduard, III 162b
Bible, IV 315b
Blackstone, I 657b, 659a, 660a, 662a
Bodin, III 19b; IV 315b, 316a
Bohemia, I 397b
Boniface VIII (Pope), IV 314a
Bosanquet, II 280a–280b
bourgeois, IV 316b
Bradley, F. H., II 415a
Bryce, I 485b
Buddhism, I 252b–253b
Burke, I 661a–661b; IV 205b
Calvinism, I 395a, 397b
Chain of Being, I 328b–329a
China, I 361a–363a, 365a, 370b
Christianity, I 405a–405b; III 671a; IV 314a, 317a
Church of England, I 405a
Cicero, I 655a; IV 313b
class, III 151b, 155a; IV 314b, 316b, 318a
classification, III 11a–12b
Clausius, II 113b–114a
common law, II 693a, 695b
communism, III 646a
community, IV 313b–314b
Comte, III 642a
conformity, IV 313a
constitutionalism, I 485b–486b
Counter-Enlightenment, II 101a, 106b, 107a, 110b
cynicism, I 629a–630a, 631b
democracy, IV 316b–317a
determinism, II 20a, 22a
Diogenes of Sinope, I 631b
discipline, IV 316a
economic history, II 47a
economics, III 151b–152a
education, III 469b–470a
elite, IV 318a–318b
emotion, IV 315a, 316b, 318b
Engels, IV 316b
Epictetus, I 655b
equality, II 143a, 145b; IV 313b–314a, 316b–318b
ethics, III 441a, 441b, 443a, 446b
evolutionism, II 180b
Figgis, IV 314a
force, IV 313a, 313b, 315a,

315b, 316b, 317a, 318a, 318b
France, I 398b–400a, 656a, 657b, 658b, 660b–662a; IV 315a, 316a
free will, II 243a
freedom, IV 317b
freedom of speech, II 252a, 252b
French Revolution (1789), IV 156a, 157a
general will, II 276a–276b, 277b, 278a, 279a–280b
Germany, I 405b, 661a, 665b
God, IV 317a, 318a
Godwin, III 470b
good, IV 180a
government by consent, III 43b–47a
Great Britain, I 397b, 656a, 656b–657b, 658b–660b, 661a, 662a–663a; IV 153b, 315a
Greece (ancient), I 487a, 652b–655a, 655b, 657a, 657b, 658a, 658b, 667a; IV 228a, 252b, 312b–313b
Green, T. H., II 415a
Grotius, IV 317a
happiness, II 379b, 380a, 381b
harmony, II 389a
Harrington, I 657a
Harris, W. T., II 415a
Hegel, II 408b, 409a–409b, 415a, 415b, 452b; III 22a, 48b–49a, 473a, 556a; IV 290b, 291b, 318a, 492b–493a
Helvétius, I 661a
Herder, III 472b
Herodotus, I 653a, 667a
historiography, II 20a, 22a; IV 147b
Hobbes, I 656a–657b; II 62a; III 20b; IV 259a, 315a, 317b
human nature, IV 315a
humanism, II 519b, 522b; IV 129b, 132b
Hume, IV 261b
ideology, IV 316b–317a, 318a
ignorance, III 472a
impressionism, II 570a, 576a
individualism, II 598a; IV 316a–318a
inequality, IV 318a
international relations, IV 313b, 315b
intolerance, IV 116a
Italy, I 665b; IV 314a,

315a, 316b
James, William, III 565b
Jefferson, I 660a, 660b; IV 317b
justice, IV 313a, 313b
Kant, II 279b; III 472b, 639b
law, II 44b, 686b–690a; III 10b–13b, 33b; IV 313a–316a, 317b
Lecky, I 655b–656a
Lenin, II 560b
liberalism, I 10a; III 37b–40a, 43b–47a, 55b–60b, 672b
liberty, IV 313b–314a, 316b, 317b
Lilburne, I 656b
Locke, I 656a, 657a–657b, 659a; II 62a; IV 120a, 258b, 317a
loyalty, III 108a, 110a–112b, 115b; IV 316b
Luther, I 396a; III 11a
Machiavelli, I 652b, 656a; II 235b; III 116a–125a; IV 132b, 314b–316b
Machiavellism, III 116b–125a
Madison, I 660b, 666a, 666b
Marx, II 59b; IV 161b, 162a, 316b
Marxism, III 148b, 151b–152a, 153a, 154b, 155a, 162b, 167a, 646a; IV 316b, 318b
Marxism-Leninism, III 155a
materialism, II 452b
Mesopotamia (ancient), IV 226b
microcosm, III 127a–127b
Middle Ages, III 116a, 319a, 319b, 320a, 320b, 323b; IV 153b, 314a–314b, 315b, 317a, 317b
Mill, James, I 662a, 662b
Mill, John Stuart, I 663a, 664a
Milton, I 657a
Montesquieu, I 656a, 657b, 659a, 660a; III 21a
More, Thomas, IV 461a
Müller, IV 206b
music, II 389a
nationalism, III 318b, 319a, 320a–326b; IV 315a, 318b
nationality, IV 315a
natural law, IV 313b
natural liberty, IV 62a, 64a, 67a, 68b–69a, 71a
natural rights, III 14a, 15a, 19b, 20b–22b
Nietzsche, IV 485a

Novalis, IV 206a, 206b
obedience, IV 316b, 317b
obligation, IV 313a, 316a–316b, 317a, 318a
organicism, III 422b
origin of the term, IV 314b–315a
Paine, I 659a–659b, 661b; IV 260b
patriotism, IV 315a, 316b, 318b
peace, III 441a, 441b, 443a, 446b
perfectibility, III 463b, 469b–473b; IV 313a, 314b
Pericles, I 653b, 654a, 654b
periodization in history, III 477b
philanthropy, III 488b, 492b
philosophy, III 153a
Plato, I 630a, 653a, 653b–654a, 655a, 658a; III 440a, 471a, 508b, 554b, 629a; IV 3b, 49b, 285b, 313b, 368b, 497a–497b
Platonism, III 508b
pleasure, II 381b
pluralism, IV 314b, 316a
politics, III 116a–125a; IV 312b–318b
Polybius, I 626a–626b, 655a, 655b, 657b
power, III 12b, 151b; IV 313a–317a, 318a, 318b
pragmatism, III 554b, 556a, 565b
primitivism, III 593b, 595a
private property, III 650b, 652a, 653a, 653b, 654b, 655a, 655b, 656a; IV 316b
progress, III 627b, 629a, 637a, 639b, 640a, 641b, 642a, 646a
prophecy, III 658a, 659a, 659b, 660b, 661a, 662a, 662b
protest movements, III 671a, 672a–673b, 676a
Protestantism, I 405a
Proudhon, II 280b; III 470b
psychology, IV 3b, 18a, 19a, 22a
Pufendorf, II 276b
quietism, I 655b
race, IV 318a
rationalism, IV 48b, 49b, 312b, 314b
reformation, IV 64a
Reformation, IV 67b
religion, IV 112b, 115a, 116a, 117b, 119a, 120a
Renaissance, IV 126b, 127a, 127b, 129b, 132b,

147b
revolution, IV 153b, 154b, 155a, 155b, 156a, 157a, 158a, 161b, 162a
Richelieu, I 399a
right, IV 180a, 313b
rights, IV 317a, 317b, 318b
Robespierre, I 661b–662a
Roman Catholic Church, I 403a–405b, 406a, 462a; IV 314a
romanticism, IV 202b–203b, 205b–206b
Rome (ancient), I 652b, 653a, 655a–655b, 657a, 658a; II 686b–690a; IV 252b, 313b–315a
Rousseau, I 656a, 657b–658a, 661a, 661b; II 276a–276b, 277b, 278a, 279b, 407b; III 21b; IV 259a, 317a
rules, IV 313a, 313b
Russia, I 665a–665b
Saint Augustine, III 11a
salvation, IV 226b, 228a
secularism, IV 317a
self-sufficiency, IV 314b
Sidney, I 657a
sin, IV 226b, 228a, 314a, 317a
Smith, Adam, II 64a
social contract, IV 251b, 252a–263b, 317a–317b
social welfare, IV 279b, 283a
socialism, IV 285b, 288a, 289a–293b, 316b–317a
society, IV 312b, 313a, 316a, 316b
Sophism, IV 313b
sovereignty, I 656b, 657a, 659a–661a; IV 314b, 315b, 316a, 318b
Switzerland, I 661a
syndicalism, III 673b
technology, IV 357b
temperance, IV 368b
Thucydides, I 653b, 655a, 656a
Tocqueville, I 663a–664a
totalitarianism, IV 407a, 407b–409a, 410a
U.S.S.R., I 665b; III 154b, 155a, 653b, 655a
U.S., I 652b, 656a, 656b, 657b, 658a, 658b–660b, 663a–664a, 665a, 666a–667a; IV 155b
Utopia, IV 459b, 461a, 462a, 462b
Victorian sentiment, IV 217b, 220b, 222a, 223b
virtù, IV 483b–485a

virtue, IV 49b, 315a
Volksgeist, IV 491a, 491b, 492b–493a, 493b, 495b
Voltaire, I 657b
vox populi, IV 497a–497b
war, I 655b–656a, 665a; IV 500b, 502a, 503b, 507b
Wilson, I 665a
witchcraft, IV 522a
women, IV 529a
work, IV 534a
Statistics
chance, I 338a
game theory, II 272a
indeterminacy, II 591a–592a
linguistics, IV 426a
numbers, IV 406a
probability, III 607a, 608b, 611b, 613b, 614b, 618b, 619b–620a
progress, III 640b
quantum mechanics, II 591a–592a
space, IV 304b
uniformitarianism, IV 426a
welfare state, IV 510b, 511a
Statius, Publius (45?–?96 A.D.), *ut pictura poesis*, IV 469a
Status
dignity, IV 141a
protest movements, III 670a, 671a, 676b
Renaissance, IV 141a, 438a
right, IV 174a
universal man, IV 438a
welfare state, IV 509a, 512b, 514b
work, IV 531a
Statutes
common law, II 692a, 692b, 694b, 695b
Greece (ancient), II 680a, 681b–685a
law, II 680a, 681b–685a; III 2a, 4a, 7b
Stead, William Thomas (1849–1912), international peace, III 453b
Steady-state theory, I 567b–568b
Stebbing, Susan, agnosticism, I 24b
Stechow, W., iconography, II 538a
Steele, Richard (1672–1729)
Burnet and, III 259a
cosmic voyages, I 529b
Enlightenment, II 89b, 91b
mountains in literature, III 259a
primitivism, III 598a, 602a

virtuoso, IV 488a, 489a–489b
Steen, Jan (1626–1679), iconography, II 532b
Stegmüller, Wolfgang, logic, III 550a
Stein, Freiherr vom, Enlightenment, II 89b
Stein, Gertrude (1874–1946), symbolism, IV 341a, 341b
Stein, K. H. von, ideal, II 551a
Stein, Lorenz von (1815–1890)
class, I 448b
inequality, I 448b
socialism, IV 291b
Stein, William B., Orientalism, III 431b
Steinbach, Erwin von, Gothic, II 371b
Steinbeck, John (1902–1968), civil disobedience, I 438a
Steiner, George, literature, III 88b
Steiner, Rudolf (1861–1925)
Faust (legend), III 251a
symbolism, IV 343a
Steinthal, Heymann (1823–1899)
evolution of literature, II 171a, 173a
Volksgeist, IV 495b
Stendhal (1783–1842)
classicism, I 450a
French Revolution, IV 157b
Machiavellism, III 119a
periodization in literary history, III 486a
realism in literature, IV 52a, 55a
Renaissance, IV 124b, 125a, 128a
revolution, IV 157b
romanticism, IV 190a–190b, 191a, 192b, 198a
Schlegel and, IV 190a
ut pictura poesis, IV 469a, 475a
Steno, Nicholaus (1638–1687), geology, III 255b, 256a
Stenzel, G. A. H., historiography, II 492a
Stephanos (c. 610–641 A.D.), I 28b–29a, 29b
Stephanus, Charles (1504–1564), mythology, III 299a
Stephanus, Robert (1503–1559), mythology, III 299a, 299b
Stephen, Leslie (1832–1904)
agnosticism, I 17b, 18b–21a, 22b–23a

atheism, I 19a
Stephens, C.A., longevity, III 93a
Sterne, Laurence (1713–1768)
Hermeticism, II 433a, 434a
irony, II 630b
literary paradox, III 77b
Stern-Gerlach experiment, II 589a
indeterminacy, II 589a
Sterry, Peter, hierarchy, II 435a
Steuart, James Denham, economic history, II 46a
Steuchius, Augustinus
Islam, II 644b
perennial philosophy, III 457b–458a, 459a–460a
Stevens, S. S.
empiricism, III 550b
logic, III 550b
psychology, III 550b
Stevens, Wallace (1879–1955), symbolism, IV 341a, 344b
Stevenson, Charles L. (1908–)
beauty, I 208a
right, IV 184a
Stevenson, Robert Louis (1850–1894)
motif, III 241b
style, IV 332b
Steward, J. H., evolutionism, II 187a
Stewart, Dugald (1753–1828)
association of ideas, I 114a
Enlightenment, II 99b, 100a
mythology, III 302a
psychology, IV 22b
society, II 99b
Stillingfleet, Benjamin (1702–1771), music, III 263b
Stillingfleet, Bishop Edward (1635–1699)
skepticism, IV 245b
causation, I 276b
Stirling, James Hutchinson (1820–1909)
Feuerbach and, II 414b
Hegel and, II 414a, 414b
Strauss and, II 414b
Stirling formula, III 609a
Stirner, Max (1806–1856)
anarchism, I 73b
Counter-Enlightenment, II 109b
irrationalism, II 638a
Marx and, IV 291a
socialism, IV 291a
Stobaeus, Joannes (late 5th century A.D.)
cynicism, I 628b

microcosm, III 128a, 129a
Stockholm papyri, I 28a
Stoicism
aesthetics, II 217a
Alexander of Aphrodisias, IV 322a
Alexander the Great, IV 320a–320b
animals, IV 319b
Aristotelianism, IV 320b, 322a
Aristotle, IV 320a, 321a
art, II 299b
asceticism, IV 320b
atomism, IV 319a
beauty, II 217a
biology, I 235a–235b
birth, IV 322a
Cato, IV 321b
causation, I 272b–273a, 275b, 290b; IV 320a
Christianity, III 590a; IV 322a, 370b
Chrysippus, III 587b; IV 321b, 322a
Cicero, II 340b; IV 50a, 319b, 321b, 322a
city-state, IV 320a
civilization, III 588a
Cleanthes, III 587b, 588a; IV 321b
Clement of Alexandria, IV 322a
community, IV 176a
consciousness, I 215a
cosmopolitanism, III 586b
the cosmos, I 62a–62b; II 340b; III 588a; IV 50a, 50b, 176a
courage, IV 320b
criticism, IV 321b
culture, I 612a; II 127b; IV 320a–320b
cycles, I 621b, 622b–624a
cynicism, I 627b; III 585b, 587b–588a; IV 320b
Cynics, III 504a
death, I 635b, 636a, 637b
deism, I 647b, 648a
democracy, I 655a, 655b
Democritus, IV 319a
design argument, I 671a
desire, IV 50a
destiny, IV 319a
determinism, II 137a, 237a, 237b, 238b
dignity, IV 136b, 137a, 137b, 138a, 139a, 142b, 143a, 144a, 146a
Diogenes of Sinope, IV 320b
disease, II 397b, 398a, 399a; IV 321a, 321b

divination, **IV** 320a
dualism, **II** 41a
duty, **IV** 50a, 176a
emotion, **IV** 176a
Enlightenment, **II** 90a, 99a
entropy, **II** 117b
environment, **II** 127b
Epictetus, **III** 590a; **IV** 319a, 321b, 322a
Epicureanism, **II** 137a; **IV** 319a
Epicurus, **IV** 321b
equality, **II** 140a, 140b; **IV** 285b
equity, **II** 150b, 151a
ethics, **III** 440b–441b; **IV** 176a, 319a–322b
evil, **II** 163a; **III** 588a; **IV** 319a, 320a, 321a
fatalism, **II** 137a
fortune, fate, and chance, **II** 228a, 230a, 232a, 234a, 234b
free will, **II** 137a, 237a, 237b, 238b, 243b, 244a, 246b; **IV** 320b
freedom, **IV** 50a
Galen, **IV** 321b
goals, **IV** 176a
God, **II** 340b, 347a–347b, 349a, 355a; **IV** 50b, 319a, 319b, 320a, 320b
Godwin, **III** 470b
good, **III** 588a; **IV** 50a, 176a, 319b–321b
Greece (ancient), **IV** 319a, 320a–320b
Grotius, **III** 441b
happiness, **II** 378a; **IV** 50a, 319b, 320b, 321a, 321b
harmony, **II** 392b
health, **II** 397b, 398a, 399a; **IV** 321a, 321b
Heraclitus, **IV** 320b
heresy, **II** 427a
historiography, **II** 469b, 470a, 471a, 509b, 510b
history, **III** 626a; **IV** 320a–320b
humanism, **II** 520a; **IV** 129a, 135a
humanitarianism, **III** 17a, 17b
imagination, **III** 210b
individualism, **I** 623b–624a; **II** 299b, 594b; **IV** 176a
Islam, **II** 641a, 646a
joy, **II** 378a; **IV** 321a
judgment, **IV** 321a
justice, **II** 653a, 656b, 658a; **IV** 320b
Kant, **IV** 322a
knowledge, **IV** 321a
language, **II** 664a; **IV** 319b,

law, **I** 290b, 487a, 487b; **II** 686a, 687b, 688a, 689a; **IV** 176a
literary criticism, **I** 596a
literary paradox, **III** 77a, 79b, 80a
logic, **IV** 319a–320b, 322a
logos, **I** 45b; **IV** 319a, 319b–321a
longevity, **III** 89b
loyalty, **III** 111a, 111b, 112a, 115a–115b
Marcus Aurelius, **II** 340b; **IV** 321b, 322a
materialism, **III** 504a
mathematics, **III** 184a
matter, **III** 190a–190b, 195a; **IV** 319a
metaphor, **III** 204a, 204b
microcosm, **III** 127a
mind, **II** 378a; **IV** 50a
monism, **II** 41a
morality, **III** 15b, 16b, 190a; **IV** 50a, 50b, 176a, 319a–322a, 478a
More, Thomas, **III** 79b
music, **II** 392b
natural rights, **III** 14a, 14b, 15b, 16b–18a, 19b
Nature, **II** 378a; **III** 15b, 588a; **IV** 49b–50a, 50b, 176a, 285b, 319a–321a
necessity, **III** 190a
neo-classicism in art, **III** 365b, 366a
Neo-Platonism, **III** 372a, 373a, 374a, 376b
norms, **III** 17a
order, **IV** 176a
pain, **IV** 320a, 321a
Panaetius, **IV** 321b
peace, **III** 440b, 441a, 441b; **IV** 176a
perennial philosophy, **III** 457b, 459b
perfectibility, **III** 465b, 466a, 468b, 469a, 470b
Petrarch, **II** 234b
philanthropy, **III** 487a
philosophy, **II** 641a, 646a; **III** 588a; **IV** 319a
physics, **IV** 319a–320b, 322a
Plato, **IV** 7a, 320a–321a
Platonism, **III** 504a; **IV** 319b, 320b
pleasure, **II** 378a; **IV** 320a, 321a
Plotinus, **III** 374a; **IV** 8b, 322a
Plutarch, **IV** 321b
pneuma, **IV** 319a, 320a
politics, **IV** 320a, 320b,

321b
Posidonius, **III** 588b; **IV** 321b
poverty, **IV** 321a
primitivism, **III** 585a, 586b, 587a, 587b–588b
progress, **III** 626a, 630a, 630b–631a, 632a–633a
providence, **IV** 319a
rationalism, **IV** 49b–50a, 50b, 51a, 176a, 319a, 320a, 320b, 321a
reformation, **IV** 60b
religion, **III** 204a, 204b, 588a
Renaissance, **IV** 129a, 135a, 136b, 137a, 137b, 138a, 139a, 142b, 143a, 144a, 146a
right, **IV** 176a
Rome (ancient), **IV** 321b–322a
Scipio Africanus, **IV** 321b–322a
self-control, **IV** 320b
self-sufficiency, **III** 585a
semitism, **IV** 320b
Seneca, **III** 588a–588b
Sextus Empiricus, **IV** 320a
signs, **IV** 237a
skepticism, **IV** 234b–240a, 241a, 244b
slavery, **III** 17a
socialism, **IV** 285b–286a, 288a
society, **IV** 320a, 320b, 322a
Socrates, **IV** 320b
soul, **II** 378a; **IV** 50a
Spinoza, **II** 238b
teleology, **IV** 51a
temperance, **IV** 369a–370b, 371b, 372b, 378a
theodicy, **IV** 380a, 380b
time, **IV** 390a, 391a–391b, 401a
tragic sense, **IV** 415a
tranquility, **IV** 176a
universality, **IV** 50a, 285b
Utopia, **IV** 460a
vice, **IV** 50a, 321a
virtue. **III** 465b; **IV** 49b–50a, 176a, 320b–322a, 378a, 478a, 478b
vox populi, **IV** 498a
wealth, **IV** 321a, 321b
wisdom, **IV** 320b
wisdom of the fool, **IV** 518b
World Spirit, **II** 392b
Zeno of Citium, **III** 587b; **IV** 7a, 319a, 320a, 320b, 321b, 322a
Stoics
Adam (Bible), **III** 583a

alchemy, **I** 28a
Alexander the Great, **IV** 7a
analogy, **I** 68b
anthropomorphism, **I** 89a
Aristotle, **IV** 7a
astrology, **I** 119b
authority, **I** 142b
behaviorism, **IV** 8a
Christianity, **IV** 8b
classification of the arts, **I** 456b
concept formation, **I** 2b
cosmology, **I** 622b–623a
earth, **IV** 7a
emotion, **IV** 8a
ethics, **IV** 8a
God, **IV** 8a
Great Year (myth), **IV** 401a
Greece (ancient), **IV** 7a
hallucinations, **IV** 7b
human nature, **III** 348a
knowledge, **IV** 8a
materialism, **IV** 7a, 8a
morality, **IV** 7a, 8a
motivation, **IV** 8a
mythology, **III** 274a–274b, 287b, 288a
natural law, **I** 129a; **III** 14a–18a, 19b; **IV** 176a
Nature, **III** 348a
nominalism, **I** 2b
perception, **I** 2b; **IV** 8a
Platonism, **III** 504b
poetry, **III** 526b
pragmatism, **III** 555b
pre-Socratics, **IV** 7b
primitivism, **III** 581a, 583a, 585b, 586a, 600b
psychology, **IV** 7a–8b, 10b, 22b
psychosomatics, **IV** 8a
rationalism, **IV** 8a
reason, **I** 2b; **III** 17a, 586a, 588a; **IV** 50a, 176a, 285b, 319a–321b
right, **III** 348a
social contract, **IV** 252a
soul, **IV** 8a
species, **I** 233a
Strato, **IV** 7a, 8a
water, **IV** 7a
Stojanović, Svetozar, Marxism, **III** 168a, 168b
Stokes, George Gabriel (1819–1903), religion, **IV** 108a
Stone, Julius
  computers, **III** 32b
  law, **III** 28a
Stone, Lucy (1818–1893), women, **IV** 526b
Stosch, Baron Phillip von, neo-classicism in art, **III** 363b, 367b
Stow, John (1525?–1605)

hierarchy, II 443b
Strabo (63 B.C.–?24 A.D.)
    custom, II 129a
    cynicism, I 631b–632a
    humanism, II 521b
    mimesis, III 226a
    primitivism, III 591b
    progress, III 631b
Strabo, Walafrid, iconography, II 527a
Strachey, Alix, war, IV 505b
Strakhov, N. N., realism in literature, IV 53a
Stramm, August, expressionism, II 208b
Strasburger, Eduard (1844–1912)
    cell division, II 286b
    chromosomes, II 286b, 287a, 287b, 289a
Strato (c. 288 B.C.)
    Aristotelianism, IV 6b–7a
    body, IV 7a
    immortality, IV 7a
    Platonism, IV 6b–7a
    psychology, IV 6b–7a, 8a
    senses, IV 7a
    soul, IV 7a
    Stoics and, IV 7a, 8a
    Theophrastus and, IV 6b
    thought, IV 7a
Strauss, David Friedrich (1808–1874)
    agnosticism, I 21b
    Bible, II 412b–413a
    Baur and, II 412b
    Christianity, I 405b; II 412b–413a
    Fichte and, II 413a
    God, II 412b
    Goethe and, II 413a
    Göschel and, II 413a
    Hegel and, II 412b–413a, 414a
    Jesus, II 412b–413a
    Michelet and, II 412b
    modernism, I 419b
    mysticism, II 412b
    mythology, II 413a; III 304b
    Rosenkranz and, II 412b
    Schleiermacher and, II 412b
    socialism, IV 291a
    Stirling and, II 414b
    work, IV 534b
Strauss, Richard (1864–1949)
    impressionism, II 575a
    ut pictura poesis, IV 473a
Stream of consciousness, IV 55a
Strich, Fritz
    baroque, I 189b, 192a
    classicism, I 451a
    romanticism, IV 197a
Strife

Empedocles, IV 2b
microcosm, III 126b
Strikes
    Marxism, III 149b, 150b–151a, 152a
    pragmatism, III 564a–564b
    protest movements, III 672a, 673b, 674b, 675a, 675b, 676b
    Sorel, III 564a–564b
Strindberg, Johan August (1849–1912), symbolism, IV 344b
Strong, E. W.
    methodology, III 390b
    Newton and, III 390b
Strong, Josiah (1847–1916), reformation, IV 69a
Structuralism, IV 322b–330a
    algorithms, IV 325a
    Althusser, IV 329a–329b
    anthropology, III 316b–317b; IV 323a–327a, 329b
    art, IV 327b, 328b
    atomism, IV 324b
    Bally, IV 323a
    Barthes, IV 327b–328b
    Baudelaire, IV 327b
    biology, IV 322b
    Cartesianism, IV 328b, 329a
    Chomsky, IV 324b–325a, 326b
    collectivism, IV 326b
    communication, IV 325b–326a
    conscious, IV 324b, 328b
    culture, IV 322b, 326b, 327a–327b, 328a
    deep structure, IV 324b
    defined, IV 322b
    Derrida, IV 329a
    Descartes, IV 328b
    diachromy, IV 323b
    Diderot, IV 328a
    Durkheim, IV 325a
    Engels, IV 326a
    epistemology, IV 326b
    ethnology, IV 325a, 326b, 327b, 329a
    etymology, IV 323b
    evolution, IV 323a–323b
    existentialism, IV 327b, 329b
    Foucault, IV 323a, 328b–329a, 329b
    France, IV 323a, 324b, 327b–329b
    Freud, IV 328b
    functionalism, IV 325b
    grammar, IV 323b, 324b
    Hegel, IV 329b
    history, IV 322b, 323a, 329b

humanism, IV 328b–329a
Humboldt, IV 324b, 325a
Husserl, IV 329a
hypotheses, IV 325a
idea, IV 322b
ideology, IV 327b, 329a–329b
Indians (American), IV 325a
individualism, IV 326b
Jakobson, IV 324a, 327b
Java, IV 325a
Karcewski, IV 324a
kinship practices, IV 327a, 328b
knowledge, IV 329a
Lacan, IV 328a, 328b, 329b
language, IV 322b, 323a–329a
langue, IV 323b–324a
Lévi-Strauss, IV 324a–329b
linguistics, IV 323a–329b
literary criticism, I 606a; IV 323a, 327a–328b
literature, IV 322b, 327b, 328b, 329b, 333a
logic, IV 329b, 330a
Malinowski, IV 325b
Marx, IV 326a, 329a–329b
Marxism, IV 326a, 327b
mathematics, IV 329b
Mauss, IV 324a, 325b
metaphysics, IV 330a
methodology, IV 323a, 327a
Montesquieu, IV 325a
Morgan, L. H., IV 325a
mythology, III 316a–317b; IV 326a–329a
Nietzsche, IV 329a
ontology, IV 326b
parole, IV 323b–324a
Peirce, IV 327a, 328a
phenomenology, IV 329a
philosophy, II 652a; IV 322b, 323a, 328b–330a
phonetics, IV 324b, 327b
phonology, IV 324a–324b, 327b
Picard, IV 327b–328a
positivism, IV 329b
primitivism, IV 326b
prosody, IV 327b
psychoanalysis, IV 326a, 327a–328b
psychology, IV 324a, 326a
Racine, IV 327b
Radcliffe-Brown, IV 325b
Reidlinger, IV 323a
Rousseau, IV 323a
Sanskrit language, IV 323a
Saussure, IV 322b–323a, 323b–324a, 328a

scholasticism, IV 329b
science, IV 323a, 324a, 326b, 328a, 329b
Sechehaye, IV 323a
semantics, IV 327b
semiology, IV 324a
signification, IV 324a
signs, IV 324a, 325b–326a, 328a
society, IV 325a, 325b
structures, IV 322b–323a, 324b
style, IV 327b, 333a
synchrony, IV 323b
syntax, IV 327b
system of differences, IV 324a
teleology, IV 324b
totemism, IV 326b
Troubetzkoy, IV 324a–324b, 326a
unconscious, IV 324b, 326a, 328b, 329a
women, IV 325b–326a
Structure
    aesthetics, II 219a
    music, III 261a
    naturalism in art, III 340b, 341a, 343b
    structuralism, IV 322b–323a, 324b
Struve, Peter
    Marxism, III 165a
    neo-Kantianism, III 165a
Strzemiński, W., aesthetics, II 222a
Stuart, James (1713–1788), neo-classicism in art, III 363a, 365b
Stubbes, Philip (fl. 1583–1591)
    Cosmic Fall, I 505b
    harmony, II 388a
Stubbs, William (1825–1901)
    historiography, II 491b, 496a
    law, II 686a
Stucken, E., mythology, III 310a
Sturm, Johannes (1507–1589), Ramism, IV 43b
Sturm und Drang
    Goethe, IV 200a
    revisionism, IV 266a
    romanticism, IV 200a, 208a–208b
Style
    adornment, IV 331a
    aesthetics, IV 330b, 331b, 332b
    Albalat, IV 332b
    Aristotle, IV 330b, 331a
    art, II 297b–298b, 567b, 570a–570b, 572a, 572b,

574a, 574b, 576a, 576b–577b, 580a, 580b, 581b, 583a
Boileau, IV 330b, 331b
Brunetière, IV 332b
Buffon, IV 330b, 331b, 332a
Burton, IV 331b
Chateaubriand, IV 332b
Cicero, IV 330a–331a
computers, IV 333a
content, IV 330b, 332a, 332b
correctness, IV 331a
Crevier, IV 332a
Dante, IV 331a
De Quincey, IV 332b
Demetrius, IV 330b, 331a
Dionysius of Halicarnassus, IV 330b, 331a
du Marsais, IV 332a
Flaubert, IV 332b
France, IV 331a, 331b, 332b
Garland, IV 331a
genius, II 316a, 321a, 321b
Geoffroi de Vinsauf, IV 331a
Gourmont, IV 332a, 332b
Greece (ancient), IV 330a, 330b, 331b
historiography, IV 147a
Horace, IV 330b, 331a
Hugo, IV 332b
idea, IV 332a
imagery, IV 331b, 333a
individualism, II 297b–298b; IV 333a
James, IV 332b
Jonson, IV 331b, 332a
Kames, IV 332a
La Bruyère, IV 331b
Laharpe, IV 332a
Lamy, IV 331b, 332a, 332b
Latin language, IV 330a
levels, IV 331a–332b
Lewes, IV 332b
literary criticism, I 606a
literature, III 88a; IV 157a, 330a–333a
Locke, IV 332a
Longinus, IV 330b, 331b, 332b
Marmontel, IV 332a
Mathieu of Vendôme, IV 331a
Middle Ages, IV 331a
mobility, II 298a
Montaigne, IV 331b
movement, IV 332a
music, II 316a, 321a, 321b; III 263b, 270a
nationalism, II 297b; IV 332a
naturalism in art, III 339a, 339b, 340b
Nature, IV 332a
neo-classicism in art, III 363b, 368b–369b, 371a
Newman, IV 332b
Newton, IV 332a
Opitz, IV 331b
organicism, III 422b
painting, II 567b, 570a–580b, 581b, 583a; IV 467a
passions, IV 332a
pastoral, IV 331a
Plato, IV 330b, 332b
Platonism, IV 330b, 331b
poetry, IV 467a
Proust, IV 330b
Quintilian, IV 330b–332a
Raleigh, IV 332b
Rapin, IV 331b
rationalism, IV 332a
Renaissance, IV 147a, 331a–331b
rhetoric, IV 167b, 168b–171a, 330a–333a
Richards, IV 332a
Robortello, IV 331a
Rollin, IV 332a
Rome (ancient), IV 330b, 331a
Ronsard, IV 331a, 331b
Sallust, IV 331b
Sanskrit language, IV 331a
Saussure, IV 333a
Scaliger, IV 331b
Schopenhauer, IV 332b
science, IV 332a, 332b
sculpture, IV 331b
Seneca, IV 331b
Socrates, IV 330b
Spencer, IV 332b
Stevenson, IV 332b
structuralism, IV 327b, 333a
Swift, IV 332a
symbolism, IV 344a
Theophrastus, IV 331a
Vergil, IV 331a
Vives, IV 331b
vocabulary, IV 331a
Voltaire, IV 332a
Wackernagel, IV 332b
Wordsworth, IV 332b
Su Shih (1036–1101), *ut pictura poesis*, IV 475b
Su Sung (A.D. 1092), time, IV 401b
Suarez, Francisco (1548–1617)
   abstraction, I 6b
   God, III 461a
   international peace, III 451b
   motion, III 461a
natural law, III 20a
perennial philosophy, III 461a
social contract, IV 254a
time, IV 392b
Subjectivism
   aesthetics, IV 355b, 356b
   Kant, II 455a
   literary criticism, I 597a, 598b, 601b
   Marxism, III 153a
   materialism, II 455a
   perennial philosophy, III 462a
   utilitarianism, IV 444b
Subject-object problem, II 590a
Sublime in external nature, IV 333a–337b
   Addison, IV 334a–335a, 335b, 336b
   aesthetics, IV 334a, 335a, 336b, 356a
   agoraphobia, IV 335a
   Akenside, IV 335a–337a
   Alps, IV 333b–334a
   Arabs, IV 334b
   architecture, IV 334b
   art, IV 334b, 336a, 336b
   astronomy, IV 336b
   beauty, IV 333b–337a
   Berkeley, IV 334b
   Boileau, IV 333b
   Burke, IV 335a, 336b–337a
   Burnet, IV 333b
   claustrophobia, IV 335a
   color, IV 335b, 336b, 337a
   Cooper, A. A., IV 334a–336b
   cosmic voyages, IV 335b, 336a–336b
   Dennis, IV 333b–334a, 335b
   eternity, IV 336b
   fear, IV 333b
   Flood, IV 333b
   France, IV 333a–333b, 334b
   gardening, IV 334b
   God, IV 334a, 335a, 336b, 337a
   Gothic, II 370a
   Great Britain, IV 333a–337b
   happiness, IV 335a
   Hume, IV 336b
   imagination, IV 334b–336b
   infinity, IV 336b
   Kant, IV 335a
   light, IV 335b, 336b, 337a–337b
   literary criticism, IV 333a, 334a
Locke, IV 334b, 336b
Longinus, IV 333b
Mallett, IV 335a–335b
microscope, IV 334b
Milton, IV 334b, 337a
mountain-origin, IV 333b
mountains in literature, III 258b; IV 333a–337b
Nature, IV 333b–336b
pain, IV 336b, 337a
painting, IV 472a, 473b
Pascal, IV 334a
planets, IV 336b
pleasure, IV 334b, 336b
poetry, IV 335a–337b, 472a, 472b, 473b
Pope, IV 333b, 337a–337b
psychology, IV 335a
rhetoric, IV 333a–333b, 334b
senses, IV 333a–337b
Seven Wonders of the World, IV 336a
space, IV 336a, 336b
stars, IV 336b
taste, IV 356a
telescope, IV 334b
Thomson, IV 335a–335b, 336b, 337a
time, IV 336b
vision, IV 334b
Young, Edward, IV 335b
Young, Thomas, IV 336a–336b, 337a
Suetonius (c. 100 A.D.), periodization in literary history, III 482a
Suffering
   animals, IV 415b
   Aristotle, IV 412a
   children, IV 415b
   good, IV 175a, 178a
   Hobbes, III 20b; IV 178a
   human nature, III 572b
   Kant, IV 382b
   Leibniz, IV 382a
   natural law, III 20a
   perfectibility, III 466a, 467b
   Plato, III 498a
   Plotinus, III 466a
   prophecy, III 664a, 665a, 669b
   retribution, IV 379b, 380b, 382a
   symbolism, IV 338a
   theodicy, IV 379b, 380b, 382a, 382b, 383a
   tragic sense, IV 412a, 412b, 413a, 413b, 414a, 415b
   wisdom, IV 413b
Suffrage
   democracy, I 660a, 662a, 664b, 665a, 666a; II 70a

equality, **II** 138b–139a, 145a, 145b
France, **I** 662a
freedom of speech, **II** 261a
general will, **II** 277b, 279b
Great Britain, **II** 138b
Greece (ancient), **II** 138b
Hegel, **II** 409b
individualism, **III** 45a–47a
natural liberty, **II** 70a
rights, **III** 45a–47a
Rome (ancient), **II** 261a
Rousseau, **II** 277b
social welfare, **IV** 280b–284a
Thoreau, **I** 437a, 437b
U.S., **I** 437a–437b, 439b, 660a, 666a; **II** 138b
Victorians, **IV** 218b
vox populi, **IV** 498b
welfare state, **IV** 509b
women, **III** 432a; **IV** 526b–527a, 528a–528b, 529a
Sufism, **II** 648a, 648b, 650a, 650b–651a
love, **III** 99b, 100a, 101a
Suger, Abbot (1081?–1151), iconography, **II** 527a–527b
Suhrawardi, **II** 645b, 650a–650b, 651b
love, **III** 99b
Suicide
Christianity, **III** 80a
Donne, **III** 80a
Egypt (ancient), **II** 256a–256b
ethics, **IV** 70a
impiety, **II** 566a
impressionism, **II** 575b
literary paradox, **III** 80a–80b
relativism, **IV** 70a
Victorian sensibility, **IV** 222b
Sulla, Lucius Cornelius (138–78 B.C.), freedom of speech, **II** 261a
Sullivan, Harry Stack (1892–1949), psychology, **IV** 14a, 28a
Sullivan, William L. (1803–18/3), modernism, **I** 424b
Sully, Duc de (1560–1641), international peace, **III** 452b
Sulzer, Johann Georg (1720–1774)
aesthetics, **II** 551a; **IV** 356a
classification of the arts, **I** 460b
genius, **II** 295a–295b
ideal, **II** 550a, 551a
Sumer
geometry, **III** 171a–172b
historiography, **II** 465a

mathematics, **III** 171a, 173a
mythology, **III** 280a
Sumner, William Graham (1840–1910)
association of ideas, **I** 115b
evolutionism, **II** 181a
individualism, **II** 596a, 601a
psychology, **IV** 25b
Social Darwinism, **II** 181a
Sun
attraction of, **I** 547a
Bode's law, **I** 552a
cosmology, **I** 535b–547a, 551a, 552a
determinism, **II** 18b–19a
disease, **II** 397b
distance from the planets, **I** 552a
eclipses, **I** 537b–538a, 539a, 539b, 540a
geology, **IV** 419a
measurement, **IV** 400b
microcosm, **III** 128a, 130b
motion, **I** 536a, 551a; **IV** 50a
mythology, **III** 278a, 280b, 282a, 282b, 287b, 291a, 303b, 307b–310b
Newton, **I** 674a
orbits, **I** 540a, 541a
relativity, **IV** 74b, 76a
size of, **I** 539a, 543b
time, **IV** 400b
velocity, **I** 537b, 540a
Sun Tsu, war, **IV** 501a
Sun Yat-sen (1866–1925), nationalism, **III** 333a, 334a
Sundwall, J., freedom of speech, **II** 260a
Sung dynasty
ut pictura poesis, **IV** 475b
Sung Wu, nationalism, **III** 334a
Superego
environment and, **II** 123b–124a
happiness, **II** 383a
wisdom of the fool, **IV** 516a–516b
Super-Hilbert space, **II** 591a
Superman
Dühren, **III** 474a
evolution, **III** 474a
Faust (legend), **III** 250b, 251a
Nietzsche, **III** 474a
perfectibility, **III** 474a
Supernatural
art, **II** 575b, 576b, 580b
Carlyle, **IV** 201a
dignity, **IV** 142b, 145a
Epicureanism, **III** 587b
Faust (legend), **III** 245a,

245b, 247b, 249b
Ficino, **IV** 145a
genius, **II** 293b
Gothic, **II** 370b
historiography, **II** 468a, 470b, 487b–488a, 488b
Huxley, **I** 18a–18b
ideal, **II** 549b, 550b, 551b
impressionism, **II** 575b, 576b, 580b
James, **III** 568a
law, **III** 10b, 27b, 29a
Man-Machine, **III** 133a
natural law, **III** 15a, 19a
naturalism, **IV** 53b
Nature, **I** 129b; **III** 346b, 347a, 347b
necessity, **III** 352b, 360a
Otto, Rudolf, **IV** 97a
poetry, **III** 531a
pragmatism, **III** 552a, 553a, 554b, 564b, 568a
primitivism, **III** 587b
progress, **III** 635b
rationalism, **IV** 46a
realism in literature, **IV** 53b
religion, **III** 95b, 97a, 99b, 106b, 111a, 142b, 145a
romanticism, **IV** 198a, 201a, 207a
Saint Thomas Aquinas, **I** 669b
symbolism, **IV** 345a
Utopia, **IV** 462a
Victorians, **IV** 218a
witchcraft, **IV** 521a
Superparticular music, **III** 262a
Superstition
China, **I** 362a
deism, **I** 647b
Diderot, **III** 644b
disease, **II** 396b
Epicureanism, **IV** 176a
ethics, **IV** 91a
evil, **II** 165a, 168b
fortune, fate and chance, **II** 226a, 234b
God, **II** 356a
happiness and pleasure, **II** 378a
health, **II** 396b
Helvétius, **III** 470a
heresy, **II** 426b
magic, **III** 246a
matter, **III** 187b
microcosm, **III** 126a–126b
mythology, **III** 302a
perfectibility, **III** 465a, 470a, 470b
progress, **III** 635b, 644b
Pythagoreans, **IV** 31b
rationalism, **IV** 48a

relativism, **IV** 71a
religion, **IV** 107a
right and good, **IV** 176a
social contract, **IV** 261a
syncretism, **I** 44b
Victorians, **IV** 218b
witchcraft, **IV** 521a, 522a
Surplus value
Bernstein, **III** 162b
capitalism, **III** 148a
Marxism, **III** 148a, 150b, 162b
Surrealism, **I** 352b
expressionism and, **II** 206a, 206b
fantasy, **III** 342b
Freud, **I** 352b
imagination, **III** 212b
irrationalism, **II** 638a
literature, **II** 638a; **III** 242b
love, **III** 107a, 107b
naturalism in art, **III** 342b
Proust, **IV** 340a
symbolism, **IV** 340a, 345a
Survival of the fittest
evolutionism, **II** 182a, 187a
perfectibility, **III** 473b
Spencer, **III** 473b
Susanna (Bible), temperance, **IV** 370b, 372b
Suso, Heinrich (1300?–1366), perfectibility, **III** 467b
Süssmilch, J. P., chance, **I** 338a
Sutherland, Arthur, constitutionalism, **I** 487b–488a
Sutter, Baroness Bertha von, international peace, **III** 449a, 453b
Sutton, Francis X., ideology, **II** 556b, 557b
Suzuki, Daisetz Teitaro
Buddhism, **I** 256b
Orientalism, **III** 436a
Sviták, Ivan, Marxism, **III** 169a, 169b
Swadesh, Morris (1909–1967), linguistics, **III** 72a; **IV** 429b–430a
Swammerdam, Jan (1637–1680)
Cosmic Fall, **I** 509a
spontaneous generation, **II** 282a–282b; **IV** 309b
Sweden
Buddhism, **I** 255a
Great Depression of the 1930s, **IV** 512a
intolerance, **IV** 113a
Jesuits, **IV** 113a
mythology, **III** 311b
religion, **IV** 113a
welfare state, **IV** 512a

Swedenborg, Emmanuel (1688–1772)
cosmic images, I 520b
symbolism, IV 339a
Swedish language, II 660b
Sweet, Henry (1845–1912), linguistics, III 70b
Sweetser, William, longevity, III 93a
Sweezy v. New Hampshire, I 12a
Swerve theory, II 136a–137a
Swift, Jonathan (1667–1745)
attitude toward antiquity, I 81a, 81b
classicism, I 453a
comedy, I 469b
cosmic voyages, I 528a, 528b, 532b, 533a–534a
irony, II 628b, 629a, 634a
literary paradox, III 77b
literature, III 84b; IV 332a
longevity, III 89b
primitivism, III 599a–599b
satire, IV 211b, 213b, 214b, 215a, 215b
style, IV 332a
Utopia, IV 464a
virtuoso, IV 489b
wisdom of the fool, IV 520a
Swindler, Mary, creativity in art, I 582a
Swineshead, Richard (fl. 1350)
humanism, IV 129a
matter, II 201a–201b; III 192a
medieval science, II 200b, 201a, 204a, 204b
Switzerland
autonomy, III 329a
capitalism, I 396b
democracy, I 661a
Enlightenment, III 329a
equality, III 329a
ethnic groups, III 328b, 329a
international peace, III 451a
intolerance, IV 113a, 117a
Italy, III 328b
Jesuits, IV 113a
language, II 660b, 671b–672a
majorities, III 328b, 329a
minorities, III 392a
music, III 267a
nationalism, III 328b, 329a, 329b, 330b, 338b
primitivism, III 600b
private property, III 655b
psychology, IV 12b–13b
race, III 328b, 329a
Ramism, IV 44b
Reformation, I 391a–392b;

IV 67b
religion, IV 109a, 113a, 117a
romanticism, IV 205b
social contract, IV 259b
space, IV 303a
State, I 661a
witchcraft, IV 522b
Sybilline writings, I 336a; III 665b, 668b–669a
Sydenham, Floyer, Platonism, III 518a
Sydenham, Thomas (1624–1689), disease, II 400a
Sydney, Algernon (1622–1683)
constitutionalism, I 488b
natural law, I 488b
See also Sidney
Sydow, C. W. von, mythology, III 316a
Syllabus of Errors (1864)
heresy, II 429b
Roman Catholic Church, II 429b
Syllogism
Descartes, III 356b
necessity, III 356b
Ramism, IV 43b
Sylvester, II, Pope (940?–1003)
Faust (legend), III 245b
harmony, II 391b
humanism, IV 130b
logic, I 381a
music, II 391b
Sylvius, Franciscus (1614–1672), alchemy, I 33a
Symbolism, IV 337b–345b
abstraction, IV 344a, 345a
Acmeists, IV 343a
Aeschylus, III 626a
aesthetics, IV 338a, 338b, 339b, 340a, 341b, 343b, 345a
Akhmatova, IV 343a
Alberti, IV 342a
allegory, I 41a, 42a; IV 338a, 339a, 341b, 342a, 342b, 344a, 345a
Alonso, IV 342b
animals, IV 338b
Annensky, IV 343b
anthropology, IV 341b
anthropomorphism, IV 338b
Aristotle, II 663a; III 273b
art, II 525a–540a, 570b, 575b, 576b, 580b–582a; IV 338b, 339a, 339b, 342a, 345a, 345b
atheism, IV 345a
axiomatization, I 169b
Bachofen, III 313b

Baird, IV 341b
Baroja, IV 342a
Barre, IV 340a
Barthes, IV 344b
Baudelaire, IV 338b, 339b, 340b, 342b, 344a–345a
beauty, IV 338a, 338b, 339a
Bely, IV 344b
Bergson, IV 344a
Blake, IV 340b, 341b
Blok, IV 343a, 344b
Campana, IV 342a
Carlyle, IV 339a, 344b
Castro, IV 341a
Chaucer, IV 341b
Child, IV 341a
Christianity, IV 341b
city, I 427a–428a, 429a–431b
Claudel, IV 340a, 340b, 344a
Coleridge, IV 338b–339a, 344b, 345a
Crane, IV 341a, 344b
Crowe, IV 344b
cubism, IV 345b
Czechoslovakia, IV 343b
D'Annunzio, IV 341a, 343a
Dante, III 511a; IV 341b
Darío, IV 342a, 344b
decline of, I 58a
defined, IV 337b–338a
drama, IV 340b, 344b
Egypt (ancient), IV 338b
Eliot, T. S., IV 341a, 344b
Emerson, IV 339a, 341b, 344b
essence, IV 338b
expressionism, IV 345a
Faulkner, IV 341a, 343a
Faust (legend), III 248a, 249a, 251a, 252b
Fet, IV 343a
Fletcher, IV 342a
formalism, IV 343a, 343b
France, III 483b; IV 339a–344a, 345a
free verse, IV 344a
Frye, IV 337b, 341b
futurism, IV 343b, 345a
Gauss, IV 341b
George, IV 342b, 344b
Germany, III 483b; IV 338a–338b, 341a, 342b–343a, 343b, 344b
Gide, IV 340b, 344b
God, IV 341b, 345a
Goethe, IV 338a, 338b, 339a, 341b, 343a, 343b
Góngora, IV 342a
Gosse, IV 340b
Gourmont, IV 341a, 342b, 344b

Great Britain, III 483b; IV 338b–339a, 340b–341a, 343b, 344b
Guillén, Jorge, IV 342a, 344b
Hartmann, IV 345a
Hauptmann, IV 344b
Hawthorne, IV 341b
Hebbel, IV 338b
Hegel, IV 338b
Heine, IV 338b, 344b
Herder, III 305a; IV 338a
Herrera y Reissig, IV 342a
hieroglyphic signs, II 529b, 530a
history, IV 337b–338a, 344a
Hlaváček, IV 343b
Hoffmann, IV 344b
Hofmannsthal, IV 342b, 344b
Hugo, IV 344a
humanism, II 521a
Huneker, IV 341a, 341b
Huysman, IV 340b
Ibsen, IV 341a, 344b
iconography, II 525a–535a, 537b, 540a
idea, II 546a; IV 338a, 339b, 342b
idealism, IV 343b
ideology, II 558a–558b
imagery, IV 338a, 341b, 343b, 344a, 345a
imagination, III 212a, 222a, 222b; IV 339b
impressionism, II 570b, 575b, 576b, 580b–582a
India (ancient), IV 338b
Ireland, IV 340b
Italy, III 484a; IV 341a, 342a, 343b
James, IV 341a, 344b
Jiménez, IV 342a
Joyce, IV 341a, 344b
Jung, IV 341a
Kafka, IV 345a
Kahn, IV 339b, 340a, 344a
Kant, IV 388a
Kayser, Wolfgang, IV 343a
language, II 662b, 663a, 668b; IV 339b, 345a
Latin America, IV 344b
Lawrence, D. H., IV 344b
Leibniz, IV 338a
literary criticism, IV 337b, 340b, 341b–342a, 344b
logic, IV 337b, 338a
Lorca, García, IV 342a
love, III 104a
Lüth, IV 342b
Luzi, María, IV 342a
Machado, IV 342a, 344b

Maeterlinck, **IV** 340a, 340b, 341a, 343a, 344b
Mallarmé, **IV** 339a, 340a, 340b, 341a, 342a, 342b, 343a, 343b, 344b, 345a
Mann, **IV** 344b
mannerism, **IV** 344a
mathematics, **III** 173a, 175b, 176a, 176b, 178a, 179a, 183b, 184b; **IV** 337b, 338b
Matthiessen, **IV** 341b
Matthisson, **IV** 338a
Melville, **IV** 341b
Merezhkovsky, **IV** 343a
metaphor, **III** 203b; **IV** 339a, 344a
Michaud, **IV** 340a, 340b
Middle Ages, **II** 580b; **IV** 341b
modernism, **IV** 343b
Moore, George, **IV** 340b
motif, **III** 242a–243a
music, **III** 226b, 268b, 269a, 270a–271b; **IV** 342b
Musil, **IV** 342b
mysticism, **IV** 343a
mythology, **III** 273b, 274a, 283a, 288a, 291b, 292a, 292b, 293a, 295a, 299a, 304b, 305a, 305b, 306b, 312b, 313a, 313b, 315b; **IV** 338b, 339a, 341b, 342a, 344b
nationalism, **IV** 343a, 344b
naturalism, **IV** 339a, 342b
naturalism in art, **III** 341b, 345b
Nature, **IV** 338a, 338b, 339a, 345a
necessity, **III** 361a
neo-romanticism, **IV** 343b
Nerval, **IV** 340b, 344a
Netherlands, **IV** 341a
Nicaragua, **IV** 342a
Nietzsche, **IV** 342b, 345a
Nordau, **IV** 341a, 343a
Novalis, **IV** 338a, 344b, 345a
numbers, **II** 527b, 546a
occultism, **IV** 345a
O'Neill, **IV** 341a, 344b
Onofri, **IV** 342a
Orientalism, **III** 431a
Orpheus (myth), **IV** 345a
Ortega y Gasset, **IV** 342b
Pascoli, **IV** 342a
Péguy, **IV** 340a
perennial philosophy, **III** 460a, 461a
periodization in literary history, **III** 483b, 484a
pessimism, **IV** 345a
Pica, **IV** 342a
Platonism, **III** 508a, 511a,

523b 524b; **IV** 341b
Poe, **IV** 341b, 345a
poetry, **IV** 338a–340a, 341a, 342a–344a, 468b, 474b
Poland, **IV** 343b
Polonsky, **IV** 343a
Portugal, **IV** 340b
positivism, **IV** 345a
post-symbolism, **IV** 345a
Pound, **IV** 341a
Procházka, **IV** 343b
progress, **III** 626a
prophecy, **III** 657b–658a
prose, **IV** 340b, 344b
Protestantism, **IV** 341b
Proust, **IV** 340a, 340b, 341a, 343a, 344b
Przesmycki, **IV** 343b
psychology, **IV** 338b
Puritanism, **IV** 341b
Quinet, **IV** 344b
Ramism, **IV** 44a
rationalism, **IV** 345a
realism, **IV** 56a, 344b
reality, **IV** 338a
Régnier, **IV** 340a, 342b
religion, **II** 581a; **III** 203b; **IV** 99b, 341b
Reyes, **IV** 342b
rhetoric, **IV** 339a, 344a
Rilke, **IV** 342b, 344b
Rimbaud, **IV** 340b, 342a, 342b
Robertson, D. W., **IV** 341b
romanticism, **IV** 195b, 196a, 197a, 338a, 338b, 341b, 343a, 344b, 345a
Rousseau, **IV** 345a
Ruskin, **IV** 339a
Saint Antoine, **IV** 340a
Šalda, F. X., **IV** 343b
Schelling, **IV** 338a–338b, 343b
schematism, **IV** 338b
Schiller, **IV** 338a
Schlegel, August Wilhelm, **IV** 338a, 339a, 345a
Schlegel, Friedrich, **IV** 338a, 339a
Schopenhauer, **IV** 345a
Shakespeare, **IV** 338a
Shelley, **II** 581a; **III** 508a
socialism, **IV** 339a–339b
Soffici, **IV** 342a
Solger, **IV** 338a
Solověv, **IV** 343a
soul, **IV** 338b
sound, **II** 662b
Souza, **IV** 340a
Sova, **IV** 343b
Spain, **IV** 341a, 342a–342b, 343b, 344b
Staël, **IV** 339a

Stein, **IV** 341a, 341b
Steiner, **IV** 343a
Stevens, **IV** 341a, 344b
Strindberg, **IV** 344b
style, **IV** 344a
suffering, **IV** 338a
supernatural, **IV** 345a
surrealism, **IV** 340a, 345a
Swedenborg, **IV** 339a
symbols, **IV** 337b–338a
Symons, **IV** 340b, 341a, 342b
synaesthesia, **IV** 344a, 344b
Taupin, **IV** 341a
temperance, **IV** 371b, 373a, 377a
Tolstoy, **IV** 343a
Trakl, **IV** 342b
transcendentalism, **IV** 345a
Tyutchev, **IV** 343a
Unamuno, **IV** 342a
Ungaretti, **IV** 342a
U.S.S.R., **IV** 341a, 343a–343b, 344b
U.S., **IV** 341a–342a, 343b, 344b
Uruguay, **IV** 342a
Valéry, **IV** 340a, 340b, 341a, 342a, 343a, 344a–345a
Vengerova, **IV** 343a
Verhaeren, **IV** 340a
Verlaine, **IV** 339b, 340b, 342a, 342b, 343a, 343b
Viélé-Griffin, **IV** 340a, 342b
Villiers de l'Isle-Adam, **IV** 340b, 343b
Vinet, **IV** 339a
Vischer, **IV** 338b, 343b
Vortriede, **IV** 344b, 345a
Wagner, **IV** 342b, 344b
Whitman, **IV** 341b
Wilson, **IV** 341a–341b
Winckelmann, **IV** 338a
Wolff, **IV** 338a, 343a
Wyspiański, **IV** 343b
Wyzéwa, **IV** 340a, 342a
Yeats, **IV** 340b–341a, 343a, 344b

Symbols
  allegory, **I** 41a, 42a
  numbers, **III** 399b, 400b, 401a, 402a, 402b, 406b
  symbolism, **IV** 337b–338a
Symeon (Bible), Jesus Christ and, **I** 413b
Symmachus (late 2nd century A.D.), Pythagorean cosmos, **IV** 406
Symmetry, **IV** 345b–353b
  Aeschylus, **IV** 348a
  aesthetics, **II** 217b; **IV** 347b, 348b, 351b
  Alcmaeon of Croton, **IV**

346b
Anaxagoras, **IV** 346b
Anaximander, **IV** 346b, 348a
antimatter, **IV** 351a
Aristotle, **IV** 346b, 347a, 349a
art, **IV** 348a
astronomy, **IV** 348b
asymmetry, **IV** 347b, 349a, 350b, 351a, 351b
automorphism, **IV** 351a–352b
beauty, **IV** 347a
Bergson, **IV** 349a
Bible, **IV** 348a
bilateral, **IV** 346a, 347b, 349b, 350b, 351a, 351b
body, **IV** 348a–348b
Brahe, **IV** 348b
broken, **IV** 352a
charge conjugation, **IV** 351a
circularity, **IV** 348b–350b
computers, **IV** 350b
Copernicus, **IV** 348b
corpuscles, **IV** 349a, 350b–351a
cosmology, **IV** 349a, 349b, 350b, 352b
Creation, **IV** 349a, 350b
de Broglie waves, **IV** 349a, 350b–351a
defined, **IV** 346a
Democritus, **IV** 346b, 348a
dilations, **IV** 351b
Droysen, **IV** 347a–347b
dualism, **IV** 346a–347a, 350b–351a
electromagnetics, **IV** 349a
electrons, **IV** 351a, 353a
ellipses, **IV** 348b–349a
Empedocles, **IV** 346b, 348a
energy, **IV** 349a, 352b
entropy, **IV** 349b, 350a
Euclid, **IV** 346b
Eudoxus, **IV** 349a
evil, **IV** 348a
evolution, **IV** 349a, 349b, 353a
Frey, Dagobert, **IV** 348a
geology, **IV** 352b–353a
geometry, **IV** 346a, 349b, 351b
God, **IV** 349a, 353b
good, **IV** 348a
gravity, **IV** 348a, 349a, 352b, 353a
Greece (ancient), **IV** 346a–348a, 349a
groups, **IV** 351b
harmony, **IV** 353a
health, **II** 399a
heat, **IV** 349b

Helmholtz, IV 352a
Heraclitus, IV 346b
Herodotus, IV 347a
Homer, IV 346a
homogeneity, IV 352a–352b
Iamblichus, IV 346b–347a
idea, IV 348a
ideal, IV 348a
invariance, IV 352b, 353a
irreversibility, IV 349b
Kepler, IV 348b
kinetics, IV 350a
Leibniz, IV 353a
Leonardo da Vinci, IV 351b
light, IV 349a
magnetism, IV 353a–353b
mathematics, IV 346b, 348b–352b
matter, IV 349a, 350a, 351a, 352b
Maxwell, IV 353a
mechanism, IV 348b, 349b, 350a
metaphysics, IV 352a
mimesis, IV 347b
mirrors, IV 346a, 348b, 351a, 351b
morality, IV 347b
motion, IV 349a, 350a
Naturalism in art, III 340b
Nature, IV 347b, 348a
Newton, IV 348b, 352b
Nicholas of Cusa, IV 352a
nonsymmetry, IV 347b
ontology, IV 348b, 351a
orbits, IV 348b
order, IV 350a
orthogonal transformation, IV 351b, 352a
painting, IV 348a, 467b
Parmenides, IV 346b
perception, IV 347b
philosophy, IV 346a–346b
physics, IV 349a, 349b–350a, 351a, 352b–353b
Plato, IV 346b, 347a, 348a, 348b, 350b
Platonism, IV 348a
Pliny, IV 345b, 346a
Plotinus, IV 347a–348a
poetry, IV 467b
positrons, IV 351a
pre-Socratics, IV 350b
probability, IV 350a
prophecy, IV 348a
protons, IV 351a
psyche, IV 349a
Ptolemy, IV 349a
Pythagoreans, IV 346b
randomness, IV 350a
rationalism, IV 346b
real numbers, IV 348a
reason, IV 349a–349b

reflection, IV 348b, 351a, 351b
relativity, IV 352b–353a
religion, IV 347b, 348a
reversibility, IV 349b, 350a
romanticism, IV 347a–347b
Rome (ancient), IV 345b–346a
Saint Augustine, IV 349a
science, IV 348b, 349a–349b, 352b
Socrates, IV 347b
solids, IV 346b
Sophists, IV 346b
space, IV 346b, 351a–353a
symmetry law, IV 352b, 353a
Thales, IV 353a–353b
theology, IV 348a, 349a, 352a
Theophrastus, IV 348a
thermodynamics, IV 350a
Thompson, D. W., IV 347b
time, IV 349a–350b
uniformitarianism, IV 353a
universe, IV 350a–350b, 351a, 352a, 352b
Vitruvius, IV 346a
waves, IV 349a, 350b–351a
Weyl, IV 347b, 348b, 351b
Wickham, Annas, IV 347b
Wigner, IV 352b, 353a
Winckelmann, IV 347a
Xenophanes, IV 348a
Zoroastrianism, IV 348a
Symmetry law, IV 352b, 353a
Symonds, John Addington (1840–1893)
evolution of literature, II 171a–171b
literary criticism, I 601a
Renaissance, IV 128a
universal man, IV 438a
Symons, Arthur (1865–1945)
irony, II 633b
symbolism, IV 340b, 341a, 342b
Sympathy
Aristotle, IV 412a
Bentham, IV 178b
empathy, II 87b
Gerard, II 87b
good, IV 178a, 178b, 182a
happiness, II 380a
Hartley, III 234b
Hume, III 232a–232b; IV 178a
Hutcheson, III 232b
Kames, II 87b
moral sense, III 232a–232b, 233b, 234b
Smith, Adam, III 233b; IV 178a

tragic sense, IV 412a
vox populi, IV 498b–499b
Syncretism
allegory, I 43b–46a
defined, I 43b
dignity, IV 144a
Ficino, IV 126b
God, II 341b
Middle Ages, I 44a
Origen, I 44b–45a
Philo Judaeus, I 44a
Pico della Mirandola, IV 126b
piety, I 44a–44b
religion, IV 93b
Renaissance, I 43b, 44a; IV 126b, 144a
Spenser, I 44a
superstition, I 44b
Syndicalism
agriculture, III 674b
bureaucracy, III 673b
democracy, I 664b
France, III 676b
Great Britain, III 677a
ideology, III 674a
industry, III 673b
organization, III 673b
protest movements, III 671a, 672a, 673a, 673b–674a, 675b, 676b, 677a
society, III 673b
Spain, III 674a
State, III 673b
violence, III 673b
Synergism, II 28a
Synesius (c. 410 A.D.)
imagination, III 212a
literary paradox, III 77b
Platonism, III 376b
Porphyry and, III 376b
Synthesis
naturalism in art, III 341a
Synthetic method
methodology, III 379a
Newton, III 379a
Sypher, Wylie
baroque in literature, I 193b
necessity, III 358a, 359a, 359b
periodization in literary history, III 484a
Syrens (myth), music, III 268b–269a
Syria
Eastern Orthodox Church, I 411a
nationalism, III 338a
Syria (ancient)
disease, II 398b
freedom of speech, II 253b–254a, 254b
Gnosticism, II 330a
God, II 333b, 335a–335b

Judaic-Christianity, I 375a
Neo-Platonism, III 372b
Szilard, Leo, entropy, II 116b

T

Ta eirēmena, law, II 680a
Taboos
Freud, IV 96b
holy, II 513b, 514a
love, III 107b
Otto, IV 97b
religion, IV 96b, 97b
Taborites
heresy, II 418b
socialism, IV 287b
Tachyons, IV 83b, 84a
Tacitus (55?–after 117 A.D.)
chance, I 336a
conservation, I 472a–472b
freedom of speech, II 260b, 261b–262a
Gothic, II 368b
historiography, II 470a–470b, 482b
humanism, II 516a
impiety, II 566b
law, II 686a
Machiavellism, III 116a
morality, III 116a
necessity, III 356a
periodization in literary history, III 482a
primitivism, III 591b
private property, III 651b
temperance, IV 370b
welfare, III 116a
Taft, William Howard (1857–1930), international peace, III 450a, 450b
Tahiti
Diderot, III 603a–603b
Great Britain, III 602a
primitivism, III 602a, 602b, 603a, 603b
Taine, Hippolyte A. (1828–1893)
art, II 308b
authority, I 155b, 156a
behaviorism, I 220a
classicism, I 450a
conservatism, I 483a
environment, II 583a
evolutionism, II 183a
genius, II 308b
historiography, II 495b
history, II 171b
impressionism, II 583a
literary criticism, I 600a–600b
Man-Machine, III 143a

modernism, I 420b
naturalism, IV 53b
psychology, IV 12a
realism in literature, IV 53b, 55a
society, II 171b
style, IV 332a
Tait, Peter Guthrie (1831–1903)
    entropy, II 116a
    time measurement, IV 404b
Talaeus, Audomarus, *see* Talon, Omer
Talbert, Ernest William, mythology, III 299a
Talleyrand, Charles Maurice de (1754–1838)
    balance of power, I 186a
    law, II 688b
Tallis, Thomas (1510?–1585)
    harmony, II 390a
Talmud
    philanthropy, III 488a
    progress, III 636a
Talon, Omer (1510–1562), Ramism, IV 42b
Tamm, I., indeterminacy, II 591a
Tammuz (myth), II 335a–335b
    Mesopotamia (ancient), IV 101b
    religion, IV 101b, 104b
Tanaquil (myth), III 313b
Tanchelm (d. 1115?), heresy, II 418b, 419a
Taney, Roger Brooke (1777–1864), law, III 8b–9a
Tantrism, longevity, III 90a
Taoism, I 355a, 355b, 357a, 367a–368b, 371a
    alchemy, III 91a
    China, I 249a, 254a
    China (ancient), IV 476a
    evolutionism, II 174b
    God, II 344b
    health, II 397a
    longevity, III 90a, 90b, 91a, 93a
    Orientalism, III 430a, 434a
    philanthropy, III 486b
    U.S., III 430a, 434a
    ut pictura poesis, IV 476a
Tarde, Gabriel (1843–1904), individualism, II 601a, 601b
Tarphon, Rabbi, equity, II 151b–152a
Tarquin, Lucius (534–510 B.C.), temperance, IV 375b
Tarski, Alfred (1902–   )
    axiomatization, I 170b
    positivism, III 547b
Tartaglia, Nicolo (1500?–1557), mathematics, II 205a

Tartars, nationalism, III 333b
Tartini, Giuseppe (1692–1770), music, III 263b
Tasso, Torquato (1544–1595)
    baroque in literature, I 189a, 190a, 192a, 195a
    Goethe and, III 84b
    Gothic, II 368b
    hedonism, III 514b
    iconography, II 531a
    mimesis, III 228b
    Platonism, III 513a–513b, 514b
    poetics, III 529a–529b, 530b
    romanticism, IV 187a, 188a, 190b, 192a, 193b
    ut pictura poesis, IV 467b, 468b, 469b
Tassoni, Alessandro (1565–1635), poetry, I 78a
Taste, IV 353b–357b
    Addison, IV 355b
    Alembert, IV 355a
    Ariosto, IV 354b
    art, II 572b, 573a; IV 353b, 355b, 356a
    Balzac, IV 354b
    Batteux, IV 355a
    Baumgarten, IV 356a
    beauty, IV 353b–356b
    behavior, IV 354b
    Bodmer, IV 356a
    Burke, IV 355b
    Caxton, IV 355b
    Cellini, IV 354b
    classicism, IV 353b, 355b
    common sense, IV 355b, 356a
    Congreve, IV 355b
    Crousaz, IV 355a
    Crusius, IV 356a
    Dacier, IV 355a
    Diderot, IV 355a
    Dolce, IV 354b
    Dubos, IV 355a, 355b
    Ebreo, IV 354b
    education, IV 354a, 355a
    Ettorri, IV 354b
    feeling, IV 353b, 354a, 354b, 355a, 356b
    Feijóo, IV 354b
    Filarete, IV 354a
    France, IV 354b–355b
    genius, II 294a, 294b, 295a, 296a, 323b; IV 356b
    Gerard, IV 355b–356a
    Germany, IV 356a–356b
    good, IV 354a, 355a, 356a, 356b
    Gothic, II 368a, 368b, 370a
    Gottsched, IV 356a
    Gracián, IV 354b
    Graziani, IV 354b

Great Britain, IV 355a, 355b–356a
    Hamann, IV 356b
    Hartley, IV 356a
    Herder, IV 356b
    Hume, III 232a; IV 355b, 356a
    Hutcheson, IV 355b
    impressionism, II 572b, 573a
    irrationalism, IV 355a, 355b, 356b
    Johnson, Samuel, IV 356a
    judgment, IV 354a, 354b, 355a, 355b, 356a, 356b
    Kant, IV 356a, 356b
    knowledge, IV 354a, 355a
    König, J. U., IV 356a
    La Bruyère, IV 355b
    La Fontaine, IV 354b
    La Rochefoucauld, IV 354b
    Leibniz, IV 356a
    Lessing, IV 356a
    literary criticism, I 597a, 597b–598a, 600a, 603a
    Malebranche, IV 355a
    Mandeville, IV 356a
    Mendelssohn, IV 356a
    Mengs, IV 356a
    Méré, IV 354b
    Michelangelo, IV 354b
    Milton, IV 355b
    Molière, IV 354b
    Montesquieu, IV 355a
    moral sense, III 232a
    morality, IV 354b, 355b, 356a, 356b
    Muratori, IV 354b
    music, II 323b
    Nature, IV 355b
    neo-classicism in art, III 370a
    perfection, IV 256a, 356b
    philosophy, IV 356a, 356b
    pleasure, IV 354a, 354b
    Priestley, IV 356a
    Rapin, IV 355a
    rationalism, IV 355b, 356a
    reason, IV 353b–356b
    relativism, IV 356a
    Renaissance, IV 354a–354b
    rhetoric, IV 172a, 172b
    Rinuccini, IV 354b
    Saint-Evremond, IV 354b–355a
    Schramm, IV 356a
    science, IV 354a, 356a
    senses, IV 355a, 355b
    Shaftesbury, IV 355b, 356a
    Spain, IV 354b
    subjectivism, IV 355b, 356b
    sublime in external nature, IV 356a
    Sulzer, IV 356b

Thomasius, IV 356a
    truth, IV 354a, 355a, 356b
    typology, IV 356a–356b
    universality, IV 354a–356b
    ut pictura poesis, IV 471b, 472a, 473b, 474a
    utility, IV 355a, 355b, 356a
    Varchi, IV 354b
    Vauvenargues, IV 355a
    Vilate, IV 355a
    Voltaire, IV 355a
    vox populi, IV 497a
    Webb, IV 355b
    Zuccolo, IV 354b
Tat (myth), hermeticism, II 431b
Tate, Allen (1899–   ), literary criticism, I 603a–603b
Tatian (2nd century A.D.)
    cycles, I 623a–623b
    death, I 643a
    immortality, I 643a
Tauler, Johannes (1300?–1361)
    Hegel and, II 412b
    perfectibility, III 467b
Taupin, René, symbolism, IV 341a
Tawney, R. H. (1880–1962)
    China, I 371b
    economic history, II 60b
    equality, II 147a
    individualism, II 596b
    liberalism, III 56b
    right, IV 177a
Taxation
    desegregation, III 13a
    economic history, II 45b
    equality, II 144a, 144b, 145b
    kingship, II 690a
    law, II 690a; III 1b
    Machiavellism, III 119b, 120a
    Marxism, III 151b
    peace, III 441a
    philanthropy, III 490a, 492a
    private property, III 653a, 654b, 655a
    Rome (ancient), II 690a
    social welfare, IV 279a, 283a
    U.S., III 11b
    utility, IV 458a
Taxonomy
    acquired characteristics, II 618a
    evolutionism, II 175b
    folklore, III 240a
    Greece (ancient), III 61b
    motif, III 240a
Taylor, Edward (1642–1729)
    baroque in literature, I 194a

psychology, IV 16b
Puritanism, IV 16b
Taylor, Henry O. (1856–1941), war, IV 505a
Taylor, Herbert, DNA, II 291b
Taylor, Jeremy (1613–1667), baroque in literature, I 193b
Taylor, John (1753–1824), democracy, I 660a–660b
Taylor, Nathaniel W. (1786–1858), religion, IV 111a
Taylor, Thomas (1758–1835), Schleiermacher and, III 519a–519b
Taylor, William (1765–1836), romanticism, IV 192a
Teaching
  academic freedom, I 10a–16b
  anti-intellectualism, I 16a
  education, II 72b, 73b, 75b, 80a–80b, 81a–81b
  freedom of speech, II 252a–252b, 258b
  salaries, I 14a–15b
  Socrates, II 80a–80b
  tenure, I 12b–14a
Technique
  creativity in art, I 577b, 578a–578b, 583b, 584a, 585a, 585b, 586a, 588b
  impressionism, II 567b, 570a–570b, 574a, 580a, 581b, 583a
  literature, IV 330b
Technology, IV 357b–365b
  abstraction, IV 361a
  Africa, IV 361a
  alchemy, IV 358a, 360a
  Arabs, IV 358b, 359a
  Arkwright, IV 362b–363a
  art, IV 358b, 359b
  artists, IV 359b
  Asia, IV 361a
  astrology, IV 360a
  Bacon, I 173b, 174b–175b; IV 361a, 361b–364b, 462a
  Black, IV 362b
  Boyle, IV 361b
  bureaucracy, IV 357b, 358a
  Carnot, IV 363b–364a
  cartography, IV 359b
  chemistry, IV 360a, 364a
  China, I 353b, 594a; IV 358b, 359a
  China (ancient), I 354a; IV 358a
  Christianity, IV 358b, 359b
  civic I 609a, 609b
  civilization, I 620a; IV 357b, 358a, 360b
  Clausius, IV 363b
  common sense, IV 361a

community, IV 357b
competition, IV 358b
cosmology, IV 364a
crisis in history, I 594a
culture, I 608b, 609a–609b, 611a, 611b–612b, 620a; IV 358b
ecology, II 122a
economic history, II 46a, 49a, 51a, 51b, 52b, 54a, 56b
economics, IV 358a, 359b, 364a
education, IV 358b, 360a
Egypt (ancient), IV 358a–358b
electromagnetics, IV 364a
empiricism, IV 361b, 363a, 364b
Enlightenment, II 90b, 91a
environment, IV 364b
Eratosthenes, IV 358a
eschatology, II 159b
Euclid, IV 359b
evil, II 168b; III 648a
experience, IV 361a
experiments, IV 361a
Faust (legend), III 250b, 251a
fear, IV 358a
France, IV 362a, 363a, 363b
Galileo, IV 361a–361b, 362a, 363b
genetic continuity, II 292a
geometry, IV 359b
Germany, IV 360a, 360b, 361a, 362a, 364a
Gibbs, IV 363b
God, II 347a; IV 358b
good, III 648a
Great Britain, IV 360b, 361b, 362a–363a
Greece (ancient), I 60b, 62a; IV 358a
Helmholtz, IV 363b
Hero, IV 358a
humanism, II 521a
Huygens, IV 362a
ideal, IV 361a
imitation, IV 358b, 364b
industry, III 150b; IV 358b, 360a, 363a, 364a
intuition, IV 361a
invention, IV 358a–364a, 364b
Italy, IV 360b, 361a, 362a
Joule, IV 363b
Kelvin, IV 363b
knowledge, IV 360b, 361b
Lenoble, IV 360a
Leonardo da Vinci, IV 360a
Lucretius, III 631a–631b

Machiavellism, III 124b
magic, IV 360a
Man-Machine, III 131b, 134a–140a, 142a, 145b, 146a
Marxism, III 147a, 147b, 150a, 150b, 153b–154a, 155b, 157a, 168b; IV 292b
mathematics, III 177a; IV 359b, 361a
matter, III 191a
measurement, IV 361a–361b
mechanism, IV 360a–364a
medicine, IV 360a
Middle Ages, IV 358a, 358b–360b
military, IV 357b, 361b
millenarianism, III 225b
mining, IV 360a, 362a
monotheism, IV 358b
morality, III 624a, 631a–631b, 645a–645b
motion, IV 359a, 360a, 361a, 361b
music, III 264a
nationalism, III 324b, 325a, 332b, 334b, 336a
natural liberty, II 63b
Nature, IV 357b–361b
necessity, III 355b
Netherlands, IV 362a
Newcomen, IV 362a, 362b
Newton, IV 359b, 361b, 362a, 363b, 364a
numbers, III 406a, 406b
Olschki, IV 360b
painting, IV 359b
Papin, IV 362a
Parent, IV 361b
peace, III 445a, 445b, 446b; IV 504b
perfectibility, III 475a
periodization in history, III 479a
philosophy, IV 359b, 360b, 361b
Plato, I 612a; III 499b–500a, 629a
Platonism, III 499b–500a; IV 359b, 361a
Poland, IV 360b
pollution, IV 364b
Portugal, IV 360b
Posidonius, III 631a
positivism, III 534b, 540b
power, IV 357b, 363a–363b
primitivism, III 580a, 597b
progress, III 624a, 625a–625b, 629a, 630b, 631a–631b, 632b, 633a, 634a, 642a, 645a–645b, 648a; IV 357b, 360b, 364b

protest movements, III 675b
Ptolemy, IV 358b
religion, IV 364b
Renaissance, IV 358a, 360a, 360b, 441b, 442a–442b
Rome (ancient), IV 358a, 358b
Russell, Bertrand, III 446b
Scandinavia, IV 360b
science, IV 357b–364b
scientific classification, I 465b
self-destruction, III 648a
Seven Wonders of the World, IV 358a
slavery, IV 358a
Smeaton, IV 362a
social welfare, IV 276a
socialism, IV 292b
society, IV 357b–358a, 358b, 361a–362a, 364a
space, IV 359b
Spain, IV 360b
State, IV 357b
theocracy, IV 357b
thermodynamics, IV 363b–364a
time, IV 359a–359b, 360b
totalitarianism, IV 406b, 408a, 409a
tragic sense, IV 414a, 414b
Trotsky, III 153b–154a
typography, IV 360b
tyranny, IV 357b
U.S.S.R., III 155b
U.S., I 594a; IV 362a–363a
universal man, IV 441b, 442a–442b
universe, IV 360b, 363b
urbanization, IV 360b
Ure, IV 363a
utilitarianism, IV 358a, 360a
utility, IV 453b
Utopia, IV 462a, 463b
Victorian sentiment, IV 220a, 221b, 222a
war, IV 501b, 504a, 504b, 506b, 508b
Watt, IV 362b
wealth, IV 357b, 361b
work, IV 533a–534b
Tehom (myth), III 281b
Teilhard de Chardin, Pierre (1881–1955)
  design argument, I 677a
  environment, II 133a
  eschatology, II 160a
  evolution, III 474b
  evolutionism, II 188a
  faith, hope, and charity, II 214a

God, II 352a
love, III 107a, 107b
Marxism, II 214a
modernism, I 425a
monad, II 448b
order, II 448b
perfectibility, III 474b
universe, II 448b
Teixeira Mendes, Raimundo,
    positivism, III 539b, 543a
Telemachus (myth), law, II
    676a
Teleology
    acquired characteristics, II
        618a, 618b, 619b, 620a
    antiquity, I 233b–236a
    Aristotle, I 234a–236b,
        272a, 300b, 301a, 302a–
        302b, 303b; II 623a; III
        90a, 354a, 354b; IV 51a,
        175a, 175b
    atomism, I 303b
    Bacon, I 301a
    Basson, I 303b
    Boyle, I 303b, 304a
    causation, I 300b–301a
    Clauberg, I 302b
    Cosmic Fall, I 511b
    Crusius, I 301a
    culture, I 609b, 611a–
        613a, 619a; II 128b, 129a
    deism, I 651b
    Descartes, I 302a, 302b,
        303b; II 381a
    determinism, II 24a
    environment, II 128b, 129a
    Epicureanism, IV 175b
    eschatology, II 156a
    evolution, II 170a; III 149b;
        IV 180a
    evolutionism, II 178b, 182b,
        183a
    existentialism, II 192a
    fortune, fate, and chance,
        II 231a
    Galileo, I 301b
    Gassendi, I 301a, 303b
    Guilinex, I 302b
    God, II 338a
    good, IV 175a, 175b,
        176b, 177a, 180a, 182a–
        182b, 184b
    happiness, II 378a, 381a
    health, II 398a
    Helmont, I 301a
    historiography, II 24a
    Hobbes, I 301b, 303a;
        IV 177a
    imagination, III 219a
    Kant, IV 382b, 383a
    Leibniz, I 303b–304a
    Lucretius, I 301a–301b
    Malebranche, I 302b–303a
    Marxism, III 149b

matter, III 188b, 192b–
    193a
natural law, III 22a
necessity, III 352b, 354a,
    354b
Neo-Platonism, I 235b,
    303b
numbers, III 406a
occasionalism, I 302b
organicism, III 425a
pangenesis, II 623a
perfectibility, III 463b
Plato, I 234a, 234b, 235a,
    271b, 272a, 303b
Platonism, III 522b
progress, III 626a, 629b,
    635b, 639b
Raei, I 302a–302b
rationalism, IV 51a
Regius, I 302b
right, IV 175a, 175b, 176b,
    177a, 180a, 182a–182b,
    184b
scholasticism, I 300b–301a,
    303b
Spinoza, I 301a, 301b,
    303a–303b; IV 177b
Stoicism, IV 51a
structuralism, IV 324b
Telesio, I 301a
theodicy, IV 381b–383b
time, IV 402a
unity of science, IV 436a–
    436b
Velthuysen, I 302b
Telepinush (c. 1500 B.C.),
    freedom of speech, II 253a–
    253b
Teles of Megara, cynicism, I
    628b
Telescope
    cosmic images, I 521b
    cosmology, I 546b
    Galileo, III 414a–415b,
        420a
    optics, III 414a–415b, 420a
    sublime in external nature,
        IV 334b
Telesio, Bernardino (1509–
    1588)
    Bacon and, I 173b, 545a
    causation, I 301a
    cosmology, I 545a
    idea, II 547a
    imagination, III 213b
    matter, III 193b
    Platonism, III 510a–510b
    teleology, I 301a
    time, IV 392b
Telford, K., tragic sense, IV
    411b
Teller, Edward, cosmology, I
    568b
Temperament

Galen, III 133b
    human nature, III 573a
Locke, III 469b
music, III 262b
perfectibility, III 469b
stars, III 288b
Temperaments (four)
    Galen, III 133b
    health, II 398b, 399a
    Man-Machine, III 133a–
        133b
    mythology, III 288b, 290b
    phrenology, IV 23b
Temperance, IV 365b–378b
    Aeschines of Sphettus, IV
        368a, 370b
    Aeschylus, IV 366b–367a,
        368b
    aesthetics, IV 368a, 369a,
        369b, 370a
    Ajax (myth), IV 367a
    Alberti, IV 377b
    Alciati, IV 377b
    Alcuin, IV 371a
    allegory, IV 377b
    anarchy, IV 366b
    Andromache (myth), IV
        365b
    animals, IV 370a, 371b,
        373a, 377a–377b
    Antigone (myth), IV 367a
    Antipater, IV 369b
    Antisthenes, IV 368a
    Apollo (myth), IV 365b,
        366a, 367a
    architecture, IV 373a, 377a
    Ariston of Chios, IV 369b
    Aristotelianism, IV 369a
    Aristotle, IV 369a–369b,
        375a, 377a
    art, IV 366a, 371a–378a
    asceticism, IV 371a
    Athena (myth), IV 367a
    Augustus Caesar, IV 370b
    balance, IV 369a
    baroque, IV 377b
    behavior, IV 366a
    Bellerophon (myth), IV
        366a
    Bible, IV 369a, 371a, 371b,
        375a, 375b
    Book of the Hours, IV
        372b
    Botticelli, IV 373b
    Brittany, Duke of, IV 375a
    Burgundy, Dukes of, IV
        375a
    Caelius, IV 370b
    Camillus, IV 377a
    Cappadocians, IV 370b
    cardinal virtues, IV 366b,
        368a–368b, 369a, 371a
    Cassian, IV 371a
    Cato the Elder, IV 370a

charity, IV 372b, 374a,
    375b
chastity, IV 367b, 370a,
    370b, 371a, 371b, 372b,
    373a, 377a
Chilon, IV 366a
Christianity, IV 370b
Chrysippus, IV 369b
Cicero, IV 365b, 370a–
    370b, 371a, 375a
Cincinnatus, IV 377a
Circe (myth), IV 365b
city-state, IV 365b, 366b,
    368b, 373b
Clarke, III 432a
class, IV 368b
Clement, IV 370b
Colombe, IV 375a
comedy, IV 370a
conduct, IV 370a
Conrad of Hirzau, IV 372b
conservatism, IV 367b
continence, IV 367b
cosmology, IV 368b
courage, IV 366b, 368b,
    369b, 370a
Crete, IV 366a
culture, IV 367a
Cynics, IV 368a, 369b
d'Amboise, IV 375a
David (Bible), IV 371b
Deianeira, IV 367a
Delphic code, IV 365b–
    366a
democracy, IV 366b, 368a
Democritus, III 576b
derivation of, IV 365b
Diogenes of Sinope, IV
    369b
discipline, IV 367b
education, IV 368b
Electra (myth), IV 367a
emblem books, IV 377a–
    377b
Ephialtes, IV 366b
epics, IV 365b
Epicureanism, IV 369b
Epicurus, IV 375b
ethics, IV 369b, 378a
Euripides, IV 367a–367b
evil, IV 371a
Evragius Ponticus, IV 371a
excess, IV 369a
faith, IV 372b, 375b
Finley, M. I., IV 365b
fortitude, IV 366b, 368b,
    369b–375b, 377a, 377b
France, IV 371b, 372b,
    373a, 374b, 375a, 378a
freedom, IV 366b
Furies (myth), IV 367a
Gaulli, IV 377b
Germany, IV 371a
gift virtues, IV 372b

Giotto, IV 372a, 373a, 373b, 374b
Glaber, IV 372a
God, IV 366a, 366b, 368b, 371a, 372b
good, IV 174b, 371a
Gothic, IV 373a, 377a
grace, IV 370b
Great Britain, IV 374b
Greece (ancient), IV 365b, 366b, 367a, 367b, 368a, 369a, 369b–370a, 371a, 373b
Gregory I (the Great), Pope, IV 371a
harmony, IV 368b
health, II 398b–399a; IV 368b
heroes, IV 365b, 366b, 367a, 367b, 370a
Herrad of Landsberg, IV 372b
Hesiod, IV 366a
historians, IV 370b
history, IV 365b, 375a, 375b
Holofernes (Bible), IV 372b, 375b
Homer, IV 365b, 366a
hope, IV 372b, 375b
Horapollo, IV 377b
Horatius Cocles, IV 377a
hubris, IV 366a, 366b, 367b, 369a
Hugo of St. Victor, IV 372b
Iron Age (myth), IV 366a
irrationalism, IV 367b, 368b
Isaeus, IV 368a
Isidore of Seville, IV 371a
isolationism, IV 367b
Italy, IV 371b, 373a–374b, 378a
Ixion (myth), IV 366a
Jesus Christ, IV 371a
John the Evangelist (Bible), IV 375b
human nature, III 576b
iconography, IV 371a–378a
Joseph (Bible), IV 371a, 375a
Judith (Bible), IV 371a, 372b, 375a
justice, IV 366b, 368b, 370a, 371a, 371b, 372b, 373a, 374a, 374b, 375a, 375b, 377a, 377b
knowledge, IV 368a, 369a
Lactantius, IV 370b
Lambert, IV 372b
Latin language, IV 365b, 370a
Leonidas, IV 377a
literature, IV 366a, 368b, 369b, 370a, 372a, 377a

Livy, IV 370b
Lorenzetti, IV 374a
love, IV 367b, 371a
Lucius Sincinnius, IV 377a
Lucretia, IV 370a
Lysias, IV 368a
Macrobius, IV 371a
macrocosm, IV 372a
Martianus Capella, IV 371a
Martin of Braga, IV 371a, 375a
masculinity, IV 366b
Medea (myth), IV 367b
microcosm, IV 372a
Middle Ages, IV 369a, 370a, 371a, 375a, 377a
mind, IV 365b, 366a
moderation, IV 365b, 366b, 367b, 369a, 370a
monasteries, IV 371a
money, IV 371a
morality, IV 366a, 368b, 369a, 369b, 370a, 371a
mythology, IV 366a, 366b, 367b, 375a
Neo-Platonism, IV 371a, 377a
Neo-Pythagoreans, IV 372b
Nero, IV 375b
Nestor (myth), IV 365b
Netherlands, IV 371a, 374b
Numa Pompilius, IV 377a
obedience, IV 367a, 368b, 369a, 373a
Oceanus (myth), IV 367a
Odysseus (myth), IV 365b
Oedipus (myth), IV 367a
oligarchy, IV 367b, 368a
orators, IV 368a
oratory, IV 369b, 370a
order, IV 370a
Origen, IV 370b
Panaetius, IV 369b–370a
passions, IV 367b
peace, IV 366b
Peleus (myth), IV 366b
Penelope (myth), IV 365b
Pericles, IV 367b, 377a
Persia (ancient), IV 366b
Perugino, IV 377a
Pesellino, IV 375b
Petrarch, IV 371b
Phaedra (myth), IV 367b
Philip III, IV 372b
Philo Judaeus, IV 372b, 375a
philosophers, IV 368a, 368b
philosophy, IV 370a, 371a
physics, IV 368b
Pietism, III 495a
piety, IV 366a, 368b
Pindar, IV 366a–366b, 368b
Pisano, IV 375a
Piso Frugi, IV 370a

Pittacus, IV 366a, 377a
Pius II (Pope), IV 375a, 375b
Plato, IV 367a–369b
Platonism, IV 369a, 369b, 370a, 371a, 378a
pleasure, IV 369a, 369b
Pliny the Elder, IV 377a
Plutarch, IV 377a
poetry, IV 365b, 366a, 366b, 368a, 369a, 371b, 372a
poets, IV 368a
politics, IV 366a, 366b, 367b, 368a, 369a, 370b, 371a, 373b, 374a, 378a
Pollaiuoli, IV 373b
Pompey, IV 370b
pre-Socratics, IV 367b, 369a
proportion, IV 369a
propriety, IV 370a
prudence, IV 371a, 371b, 372b, 373a, 374a, 374b, 375a, 375b, 377a, 377b
Prudentius, IV 371a, 371b
Pseudo-Vincent of Beauvais, IV 372b
purity, IV 370b
Quintus Fabius Maximus, IV 377a
Raffaelli, IV 377b
Raphael, IV 372a
rationalism, IV 367a–367b
reason, IV 367b
religion, IV 366b, 373b, 378a
Renaissance, IV 369a, 370a, 371a, 374a–374b
Rhadamanthys (myth), IV 366a
rhetoric, IV 369a, 370a, 371a
right, IV 174b
Ripa, IV 377b
Roman Catholic Church, IV 368b, 369b, 370b
Rome (ancient), IV 369a, 369b, 370a–371a
sacraments, IV 372b
Saint Ambrose, IV 370b, 372b
Saint Augustine, IV 370b, 372b
Saint James, IV 375b
Saint John, IV 375b
Saint Peter, IV 375b, 377b
Saint Thomas Aquinas, IV 372b
Sallust, IV 370b
Samson (Bible), IV 375a, 377a
sanity, IV 366a, 367b
Sardanapalus, IV 375b

satire, IV 369b
Scipio Africanus, IV 370a, 377a
secularism, IV 373b
self-knowledge, IV 365b, 366b, 367a, 368a
self-restraint, IV 365b, 366b, 367b, 369b, 370b
Seneca, IV 371a
Serpotta, IV 377b
seven deadly sins, IV 378a
sin, IV 372b, 378a
sobriety, IV 366a, 367b, 370b, 371b
society, IV 366a, 366b, 368b, 378a
Socrates, III 576b; IV 368a, 377a
Solomon, IV 377a
Solon, IV 366a, 377a
Sophists, IV 367a, 367b
Sophocles, IV 367a
soul, IV 368a
State, IV 368b
Stoicism, IV 369a–371b, 372b, 378a
Susanna (Bible), IV 371a, 375a
symbolism, IV 371b, 373a, 377a
Tacitus, IV 370b
Tarquin, IV 375b
Thales, IV 366a
theater, IV 370a
Theodulf of Orleans, IV 371b, 372a
Theognis of Megara, IV 366a
theology, IV 371a
Thucydides, IV 367b
tragedy, IV 366a, 366b, 367a, 367b, 369a, 370a
Trajan, IV 377a
tyranny, IV 366b
universe, IV 369a
Valeriani, IV 377b
Verginia, IV 370a
vice, IV 369a–373a, 374a, 375a, 377a
Victorians, IV 219a, 219b
Virgin Mary (Bible), IV 371a
virtue, IV 365b–378a
war, IV 366b, 367b
Waugh, IV 378a
wisdom, IV 366b, 368a, 368b, 371a
Xenophon, IV 368a
Zeno of Citium, IV 369b
Zeus (myth), IV 366a, 367a
Tempier, Etienne (fl. 1277)
  anti-Aristotle, II 199a
Temple, Frederick (1821–1902), religion, IV 107b

Temple, Archbishop William (1881–1944), welfare state, IV 514b

Temple, William (1628–1699)
art, II 305b, 307b
attitude toward antiquity, I 80b, 81a, 85a, 85b
China, I 364a
genius, II 294b, 305b, 307b
mountains in literature, III 258b

Temptation
Adam (Bible), III 583a
perfectibility, III 468a
primitivism, III 583a

Ten Commandments, IV 227a
law, III 6b, 7a, 11a

Tennant, F. R.
Creation, I 574b–575b, 576a
design argument, I 677a
God, I 574b–575b, 576a
Nature, I 574b–575a, 677a
Pelagianism, III 467a
sin, III 467a

Tennemann, W. G.
Kant and, III 518b, 522b
Plato and, III 518b, 522b

Tennyson, Alfred Lord (1809–1892)
China, I 369a
evolutionism, II 181b
longevity, III 89b
motif, III 241a
romanticism, IV 193a

Tensors, IV 89a, 89b

Terence (185–159 B.C.), motif, III 238a

Teresa, Saint (1515–1582)
literary paradox, III 80a
love, III 101a
perfectibility, III 467b
women, IV 525b

Tereus (myth), III 296a

Terman, Lewis (1877–1956), psychology, IV 26b

Terrasson, Abbé Jean
attitude toward antiquity, I 77a, 79b, 81b, 84a–84b
poetry, III 530a

Territorial imperative, III 597b

Tertullian (160?–?230 A.D.)
casuistry, I 260a
Christianity, III 589a, 590b
dignity, IV 138a
Hermeticism, II 432a
literature, III 81b
metaphor, III 205b
mimesis, III 227a–227b
mountains in literature, III 255b
motif, III 240b
poetry, III 525b

primitivism, III 582a, 583a, 589a, 590b, 595a
reformation, IV 62b
religion, III 205b
theodicy, IV 380b
women, IV 524b

Tesauro, E.
classification of the arts, I 460a
genius, II 293b
mimesis, III 228b
style, IV 331b

Testelin, Henri, aesthetics, II 218b, 221b–222a

Tetens, J. N., imagination, III 218b

Tetrachord, III 261a

Tetthmoi
law, II 681a–681b

Teyssèdrey, B., iconography, II 539b

Thackeray, William Makepeace (1811–1863)
realism in literature, IV 52b
Victorian sensibility, IV 219b–220b

Thailand, Buddhism, I 248b, 251b, 252b

Thales (640?–546 B.C.)
continuity, I 502b
eighteenth century view of, I 86a
historiography, I 502b
infinity, II 604b
matter, III 186a, 186b
metaphor, III 197a, 203a
necessity, III 352b
philosophy, III 197a
progress, III 625a
psychology, IV 2a
rationalism, IV 46b
religion, III 203a
space, IV 295b, 298a
symmetry, IV 353a–353b
temperance, IV 366a

Thanatos (myth)
Greece (ancient), III 96a
love, III 96a

Thayer, H. S., pragmatism, III 552a

Theagenes of Rhegium (fl. 530?), metaphor, III 203b

Theater
Aristotle, III 226b
beauty, I 208a
censorship, III 497b–498a
cruelty, I 208a
freedom of speech, II 258b, 259b, 261a
hierarchy, II 436b
human nature, III 572a, 573a, 574a, 575b, 576a
iconography, II 538b
love, III 103a, 105b

magic, III 246a
Middle Ages, III 528b
mimesis, III 226a, 226b
music, III 265a, 265b, 270a
mythology, III 297a, 306b, 311a
organicism, III 423a, 424b, 425b
perfectibility, III 470b, 473a
Plato, III 496b, 497b–498a, 500a, 501a
Platonism, III 496b, 497b–498a, 500a, 501a
poetry, III 528b, 530a
pragmatism, III 564a
progress, III 625a–626b, 629a
rationalism, IV 48b, 49a
religion, II 538a
romanticism, IV 207a
Rome (ancient), IV 370a
satire, IV 211a, 212b, 215b, 216a
temperance, IV 370a
theodicy, IV 379b
theriophily, IV 387a
tragic sense, IV 411b–417a
virtuoso, IV 487b, 488b, 490a–490b
wisdom of the fool, IV 519b–520a

Theft
ethics, IV 71a
law, II 688b, 689a
Rome (ancient), II 688b, 689a

Theism
Creation, I 571a–576a
free will, II 244b
God, I 571a–576a; II 351a–355b, 363b
perennial philosophy, III 458b
theodicy, IV 379a

Themis (myth), law, II 674b, 675a, 675b, 679a

Themistius (4th century A.D.), atomism, I 130b

Theocracy
Comte, III 534b
positivism, III 534b
technology, IV 357b
Utopia, IV 460a, 462a

Theocritus (3rd century B.C.)
eighteenth century view of, I 79a
magic, III 246a
primitivism, III 593b
progress, III 630a
vox populi, IV 498b

Theodicy, IV 378b–384a
aesthetics, IV 381b
Anaximander, IV 380b

Arguna, IV 379b
Aristotle, IV 380a
atheism, IV 380b, 381b
Augustinianism, IV 381b, 382a
Barth, IV 381b
Berdyaev, IV 383a
Bergson, IV 383a
Bhagavad-Gita, IV 379b
Bible, II 163b–164a
Bolingbroke, IV 382b
Brightman, IV 383a–384a
Buddha, IV 379b
Calvin, IV 381b
causation, IV 381a
China (ancient), IV 379b
Christianity, II 164a–165a; IV 379b, 380b–381b
Chrysippus, IV 380b
Clarke, IV 382b
cosmology, IV 380a, 382b, 383a
Creation, IV 381a, 381b
culture, IV 379b
Darwin, IV 383b
death, IV 381a
defined, IV 378b–379a
deism, IV 380b
disharmony, IV 381a
disteleology, IV 382b
dualism, IV 379a–380b
Duméry, IV 383a
emotion, IV 381b
empiricism, IV 382b
Enlightenment, IV 382a–383b
Epicurus, IV 380a–380b
eschatology, IV 380b
ethics, IV 379a, 380b
evil, IV 162b–165a, 166a; IV 378b–383b
evolution, IV 383b
experience, IV 381a, 382b–383a
faith, IV 379b, 380b, 381b, 383a
Fall, IV 381a, 381b
fate, IV 379a
Fichte, IV 383a
fideism, IV 381b, 383b
free will, IV 379b
freedom, IV 380b–383b
Gnosticism, IV 380b
God, IV 378b–383b
good, IV 379a–383a
grace, IV 380b
Greece (ancient), IV 379b, 380a–380b, 386b
harmony, IV 380a, 381a, 381b, 382a
Hegel, IV 383a
Henderson, IV 383b
henotheism, IV 379a
Heraclitus, IV 380a

heresy, **IV** 379b, 380b
Hick, **IV** 381a
hierarchy, **IV** 380a
history, **IV** 383a
humanism, **IV** 383b
Hume, **IV** 382a, 382b, 383b
immortality, **IV** 380a, 380b, 382a
India (ancient), **IV** 379b
individualism, **IV** 379b, 382a, 383a
injustice, **IV** 383a
Iran, **IV** 379b
Irenaeus, **IV** 381a, 383b
James, **IV** 383a–384a
Jesus Christ, **IV** 380b
Job (Bible), **IV** 379b, 380b, 381b, 383a
Judaism, **II** 163b–164a; **IV** 379b, 380b
justice, **IV** 378b, 379a, 381b, 382a, 382b, 383a
Kant, **IV** 381b–383b
knowledge, **IV** 382a
Krishna, **IV** 379b
Lactantius, **IV** 380a–380b
Last Judgment, **IV** 380b
law, **IV** 378b, 382a
Leibniz, **II** 166a–166b; **IV** 378b, 380b, 381b–383a
logic, **IV** 379a, 380a, 382a
love, **IV** 381a, 382a
loyalty, **IV** 379b
Luther, **IV** 381b
Manicheism, **IV** 380b
mathematics, **IV** 381b, 382a
matter, **IV** 380a, 380b
Mesopotamia (ancient), **IV** 379b
metaphysics, **IV** 380a, 381a, 381b, 382a
Mill, **IV** 383a–384a
monads, **IV** 382a
monotheism, **IV** 379a
mysticism, **IV** 379b, 381b
Nature, **IV** 380b, 381b, 383a, 383b
necessity, **III** 355a; **IV** 381a
Neo-Platonism, **IV** 380b, 381b, 383a
Newton, **IV** 382b
Nicholas of Cusa, **IV** 381b
obedience, **IV** 380b
order, **IV** 380a, 380b
pantheism, **IV** 379a, 379b
Pascal, **IV** 381b
perfectibility, **IV** 381a, 382b
Plato, **II** 162b; **IV** 380a, 380b
Platonism, **IV** 380b, 381a
Plotinus, **II** 163a–163b; **IV** 380a, 380b
pluralism, **IV** 379b

Plutarch, **IV** 380b
polytheism, **IV** 379a, 379b
Pope, **IV** 382b
power, **IV** 379b, 380a, 380b, 381b, 383a
prayer, **IV** 379b
pride, **IV** 379b
privation, **IV** 381a
progress, **IV** 383b
psychology, **IV** 379a
punishment, **IV** 379b, 380b
Pythagoreans, **IV** 380a
reason, **IV** 380b, 381b, 382b, 383a
Reformation, **IV** 381b–382a
responsibility, **IV** 383a
retribution, **IV** 379b, 380b, 382a
revelation, **IV** 381b
reward, **IV** 379b, 380b
Royce, **IV** 383a
Saint Augustine, **IV** 379b, 380b–381b
Saint Paul, **IV** 380b
Saint Thomas Aquinas, **IV** 380b, 381a, 382a
Schleiermacher, **IV** 381b
scholasticism, **IV** 380b, 381a
sin, **IV** 379b, 380b, 381a, 381b, 382a
skepticism, **IV** 380b, 381b, 383b
society, **IV** 379b, 383a
Spinoza, **IV** 381b
Stoicism, **IV** 380a, 380b
suffering, **IV** 379b, 380b, 382a, 382b, 383a
teleology, **IV** 381b–383b
Tertullian, **IV** 380b
theater, **IV** 379b
theism, **IV** 379a
theology, **IV** 378b, 379a, 381a, 381b, 382b
Thomism, **IV** 382a
tragedy, **IV** 379b
tragic sense, **IV** 413b
tribes, **IV** 379b
truth, **IV** 383a
Tsanoff, **IV** 383b
universality, **IV** 379b
universe, **IV** 380b, 382a
Voltaire, **IV** 382b
voluntarism, **IV** 381b
William of Ockham, **IV** 381a
wisdom, **IV** 379a, 380b, 382a, 382b, 383a
Wolff, Christian, **IV** 379a
Theodore of Mopsuestia (350?–?428), metaphor, **III** 205a
Theodorus of Cyrene (c. 4th century B.C.), impiety, **II**

565b
Theodorus of Samos (c. 6th century B.C.), art, **II** 299a
Theodosius I, Emperor (346?–395), paganism, **I** 378a
Theodosius II, Emperor (401–450 A.D.), Gnosticism, **II** 329b
Theodulf of Orleans (d. 821), temperance, **IV** 371b, 372a
Theognis of Megara (6th century B.C.)
death, **I** 635b
freedom of speech, **II** 259a
health, **II** 397a
impiety, **II** 565b
law, **II** 677a, 678b, 679a, 682a, 683a
primitivism, **III** 579a
temperance, **IV** 366a
Theology
agnosticism, **I** 17a–27a
alienation, **I** 34a–34b
allegory, **I** 41b
Anglicanism, **IV** 20a
Aristotle, **IV** 176b
Arminius, **II** 28b
atomism, **I** 495b–497b
Augustinianism, **II** 27b
Barth, **II** 29a, 30b
Bible, **II** 26b
caesaropapism, **II** 30a
Calvin, **II** 27b, 28a, 28b, 29a, 30b
Calvinism, **II** 28b–29a, 30a–30b
causation, **I** 279b–281a
Chain of Being, **I** 326a–326b
Christianity, **I** 17a–27a, 34a–37a, 52a–53a, 326a–326b; **II** 26a–31a; **III** 476b
Comte, **III** 641b
continuity, **I** 492b
Counter-Reformation, **II** 30b
Dante, **III** 511a
death, **II** 27a
deism, **I** 647a, 647b, 648b, 649b
determinism, **II** 21a, 24a
dignity, **IV** 137b–145a
discontinuity, **I** 495b–497b
double truth, **II** 31a–37b
Eastern Orthodox Church, **II** 30a
education, **II** 79a
Engels, **III** 473b
evil, **II** 26b, 27a
evolutionism, **II** 186a
fatalism, **II** 29b, 30a
Faust (legend), **III** 247a, 251a, 252a
France, **II** 30b

France, Anatole, **II** 575b
free will, **II** 26b, 27a, 29b, 30a, 242a–248b
freedom, **II** 25b–26a, 26b
Germany, **II** 30b
Gnosticism, **II** 328b–330a
God, **II** 25b–31a, 354b–366b
Gomarus, **II** 28a
Gottschalk of Orbias, **II** 27b
grace, **II** 27a
Great Britain, **II** 30b
Greece (ancient), **II** 516b
Hegel, **III** 473b, 474a; **IV** 290b
historiography, **II** 21a, 24a, 473b; **IV** 151a
history, **I** 279b–281a; **II** 21a, 24a
Huguenots, **II** 30b
humanism, **II** 515a, 515b, 516b, 517b, 520b; **IV** 129b, 130a, 131b, 132a
imagination, **III** 211b
infinity, **II** 605b, 606a, 608a, 611b, 614a, 614b, 615a
Islam, **II** 29b, 30b, 474b, 641a, 641b, 643b, 647a–648b
Jesus Christ, **II** 26a, 27a, 28b, 29a
Judaism, **II** 29b–30a
Kant, **IV** 382b
Koran, **II** 29b
law, **II** 688a
Leibniz, **IV** 378b
linguistics, **III** 61a–61b
literature, **III** 82b
Luther, **II** 27b
Man-Machine, **III** 135a, 137b
Marx, **IV** 291a
Melanchthon, **II** 28a
metaphor, **III** 204a–206a
Middle Ages, **II** 28a
More, Thomas, **II** 514b
mountains in literature, **III** 258b
Muhammad, **II** 29b
music, **III** 264b, 266b, 268a, 270a, 270b–271a, 271b
mythology, **III** 274a, 291a, 291b, 292a, 293a, 294a, 300a, 302b, 305a, 307b
natural law, **III** 18b
necessity, **III** 351b, 354b–355b, 357a, 360a, 360b
Neo-Platonism, **III** 372b, 376b, 377b, 378a
Netherlands, **II** 28a–28b, 30b
Niebuhr, **II** 29a, 30b
optics, **III** 410a, 418a
Orientalism, **III** 432b, 435a

Pelagius, II 26b–27a

perennial philosophy, III 458b–460a, 461a

perfectibility, III 463b, 464a, 464b, 468b–469a, 469b, 470b, 473b, 474a, 475a

periodization in history, III 476b, 478a

philanthropy, III 489a

Pietism, III 493b, 494a, 494b, 495a

Plato, III 510a

Platonism, III 504b, 505a, 505b, 506a–506b, 507b, 509a, 510a, 511a, 512a, 514b, 516b, 517a, 522b

poetry, III 528b, 529b, 530a, 530b

positivism, III 533a, 535b, 536a, 539b

pragmatism, III 553a, 564b, 567a, 568a

progress, III 634b–636b, 641b, 642a

prophecy, III 665b

Protestantism, II 27b–29a, 30a–30b

psychology, IV 11b, 16a, 16b

Puritanism, II 30b

Ramism, IV 45a

rationalism, IV 46b

reason, II 26b

reformation, IV 60a, 63a, 63b, 64a, 67a, 68b, 69a

Reformation, II 28a, 30b

religion, IV 97a, 101a, 108a–108b, 110b, 111a, 111b, 114a, 116a, 117b, 118b

Renaissance, IV 121b, 122a, 129b, 130a, 131b, 132a, 137b–145a, 151a, 441a, 443a

rhetoric, IV 170b

Roman Catholic Church, II 30a, 30b

romanticism, IV 201a, 209b

Saint Ambrose, II 26b

Saint Augustine, II 26a–27b, 28a, 29a; III 505b; IV 63a

Saint John Chrysostom, II 26b

science, II 29a

scientific classification, I 464b

sin, II 26a, 26b–27b, 29a

skepticism, IV 235b, 240b, 241b, 243a, 243b, 244a, 247a, 247b

socialism, II 30b; IV 285a, 287b, 290b, 291a

soul, II 26a, 26b

space, IV 295a, 302b

spontaneous generation, IV 308a–308b, 310a, 310b

symmetry, IV 348a, 349a, 352a

synergism, II 28a

temperance, IV 371a

theodicy, IV 378b, 379a, 381a, 381b, 382b

time, IV 393b, 399b

U.S., III 432b, 435a

unity of science, IV 436b

universal man, IV 441a, 443a

virtue, IV 477a

witchcraft, IV 522a, 523a

women, IV 524a, 525a, 527b

Zwingli, II 30b

Theon of Smyrna, music, III 261a

Theophilus (2nd century A.D.), primitivism, III 581b, 582a

Theophilus of Cilicia (5th century A.D.), Faust (legend), III 246b

Theophilus of Edessa (6th century A.D.), astrology, I 124a

Theophrastus (d. about 287 B.C.)

Aristotle and, IV 6b

biology, I 233a

catharsis, I 269a

creativity in art, I 584b

culture, I 611b

cynicism, I 628b

historiography, II 507a

impiety, II 565b

irony, II 627b

Islam, II 645b

loyalty, III 112a

optics, III 407a

poetry, III 526a

pre-Socratics, IV 6b

progress, III 629b–630a

psychology, IV 6b–7a

Strato and, IV 6b

symmetry, IV 348a

Theopompus of Chios (b. about 380 B.C.), historiography, II 504a–504b, 507a–507b, 509a

Theosophy, II 643a, 645b, 650b

Theriophily, IV 384a–389a

Aelian, IV 384b, 388b

Aesop, IV 384b

Anaxagoras, IV 385b

argumentation, IV 386a

Aristodemus, IV 385b

Aristophanes, IV 385b

Aristotle, IV 384a, 384b, 385b, 388b

art, IV 385a, 385b

Bergson, IV 388b

Bible, IV 384a, 384b, 386a, 388a

cannibalism, IV 385a

Charron, IV 387b

Christianity, IV 384b, 386a

Chrysippus, IV 384b

Condillac, IV 388b

Cynics, IV 384b–386a

Democritus, IV 385b

Descartes, IV 388a

Diogenes of Sinope, IV 384b–385a, 385b

entomology, IV 388b

ethics, IV 385a

evil, IV 386a–386b

Fabre, IV 388b

faith, IV 386b

folklore, IV 384b

freedom, IV 385a

God, IV 384b, 386a

happiness, IV 384a, 388a

Humane Societies, IV 388a

immortality, IV 384b

incest, IV 385a

instinct, IV 384b, 385a

intuition, IV 388b

invention, IV 385a

knowledge, IV 387a

La Fontaine, IV 384b

La Rochefoucauld, IV 388a

law, IV 385a, 385b

legends, IV 384b

Locke, IV 388b

Lorenz, IV 388b

Maximus of Tyre, IV 386b

memory, IV 385b

Menander, IV 386a

Middle Ages, IV 386a–386b

Montaigne, IV 385b, 387a–387b

morality, IV 384a, 387b, 388a

Nature, IV 384a–387a

origin of the term, IV 384a

parables, IV 384b

peasantry, IV 386b

Phaedrus, IV 384b

Philemon, IV 386a

philosophy, IV 388a–388b

Pliny, IV 384b, 386a, 386b, 387b, 388b

Plutarch, IV 385a–386b, 387b, 388b

polygamy, IV 385a

primitivism, IV 387a

psychology, IV 384b, 388a

rationalism, IV 384a, 385a, 385b, 388a, 388b

reason, IV 384a–386b, 388a

Romanes, IV 388b

Réaumur, IV 388b

satire, IV 386b

Saint Thomas Aquinas, IV 386b

Rostand, IV 387a

Saint Augustine, IV 386b

senses, IV 384a

science, IV 384b, 387b, 388a, 388b

sin, IV 386b

skepticism, IV 386b

society, IV 385a, 387a

Socrates, IV 385b

soul, IV 384b, 386a, 388a

Spenser, IV 387a

suffering, IV 388a

theater, IV 387a

virtue, IV 385a

Whitman, IV 388b

Xenophon, IV 385b

zoology, IV 388a, 388b

Thermal death theory, II 115b

Thermodynamics

Aristotle, I 495a

empiricism, III 548b

entropy, II 112b–120a

First Law, II 113a–113b

logic, III 548b

Man-Machine, III 136b

music, III 263b

Second Law, II 113a–113b, 117a, 118b; IV 350a

symmetry, IV 350a

technology, IV 363b–364a

Thermoelectric pile, III 419b

Thermometers, II 402a, 402b

Thersites (myth), freedom of speech, II 259a

Theseus (myth), III 272b, 275b, 288a

human nature, III 572a

law, II 683a

motif, III 240b

mythology, III 240b

progress, III 626a

Thesmos, law, II 680a–682a, 685a

Thibaudet, Albert (1874–1936)

literary criticism, I 604b

periodization in literary history, III 485b, 486a

Thicknesse, Philip, anti-primitivism, III 604a

Thierry, Augustin (1795–1856), romanticism, IV 203b

Thierry of Chartres, dignity, IV 139b, 140a

Thiers, Louis Adolphe (1797–1877)

French Revolution (1789), III 671b

protest movements, III 671b

revolution, IV 159b

Thimus, A. von, Pythagorean cosmos, IV 41b

Third sound, *see* Difference tone

Thirlwall, Bishop Connop (1797–1875), irony, II 629b, 632a, 632b, 634b

Thirty Years' War
determinism, II 30b
eschatology, II 157a
ethics, III 441b
freedom, II 250b
Germany, III 483a
Grotius, III 441b
history, I 400b
law, II 250b
peace, III 441b
periodization in literary history, III 483a
Roman Catholic Church, I 398b

Thomas, Dylan (1914–1953) *ut pictura poesis*, IV 470b

Thomas of Celano (c 1200–c1255), mythology, III 284b

Thomas à Kempis (1380–1471), wisdom of the fool, IV 517b

Thomasius, Christian (1655–1728)
China, I 360a
taste, IV 356a

Thomasius, Jacob, perennial philosophy, III 460b

Thomaz, Alvaro, medieval science, II 204a

Thomism
Creation, I 572b, 574b–575b
empiricism, III 20a
God, I 572b, 574b–575b; II 356b, 361b, 362a, 363a, 363b, 365a, 365b
humanism, II 520b
Islam, II 646a
justice, II 656b–657a
Marxism and, III 169a
modernism, I 420a, 422b
natural law, III 14a, 19b, 20a, 23a
necessity, III 355b
Platonism, III 514a
religion, IV 108b
theodicy, IV 382a

Thompson, D'Arcy Wentworth, symmetry, IV 347b

Thompson, Stith
folklore, III 238b, 239a–239b, 241b
iconography, II 539a

Thompson, Vance, symbolism, IV 341a

Thompson, William (1785?–1833)

anarchism, I 73a
economic history, II 60a
socialism, IV 292b

Thoms, Peter Perring, China, I 368b

Thoms, William J., longevity, III 91b

Thomson, James (1700–1748)
baroque in literature, I 191a, 193a
Chain of Being, II 446b
deism, I 651a
evil, II 167b
hierarchy, II 446b
mountains in literature, III 256b, 259a, 259b
Newton and, III 392b–396b, 398a–398b
optics, III 392b–396b, 398a–398b
primitivism, III 600a
romanticism, IV 194a, 195a
satire, IV 215a
sublime in external nature, IV 335a–335b, 336a, 337a

Thomson, William, *see* Kelvin, Lord

Thor (myth)
Nazis, III 597b
primitivism, III 597b

Thoreau, Henry David (1817–1862)
anarchy, I 72a, 436b
Brown, John, and, III 431a
Buddhism, I 256a
civil disobedience, I 434b, 435a–436b, 438b; III 431a
conservation, I 474a–474b, 475a, 476a
Emerson and, I 474a–474b; III 430b–431a
ethics, III 446a
Gandhi and, III 446a
justice, III 431a
Mexico, I 436a–436b
mysticism, III 431a
mythology, III 306b
natural rights, I 437a, 437b
Nature, I 474a–474b
organicism, III 426b
Orientalism, III 429a, 430a, 430b–431b, 433a, 433b, 439a
peace, III 446a
pragmatism, III 553b
psychology, IV 24a
rights, I 437a, 437b
self-discipline, III 431a, 431b
slavery, I 436a
suffrage, I 437a, 437b
transcendentalism, I 436a–436b; III 429a, 430a, 430b–

431b, 433a, 433b, 439a; IV 24a

Thorel, Jean, symbolism, IV 344b

Thorez, Maurice, nationalism, III 334a

Thorndike, Edward Lee (1874–1949)
association of ideas, I 115b–116a
behaviorism, I 218b, 221a, 224b, 225a, 226b, 227a
imprinting, II 585a
psychology, IV 26b, 28a

Thorndike, Lynn, Renaissance, IV 128a

Thorpe, W. H., learning, II 585a

Thorvaldsen, Bertel (1768–1844)
classicism, I 454b
mimesis, III 229b

Thoth (myth)
hermeticism, II 431a
Judgment, IV 225b
music, III 268a

Thouret, A., realism in literature, IV 52a

Thucydides (471 ?–?400 B.C.)
balance of power, I 180a
continuity, I 502b
culture, I 609b
democracy, I 653b, 655a, 656a
Enlightenment, II 95a
Euripides and, IV 367b
freedom of speech, II 258a, 259a, 259b–260
God, III 576a
historiography, II 467a, 468a, 469a, 469b, 475b, 476b, 477a, 482b, 501a, 501b–503a, 504a, 509a, 509b, 510b
history, III 576b
Hobbes and, I 656a
human nature, III 571a, 573b, 575b, 576a, 576b
humanism, II 516b
irrationalism, IV 367b
law, I 653b; I 682b–684b
liberty, II 95a
Machiavellism, III 116a
mathematics, III 180a
necessity, III 353a, 353b, 356a
Pericles and, IV 367b
philanthropy, III 487a
progress, III 627b, 628a
rationalism, IV 48a–48b, 367b
revolution, IV 152b
State, I 653b, 655a, 656a
temperance, IV 367b

virtue, IV 367b
war, IV 501b

Thumāma Ibn al-Ashras (d. 828)
causation, I 287b
God, I 287b

Thummim, the, III 658a–659b

Thünen, J. H. v., economic history, IV 50b

Thutmose III (c. 1490–1436 B.C.)
historiography, II 475a
law, III 11a

Ti (myth), II 344b
justice, II 658a

Tiamat (myth), II 336a; III 278a, 281b

Tiberius (42 B.C.–37 A.D.)
astrology, I 121a
freedom of speech, II 261b

Tibullus, Albius (54?–?18 B.C.)
humanism, II 517b
love, III 96a
primitivism, III 579b, 580b

Tickell, Thomas (1686–1740)
mythology, III 300a
pragmatism, III 552a, 553b–554a, 555b, 556a, 558a, 560b, 566a, 568a, 568b
progress, III 624a, 625a, 638a, 641b
psychology, IV 1a–3a, 6a–7b, 9a, 11a, 13a, 13b, 15a, 19a
Puritanism, IV 16b, 17b–19a
rationalism, IV 47b, 49b
religion, IV 97a, 106b
Saint Augustine, IV 9a
Santayana, III 553b–554a
science, I 465b
Spinoza, IV 434b
Strato, IV 7a
style, IV 332a

Tieck, Ludwig (1773–1853)
Counter-Enlightenment, II 109b
irony, II 629b, 630a, 630b, 632b
romanticism, IV 189a, 194b, 197a, 208a, 209b
Schlegel and, IV 208a
Weltschmerz, IV 209b

Tiedemann, Dietrich (1748–1803), Platonism, III 518a

Tieghen, Paul Van, romanticism, IV 196b

Tiele, Cornelius Petrus (1830–1902), Orientalism, III 434b

T'ien (myth), II 344b

Tiepolo, Giovanni Battista (1696–1770), impressionism, II 578b

Tilgher, Adriano, pragmatism, III 564a

Tillich, Paul (1886–1965)
  Buddhism, I 257a
  classification of the sciences, I 465b
  Creation, I 575b
  faith, II 211a
  God, I 575b; II 362b–363a
  holy, II 514a
  Marx and, III 158a
  Marxism, III 158a
  mythology, III 276a
  perennial philosophy, III 463a
  romanticism, IV 210b
  Schelling and, IV 210b
Tillotson, John (1630–1694), certainty, I 308a
Tillyard, E. M. W., baroque in literature, I 193a
Time, IV 389a–406a
  aborigines, IV 399a
  absolute space, IV 403b
  absolute time, IV 403b
  abstract, IV 400a
  aesthetics, II 223a, 223b
  aether, IV 405a
  agriculture, IV 402a
  Alexander, IV 396b
  allegory, I 47a–47b
  Anaxagoras, IV 390a
  Anaximander, IV 390a
  appearance, IV 394a, 394b
  Archytas of Tarentum, IV 390b, 400b
  Aristotelianism, IV 392a, 392b
  Aristotle, I 492b–493a; II 170a, 664a; III 189a–189b; IV 301a, 349a, 390b–391a, 391b, 393a, 393b, 400a–400b
  astrology, IV 399a, 402b
  astronomy, IV 399a, 399b, 401a, 402b, 403a, 405b
  asymmetry, IV 349a, 349b
  atomism, IV 389b–390a, 390b, 394b
  Australia, IV 399a
  Barrow, IV 393a, 403a–403b, 405a
  Barth, II 160b–161a
  becoming, IV 390a, 390b, 391a–391b, 396b
  Being, IV 389b, 390a, 391b, 393b, 395b, 398a
  Bergson, II 183a; IV 349b, 391b, 394b, 396a, 396b, 397a
  Berkeley, IV 394b, 395a
  Bible, IV 402a
  Boas, IV 395b
  Bonnet, IV 392a, 392b
  Boutroux, IV 395b, 396a, 398a

Boyle, IV 402b
Bradley, F. H., IV 393b, 394a
Broad, IV 396b
Bruno, IV 392a–394a
Burnet, IV 390a
calendar, IV 399b
cataclysms, IV 391a
catastrophism, IV 417b, 422b
causation, IV 395b, 396a, 397a
chance, II 231b, 232b, 233a; IV 395b, 398a
change, IV 389a, 390a, 390b, 391a, 392a, 392b, 393b, 394b, 395a, 396b
chaos, IV 390a
China (ancient), IV 399a, 401a, 402a
Christianity, II 155b–156b; IV 391b–392a, 402a
chronology, IV 400a
chronometry, IV 403a, 404b
chronon, IV 397b–398a
Chrysippus, IV 391b
Clarke, IV 394b
class, IV 402a
clocks, IV 399a, 401a–401b, 402b, 403a, 404a
consciousness, IV 389a, 391b, 394a, 396a
contingentism, IV 396a
continuity, IV 390a
cosmic rays, IV 405b
cosmic time, IV 405b
cosmogony, IV 399b, 400a
cosmology, I 543b, 548a, 549a, 554a–561b; IV 391b–394a, 396b, 397b, 400b, 405b
Creation, IV 392a, 393a, 394b
Croce, IV 394a
culture, I 619a–619b; IV 399a
cycles, IV 390a, 391a, 392a, 399b, 400b, 401a, 402a, 403a
Darwin, II 588a; IV 395b
d'Ascoli, IV 492b
Democritus, IV 389b–390a
Descartes, IV 393a, 394b, 395a, 402b
determinism, II 240b; IV 393b, 394a, 395b–396a, 396b, 398a
Dewey, IV 396b
Dionysius Exiguus, IV 402a
dualism, IV 391b, 393b
Duns Scotus, IV 392a
earth, IV 404a, 405a, 405b
economics, IV 402a
Eddington, IV 397a

ego, IV 395a
Egypt (ancient), IV 401a
Einstein, I 556b, 557a–557b, 558b, 559a, 559b, 561b; II 590a, 590b–591a; IV 81b, 85b, 88b–89a, 90a, 90b, 92a, 397a, 404b–405a
Eleatics, IV 389b, 390a, 390b, 391b, 393b, 394a
electromagnetics, IV 405a, 405b
Empedocles, IV 390a
empiricism, III 546b, 550a; IV 395a–395b
energy, IV 395b
Epicurus, IV 389b
epistemology, IV 390b, 395a
equivalence principle, IV 397b
eschatology, II 155b–156a, 160b–161a
eternal return, IV 392a, 395b
eternity, IV 392a, 393b, 400a
ethics, IV 392a, 395b
Eudemus of Rhodes, IV 390b
evolution, IV 395a–395b
evolution of literature, II 174a
evolutionism, II 183a
existentialism, II 189b, 192a, 193b
experience, IV 396a
experiments, IV 395a
faith, IV 392a
fate, II 231b, 232b, 233a
Fichte, IV 393b–394a, 394b
Findlay, IV 394a
fortune, II 231b, 232b, 233a
France, IV 401b
free will, II 240b; IV 392a
freedom, IV 392a
galaxies, IV 405b
Galileo, IV 393b, 402b–403a, 403b
Gassendi, IV 394b
geometry, IV 349b, 399b, 400a, 403a, 403b
gnomon, IV 400a
God, I 576b–577a; II 338a, 338b, 339a–339b, 343b, 344a; IV 390b, 391b–392a, 393b, 402b
gravity, IV 397b, 403a
Great Britain, IV 404b
Great Year (myth), IV 390a, 391a, 392a; IV 400b–401a
Greece (ancient), II 681b; IV 389a–391b, 392a, 393a–393b, 399b–401a, 402a
Greenwich, IV 404b
Harrison, IV 404b

Gregory XIII (Pope), IV 399b
Häckel, IV 395b
harmony, IV 394b
Hegel, IV 390a, 394a
Heidegger, II 193a; IV 396b
Heisenberg, IV 398a
Helmholtz, IV 395b
Heraclitus, IV 390a, 390b, 394a, 398a, 399b, 400b, 401a
Herbart, IV 394b
Hesiod, IV 399b
history, IV 392a, 393b, 394a, 395b, 402a
Homer, I 493a; IV 399b
horology, IV 399a, 401a, 401b, 402b, 403a
hours, IV 401a
hubris, IV 399b
Hume, IV 395a
Husserl, IV 396b–397a
Huygens, IV 403a
idea, II 547b, 548a; IV 390b, 391a
ideal, IV 395a
idealism, IV 393b
Incarnation, IV 392a
indeterminacy, II 588a, 590a, 590b–591a; IV 396a
Indians (American), IV 399a–399b, 402a
individualism, IV 392a
inertia, IV 397b, 404b
infinity, II 605b, 606a, 610a, 614a
irreversibility, IV 390a
Islam, IV 391b, 402a
Italy, IV 401b
James, IV 395b–396a, 396b
Jesus Christ, IV 392a, 402a
Judaism, IV 391b, 392a, 402a
Kant, II 240b, 547b, 548a; IV 393b–394a, 394b, 395a
Kelvin, IV 402b, 404b
Kepler, IV 402b
Kierkegaard, II 189b
kinematics, IV 403a
knowledge, IV 390b, 391b
Langevin, IV 397b
language, II 664a, 669a, 669b, 672a
Laplace, IV 393b, 394a, 394b, 395b, 396a, 398a
Lasalle, IV 390a
law, II 681b; III 28a
leap year correction, IV 399b
Leibniz, IV 394a–394b, 395a, 404a
light, IV 404b, 405a, 405b
literature, IV 399b

Locke, IV 394b, 395a, 397b, 404a
logic, III 546b, 550a; IV 394b, 400a
Lucretius, IV 389b
McTaggart, IV 394a, 394b
magic, IV 402a, 402b
Marxism, III 149b
mathematics, III 176b; IV 392b, 393a, 394b, 395a, 396a, 396b, 397b, 400b, 402a, 403a, 403b
matter, II! 187b, 189a–189b, 194b–195a, 196a; IV 390a
Maxwell, IV 393a
Mayer, IV 395b
measurement, IV 389b, 392b, 398b–406a
mechanism, IV 402b
meliorism, IV 396b
memory, IV 396a
mesons, IV 405b
metaphor, III 199a
metaphysics, IV 389b, 390b, 396b
metempsychosis, IV 392a
Meyerson, IV 397a
Michelson-Morley experiment, IV 405a
Middle Ages, IV 391b–392a, 393a–393b, 399a, 401b, 402a
mind, IV 391b, 393b
Minkowski, IV 397a
monads, IV 394a–394b
monasteries, IV 399a
monism, IV 393b, 394a
moon, IV 400b, 404a
morality, IV 399a
Morgan, Lloyd, IV 396b
motion, IV 389b–392b, 400a, 400b, 403a, 403b
Mumford, IV 402b
music, IV 399a, 399b, 402a
mythology, III 274a, 286b, 306b, 314a, 314b, 317a; IV 389a, 390a
natural law, III 15a, 15b
Nature, IV 390b, 393b, 396b, 398a, 399a, 399b, 402b, 404b, 405b
navigation, IV 403a
necessity, III 361a
Neo-Platonism, IV 392a
Newton, I 492b, 493a, 549a, 554a–554b, 555a, 557a; III 194b–195a, 557a; IV 75b, 76a, 77a, 84b, 86a, 391a, 392b, 393a, 394b, 395a, 397a, 397b, 403a, 403b, 404a
Nietzsche, IV 395b
nonbeing, IV 390a

numbers, III 401b; IV 390b, 391a, 399b–400b
Olbers, I 555b–556a
One, IV 390b, 393b, 394a
ontology, IV 395b
open future, IV 390b
open world, IV 398a
order, IV 393b
Oresme, IV 402b
Origen, IV 392a
Ostwald, IV 395b
Overman, IV 395b
panpsychism, IV 391b
pantheism, IV 393b
Parmenides, IV 389b, 390b, 398a, 400a
Peirce, IV 395b, 396a, 396b, 398a
perennial philosophy, III 459a
periodicity, IV 390a, 391a
periodization in history, III 476b
phenomenology, IV 395a, 396b–397a
philosophy, III 199a; IV 390b, 393a–398a, 399b, 402b
physics, IV 393a, 393b, 395b, 396a, 397a–398a, 405a, 405b
Planck's constant, IV 397b–398a
planets, IV 400b
Plato, IV 390b, 391a, 391b, 400a, 400b–401a
Platonism, III 508a, 513a
Plotinus, IV 391b, 393b
pluralism, IV 394a, 394b, 396a
Plutarch, IV 391b, 399b
Poincaré, IV 394b, 397b
power, IV 392a
pragmatism, III 553a, 557a
predestination, IV 391b, 392a
pre-Socratics, IV 390a
Protestantism, IV 392a
psychology, IV 391b, 395a–395b, 396a, 397b–398a
psychopathology, IV 395a
Pythagoras, IV 399b
Pythagoreans, IV 389a–390b, 399b, 400a, 400b
quantum theory, IV 397b
radar, IV 405b
rationalism, IV 47a
reality, IV 390b, 391a, 391b, 393b, 394b, 395b
reformation, IV 60b, 61a, 63a
Reichenbach, IV 397a
relational theory, IV 389b, 390b, 392b, 393a, 394b,

397b
relativity, IV 74b, 75b, 76a, 77a, 79b, 81b, 82b, 83b, 84a, 85a–92a, 397a–397b, 405a, 405b
religion, IV 97b–98a, 399a, 399b
Renaissance, IV 439b
Renouvier, IV 395b, 396a
rhythm, IV 399a
Robb, IV 397a
romanticism, IV 196a
Rome (ancient), IV 401a
rotation, IV 389b, 392a
Royal Observatory, IV 404b
Royce, IV 396b
Russell, IV 394b, 396b
Saint Augustine, III 355a; IV 63a, 391b
Saint Thomas Aquinas, IV 392a, 393b
Schelling, IV 394a
Schleiermacher, IV 390a
Schopenhauer, IV 394a, 395b
science, IV 392a–393a, 395b–398a, 402a, 402b, 403a, 404a
seasons, IV 402a
Sextus Empiricus, IV 389b
Shakespeare, IV 399a
Shelley, III 508a
Simplicius, IV 390a
skepticism, IV 235a
Socrates, IV 391a
solar system, IV 400b, 405b
soul, IV 391b, 392a, 399b
space, IV 301a, 303b, 389a, 389b, 393a, 394b, 397a–397b, 400a, 403b
Spencer, IV 395a, 395b
Spengler, III 361a
Spinoza, IV 393b, 394a, 395b
stars, IV 392a, 392b, 393a
Stoicism, IV 390a, 391a–391b, 401a
Su Sung, IV 401b
Suárez, IV 392b
sublime in external nature, IV 336b
sun, IV 400b
sundials, IV 401a
symmetry, IV 349a–350b
Tait, IV 404b
technology, IV 359a–359b, 360b
teleology, IV 402a
Telesio, IV 392b
theology, IV 393b, 399b
time dilatation, IV 405a, 405b
timelessness, IV 389b, 390b, 391b, 393b–394b

Torricelli, IV 403a
tragic sense, IV 413a
tychism, IV 396a
uncertainty principle, IV 398a
uniformitarianism, IV 392a–392b, 417b, 422b, 427b, 428b
universal man, IV 439b
universe, IV 390a, 390b, 391a, 395b–396a, 397a, 399b, 400a, 402a, 402b, 404b, 405b,
unity, IV 390a, 392a–392b, 396a
ut pictura poesis, IV 465b, 469b, 471a, 474a–475b
velocity, IV 404b, 405a, 505b
Vitruvius, IV 401a–401b
wave mechanics, IV 397b
wealth, IV 402a–402b
Weyl, IV 398a
Whitehead, IV 391b, 396b, 397b
Whitrow, IV 397a
William of Ockham, IV 392a
Wright, I 519a
Zeno of Citium, IV 389b
Zeno of Elea, IV 400a
zodiac, IV 402a
Zoroastrianism, IV 402a
Timiriazev, K. A., eugenics, II 620b
Timmers, J. J. M., iconography, II 535b
Timocracy
   Plato, II 22a
   pragmatism, III 554a
   Santayana, III 554a
Timofeyev, L. I., realism in literature, IV 55a–55b
Timon (c. 320–c. 230), Platonism, III 504b
Timon of Phlius (fl. c. 280 B.C.), skepticism, IV 234a, 234b–235a, 236a–236b, 237b, 238b
Timotheus (446?–357 B.C.) musical genius, II 313a, 316b
Tinctoris, Johannes (1446?–1511), musical genius, II 315a–316b
Tindal, Matthew (1657–1733), deism, I 650b–651a
Tinguely, Jean, ut pictura poesis, IV 475b
Tintoretto (1518–1594)
   genius, II 302a
   impressionism, II 577b
   mythology, III 291a

Tipper, John, virtuoso, **IV** 489a

Tiraboschi, Girolamo (1731–1794)
literature, **III** 82a
periodization in literary history, **III** 482a

Tirso de Molina (1571?–1648)
baroque in literature, **I** 192a
motif, **III** 241a

Tissot (1728–1797), health, **II** 402b–403a

Titans (myth), **III** 274a

Titchener, Edward Bradford (1867–1927)
association of ideas, **I** 116b
behaviorism, **I** 217b, 221b
empathy, **II** 85b
psychology, **IV** 27b

Tithonus (myth), longevity, **III** 89b

Titian (1477–1576)
classicism, **I** 455b
iconography, **II** 529a, 529b, 538a
impressionism, **II** 577b
mythology, **III** 291b–292b
periodization in literary history, **III** 485b
ut pictura poesis, **IV** 469a, 471a

Titmuss, Richard, welfare state, **IV** 513a, 515a

To pan
Aristotle, **IV** 300a
Homer, **IV** 300a

Tocqueville, Alexis Charles de (1805–1859)
conservatism, **I** 481a
crisis in history, **I** 591a
democracy, **II** 17a–17b; **IV** 503a–503b
despotism, **II** 1a, 2a, 17a–17b
equality, **II** 139b, 146a–146b
French Revolution, **IV** 158b–159a
historiography, **II** 494b
individualism, **II** 17b, 595a, 595b, 596a, 599a
liberalism, **III** 49b, 50a, 57a
nationalism, **III** 330b
peace, **IV** 503a
periodization in history, **III** 479a
sovereignty, **II** 17b
State, **I** 663a–664a
tyranny, **II** 17a–17b
war, **IV** 503a–503b, 505b

Todhunter, Isaac (1820–1884)
probability, **III** 605b, 609b, 612b
social welfare, **IV** 282a,

282b

Toland, John (1670–1722)
deism, **I** 650b, 651b
mythology, **III** 301b–302a
rationalism, **III** 301b–302a

Tolerance, **IV** 112b–121a
Age of Reason, **I** 400b–401a
Charles II, **I** 401b
Christianity, **I** 400b–401a
France, **I** 401b
Germany, **I** 400b
Great Britain, **I** 400b–401b
heresy, **II** 426a
Ireland, **I** 401a
liberalism, **III** 40b, 41a, 42a–42b
Louis XIV, **I** 401a
nationalism, **III** 325a
Orientalism, **III** 432b
Peace of Augsburg, **IV** 118a
periodization in history, **III** 479b
Pietism, **III** 494b
Presbyterians, **I** 401b
Protestantism, **I** 400b–401a
Roman Catholic Church, **I** 400b
Utopia, **IV** 462b

Tolman, E. C. (1886–1959)
behaviorism, **I** 217a, 223b–225a, 226a; **IV** 185a
consciousness, **I** 223b
psychology, **IV** 28b

Tolman, Richard Chace (1881–1948), cosmology, **I** 565b

Tolnay, Ch. de, iconography, **II** 538a

Tolomei, Claudio, linguistics, **III** 63b

Tolstoy, Leo (1828–1910)
anarchy, **I** 72a, 438b
beauty, **I** 209a
China, **I** 371a
civil disobedience, **I** 435a, 438a–438b, 439a
Confucianism, **I** 371a
death, **II** 193b
economy, **II** 169a
evil, **II** 168b–169a
existentialism, **II** 193b
Gandhi and, **III** 446a
God, **I** 438a
Jesus Christ, **I** 438a
love, **I** 438a; **III** 445b
music, **I** 371a
peace, **III** 441a, 445b–446a
realism in literature, **IV** 53b
Rousseau and, **III** 445b
Sermon on the Mount, **III** 445b
symbolism, **IV** 343a

Tomars, Adolf S., beauty, **I** 213b

Tomashevsky, Boris, folklore, **III** 239a

Tomb decorations, art, **II** 525b, 531b

Tombaugh, Clyde William, cosmology, **I** 552b

Tomsky, Mikhail P. (1888–1936), Marxism, **III** 165b

Tone, **II** 314a, 315b, 323b; **III** 261a, 262a, 263b, 268b
Agrippa, **II** 389b
Ficino, **II** 389b
harmony, **II** 389a

Tonnies, Ferdinand, nationalism, **III** 326b, 327a

Topos
Aristotle, **IV** 299b, 301b
motif, **III** 243a
Nicholas of Cusa, **IV** 300a–300b
Plato, **IV** 299b

Torah, mythology, **III** 283a

Tornier, E., probability, **III** 622a, 622b

Torrentinus, Herman, mythology, **III** 299a

Torri, Bartolomeo
art, **II** 301b
individualism, **II** 301b

Torricelli, Evangelista (1608–1647)
axiomatization, **I** 165b
genius, **II** 293b, 301b
imagination, **III** 218a
methodology, **III** 387b
Newton and, **III** 387b
optics, **III** 420a
time, **IV** 403a

Torture
Inquisition, **II** 689a
law, **II** 689a; **III** 567a
music, **III** 266a–266b
mythology, **III** 292a
pragmatism, **III** 567a
Rome (ancient), **II** 689a

Tory, Geoffroy (1480?–? 1533), mythology, **III** 292b

Totalitarianism, **IV** 406a–411a
absolutism, **IV** 406b, 407a, 408a, 408b
activism, **IV** 408a
Arendt, **IV** 409b
Aristotle, **IV** 406b
authority, **I** 158b–160a, 161a; **IV** 407b
autocracy, **IV** 406b, 410b
Brzezinski, **IV** 409b
Buddhism, **I** 253a
bureaucracy, **IV** 410b
capitalism, **IV** 406b, 407b
China (Communist), **IV**

409b
class, **IV** 407a, 407b, 408a, 408b, 410a, 410b
cold war, **IV** 406b, 408b, 410b
communications, **IV** 406b, 407b, 409a, 410b
communism, **IV** 406b–409a, 410b
conscription, **IV** 408a
crime, **IV** 410b
criticism, **IV** 406b, 408b, 409a
culture, **IV** 407a
defined, **IV** 406a–408a
democracy, **III** 147b; **IV** 407a, 408b, 409a, 409b, 410b
despotism, **II** 1a; **IV** 406b
dictatorship, **IV** 406a–410b
dualism, **IV** 409a, 410a
dynamism, **IV** 408b
economics, **IV** 407a, 407b, 409b
equality, **IV** 407b
etatism, **IV** 408a, 408b
evolution, **III** 646b–647a
fascism, **IV** 406a–408b, 409b, 410b
Franco, **IV** 409b
freedom, **IV** 407a, 410b
French Revolution (1789), **IV** 408a
Friedrich, **IV** 409b
Gentile, **IV** 408b
Germany, **IV** 406a, 408b, 410a
Goebbels, **IV** 408a
Hegel, **IV** 408a, 408b
history, **IV** 408a–409b, 410b
Hitler, **IV** 408b, 409a, 410a, 410b
ideology, **IV** 406b–410b
imperialism, **IV** 408b
individualism, **IV** 407a, 410b
industry, **IV** 406b
intolerance, **IV** 408a
Italy, **IV** 406a, 407a, 408a, 409b, 410a
Lassalle, **IV** 408a
Latin America, **IV** 409b
law, **II** 690b; **III** 2a, 5a; **IV** 407a, 407b, 408b, 409a, 410a
Left, **IV** 408a, 409b, 410a, 410b
Leninism, **IV** 410a
liberty, **IV** 407a
Ludendorff, **IV** 408a
Machiavellism, **III** 125a
Mao Tse-tung, **IV** 409b
Marx, **IV** 408a

445

Marxism, III 147b, 150b, 165b, 569a; IV 409b
millenarianism, IV 407b, 408a, 410b
mobilization, IV 408b, 409a
monarchy, IV 410a
monopoly, IV 407a, 407b, 410a
Müller, Adam, IV 408a
Mussolini, IV 407b–410a
nationalism, IV 407a, 410a, 410b
Nazis, IV 406a, 407a, 407b, 408b
Neumann, Franz L., IV 409b
Neumann, Sigmund, IV 409b
oligarchy, IV 408a
one-party rule, IV 407b
organization, IV 408b, 409a
Pallas, IV 418b
parliamentarism, IV 407a, 408b
perfectibility, IV 407b
persecution, IV 409a
Plato, III 554b; IV 406b
Platonism, III 520b
plebiscite, IV 407a, 409a
post-Stalinism, IV 410a
power, IV 407a–410b
pragmatism, III 553a, 554b, 569a
progress, III 646b–647a; IV 409b, 410a
proletariat, IV 409a
propaganda, IV 406b, 410b
purges, IV 401a
race, IV 408b, 410a
radicalism, IV 408a, 408b, 409b
reactionary, IV 410a
regimentation, IV 406b
religion, IV 407a, 410b
revolution, IV 407a, 408a, 408b, 409b
rhetoric, IV 408b
Right, IV 408a, 409b, 410a, 410b
Robespierre, IV 408a
Roman Catholic Church, IV 410a
rules, III 232b
Schapiro, Leonard, IV 409b
Schmitt, Carl, IV 408b
security, IV 410b
social contract, IV 255b, 257b
socialism, IV 407b
Spain, IV 409b
Stalin, II 563a; IV 406b, 407b, 409b, 410a, 410b
Stalinism, IV 406a, 409a, 409b
technology, IV 406b, 408a,
409a
terror, IV 408a, 409a, 410b
Tucker, Robert, IV 409b
typology, IV 409b
tyranny, IV 406b
U.S.S.R., II 563a; III 150b; IV 406a, 408b
utilitarianism, IV 448a
Utopia, IV 461b, 464a
violence, IV 408a
war, IV 408a, 409a, 505b, 506b
Weimar Republic, IV 408b
World War I, IV 406b–407a, 408a
World War II, IV 406b, 407b, 408a
Totemism
Freud, IV 96b
Otto, IV 97b
religion, IV 96b, 97b
structuralism, IV 326b
Toulmin, S.
matter, III 190a–190b, 195a
Newton and, III 195a
positivism, III 550b
Tower of Babel (Bible), linguistics, III 61b
Toy, Crawford Howell (1836–1919), Orientalism, III 435b
Toynbee, Arnold (1852–1883), welfare state, IV 509b
Toynbee, Arnold J. (1889–)
causation, I 283a
China, I 371b–372a
Christianity, II 213a
civilization, I 616a, 617b, 619a; II 21a–21b, 22b–23b; III 361a–361b
climate, II 369b
communism, III 647b–648a
continuity, I 503b, 504a
cycles, I 626b–627a
determinism, II 21a–23b
environment, II 23a, 131b
as historian, III 361b
liberalism, III 647b–648a
Nature, II 21b
necessity, III 360b–361b
peace, IV 508a
primitivism, III 593a
progress, III 647b–648a
revolution, IV 162b
Spengler and, III 361a
Trade
art, II 580a
China, I 354a, 354b, 356b; III 428b
common law, II 694b
degrading aspect of, II 69a–69b
economic history, II 45b,
57a
Enlightenment, II 90b, 93b
India, III 428b
law, II 686a, 687b; III 3b
Lucretius, III 587a
monopoly, II 57a
nationalism, III 330a
natural liberty, II 67a–68a
Orientalism, III 428b, 439a
painting, II 580a
Plato, III 629a
Platonism, III 506a, 507a
primitivism, III 579b, 580a, 580b, 587a
private property, III 652a, 652b, 653a, 653b, 656b
progress, III 629a, 630a, 642a
religion, IV 94a
Rome (ancient), II 686a, 687b; III 652a
social contract, IV 259a
trade names, II 662b
U.S., III 428b, 439a
virtue, IV 477a
welfare state, IV 509b
Tradition
aesthetics, II 224a
art, II 577a–577b, 579b, 581b
Bacon, I 173b–174a
China (Communist), III 334a
culture, I 621a
Darwin, III 646a
dignity, IV 144a, 145b
education, II 57a
evolution, III 646a, 646b
freedom of speech, II 260a
God, II 358b
happiness, II 379a
Hegel, II 409a, 409b, 410a, 411b
Herder, I 621a; III 327a
hierarchy, II 441b, 442a
historiography, IV 148b
holy, II 512b, 513a
humanism, II 515a, 519b; IV 131b, 135a
language, II 661a, 661b, 665a
loyalty, III 110a
metaphor, III 203b
mythology, III 272b, 275b–276a, 286b, 287a, 288b, 290a, 290b, 291a, 293a, 293b, 295a, 298a, 304a, 307b, 308b, 317a
nationalism, III 324b, 325a, 325b, 327a, 327b, 331b, 332a, 333a, 333b, 334a, 334b, 335a, 337b
naturalism in art, III 340b
painting, II 577a–577b,
579b, 581b
perennial philosophy, III 458a, 458b, 459b, 461b
Platonism, III 496a
progress, III 646a, 646b
protest movements, III 675a
rationalism, IV 48a, 48b
religion, III 203b
Renaissance, IV 131b, 135a, 144a, 145b, 148b, 438b–439a
revisionism, IV 264b
romanticism, IV 205a, 207a
skepticism, IV 238b
Socrates, IV 48b
U.S., III 329a
universal man, IV 438b–439a
Volksgeist, IV 494b, 496a
Tragedy
Aeschylus, I 267a; IV 366b
aesthetics, II 224a
Aristotle, I 264b–270a, 578b, 584b, 585a–585b, 611a; II 169b–170a, 506a, 507a, 544a–544b; III 423a, 527a, 527b, 629a; IV 411b–412a, 413a
catharsis, I 264b–270a
Cornford, I 468a
creativity in art, I 578b, 584b, 585a–585b
cynicism, I 631a
Diogenes of Sinope, I 631a
drama, III 527a, 527b, 531a
Else, I 266a, 266b, 268b
Euripides, I 266b; IV 367a–367b
evolution of literature, II 169b–170a, 171a–172a
Faust (legend), III 249b–250a, 251b, 252b
Greece (ancient), I 467b–470a; II 228a, 652b; III 347a, 527a, 527b; IV 366b
happiness, II 376b
Hegel, II 171a
human nature, III 572a, 573a
Hume, I 268a, 268b
idea, II 544b
ideal, II 551b
irony, II 627a, 627b, 628b, 630a, 631a–633b
literary criticism, I 596a
logic, I 467b
Meredith, I 468a
Milton, I 267a
mimesis, III 226b
mythology, III 311a
Nietzsche, I 626b
organicism, III 423a, 424a, 425b
parts of, IV 411b–412a

peace, III 440a
Petrusevski, I 269b–270a
Plato, II 376b; III 226b, 448a, 501a
Platonism, III 498a, 501a, 520a
poetry, III 526b, 527a, 527b, 531a
progress, III 629a
rationalism, IV 49a
romanticism, IV 187b, 190b
Saint-Évremond, I 266b
satire, IV 211a, 215b, 216a
Sophocles, I 264b; IV 367a
temperance, IV 366a, 366b, 367a, 367b, 369a, 370a
theodicy, IV 379b
tragic sense, IV 411b–417a
Utopia, IV 464b
Wilamowitz-Moellendorff, I 269a
women, III 501a
Tragic sense, IV 411a–417b
Achilles (myth), IV 413a
Adam (Bible), IV 415b, 416a
Aeschylus, IV 413b
Agamemnon (myth), IV 413a
Albee, IV 414a
Alving, Oswald (fiction), IV 416b–417a
Antigone (myth), IV 412b
Apollo (myth), IV 415a
Aristotle, IV 411b–412a, 413a
Becket, IV 417a
Beckett, IV 414b
becoming, IV 414b, 415a
belief, IV 412b, 414a
Bible, IV 415b, 416a
body, IV 414b–415b
Bunyan, IV 415a
Burke, Kenneth, IV 412b
Camus, IV 414b
Castelvetro, IV 412b
catharsis, IV 411b, 412a
Christianity, IV 411b, 413a, 415a, 415b–417a
communication, IV 411b, 414a, 414b
cosmos, IV 413b, 414a, 414b, 416b
Creation, IV 415b
Creon (myth), IV 412b
Dante, IV 415b
death, IV 414b, 415a
Demiurge, IV 415a
dignity, IV 413a, 414a, 417a
Dionysian, IV 413a–414b
Dostoevsky, IV 416b
dualism, IV 414b, 415a
Eliot, T. S., IV 417a

ethics, IV 413a, 415b, 416a
Euripides, IV 413b
Eve (Bible), IV 416a
evil, IV 411a–417a
Fall, IV 415b, 416a
fate, IV 412a–416b
Faust (legend), IV 416a–416b
fear, IV 412a, 413a, 415a
Fergusson, IV 412b
fortune, IV 413a, 416b
free will, IV 411b–412a
freedom, IV 414a, 417a
Gnosticism, IV 414b, 415a
God, IV 413a–416a
good, IV 413a, 414a, 414b, 415a, 415b
Great Year (myth), IV 415a
Greece (ancient), IV 411b–416b
guilt, IV 416a, 416b
Hamlet, IV 416b
Hardy, IV 414a
Harrison, Jane, IV 412b
Hegel, IV 411b
Heraclitus, IV 413b
heroes, IV 411b–414a, 415b, 416a
Homer, IV 413a, 413b
hybris, IV 413a, 414b
human nature, IV 414a, 416a
Ibsen, IV 416b–417a
ignorance, IV 414b, 415b
illusion, IV 414a
imitation, IV 411b
individualism, IV 415b
injustice, IV 413b, 414b, 416a
irony, IV 411b, 412b, 414b
irrationalism, IV 413b, 414a, 415a
Jansenism, IV 415a
Jaspers, IV 416a
jealousy, IV 413a, 414b
Jesus Christ, IV 416a
Job (Bible), IV 416a, 416b
Judaism, IV 415b
justice, IV 413a–414a
Karamazov family, IV 416b
Kierkegaard, IV 416b
knowledge, IV 415a
Lear, King, IV 416b
love, IV 415b
malevolence, IV 413a
Marlowe, IV 416a–416b
Melville, IV 416b
metaphor, IV 413b
metaphysics, IV 411b
Miller, Arthur, IV 414a
Milton, IV 415b
mimesis, IV 411b
monotheism, IV 415b

Murray, Gilbert, IV 412b
mythology, IV 412b–417a
Nature, IV 414a
necessity, IV 411b–412a, 413a
Neo-Platonism, IV 415a
Nietzsche, IV 414a, 415a
Orestes (myth), IV 413b
Orphic, IV 411b, 414b–415b
Pascal, IV 416b
passions, IV 413b, 415a
pathos, IV 414a
pity, IV 414b, 412a
Plato, IV 414b, 415a
power, IV 412a, 413a, 414a, 414b, 417a
Prometheus (myth), IV 413b
Puritanism, IV 415a, 415b
Racine, IV 415a
religion, IV 413a–413b, 414b
Robbe-Grillet, IV 414b
Saint Augustine, IV 415b
Saint Paul, IV 415a, 416a
Satan, IV 415b, 416a
Scaliger, IV 412b
Shakespeare, IV 416b
Shaw, IV 415b
Socrates, IV 414b–415a
Sophists, IV 413b
Sophocles, IV 412a–412b, 413b
soul, IV 414b, 415a
Stoicism, IV 415a
technology, IV 414a, 414b
terror, IV 411b, 412a, 413a
theodicy, IV 413b
time, IV 413a
truth, IV 415b
unity, IV 411b, 412b
universe, IV 414a, 415b–417a
Zeus (myth), IV 413b
Traherne, Thomas (1637?–1674), hierarchy, II 443b
Trajan (52 or 53–117)
Gnosticism, II 330a
temperance, IV 377a
Trajan Column, ut pictura poesis, IV 471a
Trakl, Georg
expressionism, II 206b, 208b
symbolism, IV 342b
Tranquility
good, IV 176a
Stoicism, II 176a
Transcendentalism
Abbot, F. E., III 429a, 434b
aesthetics, IV 24a
Alcott, IV 24a
antinomy of pure reason, I

91b, 92a
Aristotle, I 584b
Bancroft, IV 24a
beauty, I 207b
Bramo Samaj, III 429b
Buddhism, I 256a; IV 233a
Chadwick, John, III 429a
Channing, III 429a, 434b
Child, Lydia M., III 429a
China, I 368b
Christianity, IV 24a
civil disobedience, I 436a
Clarke, J. F., III 429a, 431b–434a, 435a–435b, 439a
Confucius, III 430a, 430b, 431a
Conway, M., III 429a, 431b, 434a–434b
Cooper, J. F., IV 24a
creativity in art, I 578b, 583b, 584a–584b
culture, IV 24a
Curtis, I 436a
De Berard Mills, III 434a–434b
democracy, IV 24a
eclecticism, III 429b
education, IV 24a
Egypt (ancient), IV 224b
Emerson, Mary Moody, III 429b
Emerson, Ralph, Waldo, I 436a; III 429a, 429b–430b, 431b, 432a, 433a, 433b, 439a; IV 24a
evolution, III 433b, 434a
Finney, Charles G., IV 24a
Frothingham, III 429a, 434b
Fuller, IV 24a
Gnosticism, II 330a
God, I 575b, 576a; II 356a–356b, 357b, 358b, 359b, 360b, 361a, 362b, 363a, 363b, 364a, 365b
Hafiz, III 430a
Harris, W. T., III 429a
Hegel, IV 24a
Higginson, III 429a, 431b, 434a–434b
Higher Law doctrine, 436a–436b
Hodgson, III 429b
Holmes, O. W., III 429a
humanitarianism, IV 24a
idealism, IV 24a
imagination, III 210a
India, I 368b
individualism, II 596a
industry, IV 24a
Janes, III 429a, 434b
Johnson, III 428b, 429a, 431b, 433a–434a, 434b, 435a, 439a
Jones, William, III 429b

Kant, **IV** 200a; **III** 219a, 358b, 444a
literature, **IV** 24a
Longfellow, **III** 429a, 434a–434b
materialism, **IV** 24a
mysticism, **IV** 24a
Nature, **IV** 24a
necessity, **III** 358b
Neo-Platonism, **III** 372a, 372b, 374a, 374b, 375a, 376a; **IV** 24a
Nietzsche, **III** 520b
Orientalism, **III** 429a–434b, 439a; **IV** 24a
Parker, Theodore, **I** 436a
Peabody, **IV** 24a
peace, **III** 444a
perfectibility, **III** 463b
periodization in literary history, **III** 483b
Pietism, **IV** 111b
Plato, **I** 578b, 583b, 584a–584b
Platonism, **III** 503a, 519b, 520b, 522a–522b, 523b–524a; **IV** 24a
Poe, **IV** 24a
poetry, **IV** 24a
Potter, **III** 434b
pragmatism, **III** 568a
primitivism, **IV** 24a
Protap Chunder Mozoomdar, **III** 429b
psychology, **IV** 23b–24a
religion, **IV** 111b
romanticism, **IV** 24a, 200a, 202a, 202b
Roy, **III** 429b
Saadi, **III** 430a
Sen, **III** 429b
symbolism, **IV** 345a
Thoreau, **I** 436a–436b; **III** 429a, 430a, 430b–431b, 433a, 433b, 439a; **IV** 24a
truth, **IV** 24a
Underwood, B. F., **III** 434b
Unitarianism, **III** 429a, 429b, 432a, 433a, 434a
Upanisads, **I** 256a
U.S., **II** 596a; **III** 429a–434b, 439a, 483b, 519b, 522a–522b
Whitman, **IV** 24a
Wilkins, Charles, **III** 429b
Wilson, Harold, **III** 429b
Transformism
continuity, **I** 499b, 500b
Darwin, **I** 499b
discontinuity, **I** 499b, 500b
evolutionism, **II** 177b–179a
knowledge, **I** 499b, 500b
Lamarck, **I** 499b
Nature, **I** 499b, 500b

progress, **II** 179a
progressionism, **II** 179a
Translation
Aristotle, **II** 640b
Golden Age, **II** 640b–641a
Islam, **II** 639b–641b, 643a, 649b, 650b
Kant, **III** 444a
linguistics, **III** 61b, 62a, 72a
mathematics, **III** 181b
medicine, **II** 640b
Neo-Platonism, **III** 377b
philosophy, **II** 640b
Renaissance, **III** 181b
Transmigration, **I** 644b, 645a; **II** 243b; **III** 573a
Buddhism, **I** 250b, 255a
Transmutation
evolutionism, **II** 183b
mythology, **III** 292a
Transubstantiation
Christianity, **I** 394b
faith, **II** 212b
Hobbes, **II** 212b
Trapp, Joseph, *ut pictura poesis*, **IV** 466b
Travel
Counter-Enlightenment, **II** 101b
Enlightenment, **II** 90b
primitivism, **III** 598b, 599a
Shaftesbury, **III** 598b
Traversari, Ambrogio
dignity, **IV** 143b
humanism, **II** 520b
Treason
Great Britain, **II** 689a
Inquisition, **II** 689a
law, **II** 686a, 689a
loyalty, **III** 110a, 113b–114b
Montaigne, **III** 594b
Papal Inquisition, **II** 689a
primitivism, **III** 594b
Rome (ancient), **II** 686a, 689a
witchcraft, **IV** 522a
Treaties
impiety, **II** 566b
international peace, **III** 448b, 449b, 450a, 451a, 452a, 452b, 455a, 455b
Machiavellism, **III** 122b
war, **III** 444b, 448b, 449b, 450a, 451a, 452a, 455a
Treaty of Nerchinsk, **I** 360b
Treaty of Westphalia, **I** 400b
Treitschke, Heinrich von (1834–1896), war, **IV** 503a
Trembley, Abraham (1700–1784)
Chain of Being, **I** 331b, 334a–335a
genetic continuity, **II** 284a–

284b
Trenchard, John, deism, **I** 650b–651a
Trendelenburg, Friedrich Adolf (1802–1872)
Bradley, **II** 415a
perennial philosophy, **III** 462a
Tressan, Louis de
cosmic images, **I** 518a
motion, **I** 518a
Trethowan, Dom Illtyd, Cosmic Fall, **I** 512b
Trevelyan, George Macaulay (1876–1962), crisis in history, **I** 593a
Trevor-Roper, H., periodization in history, **III** 480b
Trials, **III** 7a–7b
Greece (ancient), **II** 676a, 679b
Rome (ancient), **II** 686a, 687b, 688a–689a, 690b
Tribus, M., entropy, **II** 116b
Trigault, Father Nicolas, China, **I** 355b
Trilling, Lionel (1905–)
education, **II** 81a
genius, **II** 308b–309a
literary criticism, **I** 604a
Trinity
Calvinism, **I** 436a
Christianity, **I** 376a
civil disobedience, **I** 436a–436b
dignity, **IV** 138b, 140b, 141a
Faust (legend), **III** 246b
God, **II** 342b–343a
heresy, **II** 417a, 418a, 425a, 426b, 427b
idea, **II** 546b
microcosm, **III** 130a
religion, **IV** 103a
Renaissance, **IV** 138b, 140b, 141a
Roman Catholic Church, **I** 376a
Saint Augustine, **IV** 138b
Trissino, Giovanni Giorgio (1478–1550)
genius, **II** 293b
poetry, **III** 529a
style, **IV** 331a
Tristan (fiction), love, **III** 96a, 98b, 102a, 102b, 103a, 103b, 104b, 105a, 106a
Tritheim, Johannes (1462–1516), Faust (legend), **III** 244b–245a
Troeltsch, Ernst (1865–1923)
class, **I** 446a
Enlightenment, **II** 89a
historicism, **II** 457a–457b,

458a, 458b, 461a, 461b
historiography, **II** 496a, 496b
individualism, **II** 596b
Trojan War
ethics, **III** 440a
Greece (ancient), **II** 466b–467a
historiography, **II** 466b–467a, 483a
law, **II** 675a
primitivism, **III** 578b
Trotsky, Leon (1877–1940)
China, **I** 372a–372b
culture, **IV** 165b
economics, **III** 153b–154a
Marxism, **III** 153b–154a, 165b, 168b
nationalism, **III** 335b
perfectibility, **III** 473b
revolution, **IV** 158a, 163b, 165b
socialism, **III** 153b–154a
society, **III** 473b
technology, **III** 153b–154a
Troubadours, love, **III** 95b, 97b–99b, 101a–102b, 103b, 104a, 105a, 106a, 107b
Troubetskoy, N. S. (1890–1938)
language, **II** 672a
linguistics, **III** 71a
structuralism, **IV** 324a–324a, 326a
Trublet, Nicolas, literature, **III** 82a
Trueblood, Benjamin F., international peace, **III** 453a, 453b
Trust
Locke, **IV** 258b, 259a
Paine, **IV** 260b
philanthropy, **III** 489b, 492a
private property, **III** 655b
Truth
aesthetics, **IV** 354a, 355a, 356b
Aristotle, **II** 663a, 663b; **IV** 431b–432a
art, **I** 460b–461a; **II** 571a, 575b, 576a–576b, 582b
Beattie, **I** 317a, 317b
beauty, **I** 212a–212b
belief, **III** 562b
Blasius of Parma, **II** 35b
Christianity, **II** 582b
Cicero, **III** 16b, 227a, 587b
common sense, **I** 319b
communism, **III** 22b
Counter-Enlightenment, **II** 101a, 102a, 102b, 103a, 104b–105a
cynicism, **I** 629a

dadaists, I 322a
deism, I 647a
Descartes, IV 244b, 432b
dualism, II 39a
education, II 81b
emotion, III 562b
Engels, III 22a
Enlightenment, III 248a
ethics, IV 72b
evil, II 161b–162a, 162b
existentialism, III 160b
faith, III 563b
freedom of speech, II 254b
genius, II 313b
God, II 334b, 344a, 351b, 355a
Goethe, I 322a
good, IV 177a, 177b, 183b–184a
Greece (ancient), II 677b
happiness, II 376b, 377a
Hegel, I 37a, 319a–319b; II 410b
Herder, III 305a
heresy, II 416b, 417a
hermeticism, II 432a
Herodotus, II 513a
Hesiod, II 513a
hierarchy, II 439a, 443b, 446a
historiography, IV 149b
Hobbes, IV 177a
holy, II 513a
human nature, III 572a, 575a
humanism, IV 129b, 130a, 135a, 135b
Hume, II 101b
Husserl, I 322a–322b
idea, II 548b
ideology, II 556b
imagination, III 213b
Islam, II 643b
James, II 562b, 563a, 563b
John of Jandun, II 34b
Kant, I 315b, 319a; III 518a–518b; IV 383a, 433a
Kierkegaard, II 189b
language, II 662b–663b
law, II 677b; III 32b
Leibniz, I 315b; II 446a
literature, I 322a
Lovejoy, III 552b–553a
loyalty, II 110a, 111b, 115a
Marx, III 22a
Marxism, III 146b, 147b, 153a–153b, 160b, 161a
matter, III 188b
metaphor, III 204a, 204b, 205a, 206a
methodology, III 379a
mimesis, III 226b, 227a, 227b, 228b
Moore, G. E., I 319b
moral sense, III 233a

music, II 313b
mythology, III 273a, 273b, 274a, 274b, 275b, 290a, 300b, 301a, 302b, 303b, 304a, 304b, 305a, 307b
natural law, III 15a, 19a, 22a, 22b
Neo-Platonism, III 509b
Newton, III 379a, 394b, 398b
optics, III 408a, 416b
painting, I 322a; II 571a, 575b, 576a–576b, 582b
Parmenides, IV 47a
Peirce, III 552b–553a, 559a, 561a, 568b
perennial philosophy, III 457b, 458a, 458b, 459b, 460a, 460b, 461a, 462a, 462b
Philo Judaeus, II 513a
Pirandello, III 564a
Plato, II 582b, 662b; III 188b, 273a, 273b, 408a, 496a, 498b, 499b, 501b, 502a, 507a; IV 431b
Platonism, III 496a, 498b, 499b, 501b, 502a, 504b, 507a, 509b, 511b, 517a, 518a–518b
poetry, III 302b, 529b, 530a; Pomponazzi, II 37a
Pope, III 397a
Popper, I 323a–323b
positivism, III 535b
pragmatism, III 551b, 552b–553a, 557a, 557b, 559a, 561a, 562b, 563a, 563b, 564a, 565a, 565b, 566a, 568b
primitivism, III 587b, 595b, 596b, 599a, 599b
probability, III 606b
progress, III 636b
psychology, IV 9a, 17a, 18b, 19b, 20a, 24a
quantum theory, I 322b–322a
Ramism, IV 43a
rationalism, IV 47a
realism in literature, IV 53b
reformation, IV 64a, 67a
Reid, I 317a
relativism, IV 72b
religion, III 204a, 204b, 205a, 206a; IV 106b, 113b, 114a, 118b, 119a, 120b, 177b
Renaissance, IV 149b, 441a
rhetoric, IV 167b
right, IV 177a, 177b, 183b–184a
romanticism, III 303b–305a
Rousseau, II 104b–105a; III

595b
Royce, III 561a
Russell, I 319b–321b, 323b
Saint Augustine, III 509b; IV 9a
satire, IV 212b–213a
science, I 312a–325a
Siger of Brabant, II 32b–33b
skepticism, IV 235b, 237a, 242a, 243a, 244b, 245a, 246a, 246b, 250b, 251a
social contract, IV 258b, 259a, 260b, 261a
Socrates, III 496a, 499b
Sorel, III 565a
space, IV 305a
Spinoza, IV 246a
Swift, III 599b
taste, IV 354a, 355a, 356b
theodicy, IV 383a
theology, IV 129b, 130a, 131b, 132a
tragic sense, IV 415b
transcendentalism, IV 24a
unity of science, IV 431b–443b
universal man, IV 441a
ut pictura poesis, IV 465b, 466a, 475a
utilitarianism, IV 446b, 447a, 448b
Wilkins, I 310a; II 443b
wisdom of the fool, IV 515b, 516b, 518a, 519a
Wolff, I 315b
Zeitgeist, IV 536b
Zola, II 575b
See also Double truth
Tsanoff, R. A., theodicy, IV 383b
Tschermak, Erich, acquired characteristics, II 619a
Tschistiakoff, I., chromosomes, II 287a
Tsui-goab (myth), III 308a
Tubal-Cain (Bible), mythology, III 276b, 279b
Tucker, Benjamin R. (1854–1939), anarchism, I 73b–74a
Tucker, Josiah (1712–1799), social contract, IV 263a
Tucker, Robert
   Marxism, III 158a–159b
   totalitarianism, IV 409b
Tudor, William (1779–1830), Orientalism, III 429a
Tufts, James H., right, IV 186b
TULIP formula, II 28b
Tullock, Gordon, social welfare, IV 283b
T'ung dynasty

China (ancient), II 481a
   historiography, II 481a
Tuning, music, III 261a–263a
Tunisia
   France, III 537a
   nationalism, III 337b
   positivism, III 537a
Turberville, John, spontaneous generation, II 283a
Turgot, Anne Robert Jacques (1727–1781)
   Comte and, III 533a
   despotism, II 12a
   Enlightenment, II 90b, 93a, 93b, 98b
   eschatology, II 158b
   history, III 638a–639a
   individualism, II 600a–600b, 602a
   mythology, III 303a, 303b
   natural liberty, II 62b
   positivism, III 533a
   progress, III 637a, 638a, 638b–639a, 644b
   rationalism, III 303a, 303b
   revolution, IV 155a
   Smith and, II 62b
   social welfare, IV 277a
   unity, III 639a
   utility, IV 453a, 453b, 455b
   Utopia, IV 462b
Turkey
   Counter-Enlightenment, II 106a
   despotism, II 4b, 13a
   determinism, II 30b
   Eastern Orthodox Church, I 409a–411b
   nationalism, III 332b, 337a, 338a
   neo-classicism in art, III 365a
   Platonism, III 505b, 506a
   revolution, IV 160b, 162a
Turnbull, George, neo-classicism in art, III 365b
Turner, Frederick Jackson (1861–1932)
   historiography, II 497b
   nationalism, III 335b
Turner, Joseph M. W. (1775–1851)
   chance images, I 350b
   impressionism, II 578a, 579a–579b
   ut pictura poesis, IV 467a, 467b, 470b, 473b
Turner, L. A., entropy, II 114b
Turner, Nat (1800–1831), crisis in history, I 593b
Turner, Victor W., mythology, III 315a
Turpin, J. P. F., cell division, II 285b

Turquette, A. R., Peirce and, III 560b–561a

Turretin, J. A., skepticism, IV 242b

Tutankhamen (fl. about 1358 B.C.), freedom of speech, II 253b

Tuve, Rosemund, mythology, III 295a

Twining, Thomas, catharsis, I 267a

Tyard, Pontus de (1521–1605), mythology, III 292b

Tychism
    Peirce, II 587b; IV 396a
    pragmatism, III 560b, 561a, 569a
    time, IV 396a

Tyler, Bennett (1783–1858), religion, IV 111a

Tyler, Wat (d. 1381)
    heresy, II 427a
    primitivism, III 593a

Tylor, Edward Burnett (1832–1917)
    culture, I 617b–618a
    evolutionism, II 187a
    holy, II 513b
    Lang and, III 309a
    Müller and, III 308a, 308b
    mythology, III 307a, 308a–309a, 315a
    Nature, III 308b
    religion, IV 95a

Tymme, Thomas, hierarchy, II 438a

Tyndall, John (1820–1893)
    anthropomorphism, I 89b
    entropy, II 116a
    evolutionism, II 187a
    religion, IV 107a
    spontaneous generation, II 283b–284a; IV 308a–308b, 310a, 310b

Typography
    Ramism, IV 42b, 44a, 44b, 45b
    Renaissance, IV 149a–149b
    technology, IV 360b

Typology
    aesthetics, IV 356a–356b
    linguistics, III 66b, 67b, 68b, 71a, 71b, 72a
    romanticism, IV 188a, 189a, 191a
    taste, IV 356a–356b
    totalitarianism, IV 409b

Tyranny
    Aeschylus, IV 366b
    Antisthenes, I 629b
    Aristotle, I 625b; II 2a–2b, 4b
    Counter-Enlightenment, II 106b

democracy, I 654a, 656b, 663b, 664a
    despotism, II 1a, 2a–2b, 8a, 10b, 11b–12a, 14a, 14b, 17a–17b
    equality, II 146b
    freedom, II 250a, 250b
    freedom of speech, II 259a
    French Revolution (1789), II 409a–409b
    general will, II 276a
    Great Britain, IV 154a
    Greece (ancient), II 680b, 681b, 682a, 683a, 684b, 685a
    happiness, II 376a
    Hegel, II 409a–409b
    Hobbes, I 656b
    law, II 250a, 250b, 680b, 681b, 682a, 683a, 684b, 685a, 688b
    Locke, III 21a; IV 259a
    loyalty, III 112a, 112b
    Machiavellism, III 121a, 122b–123a, 123b
    Marxism, III 167b
    millenarianism, III 224a
    Montaigne, III 594b
    Montesquieu, II 11b
    mythology, III 281a, 287b
    natural law, III 21a
    natural liberty, II 70a
    necessity, III 354a
    Plato, I 654a; II 22a; III 498a; IV 175a
    Platonism, III 498a, 501a, 520a
    Polybius, I 625b, 626a
    primitivism, III 594b
    progress, III 631a, 638b, 647a, 647b
    prophecy, III 664b
    Renaissance, IV 126b
    revolution, IV 152b, 154a, 155b
    right, IV 175a
    Rome (ancient), II 688b
    Rousseau, II 11b–12a
    Savonarola, IV 477a–477b
    Schiller, IV 157a
    social contract, IV 253a, 254a, 255a, 259a
    Socrates, II 376a
    Staël, II 14b
    technology, IV 357b
    temperance, IV 366b
    Tocqueville, II 17a–17b
    totalitarianism, IV 406b
    U.S., IV 155b
    virtù, IV 477a–477b, 479b, 480a, 485a–485b

Tyrell, George (1861–1909)
    eschatology, I 422b

excommunication of, I 423b
    Jesus Christ, I 422b
    modernism, I 419b, 422b–423a, 423b, 424b, 425b

Tyrtaeus (middle 7th century B.C.), freedom of speech, II 258a

Tyutchev, Fëdor Ivanovich (1803–1873), symbolism, IV 343a

U

Ubertino of Casale, prophecy, III 668b

Uccello, Paolo (1397–1475) individualism, II 301b

Udall, Stewart (1920–), conservation, I 471b, 475a, 476b

Ugliness
    Aristotle, I 585a, 586a, 586b
    creativity in art, I 585a, 586a–586b
    painting, II 571a
    Plato, I 585a, 586b; II 217a
    Plotinus, I 586b
    Saint Augustine, I 586b
    ut pictura poesis, IV 468b
    utilitarianism, IV 447a

Uhland, Johann Ludwig (1787–1862), romanticism, IV 189a

Uhlhorn, Gerhrard, philanthropy, III 487b

Ui, Hakuju, Buddhism, I 247a

Ulbricht, Walter (1893–1973), Marxism, III 166b

Ullmann, W., individualism, II 598a–598b

Ulphilas, Bishop, Gothic, II 369a

Ulpian (170?–228 A.D.)
    authority, I 145b
    Bodin and, III 19b
    justice, II 656b, 688b
    law, II 687b, 688a, 688b, 689b
    natural law, III 16b, 17a, 17b, 18a, 19b
    Nature, III 17a
    pragmatism, III 554a
    progress, III 632b

Ulrich of Strassburg (fl. 13th century), beauty, II 222b

Ulysses (myth), III 273b

Unam Sanctam, I 385a

Unamuno, Miguel de (1864–

1936), symbolism, IV 342a

Uncertainty principle
    Bohr, II 589a
    Einstein, II 590a–591a
    Heisenberg, I 323a, 324a–324b; II 586b, 587b, 588b, 589a–590a, 591a
    indeterminacy, II 586b, 587b, 588b, 589a, 590a–591a, 591b
    Popper, II 591b
    Schlick, II 589b
    subject-object problem, II 590a
    time, IV 398a

Unconscious
    Jung, IV 97a
    love, III 107a
    psychology, IV 11b, 14a, 28b
    romanticism, IV 196b

Underwood, Benjamin Franklin
    Orientalism, III 434b
    transcendentalism, III 434b

Unemployment
    capitalism, III 151b
    economic history, II 58a, 58b
    Great Britain, IV 511b–512a, 512b, 513a
    Marx, IV 292b
    Marxism, III 151b
    natural liberty, II 70a–71a
    socialism, IV 289b
    U.S., II 58b, 70a–70b; IV 511b, 512a, 512b, 513a
    welfare state, IV 509b–514b

Ungaretti, Giuseppe, symbolism, IV 342a

Unger, Franz (1800–1870)
    cell division, II 286a

Uniformitarianism, IV 417b–430b
    animals, IV 418b, 419b, 420a, 425b, 427b
    archeology, IV 430a
    basalt, IV 420a–420b
    Beaumont, IV 418a
    Bible, IV 418a, 418b, 419b, 420a, 423b–424a, 426a, 427a, 427b
    biology, I 492b, 499b–500b; IV 424a, 424b, 425a–427b, 428a, 429a
    Black, Joseph, IV 419a
    Boltwood, IV 426b
    Bopp, IV 427b
    Bourbon restoration, IV 420a
    Buch, IV 418a, 421a–421b
    Buckland, IV 420a
    Burnet, IV 418b

calculus, IV 430a
Canary Islands, IV 418a, 421a
Cassirer, IV 428b
catastrophism, I 500a; IV 417b–423b, 425a
chemistry, IV 424b
Christianity, IV 419b
Columbus, IV 427b
communication, IV 426a
Comparative Method, IV 426b, 427a, 428a, 430a
continuity, I 492b, 499b–500b
Conybeare, IV 420a, 421b
Creation, IV 419b, 423b, 424a, 426a
Cuvier, IV 419b, 420a, 427b
Darwin, IV 422b–423a, 424a–425a, 428b–429b
Darwinism, IV 428a
defined, IV 417b
determinism, IV 429a
discontinuity, I 492b, 499b–500b
Du Bois-Reymond, IV 428b
earth, IV 417b–424b, 426b
education, IV 426a
Eiseley, IV 424a
electricity, IV 419a
elements, IV 423a
Enlightenment, IV 419b, 428b
evolution, IV 423a, 424a, 424b, 429a
evolutionism, II 176b
Fechner, IV 429b
Flood, IV 419b, 423b, 424a, 426a
fossils, IV 418b, 419b, 420a, 421a–422a, 425a, 425b
France, IV 420a, 421a, 421b, 422a
French Revolution (1789), IV 419b
Geiger, IV 425a
Geikie, IV 423a
geography, IV 422a
Geological Society of London, IV 419b
geologists, IV 418b–423a
geology, I 492b, 499b–500b; IV 417b–427b, 429a
Germany, IV 418a, 425a, 428b
glotto-chronology, IV 429b–430a
God, IV 424a, 424b, 426a
Great Britain, IV 418a–422a, 425a
Greek language, IV 425b, 427b
Grimm, IV 427b
Guettard, IV 420a

heat, IV 419a, 423a
Hebrew language, IV 426b, 427a
Hegel, IV 427b, 428a
Herder, IV 426b
Highet, IV 425b
historiography, IV 148a, 150b, 151b
history, IV 417b, 418a, 420b, 421b, 423a, 426b, 428a
Hoenigswald, IV 427b
Humboldt, IV 427b
Hume, IV 419b
Hutton, I 499b; IV 419a, 419b, 420a, 420b
Huxley, IV 424a, 424b, 425a, 427b, 428b
indistinguishability, IV 429b
Indo-European family, IV 426b, 427b
Ireland, IV 420b
Isle of Wight, IV 420b
Italy, IV 418b, 420b, 421b, 422a
Jespersen, IV 425b
Jones, William, IV 427b
Kelvin, IV 423a, 426b
Kruszewski, IV 425a
language, IV 424b–430a
latent heat, IV 419a
Latin language, IV 425b, 427b
Leibniz, IV 423b, 426a, 426b
liberalism, IV 419b
light, IV 419a
linguistic paleontology, IV 425a
literature, IV 425b
logic, IV 425a
Lyell, I 499b, 500a–500b; II 176b; IV 421b–425a, 426a, 427a–428a, 429b
mathematics, IV 426a, 429a, 430a
matter, IV 419a, 424a
mineralogy, IV 418b
monogenesis, IV 426b
Moses (Bible), IV 419b
mountains, IV 417b–423a
Müller, IV 424b–425a, 426b
Murchison, IV 422a
mutation, IV 424b
natural selection, IV 422b, 423a, 424a, 428a
Nature, IV 418a, 419b, 422b, 424a, 427b–429a
neogrammarianism, IV 428a–429b
Newton, III 379b
Norway, IV 421a
origin of species, IV 422b–423a

paleontology, IV 420a, 421b, 425a, 427b
Peirce, IV 429a
physics, IV 419a, 423a, 424b, 426b, 427a
Pictet, A., IV 425a
Pictet, F. J., IV 425a
plants, IV 421b, 425b, 427b
polygenesis, IV 426b
pre-Hegelianism, IV 428a
primitivism, III 599a
probability, IV 424b, 426a
progress, IV 150b
psychology, IV 428b, 429b
radioactivity, IV 423a, 426b, 430a
rationalism, IV 419b
Ray, IV 418b
reactionism, IV 419b
reason, IV 424a
Renaissance, IV 148a, 150b, 151b
religion, IV 419b, 420a
revelation, IV 424a, 426b, 427b
rocks, IV 418b, 419a, 420b, 421b, 423a, 424b, 427b
romanticism, IV 425b
Rutherford, IV 423a
Sanskrit language, IV 427b
Sapir, IV 426b
Saussure, IV 418b, 425a
Schleicher, IV 426b, 427b–428a
Schmidt, IV 428a
science, IV 417b, 419b, 420a, 422a, 423a, 423b, 424a, 425a, 426a, 426b
scientists, IV 417b, 418b
Scotland, IV 419a, 419b, 420a, 421b
Shaftesbury, III 599a
Shankara, IV 429a
Sicily, IV 421a, 421b, 422a
Smith, Adam, IV 419b
society, IV 426a
sound-change, IV 428b
sound-laws, IV 428b
space, IV 417b, 428b
species, IV 424b, 428a
specific heat, IV 419a
spirit, IV 428a
statistics, IV 426a
substratum, IV 425a
sun, IV 419a
Swadesh, IV 429b–430a
Switzerland, IV 421b
symmetry, IV 353a
Techmer, IV 425a
time, IV 392a–392b, 417b, 422b, 427b, 428b
Tower of Babel (Bible), IV 426a–426b
universe, IV 424a

Ussher, IV 426b, 427a
vocabulary, IV 430a
volcanoes, IV 417b–423a
Webster, Thomas, IV 420b
Werner, IV 418b, 419b, 420a, 420b
Whewell, IV 418a, 420b, 423b
Whitney, IV 425a, 426b, 427b
Wimsatt, IV 425b
Union of Soviet Socialist Republics
acquired characteristics, II 617b, 619a, 619b–621b
agriculture, II 620a, 621a–621b; III 152b, 155a, 653b
Albania, III 334a
animals, III 655a
anti-Semitism, III 157b
Baltic countries, III 334a
biology, II 620a, 621a
Bolshevik Party, II 559b–560a, 561a; III 152b
Bolshevism, IV 166a
Buddhism, I 253a
Bukharin, II 560a
bureaucracy, IV 158a
capitalism, III 151a, 155a, 166a
censorship, III 153a
chauvinism, III 333b
China (communist), IV 166a–166b
Civil War, II 560a, 561a
class, III 154b, 155a; IV 158a, 165a, 165b, 166a
Cold War, I 16a
collectivism, III 151a, 152b
communism, III 148a, 150b, 152a–157b, 333a–334a
Communist Party, I 665b
Constituent Assembly, II 560a
Constitution, I 486a; II 563a; III 334a
constitutionalism, I 486a
corporations, III 655a
craftsmanship, III 653b, 655a
culture, III 333b
democracy, I 665b
despotism, III 147b, 475a
dictatorship, II 560b; III 647b
Disarmament Committee, III 455b
economic history, II 59b
economics, III 150b, 151a, 153b, 154b–155b, 655a
equality, II 147a
espionage, III 157a
eugenics, II 620b
folklore, III 239a, 333b

freedom, I 486a; III 155a, 155b
genetics, II 619b–621b
Germany, II 563a
Guevara, IV 166a–166b
history, III 333b
Hungary, III 334a
ideology, II 559a–563b
imperialism, III 161b, 167a; IV 166a
industry, III 150b, 153b–155a, 334a, 655a
integration, III 333b
international peace, III 455b, 456a
justice, II 657b
language, III 333b
Lenin, II 560a, 562a
Leninism, II 562a–562b
literary criticism, I 606b
loyalty, III 114b
Marxism, III 147b, 150b, 151a, 152b–157b, 161b, 165a–169b, 645b
Marxism-Leninism, II 453b, 562b, 563b; IV 512b
materialism, II 453b, 455a; III 153a
Menshivik Party, II 559b, 560a
military, IV 506a, 507a
minorities, III 155a
Mir, III 651b
nationalism, III 167b, 332b–334a, 336b
natural liberty, II 70a
nonproliferation pact, III 456a
nuclear power, III 155a, 157a, 455b
oligarchy, II 560b, 561a, 562b
opposition to, III 334a
pangenesis, II 626b
peace, IV 506a
peaceful coexistence, III 157a
peasantry, II 620b
perfectibility, III 475a
periodization in history, III 479a
poetry, III 333b
Poland, III 334a
politics, II 560a, 561a, 620a; III 150b, 154b
polycentrism, III 114b
post-Stalinism, III 333b–334a
power, III 154b, 155b; IV 166a
pragmatism, III 565b–566a
private property, III 154b, 651b, 653b, 655a
production, III 155b

profit, III 155a–155b
progress, III 645b, 647b
psychology, IV 14a
proletariat, II 560a, 620b; III 154b
religion, II 562a
revisionism, IV 274b–275a
revolution, IV 158a, 163b, 164a, 165a–166b
Rumania, III 334a, 336b
Russian Revolution (October 1917), IV 158a, 163b, 164a, 165a
satellites, III 334a
secret police, II 561a
Social Democratic Party, II 559b
socialism, II 461b; III 152b, 153b, 155a
society, III 154b, 155a, 653b
sociology, II 620a, 621a
State, I 665b; III 154b, 155a, 653b, 655a
symbolism, IV 341a, 343a–343b, 344b
technology, III 155b
test-ban treaty, III 455b
totalitarianism, II 563a; III 150b; IV 406a, 408b
unions, III 154b
urbanization, III 334a
war, IV 506a, 507a
welfare state, IV 512b
women, IV 528a
World War II, II 563a–563b
Yugoslavia, III 334a
Unions
Bernstein, III 163b
equality, II 145b
Great Britain, III 537a
Marxism, III 148b, 154b, 163b
positivism, III 537a
progress, III 646a
revisionism, IV 267b, 268a, 271b–272a, 272b
U.S.S.R., III 154b
welfare state, IV 509b, 510a, 510b
Unitarianism
Faust (legend), III 246b
individualism, II 596a
Orientalism, III 429a, 429b, 432a, 433a, 434a
Pietism, IV 111a
psychology, IV 23b
transcendentalism, III 429a, 429b, 432a, 433a, 434a
United Nations
armaments, III 455a
Atomic Energy Commission, III 455b
Charter, III 454b–455b

Commission for Conventional Armaments, III 455b
conservation, I 471a
creation of, III 454b
diplomacy, III 454b
Disarmament Commission, III 455b
equality, II 138b, 140a, 147b; III 12a
freedom, III 12a
General Assembly, III 454b, 455b
international peace, III 449b, 451b, 452a, 454b–455a, 455b, 456b
justice, II 657b
Korea, III 454b
law, III 7b, 11b, 12a, 13a
League of Nations, III 454b
loyalty, III 113a
military observers, III 454b
nationalism, III 332a
natural law, III 26a
police force, III 454b
power, III 455a
Secretary-General, III 454b
Security Council, III 454b
Stalin, II 563b
U.S., IV 528b
Uniting for Peace Resolution, III 454b
Universal Declaration of Human Rights, I 437a, 437b; II 140a; III 7b, 12a
Universal Declaration of the Rights of Man, III 26a
war, III 449b, 451b, 452a, 454b–455a, 455b
weakness of, III 454b–455a
women, IV 528a
World Food Bank, I 371b
U.N. Disarmament Commission, international peace, III 455b
United States of America
academic freedom, I 10a–16b
activism, III 430a, 431a
aesthetics, II 219a
Agricultural Adjustment Act, I 371b
agriculture, I 367b, 371b; II 69a
Alien and Sedition Laws, III 114a
American Society, III 448b, 453a
American Peace Society of International Law, III 451a
American Society for Judicial Settlement of International Disputes, III 451a
Americanism, III 114a
anarchy, I 74a

anti-slavery, IV 529a
Arms Control and Disarmament Agency, III 455b
Attorney General, III 114b
baroque in literature, I 193a, 193b–194a, 194b
blacklisting, III 114b
blacks, I 442a, 449a, 594a; III 12b–13b, 328b–329a
Brazil, III 542b
Buddhism, I 256a, 256b–257a; III 429a, 430b, 431a, 432b, 434b, 436a, 436b–438b, 439a
Calvinism, III 429a
Carnegie Endowment for International Peace, III 449a
caste, I 442a
China, I 367b, 370b, 371b; III 428a, 428b, 430a–430b, 431a, 433a, 433b, 434a, 434b, 436a
Christianity, III 428b, 429a, 432a–434a, 436a, 436b
Church Peace Union, III 449a
city, I 432b
civil disobedience, I 435a, 436a–441a
Civil Rights Act (1964), IV 528b, 529a, 529b
Civil War, III 225b, 450a
class, I 442a, 444a, 444b, 448b–449b; IV 499b–500a
classicism, I 450a, 453a, 455a
Cold War, I 16a
collectivism, III 151a
colonialism, III 7b–8a, 329a, 483b
Committee on the Cause and Cure of War, III 449b
common law, II 696a; III 31b–32a
communism, III 151a
conservation, I 471a–476b
conservatism, I 481b, 483b–484b
Constitutional Convention (1787), III 8a, 444b
constitutionalism, I 488b–490b, 491a
cosmic voyages, I 534b
Counter-Enlightenment, II 101b
crime, I 71b
crisis in history, I 590a, 593a, 593b, 594a
Cuba, III 565b
culture, III 328b, 427b–439a, 491b
cynicism, III 347b–348a

Declaration of Rights (Virginia), III 8a
deism, I 647b, 651b, 652a
Democratic Party, III 152a
democracy, I 652b, 656a–660b, 663a–664a, 665a, 666a–667a
desegregation, III 9b, 13a
despotism, II 1a, 7a–7b, 10a
Disarmament Committee, III 455b
drama, II 208b
economic history, II 44b, 45a, 46a, 47a, 58b, 60b
Economic Opportunity Act of 1964, IV 514a
economics, I 490b; III 9a–9b, 151a, 428a, 428b, 434a
education, I 15b–16a, 440a, 440b; II 63b–64a, 83a, 147a; III 4b, 9b, 12b, 491b, 495a
empathy, II 88b
environment, II 124b
Equal Rights Amendment, IV 528b, 529a
equality, II 138b, 139a–139b, 142a, 143a, 143b, 145a, 146b, 147a; III 329a
equity, II 148a, 152a, 153a
Espionage Act, III 114a
evangelicalism, II 596a
evolution, III 433b, 434a, 435a, 438a–438b, 439a
evolution of literature, II 171b, 173a
evolutionism, II 181a
extremism, III 331a
Fair Labor Standards Act of 1938, IV 512a–512b
Fellowship of Reconciliation, III 449b
fiction, III 348a
First Continental Congress, III 8a
foundations, III 492a
founding principle, III 329a
freedom, II 251a
French Revolution (1789), IV 156a, 160b
Fugitive Slave Laws, I 436a
fundamentalism, II 429b, 430a
God, III 429b, 432b, 433b, 435a
Gothic, II 372b
Great Britain, III 428b; IV 155b
Great Depression of the 1930s, II 70a–70b; IV 511b, 512a–512b
heresy, II 429a, 429b, 430b
Hinduism, III 429a, 430a–432b, 433b, 434a, 436b,

439a
House Un-American Activities Committee, III 114b
housing, II 66b
idea, III 329a
idealism, I 408a; III 429b, 430a, 430b, 432b, 439a
impressionism, II 567b, 570b, 573b, 575a, 579b
independence, III 348a
India, III 428a, 428b, 429b, 430a, 431a, 431b, 433a, 433b, 434b, 436a
individualism, II 595a, 596a–596b
Inspirationists, IV 461a
international peace, III 449a, 449b, 450a, 451a, 451b, 453a, 453b, 454a, 455b, 456a
Islam, III 434b
isolationism, III 449b
Japan, III 428a, 437b–438b
Jay Treaty, III 450a
Jeffersonianism, II 596a
Judaism, III 432a–432b
justice, II 654b–655a, 657b
Korean War, III 114b
labor, III 151a; IV 512a–512b
language, II 660b, 661a, 661b, 669a–669b, 672a, 672b
Latin America, III 563a, 565b
law, I 292a–292b; II 148a, 152a, 153a, 251a, 686b, 689a, 690a; III 4a–5a, 5b, 7b–10a, 11b, 12a–13a, 29b, 31b–32a, 32b
League to Enforce Peace, III 454a
League of Free Nations Society, III 454a
League of Nations Association, III 449b
liberty, I 392b; III 329a
linguistics, II 247a
literary criticism, I 596a, 599a, 601b, 603a–604b; IV 341b–342a
literature, III 85a, 428a–431b, 438b
loyalty, III 113a–115a
loyalty tests, III 114b
Lutheranism, II 64b
McCarthyism, III 492a
Machiavellism, III 124a, 124b
Marxism, III 151a, 152a, 154a, 156b–157b, 160b
materialism, III 429a–429b, 430a, 433b, 438a
Medicare Act, III 114b

military, III 444a; IV 504a, 505b–506a, 507a, 508a
millenarianism, III 225b
missionaries, I 407a–407b
modernism, I 419a, 419b, 423b, 424b
monism, III 430a, 436b, 438a–438b, 439a
monopoly, III 563b, 565b
morality, III 428a–429a, 430b, 436b
Moravians, I 403a
mysticism, III 429b–431a
mythology, III 279b, 306b, 316a
National Council for the Prevention of War, III 449b
National Organization for Women, IV 528b–529b
nationalism, III 328b–329a, 330a–331a, 332a, 337a
natural law, III 5a, 21b
natural liberty, II 63b–64a, 66b, 67a, 69a, 70a–70b
natural rights, II 596a; III 21b
naturalism, III 483b; IV 54b
Nature, III 347b–348b
neo-colonialism, III 330a
New Deal, II 58b; III 9b, 654b; IV 512a
New Left, IV 529b
New York Peace Society, III 448b, 449a
New York State Legislature, III 114a
Nisei evacuation, III 114b
nonproliferation pact, III 456a
Northwest Ordinance (1787), III 8a
nuclear power, III 455b
Oneida Community, IV 461a
organicism, III 426b
Orientalism, III 427b–439b
pantheism, III 432b
peace, III 444a, 444b, 446b, 447a; IV 505b–506a
Pennsylvania Hospital, III 490b
periodization in history, III 479a
periodization in literary history, III 483b
Persia, III 430a, 430b, 431a, 433a, 434a
philanthropy, III 490b, 491a, 491b, 492a, 492b
Philippines, III 331a, 563a, 565b
phrenology, IV 23a–23b
Pietism, III 493b, 495a
Platonism, III 519b, 522a–

522b
polytheism, III 434a
positivism, III 5b, 537a, 542b, 544a, 545a, 546b, 547a, 549a, 549b
poverty, I 440b
power, III 12a–13a
pragmatism, III 551b–554a, 557a–563a, 564a, 565b, 566a–569b; IV 69a
primitivism, III 591b, 597b, 598a, 598b, 599a, 603b, 604a
private property, III 654b, 655b
Protestantism, III 432b
psychology, IV 12b, 14a, 15a, 16a–30b
Puritanism, II 596a; III 483b
racial discrimination, I 439a, 440a–440b; III 12b–13a
racial prejudice, I 16a–16b; II 139a–139b, 251a; III 9b
Ramism, IV 42b, 44b
Rappites, IV 461a
rationalism, III 429a, 429b, 432b
realism, III 483b
realism in literature, IV 52b, 54a–54b
reformation, IV 68b, 69a
Reformation, IV 396a
religion, II 64a–64b; III 428a–439a; IV 106b, 107a, 108a, 109a–112a
Renaissance, IV 125b
Republican Party, III 455b
revolution, III 329a, 428b; IV 155b–156a, 160b, 164a
rhetoric, IV 170a
rights, III 7b–10a
Roman Catholic Church, III 432b
romanticism, III 306b, 483b; IV 189a, 195a, 195b, 196b, 210b
satire, IV 212a
science, III 432b–437a, 439a
Scopes trial, II 430b
segregation, I 435a, 440a–440b; III 9b
Seven Years' War, I 402b
slavery, I 435a, 436a–437a; II 7a–7b
Smith Act of 1940, III 114b
social contract, IV 254b, 255a, 260b–261a, 262b–263a
Social Gospel movement, II 429a
Social Security Act of 1935, IV 512b

social welfare, **IV** 277b, 282a
socialism, **IV** 289b
society, **III** 428a, 428b, 434a
sovereignty, **I** 659a–660b
space, **IV** 305b
State, **I** 652b, 656a, 656b, 657b, 658a, 658b–660b, 663a–664a, 665a, 666a–667a; **IV** 155b
student unrest, **I** 16b
Subversive Activities Control Board, **III** 114b
suffrage, **I** 437a–437b, 439b, 660a, 666a; **II** 138b
symbolism, **IV** 341a–342a, 343b, 344b
Taoism, **III** 430a, 434a
taxation, **III** 11b
technology, **I** 594a; **IV** 363a
test-ban treaty, **III** 455b
theology, **III** 432b, 435a
trade, **III** 428b, 439a
tradition, **III** 329a
transcendentalism, **II** 596a; **III** 429a–434b, 439a, 483b, 519b
tyranny, **IV** 155b
unemployment, **II** 58b, 70a–70b; **IV** 511b–513a
Unitarianism, **II** 596a; **III** 429a, 429b, 432a, 433a, 434a
U.N., **IV** 528b
Universal Peace Union, **III** 449a
universality, **III** 329a
urbanization, **I** 594a
utilitarianism, **III** 433b
Utopia, **IV** 461a, 463a, 463b
Venezuela, **III** 565b
Vietnam War, **I** 435a, 440b; **II** 67a
Volksgeist, **IV** 494b–495b
vox populi, **IV** 499a–500a
war, **III** 428b, 444a; **IV** 504a, 505b–506a, 507a, 508a
Washington Conference, **III** 455b
wealth, **III** 491b–492b
welfare state, **IV** 511b–514a
witch hunt, **III** 114b
women, **IV** 526b, 528a–529b
Women's Liberation Movement, **IV** 529b
World Court, **III** 449b
World Peace Foundation, **III** 449a
World War I, **I** 665a; **III**

114a–114b, 332a
World War II, **III** 114b
World's Court League, **III** 454a
yoga, **III** 428a, 431a, 431b, 439a
Zen Buddhism, **III** 428a, 436a
United States Constitution, **I** 489a–490b, 491b, 659a–660b, 666a–666b; **II** 379b; **III** 7b–10a, 11b; **IV** 260b, 261a, 262b, 499b, 528a
Bill of Rights, **I** 437b, 490a; **III** 8a, 13a
Commerce Clause, **III** 13a
Fifth Amendment, **II** 689a; **III** 8b, 9b, 654b
First Amendment, **III** 8a, 10a, 114a
Fourteenth Amendment, **III** 8b, 9a, 9b, 12a, 654b; **IV** 528b
private property, **III** 654b
Thirteenth Amendment, **III** 12b–13a
United States Supreme Court, **I** 489a–490a
United States Declaration of Independence, **I** 64a, 571a; **II** 1a, 46a, 89a, 379b; **III** 11b, 332b; **IV** 21b–22a, 263a
Jefferson, **IV** 21b
nationalism, **III** 332b
United States National Student Association, **I** 11a
United States Supreme Court **II** 251a, **III** 12a, 12b, 114b
academic freedom, **I** 11b–13b
Adamson v. California, **III** 9b–10a
Baldwin v. Missouri, **III** 9b
The Bank of Columbia v. Okely, **III** 8b
Bolling v. Sharpe, **III** 9b
Brown v. Board of Education, **III** 9b
Chicago, Milwaukee, & St. Paul Ry. Co. v. Minnesota, **III** 9a
Constitution, **I** 489a–490a
constitutionalism, **I** 489a–490a
De Jonge v. Oregon, **I** 490a
Dred Scott v. Sandford, **III** 9a
Ex parte Milligan, **I** 489b–490a
Ferguson v. Skrupa, **III** 9a
French v. Barber Asphalt Paving Co., **III** 8b

Granger Cases, **III** 9a
Griswold v. Connecticut, **III** 9b
Hurtado v. California, **III** 10a
Jay Burns Baking Co. v. Bryan, **III** 9b
Jones v. Mayes Co., **III** 13a
justice, **II** 654b–655a
Keyishian v. Board of Regents of New York, **I** 12a
loyalty, **III** 114b
Marbury v. Madison, **I** 489b
Murray's Lessees v. The Hoboken Land & Improvement Co., **III** 8b
Nebbia v. New York, **III** 9a
Plessy v. Ferguson, **III** 12b
precedent, **III** 32a
private property, **III** 654b
psychology, **IV** 26b
Rinaldi v. Yaeger, **III** 12b
Roman Catholic Church, **III** 654b
segregation, **I** 440a
Shaughnessy v. United States ex rel. Mezei, **I** 13a–13b
Slaughter-House Cases, **III** 9a
Sweezy v. New Hampshire, **I** 12a
West Virginia State Board of Education v. Barnette, **I** 490a
Whitney v. California, **III** 9a
Williamson v. Lee Optical Co., **III** 9a
women, **IV** 528a
Unity
Aristotle, **I** 501a; **II** 623a; **III** 423a, 527a, 527b, 531a
Averroës, **II** 34b
common law, **II** 692b
Comte, **III** 641b–642a
Dewey, **III** 556b
drama, **III** 527a, 527b, 531a
Engels, **II** 455a
environment, **II** 128a, 128b
Fichte, **III** 473a
good, **IV** 176a, 176b, 180a, 184a
Hegel, **III** 556a, 556b; **IV** 180a
Heraclitus, **III** 187a
Herder, **III** 304b
hierarchy, **II** 442a, 444b, 445a, 445b, 446a, 448b
historiography, **IV** 148a
history, **III** 648a
Horace, **III** 423b
human nature, **III** 648a–648b
humanism, **IV** 132a

ideal, **II** 550b, 551b
impressionism, **II** 576a
India, **III** 338a
international peace, **III** 453a
Kant, **II** 551b; **III** 639b
Kelsen, **III** 2a–2b
language, **II** 660b
law, **III** 2b, 35a
Leibniz, **II** 446a
loyalty, **III** 115a
matter, **III** 186b, 187a, 193b
methodology, **III** 648a
music, **III** 269a
mythology, **III** 292a, 293b, 303b, 304b, 305a, 310b, 313b
nationalism, **III** 329b, 330a, 335b, 336b, 338a
naturalism in art, **III** 341b
Nature, **II** 128a, 128b
Newton, **III** 390a
numbers, **III** 403a, 403b
organicism, **III** 421a–427a
pangenesis, **II** 623a
Parmenides, **III** 187a
Peirce, **III** 556b
perennial philosophy, **III** 457b, 458a, 458b, 460a, 460b, 462b
perfectibility, **III** 473a
Plato, **III** 503b; **IV** 34a
Platonism, **III** 503b, 519b
poetics, **III** 527a, 527b, 531a
positivism, **III** 548a, 548b, 549a, 549b
pragmatism, **III** 556a, 556b
probability, **III** 605b, 608a
progress, **III** 638a–640a, 641a–642a, 648a–648b
Pythagoreans, **IV** 34a, 35b
rationalism, **IV** 46b
Renaissance, **IV** 132a, 148a, 437a, 440a, 441a
right, **IV** 176a, 176b, 180a, 184a
romanticism, **III** 303b, 304b, 305a
space, **IV** 300a
Speusippus, **IV** 35b
Spinoza, **II** 444b, 445a, 445b
Teilhard de Chardin, **II** 448b
time, **IV** 390a, 392a–392b, 396a
tragic sense, **IV** 411b, 412b
Turgot, **III** 639a
universal man, **IV** 437a, 440a, 441a
Volksgeist, **IV** 495a, 495b
Unity of science, **IV** 431a–437a
algebra, **IV** 435b, 436a

Aristotle, IV 431a–433b, 434b–436a

arithmetic, IV 431b, 435b

art, IV 431b

astronomy, IV 431b, 433b

atheism, IV 432b

Bacon, Francis, IV 431a, 432a, 433b–434a

Bacon, Roger, IV 434b

Being, IV 431b, 432a–432b, 434b

body, IV 432b, 434b

causation, IV 433b–434b

Condillac, IV 435b–436a

culture, IV 431a

Descartes, IV 432b, 433a, 435b

discovery, IV 435a

education, IV 431a, 434b

emotion, IV 434b

empiricism, IV 433a, 433b, 434b

experience, IV 432b, 433b, 435a

geometry, IV 431b, 434a, 435b

God, IV 434a–435b, 436b

good, IV 431b, 432b, 436a

Greece (ancient), IV 431a–432b

harmony, IV 431b, 436b

history, IV 434a

Hobbes, IV 434a

human nature, IV 433a

Hume, IV 432b, 433a

hypotheses, IV 431b, 435a

idea, IV 436b

ideal, IV 431a, 436a

imagination, IV 434a

indexes, IV 435b

inspiration, IV 435a

judgment, IV 433a, 433b

Kant, IV 431a, 432b, 433a–433b, 436a–436b

knowledge, IV 431a, 431b, 432a, 433b–436b

language, IV 435b–436a

learning, IV 434a, 435a

Leibniz, IV 432b–433a, 434a–436a

logic, IV 431a, 433a, 433b, 434a, 435b, 436a

Lully, IV 434b, 435a

materialism, IV 432a, 434a

mathematics, IV 431b, 432b, 433a, 435b

matter, IV 434a

mechanism, IV 432b, 434b

medicine, IV 432b, 433b, 434b

memory, IV 434a

metaphysics, IV 432a–434b, 436a

methodology, IV 431a,

434b–436a

Middle Ages, IV 432a, 436a

mind, IV 432b, 434a, 434b

morality, IV 432b, 433a, 433b–434a, 434b, 536b

motion, IV 434a

music, IV 433b

Nature, IV 432a–436b

Newton, IV 433a

ontology, IV 432a

optics, IV 433b

order, IV 435b

passions, IV 432b

philosophy, IV 431a–434b, 436a

physics, IV 432b, 433a, 433b, 434a, 434b, 436b

Plato, IV 431a–431b, 432b, 436a

pluralism, IV 435b

poetry, IV 434a

power, IV 434b

progress, IV 433b, 435b

psychology, IV 433a, 433b, 436b

reason, IV 434a, 434b, 435b, 436a, 436b

religion, IV 433a

Rome (ancient), IV 431a

Saint Thomas Aquinas, IV 432a, 434b, 435a, 436a

scholasticism, IV 432a, 432b, 433a, 436a

senses, IV 434a, 435a

signs, IV 435a, 435b

Socrates, IV 436a

Spinoza, IV 434a–434b

subject matter, IV 431a, 433b–434b, 435b

teleology, IV 436a–436b

theology, IV 436b

thought, IV 434b

truth, IV 431b–433b

universality, IV 431a, 431b, 432a, 433b, 434b, 435a, 435b, 436a

utilitarianism, IV 431b

wisdom, IV 431a

Universal Declaration of Human Rights, I 437a

Universal language, II 668a–669a

Universal man, IV 437a–443b

aesthetics, IV 439b–440a, 442b

Alberti, IV 437b–438a, 439a–442b

Alembert, IV 443a

anatomy, IV 440a

architecture, IV 439b, 440a

aristocracy, IV 441b

Aristotle, IV 439a

arithmetic, IV 438b

art, IV 437a, 437b, 438a, 439b, 440a, 441b, 442a, 443a

artists, IV 437b, 439b

astronomy, IV 438b, 440a, 441a

Bacon, Francis, IV 443a

Bacon, Roger, IV 441a

beauty, IV 440b

Bible, IV 442b

body, IV 439a

Borgia, IV 442a

bourgeois, IV 441b, 442b

Burckhardt, IV 437a–439b, 440a, 441a

capitalism, IV 442a

Cassirer, IV 440a, 441a, 443a

Castiglione, IV 439a, 442b

Cicero, IV 439a, 440b

city-state, IV 438a, 441b

class, IV 438a, 441b

cosmology, IV 440b, 442b

Counter-Reformation, IV 442a, 442b

craftsmanship, IV 437b, 441b

creativity, IV 437a

cryptography, IV 441b

culture, IV 437a–443a

dancing, IV 439a

Dante, IV 442b

death, IV 439b

Descartes, IV 443a

dialectics, IV 438b, 441a

Diderot, IV 443a

dignity, IV 439a, 441b

economics, IV 438a, 439b, 442a

education, IV 437a, 437b, 438b–441b

eloquence, IV 438b–439a

emotion, IV 437b

empiricism, IV 440b–441a, 442b, 443a

equality, IV 438a

ethics, IV 440a, 441a, 442a–442b

experience, IV 440a, 440b, 441a, 443a

freedom, IV 438a

Garin, IV 440a

geography, IV 440a

geometry, IV 438b, 440a

God, IV 443a

grammar, IV 438b, 439b

Greece (ancient), IV 438a, 441b

Guarino, IV 438b

harmony, IV 439b, 440b

Hauser, IV 442a

Heydenreich, IV 440a

history, IV 438b, 439a, 441a, 442b

humanism, IV 437b, 438b–443a

ideal, IV 438b, 439a, 439b, 440b, 441b, 443a

individualism, IV 437a, 438a, 439a

intuition, IV 440b

Italy, IV 437a–443a

Julius Caesar, IV 439a

justice, IV 440b

knowledge, IV 437a, 440b, 441a–443a

law, IV 437b

Leibniz, IV 443a

leisure, IV 438a, 439a

Leonardo da Vinci, IV 437a, 437b, 438a, 439b, 440a–441a, 442a–442b

literature, IV 437b, 439a, 439b, 440a, 441a–443a

logic, IV 438b

Machiavelli, IV 442b

Martin, IV 442a

mathematics, IV 437b, 438b, 439b–443a

measurement, IV 440a, 440b, 441a, 443a

mechanism, IV 440a, 441b

Medici, Lorenzo de', IV 442a

Medici family, IV 443a

metaphysics, IV 439b, 440b, 441a

methodology, IV 440a, 441a, 441b

Michelangelo, IV 439b, 442a, 442b–443a

Middle Ages, IV 438a, 438b, 440b, 443a

morality, IV 438b–443a

mores, IV 440b

music, IV 437b, 438b, 439a

Nature, IV 441a

Neo-Platonism, IV 442a, 442b

optics, IV 440a

oratory, IV 439a

painters, IV 439b

painting, IV 439a, 439b, 440a, 441b

perspective, IV 440a

philology, IV 440a

philosophy, IV 438b, 439a, 439b, 440a, 441a, 443a

physics, IV 437b

Plato, IV 440b

Platonism, IV 440a

Pliny, IV 437b

Plutarch, IV 439a

poetry, IV 438b, 439a

power, IV 437b, 438a, 441b

proportionality, IV 439b–440a, 440b

Ptolemy, IV 439b

rationalism, **IV** 438a, 440a, 441b, 442b, 443a
reality, **IV** 440a
reason, **IV** 439a, 441a, 443a
rhetoric, **IV** 438b, 439a, 441b
Roman Catholic Church, **IV** 442a, 442b
Rome (ancient), **IV** 441b
Saint Thomas Aquinas, **IV** 441a
Savonarola, **IV** 442b
scholasticism, **IV** 437b, 441a
science, **IV** 437a, 439b–443a
sculpture, **IV** 439b
self-realization, **IV** 438a
senses, **IV** 440a
Sforza, **IV** 442a
society, **IV** 437a, 437b, 438a, 439a, 439b, 441a–443a
soul, **IV** 439a
Spain, **IV** 442a–443a
status, **IV** 438a
surveying, **IV** 441b
Symonds, **IV** 438a
technology, **IV** 441b–442b
theology, **IV** 441a, 443a
time, **IV** 439b
tradition, **IV** 438b–439a
truth, **IV** 441a
unity, **IV** 437a, 440a, 441a
urbanization, **IV** 438a, 439b, 441b
value, **IV** 437b
Vasari, **IV** 442b
Vergil, **IV** 439a
versatility, **IV** 437a
virtue, **IV** 439a
Vitruvius, **IV** 439b
Vittorino da Feltre, **IV** 438b
wealth, **IV** 438a, 441b
Woodward, **IV** 438b, 439a
Zubov, **IV** 440a
See also Renaissance
Universal Peace Congress, **III** 449a
Universal Peace Union, **III** 449a
Universality
aesthetics, **IV** 354a–356b
Aristotle, **IV** 49b, 175b, 431b
Bacon, **IV** 432a
Buddhism, **III** 437a
Descartes, **IV** 435b
determinism, **II** 18a–19b, 587b
dignity, **IV** 145a, 145b
Ficino, **IV** 145b
Judaism, **III** 636a
Kant, **IV** 179b, 433b

knowledge, **IV** 435a
law, **II** 149b
linguistics, **III** 67b, 75b
morality, **III** 645a
motif, **III** 240a, 240b
music, **II** 388b
mythology, **III** 240a–240b, 308b, 311a
nationalism, **III** 329a, 332b
Nature, **III** 348a
Orientalism, **III** 437a
perennial philosophy, **III** 458b, 460b, 462a, 462b
Pico della Mirandola, **IV** 145b
Plato, **IV** 34b, 35b
progress, **III** 636a, 637b, 645a, 648b
Pythagoreans, **IV** 34b, 35b
rationalism, **IV** 49b, 50a
Renaissance, **IV** 145a, 145b
right, **IV** 173b, 174a, 175b, 179b
romanticism, **IV** 205b, 206a
Saint Thomas Aquinas, **IV** 432a
socialism, **IV** 285b
Socrates, **IV** 34b
Speusippus, **IV** 35b
Stoicism, **IV** 50a, 285b
taste, **IV** 354a–356b
theodicy, **IV** 379b
U.S., **III** 329a
unity of science, **IV** 431a, 431b, 432a, 433b, 434b, 435a, 435b, 436a
utilitarianism, **IV** 448b, 449a, 449b
Universe
Alain de Lille, **IV** 41a
Anaximander, **IV** 38b
angels, **IV** 40b–41a
Anselmi, **IV** 41a
anthropocentric, **II** 442b
Arabs, **IV** 41a
Archytas, **IV** 38a
Aristides Quintilianus, **IV** 39a, 40a–40b
Aristotle, **II** 175b, 438b; **III** 354a; **IV** 38a, 40a
arithmetic, **IV** 38a, 39a, 40b, 42a
astrology, **IV** 40b
astronomy, **IV** 40b
atomism, **III** 187b
Augustinianism, **II** 32a
Babylonia, **IV** 38b
Bergson, **III** 474a
Bible, **IV** 38b, 40b
big bang hypothesis, **I** 566b–567b, 569a
block-universe, **IV** 395b–

396a
Boccaccio, **II** 233b
Bode, **IV** 42a
Boethius, **IV** 40b, 41a
Boltzmann, **II** 117b
Bruno, **II** 347b, 348a, 348b, 442b–443a; **III** 194a, 510b
Buddhism, **I** 250b–251a; **II** 344a
Cassiodorus, **IV** 41a
Chalcidius, **IV** 39b
Chaldeans, **IV** 38b
chance, **II** 225b–235a
Cicero, **IV** 40a
circular, **II** 436b–438b, 442b
Copernicus, **II** 442b
cosmology, **I** 536b, 541b, 542b, 544b, 545b, 554b–556a, 559b–562b, 568b, 569a; **IV** 38b–42a, 297b
Counter-Enlightenment, **II** 103a, 103b, 108b, 109b
Creation, **IV** 38b, 39a
creativity in art, **I** 580a
Dante, **II** 233b; **IV** 41a
Demiurge, **IV** 39a–39b
Democritus, **II** 135b
Descartes, **II** 443b
design argument, **I** 671b–672a, 672b
determinism, **II** 18a–19b
Diderot, **II** 177b
dignity, **IV** 136b, 137a, 138a, 138b, 139a, 140b, 142a, 145a, 146a
disease, **II** 396b
Donne, **II** 443b
double truth, **II** 32a
Eddington, **IV** 42a
Einstein, **I** 559b–562b, 565b, 566a–566b
elements, **IV** 40a
entropy, **II** 115b, 117b
equality, **II** 138b
Er (myth), **IV** 38b, 39b, 41a
Erigena, **IV** 41a
eschatology, **II** 157a
Euclid, **IV** 39b
evil, **II** 162a
evolutionism, **II** 174a–174b, 175b, 176a–176b, 177b, 181b, 183b, 184b, 188a
expanding, **I** 561b–562b, 564b–566b; **II** 448b
fate, **II** 225b–235a
Ficino, **II** 442a, 442b; **IV** 39b, 41a
Fludd, **II** 390a; **IV** 41b
free will, **II** 243b
Galileo, **III** 193a
geometrical, **II** 443a–443b

geometry, **IV** 38a, 39a, 40a, 40b, 41b
Gnosticism, **IV** 40b–41a
God, **II** 335b, 336b, 338b, 340a, 340b, 343b, 344a, 344b, 347b, 348a, 348b; **III** 465b; **IV** 380b
Greece (ancient), **II** 675b, 677b, 681b, 682a; **IV** 38a–41a, 41b
Guillaume de Conches, **IV** 41a
Hamann, **II** 103b
harmony, **II** 388a–392b, 394a, 394b; **III** 260b, 268b, 270b; **IV** 38a–42a
Hegel, **I** 319a
heliocentric, **II** 442b
Helmholtz, **II** 115b
Heraclitus, **IV** 38b
Hermeticism, **II** 432a, 433a
hierarchy, **IV** 434b, 436a–439b, 441a–448b; **III** 192a
Hippolytus, **IV** 39a
history, **II** 18a–19b
Hobbes, **II** 443b, 444b
humanism, **II** 521a; **IV** 41a
Hume, **I** 314a
Huxley, **III** 474a
Iamblichus, **IV** 39a
ideal, **II** 550b, 551a
imagination, **III** 213a, 217b, 218b
impressionism, **II** 582a
infinity, **II** 441a–443b, 608a, 612a, 615a, 615b
Kant, **II** 447b
Kepler, **II** 443a–443b; **III** 260b, 271a; **IV** 41b
Kircher, **IV** 41b
Laplace, **II** 18b
law, **II** 226a, 227a, 675b, 677b, 681b, 682a; **III** 19a
Leibniz, **II** 445b–446a, 447b; **III** 131a; **IV** 41b, 382a
Leonardo da Vinci, **IV** 41a
Macrobius, **IV** 40a
macrocosm-microcosm, **III** 126a–127b, 128b, 129b, 130b–131a
Man-Machine, **III** 137b
Martianus Capella, **II** 229a; **IV** 40a
materialism, **II** 451a, 455a
mathematics, **II** 442b; **IV** 38a–40a
matter, **III** 187b, 190a, 191a, 192a, 192b, 193a, 194a, 194b
measurement, **IV** 399b, 400a, 402a, 402b, 404b, 405b
Mersenne, **IV** 41b

metaphor, III 203a
Middle Ages, IV 39b, 41a
motion, IV 39a, 40a
mountains in literature, III 257a
mythology, III 278a, 290a; IV 38b, 39b, 41a
natural law, III 14b, 15a, 19a
Nature, IV 38a
necessity, III 353a, 354a, 356a, 360a, 361b; IV 39b
Neo-Platonism, IV 39a, 39b, 41a
Neo-Pythagoreans, IV 39a, 39b, 42a
Newton, III 194b, 557a
Nicholas of Cusa, II 441a–441b; III 510b
nonstatic, nonempty, I 562b–564a
numbers, IV 33a, 38a–38b, 39a–39b, 42a
Numenius, IV 40b
order, II 434b, 436a–439b, 441a–448b; IV 38b
organicism, III 424a
oscillating, I 563b–565a
Parmenides, IV 38b
perfectibility, III 464b, 465b, 473b–474a
Philo Judaeus, IV 38b, 40b
Plato, I 579a, 580a, 671b–672a; II 390a; III 353a; IV 34a, 38b–41b
Platonism, III 503b, 510a, 510b, 513a
Plotinus, II 439a
Plutarch, IV 38b
Pontus de Tyard, IV 41a
pre-Socratics, IV 38b
Proclus, II 441a; IV 39b
Pseudo-Dionysius, II 441a; IV 41a
Ptolemy, IV 39b, 40b, 41b
Pythagoras, II 390a; IV 32a, 37a, 39a
Pythagorean scale, IV 39a–39b
Pythagoreans, IV 31b, 32a, 33a, 34a, 37a–42a
Ramism, IV 44a, 45a
rationalism, IV 46a, 50a
relativity, IV 74a, 74b
religion, III 203a; IV 97b
Renaissance, IV 39b, 41a–41b, 136b, 137a, 138a, 138b, 139a, 140b, 142a, 145a, 146a
romanticism, IV 200b, 204a, 204b, 205b, 206a
Saint Augustine, II 230a–230b, 441a

Saint Thomas Aquinas, III 19a
Schelling, II 108b
Schopenhauer, IV 41b
skepticism, IV 237a, 247b, 249b, 250b
space, IV 295a–306b
spatiotemporal representation of, III 14b
Spencer, III 473b–474a
Spinoza, II 445a
static, I 556a, 559b–562b, 565b, 566a–566b
steady-state theory, I 567b–568b
symmetry, IV 350a–352b
technology, IV 360b, 363b
theism, I 572b
theodicy, IV 380b, 382a
time, IV 390a, 390b, 391a, 395b–396a, 397a, 399b, 400a, 402a, 402b, 404b, 405b
uniformitarianism, IV 424a
Vico, II 103a
Whitehead, IV 42a
World Spirit, II 392b, 394a
Unzer, Ludwig, China, I 368b
Upanisads
Emerson and, I 256a
love, III 100b
necessity, III 361a
Schopenhauer and, I 255b
transcendentalism, I 256a
Upham, Thomas C. (1799–1872), psychology, IV 22b–23a
Uranus (myth), III 273b, 274b
religion, IV 93a
Uranus (planet), cosmology, I 550a, 552a–552b
Urban VIII, Pope (1568–1644), Christianity, I 398b
Urbanization
Aristotle, I 654b
Christianity, I 376a, 405b
city planning, I 431b–434a
cosmology, I 537a
crisis in history, I 594a
culture, I 613b, 616b, 617a, 617b
democracy, I 654b
environment, II 124a
Le Corbusier, I 432b, 433a–434a
nationalism, III 325a, 331a, 334a
private property, III 652b, 654a
progress, III 630a, 636b
protest movements, III 672a
Renaissance, I 429b–430a, 431a; IV 438a, 439b,

441b
revisionism, IV 264a
revolution, IV 166a
Roman Catholic Church, I 376a
technology, IV 360b, 363b
U.S.S.R., III 334a
U.S., I 594a
universal man, IV 438a, 439b, 441b
Utopia, IV 459a, 461a
Victorian sentiment, IV 217b–218b, 219b–220a
Voltaire, I 616b
vox populi, IV 499a, 499b, 500a
welfare state, IV 509b
Wright, I 433b
See also City
Ure, Andrew (1778–1857), technology, IV 363a
Urey, Harold (1893–   ) cosmology, I 507a
Urfaust, Faust (legend), III 248b, 250a
Urim, III 657b, 658a–659a
Urmson, J. O.
good, IV 184b
utilitarianism, IV 448b
Uruguay
positivism, III 543b, 545a
symbolism, IV 342a
Ussher, Archbishop James (1581–1656)
Creation, II 176b
evolutionism, II 176b
linguistics, IV 426b, 427a
Usury
Luther, I 396a–396b
Methodism, I 396b–397a
Wesley, I 396b–397a
U Thant (1904–   ), Buddhism, I 253b, 257a
Ut pictura poesis, IV 465b–476b
See also Painting; Poetry
Utilitarianism, IV 444a–449b
Aristotle, IV 444a
Austin, IV 448b
beauty, IV 446b, 447a, 448b
Beccaria, II 380b
benevolence, IV 444b, 447a, 447b
Bentham, II 97b, 380b, 381a–381b; III 234a; IV 278b–279a, 444a–446b, 447b, 449a, 453b
biology, IV 445b
Brown, IV 444b, 445b
Butler, IV 444a, 444b, 447b
China, III 433b
Counter-Enlightenment, II 102b

criticism, IV 446b, 447a, 448b, 449b
Cumberland, II 380b; IV 444a
defined, IV 444a
Dewey, II 382b; III 552b
Diderot, II 97b
dignity, IV 143a
economics, IV 447a
egoism, IV 445b
Enlightenment, II 94a, 96b–98a
equality, IV 447a, 449b
ethics, III 441a
evangelicalism, IV 218b–219a
evil, IV 447b–449a
evolution, IV 180a–180b
France, IV 444a
friendship, IV 445a
game theory, II 265a–266a
Godwin, IV 444b–445a, 447b
good, IV 178b–179a, 180a–180b, 183a, 185a, 185b, 444a, 446b–449b
Great Britain, III 538a; IV 444a, 444b
Greece (ancient), IV 444a
Green, IV 445a, 447b
happiness, II 379a–382a, 383a, 384b; IV 178b, 179a, 444a–448b, 449b
Hartley, IV 445b, 446a
hedonism, IV 180a–180b, 445b, 446a, 446b, 447a
Hegel, II 409b
Helvétius, II 380b; IV 444a
Hobbes, IV 445b, 446a
Holbach, II 380b
Hume, II 97a, 380a; III 232a, 232b, IV 444b, 448b
Hutcheson, II 97b–98a; III 231a–231b, 234a; IV 444a–444b, 447a, 448b
ideal, IV 446b, 447a
intuition, IV 445a, 445b
Jesuits, III 293b
justice, IV 179a, 448a, 449a
labor, IV 447b
language, II 660a
law, III 1a; IV 445a, 448a, 448b
Locke, IV 120a
love, IV 446b
Lovejoy, III 552b
Marx, II 381b
Mill, II 381b–382a; III 561b; IV 179a, 444b, 445b–446b, 448b–449b
misery, IV 447a
Moore, G. E., IV 446b

moral sense, III 231a–231b, 232a, 232b, 234a, 234b
morality, IV 444a–448b
natural law, III 15b, 22a; IV 444b, 445b
pain, IV 445b–447b
Paley, II 380b; IV 444b, 445b
philanthropy, III 488a
Philosophical Radicals, IV 444a
philosophy, IV 446b
pleasure, II 379a–382a, 382b, 383a, 384b; IV 178b, 179a, 185a, 444b, 445b, 446a, 446b, 447a, 448a
pragmatism, III 552b, 560b, 561b, 563b, 567a
Priestley, II 380b
psychology, IV 445a, 445b
Randall, IV 446b
Rawls, IV 448b
reason, IV 448b
Renaissance, IV 143a
restricted, IV 448a
right, IV 178b–179a, 180a–180b, 183b, 185a, 185b, 447a–449b
Rule, IV 448a–449b
self-interest, III 1a
Shaftesbury, II 97b; IV 444b
Sidgwick, IV 445a, 446b–447a
Smith, Adam, II 97a, 380a
social contract, IV 261b, 262b
social welfare, IV 278b–279a, 279b, 280a
society, IV 444b, 445b, 446a, 447b
Spencer, II 383a; IV 180b
U.S., III 433b
unity of science, IV 431b
universality, IV 448b–449b
Urmson, IV 448b
utility, IV 451a, 453b
Vico, II 102b
Victorian sentiment, IV 217b–218b, 219b–220a, 221a–222b
virtue, IV 444b, 478b–479a
Voltaire, II 97a–97b
welfare, IV 447b, 448b, 449a, 449b
work, IV 533b, 534b
Wright, III 561b
Utility, IV 450a–458b
advantage, IV 450a
aesthetics, IV 355a, 355b, 356a
agriculture, IV 453a
Aristotle, IV 450b, 451b–

452a, 453b–455b
benefit, IV 450a
Bentham, IV 277b; IV 450a, 451a, 451b, 452a, 453b, 454a, 454b, 455b
Bernoulli, IV 454a, 454b, 457a
choice, IV 453a, 456b, 457a, 457b, 458a
Christianity, IV 452a
commodities, IV 450b–452b, 453b–455a, 456b, 458a
community, IV 452b, 454a–454b
Condillac, IV 451a
Cournot, IV 452b
deism, I 651b
demand, IV 452b, 453b
democracy, I 653a
desire, IV 453a
disutility, IV 451a
Duns Scotus, IV 452a
economic history, II 48a, 51b, 52b, 59a
economics, IV 450a–458b
Edgeworth, IV 451b, 454b, 455b–456a, 457b
Enlightenment, IV 450b–451a, 452a, 452b
ethics, IV 451b, 452a
Fechner, IV 454b
Fisher, Irving, IV 456a
France, IV 453a
Friedman, M., IV 453a
Galiani, IV 450a, 452a–453b
gambling, IV 454a, 457a
geometry, IV 456a–456b
Germany, IV 453b
good, IV 450a, 451b
Great Britain, IV 453a–453b, 454b
Greece (ancient), IV 450b, 451a–452a
Halévy, IV 453b
happiness, IV 450a, 454a
hedonimeter, IV 454b, 457b
hedonism, IV 454b
hierarchy, IV 451b, 454b, 457b
income, IV 451b, 453a, 453b
indifference curve, IV 456b
individualism, IV 452a, 453b, 454a, 454b, 456b, 457a, 457b
Industrial Revolution, IV 453a,·453b
isolines, IV 456a
Jennings, Richard, IV 451b, 454b
Jevons, IV 450a, 450b, 453b, 454b, 455a, 458a

justice, IV 452a
labor, IV 453b
Law, IV 452b
Lloyd, IV 450a, 454a
luxury, IV 453a, 458a
manufacturing, IV 453b
Marshall, Alfred, IV 454a–454b
Marx, IV 452a, 452b
mathematics, IV 451a, 454a, 455a, 456a–456b, 458a
measurement, IV 450b, 451b–452a, 454a–454b, 455a, 456b, 457a, 457b
Menger, IV 450b, 453b, 454b–455a, 457b
Middle Ages, IV 452a
Mill, J. S., IV 453b
money, IV 451b, 452b, 454a, 454b
monism, IV 450b
Morgenstern, IV 457a
natural resources, IV 453a
Nature, IV 451a
Neumann, IV 457a
ophelimity, IV 450a
pain, IV 450a, 451a–451b
Pareto, IV 450a, 456b, 457a
Pindar, IV 450b
Plato, IV 450b, 451a–451b, 452b
pleasure, IV 450a, 450b, 451a–451b, 454a, 454b
price, IV 452b
Principle of Decreasing Marginal Rate of Substitution, IV 457a
Principle of Decreasing Marginal Utility, IV 454a, 454b–455a, 455b, 456a
production, IV 452b
psychogalvanometers, IV 457b
Quesnay, IV 453a
Ramsey, F. P., IV 457a–457b
Ricardo, IV 453b
Saint Antoninus, IV 452a, 452b
Saint Thomas Aquinas, IV 452a
Samuelson, IV 456b–457a
Say, IV 450b, 452b
scholasticism, IV 452a
science, IV 450b
Smith, IV 452b, 453b
social welfare, IV 277a–280b
society, IV 452a–453b
supply, IV 452b
taste, IV 355a, 355b, 356a
taxation, IV 458a

technology, IV 453b
Turgot, IV 453a, 453b, 455b
utilitarianism, IV 451a, 453b
Utopia, IV 458b
Walras, IV 453b, 455a, 458a
wants, IV 451b, 453b, 454b, 457b, 458a
Weber, E. H., IV 454b
welfare, IV 454a, 457b
work, IV 452a, 453a
Xenophon, IV 450b
Utopia, IV 459a–465b
agriculture, IV 462b
Alembert, IV 462a
alienation, IV 463b
Anderae, IV 461b–462a
anti-utopia, IV 464a
Arcadia, IV 460a
architects, IV 461a
Aristophanes, IV 464a
Aristotle, IV 459b, 460a, 461b
art, IV 462b
artists, IV 461a
astrology, IV 461b
Atlantis (myth), IV 460a
Babeuf, IV 463a
Bacon, IV 462a
behaviorism, IV 464a
Bellamy, IV 463b
Bible, IV 460a–460b
Burton, IV 462a
Butler, IV 464a
Campanella, IV 461b, 462a
China, IV 459a
Christianity, IV 460b–462b
Cicero, IV 460a
city-state, IV 459b, 461a
civilization, IV 459a
class, IV 459a, 459b, 461a, 462b
communism, IV 459b, 460b, 461b, 462b
Condorcet, IV 462b–463a
crime, IV 463b
criticism, IV 462b
culture, IV 459a
Cyrano de Bergerac, IV 462b
Dante, IV 461a
death, IV 463b
deism, IV 462b
democracy, IV 459b
derivation of, IV 458b
Diderot, IV 462a, 462b
disease, IV 463b
disorder, IV 463b
economics, IV 459a, 461a, 461b, 462b, 463b
education, IV 463a
Enlightenment, IV 462b

equality, IV 462b
Euhemerus, IV 460a
evil, IV 463b
Fourier, IV 463a
France, IV 462a, 463b
freedom, IV 459b, 460a, 463b, 464b
French Revolution (1789), IV 463a
Galileo, IV 461b
Garin, IV 461a
Germany, IV 461b
God, IV 460a, 460b
Golden Age (myth), IV 459a, 460a
good, IV 458b, 459b, 460a, 463b
Great Britain, IV 462a, 463a, 463b
Greece (ancient), IV 459a–460a
happiness, IV 460a, 463b
harmony, IV 458b, 460b, 464a
Harrington, IV 462a–462b
Hartlib, IV 462a
Helvétius, IV 462b
heresy, IV 461a
Hermeticism, IV 461b
Hesiod, IV 459a
Hippodamus of Miletus, IV 459b
history, IV 461b
Hobbes, IV 462a
Holbach, IV 462b
hope, IV 458b
human nature, IV 463a
humanism, IV 461a
Huxley, IV 464a
Hyperboreans (myth), IV 460a
idealism, IV 458b, 461a, 463b
ideology, II 555a; IV 463b
individualism, IV 463b
Iron Age (myth), IV 459a
Italy, IV 461a, 461b
Jesus Christ, IV 460b
Judaism, IV 460a–460b
justice, IV 459b
K'ang Yieu Wei, IV 459a
Kepler, IV 462a
knowledge, IV 461b, 462a
labor, IV 459b, 462b
Latin America, IV 463b
law, IV 460a
Left, IV 463b
Leonardo da Vinci, IV 461a
literature, IV 458b, 459b, 460a, 462a–464b
Lycurgus, IV 460a
Marxism, IV 463b
methodology, IV 462a
Middle Ages, IV 461a

millenarianism, IV 460b, 461b, 462a
mind, IV 463a
monarchy, IV 461a–462a
morality, IV 458b, 459a, 460a, 461a, 462b
More, III 79a–79b; IV 461a–461b
Morelly, IV 462b
Mumford, IV 459a
naturalism, IV 462a, 463a
Nature, IV 459a
navigation, IV 461a
Nicholas of Cusa, IV 461a
Oneida Community, IV 461a
optimism, I 458b, 461a
Orwell, IV 464a
Ovid, IV 460a
Owen, IV 463a
Panchaeans (myth), IV 460a
Pax Romana, IV 459b
peace, IV 459a, 459b, 460b
perfectibility, IV 458b, 463a, 464b
Phaleas of Chalcedon, IV 459b
philosophy, IV 462b, 464a
Plato, IV 459b–460a, 461a–461b
Plutarch, IV 459b, 460a
poverty, IV 461a, 463b
power, IV 459a
press, IV 463b
Prester John (legend), IV 461a
private property, III 654a; IV 459a
progress, IV 461b, 462b, 463a, 464b
propaganda, IV 464a
psychology, IV 464a
Rappites, IV 461a
rationalism, IV 458b, 459a, 462b, 463a, 464a
realism, IV 462a, 464a
Reformation, IV 460b, 461a
religion, IV 459a, 461a, 461b, 462a, 463b, 464a
Renaissance, IV 461a
republicanism, IV 462b
revolution, IV 463a
Right, IV 463b
romanticism, IV 464b
Rousseau, II 12b
Royal Society of London, IV 462a
Russell, IV 463b
Saint Peter, IV 460b
satire, IV 464a
science, IV 461a, 462a, 462b, 463b, 464a

science-fiction, IV 464a
Scotland, IV 463a
secularism, IV 461a, 462a
sin, IV 460b, 461a
Skinner, IV 464a
socialism, IV 463a, 463b
society, IV 458b, 459a, 459b, 461a, 461b, 462a, 463a, 463b, 464a
Sparta (ancient), IV 460a
stability, IV 459b
State, IV 459b, 461a, 462a, 462b
Stoicism, IV 460a
strength, IV 459b
supernatural, IV 462a
Swift, IV 464a
technology, IV 462a, 463b
theocracy, IV 460a, 462a
tolerance, IV 462b
totalitarianism, IV 461b, 464a
tragedy, IV 464b
Turgot, IV 462b
U.S., IV 461a, 463a, 463b
urbanization, IV 459a, 461a
utility, IV 458b
Vespucci, IV 461a
virtue, IV 459b
Voltaire, IV 464a
Wallace, IV 463a
war, IV 459a, 459b, 507a
Waugh, IV 464a
welfare, IV 461b
Wells, IV 464a
Wilde, IV 464a
Winstanley, IV 462a
Xenophon, IV 460a
Zamyatin, IV 464a
Zeno of Citium, IV 460a
Utopianism
Bacon, II 379b
Burke, IV 203a
Christianity, III 670b
city, I 430a, 431a–431b, 432b
deism, I 649a
despotism, II 12b
economic history, II 59b–60a
Edwards, III 225b
existentialism, III 160a
Fourier, I 433b; II 380a
happiness, II 374b, 379b–380a
historiography, IV 148a
hope, II 214b, 215a
Islam, II 649a
labor, III 676a
liberalism, III 671a
longevity, III 92b
Marx, II 59b; III 160a
Marxism, III 160a
millenarianism, III 224a,

224b, 225b; IV 61a
More, II 379b
natural law, III 22a
Owen, II 380a
perennial philosophy, III 458b
perfectibility, III 469a, 470b
philosophy, II 649a
Plato, III 554b
pragmatism, III 554b
progress, III 628a–628b, 629a, 630a
prolongevity, III 92b
protest movements, III 670b, 671a, 672b, 674b, 675a, 676a
radicalism, III 671a
reformation, IV 61a, 65a, 66a
Renaissance, IV 148a
revolution, IV 167a
romanticism, IV 203a
Rousseau, II 12b
Saint-Simon, II 380a
socialism, III 671a; IV 285a, 287b–288a, 289b, 294a
Utrecht, Treaty of, balance of power, I 183a, 184a

V

Vacca, G., pragmatism, III 557b, 560a
Vacherot, Étienne (1809–1897), progress, III 636b
Vadian, Joachim (1484–1551), musical genius, II 321a
Vaihinger, Hans (1852–1933)
axiomatization, I 166b
Holmes and, III 566a
idea, II 548b
irrationalism, II 636a
James and, III 566a
metaphor, III 199b
pragmatism, III 551b, 566a
skepticism, IV 250a
Vailati, G.
James and, III 560a
logic, III 560a
mathematics, III 560a
Peirce and, III 560a
pragmatism, III 551b, 553b, 557b, 560a
science, III 560a
Vaillant, Auguste (1840–1915), anarchy, I 72a

Valades, Didacus, hierarchy, II 436a, 436b

Valdes, Peter (fl. late 12th century), heresy, II 419a, 419b

Valentine, C. W., beauty, I 212b

Valeriano, Pierio (c. 16th century)
hermeticism, II 432b
mythology, III 289b

Valerio, Luca, continuity, I 498a

Valerius Maximus (fl. 14 A.D.), iconography, II 531a

Valéry, Paul (1871–1945)
classicism, I 455a; IV 196b
Faust (legend), III 251b–252a
literary criticism, I 605a
Platonism, III 524b
romanticism, IV 196b
symbolism, IV 340a, 340b, 341a, 342a, 343a, 344a, 344b, 345a

Valignano, Alessandro, China, I 354b, 355b

Valla, Giorgio (fl. 15th century), poetics, III 529a

Valla, Lorenzo (c. 1400–1457)
dignity, IV 142b–143b
Donation of Constantine, II 520b
Epicureanism, II 137b; IV 142b, 143a
God, IV 142b–143a
good, IV 133b
Gothic, II 367b
historiography, II 485a, 485b, 487a
human nature, IV 142b–143a
humanism, II 519a, 519b, 520a, 520b; IV 129b, 130b, 133b, 134a, 135a–135b
logic, II 519a; IV 135a–135b
love, IV 142b–143a
pleasure, IV 133b
reformation, IV 63a
virtue, IV 143a

Vallisnieri, Antonio (1661–1730)
Chain of Being, I 332a
God, I 332a
spontaneous generation, II 282b

Van Beneden, Eduard, chromosomes, II 287a, 287b

Van Buren, Paul, God, II 363b–364a

Van de Waal, H., iconography, II 532a, 538a–539b

Van der Leeuw, Gerardus
holy, II 514a
mythology, III 314b

Van Eyck, Jan (1370?–1440)
mythology, III 285a
naturalism in art, III 340a, 340b

Van Gelder, J. G., iconography, II 538a

Van Gogh, Vincent (1853–1890)
beauty, I 212a–212b
expressionism, II 207a
iconography, II 538b
imagination, III 209a
motif, III 241b

Van Tieghem, Paul, literature, III 85a

Vanderbilt, Cornelius (1794–1877), philanthropy, III 491b

Vanishing point, II 612b, 614a

Varchi, Benedetto (1503–1565)
aesthetics, IV 354b
classification of the arts, I 459a
mimesis, III 228a, 228b
taste, IV 354b

Varenius, Bernhardus (1622–?1650)
geology, III 256b
mountains in literature, III 256b

Vargas, Getúlio (1883–1954)
nationalism, III 335b
positivism, III 542a

Varona y Pera, Enrique José, positivism, III 544b

Varro, Marcus Terentius (116–27 B.C.)
city, I 428a
classification of the sciences, I 463b
cynicism, I 628b
disease, II 400a
language, II 665b

Varronian satire, IV 213b

Varuna (myth), II 338b, 343b

Vasari, Giorgio (1511–1574)
aesthetics, II 221b
architecture, II 367b–368a
art, II 298a, 301b–303b, 305a–305b, 309b; IV 123a, 124a, 150a
chance images, I 348a–348b
classification of the arts, I 459b
climate, IV 150a
cycles, IV 150b

genius, II 293b, 298a, 301b, 302a,–303b, 305a–305b, 309b
God, IV 123a
Gothic, II 367b–368a, 369b
historiography of art, IV 150a, 150b
iconography, II 524b, 534b
mimesis, III 229a
mythology, III 293a
periodization in history, III 479b
universal man, IV 442b

Vasconcelos, José (1882–1959), positivism, III 545a

Vašica, J., baroque in literature, I 193a

Vasquez, Fernando, I 69b

Vassar, Matthew (1792–1868), philanthropy, III 491b

Vattel, Emmerich de (1714–1767)
Kant and, III 442a
peace, III 442a

Vaucanson, Jacques de (1709–1782), Man-Machine, III 140a

Vaughan, Henry, Hermeticism, II 433a

Vaughn, Benjamin (1751–1835), primitivism, III 600b

Vaughan, Henry (1622–1695)
Cosmic Fall, I 509a
mountains in literature, III 254b

Vauquelin de La Fresnaye, Jean (1536–?1608), poetry, III 529b

Vauvenargues, Luc de Clapiers (1715–1747)
aesthetics, IV 355a
attitude toward antiquity, I 84a
genius, II 294a
taste, IV 355a

Vaux, Clotilde de
Comte, III 536a, 536b, 537b
Floresta and, III 540a
positivism, III 536a, 536b, 537b

Vayu (myth), II 338b

Veblen, Thorstein B. (1857–1929)
determinism, III 150a
economic history, II 60b
Marxism, III 150a
pragmatism, III 569a–569b

Veda, dualism, II 39a, 39b, 41b

Vedel, Valdemar, baroque in

literature, I 189b

Vega, Lope de (1562–1635)
baroque in literature, I 190b
poetry, III 529b

Vegetius (4th century A.D.), militarism, IV 501a

Vegio, Maffeo (1406–1458), universal man, IV 438b

Velázquez (1599–1660)
genius, II 309b
impressionism, II 577b, 578b
naturalism, III 340b, 341a

Velleius Paterculus, Marcus (c. 19 B.C.–30 A.D.)
evolution of literature, II 170a
oratory, II 170a
poetics, III 528a

Vellutello, Alessandro, rhetoric, IV 171a

Velthuysen, Lambert van (1622–1685)
causation, I 302b
teleology, I 302b

Vendôme, Matthieu de
ut pictura poesis, IV 468b

Vengerova, Zinaida (1855–1920), symbolism, IV 343a

Venice
art, II 297b
balance of power, I 180b, 181b, 182b
city, I 429b–430b
idealism, I 593a
individualism, II 297b
Machiavellism, III 120b

Venn, John (1834–1923)
chance, I 338b
probability, III 615a–616b

Venturi, Lionello, baroque in literature, I 191b

Venus (myth), III 290b, 296b, 297a, 297b, 511b
Nature, III 351a
ut pictura poesis, IV 472b, 473a

Venus (planet), III 310a
cosmology, I 538a, 539a, 540a, 540b–541a, 542a, 542b, 544b, 546b
mythology, III 287b

Verdross, Alfred, natural rights, III 25b

Verga, Giovanni (1840–1922), realism in literature, IV 53a

Vergil (70–19 B.C.)
ambiguity, I 50b–51a, 53b–54a
Christianity, III 589b
classicism, I 455b
cycles, I 623b
dignity, IV 141b

eighteenth century view of,
I 78b, 79a, 80a, 83b
Enlightenment, II 90a
genius, II 295a
Golden Age (myth), III
631b
humanism, II 516a
iconography, II 531a
impiety, II 566b
literary paradox, III 77b
magic, III 246a
Montaigne, III 594a
mountains in literature, III
253b
mythology, III 296b, 298a,
299a
poetics, III 526b, 528b,
531a, 531b
primitivism, III 580b, 581a–
581b, 589b, 591b, 593b,
594a
progress, III 624b, 631b,
632a
style, IV 331a
universal man, IV 439a
ut pictura poesis, IV 468b,
469a
vox populi, IV 498b
Vergil, Polydore (1470?–
?1555)
historiography, II 483b,
484b
mythology, III 290a
Verhaeren, Paul (1855–1916),
symbolism, IV 340a
Verlaine, Paul (1844–1896)
impressionism, II 575a
symbolism, IV 339b, 340b,
342a, 342b, 343a, 343b
ut pictura poesis, IV 472b,
473a
Vermeer, Jan (1632–1675)
ambiguity, I 56a–57a
Caravaggio and, III 340b
illusionism, III 341a
impressionism, II 578b
naturalism, III 340b, 341a
Vermeil, Edmond, modernism,
I 426b
Vernadsky, W. I.
culture, II 133a
environment, II 133a
Vernant, J. P., mythology,
III 272b, 274b
Verner, Karl Adolph (1846–
1896)
language, II 671b
linguistics, III 70a
Veron, François
certainty, I 304b, 305a
skepticism, IV 242b
Veronese, G. (1854–1917)
mathematical infinity, II
610b

Verri, Pietro, Enlightenment, II
89b, 91a
Verrocchio (1435–1488),
Ramism, IV 44a
Vertot, Abbé R. A. de (1655–
1733), revolution, IV 154a
Verworn, Max (1863–1921),
spontaneous generation, IV
311b
Vesalius, Andreas (1514–
1564)
disease, II 400b, 401a,
402a
economic history, II 45a
Man-Machine, III 135a–
135b
skepticism, IV 242a
Veselovsky, Aleksandr (1838–
1906)
evolution of literature, II
173a–173b
literature, III 84b
motif, III 237b, 238a, 239a
Vespasian (9–79 A.D.), freedom of speech, II 261b
Vespucci, Amerigo (1451–
1512)
historiography, IV 149a
skepticism, IV 241b
Utopia, IV 461a
Vettius Valens, astrology, I
121a, 122b
Vettori, Piero (1499–1585)
poetics, III 529a
Veuillot, Louis François
(1813–1883), individual-
ism, II 595a
Viau, Théophile de (1590–
1626), deism, I 649a
Vibration
Descartes, III 262b
Galileo, III 263a
music, II 389a; III 262a–
262b, 263a
optics, III 418b, 419a
Vice
Aristotle, II 237a
Cicero, IV 50a
determinism, II 237a,
237b
Diderot, III 603a
disease, II 402b
free will, II 237a, 237b
good, IV 178b
Hartley, III 234a–234b
human nature, III 571b
Hutcheson, III 231a
intolerance, IV 112b
Machiavelli, III 116b
Machiavellism, III 116b,
119a
moral sense, III 231a, 234a–
234b
primitivism, III 588b, 589b,

598a, 599b, 603a
rationalism, IV 50a
revolution, IV 152b, 154b
Rome (ancient), IV 154b
Rousseau, III 599b
Saint Ambrose, III 589b
Seneca, III 588b
Shaftesbury, III 598a
Stoicism, IV 50a, 321a
Swift, III 599b
temperance, IV 369a–371b,
372b, 373a, 374a, 375a,
377a
virtù, IV 478b, 479a, 485a
voluntariness, II 237a
welfare, IV 178b
wisdom of the fool, IV 518a
Vickrey, William S. (1914–
), social welfare, IV
280a, 280b
Vico, Giovanni Battista (1668–
1744)
art and play, I 103b
attitude toward antiquity, I
83a
Bacon and, I 172b, 176b
Cartesianism, II 102a; III
357a
causation, I 280a–280b
classification of the arts, I
460b
cosmic images, I 519b
Croce and, III 638a
Counter-Enlightenment, II
102a–103b, 105b
culture, I 615a–615b, 616b,
617a, 618a, 619b, 620a;
II 102b–103a
determinism, II 22a, 23a,
23b
empathy, II 87a
evolution of literature, II
170a
genius, II 293b
God, II 102a; III 357a
Hegel and, III 357a
historicism, II 458b–459a
historiography, II 22a, 23a,
23b, 475a, 489a, 489b
history, I 280a–280b; II
22a, 23a, 23b, 102b–103a;
III 357a, 638a–638b
Hume and, III 357b
iconography, II 538b
imagination, III 219b
individualism, II 600b
Islam, II 650a
linguistics, III 64b
mathematics, II 102a
mimesis, III 228a
mythology, II 102b; III
302a, 302b, 304a, 304b,
306b, 357a
Nature, II 102a–102b; III

357a
necessity, III 355b, 356a,
357a, 357b, 358a, 360a,
360b, 361a, 362a
pluralism, II 103a
poetry, II 102b; III 228a,
530a
primitivism, III 599a
progress, III 638a–638b
rationalism, III 302a, 302b
religion, IV 94a, 109a
Spengler and, III 361a
universe, II 103a
utilitarianism, II 102b
Volksgeist, IV 491a
Victoria, Queen (1819–1901)
periodization in literary history, III 482b–483a
Victorian sensibility, IV
220b, 223b
women, IV 526b
Victorian Sensibility and Sentiment, IV 217a–224a
aesthetics, IV 223a, 223b
agnosticism, IV 217b, 221a
alcoholism, IV 219a–219b
anarchy, IV 223b
anxiety, IV 222a
aristocracy, IV 218a, 218b,
220a–220b
Arnold, IV 222b
art, IV 219b, 221a, 221b,
223a, 223b
art and play, IV 218b, 222b,
223a
asceticism, IV 218b
astronomy, IV 221b
atheism, IV 221a
behavior, IV 218a, 222b
benevolence, IV 218b, 219b
Bible, IV 219a
biology, IV 221b–222a
Brontë, Charlotte, IV 219b
Brontë, Emily, IV 219b
censorship, IV 219b
charity, IV 219b
chastity, IV 219a
children, IV 219a, 221a
Church of England, IV 217b,
218a
class, IV 217a, 217b, 218a,
219a, 220a, 220b, 222b
common sense, IV 218a
conformity, IV 219a, 220a,
223b
conscience, IV 218b
culture, IV 217b, 219a,
222b
dandyism, IV 223a
Darwin, IV 221a–222a
Dickens, IV 219b, 221a
distribution, IV 218b
duty, IV 217b, 218a, 218b,
220b, 222a

earnestness, **IV** 217b, 220b
economics, **IV** 218a–218b, 221a, 222a, 222b
education, **IV** 218a
egoism, **IV** 218a
Eliot, George, **IV** 219b
emotion, **IV** 217a, 217b, 219b, 221b, 222a
environment, **IV** 217a, 218b–219a, 222a, 223a
ethics, **IV** 218a–218b
evangelicalism, **IV** 217b–220a, 221a, 222b
evolution, **IV** 221b
experience, **IV** 223a
faith, **IV** 217b, 218b
family, **IV** 217b–221a, 222a
fear, **IV** 220a, 222a, 222b
feeling, **IV** 217a, 217b, 218a, 221a, 221b
freedom, **IV** 218b
French Revolution, **IV** 220a
gentleman, **IV** 220a–220b, 223b
geology, **IV** 221b
goals, **IV** 218b
God, **IV** 217b, 218b, 222b
Great Britain, **IV** 217a–224a
guilt, **IV** 220a, 222b
happiness, **IV** 218a–218b
health, **IV** 222b
idealism, **IV** 219a–219b, 220a, 222b, 223b
ignorance, **IV** 218b
immortality, **IV** 221a
imperialism, **IV** 222b
impressionism, **IV** 223a
individualism, **IV** 217a–218b, 223a, 223b
industry, **IV** 217b, 218b
instinct, **IV** 217a, 222a, 222b, 223a
irrationalism, **IV** 218b
law, **IV** 218a, 218b, 219b, 222a, 222b
literature, **IV** 219b, 221a, 222a, 223a
logic, **IV** 218a, 219b
love, **IV** 219b, 221a
Malthus, **IV** 218b, 221b–222a
Methodism, **V** 217b, 220a
Mill, J. S., **IV** 220a, 221a
morality, **IV** 218a, 219a–222a, 223a, 223b
Morris, William, **IV** 223b
naturalism, **IV** 221b
Nature, **IV** 221b–223a
nonconformity, **IV** 219a, 219b, 220a, 223b
pain, **IV** 218a, 221a

painting, **IV** 221a
philanthropy, **IV** 218a, 218b, 219b
piety, **IV** 219a, 222b
pleasure, **IV** 218a
pluralism, **IV** 220a
politics, **IV** 218a, 218b, 219b, 220b, 222a, 223a–223b
population explosion, **IV** 217b, 218b, 221b–222a
poverty, **IV** 218a, 218b, 219b, 220a
power, **IV** 222a
prayer, **IV** 219a
Protestantism, **IV** 217b
psychology, **IV** 218a, 222b
Puritanism, **IV** 217b, 219a
radicalism, **IV** 220a, 223b
rationalism, **IV** 218a, 219b, 222b
reason, **IV** 217a, 221a, 221b, 222b
reform, **IV** 218a
religion, **IV** 217b–219b, 221a, 222a, 222b
respectability, **IV** 220a–220b, 223b
revolution, **IV** 220a, 222a
reward, **IV** 221a
Ricardo, **IV** 218b, 222a
romanticism, **IV** 221b, 223b
Ruskin, **IV** 221a
sabbatarianism, **IV** 219b
salvation, **IV** 218b
satire, **IV** 223a
science, **IV** 221a–222a
self-discipline, **IV** 217b, 219a
self-improvement, **IV** 219a
senses, **IV** 217a, 218a, 218b
sex, **IV** 219a–219b, 222b
sincerity, **IV** 220b
skepticism, **IV** 222b, 223a
slavery, **IV** 219b
Smith, Adam, **IV** 222a
socialism, **IV** 223b
society, **IV** 217a–219a, 220a–220b, 222a–223b
soul, **IV** 217b, 218b, 221a
State, **IV** 217b, 220b, 222a, 223b
suffrage, **IV** 218b
suicide, **IV** 222b
supernatural, **IV** 218a
superstition, **IV** 218b
sympathy, **IV** 218b
technology, **IV** 220a, 221b, 222a
temperance, **IV** 219a–219b
Thackeray, **IV** 219b, 220a–220b

theology, **IV** 217b, 219a
thought, **IV** 217a
time, **IV** 221b
tolerance, **IV** 220b
truth, **IV** 220b, 221b
universe, **IV** 221b, 222a
urbanization, **IV** 217b, 218a, 218b, 219b, 220a, 222a
utilitarianism, **IV** 217b, 218a–218b, 219b–220a, 221a, 222a, 222b
virtue, **IV** 218a, 219b, 220b, 222b
wealth, **IV** 217b, 218b, 219a, 223a
women, **IV** 219b
Vida, Marco Girolamo (1480?–1566)
  imitation, **II** 306a
  poetics, **III** 529a
  ut pictura poesis, **IV** 467b
Viélé-Griffin, Francis (1864–1937), symbolism, **IV** 340a, 342b
Vien, Joseph-Marie, neo-classicism in art, **II** 364a, 369a
Viète, François (1504–1603), mathematics, **III** 178b, 183b
Vietnam War
  civil disobedience, **I** 435a, 440b
  international peace, **III** 449b
  natural liberty, **II** 67a
Vigny, Alfred de (1797–1863)
  evolution of literature, **II** 172b
  Newton and, **IV** 201a
  romanticism, **IV** 201a, 204a, 205a, 208b
  Weltschmerz, **IV** 204a
Vilate, Cartaud de la taste, **IV** 355a
Villani, Filippo, Gothic, **II** 367b
Villani, Giovanni (c. 1275–1348)
  cycles, **I** 626a–626b
  historiography, **II** 482a
Ville, Jean
  game theory, **II** 265a
  utility, **IV** 457a
Villemain, Abel-François (1790–1870)
  comparative literature, **III** 83b–84a
  romanticism, **IV** 191a
  Sorbonne, **III** 83b–84a
Villers, Charles, romanticism, **IV** 189b
Villey, Michel, natural law, **III** 16a, 23a
Villiers, George (1592–1628)

deism, **I** 650a
mythology, **III** 297a
Puritanism, **I** 650a
Villiers de l'Isle-Adam, Philippe-August Mathias (1838–1889), symbolism, **IV** 340b, 343b
Vilmar, August (1800–1868)
  classicism, **I** 454a
  literature, **III** 83a
Vincent of Beauvais (d. before 1264)
  hierarchy, **II** 438a
  iconography, **II** 527a
  nationalism, **III** 319b
Vincent of Lérins (d. 450?)
  Church, **I** 416b
  heresy, **II** 428b
Vincent de Paul, Saint (1581?–1660), Christianity, **I** 399a
Viner, Jacob, welfare state, **IV** 515a
Vinet, Alexandre (1797–1847)
  individualism, **II** 594b
  symbolism, **IV** 339a
Vinsauf, Geoffroi de, *ut pictura poesis*, **IV** 468b
Violence
  anarchy, **I** 72a; **III** 673b
  anti-industrialism, **III** 676a
  Bergson, **III** 564b
  Christianity, **III** 670b, 671a
  civil disobedience, **I** 435b, 438a, 439b
  ethics, **IV** 71a
  fascism, **III** 674a
  French Revolution (1789), **IV** 156b, 157a, 157b
  Gandhi, **III** 446a
  Greece (ancient), **II** 677a, 679a, 683b
  Hume, **IV** 261b
  law, **II** 677a, 679a, 683b, 688a
  liberalism, **III** 672b
  Lorenz, **IV** 507b
  Machiavelli, **IV** 502a
  Marat, **II** 14a
  Marxism, **III** 148b, 149b, 160b
  the military, **IV** 502a, 502b, 504b, 507a
  millenarianism, **III** 224a
  mythology, **III** 279a, 279b
  nationalism, **III** 673a
  pragmatism, **III** 555a, 564b, 565a
  progress, **III** 647a, 649a
  prophecy, **III** 661a, 662b, 664a, 665b, 667b
  protest movements, **III** 670b, 671a, 672b, 673a, 673b, 674a, 675a, 676a

religion, IV 118b
revolution, IV 156b, 157a, 157b, 158a, 158b, 159b, 160a, 164a
Rome (ancient), II 688a
social contract, IV 261a, 261b
Sorel, III 555a, 564b, 565a
syndicalism, III 673b
Tolstoy, III 445b
totalitarianism, IV 408a
virtue, IV 483b
war, IV 502a, 502b, 504b, 507a
Viollet-le-Duc, Eugène-Emmanuel (1814–1879), Gothic, II 373a
Virchow, Rudolf (1821–1902)
cell division, II 286a
disease, II 403a, 404a, 404b, 405b
genetic continuity, II 286a
Virgil, *see* Vergil
Virgin Birth
heresy, II 429b
mythology, III 276a, 282b
Virgin Mary (Bible)
ambiguity, I 52b–53a
Assumption, III 107a
cults, III 107a
Faust (legend), III 246b, 249b
iconography, II 526a, 528a
Immaculate Conception, III 98b
love, III 98b, 107a
Mariology, III 107a, 107b
mythology, III 282a–282b
primitivism, III 596b
temperance, IV 371a
women, III 596b
Virtù, IV 476b–486a
Agathocles the Sicilian, IV 480a, 482b
Alembert, IV 484a–484b
anarchy, IV 485a–485b
animals, IV 480b, 481b–482a
audacity, IV 480b, 482a
Barberino, IV 477b
Borgia, IV 125a, 480a, 483b, 485a
Bracciolini, IV 479a
Burckhardt, IV 485a
choice, IV 477b, 481b, 482a
Cicero, IV 477b–478b
courage, IV 477a, 477b, 478b, 484b
Diderot, IV 484a–484b
Enlightenment, IV 484b
Fabius Maximus, IV 481a,

482a
Filarete, IV 477b
force, IV 479a, 484a, 485a
foreign policy, IV 484a
fortune, II 225b, 231b, 233b–236a; IV 478a, 479b, 480b–482b, 484b
Frederick the Great, IV 484a
Galen, IV 480b
God, IV 477a, 480b, 483a, 484b
good, IV 482a, 483a, 484b
Greece (ancient), IV 477a
Hannibal, IV 480a, 481b
Hegel, IV 485a
Hercules (myth), IV 477b
Hobbes, IV 484a
human nature, IV 478a–478b, 480b, 481a, 481b–482a, 483a
individualism, IV 479b, 480b–481a, 483a–483b, 485a
Julius II (Pope), IV 481a
Livy, IV 478a, 480a
Machiavellism, III 116b; IV 477a, 477b, 479a–485a
manufacturing, IV 477a
Medici family, IV 483a
Meinecke, IV 483b
necessity, IV 480b, 481b, 482a, 482b, 484b
Neo-Platonism, IV 481b
Nietzsche, IV 484b–485b
Palmieri, IV 478b–479a
papacy, IV 477a
passions, IV 482a–482b
peace, IV 483b, 484a
politics, IV 477a, 479a–485a
Pontano, IV 479a
poverty, IV 483a
power, IV 476b, 477a, 478a, 479a, 480b, 481a, 482b, 483b–485a
Roman Catholic Church, IV 477a, 479a, 483b
romanticism, IV 485a
Rome (ancient), IV 477a, 478a, 479b, 481a, 482b, 483a
Satan, IV 477a, 477b
Savonarola, IV 477a–477b, 479b, 483a
Scipio, IV 480a, 481b
secularism, IV 477a, 483a
self-realization, IV 485a
Soderini, IV 480b, 481a
State, IV 483b–484a, 485a
tyranny, IV 477a–477b, 479b, 480a, 485a–485b
utilitarianism, IV 478b–479a

vice, IV 478b, 479a, 485a
violence, IV 483b
virility, IV 477b, 478a
virtuoso, IV 482b
Voltaire, IV 484a
vox populi, IV 497a
war, IV 483a, 484a
wealth, IV 483a
Virtue
Aeschylus, IV 366b–367a, 368b
aesthetics, IV 355b, 356b
Aristotle, II 237a, 377a, 377b; IV 49b, 175b, 369a, 375a, 477a, 530b
art, II 550b; IV 371a–378a
artificial, III 232a, 232b
Balguy, III 233a
beauty, I 198b; III 231a, 233a
Bible, IV 371b
Boccaccio, IV 477a
Botticelli, IV 373b
Calvin, III 467a
cardinal, IV 366b, 368a–368b, 369a, 371a–378a
Chapman, III 294b
chastity, IV 371a–371b, 372b, 377a
Christianity, IV 370b–371a
Cicero, IV 375a
Counter-Enlightenment, II 101a, 102a, 106b
courage, IV 366b, 368b, 371b
cynicism, I 629b–630a, 632b, 633a
Dante, II 233b; IV 176b–177a, 477a, 479b
democracy, I 652b, 653a, 653b, 655b
despotism, II 13b
determinism, II 237a, 237b
dignity, IV 136a, 137a, 138b, 141a, 143a
education, II 80a–80b, 249b
Edwards, IV 109b, 110a, 111a
emblem books, IV 377a–377b
empiricism, IV 178b
ethics, I 629b–630a; IV 320b, 321a, 321b, 322a, 478b, 483b
Euripides, IV 367a–367b
evil, II 166b; IV 482a, 483a
existentialism, II 192a
faith, hope, and charity, II 211a, 211b–212a, 212b; IV 372b, 375b
fortitude, IV 366b, 368b,

369b, 370a, 371b, 372b, 373a, 374a, 374b, 375a, 375b, 377a, 377b
free will, II 237a, 237b
freedom of speech, II 256b, 259a, 260a
Giotto, IV 372a, 373a, 373b, 374b
God, II 334a
good, IV 173a–180b, 181a, 182b
happiness, II 376b, 377a, 377b, 380b
harmony, II 388b, 391a, 391b, 392a
Hartley, III 234a–234b
health, II 397a; 397b, 399a
Helvétius, III 470a
heroes, IV 413a–414a
historiography, IV 147b
Hobbes, II 212b
hubris, IV 413a
Hume, III 232a, 232b
Hutcheson, III 230b, 231a
iconography, IV 371a–378a
ideal, II 550b, 551a
illuminists, IV 109a
justice, IV 366b, 368b, 370a, 371a, 371b, 372b, 373a, 374a, 374b, 375a, 375b, 377a, 377b
Kant, II 80b; IV 179b
Kierkegaard, II 192a
knowledge, III 508b; IV 49a
Laird, IV 484a
literature, IV 368b
Luther, II 212a
Machiavelli, I 652b; II 235b, 236a; III 116b; IV 315a
Mendelssohn, II 550b
Mill, IV 179a
millenarianism, III 224a
Montesquieu, II 13b
moral sense, III 230b, 231a, 232a–234b
music, II 388b, 391a, 391b, 392a
mythology, III 274a, 286b, 287b, 288a, 288b, 291a, 294b
natural, III 232a
natural law, III 15a, 16a, 17b
Nature, III 16a, 351a
numbers, IV 372a–372b
obligation, IV 179b
perfectibility, III 464b, 465b, 466a–467a, 470a, 472a
Peripatetics, IV 478a–478b
pessimism, IV 483a
Petrarch, IV 477b, 478a, 478b, 479b–480a

piety, IV 366b, 368b
Pindar, IV 365a–366b, 368b
Pisano, IV 375a, 477b
Plato, I 612a; II 80b, 376b; III 465b, 508b; IV 49a, 49b, 195a, 368a–368b, 378a, 415a
Platonism, III 508b, 512a
Plotinus, III 466a
Price, III 233a
primitivism, III 600b, 603a
progress, III 627a, 638a, 648b
Protagoras, III 627a
prudence, IV 371a, 371b, 372b, 373a, 374a, 374b, 375a, 375b, 377a, 377b
Pseudo-Dionysius, II 210b
Raphael, IV 372a
rationalism, IV 46a, 49a, 49b–50a
reason, IV 482a
reformation, IV 63a
Releus (myth), IV 366b
religion, IV 109a, 110a, 111a, 373a, 477b
Renaissance, IV 132b, 136a, 137a, 138b, 141a, 143a, 147b, 374a–374b, 439a
respect, II 259a
results, IV 476b
revolution, IV 152b
right, IV 173a–179b, 180b, 181a, 182b
Robespierre, II 13b
Saint Augustine, III 17b; IV 63a, 138b
Saint Thomas Aquinas, I 259b; II 211a, 211b–212a; III 466b
Salutati, II 234b
salvation, IV 225a
Schopenhauer, II 166b
self-respect, II 259a
Seven Deadly Sins, IV 378a
Shaftesbury, III 230b
skepticism, IV 237a
Smith, III 233b
sobriety, IV 371b
Socrates, II 80b; III 508b, 577a; IV 49a, 174b, 414b, 415b
Sophocles, IV 367a
Spencer, IV 180b
Spinoza, IV 177b
Stoicism, III 465b; IV 49b–50a, 176a, 320b, 321a, 321b, 322a, 378a, 478a, 478b
taste, IV 355b, 356b
temperance, IV 375b, 377a, 377b, 378a

theriophily, IV 385a
thought, III 15a
Thucydides, IV 367b
tragic sense, IV 413a–415b
universal man, IV 439a
Utopia, IV 459b
Valla, IV 143a
values, IV 476b
Victorian sensibility, IV 218a, 219b, 220b, 222b
wisdom, IV 366b, 368b, 371a
wisdom of the fool, IV 518a, 519a
work, IV 530b
Virtuosa, IV 486b, 488a–490a
Behn, IV 488b
Carter, IV 489a
Cavendish, IV 488a–488b
Centlivre, IV 490a–490b
Pepys, IV 488b
Virtuoso, IV 486a–490a
Addison, IV 488a, 489a–489b
Algarotti, IV 489a
astronomy, IV 489a, 489b
Bacon, IV 486b
blood transfusions, IV 487b–488a
Boyle, IV 487a, 487b, 488b
Bruno, IV 489a
Burton, IV 486b
Charles I, IV 487b
Charlton, IV 489b
class, IV 486a
comedy, IV 488b
commerce, IV 486a
Dunton, IV 489a
education, IV 490a, 490b
Evelyn, IV 486a–487a
Fontenelle, IV 488b, 489a
France, IV 486a, 488b
Galileo, IV 489a
gentleman, IV 486a, 486b
God, IV 490a
Great Britain, IV 486a–490a
Haywood, IV 490a
Henry (Prince), IV 486b
Hooke, IV 487b, 488b
Houghton, IV 486a
Italy, IV 486a
James I, IV 486a
Lamb, IV 488a
Leadbetter, IV 489b
learning, IV 486b
leisure, IV 486a
Lennox, IV 490a
Machiavelli, IV 482b
melancholy, IV 486b
Meyer, IV 489a, 490a
Molière, IV 488b

Newbery, IV 489b
Newton, IV 489a
painting, IV 486b
Peacham, IV 486a
Pepys, IV 486b, 487a, 487b, 488a–488b
Philips, IV 489a
pleasure, IV 486b
Pope, IV 489b
satire, IV 487b–488a
science, IV 487a–487b, 489b
sculpture, IV 486b
Shadwell, IV 487b
Steele, IV 488a, 489a–489b
Swift, IV 489b
theater, IV 487b, 488b, 490a–490b
Tipper, IV 489a
utilitarianism, IV 486a
virtue, IV 482b
wealth, IV 486a
Whiston, IV 489b
women, IV 486b, 488a–490a
Viruses
genetic continuity, II 285a–285b
spontaneous generation, IV 312a
Vischer, Friedrich Theador (1807–1887)
empathy, II 86a
symbolism, IV 338b, 343b
Vischer, Robert (1847–1933), empathy, II 85b, 86a
Visconti, Ermes
classicism, I 450a
literature, IV 190b
romanticism, IV 190b
Visconti, Giangaleazzo (1351–1402), humanism, II 522b
Vishnu (myth), II 343b, 344a
salvation, IV 232a
sin, IV 232a
Vision, III 407a–421a; see Optics
Visions
harmony, IV 40a
mythology, IV 277b, 282b, 284a, 290b
prophecy, III 657b–658a, 662b, 663a, 664a, 668a
Vitalism
acquired characteristics, II 619a
analogy, I 60b, 61b–62a
Bergson, III 565b
Chain of Being, I 334a
deism, I 651b
determinism, II 238b
evolutionism, II 182b–183b,

185b–186a
free will, II 238b
Greece (ancient), I 60b, 61b–62a
irrationalism, II 636b
Man-Machine, III 141b, 144a
matter, III 187a
mythology, III 303b–304a
positivism, III 548b–549a
pragmatism, III 565b
reformation, IV 60b–61a
Sorel, III 565b
Spinoza, II 238b
Vitruvius Pollio, Marcus (1st century B.C.)
architecture, II 217a
culture, I 610b
hierarchy, II 437b
progress, III 631a, 632b
symmetry, IV 346a
time, IV 401a–401b
universal man, IV 439a
Vittorino da Feltre (1378–1446)
humanism, II 519a–519b
universal man, IV 438b
Vives, Juan Luis (1492–1540)
attitude toward antiquity, I 77b, 84b–85a
baroque in literature, I 188b
genius, II 293b
idea, I 111b
mythology, IV 299b
skepticism, IV 241b
style, IV 331b
Vivian Bible, IV 371b
Vocabulary
language, II 659b, 668b; III 63b
linguistics, III 63b, 64b; IV 430a
Plato, III 211a
Voetius, Gisbert (1588–1676), skepticism, IV 245a
Vogel, Adolf, Buddhism, I 256b
Vogrich, Max, Buddhism, I 256b
Vogt, William, conservation, I 471a, 476a
Void
atomism, III 187b
kenon, IV 298b
matter, III 186b, 187b, 195a
Newton, III 195a
Non-Being, IV 299a
space, IV 298a, 298b, 299a
Voigt, Georg, Renaissance, IV 124b, 125b
Voigt, Woldemar (1850–

1919), relativity, IV 79b, 89a
Voilquin, Jean, natural law, III 14b, 15a
Volapük language, II 669a
Volcanoes, catastrophism, IV 417b–423a
Volfius, Abbé, nationalism, III 326b
Volkelt, Johannes Immanuel (1848–1930), empathy, II 88a
Völkerpsychologie, IV 495b–496a
Volksgeist, IV 490b–496b, 535b
  anthropology, IV 496a
  Australia, IV 495a
  Bancroft, IV 495b
  blacks, IV 491b
  bourgeois, IV 494b
  Burke, Edmund, IV 491a
  Canada, IV 495a
  capitalism, IV 494a
  causation, IV 496a
  climate, IV 491a–492a
  common sense, IV 491a
  communism, IV 494b
  constitutions, IV 492a, 492b, 493a
  creativity, IV 492a, 492b, 494b
  culture, IV 491b, 492b, 495a, 496a
  custom, IV 491a, 491b, 493a, 496a
  cycles, IV 493a
  defined, IV 490b–491a
  Descartes, IV 492a
  Dewey, IV 494b
  dualism, IV 495a
  duty, IV 495b
  economics, IV 494a–494b
  education, IV 494b
  egoism, IV 494a
  empiricism, IV 496a
  experience, IV 492a, 496a
  Fiske, IV 495b
  folklore, IV 491a, 492a, 494a, 495a
  France, 493b, 494a, 495b
  freedom, IV 495b
  genetics, IV 491a, 496a
  genius, IV 491a, 491b, 493a, 493b
  Germany, IV 491a, 491b–494b, 495a–496a
  God, IV 493a, 495b
  Great Britain, IV 494a–494b, 495b
  Greece (ancient), IV 491a, 494a
  Grimm, IV 494a, 495a
  Hegel, IV 492a–493a, 493b
  Herbart, IV 495b

  Herder, III 305a; IV 203a, 492a, 494a, 495a
  Herzen, IV 494b
  hierarchy, IV 491b
  history, IV 491a–496a
  Humboldt, IV 494a
  Hume, IV 491b, 492a
  ideology, IV 493b–495a
  individualism, IV 492b, 493a, 494a, 495b, 496a
  Italy, IV 493b, 495a
  Judaism, IV 491a, 492b, 493a, 494b
  judgment, IV 491a
  Kant, IV 491b–492a
  language, IV 491a, 492a, 493a, 493b, 494a, 496a
  law, IV 491a–495b
  Leibniz, IV 491a
  liberalism, IV 494a
  liberty, IV 495a
  Lieber, IV 495a
  List, IV 494b
  literature, IV 492a, 493b, 494a
  manners, IV 491b
  methodology, IV 494a
  Michelet, IV 492b
  Mickiewicz, IV 494b
  Middle Ages, IV 493b
  monotheism, IV 493a
  Montesquieu, IV 491a–491b, 492a
  morality, IV 491a, 491b, 493a, 495b
  mores, IV 491a, 492a, 492b
  Möser, IV 491b, 493b
  Müller, Adam, IV 493b
  mythology, III 305a; IV 496a
  nationalism, IV 491b, 493b, 494a, 495a
  natural law, IV 494a, 494b, 495b
  Nature, IV 491b
  Nazism, IV 494a
  necessity, III 359a
  norms, IV 491b
  Oakeshott, IV 496a
  origin of the term, IV 492a
  Parker, Theodore, IV 495b
  patriotism, IV 491b
  philosophy, IV 492a, 492b, 493b, 494a, 494b
  poetry, IV 492a, 494a, 495a
  Poland, IV 493b, 494b
  power, IV 491a
  Protestantism, IV 494b
  psyche, IV 495b, 496a
  psychology, IV 491b, 495b–496a
  race, IV 491b, 494a, 495a
  Ranke, IV 493b
  rationalism, IV 495a

  religion, IV 491a, 491b, 492b, 494b
  Roman Catholic Church, IV 491b
  romanticism, IV 203a, 494a
  Rome (ancient), IV 491a, 492a–492b, 494a
  Russia, IV 494b
  Saint Paul, IV 491a
  Savigny, IV 493a–494a
  Schaff, IV 495a–495b
  science, IV 491a
  soul, IV 492a, 495b–496a
  Staël, IV 493b, 494a
  State, IV 491a–493b, 495b
  Steinthal, IV 495b
  tradition, IV 494b, 496a
  U.S., IV 494b–495b
  unity, IV 495a, 495b
  Vico, IV 491a
  Völkerpsychologie, IV 495b–496a
  Voltaire, IV 491b
  Von Gierke, IV 494a
  Whitman, IV 494b, 495a
  World Spirit, IV 492b, 493b
  Wundt, IV 495b–496a
Vollmar, Georg Heinrich von (1850–1922)
  Marxism, III 166a
  revisionism, IV 265b
Voltaire, (1694–1778), I 409a
  aesthetics, IV 355a
  antiprimitivism, III 604b–605a
  aristocracy, II 11a
  art, IV 124a
  attitude toward antiquity, I 86a, 86b
  Bacon and, I 177b
  Burnet and, I 511a; III 259a
  Chain of Being, I 329a, 329b–330a; II 447a, 447b
  China, I 361b, 362a, 365a
  city, I 432a
  class, IV 288a
  classicism, I 451b
  Cosmic Fall, I 511a
  cosmic voyages, I 526a, 534a–534b
  Counter-Enlightenment, II 101b, 104b, 106a, 106b
  culture, I 616a–616b, 618a, 619b; II 129b
  death, I 634a
  deism, I 651a; III 302b, 303a
  democracy, I 657b
  despotism, II 8a, 10a, 10b–11a, 13a, 13b
  dogma, IV 118b
  empiricism, I 220a
  Enlightenment, II 90a, 91a, 91b, 94b, 95a–95b, 97a–

97b, 98a; IV 155b
  environment, II 129b
  equality, II 143b; IV 288a
  Epicureanism, II 137b
  evil, II 166b
  evolution of literature, II 171b, 172a
  evolutionism, II 176b
  free will, II 137b
  freedom, II 11a
  genius, II 294b
  God, I 329b, 330a; II 353a, 356b
  Herder and, I 618a
  hierarchy, II 446b
  historicism, II 458a
  historiography, II 487b, 488b, 489b, 495a
  history, III 638a, 638b
  imagination, II 216b
  Indians (American), III 605a
  irony, II 629a
  language, II 662a
  law, II 106b
  Leibniz and, II 446b, 447a; IV 382b
  liberalism, III 45a
  liberty, II 94b, 95a
  literature, III 81b, 82a; IV 332a
  love, III 94a
  luxury, III 604b
  Machiavellism, III 120a
  Mandeville and, III 604b–605a
  mathematics, III 179a
  methodology, III 378b
  Middle Ages, I 619b
  monarchy, II 11a
  Montesquieu and, II 10a, 10b–11a
  motif, III 240b
  mountains in literature, III 259a
  mythology, III 302b, 303a
  Nature, I 330a, 615a; II 176b; III 348a, 605a
  necessity, III 358a
  neo-classicism in art, III 366a
  Newton and, III 378b
  optimism, I 329a
  Orientalism, III 428a, 638b
  philosophy, IV 155a
  periodization in history, III 477a, 477b
  periodization in literary history, III 482b–483a
  Platonism, III 516a
  pluralism, III 303a
  poetics, III 530a
  positivism, III 532b
  poverty, IV 288a

primitivism, III 604b–605a
private property, III 605a
progress, III 638a, 638b
rationalism, III 302b, 303a
reason, II 11a
religion, IV 118b, 124a
revolution, IV 155a, 155b
romanticism, IV 200b
Rousseau and, III 605a
satire, IV 213b, 214b, 215a, 215b
skepticism, IV 241b, 247b
socialism, IV 288a
society, IV 288a
spontaneous generation, IV 310b
State, I 657b
style, IV 332a
taste, IV 355a
theodicy, IV 382b
urbanization, I 616b
utilitarianism, II 97a–97b
Utopia, IV 464a
virtù, IV 484a
Volksgeist, IV 491b
wealth, IV 288a
women, IV 526a
work, IV 534b
Zeitgeist, IV 535b
Voluntarism
existentialism, III 158a
general will, II 280b
Lenin, III 152b–153a
Luther, IV 381b
Marxism and, III 152a, 152b–153a, 153b, 158a
positivism and, III 22b
pragmatism, III 563b
Sartre, III 158a
theodicy, IV 381b
welfare state, IV 509b
Vondel, Joost Van Den (1587–1679), baroque in literature, I 191b
Voronoff, Serge (1866–1951), longevity, III 93a
Vortriede, Werner, symbolism, IV 344b, 345a
Voss, Gerhard Johann, perennial philosophy, III 460b
Voss, Johann Heinrich (1751–1826), romanticism, IV 189a
Vossius, Gerhard Johannes (1577–1649)
classicism, I 453a
genius, II 295a
literary criticism, I 597a
ut pictura poesis, IV 467b
Vossius, Isaac (1618–1689), China, I 358b–359a
Vossler, Karl (1872–1949), baroque in literature, I 190b
Voting, *see* Suffrage

Vox populi, IV 496b–500b
Alcuin, IV 498a–498b
Aristotle, IV 497a–497b
art, IV 499a, 499b
Ball, IV 498a
ballads, IV 498b–499a
Bible, IV 498b
blacks, IV 497a
bourgeois, IV 499a, 500a
Cain (Bible), IV 498a
Charlemagne, IV 498a–498b
Christianity, IV 498a–498b
Cicero, IV 497b, 498a
class, IV 497a–497b, 498b, 499b–500a
democracy, IV 497a, 500a
Dickens, IV 499b
economics, IV 499b–500a
education, IV 499b
emotion, IV 499a, 500a
evil, IV 498a
France, IV 499a, 500a
French Revolution (1789), IV 499a
Gaskell, IV 497b, 499a, 499b
Germany, IV 500a
God, IV 497a, 498a, 498b
Goncourt brothers, IV 499b
grace, IV 498a
Great Britain, IV 499a, 500a
Greece (ancient), IV 497a–498a
guilt, IV 498a
health, IV 499b
Herder, IV 499a
Hesiod, IV 498b
housing, IV 499b
industry, IV 499b
Jay, IV 499a
kingship, IV 498b
Kingsley, IV 499b
labor, IV 497a–500a
law, IV 497b
leisure, IV 497b
literature, IV 497b, 498b
Livy, IV 497b
Marxism, IV 499a
Middle Ages, IV 498a–498b
military, IV 497a
monarchy, IV 497a
music, IV 498b–499a, 499b
Napoleon I, IV 499a
Nature, IV 499a
Ossian, IV 499a
peasantry, IV 498a, 498b–499a, 500a
Percy, IV 498b–499a
Philip of Macedon, IV 497a
philosophers, IV 497a
pity, IV 499b

Plato, IV 497a–497b
Plautus, IV 497b
pleasure, IV 499b
poetry, IV 498b–499a
poverty, IV 497a
power, IV 499b–500a
private property, IV 499a
race, IV 496b
reason, IV 497b
religion, IV 496b
Renaissance, IV 497b, 498b
Roman Catholic Church, IV 498b
romanticism, IV 498b
Rome (ancient), IV 497b, 498a
Saint Augustine, IV 498a
Samuel (Bible), IV 498b
Shakespeare, IV 497b
slavery, IV 497a
Solon, IV 497a
songs, IV 498b–499a
soul, IV 499a
Spain, IV 500a
State, IV 497a–497b
Stoicism, IV 498a
suffrage, IV 498b
sympathy, IV 498b–499b
taste, IV 497a
Theocritus, IV 498b
U.S., IV 499a–500a
urbanization, IV 499a–500a
Vergil, IV 498b
virtue, IV 497a
Warner, IV 499b
welfare state, IV 499b
women, IV 497a, 499a
Wordsworth, IV 499a
Zola, IV 499b
Vredeman de Vries, Hans (1527–after 1604), Gothic, II 371a
Vulcan (myth), III 294a
Vyazemsky, Prince, romanticism, IV 191b

———————

W

———————

Wachler, Ernst, literature, III 83a
Wachler, Ludwig, literature, III 85a
Wachter, J. G., linguistics, III 67a
Wackernagel, J. (1853–1938), linguistics, III 72b
Wackernagel, Wilhelm (1806–1869), style, IV 332b
Waddington, C. H. (1905–), acquired charac-

teristics, II 619a
Wages
capitalism, III 151b
economic history, II 45b, 46b, 48b–50a, 54a–57a
equality, II 146a
Marx, IV 292b
Marxism, III 151b
revisionism, IV 264b
socialism, IV 292b, 293a
welfare state, IV 509b, 510b, 511b, 512a–512b
Wagner, Adolf, historicism, II 457a
Wagner, Gabriel, perennial philosophy, III 461b
Wagner, Richard (1813–1883)
baroque in literature, I 189a
Buddhism, I 256a
Eliot and, III 236a
genius, II 325a
impressionism, II 575a
Joyce and, III 236a
leitmotiv, III 236a
love, III 104b
Mann and, III 236a
morality, III 330b
motif, III 236a, 236b
music, II 325a; III 271b
mythology, III 306b
nationalism, III 330b
Proust and, III 236a
racialism, III 330b
symbolism, IV 342b, 344b
ut pictura poesis, IV 472b
Wolzogen and, III 236a
Wahl, Jean, imagination, III 209a, 209b
Waismann, Friedrich (1896–1959), positivism, III 545b
Waitz, Georg (1813–1886), historiography, II 494a
Walcutt, Charles Child, realism in literature, IV 54b
Wald, A. (1902–1950)
game theory, II 265a, 272a
probability, III 617a, 622a
Waldensians
beliefs, II 420a
Cathars, II 423b
condemnation, II 419b
denunciation of Roman Catholic Church, II 420a
excommunication, II 420b
founder of, II 419a
heresy, II 418b, 419a–420b, 421b, 422a, 423b, 426b
Hussites, II 420b
Lollards, II 420b
poverty, II 419b–420a
Roman Catholic Church, II 420a

socialism, IV 286b
success of, II 420b
Waldmüller, Ferdinand Georg (1793–1865), naturalism in art, III 339b, 341a
Waldo, Peter (fl. late 12th century), heresy, I 383b
Wallace, Alfred R. (1823–1913)
association of ideas, I 115b
evolutionism, II 180b
Wallace, Henry A. (1888–1965), China, I 371b
Wallace, Robert, Utopia, IV 463a
Wallace, William (1844–1897)
evolution, III 473b
Hegel and, II 414a, 414b
Huxley and, III 474a
natural selection, III 473b
perfectibility, III 473b
Wallenstein, Albrecht von (1583–1634), Machiavellism, III 120b
Waller, Edmund (1606–1687)
periodization in literary history, III 483a, 485b
romanticism, IV 194a
Wallis, John (1616–1703)
Bacon and, I 177a
certainty, I 308a
infinity, II 609b, 611a
language, II 667a
methodology, III 389a
music, III 263a
Newton and, III 389a
Walpole, Horace (1717–1797)
genius, II 306a
Gothic, II 370b
Walpole, Robert (1676–1745), deism, I 651a
Walras, Léon (1834–1910)
economic history, II 47a, 50b, 52a, 52b
individualism, II 602b
social welfare, IV 277b
utility, IV 453b, 455a, 458a
Waltz, K. M., war, IV 500b
Walwyn, William, deism, I 649b
Walzel, Oskar F.
art, II 308b
baroque in literature, I 189b, 194b
genius, II 308b
periodization in literary history, III 484a
romanticism, IV 197a
Walzer, Michael, democracy, I 656b
Wambaugh, Eugene, law, III 31b
War, IV 500b–509a

aggression, IV 507a–508a
agriculture, IV 500b, 501b
air power, IV 505b
Alexander the Great, IV 502b
American Revolution, III 453a
Andreski, IV 507a
Angell, IV 507a–507b
animals, III 596a
anthropology, IV 508a
arbitration, III 449b–450b, 451b, 452b, 453b, 454a
aristocracy, IV 501b, 504b
Aristotle, IV 501b
armament-race, III 448b, 449b, 455a
armaments, IV 501b, 503b, 504a
arms control, III 456a, 456b
Arms Control and Disarmament Agency, III 455b
Aron, IV 508a
art, II 577a, 580a; IV 504b
Atomic Energy Commission, III 455b
Austria, IV 500b
balance of power, I 185a–185b; III 452a
barbarism, IV 501b, 502a
Belgium, IV 505a
Bentham, III 444b
Bernard, IV 507b
Bernhardi, IV 505a
Bethmann-Hollweg, IV 505a
biochemical, IV 501a
biology, III 448b
Bismarck, IV 505a
Bloch, IV 504a, 504b, 507a, 508a
Bodin, II 6a; IV 502a–502b, 507b
Boulding, IV 504b, 508a
Bowlby, IV 507b
Buchan, IV 507a
Burckhardt, I 591b
Burnod, IV 501a
Calvin, III 441b
causes of, III 447a, 447b
China (Communist), IV 507a
Christianity, III 448a; IV 502a, 505b
city-state, IV 501a, 502a
civil, III 443a, 450a
civilization, IV 501b, 502a, 508a
class, IV 502b, 503b, 504b, 505a, 506a
Clausewitz, IV 500b, 501a, 502a, 502b, 503a, 504a, 505b, 506b

cold, III 445a
Commission for Conventional Armaments, III 455b
communism, IV 505a, 505b
Comte, III 642a–642b
conciliation, III 450b
Congo, III 454b
conservativism, IV 502b, 504b–507a
"cooling off" principle, III 450b
Crackanthorpe, IV 504b
crisis in history, I 591b, 593b–594a, 594b
Crusades, III 452b
Cuba, III 544b
culture, III 447a; IV 506a
Cyprus, III 454b
Darwinism, IV 501a, 503b, 505a, 505b
democracy, IV 501a, 501b, 503a, 503b, 505a–507a
despotism, II 2a, 6a, 10a, 14a, 16a; IV 503a
Dewey, John, III 447a–447b, 569a
dictatorship, IV 505a
diplomacy, III 443b
disarmament, III 444b, 449b, 455a–456b
Disarmament Commission, III 455b
Disarmament Committee, III 455b
Dollard, IV 507b
economics, III 157b, 448b; IV 504a, 504b, 506a
education, IV 500b, 505a, 508a
Einstein, III 446b–447a
emancipation, III 444b
Engels, IV 506a
equality, IV 503b
Erasmus, IV 118b
ethics, III 440a–447b; IV 70a, 506a
Ethiopia, III 454a
Eve (Bible), III 582a
evil, IV 502a, 506a, 507a, 508a
evolution, III 448b
fascism, IV 505a, 505b
Ferdinand, II, IV 502a
feudalism, IV 501a, 503b
Fichte, IV 502a
Five Power Treaty, III 455b
Foch, IV 504a
France, IV 500b, 501a, 502b, 503a, 504a, 504b, 505b, 506a
Frederick the Great, IV 501a, 502b, 504a, 505a
freedom of speech, II 259a
French Revolution (1789),

IV 500b, 501a, 502b
Freud, III 447a; IV 507b
game theory, II 264a
Gandhi, III 446b
genius, II 293a
Germany, III 455a; IV 503b–505b
Glover, IV 505b
God, IV 502a
Great Britain, IV 503b, 504a, 505a, 505b, 507a
Greece, III 454b
Greece (ancient), II 678b, 683b; III 448a; IV 366b, 367b, 501a–502a
Green, T. H., IV 503b
Grotius, II 6a; III 441b–442a
gunpowder, IV 502b
Hague Peace Conferences, III 450a, 451a, 453b, 455a
Hart, Liddell, IV 502b
Hawtrey, III 445a–445b
Hegel, II 16a, 409b, 415b–416a; III 445a; IV 502a, 503a, 503b, 506a
Herder, III 326a
Hiroshima, III 455b
historiography, II 466b–469b, 472a, 473a, 474a, 480a, 482b, 492a, 496b, 498a, 500b, 501b, 503a
history, IV 504a, 508a
Hitler, IV 505a
Hobbes, I 656a; II 6a; III 441b, 442b–443a, 484a
holy, II 512b
honor, IV 505b
Huguenots, IV 113a, 116a–116b
human nature, IV 506a
Huntington, IV 506a, 506b
ideas, III 448a–448b
ideology, III 448b; IV 506a
impiety, II 566b
impressionism, II 577a, 580a, 582b
individualism, IV 503b
Industrial Revolution, IV 500b, 504a
industry, III 642a–642b; IV 503b, 504b, 506b
internationalism, III 447a; IV 502b
irrationalism, II 635a
Islam, IV 502a
Italy, III 454a; IV 505b
James, III 447a; IV 507a–507b, 508b
Japan, III 454a; IV 505b
Jaurès, IV 506a–506b
just, III 451b; IV 502a
justice, III 441b

Kant, III 442a–444a; IV 502a
Kashmir, III 454b
Keynes, IV 507a
Korea, III 454b
labor, IV 501b
law, II 678b, 683b, 687b, 689b, 690a; III 10b, 33b, 451a, 451b, 452a; IV 502a, 502b, 504b
League of Nations, III 449b, 451a, 451b, 454a, 454b, 455a, 455b
Lebanon, III 454b
Lecky, I 655b–656a
Leibniz, III 442a
liberalism, IV 502b, 503b, 504b, 505a, 506b, 507a
Liebknecht, IV 506a
Lincoln, III 444a
literature, IV 500b, 501a, 504a
Locarno Pact, III 452b
Lorenz, IV 507b
love, III 101b, 102b–103a; IV 502a
loyalty, III 114a
Lucretius, III 587b
McDougall, IV 507a
Machiavelli, III 441b; IV 501a, 502a, 502b, 507b
Machiavellism, III 120a
McNeill, IV 508a
Maistre, IV 504a
Manchuria, III 454a
Man-Machine, III 135b
Marx, I 593b–594a; III 445a
Marxism, III 149b, 150b–151a, 155a, 157a, 157b; IV 501a, 506a
mathematics, IV 502b
metallurgy, IV 501b
Middle Ages, III 448a; IV 502a–502b
Middle East, III 454b
the military, III 448a, 448b, 452a, 455a; IV 500b, 501a, 501b, 502b, 504a, 505b–506a, 506b, 507a, 508a, 508b
millenarianism, III 223b, 224b, 225b
Montaigne, III 594b
Montesquieu, II 10a; IV 500b–501a, 501b
morality, III 442a; IV 500b, 502a, 504b
moratorium, III 450b
Muirhead, IV 503a
mythology, III 280b, 281b–282a, 284b, 284b
Nagasaki, III 455b
Napoleon I, IV 502b, 503a,

504a, 505a
Napoleon III, IV 503b
nationalism, III 322b, 324a, 326a, 329b, 330a, 673a; IV 501a, 503b, 504a, 505b, 506a, 507a
nation-state, III 444a
natural law, III 18a, 24b
Nazism, III 597b
Newton, IV 502a
Nicholas II, IV 504b
Nietzsche, IV 503a
nuclear power, III 456b; IV 501a
nuclear weapons, III 449b, 455a, 455b
Nuremberg Trials, III 452a
offensive, III 441b
Orientalism, III 428b
origins of, IV 507a–508b
over-population, III 446b
pacifism, IV 502a
patriotism, III 445a; IV 503b
peasantry, IV 502a, 506b
Permanent Court of Arbitration, III 450a, 451a
philanthropy, III 491a
philosophers, IV 503a
philosophy, IV 500b, 501a, 502a, 504a, 508b
plunder, IV 501b, 507b
politics, III 448b, 451b–452a, 453a, 454b, 455a; IV 500b, 501a, 501b, 502a, 502b, 504a, 505a, 505b, 506a, 506b, 507a, 508a, 508b
Polybius, IV 501b, 508a
population explosion, IV 507b
positivism, III 544b; IV 500b, 501a
poverty, IV 507b
power, III 445a; IV 504b, 508a
pragmatism, III 569a
primitivism, III 578a, 578b, 579a, 579b, 580a, 581a, 582a, 587b, 594b, 595a, 596a, 597b
prisoners, III 441b
private property, III 652a
professionalism, IV 506a, 506b, 507a
progress, III 629b, 631b, 632a, 639a, 642a–642b, 647a, 648a, 648b, 649a
propaganda, IV 503a
prophecy, III 659a, 660b, 662b, 663a, 664b, 665a, 667b
prosperity, IV 504b
protest movements, III 673a,

675b
Prussia, IV 500b, 501a, 503a, 503b, 504b–505a, 507a
psychiatry, IV 505b
psychology, III 447a; IV 18b, 22b, 24b, 25b, 28a, 507a–508b
Pufendorf, II 6a
race, III 448b
radicalism, IV 505b
rationalism, IV 46b
relativism, IV 70a
religion, III 444a, 448b; IV 113a, 113b, 118b
republicanism, III 443a–443b
revolution, IV 155b, 166b, 503b, 504a, 505a, 506a
Roman Catholic Church, III 452b; IV 502a
Rome (ancient), II 687b, 689b, 690a; III 448a, 652a; IV 501a–502a, 502b
Rousseau, IV 502a
Russell, Bertrand, III 446b
Russia, IV 504a
Saint-Pierre, III 442a
Saxe, IV 504a
Scharnhorst, IV 504a, 505a
science, III 642b; IV 504a, 504b, 507b, 508a, 508b
self-preservation, IV 507b
sex, IV 507b
sin, IV 508a
slavery, III 441a
socialism, III 445a; IV 502b, 504b, 505a, 507a
society, III 445b; IV 500b, 501b, 502a, 503b, 504a, 504b, 506a, 507a
sociology, IV 507a
Spencer, III 642a; IV 500b, 502a, 503b, 507b
Stalin, III 157a
State, I 655b–656a, 665a; IV 500b, 502a, 503b, 507b
Strachey, IV 505b
Suárez, III 451b
Sun Tsu, IV 501a
Taylor, IV 505a
technology, IV 501b, 504a, 504b, 506b, 508b
temperance, III 366b, 367b
Thucydides, IV 501b
Tocqueville, IV 503a–503b, 505b
Tolstoy, III 445b
totalitarianism, IV 408a, 409a, 505b, 506b
Toynbee, IV 508a
tragic sense, IV 416a
treaties, III 444b, 448b,

449b, 450a, 451a, 452a, 455a
Treitschke, IV 503a
undeclared wars, III 445a
U.S.S.R., IV 506a, 507a
U.N., III 449b, 451b, 452a, 454b–455a, 455b
U.S., III 428b, 444a; IV 504a, 505b–506a, 507a, 508a
Utopia, IV 459a, 459b; IV 507a
Vagt, IV 504b, 505a, 506a
Vegetius, IV 501a
victory, IV 504b
Vietnam War, III 449b
violence, IV 502a, 502b, 504b, 507a
virtù, IV 483a, 484a
Washington Conference, III 455b
wealth, IV 501b, 504a
weapons, IV 501a, 502b, 504a, 504b, 505a, 506b, 507a, 508a
Weber, IV 507a
Whitehead, IV 504a
World War, I, IV 501a, 502b, 504a; III 449a, 449b, 450a, 452b, 453b–454a, 455a
World War II, III 449b, 452a, 454a, 455b; IV 501a
Wright, Q., IV 507a, 508a
Xenophon, IV 504a
See also Military, Peace

War of the Spanish Succession, balance of power, I 183a, 185b–186a
Warburg, Aby, iconography, II 535b, 536a
Warburton, William (Bishop) (1698–1779)
    Gothic, II 370b–371a
    mythology, III 302a
Ward, James (1843–1925)
    agnosticism, I 17a, 22b–23a
    Creation, I 573b
    God, I 573b
Ward, Lester Frank (1841–1913), psychology, IV 26a
Ward, Maisie, baroque in literature, I 193a
Ward, Mary (1585–1645), women, IV 526a
Ward, Samuel (d. 1643) hierarchy, II 434b
Ward, Seth (1617–1689), linguistics, III 74b
Ward, Wilfrid, modernism, I 425a

Warner, Amos, psychology, **IV** 26a

Warner, Joseph B., pragmatism, **III** 558a, 566a–566b

Warner, Lloyd, *vox populi*, **IV** 499b

Warren, Austin, baroque in literature, **I** 193b, 194a

Warren, Earl (Chief Justice) (1891–   ), academic freedom, **I** 11b–12a

Warren, Henry Clarke Buddhism, **I** 255b
Orientalism, **III** 434b–435a

Warren, Josiah (1798?–1874), anarchy, **I** 74a

Warren, Robert Penn (1905–   )
irony, **II** 633a
organicism, **III** 426b

Warren, William Fairfield (1833–1929), Orientalism, **III** 435b

Warsaw Pact, **III** 456b
Marxism, **III** 167a

Warton, Joseph (1722–1800)
primitivism, **III** 600a, 601a
romanticism, **IV** 194a, 195a
ut pictura poesis, **IV** 471b

Warton, Thomas (1728–1790)
Gothic, **II** 370b
periodization in literary history, **III** 482a
Renaissance, **IV** 124a
romanticism, **IV** 187b, 188a, 189b, 190b, 191b, 194a, 195a, 195b
ut pictura poesis, **IV** 471b

Washington Conference, **III** 455b

Wasil ibn 'Atā' (d. 748 A.D.) Islam, **II** 641b

Water
Empedocles, **IV** 2b
psychology, **IV** 2b, 7b
Stoics, **IV** 7a

Watkin, E. I., baroque in literature, **I** 193a

Watson, George, literary criticism, **I** 602b

Watson, J. D., DNA, **II** 289b–291a, 291b

Watson, John B. (1878–1958)
association of ideas, **I** 116b–117a
associationism, **I** 214b–215a
behaviorism, **I** 214a–215a, 216a, 217b, 218b, 220b–222b, 223a–223b, 225a, 227a; **II** 382b
empiricism, **III** 549a, 550b
happiness and pleasure, **II** 382b
idea, **I** 116b–117a
learning, **I** 222a
Man-Machine, **III** 144a
perfectibility, **III** 469b
psychology, **IV** 14a, 28a
on science, **I** 214b

Watson, W. H., positivism, **III** 550b

Watt, James (1736–1819), technology, **IV** 362b

Watteau, Jean Antoine (1684–1721)
China, **I** 363b, 364a
Nature, **III** 349b
ut pictura poesis, **IV** 467a

Watts, Alan, Buddhism, **I** 256a

Waugh, Evelyn (1903–1966) satire, **IV** 214a–215b
Utopia, **IV** 464a

Waugh, Sidney, temperance, **IV** 378a

Wave mechanics
indeterminacy, **II** 588b
Schrödinger, **II** 588b
time, **IV** 397b

Waves
optics, **III** 418a, 418b, 419b, 420b
symmetry, **IV** 349a, 350b–351a

Wayland, Francis (1796–1865), psychology, **IV** 22b

Wealth
Aristotle, **I** 625b, 654a
art, **II** 299b, 570a, 577a
Baader, **IV** 207b
Bacon, **IV** 361b
Bentham, **II** 381a; **IV** 277b
Calvinism, **III** 654a
chance, **II** 231b
Christianity, **III** 589b, 670b
despotism, **II** 12a
economic history, **II** 45a–45b, 49b, 53a, 56b, 58b, 60b
Enlightenment, **II** 91a, 99b
equality, **II** 139a, 143a, 144a, 145a
evolutionism, **II** 180b
fortune, **II** 228a, 228b, 231b
freedom of speech, **II** 260a, 261a
general will, **II** 276b, 277a, 277b, 278a, 279a
genius, **II** 299b
good, **II** 231b; **IV** 175a, 177a
happiness, **II** 377b, 379a, 381a
health, **II** 397a
human nature, **III** 575b

humanism, **IV** 133b
Hume, **II** 45a–45b
impressionism, **II** 570a, 577a, 580a
law, **II** 686a, 688b; **III** 11a, 11b
Locke, **IV** 259a
Lucretius, **III** 587b
Machiavelli, **IV** 483a
Marxism, **III** 151b
Middle Ages, **IV** 123b, 153a
millenarianism, **III** 224a
natural liberty, **II** 65a–65b, 66b
philanthropy, **III** 491b
Plato, **III** 629a; **IV** 175a
pleasure, **II** 376a, 379a, 381a
primitivism, **III** 587b, 588a, 589a, 600b
private property, **III** 650b, 651a, 653b, 654a, 655a
progress, **III** 629a, 630a, 636b, 637b
protest movements, **III** 670b, 672a
psychology, **IV** 18a, 23a
Puritanism, **IV** 18a
reformation, **IV** 63b, 65a, 65b
Renaissance, **IV** 122b, 133b, 438a, 441b
revolution, **IV** 153a
right, **IV** 175a, 177a
romanticism, **IV** 207b
Rome (ancient), **II** 686a, 688b
social contract, **IV** 256a, 259a
social welfare, **IV** 276a, 277b, 279a, 279b
socialism, **IV** 288a–289b
Stoicism, **IV** 321a, 321b
technology, **IV** 357b, 361b
U.S., **III** 491b–492b
universal man, **IV** 438a, 441b
Victorian sentiment, **IV** 217b, 218b, 219a, 223a
virtù, **IV** 483a
virtuoso, **IV** 486a
Voltaire, **IV** 288a
war, **IV** 501b, 504a
welfare state, **IV** 512a, 512b
William of Ockham, **IV** 65b
women, **IV** 525b
work, **IV** 531b, 534a

Web of life concept, **II** 128b, 133a

Webb, Beatrice (1858–1943)
Bernstein and, **III** 163b
Marxism, **III** 163b
positivism, **III** 538b
welfare state, **IV** 510b–511a

Webb, C. C. J., Cosmic Fall, **I** 512b

Webb, Daniel, *ut pictura poesis*, **IV** 472a

Webb, David
creativity in art, **I** 588a
ideal, **II** 550a

Webb, John (1611–1672), language, **I** 358a

Webb, Sidney (1859–1947), economic history, **II** 60a

Weber, Carl Maria von (1786–1826), music, **III** 264b

Weber, Ernst Heinrich (1795–1878)
behaviorism, **I** 219b
psychology, **IV** 12a, 12b, 24b
utility, **IV** 454b

Weber, Max (1864–1920)
authority, **I** 157a
Bentham and, **I** 260b
Buddhism, **I** 256a
China, **I** 368a–368b, 372b, 396a
class, **I** 444b–445a
economic history, **II** 46b
empathy, **II** 85b, 86b–87a
ethics, **I** 260b
faith, **II** 211b, 212b
good, **IV** 177a
historicism, **II** 462b–463b
historiography, **II** 496a–497a
ideology, **II** 554b
individualism, **II** 596b, 602a, 602b–603a
Kant and, **I** 260b
longevity, **III** 90b
Marx and, **II** 453a
Marxism, **III** 149b
materialism, **II** 453a
periodization in history, **III** 480b
power, **I** 445a
Protestantism, **I** 396a
revolution, **IV** 162a
right, **IV** 177a
salvation, **II** 212b
socialism, **IV** 288a–289b
war, **IV** 507a
work, **IV** 533a

Weber, Wilhelm Eduard (1804–1891), relativity, **IV** 90a

Webern, Anton von (1883–1945), imagination, **III** 208a

Webster, John (c. 17th century)
alchemy, **I** 32b
Bacon and, **III** 74b
linguistics, **III** 74b

Webster, Thomas, catastrophism, IV 420b
Wechssler, Eduard, periodization in literary history, III 485b
Wedgwood, Josiah (1730–1795), neo-classicism in art, III 366b
Weierstrass, Karl Theodor (1815–1897), infinity, II 606b
Weil, Eric, democracy, I 666b
Weil, Henri (1818–1909), catharsis, I 267a
Weimar Republic
    positivism, III 534b
    totalitarianism, IV 408b
Weinreich, Uriel (1926–1967)
    language, II 668b
    linguistics, III 72a
Weisinger, Herbert
    mythology, III 279b
    romanticism, IV 192a
Weismann, August (1834–1914)
    acquired characteristics, II 618b–619a
    genetic continuity, II 288b–289a
    James and, III 565a
    longevity, III 92b
    pangenesis, II 624b–625a, 626a, 626b
    pragmatism, III 565a
    psychology, IV 26a
    sexual reproduction, II 619a
Weiss, Albert P.
    behaviorism, I 222b–223b
    positivism, III 549a
Weiss, Johannes
    eschatology, I 420b, 422b; II 160b
    modernism, I 419b, 420b
Weitling, Wilhelm, socialism, IV 290a
Weizsäcker, C. F. von, cosmology, I 570a
Welfare
    Campanella, IV 461b
    Cicero, III 116a
    happiness, II 374b, 378a, 384b–385a
    law, II 686b, 687a, 688a, 688b, 689b
    Machiavellism, III 116a
    Marxism, III 149b, 152a
    Mill, IV 179a
    nationalism, III 318b, 319a, 320a, 320b, 321b, 322a, 322b, 323a, 325a, 333a
    right, IV 179a
    Roman Catholic Church, III 654b
    Rome (ancient), II 686b,

687a, 688a, 688b
Tacitus, III 116a
utilitarianism, IV 447b, 448b, 449a, 449b
utility, IV 454a, 457b
Utopia, IV 461b
Welfare state, IV 509a–515b
    accidents, IV 510a
    aged, IV 509b–511a, 514b
    agriculture, IV 511a
    Arnold, Matthew, IV 510a
    Asquith, IV 510b
    Australia, IV 510b
    authority, IV 509a, 510a
    Bevan, IV 513b, 514a
    Beveridge, IV 413a
    Bismarck, IV 510a, 510b
    Booth, IV 510b, 511a
    capitalism, IV 510a, 512a
    charity, IV 509b
    children, IV 510b, 511a
    Churchill, IV 510b, 511b
    class, IV 509a, 513a, 514b
    collectivism, IV 510a, 510b, 511b, 512b
    community, IV 511a, 511b
    constitutions, IV 509a
    death, IV 509b
    democracy, IV 510b
    duty, IV 511b
    economics, IV 509a–512b, 514a–515a
    education, IV 510b, 511a, 512a, 513b, 515a
    Ely, Richard T., IV 512a
    empiricism, IV 512b
    employment, IV 509b, 512a, 513a
    equality, IV 510b, 511a
    ethics, IV 512a
    factories, IV 509a, 509b
    fear, IV 513a
    France, IV 510b, 514a
    Germany, IV 509a, 510a–510b, 512b, 514a
    Great Britain, IV 509a–514a
    Great Depression (1930s), IV 511b–512b
    Green, IV 509b
    Haldane, IV 511b
    Hansen, IV 513a
    happiness, IV 509a
    health, IV 509b–511a, 512a, 513b–515a
    hierarchy, IV 510a
    Hobson, IV 511a
    housing, IV 511b, 512a, 513b
    income, IV 512a–512b, 514b, 515a
    India, IV 513b
    individualism, IV 509b–

511a, 512b, 514b
    industry, IV 509a–510b, 511b, 512b, 514b
    insurance, IV 509b, 510a–510b, 511b, 512b, 513b, 514a
    International Labour Organization, IV 513a–514a
    justice, IV 509b, 512a
    Keynes, IV 512a, 513a
    labor, IV 510a, 510b, 512a–514a, 515a
    laissez-faire, IV 509b, 510a, 511a, 512a, 514b
    Lassalle, IV 509a
    law, IV 509a, 510a, 511a, 512a, 514a
    liberalism, IV 510a
    Lloyd George, IV 511b
    malnutrition, IV 511a, 512b
    Marshall, T. H., IV 513b
    Marxism-Leninism, IV 512b
    medicine, IV 510b
    morality, IV 509b, 512a, 514b
    Myrdal, IV 512a
    New Zealand, IV 510b, 512a, 512b
    Oastler, IV 509a–509b, 510a, 511a
    obligation, IV 511a
    order, IV 510a
    patriotism, IV 510a
    pensions, IV 510b, 511a
    philanthropy, III 492a–492b; IV 510b
    politics, IV 509a–512b, 514a–515a
    poverty, IV 509a, 509b, 510b, 512b, 513a, 514a
    power, IV 509b, 510a, 513b, 514b
    private property, IV 511a, 514b
    prosperity, IV 509a, 514a
    Reeves, IV 510b
    responsibility, IV 513a
    rights, IV 510a, 512a
    Roosevelt, IV 512a–512b
    Rowntree, IV 510b, 511a
    Ruskin, IV 509b
    savings, IV 509b
    Scandinavia, IV 512a, 514a
    self-help, IV 509b, 510b
    Senior, IV 509a–509b
    services, IV 509b, 510b, 512b–514a, 514b
    socialism, IV 510a, 510b–512a, 513b, 515a
    statistics, IV 510b, 511a
    status, IV 509a, 512b, 514b
    suffrage, IV 509b
    Sweden, IV 512a
    Temple, IV 514b

511a, 512b, 514b
Toynbee, IV 509b
trade, IV 509b
Titmuss, IV 513a, 515a
unemployment, IV 509b, 510a, 510b, 511b–512a, 512b, 513a, 514a, 514b
U.S.S.R., IV 512b
unions, IV 509b–510b
U.S., IV 511b–514a
Viner, IV 515a
voluntarism, IV 509b
voluntary organizations, IV 509b
vox populi, IV 499b
wages, IV 509b, 510b, 511b, 512a–512b
wealth, IV 512a, 512b
Webb, Beatrice, IV 510b–511a
work, IV 510a, 512a, 513a, 514b
working day, IV 510b
World War I, IV 511b
World War II, IV 512b–513a
Wellcome, Henry (1854–1936), philanthropy, III 492a
Wellek, René
    evolution of literature, II 173b–174a
    expressionism, II 206a
    genius, II 304b, 307a
    romanticism, IV 195b–196a, 198b, 208b
Welles, Orson (1915–   ), cosmic voyages, I 534b
Wellhausen, Julius (1844–1918), modernism, I 419b
Wellington, Arthur W. (1st Duke of) (1769–1852), conservatism, I 477b
Wells, Herbert George (1866–1946)
    China, I 371b
    cosmic voyages, I 526a, 534b
    entropy, II 116a
    hierarchy, II 448a
    perfectibility, III 474b, 475a
    society, II 621b
    Utopia, IV 464a
Wells, S. B.
    phrenology, IV 23b
    psychology, IV 23b
Welsh language, III 63a
Welsted, Leonard, periodization in literary history, III 483a
Weltanschauung
    constituents of, III 208b
    heresy, II 419a
    ideology, II 555a
    imagination, III 208b, 219b

metaphor, **III** 198a, 199a
post-Kantianism, **IV** 209a
religion, **IV** 93b
romanticism, **IV** 198b, 208a, 209a

Weltschmerz
Baudelaire, **IV** 209b
Byron, **IV** 204a, 209b
Delacroix, **IV** 204a
evil, **IV** 209b
France, **IV** 204a
French Revolution (1789), **IV** 204a
Germany, **IV** 204a
Kleist, **IV** 209b
Leopardi, **IV** 204a, 209b
Lermontov, **IV** 209b
melancholy, **IV** 204a
Musset, **IV** 204a
Novalis, **IV** 209b
philosophy, **IV** 204a
romanticism, **IV** 204a, 209b
Schopenhauer, **IV** 204a, 209b
Tieck, **IV** 209b
Vigny, **IV** 204a

Werckmeister, Andreas, music, **III** 267a
Werner, Abraham Gottlob (1750–1817), uniformitarianism, **IV** 418b, 419b, 420a, 420b
Werner, Johann, mathematics, **III** 178b
Werner, Zacharias (1768–1823), romanticism, **IV** 189a
Wertheimer, M. (1880–1943)
positivism, **III** 549a
psychology, **IV** 14b
Wesley, Charles (1707–1788), Saint Alphonsus of Liguori and, **I** 263a–263b
Wesley, John (1703–1791)
attitude toward antiquity, **I** 85b
authority, **I** 401b
Chain of Being, **II** 446b
hierarchy, **II** 446b
Moravians, **I** 403a
pain, **III** 468a
perfectibility, **III** 468a
Pietism, **III** 493b
reformation, **IV** 68b
Saint Alphonsus of Liguori and, **I** 263a–263b
sin, **III** 468a
usury, **I** 396b–397a
Wesley, Samuel (1662–1735), cosmic voyages, **I** 528a
Wessel, C., numbers, **III** 405b
West, Benjamin (1738–1820), neo-classicism in art, **III** 368b, 369a

West, Nathanael (1903–1940), satire, **IV** 221b, 215a
West, R. B., organicism, **III** 426b
West Germany
Constitution, **I** 491a
constitutionalism, **I** 491a
Marxism, **III** 166b
Westermarck, Edward (1862–1939)
good, **IV** 184a
progress, **III** 645a, 645b
relativism, **IV** 71a
right, **IV** 184a
Westlake, John, international peace, **III** 451a
Westphalia, Treaty of, balance of power, **I** 184a
Wetter, Johannes, Gothic, **II** 373a
Weyer, John, witchcraft, **IV** 522b
Weyl, Hermann (1885–1955)
cosmology, **I** 562b
relativity, **IV** 90b–91a
symmetry, **IV** 347b, 348b
time, **IV** 398a
Whewell, William (1794–1866)
axiomatization, **I** 166a
Bacon and, **I** 178a
catastrophism, **IV** 419a, 420b
certainty, **I** 318b
linguistics, **IV** 423b
matnematics, **III** 179a
uniformitarianism, **IV** 418a, 420b, 423b
Whichcote, Benjamin (1609–1683)
Neo-Platonism, **III** 506a
Platonism, **III** 506b, 515a
Whistler, James A. McNeill (1834–1903)
art for art's sake, **I** 109b, 110a
chance images, **I** 351a–352a
impressionism, **II** 567b, 569a, 569b, 570b, 573a, 579a–579b
Whiston, William (1667–1752), virtuoso, **IV** 489b
White, Helen C., baroque in literature, **I** 193b
White, L. A., evolutionism, **II** 187a
Whitehead, Alfred North (1861–1947)
abstraction, **I** 8a
antinomy of pure reason, **I** 92b
axiomatization, **I** 168b
causation, **I** 278a

cosmic images, **I** 513b
continuity, **I** 502b
Creation, **I** 576a
design argument, **I** 677a
evolutionism, **II** 186a
God, **I** 576a; **II** 359a, 360a, 362a
infinity, **II** 611b
Marxism, **III** 150a
mathematics, **III** 176a, 176b
matter, **III** 194a
metaphor, **III** 207a
Newton and, **III** 397b, 398a
Peirce and, **III** 561a
perennial philosophy, **III** 463a
Plato and, **III** 501b
Platonism, **III** 502b, 515a, 522b
positivism, **III** 545b, 547b, 548a
Pythagorean cosmos, **IV** 42a
religion, **III** 207a; **IV** 97b, 105a
time, **IV** 391b, 396b, 397b
war, **IV** 504a
Zeitgeist, **IV** 536b
Whitelocke, Bulstrode (1605–1675), deism, **I** 649b
Whitman, Walt (1819–1892)
individualism, **II** 596a
mythology, **III** 306b
nationalism, **III** 329a
organicism, **III** 426b
pragmatism, **III** 553b
psychology, **IV** 23b, 24a
romanticism, **IV** 208b
symbolism, **IV** 341b
theriophily, **IV** 388b
transcendentalism, **IV** 24a
Volksgeist, **IV** 494b, 495a
Whitney, Geoffrey, mythology, **III** 296a
Whitney, Lois, Enlightenment, **II** 99a
Whitney, William Dwight (1827–1894)
linguistics, **IV** 425a, 426b, 427b
Orientalism, **III** 434b
Whitrow, G. J., time, **IV** 397a
Whittaker, Edmund Taylor (1873–1956)
classification of the sciences, **I** 465a
Einstein and, **IV** 79b–80a
relativity, **IV** 79b–80a
Whore of Babylon, mythology, **III** 282a
Whorf, B. L. (1897–1941), linguistics, **III** 71b
Wickham, Anna, symmetry, **IV** 347b

Wickhoff, Franz, naturalism in art, **III** 339b
Wicksell, Knut, social welfare, **IV** 283a
Wicksteed, P. H.
economic history, **II** 50b
social welfare, **IV** 283a
Widengren, G., mythology, **III** 311b
Widmann, Josef Viktor (1842–1911), Buddhism, **I** 256b
Wieland, Christoph Martin (1733–1813)
classicism, **I** 453a–453b
genius, **II** 295a
ideal, **II** 550b, 551a, 551b
Platonism, **III** 516a, 523b
Wieman, H. N., God, **II** 362a
Wiene, Robert, Gothic, **II** 372b
Wiener, Norbert (1874–1964)
computers, **III** 32b
cybernetic theory, **II** 126a
environment, **II** 126a
milieu intérieur concept, **II** 126a
Wiener, Philip P.
Buddhism, **I** 256a
pragmatism, **III** 551a–570b
Wigner, Eugene P., symmetry, **IV** 352b, 353a
Wilamowitz-Moellendorff, Ulrich von (1848–1931)
baroque in literature, **I** 189a
catharsis, **I** 269a
Wilberforce, Bishop Samuel (1805–1873)
Darwinism, **IV** 107a
religion, **IV** 107a
Wild, Friedrich, baroque in literature, **I** 191a
Wilde, Oscar (1854–1900)
art for art's sake, **I** 109b
literary criticism, **I** 601b–602a, 605a, 606a
longevity, **III** 89b
motif, **III** 238a
organicism, **III** 424a
Utopia, **IV** 464a
Wildman, Major John, deism, **I** 649b
Wilhelm, Richard (1873–1930), China, **I** 369b
Wilhelm I, Emperor (1797–1888), periodization in literary history, **III** 483a
Wilhelm II, Emperor (1859–1941), China, **I** 370b
Wilhelm V, Duke (Bavaria) musical genius, **II** 320a
Wilkes, John (1727–1797), despotism, **II** 12b
Wilkins, Charles (1749?–1836)
mythology, **III** 305b

Orientalism, III 429b
transcendentalism, III 429b
Wilkins, John (1614–1672)
  Aristotle and, I 310a
  Bacon and, I 176b, 510a
  certainty, I 304b, 308a–
    310a, 311a
  cosmic voyages, I 525a,
    528a–530a, 531b, 532b
  God, I 309a
  hierarchy, II 443b
  language, I 327b; II 668a–
    669a
  Leibniz and, II 668b–669a
  linguistics, III 74b, 75a
  skepticism, I 308a–310a,
    311a; IV 245b
  truth, I 310a; II 443b
Will
  Calvinism, III 654a
  Descartes, II 381a
  dignity, IV 138b, 142b
  Edwards, IV 109b, 110a
  evolutionism, II 182b
  Faust (legend), III 250a
  God, II 230a, 230b, 234a
  good, IV 173b, 182b
  happiness, II 379b, 380b,
    381a
  health, II 400b
  heresy, II 425a
  historicism, II 463a
  historiography, II 480b
  imagination, III 208b, 213b
  individualism, II 598b, 600a
  irrationalism, II 636a
  Machiavellism, III 119a
  mythology, III 310a
  natural law, III 18a
  private property, III 654a
  psychology, IV 8a, 10b,
    17a, 19b, 20a, 22b, 23a,
    24b, 27b
  religion, IV 109b, 110a,
    112b
  Renaissance, IV 138b,
    142b
  right, IV 173b
  romanticism, IV 204b
  Rousseau, IV 259b, 260a
  Saint Augustine, III 18a;
    IV 138b
  Schopenhauer, II 182b; IV
    202b
  social contract, IV 259b,
    260a
  See also Free Will
Will to believe
  James, III 552b, 561b, 562a,
    562b, 563a
  Lovejoy, III 552b
  Papini, III 563b
  Peirce, III 562b
  pragmatism, III 552b, 561a–

563a, 563b, 565b
Sorel, III 565b
Wright, Chauncey, III 562b
Willaert, Adrian (1480?–1562)
  musical genius, II 320a
William, N. P., Cosmic Fall, I
  512b
William of Auvergne (1180?–
  1299), Islam, II 646a
William of Auxerre, natural
  law, III 18a
William of Conches
  Chain of Being, I 326b
  dignity, IV 140a
William of Heytesbury,
  medieval science, II 200b,
  204a
William of Malmesbury (1090
  and 1096–?1143), historiography, II 473b, 478b–479a
William of Moerbeke
  despotism, II 3a, 4a
  poetics, III 528a
William of St. Amour, prophecy, III 668a
William of St. Thierry, dignity,
  IV 140a
William of Tyre (1130?–
  ?1190), historiography, II
  474a
William I, King (1027–1087)
  common law, II 693b
  iconography, II 528a
  nationalism, III 319b
William III, King (1650–
  1702), social contract, IV
  258a
William IV, Duke, reformation,
  IV 63b–64a
William IV, King (1765–
  1837), periodization in
  literary history, III 482b
William IX of Poitiers, Count-
  Duke, love, III 98a, 99a–
  99b, 100a, 102a
Williams, Bishop John (1817–
  1899), equity, II 152a–
  152b
Williams, Charles, witchcraft,
  IV 521a
Williams, Roger (1603?–
  1683), Puritanism, IV 18b
Williams, Samúel Wells
  (1812–1884), China, I
  367b
Williams, T. Harry, Machiavel-
  lism, III 124a
Williams, William Carlos
  (1883–1963)
  ut pictura poesis, IV 469b
Williamson, George (1858–
  1942), baroque in literature,
  I 193b
Wills

common law, II 691a
  law, II 686b; III 2b
  Rome (ancient), II 686b
Wilson, A. I., mythology, III
  306a
Wilson, Edmund (1895–1972)
  Gauss and, IV 341b
  Huneker and, IV 341b
  symbolism, IV 341a–341b
Wilson, Edmund B. (1856–
  1939)
  biology, I 239b
  chromosomes, II 286b–
  287a
Wilson, E. O., biology, I 241a
Wilson, F. P., baroque in
  literature, I 193a
Wilson, Horace H. (1786–
  1860)
  Orientalism, III 429b
  transcendentalism, III 429b
Wilson, James (1742–1798)
  democracy, I 660b
  freedom of speech, II 254a
  peace, II 444b
Wilson, R. W., cosmology, I
  567a
Wilson, Woodrow (1856–
  1924)
  balance of power, I 187a
  Germany and, I 665a
  loyalty, III 113a
  Machiavellism, III 124a
  State, I 665a
Wimsatt, William K., literary
  criticism, I 603b
Winch, P., ethics, IV 72b
Winckelmann, Johann
  Joachim (1717–1768)
  aesthetics, II 218b, 550a;
    IV 124b
  Albani, III 366b
  architecture, III 367b
  Aristotle and, III 365b, 366a
  art, II 297b; III 367a
  attitude toward antiquity, I
    87a
  beauty, I 200b; II 550a
    550b; III 367b
  classicism, III 367a–367b
  dichotomy, III 368a
  Enlightenment, II 89b; III
    343a
  evolution of literature, II
    170a
  genius, II 297b
  Greece (ancient), III 367a
  historicism, II 459a
  historiography, II 489b
  homosexuality, III 368a
  iconography, II 533a
  ideal, II 550a, 550b, 551a
  Klopstock and, II 550b
  mimesis, III 229b

mythology, III 304a, 304b
  naturalism in art, III 343a
  neo-classicism in art, III
    365b–368b
  Platonism, III 519a
  Richardson and, III 367b
  Shaftesbury and, III 367b
  symbolism, IV 338a
  symmetry, IV 347a
  ut pictura poesis, IV 469b,
    474a
Winckler, Hugo (1863–1913)
  mythology, III 310a
Wind, Edgar, iconography, II
  538a
Windelband, Wilhelm (1848–
  1915)
  historiography, II 496a
  Nature, III 351a
Winstanley, Gerrard (1609–
  1652)
  class, I 442a–442b
  deism, I 649b
  equality, II 143a
  radicalism, I 479b
  socialism, IV 287a, 287b
  Utopia, IV 462a
Winteler, Jost (1846–1929),
  linguistics, III 70a, 70b
Winters, Yvor, literary criticism, I 603a, 603b
Winthrop, John (1588–1649)
  psychology, IV 16b, 18b
  Puritanism, IV 16b, 18b
Wireker, Nigel, wisdom of the
  fool, IV 518a
Wirth, A. K., iconography, II
  537b
Wisdom
  Aristotle, IV 49b, 175b
  catharsis, I 267b–268a
  Counter-Enlightenment, II
    101a, 108a
  Cronus (myth), I 612a
  Democritus, III 576b
  equality, II 139a
  evil, IV 412b
  freedom of speech, II 256b
  Gnosticism, II 328b, 329b
  God, II 347a; IV 379a,
    380b, 517a, 517b
  good, IV 174b, 175b, 184b
  happiness, II 378b
  health, II 399a
  Heraclitus, III 14b
  Herder, III 304b
  hermeticism, II 431a, 431b
  human nature, III 572a,
    576b, 577a, 643b
  humanism, II 519a; IV 129b,
    132a, 133b
  ignorance, IV 174b, 517a,
    517b, 519b
  Islam, II 650a–650b

Kant, IV 382b, 383a
knowledge, II 650a–650b
law, III 27b
Leibniz, IV 379a, 382a
Locke, III 598b
loyalty, III 110a
microcosm, III 127a
millenarianism, III 223b
mimesis, III 227a
motif, III 239b
mythology, III 278b, 286b, 299b–300a, 302b, 303b, 304b, 314b, 524b
natural law, III 14b, 15a
Nature, III 347a, 349a
Nicholas of Cusa, III 510b
perennial philosophy, III 457a, 457b, 459a–460a
perfectibility, III 643b
Petrarch, IV 519b
Pico della Mirandola, IV 132a
Plato, I 612a; III 110a, 501b; IV 4a, 368b
Platonism, III 501b, 506a, 510b, 512a, 517a, 524b
primitivism, III 598b
progress, III 632b, 638a, 643b
prophecy, III 667a
psychology, IV 4a
rationalism, IV 46a, 49b
Renaissance, IV 122a, 127b, 129b, 132a, 133b
right, IV 174b, 175b, 184b
romanticism, III 303b, 304b
Saint Paul, IV 416a, 517a
skepticism, IV 238b
Socrates, III 577a; IV 174b, 517a
Spinoza, I 636b
Stoicism, IV 320b
suffering, IV 413b
temperance, IV 366b, 368a, 368b, 371a
theodicy, IV 379a, 380b, 382a, 382b, 383a
tragic sense, IV 412b, 413b, 414b, 416a
unity of science, IV 431a
virtue, IV 366b, 368b, 371a
wisdom of the fool, IV 515b–520b
Wisdom, John, imagination, III 220b
Wisdom of the fool, IV 515b–520b
Aeschylus, IV 517a
Agrippa, IV 519b
Alberti, IV 519b
Ariosto, IV 519b
art, IV 519b
artificial (professional) fool, IV 516b–517a

Athenaeus, IV 516b
authentic (natural) fool, IV 516b
authority, IV 516b
Bible, IV 517a–518a, 519a
Cervantes, IV 519b, 520a
children, IV 516a
Christianity, IV 516b–518b
dignity, IV 519b
Dostoevsky, IV 520a
education, IV 517a
empiricism, IV 515b
Epicurus, IV 518b
Erasmus, IV 518a–519b
Erigena, IV 517b
etymology, IV 515b–516a
experience, IV 519a
Fête des Fous, IV 516b, 519b
Folengo, IV 519b
François I, IV 516b
freedom, IV 516a, 516b
Freudianism, IV 516a
God, IV 516a, 517a, 517b, 518a
Greece (ancient), IV 516b, 517a
Gregory I (the Great), Pope, IV 517b
Grimmelshausen, IV 520a
happiness, IV 516a
Hauptmann, IV 520a
Heraclitus, IV 517a
Heywood, IV 520a
Holbein, IV 519b
Horace, IV 517a
human nature, IV 518b, 519a
humanism, IV 518b, 519b
id, IV 516a, 516b
ignorance, IV 517a, 517b, 519b
instinct, IV 516a, 518b
intuition, IV 516a
irony, IV 518b, 519a
irrationalism, IV 515b
Jacopone da Todi, IV 517b
Jesus Christ, IV 517a–517b, 519a–519b
Jonson, IV 519b–520a
judgment, IV 519a
knowledge, IV 515b, 517a, 517b, 519a
learning, IV 515b, 517a, 518a, 519a, 520a
literature, IV 515b, 516a, 517a, 517b–520a
love, IV 519a
Lucian, IV 516b, 519b
Lull, IV 517b
Luther, IV 518b
Lydgate, IV 518a
Melville, IV 517b
memory, IV 516a

Middle Ages, IV 516a, 516b, 517b–518a, 519b
Middleton, IV 520a
Molière, IV 520a
Montaigne, IV 517b, 519b
More, Thomas, IV 516b, 519b
Murner, IV 519b
mysticism, IV 517b
naturalism, IV 518b
Nicholas of Cusa, IV 517b, 519a
oxymoron, IV 517a, 518b
painting, IV 519b
passions, IV 519a
Petrarch, IV 519b
phallic symbols, IV 516a
piety, IV 518b
Plautus, IV 516b
pleasure, IV 516a, 518a, 518b, 519a
primitivism, IV 515b
privilege, IV 516a
proverbs, IV 515b
psychology, IV 516a
Rabelais, IV 519b
rationalism, IV 515b–516b
reason, IV 515b, 517b, 519a
Renaissance, IV 515b, 516b, 518a–520a
responsibility, IV 516a
Rome (ancient), IV 516b, 517a
Sachs, IV 519b
Saint Francis of Assisi, IV 517b
Saint Jerome, IV 518a
Saint Paul, IV 517a, 518a, 519a
salvation, IV 518a
Sanchez, IV 519b
self-love, IV 519a
senses, IV 516a
Shakespeare, IV 519b, 520a
sin, IV 518a
Skelton, IV 519b
Sociétés Joyeuses, IV 516b
society, IV 515b, 516a–516b, 518a
Socrates, IV 517a, 517b
Sophocles, IV 519a
Stoicism, IV 518b
superego, IV 516a–516b
Swift, IV 520a
theater, IV 519b–520a
Thomas à Kempis, IV 517b
truth, IV 515b, 516b, 518a, 519a
vice, IV 518a
virtue, IV 518a, 519a
Wireker, IV 518a
Xenophon, IV 516b
Yeats, IV 520a

Wise, John (1652–1725)
Puritanism, IV 19a
psychology, IV 19a
Witchcraft, IV 521a–523a
Adam (Bible), IV 521b
Africa, IV 521a, 523a
Alexander IV (Pope), IV 522a
angels, IV 521b, 523a
anthropology, IV 522b
art, IV 522b
Bible, IV 521a–522b
blacks, IV 523a
Bodin, IV 522a
Burns, IV 522b
Calvinism, IV 522b
causation, IV 521a
charms, IV 521b
Christianity, IV 521a–523a
common sense, IV 522b
crime, IV 521a, 522a, 522b
curse, IV 521b
death, IV 521a, 522a, 522b
Del Rio, IV 522a
demonology, IV 521a–522b
Diana (myth), IV 521a, 521b
disease, IV 523a
divination, IV 521a
dualism, IV 521b–523a
effect, IV 521a
Egypt (ancient), IV 521a
Ennemoser, IV 522b
evil, IV 521a, 521b, 522b, 523a
evil eye, IV 521b
Faust (legend), III 245b, 246b
France, IV 522b
Frederick II, IV 522a
folklore, IV 521a, 521b, 522b
Germany, IV 521a
God, IV 521a–523a
good, IV 521a, 523a
Goya, IV 522b
Great Britain, IV 522b
Greece (ancient), IV 521a
Hecate (myth), IV 521a
hell, IV 522a
heresy, II 426b–427a; IV 521a, 521b, 522a, 522b
Hibbert, IV 523a
history, IV 522b
idolatry, IV 521a
infidelism, IV 521a–522a
Innocent III (Pope), IV 522a
Inquisition, IV 531b, 522a, 522b
Jesus Christ, IV 521b
Judaism, IV 521a
justice, IV 522b
law, IV 521a, 522a

Lea, IV 522a, 522b
Lecky, IV 522b
literature, IV 522b
Luther, IV 522a–522b
magic, IV 521a
Melville, IV 522b
Middle Ages, IV 522b, 523a
monotheism, IV 521a
motif, III 239a
music, III 264b, 265a, 267a
Nature, IV 522a, 522b
night-riding, IV 501b
paganism, IV 521b
Platonism, III 506a
polytheism, IV 521a
power, IV 521a, 521b, 522a, 522b
Protestantism, IV 521b
psychologists, IV 523a
psychology, IV 18b
Puritanism, IV 18b
rationalism, IV 522b, 523a
reason, IV 522b
Regino of Prüm, IV 521a–521b
religion, IV 521a, 522b
Renaissance, II 426b–427a
Roman Catholic Church, IV 521a, 521b, 522a
romanticism, IV 522b
Rome (ancient), IV 521a
Sabbat, IV 522b
Saint Augustine, IV 521a, 522a
Salazar y Frias, IV 522b
Satan, IV 521a–522b
scholasticism, IV 521a, 521b
science, IV 522b
Scott, IV 522b
skepticism, IV 522b
society, IV 521a
sorcery, IV 521a–522a
soul, IV 522a
Spain, IV 522b
Sprenger, IV 521b
State, IV 522a
superstition, IV 521a, 522a
Switzerland, IV 522b
theology, IV 522a, 523a
treason, IV 522a
witches, IV 521a–522b
Witelo, Islam, II 647a
Wither, George (1588–1667)
  harmony, II 388b, 392a, 394a
Witkiewicz, Stanislaw I., aesthetics, II 219a
Wittkower, R., iconography, II 538b
Wittenberger Reformation (1545), Reformation, IV 66b
Wittfogel, Karl, China, I 372b

Wittgenstein, Ludwig (1889–1951)
  anthropomorphism, I 90a
  axiomatization, I 169a
  certainty, I 320a, 321b–322a
  ethics, IV 184a
  imagination, III 220b
  individualism, II 603b
  language, I 322a
  literary criticism, I 602b
  Man-Machine, III 145a
  mathematics, I 320a
  metaphor, III 200a, 200b, 207a
  nature of universals, I 237b
  philosophy, III 200a, 200b
  positivism, III 545b, 546b, 548a, 549b, 550b
  religion, III 207a
  Russell and, I 320a, 321b–322a
  space, IV 304b–305a
Wizards, III 657b
Wöhler, Friedrich (1800–1882), spontaneous generation, II 283b
Wolf, Erik, natural law, III 14a
Wolf, Friedrich August (1759–1824)
  aesthetics, IV 124b
  historicism, II 459a
  historiography, II 491a–491b
  mythology, III 304a
  periodization in literary history, III 482a
Wolf, Julius (1862–1935)
  economics, III 162a
  Marxism, III 162a
Wolfenstein, Martha, happiness and pleasure, II 385b
Wolff, Christian von (1679–1754)
  axiomatization, I 165b
  causation, I 290b
  cells, II 285b
  China, I 361a–361b
  dualism, II 38a
  equality, III 11b
  genetic continuity, II 285b
  genius, II 295a
  God, II 353a
  Hegel and, II 414a
  law, I 290b; III 11b
  metaphysics, II 414a
  Nature, III 11b
  natural law, III 20b
  Orientalism, III 428a
  pain, II 381a
  perennial philosophy, III 461b

Pietism, I 361b
  pleasure, II 381a
  psychology, IV 11b, 20a
  symbolism, IV 338a
  theodicy, IV 379a
  truth, I 315b
Wolff, Hans, Platonism, III 504a–504b
Wolff, Kaspar Friedrich (1733–1794)
  antinomy of pure reason, I 91b
  evolutionism, II 178a
Wölfflin, Heinrich (1864–1945)
  aesthetics, II 223b
  baroque in literature, I 189a, 189b, 190a, 191a, 191b, 192b, 193b
  classicism, I 451a
  cosmic images, I 513b
  genius, II 297b
  naturalism in art, III 339b
  periodization in history, III 479b
  romanticism, IV 197a
Wolfson, H. A., Gnosticism, II 329b, 330b
Wollaston, William Hyde (1766–1828)
  mathematics, III 179a
  optics, III 419b
Woltmann, Ludwig
  Marxism, III 163a
  revisionism, IV 269b
Wolzogen, Hans von (1848–1938)
  motif, III 236a
  Wagner and, III 236a
Women, IV 523a–530a
  Adam (Bible), III 596b
  androcentrism, IV 524a, 524b, 525b, 527a
  Anthony, IV 526b
  anthropology, IV 523b, 525b
  anti-feminity, IV 524a
  anti-slavery, IV 529a
  Aristotelianism, IV 525a, 525b
  Aristotle, IV 525a
  art, III 596b
  Barth, IV 528a
  Beauvoir, IV 523b, 529a
  behavior, III 596b
  Benedict XV (Pope), IV 526b
  Bible, IV 523b–524b, 525b, 526b
  biology, IV 523b, 525b
  blacks, IV 529a
  Blanche of Castille, IV 525b
  Blanche of Navarre, IV 525b
  Bonhoeffer, IV 528a

Catt, IV 526b
  Christianity, IV 524a, 524b, 525a, 526b
  Christine de Pisan, IV 526a
  Cleveland, IV 526b
  Clotilde, IV 525b
  Comte, IV 526b
  Condorcet, IV 526a
  conservatism, IV 528a, 529b
  creativity, IV 523a
  culture, IV 523a, 523b, 524a
  deification of, II 331b–333b
  Diderot, IV 526a
  discrimination, IV 528b, 529a, 529b
  divorce, IV 526b
  economics, III 596b; IV 523a, 523b, 524b
  education, IV 490a, 490b, 523b, 524b, 525a, 526a, 527a, 528a
  Eleanor of Aquitaine, IV 525b
  Elyot, IV 526a
  emancipation, III 596b; IV 526a, 526b, 527a
  Engels, IV 529b
  equality, IV 524b, 525b, 526b–529a
  Erasmus of Rotterdam, IV 526a
  Eve (Bible), III 596b; IV 524a, 524b
  evil, III 596b
  Fall, IV 524a
  feminine mystique, IV 523a
  feminism, IV 523b, 524b, 526a, 526b, 528a, 529a, 529b
  feudalism, IV 525b
  France, IV 526a, 528a
  freedom of speech, II 255a, 256a
  Freud, IV 528a
  Friedan, IV 529a
  Germany, IV 528a
  God, III 596b; IV 524a–525b, 526b, 527b
  Godwin, IV 526a, 526b
  Great Britain, IV 526a, 528a
  Greece (ancient), IV 524a
  Hegel, IV 526b
  Helvétius, IV 526a
  heresy, IV 526a
  historians, IV 529a
  humanism, IV 526a
  hypocrisy, IV 526a
  ideology, IV 527b, 528a
  industry, IV 529a
  inferiority, IV 524a, 525a, 526b
  infidelity, IV 523a

intuition, III 596b
Jesuits, IV 526a
Jesus Christ, III 596b; IV 524b
John XXIII (Pope), IV 527b
Judaism, IV 523b–524a
labor, IV 529a
law, II 686b; IV 524b, 526a, 528a, 528b, 529a
Leo XIII (Pope), IV 526b
literature, IV 523a–524a
Luther, IV 528a
McCarthy, IV 528b
Machiavelli, IV 483a
marriage, IV 523b, 525b, 526b, 527b
Marx, IV 528a
masculinity, IV 523b
Mead, IV 523b
Mercier, IV 526a
Middle Ages, IV 525a, 525b–526a
Mill, IV 526b, 528a
misogynism, IV 524a
Molière, IV 526a
monasteries, IV 525b
morality, IV 523b, 524a
More, Thomas, IV 526a
motherhood, IV 523b, 524b, 527b
mythology, III 278b; IV 524a
Napoleonic Code, IV 526a
National Organization for Women, IV 528b–529b
New Left, IV 529b
nunneries, IV 525b
oppression, IV 526a
Peter the Lombard, IV 525a
philosophers, IV 526b, 528a
Pius XI (Pope), IV 527a
Pius XII (Pope), IV 527a–527b
Plato, III 501a
Platonism, III 501a, 510a
politics, III 596b; IV 523a, 523b, 526a, 528a–529b
Poulain de la Barre, IV 526a
primitivism, III 596a–596b
professions, IV 528b, 529a
progress, III 636b
Protestantism, IV 528a
psychology, IV 523b
race, IV 529a–529b
radicalism, IV 529b
Reik, IV 524a
religion, IV 526b–528a, 529a
romanticism, III 596a–596b
Rome (ancient), II 686b
Renaissance, IV 526a
reproduction, IV 525a
revolution, IV 529b
rights, IV 526b, 527b, 528b

Roman Catholic Church, IV 524b, 525b, 526a–528a
Rossi, IV 529a, 529b
Saint Augustine, IV 524b
Saint Catherine of Siena, IV 525b
Saint Joan of Arc, IV 525b
Saint Paul, IV 524a–524b, 525b
Saint Teresa, IV 526a
Saint Thomas Aquinas, IV 525a–525b
saints, IV 525b
science, IV 525b, 528a
senses, IV 525a
sex, IV 524a, 527b
slavery, IV 523b
social welfare, IV 529a
society, IV 523a–529b
sociologists, IV 529a, 529b
soul, IV 525b
Stanton, IV 526b
State, IV 529a
stereotypes, IV 523a, 523b, 527b, 528a
Stone, IV 526b
structuralism, IV 325b–326a
subordination, IV 524a–524b, 525a
suffrage, III 432a; IV 526b–529a
Tertullian, IV 524b
theology, IV 524a, 525a, 527b
tragedy, III 501a
U.S.S.R., IV 528a
U.N., IV 528a
U.S., IV 526b, 528a–529b
U.S. Supreme Court, IV 528a
universe, IV 525a
Victoria, IV 526b
Victorians, IV 219b
Virgin Mary, III 596b
virtuosa, IV 486b, 488a–490a
Voltaire, IV 526a
vox populi, IV 497a, 499a
Ward, IV 526a
wealth, IV 525b
Women's Liberation Movement, IV 529b
work, IV 532b
World War II, IV 528b, 529b
Women's Liberation Movement, IV 529b
Wood, Antony à (1632–1695), cosmic voyages, I 527a
Wood, James, beauty, I 209a
Wood, Robert, mythology, III 304a
Woodger, J. H., positivism, III 550b

Woodward, William Harrison
   education, II 83a
   universal man, IV 438b, 439a
Woolf, Virginia (1882–1941),
   realism in literature, IV 55a
   symbolism, IV 343a
Woolman, John (1720–1772)
   pragmatism, III 553b
   psychology, IV 20a–20b
   Quakers, IV 20a–20b
Woolston, Thomas (1670–1733), deism, I 650b–651a
Words
   language, II 662b–663a, 666a, 670b
   literature, III 241b; IV 330b, 332a
   magic, I 43b
   motif, III 241b
   numbers, III 399b, 400a, 400b, 402a, 403a, 403b, 404a, 404b, 406b
   Shakespeare, III 241b
Wordsworth, William (1770–1850)
   alienation, I 36b
   appearance and reality, I 96b–97a, 98a, 98b
   art for art's sake, I 109a
   baroque in literature, I 191a
   Burnet and, III 259a
   children, III 596a
   Counter-Enlightenment, II 108b
   health, II 403b
   Hermeticism, II 433a
   idea, II 543a
   immortality, III 508a
   literature, IV 332b
   Macaulay and, IV 194b
   mountains in literature, III 259a, 259b–260a
   mythology, III 306b
   Nature, III 259b, 260a, 349a–349b, 351a
   peasantry, III 595a
   periodization in literary history, III 485b
   Platonism, III 507b–508a, 524a
   power of mountains, III 260a
   primitivism, III 595a, 596a
   romanticism, III 508a; IV 193a, 194a, 194b, 195a, 198b, 200a, 201a, 201b, 208b
   Schelling and, IV 201a
   style, IV 332b
   vox populi, IV 499a
Work, IV 530a–535b
   aesthetics, IV 533b
   Adam (Bible), IV 531a

Alberti, IV 532a
Alcuin, IV 531b
angels, IV 533b
Antiphon, IV 530b
aristocracy, IV 530b
Aristotle, IV 530b
asceticism, IV 531b
Augustinianism, IV 533a
authority, IV 534b
Bacon, IV 533b, 534a
becoming, IV 534a
Bede, IV 531b
Bible, IV 531a–531b
Boethius, IV 531b
Bruno, IV 532a
Calvin, IV 533a
Campanella, IV 532a, 532b
capitalism, IV 533a
Cassiodorus, IV 532a
Christianity, IV 531a–531b, 532b–533b
class, IV 534a, 534b
commodities, IV 532b, 533a, 534a, 535a
Comte, IV 534b
creativity, IV 532b
dignity, IV 136b, 531a, 532a, 533b, 534b
discipline, IV 531b, 532a
dualism, IV 530b, 532a
economics, IV 531a, 534a
education, IV 531b, 532b
Enlightenment, IV 534a
epistemology, IV 533b
equality, IV 532b
ethics, IV 533b, 534b
evil, IV 534b
experience, IV 533b
faith, IV 531a
Feuerbach, IV 534b
Fichte, IV 534a
Ficino, IV 532a, 532b
Franklin, IV 534a
free will, IV 532a, 532b, 533b, 534a
freedom, IV 531b, 532a
Galileo, IV 533b
God, IV 530b–534a
good, IV 174a, 176a, 177a
grace, IV 533a
Greece (ancient), IV 530a–531a
happiness, II 385a, 385b; IV 530b
health, IV 395b, 403a
Hegel, IV 534a, 534b
Heidegger, IV 535a
heresy, II 420a
hierarchy, IV 534b
history, IV 534a, 535a
human nature, IV 532b
humanism, IV 134b, 135a, 532a

Hume, IV 534b
Isidore of Seville, IV 531b
Jesus Christ, IV 531a–531b
Judaism, IV 531a
judgment, IV 533b
knowledge, IV 530b, 531b, 533b, 534a
learning, IV 530b, 531b, 532a, 532b
leisure, IV 532b
Leonardo da Vinci, IV 532a, 533b, 534a
love, IV 531b
Luther, IV 532b–533a
Marcuse, IV 535a
Martianus Capella, IV 531b
Marx, IV 291b, 534a–534b
Mazzini, IV 534b
methodology, IV 533b
Middle Ages, IV 531b
mind, IV 532a, 534a
Mondolfo, IV 530b
morality, IV 532b
mythology, III 278b, 279b
Nature, IV 532a, 533b, 534b
necessity, IV 534a, 534b
Palmieri, IV 532a
philosophy, IV 531b, 533a–533b
Pico della Mirandola, IV 532a
Plato, IV 530b
pleasure, II 374b; IV 533b
poverty, IV 531b
power, IV 531b, 533a–533b
predestination, IV 533a
private property, IV 534a, 534b
Prodicus of Chios, IV 530b
production, IV 533a, 534a, 535a
progress, IV 532a, 532b, 534a
prophecy, IV 531a
Protestantism, IV 532b–533a
psychology, IV 533a
Rabanus Maurus, IV 531b
reason, IV 531b, 532a
reformation, IV 63b
Reformation, IV 532b–533a
relativity, IV 82b
Renaissance, IV 134b 135a, 136b, 532a–534a
reward, IV 531a
right, IV 174a, 176a, 177a
Rousseau, IV 534b
Ruge, IV 534b
Saint Benedict, IV 531b
Saint Paul, IV 531a–531b
salvation, IV 531a

Scheler, IV 534b
science, IV 532b–534a
senses, IV 530b
sin, IV 531a, 532b
slavery, IV 530b, 532a
Smith, Adam, IV 534b
socialism, IV 285a, 287b, 291b, 293a, 534b
society, IV 530a, 530b, 532b, 533a, 534a–535a
sociology, IV 535a
Sophists, IV 530b
State, IV 534a
status, IV 531a
Strauss, D. F., IV 534b
technology, IV 533a–534b
thought, IV 530b, 532b
utilitarianism, IV 533b, 534b
value, IV 452a, 453a, 533b, 534a, 534b, 535a
virtue, IV 530b
Voltaire, IV 534b
wealth, IV 531b, 534a
Weber, IV 533a
welfare state, IV 510a, 512a, 513a, 514b
women, IV 532b
Xenophon, IV 530a–530b
Workingmen's Peace Association, III 448b
World Council of Churches, I 408b
World Court, III 449b
World Food Bank, I 371b
World Health Organization (U.N.), II 406a
World Peace Foundation, III 449a
World Spirit
alchemy, II 392b
Aristotle, II 392b
astrology, II 392b
demonology, II 393b–394a
God, II 392b
Greece (ancient), II 392a–392b
harmony, II 389a, 392a–395a
music, II 389a, 392a–395a
planets, II 392b
soul, II 392a–392b, 394a
stars, II 392b
Stoicism, II 392b
universe, II 392b, 394a
Volksgeist, IV 492b, 493b
World War I
balance of power, I 187a; III 332a
Christianity, I 407b
crisis in history, I 594b, 595b
dynasty, III 332a
Germanism, III 332a
Great Britain, IV 511b

Habsburgs, III 332a
hegemony, III 332a
historicism, II 461a, 461b
Hohenzollern, III 332a
international peace, III 449a, 449b, 450b, 452a, 453b–454a, 455a
loyalty, III 114a–114b
Marxism, III 149b, 150b–151a, 152a, 152b, 164a
nationalism, III 332a
Ottoman Empire, III 332a
periodization in history, III 479a
periodization in literary history, III 485b
progress, III 647a
protest movements, III 674a
psychology, IV 14b, 26b
republicanism, III 332a
revisionism, IV 268a, 271a, 271b, 272b–273a
revolution, IV 164a, 165a, 166a
Romanovs, III 332a
Russian Revolution (October 1917), III 332a
Slavism, III 332a
totalitarianism, IV 406a–407a, 408a
U.S., I 665a; III 114a–114b, 332a
war, III 449a, 449b, 450b, 452b, 453b–454a, 455a; IV 501a, 502b, 504a
welfare state, IV 511b
World War II
balance of power, I 187a
civil disobedience, I 435a
crisis in history, I 595b
Faust (legend), III 252a
Great Britain, IV 512b
historicism, II 462a
international peace, III 449b, 452a, 454a, 455b
justice, II 659a
loyalty, III 114b
Marxism, III 151a
nationalism, III 328b
natural liberty, II 70b
revolution, III 166a
romanticism, IV 197a
Stalin, II 563a–563b
totalitarianism, IV 406b, 407b, 408a
U.S.S.R., II 563a–563b
U.S., III 114b
war, III 449a, 449b, 450b, 452a, 452b, 453b–454a, 455a, 455b; IV 501a
welfare state, IV 512b–513a
women, IV 528b, 529b
World's Court League, III 454a

World's Student Christian Federation, IV 69a
Wormald, F. iconography, II 538b
Worringer, Wilhelm
aesthetics, II 223b
expressionism, II 207b, 208a, 208b
Gothic, II 373b
Wortman, Tunis, psychology, IV 20b
Wotton, Henry (1568–1639)
Gothic, II 368a
harmony, II 390b
mythology, III 297a
Wotton, William (1666–1727)
attitude toward antiquity, I 80b–81a, 85a
poetics, III 531b
Wren, Christopher (1632–1723)
atomism, I 138a, 139a–139b
cosmic voyages, I 529b
Gothic, II 369a
methodology, III 389a
Newton and, III 389a
Wright, Chauncey (1830–1875)
agnosticism, III 561b
Darwin and, III 561a–561b
empiricism, III 558a, 561a, 562a
evolution, III 561a–561b
evolutionism, II 184a
free will, III 562a
Haeckel and, III 556b
Hegel and, III 556b
James and, III 561a–562b, Kant and, III 555b, 562a
law, III 566b
logic, III 562a
mathematics, III 558a, 561a
methodology, III 561a
Mill and, III 561a–562a
morality, III 561b–562b
nihilism, III 561b
Peirce and, III 555b, 558a, 561a
positivism, III 561b
pragmatism, III 553a, 553b, 555b, 556b, 558a, 561a–561b, 562a, 562b, 566b, 568a
psychology, IV 26b
relativism, III 561b
religion, III 561b
responsibility, III 562a
science, III 561b, 562b
skepticism, III 561b
utilitarianism, III 561b
will to believe, III 562b

Wright, Frank Lloyd (1869–1959), city, I 433b

Wright, G. H. von, good, IV 184b

Wright, Thomas (1810–1877)
cosmic images, I 519a
cosmology, I 549b
God, I 521a
harmony, II 393a

Writing
alphabet, III 180b
Aristotle, II 663a
Babylonia, III 180b
China (ancient), III 180b–181a
dramatic, III 339a
Egypt (ancient), III 180a–180b
Greece (ancient), III 180b
India, II 670a–670b
knowledge, III 180a
language, II 661a, 663a, 666b, 670a–670b, 672a
mathematics, III 178a, 180a–181a
Mesopotamia (ancient), III 180a–180b
narrative, III 339a
naturalism in art, III 339a–339b
nature of, II 661a
neo-classicism in art, III 368b, 369a, 369b
numbers, III 400b, 406b
organicism, III 421b
organized, III 180b, 181a
phonetic, III 178a, 180a–181a
See also Handwriting

Written law, III 14a, 15a, 18b, 24a, 29a, 30a

Wu, Emperor (222–280 A.D.), historiography, II 480b

Wulf, Maurice de, allegory, I 46b

Wundt, Wilhelm (1832–1920)
association of ideas, I 116b
behaviorism, I 217b, 221b; II 382b
classification of the sciences, I 465b
Enlightenment, II 93b
idea, I 116b
mythology, III 315a
pleasure, II 382b
psychology, IV 12b, 13a, 13b, 24b, 25a, 27a, 27b
Volksgeist, IV 495b–496a

Wycherley, William (1640?–1716)
comedy, I 469b
Molière and, I 453a
satire, IV 215b

Wycliffe, John (1320?–1384)
Christianity, I 386b–387a
conservatism, I 479b
economic history, II 45a
heresy, II 417b, 418a, 419a, 421b–422a, 426b
reformation, IV 65b
socialism, IV 287a

Wyspiański, Stanisław (1869–1907), symbolism, IV 343b

Wyżewa, Téodor de, symbolism, IV 340a, 342a

X

Xenocrates (c. 396–314 B.C.)
Aristotle and, IV 35a, 36b, 37a
cynicism, I 628b
demonology, I 668a, 669a
idea, IV 35a, 36b
monad, IV 37a
morality, IV 37a
Neo-Platonism, III 372a
nous, IV 37a
number, IV 36b
Plato and, IV 34b–35a, 36b–37a
Platonism, III 504a
Pythagoreans, IV 34b–35a, 36b–37a
soul, IV 36b

Xenophanes (6th century B.C.)
Aristotle and, III 464a
cosmology, I 539a–539b
culture, I 608b; III 625a
God, III 573b, 624b, 625a
Homer and, III 573b
Hesiod and, III 573b
human nature, III 572a, 573a, 573b, 574b
immortality, III 273a
infinity, II 605b, 607b
irrationalism, II 635a
metaphor, III 203b
mythology, III 273a, 274a
nous, IV 32b
Parmenides and, III 464a
perfectibility, III 464a
Platonism, III 496a
poetry, III 526a
progress, III 624b–625a, 626b, 633a
Pythagoreans, IV 31a, 32b
rationalism, IV 46b
religion, III 203b; IV 92b–93a
skepticism, IV 234b, 235a
soul, III 573a
symmetry, IV 348a

Xenophon (434?–?355 B.C.)
allegory, I 42a
analogy, I 68b
beauty, I 196b, 201a
creativity in art, I 581b
culture, I 611b
cynicism, I 630a, 633a, 633b
despotism, II 2a
economic history, II 45a
Enlightenment, II 95a
freedom of speech, II 258a
historiography, II 503a–503b, 509a
human nature, III 577a
humanism, II 516b
liberty, II 95a
loyalty, III 112a
military, IV 504a
mimesis, III 226a, 497b
philanthropy, III 487a
Plato and, III 577a
Platonism, III 497b, 517b, 519a
progress, III 626a, 627a, 628a
social contract, IV 252b
Socrates and, III 577a
temperance, IV 368a
theriophily, IV 385b
utility, IV 450b
Utopia, IV 460a
war, IV 504a
wisdom of the fool, IV 516b
work, IV 530a–530b

Xerxes, King (519?–465 B.C.)
cynicism, I 633a
freedom of speech, II 254b
historiography, II 501a

Xylander, Wilhelm (1532–1576), mythology, III 295a

Y

Yama (myth), II 343b

Yates, Frances, Ramism, IV 44b

Yeats, William Butler (1865–1939)
creativity in art, I 579b
Platonism, III 524b–525a
Pythagoras and, I 579b
symbolism, IV 340b–341a, 343a, 344b
wisdom of the fool, IV 520a

YHWH, III 658a–662b

Yin and yang
dualism, II 41b–42a
environment, II 122b
God, II 344b
health, II 397a
love, III 96a

Yoga

longevity, III 90a
Orientalism, III 428a, 431a, 431b, 439a
U.S., III 428a, 431a, 431b, 439a

Yosher, equity, II 151a–152a

Youmans, Edward L. (1821–1887), psychology, IV 25a

Young, Arthur (1741–1820)
Counter-Enlightenment, II 104b
Enlightenment, II 98b

Young, Edward (1683–1765)
attitude toward antiquity, I 83b, 84b
Chain of Being, II 446b–447a
Cosmic Fall, I 509b
cosmic images, I 518b
creativity in art, I 587b
genius, II 295a, 295b, 306b, 307a, 307b
hierarchy, II 446b–447a
mythology, III 304a
Newton and, III 395a, 395b, 398a
sublime in external nature, IV 335b, 336a–336b, 337a

Young, Charles Augustus (1834–1908), relativity, IV 78a

Young, Michael
class, I 449b
equality, II 146b–147a

Young, Thomas (1773–1829)
continuity, I 494a
mathematics, III 179a
optics, III 419a–419b

Yugoslavia
agriculture, III 166a
baroque in literature, I 191a, 193a
class, III 154b
communism, III 154b, 334a
Marxism, III 154b, 157b, 166a, 166b–167a, 167b, 168b, 169a, 169b
nationalism, III 328b, 334a, 335a
natural liberty, II 70a
pragmatism, III 565b
revisionism, IV 274b
U.S.S.R., III 334a

Yule, Henry (1820–1889), China, I 368a

Z

Zabarella, Jacopo (1533–1589)
causation, III 382b

Man-Machine, III 135a
methodology, III 382b, 385b
Newton and, III 382b, 385b
science, II 204a
Zamagna, Bernard, cosmic voyages, I 532b
Zamyatin, Eugeni I. (1884–1937)
perfectibility, III 474b
Utopia, IV 464a
Zarathustra, *see* Zoroaster
Zarlino, Giuseppe (1517–1590)
Artusi and, III 262b
genius, II 319a, 319b
music, II 319a, 319b; III 261b–262a, 262b
Ptolemy and, III 262a
Zechariah (Bible)
God, II 337a
metaphor, III 202b
religion, III 202b
Zedekiah (Bible), mythology, III 283b
Zeigler, Jakob, baroque in literature, I 189b
Zeitgeist, IV 535b–537b
art, IV 536b
authority, IV 536a
Being, IV 536b
Collingwood, R. G., IV 536b–537a
defined, IV 535b
economics, IV 536a
experience, IV 536b
Faust (legend), IV 536a–536b
Fichte, IV 536a
freedom, IV 536b
genius, IV 535b, 536a
God, IV 536b
Goethe, IV 536a–536b
Hegel, IV 535b–536a
Heidegger, IV 536b
Herder, IV 535b
history, IV 535b–536b
individualism, IV 536a
Jaspers, IV 536b
Kant, IV 536a
literature, IV 535b, 536b
Löwith, IV 535b
Marx, IV 536a
Marxism, IV 536a
metaphysics, IV 536b–537a
Mill, J. S., IV 536b
mind, IV 536b
morality, IV 536a, 536b
Nature, IV 536b
order, IV 536b
periodization in literary history, III 484a
permissiveness, IV 536b
philosophy, IV 535b–536b

power, IV 536a
reality, IV 536a
Sartre, IV 536a
Schiller, IV 536a
science, IV 536b–537a
society, IV 535b, 536a, 536b
technology, IV 536b
truth, IV 536b
Voltaire, IV 535b
Whitehead, IV 536b
Zeller, Eduard (1814–1908)
Hegel and, II 414a
Platonism, III 521a
Zen Buddhism, I 248a–248b, 249a, 250b–251a, 253a, 253b, 256a, 256b–257a
emphasis on direct insight, I 249b
literary paradox, III 77b
Orientalism, III 428a, 436a
U.S., III 428a, 436a
Zeno of Citium (4th-3rd century B.C.)
anarchy, I 71a
antinomy of pure reason, I 91a–91b
appearance and reality, I 94a, 94b
Aristotle and, IV 301a, 320b
Chain of Being, I 329b
Chrysippus, IV 321b
cycles, I 623a–623b
cynicism, IV 320b
Diogenes of Sinope and, IV 320b
education, III 630a
Enlightenment, II 90a
ethics, III 440b; IV 319a, 320a, 320b, 321b, 322a
freedom of speech, II 260b
God, II 340b
Heraclitus and, IV 320b
influence of, IV 321b–322a
linguistics, III 62a
literary paradox, III 76b
logos, IV 320b
loyalty, III 111a
mathematics, IV 32a–32b
matter, III 187a
motion, IV 389b
mythology, III 274a
natural law, III 17b
Nature, III 17b
Parmenides and, IV 47b
peace, III 440b
perfectibility, III 465b
Plato and, IV 320b
primitivism, III 587b
psychology, IV 7a
Pythagoreans, IV 32a–32b, 37a
rationalism, IV 47b
reason, III 17b

Semitism, IV 320b
skepticism, IV 234b
Socrates and, IV 320b
space, IV 301a
Stoicism, III 587b; IV 7a, 319a, 320a, 320b, 321b, 322a
temperance, IV 369b
time, IV 389b
Utopia, IV 460a
Zeno of Elea (5th century B.C.)
continuity, I 498b, 499a
infinity, II 607b, 608b, 610a, 610b
justice, II 653b
mathematics, III 172b
Parmenides and, IV 400a
time, IV 400a
straight line, III 172b
Zeno of Verona, Saint, socialism, IV 286a
Zephaniah (Bible), prophecy, III 662b
Zermelo, Ernst (1871–1953)
entropy, II 117a–117b, 118b
game theory, II 265a
mathematics, III 176a
Zernike, F., indeterminacy, II 588a
Zetzner, Lazarus (c. 17th century), alchemy, I 31b
Zeus (myth), I 60b; II 339b–340b; III 272b, 273a, 273b, 274b, 282b, 309a, 497b
culture, I 608a
dualism, II 39a
Eden-motif, I 608a
evil, III 571b
fate, II 229a
fortune, II 229a
Gnosticism, II 329a
good, III 571b
hierarchy, II 440a
historiography, II 506b
human nature, III 571b, 572b
idea, II 545b
justice, II 652b, 653a; III 572b
law, II 674b–677b, 678b, 679a, 682a, 682b, 684b
metaphor, III 203b
music, III 268b
perfectibility, III 464a
primitivism, III 578b, 579a, 580a
psychology, IV 1b
Pythagoreans, IV 37a
Ramism, IV 44a, 44b
rationalism, IV 48b
religion, III 203b; IV 93a
temperance, IV 366a, 367a
tragic sense, IV 413b

Zeuxis (fl. late 5th century A.D.)
ideal, II 549b
individualism, II 299b
neo-classicism in art, III 368b
Zhukov, E. M., periodization in history, III 479a
Ziegler, Leopold, eschatology, II 160a
Ziehen, T., Man-Machine, III 143a
Zilsel, Edgar (1891–1943)
genius, II 293b, 294a, 295a, 317b
positivism, III 545b
Zimet, C. N., beauty, I 213b
Zimmermann, Robert von (1824–1898), aesthetics, II 217a, 218b
Zinzendorf, Graf Nikolaus Ludwig von (1700–1760), Pietism, III 493b, 495a
Zirkle, C. (1895–   )
acquired characteristics, II 617b
Zodiac
microcosm, III 128a–128b, 129a, 131a
mythology, III 287b, 288b, 291a, 310b
signs of, I 538b–539a; III 128b
time, IV 402a
Zola, Émile (1840–1902)
ambiguity, I 55a
beauty, I 208a
impressionism, II 573a, 575b, 581a, 581b
Man-Machine, III 143a
mimesis, III 229b
motif, III 242b
naturalism, II 575b; III 229b; IV 53b–54a
naturalism in art, III 339a, 339b
Nature, III 349a
realism in literature, IV 52a, 53b–54a, 55a
ut pictura poesis, IV 467a
vox populi, IV 499b
Zoogony, progress, III 627a
Zoology
cosmology, I 230a
Counter-Enlightenment, II 110a
evolutionism, II 179a
ideology, II 553b
mathematics, III 177a
mythology, III 287b
theriophily, IV 388a, 388b
Zoroaster (Zarathustra; fl. about 6th century B.C.)
astrology, I 122a

cosmic voyages, I 527a
despotism, II 13a
dualism, II 39b, 40a
evil, II 162b
Faust (legend), III 251a
Figurism, I 359b
gods, II 338a–339a
Neo-Platonism, III 510a
salvation, IV 231a–231b
sin, IV 231a–231b
Zoroastrianism
    astrology, I 122a–123a
    dualism, II 38a–43a; IV
    231a
    eschatology, II 40a, 339a;
    IV 231b

evil, II 162b, 164b, 165a;
    IV 231a, 231b
free will, IV 231a
God, II 335b, 339a, 339b
Islam, II 639a, 639b, 640b
Manicheism, II 42b
morality, II 40a; IV 231a
mythology, III 281b
Persia, I 376a
religion, IV 98a
salvation, IV 231a–231b
sin, IV 231a–231b
symmetry, IV 348a
systematic character of, II
    39a–39b
time, IV 402a

Zosimos (fl. 3rd century A.D.),
    alchemy, I 28b, 29b
Zubov, V. P., universal man,
    IV 440a
Zuccaro, Federigo (1543–
    1609)
    aesthetics, II 221b, 222b
    mythology, III 293a
Zucchi, J., mythology, III 293a
Zurvan (myth), II 338b, 339a,
    343b
    dualism, II 40a
    God, II 339a
Zwaardemaker, H., entropy, II
    117b
Zwinger, Theodor the Elder

(1533–1588), Ramism, IV
44a
Zwingli, Ulrich (1484–1531),
    I 391a–391b, 392a
    authority, I 150a
    Bible, I 390b
    city-state, I 395a
    eschatology, II 156b
    heresy, II 425b, 427b
    predestination, II 30b
    Reformation, IV 67b, 68a
    sacraments, I 391b–392a
    skepticism, IV 242b